AN MMY MONOGRAPH

Publications of
THE INSTITUTE OF MENTAL MEASUREMENTS
Edited by Oscar Krisen Buros

EDUCATIONAL, PSYCHOLOGICAL, AND PERSONALITY TESTS OF 1933 AND 1934

EDUCATIONAL, PSYCHOLOGICAL, AND PERSONALITY TESTS OF 1933, 1934, AND 1935

EDUCATIONAL, PSYCHOLOGICAL, AND PERSONALITY TESTS OF 1936

THE NINETEEN THIRTY-EIGHT MENTAL MEASUREMENTS YEARBOOK

THE NINETEEN FORTY MENTAL MEASUREMENTS YEARBOOK

THE THIRD MENTAL MEASUREMENTS YEARBOOK

THE FOURTH MENTAL MEASUREMENTS YEARBOOK

THE FIFTH MENTAL MEASUREMENTS YEARBOOK

TESTS IN PRINT

THE SIXTH MENTAL MEASUREMENTS YEARBOOK

READING TESTS AND REVIEWS

PERSONALITY TESTS AND REVIEWS

THE SEVENTH MENTAL MEASUREMENTS YEARBOOK

TESTS IN PRINT II

ENGLISH TESTS AND REVIEWS

FOREIGN LANGUAGE TESTS AND REVIEWS

INTELLIGENCE TESTS AND REVIEWS

MATHEMATICS TESTS AND REVIEWS

PERSONALITY TESTS AND REVIEWS II

READING TESTS AND REVIEWS II

SCIENCE TESTS AND REVIEWS

SOCIAL STUDIES TESTS AND REVIEWS

VOCATIONAL TESTS AND REVIEWS

VOCATIONAL
TESTS AND REVIEWS

VOCATIONAL
TESTS AND REVIEWS

A Monograph
Consisting of the Vocational Sections of the
SEVEN MENTAL MEASUREMENTS YEARBOOKS (1938–72)
and
TESTS IN PRINT II (1974)

Edited by
OSCAR KRISEN BUROS
Director, The Institute of Mental Measurements

THE UNIVERSITY OF NEBRASKA PRESS
LINCOLN AND LONDON

DESIGNED BY LUELLA BUROS

COPYRIGHT 1975 BY OSCAR KRISEN BUROS; PUBLISHED BY THE UNIVERSITY OF NEBRASKA PRESS,
901 N. 17TH ST., LINCOLN, NEBRASKA 68588. No part of this publication may
be reproduced in any form, nor may any of the contents be used in an informational storage,
retrieval, or transmission system without the prior written permission of the publisher.

LC 75–8116, ISBN 0–8032–4650–1

Manufactured in the United States of America

To
Jennie and Francis

TABLE OF CONTENTS

	PAGE
MMY TEST REVIEWERS	xi
PREFACE	xv
INTRODUCTION	xvii
VOCATIONAL TESTS	
Tests in Print II	1
VOCATIONAL TEST REVIEWS	
First Mental Measurements Yearbook	97
Second Mental Measurements Yearbook	109
Third Mental Measurements Yearbook	151
Fourth Mental Measurements Yearbook	297
Fifth Mental Measurements Yearbook	457
Sixth Mental Measurements Yearbook	603
Seventh Mental Measurements Yearbook	803
TIP II SCANNING INDEX	1002
PUBLISHERS DIRECTORY AND INDEX	1037
INDEX OF TITLES	1042
INDEX OF NAMES	1054
VOCATIONS SCANNING INDEX	1081

MMY TEST REVIEWERS

C. J. Adcock	7:977
Dorothy C. Adkins	3:690
	5:514, 5:607, 6:775
Lewis E. Albright	7:1064, 7:1066
Vera M. Amerson	3:369, 3:380
Anne Anastasi	4:715, 4:716
	5:610, 5:615, 6:773
Harvey A. Andruss	3:368, 3:373
Edgar Anstey	6:1090
Dwight L. Arnold	4:801
Alexander W. Astin	6:1070
Thomas S. Baldwin	7:976
Irol W. Balsley	6:43
Richard S. Barrett	6:1117
Brent Baxter	4:770, 4:783, 5:930
Harold P. Bechtoldt	4:711, 4:715
	5:602, 5:608, 6:771, 7:1049
George K. Bennett	3:645, 3:690, 4:739
Ralph F. Berdie	3:639, 3:640
	4:711, 4:716, 5:608
	5:613, 6:1066, 7:1041, 7:1042
Robert G. Bernreuter	3:703
Marion A. Bills	3:623, 6:638
Walter V. Bingham	1:1174
Reign H. Bittner	3:669, 3:680
	4:459, 4:725, 4:778
E. G. Blackstone	3:378
	3:382, 3:383, 3:394
Milton L. Blum	3:657, 3:660
	3:664, 4:714, 4:741
Jack L. Bodden	7:1012
Edward S. Bordin	3:638, 3:643
	3:655, 4:742, 4:747, 5:862
Arthur H. Brayfield	4:743
	5:879, 5:886, 6:1192
Ann Brewington	3:386, 3:391
Leo J. Brueckner	4:796, 4:804
Paul S. Burnham	3:636
David P. Campbell	6:1053, 6:1062
	7:1011, 7:1018, 7:1032, 7:1038
Joel T. Campbell	6:1189
John B. Carroll	4:715, 4:716
	5:605, 5:608, 6:771
Harold D. Carter	1:1170, 1:1180, 2:1679
	2:1680, 3:638, 3:655, 4:742
E. G. Chambers	3:640, 3:682, 4:723
	4:724, 4:758, 5:877, 5:885
Ruth D. Churchill	5:615
Gale W. Clark	5:512, 5:518
J. F. Clark	5:880, 5:890
Glen U. Cleeton	3:645, 3:694
Dorothy M. Clendenen	7:1037
Nancy S. Cole	7:1100
W. D. Commins	2:1664
Andrew L. Comrey	5:609, 5:901
Clyde H. Coombs	3:685
William C. Cottle	5:856
Stuart A. Courtis	4:716
Albert B. Crawford	2:1671, 2:1676
John O. Crites	6:1056, 7:1026
Lysle W. Croft	3:636, 3:637
Lee J. Cronbach	4:801
Edward E. Cureton	4:725, 4:730
Louise W. Cureton	4:729
John G. Darley	1:1171
	1:1178, 1:1179, 2:1680

EDWIN W. DAVIS 3:634
GWENDOLEN S. DICKSON 1:1170
3:642, 3:649
ROBERT H. DOLLIVER 7:1025, 7:1028
JEROME E. DOPPELT 4:812, 5:859
6:1190, 7:1059, 7:1080
ROBERT C. DROEGE 7:977
PHILIP H. DUBOIS 3:372
3:390, 3:393, 6:1137
STANLEY G. DULSKY 2:1666
3:639, 3:643, 3:644
JACK W. DUNLAP 2:1675
S. S. DUNN 6:776
MARVIN D. DUNNETTE 6:1025
BEATRICE J. DVORAK 3:389, 3:394
HENRY S. DYER 5:859
ROBERT L. EBEL 6:1137
M. H. ELLIOTT 3:689
BERTRAM EPSTEIN 4:449
LAWRENCE W. ERICKSON 6:51
6:55, 7:557, 7:559A
ELIZABETH FEHRER 3:384, 3:391
GEORGE A. FERGUSON 3:645, 3:690, 4:735
LEONARD W. FERGUSON 6:1024, 6:1045
ROBERT FITZPATRICK 7:988
JOHN P. FOLEY, JR. 6:1119, 6:1177, 7:1064
HANFORD M. FOWLER 4:742
THOMAS T. FRANTZ 7:1029, 7:1035
NORMAN FREDERIKSEN 3:641, 3:698, 4:745
4:750, 5:605, 5:614, 6:770, 7:978
FRANK S. FREEMAN 4:794
JOHN W. FRENCH 3:701, 4:810, 5:901
6:1053, 6:1060, 6:1165, 7:1012, 7:1014
CLIFFORD P. FROEHLICH 4:710
4:798, 5:609, 5:863
BENJAMIN FRUCHTER 5:610, 5:613
DOUGLAS H. FRYER 3:685, 3:686, 3:691
EDWARD J. FURST 6:1070, 7:1033
EDWIN E. GHISELLI 3:663, 3:665, 3:666
CECIL A. GIBB 7:1148, 7:1149
LEO GOLDMAN 6:781, 6:1075
LEONARD V. GORDON 6:1029, 6:1182, 6:1183
EDWARD B. GREENE 3:635, 4:714
5:518, 5:522, 5:893, 5:930
WILLIAM R. GROVE 3:658
3:662, 3:671, 3:679
JOHN W. GUSTAD 5:862
MILTON E. HAHN 3:697, 3:704
4:798, 4:824, 6:1054
GARY R. HANSON 7:1080

THOMAS W. HARRELL 3:665, 3:666
MARY T. HARRISON 7:1007, 7:1008
CHARLES M. HARSH 3:673, 3:681, 3:683
GEORGE W. HARTMANN 4:805
DAVID G. HAWKRIDGE 7:1011, 7:1015
EDWARD N. HAY 3:624, 3:630
3:631, 4:731, 4:732, 5:515
LESLIE M. HAYNES 4:460
KENNETH L. HEATON 4:803
ALICE W. HEIM 7:1034
WILLIAM H. HELME 6:774
JOHN K. HEMPHILL 6:1099, 7:975, 7:981
DAVID O. HERMAN 6:1147, 7:1028, 7:1032
JOHN R. HILLS 6:1059
ELMER D. HINCKLEY 4:737, 4:747
KENNETH B. HOYT 6:1056, 6:1057
LLOYD G. HUMPHREYS 3:668, 3:670, 3:683
4:711, 5:609, 5:891, 6:775
STEPHEN HUNKA 6:1032
THELMA HUNT 3:627, 3:630
JOHN R. JENNINGS 5:874, 5:875
A. PEMBERTON JOHNSON 5:876, 5:933
RICHARD T. JOHNSON 7:1089, 7:1090, 7:1103
CLIVE JONES 7:1034
EDWARD S. JONES 2:1669
ROBERT A. JONES 5:855
CLIFFORD E. JURGENSEN 3:681, 3:682, 4:459
4:763, 5:526, 5:955, 6:1024
HARRY W. KARN 4:781
MARTIN R. KATZ 5:864, 6:1063, 7:1036
RAYMOND A. KATZELL 3:624, 3:629
3:630, 4:752, 4:763
5:947, 5:954, 6:1025, 6:1104, 6:1108
J. A. KEATS 6:767
WILLIAM E. KENDALL 6:1173, 6:1181
WILLARD A. KERR 3:662, 4:761
6:1198, 6:1199, 6:1200
JOSEPH E. KING 3:684
FORREST A. KINGSBURY 2:1682
JOHN R. KINZER 3:661, 3:663
WAYNE K. KIRCHNER 6:1180, 6:1190
BARBARA A. KIRK 7:1024, 7:1037
BENJAMIN KLEINMUNTZ 6:773
CHARLES J. KRAUSKOPF 7:1036
PHILIP H. KRIEDT 6:1039, 6:1046
FREDERIC KUDER 2:1654
ALBERT K. KURTZ 4:729, 5:614
5:902, 6:1115, 6:1173, 6:1192
HERBERT A. LANDRY 2:1668
CHARLES R. LANGMUIR 4:779

C. H. LAWSHE, JR.   3:656, 3:659, 3:661
WILBUR L. LAYTON   4:739
                        4:740, 5:864, 5:870
RICHARD LEDGERWOOD   1:1171
D. WELTY LEFEVER   3:675, 3:687
                        3:695, 4:712, 4:726
SEYMOUR LEVY   6:1123, 6:1193
JOHN LIGGETT   5:877
ORREL E. LITTLE   3:375, 3:376
PAUL R. LOHNES   7:1024
PAUL S. LOMAX   3:396
IRVING LORGE   2:1654, 2:1655, 2:1656
JAMES LUMSDEN   5:520
JOHN N. MCCALL   7:1019, 7:1024
D. W. MCELWAIN   4:719
                        4:756, 5:884, 5:888
ARTHUR C. MACKINNEY   6:1049
                        6:1068, 7:1062
MILTON M. MANDELL   4:774, 4:785
HERSCHEL T. MANUEL   3:634
MELVIN R. MARKS   6:33
ROSS W. MATTESON   4:726
SAMUEL T. MAYO   6:1130, 6:1135, 6:1136
I. G. MEDDLETON   5:890
P. L. MELLENBRUCH   5:854, 5:943
RICHARD S. MELTON   6:1085, 6:1099
PHILIP R. MERRIFIELD   6:1130
                        6:1135, 6:1136
BERNADINE MEYER   5:523
WILLIAM B. MICHAEL   6:770
WILLIAM J. MICHEELS   5:887, 5:944
JOHN E. MILHOLLAND   6:780
J. B. MINER   2:1666, 2:1683
JOSEPH E. MOORE   3:656, 3:667, 4:731
                    4:813, 6:775, 6:1186, 6:1197
JOHN B. MORRIS   5:879, 5:954
N. W. MORTON   1:1180
                    2:1680, 2:1682, 4:766
CHARLES I. MOSIER   3:675, 3:687
LEO A. MUNDAY   7:1098
CHARLES T. MYERS   5:885
BERNARD H. NEWMAN   7:552, 7:558
WARREN T. NORMAN   6:1052
C. A. OAKLEY   2:1652, 3:635, 3:670
MARY E. OLIVERIO   5:853
                    5:955, 7:554, 7:559
JACOB S. ORLEANS   5:515, 6:51
AGNES E. OSBORNE   3:377, 3:381
JAY L. OTIS   3:672, 3:676
                    3:680, 4:750, 4:776

WILLIAM A. OWENS   6:1089, 6:1098
C. ROBERT PACE   4:805
ALBERT G. PACKARD   3:665, 3:666
JEAN M. PALORMO   6:1110, 6:1116
DONALD G. PATERSON 2:1665, 2:1669, 3:623
                3:625, 3:631, 4:824, 4:825, 4:828
DAVID A. PAYNE   7:1014
JOHN GRAY PEATMAN   2:1654, 2:1667
E. A. PEEL   4:753, 5:606
SHAILER PETERSON   3:680, 3:681
JOHN PIERCE-JONES   5:863
JAMES M. PORTER, JR.   3:669, 3:678, 3:682
LYMAN W. PORTER   6:1029, 6:1182, 6:1183
RAY G. PRICE   3:368, 3:385, 6:31
                    6:52, 6:1044, 7:554, 7:556
HUGH F. PRIEST   7:1018
M. Y. QUERESHI   7:673, 7:680
H. H. REMMERS   5:612
JAMES M. RICHARDS, JR.   7:1100
M. W. RICHARDSON   2:1655
HARRY N. RIVLIN   4:802
A. OSCAR H. ROBERTS   7:1049
ALEC RODGER   2:1652, 2:1673
                    3:661, 3:669, 4:731, 4:764
PAUL F. ROSS   6:769, 6:1110
HAROLD F. ROTHE   4:454, 4:455
JOHN W. M. ROTHNEY   7:1029
HAROLD L. ROYER   6:35
ARTHUR B. ROYSE   5:857
STANLEY I. RUBIN   6:774
FLOYD L. RUCH   3:697, 3:704
                    3:705, 4:773, 4:781
C. H. RUEDISILI   3:686, 3:687
EDWARD A. RUNDQUIST   3:372, 3:390
EVERETT B. SACKETT   1:1176
I. DAVID SATLOW   5:504
GEORGE A. SATTER   3:672
                    3:683, 4:730, 4:732
WILLIAM L. SCHAAF   4:450
ARNOLD E. SCHNEIDER   3:379, 3:387
LYLE F. SCHOENFELDT   7:1043, 7:1046
WILLIAM B. SCHRADER   5:933
DOUGLAS G. SCHULTZ 4:761, 4:764, 6:1043
                6:1044, 7:994, 7:995, 7:997
DONALD H. SCHUSTER 6:1198, 6:1199, 6:1200
RICHARD E. SCHUTZ   6:767, 7:680
MAY V. SEAGOE   4:799, 4:806
HAROLD G. SEASHORE   3:696
R. B. SELOVER   3:627, 3:628

Benjamin Shimberg   3:695, 6:1054, 7:976
Patrick Slater   3:638, 3:681
I. Macfarlane Smith   4:713, 6:1085, 6:1086
Donald Spearritt   5:853, 5:855
John M. Stalnaker   1:1171
Julian C. Stanley   4:746, 4:755, 6:766
Harry L. Stein   6:1032, 6:1041
Ruth M. Strang   2:1672, 2:1681
Dewey B. Stuit   3:668, 3:676
    3:677, 4:812, 4:813
Donald E. Super   3:640, 3:653
    3:655, 4:740, 4:744
    4:745, 5:606, 5:850, 6:1066
Edward O. Swanson   6:41
Erwin K. Taylor   3:624, 3:627
    3:631, 5:905, 6:769
Howard R. Taylor   3:694, 4:714, 4:741
Lorene Teegarden   2:1662, 2:1663
Paul W. Thayer   6:1043, 6:1046
Albert S. Thompson   1:1181, 2:1659
    2:1662, 2:1678, 4:825
    4:828, 5:902, 5:905, 6:1130
Robert L. Thorndike   4:808
David V. Tiedeman   7:1033, 7:1042
Herbert A. Tonne   1:942
    3:376, 3:380, 5:894
Herbert A. Toops   3:636
Marion R. Trabue   1:1170, 1:1171
    1:1174, 1:1181, 2:1675, 2:1679
Robert M. W. Travers   3:698, 4:792
Arthur E. Traxler   1:1171, 2:1671, 3:635
    3:641, 4:738, 4:777, 5:903
Frances O. Triggs   3:642, 3:654
William W. Turnbull   6:766
Leona E. Tyler   6:1052
C. C. Upshall   3:369, 3:379
Donald J. Veldman   7:1089, 7:1103

Philip E. Vernon   4:715
    4:716, 5:606, 5:610
Morris S. Viteles   2:1659
    2:1662, 2:1678, 3:696
William W. Waite   3:693, 3:702, 4:775
J. V. Waits   3:696
S. Rains Wallace   4:776
    4:789, 5:607, 5:948
Wimburn L. Wallace   5:515
W. Bruce Walsh   7:1025
Edwin Wandt   4:792, 4:796, 4:804
Morey J. Wantman   4:817
F. W. Warburton   4:779
Charles F. Ward   7:1125, 7:1136, 7:1140
William C. Ward   7:975
Charles F. Warnath   6:1049, 6:1068
Neil D. Warren   3:659
    3:665, 5:871, 5:873
Richard W. Watkins   7:1010
David J. Weiss   7:676
Henry Weitz   3:623, 6:52, 7:1020
A. T. Welford   4:757, 4:769
Alexander G. Wesman   4:814, 4:815, 5:932
Leonard J. West   7:559A, 7:1007
Bert W. Westbrook   7:1019, 7:1026
Haydn S. Williams   5:874, 5:875
Edmund G. Williamson   1:1181, 2:1661
John M. Willits   3:625, 3:632
William L. Winnett   7:552
Emory E. Wiseman   7:1137
Leroy Wolins   6:776
E. F. Wonderlic   3:623, 3:624
    3:626, 3:627, 3:630, 3:632
D. A. Worcester   4:799, 4:800
C. Gilbert Wrenn   2:1667
Alfred Yates   5:857
Dale Yoder   4:785
Donald G. Zytowski   7:1021, 7:1023

PREFACE

I T IS my considered belief that most standardized tests are poorly constructed, of questionable or unknown validity, pretentious in their claims, and likely to be misused more often than not. This conviction began to form 48 to 50 years ago when I was taking courses in testing at the University of Minnesota. I vividly recall presenting a paper entitled "Common Fallacies in the Use of Standardized Tests" in an advanced educational psychology class taught by Professor W. S. Miller, a paper in which I criticized some of the views of my instructors. Shortly thereafter, I had the good fortune to read a book which was a landmark in the consumer movement—*Your Money's Worth* by Stuart Chase and F. J. Schlink. It was this book which led to the founding of Consumers' Research, Inc., an organization which tests and evaluates commonly used commercial products. This book and the establishment of Consumers' Research stimulated me to begin thinking about a test users' research organization to evaluate tests.

After failing to secure financial support for the initiation of a test users' research organization, I scaled down my objectives to the establishment of a cooperative test reviewing service which would report on and evaluate standardized tests used in education, industry, and psychology. One hundred thirty-three specialists in a wide variety of disciplines cooperated by contributing "frankly critical reviews" for *The 1938 Mental Measurements Yearbook* (also called *The First Yearbook*). Later yearbooks (each volume supplementing earlier volumes)

were published in 1941, 1949, 1953, 1959, 1965, and 1972.

The objectives of the *Mental Measurements Yearbooks* (MMY's) have remained essentially the same since they were first presented in detail in *The 1940 Mental Measurements Yearbook* (also called *The Second Yearbook*): (*a*) to provide information about tests published as separates throughout the English-speaking world; (*b*) to present frankly critical test reviews written by testing and subject specialists representing various viewpoints; (*c*) to provide extensive bibliographies of verified references on the construction, use, and validity of specific tests; (*d*) to make readily available the critical portions of test reviews appearing in professional journals; and (*e*) to present fairly exhaustive listings of new and revised books on testing along with evaluative excerpts from representative reviews in professional journals.

As important as the above objectives are, I place even greater importance on these less tangible objectives: (*f*) to impel test authors and publishers to publish better tests and to provide test users with detailed information on the validity and limitations of these tests; (*g*) to inculcate in test users a keener awareness of the values and limitations of standardized tests; (*h*) to stimulate contributing reviewers to think through more carefully their own beliefs and values relevant to testing; (*i*) to suggest to test users better methods of appraising tests in light of their own particular needs; and (*j*) to impress upon test users the need to suspect all tests unaccompanied by detailed data on their construction, validity, uses, and limitations—

even when products of distinguished authors and reputable publishers.

As the number of published tests and, especially, the related literature increased tremendously over the years, the MMY's became increasingly more encyclopedic in scope. Many test users, however, are interested in only one or two areas of testing. To meet their needs, we announced in 1941 plans for publishing monographs in English, foreign languages, intelligence, mathematics, personality, reading, science, social studies, and vocations. Unfortunately, we were too optimistic; it was over a quarter of a century before we were able to finance the publication of the first monograph, *Reading Tests and Reviews* (RTR I), published in 1968.

The next monograph, *Personality Tests and Reviews* (PTR I), was published in 1970. The core of these two monographs, RTR I and PTR I, consists of a reprinting of the reading and personality sections, respectively, of the first six MMY's and a new section listing both in print and out of print tests in the area represented by the monograph.

Despite the use of a large amount of reprinted material, the preparation and publication of these two monographs turned out to be very costly. Since sales later proved insufficient to finance similar monographs in other areas, we temporarily abandoned our plans for additional monographs.

Following the publication of *The Seventh Yearbook* in early 1972, we began devoting all of our time to the completion of *Tests in Print II: An Index to Tests, Test Reviews, and the Literature on Specific Tests* (TIP II). In mid-1974, while TIP II was in press, it suddenly occurred to me that up-to-date monographs could be prepared at a manageable cost by reprinting a given section of TIP II along with the corresponding sections of the seven MMY's. As a consequence, we are now publishing monographs in nine areas: second monographs in personality and reading, and first monographs in English, foreign languages, intelligence, mathematics, science, social studies, and vocations. Hopefully, the publication of these monographs will make our material' available to many test users who might otherwise not consult the MMY's and TIP II. Broadening the readership of our test reviews will bring us closer to achieving our objectives.

This monograph, *Vocational Tests and Reviews* (VTR), is a reprinting of the business education, multi-aptitude, and vocations sections of the seven *Mental Measurements Yearbooks* and *Tests in Print II*. A tremendous amount of information and literature on specific tests published over the past fifty years has been gathered together in a single volume. [The cumulative name indexes for specific tests and the extensive end-of-the-book indexes of names and titles will greatly facilitate the use of this monograph. Even those who have access to all seven MMY's and TIP II will find it much more convenient to use VTR whenever they want information on vocational tests.]

Our bibliographies on specific vocational tests are exceptionally comprehensive. More than 6,000 references have been located and examined (except unpublished theses) to make sure that they meet our criteria of relevancy. Although these bibliographies are probably unequaled in their accuracy, comprehensiveness, and relevancy, we know of no instance where any of them has been cited in a test manual, article, or book dealing with a specific test. We would feel happier about the preparation of these costly and time-consuming bibliographies if they were cited in test manuals and the literature dealing with specific tests—citations which would normally be made for bibliographies published as journal articles.

It has been particularly hectic preparing nine MMY monographs simultaneously. Fortunately, I have been assisted by a dedicated staff. Although other people worked for shorter periods of time, there are seven whom I would like to name for special recognition: Mary Anne Miller Becker, Sandra Boxer Discenza, Doris Greene McCan, Barbara Ruis Martko, Mary T. Mooney, Joan Stein Paszamant, and Natalie J. Rosenthal Turton. I am greatly indebted to my staff colleagues for their assistance in producing these nine derivative monographs.

We plan to publish *The Eighth Mental Measurements Yearbook* in 1977, followed by *Tests in Print III* in 1978. The vocations sections of these volumes will supplement and update the material in this monograph.

OSCAR KRISEN BUROS

Highland Park, New Jersey
February 24, 1975

INTRODUCTION

For THE past 40 years we have been providing test users in education, industry, and psychology with a series of publications designed to assist them in the selection and use of tests which best meet their needs. We maintained an annual production schedule for our first four volumes (1935–38); since then, however, the intervals between books have been quite irregular with publication dates 1941, 1949, 1953, 1959, 1961, 1965, 1968, 1970, 1972, and 1974. Our publications through 1974 include three test bibliographies, seven *Mental Measurements Yearbooks,* two monographs, and two *Tests in Print.*[1] Nine derivative mono-

graphs—this volume and eight others—are being published in 1975. A brief description of our first fourteen publications follows.

FIRST THREE PUBLICATIONS

Although the earliest three publications are noncritical bibliographies, the original intent had been to prepare an annual critical review of new tests for journal publication. It soon became apparent, however, that this was far beyond the capacity of a single individual. A more modest goal was substituted, the publication of an annual bibliography of tests, as described in the Introduction to the first one:

To locate the standard tests recently published in specific areas is a laborious task. The usual bibliographic aids for locating periodical, monograph, and book publications are of little value in locating standard tests. New tests are being published so rapidly that the test technicians themselves find it difficult to locate the test titles of the past year without an inordinate amount of searching. For these reasons, the writer has undertaken the task of preparing a bibliography of psychological, achievement, character, and personality tests published in 1933 and 1934. This bibliography will be the first of a series to be published annually by the School of Education, Rutgers University.[2]

This 44-page bibliography lists 257 tests that were new, revised, or supplemented in 1933 and 1934. Many of these tests, usually revised editions, are still in print today.

Similar test bibliographies[3] were published in 1936 and 1937. During this time, attempts were being made to obtain a grant to initiate a

---

1 The first fourteen publications (1935–1974), edited by Oscar K. Buros and now published by The Gryphon Press, are listed from the most recent to the oldest:
  a) *Tests in Print II: An Index to Tests, Test Reviews, and the Literature on Specific Tests,* December 1974. Pp. xxxix, 1107. $70.
  b) *The Seventh Mental Measurements Yearbook,* Vols. I and II, 1972. Pp. xl, 935; vi, 937–1986. $70 per set.
  c) *Personality Tests and Reviews: Including an Index to The Mental Measurements Yearbooks,* 1970. Pp. xxxi, 1659. $45. For reviews, see 7:B120.
  d) *Reading Tests and Reviews: Including a Classified Index to The Mental Measurements Yearbooks,* 1968. Pp. xxii, 520. $20. For reviews, see 7:B121.
  e) *The Sixth Mental Measurements Yearbook,* 1965. Pp. xxxvii, 1714. $45. (Reprinted 1971) For reviews, see 7:B122.
  f) *Tests in Print: A Comprehensive Bibliography of Tests for Use in Education, Psychology, and Industry,* 1961. Pp. xxix, 479. $15. (Reprinted 1974) For reviews, see 6:B105.
  g) *The Fifth Mental Measurements Yearbook,* 1959. Pp. xxix, 1292. $35. (Reprinted 1961) For reviews, see 6:B104.
  h) *The Fourth Mental Measurements Yearbook,* 1953. Pp. xxv, 1163. $30. (Reprinted 1974) For reviews, see 5:B84.
  i) *The Third Mental Measurements Yearbook,* 1949. Pp. xv, 1047. $25. (Reprinted 1974) For reviews, see 4:B71.
  j) *The Nineteen Forty Mental Measurements Yearbook,* 1941. Pp. xxv, 674. $20. (Reissued 1972) For reviews, see 3:788 and 4:B70.
  k) *The Nineteen Thirty Eight Mental Measurements Yearbook,* 1938. Pp. xv, 415. $17.50. (Reissued 1972) For reviews, see 2:B858.
  l) *Educational, Psychological, and Personality Tests of 1936: Including a Bibliography and Book Review Digest of Measurement Books and Monographs of 1933–36,* 1937. Pp. 141. *Out of print.* For reviews, see 1:B326.
  m) *Educational, Psychological, and Personality Tests of 1933, 1934, and 1935,* 1936. Pp. 83. *Out of print.* For reviews, see 36:B46.
  n) *Educational, Psychological, and Personality Tests of 1933 and 1934,* 1935. Pp. 44. *Out of print.* For a review, see 36:B45.

2 *Educational, Psychological, and Personality Tests of 1933 and 1934,* p. 5.
3 *Educational, Psychological, and Personality Tests of 1933, 1934, and 1935.*
Educational, Psychological, and Personality Tests of 1936.

research organization which would serve as a bureau of standards for the evaluation of educational and psychological tests. It was only after we despaired of raising such funds that we decided to set up a test reviewing service.

THE SEVEN MMY'S

Since tests, unlike books, were rarely reviewed in professional journals, it was a revolutionary step forward when we published *The 1938 Mental Measurements Yearbook* 37 years ago. In his Foreword, Clarence E. Partch's comments reflect our excitement and mood in those early days:

The publication of *The 1938 Mental Measurements Yearbook of the School of Education, Rutgers University* is likely to prove a landmark of considerable importance in the history of tests and measurements. Heretofore, despite the obvious need of test users for frank evaluations of tests by competent reviewers, few standardized tests have been critically appraised in the professional journals and textbooks for students of education and psychology. Now, for the first time, a large number of frankly evaluative reviews by able test technicians, subject-matter specialists, and psychologists are available to assist test users in making more discriminating selections from among the hundreds of tests on the market.[4]

Except for a few test authors and publishers who objected to unfavorable reviews, *The 1938 Yearbook* (also referred to as *The First Yearbook*) was enthusiastically acclaimed in this country and abroad. It took some time, however, before most of the protesting publishers were able to accept unfavorable test reviews with equanimity.

Before *The 1938 Yearbook* was off the press, we began sending out invitations to review tests for a 1939 yearbook. Unfortunately, because of financing and production problems, we were unable to maintain our annual production schedule. It took us over two years to publish the next volume, *The 1940 Mental Measurements Yearbook*.

Much enlarged and greatly improved over its predecessor, *The 1940 Yearbook* (also referred to as *The Second Yearbook*) has been the prototype for all later yearbooks. In addition to the increased number of tests, reviews, and references, there were many qualitative changes: (*a*) The objectives which have characterized all MMY's were presented in detail for the first time. (*b*) The format was standardized. (*c*) The classification of tests was

4 *The 1938 Mental Measurements Yearbook*, p. xi.

changed from 40 specific categories to 12 broad categories. (*d*) The practice of including very short reviews of 100 words or less was discontinued. (*e*) The review coverage was extended to old tests and to tests previously reviewed as well as new tests. (*f*) The instructions given to reviewers concerning the preparation of their test reviews were presented. (*g*) The reactions of test authors and publishers—most of them objecting strenuously to unfavorable reviews—were reprinted for the first and last time.

In the Preface of *The 1940 Yearbook* we announced that the yearbooks would be published every two years. Because of World War II, however, *The Third Mental Measurements Yearbook* was not published until 1949. Except for its larger size and more thorough preparation, *The Third Yearbook*—like all later yearbooks—is very similar in its coverage, format, indexing, and organization to *The 1940 Yearbook*. There were, however, several improvements: (*a*) The "Classified Index of Tests," an expanded table of contents, was introduced. (*b*) Stars and asterisks were used preceding test titles to indicate, respectively, tests listed in a yearbook for the first time and tests revised or supplemented since last listed. (*c*) Asterisks were used at the end of a reference to indicate that the reference had been examined personally for accuracy and relevance. (*d*) Whenever possible, the abstract in *Psychological Abstracts* was cited for each reference. (*e*) Two improvements were made in the name index. Previously authors of references for specific tests had been indexed merely by citing the test for which the reference appears. After locating the test, one then had to search through the references to find those by that author. The new index eliminated this searching by citing each reference both to the test number and the reference number. Secondly, the index was converted into an "analytic index" in which *"test," "rev," "exc," "bk,"* and *"ref"* were used to indicate whether a citation referred to authorship of a test, review, excerpted review, book, or reference. These five features have been included in all later yearbooks.

In *The Fourth Mental Measurements Yearbook,* published in 1953, our review coverage was extended for the first time to many tests restricted to testing programs administered by organizations such as the College Entrance Examination Board. Six years later, in 1959, *The Fifth Yearbook* was published. Upon the completion of that volume, we were concerned that some cutbacks would be necessary to stem the phenomenal growth of production costs, as well as the ever increasing length of each MMY. As a result, we decided to discontinue specific test bibliographies and almost all reviews of foreign tests. The appreciative reviews *The Fifth Yearbook* received, however, especially those mentioning the value of the specific bibliographies to students of testing, caused us to reconsider. Consequently, despite the expanding literature on specific tests, we decided to continue all features of the earlier volumes. As a result, it took us six years to publish in 1965 *The Sixth Mental Measurements Yearbook,* a 1,751-page volume, approximately one-third larger than the previous yearbook. In addition to its more extensive coverage, *The Sixth Yearbook* presents a comprehensive listing of all tests in print as of mid-1964. The latest yearbook to date, *The Seventh Yearbook,* was published in 1972. This massive two-volume work of 2,032 pages may well be considered the zenith of the MMY's.

Like all other volumes published since 1938, *The Seventh Yearbook* supplements rather than supplants earlier yearbooks. For complete coverage, therefore, a reader must have access to all seven MMY's. A person using only the latest, *The Seventh Yearbook,* will miss a tremendous amount of valuable information in the six earlier volumes. Although the more recent yearbooks—especially the last three—are of greatest value, the third and fourth yearbooks also contain much useful information on many in print tests. Even though the first two yearbooks are mainly of historical interest, they also include some critical information on currently used tests. Our faith in the value of the first four MMY's, published between 1938 and 1953, is attested to by our reissuing of the first and second yearbooks in 1972 and reprinting of the third and fourth in 1974. Consequently, all seven yearbooks are now in print.

EARLIER MMY MONOGRAPHS

It is with amusement and wonder that we look back at some of the dreams of our youth. *The 1940 Mental Measurements Yearbook* was the first yearbook published by my wife and myself. In those depression days, money was scarce but printing was cheap and penny postcards could be used for advertising. Borrowed capital of $3,500 was sufficient to launch us into book publishing. Even before our first book was off the press we were planning to publish not only a new MMY every two years, but also a series of derivative monographs. Our plans were confidently announced in the Preface of *The 1940 Yearbook* thus:

In order to make the material in the yearbooks more easily accessible to individuals who are interested in only a small part of each volume, a new series of monographs is being planned. If the first two or three monographs prove successful, others will eventually be prepared to cover tests in each of the following fields: business education, English and reading, fine arts, foreign languages, health and physical education, home economics, industrial arts, intelligence, mathematics, sciences, social studies, and vocational aptitudes. The first publication in each field will include: a comprehensive bibliography of all standard tests in print in that area; a reprinting, in part or in full, of all reviews of these tests which have appeared in previous yearbooks or in the journal literature; new reviews written especially for the monograph (to be, in turn, reprinted, in part or in full, in the following yearbook); and an extensive list of references on the construction, validation, use, and limitations of the tests. Separates in each field will be issued every four, six, or eight years depending upon the frequency of test publication. These monographs will range in size from fifty to two hundred pages. This new series will make it possible for an individual to purchase, at a nominal cost, every four, six, or eight years a monograph devoted solely to the tests and reviews of most interest to him.[5]

However, the publishing of the MMY's alone, even at intervals of 4 to 8 years, proved to be so time consuming and difficult that initiating the monograph series had to be continually postponed. But the dreams were never abandoned.

In 1968, 27 years after the monograph series was initially announced, the first monograph, *Reading Tests and Reviews* (RTR I), was published. This 542-page volume consists of a comprehensive bibliography of reading tests as of May 1968 and a reprinting of the reading sections of the first six MMY's. A second monograph, *Personality Tests and Reviews* (PTR I), was published two years later. This 1,695-page volume lists all personality tests as of June 1969 and provides a reprinting of the personality sections of the first six MMY's. The preparation of these two monographs turned out to be too costly and time consuming to justify working on monographs in other areas.

5 *The 1940 Mental Measurements Yearbook*, p. xx.

TIP I AND TIP II

In 1961, we published the ninth volume in the MMY series: *Tests in Print: A Comprehensive Bibliography of Tests for Use in Education, Psychology, and Industry*. The objectives and nature of *Tests in Print* (hereafter called *Tests in Print I* or TIP I) are described in its Introduction as follows:

The objectives of *Tests in Print* are threefold: first, to present a comprehensive bibliography of tests—achievement, aptitude, intelligence, personality, and certain sensory-motor skills—published as separates and currently available in English-speaking countries; second, to serve as a classified index and supplement to the volumes of the *Mental Measurements Yearbook* series published to date; third, to give a wider distribution to the excellent recommendations for improving test manuals made by committees of the American Psychological Association, the American Educational Research Association, and the National Council on Measurements Used in Education.[6]

TIP I lists 2,967 tests—2,126 in print and 841 out of print as of early 1961, and also serves as a master index to the contents of the first five MMY's. Originally, we had planned to publish a new edition of TIP shortly after the publication of each new MMY, but poor sales of TIP I caused these plans to be abandoned. *The Sixth Yearbook,* in effect, served as a new edition of *Tests in Print* by referring to the tests in TIP I which were still in print as of mid-1964. Surprisingly, however, sales of the 1961 *Tests in Print* began to pick up after publication of *The Sixth Yearbook* in 1965. This unexpected upturn encouraged us to begin devoting all of our time to the preparation of a new edition of TIP immediately after approving the last proofs for *The Seventh Yearbook.*

Tests in Print II: An Index to Tests, Test Reviews, and the Literature on Specific Tests (TIP II) was published in December 1974. Like the 1961 volume, *Tests in Print II* presents: (*a*) a comprehensive bibliography of all known tests published as separates for use with English-speaking subjects; (*b*) a classified index to the contents of the test sections of the seven *Mental Measurements Yearbooks* published to date; and (*c*) a reprinting of the 1974 APA-AERA-NCME *Standards for Educational and Psychological Tests.*

In addition, TIP II introduces the following new features: (*d*) comprehensive bibliographies through 1971 on the construction, use,

6 *Tests in Print*, p. xv.

and validity of specific tests; (*e*) a classified list of tests which have gone out of print since TIP I; (*f*) a cumulative name index for each test with references; (*g*) a title index covering in print and out of print tests, as well as inverted, series, and superseded titles in the MMY's and monographs; (*h*) an analytic name index covering all authors of tests, reviews, excerpts, and references in the MMY's and monographs; (*i*) a publishers directory with a complete listing of each publisher's test titles; (*j*) a classified scanning index which describes the population for which each test is intended; (*k*) identification of foreign tests and journals by presenting the country of origin in brackets immediately after a test entry or journal title; (*l*) inclusions of factual statements implying criticism such as "1971 tests identical with tests copyrighted 1961 except for format," and "no manual"; (*m*) listing of test titles at the foot of each page to permit immediate identification of pages consisting only of references or names; and (*n*) directions on how to use the book and an expanded table of contents printed on the endpages to greatly facilitate its use.

TIP II contains 2,467 in print test entries, 16.0 percent more than in TIP I. Table 1 presents a breakdown of the number of tests and new references in TIP II by classification. Personality—the area in which we know the least about testing—has, as it did in 1961, the greatest number of tests. Although the percentage of personality tests is 17.9, 44.9 percent of the TIP II references are for personality tests. Three categories—intelligence, personality, and

TABLE 1
TESTS AND NEW REFERENCES
IN TESTS IN PRINT II

Classification	Tests		References	
	Number	Percent	Number	Percent
Achievement Batteries	50	2.0	438	2.6
English	131	5.3	220	1.3
Fine Arts	35	1.4	229	1.4
Foreign Languages	105	4.3	81	.5
Intelligence	274	11.1	4,039	24.4
Mathematics	168	6.8	166	1.0
Miscellaneous	291	11.8	866	5.2
Multi-Aptitude	26	1.1	235	1.4
Personality	441	17.9	7,443	44.9
Reading	248	10.1	837	5.1
Science	97	3.9	72	.4
Sensory-Motor	62	2.5	382	2.3
Social Studies	85	3.4	49	.3
Speech and Hearing	79	3.2	216	1.3
Vocations	375	15.2	1,301	7.8
Total	2,467	100.0	16,574	99.9

vocations—make up 44.2 percent of tests and 77.1 percent of the references in TIP II.

VOCATIONAL TESTS AND REVIEWS

This monograph consists of the business education, multi-aptitude, and vocations sections of the seven *Mental Measurements Yearbooks* (1938–72) and *Tests in Print II* (December 1974). In addition to the 96-page reprint from TIP II and the 905-page section of reprints from the seven MMY's, *Vocational Tests and Reviews* (VTR) includes a publishers directory, title index, name index, and a vocations scanning index. The TIP II scanning index is reprinted in full also.

TIP II TESTS REPRINT

The section of this volume reprinted from *Tests in Print II*, TIP II Tests, contains a bibliography of in print vocational tests, references for specific tests, cumulative name indexes for specific tests having references, and lists of tests which have gone out of print since appearing in TIP I. (The out of print tests are listed alphabetically following each subsection: Business Education, Multi-Aptitude Batteries, General, Clerical, Interests, Manual Dexterity, Mechanical Ability, Miscellaneous, Selection and Rating Forms, and the 14 subdivisions under Specific Occupations.) The first three of these categories will be described in more detail.

VOCATIONAL TESTS

The TIP II reprint section lists 429 tests in print as of early 1974—19.2 percent more tests than were listed 14 years ago in TIP I (Table 2). The four categories with the most tests follow: Specific Vocations, 155 tests (36.1 percent); Clerical and Business Education, 78 tests (18.2 percent); Interests, 54 tests (12.6 percent); and Mechanical Ability, 36 tests (8.4 percent). Forty-seven tests (11.0 percent) are new and 103 (24.0 percent) have been revised or supplemented since the 7th MMY. Over half (52.7 percent) are new since the 1961 *Tests in Print*.

Unlike the long test entries in the *Mental Measurements Yearbooks,* the TIP II entries in this volume are short entries supplying the following information:

a) TITLE. Test titles are printed in boldface type. Secondary or series titles are set off from main titles by a colon. Titles are always presented exactly as reported in the test materials. Stars precede titles of tests listed for the first time in TIP II; asterisks precede titles of tests which have been revised or supplemented since last listed.

b) TEST POPULATION. The grade, chronological age, or semester range, or the employment category is usually given. Commas are used to indicate separate grade levels. "Grades 1.5–2.5, 2–3, 4–12, 13–17" means that there are four test booklets: a booklet for the middle of the first grade through the middle of the second grade, a booklet for the beginning of the second grade through the end of the third grade, a booklet for grades 4 through 12 inclusive, and a booklet for undergraduate and graduate students in colleges and universities. "First, second semester" means that there are two test booklets: one covering the work of the first semester, the other covering the work of the second semester. "1, 2 semesters" indicates that the second booklet covers the work of the two semesters. "Ages 10-2 to 11-11" means ages 10 years 2 months to 11 years 11 months and "Grades 4-6 to 5-9" means the sixth month in the fourth grade through the ninth month in the fifth grade. "High school and college" denotes a single test booklet for both levels; "High school, college" denotes two test booklets, one for high school and one for college.

c) COPYRIGHT DATE. The range of copyright dates (or publication dates if not copyrighted) includes the various forms, accessories, and editions of a test. When the publication date differs from the copyright date, both dates are given; e.g., "1971, c1965–68" means that the test materials were copyrighted between 1965 and 1968 but were not published until 1971. Publication or copyright dates enclosed in brackets do not appear on the test materials but were obtained from other sources.

d) ACRONYM. An acronym is given for many tests. Following the alphabetical sequence of test titles in the Index of Titles, there is an alphabetical listing of acronyms for tests with 10 or more references.

e) SPECIAL COMMENTS. Some entries contain special notations, such as: "for research use only"; "revision of the *ABC Test*"; "tests administered monthly at centers throughout the United States"; "subtests available as separates"; and "verbal cre-

TABLE 2

IN PRINT VOCATIONAL TESTS IN TIP II AND TIP I

Classification	TIP II		TIP I	
	Number	Percent	Number	Percent
General	17	4.0	9	2.5
Clerical and Business Education [1]	78	18.2	80	22.2
Interests	54	12.6	41	11.4
Manual Dexterity	15	3.5	16	4.4
Mechanical Ability	36	8.4	40	11.1
Miscellaneous	20	4.7	23	6.4
Multi-Aptitude	26	6.1	20	5.6
Selection and Rating Forms	28	6.5	18	5.0
Specific Vocations	155	36.1	113	31.4
Total	429	100.1	360	100.0

[1] Although listed separately in the reprint sections of this monograph, "Clerical" and "Business Education" have been combined in this table.

ativity." "For research use only" should be interpreted to mean that the *only* use of the test should be in research designed to assess its usefulness; contrary to what the implications seem to be, "for research use only" does not mean that a test has any use, whatsoever, as a research instrument. Tests used in research studies should have demonstrated validity before being selected as research tools. A statement such as "verbal creativity" is intended to further describe what the test claims to measure.

f) PART SCORES. The number and description of part scores is presented.

g) FACTUAL STATEMENTS IMPLYING CRITICISM. Some of the test entries include factual statements which imply criticism of the test, such as "1970 test identical with test copyrighted 1960" and "no manual."

h) AUTHOR. For most tests, all authors are reported. In the case of tests which appear in a new form each year, only authors of the most recent forms are listed. Names are reported exactly as printed on test materials. Names of editors are generally not reported.

i) PUBLISHER. The name of the publisher or distributor is reported for each test. Foreign publishers are identified by listing the country in brackets immediately following the name of the publisher. The Publishers Directory and Index must be consulted for a publisher's address.

j) FOREIGN ADAPTATIONS. Revisions and adaptations of tests for foreign use are listed in parentheses following the description of the original edition.

k) CLOSING ASTERISK. An asterisk following the publisher's name indicates that the entry was prepared from a first-hand examination of the test materials.

l) SUBLISTINGS. Levels, editions, subtests, or parts of a test which are available in separate booklets are sometimes presented as sublistings with titles set in small capitals. Sub-sublistings are indented with titles set in italic type.

m) CROSS REFERENCES. Except for tests being listed for the first time, a test entry includes a second paragraph with cross references to relevant material which may be found in the MMY reprint sections in this volume, or, in rare instances, the material in other sections of the MMY's. These cross references may be to "additional information" reported in longer entries, or to reviews, excerpts, and references for specific tests.

REFERENCES

The specific test bibliographies in this monograph contain 6,652 references on the construction, use, and validity of specific tests—6,262 (94.1 percent) of these references for tests currently in print (Table 3). Thirty-one percent of the references for in print tests are for the last six years reported on, 1966–71.

Table 3 presents reference counts for the 37 tests currently in print having 25 or more references. The *Strong Vocational Interest Blank for Men,* first published in 1927, leads with 1,231 references—42.0 percent more than its nearest competitor, the *Kuder Preference Record—Vocational.* The five tests with more than 300 references, responsible for 51.8 percent of the references for all in print tests, are: *Strong Vocational Interest Blank for Men,*

1,231 references; *Kuder Preference Record— Vocational,* 867; *General Aptitude Test Battery,* 447; *SRA Primary Mental Abilities,* 368; and *Differential Aptitude Tests,* 331. The 37 tests with 25 or more references account for 86.5 percent of all references for in print vocational tests.

Current trends in the literature output for specific tests are shown in Table 4. In the three years 1969–71, SVIB for Men generated an average of 74 references per year—nearly three times as many references as its nearest competitor, the GATB. The 16 tests averaging five or more references per year in 1969–71 account for 73.8 percent of the references for all vocational tests during this period. In the last three trienniums for which references are reported, the average number of references per year has increased from 225 in the years 1963–65 to 338 in 1969–71. The current rate is probably 400 or more references per year.

TABLE 3
VOCATIONAL TESTS
WITH 25 OR MORE REFERENCES THROUGH 1971

Test (Rank)	References
Strong Vocational Interest Blank for Men (1)	1,231
Kuder Preference Record—Vocational (2)	867
General Aptitude Test Battery (3)	447
SRA Primary Mental Abilities (4)	368
Differential Aptitude Tests (5)	331
Strong Vocational Interest Blank for Women (6)	201
Revised Minnesota Paper Form Board Test (7)	196
Medical College Admission Test (8)	145
Leader Behavior Description Questionnaire (9)	143
Bennett Mechanical Comprehension Test (10)	139
Minnesota Clerical Test (11)	119
MacQuarrie Test for Mechanical Ability (12)	96
Purdue Pegboard (13)	92
Minnesota Rate of Manipulation Test (14)	71
Occupational Interest Inventory (15)	68
Leader Behavior Description Questionnaire, Form 12 (16)	67
Leadership Opinion Questionnaire (17)	62
O'Connor Finger Dexterity Test (18)	61
Minnesota Vocational Interest Inventory (19)	56
Guilford-Zimmerman Aptitude Survey (21)	51
How Supervise? (21)	51
Minnesota Spatial Relations Test (21)	51
O'Connor Tweezer Dexterity Test (23.5)	45
Work Values Inventory (23.5)	45
Dental Admission Testing Program (25)	44
Law School Admission Test (26)	43
Minnesota Importance Questionnaire (27)	37
Career Maturity Inventory (28)	35
Kuder Occupational Interest Survey (29)	32
Short Employment Tests (30)	31
Geist Picture Interest Inventory (31.5)	30
O'Connor Wiggly Block (31.5)	30
Minnesota Satisfaction Questionnaire (33)	29
American Institute of Certified Public Accountants Testing Programs (34)	28
NLN Pre-Nursing and Guidance Examination (35)	26
Hackman-Gaither Vocational Interest Inventory (36.5)	25
RAD Scales (36.5)	25
Total for the 37 in print tests	5,418
Total for the remaining 392 in print tests	844
Grand total for all in print tests	6,262

TABLE 4
VOCATIONAL TESTS
WITH 15 OR MORE REFERENCES
IN THE TRIENNIUM 1969-71

Test (Rank)	'69-71	'66-68	'63-65
Strong Vocational Interest Blank for Men (1)	222	203	149
General Aptitude Test Battery (2)	78	59	40
Kuder Preference Record—Vocational (3)	57	86	99
Strong Vocational Interest Blank for Women (4)	55	40	15
Leader Behavior Description Questionnaire (5)	54	34	22
Differential Aptitude Tests (6)	50	61	66
SRA Primary Mental Abilities (7)	42	45	38
Leader Behavior Description Questionnaire, Form 12 (8)	28	19	8
Leadership Opinion Questionnaire (9)	26	14	11
Medical College Admission Test (10)	25	31	33
Kuder Occupational Interest Survey (11)	21	10	1
Purdue Pegboard (12)	20	17	5
Minnesota Satisfaction Questionnaire (13)	19	9	1
Minnesota Importance Questionnaire (14)	18	14	5
Career Maturity Inventory (15)	17	11	6
Work Values Inventory (16)	16	14	8
Total for the 16 in print tests	748	667	507
Total for the remaining 413 in print tests	265	243	167
Grand total for all in print tests	1,013	910	674

These specific test bibliographies cover not only the literature of the English-speaking world, but also the literature in English published in non-English-speaking countries. Our goal has been to include all published material —articles, books, chapters, and research monographs—as well as unpublished theses. We do not list as references research reports prepared for internal organizational use, prepublication reports, ERIC material, or abstracts of documents which are reproduced only on receipt of a purchase order (e.g., JSAS manuscripts). Secondary sources (e.g., *Psychological Abstracts*) may provide leads, but if the original publication cannot be located and examined, the reference is not used. We do, however, rely on secondary sources (primarily *Dissertation Abstracts International*) for unpublished theses. Except for doctoral dissertations abstracted in DAI, in recent years all thesis entries have been checked for accuracy by the degree-granting institutions.

References for a given test immediately follow the test entry. They are numbered consecutively for each test as they appear in the first through the seventh MMY and TIP II. References which appeared in earlier volumes are referred to but not repeated; e.g., "96-124. See 5:884" means references 96-124 can be found following test 884 in the section "Fifth MMY Reviews" in this volume.

References are arranged in chronological order by year of publication and alphabetically by authors within years. No references later than 1971 have been included. Supplementary bibliographies will be provided in the forthcoming 8th MMY for those tests which are listed again in that volume; the bibliographies for other tests will be brought up to date in *Tests in Print III,* scheduled for publication after the 8th MMY.

CUMULATIVE NAME INDEXES

A cumulative name index has been provided for every in print test having references to facilitate the search for an author's writings relevant to that test. To simplify indexing, forenames were reduced to initials. Authors not consistent in reporting their names will find their publications listed under two or more citations. On the other hand, a given name may represent two or more persons. In all cases, however, the references present names exactly as they appear in the publication referenced.

MMY REVIEWS REPRINT

This chapter is a reprinting of the business education, multi-aptitude, and vocations sections of the seven *Mental Measurements Yearbooks,* presented in their order of publication: 1st MMY (1938, 12 pages), 2nd MMY (1941, 42 pages), 3rd MMY (1949, 146 pages), 4th MMY (1953, 160 pages), 5th MMY (1959, 146 pages), 6th MMY (1965, 200 pages), and 7th MMY (1972, 199 pages). This chapter brings together in a single well-indexed volume a tremendous amount of information on vocational testing covering the past 50 years and more.

This chapter presents 675 original test reviews written by 278 specialists, 65 excerpted test reviews, and 5,088 references on the construction, use, and validity of specific tests (Table 5). Of the 740 reviews and excerpts, 66.0 percent are for tests currently in print, although not always the most recent editions. Of the 6,652 references in this chapter and the preceding chapter, 94.1 percent are for tests in print.

The contributing reviewers represent a wide range of interests and viewpoints. Every effort was made to select reviewers who would be

TABLE 5

REVIEWS, EXCERPTS, AND REFERENCES
FOR THE 649 VOCATIONAL TESTS
IN THIS VOLUME

Reprint	Tests	Rev's	Exc's	Ref's
TIP II	429			1,564
7th MMY	200	95	22	1,679
6th MMY	224	121	12	941
5th MMY	153	97		978
4th MMY	139	126	3	734
3rd MMY	119	177	16	550
2nd MMY	61	40	8	203
1st MMY	26	19	4	3
Total	649 1	675	65	6,652

1 The total number of different tests in all publications is 649 —429 in print and 220 out of print.

considered highly competent by a sizable group of test users. Our practice of publishing multiple reviews of given tests makes it possible to give representation to differing viewpoints among reviewers. The test reviews in a given yearbook are not limited to new and revised tests; old tests, especially those generating considerable research and writing, are frequently reviewed in successive yearbooks.

In order to make sure that persons invited to review would know what was expected of them, a sheet entitled "Suggestions to MMY Reviewers" was enclosed with each letter of invitation. The suggestions follow:

1. Reviews should be written with the following major objectives in mind:
   a) To provide test users with carefully prepared appraisals of tests for their guidance in selecting and using tests.
   b) To stimulate progress toward higher professional standards in the construction of tests by commending good work, by censuring poor work, and by suggesting improvements.
   c) To impel test authors and publishers to present more detailed information on the construction, validity, reliability, uses, and possible misuses of their tests.
2. Reviews should be concise, the average review running from 600 to 1,200 words in length. The average length of the reviews written by one person generally should not exceed 1,000 words. Except for reviews of achievement batteries, multi-factor batteries, and tests for which a literature review is made, longer reviews should be prepared only with the approval of the Editor.
3. Reviews should be frankly critical, with both strengths and weaknesses pointed out in a judicious manner. Descriptive comments should be kept to the minimum necessary to support the critical portions of the review. Criticism should be as specific as possible; implied criticisms meaningful only to testing specialists should be avoided. Reviews should be written primarily for the rank and file of test users. An indication of the relative importance and value of a test with respect to competing tests should be presented whenever possible. If a reviewer considers a competing test better than the one being reviewed, the competing test should be specifically named.
4. If a test manual gives insufficient, contradictory, or ambiguous information regarding the construction,

validity, and use of a test, reviewers are urged to write directly to authors and publishers for further information. Test authors and publishers should, however, be held responsible for presenting adequate data in test manuals—failure to do so should be pointed out. For comments made by reviewers based upon unpublished information received personally from test authors or publishers, the source of the unpublished information should be clearly indicated.
5. Reviewers will be furnished with the test entries which will precede their reviews. Information presented in the entry should not be repeated in reviews unless needed for evaluative purposes.
6. The use of sideheads is optional with reviewers.
7. Each review should conclude with a paragraph presenting a concise summary of the reviewer's overall evaluation of the test. The summary should be as explicit as possible. Is the test the best of its kind? Is it recommended for use? If other tests are better, which of the competing tests is best?
8. A separate review should be prepared for each test. Each review should begin on a new sheet. The test and forms reviewed should be clearly indicated. Your name, title, position, and address should precede each review, e.g.: John Doe, Professor of Education and Psychology, University of Maryland, College Park, Maryland. The review should begin a new paragraph immediately after the address.
9. All reviews should be typed double spaced and in triplicate. Two copies of each review should be submitted to the Editor; one copy should be retained by the reviewer.
10. If for any reason a reviewer thinks he is not in a position to write a frankly critical review in a scholarly and unbiased manner, he should request the Editor to substitute other tests for review.
11. Reviewers may not invite others to collaborate with them in writing reviews unless permission is secured from the Editor.
12. Most tests will be reviewed by two or more persons in order to secure better representation of various viewpoints. Noncritical content which excessively overlaps similar materials presented by another reviewer may be deleted. Reviews will be carefully edited, but no important changes will be made without the consent of the reviewer. Galley proofs (unaccompanied by copy) will be submitted to reviewers for checking.
13. The Editor reserves the right to reject any review which does not meet the minimum standards of the MMY series.
14. Each reviewer will receive a complimentary copy of *The Seventh Mental Measurements Yearbook*.

The long test entries in the section Seventh MMY Reviews contain all the information in the short TIP II entries plus the following:

a) INDIVIDUAL OR GROUP TEST. All tests are group tests unless otherwise indicated.
b) FORMS, PARTS, AND LEVELS. All available forms, parts, and levels are listed with copyright dates.
c) PAGES. The number of pages on which print occurs is reported for test booklets, manuals, technical reports, profiles, and other nonapparatus accessories.
d) FACTUAL STATEMENTS IMPLYING CRITICISM. Much more so than short entries, the long entries include factual statements implying criticism of the following type: "no data on reliability," "no data on validity," "no norms," "norms for grade 5 only," "no description of the normative population," "no norms for difference scores," "test copyrighted in 1970 identical with test copyrighted in 1960," and "statistical data based on earlier forms."
e) MACHINE SCORABLE ANSWER SHEETS. All types of

machine scorable answer sheets available for use with a specific test are reported: Digitek (OpScan Test Scoring and Document Scanning System), IBM 805 (IBM Test Scoring Machine), IBM 1230 (IBM Optical Mark Reader), MRC (MRC Scoring and Reporting Service), NCS (NCS Scoring and Reporting Service), and NCS Sentry/70, and a few other answer sheets less widely used.

f) COST. Price information is reported for test packages (usually 20 to 35 tests), answer sheets, all other accessories, and specimen sets. The statement "$5.20 per 35 tests" means that all accessories are included unless separate prices are given for accessories. The statement also means 35 tests of one level, one edition, or one part unless stated otherwise. Quantity discounts and special discounts are not reported. Specimen set prices include copies of each level and part—but not all forms—unless otherwise indicated. Since 1970 prices are reported, the latest catalog of a test publisher should be consulted for current prices.

g) SCORING AND REPORTING SERVICES. Scoring and reporting services provided by publishers are reported along with information on costs. Special computerized scoring and interpretation services are sometimes given in separate entries immediately following the test entry.

h) TIME. The number of minutes of actual working time allowed examinees and the approximate length of time needed for administering a test are provided whenever obtainable. The latter figure is always enclosed in parentheses. Thus, "50(60) minutes" indicates that the examinees are allowed 50 minutes of working time and that a total of 60 minutes is needed to administer the test. When the time necessary to administer a test has been obtained through correspondence with the test publisher or author, the time is enclosed in brackets.

RUNNING HEADS AND FEET

To use this volume most efficiently, it is important to take advantage of the information given at the top and bottom of each page in the test and review sections. Both test entry and page numbers are given in the running heads. However, since all citations in the indexes and cross references are to entry numbers, these numbers, found next to the outside margins on facing pages, can be used as guide numbers in locating a particular test. The entry number on the left-hand page corresponds to the test embodying the first line of type on that page; the entry number on the right-hand page refers to the test containing the last line of type on that page. The test titles corresponding to these guide numbers are given in the running feet at the bottom of the page. Thus, the reader can quickly identify the first and last test discussed on each pair of facing pages.

The first reprint section, from *Tests in Print II*, has guide numbers in the range 775 to 2476, the second reprint section, from the seven MMY's, has the successive ranges: 1 :935

to 1 :1181, 2 :1476 to 2 :1684, 3 :367 to 3 :705, 4 :443 to 4 :830, 5 :502 to 5 :957, 6 :28 to 6 :1200, and 7 :552 to 7 :1155. The digit preceding the colon in the guide number corresponds to the number of the yearbook being reprinted. The numbers following the colon are the test entry numbers within that yearbook.

TIP II SCANNING INDEX

The complete TIP II Scanning Index, a classified listing of all tests in TIP II, has been reprinted to provide readers with an overview of tests available in areas other than vocations. The 2,467 tests are divided into the categories delineated in Table 1 of this Introduction. Since the vocations sections of the TIP II Scanning Index will be of most interest to readers of this monograph, we have reprinted that section (entitled Vocations Scanning Index) at the end of this volume for convenient reference. This end-of-the-book index is especially useful for locating tests suitable for a given population, since descriptions of these populations are reported immediately following the test titles.

PUBLISHERS DIRECTORY AND INDEX

Instead of giving only the entry numbers of the tests of a given publisher, as in our earlier publications, this Publishers Directory and Index gives both test titles and entry numbers. Stars denote the 32 publishers with test catalogs listing 10 or more tests (not necessarily vocations tests). Tests not originating in the country of publication are identified by listing in brackets the country in which the test was originally prepared and published.

All addresses have been checked by the publishers (except for one publisher who did not reply to our four requests for verification), and are accurate through 1973. However, with such a large number of publishers (including many author-publishers), some address changes must be expected.

The directory lists 116 publishers of vocational tests, 38.8 percent of which publish only one vocational test. Their geographical distribution covers five foreign countries: Great Britain, 7 publishers; Canada, 2; South Africa, 2; Australia, 1; and India, 1.

The ten publishers with 10 or more vocational

tests are: Psychological Corporation, 34 tests; Science Research Associates, Inc., 28; Psychometric Affiliates, 21; NFER Publishing Co. Ltd., 16; Instructional Materials Laboratory, Ohio State University, 14; Martin M. Bruce, Publishers, 13; College Entrance Examination Board, 12; McCann Associates, 11; National Institute for Personnel Research, 11; and Richardson, Bellows, Henry & Co., 10.

INDEX OF TITLES

This cumulative title index includes vocational tests in print as separates as of February 1, 1974, and out of print or status unknown vocational tests.

Citations are to test entry numbers, not to pages. Numbers without colons refer to in print tests listed in the first reprint section (TIP II Tests) in this volume; numbers with colons refer to tests out of print, status unknown, or reclassified since last listed with vocational tests. Unless preceded by the word *"consult,"* all numbers containing colons refer to tests in this volume. To obtain the latest information on a test no longer classified with vocational tests, the reader is directed to consult the last yearbook in which the test appeared. For example, "Minnesota Teacher Attitude Inventory, 4:801; reclassified, *consult* T2:868" indicates that the test was listed as a vocational test in the *Fourth Yearbook* but has been reclassified and for the latest information available, the reader must consult test 868 in *Tests in Print II*. Superseded titles are listed with cross references to the current title. Tests which are part of a series are listed under their individual titles and also their series titles.

INDEX OF NAMES

This cumulative index is an analytical index distinguishing between authorship of a test, test review, excerpted review, or reference dealing with a specific test. Furthermore, the index indicates whether the relevant test is in print or out of print. Numbers with colons refer to out of print or status unknown tests. Unless preceded by the word "consult," all numbers containing colons refer to tests in this volume.

Forenames have been reduced to initials to lower the cost of indexing. Since authors are not always consistent in how they list their names, two or more listings may refer to the same person. On the other hand, the use of initials sometimes results in one name representing two or more persons. Reference to the cited material in the text will resolve these difficulties in almost all cases.

Except for test authors, the use of the Index of Names is a two-step process. For example, if the name index reports *"rev, 2214"* for D. E. Super, the reader must look at the cross reference for test 2214 in the TIP II Tests section of this volume to learn where Super's review may be found in the yearbook reprints. Similarly, if the name index reports *"ref, 1069"* for G. K. Bennett, the reader must look at the Cumulative Name Index for test 1069 to learn where, in this volume, Bennett's reference or references on that test may be found. The Cumulative Name Index for test 1069 indicates that Bennett is the author of 10 references for this test, each cited by number, so the reader can quickly locate them in the list of references under the test entry.

VOCATIONAL
TESTS AND REVIEWS

BUSINESS EDUCATION – TIP II

[775]
Bookkeeping: Achievement Examinations for

Secondary Schools. High school; 1951–54; Form 4 ('54) of a series of tests, currently (1973) entitled

Bookkeeping: Minnesota High School Achievement Examinations (see 776), issued annually for May testing; Helen Haberman; Bobbs-Merrill Co., Inc. *

For additional information concerning later and earlier forms, see 776, 7:553, 6:35 (1 review), 5:502, and 5:504 (1 review).

[776]

*Bookkeeping: Minnesota High School Achievement Examinations. High school; 1951-70; a new, revised, or previously inactive form issued each May; Achievement Examinations for Secondary Schools, High School Achievement Examinations, and Midwest High School Achievement Examinations have also been used as series titles; Form GJ Rev ('70) used in 1970 and 1973 testings; Form 4 ('54), entitled *Bookkeeping: Achievement Examinations for Secondary Schools* (see 775), is available from another publisher; edited by V. L. Lohmann; American Guidance Service, Inc. *

For additional information concerning out of print and inactive forms, see 7:553 and 5:502; for a review by Harold L. Royer of Form F (1963), see 6:35; for a review by I. David Satlow of Form A (1955) and Form B (1952), see 5:504.

[777]

*Bookkeeping Test: National Business Entrance Tests. Grades 11-16 and adults; 1938-72; National Business Education Association. * For the complete battery entry, see 786.

For additional information, see 6:36; for reviews by Harvey A. Andruss and Ray G. Price of an earlier form, see 3:368. For reviews of the complete battery, see 6:33 (1 review), 5:515 (3 reviews), and 3:396 (1 review).

[778]

*Business Fundamentals and General Information Test: National Business Entrance Tests. Grades 11-16 and adults; 1938-72; National Business Education Association. * For the complete battery entry, see 786.

For additional information, see 6:30; for reviews by Vera M. Amerson and C. C. Upshall of an earlier form, see 3:369. For reviews of the complete battery, see 6:33 (1 review), 5:515 (3 reviews), and 3:396 (1 review).

[779]

*Business Relations and Occupations: Achievement Examinations for Secondary Schools. High school; 1951-61; a new, revised, or previously inactive form was issued each May from 1951 through 1961; Form 4 ('54) is the only form in print; High School Achievement Examinations and Midwest High School Achievement Examinations have also been used as series titles; A. Donald Beattie; Bobbs-Merrill Co., Inc. *

For additional information concerning later and earlier forms, see 5:509-10.

[780]

Clerical Aptitude Test: Acorn National Aptitude Tests. Grades 7-16 and adults; 1943-50; 4 scores: business practice, number checking, date-name-address checking, total; 1950 test materials identical with those copyrighted 1943; Andrew Kobal, J. Wayne Wrightstone, and Karl R. Kunze; Psychometric Affiliates. *

For additional information, see 5:847 (1 reference); for reviews by Marion A. Bills, Donald G. Paterson, Henry Weitz, and E. F. Wonderlic, see 3:623.

REFERENCES THROUGH 1971

1. See 5:847.

CUMULATIVE NAME INDEX

Bair, J. T.: 1
Bills, M. A.: *rev*, 3:623
Paterson, D. G.: *rev*, 3:623
Weitz, H.: *rev*, 3:623
Wonderlic, E. F.: *rev*, 3:623

[781]

*Clerical Speed and Accuracy: Differential Aptitude Tests. Grades 8-12 and adults; 1947-73; 2 editions; George K. Bennett, Harold G. Seashore, and Alexander G. Wesman; Psychological Corporation. * For the complete battery entry, see 1069.

a) FORM A. 1947-59. *Out of print.*

b) FORM T. 1947-73; 1972 test (Part I) identical with tests copyrighted 1947 and 1961 (i.e., Forms A, B, L, and M).

For reviews of the complete battery, see 7:673 (1 review, 1 excerpt), 6:767 (2 reviews), 5:605 (2 reviews), 4:711 (3 reviews), and 3:620 (1 excerpt).

REFERENCES THROUGH 1971

1. "Results of the Space Relations, Mechanical Reasoning, and Clerical Speed and Accuracy Tests of the Differential Aptitude Test Battery in Six Public Schools." *Ed Rec B* 58:79-84 F '52. * (*PA* 26:7240)
2. GARNER, GLENN LAMAR. *High School Freshmen DAT Clerical Speed and Accuracy Scores and English Grades as Predictors of Success in Business Courses.* Master's thesis, Millersville State College (Millersville, Pa.), 1969.

CUMULATIVE NAME INDEX

Garner, G. L.: 2

[781A]

Clerical Tests FG and 2. Ages 12-0 to 13-11; 1952-54; 2 tests; published for the National Foundation for Educational Research in England and Wales; Ginn & Co. Ltd. [England]. *

a) CLERICAL TEST FG. Ages 12-0 to 13-11; 1952-53; formerly called *Clerical Test 1*; M. K. B. Richards.

b) CLERICAL TEST 2. Ages 12-3 to 13-1; 1953-54; distribution restricted to directors of education; G. A. V. Morgan.

For additional information, see 5:848.

[782]

Detroit Clerical Aptitudes Examination. Grades 9-12; 1937-44; 12 scores: motor (circles, classification, total), visual imagery (likenesses and differences, disarranged pictures, total), trade information, educational (handwriting, arithmetic, alphabetizing, total), total; includes *Ayres Measuring Scale for Handwriting*; Harry J. Baker and Paul H. Voelker; Bobbs-Merrill Co., Inc. *

For additional information and a review by E. F. Wonderlic, see 3:626 (1 reference); for reviews by Irving Lorge and M. W. Richardson of an earlier edition, see 2:1655.

REFERENCES THROUGH 1971

1. See 3:626.
2. GUINN, MARY PAULINE. *Aids for the Prognosis of Success in Typewriting.* Master's thesis, Kansas State Teachers College (Pittsburg, Kan.), 1948.
3. BAIR, JOHN T. "Factor Analysis of Clerical Aptitude Tests." *J Appl Psychol* 35:245-9 Ag '51. * (*PA* 26:3067)
4. COOK, FRED SOLOMON. *A Study to Determine the Predictive Value of the Detroit Clerical Aptitudes Examination.* Doctor's thesis, University of Michigan (Ann Arbor, Mich.), 1953. (*DA* 13:333)

CUMULATIVE NAME INDEX

Anderson, R. N.: 1
Bair, J. T.: 3
Cook, F. S.: 4
Guinn, M. P.: 2
Lorge, I.: *rev*, 2:1655
Richardson, M. W.: *rev*, 2:1655
Wonderlic, E. F.: *rev*, 3:626

[783]

*General Office Clerical Test: National Business Entrance Tests. Grades 11-16 and adults; 1948-72; National Business Education Association. * For the complete battery entry, see 786.

For additional information, see 6:32 (1 reference). For reviews of the complete battery, see 6:33 (1 review), 5:515 (3 reviews), and 3:396 (1 review).

REFERENCES THROUGH 1971
1. See 6:32.

CUMULATIVE NAME INDEX
Hamilton, H. A.: 1

[784]

Hiett Simplified Shorthand Test (Gregg). 1, 2 semesters high school; 1951–63; an identical edition, entitled *Hiett Diamond Jubilee Shorthand Test* ('63), is available without a manual; Victor C. Hiett and H. E. Schrammel (manual); Bureau of Educational Measurements. *

For additional information, see 7:555; for a review by Gale W. Clark, see 5:512.

[785]

***Machine Calculation Test: National Business Entrance Tests.** Grades 11–16 and adults; 1941–72; earlier tests called *Key-Driven Calculating Machine Ability Test;* National Business Education Association. * For the complete battery entry, see 786.

For additional information, see 6:39; for a review by Dorothy C. Adkins of earlier forms, see 5:514; for a review by Elizabeth Fehrer, see 3:384. For reviews of the complete battery, see 6:33 (1 review), 5:515 (3 reviews), and 3:396 (1 review).

[786]

***National Business Entrance Tests.** Grades 11–16 and adults; 1938–72; formerly called *National Clerical Ability Tests* and *United-NOMA Business Entrance Tests;* subtests available as separates; 3 series; National Business Education Association. *
a) [GENERAL TESTING SERIES (SERIES 2500).] 1938–72; 6 tests.
   1) *Business Fundamentals and General Information Test.* 1938–72.
   2) *Bookkeeping Test.* 1938–72.
   3) *General Office Clerical Test.* 1948–72.
   4) *Machine Calculation Test.* 1941–72.
   5) *Stenographic Test.* 1938–72.
   6) *Typewriting Test.* 1941–72.
b) [SHORT FORM SERIES.] 1938–55; 2 tests. *Out of print.*
   1) *Stenographic Test.* 1938–55.
   2) *Typewriting Test.* 1941–55.
c) [OFFICIAL TESTING SERIES (SERIES 2000 AND 2100).] 1938–65; administered only at NBET Centers which may be established in any community; 1965 tests identical with tests copyrighted 1959 (2000 series) and 1960 (2100 series) except for deletion of authorship; 6 tests.
   1) *Business Fundamentals and General Information Test.* 1938–65.
   2) *Bookkeeping Test.* 1938–65.
   3) *General Office Clerical Test.* 1948–65.
   4) *Machine Calculation Test.* 1941–65.
   5) *Stenographic Test.* 1938–65.
   6) *Typewriting Test.* 1941–65.
For additional information and a review by Melvin R. Marks, see 6:33 (5 references); for reviews by Edward N. Hay, Jacob S. Orleans, and Wimburn L. Wallace of earlier forms, see 5:515; see also 4:453 (1 reference); for a review by Paul S. Lomax, see 3:396; see also 2:1476 (9 references). For a review of the typewriting test, see 6:55; earlier editions of the machine calculation test, see 5:514 (1 review) and 3:384 (1 review); the stenographic test, see 5:522 (1 review) and 3:391 (2 reviews); the typewriting test, see 5:526

(1 review) and 3:394 (2 reviews); the bookkeeping test, see 3:368 (2 reviews); the business fundamentals test, see 3:369 (2 reviews); and the clerical test, see 3:379 (2 reviews).

REFERENCES THROUGH 1971
1–9. See 2:1476.
10. See 4:453.
11–16. See 6:33.

CUMULATIVE NAME INDEX
Baird, M. W.: 15
Brigham, L. H.: 2
Cowan, H. E.: 3
Crissy, W. J.: 11
Eastern Commercial Teachers' Association: 1
Ford, G. C.: 7
Hay, E. N.: *rev,* 5:515
Hittler, G. M.: 8
Joint Committee on Tests: 4
Liles, P.: 13
Lomax, P. S.: *rev,* 3:396
Marks, M. R.: *rev,* 6:33
Nelson, J. H.: 10, 12
Orleans, J. S.: *rev,* 5:515
Slaughter, R. E.: 14
Wallace, W. L.: *rev,* 5:515
Wantman, M. J.: 11

[787]

***National Teacher Examinations: Business Education.** College seniors and teachers; 1956–73; an inactive form (1966) entitled *Teacher Education Examination Program: Business Education* is available to colleges for local administration; another inactive form (1968) entitled *Specialty Examinations: Business Education* is available to school systems for local use as part of the program entitled *School Personnel Research and Evaluation Services;* Educational Testing Service. * For the testing program entry, see 869.

For additional information and a review by Ray G. Price of an earlier form, see 7:556. For reviews of the testing program, see 7:582 (2 reviews), 6:700 (1 review), 5:538 (3 reviews), and 4:802 (1 review).

[788]

★**Office Information and Skills Test: Content Evaluation Series.** High school; 1971–72; 4 scores: office information, error location and correction, typewriting, transcription; G. Elizabeth Ripka; Houghton Mifflin Co. *

[789]

Reicherter-Sanders Typewriting I and II. 1, 2 semesters high school; 1962–64; first published 1962–63 in the Every Pupil Scholarship Test series; Richard F. Reicherter and M. W. Sanders; Bureau of Educational Measurements. *

For additional information and a review by Lawrence W. Erickson, see 7:557.

[790]

Russell-Sanders Bookkeeping Test. 1, 2 semesters high school; 1962–64; first published 1962–63 in the Every Pupil Scholarship Test series; Raymond B. Russell and M. W. Sanders; Bureau of Educational Measurements. *

For additional information and a review by Bernard H. Newman, see 7:558.

[791]

SRA Clerical Aptitudes. Grades 9–12 and adults; 1947–50; 4 scores: office vocabulary, office arithmetic, office checking, total; Richardson, Bellows, Henry & Co., Inc.; Science Research Associates, Inc. *

For additional information and reviews by Edward N. Hay and G. A. Satter, see 4:732.

REFERENCES THROUGH 1971
1. SEASHORE, HAROLD G. "Validation of Clerical Testing in Banks." *Personnel Psychol* 6:45–56 sp '53. * (*PA* 28:1670)
2. HAY, EDWARD N. "Comparative Validities in Clerical Testing." *J Appl Psychol* 38:299–301 O '54. * (*PA* 29:6351)

CUMULATIVE NAME INDEX
Hay, E. N.: 2; *rev,* 4:732
Satter, G. A.: *rev,* 4:732
Seashore, H. G.: 1

SRA Clerical Aptitudes

[792]

SRA Typing Skills. Grades 9–12 and adults; 1947; 2 scores: speed, accuracy; Marion W. Richardson and Ruth A. Pedersen; Science Research Associates, Inc. *

For additional information and reviews by Lawrence W. Erickson and Jacob S. Orleans, see 6:51 (2 references).

REFERENCES THROUGH 1971

1–2. See 6:51.
3. THUMIN, FRED J., AND BOERNKE, CAROL. "Ability Scores as Related to Age Among Female Job Applicants." *J Gerontol* 21:369–71 Jl '66. *

CUMULATIVE NAME INDEX

Ash, P.: 2
Boernke, C.: 3
Erickson, L. W.: *rev,* 6:51
Orleans, J. S.: *rev,* 6:51
Skula, M.: 1
Spillane, R. F.: 1
Thumin, F. J.: 3

[793]

Shorthand Aptitude Test. High school; 1953–54; V. Brownless, S. Dunn, and the Queensland Department of Public Instruction; Australian Council for Educational Research [Australia]. *

For additional information and a review by James Lumsden, see 5:520.

[794]

Stenographic Aptitude Test. Grades 9–16; 1939–46; 3 scores: transcription, spelling, total; George K. Bennett; Psychological Corporation. *

For additional information and reviews by Philip H. DuBois and Edward A. Rundquist, see 3:390 (1 reference); see also 2:1677 (1 reference).

REFERENCES THROUGH 1971

1. See 2:1677.
2. See 3:390.
3. SEASHORE, HAROLD G. "Psychological Testing With Phonograph Recordings." Abstract. *Am Psychologist* 1:248 Jl '46. * (*PA* 20:3932, title only)
4. WIGHTWICK, BEATRICE. *The Effect of Retesting on the Predictive Power of Aptitude Tests.* Doctor's thesis, New York University (New York, N.Y.), 1949.

CUMULATIVE NAME INDEX

Barrett, D. M.: 2
Bennett, G. K.: 1
DuBois, P. H.: *rev,* 3:390
Rundquist, E. A.: *rev,* 3:390
Seashore, H. G.: 3
Wightwick, B.: 4

[795]

*Stenographic Test: National Business Entrance Tests. Grades 11–16 and adults; 1938–72; earlier tests called *Stenographic Ability Tests;* National Business Education Association. * For the complete battery entry, see 786.

For additional information, see 6:47 (1 reference); for a review by Edward B. Greene of earlier forms, see 5:522; for reviews by Ann Brewington and Elizabeth Fehrer, see 3:391. For reviews of the complete battery, see 6:33 (1 review), 5:515 (3 reviews), and 3:396 (1 review).

REFERENCES THROUGH 1971

1. See 6:47.
2. NATALE, GLORIA MARIE. *Measurement Aspects of the Stenographic and Typewriting Tests of the National Business Entrance Tests.* Doctor's thesis, Columbia University (New York, N.Y.), 1963. (*DA* 24:1887)
3. ROTHWELL, WADE BROWNELL. *The Relationship of Certain Predictive Factors Including Personality Traits to Job Success of Graduates of Stenographic and Secretarial Programs of Public Supported Technical Institutes and Junior Colleges in the State of Alabama.* Doctor's thesis, Auburn University (Auburn, Ala.), 1970. (*DAI* 31:4055A)
4. REID JAYNE. *The Relationship of Selected Aspects of Attitude, Personality, and Achievement to the Post-High School Employment of Senior Stenographic Students.* Doctor's thesis, University of Cincinnati (Cincinnati, Ohio), 1971. (*DAI* 32:3570A)

CUMULATIVE NAME INDEX

Brewington, A.: *rev,* 3:391
Fehrer, E.: *rev,* 3:391
Greene, E. B.: *rev,* 5:522
Natale, G. M.: 2
Nelson, J. H.: 1
Reid, J.: 4
Rothwell, W. B.: 3

[796]

*The Tapping Test: A Predictor of Typing and Other Tapping Operations. High school; 1959–70; John C. Flanagan, Grace Fivars (manual), Shirley A. Tuska (manual), and Carol F. Hershey (manual); Psychometric Techniques Associates. *

For additional information and reviews by Ray G. Price and Henry Weitz, see 6:52 (2 references).

REFERENCES THROUGH 1971

1–2. See 6:52.
3. FLANAGAN, JOHN C., AND FIVARS, GRACE. "Predicting Success in Typewriting." *Balance Sheet* 46:7–9 S '64. *
4. FLANAGAN, JOHN C., AND FIVARS, GRACE. "The Tapping Test—A New Tool to Predict Aptitude for Typing." *Delta Pi Epsilon J* 6:33–9 F '64. *
5. WILEY, EDITH S. *An Evaluation of the Effectiveness of the Flanagan Tapping Test as a Predictor of Typing Achievement in Adult Classes.* Master's thesis, California State College (Hayward, Calif.), 1969.

CUMULATIVE NAME INDEX

Banas, P.: 2
Fivars, G.: 1, 3–4
Flanagan, J. C.: 1, 3–4
Kirchner, W. K.: 2
Price, R. G.: *rev,* 6:52
Tuska, S. A.: 1
Weitz, H.: *rev,* 6:52
Wiley, E, S.: 5

[797]

*Teacher Education Examination Program: Business Education. College seniors preparing to teach secondary school; 1957–72; reprinting of inactive 1966 form of *National Teacher Examinations: Business Education;* test available to colleges for local administration; Educational Testing Service. * For the testing program entry, see 898.

For additional information concerning an earlier form, see 6:29. For a review of the testing program, see 5:543. For reference to a review of the *National Teacher Examinations: Business Education,* see 787.

[798]

Turse Shorthand Aptitude Test. Grades 8 and over; 1937–40; 8 scores: stroking, spelling, phonetic association, symbol transcription, word discrimination, dictation, word sense, total; Paul L. Turse; Harcourt Brace Jovanovich, Inc. *

For additional information and a review by Leslie M. Haynes, see 4:460 (5 references); for a review by Philip H. DuBois, see 3:393.

REFERENCES THROUGH 1971

1–5. See 4:460.
6. HOLMES, JACK A. "Factors Underlying Major Reading Disabilities at the College Level." *Genetic Psychol Monogr* 49:3–95 F '54. * (*PA* 28:8982)
7. STRICKLAND, ESTHER HEDGES. *Criteria for Predicting Success in Shorthand at East High School, Columbus, Ohio.* Master's thesis, Ohio State University (Columbus, Ohio), 1957.
8. BENDER, W. R. G., AND LOVELESS, H. E. "Validation Studies Involving Successive Classes of Trainee Stenographers." *Personnel Psychol* 11:491–508 w '58. * (*PA* 34:2143)
9. DI BONA, LUCILLE J. "Predicting Success in Shorthand." *J Bus Ed* 35:213–4 F '60. *
10. PAUK, WALTER. "Comparison of the Validities of Selected Test Procedures to Predict Shorthand Success." *Ed & Psychol Meas* 23:831–5 w '63. *
11. PAUK, WALTER. "What's the Best Way to Predict Success in Shorthand?" *Bus Ed World* 43:7–8+ Ap '63. *
12. DAVIS, ROSE ANNE. "Will Half a Turse Do Just as Well?" *Bus Ed World* 46:11–2 Ja '66. *
13. HANSON, ROBERT NELTON. *Visual Stimulus Versus Combined Audio-Visual Stimuli for Out-of-Class Practice in First-Semester College Gregg Shorthand.* Doctor's thesis, University of North Dakota (Grand Forks, N.D.), 1966. (*DA* 27:3224A)
14. HEEMSTRA, JOYCE J. "Shorthand Prognosis: Can We Be Sure?" *Bus Ed Forum* 20:21+ F '66. *
15. O'CONNELL, MARY MARGARET, AND HOSLER, RUSSEL J. "Predictors of Success in Shorthand." *J Bus Ed* 44:96–8 D '68. *

16. Pehrson, Patricia J. *A Comparison of Student Achievement in Shorthand and Performance on the Turse Test and the ACT Test at Mankato State College.* Master's thesis, Mankato State College (Mankato, Minn.), 1970.

CUMULATIVE NAME INDEX

Barrett, D. M.: 3
Bender, W. R. G.: 8
Davis, R. A.: 12
Department of Educational Research, Ontario College of Education, University of Toronto: 5
Di Bona, L. J.: 9
DuBois, P. H.: *rev,* 3:393
Hanson, R. N.: 13
Haynes, L. M.: *rev,* 4:460
Heemstra, J. J.: 14

Holmes, J. A.: 6
Hosler, R. J.: 4, 15
Loveless, H. E.: 8
O'Connell, M. M.: 15
Ontario Commercial Teacher's Association: 5
Pauk, W.: 10–1
Pehrson, P. J.: 16
Strickland, E. H.: 7
Tuckman, J.: 2
Turse, P. L.: 1

[799]

*Typewriting Test: National Business Entrance Tests. Grades 11–16 and adults; 1941–72; earlier tests called *Typing Ability Test;* National Business Education Association. * For the complete battery entry, see 786.

For additional information and a review by Lawrence W. Erickson, see 6:55 (1 reference); for a review by Clifford E. Jurgensen of earlier forms, see 5:526; for reviews by E. G. Blackstone and Beatrice J. Dvorak, see 3:394. For reviews of the complete battery, see 6:33 (1 review), 5:515 (3 reviews), and 3:396 (1 review).

REFERENCES THROUGH 1971

1. See 6:55.
2. Natale, Gloria Marie. *Measurement Aspects of the Stenographic and Typewriting Tests of the National Business Entrance Tests.* Doctor's thesis, Columbia University (New York, N.Y.), 1963. (*DA* 24:1887)

CUMULATIVE NAME INDEX

Blackstone, E. G.: *rev,* 3:394
Dvorak, B. J.: *rev,* 3:394
Erickson, L. W.: *rev,* 6:55

Jurgensen, C. E.: *rev,* 5:526
Natale, G. M.: 2
Nelson, J. H.: 1

[800]

*The Undergraduate Program Field Tests: Business Test. College; 1969–73; formerly called *The Undergraduate Record Examinations: Business Test;* test available to colleges for local administration; Educational Testing Service. * For the testing program entry, see 1062.

For additional information concerning an earlier form, see 7:1086. For reviews of the testing program, see 7:671 (2 reviews).

[801]

United Students Typewriting Tests, Volume 14. 1, 2, 3, 4 semesters; 1932–58; Committee on Tests, UBEA Research Foundation; National Business Education Association. *

For additional information, see 5:527.

[Out of Print Since TIP I]

Bookkeeping Achievement Test: Business Education Achievement Test Series, 7:552 (2 reviews)
Bookkeeping: Every Pupil Scholarship Test, 6:34
Byers' First-Year Shorthand Aptitude Tests, 6:41 (1 review, 1 reference)
Commercial Law: Every Pupil Scholarship Test, 6:38
First-Year Bookkeeping: Every Pupil Test, 6:37
First-Year Shorthand: Every Pupil Test, 6:42
First-Year Typewriting: Every Pupil Test, 6:49
General Business Achievement Test: Business Education Achievement Test Series, 7:554 (2 reviews)
General Business: Every Pupil Scholarship Test, 6:31 (1 review)
Revised Standard Graded Tests for Stenographers, 6:44
SRA Typing Adaptability Test, 5:518 (2 reviews)
Stanford Achievement Test: High School Business and Economics Test, 7:559 (1 review)
Typewriting Achievement Test: Business Education Achievement Test Series, 7:559A (2 reviews)
Typewriting I and II: Every Pupil Scholarship Test, 6:54

MULTI-APTITUDE BATTERIES – TIP II

[1063]

Academic Promise Tests. Grades 6–9; 1959–69; APT; 7 scores: abstract reasoning, numerical, nonverbal total, language usage, verbal, verbal total, total; George K. Bennett, Marjorie G. Bennett, Dorothy M. Clendenen, Jerome E. Doppelt, James H. Ricks, Jr., Harold G. Seashore, and Alexander G. Wesman; Psychological Corporation. *

For additional information, see 7:672 (6 references); for reviews by Julian C. Stanley and William W. Turnbull, see 6:766.

REFERENCES THROUGH 1971

1–6. See 7:672.
7. Morse, John L. "The Adaptation of a Non-Verbal Abstract Reasoning Test for Use With the Blind." *Ed Visually Handicapped* 2(3):79–80 O '70. * (*PA* 46:1795)

CUMULATIVE NAME INDEX

Beymer, C. L.: 1	Proger, B. B.: 5
Church, J. J.: 4	Stanley, J. C.: *rev*, 6:766
Dungan, R. H.: 5	Taylor, R. G.: 5
Johnson, H. S.: 2	Tidey, W. J.: 5
Mann, L.: 5	Turnbull, W. W.: *rev*, 6:766
Morse, J. L.: 6–7	Willard, L. A.: 3

[1064]

★**Academic-Technical Aptitude Tests.** "Coloured pupils" in standards 6–8; 1970; ATA; the coordination and writing speed tests are taken from the *N.B. Aptitude Tests (Junior);* 10 scores: verbal reasoning, nonverbal reasoning, computations, spatial perception (2-D), mechanical reasoning, language comprehension, spatial perception (3-D), comparison, coordination, writing speed; all test materials are in both English and Afrikaans except the Technical Report which is in Afrikaans; K. Owen (7 tests and manual) and C. P. Celliers (language comprehension test); Human Sciences Research Council [South Africa]. *

[1065]

★**Aptitude Test for Junior Secondary Pupils.** Bantus in Form I; 1970–72; AJB; formerly called *Aptitude Test for Junior Secondary Bantu Pupils in Form I;* 6–11 scores: core battery (English, spatial perception, nonverbal reasoning, mathematics, Afrikaans, verbal reasoning), supplementary battery (comparison, numerical, mechanical insight, eye-hand coordination, writing speed); some subtests in both English and Afrikaans; test by J. D. van Staden, J. P. du Toit, F. W. Gericke, R. R. C. Horne, and D. P. Lombard; manual by G. J. Ligthelm; Human Sciences Research Council [South Africa]. *

[1066]

Aptitude Tests for Occupations. Grades 9–13 and adults; 1951; 6 tests; Wesley S. Roeder and Herbert B. Graham; CTB/McGraw-Hill. *

a) PERSONAL-SOCIAL APTITUDE.
b) MECHANICAL APTITUDE.
c) GENERAL SALES APTITUDE.
d) CLERICAL ROUTINE APTITUDE.
e) COMPUTATIONAL APTITUDE.
f) SCIENTIFIC APTITUDE.

For additional information and a review by Lloyd G. Humphreys, see 5:891; for a review by Clifford P. Froehlich and an excerpted review by Laurance F. Shaffer, see 4:710.

REFERENCES THROUGH 1971

1. Cureton, Edward E. "Service Tests of Multiple Aptitudes." *Proc Inv Conf Testing Probl* 1955:22–39 '56. * (*PA* 31:3017)
2. Durflinger, Glenn W. "Personality Correlates of Success in Student-Teaching." *Ed & Psychol Meas* 23:383–90 su '63. * (*PA* 38:1427)
3. Price, Thomas Hugh. *Psychological Case Studies of Successful Workers in the Field of Retailing.* Doctor's thesis, University of North Carolina (Chapel Hill, N.C.), 1967. (*DA* 28:4790B)

CUMULATIVE NAME INDEX

Cureton, E. E.: 1	Humphreys, L. G.: *rev*, 5:891
Durflinger, G. W.: 2	Price, T. H.: 3
Froehlich, C. P.: *rev*, 4:710	Shaffer, L. F.: *exc*, 4:710

[1067]

★**Armed Services Vocational Aptitude Battery.** High school (some seniors must be included); 1967–73; ASVAB; administered free of charge at participating high schools by Department of Defense personnel; for use in counseling and to stimulate "student interest in service job and training opportunities"; a battery of 9 tests "selected to represent 'common' content among the military service classification batteries"; 9 scores: coding speed, word knowledge, arithmetic reasoning, tool knowledge, space perception, mechanical comprehension, shop information, automotive information, electronics information plus 5 aptitude composites: general-technical, clerical, electronics, general mechanics, motor mechanics; Armed Forces Vocational Testing Group. *

REFERENCES THROUGH 1971

1. Bayroff, A. G., and Fuchs, Edmund F. "The Armed Services Vocational Aptitude Battery." Abstract. *Proc 76th Ann Conv Am Psychol Assn* 3:635–6 '68. * (*PA* 43:125, title only)

CUMULATIVE NAME INDEX

Bayroff, A. G.: 1	Fuchs, E. F.: 1

[1068]

Detroit General Aptitudes Examination. Grades 6–12; 1938–54; assembled from *Detroit Mechanical Aptitudes Examination, Detroit Clerical Aptitudes Examination, Detroit General Intelligence Examination,* and *Detroit Advanced Intelligence Test;* 20 scores: intelligence, mechanical, clerical, total, and 16 subtest scores; 1954 manual identical with manual copyrighted

1941 except for minor changes; Harry J. Baker, Alex C. Crockett, and Paul H. Voelker; Bobbs-Merrill Co., Inc. *

For additional information, see 5:603; for reviews by G. Frederic Kuder, Irving Lorge, and John Gray Peatman, see 2:1654.

REFERENCES THROUGH 1971

1. WOODY, CLIFFORD. *Aptitudes, Achievements and Interests of High School Pupils.* University of Michigan, Bureau of Educational Reference and Research Bulletin No. 157. Ann Arbor, Mich.: School of Education, the University, 1945. Pp. vi, 159. *

2. ROSENZWEIG, SAUL; WITH THE COLLABORATION OF KATE LEVINE KOGAN. *Psychodiagnosis: An Introduction to Tests in the Clinical Practice of Psychodynamics,* pp. 76-80. New York: Grune & Stratton, Inc., 1949. Pp. xii, 380. * (PA 23:3761)

3. CHRISTEL, ROBERT I. *A Correlation Study of General Mental Ability, Mechanical Aptitude and Clerical Aptitude as Measured by the Detroit General Aptitudes Examination, Form A, With Teachers' Marks in Sophomore Exploratory and Junior-Senior Industrial Arts Subjects in the Springfield, Ohio, Senior High School.* Master's thesis, Miami University (Oxford, Ohio), 1958.

CUMULATIVE NAME INDEX

Christel, R. I.: 3   Peatman, J. G.: *rev,* 2:1654
Kogan, K. L.: 2   Rosenzweig, S.: 2
Kuder, G. F.: *rev,* 2:1654 Woody, C.: 1
Lorge, I.: *rev,* 2:1654

[1069]

*Differential Aptitude Tests. Grades 8-12 and adults; 1947-73; DAT; 3 editions; George K. Bennett, Harold G. Seashore, and Alexander G. Wesman; Psychological Corporation. *

a) FORMS A AND B. 1947-59; 9 scores: verbal reasoning, numerical ability, total (scholastic aptitude), abstract reasoning, clerical speed and accuracy, mechanical reasoning, space relations, language usage (spelling, sentences). *Out of print.*

b) FORMS L AND M. 1947-67; 2 booklets.

1) *Booklet 1.* 5 scores: verbal reasoning, numerical ability, total, abstract reasoning, clerical speed and accuracy; verbal reasoning and numerical ability also available in a single booklet; 1961 tests identical with Forms A and B copyrighted 1947 except for number of response options in verbal reasoning test.

2) *Booklet 2.* 4 scores: mechanical reasoning, space relations, spelling, grammar; 1962 mechanical reasoning and spelling tests identical with Forms A and B copyrighted 1947.

c) FORMS S AND T. 1947-73; 1972 tests in abstract reasoning identical with tests copyrighted 1947 and 1961 except for sequence of items; 1972 test in space relations identical with earlier forms copyrighted 1962 except for sequence of items; part 1 of the clerical speed and accuracy test identical in all forms (A, B, L, M, S, and T), part 2 identical in all forms except Form T and a different item sequence in Forms B and M; 9 scores: verbal reasoning, numerical ability, total, abstract reasoning, clerical speed and accuracy, mechanical reasoning, space relations, spelling, language usage; subtests available as separates.

For additional information, a review by M. Y. Quereshi, and an excerpted review by Jack C. Merwin of *b,* see 7:673 (139 references); for reviews by J. A. Keats and Richard E. Schutz, see 6:767 (52 references); for reviews by John B. Carroll and Norman Frederiksen of *a,* see 5:605 (49 references); for reviews by Harold Bechtoldt, Ralph F. Berdie, and Lloyd G. Humphreys, see 4:711 (27 references); for an excerpted review, see 3:620.

REFERENCES THROUGH 1971

1-28. See 4:711.
29-77. See 5:605.
78-129. See 6:767.
130-268. See 7:673.
269. BARRATT, ERNEST S. "The Space-Visualization Factors

Related to Temperament Traits." *J Psychol* 39:279-87 Ap '55. * (PA 29:8424)

270. MENDICINO, LORENZO. *The Effect of Certain Educational Experiences Upon Achievement in Mechanical Reasoning and Space Perception.* Doctor's thesis, University of Pittsburgh (Pittsburgh, Pa.), 1955. (DA 16:65)

271. BAIR, JOHN T.; LOCKMAN, ROBERT F.; AND MARTOCCIA, CHARLES T. "Validity and Factor Analyses of Naval Air Training Predictor and Criterion Measures." *J Appl Psychol* 40:213-9 Ag '56. * (PA 31:6701)

272. DRESSEL, PAUL L. "Working With Youth of Below Average Ability." *Personnel & Guid J* 34:348-50 F '56. * (PA 31:3745)

273. FROEHLICH, CLIFFORD P. "Must Counseling Be Individual?" *Ed & Psychol Meas* 18:681-9 w '58. * (PA 34:2079)

274. WALCH, SHELBY LEWIS. *Self-Estimates of Aptitudes and Preferences and Test-Score Defensiveness.* Doctor's thesis, University of Texas (Austin, Tex.), 1959. (DA 20:210)

275. FRANKEL, EDWARD. "A Comparative Study of Achieving and Underachieving High School Boys of High Intellectual Ability." *J Ed Res* 53:172-80 Ja '60. * (PA 35:7115)

276. PAUK, WALTER J. "Are Present Reading Tests Valid for Both Girls and Boys?" *J Ed Res* 53:279-80 Mr '60. *

277. ROBERTSON, MALCOLM H. "Test Scores and Self-Estimates of Two Curricula Groups." *Personnel & Guid J* 38:746-50 My '60. * (PA 35:2767)

278. WESMAN, ALEXANDER G. "Some Effects of Speed in Test Use." *Ed & Psychol Meas* 20:267-74 su '60. * (PA 35:6396)

279. AIKEN, LEWIS R., JR., AND DREGER, RALPH MASON. "The Effect of Attitudes on Performance in Mathematics." *J Ed Psychol* 52:19-24 F '61. * (PA 36:2KD19A)

280. McGUIRE, CARSON. "Sex Role and Community Variability in Test Performances." *J Ed Psychol* 52:61-73 Ap '61. * (PA 38:3207)

281. SEASHORE, HAROLD G. "Women Are More Predictable Than Men." *J Counsel Psychol* 9:261-70 f '62. * (PA 38:3194)

282. D'AOUST, THÉRÈSE. *Predictive Validity of Four Psychometric Tests in a Selected School of Nursing.* Master's thesis, Catholic University of America (Washington, D.C.), 1963.

283. HUGHES, HERBERT H., AND NELSON, WILLARD H. "The Effect of Reward on Expectancy and Test Performance of Low and High Achievers With High Ability Scores." *J Res Services* 3:22-9 D '63. *

284. RUTT, ROBERT JAMES. *A Study in Predicting Student Success in Plane Geometry Classes of a Minneapolis Senior High School.* Master's thesis, St. Cloud State College (St. Cloud, Minn.), 1963.

285. MOLOMO, RAYMOND R-S. *Two Spatial Factors in Two-Dimensional and Three-Dimensional Spatial Aptitude.* Master's thesis, University of Ottawa (Ottawa, Ont., Canada), 1964.

286. PETERSON, AUDREY J. *A Statistical Analysis of Selected Factors for Predicting Academic Success at Wheaton Community High School, Central.* Master's thesis, Northern Illinois University (DeKalb, Ill.), 1964.

287. SUMMERS, BARBARA L. *A Study of Predictive Devices for Placement in Ninth-Grade English and Algebra Classes for Wheaton Community High School-Central.* Master's thesis, Northern Illinois University (DeKalb, Ill.), 1964.

288. TRITES, DAVID K., AND COBB, BART B. "Problems in Air Traffic Management: 4, Comparison of Pre-Employment, Job Related Experience With Aptitude Tests as Predictors of Training and Job Performance of Air Traffic Control Specialists." *Aerospace Med* 35:428-36 My '64. *

289. CHAUDHRY, GHULAM MOHAMMED, AND KAYANI, MOHAMMED RASHID. "A Comparative Study of the DAT Verbal Reasoning, ACE Psychological Examination and Cooperative English Comprehension Tests as Predictors of Academic Success in the Institute of Education and Research, University of the Panjab." *B Ed & Res* (Pakistan) 4(2):1-21 '65. *

290. KOSAI, JOSEPH HIDEO. *A Proposed Basis for Predicting the Grades in Elementary Algebra of Tenth Grade Students at Stadium High School.* Master's thesis, University of Puget Sound (Tacoma, Wash.), 1965.

291. PETERSON, DONALD FREDERICK. *A Predictive Study of Success in First Year Bookkeeping.* Master's thesis, San Diego State College (San Diego, Calif.), 1965.

292. PETIT, JEAN L. *Selecting Variables Found in the Cumulative Folder of Belvidere High School Students Predicting Academic Success.* Master's thesis, Northern Illinois University (DeKalb, Ill.), 1965.

293. STILLWELL, DOUGLAS JAMES. *A Study of Some Relationships Between the Differential Aptitude Test Scores and Course Marks of Students in the Elk River Public Schools.* Master's thesis, St. Cloud State College (St. Cloud, Minn.), 1965.

294. TAYLOR, JEAN. *An Examination of the Relationships Between Test Scores and Grades in Eleventh Grade English Groups at Hillcrest High School.* Master's thesis, University of Utah (Salt Lake City, Utah), 1965.

295. WHITTEMORE, ROBERT G.; ECHEVERRIA, BEN P.; AND GRIFFIN, JOHN V. "Can We Use Existing Tests for Adult Basic Education?" *Adult Ed* 17:19-29 au '66. *

296. BUIKEMA, ROGER J. *The Development of a Multiple Regression Equation for Predicting Ninth Grade English Grades*

at Morrison Community High School. Master's thesis, Northern Illinois University (DeKalb, Ill.), 1967.

297. COXFORD, LOLA MAE. *A Predictive Study of Success in Shorthand at Mayfair High School.* Master's thesis, California State College (Long Beach, Calif.), 1967.

298. HUDSON, DONALD K. *Relationship of Student Aptitude and Extra-Class Participation to Student Success.* Master's thesis, Illinois State University (Normal, Ill.), 1967.

299. HUFF, BETTY. *The Predictive Value of Standardized Testing in Relation to Mathematical Achievement at Virginia High School.* Master's thesis, East Tennessee State University (Johnson City, Tenn.), 1967.

300. KARPOFF, JOHN T. *Aptitudes for Achievement in the Vocational Programs of One Composite High School in Alberta.* Master's thesis, University of Alberta (Edmonton, Alta., Canada), 1967.

301. MARTIN, BERNARD L. "Spatial Visualization Abilities of Prospective Mathematics Teachers." *J Res Sci Teach* 5(1):11-9 '67. *

302. WOOD, SUSAN. *An Evaluation of Published English Tests,* pp. 23-5. Madison, Wis.: Wisconsin Department of Public Instruction, 1967. Pp. 91. *

303. BOCK, R. DARRELL, AND VANDENBERG, STEVEN G. Chap. 14, "Components of Heritable Variation in Mental Test Scores," pp. 233-60. In *Progress in Human Behavior Genetics.* Edited by Steven G. Vandenberg. Baltimore, Md.: Johns Hopkins Press, 1968. Pp. xi, 356. *

304. CHANCELLOR, GEORGE A., JR. *Standardized Tests as Predictors of Academic Success in Either One or Two Forms of High School Biology.* Master's thesis, Stetson University (DeLand, Fla.), 1968.

305. BEVERIDGE, MARTIN DOYLE. *The Correlation of Selected Characteristics to Achievement in Orthographic Projection.* Master's thesis, California State College (California, Pa.), 1969.

306. LUCAS, ROBERT J., AND SHROCK, JOHN G. "Identifying Socially Sensitive Applicants for Dental Schools." *J Pub Health Dent* 29(2):92-5 sp '69. *

307. SHADEED, CHARLES T. *A Study of Available Criteria for Predicting Success in Algebra.* Master's thesis, Western Connecticut State College (Danbury, Conn.), 1969.

308. DE MARTINO, ALICE J. *The Relations Among Adaptive Regression, Independence, and Creativity in Adolescents.* Doctor's thesis, New York University (New York, N.Y.), 1970. (*DAI* 32:539B)

309. FLYE, LINDA M. *Knowledge of Aptitude as a Source of Change in Inventoried Interests.* Master's thesis, East Tennessee State University (Johnson City, Tenn.), 1970.

310. KALOGER, JAMES HERACLES. *Characteristics of Grosse Pointe High School Students in Advanced Placement Programs.* Doctor's thesis, University of Michigan (Ann Arbor, Mich.), 1970. (*DAI* 31:6440A)

311. SIMPSON, D. "The Aptitudes of Computer Programmers." *Computer B* (England) 14(2):37-40 F '70. *

312. STEVENS, NORMA YOUNG. *A Longitudinal Study of Biographical, Intelligence, and Personality Variables in Predicting Achievement of Mexican Theological Students.* Doctor's thesis, University of Georgia (Athens, Ga.), 1970. (*DAI* 31:4564A)

313. ZUPKA, ANSELM J. *The Development of Expectancy Tables to Estimate the Probable Success of Freshmen Students at Benedictine High School Utilizing Selected Parts of the Differential Aptitude Tests and Grades in Specified Subject Areas.* Master's thesis, John Carroll University (Cleveland, Ohio), 1970.

314. ADCOCK, C. J., AND WEBBERLEY, M. "Primary Mental Abilities." *J General Psychol* 84(2):229-43 Ap '71. * (*PA* 46:4979)

315. ANDERSON, RUTH. *A Study of the Predictability of High School Grades and the Differential Aptitude Tests for Success in Vocational Programs in Health Careers.* Master's thesis, University of Wisconsin (LaCrosse, Wis.), 1971.

316. ARMSTRONG, KENNETH EUGENE. *A Comparative Validity Study of the General Aptitude Test Battery, Differential Aptitude Tests, and the Iowa Tests of Educational Development in Idaho Area Vocational Schools.* Doctor's thesis, University of Idaho (Moscow, Idaho), 1971. (*DAI* 32:3613B)

317. BRADLEY, RICHARD W., AND SANBORN, MARSHALL P. "Using Tests to Predict Four-Year Patterns of College Grade Point." *J Col Stud Personnel* 12(2):138-42 Mr '71. * (*PA* 46:5699)

318. FRYETT, HOWARD LESLIE. *An Interpretation of Student Self Concept and Analysis of Relationships Between the Self and Selected Characteristics of Business Education Students Enrolled in Minnesota Area Vocational-Technical Schools.* Doctor's thesis, University of North Dakota (Grand Forks, N.D.), 1971. (*DAI* 33:76A)

319. HALL, LUCIEN T., JR. "The Prediction of Success in Each of Six Four-Year Selections of Secondary Mathematics Courses." *Sch Sci & Math* 71(8):693-6 N '71. *

320. HELWIG, CARL, AND PENDERGRAPH, ANITA. "Data Processing—Success or Failure?" *J Bus Ed* 47(3):99-100 D '71. *

321. HOOD, DUANE. *A Study of Selected Factors Related to Achievement in Applied and Abstract Mathematics for College*

Juniors and Seniors. Doctor's thesis, East Texas State University (Commerce, Tex.), 1971. (*DAI* 32:4985A)

322. KING, MICHAEL, AND KING, JOHANNA. "Some Correlates of University Performance in a Developing Country: The Case of Ethiopia." *J Cross-Cultural Psychol* 2(3):293-300 S '71. * (*PA* 47:7735)

323. LANSDELL, H. "A General Intellectual Factor Affected by Temporal Lobe Dysfunction." *J Clin Psychol* 27(2):182-4 Ap '71. * (*PA* 46:7303)

324. MEEKER, MARY, AND MEYERS, C. E. "Memory Factors and School Success of Average and Special Groups of Ninth-Grade Boys." *Genetic Psychol Monogr* 83(2):275-308 My '71. * (*PA* 46:5673)

325. MOORE, TELFORD IRA. *The Relationship Among Differentiated Cognitive Abilities, Field Dependency, Achievement, and Rated Classroom Behavior of Ninth Grade Junior High School Students.* Doctor's thesis, University of Southern California (Los Angeles, Calif.), 1971. (*DAI* 32:249A)

326. PETERSON, JOANNE E. *A Comparative Investigation of Student Scores on the Numerical Ability Section of the Differential Aptitude Test and the Same Students' First Semester Grades in Algebra at Keithley Junior High School.* Master's thesis, Pacific Lutheran University (Tacoma, Wash.), 1971.

327. SIMPSON, D. "An Analysis of the Aptitudes of HND Business Studies Students." *Voc Aspect Ed* (England) 23(56):127-36 N '71. *

328. SMITH, RICHARD LEE. *A Factor-Analytic Study of Critical Reading/Thinking, Influenceability, and Related Factors.* Doctor's thesis, University of Maine (Orono, Me.), 1971. (*DAI* 32:6229A)

329. SOUTHALL, BARBARA J. *A Comparative Investigation of the Relationship Between Algebra Grades and Differential Aptitude Test Subtests to Geometry Grades.* Master's thesis, University of Richmond (Richmond, Va.), 1971.

330. SUMMERS, GENE F.; BURKE, MARIANNE; SALTIEL, SUZANNE; AND CLARK, JOHN P. "Stability of the Structure of Work Orientations Among High School Students." *Multiv Behav Res* 6(1):35-50 Ja '71. * (*PA* 46:9686)

331. TAYLOR, ALTON L. "Regression Analysis of Antecedent Measures of Slow Sections in High School Biology." *Sci Ed* 55(3):395-402 Jl–S '71. *

332. TSAI, LOH SENG, AND HAINES, RICHARD B. "Tsai Number-Joining Test Scores Correlated With College Students' Performance on WAIS and DAT." *Percept & Motor Skills* 33(1):35-44 Ag '71. * (*PA* 47:3643)

CUMULATIVE NAME INDEX

Adcock, C. J.: 314
Aijaz, S. M.: 124
Aiken, L. R.: 279
Alvi, S. A.: 125
Anant, S. S.: 236
Anderson, R.: 315
Armbrust, R.: 247
Armstrong, K. E.: 316
Bae, A. Y.: 174, 214
Bair, J. T.: 271
Baroya, G. M.: 196
Barratt, E. S.: 269
Barrett, R. S.: 242
Barry, J. R.: 197
Beamer, G. C.: 42
Bechtoldt, H.: *rev,* 4:711
Bennett, G. K.: 1-4, 20, 22, 29, 33, 54, 65
Berdie, R. F.: 6, 21; *rev,* 4:711
Berg, O. D.: 175
Beveridge, M. D.: 305
Bhatt, L. J.: 198
Bingman, R. M.: 215, 237
Blanton, W. L.: 153
Bloom, T. K.: 176
Blosser, G. H.: 126
Bock, R. D.: 303
Boney, J. D.: 154, 199
Bourne, R. K.: 100
Bowen, C. W.: 238
Bradley, R. W.: 317
Bray, D. W.: 265
Brayfield, A. H.: 69
Brim, C. W.: 109
Bromer, J. A.: 116
Buikema, R. J.: 296
Burke, M.: 330
Busby, W. A.: 177
Cain, R. W.: 155, 200
Calia, V. F.: 87, 101
Carmical, L.: 156
Carmical, L.: 143
Carroll, J. B.: *rev,* 5:605
Cassel, R. N.: 102
Cattell, R. B.: 84
Chancellor, G. A.: 304

Chase, C. I.: 157-8
Chaudhry, G. M.: 289
Cheney, T. M.: 127
Cheong, G. S. C.: 262
Chothia, R. S.: 78
Clark, J. P.: 330
Clarke, R. B.: 216
Clarke, W. V.: 118, 187, 210, 257
Cobb, B. B.: 117, 159, 233, 288
Cooley, D. B.: 178
Cooley, W. W.: 179
Cottle, W. C.: 5, 7
Coughlin, G. J.: 12
Coxford, L. M.: 297
Crites, J. O.: 122
Cronbach, L. J.: 263
Crouch, M. S.: 43
Cureton, E. E.: 79
D'Aoust, T.: 282
Dayal, P.: 160, 180, 201
De Martino, A. J.: 308
Dirr, P. M.: 202
Dixon, A. S.: 248
Dole, A. A.: 105
Doppelt, J. E.: 2, 13, 22-3, 34, 88-9
Dosajh, N. L.: 239
Dreger, R. M.: 279
Dressel, P. L.: 272
Dunnette, M. D.: 72
Dutt, K. F.: 249
Dworkin, S. F.: 264
Echeverria, B. P.: 295
Edington, E. D.: 144
Eells, K.: 110
Elton, C. F.: 66
Embree, R. B.: 14
Ewald, H. H.: 111
Ewen, R. B.: 242
Fangman, E. G.: 161
Filella, J. F.: 103
Fink, D. D.: 148
Flye, L. M.: 309
Foote, R. P.: 104
Frandsen, A. N.: 250

Frankel, E.: 136, 275
Frary, R. B.: 252
Frederiksen, N.: rev, 5:605
Friesen, D.: 90
Froehlich, C. P.: 50, 273
Fruchter, B.: 35
Frye, R. L.: 99
Fryett, H. L.: 318
Fulkerson, S. C.: 197
Garland, K. E.: 217
Garner, G. L.: 251
Gavurin, E. I.: 218
Gelatt, H. B.: 216
Giles, G. C.: 162
Gillam, E. S.: 203
Glaser, R.: 24-6, 36, 51
Goldman, L.: 15, 27
Goodish, N.: 127
Goolsby, T. M.: 252
Grant, D. L.: 265
Gray, B.: 181
Griffin, J. V.: 295
Grobman, H.: 182
Guilford, J. P.: 183
Gwydir, R. R.: 133
Hager, C. W.: 112
Hahn, M. S.: 219
Haines, R. B.: 332
Hall, C. E.: 118
Hall, L. T.: 253, 319
Hall, R. C.: 52, 70
Halsey, H.: 67
Hanna, G. S.: 220
Harootunian, B.: 141
Harris, Y. Y.: 105
Harrison, R.: 55
Hartlage, L. C.: 254
Hascall, E. O.: 91, 113
Hashmi, S. A.: 204
Hawkes, N. J.: 221
Helm, C. R.: 222
Helwig, C.: 320
Heriot, M. R.: 223
Hewick, W. E.: 255
Hindsman, E.: 145
Hodges, J. M.: 37
Hoepfner, R.: 183
Holder, J. R.: 250
Hollenbeck, G. P.: 224
Hood, D.: 321
Horn, F. M.: 138
Hudson, D. K.: 298
Huff, B.: 299
Hughes, H. H.: 106, 283
Humphreys, L. G.: rev, 4:711
Hunt, W.: 55
Hunter, N. W.: 240
Irvine, F. R.: 241
Irwin, J. T.: 163
Jackson, C. W.: 121
Jackson, T. A.: 55
Jacobs, J. N.: 80, 92
Jacobs, O.: 51
Jacobsen, G.: 187, 210, 257
Jayalakshmi, G.: 93
Jenkins, F. T.: 256
Jenkins, T. V.: 142
Jennings, E.: 145
Jenson, R. E.: 56
Jex, F. B.: 205
Johnson, H. S.: 184
Johnson, J. M.: 116
Jones, C. W.: 185
Kaloger, J. H.: 310
Karp, R. E.: 206
Karpoff, J. T.: 300
Katzell, R. A.: 242
Kayani, M. R.: 289
Keats, J. A.: rev, 6:767
Kebbon, L.: 186
Kermeen, B. G.: 30
King, C. E.: 225
King, F. J.: 145
King, J.: 322
King, M.: 322
Kinsey, D. R.: 266
Kirchner, W. K.: 72
Kirkpatrick, J. J.: 242
Kohli, P. E.: 243
Kornhaus, D. C.: 164
Kosai, J. H.: 290
Kurek, A.: 233
Lansdell, H.: 323
Lasco, R. A.: 252

Layton, W. L.: 73
LeBold, W. K.: 134, 246
Littrell, R. T.: 135
Lockman, R. F.: 271
Lopez, F. M.: 207
Loughridge, R. E.: 208
Lucas, R. J.: 306
Ludlow, H. G.: 16, 157-8
Lundquist, J. N.: 131
Lundy, C. T.: 128
McClintic, S. A.: 68
McGuire, C.: 114, 145, 280
McMillen, D.: 185
McNemar, Q.: 165
Marsh, M. M.: 69
Martens, W. L.: 74
Martin, B. L.: 209, 301
Martin, W. T.: 226
Martoccia, C. T.: 271
Massey, H. W.: 82
Mearig, J. S.: 166
Meeker, M.: 324
Meleika, L. K.: 17, 38
Melton, R. S.: 129
Mendicino, L.: 75, 270
Merenda, P. F.: 118, 187, 210, 257
Merwin, J. C.: 188; exc, 7:673
Meyers, C. E.: 324
Milholland, J. E.: 189
Miller, J. D.: 179
Milton, O.: 107
Molomo, R. R-S.: 285
Moore, T. I.: 325
Morris, D.: 66
Morrison, M. M.: 98
Moser, W. E.: 50
Moshin, S. M.: 94
Mueller, D. E.: 167
Mukherjee, B. N.: 119
Myers, M.: 85
Nash, M. J.: 149
Naughton, J.: 244
Nelson, L. T.: 245
Nelson, W. H.: 283
Norton, D. P.: 95
Nugent, F. A.: 115
Oakes, J.: 96
Odgers, J. G.: 89
O'Hara, R. P.: 139, 227
Ojha, J. M.: 198
Osburn, H. G.: 129
Ota, Y. K.: 190
Parmenter, W. H.: 211
Parmon, R. E.: 258
Parton, N. W.: 42
Pascale, A. C.: 118
Pasricha, P.: 150
Pauk, W. J.: 57, 276
Peck, R. F.: 153
Pedersen, E. C.: 191
Peel, R. A.: 192
Pender, F. R.: 42
Pendergraph, A.: 320
Perrine, M. W.: 58
Petersen, H.: 183
Peterson, A. J.: 286
Peterson, D. F.: 291
Peterson, J. E.: 326
Petit, J. L.: 292
Pippert, R. R.: 140
Plummer, R. H.: 28
Pomeroy, M. C.: 158
Pugh, R. C.: 157-8
Quereshi, M. Y.: rev, 7:673
Quidwai, A. A.: 168
Rector, A. P.: 130
Reinhart, W. C.: 267
Rice, V.: 228
Richman, J. T.: 193
Riddle, C. W.: 194
Robertson, G. J.: 229
Robertson, M. H.: 277
Robey, D. L.: 151
Robinson, F. K.: 195
Rosinski, E. F.: 108
Ross, D. R.: 230
Rothney, J. W. M.: 100
Rubin, R. A.: 146
Rudd, J. P.: 120
Rutt, R. J.: 284
Sakalosky, J. C.: 268
Saltiel, S.: 330

Sanborn, M. P.: 317
Scheier, I. H.: 84
Schreck, T. C.: 169
Schroth, M. L.: 231
Schulman, J.: 59
Schusler, M. M.: 212
Schutz, R. E.: rev, 6:767
Seashore, H.: 3, 53, 60
Seashore, H. G.: 4, 8, 11, 20, 29, 33, 44, 65, 88-9, 281
Sevransky, P.: 116
Shadeed, C. T.: 307
Shappell, D. L.: 259
Sheldon, F. A.: 31
Shertzer, B.: 128
Shrock, J. G.: 306
Shukla, N. N.: 137
Simpson, D.: 311, 327
Sininger, R. A.: 81
Skelly, C. G.: 147
Smith, D. D.: 76, 86, 97
Smith, G.: 266
Smith, R. L.: 328
Southall, B. J.: 329
Springob, H. K.: 121
Stafford, R. E.: 213
Stancik, E. J.: 102
Stevens, N. Y.: 312
Stewart, L. H.: 71
Stilgebauer, L. K.: 232
Stillwell, D. J.: 293
Stinson, P. J.: 39, 98
Stockstill, K.: 99
Stoughton, R. W.: 61
Stritch, T. M.: 99
Summers, B. L.: 287

Summers, G. F.: 330
Super, D. E.: 9, 65, 122
Sutherland, K.: 260
Swanson, E. O.: 73
Tate, M. W.: 141
Taylor, A. L.: 331
Taylor, J.: 294
Thomson, W. D.: 261
Tiedeman, D. V.: 139
Townsend, A.: 18
Tremel, J. G.: 152
Trites, D. K.: 170, 233, 288
Tsai, L. S.: 332
Tucker, W. F.: 234
Unruh, L. D.: 171
Vandenberg, S. G.: 303
Vineyard, E. E.: 62, 77, 82
Wakeland, W. F.: 172
Walch, S. L.: 274
Webberley, M.: 314
Weeks, W. R.: 83
Wesman, A.: 10
Wesman, A. G.: 4, 11, 20, 23, 29, 33-4, 40, 65, 278
Whittemore, R. G.: 295
Wilkerson, C. D.: 235
Williams, N.: 41
Wolking, W. D.: 63
Womer, F. B.: 189
Wood, D. A.: 246
Wood, S.: 302
Young, C. R.: 123
Young, D. M.: 45
Zimmer, J. H.: 173
Zuckman, L.: 132
Zupka, A. J.: 313

[1070]

Differential Test Battery. Ages 11 to "top university level" (range for Test 1 extends downward to age 7); 1955–59; 12 tests in 7 booklets; J. R. Morrisby; distributed by Educational and Industrial Test Services [England]. *

a) TEST 1, COMPOUND SERIES TEST. Ages 7 and over; "mental work power"; 1955.

b) GENERAL ABILITY TESTS. Ages 11 and over; 1955; 3 tests.

  1) *Test 2, General Ability Tests: Verbal.*
  2) *Test 3, General Ability Tests: Numerical.*
  3) *Test 4, General Ability Tests: Perceptual.*

c) TEST 5, SHAPES TEST. Ages 11 and over; 1955; spatial ability.

d) TEST 6, MECHANICAL ABILITY TEST. Ages 11 and over; 1955.

e) SPEED TESTS. Ages 11 and over; 1955–59; 6 tests in a single booklet.

  1) *Test 7 (Speed Test 1), Routine Number and Name Checking.*
  2) *Test 8 (Speed Test 2), Perseveration.*
  3) *Test 9 (Speed Test 3), Word Fluency.*
  4) *Test 10 (Speed Test 4), Ideational Fluency.*
  5) *Test 11 (Speed Test 5), Motor Speed.*
  6) *Test 12 (Speed Test 6), Motor Skill.*

For additional information, see 6:768; for reviews by E. A. Peel, Donald E. Super, and Philip E. Vernon, see 5:606.

REFERENCES THROUGH 1971

1. MORRISBY, J. R. "The Differential Test Battery: A Preliminary Notice." *B Nat Found Ed Res Engl & Wales* (England) (6):27–31 N '55. *
2. BEARD, RUTH M.; LEVY, P. M.; AND MADDOX, H. "Academic Performance at University: Test Performance, Motivation and Course of Training." *Ed R* (England) 16:163–74 Je '64. *
3. EL-SHARKAWY, M. K. L., AND LEE, D. M. "A Study of Some Contributions of the Morrisby Differential Test Battery to Vocational Selection." *Brit J Ed Psychol* 35:223–41 Je '65. * (*PA* 39:15227)
4. LEWIS, D. G. "Ability in Science at Ordinary Level of the General Certificate of Education." *Brit J Ed Psychol* 37:361–70 N '67. * (*PA* 42:6146)
5. SMITH, I. MACFARLANE. "The Use of Diagnostic Tests for Assessing the Abilities of Overseas Students Attending Insti-

tutions of Further Education, Part I." *Voc Aspect Ed* (England) 22(51):1–8 Mr '70. *

6. SMITH, I. MACFARLANE. "The Use of Diagnostic Tests for Assessing the Abilities of Overseas Students Attending Institutions of Further Education, Part II." *Voc Aspect Ed* (England) 23(54):39–48 Ap '71. *

CUMULATIVE NAME INDEX

Beard, R. M.: 2
El-Sharkawy, M. K. L.: 3
Lee, D. M.: 3
Levy, P. M.: 2
Lewis, D. G.: 4
Maddox, H.: 2
Morrisby, J. R.: 1
Peel, E. A.: *rev*, 5:606
Smith, I. M.: 5–6
Super, D. E.: *rev*, 5:606
Vernon, P. E.: *rev*, 5:606

[1071]

Employee Aptitude Survey. Ages 16 and over; 1952–63; EAS; 10 tests; G. Grimsley (*a–h*), F. L. Ruch (*a–g, i, j*), N. D. Warren (*a–g*), and J. S. Ford (*a, c, e–g, j*); Psychological Services, Inc. *
a) TEST 1, VERBAL COMPREHENSION. 1952–63.
b) TEST 2, NUMERICAL ABILITY. 1952–63.
c) TEST 3, VISUAL PURSUIT. 1956–63.
d) TEST 4, VISUAL SPEED AND ACCURACY. 1952–63.
e) TEST 5, SPACE VISUALIZATION. 1952–63.
f) TEST 6, NUMERICAL REASONING. 1952–63.
g) TEST 7, VERBAL REASONING. 1952–63.
h) TEST 8, WORD FLUENCY. 1953–63.
i) TEST 9, MANUAL SPEED AND ACCURACY. 1953–63.
j) TEST 10, SYMBOLIC REASONING. 1956–63.

For additional information, reviews by Paul F. Ross and Erwin K. Taylor, and an excerpted review by John O. Crites, see 6:769 (4 references); for reviews by Dorothy C. Adkins and S. Rains Wallace, see 5:607.

REFERENCES THROUGH 1971

1–4. See 6:769.
5. BARRATT, ERNEST S. "The Space-Visualization Factors Related to Temperament Traits." *J Psychol* 39:279–87 Ap '55. * (PA 29:8424)
6. FOY, GLENN ARTHUR. *A Study of the Relationship Between Certain Factor-Analyzed Ability Measures and Success in College Engineering.* Doctor's thesis, University of Southern California (Los Angeles, Calif.), 1959. (DA 20:368)
7. BROE, JOHN RICHARD. *Prediction of Success in Training Among Electronics Technicians.* Doctor's thesis, University of Southern California (Los Angeles, Calif.), 1962. (DA 23:2417)
8. GUION, ROBERT M. "Synthetic Validity in a Small Company: A Demonstration." *Personnel Psychol* 18:49–63 sp '65. * (PA 39:16490)
9. RUDE, H. NEIL, AND KING, DONALD C. "Aptitude Levels in a Depressed Area." *Personnel & Guid J* 43:785–9 Ap '65. * (PA 39:14918)
10. LUNNEBORG, CLIFFORD E., AND LUNNEBORG, PATRICIA W. "Uniqueness of Selected Employment Aptitude Tests to a General Academic Guidance Battery." *Ed & Psychol Meas* 27:953–60 w '67. * (PA 42:9425)
11. THUMIN, FRED J. "Ability Scores as Related to Age Among Male Job Applicants." *J Gerontol* 23:390–2 Jl '68. *
12. CARLSON, ROBERT E.; DAWIS, RENE V.; AND WEISS, DAVID J. "The Effect of Satisfaction on the Relationship Between Abilities and Satisfactoriness." *Occup Psychol* (England) 43(1):39–46 '69. * (PA 44:17573)
13. DUBIN, JERRY A.; OSBURN, HOBART; AND WINICK, DARVIN M. "Speed and Practice: Effects on Negro and White Test Performances." *J Appl Psychol* 53:19–23 F '69. * (PA 43:7254)
14. DUBIN, JERRY ALAN. *Effects of Practice and Speed on Negro and White Mental Ability Test Performances.* Doctor's thesis, University of Houston (Houston, Tex.), 1969. (DAI 30:367B)
15. TENOPYR, MARY L. "The Comparative Validity of Selected Leadership Scales Relative to Success in Production Management." *Personnel Psychol* 22(1):77–85 sp '69. * (PA 43:14924)
16. WIGGINS, NANCY; HOFFMAN, PAUL J.; AND TABER, THOMAS. "Types of Judges and Cue Utilization in Judgments of Intelligence." *J Pers & Social Psychol* 12(1):52–9 My '69. * (PA 43:11266)
17. POUNDERS, CEDRIC J. "The Admissions Test for Graduate Study in Business: A Factor Analytic Study." *Ed & Psychol Meas* 30(2):469–73 su '70. * (PA 45:2955)
18. BETZ, ELLEN L. "An Investigation of Job Satisfaction as a Moderator Variable in Predicting Job Success." *J Voc Behav* 1(2):123–8 Ap '71. * (PA 47:11882)

CUMULATIVE NAME INDEX

Adkins, D. C.: *rev*, 5:607
Barratt, E. S.: 5
Betz, E. L.: 18
Broe, J. R.: 7

Carlson, R. E.: 12
Crites, J. O.: *exc*, 6:769
Dawis, R. V.: 12
Dubin, J. A.: 13–4
Foy, G. A.: 6
Gershon, A.: 3–4
Guion, R. M.: 8
Haney, R.: 3–4
Hoffman, P. J.: 16
King, D. C.: 9
Lunneborg, C. E.: 10
Lunneborg, P. W.: 10
Michael, W. B.: 3–4
Osburn, H.: 13
Pounders, C. J.: 17
Ross, P. F.: *rev*, 6:769
Ruch, F. L.: 1–2
Ruch, W. W.: 2
Rude, H. N.: 9
Taber, T.: 16
Taylor, E. K.: *rev*, 6:769
Tenopyr, M. L.: 15
Thumin, F. J.: 11
Wallace, S. R.: *rev*, 5:607
Weiss, D. J.: 12
Wiggins, N.: 16
Winick, D. M.: 13

[1072]

Flanagan Aptitude Classification Tests. Grades 9–12, 10–12 and adults; 1951–60; FACT; 2 editions; John C. Flanagan; Science Research Associates, Inc. *
a) SEPARATE BOOKLET 16-TEST EDITION. Grades 10–12 and adults; 1951–60; 16 tests.
1) *FACT 1A, Inspection.* 1953–56.
2) *FACT 2A and 2B, Coding.* 1953–56.
3) *FACT 3A and 3B, Memory.* 1953–56.
4) *FACT 4A, Precision.* 1953–56.
5) *FACT 5A, Assembly.* 1953–56.
6) *FACT 6A, Scales.* 1953–56.
7) *FACT 7A, Coordination.* 1953–56.
8) *FACT 8A, Judgment and Comprehension.* 1953–56.
9) *FACT 9A, Arithmetic.* 1953–56.
10) *FACT 10A, Patterns.* 1953–56.
11) *FACT 11A, Components.* 1953–56.
12) *FACT 12A, Tables.* 1953–56.
13) *FACT 13A and 13B, Mechanics.* 1953–56.
14) *FACT 14A. Expression.* 1953–56.
15) *FACT 15A, Reasoning.* 1957–60.
16) *FACT 16A, Ingenuity.* 1957–60.
b) 19-TEST EDITION. Grades 9–12; 1957–60; 19 tests (same as for *a* plus vocabulary, planning, alertness) in 2 booklets.

For additional information and an excerpted review by Harold D. Murphy (with John P. McQuary), see 7:675 (10 references); for reviews by Norman Frederiksen and William B. Michael, see 6:770 (7 references); for reviews by Harold P. Bechtoldt, Ralph F. Berdie, and John B. Carroll, see 5:608.

REFERENCES THROUGH 1971

1–7. See 6:770.
8–17. See 7:675.
18. LATHAM, ELLEN DIXON. *An Investigation of the Influence of Instructional Sets Upon the Test Performance, Expectancy Levels, and Post-Performance Estimates of Selected Students at Western Carolina University.* Doctor's thesis, University of North Carolina (Chapel Hill, N.C.), 1971. (DAI 32:2486A)

CUMULATIVE NAME INDEX

Alford, M. L.: 11
Altman, J. W.: 8
Anderson, R. C.: 14
Bechtoldt, H. P.: *rev*, 5:608
Berdie, R. F.: *rev*, 5:608
Bolton, F. B.: 7
Carroll, J. B.: *rev*, 5:608
Cooley, W. W.: 12
Cureton, E. E.: 4
Flanagan, J. C.: 3, 5, 9, 17
Frederiksen, N.: *rev*, 6:770
Guilliams, C. I.: 15
Jex, F. B.: 10
Latham, A. J.: 1
Latham, E. D.: 18
Little, E. N.: 16
McQuary, J. P.: *exc*, 7:675
Michael, W. B.: *rev*, 6:770
Morgart, H. S.: 13
Murphy, H. D.: *exc*, 7:675
Phipps, G. T.: 13
Scott, R. H.: 13
Volkin, L. A.: 2
White, A. J.: 6

[1073]

General Aptitude Test Battery. Grades 9–12 and adults; 1946–73; GATB; for a nonreading adaptation, *Nonreading Aptitude Test Battery,* see 1086; developed by the United States Employment Service for use in its occupational counseling program and released for use by State Employment Services; orders for test materials must be cleared through a State Employment Service office; test booklets and manuals distributed by United States Government Printing Office. *

a) SCREENING DEVICE AND PRETESTING EXERCISES. 1966–73.

1) *GATB-NATB Screening Device.* 1966–73; test sheet title is *Wide-Range Scale;* to identify examinees who are deficient in reading and arithmetic skills and should be tested with *Nonreading Aptitude Test Battery.*

2) *USES Pretesting Orientation Exercises.* 1968; test-taking practice for disadvantaged persons.

b) GATB, B-1001, [EXPENDABLE BOOKLET EDITION]. *Out of print.*

c) GATB, B-1002, [SEPARATE ANSWER SHEET EDITION]. 1952–70; 9 scores: intelligence, verbal, numerical, spatial, form perception, clerical perception, motor coordination, finger dexterity, manual dexterity; 12 tests: 8 paper and pencil tests plus 4 performance tests.

1) *Book 1.* 1965 test identical with test published 1952; 4 tests: name comparison, computation, three-dimensional space, vocabulary.

2) *Book 2.* 3 tests: tool matching, arithmetic reasoning, form matching.

3) *Part 8 [Mark Making].* 1965.

4) *Pegboard.* 2 tests: place, turn; K & W Products Co., Inc., Specialty Case Manufacturing Co., and Warwick Products Co.

5) *Finger Dexterity Board.* 2 tests: assemble, disassemble; K & W Products Co., Inc., Specialty Case Manufacturing Co., and Warwick Products Co.

For additional information and a review by David J. Weiss, see 7:676 (138 references); for reviews by Harold P. Bechtoldt and John B. Carroll of earlier forms, see 6:771 (55 references); for reviews by Andrew L. Comrey, Clifford P. Froehlich, and Lloyd G. Humphreys, see 5:609 (176 references); for reviews by Milton L. Blum, Edward B. Greene, and Howard R. Taylor, see 4:714 (33 references).

REFERENCES THROUGH 1971

1–33. See 4:714.
34–209. See 5:609.
210–264. See 6:771.
265–402. See 7:676.
403. HERON, ALASTAIR. "The Objective Assessment of Personality Among Factory Workers." *J Social Psychol* 39:161–85 My '54. * (*PA* 29:4728)
404. TRATTNER, MARVIN H.; FINE, SIDNEY A.; AND KUBIS, JOSEPH F. "A Comparison of Worker Requirement Ratings Made by Reading Job Descriptions and by Direct Job Observation." *Personnel Psychol* 8:183–94 su '55. * (*PA* 30:5309)
405. AYRES, A. JEAN. "A Study of the Manual Dexterity and Workshop Wages of Thirty-Nine Cerebral Palsied Trainees." *Am J Phys Med* 36:6–10 F '57. * (*PA* 32:4463)
406. CAIRD, W. K.; SLOANE, BRUCE; AND INGLIS, JAMES. "The Effects of Nialamide and Ethyl Alcohol on Some Personality, Cognitive and Psychomotor Variables in Normal Volunteers." *J Neuropsychiatry* 2:31–4 S–O '61. *
407. INGLIS, J.; CAIRD, W. K.; AND SLOANE, R. B. "An Objective Assessment of the Effects of Nialamide on Depressed Patients." *Can Med Assn J* 84:1059–63 My 13 '61. *
408. WILLIAMS, RUTH. "A Preliminary Report on the Validity of Aptitude Tests as a Predictor of Success in Medical Technology." *Am J Med Technol* 29:157–62 My–Je '63. *
409. DVORAK, BEATRICE J. "Changing Emphasis in Occupational Test Development." *Employ Service R* 2:45–7 Ag '65. *
410. DVORAK, BEATRICE J. "Program Research on Effectiveness of USES Tests." *Employ Service R* 2:62–4 O '65. *
411. PASKEWITZ, DORIS L. *A Prediction Study of Senior High Course Grades and Test Scores.* Master's thesis, Stetson University (DeLand, Fla.), 1965.
412. ROZYNKO, VITALI, AND WENK, ERNEST. "Intellectual Performance of Three Delinquent Groups of Different Ethnic Origin." Abstract. *J Consult Psychol* 29:282 Je '65. * (*PA* 39:12810)
413. SEILER, JOSEPH. "Abilities for ADP Occupations: Assessment of High and Low Education Job Applicants." *Proc Ann Computer Personnel Res Conf* 3:52–9 '65. *
414. WILLIAMS, RUTH. "Aptitude Tests for Med. Tech. Recruits?" *Hosp Progr* 46:30+ O '65. *
415. WHITTEMORE, ROBERT G.; ECHEVERRIA, BEN P.; AND GRIFFIN, JOHN V. "Can We Use Existing Tests for Adult Basic Education?" *Adult Ed* 17:19–29 au '66. *

416. BENDER, LLOYD D.; HOBBS, DARYL J.; AND GOLDEN, JAMES F. "Congruence Between Aspirations and Capabilities of Youth in a Low-Income Rural Area." *Rural Sociol* 32:278–89 S '67. * (*PA* 41:16572)
417. MONTGOMERY, TRAVIS. "Use of the GATB in Predicting Success on the High School Equivalency Tests." *J Employ Counsel* 4:117–21 D '67. *
418. SOUTHWICK, RICHARD NEPHI. *Relationship of Intelligence to Vocational Adjustment.* Master's thesis, University of Utah (Salt Lake City, Utah), 1967.
419. WILLIAMS, RUTH; KONECNY, PATRICIA WARNER; AND CHAMPION, JOAN. "Validity and Predictive Studies on the General Aptitude Test Battery." *Am J Med Technol* 33:142–7 Mr–Ap '67. *
420. BAIRD, ROBERT G. *A Comparison of Success Predictions With Performance of Disadvantaged Apprenticeship Candidates.* Master's thesis, Seattle University (Seattle, Wash.), 1969.
421. BOYD, HELEN L. *Freedom to Vary: Environment and Perceptual Aptitude; the General Aptitude Test Battery.* Master's thesis, East Texas State University (Commerce, Tex.), 1970.
422. KASL, STANISLAV V.; BROOKS, GEORGE W.; AND RODGERS, WILLARD L. "Serum Uric Acid and Cholesterol in Achievement Behavior and Motivation: 1, The Relationship to Ability, Grades, Test Performance, and Motivation." *J Am Med Assn* 213(7):1158–64 Ag 17 '70. * (*PA* 45:9556)
423. MYERS, RICHARD WAYNE. *Effects of Motivational Incentives on GATB "F" and "M" Subtest Performance With Hospitalized Neuropsychiatric Patients.* Doctor's thesis, Iowa State University (Ames, Iowa), 1970. (*DAI* 31:4470A)
424. NOLEN, DONOVAN R. *Validation of the GATB Tests for Predicting LPN State Board Examination Success.* Master's thesis, University of Tennessee (Knoxville, Tenn.), 1970.
425. SUBBERT, DWIGHT C. *Predicting School Success Through the Use of GATB Scores and Core Area Grades.* Master's thesis, Drake University (Des Moines, Iowa), 1970.
426. TURNER, JEANINE F. *A Comparison of the General Aptitude Test Battery Scores of Disadvantaged and Non-Disadvantaged Individuals.* Master's thesis, Gonzaga University (Spokane, Wash.), 1970.
427. ARMSTRONG, KENNETH EUGENE. *A Comparative Validity Study of the General Aptitude Test Battery, Differential Aptitude Tests, and the Iowa Tests of Educational Development in Idaho Area Vocational Schools.* Doctor's thesis, University of Idaho (Moscow, Idaho), 1971. (*DAI* 32:3613B)
428. BEARD, R. B., AND BLACKBURN, H. L. "Factors Affecting General Aptitude Test Battery Scores Among Schizophrenic Patients." *Newsl Res Psychol* 13(3):3–4 Ag '71. *
429. BEMIS, STEPHEN E. "Use of Aptitude Scores as Predictors of Success in Occupational Training Under the MDTA." *J Employ Counsel* 8(1):11–8 Mr '71. * (*PA* 47:11868)
430. CASSEL, RUSSELL N., AND REIER, GEROLD W. "Comparative Analysis of Concurrent and Predictive Validity for the GATB Clerical Aptitude Test Battery." *J Psychol* 79(1):135–40 S '71. * (*PA* 47:5603)
431. FOZARD, JAMES L., AND NUTTALL, RONALD L. "General Aptitude Test Battery Scores for Men Differing in Age and Socioeconomic Status." *J Appl Psychol* 55(4):372–9 Ag '71. * (*PA* 47:3835)
432. GOLDMAN, ROBERT CHARLIE. *The General Aptitude Test Battery as a Predictor of Student Success in Seven Area Vocational-Technical Schools in Arkansas.* Doctor's thesis, University of Mississippi (University, Miss.), 1971. (*DAI* 32:3686A)
433. GRINA, ALONDA A. *Effectiveness of the GATB in Predicting Training Success of Practical Nurse Students When the Confidence Band Principle Is Employed.* Master's thesis, Duquesne University (Pittsburgh, Pa.), 1971.
434. HENDEL, DARWIN D. "Test Format and Administration Variables as Related to the Performance of Mentally Retarded Adults on Multifactor Tests of Vocational Abilities." Abstract. *Proc 79th Ann Conv Am Psychol Assn* 6(2):615–6 '71. * (*PA* 46:5374)
435. KAPES, JEROME THEODORE. *The Relationship Between Selected Characteristics of Ninth Grade Boys and Curriculum Selection and Success in Tenth Grade.* Doctor's thesis, Pennsylvania State University (University Park, Pa.), 1971. (*DAI* 32:6131A)
436. MARTIN, GEORGE E. *The General Aptitude Test Battery in Enrolling Vocational Students at Haskell Institute.* Master's thesis, Kansas State Teachers College (Emporia, Kan.), 1971.
437. MAZUR, JAMES MATTHEW. *A Study of Predictive Validity of Standardized Tests Used for Placement of Vocational Students at Rockingham Community College.* Master's thesis, North Carolina State University (Raleigh, N.C.), 1971.
438. MILLER, DELBERT G. *A Comparative Study of the Rorschach F+ Per Cent to the General Aptitude Test Battery Subtests S, Spatial Aptitude and P, Form Perception.* Master's thesis, University of Idaho (Moscow, Idaho), 1971.
439. NUTTALL, RONALD L., AND FOZARD, JAMES L. "A Re-examination of the Structure of the General Aptitude Test Battery Aptitudes." *Indus Gerontol* 8:1–18 w '71. * (*PA* 46:11781)
440. NUTTALL, RONALD L.; FOZARD, JAMES L.; ROSE, CHARLES L.; AND BURNEY, SPENCER W. "Ages of Man: Ability Age,

Personality Age, and Biochemical Age." Abstract. *Proc 79th Ann Conv Am Psychol Assn* 6(2):605-6 '71. * (*PA* 46:4729)

441. PRIMMER, RICHARD D., AND TIPTON, ROBERT M. "Effects on Test Performance of Test Apparatus Boards Made of Different Material." *Percept & Motor Skills* 32(3):916-8 Je '71. * (*PA* 47:39)

442. ROSENAU, CHARLES B., AND WILLIAMS, JOHN D. "A Comparison of the Lorge-Thorndike Intelligence Test Total IQ and the General Aptitude Test Battery Aptitude G." *Col Ed Rec Univ N Dak* 56(9):167-70 Je '71. *

443. WANGER, RUTH SCHWARTZ. *The Relationship of Selected Variables to the Performance and Persistence of Career-Oriented Community College Students.* Doctor's thesis, George Washington University (Washington, D.C.), 1971. (*DAI* 32:3044A)

444. WEBER, THOMAS R. "An Evaluation of the Effectiveness of SATB Norms in MDTA Selection." *J Employ Counsel* 8(1):2-10 Mr '71. * (*PA* 47:11878)

445. WENK, ERNEST A.; ROZYNKO, VITALI V.; SARBIN, THEODORE R.; AND ROBISON, JAMES O. "The Effect of Incentives Upon Aptitude Scores of White and Negro Inmates." *J Res Crime & Del* 8(1):53-64 Ja '71. *

446. WILHIDE, EARLE R. *An Investigation of the Usefulness of the GATB for Beginning Tenth Grade Vocational Students.* Master's thesis, Western Maryland College (Westminster, Md.), 971.

447. ZIEGLER, ELWOOD. "An Evaluation of the Effect of Pre-Testing Orientation on GATB Scores." *J Employ Counsel* 8(1):31-6 Mr '71. * (*PA* 47:11867)

CUMULATIVE NAME INDEX

Akerman, R. H.: 315
Alexakos, C. E.: 379
Anderson, M. R.: 54
Anderson, P. K.: 212
Armstrong, K. E.: 427
Ashe, M. R.: 37
Aucker, J. R.: 381
Ayers, L. D.: 299
Ayres, A. J.: 405
Baird, R. G.: 420
Banas, P. A.: 274, 300
Beamer, G. C.: 211, 224
Beard, R. B.: 428
Bechtoldt, H. P.: *rev,* 6:771
Bell, F. O.: 260, 275
Bellamy, R. Q.: 371
Bellucci, J. T.: 382
Bemis, S.: 388
Bemis, S. E.: 334, 355, 429
Bender, L. D.: 416
Bidwell, G. P.: 353
Bierbaum, W. B.: 35
Biggers, A. F.: 287
Bird, R. G.: 20
Bischof, L. J.: 21
Blackburn, H. L.: 428
Blackburn, J. B.: 110
Blackburn, J. R.: 29
Blum, M. L.: *rev,* 4:714
Bookout, D. V. T.: 354
Botterbusch, K. F.: 355
Boulger, J. R.: 38, 46
Boyd, H. L.: 421
Brenna, D. W.: 356
Briggs, P. F.: 301
Broman, H. J.: 362
Brooks, G. W.: 422
Brown, C. M.: 9
Burney, S. W.: 440
Burt, S. M.: 261
Busse, W.: 325
Caird, W. K.: 406-7
Carbuhn, W. M.: 383
Carlson, R. E.: 288, 357
Carroll, J. B.: *rev,* 6:771
Cassel, R. N.: 430
Champion, J.: 419
Cheney, T. M.: 346, 369
Cobb, K. C.: 384
Colmen, J. G.: 29
Comrey, A. L.: *rev,* 5:609
Cook, G. L.: 358
Cooley, W. W.: 289
Crambert, A. C.: 262
Crawford, J. M.: 28
Crites, J. O.: 259
Cronbach, L. J.: 385
Culhane, M. M.: 276
Cullum, F. W.: 290
Cureton, E. E.: 213
Currie, C.: 267
Dawis, R. V.: 313, 357
Deabler, H. L.: 316, 322-3
Densley, K. G.: 317

Desmond, R. E.: 386
Dreiling, T. C.: 318
Droege, R. C.: 253, 262, 291-2, 302-3, 319-20, 330, 335-8, 355, 377, 387-8
Dutt, K. F.: 359
Dvorak, B. J.: 2-3, 32, 39, 111, 140-2, 292, 409-10
Echeverria, B. P.: 415
Edington, E. D.: 294
Eisen, I.: 277, 321
England, G. W.: 313
Enneis, W. H.: 265
Fatzinger, F. A.: 331
Feingold, W.: 277
Fiedler, G. O.: 29
Finch, C. R.: 339
Fine, S. A.: 404
Flanagan, J.: 360
Fleming, S. V.: 389
Floyd, W. A.: 278
Fox, F. C.: 39
Fozard, J. L.: 390, 397, 431, 439-40
Froehlich, C. P.: *rev,* 5:609
Gagni, A. O.: 340
Gavurin, E.: 263
Gay, R. A.: 324
Gerber, V. R.: 47
Gibson, A. M.: 30
Gjernes, D.: 112
Goble, R. L.: 341
Golden, J. F.: 304, 416
Goldman, R. C.: 432
Gordon, O. J.: 22
Grant, G. V.: 305
Grant, W. V.: 23
Greene, E. B.: *rev,* 4:714
Griess, J. A.: 306
Griffin, J. V.: 415
Grina, A. A.: 433
Harford, T. C.: 322-3
Harmon, J. S.: 361
Hasler, K. R.: 321
Hawk, J.: 387-8
Hawk, J. A.: 355, 391
Hay, J. E.: 203
Heggen, J. R.: 342
Hendel, D. D.: 434
Henkin, J. B.: 262
Heron, A.: 403
Hirt, M.: 222-3
Hirt, M. L.: 215, 279
Hobbs, D. J.: 416
Hoff, A. L.: 260, 275
Hollender, J. W.: 362
Hosford, R. E.: 354
Hountras, P. T.: 343
Howell, M. A.: 324
Hoyt, K. B.: 260, 275
Huddy, J. A.: 344
Humphreys, L. G.: *rev,* 5:609
Hunter, N. W.: 345
Impellitteri, J. T.: 363

Ingersoll, R. W.: 280, 307
Inglis, J.: 406-7
Isaacson, L. E.: 40
Jeremias, H. I.: 308
Jex, F. B.: 48, 214, 309
Jones, R. D.: 364
Kapes, J. T.: 363, 435
Kasl, S. V.: 422
Kauppi, D. R.: 365
Kebbon, L.: 293
Kish, G. B.: 325, 346, 366-9, 392-4
Klein, F.: 370, 395
Klugman, S. F.: 281
Konecny, P. W.: 419
Kooker, E. W.: 371
Kubis, J. F.: 404
Kuntz, R. H.: 294
Lehmann, I. J.: 373
Lewis, G.: 360
Lewis, H. J.: 310
Lofgreen, J. C.: 347
Lofquist, L. H.: 313
Loudermilk, K. M.: 282, 311
Lucas, D. H.: 326
Lunneborg, C. E.: 327
Lunneborg, P. W.: 327
McDaniel, E. D.: 254
McDonald, K. L.: 372
McKinley, M. M.: 396
McNamara, T. A.: 256
Madden, G. J.: 113
Malecki, H. R.: 49
Mapou, A.: 50, 114
Martin, G. E.: 436
Mathis, H. I.: 348
Mazur, J. M.: 437
Meadow, L.: 283
Mehrens, W. A.: 373
Meigh, C.: 32, 39
Metwally, A.: 255
Miller, D. G.: 438
Minnesota State Employment Service: 55-6
Montag, G. M.: 396
Montgomery, T.: 417
Morgan, J. P.: 51
Morgan, M.: 36
Mouly, G. J.: 10
Mueller, D. E.: 284
Mullen, R. A.: 271
Myers, R. W.: 402, 423
Nash, A. N.: 300
Nesbitt, J. D.: 374
Nicksick, T.: 173, 224
Ninemeier, J. D.: 396
Nitardy, J. R.: 375
Nolen, D. R.: 424
Nuttall, R. L.: 390, 397, 431, 439-40
O'Connor, N.: 28, 31, 41
Odell, C. E.: 32, 34
Ohio Employment Service, State Testing Staff: 11
Orr, B.: 4
Paskewitz, D. L.: 411
Perrone, P. A.: 285
Peters, H. J.: 307
Peterson, C. D.: 375
Peterson, M. A.: 328
Petty, G. C.: 12
Pickett, L. M.: 216, 225
Pockell, N. E.: 263
Primmer, R. D.: 441
Pugh, R. C.: 329
Ralph, R. B.: 13, 24, 42
Ralph, S.: 6
Rawlings, T. D.: 266
Reier, G. W.: 430
Reitan, H. M.: 25
Renick, C. P.: 7
Robinson, L. G. M.: 14
Robison, J. O.: 445
Rodgers, W. L.: 422
Rose, C. L.: 440
Rose, T.: 211
Rosen, M. H.: 269
Rosenau, C. B.: 442
Ross, J. E.: 398

Rotman, C. B.: 272
Rozynko, V.: 412
Rozynko, V. V.: 445
Russo, J. R.: 257
Sadnavitch, J. M.: 268
Sakalosky, J. C.: 399
Samuelson, C. O.: 143
Sandmann, C. W.: 376
Sarbin, T. R.: 445
Schenkel, K. F.: 52
Seiler, J.: 292, 413
Seitz, M. J.: 15
Senior, N.: 115, 210
Sharp, H. C.: 225
Sherr, R. D.: 349
Shipman, V. C.: 400
Shore, T. C.: 401
Showler, W.: 388
Showler, W. K.: 330, 377
Sloane, B.: 406
Sloane, R. B.: 407
Smith, W. R.: 26
Sommerfeld, D.: 331
Sorenson, A. G.: 48
Sorenson, G.: 115
Soueif, M. I.: 255
Southwick, R. N.: 418
Spencer, S. J.: 350
Spergel, P.: 351
Steffen, H. H. J.: 270
Stein, C. I.: 258
Stephenson, H. W.: 254
Stone, T. C.: 378
Storrs, S.: 44
Storrs, S. V.: 43
Strowig, R. W.: 379
Subbert, D. C.: 425
Sullivan, T. W.: 332
Summers, M. D.: 295
Super, D. E.: 16, 259
Tate, F. E.: 296
Tate, J. R.: 333
Taylor, C. W.: 24, 33, 42
Taylor, E. S.: 45
Taylor, F. R.: 264
Taylor, H. R.: *rev,* 4:714
Tellegen, A.: 297
Thiel, P. G.: 343
Thompson, J. W.: 27
Thurman, C. G.: 17
Tipton, R. M.: 441
Tizard, J.: 28, 31
Traeger, C.: 116
Trattner, M. H.: 404
Traxler, H. W.: 312
Trione, V.: 395
Triplett, B.: 8
Turner, J. F.: 426
United States Employment Service: 5, 57-108, 117-39, 144-72, 174-202, 204-9, 217-21, 226-52
Vincent, J. W.: 324
Wallner, C. A.: 352
Wanger, R. S.: 443
War Manpower Commission, Division of Occupational Analysis, Staff: 1
Warman, R. E.: 402
Watson, G. E.: 8
Weber, T. R.: 444
Weiner, M.: 273, 286
Weiss, D. J.: 313, 357, 365, 375, 386; *rev,* 7:676
Wenk, E.: 412
Wenk, E. A.: 445
Westwood, D.: 18
Whittemore, R. G.: 415
Wilhide, E. R.: 446
Williams, J. D.: 442
Williams, R.: 408, 414, 419
Willis, C. H.: 316, 322-3
Wise, R. M.: 109
Woodhead, M. J.: 19
Woods, N. J.: 380
Woolington, J. M.: 314
Wysong, H. E.: 298
Yater, A. C.: 301
Ziegler, E.: 447

[1074]

The Guilford-Zimmerman Aptitude Survey. Grades 9-16 and adults; 1947-56; GZAS; 7 parts; J. P.

General Aptitude Test Battery

Guilford and Wayne S. Zimmerman; Sheridan Psychological Services, Inc. *

a) PART 1, VERBAL COMPREHENSION.
b) PART 2, GENERAL REASONING.
c) PART 3, NUMERICAL OPERATIONS.
d) PART 5, PERCEPTUAL SPEED.
e) PART 5, SPATIAL ORIENTATION.
f) PART 6, SPATIAL VISUALIZATION.
g) PART 7, MECHANICAL KNOWLEDGE.

For additional information, see 6:772 (17 references); for reviews by Anne Anastasi, Harold Bechtoldt, John B. Carroll, and P. E. Vernon, see 4:715 (15 references).

REFERENCES THROUGH 1971

1-15. See 4:715.
16-32. See 6:772.
33. BARRATT, ERNEST S. "The Space-Visualization Factors Related to Temperament Traits." *J Psychol* 39:279–87 Ap '55. * (PA 29:8424)
34. BAIR, JOHN T.; LOCKMAN, ROBERT F.; AND MARTOCCIA, CHARLES T. "Validity and Factor Analyses of Naval Air Training Predictor and Criterion Measures." *J Appl Psychol* 40:213–9 Ag '56. * (PA 31:6701)
35. DREWES, HENRY WALTER. *An Experimental Study of the Relationship Between Electroencephalographic Imagery Variables and Perceptual-Cognitive Processes.* Doctor's thesis, Cornell University (Ithaca, N.Y.), 1958. (DA 19:87)
36. FRANCESCO, E. "The General Orientations Profile (GOP)." *Psychol Rep* 5:561–9 S '59. * (PA 38:4264)
37. BALLANTYNE, ROBERT HUBBARD. *An Analysis of Criteria for Selecting Freshmen Students for an Honors Program at Washington State University.* Doctor's thesis, Washington State University (Pullman, Wash.), 1962. (DA 23:2439)
38. DE MILLE, RICHARD. "Intellect After Lobotomy in Schizophrenia: A Factor Analytic Study." *Psychol Monogr* 76(16): 1–18 '62. * (PA 38:2784)
39. LOCKE, EDWIN A. "Some Correlates of Classroom and Out-of-Class Achievement in Gifted Science Students." *J Ed Psychol* 54:238–48 O '63. * (PA 38:4649)
40. PIMSLEUR, PAUL. "A Study of Foreign Language Learning Ability: Parts 1 and 2," pp. 57–72. In *Report of the Twelfth Annual Round Table Meeting on Linguistics and Language Studies.* Edited by Michael Zarechnak. Washington, D.C.: Georgetown University Press, 1963. Pp. 132. *
41. RONAN, W. W. "Evaluation of Skilled Trades Performance Predictors." *Ed & Psychol Meas* 24:601–8 f '64. * (PA 39:6074)
42. COLLIER, BOY N., AND NUGENT, FRANK A. "Characteristics of Self-referred, Staff-referred, and Non-Counseled College Students." *J Counsel Psychol* 12:208–12 su '65. * (PA 39:12609, title only)
43. SCOTT, RUSSELL H.; PHIPPS, GRANT T.; AND MORGART, HELEN S. "Prediction of Success in a Dental Assisting Course." *J Dental Ed* 29:348–57 D '65. *
44. GETZELS, J. W., AND CSIKSZENTMIHALYI, M. Chap. 15, "The Study of Creativity in Future Artists: The Criterion Problem," pp. 349–68. In *Experience, Structure and Adaptability.* Edited by O. J. Harvey. New York: Springer Publishing Co., Inc., 1966. Pp. ix, 406. *
45. NEEDHAM, WALTER EVANS. *Intellectual, Personality and Biographical Characteristics of Southern Negro and White College Students.* Doctor's thesis, University of Utah (Salt Lake City, Utah), 1966. (DA 27:1609B)
46. SINAY, RUTH DORIS. *Creative Aptitude Patterns of College Honors Students.* Doctor's thesis, University of Southern California (Los Angeles, Calif.), 1967. (DA 28:5212B)
47. VERY, PHILIP S. "Differential Factor Structures in Mathematical Ability." *Genetic Psychol Monogr* 75:169–207 My '67. * (PA 41:10451)
48. LUNNEBORG, CLIFFORD E., AND LUNNEBORG, PATRICIA W. "Architecture School Performance Predicted From ASAT, Intellective, and Nonintellective Measures." *J Appl Psychol* 53(3):209–13 Je '69. * (PA 43:11928)
49. HAYNES, JACK R. "Factor-Analytic Study of Performance on the Bender-Gestalt." *J Consult & Clin Psychol* 34(3):345–7 Je '70. * (PA 44:13618)
50. HAYNES, JACK R., AND CARLEY, JOHN W. "Relation of Spatial Abilities and Selected Personality Traits." *Psychol Rep* 26(1):214 F '70. * (PA 45:4238)
51. VINCENT, WILLIAM J., AND ALLMANDINGER, MICHAEL F. "Relationships Among Selected Tests of Spatial Orientation Ability." *J Motor Behav* 3(3):259–64 S '71. * (PA 48:8830)

CUMULATIVE NAME INDEX

Allmandinger, M. F.: 51
Anastasi, A.: *rev*, 4:715
Bair, J. T.: 34
Ball, J. M.: 16, 24
Ballantyne, R. H.: 37
Barratt, E. S.: 33
Bechtoldt, H.: *rev*, 4:715
Berger, R. M.: 21
Blakemore, A.: 14
Borko, H.: 5

Buchanan, P. C.: 10
Carley, J. W.: 50
Carroll, J. B.: *rev*, 4:715
Christensen, P. R.: 21, 31
Collier, B. N.: 42
Cottle, W. C.: 23
Csikszentmihalyi, M.: 44
Cureton, E. E.: 19
de Mille, R.: 38
Drewes, H. W.: 35
Francesco, E.: 36
Frick, J. W.: 31
Getzels, J. W.: 44
Guilford, J. P.: 1–4, 11, 15, 20–1, 26, 31
Haney, R.: 27–8
Haynes, J. R.: 49–50
Hills, J. R.: 22
Jones, R. A.: 27–8
Locke, E. A.: 39
Lockman, R. F.: 34
Long, J. M.: 30
Lunneborg, C. E.: 48
Lunneborg, P. W.: 48
Martin, G. C.: 17

Martoccia, C. T.: 34
Merrifield, P. R.: 31
Michael, W. B.: 3, 6, 11, 15, 27–8
Miller, R. S.: 23
Morgart, H. S.: 43
Needham, W. E.: 45
Nugent, F. A.: 42
Phipps, G. T.: 43
Pimsleur, P.: 40
Razor, B. A. L.: 12
Ronan, W. W.: 41
Scott, R. H.: 43
Sinay, R. D.: 46
Stinson, P. J.: 25
Thompson, P. O.: 13
Tomkins, S. S.: 18
Vernon, P. E.: *rev*, 4:715
Very, P. S.: 47
Vincent, W. J.: 51
Wilson, J. E.: 29
Zimmerman, W. S.: 2, 4, 7, 11, 15
Zubin, J.: 18

[1075]

*High Level Battery: Test A/75.** Adults with at least 12 years of education; 1960–72; formerly listed as *National Institute for Personnel Research High Level Battery;* 6 tests in a single booklet: mental alertness, arithmetical problems, reading comprehension (English, Afrikaans), vocabulary (English, Afrikaans); manual by D. P. M. Beukes; National Institute for Personnel Research [South Africa]. *

For additional information, see 6:778 (1 reference).

REFERENCES THROUGH 1971

1. See 6:778.

CUMULATIVE NAME INDEX

Schepers, J. M.: 1

[1076]

★International Primary Factors Test Battery. Grades 5 and over; 1973; also called IPF; 17 scores: vocabulary (subtest 1), word fluency (2), memory [words (3), numbers (4), designs (5)], mazes (6), reasoning [designs (7), letters and numbers (8)], hidden designs (9), space (10), mutilated pictures (11), mutilated words (12), spelling (13), addition (14), comparison [words (15), numbers (16)], total, plus 6 "potential" scores based upon overlapping combinations of subtests in 6 areas: mathematics (subtests 1, 7, 8, 13, 14), English (1, 2, 8, 12, 13), clerical (12–16), technological (1, 7–10), practical (6, 7, 9–11), fluid intelligence (3–7); W. O. Horn; International Tests, Inc. *

[1077]

*The Jastak Test of Potential Ability and Behavior Stability.** Ages 11.5–14.5; 1958–67; the publisher's catalog lists this test under a new title, *Wide Range Intelligence and Personality Test* (for ages 9.5–54), but all currently available test materials bear the original title; test booklet title is *The Jastak Test;* 1967 test identical with test copyrighted 1959 except for the title page; 16 scores: 10 direct scores (vocabulary, number series, coding, picture reasoning, space series, verbal reasoning, social concept, arithmetic, space completion, spelling) and 6 derived scores (language, reality, motivation, psychomotor, intelligence, capacity); J. F. Jastak; Guidance Associates of Delaware, Inc. *

For additional information, reviews by Anne Anastasi and Benjamin Kleinmuntz, and excerpted reviews by Edward S. Bordin and Earl C. Butterfield, see 6:773 (3 references).

REFERENCES THROUGH 1971

1–3. See 6:773.

CUMULATIVE NAME INDEX

Anastasi, A.: *rev*, 6:773
Bordin, E. S.: *exc*, 6:773
Butterfield, E. C.: *exc*, 6:773
Condell, J. F.: 2

Kleinmuntz, B.: *rev*, 6:773
O'Block, F. R.: 3
Stretch, L. B.: 1

[1078]

Job-Tests Program. Adults; 1947–60; battery of aptitude tests, personality tests, and biographical forms used in various combinations in different jobs in business and industry; 3 series; Industrial Psychology, Inc. *

a) FACTORED APTITUDE SERIES. 1947–60; also called *Aptitude-Intelligence Tests;* 15 tests; Joseph E. King (1–2, 4–15) and H. B. Osborn, Jr. (3).

1) *Office Terms.* 1947–60.
2) *Sales Terms.* 1948–60.
3) *Factory Terms.* 1957–60.
4) *Tools.* 1948–60.
5) *Numbers.* 1947–60.
6) *Perception.* 1948–60.
7) *Judgment.* 1947–60.
8) *Precision.* 1947–60.
9) *Fluency.* 1947–60; 2 scores: words ending in tion and jobs, or words beginning with pre and equipment.
10) *Memory.* 1948–60.
11) *Parts.* 1949–60.
12) *Blocks.* 1948–60; adapted from *Army General Classification Test.*
13) *Dimension.* 1947–60.
14) *Dexterity.* 1949–60; 3 scores: maze, checks, dots.
15) *Motor.* 1948–60.

b) EMPLOYEE ATTITUDE SERIES. 1954–60; 3 tests; R. B. Cattell, J. E. King (1–2), and A. K. Schuettler (1–2).

1) *CPF.* 1954; also published by Institute for Personality and Ability Testing as Form A of *IPAT Contact Personality Factor Test.*
2) *NPF.* 1954; also published by Institute for Personality and Ability Testing as *IPAT Neurotic Personality Factor Test* with 1955 copyright.
3) *16 PF.* 1956–60; special printing with new item format, labeled Industrial Edition A, of *Sixteen Personality Factor Questionnaire,* 1956 edition of Form C.

c) APPLICATION-INTERVIEW SERIES. 1948–60; questions in 8 areas: job stability, job experience, education, financial maturity, health-physical condition, family, domestic, outside activities; 5 biography booklets; Joseph E. King.

1) *Biography-Clerical.*
2) *Biography-Mechanical.*
3) *Biography-Sales.*
4) *Biography-Technical.*
5) *Biography-Supervisor.*

For additional information and reviews by William H. Helme and Stanley I. Rubin, see 6:774; for a review by Harold P. Bechtoldt of the *Factored Aptitude Series,* see 5:602; for a review by D. Welty Lefever and an excerpted review by Laurance F. Shaffer of an earlier edition of this series, see 4:712 (1 reference). For reviews of the personality tests, see 6:174 (1 review), 5:71 (2 reviews), 5:74 (2 reviews), 5:112 (1 review), and 4:87 (3 reviews).

REFERENCES THROUGH 1971

1. See 4:712.
2. KNIEVEL, WILLIAM R. "A Vocational Aptitude Test Battery for the Deaf." *Am Ann Deaf* 99:314–9 My '54. * (*PA* 29:4595)
3. ASH, PHILIP. "Claimed and Reported Use of an Industrial Aptitude Test Battery." Abstract. *Am Psychologist* 10:473 Ag '55. *
4. CURETON, EDWARD E. "Service Tests of Multiple Aptitudes." *Proc Inv Conf Testing Probl* 1955:22–39 '56. * (*PA* 31:3017)
5. KIRCHNER, WAYNE K.; LAW, MARY L.; AND DUNNETTE, MARVIN D. "Validity Information Exchange, No. 9-46; D.O.T.

Code 1-86.10, Salesman (Machinery, Equipment, & Supplies)." *Personnel Psychol* 9:525 w '56. *
6. KING, JOSEPH E. "Factored Aptitude Series of Business and Industrial Tests." Comments by Donald E. Super. *Personnel & Guid J* 35:351–60 F '57. * (*PA* 32:998)
7. SHORE, RICHARD P. "Validity Information Exchange, No. 11-22: D.O.T. Code 1-02.01, Bookkeeping-Machine Operator (Banking)." *Personnel Psychol* 11:435–6 au '58. *
8. SHORE, RICHARD P. "Validity Information Exchange, No. 11-23: D.O.T. Code 1-06.02, Teller." *Personnel Psychol* 11:437 au '58. *
9. SHORE, RICHARD P. "Validity Information Exchange, No. 11-24: D.O.T. Code 1-25.68, Proof-Machine Operator." *Personnel Psychol* 11:438–9 au '58. *
10. MACKINNEY, ARTHUR C., AND WOLINS, LEROY. "Validity Information Exchange, No. 12-19: D.O.T. Code 1-36.05, Coding Clerk; 1-17.02, File Clerk II, Circulation Clerk." *Personnel Psychol* 12:482–3 au '59. *
11. BILASKI, I., AND ZUBEK, JOHN P. "The Effects of Age on Factorially 'Pure' Mental Abilities." *J Gerontol* 15:175–82 Ap '60. * (*PA* 35:6223)
12. RONAN, W. W. "Evaluation of Skilled Trades Performance Predictors." *Ed & Psychol Meas* 24:601–8 f '64. * (*PA* 39:6074)
13. CARRON, THEODORE J. "Validity of Tests for Chemical Plant Personnel." *Personnel Psychol* 22(3):307–12 au '69. * (*PA* 44:9414)

CUMULATIVE NAME INDEX

Ash, P.: 3
Bechtoldt, H. P.: *rev*, 5:602
Bilaski, I.: 11
Carron, T. J.: 13
Cureton, E. E.: 4
Dunnette, M. D.: 5
Helme, W. H.: *rev*, 6:774
King, J. E.: 1, 6
Kirchner, W. K.: 5
Knievel, W. R.: 2

Law, M. L.: 5
Lefever, D. W.: *rev*, 4:712
MacKinney, A. C.: 10
Ronan, W. W.: 12
Rubin, S. I.: *rev*, 6:774
Shaffer, L. F.: *exc*, 4:712
Shore, R. P.: 7–9
Super, D. E.: 6
Wolins, L.: 10
Zubek, J. P.: 11

[1079]

★**Junior Aptitude Tests for Indian South Africans.** Standards 6–8; 1971; JATISA; 10 scores: verbal reasoning, series completion, social insight, language usage, numerical reasoning, spatial perception (2 dimensional, 3 dimensional), visual arts, clerical speed and accuracy, mechanical insight; S. Oosthuizen; Human Sciences Research Council [South Africa]. *

[1080]

Measurement of Skill: A Battery of Placement Tests for Business, Industrial and Educational Use. Adults; 1956–67; MOS; 8 tests; Walter V. Clarke Associates, Inc.; AVA Publications, Inc. *

a) SKILL WITH VOCABULARY.
b) SKILL WITH NUMBERS.
c) SKILL WITH SHAPE.
d) SPEED AND ACCURACY.
e) SKILL IN ORIENTATION.
f) SKILL IN THINKING.
g) SKILL WITH MEMORY. 1966 test identical with test copyrighted 1960 except for format.
h) SKILL WITH FINGERS.

For additional information, see 7:677 (4 references); for reviews by Dorothy C. Adkins, Lloyd G. Humphreys, and Joseph E. Moore, see 6:775 (2 references).

REFERENCES THROUGH 1971

1–2. See 6:775.
3–6. See 7:677.

CUMULATIVE NAME INDEX

Adkins, D. C.: *rev*, 6:775
Bailey, W. M. B.: 4
Clarke, W. V.: 2–3, 5–6
Hall, C. E.: 2
Humphreys, L. G.: *rev*, 6:775

Jacobsen, G.: 3, 5–6
Merenda, P. F.: 1–3, 5–6
Moore, J. E.: *rev*, 6:775
Pascale, A. C.: 2

[1081]

The Multi-Aptitude Test. College courses in testing; 1955; miniature battery of 10 tests for instructional use; Edward E. Cureton, Louise Witmer Cureton, and students; Psychological Corporation. *

For additional information and a review by H. H. Remmers, see 5:612 (1 reference).

REFERENCES THROUGH 1971
1. See 5:612.

CUMULATIVE NAME INDEX
Remmers, H. H.: *rev*, 5:612   Wesman, A. G.: 1

[1082]

Multiple Aptitude Tests, 1959 Edition. Grades 7–13; 1955–60; tests identical with those of 1955 edition except for booklet organization; 14 scores: scholastic potential plus 13 scores listed below; 9 tests in 4 booklets; David Segel and Evelyn Raskin; CTB/McGraw-Hill. *

a) FACTOR 1, VERBAL COMPREHENSION. 3 scores: word meaning, paragraph meaning, total.

b) FACTOR 2, PERCEPTUAL SPEED. 3 scores: language usage, routine clerical facility, total.

c) FACTOR 3, NUMERICAL REASONING. 3 scores: arithmetic reasoning, arithmetic computation, total.

d) FACTOR 4, SPATIAL VISUALIZATION. 4 scores: applied science and mechanics, 2-dimensional spatial relations, 3-dimensional spatial relations, total.

For additional information, reviews by S. S. Dunn and Leroy Wolins, and an excerpted review by Laurence Siegel, see 6:776 (8 references) ; for reviews by Ralph F. Berdie and Benjamin Fruchter of the original edition, see 5:613.

REFERENCES THROUGH 1971
1–8. See 6:776.
9. SILVERMAN, RONALD H. *Comparing the Effects of Two Versus Three-Dimensional Art Activity Upon Spatial Visualization, Aesthetic Judgment, and Art Interest.* Doctor's thesis, Stanford University (Stanford, Calif.), 1962. (*DA* 23:2017)
10. BOWERS, ORVON REX. *The Effects of Varied Amounts of Pre-Test Orientation and Types of Post-Test Interpretation on the Accuracy of Students' Vocational Self-Perception.* Doctor's thesis, University of Missouri (Columbia, Mo.), 1963. (*DA* 24:4535)
11. CAPLAN, STANLEY W., AND RUBLE, RONALD A. "A Study of Culturally Imposed Factors on School Achievement in a Metropolitan Area." *J Ed Res* 58:16–21 S '64. *
12. CHANSKY, NORMAN M. "Race, Aptitude and Vocational Interests." *Personnel & Guid J* 43:780–4 Ap '65. * (*PA* 39:16499)
13. CHASE, CLINTON I. *The University Freshman Dropout.* Indiana University, Monoraph of the Bureau of Educational Studies and Testing, Indiana Studies in Prediction, No. 6. Bloomington, Ind.: the Bureau, 1965. Pp. 36. *
14. GARBER, JOHN RODNEY. *Characteristics of Students Enrolled in the Guided Studies Program at Rockingham Community College and Their Implications for Curriculum Development.* Doctor's thesis, North Carolina State University (Raleigh, N.C.), 1971. (*DAI* 32:3555A)

CUMULATIVE NAME INDEX
Berdie, R. F.: *rev*, 5:613	Garber, J. R.: 14
Bowers, O. R.: 10	Khan, L.: 5, 7
Bryant, J. H.: 4	Mendenhall, G. V.: 1
Caplan, S. W.: 8, 11	Miner, J. B.: 6
Chansky, N. M.: 12	Prahl, M. R.: 4
Chase, C. I.: 13	Ruble, R. A.: 8, 11
Cureton, E. E.: 2	Segel, D.: 3, 8
D'Amico, L. A.: 4	Siegel, L.: *exc*, 6:776
Dunn, S. S.: *rev*, 6:776	Silverman, R. H.: 9
Fruchter, B.: *rev*, 5:613	Wolins, L.: *rev*, 6:776

[1083]

N.B. Aptitude Tests (Junior). Standards 4–8; 1961–62; 12 scores: reasoning, classification, computations, spare parts, synonyms, squares, name comparison, figure perception, memory for names and faces, word fluency, coordination, writing speed; Human Sciences Research Council [South Africa]. *

For additional information, see 6:777.

[1084]

National Institute for Personnel Research Intermediate Battery. Standards 7–10 and job applicants with 9–12 years of education; 1964–69; 7 tests in a single booklet: mental alertness, arithmetical problems, computation, spot-the-error (speed, accuracy), reading comprehension, vocabulary, spelling; manual by Anne-Marie Wilcocks; National Institute for Personnel Research [South Africa]. *

For additional information, see 7:678.

REFERENCES THROUGH 1971
1. GIESEKE, MARTHA. "Predicting the Ability to Learn a Foreign Language." *Psychologia Africana* (South Africa) 13(2–3):218–21 O '70. * (*PA* 46:6812)

CUMULATIVE NAME INDEX
Gieseke, M.: 1

[1085]

*National Institute for Personnel Research Normal Battery. Standards 6–10 and job applicants with 8–11 years of education; 1960–73; 1973 metricated battery identical with battery copyrighted 1960 except for 8 revised items; 5 tests in a single booklet: mental alertness, reading comprehension, vocabulary, spelling, computation; manual by S. M. A. Waterhouse; National Institute for Personnel Research [South Africa]. *

For additional information concerning an earlier edition, see 6:779.

REFERENCES THROUGH 1971
1. MACARTHUR, R. S.; IRVINE, S. H.; AND BRIMBLE, A. R. *The Northern Rhodesia Mental Ability Survey 1963.* Rhodes-Livingstone Communication No. 27. Lusaka, Zambia: Rhodes-Livingstone Institute, 1964. Pp. ix, 100. *
2. IRVINE, S. H. "Factor Analysis of African Abilities and Attainments: Constructs Across Cultures." *Psychol B* 71(1):20–32 Ja '69. * (*PA* 43:7553)

CUMULATIVE NAME INDEX
Brimble, A. R.: 1	MacArthur, R. S.: 1
Irvine, S. H.: 1–2	

[1086]

*Nonreading Aptitude Test Battery, 1969 Edition. Disadvantaged grades 9–12 and adults; 1965–73; NATB; nonreading adaptation of the *General Aptitude Test Battery;* 9 scores: intelligence, verbal, numerical, spatial, form perception, clerical perception, motor coordination, finger dexterity, manual dexterity; 14 tests: 10 paper and pencil tests plus 4 performance tests; United States Employment Service; orders for test materials must be cleared through a State Employment Service office; manuals, accessóries and GATB Part 8 distributed by United States Government Printing Office; Books 1–8 and scoring keys distributed by NCS Interpretive Scoring Systems. *

a) GATB-NATB SCREENING DEVICE. 1972–73; test sheet title is *Wide-Range Scale;* to identify examinees who are sufficiently skilled in reading and arithmetic to be tested with the *General Aptitude Test Battery.*

b) BOOK 1, PICTURE WORD MATCHING.

c) BOOK 2, COIN MATCHING.

d) BOOK 3, MATRICES.

e) BOOK 4, TOOL MATCHING.

f) BOOK 5, THREE-DIMENSIONAL SPACE.

g) BOOK 6, FORM MATCHING.

h) BOOK 7, COIN SERIES.

i) BOOK 8, NAME COMPARISON.

j) GATB PART 8 [MARK MAKING].

k) PEGBOARD. 2 tests: place, turn; K & W Products Co., Inc., Specialty Case Manufacturing Co., and Warwick Products Co.

l) FINGER DEXTERITY BOARD. 2 tests: assemble, disassemble; K & W Products Co., Inc., Specialty Case Manufacturing Co., and Warwick Products Co.

For additional information, see 7:679 (3 references).

REFERENCES THROUGH 1971
1–3. See 7:679.

CUMULATIVE NAME INDEX

Bemis, S.: 3　　　　　　Hawk, J.: 2–3
Droege, R. C.: 1–3　　　Seiler, J.: 1
Dvorak, B. J.: 1　　　　Showler, W.: 3

[1087]

SRA Primary Mental Abilities, 1962 Edition.
Grades kgn–1, 2–4, 4–6, 6–9, 9–12, adults; 1946–69;
PMA; earlier editions entitled *Tests of Primary Mental
Abilities* and *Chicago Tests of Primary Mental Abilities;* 6 levels; L. L. Thurstone (earlier editions) and
Thelma Gwinn Thurstone; Science Research Associates, Inc. *

a) GRADES KGN–1. 1946–65; 5 scores: verbal meaning,
perceptual speed, number facility, spatial relations, total.
b) GRADES 2–4. 1946–65; 5 scores: same as for grades
kgn–1.
c) GRADES 4–6. 1946–69; 6 scores: same as for grades
kgn–1 plus reasoning.
d) GRADES 6–9. 1946–69; 5 scores: verbal meaning,
number facility, reasoning, spatial relations, total.
e) GRADES 9–12. 1946–69; 5 scores: same as for grades
6–9.
f) ADULT. 1946–69; 5 scores: same as for grades 6–9;
1965 test identical with test copyrighted 1962 for grades
9–12 except for title.

For additional information and reviews by M. Y.
Quereshi and Richard E. Schutz, see 7:680 (98 references); for a review by John E. Milholland of *a–e*, see
6:780 (50 references); for reviews by Norman Frederiksen and Albert K. Kurtz of an earlier edition, see
5:614 (58 references); for reviews by Anne Anastasi,
Ralph F. Berdie, John B. Carroll, Stuart A. Courtis,
and P. E. Vernon, see 4:716 (42 references); for reviews by Cyril Burt, James R. Hobson, and F. L. Wells,
see 3:225 (52 references); for a review by Florence L.
Goodenough of *a*, see 3:264; for reviews by Henry E.
Garrett, Truman L. Kelley, C. Spearman, Godfrey H.
Thomson, and Robert C. Tryon and excerpted reviews
by A. B. Crawford and John M. Stalnaker, see 2:1427
(11 references). For excerpts from related book reviews, see 2:B1099 (9 excerpts) and 1:B503 (4 excerpts).

REFERENCES THROUGH 1971

1–10. See 2:1427.
11–60. See 3:225.
61–102. See 4:716.
103–161. See 5:614.
162–211. See 6:780.
212–309. See 7:680.
310. JOHNSON, J. T. "On the Nature of Problem-Solving in
Arithmetic." *J Ed Res* 43:110–5 O '49. * (*PA* 24:2791)
311. EELLS, KENNETH; DAVIS, ALLISON; HAVIGHURST, ROBERT J.; HERRICK, VERGIL E.; AND TYLER, RALPH W. *Intelligence and Cultural Differences: A Study of Cultural Learning
and Problem Solving.* Chicago, Ill.: University of Chicago Press,
1951. Pp. xii, 388. * (*PA* 27:5738)
312. HIMMELWEIT, HILDE T., AND SUMMERFIELD, ARTHUR.
"Student Selection—An Experimental Investigation: II." *Brit J
Sociol* 2:59–75 Mr '51. * (*PA* 26:542)
313. LEE, EVERETT S. "Negro Intelligence and Selective
Migration: A Philadelphia Test of the Klineberg Hypothesis."
Am Sociol R 16:227–33 Ap '51. * (*PA* 27:1093)
314. O'BRIEN, MARY C. *A Computation of Norms for Science
Research Associates Primary Mental Abilities Test for the
State of West Virginia.* Master's thesis, West Virginia University (Morgantown, W.Va.), 1953.
315. DUNHAM, RALPH E. "Factors Related to Recidivism in
Adults." *J Social Psychol* 39:77–91 F '54. * (*PA* 28:8866)
316. RUSSELL, DAVID H. "A Second Study of Characteristics
of Good and Poor Spellers." *J Ed Psychol* 46:129–41 Mr '55. *
(*PA* 30:1531)
317. BINDER, ARNOLD. "Schizophrenic Intellectual Impairment: Uniform or Differential?" *J Abn & Social Psychol*
52:11–8 Ja '56. * (*PA* 31:3444)
318. DREVDAHL, JOHN E. "Factors of Importance for Creativity." *J Clin Psychol* 12:21–6 Ja '56. * (*PA* 30:4160)
319. DURLING, DOROTHY, AND ESEN, FATMA MUNIRE. "Irregular Test Profiles Correlated With Personality Traits." *Am J
Mental Def* 61:409–12 O '56. * (*PA* 32:1772)
320. TALLENT, NORMAN. "Behavioral Control and Intellectual

Achievement of Secondary School Boys." *J Ed Psychol* 47:
490–503 D '56. * (*PA* 32:4624)
321. HOFSTAETTER, PETER R.; O'CONNOR, JAMES P.; AND
SUZIEDELIS, ANTANAS. "Sequences of Restricted Associative
Responses and Their Personality Correlates." *J General Psychol*
57:219–27 O '57. * (*PA* 33:9818)
322. OVERTON, ELEAZER C. "Factors That Influence Personality Behavior of High School Students." *Optom Weekly* 48:
583–6 Mr 28 '57. * (*PA* 32:2464)
323. GARRISON, MORTIMER, JR. "A Comparison of Psychological Measures in Mentally Retarded Boys Over a Three-Year
Period as a Function of Etiology." *Training Sch B* 55:54–60
N '58. * (*PA* 34:1664)
324. WRIGLEY, CHARLES; SAUNDERS, DAVID R.; AND NEUHAUS,
JACK O. "Application of the Quartimax Method of Rotation to
Thurstone's Primary Mental Abilities Study." *Psychometrika*
23:151–70 Je '58. * (*PA* 33:7329)
325. CLARK, JAMES W. "The Aging Dimension: A Factorial
Analysis of Individual Differences With Age on Psychological
and Physiological Measurements." *J Gerontol* 15:183–7 Ap '60. *
(*PA* 35:6227)
326. GROVER, V. M. "The Basis of Reading Disability in the
Elementary School Years." *J Social Res* (South Africa) 13:
29–38 D '62. * (*PA* 38:9229)
327. PETERS, HERBERT D. "Performance of Hopi Children on
Four Intelligence Tests." *J Am Indian Ed* 2:27–31 Ja '63. *
328. RANDECKER, HELEN. *A Study to Determine if Chronological Age, Mental Age Scores, and Reading Readiness Tests
Predict the Probable Achievement in Reading of First Grade
Pupils.* Master's thesis, Wisconsin State University (Whitewater, Wis.), 1963.
329. ANASTASIOW, NICHOLAS J. "Maximizing Identification
of the Gifted." *J Ed Res* 57:538–41 Jl–Ag '64. *
330. PETERSON, DONALD FREDERICK. *A Predictive Study of
Success in First Year Bookkeeping.* Master's thesis, San Diego
State College (San Diego, Calif.), 1965.
331. VANDENBERG, STEVEN G. "Multivariate Analysis of Twin
Differences," pp. 29–43. In his *Methods and Goals in Human
Behavior Genetics.* New York: Academic Press Inc., 1965.
Pp. xiii, 351. *
332. FREYBERG, P. S. "Concept Development in Piagetian
Terms in Relation to School Attainment." *J Ed Psychol* 57:
164–8 Je '66. * (*PA* 40:9223)
333. HOLMES, JACK A., AND SINGER, HARRY. *Speed and
Power of Reading in High School.* Cooperative Research Monograph No. 14. Washington, D.C.: United States Government
Printing Office, 1966. Pp. xii, 183. *
334. ORPET, R. E., AND MEYERS, C. E. "Six Structure-of-
Intellect Hypotheses in Six-Year-Old Children." *J Ed Psychol*
57:341–6 D '66. * (*PA* 41:1416)
335. OWENS, CHARLES D. *Development of a Regression
Equation for Predicting Academic Achievement in the Lake
City, Arkansas, High School.* Master's thesis, Arkansas State
College (State University, Ark.), 1966.
336. VANDENBERG, STEVEN G. "Hereditary Factors in Psychological Variables in Man, With a Special Emphasis on
Cognition," pp. 99–133. In *Genetic Diversity and Human
Behavior.* Viking Fund Publications in Anthropology No. 45.
Edited by J. N. Spuhler. Chicago, Ill.: Aldine Publishing Co.,
1967. Pp. xi, 291. *
337. BURNHAM, RUTH ELIZABETH. *The Relationship Between
the Intelligence Quotient and the Creative Ability of Second
Grade Children in the Villa Park School System.* Master's thesis,
Northern Illinois University (DeKalb, Ill.), 1968.
338. FREYBERG, P. S. "Fluctuations in Children's Cognitive
Test Scores Over a Two-Year Period." *Brit J Ed Psychol* 38:
82–6 F '68. * (*PA* 42:12731)
339. LOEHLIN, JOHN C., AND VANDENBERG, STEVEN G. Chap.
15, "Genetic and Environmental Components in the Covariation
of Cognitive Abilities: An Additive Model," pp. 261–78. In
Progress in Human Behavior Genetics. Edited by Steven G.
Vandenberg. Baltimore, Md.: Johns Hopkins Press, 1968. Pp.
xi, 356. *
340. ROUDABUSH, GLENN E. Chap. 17, "Analyzing Dyadic
Relationships," pp. 303–32. In *Progress in Human Behavior
Genetics.* Edited by Steven G. Vandenberg. Baltimore, Md.:
Johns Hopkins Press, 1968. Pp. xi, 356. *
341. SCHAIE, K. W., AND STROTHER, C. R. "Limits of
Optimal Functioning in Superior Old Adults." Discussion by
Joseph H. Britton. *Interdiscipl Topics Gerontol* 1:132–53 '68. *
342. SCHAIE, K. WARNER, AND STROTHER, CHARLES R. "Cognitive and Personality Variables in College Graduates of
Advanced Age," pp. 281–308. (*PA* 43:15628, title only) In
*Human Aging and Behavior: Recent Advances in Research
and Theory.* Edited by George A. Talland. New York: Academic
Press Inc., 1968. Pp. xiii, 322. *
343. KING, F. J.; ROBERTS, DENNIS; AND KROPP, RUSSELL P.
"Relationship Between Ability Measures and Achievement
Under Four Methods of Teaching Elementary Set Concepts."
J Ed Psychol 60(3):244–7 Je '69. * (*PA* 43:13392)
344. DIELMAN, T. E., AND FURUNO, SETSU. "Interrelationships
Among Selected Environmental, Cognitive, and Achievement
Variables: A Further Analysis of the Ten-Year Follow-Up of

Nonreading Aptitude Test Battery

the Children of the Kauai Pregnancy Study." *Personality* 1(3):185–99 au '70. * (*PA* 47:9797)

345. MARJORIBANKS, KEVIN MCLEOD. *Ethnic and Environmental Influences on Levels and Profiles of Mental Abilities.* Doctor's thesis, University of Toronto (Toronto, Ont., Canada), 1970. (*DAI* 32:6052A)

346. RENNELS, MAX RAYMOND. "The Effects of Instructional Methodology in Art Education Upon Achievement on Spatial Tasks by Disadvantaged Negro Youths." *J Negro Ed* 39(2):116–23 sp '70. * (*PA* 46:7841)

347. RIVERS, LARRY WENDELL. *The Stability of Differential Patterns of Mental Abilities in Children From Different Ethnic Groups.* Doctor's thesis, St. Louis University (St. Louis, Mo.), 1970. (*DAI* 32:1194B)

348. VAN CAMP, SARAH STREET. *An Auditory and Visual Discrimination Test for Kindergarten and First Grade Children: A New Approach.* Doctor's thesis, University of Massachusetts (Amherst, Mass.), 1970. (*DAI* 31:5680A)

349. WOOD, MILDRED HOPE. *A Longitudinal Study of the Effectiveness of Certain Kindergarten Tests in Predicting Reading Achievement, School Failure, and the Need for Special Services.* Doctor's thesis, Indiana University (Bloomington, Ind.), 1970. (*DAI* 31:5683A)

350. BALTES, PAUL B.; SCHAIE, K. WARNER; AND NARDI, ANNE H. "Age and Experimental Mortality in a Seven-Year Longitudinal Study of Cognitive Behavior." *Develop Psychol* 5(1):18–26 Jl '71. * (*PA* 46:8800)

351. CRARY, HELEN L., AND RIDGWAY, ROBERT W. "Relationships Between Visual Form Perception Abilities and Reading Achievement in the Intermediate Grades." *J Exp Ed* 40(1):17–22 f '71. * (*PA* 47:9796)

352. JOHNSON, THEOLA GAE. *Influence of Selected Factors on the Ability of Fourth, Fifth, and Sixth Graders to Read Graphs.* Doctor's thesis, University of Southern California (Los Angeles, Calif.), 1971. (*DAI* 32:726A)

353. LAVELY, ROBERT HENRY. *An Investigation Comparing Primary Mental Abilities of Trainable Mentally Retarded Children, Educable Mentally Retarded Children, and Normal Children With Comparable Mental Ages.* Doctor's thesis, Ohio State University (Columbus, Ohio), 1971. (*DAI* 32:3823A)

354. LOO, CHALSA, AND WENAR, CHARLES. "Activity Level and Motor Inhibition: Their Relationship to Intelligence-Test Performance in Normal Children." *Child Develop* 42(3):967–71 S '71. * (*PA* 47:6495)

355. MCGILLIGAN, ROBERT PATRICK. *Psychological Differentiation, Abilities and Personality.* Doctor's thesis, St. Louis University (St. Louis, Mo.), 1971. (*DAI* 33:1291B)

356. MARJORIBANKS, KEVIN. "Environmental Correlates of Diverse Mental Abilities." *J Exp Ed* 39(4):64–8 su '71. * (*PA* 47:655)

357. MARJORIBANKS, KEVIN. "The Learning Environment of the Home—An Instrument." *Austral & N Zeal J Sociol* (Australia) 7(2):69–77 O '71. *

358. MARTIN, WILLIAM A. "Word Fluency—Intellect or Personality?" *J Genetic Psychol* 118(1):17–24 Mr '71. * (*PA* 46:8848)

359. MUSSIO, JERRY J., AND WAHLSTROM, MERLIN W. "Predicting Performance of Programmer Trainees in a Post-High School Setting." Discussion by Charles D. Lothridge. *Proc Ann Computer Personnel Res Conf* 9:26–53 '71. *

360. MYKLEBUST, HELMER R.; BANNOCHIE, MARGARET N.; AND KILLEN, JAMES R. Chap. 9, "Learning Disabilities and Cognitive Processes," pp. 213–51. In *Progress in Learning Disabilities, Vol. 2.* Edited by Helmer R. Myklebust. New York: Grune & Stratton, Inc., 1971. Pp. ix, 404. *

361. NELSON, JOHN CLEMENT. *Relating Student and Teacher Personality and Cognitive Characteristics With School Achievement of Educable Mentally Retarded Children.* Doctor's thesis, George Peabody College for Teachers (Nashville, Tenn.), 1971. (*DAI* 32:1948A)

362. PARKER, HARRY J.; STERNLOF, RICHARD E.; AND MCCOY, JOHN F. "Objective Versus Individual Mental Ability Tests With Former Head Start Children in the First Grade." *Percept & Motor Skills* 32(1):287–92 F '71. * (*PA* 46:3868)

363. RAJU, VIJAYA, AND RAMAMURTHI, P. V. "Verbal Ability and Educational Achievement." *Indian J Appl Psychol* 8(2):59–60 Jl '71. *

364. SCOTT, RALPH, AND SATTEL, LUDWIG. "School and Home: Not Either-Or." *Merrill-Palmer Q* 17(4):335–45 O '71. *

365. UPCHURCH, WINIFRED BROOK. *The Relationship Between Perceptual-Motor Skills and Word Recognition Achievement at the Kindergarten Level.* Doctor's thesis, Syracuse University (Syracuse, N.Y.), 1971. (*DAI* 32:4497A)

366. VARNER, DONALD GILES. *The Relationship of Selected Cumulative Grade Point Averages to Intelligence Quotient.* Master's thesis, Eastern Illinois University (Charleston, Ill.), 1971.

CUMULATIVE NAME INDEX

Abrams, E. N.: 86
Adkins, D. C.: 10, 17–8
Alexander, D.: 264
Allebach, N. L.: 130
Amundson, G. J.: 236
Anant, S. S.: 231, 237, 274
Anastasi, A.: 131; *rev*, 4:716
Anastasiow, N. J.: 329
Ansbacher, H. L.: 106
Asbury, C. A.: 292, 306
Attwell, A. A.: 202, 286
Auria, C.: 226

Avakian, S. A.: 104, 192
Baker, E. H.: 132
Ball, F. J.: 19
Baltes, P. B.: 350
Bannochie, M. N.: 360
Battle, E. S.: 307
Baughman, E. E.: 275
Bechtel, R.: 107
Beck, I. H. H.: 224
Becker, G. J.: 63
Beery, K. E.: 276
Bellows, R. M.: 32
Bendig, A. W.: 195, 206
Berdie, R. F.: 142; *rev*, 4:716
Bernreuter, R. G.: 11, 26
Binder, A.: 213, 317
Blewett, D. B.: 133
Blumenfeld, E. R.: 232
Blumenfeld, W. S.: 232
Bond, G. L.: 143
Bonfield, J. R.: 277
Bouthilet, L.: 64
Breese, F. H.: 56b
Brendemuehl, F. L.: 265
Brennan, J. T.: 258
Britton, J. H.: 341
Brody, A. B.: 87
Broverman, D. M.: 238
Brozek, J.: 57a
Bruce, M. M.: 151
Bruininks, R. H.: 293
Burgess, T. C.: 193
Burnham, P. S.: 55
Burnham, R. E.: 337
Burrall, L.: 119, 134
Burt, C.: *rev*, 3:225
Busse, T. V.: 278
Butcher, H. J.: 279, 294–5
Byrne, N. M.: 64, 95, 101
Cain, L. F.: 12
Canisia, M.: 197
Carroll, J. B.: *rev*, 4:716
Carter, L.: 72
Cassel, R. H.: 73, 88
Cattell, R. B.: 207, 279
Cawley, J. F.: 280
Center, W. R.: 208
Chambers, E. G.: *exc*, 2:B1099
Chambers, J. A.: 174
Chambers, J. R.: 120
Chansky, N. M.: 259
Chase, C. I.: 185
Clark, J. W.: 221, 325
Clark, M. P.: 50
Clark, P. J.: 194
Clausen, J.: 246
Cleland, D. L.: 198
Clymer, T. W.: 143
Cohen, S. A.: 247
Coleman, J. C.: 175
Connery, T. F.: 167
Conry, R.: 248
Coombs, C. H.: 27
Corter, H. M.: 74, 108
Courtis, S. A.: *rev*, 4:716
Crandall, V. C.: 307
Crary, H. L.: 351
Crawford, A. B.: 8, 55; *exc*, 2:1427
Crites, J. O.: 203
Cronholm, B.: 281
Cropley, A. J.: 296
Cureton, E. E.: 162
Dahlstrom, W. G.: 275
Danenhower, H. S.: 73, 88
Davidson, K. S.: 191
Davis, A.: 311
Davis, M. R.: 282
Davis, W. A.: 65
Dean, D. A.: 89
Delancy, E. O.: 135
Delman, L.: 66
Derrick, M. W.: 199
Devlin, J. P.: 90
Dielman, T. E.: 344
Dingman, H. F.: 202
Donald, M. W.: 200
Drake, D. J.: 121, 131
Drevdahl, J. E.: 214, 318
Driscoll, A. M.: 13
Dunham, R. E.: 315
Durkin, D.: 186
Durling, D.: 319

Edgerton, H. A.: 28
Eells, K.: 311
Elias, J. Z.: 96
Ellison, M. L.: 28
Emm, M. E.: 176
Ertl, J. P.: 297
Esen, F. M.: 319
Eysenck, H. J.: *exc*, 2:B1099
Farrant, R. H.: 239
Farrell, M. L.: 14
Faubion, R.: 20, 30
Ferguson, L. R.: 260
Fiedler, E. R.: 298
Finley, P. J.: 240
Fiske, D. W.: 97
Ford, A. H.: 91
Frank, H.: 298
Frederiksen, N.: *rev*, 5:614
Freeman, J. A.: 266, 283, 308
French, T. M.: *exc*, 2:B1099
Freyberg, P. S.: 332, 338
Fruchter, B.: 56, 67
Frye, U. C.: 152
Furuno, S.: 344
Gale, D. F.: 267
Gardner, R. C.: 249
Garrett, H. E.: *rev*, 2:1427; *exc*, 2:B1099
Garrison, M.: 323
Gaspar, M. A.: 299
Gibney, E. F.: 75
Godin, M. A.: 199
Goldberg, L. R.: 178
Goodenough, F. L.: *rev*, 3:264
Goodman, C. H.: 26, 29, 48–9, 51
Goodman, C. M.: 15
Goodman, J. O.: 280
Grover, V. M.: 326
Guetzkow, H.: 57a
Guilford, J. P.: 100
Hall, W. E.: 61
Harbilas, J. N.: 187
Harrell, W.: 20, 30
Harris, D. B.: 177
Havighurst, R. J.: 57b, 65, 311
Hay, E. N.: *exc*, 1:B503
Herrick, V. E.: 311
Herzberg, F.: 136
Hessemer, M.: 40
Himmelweit, H. T.: 312
Hobson, J. R.: 58; *rev*, 3:225
Hodges, J. M.: 109
Hofstaetter, P. R.: 321
Holloway, H. D.: 122, 137
Holmes, J. A.: 333
Horst, P.: 165
Hudson, H. H.: 46
Humphreys, L. G.: 268
Hundleby, J. D.: 284
Hutcheon, J. F.: 110
Huttner, L.: 166
Jacobs, R.: 60
Jacobs, R. E.: 188
Jeffries, L. A.: 68
Johnson, A. P.: 41–2
Johnson, J. T.: 310
Johnson, R. W.: 111
Johnson, T. G.: 352
Junkala, J. B.: 250, 261
Kaczkowski, H. R.: 167
Kamin, L. J.: 156
Kanderian, S. S.: 300
Kaplan, H. K.: 220
Kashiwagi, S.: 233
Kebbon, L.: 251
Kelley, T. L.: *rev*, 2:1427
Kelly, E. L.: 97, 178
Kerr, W. D.: 262
Ketcham, W. A.: 237
Killen, J. R.: 360
Kilman, M. D.: 301
King, F. J.: 343
Kingsley, R. F.: 241
Koch, M. L.: 138
Kolstoe, O. P.: 139, 212
Krebs, E. G.: 302
Kropp, R. P.: 343
Kuder, G. F.: 18, 33
Kurtz, A. K.: *rev*, 5:614
Lagan, M.: 200
Lambert, W. E.: 249
Lapp, C. J.: 34

Larson, A. A.: 263
Lavely, R. H.: 353
Lee, E. S.: 313
Lepkin, M.: 136
Levine, S.: 98
Lewis, D. G.: 242
Lewis, L. H.: 285
Lighthall, F. K.: 191
Lloyd, C. J.: 168
Loehlin, J. C.: 339
Long, J. R.: 157
Loo, C.: 354
Loranger, A. W.: 179, 189
Lothridge, C. D.: 359
Lundberg, G. A.: exc, 1:B503
Maccoby, E. E.: 260
McCormick, J. H.: 234
McCoy, J. F.: 362
McElwee, A. R.: 43
McFarland, R. L.: 201
McGilligan, R. P.: 355
McKee, J. P.: 112
McNemar, Q.: exc, 2:B1099
McTaggart, H. P.: 180
Mangan, G. L.: 221
Marjoribanks, K.: 356-7
Marjoribanks, K. M.: 345
Marquis, F. N.: 113
Martin, W. A.: 303, 358
Maslany, G. W.: 296
Mearig, J. S.: 243
Melton, R. S.: 209
Meredith, P.: 144
Meyer, H. H.: 99
Meyer, W. J.: 190, 195, 206
Meyers, C. E.: 257, 286, 334
Meyers, E.: 202
Michael, W. B.: 76, 100
Micheli, G. S.: 114
Milholland, J. E.: rev, 6:780
Mill, C. R.: 145
Misiak, H.: 179, 189
Mitchell, J. V.: 153
Moffie, D. J.: 21-2, 44
Money, J.: 264
Moody, C. B.: 115
Mueller, M. W.: 252-3, 287, 304
Mukherjee, B. N.: 254
Murray, J. E.: 77
Mussio, J. J.: 359
Myklebust, H. R.: 360
Nardi, A. H.: 350
Nelson, C. L.: 201
Nelson, J. C.: 361
Neuhaus, J. O.: 324
Nicholls, J. G.: 269
Nixon, M.: 72
Novack, H. S.: 222
O'Brien, M. C.: 314
O'Connor, J. P.: 321
Olson, D. J.: 105
Orpet, R. E.: 202, 286, 334
Osburn, H. G.: 209
Overton, E. C.: 322
Owens, C. D.: 335
Pankaskie, M.: 31
Parker, H. J.: 362
Perlman, R. M.: 124

Perry, J. O.: 229
Peters, H. D.: 327
Peterson, D. F.: 330
Plant, W. T.: 248
Pont, H. B.: 295
Pooler, M. H.: 146
Poteet, J. A.: 309
Pouncey, A. T.: 215
Proctor, C. H.: 194
Quereshi, M. Y.: rev, 7:680
Racky, D. J.: 181
Rainey, R. G.: 255
Raju, V.: 363
Ramamurthi, P. V.: 363
Ramaseshan, R. S.: 92
Randecker, H.: 328
Rawlings, T. D.: 218
Reddig, G. L.: 256
Reining, H.: 45
Rennels, M. R.: 346
Ridgway, R. W.: 351
Rivers, L. W.: 347
Roberts, D.: 343
Roberts, S. O.: 116
Robinson, F. P.: 61
Robinson, J. B.: 32
Robinson, J. M.: 116
Rochlin, I.: 117
Rogers, C. A.: 154
Ronan, W. W.: 244
Rosenthal, F.: 124
Rossi, A. M.: 201
Rothney, J. W. M.: 140
Roudabush, G. E.: 340
Rowan, T. C.: 164
Ruebush, B. K.: 191
Russell, D. H.: 316
Sanders, J. R.: 93
Sanders, R. M.: 210
Sarason, S. B.: 191
Sattel, L.: 364
Satter, G.: 147
Saunders, D. R.: 324
Schaefer, W. C.: 23
Schafer, E. W. P.: 297
Schaffer, M. C.: 305
Schaie, K. W.: 124, 148, 165, 169-70, 182, 288-9, 341-2, 350
Schalling, D.: 281
Schmidt, L. G.: 78, 125, 140
Schutz, R. E.: rev, 7:680
Scott, R.: 364
Seashore, H. G.: 85
Shalloe, M. P.: 141
Shanner, W. M.: 6, 33, 52
Shaw, D. C.: 69, 79
Shinn, E. O.: 155
Shofstall, W. P.: exc, 2: B1099
Silverstein, A. B.: 196
Simonian, K.: 272, 290
Singer, H.: 333
Smith, A. E.: 80
Smith, C. E.: exc, 1:B503
Smith, D. D.: 160, 171
Smith, G. R.: 225
Smith, H. C.: 8
Smith, R. S.: 272, 290

Spaulding, G.: 118
Spearman, C.: rev, 2:1427
Spivey, G. M.: 94
Stalnaker, J. M.: 7, 9; exc, 2:1427
Staveley, B.: 270
Stempel, E. F.: 126
Stene, D. M.: 166
Sternlof, R. E.: 362
Stier, L. D.: 205
Stonesifer, F. A.: 219
Stonesifer, J. N.: exc, 2: B1099
Stromsen, K. E.: 45
Strother, C. R.: 148, 165, 288-9, 341-2
Stuit, D. B.: 34, 46
Summerfield, A.: 312
Super, D. E.: 82, 203
Sutherland, T. E.: 216
Suziedelis, A.: 321
Tallent, N.: 320
Taylor, P. L.: 163
Thomson, G. H.: rev, 2:1427
Thurstone, L. L.: 1-5, 24, 35, 53-4, 57, 70, 83
Thurstone, T. G.: 25, 35-6, 62, 71, 84, 95, 101, 159
Toussaint, I. H.: 198, 227
Townsend, A.: 59, 118
Traxler, A. E.: 37
Tredick, V. D.: 16
Trumbull, R.: 127
Tryon, R. C.: rev, 2:1427
Tuel, J. K.: 257
Turner, C. J.: 145
Tutt, M. L.: 245
Tyler, L. E.: 102, 128, 172

Tyler, R. W.: 311
Upchurch, W. B.: 365
Van Camp, S. S.: 348
Vandenberg, S. G.: 183, 194, 217, 230, 271, 331, 336, 339
Van Voorhis, W. R.: 38
Varner, D. G.: 366
Vernon, P. E.: rev, 4:716
Wagner, R. M.: 204
Wahlstrom, M. W.: 359
Waite, R. R.: 191
Walters, R. H.: 161
Weise, P.: 257
Wellington, J. A.: 149
Wellman, F. E.: 158
Wells, F. L.: rev, 3:225
Wenar, C.: 354
Werner, E. E.: 272, 290
Wesman, A. G.: 85
Weston, L. D.: 291
Wheatley, M. M.: 103
White, H. G.: 211
White, I. W.: 47
Wilkins, W. F.: 184
Willis, W. K.: 262
Wilson, J. A. R.: 173, 205
Wilson, R. C.: 223, 228
Wolking, W. D.: 150
Wood, M. H.: 349
Wright, R. E.: 7.1
Wrigley, C.: 324
Yates, L. G.: 273
Young, E. F.: exc, 1:B503
Yum, K. S.: 39
Zaidi, S. W. H.: 235
Zimmerman, W. S.: 100, 129
Zubin, J.: exc, 2:B1099

[1088]

*Senior Aptitude Tests. Standards 8–10 and college and adults; 1969–71; SAT; 12 scores: verbal comprehension, numerical fluency, word fluency, visual perception speed, reasoning (deductive, inductive), spatial visualization (2 dimensional, 3 dimensional), memory (paragraphs, symbols), psychomotor coordination, writing speed; F. A. Fouche and N. F. Alberts; Human Sciences Research Council [South Africa]. *

For additional information, see 7:681.

[Out of Print Since TIP I]

Differential Ability Tests, 5:604
Experimental Comparative Prediction Batteries, 7:674 (3 references)
Fife Tests of Ability, 4:713 (2 reviews, 3 references)
Holzinger-Crowder Uni-Factor Tests, 5:610 (3 reviews, 3 references)
United States Employment Service Special Aptitude Tests, 4:717
Vocational Guidance Program, 6:781 (1 review)
Yale Educational Aptitude Test Battery, 5:615 (2 reviews, 11 references)

VOCATIONS – TIP II

[2100]

★**ACT Assessment of Career Development.** Grades 8–11; 1973, c1972–73; ACD; "career development behavior generally thought to be of practical significance in evaluating and modifying school career guidance programs"; "interpretation of ACD scores to individual students is not recommended"; 11 scores: occupational knowledge (occupational characteristics, occupational preparation requirements), exploratory occupational experiences (social-health-personal services, business sales and management, business operations, technologies and trades, natural-social-medical sciences, creative and applied arts, total), career planning (knowledge, involvement), plus statistical summaries of responses to 42 specific items and up to 19 locally developed items; Dale Prediger in conjunction with Bert Westbrook and John Roth; American College Testing Program. *

[2101]

★**ACT Career Planning Program.** Entrants to postsecondary educational institutions; 1970–73; CPP; test booklet title is *Career Planning Profile;* a battery of interest, ability, and background measures which may be administered by participating institutions; in addition to the scores and biographical details listed below, the Student Report lists ratings of interests, competencies, abilities, and expectancies of educational success in each of the 8 vocational interest areas; optional institutional summary available; colleges which administer the *Student Follow-Up Questionnaire* at the end of the first term may also receive an optional institutional report presenting local validity data on the CPP; 3 parts; American College Testing Program. *
a) VOCATIONAL INTEREST PROFILE. 8 scores: trades, technical, science, health, arts, social service, business contact, business detail.
b) ABILITY MEASURES. 8 scores: mechanical reasoning, numerical computation, mathematics usage, space relations, reading skills, language usage, clerical skills, nonverbal reasoning.
c) STUDENT INFORMATION SECTION. Background, educational plans, student concerns, work orientation, and career-related competencies.

REFERENCES THROUGH 1971

1. *Handbook for the ACT Career Planning Profile, 1970–71 Edition.* Iowa City, Iowa: ACT Publications, 1970. Pp. viii, 52. *
2. *Career Planning Profile National Norms for Vocational-Technical Students Beyond High School.* Iowa City, Iowa: American College Testing Program, Inc., 1971. Pp. vii, 31, plus unnumbered appendices. *
3. COLE, NANCY S., AND HANSON, GARY R. "An Analysis of the Structure of Vocational Interests." *ACT Res Rep* 40:1–17 Ja '71. * (*PA* 47:1843)
4. COLE, NANCY S., AND HANSON, GARY R. "An Analysis of the Structure of Vocational Interests." *J Counsel Psychol* 18(5): 478–86 S '71. * (*PA* 47:3679)

CUMULATIVE NAME INDEX

Cole, N. S.: 3–4   Hanson, G. R.: 3–4

[2102]

*[**Aptitude Inventory.**] Employee applicants; 1957–71; 1 test published in the same form under 3 titles; 4 scores for each test: intelligent job performance,

leadership qualities, proper job attitude, relations with others; John C. Denton; Psychological Business Research. *
a) MANAGEMENT APTITUDE INVENTORY. Applicants for management and supervisory positions; 1957–71; MAI.
b) EMPLOYMENT APTITUDE INVENTORY. Applicants for office and factory positions; 1957–61; EAI.
c) SALES APTITUDE INVENTORY. Applicants for sales positions; 1957–63; SAI.
For additional information, reviews by Leonard W. Ferguson and C. E. Jurgensen, and an excerpted review by Laurence Siegel, see 6:1024 (1 reference).

REFERENCES THROUGH 1971

1. See 6:1024.
2. GUION, ROBERT M. "Synthetic Validity in a Small Company: A Demonstration." *Personnel Psychol* 18:49–63 sp '65. * (*PA* 39:16490)

CUMULATIVE NAME INDEX

Denton, J. C.: 1   Jurgensen, C. E.: *rev*, 6:1024
Ferguson, L. W.: *rev*, 6:1024   Siegel, L.: *exc*, 6:1024
Guion, R. M.: 2

[2103]

★**Career Maturity Inventory.** Grades 6–12; 1973; CMI; formerly called *Vocational Development Inventory;* 2 tests; John O. Crites; CTB/McGraw-Hill. *
a) ATTITUDE SCALE.
b) COMPETENCE TEST, RESEARCH EDITION. 5 scores: self-appraisal, occupational information, goal selection, planning, problem solving.

REFERENCES THROUGH 1971

1. DAS, AJIT KUMAR. *The Effect of Counseling on the Vocational Maturity of a Group of Potential Drop-Outs From High School.* Doctor's thesis, State University of Iowa (Iowa City, Iowa), 1962. (*DA* 23:2788)
2. HALL, DONALD W. "The Vocational Development Inventory: A Measure of Vocational Maturity in Adolescence." *Personnel & Guid J* 41:771–5 My '63. *
3. JESSEE, BILLY EUGENE. *The Effects of Individual Counseling and Group Guidance With Eighth Grade Boys on Their Vocational Maturity the Following Year.* Doctor's thesis, Arizona State University (Tempe, Ariz.), 1963. (*DA* 25:6389)
4. HARLAN, GRADY EDWARD. *A Comparison of Differences in Selected Characteristics Among High School Seniors, College Freshmen, Trade School Students, Technical School Students, and Business School Students.* Doctor's thesis, State University of Iowa (Iowa City, Iowa), 1964. (*DA* 25:5016)
5. CRITES, JOHN O. "Measurement of Vocational Maturity in Adolescence: 1, Attitude Test of the Vocational Development Theory." *Psychol Monogr* 79(2):1–36 '65. * (*PA* 39:10869)
6. DRAHOZAL, EDWARD CHARLES. *A Study of Selected Characteristics of Senior High School Students and Their Perceptions of Their Counselor's Role in the Post High School Decision.* Doctor's thesis, State University of Iowa (Iowa City, Iowa), 1965. (*DA* 26:2544)
7. JESSEE, BILL E., AND HEINMANN, ROBERT A. "The Effects of Counseling and Group Guidance on the Vocational Maturity of Ninth Grade Boys." *J Ed Res* 59:68–72 O '65. * (*PA* 40: 3397)
8. HARRIS, JOHN WILLIAM, JR. *The Effect of Vocational Development and Family Social Status on the Academic Performance of Male Freshmen at Middle Tennessee State University.* Doctor's thesis, University of Tennessee (Knoxville, Tenn.), 1966. (*DA* 27:2828A)
9. MALONE, FRANCIS EDWARD, JR. *A Study of Students Enrolled in Post-High School Public Vocational Education Programs in Iowa During the 1964–1965 School Year.* Doctor's thesis, University of Iowa (Iowa City, Iowa), 1966. (*DA* 27: 678A)
10. MYERS, WAYNE PRUITT. *The Effect of Neighborhood Youth Corps Upon Vocational Development Variables of Rural Southern*

Appalachian Youth. Doctor's thesis, University of Tennessee (Knoxville, Tenn.), 1966. (*DA* 27:650A)

11. BARTLETT, WILLIS EDWARD. *Psychological Needs and Vocational Maturity of Manpower Trainees.* Doctor's thesis, Ohio State University (Columbus, Ohio), 1967. (*DA* 28:3456A)

12. CRITES, JOHN O., AND SEMLER, IRA J. "Adjustment, Educational Achievement, and Vocational Maturity as Dimensions of Development in Adolescence." *J Counsel Psychol* 14:489-96 N '67. * (*PA* 42:3783)

13. WILLIAMS, RODNEY HOWE. *The Relationship Between the Vocational Development and Scholastic Achievement of Male College Students: A Correlational Analysis and Evaluation of the Relationship Between Scores of Vocational Maturity, Vocational Maladjustment, Intellectual Capacity, and Scholastic Index.* Doctor's thesis, New York University (New York, N.Y.), 1967. (*DA* 28:1318A)

14. ASHBURY, FRANK A. "Vocational Development of Rural Disadvantaged Eighth-Grade Boys." *Voc Guid Q* 17:109-13 D '68. *

15. BARTLETT, WILLIS E. "Vocational Maturity and Personality Variables of Manpower Trainees." *Voc Guid Q* 17:104-8 D '68. *

16. COX, STEVEN GRAHN. *A Study of Relationships Between Student Scores on Various Predictor Measures and Vocational Success of Students Who Were Followed Up One and Five Years Following Training in Selected Private Trade, Technical, and Business Schools.* Doctor's thesis, University of Iowa (Iowa City, Iowa), 1968. (*DA* 29:3827A)

17. OSIPOW, SAMUEL H., AND ALDERFER, RICHARD D. "The Effects of a Vocationally Oriented Speech Course on the Vocational Planning Behavior of High School Students." *Personnel & Guid J* 47:244-8 N '68. *

18. SHIRTS, ROBERT GARRY. *Response Style in the Vocational Development Inventory.* Doctor's thesis, University of Utah (Salt Lake City, Utah), 1968. (*DA* 29:761B)

19. CONDUFF, ELIZABETH. *Personality Characteristics and Adjustment of Adolescents With Regard to Vocational Maturity.* Master's thesis, University of Tennessee (Knoxville, Tenn.), 1969.

20. NICHOL, JOHN STEWART. *The Use of Vocational Discussion in Small Groups to Increase Vocational Maturity.* Doctor's thesis, Arizona State University (Tempe, Ariz.), 1969. (*DAI* 30:3733A)

21. ANSELL, EDGAR MERLE. *An Assessment of Vocational Maturity of Lower-Class Caucasians, Lower-Class Negroes and Middle-Class Caucasians in Grades Eight Through Twelve.* Doctor's thesis, State University of New York (Buffalo, N.Y.), 1970. (*DAI* 31:2094A)

22. DOMENICHETTI, MADONNA. *Work Values in Adolescence as a Function of Vocational Maturity.* Doctor's thesis, Catholic University of America (Washington, D.C.), 1970. (*DAI* 31:1574A)

23. HANLEY, DENNIS EUGENE. *The Effects of Short-Term Counseling Upon High School Underachievers' Measured Self-Concepts, Academic Achievement, and Vocational Maturity.* Doctor's thesis, Purdue University (Lafayette, Ind.), 1970. (*DAI* 31:5125A)

24. JALKANEN, ARTHUR WILHELM. *A Comparison of Vocational Attitudes and Job Aspirations of Urban and Suburban School Students.* Doctor's thesis, Wayne State University (Detroit, Mich.), 1970. (*DAI* 31:4464A)

25. MAYNARD, PETER E., AND HANSEN, JAMES C. "Vocational Maturity Among Inner-City Youths." *J Counsel Psychol* 17(5): 400-4 S '70. * (*PA* 45:3005)

26. MAYNARD, PETER ELWOOD. *Assessing the Vocational Maturity of Inner-City Youths.* Doctor's thesis, State University of New York (Buffalo, N.Y.), 1970. (*DAI* 31:4468A)

27. MUNSON, PAUL JONATHAN. *An Investigation of the Relationship of Values, and Curriculum Selection to Vocational Maturity.* Doctor's thesis, University of Virginia (Charlottesville, Va.), 1970. (*DAI* 31:4470A)

28. SCHRADER, CHARLES HENRY. *Vocational Choice Problems: Indecision vs. Indecisiveness.* Doctor's thesis, University of Iowa (Iowa City, Iowa), 1970. (*DAI* 31:3694B)

29. COX, STEVEN G. "Do Educational Measures Predict Vocational Success?" *Voc Guid Q* 19(4):271-4 Je '71. * (*PA* 48: 1981)

30. CRITES, JOHN O. "Acquiescence Response Style and the Vocational Development Inventory." *J Voc Behav* 1(2):189-200 Ap '71. * (*PA* 47:11693)

31. CRITES, JOHN O. *The Maturity of Vocational Attitudes in Adolescence.* APGA Inquiry Series Number 2. Washington, D.C.: American Personnel and Guidance Association, 1971. Pp. 112. *

32. DONAHUE, MICHAEL A. *College Placement: An Exploratory Investigation of the Employment Selection Process and Certain Correlates of Vocational Development.* Doctor's thesis, Purdue University (Lafayette, Ind.), 1971. (*DAI* 32:735A)

33. KAPES, JEROME THEODORE. *The Relationship Between Selected Characteristics of Ninth Grade Boys and Curriculum Selection and Success in Tenth Grade.* Doctor's thesis, Pennsylvania State University (University Park, Pa.), 1971. (*DAI* 32: 6131A)

Career Maturity Inventory

34. MEERBACH, JOHN CALVIN. *A Study of the Relationship of Creativity, Vocational Maturity and Vocational Choice Among Eighth Grade Students.* Doctor's thesis, University of Toledo (Toledo, Ohio), 1971. (*DAI* 32:3695A)

35. STENSON, ORVIS J. *The Effect of Multi-Type Short Term Counseling on the Vocational Maturity of Male Tenth Grade Vocational Students.* Doctor's thesis, University of Montana (Missoula, Mont.), 1971. (*DAI* 32:2425A)

CUMULATIVE NAME INDEX

Alderfer, R. D.: 17	Heinmann, R. A.: 7
Ansell, E. M.: 21	Jalkanen, A. W.: 24
Ashbury, F. A.: 14	Jessee, B. E.: 3, 7
Bartlett, W. E.: 11, 15	Kapes, J. T.: 33
Conduff, E.: 19	Malone, F. E.: 9
Cox, S. G.: 16, 29	Maynard, P. E.: 25-6
Crites, J. O.: 5, 12, 30-1	Meerbach, J. C.: 34
Das, A. K.: 1	Munson, P. J.: 27
Domenichetti, M.: 22	Myers, W. P.: 10
Donahue, M. A.: 32	Nichol, J. S.: 20
Drahozal, E. C.: 6	Osipow, S. H.: 17
Hall, D. W.: 2	Schrader, C. H.: 28
Hanley, D. E.: 23	Semler, I. J.: 12
Hansen, J. C.: 25	Shirts, R. G.: 18
Harlan, G. E.: 4	Stenson, O. J.: 35
Harris, J. W.: 8	Williams, R. H.: 13

[2104]

★**Classification Test Battery.** Illiterate and semi-literate applicants for unskilled and semiskilled mining jobs; 1970-71; CTB; replaces *General Adaptability Battery;* nonverbal reasoning and spatial ability; tests administered at centers established by firms employing the publisher's consultation and training services; 4 tests, 4 scores: 3 scores listed below (*b, c, d*), total; pre-test instructions in any of 9 African languages or in English, all test instructions presented by silent motion pictures; National Institute for Personnel Research [South Africa]. *

a) COLOURED PEG BOARD. Unscored "buffer test."

b) PATTERN REPRODUCTION TEST.

c) CIRCLES TEST.

d) FORM SERIES TEST.

[2105]

The Dailey Vocational Tests. Grades 8-12 and adults; 1964-65; DVT; 3 tests; John T. Dailey and Kenneth B. Hoyt (manual); Houghton Mifflin Co. *

a) TECHNICAL AND SCHOLASTIC TEST. See 974.

b) SPATIAL VISUALIZATION TEST. See 2270.

c) BUSINESS ENGLISH TEST. See 57.

For additional information, reviews by Thomas S. Baldwin and Benjamin Shimberg, and excerpted reviews by Betty W. Ellis and Jack C. Merwin, see 7:976 (5 references).

REFERENCES THROUGH 1971

1-5. See 7:976.

6. COX, STEVEN G. "Do Educational Measures Predict Vocational Success?" *Voc Guid Q* 19(4):271-4 Je '71. * (*PA* 48: 1981)

CUMULATIVE NAME INDEX

Baldwin, T. S.: *rev*, 7:976	Merwin, J. C.: *exc*, 7:976
Cox, S. G.: 3, 6	Passmore, J. L.: 4
Doerr, J. J.: 2	Shimberg, B.: *rev*, 7:976
Ellis, B. W.: *exc*, 7:976	Stone, T. C.: 5
Malone, F. E.: 1	

[2106]

*ETSA Tests.** Job applicants; 1960-73, c1957-66; formerly called *Aptitest;* 8 tests; publisher recommends use of Tests 1A, 8A, and one other; manual and technical handbook by S. Trevor Hadley and George A. W. Stouffer, Jr.; tests by Psychological Services Bureau; Educators'-Employers' Tests & Services Associates. *

a) ETSA TEST 1A, GENERAL MENTAL ABILITY TEST. See 378.

b) ETSA TEST 2A, OFFICE ARITHMETIC TEST. See 726.

c) ETSA TEST 3A, GENERAL CLERICAL ABILITY TEST. See 2128.

d) ETSA TEST 4A, STENOGRAPHIC SKILLS TEST. See 2160.
e) ETSA TEST 5A, MECHANICAL FAMILIARITY TEST. See 2417.
f) ETSA TEST 6A, MECHANICAL KNOWLEDGE TEST. See 2419.
g) ETSA TEST 7A, SALES APTITUDE TEST. See 2405.
h) ETSA TEST 8A, PERSONAL ADJUSTMENT INDEX. See 1312.

For additional information and reviews by Marvin D. Dunnette and Raymond A. Katzell, see 6:1025.

[2107]

Flanagan Industrial Tests. Business and industry; 1960–70; FIT; adaptation for business use of the *Flanagan Aptitude Classification Tests;* 2 series; John C. Flanagan; Science Research Associates, Inc. *
a) FORM A SERIES. Job applicants and employees; 1960–65; 18 tests.
  1) *Arithmetic.*
  2) *Assembly.*
  3) *Components.*
  4) *Coordination.*
  5) *Electronics.*
  6) *Expression.*
  7) *Ingenuity.*
  8) *Inspection.*
  9) *Judgment and Comprehension.*
  10) *Mathematics and Reasoning.*
  11) *Mechanics.*
  12) *Memory.*
  13) *Patterns.*
  14) *Planning.*
  15) *Precision.*
  16) *Scales.*
  17) *Tables.*
  18) *Vocabulary.*
b) FORM AA SERIES. Entry level job applicants; 1960–70; 7 tests; this revision of the Form A series involves changes in time limits and directions and the rewording, rearrangement, and omission of items to make the tests more suitable for entry level job applicants; no manual.
  1) *Assembly.*
  2) *Components.*
  3) *Electronics.*
  4) *Ingenuity.*
  5) *Inspection.*
  6) *Memory.*
  7) *Scales.*
For additional information, reviews by C. J. Adcock and Robert C. Droege, and an excerpted review by John L. Horn, see 7:977 (1 reference).

REFERENCES THROUGH 1971
1. See 7:977.

CUMULATIVE NAME INDEX
Adcock, C. J.: *rev,* 7:977   Horn, J. L.: *exc,* 7:977
Droege, R. C.: *rev,* 7:977   Penfield, R. V.: 1

[2108]

Individual Placement Series. High school (*h* only) and adults; 1957–66; 8 tests, also listed separately; J. H. Norman: Personnel Research Associates, Inc. *
a) ACADEMIC ALERTNESS "AA." 1957–66; 7 scores: general knowledge, arithmetic, vocabulary, reasoning ability, logical sequence, accuracy, total.
b) PERFORMANCE ALERTNESS "PA" (WITH PICTURES). 1961–66.
c) READING ADEQUACY "READ" TEST. 1961–66; 3 scores: reading rate, comprehension, corrected reading rate.
d) SURVEY OF CLERICAL SKILLS "SOCS." 1959–66; 5 scores: spelling, office math, office terms, filing, grammar.

e) TYPING TEST. 1959–66.
f) SHORTHAND TEST. 1960–66.
g) SURVEY OF PERSONAL ATTITUDE "SPA" (WITH PICTURES). 1960–66; 3 scores: social attitude, personal frankness, aggressiveness.
h) OCCUPATIONAL INTEREST SURVEY "OIS" (WITH PICTURES). High school and adults; 1959–66; 9 scores: scientific, social service, literary, agricultural, business, mechanical, musical, clerical, artistic.

For additional information, see 7:979. For reviews of the personal attitude test, see 7:147 (2 reviews); the academic alertness test, see 7:332 (1 review); the performance alertness test, see 7:372 (1 review); the reading adequacy test, see 7:773 (1 review); the typing test, see 7:1008 (1 review); and the occupational interest test, see 7:1028 (2 reviews).

[2109]

★**New Mexico Career Education Test Series.** Grades 9–12; 1973; "designed to assess specific learner objectives in the area of career education"; 6 tests; Charles C. Healy and Stephen P. Klein; Monitor. *
a) NM ATTITUDE TOWARD WORK TEST.
b) NM CAREER PLANNING TEST.
c) NM CAREER ORIENTED ACTIVITIES CHECKLIST.
d) NM KNOWLEDGE OF OCCUPATIONS TEST.
e) NM JOB APPLICATION PROCEDURES TEST.
f) NM CAREER DEVELOPMENT TEST.

[2110]

Personal History Index. Job applicants; 1963–67; PHI; for research use only; 8 scores: school achievement, higher educational achievement, drive, leadership and group participation, financial responsibility, early family responsibility, parental family adjustment, stability; Melany E. Baehr, Robert K. Burns, and Robert N. McMurry; Industrial Relations Center, University of Chicago. *

For additional information and a review by John K. Hemphill, see 7:981 (5 references).

REFERENCES THROUGH 1971
1–5. See 7:981.

CUMULATIVE NAME INDEX
Baehr, M. E.: 1–3   Huber, N. A.: 4
Froemel, E. C.: 3   Marks, L. G.: 5
Furcon, J. E.: 3   Williams, G. B.: 1–2
Hemphill, J. K.: *rev,* 7:981

[2111]

Steward Basic Factors Inventory (1960 Edition). Applicants for sales and office positions; 1957–63; revision of *Steward Sales Aptitude Inventory;* originally called *Steward Vocational Fitness Inventory;* 14 scores: business knowledge (vocabulary, arithmetic, total), dominance, personal adjustment, occupational interests (clerical, artistic, supervisory, accounting, writing, selling, mechanical, total), total; Verne Steward; Steward-Mortensen & Associates. *
For additional information and reviews by Leonard V. Gordon and Lyman W. Porter, see 6:1182.

[2112]

Steward Personnel Tests (Short Form), 1958 Edition. Applicants for sales and office positions; 1957–58; abbreviated version of *Steward Sales Aptitude Inventory* and *Steward Vocational Fitness Inventory;* 10 scores: business knowledge, arithmetic, occupational interests (clerical, artistic, supervisory, accounting, writing, selling, mechanical, selling activities); Verne Steward; Steward-Mortensen & Associates. *
For additional information and reviews by Leonard V. Gordon and Lyman W. Porter, see 6:1029.

[2113]

TAV Selection System. Adults; 1963–68; TAV; vocational selection and counseling; 7 tests; R. R. Morman; TAV Selection System. *
a) TAV ADJECTIVE CHECKLIST. 1963–68; 3 scores: toward people (T), away from people (A), versus people (V).
b) TAV JUDGMENTS. 1964–68; 3 scores: same as in *a.*
c) TAV PERSONAL DATA. 1964–68; 3 scores: same as in *a.*
d) TAV PREFERENCES. 1963–68; 3 scores: same as in *a.*
e) TAV PROVERBS AND SAYINGS. 1966–68; 3 scores: same as in *a.*
f) TAV SALESMAN REACTIONS. 1967–68; 3 scores: same as in *a.*
g) TAV MENTAL AGILITY. 1965–68; 3 scores: follow directions and carefulness, weights and balances, verbal comprehension.
For additional information and an excerpted review by John O. Crites, see 7:983 (1 reference); see also P:263A (11 references).

REFERENCES THROUGH 1971
1–11. See P:263A.
12. See 7:983.
13. MORMAN, ROBERT R.; HANKEY, R. O.; JONES, E.; AND LIDDLE, L. R. "Adjuster Selection by Prediction." *Best's Insur News (Fire & Cas)* 68:38+ Je '67. *
14. BRAUN, JOHN R. "Effects of Faking Instructions on the TAV Adjective Check List." *Psychol Rep* 29(2):496 O '71: * (PA 47:8943)
15. LIDDLE, L. ROGERS; HEYWOOD, HAROLD L.; HANKEY, RICHARD O.; AND MORMAN, ROBERT R. "Predicting Baccalaureate Degree Attainment for Nursing Students: A Theoretical Study Using the TAV Selection System." *Nursing Res* 20(3): 258–61 My–Je '71. * (PA 51:3250)

CUMULATIVE NAME INDEX
Braun, J. R.: 14
Crites, J. O.: *exc*, 7:983
Duvlick, J.: 4
Goldwhite, M.: 9
Hankey, R. O.: 1–4, 7–9, 11–3, 15
Heywood, H.: 3, 10
Heywood, H. C.: 12
Heywood, H. L.: 1–2, 4–7, 9, 11, 15
Jones, E.: 13
Jones, E. M.: 8
Kennedy, P.: 1–2
Kennedy, P. K.: 3, 5, 8, 12
Liddle, L. R.: 4–7, 9–11, 13, 15
Morman, R.: 10
Morman, R. R.: 1–9, 11–3, 15

[2114]

Vocational Planning Inventory. Vocational students in grades 8–10, 11–12 and grade 13 entrants; 1968–70, c1954–70; VPI; the battery consists of the *SRA Arithmetic Index, SRA Pictorial Reasoning Test, SRA Verbal Form, Survey of Interpersonal Values, Survey of Personal Values,* Mechanics subtest of the *Flanagan Aptitude Classification Test,* and the following subtests of the *Flanagan Industrial Tests:* Arithmetic, Assembly (*a*), Expression (*a*), Memory (*a*), Scales (*b*), and Tables (*b*); tests cannot be scored locally; the student's copy of his test report presents predicted grades in 9 or 10 areas: agriculture (*a* only), business, construction trades, drafting and design, electronics and electrical trades, home economics and health, mechanics and mechanical maintenance, metal trades, general academic, general vocational; the counselor's copy of an individual test report also presents national percentile rank norms for the component tests: single scores for the 7 (or 8) nonpersonality tests and 12 value scores (practical mindedness, achievement, variety, decisiveness, orderliness, goal orientation, support, conformity, recognition, independence, benevolence, leadership) on the 2 personality tests; 2 levels; Science Research Associates, Inc. *
a) HIGH SCHOOL PREDICTION PROGRAM. Vocational students in grades 8–10; 1968–70, c1954–70; for predicting success in grades 9–12 in areas listed above.
b) POST-HIGH SCHOOL PREDICTION PROGRAM. Vocational students in grades 11–12 and grade 13 entrants; 1968,

c1954–68; for predicting success in grade 13 in areas listed above.
For additional information, see 7:984.

[2115]

WLW Employment Inventory, Short Form. Adults; 1957–64; 4 scores: general knowledge, emotional stability, humility, friendliness; manual by Robert W. Henderson; William, Lynde & Williams. *
For additional information, see 7:985.

[2116]

★Wide Range Employment Sample Test. Ages 16–35 (normal and handicapped); 1973; WREST; manual refers to the test as *The Jastak-King Work Samples;* originally developed for use with "mentally and physically handicapped" persons enrolled in a rehabilitation workshop; 12 scores: folding, stapling, bottle packaging, rice measuring, screw assembly, tag stringing, swatch pasting, collating, color and shade matching, pattern matching, total performance, total errors; J. F. Jastak and Dorothy E. King; Guidance Associates of Delaware, Inc. *

[Out of Print Since TIP I]
Airman Qualifying Examination, 6:1023 (1 reference)
General Adaptability Battery, 6:1026 (1 reference)
Personnel Selection and Classification Test, 3:690 (3 reviews)
RBH Industrial Questionnaire, 7:982
Screening Tests for Apprentices, 6:1028
Vocational Aptitude Examination, 3:695 (4 reviews, 4 references)

CLERICAL

[2117]

ACER Short Clerical Test—Form C. Ages 13 and over; 1953–67; 2 scores: checking, arithmetic; 1966 form essentially the same as form copyrighted 1956 except for conversion to decimal currency; Australian Council for Educational Research [Australia]. *
For additional information, see 7:986.

[2118]

A.C.E.R. Speed and Accuracy Tests. Ages 13.5 and over; 1942–62; 2 scores: number checking, name checking; revised manual by T. M. Whitford; Australian Council for Educational Research [Australia]. *
For additional information, see 6:1031 (2 references); for a review by D. W. McElwain of an earlier form, see 4:719.

REFERENCES THROUGH 1971
1–2. See 6:1031.
3. BILES, DAVID. "Test Performance and Imprisonment." *Austral & N Zeal J Criminol* (Australia) 1:46–58 Mr '68. *
CUMULATIVE NAME INDEX
Biles, D.: 3
Bucklow, M.: 2
Doughty, P.: 2
Hohne, H. H.: 1
McElwain, D. W.: *rev*, 4:719

[2119]

APT Dictation Test. Stenographers; 1955; Associated Personnel Technicians, Inc. *
For additional information, see 6:40.

[2120]

★Appraisal of Occupational Aptitudes. High school and adults; 1971; AOA; "for predicting success in . . . . office occupations"; 8 scores: checking letters, checking numbers, filing names, filing numbers, posting names, posting numbers, arithmetical computation and reasoning, desk calculator (norms for women only) ; Aurelius A. Abbatiello ; Houghton Mifflin Co. *

[2121]

Clerical Skills Series. Clerical workers and applicants ; 1966–69 ; CSS ; 10 tests ; Martin M. Bruce ; Martin M. Bruce, Ph.D., Publishers. *
a) ALPHABETIZING-FILING. 1966.
b) ARITHMETIC. 1966–69 ; 1969 test identical with test copyrighted 1966.
c) CLERICAL SPEED AND ACCURACY. 1966.
d) CODING. 1966.
e) EYE-HAND ACCURACY. 1966.
f) GRAMMAR AND PUNCTUATION. 1966.
g) SPELLING. 1966–69 ; 1969 test identical with test copyrighted 1966.
h) SPELLING-VOCABULARY. 1966.
i) VOCABULARY. 1966.
j) WORD FLUENCY. 1966.
For additional information and a review by Robert Fitzpatrick, see 7 :988.

[2122]

Clerical Tests. Applicants for clerical positions ; 1951–66 ; 6 tests ; no manual ; Stevens, Thurow & Associates, Inc. *
a) INVENTORY J, ARITHMETICAL REASONING. 1966.
b) INVENTORY K, ARITHMETICAL PROFICIENCY. 1951–66.
c) INVENTORY M, INTERPRETATION OF TABULATED MATERIAL. 1951–66.
d) INVENTORY R, INTERPRETATION OF TABULATED MATERIAL. 1951–66.
e) INVENTORY S, ALPHABETICAL FILING. 1951–66.
f) INVENTORY Y, GRAMMAR. 1951–66.
For additional information, see 7 :989.

[2123]

Clerical Tests, Series N. Applicants for clerical positions not involving frequent use of typewriter or verbal skill ; 1940–59 ; 5 scores : comparing names and numbers, copying names, copying numbers, addition and multiplication, mental ability ; 5 tests and 1 application form ; Stevens, Thurow & Associates, Inc. *
a) INVENTORY E, COMPARING NAMES AND NUMBERS.
b) INVENTORY F, COPYING NUMBERS.
c) INVENTORY G, ADDITION AND MULTIPLICATION.
d) INVENTORY H, COPYING NAMES.
e) INVENTORY NO. 2. Mental ability. See 393.
f) APPLICATION FOR POSITION. See 2318.
For additional information, see 6 :1036.

[2124]

Clerical Tests, Series V. Applicants for typing and stenographic positions ; 1940–59 ; 5 scores : grammar, spelling, vocabulary, typing (words per minute), mental ability ; 5 tests and 1 application form ; Stevens, Thurow & Associates, Inc. *
a) INVENTORY A, GRAMMAR.
b) INVENTORY B, SPELLING.
c) INVENTORY C, VOCABULARY.
d) TEST OF TYPEWRITING ABILITY.
e) INVENTORY NO. 2. Mental ability. See 393.
f) APPLICATION FOR POSITION. See 2318*b*.
For additional information, see 6 :1037.

[2125]

Clerical Worker Examination. Clerical workers ; 1962–63 ; test booklet title is *Clerical Worker* ; 5 scores : clerical speed and accuracy, verbal ability,

quantitative ability, total ability, total ; McCann Associates. *
For additional information, see 6 :1038.

[2126]

Cross Reference Test. Clerical job applicants ; 1959 ; James W. Curtis ; Psychometric Affiliates. *
For additional information and a review by Philip H. Kriedt, see 6 :1039.

[2127]

Curtis Verbal-Clerical Skills Tests. Applicants for clerical positions ; 1963–65 ; 4 tests : computation, checking, comprehension, logical reasoning ability ; James W. Curtis ; Psychometric Affiliates. *
For additional information, see 7 :990.

[2128]

***General Clerical Ability Test: ETSA Test 3A.** Job applicants ; 1960–72, c1957–59 ; manual and technical handbook by S. Trevor Hadley and George A. W. Stouffer, Jr. ; test by Psychological Services Bureau ; Educators'-Employers' Tests & Services Associates. * For the complete battery entry, see 2106.
For reviews of the complete battery, see 6 :1025 (2 reviews).

[2129]

***General Clerical Test.** Grades 9–16 and clerical job applicants ; 1944–72 ; formerly called *Psychological Corporation General Clerical Test* ; 4 scores : clerical speed and accuracy, numerical ability, verbal facility, total ; Psychological Corporation. (British adaptation : NFER Publishing Co. Ltd. [England].) *
For additional information and reviews by Edward E. Cureton and G. A. Satter, see 4 :730 (4 references) ; for reviews by Edward N. Hay, Thelma Hunt, Raymond A. Katzell, and E. F. Wonderlic, see 3 :630.

REFERENCES THROUGH 1971

1–4. See 4 :730.
5. BARNETTE, W. LESLIE, JR. "Occupational Aptitude Pattern Research." *Occupations* 29 :5–12 O '50. * (*PA* 25 :3239)
6. KERNAN, JOHN P. *An Empirical Determination of Test Reliability by Different Experimental Designs.* Master's thesis, Fordham University (New York, N.Y.), 1951.
7. BENNETT, GEORGE K. "Research Upon Item Types and Its Implications for Test Improvement." *Yearb Nat Council Meas Used Ed* 9 :114–5 '52. *
8. HANNA, JOSEPH V. "Use of Speed Tests in Guidance." *Occupations* 30 :329–31 F '52. * (*PA* 26 :6355)
9. WESMAN, ALEXANDER G., AND KERNAN, JOHN P. "An Experimental Comparison of Test-Retest and Internal Consistency Estimates of Reliability With Speeded Tests." *J Ed Psychol* 43 :292–8 My '52. * (*PA* 27 :3154)
10. SEASHORE, HAROLD G. "Validation of Clerical Testing in Banks." *Personnel Psychol* 6 :45–56 sp '53. * (*PA* 28 :1670)
11. HUGHES, J. L., AND MCNAMARA, W. J. "Relationship of Short Employment Tests and General Clerical Tests." *Personnel Psychol* 8 :331–7 au '55. * (*PA* 30 :7828)
12. MISKO, ALOYSIUS EDWARD. *An Investigation Into the Validity of Three Employment Tests of a Clerical Personnel Selection Program.* Doctor's thesis, University of Michigan (Ann Arbor, Mich.), 1962. (*DA* 23 :3170)
13. DICKEN, CHARLES F., AND BLACK, JOHN D. "Predictive Validity of Psychometric Evaluations of Supervisors." *J Appl Psychol* 49 :34–47 F '65. * (*PA* 39 :8793)
14. PARRY, MARY ELLEN. "Ability of Psychologists to Estimate Validities of Personnel Tests." *Personnel Psychol* 21 :139–47 su '68. * (*PA* 42 :14727)
15. WILLE, GLENN R. *An Investigation of the Relationship Between the Wonderlic Personnel Tests, Form I, and the General Clerical Test; the Relationship Between the Wonderlic Personnel Test, Form I, and Employee Job Performance.* Master's thesis, Wisconsin State University (Oshkosh, Wis.), 1969.

CUMULATIVE NAME INDEX

Bair, J. T. : 3
Barnette, W. L. : 1, 4–5
Bennett, G. K. : 7
Black, J. D. : 13
Cureton, E. E. : *rev,* 4 :730
Dicken, C. F. : 13
Giese, W. J. : 2
Hanna, J. V. : 8
Hay, E. N. : *rev,* 3 :630
Hughes, J. L. : 11
Hunt, T. : *rev,* 3 :630
Katzell, R. A. : *rev,* 3 :630

General Clerical Test

Kernan, J. P.: 6, 9
McNamara, W. J.: 11
Misko, A. E.: 12
Parry, M. E.: 14
Satter, G. A.: *rev, 4:730*

Seashore, H. G.: 10
Wesman, A. G.: 9
Wille, G. R.: 15
Wonderlic, E. F.: *rev, 3:630*

[2130]

*Group Test 20. Ages 15 and over; 1936–72; checking of names and numbers; 2 scores: speed, accuracy; National Institute of Industrial Psychology; NFER Publishing Co. Ltd. [England]. *

For additional information and a review by E. G. Chambers, see 4:723 (2 references).

REFERENCES THROUGH 1971

1–2. See 4:723.
3. LEE, TERENCE. "The Selection of Student Nurses: A Revised Procedure." *Occup Psychol* (England) 33:209–16 O '59. *

CUMULATIVE NAME INDEX

Chambers, E. G.: *rev, 4:723*
Kerr, G.: 1

Lee, T.: 3
Shuttleworth, C. W.: 2

[2131]

*Group Tests 61A, 64, and 66A. Clerical applicants; 1956–72; 1972 manual identical with manual copyrighted 1971 except for revised norms for *c;* 3 tests; National Institute of Industrial Psychology; NFER Publishing Co. Ltd. [England]. *

a) GROUP TEST 61A. 1956–71; decimalized version of *Group Test 61;* filing, classification, and checking; 2 scores: speed, accuracy.

b) GROUP TEST 64. 1957–71; spelling.

c) GROUP TEST 66A. 1957–72; decimalized version of *Group Test 66;* arithmetic; 2 scores: basic operations, problems.

For additional information, see 7:991.

[2132]

*[Hay Clerical Test Battery.] Applicants for clerical positions; 1941–72; formerly called *Hay Tests for Clerical Aptitude;* 4 tests; 1971 tests identical with tests copyrighted 1947–55; Edward N. Hay; Aptitude Test Service, Inc. *

a) TEST I: THE WARM UP. 1945–72.

b) NUMBER PERCEPTION TEST. 1947–72.

c) NAME FINDING TEST. 1941–72.

d) NUMBER SERIES COMPLETION TEST. 1941–72.

For additional information, see 5:849 (2 references); for reviews by Reign H. Bittner and Edward E. Cureton, see 4:725 (8 references).

REFERENCES THROUGH 1971

1–8. See 4:725.
9–10. See 5:849.
11. MACKINNEY, ARTHUR C., AND WOLINS, LEROY. "Validity Information Exchange, No. 12–19: D.O.T. Code 1-36.05, Coding Clerk; 1-17.02, File Clerk II, Circulation Clerk." *Personnel Psychol* 12:482–3 au '59. *
12. HARKER, JOHN B. "Cross-Validation of an IBM Proof Machine Test Battery." *J Appl Psychol* 44:237–40 Ag '60. * (*PA* 35:4055)

CUMULATIVE NAME INDEX

Bittner, R. H.: *rev, 4:725*
Blakemore, A.: 7
Cureton, E. E.: *rev, 4:725*
Doub, B. A.: 2
Harker, J. B.: 12

Hay, E. N.: 1, 3–5, 8, 10
MacKinney, A. C.: 11
Miller, R. B.: 6
Seashore, H. G.: 9
Wolins, L.: 11

[2133]

[L & L Clerical Tests.] Applicants for office positions; 1964; 5 tests; no manual; distribution restricted to business firms; L & L Associates. *

a) ARITHMETIC REVIEW.

b) CHECK LIST REVIEW.

c) OFFICE ABILITY REVIEW. 6 scores: spelling, grammar and punctuation, arithmetic, filing, business terms, total.

General Clerical Test

d) SPELLING REVIEW.

e) TYPING REVIEW.

For additional information, see 7:992.

[2134]

[McCann Typing Tests.] Applicants for typing positions; 1961–64; 3 scores: speed, accuracy, total; McCann Associates. *

For additional information, see 6:50.

[2135]

Minnesota Clerical Test. Grades 8–12 and adults; 1933–59; formerly called *Minnesota Vocational Test for Clerical Workers;* 2 scores: number comparison, name comparison; Dorothy M. Andrew, Donald G. Paterson, and Howard P. Longstaff (test); Psychological Corporation. *

For additional information, see 6:1040 (10 references); for a review by Donald E. Super, see 5:850 (46 references); for reviews by Thelma Hunt, R. B. Selover, Erwin K. Taylor, and E. F. Wonderlic, see 3:627 (22 references); for a review by W. D. Commins, see 2:1664 (18 references).

REFERENCES THROUGH 1971

1–18. See 2:1664.
19–40. See 3:627.
41–86. See 5:850.
87–96. See 6:1040.
97. QUAYLE, MARGARET SIDNEY. "A Study of Some Aspects of Satisfaction in the Vocation of Stenography." *Teach Col Contrib Ed* 659:1–121 '35. * (*PA* 10:2644)
98. BRENTLINGER, W. H. "The Abilities and Occupational History of Transients: A Preliminary Study." *J Appl Psychol* 20:105–13 F '36. * (*PA* 10:3673)
99. OTIS, JAY L. "The Prediction of Success in Power Sewing Machine Operating." *J Appl Psychol* 22:350–66 Ag '38. * (*PA* 13:1688)
100. SUPER, DONALD E.; BRAASCH, WILLIAM F., JR.; AND SHAY, JOSEPH B. "The Effect of Distractions on Test Results." *J Ed Psychol* 38:373–7 O '47. * (*PA* 22:2159)
101. CARRUTHERS, JOHN B. "Tabular Summary Showing Relation Between Clerical Test Scores and Occupational Performance." *Occupations* 29:40–50 O '50. * (*PA* 25:3450)
102. GUEST, LESTER, AND NUCKOLS, ROBERT. "A Laboratory Experiment in Recording in Public Opinion Interviewing." *Int J Opin & Attitude Res* (Mexico) 4:336–52 f '50. * (*PA* 25:7387)
103. DUNHAM, RALPH E. "Factors Related to Recidivism in Adults." *J Social Psychol* 39:77–91 F '54. * (*PA* 28:8866)
104. STOREY, JOHN STUART. *The Validity of Counseling Variables Considered in the Advisement of Disabled Veterans Entering Terminal Business Training.* Doctor's thesis, Michigan State University (East Lansing, Mich.), 1955. (*DA* 15:1019)
105. BAIR, JOHN T.; LOCKMAN, ROBERT F.; AND MARTOCCIA, CHARLES T. "Validity and Factor Analyses of Naval Air Training Predictor and Criterion Measures." *J Appl Psychol* 40:213–9 Ag '56. * (*PA* 31:6701)
106. HABER, WILFRED. *The Contribution of Selected Variables to Success or Failure in a Vocational Rehabilitation Evaluation.* Doctor's thesis, New York University (New York, N.Y.), 1959. (*DA* 20:4171)
107. MATTHEWS, ROMINE ELLWOOD. *Certain Personality Variables Related to Success in Veterans' Rehabilitation Training in Clerical Occupations.* Doctor's thesis, University of Minnesota (Minneapolis, Minn.), 1960. (*DA* 21:127)
108. EDINGTON, EVERETT D. *Abilities and Characteristics of Young Adult Dairy Farmers in Pennsylvania Which Are Associated With Successful Farm Management.* Doctor's thesis, Pennsylvania State University (University Park, Pa.), 1961. (*DA* 22:3791)
109. LOCKE, EDWIN A. "Some Correlates of Classroom and Out-of-Class Achievement in Gifted Science Students." *J Ed Psychol* 54:238–48 O '63. * (*PA* 38:4649)
110. MORRISON, WILLIAM E. *The Effectiveness of the Minnesota Clerical Test and the Wonderlic Personnel Test in the Selection of Clerk Typists and File Clerks.* Master's thesis, Springfield College (Springfield, Mass.), 1963.
111. HAFEEZ, A., AND YAKUB, SYED. "A Study of Clerical Ability." *J Indian Acad Appl Psychol* 1:77–80 S '64. * (*PA* 39:8781)
112. DICKEN, CHARLES F., AND BLACK, JOHN D. "Predictive Validity of Psychometric Evaluations of Supervisors." *J Appl Psychol* 49:34–47 F '65. * (*PA* 39:8793)
113. STEIGELMAN, GEORGE W. *The Effect of Controlled Distractions Upon the Minnesota Clerical Test Results of Eighth*

Graders in Charleston, Illinois. Master's thesis, Eastern Illinois University (Charleston, Ill.), 1966.

114. MOSKOVIS, LEFTERIE MICHAEL. *An Identification of Certain Similarities and Differences Between Successful and Unsuccessful College Level Beginning Shorthand Students and Transcription Students.* Doctor's thesis, Michigan State University (East Lansing, Mich.), 1967. (*DA* 28:4826A)

115. BLANK, STANLEY S. "An Examination of the Usefulness of Various Psychological Instruments for Predicting Department Managers' Ratings of Clerical Sales Personnel." *Can Counsellor* 2:46–50 Ja '68. *

116. GEORGAS, JAMES G.; BRAMOS, IRENE; AND BAKIRDGIS, IOANNA. "The Minnesota Clerical Test in Greece: A Validation Study." *Personnel Psychol* 21:79–83 sp '68. * (*PA* 42:16172)

117. RAFFEL, SHERMAN C.; SWINK, RICHARD; AND LAMPTON, T. D. "The Influence of Chlorphenesin Carbamate and Carisoprodol on Psychological Test Scores." *Curr Ther Res* 11(9): 553–60 S '69. *

118. LLEWELLYN, HOWARD CHARLES. *The Relationship Between Selected Silent Word Perception Skills and Achievement in First-Year High School Typewriting.* Doctor's thesis, University of North Dakota (Grand Forks, N.D.), 1970. (*DAI* 31: 6454A)

119. MOSKOVIS, L. MICHAEL. "Similarities and Differences of College-Level Successful and Unsuccessful Shorthand Students." *Delta Pi Epsilon J* 12(2):12–6 F '70. *

CUMULATIVE NAME INDEX

Achard, F. H.: 44
American Gas Association, Personnel Committee: 70
Anderson, R. G.: 72
Anderson, R. N.: 30
Andrew, D. M.: 2–3, 9
Bair, J. T.: 50, 65, 105
Bakirdgis, I.: 116
Barnette, W. L.: 18
Barrett, D. M.: 38
Beamer, G. C.: 49
Beldo, L. A.: 86
Bellows, R. M.: 42
Bender, W. R. G.: 88
Bennett, G. K.: 39
Bergen, G. L.: 4
Berkshire, R.: 58
Berman, I. R.: 8
Bingham, W. V. D.: 10
Black, J. D.: 112
Black, M. H.: 51
Blakemore, A.: 66
Blakemore, A. M.: 27, 32
Blanchard, H. L.: 52
Blank, S. S.: 115
Blum, M.: 11
Blum, M. L.: 21
Bond, G. L.: 62
Borg, W. R.: 59
Braasch, W. F.: 100
Bramos, I.: 116
Brayfield, A. H.: 73
Brentlinger, W. H.: 98
Candee, B.: 11, 21
Capwell, D. F.: 53
Carpenter, E. K.: 46
Carruthers, J. B.: 101
Carter, L.: 54
Cass, J. C.: 93
Champion, J. M.: 89
Clarke, F. H.: 44
Commins, W. D.: *rev,* 2:1664
Cooper, J. H.: 42
Copeland, H. A.: 7, 12
Cox, K. J.: 45
Coyle, F. P.: 76
Crane, W. J.: 95
Crissey, O. L.: 43
Crites, J. O.: 96
Davidson, C. M.: 13–4
Dicken, C. F.: 112
Dodge, A. F.: 5
Dudycha, G. J.: 17
Dunham, R. E.: 103
Dvorak, B. J.: 6, 42
Edington, E. D.: 108
Edmonson, L. D.: 49
Endler, O. L.: 42
Engelhardt, O. E. de C.: 60
Erickson, I. P.: 20
Fife, I. E.: 40
Fleet, D.: 58
Forster, C. R.: 83
Garrett, W. S.: 94
Georgas, J. G.: 116
Ghiselli, E. E.: 22, 25–6

Graham, W. R.: 77
Green, H. J.: 8
Guest, L.: 102
Haber, W.: 106
Hackman, R. C.: 41
Hafeez, A.: 111
Hahn, M. E.: 47
Hales, W. M.: 15
Hay, E. N.: 27, 31–2, 61, 67
Hunt, T.: *rev,* 3:627
Jackson, J.: 55
Jenkins, J. J.: 74
Johnson, R. H.: 62
Kendall, W. E.: 47
Kirkpatrick, D. L.: 84
Klugman, S. F.: 33–4, 36
Kolbe, L. E.: 42
Lampton, T. D.: 117
Lee, M. C.: 63, 71
Lee, P. J.: 78
Llewellyn, H. C.: 118
Locke, E. A.: 109
Lockman, R. F.: 105
Loevinger, J.: 19
Longstaff, H. P.: 79, 86
Loveless, H. E.: 88
Lowe, L. M.: 80
McGehee, W.: 28
Maher, H.: 40
Martin, F.: 81
Martoccia, C. T.: 105
Matthews, R. E.: 107
Miller, R. B.: 64
Moffie, D. J.: 28
Morrison, W. E.: 110
Morrow, R. S.: 23
Moskovis, L. M.: 114, 119
Nixon, M.: 54
Nuckols, R.: 102
Osborne, H. F.: 42
Otis, J. L.: 42, 99
Paterson, D. G.: 2, 8, 16, 29
Petrie, A.: 68
Petro, P. K.: 87
Pond, M.: 1
Powell, M. B.: 68
Purdy, B. F.: 69
Quayle, M. S.: 97
Raffel, S. C.: 117
Rusmore, J.: 81
Sawyer, J.: 85
Schneidler, G. G.: 16, 24, 29
Seashore, H. G.: 75
Selover, R. B.: *rev,* 3:627
Shartle, C. L.: 42
Shay, J. B.: 100
Shore, R. P.: 90–2
Shuman, J. T.: 35
Stead, W. H.: 42
Steigelman, G. W.: 113
Storey, J. S.: 104
Strong, E. K.: 48
Strother, G. B.: 49
Super, D. S.: 56, 96, 100; *rev,* 5:850
Swem, B. R.: 37

Swink, R.: 117
Taylor, E. K.: *rev,* 3:627
Tiedeman, D. V.: 93
Trabue, M. R.: 8
Ward, R. S.: 42
Wesman, A. G.: 39

Wightwick, B.: 57
Williamson, E. G.: 16
Wonderlic, E. F.: *rev,* 3:627
Yakub, S.: 111
Young, M. B.: 82

[2136]

Office Skills Achievement Test. Employees; 1962–63; 7 scores: business letter, grammar, checking, filing, arithmetic, written directions, total; Paul L. Mellenbruch; Psychometric Affiliates. *

For additional information and reviews by Douglas G. Schultz and Paul W. Thayer, see 6:1043.

[2137]

*****Office Worker Test.** Office workers; 1956–72; 11 scores: reading, vocabulary, reasoning, arithmetic, checking, filing, spelling, punctuation, usage, information, total; distribution restricted to member public personnel agencies and nonmember agencies approved by the publisher; International Personnel Management Association. *

For additional information and reviews by Ray G. Price and Douglas G. Schultz, see 6:1044.

[2138]

O'Rourke Clerical Aptitude Test, Junior Grade. Applicants for clerical positions; 1926–58; 2 parts; no manual; L. J. O'Rourke; O'Rourke Publications. *
a) CLERICAL PROBLEMS. 1926–35.
b) REASONING TEST. 1926–58; 1958 test essentially the same as test copyrighted 1936 except for changes in a few items.

For additional information, see 5:851 (1 reference); for a review by Raymond A. Katzell, see 3:629 (3 references).

REFERENCES THROUGH 1971

1–3. See 3:629.
4. See 5:851.
5. WOODY, CLIFFORD. *Aptitudes, Achievements and Interests of High School Pupils.* University of Michigan, Bureau of Educational Reference and Research Bulletin No. 157. Ann Arbor, Mich.: School of Education, the University, 1945. Pp. vi, 159. *

CUMULATIVE NAME INDEX

Anderson, R. N.: 2
Bair, J. T.: 4
Copeland, H. A.: 1

Katzell, R. A.: *rev,* 3:629
Woody, C.: 3, 5

[2139]

[Personnel Institute Clerical Tests.] Clerical personnel and typists-stenographers-secretaries; 1922–67; 12 tests; Personnel Institute, Inc. *
a) PRELIMINARY SCREENING INTERVIEW. 1957–67.
b) CONFIDENTIAL PERSONAL HISTORY INVENTORY. 1957–67.
c) DIAGNOSTIC INTERVIEWER'S GUIDE. 1956–67.
d) WORK REFERENCE INVESTIGATION. 1957–67.
e) MENTAL ALERTNESS TEST. 1922; formerly called *EM-AY Inventory;* reprint of the *Otis Employment Test.*
f) VOCABULARY TEST. 1954–67; 1967 test identical with tests copyrighted 1954 and 1956.
g) COMPARING NAMES TEST. 1957–67; 1967 test identical with test copyrighted 1957.
h) COPYING NUMBERS TEST. 1957–67; 1967 test identical with tests copyrighted 1957 and 1962.
i) ARITHMETIC TEST. 1957–67; 1967 test identical with tests copyrighted 1957 and 1963.
j) GRAMMAR TEST. 1957–67; 1967 test identical with tests copyrighted 1957 and 1960.
k) SPELLING TEST. 1957–67; 1967 test identical with tests copyrighted 1957 and 1963.
l) TYPING TEST. 1957–67; 1967 test identical with tests copyrighted 1957 and 1960.

For additional information, see 7:993.

[2140]

[Personnel Research Institute Clerical Battery.] Applicants for clerical positions; 1945–48; 7 tests; Personnel Research Institute. *

a) NUMBER COMPARISON TEST FOR CLERICAL AND INDUSTRIAL INSPECTION OPERATIONS. 1945–46; Jay L. Otis and Louise W. Garman.

b) NAME COMPARISON TEST FOR CLERICAL AND INDUSTRIAL INSPECTION OPERATIONS. 1945–46; Jay L. Otis and Louise W. Garman.

c) TABULATION TEST. 1947; Jay L. Otis and David J. Chesler.

d) FILING TEST. 1947; Jay L. Otis and David J. Chesler.

e) ALPHABETIZING TEST. 1947; David J. Chesler.

f) ARITHMETIC REASONING TEST. See 699.

g) SPELLING TEST FOR CLERICAL WORKERS. See 159.

For additional information and reviews by Louise Witmer Cureton and Albert K. Kurtz, see 4:729. For reference to a review of the spelling test, see 159.

REFERENCES THROUGH 1971

1. HILTON, ANDREW C.; BOLIN, STANLEY F.; PARKER, JAMES W., JR.; TAYLOR, ERWIN K.; AND WALKER, WILLIAM B. "The Validity of Personnel Assessments by Professional Psychologists." *J Appl Psychol* 39:287–93 Ag '55. * *(PA* 30:5294)
2. CAMPBELL, JOEL T., AND PRIEN, ERICH P., JR. "Normative Data Information Exchange, Nos. 11–19, 11–20." *Personnel Psychol* 11:449–50 au '58. *
3. CAMPBELL, JOEL T., AND PRIEN, ERICH P., JR. "Normative Data Information Exchange, Nos. 11–21, 11–22." *Personnel Psychol* 11:451–2 au '58. *
4. CAMPBELL, JOEL T., AND PRIEN, ERICH P., JR. "Normative Data Information Exchange, Nos. 11–29, 11–30." *Personnel Psychol* 11:595–6 w '58. *
5. CAMPBELL, JOEL T., AND PRIEN, ERICH P., JR. "Normative Data Information Exchange, Nos. 11–31, 11–32." *Personnel Psychol* 11:597–8 w '58. *
6. CAMPBELL, JOEL T.; PRIEN, ERICH P.; AND BRAILEY, LESTER B. "Predicting Performance Evaluations." *Personnel Psychol* 13:435–40 w '60. * *(PA* 36:1LD35C)

CUMULATIVE NAME INDEX

Bixler, H. H.: *rev,* 4:211
Bolin, S. F.: 1
Brailey, L. B.: 6
Campbell, J. T.: 2–6
Cureton, L. W.: *rev,* 4:729
Hilton, A. C.: 1
Kurtz, A. K.: *rev,* 4:729
Parker, J. W.: 1
Prien, E. P.: 2–6
Taylor, E. K.: 1
Walker, W. B.: 1

[2141]

Personnel Research Institute Test of Shorthand Skills. Stenographers; 1951–54; title on test is *Otis and Laurent Test of Shorthand Skills;* 2 scores: transliteration, transcription; Jay L. Otis and Harry Laurent; Personnel Research Institute. *

For additional information and a review by Irol Whitmore Balsley, see 6:43.

[2142]

Purdue Clerical Adaptability Test, Revised Edition. Applicants for clerical positions; 1949–56; 6 scores: spelling, computation, checking, word meaning, copying, reasoning; C. H. Lawshe, Joseph Tiffin, and Herbert Moore; distributed by University Book Store. *

For additional information and reviews by Mary Ellen Oliverio and Donald Spearritt, see 5:853 (2 references); for reviews by Edward N. Hay, Joseph E. Moore, and Alec Rodger of an earlier edition, see 4:731.

REFERENCES THROUGH 1971

1–2. See 5:853.
3. RAUBENHEIMER, I. VAN W. "Influence of Group and Situational Differences on the Applicability of a Personnel Test." *J Appl Psychol* 54(3):214–6 Je '70. * *(PA* 44:13464)
4. RAUBENHEIMER, I. VAN W., AND TIFFIN, JOSEPH. "Personnel Selection and the Prediction of Error." *J Appl Psychol* 55(3):229–33 Je '71. * *(PA* 46:9844)

CUMULATIVE NAME INDEX

Hay, E. N.: *rev,* 4:731
Lawshe, C. H.: 2
Moore, J. E.: *rev,* 4:731
Oliverio, M. E.: *rev,* 5:853
Raubenheimer, I. van W.: 3–4
Rodger, A.: *rev,* 4:731
Sinclair, G. R.: 1
Spearritt, D.: *rev,* 5:853
Steinberg, M. D.: 2
Tiffin, J.: 4

[2143]

RBH Checking Test. Applicants for clerical and stenographic positions; 1948–63; catalog uses the title *The RBH Coding Test;* Richardson, Bellows, Henry & Co., Inc. *

For additional information and a review by Douglas G. Schultz, see 7:994.

[2144]

RBH Classifying Test. Business and industry; 1950–63; 3 scores: speed, accuracy, rights minus wrongs; 1961 test identical with test copyrighted 1950 except for cover; Richardson, Bellows, Henry & Co., Inc. *

For additional information and a review by Douglas G. Schultz, see 7:995.

[2145]

RBH Number Checking Test. Business and industry; 1957–63; 2 scores: checking forward, checking backward; Richardson, Bellows, Henry & Co., Inc. *

For additional information and a review by Douglas G. Schultz, see 7:997.

[2146]

*RBH Test of Dictation Speed. Stenographers; 1958–63; no manual; Richardson, Bellows, Henry & Co., Inc. *

For additional information, see 6:48.

[2147]

RBH Test of Typing Speed. Applicants for clerical positions; 1958–63; 2 scores: net speed, accuracy; Richardson, Bellows, Henry & Co., Inc. *

For additional information, see 6:53.

[2148]

The Seashore-Bennett Stenographic Proficiency Test: A Standard Recorded Stenographic Worksample. Adults; 1946–56; Harold Seashore and George K. Bennett; Psychological Corporation. *

For additional information, see 5:519 (2 references); for a review by Harold F. Rothe, see 4:455 (1 reference); for a review by Ann Brewington, see 3:386.

REFERENCES THROUGH 1971

1. See 4:455.
2–3. See 5:519.

CUMULATIVE NAME INDEX

Bennett, G. K.: 1
Brewington, A.: *rev,* 3:386
McCarty, J. J.: 3
Rothe, H. F.: *rev,* 4:455
Seashore, H. G.: 1

[2149]

Secretarial Performance Analysis. Employees; 1969; SPA; ratings by supervisors; 4 scores: basic skills, executive skills, personal attributes, total; William T. Martin; Psychologists and Educators, Inc. *

For additional information, see 7:998.

[2150]

Selection Tests for Office Personnel. Insurance office workers and applicants; 1962–64; STOP; 10 tests; Walter A. Eggert and Albert H. Malo; distributed by Kemper Psychological Services. *

a) LANGUAGE SKILLS 1A.

b) DATA PERCEPTION 2A.

c) ARITHMETIC 3A.

d) CODING 4A.
e) RATING 5A.
f) PERSONALITY 6A.
g) FILING 7A.
h) STENOGRAPHY 8A.
i) SPELLING 9A.
j) TYPING 10A.
    For additional information, see 7:999.

[2151]

*The Short Employment Tests. Applicants for clerical positions; 1951–72; SET; 3 tests; distribution of Form 1 restricted to banks which are members of the American Bankers Association; George K. Bennett and Marjorie Gelink; Psychological Corporation. *
a) V [VERBAL].
b) N [NUMERICAL].
c) CA [CLERICAL].
    For additional information and a review by Leonard W. Ferguson, see 6:1045 (9 references); for a review by P. L. Mellenbruch, see 5:854 (16 references).

REFERENCES THROUGH 1971
1–16. See 5:854.
17–25. See 6:1045.
26. MILLER, MARTIN M. *A Validation of the Short Employment Test on Secretarial Personnel at the University of Tennessee.* Master's thesis, University of Tennessee (Knoxville, Tenn.), 1964.
27. KIRCHNER, WAYNE K. "Analysis Prediction of Performance of Experienced Key-Punch Operators." *J Indus Psychol* 4(2):48–52 '66. *
28. THUMIN, FRED J., AND BOERNKE, CAROL. "Ability Scores as Related to Age Among Female Job Applicants." *J Gerontol* 21:369–71 Jl '66. *
29. KIRKPATRICK, JAMES J.; EWEN, ROBERT B.; BARRETT, RICHARD S.; AND KATZELL, RAYMOND A. *Testing and Fair Employment: Fairness and Validity of Personnel Tests for Different Ethnic Groups,* pp. 17, 25–7, 43–50. New York: New York University Press, 1968. Pp. x, 145. *
30. THUMIN, F., AND GOLDMAN, SUE. "Comparative Test Performance of Negro and White Job Applicants." *J Clin Psychol* 24:455–7 O '68. * (*PA* 43:4565)
31. PRIEN, ERICH P. "Measuring Performance Criteria of Bank Tellers." *J Indus Psychol* 5(1):29–36 Mr '70. * (*PA* 45:7135)

CUMULATIVE NAME INDEX

Ash, P.: 23
Banas, P.: 25
Barrett, R. S.: 29
Bennett, G. K.: 1, 9
Boernke, C.: 28
Buel, W. D.: 21
Doppelt, J. E.: 9
Dunnette, M. D.: 16
Ewen, R. B.: 29
Ferguson, L. W.: *rev,* 6:1045
Fitzpatrick, E. D.: 4–7, 10
Gelink, M.: 1
Goldman, S.: 30
Harker, J. B.: 24
Hughes, J. L.: 8
Katzell, R. A.: 29
Kirchner, W. K.: 16, 25, 27
Kirkpatrick, J. J.: 29
McCarty, J. J.: 4–7, 10, 12–5
McNamara, W. J.: 8
Martin, F.: 3
Mellenbruch, P. L.: *rev,* 5: 854
Miller, M. M.: 26
Prien, E. P.: 31
Rusmore, J.: 3
Shore, R. P.: 17–20, 22
Stevens, S. N.: 21
Thumin, F.: 30
Thumin, F. J.: 28
Walker, F. C.: 11
Westberg, W. C.: 4–6
Wilkinson, B.: 2

[2152]

Short Occupational Knowledge Test for Bookkeepers. Job applicants; 1970; score is pass, fail, or unclassifiable; Bruce A. Campbell and Suellen O. Johnson; Science Research Associates, Inc. *
    For additional information, see 7:1000.

[2153]

Short Occupational Knowledge Test for Office Machine Operators. Job applicants; 1970; score is pass, fail, or unclassifiable; Bruce A. Campbell and Suellen O. Johnson; Science Research Associates, Inc. *
    For additional information, see 7:1001.

[2154]

Short Occupational Knowledge Test for Secretaries. Job applicants; 1969–70; score is pass, fail, or unclassifiable; Bruce A. Campbell and Suellen O. Johnson; Science Research Associates, Inc. *
    For additional information, see 7:1002.

[2155]

Short Tests of Clerical Ability. Applicants for office positions; 1959–60; 7 tests; Jean Maier; Science Research Associates, Inc. *
a) CODING.
b) CHECKING.
c) FILING.
d) DIRECTIONS—ORAL AND WRITTEN.
e) ARITHMETIC. 3 scores: computation, business arithmetic, total.
f) BUSINESS VOCABULARY.
g) LANGUAGE.
    For additional information and reviews by Philip H. Kriedt and Paul W. Thayer, see 6:1046.

[2156]

Shorthand Test: Individual Placement Series. Adults; 1960–66; J. H. Norman; Personnel Research Associates, Inc. *
    For additional information, see 7:1003.

[2157]

Skill in Typing: Measurement of Skill Test 9. Job applicants; 1966–68; MOS 9; Walter V. Clarke Associates, Inc.; AVA Publications, Inc. *
    For additional information, see 7:1004.

[2158]

Stenographic Dictation Test. Applicants for stenographic positions; 1962–64; McCann Associates. *
    For additional information, see 6:46.

[2159]

*Stenographic Skill-Dictation Test. Applicants for stenographic positions; 1950–73; formerly called *Test for Stenographic Skill;* 1972 test essentially the same as test copyrighted 1950 except for title and deletion from manual of one paragraph and a sample application-scoring sheet; Edward N. Hay; Aptitude Test Service, Inc. *
    For additional information and reviews by Reign H. Bittner and Clifford E. Jurgensen, see 4:459.

[2160]

*Stenographic Skills Test: ETSA Test 4A. Job applicants; 1960–72, c1957–59; manual and technical handbook by S. Trevor Hadley and George A. W. Stouffer, Jr.; test by Psychological Services Bureau; Educators'-Employers' Tests & Services Associates. *
    For the complete battery entry, see 2106.
    For reviews of the complete battery, see 6:1025 (2 reviews).

[2161]

Survey of Clerical Skills: Individual Placement Series. Adults; 1959–66; SOCS; 5 scores: spelling, office math, office terms, filing, grammar; J. H. Norman; Personnel Research Associates, Inc. *
    For additional information, see 7:1006.

[2162]

Thurstone Employment Tests. Applicants for clerical and typing positions; 1922; 2 tests, 3 scores for each test: speed, accuracy, total; L. L. Thurstone; Harcourt Brace Jovanovich, Inc. *

a) EXAMINATION IN CLERICAL WORK.
b) EXAMINATION IN TYPING.

For additional information and reviews by John M. Willits and E. F. Wonderlic of *a*, see 3:632 (6 references).

REFERENCES THROUGH 1971

1-6. See 3:632.
7. STEDMAN, MELISSA BRANSON. "A Study of the Possibility of Prognosis of School Success in Typewriting." *J Appl Psychol* 13:505–15 O '29. * (*PA* 4:891)
8. CARRUTHERS, JOHN B. "Tabular Summary Showing Relation Between Clerical Test Scores and Occupational Performance." *Occupations* 29:40–50 O '50. * (*PA* 25:3450)

CUMULATIVE NAME INDEX

Carruthers, J. B.: 8	Stedman, M. B.: 2, 7
Davidson, C. M.: 4–5	Thurstone, L. L.: 1
Hales, W. M.: 6	Willits, J. M.: *rev*, 3:632
Jorgensen, C.: 3	Wonderlic, E. F.: *rev*, 3:632

[2163]

*Typing Skill. Typists; 1952–71; formerly called *Test for Typing Skill;* Edward N. Hay; Aptitude Test Service, Inc. *

For additional information and a review by Bernadine Meyer, see 5:523.

[2164]

Typing Test for Business. Applicants for typing positions; 1967–68; TTB; 5 tests plus practice test (*a*); distribution restricted to personnel departments; Psychological Corporation (test), Jerome E. Doppelt (manual), Arthur D. Hartman (manual), and Fay B. Krawchick (manual); Psychological Corporation. *
a) PRACTICE COPY.
b) STRAIGHT COPY. 2 scores: speed, accuracy.
c) LETTERS.
d) REVISED MANUSCRIPT.
e) NUMBERS.
f) TABLES.

For additional information and reviews by Mary T. Harrison and Leonard J. West, see 7:1007.

[2165]

Typing Test: Individual Placement Series. Adults; 1959–66; J. H. Norman; Personnel Research Associates, Inc. *

For additional information and a review by Mary T. Harrison, see 7:1008.

[2166]

USES Clerical Skills Tests. Applicants for clerical positions; 1968; 6 tests; distribution restricted to State Employment Services affiliated with the United States Employment Service; published by United States Employment Service and distributed by United States Government Printing Office. *
a) TYPING TEST. 2 scores: speed, accuracy.
b) DICTATION TEST.
c) SPELLING TEST.
d) STATISTICAL TYPING TEST. 2 scores: speed, accuracy.
e) MEDICAL SPELLING TEST.
f) LEGAL SPELLING TEST.

For additional information, see 7:1009 (1 reference).

REFERENCES THROUGH 1971

1. See 7:1009.

CUMULATIVE NAME INDEX

Crambert, A. C.: 1

[Out of Print Since TIP I]

Beginner's Clerical Test, 6:1032 (2 reviews)
Business Career Aptitude Test (status unknown), 7:987
Cardall Test of Clerical Perception (status unknown), 6:1033

Thurstone Employment Tests

Clerical Perception Test, 3:624 (4 reviews, 1 excerpt)
Clerical Test D (status unknown), 3:625 (2 reviews)
Group Test 25 (Clerical), 4:724 (1 review, 1 reference)
Martin Office Aptitude Tests (status unknown), 4:726 (2 reviews)
National Institute of Industrial Psychology Clerical Test, 6:1041 (3 reviews, 6 references)
RBH Language Skills and Dictation Test, 7:996
Spot-the-Error Test, 7:1005
Stenogauge (status unknown), 3:389 (1 review)
Survey of Working Speed and Accuracy, 3:631 (3 reviews)
Turse Clerical Aptitudes Test, 5:855 (2 reviews, 1 reference)

INTERESTS

[2167]

The ACT Guidance Profile, Two-Year College Edition. Junior college; 1965–69; GP; the occupational interests section is the same as the *Vocational Preference Inventory;* self-administered inventory in 5 areas of which 3 (*c-e*) are profiled; Research and Development Division, American College Testing Program; the Program. *
a) AMBITIONS AND PLANS.
b) SELF-ESTIMATES.
c) OCCUPATIONAL INTERESTS. 7 scores: technical-realistic, scientific-intellectual, artistic, social, enterprising, clerical-conventional, infrequency.
d) POTENTIALS. 8 scores: technical, scientific, artistic, musical, literary, dramatic, social-enterprising, clerical.
e) COMPETENCIES. 10 SCORES: skilled trades (technical), home economics (technical), scientific, artistic, social (community service), business (enterprising), leadership (enterprising), clerical, sports, language.

For additional information and a review by Richard W. Watkins, see 7:1010 (2 references).

REFERENCES THROUGH 1971

1-2. See 7:1010.
3. McCLUNG, RAY O. *Differences in Student Characteristics and Perceptions of the College Environment Between Junior College Students Classified by Level of Satisfaction With Environment, Educational Classification and Sex.* Doctor's thesis, North Texas State University (Denton, Tex.), 1970. (*DAI* 31:5770A)
4. BRUE, ELDON J.; ENGEN, HAROLD B.; AND MAXEY, E. JAMES. "How Do Community College Transfer and Occupational Students Differ?" *ACT Res Rep* 41:1–33 F '71. * (*PA* 47:1775)

CUMULATIVE NAME INDEX

Brue, E. J.: 4	McClung, R. O.: 3
Engen, H. B.: 4	Maxey, E. J.: 4
Kee, B. E.: 2	Watkins, R. W.: *rev*, 7:1010
Lutz, S. W.: 1	

[2168]

A.P.U. Occupational Interests Guide: Intermediate Version. Ages 14–18; 1966–69; OIG; 8 scores: scientific, social service, clerical/sales, literary, artistic, computational, practical, outdoor; S. J. Closs, W. T. G. Bates (manual), M. C. Killcross (manual), and D. McMahon (manual); University of London Press Ltd. [England]. *

For additional information and reviews by David P. Campbell and David G. Hawkridge, see 7:1011 (1 reference).

REFERENCES THROUGH 1971

1. See 7:1011.
2. BATES, W. T. G.; KILLCROSS, M. C.; AND McMAHON, D. "Some Aspects of the Validation of a Measure of Occupa-

tional Interest." *Proc Inter Congr Appl Psychol* 16:717-20 '68. *

3. Preston, L. R.; Openshaw, Joan M.; and Stockbridge, H. C. W. "Measurement of Army Interests With APU Occupational Interests Guide." *Occup Psychol* (England) 45(3-4):243-51 '71. * (*PA* 48:12318)

CUMULATIVE NAME INDEX

Bates, W. T. G.: 1-2
Campbell, D. P.: *rev*, 7:1011
Hawkridge, D. G.: *rev*, 7: 1011
Killcross, M. C.: 1-2

McMahon, D.: 2
Openshaw, J. M.: 3
Preston, L. R.: 3
Stockridge, H. C. W.: 3

[2169]

The Applied Biological and Agribusiness Interest Inventory. Grade 8; 1965-71; revision of *Vocational Agriculture Interest Inventory;* 5 scores: animals, plants, mechanics, business, total; Robert W. Walker and Glenn Z. Stevens; Interstate Printers & Publishers, Inc. *

For additional information and a review by David P. Campbell of the original edition, see 7:1038 (4 references).

REFERENCES THROUGH 1971

1-4. See 7:1038.

CUMULATIVE NAME INDEX

Campbell, D. P.: *rev*, 7:1038
McCarley, W. W.: 4

Robinson, W. A.: 3
Walker, R. W.: 1-2

[2170]

*California Occupational Preference Survey. Grades 9-16 and adults; 1966-71; COPS; 14 scores: science professional, science skilled, technical professional, technical skilled, outdoor, business professional, business skilled, clerical, linguistic professional, linguistic skilled, aesthetic professional, aesthetic skilled, service professional, service skilled; Robert R. Knapp, Bruce Grant, and George D. Demos; Educational and Industrial Testing Service. *

For additional information, reviews by Jack L. Bodden and John W. French, and an excerpted review by Robert H. Bauernfeind, see 7:1012 (1 reference).

REFERENCES THROUGH 1971

1. See 7:1012.
2. Seder, Robin Walter. *An Investigation of the Relationship Between Inventoried Interest and Academic Major.* Master's thesis, California State College (Long Beach, Calif.), 1969.
3. Huang, David Darming. *An Investigation of Probationary and Non-Probationary Engineering Students' Self Perceived Versus Measured Temperaments, Values and Vocational Preferences.* Doctor's thesis, Purdue University (Lafayette, Ind.), 1971. (*DAI* 32:3030A)

CUMULATIVE NAME INDEX

Bauernfeind, R. H.: *exc*, 7: 1012
Bodden, J. L.: *rev*, 7:1012
Freeberg, N. E.: 1

French, J. W.: *rev*, 7:1012
Huang, D. D.: 3
Seder, R. W.: 2

[2171]

California Pre-Counseling Self-Analysis Protocol Booklet. Student counselees; 1965; unscored survey of information and interests to be completed by student prior to counseling; no manual; George D. Demos and Bruce Grant; Western Psychological Services. *

For additional information, see 7:1013.

[2172]

★Career Guidance Inventory. Grades 7-13 students interested in trades, services and technologies; 1972; CGI; 25 scores: 14 engineering related trades (carpentry and woodworking, masonry, mechanical repair, painting and decorating, plumbing and pipefitting, printing, tool and die making, sheet metal and welding, drafting and design, mechanical engineering, in-

dustrial production, civil and architectural engineering, electrical engineering, chemical and laboratory) and 11 nonengineering related services (environmental health, agriculture and forestry, business management, communications, data processing, sales, transportation services, protective services, medical laboratory, nursing, food service); James E. Oliver; Educational Guidance, Inc. *

[2173]

Chatterji's Non-Language Preference Record. Ages 11-16; 1962; 10 scores: fine arts, literary, scientific, medical, agricultural, mechanical, crafts, outdoor, sports, household work; S. Chatterji; distributed by Manasayan [India]. *

For additional information, see 6:1050.

REFERENCES THROUGH 1971

1. Chatterji, S., and Mukerjee, Manjula. "Stability of Measured Interests." *J Voc & Ed Guid* (India) 10:10-4 F '64. * (*PA* 39:1722)
2. Rohila, Pritam; Shankhdhar, S. C.; and Sharma, Vijay. "Comparison of a Non-Verbal Interest Inventory With Its Verbal Equivalent." *J Psychol Res* (India) 10:32-6 Ja '66. * (*PA* 40:7719)
3. Bayti, Jamna Lal. "A Study of Vocational Preferences, Job Values and Occupational Choices of Secondary School Leavers." *J Ed Res & Exten* (India) 3:131-5 Ap '67. *
4. Banerjee, Chhabi; Dutta, Anath; Chatterji, S.; and Mukerjee, M. "An Investigation Into the Interest Pattern of Deaf Children." *Psychol Ann* 4:40-4 Mr '70. * (*PA* 46:3545)
5. Bose, Utpala; Sinha, S.; Chatterji, S.; and Mukerjee, Manjula. "An Investigation Into the Interest Patterns of the Students in Science, Humanities and Commerce Streams at the Higher Secondary Level." *J Psychol Res* (India) 14(1):14-21 Ja '70. *
6. Chatterji, S.; Mukerjee, Manjula; Mitra, Sadhana; and Dutta, A. "A Comparative Study of the Interest Patterns of the Inmates of the House of Detention, Normal School Children and Children Living in a Slum Area." *Indian J Appl Psychol* 7(2):56-62 Jl '70. *

CUMULATIVE NAME INDEX

Banerjee, C.: 4
Bayti, J. L.: 3
Bose, U.: 5
Chatterji, S.: 1, 4-6
Dutta, A.: 4, 6
Mitra, S.: 6

Mukerjee, M.: 1, 4-6
Rohila, P.: 2
Shankhdhar, S. C.: 2
Sharma, V.: 2
Sinha, S.: 5

[2174]

College Interest Inventory. Grades 11-16; 1967; CII; 16 scores: agriculture, home economics, literature and journalism, fine arts, social science, physical science, biological science, foreign language, business administration, accounting, teaching, civil engineering, electrical engineering, mechanical engineering, law, total; Robert W. Henderson; Personal Growth Press. *

For additional information and reviews by John W. French and David A. Payne, see 7:1014.

[2175]

Connolly Occupational Interests Questionnaire. Ages 15 and over; 1967-70; COIQ; 7 scores: scientific, social welfare, persuasive, literary, artistic, clerical-computational, practical; T. G. Connolly and Joshua Fox (supplementary manual); Careers Research and Advisory Centre [England]. *

For additional information and a review by David G. Hawkridge, see 7:1015 (2 references).

REFERENCES THROUGH 1971

1-2. See 7:1015.

CUMULATIVE NAME INDEX

Connolly, T. G.: 1
Hawkridge, D. G.: *rev*, 7:1015

Morea, P. C.: 2

[2176]

*Crowley Occupational Interests Blank. Ages 13 and over of average ability or less; 1970-72; COIB;

10 scores: 5 interest areas (active-outdoor, office, social, practical, artistic) and 5 sources of job satisfaction (financial gain, stability-security, companionship, working conditions, interest); A. D. Crowley; Careers Research and Advisory Centre [England]. *

For additional information, see 7:1016.

[2177]

Curtis Interest Scale. Grades 9–16 and adults; 1959; 10 scores (business, mechanics, applied arts, direct sales, production, science, entertainment, interpersonal, computation, farming) and 1 rating (desire for responsibility); James W. Curtis; Psychometric Affiliates. *

For additional information and reviews by Warren T. Norman and Leona E. Tyler, see 6:1052.

REFERENCES THROUGH 1971
1. KELLEHER, EDWARD J.; KERR, WILLARD A.; AND MELVILLE, NORBERT T. "The Prediction of Subprofessional Nursing Success." *Personnel Psychol* 21:379–88 au '68. * (*PA* 43:4063)

CUMULATIVE NAME INDEX

Kelleher, E. J.: 1	Norman, W. T.: *rev,* 6:1052
Kerr, W. A.: 1	Tyler, L. E.: *rev,* 6:1052
Melville, N. T.: 1	

[2178]

*Educational Interest Inventory. Grades 11–13 and adults; 1962–71; EII; 18 (females) or 19 (males) scores: literature, music, art, communication, education, business administration (males), engineering (males), industrial arts (males), agriculture (males), secretarial arts (females), nursing (females), library arts (females), home economics (females), botany, zoology, physics, chemistry, earth science (males), history and political science, sociology, psychology, economics, mathematics; James E. Oliver, Thomas C. Oliver (validity report), and Warren K. Willis (validity report); Educational Guidance, Inc. *

For additional information, see 7:1017 (6 references).

REFERENCES THROUGH 1971
1–6. See 7:1017.
7. WANDZEK, FRANK P. "Effects of Positive Verbal Reinforcements on Interest Selections." *Psychol Rep* 24(2):407–12 Ap '69. * (*PA* 43:15178)

CUMULATIVE NAME INDEX

Meisgeier, C. H.: 2	Thomas, D. L.: 4
Miller, C. D.: 4–6	Thomas, L. E.: 5–6
Morrill, W. H.: 5–6	Wandzek, F. P.: 7
Rishel, D. F.: 1	Weiser, J. C.: 3

[2179]

The Factorial Interest Blank. Ages 11–16; 1967; FIB; 8 scores: rural-practical, sociable, humanitarian, entertainment, physical, literate, aesthetic, scientific-mechanical; P. H. Sandall; distributed by NFER Publishing Co. Ltd. [England]. *

For additional information and reviews by David P. Campbell and Hugh F. Priest, see 7:1018 (1 reference).

REFERENCES THROUGH 1971
1. See 7:1018.
2. ZAHRAN, HAMED A. S. "The Self-Concept in the Psychological Guidance of Adolescents." *Brit J Ed Psychol* 37:225–40 Je '67. * (*PA* 41:15077)

CUMULATIVE NAME INDEX

Campbell, D. P.: *rev,* 7:1018	Sandall, P. H.: 1
Priest, H. F.: *rev,* 7:1018	Zahran, H. A. S.: 2

[2180]

*The Geist Picture Interest Inventory. Grades 8–16 and adults; 1959–71; GPII; 18 (males) or 19 (females) scores: 11 or 12 interest scores (persuasive, clerical, mechanical, musical, scientific, outdoor,

Crowley Occupational Interests Blank

literary, computational, artistic, social service, dramatic, personal service—females only) and 7 motivation scores (family, prestige, financial, intrinsic and personality, environmental, past experience, could not say); Harold Geist; Western Psychological Services. *

For additional information, reviews by Milton E. Hahn and Benjamin Shimberg, and an excerpted review by David V. Tiedeman, see 6:1054 (12 references).

REFERENCES THROUGH 1971
1–12. See 6:1054.
13. MONTESANO, NICHOLAS RAYMOND. *Interest Bases Differentials Between Ninth and Twelfth Grade Boys.* Doctor's thesis, Stanford University (Stanford, Calif.), 1962. (*DA* 23:4228)
14. GEIST, HAROLD. "Socio-Economic Status and Culture, and Occupational Aspiration and Choice." *Congreso Interamericano de Psicologia* (Mexico) 7:284–7 '63. *
15. MONTESANO, NICHOLAS, AND GEIST, HAROLD. "Differences in Occupational Choice Between Ninth and Twelfth Grade Boys." *Personnel & Guid J* 43:150–4 O '64. * (*PA* 39:9851)
16. BURG, BILLIE WALCUTT, AND BARRETT, ALBERT M. "Interest Testing With the Mentally Retarded: A Bi-Sensory Approach." *Am J Mental Def* 69:548–52 Ja '65. * (*PA* 39:10571)
17. CONNORS, MAUREEN. *A Comparative Study of the Occupational Interests of Negro and White Adolescent Boys.* Doctor's thesis, Catholic University of America (Washington, D.C.), 1965. (*DA* 26:6508)
18. GEIST, HAROLD. "Vocational Interests in Different Countries." Abstract. *Congr Inter-Am Soc Psychol* 9(1964):633–4 ['65].
19. HAYES, MARY P. *The Variability of Occupational Interest Patterns of Catholic, Public, and Training School Girls as Measured by the Geist Picture Interest Inventory.* Master's thesis, Catholic University of America (Washington, D.C.), 1965.
20. BLAKE, RICHARD HALEY. *A Comparison of the Test-Retest Reliability of Picture and Verbal Forms of Occupational Interest Inventories.* Doctor's thesis, University of Missouri (Columbia, Mo.), 1966. (*DA* 27:2868A)
21. KENNEDY, LEO THOMAS. *A Study of the Vocational Interest Differences Between Hearing and Non-Hearing Secondary School Students as Determined by the Geist Picture Interest Inventory.* Master's thesis, Catholic University of America (Washington, D.C.), 1967.
22. GEIST, H. "A Comparison of Occupational Choice in Various Cultures." *Proc Inter Congr Appl Psychol* 16:724–31 '68. *
23. GEIST, HAROLD. "A Comparison of Occupational Choice in Various Cultures." *Int J Exp Res Ed* 5(2):200–12 '68. *
24. GEIST, HAROLD. "A 10 Year Follow-Up of the Geist Picture Interest Inventory." *Calif J Ed Res* 19:198–206 S '68. * (*PA* 43:5924)
25. KRONENBERGER, EARL J., AND QUATMAN, GERALD L. "Performance of Institutionalized Juvenile Delinquents on the Geist Picture Interest Inventory." *Psychol Rep* 22:185–6 F '68. * (*PA* 42:10756)
26. BLAKE, RICHARD. "Comparative Reliability of Picture Form and Verbal Form Interest Inventories." *J Appl Psychol* 53(1):42–4 F '69. * (*PA* 43:7416)
27. GEIST, HAROLD. "A Comparison of Vocation Interests in Various Countries in Latin America." *Interam J Psychol* (Mexico) 3(3):169–76 S '69. * (*PA* 44:9293)
28. GEIST, HAROLD. "A Comparison of Vocational Interests at Different Levels in Schools in Japan and a Comparison With United States Counterparts." *Psychologia* (Japan) 12(3–4):227–31 D '69. * (*PA* 45:2998)
29. GEIST, HAROLD, AND GULATI, KRISHNA. "A Comparison of Vocation Interests in India and the United States." *Indian Psychol R* 7(1):67–70 Jl '70. *
30. MORRIS, J. L., AND PARKINSON, M. "Vocational Interests of Computer Programmers." *Austral Computer J* 2(3):139–42 Ag '70. *

CUMULATIVE NAME INDEX

Abdel-Meguid, S. G. M.: 1	Kennedy, L. T.: 21
Barrett, A. M.: 16	Kronenberger, E. J.: 25
Blake, R.: 26	McDaniel, H. B.: 2
Blake, R. H.: 20	Magary, J. F.: 7
Burg, B. W.: 16	Montesano, N.: 15
Clarke, C. T.: 3	Montesano, N. R.: 13
Connors, M.: 17	Morris, J. L.: 30
Geist, H.: 2, 4–6, 8–12, 14–5, 18, 22–4, 27–9; *exc,* 6:1054	Parkinson, M.: 30
	Quatman, G. L.: 25
Gulati, K.: 29	Shimberg, B.: *rev,* 6:1054
Hahn, M. E.: *rev,* 6:1054	Tiedeman, D. V.: *exc,* 6:1054
Hayes, M. P.: 19	

[2181]

Geist Picture Interest Inventory: Deaf Form: Male. Deaf and hard of hearing males (grades 7–16 and adults) ; 1962; adaptation of *Geist Picture Interest Inventory;* 10 scores: persuasive, clerical, mechanical, scientific, outdoor, literary, computational, artistic, social service, dramatic; Harold Geist; Western Psychological Services. *

For additional information, see 6:1055 (1 reference).

REFERENCES THROUGH 1971

1. See 6:1055.
2. BOLTON, BRIAN. "A Critical Review of the Geist Picture Interest Inventory: Deaf Form: Male." *J Rehabil Deaf* 5(2): 21–9 O '71. *

CUMULATIVE NAME INDEX

Bolton, B.: 2   Geist, H.: 1

[2182]

Gordon Occupational Check List. High school students not planning to enter college; 1961–67; 5 or 11 scores: business, outdoor, arts, technology, service, and 6 optional response summarization scores (preceding 5 areas and total) ; Leonard V. Gordon; Harcourt Brace Jovanovich, Inc. *

For additional information and reviews by John N. McCall and Bert W. Westbrook, see 7:1019; for reviews by John O. Crites and Kenneth B. Hoyt, see 6:1056.

[2183]

Gregory Academic Interest Inventory. Grades 13–16; 1946; 28 scores: agriculture, architecture, biological sciences, business administration, chemistry, civil engineering, commercial arts, electrical engineering, elementary education, English, fine arts, geology, history, home economics, journalism, languages, mathematics, mechanical engineering, military science, music, physics, physical education, psychology, public service engineering, religion, secondary education, sociology, speech; W. S. Gregory; Sheridan Psychological Services, Inc. *

For additional information and reviews by Paul S. Burnham, Lysle W. Croft, and Herbert A. Toops, see 3:636 (1 reference).

REFERENCES THROUGH 1971

1. See 3:636.
2. RICHARD, WILMA A. *Effectiveness of the Gregory Academic Interest Inventory in the Prediction of Academic Success of Home Economics Freshmen.* Master's thesis, University of Nebraska (Lincoln, Neb.), 1952.
3. SHAPPELL, DEAN L.; ARNOLD, FRANK C.; AND GREGORY, WILBUR S. "Differentiation of Academic Interests." *Ed & Psychol Meas* 29(2):473–8 su '69. * (*PA* 44:17427)

CUMULATIVE NAME INDEX

Arnold, F. C.: 3   Richard, W. A.: 2
Burnham, P. S.: *rev,* 3:636   Shappell, D. L.: 3
Croft, L. W.: *rev,* 3:636   Toops, H. A.: *rev,* 3:636
Gregory, W. S.: 1, 3

[2184]

The Guilford-Shneidman-Zimmerman Interest Survey. Grades 9–16 and adults; 1948; 18 scores: artistic (appreciative, expressive), linguistic (appreciative, expressive), scientific (investigatory, theoretical), mechanical (manipulative, designing), outdoor (natural, athletic), business-political (mercantile, leadership), social activity (persuasive, gregarious), personal assistance (personal service, social welfare), office work (clerical, numerical); J. P. Guilford, Edwin Shneidman, and Wayne S. Zimmerman; Sheridan Psychological Services, Inc. *

For additional information and reviews by George K. Bennett and Wilbur L. Layton, see 4:739 (2 references).

REFERENCES THROUGH 1971

1–2. See 4:739.
3. McCARTHY, MARY VITERBO. "An Empirical Study of the Personality Profiles Characterizing Differential Quantitative

and Linguistic Ability." *Studies Psychol & Psychiatry* 8(4):1–45 Je '53. * (*PA* 28:4043)
4. SHNEIDMAN, EDWIN S. "The Case of El: Psychological Test Data." *J Proj Tech* 25:131–54 Je '61. * (*PA* 36:21K31S)

CUMULATIVE NAME INDEX

Bennett, G. K.: *rev,* 4:739   McCarthy, M. V.: 3
Foster, K. E.: 1   Shneidman, E. S.: 2, 4
Guilford, J. P.: 2   Zimmerman, W. S.: 2
Layton, W. L.: *rev,* 4:739

[2185]

The Guilford-Zimmerman Interest Inventory. Grades 10–16 and adults; 1962–63; 10 scores: mechanical, natural, aesthetic, service, clerical, mercantile, leadership, literary, scientific, creative; Joan S. Guilford and Wayne S. Zimmerman; Sheridan Psychological Services, Inc. *

For additional information and a review by Kenneth B. Hoyt, see 6:1057.

REFERENCES THROUGH 1971

1. GUILFORD, J. P.; CHRISTENSEN, PAUL R.; BOND, NICHOLAS A., JR.; AND SUTTON, MARCELLA A. "A Factor Analysis Study of Human Interests." *Psychol Monogr* 68(4):1–38 '54. * (*PA* 29:4727)
2. GITLIN, SIDNEY. *A Study of the Interrelationships of Parents' Measured Interest Patterns and Those of Their Children.* Doctor's thesis, Temple University (Philadelphia, Pa.), 1958. (*DA* 19:3352)
3. GUILFORD, J. P. *Personality.* New York: McGraw-Hill Book Co., Inc., 1959. Pp. xiii, 562. *
4. ABDEL-GHAFFAR, ABDEL-SALAM ABDEL-KADER. *Relationships Between Selected Creativity Factors and Certain Non-Intellectual Factors Among High School Students.* Doctor's thesis, University of Denver (Denver, Colo.), 1963. (*DA* 25:1728)
5. FLAX, MORTON LEWIS. *The Stability of Relationships Between Creativity and Personality Variables.* Doctor's research study No. 1, Colorado State College (Greeley, Colo.), 1966. (*DA* 27:2857B)
6. BLANKENSHIP, KARL RICHARD. *The Relationship of Divergent Production Ability to the Interests of Selected Male Junior High School Students.* Doctor's thesis, University of Denver (Denver, Colo.), 1968. (*DA* 29:3761A)
7. SIMMS, JEANNE THOMAS. *An Investigation of the Differences Between Creative High Socio-Economic College Freshmen and Creative Low-Socio-Economic College Freshmen on Measures of Vocational Interests and Certain Motivational Factors.* Doctor's thesis, Catholic University of America (Washington, D.C.), 1970. (*DAI* 31:2693A)

CUMULATIVE NAME INDEX

Abdel-Ghaffar, A. S. A. K.: 4   Gitlin, S.: 2
Blankenship, K. R.: 6   Guilford, J. P.: 1, 3
Bond, N. A.: 1   Hoyt, K. B.: *rev,* 6:1057
Christensen, P. R.: 1   Simms, J. T.: 7
Flax, M. L.: 5   Sutton, M. A.: 1

[2186]

Hackman-Gaither Vocational Interest Inventory: Standard Edition. Grades 9–12 and adults; 1962–68; HGVII; positive (like), negative (dislike), and total scores for each of 8 areas: business contact, artistic, scientific-technical, health and welfare, business-clerical, mechanical, service, outdoor; 1968 form identical with form copyrighted 1965; Roy B. Hackman and James W. Gaither; Psychological Service Center of Philadelphia. *

For additional information and a review by Henry Weitz, see 7:1020 (21 references) ; see also 6:1058 (4 references).

REFERENCES THROUGH 1971

1–4. See 6:1058.
5–25. See 7:1020.

CUMULATIVE NAME INDEX

Arns, J.: 1   Gash, I. A.: 15
Berrier, J. G.: 2   Hess, A. W.: 10
Buckalew, R. J.: 5   Jeremias, H. I.: 16
Cohen, L. M.: 4   Kline, G. R.: 11
Cook, K. L.: 20   Llana, A.: 12
Creamer, W.: 18   Logue, J. J.: 17
DeCencio, D. V.: 14   Lubetkin, A. I.: 7
Dressler, R. M.: 21   Miller, J.: 8
Eddins, E. L.: 6   Reiter, R. G.: 13
Gaither, J. W.: 3   Sherr, R. D.: 22

Silverman, E. H.: 9   Sullivan, J. W.: 24
Smith, J. A.: 19   Weitz, H.: *rev*, 7:1020
Spergel, P.: 23   Ziegler, D. J.: 25

[2187]

*Hall Occupational Orientation Inventory, Second Edition. Grades 7–16 and adults; 1968–71, c1965–71; HOOI; 22 scores: creativity-independence, risk, information-knowledge, belongingness, security, aspiration, esteem, self-actualization, personal satisfaction, routine-dependence, data orientation, things orientation, people orientation, location concern, aptitude concern, monetary concern, physical abilities concern, environment concern, co-worker concern, qualifications concern, time concern, defensiveness; L. G. Hall, R. B. Tarrier (manual), and D. L. Shappell (manual); Scholastic Testing Service, Inc. *

For additional information and a review by Donald G. Zytowski of the earlier edition, see 7:1021 (4 references).

REFERENCES THROUGH 1971

1–4. See 7:1021.
5. YOUNGER, JESSAMINE GRIMES. *The Effect of Vocational Choice Counseling on Vocational Maturity in Selected First Year University Students.* Master's thesis, Southern Methodist University (Dallas, Tex.), 1969.
6. DIXON, DANA H. *A Comparison of the Personality Adjustment and the Occupational Needs of Black College Women.* Master's thesis, Wake Forest University (Winston-Salem, N.C.), 1971.
7. SHAPPELL, DEAN L.; HALL, LACY G.; AND TARRIER, RANDOLPH B. "Perceptions of the World of Work: Inner-City Versus Suburbia." *J Counsel Psychol* 18(1):55–9 Ja '71. * (*PA* 45:8956)

CUMULATIVE NAME INDEX

Dixon, D. H.: 6   Tarrier, R. B.: 2, 4, 7
Hall, L. G.: 1, 4, 7   Younger, J. G.: 5
Shappell, D. L.: 3–4, 7   Zytowski, D. G.: *rev*, 7:1021

[2188]

Henderson Analysis of Interest, [Second Edition]. Grades 9–16 and adults; 1950; occupational preferences in 14 areas: business service, clerical, accounting and statistics, persuasive, managerial, social science, physical science, biological science, engineering, art and music, teaching, writing, mechanical, manual; Robert W. Henderson; [Personal Growth Press]. *

For additional information and reviews by Wilbur L. Layton and Donald E. Super, see 4:740.

[2189]

How Well Do You Know Your Interests. High school, college, adults; 1957–70; 54 scores: numerical, clerical, retail selling, outside selling, selling real estate, one-order selling, sales complaints, selling intangibles, buyer, labor management, production supervision, business management, machine operation, repair and construction, machine design, farm or ranch, gardening, hunting, adventure, social service, teaching service, medical service, nursing service, applied chemistry, basic chemical problems, basic biological problems, basic physical problems, basic psychological problems, philosophical, visual art appreciative, visual art productive, visual art decorative, amusement appreciative, amusement productive, amusement managerial, literary appreciative, literary productive, musical appreciative, musical performing, musical composing, sports appreciative, sports participative, domestic service, unskilled labor, disciplinary, power seeking, propaganda, self-aggrandizing, supervisory initiative, bargaining, arbitrative, persuasive, disputatious, masculinity (for males only) or femininity (for females only); Thomas N. Jenkins, John H. Coleman (manual), and Harold T. Fagin (manual); Executive Analysis Corporation. *

For additional information, see 7:1022 (2 references); for a review by John R. Hills and an excerpted review by Gordon V. Anderson, see 6:1059 (1 reference); for reviews by Jerome E. Doppelt and Henry S. Dyer, see 5:859.

REFERENCES THROUGH 1971

1. See 6:1059.
2–3. See 7:1022.

CUMULATIVE NAME INDEX

Anderson, G. V.: *exc*, 6:1059   Hills, J. R.: *rev*, 6:1059
Doppelt, J. E.: *rev*, 5:859   Levine, H.: 2
Dyer, H. S.: *rev*, 5:859   Mendelson, M. A.: 1
Griggs, S. A.: 3   Schwartz, M. M.: 2

[2190]

*Interest Check List. Grades 9 and over; 1946–67; ICL; interviewing aid; 1967 revision identical with 1957 edition except for instructions and coding structure; developed by the United States Employment Service; United States Government Printing Office. *

For additional information on the 1957 edition, see 5:860; for reviews by Milton L. Blum and Howard R. Taylor of the original edition, see 4:741.

REFERENCES THROUGH 1971

1. HENDERSON, BRUCE, AND MADAY, DAVID. "Interest Check List Responses of Three Youth Groups." *J Employ Counsel* 4:122–6 D '67. *
2. DAVIS, STEPHEN P. "Analysis of the Interest Check List for Indications of Bias." *J Employ Counsel* 8(2):50–8 Je '71. * (*PA* 47:11865)

CUMULATIVE NAME INDEX

Blum, M. L.: *rev*, 4:741   Maday, D.: 1
Davis, S. P.: 2   Taylor, H. R.: *rev*, 4:741
Henderson, B.: 1

[2191]

★Interest Questionnaire for Indian South Africans. Standards 6–10; 1969–71; IQISA; 7 scores: language, arts, social service, science, mechanics, business, office work; S. Oosthuizen; Human Sciences Research Council [South Africa]. *

[2192]

Inventory of Vocational Interests: Acorn National Aptitude Tests. Grades 7–16 and adults; 1943–60; 5 scores: mechanical, academic, artistic, business and economic, farm-agricultural; 1957 test identical with test copyrighted 1943; 1960 manual identical with manual copyrighted 1943; Andrew Kobal, J. Wayne Wrightstone, and Karl R. Kunze; Psychometric Affiliates. *

For additional information and a review by John W. French, see 6:1060; for reviews by Marion A. Bills, Edward S. Bordin, Harold D. Carter, and Patrick Slater, see 3:638.

[2193]

Kuder General Interest Survey. Grades 6–12; 1934–70; KGIS; also called *Kuder E*; revision and downward extension of *Kuder Preference Record—Vocational*, Form C; 11 scores: outdoor, mechanical, computational, scientific, persuasive, artistic, literary, musical, social service, clerical, verification; G. Frederic Kuder; Science Research Associates, Inc. *

For additional information, reviews by Barbara A. Kirk, Paul R. Lohnes, and John N. McCall, and excerpted reviews by T. R. Husek and Robert F. Stahmann, see 7:1024 (8 references).

REFERENCES THROUGH 1971

1–8. See 7:1024.

CUMULATIVE NAME INDEX

Carrett, P.: 7   Kirk, B. A.: *rev*, 7:1024
Cronbach, L. J.: 8   Lohnes, P. R.: *rev*, 7:1024
Husek, T. R.: *exc*, 7:1024   McCall, J. N.: *rev*, 7:1024

Mooney, R. F.: 2, 5
Plotkin, A. L.: 1
Replogle, J. R.: 3
Schneider, D. L.: 4

Shann, M. H.: 6
Shapiro, R. M.: 7
Stahmann, R. F.: *exc,* 7:1024
Tillinghast, B. S.: 7

[2194]

Kuder Occupational Interest Survey. Grades 11–16 and adults; 1956–70; KOIS; also called *Kuder DD;* items same as those in *Kuder Preference Record—Occupational* but differently scored; 106 scales for men: 77 occupational, 29 college major; 84 scales for women: 57 occupational, 27 college major; G. Frederic Kuder; Science Research Associates, Inc. *

For additional information, reviews by Robert H. Dolliver and W. Bruce Walsh, and excerpted reviews by Frederick G. Brown and Robert F. Stahmann, see 7:1025 (19 references).

REFERENCES THROUGH 1971

1–19. See 7:1025.
20. JOHNSON, CLARICE WELLS. *Nonintellective Factors Related to College Achievement and Attrition.* Doctor's thesis, University of South Carolina (Columbia, S.C.), 1970. (*DAI* 31:5129A)
21. COLE, NANCY S., AND HANSON, GARY R. "An Analysis of the Structure of Vocational Interests." *ACT Res Rep* 40:1–17 Ja '71. * (*PA* 47:1843)
22. COLE, NANCY S., AND HANSON, GARY R. "An Analysis of the Structure of Vocational Interests." *J Counsel Psychol* 18(5): 478–86 S '71. * (*PA* 47:3679)
23. DIAMOND, ESTHER E. "Occupational Interests: Male-Female or High Level-Low Level Dichotomy." *J Voc Behav* 1(4):305–15 O '71. * (*PA* 48:5928)
24. FLOWERS, HENRY MOSES. *The Relationship of Parental Identification to Parental Vocational Interest Similarity.* Doctor's thesis, University of Kansas (Lawrence, Kan.), 1971. (*DAI* 32:1851A)
25. GOLDMAN, BERT A., AND VICINANZA, PAUL. "A Scoring System for Measuring College Interest With the Kuder Occupational Interest Survey Form DD." *J Ed Res* 65(3):101–2 N '71. * (*PA* 48:1734)
26. HARRINGTON, THOMAS F.; LYNCH, MERVIN D.; AND O'SHEA, ARTHUR J. "Factor Analysis of Twenty-Seven Similarly Named Scales of the Strong Vocational Interest Blank and the Kuder Occupational Interest Survey, Form DD." *J Counsel Psychol* 18(3):229–33 My '71. * (*PA* 46:5555)
27. HAVENS, JANET M. *Relationship Between Some Intellective and Nonintellective Factors of Disadvantaged High Risk Students and Their Success in College.* Doctor's thesis, Rutgers—The State University (New Brunswick, N.J.), 1971. (*DAI* 32:6201A)
28. HORNADAY, JOHN A., AND ABOUD, JOHN. "Characteristics of Successful Entrepreneurs." *Personnel Psychol* 24(2):141–53 su '71. * (*PA* 49:3400)
29. JOHNSON, RICHARD W. "Congruence of Strong and Kuder Interest Profiles." *J Counsel Psychol* 18(5):450–5 S '71. * (*PA* 47:3697)
30. LOADMAN, WILLIAM EARL, II. *A Comparison of Several Methods of Scoring the Kuder Occupational Interest Survey.* Doctor's thesis, Michigan State University (East Lansing, Mich.), 1971. (*DAI* 32:6810A)
31. NELSON, A. GORDON. "Discrepancy Between Expressed and Inventoried Vocational Interests." *Voc Guid Q* 20(1):21–4 S '71. * (*PA* 48:1755)
32. PLATA, MAXIMINO. *A Comparative Study of the Occupational Aspirations and Interests of High School Age Emotionally Disturbed, Vocational-Technical and Regular Academic Students.* Doctor's thesis, University of Kansas (Lawrence, Kan.), 1971. (*DAI* 32:5684A)

CUMULATIVE NAME INDEX

Aboud, J.: 28
Anderson, T. E.: 5
Brown, F. G.: *exc,* 7:1025
Bunker, C. S.: 17
Cain, E. T.: 12
Clemans, W. V.: 6
Cole, N. S.: 21–2
Dauw, D. C.: 3
Diamond, E. E.: 7, 16, 23
Dolliver, R. H.: *rev,* 7:1025
Drum, D. J.: 13
Flowers, H. M.: 24
Goldman, B. A.: 25
Hanson, G. R.: 21–2
Harrington, T. F.: 19, 26
Havens, J. M.: 27
Hornaday, J. A.: 17, 28
Johnson, C. W.: 20

Johnson, R. W.: 29
Kaiser, H. E.: 10
Kuder, F.: 14
Kuder, G. F.: 2
Lefkowitz, D. M.: 18
Loadman, W. E.: 30
Lynch, M. D.: 26
Nelson, A. G.: 31
O'Shea, A. J.: 19, 26
Plata, M.: 32
Richard, J. T.: 8
Ritchie, C. M.: 9
Stahmann, R. F.: *exc,* 7:1025
Vicinanza, P.: 25
Viswanathan, K.: 1
Walsh, W. B.: *rev,* 7:1025
Wilson, R. N.: 4, 10
Zytowski, D. G.: 11, 15

[2195]

Kuder Preference Record—Vocational. Grades 9–16 and adults; 1934–70; KPR-V; G. Frederic Kuder; Science Research Associates, Inc. *
a) FORM B. 1934–60; also called *Kuder B;* 9 scores: mechanical, computational, scientific, persuasive, artistic, literary, musical, social service, clerical; masculinity-femininity score also obtainable. *Out of print.*
b) FORM C. 1934–70; also called *Kuder C;* for revision and downward extension, see 2193; 11 scores: same as for Form B plus outdoor, verification.

For a review by Martin Katz, see 6:1063 (148 references); for reviews by Clifford P. Froehlich and John Pierce-Jones, see 5:863 (211 references); for reviews by Edward S. Bordin, Harold D. Carter, and H. M. Fowler, see 4:742 (144 references); for reviews by Ralph F. Berdie, E. G. Chambers, and Donald E. Super and an excerpted review by Arthur H. Brayfield of *a,* see 3:640 (60 references); for reviews by A. B. Crawford and Arthur E. Traxler of an earlier edition, see 2:1671 (2 references).

REFERENCES THROUGH 1971

1–2. See 2:1671.
3–62. See 3:640.
63–208. See 4:742.
209–419. See 5:863.
420–567. See 6:1063.
568. SHULTZ, IRVIN T., AND RUSH, HARVEY. "Comparison of the Occupational Ranking and Interests, Education and Intelligence of Patients at Sunnyside Sanatorium." *J Appl Psychol* 26:218–26 Ap '42. * (*PA* 16:4184)
569. FRANDSEN, ARDEN. "Appraisal of Interests in Guidance." *J Ed Res* 39:1–12 S '45. * (*PA* 20:555)
570. WOODY, CLIFFORD. *Aptitudes, Achievements and Interests of High School Pupils.* University of Michigan, Bureau of Educational Reference and Research Bulletin No. 157. Ann Arbor, Mich.: School of Education, the University, 1945. Pp. vi, 159. *
571. LARSEN, ARTHUR H.; LOVELASS, HARRY D.; AND WALTER, LOWELL. "Some Characteristics of Veterans Applying for Vocational Rehabilitation." *Sch & Soc* 66:299–303 O 18 '47. * (*PA* 22:2645)
572. HAYES, SAMUEL P. "An Interest Inventory for the Educational and Vocational Guidance of the Blind." *Outl Blind* 42:95–104 Ap '48. * (*PA* 22:5553)
573. SPAULDING, V. V. "A Study of Nurse and Police Applicants." *Delaware State Med J* 20:177–8 Ag '48. * (*PA* 23: 2945)
574. HAYES, SAMUEL P. "What Mental Tests Should We Use?" *Outl Blind* 43:271–9 D '49. * (*PA* 24:3355)
575. BARNETTE, W. LESLIE, JR. "Occupational Aptitude Pattern Research." *Occupations* 29:5–12 O '50. * (*PA* 25:3239)
576. COTTLE, WM. C. "A Factorial Study of the Multiphasic, Strong, Kuder, and Bell Inventories Using a Population of Adult Males." *Psychometrika* 15:25–47 Mr '50. * (*PA* 24:4492)
577. OSBORNE, R. T.; GREENE, J. E.; AND SANDERS, WILMA B. "Are Disabled Veterans Significantly Different From Nondisabled Veterans in Occupational Preferences, Employment Histories, Aptitudes, and College Achievements?" *Sch & Soc* 72: 8–11 Jl 1 '50. * (*PA* 26:2992)
578. CAMPBELL, JESSE FRANK. *Determination of the Predictive Relationship of Selected Factors to the Scholastic Achievement of 456 Veterans With Service-Connected Disabilities.* Doctor's thesis, University of Michigan (Ann Arbor, Mich.), 1952. (*DA* 12:148)
579. HEALY, IRENE, AND BORG, WALTER R. "Personality and Vocational Interests of Successful and Unsuccessful Nursing School Freshmen." *Ed & Psychol Meas* 12:767–75 w '52. * (*PA* 27:6221)
580. PEARLMAN, SAMUEL. *An Investigation of the Problem of Academic Underachievement Among Intellectually Superior College Students.* Doctor's thesis, New York University (New York, N.Y.), 1952. (*DA* 12:599)
581. PRINCENTHAL, HERMAN H. *Response to Vocational Guidance: Veterans With Functional Psychiatric Disorders Compared With Other Disabled Veterans.* Doctor's thesis, New York University (New York, N.Y.), 1952. (*DA* 13:127)
582. WHITTOCK, JOHN MELVILLE, JR. *Study of the Interests of the Female Students Enrolled in the School of Library Science, Drexel Institute of Technology, as Measured by the Strong Vocational Interest Blank and the Kuder Preference Record.* Master's thesis, Drexel Institute of Technology (Philadelphia, Pa.), 1952. *
583. DELISLE, FRANCES HELEN. *A Study of the Relationship of the Self-Concept to Adjustment in a Selected Group of College*

Women. Doctor's thesis, Michigan State College (East Lansing, Mich.), 1953. (*DA* 13:719)

584. KULICK, WILLIAM. *Personality Traits and Academic Standing of Probationary Engineering Students Before and After Counseling: An Evaluation of the Effectiveness of Non-Directive Counseling by Means of the Rorschach Test.* Doctor's thesis, New York University (New York, N.Y.), 1953. (*DA* 13:584)

585. McCARTHY, MARY VITERBO. "An Empirical Study of the Personality Profiles Characterizing Differential Quantitative and Linguistic Ability." *Studies Psychol & Psychiatry* 8(4):1–45 Je '53. * (*PA* 28:4043)

586. MARTINSON, FLOYD M. *Some Personality Adjustment Differences of Rural Nonmigrants and Migrants.* Doctor's thesis, University of Minnesota (Minneapolis, Minn.), 1953. (*DA* 13: 1291)

587. BITNER, HAROLD MILLER. *Ethnic Inter-Group Differences in Personality, General Culture, Academic Ability, and Interests in a Geographically Restricted Area.* Doctor's thesis, Ohio State University (Columbus, Ohio), 1954. (*DA* 20:772)

588. CAREY, JOAN. *An Analysis of Certain Traits as Exhibited by a Group of Women Selected for Elementary Education at Syracuse University.* Doctor's thesis, Syracuse University (Syracuse, N.Y.), 1954. (*DA* 15:1356)

589. HILL, JULIUS MATHEW. *The Effects of Artificially Measured Low Aptitude Test Scores on Change in Vocational Interest.* Doctor's thesis, University of Michigan (Ann Arbor, Mich.), 1954. (*DA* 14:781)

590. LaBue, ANTHONY CHARLES. *An Analysis of Some Factors Associated With Persistence of Interest in Teaching as a Vocational Choice.* Doctor's thesis, Syracuse University (Syracuse, N.Y.), 1954. (*DA* 14:2001)

591. TANNER, WILLIAM C., JR. "Personality Bases in Teacher Selection." *Phi Delta Kappan* 35:271–4+ Ap '54. *

592. ARMSTRONG, MARION ELIZABETH. *A Comparison of the Interests and Social Adjustment of Underachievers and Normal Achievers at the Secondary School Level.* Doctor's thesis, University of Connecticut (Storrs, Conn.), 1955. (*DA* 15:1349)

593. CARMAN, PHILIP McCELLAN. *The Relationship of Individual and Husband-Wife Patterns of Personality Characteristics to Marital Stability.* Doctor's thesis, University of Washington (Seattle, Wash.), 1955. (*DA* 15:113)

594. GENGERELLI, J. A., AND BUTLER, BRUCE V. "A Method for Comparing the Profiles of Several Population Samples." *J Psychol* 40:247–68 O '55. * (*PA* 30:6534)

595. HYMAN, BERNARD. *The Relationship of Social Status and Vocational Interest.* Doctor's thesis, Columbia University (New York, N.Y.), 1955. (*DA* 15:1354)

596. JOHNSON, RALPH HAAKON. *Factors Related to the Success of Disabled Veterans of World War II in the Rehabilitation Training Program Approved for Mechanics and Repairmen, Motor Vehicle.* Doctor's thesis, University of Minnesota (Minneapolis, Minn.), 1955. (*DA* 15:2460)

597. LODATO, FRANCIS JOSEPH. *The Relationship Between Interest and Personality as Measured by the Kuder and the Heston and Gordon Inventories.* Doctor's thesis, St. John's University (Jamaica, N.Y.), 1955.

598. MARTINSON, FLOYD M. "Ego Deficiency as a Factor in Marriage." *Am Sociol R* 20:161–4 Ap '55. * (*PA* 31:912)

599. STOREY, JOHN STUART. *The Validity of Counseling Variables Considered in the Advisement of Disabled Veterans Entering Terminal Business Training.* Doctor's thesis, Michigan State University (East Lansing, Mich.), 1955. (*DA* 15:1019)

600. GORMAN, WILLIAM EDWARD. *The Effect of Occupational Information in English Classes on High School Juniors.* Doctor's thesis, Northwestern University (Evanston, Ill.), 1956. (*DA* 17:301)

601. KNAAK, NANCY KATHERINE. *A Study of the Characteristics of Academically Successful and Unsuccessful Freshmen Women Who Entered Northwestern University in the Fall of 1954.* Doctor's thesis, Northwestern University (Evanston, Ill.), 1956. (*DA* 17:304)

602. LEE, MARILYN CAIRNS. *Configural vs. Linear Prediction of Collegiate Academic Performance.* Doctor's thesis, University of Illinois (Urbana, Ill.), 1956. (*DA* 17:397)

603. PATTERSON, C. H. "A Kuder Pattern for Bakers and Baking Students." *Personnel & Guid J* 35:110–1 O '56. * (*PA* 31:8188)

604. POLLAN, WILLIAM D. *Stability of Interest of College Students.* Doctor's thesis, North Texas State College (Denton, Tex.), 1956. (*DA* 17:673)

605. VAN DALSEM, ELIZABETH LOU. *Factors Related to Low Achievement in High School English.* Doctor's thesis, Stanford University (Stanford, Calif.), 1956. (*DA* 16:1233)

606. CURRIE, CAROLINE. *The Relationship of Certain Selected Factors to Achievement in Freshman Composition.* Doctor's thesis, Northwestern University (Evanston, Ill.), 1957. (*DA* 18:884)

607. DIENER, CHARLES L. *A Comparison of Over-Achieving and Under-Achieving Students at the University of Arkansas.* Doctor's thesis, University of Arkansas (Fayetteville, Ark.), 1957. (*DA* 17:1692)

608. JENSEN, VERN HARMON. *An Analysis and Comparison of the Adjustment Problems of Nonachieving College Students of Low Scholastic Ability and Other Groups of Achieving and Nonachieving Students.* Doctor's thesis, University of Colorado (Boulder, Colo.), 1957. (*DA* 19:70)

609. KEMP, CLARENCE GRATTON. *Changes in Patterns of Personal Values in Relation to Open-Closed Belief Systems.* Doctor's thesis, Michigan State University (East Lansing, Mich.), 1957. (*DA* 19:271)

610. LAY, ARCHIE WILSON. *A Study of the Influence of an Interest Inventory on Choice of Major and Subsequent Academic Behavior.* Doctor's thesis, University of Houston (Houston, Tex.), 1957. (*DA* 17:1707)

611. PATTERSON, C. H. "Interest Tests and the Emotionally Disturbed Client." *Ed & Psychol Meas* 17:264–80 su '57. * (*PA* 32:5620)

612. ROOKS, ILA. *Teaching Satisfaction in Relation to Intelligence, Interests, and Grade-Point Average of Selected University of Georgia Graduates.* Doctor's thesis, University of Georgia (Athens, Ga.), 1957. (*DA* 17:1953)

613. ROWE, FREDERICK B. *The Selection of Psychiatric Aides: Criterion Development and Prediction.* Doctor's thesis, University of Maryland (College Park, Md.), 1957. (*DA* 17:2674)

614. SIDNEY, GEORGE PAUL. *A Study of Psychological Test and Biographical Variables as Possible Predictors of Successful Psychiatric Aide Performance.* Doctor's thesis, Pennsylvania State University (University Park, Pa.), 1957. (*DA* 18:289)

615. SMITH, ROBIN NELSON. *The Evaluation of a Less Structured Form of Interest Test Item.* Doctor's thesis, Columbia University (New York, N.Y.), 1957. (*DA* 17:1709)

616. BRADLEY, ARTHUR DICKINSON. *Estimating Success in Technical and Skilled Trade Courses Using a Multivariate Statistical Analysis.* Doctor's thesis, University of Minnesota (Minneapolis, Minn.), 1958. (*DA* 21:313)

617. CANNON, DEORE J. *The Concepts of Interest and Need Held by Two Occupational Groups.* Doctor's thesis, University of Texas (Austin, Tex.), 1958. (*DA* 19:2283)

618. FRANKEL, EDWARD. *A Comparative Study of Achieving and Underachieving High School Boys of High Intellectual Ability.* Doctor's thesis, Yeshiva University (New York, N.Y.), 1958. (*DA* 20:956)

619. HENNESSY, THOMAS, AND BLUHM, HAROLD. "Using Interest Inventories in Religious and Sacerdotal Counseling." *Cath Counselor* 2:46–9 w '58. *

620. MAHONEY, STANLEY C., AND AUSTON, CHARLES A. "The Empathy Test and Self-Awareness of Kuder Interest Pattern." *Psychol Rep* 4:422 S '58. * (*PA* 33:6265)

621. REINHARD, NORMAN F. *The Validation of Several Procedures for Selecting Student Leaders in a Secondary School Level Naval Military Academy.* Doctor's thesis, Temple University (Philadelphia, Pa.), 1958. (*DA* 19:357)

622. BARSHAY, HELEN BERNADETTE. *An Evaluation of the Contribution of Selected Factors to the Job Satisfaction of Transcribing Typists Who Are Blind.* Doctor's thesis, New York University (New York, N.Y.), 1959. (*DA* 20:1221)

623. BERRYESSA, MAX JOSEPH. *Factors Contributing to the Competency of Elementary Teachers in Teaching Science.* Doctor's thesis, Stanford University (Stanford, Calif.), 1959. (*DA* 20:558)

624. GORDON, BARBARA JANE ARTHUR. *The Determination and Study of Academic Underachievement in the New York State College of Home Economics at Cornell University With Implications for Counseling and Admissions.* Doctor's thesis, Cornell University (Ithaca, N.Y.), 1959. (*DA* 20:1675)

625. MORTOLA, DORIS S. *A Study Employing the Kuder Preference Record for the Purpose of Comparing the Interest Patterns of Two Groups of College Freshmen: Accounting Majors and Marketing Majors.* Master's thesis, Fordham University (New York, N.Y.), 1959.

626. O'HARA, ROBERT P., AND TIEDEMAN, DAVID V. "The Vocational Self-Concept in Adolescence." *J Counsel Psychol* 6:292–301 w '59. * (*PA* 35:3279)

627. VILLEME, MELVIN G. *A Study of the Problems Associated With Various Types of Interest Patterns on the Kuder Preference Record as Indicated by the Mooney Problem Checklist.* Master's thesis, University of Kansas (Lawrence, Kan.), 1959.

628. WALCH, SHELBY LEWIS. *Self-Estimates of Aptitudes and Preferences and Test-Score Defensiveness.* Doctor's thesis, University of Texas (Austin, Tex.), 1959. (*DA* 20:210)

629. BELL, MYRTLE LEE. *The Relationship of Selected Variables to Success of Part-Time Recreation Personnel Employed as Summer Playground Leaders.* Doctor's thesis, University of Texas (Austin, Tex.), 1960. (*DA* 21:2528)

630. FRANKEL, EDWARD. "A Comparative Study of Achieving and Underachieving High School Boys of High Intellectual Ability." *J Ed Res* 53:172–80 Ja '60. * (*PA* 35:7115)

631. GRAY, BENJAMIN GALBREATH. *Characteristics of High and Low Achieving High School Seniors of High Average Academic Aptitude.* Doctor's thesis, University of Southern California (Los Angeles, Calif.), 1960. (*DA* 21:1459)

632. NAUSS, ALLEN HENRY. *Scholastic Ability, Self-Concept and Occupational Plans.* Doctor's thesis, University of Missouri (Columbia, Mo.), 1960. (*DA* 21:2596)

633. ROSEN, MORTON HAROLD. *The Relationship Between Unevenness of Cognitive Functioning as Derived From Verbal-Spatial Discrepancy Scores and Measures of Personality Func-*

Kuder Preference Record—Vocational

tioning. Doctor's thesis, New York University (New York, N.Y.), 1960. (*DA* 20:4724)

634. WAGNER, EDWIN E. "Predicting Success for Young Executives From Objective Test Scores and Personal Data." *Personnel Psychol* 13:181–6 su '60. * (*PA* 36:2LD81W)

635. CAMPBELL, MARY GREGORY. *A Comparative Study of Mental Ability, Personality, and Interests of First-Year Nursing Students in the Diploma and the Baccalaureate Programs.* Doctor's thesis, Fordham University (New York, N.Y.), 1961. (*DA* 26:7152)

636. CARMICAL, LaVERNE LATHROP. *The Identification of Certain Characteristics of Selected Achievers and Underachievers of Bellaire Senior High School.* Doctor's thesis, University of Houston (Houston, Tex.), 1961. (*DA* 22:2244)

637. DARTER, CLARENCE LESLIE, JR. *A Comparative Study of Over-Achieving and Under-Achieving Ninth-Grade Students.* Doctor's thesis, Texas Technological College (Lubbock, Tex.), 1961. (*DA* 22:1462)

638. FIRKINS, CURTIS JAMES. *Factors Related to Change of Major by College Students.* Doctor's thesis, North Texas State College (Denton, Tex.), 1961. (*DA* 22:2287)

639. GOLBURGH, STEPHEN JON. "Vocational Interests of Psychiatric Patients." *Rehabil Counsel B* 4:130–2 S '61. *

640. RISHEL, DARRELL FRED. *The Development and Validation of Instruments and Techniques for the Selective Admission of Applicants for Graduate Studies in Counselor Education.* Doctor's thesis, Pennsylvania State University (University Park, Pa.), 1961. (*DA* 22:2271)

641. SHNEIDMAN, EDWIN S. "The Case of El: Psychological Test Data." *J Proj Tech* 25:131–54 Je '61. * (*PA* 36:21K31S)

642. ABRAHAMS, INA. "Vocational Interests of Selected Indian College Students as Measured by the Kuder Preference Record." *J Am Indian Ed* 2:20–4 O '62. *

643. FRINSKO, WILLIAM. *Experimental Post-Degree Program at Wayne State University—An Analysis of the Selective and Predictive Factors in Student Teaching.* Doctor's thesis, Wayne State University (Detroit, Mich.), 1962. (*DA* 24:1901)

644. JONES, J. B. "Some Personal-Social Factors Contributing to Academic Failure at Texas Southern University," pp. 135–6. (*PA* 37:5606) In *Personality Factors on the College Campus: Review of a Symposium.* Edited by Robert L. Sutherland and Others. Austin, Tex.: Hogg Foundation for Mental Health, 1962. Pp. xxii, 242. * (*PA* 37:5621)

645. MARSH, STEWART H. "Validating the Selection of Deputy Sheriffs." *Pub Personnel R* 23:41–4 Jl '62. * (*PA* 37:2051)

646. PERRY, JAMES OLDEN. *A Study of a Selective Set of Criteria for Determining Success in Secondary Student Teaching at Texas Southern University.* Doctor's thesis, University of Texas (Austin, Tex.), 1962. (*DA* 23:1617)

647. POOR, FREDERICK ALBERT. *The Similarities and Differences in the Successful and Unsuccessful Second-Semester Accounting Students at Northern Illinois University.* Doctor's thesis, University of Minnesota (Minneapolis, Minn.), 1962. (*DA* 23:2381)

648. TERWILLIGER, JAMES SHAW. *Dimensions of Occupational Preference.* Doctor's thesis, University of Illinois (Urbana, Ill.), 1962. (*DA* 23:4424)

649. BECKER, JAMES A. "Interest Pattern Faking by Female Job Applicants." *J Indus Psychol* 1:51–4 Je '63. * (*PA* 38:10455)

650. D'AOUST, THÉRÈSE. *Predictive Validity of Four Psychometric Tests in a Selected School of Nursing.* Master's thesis, Catholic University of America (Washington, D.C.), 1963.

651. DUSTAN, LAURA CORBIN. *Characteristics of Students in Three Types of Nursing Education Programs.* Doctor's thesis, University of California (Berkeley, Calif.), 1963. (*DA* 24:3697)

652. MACLEAN, MURDOCH JOSEPH. *An Investigation of the Factors Influencing the Occupational Choices of Selected College Students.* Doctor's thesis, Fordham University (New York, N.Y.), 1963. (*DA* 25:2351)

653. MAGEE, PAULINE CECILIA. *Cooperation, Background Factors, Personality, and Interests of Senior and Junior College Students in Three Achievement Categories.* Doctor's thesis, Fordham University (New York, N.Y.), 1963. (*DA* 24:630)

654. RICHARDSON, JOHN FRANCIS, III. *A Comparison of Certain Characteristics of a Group of Negro Education and Non-Education College Students: An Investigation to Determine the Nature and Significance of the Differences in Various Characteristics Between Negro College Students Who Select Teaching and Those Who Choose Other Vocational Goals.* Doctor's thesis, New York University (New York, N.Y.), 1963. (*DA* 24:2789)

655. WOOD, PAUL LESLIE. *The Relationship of the College Characteristics Index to Achievement and Certain Other Variables for Freshmen Women in the College of Education at the University of Georgia.* Doctor's thesis, University of Georgia (Athens, Ga.), 1963. (*DA* 24:4558)

656. WYNN, DAN CAMP. *Factors Related to Gain and Loss of Scientific Interest During High School.* Doctor's thesis, University of Georgia (Athens, Ga.), 1963. (*DA* 24:4491)

657. ATTY, JAMES CHARLES. *A Study of the Scatter of Kuder Preference Scores and Their Relationship to Academic Achievement and Mental Ability.* Doctor's thesis, University of Pittsburgh (Pittsburgh, Pa.), 1964. (*DA* 26:485)

658. BALL, MARY K. *The Relation of Identification to Voca-*

tional Interest Development. Master's thesis, Ohio University (Athens, Ohio), 1964.

659. BUCK, JAMES R., JR. *Some Identifiable Characteristics of Students Entering Negro Senior Colleges in Mississippi.* Doctor's thesis, George Peabody College for Teachers (Nashville, Tenn.), 1964. (*DA* 25:5039)

660. CALLIS, ROBERT; WEST, DORAL N.; AND RICKSECKER, E. L. *The Counselor's Handbook: Profile Interpretation of the Strong Vocational Interest Blanks.* Urbana, Ill.: R. W. Parkinson & Associates, 1964. Pp. 100. *

661. CARMICAL, LAVERNE. "Characteristics of Achievers and Under-achievers of a Large Senior High School." *Personnel & Guid J* 43:390–5 D '64. * (*PA* 39:10711)

662. CHATTERJI, S., AND MUKERJEE, MANJULA. "Stability of Measured Interests." *J Voc & Ed Guid* (India) 10:10–4 F '64. * (*PA* 39:1722)

663. DENTON, MARY JANE. *Identification of Characteristics Associated With Discrepancy Between Self-Estimated and Measured Interests.* Doctor's thesis, Oklahoma State University (Stillwater, Okla.), 1964. (*DA* 26:1474)

664. DRASGOW, JAMES, AND CARKHUFF, ROBERT R. "Kuder Neuropsychiatric Keys Before and After Psychotherapy." Comments by Robert S. Waldrop. *J Counsel Psychol* 11:67–71 sp '64. * (*PA* 38:8485)

665. DREW, ALFRED S. "The Relationship of General Reading Ability and Other Factors to School and Job Performance of Machine Apprentices." *J Indus Teach Ed* 2:47–60 f '64. *

666. DUSTAN, LAURA C. "Characteristics of Students in Three Types of Nursing Programs." *Nursing Res* 13:159–66 sp '64. *

667. EDENS, LESTER WILLIAM. *An Analysis of Certain Socio-Psychological Characteristics of Unwed Mothers Referred to Private Agencies in Washington and Idaho.* Doctor's thesis, University of Idaho (Moscow, Idaho), 1964. (*DA* 25:5730)

668. FANGMAN, ELMER G. *A Comparison of Kuder Preference Record-Vocational Scores for Groups of Ninth Grade Boys and Girls Who Differ in Aptitude on Two Scales of the Differential Aptitude Tests.* Master's thesis, University of Kansas (Lawrence, Kan.), 1964.

669. FEINBERG, M. R., AND PENZER, W. N. "Factor Analysis of a Sales Selection Battery." *Personnel Psychol* 17:319–24 au '64. * (*PA* 39:8794)

670. FINLEY, PETER J. "Performance of Male Juvenile Delinquents on Four Psychological Tests." *Training Sch B* 60:175–83 F '64. * (*PA* 39:5704)

671. FORNESS, STEPHEN R., AND MIMS, THOMAS S. "A Comparison of Interest Areas on the Kuder Preference Record With Responses on an Educational Planning Questionnaire for Ninth Grade Students." *J Res Services* 4:21–2 D '64. *

672. GOBETZ, WALLACE. "Suggested Personality Implications of Kuder Preference Record (Vocational) Scores." *Personnel & Guid J* 43:159–66 O '64. *

673. HOLTAN, BOYD. "Motivation and General Mathematics Students." *Math Teach* 57:20–5 Ja '64. *

674. HUGHES, HEIDI B., AND DOLEYS, ERNEST J. "Interest, Set, and Incidental Learning." *Psychol Rep* 15:47–51 Ag '64. * (*PA* 39:587)

675. JONES, KENNETH J. "Interest, Motivation, and Achievement in Science." *J Exp Ed* 33:41–53 f '64. * (*PA* 39:6097)

676. KLUGMAN, SAMUEL F. "Intra-Individual Variability Findings for a Psychotic Population on Vocational Interest Inventories." *J Counsel Psychol* 11:191–3 su '64. *

677. KOBLER, FRANK J. "Screening Applicants for Religious Life." *J Relig & Health* 3:161–70 Ja '64. * (*PA* 40:1793)

678. KRAUSKOPF, C. J.; ELDER, DOROTHY; AND MAPELI, DELIA. "Some Characteristics of Students Who Transfer From Engineering to Arts and Sciences." *Voc Guid Q* 12:187–91 sp '64. * (*PA* 39:5981)

679. KUNZLER, H. GRANT. *Self Rated Vocational Interests vs. Measured Vocational Interests and Implications for High School Guidance.* Master's thesis, University of Utah (Salt Lake City, Utah), 1964.

680. LISKE, RALPH E.; ORT, ROBERT S.; AND FORD, AMASA B. "Clinical Performance and Related Traits of Medical Students and Faculty Physicians." *J Med Ed* 39:69–80 Ja '64. *

681. LONG, JOHN M. "Sex Differences in Academic Prediction Based on Scholastic, Personality and Interest Factors." *J Exp Ed* 32:239–48 sp '64. * (*PA* 39:6058)

682. McMAHON, WILLIAM JOSEPH. *Differential Analysis of Nonintellective Factors Associated With Identified Scholastic Talent in a High School.* Doctor's thesis, Fordham University (New York, N.Y.), 1964. (*DA* 26:873)

683. MAYESKE, GEORGE W. "The Validity of Kuder Preference Record Scores in Predicting Forester Turnover and Advancement." *Personnel Psychol* 17:207–10 su '64. *

684. MEYER, PRISCILLA R. "The Kuder 'V' Scale as a Predictor of Discharge and Rehospitalization." *Newsl Res Psychol* 6:48 Ag '64. *

685. MILLSAP, CARL SHELBY. *Selected Characteristics and Post-Secondary School Educational Plans of Polk County Secondary Public School Graduates.* Doctor's thesis, University of Missouri (Columbia, Mo.), 1964. (*DA* 25:5639)

686. NEAL, CAROLYN MAE. *A Study of the Relationship of Personality Variables to Reading Ability Utilizing Tests Adminis-*

Kuder Preference Record—Vocational

tered College Freshmen. Doctor's thesis, University of Illinois (Urbana, Ill.), 1964. (*DA* 25:4480)

687. POOL, DONALD A., AND BROWN, ROBERT A. "Kuder-Strong Discrepancies and Personality Adjustment." *J Counsel Psychol* 11:63–6 sp '64. * Supplementary letter to the editor. 11:298 f '64. * (*PA* 38:8596)

688. RONAN, W. W. "Evaluation of Skilled Trades Performance Predictors." *Ed & Psychol Meas* 24:601–8 f '64. * (*PA* 39:6074)

689. SPITZER, MORTON EDWARD, AND MCNAMARA, WALTER J. "A Managerial Selection Study." *Personnel Psychol* 17:19–40 sp '64. * (*PA* 39:2945)

690. STEPHAN, EARL E. *A Study of the Relationship of the Social Status of Ninth Grade Students and Their Interests as Measured by the Kuder Preference Record.* Master's thesis, Winona State College (Winona, Minn.), 1964.

691. SWEENEY, ROBERT HOWARD. *Testing Seminarians With the MMPI and Kuder: A Report of Ten Years of Testing.* Master's thesis, Loyola University (Chicago, Ill.), 1964.

692. TILLMAN, KENNETH GENE. *The Relationship Between Physical Fitness and Selected Personality Traits.* Doctor's thesis, University of New Mexico (Albuquerque, N.M.), 1964. (*DA* 25:276)

693. TURO, JOANN K. *The Relationship of Differential Value and Interest Patterns to Authoritarian Attitudes.* Master's thesis, Ohio University (Athens, Ohio), 1964.

694. TYLER, LEONA E. "The Antecedents of Two Varieties of Vocational Interests." *Genetic Psychol Monogr* 70:177–227 N '64. * (*PA* 39:10878)

695. WAGMAN, MORTON. "Persistence in Ability-Achievement Discrepancies and Kuder Scores." *Personnel & Guid J* 43:383–9 D '64. * (*PA* 39:10730)

696. WINICK, CHARLES. "Personality Characteristics of Embalmers." *Personnel & Guid J* 43:262–6 N '64. * (*PA* 39:10222)

697. ZECH, JAMES C. *The Kuder Preference Record as a Predictor of Occupational Choice.* Master's thesis, State College of Iowa (Cedar Falls, Iowa), 1964.

698. BALL, MARY K., AND RUSSELL, DAVID L. "Relationships Between Measures of Identification and Vocational Interests." Abstract. *Proc Ann Conv Am Psychol Assn* 73:339–40 '65. * (*PA* 39:16497)

699. DENT, ORAN B., AND ELDER, R. F. "A Vocational Preference Rank Technique." *Personnel & Guid J* 43:801–3 Ap '65. *

700. DRASGOW, JAMES, AND DREHER, ROBERT G. "Predicting Client Readiness for Training and Placement in Vocational Rehabilitation." *Rehabil Counsel B* 8:94–8 Mr '65. *

701. HANNA, GERALD STANLEY. *An Investigation of Selected Ability, Aptitude, Interest. and Personality Characteristics Relevant to Success in High School Geometry.* Doctor's thesis, University of Southern California (Los Angeles, Calif.), 1965. (*DA* 26:3152)

702. HARRANGUE, M. DAMIAN. *Developmental Changes in Vocational Interests and Work Values as Related to the Vocational Choices of College Women.* Doctor's thesis, Catholic University of America (Washington, D.C.), 1965. (*DA* 26:2050)

703. HARTMAN, BERNARD J. "A Comparison of Implied Interest and Measured Interest." *J Ed Res* 58:380 Ap '65. *

704. IVEY, ALLEN E., AND PETERSON, MARK B. "Vocational Preference Patterns of Communications Graduates." *Ed & Psychol Meas* 25:849–56 au '65. * (*PA* 40:3422)

705. JOHANSEN, ANSGAR NICHOLAS. *An Investigation of the Relationship of Childhood Identification to Language Interest and Ability.* Doctor's thesis, University of North Dakota (Grand Forks, N.D.), 1965. (*DA* 26:5869)

706. KNUDSEN, ROBERT G. *A Study of the Relationship Between Personality as Measured by the Minnesota Multiphasic Personality Inventory and Interest as Measured by the Kuder Preference Record-Form C.* Master's thesis, Utah State University (Logan, Utah), 1965.

707. LAWSON, EDWIN D. "Faking on the Kuder Preference Record." *B Maritime Psychol Assn* 14:3–8 sp '65. * (*PA* 39:15245)

708. MCCALL, JOHN N., AND MOORE, GILBERT D. "Do Interest Inventories Measure Estimated Abilities?" *Personnel & Guid J* 43:1034–7 Je '65. * (*PA* 39:15365)

709. MOUL, EDWARD CLINTON. *Analysis of Scores Made on the Kuder Preference Record, Vocational, by a Group of Negro High School Students.* Master's thesis, University of Texas (Austin, Tex.), 1965.

710. MURTAUGH, JAMES J. *A Longitudinal Study Investigating the Predictability of the MMPI and Kuder for Diocesan Seminaries.* Master's thesis, Loyola University (Chicago, Ill.), 1965.

711. NASH, ALLAN N. "Vocational Interests of Effective Managers: A Review of the Literature." *Personnel Psychol* 18:21–37 sp '65. * (*PA* 39:16589)

712. PALMER, DENSLEY HARLEY. *A Comparison of the Consistency of the Self-Judgments of Physically Disabled and Non-Disabled Male College Students.* Doctor's thesis, University of Oregon (Eugene, Ore.), 1965. (*DA* 26:4456)

713. PEDERSEN, DARHL M. "The Measurement of Individual Differences in Perceived Personality-Trait Relationships and Their Relation to Certain Determinants." *J Social Psychol* 65:233–58 Ap '65. * (*PA* 39:14976)

714. PHILLIPS, LEONARD WARREN. *A Study of the Relations*

Between Tentative Occupational Choice-Vocational Interests Congruency and Selected Variables. Doctor's thesis, Michigan State University (East Lansing, Mich.), 1965. (*DA* 26:4507)

715. POOL, DONALD A. "The Kuder Social Service Scale and Hospitalization." *Rehabil Counsel B* 9:47–52 D '65. *

716. RAYGOR, ALTON L., AND WATLEY, DONIVAN J. "Height and Weight in Relation to the Development of Vocational Interests." *J Ed Res* 59:73–5 O '65. * (*PA* 40:2667)

717. SAVASTANO, HELENA. "Interests of a Group of Dental Medicine Students Studied Through the Kuder Preference Record—Some Reasons for Choosing Their Profession." *Congr Inter-Am Soc Psychol* 9(1964):628–32 ['65]. *

718. SLAYTON, WILFRED GEORGE. *A Comparison of Successful and Unsuccessful Bible College Students With Respect to Selected Personality Factors.* Doctor's thesis, University of Arizona (Tucson, Ariz.), 1965. (*DA* 26:1487)

719. SPIERS, DUANE EDWIN. *A Study of the Predictive Validity of a Test Battery Administered to Theological Students.* Doctor's thesis, Purdue University (Lafayette, Ind.), 1965. (*DA* 26:1488)

720. STAPLES, JOHN DIXON. *An Experimental Study to Identify the Basic Abilities Needed to Detect Typescript Errors With Implications for the Improvement of Instruction in Typewriting.* Doctor's thesis, University of North Dakota (Grand Forks, N.D.), 1965. (*DA* 27:1693A)

721. TARPEY, M. SIMEON. "Personality Factors in Teacher Trainee Selection." *Brit J Ed Psychol* 35:140–9 Je '65. * (*PA* 39:16480)

722. TILLMAN, KENNETH. "Relationship Between Physical Fitness and Selected Personality Traits." *Res Q* 36:483–9 D '65. * (*PA* 40:4613)

723. TRAVERS, KENNETH JOSEPH DEAN. *Forced-Choice Preferences for Problem-Solving Situations in Mathematics.* Doctor's thesis, University of Illinois (Urbana, Ill.), 1965. (*DA* 26:7161)

724. VERGER, DON MARSHALL. *A Study of the Relationships of Birth Order to the Development of Interests.* Doctor's thesis, University of Oregon (Eugene, Ore.), 1965. (*DA* 26:5544)

725. WIESNER, EUGENE FRANCIS. *Multilevel Personality Descriptions of Domiciled Men With Selected Kuder Preference Record-Vocational Profiles: A Predictive Study in Interpersonal Theory.* Doctor's thesis, University of Kansas (Lawrence, Kan.), 1965. (*DA* 26:3159)

726. ZYTOWSKI, DONALD G. "Characteristics of Male University Students With Weak Occupational Similarity on the Strong Vocational Interest Blank." *J Counsel Psychol* 12:182–5 su '65. * (*PA* 39:12374)

727. BANKS, ROBERT RICHARD. *Selected Social and Psychological Variables Related to Role Satisfaction Among Graduate Ministerial Students in a Seventh-Day Adventist Seminary.* Doctor's thesis, University of Notre Dame (Notre Dame, Ind.), 1966. (*DA* 27:2384A)

728. BARE, CAROLE E. "Counselor Sensitivity to the Counselor-Client Communication Process." Abstract. *Proc 74th Ann Conv Am Psychol Assn* 1:301–2 '66. * (*PA* 41:6145)

729. BEATON, MARY ANNE. *A Study of Underachievers in Mathematics at the Tenth Grade Level in Three Calgary High Schools.* Doctor's thesis, Northwestern University (Evanston, Ill.), 1966. (*DA* 27:3215A)

730. BELL, EVERETTE LYLE. *Factors Relating to Employment of Graduates of Des Moines Technical High School.* Doctor's thesis, Iowa State University (Ames, Iowa), 1966. (*DA* 27:892A)

731. BROADBENT, LEE ARTHUR. *The Relationship Between Self-Ratings of Interests and Measured Interests.* Master's thesis, University of California (Los Angeles, Calif.), 1966.

732. DRISCOLL, JOHN. *The Dimensions of Satisfaction With the Religious Life Among Scholastics in a Community of Teaching Brothers: A Descriptive Study.* Doctor's thesis, University of Notre Dame (Notre Dame, Ind.), 1966. (*DA* 27:1653A)

733. FINCO, ARTHUR ANTHONY. *Mathematics Majors and Transfers From the Mathematics Major at Purdue University: Temperament, Interest, Value, and Student Questionnaire Differences at the Exploratory Stage.* Doctor's thesis, Purdue University (Lafayette, Ind.), 1966. (*DA* 27:327A)

734. GASH, IRA ARNOLD. *The Stability of Measured Interests as Related to the Clinical Improvement of Hospitalized Psychiatric Patients.* Doctor's thesis, Temple University (Philadelphia, Pa.), 1966. (*DA* 27:1290B)

735. GOLDEN, JAMES FRANKLIN. *Aspirations and Capabilities of Rural Youth in Selected Areas of Arkansas in Relation to Present and Projected Labor Market Requirements.* Doctor's thesis, University of Arkansas (Fayetteville, Ark.), 1966. (*DA* 27:1199A)

736. GOSS, ALLEN MILES. *Predicting Work Success for Patients on an Industrial Rehabilitation Ward in a Neuropsychiatric Setting.* Doctor's thesis, University of Texas (Austin, Tex.), 1966. (*DA* 27:2511B)

737. HANNA, GERALD S. "An Attempt to Validate an Empirically-Derived Interest Scale and Standard Kuder Scales for Predicting Success in High School Geometry." *Ed & Psychol Meas* 26:445–8 su '66. * (*PA* 40:12781)

738. HARDING, WILLIAM THOMAS. *Differential Verbal and Quantitative Scores and Interests.* Master's thesis, Illinois State University (Normal, Ill.), 1966.

Kuder Preference Record—Vocational

739. HOLMES, JACK A., AND SINGER, HARRY. *Speed and Power of Reading in High School.* Cooperative Research Monograph No. 14. Washington, D.C.: United States Government Printing Office, 1966. Pp. xii, 183. *

740. IVANOFF, JOHN M.; MONROE, GERALD D.; AND MARITA, M. "Use of Intellective and Non-Intellective Factors in Classifying Female Elementary and Secondary Teacher Trainees." *J Exp Ed* 34:55–61 su '66. * (*PA* 40:11511)

741. KEIM, LAWRENCE. *A Study of Psychometric Profile Patterns of Selected Associate Degree Technology Majors.* Doctor's thesis, Purdue University (Lafayette, Ind.), 1966. (*DA* 27: 2049A)

742. KERR, WILLIAM D., AND WILLIS, WARREN K. "Interest and Ability: Are They Related?" *Voc Guid Q* 14:197–200 sp '66. * (*PA* 40:10493)

743. KLUGMAN, SAMUEL F. "Differential Preference Patterns Between Sexes for Schizophrenic Patients." *J Clin Psychol* 22: 170–2 Ap '66. * (*PA* 40:7911)

744. LEWIS, LESLIE. *A Multivariate Analysis of Variables Associated With Academic Success Within a College Environment.* Doctor's thesis, Oklahoma State University (Stillwater, Okla.), 1966. (*DA* 27:4134A)

745. MICHAL, ROBERT D. *A Study of the Prediction of Interest Stability Using Multivariate Procedures.* Doctor's thesis, University of Kansas (Lawrence, Kan.), 1966. (*DA* 28:969A)

746. MILLER, ADAM W., JR. "Proposals for Interest Test Development and Experimentation." *Personnel & Guid J* 45: 231–7 N '66. *

747. PARKER, ADAH DONOHUE. *Projections for the Selection, Training and Retention of Sub-Professional Recreation Leaders Based on an Analysis of Personality, Interest, Aptitude, and Preference Data.* Doctor's thesis, University of Illinois (Urbana, Ill.), 1966. (*DA* 27:2059A)

748. RENFER, MARY EMMA FEWELL. *Predicting Success in the Study of Descriptive Linguistics.* Doctor's thesis, University of Southern California (Los Angeles, Calif.), 1966. (*DA* 27:1268A)

749. RYDER, ANN D. *An Inquiry Into the Kuder Preference Record-Vocational Verification Scale and the Guilford-Zimmerman Temperament Survey Falsification Scale.* Master's thesis, University of Richmond (Richmond, Va.), 1966.

750. SAVASTANO, HELENA. "Interests of a Group of Dental Medicine Students Studied Through the Kuder Preference Record: Some Reasons for Choosing Their Profession." *Revista de Psicologia Normal e Patológica* 11:67–89 Ja–S '66. * (*PA* 41: 849, title only)

751. STALANS, VIRGIL, JR. *A Comparative Study of Characteristics of Students Who Made a Low Invalid V-Score and a Valid V-Score on the Kuder Preference Record.* Master's thesis, University of Tennessee (Knoxville, Tenn.), 1966.

752. VAUGHAN, RICHARD P. "Personality Characteristics of Exceptional College Students." Abstract. *Proc 74th Ann Conv Am Psychol Assn* 1:281–2 '66. * (*PA* 41:6255)

753. WEIS, SUSAN F. *An Exploratory Study of the Nature of the Occurrence of Creativity and Self Actualization Among College Students Making Vocational Selections in Home Economics Fields.* Master's thesis, Pennsylvania State University (University Park, Pa.), 1966.

754. WHITTEMORE, ROBERT G.; ECHEVERRIA, BEN. P.; AND GRIFFIN, JOHN V. "Can We Use Existing Tests for Adult Basic Education?" *Adult Ed* 17:19–29 au '66. *

755. BENTZ, V. JON. Chap. 7, "The Sears Experience in the Investigation, Description, and Prediction of Executive Behavior," pp. 147–205; critique by Ross Stagner, pp. 206–27. In *Measuring Executive Effectiveness.* Edited by Frederic R. Wickert and Dalton E. McFarland. New York: Appleton-Century-Crofts, 1967. Pp. viii, 242. *

756. BINGMAN, RICHARD MARVIN. "Aptitude and Interest Profiles of Biology Participants in Montgomery County (Pennsylvania) Science Fairs." *J Res Sci Teach* 5(2):245–52 '67–68 ['68]. *

757. BINGMAN, RICHARD MARVIN. *Aptitude and Interest Profiles of Tenth Grade Biology Students Participating in the Montgomery County, Pennsylvania Science Fairs (1962–1966).* Doctor's thesis, Temple University (Philadelphia, Pa.), 1967. (*DA* 28:4039A)

758. CASTRICONE, NICHOLAS RAYMOND. *A Study of Intrateacher Group Variations: The Measured Interests of Teachers of the Educable Mentally Handicapped.* Doctor's thesis, University of Virginia (Charlottesville, Va.), 1967. (*DA* 28:3879A)

759. GOSS, ALLEN M., AND PATE, KENTON D. "Predicting Vocational Rehabilitation Success for Psychiatric Patients With Psychological Tests." *Psychol Rep* 21:725–30 D '67. * (*PA* 42:7550)

760. HUSTON, BEATRICE MOORE. *A Normative Survey of the Personal and Academic Characteristics of the Freshmen Women Students Enrolled in Mary Hardin-Baylor College, 1966–1967.* Doctor's thesis, Baylor University (Waco, Tex.), 1967. (*DA* 28:1209A)

761. KARPOFF, JOHN T. *Aptitudes for Achievement in the Vocational Programs of One Composite High School in Alberta.* Master's thesis, University of Alberta (Edmonton, Alta., Canada), 1967.

762. KISH, GEORGE B., AND BUSSE, WILLIAM. "Interest and Stimulus-Seeking." *Newsl Res Psychol* 9:13–5 N '67. *

763. LUCAS, DONALD HERBERT. *Personality Correlates of Agreement and Nonagreement Between Measures of Ability and Interest for Two Groups of Institutionalized Males.* Doctor's thesis, University of Kansas (Lawrence, Kan.), 1967. (*DA* 28:2986A)

764. MCGUNNIGAL, JAMES V. *An Investigation to Determine the Relationship Between Science Achievement and Scientific Interest as Expressed by the Kuder Preference Record-Vocational.* Master's thesis, Northern Illinois University (DeKalb, Ill.), 1967.

765. MADAUS, GEORGE F., AND O'HARA, ROBERT P. "Contrasts Between High School Boys Choosing the Priesthood as Their Occupational Choice and Boys Choosing Eight Other Occupational Categories." *Cath Psychol Rec* 5:41–51 sp '67. *

766. MADAUS, GEORGE F., AND O'HARA, ROBERT P. "Vocational Interest Patterns of High School Boys: A Multivariate Approach." *J Counsel Psychol* 14:106–12 Mr '67. * (*PA* 41: 7885)

767. MARGOLIS, VICTOR HERBERT. *Kuder-Strong Discrepancy in Relation to Conflict and Congruence of Vocational Preference.* Doctor's thesis, Columbia University (New York, N.Y.), 1967. (*DA* 28:1685B)

768. MARSDEN, RALPH DAVENPORT. *Topological Representation and Vector Analysis of Interest Patterns.* Doctor's thesis, Utah State University (Logan, Utah), 1967. (*DA* 28:4004A)

769. MOWBRAY, JEAN K., AND TAYLOR, RAYMOND G. "Validity of Interest Inventories for the Prediction of Success in a School of Nursing." *Nursing Res* 16:78–81 w '67. * (*PA* 42:4634)

770. NEAL, CAROLYN M. "The Relationship of Personality Variables to Reading Ability." *Calif J Ed Res* 18:133–44 My '67. * (*PA* 41:12578)

771. NEAL, CAROLYN M. "Student Ability: Its Effect on Reading-Personality Relationships." *Ed & Psychol Meas* 27: 1145–53 w '67. * (*PA* 42:8985)

772. O'HARA, ROBERT P. "Vocational Self Concepts of Boys Choosing Science and Non-Science Careers." *Ed & Psychol Meas* 27:139–49 sp '67. * (*PA* 41:9476)

773. PEDERSEN, DARHL M. "Acquiescence and Social Desirability Response Sets and Some Personality Correlates." *Ed & Psychol Meas* 27:691–7 au '67. * (*PA* 42:739)

774. REZLER, AGNES G. "Characteristics of High School Girls Choosing Traditional or Pioneer Vocations." *Personnel & Guid J* 45:659–65 Mr '67. * (*PA* 41:9472)

775. REZLER, AGNES G. "The Joint Use of the Kuder Preference Record and the Holland Vocational Preference Inventory in the Vocational Assessment of High School Girls." *Psychol Sch* 4:82–4 Ja '67. * (*PA* 41:5031)

776. SINGH, N. P. "A Hindi Adaptation of Kuder Preference Record-Vocational Form CH." *Manas* (India) 14:81–9 D '67. * (*PA* 43:11959)

777. SLAUGHTER, KENNETH BROOKS. *A Study of Male Dropouts From Selected Public Secondary Schools of Mississippi.* Doctor's thesis, University of Southern Mississippi (Hattiesburg, Miss.), 1967. (*DA* 28:3443A)

778. STEIN, KENNETH B. "Correlates of the Ideational Preference Dimension Among Prison Inmates." *Psychol Rep* 21:553–62 O '67. * (*PA* 42:5757)

779. SWANSON, FERN TALENT. *Typewriting Achievement of Post-Secondary Students at the American Institute of Business Compared With Reading Scores, IQ's, and Academic Interests.* Master's thesis, State College of Iowa (Cedar Falls, Iowa), 1967.

780. THOMPSON, JAMES NEWTON. *Stability and Change in Measured Attitudes and Vocational Interests of Women in a Teacher Education Program.* Doctor's thesis, University of Missouri (Columbia, Mo.), 1967. (*DA* 28:4035A)

781. WINDHOLZ, GEORGE. *Divergent and Convergent Abilities of Semantic Content as Related to Some Personality Traits of College Students.* Doctor's thesis, Columbia University (New York, N.Y.), 1967. (*DA* 28:2130B)

782. WINDHOLZ, GEORGE. "Divergent and Convergent Abilities of Semantic Content as Related to Some Personality Traits of College Students." *Ed & Psychol Meas* 27:1015–23 w '67. * (*PA* 42:8976)

783. WINTER, GERALD DAVID. *Intelligence, Interest, and Personality Characteristics of a Selected Group of Students: A Description and Comparison of White and Negro Students in a Vocational Rehabilitation Administration Program in Bassick and Harding High Schools, Bridgeport, Connecticut.* Doctor's thesis, Columbia University (New York, N.Y.), 1967. (*DA* 28: 4920A)

784. ANDERSON, THOMAS EDWIN, JR. *The Effect of Reading Skill on the Comparability of the Kuder Preference Record and the Occupational Interest Survey.* Master's thesis, University of Texas (Austin, Tex.), 1968.

785. ATKINSON, GILBERT, AND LUNNEBORG, CLIFFORD E. "Comparison of Oblique and Orthogonal Simple Structure Solutions for Personality and Interest Factors." *Multiv Behav Res* 3:21–35 Ja '68. * (*PA* 42:11349)

786. BAGGALEY, ANDREW R. "Congruent Validity of the Milwaukee Academic Interest Inventory." *Ed & Psychol Meas* 28:1207–11 w '68. * (*PA* 44:6786)

787. BENTZ, V. JON. Chap. 3, "The Sears Experience in the Investigation, Description and Prediction of Executive Be-

havior," pp. 59–152. In *Predicting Managerial Success*. Edited by John A. Myers, Jr. Ann Arbor, Mich.: Foundation for Research on Human Behavior, April 1968. Pp. v, 173. *

788. BLANK, STANLEY S. "An Examination of the Usefulness of Various Psychological Instruments for Predicting Department Managers' Ratings of Clerical Sales Personnel." *Can Counsellor* 2:46–50 Ja '68. *

789. BRADSHAW, OTTIE LEON. *The Relationship of Selected Measures of Aptitude, Interest, and Personality to Academic Achievement in Engineering and Engineering Technology*. Doctor's thesis, Oklahoma State University (Stillwater, Okla.), 1968. (*DAI* 30:979A)

790. CAHOON, D. D.; PETERSON, LARS P.; AND WATSON, CHARLES G. "Relative Effectiveness of Programmed Text and Teaching Machine as a Function of Measured Interests." *J Appl Psychol* 52:454–6 D '68. * (*PA* 43:3145)

791. CLEMANS, WILLIAM V. "Interest Measurement and the Concept of Ipsativity." *Meas & Eval Guid* 1:50–5 sp '68. * (*PA* 44:7280)

792. COTTLE, WILLIAM C. *Interest and Personality Inventories*, pp. 30–49, 56–60. Guidance Monograph Series, Series 3, Testing, [No. 6]. Boston, Mass.: Houghton Mifflin Co., 1968. Pp. xi, 116. *

793. FINEGAN, ANNE L. *A Comparison Between the Cleeton Vocational Interest Inventory and the Kuder Preference Record in Assessing the Interests of College Freshmen*. Master's thesis, Colgate University (Hamilton, N.Y.), 1968.

794. FRANDSEN, ARDEN, AND SORENSON, MAURICE. "Interests as Motives in Academic Achievement." *J Sch Psychol* 7(1):52–6 '68–69. * (*PA* 43:10415)

795. GOSS, ALLEN M. "Importance of Diagnostic Categories in Evaluating Psychological Data." *J Counsel Psychol* 15:476–8 S '68. * (*PA* 42:19121)

796. GOSS, ALLEN M. "Predicting Work Success for Psychiatric Patients With the Kuder Preference Record." *Ed & Psychol Meas* 28:571–6 su '68. * (*PA* 42:19110)

797. HALL, SIDNEY G. *The Kuder Preference Record-Vocational and Its Relationship to Academic Success*. Master's thesis, East Tennessee State University (Johnson City, Tenn.), 1968.

798. HEDLEY, CAROLYN NEAL. "Learning Relationship Differences and Curriculum Choice." *Improving Col & Univ Teach* 16:268–72 au '68. *

799. HEDLEY, CAROLYN NEAL. "The Relationship of Personality Factors to Scientific and Mathematical Ability Factors." *Sch Sci & Math* 68:265–71 Ap '68. *

800. HEIBERG, DAVID ALLISON. *Psychometric Correlates Within a Youthful Offender Population*. Doctor's thesis, University of Minnesota (Minneapolis, Minn.), 1968. (*DAI* 30:382B)

801. HEILMAN, HENRIETTA. *A Study of the Relationships Between Certain Factors Associated With Employability and the Rehabilitation Status of Selected Psychiatric Clients in a Vocational Rehabilitation Program*. Doctor's thesis, New York University (New York, N.Y.), 1968. (*DA* 29:2564A)

802. LoMONACO, LEON JOHN. *Response Levels of Disadvantaged Ninth-Grade Negro Boys to Both Standard and Oral-Visual Administrations of Two Vocationally Relevant Instruments*. Doctor's thesis, New York University (New York, N.Y.), 1968. (*DA* 29:3004A)

803. MEHROTRA, CHANDRA MOHAN NATH. *Behavioral Cognition as Related to Interpersonal Perception and Some Personality Traits of College Students*. Doctor's thesis, Ohio State University (Columbus, Ohio), 1968. (*DAI* 30:372B)

804. NEAL, CAROLYN M. "Sex Differences in Personality and Reading Ability." *J Read* 11:609–14 My '68. * (*PA* 42:17204)

805. NUGENT, FRANK A. "Relationship of Kuder Preference Record Verification Scores to Adjustment: Implications for Vocational Development Theory." *J Appl Psychol* 52:429–31 D '68. * (*PA* 42:3082)

806. PALLONE, NATHANIEL J., AND BANKS, R. RICHARD. "Vocational Satisfaction Among Ministerial Students." *Personnel & Guid J* 46:870–5 My '68. * (*PA* 42:16191)

807. STAUFFER, E. "The Validity of Measured Vocational Interests in the Selection of Nonprofessional Trainees." *Proc Inter Congr Appl Psychol* 16:316–21 '68. *

808. STEIN, FRANKLIN. *Consistency of Cognitive, Interest, and Personality Variables With Academic Mastery: A Study of Field-Dependence-Independence, Verbal Comprehension, Self-Perception, and Vocational Interest in Relation to Academic Performance Among Male Juniors Attending an Urban University*. Doctor's thesis, New York University (New York, N.Y.), 1968. (*DA* 29:1429A)

809. TALLMADGE, G. K. "Relationships Between Training Methods and Learner Characteristics." *J Ed Psychol* 59:32–6 F '68. * (*PA* 42:7932)

810. TARRIER, RANDOLPH BRENAN. *Vocational Counseling: A Comparative Study of Different Methods*. Doctor's thesis, Case Western Reserve University (Cleveland, Ohio), 1968. (*DAI* 30:938A)

811. WILSON, ROBERT N., AND KAISER, HERBERT E. "A Comparison of Similar Scales on the SVIB and the Kuder, Form DD." *J Counsel Psychol* 15:468–70 S '68. * (*PA* 42:19287)

812. WINDHOLZ, GEORGE. "The Relation of Creativity and Intelligence Constellations to Traits of Temperament, Interest,

and Value in College Students." *J General Psychol* 79:291–9 O '68. * (*PA* 43:3998)

813. BAILEY, HOWARD CLARK. *The Kuder Preference Record as an Instrument for Diagnosing Maladjustment in Prospective Members of the Helping Professions*. Doctor's thesis, Florida State University (Tallahassee, Fla.), 1969. (*DAI* 32:550B)

814. BATEMAN, HILMA B. *Stability of Interests and Direction of Change in Brigham Young University Seniors*. Master's thesis, Brigham Young University (Provo, Utah), 1969.

815. BENJAMIN, JEANETTE ANN. *A Study of the Social Psychological Factors Related to the Academic Success of Negro High School Students*. Doctor's thesis, Northwestern University (Evanston, Ill.), 1969. (*DAI* 30:3543A)

816. BIDWELL, GLORIA P. "Ego Strength, Self-Knowledge, and Vocational Planning of Schizophrenics." *J Counsel Psychol* 16(1):45–9 Ja '69. * (*PA* 43:5726)

817. BUTCHER, H. J. "The Structure of Abilities, Interests and Personality in 1,000 Scottish School Children." *Brit J Ed Psychol* 39(2):154–65 Je '69. * (*PA* 44:7217)

818. BUTCHER, H. J., AND PONT, H. B. "Predicting Arts and Science Specialisation in a Group of Scottish Secondary School Children: Some Preliminary Results." *Scottish Ed Studies* 1(3):3–10 Je '69. *

819. CARRON, THEODORE J. "Validity of Tests for Chemical Plant Personnel." *Personnel Psychol* 22(3):307–12 au '69. * (*PA* 44:9414)

820. FOREMAN, MILTON E., AND JAMES, LEONARD E. "Vocational Relevance and Estimated and Measured Test Scores." *J Counsel Psychol* 16(6):547–50 N '69. * (*PA* 44:4197)

821. HARRINGTON, JOSEPH ANDREW. *Multivariate Test Score Patterns on the KPR-V, the KPR-P, and Both Combined for College Women in Four Curriculum Groups and College Men in Five Curriculum Groups*. Doctor's thesis, Boston College (Chestnut Hill, Mass.), 1969. (*DAI* 30:3784A)

822. HUCKABEE, MALCOM W. "Personality and Academic Aptitude Correlates of Cognitive Control Principles." *South J Ed Res* 3(1):1–9 Ja '69. *

823. KISH, GEORGE B. "Obscure Figures Test (OFT): 4, Relationships With Kuder-Measured Interests." *Newsl Res Psychol* 11(2):18 My '69. *

824. KISH, GEORGE B., AND DONNENWERTH, GREGORY V. "Interests and Stimulus Seeking." *J Counsel Psychol* 16(6):551–6 N '69. * (*PA* 44:4260)

825. KISH, GEORGE B., AND LEAHY, LOUIS. "Stimulus-Seeking, Interests, and Aptitudes: A Replication." *Newsl Res Psychol* 11(4):22–4 N '69. *

826. LaGRONE, C. W. "Sex and Personality Differences in Relation to Feeling for Direction." *J General Psychol* 81(1):23–33 Jl '69. * (*PA* 44:5150)

827. LATHROP, ROBERT CHARLES. *A Study of Various Characteristics of Vocational-Technical Students and Community College Students*. Doctor's thesis, Washington State University (Pullman, Wash.), 1969. (*DAI* 30:4225A)

828. MORTON, JOYCE. *Stability of High School Kuder Vocational Interests as Related to Edwards Personality Needs*. Master's thesis, East Tennessee State University (Johnson City, Tenn.), 1969.

829. POSTON, WILLIAM KENNETH, JR. *Educational Administrator Job Performance and Training Program Admission Criteria*. Doctor's thesis, Arizona State University (Tempe, Ariz.), 1969. (*DAI* 30:532A)

830. RAVENSBORG, MILTON R. "Psychiatric Technicians' Ranking of Five Potential Employment Screening Tests." *Personnel J* 48(1):39–41 Ja '69. * (*PA* 44:2910)

831. SINGH, R. P. "Stability of Interest Patterns." *Indian Psychol R* 6(1):14–5 Jl '69. * (*PA* 46:11594)

832. STALLINGS, WILLIAM M., AND ANDERSON, FRANCES E. "Some Characteristics and Correlates of the Meier Art Test of Aesthetic Perception Under Two Systems of Scoring." *J Ed Meas* 6(3):179–85 f '69. * (*PA* 44:14571)

833. WALKER, RONALD E.; NICOLAY, ROBERT C.; KLUCZNY, RITA; AND RIEDEL, ROBERT G. "Psychological Correlates of Smoking." *J Clin Psychol* 25(1):42–4 Ja '69. * (*PA* 43:9698)

834. WILLMARTH, JOHN GARY. *Factors Affecting the Vocational Choice of Women of Different Ages Selecting Clerical and Secretarial Occupations*. Doctor's thesis, Washington State University (Pullman, Wash.), 1969. (*DAI* 30:991A)

835. CARLSON, STANLEY LLOYD. *Differences in Aptitude, Previous Achievement, and Nonintellectual Traits (Personality, Values, Interest, and Attitude Toward Mathematics) of Freshmen Mathematics Majors and Transfers From the Mathematics Major at the University of Northern Colorado*. Doctor's thesis, University of Northern Colorado (Greeley, Colo.), 1970. (*DAI* 31:3768A)

836. CRONBACH, LEE J. *Essentials of Psychological Testing, Third Edition*, pp. 457–86. New York: Harper & Row, Publishers, Inc., 1970. Pp. xxxix, 752. *

837. CROWELL, ORVILLE. *An Analysis of the Relationship of Measured Interests of Entering College Freshmen to Choice of Occupation Approximately Forty-Four Months Later*. Doctor's thesis, University of Arkansas (Fayetteville, Ark.), 1970. (*DAI* 31:2680A)

838. DUNHAM, PHIL RANDOLPH. *A Comparison of Interests for Selected College Majors at Southeastern State College*. Doc-

tor's thesis, Oklahoma State University. (Stillwater, Okla.), 1970. (*DAI* 31:5122A)

839. ELDERFELD, STEPHAN, AND LOVE, BETHOLENE. "Identification of Aptitude Criteria for Medical Technology." *Am J Med Technol* 36(8):388–99 Ag '70. *

840. FLYE, LINDA M. *Knowledge of Aptitude as a Source of Change in Inventoried Interests.* Master's thesis, East Tennessee State University (Johnson City, Tenn.), 1970.

841. HAKANSON, IRVING STEARNS. *Influences of Parent Education and Occupation Upon Eventual Occupational Choice and Interest Patterns of Students.* Doctor's thesis, University of Oregon (Eugene, Ore.), 1970. (*DAI* 32:176A)

842. JONES, KENNETH J., AND JONES, PRISCILLA P. "Contribution of the Rorschach to Description of Personality Structure Defined by Several Objective Tests." *Psychol Rep* 26(1):35–45 F '70. * (*PA* 45:4281)

843. KEOUGH, M. ADRIENNE. *Dimensionalities and Discrepancies in Maternal Perception of the Vocational Interests of Caucasian and Negro Mothers.* Doctor's thesis, Catholic University of America (Washington, D.C.), 1970. (*DAI* 31:2109A)

844. KISH, GEORGE B. "Cognitive Innovation and Stimulus-Seeking: A Study of the Correlates of the Obscure Figures Test." *Percept & Motor Skills* 30(1):95–101 F '70. * (*PA* 46:9304)

845. KISH, GEORGE B. "Oral Passivity, Interests, and Aptitudes." *Newsl Res Psychol* 12(1):22–3 F '70. *

846. KISH, GEORGE B., AND LEAHY, LOUIS. "Stimulus-Seeking, Age, Interests, and Aptitudes: An Amplification." *Percept & Motor Skills* 30(2):670 Ap '70. * (*PA* 46:7567)

847. LAHEY, HENRY CHARLES. *Personality Differentiation of Elevated Outdoor and Literary Kuder Preference Record Scales in an Urban Population.* Doctor's thesis, University of Connecticut (Storrs, Conn.), 1970. (*DAI* 31:1014A)

848. LINDEMAN, ROBERT PAUL. *A Study of Selected Nonintellectual Variables Among Classes of Students in a College of Engineering.* Doctor's thesis, Oklahoma State University (Stillwater, Okla.), 1970. (*DAI* 31:5852A)

849. NICOL, DONALD D., AND WARD, GEORGE, II. "A Canonical Correlation Analysis of the Minnesota Multiphasic Personality Inventory and the Kuder Preference Record." *Proc W Va Acad Sci* 41(1969):214–8 '70. *

850. REFICE, RONALD J. *A Study of the Relationship of Interest and Personality Variables Using a Multimethod Factor Analysis.* Doctor's thesis, University of Kansas (Lawrence, Kan.), 1970. (*DAI* 31:5777A)

851. RESNICK, HARVEY; FAUBLE, MARIANNE LEESON; AND OSIPOW, SAMUEL H. "Vocational Crystallization and Self-Esteem in College Students." *J Counsel Psychol* 17(5):465–7 S '70. * (*PA* 45:3008)

852. SMITH, I. MACFARLANE. "The Use of Diagnostic Tests for Assessing the Abilities of Overseas Students Attending Institutions of Further Education, Part I." *Voc Aspect Ed* (England) 22(51):1–8 Mr '70. *

853. WRIGHT, FRED H., AND L'ABATE, LUCIANO. "On the Meaning of the MMPI Mf and SVIB MF Scales." *Brit J Social & Clin Psychol* 9(2):171–4 Je '70. * (*PA* 44:16718)

854. ZENGER, WELDON F. *A Study of the Influence of Vocational and Occupational Exploration and Self-Appraisal Activities Upon the Vocational Choices and Vocational Interests of High School Seniors.* Doctor's thesis, University of Kansas (Lawrence, Kan.), 1970. (*DAI* 32:2627A)

855. BESWICK, DAVID G., AND TALLMADGE, G. KASTEN. "Reexamination of Two Learning Style Studies in the Light of the Cognitive Process Theory of Curiosity." *J Ed Psychol* 62(6):456–62 D '71. * (*PA* 47:8153)

856. BREIDENBAUGH, BARRY E., AND BROZOVICH, RICHARD W. "Self-Rated and Test Interest Patterns Among Students Referred for Vocational Rehabilitation Services." *Sch Counselor* 18(3):185–8 Ja '71. *

857. DORRIS, COLEEN WALL. *An Investigation of Vocational Interests Patterns Associated With Perceived Parent-Child Relationships of High School Adolescents of Clarksville-Montgomery County, Tennessee.* Master's thesis, University of Tennessee (Knoxville, Tenn.), 1971.

858. GABLE, ROBERT KEITH. *A Multivariate Study of Work Value Orientations.* Doctor's thesis, State University of New York (Albany, N.Y.), 1971. (*DAI* 32:1997A)

859. GARBER, JOHN RODNEY. *Characteristics of Students Enrolled in the Guided Studies Program at Rockingham Community College and Their Implications for Curriculum Development.* Doctor's thesis, North Carolina State University (Raleigh, N.C.), 1971. (*DAI* 32:3555A)

860. HARDY, RICHARD E., AND CULL, JOHN G. "Vocational Satisfaction Among Alcoholics." *Q J Studies Alcohol* 32(1A):180–2 Mr '71. * (*PA* 46:7098)

861. LEVITT, EUGENE E.; LUBIN, BERNARD; AND DeWITT, KATHRYN N. "An Attempt to Develop an Objective Test Battery for the Selection of Nursing Students." *Nursing Res* 20(3):255–8 My–Je '71. * (*PA* 51:3969)

862. LINN, MOTT ROBERTSON. *Achievement, Aptitude, Interest, and Personality Variables as Predictors of Curriculum, Graduation, and Placement.* Doctor's thesis, University of Pennsylvania (Philadelphia, Pa.), 1971. (*DAI* 32:1857A)

863. MORRIS, J. L., AND PARKINSON, M. "Vocational Interests

of Data Processing Personnel." *Austral Psychologist* 6(1):19–25 Mr '71. * (*PA* 47:3839)

864. MORRISON, JOHN WESLEY, JR. *An Investigation of Relationships Between the Experiences of High School Students and Changes in Their Vocational Interest Profiles.* Doctor's thesis, University of Connecticut (Storrs, Conn.), 1971. (*DAI* 33:2770A)

865. MULDER, FRANS. "Characteristics of Violators of Formal Company Rules." *J Appl Psychol* 55(5):500–2 O '71. * (*PA* 47:7906)

866. SAMPLE, DUANE, AND HOTCHKISS, SALLY M. "An Investigation of Relationships Between Personality Characteristics and Success in Instrumental Study." *J Res Music Ed* 19(3):307–13 f '71. * (*PA* 48:5871)

867. SMITH, I. MACFARLANE. "The Use of Diagnostic Tests for Assessing the Abilities of Overseas Students Attending Institutions of Further Education, Part II." *Voc Aspect Ed* (England) 23(54):39–48 Ap '71. *

868. VANDER WOUDE, JACK DALE. *The Relationship Between an Electro-Oculographic Measure of Interest and a Measure of Expressed and Inventoried Interests.* Doctor's thesis, University of Kansas (Lawrence, Kan.), 1971. (*DAI* 32:5685A)

869. WILKINSON, A. EARL; PRADO, WILLIAM M.; WILLIAMS, WOODROW O.; AND SCHNADT, FREDERICK W. "Psychological Test Characteristics and Length of Stay in Alcoholism Treatment." *Q J Studies Alcohol* 32(1A):60–5 Mr '71. * (*PA* 46:7116)

CUMULATIVE NAME INDEX

Abrahams, I.: 642
Adams, F. J.: 389
Adjutant General's Office, Personnel Research and Procedures Branch, Personnel Research Section Staff: 65
Adkins, D. C.: 3–4
Allen, C. L.: 83
Allen, R. J.: 501
American Nurses' Association, Research Department: 36
Anastasi, A.: 502
Anderson, C. L.: 158, 478
Anderson, F. E.: 832
Anderson, M. E.: 487
Anderson, R. G.: 267
Anderson, T. E.: 784
Angers, W. P.: 542
Anikeeff, A. M.: 436
Arbuckle, D. S.: 364
Armstrong, M. E.: 592
Arnold, D. L.: 408
Atkinson, E.: 345
Atkinson, G.: 785
Atkinson, J. A.: 528
Atty, J. C.: 657
Auston, C. A.: 620
Ausubel, D. P.: 268
Baas, M. L.: 116, 159
Bachner, V. M.: 506
Baer, B. S.: 269
Baggaley, A. R.: 71, 786
Baier, D. E.: 274
Bailey, H. C.: 813
Ball, M. K.: 658, 698
Banks, R. R.: 727, 806
Bare, C. E.: 728
Barnette, W. L.: 117, 135, 187–8, 575
Baron, S.: 345
Barrett, R. E.: 237
Barrett, R. S.: 409
Barrilleaux, L. E.: 503
Barry, C. M.: 19
Barshay, H. B.: 622
Bateman, H. B.: 814
Bateman, R. M.: 118
Bath, J. A.: 216
Bauernfeind, R. H.: 529, 548
Baxter, J. L.: 463
Bayley, N.: 119, 189
Beamer, G. C.: 72, 84, 270, 390
Beaton, M. A.: 729
Beaver, A. P.: 271, 365
Becker, J. A.: 549, 649
Bell, E. L.: 730
Bell, M. L.: 629
Belman, H. S.: 160, 190
Bendig, A. W.: 298, 391, 449, 550
Benjamin, J. A.: 815
Bentz, V. J.: 755, 787
Berdie, R. F.: 161; *rev*, 3:640
Berg, I. A.: 47, 66

Bernard, J.: 299
Berryessa, M. J.: 623
Beswick, D. G.: 855
Bidwell, G. P.: 816
Billing, P. S.: 212, 239
Bingman, R. M.: 756–7
Bitner, H. M.: 587
Blank, S. S.: 788
Bluhm, H.: 619
Bolanovich, D. J.: 20–1
Bond, G. L.: 220
Bond, N. A.: 316
Bone, J. H.: 392
Booth, M. D.: 431
Bordin, E. S.: 48, 114, 272; *rev*, 4:742
Borg, W. R.: 162–3, 281, 579
Bourdo, E. A.: 300
Bouton, A.: 318–9
Bouton, A. S.: 238
Bradfield, A. F.: 164
Bradley, A. D.: 616
Bradshaw, O. L.: 789
Brayfield, A. H.: 273, 393; *exc*, 3:640
Breidenbaugh, B. E.: 856
Brewer, J. M.: 14
Bridgman, C. S.: 504
Broadbent, L. A.: 731
Brody, D. S.: 165, 394
Brogden, H. E.: 274
Brooks, M. S.: 301
Brown, M. N.: 166, 191, 225
Brown, R. A.: 687
Brown, T. E.: 505
Brown, W. E.: 120
Brozovich, R. W.: 856
Bruce, M. M.: 302, 395
Bryan, J. G.: 340
Bryan, J. L.: 303, 436
Buck, J. R.: 659
Buckalew, R. J.: 530
Budd, W. C.: 450
Buegel, H. F.: 239
Buel, W. D.: 506
Burdette, W. E.: 213
Bursch, C. W.: 192, 240, 304
Busse, W.: 762
Butcher, H. J.: 565, 817–8
Butler, B. V.: 594
Cahoon, D. D.: 790
Calia, V. F.: 451, 484
Callis, R.: 305, 660
Campbell, J. F.: 578
Campbell, M. G.: 635
Campbell, R. E.: 531
Canfield, A. A.: 275
Cannon, D. J.: 617
Cannon, W. M.: 452
Capwell, D. F.: 121
Carey, J.: 588
Carkhuff, R. R.: 664
Carlson, S. L.: 835
Carman, P. M.: 593
Carmical, L.: 661

Carmical, L. L.: 636
Carron, T. J.: 819
Carse, D.: 217
Carter, G. C.: 241, 306
Carter, H. D.: 334; rev, 4: 742
Carter, L.: 122
Case, H. W.: 242
Casey, E. W.: 524
Casner, D.: 218
Cass, J. C.: 485
Cassel, R. N.: 551
Castricone, N. R.: 758
Cerf, A. Z.: 73
Chambers, E. G.: rev, 3:640
Champion, J. M.: 437
Chase, J. B.: 219
Chatterji, S.: 532, 662
Christensen, C. M.: 533
Christensen, P. R.: 316
Christensen, T. E.: 37
Clark, K. E.: 486
Clemans, W. V.: 791
Coats, J. E.: 507
Cockrum, L. V.: 243
Cohen, L. M.: 453
Comer, J. E.: 123
Comrey, A. L.: 346
Conner, H. T.: 307
Coomb, W. A.: 67
Cooper, M. N.: 347
Corey, D.: 82
Corey, D. Q.: 186
Costello, C. G.: 487
Cottingham, H. F.: 5
Cottle, W. C.: 85, 124-6, 167, 576, 792
Coulson, R. W.: 438
Coutts, R. L.: 534
Cox, K. J.: 63
Crane, W. J.: 535
Craven, E. C.: 410, 508
Crawford, A. B.: rev, 2:1671
Crawford, L. E.: 230
Crites, J. O.: 546
Cronbach, L. J.: 836
Crosby, R. C.: 6-7, 15
Cross, O. H.: 86, 168
Crowell, O.: 837
Crumrine, W. M.: 254
Cull, J. G.: 860
Cumings, R.: 379
Cummings, I. M.: 68
Curran, J. P.: 308
Currie, C.: 606
Dabelstein, D. H.: 49
Daly, J. M.: 87, 226
D'Aoust, T.: 650
D'Arcy, P. F.: 421, 536
Darter, C. L.: 637
Davis, S. S.: 309
Day, J. F.: 127
Day, M. E.: 396
DeLisle, F. H.: 583
Dent, O. B.: 699
Denton, M. J.: 663
Detchen, L.: 38
DeWitt, K. N.: 861
Diamond, S.: 88
Diener, C. L.: 488, 607
DiMichael, S. G.: 49, 128-9
Doleys, E. J.: 674
Donnenwerth, G. V.: 824
Dorris, C. W.: 857
Downie, N. M.: 366
Drasgow, J.: 664, 700
Dreher, R. G.: 700
Dressel, P. L.: 244
Drew, A. S.: 537, 665
Driscoll, J.: 732
Dulsky, S. G.: 169
Dunham, P. R.: 838
Dunlap, J. W.: 183
Durnall, E. J.: 310
Dustan, L. C.: 651, 666
Echeverria, B. P.: 754
Edens, L. W.: 667
Edmonson, L. D.: 84
Eimicke, V. W.: 130, 193
Elberfeld, S.: 839
Elder, D.: 678
Elder, R. F.: 699
Engram, W. C.: 305
Entwisle, F. N.: 542

Erlandson, F. L.: 461
Evans, C. E.: 39
Evans, M. C.: 89
Evans, R. N.: 160, 190
Ewens, W. P.: 131, 367, 378, 552
Fangman, E. G.: 668
Farber, R. H.: 194
Farrow, E. G.: 276
Fattu, N. A.: 563
Fauble, M. L.: 851
Feather, D. B.: 170
Feder, D. D.: 18
Feinberg, M. R.: 669
Finco, A. A.: 733
Finegan, A. L.: 793
Finley, P. J.: 670
Firkins, C. J.: 638
Fiske, D. W.: 198
Fitzpatrick, E. D.: 329, 342-3
Fleming, W. G.: 454
Flye, L. M.: 840
Foley, A. W.: 348
Foote, R. P.: 489
Force, R. C.: 349, 411
Ford, A. B.: 680
Ford, A. H.: 171
Foreman, M. E.: 820
Forer, B. R.: 195, 350
Forness, S. R.: 671
Forrest, G. M.: 565
Forster, C. R.: 351
Fosselius, E. E.: 22
Fowler, H. M.: rev, 4:742
Fox, W. H.: 74
Frandsen, A.: 50, 569, 794
Frandsen, A. N.: 245, 277
Frankel, E.: 618, 630
Freehill, M. F.: 246, 278
Freeman, F. S.: 538
French, J. L.: 412
Fricke, B. G.: 426
Frinsko, W.: 643
Froehlich, C. P.: 69; rev, 5: 863
Furst, E. J.: 425-6
Gable, R. K.: 858
Gadel, M. S.: 323
Gage, N. L.: 104, 146
Garber, J. R.: 859
Garner, R. G.: 507
Garrett, G. A.: 427, 509
Gash, I. A.: 734
Gehman, W. S.: 368, 455-6
Gengerelli, J. A.: 594
George, C. E.: 378
Getzels, J. W.: 371
Giblette, J. F.: 490
Gilbert, J.: 553
Gitlin, S.: 439
Givens, P. R.: 279
Glazer, S. H.: 413
Gobetz, W.: 672
Goche, L. N.: 311
Golburgh, S. J.: 491, 639
Golden, J. F.: 735
Goldstein, A. P.: 369, 492
Goodman, C. H.: 21
Gordon, B. J. A.: 624
Gordon, H. C.: 8, 10
Gorman, J. R.: 510
Gorman, W. E.: 600
Goshorn, W. M.: 172
Goss, A. M.: 736, 759, 795-6
Gowan, J. C.: 312, 370, 397-8, 432
Grant, D. L.: 313-4
Gray, B. G.: 631
Green, R. F.: 132, 196
Greene, J. E.: 577
Griffin, J. V.: 754
Guazzo, E. J.: 315
Guba, E. G.: 371
Guilford, J. P.: 247, 316, 457
Gunter, L. M.: 335
Hadley, J. M.: 133, 140
Hahn, M. E.: 32-3, 76, 209
Hakanson, I. S.: 841
Hake, D. T.: 134
Hale, P. P.: 248, 372, 440
Hall, S. G.: 797
Hammill, D.: 317
Hanna, G. S.: 701, 737
Hanna, J. V.: 135

Hannum, T. E.: 558
Harding, W. T.: 738
Hardy, R. E.: 860
Harmon, L. R.: 249
Harrangue, M. D.: 702
Harrington, J. A.: 821
Harrison, L.: 136
Hartman, B. J.: 703
Hascall, E. O.: 458, 511
Haselkorn, H.: 280, 373
Hayes, S. P.: 572, 574
Headlee, M. K.: 90
Healy, I.: 281, 579
Hedley, C. N.: 798-9
Heiberg, D. A.: 800
Heilman, H.: 801
Henderson, E. C.: 374
Hennessy, T.: 619
Henry, W. O.: 137
Herkness, W. W.: 8, 10
Herzberg, F.: 262, 282, 318-9
Hester, R.: 257
Heston, J. C.: 51, 91
High, W. S.: 346
Hill, G. E.: 414-5
Hill, J. M.: 589
Hillman, C.: 227
Hirt, M.: 459
Hole, R. M.: 375, 414
Holland, J. L.: 283
Hollenbeck, G. P.: 504
Holmes, J. A.: 739
Holtan, B.: 673
Hoover, K. H.: 376
Hornaday, J. A.: 512, 554
Hosford, P. M.: 513
Hotchkiss, S. M.: 866
Huckabee, M. W.: 822
Huffman, W. J.: 228
Hughes, H. B.: 674
Hughes, J. B.: 298
Huston, B. M.: 760
Hyman, B.: 377, 595
Isaacson, L. E.: 250
Ivanoff, J. M.: 740
Ivey, A. E.: 555, 704
Izard, C. E.: 336
Jackson, C. W.: 545
Jackson, J.: 75
Jacobs, R.: 138, 197, 320, 422
James, L. E.: 820
Jensen, G. L.: 139
Jensen, V. H.: 608
Johansen, A. N.: 705
Johnson, A. P.: 542
Johnson, J. M.: 173
Johnson, R. H.: 220, 596
Jones, J. B.: 644
Jones, K. J.: 556, 675, 842
Jones, P. P.: 842
Kahn, R. L.: 92, 133, 140
Kaiser, H. E.: 811
Karpoff, J. T.: 761
Katz, M.: 539; rev, 6:1063
Katzenmeyer, W. G.: 456
Kegan, E. O.: 321
Keim, L.: 741
Kelley, E. P.: 352
Kelly, E. L.: 198
Kelly, J. G.: 322
Kelso, N. E.: 93
Kemp, C. G.: 609
Kendall, W. E.: 76
Kennedy, E. C.: 441
Kenney, C. E.: 460
Keough, M. A.: 843
Kermeen, B. G.: 229
Kern, D. W.: 284
Kerns, R. D.: 251
Kerr, W. D.: 742
Kimbell, F. T.: 493
Kimber, J. A. M.: 77
King, D. C.: 523
King, P.: 461, 557
Kingston, A. J.: 378
Kish, G. B.: 762, 823-5, 844-6
Kline, M. V.: 379
Kluczny, R.: 833
Klugman, S. F.: 174, 353, 399, 462, 494, 676, 743
Knaak, N. K.: 601
Knudsen, R. G.: 706

Kobler, F. J.: 677
Kohn, N.: 94-5
Kopp, T.: 52
Krause, A. H.: 283, 463
Krauskopf, C. J.: 678
Kraybill, E. K.: 456
Kriedt, P. H.: 323
Krout, M. H.: 169
Krumm, R. L.: 252
Kuder, G. F.: 2, 4, 23, 141, 199, 230, 291, 400, 512
Kulick, W.: 584
Kunzler, H. G.: 679
Kutner, M.: 78
L'Abate, L.: 853
LaBue, A. C.: 590
LaGrone, C. W.: 826
Lahey, H. C.: 847
Laird, J. T.: 401
Lane, P. A.: 464
Lange, H. M.: 380
Lanna, M. G.: 540
Larsen, A. H.: 571
Lathrop, R. C.: 827
Lattin, G. W.: 175
Lauro, L.: 96
Lawrence, R. M.: 176
Lawson, E. D.: 707
Lay, A. W.: 610
Leach, K. W.: 324
Leahy, L.: 825, 846
LeBlanc, C. R.: 495
Ledbetter, E. W.: 390
Lee, M. C.: 602
Lee, P. J.: 325
Lehman, R. T.: 24
Leonard, R. J.: 372
Leshner, S. S.: 210
Lessing, E. E.: 465
Levine, P. R.: 326
Levinson, B. M.: 514
Levitt, E. E.: 861
Lewis, E. C.: 497, 515
Lewis, J. A.: 53
Lewis, L.: 744
Lindeman, R. P.: 848
Lindgren, H. C.: 79
Linn, M. R.: 862
Lipsett, L.: 54, 327
Liske, R. E.: 680
Livingston, C. D.: 381
Livingston, E.: 285
Lodato, F. J.: 597
LoMonaco, L. J.: 802
Long, J. M.: 681
Long, L.: 286
Longstaff, H. P.: 97
Love, B.: 839
Lovelass, H. D.: 571
Lowrie, K. H.: 11
Lubin, B.: 861
Lucas, D. H.: 763
Lucio, W. H.: 433
Lunneborg, C. E.: 785
Luton, J. N.: 424
McCall, J. N.: 708
McCall, W. C.: 9
McCarthy, M. V.: 585
McCarthy, T. N.: 420
McCarty, J. J.: 328-9, 342-3, 402
McCoy, R. A.: 330
McCully, C. H.: 331, 354
McDonagh, A. J.: 516
McGowan, J. F.: 305
McGunnigal, J. V.: 764
MacKinney, A. C.: 515, 527
MacLean, M. J.: 652
McMahon, W. J.: 682
McMillen, D. M.: 517
McNamara, W. J.: 689
MacPhail, A. H.: 200
McRae, G. G.: 466
Madaus, G. F.: 765-6
Magee, P. C.: 653
Magill, J. W.: 253, 355
Mahoney, S. C.: 620
Maier, G. E.: 403
Malcolm, D. D.: 98, 177
Mallinson, G. G.: 254
Manzano, I. B.: 231
Mapeli, D.: 678
Margolis, V. H.: 767
Marita, M.: 740

Marsden, R. D.: 768
Marsh, M. M.: 393
Marsh, S. H.: 645
Martin, G. C.: 232
Martinson, F. M.: 586, 598
Matteson, R. W.: 244
Mayeske, G. W.: 683
Meek, C. R.: 332
Mehrotra, C. M. N.: 803
Meleika, L. K.: 255
Meyer, P. R.: 684
Meyer, W. J.: 550
Meyers, E. S.: 34
Michal, R. D.: 745
Michaux, W.: 100
Micka, H. K.: 376
Miles, R. W.: 101
Miller, A. D.: 102
Miller, A. W.: 746
Miller, W. G.: 558
Millsap, C. S.: 685
Mims, T. S.: 671
Miner, J. B.: 496
Mink, O. G.: 518
Moffett, C. R.: 423
Monroe, G. D.: 740
Monroe, M. B.: 80
Moore, C. W.: 416
Moore, G. D.: 708
Moorman, J. D.: 559
Morey, E. A.: 142
Morris, J. L.: 863
Morrison, J. W.: 864
Mortola, D. S.: 625
Morton, J.: 828
Moser, W. E.: 256
Motto, J. J.: 467
Moul, E. C.: 709
Mowbray, J. K.: 769
Mugaas, H. D.: 257
Mukerjee, M.: 532, 662
Mulder, F.: 865
Munson, H. R.: 468
Murtaugh, J. J.: 710
Namani, A. K.: 442
Nash, A. N.: 711
Nauss, M. W.: 632
Neal, C. M.: 686, 770–1, 804
Neumann, T. M.: 221
Newman, J.: 356
Nicol, D. D.: 849
Nicolay, R. C.: 833
Nixon, M.: 122
Nixon, M. E.: 283
Norrell, G.: 461, 557
North, A. J.: 208
North, R. D.: 143, 178
Novak, B. J.: 201
Novak, D. F.: 519
Nugent, F. A.: 520, 805
Nunnery, M. Y.: 469
Oakes, F.: 470
O'Hara, R. P.: 541, 626, 765–6, 772
Oliver, J. A.: 206
O'Loughlin, D. R.: 521
Onarheim, J.: 55
Ort, R. S.: 680
Osborne, R. T.: 145, 577
Osipow, S. H.: 851
Ostlund, L. A.: 443
Overall, J. E.: 560
Pallone, N. J.: 806
Palmer, D. H.: 712
Parker, A. D.: 747
Parker, J. W.: 287
Parkinson, M.: 863
Parton, N. W.: 270
Pate, K. D.: 759
Paterson, D. G.: 40
Patterson, C. H.: 357, 471, 603, 611
Paulson, B. B.: 141, 199
Pearlman, S.: 580
Pearson, D. T.: 382
Pedersen, D. M.: 713, 773
Pemberton, C. L.: 233
Pender, F. R.: 270
Penzer, W. N.: 669
Perrine, M. W.: 358
Perry, J. D.: 103, 286
Perry, J. O.: 646
Perry, M. L.: 561
Pervin, D. W.: 144

Peters, E. F.: 12
Petersen, L. P.: 790
Peterson, M. B.: 704
Peterson, M. E.: 472
Petro, P. K.: 434
Phelan, R. F.: 295
Phillips, L. W.: 714
Phillips, W. S.: 145
Pierce-Jones, J.: 333–4, 473–4, 522; rev, 5:863
Piotrowski, Z. A.: 41
Plummer, R. H.: 202
Pollan, W. D.: 604
Pont, H. B.: 818
Pool, D. A.: 687, 715
Poor, F. A.: 647
Poston, W. K.: 829
Powell, J. O.: 126
Powers, G. P.: 557
Prado, W. M.: 869
Princenthal, H. H.: 581
Quimby, N. F.: 25
Racky, D. J.: 475
Radcliffe, J. A.: 562
Ravensborg, M. R.: 830
Raygor, A. L.: 716
Redlener, J.: 214
Reed, W. W.: 497
Refice, R. J.: 850
Reid, J. W.: 203, 234, 542
Reinhard, N. F.: 621
Remmers, H. H.: 104, 146
Renfer, M. E. F.: 748
Renke, W. W.: 258
Resnick, H.: 851
Rezler, A. G.: 774–5
Richardson, J. F.: 654
Ricksecker, E. L.: 660
Riedel, R. G.: 833
Risch, F.: 433
Rishel, D. F.: 640
Risher, C. C.: 444
Robb, G. P.: 288
Robbins, A.: 289
Robbins, J. E.: 523
Roberts, J. P.: 361
Roberts, S. O.: 335
Roberts, W. H.: 70
Roeber, E. C.: 105, 147
Rogge, H.: 415
Rogge, H. J.: 259
Rohrs, D. K.: 543
Rollins, R. W.: 35
Romney, A. K.: 179
Ronan, W. W.: 688
Rooks, I.: 612
Rose, W.: 106
Rosen, M. H.: 633
Rosenberg, N.: 290, 336
Rosenberg, P.: 260
Ross, G. R.: 180
Rowe, F. B.: 613
Ruedisili, C. H.: 134
Rupiper, O. J.: 544
Rush, H.: 568
Russell, D.: 261–2, 282
Russell, D. L.: 698
Ryder, A. D.: 749
Sample, D.: 866
Samuelson, C. O.: 382, 417
Sanders, W. B.: 577
Sartain, A. Q.: 42
Sassenrath, J. M.: 563
Savastano, H.: 717, 750
Scarborough, B. B.: 419
Scheuhing, M. A.: 107, 201
Schiff, H. M.: 268
Schnadt, F. W.: 869
Schnebly, L. M.: 235
Schneider, D. E.: 339
Seagoe, M.: 398
Seibert, E. W.: 43
Sessions, A. D.: 277
Shaffer, R. H.: 148–9, 291
Shah, S. A.: 404
Shaw, C. B.: 337
Sherman, E. C.: 236
Shierson, H. E.: 64
Shinn, E. O.: 383
Shneidman, E. S.: 641
Shoemaker, W. L.: 359, 476
Shultz, I. T.: 568
Shuttleworth, F. K.: 103
Sidney, G. P.: 614

Silver, R. J.: 524
Silvey, H. M.: 150, 205
Singer, H.: 739
Singh, N. P.: 776
Singh, R. P.: 831
Sininger, R. A.: 435
Sinnett, E. R.: 384
Slaughter, K. B.: 777
Slaymaker, R. R.: 56
Slayton, W. G.: 718
Smith, D. D.: 418, 445, 477
Smith, D. E.: 151
Smith, I. M.: 852, 867
Smith, R. N.: 615
Sorenson, M.: 794
Southern, J. A.: 368
Spaulding, V. V.: 573
Speer, G. S.: 58, 108–12
Spiers, D. E.: 719
Spitzer, M. E.: 689
Spivey, G. M.: 181
Springob, H. K.: 545, 564
Stagner, R.: 755
Stalans, V.: 751
Stallings, W. M.: 832
Stanley, J. C.: 263
Staples, J. D.: 720
Stauffacher, J. C.: 478
Stauffer, E.: 807
Steffire, B.: 57
Stein, F.: 808
Stein, K. B.: 778
Steinberg, A.: 264
Steiner, B. J.: 319
Stephan, E. E.: 690
Stephans, P.: 527
Sternberg, C.: 292–3, 360, 385
Sterne, D. M.: 498
Stewart, B.: 82
Stewart, B. M.: 186
Stewart, L. H.: 361, 405
Stinson, M. C.: 182
Stinson, P. J.: 446
Stone, S.: 406
Stoops, J. A.: 294
Storey, J. S.: 599
Stowe, E. W.: 362
Strong, E. K.: 152
Strother, G. B.: 84
Super, D. E.: 59, 153, 183, 546; rev, 3:640
Sutter, C. R.: 525
Sutton, M. A.: 316
Swanson, F. T.: 779
Sweeney, F. J.: 338
Sweeney, R. H.: 691
Tallmadge, G. K.: 809, 855
Tanner, W. C.: 591
Tarpey, M. S.: 721
Tarrier, R. B.: 810
Tavris, E. C.: 479
Taylor, E. K.: 274, 339
Taylor, P. L.: 428
Taylor, R. G.: 769
Terwilliger, J. S.: 648
Tharpe, F. D.: 386
Thomas, P. L.: 349, 447
Thompson, C. E.: 26, 81
Thompson, J. N.: 780
Thrash, P. A.: 480
Thurstone, L. L.: 1
Tiedeman, D. V.: 340, 484–5, 626
Tiffin, J.: 295
Tillman, K.: 722
Tillman, K. G.: 692
Topetzes, N. J.: 407
Townsend, A.: 44
Travers, K. J. D.: 723
Traxler, A. E.: 9, 16, 45, 320, 341, 422; rev, 2:1671
Trembath, M. F.: 283
Triggs, F. O.: 17–8, 27–8, 60–1, 113, 211, 296
Troxel, L. L.: 154

Tuckman, J.: 29
Turo, J. K.: 693
Tussing, L.: 52
Tutton, M. E.: 363
Tyler, F. T.: 62
Tyler, L. E.: 694
Uecker, A. E.: 265
Urschalitz, M. O.: 429
Van Dalsem, E. L.: 605
Vander Woude, J. D.: 868
Vaughan, G. E.: 222
Vaughan, L. E.: 481
Vaughan, R. P.: 752
Verger, D. M.: 724
Villeme, M. G.: 627
Voas, R. B.: 482
Vopatek, S. H.: 387
Wagman, M.: 695
Wagner, E. E.: 483, 499, 634
Walch, S. L.: 628
Waldrop, R. S.: 263, 664
Walker, R. E.: 833
Walker, R. O.: 184
Wallace, S. R.: 155
Wallen, R.: 326
Walter, L.: 571
Warburton, F. W.: 565
Ward, G.: 849
Watkins, R. W.: 185
Watley, D. J.: 716
Watson, C. G.: 790
Wauck, L.: 430
Way, H. H.: 297
Webster, E. C.: 206
Weis, S. F.: 753
Welna, C. T.: 500
Wesley, S. M.: 82, 186
West, D. N.: 660
Westberg, W. C.: 329, 342–3
Westmoreland, L.: 30
Weynand, R. S.: 223, 301
White, H. G.: 566
White, R. M.: 448
Whittemore, R. G.: 754
Whittock, J. M.: 582
Wiener, D. N.: 207
Wiesner, E. F.: 725
Wiggins, R. E.: 46
Wilkinson, A. E.: 869
Williams, C. T.: 33
Williams, W. O.: 869
Willis, W. K.: 742
Willmarth, J. G.: 834
Wilson, E.: 114
Wilson, E. H.: 215, 272
Wilson, J. W.: 327
Wilson, R. N.: 811
Windholz, G.: 781–2, 812
Winick, C.: 696
Winn, A.: 206
Winn, J. C.: 156
Winsor, A. L.: 7
Winter, G. D.: 783
Wisdom, J. R.: 224
Witherspoon, R. P.: 526
Wittenborn, J. R.: 18
Wolff, W. M.: 208
Wolins, L.: 497, 527
Womer, F. B.: 425
Wood, P. L.: 655
Woods, W. A.: 115
Woodward, C. L.: 266
Woody, C.: 31, 570
Wright, F. H.: 853
Wright, J. C.: 419
Wright, R. L.: 344
Wynn, D. C.: 656
Yum, K. S.: 13
Zech, J. C.: 697
Zeleny, M. P.: 268
Zenger, W. F.: 854
Zenti, R. N.: 388
Zimmerer, A. M.: 567
Zwilling, V. T.: 157
Zytowski, D. G.: 726

[2196]

★**Milwaukee Academic Interest Inventory.** Grades 12–14; 1973; MAII; 8 scores: 6 "field variable" scores (physical science, healing occupations, behavorial science, economics, humanities-social studies, elementary education) plus 2 "discriminant variable" scores (commercial vs. nurturant interests, natural science vs. social studies interests) ; Andrew R. Baggaley ; Western Psychological Services. *

REFERENCES THROUGH 1971

1. BAGGALEY, ANDREW R. "Development of a Predictive Academic Interest Inventory." *J Counsel Psychol* 10:41–6 sp '63. * (*PA* 38:10151)
2. BAGGALEY, ANDREW R., AND CAMPBELL, JAMES P. "Multiple-Discriminant Analysis of Academic Curricula by Interest and Aptitude Variables." *J Ed Meas* 4:143–9 f '67. * (*PA* 42:4434)
3. BAGGALEY, ANDREW R. "Congruent Validity of the Milwaukee Academic Interest Inventory." *Ed & Psychol Meas* 28:1207–11 w '68. * (*PA* 44:6786)
4. CAMPBELL, JAMES P. "Test-Space Prediction of Major Field of Study." *Ed & Psychol Meas* 28:887–9 au '68. * (*PA* 43:4460)

CUMULATIVE NAME INDEX

Baggaley, A. R.: 1–3　　　　Campbell, J. P.: 2, 4

[2197]

Minnesota Vocational Interest Inventory. Males ages 15 and over not planning to attend college ; 1965–66 ; MVII ; abbreviated version of *Navy Vocational Interest Inventory;* 30 scores : 21 occupational scales (baker, food service manager, milk wagon driver, retail sales clerk, stock clerk, printer, tabulating machine operator, warehouseman, hospital attendant, pressman, carpenter, painter, plasterer, truck driver, truck mechanic, industrial education teacher, sheet metal worker, plumber, machinist, electrician, radio-TV repairman) and 9 area scales (mechanical, health service, office work, electronics, food service, carpentry, sales-office, clean hands, outdoors) ; Kenneth E. Clark and David P. Campbell (manual) ; Psychological Corporation. *

For additional information, reviews by John O. Crites and Bert W. Westbrook, and excerpted reviews by Donald W. Hall and John W. M. Rothney (reply by David P. Campbell), see 7:1026 (45 references). For excerpts from related book reviews, see 6:B126 (2 excerpts).

REFERENCES THROUGH 1971

1–45. See 7:1026.
46. CLARK, KENNETH E., AND GEE, HELEN H. "Selecting Items for Interest Inventory Keys." *J Appl Psychol* 38:12–7 F '54. * (*PA* 29:1044)
47. MAYO, GEORGE DOUGLAS, AND THOMAS, DAVID S. "Agreement Between Counselor-Counselee Vocational Decisions and Interest Inventory Scores." *Personnel & Guid J* 35:37–8 S '56. * (*PA* 31:8183)
48. MAYO, GEORGE DOUGLAS, AND GUTTMAN, ISAIAH. "Faking in a Vocational Classification Situation." *J Appl Psychol* 43:117–21 Ap '59. * (*PA* 34:2776)
49. CHRISTIANSEN, HARLEY D. "Inventoried and Claimed Interests." *Voc Guid Q* 9:128–30 w '60–61. *
50. SPIES, CARL JOSEPH. *Some Non-Intellectual Predictors of Classroom Success.* Doctor's thesis, Washington University (St. Louis, Mo.), 1965. (*DA* 26:7442)
51. LAROSE, MICHAEL JOSEPH. *The Effect of Occupational Information and Counseling Upon the Vocational Interest Patterns of Adolescent Boys in a High School Special Education Program for Educable Mentally Retarded.* Master's thesis, Catholic University of America (Washington, D.C.), 1968.
52. COLE, NANCY S., AND HANSON, GARY R. "An Analysis of the Structure of Vocational Interests." *ACT Res Rep* 40:1–17 Ja '71. * (*PA* 47:1843)
53. COLE, NANCY S., AND HANSON, GARY R. "An Analysis of the Structure of Vocational Interests." *J Counsel Psychol* 18(5):478–86 S '71. * (*PA* 47:3679)
54. KAUPPI, DWIGHT RANDOLPH. *The Development of Instrument-Specific Reading and Comprehension Pre-Tests for Standardized Questionnaires and Inventories.* Doctor's thesis, University of Minnesota (Minneapolis, Minn.), 1971. (*DAI* 32:4844B)
55. LAU, ALAN W., AND ABRAHAMS, NORMAN M. "Stability of Vocational Interests Within Nonprofessional Occupations." *J Appl Psychol* 55(2):143–50 Ap '71. * (*PA* 46:3902)
56. RYAN, JOSEPH ADRIAN. *Vocational Preferences of Public School Special Class Students.* Doctor's thesis, Boston College (Chestnut Hill, Mass.), 1971. (*DAI* 32:1367A)

CUMULATIVE NAME INDEX

Abrahams, N. M.: 55　　　　Blank, P. M.: 43
Barclay, J. R.: 26　　　　　Bonfield, J.: 31
Barnette, W. L.: 22, 45　　　Bradley, A. D.: 7
Beal, L. E.: 39　　　　　　Campbell, D.: 16, 18
Campbell, D. P.: 10, 19–20, 23, 25; *exc*, 7:1026
Cardon, B. W.: 32
Christiansen, H. D.: 8, 49
Clark, K. E.: 1, 13, 46
Cole, N. S.: 52–3
Crites, J. O.: *rev*, 7:1026
Dawis, R. V.: 37
Doerr, J. J.: 27
French, J. L.: 32
Gee, H. H.: 3, 46
Ghei, S.: 9, 11
Guttman, I.: 48
Hale, P. P.: 39
Hall, D. W.: *exc*, 7:1026
Hanson, G. R.: 52–3
Johnson, R. W.: 35, 44
Kauppi, D. R.: 40–1, 54
Larose, M. J.: 51
Lau, A. W.: 55
Lowman, C. L.: 28
McCall, J. N.: 22, 24
Mahlman, R. W.: 14
Martin, G. R.: 33
Mayo, G. D.: 47–8
Messman, W. B.: 21
Michie, J.: 34
Nelson, H. F.: 17
Norman, W. T.: 6, 12
Olson, D. W.: 35
Passmore, J. L.: 36
Perry, D. K.: 4–5
Ravensborg, M. R.: 42
Rothney, J. W. M.: *exc*, 7:1026
Ryan, J. A.: 56
St. John, D. E.: 44
Schenkel, K. F.: 2
Scott, T. B.: 15
Silver, H. A.: 29, 45
Sorenson, W. W.: 19
Spies, C. J.: 50
Stafford, R. E.: 30
Thomas, D. S.: 47
Thorndike, R. M.: 37
Trockman, R. W.: 20
Vandenberg, S. G.: 30
Weiss, D. J.: 37, 40–1
Westbrook, B. W.: *rev*, 7:1026
Zytowski, D. G.: 38

[2198]

19 Field Interest Inventory. Standards 8–10 and college and adults ; 1970–71 ; 19FII ; 21 scores : fine arts, performing arts, language, historical, service, social work, sociability, public speaking, law, creative thought, science, practical-male, practical-female, numerical, business, clerical, travel, nature, sport, work-hobby, active-passive ; F. A. Fouché and N. F. Alberts ; Human Sciences Research Council [South Africa]. *

For additional information, see 7:1027.

[2199]

Occupational Interest Inventory, 1956 Revision. Grades 7–16 and adults, 9–16 and adults ; 1943–58 ; 10 scores grouped in 3 categories : fields of interests (personal-social, natural, mechanical, business, the arts, the sciences), types of interests (verbal, manipulative, computational), level of interest ; Edwin A. Lee and Louis P. Thorpe ; CTB/McGraw-Hill. *

For additional information, see 6:1064 (6 references) ; for reviews by Martin Katz and Wilbur L. Layton, see 5:864 (20 references) ; for a review by Arthur H. Brayfield of the original edition, see 4:743 (19 references) ; for reviews by Edward S. Bordin and Stanley G. Dulsky, see 3:643.

REFERENCES THROUGH 1971

1–20. See 4:743.
21–40. See 5:864.
41–46. See 6:1064.
47. HUTSON, BILLY T., AND VINCENT, NICHOLAS M. "Motivation and Prognosis in Shorthand." *J Bus Ed* 33:29–31 O '57. *
48. BONNEY, WARREN CHESTER. *An Investigation of Factors Associated With Changes in Inventoried Interests During the First Semester of College.* Doctor's thesis, University of Texas (Austin, Tex.), 1958. (*DA* 18:1718)
49. SWANSON, ROBERT ALLEN. *A Study of Factors Related to the Distortion of Interest Inventory Information Interpreted to Individuals and to Groups.* Doctor's research study No. 1, Colorado State College (Greeley, Colo.), 1963. (*DA* 25:304)
50. HELTON, WILLIAM BERNARD. *A Comparative Analysis of Selected Characteristics of Intellectually Superior Male Students Who Persist and Those Who Do Not Persist in an Advanced Placement Program.* Doctor's thesis, North Texas State University (Denton, Tex.), 1964. (*DA* 25:3394)
51. KLUGMAN, SAMUEL F. "Intra-Individual Variability Findings for a Psychotic Population on Vocational Interest Inventories." *J Counsel Psychol* 11:191–3 su '64. *
52. MORRIS, RUBY PEARL. *A Comparative Analysis of Selected Characteristics of Intellectually Superior Female Students Who Persisted and Those Who Did Not Persist in an Advanced Placement Program.* Doctor's thesis, North Texas State University (Denton, Tex.), 1964. (*DA* 25:3402)
53. STOKER, H. W.; KROPP, R. P.; AND BASHAW, W. L. "A Comparison of Scores Obtained Through Normal and Visual Administrations of the Occupational Interest Inventory." *Fla J Ed Res* 6:63–72 Ja '64. *
54. STRATTON, HERBERT B. *A Study of Vocational Interest Stability of Secondary School Students.* Master's thesis, Brigham Young University (Provo, Utah), 1964.

55. BELL, EVERETTE LYLE. *Factors Relating to Employment of Graduates of Des Moines Technical High School.* Doctor's thesis, Iowa State University (Ames, Iowa), 1966. (*DA* 27:892A)

56. BISSETT, SHIRLEY JEFFREYS. *The Relationship of Occupational Value Orientation to Vocational Choice.* Master's thesis, Southern Methodist University (Dallas, Tex.), 1967.

57. MARSDEN, RALPH DAVENPORT. *Topological Representation and Vector Analysis of Interest Patterns.* Doctor's thesis, Utah State University (Logan, Utah), 1967. (*DA* 28:4004A)

58. PRICE, THOMAS HUGH. *Psychological Case Studies of Successful Workers in the Field of Retailing.* Doctor's thesis, University of North Carolina (Chapel Hill, N.C.), 1967. (*DA* 28:4790B)

59. STAHMANN, ROBERT F. *Choice of Major Field: A Study of Four Systems of University Entrance Data as Predictors of Major Field at Graduation.* Doctor's thesis, University of Utah (Salt Lake City, Utah), 1967. (*DA* 28:2571A)

60. CLARK, JAMES VAL. *Characteristics Related to Preferences for Different Procedural Approaches to Counseling.* Doctor's thesis, University of Texas (Austin, Tex.), 1968. (*DA* 29:476A)

61. FREEDMAN, SAUL. *The Relationship Between Selected Variables and Success in Transcribing Typing for Trainees Who Are Blind.* Doctor's thesis, New York University (New York, N.Y.), 1968. (*DA* 29:3000A)

62. MAZUREK, FREDERICK H. *The Occupational Interests of Superior Ninth-Grade Boys as Related to Their Aspects of Adjustment.* Master's thesis, Catholic University of America (Washington, D.C.), 1968.

63. NADEL, ROBERT S. *Social Responsibility as a Criterion for the Prediction of Success of Volunteers: A Study of the Characteristics of People Who Volunteer to Serve.* Doctor's thesis, New York University (New York, N.Y.), 1969. (*DAI* 30:3549A)

64. SHERMAN, LILLIAN LASKAW. *Movers and Perseverers in Education: An Investigation of Interests, Values, Personality Factors, Self-Actualization, Need Satisfaction and Job Satisfaction Among Movers Into Counseling and Into Administration and Among Perseverers in Teaching.* Doctor's thesis, New York University (New York, N.Y.), 1969. (*DAI* 31:1023A)

65. STAHMANN, ROBERT F. "Occupational Interest Inventory 'Fields of Interests' Scores and Major Field of Study." *Ed & Psychol Meas* 29(4):987–91 w '69. * (*PA* 44:21005)

66. STAHMANN, ROBERT F. "Predicting Graduation Major Field From Freshman Entrance Data." *J Counsel Psychol* 16(2):109–13 Mr '69. * (*PA* 43:10376)

67. LEUNES, ARNOLD, AND CHRISTENSEN, LARRY. "Reliability and Inmate Test Results." *Correct Psychologist* 4(3):85–93 N–D '70. * (*PA* 49:2670)

68. NICHOLSON, EVERARD. *Final Report of the Study of Success and Admission Criteria for Potentially Successful Risks.* Providence, R.I.: Brown University, 1970. Pp. iv, 264. *

69. JACKSON, ARTHUR MELLS. *The Effects of Three Group Approaches in Effecting Change Among Black Students.* Doctor's thesis, Indiana University (Bloomington, Ind.), 1971. (*DAI* 32:4351A)

CUMULATIVE NAME INDEX

Ausubel, D. P.: 32
Barksdale, A.: 21
Bashaw, W. L.: 53
Bell, E. L.: 55
Bissett, S. J.: 56
Bond, G. L.: 23
Bonney, W. C.: 48
Bordin, E. S.: *rev,* 3:643
Boykin, L. L.: 42
Brayfield, A. H.: *rev,* 4:743
Brazziel, W. F.: 42
Bridge, L.: 33
Brown, M. N.: 18–9, 24
Brown, W. E.: 8
Cassel, R. N.: 12, 45
Christensen, L.: 67
Clark, J. V.: 60
Congdon, R. G.: 40
Dressel, P.: 40
Dulsky, S. G.: *rev,* 3:643
Dunn, F. E.: 46
Eastman, F.: 1
Fauquier, W.: 2
Ferson, R. F.: 25
Freedman, S.: 61
George, C. E.: 36
Gilberg, R. L.: 37
Glaser, R.: 9
Helton, W. B.: 50
Hendsch, G.: 45
Hutson, B. T.: 47
Irwin, I. A.: 13–4
Jackson, A. M.: 69
Jacobs, R.: 20
Jervis, F. M.: 40
Johnson, R. H.: 23
Katz, M.: *rev,* 5:864

Kingston, A. J.: 36
Klugman, S. F.: 51
Kropp, R. P.: 53
Layton, W. L.: *rev,* 5:864
LeUnes, A.: 67
Lien, A. J.: 27
Lindgren, H. C.: 3, 37
MacKinney, A. C.: 44
MacPhail, A. H.: 28, 34
Malcolm, D. D.: 5, 15
Marsden, R. D.: 57
Masten, F. D.: 29
Mazurek, F. H.: 62
Miller, C. H.: 16
Morris, R. P.: 52
Morson, M.: 33
Nadel, R. S.: 63
Nair, R. K.: 17
Nash, P. G.: 41
Nicholson, E.: 68
Price, T. H.: 58
Prideaux, G. G.: 22
Ramey, W. S.: 39
Roeber, E. C.: 7, 10
Schiff, H. M.: 32
Sherman, L. L.: 64
Shierson, H. E.: 2
Singer, S. L.: 35
Smith, J. A.: 41
Stahmann, R. F.: 59, 65–6
Stefflre, B.: 4, 35, 38
Stoker, H. W.: 53
Stratton, H. B.: 54
Super, D. E.: 11
Swanson, R. A.: 49
Thompson, G. R.: 28
Torr, D. V.: 30

Vaccaro, J. J.: 26
Vincent, N. M.: 47
Weaver, S. J.: 43

Wolins, L.: 44
Woodward, C. L.: 31
Zeleny, M. P.: 32

[2200]

Occupational Interest Survey (With Pictures): Individual Placement Series. Industrial applicants and employees; 1959–66; OIS; 9 scores: scientific, social service, literary, agricultural, business, mechanical, musical, clerical, artistic; J. H. Norman; Personnel Research Associates, Inc. *

For additional information and reviews by Robert H. Dolliver and David O. Herman, see 7:1028.

[2201]

*****Ohio Vocational Interest Survey.** Grades 8–12; 1969–72; OVIS; 24 scores: manual work, machine work, personal services, caring for people or animals, clerical work, inspecting and testing, crafts and precise operations, customer services, nursing and related technical services, skilled personal services, training, literary, numerical, appraisal, agriculture, applied technology, promotion and communication, management and supervision, artistic, sales representative, music, entertainment and performing arts, teaching-counseling-social work, medical; Ayres G. D'Costa, David W. Winefordner, John G. Odgers, and Paul B. Koons, Jr.; Harcourt Brace Jovanovich, Inc. *

For additional information and reviews by Thomas T. Frantz and John W. M. Rothney, see 7:1029 (4 references).

REFERENCES THROUGH 1971

1–4. See 7:1029.

5. FERENCE, CAMILLE. *Prediction of Creativity by Means of Interest Measures.* Doctor's thesis, Ohio State University (Columbus, Ohio), 1971. (*DAI* 32:3685A)

6. HOUSLEY, WARREN FRANK. *The Narrowing Process of Vocational Decision-Making as a Function of Rejecting Attitudes.* Doctor's thesis, University of Arkansas (Fayetteville, Ark.), 1971. (*DAI* 32:2418A)

7. KARLSON, LARRY AXEL. *A Comparison of Vocational Interests of High School Juniors With Projected Manpower Needs.* Doctor's thesis, Washington State University (Pullman, Wash.), 1971. (*DAI* 32:2420A)

CUMULATIVE NAME INDEX

D'Costa, A.: 2
D'Costa, A. G. J. E.: 1
Ference, C.: 5
Frantz, T. T.: *rev,* 7:1029
Housley, W. F.: 6
Karlson, L. A.: 7

Morrison, J. S.: 3
Rothney, J. W. M.: *rev,* 7:1029
Winefordner, D.: 2
Winefordner, D. W.: 4

[2202]

Phillips Occupational Preference Scale. Ages 14 and over; 1959–65; POPS; 10 scores: clerical, computational, practical, scientific, mechanical (males), medical (females), persuasive, social service, literary, artistic, outdoor; G. R. Phillips; Australian Council for Educational Research [Australia]. *

For additional information, see 7:1030.

[2203]

Pictorial Interest Inventory. Adult males, particularly poor readers and nonreaders; 1959; for research use only; 11 scores: clerical and sales, personal service, protective and custodial, farming, mechanical, building and maintenance, skilled-sedentary, vehicle operators, electrical workers, natural processors, assembly line workers; Barron B. Scarborough; the Author. *

REFERENCES THROUGH 1971

1. YOUNG, G. W. *Preliminary Standardization of an Interest Inventory for Use in a Correctional Institution.* Master's thesis, Florida State University (Tallahassee, Fla.), 1961.

2. SCARBOROUGH, B. B. "Measurement of Interest With Pictures." *Percept & Motor Skills* 15:122 Ag '62. * (*PA* 37:4994)

3. CHANSKY, NORMAN M. "Race, Aptitude and Vocational

Interests." *Personnel & Guid J* 43:780–4 Ap '65. * (*PA* 39:16499)

4. ZURICK, GEORGE T. *The Relationship of the Pictorial Test of Intelligence With Reading Achievement.* Master's thesis, Pennsylvania State University (University Park, Pa.), 1968.

CUMULATIVE NAME INDEX

Chansky, N. M.: 3   Young, G. W.: 1
Scarborough, B. B.: 2   Zurick, G. T.: 4

[2204]

★**Pictorial Inventory of Careers.** Grades 3–14 and disadvantaged adults; 1972; PIC; developmental edition called *Pictorial Inventory of Occupational Training Interest;* 21 scores: agriculture, business and office (data processing, secretarial), communications (fine arts, media), criminal justice, electrical/electronics, engineering technology (applied, civil/drafting), environmental and natural resources, health services, home economics and food service, mid-management and supervision, science and laboratory, service (air transportation, fire science, personal, public), trade and industry construction, mechanics, metal trades; slide projector necessary for administration; Tom Kosuth and Earl Clancy; Educators Assistance Institute. *

[2205]

Picture Interest Inventory. Grades 7 and over; 1958; PII; 9 scores: interpersonal service, natural, mechanical, business, esthetic, scientific, verbal, computational, time perspective; Kurt P. Weingarten; CTB/McGraw-Hill. *

For additional information, reviews by Ralph F. Berdie and Donald E. Super, and an excerpted review by Laurence Siegel, see 6:1066 (4 references).

REFERENCES THROUGH 1971

1–4. See 6:1066.
5–6. HOUSTON, LAWRENCE N. "Vocational Interest Patterns of Institutionalized Youthful Offenders as Measured by a Nonverbal Inventory." *J Clin Psychol* 21:213–4 Ap '65. * (*PA* 39:12778)
7. BLAKE, RICHARD HALEY. *A Comparison of the Test-Retest Reliability of Picture and Verbal Forms of Occupational Interest Inventories.* Doctor's thesis, University of Missouri (Columbia, Mo.), 1966. (*DA* 27:2868A)
8. CHANSKY, NORMAN M. "Sex Differences and the Picture Interest Inventory." *Voc Guid Q* 15:71–4 S '66. *
9. CHANSKY, NORMAN M. "Work-Oriented Interest Scales." *Percept & Motor Skills* 23:1189–90 D '66. * (*PA* 41:5256)
10. MIHALKA, JOSEPH ALEXANDER. *Interests and the Disadvantaged.* Master's thesis, Ohio State University (Columbus, Ohio), 1966.
11. BLAKE, RICHARD. "Comparative Reliability of Picture Form and Verbal Form Interest Inventories." *J Appl Psychol* 53(1):42–4 F '69. * (*PA* 43:7416)
12. RAVENSBORG, MILTON R. "Psychiatric Technicians' Ranking of Five Potential Employment Screening Tests." *Personnel J* 48(1):39–41 Ja '69. * (*PA* 44:2910)

CUMULATIVE NAME INDEX

Berdie, R. F.: *rev,* 6:1066   Houston, L. N.: 4–5
Blake, R.: 11   Mihalka, J. A.: 10
Blake, R. H.: 7   Ravensborg, M. R.: 12
Cassel, R. N.: 3   Siegel, L.: *exc,* 6:1066
Chansky, N. M.: 8–9   Super, D. E.: *rev,* 6:1066
Hendsch, G.: 3   Weingarten, K. P.: 1–2

[2206-7]

Preference Analysis. Standards 8 and over; 1968–69; PA; 11 or 13 scores: adventurous, outdoors, clerical, domestic-decorative (females only), domestic routine (females only), fine arts and music, natural sciences, persuasion, social sciences, technical, altruistic, verbal, mathematical interest; P. Lourens; National Institute for Personnel Research [South Africa]. *

For additional information, see 7:1031.

[2208]

Rothwell-Miller Interest Blank. Ages 13 and over; 1958; RMIB; formerly called *Rothwell Interest Blank, Miller Revision;* 12 scores: outdoor, mechanical, computational, scientific, personal contact, aesthetic, literary, musical, social service, clerical, practical, medical; Kenneth M. Miller and J. W. Rothwell; Australian Council for Educational Research [Australia]. *

For additional information, see 5:867.

[2209]

Rothwell-Miller Interest Blank, [British Edition]. Ages 11 and over; 1958–68; British adaptation of original Australian edition; 12 scores: outdoor, mechanical, computational, scientific, persuasive, aesthetic, literary, musical, social service, clerical, practical, medical; original test by J. W. Rothwell; 1958 and 1968 revisions by Kenneth M. Miller; NFER Publishing Co. Ltd. [England]. *

For additional information and reviews by A. W. Heim and Clive Jones, see 7:1034 (2 references).

REFERENCES THROUGH 1971

1–2. See 7:1034.

CUMULATIVE NAME INDEX

Heim, A. W.: *rev,* 7:1034   Miller, K. M.: 1
Jones, C.: *rev,* 7:1034   Nelson, D. M.: 2

[2210]

Safran Student's Interest Inventory. Grades 8–12; 1960–69; SSII; revision of *Safran Vocational Interest Test;* 11 scores: 7 interest scores (economic, technical, outdoor, service, humane, artistic, scientific) and 4 ability self-ratings (academic, mechanical, social, clerical); Carl Safran and Edgar N. Wright; Thomas Nelson & Sons (Canada) Ltd. [Canada]. *

For additional information and a review by Thomas T. Frantz, see 7:1035; see also 6:1069 (1 reference).

REFERENCES THROUGH 1971

1. See 6:1069.

CUMULATIVE NAME INDEX

Frantz, T. T.: *rev,* 7:1035   Stewart, J. A.: 1
Safran, C.: 1

[2211]

★**The Self Directed Search: A Guide to Educational and Vocational Planning.** High school and college and adults; 1970–73; SDS; "a self-administered, self-scored, and self-interpreted vocational counseling tool"; 18 scores: 6 scores (realistic, investigative, artistic, social, enterprising, conventional) for each of 3 scales (activities, competencies, occupations); John L. Holland; Consulting Psychologists Press, Inc. *

REFERENCES THROUGH 1971

1. HOLLAND, JOHN L. "A Theory-Ridden, Computerless, Impersonal Vocational Guidance System." *J Voc Behav* 1(2):167–76 Ap '71. * (*PA* 47:11854)

CUMULATIVE NAME INDEX

Holland, J. L.: 1

[2212]

Strong Vocational Interest Blank for Men. Ages 16 and over; 1927–71; SVIB; 84 scoring scales (22 basic interests, 54 occupational, 8 nonoccupational) and 6 administrative indices; BASIC INTERESTS: adventure ('69), agriculture ('69), art ('69), business management ('69), law/politics ('69), mathematics ('69), mechanical ('69), medical service ('69), merchandising ('69), military activities ('69), music ('69), nature ('69), office practices ('69), public speaking ('69), recreational leadership ('69), religious activities ('69), sales ('69), science ('69), social service ('69), teaching ('69), technical supervision ('69), writing ('69); OCCUPATIONAL: *group 1, biological science:* dentist ('32–66), osteopath ('47–66), veterinarian ('49–66, original scale by T. E. Hannum), physician ('28–66), psychiatrist ('52–66), psychologist ('28–66, original scale by

P. H. Kriedt), biologist ('62–66, original scale by Carl A. Lindsay, Louis M. Herman, and Martin L. Ziegler) ; *group 2, physical science:* architect ('28–66), mathematician ('30–66), physicist ('30–66), chemist ('28–66), engineer ('28–66) ; *group 3, technical supervision:* production manager ('38–66), army officer ('52–66), air force officer ('66) ; *group 4, technical and skilled trades:* carpenter ('33–66), forest serviceman ('38–66), farmer ('28–66), math-science teacher ('38–66), printer ('38–66), policeman ('34–66) ; *group 5, social service:* personnel director ('28–66), public administrator ('44–66), rehabilitation counselor ('50–66, original scale entitled vocational counselor by Nathan E. Acree), YMCA secretary ('28–66), social worker ('54–66), social science teacher ('38–66), school superintendent ('30–66), minister ('28–66) ; *group 6, aesthetic-cultural:* librarian ('63–66), artist ('33–66), musician performer ('33–66), music teacher ('54–66) ; *group 7, CPA owner:* CPA owner ('49–66) ; *group 8, business and accounting:* senior CPA ('49–66), accountant ('32–66), office worker ('30–66), purchasing agent ('28–66), banker ('38–66), pharmacist ('49–66, original scale by Milton Schwebel), mortician ('46–66) ; *group 9, sales:* sales manager ('38–66), real estate salesman ('28–66), life insurance salesman ('28–66) ; *group 10, verbal-linguistic:* advertising man ('28–66), lawyer ('28–66), author-journalist ('28–66) ; *group 11, president, manufacturing concern:* president, manufacturing ('38–66) ; *group 12, supplementary occupational:* credit manager ('59–66), chamber of commerce executive ('62–66), physical therapist ('58–66), computer programmer ('66), business education teacher ('59–66, original scale by Robert V. Bacon), community recreation administrator ('66) ; NONOCCUPATIONAL: academic achievement ('66), age related interests ('69), diversity of interests ('69), masculinity-femininity II ('34–69), managerial orientation ('69), occupational introversion-extroversion ('66), occupational level ('39–66), specialization level ('52–66, original scale by Milton G. Holmen) ; ADMINISTRATIVE INDICES : total responses ('69), unpopular responses ('69), form check ('69), like percentage ('69), indifferent percentage ('69), dislike percentage ('69) ; Edward K. Strong, Jr. (except 1969 supplement), David P. Campbell, Ralph F. Berdie (1966 test), and Kenneth E. Clark (1966 test) ; Stanford University Press. *

For additional information, reviews by Martin R. Katz and Charles J. Krauskopf, and excerpted reviews by David P. Campbell and John W. M. Rothney, see 7:1036 (485 references) ; for reviews by Alexander W. Astin and Edward J. Furst of earlier editions, see 6:1070 (189 references) ; see also 5:868 (153 references) ; for reviews by Edward S. Bordin and Elmer D. Hinckley, see 4:747 (98 references) ; see also 3:647 (102 references) ; for reviews by Harold D. Carter, John G. Darley, and N. W. Morton, see 2:1680 (71 references) ; for a review by John G. Darley, see 1:1178. For excerpts from related book reviews, see 7:B127 (1 excerpt), 6:B304 (2 excerpts), 6:B305 (2 excerpts), 5:B115 (5 excerpts), 5:B414 (4 excerpts), 4:748 (2 excerpts), 3:648 (2 excerpts), 3:650 (1 excerpt), and 3:652 (11 excerpts).

REFERENCES THROUGH 1971

1–71. See 2:1680.
72–175. See 3:647.
176–273. See 4:747.
274–426. See 5:868.
427–614. See 6:1070.
615–1099. See 7:1036.
1100. OLIVER, R. A. C. "The Traits of Extroverts and Introverts." *J Social Psychol* 1:345–66 Ag '30. * (*PA* 5:308)
1101. ROSENSTEIN, ISABEL. *The Vocational Interests of Freshmen Engineers and the Development of a Short Method for*

Scoring Strong's Vocational Interest Test. Master's thesis, University of Minnesota (Minneapolis, Minn.), 1930.
1102. ALLEN, GRACE E. "Plane Geometry and Character Education." *J Ed Sociol* 7:254–8 D '33. * (*PA* 8:2254)
1103. SEGEL, DAVID. "Differential Prediction of Scholastic Success." *Sch & Soc* 39:91–6 Ja 20 '34. *
1104. DYER, DOROTHY TUNELL. *The Relation Between Vocational Interests of Men in College and Their Subsequent Occupational Histories for Ten Years.* Master's thesis, University of Minnesota (Minneapolis, Minn.), 1937.
1105. FINCH, F. H., AND ODOROFF, M. E. "Sex Differences in Vocational Interests." *J Ed Psychol* 30:151–6 F '39. * (*PA* 13:4353)
1106. THOMSON, WILLIAM A. "An Inventory for Measuring Socialization—Self-Seeking and Its Relationship to the Study of Values Test, the ACE Psychological Examination, and the Strong Vocational Interest Blank." *J Appl Psychol* 25:202–12 Ap '41. * (*PA* 15:4285)
1107. ARSENIAN, SETH. "Own Estimate and Objective Measurement." *J Ed Psychol* 33:291–302 Ap '42. * (*PA* 17:934)
1108. SPOERL, DOROTHY TILDEN. "The Academic and Verbal Adjustment of College Age Bilingual Students." *J Genetic Psychol* 64:139–57 Mr '44. * (*PA* 18:2275)
1109. TODD, J. E. "Measurement in the Continuous Selection and Counseling of Students in a College of Physical Education and Social Work." *Ed & Psychol Meas* 4:233–43 au '44. * (*PA* 19:1810)
1110. FRANDSEN, ARDEN. "Appraisal of Interests in Guidance." *J Ed Res* 39:1–12 S '45. * (*PA* 20:555)
1111. GORY, ADRIAN E., AND McCLELLAND, DAVID C. "Characteristics of Conscientious Objectors in World War II." *J Consult Psychol* 11:245–57 S–O '47. * (*PA* 22:604)
1112. GUEST, LESTER. "A Study of Interviewer Competence." *Int J Opin & Attitude Res* (Mexico) 1:17–30 S '47. * (*PA* 22:4361)
1113. TERMAN, LEWIS M., AND OGDEN, MELITA H. Chap. 15, "Vocational Interests Tests," pp. 196–203. In their *Genetic Studies of Genius: Vol. 4, The Gifted Child Grows Up.* Stanford, Calif.: Stanford University Press, 1947. Pp. xiv, 448. *
1114. COTTLE, WM. C. "A Factorial Study of the Multiphasic, Strong, Kuder, and Bell Inventories Using a Population of Adult Males." *Psychometrika* 15:25–47 Mr '50. * (*PA* 24:4492)
1115. ADAMSON, DERYCK. "Selection and Appraisal of Engineering Graduates: A Case Study." *Personnel* 29:175–93 S '52. * (*PA* 27:3797)
1116. SHAW, JACK. "The Function of the Interview in Determining Fitness for Teacher-Training." *J Ed Res* 45:667–81 My '52. * (*PA* 27:3007)
1117. McCORNACK, ROBERT, AND KIDNEIGH, JOHN C. "The Vocational Interest Patterns of Social Workers." *Social Work J* 35:160–3 O '54. * (*PA* 29:6448)
1118. CROSS, THEODORE RYLAND. *An Exploratory Investigation of the Personality and Background Factors Characterizing Entering College Men Who Possess a Low Intensity of Vocational Interests.* Doctor's thesis, University of Minnesota (Minneapolis, Minn.), 1955. (*DA* 15:2467)
1119. PERSON, GERALD ALTON. *A Comparative Study of University of Minnesota Physical Education Graduates Employed in Related Occupations and Those in Other Vocations.* Doctor's thesis, University of Minnesota (Minneapolis, Minn.), 1955. (*DA* 16:705)
1120. GOSWITZ, CHARLES R. *An Evaluation of the Simplified Method for Scoring the Strong Vocational Interest Blank.* Master's thesis, University of Arizona (Tucson, Ariz.), 1956.
1121. JONES, ROBERT L. "A Psychometric Study of Minnesota Industrial Editors." *Journalism Q* 34:253–5 sp '57. * (*PA* 32:5616)
1122. YESLIN, ARTHUR R.; VERNON, LEROY N.; AND KERR, WILLARD A. "The Significance of Time Spent in Answering Personality Inventories." *J Appl Psychol* 42:264–6 Ag '58. * (*PA* 33:9369)
1123. WHERRY, ROBERT J. "An Evaluative and Diagnostic Forced-Choice Rating Scale for Servicemen." *Personnel Psychol* 12:227–36 su '59. * (*PA* 34:3632)
1124. HANNUM, THOMAS E. "Correlates of Achievement in a Veterinary Medicine Curriculum." *Proc Iowa Acad Sci* 67:459–62 '60. *
1125. HERMAN, LOUIS M., AND ZEIGLER, MARTIN L. "Comparison of Academic Achievement, Aptitudes, and Interest Patterns of Two-Year Technical Students and Four-Year Degree Candidates in Engineering." *J Exp Ed* 29:81–7 S '60. * (*PA* 36:2KL81H)
1126. SHEEHAN, JOSEPH G.; HADLEY, ROBERT G.; AND WHITE, GERALD R. "The Speech Pathologist: His Interests, Activities and Attitudes." *J Speech & Hearing Disorders* 25:317–22 N '60. * (*PA* 35:3762)
1127. SHNEIDMAN, EDWIN S. "The Case of El: Psychological Test Data." *J Proj Tech* 25:131–54 Je '61. * (*PA* 36:21K31S)
1128. MARKS, EDMOND; VAIRO, JOHN D.; AND ZEIGLER, MARTIN L. "Scholastic Aptitudes, Vocational Interests, and Personality Characteristics of Journalism Students." *J Ed Res* 56:37–40 S '62. *
1129. GOSNEY, CHARLES ALAN. *Vocational Interest Patterns of Indiana County Agricultural Extension Agents.* Master's thesis, Purdue University (Lafayette, Ind.), 1963.

Strong Vocational Interest Blank for Men

1130. GOTTERER, MALCOLM, AND STALNAKER, ASHFORD W. "Predicting Programmer Performance Among Non-Preselected Trainee Groups." *Proc Ann Conf Computer Personnel Group* 2:29–44 '64. *

1131. CANNON, W. M. "Toward A New Vocational Interest Scale for Computer Programmers—A Procedural Report." *Proc Ann Computer Personnel Res Conf* 3:60–7 '65. *

1132. HEATH, DOUGLAS H.; WITH THE ASSISTANCE OF HARRIET E. HEATH. *Explorations of Maturity: Studies of Mature and Immature College Men.* New York: Appleton-Century-Crofts, 1965. Pp. xv, 423. * (*PA* 39:12057)

1133. PERRY, DALLIS K., AND CANNON, WILLIAM M. *Heterogeneous Key Development: Vocational Interests of Computer Programmers.* Technical Memorandum TM-2655/003/33. Santa Monica, Calif.: System Development Corporation, 1965. Pp. 11. *

1134. RYDEN, E. R. "Predicting Successful Performance." *J Coop Exten* 3:103–9 su '65. *

1135. BERDIE, RALPH F., AND STEIN, JUNE. "A Comparison of New University Students Who Do and Do Not Seek Counseling." *J Counsel Psychol* 13:310–7 f '66. * (*PA* 40:12631)

1136. CANNON, WILLIAM M., AND PERRY, DALLIS K. "A Vocational Interest Scale for Computer Programmers." *Proc Ann Computer Personnel Res Conf* 4:61–82 '66. *

1137. MILLER, ADAM W., JR. "Proposals for Interest Test Development and Experimentation." *Personnel & Guid J* 45: 231–7 N '66. *

1138. PERRY, DALLIS K., AND CANNON, WILLIAM M. *Relationships Among Programmers' Background and Interest Characteristics: Vocational Interests of Computer Programmers.* Technical Memorandum TM-2655/004/00. Santa Monica, Calif.: System Development Corporation, 1966. Pp. 33. *

1139. PERRY, DALLIS K., AND CANNON, WILLIAM M. *Vocational Interests of Female Computer Programmers.* Technical Memorandum TM-2655/005/00. Santa Monica, Calif.: System Development Corporation, 1966. Pp. 22. *

1140. DEB, MAYA. "Interest Patterns of High Achievers in Natural Science Course." *Indian J Psychol* 42(1–4):97–100 '67. *

1141. MAYER, DAVID B., AND STALNAKER, ASHFORD W. "Computer Personnel Research—Issues and Progress in the 60's." *Proc Ann Computer Personnel Res Conf* 5:6–41 '67. *

1142. TILLMAN, CARROLL ALTON. *Interest Patterns of Industrial Engineers as Measured by the Strong Vocational Interest Blank.* Master's thesis, Sacramento State College (Sacramento, Calif.), 1967.

1143. AMICUCCI, EDWARD. *Masculinity Interest in High School Athletes.* Master's thesis, Allegheny College (Meadville, Pa.), 1968.

1144. ATHELSTAN, GARY T. *The Vocational Interests, Values, and Career Development of Specialists in Physical Medicine and Rehabilitation.* CEPM&R Bulletin 9. Minneapolis, Minn.: Commission on Education in Physical Medicine and Rehabilitation, 1968. Pp. vii, 63. *

1145. BERGER, RAYMOND M. "Selection of Systems Analysts and Programmer Trainees." *Proc Ann Computer Personnel Res Conf* 6:44–63 '68. *

1146. MALONE, JAMES H. *Interests and Effectiveness of Residence Hall Counselors.* Master's thesis, Kent State University (Kent, Ohio), 1968.

1147. CAMPBELL, DAVID. "A Psychological Profile of the Money Manager." *Institutional Investor* 3(9):29–36 S '69. *

1148. McCUNE, CORNELIA D., AND RAUSCH, VERNA L. "Vocational Interests of Pre-Medical Technology Students." *Am J Med Technol* 35(10):634–51 O '69. *

1149. SLIVINSKI, L. W., AND DESBIENS, B. "Interests of Managers in the Canadian Public Service." *Studies Personnel Psychol* 1(2):93–120 O '69. *

1150. WILEY, NANCY NEWELL. *A Comparison of Certain Personality Traits and Academic Performance in Freshman Students Who Do and Do Not Seek Counseling.* Master's thesis, Southern Methodist University (Dallas, Tex.), 1969.

1151. ANDERSON, RICHARD J. "Stability of Student Interests in General Psychology." *Am Psychologist* 25(7):630–2 Jl '70. * (*PA* 45:1365)

1152. BALLOU, SUSAN I.; ALSIP, JONATHAN E.; AND HANNUM, THOMAS E. "A Longitudinal Study of the Interests of Veterinarians." *Proc Iowa Acad Sci* 77:322–30 '70. *

1153. BIEDENKAPP, MILDRED SPIER. *Measured Masculinity and Related Variables of a Group of Male Elementary School Educators.* Doctor's thesis, University of Maryland (College Park, Md.), 1970. (*DAI* 31:4375A)

1154. BRASINGTON, CHOLTON REGINALD. *Comparison of the Predictive Validity of the SVIB With Achievement and Aptitude Variables for University of South Carolina Freshman Males.* Doctor's thesis, University of South Carolina (Columbia, S.C.), 1970. (*DAI* 31:5117A)

1155. CARROLL, DELBERT L. *An Investigation of the Relationship Between Undergraduate GPA and High and Low Scorers on the Specialization Level Scale of the Strong Vocational Interest Blank Among Male Psychology Majors at East Tennessee State University.* Master's thesis, East Tennessee State University (Johnson City, Tenn.), 1970.

1156. CASSON, ABRAHAM MORTIMER. *The Negro Law Student: His Childhood Experience, Vocational Interests and Professional Concerns.* Doctor's thesis, University of Michigan (Ann Arbor, Mich.), 1970. (*DAI* 31:7590B)

1157. FLOM, PENELOPE KEGEL. *Performance in the Medical Internship.* Doctor's thesis, University of California (Berkeley, Calif.), 1970. (*DAI* 32:1188B)

1158. FOSTER, JAMES ANDREW. *An Exploratory Study of Holland's Theory of Vocational Choice and Rotter's Social Learning Theory.* Doctor's thesis, University of North Dakota (Grand Forks, N.D.), 1970. (*DAI* 31:4458A)

1159. GERSTEIN, OFFRA BILHA. *The Relationship Between Perception of Parental Behavior, Level of Dependency, and Vocational Interest Pattern in Hemophilic Young Adults.* Doctor's thesis, New York University (New York, N.Y.), 1970. (*DAI* 31:6401A)

1160. HANSON, GARY RANDALL. *Empirical Exploration of the Correlates of Academic Predictability.* Doctor's thesis, University of Minnesota (Minneapolis, Minn.), 1970. (*DAI* 32:177A)

1161. HARRINGTON, CHARLES CHRISTOPHER. *Errors in Sex-Role Behavior in Teen-Age Boys.* New York: Teachers College Press, 1970. Pp. viii, 109. * (*PA* 44:21190, title only)

1162. HOLLAND, PAUL LAVERNE. *A Study of Factors Predictive of Persistence in the Parish Ministry of United Presbyterian Clergymen.* Doctor's thesis, University of Illinois (Urbana, Ill.), 1970. (*DAI* 31:6426A)

1163. IM, IN JAE. *A Multivariate Analysis of the Relationship of Academic, Personality, and Family Background Variables to the Different Patterns of Collegiate Attendance.* Doctor's thesis, University of Minnesota (Minneapolis, Minn.), 1970. (*DAI* 32:240A)

1164. IRWIN, TOM JAY. *An Investigation of the Expression of Empathy of A and B Therapists in a Quasi-Therapeutic Encounter.* Doctor's thesis, University of Missouri (Columbia, Mo.), 1970. (*DAI* 31:5128A)

1165. JOHNSON, JAMES CLIFTON. *Differences in the Vocational Interests of Engineers Engaged in Research, Development, Production, and Sales Functions.* Doctor's thesis, University of Minnesota (Minneapolis, Minn.), 1970. (*DAI* 31:5687B)

1166. LEE, DAVID LAWRENCE. *Selected Interest Factors Related to Academic Achievement at the University of North Dakota.* Doctor's thesis, University of North Dakota (Grand Forks, N.D.), 1970. (*DAI* 32:6762A)

1167. LEON, HERMAN. *Factors Predictive of Successful Educational Performance in Social Work School.* Doctor's thesis, Columbia University (New York, N.Y.), 1970. (*DAI* 31:6724A)

1168. LIBBY, BRUCE C. *The AB Dimension in a Counseling Analogue.* Doctor's thesis, University of Minnesota (Minneapolis, Minn.), 1970. (*DAI* 31:6262B)

1169. McARTHUR, CHARLES. "Vocational Guidance in the Ivy League," pp. 111–23. *Int Psychiatric Clinic* 7(3):83–131 '70. *

1170. MORRIS, J. L., AND PARKINSON, M. "Vocational Interests of Computer Programmers." *Austral Computer J* 2(3):139–42 Ag '70. *

1171. NAOR, NEHAMA KLIBAN. *Configurational Analysis of the Strong Vocational Interest Blank (SVIB) and Concomitant Personality Correlates.* Doctor's thesis, University of North Carolina (Chapel Hill, N.C.), 1970. (*DAI* 31:6908B)

1172. QUIRING, RICHARD G. *The A.A.C.H. Scale on the Strong Vocational Interest Blank.* Master's thesis, Fresno State College (Fresno, Calif.), 1970.

1173. SCHILLINGER, MORTON. *Cotherapist Value Similarity as a Determinant of Combined Therapy Outcome.* Doctor's thesis, New York University (New York, N.Y.), 1970. (*DAI* 31:7612B)

1174. SCHULZETENBERGE, ANTHONY C. *Interests and Background Variables Characterizing Secondary School Librarians Who Work With Teachers in Curriculum Development and Improvement of Instruction.* Doctor's thesis, University of North Dakota (Grand Forks, N.D.), 1970. (*DAI* 32:7019A)

1175. STEPHENSON, PATRICIA M. *The Relationship of Personality Congruence and Achievement Profile to Upper-Division Change of Major.* Doctor's thesis, Florida State University (Tallahassee, Fla.), 1970. (*DAI* 31:4497A)

1176. THOMAS, CAROLINE BEDELL; FARGO, ROGER; AND ENSLEIN, KURT. "Personality Characteristics of Medical Students as Reflected by the Strong Vocational Interest Test With Special Reference to Smoking Habits." *Johns Hopkins Med J* 127(6): 323–35 D '70. *

1177. WARD, WILLIAM P. *A Study of the Interests of the Priests of Diocese of Scranton Using the Strong Vocational Interest Blank and Catholic Priest Scale.* Master's thesis, University of Scranton (Scranton, Pa.), 1970.

1178. WILLOUGHBY, THEODORE C. "Needs, Interests, and Reinforcer Preferences of Data Processing Personnel." *Proc Ann Computer Personnel Res Conf* 8:119–43 '70. *

1179. ABRAHAMS, N. M.; NEUMANN, IDELL; AND GITHENS, W. H. "Faking Vocational Interests: Simulated Versus Real Life Motivation." *Personnel Psychol* 24(1):5–12 sp '71. * (*PA* 47:3671)

1180. ANDERSON, SUSAN C., AND APOSTAL, ROBERT A. "Occupational Introversion-Extroversion and Size of Hometown." *Voc Guid Q* 20(2):138–40 D '71. *

1181. ATHELSTAN, GARY T., AND PAUL, GERALD J. "New Approach to the Prediction of Medical Specialization: Student-Based Strong Vocational Interest Blank Scales." *J Appl Psychol* 55(1):80–6 F '71. * (*PA* 46:1249)

1182. BAILEY, ROGER L. "Testing Holland's Theory." *Meas & Eval Guid* 4(2):107–14 Jl '71. *

1183. BENJAMIN, DARRELL R. "On Engineers' Interest Patterns." Letter. *Meas & Eval Guid* 4(2):69 Jl '71. *

1184. BENTON, ARTHUR LOUIS. *The Inventoried Interests of Cartographers.* Doctor's thesis, American University (Washington, D.C.), 1971. (*DAI* 32:6093B)

1185. BORGEN, FRED H. "Predicting Career Choices of Able College Men From Occupational and Basic Interest Scales of the SVIB." *NMSC Res Rep* 7(9):1–14 '71. * (*PA* 47:5870)

1186. CAMPBELL, DAVID P. "Admissions Policies: Side Effects and Their Implications." *Am Psychologist* 26(7):636–47 Jl '71. * (*PA* 47:11560)

1187. CHARTIER, GEORGE M. "A-B Therapist Variable: Real or Imagined?" *Psychol B* 75(1):22–33 Ja '71. * (*PA* 45:8313)

1188. CLAR, PHILIP NORMAN. *The Relationship of Psychological Differentiation to Client Behavior in Vocational Choice Counseling.* Doctor's thesis, University of Michigan (Ann Arbor, Mich.), 1971. (*DAI* 32:1837B)

1189. COLE, NANCY S., AND HANSON, GARY R. "An Analysis of the Structure of Vocational Interests." *ACT Res Rep* 40:1–17 Ja '71. * (*PA* 47:1843)

1190. COLE, NANCY S., AND HANSON, GARY R. "An Analysis of the Structure of Vocational Interests." *J Counsel Psychol* 18(5):478–86 S '71. * (*PA* 47:3679)

1191. COLLINS, JAMES AMBROSE. *A Configural Approach to the Strong Vocational Interest Blank.* Doctor's thesis, University of Minnesota (Minneapolis, Minn.), 1971. (*DAI* 32:2996B)

1192. FERENCE, CAMILLE. *Prediction of Creativity by Means of Interest Measures.* Doctor's thesis, Ohio State University (Columbus, Ohio), 1971. (*DAI* 32:3685A)

1193. FRANK, AUSTIN C. "Men's Strong Vocational Interest Blank Academic Achievement Scale: An Attempted Validation." *J Counsel Psychol* 18(4):324–31 Jl '71. * (*PA* 46:11572)

1194. GANTZ, BENJAMIN S., JR.; ERICKSON, CLARA; AND STEPHENSON, ROBERT W. "Measuring the Motivation to Manage in a Research and Development Population." Abstract. *Proc 79th Ann Conv Am Psychol Assn* 6(1):129–30 '71. * (*PA* 46:3949)

1195. GROSZ, RICHARD D. "Vocational Interests of Freshman Engineering, Business, and Arts and Sciences Students." *Eng Ed* 62(3):297–8 D '71. *

1196. HAAKENSTAD, KENNETH W., AND APOSTAL, ROBERT A. "Acquiescence and Nonoccupational Interests." Abstract. *J Counsel Psychol* 18(5):501–2 S '71. * (*PA* 47:3602)

1197. HAASE, RICHARD F. "Canonical Analysis of the Vocational Preference Inventory and the Strong Vocational Interest Blank." *J Counsel Psychol* 18(2):182–3 Mr '71. * (*PA* 46:1819)

1198. HAGER, PAUL C., AND ELTON, CHARLES F. "The Vocational Interests of Black Males." *J Voc Behav* 1(2):153–8 Ap '71. * (*PA* 47:11701)

1199. HALL, DAVID HENRY. *The Effect of Occupational Information on the Inventoried Interests of Eleventh Grade Boys.* Doctor's thesis, Columbia University (New York, N.Y.), 1971. (*DAI* 32:3682B)

1200. HARRINGTON, THOMAS F.; LYNCH, MERVIN D.; AND O'SHEA, ARTHUR J. "Factor Analysis of Twenty-Seven Similarly Named Scales of the Strong Vocational Interest Blank and the Kuder Occupational Interest Survey, Form DD." *J Counsel Psychol* 18(3):229–33 My '71. * (*PA* 46:5555)

1201. HUGHES, HENRY MICHAEL, JR. *Vocational Choice Level, and Consistency: A Test of Holland's Theory on an Employed Sample.* Doctor's thesis, State University of New York (Albany, N.Y.), 1971. (*DAI* 32:1999A)

1202. HULTGREN, DAYTON DELANO. *Interests and Job Activities of Ministers in a Variety of Preferred Roles.* Doctor's thesis, University of Minnesota (Minneapolis, Minn.), 1971. (*DAI* 32:5038A)

1203. IVERS, KENNETH JOHN. *An Investigation of Holland's (S) Social and (A) Artistic Personality Types With Music and Art Education Majors, and Applied Music and Art Majors.* Doctor's thesis, University of Kansas (Lawrence, Kan.), 1971. (*DAI* 32:1854A)

1204. JACKSON, DOUGLAS N. "The Dynamics of Structured Personality Tests: 1971." *Psychol R* 78(3):229–48 My '71. * (*PA* 46:4995)

1205. JOHANSSON, CHARLES B. "Cognitive Interest Styles of Students." *Meas & Eval Guid* 4(3):176–83 O '71. * (*PA* 49:11957)

1206. JOHANSSON, CHARLES B., AND CAMPBELL, DAVID P. "Stability of the Strong Vocational Interest Blank for Men." *J Appl Psychol* 55(1):34–6 F '71. * (*PA* 46:1925)

1207. JOHANSSON, CHARLES B., AND ROSSMANN, JACK E. "Interest Patterns Among Economists." *J Counsel Psychol* 18(3):255–61 My '71. * (*PA* 46:5827)

1208. JOHANSSON, CHARLES B.; CHAPMAN, CAROL R.; AND CAMPBELL, DAVID P. "College Professors—Their Likes and Dislikes." *Am Psychologist* 26(5):486–8 My '71. * (*PA* 47:3734)

1209. JOHNSON, RICHARD W. "Measurement of Sex and Age Differences on the Strong Vocational Interest Blank for Men." Abstract. *J Counsel Psychol* 18(5):498–500 S '71. * (*PA* 47:3698)

1210. KEMP, DAVID E., AND STEPHENS, JOSEPH H. "Which AB Scale? A Comparative Analysis of Several Versions." *J Nerv & Mental Dis* 152(1):23–30 Ja '71. * (*PA* 46:9381)

1211. KIRK, KENNETH W.; OHVALL, RICHARD A.; AND JOHNSON, RICHARD W. "Vocational Interests of Pharmacy Students." *Am J Pharm Ed* 35(4):564–70 N '71. *

1212. LANTAY, GEORGE CHARLES VON WAGNER. *Academic Underachievement: When It Appears in Male Junior High School Students of Superior Intelligence, Correlates Significantly With Poor Father Identification as Measured by the Strong Vocational Interest Blank.* Master's thesis, University of Illinois (Urbana, Ill.), 1971.

1213. LIPS, ORVILLE JAMES. *An Empirical Test of Hershenson and Roth's Vocational Decision Process Model.* Doctor's thesis, Iowa State University (Ames, Iowa), 1971. (*DAI* 32:4845B)

1214. MIRELS, HERBERT L., AND GARRETT, JAMES B. "The Protestant Ethic as a Personality Variable." *J Consult & Clin Psychol* 36(1):40–4 F '71. * (*PA* 45:9987)

1215. MUSSIO, JERRY J., AND WAHLSTROM, MERLIN W. "Predicting Performance of Programmer Trainees in a Post-High School Setting." Discussion by Charles D. Lothridge. *Proc Ann Computer Personnel Res Conf* 9:26–53 '71. *

1216. NAVRAN, LESLIE, AND KENDALL, LORNE M. "A Canonical Correlational Analysis of the Strong Vocational Interest Blank, the Holland Vocational Preference Inventory, and the Edwards Personal Preference Schedule." *J Counsel Psychol* 18(6):514–9 N '71. * (*PA* 47:7653)

1217. OSTRAND, JANET LOUISE. *Change in Counselor Trainee Personality Variables After Practicum as Measured by the California Psychological Inventory and Subjects Most Amenable to Change According to Interests Measured by the Strong Vocational Interest Blank.* Master's thesis, University of Illinois (Urbana, Ill.), 1971.

1218. PAGE, MARY JEAN. *A Descriptive Analysis of Selected Attitudes, Interests, and Personality Characteristics of Mature College Women.* Doctor's thesis, North Texas State University (Denton, Tex.), 1971. (*DAI* 32:3699A)

1219. RAZIN, ANDREW M. "A-B Variable in Psychotherapy: A Critical Review." *Psychol B* 75(1):1–21 Ja '71. * (*PA* 45:8344)

1220. ROHLF, RICHARD J. "A Higher-Order Alpha Factor Analysis of Interest, Personality, and Ability Variables, Including an Evaluation of the Effect of Scale Interdependency." *Ed & Psychol Meas* 31(2):381–96 su '71. * (*PA* 46:11516)

1221. ROSSMANN, JACK E.; LIPS, ORVILLE J.; AND CAMPBELL, DAVID P. "Vocational Interests of Political Scientists." *J Appl Psychol* 55(2):135–7 Ap '71. * (*PA* 46:3904)

1222. ROTH, NEIL CHARLES. *An Investigation of the Effects of Cognitive Dissonance Upon the Variables: Basic Values, Vocational Interest, and Vocational Choice.* Doctor's thesis, University of Idaho (Moscow, Idaho), 1971. (*DAI* 32:3039A)

1223. SHEPPARD, NATHANIEL ALAN. *Educational-Vocational Decision and Indecision in College Freshmen.* Doctor's thesis, Ohio State University (Columbus, Ohio), 1971. (*DAI* 32:3040A)

1224. SIESS, THOMAS F., AND JACKSON, DOUGLAS N. Chap. 6, "The Personality Research Form and Vocational Interest Research," pp. 109–32. In *Advances in Psychological Assessment, Vol. 2.* Edited by Paul McReynolds. Palo Alto, Calif.: Science and Behavior Books, Inc., 1971. Pp. xii, 395. *

1225. WAGMAN, MORTON. "Clinical and Research Use of the Strong Vocational Interest Blank Academic Achievement Scale." *J Counsel Psychol* 18(4):337–430 Jl '71. * (*PA* 46:11599)

1226. WEINERT, JANE ROSE. *A Factor Analytic Comparison of the Structure of Form M and Form T of the Strong Vocational Interest Blank.* Master's thesis, Boston College (Chestnut Hill, Mass.), 1971.

1227. WELSH, GEORGE S. "Vocational Interests and Intelligence in Gifted Adolescents." *Ed & Psychol Meas* 31(1):155–64 sp '71. * (*PA* 46:10645)

1228. WHITTAKER, DAVID. "The Psychological Adjustment of Intellectual, Nonconformist, Collegiate Dropouts." *Adolescence* 6(24):415–24 w '71. * (*PA* 48:7723)

1229. WIGGINS, JERRY S.; GOLDBERG, LEWIS R.; AND APPELBAUM, MARK. "MMPI Content Scales: Interpretative Norms and Correlations With Other Scales." *J Consult & Clin Psychol* 37(3):403–10 D '71. * (*PA* 47:8950)

1230. WILLOUGHBY, THEODORE CRAWFORD. *Needs, Interests, Reinforcer Patterns and Satisfaction of Data Processing Personnel.* Doctor's thesis, University of Minnesota (Minneapolis, Minn.), 1971. (*DAI* 32:5421A)

1231. WRIGHT, WILBERT. "Vocational and Learning Attitudes of Black Students." *J Col Stud Personnel* 12(4):253–8 Jl '71. * (*PA* 47:7674)

1232. YURA, MICHAEL THOMAS. *The Personality Traits and Vocational Interests of Guidance Students.* Doctor's thesis, Ohio State University (Columbus, Ohio), 1971. (*DAI* 32:3711A)

CUMULATIVE NAME INDEX

Abrahams, N.: 686
Abrahams, N. M.: 724, 827, 965, 1179
Abramowitz, E.: 177
Achard, F. H.: 119, 183
Achilles, P. S.: 27
Ackerman, B. R.: 725
Adams, J. F.: 726
Adamson, D.: 1115
Adinolfi, A. A.: 1042–3

Agee, K. M.: 966
Aldag, J. C.: 1044
Aldag, J. C. K.: 967
Allen, B. V.: 704
Allen, C. L.: 198
Allen, G. E.: 1102
Alsip, J. E.: 773, 1152
Alteneder, L. E.: 89, 92
Althouse, R.: 1017
Amicucci, E.: 1143

Anastasi, A.: 512
Anderson, G. W.: 968
Anderson, H. C.: 138
Anderson, H. E.: 727
Anderson, M. R.: 289
Anderson, R. J.: 1151
Anderson, R. N.: 24
Anderson, S. C.: 1180
Anderson, W.: 675, 828, 894
Anker, J.: 675
Anker, J. M.: 582
Apostal, R. A.: 774, 895, 1180, 1196
Appelbaum, M.: 1229
Arden, W.: 12
Armatas, J. P.: 454, 543
Arsenian, S.: 1107
Ashby, J. D.: 775, 883
Astin, A. W.: 554; rev, 6:1070
Athelstan, G. T.: 776, 1144, 1181
Atkinson, G.: 896
Aylward, M. S.: 390
Bacon, R. V.: 436
Baggaley, A. R.: 897
Bailey, R. L.: 1045, 1182
Ballou, S. I.: 1152
Banas, P. A.: 676
Barnabas, B.: 159, 199
Barnett, G. J.: 240, 290, 318
Barnette, W. L.: 141
Barocas, R.: 898
Barrows, G. A.: 476
Barry, J. R.: 727
Barthol, R. P.: 387
Bates, C. O.: 663
Bauer, R.: 899, 944
Bazik, A. M.: 969
Beamer, G. C.: 186
Bechtel, R. D.: 664
Bednar, R. L.: 1046
Bedrosian, H.: 544, 677
Bellows, R. M.: 103, 115
Bendig, A. W.: 583
Benjamin, D. R.: 829, 1183
Benson, D.: 492
Bentley, J. C.: 1030
Benton, A. L.: 200, 1184
Berdie, R. F.: 66, 120, 142–3, 150–1, 241, 363, 477–8, 716, 728, 900, 1047, 1135
Berg, I. A.: 306
Bergen, G. L.: 38
Berger, R. M.: 1145
Berman, I. R.: 28
Bernstein, A. J.: 319
Bertness, H. J.: 625
Berzins, J. I.: 984, 1048
Betz, B. J.: 511
Bidlake, L. A.: 78
Biedenkapp, M. S.: 1153
Biggs, D. A.: 1049
Bills, M. A.: 43, 50–1, 104, 291, 320
Bingham, W. V. D.: 46
Black, J. D.: 734
Blocher, D. H.: 535
Bluett, C. G.: 156
Bluhm, H.: 635
Blum, L. P.: 187
Bodden, J. L.: 970
Bohn, M. J.: 665, 777–8, 901
Bolin, S. F.: 432a
Bond, G. L.: 278
Bond, P. J.: 647
Bondy, S.: 766
Bondy, S. B.: 819, 879
Bordin, E. S.: 144, 171, 209; rev, 4:747
Borg, W. R.: 242
Borgen, F. H.: 908, 1185
Boyce, E. M.: 627
Boyd, J. B.: 513
Boyd, J. D.: 729
Boyd, R. E.: 971
Braasch, W. F.: 337
Bradfield, A. F.: 243
Bradley, A. D.: 750
Brams, J. M.: 404
Brandt, J. E.: 830–1, 902, 947
Brasington, C. R.: 1154
Braskamp, L. A.: 947

Brayfield, A. H.: 121
Bredemeier, R. A.: 972
Breimeier, K. H.: 832
Bretnall, E. P.: 40
Brewer, B.: 702, 804
Brewer, J. M.: 145
Brintle, S. L.: 32
Bronson, L.: 930
Brown, D. J.: 479
Brown, F. G.: 514, 584, 833
Brown, J. E.: 93
Brown, M. N.: 281, 338
Brown, R. A.: 708, 779
Brown, T. E.: 903
Bruening, J. H.: 834
Bruno, F. B.: 904
Bryan, W. E.: 905
Buck, C. W.: 973, 1050
Burack, B.: 515
Burdock, E. I.: 480
Burgess, E.: 321, 388
Burk, K. W.: 545
Burke, H. R.: 188
Burnham, P. S.: 39, 82, 122
Burton, R. L.: 1051
Buttenwieser, P.: 85
Callahan, D. M.: 561
Callis, R.: 518, 614, 1014; exc, 6:B304
Cameron, A. R.: 730
Campbell, D.: 585, 1147
Campbell, D. P.: 678, 716, 731–2, 780–4, 873, 900, 906–9, 924, 974–6, 1033, 1052, 1099, 1186, 1206, 1208, 1221; exc, 7:1036
Campbell, R. K.: 94
Canning, L.: 105
Canning, L. B.: 106
Cannon, W. M.: 755–6, 870, 950, 1131, 1133, 1136, 1138–9
Carkhuff, R. R.: 586
Carlson, R.: 977
Carlton, S.: 552
Carnes, G. D.: 437, 679
Carroll, D. L.: 1155
Carson, R. C.: 835, 855
Carter, H. D.: 25, 40, 42, 52, 65.1, 76, 105–6, 152; rev, 2:1680; exc, 3:652
Casson, A. M.: 1156
Castor, M.: 803
Cerf, A. Z.: 189
Chaffee, G. A.: 836
Chambers, R. M.: 761
Chaney, F. B.: 656, 680
Chaplin, C. L.: 218
Chapman, C. B.: 1073
Chapman, C. R.: 1208
Chappell, J. S.: 837
Chartier, G. M.: 1187
Cheek, F.: 480
Chille, R. A.: 339
Christensen, D.: 898
Christenson, M.: 978
Cisney, H. N.: 180, 184
Clar, P. N.: 1188
Clark, A. B.: 681, 785
Clark, K. E.: 340, 481, 716
Clark, P. N.: 292
Clarke, F. H.: 183
Clemans, W. V.: 910
Clemens, B.: 1053
Clemens, B. T.: 979, 1054
CoBabe, T. A.: 838
Coblentz, I.: 123
Cofer, C. N.: 203
Coffield, W.: 552
Cohen, D.: 633
Cohen, J.: 811, 885–6
Cohen, T. R.: 839
Cole, N. S.: 1189–90
Collins, C. S.: 364
Collins, J. A.: 1191
Collister, E. G.: 341, 543; exc, 5:B414
Combs, H. T.: 1055
Cooley, W. W.: 587
Cooper, A. C.: 342, 415
Cooper, C. E.: 322
Cordrey, L. J.: 733
Corey, S. M.: exc, 3:652
Cottle, W. C.: 201, 219–21,

244, 343, 911, 1114; exc, 5:B115
Cowdery, K. M.: 1
Cranny, C. J.: 840
Crawford, A. B.: 39
Crissey, O. L.: 98
Crites, J. O.: 433, 455, 482, 546, 576, 588
Croft, L. W.: 53
Croftchik, V. P.: 456
Cronbach, L. J.: 1056
Cross, T. R.: 1118
Crowder, D. G.: 457
Crutchfield, R. S.: 1068–9
Cummings, R. W.: 527, 547, 597
Curtis, J. T.: 1057
Daley, R. F.: 276
D'Arcy, P. F.: 432, 548
Darley, J. G.: 28, 54, 107–8, 365, 483; rev, 2:1680, 1: 1178; exc, 3:652
David, K. H.: 996
Davidson, C. M.: 51
Davis, C. E.: 912
Davis, S. E.: 913
Dawis, R. V.: 880, 958
Dayley, A. J.: 682
Deabler, H. L.: 850–1
Dean, J. W.: 628
Deb, M.: 1140
DeCencio, D. V.: 786
Decker, C. E.: 74
DeGideo, J.: 417
Dekker, J. H.: 683
Denenberg, V. H.: 761
Denison, W. M.: 980
Desbiens, B.: 1149
De Sena, P. A.: 589, 684
Deutsch, S.: 300
Deutscher, J. C.: 787
Dick, W.: 1005
Dick, W. W.: 685, 788
Dicken, C. F.: 734
DiGiorgio, A. J.: 981
Dodd, W. E.: 1058
Dolliver, R. H.: 789, 841, 914–5, 982–3
Domino, G.: 842
Donnenwerth, G. V.: 1009–10
Doppelt, J. E.: 190
Doré, R. L.: 1059
Drake, J. D.: 389
Drasgow, J.: 586
Dreffin, W. B.: 202
Dubin, W.: 634
Dublin, J. E.: 984
DuBois, P. H.: 245, 344
Dubrow, M.: 639
Duda, W. B.: 516
Dunkleberger, C. J.: 517
Dunlap, J. W.: 95, 114, 153, 256
Dunn, D. C.: 1060
Dunnette, M. D.: 390, 405, 416–7, 484, 590, 686, 931
Dunteman, G. H.: 790
Durflinger, G. W.: 591
Dvorak, B.: 73
Dwyer, P. S.: 55
Dyer, D. T.: 65, 1104
Eaddy, M. L.: 549
Eastes, S. H.: 908
Eddy, B.: 1096
Eddy, R. T.: 485
Educational Records Bureau: 29
Eichsteadt, A. C.: 222
Eide, L. J.: 985
Ekblad, R. L.: 916
Elder, D.: 701
Elder, G. H.: 917–8
Elliott, E. S.: 843
Elton, C. F.: 592, 984, 1087, 1198
Engel, I. M.: 550
Engen, H. B.: 986
England, G. W.: 391, 418, 486
Enright, J. B.: 366
Enslein, K.: 1176
Erickson, C.: 1061, 1194
Erickson, P.: 687

Erlandson, F. L.: 323
Escalona, S. K.: 441
Estabrooks, G. H.: 49, 72
Estenson, L. O.: 293
Estes, S. G.: 64
Evans, C. E.: 166
Eyde, L. D.: 532
Fagin, W. B.: 246
Fair, D. C.: 688, 735
Falck, F. E.: 791
Fargo, R.: 1176
Farnsworth, P. R.: 227, 427
Fassett, K. K.: 247
Fast, I.: 991
Faunce, P. S.: 919
Feder, D. D.: 149
Fehrer, E.: 203
Feil, M. H.: 223
Fein, A.: 592
Feist, J.: 689, 792
Ference, C.: 1192
Ferguson, L. W.: 109, 438
Field, L. W.: 345
Fielder, D. W.: 690
Filbeck, R. W.: 458, 518
Finch, F. H.: 83, 1105
Fisher, E. J.: 204
Fisher, S.: 428
Fiske, D. W.: 251, 258
Flanagan, J. C.: exc, 5:B414
Flemming, C. W.: 167
Flemming, E. G.: 167
Flinner, I. A.: 44
Flom, P. K.: 1157
Foreman, M. E.: 666, 987
Forer, B. R.: 519
Formica, L. A.: 439
Forrest, D. V.: 793, 844
Forster, M. C.: 75
Fosshage, J. L.: 920
Foster, J. A.: 1158
Frandsen, A.: 1110
Frank, A. C.: 961, 988, 1062–3, 1193
Frederick, M. L.: 406
Frederiksen, N.: 260, 294, 302, 346, 487, 552, 794
Freeburn, P. P.: 921
Freeman, F. S.: 551
Fresco, R.: 1064
Friedl, F. P.: 429
Frinsko, W.: 657
Fullerton, J. R.: 989
Funkenstein, D. H.: 593
Furst, E. J.: rev, 6:1070
Gahlhoff, P. E.: 990
Galinsky, M. D.: 991
Gamble, A. O.: exc, 5:B414
Gantz, B. S.: 1061, 1194
Gardner, P. L.: 640
Gareis, F. E.: 667
Garman, G. D.: 347, 419
Garrett, G. A.: 520
Garrett, J. B.: 1214
Garrison, M. L.: 845
Garry, R.: 324
Garry, R. J.: 282
Gash, I. A.: 795
Gaubinger, J. R.: 846
Gee, H. H.: 340
Gehlhausen, P. E.: 992
Gehlmann, F.: 129
Gehman, W. S.: 407
Gerstein, O. B.: 1159
Gerum, E.: 15
Gewirtz, H.: 557
Ghiselli, E. E.: 124
Giesz, W. G.: 691
Gilberg, R. L.: 372
Gilbert, A. C. F.: 487
Gilkinson, H.: 90, 110
Githens, W. H.: 965, 1179
Glass, C. F.: 79
Glick, W. P.: 97
Gold, J. A.: 868, 948
Goldberg, L. R.: 462, 641, 1229
Goldschmid, M. L.: 736, 847
Golisch, J. E. W.: 993
Goodfellow, L. D.: 19
Goodling, R. A.: 392, 451
Goodner, S.: 866
Goodstein, L. D.: 521, 527
Gordon, B. J. A.: 642

Gordon, H. C.: 111, 125
Gordon, J. H.: 994
Gory, A. E.: 1111
Gosney, C. A.: 1129
Goswitz, C. R.: 1120
Gotterer, M.: 1130
Grace, E. R.: 995
Graff, F. A.: 408
Grant, J. N.: 922
Grater, H.: 499
Gray, C. W.: 459
Green, H. B.: 699
Green, H. J.: 22
Green, S.: 493
Greene, E. B.: exc, 3:650
Greene, J. E.: 224
Greenwald, A. F.: 848
Gregorio, L. J.: 785
Grenfell, J. E.: 796
Gresham, M.: 203
Griffin, J. J.: 1065
Griffiths, D. E.: 552
Gross, M. C.: 1066
Grosz, R. D.: 1195
Guest, L.: 1112
Guilford, J. P.: 295, 460
Gundlach, R. H.: 15
Gustad, J. W.: 257, 296, 348
Gutekunst, J. G.: 461
Guthrie, G. M.: 594, 849
Gysbers, N. C.: 500
Haag, R. A.: 996
Haakenstad, K. W.: 1196
Haase, R. F.: 1197
Hackett, H. R.: 597
Hadley, R. G.: 862, 1126
Hagenah, T.: 325, 365, 488
Hager, P. C.: 1198
Hahn, M. E.: 191, 274
Hall, D. H.: 1199
Hall, W. B.: 997
Hall, W. J.: 668
Hammidi, B. C.: 709
Hampton, P. J.: 326
Handelsman, I.: 290
Hankes, E. J.: 196
Hannum, T. E.: 225, 277, 349, 367, 1124, 1152
Hanson, G. R.: 1095, 1160, 1189-90
Hanson, R.: 492
Harford, T.: 1096
Harford, T. C.: 850-1
Harker, J. B.: 923
Harmon, L. W.: 923-4, 998
Harper, B. P.: 153; exc, 3: 648
Harrell, T. W.: 489, 722, 999, 1067
Harrell, W.: 96
Harrington, C.: 1000
Harrington, C. C.: 1161
Harrington, T. F.: 1200
Harrison, R.: 368
Hartmann, E. L.: 1051
Hartmann, G. W.: 77
Hartshorn, H. H.: 226
Haselkorn, H.: 327, 393
Havighurst, R. J.: exc, 3:652
Havlicek, L. L.: 737
Hayes, A. B.: 692
Healy, C. C.: 852, 925
Heath, D. H.: 1132
Heath, H. E.: 1132
Heilbrun, A. B.: 1001
Heist, P.: 490, 522-3
Helmick, K. D.: 926
Helper, M. M.: 328
Helson, R.: 927, 1068-9
Hemphill, J. K.: 552
Henderson, H. L.: 440
Hendrix, O. R.: 329
Hennessy, T.: 635
Herkness, W. W.: 111, 125
Herman, L. M.: 553, 1125
Hersch, P. D.: 1002
Hershenson, D. B.: 928
Hesch, G. P.: 929
Heston, J. C.: 205
Hewer, V. H.: 350, 394, 410, 738
Hillis, D. J.: 283
Hilton, A. C.: 432a
Hinckley, E. D.: rev, 4:747

Hinds, E.: 428
Hinman, S. L.: 853
Hinton, B. L.: 797, 1070
Hodge, S. E.: 693
Hoffman, E. G.: 700
Hoffman, E. L.: 206
Hogan, J.: 746
Hogg, M. I.: 8
Holcomb, G. W.: 20
Holland, J.: 554, 595
Holland, P. L.: 1162
Holmen, M. G.: 297, 351
Holt, R. R.: 298, 441
Holzberg, J. D.: 557
Hood, A. B.: 739, 830, 902
Horn, D.: 64
Horsman, V. G.: 694
Howard, L. H.: 740
Howland, R. H.: 695
Hoyt, D. P.: 491
Hudesman, J.: 1071
Hughes, H. M.: 1201
Hughes, J. L.: 420
Hull, J. S.: 1003
Hultgren, D. D.: 1202
Hummel, R.: 741
Humphreys, L. G.: 109
Hunt, W.: 368
Hutchins, E. B.: 696, 798
Huttner, L.: 442
Iannaccone, L.: 552
Im, I. J.: 1047, 1163
Irvin, F. S.: 1004
Irwin, I. A.: 248-9
Irwin, T. J.: 1164
Isabelle, L. A.: 788, 1005
Ivers, K. J.: 1203
Jackson, D. N.: 877, 1091, 1204, 1224
Jackson, T. A.: 368
Jacobs, R.: 362
Jacobsen, C. F.: 126, 185
James, L. E.: 987
James, N. E.: 930
Jenson, P. G.: 369, 421
Jerdee, T. H.: 530, 648
Johansson, C. B.: 784, 908-9, 1006, 1072-3, 1205-8
John, E. R.: 750
Johnson, A. P.: 127-8
Johnson, B. R.: 137
Johnson, D. E.: 697
Johnson, D. G.: 798
Johnson, G. K.: 207
Johnson, J. C.: 931, 1165
Johnson, R. H.: 278, 750
Johnson, R. W.: 524, 742, 1007, 1209, 1211
Jones, M. C.: 52
Jones, R. L.: 1121
Joselyn, E. G.: 932
Joseph, M. P.: 525
Kahn, E. M.: 933
Kaiser, H. E.: 962
Kaplon, M. D.: 103
Karr, B.: 854
Kassarjian, H. H.: 743
Kassarjian, W. M.: 743
Kates, S. L.: 250
Katz, M.: 1008
Katz, M. R.: rev, 7:1036
Kearney, D. L.: 799
Kelley, T. L.: 30
Kellogg, R. L.: 934
Kelly, E. L.: 251, 258, 370, 462, 698
Kelly, L.: 720
Kelso, D. F.: 208-9
Kelso, N. E.: 210
Kemp, C. G.: 630
Kemp, D. E.: 855, 1210
Kendall, L. M.: 1216
Kendall, W. E.: 172, 191
Kennedy, E. C.: 443
Kenney, C. E.: 463
Kenworthy, J. A.: 935
Kerr, W. A.: 1122
Kidneigh, J. C.: 1117
Kiev, A.: 604
Kilburn, K. L.: 1074
King, L. A.: 411, 422, 629
King, P.: 572, 596
King, P. T.: 718
Kinnane, J. F.: 555

Kinslinger, H. J.: 800
Kirchner, W.: 492
Kirchner, W. K.: 416-7, 484, 526
Kirk, B. A.: 387, 521, 527, 597, 825, 961, 988, 1062-3; exc, 5:B115
Kirk, D.: 464
Kirk, J. P.: 643
Kirk, K. W.: 1211
Kish, G. B.: 1009-10
Klein, F. L.: 556
Kleist, M.: 227
Kleist, M. E.: 192
Kloster, C. G.: 395
Klugman, S. F.: 146
Knapp, R. H.: 493, 557, 699-700
Knapp, T. R.: 801
Knauft, E. B.: 259
Knower, F. H.: 90, 110
Knowles, R. H.: 444
Kodama, H.: 658
Kogan, K. L.: 234
Kogan, L.: 129
Kohlan, R. G.: 802, 936
Kohler, A. T.: 1011
Kohn, N.: 211
Kolb, A.: 430
Kole, D. M.: 598, 659, 744
Kopas, J. S.: 56
Koprowski, E. J.: 660
Korn, H. A.: 558-9
Kornhauser, S. I.: 200
Kramer, H. C.: 1075
Krauskopf, C. J.: 701; rev, 7: 1036
Kriedt, P. H.: 228-9, 267, 299
Kriegsfeld, M.: 1076
Krienke, J. W.: 1012
Kroger, R. O.: 856, 937, 1077
Kuder, G. F.: 154; exc, 3:652
Kulberg, G. E.: 494
Kulik, J. A.: 1002
Kunce, J.: 702, 803
Kunce, J. T.: 804-5, 857-8, 1013-4
Kurtz, A. K.: 193
Kutner, M.: 194
L'Abate, L.: 1097
LaBue, A. C.: 618
Laime, B. F.: 599
Lanna, M. G.: 560
Lantay, G. C. von W.: 1212
Lasch, H. A.: 423
Laslett, H. R.: 20
Launer, P. T.: 600
Lawshe, C. H.: 300
Layton, W. L.: 252, 301, 371, 424, 495
Leafgren, F.: 572
Lee, D. L.: 1166
Lee, E. C.: 601
Lee, R. J.: 745
Lefkowitz, D. M.: 1015, 1078
Leigh, M. B.: 1016
Leon, H.: 1167
Lepak, R. C.: 938-9
Lester, H.: 130
Lester, R. A.: 602
Lewis, E. C.: 528, 746
Lewis, R.: 1037
Lezotte, L.: 879
Lhota, B.: 212
Libby, B. C.: 1168
Lief, H. I.: 747
Lief, V. F.: 747
Lind, A.: 603
Linden, J.: 1058
Lindgren, H. C.: 372
Lindsay, C. A.: 553, 1017
Lips, O.: 873
Lips, O. J.: 1213, 1221
Lipton, L.: 592
Liu, P. Y. H.: 1018
Long, L.: 157, 330
Longhofer, P.: 803
Longstaff, H. P.: 213
Lonner, W. J.: 859, 940
Loper, R. G.: exc, 7:B127
Lorimer, M. W.: 147
Lorr, M.: 556, 561
Lothridge, C. D.: 1215

Lowrie, K. H.: 131
Luborsky, L.: 298, 441
Lucas, J. R.: 615
Lunneborg, C. E.: 896
Lyerly, S. B.: 412
Lynch, M. D.: 1200
Lyon, J. B.: 644
McArthur, C.: 352, 373-4, 748, 1169
McCampbell, M. K.: 806
McCarthy, T. N.: 431
McClelland, D. C.: 1111
McCollum, E. L.: 353
McConnell, T. R.: 522
McCornack, R.: 1117
McCornack, R. L.: 354, 396, 465
McCune, C. D.: 1148
McDole, G.: 1074
McDougal, L.: 1026
McIff, L. H.: 749
MacIntosh, A.: 331
McKendry, M. S.: 594
MacKenzie, H.: 14
MacKinney, A. C.: 496, 528
MacKinnon, D. W.: 529, 997
McNair, D. M.: 556, 561
McNamara, W. J.: 420, 1058
McNeely, J. B.: 1079
McQuitty, L. L.: 57, 328
Maffia, L. A.: 619
Magoon, T. M.: exc, 6:B304
Mahoney, T. A.: 530, 648
Maier, G. E.: 413
Malcolm, D. D.: 214, 253
Malone, J. H.: 1146
Malone, K. H.: 445
Mann, C. V.: 31
Mapeli, D.: 701
Margolis, V. H.: 860
Maricle, L. R.: 91
Marks, E.: 1128
Marks, P. A.: 570
Markwardt, F. C.: 497
Marsden, R. D.: 861
Marsh, J. S.: 230
Marshall, J. C.: 941-2
Martin, A. M.: 562, 703
Martin, H. T.: 578
Martucci, L. G.: 653
Martyn, M. M.: 862
Masih, L. K.: 661, 863
Matarazzo, J. D.: 598, 704, 744
Mather, M. E.: 132
Matzler, F.: 522
Mayer, D. B.: 1141
Mayfield, E. C.: 498
Mazak, R. M. J.: 864
Meadows, M. E.: 807, 943
Medsker, L. L.: 959
Mehenti, P. M.: 620
Mehrens, W. A.: 899, 944
Melton, R. S.: 375
Melville, S. D.: 260, 294, 302, 346
Mendoza, B. F. H.: 865, 945
Merenda, P. F.: exc, 6:B305
Merrill, K. E.: 705
Merritt, C. B.: 254
Merwin, J. C.: 750, 816
Metzger, P. L.: 446
Milam, A. T.: 355
Millar, A. C.: 808
Miller, A. W.: 1137
Miller, C. D.: 809
Miller, C. W.: 97
Miller, L. A.: 986
Miller, L. D.: 946
Miller, P. G.: 1019
Mills, D. H.: 1041
Milton, C. R.: 303
Mirels, H. L.: 1214
Mitchell, W. M.: 279
Moffie, D. J.: 133, 303, 866
Moore, B. V.: 112
Morgan, H. H.: 284, 304
Morril, R. A.: 1080
Morris, J. L.: 1170
Morrison, J. S.: 662
Morrow, W. R.: 441
Morse, P. K.: 563
Mortensen, D. G.: 255
Morton, N. W.: rev, 2:1680

Moser, H. P.: 510
Mosier, C. I.: 47
Mowbray, J. K.: 867
Mowrer, G. E.: 941–2
Munday, L. A.: 947
Murphy, P. S.: 1098
Murphy, R. O.: 649
Murray, J. B.: 434, 645
Murray, S.: 261
Mussen, P.: 531
Mussio, J. J.: 1215
Myers, C. S.: exc, 3:652
Namani, A. K.: 447
Nance, R. D.: 231
Naor, N. K.: 1171
Nash, A. N.: 530, 648, 669, 751–2, 810
Nauss, A. H.: 650
Navran, L.: 1081, 1085, 1216
Neal, R. G.: 915
Nelson, K. G.: 305, 332
Neumann, I.: 965, 1179
Nicholson, E.: 1082
Nickels, J. B.: 466
Nielson, C. L.: 1020
Nolan, E. G.: 467
Norenberg, C. D.: 1083
Norrell, G.: 499, 596
Norton, E. D.: 670
O'Connor, J. P.: 582
Odoroff, M. E.: 1105
Oelke, M. C.: 943
Ogden, M. H.: 1113
Ogden, W. E.: 753
Ohlsen, M. M.: 378
Ohvall, R. A.: 1211
Older, H. J.: 181
Olheiser, M. D.: 564
Oliver, J. A.: 273
Oliver, R. A. C.: 1100
Ortenzi, A.: 754
Ortmeyer, D.: 811, 885
Ortmeyer, D. H.: 886
Osborne, R. T.: 224
O'Shea, A. J.: 1200
Osipow, S. H.: 775, 868, 883, 948
Ostrand, J. L.: 1217
Ostrom, S. R.: 215, 232–3
O'Toole, J. J.: 1021
Owens, W. A.: 494, 680
Paepe, C.: 1041
Page, M. J.: 1218
Palubinskas, A. L.: 532, 706
Pappas, A. J.: 500
Parker, E. B.: 559
Parker, J. W.: 432a
Parkinson, M.: 1170
Parry, D. F.: 134–5
Parsons, R. T.: 178
Pasewark, R. A.: 949
Paterson, D. G.: 28, 58, 168, 299, 418, 565
Patterson, C. H.: 566, 631
Paul, G. J.: 1181
Penfield, R. V.: 812
Pennington, A. L.: 1022–3
Peres, S. H.: 709
Perry, D.: 501
Perry, D. K.: 333, 376, 755–6, 869–70, 950, 1133, 1136, 1138–9
Perry, J. D.: 330
Person, G. A.: 1119
Pesci, M. L.: 1084
Peters, E. F.: 136
Petersen, D. F.: 707
Peterson, B. M.: 114
Peterson, C. A.: 813
Peterson, R. A.: 908, 1022–3
Petrik, N. D.: 757, 871, 1024
Phelps, H. R.: 195
Phillips, M.: 1037
Pierson, J. S.: 758
Pierson, R. R.: 285
Pilapil, B.: 1047
Pinneau, S. R.: 366
Poe, C.: 771
Poe, W. A.: 306
Pollack, I. W.: 604
Pool, D. A.: 708, 779
Porter, A.: 533, 567, 605
Posthuma, A. B.: 1081, 1085
Powell, F. V.: 377

Powell, J. O.: 221
Powers, G. P.: 596
Powers, M. K.: 356, 397
Priebe, D. W.: 951, 1025
Pyles, M. K.: 40
Quiring, R. G.: 1172
Rabinowitz, W.: 425
Raju, N. S.: 534
Raley, C. L.: 502
Rapaport, D.: 441
Rausch, V. L.: 1148
Razin, A. M.: 1219
Redlener, J.: 275
Redmond, J. F.: 636
Reinstedt, R. N.: 709
Reitz, W. E.: 1026
Rhode, J. G.: 1027
Rhodes, G. S.: 398
Ricard, E. L.: 709
Richmond, A. M.: 759
Ricksecker, E. L.: 614
Rishel, D. F.: 654
Ritchie, C. M.: 952
Rittenhouse, C. H.: 227
Roadman, H. E.: 621
Roberts, B. B.: 953
Roberts, F. M.: 1086
Roberts, R. K.: 1028
Robinson, H. A.: exc, 4:748
Robinson, J. B.: 115
Rock, D. A.: 760
Rock, R. T.: 80
Rodgers, F. P.: 468
Roeber, E. C.: 216
Roehlke, A.: 771
Rohila, P. K.: 1029
Rohlf, R. J.: 954, 1220
Rohrer, J. H.: 217
Romero, T. D.: 179
Rose, H. A.: 1087
Rosen, E.: 262
Rosen, J.: 814, 872
Rosenbaum, I.: 425
Rosenstein, I.: 1101
Rosenzweig, S.: 234
Ross, J.: 715
Ross, S.: 761
Rossmann, J. E.: 873, 1030, 1207, 1221
Roth, J. D.: 1049
Roth, N. C.: 1222
Rothney, J. W. M.: exc, 7: 1036
Roys, K. B.: 762, 874
Rudloff, J. S.: 1031
Rulon, P. J.: 12
Rupiper, O. J.: 568
Rust, R. M.: 357
Ryan, F. J.: 263, 357
Ryan, T. A.: exc, 5:B115
Ryan, T. G.: 137
Ryden, E. R.: 1134
Saddler, L. E.: 235
Saguiguit, G. F.: 646
Salva, D. M.: 955
Sanders, W. B.: 224
Sarbin, T. R.: 66, 138
Saslow, G.: 704
Satterfield, A. E.: 88
Saunders, D. R.: 399
Sawyer, R. N.: 949
Scheibe, K. E.: 1002
Schell, R. E.: 882
Scheller, T. G.: 875
Schillinger, M.: 1173
Schissel, R. F.: 876, 956
Schletzer, V. M.: 671, 815
Schneidler, G. G.: 58
Schofield, W.: 816
Scholl, C. E.: 435
Schrader, C. H.: 1088
Schultz, R. E.: 378
Schultz, R. S.: 27, 86
Schulzetenberge, A. C.: 1174
Schumacher, C. F.: 606, 710
Schutz, R. A.: 469, 535
Schutz, R. E.: 569
Schweble, M.: 264
Scott, D. A.: 833
Scott, T. B.: 655
Seagoe, M. V.: 158
Seaquist, D. L.: 1089
Seder, M.: 67–70
Seeman, W.: 570

Segal, D.: 32
Segal, S. J.: 622, 379
Segel, D.: 1103
Seidman, E.: 1048
Shaffer, L. F.: exc, 4:748
Shah, I.: 1090
Shardlow, G. W.: 957
Shartle, C. L.: exc, 3:652
Shaw, J.: 1116
Shazo, D. D.: 763
Sheehan, J.: 862
Sheehan, J. G.: 1226
Shellow, S. M.: 15
Shepler, B. F.: 265
Sheppard, R. N. A.: 1223
Sherry, N. M.: 607
Shertzer, B.: 1058
Shirley, J. H.: 503
Shlaudeman, K. W.: 87
Shneidman, E. S.: 1127
Shoemaker, H. A.: 217
Shultz, I. T.: 159
Siess, T. F.: 711, 877, 1091, 1224
Simes, F. J.: 286
Simkevich, J. C.: 59
Sinay, R. D.: 878
Sinnett, E. R.: 400
Sirota, L. M.: 632
Skodak, M.: 98
Slife, W. G.: 571
Slivinski, L. W.: 1149
Sloan, C. M.: 928
Smith, L. M.: 608
Smith, R. E.: 1074
Smith, S. E.: 504
Spiegel, J. A.: 1032
Spoerl, D. T.: 1108
Sprinkle, R. L.: 536
Sprinthall, N.: 741
Staats, A. W.: 569
Staats, C. K.: 569
Stalnaker, A. W.: 1130, 1141
Stanfiel, J. D.: 1092
Starbuck, E. O.: 60
Steen, F. H.: 72
Steffire, B.: 173, 572
Steimel, R. J.: 448, 505, 609, 611
Stein, J.: 1135
Steiner, A. F.: 1093
Steinmetz, H. C.: 21
Stene, D. M.: 442
Stephens, D. H.: 206
Stephens, J. H.: 1210
Stephenson, N. L.: 1094
Stephenson, P. M.: 1175
Stephenson, R. R.: 470, 537–9, 573, 665
Stephenson, R. W.: 1061, 1194
Stevens, J. H.: 909
Stevens, L. R.: 374
Stewart, L. H.: 266, 290, 318, 449, 471–2, 506, 574, 712–4; exc, 5:B115, 6:B305
Stice, G.: 552
Stoler, N.: 817
Stone, C. H.: 267, 299
Stone, V. W.: 507, 540
Stone, W. H.: exc, 3:652
Stordahl, K. E.: 334, 358–9
Stricker, L. J.: 715, 818
Strong, E. K.: 2–7, 9, 11, 13–4, 17, 22, 25–6, 33–7, 41–2, 45, 81, 148, 160–2, 169, 174, 176, 196, 236–7, 268–70, 287, 307–11, 335–6, 360, 380–2, 414, 508–9, 575, 577, 610, 637, 716
Strong, F. W.: 109
Strong, S. R.: 1049
Strunk, O.: 473
Stufflebeam, D. L.: 764
Stuit, D. B.: 61
Sturman, J.: 803
Sumner, F. C.: 355
Sundberg, N. D.: 312
Super, D. E.: 71, 99, 116, 163, 175, 238, 256, 290, 318, 510, 576; exc, 3:648, 3:652, 5:B115, 5:B414
Surette, R. F.: 765
Suziedelis, A.: 555, 609, 611
Tanner, W. C.: 623

Taylor, D. W.: 612
Taylor, E. K.: 432a
Taylor, G. J.: 100
Taylor, G. M.: 626
Taylor, J. G.: 320
Taylor, K. V. F.: 105–6, 139
Taylor, R. G.: 766, 819, 867, 879, 1033, 1095
Terman, L. M.: 85, 624, 1113
Thomas, C. B.: 820, 1176
Thomas, D. L.: 809
Thomas, E. R.: 450
Thomas, R. R.: 383
Thomas, S. D.: 1034
Thompson, J. S.: 401
Thomson, R. W.: 717
Thomson, W. A.: 1106
Thoresen, C. E.: 821
Thorndike, R. M.: 880, 958
Thrall, J. B.: 367
Thrall, J. R.: 349
Thrush, R. S.: 718
Thurstone, L. L.: 18
Tillman, C. A.: 1142
Todd, J. E.: 1109
Toews, J. M.: 767
Tollefson, N. F.: 768
Toronto, R. S.: 881
Torr, D. V.: 313
Townsend, A.: 164, 170
Townsend, J. C.: 582
Traphagen, A. L.: 314
Traxler, A. E.: 62, 130, 197, 271
Trent, J. W.: 959
Triggs, F. O.: 149, 155
Trimble, J. T.: 769
Trinkaus, W. K.: 361
Trueblood, G. E.: 315
Tucker, A. C.: 311, 384, 577
Turnbull, W.: 1077
Tussing, L.: 117, 140
Tuthill, C. E.: 203
Tyler, L. E.: 165, 288, 474, 517, 719
Uhlenhuth, E. H.: 909
Uhr, L.: 419
Uhrbrock, R. S.: 182
Uray, R. M.: 672
Vairo, J. D.: 1128
Vandenberg, S. G.: 720
Van Dusen, A. C.: 101
Verburg, W. A.: 272, 316
Verda, M. M.: 721
Vernon, L. N.: 1122
Villaveces, H. J.: 1035
Vinitsky, M. H.: 1036
Vinsonhaler, J. F.: 899, 944
Vogel, B. S.: 882
Wagman, M.: 822, 1225
Wagner, P. D.: 912
Wahlstrom, M. W.: 1215
Walker, T. H.: 770
Walker, W. B.: 432a
Wall, H. W.: 775, 883
Wallace, W. L.: 239
Wallar, G. A.: 118
Walsh, J. A.: 893
Ward, L. W.: 43
Ward, W. P.: 1177
Warman, R. E.: 638
Watley, D. J.: 541, 578, 823
Watson, R. I.: 245, 344
Webb, S. C.: 451
Webster, E. C.: 273
Wegner, K. W.: 542
Weigel, R.: 771
Weigel, R. G.: 1037
Weinert, J. R.: 1226
Weir, J. R.: 616
Weise, I. B.: 824
Weise, P.: 884
Weiss, D. J.: 880, 958
Weissman, M. P.: 452
Welch, R. D.: 1048
Welkowitz, J.: 811, 885–6
Welsch, L. A.: 887
Welsh, G. S.: 888, 1038, 1227
Wernimont, P.: 686
Werts, C. E.: 960
West, D. N.: 614
Wherry, R. J.: 1123
White, G. R.: 1126
Whitehorn, J. C.: 511

Whitlock, G. E.: 475, 579, 613
Whitney, D. R.: 1039
Whittaker, D.: 1128
Whittaker, D. N. E.: 889
Whittock, J. M.: 617
Wiens, A. N.: 704
Wientge, K. M.: 608
Wiggins, J. S.: 1229
Wiley, N. N.: 1150
Wilkinson, M. A.: 362
Williams, C. L.: 673
Williams, F. J.: 651, 722
Williams, P.: 522
Williams, P. A.: 523, 723, 825, 961
Williams, R. E.: 426
Williamson, E. G.: 48, 58, 63
Willis, C. H.: 850-1, 1096
Willoughby, T. C.: 1178, 1230
Wilson, R. N.: 890, 962
Winn, A.: 273
Winter, F.: 674
Winters, J. S.: 580
Wisdom, J. R.: 280
Witkin, A. A.: 402-3
Wittenborn, J. R.: 149
Woehr, H. J.: 385

Wolins, L.: 496, 746
Wollowick, H. B.: 1058
Wood, B. D.: 23
Woods, J. E.: 581
Woodward, C. L.: 317
Woolf, J. A.: 386
Woolf, M. D.: 386
Woo-Sam, J. M.: 652
Worley, B.: 858
Worley, B. H.: 805
Wrenn, C. G.: 202
Wright, F. H.: 1097
Wright, R. M.: 453
Wright, W.: 1231
Wynne, J. T.: 1098
Yanis, M.: 826
Yeslin, A. R.: 1122
Young, C. W.: 49
Young, K. M.: 747
Yura, M. T.: 1232
Zahn, J. C.: 891
Zeigler, M. L.: 553, 1125, 1128
Zektick, I. N.: 849
Zubin, J.: 480
Zuckerman, M.: 476
Zytowski, D. G.: 599, 772, 892-3, 963, 1040-1

[2213]

Strong Vocational Interest Blank for Women.
Ages 16 and over; 1933-71; SVIB-W; 81 scoring scales (19 basic interests, 58 occupational, 4 nonoccupational) and 6 administrative indices; BASIC INTERESTS: art ('69), biological science ('69), homemaking ('69), law/politics ('69), mechanical ('69), medical service ('69), merchandising ('69), music ('69), numbers ('69), office practices ('69), outdoors ('69), performing arts ('69), physical science ('69), public speaking ('69), religious activities ('69), social service ('69), sports ('69), teaching ('69), writing ('69); OCCUPATIONAL: *group 1, music-performing:* music teacher ('54-69), entertainer ('69), musician performer ('54-69), model ('69); *group 2, art:* art teacher ('69), artist ('35-69), interior decorator ('69); *group 3, verbal-linguistic:* newswoman ('35-69, original scale entitled author), English teacher ('35-69), language teacher ('69); *group 4, social service:* YWCA staff member ('35-69, original scale entitled YWCA secretary), recreation leader ('69), director-Christian education ('69), nun-teacher ('62-69, original scale entitled sister teacher by Sister Mary David Olheiser), guidance counselor ('69), social science teacher ('35-69), social worker ('35-69); *group 5, verbal-scientific:* speech pathologist ('66-69), psychologist ('46-69), librarian ('35-69), translator ('69); *group 6, scientific:* physician ('35-69), dentist ('35-69), medical technologist ('69), chemist ('69), mathematician ('69), computer programmer ('67-69), math-science teacher ('35-69), engineer ('54-69); *group 7, military-managerial:* army-enlisted ('69), navy-enlisted ('69), army-officer ('69), navy-officer ('69); *group 8, business:* lawyer ('35-69), accountant ('69), bankwoman ('69), life insurance underwriter ('35-69, original scale entitled life insurance saleswoman), buyer ('46-69), business education teacher ('38-69, original scale by H. F. Koepke); *group 9, home economics:* home economics teacher ('46-69), dietician ('46-69); *group 10, health-related services:* physical education teacher ('41-69, original scale by Patricia Collins), occupational therapist ('46-69), physical therapist ('58-69), public health nurse ('35-69), registered nurse ('35-69), licensed practical nurse ('35-69), radiologic technologist ('69), dental assistant ('69); *group 11, nonprofessional:* executive housekeeper ('69), elementary teacher ('41-69, original scale by Ralph Bedell), secretary ('35-69, original scale entitled stenographer-secretary), saleswoman ('69), telephone operator ('69), instrument assembler ('69), sewing machine operator ('69), beau-

tician ('69), airline stewardess ('69); NONOCCUPATIONAL: academic achievement ('66-69), diversity of interests ('69), femininity-masculinity II ('35-69), occupational introversion-extroversion; ADMINISTRATIVE INDICES: total responses ('69), unpopular responses ('69), form check ('69), like percentage ('69), indifferent percentage ('69), dislike percentage ('69); Edward K. Strong, Jr. (except supplement) and David P. Campbell; Stanford University Press. *

For additional information and reviews by Dorothy M. Clendenen and Barbara A. Kirk, see 7:1037 (92 references); see also 6:1071 (12 references) and 5:869 (19 references); for a review by Gwendolen Schneidler Dickson of an earlier edition, see 3:649 (38 references); for a review by Ruth Strang, see 2:1681 (10 references); for a review by John G. Darley, see 1:1179. For excerpts from related book reviews, see 7:B127 (1 excerpt), 6:B304 (2 excerpts), 6:B305 (2 excerpts), 3:650 (1 excerpt), and 3:652 (11 excerpts).

REFERENCES THROUGH 1971

1–9. See 2:1681.
10–45. See 3:649.
46–64. See 5:869.
65–76. See 6:1071.
77–168. See 7:1037.
169. NOTTINGHAM, RUTH D. "A Psychological Study of Forty Unmarried Mothers." *Genetic Psychol Monogr* 19:157–228 My '37. * (PA 11:4670)
170. BEDELL, RALPH. "The Science Interests of Successful Elementary Teachers." *Sci Ed* 24:193–9 Ap '40. *
171. CARTER, H. D.; TAYLOR, K. VON F.; AND CANNING, L. B. "Vocational Choices and Interest Test Scores of High School Students." *J Psychol* 11:297–306 Ap '41. * (PA 15:3573)
172. McCARTHY, MARY VITERBO. "An Empirical Study of the Personality Profiles Characterizing Differential Quantitative and Linguistic Ability." *Studies Psychol & Psychiatry* 8(4):1–45 Je '53. * (PA 28:4043)
173. McCORNACK, ROBERT, AND KIDNEIGH, JOHN C. "The Vocational Interest Patterns of Social Workers." *Social Work J* 35:160–3 O '54. * (PA 29:6448)
174. LEAHY, DOROTHY M. "The Need for Selective Recruitment in Home Economics." *J Ed Res* 52:293–8 Ap '59. *
175. KENTZ, MARY JOAN. *The Relationship of Masculine and Feminine Interests to Adjustment in Career-Orientated Women.* Master's thesis, Catholic University of America (Washington, D.C.), 1965.
176. LUNDGREN, ELIZABETH J. "Predicting Student Success in Medical Technology and Clinical Laboratory Assistant Programs." *Am J Med Technol* 34:349–61 Je '68. *
177. GREENWOOD, KATHRYN B. *A Study of Personality Traits and Interest of Prospective Teachers.* Master's thesis, University of Tennessee (Knoxville, Tenn.), 1969.
178. WILLIAMS, HELEN B. *Interests and Prediction of Academic Performance of Associate Degree Nursing Students.* Master's thesis, Alfred University (Alfred, N.Y.), 1969.
179. BOAZ, JACQUELYN ANNE. *A Comparison of the Interests of Female Professional Personnel in Community Recreation to Other Occupations Described by the Strong Vocational Interest Blank for Women.* Doctor's thesis, University of Minnesota (Minneapolis, Minn.), 1970. (DAI 31:5220A)
180. HUGHES, LOIS JUNE. *Selected Factors as Related to Success in Student Teaching of Home Economics.* Doctor's thesis, University of Missouri (Columbia, Mo.), 1970. (DAI 31:5249A)
181. KOELLING, JOHN ALBERT. *A Differential Study of Prospective Elementary School Teachers at the University of Oregon: A Comparison of Those Preferring Lower and Upper Teaching Levels.* Doctor's thesis, University of Oregon (Eugene, Ore.), 1970. (DAI 31:5251A)
182. KOLPACK, KAREN CARLA. *The Relationship Between Vocational Interest Patterns and Performance Appraisals of Women Resident Assistants on the Wisconsin State University-Oshkosh Campus.* Master's thesis, Wisconsin State University (Oshkosh, Wis.), 1970.
183. LEON, HERMAN. *Factors Predictive of Successful Educational Performance in Social Work School.* Doctor's thesis, Columbia University (New York, N.Y.), 1970. (DAI 31:6724A)
184. OKUN, BARBARA FRANK. *A Study of the Variables Affecting the Occupational Choice of Women 12-20 Years After College Graduation.* Doctor's thesis, Northwestern University (Evanston, Ill.), 1970. (DAI 31:5960A)
185. PRATT, ANN BOGUE. *Meanings of Popular and Unpopular Occupations on the Strong Vocational Interest Blank for Women.* Doctor's thesis, University of Minnesota (Minneapolis, Minn.), 1970. (DAI 31:6317B)
186. SCHILLINGER, MORTON. *Cotherapist Value Similarity as a Determinant of Combined Therapy Outcome.* Doctor's thesis, New York University (New York, N.Y.), 1970. (DAI 31:7612B)

187. Schulzetenberge, Anthony C. *Interests and Background Variables Characterizing Secondary School Librarians Who Work With Teachers in Curriculum Development and Improvement of Instruction.* Doctor's thesis, University of North Dakota (Grand Forks, N.D.), 1970. (*DAI* 32:7019A)

188. Anderson, Susan C., and Apostal, Robert A. "Occupational Introversion-Extroversion and Size of Hometown." *Voc Guid Q* 20(2):138–40 D '71. *

189. Becker, Steven Joel. *A Comparison of Body Attitudes in Women With Masculine Vocational Interests and Those With Feminine Vocational Interests.* Doctor's thesis, University of Maryland (College Park, Md.), 1971. (*DAI* 32:5421B)

190. Campbell, David P. "Admissions Policies: Side Effects and Their Implications." *Am Psychologist* 26(7):636–47 Jl '71. * (*PA* 47:11560)

191. Cockriel, Irvin W. "A Question About the Usefulness of the SVIB's Academic Achievement Scale for Women in Education." *J Stud Pers Assn Teach Ed* 10(1):14–5 f '71. *

192. Faunce, Patricia Spencer. "Vocational Interests of High Ability College Women." *J Col Stud Personnel* 12(6):430–7 N '71. * (*PA* 47:9758)

193. Harmon, Lenore W. "The Childhood and Adolescent Career Plans of College Women." *J Voc Behav* 1(1):45–56 Ja '71. * (*PA* 47:3693)

194. Johnson, Richard W. "Congruence of Strong and Kuder Interest Profiles." *J Counsel Psychol* 18(5):450–5 S '71. * (*PA* 47:3697)

195. Sharf, Richard S. "Computer-Based Report for the Strong Vocational Interest Blank for Women." *Meas & Eval Guid* 4(1):9–17 Ap '71. *

196. Steele, Carolyn I. "Sexual Identity Problems Among Adolescent Girls in Institutional Placement." *Adolescence* 6(24):509–22 w '71. * (*PA* 48:7393)

197. Stroops, Sylvia Lynn. *Personality Types and Vocational Interests of Women Students Majoring in Two Different Areas of Teacher Education.* Doctor's thesis, University of Alabama (University, Ala.), 1971. (*DAI* 32:5027A)

198. Wong, John C. *The Effect of Instruction in Health Occupations and of Vocational Interest Appraisal on the Preference of Health Occupations Among Female College Freshmen and Sophomores.* Doctor's thesis, University of Missouri (Columbia, Mo.), 1971. (*DAI* 33:233A)

CUMULATIVE NAME INDEX

Achauer, M. P.: 21
Aldag, J. C.: 153
Aldag, J. C. K.: 136
Allen, C. L.: 49
Alteneder, L. E.: 11, 16
Althouse, R.: 148
Anderson, H. E.: 92
Anderson, M. R.: 58
Anderson, S. C.: 188
Andrews, M. E.: 22
Apostal, R. A.: 188
Athelstan, G. T.: 152
Bailey, J. P.: 116, 137
Barrett, D. M.: 39
Becker, J. A.: 85
Becker, S. J.: 189
Bedell, R.: 17, 19, 170
Berman, I. R.: 1
Bingham, W. V. D.: 2
Bird, D. J.: 65
Boaz, J. A.: 179
Bohn, M. J.: 155
Bondy, S. B.: 135
Bott, M. M.: 123
Brooks, E.: 10
Brown, N. W.: 97
Buchanan, B. F.: 124
Burgemeister, B. B.: 17a
Callis, R.: *exc*, 6:B304
Campbell, D. P.: 111–2, 125, 138, 167, 190
Canning, L. B.: 171
Carter, H. D.: 3, 6.1, 30, 33, 171; *exc*, 3:652
Cawley, A.: 113
Cawley, A. M.: 45
Cisney, H. N.: 34
Clendenen, D. M.: *rev*, 7:1037
Cockriel, I. W.: 191
Collins, P. J.: 23
Compton, N. H.: 139
Corey, S. M.: *exc*, 3:652
Crider, B.: 31
Crissey, O. L.: 27
Crissy, W. J. E.: 6, 7, 13
Daniel, W. J.: 6
Darley, J. G.: 1; *rev*, 1:1179; *exc*, 3:652
DeWolfe, A. S.: 154
Dickson, G. S.: *rev*, 3:649

Donnenwerth, G.: 131
Donnenwerth, G. V.: 147
Dreffin, W. B.: 50
Duffy, E.: 7, 13
Dunlap, J. W.: 20a, 24
Dunteman, G. H.: 98, 114–6, 137
Durflinger, G. W.: 75
Espenschade, A.: 51
Farmer, H. S.: 155
Farnsworth, K. E.: 126, 140
Farnsworth, P. R.: 53
Faunce, P. S.: 99, 192
Flint, R. T.: 156
France-Kelly, K.: 141
Frank, A. C.: 157–8
Friedersdorf, N. W.: 142
Gernes, E.: 18
Gerstein, A. I.: 93
Gilkinson, H.: 14
Glick, R.: 94
Glosser, E. A.: 100
Glotzbach, C. J.: 79
Golden, M. C.: 101
Greenberg, E. S.: 121
Greene, E. B.: *exc*, 3:650
Greenwood, K. B.: 177
Gunnell, D. C.: 63
Gysbers, N. C.: 127
Hall, O. A.: 66
Hall, W. J.: 86
Hammer, M.: 128
Harmon, L. A. W.: 95
Harmon, L. W.: 117–8, 138, 143–4, 159, 193
Harper, B. P.: 24
Havighurst, R. J.: *exc*, 3:652
Helson, R.: 102, 129
Herkenhoff, L. H.: 103
Hersch, P. D.: 145
Higginbottom, A. R.: 20
Hilgard, J. R.: 15
Hornung, P. E.: 146
Hoyt, D. P.: 64
Hughes, L. J.: 180
Hutchinson, J. C.: 77
Isenberger, W.: 67
Isenberger, W. E.: 80
Jantzen, A. C.: 137
Johnson, R. J.: 161

Johnson, R. W.: 160, 168, 194
Johnston, J. A.: 127
Jones, M. C.: 3
Joselyn, E. G.: 130
Kennedy, C. E.: 64
Kentz, M. J.: 175
Kidneigh, J. C.: 173
Kirk, B. A.: 157–8; *rev*, 7:1037
Kish, G. B.: 131, 147
Klahn, J. E.: 104
Kleist, M.: 53
Klugman, S. F.: 35, 40–1
Knower, F. H.: 14
Koelling, J. A.: 181
Koepke, H. F.: 36
Kolpack, K. C.: 182
Kuder, G. F.: *exc*, 3:652
Kulik, J. A.: 145
Kutner, M.: 47
Laime, B. F.: 76
Laleger, G. E.: 25
Leahy, D. M.: 174
Leon, H.: 183
Leonard, L. C.: 161
Lewis, E. C.: 91
Lind, A. I.: 162
Lindsay, C. A.: 148
Linnick, I.: 52
Loper, R. G.: *exc*, 7:B127
Lundgren, E. J.: 176
McArthur, C.: 64
McCall, R. J.: 74
McCarthy, M. K.: 74, 82
McCarthy, M. V.: 172
McCornack, R.: 173
McGann, J. R.: 87
Madaus, G. F.: 107
Magoon, T. M.: *exc*, 6:B304
Matis, E. E.: 132
Mayer, W. K.: 105
Meadow, L.: 81, 89
Mercer, M.: 26
Merenda, P. F.: *exc*, 6:B305
Merkle, R. W.: 133
Miller, C. D.: 163
Miller, D. I.: 96, 106
Mitzel, H. E.: 59
Morey, E. A.: 54
Morrill, W. H.: 163
Mydelle, E. K.: 48
Myers, C. S.: *exc*, 3:652
Navran, L.: 60
Nolting, E.: 119, 164
Nottingham, R. D.: 169
Nutting, R. E.: 63
Nuzum, R. E.: 165
Obst, F.: 68
Okun, B. F.: 184
Olheiser, M. D.: 83

O'Neil, P. M.: 107
Parker, A. W.: 72, 108
Parsons, R. T.: 46
Paterson, D. G.: 1, 4
Peterson, B. M.: 20a
Peterson, M. E.: 69
Petrik, N. D.: 149
Pratt, A. B.: 185
Rittenhouse, C. H.: 53, 55
Roberts, F. M.: 166
Rossmann, J. E.: 88
Rudloff, J. S.: 109
Scheibe, K. E.: 145
Schillinger, M.: 186
Schneider, G. G.: 4
Schuell, H.: 112
Schulzetenberge, A. C.: 187
Seagoe, M. V.: 42–3
Seder, M.: 8–9, 12
Sedlacek, C. G.: 134
Shanks, J. L.: 150
Sharf, R. S.: 195
Shartle, C. L.: *exc*, 3:652
Shepler, B. F.: 56
Siegel, H. J.: 120
Skodak, M.: 27
Snyder, D. F.: 62
Soliman, A. M.: 125
Steele, C. I.: 151, 196
Stewart, L. H.: *exc*, 6:B305
Stone, T. H.: 152
Stone, W. H.: *exc*, 3:652
Strang, R.: *rev*, 2:1681
Strong, E. K.: 32
Stroops, S. L.: 197
Stuit, D. B.: 5
Super, D. E.: *exc*, 3:652
Tanner, W. C.: 78
Taylor, K. von F.: 28–30, 171
Taylor, R. G.: 135
Thomas, L. E.: 163
Tomedy, F. J.: 61
Triggs, F. O.: 37
Tyler, L. E.: 90
Vernson, E. E.: 57
Vetter, L.: 91
Warren, P. A.: 70
Wegner, K. W.: 73
Werkman, S. L.: 121
White, B. J.: 71
Whittaker, D. N. E.: 122
Wightwick, M. I.: 38, 44
Wilkins, P. E.: 110
Williams, H. B.: 178
Williamson, E. G.: 4
Wong, J. C.: 198
Wrenn, C. G.: 50
Zissis, C.: 84
Zytowski, D. G.: 76

[2214]

Thurstone Interest Schedule. Grades 9–16 and adults; 1947; 10 scores: physical science, biological science, computational, business, executive, persuasive, linguistic, humanitarian, artistic, musical; L. L. Thurstone; Psychological Corporation. *

For additional information and reviews by Norman Frederiksen and Donald E. Super, see 4:745 (1 reference).

REFERENCES THROUGH 1971

1. See 4:745. *
2. Thurstone, L. L. "A Vocational Interest Schedule." Abstract. *Psychol B* 32:719 N '35. * (*PA* 10:1152, title only)
3. Laycock, S. R., and Hutcheon, N. B. "A Preliminary Investigation Into the Problem of Measuring Engineering Aptitude." *J Ed Psychol* 30:280–8 Ap '39. * (*PA* 13:5899)
4. Roeber, Edward C. "A Comparison of Seven Interest Inventories With Respect to Word Usage." *J Ed Res* 42:8–17 S '48. * (*PA* 23:2915)
5. José, Alicia B. *A Study of the Vocational and Avocational Interests of Eleventh-Grade Pupils in a Diocesan High School.* Doctor's thesis, Fordham University (New York, N.Y.), 1950.
6. Daly, Joan M. *A Comparison of the Relation of the Thurstone Interest Schedule to the Kuder Preference Record and to Self-Estimated Interests.* Master's thesis, Fordham University (New York, N.Y.), 1951.
7. Newman, Sidney H.; French, John W.; and Bobbitt, Joseph M. "Analysis of Criteria for the Validation of Selection Measures at the United States Coast Guard Academy." *Ed & Psychol Meas* 12:394–407 au '52. * (*PA* 27:6159)

8. SKARD, ØYVIND. "Measurement of Students' Interests." *Acta Psychologica* (Netherlands) 8(4):264–78 '52. * (*PA* 27:5400)

9. TORR, DONALD V. "A Factor Analysis of Selected Interest Inventories." Abstract. *Am Psychologist* 7:296 Jl '52. *

10. SKARD, ØYVIND; AURSAND, INGER MARIE; AND BRAATEN, LEIF J. "Development and Application of Tests for University Students in Norway: A Report on Parts of a Research Project." *Psychol Monogr* 68(12):1–54 '54. * (*PA* 29:7971)

11. KEELER, HAROLD JAY. *Predicting Teacher Effectiveness of Graduates of the State University of New York Teachers Colleges.* Doctor's thesis, Cornell University (Ithaca, N.Y.), 1956. (*DA* 17:545)

12. EASTON, JUDITH C. "Some Personality Traits of Underachieving and Achieving High School Students of Superior Ability." *B Maritime Psychol Assn* 8:34–9 Ap '59. * (*PA* 34:4786)

13. SPRINGFIELD, FRANKLYN BRUCE. *Concept of Father and Ideal Self in a Group of Criminals and Non-Criminals.* Doctor's thesis, New York University (New York, N.Y.), 1960. (*DA* 21:1258)

14. FISHER, SEYMOUR. "Front-Back Differentiations in Body Image and Body Reactivity." *J General Psychol* 64:373–9 Ap '61. * (*PA* 36:1HE73F)

15. PHILIPPUS, MARION JOHN. *A Study of Personality, Value and Interest Patterns of Student Teachers in the Areas of Elementary, Secondary and Special Education.* Doctor's thesis, University of Denver (Denver, Colo.), 1961. (*DA* 22:3926)

16. PHILIPPUS, MARION JOHN, AND FLEIGLER, LOUIS. "A Study of Personality, Value and Interest Patterns of Student Teachers in the Areas of Elementary, Secondary, and Special Education." *Sci Ed* 46:247–52 Ap '62. *

17. BARBERA, RICHARD CARLTON. *The Influence of the Use of Gestalt Teaching Methods Upon the Achievement of Certain Outcomes of Instruction in Junior High School Physical Science.* Doctor's thesis, Boston University (Boston, Mass.), 1968. (*DAI* 30:611A)

18. BARRY, JOHN R.; DUNTEMAN, GEORGE H.; AND WEBB, MARVIN W. "Personality and Motivation in Rehabilitation." *J Counsel Psychol* 15:237–44 My '68. * (*PA* 42:12535)

19. ROSEN, JULIUS. "School Counselor Dogmatism and Vocational Identity." *Psychol Rep* 23:24–6 Ag '68. * (*PA* 43:7350)

20. ISABELLE, LAURENT A., AND DICK, WILLIAM. "Clarity of Self-Concepts in the Vocational Development of Male Liberal Arts Students (An Abstract)." *Can Psychologist* 10(1):20–31 Ja-F '69. * (*PA* 43:16396)

21. KUMAR, K. "Influence of Intelligence on the Vocational Interests of School Children." *J Ed Res & Exten* (India) 8(1):1–8 Jl '71. *

CUMULATIVE NAME INDEX

Aursand, I. M.: 10
Barbera, R. C.: 17
Barry, J. R.: 18
Bobbitt, J. M.: 7
Braaten, L. J.: 10
Daly, J. M.: 6
Dick, W.: 20
Dunteman, G. H.: 18
Easton, J. C.: 12
Fisher, S.: 14
Fleigler, L.: 16
Frederiksen, N.: *rev*, 4:745
French, J. W.: 7
Hutcheon, N. B.: 3
Isabelle, L. A.: 20
José, A. B.: 5
Keeler, H. J.: 11
Kumar, K.: 21
Laycock, S. R.: 3
Newman, S. H.: 7
Philippus, M. J.: 15–6
Roeber, E. C.: 4
Rosen, J.: 19
Skard, O.: 8, 10
Springfield, F. B.: 13
Super, D. E.: *rev*, 4:745
Thurstone, L. L.: 2
Torr, D. V.: 9
Webb, M. W.: 18
Zwilling, V. T.: 1

[2215]

VALCAN Vocational Interest Profile (VIP). Ages 15 and over; 1960–61; title on manual and profile is *PSYCAN Vocational Interest Profile*; formerly called *WIPCO Vocational Interest Profile*; 9 scores: numerical, mechanical, scientific, clerical, persuasive, musical, literary, artistic, service; 1961 test essentially the same as 1960 research edition; R. N. Smith and J. R. McIntosh; distributed by University of British Columbia Bookstore [Canada]. *

For additional information, see 6:1072.

[2216]

The Vocational Apperception Test: Advanced Form. College; 1949; VAT; 2 forms; Robert B. Ammons, Margaret N. Butler, and Sam A. Herzig; Psychological Test Specialists. *

a) [FORM FOR MEN.] Preferences in 8 areas: teacher, executive or office worker, doctor, lawyer, engineer, personnel or social worker, salesman, laboratory technician.

b) [FORM FOR WOMEN.] Preferences in 10 areas: laboratory technician, dietician, buyer, nurse, teacher, artist, secretary, social worker, mother, housewife.

For additional information, see P:492 (3 references); for reviews by Benjamin Balinsky and William E. Henry and an excerpted review by George S. Rhodes, see 4:146 (1 reference).

REFERENCES THROUGH 1971

1. See 4:146.
2–4. See P:492.

CUMULATIVE NAME INDEX

Ammons, R. B.: 1
Balinsky, B.: *rev*, 4:146
Butler, M. N.: 1
Clark, E. T.: 4
Goldstein, A. P.: 3
Henry, W. E.: *rev*, 4:146
Herzig, S. A.: 1
Rhodes, G. S.: *exc*, 4:146
Stowe, E. W.: 2

[2217]

Vocational Interest and Sophistication Assessment. Retarded adolescents and young adults; 1967–68; VISA; 2 forms; Joseph J. Parnicky, Harris Kahn, and Arthur D. Burdett; Joseph J. Parnicky. *

a) FORM FOR MALES. Interest and knowledge scores in each of 7 areas: garage, laundry, food service, maintenance, farm and grounds, materials handling, industry.

b) FORM FOR FEMALES. Interest and knowledge scores in each of 4 areas: business and clerical, housekeeping, food service, laundry and sewing.

For additional information, see 7:1039 (2 references).

REFERENCES THROUGH 1971

1–2. See 7:1039.
3. PARNICKY, JOSEPH J.; KAHN, HARRIS; AND BURDETT, ARTHUR D. "Standardization of the VISA (Vocational Interest and Sophistication Assessment) Technique." *Am J Mental Def* 75(4):442–8 Ja '71. * (*PA* 46:3618)

CUMULATIVE NAME INDEX

Burdett, A.: 1, 3
Burdett, A. D.: 2
Kahn, H.: 1–3
Parnicky, J. J.: 1–3

[2218]

Vocational Interest Profile. Ages 15 and over; 1960–66; VIP; 9 scores: numerical, mechanical, scientific, clerical, persuasive, musical, artistic, literary, service; Robin N. Smith and J. R. McIntosh (test and user's guide); distributed by University of British Columbia Bookstore [Canada]. *

For additional information, see 7:1040 (1 reference).

REFERENCES THROUGH 1971

1. See 7:1040.

CUMULATIVE NAME INDEX

Henry, S.: 1

[2219]

★**Wide Range Interest-Opinion Test.** Grades 8–12 and adults; 1970–72; WRIOT; 25 scores: 18 occupational interests (art, literature, music, drama, sales, management, office work, personal service, protective service, social service, social science, biological science, physical science, number, mechanics, machine operation, outdoor, athletics), 7 vocational attitudes (sedentariness, risk, ambition, chosen skill level, activity by sex, agreement, interest spread); Joseph F. Jastak and Sarah R. Jastak; Guidance Associates of Delaware, Inc. *

[2220]

*****William, Lynde & Williams Analysis of Interest.** Male adults; 1956–71; 8 scores: management, accounting, engineering, mechanical, sales, service, teaching, writing; R. W. Henderson; William, Lynde & Williams. *

For additional information and a review by Ralph F. Berdie, see 7:1041.

[2221]

Work Values Inventory. Grades 7–16 and adults; 1968–70; WVI; 15 scales: altruism, esthetics, creativity, intellectual stimulation, independence, achievement, prestige, management, economic returns, security, surroundings, supervisory relations, associates, variety, way of life; Donald E. Super; Houghton Mifflin Co. *

For additional information, reviews by Ralph F. Berdie and David V. Tiedeman, and an excerpted review by John W. French, see 7:1042 (33 references).

REFERENCES THROUGH 1971

1–33. See 7:1042.

34. WOODBURY, ROGER WILLIAM. *Sex Differences, Parental Occupational Level, and Intelligence as Measured by Super's Work Values Inventory on 379 Southern Rural, Caucasian, Protestant 9th Graders of North Carolina.* Master's thesis, North Carolina State University (Raleigh, N.C.), 1966.

35. JORDAN, MARCELLA JULIE. *The Relationship of Life Values and Work Values of College Women to Their Vocational Preferences.* Master's thesis, Catholic University of America (Washington, D.C.), 1967.

36. BROWN, FREDERICK G. "Work Values Inventory: A Review." *Meas & Eval Guid* 4(3):189–90 O '71. *

37. DENDALUCE, IGNATIUS. *Industrialization Level, Socioeconomic Class and Work Values.* Doctor's thesis, Columbia University (New York, N.Y.), 1971. (DAI 32:5470B)

38. DONAHUE, MICHAEL A. *College Placement: An Exploratory Investigation of the Employment Selection Process and Certain Correlates of Vocational Development.* Doctor's thesis, Purdue University (Lafayette, Ind.), 1971. (DAI 32:735A)

39. GABLE, ROBERT K., AND PRUZEK, ROBERT M. "Super's Work Values Inventory: Two Multivariate Studies of Interitem Relationships." *J Exp Ed* 40(1):41–50 f '71. *

40. GABLE, ROBERT KEITH. *A Multivariate Study of Work Value Orientations.* Doctor's thesis, State University of New York (Albany, N.Y.), 1971. (DAI 32:1997A)

41. HALL, JOHN ARLIS. *The Influence of School Desegregation on the Work Values and Occupational Aspiration Levels of Twelfth-Grade Negro Males in Texas Public High Schools.* Doctor's thesis, East Texas State University (Commerce, Tex.), 1971. (DAI 32:5545A)

42. LUCIANO, WILSON. *A Comparative Analysis of the Occupational Values of Male High School Seniors in Urban and Rural Areas of Puerto Rico.* Doctor's thesis, University of New Mexico (Albuquerque, N.M.), 1971. (DAI 32:741A)

43. SHEPPARD, NATHANIEL ALAN. *Educational-Vocational Decision and Indecision in College Freshmen.* Doctor's thesis, Ohio State University (Columbus, Ohio), 1971. (DAI 32:3040A)

44. TEBO, JACK. *An Assessment of Work Values Held by Future, Junior, Field, and Senior Grade Air Force Officers in Flying and Non-Flying Categories.* Doctor's thesis, Florida State University (Tallahassee, Fla.), 1971. (DAI 32:5556A)

45. UNDERWOOD, K. L. "Work Values of University Entrants." *J Col Stud Personnel* 12(6):455–9 N '71. * (PA 47:9626)

CUMULATIVE NAME INDEX

Anker, J. M.: 8
Bannon, M. M.: 12
Beilin, H.: 10
Berdie, R. F.: *rev*, 7:1042
Bernstein, B. H.: 24
Brown, F. G.: 36
Carruthers, T. E.: 25
Cotnam, J. D.: 28
Dendaluce, I.: 37
Donahue, M. A.: 38
Drahozal, E. C.: 13
French, J. W.: *exc*, 7:1042
Gable, R. K.: 39–40
Gaubinger, J. R.: 10
Goss, A.: 16
Goss, A. M.: 19, 26
Hall, J. A.: 41
Hana, A. M.: 1
Harlan, G. E.: 11
Harrangue, M. D.: 14
Hendrix, V. L.: 27
Humbert, J. T.: 17
Hurley, R. B.: 32
Ivey, A. E.: 9
Jordan, M. J.: 35
Kaplan, H. H.: 23
Kinnane, J. F.: 3–5, 10, 12

Luciano, W.: 42
Madaus, G. F.: 20
Malone, F. E.: 18
Margulies, N.: 29
Moses, R. G.: 30
Mowry, J. G.: 7
Normile, R. H.: 21
O'Connor, J. P.: 3, 8
O'Hara, R. P.: 2, 20, 22
Pable, M. W.: 4
Pallone, N. J.: 32
Pate, K. D.: 16, 19
Pruzek, R. M.: 39
Rickard, F. S.: 32
Rim, R. J.: 32
Shah, U. D.: 31
Sheppard, N. A.: 43
Super, D. E.: 6–7, 23, 27
Surette, R. F.: 15
Suziedelis, A.: 5
Tebo, J.: 44
Tiedeman, D. V.: 2; *rev*, 7:1042
Tirman, R. J.: 32
Townsend, J. C.: 8
Underwood, K. L.: 45
Woodbury, R. W.: 34
Zytowski, D. G.: 33

[Out of Print Since TIP I]

Analysis of Choices (status unknown), T:1855
Brainard Occupational Preference Inventory, 5:856 (7 reviews, 9 references)
Burke Inventory of Vocational Development, 6:1048
Career Finder (status unknown), 6:1049 (2 reviews)
Cleeton Vocational Interest Inventory, 3:635 (8 reviews, 2 excerpts, 19 references)
College Planning Inventory, 6:1051
Devon Interest Test, 5:857 (2 reviews, 3 references)
Edmiston RO Inventory, T:1863
Fields of Occupational Interest, T:1864
Fowler-Parmenter Self-Scoring Interest Record, 6:1053 (2 reviews, 2 references)
Interest Questionnaire for High School Students, 3:637 (1 review, 6 references)
Kuder Preference Record—Occupational, 6:1062 (3 reviews, 13 references)
Motivation Indicator, 3:641 (2 reviews, 1 excerpt)
Occupational Interest Comparisons, T:1877
Occupational Interests: Self Analysis Scale (status unknown), 3:644 (1 review)
Occupational Satisfactions Inventory, T:1881
Office Occupational Interests of Women, T:1882
Primary Business Interests Test (status unknown), 6:1067 (3 reviews, 2 references)
Qualifications Record (status unknown), 6:1068 (2 reviews)
RBH Job Choice Inventory, 7:1032 (2 reviews)
Rating Scales of Vocational Values, Vocational Interests and Vocational Aptitudes, 7:1033 (2 reviews)
Vocational Interest Analyses, 5:870 (2 reviews, 1 reference)
Vocational Sentence Completion Blank, 6:1073 (4 references)
Your Educational Plans, 6:1075 (1 review, 1 excerpt, 1 reference)

MANUAL DEXTERITY

[2222]

*APT Manual Dexterity Test. Automobile and truck mechanics and mechanics' helpers; 1960–63; Bentley Barnabas (supplement); Associated Personnel Technicians, Inc. *

For additional information, see 6:1076.

[2223]

Crawford Small Parts Dexterity Test. High school and adults; 1946–56; 2 scores: pins and collars, screws; John E. Crawford and Dorothea M. Crawford; Psychological Corporation. *

For additional information and a review by Neil D. Warren, see 5:871 (8 references); for a review by Raymond A. Katzell, see 4:752; for a review by Joseph E. Moore, see 3:667.

REFERENCES THROUGH 1971

1–8. See 5:871.

9. CRAWFORD, JOHN E., AND CRAWFORD, DOROTHEA M. "Small Parts Dexterity Test." Comment by Walter R. Miles. *Meth Med Res* 3:195–7 '50. * (PA 26:3238)

10. OLLRICH, ARTHUR H. *A Validation of the Stromberg Manual Dexterity Test and the Crawford Small Parts Test (Pins and Collars) for Use in Selecting Female Packaging and Packing Employees.* Master's thesis, Drake University (Des Moines, Iowa), 1962.

11. RIM, Y. "The Predictive Validity of Seven Manual Dexterity Tests." *Psychologia* (Japan) 5:52–5 Mr '62. * (PA 38:1417)

12. PETERSON, FLOYD E. "Identification of Sub-Groups for Test Validation Research." *J Indus Psychol* 2:98–101 D '64. * (PA 40:10636)

13. KEBBON, LARS. *The Structure of Abilities at Lower Levels of Intelligence: A Factor-Analytical Study.* Stockholm, Sweden: Skandinaviska Testförlaget AB, 1965. Pp. 112. *

14. JONES, D.; BENTON, A. L.; AND MacQUEEN, J. C. "Hand Preference and Manipulative Dexterity in Normal and Retarded Children." *J Mental Def Res* 11:49–53 Mr '67. * (PA 41:14118)

15. ELKIN, LORNE. "Predicting Performance of the Men-

tally Retarded on Sheltered Workshop and Non-Institutional Jobs." *Am J Mental Def* 72:533–9 Ja '68. * (*PA* 42:7638)

16. ZIMMERMAN, JOHN JAMES. *Relationships Among Scholastic Aptitude, Attitudes Toward Various Facets of College Life, and Academic Performance of Students at Lycoming College.* Doctor's thesis, Pennsylvania State University (University Park, Pa.), 1969. (*DAI* 30:4792A)

17. GRANT, DONALD L., AND BRAY, DOUGLAS W. "Validation of Employment Tests for Telephone Company Installation and Repair Occupations." *J Appl Psychol* 54(1):7–14 F '70. * (*PA* 44:5738)

18. NORDÉN, K. "The Structure of Abilities in a Group of Deaf Adolescents." *Ed & Psychol Interactions* (Sweden) 32:1–22 '70. * (*PA* 44:15094)

19. MECKLER, ROY STEWART. *The Effects of Perceptual-Motor Training on the Development of Fine Motor Proficiency of Trainable Mentally Retarded Adolescents.* Doctor's thesis, George Peabody College for Teachers (Nashville, Tenn.), 1971. (*DAI* 32:1946A)

20. ZULLO, THOMAS G. "A Factor Analysis of Perceptual and Motor Abilities of Dental Students." *J Dental Ed* 35(6): 356–61 Je '71. *

CUMULATIVE NAME INDEX

Bauman, M. K.: 8	Meckler, R. S.: 19
Benton, A. L.: 14	Miles, W. R.: 9
Bray, D. W.: 17	Moore, J. E.: *rev*, 3:667
Bruce, M. M.: 1, 3–4	Nordén, K · 18
Crawford, D. M.: 9	Ollrich, A. H.: 10
Crawford, J. E.: 9	Osborne, R. T.: 5
Elkin, L.: 15	Peterson, F. E.: 12
Fitzpatrick, E. D.: 2	Rim, Y.: 11
Grant, D. L.: 17	Sanders, W. B.: 5
Jones, D.: 14	Speer, G. S.: 7
Katzell, R. A.: *rev*, 4:752	Walker, F. C.: 6
Kebbon, L.: 13	Warren, N. D.: *rev*, 5:871
McCarty, J. J.: 2	Zimmerman, J. J.: 16
MacQueen, J. C.: 14	Zullo, T. G.: 20

[2224]

Crissey Dexterity Test. Job applicants; 1964; CDT; Orlo L. Crissey; Psychological Services, Inc. *

For additional information and a review by Lyle F. Schoenfeldt, see 7:1043 (1 reference).

REFERENCES THROUGH 1971

1. See 7:1043.

CUMULATIVE NAME INDEX

Crissey, O. L.: 1	Schoenfeldt, L. F.: *rev*, 7:1043

[2225]

Hand-Tool Dexterity Test. Adolescents and adults; 1946–65; HTDT; George K. Bennett; Psychological Corporation. *

For additional information, see 7:1044 (4 references); for reviews by C. H. Lawshe, Jr. and Neil D. Warren, see 3:659 (2 references).

REFERENCES THROUGH 1971

1–2. See 3:659.
3–6. See 7:1044.

CUMULATIVE NAME INDEX

Bennett, G. K.: 1–2	Payton, O. D.: 6
Elkin, L.: 5	Rim, Y.: 4
Fear, R. A.: 1	Warren, N. D.: *rev*, 3:659
Laney, A. R.: 3	Wesman, A. G.: 2
Lawshe, C. H.: *rev*, 3:659	

[2226]

Manipulative Aptitude Test. Grades 9–16 and adults; 1967; MAT; 3 scores: left hand, right hand, total; Wesley S. Roeder; distributed by Western Psychological Services. *

For additional information, see 7:1045.

[2227]

Minnesota Rate of Manipulation Test, 1969 Edition. Grade 7 to adults; 1931–69; MRMT; revision of *Minnesota Manual Dexterity Test;* 5 scores: placing, turning, displacing, 1-hand turning and placing, 2-hand turning and placing; test by Minnesota Employment Stabilization Research Institute; American Guidance Service, Inc. *

For additional information and a review by Lyle F. Schoenfeldt, see 7:1046 (10 references); see also 6:1077 (24 references); for reviews by Edwin E. Ghiselli and John R. Kinzer and an excerpted review, see 3:663 (23 references); for reviews by Lorene Teegarden and Morris S. Viteles, see 2:1662 (4 references).

REFERENCES THROUGH 1971

1–4. See 2:1662.
5–26. See 3:663.
27–50. See 6:1077.
51–60. See 7:1046.

61. SHEPARD, EUGENE L. "Measurements of Certain Nonverbal Abilities of Urban and Rural Children." *J Ed Psychol* 33:458–62 S '42. * (*PA* 17:809)

62. STEEL, MARION; BALINSKY, BENJAMIN; AND LANG, HAZEL. "A Study on the Use of a Work Sample." *J Appl Psychol* 29:14–21 F '45. * (*PA* 19:1779)

63. ELLIS, DOUGLAS S. "Speed of Manipulative Performance as a Function of Work-Surface Height." *J Appl Psychol* 35:289–96 Ag '51. * (*PA* 26:3078)

64. HOFFMAN, SIMON. "Some Predictors of the Manual Work Success of Blind Persons." *Personnel & Guid J* 36:542–4 Ap '58. * (*PA* 33:8922)

65. CANTOR, GORDON N. "Motor Performance of Defectives as a Function of Competition With Same- and Opposite-Sex Opponents." *Am J Mental Def* 65:358–62 N '60. * (*PA* 35:3775)

66. DREWES, DONALD W. "Development and Validation of Synthetic Dexterity Tests Based on Elemental Motion Analysis." *J Appl Psychol* 45:179–85 Je '61. *

67. WASSENAAR, G. M. C. "The Effect of General Anxiety as an Index of Lability on the Performance of Various Psychomotor Tasks." *J General Psychol* 71:351–7 O '64. * (*PA* 39:3667)

68. ZIMMERMAN, JOHN JAMES. *Relationships Among Scholastic Aptitude, Attitudes Toward Various Facets of College Life, and Academic Performance of Students at Lycoming College.* Doctor's thesis, Pennsylvania State University (University Park, Pa.), 1969. (*DAI* 30:4792A)

69. DAVIDS, ANTHONY, AND BRENNER, DAVID. "Competition and the Premedical Student." *J Consult & Clin Psychol* 37(1): 67–72 Ag '71. * (*PA* 47:1722)

70. ZULLO, THOMAS G. "A Factor Analysis of Perceptual and Motor Abilities of Dental Students." *J Dental Ed* 35(6):356–61 Je '71. *

CUMULATIVE NAME INDEX

Balinsky, B.: 62	Hempel, W. E.: 38
Barre, M. F.: 9	Hoffman, S.: 64
Bauman, M. K.: 15, 21, 34, 40	Jayalakshmi, G.: 45–6
	Johnson, D. L.: 18
Bellows, R. M.: 6	Jurgensen, C. E.: 13
Bennett, G. K.: 8	Kinzer, J. R.: *rev*, 3:663
Bergen, G. L.: 1	Kivitz, M. S.: 59
Berman, I. R.: 2	Kolbe, L. E.: 6
Bialer, I.: 60	Lang, H.: 62
Bingham, W. V. D.: 3	McCoy, W. L.: 58
Blum, M.: 7	MacKinney, A. C.: 50
Bodley, E. A.: 36	McMurray, R. M.: 18
Bourassa, G. L.: 43	Moore, J. E.: 27
Brenner, D.: 69	Osborne, H. F.: 6
Candee, B.: 7	Otis, J. L.: 6
Cantor, G. N.: 65	Oxlade, M. N.: 23, 30
Clark, G. R.: 59	Parker, J. F.: 47
Clawson, L. E.: 56–7	Paterson, D. G.: 4
Cook, D. W.: 9	Peterson, F. E.: 55
Cooper, J. H.: 6	Rim, Y.: 52
Crites, J. O.: 49	Roberts, J. R.: 15
Cruikshank, R. M.: 8	Rogers, H. B.: 29
Davids, A.: 69	Rosen, M.: 59
Deutsch, M. R.: 60	Sartain, A. Q.: 31
Distefano, M. K.: 41	Schneidler, G. G.: 4
Drewes, D. W.: 66	Schoenfeldt, L. F.: *rev*, 7:1046
Drussell, R. D.: 44	
Dvorak, B. J.: 6	Seashore, H. G.: 25–6
Ellis, D. S.: 63	Shartle, C. L.: 6
Ellis, N. R.: 41	Shepard, E. L.: 61
Ellison, G. D.: 48	Shore, R. P.: 42
Endler, O. L.: 6	Sloan, W.: 41
Finley, P. J.: 54	Sprague, A. L.: 51
Fleishman, E. A.: 37–8, 47–8	Stead, W. H.: 6
	Steel, M.: 62
Floor, L.: 59	Sternlicht, M.: 60
Geist, H.: 32	Strange, J. R.: 31
Ghiselli, E. E.: 10, 12; *rev*, 3:663	Super, D. E.: 33, 49
	Surgent, L. V.: 24
Green, H. J.: 2	Teegarden, L.: 11, 11a, 14; *rev*, 2:1662
Guion, R. M.: 43	
Hackman, R. C.: 28	Tiffin, J.: 29
Harrell, W.: 5	Topetzes, N. J.: 39

Tuckman, J.: 16–7, 22
Viteles, M. S.: *rev*, 2:1662
Walker, K. F.: 23, 30
War Manpower Commission, Division of Occupational Analysis, Staff: 19
Ward, R. S.: 6
Wassenaar, G. M. C.: 67

Williamson, E. G.: 4
Wilson, G. M.: 20
Winschel, J. F.: 53
Wolins, L.: 50
Wyndham, A. S.: 35
Zimmerman, J. J.: 68
Zullo, T. G.: 70

[2228]

O'Connor Finger Dexterity Test. Ages 14 and over; 1920–26(?); Johnson O'Connor; Stoelting Co. (Also published by Lafayette Instrument Co.) *

For additional information, see 6:1078 (32 references); for a review by Morris S. Viteles, see 2:1659 (15 references).

REFERENCES THROUGH 1971

1–15. See 2:1659.
16–47. See 6:1078.
48. OTIS, JAY L. "The Prediction of Success in Power Sewing Machine Operating." *J Appl Psychol* 22:350–66 Ag '38. * (*PA* 13:1688)
49. WELLS, F. L. "Clinical Aspects of Functional Transfer. (Psychometric Practice in Adults of Superior Intelligence, IV.)" *Am J Orthopsychiatry* 9:1–22 Ja '39. * (*PA* 13:3317)
50. STEEL, MARION; BALINSKY, BENJAMIN; AND LANG, HAZEL. "A Study on the Use of a Work Sample." *J Appl Psychol* 29: 14–21 F '45. * (*PA* 19:1779)
51. JOHNSON, RALPH HAAKON. *Factors Related to the Success of Disabled Veterans of World War II in the Rehabilitation Training Program Approved for Mechanics and Repairmen, Motor Vehicle.* Doctor's thesis, University of Minnesota (Minneapolis, Minn.), 1955. (*DA* 15:2460)
52. KEBBON, LARS. *The Structure of Abilities at Lower Levels of Intelligence: A Factor-Analytical Study.* Stockholm, Sweden: Skandinaviska Testförlaget AB, 1965. Pp. 112. *
53. ELKIN, LORNE. "Predicting Performance of the Mentally Retarded on Sheltered Workshop and Non-Institutional Jobs." *Am J Mental Def* 72:533–9 Ja '68. * (*PA* 42:7638)
54. ZIMMERMAN, JOHN JAMES. *Relationships Among Scholastic Aptitude, Attitudes Toward Various Facets of College Life, and Academic Performance of Students at Lycoming College.* Doctor's thesis, Pennsylvania State University (University Park, Pa.), 1969. (*DAI* 30:4792A)
55. NORDÉN, K. "The Structure of Abilities in a Group of Deaf Adolescents." *Ed & Psychol Interactions* (Sweden) 32:1–22 '70. * (*PA* 44:15094)
56. CORLETT, E. N.; SALVENDY, G.; AND SEYMOUR, W. D. "Selecting Operators for Fine Manual Tasks: A Study of the O'Connor Finger Dexterity Test and the Purdue Pegboard." *Occup Psychol* (England) 45(1):57–65 '71. * (*PA* 48:3929)
57. DAVIS, LEO J., JR., AND MUENTER, MANFRED D. "Psychomotor Performances of Patients Undergoing L-Dopa Therapy." *Percept & Motor Skills* 33(3):1303–8 D '71. * (*PA* 48:3518)
58. GLUSKINOS, URY, AND BRENNAN, THOMAS F. "Selection and Evaluation Procedure for Operating Room Personnel." *J Appl Psychol* 55(2):165–9 Ap '71. * (*PA* 46:3909)
59. INSKEEP, GORDON C. "The Use of Psychomotor Tests to Select Sewing Machine Operators—Some Negative Findings." *Personnel Psychol* 24(4):707–14 w '71. *
60. NEEMAN, RENATE L. "Manipulative Dexterity and Perceptual-Motor Abilities of Mentally Retarded Adolescents and Young Adults: Perceptual-Motor Attributes of Mental Retardates, Part II." *Am J Occup Ther* 25(6):309–12 S '71. * (*PA* 49:10347)
61. ZULLO, THOMAS G. "A Factor Analysis of Perceptual and Motor Abilities of Dental Students." *J Dental Ed* 35(6): 356–61 Je '71. *

CUMULATIVE NAME INDEX

Balinsky, B.: 50
Bellows, R. M.: 20
Bennett, G. K.: 25
Bergen, G. L.: 4
Berman, I. R.: 6
Bingham, W. V. D.: 8
Blum, M.: 10, 21
Blum, M. L.: 15, 22
Bodley, E. A.: 37
Bourassa, G. L.: 41
Brennan, T. F.: 58
Brown, F.: 9
Candee, B.: 10, 21–2
Cooper, J. H.: 20
Corlett, E. N.: 56
Crites, J. O.: 47
Cruikshank, R. M.: 25
Darley, J. G.: 7
Davis, L. J.: 57
Douglass, H. R.: 11

Dvorak, B. J.: 5, 20
Elkin, L.: 53
Elliott, R. M.: 7
Ellison, G. D.: 45
Endler, O. L.: 20
Fleishman, E. A.: 38–9, 44–5
Ghiselli, E. E.: 26, 28
Gluskinos, U.: 58
Green, H. J.: 6
Greenly, R. J.: 14
Guion, R. M.: 41
Hackman, R. C.: 18
Hayes, E. G.: 3
Hempel, W. E.: 39
Hines, M.: 1
Inskeep, G. C.: 59
Jacobsen, E. E.: 29
Jayalakshmi, G.: 42–3
Johnson, R. H.: 51
Kebbon, L.: 52

Kolbe, L. E.: 20
Laney, A. R.: 36
Lang, H.: 50
McCullough, C. M.: 16
Morrow, R. S.: 23
Muenter, M. D.: 57
Neeman, R. L.: 60
Nordén, K.: 55
O'Connor, J.: 1–2, 12, 19, 24, 30
Osborne, H. F.: 20
Otis, J. L.: 20, 48
Parker, J. F.: 44
Paterson, D. G.: 7, 13
Prakash, J. C.: 40
Rim, Y.: 46
Rinsland, H. D.: 34

Ross, L. W.: 31
Salvendy, G.: 56
Schneidler, G. G.: 13
Seymour, W. D.: 56
Shartle, C. L.: 20
Stead, W. H.: 20
Steel, M.: 50
Super, D. E.: 35, 47
Surgent, L. V.: 32
Thompson, C. E.: 17, 27
Tiffin, J.: 14, 33
Viteles, M. S.: *rev*, 2:1659
Ward, R. S.: 20
Wells, F. L.: 49
Williamson, E. G.: 13
Zimmerman, J. J.: 54
Zullo, T. G.: 61

[2229]

O'Connor Tweezer Dexterity Test. Ages 14 and over; 1920–28(?); Johnson O'Connor; Stoelting Co. (Also published by Lafayette Instrument Co.) *

For additional information, see 6:1079 (23 references); for a review by Morris S. Viteles, see 2:1678 (13 references).

REFERENCES THROUGH 1971

1–13. See 2:1678.
14–36. See 6:1079.
37. OTIS, JAY L. "The Prediction of Success in Power Sewing Machine Operating." *J Appl Psychol* 22:350–66 Ag '38. * (*PA* 13:1688)
38. WELLS, F. L. "Clinical Aspects of Functional Transfer. (Psychometric Practice in Adults of Superior Intelligence, IV.)" *Am J Orthopsychiatry* 9:1–22 Ja '39. * (*PA* 13:3317)
39. STEEL, MARION; BALINSKY, BENJAMIN; AND LANG, HAZEL. "A Study on the Use of a Work Sample." *J Appl Psychol* 29: 14–21 F '45. * (*PA* 19:1779)
40. JOHNSON, RALPH HAAKON. *Factors Related to the Success of Disabled Veterans of World War II in the Rehabilitation Training Program Approved for Mechanics and Repairmen, Motor Vehicle.* Doctor's thesis, University of Minnesota (Minneapolis, Minn.), 1955. (*DA* 15:2460)
41. KAPOOR, K. "A Study on Relation Between Tests of Manual Dexterity and General Mental Ability." *Indian J Psychol* 39:59–64 Je '64. *
42. PETERSON, FLOYD E. "Identification of Sub-Groups for Test Validation Research." *J Indus Psychol* 2:98–101 D '64. * (*PA* 40:10636)
43. GEORGE, E. I., AND DEVADASAN, K. "A Comparative Study of Tweezer Dexterity in Two Selected Groups." *J Ed & Psychol* (India) 26:149–52 Jl '68. *
44. ZIMMERMAN, JOHN JAMES. *Relationships Among Scholastic Aptitude, Attitudes Toward Various Facets of College Life, and Academic Performance of Students at Lycoming College.* Doctor's thesis, Pennsylvania State University (University Park, Pa.), 1969. (*DAI* 30:4792A)
45. ZULLO, THOMAS G. "A Factor Analysis of Perceptual and Motor Abilities of Dental Students." *J Dental Ed* 35(6):356–61 Je '71. *

CUMULATIVE NAME INDEX

Albright, L. E.: 30–1
Balinsky, B.: 39
Beamer, G. C.: 27
Bellows, R. M.: 18
Bennett, G. K.: 21
Bergen, G. L.: 3
Berman, I. R.: 5
Bingham, W. V. D.: 7
Blum, M.: 9
Blum, M. L.: 13
Bourassa, G. L.: 33
Brown, F.: 8
Candee, B.: 9
Cooper, J. H.: 18
Crissey, O. L.: 22
Crites, J. O.: 36
Cruikshank, R. M.: 21
Darley, J. G.: 6
Devadasan, K.: 43
Dvorak, B. J.: 4, 18
Edmonson, L. D.: 27
Elliott, R. M.: 6
Endler, O. L.: 18
George, E. I.: 43
Green, H. J.: 5
Guion, R. M.: 33
Hackman, R. C.: 16
Harris, A. J.: 10
Jacobsen, E. E.: 24
Johnson, R. H.: 40

Kapoor, K.: 41
Kolbe, L. E.: 18
Lang, H.: 39
Lee, T.: 34
McCullough, C. M.: 14
Morrow, R. S.: 19
O'Connor, J.: 1, 11, 17, 20, 25
Osborne, H. F.: 18
Otis, J. L.: 18, 37
Paterson, D. G.: 6, 12
Peterson, F. E.: 42
Petrie, A.: 29
Powell, M. B.: 29
Prakash, J. C.: 32
Rim, Y.: 35
Schneidler, G. G.: 12
Shartle, C. L.: 18
Stead, W. H.: 18
Steel, M.: 39
Strother, G. B.: 27
Super, D. E.: 28, 36
Surgent, L. V.: 26
Thompson, C. E.: 15, 23
Viteles, M. S.: *rev*, 2:1678
Ward, R. S.: 18
Wells, F. L.: 2, 38
Williamson, E. G.: 12
Zimmerman, J. J.: 44
Zullo, T. G.: 45

[2230]

★**One Hole Test.** Job applicants; 1972; OHT; 2 machines; Gavriel Salvendy and W. Douglas Seymour; Lafayette Instrument Co., Inc. *
a) LEVEL ONE. 3 scores: number of pins inserted in first and last of 7 or 15 one-minute trials, total.
b) LEVEL TWO. 9 scores: same as above plus first and last trial time for each of 3 categories (grasp, position, reach and move).

REFERENCES THROUGH 1971
1. SALVENDY, GAVRIEL; SEYMOUR, W. DOUGLAS; AND CORLETT, E. NIGEL. "Comparative Study of Static Versus Dynamic Scoring of Performance Tests for Industrial Operators." *J Appl Psychol* 54(2):135-9 Ap '70. * (*PA* 44:11490)

CUMULATIVE NAME INDEX
Corlett, E. N.: 1   Seymour, W. D.: 1
Salvendy, G.: 1

[2231]

Pennsylvania Bi-Manual Worksample. Ages 16 and over; 1943-45; 2 scores: assembly, disassembly; John R. Roberts; American Guidance Service, Inc. *
For additional information and reviews by Edwin E. Ghiselli, Thomas W. Harrell, Albert Gibson Packard, and Neil D. Warren, see 3:665 (3 references).

REFERENCES THROUGH 1971
1-3. See 3:665.
4. GEIST, HAROLD. "The Performance of Amputees on Motor Dexterity Tests." *Ed & Psychol Meas* 9:765-72 w '49. * (*PA* 26:2950)
5. BAUMAN, MARY K. Chap. 8, "Mechanical and Manual Ability Tests for Use With the Blind," pp. 97-113. (*PA* 26:487) In *Psychological Diagnosis and Counseling of the Adult Blind: Selected Papers From the Proceedings of the University of Michigan Conference for the Blind, 1947.* Edited by Wilma Donahue and Donald Dabelstein. New York: American Foundation for the Blind, Inc., 1950. Pp. vii, 173. * (*PA* 26:493)
6. BAUMAN, MARY K. *A Manual of Norms for Tests Used in Counseling Blind Persons.* AFB Publications, Research Series, No. 6. New York: American Foundation for the Blind, Inc., 1958. Pp. 40. * (*PA* 32:1949)
7. HOFFMAN, SIMON. "Some Predictors of the Manual Work Success of Blind Persons." *Personnel & Guid J* 36:542-4 Ap '58. * (*PA* 33:8922)
8. RIM, Y. "The Predictive Validity of Seven Manual Dexterity Tests." *Psychologia* (Japan) 5:52-5 Mr '62. * (*PA* 38:1417)
9. RONAN, W. W. "Evaluation of Skilled Trades Performance Predictors." *Ed & Psychol Meas* 24:601-8 f '64. * (*PA* 39:6074)
10. GHOSH, S. N., AND TRIPATHI, R. C. "Perceptual—Motor Speed Ratio and Accident Proneness." *Indian J Appl Psychol* 2:10-6 Ja '65. * (*PA* 39:10937)
11. FREEBERG, NORMAN E. "Construct Validity of a Paper-and-Pencil Test of Manual Dexterity." *Percept & Motor Skills* 22:200 F '66. * (*PA* 40:4761)

CUMULATIVE NAME INDEX
Bauman, M. K.: 1-2, 5-6   Maher, H.: 3
Fife, I. E.: 3   Packard, A. G.: *rev,* 3:665
Freeberg, N. E.: 11   Rim, Y.: 8
Geist, H.: 4   Roberts, J. R.: 1
Ghiselli, E. E.: *rev,* 3:665   Ronan, W. W.: 9
Ghosh, S. N.: 10   Tripathi, R. C.: 10
Harrell, T. W.: *rev,* 3:665   Warren, N. D.: *rev,* 3:665
Hoffman, S.: 7

[2232]

Practical Dexterity Board. Ages 8 and over; 1962; John G. Miller; SPECO Educational Systems. *
For additional information, see 7:1047.

[2233]

*****Purdue Hand Precision Test.** Ages 17 and over; 1941; 3 scores: attempts, correct responses, error time; Joseph Tiffin; Lafayette Instrument Co. *
For additional information, see 6:1080 (2 references).

REFERENCES THROUGH 1971
1-2. See 6:1080.

CUMULATIVE NAME INDEX
Rogers, H. B.: 1   Tiffin, J.: 1-2

[2234]

*****Purdue Pegboard.** Grades 9-16 and adults; 1941-68; PP; 5 scores: right hand, left hand, both hands, right plus left plus both hands, assembly; Purdue Research Foundation under the direction of Joseph Tiffin; Science Research Associates, Inc. *
For additional information, see 6:1081 (15 references); for a review by Neil D. Warren, see 5:873 (11 references); see also 4:751 (12 references); for reviews by Edwin E. Ghiselli, Thomas W. Harrell, and Albert Gibson Packard, see 3:666 (3 references).

REFERENCES THROUGH 1971
1-3. See 3:666.
4-15. See 4:751.
16-26. See 5:873.
27-41. See 6:1081.
42. BARNETTE, W. LESLIE, JR. "Occupational Aptitude Pattern Research." *Occupations* 29:5-12 O '50. * (*PA* 25:3239)
43. KING, H. E., AND CLAUSEN, J. "Finger Dexterity." *Meth Med Res* 3:193-4 '50. * (*PA* 26:3242)
44. CHRISWELL, M. IRVING. "Validity of a Structural Dexterity Test." *J Appl Psychol* 37:13-5 F '53. * (*PA* 28:1618)
45. DUNHAM, RALPH E. "Factors Related to Recidivism in Adults." *J Social Psychol* 39:77-91 F '54. * (*PA* 28:8866)
46. KAPLAN, HARRY A.; MACHOVER, SOLOMON; AND RABINER, ABRAHAM. "A Study of the Effectiveness of Drug Therapy in Parkinsonism." *J Nerv & Mental Dis* 119:398-411 My '54. * (*PA* 29:4555)
47. VAN BILJON, I. J. "The Influence of Emotional Tension and Lability Upon the Performance of Certain Aptitude Tests." *J Social Res* (South Africa) 5:51-9 Je '54. * (*PA* 30:2331)
48. SEYMOUR, JOHN H. *Some Changes in Psychometric, Perceptual and Motor Performance as a Function of Sleep Deprivation.* Doctor's thesis, New York University (New York, N.Y.), 1956. (*DA* 16:2216)
49. HOFFMAN, SIMON. "Some Predictors of the Manual Work Success of Blind Persons." *Personnel & Guid J* 36:542-4 Ap '58. * (*PA* 33:8922)
50. HABER, WILFRED. *The Contribution of Selected Variables to Success or Failure in a Vocational Rehabilitation Evaluation.* Doctor's thesis, New York University (New York, N.Y.), 1959. (*DA* 20:4171)
51. KIESSLING, RALPH J., AND MAAG, CLINTON H. "Performance Impairment as a Function of Nitrogen Narcosis." *J Appl Psychol* 46:91-5 Ap '62. * (*PA* 38:8922)
52. CLARK, MERVIN L.; RAY, THOMAS S.; AND RAGLAND, ROBERT E. "Chlorpromazine in Chronic Schizophrenic Women: Rate of Onset and Rate of Dissipation of Drug Effects." *Psychosom Med* 25:212-7 My-Je '63. * (*PA* 38:4397)
53. COSTA, LOUIS D.; SCAROLA, LOUISE M.; AND RAPIN, ISABELLE. "Purdue Pegboard Scores for Normal Grammar School Children." *Percept & Motor Skills* 18:748 Je '64. * (*PA* 39:5045)
54. TAYLOR, JAMES BENTLEY. "The Structure of Ability in the Lower Intellectual Range." *Am J Mental Def* 68:766-74 My '64. * (*PA* 39:1793)
55. SCHWARTZ, ALFRED H. "Pegboard Changes." Letter and reply by Ronald M. Schwartz. *Am Psychologist* 20:366 My '65. *
56. EIDLE, WILLIAM REYNOLDS. *The Effects of a Mild Alcohol Dose on Tactual Vernier Acuity, Simple Addition, and Purdue Pegboard Performance.* Doctor's thesis, Fordham University (New York, N.Y.), 1966. (*DA* 27:622B)
57. FERNALD, L. DODGE, JR.; FERNALD, PETER S.; AND RINES, W. BRIAN. "Purdue Pegboard and Differential Diagnosis." Abstract. *J Consult Psychol* 30:279 Je '66. * (*PA* 40:8253, title only)
58. FREEBERG, NORMAN E. "Construct Validity of a Paper-and-Pencil Test of Manual Dexterity." *Percept & Motor Skills* 22:200 F '66. * (*PA* 40:4761)
59. PAREDES, ALFONSO; BAUMGOLD, JOHN; PUGH, LAWRENCE A.; AND RAGLAND, ROBERT. "Clinical Judgment in the Assessment of Psychopharmacological Effects." *J Nerv & Mental Dis* 142:153-60 F '66. * (*PA* 40:11294)
60. RAPIN, ISABELLE; TOURK, LESTER M.; AND COSTA, LOUIS D. "Evaluation of the Purdue Pegboard as a Screening Test for Brain Damage." *Develop Med & Child Neurol* (England) 8:45-54 F '66. * (*PA* 40:6962)
61. CLAWSON, LAVERE EDWIN. *A Study of the Clawson Worksample Tests for Measuring Manual Dexterity of the Blind.* Doctor's thesis, University of Utah (Salt Lake City, Utah), 1967. (*DA* 28:2548A)
62. KAHN, HARRIS, AND BURDETT, ARTHUR D. "Interaction of Practice and Rewards on Motor Performance of Adolescent Mental Retardates." *Am J Mental Def* 72:422-7 N '67. * (*PA* 42:7649)
63. MAYHUGH, JAMES CARROL. *The Relationship Between Normals and Subnormals Involving Tapping, the Purdue Pegboard, and Simple and Complex Reaction Times.* Doctor's thesis, University of Oklahoma (Norman, Okla.), 1967. (*DA* 28:1231B)

64. Phillips, Beatrice K., and Holden, Raymond H. "Relationship Between Fine Manipulative Ability and Intelligence in Adults in a Vocational Rehabilitation Setting." *Voc Guid Q* 15:213–6 Mr '67. * (*PA* 42:9542)

65. Rapin, I.; Scarola, L. M.; and Costa, L. D. "The Purdue Pegboard as a Screening Test for Brain Damage and Mental Retardation in Nonverbal Children." *Volta R* 69:635–8 D '67. *

66. Wagner, Hilmar Ernest. *A Study of Physical, Mental and Musical Characteristics of Selected Band Members.* Doctor's thesis, North Texas State University (Denton, Tex.), 1967. (*DA* 28:2285A) [Reviewed by James M. Shugert, *Council Res Music Ed B* 24:27–35 sp '71. *]

67. Clawson, LaVere E. "A Study of the Clawson Worksample Tests for Measuring the Manual Dexterity of the Blind." *New Outl Blind* 62:182–7+ Je '68. *

68. Elkin, Lorne. "Predicting Performance of the Mentally Retarded on Sheltered Workshop and Non-Institutional Jobs." *Am J Mental Def* 72:533–9 Ja '68. * (*PA* 42:7638)

69. Freedman, Saul. *The Relationship Between Selected Variables and Success in Transcribing Typing for Trainees Who Are Blind.* Doctor's thesis, New York University (New York, N.Y.), 1968. (*DA* 29:3000A)

70. Gilberstadt, Harold. "Relationships Among Scores of Tests Suitable for the Assessment of Adjustment and Intellectual Functioning." *J Gerontol* 23:483–7 O '68. *

71. Pelosi, John William. *A Study of the Effects of Examiner Race, Sex, and Style on Test Responses of Negro Examinees.* Doctor's thesis, Syracuse University (Syracuse, N.Y.), 1968. (*DA* 29:4105A)

72. Repovich, Lieber Don. *Effect of Practice Upon Motor Skills and Spatial Relationship of Hard-Core Poverty Adult Basic Education Trainees.* Doctor's thesis, University of Mississippi (University, Miss.), 1968. (*DA* 29:3008A)

73. Aftanas, M. S., and Royce, J. R. "A Factor Analysis of Brain Damage Tests Administered to Normal Subjects With Factor Score Comparisons Across Ages." *Multiv Behav Res* 4(4):459–81 O '69. * (*PA* 44:11030)

74. Costa, Louis D.; Vaughan, Herbert G., Jr.; Horwitz, Morton; and Ritter, Walter. "Patterns of Behavioral Deficit Associated With Visual Spatial Neglect." *Cortex* (Italy) 5(3):242–63 S '69. * (*PA* 44:13142)

75. Mack, James L. "Validity of the Purdue Pegboard as a Screening Test for Brain Damage in a Psychiatric Population." *Percept & Motor Skills* 28(3):832–4 Je '69. * (*PA* 43:17622)

76. Shih, Wei-tun. *The Correlation Among Factors Related to Measuring Ability.* Doctor's thesis, Texas A & M University (College Station, Tex.), 1969. (*DAI* 30:4804A)

77. Sterne, David M. "The Purdue Pegboard and MacQuarrie Tapping and Dotting Tasks as Measures of Motor Functioning." *Percept & Motor Skills* 28(2):556 Ap '69. * (*PA* 43:15143)

78. Vega, Arthur. "Use of Purdue Pegboard and Finger Tapping Performance as a Rapid Screening Test for Brain Damage." *J Clin Psychol* 25(3):255–8 Jl '69. * (*PA* 44:4019)

79. Zimmerman, John James. *Relationships Among Scholastic Aptitude, Attitudes Toward Various Facets of College Life, and Academic Performance of Students at Lycoming College.* Doctor's thesis, Pennsylvania State University (University Park, Pa.), 1969. (*DAI* 30:4792A)

80. Burgess, Michael M.; Kodanaz, Altan; and Ziegler, Dewey K. "Prediction of Brain Damage in a Neurological Population With Cerebrovascular Accidents." *Percept & Motor Skills* 31(2):595–601 O '70. * (*PA* 45:6841)

81. Burgess, Michael M.; Kodanaz, Altan; Ziegler, Dewey; and Greenburg, Howard. "Prediction of Brain Damage in Two Clinical Populations." *Percept & Motor Skills* 30(2):523–32 Ap '70. * (*PA* 46:7299)

82. McCoy, Wesley Lawrence. *A Comparison of Select Psychomotor Abilities of a Sample of Undergraduate Instrumental Music Majors and a Sample of Undergraduate Non-Music Majors.* Doctor's thesis, Louisiana State University (Baton Rouge, La.), 1970. (*DAI* 31:1833A)

83. Philbrick, Barbara Brinkman. *Self-Concept and Its Relation to Selected Movement Performances of 4th Grade Girls.* Doctor's thesis, Purdue University (Lafayette, Ind.), 1970. (*DAI* 31:1605A)

84. Pittman, Frank Mallory, Jr. *An Investigation of the Predictive Value of Selected Factors on Achievement in Beginning Woodworking, Metalworking, and Electricity-Electronics Courses at the College Level.* Doctor's thesis, Texas A & M University (College Station, Tex.), 1970. (*DAI* 31:2149A)

85. Rosen, Marvin; Kivitz, Marvin S.; Clark, Gerald R.; and Floor, Lucretia. "Prediction of Postinstitutional Adjustment of Mentally Retarded Adults." *Am J Mental Def* 74(6):726–34 My '70. * (*PA* 44:17195)

86. Salvendy, Gavriel; Seymour, W. Douglas; and Corlett, E. Nigel. "Comparative Study of Static Versus Dynamic Scoring of Performance Tests for Industrial Operators." *J Appl Psychol* 54(2):135–9 Ap '70. * (*PA* 44:11490)

87. Bolton, Brian. "A Factor Analytic Study of Communication Skills and Nonverbal Abilities of Deaf Rehabilitation Clients." *Multiv Behav Res* 6(4):485–501 O '71. * (*PA* 47:11373)

88. Corlett, E. N.; Salvendy, G.; and Seymour, W. D. "Selecting Operators for Fine Manual Tasks: A Study of the O'Connor Finger Dexterity Test and the Purdue Pegboard." *Occup Psychol* (England) 45(1):57–65 '71. * (*PA* 48:3929)

89. Davis, Leo J., Jr. and Muenter, Manfred D. "Psychomotor Performances of Patients Undergoing L-Dopa Therapy." *Percept & Motor Skills* 33(3):1303–8 D '71. * (*PA* 48:3518)

90. Neeman, Renate L. "Manipulative Dexterity and Perceptual-Motor Abilities of Mentally Retarded Adolescents and Young Adults: Perceptual-Motor Attributes of Mental Retardates, Part II." *Am J Occup Ther* 25(6):309–12 S '71. * (*PA* 49:10347)

91. Tarter, Ralph E., and Jones, Ben M. "Motor Impairment in Chronic Alcoholics." *Dis Nerv System* 32(9):632–6 S '71. * (*PA* 48:1249)

92. Zullo, Thomas G. "A Factor Analysis of Perceptual and Motor Abilities of Dental Students." *J Dental Ed* 35(6):356–61 Je '71. *

CUMULATIVE NAME INDEX

Aftanas, M. S.: 73
Albright, L. E.: 23–4
Alderman, E.: 7
Asher, E. J.: 6
Barnette, W. L.: 8, 13, 42
Bass, B. M.: 14
Baumgold, J.: 59
Bluett, C. G.: 4
Bolton, B.: 87
Bourassa, G. L.: 28
Bruce, M. M.: 19
Burdett, A. D.: 62
Burdock, E. I.: 35
Burgess, M. M.: 80–1
Cantor, G. N.: 15
Chriswell, M. I.: 44
Clark, G. R.: 85
Clark, M. L.: 52
Clausen, J.: 43
Clawson, L. E.: 61, 67
Comrey, A. L.: 16, 20–1
Corlett, E. N.: 86, 88
Costa, L. D.: 39, 41, 53, 60, 65, 74
Crites, J. O.: 38
Curtis, J. W.: 12
Davis, L. J.: 89
Deskin, G.: 20–1
Dingman, H. F.: 29
Dunham, R. E.: 45
Eidle, W. R.: 56
Elkin, L.: 68
Ellison, G. D.: 36
Eyman, R. K.: 29
Farber, N.: 41
Fernald, L. D.: 57
Fernald, P. S.: 57
Fleishman, E. A.: 22, 31, 36
Floor, L.: 85
Freeberg, N. E.: 58
Freedman, S.: 69
Geist, H.: 9
Ghiselli, E. E.: rev, 3:666
Gilberstadt, H.: 70
Gorelick, J.: 32
Greenburg, H.: 81
Guion, R. M.: 28
Haber, W.: 50
Harrell, T. W.: rev, 3:666
Hempel, W. E.: 22
Hill, J.: 1
Hirschhorn, B.: 26
Hoag, R. L.: 33
Hoffman, S.: 49
Holden, R. H.: 64
Horwitz, M.: 74
Jones, B. M.: 91
Kahn, H.: 62
Kaplan, H. A.: 46
Kiessling, R. J.: 51
King, H. E.: 43
Kivitz, M. S.: 85
Kodanaz, A.: 80–1
Levita, E.: 41
Long, L.: 1
Maag, C. H.: 51
McCoy, W. L.: 82
Machover, S.: 46

Mack, J. L.: 75
MacKinney, A. C.: 40
Maxfield, K. E.: 30
Mayhugh, J. C.: 63
Moffie, D. J.: 34
Muenter, M. D.: 89
Neeman, R. L.: 90
Packard, A. G.: rev, 3:666
Paredes, A.: 59
Parker, J. F.: 31
Pelosi, J. W.: 71
Peretz, D.: 35
Perry, J. D.: 30
Philbrick, B. B.: 83
Phillips, B. K.: 64
Pittman, F. M.: 84
Pugh, L. A.: 59
Rabiner, A.: 46
Radley, S.: 17
Ragland, R.: 59
Ragland, R. E.: 52
Rapin, I.: 53, 60, 65
Ray, T. S.: 52
Repovich, L. D.: 72
Rim, Y.: 37
Rines, W. B.: 57
Rinsland, H. D.: 10
Ritter, W.: 74
Rosen, M.: 85
Royce, J. R.: 73
Salvendy, G.: 86, 88
Salzinger, K.: 35
Salzinger, S.: 35
Sartain, A. Q.: 5
Scarola, L. M.: 53, 65
Schwartz, A. H.: 55
Seymour, J. H.: 48
Seymour, W. D.: 86, 88
Shih, W.: 76
Shimota, H. E.: 25
Shore, R. P.: 27
Shugert, J. M.: 66
Siegel, M.: 26
Soper, M. E.: 18
Stacey, C. L.: 15
Sterne, D. M.: 77
Strange, J. R.: 5
Stucki, R. E.: 14
Super, D. E.: 11, 38
Surgent, L. V.: 2
Sutton, S.: 35
Tarter, R. E.: 91
Taylor, J. B.: 54
Tiffin, J.: 3, 6
Tobias, J.: 32
Tourk, L. M.: 60
van Biljon, I. J.: 47
Vaughan, H. G.: 39, 41, 74
Vega, A.: 78
Wagner, H. E.: 66
Warren, N. D.: rev, 5:873
Windle, C.: 29
Wolins, L.: 40
Ziegler, D.: 81
Ziegler, D. K.: 80
Zimmerman, J. J.: 79
Zubin, J.: 35
Zullo, T. G.: 92

[2235]

Stromberg Dexterity Test. Trade school and adults; 1945–51; SDT; Eleroy L. Stromberg; Psychological Corporation. *

For additional information and a review by Julian C. Stanley, see 4:755 (1 reference).

REFERENCES THROUGH 1971

1. See 4:755.
2. ELDEEN, MUSTAFA HUSAM, AND TARVIN, JOHN C. "Validity Information Exchange, No. 9–14: D.O.T. Code 5–24, Mason." *Personnel Psychol* 9:123 sp '56. *
3. ELDEEN, MUSTAFA HUSAM, AND TARVIN, JOHN C. "Validity Information Exchange, No. 9–19: D.O.T. Code 7–88.410, Lift Truck Operator." *Personnel Psychol* 9:129 sp '56. *
4. BOLIN, S. F. "Validity Information Exchange, No. 13–04: D.O.T. Code 6–001A, Trainees in Basic Metal Work." *Personnel Psychol* 13:451–3 w '60. *
5. OLLRICH, ARTHUR H. *A Validation of the Stromberg Manual Dexterity Test and the Crawford Small Parts Test (Pins and Collars) for Use in Selecting Female Packaging and Packing Employees.* Master's thesis, Drake University (Des Moines, Iowa), 1962.
6. RIM, Y. "The Predictive Validity of Seven Manual Dexterity Tests." *Psychologia* (Japan) 5:52–5 Mr '62. * (*PA* 38:1417)
7. PETERSON, FLOYD E. "Identification of Sub-Groups for Test Validation Research." *J Indus Psychol* 2:98–101 D '64. * (*PA* 40:10636)
8. TAYLOR, JAMES BENTLEY. "The Structure of Ability in the Lower Intellectual Range." *Am J Mental Def* 68:766–74 My '64. * (*PA* 39:1793)
9. KAHN, HARRIS, AND BURDETT, ARTHUR D. "Interaction of Practice and Rewards on Motor Performance of Adolescent Mental Retardates." *Am J Mental Def* 72:422–7 N '67. * (*PA* 42:7649)

CUMULATIVE NAME INDEX

Bolin, S. F.: 4
Burdett, A. D.: 9
Eldeen, M. H.: 2–3
Kahn, H.: 9
Ollrich, A. H.: 5
Peterson, F. E.: 7

Rim, Y.: 6
Stanley, J. C.: *rev,* 4:755
Stromberg, E. L.: 1
Tarvin, J. C.: 2–3
Taylor, J. B.: 8

[2236]

Yarn Dexterity Test. Textile workers and applicants; 1964–65; YDT; Robert L. Brown; Brown & Associates, Inc.*

For additional information, see 7:1048.

[Out of Print Since TIP I]

Benge Han-Dexterity Test (status unknown), 3:656 (2 reviews)
Martin Peg Board (Finger Dexterity Test) (status unknown), 4:749
Mellenbruch Curve-Block Series, 3:662 (2 reviews, 1 reference)
Minnesota Manual Dexterity Test, T:1902; for a revision, see *Minnesota Rate of Manipulation Test,* 2227
Motor Skills Tests Adapted to the Blind, T:1905

MECHANICAL ABILITY

[2237]

A.C.E.R. Mechanical Comprehension Test. Ages 13.5 and over; 1942–53; Australian Council for Educational Research [Australia].*

For additional information and reviews by John R. Jennings and Hayden S. Williams, see 5:874 (2 references); for a review by D. W. McElwain, see 4:756.

REFERENCES THROUGH 1971

1–2. See 5:874.

CUMULATIVE NAME INDEX

Hohne, H. H.: 2
Jennings, J. R.: *rev,* 5:874
McElwain, D. W.: *rev,* 4:756

Oxlade, M.: 1
Williams, H. S.: *rev,* 5:874

[2238]

A.C.E.R. Mechanical Reasoning Test. Ages 13-9 and over; 1951–62; abbreviated adaptation of *A.C.E.R. Mechanical Comprehension Test;* T. M. Whitford (revised manual) and Research and Guidance Branch, Queensland Department of Public Instruction (test);

Australian Council for Educational Research [Australia]. *

For additional information, see 6:1082; for reviews by John R. Jennings and Hayden S. Williams, see 5:875.

REFERENCES THROUGH 1971

1. CHAPPEL, SUSAN. "Pre-Selection of Apprentice Motor Mechanics—A Preliminary Validation Study." *Personnel Prac B* (Australia) 23:204–13 S '67. *
2. STAVELEY, BRYAN. *The Abilities and Interests of Craft and Technician Students of Mechanical Engineering.* Master's thesis, University of Manchester (Manchester, England), 1967. (Abstract: *Brit J Ed Psychol* 38:324)
3. BILES, DAVID. "Test Performance and Imprisonment." *Austral & N Zeal J Criminol* (Australia) 1:46–58 Mr '68. *

CUMULATIVE NAME INDEX

Biles, D.: 3
Chappel, S.: 1
Jennings, J. R.: *rev,* 5:875

Staveley, B.: 2
Williams, H. S.: *rev,* 5:875

[2239]

Bennett Mechanical Comprehension Test. Grades 9–12 and adults; 1940–70; BMCT; revision of *Tests of Mechanical Comprehension,* Forms AA, BB, W1; Form CC (entitled *Mechanical Comprehension Test*) for men in engineering schools, is still available; George K. Bennett and William A. Owens (Form CC); Psychological Corporation. (British manuals: 1973; Peter Saville; NFER Publishing Co. Ltd. [England].) *

For additional information, reviews by Harold P. Bechtoldt and A. Oscar H. Roberts, and an excerpted review by Ronald K. Hambleton, see 7:1049 (22 references); see also 6:1094 (15 references) and 5:889 (46 references); for a review by N. W. Morton of earlier forms, see 4:766 (28 references); for reviews by Charles M. Harsh, Lloyd G. Humphreys, and George A. Satter, see 3:683 (19 references).

REFERENCES THROUGH 1971

1–19. See 3:683.
20–47. See 4:766.
48–93. See 5:889.
94–108. See 6:1094.
109–130. See 7:1049.
131. LANE, G. GORHAM. "Studies in Pilot Selection: 1, The Prediction of Success in Learning to Fly Light Aircraft." *Psychol Monogr* 61(5):1–17 '47. * (*PA* 22:5166)
132. BARNETTE, W. LESLIE, JR. "Occupational Aptitude Pattern Research." *Occupations* 29:5–12 O '50. * (*PA* 25:3239)
133. WEIDER, ARTHUR. "Some Aspects of an Industrial Mental Hygiene Program." *J Appl Psychol* 35:383–5 D '51. * (*PA* 26:6560)
134. DUNHAM, RALPH E. "Factors Related to Recidivism in Adults." *J Social Psychol* 39:77–91 F '54. * (*PA* 28:8866)
135. JOHNSON, RALPH HAAKON. *Factors Related to the Success of Disabled Veterans of World War II in the Rehabilitation Training Program Approved for Mechanics and Repairmen, Motor Vehicle.* Doctor's thesis, University of Minnesota (Minneapolis, Minn.), 1955. (*DA* 15:2460)
136. KIRKPATRICK, JAMES J. "Validation of a Test Battery for the Selection and Placement of Engineers." *Personnel Psychol* 9:211–27 su '56. * (*PA* 31:8964)
137. YESLIN, ARTHUR R.; VERNON, LEROY N.; AND KERR, WILLARD A. "The Significance of Time Spent in Answering Personality Inventories." *J Appl Psychol* 42:264–6 Ag '58. * (*PA* 33:9369)
138. FOREHAND, G. A., JR., AND McQUITTY, LOUIS L. "Configurations of Factor Standings as Predictors of Educational Achievement." *Ed & Psychol Meas* 19:31–43 sp '59. * (*PA* 34:119)
139. SPARKS, CHARLES P. "Validity of Psychological Tests." *Personnel Psychol* 23(1):39–46 sp '70. * (*PA* 44:17556)

CUMULATIVE NAME INDEX

Albright, L. E.: 94
Anderson, R. G.: 17, 20
Ash, P.: 98
Barnabas, B.: 12
Barnette, W. L.: 27, 43, 132
Barrett, R. S.: 91
Bechtoldt, H. P.: *rev,* 7:1049
Bennett, G. K.: 2–3, 5, 18
Berg, I. A.: 59
Black, J. D.: 119

Bond, G. L.: 48
Borg, W. R.: 35–6
Bradley, A. D.: 112
Bradshaw, O. L.: 126
Bray, D. W.: 130
Bruce, M. M.: 60, 64–5, 81–2, 109
Campbell, J. T.: 107
Carter, G. C.: 52
Carter, L.: 29

Case, H. W.: 53
Cass, J. C.: 99
Chandler, R. E.: 111
Clegg, H. D.: 102
Cohen, R. M.: 45
Coleman, W.: 61
Cottingham, H. F.: 22, 25
Crane, W. J.: 103
Crannell, C. W.: 34
Crites, J. O.: 105
Cronbach, L. J.: 55, 129
Cruikshank, R. M.: 2–3
Cuomo, S.: 72–4
Decker, R. L.: 92, 102
Dicken, C. F.: 119
Drew, A. S.: 104, 115
DuBois, P. H.: 37, 66
Dunham, R. E.: 134
Durrett, H. L.: 101
Ewing, T. N.: 55
Fear, R. A.: 5
Ferson, R. F.: 50
Finch, C. R.: 127
Fiske, D. W.: 23
Fitzpatrick, E. D.: 70, 75, 83
Fletcher, F. M.: 38, 45
Forehand, G. A.: 138
Forster, C. R.: 76
Gilbert, H. B.: 44, 54
Gilbert, W. M.: 55
Glennon, J. R.: 94
Goodner, S.: 124
Gordon, T.: 30
Grant, D. L.: 130
Greene, R. R.: 21
Grohsmeyer, F. A.: 67
Halliday, R. W.: 38, 45
Halstead, H.: 39
Hambleton, R. K.: *exc,* 7:1049
Hanes, B.: 110
Harrison, R.: 77
Harsh, C. M.: *rev,* 3:683
Hinman, S. L.: 122
Hodgson, R. W.: 116
Holmes, J. L.: 71
Hueber, J.: 68
Humphreys, L. G.: *rev,* 3:683
Hunt, W.: 77
Jackson, T. A.: 77
Jacobsen, E. E.: 6
Jensen, M. B.: 19
Johnson, D. L.: 10
Johnson, R. H.: 48, 84, 135
Juergenson, E. M.: 95
Jurgensen, C. E.: 26
Kazmier, L. J.: 96
Kerr, W. A.: 137
Kirkpatrick, J. J.: 136
Krathwohl, D. R.: 55
Lane, G. G.: 15, 131
Laney, A. R.: 46
Lee, M. C.: 49, 56
Lingwood, J.: 57
Lipsman, C. K.: 123
Littleton, I. T.: 58

McCarty, J. J.: 69–70, 75, 83, 87
McDaniel, J. W.: 8
McElheny, W. T.: 28
McGehee, W.: 4
MacKinney, A. C.: 100
McMurry, R. N.: 10
MacNaughton, J. F.: 128
McQuitty, L. L.: 138
Meadow, L.: 117
Meyer, H. H.: 73–4
Miller, G. E.: 51
Moffie, D. J.: 4, 124
Mollenkopf, W. G.: 88
Moore, B. V.: 1
Moore, C. L.: 128
Morton, N. W.: *rev,* 4:766
Nair, R. K.: 40
Nixon, M.: 29
North, A. J.: 47
Onarheim, J.: 24
Osburn, H. G.: 128
Otterness, W. B.: 84
Owens, W. A.: 41, 97
Patterson, C. H.: 78, 84–5
Penfield, R. V.: 120
Peterson, L. R.: 84
Poe, W. A.: 59
Reynolds, W. A.: 8
Riland, L. H.: 93
Rinsland, H. D.: 31
Roberts, A. O. H.: *rev,* 7:1049
Ronan, W. W.: 118
Rotter, J. B.: 19
Sartain, A. Q.: 11, 16
Satter, G. A.: *rev,* 3:683
Saunders, W. J.: 89
Schmitz, R. M.: 71
Shukla, N. N.: 113
Shultz, I. T.: 12
Shuman, J. T.: 9, 13–4
Smith, O. B.: 79
Smith, W. J.: 94
Sorenson, W. W.: 121
Sparks, C. P.: 139
Super, D. E.: 32, 105
Taylor, D. W.: 108
Tiedeman, D. V.: 99
Topetzes, N. J.: 90
Torres, L.: 114
Travers, R. M. W.: 42
Traxler, A. E.: 7
Upshall, C. C.: 93
Vernon, L. N.: 137
Vernon, P. E.: 33
Walker, F. C.: 86
Wallace, W. L.: 42
Watson, R. I.: 37, 66
Weider, A.: 133
Welsch, L. A.: 125
Wesman, A. G.: 18
Westberg, W. C.: 70
Whitlock, J. B.: 34
Wolff, W. M.: 47
Wolins, L.: 100
Yeslin, A. R.: 137

[2240]

Chriswell Structural Dexterity Test. Grades 7-9; 1953–63; manual title is *Structural Dexterity Test of Mechanical Ability;* 1963 revision identical with 1953 edition except for additional norms and technical data in manual; M. Irving Chriswell; Vocational Guidance Service. *

For additional information, see 6:1083 (1 reference); for a review by A. Pemberton Johnson, see 5:876.

REFERENCES THROUGH 1971
1. See 6:1083.

CUMULATIVE NAME INDEX
Chriswell, M. I.: 1   Johnson, A. P.: *rev,* 5:876

[2241]

College Placement Test in Spatial Relations. Entering college freshmen; 1962–72, c1954–72; reprintings of inactive 1954 and 1955 forms of *College Board Special Aptitude Test in Spatial Relations;*

Bennett Mechanical Comprehension Test

test available to colleges for local administration; program administered for the College Entrance Examination Board by Educational Testing Service. * For the testing program entry, see 1051.

For additional information, see 7:1050; see also 6:1084 (4 references). For a review of the testing program, see 7:665. For a review of the *College Board Special Aptitude Test in Spatial Relations,* see 4:808.

REFERENCES THROUGH 1971
1–4. See 6:1084.

CUMULATIVE NAME INDEX
Blade, M. F.: 3–4   Newman, S. H.: 1
Bobbitt, J. M.: 1   Thorndike, R. L.: *rev,* 4:808
French, J. W.: 1   Watson, W. S.: 3–4
Myers, C. T.: 2

[2242]

[Cox Mechanical and Manual Tests.] Boys ages 10 and over, 11–14, 14 and over; 1928–34; 6 tests; J. W. Cox; Charles J. Cox [England]. *
a) COX MECHANICAL TEST M. Ages 11–14, 14 and over.
b) MECHANICAL DIAGRAMS TEST. Ages 14 and over.
c) MECHANICAL EXPLANATION TEST I. Ages 14 and over.
d) COX EYEBOARD TEST NO. 2. Ages 10 and over.
e) COX NAILBOARD TEST. Ages 10 and over.
f) COX NAILSTICK TEST. Ages 10 and over.

For additional information and reviews by C. A. Oakley and Alec Rodger, see 2:1652 (4 references). For excerpts from related book reviews, see 2:B872.1 (2 excerpts) and 1:B336 (12 excerpts).

REFERENCES THROUGH 1971
1–4. See 2:1652.
5. HOLLIDAY, FRANK. "An Investigation Into the Selection of Apprentices for the Engineering Industry." *Occup Psychol* (England) 14:69–81 Ap '40. * (*PA* 14:3710)
6. SLATER, PATRICK. "Some Group Tests of Spatial Judgment or Practical Ability." *Occup Psychol* (England) 14:40–55 Ja '40. * (*PA* 14:2644)
7. BRUSH, EDWARD N. "Mechanical Ability as a Factor in Engineering Aptitude." *J Appl Psychol* 25:300–12 Je '41. * (*PA* 15:4377)
8. KERR, GEORGE. "Aptitude Testing for Secondary Courses: An Essay in Control Under War-Time Difficulties." *Occup Psychol* (England) 16:73–8 Ap '42. * (*PA* 16:3290)
9. SHUTTLEWORTH, CLIFFORD W. "Tests of Technical Aptitude." *Occup Psychol* (England) 16:175–82 O '42. *
10. OXLADE, M. "An Experiment in the Use of Psychological Tests in the Selection of Women Trainee Telephone Mechanics." *B Indus Psychol & Personnel Prac* 2:26–32 Mr '46. * (*PA* 20:4838)
11. VERNON, P. E. "The Structure of Practical Abilities." *Occup Psychol* (England) 23:81–96 Ap '49. * (*PA* 23:5313)
12. YELA, MARIANO. "Application of the Concept of Simple Structure to Alexander's Data." *Psychometrika* 14:121–35 Je '49. * (*PA* 24:1066)

CUMULATIVE NAME INDEX
Blackburn, J. M.: *exc,* 1:B336   Oakley, C. A.: *rev,* 2:1652
Brush, E. N.: 7   Oberlin, K. W.: *exc,* 1:B336
Cox, J. W.: 1, 3   Oxlade, M.: 10
Earle, F. M.: *exc,* 1:B336   Pear, T. H.: *exc,* 1:B336
Garrett, H. E.: *exc,* 1:B336   Rodger, A.: *rev,* 2:1652
Greene, E. B.: *exc,* 1:B336   Shuttleworth, C. W.: 9
Harvey, O. L.: 2   Slater, P.: 6
Holliday, F.: 5   Slocombe, C. S.: *exc,* 1:B336
Hutcheon, N. B.: 4   Vernon, P. E.: 11; *exc,* 1:B336
Kerr, G.: 8   Yela, M.: 12
Laycock, S. R.: 4
Martin, A. H.: *exc,* 1:B336

[2243]

[Curtis Object Completion and Space Form Tests.] Applicants for mechanical and technical jobs; 1960–61; 2 tests; James W. Curtis; Psychometric Affiliates. *
a) OBJECT-COMPLETION TEST.
b) SPACE FORM TEST.

For additional information and reviews by Richard S. Melton and I. Macfarlane Smith, see 6:1085.

[2244]

Detroit Mechanical Aptitudes Examination, Revised. Grades 7–16; 1928–39; 12 scores: motor (circles, classification, total), visual imagery (disarranged pictures, sizes, pulleys, total), mechanical information (tool recognition, tool information, total), arithmetic, total; Harry J. Baker, Paul H. Voelker, and Alex C. Crockett; Bobbs-Merrill Co., Inc. *

For additional information and reviews by Lloyd G. Humphreys and Dewey B. Stuit, see 3:668 (4 references); for a review by Irving Lorge and an excerpted review by J. Wayne Wrightstone, see 2:1656.

REFERENCES THROUGH 1971

1–4. See 3:668.
5. MILLER, ANDREW J., AND MANWILLER, C. E. "A Study of Trade School Pupils." *Pittsburgh Sch* 6:219–69 My–Je '32. *
6. WILLIAMS, RAY A. *The Prognostic Value of the Detroit Mechanical Aptitude Test Battery in the Vocational Education of the American Indian.* Master's thesis, University of South Dakota (Vermillion, S.D.), 1934.
7. MURPHY, LAURA WHITE. "The Relation Between Mechanical Ability Tests and Verbal and Non-Verbal Intelligence Tests." *J Psychol* 2:353–66 Mr '36. * (PA 11:3928)
8. GARRISON, K. C. "The Use of Psychological Tests in the Selection of Student-Nurses." *J Appl Psychol* 23:461–72 Ag '39. * (PA 13:6426)
9. NEMZEK, CLAUDE L., AND DE HEUS, JOHN H. "The Prediction of Academic and Non-Academic Marks in Junior High Schools." *Sch & Soc* 50:670–2 N 18 '39. * (PA 14:1598)
10. BOWN, MAX DUANE. "Variability as a Function of Ability and Its Relation to Personality and Interests." *Arch Psychol* 262:1–45 Jl '41. * (PA 16:493)
11. COTTINGHAM, HAROLD F. *The Predictive Value of Certain Paper and Pencil Mechanical Aptitude Tests in Relation to Woodworking Achievement of Junior High School Boys.* Doctor's thesis, Indiana University (Bloomington, Ind.), 1947.
12. BROADHURST, JOHN C. *A Differential Prediction of Success in Vocational-Technical and Vocational-Industrial Courses in a Vocational High School.* Doctor's thesis, New York University (New York, N.Y.), 1948.
13. COTTINGHAM, H. F. "Paper-and-Pencil Tests Given to Students in Woodworking." *Occupations* 27:95–9 N '48. * (PA 23:4408)
14. NAIR, RALPH KENNETH. *Predictive Value of Standardized Tests and Inventories in Industrial Arts Teacher Education.* Doctor's thesis, University of Missouri (Columbia, Mo.), 1950. (DA 10:77)
15. CANTONI, LOUIS J. "High School Tests and Measurements as Predictors of Occupational Status." *J Appl Psychol* 39:253–5 Ag '55. * (PA 30:4722)

CUMULATIVE NAME INDEX

Baker, H. J.: 1	Manwiller, C. E.: 5
Bennett, G. K.: 2	Miller, A. J.: 5
Bown, M. D.: 10	Murphy, L. W.: 7
Broadhurst, J. C.: 12	Nair, R. K.: 14
Cantoni, L. J.: 15	Nemzek, C. L.: 9
Cottingham, H. F.: 11, 13	Portenier, L. G.: 4
Cruikshank, R. M.: 2	Preische, W. A.: 3
de Heus, J. H.: 9	Stuit, D. B.: rev, 3:668
Garrison, K. C.: 8	Williams, R. A.: 6
Humphreys, L. G.: rev, 3:668	Wrightstone, J. W.: exc, 2:1656
Lorge, I.: rev, 2:1656	

[2245]

Flags: A Test of Space Thinking. Industrial employees; 1959, c1956–59; L. L. Thurstone (test), T. E. Jeffrey (test), and Measurement Research Division, Industrial Relations Center, University of Chicago (manual); the Center. * [The publisher has not replied to our four requests to check the accuracy of this entry.]

For additional information and a review by I. Macfarlane Smith, see 6:1086.

REFERENCES THROUGH 1971

1. EL-ABD, HAMED A. "The Intellect of East African Students." *Multiv Behav Res* 5(4):423–33 O '70. * (PA 45:8037)

CUMULATIVE NAME INDEX

El-Abd, H. A.: 1	Smith, I. M.: rev, 6:1086

[2246]

Form Perception Test. Illiterate and semiliterate adults; 1966–68; J. M. Schepers; National Institute for Personnel Research [South Africa]. *

For additional information, see 7:1051.

[2247]

Form Relations Group Test. Ages 14 and over; 1926–46; National Institute of Industrial Psychology; NFER Publishing Co. Ltd. [England]. *

For additional information and a review by A. T. Welford, see 4:757 (10 references).

REFERENCES THROUGH 1971

1–10. See 4:757.
11. MEHROTRA, S. N. "Predicting Intermediate Examination Success by Means of Psychological Tests: A Follow-Up Study." *J Voc & Ed Guid* (India) 4:157–65 My '58. * (PA 34:3442)
12. FRISBY, C. B.; VINCENT, D. F.; AND LANCASHIRE, RUTH. *Tests for Engineering Apprentices: A Validation Study.* National Institute of Industrial Psychology, Report 14. London: the Institute, 1959. Pp. iii, 24. *
13. MEHROTRA, S. N. "An Educational-Vocational Guidance Project for Intermediate Students: A Follow-Up Study." *Indian J Psychol* 34:148–62 pt 3 '59. * (PA 36:4KJ48M)
14. VENABLES, ETHEL C. "Placement Problems Among Engineering Apprentices in Part-Time Technical College Courses: Part II, Level of Ability Needed for Success in National Certificate Courses." *Brit J Ed Psychol* 31:56–8 F '61. * (PA 36:1KJ56V)
15. MONTGOMERY, G. W. G. "Predicting Success in Engineering." *Occup Psychol* (England) 36:59–68 Ja–Ap '62. *
16. ROSS, JEAN. "Predicting Practical Skill in Engineering Apprentices." *Occup Psychol* (England) 36:69–74 Ja–Ap '62. *
17. JOG, R. N. "An Attempt to Predict Success at the 'First Year Engineering Examination.'" *J Voc & Ed Guid* (India) 9:142–8 Ag '63. * (PA 38:6643)
18. JOG, R. N., AND AGA, H. "A Comparative Study of the Prediction of Academic Achievement of Engineering." *J Voc & Ed Guid* (India) 12:45–50 My '66. *
19. MILLER, EDGAR. "Handedness and the Pattern of Human Ability." *Brit J Psychol* 62(1):111–2 F '71. * (PA 46:795)

CUMULATIVE NAME INDEX

Aga, H.: 18	Miller, E.: 19
Frisby, C. B.: 12	Montgomery, G. W. G.: 15
Harding, D. W.: 8	Moore, B. G. R.: 10
Holliday, F.: 2, 4–5, 9	Peel, E. A.: 10
Hutcheon, N. B.: 1	Ross, J.: 16
Jog, R. N.: 17–8	Shuttleworth, C. W.: 7
Kerr, G.: 6	Slater, P.: 3
Lancashire, R.: 12	Venables, E. C.: 14
Laycock, S. R.: 1	Vincent, D. F.: 12
Mehrotra, S. N.: 11, 13	Welford, A. T.: rev, 4:757

[2248]

Group Test 80A. Ages 15 and over; 1943–51; spatial perception; National Institute of Industrial Psychology; NFER Publishing Co. Ltd. [England]. *

For additional information and reviews by E. G. Chambers and John Liggett, see 5:877.

REFERENCES THROUGH 1971

1. FOULDS, G. A., AND CAINE, T. A. "Personality Factors and Performance on Timed Tests of Ability." *Occup Psychol* (England) 32:102–5 Ap '58. *
2. FRISBY, C. B.; VINCENT, D. F.; AND LANCASHIRE, RUTH. *Tests for Engineering Apprentices: A Validation Study.* National Institute of Industrial Psychology, Report 14. London: the Institute, 1959. Pp. iii, 24. *

CUMULATIVE NAME INDEX

Caine, T. A.: 1	Lancashire, R.: 2
Chambers, E. G.: rev, 5:877	Liggett, J.: rev, 5:877
Foulds, G. A.: 1	Vincent, D. F.: 2
Frisby, C. B.: 2	

[2249]

Group Test 81. Ages 14 and over; 1949; spatial perception; National Institute of Industrial Psychology; NFER Publishing Co. Ltd. [England]. *

For additional information and a review by E. G. Chambers, see 4:758 (5 references).

REFERENCES THROUGH 1971

1–5. See 4:758.
6. SHUTTLEWORTH, CLIFFORD W. "Tests of Technical Aptitude." *Occup Psychol* (England) 16:175–82 O '42. *

7. WRIGLEY, JACK. "The Factorial Nature of Ability in Elementary Mathematics." *Brit J Ed Psychol* 28:61–78 F '58. * (*PA* 33:6845)

8. LEWIS, D. G. "The Factorial Nature of Attainment in Elementary Science." *Brit J Ed Psychol* 34:1–9 F '64. * (*PA* 38:9173)

9. JAMIESON, G. H. "Psychological Aspects of Craftsmanship in Pottery-Making at a Secondary School." *Brit J Ed Psychol* 35:179–82 Je '65. * (*PA* 39:16457)

10. SMITH, I. MACFARLANE. "The Use of Diagnostic Tests for Assessing the Abilities of Overseas Students Attending Institutions of Further Education, Part I." *Voc Aspect Ed* (England) 22(51):1–8 Mr '70. *

11. SMITH, I. MACFARLANE. "The Use of Diagnostic Tests for Assessing the Abilities of Overseas Students Attending Institutions of Further Education, Part II." *Voc Aspect Ed* (England) 23(54):39–48 Ap '71. *

CUMULATIVE NAME INDEX

Chambers, E. G.: *rev*, 4:758
Holliday, F.: 1, 3–5
Jamieson, G. H.: 9
Lewis, D. G.: 8
Shuttleworth, C. W.: 6
Slater, P.: 2
Smith, I. M.: 10–1
Wrigley, J.: 7

[2250]

Group Test 82. Ages 14.5 and over; 1959–70; subtest of *N.I.I.P. Engineering Apprentice Selection Test Battery;* spatial perception; National Institute of Industrial Psychology; NFER Publishing Co. Ltd. [England]. * For the complete battery entry, see 2345. For additional information, see 7:1052.

[2251]

MacQuarrie Test for Mechanical Ability. Grades 7 and over; 1925–43; 8 scores: tracing, tapping, dotting, copying, location, blocks, pursuit, total; T. W. MacQuarrie; CTB/McGraw-Hill. *

For additional information, see 4:759 (15 references) ; for reviews by John R. Kinzer, C. H. Lawshe, Jr., and Alec Rodger, see 3:661 (43 references). For an excerpt from a related book review, see 4:760.

REFERENCES THROUGH 1971

1–43. See 3:661.
44–58. See 4:759.
59. FULLER, FLORENCE D. "A Study of the Minnesota Paper Formboard Test." *Ed Res B* (Los Angeles City Schools) 7:4–5 Je '28. *

60. WALTON, MAUD SMITH. "The Correlation of Teacher Ratings in Vocational Exploratory Courses With Test Scores of Mechanical Ability." *Ed Res B* (Los Angeles City Schools) 8:2–4 O '28. *

61. LINDSEY, T. T. "Do the White and Colored Races Differ in Mechanical Ability?" *Peabody J Ed* 7:160–3 N '29. *

62. STEDMAN, MELISSA BRANSON. "A Study of the Possibility of Prognosis of School Success in Typewriting." *J Appl Psychol* 13:505–15 O '29. * (*PA* 4:891)

63. GARRETSON, OLIVER KELLEAM. "Relationships Between the Expressed Preferences and the Curricular Abilities of Ninth Grade Boys." *J Ed Res* 23:124–32 F '31. * (*PA* 5:2537)

64. EELLS, WALTER CROSBY. "Mechanical, Physical, and Musical Ability of the Native Races of Alaska." *J Appl Psychol* 17:493–506 O '33. * (*PA* 8:2669)

65. ANDERSON, H. DEWEY, AND EELLS, WALTER CROSBY. *Alaska Natives: A Survey of Their Sociological and Educational Status,* pp. 298–370. Stanford, Calif.: Stanford University Press, 1935. Pp. xvi, 472. * (*PA* 9:2346)

66. HOWARD, JOSEPHINE THEO. *The Mechanical Aptitudes of Indian Boys of the Southwest.* Master's thesis, George Washington University (Washington, D.C.), 1940.

67. GUINN, MARY PAULINE. *Aids for the Prognosis of Success in Typewriting.* Master's thesis, Kansas State Teachers College (Pittsburg, Kan.), 1948.

68. HELLEBRANDT, F. A.; HOUTZ, SARA JANE; AND PEDERSEN, THELMA. "Sex and Age Differences in the Mechanical Ability of Physical Therapy Matriculants." *Arch Phys Med* 32:567–71 S '51. *

69. MARTIN, GLENN C. "Test Batteries for Trainees in Auto Mechanics and Apparel Design." *J Appl Psychol* 35:20–2 F '51. * (*PA* 25:7123)

70. AMERICAN GAS ASSOCIATION, PERSONNEL COMMITTEE. *Personnel Testing in the Gas Industry.* New York: the Association, January 1952. Pp. 10. *

71. BALINSKY, BENJAMIN, AND HUJSA, CHARLES. "Performance of College Students on a Mechanical Knowledge Test." *J Appl Psychol* 38:111–2 Ap '54. * (*PA* 29:3028)

72. HELLEBRANDT, F. A., AND HOUTZ, SARA JANE. "Applications of the MacQuarrie Test for Mechanical Ability." *Am J Occup Ther* 9:259–63+ N–D '55. * (*PA* 30:7198)

73. LIPTON, ROBERT LAWRENCE. "A Study of the Effect of Exercise in a Simple Mechanical Activity on Mechanical Aptitude as Is Measured by the Subtests of the MacQuarrie Test for Mechanical Ability." *Psychol Newsl* 7:39–42 Ja–F '56. * (*PA* 31:1758)

74. SINICK, DANIEL. "Encouragement, Anxiety, and Test Performance." *J Appl Psychol* 40:315–8 O '56. * (*PA* 31:7972)

75. JAEGER, MARTHA. *Some Aspects of Relationship Between Motor Coordination and Personality in a Group of College Women.* Doctor's thesis, Columbia University (New York, N.Y.), 1957. (*DA* 17:2065)

76. ARNOLDI, J. "The Vocational Choices, Interests, and Aptitudes of Secondary School Boys, With Special Reference to the Consistency of These Factors." *J Social Res* (South Africa) 9:1–22 My '58. * (*PA* 34:6552)

77. SHORE, RICHARD P. "Validity Information Exchange, No. 11-22: D.O.T. Code 1-02.01, Bookkeeping-Machine Operator (Banking)." *Personnel Psychol* 11:435–6 au '58. *

78. SHORE, RICHARD P. "Validity Information Exchange, No. 11-23: D.O.T. Code 1-06.02, Teller." *Personnel Psychol* 11:437 au '58. *

79. SHORE, RICHARD P. "Validity Information Exchange, No. 11-24: D.O.T. Code 1-25.68, Proof-Machine Operator." *Personnel Psychol* 11:438–9 au '58. *

80. BUSCH, ALLEN C., AND WOODWARD, RICHARD H. "Validity Information Exchange, No. 12-18: D.O.T. Code 0-18.01, Industrial Engineer." *Personnel Psychol* 12:481 au '59. *

81. HANEY, RUSSELL; MICHAEL, WILLIAM B.; AND JONES, ROBERT A. "Identification of Aptitude and Achievement Factors in the Prediction of the Success of Nursing Trainees." *Ed & Psychol Meas* 19:645–7 w '59. * (*PA* 34:6164)

82. MICHAEL, WILLIAM B.; JONES, ROBERT A.; AND HANEY, RUSSELL. "The Development and Validation of a Test Battery for Selection of Student Nurses." *Ed & Psychol Meas* 19:641–3 w '59. * (*PA* 34:6171)

83. RACKY, DONALD J. "Predictions of Ninth Grade Woodshop Performance From Aptitude and Interest Measures." *Ed & Psychol Meas* 19:629–36 w '59. * (*PA* 34:6572)

84. GARRETT, WILEY S. "Prediction of Academic Success in a School of Nursing." *Personnel & Guid J* 38:500–3 F '60. * (*PA* 35:3954)

85. MARTIN, JACK R. "The Correlation Between Preadmission Tests and Graduation From Nursing School." *J Nursing Ed* 1:3–4+ D '62. *

86. SUPER, DONALD E., AND CRITES, JOHN O. *Appraising Vocational Fitness by Means of Psychological Tests, Revised Edition,* pp. 256–72. New York: Harper & Brothers, 1962. Pp. xv, 688. * (*PA* 37:2038)

87. MATTSON, DALE E.; REILLY, ROBERT R.; AND STACHNIAK, JOSEPH J. "The MacQuarrie Test of Mechanical Ability as a Predictor of Technic Course Grades in Dental School." *J Dental Ed* 27:327–31 D '63. *

88. TAYLOR, JAMES BENTLEY. "The Structure of Ability in the Lower Intellectual Range." *Am J Mental Def* 68:766–74 My '64. * (*PA* 39:1793)

89. DARBES, ALEX. "Some Test Characteristics of Female Student Beauticians." *Proc W Va Acad Sci* 37:286–8 F '66. * (*PA* 40:8250)

90. MCRAE, JAMES A. *The Relationship of Mathematical Ability and Physical Coordination.* Master's thesis, North Carolina State University (Raleigh, N.C.), 1966.

91. PETERSON, MARVIN ANHILM. *Correlates of Size of Course Offerings in California's Public Junior Colleges.* Doctor's thesis, Stanford University (Stanford, Calif.), 1967. (*DA* 29:518A)

92. O'CONNOR, GAIL. "Problems of Optimum Selection." *Percept & Motor Skills* 27:715–20 D '68. * (*PA* 43:7528)

93. STOCK, WILLIAM H., JR. *Some Psychological and Physiological Factors Affecting Excellence in Acting.* Doctor's thesis, Michigan State University (East Lansing, Mich.), 1968. (*DA* 29:3716A)

94. STERNE, DAVID M. "The Purdue Pegboard and MacQuarrie Tapping and Dotting Tasks as Measures of Motor Functioning." *Percept & Motor Skills* 28(2):556 Ap '69. * (*PA* 43:15143)

95. MCCOY, WESLEY LAWRENCE. *A Comparison of Select Psychomotor Abilities of a Sample of Undergraduate Instrumental Music Majors and a Sample of Undergraduate Non-Music Majors.* Doctor's thesis, Louisiana State University (Baton Rouge, La.), 1970. (*DAI* 31:1833A)

96. STRAUSS, RALPH JOSEPH. *Biographical Factors and Performance: How Are They Related? A Study of the Relationship Between Various Subcultural Factors, Aptitude Test Performance and Job-Success Ratings of Repair and Assembly Workers.* Doctor's thesis, New York University (New York, N.Y.), 1971. (*DAI* 32:5899A)

CUMULATIVE NAME INDEX

American Gas Association, Personnel Committee: 70
Anderson, H. D.: 65
Anderson, R. G.: 40, 48
Arnoldi, J.: 76
Babcock, H.: 17, 54
Balinsky, B.: 71
Barrett, D. M.: 36

Beamer, G. C.: 50
Bellows, R. M.: 22, 25
Bennett, G. K.: 26
Bingham, W. V.: 13
Bingham, W. V. D.: 15
Blum, M. L.: 30
Burr, M.: 11
Busch, A. C.: 80

Chapman, R. L.: 51
Cooper, J. H.: 22
Crawford, J. E.: 23
Crites, J. O.: 86
Cruikshank, R. M.: 26
Curtis, H. S.: 27
Darbes, A.: 89
Duran, J. C.: 55
Dvorak, B. J.: 22
Edmonson, L. D.: 50
Eells, W. C.: 64-5
Emerson, M. R.: 17
Endler, O. L.: 22
Faubion, R.: 21
Fife, I. E.: 43
Fuller, F. D.: 59
Garretson, O. K.: 63
Garrett, W. S.: 84
Ghiselli, E. E.: 24, 28
Goodman, C. H.: 37, 41-2, 56
Griffitts, C. H.: 9
Guinn, M. P.: 67
Haney, R.: 81-2
Harrell, W.: 16, 19-21
Hellebrandt, F. A.: 68, 72
Holcomb, G. W.: 10
Horning, S. D.: 1
Houtz, S. J.: 68, 72
Howard, J. T.: 66
Hujsa, C.: 71
Jaeger, M.: 75
Jones, R. A.: 81-2
Jorgensen, C.: 12
Kefauver, G. N.: 5
Kinzer, J. R.: rev, 3:661
Klugman, S. F.: 31
Kolbe, L. E.: 22
Lackey, F. W.: 18
Laney, A. R.: 58
Laslett, H. R.: 10
Lawshe, C. H.: rev, 3:661
Lindsey, T. T.: 61
Lipton, R. L.: 73
McCoy, W. L.: 95
McDaniel, J. W.: 32
MacQuarrie, T. W.: 2
McRae, J. A.: 90
Maher, H.: 43
Martin, G. C.: 69

Martin, J. R.: 85
Mattson, D. E.: 87
Mercer, M.: 46
Michael, W. B.: 81-2
Mitrano, A. J.: 29
Moodie, M.: 47
Morgan, W. J.: 33
Murphy, L. W.: 45
O'Connor, G.: 92
Osborne, H. F.: 22
Otis, J. L.: 22
Pedersen, T.: 68
Peterson, M. A.: 91
Racky, D. J.: 83
Raubenheimer, A. S.: 6
Reilly, R. R.: 87
Reynolds, W. A.: 32
Robinson, J. B.: 25
Rodger, A.: rev, 3:661
Sartain, A. Q.: 35, 38
Scudder, C. R.: 6
Shaffer, L. F.: exc, 4:760
Shartle, C. L.: 22
Shore, R. P.: 77-9
Shultz, I. T.: 49
Sinick, D.: 74
Skolnik, R. F.: 14
Stachniak, J. J.: 87
Stannard, C.: 44
Stead, W. H.: 22
Stedman, M. B.: 7, 62
Stein, M. L.: 3
Sterne, D. M.: 94
Stock, W. H.: 93
Stoy, E. G.: 4
Strauss, R. J.: 96
Strother, G. B.: 50
Super, D. E.: 52, 86
Taylor, D. H.: 8
Taylor, J. B.: 88
Thompson, C. E.: 34
Travers, R. M. W.: 57
Tuckman, J.: 39
Wallace, W. L.: 57
Walton, M. S.: 60
Ward, R. S.: 22
Woodward, R. H.: 80
Zakolski, F. C.: 53

[2252]

Mechanical Aptitude Test: Acorn National Aptitude Tests. Grades 7–16 and adults; 1943–52; 5 scores: comprehension of mechanical tasks, use of tools and materials (verbal), matching tools and operations, use of tools and materials (nonverbal), total; 1952 test identical with test copyrighted 1943; Andrew Kobal, J. Wayne Wrightstone, and Karl R. Kunze; Psychometric Affiliates. *

For additional information, see 5:878; for reviews by Reign H. Bittner, James M. Porter, Jr., and Alec Rodger, see 3:669.

[2253]

Mechanical Comprehension Test, Second Edition. Male technical apprentices and trainee engineer applicants; 1966–68; manual by P. D. Griffiths; National Institute for Personnel Research [South Africa]. *

For additional information, see 7:1053.

[2254]

Mechanical Information Test. Ages 15 and over; 1948–70; MIT; subtest of *N.I.I.P. Engineering Apprentice Selection Test Battery;* National Institute of Industrial Psychology; NFER Publishing Co. Ltd. [England]. * For the complete battery entry, see 2345. For additional information, see 7:1054 (1 reference).

REFERENCES THROUGH 1971

1. See 7:1054.

CUMULATIVE NAME INDEX

Frisby, C. B.: 1
Lancashire, R.: 1
Vincent, D. F.: 1

[2255]

Mechanical Movements: A Test of Mechanical Comprehension. Industrial employees; 1959–63, c1956–63; abbreviated version of a Thurstone test developed about 1918; L. L. Thurstone (test), T. E. Jeffrey (test), and Measurement Research Division, Industrial Relations Center, University of Chicago (manual); the Center. * [The publisher has not replied to our four requests to check the accuracy of this entry.]

For additional information and a review by William A. Owens, see 6:1089.

[2256]

*****Mechanical Reasoning: Differential Aptitude Tests.** Grades 8–12 and adults; 1947–73; 2 editions; George K. Bennett, Harold G. Seashore, and Alexander G. Wesman; Psychological Corporation. * For the complete battery entry, see 1069.
a) FORM A. 1947–59. *Out of print.*
b) FORM T. 1947–73; revision of Forms L and M ('62).

For reviews of the complete battery, see 7:673 (1 review, 1 excerpt), 6:767 (2 reviews), 5:605 (2 reviews), 4:711 (3 reviews), and 3:620 (1 excerpt).

REFERENCES THROUGH 1971

1. "Results of the Space Relations, Mechanical Reasoning, and Clerical Speed and Accuracy Tests of the Differential Aptitude Test Battery in Six Public Schools." *Ed Rec B* 58:79–84 F '52. * (*PA* 26:7240)
2. "Validity Information Exchange, No. 7-094: D.O.T. Code 7-80.120, Beginner Mechanics." *Personnel Psychol* 7:572 w '54. *
3. "Validity Information Exchange, No. 7-095: D.O.T. Code 7-94.112 and 7-94.100, Tool and Die and Machinist Apprentice." *Personnel Psychol* 7:573 w '54. *
4. "Validity Information Exchange, No. 7-096: D.O.T. Code 9-03.01, Riveter Assistants (Rivet-Buckers)." *Personnel Psychol* 7:574 w '54. *
5. MENDICINO, LORENZO. "Mechanical Reasoning and Space Perception: Native Capacity or Experience." *Personnel & Guid J* 36:335–8 Ja '58. * (*PA* 33:6837)
6. JAYALAKSHMI, G. "Correlation of Tests of Psychomotor Ability With Intelligence and Non-motor Tests." *J Psychol Res* (India) 3:78–84 S '59. *
7. FOOTE, RICHARD PAUL. *The Prediction of Success in Automotive Mechanics in a Vocational-Industrial Curriculum on the Secondary School Level.* Doctor's thesis, New York University (New York, N.Y.), 1960. (*DA* 21:3014)
8. McGUIRE, CARSON. "The Prediction of Talented Behavior in the Junior High School." *Proc Inv Conf Testing Probl* 1960: 46–67 '61. *
9. JONES, CHARLES W., AND McMILLEN, DAN. "Engineering Freshman Norms for the D.A.T. Mechanical Reasoning and Space Relations Tests Utilizing Fifteen-Minute Time Limits." *Ed & Psychol Meas* 25:459–64 su '65. * (*PA* 39:16507)
10. PARMENTER, WILLIAM H. *An Investigation of the Predictive Validity of the Spatial and Mechanical Tests of the Differential Aptitude Tests in Regard to Success in Industrial Arts.* Master's thesis, California State College (Long Beach, Calif.), 1966.
11. IRVINE, FLEET RAYMOND. *A Study of Creative Thinking Ability, and Its Relationship to Psychomotor Ability, Mechanical Reasoning Ability, and Vocational Aptitude of Selected High School Industrial Arts Students.* Doctor's thesis, Utah State University (Logan, Utah), 1968. (*DA* 29:1768A)

CUMULATIVE NAME INDEX

Foote, R. P.: 7
Irvine, F. R.: 11
Jayalakshmi, G.: 6
Jones, C. W.: 9
McGuire, C.: 8
McMillen, D.: 9
Mendicino, L.: 5
Parmenter, W. H.: 10

[2257]

Mellenbruch Mechanical Motivation Test. Grades 6–16 and adults; 1944–57; formerly called *Mellenbruch Mechanical Aptitude Test for Men and Women;* P. L. Mellenbruch; Psychometric Affiliates. *

For additional information and reviews by Arthur H. Brayfield and John B. Morris, see 5:879; for reviews by Lloyd G. Humphreys and C. A. Oakley of the original edition, see 3:670.

REFERENCES THROUGH 1971

1. COTTINGHAM, HAROLD F. *The Predictive Value of Certain Paper and Pencil Mechanical Aptitude Tests in Relation to Wood-*

working Achievement of Junior High School Boys. Doctor's thesis, Indiana University (Bloomington, Ind.), 1947.

2. COTTINGHAM, H. F. "Paper-and-Pencil Tests Given to Students in Woodworking." *Occupations* 27:95–9 N '48. * (*PA* 23: 4408)

CUMULATIVE NAME INDEX

Brayfield, A. H.: *rev,* 5:879　　Morris, J. B.: *rev,* 5:879
Cottingham, H. F.: 1–2　　　Oakley, C. A.: *rev,* 3:670
Humphreys, L. G.: *rev,* 3:670

[2258]

Minnesota Spatial Relations Test. Ages 11 and over; 1930; revision of H. C. Link's *Spatial Relations Test* ('19); 2 scores: time, error; M. R. Trabue, Donald G. Paterson, Richard M. Elliott, L. Dewey Anderson, Herbert A. Toops, and Edna Heidbreder; American Guidance Service. *

For additional information and a review by Milton L. Blum, see 3:664 (18 references); for a review by Lorene Teegarden, see 2:1663 (10 references).

REFERENCES THROUGH 1971

1–10. See 2:1663.
11–28. See 3:664.
29. VANDEN BOOGERT, ALYCE W. *The Significance of the Minnesota Spatial Relations Test With a Group of First and Second-Grade Children.* Master's thesis, University of Michigan (Ann Arbor, Mich.), 1934.
30. BRODY, DAVID. "Twin Resemblances in Mechanical Ability, With Reference to the Effects of Practice on Performance." *Child Develop* 8:207–16 S '37. * (*PA* 12:565)
31. GREENE, EDWARD B. "Practice Effects on Various Types of Standard Tests." *Am J Psychol* 49:67–75 Ja '37. * (*PA* 11:2482)
32. PRITCHARD, MIRIAM C. "The Mechanical Ability of Subnormal Boys." *Teach Col Contrib Ed* 699:1–73 '37. * (*PA* 11: 4608)
33. OTIS, JAY L. "The Prediction of Success in Power Sewing Machine Operating." *J Appl Psychol* 22:350–66 Ag '38. * (*PA* 13:1688)
34. HACKMAN, RAY CARTER. *The Differential Prediction of Success in Two Contrasting Vocational Areas.* Doctor's thesis, University of Minnesota (Minneapolis, Minn.), 1940.
35. SHEPARD, EUGENE L. *Measurements of Certain Nonverbal Abilities of Urban and Rural Children.* Doctor's thesis, New York University (New York, N.Y.), 1940.
36. CRISSEY, ORLO L. "Test Predictive of Success in Occupation of Job-Setter." Abstract. *Psychol B* 39:436 Jl '42. * (*PA* 16:4971, title only)
37. ROSS, LAWRENCE W. "Results of Testing Machine-Tool Trainees." *Personnel J* 21:363–7 Ap '43. * (*PA* 17:2459)
38. STEEL, MARION; BALINSKY, BENJAMIN; AND LANG, HAZEL. "A Study on the Use of a Work Sample." *J Appl Psychol* 29: 14–21 F '45. * (*PA* 19:1779)
39. WITTENBORN, J. R. "Mechanical Ability, Its Nature and Measurement: 1, An Analysis of the Variables Employed in the Preliminary Minnesota Experiment." *Ed & Psychol Meas* 5: 241–60 au '45. * (*PA* 20:2925)
40. WITTENBORN, J. R. "Mechanical Ability, Its Nature and Measurement: 2, Manual Dexterity. *Ed & Psychol Meas* 5:395– 409 w '45. * (*PA* 20:2926)
41. HALSTEAD, H., AND SLATER, PATRICK. "An Experiment in the Vocational Adjustment of Neurotic Patients." *J Mental Sci* (England) 92:509–15 Jl '46. * (*PA* 21:281)
42. BARNETT, ALBERT. "A Note on Mechanical Aptitude of West Texans." *J Appl Psychol* 33:316–8 Ag '49. * (*PA* 24:2363)
43. GEIST, HAROLD. "The Performance of Amputees on Motor Dexterity Tests." *Ed & Psychol Meas* 9:765–72 w '49. * (*PA* 26:2950)
44. RINSLAND, HENRY D. "The Prediction of Veterans' Success From Test Scores at the University of Oklahoma." Part 1, pp. 59–72. In *The Sixth Yearbook of the National Council on Measurements Used in Education, 1948–1949.* Fairmont, W.Va.: the Council, Fairmont State College, 1949. Pp. v, 140. *
45. SUPER, DONALD E. *Appraising Vocational Fitness by Means of Psychological Tests,* pp. 285–97. New York: Harper & Brothers, 1949. Pp. xxiii, 727. * (*PA* 24:2130)
46. LANEY, ARTHUR R., JR. "Validity of Employment Tests for Gas-Appliance Service Personnel." *Personnel Psychol* 4:199– 208 su '51. * (*PA* 26:1735)
47. TIZARD, J., AND LOOS, F. M. "The Learning of a Spatial Relations Test by Adult Imbeciles." *Am J Mental Def* 59:85–90 Jl '54. * (*PA* 29:4278)
48. JOHNSON, RALPH HAAKON. *Factors Related to the Success of Disabled Veterans of World War II in the Rehabilitation Training Program Approved for Mechanics and Repairmen, Motor Vehicle.* Doctor's thesis, University of Minnesota (Minneapolis, Minn.), 1955. (*DA* 15:2460)
49. SUPER, DONALD E., AND CRITES, JOHN O. *Appraising Vocational Fitness by Means of Psychological Tests, Revised Edition,*

pp. 281–90. New York: Harper & Brothers, 1962. Pp. xv, 688. * (*PA* 37:2038)
50. FINLEY, PETER J. "Performance of Male Juvenile Delinquents on Four Psychological Tests." *Training Sch B* 60:175–83 F '64. * (*PA* 39:5704)
51. ZIMMERMAN, JOHN JAMES. *Relationships Among Scholastic Aptitude, Attitudes Toward Various Facets of College Life, and Academic Performance of Students at Lycoming College.* Doctor's thesis, Pennsylvania State University (University Park, Pa.), 1969. (*DAI* 30:4792A)

CUMULATIVE NAME INDEX

Anderson, L. D.: 1–2　　Laney, A. R.: 46
Balinsky, B.: 38　　　　Lang, H.: 38
Barnett, A.: 42　　　　Loos, F. M.: 47
Bates, J.: 24　　　　　Morrow, R. S.: 18
Bellows, R. M.: 14　　Myklebust, H. R.: 28
Bennett, G. K.: 19　　Osborne, H. F.: 14
Bergen, G. L.: 5　　　Otis, J. L.: 14, 33
Berman, I. R.: 7　　　Page, M. L.: 11
Bingham, W. V. D.: 8　Paterson, D. G.: 2, 7, 10
Blum, M. L.: *rev,* 3:664　Pritchard, M. C.: 32
Brody, D.: 30　　　　Rinsland, H. D.: 44
Brown, F.: 9　　　　Ross, L. W.: 37
Brush, E. N.: 15　　Schieffelin, B.: 3
Cooper, J. H.: 14　　Schneidler, G. G.: 10
Crissey, O. L.: 36　　Schwesinger, G. C.: 3
Crites, J. O.: 49　　Shartle, C. L.: 14
Cruikshank, R. M.: 19　Shepard, E. L.: 35
Dvorak, B. J.: 6, 14　Slater, P.: 26, 41
Elliott, R. M.: 2　　Stanton, M. B.: 12
Endler, O. L.: 14　　Stead, W. H.: 14
Finley, P. J.: 50　　Steel, M.: 38
Geist, H.: 43　　　Super, D. E.: 45, 49
Ghiselli, E. E.: 16　Teegarden, L.: 22–3, 25; *rev,*
Green, H. J.: 7　　　　2:1663
Greene, E. B.: 31　　Tizard, J.: 47
Hackman, R. C.: 34　Toops, H. A.: 2
Halstead, H.: 26, 41　Trabue, M. R.: 7
Harmon, J. B.: 17　　Vanden Boogert, A. W.: 29
Harmon, L. R.: 17　　Wallace, M.: 24
Harrell, W.: 13　　　War Manpower Commission,
Harvey, O. L.: 4　　　Division of Occupational
Heidbreder, E.: 2　　　Analysis, Staff: 27
Henderson, M. T.: 24　Ward, R. S.: 14
Johnson, A. P.: 20–1　Williamson, E. G.: 10
Johnson, R. H.: 48　　Wittenborn, J. R.: 39–40
Kolbe, L. E.: 14　　　Zimmerman, J. J.: 51

[2259]

O'Connor Wiggly Block. Ages 16 and over; 1928– 51; Johnson O'Connor; Stoelting Co. (Also published by Lafayette Instrument Co.) *

For additional information, see 6:1091 (27 references).

REFERENCES THROUGH 1971

1–27. See 6:1091.
28. LINDSEY, T. T. "Do the White and Colored Races Differ in Mechanical Ability?" *Peabody J Ed* 7:160–3 N '29. *
29. GOODRICH, JOHN RICHARD. *The Prediction of Mechanical Ability in Ninth Grade Boys by Means of a Block Assembly Test.* Master's thesis, University of Cincinnati (Cincinnati, Ohio), 1935.
30. WELLS, F. L. "Clinical Aspects of Functional Transfer. (Psychometric Practice in Adults of Superior Intelligence, IV.)" *Am J Orthopsychiatry* 9:1–22 Ja '39. * (*PA* 13:3317)

CUMULATIVE NAME INDEX

Bates, J.: 16　　　　Kjerland, R. N.: 25–7
Bennett, G. K.: 14　Lauer, A. R.: 21, 25
Bittel, J.: 22　　　Licht, M.: 18–9
Brush, E. N.: 12　　Lindsey, T. T.: 28
Bunch, R. H.: 25　　McIntosh, W. J.: 24
Cruikshank, R. M.: 14　Miller, C.: 21
Estes, S. G.: 15　　O'Connor, J.: 1, 5, 17
Foley, J.: 23　　　Philip, B. R.: 6
Frye, E. K.: 8　　Phillips, J. J.: 27
Giese, W. J.: 13　　Remmers, H. H.: 3, 7
Goodrich, J. R.: 29　Schell, J. W.: 3
Green, M. C.: 27　　Smith, J. M.: 7
Harrell, W.: 9, 11　Stoy, E. G.: 2
Harris, A. J.: 10　Viteles, M. S.: 4
Henderson, M. T.: 16　Wallace, M.: 16
Keane, F. L.: 1　　Wells, F. L.: 30
Khan, H. I. A.: 20

[2260]

O'Rourke Mechanical Aptitude Test. Grades 7–12 and adults; 1926–57; some forms entitled *O'Rourke*

Mechanical Aptitude Test—Junior Grade; L. J. O'Rourke; O'Rourke Publications. *

For additional information, see 5:882; for reviews by Jay L. Otis and George A. Satter, see 3:672 (8 references); for a review by Herbert A. Landry, see 2:1668.

REFERENCES THROUGH 1971

1–8. See 3:672.
9. SUPER, DONALD E., AND CRITES, JOHN O. *Appraising Vocational Fitness by Means of Psychological Tests, Revised Edition,* pp. 232–42. New York: Harper & Brothers, 1962. Pp. xv, 688. * (PA 37:2038)

CUMULATIVE NAME INDEX

Bennett, G. K.: 3
Bingham, W. V. D.: 2
Crites, J. O.: 9
Cruikshank, R. M.: 3
Hanman, B.: 4
Landry, H. A.: *rev,* 2:1668
Lawshe, C. H.: 5
McDaniel, J. W.: 6
Otis, J. L.: *rev,* 3:672
Raubenheimer, A. S.: 1
Reynolds, W. A.: 6
Sartain, A. Q.: 8
Satter, G. A.: *rev,* 3:672
Scudder, C. R.: 1
Super, D. E.: 9
Thornton, G. R.: 5
Tuckman, J.: 7

[2261]

Perceptual Battery. Job applicants with at least 10 years of education; 1961–63; spatial relations; National Institute for Personnel Research [South Africa]. *

For additional information, see 7:1055.

[2262]

Primary Mechanical Ability Tests. Applicants for positions requiring mechanical ability; 1940–50; 4 tests, 5 scores: 4 scores listed below, total; J. H. Hazelhurst; Stevens, Thurow & Associates, Inc. *

a) TEST 1, CROSSES.
b) TEST 2, BOLTS.
c) TEST 3, TOOLS.
d) TEST 4, MISSING LINES.

For additional information, see 6:1087.

[2263]

Purdue Mechanical Adaptability Test. Males ages 15 and over; 1945–50; C. H. Lawshe, Jr. and Joseph Tiffin; University Book Store. *

For additional information, see 4:762 (6 references); for reviews by Jay L. Otis and Dewey B. Stuit, see 3:676.

REFERENCES THROUGH 1971

1–6. See 4:762.
7. BRUCE, MARTIN M. "Validity Information Exchange, No. 7-079: D.O.T. Code 7-83.058, Electrical Appliance Serviceman." *Personnel Psychol* 7:425–6 au '54. *
8. HUEBER, JOANNE. "Validity Information Exchange, No. 7-089: D.O.T. Code 5-83.641, Maintenance Mechanic II." *Personnel Psychol* 7:565–6 w '54. *
9. DREW, ALFRED STANISLAUS. *The Relationship of General Reading Ability and Other Factors to School and Job Performance of Machinist Apprentices.* Doctor's thesis, University of Wisconsin (Madison, Wis.), 1962. (DA 23:1261)
10. CAMPBELL, JOEL T. "Validity Information Exchange, No. 16-04: D.O.T. Code 7-36.250, Gas Deliveryman." *Personnel Psychol* 16:181–3 su '63. *
11. DREW, ALFRED S. "The Relationship of General Reading Ability and Other Factors to School and Job Performance of Machine Apprentices." *J Indus Teach Ed* 2:47–60 f '64. *

CUMULATIVE NAME INDEX

Belman, H. S.: 4
Bruce, M. M.: 7
Campbell, J. T.: 10
Drew, A. S.: 9, 11
Evans, R. N.: 4
Hueber, J.: 8
Lawshe, C. H.: 1–2
Otis, J. L.: *rev,* 3:676
Rothe, H. F.: 5
Semanek, I. A.: 1
Stuit, D. B.: *rev,* 3:676
Super, D. E.: 3
Tiffin, J.: 1–2
Wells, R. G.: 6

[2264]

RBH Three-Dimensional Space Test. Industrial workers in mechanical fields; 1950–63; Richardson, Bellows, Henry & Co., Inc. *

For additional information, see 6:1095.

[2265]

RBH Two-Dimensional Space Test. Business and industry; 1948–63; Richardson, Bellows, Henry & Co., Inc. *

For additional information, see 6:1097.

[2266]

Revised Minnesota Paper Form Board Test. Grades 9–16 and adults; 1930–70; original test by Donald G. Paterson, Richard M. Elliott, L. Dewey Anderson, Herbert A. Toops, and Edna Heidbreder; revision by Rensis Likert and William H. Quasha; Psychological Corporation. *

For additional information, see 7:1056 (19 references); see also 6:1092 (16 references); for a review by D. W. McElwain, see 5:884 (29 references); for reviews by Clifford E. Jurgensen and Raymond A. Katzell, see 4:763 (38 references); for a review by Dewey B. Stuit, see 3:677 (48 references); for a review by Alec Rodger, see 2:1673 (9 references).

REFERENCES THROUGH 1971

1–9. See 2:1673.
10–57. See 3:677.
58–95. See 4:763.
96–124. See 5:884.
125–140. See 6:1092.
141–159. See 7:1056.
160. STOY, E. G. "Tests for Mechanical Drawing Aptitude." *Personnel J* 6:93–101 Ag '27. * (PA 2:816)
161. CARTER, HAROLD DEAN. "The Organization of Mechanical Intelligence." *J Genetic Psychol* 35:270–85 Je '28. * (PA 2:3743)
162. FULLER, FLORENCE D. "A Study of the Minnesota Paper Formboard Test." *Ed Res B* (Los Angeles City Schools) 7:4–5 Je '28. *
163. PETERSON, JOSEPH, AND LANIER, LYLE H. Part 2, "Comparisons of Certain Mental Abilities in White and Negro Adults," pp. 103–56. In their *Studies in the Comparative Abilities of Whites and Negroes.* Mental Measurements Monographs. Serial No. 5. Baltimore, Md.: Williams & Wilkins Co., 1929. Pp. vi, 156. * (PA 3:2316)
164. HALL, O. MILTON. "An Aid to the Selection of Pressman Apprentices." *Personnel J* 9:77–85 Je '30. * (PA 4:3994)
165. GARRETSON, OLIVER KELLEAM. "Relationships Between the Expressed Preferences and the Curricular Abilities of Ninth Grade Boys." *J Ed Res* 23:124–32 F '31. * (PA 5:2537)
166. DUBOIS, PHILIP HUNTER. "A Speed Factor in Mental Tests." *Arch Psychol* 141:1–38 Je '32. * (PA 7:3591)
167. RUGGLES, EDWARD W. "An Analytical Study of Various Factors Relating to Juvenile Crime." *J Juvenile Res* 16:125–32 Ap '32. * (PA 6:4501)
168. SORENSON, HERBERT. "Some Factors for Pupil Control Measured and Related." *J Ed Psychol* 23:1–10 Ja '32. * (PA 6:2027)
169. PRITCHARD, MIRIAM C. "The Mechanical Ability of Subnormal Boys." *Teach Col Contrib Ed* 699:1–73 '37. * (PA 11:4608)
170. OTIS, JAY L. "The Prediction of Success in Power Sewing Machine Operating." *J Appl Psychol* 22:350–66 Ag '38. * (PA 13:1688)
171. MORRIS, CHARLES M. "A Critical Analysis of Certain Performance Tests." *J Genetic Psychol* 54:85–105 Mr '39. * (PA 13:5387)
172. BOWN, MAX DUANE. "Variability as a Function of Ability and Its Relation to Personality and Interests." *Arch Psychol* 262:1–45 Jl '41. * (PA 16:493)
173. BEAN, KENNETH L. "Negro Responses to Verbal and Non-Verbal Test Materials." *J Psychol* 13:343–53 Ap '42. * (PA 16:3487)
174. SHEPARD, EUGENE L. "Measurements of Certain Non-verbal Abilities of Urban and Rural Children." *J Ed Psychol* 33:458–62 S '42. * (PA 17:809)
175. EBERT, ELIZABETH, AND SIMMONS, KATHERINE. *The Brush Foundation Study of Child Growth and Development: 1, Psychometric Tests.* Monographs of the Society for Research in Child Development, Vol. 8, No. 2, Serial No. 35. Washington, D.C.: the Society, National Research Council, 1943. Pp. xiv, 113. * (PA 18:3322)
176. OSBORNE, AGNES ELIZABETH. "The Relationship Between Certain Psychological Tests and Shorthand Achievement." *Teach Col Contrib Ed* 873:1–58 '43. *
177. BARNETTE, W. LESLIE, JR. "Occupational Aptitude Pattern Research." *Occupations* 29:5–12 O '50. * (PA 25:3239)
178. LEE, EVERETT S. "Negro Intelligence and Selective Migration: A Philadelphia Test of the Klineberg Hypothesis." *Am Sociol R* 16:227–33 Ap '51. * (PA 27:1093)

179. DUNHAM, RALPH E. "Factors Related to Recidivism in Adults." *J Social Psychol* 39:77–91 F '54. * (*PA* 28:8866)

180. ABRAMSON, H. A.; JARVIK, M. E.; HIRSCH, M. W.; AND EWALD, A. T. "Lysergic Acid Diethylamide (LSD-25): 5, Effect on Spatial Relations Abilities." *J Psychol* 39:435–42 Ap '55. * (*PA* 29:8316)

181. BARRATT, ERNEST S. "The Space-Visualization Factors Related to Temperament Traits." *J Psychol* 39:279–87 Ap '55. * (*PA* 29:8424)

182. JOHNSON, RALPH HAAKON. *Factors Related to the Success of Disabled Veterans of World War II in the Rehabilitation Training Program Approved for Mechanics and Repairmen, Motor Vehicle.* Doctor's thesis, University of Minnesota (Minneapolis, Minn.), 1955. (*DA* 15:2460)

183. RABE, AUSMA. "Individual Differences in Orientation in Perceptual and Cognitive Tasks." *Can J Psychol* 9:149–54 S '55. * (*PA* 30:3923)

184. BAIR, JOHN T.; LOCKMAN, ROBERT F.; AND MARTOCCIA, CHARLES T. "Validity and Factor Analyses of Naval Air Training Predictor and Criterion Measures." *J Appl Psychol* 40:213–9 Ag '56. * (*PA* 31:6701)

185. WITHERSPOON, Y. T. "The Measurement of Indian Children's Achievement in the Academic Tool Subjects." *J Am Indian Ed* 1:5–9 My '62. *

186. LEVITA, ERIC; RIKLAN, MANUEL; AND COOPER, IRVING S. "Cognitive and Perceptual Performance in Parkinsonism as a Function of Age and Neurological Impairment." *J Nerv & Mental Dis* 139:516–20 D '64. * (*PA* 39:10554)

187. MOLOMO, RAYMOND R-S. *Two Spatial Factors in Two-Dimensional and Three-Dimensional Spatial Aptitude.* Master's thesis, University of Ottawa (Ottawa, Ont., Canada), 1964.

188. DAWSON, JOHN L. M. "Cultural and Physiological Influences Upon Spatial-Perceptual Processes in West Africa, Part II." *Int J Psychol* (France) 2(3):171–85 '67. * (*PA* 43:5194)

189. GEORGE, E. I.; PILLAY, P. GOPALA; AND DHARMANGADAN, B. "Effect of Physical Disability on Personality Adjustment and Achievement of Secondary School Pupils." *J Ed & Psychol* (India) 24:180–7 Ja '67. *

190. MARTIN, BERNARD L. "Spatial Visualization Abilities of Prospective Mathematics Teachers." *J Res Sci Teach* 5(1):11–9 '67. *

191. BILES, DAVID. "Test Performance and Imprisonment." *Austral & N Zeal J Criminol* (Australia) 1:46–58 Mr '68. *

192. WIGGINS, NANCY; HOFFMAN, PAUL J.; AND TABER, THOMAS. "Types of Judges and Cue Utilization in Judgments of Intelligence." *J Pers & Social Psychol* 12(1):52–9 My '69. * (*PA* 43:11266)

193. DEE, H. L. "Visuoconstructive and Visuoperceptive Deficit in Patients With Unilateral Cerebral Lesions." *Neuropsychologia* (England) 8(3):305–14 Jl '70. * (*PA* 44:21403)

194. BOLTON, BRIAN. "A Factor Analytic Study of Communication Skills and Nonverbal Abilities of Deaf Rehabilitation Clients." *Multiv Behav Res* 6(4):485–501 O '71. * (*PA* 47:11373)

195. WERNER, LAWRENCE KURT. *The Relationships Among the Psycho-Motor, Motor Coordination, Personality, and Intellectual Domains of Development in Preadolescent Children.* Doctor's thesis, Purdue University (Lafayette, Ind.), 1971. (*DAI* 32:4435A)

196. ZULLO, THOMAS G. "A Factor Analysis of Perceptual and Motor Abilities of Dental Students." *J Dental Ed* 35(6):356–61 Je '71. *

CUMULATIVE NAME INDEX

Abramson, H. A.: 180
Achard, F. H.: 66
Albright, L. E.: 128–9
Alteneder, L. E.: 12, 16
Anderson, L. D.: 1–2
Anderson, R. G.: 56, 70
Angers, W. P.: 137
Ash, P.: 130
Bair, J. T.: 184
Baldwin, E. F.: 41
Balinsky, B.: 105
Barnett, A.: 80
Barnette, W. L.: 81, 92, 177
Barratt, E. S.: 181
Barratt, D. M.: 48
Barrett, R. S.: 124
Bates, J.: 37
Beamer, G. C.: 73
Bean, K. L.: 173
Bellows, R. M.: 17
Bennett, G. K.: 26
Berdie, R. F.: 88
Biles, D.: 191
Bingham, W. V. D.: 6
Blanchard, H. L.: 82
Bobbitt, J. M.: 100
Bodley, E. A.: 101
Bolton, B.: 194
Bown, M. D.: 172
Bradley, A. D.: 144

Branson, B. D.: 142
Broadhurst, J. C.: 74
Bruce, M. M.: 118, 121–2
Brush, E. N.: 19
Bryan, A. I.: 27
Cantoni, L. J.: 110
Carter, H. D.: 161
Casey, D. L.: 134
Cass, J. C.: 131
Chothia, F. S.: 125
Clarke, F. H.: 66
Coleman, W.: 102
Cooper, I. S.: 186
Cooper, J. H.: 17
Crawford, J. E.: 20, 28
Crites, J. O.: 139
Cruikshank, R. M.: 26
Cuomo, S.: 111
Dawson, J. L. M.: 188
Dee, H. L.: 155, 193
Dejmek, F. W.: 75
Dharmangadan, B.: 189
Dreffin, W. B.: 76
DuBois, P. H.: 89, 106, 166
Dunham, R. E.: 179
Dvorak, B. J.: 17
Ebert, E.: 175
Edmonson, L. D.: 73
Edwards, K. D.: 96
Elliott, R. M.: 2

Endler, O. L.: 17
Entwisle, F. N.: 137
Erickson, I. P.: 14
Estes, S. G.: 29
Ewald, A. T.: 180
Ferson, R. F.: 97
Finch, C. R.: 153
Frank, A. C.: 156
French, J. W.: 100
Fuller, F. D.: 162
Garretson, O. K.: 165
Garrett, H. E.: 3
Gavurin, E. I.: 152
George, E. I.: 189
Ghiselli, E. E.: 21, 30
Glennon, J. R.: 128–9
Graham, L. F.: 113
Guazzo, E. J.: 107
Habegger, O. F.: 77
Hackman, R. C.: 61
Hakkinen, S.: 132
Hall, O. M.: 164
Hanes, B.: 141
Hanman, B.: 31
Havighurst, R. J.: 64, 67
Heidbreder, E.: 2
Henderson, M. T.: 37
Hirsch, M. W.: 180
Hoffman, P. J.: 192
Hohne, H. H.: 112
Holmes, J. L.: 109
Hueber, J.: 108
Hujsa, C.: 105
Jacobsen, E. E.: 38
Janke, L. L.: 64, 67
Janus, S.: 65
Jarvik, M. E.: 180
Jenkins, J. J.: 103
Johnson, A. P.: 32–3, 137
Johnson, R. H.: 119, 182
Jurgensen, C. E.: *rev*, 4:763
Katzell, R. A.: *rev*, 4:763
Kirk, B. A.: 156
Klugman, S. F.: 39
Kolbe, L. E.: 17
Laney, A. R.: 93
Lanier, L. H.: 163
Lapp, C. J.: 24
Lauer, A. R.: 71
LeBold, W. K.: 143
Lee, E. S.: 178
Levita, E.: 186
Likert, R.: 4, 7
Littleton, I. T.: 98
Lockman, R. F.: 184
Lorencki, S. F.: 157
McElwain, D. W.: *rev*, 5:884
McGehee, W.: 34
MacKinney, A. C.: 133
Malloy, J. P.: 113
Martin, B. L.: 150, 190
Martin, H. T.: 140
Martoccia, C. T.: 184
Mason, P. L.: 134
Melberg, M. E.: 83
Mercer, M.: 60
Meyer, H. H.: 111
Miller, A. J.: 151
Miller, C. R.: 99
Milton, C. R.: 99
Mitrano, A. J.: 35
Moffie, D. J.: 34, 99
Molomo, R. R-S.: 187
Moore, B. V.: 22
Morgan, W. J.: 42–3
Morris, C. M.: 59, 171
Morrow, R. S.: 23
Murphy, L. W.: 58
Murray, J. E.: 84
Myklebust, H. R.: 54
Nair, R. K.: 90
Newall, K.: 126
Newman, S. H.: 100
Novak, B. J.: 94
Osborne, A. E.: 176
Osborne, H. F.: 17

Otis, J. L.: 17, 170
Otterness, W. B.: 119
Oxlade, M. N.: 72, 78, 95
Paterson, D. G.: 2, 8
Patterson, C. H.: 14, 119–20
Perrine, M. W.: 115
Peterson, J.: 163
Peterson, L. R.: 119
Phillips, G. R.: 147
Pillay, P. G.: 189
Poidevin, B.: 116
Pritchard, M. C.: 169
Quasha, W. H.: 7
Quasha, W. R.: 5
Rabe, A.: 183
Reichard, S.: 44
Reid, J. W.: 137
Riklan, M.: 186
Rinsland, H. D.: 85
Rodger, A.: *rev*, 2:1673
Ronan, W. W.: 148, 159
Ross, L. W.: 63
Ruggles, E. W.: 167
Sartain, A. Q.: 49, 55
Saxena, K. N.: 138
Scheuhing, M. A.: 79, 94
Schmitz, R. M.: 109
Schneck, M. R.: 3
Schneidler, G. G.: 8
Schultz, R. S.: 9
Shartle, C. L.: 17
Shepard, E. L.: 62, 174
Shih, W.: 158
Shukla, N. N.: 145
Shuman, J. T.: 45, 50–1
Simmons, K.: 175
Skolnicki, J.: 127
Smith, L. F.: 41
Smith, O. B.: 117
Smith, W. J.: 128–9
Sorenson, H.: 168
Speer, G. S.: 123
Stanton, M. B.: 13
Stead, W. H.: 17
Stephens, E. W.: 52
Sterne, D. M.: 154
Stoy, E. G.: 160
Strother, G. B.: 73
Stuit, D. B.: 18, 24; *rev*, 3: 677
Super, D. E.: 86, 139
Sutter, N. A.: 88
Taber, T.: 192
Tandon, R. K.: 149
Taylor, D. H.: 10
Thompson, C. E.: 15, 36
Tiedeman, D. V.: 131
Tinker, M. A.: 46
Toivainen, Y.: 132
Toops, H. A.: 2
Torres, L.: 146
Travers, R. M. W.: 91
Traxler, A. E.: 40
Tuckman, J.: 47, 57
Tyler, D. J.: 135
Viteles, M. S.: 11
Walker, K. F.: 72
Wallace, M.: 37
Wallace, W. L.: 91
War Manpower Commission, Division of Occupational Analysis, Staff: 53
Ward, R. S.: 17
Watley, D. J.: 136, 140
Watson, R. I.: 89, 106
Watts, F. P.: 25
Werner, L. K.: 195
Wiggins, N.: 192
Wightwick, B.: 87
Williamson, E. G.: 8
Witherspoon, Y. T.: 185
Wittenborn, J. R.: 68–9
Wolins, L.: 133
Wrenn, C. G.: 76
Wysocki, B.: 113
Zullo, T. G.: 196

[2267]

SRA Mechanical Aptitudes. Grades 9–12 and adults; 1947–50; 4 scores: mechanical knowledge, space relations, shop arithmetic, total; Richardson, Bellows, Henry & Co., Inc.; Science Research Associates, Inc. *

Revised Minnesota Paper Form Board Test

For additional information and reviews by Alec Rodger and Douglas G. Schultz, see 4:764.

REFERENCES THROUGH 1971

1. FERSON, REGIS F. *The Probabilities of Success in Trade Training as Estimated by Standardized Tests.* Doctor's thesis, University of Pittsburgh (Pittsburgh, Pa.), 1951.
2. LITTLETON, ISAAC T. "Prediction in Auto Trade Courses." *J Appl Psychol* 36:15–9 F '52. * (*PA* 26:7256)
3. BALINSKY, BENJAMIN, AND HUJSA, CHARLES. "Performance of College Students on a Mechanical Knowledge Test." *J Appl Psychol* 38:111–2 Ap '54. * (*PA* 29:3028)
4. VOPATEK, S. H. "Normative Data Information Exchange, No. 36." *Personnel Psychol* 9:551 w '56. *
5. FOOTE, RICHARD PAUL. *The Prediction of Success in Automotive Mechanics in a Vocational-Industrial Curriculum on the Secondary School Level.* Doctor's thesis, New York University (New York, N.Y.), 1960. (*DA* 21:3014)
6. MACKINNEY, ARTHUR C., AND WOLINS, LEROY. "Validity Information Exchange, No. 13–01, Foreman II, Home Appliance Manufacturing." *Personnel Psychol* 13:443–7 w '60. *
7. FRITZ, KENTNER V., AND FRITZ, MARTIN F. "Untimed Norms for the SRA Mechanical Knowledge and Shop Arithmetic Tests." *J Psychol* 72(1):115–8 My '69. * (*PA* 43:16495)
8. PITTMAN, FRANK MALLORY, JR. *An Investigation of the Predictive Value of Selected Factors on Achievement in Beginning Woodworking, Metalworking, and Electricity-Electronics Courses at the College Level.* Doctor's thesis, Texas A & M University (College Station, Tex.), 1970. (*DAI* 31:2149A)

CUMULATIVE NAME INDEX

Balinsky, B.: 3
Ferson, R. F.: 1
Foote, R. P.: 5
Fritz, K. V.: 7
Fritz, M. F.: 7
Hujsa, C.: 3
Littleton, I. T.: 2

MacKinney, A. C.: 6
Pittman, F. M.: 8
Rodger, A.: *rev*, 4:764
Schultz, D. G.: *rev*, 4:764
Vopatek, S. H.: 4
Wolins, L.: 6

[2268]

*Space Relations: Differential Aptitude Tests. Grades 8–12 and adults; 1947–73; 2 editions; George K. Bennett, Harold G. Seashore, and Alexander G. Wesman; Psychological Corporation. * For the complete battery entry, see 1069.
a) FORM A. 1947–59. *Out of print.*
b) FORM T. 1947–73; 1972 test identical with Form M copyrighted 1962 except for item sequence.

For reviews of the complete battery, see 7:673 (1 review, 1 excerpt), 6:767 (2 reviews), 5:605 (2 reviews), 4:711 (3 reviews), and 3:620 (1 excerpt).

REFERENCES THROUGH 1971

1. GLASER, ROBERT. "The Application of the Concepts of Multiple-Operation Measurement to the Response Patterns on Psychological Tests." *Ed & Psychol Meas* 11:372–82 au '51. * (*PA* 27:5522)
2. GLASER, ROBERT. "Predicting Achievement in Medical School." *J Appl Psychol* 35:272–4 Ag '51. * (*PA* 26:3046)
3. GLASER, ROBERT. "The Validity of Some Tests for Predicting Achievement in Medical School." Abstract. *Am Psychologist* 6:298 Jl '51. *
4. "Results of the Space Relations, Mechanical Reasoning, and Clerical Speed and Accuracy Tests of the Differential Aptitude Test Battery in Six Public Schools." *Ed Rec B* 58:79–84 F '52. * (*PA* 26:7240)
5. GLASER, ROBERT. "The Reliability of Inconsistency." *Ed & Psychol Meas* 12:60–4 sp '52. * (*PA* 27:5523)
6. GLASER, ROBERT, AND JACOBS, OWEN. "Predicting Achievement in Medical School: A Comparison of Preclinical and Clinical Criteria." *J Appl Psychol* 38:245–7 Ag '54. * (*PA* 29:6271)
7. HARRISON, ROSS; HUNT, WINSLOW; AND JACKSON, THEODORE A. "Profile of the Mechanical Engineer: 1, Ability." *Personnel Psychol* 8:219–34 su '55. * (*PA* 30:5414)
8. MENDICINO, LORENZO. "Mechanical Reasoning and Space Perception: Native Capacity or Experience." *Personnel & Guid J* 36:335–8 Ja '58. * (*PA* 33:6837)
9. HORN, FERN MAY. *A Study of the Relationships Between Certain Aspects of Clothing and the Ability to Handle Selected Clothing Construction Tools With the Developmental Levels of Early Adolescent Girls.* Doctor's thesis, Michigan State University (East Lansing, Mich.), 1959. (*DA* 20:3278)
10. JAYALAKSHMI, G. "Correlation of Tests of Psychomotor Ability With Intelligence and Non-motor Tests." *J Psychol Res* (India) 3:78–84 S '59. *
11. JONES, CHARLES W., AND MCMILLEN, DAN. "Engineering Freshman Norms for the D.A.T. Mechanical Reasoning and Space Relations Tests Utilizing Fifteen-Minute Time Limits." *Ed & Psychol Meas* 25:459–64 su '65. * (*PA* 39:16507)
12. MARTIN, BERNARD LOYAL. *Spatial Visualization Abilities of Central Washington State College Prospective Elementary and Secondary Teachers of Mathematics.* Doctor's thesis, Oregon State University (Corvallis, Ore.), 1966. (*DA* 27:2427A)
13. PARMENTER, WILLIAM H. *An Investigation of the Predictive Validity of the Spatial and Mechanical Tests of the Differential Aptitude Tests in Regard to Success in Industrial Arts.* Master's thesis, California State College (Long Beach, Calif.), 1966.
14. MARTIN, BERNARD L. "Spatial Visualization Abilities of Prospective Mathematics Teachers." *J Res Sci Teach* 5(1):11–9 '67. *
15. ROSS, DONALD RUFUS. *Test Performance of Deaf Adults Under Two Modes of Test Administration.* Doctor's thesis, University of Arizona (Tucson, Ariz.), 1967. (*DA* 28:2992A)
16. SCHROTH, MARVIN L. "Spatial Aptitude and Its Relationship to Art Judgment." *Percept & Motor Skills* 24:746 Je '67. * (*PA* 41:13608, title only)
17. NELSON, LEONARD THEODORE, JR. *The Relationship Between Verbal, Visual-Spatial, and Numerical Abilities and the Learning of the Mathematical Concept of Function.* Doctor's thesis, University of Michigan (Ann Arbor, Mich.), 1968. (*DAI* 30:218A)
18. HARTLAGE, LAWRENCE C. "Nonvisual Test of Spatial Ability." Abstract. *Proc 77th Ann Conv Am Psychol Assn* 4(1):163–4 '69. * (*PA* 43:16635)

CUMULATIVE NAME INDEX

Glaser, R.: 1–3, 5–6
Harrison, R.: 7
Hartlage, L. C.: 18
Horn, F. M.: 9
Hunt, W.: 7
Jackson, T. A.: 7
Jacobs, O.: 6
Jayalakshmi, G.: 10

Jones, C. W.: 11
McMillen, D.: 11
Martin, B. L.: 12, 14
Mendicino, L.: 8
Nelson, L. T.: 17
Parmenter, W. H.: 13
Ross, D. R.: 15
Schroth, M. L.: 16

[2269]

Spatial Tests EG, 2, and 3. Ages 10-0 to 13-11 and 15-0 to 18-0; 1950–63; 3 tests; published for the National Foundation for Educational Research in England and Wales; Ginn & Co. Ltd. [England]. *
a) SPATIAL TEST EG. Ages 11-0 to 13-11; 1950–59; formerly called *Spatial Test 1*; I. Macfarlane Smith.
b) SPATIAL TEST 2 (THREE-DIMENSIONAL). Ages 10-7 to 13-11; 1950–56; distribution restricted to directors of education and colleges of further education; A. F. Watts with the assistance of D. A. Pidgeon and M. K. B. Richards.
c) SPATIAL TEST 3 (NEWCASTLE SPATIAL TEST). Ages 10-0 to 11-11 and 15-0 to 18-0; 1958–63; distribution restricted to directors of education and colleges of further education; I. Macfarlane Smith and J. S. Lawes.

For additional information, see 7:1057 (1 reference); see also 6:1093 (4 references); for reviews by E. G. Chambers and Charles T. Myers of tests 1 and 2, see 5:885; for a review by E. A. Peel of test 1, see 4:753.

REFERENCES THROUGH 1971

1–4. See 6:1093.
5. See 7:1057.
6. SMITH, I. MACFARLANE. "The Development of a Spatial Test." *Durham Ed R* (England) 1(5):19–33 S '54. * (*PA* 29:7298)
7. BULL, K. R. "An Investigation Into the Relationship Between Physique, Motor Capacity and Certain Temperamental Traits." *Brit J Ed Psychol* 28:149–54 Je '58. * (*PA* 33:7655)

CUMULATIVE NAME INDEX

Bull, K. R.: 7
Chambers, E. G.: *rev*, 5:885
Lawes, J. S.: 4
Myers, C. T.: *rev*, 5:885

Peel, E. A.: *rev*, 4:753
Smith, I. M.: 1–2, 6
Taylor, C. C.: 3
Vandenberg, S. G.: 5

[2270]

Spatial Visualization Test: The Dailey Vocational Tests. Grades 8–12 and adults; 1964–65; SVT; John T. Dailey and Kenneth B. Hoyt (manual); Houghton Mifflin Co. * For the complete battery entry, see 2105.

For reviews of the complete battery, see 7:976 (2 reviews, 2 excerpts).

[2271]

Vincent Mechanical Diagrams Test. Ages 15 and over; 1936–70; VMD; based upon *The Vincent Mechanical Models Test A;* subtest of *N.I.I.P. Engineering Apprentice Selection Test Battery;* National Institute of Industrial Psychology; NFER Publishing Co. Ltd. [England]. * For the complete battery entry, see 2345.

For additional information, see 7:1058.

[2272]

Weights and Pulleys: A Test of Intuitive Mechanics. Engineering students and industrial employees; 1959, c1956–59; L. L. Thurstone (test), T. E. Jeffrey (test), and Measurement Research Division, Industrial Relations Center, University of Chicago (manual); the Center. * [The publisher has not replied to our four requests to check the accuracy of this entry.]

For additional information and a review by William A. Owens, see 6:1098.

[Out of Print Since TIP I]

Mechanical Information Questionnaire (status unknown), 6:1088
Mechanical Knowledge Test, T:1925
Minnesota Assembly Test, 3:671 (1 review, 11 references)
Moray House Space Test 2, 6:1090 (1 review, 4 references)
N.I.I.P. Squares Test, 5:880 (1 review, 9 references)
Paper Puzzles: A Test of Space Relations, T:1935
Prognostic Test of Mechanical Abilities, 4:761 (2 reviews, 1 excerpt, 1 reference)
Purdue Mechanical Performance Test, 5:883 (1 reference)
RBH Tool Knowledge Test, 6:1096
Stenquist Mechanical Assembling Test, 3:679 (1 review, 10 references)
Survey of Mechanical Insight, 5:886 (4 reviews, 3 references)
Survey of Object Visualization, 5:887 (5 reviews, 5 references)
Survey of Space Relations Ability, 5:888 (4 reviews, 4 references)
Tool Knowledge Test, 5:890 (2 reviews)
V.G.C. Object Visualization Indicator, 4:767
V.G.C. Space Relations Ability Indicator, 4:768
Vincent Mechanical Models Test A (Industrial), 4:769 (1 review, 7 references)

MISCELLANEOUS

[2273]

Alpha Biographical Inventory. Grades 9–12; 1968, c1966–68; ABI; earlier experimental editions called *Biographical Inventory,* Forms A, B, C, C–1, J, K, L, M, N, O; 2 scores: creativity, academic performance in college; Institute for Behavorial Research in Creativity. *

For additional information and reviews by John K. Hemphill and William C. Ward, see 7:975 (16 references).

REFERENCES THROUGH 1971

1–16. See 7:975.
17. Counts, Perry Dalmond. *A Study of the Relationship Between Academic Achievement and Creativity.* Doctor's thesis, University of Tennessee (Knoxville, Tenn.), 1971. (*DAI* 32:4342A)
18. Davis, Gary A., and Belcher, Terence L. "How Shall Creativity Be Measured? Torrance Tests, RAT, Alpha Biographical, and IQ." *J Creative Behav* 5(3):153–61 '71. *

19. Lunneborg, C. E. "Alpha Biographical Inventory: A Review." *J Ed Meas* 8(3):233–4 f '71. *

CUMULATIVE NAME INDEX

Abe, C.: 2, 13
Belcher, T. L.: 18
Carron, T. J.: 15
Cline, V. B.: 2, 4, 9
Counts, P. D.: 17
Damm, V. J.: 14
Davis, G. A.: 18
Ellison, R. L.: 1, 3, 5, 8, 10, 15–6
Fox, D. G.: 16
Goodner, S.: 7
Harrington, C.: 11
Hemphill, J. K.: *rev,* 7:975
Hinman, S. L.: 6
James, L. R.: 10, 15–6
Lunneborg, C. E.: 19
McDonald, B. W.: 10
Moffie, D. J.: 7
Mulaik, S. A.: 4
Price, J. S.: 12
Richards, J. M.: 2
Schmitt, J. R.: 9
Taylor, C. W.: 5, 8, 10, 16
Tucker, M. F.: 4–5, 9
Ward, W. C.: *rev,* 7:975

[2274]

The Biographical Index. College and industry; 1961–62; 5 scores: drive to excel, financial status, human relations orientation, personal adjustment, stability; Willard A. Kerr; Psychometric Affiliates. *

For additional information and reviews by John K. Hemphill and Richard S. Melton, see 6:1099.

[2275]

Business Judgment Test, Revised. Adults; 1953–69; BJT; Martin M. Bruce; Martin M. Bruce, Ph.D., Publishers. *

For additional information, a review by Jerome E. Doppelt, and an excerpted review by Kenneth D. Orton, see 7:1059 (1 reference); see also 6:1101 (4 references); for a review by Edward B. Greene, see 5:893.

REFERENCES THROUGH 1971

1–4. See 6:1101.
5. See 7:1059.
6. Bass, Bernard M. "Validity Information Exchange, No. 10–25; D.O.T. Code 1–85.22, Salesman, Foodstuffs." *Personnel Psychol* 10:343–4 au '57. *

CUMULATIVE NAME INDEX

Bass, B. M.: 6
Bruce, M. M.: 1–2
Doppelt, J. E.: *rev,* 7:1059
Friesen, E. P.: 2
Greene, E. B.: *rev,* 5:893
Martin, H. T.: 4
Orton, K. D.: *exc,* 7:1059
Watley, D. J.: 3–5

[2276]

*The Conference Evaluation.** Conference participants; 1969–71; ratings by participants; Psychologists and Educators, Inc. *

For additional information, see 7:1060.

[2277]

Conference Meeting Rating Scale. Conference leaders and participants; 1959; B. J. Speroff; Psychometric Affiliates. *

For additional information, see 6:1103.

[2278-9]

★**Continuous Letter Checking and Continuous Symbol Checking.** Ages 12 and over; 1967–72; "capacity to stick to a tedious task"; 2 tests; 7 scores: speed, accuracy, neatness, curve of work (4 scores); H. Reuning; National Institute for Personnel Research [South Africa]. *
a) continuous letter checking. High school educational level; 1967–72; CLC.
b) continuous symbol checking. Any educational level; 1972; CSC.

[2280]

Gullo Workshop and Seminar Evaluation. Workshop and seminar participants; 1969; ratings by participants; John M. Gullo; Psychologists and Educators, Inc. *

For additional information, see 7:1061.

[2281]

Job Attitude Analysis. Production and clerical workers; 1961–70; an inventory for employment interviewing and vocational counseling; 1970 test materials identical with materials published 1965 except for cover design; P. L. Mellenbruch; Psychometric Affiliates. *

For additional information, see 7:980 (1 reference).

REFERENCES THROUGH 1971

1. See 7:980.

CUMULATIVE NAME INDEX

Mellenbruch, P. L.: 1

[2282]

Mathematical and Technical Test. Ages 11 and over; 1948; also called *M-T Test;* 11 scores: completing pictures, copying models, calculations, completing the series, continuing patterns, filling up gaps, technical insight, figure series, geometrical figures, remembering drawings, total; manual out of print; J. Luning Prak; George G. Harrap & Co. Ltd. [England]. *

For additional information and reviews by Charles R. Langmuir and F. W. Warburton, see 4:779.

[2283]

Minnesota Importance Questionnaire, 1967 Revision. Vocational counselees; 1967–71; MIQ; intrapersonal vocational needs of an individual for specified job-related reinforcers; 21 scores (20 of which parallel scores of *Minnesota Job Description Questionnaire* and *Minnesota Satisfaction Questionnaire*): ability utilization, achievement, activity, advancement, authority, company policies and practices, compensation, coworkers, creativity, independence, moral values, recognition, responsibility, security, social service, social status, supervision—human relations, supervision—technical, variety, working conditions, validity; David J. Weiss, Rene V. Dawis, Lloyd H. Lofquist, Evan G. Gay, and Darwin D. Hendel (manual); Vocational Psychology Research. *

For additional information, see 7:1063 (29 references).

REFERENCES THROUGH 1971

1–29. See 7:1063.
30. ELO, MARGARET REED. *The Relationship of Counselor and Client Needs to Occupational Outcomes.* Doctor's thesis, University of Minnesota (Minneapolis, Minn.), 1970. (*DAI* 32: 1838B)
31. WARREN, LYNDA WALKER. *The Prediction of Job Satisfaction as a Function of the Correspondence Between Vocational Needs and Occupational Reinforcers.* Doctor's thesis, University of Minnesota (Minneapolis, Minn.), 1970. (*DAI* 32:608B)
32. WILLOUGHBY, THEODORE C. "Needs, Interests, and Reinforcer Preferences of Data Processing Personnel." *Proc Ann Computer Personnel Res Conf* 8:119–43 '70. *
33. GAY, EVAN G.; WEISS, DAVID J.; HENDEL, DARWIN D.; DAWIS, RENÉ V.; AND LOFQUIST, LLOYD H. *Manual for the Minnesota Importance Questionnaire.* University of Minnesota Industrial Relations Center Bulletin 54; Minnesota Studies in Vocational Rehabilitation 28. Minneapolis, Minn.: the Center, June 1971. Pp. x, 83. *
34. KAUPPI, DWIGHT RANDOLPH. *The Development of Instrument-Specific Reading and Comprehension Pre-Tests for Standardized Questionnaires and Inventories.* Doctor's thesis, University of Minnesota (Minneapolis, Minn.), 1971. (*DAI* 32:4844B)
35. LYBARGER, ALVIN EUGENE. *A Comparison of Job Satisfaction Needs of Selected Rural and Urban Industrial Education Students in the State of Utah.* Doctor's thesis, Utah State University (Logan, Utah), 1971. (*DAI* 32:3746A)
36. SIMPSON, ALAN ROGER. *A Comparison of Selected Characteristics of Counselors Leaving the State Rehabilitation Agency With Counselors Who Stay.* Doctor's thesis, University of Iowa (Iowa City, Iowa), 1971. (*DAI* 32:4362A)
37. WILLOUGHBY, THEODORE CRAWFORD. *Needs, Interests, Reinforcer Patterns and Satisfaction of Data Processing Personnel.* Doctor's thesis, University of Minnesota (Minneapolis, Minn.), 1971. (*DAI* 32:5421A)

CUMULATIVE NAME INDEX

Anderson, L. L.: 2
Betz, E. L.: 10, 20
Borgen, F. H.: 11
Carlson, R. E.: 2
Dauw, D. C.: 4, 6
Davis, R. V.: 2–3, 5–6, 8–9, 11, 13–4, 18–9, 33
Dressler, R. M.: 12
Elo, M. R.: 30
Elster, R. S.: 2–3, 5
England, G. W.: 2–3, 5, 8
Fisher, S. T.: 13
Gay, E. G.: 25, 33
Graen, G. B.: 14
Hendel, D. D.: 15, 26–7, 33
Katz, M.: 21
Kauppi, D. R.: 22, 34
Kohlan, R. G.: 7, 16
Lofquist, L. H.: 2–3, 5, 8, 11, 33
Lybarger, A. E.: 35
Muthard, J. E.: 23
Richardson, B. K.: 24
Salomone, P. R.: 17, 23
Shapiro, S.: 1
Simpson, A. R.: 36
Stone, G. V.: 28
Thorndike, R. M.: 9, 18–9
Tinsley, H. E. A.: 11
Warren, L. W.: 31
Weiss, D. J.: 2–3, 5, 8–9, 11, 13–5, 18–9, 22, 25–7, 33
Willoughby, T. C.: 32, 37
Zytowski, D. G.: 29

[2284]

★Minnesota Job Description Questionnaire. Employees and supervisors; 1967–68; MJDQ; for research use only; primarily for group measurement of occupational reinforcer patterns (ORP's) to match with intrapersonal vocational needs as measured by *Minnesota Importance Questionnaire;* 22 scores (20 of which parallel scores of *Minnesota Importance Questionnaire* and *Minnesota Satisfaction Questionnaire*): ability utilization, achievement, activity, advancement, authority, company policies and practices, compensation, coworkers, creativity, independence, moral values, recognition, responsibility, security, social service, social status, supervision—human relations, supervision—technical, variety, working conditions, autonomy, neutral point; separate forms for employees, supervisors; Fred H. Borgen, David J. Weiss, Howard E. A. Tinsley, Rene V. Dawis, and Lloyd H. Lofquist; Vocational Psychology Research. *

REFERENCES THROUGH 1971

1. BORGEN, FRED H., AND WEISS, DAVID J. "Application of the Method of Multiple-Rank Orders to the Scaling of Environmental Characteristics." Abstract. *Proc 76th Ann Conv Am Psychol Assn* 3:197–8 '68. * (*PA* 43:52, title only)
2. BORGEN, FRED H.; WEISS, DAVID J.; TINSLEY, HOWARD E. A.; DAWIS, RENE V.; AND LOFQUIST, LLOYD H. *The Measurement of Occupational Reinforcer Patterns.* University of Minnesota, Industrial Relations Center, Bulletin 49; Minnesota Studies in Vocational Rehabilitation 25. Minneapolis, Minn.: the Center, October 1968. Pp. x, 89. * (*PA* 43:4560)
3. BORGEN, FRED H.; WEISS, DAVID J.; TINSLEY, HOWARD E. A.; DAWIS, RENE V.; AND LOFQUIST, LLOYD H. *Occupational Reinforcer Patterns (First Volume).* University of Minnesota, Industrial Relations Center, Bulletin 48; Minnesota Studies in Vocational Rehabilitation 24. Minneapolis, Minn.: the Center, October 1968. Pp. x, 263. *
4. BETZ, ELLEN L. "Need-Reinforcer Correspondence as a Predictor of Job Satisfaction." *Personnel & Guid J* 47(9):878–83 My '69. *
5. STONE, GAYLE VAUGHN. *The Relationship Between Personality and Work Need-Reinforcer Correspondence.* Doctor's thesis, University of Minnesota (Minneapolis, Minn.), 1970. (*DAI* 31:4346B)
6. WILLOUGHBY, THEODORE C. "Needs, Interests, and Reinforcer Preferences of Data Processing Personnel." *Proc Ann Computer Personnel Res Conf* 8:119–43 '70. *
7. TINSLEY, HOWARD E. A., AND WEISS, DAVID J. "A Multitrait-Multimethod Comparison of Job Reinforcer Ratings of Supervisors and Supervisees." *J Voc Behav* 1(3):287–99 Jl '71. * (*PA* 48:3967)
8. WILLOUGHBY, THEODORE CRAWFORD. *Needs, Interests, Reinforcer Patterns and Satisfaction of Data Processing Personnel.* Doctor's thesis, University of Minnesota (Minneapolis, Minn.), 1971. (*DAI* 32:5421A)

CUMULATIVE NAME INDEX

Betz, E. L.: 4
Borgen, F. H.: 1–3
Dawis, R. V.: 2–3
Lofquist, L. H.: 2–3
Stone, G. V.: 5
Tinsley, H. E. A.: 2–3, 7
Weiss, D. J.: 1–3, 7
Willoughby, T. C.: 6, 8

[2285]

Minnesota Satisfaction Questionnaire. Business and industry; 1963–67; MSQ; satisfaction with specific aspects of work and work environments; 2 editions; David J. Weiss, Rene V. Dawis, George W. England, and Lloyd H. Lofquist; Vocational Psychology Research. *

a) LONG FORM. 21 scores (20 of which parallel scores of *Minnesota Importance Questionnaire* and *Minnesota Job Description Questionnaire*): ability utilization, achievement, activity, advancement, authority, company policies and practices, compensation, coworkers, creativity, independence, moral values, recognition, responsibility, security, social service, social status, supervision—human relations, supervision—technical, variety, working conditions, general satisfaction.

b) SHORT FORM. 3 scores: intrinsic, extrinsic, general.

For additional information and reviews by Lewis E. Albright and John P. Foley, Jr., see 7:1064 (18 references).

REFERENCES THROUGH 1971

1–18. See 7:1064.

19. ELO, MARGARET REED. *The Relationship of Counselor and Client Needs to Occupational Outcomes.* Doctor's thesis, University of Minnesota (Minneapolis, Minn.), 1970. (*DAI* 32:1838B)

20. LEE, LA JUANA WILLIAMS. *Personality Characteristics and Job Satisfactions of Certified Professional Secretaries and Non-Certified Secretaries.* Doctor's thesis, University of Northern Colorado (Greeley, Colo.), 1970. (*DAI* 31:6220A)

21. MACE, RICHARD EDWARD. *Factors Influencing the Decisions of Teachers to Become Administrators: A Study of the Differences in Self-Actualization and Job Satisfaction Occurring Between Future Administrators and Career Teachers.* Doctor's thesis, Syracuse University (Syracuse, N.Y.), 1970. (*DAI* 32:132A)

22. WARREN, LYNDA WALKER. *The Prediction of Job Satisfaction as a Function of the Correspondence Between Vocational Needs and Occupational Reinforcers.* Doctor's thesis, University of Minnesota (Minneapolis, Minn.), 1970. (*DAI* 32:608B)

23. WILLOUGHBY, THEODORE C. "Needs, Interests, and Reinforcer Preferences of Data Processing Personnel." *Proc Ann Computer Personnel Res Conf* 8:119–43 '70. *

24. BETZ, ELLEN L. "An Investigation of Job Satisfaction as a Moderator Variable in Predicting Job Success." *J Voc Behav* 1(2):123–8 Ap '71. * (*PA* 47:11882)

25. GRAY, BONNIE L., AND WEISS, DAVID J. "Pilot Study of the Measurement of Job Satisfaction of Mentally Retarded Adults." Abstract. *Proc 79th Ann Conv Am Psychol Assn* 6(2):611–2 '71. * (*PA* 46:5373, title only)

26. HERSHEY, GERALD LEE. *Experiential Attributes and Attitudinal Postures of Indiana University Academic Secretaries.* Doctor's thesis, Indiana University (Bloomington, Ind.), 1971. (*DAI* 32:4180A)

27. KARASICK, BERNARD WOLFE. *Organizational Climate and Its Relationship to Managerial Behavior.* Doctor's thesis, Purdue University (Lafayette, Ind.), 1971. (*DAI* 32:1266B)

28. MACTAGGERT, DONALD STUART. *Job Satisfaction and Organizational Openness as Perceived by Elementary Teachers in a Florida School System.* Doctor's thesis, University of Miami (Coral Gables, Fla.), 1971. (*DAI* 32:3622A)

29. WILLOUGHBY, THEODORE CRAWFORD. *Needs, Interests, Reinforcer Patterns and Satisfaction of Data Processing Personnel.* Doctor's thesis, University of Minnesota (Minneapolis, Minn.), 1971. (*DAI* 32:5421A)

CUMULATIVE NAME INDEX

Albright, L. E.: *rev*, 7:1064
Anderson, L. M. L.: 11
Bates, G. L.: 12, 18
Becvar, R. J.: 13
Betz, E.: 4
Betz, E. L.: 7, 14, 24
Carlson, R. E.: 15
Dawis, R. V.: 1, 3–4, 6, 9, 15
Elo, M. R.: 19
Elster, R. S.: 1
England, G. W.: 1, 3, 6
Foley, J. P.: *rev*, 7:1064
Golie, B. N.: 8
Graen, G. B.: 9
Gray, B. L.: 25
Hamlin, M. M.: 2

Hershey, G. L.: 26
Karasick, B. W.: 27
Lee, L. J. W.: 20
Lofquist, L. H.: 1, 3–4, 6
McCoy, J. F.: 18
Mace, R. E.: 21
MacTaggert, D. S.: 28
Olson, H.: 5, 18
Parker, H. J.: 18
Poley, J. P.: *rev*, 7:1064
Taylor, K. E.: 17
Warren, L. W.: 22
Weiss, D. J.: 1, 3–4, 6, 9–10, 15, 17, 25
Willoughby, T. C.: 23, 29

[2286]

Per-Flu-Dex Tests. College and industry; 1955; 7 tests; Frank J. Holmes; Psychometric Affiliates. *

a) PER-SYMB TEST. Symbol number substitution.
b) PER-VERB TEST. Letter perception and counting.
c) PER-NUMB TEST. Number counting and perception.
d) FLU-VERB TEST. Word completion and verbal fluency.
e) FLU-NUMB TEST. Arithmetic computation.
f) THE DEX-MAN SCALE. Manual speed of movement.

g) DEX-AIM TEST. Aiming accuracy and speed.

For additional information and reviews by Andrew L. Comrey and John W. French, see 5:901.

REFERENCES THROUGH 1971

1. KERR, WILLARD A., AND McGEHEE, EDWARD M. "Creative Temperament as Related to Aspects of Strategy and Intelligence." *J Social Psychol* 62:211–6 Ap '64. * (*PA* 39:5126)

2. KELLEHER, EDWARD J.; KERR, WILLARD A.; AND MELVILLE, NORBERT T. "The Prediction of Subprofessional Nursing Success." *Personnel Psychol* 21:379–88 au '68. * (*PA* 47:4063)

CUMULATIVE NAME INDEX

Comrey, A. L.: *rev*, 5:901
French, J. W.: *rev*, 5:901
Kelleher, E. J.: 2

Kerr, W. A.: 1–2
McGehee, E. M.: 1
Melville, N. T.: 2

[2287]

RBH Breadth of Information. Business and industry; 1957–63; "practical intelligence and attention to the ordinary happenings of the world"; Richardson, Bellows, Henry & Co., Inc. *

For additional information, see 6:1100.

[2288]

A Self-Rating Scale for Leadership Qualifications. Adults; 1942–48; E. J. Benge; National Foremen's Institute, Inc. *

For additional information, see 5:906.

[2289]

The Tear Ballot for Industry. Employees in industry; 1944–62; TBI; job satisfaction questionnaire; Willard A. Kerr; Psychometric Affiliates. *

For additional information and an excerpted review by John O. Crites, see 7:1065; for a review by Raymond A. Katzell, see 6:1108 (5 references); for a review by Brent Baxter, see 4:783 (4 references).

REFERENCES THROUGH 1971

1–4. See 4:783.

5–9. See 6:1108.

10. GROVE, BYRON A., AND KERR, WILLARD A. "Specific Evidence of Origin of Halo Effect in Measurement of Employee Morale." *J Social Psychol* 34:165–70 N '51. * (*PA* 26:5871)

CUMULATIVE NAME INDEX

Baxter, B.: *rev*, 4:783
Crites, J. O.: *exc*, 7:1065
Griffith, J. W.: 1
Grove, B. A.: 10
Katzell, R. A.: *rev*, 6:1108
Kerr, W. A.: 1–2, 4–5, 8, 10
Koppelmeier, G. J.: 2

Mayo, T. B.: 1
Pressel, G. L.: 7
Speroff, B. J.: 9
Sullivan, J. J.: 2
Topal, J. R.: 1, 6
Van Zelst, R.: 3
Zintz, F. R.: 4

[2290]

Test Orientation Procedure. Job applicants and trainees; 1967; TOP; job applicants needing practice taking tests; no scores; George K. Bennett and Jerome E. Doppelt with the assistance of A. B. Madans and R. G. Buchanan; Psychological Corporation. *

For additional information and a review by Lewis E. Albright, see 7:1066.

[2291]

[Tests A/9 and A/10.] Applicants for technical and apprentice jobs; 1955–57; interest in scientific fields; 2 parts; tests in English and Afrikaans; no manual; National Institute for Personnel Research [South Africa]. *

a) TEST A/9: [TECHNICAL AND SCIENTIFIC KNOWLEDGE].
b) TEST A/10: [TECHNICAL READING COMPREHENSION].

For additional information, see 6:1109.

[2292]

Whisler Strategy Test. Business and industry; 1959–61, c1955–61; "intelligent action"; 6 scores: 4 direct scores (number circled-boldness, number attempted-speed, number right-accuracy, net strategy) and 2 derived scores (caution, hypercaution) ; Laurence D. Whisler ; Psychometric Affiliates. *

For additional information and reviews by Jean Maier Palormo and Paul F. Ross, see 6:1110 (1 reference).

REFERENCES THROUGH 1971

1. See 6:1110.
2. KERR, WILLARD A., AND MCGEHEE, EDWARD M. "Creative Temperament as Related to Aspects of Strategy and Intelligence." *J Social Psychol* 62:211–6 Ap '64. * (*PA* 39:5126)

CUMULATIVE NAME INDEX

Abrams, P.: 1   Palormo, J. M.: *rev,* 6:1110
Kerr, W. A.: 1–2   Ross, P. F.: *rev,* 6:1110
McGehee, E. M.: 2

[2293]

Work Information Inventory. Employee groups in industry ; 1958 ; morale ; Raymond E. Bernberg ; Psychometric Affiliates. *

For additional information, see 6:1111.

[Out of Print Since TIP I]

Cancellation Test, 5:894 (2 reviews)
Cardall Test of Practical Judgment (status unknown), 6:1102 (2 reviews, 10 references)
Dartnell Self-Administered Employee Opinion Unit, 6:1104 (1 review)
Diagnostic Counseling Form for Educational, Preventive, and Remedial Counseling, T :1957
Employee Opinion Survey, 6:1105
Five Factor Inventory, T :1959
General Information Survey, T :1960
Guidance Summary Form for Use in Vocational and Educational Counseling, 3:446 (1 review, 1 excerpt)
Jenkins Job Attitudes Survey, 7:1062 (1 review, 4 references)
Labor Turnover Tests, T :1962
Observation Test, T :1964
Organization Survey (status unknown), 6:1107
Q-Sort Cards for Executive Position, T :1967
SRA Employee Inventory, 5:905 (2 reviews, 10 references)

SELECTION AND RATING FORMS

[2294]

APT Controlled Interview. Applicants for employment ; 1945–56 ; revision of *APT Quick Screening Interview;* 19 ratings : job experience (2 ratings), work history, financial status (2 ratings), marital status, voice (3 ratings), appearance (4 ratings), health (2 ratings), family background, relations with the law, social history, total ; distribution restricted to clients ; Associated Personnel Technicians, Inc. *

For additional information, see 6:1112.

[2295]

Application Interview Screening Form. Job applicants ; 1965 ; 10 ratings by interviewer : work experience, previous education and training, job knowledge, intelligence, sociability, ambition, emotional stability, fluency, maturity, leadership capacity ; Psychological Publications Press. *

For additional information, see 7:1067.

[2296]

Career Counseling Personal Data Form. Vocational counselees ; 1962 ; no manual ; John B. Ahrens ; Martin M. Bruce, Ph.D., Publishers. *

For additional information, see 6:1113.

[2297]

Employee Competency Scale. Employees ; 1969 ; ECS ; ratings by supervisors ; 6 scores : communication, dependability, attitude, job competence, leadership, total ; William T. Martin ; Psychologists and Educators, Inc. *

For additional information, see 7:1068.

[2298]

Employee Evaluation Form for Interviewers. Adults ; 1943 ; Richard A. Fear and Byron Jordan ; Psychological Corporation. *

For additional information, reviews by Douglas H. Fryer and C. H. Ruedisili, and excerpted reviews by Kenneth Byers and Martin L. Reymert, see 3 :686.

[2299]

Employee Performance Appraisal. Business and industry ; 1962 ; 7 merit ratings by supervisors : quantity of work, quality of work, job knowledge, initiative, inter-personal relationships, dependability, potential ; no manual ; Martin M. Bruce, Ph.D., Publishers. *

For additional information and a review by Jean Maier Palormo, see 6:1116.

[2300]

★**Employee Progress Appraisal Form.** Rating of office employees ; 1944 ; Albert N. Gillett ; National Foremen's Institute, Inc. *

[2301]

*****[Employee Rating and Development Forms.]** Executive, industrial, office, and sales personnel ; 1950–65 ; all current forms, except *c,* identical with forms copyrighted 1950–59 ; Robert N. McMurry ; Dartnell Corporation. *

a) [PATTERNED MERIT REVIEW FORMS.] 1950–64 ; 5 forms ; no manual.
  1) *Patterned Merit Review—Executive.* 1955–59.
  2) *Patterned Merit Review Form—Plant and Office.* 1950–64.
  3) *Patterned Merit Review—Sales.* 1955–59.
  4) *Patterned Merit Review—Technical, Office, Special Skills.* 1956–64.
  5) *Statement of Supervisory Expectancies.* 1958–64.
b) PATTERNED EXIT INTERVIEW. 1953–65.
c) PERSONAL HISTORY REVIEW FORM. 1957 ; no manual.

For additional information and a review by Richard S. Barrett, see 6:1117 ; for reviews by Harry W. Karn and Floyd L. Ruch, see 4:781.

[2302]

*****[Executive, Industrial, and Sales Personnel Forms.]** Applicants for executive, industrial, office, or sales positions ; 1949–68 ; most current forms are essentially the same as or identical with earlier forms ; Robert N. McMurry ; Dartnell Corporation. *

a) [EXECUTIVE PERSONNEL FORMS.] 1949–68 ; 7 forms.
  1) *Application for Executive Position.* 1949–64.
  2) *Patterned Interview Form—Executive Position.* Applicants for management positions ; 1949–65.
  3) *Patterned Interview Form.* Applicants for positions of supervisor, foreman, engineer ; 1955–68.
  4) *Telephone Check on Executive Applicant.* 1950–64.
  5) *Selection and Evaluation Summary.* 1950–64.
  6) *Position Analysis.* 1956–58.
  7) *Physical Record.* 1958.
b) [INDUSTRIAL PERSONNEL FORMS.] 1949–64 ; 10 forms.
  1) *Application for Position.* 1950–64.
  2) *Application for Employment.* 1950–59.
  3) *Application for Office Position.* 1953–64.

4) *Patterned Interview (Short Form).* 1949–64.
5) *Patterned Interview Form.* Same as *a*(3) above.
6) *Telephone Check [With Previous Employers].* 1949–59.
7) *Telephone Check With Schools.* 1949–57.
8) *Selection and Evaluation Summary.* Same as *a*(5) above.
9) *Position Analysis.* Same as *a*(6) above.
10) *Physical Record.* Same as *a*(7) above.
c) [SALES PERSONNEL FORMS.] 1949–68; 10 forms.
  1) *Application for Sales Position.* 1950–67.
  2) *Patterned Interview Form—Sales Position.* 1950–64.
  3) *Telephone Check on Sales Applicant.* 1949–64.
  4) *Sales Application Verification.* 1953–59.
  5) *Home Interview Report Form.* 1954–59.
  6) *Selection and Evaluation Summary.* Same as *a*(5) above.
  7) *Sales Position Analysis.* 1962–65.
  8) *Physical Record.* Same as *a*(7) above.
  9) *Salesman Performance Inventory.* 1965; 20 scores: general appraisal, physical and personal factors, external influences, job knowledge, motivational factors, identification with the company, company policies, planning and organization, administrative duties, personal relationships, prospecting, sales approaches, analyzing prospect needs, product presentation, handling objections, closing skills, follow-ups and call-backs, customer relations, special situations, related duties.
  10) *Man Specification Sheet—Sales.* 1968.
For additional information and a review by John P. Foley, Jr., see 6:1119 (1 reference); for a review by Floyd L. Ruch, see 4:773.

REFERENCES THROUGH 1971
1. See 6:1119.

CUMULATIVE NAME INDEX
Foley, J. P.: *rev,* 6:1119   Ruch, F. L.: *rev,* 4:773
McMurry, R. N.: 1

[2303]
*[Job Application Forms.] Job applicants and employees; 1957–71; 8 application forms; no manual for *b-h;* Hilton Shepherd Co., Inc. *
a) JOB APPLICATION FORM. Job applicants; [1960].
b) PERSONNEL INVENTORY FORM. Employees being considered for transfer or promotion; [1960].
c) EMPLOYMENT APPLICATION FORM. Job applicants; 1960–66.
d) PERSONNEL RECORD FOLDER. 1960–68.
e) CONTENT CONTROL SHEET. 1960–68.
f) MEDICAL EMPLOYMENT FORM. Administrators, nurses, and technologists; 1960–67.
g) EMPLOYMENT APPLICATION. Nonmedical personnel; 1960–67.
h) BANK EMPLOYMENT FORM. Applicants for positions in banks and financial institutions; 1971.
For additional information, see 7:1069.

[2304]
Lawshe-Kephart Personnel Comparison System. For rating any aspect of employee performance by the paired comparison technique; 1946–48; C. H. Lawshe, Jr. and N. C. Kephart; Village Book Cellar. *
For additional information and a review by Reign H. Bittner, see 4:778 (1 reference).

REFERENCES THROUGH 1971
1. See 4:778.

CUMULATIVE NAME INDEX
Bittner, R. H.: *rev,* 4:778   Lawshe, C. H.: 1
Kephart, N. C.: 1   McCormick, E. J.: 1

[2305]
★**The McCormick Job Performance Measurement "Rate-$-Scales."** Employees; 1971; 5 ratings by supervisors: responsibility, attitude, time in grade, efficiency, total; Ronald R. McCormick; Trademark Design Products, Inc. *

[2306]
The McQuaig Manpower Selection Series. Applicants for office and sales positions; 1957; 4 parts in 2 booklets; no manual; Jack H. McQuaig; McQuaig Institute of Executive Development. *
a) [PARTS 1–3.]
  1) *Part 1, The McQuaig Telephone Reference Check List.*
  2) *Part 2, The McQuaig Screening Interview Guide.*
  3) *Part 3, Personal History and Experience Record.*
b) PART 4, THE MC QUAIG OCCUPATIONAL TEST.
For additional information, see 6:1122.

[2307]
*★The Martin Performance Appraisal. Employees; 1966–69; MPA; ratings by supervisors; William T. Martin; Western Psychological Services. *
For additional information, see 7:1070.

[2308]
Merit Rating Series. Industry; 1948–59; formerly called *Employee Evaluation Series;* 5 scales; Joseph E. King; Industrial Psychology, Inc. *
a) PERFORMANCE: CLERICAL. 1956; 5 scores: quantity, accuracy, job knowledge, personal-work habits, overall.
b) PERFORMANCE: MECHANICAL. 1953–57; 5 scores: production, quality, job knowledge, personal-work habits, overall.
c) PERFORMANCE: SALES. 1953–57; 5 scores: volume, accuracy, job knowledge, personal-work habits, overall.
d) PERFORMANCE: TECHNICAL. 1953–57; 5 scores: same as for *b.*
e) PERFORMANCE: SUPERVISOR. 1953–57; 4 scores: department operation, employee relations, job knowledge, personal-work habits.
For additional information and a review by Seymour Levy, see 6:1123; for a review by Brent Baxter of the original series, see 4:770 (1 reference).

REFERENCES THROUGH 1971
1. See 4:770.

CUMULATIVE NAME INDEX
Baxter, B.: *rev,* 4:770   Levy, S.: *rev,* 6:1123
King, J. E.: 1

[2309]
The Nagel Personnel Interviewing and Screening Forms. Job applicants; 1963; 4 forms; Jerome H. Nagel Associates; Western Psychological Services. *
a) THE NAGEL INITIAL INTERVIEW DATA FORM. 10 ratings: first impression, physical appearance, voice and speech, educational background, poise and self-confidence, ambition-motivation, intelligence, knowledge of company, maturity, total impression.
b) THE NAGEL PERSONAL HISTORY INVENTORY.
c) THE NAGEL DEPTH INTERVIEW FORM. Ratings in 8 areas: work factors, social and educational factors, economic factors and goals, personal factors, ability to do job, motivation to do job, likelihood to remain on job, suitability of personality.
d) THE NAGEL EMPLOYMENT REFERENCE CHECK.
For additional information, see 6:1124.

[2310]
[Performance Review Forms.] Employees, managers; 1960–61; 2 forms; Seymour Levy; Martin M. Bruce, Ph.D., Publishers. *

a) COUNSELING INTERVIEW SUMMARY. Employees, managers; 1960; for summarizing a performance review interview; 2 editions: forms for employees, managers.

b) MANAGERIAL PERFORMANCE REVIEW. Managers; 1961; ratings by supervisors preparatory to performance review interview.

For additional information, see 6:1125.

[2311]

Personal Data Blank. Counselees ages 15 and over; 1934–52; J. Gustav White; Consulting Psychologists Press, Inc. *

For additional information and a review by Arthur E. Traxler, see 5:903; for reviews by Edward S. Jones and Donald G. Paterson of an earlier edition, see 2:1669.

[2312]

[Personnel Interviewing Forms.] Business and industry; 1956; 4 forms; no manual; Judd-Safian Associates; Martin M. Bruce, Ph.D., Publishers. *

a) INITIAL INTERVIEW TABULATION. For recording ratings in 10 areas: appearance, voice and speech, poise, health, education, manner, responsiveness, experience, job stability, motivation.

b) PERSONAL HISTORY AUDIT. Job applicants.

c) DEPTH INTERVIEW PATTERN. For interviewing in 5 areas: work evaluation, educational and social evaluation, economic evaluation, personality evaluation, ambitions evaluation.

d) EMPLOYMENT REFERENCE INQUIRY. For securing employee evaluation from previous employers.

For additional information, see 6:1127.

[2313]

Personnel Rating Scale. Employees; 1965–66; 11 ratings by supervisors: cooperativeness, quality of work, adaptability, dependability, emotional stability, quantity of work, sociability, persistence, initiative, work knowledge, overall; Psychological Publications Press. *

For additional information, see 7:1071.

[2314]

RBH Individual Background Survey. Business and industry; 1949–69; 3 editions; Richardson, Bellows, Henry & Co., Inc. *

a) FORM T. Business and industry; 1952–63; 4 scoring keys: female clerical, male clerical, male industrial, male sales-supervisory-professional.

b) FORM M-E. Managers and executives; 1962. *Out of print.*

c) FORM W-E. Wage earner level applicants; 1965–69.

For additional information, see 7:1072 (2 references).

REFERENCES THROUGH 1971
1–2. See 7:1072.

CUMULATIVE NAME INDEX
Harrell, T. W.: 1–2

[2315]

San Francisco Vocational Competency Scale. Mentally retarded adults; 1968; SFVCS; for rating workers in "sheltered workshops"; Samuel Levine and Freeman F. Elzey; Psychological Corporation. *

For additional information and an excerpted review by N. M. Downie, see 7:1073.

REFERENCES THROUGH 1971
1. LEVINE, SAMUEL, AND ELZEY, FREEMAN F. "Factor Analysis of the San Francisco Vocational Competency Scale." *Am J Mental Def* 73:509–13 N '68. * (*PA* 43:8592)

CUMULATIVE NAME INDEX
Downie, N. M.: *exc,* 7:1073   Levine, S.: 1
Elzey, F. F.: 1

[2316]

[Selection Interview Forms.] Business and industry; 1962; 2 forms; Benjamin Balinsky; Martin M. Bruce, Ph.D., Publishers. *

a) SELECTION INTERVIEW FORM.

b) INTERVIEW RATING FORM.

For additional information, see 6:1128.

[2317]

Speech-Appearance Record. Job applicants; 1967; SAR; evaluation of young adults for employability; George K. Bennett and Jerome E. Doppelt with the assistance of A. B. Madans; Psychological Corporation. *

For additional information, see 7:1074.

[2318]

***[Stevens-Thurow Personnel Forms.]** Business and industry; 1951–72; 12 record and rating forms; Stevens, Thurow & Associates, Inc. *

a) PERSONAL HISTORY RECORD. Applicants, employees; 1951–72; 1972 form essentially the same as form copyrighted 1967 except for 4 new items and adaptation of 2 items concerning age.

b) APPLICATION FOR POSITION. Applicants for clerical positions; 1951.

c) APPLICATION FOR EMPLOYMENT. Applicants for shop or plant positions; 1951.

d) PRELIMINARY INTERVIEW. Prospective employees; 1954.

e) INTERVIEWER'S GUIDE AND RATING FORM FOR PROSPECTIVE EMPLOYEES. Prospective employees; 1956–67; 1963 form essentially the same as form published 1956.

f) EMPLOYMENT INTERVIEW SCHEDULE. Prospective employees; 1956.

g) WORK REFERENCE INVESTIGATION. 1951–63.

h) JOB DESCRIPTION [SHORT FORM]. 1956.

i) JOB DESCRIPTION QUESTIONNAIRE [LONG FORM]. 1952.

j) APPRAISAL REPORT FOR MANAGEMENT PERSONNEL. Manager's rating of employees; 1959.

k) APPRAISAL REPORT FOR MANAGEMENT PERSONNEL (SUPPLEMENTARY FORM FOR SALES MANAGERS). 1959.

l) WORK BEHAVIOR INVENTORY. Supervisor's rating of employees; 1951–63.

For additional information, see 6:1129.

[2319]

★Tickmaster. Job applicants; 1954–65; environmental conditions under which applicant will be most productive; Roland Ballen; the Author. *

[2320]

Wonderlic Personnel Selection Procedure. Applicants for employment; 1967–69; WPSP; 8 parts; E. F. Wonderlic & Associates. *

a) P-1: INTRODUCTORY APPLICATION.

b) P-2: PERSONNEL APPLICATION.

c) P-3: WONDERLIC PERSONNEL TEST, FORM 1. See 482.

d) P-4: PERSONNEL INTERVIEWER'S GUIDE. 1967 guide identical with *Diagnostic Interviewer's Guide* copyrighted 1937 and 1942.

e) P-5: HEALTH QUESTIONNAIRE.

f) P-6: [WRITTEN REFERENCE REPORTS].

g) P-7: TELEPHONE REFERENCE CHECK.

h) P-8: PRE-EMPLOYMENT SUMMARY.

For additional information, see 7:1075.

[2321]

Work Reference Check. Job applicants; 1965; information and ratings by former employer; Psychological Publications Press. *

For additional information, see 7:1076.

[Out of Print Since TIP I]

Application-Interview Series, 5:892
Cardall Interviewing Aids (status unknown), 6:1114
Diagnostic Interviewer's Guide, 6:1115 (3 reviews, 2 references)
Employee Merit Report, 4:771
Employee Rating Forms, 6:1118
Hiring Summary Worksheet, 5:898
Job Description Forms, T:1983
Job Description Questionnaire, 6:1121
Occupational Adjustment Forms, T:1988
Performance Record, 5:902 (2 reviews, 1 reference)
Personal History Record [Richardson, Bellows, Henry & Co., Inc.], 6:1126

SPECIFIC VOCATIONS

[Out of Print Since TIP I]

Probst Rating System, 4:785 (2 reviews, 2 references)

ACCOUNTING

[2322]

Account Clerk Test. Job applicants; 1957–66; 1966 edition identical with test copyrighted 1959; distribution restricted to member public personnel agencies and nonmember agencies approved by the publisher; International Personnel Management Association. *

For additional information, see 7:1077.

[2323]

*American Institute of Certified Public Accountants Testing Programs. Grades 13–16 and accountants; 1946–72; 2 programs: College Accounting Testing Program (tests available at any time) and Professional Accounting Testing Program (tests available to accountant employers at any time and also administered at regional testing centers); 3 tests; Committee on Personnel Testing, American Institute of Certified Public Accountants; distributed by Psychological Corporation. *
a) ORIENTATION TEST. 3 scores: verbal, quantitative, total.
b) ACHIEVEMENT TEST: LEVELS 1 AND 2.
c) STRONG VOCATIONAL INTEREST BLANK FOR MEN. See 2212; scored for 34 scales and plotted on an accountant's profile.

For additional information concerning earlier forms, see 5:911 (6 references); see also 4:787 (15 references).

REFERENCES THROUGH 1971
1–15. See 4:787.
16–21. See 5:911.
22. BEAMER, GEORGE C., AND ROSE, TOM. "The Use of the GATB and the AIA Tests in Predicting Success in Accounting." *Acctg R* 30:533–5 Jl '55. *
23. NORTH, ROBERT D. "Relation Between Scores on the AIA Elementary and Advanced Accounting Achievement Tests." *Acctg R* 31:50–5 Ja '56. *
24. RILEY, ROBERT C. "Comparison of Results of AIA Achievement Test and ACE Psychological Examination." *Acctg R* 33:128–30 Ja '58. *
25. TRAXLER, ARTHUR E. "Testing for the Professions: Accounting." *J Exp Ed* 27:341–6 Je '59. * (*PA* 35:1280)
26. COOPER, CHARLES LEWIS. *A Study of the Relationship of*

the American Institute of Certified Public Accountants College Tests and Other Selected Factors to Success in Accounting. Doctor's thesis, University of Pittsburgh (Pittsburgh, Pa.), 1961. (*DA* 22:3545)
27. AHOLA, VIRGINIA I. *Achievement and Aptitude in Accounting of Junior College Accounting of Junior College Transfer Students and SDSC Students.* Master's thesis, San Diego State College (San Diego, Calif.), 1967.
28. DAILY, VICTORIA LEE DEFORE. *The Effect of Programmed Instruction in the Teaching of Principles of Accounting.* Doctor's thesis, Colorado State College (Greeley, Colo.), 1969. (*DAI* 30:4061A)

CUMULATIVE NAME INDEX

Ahola, V. I.: 27	Jacobs, R.: 7, 11, 15, 18
American Institute of Accountants, Committee on Selection of Personnel: 2	Morici, A. R.: 20
	Nissley, W. W.: 5
Ankers, R. G.: 13	North, R. D.: 21, 23
Beamer, G. C.: 22	Riley, R. C.: 24
Budd, T. A.: 3	Rose, T.: 22
Caffyn, H. R.: 6, 10	Schmidt, L. A.: 8
Cooper, C. L.: 26	Strong, E. K.: 9
Daily, V. L. D.: 28	Traxler, A. E.: 1, 4-5, 10, 14–15, 25
Frederick, M. L.: 19	Ward, L. B.: 12
Hassler, R. H.: 12	Wood, B. D.: 5
Hendrix, O. R.: 16–7	

[2324]

*CLEP Subject Examination in Introductory Accounting. 1 year or equivalent; 1970–73; for college accreditation of nontraditional study, advanced placement, or assessment of educational achievement; tests administered monthly at centers throughout the United States; program administered for the College Entrance Examination Board by Educational Testing Service. * For the testing program entry, see 1050.

For additional information, see 7:1079. For reviews of the testing program, see 7:664 (3 reviews).

[Out of Print Since TIP I]

Accounting Orientation Test, 7:1078 (5 references)

BUSINESS

[2325]

*Admission Test for Graduate Study in Business. Business graduate students; 1954–73; ATGSB; test administered 4 times annually (January, March, July, November) at centers established by the publisher; 3 scores: quantitative, verbal, total; Educational Testing Service. *

For additional information and reviews by Jerome E. Doppelt and Gary R. Hanson, see 7:1080 (10 references).

REFERENCES THROUGH 1971
1–10. See 7:1080.
11. FOSTER, PHILLIP B. "Management Perspective: Predicting Academic Performance of Foreign and Non-Foreign Students in Graduate Business School." *Acad Mgmt J* 8:319–23 D '65. *
12. BASS, BERNARD M. "Ability, Values, and Concepts of Equitable Salary Increases in *Exercise Compensation*." *J Appl Psychol* 52:299–303 Ag '68. * (*PA* 42:16239)
13. BASS, BERNARD M. "How to Succeed in Business According to Business Students and Managers." *J Appl Psychol* 52:254–62 Je '68. * (*PA* 42:12889)
14. PAGE, ALFRED N., AND WEST, RICHARD R. "Evaluating Student Performance in Graduate Schools of Business." *J Bus* 42(1):36–41 Ja '69. *
15. CRAVENS, DAVID W. "Predicting Performance of Information Specialists." *J Am Soc Inf Sci* 22(1):5–11 Ja–F '71. *

CUMULATIVE NAME INDEX

Bass, B. M.: 12–3	Hinton, B. L.: 7
Cravens, D. W.: 15	Lewis, J. W.: 4–6
Curtis, K. C.: 9	Mittman, A.: 6
Doppelt, J. E.: *rev*, 7:1080	Page, A. N.: 14
Foster, P. B.: 11	Pounders, C. J.: 10
Gruber, E. C.: 2	Rudman, J.: 3
Hanson, G. R.: *rev*, 7:1080	West, R. R.: 14
Harrell, T. W.: 1	

[2326]

*CLEP Subject Examination in Introduction to Business Management. I semester or equivalent; 1969–73; for college accreditation of nontraditional study, advanced placement, or assessment of educational achievement; tests administered monthly at centers throughout the United States; program administered for the College Entrance Examination Board by Educational Testing Service. * For the testing program entry, see 1050.

For additional information, see 7:1081. For reviews of the testing program, see 7:664 (3 reviews).

[2327]

*CLEP Subject Examination in Introductory Business Law. I semester or equivalent; 1970–73; for college accreditation of nontraditional study, advanced placement, or assessment of educational achievement; tests administered monthly at centers throughout the United States; program administered for the College Entrance Examination Board by Educational Testing Service. * For the testing program entry, see 1050.

For additional information, see 7:1082. For reviews of the testing program, see 7:664 (3 reviews).

[2328]

*CLEP Subject Examination in Introductory Marketing. I semester or equivalent; 1968–73; for college accreditation of nontraditional study, advanced placement, or assessment of educational achievement; tests administered monthly at centers throughout the United States; program administered for the College Entrance Examination Board by Educational Testing Service. * For the testing program entry, see 1050.

For additional information, see 7:1083. For reviews of the testing program, see 7:664 (3 reviews).

[2329]

*CLEP Subject Examination in Money and Banking. I semester or equivalent; 1967–73; for college accreditation of nontraditional study, advanced placement, or assessment of educational achievement; tests administered monthly at centers throughout the United States; program administered for the College Entrance Examination Board by Educational Testing Service. * For the testing program entry, see 1050.

For additional information, see 7:1084. For reviews of the testing program, see 7:664 (3 reviews).

[2330]

Organizational Value Dimensions Questionnaire: Business Form. Adults; 1965–66; OVDQ; for research use only; attitudes toward business and industrial firms in general; manual title is *Value Scale—The Business Firm;* 9 scores: organizational magnitude and structure, internal consideration, competition and strategy, social responsibility, quality, change, member identification and control, external political participation, member equality and participation; Carroll L. Shartle and Ralph M. Stogdill; University Publications Sales, Ohio State University. *
For additional information, see 7:1085.

COMPUTER PROGRAMMING

[2331]

Aptitude Assessment Battery: Programming. Programmers and trainees; 1967–69; AABP; no manual; distribution restricted to employers of programmers, not available to school personnel; Jack M. Wolfe; Programming Specialists, Inc. *
For additional information, see 7:1087 (1 reference).

REFERENCES THROUGH 1971
1. See 7:1087.
CUMULATIVE NAME INDEX
Wolfe, J. M.: 1

[2332]

*CLEP Subject Examination in Computers and Data Processing. I–2 semesters or equivalent; 1968–73; for college accreditation of nontraditional study, advanced placement, or assessment of educational achievement; tests administered monthly at centers throughout the United States; program administered for the College Entrance Examination Board by Educational Testing Service. * For the testing program entry, see 1050.

For additional information, see 7:1088. For reviews of the testing program, see 7:664 (3 reviews).

[2333]

★CLEP Subject Examination in Elementary Computer Programming—Fortran IV. I semester or equivalent; 1971–73; for college accreditation of nontraditional study, advanced placement, or assessment of educational achievement; tests administered monthly at centers throughout the United States; program administered for the College Entrance Examination Board by Educational Testing Service. * For the testing program entry, see 1050.

[2334]

*Computer Programmer Aptitude Battery. Applicants for computer training or employment; 1964–67; CPAB; 6 scores: verbal meaning, reasoning, letter series, number ability, diagramming, total; Jean Maier Palormo; Science Research Associates, Inc. (British edition: 1964–71; standardization supplement by Peter Saville; NFER Publishing Co. Ltd. [England].) *
For additional information and reviews by Richard T. Johnson and Donald J. Veldman of *a,* see 7:1089 (2 references).

REFERENCES THROUGH 1971
1–2. See 7:1089.
3. MARTIN, MAURICE A. "A Study of the Concurrent Validity of the Computer Programmer Aptitude Battery." *Studies Pers Psychol* (Canada) 3(1):69–76 Ap '71. * (*PA* 46:11831)
4. MUSSIO, JERRY J., AND WAHLSTROM, MERLIN W. "Predicting Performance of Programmer Trainees in a Post-High School Setting." Discussion by Charles D. Lothridge. *Proc Ann Computer Personnel Res Conf* 9:26–53 '71. *

CUMULATIVE NAME INDEX
Cronbach, L. J.: 2   Mussio, J. J.: 4
Johnson, R. T.: *rev,* 7:1089   Palormo, J. M.: 1
Lothridge, C. D.: 4   Veldman, D. J.: *rev,* 7:1089
Martin, M. A.: 3   Wahlstrom, M. W.: 4

[2335]

The Diebold Personnel Tests. Programmers and systems analysts for automatic data processing and computing installations; 1959; 5 tests; John Diebold & Associates. *
a) SYMBOLS BLOCK DIAGRAM TEST.
b) CODE INDEX TEST.
c) RELATIONS IN NUMBERS TEST.
d) CODE MATCHING TEST.
e) WORD SEQUENCE TEST.
For additional information, see 6:1142.

[2336]

★Programmer Aptitude/Competence Test System. Computer programmers and applicants for programmer training; 1970; PACTS; 2 tests; Haverly Systems Inc. *

a) PACTS APTITUDE TEST. Applicants for programmer training; "ability to learn programming"; 3 scores (correctness, quality, overall grade) for each of 15 problems plus a single overall aptitude rating.

b) PACTS COMPETENCE TEST. Experienced programmers; tests tailored to meet individual needs, local objectives, and time available by selecting 5 to 9 problems in programming (a maximum of 20 may be selected) out of 30 available; a work performance test which requires the use of computer facilities; 5 scores (percent correct, percent of objective, straight score, numeric grade, letter grade) for each problem and 3 final scores (straight score, numeric grade, letter grade).

REFERENCES THROUGH 1971

1. SEINER, J. P. "Programmer Aptitude and Competence Test System (PACTS)." Discussion by Charles D. Lothridge. *Proc Ann Computer Personnel Res Conf* 9:3-25, 47-53 '71. *

CUMULATIVE NAME INDEX

Lothridge, C. D.: 1   Seiner, J. P.: 1

[Out of Print Since TIP I]

Aptitude Test E51 for Electronic Data-Processing Programmers (status unknown), T:2015
Card Punch Operator Aptitude Test, 7:1103 (2 reviews, 4 references)
IBM Aptitude Test for Programmer Personnel, 7: 1090 (1 review, 14 references)
Punched Card Machine Operator Aptitude Test, 5:941
Revised Programmer Aptitude Test, 6:1153 (2 references)

DENTISTRY

[2337]

*Dental Admission Testing Program. Dental school applicants; 1946-72; DATP; formerly called *Dental Aptitude Testing Program;* tests administered 3 times annually (January, April, September or October) at centers established by the publisher; 4 tests, 12 scores: 11 scores listed below and academic average (average of *a-c*); Division of Educational Measurements, Council on Dental Education, American Dental Association. *

a) SURVEY OF THE NATURAL SCIENCES. 1951-72; 4 scores: biology, inorganic chemistry, organic chemistry, total.

b) READING COMPREHENSION. 1953-69; 2 forms.
   1) *Reading Comprehension in the Natural Sciences.* 1953-65.
   2) *Reading Comprehension in the Basic Sciences.* 1968-69.

c) COOPERATIVE SCHOOL AND COLLEGE ABILITY TESTS. 1961; 3 scores: quantitative reasoning, verbal reasoning, total.

d) PERCEPTUAL-MOTOR ABILITY TEST. 1968-72; 3 scores: 2-dimensional problem solving, 3-dimensional problem solving, average.

For additional information, see 7:1091 (28 references); see also 5:916 (6 references) and 4:788 (2 references).

REFERENCES THROUGH 1971

1-2. See 4:788.
3-8. See 5:916.
9-36. See 7:1091.
37. PETERSON, SHAILER. "Dental Aptitude Testing Program: A Report of Progress." *J Am Dental Assn* 35:175-84 Ag 1 '47. *
38. PETERSON, SHAILER. "The Aptitude Testing Program of the American Dental Association." *Col & Univ* 23:212-6 Ja '48. * (*PA* 22:4671)

39. PETERSON, SHAILER. "Forecasting the Success of Freshman Dental Students Through the Aptitude Testing Program." *J Am Dental Assn* 37:259-65 S '48. *
40. DWORKIN, SAMUEL F. "Further Correlational and Factor Analyses of the DAT as a Predictor of Performance: Conclusions and Summary." *J Dental Ed* 34(4):358-64 D '70. *
41. FULL, CLEMANS A., AND FOLEY, WALTER J. "Selection and Performance: A Factorial Study of Dental Students." *J Dental Ed* 35(9):563-6 S '71. *
42. PYSKACEK, ROBERT A. "The Dental Admission Testing Program and Proposed Changes." *J Dental Ed* 35(4):237-41 Ap '71. *
43. ZULLO, THOMAS G. "A Factor Analysis of Perceptual and Motor Abilities of Dental Students." *J Dental Ed* 35(6):356-61 Je '71. *
44. ZULLO, THOMAS G. "Principal Components Analysis of the Dental Aptitude Test Battery." *J Dental Ed* 35(3):144-8 Mr '71. *

CUMULATIVE NAME INDEX

Anderson, A. V.: 5
Carson, R. L.: 20
Chen, M. K.: 24, 32
DeRevere, R. E.: 13
Douglas, B. L.: 20
Dworkin, S. F.: 34, 40
Endey, M. W.: 14
Ference, L. W.: 35
Fernandez-Pabon, J. J.: 25
Fishman, R.: 28
Foley, W. J.: 41
Fredericks, M. A.: 26
Friedman, S.: 5
Full, C. A.: 41
Ginley, T. J.: 22
Gough, H. G.: 36
Gruber, E. C.: 16
Hall, D. S.: 23
Heller, D. B.: 20
Hood, A. B.: 17
Huck, F. T.: 9
Hutton, J. G.: 29
Kirk, B. A.: 36
Kreit, L. H.: 27
Land, M.: 18
Layton, W. L.: 7
Lorencki, S. F.: 30
McDonald, R. E.: 27
Manhold, B. S.: 19, 21
Manhold, J. H.: 19, 21
Marles, L.: 3
Mundy, P.: 26
Parkins, G. L.: 10
Peterson, S.: 1, 2, 4, 37-9
Phillip, P. J.: 31
Phipps, G. T.: 28
Podshadley, D. W.: 24, 32
Pyskacek, R. A.: 42
Reinke, B. C.: 14
Rudman, J.: 15
Scott, R. H.: 28
Shrock, J. G.: 24, 32
Thomassen, P. R.: 14
Timmons, G. D.: 11
Tocchini, J. J.: 14
Vinton, P. W.: 19
Webb, S. C.: 8, 12
Weiss, I.: 6
Zimmerman, J. J.: 33
Zullo, T. G.: 43-4

[2338]

Dental Hygiene Aptitude Testing Program. Dental hygiene school applicants; 1947-72; DHATP; tests administered 3 times anually (February, May, November) at centers established by the American Dental Hygienists' Association; 4 scores: numerical ability, study-reading, science, general information; prepared for the American Dental Hygienists' Association by Psychological Corporation. *

For additional information, see 7:1092.

[2339]

★Ohio Dental Assisting Achievement Test. Grades 11-12; 1970-73; ODAAT; available only as a part of the *Ohio Trade and Industrial Education Achievement Test Program* (see 2431 for more complete information); 16 scores: orientation, ethics, dental anatomy, dental and laboratory materials, microbiology and sterilization, preventive dentistry, operative-chairside assisting, specialties-chairside assisting, radiology, pharmacology, oral pathology, diet and nutrition, first aid and dental emergencies, human relations, office practice, total; Instructional Materials Laboratory, Ohio State University. *

ENGINEERING

[2340]

AC Test of Creative Ability. Engineers and supervisors; 1953-60; 9 scores: quantity (3 scores), uniqueness (4 scores), quality, total; subtests yielding quantity scores may be administered alone for quantity scores only; Richard H. Harris (test), A. L. Simberg (test), and Measurement Research Division, Industrial

Relations Center, University of Chicago (manual); the Center. * [The publisher has not replied to our four requests to check the accuracy of this entry.]

For additional information and reviews by Samuel T. Mayo, Philip R. Merrifield, and Albert S. Thompson, see 6:1130 (1 reference).

REFERENCES THROUGH 1971

1. See 6:1130.
2. MAIZELL, ROBERT EDWARD. *Information Gathering Patterns and Creativity: A Study of Research Chemists in an Industrial Research Laboratory.* Doctor's thesis, Columbia University (New York, N.Y.), 1957. (*DA* 18:1802)
3. MEADOW, ARNOLD, AND PARNES, SIDNEY J. "Evaluation of Training in Creative Problem-Solving." *J Appl Psychol* 43:189–94 Je '59. * (*PA* 34:5568)
4. MEADOW, ARNOLD; PARNES, SIDNEY J.; AND REESE, HAYNE. "Influence of Brainstorming Instructions and Problem Sequence on a Creative Problem Solving Test." *J Appl Psychol* 43:413–6 D '59. * (*PA* 34:7338)
5. ANTLEY, ELIZABETH MARTIN. *Creativity in Educational Administration.* Doctor's thesis, University of Southern Mississippi (Hattiesburg, Miss.), 1962. (*DA* 23:3707)
6. LOCKE, EDWIN A. "Some Correlates of Classroom and Out-of-Class Achievement in Gifted Science Students." *J Ed Psychol* 54:238–48 O '63. * (*PA* 38:4649)
7. DUNNETTE, MARVIN D.; WERNIMONT, PAUL; AND ABRAHAMS, NORMAN. "Further Research on Vocational Interest Differences Among Several Types of Engineers." *Personnel & Guid J* 42:484–93 Ja '64. * (*PA* 39:6040)
8. GERLACH, VERNON S.; SCHUTZ, RICHARD E.; BAKER, ROBERT L.; AND MAZER, GILBERT E. "Effects of Variations in Test Direction on Original Test Response." *J Ed Psychol* 55:79–83 Ap '64. * (*PA* 39:734)
9. RAPP, MARJORIE LEE. *Factors Related to the Impressions Made on One Another by Members of a Discussion Group.* Doctor's thesis, University of California (Los Angeles, Calif.), 1965. (*DA* 25:7087)
10. TUCKER, CASEY ALLEN. *Creativity and Its Relationship to Success in College as Measured by the Grade Point Average.* Doctor's research study No. 1, Colorado State College (Greeley, Colo.), 1965. (*DA* 26:5275)
11. WHITTEMORE, ROBERT G., JR., AND HEIMANN, ROBERT A. "Modification of Originality Responses." *J Counsel Psychol* 13:213–8 su '66. * (*PA* 40:8833)
12. CRAFT, CLYDE O'BRIEN. *Creativity in Engineering Graphics: An Experimental Comparison of Two Types of Graphics Problems.* Doctor's thesis, Texas A & M University (College Station, Tex.), 1967. (*DA* 28:2435A)
13. MAGOWAN, ROBERT EVAN. *A Comparison of Pragmatical and Hypothetical Problems for Developing Creativity in Design.* Doctor's thesis, Texas A & M University (College Station, Tex.), 1967. (*DA* 28:1992A)
14. MILES, DAVID T. *An Experimental Investigation of Programed Creativity.* Doctor's thesis, Southern Illinois University (Carbondale, Ill.), 1967. (*DA* 28:2099A)
15. BUCKEYE, DONALD ANDREW. *The Effects of a Creative Classroom Environment on the Creative Ability of Prospective Elementary Mathematics Teachers.* Doctor's thesis, Indiana University (Bloomington, Ind.), 1968. (*DA* 29:1801A)
16. TURNER, THOMAS B. "The Creative Process." *J Creative Behav* 2:63–70 w '68. * (*PA* 42:13766)
17. BAEHR, MELANY E.; FURCON, JOHN E.; AND FROEMEL, ERNEST C. *Psychological Assessment of Patrolman Qualifications in Relation to Field Performance.* Washington, D.C.: United States Government Printing Office, 1969. Pp. vii, 246. *
18. GOODMAN, P.; FURCON, J.; AND ROSE, J. "Examination of Some Measures of Creative Ability by the Multitrait-Multimethod Matrix." *J Appl Psychol* 53(3):240–3 Je '69. * (*PA* 43:11327)
19. CARLETON, FREDERICK O. "Relationships Between Follow-Up Evaluations and Information Developed in a Management Assessment Center." Abstract. *Proc 78th Ann Conv Am Psychol Assn* 5(2):565–6 '70. * (*PA* 44:19655)
20. ERICKSON, CLARA; GANTZ, BENJAMIN S.; AND STEPHENSON, ROBERT W. "Logical and Construct Validation of a Short-Form Biographical Inventory Predictor of Scientific Creativity." Abstract. *Proc 78th Ann Conv Am Psychol Assn* 5(1):151–2 '70. * (*PA* 44:18715)
21. MCNEILL, JOSEPH GERARD. *The Development of Creative Abilities of Personnel in Professional Occupations.* Doctor's thesis, Rutgers—The State University (New Brunswick, N.J.), 1970. (*DAI* 32:674A)
22. REESE, HAYNE W., AND PARNES, SIDNEY J. "Programming Creative Behavior." *Child Develop* 41(2):413–23 Je '70. * (*PA* 44:15509)
23. ROSSITER, CHARLES M., JR. "Creativity and Achievement in Speech." *Today's Speech* 18(3):15–7 su '70. *
24. GLUSKINOS, URY M. "Criteria for Student Engineering Creativity and Their Relationship to College Grades." *J Ed Meas* 8(3):189–95 f '71. *

CUMULATIVE NAME INDEX

Abrahams, N.: 7	Maizell, R. E.: 2
Antley, E. M.: 5	Mayo, S. T.: *rev*, 6:1130
Baehr, M. E.: 17	Mazer, G. E.: 8
Baker, R. L.: 8	Meadow, A.: 1, 3–4
Buckeye, D. A.: 15	Merrifield, P. R.: *rev*, 6:1130
Carleton, F. O.: 19	Miles, D. T.: 14
Craft, C. O.: 12	Parnes, S. J.: 1, 3–4, 22
Dunnette, M. D.: 7	Rapp, M. L.: 9
Erickson, C.: 20	Reese, H.: 4
Froemel, E. C.: 17	Reese, H. W.: 22
Furcon, J.: 18	Rose, J.: 18
Furcon, J. E.: 17	Rossiter, C. M.: 23
Gantz, B. S.: 20	Schutz, R. E.: 8
Gerlach, V. S.: 8	Stephenson, R. W.: 20
Gluskinos, U. M.: 24	Thompson, A. S.: *rev*, 6:1130
Goodman, P.: 18	Tucker, C. A.: 10
Heimann, R. A.: 11	Turner, T. B.: 16
Locke, E. A.: 6	Wernimont, P.: 7
McNeill, J. G.: 21	Whittemore, R. G.: 11
Magowan, R. E.: 13	

[2341]

Engineering Aide Test. Engineering aides; 1957–60; distribution restricted to member public personnel agencies and nonmember agencies approved by the publisher; International Personnel Management Association. *

For additional information, see 6:1131.

[2342]

***Garnett College Test in Engineering Science.** 1–2 years technical college; 1966–71; GCTES; 3 scores: mechanics, heat-electricity-magnetism, total; I. Macfarlane Smith; NFER Publishing Co. Ltd. [England]. *

For additional information concerning the earlier edition, see 7:1093.

[2343]

***The Graduate Record Examinations Advanced Engineering Test.** Graduate school candidates; 1939–73; 3 scores: engineering, mathematics usage, total; Educational Testing Service. * For the testing program entry, see 1053.

For additional information concerning earlier forms, see 7:1094. For reviews of the testing program, see 7:667 (1 review) and 5:601 (1 review).

[2344]

Minnesota Engineering Analogies Test. Candidates for graduate school and industry; 1954–70; MEAT; distribution restricted and test administered at specified licensed university centers; Marvin D. Dunnette; Psychological Corporation. *

For additional information, see 7:1095 (2 references); see also 6:1133 (2 references); for reviews by A. Pemberton Johnson and William B. Schrader, see 5:933 (6 reviews).

REFERENCES THROUGH 1971

1–6. See 5:933.
7–8. See 6:1133.
9–10. See 7:1095.

CUMULATIVE NAME INDEX

Abrahams, N.: 9	Pesci, M. L.: 10
Aylward, M. S.: 5	Reynolds, H. J.: 8
Dunnette, M. D.: 1–5, 9	Schrader, W. B.: *rev*, 5:933
Johnson, A. P.: *rev*, 5:933	Spencer, G. M.: 8
MacKinnon, D. W.: 7	Wernimont, P.: 9
Owen, M. L.: 6	

[2345]

***N.I.I.P. Engineering Apprentice Selection Test Battery.** Engineering apprentices; 1936–72; 6 tests, 7 scores: 6 scores listed below and combined score for *a–e*; subtests available only as separates; National Institute of Industrial Psychology; NFER Publishing Co. Ltd. [England]. *

a) GROUP TEST 82. Spatial perception; see 2250.

b) GROUP TESTS 90A AND 90B. Verbal intelligence; see 390.

c) GROUP TESTS 70 AND 70B. Nonverbal intelligence; see 388.

d) ARITHMETIC TESTS EA2A AND EA4. Arithmetic attainment; see 702.

e) VINCENT MECHANICAL DIAGRAMS TEST. Mechanical ability; see 2271.

f) MECHANICAL INFORMATION TEST. See 2254.

For additional information, see 7:1096 (1 reference).

REFERENCES THROUGH 1971
1. See 7:1096.

CUMULATIVE NAME INDEX
Frisby, C. B.: 1   Vincent, D. F.: 1
Lancashire, R.: 1

[2346]
*National Engineering Aptitude Search Test: The Junior Engineering Technical Society. Grades 9–12; 1963–71, c1947–68; tests administered each spring at chapter centers of the Junior Engineering Technical Society; 5 scores: verbal, numerical, science, total, mechanical comprehension; Psychological Corporation. *

For additional information concerning an earlier form, see 6:1134.

[2347]
Purdue Creativity Test. Applicants for engineering positions; 1960, c1957–60; test booklet title is *Creativity Test;* 3 scores: fluency, flexibility, total; C. H. Lawshe and D. H. Harris; distributed by University Book Store. *

For additional information and reviews by Samuel T. Mayo and Philip R. Merrifield, see 6:1136 (2 references).

REFERENCES THROUGH 1971
1–2. See 6:1136.
3. GLUSKINOS, URY M. "Criteria for Student Engineering Creativity and Their Relationship to College Grades." *J Ed Meas* 8(3):189–95 f '71. *

CUMULATIVE NAME INDEX
Gluskinos, U. M.: 3   Mayo, S. T.: *rev,* 6:1136
Harris, D.: 2   Merrifield, P. R.: *rev,* 6:1136
Harris, D. H.: 1

[2348]
*The Undergraduate Program Field Tests: Engineering Test. College; 1969–73; formerly called *The Undergraduate Record Examinations: Engineering Test;* test available to colleges for local administration; Educational Testing Service. * For the testing program entry, see 1062.

For additional information concerning an earlier form, see 7:1097. For reviews of the testing program, see 7:671 (2 reviews).

[Out of Print Since TIP I]
Engineering Aide Test, 6:1131
Engineering and Physical Science Aptitude Test, 4:810 (3 reviews, 6 references)
Engineering Interest Comparisons, T:2002
Owens' Creativity Test for Machine Design, 6:1135 (2 reviews, 1 reference)
Pre-Engineering Ability Test, 4:812 (2 reviews, 11 references)
Professional Employee Inventory, T:2007
Stanford Scientific Aptitude Test, 4:813 (3 reviews, 7 references)

LAW

[2349]
*Law School Admission Test. Law school applicants; 1948–73; LSAT; 2 scores: aptitude (commonly referred to as the LSAT score), writing ability; test administered 5 times annually (February, April, July, October, December) at centers established by the publisher; Educational Testing Service. *

For additional information and a review by Leo A. Munday of earlier forms, see 7:1098 (23 references); see also 5:928 (7 references); for a review by Alexander G. Wesman, see 4:815 (6 references).

REFERENCES THROUGH 1971
1–6. See 4:815.
7–13. See 5:928.
14–36. See 7:1098.
37. BURNHAM, PAUL S., AND CRAWFORD, ALBERT B. "Law School Prediction at Mid-Century (With Particular Reference to Experience at Yale)." *J Legal Ed* 10(2):189–200 '58. *
38. FREEDMAN, MONROE H. "Testing for Analytic Ability in the Law School Admission Test." *J Legal Ed* 11(1):24–42 '58. *
39. HILLS, JOHN R., AND RAINE, WALTER J. "Pair-Comparisons Consistency and Grades in Law School." *J Appl Psychol* 44:94–6 Ap '60. * (PA 35:3956)
40. LUNNEBORG, CLIFFORD E., AND LUNNEBORG, PATRICIA W. "Relations of Background Characteristics to Success in the First Year of Law School." *J Legal Ed* 18(4):425–36 '66. *
41. LUNNEBORG, PATRICIA W., AND RADFORD, DONNA. "The LSAT: A Survey of Actual Practice." *J Legal Ed* 18(3):313–24 '66. *
42. GOOLSBY, THOMAS M., JR.; FRARY, ROBERT B.; AND LASCO, RICHARD A. "Factorial Structure and Principal Correlates of the Florida Bar Examination." *Ed & Psychol Meas* 28:427–32 su '68. * (PA 42:19400)
43. KLEIN, STEPHEN P.; ROCK, DONALD A.; AND EVANS, FRANKLIN R. "Predicting Success in Law School With Moderators." *J Legal Ed* 21(3):304–13 '69. *

CUMULATIVE NAME INDEX
Andrulis, R. S.: 31	Lasco, R. A.: 42
Bass, B. M.: 14	Lewis, J. W.: 21
Braden, G. D.: 2	Ludlow, H. G.: 29
Braskamp, L.: 21	Lunneborg, C. E.: 26–8, 40
Breslow, E.: 13	Lunneborg, P. W.: 26–8, 40–1
Buckton, L.: 9	Miller, P. V. R.: 22
Burnham, P. S.: 37	Munday, L. A.: *rev,* 7:1098
Chase, C. I.: 29	Olsen, M. A.: 1, 4, 7–8, 11–2
Crawford, A. B.: 37	Pugh, R. C.: 29, 36
Demaree, R. G.: 20	Radford, D.: 41
Distefano, M. K.: 14	Raine, W. J.: 39
Doppelt, J. E.: 9	Ramsey, R. R.: 16–7
Evans, F. R.: 33, 35, 43	Rees, V. M.: 23
Feeney, B. J.: 5	Rock, D. A.: 35, 43
Frary, R. B.: 42	Rudman, J.: 19
Freedman, M. H.: 38	Schrader, W. B.: 4, 8
Fricke, B. G.: 15	Schweiker, R. F.: 20
Goolsby, T. M.: 32, 42	Shah, M.: 20
Gruber, E. C.: 18	Statler, C.: 21
Halfter, I. T.: 25	Thomson, J. E.: 30
Hart, F. M.: 34	Warkov, S.: 24
Hills, J. R.: 39	Wesman, A. G.: *rev,* 4:815
Johnson, A. P.: 3, 6–7, 10–1	Winterbottom, J. A.: 11
Klein, S. P.: 33–5, 43	

[Out of Print Since TIP I]
Iowa Legal Aptitude Test, 4:814 (1 review, 5 references)

MEDICINE

[2350]
★CLEP Subject Examination in Clinical Chemistry. Medical technologists; 1972–73; for college accreditation of nontraditional study, advanced placement, or assessment of educational achievement; tests administered monthly at centers throughout the United States; program administered for the College Entrance Examination Board by Educational Testing Service. * For the testing program entry, see 1050.

[2351]

★**CLEP Subject Examination in Hematology.**
Medical technologists; 1972–73; for college accreditation of nontraditional study, advanced placement, or assessment of educational achievement; tests administered monthly at centers throughout the United States; program administered for the College Entrance Examination Board by Educational Testing Service. * For the testing program entry, see 1050.

[2352]

★**CLEP Subject Examination in Immunohematology and Blood Banking.** Medical technologists; 1972–73; for college accreditation of nontraditional study, advanced placement, or assesment of educational achievement; tests administered monthly at centers throughout the United States; program administered for the College Entrance Examination Board by Educational Testing Service. * For the testing program entry, see 1050.

[2353]

★**CLEP Subject Examination in Microbiology.**
Medical technologists; 1972–73; for college accreditation of nontraditional study, advanced placement, or assessment of educational achievement; tests administered monthly at centers throughout the United States; program administered for the College Entrance Examination Board by Educational Testing Service. * For the testing program entry, see 1050.

[2354]

✻**Colleges of Podiatry Admission Test.** Grades 14 and over; 1968–72; CPAT; tests administered 3 times annually (February, June, October) at centers established by the publisher; 4 scores: verbal aptitude, quantitative aptitude, natural science, spatial relations; program administered for The American Association of Colleges of Podiatric Medicine by Educational Testing Service (Midwestern Office). *
For additional information, see 7:1099.

[2355]

✻**Medical College Admission Test.** Applicants for admission to member colleges of the Association of American Medical Colleges; 1946–74; MCAT; 4 scores: verbal, quantitative, general information, science; administered 2 times annually (spring, fall) at centers established by the publisher; program administered for the Association of American Medical Colleges by American College Testing Program.
For additional information and reviews by Nancy S. Cole and James M. Richards, Jr. of earlier forms, see 7:1100 (57 references); for reviews by Robert L. Ebel and Philip H. DuBois, see 6:1137 (43 references); for a review by Alexander G. Wesman, see 5:932 (4 references); for a review by Morey J. Wantman, see 4:817 (11 references).

REFERENCES THROUGH 1971

1–11. See 4:817.
12–15. See 5:932.
16–58. See 6:1137.
59–115. See 7:1100.
116. STALNAKER, JOHN M. "The Study of Applicants for Admission to United States Medical Colleges, Class Entering in 1952–1953." *J Med Ed* 28:21–8 F '53. *
117. STALNAKER, JOHN M. "The Study of Applicants for Admission to United States Medical Colleges, Class Entering in 1953–54." *J Med Ed* 29:13–20 Ap '54. *
118. DYKMAN, ROSCOE A., AND STALNAKER, JOHN M. "The History of the 1949–50 Freshman Class." *J Med Ed* 30:611–21 N '55. * (*PA* 30:5234)
119. GEE, HELEN HOFER, AND COWLES, JOHN T., EDITORS. *The Appraisal of Applicants to Medical Schools: Report of the Fourth Teaching Institute, Association of American Medical Colleges, Colorado Springs, Colorado, November 7–10, 1956.*

Evanston, Ill.: Association of American Medical Colleges, 1957. Pp. xix, 228. * (*PA* 32:3345)
120. ANDERSON, DONALD O., AND RICHES, ELEANOR. "A Decade of Experience With Medical School Applicants at the University of British Columbia." *Can Med Assn J* 88:693–700 Ap 6 '63. *
121. JAMES, FLEMING, III. "A Study of the Relationship Between Grades in Medical School and Certain Predictor Variables." Abstract. *Univ Va Ed R* 1:94–5 '63. *
122. WEITMAN, MORRIS. "A Study of Long-Term Retention in Medical Students." *J Exp Ed* 33:87–91 f '64. * (*PA* 39: 3959)
123. JOHNSON, DAVIS G. "The Study of Applicants, 1964–65." *J Med Ed* 40:1017–30 N '65. *
124. SCHOTTSTAEDT, WILLIAM W. "Some Factors Affecting Performance in Medical School." *Trans Am Clin & Climatol Assn* 77:137–49 '65. *
125. ANDERSON, DONALD O.; RICHES, ELEANOR; AND EVANS, ROBERT K. "Applications and Enrollments at the Western Medical Schools: A Study of Medical Matriculants for 1964." *Can Med Assn J* 95:1368–74 D 24 & 31 '66. *
126. "Relationship Between Number of Applications, MCAT Performance and Admission to Medical Schools." *J Med Ed* 43:1268–9 D '68. *
127. JARECKY, ROY K.; JOHNSON, DAVIS G.; AND MATTSON, DALE E. "The Study of Applicants, 1967–68." *J Med Ed* 43: 1215–28 D '68. *
128. "Application Activity and MCAT Data of Applicants to the Class of 1969–70." *J Med Ed* 45(12):1071–3 D '70. *
129. CARTWRIGHT, LILLIAN KAUFMAN. *Women in Medical School.* Doctor's thesis, University of California (Berkeley, Calif.), 1970. (*DAI* 31:6237B)
130. FLOM, PENELOPE KEGEL. *Performance in the Medical Internship.* Doctor's thesis, University of California (Berkeley, Calif.), 1970. (*DAI* 32:1188B)
131. GALLAGHER, RICHARD EUGENE. *An Exploration of the Prediction of Academic Performance in Medical School Through the Use of Adjusted Pre-Medical Grades.* Doctor's thesis, Ohio State University (Columbus, Ohio), 1970. (*DAI* 31:4488A)
132. MENSH, IVAN N. "Orientation of Social Values in Medical Student Assessment." *Social Sci & Med* (England) 3(3): 339–48 Ja '70. *
133. NELSON-JONES, RICHARD, AND FISH, DAVID G. "Social Characteristics of Applicants to Canadian Medical Schools." *J Med Ed* 45(11):918–28 N '70. *
134. NELSON-JONES, RICHARD, AND FISH, DAVID G. "Women Students in Canadian Medical Schools." *Brit J Med Ed* 4(2): 97–108 Je '70. *
135. "Medical College Admission Test." *J Med Ed* 46(5): 472–4 My '71. *
136. BEST, WILLIAM R.; DIEKEMA, ANTHONY J.; FISHER, LAWRENCE A.; AND SMITH, NAT E. "Multivariate Predictors in Selecting Medical Students." *J Med Ed* 46(1):42–50 Ja '71. *
137. BRADING, PAUL LEE. *The Relationship Between Success in Medical School and Both Selected Academic and Non-Academic Prediction Factors.* Doctor's thesis, University of Southern California (Los Angeles, Calif.), 1971. (*DAI* 32:747A)
138. DUBE, W. F.; STRITTER, FRANK T.; AND NELSON, BONNIE C. "Study of U.S. Medical School Applicants, 1970–71." *J Med Ed* 46(10):837–57 O '71. *
139. ERDMANN, JAMES B.; MATTSON, DALE E.; HUTTON, JACK G., JR.; AND WALLACE, WIMBURN L. "The Medical College Admission Test: Past, Present, Future." *J Med Ed* 46(11): 937–46 N '71. *
140. HALEY, HAROLD B.; JUAN, ISABEL E.; AND PAIVA, ROSALIA E. A. "MCAT Scores in Relation to Personality Measures and Biographical Variables." *J Med Ed* 46(11):947–58 N '71. *
141. HAMBERG, RONALD L.; SWANSON, AUGUST G.; AND DOHNER, CHARLES W. "Perceptions and Usage of Predictive Data for Medical School Admissions." *J Med Ed* 46(11):959–63 N '71. *
142. MOFFATT, D. J.; JACOBS, A. W.; AND METCALF, W. K. "Predictors of Academic Performance in Gross Anatomy." *J Med Ed* 46(6):545–8 Je '71. *
143. PAIVA, ROSALIA E. A., AND HALEY, HAROLD B. "Intellectual, Personality, and Environmental Factors in Career Specialty Preferences." *J Med Ed* 46(4):281–9 Ap '71. * (*PA* 46:6947)
144. STEFANU, CONSTANTINE, AND FARMER, T. ALBERT, JR. "The Differential Predictive Validity of Science MCAT in the Admissions Process." *J Med Ed* 46(5):461–3 My '71. *
145. STRITTER, FRANK T.; HUTTON, JACK G., JR.; AND DUBE, W. F. "Study of U.S. Medical School Applicants, 1969–70." *J Med Ed* 46(1):25–41 Ja '71. *

CUMULATIVE NAME INDEX

Adsett, C. A.: 94
Allender, J. S.: 65
Anderson, D. O.: 62, 91, 120, 125
Badgley, R. F.: 61
Banghart, F. W.: 71
Bartlett, J. W.: 92
Beiser, H. R.: 65, 93
Best, W. R.: 136

Bird, H. B.: 94
Brading, P. L.: 137
Brenkus, P. M.: 16
Bruhn, J. G.: 94
Buckton, L.: 14
Buehler, J. A.: 37
Buxbaum, R. C.: 74
Cameron, D. F.: 85
Cartwright, L. K: 129

Ceithaml, J.: 38
Chapman, J. E.: 84
Coisman, F. G.: 80
Cole, N. S.: *rev*, 7:1100
Colten, T.: 63
Conger, J. J.: 51
Cowles, J. T.: 119
Crowder, D. G.: 23
Davis, J. R.: 15
Diekema, A. J.: 136
Dohner, C. W.: 141
Doppelt, J. E.: 14
Dube, W. F.: 138, 145
DuBois, P. H.: *rev*, 6:1137
Dykman, R. A.: 60, 118
Ebel, R. L.: *rev*, 6:1137
Erdmann, J. B.: 139
Evans, L. R.: 82, 97
Evans, R. K.: 125
Farmer, T. A.: 144
Faterson, H. F.: 109
Fish, D. G.: 113, 133–4
Fisher, L. A.: 136
Fitz, R. H.: 51
Flom, P. K.: 130
Flowers, J. F.: 114
Fredericks, M. A.: 75, 95–6, 111
Funkenstein, D. H.: 76, 83
Gallagher, R. E.: 131
Garfield, S. L.: 31
Gee, H. H.: 20, 25, 28–9, 32, 34, 39, 42, 59, 119
Geertsma, R. H.: 84
Geiger, J.: 63
Gilbert, J. A. L.: 85
Glaser, R.: 8
Glaser, R. J.: 21
Gough, H. G.: 52, 66
Graves, G. O.: 67, 77, 97
Groff, M.: 40
Gruber, E. C.: 40
Hain, J. D.: 71
Haley, H. B.: 112, 140, 143
Hall, W. B.: 52, 66
Hamberg, R. L.: 141
Harris, R. E.: 52
Hetherington, R. W.: 61
Hill, J. K.: 24
Hoffman, E. L.: 53
Howell, M. A.: 98
Hunka, S.: 85
Hunter, R. C. A.: 35, 47–8
Hurd, A. W.: 4
Hutchins, E. B.: 32, 41–2, 54–6, 58, 86, 88, 89
Hutton, J. G.: 139, 145
Ingersoll, R. W.: 67, 77, 82, 97
Jackson, G. G.: 22
Jacobs, A. W.: 142
Jacobson, M. D.: 104
James, F.: 121
Jarecky, R. K.: 127
Johnson, D. G.: 27, 43, 86, 107, 123, 127
Juan, I. R.: 112, 140
Kellow, W. F.: 22
Kelly, E. L.: 69
Klinger, E.: 25, 28, 59
Korman, M.: 106
Kosa, J.: 111
Levitt, E. E.: 44
Lief, H. I.: 53, 78
Lief, V. F.: 78
Little, J. M.: 29

Lohrenz, J. G.: 47–8
Lyden, F. J.: 63
McGuire, F. L.: 70
Macleod, J. W.: 61
Martin, L. W.: 106
Mattson, D. E.: 107, 127, 139
Mensh, I. N.: 132
Merwin, J. C.: 88
Metcalf, W. K.: 142
Michael, W. B.: 100
Moffatt, D. J.: 142
Moldowski, E. W.: 109
Moldowski, L. H. K.: 109
Moore, R. A.: 45
Morris, W. W.: 9, 56, 87, 99
Mundy, P.: 95–6, 111
Nelson, B. C.: 138
Nelson-Jones, R.: 113, 133–4
Netsky, M. G.: 71, 104
Novick, M. R.: 29
Opdyke, D.: 103
Paiva, R. E. A.: 140, 143
Peterson, O. L.: 63, 74
Pierson, G. A.: 3
Pollack, S.: 100
Price, P. B.: 46
Prince, R. H.: 35
Ralph, R. B.: 5, 12
Richards, J. M.: 33, 46; *rev*, 7:1100
Riches, E.: 62, 91, 120, 125
Robertson, L. S.: 111
Roemer, R. E.: 79
Rohrer, J. H.: 2
Rothman, A. I.: 114
Rudman, J.: 57
Sanazaro, P. J.: 58
Schofield, W.: 88, 115
Schottstaedt, W. W.: 124
Schultz, D. G.: 10
Schumacher, C. F.: 34, 39, 72
Schwartzman, A. E.: 35, 47–8
Scott, J. A.: 16
Scott, W.: 70
Sedlacek, W. E.: 89, 101–2, 107
Shatin, L.: 103
Shoemaker, H. A.: 2
Smith, E. J.: 82
Smith, N. E.: 136
Solkoff, N.: 108
Stalnaker, J. M.: 6, 11, 13, 17–8, 116–8
Stefanu, C.: 144
Stritter, F. T.: 138, 145
Stubblefield, R. L.: 106
Swanson, A. G.: 141
Taylor, C. W.: 5, 7, 12, 33, 46
Trainer, J. B.: 37
Tyler, E. A.: 44
Vaughn, K. W.: 1
Vincent, J. W.: 98
Wallace, W. L.: 139
Wantman, M. J.: *rev*, 4:817
Watson, R. I.: 19
Weitman, M.: 80, 122
Wesman, A. G.: *rev*, 5:932
Wilson, J. W. D.: 60
Wing, C. W.: 53
Wolpin, M.: 31
Woods, B. T.: 104
Work, H. H.: 49
Young, K. M.: 78
Young, R. H.: 3
Zickmantel, R.: 62

[2356]
Medical School Instructor Attitude Inventory.
Medical school faculty members; 1961; 6 scores: democratic-autocratic attitude toward teaching, critical-complimentary attitude toward medical schools, liberal-traditional attitude toward medical education, appreciative-depreciative attitude toward medical students, favorable-unfavorable attitude toward full-time teachers, favorable-unfavorable attitude toward part-time teachers; Edwin F. Rosinski; the Author. *
For additional information, see 6:1138 (1 reference).

REFERENCES THROUGH 1971
1. See 6:1138.

Medical College Admission Test

Rosinski, E. F.: 1

[2357]
★**Optometry College Admission Test.** Optometry college applicants; 1971–73; OCAT; tests administered 3 times annually (January, March, November) at centers established by the publisher; 6 scores: verbal ability, quantitative ability, biology, chemistry, physics, study-reading; sponsored by the Association of Schools and Colleges of Optometry; prepared and administered by Psychological Corporation. *

[2358]
★**Veterinary Aptitude Test.** Veterinary school applicants; 1951–73; VAT; tests administered at centers established by the publisher; 5 scores: reading comprehension, quantitative ability, science information, verbal memory, total; original test by William A. Owens and Loyal C. Payne; Psychological Corporation. *
For additional information, see 7:1101; see also 6:1139 (3 references) and 5:957 (3 references).

REFERENCES THROUGH 1971
1–3. See 5:957.
4–6. See 6:1139.
7. OWENS, WILLIAM A. "Development of a Test of Aptitude for Veterinary Medicine." Abstract. *Am Psychologist* 4:240 Jl '49. * (PA 23:6530, title only)

CUMULATIVE NAME INDEX
Brown, F. G.: 5   Payne, L. C.: 3
Layton, W. L.: 2   Ray, D. K.: 6
Owens, W. A.: 1, 4, 7

[Out of Print Since TIP I]
Medical Preference Inventory, T:2012

MISCELLANEOUS

[2359]
★**Architectural School Aptitude Test.** Architectural school applicants; 1963–73; ASAT; tests administered 2 times annually (February, December) at centers established by the publisher; program administered for the Association of Collegiate Schools of Architecture by Educational Testing Service. *
For additional information, see 7:1102 (2 references).

REFERENCES THROUGH 1971
1–2. See 7:1102.

CUMULATIVE NAME INDEX
Lunneborg, C. E.: 1–2   Lunneborg, P. W.: 1–2

[2360]
Chemical Operators Selection Test, Revised Edition. Chemical operators and applicants; 1958–71; test by M. A. Storr, J. H. McPherson, P. A. Maschino, and R. G. Garner; manual by J. I. Wegener; Dow Chemical Co. *
For additional information, see 7:1104; see also 6:1141 (1 reference).

REFERENCES THROUGH 1971
1. See 6:1141.

CUMULATIVE NAME INDEX
Coats, J. E.: 1   Garner, R. G.: 1

[2361]
Fire Promotion Tests. Prospective firemen promotees; 1960–69; 5 tests; McCann Associates. *
a) LIEUTENANT. 1962–69; 4 scores: pre-fire practices, extinguishment practices, fire supervision, total.
b) CAPTAIN. 1962–69; 5 scores: pre-fire practices, extinguishment practices, overhaul-salvage-rescue, fire supervision, total.

c) ASSISTANT FIRE CHIEF. 1961–69; 5 scores: fire administration, firefighting knowledge, fire prevention, fire supervision, total.
d) DEPUTY FIRE CHIEF. 1967–69; test also used for battalion chief; 5 scores: same as for *c*.
e) FIRE CHIEF. 1969; 5 scores: same as for *c*.
For additional information, see 7:1106.

[2362]
***Firefighter Test.** Prospective firemen; 1954–72; distribution restricted to member public personnel agencies and nonmember agencies approved by the publisher; International Personnel Management Association. *
For additional information, see 6:1143.

[2363]
Fireman Examination. Prospective firemen; 1961–62; 8 or 9 scores: learning ability (verbal, quantitative, total), fireman aptitude (interest, common sense, mechanical, total), easy verbal learning (form 70 only), total; distribution restricted to civil service commissions and municipal officials; McCann Associates. *
For additional information, see 6:1145.

[2364]
General Municipal Employees Performance (Efficiency) Rating System. Municipal employees; 1967–69; ratings by immediate supervisors; 8 summary ratings: quality of work, quantity of work, work habits, personal traits, relationships with people, supervisory ability, administrative ability, total; McCann Associates. *
For additional information, see 7:1107.

[2365]
Journalism Test. High school; 1957; 16 scores: news values, arrangement of facts, paragraphing, sentence variety, news source, sports, feature values, speech-interview, editorials, news style, columns, advertising, makeup, headlines, terminology, copyreading; no manual; Frances Miller and Kenneth Stratton; Stratton-Christian Press. *
For additional information, see 7:1108.

[2366]
★**Law Enforcement Perception Questionnaire.** Law enforcement personnel; 1970; LEPQ; attitudes toward law enforcement and law enforcement personnel; Frank Lee; Psychometric Affiliates. *

[2367]
Memory and Observation Tests for Policeman. Prospective policemen; 1962; for use with *Policeman Examination*; 2 tests; distribution restricted to civil service commissions and municipal officials; McCann Associates. *
a) MEMORY TEST FOR POLICEMAN.
b) OBSERVATION TEST FOR POLICEMAN.
For additional information, see 6:1146.

[2368]
Police Performance Rating System. Policemen; 1964–69; PPRS; ratings by immediate supervisors; 7 summary ratings: quality of work, interpersonal relationship traits, quantity of work, character traits, quality of supervision given, quality of administrative work, total; McCann Associates. *
For additional information, see 7:1109.

[2369]
Police Promotion Tests. Prospective policemen promotees; 1960–69; 6 tests; McCann Associates. *

a) SERGEANT. 1962–69; 6 or 7 scores: patrol, other police knowledges, crime investigation, law, supervision, reading comprehension (Form B only), total.
b) LIEUTENANT. 1962–69; 6 or 8 scores: same as for *a* plus administration (Form B only).
c) DETECTIVE. 1962–69; 4 scores: crime investigation, investigative judgment, law, total.
d) CAPTAIN. 1962–68; 6 scores: police supervision, police administration, crime investigation, other police knowledges, law (Form A only), reading comprehension (Form B only), total.
e) ASSISTANT CHIEF. 1968–69; 6 scores: same as for *d*.
f) CHIEF OF POLICE. 1960–69; 6 scores: same as for *d*.
For additional information, see 7:1110.

[2370]
Policeman Examination. Prospective policemen; 1960–62; 8 or 9 scores: learning ability (verbal, quantitative, total), police aptitude (interest, common sense, public relations, total), easy verbal learning (forms 70 only), total; distribution restricted to civil service commissions and municipal officials; McCann Associates. *
For additional information, see 6:1150.

[2371]
Policeman Test. Policemen and prospective policemen; 1953–65; distribution restricted to member public personnel agencies and nonmember agencies approved by the publisher; International Personnel Management Association. *
For additional information, see 7:1111.

[2372]
The Potter-Nash Aptitude Test for Lumber Inspectors and Other General Personnel Who Handle Lumber. Employees in woodworking industries; 1958; test booklet title is *The P-N Test;* arithmetic; F. T. Potter and N. Nash; N. Nash. *
For additional information, see 6:1152.

[2373]
★**Test for Firefighter B-1.** Firemen and prospective firemen; 1973; test booklet title is *Firefighter;* no manual; test rented to member public personnel agencies and nonmember agencies approved by the publisher; International Personnel Management Association. *

[2374]
★**Test for Police Officer A-1.** Policemen and prospective policemen; 1973; test booklet title is *Police Officer A-1;* no manual; test rented to member public personnel agencies and nonmember agencies approved by the publisher; International Personnel Management Association. *

[2375]
Visual Comprehension Test for Detective. Prospective police detectives; 1963; no manual; McCann Associates. *
For additional information, see 6:1154.

[Out of Print Since TIP I]
Air Force Preference Inventory, T:2014
Fire Performance Rating System, 7:1105
NCR Test Battery for Prospective Check-Out Cashiers (status unknown), 6:1147 (1 review)
P-L-S Journalism Test, 3:149
Personnel Service Rating Report, 5:939
Store Personnel Test, 5:954 (2 reviews, 1 reference)

NURSING

[2376]

Achievement Tests in Nursing. Students in schools of registered nursing; 1952–71; tests administered at any time by individual schools; 14 tests; Psychological Corporation. *
a) ANATOMY AND PHYSIOLOGY. 1953–68.
b) CANCER NURSING. 1967.
c) GENERAL CHEMISTRY. 1954–64.
d) ORGANIC AND INORGANIC CHEMISTRY. 1964.
e) COMMUNICABLE DISEASES. 1953–61.
f) MEDICAL NURSING. 1952–68.
g) MICROBIOLOGY. 1952–68.
h) NUTRITION AND DIET THERAPY. 1952–68.
i) OBSTETRICAL NURSING. 1952–68.
j) PEDIATRIC NURSING. 1952–68.
k) PHARMACOLOGY. 1952–68.
l) PSYCHIATRIC NURSING. 1952–71.
m) PSYCHOLOGY AND SOCIOLOGY. 1957–68.
n) SURGICAL NURSING. 1952–68.
For additional information, see 7:1112.

[2377]

Achievement Tests in Practical Nursing. Practical nursing students; 1957–67; tests administered at any time by individual schools; Psychological Corporation. *
For additional information, see 7:1113 (1 reference).

REFERENCES THROUGH 1971
1. See 7:1113.
CUMULATIVE NAME INDEX
Cavallo, M.: 1   Sternlicht, M.: 1

[2378]

Empathy Inventory. Nursing instructors; 1966–70; EI; empathy for nursing school students; John R. Thurston, Helen L. Brunclik, and John F. Feldhusen (manual); Nursing Research Associates. *
For additional information, see 7:1114 (2 references).

REFERENCES THROUGH 1971
1–2. See 7:1114.
CUMULATIVE NAME INDEX
Brunclik, H.: 1   Feldhusen, J. F.: 2
Brunclik, H. L.: 2   Thurston, J. R.: 1–2
Feldhusen, J.: 1

[2379]

Entrance Examination for Schools of Nursing. Nursing school applicants; 1938–70; EESN; tests administered at centers established by the publisher; 13 scores: 7 ability scores (verbal, numerical, science, reading comprehension, arithmetic processes, general information, scholastic aptitude total) and 6 personality scores (achievement, orderliness, persistence, congeniality, altruism, respectfulness); Psychological Corporation. *
For additional information, see 7:1115 (3 references); see also 6:1156 (2 references).

REFERENCES THROUGH 1971
1–2. See 6:1156.
3–5. See 7:1115.
6. NLN MEASUREMENT AND EVALUATION SERVICE. "The Predictive Validity of Two Entrance Examinations in a School of Practical Nursing." *Nursing Outl* 19(9):611 S '71. *
CUMULATIVE NAME INDEX
Carruth, M. S.: 1   NLN Measurement and Eval-
Lyman, H. B.: 5   uation Service: 6
Meadow, L.: 3   Sartain, A. Q.: 2
Mueller, E. J.: 4–5

[2380]

Entrance Examination for Schools of Practical Nursing. Practical nursing school applicants; 1942–69; tests administered at regional centers established by the publisher; 12 scores: 6 ability scores (verbal, numerical, science, reading, arithmetic fundamentals, total) and 6 personality scores (achievement, orderliness, persistence, congeniality, altruism, respectfulness); Psychological Corporation. *
For additional information, see 7:1116 (2 references).

REFERENCES THROUGH 1971
1–2. See 7:1116.
CUMULATIVE NAME INDEX
Cavallo, M.: 1   Sternlicht, M.: 1
Sitzmann, M. R.: 2

[2381]

George Washington University Series Nursing Tests. Prospective nurses; 1931–50; 5 tests; Thelma Hunt; Center for Psychological Service. *
a) APTITUDE TEST FOR NURSING. 1931–50; F. A. Moss (Form 1).
b) ARITHMETIC TEST FOR PROSPECTIVE NURSES. 1940–50.
c) READING COMPREHENSION TEST FOR PROSPECTIVE NURSES. 1940–50.
d) GENERAL SCIENCE TEST FOR PROSPECTIVE NURSES. 1944–50.
e) INTEREST-PREFERENCE TEST FOR PROSPECTIVE NURSES. 1944–50.
For additional information, see 4:818 (2 references); see also 3:699 (6 references).

REFERENCES THROUGH 1971
1–6. See 3:699.
7–8. See 4:818.
9. FAHRIG, MARJORIE W. *A Preliminary Study of the Aptitude Test (Form 2) of the George Washington University Series of Nursing Tests, in Five Canadian Hospitals.* Master's thesis, Dalhousie University (Halifax, N.S., Canada), 1951.
10. LEPLEY, WILLIAM M. "Predicting Success in Nurses Training." *J Psychol* 48:121–4 Jl '59. * (*PA* 34:6169)
11. GARRETT, WILEY S. "Prediction of Academic Success in a School of Nursing." *Personnel & Guid J* 38:500–3 F '60. * (*PA* 35:3954)
CUMULATIVE NAME INDEX
Berg, I. A.: 6–7   Lepley, W. M.: 10
Douglass, H. R.: 5   McCullough, C. M.: 5
Fahrig, M. W.: 9   Merrill, R. A.: 2, 5
Fiss, C. B.: 3   Rhinehart, J. B.: 1
Ford, A. H.: 8   Stover, R. D.: 3
Garrett, W. S.: 11   Williamson, E. G.: 3
Kraft, L.: 4

[2382]

Luther Hospital Sentence Completions. Prospective nursing students; 1959–70; LHSC; nonquantitative interpretations of responses in 7 attitudinal areas: nursing, self, home-family, responsibility, others, classwork and studies, love and marriage; an abbreviated edition, consisting of 40 of the 90 items, is also available under the title *Nursing Sentence Completions* (NSC); these 40 items may be scored quantitatively in either edition to obtain a score for predicting success in training; the authors refer to the scoring key as the *Nursing Education Scale* (NES); John R. Thurston, Helen L. Brunclik, P. A. Finn (test), and John Feldhusen (manual); Nursing Research Associates. *
For additional information, see 7:1117 (5 references).

REFERENCES THROUGH 1971
1–5. See 7:1117.
6. THURSTON, JOHN R.; FINN, PATRICIA A.; AND BRUNCLIK, HELEN L. "A Method for Evaluating the Attitudes of Prospective Nursing Students." *J Nursing Ed* 2:3–7+ My–Je '63. *
7. LOWE, BARBARA W. *A Comparison of Responses on Selected Items From the Luther Hospital Sentence Completions Form for a Group of Successful Nursing Students and Drop-Outs.* Master's thesis, University of Tennessee (Knoxville, Tenn.), 1971.

CUMULATIVE NAME INDEX

Brunclik, H. L.: 1–6
Feldhusen, J. F.: 3–5
Finn, P. A.: 6

Lowe, B. W.: 7
Thurston, J. R.: 1–6

[2383]

*NLN Achievement Tests for Schools Preparing Registered Nurses. Students in state-approved schools preparing registered nurses; 1943–73; tests loaned to schools for their own use; 3 levels; National League for Nursing, Inc. *

a) [BASIC ACHIEVEMENT TESTS.] Course-end tests; 1943–73; 9 tests.

1) *Anatomy and Physiology.* 1943–64.
2) *Chemistry.* 1943–63; 4 scores: inorganic, organic, biochemistry, total.
3) *Microbiology.* 1943–71.
4) *Normal Nutrition.* 1946–72; formerly called *Nutrition and Diet Therapy.*
5) *Basic Pharmacology.* 1944–67; formerly called *Pharmacology and Therapeutics.*
6) *Medical-Surgical Nursing.* 1956–62; 4 scores: medical nursing, surgical nursing, medical-surgical nursing, total.
7) *Obstetric Nursing.* 1945–68; 4 scores: antepartal care, partal and postpartal care of mothers, care of newborn, total.
8) *Nursing of Children.* 1945–68; 3 scores: growth and development, care of the sick child, total.
9) *Psychiatric Nursing.* 1945–73; 3 scores: psychiatric nursing practices, facts and principles, total.

b) COMPREHENSIVE ACHIEVEMENT TESTS. Students about to graduate; 1957–68; 8 tests.

1) *Diet Therapy and Applied Nutrition.* 1962.
2) *Pharmacology in Clinical Nursing (Application of Facts and Principles).* 1960–67.
3) *Natural Sciences in Nursing.* 1957–68; 3 scores: facts and principles (knowledge, application, total).
4) *Maternity and Child Nursing.* 1958–67; 3 scores: care of the normal pregnant woman and normal child, care of sick children, total.
5) *Disaster Nursing.* 1961; 3 scores: general nursing applied to disasters, facts and principles of disasters and disaster nursing, total.
6) *Medical-Surgical Nursing, Part 1.* 1961; 4 scores: orthopedic nursing, neurological-neurosurgical nursing, eye-ear-nose-and-throat nursing, total.
7) *Medical-Surgical Nursing, Part 2.* 1962; 3 scores: medical nursing, surgical nursing, total.
8) *Communicable Disease Nursing.* 1946–63; 3 scores: prevention and transmission, disease manifestations and other aspects, total.

c) [BACCALAUREATE LEVEL TESTS.] For baccalaureate programs only; 1956–73; 5 tests.

1) *Maternal-Child Nursing.* 1964; 4 scores: growth and development (including pregnancy), conditions and care of the sick child, other relevant aspects, total.
2) *Medical-Surgical Nursing.* 1967; 4 scores: part A, part B, knowledge, application.
3) *Applied Natural Sciences.* 1967; 4 scores: part A, part B, knowledge, application.
4) *Community Health Nursing.* 1956–73; earlier forms called *Public Health Nursing;* 4 scores: family health, community health, science and general information, total.
5) *Psychiatric Nursing.* 1972; 3 scores: facts and principles, psychiatric nursing practice, total.

For additional information, see 7:1118 (10 references); see also 6:1157 (1 reference).

REFERENCES THROUGH 1971

1. See 6:1157.
2–11. See 7:1118.

12. "Science and Nursing Knowledge of Graduate Students." *Nursing Outl* 15:53 D '67. *
13. "A Study Which Used the NLN Microbiology Achievement Test." *Nursing Outl* 15:73 Je '67. *
14. "The Relationship of State Boards and Achievement Test Performance." *Nursing Outl* 18(8):61 Ag '70. *
15. MUHLENKAMP, ANN F. "Prediction of State Board Scores in a Baccalaureate Program." *Nursing Outl* 19(1):57 Ja '71. *

CUMULATIVE NAME INDEX

Baldwin, J. P.: 6
Baziak, A. T.: 7
Brandt, E. M.: 5
Cavallo, M.: 3
Flitter, H.: 2
Hastie, B.: 5
Ledbetter, P. J.: 8
Lyman, H. B.: 9
Mowbray, J. K.: 6
Mueller, E. J.: 9

Muhlenkamp, A. F.: 15
NLN Measurement and Evaluation Services: 10
National League for Nursing: 11
Schumann, D.: 5
Sternlicht, M.: 3
Taylor, R. G.: 6
Thomas, M. J.: 4
Weinstein, A. S.: 4

[2384]

NLN Aide Selection Test. Applicants for aide positions in hospitals and home health agencies; 1970; AST; National League for Nursing, Inc. *

For additional information, see 7:1119.

[2385]

NLN Practical Nursing Achievement Tests. Students in state-approved schools of practical nursing; 1950–64; tests loaned to schools for their own use; 3 tests; National League for Nursing, Inc. *

a) THREE UNITS OF CONTENT. 1957–64; TUC; 4 scores: body structure and function, basic nursing procedures, nutrition and diet therapy, total.
b) NURSING INCLUDING ASPECTS OF PHARMACOLOGY. 1950–64; NIP; 4 scores: medical-surgical, maternal-child, pharmacology, total.
c) ELEMENTARY PSYCHIATRIC NURSING. 1958; for aide-training programs.

For additional information, see 7:1120 (1 reference).

REFERENCES THROUGH 1971

1. See 7:1120.
2. "Factors in the Success of Students in Schools of Practical Nursing." *Nursing Outl* 2:423–7 Ag '54. *
3. THOMAS, MARTHA J., AND WEINSTEIN, ABBOTT S. "Comparison of Test Scores in Psychiatric Nursing." *Nursing Outl* 13:38–41 My '65. *

CUMULATIVE NAME INDEX

National League for Nursing: 1

Thomas, M. J.: 3
Weinstein, A. S.: 3

[2386]

NLN Pre-Admission and Classification Examination. Practical nursing school entrants; 1950–63; PACE; tests administered throughout the year at centers established by the publisher; 2 tests, 8 scores: 7 scores listed below, composite; National League for Nursing, Inc. *

a) GENERAL INFORMATION AND JUDGMENT TEST. 4 scores: science and health, general information, arithmetic, total.
b) VOCABULARY AND READING TEST. 3 scores: vocabulary, reading, total.

For additional information, see 6:1161 (1 reference).

REFERENCES THROUGH 1971

1. See 6:1161.
2. "Factors in the Success of Students in Schools of Practical Nursing." *Nursing Outl* 2:423–7 Ag '54. *
3. MEADOW, LLOYD. "Assessment of Students for Schools of Practical Nursing." *Nursing Res* 13:222–9 su '64. *
4. BAILEY, LARRY J. "Factors Related to Success in Practical Nursing Programs." *Nursing Outl* 16:59 N '68. *
5. "The Interpretation of Scores on the NLN Pre-Admission and Classification Examination." *Nursing Outl* 18(12):47 D '70. *
6. NLN MEASUREMENT AND EVALUATION SERVICE. "The Predictive Validity of Two Entrance Examinations in a School of Practical Nursing." *Nursing Outl* 19(9):611 S '71. *

CUMULATIVE NAME INDEX

Bailey, L. J.: 4
Heslin, P.: 1
Katzell, M.: 1

Meadow, L.: 3
NLN Measurement and Evaluation Service: 6

[2387]

*NLN Pre-Nursing and Guidance Examination.
Applicants for admission to state-approved schools preparing registered nurses; 1941–72; PNG; tests administered throughout the year at centers established by the publisher; 4 tests, 7 scores: 6 scores listed below, composite; National League for Nursing, Inc. *
a) NLN TEST OF ACADEMIC APTITUDE. Special printing of level 1 (for grades 12–14) of *Cooperative School and College Ability Tests: Series 2;* 3 scores: quantitative, verbal, total.
b) NLN READING TEST. Special printing of level 1 (for grades 12–14) of *Sequential Tests of Educational Progress, Series 2: Reading.*
c) NLN SCIENCE TEST. Special printing of level 1 (for grades 12–14) of *Sequential Tests of Educational Progress, Series 2: Science.*
d) NLN SOCIAL STUDIES TEST. Special printing of level 1 (for grades 12–14) of *Sequential Tests of Educational Progress, Series 2: Social Studies.*

For additional information, see 6:1162 (8 references).

REFERENCES THROUGH 1971

1–8. See 6:1162.
9. JOEL, M. LAMPEN. *The Validity of the NLN PNG Examination and Some Other Factors in a School of Nursing.* Doctor's thesis, Loyola University (Chicago, Ill.), 1964.
10. NATIONAL LEAGUE FOR NURSING. *The NLN Pre-Nursing and Guidance Examination, Fourth Edition.* The Use of Tests in Schools of Nursing, Pamphlet No. 1. New York: the League, 1965. Pp. vii, 37. *
11. MADAUS, GEORGE F. "The Predictive Validity of the National League for Nursing, Pre-Nursing and Guidance Examination for Different Criteria of Success in a Three Year Diploma Program." *Ed & Psychol Meas* 26:431–7 su '66. * (*PA* 40:12764)
12. "The Interpretation of Scores on the NLN Pre-Nursing and Guidance Examination." *Nursing Outl* 15:51 Mr '67. *
13. "Multiple Regression and Multiple Cutoffs." *Nursing Outl* 15:61 O '67. *
14. "PNG, HSR, and Licensure Examination Results." *Nursing Outl* 15:66 N '67. *
15. BAZIAK, ANNA T. "Developing Reliable Indices to Predict Success on Psychiatric Nursing State Board Examinations." *J Psychiatric Nursing* 6:79–85 Mr–Ap '68. * (*PA* 42:18848)
16. CRUTCHLOW, MARY ANN. "Validation of Entrance Examination by School Faculties." *Nursing Outl* 16:58–9 O '68. *
17. KIRKPATRICK, JAMES J.; EWEN, ROBERT B.; BARRETT, RICHARD S.; AND KATZELL, RAYMOND A. *Testing and Fair Employment: Fairness and Validity of Personnel Tests for Different Ethnic Groups,* pp. 22–3, 25–7, 95–122. New York: New York University Press, 1968. *
18. THURSTON, JOHN R.; BRUNCLIK, HELEN L.; AND FELDHUSEN, JOHN F. "The Relationship of Personality to Achievement in Nursing Education, Phase 2." *Nursing Res* 17:265–8 My–Je '68. * (*PA* 42:17997)
19. MIKAN, CAROLYN JANE. *High School Biology and Chemistry Grades and the NLN Pre-Nursing and Guidance Examination as Predictors of Achievement in a Diploma School of Nursing.* Master's thesis, St. Joseph College (West Hartford, Conn.), 1969.
20. NLN MEASUREMENT AND EVALUATION SERVICES. "The Relationship of PNG and Achievement Test Scores." *Nursing Outl* 17(3):52 Mr '69. *
21. NLN MEASUREMENT AND EVALUATION SERVICES. "PNG Performance and Academic Ratings." *Nursing Outl* 18(5):66 My '70. *
22. NLN MEASUREMENT AND EVALUATION SERVICES. "PNG Performance and Performance in a School of Nursing." *Nursing Outl* 18(4):55 Ap '70. *
23. NLN MEASUREMENT AND EVALUATION SERVICES. "PNG Performance and Race." *Nursing Outl* 18(7):41 Jl '70. *
24. NLN MEASUREMENT AND EVALUATION SERVICES. "Performance on the PNG and the State Board of Examination." *Nursing Outl* 18(6)62–3 Je '70. *
25. NLN MEASUREMENT AND EVALUATION SERVICES. "The Validity of NLN Pre-Nursing and Guidance Examination." *Nursing Outl* 18(3):56 Mr '70. *
26. NATIONAL LEAGUE FOR NURSING. *A Validation Study of the NLN Pre-Nursing and Guidance Examination and Related Studies Emerging From Data Gathered From the Validation Study.* New York: the League, 1970. Pp. v, 58. *

CUMULATIVE NAME INDEX

Barrett, R. S.: 17
Baziak, A. T.: 15
Brunclik, H. L.: 18
Bruton, F. E.: 2
Crutchlow, M. A.: 16
Ewen, R. B.: 17
Feldhusen, J. F.: 18
Ferguson, R. H.: 5
Heyward, R. W.: 6
Joel, M. L.: 9
Katzell, R. A.: 17

Kirkpatrick, J. J.: 17
Madaus, G. F.: 11
Meyer, B.: 4
Mikan, C. J.: 19
NLN Measurement and Evaluation Services: 20–5
National League for Nursing: 3, 7, 10, 26
Rowe, H. R.: 8
Shaycoft, M. F.: 1
Thurston, J. R.: 18

[2388]

Netherne Study Difficulties Battery for Student Nurses. Student nurses; 1964–69; SDB; also called *Study Difficulties Battery;* 15 scores: understanding of words, use of words, scientific information, learning from a text, checking correctness of spelling, checking accuracy of numbers, checking accuracy of names, learning from a diagram, summarizing a paragraph, following directions, summarizing drawings and diagrams, speed of associations, speed and legibility of handwriting, speed and accuracy of freehand drawing, total; James Patrick S. Robertson; Psychological Research Department, Netherne Hospital; distributed by NFER Publishing Co. Ltd. [England]. *

For additional information, see 7:1121.

[2389]

Nurse Attitudes Inventory. Prospective nursing students; 1965–70; NAI; a multiple choice test based upon *Luther Hospital Sentence Completions;* 9 scores: attitudes (nursing, self, home-family, responsibility, others-love-marriage, academic), verification (V-1, V-2), total; the authors refer to the scoring key used to obtain the total score as the *Nursing Education Scale,* abbreviated NES-NAI to distinguish it from the *Nursing Education Scale* based upon either the *Luther Hospital Sentence Completions* or the *Nursing Sentence Completions;* John R. Thurston, Helen L. Brunclik, and John F. Feldhusen (manual); Nursing Research Associates. *

For additional information, see 7:1122 (5 references).

REFERENCES THROUGH 1971

1–5. See 7:1122.

CUMULATIVE NAME INDEX

Behring, D. W.: 3
Brunclik, H. L.: 1–2, 4
Feldhusen, J. F.: 2, 4–5

Owen, S. V.: 5
Thurston, J. R.: 1–2, 4–5

[2390]

*PSB-Aptitude for Practical Nursing Examination. Applicants for admission to practical nursing schools; 1961–72; revision of *PSB-Entrance Examination for Schools of Practical Nursing;* 5 scores: general mental ability, spelling, natural sciences, judgment in practical nursing situations, personal adjustment index; Anna S. Evans, Joan R. Yanuzzi, and George A. W. Stouffer, Jr., with the technical assistance of the Psychological Services Bureau; the Bureau. *

For additional information concerning the earlier edition, see 6:1163.

[Out of Print Since TIP I]

Basic Nursing Procedures and Elementary Nutrition: NLN Achievement Tests for Psychiatric Aides, 6:1158b
NLN Graduate Nurse Examination, 6:1159 (4 references)

RESEARCH

[2391]

Research Personnel Review Form. Research and engineering and scientific firms; 1959–60; for supervisor's evaluation of research personnel in preparation for a performance review interview; Morris I. Stein; the Author. *

For additional information, see 6:1164.

[2392]

Supervisor's Evaluation of Research Personnel. Research personnel; 1960; SERP; ratings by supervisors; William D. Buel; Byron Harless, Schaffer, Reid & Associates, Inc. *

For additional information, a review by John W. French, and an excerpted review by Laurence Siegel, see 6:1165 (3 references).

REFERENCES THROUGH 1971

1–3. See 6:1165.
4. BUEL, WILLIAM D. "Biographical Data and the Identification of Creative Research Personnel." *J Appl Psychol* 49:318–21 O '65. * (*PA* 40:787)
5. BUEL, WILLIAM D.; ALBRIGHT, LEWIS E.; AND GLENNON, J. R. "A Note on the Generality and Cross-Validity of Personal History for Identifying Creative Research Scientists." *J Appl Psychol* 50:217–9 Je '66. * (*PA* 40:8829)

CUMULATIVE NAME INDEX

Albright, L. E.: 5   French, J. W.: *rev*, 6:1165
Bachner, V. M.: 3   Glennon, J. R.: 5
Buel, W. D.: 1–5   Siegel, L.: *exc*, 6:1165

[2393]

Surveys of Research Administration and Environment. Research and engineering and scientific firms; 1959–60; 2 forms for gathering information and opinions on the company and its research activities; Morris I. Stein; the Author. *

a) STEIN SURVEY FOR ADMINISTRATORS. Supervisors and administrators; also part of *Technical Personnel Recruiting Inventory.*

b) STEIN RESEARCH ENVIRONMENT SURVEY. Research and technical personnel.

For additional information, see 6:1166.

[2394]

Technical Personnel Recruiting Inventory. Research and engineering and scientific firms; 1959–60; 3 parts; Morris I. Stein; the Author. *

a) INDIVIDUAL QUALIFICATION FORM. Supervisors; description of an available research position.

b) PERSONAL DATA FORM FOR SCIENTIFIC, ENGINEERING, AND TECHNICAL PERSONNEL. Job applicants.

c) STEIN SURVEY FOR ADMINISTRATORS. Administrators; description of company's research environment; also part of *Surveys of Research Administration and Environment.*

For additional information, see 6:1167.

SELLING

[2395]

Aptitudes Associates Test of Sales Aptitude: A Test for Measuring Knowledge of Basic Principles of Selling. Applicants for sales positions; 1947–60; for a revised edition, see 2406; 1960 manual identical with manual copyrighted 1958 excerpt for format, modification in some normative tables, and extension of bibliography; Martin M. Bruce; Martin M. Bruce, Ph.D., Publishers. *

For additional information, see 6:1169 (6 references); for reviews by Milton E. Hahn and Donald G. Paterson, see 4:824. For reference to a review of the revised edition, see 2406.

REFERENCES THROUGH 1971

1–6. See 6:1169.

CUMULATIVE NAME INDEX

Bruce, M. M.: 1, 4   Rosen, J. C.: 3
Gray, E. J.: 3   Speer, G. S.: 5
Hahn, M. E.: *rev*, 4:824   United States Employment
Harless, B. B.: 4   Service: 2
Paterson, D. G.: *rev*, 4:824

[2396]

Combination Inventory, Form 2. Prospective debit life insurance salesmen; 1954–66; CI; 6 scores: arithmetic, general knowledge, sales aptitude (interest, reaction, personal history, total); interest items selected from *Strong Vocational Interest Blank for Men, Revised;* distribution restricted to home offices of member life insurance companies; Life Insurance Agency Management Association. *

For additional information, see 7:1123; see also 6:1170 (1 reference).

REFERENCES THROUGH 1971

1. See 6:1170.

CUMULATIVE NAME INDEX

Ferguson, L. W.: 1

[2397]

Detroit Retail Selling Inventory. Candidates for training in retail selling; 1940, c1939; 5 scores: personality, intelligence, checking, arithmetic, total; Harry J. Baker and Paul H. Voelker; Bobbs-Merrill Co., Inc. *

For additional information, reviews by Milton E. Hahn and Floyd L. Ruch, and excerpted reviews by William J. Jones and one other, see 3:697.

REFERENCES THROUGH 1971

1. BOUCK, WALTER C. *The Predictive Value of the Detroit Retail Selling Inventory for Success in the College of Business Administration at the University of Toledo.* Master's thesis, University of Toledo (Toledo, Ohio), 1953.
2. STOTSKY, BERNARD A. "Vocational Tests as Measures of Performance of Schizophrenics in Two Rehabilitation Activities." *J Clin Psychol* 12:236–42 Jl '56. * (*PA* 31:6447)

CUMULATIVE NAME INDEX

Bouck, W. C.: 1   Ruch, F. L.: *rev*, 3:697
Hahn, M. E.: *rev*, 3:697   Stotsky, B. A.: 2
Jones, W. J.: *exc*, 3:697

[2398]

The Evaluation Record. Prospective life insurance agency managers; 1947–63; combination of evaluation procedures yielding a composite score; 3 parts; distribution restricted to home offices of member life insurance companies; Life Insurance Agency Management Association. *

a) EXPERIENCE FORM. Completed by candidates.

b) STRONG VOCATIONAL INTEREST BLANK FOR MEN. See 2212; scored for production manager only.

c) HOME OFFICE RATING CHART. Ratings of personal qualities by 1–3 supervisors.

For additional information, see 6:1172.

[2399]

Hall Salespower Inventory. Salesmen; 1946–57; test booklet title is *Salespower Inventory;* 10 scores: background, intelligence, aggressiveness, dominance, sales temperament, sales interest, introversion-extroversion, motivation, emotional, total; Clifton W. Hall and Richard M. Page; Hall & Liles. *

For additional information, see 5:924.

[2400]

Hanes Sales Selection Inventory, Revised Edition. Insurance and printing salesmen; 1954–55; 3 scores: verbal, personality, drive; Bernard Hanes; Psychometric Affiliates. *

For additional information and reviews by William E. Kendall and Albert K. Kurtz, see 6:1173.

[2401]

*Information Index. Life and health insurance agents; 1951–72; 2 editions; distribution restricted to home offices of member life and health insurance companies; Life Insurance Agency Management Association. *
a) LIFE EDITION. 1951–72; life insurance information.
b) HEALTH EDITION. 1966; health insurance information.

For additional information regarding an earlier edition of a, see 6:1174 (1 reference); see also 5:927 (3 references).

REFERENCES THROUGH 1971

1–3. See 5:927.
4. See 6:1174.
5. THAYER, PAUL W.; ANTOINETTI, JOHN A.; AND GUEST, THEODORE A. "Product Knowledge and Performance—A Study of Life Insurance Agents." *Personnel Psychol* 11:411–8 au '58. * (*PA* 33:11230)

CUMULATIVE NAME INDEX

Antoinetti, J. A.: 5   Guest, T. A.: 1, 5
Baier, D. E.: 2–4   Thayer, P. W.: 5
Dugan, R. D.: 2–4

[2402]

LIAMA Inventory of Job Attitudes. Life insurance field personnel; 1956–70; IJA; group measurement of company performance; job attitude scores in 10 areas; distribution restricted to home offices of member life insurance companies and research personnel; Life Insurance Agency Management Association. *

For additional information, see 7:1124.

[2403]

Personnel Institute Hiring Kit. Applicants for sales positions; 1954–62; 1957 manual identical with manual copyrighted 1956 except for one minor change; Personnel Institute, Inc. *
a) PRELIMINARY SCREENING INTERVIEW. 1957.
b) PERSONAL HISTORY INVENTORY. 1957–62; 1962 form identical with form copyrighted 1957.
c) DIAGNOSTIC INTERVIEWER'S GUIDE. 1956–57.
d) PERSONAL OR TELEPHONE WORK REFERENCE INVESTIGATION. 1957–59; formerly called *Work Reference Investigation.*
e) SELECTOR TEST BATTERY. Applicants for routine selling jobs; 1955–57; 3 tests.
  1) *EM-AY Inventory.* Reprint of *Otis Employment Tests,* Test 2, Form A ('22); mental alertness.
  2) *ESS-AY Inventory.* Sales aptitude.
  3) *The Personality Inventory.* See 1320; 4 scores: extroversion, dominance, self-confidence, social dependence.
f) COMPREHENSIVE TEST BATTERY. Applicants for complex selling jobs; 1954–62; 6 tests.
  1) Same as e(1) above.
  2) Same as e(2) above.
  3) Same as e(3) above.
  4) *Vocabulary Inventory.* 1956 test identical with test copyrighted 1954.
  5) *ESS-EYE Inventory.* Reprint of the SP (Special) Edition of the *Social Intelligence Test: George Washington University Series, Revised Form* ('47); 3 scores: social judgment, social observation, total.
  6) *B-B-ESS Inventory.* Business skills; 8 scores: comparing, computation, reading, spelling, vocabulary, arithmetical reasoning, English, total; 1956 test identical with test copyrighted 1954.
For additional information, see 6:1176 (3 references).

REFERENCES THROUGH 1971

1–3. See 6:1176.
4. BRUCE, MARTIN MARC. *The Importance of Certain Personality Characteristics, Skills and Abilities in Effectiveness as a*

Factory Foreman. Doctor's thesis, New York University (New York, N.Y.), 1952. (*DA* 13:116)

CUMULATIVE NAME INDEX

Bruce, M. M.: 1–4

[2404]

SRA Sales Attitudes Check List. Applicants for sales positions; 1960; modification of *Sales Personnel Description Form;* Erwin K. Taylor and the Personnel Research & Development Corporation; Science Research Associates, Inc. *

For additional information and a review by John P. Foley, Jr., see 6:1177.

[2405]

*Sales Aptitude Test: ETSA Test 7A. Job applicants; 1960–72, c1957–59; 8 scores: sales judgment, interest in selling, personality factors, occupational identification, level of aspiration, insight into human nature, awareness of sales approach, total; manual and technical handbook by S. Trevor Hadley and George A. W. Stouffer, Jr.; test by Psychological Services Bureau; Educators'-Employers' Tests & Services Associates. * For the complete battery entry, see 2106.

For reviews of the complete battery, see 6:1025 (2 reviews).

[2406]

*Sales Comprehension Test. Applicants for sales positions; 1947–71; revision of the still-in-print *Aptitudes Associates Test of Sales Aptitude;* 1971 test identical with test copyrighted 1953 except for format and 1 new item; Martin M. Bruce; Martin M. Bruce, Ph.D., Publishers. *

For additional information, see 6:1178 (7 references); for a review by Raymond A. Katzell, see 5:947 (10 references). For reference to reviews of the original edition, see 2395.

REFERENCES THROUGH 1971

1–10. See 5:947.
11–17. See 6:1178.
18. BASS, BERNARD M. "Validity Information Exchange, No. 10-25: D.O.T. Code 1-85.22, Salesman, Foodstuffs." *Personnel Psychol* 10:343–4 au '57. *
19. BLANK, STANLEY S. "An Examination of the Usefulness of Various Psychological Instruments for Predicting Department Managers' Ratings of Clerical Sales Personnel." *Can Counsellor* 2:46–50 Ja '68. *
20. DEWITT, CHARLES JAY. *A Study of Selected Variables in Discriminating Between Contrasting Levels of Student Teaching Performance.* Doctor's thesis, University of Virginia (Charlottesville, Va.), 1969. (*DAI* 31:260A)

CUMULATIVE NAME INDEX

Albright, L. E.: 8, 10   Dugan, R. D.: 16
Aron, J.: 11   Friesen, E. P.: 4
Ash, P.: 14–5   Glennon, J. R.: 8, 10
Bass, B. M.: 17–8   Hecht, R.: 6, 11
Blank, S. S.: 19   Katzell, R. A.: *rev,* 5:947
Bruce, M. M.: 1–7, 9, 12–3   Murray, L. E.: 7, 12–3
DeWitt, C. J.: 20   Smith, W. J.: 8, 10

[2407]

*Sales Method Index. Life insurance agents; 1948–71; continuous work-diary record of specific sales procedures and effectiveness for supervisory and self-analysis; distribution restricted to home offices of member life insurance companies; Life Insurance Agency Management Association. *

[2408]

*Sales Motivation Inventory, Revised. Applicants for sales positions; 1953–69; SMI; Martin M. Bruce; Martin M. Bruce, Ph.D., Publishers. *

For additional information and a review by S. Rains Wallace, see 5:948 (2 references).

REFERENCES THROUGH 1971

1-2. See 5:948.
3. BRUCE, MARTIN M. "Normative Data Information Exchange, No. 12-24." *Personnel Psychol* 12:506 au '59. *
4. MURRAY, L. E., AND BRUCE, MARTIN M. "Normative Data Information Exchange, No. 12-18." *Personnel Psychol* 12:334 su '59. *
5. MURRAY, LESTER E., AND BRUCE, MARTIN M. "A Study of the Validity of the Sales Comprehension Test and Sales Motivation Inventory in Differentiating High and Low Production in Life Insurance Selling." *J Appl Psychol* 43:246-8 Ag '59. * (*PA* 34:6609)
6. BRAUN, JOHN R., AND ASTA, PATRICIA. "Effects of Faking Instructions on Sales Motivation Inventory Scores." *J Ed Meas* 5:339-40 w '68. * (*PA* 44:11210)
7. DEWITT, CHARLES JAY. *A Study of Selected Variables in Discriminating Between Contrasting Levels of Student Teaching Performance.* Doctor's thesis, University of Virginia (Charlottesville, Va.), 1969. (*DAI* 31:260A)

CUMULATIVE NAME INDEX

Asta, P.: 6	DeWitt, C. J.: 7
Braun, J. R.: 6	Murray, L. E.: 2, 4-5
Bruce, M. M.: 1-5	Wallace, S. R.: *rev*, 5:948

[2409]
The Sales Sentence Completion Blank. Applicants for sales positions; 1961; Norman Gekoski; Martin M. Bruce, Ph.D., Publishers. *
For additional information, a review by William E. Kendall, and an excerpted review by John O. Crites, see 6:1181.

[2410]
Steward Life Insurance Knowledge Test. Applicants for life insurance agent or supervisory positions; 1952-56; 5 scores: arithmetic, vocabulary, principles, functions, total; Verne Steward; Steward-Mortensen & Associates. *
For additional information, see 5:950.

[2411]
Steward Occupational Objectives Inventory, 1957 Edition. Applicants for supervisory positions in life insurance companies or agencies; 1956-57; formerly called *Steward Supervisory Personnel Inventory;* ratings in 8 areas: caliber level, life insurance knowledge, selling skills, leadership ability, supervisory skills, personal adjustment, survival on job, supplementary items; Verne Steward; Steward-Mortensen & Associates. *
For additional information, see 5:951.

[2412]
Steward Personal Background Inventory (1960 Revised Edition). Applicants for sales positions; 1949-60; revision of *Personal Inventory of Background Factors;* ratings of 5 factors (caliber, aptitude, adjustment, survival, supplementary) in 7 areas (health, education, experience, financial status, activities, family status, miscellaneous); 1960 manual identical with manual copyrighted 1957 except for minor changes; Verne Steward; Steward-Mortensen & Associates. *
For additional information and reviews by Leonard V. Gordon and Lyman W. Porter, see 6:1183.

[2413]
Test for Ability to Sell: George Washington University Series. Grades 7-16 and adults; 1929-50; F. A. Moss, Herbert Wyle, William Loman, William Middleton, Thelma Hunt, Robert George, and William Schnell; Center for Psychological Service. *
For additional information, see 4:829; for a review by Floyd L. Ruch, see 3:705.

[2414]
★**Test of Retail Sales Insight.** Retail clerks and students; 1960-71; TRSI; earlier form called *Test of Sales Insight;* 6 scores: sales knowledge, customer

motivation, merchandise procurement, sales promotion, sales closure, total; Russell Cassel; Psychologists and Educators, Inc. *

[Out of Print Since TIP I]
Aptitude Index Selection Procedure, 6:1168 (2 reviews, 21 references)
Bigelow Hiring Kit (status unknown), 4:826
Dealer Inventory (status unknown), 6:1171
How to Develop Sales Ability, T:2053
Interviewer's Impressions—Sales Applicants (status unknown), 6:1175
Measure of Consociative Tendency, 5:931
Personnel Research Institute Area Interview, T:2059
Sales Employee Inventory (status unknown), 6:1179
Sales Personnel Description Form, 6:1180 (1 review, 2 references)
Sales Situation Test, 4:827 (1 reference)
Test of Sales Ability, T:2074
Test of Sales Judgment (status unknown), 4:830
Word Check Forms (status unknown), 6:1184

SKILLED TRADES

[2415]
Electrical Sophistication Test. Job applicants; 1963-65; Stanley G. Ciesla; Psychometric Affiliates. *
For additional information and a review by Charles F. Ward, see 7:1125.

[2416]
The Fiesenheiser Test of Ability to Read Drawings. Trade school and adults; 1955; Elmer I. Fiesenheiser; Psychometric Affiliates. *
For additional information and a review by Joseph E. Moore, see 6:1186.

[2417]
*****Mechanical Familiarity Test: ETSA Test 5A.** Job applicants; 1960-72, c1957-59; manual and technical handbook by S. Trevor Hadley and George A. W. Stouffer, Jr.; test by Psychological Services Bureau; Educators'-Employers' Tests & Services Associates. * For the complete battery entry, see 2106.
For reviews of the complete battery, see 6:1025 (2 reviews).

[2418]
Mechanical Handyman Test. Maintenance workers; 1957-65; distribution restricted to member public personnel agencies and nonmember agencies approved by the publisher; International Personnel Management Association. *
For additional information, see 7:1126.

[2419]
*****Mechanical Knowledge Test: ETSA Test 6A.** Job applicants; 1960-72, c1957-59; manual and technical handbook by S. Trevor Hadley and George A. W. Stouffer, Jr.; test by Psychological Services Bureau; Educators'-Employers' Tests & Services Associates. * For the complete battery entry, see 2106.
For reviews of the complete battery, see 6:1025 (2 reviews).

[2420]
*****Ohio Auto Body Achievement Test.** Grades 11-12; 1969-73; OABAT; available only as a part of the *Ohio Trade and Industrial Education Achievement Test Program* (see 2431 for more complete information); 16 scores: welding, metal forming, body filler,

refinishing, trim and hardware, parts replacement, alignment, glass replacement, fiber glass repair, frame and unit body, electrical system, cooling and conditioning, shop management, applied science, applied math, total; Instructional Materials Laboratory, Ohio State University. *

For additional information, see 7:1127.

[2421]
*Ohio Automotive Mechanics Achievement Test. Grades 11–12; 1959–73; OAMAT; available only as a part of the *Ohio Trade and Industrial Education Achievement Test Program* (see 2431 for more complete information); 15 scores: applied math, basic operations, general service, engine, cooling system, electrical system, applied science, fuel system, emission system, power train, suspension system, steering system, brakes, ventilation, total; Instructional Materials Laboratory, Ohio State University. *

[2422]
★Ohio Carpentry Achievement Test. Grades 11–12; 1970–73; OCAT; available only as a part of the *Ohio Trade and Industrial Education Achievement Test Program* (see 2431 for more complete information); 14 scores: orientation, blueprint reading, applied math, applied science, foundations, floor framing, roofing, insulation, exterior finish, interior finish, wall framing, roof framing, special operations, total; Instructional Materials Laboratory, Ohio State University. *

[2423]
★Ohio Communication Products Electronics Achievement Test. Grades 11–12; 1973; OCPEAT; available only as a part of the *Ohio Trade and Industrial Education Achievement Test Program* (see 2431 for more complete information); 12 scores: orientation, D/C electricity, A/C electricity, electron tubes, semi-conductors, vacuum tube and solid state circuitry, audio devices, receivers, transmitters, television, business practices, total; Instructional Materials Laboratory, Ohio State University.

[2424]
★Ohio Construction Electricity Achievement Test. Grades 11–12; 1973; OCEAT; available only as a part of the *Ohio Trade and Industrial Education Achievement Test Program* (see 2431 for more complete information); 19 scores: orientation, D/C electricity, magnetism, D/C power sources, D/C motors and controllers, instrumentation, A/C electricity, A/C circuits, three-phase A/C electricity, transformers, A/C motors and starters, electronics, planning and layout, branch circuits, wiring methods, lighting, heating and air conditioning, low-voltage systems, total; Instructional Materials Laboratory, Ohio State University.

[2425]
*Ohio Cosmetology Achievement Test. Grades 11–12; 1967–73; OCAT; available only as a part of the *Ohio Trade and Industrial Education Achievement Test Program* (see 2431 for more complete information); 14 scores: scalp, hands and feet, hair, hair tints and bleach, face information, facial, make-up, sanitation and bacteriology, applied science, anatomy and physiology, shop management, trade math, legal guidance, total; Instructional Materials Laboratory, Ohio State University. *

For additional information, see 7:1129.

Ohio Auto Body Achievement Test

[2426]
★Ohio Industrial Electronics Achievement Test. Grades 11–12; 1973; OIEAT; available only as a part of the *Ohio Trade and Industrial Education Achievement Test Program* (see 2431 for more complete information); 19 scores: orientation, D/C electricity, A/C electricity, electron tubes, semi-conductors, schematic drawings, power supplies, D/C timers, A/C timers, heavy current conductors, sequence timers, welding, sensors, heaters, magnetics, rotating machinery, servos, logic systems, total; Instructional Materials Laboratory, Ohio State University.

[2427]
*Ohio Machine Trades Achievement Test. Grades 11–12; 1958–73; OMTAT; available only as a part of the *Ohio Trade and Industrial Education Achievement Test Program* (see 2431 for more complete information); 18 scores: applied math, layout, hand tools, measuring, power sawing, drilling, shaping, heat treating, trade science, machining-lathe, milling, blueprint reading, grinding (bench, surface, tool and cutter, cylindrical, internal), total; Instructional Materials Laboratory, Ohio State University. *

For additional information, see 7:1130.

REFERENCES THROUGH 1971
1. KAPES, JEROME T., AND LONG, THOMAS E. "An Assessment of the Criterion-Related Validity of the Ohio Trade and Industrial Education Achievement Test Battery." *J Indus Teach Ed* 9(1):6–14 f '71. *
2. RAU, GERALD NORMAN. *The Relationship of Occupational Experience and Professional Preparation of Machine-Trades Teachers to the Achievement of Machine-Trades Students.* Doctor's thesis, University of Missouri (Columbia, Mo.), 1971. (*DAI* 32:3175A)

CUMULATIVE NAME INDEX
Kapes, J. T.: 1   Rau, G. N.: 2
Long, T. E.: 1

[2428]
*Ohio Mechanical Drafting Achievement Test. Grades 11–12; 1962–73; OMDAT; available only as a part of the *Ohio Trade and Industrial Education Achievement Test Program* (see 2431 for more complete information); 19 scores: materials and equipment, dimensioning, auxiliary views, threads and fasteners, production or working drawings, machine elements, auxiliary information, industrial processes, materials of industry, applied science, orthographic projection, sectional views, pictorial drawings, intersections and developments, goemetric drawing, lettering, reproduction of drawings, functions of mathematics, total; Instructional Materials Laboratory, Ohio State University. *

For additional information, see 7:1131.

REFERENCES THROUGH 1971
1. KAPES, JEROME T., AND LONG, THOMAS E. "An Assessment of the Criterion-Related Validity of the Ohio Trade and Industrial Education Achievement Test Battery." *J Indus Teach Ed* 9(1):6–14 f '71. *

CUMULATIVE NAME INDEX
Kapes, J. T.: 1   Long, T. E.: 1

[2429]
*Ohio Printing Achievement Test. Grades 11–12; 1963–73; OPAT; available only as a part of the *Ohio Trade and Industrial Education Achievement Test Program* (see 2431 for more complete information); 17 scores: orientation, printing planning, composition (hand, machine, photo), camera operation, film processing, letterpress (platemaking, presswork), applied science, lithograph (stripping and platemaking, presswork), bindery work, paper technology, ink tech-

nology, applied math, total; Instructional Materials Laboratory, Ohio State University. *
For additional information, see 7:1132.

REFERENCES THROUGH 1971
1. KAPES, JEROME T., AND LONG, THOMAS E. "An Assessment of the Criterion-Related Validity of the Ohio Trade and Industrial Education Achievement Test Battery." *J Indus Teach Ed* 9(1):6–14 f '71. *

CUMULATIVE NAME INDEX
Kapes, J. T.: 1   Long, T. E.: 1

[2430]
*Ohio Sheet Metal Achievement Test.** Grades 11–12; 1964–73; OSMAT; available only as a part of the *Ohio Trade and Industrial Education Achievement Test Program* (see 2431 for more complete information); 15 scores: blueprint reading, applied science, applied math, hand tool operations, machine operations, soldering, special operations, mechanical drawing, free-hand sketching, metals, non-metallic, layout, fabricating, welding, total; Instructional Materials Laboratory, Ohio State University. *
For additional information, see 7:1133.

REFERENCES THROUGH 1971
1. KAPES, JEROME T., AND LONG, THOMAS E. "An Assessment of the Criterion-Related Validity of the Ohio Trade and Industrial Education Achievement Test Battery." *J Indus Teach Ed* 9(1):6–14 f '71. *

CUMULATIVE NAME INDEX
Kapes, J. T.: 1   Long, T. E.: 1

[2431]
*Ohio Trade and Industrial Education Achievement Test Program.** Grades 11–12; 1958–73; tests administered annually in March at participating schools; each student must take 2 tests: the intelligence test and a trade test; Instructional Materials Laboratory, Ohio State University.
a) INTELLIGENCE TEST. *Short Form Test of Academic Aptitude,* Level 5 (grades 9–12); see 458.
b) TRADE TESTS. 1958–73; 13 tests based on course outlines prepared for use in Ohio.
   1) *Ohio Auto Body Achievement Test.* See 2420. *
   2) *Ohio Automotive Mechanics Achievement Test.* See 2421. *
   3) *Ohio Carpentry Achievement Test.* See 2422. *
   4) *Ohio Cosmetology Achievement Test.* See 2425. *
   5) *Ohio Dental Assisting Achievement Test.* See 2339. *
   6) *Ohio Mechanical Drafting Achievement Test.* See 2428. *
   7) *Ohio Construction Electricity Achievement Test.* See 2424. *
   8) *Ohio Communication Products Electronics Achievement Test.* See 2423.
   9) *Ohio Industrial Electronics Achievement Test.* See 2426.
   10) *Ohio Machine Trades Achievement Test.* See 2427. *
   11) *Ohio Printing Achievement Test.* See 2429. *
   12) *Ohio Sheet Metal Achievement Test.* See 2430. *
   13) *Ohio Welding Achievement Test.* See 2432. *
For additional information, see 7:1134.

REFERENCES THROUGH 1971
1. KAPES, JEROME T., AND LONG, THOMAS E. "An Assessment of the Criterion-Related Validity of the Ohio Trade and Industrial Education Achievement Test Battery." *J Indus Teach Ed* 9(1):6–14 f '71. *

CUMULATIVE NAME INDEX
Kapes, J. T.: 1   Long, T. E.: 1

[2432]
*Ohio Welding Achievement Test.** Grades 11–12; 1969–73; OWAT; available only as a part of the *Ohio Trade and Industrial Education Achievement Test Program* (see 2431 for more complete information); 12 scores: blueprint reading, flame cutting, oxy-acetylene, arc welding, resistance welding, gas tungsten—arc welding process, gas metal arc welding, equipment, labor and management, applied math, applied science, total; Instructional Materials Laboratory, Ohio State University. *
For additional information, see 7:1135.

[2433]
Purdue Industrial Training Classification Test. Grades 9–12 and adults; 1942; shop mathematics; C. H. Lawshe and A. C. Moutoux; University Book Store. *
For additional information and reviews by D. Welty Lefever and Charles I. Mosier, see 3:675 (2 references).

REFERENCES THROUGH 1971
1–2. See 3:675.
3. LITTLETON, ISAAC T. "Prediction in Auto Trade Courses." *J Appl Psychol* 36:15–9 F '52. * (PA 26:7256)
4. LAWSHE, C. H., AND PATINKA, PAUL J. "An Empirical Comparison of Two Methods of Test Selection and Weighting." *J Appl Psychol* 42:210–2 Je '58. * (PA 33:9093)

CUMULATIVE NAME INDEX
Lawshe, C. H.: 1–2, 4   Mosier, C. I.: *rev,* 3:675
Lefever, D. W.: *rev,* 3:675   Patinka, P. J.: 4
Littleton, I. T.: 3   Thornton, G. R.: 2

[2434]
Purdue Interview Aids. Applicants for industrial employment; 1943; 3 tests; C. H. Lawshe; distributed by University Book Store. *
a) CAN YOU READ A WORKING DRAWING?
b) CAN YOU READ A MICROMETER?
c) CAN YOU READ A SCALE?
For additional information and a review by William W. Waite, see 4:775.

[2435]
Purdue Trade Information Test for Sheetmetal Workers. Sheetmetal workers; 1958; Joseph Tiffin, B. R. Modisette, and Warren B. Griffin; University Book Store. *
For additional information, see 5:942.

[2436]
Purdue Trade Information Test in Carpentry. Vocational school and adults; 1952; Joseph Tiffin and Robert F. Mengelkoch; University Book Store. *
For additional information and a review by P. L. Mellenbruch, see 5:943 (1 reference).

REFERENCES THROUGH 1971
1. See 5:943.

CUMULATIVE NAME INDEX
Mellenbruch, P. L.: *rev,* 5:943   Mengelkoch, R. F.: 1

[2437]
Purdue Trade Information Test in Engine Lathe Operation. Vocational school and adults; 1955; Robert Cochran and Joseph Tiffin; University Book Store. *
For additional information and a review by William J. Micheels, see 5:944.

[2438]
Purdue Trade Information Test in Welding, Revised Edition. Vocational school and adults; 1952;

Joseph Tiffin and Warren B. Griffin; distributed by University Book Store.*

For additional information, see 5:945.

REFERENCES THROUGH 1971

1. GRIFFIN, WARREN B. *A Trade Information Test for Welders.* Master's thesis, Purdue University (Lafayette, Ind.), 1952.

CUMULATIVE NAME INDEX

Griffin, W. B.: 1

[2439]

Short Occupational Knowledge Test for Auto Mechanics. Job applicants; 1969–70; score is pass, fail, or unclassifiable; Bruce A. Campbell and Suellen O. Johnson; Science Reasearch Associates, Inc.*

For additional information and a review by Emory E. Wiseman, see 7:1137.

[2440]

Short Occupational Knowledge Test for Carpenters. Job applicants; 1969–70; score is pass, fail, or unclassifiable; Bruce A. Campbell and Suellen O. Johnson; Science Research Associates, Inc.*

For additional information, see 7:1138.

[2441]

Short Occupational Knowledge Test for Draftsmen. Job applicants; 1969–70; score is pass, fail, or unclassifiable; Bruce A. Campbell and Suellen O. Johnson; Science Research Associates, Inc. *

For additional information, see 7:1139.

[2442]

Short Occupational Knowledge Test for Electricians. Job applicants; 1969–70; score is pass, fail, or unclassifiable; Bruce A. Campbell and Suellen O. Johnson; Science Research Associates, Inc.*

For additional information and a review by Charles F. Ward, see 7:1140.

[2443]

Short Occupational Knowledge Test for Machinists. Job applicants; 1969–70; score is pass, fail, or unclassifiable; Bruce A. Campbell and Suellen O. Johnson; Science Research Associates, Inc. *

For additional information, see 7:1141.

[2444]

Short Occupational Knowledge Test for Plumbers. Job applicants; 1970; score is pass, fail, or unclassifiable; Bruce A. Campbell and Suellen O. Johnson; Science Research Associates, Inc. *

For additional information, see 7:1142.

[2445]

Short Occupational Knowledge Test for Tool and Die Makers. Job applicants; 1970; score is pass, fail, or unclassifiable; Bruce A. Campbell and Suellen O. Johnson; Science Research Associates, Inc.*

For additional information, see 7:1143.

[2446]

Short Occupational Knowledge Test for Welders. Job applicants; 1969–70; score is pass, fail, or unclassifiable; Bruce A. Campbell and Suellen O. Johnson; Science Research Associates, Inc. *

For additional information, see 7:1144.

[2447]

Technical Tests. Standards 6–8 (ages 13–15); 1962; 5 scores: arithmetic, mechanical insight, spatial relations (2 scores), tool test; Human Sciences Research Council [South Africa].*

For additional information, see 6:1187.

Purdue Trade Information Test in Welding

[Out of Print Since TIP I]

Automotive Mechanic Test, 6:1185
Garage Mechanic Test, 5:573
Ohio Basic Electricity and Electronics Achievement Tests, 7:1128
Purdue Blueprint Reading Test, 4:782
Purdue Test for Electricians, 7:1136 (2 reviews)
Purdue Test for Machinists and Machine Operators, 4:816 (1 review)
Written Trade Tests, 6:1188

SUPERVISION

[2448]

*****How Supervise?** Supervisors; 1943–71; Quentin W. File and H. H. Remmers (manual); Psychological Corporation. (Australian edition: Australian Council for Educational Research [Australia]). *

For additional information and a review by Joel T. Campbell, see 6:1189 (9 references); see also 5:926 (18 references); for a review by Milton M. Mandell, see 4:774 (8 references); for reviews by D. Welty Lefever, Charles I. Mosier, and C. H. Ruedisili, see 3:687 (5 references).

REFERENCES THROUGH 1971

1–5. See 3:687.
6–13. See 4:774.
14–31. See 5:926.
32–40. See 6:1189.
41. WYLAND, ROBERT R. "A Way to Measure the Results of Supervisory Training." *Factory Mgmt & Maint* 110:110–1 Ja '52. * (*PA* 26:6588)
42. DI VESTA, FRANCIS J. "Instructor-Centered and Student-Centered Approaches in Teaching a Human Relations Course." *J Appl Psychol* 38:329–35 O '54. * (*PA* 29:6161)
43. JOHNSON, ROSSALL J. "Relationship of Employee Morale to Ability to Predict Responses." *J Appl Psychol* 38:320–3 O '54. * (*PA* 29:6372)
44. BASS, BERNARD M. "Validity Information Exchange, No. 10-25: D.O.T. Code 1-85.22, Salesman, Foodstuffs." *Personnel Psychol* 10:343–4 au '57. *
45. MOSEL, JAMES N., AND TSACNARIS, HARRY J. "Evaluating the Supervisors Training Program." *Eng & Ind Psychol* 1:18–23 sp '59. * (*PA* 34:4852)
46. DICKEN, CHARLES F., AND BLACK, JOHN D. "Predictive Validity of Psychometric Evaluations of Supervisors." *J Appl Psychol* 49:34–47 F '65. * (*PA* 39:8793)
47. HESTER, EDWARD J. *A New Method of Scoring the How Supervise Test.* Master's thesis, Loyola University (Chicago, Ill.), 1965.
48. PEARSON, WILLIAM W. *Creating Change in Performance of Supervisors in the Electrical Trades Through Human Relations Training.* Doctor's thesis, New York University (New York, N.Y.), 1967. (*DA* 28:4749B)
49. PARRY, MARY ELLEN. "Ability of Psychologists to Estimate Validities of Personnel Tests." *Personnel Psychol* 21:139–47 su '68. * (*PA* 42:14727)
50. RONAN, W. W. "Evaluation of Three Criteria of Management Performance." *J Indus Psychol* 5(1):18–28 Mr '70. * (*PA* 45:7148)
51. HAYES, WILLIAM G., AND WILLIAMS, EUGENE I. "Supervisory Training—An Index of Change." *Training & Develop J* 25(4):34–8 Ap '71. *

CUMULATIVE NAME INDEX

Albright, L. E.: 34–5	Hayes, W. G.: 51
Barthol, R. P.: 25	Hester, E. J.: 47
Bass, B. M.: 44	Hilton, A. C.: 32
Belman, H. S.: 10–1	Holmes, F. J.: 14
Black, J. D.: 46	Johnson, R. J.: 23, 43
Bolin, S. F.: 32	Jurgensen, C. E.: 7
Campbell, J. T.: *rev,* 6:1189	Karn, H. W.: 8
Canter, R. R.: 12	Katzell, R. A.: 6
Carter, G. C.: 16	Kirchner, W. K.: 31
Cook, J. M.: 28	Lefever, D. W.: *rev,* 3:687
Decker, R. L.: 26, 36	McCormick, E. J.: 27
Dicken, C. F.: 46	Maloney, P. W.: 17
Di Vesta, F. J.: 42	Mandell, M. M.: *rev,* 4:774
Dunn, R. E.: 37	Meyer, H. H.: 33
Dunnette, M. D.: 31	Middaugh, R. W.: 27
Evans, R. N.: 10–1	Millard, K. A.: 18
Farbro, P. C.: 28	Miller, F. G.: 15
File, Q. W.: 1–3	Mosel, J. N.: 45
Glennon, J. R.: 34–5	Mosier, C. I.: *rev,* 3:687

Mowry, H. W.: 29
Neel, R. G.: 37
Nuckols, R. C.: 21
Parker, J. W.: 32
Parry, M. E.: 49
Patton, W. M.: 24
Pearson, W. W.: 48
Pond, B. B.: 13
Remmers, H. H.: 3, 9, 15
Remmers, L. J.: 9
Ronan, W. W.: 50
Rosen, N. A.: 38–9
Ruedisili, C. H.: *rev*, 3:687

Sartain, A. Q.: 4
Saunders, W. J.: 30
Slocombe, C. S.: 2, 5
Smith, W. J.: 34–5
Taylor, E. K.: 32
Tsacnaris, H. J.: 45
Walker, W. B.: 32
Weitz, J.: 21
Wickert, F. R.: 19–20
Wiener, D. N.: 40
Williams, E. I.: 51
Wyland, R. R.: 41
Zeigler, M.: 25

[2449]
Ideal Leader Behavior Description Questionnaire. Supervisors; 1957; ILBDQ; employee ratings of a supervisor; test booklet title is *Ideal Leader Behavior (What You Expect of Your Leader)*; same as *Leader Behavior Description Questionnaire* except that the responses indicate what a supervisor ought to be rather than what he is; original edition by John K. Hemphill and Alvin E. Coons; current edition by Personnel Research Board, Ohio State University; University Publications Sales, Ohio State University. *

For additional information, see 7:1145 (10 references).

REFERENCES THROUGH 1971
1–10. See 7:1145.
11. MORROW, HOWARD GLENN. *Consensus of Observed Leader Behavior and Role Expectations of the Elementary School Principal.* Doctor's thesis, University of Oklahoma (Norman, Okla.), 1970. (*DAI* 31:5856A)
12. DALTON, SAMUEL L. *Perception of the Leadership Behavior of the School Business Manager: A Team Approach.* Doctor's thesis, Miami University (Coral Gables, Fla.), 1971. (*DAI* 32:2338A)
13. JOHNSON, MARY MAGDALENE. *Role Expectations That Supervisors, Teachers and Elementary School Principals Have for the Supervisor of Special Classes for Mentally Retarded Children.* Doctor's thesis, University of Maryland (College Park, Md.), 1971. (*DAI* 32:3613A)
14. MCLENNAN, THOMAS DAVID. *An Analysis of the Leader-Behavior Preferences of Selected Suburban Residents From Three Socio-Economic Levels.* Doctor's thesis, Wayne State University (Detroit, Mich.), 1971. (*DAI* 32:2358A)
15. REED, ROY LAWRENCE. *A Study of Relationships Among Certain Aspects of Teacher Perceived Role Discrepancies of Western New York Secondary Principals, Teachers' Stated Satisfaction With Work, and Certain Self-Reported Factual Data About Teachers.* Doctor's thesis, State University of New York (Buffalo, N.Y.), 1971. (*DAI* 32:1808A)
16. SWENSON, JAMES KENNETH. *An Analysis of Leader Behavior and Organizational Climate of the Central Office Administration in a North Dakota School District.* Doctor's thesis, University of North Dakota (Grand Forks, N.D.), 1971. (*DAI* 33:128A)

CUMULATIVE NAME INDEX
Beer, M.: 6
Black, D. O.: 9
Bryant, G. W.: 8
Coady, N. P.: 10
Dalton, S. L.: 12
Gott, C. M.: 7
Halpin, A. W.: 1, 3
Hemphill, J. K.: 2, 4

Johnson, M. M.: 13
Luckie, W. R.: 5
McLennan, T. D.: 14
Morrow, H. G.: 11
Reed, R. L.: 15
Stogdill, R. M.: 10
Swenson, J. K.: 16

[2450]
★In-Basket Test. Applicants for high level executive positions; 1961–66; managerial ability; no manual; National Institute for Personnel Research [South Africa]. *

[2451]
Leader Behavior Description Questionnaire. Supervisors; 1957; LBDQ; for a later edition, see 2452; employee ratings of a supervisor; 2 scores: consideration, initiating structure; scores are based upon responses by 4 to 10 raters; original edition by John K. Hemphill and Alvin E. Coons; manual by Andrew W. Halpin; current edition by Personnel Research Board, Ohio State University; University Publications Sales, Ohio State University. *

For additional information, see 7:1146 (108 references).

REFERENCES THROUGH 1971
1–108. See 7:1146.
109. FLEISHMAN, EDWIN A. *The Relationship Between Leadership Climate and Supervisory Behavior.* Doctor's thesis, Ohio State University (Columbus, Ohio), 1951.
110. HALPIN, ANDREW W. "The Superintendent's Effectiveness as a Leader." *Administrator's Notebook* 7(2):1–4 O '58. *
111. BAILEY, BENJAMIN H. "Personality Rigidity, Patterns of Operation and Leadership Effectiveness of Secondary School Principals." *Fla J Ed Res* 2:1–7 Ja '60. *
112. BARNHART, ALVIN E., AND WISCH, PAUL J. "Perceptual Behavior Patterns and the Influence of Value Systems." *J Res Services* 4:9–14 D '64. *
113. STOGDILL, RALPH M.; GOODE, OMAR S.; AND DAY, DAVID R. "The Leader Behavior of Presidents of Labor Unions." *Personnel Psychol* 17:49–57 sp '64. * (*PA* 39:2971)
114. CROFT, JOHN C. "Dogmatism and Perceptions of Leader Behavior." *Ed Adm Q* 1:60–71 au '65. *
115. THORNTON, MERVIN F. *Values and the Perception of Leader Behavior.* Master's thesis, University of Alberta (Edmonton, Alta., Canada), 1967.
116. LOWIN, AARON; HRAPCHAK, WILLIAM J.; AND KAVANAGH, MICHAEL J. "Consideration and Initiating Structure: An Experimental Investigation of Leadership Traits." *Adm Sci Q* 14(2):238–53 Je '69. * (*PA* 44:11503)
117. COOK, RICHARD PAUL. *The Relationship of Principal Leader Behavior and Teacher Morale to Certain Other Variables in Selected Urban Elementary Schools.* Doctor's thesis, Purdue University (Lafayette, Ind.), 1970. (*DAI* 31:5063A)
118. COTTRELL, DAVID ALTON. *The Relationship Between Superintendents' Role Conflict Resolution Orientation and Their Perceived Leader Behavior.* Doctor's thesis, University of Akron (Akron, Ohio), 1970. (*DAI* 32:119A)
119. DOWNEY, RICHARD DELAINE. *A Study of the Leader Behavior of Special Education Administrators in Illinois Public Schools.* Doctor's thesis, Southern Illinois University (Carbondale, Ill.), 1970. (*DAI* 31:5065A)
120. GREEN, PAUL C., JR. *The Effectiveness of Supervisory Style When Leader, Group and Situational Variables Are Considered.* Doctor's thesis, Memphis State University (Memphis, Tenn.), 1970. (*DAI* 31:7659B)
121. JOHNSON, PAUL O'NEAL. *Relationships Between the Morale of Georgia Extension Agents and the Leader Behavior of Georgia County Agent Chairman.* Doctor's thesis, University of Georgia (Athens, Ga.), 1970. (*DAI* 31:5748A)
122. LUCIETTO, LENA L. "Speech Patterns of Administrators." *Administrator's Notebook* 18(5):1–4 Ja '70. *
123. MAGLARAS, TOM. *Leadership Traits and Characteristics of Principals in Secondary Schools of Varying Degrees of Effectiveness.* Doctor's thesis, University of Colorado (Boulder, Colo.), 1970. (*DAI* 31:4423A)
124. MORROW, HOWARD GLENN. *Consensus of Observed Leader Behavior and Role Expectations of the Elementary School Principal.* Doctor's thesis, University of Oklahoma (Norman, Okla.), 1970. (*DAI* 31:5856A)
125. OBORNY, WILLIAM JOSEPH. *The Relationship of Teachers' Perceptions of Their Professionalism, the Organizational Structure of Schools, and the Leadership Behavior of Their Principals.* Doctor's thesis, Oklahoma State University (Stillwater, Okla.), 1970. (*DAI* 31:5090A)
126. SULLIVAN, BLOOMER DON. *The Correlates of Leadership Behavior of Chief Administrative Officers in Selected Junior Colleges.* Doctor's thesis, University of Missouri (Columbia, Mo.), 1970. (*DAI* 31:5736A)
127. VROOMAN, THEODORE HERBERT. *The Perceptions and Expectations of Superintendents and Their High School Principals With Regard to Leadership Style and Delegated Formal Task-Performance.* Doctor's thesis, Syracuse University (Syracuse, N.Y.), 1970. (*DAI* 31:6326A)
128. BEATTY, RICHARD W. "First- and Second-Level Supervision and the Job Performance of the Hard-Core Unemployed." Abstract. *Proc 79th Ann Conv Am Psychol Assn* 6(1):479–80 '71. * (*PA* 46:5873)
129. BRICKNER, CHARLES ELIAS. *An Analysis of Organizational Climate and Leader Behavior in a North Dakota School System.* Doctor's thesis, University of North Dakota (Grand Forks, N.D.), 1971. (*DAI* 33:96A)
130. CORPUS, MARY CYRIL. *Leader Behavior, Teachers' Behavior, and Organizational Climate in St. Paul Secondary Schools.* Doctor's thesis, Catholic University of America (Washington, D.C.), 1971. (*DAI* 32:1214A)
131. DALTON, SAMUEL L. *Perception of the Leadership Behavior of the School Business Manager: A Team Approach.* Doctor's thesis, Miami University (Coral Gables, Fla.), 1971. (*DAI* 32:2338A)
132. GILLESPIE, JOHN OWEN. *Administrative Theory and Policy Patterns of Secondary School Administrators as Factors in Administrative Performance.* Doctor's thesis, West Virginia University (Morgantown, W.Va.), 1971. (*DAI* 32:4283A)
133. HOUSE, ROBERT J.; FILLEY, ALAN C.; AND GUJARATI, DAMODAR N. "Leadership Style, Hierarchical Influence, and the

Satisfaction of Subordinate Role Expectations: A Test of Likert's Influence Proposition." *J Appl Psychol* 55(5):422–32 O '71. * (*PA* 47:7914)

134. HOUSE, ROBERT J.; FILLEY, ALAN C.; AND KERR, STEVEN. "Relation of Leader Consideration and Initiating Structure to R and D Subordinates' Satisfaction." *Adm Sci Q* 16(1):19–30 Mr '71. *

135. LANDSWERK, DAVID RICHARD. *A Study of the Self Perceptions of School Executives and Their Perceptions of Corporate Executives, and the Self Perceptions of Corporate Executives and Their Perceptions of School Executives in Owatonna, Minnesota.* Doctor's thesis, University of Iowa (Iowa City, Iowa), 1971. (*DAI* 32:1229A)

136. LONG, CLIFFORD DAYTON. *Leader Behavior as Perceived by Junior College Professionals.* Doctor's thesis, University of Tulsa (Tulsa, Okla.), 1971. (*DAI* 32:1231A)

137. MCGHEE, PAUL RALPH. *An Investigation of the Relationship Between Principals' Decision-Making Attitudes, Leader Behavior and Teacher Grievances in Public Schools.* Doctor's thesis, Syracuse University (Syracuse, N.Y.), 1971. (*DAI* 32:4294A)

138. OUSLEY, JACK M. *Behavior Patterns and Operational Effectiveness of Foremen: An Inter-Organizational Analysis.* Doctor's thesis, Boston University (Boston, Mass.), 1971. (*DAI* 32:1833A)

139. REED, ROY LAWRENCE. *A Study of Relationships Among Certain Aspects of Teacher Perceived Role Discrepancies of Western New York Secondary Principals, Teachers' Stated Satisfaction With Work, and Certain Self-Reported Factual Data About Teachers.* Doctor's thesis, State University of New York (Buffalo, N.Y.), 1971. (*DAI* 32:1808A)

140. SIMPSON, DOUGLAS BARRY. *Leadership Behavior, Need Satisfactions, and Role Perceptions of Labor Leaders: A Behavorial Analysis.* Doctor's thesis, University of Washington (Seattle, Wash.), 1971. (*DAI* 32:2248A)

141. SWENSON, JAMES KENNETH. *An Analysis of Leader Behavior and Organizational Climate of the Central Office Administration in a North Dakota School District.* Doctor's thesis, University of North Dakota (Grand Forks, N.D.), 1971. (*DAI* 33:128A)

142. WALTER, JOHN EDWARD. *The Relationships Between the Personality Characteristics, Personal Factors, and Effectiveness of Community School Directors.* Doctor's thesis, Utah State University (Logan, Utah), 1971. (*DAI* 32:3644A)

143. WASDYKE, RAYMOND G. *Self Role Perception and Leadership Behavior of Area Vocational School Principals in New Jersey.* Doctor's thesis, Rutgers—The State University (New Brunswick, N.J.), 1971. (*DAI* 33:129A)

CUMULATIVE NAME INDEX

Anderson, J. W.: 56
Anderson, L. R.: 50
Anderson, R. M.: 38
Andrews, J. H. M.: 19, 33
Bailey, B. H.: 15, 111
Bailey, H. D.: 51
Barden, J. W.: 101
Barnhart, A. E.: 23, 112
Bass, B. M.: 7
Beatty, R. W.: 128
Benevento, P.: 6
Black, D. O.: 83
Blood, M. R.: 75
Bowman, H. J.: 39
Brickner, C. E.: 129
Britton, J. O.: 96
Campbell, O. L.: 18
Carlson, J. W.: 84
Carson, J.: 24, 40
Carter, C. E.: 57
Claye, C. M.: 25
Cook, E. V.: 49
Cook, R. P.: 117
Coons, A. E.: 11, 14
Corpus, M. C.: 130
Cottrell, D. A.: 118
Croft, J. C.: 41, 114
Croghan, J. H.: 85
Crook, R.: 22
Dalton, S. L.: 131
Day, D. R.: 113
Downey, R. D.: 119
Dropkin, S.: 22
Evans, M. G.: 70
Feeley, A. L.: 26
Filley, A. C.: 74, 133-4
Fleishman, E. A.: 44, 109
Flocco, E. C.: 71
Fogarty, B. M.: 42
Garner, W. K.: 86
Gillespie, J. O.: 132
Glasgow, A. D.: 102
Glogau, L. F.: 87
Goode, O. S.: 113

Gordon, B. K.: 58
Gott, C. M.: 52
Green, P. C.: 120
Greenfield, T. B.: 19, 31, 72
Grinberg, B.: 64
Gujarati, D. N.: 133
Halpin, A. W.: 2-4, 8-9, 110
Harmes, H. M.: 16
Hatch, R. H.: 43
Hays, B. B.: 59
Hemphill, J. K.: 5, 10-1
Herod, J.: 73
Hills, R. J.: 32
Hiltenbrand, R. E.: 103
Hobbs, P. J.: 88
Holloman, C. R.: 60
House, R. J.: 74, 133-4
Howard, J. M.: 104
Hrapchak, W. J.: 116
Hunt, J. E.: 61
Hutton, D. E.: 89
Incardona, J. S.: 62
Johnson, P. O.: 121
Kavanagh, M. J.: 116
Keeler, B. T.: 20, 33
Kelada, F. S.: 90
Kerr, S.: 134
Keys, S. R.: 17
Kline, C. E.: 91
Kokovich, S.: 92
Korman, A. K.: 53
Landswerk, D. R.: 135
Law, L. E.: 27
Lindemuth, M. H.: 93
Long, C. D.: 136
Lowin, A.: 116
Lucietto, L. L.: 122
Luckie, W. R.: 34
McDonald, C. O.: 63
McGhee, P. R.: 137
Maglaras, T.: 123
Mannheim, B. F.: 64
Mathews, J. E.: 35
Mitchell, L. L.: 94

Mitchell, T. R.: 105
Moloney, M. A.: 65
Morrow, H. G.: 124
Moullette, J. B.: 106
Murphy, M. D.: 95
Nalder, W. K.: 66
Nealy, S. M.: 75
Newman, W. H.: 21
Newport, G.: 28
Niemeyer, K. P.: 76
Oaklander, H.: 44
Oborny, W. J.: 125
Ousley, J. M.: 138
Pacinelli, R. N.: 77, 96
Parsons, G. E.: 36
Patterson, J. W.: 97
Peirce, J. R.: 107
Peterson, G. D.: 78
Reed, R. L.: 139
Rim, Y.: 142
Robinson, H. W.: 79
Rousey, N. S.: 80
Rush, C. H.: 1, 12
St. Clair, J. K.: 29
Schneider, F. A.: 81
Schroeder, G. B.: 98

Schultz, R. E.: 40
Seeman, M.: 13
Simpson, D. B.: 140
Smith, L. M.: 45
Sommers, N. L.: 99
Spencer, R. L.: 46
Stogdill, R. M.: 14, 67, 100, 113
Stromberg, R. P.: 54
Sullivan, B. D.: 126
Swenson, J. K.: 141
Taylor, M.: 22
Thornton, M. F.: 115
Trimble, C.: 68
Verbeke, M. G.: 55
Vrooman, T. H.: 127
Walker, J. E.: 142
Wasdyke, R. G.: 143
Watts, C. B.: 47
Weber, R. G.: 37
Wells, W. S.: 48
Wisch, P. J.: 30, 112
Woodall, M. V.: 82
Wray, J. F.: 69
Yukl, G.: 108

[2452]

Leader Behavior Description Questionnaire, Form 12. Supervisors; 1957–63; LBDQ–12; revision of still-in-print *Leader Behavior Description Questionnaire* with 10 additional scores; for research use only; employee ratings of a supervisor; 12 scores: representation, demand reconciliation, tolerance of uncertainty, persuasiveness, initiation of structure, tolerance of freedom, role assumption, consideration, production emphasis, predictive accuracy, integration, superior orientation; scores are based upon responses of 4 to 10 raters; original edition by John K. Hemphill and Alvin E. Coons; manual by Ralph M. Stogdill; current edition by Bureau of Business Research, Ohio State University; University Publications Sales, Ohio State University. *

For additional information, see 7:1147 (48 references).

REFERENCES THROUGH 1971

1–48. See 7:1147.

49. STOGDILL, RALPH M.; GOODE, OMAR S.; AND DAY, DAVID R. "The Leader Behavior of Presidents of Labor Unions." *Personnel Psychol* 17:49–57 sp '64. * (*PA* 39:2971)

50. STOGDILL, RALPH M.; IN COLLABORATION WITH DAVID R. DAY, DONALD A. GAAL, NORMAN GEORGE, AND OMAR S. GOODE. *Managers, Employees, Organizations: A Study of 27 Organizations.* Bureau of Business Research Monograph No. 125. Columbus, Ohio: Bureau of Business Research, Ohio State University, 1965. Pp. xiii, 315. *

51. SERGIOVANNI, THOMAS J.; METZCUS, RICHARD; AND BURDEN, LARRY. "Toward a Particularistic Approach to Leadership Style: Some Findings." *Am Ed Res J* 6(1):62–79 Ja '69. * (*PA* 44:13356)

52. FEITLER, FRED CROOHE. *A Study of Relationships Between Principal Leadership Styles and Organizational Characteristics of Elementary Schools.* Doctor's thesis, Syracuse University (Syracuse, N.Y.), 1970. (*DAI* 32:123A)

53. SCHOTT, JAMES LAWRENCE. *The Leader Behavior of Non-White Principals in Inner-City Elementary Schools With Integrated Teaching Staffs Under Conditions of High and Low Morale.* Doctor's thesis, Purdue University (Lafayette, Ind.), 1970. (*DAI* 31:5097A)

54. BRAINARD, STEPHEN RICHARD. *Correlates of Leadership Effectiveness in Personnel Assistants.* Doctor's thesis, University of Missouri (Columbia, Mo.), 1971. (*DAI* 32:2542A)

55. CELASCHI, DONALD ALBERT. *The Relationships Between the Receptivity-to-Change of Public Elementary School Principals in Montgomery County and Their Ages, Sex, and Lengths of Tenure in Their Present Positions.* Doctor's thesis, American University (Washington, D.C.), 1971. (*DAI* 32:6703A)

56. DOW, JOHN, JR. *A Comparative Study of Inner-City Elementary Teachers' and Principals' Perceptions of and Role Expectations for the Leadership Behavior of Selected Inner-City Elementary Principals.* Doctor's thesis, Michigan State University (East Lansing, Mich.), 1971. (*DAI* 32:4869A)

57. FOLEY, GERALD FRANCIS. *A Study of the Relationships Between Team Leaders' Leadership Behavior and the Morale and Effectiveness of Their Team Members.* Doctor's thesis, State University of New York (Buffalo, N.Y.), 1971. (*DAI* 32:2944A)

58. FULTINEER, JAMES DEAN. *School Principals Look at Leader Behavior: The Problem of Interpersonal Needs.* Doctor's thesis, West Virginia University (Morgantown, W.Va.), 1971. (*DAI* 32:6036A)

59. GUBASTA, JOSEPH LEE. *The Leader and Planning Behaviors of College and University Chief Executives.* Doctor's thesis, University of Wisconsin (Madison, Wis.), 1971. (*DAI* 32:5497A)

60. HEFTY, JOHN CHARLES. *The Relationships Between the Value Orientations, Leader Behavior, and Effectiveness of Secondary School Principals in Selected Middle Sized School Systems.* Doctor's thesis, University of Wisconsin (Madison, Wis.), 1971. (*DAI* 32:4286A)

61. LEDGERWOOD, LESLIE BRYANT. *An Analysis of the Leader Behavior of Middle Managers in Selected Public Four-Year Colleges.* Doctor's thesis, University of Oklahoma (Norman, Okla.), 1971. (*DAI* 32:1881A)

62. NULL, ELDON J., AND SMEAD, WILLIAM M. "Relationships Between the Political Orientation of Superintendents and Their Leader Behavior as Perceived by Subordinates." *J Ed Res* 65(3): 103–6 N '71. * (*PA* 48:1776)

63. PRYER, MARGARET W., AND DISTEFANO, M. K., JR. "Perceptions of Leadership Behavior, Job Satisfaction, and Internal-External Control Across Three Nursing Levels." *Nursing Res* 20(6):534–7 N–D '71. * (*PA* 48:3086)

64. SOLBACH, M. THERESA. *Elementary School Principals' Perception of Their Administrative Performance as Related to Their Staff's Perception of Their Leader Behavior.* Doctor's thesis, Purdue University (Lafayette, Ind.), 1971. (*DAI* 32:2983A)

65. SPENCE, BETTY A. *Sex of Teachers as a Factor in Their Perception of Selected Leadership Characteristics of Male and Female Elementary School Principals.* Doctor's thesis, Purdue University (Lafayette, Ind.), 1971. (*DAI* 32:2985A)

66. VAN MEIER, EDWARD JAMES, JR. *Leadership Behavior of Male and Female Elementary School Principals.* Doctor's thesis, Northern Illinois University (DeKalb, Ill.), 1971. (*DAI* 32:3643A)

67. WHITE, RICHARD KENNETH. *The Relationship Among Secondary School Teachers' and Departmental Chairmen's Educational Attitudes, Teacher Perceptions of Leadership Style, and Teacher Ratings of the Chairman.* Doctor's thesis, New York University (New York, N.Y.), 1971. (*DAI* 33:131A)

CUMULATIVE NAME INDEX

Anderson, B. D.: 19
Andrews, J. H. M.: 17
Ash, W. E.: 38
Ashbrook, J. B.: 16, 25
Beer, M.: 20
Blatt, C. A.: 21
Bostic, C. R.: 39
Brainard, S. R.: 54
Brown, A. F.: 26
Burden, L.: 51
Campbell, D. T.: 3
Castore, C. H.: 36
Celaschi, D. A.: 55
Christner, C. A.: 1
Coons, A. E.: 7
Day, D. R.: 10, 12, 14–5, 49–50
Distefano, M. K.: 63
Dow, J.: 56
Feitler, F. C.: 52
Foley, G. F.: 57
Fultineer, J. D.: 58
Gaal, D. A.: 50
Garrison, J. M.: 31
George, N.: 50
Good, C. G.: 40
Goode, O. S.: 12, 14–5, 49–50
Greenfield, T. B.: 32
Grimsley, W. G.: 41
Gubasta, J. L.: 59
Halpin, A. W.: 6
Harris, E. H.: 33
Hastings, R. E.: 13
Hefty, J. C.: 60
Hemphill, J. K.: 1
Holloway, J.: 42
Ignatovich, F. R.: 44
Jacobs, J. W.: 18

Jaynes, W. E.: 4–5, 8
Kelley, W. R.: 27
Larsen, J. L.: 22
Ledgerwood, L. B.: 61
Mansour, J. M.: 34
Marder, E.: 9
Metzcus, R.: 51
Morsink, H. M.: 23
Neary, J. R.: 28
Null, E. J.: 62
Olafson, G. A. A.: 43
Parks, D. J.: 45
Peak, L. N.: 24
Pryer, M. W.: 63
Rawlings, J. S.: 46
Rooker, J. L.: 29
Saris, R. J.: 47
Schmidt, W. G.: 30
Schott, J. L.: 53
Schreiner, J. O.: 35
Scott, E. L.: 4, 8
Sergiovanni, T. J.: 51
Shartle, C. L.: 2
Sindwani, K. L.: 11
Smead, W. H.: 62
Solbach, M. T.: 64
Spence, B. A.: 65
Stogdill, R. M.: 2, 4–5, 7–8, 12, 14–5, 49–50
Streufert, S.: 36
Streufert, S. C.: 36
Tarallo, J. J.: 37
Van Meier, E. J.: 66
Wall, C. C.: 48
Wherry, R. J.: 5
White, R. K.: 67
Winer, B. J.: 6

[2453]

Leadership Evaluation and Development Scale. Prospective supervisors; 1964–65; LEADS; Harley W. Mowry (question booklet and casebook, from materials prepared by the Armstrong Cork Company); Psychological Services, Inc. *

For additional information and a review by Cecil A. Gibb, see 7:1148 (1 reference).

REFERENCES THROUGH 1971

1. See 7:1148.

[2454]

Leadership Opinion Questionnaire. Supervisors and prospective supervisors; 1960–69; LOQ; 2 scores: consideration, structure; Edwin A. Fleishman; Science Research Associates, Inc. *

For additional information and a review by Cecil A. Gibb, see 7:1149 (41 references); for reviews by Jerome E. Doppelt and Wayne K. Kirchner, see 6: 1190 (6 references).

REFERENCES THROUGH 1971

1–6. See 1190.

7–47. See 7:1149.

48. FLEISHMAN, EDWIN A. *The Relationship Between Leadership Climate and Supervisory Behavior.* Doctor's thesis, Ohio State University (Columbus, Ohio), 1951.

49. ARKOFF, ABE, AND SHEARS, LOYDA M. "Conceptions of 'Ideal' Leadership in Accepted and Rejected Principal Training Candidates." *J Ed Res* 55:71–4 O '61. *

50. PERRY, SIMON D., AND WARD, GEORGE, II. "An Evaluation of the Leadership Opinion Questionnaire as Related to Dogmatism and Authoritarianism." *Proc W Va Acad Sci* 35(1963): 216–8 '64. *

51. ASQUITH, RONALD H., AND HEDLUND, DALVA E. "Laboratory Training and Supervisory Attitudes." *Psychol Rep* 20:618 Ap '67. * (*PA* 41:9496)

52. BONS, PAUL M.; BASS, ALAN R.; AND KOMORITA, S. S. "Changes in Leadership Style as a Function of Military Experience and Type of Command." *Personnel Psychol* 23(4):551–68 w '70. * (*PA* 46:7893)

53. CUMMINS, ROBERT CRAIG. *An Investigation of a Model of Leadership Effectiveness.* Doctor's thesis, Purdue University (Lafayette, Ind.), 1970. (*DAI* 31:6313B)

54. FLORESTANO, THOMAS E. *The Relationship of College Leadership and Post-College Leadership as Measured by the Leadership Opinion Questionnaire and a Leadership Inventory.* Doctor's thesis, University of Maryland (College Park, Md.), 1970. (*DAI* 32:173A)

55. STELTER, MERVYN WALTER. *Changes in Self-Perception, Interpersonal Orientation, and View of the Nature of Man of Residence Hall Personnel.* Doctor's thesis, East Texas State University (Commerce, Tex.), 1970. (*DAI* 31:4476A)

56. BEATTY, RICHARD W. "First- and Second-Level Supervision and the Job Performance of the Hard-Core Unemployed." Abstract. *Proc 79th Ann Conv Am Psychol Assn* 6(1):479–80 '71. * (*PA* 46:5873)

57. CUMMINS, ROBERT C. "Relationship of Initiating Structure and Job Performance as Moderated by Consideration." *J Appl Psychol* 55(5):489–90 O '71. * (*PA* 47:7898)

58. DENNIS, JAMES MERCER. *Administrative Behavior of Successful and Unsuccessful Athletic Directors in Small Colleges and Universities.* Doctor's thesis, University of Southern California (Los Angeles, Calif.), 1971. (*DAI* 32:5015A)

59. NIEBUHR, HAROLD EMIL. *Effects of Short Term Rational Counseling in an Industrial Setting.* Doctor's thesis, East Texas State University (Commerce, Tex.), 1971. (*DAI* 32:5551A)

60. OUSLEY, JACK M. *Behavior Patterns and Operational Effectiveness of Foremen: An Inter-Organizational Analysis.* Doctor's thesis, Boston University (Boston, Mass.), 1971. (*DAI* 32:1833A)

61. TRANG, MYRON LEE. *The Effects of a Small Group Leadership Experience Upon Selected Upper Division Education Students at Washington State University.* Doctor's thesis, Washington State University (Pullman, Wash.), 1971. (*DAI* 32:4386A)

62. TURNER, JOHN NICHOLAS. *Relationship Between Supervisors' Orientation and Correlations Between Ratings Given and Objective Production Data.* Doctor's thesis, Wayne State University (Detroit, Mich.), 1971. (*DAI* 32:3052B)

CUMULATIVE NAME INDEX

Ahnell, I. V.: 28
Arkoff, A.: 49
Asquith, R. H.: 51
Ayers, A. W.: 13
Bass, A. R.: 52
Bass, B. M.: 4, 8
Beatty, R. W.: 56
Berlfein, H. P.: 33
Biggs, D. A.: 20
Bons, P. M.: 52
Capelle, M. H.: 21
Carron, T. J.: 14
Cummins, R. C.: 43, 53, 57
Delaney, J. J.: 20
Dennis, J. M.: 58
Doppelt, J. E.: *rev*, 6:1190
Florestano, E. A.: 1–3, 6–7, 16, 48

Florestano, T. E.: 54
Gibb, C. A.: *rev*, 7:1149
Gorham, W. A.: 44
Greenwood, J. M.: 34
Gruenfeld, L. W.: 22, 27
Harrell, T. W.: 35, 45
Harris, E. F.: 7
Hawkins, R. E.: 46
Hay, J. E.: 15
Hedlund, D. E.: 51
Hinrichs, J. R.: 36
Hooper, D. B.: 29
Huneryager, S. G.: 21
Jabs, M. L.: 37
Kernan, J. P.: 10
Kirchner, W. K.: *rev*, 6:1190
Komorita, S. S.: 52
Korman, A. K.: 23

Litzinger, W. D.: 11, 18
McClung, J. A.: 24
McNamara, W. J.: 17, 34, 41
Mann, W. G.: 44
Niebuhr, H. E.: 59
Oaklander, H.: 16
Ousley, J. M.: 60
Parker, T. C.: 9, 12
Peirce, J. R.: 47
Penfield, R. V.: 25
Perry, S. D.: 50
Peters, D. R.: 6
Rim, Y.: 19
Rowland, K. M.: 30
Schenk, K. N.: 38
Scott, W. E.: 30

Seiler, D. A.: 31
Shears, L. M.: 49
Siegel, J. P.: 32
Skinner, E. W.: 39
Spitzer, M. E.: 17
Stanton, E. S.: 5
Stelter, M. W.: 55
Stephenson, H. B.: 26
Tenopyr, M. L.: 40
Trang, M. L.: 51
Turner, J. N.: 62
Ward, G.: 50
Weissenberg, P.: 22, 27
Wollowick, H. B.: 41
Yeager, J. C.: 42

[2455]

★Leadership Practices Inventory. Supervisors; 1955–67; LPI; for use with the author's management development program in leadership and communication; 2 scores (desirable practices marked as ideal, desirable practices marked as in actual practice) for each of: 4 leadership styles (using style answer form), 5 management areas (using area answer form), and 2 derived totals; Charles W. Nelson; Management Research Associates. *

[2456]

Managerial Scale for Enterprise Improvement. Supervisors; 1955; job satisfaction; Herbert A. Kaufman, Jr.; Psychometric Affiliates. *
For additional information and reviews by Brent Baxter and Edward B. Greene, see 5:930.

[2457]

The RAD Scales. Supervisors; 1957; RAD; self-ratings of perceived degrees of responsibility, authority, and delegation of authority; 3 scores: responsibility, authority, delegation; Ralph M. Stogdill; University Publications Sales, Ohio State University. *
For additional information, see 7:1150 (20 references).

REFERENCES THROUGH 1971

1–20. See 7:1150.
21. BROWNE, C. G. "Study of Executive Leadership in Business: 4, Sociometric Pattern." *J Appl Psychol* 35:34–7 F '51. * (*PA* 25:7151)
22. OTIS, JAY L.; CAMPBELL, JOEL; AND PRIEN, ERIC. Sect. 7, "Leadership Characteristics of Chief Executives," pp. 149–77. In *Small Business Success: Operating and Executive Characteristics: A Study of 110 Successful Metalworking Plants in Ohio.* Edited by Kenneth Lawyer. Cleveland, Ohio: Bureau of Business Research, School of Business, Western Reserve University, 1963. Pp. xii, 183. *
23. STOGDILL, RALPH M.; IN COLLABORATION WITH DAVID R. DAY, DONALD A. GAAL, NORMAN GEORGE AND OMAR S. GOODE. *Managers, Employees, Organizations: A Study of 27 Organizations.* Bureau of Business Research Monograph No. 125. Columbus, Ohio: Bureau of Business Research, Ohio State University, 1965. Pp. xiii, 315. *
24. DENNIS, JAMES MERCER. *Administrative Behavior of Successful and Unsuccessful Athletic Directors in Small Colleges and Universities.* Doctor's thesis, University of Southern California (Los Angeles, Calif.), 1971. (*DAI* 32:5015A)
25. PFANSTIEL, EVERETT EARL, JR. *A Discriminant Analysis of the Orientation of Principals and Teachers in Changing and Stable Schools.* Doctor's thesis, University of Kentucky (Lexington, Ky.), 1971. (*DAI* 32:4898A)

CUMULATIVE NAME INDEX

Bowman, H. J.: 14
Browne, C. G.: 1, 3–4, 21
Campbell, D. T.: 6
Campbell, J.: 22
Coons, A. E.: 11
Day, D. R.: 23
Dennis, J. M.: 24
Fleishmann, E. A.: 7
Gaal, D. A.: 23
George, N.: 23
Glogau, L. F.: 18
Goode, O. S.: 23
Jaynes, W. E.: 10–2

Morsink, H. M.: 15
Neitzel, B. J.: 4
Otis, J. L.: 22
Pfanstiel, E. E.: 25
Prien, E.: 22
Schroeder, G. B.: 19
Scott, E. L.: 8, 10–1, 13
Shartle, C. L.: 2, 5, 9, 11
Stogdill, R. M.: 2, 5, 9–13, 17, 23
Tribble, J. S.: 20
Wherry, R. J.: 12
Zinn, L. A.: 16

Leadership Opinion Questionnaire

[2458]

RBH Test of Supervisory Judgment. Business and industry; 1949–63; Richardson, Bellows, Henry & Co., Inc. *
For additional information, see 6:1195.

REFERENCES THROUGH 1971

1. SPITZER, MORTON EDWARD, AND MCNAMARA, WALTER J. "A Managerial Selection Study." *Personnel Psychol* 17:19–40 sp '64. * (*PA* 39:2945)

CUMULATIVE NAME INDEX

McNamara, W. J.: 1   Spitzer, M. E.: 1

[2459]

Supervisory Index. Supervisors; 1960–69; SI; 5 attitude scores: management, supervision, employees, human relations practices, total; Norman Gekoski and Solomon L. Schwartz; Science Research Associates, Inc. *
For additional information, see 7:1151 (1 reference); for reviews by Arthur H. Brayfield and Albert K. Kurtz, see 6:1192 (1 reference).

REFERENCES THROUGH 1971

1. See 6:1192.
2. See 7:1151.
3. ASQUITH, RONALD H., AND HEDLUND, DALVA E. "Laboratory Training and Supervisory Attitudes." *Psychol Rep* 20:618 Ap '67. * (*PA* 41:9496)

CUMULATIVE NAME INDEX

Asquith, R. H.: 3
Brayfield, A. H.: *rev*, 6:1192
Gekoski, N.: 1

Hedlund, D. E.: 3
Kurtz, A. K.: *rev*, 6:1192
Schwartz, S. L.: 1–2

[2460]

★Supervisory Inventory on Communication. Supervisors and prospective supervisors; 1965–72; SIC; Donald L. Kirkpatrick; the Author. *
For additional information, see 7:1152 (1 reference).

REFERENCES THROUGH 1971

1. See 7:1152.

CUMULATIVE NAME INDEX

Kirkpatrick, D. L.: 1

[2461]

★Supervisory Inventory on Discipline. Supervisors; 1973; manual subtitle is (*For Union and Non-Union Firms*); SID; Earl J. Wyman; the Author. *

[2462]

★Supervisory Inventory on Grievances. Supervisors; 1970; SIG; Earl J. Wyman and Donald L. Kirkpatrick; Earl J. Wyman. *

[2463]

★Supervisory Inventory on Human Relations. Supervisors and prospective supervisors; 1960–72; SIHR; Donald L. Kirkpatrick and Earl Planty (test); Donald L. Kirkpatrick. *
For additional information and a review by Seymour Levy of the original edition, see 6:1193 (1 reference).

REFERENCES THROUGH 1971

1. See 6:1193.
2. THUMIN, F. J., AND PAGE, D. S. "A Comparative Study of Two Tests of Supervisory Knowledge." *Psychol Rep* 18:535–8 Ap '66. * (*PA* 40:8273)

CUMULATIVE NAME INDEX

Benson, D.: 1
Hanson, R.: 1
Kirchner, W.: 1

Levy, S.: *rev*, 6:1193
Page, D. S.: 2
Thumin, F. J.: 2

[2464]

★**Supervisory Inventory on Labor Relations.**
Supervisors in unionized firms; 1972; SILR; Earl J.
Wyman; the Author. *

[2465]

Supervisory Inventory on Safety. Supervisors and
prospective supervisors; 1967–69; SIS; Donald L.
Kirkpatrick; the Author. *
For additional information, see 7:1153.

[2466]

Supervisory Practices Test. Supervisors; 1957–64;
SPT; Martin M. Bruce; Martin M. Bruce, Ph.D.,
Publishers. *
For additional information, see 6:1194 (4 refer-
ences); for reviews by Clifford E. Jurgensen and
Mary Ellen Oliverio, see 5:955.

REFERENCES THROUGH 1971

1–4. See 6:1194.
5. BRUCE, ROBERT LEE. *Predicting Administrative-Supervisory
Effectiveness in Senior County Agricultural Extension Agents.*
Doctor's thesis, Cornell University (Ithaca, N.Y.), 1962. (DA
23:3221)
6. THUMIN, F. J., AND PAGE, D. S. "A Comparative Study of
Two Tests of Supervisory Knowledge." *Psychol Rep* 18:535–8
Ap '66. * (PA 40:8273)

CUMULATIVE NAME INDEX

Bruce, M. M.: 1–2   Oliverio, M. E.: *rev,* 5:955
Bruce, R. L.: 5   Page, D. S.: 6
Jurgensen, C. E.: *rev,* 5:955   Thumin, F. J.: 6
Learner, D. B.: 2   Watley, D. J.: 3–4
Martin, H. T.: 4

[2467]

★**Survey of Management Perception.** Supervisors;
1956–58; SMP; a projective test requiring the subject to write stories (setting, characters, plot, outcome) about 9 pictures and a story "that could happen
in your own company"; no manual; Charles W.
Nelson; Management Research Associates. *

[2468]

**The WPS Supervisor-Executive Tri-Dimen-
sional Evaluation Scales.** Supervisors; 1966; TES;
the same questions about the individual being rated
are answered by 3 persons—his supervisor, a colleague, and himself; 12 scores for each of the 3 forms:
knowledge, planning, results, delegating, leadership,
morale, training, adaptability, communication, emotionality, growth, total; Western Psychological Services. *
For additional information, see 7:1154.

[Out of Print Since TIP I]

Chart for the Rating of a Foreman (status unknown),
5:915
Personal Development Record, 6:1191
Supervisory Aptitude Test, T:2093
Test of Supervisory Ability, T:2098
WLW Supervisor Survey, 6:1196

TRANSPORTATION

[2469]

[American Transit Association Tests.] Transit
operating personnel; 1941–51; 4 tests; Glen U.
Cleeton, Merwyn A. Kraft, and Robert F. Royster;
American Transit Association. *
a) STANDARD EXAMINATION FOR TRANSIT EMPLOYEES.
1941–46; intelligence.
b) PERSONAL REACTION TEST FOR TRANSIT EMPLOYEES.
1943–46; personality.

c) THE PLACEMENT INTERVIEW FOR TRANSIT EMPLOYEES.
1946; 9 ratings (moral character, mental ability,
motor ability, health, motivation, stability, maturity,
sociability, manner and appearance) in 3 areas (work
experience, schooling and childhood, personal history).
d) A STANDARDIZED ROAD TEST FOR BUS OPERATORS. 1951.
For additional information, see 5:912; for reviews
by Harold G. Seashore, Morris S. Viteles, and J. V.
Waits of *a-c,* see 3:696 (1 reference).

REFERENCES THROUGH 1971

1. See 3:696.
2. SEELEY, W. H. C., AND KRAFT, MERWYN A. "Selecting
Transit Operators." *Mgmt Rec* 10:191–3 Mr '48. *

CUMULATIVE NAME INDEX

Kraft, M. A.: 2   Viteles, M. S.: *rev,* 3:696
Seashore, H. G.: *rev,* 3:696   Waits, J. V.: 1; *rev,* 3:696
Seeley, W. H. C.: 2

[2470]

*****[Driver Selection Forms and Tests.]** Truck
drivers; 1943–73; all revised forms essentially the
same as or identical with earlier forms; no manual;
Dartnell Corporation. *
a) EMPLOYMENT APPLICATION. 1946–64.
b) TELEPHONE CHECK. 1946–73; Robert N. McMurry.
c) DRIVER INTERVIEW. 1946–64.
d) PHYSICAL EXAMINATION RECORD. 1946–54.
e) SELECTION AND EVALUATION SUMMARY. 1950–72;
Robert N. McMurry.
f) STANDARDIZED TEST: TRAFFIC AND DRIVING KNOW-
LEDGE FOR DRIVERS OF MOTOR TRUCKS. 1946–64; Amos
E. Neyhart and Helen L. Neyhart.
g) ROAD TEST IN TRAFFIC FOR TESTING, SELECTING,
RATING, AND TRAINING TRUCK DRIVERS. 1943–64; 3
scores: specific driving skills, general driving habits
and attitudes, total; Amos E. Neyhart.
For additional information and a review by Joseph
E. Moore, see 6:1197; for a review by S. Rains Wallace, Jr., see 4:789.

[2471]

**[McGuire Safe Driver Scale and Interview
Guide.]** Prospective motor vehicle operators; 1961–
62; 2 parts; Frederick L. McGuire; Western Psychological Services. *
a) THE MCGUIRE SAFE DRIVER SCALE. Test booklet title
is *The McGuire S D Scale;* items selected in part
from *Kuder Preference Record—Personal* and *Minnesota Multiphasic Personality Inventory.*
b) THE MCGUIRE SAFE DRIVER INTERVIEW GUIDE.
For additional information and reviews by Willard
A. Kerr and D. H. Schuster, see 6:1198 (1 reference).

REFERENCES THROUGH 1971

1. See 6:1198.
2. McGUIRE, FREDERICK. "Psychological Comparison of Automobile Drivers: Accident- and Violation-Free Versus Accident-
Violation-Incurring Drivers." *U S Armed Forces Med J* 7:1741–
8 D '56. * (PA 31:3949)

CUMULATIVE NAME INDEX

Kerr, W. A.: *rev,* 6:1198   McGuire, F. L.: 1
McGuire, F.: 2   Schuster, D. H.: *rev,* 6:1198

[2472]

**Road Test Check List for Testing, Selecting,
Rating, and Training Coach Operators.** Bus drivers; 1958; 3 or 4 scores: general attitude and driving
practices, specific driving errors, total, errors on an
actual bus run (optional); Amos E. Neyhart; published jointly by American Automobile Association
and Institute of Public Safety. *
For additional information, see 5:946.

[2473]
Road Test in Traffic for Testing, Selecting, Rating and Training Truck Drivers [1955 Revision]. Truck drivers; 1943–55; 3 scores: specific skills, general habits and attitudes, total; Amos E. Neyhart; published jointly by American Automobile Association and Institute of Public Safety. *
For additional information, see 4:790.

[2474]
Short Occupational Knowledge Test for Truck Drivers. Job applicants; 1970; score is pass, fail, or unclassifiable; Bruce A. Campbell and Suellen O. Johnson; Science Research Associates, Inc. *
For additional information, see 7:1155.

[2475]
★Truck Driver Test. Drivers of light and medium trucks; 1957–72; distribution restricted to member public personnel agencies and nonmember agencies approved by the publisher; International Personnel Management Association. *

For additional information and reviews by Willard A. Kerr and D. H. Schuster of an earlier form, see 6:1199.

[2476 1]
*Wilson Driver Selection Test. Prospective motor vehicle operators; 1961–72; 6 scores (visual attention, depth visualization, recognition of simple detail, recognition of complex detail, eye-hand coordination, steadiness) and safety aptitude rating (based on number of subtests passed); Clark L. Wilson; Martin M. Bruce, Ph.D., Publishers. *
For additional information and reviews by Willard A. Kerr and D. H. Schuster, see 6:1200.

1 After all tests were numbered, 11 additional test entries were inserted and 20 were deleted, leaving a total of 2467 test entries in this volume. The inserted entries are 63A, 341A, 386A, 419A, 560A, 781A, 997A, 1025A, 1040A, 1354A, and 2027A. The deleted test entries are indicated by the compound numbers assigned to the immediately preceding entries: 93-4, 108-9, 365-6, 376-7, 666-7, 732-3, 748-9, 956-66, 2063-4, 2206-7, and 2278-9.

VOCATIONS—FIRST MMY

REVIEWS BY *Walter V. Bingham, Harold D. Carter, John G. Darley, Richard Ledgerwood, N. W. Morton, Everett B. Sackett, Gwendolen Schneidler, John M. Stalnaker, Albert S. Thompson, Herbert A. Tonne, Marion R. Trabue, Arthur E. Traxler, and Edmund G. Williamson.*

BUSINESS EDUCATION

[935]

Bookkeeping Test: State High School Tests for Indiana, 1936–1937 Edition. First, second, third, fourth semesters; p1936–37; 4 levels; a new first-semester form is scheduled for publication each December; a new second-semester form is scheduled for publication each March; new third- and fourth-semester forms are scheduled for publication irregularly; mimeographed; 2¢ per test; 15¢ per sample test; 40(45) minutes; M. E. Studebaker, B. M. Swinford, V. H. Carmichael, F. R. Botsford, C. Puckett, and R. Burkhart; edited by H. H. Remmers; Division of Educational Reference.

[936]

Commercial Education Survey Tests. 1–2 years of shorthand in high school; p1933; 1 form; $1 per 25 of either the junior or senior test; 25¢ per teacher's manual and key; 40¢ per sample set; 55 minutes plus time for transcription of shorthand notes; E. V. Bisbee; Public School Publishing Co.
a) JUNIOR SHORTHAND. 1 year of shorthand in high school.
b) SENIOR SHORTHAND. 2 years of shorthand in high school.
References: Bisbee, E. V. "Testing Program for Junior Shorthand." *Commercial Education,* 17:4–9; October 1931. ¶ *Wisconsin State-Wide Commercial Education Survey.* Bulletin, Serial No. 158. Whitewater, Wis.: State Teachers College, January 1931.

Teach Col J 5:267–8 Jl '34. E. L. Abell. These tests aim to cover the three most fundamental phases of shorthand: 1. knowledge of subject matter; 2. ability to take dictation; 3. ability of students to read their own notes. * The tests seem to be carefully prepared and should prove very useful. The recording sheet is especially helpful in filing and interpreting the scores. Tentative norms *

[937]

General Clerical: Every Pupil Test, December 1937 and April 1938. High school and clerical applicants; p1937–38; a new form is scheduled for publication each December and April; 2¢ per test; 1¢ per key; specimen set free; 12(17) minutes; H. A. Copeland; Ohio Scholarship Tests.

[938]

Shemwell-Whitcraft Bookkeeping Test. First, second semesters: high school; p1937–38; 2 forms; 2 levels (Test I, first semester; Test II, second semes-

ter) ; 60¢ per 25 tests, postpaid; 15¢ per specimen set; 40(45) minutes; E. C. Shemwell, J. E. Whitcraft, and H. E. Schrammel; Bureau of Educational Measurements.

[939]

Shorthand I: Every Pupil Test, April 1938. High school; p1938; dictation is given at the rate of 50, 60, and 70 words a minute; a new form is scheduled for publication each April; 2¢ per test; 1¢ per key; specimen set free; 5 minutes for dictation; 25 minutes for transcription; R. D. Purdy and Commercial Teachers of Fairfield County; Ohio Scholarship Tests.

[940]

Shorthand II: Every Pupil Test, December 1937 and April 1938. High school; p1937–38; dictation is given at the rate of 70 words a minute for the December form and 80, 90, and 100 words a minute for the April form; a new form is scheduled for publication each December and April; 2¢ per test; 1¢ per key; specimen set free; 5 minutes for dictation; December form: 16 minutes for transcription; April form: 21 minutes for transcription; R. D. Purdy and Commercial Teachers of Fairfield County; Ohio Scholarship Tests.

[941]

Shorthand Test: State High School Tests for Indiana, 1936–37 Edition. First, second, third, fourth semesters; p1936–37; 4 levels; new second- and fourth-semester forms are scheduled for publication each March; new first- and third-semester forms are scheduled for publication each December; mimeographed; 3½¢ per test; 15¢ per sample test; 40(45) minutes; M. E. Studebaker, B. M. Swinford, V. H. Carmichael, F. R. Botsford, C. Puckett, and R. Burkhart; edited by H. H. Remmers; Division of Educational Reference.

[942]

Thompson Business Practice Test. Junior and senior high schools; c1937; 2 forms; 80(90) minutes; $1.50 per 25 tests; 20¢ per specimen set; J. M. Thompson; World Book Co.

Herbert A. Tonne, New York University. While a considerable number of tests in general business information have been set up for use in connection with specific texts, the *Thompson Business Practice Test* is the first set up without this objective in mind. This is surprising indeed, considering the fact that junior business training has had a period of over fifteen years of continuous growth.

This test has been organized in terms of the content of more frequently used texts in the subject. Far more sufficient test items were developed and demonstrated to students. Upon the basis of this preliminary test the material was then organized into two forms which were given to students in all parts of the country. The correlation between the two test forms, .90, indicates the high degree of reliability of the test. The method by which the test material was secured gives some indication of its validity. Each test form can be given in about two forty-minute class periods.

The test is useful for preteaching purposes and, therefore, should have considerable diagnostic value. The accomplishment in the class can be measured quite well by the use of the other form as a final test.

[943]

Typewriting I: Every Pupil Test, April 1938. High school; p1938; a new form is scheduled for publication each April; 2¢ per test; 1¢ per key; specimen set free; 39(50) minutes; R. D. Purdy and Commercial Teachers of Fairfield County; Ohio Scholarship Tests.

[944]

Typewriting II: Every Pupil Test, December 1937 and April 1938. High school; p1937–38; a new form is scheduled for publication each December and April; 2¢ per test; 1¢ per key; specimen set free; December form: 35(40) minutes; April form: 45(50) minutes; R. D. Purdy and Commercial Teachers of Fairfield County; Ohio Scholarship Tests.

[945]

Typewriting Test: State High School Tests for Indiana, 1936–1937 Edition. First, second, third, fourth semesters; p1936–37; 4 levels; new first- and third-semester forms are scheduled for publication each December; new second- and fourth-semester forms are scheduled for publication each March; mimeographed; 2¢ per test; 15¢ per sample test; 30(35) minutes; M. E. Studebaker, B. M. Swinford, V. H. Carmichael, F. R. Botsford, C. Puckett, and R. Burkhart; edited by H. H. Remmers; Division of Educational Reference.

VOCATIONS

[1167]

Dynamicube Test of Power to Visualize. Grades 11–12 and freshmen in engineering or architectural colleges; c1937; 8 forms; a test of ability to think in terms of three-dimensional spatial relationships; 60(70) minutes; $1 per 25 nonconsumable tests; sample tests are not obtainable; C. V. Mann; Missouri Educational Test Co.

[1168]

Gordon-Douglass Fraction Test for Beginning Students of Nursing. c1937; 1 form; 25(30) minutes; $1 per 25 tests; $3 per 100; 25¢ per specimen set; P. Gordon and H. R. Douglass; University of Minnesota Press.

Am J Nursing 37:1442 D '37. * devised to increase accuracy in predicting the probable scholastic success of beginning or prospective student nurses and to aid in determining which ones should improve their abilities in mathematics before or immediately upon entering the nursing school. *

[1169]

Information Blanks: For Obtaining Data About Vocational Plans and Problems of High School Students. c1937; 1¢ per blank; 90¢ per 100; $4 per 500; M. W. A. Dane; the Author, 1 Bennington Road, Lexington, Mass.

[1170]

Kefauver-Hand Guidance Tests and Inventories. Grades 7–14; c1937; 8 parts; 50¢ per 25 student profile charts; 15¢ per manual; G. N. Kefauver, H. C. Hand, V. L. Block (parts *a, b, e, f, g* only) and W. M. Proctor (part *h* only); World Book Co.

a) EDUCATIONAL GUIDANCE TEST. 1 form; $1.20 per 25 tests; 15¢ per specimen set; (30) minutes.

b) HEALTH GUIDANCE TEST. 1 form; $1 per 25 tests; 10¢ per specimen set; (25) minutes.

c) INVENTORY OF STUDENT PLANS. 1 form; $1.30 per 25 inventories; 5¢ per specimen set; (30) minutes.

d) INVENTORY OF STUDENT SELF-RATINGS. 1 form; $1.20 per 25 inventories; 5¢ per specimen set; (30) minutes.

e) RECREATIONAL GUIDANCE TEST. 1 form; $1 per 25 tests; 10¢ per specimen set; (25) minutes.

f) SOCIAL-CIVIC GUIDANCE TEST. 1 form; $1.20 per 25 tests; 15¢ per specimen set; (25) minutes.

g) STUDENT-JUDGMENT GUIDANCE TEST. 1 form; $1 per 25 tests; 10¢ per specimen set; (25) minutes.

h) VOCATIONAL GUIDANCE TEST. 1 form; $1 per 25 tests; 10¢ per specimen set; (25) minutes.

Harold D. Carter, University of California. The manual gives an adequate account of the theoretical basis for the tests. Apparently they are reliable and efficiently constructed, with a selection of items suitable for general use throughout the senior high school. Experience may show that the tests include too many very easy items. Since the tests measure information essential in several areas of adjustment to school and community conditions, they should furnish a sound basis for cooperation between counselors and pupils.

Gwendolen Schneidler, Goucher College. This battery of "guidance tests and inventories" does not, as the name might indicate, consist of tests of intelligence, special aptitudes, interests, etc., which are an essential part of any adequate guidance program. Instead, its purpose is to evaluate the effectiveness of the guidance program for the school as a whole and for the individual student who has been "exposed" to the guidance program.

The authors base their claims for the validity of the battery upon their exhaustive study of the objectives of student guidance. They determined upon these objectives by consulting the literature on guidance and persons considered to be experts in the field. This technique for attempting to construct a valid measuring device by the careful selection of items themselves considered to be valid is similar to that used in constructing the best achievement tests. This method of validation has its limitations, however, but it is acceptable here in lieu of information as to whether students who score high on the tests actually make better educational, vocational, personal, etc., adjustments. One limitation of this method of validation is that objectives and items may be incorporated when they represent outmoded and inadequate present practices as revealed in the literature and by experts, whereas more desirable and up-to-date practices which may not be so well established or wide spread may not be respresented. For example, the examinee is not asked to indicate what psychological tests, if any, formed a part of the guidance program which is being evaluated. The authors, however, specifically state that the battery is not complete and that "other tests and inventories are in the process of construction by the authors."

Fortunately, the authors supplement information regarding the reliability of the tests by giving the probable errors of the obtained scores. These probable errors indicate a fairly high degree of reliability for most of the six tests. Since several objectives have usually been incorporated and measured by a single test, however, the assurance which one has of obtaining a reliable indication of any single objective (as, for example, the student's information about occupations) is reduced. This could be increased by increasing the number of items covering each objective.

No norms are presented as the authors rightly feel that present practice among a large group of unselected schools may not represent desirable goals towards which other schools should aim.

The two inventories are not tests and cannot be scored objectively. They seem to be devices to supplement the interview in the guidance situation rather than techniques for the evaluation of the guidance program.

Despite any limitations which these tests may have, they have been constructed with great care and attention to proper methods of test construction. They represent an encouraging advancement towards the development of a means for evaluating objectively the guidance program of the secondary school.

M. R. Trabue, Pennsylvania State College. Data presented in the manual indicate that Form 1 and Form 2 of the tests have correlations of from .77 (in vocational guidance) to .89 (in educational guidance). The apparent purpose of the tests and inventories is to help the student to discover whether he has the background of information and sources of information necessary for making intelligent judgments and decisions in these various fields. It seems probable that information of this type would be valuable to the student and to the guidance officers who work with him. After it has become clear that the student has, or has not, adequate background knowledge, the task of the teacher or guidance officer is clarified to that extent.

Occupations 16:496–7 F '38. J. C. Flanagan. * While the Guidance Tests survey the extent of the student's knowledge about various types of activity, the Inventories make possible the systematic recording of the individual's plans of self-development along various lines and the self-appraisal of individual capacities. Neither is designed to provide measures of such important characteristics of the individual as his aptitudes, interests, and emotional adjustment. The authors report reliability coefficients from .77 to .89, with an average value of .82 for the various guidance tests. These coefficients were obtained from a group composed of junior high school, senior high school, and junior college students. Coefficients are not reported for a single grade range. The scoring of all sections, including the true-false, is in terms of number right. Norms are not reported for these tests. The authors state that norms have sometimes been erroneously accepted as standards and further add that there is now no way of determining just what scores students should have before it can be said that they attained a desirable standard. They, therefore, recommend that the scores be interpreted in terms of the particular situation. The authors' remarks concerning the misuse of norms and standards are certainly true, and it must remain the responsibility of the individual administering and interpreting the tests to select the most suitable bases for the interpretation of the scores made by an individual or a group. However, it seems reasonable to suppose that knowledge of the standards considered desirable by those who have spent most time with these materials and information concerning what other workers have been able to attain should result in more intelligent interpretation. * their tests should prove valuable in appraising the success of a particular method of providing these types of information.

Teach Col J 8:59 My '37. E. L. Abell. * The tests seem to be very carefully constructed * the value of the tests as instruments of measurement seems well established. In the earlier days of the measurement movement efforts were centered upon the academic achievement of children because that was most easily measured. Continuous extension into new fields and refinement of technique has in recent years enabled scientific measurement to make a valuable contribution to every objective of education. In the improvement of the student's personality and in his efforts to make successful adjustments there is need for diagnosis, analysis, and reconstruction. Any helps such as these new tests should be welcomed by all teachers who are interested in guidance. Their use should lead to a greater measure of self-guidance on the part of the student.

[1171]

Michigan Adult Profile. High school and college; c1937; 4 parts; E. B. Greene; published by the Author.
a) EDUCATIONAL PROGRESS SHEET. Printed on the last page of the 4-page Michigan Occupational Preferences Check List listed below; (5) minutes.
b) MICHIGAN OCCUPATIONAL PREFERENCES CHECK LIST. This 3-page list and the 1-page Educational Progress Sheet are printed together on a 4-page folder; (15) minutes for the check list; 10¢ per sample copy.
c) MICHIGAN VOCABULARY PROFILE. 2 forms; (40–60) minutes; $5 per 25 tests (nonconsumable); 25¢ per sample copy; 75¢ per 25 answer sheets.
d) MICHIGAN NONVERBAL SERIES (1937 REVISION). 4 parts (aiming, tapping, feature discrimination, and pencil maze); 29(45) minutes; 75¢ per 25 aiming and tapping tests; $1 per 25 feature discrimination tests; 75¢ per 25 pencil maze tests; 30¢ per sample set of all four parts.
e) MICHIGAN SPEED OF READING. 2 forms; 7(10) minutes; $1 per 25 tests; 10¢ per sample test.

Richard Ledgerwood, Ohio State University. [*Review of the total battery.*] A collection of

materials designed to provide "for suitable use of educational facilities" by comparing a person's educational advancement, occupational preferences, and tested performance. It consists of (1) a blank for recording amount of schooling in various fields, (2) check lists for indicating occupational preferences not only by name but also conditions of work, wages, and location desired, (3) a vocabulary profile which yields separate scores in eight different fields of information, (4) a speed of reading test, and a battery of four nonverbal tests, consisting of (5) an aiming test, (6) a tapping test, (7) a feature discrimination test, and (8) a pencil maze test. The record chart for assembling these data provides spaces for entering various other test information.

(1) Five minutes are sufficient for administering the *Educational Progress Sheet,* in which are distinguished 13 fields paralleling the classification of occupations. A total score is found for each field and recorded on the summary chart. (2) The *Occupational Preferences Check List* consists of 182 occupations grouped by name into 11 classes. Three categories of response are provided for, namely L, ?, D. In front of each item the years of training required for average success are indicated. Scores suggested are order of preference determined by proportion of L responses to number of items in a group and average number of years' training required for the occupations marked L. Fifteen minutes are sufficient for administering.

(3) The *Michigan Vocabulary Profile* consists of a nonconsumable test booklet provided with a replaceable answer sheet, and is available in two equivalent forms. It was "designed to give a profile of an adult's vocabulary in eight fields of information which are considered to be important and independent to a marked degree." "A test of information was desired which would be affected as little as possible by reasoning processes." Arranged in ten levels of difficulty, there are thirty items each in human relations, commerce, government, physical sciences, biological sciences, mathematics, fine arts, and sports. The items included were subjected to a fairly rigid process of selection. Each item consists of a definition preceded by four words, to only one of which the definition properly applies. The test is self-administering

and no time limit is imposed, but 50 minutes are usually sufficient. The test is scored by turning over the answer sheet and holding it to the light, counting the parentheses which have pencil marks in them. The score is number of right answers minus one-third the number of wrong answers, providing a correction for chance successes which has been shown to be unnecessary for a work-limit test such as this is. A supplementary score of vocabulary confidence may be obtained. A mean correlation of .91 between two 30-items tests in the same field is reported.

(4) The *Michigan Speed of Reading Test* consists of 75 short paragraphs. The subject is required to cross out the incongruous word in the latter part of each paragraph. The test is scored by unfolding the leaflet and holding it to the light, counting the number of cross-marks which appear in circles. Unfortunately for the mechanical adequacy of this ingenious device, many of these circles show through on the front side.

The *Michigan Non-Verbal Series* allows 8 minutes for an aiming test, 1 minute for a tapping test, and 10 minutes each for a feature discrimination test and a pencil maze test. The most interesting of these is the feature discrimination test, which requires a methodical search to find a unique feature in a row of small geometrically schematized faces. Two levels of complexity are measured separately. They have been found to be of contrasting significance, the simpler test correlating .74 with *Army Alpha* on a group of 90 white adults, the more complex test correlating −.04. The pencil mazes similarly measure two distinct levels of complexity. It may be remarked that indistinct printing marks the scoring key for level number 2 almost impossible to decipher.

Forty-five minutes' time over all is required for giving the non-verbal battery. The validity of the tests for specific purposes is indicated by the following correlations: with school marks, maze and feature test +.46 (mean), aiming +.10, tapping +.03; with *Detroit Intelligence Alpha,* composite +.68 compared with a correlation of +.55 between *Detroit Intelligence Alpha* and school success. Three of the four tests in this series are suggested as indicators of an attitude of carefulness. Just why such a trait (if it is a trait) should be weighted so heavily is not clear.

For each of the tests in the non-verbal series norms are provided in terms of standard scores and centile ranks for each school grade from the third to the college senior year, together with IQ equivalents and letter marks. The summary record form presents norms for all the tests in terms of a standard group of second-year college students. Several discrepancies appear in this chart that should be corrected.

With the exception of the vocabulary tests, these materials are lithoprinted.

This series of tests is evidently still in process of development. It would be helpful if the author would illustrate the actual use of the tests in concrete guidance situations. Some discussion of the justification for combining these particular tests into a battery is in order, either in terms of the primary abilities which they purport to measure or in terms of their significance for the prediction of particular performances. This suggestion pertains especially to the non-verbal series.

The vocabulary profile and the feature discrimination test are novel in conception, and the tests embody some very useful scoring devices. The minor defects in production noted should be easily corrected. It is to be hoped that it may be found possible to rearrange these materials in somewhat more orderly fashion so that acquaintance may be gained with less arduous effort.

M. R. Trabue, Pennsylvania State College. [*Review of the total battery.*] This interesting series of tests contains internal evidence of having been thoughtfully planned, but hastily executed. The variety of measures provided is greatly to be commended, although there is not available yet sufficient scientific evidence to indicate the specific traits that should always be measured, and one cannot, therefore, believe that Greene has provided tests in all the most important fields. The battery includes two forms of a speed of reading test, two forms of a very suggestive English vocabulary test, an occupational preference sheet, a pencil maze, a feature discrimination test, and tests of ability in aiming and tapping. The author has attempted by these measures to make it possible to compare three aspects of an individual's total educational status: "progress, interests, and tested achievement."

Each form of the speed of reading test

contains seventy-five paragraphs, in each of which the youth is to cross out "one word which spoils the meaning." The second illustrative paragraph reads as follows: "2. The football and baseball teams of our school get more notice than the debating and hockey teams. This shows that debating is a more popular activity than baseball." In the instructions, the examiner is to say, "*More* spoils the meaning of the first part so cross it out." Thoughtful individuals taking this test will be likely to spend a considerable amount of time trying to decide whether to cross out *more, debating,* or *popular*. Such opportunities to waste time should be eliminated from a "speed of reading test." Another apparent fault of this test arises from the poor quality of the paper used and the rather inadequate printing job, which allows a clever youth to determine which word the author intended to have marked out by merely observing the ring printed on the other side of the sheet.

Somewhat similar evidence of hasty construction appears in the aiming test. The subjects are told to begin with Section 1, but they are not told whether to work from right to left or from top to bottom. After working for sixty seconds, they are told to begin with "the next group (marked Section 6), although the next group of smaller circles on the reviewer's copy begins in Section 7. The instructions for the tapping test are to "point to the top square on the right hand side of the page." Unfortunately, this page of squares was not included in the set supplied to the reviewer.

The graduated maze test and the feature discrimination test are worthy of extensive study and experimentation, although a question may be raised regarding the advisability of Greene's scheme of printing the key on the back of the feature discrimination test.

In the opinion of the reviewer, Greene's most significant contribution in this series is the *Michigan Vocabulary Profile*. Thirty descriptive phrases are presented in each of eight different fields, making a total of two hundred forty terms to be checked in each form. The youth is asked in each case to check that one of four words which is most nearly defined by the printed phrase. The ultimate usefulness of this test remains to be demonstrated, but it will undoubtedly be wide.

Greene has recognized clearly the importance of knowing many different phases of an individual's personality before giving him educational guidance, but he has not provided the great variety of highly-reliable measuring instruments needed for complete educational diagnosis.

John G. Darley, University of Minnesota. [*Review of Educational Progress Sheet, Michigan Occupational Preferences Check List, and the Michigan Vocabulary Profile.*] This battery is designed to measure specific vocabulary achievement in defined fields. In addition to this, it summarizes in profile form comparable measures of claimed occupational preferences and amount of training in the fields in which vocabulary is tested. New norms have recently been made available that extend the possible range of the test. Our question about this instrument involves, first, the relation between specific vocabulary knowledge and general academic ability. In local research, these correlations with the American Council Psychological Examination, in an extremely homogeneous population, are for men and women in the range .60 through .80. This raises the question of the identity of the vocabulary achievement test with our more common measures of general academic ability.

Another question involves the relation of specifically claimed occupational preferences with more validly measured occupational interest patterns. Studies are being made of this relationship but are not available for use. Prior evidence, however, about the relation between claimed and measured interests may tend to indicate the relative inadequacy of claimed interests alone.

The *Michigan Adult Profile* has the possibility of valid use insofar as it contrasts or compares measures of knowledge, training and preferences. It remains to be seen, however, if these three separate measures are sufficiently valid for use in this much-needed comparison.

John M. Stalnaker, Princeton University. [*Review of the Michigan Vocabulary Profile.*] This vocabulary test is arranged to facilitate scoring and to reduce the cost of administration without the use of complicated forms or directions. The test booklet may be used repeatedly, although a new single scoring sheet must be inserted for each use. The test, now

Michigan Adult Profile

available in two forms, consists of thirty items in each of eight fields: human relations, commerce, government, mathematics, physical sciences, biological sciences, fine arts, and sports. Each item consists of a definition and four words or phrases. The subject indicates which word is the correctly defined one by placing a mark in the appropriate space on the answer sheet, which may be adjusted so that the spaces for marking fit next to the items being considered. If the subject is sure that his answer is correct, he marks S; if he is doubtful he marks D.

A description of the development of the test, given on the cover of the test booklet, includes items of interest and value to the users of the test. It does not indicate the actual correlations among the parts of the test although it states that the fields are considered to be independent to a marked degree.

In computing the part scores, the usual correction for guessing is made; no distinction is made between responses marked D and those marked S. The total score is obtained by adding the part scores. A score of "self-criticism" may be obtained by taking the ratio between the number of responses marked S which are correct and the total number of responses marked S. The self-criticism score and the total score are reported to give a correlation of .68. More information about the meaning and significance of this index is needed. It might be revised to include the proportion of answers marked S.

The test has no time limit although fifty minutes has been found to be adequate for most college students. Norms are given for second-year college students.

A vocabulary test of this type, when developed as carefully as this one was, should prove to be of value for certain counseling work in college. The results of further work with the test will indicate more definitely what its uses are, but other evidence suggests that differential vocabulary tests offer a promising means of determining a composite of interest, aptitude, and ability.

Authur E. Traxler, Educational Records Bureau. [*Review of the Michigan Vocabulary Profile.*] This test is designed to give a vocabulary profile in the following eight fields which factor analysis studies have shown to be independent to a considerable degree: human relations, commerce, government, mathematics, physical sciences, biological sciences, fine arts, and sports. Each test item consists of a definition, followed by four words, one of which corresponds with the definition. The test is completely objective and could readily be adapted for machine scoring. The publishers report that the average reliability of the eight sections is .91. The test should meet a real need for a diagnostic test of vocabulary at the high school and college levels.

[1172]
Mooseheart Graphic Rating Scale for House-mothers and Housefathers. For rating institutional housemothers and housefathers; 1937; 6¢ per rating scale; 5¢ per individual record and summary card; 20¢ per manual; 35¢ per specimen set; M. L. Reymert and H. A. Kohn; Public School Publishing Co.

[1173]
Mutilated Cubes Test of Power to Visualize. Grades 9-12 and freshmen in engineering colleges; c1936-37; 2 forms printed together in a single booklet; 100(110) minutes; 25 or more copies, 15¢ per nonconsumable test; test booklets may be rented; sample tests are not obtainable; C. V. Mann; Missouri Educational Test Co.
Reference: Mann, C. V. *Objective Type Tests in Engineering Education.* New York and London: McGraw-Hill Book Co., Inc., 1930.

[1174]
Occupational Interest Blank. Boys of high school age; [p1937]; 1 form; (10) minutes; 75¢ per 25 blanks; $2.50 per 100; 15¢ per specimen set; B. V. LeSuer; Psychological Corporation.

W. V. Bingham, Stevens Institute of Technology. Designed for use with boys who come to a placement office seeking employment but who have only vague notions as to which occupation they should try to enter, this blank is inexpensive, quickly scored, and provides the interviewer with a rough indication of the occupational area within which the boy's interests tend to cluster. Among the hundred occupations listed are ten representative of each of the following fields: professional, technical, clerical, sales, arts, skilled trades, semiskilled trades, advertising, personal service and agricultural. It is so printed that the interviewer can readily identify the responses made to the ten occupations in any field, and can also summarize the results in a way to indicate whether the boy's interests are limited or extensive, specialized or diversified. When a clustering of interests in one area is noted, the specific responses within that area can be inspected to see what sorts of occupation have appealed to the boy. The blank has also been used to ascertain group differences of occupational interest between high school boys following different curricula: commercial, technical and industrial.

In appraising a vocational interest schedule, it is pertinent to ask: (1) Is it more effective than other available blanks in inducing thoughtful self-appraisal on the part of the person who fills it out? (2) Does it yield scores which are more closely relevant to problems of educational and occupational planning? (3) Is it more likely to draw attention to areas of possible vocational interest which otherwise might escape consideration? (4) Are the scores more reliable? (5) Are they more valid indicators of stable occupational interests? (6) Is it more economical of time and money?

Only in this last respect can it be said that LeSuer's blank appears to be superior. Because it is easily scored it invites comparison with E. B. Greene's *Occupational Preferences Check List* [see test No. 1171] which, to be sure, costs a few cents more but which then provides an interest profile to be studied in comparison with two analogous profiles, one showing the *Michigan Vocabulary Test* score in each of the fields of vocational differentiation, the other showing the length of educational exposure in each of these areas of interest.

As a first aid to a counseling interview incidental to the work of a placement office, a blank like LeSuer's may have its place. The reviewer questions, however, whether the saving in cost outweighs the cost of the counselor's time, when it is recalled that a check list like Greene's, also easy to score, yields information which would appear to be more reliable, more valid, and more readily comparable with other significant indicators of aptitude.

M. R. Trabue, Pennsylvania State College. This single-page blank lists one hundred occupations, each of which the young person is asked to check to show whether he likes it, dislikes it, or is indifferent to it. Even though one makes the doubtful assumption that such terms as teacher, rigger, estimator, merchant, and explorer refer to definite occupations and mean the same things to different people, too much weight can easily be given to a young person's checking of such a term. Unfortunately this is one of those easily prepared interest inventories that get printed and dis-

tributed commercially before they have been adequately checked and evaluated. Similar lists have been found to be very low in validity.

[1175]

Placement Examination in General Engineering Drawing, Revised edition. Students entering a college course in general engineering drawing; c1929, p1937; 1 form; $3.75 per 25 tests; sample tests are not obtainable; 100(110) minutes; C. V. Mann; Missouri Educational Test Co.
Reference: Mann, C. V. *Objective Type Tests in Engineering Education.* New York and London: McGraw-Hill Book Co., Inc., 1930.

[1176]

Specific Interest Inventory: For Educational Diagnosis and Guidance. Age 10 and over; c1932; 2 levels for each sex; (30) minutes; 6¢ per test; $5 per 100 tests; 50¢ per specimen set; P. P. Brainard and F. G. Stewart; Psychological Corporation.
a) FORM B. Boys, 10 to 16 years of age.
b) FORM G. Girls, 10 to 16 years of age.
c) FORM M. Men, over 16 years of age.
d) FORM W. Women, over 16 years of age.

Everett B. Sackett, University of New Hampshire. This inventory has both possibilities and limitations. Experience with it in a state-wide investigation shows that as an indication of the relative interest in different fields of an individual or of a group of individuals the device has some validity. But if the inventory fulfills the authors' claim that it measures interest quantitatively, then the children of one of the most select residential communities in the country are dangerously close to lacking ambition—on the standard given in the manual—while one of the most ambitious and enthusiastic groups of children in one of our most populous states is found in a mill town where relief checks are a major source of family income. The evidence of the inventory may be right, but more reasonable seems to be the explanation that the child with high intelligence and rich experience replies more discriminatingly, and hence expresses unqualified enthusiasm less frequently, than does the child of low intelligence and meager experience.

Brainard, in the inventory manual and in the *Vocational Guidance Magazine* (Volume 6, page 156), has cited limited statistical evidence that the inventory has prognostic value in vocational guidance, but he also cites as supporting evidence tales of the "I know a boy who . . ." type.

Ruth Eckert, of the Cooperative Test Service, has developed a new method of interpreting the results of the inventory, based on sigma deviations of the scores in each field of interest from the mean score for all fields. Using some such method of interpretation to correct for the varying degrees of discrimination of those checking the inventory promises to make the inventory useful not only for measuring the relative interests of individuals but also for comparing the relative individuals and groups.

[1177]

Staticube Test of Power to Visualize. Freshmen in engineering or architectural colleges; c1937; 4 forms; 90(100) minutes; $1 per 25 nonconsumable tests; sample tests are not obtainable; C. V. Mann; Missouri Educational Test Co.

[1178]

Vocational Interest Blank for Men. High school, college, and adults; c1927–37; 2 editions (Form A is for adults who have been out of school for several years and Form B is for students; these forms differ only with regard to the first page); scoring scales are now available for measuring maturity of interest, masculinity-femininity, studiousness (Young-Estabrooks scale), and the thirty following occupations: accountant, advertiser, architect, artist, boy scout master, carpenter, certified public accountant, chemist, city school superintendent, dentist, engineer, farmer, journalist (newspaper editor), lawyer, life insurance salesman, mathematician, minister, musician, office clerk, personnel manager, physician and surgeon, physicist, policeman, psychologist, purchasing agent, real estate salesman, school teacher and administrator, vacuum cleaner salesman, Y.M.C.A. general secretary, and Y.M.C.A. physical director; $2 per 25 blanks; $3.50 per 50; $6 per 100; 500 or more, $5 per 100; $1 per scoring scale (a separate scoring scale is required for each vocation to be tested); 2 to 9 scales, 80¢ each; 10 or more scales, 70¢ each; E. K. Strong, Jr.; Stanford University Press.

John G. Darley, University of Minnesota. This test is still the outstanding and indispensable measure of vocational interests from the junior and senior high school years up through college years and adult guidance. Our clinical experience with the test indicates that it is most efficiently used in terms of the patterns of occupational interests isolated by factor analysis methods. This method of interpretation, although more difficult to grasp by the counselor, is superior to interpretations in terms of specific keys. Interpretation in terms of patterns means that the specific keys may be used as examples of types of occupations rather than hard and fast occupational niches. Recent and as yet unpublished research shows a relation between types of interest patterns and attitude and adjustment tests that may open up a field for future research to expand the occupational ability profile concept to include personality measures.

[1179]

Vocational Interest Blank for Women. High school, college, and adults; c1934–36; 2 editions (Form WA is for adults who have been out of school several years and Form WB is for students; these forms differ only with regard to the first page); scoring scales are now available for measuring masculinity-femininity and the following occupations: artist, author, dentist, housewife, lawyer, librarian, life insurance, saleswoman, nurse, office worker, physician, social worker, stenographer-secretary, Y.W.C.A. general secretary, general high-school teacher, and high-school teacher of each of the following subjects: English, mathematics, physical science, and social science; $2 per 25 blanks; $3.50 per 50; $6 per 100; 500 or more, $5 per 100; $1 per scoring scale (a separate scoring scale is required for each vocation to be tested); 2 to 9 scales, 80¢ each; 10 or more scales, 70¢ each; E. K. Strong, Jr.; Stanford University Press.

John G. Darley, University of Minnesota. This test has overcome most of the technical errors in the previous work on measurement of women's interests. However, even with a technically adequate instrument, we have found that women's occupational interests are less channelized and less clear-cut or professionalized than is the case with men. We have recently completed a factor analysis of the tables of correlation for this test, published by Mr. Strong, and it now becomes possible to use pattern interpretation with this test, as well as with the men's test. Specific educational and occupational guidance of women, however, in terms of measured occupational interests, is still difficult because of an apparent sex difference producing a greater range of interests in women, with apparent less certainty of permanence of interests and specificity of interests. The test is still indispensable, however, and must be used in counseling with more caution and considerable clinical skill.

[1180]

Vocational Interest Schedule, 1935 Edition. College students; c1935; 1 form; $2 per 25 schedules; $5 per 100 schedules; 50¢ per specimen set; (30) minutes; L. L. Thurstone; distributed by Psychological Corp.

Harold D. Carter, University of California. The test is extremely short, consisting of only 72 items; most subjects will take it in ten minutes. It is scored to yield seven interest ratings, following a procedure based upon factor analysis. The names of the seven ratings and the numbers of items upon which they are based are as follows: descriptive, 20 items; commercial, 18; academic, 12; scientific, 11; biological, 9; legal, 16; and athletic, 11. These interest factors are supposed to have practical significance.

Empirical evidence of reliability and validity is lacking. Examination of the test itself, its nature and its length, indicates low reliability and lower validity. The schedule obviously satisfies the ever-present unscientific lay demand for an ultra-brief measuring instrument.

The 72 items are all names of occupations. Such items are usually heavily weighted in the scoring of vocational interest blanks, but they are especially subject to a particular kind of error. Persons taking such tests may deceive themselves and others when the significance of the items is too evident. Inclusion of other types of items is even more important in the interests of validity than in the interests of reliability.

Item analysis enables shortening of tests up to a certain point without loss, but when the shortening is so extreme the evidence of reliability should be furnished. The method of factor analysis can make important contributions in the interests of economy and scientific truth, but here as elsewhere we must insist on a *posteriori* evidence, clinical, statistical, or otherwise, of the validity of the product. The reviewer has the highest respect for the author's research genius; this test may serve as a useful model in certain research problems. It appears inadequate for use in practical personnel work.

N. W. Morton, McGill University. The Thurstone *Vocational Interest Schedule* contains a list of 80 occupations, principally of a business or professional nature. These are checked to signify like, dislike, or indifference. The schedule is then scored to determine how far the individual subject's interests run along the line of descriptive (humanistic), commercial, academic, physical science, biological, legal or athletic types of occupations. The scoring is carried out separately for each interest-group but is very simple and rapid, and involves for each such group the use of positive or indifferent indications only, for from 9 to 20 occupations of the total of 80. The raw scores are transmuted into standard values which may be shown in convenient profile form.

The grouping of occupations and the scoring are based upon the responses of 3400 students of liberal arts, engineering, architecture, and agriculture in several universities. These sub-

jects' preferences were intercorrelated, and a multiple factor analysis made of the results by the centroid method. Eight factors (including one for art, not used in practice) were found to be sufficient to account for the intercorrelations. These factors are mostly independent, although a few correlations between pairs of them amount to .25 to .30.

It is apparent that the Thurstone interest schedule may be used in either or both of two ways: first, as a check-list of 80 occupations appropriate for students at a college level and as a basis for discussion without any statistical analysis; and secondly, for the purpose of determining the subject's major type of interest. The latter constitutes, potentially, a very useful service to the vocational counsellor.

In the opinion of the writer, however, the research value of this instrument as a means of determining characteristic relationships amongst students' occupational preferences is superior to its practical value for vocational guidance purposes. In the first place, he is inclined to question the utility of presenting to the probably relatively uninformed student a simple list of occupational titles alone, unless these be used as a springboard for discussion in the course of an interview aimed at discovering the causes of such stated preferences. This, however, is a qualitative rather than a quantitative type of analysis. It is apt to be associated with an examination of likes and dislikes for various kinds of working conditions, and with an evaluation of the subject's qualities of character and temperament.

Moreover, it remains to be demonstrated that the way in which students' vocational interests may be grouped or typified bears a close relationship to the overlapping of interests of persons actually engaged in such occupations. For example, Thurstone demonstrates that in students' thinking advertising and printing are linked together by double bonds of "descriptive" and "commercial" factors. Is there in fact such a community of interests amongst those occupied in these vocations? Such a question can be settled only by comparative analysis of the relationships of students' and workers' interests. This question, however, the writer believes, is apt to be overlooked.

As a matter of fact, a comparison of the factorial analysis of the 80 occupations in the Thurstone schedule with a similar analysis of those to which the Strong *Vocational Interest Inventory* has been applied [1] suggests a fair agreement between the two. Of 12 comparisons possible, 7 seem to show agreement, 2 are dubious, and 3 seemingly disagree. It is recognized, of course, that this comparison is itself not wholly legitimate.

The factor loadings of certain occupations are rather intriguing. Clergyman and public speaker are represented only by the "legal" factor, foreign correspondent by "descriptive" and "legal," radio announcer by "descriptive" and "athletic." These are surely somewhat unsuspected considerations which the Thurstone schedule has brought to light. Its further use with other student groups and with members of the professions in question may involve additional interesting discoveries.

[1181]

Vocational Interest Inventory. Grades 9–16 and adults; c1937; separate inventories for men and women; (45–55) minutes; 10¢ per inventory; 75¢ per 12; $4.50 per 100; 25¢ per manual; G. U. Cleeton; McKnight and McKnight.

Albert S. Thompson, University of Pennsylvania. Vocational counsellors and industrial psychologists are alert for any new inventory which can show "just cause" why it should be preferred over its predecessors.

The reviewer considers the following to be significant factors in comparing Cleeton's *Vocational Interest Inventory* with those already published.

(1) Like the Strong inventory, it includes items other than mere names of occupations. Besides the 180 occupations listed there are (in the Men's Form) 71 school subjects, 17 magazines, various school and leisure activities, general work activities, characteristics of people, and personal characteristics, totalling 670 items in all. This is in accordance with the theory behind interest testing that occupational groups have characteristic interests. This also helps to reduce what Bingham, in his *Aptitudes and Aptitude Testing,* calls the "information error."

(2) Like the Thurstone inventory, it results in a profile representing the interest rating of the subject in occupational groups comparable to Thurstone's interest factors. It accomplishes this end by grouping 630 of the items into nine

1 Thurstone, L. L. "A Multiple Factor Study of Vocational Interests." *Personnel Journal* 10:198–205; October 1931.

occupational classifications. A rating is then obtained for each classification.

(3) Unlike any of the other mentioned inventories, the Cleeton inventory uses a point-score technique in which the subjects indicate only like or dislike. A score is obtained for each of the nine sections merely by counting the number of plus (like) marks, a rapid procedure compared to the time-consuming method of the Strong inventory.

(4) Reliability coefficients obtained by the odd-even technique on groups as large as 1000 range from .822 to .910. With a group of 100 given a second administration of the inventory one month later it was found that only 6.1% of the item responses were reversed.

(5) Validity of interest scales is usually determined by analysis of scores obtained by persons successfully engaged in standard occupations. In a study of this type Mr. Cleeton reports that 76% of the 724 cases studied received the highest rating in their occupation, 82% the highest or second highest, and 95% at least the third highest.

(6) By careful selection of significant items before compiling the final lists, the author has set up one table of norms to apply to all occupational sections for each age level. Critical scores for A, B, C, D, and E ratings are given which yield a profile of the subject's interests. The author considers the inventory to be a sampling device rather than a test and suggests that the chief value of the ratings is derived from their individual profile relationships. They are not comparable, therefore, to the Strong ratings.

(7) The reviewer questions the addition of the final section of only 40 items in an effort to obtain an index of the subject's social traits. One-third of the 40 items are already directly or indirectly included in the occupational sections. The personality rating, at best, would probably be inferior to that obtained from an already-established personality test.

(8) Practical considerations: the excellent manual of directions for the counsellor; the wide range of items to stimulate the subject; the complete front page for listing data and ratings.

It is too soon, of course, for a final judgment to be made. The simplified scoring method, occupational family group ratings, and wide range of interest items are certainly desirable features, combined in a new way. If future use proves the inventory's reliability and validity, research in interest testing will have been given another valuable tool.

M. R. Trabue, Pennsylvania State College. This inventory of sixteen pages is quite similar to that upon which E. K. Strong has been experimenting for many years, although Cleeton has so far confined his efforts to indicating nine general fields of vocational interest rather than specific professions and vocations. The manual of directions includes data regarding the reliability of the scores and indicates that records of more than seven thousand successful workers have been analyzed. The items to be checked consist chiefly of acts that people perform and of rather fully described traits, although a great variety of occupations have been listed by name. Comparative studies of the long-time validity and practical usefulness of these inventories are very much needed. Although Cleeton has insisted that scientific caution be used in the interpretation of scores, there are grave dangers that the results may be misused frequently, just as the results of other good tests have been used in ways that the authors never intended them to be used.

E. G. Williamson, University of Minnesota. Separate inventories of interests were developed for men and women (high school and college) from the list used at the Carnegie Institute of Technology in 1919–1920. The author arranged the items by occupational groupings in order to derive interest scores for the following: (for men) biological sciences, specialized selling fields, physical sciences, social service occupations, business administration, legal and literary occupations, mechanical occupations, finance occupations, artistic, creative and public performance occupations. The groupings for women include: office work, selling occupations, natural sciences, social service, creative occupations, teacher, performance and

personal service occupations, mechanical and household occupations. A single score is derived for each of these groups and not for each occupation. Many of these groups are so unusual (e.g., "manicurist, actress, dancer, singer and other performance and personal service occupations") as to cause the reader to wish that the author had published sufficient data on item analysis and group comparisons to afford the reader understanding, if not conviction, of validity.

There are 670 items in the inventory for men and 670 in the one for women. The author states: "Typical reliability coefficients (odd vs. even items) for groups ranging in number from 150 to 1000: .867, .874, .903, .847, .875, .910, .901, .822. For a test-retest group only six per cent of the responses changed significantly."

The scales were given to 7424 adults in "standard" occupations. The method of selection and the characteristics of these criterion groups are not described except by the term "successfully engaged." In 76 per cent of these cases the highest inventory rating agrees with the occupation engaged in by these cases; 82 per cent rate either first or second on the appropriate occupational score and 95 per cent rate first, second or third.

Too little clinical use of these inventories has been reported to formulate an appraisal of its usefulness, and to demonstrate their advantage over other interest tests. Moreover, the author has not yet published sufficient details of his statistical validation on which to form a judgment.

Especially needed for purposes of evaluation are: (1) data on the extent to which each of the author's scales (total score) differentiates the appropriate occupational group from other groups answering items on the same scale; (2) characteristics of the criterion groups and methods of selection; (3) the extent to which each *item* on each scale differentiates each occupational group from other groups.

BUSINESS EDUCATION – SECOND MMY

[1476]

Bookkeeping Ability Tests: National Clerical Ability Tests, Series 1939. Bookkeepers; 1939; a new form is scheduled for publication each May for use in the annual testing program of the Joint Committee on Tests of the National Office Management Association and the National Council of Business Education; $1.35 per examinee is the fee charged for the administration and scoring of this "vocational ability test" along with the *Fundamentals Test* (*see* 1484) and the *General Information Test* (*see* 1485); 25 or more copies, 20¢ per copy (Series 1939); 50¢ per sample copy (Series 1939); $1.55 per set of sample copies of all National Clerical Ability Tests (Series 1939); 180(190) minutes; Cambridge, Mass.: Joint Committee on Tests, 16 Lawrence Hall, Kirkland St.

REFERENCES

1 Eastern Commercial Teachers' Association. *Measuring for Vocational Ability in the Field of Business Education.* Tenth Yearbook. Edited by Clinton A. Reed. New York: New York University Book Store, 1937. Pp. xx, 442, $2.00.

2 Brigham, Lester H. "National Clerical Ability Tests." *J Bus Ed* 15:25 O '39.

3 Cowan, Harold E. "Popularity of National Clerical Ability Tests." *J Bus Ed* 15:30 S '39.

4 Joint Committee on Tests. *National Clerical Ability Tests*: Sponsored by National Office Management Association and National Council of Business Education As a Service to Trainers and Employers of Office Workers. Bulletin No. 1. Cambridge, Mass.: Joint Committee on Tests, Lawrence Hall, Kirkland St., November 1939. Pp. iv, 40. Gratis. Paper, mimeographed.

5 "National Clerical Ability Tests." *Bus Ed World* 20:117-8 O '39.

6 "National Clerical Ability Tests: Comments and Suggestions for Their Improvement Made by Sponsors of Test Centers and Teachers of Testees with Reactions of Joint Committee on Tests." *J Bus Ed* 15:28-31 D '39.

7 Ford, Gertrude C. "Implications of the National Clerical Ability Tests for Teacher-Training Institutions," pp. 3-6. In *Proceedings of the Twelfth Annual Conference of the National Association of Business Teacher-Training Institutions*, Cleveland, February 25, 1939. Edited by A. Brewington. Bulletin 17. Akron, Ohio: the Association (c/o H. M. Doutt, Sec., University of Akron), 1939. Pp. 34.

8 Hittler, George M. "Our Experience with the National Clerical Ability Tests." *Bus Ed World* 20:715-7 Ap '40.

9 "List of Schools Giving the Tests in 1939." *J Bus Ed* 15:28 F '40.

[1477]

Breidenbaugh Bookkeeping Tests: Division I, Single Proprietorship. High school; 1936; 1 form, 4 parts; 35¢ per specimen set; V. E. Breidenbaugh; Bloomington, Ill.: Public School Publishing Co.

a) TEST I, FIRST HALF OF COURSE. $1 per 25; 6¢ per key; nontimed (50-60) minutes.

b) TEST 2, FIRST HALF OF COURSE. 50¢ per 25; 4¢ per key; nontimed (50-60) minutes.

c) TEST 3, SECOND HALF OF COURSE. $1 per 25; 6¢ per key; nontimed (50-60) minutes.

d) TEST 4, SECOND HALF OF COURSE. $1.50 per 25; 8¢ per key; nontimed (100) minutes.

Bus Ed World 19:434 Ja '39. Jessie Graham. These tests, designed for the single-proprietorship high school bookkeeping course, may be used with any textbook. The tests cover journalizing, adjustments, balance sheet, statement of profit and loss, closing entries, and work sheet. They are of the completion, true-false, matching, and equation type. They are easily scored with use of the key. Tentative norms are provided. Instructions for calculating medians are printed on the record sheet. Self-check sheets for pupils' remedial work are included. Teachers using these tests will get the benefit of the large amount of preliminary work done by Mr. Breidenbaugh in constructing, trying out, and improving these tests.

[1478]

Business Backgrounds Test. High school; 1939; 1 form; $1 per 25; 10¢ per specimen set; 60(70) minutes; Mathilde Hardaway; El Paso, Tex.: the author, Austin High School.

REFERENCES

1 Hardaway, Mathilde. "A Business Backgrounds Test." *Balance Sheet* 21:244-7, 279, 292-4, 336 F, Mr '40.

Balance Sheet 21:90 O '39. * Designed to cover the type of general business knowledge which an independent consumer should possess. * Teachers interested in evaluating their commercial courses to determine how well they are imparting the consumer type of general business knowledge will find this test a valuable aid.

[1479]

Clinton-LeMaster Commercial and Business Law Test. High school and college; 1936; 2 forms; $2.40 per 25; 15¢ per specimen set; nontimed (60) minutes J. Lloyd LeMaster and R. J. Clinton; Corvallis, Ore.: O. S. C. Cooperative Association.

[1480]

Commercial Education Survey Tests. First-, second-year typewriting; [1931]; 1 form, 2 levels; $1 per 25; 25¢ per manual; 40¢ per specimen set; Jane E. Clem; Bloomington, Ill.: Public School Publishing Co.

a) JUNIOR TYPEWRITING. First-year typewriting; 95(105) minutes.

b) SENIOR TYPEWRITING. Second-year typewriting; 120(130) minutes.

Bus Ed World 19:523 F '39. Jessie Graham. The Horn list of 1,000 commonest words was drawn upon for 73 per cent of the material in these stroking tests (Test 1). Each word is numbered in the key to the end that scoring is very easily done. Test 2 deals with the mechanics of the business letter and the ability to follow instructions. In the Senior Test, the pupil is required to supply capitals and punctuation marks. Test 3 is based on typewriter mechanics and typescript arrangements. Test 4 is on placement and tabulation test. Test 5 deals with centering and rough drafts. Each of these tests is issued in both junior and senior form. Final medians for some tests and tentative medians for others are reported. If you are familiar with Miss Clem's book, "The Technique of Teaching Typewriting" (Gregg), you will know that these are well-constructed tests of typing ability.

[1481]

Diagnostic Test of Letter-Writing Ability. High school students, teachers, and adults; 1939; 7¢ per test; $2 per test including scoring and a personal diagnosis by the test author; nontimed; Ralph R. Rice; Oakland, Calif.: the Author, 291 Lester Ave.

Bus Ed World 19:523-4 F '39. Jessie Graham. Teachers of business correspondence who take this test will reap not only benefits for themselves but, also, many ideas that will help to objectify their teaching. They will also have a good time while they are taking the test. The test is designed to measure letter-writing ability. It is not a check chart for letter copy. Persons who take the test learn why their letters do not function as they should, and are offered ways and means to overcome this ineffectiveness. The test also reveals natural abilities and provides personal information that enables the counselor to make recommendations for developing those abilities to the utmost. There are 17 pages of test material, comprising everything from copy reading to the construction of a technical letter. * The teacher who takes this test and has the results evaluated will gain self-assurance in teaching business correspondence. Mr. Rice is both a teacher and a specialist in the writing of business letters. His diagnoses are, therefore, reliable.

[1482]
Dictating Machine Transcription Test: National Clerical Ability Tests, Series 1939. Stenographers; 1939; a new form is scheduled for publication each May for use in the annual testing program of the Joint Committee on Tests of the National Office Management Association and the National Council of Business Education; $1.35 per examinee is the fee charged for the administration and scoring of this "vocational ability test" along with the *Fundamentals Test* (*see* 1484) and the *General Information Test* (*see* 1485); 25 or more copies, 20¢ per copy (Series 1939); 50¢ per sample copy (Series 1939); $1.55 per set of sample copies of all National Clerical Ability Tests (Series 1939); 60(65) minutes; Cambridge, Mass.: Joint Committee on Tests, 16 Lawrence Hall, Kirkland St.

REFERENCES

Same as for 1476.

[1483]
Filing Test: National Clerical Ability Tests, Series 1939. File clerks; 1939; a new form is scheduled for publication each May for use in the annual testing program of the Joint Committee on Tests of the National Office Management Association and the National Council of Business Education; $1.35 per examinee is the fee charged for the administration and scoring of this "vocational ability test" along with the *Fundamentals Test* (*see* 1484) and the *General Information Test* (*see* 1485); 25 or more copies, 20¢ per copy (Series 1939); 50¢ per sample copy (Series 1939); $1.55 per set of sample copies of all National Clerical Ability Tests (Series 1939); 120(130) minutes; Cambridge, Mass.: Joint Committee on Tests, 16 Lawrence Hall, Kirkland St.

REFERENCES

Same as for 1476.

[1484]
Fundamentals Test: National Clerical Ability Tests, Series 1939. Applicants for office work; a new form is scheduled for publication each May for use in the annual testing program of the Joint Committee on Tests of the National Office Management Association and the National Council of Business Education; $1.35 per examinee is the fee charged for the administration and scoring of one vocational ability test (*see* 1476, 1482-3, 1487, and 1490-1), the General Information Test (*see* 1485), and this test; 25 or more copies, 20¢ per copy (Series 1939); 50¢ per sample copy (Series 1939); $1.55 per set of sample copies of all National Clerical Ability Tests (Series 1939); 120(130) minutes; Cambridge, Mass.: Joint Committee on Tests, 16 Lawrence Hall, Kirkland St.

REFERENCES

Same as for 1476.

[1485]
General Information Test: National Clerical Ability Tests, Series 1939. Applicants for office work; 1939; a new form is scheduled for publication each May

for use in the annual testing program of the Joint Committee on Tests of the National Office Management Association and the National Council of Business Education; $1.35 per examinee is the fee charged for the administration and scoring of one vocational ability test (*see* 1476, 1482-3, 1487, and 1490-1), the Fundamentals Test (*see* 1484), and this test; 25 or more copies, 20¢ per copy (Series 1939); 50¢ per sample copy (Series 1939); $1.55 per set of sample copies of all National Clerical Ability Tests (Series 1939); 40(45) minutes; Phillip J. Rulon, Henry S. Dyer, and George B. Simon; Cambridge, Mass.: Joint Committee on Tests, 16 Lawrence Hall, Kirkland St.

REFERENCES

Same as for 1476.

[1486]
Grading Scales for Typewriting Tests. 18 to 72 weeks of instruction; 1939; a 28-page booklet for converting stroke and error scores into words typed per minute and percentage grades; 75¢; Howard Z. Stewart; Champaign, Ill.: Garrard Press.

Bus Ed World 22:165-6 O '39. Marion M. Lamb. The twenty-two grading scales, with directions for use, found in this book have been designed to assist the instructor in objectively grading the timed writings of high school students. The twenty-two scales cover two years of typewriting instruction. The person checking need only follow down the "Strokes" column until he finds the range in which lies the number of strokes written. Upon moving to the right to the proper "Error" column, he finds the net rate per minute and the percentage grade. At the discretion of the teacher, the letter grade equivalent for the percentage grade may be used. Those progressive teachers of typewriting who have adopted the plan of permitting students properly and neatly to erase errors and insert the correct letter or character will find the scales may be used successfully, for as the errors decrease through erasing, the strokes decrease proportionally. Thus, improved erasing efficiency will result in higher percentage grades. Probably the most important among the several values to be found in the use of the scales lies in the opportunity given students to know how they rank in such tests because the scales are objective statements of student achievement in proportion to the weeks spent in study.

[1487]
Key-Driven Calculating Machine Ability Test: National Clerical Ability Tests, Series 1939. Electric- or hand-operated machine calculators; 1939; a new form is scheduled for publication each May for use in the annual testing program of the Joint Committee on Tests of the National Office Management Association and the National Council of Business Education; $1.35 per examinee is the fee charged for the administration and scoring of this "vocational ability test" along with the *Fundamentals Test* (*see* 1484)

and the *General Information Test* (*see* 1485) ; 25 or more copies, 20¢ per copy (Series 1939) ; 50¢ per sample copy (Series 1939) ; $1.55 per set of sample copies of all National Clerical Ability Tests (Series 1939) ; 120(130) minutes; Cambridge, Mass.: Joint Committee on Tests, 16 Lawrence Hall, Kirkland St.

REFERENCES
Same as for 1476.

[1488]
Qualifying Test for Ediphone Voice Writing. Typists; 1938; 1 form; 40¢ per 12 tests; to schools, 30¢ per 12 tests; 24(40) minutes; Raymond C. Goodfellow and Ediphone Educational Committee; West Orange, N. J.: Thomas A. Edison, Inc.

[1489]
Scale of Problems in Commercial Arithmetic. High school; [1926]; 3 levels; $1 per 25; 25¢ per specimen set; Lucien B. Kinney; Bloomington, Ill.: Public School Publishing Co.
a) SCALE A, PART 1. First 10 weeks; 20(25) minutes.
b) SCALE A, PART 2. First 10 weeks; 10(15) minutes.
c) SCALE B. First semester; 2 forms; 40(45) minutes.
d) SCALE C. Second semester; 2 forms; 40(45) minutes.

REFERENCES
1 KINNEY, LUCIEN B. "A Program for the Determination of the Mathematical Requirements of Commercial Positions Taken by High School Graduates," pp. 60-75. In *Research Studies in Commercial Education, III.* Edited by E. G. Blackstone. University of Iowa Monographs in Education, No. 9. Iowa City, Iowa: the University, 1928. Pp. 230. $0.75. Paper.
2 KINNEY, LUCIEN B. *The Mathematical Requirements of Commercial Positions Open to High School Commercial Graduates.* Unpublished doctor's thesis, University of Minnesota, 1931.
3 KINNEY, LUCIEN B. "The Relationship of Certain Factors to Success in Clerical Positions." *J Appl Psychol* 17:55-62 F '33.

Bus Ed World 19:434 Ja '39. Jessie Graham. Although these tests are designed to be used at various stages of a one-year course in commercial arithmetic, they could be used equally well for diagnosis of pupils' needs in schools in which commercial arithmetic, as such, is not a part of the curriculum. Provision is made for retesting after the remedial drill following the first testing. Directions for giving the tests, answer keys, and record sheets are included. Tentative norms are reported. Space is provided for self-analysis by pupils. Problems range from those in the four fundamental processes to interest and percentage. The problems represent a good sampling of the entire commercial-arithmetic course.

[1490]
Stenographic Ability Tests: National Clerical Ability Tests, Series 1939. Stenographers; 1939; a new form is scheduled for publication each May for use in the annual testing program of the Joint Committee of Tests of the National Council of Business Education; $1.35 per examinee is the fee charged for the administration and scoring of this "vocational ability test" along with the *Fundamentals Test* (*see* 1484) and the *General Information Test* (*see* 1485) ; 25 or more copies, 20¢ per copy (Series 1939) ; 50¢ per sample copy (Series 1939) ; $1.55 per set of sample copies of all National Clerical Ability Tests (Series 1939) ; 180(190) minutes; Cambridge, Mass.: Joint Committee on Tests, 16 Lawrence Hall, Kirkland St.

REFERENCES
Same as for 1476.

[1490.1]
Turse Shorthand Aptitude Test. 1937-40; 1 form; $1.30 per 25; 10¢ per specimen set; 45(50) minutes; Paul L. Turse; Yonkers, N. Y.: World Book Co.

[1491]
Typing Ability Test: National Clerical Ability Tests, Series 1939. Typists; 1939; a new form is scheduled for publication each May for use in the annual testing program of the Joint Committee of Tests of the National Office Management Association and the National Council of Business Education; $1.35 per examinee is the fee charged for the administration and scoring of this "vocational ability test" along with the *Fundamentals Test* (*see* 1484) ; and the *General Information Test* (*see* 1485) ; 25 or more copies, 20¢ per copy (Series 1939) ; 50¢ per sample copy (Series 1939) ; $1.55 per set of sample copies of all National Clerical Ability Tests (Series 1939) ; 120(130) minutes; Cambridge, Mass.: Joint Committee on Tests, 16 Lawrence Hall, Kirkland St.

REFERENCES
Same as for 1476.

Key-Driven Calculating Machine Ability Test

VOCATIONS — SECOND MMY

Reviews by Harold D. Carter, A. B. Crawford, W. D. Commins, John G. Darley, Stanley G. Dulsky, Jack W. Dunlap, Edward S. Jones, Forrest A. Kingsbury, G. Frederic Kuder, Herbert A. Landry, Irving Lorge, J. B. Miner, N. W. Morton, C. A. Oakley, Donald G. Paterson, John Gray Peatman, M. W. Richardson, Alec Rodger, Ruth Strang, Lorene Teegarden, Albert S. Thompson, M. R. Trabue, Arthur E. Traxler, Morris S. Viteles, E. G. Williamson, and C. Gilbert Wrenn.

[1643]

ABC Occupational Inventory. Grades 9 and over; 1935; 1 form; $1.44 per 30; 10¢ per specimen set; nontimed; N. A. Lufburrow; Baltimore, Md.: the Author, 3112 Milford Ave.

[1644]

Adjusted Graphic Analysis Chart. Applicants for professional and sub-professional positions; 2¢ per chart; 10¢ per specimen set; R. E. Dunford; Knoxville, Tenn.: the Author, University of Tennessee.

REFERENCES

1 DUNFORD, R. E. "The Adjusted Graphic Analysis Chart." *J Appl Psychol* 23:623-9 O '39.

[1645]

Aids to Self-Analysis and Vocational Planning Inventory. Grades 9-12; 1940; 8¢ per test; H. D. Richardson; Chicago, Ill.: Science Research Associates.

REFERENCES

1 RICHARDSON, H. D. *Analytical Devices in Guidance and Counseling.* Basic Occupational Plans, No. 3. Chicago, Ill.: Science Research Associates, 1940. Pp. 63. $1.00. Paper, lithotyped.

[1646]

Aptitude Index for Life Insurance Salesmen. Prospective life insurance agents; 1938; distribution restricted to life insurance companies which are members of the Life Insurance Sales Bureau; Hartford, Conn.: Life Insurance Sales Research Bureau.

REFERENCES

1 Life Insurance Sales Research Bureau. *Rating Prospective Agents.* Hartford, Conn.: the Bureau, 1937. Pp. 16. Privately distributed. Paper.
2 Life Insurance Sales Research Bureau. *Selection of Agents:* A Method of Relating Personal History Information to Probable Success in Life Insurance Selling. Hartford, Conn.: the Bureau, 1937. Pp. 24. Privately distributed. Paper.
3 Life Insurance Sales Research Bureau. *Measuring Aptitude for Life Insurance Selling.* Hartford, Conn.: the Bureau, 1938. Pp. 22. Privately distributed. Paper.
4 Life Insurance Sales Research Bureau. *The Prospective Agents Rating Plan in Use:* Report of Session on Selection of Agents, at Research Bureau Conference, Hartford, Connecticut, March 22, 1938. New Haven, Conn.: the Bureau, 1938. Pp. 44. Privately distributed. Paper.
5 KURTZ, ALBERT K. "Evaluating Selection Tests." *Managers Mag* 14:12-6 My-Je '39.

[1647]

Basic Interest Questionnaire: For Selecting Your Vocation or Avocation. Grades 9-16 and adults; 1938-39; 1 form; $2.50 per 25; key, $5; nontimed (75) minutes; Keith Van Allyn; Los Angeles, Calif.: National Institute of Vocational Research.

[1648]

Career Incentive and Progress Blank. For recording data concerning counselees in grades 9-16 and placement offices; 1939; $1.68 per 30; 10¢ per specimen set; N. A. Lufburrow; Baltimore, Md.: the Author, 3112 Milford Ave.

[1649]

Check List for Self-Guidance in Choosing an Occupation. Grades 9-16 and adults; 1940; $1.25 per 25; 15¢ per specimen set; Robert Hoppock; New York: Psychological Corporation.

[1650]

Check List of Occupations. High school and college; 1940; $1 per 25; 15¢ per specimen set; nontimed; Margaret E. Hoppock; New York: Psychological Corporation.

[1651]

Composite Inventory and Examination, Revised. Prospective salesman; 1940; 2 editions; $1 per specimen set; Verne Steward; Los Angeles, Calif.: Verne Steward & Associates, 5471 Chesley Ave.
a) FORM A. A 12-page booklet containing the following sections: (1) Mental Ability, (2) Personality Traits, (3) General Knowledge, (4) Vocational Interests, (5) Personality Trait Illustrations, (6) Personal History, and (7) Rating Form; $3 per 10; $7 per 25; (90-100) minutes.
b) FORM B. An 8-page booklet containing Sections 1, 5, 6, and 7 of Form A; $2.40 per 10; $5.50 per 25; (45-60) minutes.

REFERENCES

1 STEWARD, VERNE. *The Use and Value of Special Tests in the Selection of Life Underwriters.* Los Angeles, Calif.: Steward and Associates, 5471 Chesley Ave., 1934. Pp. 93. $2.50.
2 STEWARD, VERNE. *Selection of Sales Personnel.* Los Angeles, Calif.: Verne Steward and Associates, 5471 Chesley Ave., 1936. Pp. 48. $2.75.

3 STEWARD, VERNE. "The Development of a Selection System for Salesmen." *Personnel* 16:124-36 F '40.

[1652-3]

[Cox Mechanical Aptitude and Manual Dexterity Tests.] Ages 11 and over; 1928-34; individual; according to the publisher, D. Draycon, Tests M1, D, and E constitute the battery usually employed in secondary and technical schools; J. W. Cox; Enfield, England: D. Draycon; London: National Institute of Industrial Psychology.

a) COX MECHANICAL MODELS TEST M1. Ages 14 and over. DRAYCON: £2 12*s*. per 10 wooden models; £6 13*s*. 4*d*. per 10 aluminum models; 6*s*. per 12 diagram booklets; 4*s*. per 50 answer sheets. N. I. I. P.: £6 13*s*. 4*d*. per set of metal models in box for transportation; 6*d*. per diagram booklet; 4*s*. per 50 answer sheets.

b) COX MECHANICAL MODELS TEST M2. DRAYCON: £3 5*s*. per 10 wooden models, more difficult than M1 (less 10*s*. if M1 and M2 are ordered together); 6*s*. per 12 diagram booklets; 4*s*. per 50 answer sheets.

c) COX MECHANICAL MODELS TEST M. Ages 11-14. DRAYCON: £2 per 5 wooden models constituting Part 1; £1 10*s*. per 5 wooden models constituting Part 2; 6*s*. per 12 diagram booklets for either part; 4*s*. per 50 answer sheets for either part; (20) minutes for Part 1.

d) COX MECHANICAL DIAGRAMS TEST D. DRAYCON: £2 2*s*. per 6 cardboard diagrams; £3 3*s*. per 6 linen diagrams; 6*s*. per 12 question booklets; 4*s*. per 50 answer sheets. N. I. I. P.: £3 3*s*. per 6 diagrams; 14*s*. per 50 question booklets.

e) COX MECHANICAL EXPLANATION TEST E. DRAYCON: 9*s*. 6*d*. per 12 test booklets; 4*s*. per 50 answer sheets.

f) COX EYEBOARD TEST. DRAYCON: 17*s*. 6*d*. N. I. I. P.: 17*s*. 6*d*.

g) COX NAILBOARD TEST. DRAYCON: 5*s*. 6*d*.

h) COX NAIL-STICK TEST. DRAYCON: 5*s*. 6*d*.

REFERENCES

1 Cox, J. W. *Mechanical Aptitude*: Its Existence, Nature and Measurement. London: Methuen & Co., Ltd., 1928. Pp. xiii, 209. 7*s*. 6*d*.
2 HARVEY, O. L. "Mechanical 'Aptitude' or Mechanical 'Ability'? A Study In Method." *J Ed Psychol* 22:517-22 O '31.
3 Cox, J. W. *Manual Skill*: Its Organizations and Development. London: Cambridge University Press, 1934. Pp. xx, 247. 16*s*. (New York: Macmillan Co. $5.00).
4 LAYCOCK, S. R., AND HUTCHEON, N. B. "A Preliminary Investigation into the Problem of Measuring Engineering Aptitude." *J Ed Psychol* 30:280-8 Ap '39.

C. A. Oakley, Scottish Area Officer of the British Air Ministry; in civil life, Scottish Divisional Director of the National Institute of Industrial Psychology, Glasgow, Scotland. In Scotland the best-known of the Cox tests is the Mechanical Models Test. Unfortunately until recently the test suffered from the unsatisfactory construction both of the wooden models and of the booklets. These matters have recently received the attention of the National Institute of Industrial Psychology.

The test (and other Cox mechanical tests, particularly the Diagrams Test) has the advantage of being a group test. Its disadvantage is that the instructions are complicated and difficult to follow. In practice this has led certain teachers to try to improve on the instructions—particularly by repeating difficult

sections—without realising that they are invalidating the test.

Cox has standardised the tests with small groups but I have found his norms reasonably satisfactory. As few of the Scottish pupils to whom the tests have been given have done any other mechanical tests it is not possible to comment upon their validity.

Cox has, in my opinion, developed a useful technique but the tests themselves need revision to meet practical requirements in schools.

The Cox Eye-Board Test also has some defects in construction. It is inclined to warp and the eye-screws are easily broken or twisted out of position. For these reasons I have stopped using it, but again I should add that the general principles on which the test has been devised seem to me to be sound.

Alec Rodger, Head of the Vocational Guidance Department, National Institute of Industrial Psychology, London, England. Cox is a protagonist of Spearman's two-factor theory of ability. It is essential that this fact should be realized by those who make inquiries about his tests. He has aimed at producing measuring instruments for a "routine" manual dexterity which can be shown to be (*a*) relatively independent of such nonmanual abilities as general intelligence and mechanical aptitude and (*b*) useful for manual occupations.

No one is likely to dispute the fact that he has performed an important task with a most admirable degree of scientific ardour and detachment. In the reviewer's opinion, his work on manual dexterity and mechanical aptitude has been more searching than that of any other investigator or team of investigators. It would seem, however, that his research methods are probably of more importance than his research findings; the groups he used in his experiment were too small to warrant the formulation of anything more than broad conclusions.

Cox deals only briefly with a problem which arises in all testing work, but which is of almost paramount importance in manual dexterity testing; namely, the problem of incentives. He omits consideration of one aspect of this problem which seems to call for discussion. The reviewer has had a good deal of experience both in the use of Cox's eyeboard test and in the training of others in its use, and he is firmly of the opinion that the degree of "urgency" suggested by the tester's actions, voice inflections and so on, is nearly always very influential in the testing situation. A quiet, easygoing student who gives the test instructions in a deliberate way will tend to obtain a set of lower scores than a brisk, businesslike student (dealing with a comparable group) whose methods make the subjects feel "keyed up." Consequently, the reviewer holds the view that each tester should build up his own norms for this (and the other) Cox manual dexterity tests; the use of tables compiled by others is definitely unsatisfactory. Few testers are likely to be in a position to do this adequately.

For this reason—and, perhaps, for the additional reason that the variations shown by testers in their ability to time these tests play a substantial part in the determination of scores—the reviewer wonders whether other investigators, pursuing similar methods, using similar test material and testing similar subjects, might not reach rather different conclusions.

Briefly: the method by which Cox produced these tests was admirably scientific, but for the present it must be doubted whether their value can be taken as proven; in any case, they seem to be in some respects unsuitable for general or occasional use. It is to be hoped that research workers who are in a position to do so will include them in experimental "batteries" of tests.

[1654]

Detroit General Aptitudes Examination. Grades 6-12; 1938; 1 form; $2.00 per 25; 18¢ per *Ayres Handwriting Scale: Gettysburg Edition*; 25¢ per manual; 45¢ per specimen set; 60(85-90) minutes; Harry J. Baker, Paul H. Voelker, and Alex C. Crockett; Bloomington, Ill.: Public School Publishing Co.

G. Frederic Kuder, Examiner, Board of Examinations, The University of Chicago. The examination blank consists of sixteen tests—one to a page. Scores from different combinations of the various tests are added together to give scores for intelligence, mechanical aptitude, and clerical aptitude. The intelligence score is obtained from ten of the tests. The mechanical aptitude and clerical aptitude scores are each obtained from nine tests. More than half the tests in each battery are common with one of the other batteries. Four of the tests are included in all three batteries. Four others are common to two batteries. The intercorrelations of the three batteries are high, as might be

expected in view of the overlapping. These intercorrelations are .80, .78, and .73 for the intelligence-mechanical, intelligence-clerical, and mechanical-clerical pairs, respectively.

The high intercorrelations raise the question as to whether the overlapping is not so large as to make obtaining all three different scores superfluous. The best answer to this question would ordinarily be the size of the intercorrelations corrected for attenuation which would indicate the extent to which each pair of batteries measure the same thing. These coefficients, obtained by the usual formula, are .94, .93, and .82. However, the usual formula for attenuation is hardly applicable in this case since it rests on the assumption of uncorrelated errors—an assumption which is not met in the case of overlapping measures. If allowance is made for estimated identical errors, the correlation between true scores on the intelligence and mechanical batteries is about .87. The estimate of the extent to which the intelligence and clerical batteries measure the same thing is about .85, and for the mechanical and clerical batteries the correlation of true scores is .74. These figures were obtained on the assumption that for purposes of estimation, the standard deviations of the batteries are approximately equal and that the common error variance is about .07 of the total variance of each test. This latter estimate appears reasonable when it is considered that the total error variance is .200, .102, and .122 for the three tests, respectively, and that more than half of each test is common to each of the others.

From these figures it appears that the intelligence variance is so well accounted for by the other two scores that use of the test is superfluous if the others are used. Another consideration militating against use of the intelligence test is its reliability of .80 as compared with reliabilities of about .90 for most intelligence tests on the market. The effort of the authors to use relatively little verbal material in the intelligence test seems to have lowered the reliability usually obtained for tests of this type and to have driven the particular measure used close to the clerical and mechanical aptitude tests. It samples essentially the same things as the other two measures and does a poor job of it at that.

The case for the mechanical and clerical measures is much better. The two measures are unrelated enough to justify the use of both, and the reliabilities are satisfactory (.90 for mechanical aptitude, and .88 for clerical aptitude). It should be remembered that neither clerical nor mechanical ability has been demonstrated to be a unitary trait; the scores obtained are vectors in the respective fields which have been found to have some relation with other measures acknowledged to be of a mechanical or clerical nature.

Use of the page scores for individual diagnosis is urged in the directions for using the record form. This practice is hardly justified by the relatively low reliabilities of most of the single tests. The reliabilities range from .57 to .88 and have a median of .76. The reliabilities of the subsections (composed of two or more single tests) such as "motor," "visual imagery," "verbal," "educational," et cetera, are not given. However, judging from the reliabilities of the component tests, it is likely that some of these do have reliabilities high enough to justify use of their scores for individual measurement. The authors observe that the reliabilities of the single-page tests are very good considering the shortness of the tests. This statement is true, but it does not make the reliabilities high enough to justify use of the page scores in individual measurement.

The authors state that "among large groups of children representing a wide range of abilities, there tend to be rather high correlations between intelligence, mechanical, and clerical aptitudes. In individual cases there are many marked differences and this is particularly true within the individual pages or subparts of the entire test." It should be added that even when tests measure the same thing marked differences are inevitable if the tests are unreliable.

SUMMARY. The mechanical and clerical aptitude batteries are reliable measures which have been demonstrated to have some validity. They deserve consideration for measurement in their respective fields. Use of the intelligence test is hardly justified in view of the fact that there are much more reliable intelligence tests on the market. Even for purposes of predicting some criterion, use of the intelligence test can hardly be justified since its variance is almost entirely accounted for by the mechanical and clerical aptitude tests. It is unfortunate that the use of scores on individual tests is recommended for individual diagnosis in view of the inadequate reliabilities of most of the single tests.

Irving Lorge, Executive Officer of the Division of Psychology, Institute of Educational Research and Associate Professor of Education, Columbia University. The examination consists of sixteen subtests with time limits from 3 to 5 minutes each as follows: (1) handwriting; (2) general information; (3) arithmetic fundamentals; (4) motor speed (circles); (5) tool recognition; (6) disarranged pictures; (7) verbal opposites; (8) spelling errors; (9) size discrimination; (10) verbal analogies; (11) same-different for numbers, figures, etc.; (12) tool information; (13) classification; (14) belt and pulley; (15) disarranged sentences; (16) alphabetizing.

The scoring of the examination gives each subtest a maximum score ranging from 30 to 53 points. These scores are grouped into three subscores for intelligence, clerical aptitude, and mechanical aptitude. The intelligence score is the sum of Subtests 2, 3, 4, 6, 7, 8, 10, 13, 14, 15; the mechanical aptitude score is the sum of Subtests 1, 3, 4, 5, 6, 9, 12, 13, 14; and the clerical aptitude score is the sum of Subtests 1, 3, 4, 6, 8, 11, 13, 15, 16. It is regrettable so much overlap was allowed among these three group scores, five tests are common to intelligence and mechanical aptitude, six tests are common to intelligence and clerical aptitude, and five tests are common to clerical and mechanical aptitude. The commonality among scores is shown by reported correlations of .80, .70 and .73 between the group scores which if corrected for attenuation might indicate that the three group scores are probably measuring the same basic set of factors.

The intelligence group score was validated against the *Detroit Advanced Intelligence Test* (r = .90 for 188 twelfth grade pupils); estimated IQ's were correlated against 1916 Stanford Binet IQ's as criterion (r = .652 for 188 twelfth grade pupils) and the clerical group score was validated against *Detroit Advanced Intelligence Test* (r = .739 for 188 twelfth grade pupils). As far as the essential purpose of the examination is concerned, the authors have not demonstrated the validity of either the clerical or the mechanical aptitude scores. Basically, the authors demonstrate that the group scores are measures of intelligence.

Retest reliabilities for the group scores after six weeks are reported as .80 for intelligence, .90 for mechanical aptitude and .88 for clerical.

Detroit General Aptitudes Examination

The subtest retest reliabilities range from .57 to .88 (259 eighth grade pupils).

Age norms are provided (based on 10,000 cases) for each of the group scores, and for each subtest score, as well as for another classification of subtest scores into verbal, educational, motor, mechanical information, visual imagery, etc., scores.

Since the authors have failed to demonstrate the differential validity of the clerical or mechanical aptitude scores, and, further, since they have failed to show the validity of other scores such as visual images, etc., the test must be used cautiously in guidance and in classification.

The test is not printed too well. Examination of several test copies shows differences in blackness, particularly in Subtests 4, 6, 9, 11, and 14. Subtest 5 is difficult for school children to take in its present format. Subtest 6 is badly drawn, and poorly reproduced. Subtest 9 is poor in format.

This test will not provide the ordinary guidance worker with those "aptitude facts essential to a direction of instruction-guidance of pupils in the first two years of high school" which are different from those measured by a good intelligence test.

John Gray Peatman, Assistant Professor of Psychology, The College of the City of New York. This aptitude examination has the useful feature of combining into one booklet of 16 pages, tests for three general areas of aptitude, viz., "intelligence, mechanical, and clerical." The superficial character of all of these areas is fairly clear, but it might have been more to the point to have named the first area "general scholastic aptitude," especially since the whole test is designed for school grades 6 to 12. Throughout the accompanying teacher's handbook, the authors employ the phrase "intelligence, mechanical, and clerical"—thus using the noun form for one aptitude area and the adjectival for the other two.

"Economy of testing has been achieved by using certain pages or tests in more than one type of aptitude. For example, if motor speed and skill are important in intelligence, in mechanical, and in clerical, two pages such as 4 and 13 accomplish this result for all three types of aptitudes. Other pages serve for two aptitudes while eight of the sixteen pages are used in only one of any of the three major

aptitudes." This statement from the handbook further indicates something of the character of the authors' approach to the problem of standardizing the examination. Their selection and weighting of the various tests employed in each one of the three areas is evidently made chiefly on the basis of rational considerations. At least no satisfactory evidence of an empirical kind is cited to support the choices made. If it is argued that it is obvious that a symbol-checking test of paired items and a filing test (using word material) are especially relevant to clerical aptitudes but not to "intelligence and mechanical"; or that tests of general information, vocabulary and verbal analogies are obviously relevant to "intelligence" but not to "mechanical and clerical"; or that tests of tool and mechanical information and of form discrimination are especially relevant to "mechanical" but not to "intelligence and clerical," it should be clear that this is exactly the point. Argument and the appeal to reasonableness are indispensable to the empirical development of an aptitude test but they are not sufficient to warrant the public sale of such tests as presumably finished products. Of course this booklet of tests doesn't come first-born out of the blue; there is a precedent in the works of previous investigators for some of the choices of types of tests used. However it is not to the credit of the authors of the handbook that their booklet of 16 tests is made for sale to teachers *as if* it will measure all intended things in a functionally adequate manner. Presumably, all the teacher has to do is to follow the explicit directions for administration and scoring, consult the tables of norms at the end of the handbook and thereby be in a very good position to classify students or to execute the purposes of "individual counseling in cases of educational disability, in cases of uneven educational accomplishments, for educational guidance, and for possible causes of emotional or social maladjustment." It is to be hoped that the teacher or administrator who obtains this aptitude examination for any of these purposes is psychologically well-trained for the responsibility. This is probably but a pious hope, at least for the present. Sometime the day may dawn when the progenitors of this or that psychological test will not wish to put their premature offspring into the hands of our well-meaning but psychologically untrained school teachers.

More specifically, the handbook presents 13

Detroit General Aptitudes Examination

tables of norms: letter ratings and mental age norms for each one of the 3 areas of aptitude, as well as mental age norms for each separate test and various test combinations. These norms are described as "based on 10,000 scores, chiefly the unselected groups of pupils at the eighth and ninth grade levels in Detroit." Whether this was a sample of 10,000 different pupils is not clearly stated nor do we learn anything further about the nature of the population used except that several hundred mentally subnormal children, some normal fifth- and sixth-grade pupils, and small groups in the senior high school were possibly used in the development of the norms. Separate norms for the sexes were not developed since, according to the authors, no appreciable differences could be detected between median values. Inasmuch as the examination is published for use considerably beyond the bounds of Detroit, and since all norms are evidently developed mainly in relation to the rankings of the individuals within the various age groups, and not at all with respect to really functional criteria, the nature of the sampling is obviously of fundamental importance.

Functional criteria in terms of later achievement in each one of the three areas of aptitude are nowhere in evidence. The possible validity of the scale is dealt with rather summarily. Later scholastic achievement records as relevant criteria for a validation analysis of the intelligence area (particularly as scholastic aptitude) are not even mentioned. The authors' case for the validation of the mechanical and clerical aptitude areas is just as inadequate and misleading. That something is being measured in a fairly reliable manner by these three aptitude groupings of the examination is suggested by retest reliability coefficients for a sample of 259 eighth grade pupils, evidently heterogeneous in age—the examination being repeated with them after an interval of six weeks. The coefficients range from .80 to .90. A good deal of attention has presumably been paid to item validation (using internal criteria). But this attention to important aspects of test construction and the possibly satisfactory reliability of the three test groupings obviously do not alter the fundamental fact that we have here a group of neatly arranged tests for which we discover practically no evidence that they are satisfactorily differentiating pupils' *aptitudes* for intellectual, mechanical, and

clerical *achievement*. It is lamentable, to say the least, that an examination in this condition has been made generally available to school teachers and other test administrators. Nor is the fact that previous publishers of tests have sinned likewise a legitimate excuse.

[1655]

Detroit Clerical Aptitudes Examination. High school; 1937-38; 1 form; $4.50 per 100; 20¢ per specimen set; 30(40) minutes; Harry J. Baker and Paul H. Voelker; Bloomington, Ill.: Public School Publishing Co.

Irving Lorge, Executive Officer of the Division of Psychology, Institute of Educational Research and Associate Professor of Education, Columbia University. The test is offered as a means of measuring the special aptitudes required in commercial courses. It consists of eight subtests as follows: (1) rate and quantity of handwriting; (2) rate and accuracy in checking; (3) arithmetic fundamentals; (4) motor speed and accuracy; (5) commercial vocabulary; (6) disarranged pictures; (7) classification; and (8) alphabetizing. Seven of these subtests are common to the *Detroit General Aptitude Examination,* Form A as follows: $1 = 1$, $2 = 11$, $3 = 3$, $4 = 4$, $6 = 6$, $7 = 13$, and $8 = 16$ of the General Aptitudes Examination. Subtest 5 is not in the larger examination.

The scoring of the examination gives each subtest a maximum score ranging from 30 to 53 points. The examination should be easy to administer and to score.

The validity is given in terms of correlations of the examination with scholarship in commercial courses as .56 in bookkeeping, .37 in shorthand, and .32 for typewriting. The correlation between the examination and the *Detroit Advanced Intelligence Test* is reported as .44. The authors also report the inter-subtest correlations as well as the correlations of each subtest with the intelligence criterion as ranging from .26 to .53. The reviewer undertook a Hotelling component analysis of the intercorrelations which shows that about 41 per cent of the variance of the examinations scores may be attributed to a single factor which is common to intelligence tests. The factor loadings with the first factor for each subtest are: 1, .51; 2, .75; 3, .69; 4, .41; 5, .56; 6, .47; 7, .72; 8, .77; and the *Detroit Advanced Intelligence Test*, .77. A second factor accounts for about 11.5 per cent of the score variance. The factor loadings are: 1, .38; 2, .20; 3, −.14; 4, .45; 5,

−.41; 6, −.45; 7, .34; 8, .08; and *Detroit Advanced Intelligence Test,* −.39.

The second factor seems to be related to speed as opposed to information. There will be other factors in the test, but they will be unreliable. Basically, the test measures factors common to intelligence tests and to speed tests.

Retest reliability for a three weeks interval is reported as .85 which is satisfactory for group differentiation, but hardly high enough for individual prognosis or guidance.

Age norms are provided for the range 8-0 years to 21-11 years. The age norms are unusual in that almost uniformly through the range two points correspond to a month of chronological age.

The test is not printed well. Subtests 2, 4 and 6 particularly are badly reproduced. This test may contribute some basis for understanding and guiding pupils that will not be given by an intelligence test, but that contribution must wait upon a reweighting of the subtests. In its present form, it does not seem to be differentiating between a hypothetical clerical aptitude and general intellectual ability.

M. W. Richardson, United States Civil Service Commission, Washington, D. C. The eight subtests of which this examination is composed are (*a*) rate and quality of handwriting, (*b*) rate and accuracy in checking, (*c*) simple arithmetic, (*d*) motor speed and accuracy, (*e*) simple commercial terms, (*f*) visual imagery, (*g*) classification, and (*h*) alphabetical filing.

The total examination requires only thirty minutes; the separate subtests require two to five minutes each. Although perhaps eight different factors are not involved, nevertheless several different abilities basic to clerical proficiency are sampled. The test is designed to predict success in subsequent commercial courses in high school; it is not designed to select individuals for clerical positions.

The subtests seem to be well designed for their purpose. Moreover, the examination as a whole bears facial evidence of careful test construction.

Adequate norms are provided for each age group from 10 to 16 inclusive. The table of norms suggests that the correlation of the examination with chronological age is perhaps higher than its correlation with bookkeeping, shorthand, or typewriting. This circumstance adds a special difficulty to the interpretation of

the results. The user of the test may legitimately raise several questions on the matter of equivalence of scores as predicting success in clerical courses given in the table of letter ratings furnished by the authors. Not enough information is given by the authors on this point, and the obvious pitfalls in the interpretation of such tables are not sufficiently pointed out.

It is this reviewer's opinion that too many subtests are included for a thirty-minute test. The question is whether the amount of increase in validity gained by wide sampling of test materials is not lost by lowered reliability due to timing, bad starts, and other accidental factors. It is at least possible that two or three well-chosen subtests, lengthened to fill thirty minutes, would predict success in commercial courses quite as well. The examination is, perhaps necessarily, loaded with speed. No separate measures of speed and quality are provided, presumably because they are not necessary in the use of an empirical selection device.

The authors promise age norms for each part of the test, "so that special diagnosis of detailed abilities, as well as the general ability, may be made." It is questionable whether an interpretation of individual part-scores is worth while, since the reliability of each part-score is necessarily low, because of the short time limit.

[1656]
Detroit Mechanical Aptitudes Examination, Revised. Grades 7-16; 1928-39; 1 form; $3 per 100; 15¢ per specimen set; 31(40) minutes; Harry J. Baker, Paul H. Voelker, and Alex Crockett; Bloomington, Ill.: Public School Publishing Co.

REFERENCES

1 BAKER, HARRY J. "A Mechanical Aptitude Test." *Detroit Ed B* 12:5-6 Ja '29.

Irving Lorge, Executive Officer of the Division of Psychology, Institute of Educational Research and Associate Professor of Education, Columbia University. The examination is offered as a means of estimating mechanical aptitude. It consists of 8 subtests as follows: (1) tool recognition; (2) motor speed; (3) size discrimination; (4) arithmetic fundamentals; (5) disarranged pictures; (6) tool information; (7) belt and pulley; (8) classification. All of the subtests are common to the *Detroit General Aptitudes Examination* as follows: 1 = 5, 2 = 4, 3 = 9, 4 = 3, 5 = 6, 6 = 12, 7 = 14, and 8 = 13.

The scoring of the examination gives each subtest a maximum ranging from 31 to 53 points. The test should be fairly easy to administer and to score with possible exception of Subtest 7 (direction of pulleys). In this test, the pupil may be able to visualize whether the second wheel will be turning in the same or a different direction from the first, but may not be able to report correctly the direction of the second wheel if he changes orientation. For instance, if the arrow is considered to be applying to the movement at the bottom of the wheel, then the key would be wrong. The directions could be improved by telling the pupil that the directions refer to movement of the upper halves of the wheels.

The validity of the test is reported in terms of correlation with the *Detroit Advanced Intelligence Test* as .65. The items were presumably validated against the trial score as criterion.

The retest reliability is reported as .90 for an interval of six weeks, with the subtest reliabilities ranging from .57 to .88.

The age norms are given for the total score, for subtest scores, and for subtest groups for motor, visual, imagery and mechanical information.

The format of Subtest 1 could be improved. The reproduction of Subtest 3 and Subtest 5 is generally a poor printing job.

The authors have made a test of an undefined kind of aptitude called "mechanical aptitudes." By failing to show what the criterion is, the test consumer is at a loss in deciding whether he needs or can use the examination. It is hoped that sooner or later the authors will demonstrate what the test measures that is different from general intelligence.

Ed Res B 19:59 Ja 17 '40. J. Wayne Wrightstone. * The title of this test seems a misnomer because no evidence is provided to show that the examination does measure any vital or important mechanical aptitudes. As a sort of information test on tools and picture puzzles it may be interesting and informative, but as a basis for serious guidance in providing reliable indexes of mechanical aptitudes, the adequacy of this test must be questioned until the authors provide more convincing evidence that it measures mechanical aptitudes validly and reliably.

[1657]

Diagnostic Interviewer's Guide. For the selection of employees; 1937; 1 form; $1.50 per 50; 75¢ per specimen set; E. F. Wonderlic and S. N. Stevens; Chicago, Ill.: E. F. Wonderlic, 919 N. Michigan Ave.

REFERENCES

1 LAIRD, DONALD A. *The Psychology of Selecting Employees,* Third edition, pp. 114-8. New York: McGraw-Hill Book Co., Inc., 1937. Pp. xiv, 316. $4.00. (London: McGraw-Hill Publishing Co., Ltd. 24s.)
2 HOVLAND, CARL IVER, AND WONDERLIC, E. F. "Prediction of Industrial Success from a Standardized Interview." *J Appl Psychol* 23:537-46 O '39.

[1658]

Entrance Questionnaire and Experience Record. High school entrants; 1940; 8¢ per copy; H. D. Richardson; Chicago, Ill.: Science Research Associates.

REFERENCES

1 RICHARDSON, H. D. *Analytical Devices in Guidance and Counseling.* Basic Occupational Plans, No. 3. Chicago, Ill.: Science Research Associates, 1940. Pp. 63. $1.00. Paper, lithotyped.

[1659]

Finger Dexterity Test: Worksample No. 16. Ages 14 and over; 1926; 1 form; individual; worklimit (10-20) minutes; Johnson O'Connor; rents for $60 for the first year and $30 a year thereafter; the *Finger Dexterity Test* and the *Tweezer Dexterity Test* together rent for $90 the first year and $45 a year thereafter; Boston, Mass.: Human Engineering Laboratory. ($25 (No. 42069); Chicago, Ill.: C. H. Stoelting Co.) ($11; Minneapolis, Minn.: Mechanical Engineering Department, University of Minnesota.)

REFERENCES

1 HINES, MILDRED, AND O'CONNOR, JOHNSON. "*A Measure of Finger Dexterity.*" *Personnel J* 4:379-82 Ja-F '26.
2 O'CONNOR, JOHNSON. *Born That Way,* pp. 21-3, 54-6, 141-2, 173-4 178-9, 181-2, 185-8, 191-9, 201-4, 213-5. Baltimore, Md.: Williams & Wilkins Co., 1928. Pp. 323. $2.00.
3 HAYES, ELINOR G. "Selecting Women for Shop Work." *Personnel J* 11:69-85 Ag '32.
4 BERGEN, GARRET L. *Use of Tests in the Adjustment Service,* p. 45. Adjustment Service Series Report [No.] 4. New York: American Adult Association for Adult Education, 1935. Pp. 70. Paper. Out of print.
5 DVORAK, BEATRICE JEANNE. *Differential Occupational Ability Patterns.* Publications of the Employment Stabilization Research Institute, University of Minnesota, Vol. 3, No. 8. Minneapolis, Minn.: University of Minnesota Press, February 1935. Pp. 46. $1.00. Paper.
6 GREEN, HELEN J., AND BERMAN, ISABEL R.; under the direction of Donald G. Paterson and M. R. Trabue. *A Manual of Selected Occupational Tests for Use in Public Employment Offices,* pp. 5-7, 9-10, 23-31. University of Minnesota, Bulletins of the Employment Stabilization Research Institute, Vol. 2, No. 3. Minneapolis, Minn.: University of Minnesota Press, July 1936. Pp. 31. $0.50. Paper.
7 PATERSON, DONALD G., AND DARLEY, JOHN G., with the assistance of Richard M. Elliott. *Men, Women, and Jobs.* Minneapolis, Minn.: University of Minnesota Press, 1936. Pp. v, 145. $2.00. (London: Oxford University Press. 9s.)
8 BINGHAM, WALTER VAN DYKE. *Aptitudes and Aptitude Testing,* pp. 281-284. New York and London: Harper & Brothers, 1937. Pp. ix, 390. $3.00; 10s. 6d.
9 BROWN, FRED. "Selective Tests for Dental School Candidates." *Oral Hyg* 27:1172-7 S '37.
10 CANDEE, BEATRICE, AND BLUM, MILTON. "Report of a Study Done in a Watch Factory." *J Appl Psychol* 21:572-82 O '37.
11 DOUGLASS, HARL R. "Means of Predicting Scholastic Success in the College of Dentistry at the University of Minnesota," pp. 204-9. In *The Role of Research in Educational Progress:* Official Report, American Educational Research Association, A Department of the National Education Association, New Orleans, Louisiana, February 20-24, 1937. Washington, D. C.: the Association, May 1937. Pp. 255. $1.50. Paper.
12 O'CONNOR, JOHNSON. *Administration and Norms for the Finger Dexterity Test, Worksample 16, and the Tweezer Dexterity Test, Worksample 18.* Human Engineering Laboratory, Technical Report, No. 16. Boston, Mass.: the Laboratory, 1938. Pp. x, 136. $1.00. Paper, mimeographed.
13 PATERSON, DONALD G.; SCHNEIDLER, GWENDOLEN G.; AND WILLIAMSON, EDMUND G. *Student Guidance Techniques,* pp. 235-7. New York: McGraw-Hill Book Co., Inc., 1938. Pp. xviii, 316. $3.00. (London: McGraw-Hill Publishing Co., Ltd. 18s.)
14 TIFFIN, JOSEPH, AND GREENLY, R. J. "Employee Selection Tests for Electrical Fixture Assemblers and Radio Assemblers." *J Appl Psychol* 23:240-63 Ap '39.
15 BLUM, MILTON L. "A Contribution to Manual Aptitude Measurement in Industry: The Value of Certain Dexterity Measures for the Selection of Workers in a Watch Factory." *J Appl Psychol* 24:381-416 Ag '40.

Morris S. Viteles, Associate Professor of Psychology, and Albert S. Thompson, Instructor of Psychology, The University of Pennsylvania. The *Finger Dexterity Test*, one of the so-called worksamples developed by O'Connor, is so well known that it need not be described here. Since about 1925 it has had a prominent place in programs of industrial selection and vocational guidance.

Despite its wide use, relatively little was known about the reliability and validity of the test until recent years. Early references to the test by O'Connor [2] were divided between vague generalizations and categorical statements. Claims were made as to its value in forecasting industrial success in various occupations without adequate supporting data.

During recent years considerable data in the way of norms and of information on reliability and validity have been made available. These suggest that the test can be of service as an instrument in forecasting achievement in certain occupations. Bingham [8] reports differential norms for six manual occupations. The University of Minnesota Employment Stabilization Research Institute [5, 6, 7] has provided norms for an adult population and has used the test in developing occupational ability patterns. Independent studies [3, 10, 14] have shown the *Finger Dexterity Test* to be useful in the selecting of competent women shopworkers, watchmakers, and workers for various assembly jobs.

Although evidence is available to show that the test can be useful, the practitioner is handicapped by the absence of a satisfactory manual which brings into usable form the data which has accumulated over the past 10 years. Technical Report No. 16,[12] published in 1938 by the Human Engineering Laboratory of Stevens Institute of Technology, might have been expected to satisfy this need. Instead, in accordance with O'Connor's usual practice, this report is characterized by a complete disregard of the really significant work done outside the Laboratory. Its 138 mimeographed pages present a mass of improvement curves, age factors, and norms based on small age-group populations. No data on reliability are given and a few generalizations on validity are provided in a short paragraph, referring back to O'Connor's 1928 *Born That Way* and to a study of graduate nurses for further information. The chief value of the report is perhaps

in the presentation of tentative age norms—although the narrow range of differences between the ages of 14 and 19 make them of somewhat doubtful value in everyday practice.

Despite all these limitations, the test should receive the attention of the practicing psychologist. The Minnesota norms were carefully obtained; Bingham presents a few occupational norms; independent studies have shown that the test has an acceptable degree of validity for certain jobs involving rapid manipulation of small objects, etc. If information were assembled in convenient and standard form by a competent psychologist and critically presented, the usefulness of the *Finger Dexterity Test* as an experimental and practical instrument could be considerably increased.

[1659.1]

Guidance Questionnaire. High school; 1937; 1 form; 50¢ per 25; $1.25 per 100; 5¢ per specimen set; nontimed (25) minutes; Anthony J. Scholter; Milwaukee, Wis.: Department of Education, Archdiocese of Milwaukee.

[1660]

Individual Guidance Record. Grades 9-12; 1940; 8¢ per copy; H. D. Richardson; Chicago, Ill.: Science Research Associates.

REFERENCES

1 RICHARDSON, H. D. *Analytical Devices in Guidance and Counseling.* Basic Occupational Plans, No. 3. Chicago, Ill.: Science Research Associates, 1940. Pp. 63. $1.00. Paper, lithotyped.

[1661]

Kefauver-Hand Guidance Tests and Inventories. Grades 7-14; 1937; 8 parts; 50¢ per 25 student profile charts; 15¢ per manual; nontimed; Grayson N. Kefauver, Harold C. Hand, Virginia Lee Block, and William M. Proctor; Yonkers, N. Y.: World Book Co.
a) EDUCATIONAL GUIDANCE TEST. 1 form; $1.20 per 25 tests; 15¢ per specimen set; (30) minutes.
b) HEALTH GUIDANCE TEST. 1 form; $1 per 25 tests; 10¢ per specimen set; (25) minutes.
c) INVENTORY OF STUDENT PLANS. 1 form; $1.30 per 25 inventories; 5¢ per specimen set; (30) minutes.
d) INVENTORY OF STUDENT SELF-RATINGS. 1 form; $1.20 per 25 inventories; 5¢ per specimen set; (30) minutes.
e) RECREATIONAL GUIDANCE TEST. 1 form; $1 per 25 tests; 10¢ per specimen set; (25) minutes.
f) SOCIAL-CIVIC GUIDANCE TEST. 1 form; $1.20 per 25 tests; 15¢ per specimen set; (25) minutes.
g) STUDENT-JUDGMENT GUIDANCE TEST. 1 form; $1 per 25 tests; 10¢ per specimen set; (25) minutes.
h) VOCATIONAL GUIDANCE TEST. 1 form; $1 per 25 tests; 10¢ per specimen set; (25) minutes.

E. G. Williamson, Coordinator of Student Personnel Services and Associate Professor of Psychology, The University of Minnesota. This battery of six tests and two inventories may be used with students in grades 7 through 14. The Educational Guidance Test consists of selected questions concerning the purposes of secondary education and of specific courses;

the student's judgment of the relative difficulty of specific subjects; the student's knowledge of the specific courses offered in his own school. The latter two sections must be scored by means of a scoring key developed locally for each school; presumably the local teacher's judgment will determine the correct answers to questions about the relative difficulty of local courses, a characteristic of inventories and questionnaires rather than of standardized tests. The Health Guidance Test measures information of the importance of factors involved in physical and mental health. The Recreational Guidance Test includes questions on the importance and values of recreation and the facilities available in the local communities. The Social-Civic Guidance Test inventories the student's knowledge of general socio-economic conditions, the student's judgment of the importance of citizenship conditions in the local school and judgment of the number of "citizens" who "would have their well-being favorably affected (directly or indirectly) by each of the types of social action." The Vocational Guidance Test samples the student's knowledge of occupational trends, employment statistics and the duties of workers in a small number of occupations. The Student-Judgment Guidance Test contains questions on methods of character analysis and advertisements of proprietary training courses to be judged false or true. In each test, except the Educational Guidance Test, students are asked to indicate whom they should interview to secure assistance or information concerning a number of questions or problems.

The Inventory of Student Plans requires that the student name and give reasons for the selection of each school subject, the curriculum, extracurricular activities and his plans for future training beyond high school, his occupational choice and reasons for that choice, recreational and social-civic activities and plans for establishing a home. The Inventory of Student Self-Ratings requires that the student record his estimate of his capabilities in various subjects and activities and the extent to which he has learned to enjoy certain activities, his estimate of abilities to succeed in certain occupations and his physical disabilities.

Items and questions in both the tests and the inventories have been carefully selected by means of criticisms and judgments of guidance workers and by actual tryout in a number of

survey-investigations. All items were selected in line with the definitive objectives of guidance activities. Questions in the six tests were subjected to item analysis to determine their differentiating values in terms of the total score. The test-retest (Form A vs. B) reliability coefficients for the six tests range from .77 to .89. The two forms have been equated. Although the manual states that a second form would be published in 1937, only one form is available at this time (fall, 1939).

The authors recommend that total raw scores be converted into percentages of the total possible scores. No norms are reported because the authors contend that local guidance workers might uncritically accept these norms as standards and because no one knows what score should be attained. As a matter of fact, all types of test norms could be misused in a similar manner. One wonders if the authors' investigations revealed such low standards of guidance activities as to make this danger of misuse of norms a special condition in this area of education.

These instruments make possible the collection of more or less objective data with which to identify the outcomes or effectiveness of the school's guidance activities. The authors advocate that the tests and inventories be given before and after the instituting of new types of guidance services. Such instruments are of self-evident importance in any serious attempt to evaluate objectively a guidance program and its many specific phases. It is to be hoped that these instruments will be used to determine whether widely used methods and techniques actually do produce the desirable effects claimed by many guidance workers. Specifically, experiments are needed to determine the outcomes of counseling, homerooms, extracurricular activities, and group guidance courses. Experiments are also needed to determine if these tests and inventories sample all of the important outcomes of guidance activities.

For reviews by Harold D. Carter, Gwendolen Schneidler, and M. R. Trabue, see 1170.

[1662]

Minnesota Rate of Manipulation Test. For selecting office and shop workers; 1933; a revision of the *Minnesota Manual Dexterity Test;* individual; $7.75 per testing outfit; worklimit (10-15) minutes; W. A. Ziegler; Minneapolis, Minn.: Educational Test Bureau, Inc. (*Minnesota Manual Dexterity Test*: $11;

Minneapolis, Minn.: Mechanical Engineering Department, University of Minnesota.)

REFERENCES

1 BERGEN, GARRET L. *Use of Tests in the Adjustment Service*, p. 47. Adjustment Service Series Report [No.] 4. New York: American Association for Adult Education, 1935. Pp. 70. Paper. Out of print.

2 GREEN, HELEN J., AND BERMAN, ISABEL R.; under the direction of Donald G. Paterson and M. R. Trabue. *A Manual of Selected Occupational Tests for Use in Public Employment Offices*, pp. 5-7, 10-11, 23-31. University of Minnesota, Bulletins of the Employment Stabilization Research Institute, Vol. 2, No. 3. Minneapolis, Minn.: University of Minnesota Press, July, 1936. Pp. 31. $0.50. Paper.

3 BINGHAM, WALTER VAN DYKE. *Aptitudes and Aptitude Testing*, pp. 278-81. New York and London: Harper & Brothers, 1937. Pp. ix, 390. $3.00; 10s. 6d.

4 PATERSON, DONALD G.; SCHNEIDLER, GWENDOLEN, G.; AND WILLIAMSON, EDMUND G. *Student Guidance Technique*, pp. 240-2. New York: McGraw-Hill Book Co., Inc., 1938. Pp. xviii, 316. $3.00. (London: McGraw-Hill Publishing Co., Ltd. 18s.)

Lorene Teegarden, Psychological Examiner, Public Schools, Cincinnati, Ohio. This test is intended to measure rapidity of movement in working with the hands and fingers. The long narrow board contains 60 holes in four rows of 15 each, into which fit 60 cylindrical blocks with one-sixteenth inch clearance. The test includes two parts, Placing and Turning, which are separate tests.

In Placing, the blocks are placed into the holes as rapidly as possible, following a definite procedure, and using one hand. The procedure is simple, and is readily learned in the first or practice trial. The score is a rating based upon the total time required for the second, third, fourth, and fifth trials. This is a measure of rapidity of movements involving the hand and arm, and not dependent upon co-ordination of the two hands working together, nor upon very delicate neuromuscular control.

Turning, the second test, measures rapidity and dexterity in manipulations requiring two-hand co-ordination. The board is presented with the blocks in place, and the subject picks up each block with one hand, turns the block over, and replaces with the other hand. With each change of rows the movement changes in direction, and the hands exchange functions. The first trial is used for practice, and the score is based upon time for the next four trials. Norms are given for adults, based upon the records of more than 5,000 employed workers. No appreciable sex difference is indicated. Time scores may be interpreted as a "percentile rank" (estimated from Z-scores) or as "per cent placement," (i.e., transmuted scores having a mean of 50 and a standard deviation of 10) in a ten quartile range.

Both parts of the test are useful for rating workers for routine manipulative operations.

Mean scores made by groups of packers, wrappers, and cartoners are reported to be distinctly above the median for the general population. For jobs requiring attention to numerous and varying details, it should be supplemented by some test, such as the *Minnesota Spatial Relations Test*, which involves reaction to observed details. For jobs requiring exact movements in the placing of small parts, it should be supplemented by some test of finger, tweezer, or plier dexterity. Few tests give so clear a picture of two-hand co-ordination as does the second part of the *Minnesota Rate of Manipulation Test*.

Morris S. Viteles, Associate Professor of Psychology, and Albert S. Thompson, Instructor in Psychology, The University of Pennsylvania. This test was devised by W. A. Ziegler to measure speed of rather gross movements of hand and fingers, of the kind frequently employed in occupational tasks calling for rapid manipulation of tools and materials. In its present form the *Minnesota Rate of Manipulation Test* is composed of a board containing 60 circular holes into which 60 slightly smaller circular blocks can be placed.

Two test situations are presented with the one board: (a) a "placing test," in which the blocks are transferred with one hand from a pre-positioned place on the table to their appropriate recesses in a set order; and (b) a "turning test," in which the blocks are lifted out of their holes, turned over by a two-handed operation, and replaced in the same holes. The "placing test," according to Ziegler, measures speed of hand manipulation; the "turning test" measures speed of finger manipulation, and a "speed index" is obtained by averaging the ratings on the two tests. Five trials of each test are given. The first trial is considered as a practice trial. The score is the sum of the times taken for the four test trials. About 20 minutes are required to administer the test.[2]

The test, in its present form, is a modification of the original *Minnesota Manual Dexterity Test* developed by Ziegler for the University of Minnesota Employment Stabilization Research Institute in order to determine "how much of the time required for the Minnesota Spatial Relations Test is consumed in the mere movement of the blocks."[2] In the original test 58 blocks and holes were provided. Only 4 trials were given and the score was the sum of all four trials. In addition to increasing the number of blocks to 60, Ziegler has made the instructions more specific, has increased the number of trials to 5, and has introduced an incentive by telling the subject the time for each trial. These modifications seem designed to increase the reliability of the test, which has been standardized on 2,000 adults engaged in a wide variety of occupations, tested by the University of Minnesota Employment Stabilization Institute during 1931 and 1932.

Just how reliable the revised test actually is, is not clear from the data supplied by the author in the manual accompanying the test. As a matter of fact, the entire treatment of "standards and interpretation" is confused by the assignment of unconventional and even novel meanings to everyday statistical concepts. So, for example, after wading through an involved discussion of "10 quartile ranges" and "per cent placements," the reader finally realizes that the latter represent "scores" obtained by transmuting raw scores to a scale with a mean of 50 and a probable error of 10 and a total range of ± 5PE's. The per cent placement score is obtained, however, by a counting process that makes no allowance for the skewness of the distribution which, in fact, appears, from inspection, to be a factor worthy of consideration in the case of the "turning test."

Data on the validity of the test are scarce. The Minnesota norms apply only to the original board and method of scoring.[2] Bingham presents occupational norms but these are also based on the original board, but with a different method of scoring.[3] Ziegler presents a table showing the range and median of speed indexes for 5 occupational groups including respectively 12 office workers; 60 package wrappers; 12 packet stuffers; 32 small parts factory assemblers, and 123 typing and stenographic students. In every case the mean is considerably higher than for the entire population and the range is within that of the better 50 per cent of adults. However, further analysis of the data is needed.

The test seems to have a fairly wide use in clinical practice. To the reviewers it appears to represent material for further experimental evaluation in specific selection and guidance situations.

[1663]

Minnesota Spatial Relations Test. Ages 11 and over; 1930; a revision of H. C. Link's *Spatial Relations Test*; 1 form; individual; $38 per testing outfit; worklimit (15-45) minutes; Donald G. Paterson,

Richard M. Elliott, L. Dewey Anderson, Herbert A. Toops, and Edna Heidbreder; Marietta, Ohio: Marietta Apparatus Co.

REFERENCES

1 ANDERSON, L. DEWEY. "The Minnesota Mechanical Ability Tests." *Personnel J* 6:473-8 Ap '28.
2 PATERSON, DONALD G.; ELLIOTT, RICHARD M.; ANDERSON, L. DEWEY; TOOPS, HERBERT A.; AND HEIDBREDER, EDNA. *Minnesota Mechanical Ability Tests*: The Report of a Research Investigation Subsidized by the Committee on Human Migrations of the National Research Council and Conducted in the Department of the University of Minnesota, pp. 59-61, 73-93, 109, 141, 204-19, 229-33, 235, 238-44, 250-4, 271-83, 291, 311-2, 339-45, 431-3, 461-6, 508-10, 531-2. Minneapolis, Minn.: University of Minnesota Press, 1930. Pp. xxii, 586. $5.00.
3 SCHIEFFELIN, BARBARA, AND SCHWESINGER, GLADYS C. *Mental Tests and Heredity*: Including a Survey of Non-Verbal Tests, pp. 216-7. New York: Galton Publishing Co., Inc. 1930. Pp. ix, 298. Out of print.
4 HARVEY, O. L. "Mechanical 'Aptitude' or Mechanical 'Ability'? A Study in Method." *J Ed Psychol* 22:517-22 O '31.
5 BERGEN, GARRET L. *Use of Tests in the Adjustment Service*, pp. 49-50. Adjustment Service Series Report [No.] 4. New York: American Association for Adult Education, 1935. Pp. 70. Paper. Out of print.
6 DVORAK, BEATRICE JEANNE. *Differential Occupational Ability Patterns*. Publications of the Employment Stabilization Research Institute, University of Minnesota, Vol. 3, No. 8. Minneapolis, Minn.: University of Minnesota Press, February 1935. Pp. 46. $1.00. Paper.
7 GREEN, HELEN J., AND BERMAN, ISABEL R.; under the direction of Donald G. Paterson and M. R. Trabue. *A Manual of Selected Occupational Tests for Use in Public Employment Offices*, pp. 5-7, 17-19, 23-31. University of Minnesota, Bulletins of the Employment Stabilization Research Institute, Vol. 2, No. 3. Minneapolis, Minn.: University of Minnesota Press, July, 1936. Pp. 31. $0.50. Paper.
8 BINGHAM, WALTER VAN DYKE. *Aptitudes and Aptitude Testing*, pp. 309-11. New York and London: Harper & Brothers, 1937. Pp. ix, 390. $3.00; 10s. 6d.
9 BROWN, FRED. "Selective Tests for Dental School Candidates." *Oral Hyg* 27:1172-7 S '37.
10 PATERSON, DONALD G.; SCHNEIDLER, GWENDOLEN G.; AND WILLIAMSON, EDMUND G. *Student Guidance Techniques*, pp. 225-7. New York: McGraw-Hill Book Co., Inc., 1938. Pp. xviii, 316. $3.00. (London: McGraw-Hill Publishing Co., Ltd. 18s.)

Lorene Teegarden, Psychological Examiner, Public Schools, Cincinnati, Ohio. This test was developed by the Employment Stabilization Research Institute of the University of Minnesota, from an earlier formboard devised by H. C. Link. It consists of a series of four boards, each with 58 holes of different shapes, into which 58 blocks are to be fitted. For the first two boards, A and B, the same blocks are used, the arrangement and spatial orientation being different in B from what it is in A, so that details of form and position must be observed anew in Board B. The last two boards, C and D, use a second set of blocks, slightly more difficult to discriminate and place than the first set. The time required is from 15 to 25 minutes.

The score is a percentile rank or standard score rating based upon the total time required for completion of B, C, and D, Board A being used as an introduction. This method is recommended as giving the highest reliability and being the most effective for individual diagnosis. There are separate norms for men and women based upon this method of scoring. Additional published norms include age norms for boys for each pair of boards and for the four boards combined; and grade norms for boys in grades 7 to 12, and for university groups. Reliability is quoted as .81 for boys, .91 for men, and .89 for women. Mean scores made by groups of workers in a number of different occupations are also given, including commercial, clerical, mechanical, and other occupations. The evidence given indicates a tendency to superior scores in mechanical occupations.

This test measures speed and accuracy in reacting to details of spatial relations. It gives a measure of the ability to work with a variety of details in handling things and materials. Since the score is influenced somewhat by rapidity of movement, it is important that the performance be so motivated as to secure the best possible interest, concentration, and effort, as indifference or distraction may appreciably increase the time and reduce the rating.

As a tryout for jobs requiring resourcefulness in solving problems of a mechanical nature it is probably surpassed by the Kent-Shakow or some other formboard which involves a series of graded problems. For jobs requiring the handling of small parts, or placement with great exactness, it should be supplemented by some test requiring fine neuromuscular control.

[1664]

Minnesota Vocational Test for Clerical Workers. Ages 17 and over for women and ages 19 and over for men; 1933-38; 1 form; $3 per 100; 25¢ per specimen set; 15(20) minutes; Dorothy M. Andrew under the direction of Donald G. Paterson and Howard P. Longstaff; New York: Psychological Corporation.

REFERENCES

1 POND, MILLICENT. "What Is New in Employment Testing." *Personnel J* 11:10-6 Je '32.
2 ANDREW, DOROTHY M., under the direction of Donald G. Paterson. *Measured Characteristics of Clerical Workers.* University of Minnesota Bulletins of the Employment Stabilization Research Institute, Vol. 3, No. 1. Minneapolis, Minn.: University of Minnesota Press, July 1934. Pp. 60. $1.00. Paper.
3 ANDREW, D. M. *"An Analysis of the Minnesota Vocational Test for Clerical Workers."* Unpublished doctor's thesis, University of Minnesota, 1935.
4 BERGEN, GARRET L. *Use of Tests in the Adjustment Service,* pp. 43-4. Adjustment Service Series Report [No.] 4. New York: American Association for Adult Education, 1935. Pp. 70. Paper. Out of print.
5 DODGE, ARTHUR F. *Occupational Ability Patterns.* Columbia University, Teachers College, Contributions to Education, No. 658. Harry Dexter Kitson, faculty sponsor. New York: Bureau of Publications, the College, 1935. Pp. v, 97. $1.60.
6 DVORAK, BEATRICE JEANNE. *Differential Occupational Ability Patterns.* Publications of the Employment Stabilization Research Institute, University of Minnesota, Vol. 3, No. 8. Minneapolis, Minn.: University of Minnesota Press, February 1935. Pp. 46. $1.00. Paper.
7 COPELAND, HERMAN A. "Some Characteristics of Three Tests Used to Predict Clerical Success." *J Appl Psychol* 20:461-70 Ag '36.
8 GREEN, HELEN J., AND BERMAN, ISABEL R.; under the direction of Donald G. Paterson and M. R. Trabue. *A Manual of Selected Occupational Tests for Use in Public Employment Offices,* pp. 5-9, 23-31. University of Minnesota, Bulletins of the Employment Stabilization Research Institute, Vol. 2, No. 3. Minneapolis, Minn.: University of Minnesota Press, July 1936. Pp. 31. $0.50. Paper.
9 ANDREW, DOROTHY M. "An Analysis of the Minnesota Vocational Test for Clerical Workers." *J Appl Psychol* 21:18-47, 139-72 F, Ap '37.
10 BINGHAM, WALTER VAN DYKE. *Aptitudes and Aptitude Testing,* pp. 322-7. New York and London: Harper & Brothers, 1937. Pp. ix, 390. $3.00; 10s. 6d.
11 CANDEE, BEATRICE, AND BLUM, MILTON. "A New Scoring System for the Minnesota Clerical Test." *Psychol B* 34:545 O '37.
12 COPELAND, HERMAN A. "Validating Two Tests for Census Enumeration." *J Appl Psychol* 21:230-2 Ap '37.
13 DAVIDSON, CHARLES M. "Analysis of Clerical Tests." *Personnel J* 16:95-8 S '37.
14 DAVIDSON, CHARLES M. "Evaluation of Clerical Tests." *Personnel J* 16:57-64 Je '37.
15 HALES, W. M. "Clerical Tests in State Reformatory." *Personnel J* 16:316-24 Ap '38.
16 PATERSON, DONALD G.; SCHNEIDLER, GWENDOLEN G.; AND WILLIAMSON, EDMUND G. *Student Guidance Techniques,* pp. 206-9. New York: McGraw-Hill Book Co., Inc., 1938. Pp. xviii, 316. $3.00. (London: McGraw-Hill Publishing Co., Ltd. 18s.)
17 DUDYCHA, GEORGE J. "Dependability and Clerical Aptitude." *J Appl Psychol* 23:332-6 Je '39.
18 BARNETTE, W. LESLIE. "Norms of Business College Students on Standardized Tests: Intelligence, Clerical Ability, English." *J Appl Psychol* 24:237-44 Ap '40.

W. D. Commins, Assistant Professor of Psychology, The Catholic University of America. The present test is accompanied by an illuminating manual containing many items relevant to the validity of the test, something that is sure to be appreciated by those interested in tests. There are data on the relation of test results to ratings, grades in accounting, speed of typing, employed vs. unemployed clerical workers, classes of clerical workers, future success, other clerical tests, age, sex, experience and training, formal education, intelligence, and speed of reading. Because of the generally favorable nature of this summary, as well as the convenience of having it at hand, one is impressed favorably by the test at the start. Correlations with intelligence, formal education, and experience and training are in general low, which offers considerable justification for the authors' claim that the test measures "an aptitude which is related positively to the abilities to discriminate small differences rapidly, to observe and compare, to adjust to a new situation, and to give attention to a problem." These, of course, are to be interpreted, for want of further evidence, in relation to the tasks imposed by the test, viz., number checking and name checking. Name checking correlates with speed of reading .45, and with spelling .65. Number checking correlates with verifying arithmetical computations .51. From an academic point of view, these results may be confusing if we think of the possible "uniqueness" of the test or the ability underlying it. It is just possible that we should not need a "clerical" test if we could identify the various mental "factors" in terms of certain fundamental operations. But until the day arrives when we can feel sure of our mental analysis, there will be a need of certain "on-the-job" specific tests which will have their justification in the practical selection of employees and promising workers. The present test ought to give considerable satisfaction in this respect, particularly because of its simple construction and relative ease of scoring. One might expect, however, that a more varied test, touching upon more aspects of clerical work, would ultimately be more satisfactory, although we do not now have adequate scientific data that such would be the case.

[1665]

N.I.I.P. Clerical Test: American Revision. Ages 16 and over; 1934; 1 form; $5 per 100; 25¢ per specimen set; (30) minutes; a revision of the *National Institute of Industrial Psychology Clerical Test, Series* 25; revision by Herbert Moore; New York: Psychological Corporation.

REFERENCES

1 MOORE, HERBERT. "The Institute's Clerical Test in America." *Human Factor* 7:407-9 N '33.
2 MOORE, HERBERT. "The Institute's Clerical Test in the Westinghouse Electric Company." *Human Factor* 10:221-4 Je '36.

Donald G. Paterson, Professor of Psychology, The University of Minnesota. This clerical test is printed in an 8-page booklet and consists of seven subtests as follows: Test I, Following oral instructions, seven statements with two questions each; Test II, Classification, each of 40 miscellaneous items is to be checked with reference to which of six categories of expense it is chargeable; Test III, Arithmetic, six simple addition problems and three problems each involving subtraction, multiplication, and division; Test IV, Copying 20 names and symbols; Test V, Checking names and numbers indicating in the case of each of 48 pairs of names and numbers whether the two members of a pair are the same or different; Test VI, Filing, two parts, one involving the arrangement of 17 numbers in increasing size, the other involving the arrangement of 17 names in alphabetical order; Test VII, Problems, 12 problems involving reasoning, number series completion, following printed directions, etc. Speed is emphasized in the general directions. The test can be administered in 30 minutes and corrected in 5. Only one form of the test is provided. It is designed for use with people whose academic training his reached the college level although norms are also provided for high school seniors.

Decile norms are provided for an unspecified number of high school seniors and college seniors and the median score for these two groups is given for each subtest. No norms for employed clerical workers are provided. Data regarding reliability are absent and little evidence bearing on validity is given. The correlation between intelligence and this test as a whole or the subtests is not given. The interrelation of the subtests is not given. There is a statement that secretarial workers would do well on all parts of the test whereas routine office workers would make a poor score on Tests I and VII and occasionally on Test V. Test V is mentioned as being of value in selecting persons for work involving close attention.

Neither the printed test nor the poorly mimeographed manual of directions mentions the publisher or distributor or cost. No references are given.

Judging solely on the basis of the test itself and the inadequate manual of directions, one is forced to suspend judgment as to the value of this test. Presumably, the present test is an experimental edition not intended for practical use in guidance and employment work, otherwise the author would supply sufficient information and data to permit a prospective consumer to judge its value for a given purpose.

[1665.1]

Occupational Analysis Form. For use with "Your Life Work Film" produced by Vocational Films, Inc., Des Moines, Iowa; 1940; 1 form; 50¢ per 25; Arthur P. Twogood; Bloomington, Ill.: McKnight & McKnight.

[1666]

Occupational Interest Blank. Boys of high school age; [1937]; 1 form; 75¢ per 25; 15¢ per specimen set; nontimed (10) minutes; Bruce V. Le Suer; New York: Psychological Corporation.

Stanley G. Dulsky, Chief Psychologist, Rochester Guidance Center, Rochester, New York. This is a one-page inventory consisting of 100 occupations to each of which the subject responds by circling *like, indifferent,* or *dislike.* The occupations are classified in ten groups: professional, technical, clerical, mercantile and sales, artistic or creative, skilled trades, semi-skilled occupations, adventuresome occupations, personal service, and agricultural occupations. There are ten occupations in each of the ten groups. A quick scoring method enables the user of the blank to determine the number of likes for each of the ten groups.

With respect to interpretation, the manual states: "No set rules can be given for the interpretation of scores. The information gained from the *Occupational Interest Blank* should be used to supplement information secured from other sources. The reactions to the individual items, and the summary of the responses should be examined critically and used as the basis for further discussion."

The question of paramount importance to a vocational counselor is: Can I do a more effective job of counseling by administering this blank to the counselee? The five-page manual accompanying the blank does not answer this question; in the reviewer's opinion the answer is a dubious "perhaps." The most serious objection to Le Suer's blank is a general one applying to all occupational interest blanks: Of what value is a response to the name of an occupation if the actual activities involved in pursuing that occupation are completely or partially unknown to the subject? The response is usually made on the basis of factors which the counselor can neither determine nor evaluate.

Comments specific to this occupational interest blank are:

(a) Three categories—like, indifferent, and dislike—are too few for anything but the crudest distinctions. A five-step scale might be better.

(b) Of what value is an occupation classification based mainly on census reports? Such a classification has no psychological basis. Why not a psychological classification of occupations for psychologists? Why consider a physician in the same category with a lawyer merely because both medicine and law are called professions? Aren't the psychological requirements and duties of a chauffeur (personal service occupation) more similar to those of a truck driver (semiskilled occupation) than to those of a barber (also personal service)?

(c) "The blank may be used without scoring, just as any similar form is used, but scoring increases its effectiveness by revealing the general trend of an individual's vocational interests as well as his specific job preferences." I disagree with the author. Because of the census classification employed, I believe one will learn more by merely inspecting the blank than by scoring it because scoring might easily mask important similarities. Circling "like" for occupations of chauffeur, machinist, auto mechanic, lathe hand, truck driver, and welder is important even though it represents three occupational groups. Certainly, those occupations have more in common than chauffeur, barber, bellboy, and soda dispenser (all classified as personal service).

The author states that information from this blank should supplement information obtained from other sources. I would caution that information from this blank should never be used without a thorough discussion of it in a vocational interview. Finally, is the expenditure of money, time, and effort justified by the results secured from this blank? To this question I would reply: The author has given us no evidence that it is.

J. B. Miner, Professor of Psychology and Director of the Personnel Bureau, University of Kentucky. A boy of high school age checks L, I, or D through a list of 100 occupations and jobs. A comparison of the number of likes out of ten jobs in each of ten groups is assumed to indicate relative preferences for fields of work such as professional, clerical, skilled trades, etc. The blank might be of some use to introduce an interview, but the attempt to quantify the results is unfortunate and misleading. With so small a number as ten choices in a group, the difference between checking three or checking seven out of ten would not be statistically significant since the checks might differ this much if made and controlled by chance alone. The instructions for interpretation attempt to guard against misuse by a counselor who does not understand the fact that neither reliability nor validity of the scores is known. The author has used the blank to discover instances for interviews when a boy's choice of course in school seems to be out of line with a pronounced record as to his field of interest.

For reviews by W. V. Bingham and M. R. Trabue, see 1174.

[1667]
Occupational Orientation Inquiry. Grades 12-16; 1939; 1 form; $1.00 per 25; 15¢ per specimen set; nontimed (40-80) minutes; G. A. Wallar and S. L. Pressey; New York: Psychological Corporation.

REFERENCES

1 WALLAR, GENE A. "The Occupational Orientation Inquiry." *Sch and Soc* 46:507-10 O 16 '37.

John Gray Peatman, Assistant Professor of Psychology, The College of the City of New York. This inquiry is chiefly useful as a systematic aid in getting from a student a good deal of relevant information for vocational guidance purposes prior to the actual vocational counseling interview. On the first page, of the 4-page blank, the student is asked to review his vocational interests and experiences. Then on the two inside pages, two hundred and twenty-four occupations are listed in alphabetical order and self-estimates are asked for each—the student indicating his relative degree (on a 5-point scale) of knowledge, interest, ability, and opportunity for placement. Finally, on the back page, the student is asked to evaluate his vocational problems in the light of the preceding considerations. In the hands of a competent counselor, this inquiry should prove useful. Its chief improvement over most other occupational inventories is its use of the four categories of knowledge, interest, ability, and opportunity for each job self-estimate. The authors emphasize the value of the inquiry as a qualitative rather than a quantitative instrument. It is unfortunate that they do not confine themselves to this and forego the unhappy custom of citing as "first norms" data which have little or no normative value. The data they present will certainly be misleading to some and misused by others, and they are of practically no use to the competent counselor.

The table of so-called norms gives decile values for three groups of men and women students whom we are told are high school seniors, college freshmen, or college seniors. That is all we learn about their background except that the suggestion is made that the college groups resided in several sections of the country—"to insure against provinciality." The decile values are calculated for distributions of the *number* of jobs or occupations receiving a self-rating of "much" (4 points) or "above average" (3 points). At least the distributions for knowledge, interest, ability, and opportunity are presented separately which is more than can be said of a second table of data presented in the mimeographed manual of directions. In this second table, the authors present four lists of 20 occupations "ranking highest according to the sum of *total* ratings by (*a*) men and (*b*) women freshmen in (1) the science division of a technical college and (2) the college of education in a large university." These results are presented as a matter of "interest" in "showing the occupations rated highest by 400 freshmen in a college of education and by 200 freshmen in a science division of a technical college." Unfortunately, however, these results are *totally* ambiguous inasmuch as they are based on a summation of all four types of self-estimates, i.e., knowledge, inter-

est, ability, and opportunity are all thrown together. This hodgepodge of four very different kinds of self-estimates presents some results, especially among the men students, which at first glance are startling. Thus, for the men's technical college group, the occupations of gas station attendant, grocer, truck driver, and life guard rank 5th, 7th, 10th, and 17th respectively. And for the men's college of education group, grocer follows teacher and athletic director as the third highest ranking occupation in the group, with gas station attendant reduced to 10th position and truck driver to 16th. Since it is impossible to disentangle knowledge, interest, ability, and opportunity self-estimates from this ambiguous mass, the uselessness of this table of data should be apparent.

On the other hand, provided the inquiry will be found to have adequate reliability and functional value when used with groups of students, both tables of data indicate a possible usefulness of the inquiry in group surveys. Thus, it may be found to be helpful in ascertaining the occupational orientation of various kinds of groups, in terms of their own self-estimates of knowledge, ability, interest, and opportunities. But as for *norms*—why even try to simulate them for an instrument of this type?

The fact remains that this kind of instrument has its chief value in counseling as a systematic, timesaving device for getting information relevant to the particular student's vocational problems. As the authors themselves state—before giving way to a consideration of "norms"—"Interpretation of the scores on the *Occupational Orientation Inquiry* must ultimately be based on intensive study of the entire blank and is thus qualitative and largely an individual matter."

C. *Gilbert Wrenn, Professor of Educational Psychology, The University of Minnesota.* This 4-page blank is an aid to the interview and not a test or even a weighted inventory. This the authors wish to make very clear. The first page calls for a brief vocational history and the last page calls for the student's subjective analysis of what he considers to be his best occupational field. These two pages comprise something of an occupational autobiography. The two inside pages are taken up with columns of 224 occupations, opposite each of which the student is supposed to place his judgment as to his knowledge, interest, ability, and the opportunity for placement. The form of these inside pages looks somewhat complicated to the reviewer since each of these four ratings carry four possible steps, and it is necessary for the student to go back in his reading to the key at the top of the page until he has at least memorized the four steps under the four ratings. The blank makes a contribution in questioning the student on his opinion of his "knowledge" of each of these occupations and "the opportunity for placement" in addition to the ordinarily requested reactions on interest and ability.

If used by the counselor and not by the student, this blank can be helpful. Its real danger lies in the fact that the student may take his own judgment as prima facie evidence. The basic concept is that of self-analysis although the authors hope this will always be followed by counselor judgment and reaction. It is more specific in nature than Achilles' *Aids to the Vocational Interview* (*see* 493) although following the same general form of the provision of ideas suggested by the student that can be used in counseling with him. It may or may not be more helpful than the *Kefauver-Hand Guidance Tests and Inventories*, although subject to the same emphasis on self-analysis. The fault does not lie in the authors' concept of the use of such instruments, but in the student's unconscious or conscious assumption that what he thinks about himself is correct. It should be helpful to a counselor to know of what occupations the student thinks he has knowledge, opportunity for placement, ability, and interest, for this may provide the very point at which counseling begins, namely, the correction of false assumptions.

The total scores on such a blank as this are probably meaningless, for a summation of checks of unknown validity does not produce a score that has very much meaning. The reviewer does not see, therefore, much value in the percentile norms that are tentatively suggested. The blanks may, on the other hand, be of real value to a counselor as a basis for interviewing and as a technique for stimulating the student to think along certain specific vocational lines. It is built for and has been tried out with college students. The opportunity given for a statement and an evaluation of vocational history, when made in connection with a student's consideration of 224 specific occupations, may be the most valuable part of the blank.

[1668]

O'Rourke Mechanical Aptitude Test: Junior Grade. Grades 7-12; 1926-39; 3 forms; 5¢ per test; 10¢ per specimen set; 61(70) minutes; L. J. O'Rourke; Washington, D. C.: Psychological Institute.

REFERENCES

1 BINGHAM, WALTER VAN DYKE. *Aptitudes and Aptitude Testing*, pp. 318-20. New York and London: Harper & Brothers, 1937. Pp. ix, 390. $3.00; 10s. 6d.

Herbert A. Landry, Research Assistant, Bureau of Reference, Research and Statistics, Public Schools, New York, New York. This is essentially a test of mechanical information. The justification for its use as a measure of mechanical aptitude undoubtedly rests on the hypothesis that the amount of mechanical information possessed by an individual is an indirect measure of his interest in the realm of mechanical things. This interest is assumed to arise from the existence of mechanical aptitude. While it seems reasonable to believe that these assumptions are sound, conclusive proof has not been demonstrated.

It must be remembered that such inferential measurements rest upon the assumption that all individuals so measured have been subjected to uniformly operating environmental factors. It can be readily shown that this is not true. Variations of opportunity for contact with mechanical things are exceedingly marked. Any scores obtained, therefore, must be carefully interpreted in the light of the individual's opportunities and experience.

In presenting data concerning the validity of the tests, the author cites relationships obtained between test scores and shop ratings. While the exact nature of these ratings is not stated, it is assumed that they are either the periodic or end marks or ranks given by instructors since these are the most commonly used criteria. The coefficients of correlation obtained range from .64 to .84. From the limited data given, it would appear that the test can predict achievement in the types of courses mentioned with reasonable success.

Unlike the other pencil-and-paper tests of mechanical aptitude, this test limits itself to the measurement of a narrow sector of the total of these elements that constitute mechanical aptitude. For instance the *MacQuarrie Test for Mechanical Ability*, the *Detroit Mechanical Aptitudes Examinations*, and the tests devised by Cox, all seek to measure on a broader base. They include tests designed to measure power of visualization, ability to recognize spatial relationships, perception of mechanical relationships, hand-and-eye coordinations, etc. They attempt to measure a broader pattern of activities since inquiries into the nature of mechanical aptitude have shown that it is a complex of several elements among the important of which are those mentioned. The O'Rourke tests, however, restrict their area of measurement to that of information concerning tools and mechanical processes. Accordingly this must be held in mind and any results used within this limitation.

The reliability of the test is not known since it is not given on the single explanatory sheet which accompanies the test.

Percentile norms which are based upon scores made by 70,000 workmen who applied for mechanical jobs are provided. In addition average scores and standard deviations are given for thirty-three occupational groups (mechanical). The norms as such are limited in their use since they do not represent unselected cases. There is no way of knowing how much better these individuals scored on the test than unselected groups. It is reasonable to assume that the test performance of these 70,000 cases would be better than that of an unselected group because of their mechanical training and experience as well as their possible higher initial mechanical aptitude. While special occupational norms have some value, general norms based on unselected cases would be of greater value. For use in the secondary school grades, age norms would be especially useful, since most tests of mechanical aptitude have shown definite score increases with age up through the secondary school level.

About one-half the items of Part I are of the matching type. In all of the six groups there are the same number of stimuli and response items. Generally it is considered advisable to include more responses than stimuli items in order to avoid the selection of the last responses on an elimination basis. Aside from this, the structure of the items is satisfactory.

Physically the illustrations in Part I could be improved. To begin with they are all very small. Accordingly the details are frequently so fine as to make for difficulty of identification. In several instances the two related drawings differ considerably in proportion. This is apt to be confusing.

The test is simple to administer and should not present any difficulties to the individuals who are given the tests. The content has considerable interest value. The directions are clear and explicit.

It is to be regretted that there is so little information provided which is descriptive of the test. While the publishers may counter that few test users make use of the information this is no excuse for its omission. No doubt some less critical test users are willing to take a test on faith, many others, however, have a real desire to know "what it is all about," without implying any lack of confidence in the author or his test.

[1669]

Personal Data Blank. Counselees of high school age and over; 1934-38; $2 per 25; specimen set free; J. Gustav White; Stanford University, Calif.: Stanford University Press.

Edward S. Jones, Professor of Psychology and Director of Personnel Research, The University of Buffalo. This report is obviously designed for Y.M.C.A.'s and other institutions concerned with the guidance of youth. It would normally fit those in the upper high school level or in college. It includes the following sections: (a) Personal History which contains items about the family, health, and the finances of the person; (b) Your Problems; (c) Your Interests and Traits; (d) Your Education; (e) Your Occupation; and (f) Summary of Counseling Blanks and Discussion. It is not a test, but an inventory of items designed to help and guide the counselor to evaluate a student more completely. I see no objection to this sort of data blank, provided it is used with discretion. It is obviously an attempt to systematize a personal history or case study of the individual. No doubt White would agree that much of the material cannot be used at face value, since it is quite subjective, raising questions about attitudes, problems, and interests. In the section Your Problems, the student is asked to write on "what seems to be your particular problem, no matter in what area of life. Mention frankly any ambitions, difficulties, or doubts, though they may seem now relatively unimportant."

One can doubt the value of this sort of approach. Many students have been known to write nothing and others who would write extensively without any particular discrimination. There is not a clear enough directional instruction to the item. There is also the item, "What have you done to solve your problem?" This

---

O'Rourke Mechanical Aptitude Test

again may very easily lead to no response or to an indefinite amount of writing, which may be quite revealing.

The blank as a whole assumes at best a great deal of insight on the part of the student or inquirer and presumes a much more aggressive attitude than is present in a good many college freshmen and sophomores.

There is one check list, asking the individual to check once or twice his outstanding abilities, including such things as mechanical traits, dramatic ability, and management of finances. The reviewer is very skeptical of the value of a list of this sort. Most people do not have any basis of estimating abilities of this kind. In the reviewer's estimation a blank half as long with well-selected items, for the most part fairly objective ones, would probably be fully as useful. The last page of the blank contains a "Summary of Counseling Blanks and Discussions," which can be duplicated, a second copy to be used by other advisors. Most of this is quite objective data, and should be very useful to a person trained to evaluate the data properly.

Donald G. Paterson, Professor of Psychology, The University of Minnesota. The *Personal Data Blank* is designed to permit a counselee to record confidential case history information about himself and his problems prior to a counseling interview and thus to save the time of a counselor in securing pertinent data.

The blank is an eight-page booklet, 8½ by 11 inches. The first six pages are to be filled in by the counselee as a preliminary step in securing the help of a competent counselor. The data to be recorded are as follows: identifying information and family background; health data; data about finances; statement of problems prompting consultation; statement of present hobbies, interests, and characteristics together with an evaluation of accomplishments and failures; detailed record of educational history; and a detailed record of occupational history together with statements in regard to occupational information possessed and needed, vocational choice and self-estimates of vocational aptitudes, abilities, aims and ambitions. Page 7 is reserved for the counselor who is to use it to summarize his interpretation of the data, to record the highlights of the interview, and to list the specific and general recommenda-

tions made to the counselee. Page 8 is blank and can be used for recording additional case notes.

In addition to the eight-page booklet a duplicate of Page 7 accompanies the blank so that the counselor may make a carbon copy of his summary and give it to the counselee to serve as a memorandum of the interview.

The device for summarizing the interview is especially praiseworthy since it forces the counselor to record available test data in regard to abilities and interests, to interpret these in the light of the problem-areas in which the counselee is having difficulty and to formulate definite suggestions and recommendations to be followed by the counselee in attempting to solve his problems.

A one-page manual of suggestions for the counselor's use of the *Personal Data Blank* is also provided. These suggestions include a letter code for listing the areas in which the difficulty lies. Thirteen problem areas are specified including the need for: expert information, financial aid, employment placement, vocational guidance, educational guidance, health guidance, socialization, sex adjustment, moral and religious adjustment, and mental hygiene treatment.

The blank is comprehensive in its coverage without being loaded with a large number of items of doubtful value.

One may criticize the blank for not providing sufficient space for the recording of test data. It appears to be geared to a minimum battery of tests such as one mental test, two personality tests, and two vocational interest tests although provision is made for recording the scores from additional tests. This is in contrast to the counseling advantage to be found in a flexible profile form for recording a greater number and variety of test scores such as is found in the Psychological Corporation's *Aids to the Vocational Interview* (*see* 493). There is also the danger that an amateur counselor may become too dependent upon the blank as a basis for counseling. Such a counselor would tend to oversimplify his procedure and would tend to accept the recorded information *at face value* without adequate independent checks and attempts at verification. But this type of criticism is a bit unfair to the blank because the author of the blank rightly assumed that it would be used in conjunction with interview observations, psychological test results, and other sources of data by properly trained and competent counselors.

In the reviewer's opinion, this blank incorporates the good features of similar case history blanks and may be listed among the useful tools now available for systematizing the counseling interview and providing a permanent record of such interviews. Hence, this blank, when used properly, should lead to improved counseling work and should provide a partial basis for follow-up and evaluation studies which are so urgently needed in this type of service.

[1670]

Personal History. Prospective life insurance agents; 1937; this rating chart is also included as Part 1 of the *Aptitude Index for Life Insurance Salesmen*; distribution restricted to life insurance companies which are members of the Life Insurance Sales Bureau; Hartford, Conn.: Life Insurance Sales Research Bureau.

REFERENCES

1 Life Insurance Sales Research Bureau. *Rating Prospective Agents.* Hartford, Conn.: the Bureau, 1937. Pp. 16. Privately distributed. Paper.

2 Life Insurance Sales Research Bureau. *Selection of Agents*: A Method of Relating Personal History Information to Probable Success in Life Insurance Selling. Hartford, Conn.: the Bureau, 1937. Pp. 24. Privately distributed. Paper.

3 Life Insurance Sales Research Bureau. *Measuring Aptitude for Life Insurance Selling.* Hartford, Conn.: the Bureau, 1938. Pp. 22. Privately distributed. Paper.

4 Life Insurance Sales Research Bureau. *The Prospective Agents Rating Plan in Use*: Report of Session on Selection of Agents, at Research Bureau Conference, Hartford, Connecticut, March 22, 1938. New Haven, Conn.: the Bureau, 1938. Pp. 44. Privately distributed. Paper.

5 KURTZ, ALBERT K. "Evaluating Selection Tests." *Managers Mag* 14:12-6 My-Je '39.

[1671]

Preference Record. Grades 9-16; 1939; 1 form, 3 editions (differing only in the method of scoring); $1.25 per 25 forms for reporting scores and profiles to students; 50¢ per sample copy of any one edition; nontimed (40-60) minutes; G. Frederic Kuder; Chicago, Ill.: University of Chicago Bookstore.

a) FORM AM, EDITION FOR MACHINE-SCORING. $5.25 per 25; $2.50 per 100 answer sheets; $6.00 per set of scoring stencils.

b) FORM AH, EDITION FOR SCORING BY STENCILS. $5.00 per 25; $1.25 per 100 answer sheets; $2.00 per set of scoring stencils.

c) FORM AS, EDITION FOR SELF-SCORING. $6.00 per 25; $5.00 per 100 answer pads; $1.25 per 100 profile sheets.

REFERENCES

1 THURSTONE, L. L. "A Multiple Factor Study of Vocational Interests." *Personnel J* 10:198-205 O '31.

2 KUDER, G. F. "The Stability of Preference Items." *J Social Psychol* 10:41-50 F '39.

A. B. Crawford, Director of the Department of Personnel Study and Bureau of Appointments and Professor of Psychology, Yale University. Evaluation of this instrument is restricted, by lack of further evidence concerning its usefulness, to that offered in Kuder's own manual. The latter, however, presents such a clear picture of well-designed and carefully controlled experimentation, over a period of some six years, as to warrant distinct confi-dence in its possibilities and reported findings. Few of the many devices designed for guidance purposes have been as thoroughly tested and studied in advance of their release for general use, as this seems to have been.

The reviewer's opportunity actually to experiment with the *Preference Record* thus far has been limited to (*a*) a current study of 70 Yale freshmen, for which results are as yet incomplete and (*b*) an earlier administration to a few personal acquaintances. His opinions regarding its possible merits are, therefore, largely subjective. However, preliminary data on the freshman group indicate possibilities of differentiating arts, science, and engineering students rather clearly on some sections of the *Preference Record*. Moreover, test profiles of the other individuals well known to him did conform rather strikingly with his own estimates, and with those of several other qualified judges, as to the scores which these acquaintances might have been expected (in view of their known interests) to make. (Possibly the writer was unduly influenced in favor of the *Preference Record's* validity by the appropriately high "persuasive" rating of his wife.)

Although these various data, including such as have thus far been obtained concerning freshman students, are insufficient for statistically dependable conclusions, he can nevertheless endorse the primary aim of this device for "obtaining measures of motivation in various lines of study and of work." The premise that application or release of individual abilities and aptitudes is strongly affected by *motivation*—in plain words, that a person will "do his damnedest" at what he most enjoys—seems wholly reasonable. Interest in any task, whether educational or vocational, supplies a natural drive for converting potentialities into effective achievement.

It is upon this premise that the work of Strong and others, in attempting to measure interest factors, has been founded. Kuder's objective is in the same direction, though his approach and methods are different. Strong developed and standardized the *Vocational Interest Blank* through its administration to successful representatives of various occupations. Thurstone [1] has shown that human interests are not actually classifiable into as many separate compartments as the Strong scales suggest; but instead fall into broader categories, each embracing certain *clusters* of the *Vocational*

Interest Blank groups. This is another way of saying that people cannot be specifically and individually labeled, respecting either their aptitudes or their interests, with the same manifold tags which distinguish vocations. The latter reflect far too much overlapping among the individual functions and abilities which they demand to parallel an occupational census. Hence, the Kuder approach, directed as it is toward identification of certain generalized activity patterns—each of which may find many career outlets—seems more fundamental in terms of observable human differences, than any preceding attempt to measure the motivating force of interests per se.

Kuder has proceeded, by the processes of experimental tryout and progressive analysis of many items, to develop a series of scores differentiating the following types of activity preferences: scientific, computational, musical, artistic, literary, social service, and "persuasive." His *Preference Record*, employing the technique of paired comparison, requires a preferential choice of one activity or interest versus another—e.g., "Go as a medical missionary to Africa" or "Establish a medical office in a fashionable suburb"; "Belong to an amateur astronomy club" or "Belong to a religious discussion group"; "Visit the Senate of the United States" or "Visit a museum of science"; "Own a good selection of tools" or "Own an encyclopedia"; "Browse in a library" or "Visit an art gallery." This method forces a selection even between "preferences" which, in fact, may be almost equally immaterial, attractive or repellent to the subject: he is offered no escape through such symbols as "I" (indifferent) or "?," as he is in most interest tests. No direct evidence is available as to relative validity of the two methods; but Kuder's recent article [2] discussing methods of selecting items for his *Preference Record* and their "stability" is well worth reading.

His immediate objective is educational guidance, although this is definitely associated with vocational choice. For each activity pattern suggestions are offered as to the occupations presumably offering it most scope. It is here that Kuder's work thus far is most vulnerable: the vocational groupings are admittedly speculative and include here and there some rather curious bedfellows. As yet, this instrument has not been validated in the occupational field at all, and its utility for the purposes in view is, therefore, still open to question. Kuder's manual states: "These studies are being extended to people actually engaged in various occupations. In the course of time, it is expected to develop indexes which will reflect the degree to which a person's pattern of scores is characteristic of that of people in each of a number of occupations and of students in each of a number of curricula."

Reliability coefficients reported in the manual range from .85 to .90 for the several scales. The instrument is designed to permit repeated use of the test booklet itself, with independent answer sheets. The latter may be obtained in either machine, stencil, or self-scoring forms; with cost varying (according to the form of answer sheet and extent of re-use for the question booklet itself) from around 2 to 10 cents per student.

It is interesting, and indeed essential, to compare Kuder's subjectively chosen occupational clusters with those obtained from the Strong *Vocational Interest Blank* by Thurstone's objective factorial analysis. The latter yielded four interest groups, respectively associated with science, language, people, and business. Apart from Kuder's aesthetic categories (musical and artistic, which were insufficiently represented in the *Vocational Interest Blank* scores analyzed by Thurstone to yield recognizable factors), the two groupings—though bearing somewhat different sets of necessarily arbitrary labels—correspond rather closely. We can, indeed, pair them off as follows: science—scientific; language—literary; people—social service and persuasive; business—computational. Considering the fact that Strong has worked downwards toward the student body from already well-established representatives of their respective vocations; while Kuder is attempting to identify interest and activity patterns among youth directly, and feeling his way upwards toward their occupational significance, the degree of correspondence just noted between the two systems of classification is striking. As a result, at least a reasonable presumption of validity may be credited to both Kuder's system and Thurstone's factorial grouping of the Strong categories into analogous clusters. If the high promise thus far offered by Kuder's approach can in time be substantiated by further evidence and its discriminating power, his contribution toward guidance purposes should prove of undoubted significance.

This test appears to be more realistic and direct in procedure than its particular fore-runners, and is certainly much easier and more economical to score. Its use, at least experimentally, is recommended, although care should naturally be exercised in the interpretation of results. Kuder reports low intercorrelations between scores on Thurstone's *Tests for Primary Mental Abilities* and scores on the *Preference Record* and states: "It is apparent that *Preference Record* scores in general are not sufficient evidence of ability in the fields measured by the *Primary Abilities Tests*, nor is the converse true. The results suggest that, in guidance, use of the preference profile should always include a consideration of measures of ability." The latter measure may indeed effectively *supplement* (but not replace) aptitude or ability tests and, therefore, has a logical place in any comprehensive "evaluation" battery.

Arthur E. Traxler, Assistant Director, Educational Records Bureau, New York, New York. The measurement of interests has been hampered by various factors, two of the most important of which are the difficulty of obtaining scores that have high reliability and the instability of responses when the form of the items and the context in which they appear is changed. In view of this fact, it is surprising that in few of the many attempts that have been made to measure interests or motivation in recent years has any attention been given to the preference type of item, for this kind of item permits wide sampling per unit of time and is therefore conducive to increased reliability, and it is also promising from the standpoint of stability.

In a test that employs the preference type of item, either the rank-order or the paired-comparison technique may be used. If the rank-order procedure is followed, the kinds of activity are grouped and the subject is instructed to rank those in each group in order of preference. In the paired-comparison procedure, each activity included in the test is paired with every other activity and the subject indicates the one in each pair which he prefers. In the past, Miner, Plechaty, Furfey, Vernon and Allport, Sullivan, Hartson, and Weedon have used one or the other of these techniques. Recently, Kuder has experimented with both procedures and has constructed a

Preference Record which utilizes the paired-comparison type of item.

Kuder's purpose in the preparation of his *Preference Record* was "to develop a number of independent measures in the field of motivation." Briefly stated, the procedure followed in the preparation of the *Preference Record* was to start with a group of items that have psychological meaning and to develop and refine a series of scales, the items of which had high correlation with their own scale and low correlation with the other scales.

The Kuder *Preference Record* consists of 330 paired-comparison items arranged and scored in such a manner that a profile of preference scores is obtained with respect to scientific, computational, musical, artistic, literary, social service, and persuasive activities. Provision is made for showing the results of these seven scales both graphically and in the form of percentile ranks. It should be clearly understood that the scores are intended to show preference alone and are not expected to show anything concerning the ability of the individual in these fields.

The *Preference Record* is designed for use with both high school and college students. There is no time limit, but most persons can finish it within a class period of forty minutes.

The unique format of the *Preference Record* is worthy of comment. The test itself consists of a directions page and eleven pages of test items which are attached permanently by means of ten small rings within a heavy cardboard cover. A detachable answer sheet containing eleven columns corresponding to the eleven pages of the test rests inside the back cover. The pages of the test booklet are of unequal width so that when the subject turns from one page to the next the appropriate column of the answer sheet is exposed adjacent to the margin.

Used answer sheets may be removed and new ones inserted, and thus each test booklet may be used repeatedly. There are three types of answer sheets—one for hand-scoring, one for machine-scoring, and one for self-scoring. The self-scoring feature will appeal to schools with limited clerical resources. The reviewer has found by trial with several individuals that the self-scoring form works satisfactorily.

Kuder is to be commended in that he has provided more statistical data concerning his *Preference Record* than usually is available for a new test. He has shown that the preference type of item is fairly stable in that it measures about the same thing when set up in different form and context. He has also shown that when academic aptitude scores and average college grades were used as criteria of validity, the validity of items originally selected in rank-order form will, when tried out with a different group, hold up about as well in paired-comparison form as in the original form. In other words, "the preference item seems to be less sensitive to rather violent treatment than some other more common varieties of personality item." [2]

In the manual of directions, Kuder reports the following reliability coefficients for the different scales: scientific, .87; computational, .85; musical, .88; artistic, .90; literary, .90; social service, .84; persuasive, .90. On the surface, these reliability coefficients indicate that the *Preference Record* should be fairly satisfactory for individual diagnosis, although not highly so. However, it should be pointed out that these reliabilities were found by a method that is reputed to yield about the same results as the Spearman-Brown method. Since it is known that prediction of reliability with the Spearman-Brown formula sometimes gives spurious high results, it would be helpful if the author would check the reliabilities, as reported, by a test-retest procedure.

In the manual of directions, Kuder states further that the intercorrelations of the seven scores obtained by a form similar to the present one were all low (less than .30). This of course is highly desirable, for if the scores are to have real value in guidance they should be relatively independent. Kuder also presents data from preliminary studies which suggest that the *Preference Record* may have some validity for predicting marks in certain curricula. It also appears that there is considerable relation between patterns of scores and occupational choice.

The most crucial question that can be raised about the *Preference Record* is of course concerned with its validity. Are the scores obtained actually indicative of preference with respect to the seven fields it is designed to cover? Naturally there is no definite answer to the question, for there is no perfect criterion of validity. It is believed, however, that the considered judgment of mature persons concerning their preference for the seven general kinds of activity should have some value as a criterion. With this thought in mind, the reviewer asked twenty-one adults to rate the seven fields in order of their preference and then obtained their scores on the *Preference Record*. He then computed Spearman correlations between the rank order of the expressed preferences of each individual and the rank order of his preferences as indicated by the record. The median of the twenty-one correlation coefficients was .75. All but one of the correlations were positive and all but six were above .60. The correlations for three individuals were .96. This procedure of evaluations was admittedly crude, but the results do offer three suggestions: (a) on the average there seems to be fairly high agreement between the expressed preferences and the tested preferences of adults for the seven groups of activities; (b) the agreement is very high for certain individuals; (c) for some individuals the results of the *Preference Record* either agree very poorly or are at variance with their expressed preferences.

The poor agreement in certain instances may have been due to misunderstanding on the part of these subjects concerning what their true interests were, although this is doubtful, for some of the most experienced persons had the lowest correlations. Another possible factor is that the items contributing to the scores may have been inadequate indices of interest in the different areas so far as certain individuals were concerned. For example, several of the subjects criticized the "persuasive" scale. They felt that it was more nearly indicative of interest in salesmanship than of interest in the broad field of persuasive activities, some of the most effective of which are exceedingly indirect and subtle. A study of the items contributing to the score for the persuasive field lends some support to this viewpoint, for 49 items, or 51 per cent of the 96 items contributing to the persuasive scale, deal with salesmanship or closely related persuasive activities, such as soliciting for charity, publicity, and so forth.

Notwithstanding a number of detailed criticisms of this kind that could be made concerning the different scales, the fact remains that Kuder has constructed one of the most interesting evaluative devices that has yet appeared in the broad field of interest and motivation and that he has made a laudatory attempt to build it on a sound basis of experimentation and to evaluate the finished product critically. At its present stage, no reviewer could more than guess at its probable value in guidance, but this one feels that the *Preference Record* is worthy of use in an experimental way by psychologists, counselors, and others who serve as advisers for students at the secondary school and college levels.

[1672]
Rating Forms for Use of Interviewers and Oral Examinations. Applicants for employment; 1938; 50¢ per 25; 5¢ per sample copy; W. V. Bingham; New York: Psychological Corporation.

REFERENCES

1 BINGHAM, W. V. *Oral Examinations in Civil Service Recruitment*: With Special Reference to Experiences in Pennsylvania. Civil Service Assembly of the United States and Canada, Pamphlet No. 13. Chicago, Ill.: the Assembly, February 1939. Pp. 30. $0.50. Paper.

Ruth Strang, Professor of Education, Columbia University. This rating form is an attempt to standardize the observational aspects of the interview. It calls the interviewer's attention to important, precisely described, nonverbal data obtainable in an employment interview. Moreover, it provides space for some descriptive support of the quantitative ratings given. In all these respects the form is commendable and would meet the approval of certain writers who believe that the kind of data in which interviewers are interested should be obtained through standardized methods.

Other writers in this field, on the contrary, believe that many of the impressions recorded in interviews are hardly susceptible of standardized measurements. Moreover, in directing the interviewer's attention to specific points, the blank may cause him to miss the most crucial evidence and its relation to the total situation. Even if the important impression was not lost, the task still remains of relating the specific items obtained on the form to the complex structure of the candidate's personality in relation to the job.

For the novitiate in the field, this form is a useful guide to observation. But it may hamper the expert interviewer in getting a total, properly high-lighted impression of the candidate's fitness for the position.

[1673]
Revised Minnesota Paper Formboard. Ages 9 and over; 1934; 2 forms, 2 editions; $3.50 per 100; 15¢ per specimen set; 14(30) minutes; Rensis Lickert and William H. Quasha; New York: Psychological Corporation.
a) SERIES AA AND BB. 1934; $3.50 per 100.
b) SERIES MA AND MB. 1940; $1.50 per 25; $5 per 100; $1.50 per 100 machine-scorable answer sheets.

REFERENCES

1 ANDERSON, L. DEWEY. "The Minnesota Mechanical Ability Tests." *Personnel J* 6:473-8 Ap '28.
2 PATERSON, DONALD G.; ELLIOTT, RICHARD M.; ANDERSON, L. DEWEY; TOOPS, HERBERT A.; AND HEIDBREDER, EDNA. *Minnesota Mechanical Ability Tests*: The Report of a Research Investigation Subsidized by the Committee on Human Migrations of the National Research Council and Conducted in the Department of the University of Minnesota, pp. 57-61, 73-6, 81-3, 93-101, 109-10, 141-3, 204-19, 227-44, 251-3, 271-83, 291, 299-305, 310-12, 335-9, 430-2, 467-76, 508-10, 531-2. Minneapolis, Minn.: University of Minnesota Press, 1930. Pp. xxii, 586. $5.00.
3 GARRETT, HENRY E., AND SCHNECK, MATTHEW R. *Psychological Tests, Methods, and Results*, pp. 84-6. New York and London: Harper and Bros., 1933. Pp. x, 137, 235. $2.75; 10s. 6d.
4 LICKERT, RENSIS. "A Multiple-Choice Revision of the Minnesota Paper Form Board." *Psychol B* 31:674 N '34.
5 QUASHA, W. R. *The Revised Minnesota Paper Form Board Test*: An Experiment in Test Construction. Unpublished master's thesis, New York University, 1935.
6 BINGHAM, WALTER VAN DYKE. *Aptitudes and Aptitude Testing*, pp. 312-3. New York and London: Harper & Brothers, 1937. Pp. ix, 390. $3.00; 10s. 6d.
7 QUASHA, WILLIAM H., AND LICKERT, RENSIS. "The Revised Minnesota Paper Form Board Test." *J Ed Psychol* 28:197-204 Mr '37.
8 PATERSON, DONALD G.; SCHNEIDLER, GWENDOLEN G.; AND WILLIAMSON, EDMUND G. *Student Guidance Techniques*, pp. 227-9. New York: McGraw-Hill Book Co., Inc., 1938. Pp. xviii, 316. $3.00. (London: McGraw-Hill Publishing Co., Ltd. 18s.)
9 SCHULTZ, RICHARD S. "Preliminary Study of an Industrial Revision of the Revised Minnesota Paper Form Board Test." *J Appl Psychol* 24:463-7 Ag '40.

Alec Rodger, Head of the Vocational Guidance Department, National Institute of Industrial Psychology, London, England. The second revision of this well-known test is characterised, it is claimed, by greater objectivity and by a reduction in scoring time. The claim is a just one. But there are matters, at least as important as these, which do not appear to have received marked attention from the authors.

In the first place, the occupational significance of the test is not discussed in the literature which accompanies the booklets. Norms, derived from the scores obtained by approximately 5,000 subjects, representative of various age and educational groups, are presented. No doubt the prospective user of the test is intended to draw his own broad conclusions about its occupational significance from the fact that groups of engineering students were found to produce higher average scores than groups of nonengineering students. The reviewer is well acquainted with the practical difficulties usually experienced by test constructors in establishing the value of their tests for vocational guidance or selection purposes, but he feels that such difficulties should, whenever possible, be faced more resolutely than they appear to have been faced by the Minnesota investigators.

Secondly, no indication is given by the authors of the extent to which success in this test is correlated with success in other tests for mechanical ability or with success in tests for general intelligence. Correlational data contained in the original report of their work is not directly relevant to this point, for the test now available is not the same as the original test. The reviewer is inclined to suspect that (on a two-factor theory of ability) the *g* saturation of the test may be quite as high as its saturation with any other factor, and his suspicions will not be removed until he is given reasonable evidence of the insecurity of their foundation. It has been found in other investigations that tests of this kind are often to a considerable extent merely nonverbal *g* tests.

A third, but relatively unimportant, flaw in the literature is to be found in its bare statement that the norms for the AA and BB series of the test are "identical." If the statement is perfectly true, it should, surely, be accompanied by a note drawing attention to this very remarkable phenomenon; if it is only approximately true, it should be modified. Doubtless the authors intended merely to suggest—perhaps very justifiably—that, for most practical purposes, the norms for the two series could be regarded as identical.

These criticisms are not intended to be purely destructive. It is clear from the data available that the test is an extremely interesting one from the vocational psychologist's point of view, and that it is worthy of very careful investigation. Could not the authors be persuaded to publish more information about it?

[1674]

Self-Administering Vocational Interest Locator, Revised Edition. Grades 9 and over; 1933-38; $1.68 per 30; 10¢ per specimen set; nontimed (30-40) minutes; N. A. Lufburrow; Baltimore, Md.: the Author, 3112 Milford Ave.

[1675]

Specific Interest Inventory: For Educational Diagnosis and Guidance. Ages 10 and over; 1932; 2 levels for each sex; $5.00 per 100; 50¢ per specimen set; nontimed (30-40) minutes; Paul P. Brainard and Frances G. Stewart; New York: Psychological Corporation.
a) FORM B. Boys: ages 10-16.
b) FORM G. Girls: ages 10-16.
c) FORM M. Men: ages 16 and over.
d) FORM W. Women: ages 16 and over.

REFERENCES

1 BRAINARD, P. P. "Interest Tests in Vocational Guidance." *Voc Guid Mag* 6:156-9 Ja '28.
2 ANDERSON, ROY N. "A Comparative Study of Three Vocational Interest Tests." *Psychol Clinic* 22:117-27 Je-Ag '33.
3 BILLINGS, ELIZABETH LOUISE. *The Use of Brainard's Specific Interest Inventories in a Secondary School.* Unpublished master's thesis, Columbia University, 1936.
4 FRYER, DOUGLAS. *The Measurement of Interests,* pp. 33-8, New York: Henry Holt and Co., Inc. 1931. Pp. xxxvi, 488. $4.50; student edition, $3.60. (London: George G. Harrap & Co., Ltd., 1937. 10s. 6d.)

Jack W. Dunlap, Associate Professor of Educational Psychology, The University of Rochester. Each of the four forms of the inventory consists of 20 groups of five items each, constructed to measure the individual's interest in a particular *mode* of expressing activity, such as physical work, mechanical work, vocal expression, experimenting, creative imagination, etc. The items in the adult forms differ from those in the adolescent forms only in that they are stated in more mature language. The forms for males are not identical in the groups of human modes of expression with those for females, and where the identical mode is used, the form of the statements is changed.

The subject is required to indicate his reaction to each item on a five point scale, where 1 means "dislike very much"; 2, "dislike it somewhat"; 3, "neutral or indifferent"; 4, "like it somewhat"; and 5, "like it very much." The average time for marking the blank is 30 minutes, and it may be filled out without supervision. In addition to the 100 items mentioned above, there are in each form 10 groups of statements with identical headings in which the subject is to underline those statements he is interested in and to double underline those of particular interest. The phrases are identical for the B and M blanks, and for the G and W blanks.

A score is determined for each mode of expression, and twenty modes are then ranked in descending order as to score. The examiner then looks at the first three or four modes, sees what general field is suggested, and notes this on a special blank. The next three modes are also examined and again the suggested field recorded. Finally, those modes are located that are least liked, i.e., have the smallest score. Special consideration is given those items marked 4 and 5 in the modes headed outdoor, scientific, experiment, observation, and creative imagination. Finally, the items underlined are examined and those that seem to fit in with the vocations suggested are recorded. The author states, "A definite vocational pattern now emerges, consisting of certain combinations of likes, limited by certain dislikes, and supported by items throughout the test marked 4 or 5, and by underlines. Select the occupation suggested most consistently by all factors, and apply other criteria such as intelligence, finances, personality, etc."

For the men's and boy's blanks a more mechanical method of scoring is proposed for various occupations. Certain items have been designated as indicative of interest in a given field, for example, 37 items supposedly indicate interest in agriculture. The number of items allocated to this group that the subject has marked with a 4 or 5 are determined and divided by 37 to give an indication of "fitness for the field." "Eighty per cent is considered to be standard. Anything less than that indicates same lack in the field."

No objective data are given as to the reliability or validity of the blank. However, some evidence as to reliability is given in terms of consistency of individuals as to order of groups on two testings. For sixty ninth-graders, foot-rule coefficients of consistency varied from .13 to .94 with an average of .68.

In view of the evidence given by the author, and a careful examination of the forms, the following conclusions are drawn: (a) The blank has merit and deserves consideration as a measure of interest. (b) More objective data as to the statistical validity, reliability, and the results of using the tests should be given. (c) The test is relatively simple to score, but will require care in recording underlined items and items marked 4 or 5. (d) It would appear that considerable instruction and practice is needed to interpret the results. A set of sample results to be interpreted by the prospective administrator, together with the authors' interpretation, would be valuable. (e) Data as to norms should be provided for the so-called "mathematical scores."

M. R. Trabue, Dean of the School of Education, The Pennsylvania State College. The publisher's catalogue describes the *Specific Interest Inventory* as follows: "An instrument to analyze tendencies which are significant in vocations. Each form includes 20 groups of 5 questions each, covering different phases of a particular mode of expression, and stated in terms of specific experiences."

The multigraphed four-page manual distributed with the test blanks suggests that the individual's record be listed under each head— "Outdoor, Scientific, Experiment, Observation, Creative Imagination," and the like. "A definite vocational pattern now emerges, consisting of certain combinations of likes, limited by certain dislikes, and supported by items

throughout the test marked 4 or 5, and by underlines. Select the occupation suggested most consistently by all factors, and apply other criteria such as intelligence, finances, personality, etc." One magazine article is cited, in which a study is reported of the persistence of 300 men in an engineering school—"43 engineers dropped out whose interest scores were above median and 62 dropped out whose scores were below median."

In the judgment of the reviewer, these inventories should not have been released for general use by untrained examiners. No group of five questions is likely to provide a highly reliable index of the amount of "Outdoor" interest or of "Scientific" interest. Even if these "basic interest groups" were each known to be reliably indicated by one's responses to five questions, not enough is known yet regarding the combinations of different "basic interest groups" that make success possible in various vocations. Relatively untrained and inexperienced persons will tend to take the scores of such instruments as these entirely too seriously or to give them no confidence at all. These and similar tools need extensive study, experimentation, and improvement at the hands of competent vocational psychologists before they are distributed for general use. It is unfortunate that those who make tests feel the financial necessity of selling them before adequate scientific evidence of their values and limitations has been collected and published.

For a review by Everett B. Sackett, see 1176.

[1676]

Stanford Scientific Aptitude Test. Entrants to schools of engineering and science; 1929-30; 1 form; $4 per 25; 50¢ per specimen set; nontimed (60-120) minutes; D. L. Zyve; Stanford University, Calif.: Stanford University Press.

REFERENCES

1 ZYVE, D. L. *An Experimental Study of Scientific Aptitude.* Unpublished doctor's thesis, Stanford University, 1926.
2 ZYVE, D. L. "A Test of Scientific Aptitude." *J Ed Psychol* 18:525-46 N '27.
3 BINGHAM, WALTER VAN DYKE. *Aptitudes and Aptitude Testing,* pp. 348-9. New York and London: Harper & Brothers, 1937. Pp. ix, 390. $3.00; 10s. 6d.

A. B. Crawford, Director of the Department of Personnel Study and Bureau of Appointments and Professor of Psychology, Yale University. The *Stanford Scientific Aptitude Test* (also called the Zyve test after its author) represents an ingenious attempt to measure directly certain mental factors or thought-processes presumably important for success in science. The test is composed of numerous exercises, each presenting problems designed to sample students' judgment, observation, reasoning power, etc., in ways which appraise not their *present* scientific achievement or knowledge; but rather their aptitude for acquiring such knowledge and consequently for contributing to *future* achievements in this division of learning. It is, therefore, essentially intended to serve as an index of educability in that particular area.

The various subtests employed in the hope of providing a composite measure of scientific aptitude (considered in the author's Explanatory Booklet to be a "complex conglomerate of mental and character traits") bear the following descriptive labels or titles: Experimental Bent; Clarity of Definition; Suspended versus Snap Judgment; Reasoning; Inconsistencies; Fallacies; Induction, Deduction, and Generalization; Caution and Thoroughness; Discrimination of Values in Selecting and Arranging Experimental Data; Accuracy of Interpretation; and Accuracy of Observation. The relative weights of subtest scores on these sections, as contributions to the total score, range from two to seven. There is no evidence that these weightings are other than arbitrary.

A mere glance at the titles just quoted shows what a wide and ambitious extent of mental traits—quite variant in specificity—this instrument purports to measure; and all within the space of 14 pages! Its reach far exceeds its grasp, as might be expected from the small number of individual items or problems allotted to each of the dozen subtests. There lies the undeniable weakness of this project. Even if its components had true separate significance, which is doubtful (compare the merger of "induction, deduction, and generalization" in Exercise S, with Thurstone's segregation of inductive and deductive reasoning), each of them would have to be extended, for satisfactory results, much beyond its present content of a few items only. One might surmise that adequate coverage of all the complex thinking abilities which this test sets out to evaluate in two hours could hardly be accomplished with success in less than six or eight. The consequence of its attempting so wide a range within such brief compass is to chop its contents up into subtests so short that their individual or total yield is quite unreliable.

The Explanatory Booklet concerning this test barely mentions reliability (in a footnote and with no indication of how the coefficients, there rather questionably employed to "correct" the validity coefficient for attenuation, were derived). Some evidence, based upon rather small numbers of subjects, is offered as to its validity; determined (*a*) through correlating test scores with the subjective ranking of 50 research students (21 in chemistry, 10 in physics, and 19 in electrical engineering) by 6 faculty representatives of those departments; and (*b*) through comparison of these "criterion group" scores on the test, with those made by "unselected" Stanford freshmen and by 79 other first-year students "intending to major either in science or engineering." While scores of the more advanced (criterion group) research scholars were distinctly higher than those of either freshman group, distributions of the "unselected" and the "science or engineering" freshmen, respectively, showed practically no difference. By an extraordinary *tour de force*, or sheer naïveté, Zyve deduces from these data "satisfactory proof of the validity of the SAT." But if the latter is intended to show *aptitude* for scientific studies, the performance of advanced "research" students or faculty members (21 in number who made the highest scores reported thereon) scarcely seems an appropriate index of its validity. Moreover, if Stanford freshmen expecting to enter science or engineering show no more educational aptitude (as thus measured) for these rather specialized fields than do "unselected" freshmen, something is curiously wrong either with matriculation guidance at Stanford or with this test. The reviewer, having both a high respect for Stanford and personal experience with the test in question, unhesitatingly attributes to the latter this anomaly.

Experimental administration of the Zyve test some years ago to a representative group of Yale freshmen (143 in number; considerably larger than the "criterion group" utilized originally for validation of this instrument) yielded the following results: (*a*) Validity— .30 (as indicated by correlation of test-scores in the fall with subsequent year-grades in science or pre-engineering courses). (*b*) Reliability—.60 (for *entire* test, by the method either of split-half, or of paired successive subtest, scores). Reliabilities for these separate subdivisions, where obtainable at all (i.e., when the number of individual items in an exercise permitted such an estimate) were still lower.

As stated earlier, the Zyve test is ingenious, and has interesting, provocative features. Unfortunately, it seems not to have been adequately "tried and proven" initially; nor has it ever been revised. No further data as to its validity (such as might, for example, have been sought through follow-up studies of the Stanford freshmen whose score distributions are depicted in the Explanatory Booklet; or its later administration to other groups) has been published since the test and Explanatory Booklet first appeared ten years ago. In fact, neither has been altered from its original form. Improvement of this instrument through further experimentation, item-analyses, and extension of its most promising sections is both desirable and necessary if it is to serve dependably the purpose for which it was designed. As the test stands, without either change in its content, or new evidence adduced in support of its value, it cannot be recommended. The chief beneficiary of its continued distribution would seem to be the Stanford University Press, whose announcements concerning it are as perennially optimistic as florid seed catalogues. Indeed, on the very day this review was written, there arrived from that press a "new test catalogue" advertising this same Stanford (Zyve) Scientific Aptitude Test as follows: "A test to detect those basic traits which comprise an aptitude for science or engineering." A measure which actually performed that function would be invaluable; but evidence as to the power of this particular instrument to do so is negative rather than positive. Consequently, neither students nor their educational advisors should place any reliance thereon. However, it will no doubt continue to be used (even if unimproved for still another decade) by vocational counselors and commercial "guidance" bureaus, since it is relatively inexpensive and easy to administer. Furthermore, it is ostensibly endorsed by Stanford University, which must give psychologists there—if they know about it—some troubled nights. That this initially promising experiment could not have been carried on to more valid and reliable forms is regrettable; that its sale in the original, unsatisfactory form is still being pushed (even by the Psychological Corporation), seems curious, to say the least.

Stanford Scientific Aptitude Test

[1677]

Stenographic Aptitude Test. Beginning secretarial students; 1939; 1 form; $4 per 100; 20¢ per specimen set; (22) minutes; George K. Bennett; New York: Psychological Corporation.

REFERENCES

1 BENNETT, GEORGE K. *Differential Aptitude Prognosis*, pp. 85-114. Unpublished doctor's thesis, Yale University, 1935.

[1678]

Tweezer Dexterity Test: Worksample No. 17. Ages 14 and over; [1928?]; 1 form; individual; worklimit (10-20) minutes; Johnson O'Connor; rents for $60 for the first year and $30 a year thereafter; the *Tweezer Dexterity Test* and the *Finger Dexterity Test* together rent for $90 the first year and $45 a year thereafter; Boston, Mass.: Human Engineering Laboratory. ($20(No. 42070); Chicago, Ill.: C. H. Stoelting Co.) ($11; Minneapolis, Minn.: Mechanical Engineering Department, University of Minnesota.)

REFERENCES

1 O'CONNOR, JOHNSON. *Born That Way*, pp. 56-9, 174-5, 179-180, 182-204, 216-7. Baltimore, Md.: Williams & Wilkins Co., 1928. Pp. 323. $2.00.
2 WELLS, F. L. "Comparative Reliability in Tests of Motor Aptitude." *J Genetic Psychol* 37:318-20 Je '30.
3 BERGEN, GARRET L. *Use of Tests in the Adjustment Service*, p. 46. Adjustment Service Series Report [No.] 4. New York: American Association for Adult Education, 1935. Pp. 70. Paper. Out of print.
4 DVORAK, BEATRICE JEANNE. *Differential Occupational Ability Patterns*. Publications of the Employment Stabilization Research Institute, University of Minnesota, Vol. 3, No. 8. Minneapolis, Minn.: University of Minnesota Press, February 1935. Pp. 46. $1.00. Paper.
5 GREEN, HELEN J., AND BERMAN, ISABEL R.; under the direction of Donald G. Paterson and M. R. Trabue. *A Manual of Selected Occupational Tests for Use in Public Employment Office*, pp. 5-7, 9, 23-31. University of Minnesota, Bulletins of the Employment Stabilization Research Institute, Vol. 2, No. 3. Minneapolis, Minn.: University of Minnesota Press, July 1936. Pp. 31. $0.50. Paper.
6 PATERSON, DONALD G., AND DARLEY, JOHN G., with the assistance of Richard M. Elliott. *Men, Women, and Jobs.* Minneapolis, Minn.: University of Minnesota Press, 1936. Pp. v, 145. $1.50. (London: Oxford University Press. 9s.)
7 BINGHAM, WALTER VAN DYKE. *Aptitudes and Aptitude Testing*, pp. 284-286. New York and London: Harper & Brothers, 1937. Pp. ix, 390. $3.00; 10s. 6d.
8 BROWN, FRED. "Selective Tests for Dental School Candidates." *Oral Hyg* 27:1172-7 S '37.
9 CANDEE, BEATRICE, AND BLUM, MILTON. "Report of a Study Done in a Watch Factory." *J Appl Psychol* 21:572-82 O '37.
10 HARRIS, ALBERT J. "The Relative Significance of Measures of Mechanical Aptitude, Intelligence, and Previous Scholarship for Predicting Achievement in Dental School." *J Appl Psychol* 21:513-21 O '37.
11 O'CONNOR, JOHNSON. *Administration and Norms for the Finger Dexterity Test, Worksample 16, and the Tweezer Dexterity Test, Worksample 18.* Human Engineering Laboratory, Technical Report, No. 16. Boston, Mass.: the Laboratory, 1938. Pp. x, 136. $1.00. Paper, mimeographed.
12 PATERSON, DONALD G.; SCHNEIDLER, GWENDOLEN G.; AND WILLIAMSON, EDMUND G. *Student Guidance Techniques*, pp. 237-40. New York: McGraw-Hill Book Co., Inc., 1938. Pp. xviii, 316. $3.00. (London: McGraw-Hill Publishing Co., Ltd. 18s.)
13 BLUM, MILTON L. "A Contribution to Manual Aptitude Measurement in Industry: The Value of Certain Dexterity Measures for the Selection of Workers in a Watch Factory." *J Appl Psychol* 24:381-416 Ag '40.

Morris S. Viteles, Associate Professor Psychology, and Albert S. Thompson, Instructor in Psychology, The University of Pennsylvania. This test, like O'Connor's *Finger Dexterity Test*, is well known and has had a somewhat similar history. Since the *Tweezer Dexterity Test* is considered a companion to the *Finger Dexterity Test*, the two have often been included in the same test battery.

Reports by the University of Minnesota Employment Stabilization Research Institute [4, 5, 6] and Bingham's text [7] represent the best sources of information on this test. Recent studies [9, 10] have shown the test to be of little value in predicting achievement in dental school but to be of considerable value in differentiating watchmakers from the general population.

The present equivocal position of the test as an instrument for forecasting vocational achievement is well reflected in Bingham's statement that "with the exception of workers engaged in fine instrument assembly jobs, the actual test achievements of large numbers of people succeeding or failing in . . . occupations have not been published; and so the counselor has to rely largely on his good sense to guide him when considering what level of tweezer dexterity might be desirable in a specific occupation." [7]

One major handicap to the use of the test is uncertainty as to its reliability. In 1930 F. L. Wells suggested modifications of the board and of administrative procedures designed to reduce the variability of the scores. [2] Practically all the studies, nevertheless, have been made with the original board (known as O'Connor's *Worksample No. 17*) and instructions. A 1938 report [11] of the Human Engineering Laboratory of the Stevens Institute of Technology, reports the development of *Worksample No. 18*—a board constructed in line with Wells' suggestions, and including countersunk holes to reduce the possibility of jamming or catching of sleeves on the inserted pins— and in the future this will be the type of board leased or rented for use by the Human Engineering Laboratory. However, adequate data on the reliability of the new board, as on that of the old, is yet to be furnished. In general, much remains to be done with this test in the way of acceptable experimental analysis to make it a useful instrument in psychological practice.

[1679]

Vocational Aptitude Examination. Male high school graduates; 1935; 1 form; $4.00 per 25; $1.00 for manual, keys, and norms; 25¢ per sample test; part nontimed (85-100) minutes; Glen U. Cleeton and C. W. Mason; New York, N. Y.: Psychological Corporation.

REFERENCES

1 MASON, CHARLES W. *The Possibilities of an Objective Executive Aptitude Test.* Unpublished master's thesis, University of Buffalo, 1930. Pp. 65.
2 CLEETON, GLEN U., AND MASON, CHARLES W. *Executive Ability*: Its Discovery and Development. Yellow Springs, Ohio: Antioch Press, 1934. Pp. xvi, 210. $2.00.

3 MASON, CHARLES W., AND CLEETON, GLEN U. "Measuring Executive Ability." *Personnel J* 13:277-9 F '35.

Harold D. Carter, Research Associate, Institute of Child Welfare, The University of California. This examination was developed primarily for the measurement of executive ability. It appears to consist of a hard group test of intelligence, plus some information tests, an interest inventory, and a personality inventory. Those wishing to understand the method of approach will have to buy the authors' book entitled *Executive Ability.* In this book, analysis of the actual duties of modern executives furnishes an explanation of the choice of tests. Considerable thought has been given to the problem of measurement of executive ability, and the tests have a sound basis in job analysis and test work aimed at suitable quantification of the data needed for selection of executives. As the authors make clear, the tests are not quite adequate for the selection of men for executive positions, but they serve as a good basis for the elimination of those definitely without executive ability. This statement seems to be substantiated. However, such a claim could be made for any one of several tests.

Users of the test will be inconvenienced because the test is expensive and is not accompanied by a properly organized manual. The general explanations, scoring keys, instructions for administering, and interpretative material are not combined into a single booklet. Furthermore, the method of construction and validation is not made clear until one buys and studies a book and reads articles available only in scattered periodicals. Since the timed parts of the test take 61 minutes actual working time, the examination will be unsuitable for administration in most college classes. The scoring is objective, and can be made fairly rapid, but in the interests of convenience the user must make his own stencils and keys. The mimeographed set of keys is rather bulky, somewhat inconvenient, not perfectly accurate, and not arranged in a form which permits efficient scoring.

The materials offered for the interpretation of the test scores are not adequate. Apparently the reliability of this test is not known, and its validity is most inadequately expressed. There is, of course, no indication of the probable error of a score. The test has not been widely used, and the tentative norms are obviously inadequate. Medians are given for the separate tests and for the total score, for college students, for a group of accountants, and for a small group of business executives. These medians alone are not particularly useful, and the few sentences given in explanation are not convincing. Research has indicated to the authors some tendencies in scores of different groups, but data furnished with the tests are insufficient for fusing these indications into a definite judgment suitable for use by counselors. The norms are insufficiently quantified; larger groups should be tested, and percentile scores or standard scores should be furnished. High scores on the tests in general may be interpreted as indicating executive aptitude. High scores on Test 3 may indicate aptitude for sales work, especially if accompanied by lower scores on Tests 1, 2, 4, 5, and 6. High scores on Tests 1, 2, 4, 5, and 6 may indicate aptitude for technical work, especially if accompanied by lower scores on the parts of Test 8. But these tendencies which may be revealed by study of means for groups may lead to serious error in the classification of individuals. In the absence of definite correlational evidence of the reliability of the test, one is justified in questioning the reliability of such indications based upon the use of test score differences.

However, this test should not be lightly dismissed. Much care has gone into its construction, and enough work has been done to justify the belief that the test measures executive ability. Examination of the test suggests that it may turn out to be very practical, and widely useful. It may permit classification of individuals into executive groups, sales groups, technical groups, and clerical groups. Although the test looks promising, some spade work remains to be done before these values can be regarded as demonstrated.

M. R. Trabue, Dean of the School of Education, The Pennsylvania State College. This test includes eight different subtests, one of which is further subdivided into five distinct parts. Each of the twelve subtests is to be given a separate score and is to have its own local distribution of scores made, from which local norms are to be determined. A mimeographed report, supplied with the examination, gives the following "data on 450 miscellaneous cases, including executives, salesmen, accountants, engineers, and research workers":

median, third quartile, lower quartile, standard deviation, and reliability coefficient. The reliability coefficients given for the various tests range from .80 to .86; and for the total of Tests 1-6 inclusive, .94 is the reported reliability.

The mimeographed "Suggestions for interpretation of score patterns" attempts to give the user of the tests aid in their practical interpretation by such notes as the following: "Executives with general administrative and supervisory responsibilities tend to score above the median on Tests 1 to 6 inclusive." "Sales aptitude for fields requiring limited general ability is indicated when the median comparisons for Tests 1 and 3 are more favorable than the average for Tests 1, 2, 5, and 6." "Engineers, research, and technical groups tend to exceed the medians on Tests 2 and 4."

In the hands of a competent psychologist, such suggestions would be very useful, although less helpful than the actual distributions of scores made by general executives, salesmen of limited general ability, and other groups. In the hands of persons of less experience in psychological testing, suggestions of this type may lead to mechanical interpretations that cannot possibly be justified by the facts.

If one could be sure that no guidance or actual employment of men would be based on the results of these tests, except by persons who had read and fully understood the book entitled *Executive Ability: Its Discovery and Development,* [2] one could be more optimistic about the usefulness of the examination scores, for the authors have presented in the book most of the warnings needed in using such tests. The test forms now for sale are not, however, those directly reported upon in the text.

The authors have faced squarely an important task: the development of instruments for the selection of executives. They have approached the problem intelligently and have produced a trial form of an examination that offers considerable promise of being helpful in the selection of executives. The examination is only in tentative form, however, and cannot be turned over without many warnings to untrained examiners. The authors cannot be criticized for wanting to obtain test records from many different executives, but they have run a real risk in assuming that everyone who tries to use the examination will be familiar with their suggestions for caution in interpretation, which appear in the book only. Their plans for further validation and improvement of the examination are, in this reviewer's judgment, quite sound, but the administration and interpretation of the tests should not be turned over to inexperienced and untrained examiners.

[1679.1]

Vocational Guidance Questionnaire. High school; 1940; 1 form; 75¢ per 25; $2 per 100; 10¢ per specimen set; nontimed; Anthony J. Scholter; Milwaukee, Wis.: Department of Education, Archdiocese of Milwaukee.

[1680]

Vocational Interest Blank for Men, Revised. Ages 17 and over; 1927-38; revised scoring scales are available for measuring maturity of interest, masculinity-femininity, studiousness, thirty-five occupations, and six occupational groups (I, II, V, VIII, IX, X): Group I: artist, psychologist, architect, physician, and dentist; Group II: mathematician, engineer, chemist; Group III: production manager; Group IV: farmer, carpenter, printer, mathematics-physical science teacher, policeman, forest service man; Group V: Y.M.C.A. physical director, personnel manager, Y.M.C.A. secretary, city school superintendent, minister; Group VI: musician; Group VII: certified public accountant; Group VIII: accountant, office man, purchasing agent, banker; Group IX: sales manager, real estate salesman, life insurance salesman; Group X: advertising man, lawyer, author-journalist; Group XI: president of a manufacturing concern; 1 form; $2.00 per 25; 50¢ per 25 report blanks; $1 per scoring scale; 2 to 9 scales, 80¢ each; 10 or more scales, 70¢ each; $2.25 per 100 machine-scorable answer sheets; $5.00 per machine-scorable scale; nontimed (40) minutes; Edward K. Strong, Jr.; Stanford University, Calif.: Stanford University Press.

REFERENCES

1 COWDERY, KARL M. "Measurement of Professional Attitudes: Differences between Lawyers, Physicians and Engineers." *J Personnel Res* 5:131-41 Ag '26.
2 STRONG, EDWARD K., JR. "Interest Analysis of Personnel Managers." *J Personnel Res* 5:235-42 S '26.
3 STRONG, EDWARD K., JR. "An Interest Test for Personnel Managers." *J Personnel Res* 5:194-203 S '26.
4 STRONG, EDWARD K., JR. "Differentiation of Certified Public Accountants from Other Occupational Groups." *J Ed Psychol* 18:227-38 Ag '27.
5 STRONG, EDWARD K., JR. "Vocational Guidance of Engineers." *Ind Psychol* 2:291-8 Je '27.
6 STRONG, EDWARD K., JR. "Vocational Guidance of Executives." *J Appl Psychol* 11:331-47 O '27.
7 STRONG, EDWARD K., JR. "Vocational Interest Test." *Ed Rec* 8:107-21 Ap '27.
8 HOGG, MARY I. "Occupational Interests of Women." *Personnel J* 6:331-7 F '28.
9 STRONG, EDWARD K., JR. "Diagnostic Value of the Vocational Interest Test." *Ed Rec* 10:59-68 Ja '29.
11 STRONG, EDWARD K., JR. "Interests of Engineers: A Basis for Vocational Guidance." *Personnel J* 7:441-54 Ap '29.
12 RULON, PHILLIP JUSTIN, AND ARDEN, WESLEY. "A Scoring Technique for Tests Having Multiple Item-Weightings." *Personnel J* 9:235-41 O '30.
13 STRONG, EDWARD K., JR. "Procedure for Scoring an Interest Test." *Psychol Clinic* 19:63-72 Ap '30.
14 STRONG, EDWARD K., JR., AND MACKENZIE, HOPE. "Permanence of Interests of Adult Men." *J Social Psychol* 1:152-9 F '30.
15 GUNDLACH, RALPH H., AND GERUM, ELIZABETH. "Vocational Interests and Types of Ability." *J Ed Psychol* 22:505-11 O '31.
16 SHELLOW, SADIE MYERS. "Vocational Interest Blank as an Aid to Interviewing," *Personnel J* 9:379-84 F '31.
17 STRONG, EDWARD K., JR. *Change of Interests with Age:* Based on Examinations of More Than Two Thousand Men between the Ages of Twenty and Sixty Representing Eight Occupations. Foreword by Walter R. Miles. Stanford University, Calif.: Stanford University Press, 1931. Pp. xix, 235. $4.00. (London: Oxford University Press. 18s.)

18 THURSTONE, L. L. "A Multiple Factor Study of Vocational Interests." *Personnel J* 10:198-205 O '31.
19 GOODFELLOW, LOUIS D. "A Study of the Interests and Personality Traits of Prospective Teachers." *Ed Adm and Sup* 18:649-58 D '32.
20 HOLCOMB, G. W., AND LASLETT, H. R. "A Prognostic Study of Engineering Aptitude." *J Appl Psychol* 16:107-15 Ap '32.
21 STEINMETZ, HARRY CHARLES. "Measuring Ability to Fake Occupational Interest." *J Appl Psychol* 16:123-30 Ap '32.
22 STRONG, EDWARD K., JR., AND GREEN, HELEN J. "Short Cuts to Scoring an Interest Test." *J Appl Psychol* 16:1-8 F '32.
23 WOOD, BEN D. "New Method for Scoring the Strong Interest Test." *Sch and Soc* 36:718 D 3 '32.
24 ANDERSON, ROY N. "A Comparative Study of Three Vocational Interest Tests." *Psychol Clinic* 22:117-27 Je-Ag '33.
25 CARTER, HAROLD D., AND STRONG, E. K., JR. "Sex Differences in Occupational Interests of High School Students." *Personnel J* 12:166-75 O '33.
26 STRONG, EDWARD K., JR. "Interest Maturity." *Personnel J* 12:77-90 Ag '33.
27 ACHILLES, P. S., AND SCHULTZ, R. S. "Characteristics of Life Insurance Salesmen." *Personnel J* 12:260-3 F '34.
28 BERMAN, ISABEL R.; DARLEY, JOHN G.; AND PATERSON, DONALD G. *Vocational Interest Scales*: An Analysis of Three Questionnaires in Relation to Occupational Classification and Employment Status, pp. 5-23, 34-5. University of Minnesota, Bulletins of the Employment Stabilization Research Institute, Vol. 3, No. 5. Minneapolis, Minn.: University of Minnesota Press, August 1934. Pp. 35. $0.50. Paper.
29 Educational Records Bureau. *1934 Achievement Test Program in Independent Schools*: A Summary of the Results of Achievement Tests Given in Elementary and Secondary Independent Schools in April, 1934, pp. 8-13. Educational Records Bulletin No. 13. New York: the Bureau, 1934. Pp. iii, 64, 9. $1.50. Paper, lithotyped.
30 KELLEY, TRUMAN L. "The Scoring of Alternative Responses with Reference to Some Criterion." *J Ed Psychol* 25:504-10 O '34.
31 MANN, CLAIR V. *Experimentation to Discover Measurable Aptitudes for Engineering*, pp. 14-18 and charts 23-34. Journal of Educational Research, Vol. 1, No. 2. Rolla, Mo.: the Author, 210 East Eighth St., June 1934. Pp. 37. $0.50. Paper.
32 SEGAL, DAVID, AND BRINTLE, S. L. "The Relation of Occupational Interest Scores as Measured by the Strong Interest Blank to Achievement Test Results and College Marks in Certain College Subject Groups." *J Ed Res* 27:442-5 F '34.
33 STRONG, EDWARD K., JR. "Aptitudes versus Attitudes in Vocational Guidance." *J Appl Psychol* 18:501-15 Ag '34.
34 STRONG, EDWARD K., JR. "Classification of Occupations by Interests." *Personnel J* 12:301-13 Ap '34.
35 STRONG, EDWARD K., JR. "Interests and Sales Ability." *Personnel J* 13:204-16 D '34.
36 STRONG, EDWARD K., JR. "Permanence of Vocational Interests." *J Ed Psychol* 25:336-44 My '34.
37 STRONG, EDWARD K., JR. "Vocational Interest Test." *Occupations* 12:49-56 Ap '34.
38 BERGEN, GARRET L. *Use of Tests in the Adjustment Service*, pp. 52-4. Adjustment Service Series Report [No.] 4. New York: American Association for Adult Education, 1935. Pp. 70. Paper. Out of print.
39 BURNHAM, PAUL S., AND CRAWFORD, ALBERT B. "The Vocational Interests and Personality Test Scores of a Pair of Dice." *J Ed Psychol* 26:508-12 O '35.
40 CARTER, H. D.; PYLES, M. K.; AND BRETNALL, E. P. "A Comparative Study of Factors in Vocational Interest Scores of High School Boys." *J Ed Psychol* 26:81-98 F '35.
41 STRONG, EDWARD K., JR. "Predictive Value of the Vocational Interest Test." *J Ed Psychol* 26:331-49 My '35.
42 STRONG, E. K., JR., AND CARTER, H. D. "Efficiency Plus Economy in Scoring an Interest Test." *J Ed Psychol* 26:579-86 N '35.
43 BILLS, MARION A., AND WARD, L. W. "Testing Salesmen of Casualty Insurance." *Personnel J* 15:55-8 Je '36.
44 FLINNER, IRA A. "The Strong Vocational Interest Test and Its Use in Secondary Schools." *Ed Rec* 17:Sup 9:138-40 Ja '36.
45 STRONG, EDWARD K., JR. "Interests of Men and Women." *J Social Psychol* 7:49-67 F '36.
46 BINGHAM, WALTER VAN DYKE. Aptitudes and Aptitude Testing, pp. 72-5, 78-80, 354-7. New York and London: Harper and Brothers, 1937. Pp. ix, 390. $3.00; 10s. 6d.
47 MOSIER, CHARLES, I. "Factors Influencing the Validity of a Scholastic Interest Scale." *J Ed Psychol* 28:188-96 Mr '37.
48 WILLIAMSON, E. G. "An Analysis of the Young-Estabrooks Studiousness Scale." *J Appl Psychol* 21:260-4 Je '37.
49 YOUNG, C. W., AND ESTABROOKS, G. H. "Report on the Young-Estabrooks Studiousness Scale for Use with the Strong Vocational Interest Blank for Men." *J Ed Psychol* 28:176-87 Mr '37.
50 BILLS, MARION A. "Relation of Scores in Strong's Interest Analysis Blanks to Success in Selling Casualty Insurance." *J Appl Psychol* 22:97-104 F '38.
51 BILLS, MARION A., AND DAVIDSON, CHARLES M. "Study of Inter-relation of Items on Bernreuter Personality Inventory and Strong's Interest Analysis Test, Part VIII, and their Relation to Success and Failure in Selling Casualty Insurance." *Psychol B* 35:677 N '38.

52 CARTER, HAROLD D., AND JONES, MARY COVER. "Vocational Attitude Patterns in High-School Students." *J Ed Psychol* 29:321-34 My '38.

53 CROFT, LYSLE W. *An Empirical Comparison of the Thurstone Vocational Interest Schedule and the Strong Vocational Interest Blank Among Senior High School and Freshmen College Students.* Unpublished doctor's thesis, University of Kentucky, 1938.

54 DARLEY, JOHN G. "A Preliminary Study of Relations between Attitude, Adjustment, and Vocational Interest Tests." *J Ed Psychol* 29:467-73 S '38.

55 DWYER, PAUL S. "An Analysis of 19 Occupational Scores of the Strong Vocational Interest Test Given to 418 Students Entering the University of Michigan Medical School during the Years 1928, 1929, 1930." *J Appl Psychol* 22:8-16 F '38.

56 KOPAS, JOSEPH S. "The Point-Tally: A Modified Method of Scoring the Strong's Vocational Interest Blank." *J Appl Psychol* 22:426-36 Ag '38.

57 McQUITTY, LOUIS L. "An Approach to the Measurement of Individual Differences in Personality." *Char and Pers* 7:81-95 S '38.

58 PATERSON, DONALD G.; SCHNEIDLER, GWENDOLEN G.; AND WILLIAMSON, EDMUND G. *Student Guidance Techniques,* pp. 175-81. New York: McGraw-Hill Book Co., Inc., 1938. Pp. xviii, 316. $3.00. (London: McGraw-Hill Publishing Co., Ltd. 18s.)

59 SIMKEVICH, JOHN CHARLES. *An Item-Analysis of Strong's Interest Inventory:* With Recommendations for Lowering the Age Level to Which It May Be Applied. Unpublished master's thesis, Brown University, 1938. Pp. 36.

60 STARBUCK, EDMUND O. *Short-Cut Scoring of the Strong Vocational Interest Blank.* Unpublished master's thesis, Ohio State University, 1938. Pp. 57.

61 STUIT, DEWEY B. "A Study of the Vocational Interests of a Group of Teachers College Freshmen." *J Appl Psychol* 22:527-33 O '38.

62 TRAXLER, ARTHUR E. "Ratings of High School Boys on the Musician Scale of the Strong Vocational Interest Blank," pp. 57-8. In *1938 Achievement Testing Program in Independent Schools.* By Educational Records Bureau. Educational Records Bulletin No. 24, New York: the Bureau, June 1938. Pp. xi, 59, 14. $1.50. Paper, lithotyped.

63 WILLIAMSON, E. G. "A Further Analysis of the Young-Estabrooks Studiousness Scale." *J Appl Psychol* 22:105 F '38.

64 ESTES, S. G. AND HORN, D. "Interest Patterns as Related to Fields of Concentration among Engineering Students." *J Psychol* 7:29-36 Ja '39.

65 DYER, DOROTHY T. "The Relation between Vocational Interests of Men in College and Their Subsequent Occupational Histories for Ten Years." *J Appl Psychol* 23:280-8 Ap '39.

65.1 CARTER, HAROLD D. "The Development of Vocational Attitudes." *J Consulting Psychol* 4:185-91 S-O '40.

66 SARBIN, THEODORE R., AND BERDIE, RALPH F. "Relation of Measured Interests to the Allport-Vernon Study of Values." *J Appl Psychol* 24:287-96 Je '40.

67 SEDER, MARGARET. "Group Scales versus Occupational Scales for the Strong Vocational Interest Blank," pp. 51-6. In *1940 Achievement Testing Program in Independent Schools and Supplementary Studies.* Educational Records Bureau Staff. Educational Records Bulletin, No. 30. New York: the Bureau, June 1940. Pp. xii, 76. $1.50. Paper, lithotyped.

68 SEDER, MARGARET. "Some Data on the Revised Strong Vocational Interest Blank," pp. 48-50. In *1939 Fall Testing Program in Independent Schools and Supplementary Studies.* Educational Records Bulletin, No. 29. New York: Educational Records Bureau, January 1940. Pp. x, 50. $1.00. Paper.

69 SEDER, MARGARET. "Vocational Interests of Professional Women: Part I." *J Appl Psychol* 24:130-43 Ap '40.

70 SEDER, MARGARET. "The Vocational Interests of Professional Women: Part II." *J Appl Psychol* 24:265-72 Je '40.

71 SUPER, DONALD E. *Avocational Interest Patterns:* A Study in the Psychology of Avocations. Stanford University, Calif.: Stanford University Press, 1940. Pp. xiv, 148. $2.25. (London: Oxford University Press. 14s.)

Harold D. Carter, Research Associate, Institute of Child Welfare, The University of California. This test is based upon twenty years of research on the measurement of interests, and is at present the most outstanding of the several inventories of its type. Its advantages and limitations are primarily those inherent in the method of approach. It is undoubtedly of value in educational and vocational guidance, but the intelligent use of it demands some understanding of the technique, and some knowledge of the accumulated facts now available concerning interests, abilities, occupations, and the significance of vocational adjustment as a factor in the integration of personality.

The manual for the inventory contains a great store of information. It states clearly the purpose of the test, explains the technique, describes the standardization, contains instructions for administering and scoring, and furnishes devices for the interpretation of scores. The test may be scored by 35 different occupational scales, for which the intercorrelations are given in the manual along with a summary of the evidence on the reliability, validity, and general stability of the measures. The average reliability coefficient is .88 by the odd-even technique, .87 by the test-retest method with one week intervening, and .75 by the test-retest method with five years intervening. Norms are furnished with each published scale. In the manual is a bibliography of 35 references which furnish detailed information concerning particular aspects of the technique, and specific limitations, advantages, and applications of the test.

The test itself contains 400 items and takes about forty minutes to administer to the average person. It is not timed. The arrangement of the revised test is much more convenient than that of the earlier forms, both for persons taking the test and for those scoring it. The test is not too long; briefer inventories of this type are almost certain to be less reliable, less valid, and more liable to self-deception on the part of subjects. The type of item is not entirely self-explanatory; hence, mere inspection is no adequate basis for insight into the meaning of the scores. Persons wishing to use the test to full advantage are urged to read the manual most carefully and to read as many of the accompanying references as possible.

Psychologists who have made extensive use of this inventory in practical vocational guidance situations have reported that it has great value. This viewpoint is supported by results in the literature. The scoring is somewhat expensive, but unpublished studies by the writer indicate that about 80 per cent of those who take the test are benefited by it and feel that they get their money's worth. About 20 per cent are adversely critical. Comments by students who cooperate in such experiments indicate that in a majority of cases the test provides a correct appraisal of their attitudes. The inference is made that it provides a basis for insights which counselors could gain otherwise only through long acquaintance. I believe that the test reflects the cultural values assimilated by the individual during his life prior to the examination, and that the measures are useful in vocational guidance. Although primarily useful at the college level and with older persons, it is probably also of value when employed with selected high school students. The test results furnish some basis for insight into personality, but the method is technical and requires the good judgment and interpretative abilities of the trained psychologist. It is in a sense a projective method.

This test is a specific instrument to aid the vocational counselor, and not a panacea for all his ills. It is intended to indicate the vocation in which the individual is likely to be best satisfied in view of his interests. It is not intended to replace ability tests or aptitude tests, but rather to supplement them. It summarizes one's attitudes in terms of occupational significance, and for this purpose it is the best available test.

John G. Darley, Director of the University Testing Bureau and Assistant Professor of Psychology, The University of Minnesota. Since the last issue of the *Mental Measurements Yearbook* appeared, the revision of Strong's test has been made available. The revision includes: reduction of items from 420 to 400; increase in the number of specific occupational keys from 30 to 34; increases in the number of cases in each standardizing group; introduction of six so-called "group keys" and one new non-occupational key called "occupational level"; reduction in the range of score weights to plus 4 to minus 4. The specific occupational keys are located in functionally similar groupings by factor analysis techniques; there are more such functionally similar groupings than there were for the old form of the test. The six "group keys" now available are based on the item differentials between "men in general" and equal proportions of the representatives of specific occupations whose specific occupational keys fall together in the factor analysis. Thus, the responses of equal numbers of sales managers, life insurance salesmen, and real estate salesmen are compared with the responses of "men in general" to derive a "group key" that might

be given the general title of "business contact" or "sales" interests.

Our clinical experience with the revised test was checked in conferences with Mr. Strong. The following conclusions seem justified.

Two factors seem to operate to produce a higher proportion of A and B scores on the revised blank. These are: increases in the size (and presumably heterogeneity) of the standardizing groups; selection of a "men in general" sample more nearly proportional to United States census figures, where earlier "men in general" groups were loaded with representatives of upper-level jobs. These factors seem to offset the statistical effect of using one-half sigma rather than the semi-interquartile range as the starting point of the A grade range.

The "group keys" need further experimentation before being substituted for the specific occupational keys for this reason: even though certain keys show high intercorrelations in one group of subjects, the averages of a new group of subjects on a derived group key may be so divergent as to prevent certain of the new subjects from getting their expected proportion of A and B grades in the "group key" presumably as typical of their interests as of the interests of representatives of functionally similar occupations. The concept of the "group key" or "pillar key" is still promising, however, and if the present technical difficulty can be resolved, it may be possible to score the test first for "group keys" as a lead to dominant interests, following this with scoring for the specific keys indicated by the highest "group interests."

The "occupational level" key at present seems to this reviewer to give a clinically significant quantitative statement of "level of aspiration." Students with significantly low occupational level scores will probably find a satisfying adjustment in activities making relatively fewer demands on the worker than the more professionalized and exacting occupations in the upper ranges of socio-economic status.

Another clinical phase of interest measurement has evolved in our growing awareness of cases with no significant interest patterns, however often they may be tested. In such cases, guidance is extremely difficult and underachievement, transiency, or other symptoms may also appear. In this connection, it is to be hoped that the new interest-maturity scale will soon be available, since its use on the old form of the test made possible some diagnosis of lacking interests attributable primarily to maturity factors, rather than to more deep-seated conditions within the individual.

With this new scale—an improvement of an already invaluable measuring instrument—it seems even more imperative for users to stress pattern analyses rather than specific occupational keys, since the pattern analysis increases guidance usefulness by embracing a wider range of occupations that are functionally alike, even though specific keys are not now available for such a range. Furthermore, pattern analysis permits adjustments to be made for individual cases in terms of levels of the necessary abilities and aptitudes which will permit the realization of basic interests in actual job adjustments.

N. W. Morton, Assistant Professor of Psychology, McGill University. The immediate question for most persons concerned with the new Strong *Vocational Interest Blank* will be, "To what extent is it an improvement over the 1927 and 1930 forms?" The answer to this query, the reviewer believes, will depend largely upon whether one was convinced of the value of the Strong blank for one's own purposes in the first place. Some vocational psychologists have regarded it as undesirably rigid, laborious to score, costly in use and (because it deals only with *some* occupations of many) limited in significance. For them, there are grains of solace in the facts that the size of the scoring weights has been reduced whenever possible (and the time for scoring lessened a shade thereby), and one can now utilize the benefits of factor analysis by scoring for groups of psychologically related occupations rather than each occupation by itself. But in general the form and method are the same, and will doubtless be regarded by this group in much the same way. For other persons, more inclined to suffer its cumbrousness and other disadvantages for the sake of its positive values of thorough organization of material, extensive study of its validity, and knowledge about its relation to other psychological measurements, this new form will be attractive in several ways. First, it is more pleasingly and clearly printed. Second, odd points of inconvenience, such as the scoring of unchecked items in Part VI, have been dealt with. Third, a graphic

scheme of report is now provided which gives a more rapid picture of an individual's status, and which at the same time furnishes an idea of the better-than-chance value of his scores. Fourth, the old percentile values for each scale are replaced by the statistically more defensible standard scores, although for practical purposes letter-grades are emphasized as being easier to interpret, and as being safer anyway, since there is apparently no correlation with ability *within* the "A" group. Fifth, the size of the criterion samples has been increased to a minimum of 250 men, the number of occupations represented has been augmented, and other additions made, such as the aforementioned occupational groups and a scoring for occupational level. By this last is meant a measurement of distinction between laboring men's and business and professional men's interests (which is not individually diagnostic). The simplification of scoring by elimination of extreme weights has already been noted. This reviewer detects no deficiencies not already apparent in older forms.

There are given in the new manual no fresh data upon the validity of the *Vocational Interest Blank,* except as already published elsewhere. In this connection it is perhaps to be hoped that as time passes, data of a genetic kind are accumulating which will throw more direct light on the predictive value of the scales.

For a review by John G. Darley of an earlier edition, see 1178.

1681

Vocational Interest Blank for Women. Ages 17 and over; 1933-38; 1 form, 2 editions; scoring scales are available for measuring masculinity-femininity, and the following occupations: artist, author, dentist, housewife, lawyer, librarian, life insurance saleswoman, nurse, office worker, physician, social worker, stenographer-secretary, and high school teachers of each of the following subjects: English, mathematics-physical science, and social science; $2.00 per 25; 50¢ per 25 report blanks; $1.00 per scoring scale; $2.25 per 100 machine-scorable answer sheets; 2 to 9 scales, 80¢ each; 10 or more scales, 70¢ each; $5.00 per machine-scorable scale; Edward K. Strong, Jr.; Stanford University, Calif.: Stanford University Press.

REFERENCES

1 BERMAN, ISABEL R.; DARLEY, JOHN G.; AND PATERSON, DONALD G. *Vocational Interest Scales:* An Analysis of Three Questionnaires in Relation to Occupational Classification and Employment Status, pp. 5-6, 24-8, 35. University of Minnesota, Bulletins of the Employment Stabilization Research Institute, Vol 3, No. 5. Minneapolis, Minn.: University of Minnesota Press, August 1934. Pp. 35. $0.50. Paper.
2 BINGHAM, WALTER VAN DYKE. *Aptitudes and Aptitude Testing,* pp. 354-7. New York and London: Harper & Brothers, 1937. Pp. ix, 390. $3.00; 10s. 6d.
3 CARTER, HAROLD D., AND JONES, MARY COVER. "Vocational Attitude Patterns in High-School Students." *J Ed Psychol* 29:321-34 My '38.
4 PATERSON, DONALD G.; SCHNEIDLER, GWENDOLEN G.; AND WILLIAMSON, EDMUND G. *Student Guidance Techniques,* pp. 181-3. New York: McGraw-Hill Book Co., Inc., 1938. Pp. xviii, 316. $3.00. (London: McGraw-Hill Publishing Co., Ltd. 18s.)

5 STUIT, DEWEY B. "A Study of the Vocational Interests of a Group of Teachers College Freshmen." *J Appl Psychol* 22:527-33 O '38.

6 CRISSY, W. J. E., AND DANIEL, W. J. "Vocational Interest Factors in Women." *J Appl Psychol* 23:488-94 Ag '39.

6.1 CARTER, HAROLD D. "The Development of Vocational Attitudes." *J Consulting Psychol* 4:185-91 S-O '40.

7 DUFFY, ELIZABETH, AND CRISSY, W. J. E. "Evaluative Attitudes as Related to Vocational Interests and Academic Achievement." *J Abn and Social Psychol* 35:226-45 Ap '40.

8 SEDER, MARGARET. "Vocational Interests of Professional Women: Part I." *J Appl Psychol* 24:130-43 Ap '40.

9 SEDER, MARGARET. "The Vocational Interests of Professional Women: Part II." *J Appl Psychol* 24:265-72 Je '40.

Ruth Strang, Professor of Education, Columbia University. The *Vocational Interest Blank for Women* is not an aptitude test; it merely shows the degree of similarity between interests expressed by people taking the test and "successful" people in a limited number of occupations. A score of *A* in a particular occupation means similarity in interests and predicts a liking for the occupation, not success in it. This distinction between interests and success is quite understandable because many people succeed in occupations which they do not like.

The reported coefficients of reliability of the blank for five hundred married women, using the "odd versus even" technique stepped up by the Spearman-Brown formula, range from .74 to .94. As the reliability coefficients would undoubtedly vary with each group studied, they should be obtained for different age and occupational groups. No adequate information or validity of the blank has yet been obtained.

The following are difficulties involved in the development of the blank for women, many of which have been recognized by the author of the blank: (*a*) Women enter and continue in certain occupations for reasons other than interest in the occupation, and for that reason the criteria of success in the occupations is not entirely adequate. (*b*) The scale is standardized on adult women, whereas it is used for counseling purposes largely with young women whose interests are probably different from those of the older women. (*c*) A limited number of occupations are scaled—only seventeen, whereas the average person may be interested in as many as fifty and may possibly choose one of five hundred occupations. (*d*) The occupational groups on which the scales are validated are not homogeneous; they include a variety of positions having widely different interest values, as for example, the school nurse, the nurse in the hospital, and the visiting nurse—all of whom are included in the category, *nurse.*

In view of these limitations of the *Vocational Interest Blank for Women,* three courses of action are open to counselors of women. The first is to experiment with the more adequately developed blank for men. The second is to use the blank only in counseling women who do not know what kind of work they want to do and use the scores merely to suggest occupations for them to explore. The third course is to use the subject's responses on individual questions, rather than the scale scores, in order to obtain a general pattern of interests and leads for interviewing.

For a review by John G. Darley, see 1179.

[1682]

Vocational Interest Inventory. Grades 9-16 and adults; 1937-39; 1 form, separate inventories for men and women; $4.50 per 100; 25¢ per manual; 2¢ per machine-scorable answer sheet; nontimed (45-55) minutes; Glen U. Cleeton; Bloomington, Ill.: McKnight & McKnight.
a) MEN.
b) WOMEN.

Forrest A. Kingsbury, Associate Professor of Psychology, The University of Chicago. This inventory, designed for use in counseling high school students, but also usable with college students and adults, endeavors to rate the subject's interests in terms not of single occupations but of 9 types of related occupations. Two forms are provided, A for men, B for women, each in a 16-page pamphlet of which 3 pages are instructions; the remaining 13 pages contain 670 items, each to be marked + (yes or like) or 0 (no or dislike). A machine-scorable form is also available. The 670 items are grouped into 9 sections of 70 items each, based on occupational similarity, while a tenth "S-R" section lists 40 typical introversion-extraversion items. The inventory thus yields 10 scores, the introversion score for which a special key is provided, and 9 scores on occupational types, obtained by totaling the number of plus marks in any section.

A high score on any section indicates interests similar to those of persons of related occupations. For men these occupations are as follows: biological sciences (e.g., physician); selling (various fields); physical sciences (e.g., engineer, technologist, chemist, mathematician); social sciences (e.g., teacher, minister, social or YMCA worker); business administration (e.g., purchasing agent, business manager, clerk); legal and literary occupations (e.g., lawyer, journalist); mechanical occupations (e.g., various skilled trades); finance (e.g., accountant, statistician, banker, broker); creative or public performance occupations (e.g., actor, musician, artist). The women's inventory gives a somewhat different grouping. Letter-grade and percentile norms are provided for each form for grades 9, 10, 11, 12, college freshmen, and adults. Norms, it is implied, are identical for each of the 9 sections, although no information is given on this point. Reliability coefficients (odd vs. even) for 8 groups numbering from 150 to 1,000 range from .822 to .910, median .875. (Presumably, although not explicitly stated, these are corrected, and for the total form of 670 items, not for separately scored sections.) Repetition of administration after a month's interval showed a change of 6.1 per cent of the responses from 0 to +, or from + to 0.

Validity is inferred from the manner of selecting items. The inventory, we are told, was developed from items included in the original *Carnegie Interest Inventory*. New items were selected and classified on the basis of agreement with items of known significance. In addition, performance of 7,424 persons "successfully engaged in standard occupations" was analyzed to determine their relative standing on the 9 scales of the inventory. The highest inventory rating of each agreed with his actual occupation in 76 per cent of the cases; the first or second inventory rating, 82 per cent of the cases; and the first, second, or third inventory rating, 95 per cent.

The 24-page manual offers practical suggestions as to the use and interpretation of results in counseling and guidance. The author's position seems reasonable and moderate; he makes neither exaggerated claims for what it will do nor apologies for its inevitable limitations; but regards scores as bits of contributory evidence for the counselor.

A few errors in the edition examined will doubtless be corrected. The use of "page" when "section" is meant, both in manual and inventory, is confusing; so also is the 3-times misprint ECF for EFC on page 17. It would be interesting also to have more explicit information as to how the grouping of occupations into 9 types was effected, whether on the basis of occupational weightings of each item in other scales, or of inter-occupational correlations, or of factorial analyses of occupational interests, or otherwise.

This instrument appears to the reviewer to be a valuable and promising contribution to the techniques of counseling, yielding information which is sufficiently definite for most purposes, and at the same time obtained with sufficient ease and reliability to make it practicable and widely useful.

N. W. Morton, Assistant Professor of Psychology, McGill University. This inventory represents a successful attempt to provide in usable form a basis for judging vocational interests in terms of certain broad categories of occupations, such as biological science, selling, legal and literary occupations, etc. In accordance with much current research data and other vocational psychologists' views, the author has concluded that these broad categories offer a more valid means of estimating preferences than any attempt to specify at the outset particular callings. Like Strong's better-known *Vocational Interest Blank* the inventory utilizes, however, items referring to individual occupations as part of its material. The remaining items concern personal habits of feeling and acting, and likes and dislikes for people, things, and activities.

Each occupational group is dealt with in a subsection by itself. This has the effect of facilitating scoring, although how it may modify the attitudes of the person taking the test is a matter for conjecture. The basis of apportioning items to these subsections consists largely in the fruits of previously validated scales, such as Strong's and Manson's. New items, however, have been added by the device of considering their relation to older, well-tried ones. This occasionally results in a distribution of items difficult to rationalize, as when the item "watchmaker" is placed under the heading "biological sciences" rather than "physical science" or "mechanical occupations."

Among the more apparent assets which these inventories possess are the facts that they are put out in a handy, well-printed booklet form, are quickly scored by totaling positive responses for each section without weighting or use of minus values, and are readily interpreted. By some statistical magic or other device, raw point-scores on the nine main subsections of each form are directly comparable, as they have exactly equivalent letter grades or percentiles. No explanation is given of how this is accomplished. By way of deficiencies, either in the test itself or in the provision in the manual of information about it, there may be listed the lack of a middle category for "doubtful" responses (this is perhaps partially a consequence of the simplified method of scoring), the absence of any handy profile chart in the test booklet (which would readily fall in with the equivalent score device), and the failure of the author to give any data as to the intercorrelation between scores on each of the nine principal sections.

Determinations of the reliability of the individual scales by the split-half method indicate it to be in the neighborhood of .8 or .9, which is satisfactory, considering the nature of the functions measured. Although there is no indication as to the source of the agreement (whether a consequence of training, experience or temperament), there is demonstrated for employed adults a high degree of correlation between occupation followed and measured interest. Ninety-five per cent of the group have either their first, second, or third highest scores in the inventory scale corresponding to their occupation.

This reviewer feels that in Cleeton's *Vocational Interest Inventory*, taken altogether, we have a reasonably practical and useful addition to measuring instruments of this type. It would be desirable eventually to have information from genetic sources as to its prognostic value, but it is yet too early to expect this.

Occupations 18:347-52 F '40. Nora A. Congdon. "A Study of Cleeton's Vocational Interest Inventory." * The results of this study show that, although it is far from perfect, Cleeton's Vocational Interest Inventory is valuable as a guide in counseling students. The results of a reliable intelligence test should be used in connection with the results of the Inventory. The SR section, purporting to measure social adjustment, seems to have very little value. As an index of success in teaching, the intelligence test score appears to be the most valuable single factor for the men. For the women the Interest Inventory is quite valuable and should be used in connection with an intelligence test score. However, these results are not very reliable because they were based on small populations. In actual practice Cleeton's Inventory has proved especially valuable, when used

with intelligence and achievement tests, for counseling certain groups of students: (*a*) Those who cannot meet the requirements for the preparation of teachers. In attempting to persuade a student to change his vocational choice, objective scores and ratings such as these are often more convincing than subjective opinion. (*b*) Students who desire to teach in high school because of better salaries, but who are obviously better fitted to teach younger children. (*c*) Students who have no definite vocational goal or who have chosen a vocation for which they can not meet the preparation requirements. (*d*) Individual problem cases.

For reviews by Albert S. Thompson, M. R. Trabue, and E. G. Williamson, see 1181.

[1683]

Vocational Interest Schedule. College students; 1935-39; 1 form, 2 editions; nontimed (10-30) minutes; L. L. Thurstone; New York: Psychological Corporation.
a) 1935 EDITION. 1935; $2.00 per 25; 50¢ per specimen set.
b) MACHINE-SCORED FORM. 1939; $1.25 per 25 machine-scorable test-answer sheets; 25¢ per specimen set.

REFERENCES

1 THURSTONE, L. L. "A Multiple-Factor Study of Vocational Interests." *Personnel J* 10:198-205 O '31.
2 BINGHAM, WALTER VAN DYKE. *Aptitudes and Aptitude Testing,* pp. 75-80. New York and London: Harper & Brothers, 1937. Pp. ix, 390. $3.00; 10s. 6d.
3 CROFT, LYSLE W. *An Empirical Comparison of the Thurstone Vocational Interest Schedule and the Strong Vocational Interest Blank Among Senior High School and Freshman College Students.* Unpublished doctor's thesis, University of Kentucky, 1938.
4 LAYCOCK, S. R., AND HUTCHEON, N. B. "A Preliminary Investigation into the Problem of Measuring Engineering Aptitude." *J Ed Psychol* 30:280-8 Ap '39.

J. B. Miner, Professor of Psychology and Director of the Personnel Bureau, University of Kentucky. [Review of the 1935 Edition.] While it is useful for guidance to narrow choices to certain fields of related occupations, such value as Thurstone's blank might have in this respect is now superseded by provision for scoring the revised form of Strong's *Vocational Interest Blank* for eleven different groups. Strong's blank has the advantage that its reliability is known, and its data have been gathered from adults actually in the occupations.

The construction of Thurstone's blank and scoring method on the basis of factor analysis makes it a worth-while venture in research that has been decidedly valuable for later efforts in this direction. The self-consistency of the procedure for his group of college students leaves quite uncertain as yet its prediction value for interests in occupations they may later enter. How far interests are stabilized at the high school level is still so uncertain that the use of such blanks at that level is merely suggestive.

Unpublished results here on 350 high school seniors and college freshmen scored on both Thurstone's and Strong's blanks show that, when the occupations for Strong's blank are grouped as suggested by the Thurstone factors, the correlations between the median scores for the same individuals on the vocational groups ranged from −.03 to +.32. Without further evidence, it does not seem safe to assume that scores for a group of occupations named by Thurstone will correspond to a group of the same occupations scored on the Strong blank. It was also found that plus scores in Thurstone's groups are about as likely to agree with any one as another of seven out of twenty-one of Strong's occupations, for which both blanks were scored. The plan of the Strong blank is clearly more discriminative.

Thurstone's *Vocational Interest Schedule* is inexpensive, can be completed in fifteen minutes, and is easily scored. It might be used to introduce a vocational interview, but would be less useful for that purpose than the more comprehensive *Preference Record* of Kuder, or the *Basic Interest Questionnaire* of the National Institute of Vocational Research. Without further evidence the scores on it should not be assumed to predict scores on Strong's

blank or motivational interest in the actual vocations. Above all, a vocational counselor must be exceedingly cautious not to jump from vocational interest to the conclusion of vocational ability. It is even possible that a person's understanding of his own deep and persistent desire to enter a particular occupation would bring special success along some branch of the occupation not developed by those in the field whose interests were unlike his. He would be doing something different and distinctive in the field. For those who have had prolonged interests in one direction, their own choice of occupation may be quite as significant as their score on the interest blanks. This means that vocational interest blanks are mainly useful for those who are quite undecided. They should be used to direct attention to fields of work to be considered.

For reviews by Harold D. Carter and N. W. Morton, see 1180.

[1684*]

Vocational Inventory. Grades 8-16 and adults; 1940; 1 form; 10¢ per inventory; 5¢ per individual analysis reports; 25¢ per specimen set; nontimed (150) minutes; Curtis G. Gentry; Minneapolis, Minn.: Educational Test Bureau, Inc.

REFERENCES

1 GENTRY, CURTIS G. "Knoxville's Seven-Point Vocational Guidance Program." *Sch Executive* 59:10-2 Ap '40.

* In order to have the entry numbers continuous with the earlier publications in this series, the first entry number in the test section is 1182. The addition of 22 new entries—assigned fractional numbers—and the assignment of a double number to one test make the total number of tests listed in this volume 524.

BUSINESS EDUCATION—THIRD MMY

REVIEWS BY *Vera M. Amerson, Harvey A. Andruss, E. G. Blackstone, Ann Brewington, Philip H. DuBois, Beatrice J. Dvorak, Elizabeth Fehrer, Orrel E. Little, Paul S. Lomax, Agnes E. Osborne, Ray G. Price, Edward A. Rundquist, Arnold E. Schneider, Herbert A. Tonne, and C. C. Upshall.*

[367]

★Bookkeeping Test: State High School Tests for Indiana. First, second, third, fourth semesters high school; 1942–45; 4 levels; Form A (1st and 3rd semesters); Form N (2nd and 4th semesters); 4¢ per test; 15¢ per sample test; 40(45) minutes; M. E. Studebaker, B. M. Swinford, Vernal H. Carmichael, Frances R. Botsford, and Russell Burkhart; State High School Testing Service, Purdue University.

[368]

Bookkeeping Test: United-NOMA Business Entrance Tests. Schools and industry; 1939–47; new form usually available annually; prior to 1947, the series title was National Clerical Ability Tests; $5 per 25; $1 per test when scoring service and certificates for acceptable work are desired; $2 per specimen set of the 6 tests in the series; 120(130) minutes; prepared by the Joint Committee on Tests representing the United Business Education Association and the National Office Management Association; National Office Management Association.

Harvey A. Andruss, President, State Teachers College, Bloomsburg, Pennsylvania. [Review of the 1946 Form.] This test *assumes that a bookkeeper must be able to keep books*, not merely to post or record sales, or enter cash items, or do other routine clerical work. Time allowance is two hours, but a bonus is given for doing the work in less time.

The *1946 Bookkeeping Test* seeks to determine fitness for bookkeeping work through: (*a*) an understanding of principles and practice; (*b*) ability to follow instructions; and (*c*) neatness. A large part involves correcting incorrect entries made in the Cash Book and Journal through careful reading of the explanations, also to correcting incorrect postings, after which a new trial balance of the General Ledger, with schedules of Accounts Receivable and Accounts Payable, is required.

The test presents a handwritten set of books. However, it should be remembered that bookkeeping is a matter of recording rather than reviewing (auditing) and reporting (accounting). It would seem that the correction of incorrect entries smacks of the type of verification that is usually a function of the auditor, while the construction of a trial balance and the supporting schedules is certainly a very elementary accounting task and the making of a trial balance is the job of every bookkeeper —it is, in fact, the beginning of the reporting activity of the accountant.

In the key to the bookkeeping test, point credits for finding errors vary from 5 to 10, while a 2-point bonus is credited for each full five minutes saved. No particular credit for recopying or taking a new trial balance appears to be given. This would seem to be provided for in the bonus given for completing the whole test in less than two hours time.

The point of view of those making the Bookkeeping Test as it appears in the latest (1947) announcement of the United–NOMA Business Entrance Tests is as follows:

Statements, adjusting, and closing entries are not complete bookkeeping tests . . . the ability to make these entries and statements is not expected of a beginning bookkeeper, as much as the ability to keep

records, and find and correct errors. . . . If a person can make and post entries, the facts do not prove that he can locate and correct inaccuracies, but if he can locate and *correct* inaccuracies, that is proof that he can also do the original work. Therefore, the U-N bookkeeping test is one involving locating and correcting inaccuracies.

Ray G. Price, Associate Professor of Education, The University of Minnesota, Minneapolis, Minnesota. [Review of the 1946 Form.] This test is intended to measure ability to do the work required of a bookkeeper. The testee is provided with a cash book, journal, general ledger, abstracts, trial balance, and subsidiary ledger. The original work is completely provided for in the form of entries, postings, and a trial balance. However, there are several entries that are incorrectly made; others are incorrectly posted. These errors cause the trial balance and abstracts to be inaccurate. The testee is to locate and correct the incorrect entries and postings; and finally to rewrite the trial balance and abstracts. The test requires two hours. It is easy to administer. The form is excellent, meeting all the requirements and usual practices of such a test. Percentile norms are provided.

The difficulty of adequately measuring a student's ability in handling a set of books in a short time is recognized, yet the fact that this test requires two hours to administer presents a serious obstacle to its use in most high school classes 45 to 60 minutes in length.

No validity is reported. The sponsors say that they "are fully aware of the fact that much additional work must be done before the full validity of these tests is established. . . . All that is claimed for the tests is that they are true samples of office work." This reviewer would question somewhat the validity of the test from the standpoint of its adequacy to measure ability to do the ordinary routine work of a bookkeeper. Rather it tends to measure ability to do auditing.

No reliability for the test is reported. An earlier form of the test (1941) had an estimated coefficient of reliability of .90. However, the form of the test was so changed that another statistical analysis will have to be made in order to estimate the reliability of the present form.

Objectivity in scoring may be questioned; for instance, 10 points of credit are allotted for "high grade of neatness," while 5 points are allotted for "average neatness." The basis for the point system of scoring is not clear. How the weighting of points of credit was determined is not explained. For example, for finding and correcting an error in the posting of the wrong amount, 5 points are allowed, while for finding and correcting an error in posting to the wrong account, a credit of 10 points is awarded. How to handle part credit is another aspect of the scoring that is not explained. For instance, Item 8 of the key states: "Journal, March 11, Notes Payable debit should be on $2,750, instead of $2,777.50 and a debit should appear to Notes Interest and Discount Expense, $27.50, 10 points." What should be the score for a student who corrected the debit to Notes Payable but who did not make the entry to Notes Interest and Discount?

There is a total of 85 points on the test, not including a bonus of 2 points for each 5 minutes saved under the two-hour time for taking the test. The minimum acceptable mark on the test is 31. No mention is made as to how this minimum score was determined. This seems unusually low since it would be possible for a testee to get 24 of the needed 31 points by the very simple expedient of handing in his paper at the end of one hour of time.

Where the test is given on a national basis at properly sponsored centers as a means for issuing certificates to adequately qualified students the test may have some value. For the ordinary bookkeeping teacher to use in her class, the test has very limited value.

[369]

Business Fundamentals and General Information Test: United-NOMA Business Entrance Tests. Schools and industry; 1939–47; new form usually available annually; prior to 1947, the series title was National Clerical Ability Tests; $5 per 25; $1 per test when scoring service and certificates for acceptable work are desired; $2 per specimen set of the 6 tests in the series; 45(55) minutes; prepared by the Joint Committee on Tests representing the United Business Education Association and the National Office Management Association; National Office Management Association.

Vera M. Amerson, Manager, Walsh School of Business Science, Miami Beach, Florida. [Review of the 1946 Form.] The *1946 Business Fundamentals and General Information Test* is required of every one who takes one or more of the vocational tests included in the National Clerical Ability Test series. The fundamentals part is designed to measure command of such skills and knowledges as spelling, use of the apostrophe, plurals, arithmetic, and social science. The general information part, in contrast with the school-taught knowledge covered in the fundamentals part, covers information gained from events reported by radio and newspaper and from common customs.

Thirty-five minutes is allowed for the Business Fundamentals Test and twenty-five minutes for the General Information Test. Each part in the Business Fundamentals Test is timed separately in order to make sure that slow pupils do something in each part. If a person finishes a given part before the time is called, he is expected to go on at once to the next part. A five-minute recess is allowed between the Business Fundamentals Test and the General Information Test. Those who finish the General Information Test before time is called may hand in their papers. Most testees have adequate time to try all the items in both tests.

Although each part restates the directions for recording answers on the separate answer sheet, the testee is given no opportunity for working out examples before taking any part of the test. In all parts of the Business Fundamentals Test, except one, the testee is given only one example. Furthermore, the code for recording the answers changes from a b c for the first 10 items to C I for the next 10, to a b N for the next 6, to a b c N for the next 5, to a b c for the next 9, and to 1 2 3 4 for the remaining 24. The arrangement of the example in Part A is different from the actual exercise, and in both Parts A and B the first example corresponds with the actual answer for the first item in each of these parts. "N" for the "none" answer is omitted in the example in Part E. These mechanical inconsistencies are supplemented by inconsistencies in capitalization, arrangement of items, and use of commas in amounts and after dates, indicating the probability of a hasty job of editing. Item 4 in Part C is weak in that the spelling of both choices is correct while the instructions read "One word in each of the following groups of plurals is correctly spelled."

A desirable characteristic of the test is the large proportion of functional information included in the test. Another desirable feature is the ease with which the test may be administered and scored.

The reliability and validity of the test have not been checked since a careful analysis a few years ago resulted in the finding that the NCA tests were highly reliable and valid. The form of the test has been maintained over the years so as to retain the qualities of reliability and validity. Plans have been laid for another checking of these two qualities at an early date.

C. C. Upshall, Psychologist, Industrial Relations Department, Eastman Kodak Company, Rochester, New York. [Review of the 1946 Form.] The business fundamentals test includes short sections on (*a*) spelling (10 questions), (*b*) apostrophe (10 points), (*c*) plurals (6 points), (*d*) arithmetic (5 questions), and (*e*) social science (9 questions). The general information test has 24 questions; a majority of them are on subjects of current interest.

The coefficients of reliability computed by the split-half technique for similar sections of the 1941 edition of the test were: General Information, $r = .84$; Business Arithmetic, $r = .75$; and English, $r = .84$.

The scores from these tests are not to be considered by themselves but are combined with scores from any of the five skill tests, to give a composite score for any particular skill. For example, the score for the filing test would be based on the score made on the filing test plus the scores made on the *Business Fundamentals and General Information Test*. This procedure is justified on the basis that employers are reported to feel that English and arithmetic fundamentals and business and general information are things that should be taken into consideration when hiring a person for any of the jobs covered by the five tests. The weights given to the business fundamentals and general information test scores vary according to the skill test score with which they are combined. The weights are determined by the "pooled subjective judgments of experienced business teachers and office managers" made effective by appropriate statistical treatment.

The questions under social science do not seem to be essentially different from those under general information except that one provides three choices and the other four. Thus, the question "The Louisiana Purchase was ——" (three choices) is placed under social science while "Blessed are the peacemakers ——" (four choices) is part of the general informa-

tion test. General Information might serve as a title for both sections.

Studies of the validity of the various skill tests combined with the fundamentals and general information tests have been promised. Objective on-the-job checks on the appropriateness of the weights given to the fundamentals and general information tests by the experts are also needed. How much, for instance, does knowledge of English, arithmetic fundamentals, and general information contribute to success on the job of file clerks?

At present, certificates of proficiency are awarded on the basis of the test results. More knowledge of the value of the tests for predicting success on the job should be obtained before the Certificate of Proficiency may be regarded as the main qualification for securing a position. This necessary knowledge can be gained more quickly if business firms will encourage schools of business to give the tests and report the scores to the firms who employ the graduates. Follow-up studies should be made and reported as soon as possible.

[370]

★**Commercial Arithmetic Test: State High School Tests for Indiana.** High school; 1945–46; Form A; 4¢ per test; 15¢ per sample test; 40(45) minutes; Charlotte Henderson and Philip Peak; State High School Testing Service, Purdue University.

[371]

★**Cooperative Commercial Arithmetic Test.** 1-2 semesters high school; 1944–47; IBM; Forms U, X; separate answer sheets must be used; $1.75 per 25; 40¢ per 25 machine-scorable answer sheets; 15¢ per scoring stencil; 25¢ per specimen set, postpaid; 40(45) minutes; prepared by the staff of the Cooperative Test Service; Cooperative Test Service.

[372]

★**E.R.C. Stenographic Aptitude Test.** Grades 9 and over; 1944; preliminary manual; 1 form; $3.65 per 25; 50¢ per specimen set; 33(45) minutes; Walter L. Deemer, Jr.; Science Research Associates.

REFERENCES

1. HOSLER, RUSSELL J. "Aptitude Testing in Shorthand." *J Bus Ed* 22:25 My '47. * (*PA* 22:834)

Philip H. DuBois, Professor of Psychology, Washington University, St. Louis, Missouri. This test appears to be an excellent prognostic instrument, constructed on sound plan and presenting evidence of careful development and validation.

Only one of the five subtests, speed of writing, is a speed test. The others, word discrimination, phonetic spelling, vocabulary and sentence dictation, have sufficiently long-time limits that the speed factor is considered of negligible importance.

The material appears to sample adequately the skills required in learning shorthand. The validity coefficient of .70 between total score and accuracy of transcription of material dictated at more than 80 words per minute at the end of two years of shorthand study indicates that the test measures what it purports to measure.

One paragraph in the manual of directions merits quotation even in a short review: "No reliability coefficients are reported for this test because it is felt that they add nothing to the reported validity coefficients. If the validity coefficient is satisfactory, the reliability coefficient must be satisfactory. On the other hand, a test with high reliability may have low validity, in which case the high reliability is of no value. The value of an aptitude test should be assessed by its validity coefficients, not by its reliability."

While the position taken by the author is logical and may help to reduce our ritualism in regard to reliability coefficients (many of which are spuriously high anyway), this reviewer hopes that other test constructors will not follow Dr. Deemer's lead in omitting reliability coefficients from their reports. A properly computed reliability coefficient giving the consistency of the test as it exists is an inverse indication of the extent to which further work with the approach used by an author is justified. The validity gives the usefulness of an instrument only as it exists. If the reliability by test-retest or by alternate forms is high, say .92 or over, little would be gained by further development along the same lines. If on the other hand, the reliability is in the .80's, test consumers have the right to expect the author to perfect his instrument still further. A test constructor who fails to report reliability information fails to provide the test user with information essential to intelligent appreciation of the instrument.

Edward A. Rundquist, Assistant Director of Personnel Research, Owens–Illinois Glass Company, Toledo, Ohio. This test would be better termed a shorthand aptitude test since it is specifically designed to predict ability to learn and transcribe shorthand—which is but one phase of stenographic proficiency. It contains five subtests: I, Speed of Writing; II, Word Discrimination; III, Phonetic Spelling; IV, Vocabulary; and V, Sentence Dictation. It is similar in content and aim to the *Turse Shorthand Aptitude Test.*

The test has been carefully validated against objective measures of shorthand transcription. Errors in spelling, punctuation, and capitalization are not counted in scoring the transcription tests. This procedure emphasizes the aim of the author to predict shorthand transcription and not general stenographic proficiency. The test given at the beginning of a shorthand course correlates with accuracy of transcription measured at intervals of one and two years later from .54 to .70. These are substantial correlations and are of the order reported for the Turse test. Speed of accurate transcription is predicted less well, two correlations of .35 being reported.

The omission of some important statistical information detracts from an otherwise clearly written manual. It is known that 500 cases were involved in all the validity studies. But N's, means, and sigmas are not reported for the specific correlations obtained. Validity is reported only for total score. No validities or intercorrelations of the subtests are given to facilitate interpretation.

The test score is interpreted by means of a table of predicted criterion scores (for each of the seven criteria) for twenty-point test score intervals. Percentile norms are given for the five subtests. Since norms usually vary widely according to age, selection, and previous experience, the absence of total score norms is unfortunate. The percentile norms for the subtests would have much more value if the subtest validities and intercorrelations were reported.

With the exception of the dictation subtest, this test is easily administered and scored. It will take some practice to give this subtest correctly. The problem is of greatest moment to the occasional user. The scoring of this test is laborious, involving the counting of syllables omitted, inserted, or substituted. While this subtest appears to involve an element important to stenographic proficiency, one wonders whether as good a prediction might not be obtained with a more easily scored test. Omission of validities and intercorrelations of the subtests prevents any judgment on this point. Some modification to simplify scoring would be welcomed by the users of the test.

E.R.C. Stenographic Aptitude Test

No reliabilities are reported, but this is unimportant in view of the validities reported.

These criticisms should not obscure the major fact that the test possesses substantial validity. In the reviewer's opinion it can be used with profit in the selection and classification of tenth and eleventh grade shorthand pupils. Whether its difficulty level will make it equally valuable for older persons in private secretarial schools is a matter for further study.

[373]

★**Examination in Bookkeeping and Accounting.** First, second years high school; 1944-45; 1 form (usually called Form B); 2 levels; separate answer booklets must be used; the test is not machine-scorable; $1.75 per 25 answer booklets of either level; 10¢ per scoring key for either level; 30¢ per specimen set of either level, postpaid; 180(190) minutes, either level; prepared by the Examinations Staff of the United States Armed Forces Institute; published by the American Council on Education; distributed by Cooperative Test Service. (Also distributed by Science Research Associates: $2 per 25; $3 per 25 answer booklets; 50¢ per key; 50¢ per specimen set.)
a) FIRST YEAR: SECONDARY SCHOOL. 1944; Form SBk-Ag-1-B-4; $2 per 25.
b) SECOND YEAR: SECONDARY SCHOOL. 1945; Form SBkAg-2-B-4; $1.75 per 25.

Harvey A. Andruss, President, State Teachers College, Bloomsburg, Pennsylvania. The first-year test consists of four subtests: (*a*) Accounting Terms, Facts, and Principles—40 minutes; (*b*) Adjusting and Closing Entries—20 minutes; (*c*) Preparation of Accounting Entries—75 minutes; and (*d*) Preparation of a Work Sheet—45 minutes. Approximately two-thirds of the testing time is devoted to practical work as against knowledge and principles. No provision is made for the correction of bookkeeping entries. The scoring key does not show the year dates, only rulings. The Cash Receipts and Cash Payments Journals do not show posting recapitulations.

The second-year test consists of four subtests: (*a*) Accounting Terms, Facts, and Principles—40 minutes; (*b*) Features of Various Forms of Business Ownership—10 minutes; (*c*) Preparation of Accounting Entries—65 minutes; (*d*) Preparation of a Work Sheet—45 minutes.

These tests seem to be comprehensive and worthy of consideration.

[374]

★**Examination in Business Arithmetic.** High school; 1944; IBM; Form SBuAr-1-B-4 (usually called Form B); separate answer sheets must be used; $1.75 per 25; 40¢ per 25 machine-scorable answer

sheets; 15¢ per scoring key; 25¢ per specimen set, postpaid; 135(145) minutes; prepared by the Examinations Staff of the United States Armed Forces Institute; published by the American Council on Education; distributed by Cooperative Test Service. (Also distributed by Science Research Associates: $2 per 25; 65¢ per 25 machine-scorable answer sheets; 50¢ per key; 50¢ per specimen set.)

[375]

★**Examination in Business English—High School Level.** Grades 11-12; 1944; IBM; Form SBuE-1-B-4 (usually called Form B); separate answer sheets must be used; $2 per 25; 40¢ per 25 machine-scorable answer sheets; 15¢ per scoring key; 25¢ per specimen set, postpaid; 120(125) minutes; prepared by the Examinations Staff of the United States Armed Forces Institute; published by the American Council on Education; distributed by Cooperative Test Service. (Also distributed by Science Research Associates: $2 per 25; 65¢ per 25 machine-scorable answer sheets; 50¢ per key; 50¢ per specimen set.)

Orrel E. Little, Associate Professor of English, Manchester College, North Manchester, Indiana. This is a comprehensive yet simple and therefore desirable examination, testing in its five separate sections the achievement of objectives usually set for high school courses in business English. As the publishers state, they do measure more "than memory of facts . . . Numerous exercises represent problem situations, involving for their successful solution applications of knowledge and the functioning of critical thinking."

Section I directs the student to select the misspelled words in a well-chosen list of 100. While these are above the minimum-essential level for general spelling usage, they are essential to ordinary business communication and include applications of troublesome spelling principles, such as doubling the final consonant, *referred,* and dropping a silent *e* before a suffix, *wholly,* choosing the correct prefix—*dis* or *de, per* or *pre, perspiration,* etc.

The Word Usage section tests diction or word choice by giving in sentence situations 25 pairs of words frequently confused in business. These range from the ever-present *principal-principle* team to such puzzlers as *accede* and *exceed.*

Section III uses multiple-choice groupings to test 20 such matters of form and usage as the correct arrangement, punctuation, and wording of the typed letterhead, the inside address, the salutation, the complimentary close, and identifying information in letters. Excepting one question concerning hanging indentations, the situations used are typical of those met in most offices.

E.R.C. Stenographic Aptitude Test

In the fourth part an effective column arrangement of error-packed sentences from the body of a business letter provides multiple choices in grammar, punctuation, and diction, from which the student is to select "from the point of view of accuracy, style, or tone." Most of these also are typical of lessons to be mastered by a high school student: word division at the ends of lines, run-on sentences, agreement of subject and verb, wordiness, and confusion of adjectives and adverbs. However, there are included some controversial problems often taught today but not tested, such as the rigid placement of commas and periods within quotation marks regardless of the thought and the determination of paragraphing and parenthetical expressions, which are too often matters of interpretation.

The last section, carefully designed to test the recognition of effectiveness, consists of three short letters—a complaint, a reply to a request for information, and a recommendation. Each sentence in them is given in three different forms: one lively but crude; another affected and wordy; another simple, direct, and sincere. The student is given good opportunity to apply his knowledge and critical reflective thinking in deciding which of the three is the best.

The publishers state that the tentative norms determined from over twelve hundred cases in thirty-two schools will be improved as more data are received. Stressing the desirability of relating varying degrees of achievement on the tests to the scholastic standards of the local institution, the editors give specific suggestions for turning the scores into letter grades. The diagnostic values of the test are enhanced by the availability of norms for both part and total scores. Analysis of the parts of the tests and of the scores will help the teacher evaluate her course, plan remedial work, and counsel the students.

[376]

★Examination in Commercial Correspondence—College Level. Grades 13-14; 1944; IBM; Form CCmC-1-B-4 (usually called Form B); separate answer sheets must be used; $2 per 25; 50¢ per 25 machine-scorable answer sheets; 30¢ per scoring key; 35¢ per specimen set, postpaid; 120(125) minutes; prepared by the Examinations Staff of the United States Armed Forces Institute; published by the American Council on Education; distributed by Cooperative Test Service. (Also distributed by Science Research Associates: $2 per 25; 65¢ per 25 machine-scorable answer sheets; 50¢ per key; 50¢ per specimen set.)

Orrel E. Little, Associate Professor of English, Manchester College, North Manchester, Indiana. The first four sections of this examination are planned to measure the mechanics of business communication, whereas the last section attempts the more difficult judgment of effective arrangement and style.

Section 1 lists 100 words in the college business person's vocabulary, from which the student is to select the misspelled forms. The authors have included examples of the common types of errors, as *omitting, dining, originally,* and words which the correspondent uses freely, such as, *competitors, notary, assessment.* The Word Usage section tests diction by giving in sentences 25 pairs of words frequently confused, from each of which the student is to select the appropriate one. He must distinguish between *personal* and *personnel, cessation* and *secession.* One pair—*further* and *farther*—should have been omitted.

Section 3 uses multiple-choice groupings to test 20 such matters of form and usage as the correct arrangement, punctuation, and wording of the typed letterhead, the inside address, the salutation, the complimentary close, and identification information in letters. Some teachers will object to the fact that semiblocked style is disapproved in one instance. In the fourth part an effective column arrangement of error-packed sentences from the body of a letter provide multiple choices in grammar, punctuation, and diction, from which the student is to select "from the point of view of accuracy, style, or tone." While most of these 74 situations are real and essential, at least 7 are objectionable because they are controversial, such as the illogical placement of the period within quotation marks, the substitution of *this* for *which,* and the use of a comma before *and* between subordinate clauses.

The problems in Section 5 attempt by three different methods to lead the student to judge the effectiveness of several letters. First he is to rearrange the jumbled sentences of two letters. The method to be followed—selecting from the multiple choices numbers representing the sentences—is so highly confusing as to render "critical reflective thinking" impossible. Then the student is asked to label as true, false, or doubtful critical remarks about a given "effective sales letter." Again his thinking is blocked, this time by the fact that the letter is not really effective. The final exercise is clear and worth while: The student, after comparing the tone of five versions of a business letter, is to label each as satisfactory, too negative, not concise enough, etc.

The publishers state that the tentative norms for both part and total scores determined from 465 cases in twenty-three schools will be improved as more data are received. Stressing the desirability of relating varying degrees of achievement on the tests to the scholastic standards of the local institution, the editors give specific suggestions for turning the scores into letter grades. Although the weaknesses of the fourth and fifth parts render the norms for them of questionable value, analysis of the parts of the tests and of the scores will help the teacher evaluate her course, plan remedial work, and counsel her students.

Herbert A. Tonne, Editor, The Journal of Business Education, and Professor of Education, New York University, New York, New York. This test consists of five sections. Sections 1 (Spelling), 2 (Word Usage), and 4 (Grammar, Punctuation, and Diction) are general in nature and deal with phases of ability to use English common to all communication situations rather than just to business correspondence. Sections 3 (Letter Form and Usage) and 5 (Recognition of Effective Letter Writing) give specialized consideration to business letter writing. All sections of the test are well constructed, avoid trick questions, and deal with the most important elements of the subject covered.

No evidence of reliability is given, but it is quite likely that it is high. Norms are given in terms of percentile ratings for almost five hundred students for each form. In addition, percentile ranks are also given for each section of the test. As evidence of understanding of the essential elements of good letter writing, the test is quite evidently valid. As final evidence of ability to write effective business letters, its validity is far more open to question. It would be interesting to compare the scores on this test of a large number of writers of effective business letters with those of little ability. The degree to which ability to recognize good letter writing correlates with actual ability to write good letters is of great consequence, and some evidence would be secured from this type of comparison. This comment should not be considered a condemnation of the test, for in the

final analysis there is no means of testing ability to write good business letters or any other kind of good writing other than that of actually having testees write letters and subjectively determining their effectiveness.

The test is, in this commentator's opinion, the best objective measure of business writing ability at present available. While it has been aimed at college level students, it has considerable value in measuring the results of work in the secondary schools and in private business schools. In these cases, of course, the tentative norms given for the test would not be valid.

It is to be hoped that the publisher will secure data on the reliability of the test and give some evidence of its validity, when and if another edition is produced.

[377]

★Examination in Gregg Shorthand. First year high school; 1944; Form SGS-1-B-4 (usually called Form B); $2 per 25; 5¢ per scoring key; 25¢ per specimen set, postpaid; (120) minutes; prepared by the Examinations Staff of the United States Armed Forces Institute; published by the American Council on Education; distributed by Cooperative Test Service. (Also distributed by Science Research Associates: $2 per 25; 50¢ per key; 50¢ per specimen set.)

Agnes E. Osborne, Assistant Professor, The City College of New York, New York, New York. This examination is not intended to test a student's ability for a *stenographic position.* In no way does the examination test an individual's ability to typewrite in acceptable form at vocational speed when shorthand notes are the stimuli. This is the standard for a stenographic position. However, the test is fairly representative of the materials covered in first-year shorthand classes in many schools and of the skills obtained in one year's time. The general form of the test is good. The directions to the student are concise but explicit, and the instructions for administering the test are sufficiently detailed to insure expert administration.

The test is divided into three sections. In Section A, 175 printed words and phrases are to be written in shorthand. Inasmuch as the value of shorthand lies in the writer's ability to record outlines when spoken words, not printed words, are the stimuli, this section of the test does not measure the knowledge and skill required in recording notes when sound, not sight, is the stimulus. Entirely different scores would no doubt be obtained if the words and phrases were written from dictation. This procedure would give a truer measure of the student's shorthand knowledge and skill. For the Shorthand Reading Test, which is Section B, the student is required to transcribe into longhand a shorthand article of 300 words. Some device should have been worked out to test reading ability with far less transcribing to be done. For example, there is no advantage in having a student transcribe the word "the" the number of times it appears in the article. The method of scoring the reading test may also be criticized. As one of the directions for scoring the transcript is to count ⅓ point for each correct word, repetitions receive the same credit as the first form. The word "the," for example, receives credit each time it appears, and receives the same credit each time as the words "foreign," "monuments," and "resources," which occur only once in the article. Section C consists of the dictation of three letters at different rates of speed—the first letter at 50 words per minute, the second at 60, and the third at 70. A phonograph record is available for the letter dictation. If it is not possible to obtain the phonograph record, the administrator may read from the printed material, which has been marked for timing. Explicit directions have been given to insure natural rather than artificial dictation.

The manual that accompanies the test gives no analytical or statistical data for the shorthand test, but deals with the general testing program of the United States Armed Forces Institute. Reliability and validity coefficients for the shorthand test are not given. The percentile norms and equivalence tables for Forms A and B are made available to those who purchase tests. The teacher who uses the tests would find it helpful if more information were given regarding the construction of the tests, especially regarding the criteria used for the selection of the vocabulary. An analysis made by the writer of this review shows that the test words in Section A (Shorthand Vocabulary) cover practically all the major principles illustrated in the Gregg manual. Therefore, the teacher who wishes to use Section A for diagnostic purposes will have a basis for specific remedial teaching.

The shorthand outlines on the scoring key lack uniformity and fluency, and they are exceedingly heavy and very large. It would be impossible to evaluate a student's notes correctly if the notes in the scoring key were used as models of Gregg shorthand. Inasmuch as the scoring directions are to "Allow credit even

though size and slant of examinee's outline differ from the outline in the key," the emphasis is evidently placed on the application of shorthand principles and not on quality of penmanship.

This test was constructed under the auspices of experts and has probably been subjected to more scientific treatment than any other elementary shorthand test. It deserves further use and should be supplemented with results presented in a revised manual, which should contain more specific information regarding the construction of the test, the validation, the reliability, and the interpretation of scores for shorthand learners.

[378]

★**Examination in Typewriting.** First, second years high school; 1944; 1 form (usually called Form B); 2 levels; separate answer booklets must be used; the test is not machine-scorable; $2 per 25; 25¢ per scoring key for either form; 45¢ per specimen set of either form, postpaid; prepared by the Examinations staff of the United States Armed Forces Institute; published by the American Council on Education; distributed by Cooperative Test Service. (Also distributed by Science Research Associates: $2 per 25; $3 per 25 answer booklets; 50¢ per key; 50¢ per specimen set.)
a) FIRST YEAR: SECONDARY SCHOOL. Form STy-1-B-4; $2 per 25 answer booklets; (130) minutes.
b) SECOND YEAR: SECONDARY SCHOOL. Form STy-2-B-4; $3 per 25 answer booklets; (115) minutes.

E. G. Blackstone, Professor of Business Education, The University of Southern California, Los Angeles, California. This test is designed for use by educational institutions to enable them to become familiar with the levels of achievement required in the Armed Forces Institute, and to facilitate the just evaluation of the educational experiences in typewriting of returning service men and women. The tests were constructed by having specialists meet with teachers of typing to identify the educational objectives to be attained; to specify the kinds of exercises to be included in the test; by preparing enough exercises to provide for two forms of the test; and by trying out the test with groups of students in high school and college. The tests were then submitted to one or more critics nominated by a professional organization of business teachers, who checked the tests for comprehensiveness of coverage, for accuracy of material, and for validity of exercises. Then the tests were revised and given another tryout in schools. One form was kept for use by the Armed Forces Institute and the other was made available to high schools and colleges.

The test consists of two five-minute timed

writings with credit to be given for the higher score of the two; a typing of corrected rough draft; a letter to be set up in modified block form from running copy; a simple tabulation; and an objective test of 30 items covering punctuation and other information in connection with the use of the typewriter.

A special scoring key is used with the timed writings which gives illustrations of the types of errors to be marked. Ten words per minute are deducted for each error.

For the rough draft, the letter, and the tabulation exercises, transparent scoring keys are provided to determine if the placement is correct and to indicate penalties for degrees of error in placement. Errors in typing are also penalized. The objective test may be marked with special pencil for machine scoring, or with ordinary writing instrument for hand scoring.

The tests may be interpreted by means of a set of percentile scores taken from more than 1,700 cases in more than 40 schools. No data are given as to reliability or validity.

The tests appear to be fairly comprehensive in form; at least enough so to be usable for the determination of credit to be allowed. The objective section is particularly ingenious and good.

It appears from the distributions of raw scores that are supplied with the norms for this examination that the step intervals used are too wide to yield discriminative scores at the upper levels.

[379]

Filing Test: United-NOMA Business Entrance Tests. Schools and industry; 1939–47; new form usually available annually; prior to 1947, the series title was National Clerical Ability Tests; $5 per 25; $1 per test when scoring service and certificates for acceptable work are desired; $2 per specimen set of the 6 tests in the series; 120(130) minutes; prepared by the Joint Committee on Tests representing the United Business Education Association and the National Office Management Association; National Office Management Association.

Arnold E. Schneider, Head, Department of Business Education, Western Michigan College of Education, Kalamazoo, Michigan. [Review of the 1946 Form.] The introductory statement on this test to the effect that "this test is to measure ability to arrange and file letters correctly under office conditions as nearly as those conditions can be reproduced" sets up the testing objective clearly. This is a performance test. It is true that the performance takes place under simulated conditions and is to some extent of

a paper-and-pencil variety, but nevertheless, it does attempt to measure performance in this vocational area. This is an efficient test and represents a long step forward in helping to solve the problem of vocational clerical testing.

The test measures up well in terms of accepted testing practices. In the main the directions are clear and concise. The directions under Part I could be restated with more clarity and effectiveness. It would be well if the sample item were separated from the main body of the test questions in Part I. This would make it much easier for the student to grasp what is required of him in this section.

A question could be raised as to the format on page I. A long list comprising 85 names is presented on three pages with the request that names from list B be entered between the names on the long list spread over three pages. This is an awkward testing situation, particularly since the time element is involved. It may be that the writers were attempting to check for "paper shuffling" ability, but this is a mere conjecture.

A manual for administration accompanies the test and clearly defines the work of the test administrator. This is particularly good for this type of test as it aids in the standardization of the administration of the test. It gives to the scores a greater degree of validity since the conditions under which the tests are administered are, for the most part, predetermined.

Parts 2, 3, 4, and 5 of the test employ the use of sample form letters. These letters are on sheets approximately 3½ by 5½ inches. Actual letters on standard-sized letterhead of 8½ by 11 inches were photographed and reduced to the size mentioned. This, of course, has reduced the size of the type considerably. This opens up two possible criticisms which may or may not be serious. One of them is that the individual who has less than 20/20 vision may be penalized more for eyesight than for ability. This may have a bearing on the test performance when one relates it to the high percentage of eye difficulties to be found in a normal population as shown by the figures among draftees during the past war. It is also possible that some individuals may find it difficult to shuffle, arrange, and rearrange the small sheets of paper which simulate actual letterhead size. It might well be that actual letter-sized sheets would improve the efficiency of the tests and add no difficulty to the problems inherent in the construction of this type of test.

Examination in Typewriting

An answer key is furnished in the manual for administration. It is suggested in the bulletin describing the tests that the tests are to be returned to the central office for scoring. This insures uniform scoring and proper analysis of each paper. A statement is also made that the tests may be corrected by the teacher. The scoring key provided in the administration manual does not lend itself to efficient use on the part of the teacher who would attempt to correct the tests locally.

No claim is made as to statistical validity. There is an a priori claim that the tests do measure actual office performance in this area. This claim has been substantiated by the businessmen and business teachers who have aided in the selection of the test items. There is no reason to question the statement that the tests are valid in that they are sample performance tests for the specific vocational area of filing. Percentile tables are furnished, based upon a wide sampling.

It must be remembered that this test is one of a battery of six tests which attempts to determine vocational clerical ability. Although each individual test is a separate measuring instrument, nevertheless the composite effect or picture of the test scores might conceivably present a performance picture which would more accurately portray the abilities of the testee than could individual tests. This test should be judged, in the long run, in terms of the entire battery of the United–NOMA Business Entrance Tests.

C. C. Upshall, Psychologist, Industrial Relations Department, Eastman Kodak Company, Rochester, New York. [Review of the 1946 Form.] This filing test is designed as a test of achievement of people who have studied filing or have had filing experience. It is not intended to be a test of aptitude or trainability. The scores from this test are not given apart from the scores on a test of general information and English and arithmetic fundamentals. These two tests are considered a valuable part of each of the six tests of office skills published by the National Council for Business Education and the Office Management Association. A composite score for the filing test is based on the weighted scores of this test plus those from the general information and fundamentals test. The importance of each of these tests is determined by the "pooled subjective judgments of experienced business teachers and office managers." The standard deviation of the scores, the reliability coefficient of the tests, and the coefficient of alienation between the separate parts are used to assign numerical weights that will reflect the judgments of the experienced teachers and managers.

The filing test is made up of five parts, four of which must be answered by the testee. The parts are: (*a*) filing each of a list of 50 names of people and companies in another alphabetized list; (*b*) filing 50 letters alphabetically according to name; (*c*) filing the same 50 letters alphabetically according to location; (*d*) sorting for triple check automatic filing; and (*e*) labeling folders for filing.

A choice is given between Parts (*d*) and (*e*). Fifty pages of correspondence, reduced in size to 3¾ x 5¾ inches, serve as the material to be alphabetized in Parts (*b*) and (*c*). Accuracy is stressed more than speed. A small bonus is allowed for each minute saved by finishing before the two hours assigned to the test are up.

It is claimed that the test will measure "production speed" rather than "spurt speed," but little proof for the statement is given apart from the fact that a candidate may take two hours to complete the test. It is doubtful whether a test of two hours will show "production speed" much better than a half-hour or an hour of testing. "Production speed" is based on many more factors than can be included in a two-hour test.

Most employment departments in industry will find the testing time of two hours for the filing test plus the hour or more for the general information and fundamentals test too long to devote to gathering information about file clerks, at least until clear evidence is given of the high validity of these tests. The use of the tests at the end of a training period is to be recommended. Employment departments might well encourage business schools to give these tests and report the results to the firms that hire their graduates.

The filing test may well prove to be one of the most valid now available.

[380]

★General Test of Business Information. Grades 9-16; 1942–43; Forms A, B; $1.15 per 25, postpaid; 20¢ per specimen set, postpaid; 40(45) minutes; Stephen J. Turille; Bureau of Educational Measurements, Kansas State Teachers College of Emporia.

Vera M. Amerson, Manager, Walsh School of Business Science, Miami Beach, Florida. This test is an effort to measure a high school or college student's ability to recall information about consumer business education and to solve certain practical problems. The test includes such fields as record keeping, business papers, business English, buying habits, basic legal principles, and business dress.

The test consists of three major sections and a total of 112 items. Sections I and II, consisting of 37 and 12 items respectively, carry the traditional titles of "True-False Test" and "Multiple Choice Test" instead of titles indicating the kind or kinds of information being tested. Since the test is named *General Test of Business Information,* some may question the inclusion of Items 1 and 38, which deal with club records. Some may also prefer "journal," "ledger," or some other business term to the use of the word "diary" in Item 23. No doubt the word "mailed" in Item 42 ("A package valued at $150.00 to be mailed third class should be (1) airmailed, (2) expressed, (3) freighted, (4) registered.") will be changed in future editions, since it weakens responses (2) and (3).

Section III, Business Problems Test, consists of 63 short answers to be filled in by the student. Since only one example is given for this section on the front page of the test, the student is likely to gain from the problem given the idea that the entire section consists of mathematical problems. When work is actually begun, the student will find that in addition to mathematical problems he has to do such tasks as filling in a check, writing an endorsement, checking a list of items, and answering information questions such as "What do the letters C.O.D. stand for in the business world?" and "At least how often should personal property inventories be taken?"

Although the test is intended for college students as well as for high school students, statistical data are given only for high school students.

Herbert A. Tonne, Editor, The Journal of Business Education, and Professor of Education, New York University, New York, New York. This comprehensive test of the minimum essentials of consumer business information covers such areas as check writing and endorsements, business papers, notes and drafts, basic legal principles, recording, and personal-use business information and buying practices. Each form is composed of 112 items. The reliability

coefficient is listed as being .91 with low probable error. This would make the test unusually reliable as classroom tests of this type go. The validity of any test of this type is, of course, subjective, but care seems to have been taken to insure adequate coverage of subject matter by checking available texts and syllabi and by submission of the material to thoughtful critics.

The test seems broader in scope than the *Thompson Business Practice Test* (38:942) and about as reliable and useful for classroom and testing purposes. Some of the test items are open to dual interpretation and a few of the answers given in the key are not correct. This, however, is not at all unusual in teacher service material of this kind.

A comparison is given of scores made by 539 pupils on Form A at midyear with scores of 465 pupils on Form B at the end of the year. No indication is given, however, of whether these pupils were the same persons, and whether they had taken a subject such as junior business training during this interval. This hardly makes possible the "intelligent interpretation" which the manual of direction suggests is provided. Moreover, a pattern is given for translating the scores into school marks without reference to subject taken, age of student, or intelligence. Scores which are satisfactory for low-intelligence students would hardly be adequate for those of higher intellectual capacity; scores which might be high for a high school freshman would be very unsatisfactory for a college senior; yet the test description indicates that the test "covers the minimal essentials of consumer business information that a high school or college student should possess." It is possible, however, that these weaknesses are the fault of the publisher rather than the author. As most classroom teachers at present must construct tests, the publisher has a serious responsibility for eliminating those weaknesses in a test which, while they are quite tolerable when used in the author's classes for his own use, make the test unsatisfactory when presented for nation-wide distribution.

Nevertheless considering the dearth of standardized materials in the subject matter of general business, this test must be considered a distinct contribution. If the teacher ignores some of the suggestions for translating test scores into marks and is careful in the use of the key, the test will be found a valuable aid in determining classroom achievement in a general business class and will provide at least a partial basis for diagnosis for remedial teaching.

[381]
Hiett Stenography Test (Gregg). First, second semesters high school; 1938–39; Forms B, C; 2 levels; $1.15 per 25, postpaid; 15¢ per specimen set, postpaid; 40(45) minutes; Victor C. Hiett and H. E. Schrammel; Bureau of Educational Measurements, Kansas State Teachers College of Emporia.
a) TEST I. First semester.
b) TEST II. Second semester.

Agnes E. Osborne, Assistant Professor, The City College of New York, New York, New York. Test I covers the work of the first semester and Test II covers the entire year's work. The same kind of test items is used in each test and each test consists of five parts. Part I consists of a list of 50 printed words which are to be reproduced in shorthand in blanks provided for that purpose. No criteria for the selection of the words are given for this part of the test or for the remaining parts. Part II consists of a list of 40 shorthand symbols which are to be transcribed on blank lines provided for that purpose. In Part II, not enough space has been provided for the student's longhand transcript while more than enough has been provided for the shorthand outlines in Part I. The authors probably experienced difficulty in arranging these two parts on the same page. Part III contains a list of 20 shorthand sentences, and opposite each sentence is a group of 4 words, one of which is to be chosen to complete the meaning of the shorthand sentence. The groups of words opposite the first 10 shorthand sentences are in longhand, and those opposite the last 10 sentences are in shorthand. In this section of the test, an attempt has been made to test the student's reading ability without resorting to the requirement of a complete transcript of the material. Part IV is a printed article of 200 words. The student is to write the shorthand outlines on the line immediately above each word. This test requires a skill that has not been practiced in the average shorthand class, and it remains to be determined whether writing outlines directly above printed words that are in context is indicative of shorthand skill. Part V consists of an exercise in letter dictation and longhand transcription. This part is to be graded only for accuracy of transcription. As the dictation for Part V is to be given in 3 minutes at the beginning of the testing period and 40 minutes is allowed for the remaining parts of the test, including the longhand

transcription of the letter, it is evident that no attempt has been made to find out how fast the student transcribes. Because of the way the time is allotted, it is quite possible that students may not reach this practical section of the test—the transcription test, which approaches more closely than any other part of the test the objective of the shorthand course.

The manual that accompanies the test consists of 2 pages of information. The authors are vague concerning the construction of the test. Insufficient analytical and statistical data regarding the important phases of selection of test items, scoring, weighting of parts, length of parts, and timing are submitted. The only data available on the reliability of the test are stated in one sentence: "Various components of parts yielded reliability coefficients for the several forms of the test from .65 to .85, average .75." These figures would seem to indicate fairly low reliability. Further information on the number of cases and the distribution of the scores is desirable if one is to get a very precise idea of reliability. Norms for the test are given in the form of percentile scores and were computed from the scores made by 5,296 students in 358 schools.

The materials for this test have been assembled in a 4-page booklet. Parts I and II are on the front page—evidently it is immaterial whether all students begin working on the test at exactly the same time. Some may fill in the information in the heading more quickly than others do and begin the test immediately or, at least, see the test material before the others do.

The scoring key and the directions for administering the test have been reproduced by a duplicating process and are therefore more difficult to read than print would be. Some of the shorthand outlines on the scoring key are not discernible, and on some copies the directions are difficult to decipher. The shorthand outlines on the test forms are fairly good. The directions for administering are brief and too indefinite to insure the same performance by each administrator. It is quite possible that students would feel the necessity for asking questions on Part III, especially where the performance varies from the average activity in the classroom. A sample answer is advisable for this part.

[382]
Kauzer Typewriting Test. First, second, fourth semesters high school; 1934; 3 levels; 90¢ per 25, postpaid; 15¢ per specimen set, postpaid; 15(25) minutes;

Adelaide Kauzer and H. E. Schrammel; Bureau of Educational Measurements, Kansas State Teachers College of Emporia.

a) TEST I, FORM A. First semester.
b) TEST I, FORM B. Second semester.
c) TEST II, FORM A. Fourth semester.

E. G. Blackstone, Professor of Business Education, The University of Southern California, Los Angeles, California. There are three of these tests. Test I, Form A, designed for use at the end of one-half year of instruction, consists of a timed writing and a paragraph copying exercise. Test I, Form B, designed for use at the end of one year of instruction, consists of a timed writing exercise and a paragraph that is to be centered on the page. Test II, Form A, to be used at the end of two years, consists of a timed writing and a simple tabulation. The timed writings are 15 minutes in length, and are scored by International Rules.

Percentile charts are provided for interpreting each part of each test. The timed writings of Forms A and B of Test I are supposed to be of equal difficulty, but no statement is given as to how they were equated. No statement is given on reliability or validity.

It appears that an effort has been made in the timed writings to provide material of little difficulty. Very few numbers or special characters are included, hence such factors are not measured. The accuracy grade is determined by multiplying the errors by 3 and subtracting from 100. Why this particular penalty is used is not clear. The speed grade, determined by International Contest Rules, is transposed by means of a table into scores from 100 down.

Teachers using these tests will need to learn how to interpret such scores, for the old method of using net words per minute does not apply. Perhaps this is an advantage. The scores in the other parts of the tests than the timed writings are combined with the timed writing scores by adding the totals and dividing by three. These may then be interpreted by means of percentile charts. Why this particular weighting of the parts is used is not justified.

The use of International Contest Rules for scoring seems to be a doubtful method, since those rules have been subjected to much criticism as being arbitrary, contrary to business office practices, and unscientific in nature. There seems to be no effort made in the test results to make possible any comparison of student scores and business standards.

The tests are rather similar to those with which teachers are familiar but have the same faults that most previous typing tests have had, namely, uncertainty as to the difficulty of copy, failure to test all characters on the keyboard, and an arbitrary grading scheme.

[383]

★**Kimberly-Clark Typing Ability Analysis.** Grades 9-12 and adults; 1942; preliminary manual; 1 form; out of print; nontimed (60) minutes; Clifford E. Jurgensen; Science Research Associates.

REFERENCES

1. JURGENSEN, CLIFFORD E. "A Test for Selecting and Training Industrial Typists." *Ed & Psychol Meas* 2:409-25 O '42. * (*PA* 17:1350)

E. G. Blackstone, Professor of Business Education, The University of Southern California, Los Angeles, California. These tests were designed either as an employee selection aid or for training purposes. The booklet contains four exercises: typing a corrected copy of a rough draft, typing a simple tabulation, typing a short business letter from penwritten copy, and a tabulation of three columns requiring the student to rearrange and alphabetize the copy.

The grading is based on a time score and an error score. The time is the number of minutes required to complete the test. The error score is based on three types of errors that are penalized at increasing rates: corrected errors, minor errors, and gross errors. A chart is provided to aid the teacher in classifying errors.

Speed and accuracy scores may be combined into one score by use of an Error Score Converting Chart which seems to have been devised by approved statistical methods. Combined scores may be determined in three ways: one by giving equal weight to speed and accuracy; one giving speed twice as much weight as accuracy; and one giving accuracy twice as much weight as speed. Percentile charts make it possible to interpret scores for speed alone, for accuracy alone, or for any one of the three combinations of speed and accuracy. The chart gives percentiles for office typists and for high school seniors.

Careful attention has been given to statistical treatment. The items were determined by conferences with office supervisors, then preliminary forms were prepared and tried out. Then comparisons were made of the test results and efficiency ratings of office typists. The test sections retained were chosen on the basis of high correlation with the criteria and low intercorrelations.

Reliability coefficients range from .72 to .84,

depending upon the method used for combining speed and accuracy. These are fairly high correlations. Validity correlations between total test scores and office efficiency ratings were .957, which is almost unbelievably high and could be possible only by chance or by means of far better efficiency ratings than are ordinarily available. The validity correlations of the various elements are: time, .79; converted errors, .71; raw errors, .65; gross errors, .45; minor errors, .55; and corrected errors, .33.

These tests attempt to measure elements of typing other than straight copy elements, although straight copy is involved to a degree. They have been given careful and complete statistical treatment of a type that may well be recommended to other testmakers.

[384]

Machine Calculation Test: United-NOMA Business Entrance Tests. Schools and industry; 1939–47; new form usually available annually; prior to 1947, the series title was National Clerical Ability Tests; $5 per 25; $1 per test hen scoring service and certificates for acceptable work are desired; $2 per specimen set of the 6 tests in the series; 120(130) minutes; prepared by the Joint Committee on Tests representing the United Business Education Association and the National Office Management Association; National Office Management Association.

Elizabeth Fehrer, Associate Professor of Psychology, Michigan State College, East Lansing, Michigan. [Review of the 1946 Form.] This test, like the others in the series, is an achievement test intended for evaluation of the student at the end of a business training course and for selection and evaluation of calculating machine operators. The test is designed to be a production-speed test in contrast to a spurt-speed test. Two hours are allowed for administration, and consequently the ability to do sustained accurate work is required. Either an electrically operated or a hand-operated machine may be used.

The test measures proficiency in the four fundamentals and in normal fractions and percentages. The majority of items are in the form of specific problems. Many are fairly long and involve considerable computation before the final value, which alone is scored, can be computed. The items were selected to sample actual office work, and they cover a wide variety of problems. On the basis of the length, complexity, and representativeness of the items, the face validity of the test seems to be high.

A new form of the test is prepared each year;

and although "the exact steps taken in the construction of the tests vary somewhat from year to year," the construction of the tests apparently adheres to sound procedures. A preliminary form is tried out on a sample of students and office workers. Analysis of the tryout results includes a study of the reliability of the scoring procedure and an item analysis with a discard of all nondiscriminating items.

Experimental evidence concerning the validity of the test is lacking at present although a follow-up study is in progress "to ascertain the business success of those who took the tests in 1937 and 1938 and to determine whether or not the certificate holders are making good, whether or not those who failed to win a certificate had any great difficulty in making good in jobs for which the tests said they were not qualified, and whether or not the certificate was helpful in securing employment." Because of the similarity of the successive forms, the results for the earlier editions would presumably apply to subsequent editions of the test.

Reliability, although not determined for each edition of the test, is probably high. A study of the 1941 edition indicated a split-half reliability coefficient of .96.

This test, like the others in the series, is administered only in certified test centers on specified dates and under adequate supervision. Test papers are returned to the central office where they are scored and results later reported to schools or employers. Norms based on those taking the test are in terms of percentiles. A minimum acceptable score on each test is specified, but the basis for determining this critical score is not described. Successful candidates are sent a certificate of proficiency in the subject.

Earlier forms of the test are available for practice or training purposes.

[385]

Parke Commercial Law Test. High school; 1933; 1 form; 90¢ per 25, postpaid; 15¢ per specimen set, postpaid; 40(45) minutes; L. A. Parke; Bureau of Educational Measurements, Kansas State Teachers College of Emporia.

Ray G. Price, Associate Professor of Education, The University of Minnesota, Minneapolis, Minnesota. This test was "originally constructed for use in the Nation-wide Every Pupil Scholarship Test of April, 1933." The test, consisting of 120 items, is easily administered. The typography and make-up are not superior; however, they are satisfactory even though the print is rather small. Percentile norms are provided, based on 623 cases.

No statistical evaluation is given of the validity of the test. "The test is based on the content of a number of respectable textbooks used in high school classes. The distribution of items is based on textbook content and judgment of commerce teachers."

The test does not use the preferred technique of arranging the items in the order of ascending difficulty. The true-false section of the test contains 34 false items and only 16 true items. It would seem desirable to have a better balance of true and false items.

Numerous clues and suggestions occur that, by the alert student, could be used to determine the correct response even though he were not familiar with the subject matter. Two examples from the matching items will illustrate this point : (a) "A condensed history or synopsis of a title to real estate." Answer, "Abstract of title." (b) "Statutes limiting the time within which law suits to recover damages may be brought." Answer, "Statutes of limitation." The rather consistent use of such terms as "all, "not," "always," "never," and "must" in the negative forms of items are other recognizable clues.

This is a rather comprehensive test covering the essential principles of an elementary course in commercial law. It is easy to give and to score. It would be of value to the teacher who wished to evaluate the attainment of her class. The test should, however, be revised in the light of the content changes in business law since 1933 when the test was first published.

[386]

★Seashore-Bennett Stenographic Proficiency Tests: A Standard Recorded Stenographic Worksample. Adults; 1946; Forms B-1, B-2; Transcription Style (33⅓ rpm): $16 per set, postpaid; Standard Record Style: $17 per set, postpaid; $2 per 100 summary charts, postpaid; 35¢ per manual, postpaid; (50-60) minutes; Harold Seashore and George K. Bennett; Psychological Corporation.

Ann Brewington, Associate Professor of Business Education, School of Business, The University of Chicago, Chicago, Illinois. These phonographically-recorded proficiency tests are worksamples which can be used by business firms, schools, and employment agencies in setting their own standards. Business firms can use them advantageously in hiring stenographic employees, in promoting on a work-production basis, and in setting achievement standards in

training programs within the firm. In fact, one of the two forms is sold only to business firms in order to guarantee that testees will not have had access to the tests in schools or at employment agencies.

While careful preliminary work is evidenced in the selection of subject matter, in the length and form of the letters, and in determining what constitutes mailability, the most significant work has been on the problem of measuring rate. The use of records controls rate and at the same time eliminates the human factors influencing the two people constituting the dictation situation. Scoring omitted, mutilated, and substituted words and limiting the transcription time measure rate and make it possible for the weighting of each of the other five factors of mailability to vary from job to job. The "just graduated" are differentiated from the experienced; the unemployable, from the "can learn," the competent, and the eminently competent. These procedures should facilitate the solution of a difficult problem—how to weight the various kinds of errors in stenographic tests which vitiate the significance of a single-number score.

Total dictation time for the five letters is approximately 20 minutes; total transcription time, 30 minutes. From one to fifty people can take dictation at the same time. Norms are not yet available. New forms will be added to the series as the tests become well known.

[387]

Shemwell-Whitcraft Bookkeeping Test. First, second semesters high school; 1937–38; Forms A, B; 2 levels; 90¢ per 25, postpaid; 15¢ per specimen set, postpaid; 40(45) minutes; E. C. Shemwell, John E. Whitcraft, and H. E. Schrammel; Bureau of Educational Measurements, Kansas State Teachers College of Emporia.
a) TEST I. First semester.
b) TEST II. Second semester.

Arnold E. Schneider, Head, Department of Business Education, Western Michigan College of Education, Kalamazoo, Michigan. Although the objective type of bookkeeping test has been in common use during the past two decades, nevertheless few innovations or new and challenging objective-test devices or situations have been devised. It may be stated that the *Shemwell–Whitcraft Bookkeeping Test* follows a too often repeated pattern. The tests are, at best, mediocre measuring instruments of the subject matter at this level.

This test is designed to measure the achievement of pupils at the end of the first semester and the second semester of the first year of bookkeeping. The tests are supplied in alternate Forms A and B for each semester.

The four tests comprising the series are constructed on the following pattern: 50 true-false items, 25 multiple matching items, 25 completion, 25 matching, and 5 problems, a total of 130 items with a score potential of 150. The faultiness of this distribution of test items lies in the fact that the measuring instrument is relying heavily on a type of test item the validity of which, for purposes of measuring bookkeeping skill, is open to question. This is particularly true of the 50 true-false items and the 25 completion items.

Apparently no attempt is made to test, in a comprehensive objective fashion, several of the basic concepts which the student of bookkeeping should grasp during his first year's work. Certainly some means of measuring the student's knowledge, skill, and abilities in dealing with adjusting and closing entries, the working sheet, the profit and loss statement, and the balance sheet should have been devised and included in the test. The only two specific areas of bookkeeping performance which are actually tested are recognition and selection of proper journal entries and recognition for the purposes of account classification.

A careful reading of the test items leaves much to be desired in the way of sharp and clear word usage. There is a good deal of ambiguity in many of the questions. The phraseology is not sharp and clear cut. Many of the questions are highly irrelevant. The claim for validity is based upon "common content of several leading textbooks and courses of study," but a study of the questions used in the true-false sections and the completion sections would suggest that many of the test items were built on a basis of testing over those areas which lent themselves to test construction.

The fact that forms are supplied, that reliability coefficients for the tests have been determined, and finally that percentile scores for an adequate population are supplied makes this test of limited value to the classroom teacher of high school bookkeeping. It does provide a comparative measure of those areas which the test does test. It is doubtful whether the test does, as the writers claim, determine pupil achievement, check the efficiency of instruction, or analyze pupil and class weaknesses. The alert and competent classroom teacher, who is not too overworked, should be readily able to construct a test which, for her purposes, would measure achievement more accurately than does this test.

[388]
★Shorthand Test: State High School Tests for Indiana. First, second, third, fourth semesters high school; 1945–46; Form A; 5¢ per test; 15¢ per sample test; 22(40) minutes; M. E. Studebaker, B. M. Swinford, Vernal H. Carmichael, Frances R. Botsford, and Russell Burkhart; State High School Testing Service, Purdue University.

[388a]
★SRA Clerical Aptitudes. High school and adults; 1947; Forms AH, BH; separate answer pads must be used; 43¢ per 25 profile sheets; 75¢ per specimen set; 25(35) minutes; prepared by Richardson, Bellows, Henry and Co., Inc.; Science Research Associates.

[388b]
★SRA Dictation Skills. High school and adults; 1947; separate answer pads must be used; the Accuracy Album includes two 12-inch records (78 rpm) presenting 1 practice and 5 test letters for measuring dictation accuracy; the Speed Album includes four 12-inch records (78 rpm) presenting 1 practice and 8 test letters for measuring dictation speed; $18.75 per set of albums; 45¢ per test booklet with answer pad; $1.65 per 25 answer pads; (60) minutes; Marion W. Richardson and Ruth A. Pedersen; Science Research Associates.

[388c]
★SRA Language Skills. Stenographers; 1947; 1 form; $1.90 per 25; 50¢ per specimen set; 15(20) minutes; Marion W. Richardson and Ruth A. Pedersen; Science Research Associates.

[388d]
★SRA Typing Skills. High school and adults; 1947; $1.90 per 25; 50¢ per specimen set; 10(15) minutes; Marion W. Richardson and Ruth A. Pedersen; Science Research Associates.

[389]
Stenogauge. Stenographers; 1922; $3 per introductory set including 10 tests, postpaid; 4¢ per extra test, postpaid; introductory sets may be ordered on approval; (12-20) minutes; Eugene J. Benge; Management Service Co.

Beatrice J. Dvorak, Chief, Worker Analysis Section, U. S. Employment Service, Washington, D. C. The *Stenogauge* is a proficiency test for stenographers and typists. It measures dictation speed, transcription speed, transcription accuracy, and spelling accuracy for stenographers; and typing speed, typing accuracy, and spelling accuracy for typists. These elements enter into a single composite score, which is converted to a percentile rank. The user is instructed to test his stenographers and typists to find the average rank in his own organization, and to compare the scores or ranks of applicants with those of employees with whose work he is familiar.

A practice period is provided, if necessary, for the applicant to become familiar with the typewriter which is to be used during the test.

The dictation is not read at a standardized speed, but at a speed "which presses the applicant slightly." The material dictated consists of a business letter, about 200 words long. Its tone may appeal to a few employers. A typical sentence is: "In the second place you insinuate that I, personally, have a grudge against you." The punctuation is also dictated. Following the dictation, a 50-word spelling test (requiring that the words which are misspelled—about 25—be identified) is interjected. The dictated material is transcribed after the completion of the spelling test.

The test for typists is similar to the test for stenographers, except that the dictation test is omitted, and the typing is from a perfect copy. For typists, the composite score is the sum of the typing rate per minute, the percentage of typing accuracy, and the spelling accuracy. The norms, or percentile ranks, were established, according to the author, in the period about 1922 after validating the test by comparing test scores with ratings of stenographic ability. A question arises regarding the weighting of the elements tested. For stenographers the composite score is the sum of the dictation rate (words per minute), the transcription rate (words per minute), the transcription accuracy (per cent of dictation correctly transcribed), and spelling accuracy (per cent of correctly recognized spelling and misspellings.) By what criterion it was determined that each of these elements should have unit weight, in terms of the indicated units of measurement, is not indicated. It is very unlikely that these are the most valid or the optimum weights. In any event, norms for each of the elements separately might have been more appropriate for placement purposes.

[390]

Stenographic Aptitude Test. Grades 9-16; 1939; 1 form; $1.60 per 25, postpaid; 35¢ per specimen set, postpaid; (25) minutes; George K. Bennett; Psychological Corporation.

REFERENCES

1. BARRETT, DOROTHY M. "Prediction of Achievement in Typewriting and Stenography in a Liberal Arts College." *J Appl Psychol* 30:624-30 D '46. * (PA 21:1624)

Philip H. DuBois, Professor of Psychology, Washington University, St. Louis, Missouri. Compared with other available tests in the same field (the *Turse Shorthand Aptitude Test* and the *E. R. C. Stenographic Aptitude Test*),

Bennett's *Stenographic Aptitude Test* does not attempt to include as wide a variety of functions in its measurement of the abilities required to master shorthand. Consequently, perhaps, its reported validity is not as high as those stated by the authors of the tests mentioned above. Actually no validity coefficient for the entire test is reported, the validities of the transcription score being of the order of .27 and of the spelling score .48 (both point biserials), with a negligible correlation being found between the two parts. The multiple correlation between the test as a prognostic instrument and later success in a private secretarial school would appear to be of the order of .55.

The manual states that an early study of the prediction of success in typing and shorthand showed that little reliance could be placed on standard intelligence test scores or on special manipulative tests. It is therefore somewhat surprising to find a number of correlations of the subtests with Alpha scores, based upon investigations in 1939 and 1945. Certainly correlations of any aptitude tests with other published tests are of interest to workers in the test field, but this information presented without interpretation under the heading of "Standardization" appears to be gratuitous.

A more workmanlike job could have been done in presenting the validity information. Since the point biserial is affected by the point of the dichotomy, some indication should have been given about the division of the group as to success or failure in training. As success in a secretarial school is probably not an all-or-none affair, the Pearsonian biserial instead of the point biserial could have been justified (and would have yielded higher coefficients!).

The reliability reported for the transcription test (.975) is perhaps spuriously high because of the way it was computed, namely, by correlating the scores made in odd minutes with those made in even minutes. The test requires substituting arbitrary symbols for five digits and, on a second page, translating the symbols back to the original digits. A high degree of learning is probably involved, which could easily boost the reliability. A more conservative estimate of the reliability could have been obtained either by separately timed halves or by development of an alternative form.

Edward A. Rundquist, Assistant Director of Personnel Research, Owens–Illinois Glass Com-

pany, Toledo, Ohio. This is a well-constructed test of model simplicity in administration and scoring. In this respect, as well as in its brief time limits, it is markedly superior to such tests as the *E. R. C. Stenographic Aptitude Test* and the *Turse Shorthand Aptitude Test.* Unfortunately, its validity cannot be accurately ascertained from the published data.

There are two subtests—a substitution test involving the translation of numbers to symbols and vice versa and a test of ability to identify and correct misspelled words. Validity was obtained by testing some seven hundred entrants to a private secretarial school and obtaining a measure of success or failure about nine months later. The criterion is broader but less objective than that of objective tests of shorthand transcription used to validate the tests mentioned above. The use of this criterion is in line with the author's purpose of predicting success in learning both typing and shorthand. It probably includes more than this. It is probably more closely related to job success than to the narrower criterion of ability to transcribe shorthand. The effort to collect such a criterion is difficult but, if successful, pays dividends. The difficulty in this instance is that the resulting validity coefficients are not capable of interpretation from the published data. Validity coefficients of .27 and .47 for the substitution and spelling tests are reported in point-biserial terms. These coefficients are the same for groups with and without typing or shorthand experience. These coefficients vary markedly with the percentage in the success and failure groups. No information is given on this point, nor are success and failure defined in any way. A further barrier to interpretation is that of the 700 students tested some 200 were eliminated for lack of an unambiguous record of success or failure. Where these cases are located on the criterion distribution will make a considerable difference in the results obtained. No test scores for the eliminated group or reasons for lack of unambiguous criteria data are presented to permit evaluation of this point.

No validity is presented for total test score although the norms are in these terms. The product moment correlation between the subtests is around zero, so the tests will combine to yield maximum prediction. Could the point-biserials be taken at face value, the multiple would be substantially greater than the .47 obtained for the spelling test, but in the absence of meaningful basic correlations, there is no incentive to make the calculation.

The author makes moderate claims for the test. In the reviewer's experience with the prediction of shorthand success from spelling tests, he would anticipate a correlation in the neighborhood of .4. From the published data, however, we cannot tell whether the validity is higher or lower than that reported.

The test is highly reliable. The manual is clearly written and directions for administration easy to follow. Norms are presented for a wide range of groups. In view of the many good features of this test further validation studies are well warranted.

[391]

Stenographic Test: United-NOMA Business Entrance Tests. Schools and industry; 1939–47; new form usually available annually; prior to 1947, the series title was National Clerical Ability Tests; $5 per 25; $1 per test when scoring service and certificates for acceptable work are desired; $2 per specimen set of the 6 tests in the series; 125(140) minutes; prepared by the Joint Committee on Tests representing the United Business Education Association and the National Office Management Association; National Office Management Association.

Ann Brewington, Associate Professor of Business Education, School of Business, The University of Chicago, Chicago, Illinois. [Review of the 1946 Form.] This test is one of a group of six worksample tests jointly constructed and administered annually by the National Office Management Association and The United Business Education Association, in an effort to lessen the differences between school standards and office standards. It is an attempt to measure the degree of "readiness for work" of skilled but uninitiated workers.

With no significant change in the structure, content, or scoring, the proportion of testees from approximately 200 high schools and colleges during an eight-year period receiving certificates has ranged from 24 to 76 per cent. Approximately 3,200 Stenographic Certificates have been issued to testees passing the test.

The dictation time is 30 minutes plus 5 minutes for redictation as necessary, at varying speeds, followed by a 90-minute transcription period. The maximum score is 230 points; the minimum acceptable score is 69 points. The reliability is .90. The validity is yet to be established.

Elizabeth Fehrer, Associate Professor of Psychology, Michigan State College, East Lansing, Michigan. [Review of the 1946 Form.] This is a shorthand achievement test "built on the assumption that a stenographer must be able to take ordinary dictation for reasonably long stretches at a time and get out her notes promptly and acceptably. Hence the candidate is subjected to a 35-minute dictation test and a 90-minute transcription test."

The test aims to approximate work under actual office conditions and appears to do so. The items to be dictated consist of nine letters which are to be transcribed in mailable form and straight matter to be typed in the form of a first draft. Specialized vocabulary has been avoided. The dictation is given at an average speed of 75 words a minute and simulates natural original dictation as distinguished from stenographically phrased, quarter-minute marked school dictation. At the end of certain items a short time is allowed for redictation. In transcribing, a dictionary is allowed. Transcripts must make the sense intended by the dictator, but the words dictated and those transcribed need not be identical in all cases.

A new edition of the test is prepared each year. Determination of the reliability of the test is not made for each edition. For the 1941 edition the reliability coefficient was .90 which is satisfactory. The very length of the test seems sufficient to insure comparable reliability for the more recent editions, although this is something that could easily be verified for each new form.

The validity of an earlier form of the test was studied by comparing the scores of fifty high school students with those of fifty employed stenographers. The results (which are not available in their details) indicated that "the high school young people did superior work in stenography in the matter of placement, neatness, and accuracy as far as they went; but by the time they reached the middle of the test they faltered and either did not finish or jumbled their transcription so as to be unusable. The working young people had the stamina and finished the test easily but with a lower quality." This brief validity study suggests that the test probably does in fact measure proficiency on the job and that the test score will indicate the immediate usefulness of an applicant. Use of the test might also have value in making the business school course in

shorthand more practical if, in order to prepare students for the test, office practices are more closely duplicated in the classroom.

Like the other tests in the series, this test is given only on specified dates in approved test centers and under competent supervision. Papers are returned to the central office for scoring. Percentile norms based on those taking the test are later reported to schools and business firms. A certificate of proficiency is sent to those students or employees passing the test.

Earlier forms of the test are available for practice or training purposes.

[392]

★Turse-Durost Shorthand Achievement Test (Gregg). 1-2 years high school; 1941–42; Form A; $1.20 per 25; 35¢ per specimen set, postpaid; (60) minutes; Paul L. Turse and Walter N. Durost; World Book Co.

REFERENCES

1. TURSE, PAUL L. "Problems in Shorthand Prognosis." *J Bus Ed* 13:17-8+ My '38. *
2. TUCKMAN, JACOB. "Study of the Turse Shorthand Aptitude Test." *J Bus Ed* 19:17-8 N '43. *
3. BARRETT, DOROTHY M. "Prediction of Achievement in Typewriting and Stenography in a Liberal Arts College." *J Appl Psychol* 30:624-30 D '46. * (PA 21:1624)
4. HOSLER, RUSSELL J. "Aptitude Testing in Shorthand." *J Bus Ed* 22:25 My '47. * (PA 22:834)

J Bus Ed 17:39–40 Je '42. * should prove valuable to teachers and administrators in assigning grades, sectioning and diagnosing difficulties, as well as in determining how their students stand in relation to other high schools and which of their students are ready to take positions in business or industry.

[393]

Turse Shorthand Aptitude Test. Grades 8-10; 1940; 1 form; $1.70 per 25; 35¢ per specimen set, postpaid; 45(50) minutes; Paul L. Turse; World Book Co.

Philip H. DuBois, Professor of Psychology, Washington University, St. Louis, Missouri. This test consists of seven subtests which involve activities that are reasonably close to the work of the stenographer: stroking, which involves manual dexterity; spelling of words commonly misspelled; phonetic association in which words spelled approximately as they are pronounced are to be transcribed into conventional spelling; symbol transcription, in which material involving 14 arbitrary symbols is to be deciphered; word discrimination; longhand writing from rapid dictation; and word sense, or reconstruction of words from abbreviations and context. The material was devised after a job analysis of stenographic work and, as might well be expected, has been found to be definitely predictive of success in training. For

268 cases, the total score correlates .67 with the *Durost–Turse Correction-Transcription Test of Stenographic Achievement,* after two years of shorthand.

The reported odd-even reliability is .98. Since all the subtests have short time limits and since there is no indication in the Manual of Directions of the difficulties of the items, this reliability may be spuriously high. However, the fact that the validity is satisfactory indicates that the instrument is useful and may be recommended in screening applicants for stenographic training and for educational guidance.

[394]

Typing Test: United-NOMA Business Entrance Tests. Schools and industry; 1939-47; new form usually available annually; prior to 1947, the series title was National Clerical Ability Tests; $5 per 25; $1 per test when scoring service and certificates for acceptable work are desired; $2 per specimen set of the 6 tests in the series; 120(130) minutes; prepared by the Joint Committee on Tests representing the United Business Education Association and the National Office Management Association; National Office Management Association.

E. G. Blackstone, Professor of Business Education, The University of Southern California, Los Angeles, California. [Review of the 1946 Form.] This test includes exercises in typing a corrected rough draft, the setting-up of a letter from running copy, a simple tabulation on a form, a simple tabulation on a plain sheet of paper, and the typing of a form letter with parts to be filled in. Two hours are allowed for the test. The test is scored for form and arrangement of typed matter, accuracy, time consumed, and ability to follow instructions. Any uncorrectible error causes an exercise to be rejected; correctible errors are accepted but penalized. Neat erasures are accepted. All scoring of papers is done at the central office; a teacher is not able to score them.

The reliability of the test is *estimated* to be .90. What its actual reliability is has not been determined. No figures are available for validity. Certificates of proficiency are awarded to those whose scores are "as high as, or higher than the score representing the minimum of office acceptability," and whose "composite score is as high as, or higher than the composite score equivalent to the minimum acceptable skill score." How these minima are determined is not announced.

The test seems to be an improvement over the typical copying test because it covers a longer period of time and because it includes several types of rather typical typing tasks. It is unfortunate that the test does not include instructions that would enable a typing teacher to score and interpret test results. Perhaps the tests were not designed as instructional tests to be used in schools, but they would be more useful if they could be so used.

It is believed by the reviewer that every honest effort possible has been made to make the tests objective, but they are still lacking in statistical evidence that they are reliable or valid, that the method of computing a composite score is statistically sound, or that the method of determining what scores shall be given the award of proficiency is justifiable. Perhaps such statistical justification may be attained in the future—but the tests have been on the market for a number of years, and such justifications seem to be slow in coming.

Beatrice J. Dvorak, Chief, Worker Analysis Section, U. S. Employment Service, Washington, D. C. [Review of the 1946 Form.] This test is a two-hour proficiency test, designed to measure "ability to do practical typing work." It consists of five specific typing jobs: typing from rough draft, typing numerical data in a table (the table form has been set up for the examinee), determining the arrangement of a letter on a page, tabulating lists of words, and filling in a form letter and preparing it for mailing. Credit is allowed for every minute less than two hours required by the examinee. The score is a composite based on the form and arrangement of the typed matter, the accuracy of typing, and the time consumed. Failure to follow directions is penalized heavily. A table of percentile norms, based on high school students, is provided to interpret the composite score. A critical score, which approximately 90 per cent of the students exceed, is presented.

According to the copyright holder, the validity of the test was established by administering it to a sample of high school young people ready for work and to a sample of office employees of from six to eighteen months experience. It was found that the employed sample did considerably better than the high school sample.

The reviewer's preference is for separate speed and accuracy norms—appearance, to the extent that it can be reliably measured, being thrown in with accuracy—rather than for composite norms. Speed compared with accuracy is not important for many typing jobs—typing insurance policies, for instance. An insurance company might not want a low accuracy score to be obscured in the total score by a high speed score.

The test is too time-consuming for widespread practical use in employment selection.

[395]

★**Typewriting Test: State High School Tests for Indiana.** First, second, third, fourth semesters high school; 1942–44; Form A (1st, 3rd semesters); Form N (2nd, 4th semesters); 4¢ per test; 15¢ per sample test; 30(35) minutes; M. E. Studebaker, B. M. Swinford, Vernal H. Carmichael, Frances R. Botsford, and Russell Burkhart; State High School Testing Service, Purdue University.

[396]

United-NOMA Business Entrance Tests. Schools and industry; 1939–47; 6 tests; new forms usually available annually; prior to 1947, this series of tests was entitled National Clerical Ability Tests; $5 per 25 of any one test; $1 per test when scoring service and certificates for acceptable work are desired; $2 per specimen set; prepared by the Joint Committee on Tests representing the United Business Education Association and the National Office Management Association; National Office Management Association.
a) BOOKKEEPING TEST. 120(130) minutes. *For reviews, see 368.*
b) BUSINESS FUNDAMENTALS AND GENERAL INFORMATION TEST. 45(55) minutes. *For reviews, see 369.*
c) FILING TEST. 120(130) minutes. *For reviews, see 379.*
d) MACHINE CALCULATION TEST. 120(130) minutes. *For a review, see 384.*
e) STENOGRAPHIC TEST. 125(140) minutes. *For reviews, see 391.*
f) TYPING TEST. 120(130) minutes. *For reviews, see 394.*

REFERENCES

1-9. *See 40:1476.*

Paul S. Lomax, Professor of Education and Chairman, Department of Business Education, New York University, New York, New York. The United–NOMA Business Entrance Tests are the same as the former National Clerical Ability Tests. The change in name is due to the discontinuance of the former National Council for Business Education and the taking over of its testing program by the United Business Education Association, a newly reorganized department of the National Education Association. The production and management of these tests continue under the same joint committee representing the National Office Management Association and the United Business Education Association.

The 1946 United–NOMA Business Entrance Tests are intended to measure the competencies of business-trained students for initial employment in one or more of the following kinds of office work: typewriting, filing, bookkeeping, stenography, and machine calculation. Each person who takes one or more of these vocational tests is also expected to take the *Business Fundamentals and General Information Test.* The business fundamentals part of the test deals with spelling, the apostrophe, plurals, arithmetic, and social science, all of which are assumed to be representative of school-taught information. The general information section of the test deals with current events, which are assumed not to be school-taught information. Two hours is allowed for each of the vocational tests; one hour for the *Business Fundamentals and General Information Test.*

The five vocational tests are designed to be valid measures of actual office work. The tests may or may not be valid measures of actual office training programs in schools, since the curricular validity of the tests apparently has not been determined. We are not told how adequately each of the tests covers all important phases of relevant office work. Nor are we informed how widely accepted by office managers are the standards of competency set up in the tests, as, for example, the dictation rate of not over 75 words a minute on an average for a period of thirty minutes in the stenographic test.

Inadequate data are provided concerning the comparability of the various annual series of the tests and the norms of achievement resulting therefrom. The criteria of objectivity, administrability, and scorability have been well observed in the construction of the tests. The utility of the tests still requires much further study. No extensive study has yet been made to determine how well persons, who have passed the previous series of the tests, have succeeded in their office work. Nor do we know what practical improvements have resulted from the use of the tests both in upgrading the vocational caliber of office-training programs in the schools and in upgrading the quality of employment testing. Nevertheless, these tests, which were first initiated in 1937, are probably the best business entrance tests that are yet available; hence, they merit widespread use by schools and offices and careful study for progressive improvement and standardization of the tests.

VOCATIONS — THIRD MMY

Reviews by *Dorothy C. Adkins, George K. Bennett, Ralph F. Berdie, Robert G. Bernreuter, Marion A. Bills, Reign H. Bittner, Milton L. Blum, Edward S. Bordin, Paul S. Burnham, Harold D. Carter, E. G. Chambers, Glen U. Cleeton, Clyde H. Coombs, Lysle W. Croft, Edwin W. Davis, Gwendolen Schneidler Dickson, Stanley G. Dulsky, M. H. Elliott, George A. Ferguson, Norman Frederiksen, John W. French, Douglas H. Fryer, Edwin E. Ghiselli, Edward B. Greene, William R. Grove, Milton E. Hahn, Thomas W. Harrell, Charles M. Harsh, Edward N. Hay, Lloyd G. Humphreys, Thelma Hunt, Clifford E. Jurgensen, Raymond A. Katzell, Willard A. Kerr, Joseph E. King, John R. Kinzer, C. H. Lawshe, Jr., D. Welty Lefever, Herschel T. Manuel, Joseph E. Moore, Charles I. Mosier, C. A. Oakley, Jay L. Otis, Albert Gibson Packard, Donald G. Paterson, Shailer Peterson, James M. Porter, Jr., Alec Rodger, Floyd L. Ruch, C. H. Ruedisili, George A. Satter, Harold G. Seashore, R. B. Selover, Benjamin Shimberg, Patrick Slater, Dewey B. Stuit, Donald E. Super, Erwin K. Taylor, Howard R. Taylor, Herbert A. Toops, Robert M. W. Travers, Arthur E. Traxler, Frances Oralind Triggs, Morris S. Viteles, William W. Waite, J. V. Waits, Neil D. Warren, Henry Weitz, John M. Willits, E. F. Wonderlic.*

[620]

★Differential Aptitude Tests. Grades 8-12; 1947; IBM; 2 forms, 8 tests in 7 booklets; separate answer sheets must be used; all prices include postage; $19.50 per 25 sets of the 7 booklets; $1.50 per 50 machine-scorable answer sheets for any one booklet; $1.25 per 50 individual report forms; $1.25 per set of 14 scoring stencils (specify whether hand- or machine-scoring); $1.75 per manual; $2.50 per specimen set; 186(240-270) minutes, entire battery; George K. Bennett, Harold G. Seashore, and Alexander G. Wesman; Psychological Corporation.

a) VERBAL REASONING. $2.75 per 25; 30(40) minutes.
b) NUMERICAL ABILITY. $2 per 25; 30(35) minutes.
c) ABSTRACT REASONING. $2.75 per 25; 25(30) minutes.
d) SPACE RELATIONS. $3 per 25; 30(40) minutes.
e) MECHANICAL REASONING. $3.50 per 25; 30(35) minutes.
f) CLERICAL SPEED AND ACCURACY. $2.75 per 25; 6(15) minutes.
g) LANGUAGE USAGE. Includes Spelling and Sentences tests; $2.75 per 25; 35(45) minutes.

J Consult Psychol 12:62 Ja-F '48. The publication of *Differential Aptitude Tests* is a major psychometric event. The battery stresses the significance of *abilities* rather than "ability" as the basis for prediction and guidance at the secondary school level. The parts, other than the clerical, are power tests rather than speed tests. Average reliabilities (except for that of girls on mechanical reasoning, which is .71) range from .85 to .93. Separate percentile norms are given for boys and girls from grades 8 to 12, based on national selections of from 750 to 2,000 cases for each grade-sex group for Form A, 350 to 1,100 for Form B. Profiles of percentiles and standard scores are drawn, and illustrative case studies offer some assistance to counselors in the use of results. The loose-leaf manual is convenient for reference, and for the addition of further data as they become available. Although there are many immediate applications for tests of this type, much research is needed on the validity of profiles for predicting various sorts of educational and vocational success.

[621]

★Guilford-Zimmerman Aptitude Survey. Grades 9-16 and adults; 1947; IBM for Parts 1-2, 5-7; Form A; 8 tests in 7 parts; separate answer sheets need not be used; $1 per key for scoring any one part; 50¢ per key for scoring answer sheets for any one of parts 1-2, 5-7; 2¢ per machine-scorable answer sheet for any one part; 25¢ per manual; 143(188) minutes; J. P. Guilford and Wayne S. Zimmerman; Sheridan Supply Co.

a) PART 1, VERBAL COMPREHENSION. IBM; $2 per 25; 25(30) minutes.
b) PART 2, GENERAL REASONING. IBM; $2 per 25; 35(40) minutes.
c) PART 3, NUMERICAL OPERATIONS. $2 per 25; 8(13) minutes.
d) PART 4, PERCEPTUAL SPEED. $2 per 25; 5(10) minutes.
e) PART 5, SPATIAL ORIENTATION. IBM; $3.50 per 25; 10(20) minutes.
f) PART 6, SPATIAL VISUALIZATION. IBM; $5 per 25; 30(40) minutes.
g) PART 7, MECHANICAL KNOWLEDGE. IBM; $3.50 per 25; 30(35) minutes.

REFERENCES
1. GUILFORD, J. P., AND ZIMMERMAN, WAYNE S. "Some A.A.F. Findings Concerning Aptitude Factors." *Occupations* 26:154-9 D '47. * (PA 22:2198)

[622]

★Yale Educational Aptitude Tests. Grades 9-16; 1947; 7 tests in 2 booklets; IBM except for one brief section; $1.75 per set of testing materials; $2.50 per set of testing materials including the scoring and reporting of individual results; (45) minutes per test if practice booklets are administered previously, otherwise (60) minutes per test; Albert B. Crawford; distributed by Educational Records Bureau.

REFERENCES
1. VAUGHN, K. W. "The Yale Scholastic Aptitude Tests as Predictors of Success in the College of Engineering." *J Eng Ed* 34:572-82 Ap '44. *

2. CRAWFORD, ALBERT B., AND BURNHAM, PAUL S. *Forecasting College Achievement: A Survey of Aptitude Tests for Higher Education: Part I, General Considerations in the Measurement of Academic Promise*, pp. 134-69, 199-201, 253-71. New Haven, Conn.: Yale University Press, 1946. Pp. xxi, 291. $3.75. * (London: Oxford University Press, 1946. 25s.) (*PA* 20:4331)

CLERICAL

[623]

★Clerical Aptitude Test: Acorn National Aptitude Tests. Grades 7 and over; 1943; 1 form; $2.00 per 25; 50¢ per specimen set; 40(45) minutes; Andrew Kobal, J. Wrightstone, and Karl R. Kunze; Acorn Publishing Co.

Marion A. Bills, Assistant Secretary, Aetna Life Insurance Company, Hartford, Connecticut. This is a 3-part test of 40 minutes. The three parts are timed separately. They are intended to measure business practice, spelling, number checking, and name checking. The test was standardized on 576 employed persons. About the average relationship between test scores and ratings of the employees was found. Norms were worked out on this group and on a large number of grade and high school pupils. The scoring directions are clear and the interpretation is given definitely.

This is a clerical, not a mental alertness test. The score apparently improves with training, and therefore previous experience of the individual must be taken into account in evaluating the score. It falls into the class of a trade test and should give indication of immediate ability to perform simple clerical operations; it should not be used before training to predict probable success after training.

The test is long enough to indicate somewhat the "staying" ability of the applicant and therefore may give more information concerning the applicant than a shorter test of the same nature.

Donald G. Paterson, Professor of Psychology, University of Minnesota, Minneapolis, Minnesota. This is an 8-page test composed of three parts and provision is made to record three part scores and a total score. Part 1, containing 27 multiple-choice items plus 13 spelling items, is devoted to knowledge of business practice. Part 2 is labeled "number checking" and is composed of 4 subparts: 10 items requiring subject to check the smallest number in a group of 5 (6 to 9 digits in length); 10 items requiring subject to check the second largest number in a group of 5 (6 to 9 digits in length); 10 items requiring subject to check the number which is the second smallest in a group of 5 (3 to 9 digits in length); and 26 items of the well-known number checking variety, subject being required to compare 26 pairs of numbers and to put a check mark between each pair which is exactly alike. Part 3 is labeled "date and name and address checking" and is composed of two subparts: 12 items requiring subject to check the date which is next to the latest date in each group of six dates (month, day, year); 25 items each consisting of a complex name and number checking item, subject being required to compare pairs of three items (name of company, street address, and city address) and to check those pairs that are exactly alike.

The test appears to be primarily a test of accuracy of work (40 minutes working time) with speed of work being secondary, although the authors state "the allotted time is an essential part of qualitative and quantitative scoring."

A 3-page manual is provided. The test is designed to "measure abilities necessary for a successful performance of skills required in commercial courses and subsequent clerical work." It is strange to see an "achievement type of test" included as part of an aptitude test as is done in Part 1. The remaining two parts appear on inspection to be of the aptitude type. The test is longer than the usual employment test. The directions for scoring are ingenious, utilizing a method of scoring by key words which can be readily memorized. Reliability, by the test-retest method, for a total of 4,141 students in grades 7 to 12, is shown to range from .83 to .93 for each of these grades. There is a systematic drop in these r's from grades 7, 8, and 9 to an r of .83 for grade 12. A validity study shows r's from .27 to .71 between total scores for 576 clerks and ratings obtained from cumulative records and ratings by supervisors. The r of .71 between "accuracy ratings" of supervisors and total score is remarkably high. The r of .62 between "speed ratings" and total score is also quite high. One cannot help but wish that these validity coefficients were presented for the part scores as well as for total scores. In that way one could ascertain the extent to which "proficiency" measured in Part 1 and aptitudes as measured in Parts 2 and 3 are responsible for these high r's.

Percentile norms are provided for total scores only for grades 7 to 12 separately and for 576 trained clerks. Failure to provide norms for male and female students and for male and female trained clerks separately is a serious drawback in view of known sex differences in clerical aptitude. Failure to provide norms by age as well as sex is also unfortunate. The norms should also be broken down by part score as well as total score, and these in turn should be provided for the general population, for different types of clerical workers, and for other occupational groups. Correlations should also be presented between part scores and total scores and standard intelligence tests for various typical norm groups. Such additional information is essential to an adequate interpretation of the test results when used for selection or for guidance purposes.

In the reviewer's opinion, this is a most promising test of clerical aptitude (if scores on Parts 2 and 3 are utilized). Intensive research is needed to provide the data needed to evaluate the real usefulness of the test.

Henry Weitz, Director, Psychological Services Center, University of Delaware, Newark, Delaware. This test purports "to indicate and measure abilities necessary for a successful performance of skills required in commercial courses and subsequent clerical work." The manual states that the test does not measure intelligence or personality, both of which constitute essential factors in clerical ability, although it offers no evidence to support the idea that the items are unrelated to intelligence or personality.

Evidence for the validity of the test is given in the relationship between test scores and shop ratings. Correlations of .71 with supervisors' accuracy ratings, of .62 with supervisors' speed ratings, and .52 with over-all shop ratings are reported for the total scores of 576 male and female clerks. Since no adequate description of the group is given, and since the nature and purpose of the ratings are not reported, it is impossible to accept these validity coefficients with any degree of confidence. The fact that mean scores rise from grade to grade is offered as further evidence of the validity of the test. A test which indicates that a behavior segment becomes more efficient as additional behavior patterns are accumulated through age, maturity, and experience is not necessarily measuring a particular "aptitude" or ability pattern. No evidence is offered to support the contention that the test scores are related to achievement in key commercial courses.

Reported reliability coefficients range from 93 for eighth grade students to .83 for a group

of clerks, with the median reliability of .91. The standard error of a score is reported as 3.4. If this latter statistic is applied to the table of norms for trained clerks, it may be said that the odds are 19 to 1 that a subject whose score is found to be 86 (the 40th percentile for this group) has a truly determined score between 93 and 80. According to the manual's interpretive scale a score of 93 falls in the "superior" group and a score of 80 falls in the "inferior" group.

A key-word scoring system is used in which an item is scored correct if any letter of the key word is recorded or checked by the subject. The publishers state that this system of scoring saves time and increases the accuracy of scoring and that they use this procedure in many of their tests. The use of lower-case letters for the purpose of recording responses in 40 of the 102 items may lead to errors especially when, for example, the selection is between alternatives labeled "h" and "k." Two sections of the test representing about one fifth of the total score involve the checking of matched and unmatched materials. The use of the key-word scoring procedure permits only correctly matched items to be scored. Thus, if a subject marked all items in these sections as correctly matched, he would receive a perfect score. One of the authors states in an unpublished communication that a study of 280 cases revealed no instance where a subject placed check marks indiscriminately, and it was, therefore, decided not to deduct credit for errors in order that the keyword scoring procedure might be retained. There is reason to believe, however, that there is sufficient variability among subjects in the degree to which they mark unmatched materials as matched to warrant a consideration of the possibility of including some measure of this behavior in the score.

Fundamentally the test items appear to be most closely related to routine clerical activities. Even the section on business practices involving some 27 items contains 14 items which are no more than vocabulary items, while only the remaining 13 require some knowledge of business operations and related information. Since clerical work is such a broad field involving so varied a configuration of skills and requiring so great a variety of traits, it is doubted that tests of this type can do much more than offer minor assistance in the selection of routine clerical workers.

Clerical Aptitude Test

E. F. Wonderlic, Vice-President, General Finance Corporation, Chicago, Illinois. This test is composed of three parts, requiring three separate timing intervals. Its construction and standardization as well as the administrative directions make it much more adaptable to educational and vocational guidance fields than to application in the field of personnel selection. It contains several original methods in the directions for scoring. At some points these seem confusing to the ordinary test administrator. Published norms are given for only one group of employed clerks. Several norms are available for high school students. Sex differences are not reported although most research workers in the field of clerical testing have reported pronounced differences in favor of female subjects both with experienced clerical workers and with totally unselected groups. The author reports that "a study of scores obtained on the Clerical Aptitude Test and a comparative rating on the job for purposes of correlation warrants selection of clerical employees on the basis of test scores" and further gives interpretative ratings by letter grades.

This reviewer recommends considerable caution be used before accepting these critical scores in other employment situations. The reported experience of most research workers is that careful standardization of tests of this nature are necessary in each business organization, and norms must be based on both applicants and employed workers before selection is recommended on the basis of test scores. Such information is not readily available on this clerical aptitude test.

[624]

★**Clerical Perception Test.** Grades 9 and over; 1947; 1 form; 75¢ per 25; 15¢ per specimen set, postpaid; 15(20) minutes; G. Bernard Baldwin; Educational Test Bureau.

Edward N. Hay, Personnel Officer, The Pennsylvania Company for Banking and Trusts; and President, Edward N. Hay and Associates, Inc.; Philadelphia, Pennsylvania. This test was constructed to give an indication of an individual's "ability to discriminate the small differences in numeral and verbal materials that comprise a large part of the work in offices." This ability has been called clerical perception and has already been found to play an important role in the prediction of machine bookkeeping.

At the same time the author has undertaken to measure ciliary muscle fatigue and has divided both number and name checking tests into two parts, giving the subject an opportunity to note how many items he has attempted in the first period, and to estimate how many he expects to be able to do in the second. Emphasizing speed in this way and providing small print and a cramped typographical arrangement probably draws attention to the resulting eye fatigue, the degree of which is reflected in the decrease in scores from one section of the test to the next. A small group of high school students, examined with and without glasses, showed significantly higher scores when glasses were worn, but the data are ambiguously presented, with no information about how the differences in these scores compared with test-retest scores of students whose eyes were normal.

Because the test has been condensed to a single page, directions have been reduced to a minimum, and practice exercises are carefully fitted into the space remaining. The test would be easier to administer if it were less compactly arranged. A further improvement could be made in the directions to examiners, where limitations of space have again caused too great condensation.

As a clerical test "validity was established by using the test to select the student clerical staff for scoring the tests of a six hour battery administered to ten thousand students in . . . high schools" and those chosen "from the upper twenty-five per cent of scores . . . required only half the time" of those chosen at random. The number of students involved in the scoring and the type of production record obtained are not mentioned. There has apparently been no attempt to validate the test for business situations.

Reliability for each of the parts in a single grade range is stated to be approximately .93 using Froehlich's form of the Kuder–Richardson formula. Since this does not, however, take into consideration the factor of speed, which is an important part of a test of this kind, another type of reliability coefficient should have been obtained. Norms for high school grades are provided. The author combines boys' and girls' scores in a single table, since "competition in clerical occupations is also with combined sex groups." It is questionable whether this is actually the case in business houses, but

Clerical Aptitude Test

under any circumstances it would seem desirable to have separate norms for each sex.

The author wisely recommends that school counselors use the *Clerical Perception Test* only in a battery and says that for occupational selection critical scores must be determined by job requirements. The attempt to measure eye fatigue is interesting and should be pursued, but a better clerical test would result if the two factors were not measured simultaneously.

Raymond A. Katzell, Associate Professor of Psychology, The University of Tennessee, Knoxville, Tennessee. Two subtests are included in this test. The items of the first are composed of pairs of numbers which are to be compared with respect to identity to one another. The items of the second subtest are made up of pairs of names which are likewise to be checked for similarity.

The test is economically designed to fit on a single sheet of paper. Instructions are concise, but in one or two places are obscure.

In single high school grade ranges, the reliabilities of the subtests are above .90, computed by the Kuder–Richardson formula 20. The reliabilities are probably overestimates, since this formula is not exactly applicable to simple, highly speeded tests like the present one. The results of a single study tend to support the validity of the test for routine clerical duties. Norms in integral standard deviation units are furnished separately for the four high school grades and are based on hundreds of cases in each grade.

The test is very similar in essence to the *Minnesota Vocational Test for Clerical Workers.* Like its well-known predecessor, the *Clerical Perception Test* seems to measure aptitudes related to speed and accuracy of discrimination of visually presented details. The usefulness of such measures for the appraisal of suitability for routine clerical work has been established in numerous instances.

In addition, the *Clerical Perception Test* is claimed to have value in the detection of defective vision. Evidence furnished for this claim includes the fact that 48 students, who ordinarily wore eyeglasses, showed significantly higher mean scores when tested with glasses than when retested without them. No mention is made of checks on the extent to which the decrement may have been due to normal fatigue, loss in interest, or other extraneous influences.

Other evidence is that these subjects showed a greater loss from the first to the second subtest when working without glasses than when working with them. The statistical reliability of this difference is not reported.

Granted, however, that imperfect vision has some adverse effect on performance on this test, the question remains of how useful the test is in the detection of such defects. It is proposed in the test manual that people getting scores below one standard deviation below the mean be suspected of visual deficiency and **given an optical examination. However, if low** scores on the test are to be strongly indicative of defective vision, individual differences in test performance must depend primarily on visual factors. But there is every reason to believe that nonvisual aptitudes play a very significant role in determination of the score. It is interesting in this connection that the mean scores of the 48 visually defective subjects, when tested without glasses, exceeded the mean scores of the general normative population on both subtests.

In general, then, the evidence does not ensure that the *Clerical Perception Test,* when used in the proposed manner, will have much practical utility for the indication of defective vision. Nor do there seem to be any technical reasons for preferring this test to the earlier and similar *Minnesota Vocational Test for Clerical Workers* as a measure of aptitude for performing routine aspects of clerical work. Indeed the more diversified standardization and validation of the Minnesota test are distinctly in its favor.

Erwin K. Taylor, Chief, Performance Evaluation and Criterion Research Unit, Personnel Research Section, The Adjutant General's Office, Washington, D. C. Except that it contains half as many items, is printed in somewhat smaller type, and is more difficult to score, the *Clerical Perception Test* is merely a copy of the *Minnesota Vocational Test for Clerical Workers.* A Kuder–Richardson reliability of .93 on an unknown number of cases is reported on the instruction and scoring sheet. Since the use of the Kuder–Richardson formulae on speed tests is entirely inappropriate, the reliability of the instrument remains an unknown quantity. The validity of the test, according to the manual, was "established" by the finding that schools that selected their clerical workers from the upper 25 per cent of the scores required only half the time for the same job that was required when workers were selected at random. No mention is made of the number of cases involved, nor of any of the numerous possible contaminants which may have entered into the situation. Some data based on 48 cases indicate that people who need glasses do better on the test when they wear them than when they do not. Norms based on high school students are available on sizable samples. No data are presented on employed groups.

The reviewer is in full accord with the statement in the manual to the effect that critical scores for occupational selection will need to be determined by job requirements. Unless this is intended as mere lip service or as an appeal to face validity, it is essential that basic validation research be performed before this test, or any other clerical test, can be safely employed to select workers. The greater length of the *Minnesota Vocational Test for Clerical Workers,* and the fact that considerably more is known of the Minnesota Test than of the present instrument, would indicate that the longer test is to be preferred for inclusion in an experimental selection battery. The test in its present state of development is not suitable for guidance purposes.

E. F. Wonderlic, Vice-President, General Finance Corporation, Chicago, Illinois. This test was standardized on the work of high school students. Therefore, its use in business and industry is limited. Standardization and validity in business and industrial situations with adult subjects are not reported by the author. This test is not in general use in business personnel situations as a selective device. For this purpose it is difficult to administer. It consists of four subtests, each requiring separate timing, and thus demands close attention of the test administrator. Occupational norms by employed clerical workers from industry are not available in the author's published material. Data in the Directions for Administration suggest that interpretative value can result from scores when the test is used for a measure of vision, with or without normal use of glasses, with high school groups. Sex and educational differences are also demonstrated for high school students. Its use in industry must be considered purely experimental.

Clerical Perception Test

J Consult Psychol 11:156 My-Je '47. * Level of aspiration scores are obtained for Part B of each test, but these are not discussed in the manual. *

[625]
Clerical Test D: Extending—Verifying—Checking—Classifying. Ages 14 and over; 1922; $3 per introductory set including 10 tests, postpaid; 5¢ per extra test, postpaid; introductory sets may be ordered on approval; 12(20) minutes; Eugene J. Benge; Management Service Co.

Donald G. Paterson, Professor of Psychology, University of Minnesota, Minneapolis, Minnesota. This test is printed on a 4-page leaflet 8½ × 11 inches. The first page is devoted to instructions and practice exercises. The next three pages are devoted to 100 items, presented in cycle-omnibus form, classified as Extending (10 arithmetical reasoning items), Verifying (40 fundamentals-of-arithmetic items presented in true-false form), Number Checking (30 pairs of numbers to be labeled Same or Different), and Classifying (20 topical sentences taken from correspondence, each to be classified as to type and kind by multiple choice). Working time is 12 minutes. Speed and accuracy are emphasized alike. A cardboard scoring stencil is provided. There is only one form of the test.

A 1-page mimeographed manual is provided, supplemented by an additional mimeographed page which purports to give as an addendum a "refinement in scoring" the Extending items. The purpose of the test is presented in one paragraph and the user is advised not to hire those making "a low score in the test," but no hint is given as to what "a low score" is. Another one sentence paragraph states that the test is to be used to eliminate unfit applicants.

Instructions are supplied for giving and scoring the test. Score is the number of items tried minus the number wrong, and a percentile scale is given for converting the raw score into a score by "rank." A percentage right score is also advocated with the statement that accuracy should be 95 per cent or better but that applicants for juniors should *average* 93 per cent in accuracy.

The number and kind of applicants upon which the percentile rank table is based is not indicated. No norms for employed clerical workers are provided. Data regarding reliability are absent and no evidence in regard to validity is presented. The correlation between intelligence and this test as a whole or the sub-tests is not given. The reliabilities and interre-lations of the subtests are not given. No refer-ences are given.

Judging solely on the basis of the test itself and the inadequate manual of directions, one is forced to conclude that all of the aims and objectives of the *Mental Measurement Year-books* have been violated. Judging on the basis of knowledge of the field of aptitude testing, it is apparent that the test is a mixture of num-ber ability (fundamentals) measured unrelia-bly, of number-checking ability measured un-reliably, and of two components of the usual type of intelligence test (arithmetical reasoning and topical classifying) measured with un-known reliability. Only the uninformed and inadequately trained personnel worker would be likely to adopt this test in practice.

John M. Willits, Associate Professor of Psy-chology, Graduate School of Business, Stan-ford University, Stanford, California. The con-tent of this brief test may be appropriate to a number of clerical situations. Its four types of items all have a reasonable resemblance to com-mon, simple clerical tasks. And all of the item content is general enough to make it an aptitude rather than an achievement test.

Mechanically, the test is adequately designed and printed. There are 10 sample items and 5 practice items, adequately covering the test con-tent. Scoring is mechanically simple, with a single strip key that is accurately fitted, legible, and durable.

The chief disadvantages of the test appear to be: (*a*) the inadequacy of the data in its manual; (*b*) the shortness of the test, for statistical re-liability; and (*c*) the lack of part-scores on the different types of item.

(*a*) The "manual" consists of a single type-written (mimeographed) page, plus a one-page "addendum to scoring instructions" (discussed below). This "manual" properly cautions the user that job success probably requires other attributes besides those measured by the test; and it gives simple, concise directions for ad-ministration and scoring. But there is no men-tion of either reliability or validity and only a single abbreviated set of percentile norms, with population also unmentioned. From the norms table, which is grouped in intervals of 5 raw-score points, only fourteen different percentile

ranks can be read directly without interpo-lation.

(*b*) The test has only 100 items, all with unit weight in scoring. There is no correction for guessing; the printed instructions properly advise the examinee to guess. As 70 of the items are in two-choice form, and 20 more are four-choice, both with approximately balanced distribution of right answers, a chance score of 40 points is quite possible. This fact is rec-ognized in the norms table, which gives the per-centile rank of 1 to all raw scores below 40. Thus, the effective range is only 60 raw-score points.

Thirty of the items are number-checking items, much like those of the *Minnesota Voca-tional Test for Clerical Workers*. The manual for that test reports an odd-even reliability coefficient of .86 for its 200 items of this type. If the length were reduced to 30 items, this reliability would be expected to shrink to .48. The reliability of the 30 similar items in the present test is probably no higher. No two of these items are presented adjacent to each other, while in the Minnesota test all 200 items are consecutive.

Ten of the items in the present test are arith-metic problems in the extension of invoice and payroll entries. They are fairly similar to at least part of the problems in Part V of the *Psychological Corporation General Clerical Test,* where 16 problems have given a split-half reliability of .63. The expected shrinkage here, in a reduction to 10 problems, would give a reliability of .52.

(*c*) All four types of items (the other two are classifying topic sentences from business letters and verifying simple arithmetic equa-tions) are different enough to suggest low in-tercorrelations among them. If the test were of reliable length, an average intercorrelation not higher than .40 might be expected, on the basis of other data on somewhat similar mate-rials. Given a clerical force large enough to permit *differential* placement of selected appli-cants, reliable part scores would be valuable on test materials as dissimilar as these. But such scores would require more than the present 12 minutes of testing time, and several times 100 items, besides rearrangement of material and sectional timing.

The "addendum to scoring directions" seeks to overcome one defect of many spiral-omnibus tests, by setting up a scale of progressive penal-

Clerical Test D

ties for omission of difficult items—in this case, items of the "invoice-extension" type. But these penalties, of which the examinee is not warned, are not in harmony with the printed instructions which tell him, "If you cannot solve any item readily, pass on to the next." Also the scale implies a steeper difficulty gradient in these items than in other types, although the others are also evidently arranged in graded difficulty. The "addendum" does not state whether the scale is arbitrary or based, as it should be, on accurate time studies of actual working times.

[626]

Detroit Clerical Aptitudes Examination. High school; 1937–44; 1 form; $5.40 per 100; 24¢ per specimen set, postpaid; 30(40) minutes; Harry J. Baker and Paul H. Voelker; Public School Publishing Co.

REFERENCES

1. ANDERSON, ROY N. "Review of Clerical Tests (1929–1942)." *Occupations* 21:654-60 My '43. * (PA 17:3218)

E. F. Wonderlic, Vice-President, General Finance Corporation, Chicago, Illinois. This clerical aptitude test was developed on a large number of school students and for school purposes may be very desirable. Reliability and validity in school situations is high. However, it has not been standardized for industrial and business use. Before it could be useful in the employment department, it would require standardization on adults, both those working at clerical work and applicants for those positions. It is possible that it would have predictive value if this were done.

The test is made up of eight parts, which require close administrative attention and which would make it difficult to administer in the typical employment office.

For reviews by Irving Lorge and M. W. Richardson, see 40:1655.

[627]

Minnesota Clerical Test. Grades 8-12 and adults; 1933–46; formerly called *Minnesota Vocational Test for Clerical Workers*; 1 form; manual only revised in 1946; $1.25 per 25, postpaid; 35¢ per specimen set, postpaid; Dorothy M. Andrew, Donald G. Paterson, and Howard P. Longstaff; Psychological Corporation.

REFERENCES

1-18. See 40:1664.
19. LOEVINGER, J. *An Analysis of Verbal and Numerical Abilities at the Junior High School Level.* Unpublished master's thesis, University of Minnesota, 1938.
20. ERICKSON, IRVING PETER. *Number and Spatial Ability in Mathematics and Intelligence.* Unpublished master's thesis, Clark University, 1939. (*Abstracts of Dissertations . . . 1939,* pp. 151-2.)
21. BLUM, MILTON L., AND CANDEE, BEATRICE. "The Selection of Department Store Packers and Wrappers With the Aid of Certain Psychological Tests: Study II." *J Appl Psychol* 25:291-9 Je '41. * (PA 15:4336)

22. GHISELLI, EDWIN E. "Tests for the Selection of Inspector-Packers." Abstract. *Psychol B* 38:735 O '41. * (PA 16:728, title only)
23. MORROW, ROBERT S. "An Experimental Analysis of the Theory of Independent Abilities." *J Ed Psychol* 32:495-512 O '41. * (PA 16:2209)
24. SCHNEIDLER, GWENDOLEN G. "Grade and Age Norms for the Minnesota Vocational Test for Clerical Workers." *Ed & Psychol Meas* 1:143-56 Ap '41. * (PA 15:4416)
25. GHISELLI, EDWIN E. "A Comparison of the Minnesota Vocational Test for Clerical Workers With the General Clerical Battery of the United States Employment Service." *J Appl Psychol* 26:75-80 F '42. * (PA 16:2453)
26. GHISELLI, EDWIN E. "Tests for the Selection of Inspector-Packers." *J Appl Psychol* 26:468-76 Ag '42. * (PA 17:2127)
27. HAY, EDWARD N., AND BLAKEMORE, ARLINE MANCE. "Testing Clerical Applicants." *J Appl Psychol* 26:852-5 D '42. * (PA 17:2854)
28. McGEHEE, WILLIAM, AND MOFFIE, D. J. "Psychological Tests in the Selection of Enrollees in Engineering, Science, Management, Defense Training Courses." *J Appl Psychol* 26:584-6 O '42. * (PA 17:2186)
29. SCHNEIDLER, GWENDOLEN G., AND PATERSON, DONALD G. "Sex Differences in Clerical Aptitude." *J Ed Psychol* 33:303-9 Ap '42. * (PA 17:973)
30. ANDERSON, ROY N. "Review of Clerical Tests (1929-1942)." *Occupations* 21:654-60 My '43. * (PA 17:3218)
31. HAY, EDWARD N. "Predicting Success in Machine Bookkeeping." *J Appl Psychol* 27:483-93 D '43. * (PA 18:1877)
32. HAY, EDWARD N., AND BLAKEMORE, ARLINE M. "The Relationship Between Clerical Experience and Scores on the Minnesota Vocational Test for Clerical Workers." *J Appl Psychol* 27:311-5 Ag '43. * (PA 18:291)
33. KLUGMAN, SAMUEL F. "Test Scores and Graduation." *Occupations* 21:389-93 Ja '43. * (PA 17:1354)
34. KLUGMAN, SAMUEL F. "Test Scores for Clerical Aptitude and Interests Before and After a Year of Schooling." *J Genetic Psychol* 65:89-96 S '44. * (PA 19:550)
35. SHUMAN, JOHN T. *An Investigation Into the Value of Certain Tests in the Selection and Upgrading of Personnel in Aircraft Engine and Propeller Industries.* Unpublished doctor's thesis, Pennsylvania State College, 1944. Pp. 251. (*Abstracts of Doctoral Dissertations . . . 1944,* 1945, pp. 160-76.)
36. KLUGMAN, SAMUEL F. "The Effect of Schooling Upon the Relationship Between Clerical Aptitude and Interests." *J Genetic Psychol* 66:255-8 Je '45. * (PA 19:3499)
37. SWEM, BOYD R. "'Accounting Aptitude' and 'Home Work.'" *Occupations* 23:218-9 Ja '45. * (PA 19:1351)
38. BARRETT, DOROTHY M. "Prediction of Achievement in Typewriting and Stenography in a Liberal Arts College." *J Appl Psychol* 30:624-30 D '46. * (PA 21:1624)
39. BENNETT, GEORGE K., AND WESMAN, ALEXANDER G. "Industrial Test Norms for a Southern Plant Population." *J Appl Psychol* 31:241-6 Je '47. * (PA 21:4095)
40. MAHER, HOWARD, AND FIFE, ISABELLE E. "A Biological-Pharmaceutical Checker Selection Program." *J Appl Psychol* 31:469-76 O '47. * (PA 22:3665)

Thelma Hunt, Professor of Psychology, The George Washington University, Washington, D. C. This test is a brief, easily administered, easily scored measuring instrument. It is a test of speed and accuracy in two types of performance—number checking and name checking. Underlying the speed and accuracy of performance it can also be presumed that the test measures qualities of attention to a stated problem, ability to determine small differences, and attention to detail. There are absent from this test the more complex performances found in so many other tests labeled "clerical" or "clerical aptitude" tests, such as the parts measuring spelling ability, alphabetizing ability, arithmetical calculation or reasoning ability, reading ability, and vocabulary. Despite its more limited nature, in general studies have indicated a relatively high validity for the Minnesota test as compared with the more complex tests. Many users should welcome this simple speed and accuracy test. The other factors so often covered in the clerical tests can be measured by separate arithmetic, spelling, reading, or intelligence tests where desired.

The manual contains far more information about the test than is included in the usual test manual, a fact for which the authors are to be commended. The test was originally developed through extensive research by the Employment Stabilization Research Institute at the University of Minnesota. The studies made by this Institute are summarized. Since the publication of *The 1940 Mental Measurements Yearbook,* a revised manual for the *Minnesota Vocational Test for Clerical Workers* (now called *Minnesota Clerical Test*) has appeared. It contains a summary of several additional studies of reliability and validity and much more information on norms than was contained in the earlier manual. The reliability of the test, as attested by statistical studies presented, is high. A satisfactory validity is indicated by correlations of the test with ratings of clerical workers, ratings of clerical abilities of commercial students, grades of students in accounting, and speed of typing by typing students. Information is presented to indicate that the clerical test scores predict performances in such clerical fields as accounting and typing better than do customary academic ability measures. Low correlations reported between the test and years of clerical experience, amount of commercial training, grade of school completed, and intelligence suggest that the test is measuring something other than the academic and experience factors so often measured in vocational tests.

Some comment should be made upon the extensive norms presented in the new manual. There are norms according to school grade for grades 8 through 12, with additional norms for grades 11 and 12 for New England groups. For adult groups there are norms for employed clerical workers (in general and broken down into types of clerical workers), for clerical applicants, for unemployed clerical workers, and for adults gainfully employed (but not in clerical work). All the norms are presented separately for men and women, and all in terms of percentile ratings. The extensive norms may seem confusing. They are of most use only when the user can carefully study his own problem and relate the performance of those tested to the most applicable group. In voca-

tional guidance a counselor is chiefly interested in the abilities of an individual in comparison with the abilities of persons in general, so that among all the aptitudes of the individual he may find those which are the most outstanding. On the other hand, the employer using the Minnesota test is likely to be most interested in the comparison of the performance of his applicants with other clerical workers. In the case of the employer using this test, as well as any other clerical test, it should be pointed out that norms should be carefully scrutinized for comparability of the groups on which the authors' norms are based with the employer's own workers. Even with the best situation in respect to published norms, many users will find it desirable to set up their own norms.

On the whole, the *Minnesota Clerical Test* can be recommended as a very usable test for selecting promising clerical workers, or for guidance in the selection of students for clerical training. In many instances it may need to be supplemented by more complex tests covering other qualities, but there is an advantage in having separately the simpler measures yielded by the Minnesota test. The examination has stood the test of wide use and acceptability over a period of fifteen years.

R. B. Selover, Assistant Personnel Director, The Prudential Insurance Company of America, Newark, New Jersey. This test was constructed for selecting clerical employees and for advising persons who wish to secure training in the clerical field. The test consists of two parts, number checking and name checking. In each part there are 200 items, 100 of which are identical pairs and 100 of which are dissimilar pairs. The numbers range from 3 through 12 digits; the names range from 7 through 16 letters. The tests are timed separately at 8 and 7 minutes. The score is the number right minus the number wrong.

The manual revised in 1946 reports information concerning reliability, validity, relationships with other tests, and extensive norms. The reliability of the total test, determined by administering comparable forms at one testing, is .90. Retest reliability coefficients are about .85 for combined performance and somewhat lower for the separate tests. High and significant relationships are reported between performance on this test and commercial teachers' ratings of students, grades in accounting, ratings of general clerical workers, and ratings of file clerks. Association is reported between test performance and speed of typing. Significant differences are reported between clerical workers and other groups. Although the two tests show considerable relationship, quite obviously separate skills are measured. The name checking test is more closely related to speed of reading, spelling, and conventional measures of intelligence, while the number checking test is more closely related to verifying arithmetic computations. Studies indicate that test performance is only slightly related to experience on clerical jobs and amount of formal education. A factor analysis by one of the authors indicates that "Number Checking measures more of a numerical factor and Name Checking more of a verbal factor."

There is a possibility that the prospective user of this test may be confused by some of the information reported in the revised manual. From the fact that clerical groups frequently show small and nonsignificant differences in test performance, it is concluded "that the clerical test used alone or in combination with intelligence tests can do no more than serve as a guide toward or away from clerical occupations as a group." The reader might quite properly ask to see relationships between test scores and criterion data for separate groups before accepting this conclusion. In explaining the relationships found between clerical test scores and intelligence for heterogeneous groups, the problem might be dealt with more effectively by reporting the authors' previous work showing how little relationship remains when speed of reading is held constant.

It is the reviewer's opinion that this clerical test is valuable for selecting certain clerical employees, as well as for advising students with respect to commercial training. Progress in the refinement of measures of clerical abilities will probably be made by continuing such attempts to measure specific abilities which show significant relationships to criterion data.

Erwin K. Taylor, Chief, Performance Evaluation and Criterion Research Unit, Personnel Research Section, The Adjutant General's Office, Washington, D. C. The *Minnesota Vocational Test for Clerical Workers* (now called *Minnesota Clerical Test*), consisting of 200 number checking and 200 name checking items, is too well known to test users generally to require elaborate description here. A total of 15 minutes is required for the administration of the test which is hand scored with a key supplied by the publisher.

While it has become an almost accepted doctrine in industrial psychology that name and number checking constitute valid measures of clerical success, it appears to the writer to be somewhat presumptuous to imply, as does the title of this test, that these two elements are adequate for exclusive use in the selection of clerical workers. The prediction of clerical success would undoubtedly be improved if the name and number checking were supplemented by tests of verbal intelligence and computational ability.

Neither the reliability nor validity data published in the test manual can be accepted as adequate to justify the use of this test without further research in each given instance. Reliabilities of .86, .93 and .90 are given for the number checking, name checking and a combination of the two, respectively. These are odd-even reliabilities based on less than 150 cases. Since the test is essentially a speed test, these figures must be taken as gross exaggerations of the true reliability of the instrument. Test-retest reliabilities on 48 business students (university) and 28 individuals in a clerical training group range from .76 to .93, but are based on so small a sample as to preclude the drawing of any conclusions on the basis of these data.

Since the validity of a test is crucial to its usefulness, the writer is much more concerned with the published data in this area than with reliability. Here again the outstanding feature of the manual is a scarcity of acceptable data. The product-moment correlation between personal history ratings based on education, experience and training, and age at leaving school is .65 for a group of 138 cases. These, however, cannot be considered valid vocational criteria. Where supervisors ratings were obtained, contingency coefficients ranged from .28 to .42 on groups varying in size from 22 to 97. The ratings, consisting of a combination of personal history and supervisors' ratings, yielded contingency coefficients ranging from .54 to .64 on equally small groups. In no case is there a description of the positions for which the test was "validated."

Norms on the following employable groups are presented in the manual: (*a*) employed clerical workers, 284 women and 120 men; (*b*) gainfully occupied adults, 232 women and 500 men; (*c*) eastern clerical applicants, approximately 1,500 women and 750 men; and (*d*) southern clerical applicants, 162 women. In addition nine sets of distributions of employed clerical workers and six sets of unemployed clerical workers by classification are presented. These groups vary in size from 17 male bank tellers to 121 female stenographers and typists. War Department research with civilian clerical employees has indicated such norms to be highly unstable, varying from job to job and between similar installations. Forty-four distributions of scores made by various groups of school children are also presented.

Under these circumstances, it is doubted whether the data presented in the test manual can be of much real value in using the test either as a selection or guidance instrument. Surely not enough in the way of validity studies have as yet been published to render the *Minnesota Vocational Test for Clerical Workers* a device upon which any considerable reliance can be placed for guidance purposes. The one possible exception occurs in the case of those who score in the lowest decile on the two tests. One could be reasonably certain that such individuals would be unlikely to succeed in clerical operations in which elements common to the test were heavily weighted. With respect to selection, the situation is somewhat happier. Where it is feasible to continue research for the selection of clerical workers, it might be well to include a test such as this in a preliminary battery to be validated.

E. F. Wonderlic, Vice-President, General Finance Corporation, Chicago, Illinois. This is the most widely used clerical test in business and industry. It has proved useful in many companies for the selection of various types of clerical workers. Some personnel research workers have found that test results are also predictive of success in other than clerical occupations. The latest manual, revised in 1946, gives much significant data and summaries of experiences with this test. Psychotechnical standards are clearly met in this publication.

The simplicity of the test when casually examined may mislead the uninformed. While it is simple to administer and to score, its interpretation requires study and practice. Sex and educational differences are pronounced. Age factor, over 40 years, is important.

The timing is a little awkward. Number Checking requires 8 minutes and Name Checking requires 7 minutes. These differences in time intervals are easily overlooked or reversed by clerical test administrators and thus cause errors in the final scores and resulting interpretations.

The consistent use of this test is a satisfactory indication of its acceptance and value in personnel administration.

For a review by W. D. Commins, see 40:1664.

[628]
N.I.I.P. Clerical Test: American Revision. Ages 16 and over; 1934; an American revision of the *National Institute of Industrial Psychology Clerical Test,* Series 25; $2.10 per 25, postpaid; 35¢ per specimen set, postpaid; (30) minutes; American revision by Herbert Moore; distributed by Psychological Corporation.

REFERENCES
1-2. *See* 40:1665.
3. OBERHEIM, GRACE M. "A New Use for the Institute's Clerical Test in America." *Occupational Psychol* 16:83-6 Ap '42. * (*PA* 16:3297)
4. OBERHEIM, GRACE M. "The Prediction of Success of Student Assistants in College Library Work." *Ed & Psychol Meas* 22:379-85 O '42. * (*PA* 17:1364)
5. SLATER, PATRICK. "Notes on Testing Groups of Young Children." *Occupational Psychol* 16:31-8 Ja '42. *
6. OBERHEIM, GRACE M. "The Relationship Between Scores on a Clerical Test and Clerical Proficiency in Library Work." *J Ed Psychol* 35:493-9 N '44. * (*PA* 19:1020)

R. B. Selover, Assistant Personnel Director, The Prudential Insurance Company of America, Newark, New Jersey. This test is an attempt to measure general clerical ability by combining performance from seven short subtests. The subtests present problems in immediate recall of information presented orally, classification of miscellaneous items according to six headings: arithmetic computation, copying names and symbols, checking names and numbers, filing, and reasoning. The subtests are administered with separate time limits ranging from 2 to 5 minutes each. The total test can be administered in 30 minutes and corrected in 5 minutes.

The manual reports deciles for high school students and college seniors. Median scores on the subtests are reported for high school seniors and college seniors. No information is given in regard to the reliability or validity of this test for selecting clerical workers. The test items show evidence of care in construction; much of the material presents considerable surface validity.

It is not probable that seven separate abilities are measured by the subtests, although several abilities are probably sampled. Speed is apparently an important factor in most of the tasks. The subtests are probably too short to be used individually with much confidence. Apparently this test was constructed by arbitrarily adding together performance on the separate tasks without reference to either the interrelationships of the subtests or the relationships between the subtests and criterion data. It is the reviewer's opinion that the test could be improved by the careful selection of fewer subtests of greater length.

For a review by Donald G. Paterson, see 40:1665.

[629]
O'Rourke Clerical Aptitude Test, Junior Grade. Applicants for clerical positions; 1926–36; 2 parts; $1.75 per 50 of either part, postpaid; 25¢ per specimen set of either part, postpaid; L. J. O'Rourke; Psychological Institute.
a) CLERICAL PROBLEMS. 1926–35; Form 1; 25(30) minutes.
b) REASONING TEST. 1926–36; Form A; 20(25) minutes.

REFERENCES
1. COPELAND, HERMAN A. "Some Characteristics of Three Tests Used to Predict Clerical Success." *J Appl Psychol* 20:461-70 Ag '36. * (*PA* 11:421)
2. ANDERSON, ROY N. "Review of Clerical Tests (1929–1942)." *Occupations* 21:654-60 My '43. * (*PA* 17:3218)
3. WOODY, CLIFFORD. *Guidance Implications From Measurements of Achievements, Aptitudes and Interests.* University of Michigan, School of Education, Bureau of Educational Reference and Research, Bulletin No. 156. Ann Arbor, Mich.: the School, September 1, 1944. Pp. viii, 162. Paper. $1.25. * (*PA* 20:573)

Raymond A. Katzell, Associate Professor of Psychology, The University of Tennessee, Knoxville, Tennessee. This is a battery of two tests, including a reasoning test and a clerical problems test. The two tests are published separately and could be used independently if desired.

The reasoning test contains a total of 45 items, which are grouped roughly according to the following types: following directions, general information, interpretation of proverbs, spelling, verbally stated arithmetic problems, word usage, and word relations. The test therefore seems to be essentially an intelligence test which measures mainly verbal factors. It is geared in difficulty and context to an average adult population.

The test is printed on both sides of a single sheet of paper and has no cover page. Thus, there are opportunities for examinees to read some of the items prior to the starting signal. This is of some consequence in view of the fact

that there is a short time limit. Present users of the test will face a problem in handling Item 6, which is based on postal rates. These rates were recently changed so that the answer which is now correct does not appear among the five alternatives offered.

The clerical problems test consists of 6 parts: (*a*) alphabetical filing; (*b*) arithmetic; (*c*) classification; (*d*) checking names and numbers; (*e*) arithmetic computations; (*f*) alphabetical filing as in part (*a*). There is a single time limit during which the examinee is to work on the 6 parts in succession.

A table of percentile norms is provided for each test separately and for the sum of the score on the clerical problems test plus ten times the score on the reasoning test. The basis for this weighting is not indicated. The norms were computed for a group of 792 "typical" applicants for clerical positions. Although no further information is given concerning the applicants or the jobs for which they applied, these norms are probably more useful for vocational guidance and selection than the oft-found norms based on school or general populations.

Unfortunately, no data are provided on the construction, reliability, or validity of these two tests. Anderson (2) cites a letter from the tests' author which indicates satisfactory reliability and validity with groups of clerical workers in industry. But such information is of limited value unless supplied directly to prospective users. Also, unelaborated citations of validity coefficients are not enough; the information furnished should include characteristics of the population studied, the jobs they filled, and the criteria of success used. The intelligent selection of tests is so severely handicapped by the absence of these data that every author of an occupational aptitude test should feel obliged to furnish them when the test is offered for general sale.

On the whole, the battery of two tests seems to have been designed in line with the common practice of measuring aptitude for clerical work in terms of general abstract intelligence and ability to perform simple detailed tasks speedily and accurately. There have been a number of demonstrations of good results through this approach.

However, the question may be raised whether a single general alertness score like that yielded by the reasoning test is really the most useful for clerical placement. Since different clerical positions involve different relative amounts of verbal and arithmetical aptitudes, it would be advantageous to have a test that would yield separate scores for these two areas. Such a breakdown can aid in differential placement and also, through multiple regression weighting of the two scores, enhance the validity of the test for any one job. This worth-while feature is incorporated in several recent measures of clerical aptitude, such as the *Psychological Corporation General Clerical Test.*

The arrangement of the clerical problems test may be objectionable to those who would prefer a test with separate scores for each of the parts as an aid to differential diagnosis. However, the inclusion of this feature would necessitate the lengthening of each part and would add considerably to the total time consumption. Since the test as it stands probably measures mainly a group of aptitudes related to speed, perception, and manipulation of simple details, all of which enter into a number of the more routine clerical jobs, it should be quite useful in providing a quick over-all appraisal of this important aspect of clerical aptitude.

[630]

★Psychological Corporation General Clerical Test. Grades 9 and over; 1944; revision of General Clerical Test, PCI Selection Form 20 (1942) ; 1 form; $3.25 per 25, postpaid; 35¢ per specimen set, postpaid; 46(50) minutes; this test is also available in two separate booklets (Partial Booklet A, Speed and Number; and Partial Booklet B, Verbal) at $1.80 per 25; Psychological Corporation.

Edward N. Hay, Personnel Officer, The Pennsylvania Company for Banking and Trusts; and President, Edward N. Hay and Associates, Inc.; Philadelphia, Pennsylvania. This test is well designed for use in counseling situations. It gives three types of scores: an over-all score which, according to the authors, "may be regarded as an index of general clerical aptitude (and which) correlates quite highly with the scores of general intelligence tests"; three section scores for "routine clerical aptitude, proficiency in mathematics, and verbal facility"; and 9 part scores, each resulting "from a specific type of clerical performance." Theoretically, the counselor should be able to guide the subject into that aspect of clerical work for which he is best fitted.

At present, however, the test offers no norms for specific occupations. Validity is merely suggested by the difference between percentile scores for high school students, industrial workers, and office workers—type unspecified. No information about interpreting scores has been included in the manual.

The test is not practical for an employment situation. It is too long, requiring over 45 minutes for administration. The authors state that it is permissible to administer and score the subtests independently; but since they are printed together in booklet form, it is impractical to do so. The reported correlation of .74 between the over-all score and a test of general intelligence indicates that it would be repetitious to include both tests in a selection battery; but if the clerical test were given alone, there would be no way of determining how much of the applicant's score could be attributed to mental alertness and how much to the ability to handle routine clerical tasks. Finally, the fact that there has been no validation of the test in business situations militates against its use for employment.

The format of test and manual are pleasing, and the authors have supplied additional norms to supplement those originally printed. They have also made a factor analysis, in which they found that Parts 1 and 2 are "true" measures of "clerical" ability, in that they are relatively free of both the verbal factor, which is loaded in Parts 6, 7, 8, and 9, and the numerical factor, loaded heavily in Parts 3, 4, and 5. The logical application for this information would be to simplify the test.

It is unfortunate that the authors have made the test available before it has been validated and that they have not recognized the fact that the best procedure in employment situations is to use a mental ability test for range of ability and an indication of promotability, supplemented by pure tests of aptitude for handling verbal and numerical material, having minimal correlation with mental ability items.

Thelma Hunt, Professor of Psychology, The George Washington University, Washington, D. C. This is a relatively new clerical test. In nature of the test items, however, it follows the general pattern of earlier ones of the more complex clerical tests. There are nine parts to the test, each timed separately. The parts involve identification of errors in a copy of original material, identification of errors in an arithmetical table, alphabetizing, arithmetic computation, arithmetic reasoning, spelling, reading, vocabulary, and grammar. By suggestions for use as given in the manual, and by norms, these nine parts are grouped into three sections (from which section scores are derived) covering, respectively, routine clerical aptitude, proficiency in mathematics, and verbal facility. This availability of the three section scores would seem to be one of the chief advantages of this test over other similar clerical tests. Since clerical workers constitute by no means a unitary group in respect to duties, many users may find it helpful to weight ratings on these three subparts of the test in proportion to their importance in particular jobs. The authors suggest the feasibility of utilizing the test as a whole, or in any of its three sections or nine parts. Users should exercise some caution, however, in utilizing alone some of the nine separate parts, since reliabilities are of marginal adequacy.

The statistical information on the test supplied in the manual includes: (a) intercorrelations between the nine parts, which are for the most part between .30 and .50; (b) reliabilities for the nine separate parts; (c) correlations of the test with *Modified Alpha Examination Form 9;* and (d) norms for high school senior girls (commercial students), clerical employees, draftsmen, and miscellaneous industrial workers. There is also a statement that factorial analyses have indicated factors agreeing with the three divisions of the test as indicated in the section scoring. The correlation of the total clerical test with the *Modified Alpha Examination* is .74, the verbal subsection correlating higher than the other two sections with the intelligence test. No information is given on validity of the test in actual use either in vocational guidance or in employment work. No references to reported studies in the literature are given. The test is as yet too new to expect many follow-up studies to be available. It is to be feared that there is nothing unusual enough in its nature or make-up to stimulate rapid research on it or study of it.

One could well afford to give the test serious consideration if looking for one of the more complex types of clerical tests. The directions for giving and scoring are clear, the test layout and printing are attractive and of such a nature as to minimize the testees' problems in following through a test. To many, the advantages of the three sectional scores will be a desirable feature.

Raymond A. Katzell, Associate Professor of Psychology, The University of Tennessee, *Knoxville, Tennessee.* This test is evidently based on the concept that there exist several aptitudes which, in different patterns, enter into different types of clerical jobs. It has therefore been designed to measure various aspects of clerical aptitude and to express them in separate scores. This reviewer believes that such an approach has two very important advantages: it makes provision for maximizing the validity of the test for any one type of job by making possible optimum weighting of the various aspects measured, and it permits differential diagnosis of an individual's suitability relative to different types of clerical positions.

The *General Clerical Test* comprises nine parts published together in a single booklet. Each part is a subtest having its own directions, time limit, and score. The contents of the parts may be described as follows: 1, checking names and numbers; 2, alphabetical filing; 3, arithmetic computations; 4, arithmetical checking; 5, arithmetical problem solving; 6, spelling; 7, paragraph comprehension; 8, vocabulary; 9, grammar. Past research on clerical aptitudes has demonstrated the usefulness of such types of tests.

The printing and format of the test booklet are excellent. Instructions are concise and generally clear, with the exception of those to Part 4. In this instance the instructions are somewhat lengthy, but, in spite of this, experience with clerical applicants in industry has shown that they sometimes have difficulty in understanding exactly what is to be done until given further explanation. This can probably be attributed in part to the rather unusual nature of the task itself. Part 9 also may present some problems to the user. A few of the items, which are of the free-choice type, may have more than one conceivable answer, although only one is given on the scoring key. Items 1, 9, and 17 seem to fall in this category.

The test provides for the computation of a total score which is the sum of the number of correct answers in all parts. It will be possible, of course, for each user of the test to develop on the basis of the subtests a multiple regression equation for predicting success in each particular job in which he may be interested. This procedure would make possible the computation of a weighted total score that would be a more valid indicator of aptitude for that job than the unweighted score now yielded by the test.

Provisions are made for the computation of

three subtotal or section scores. The "routine clerical" subtotal is the sum of the scores on Parts 1 and 2. The "numerical" subtotal is the sum of the scores on Parts 3, 4, and 5. The "verbal" subtotal is the sum of the scores on the remaining 4 parts. Two separate factorial analyses were performed in an effort to check on the authenticity of these groupings. Dr. G. K. Bennett kindly made available to the reviewer a copy of the rotated factor loadings. The results of the two analyses are not in very close accord, which is probably due in part to the relatively small number of cases in each sample (108 and 120). However, the results generally support the legitimacy of the three groupings. The subtotals overlap considerably with respect to the factors measured, but each does seem to emphasize the area of aptitude ascribed to it in its title.

For practical purposes, the test is somewhat long and perhaps unnecessarily so in view of the overlap existing among several of its parts. For example, Parts 1 and 2 are factorially similar to each other. The same can be said for Parts 3, 4, and 5; for Parts 6 and 9; and for Parts 7 and 8. One wonders whether a test composed of one of the parts from each of these sets, say Parts 2, 3, 6, and 8, might not be substantially as effective as the total battery. Of course, when the test is validated for any particular job, the results will indicate which parts, if any, may be eliminated without seriously reducing validity.

With the exception of Part 5, the parts all have split-half reliabilities above .75 (corrected for length). Those of Parts 1 through 4 are probably overestimates of their true reliability, since these subtests are highly speeded. The split-half reliability of Part 5 is only .63. The reliabilities of the total and subtotal scores are not reported, but are probably all above .8.

Norms based on several different kinds of occupational groups are provided for total, subtotal, and part scores.

Unfortunately, no decisive data on validity are reported with the test. However, for maximum utility, a test of this sort should be validated and standardized locally for each type of position for which it is to be employed. Once this preliminary research is done, the user will probably be in possession of an effective instrument for the placement of clerical personnel.

E. F. Wonderlic, Vice President, General Finance Corporation, Chicago, Illinois. This test is made up of nine subtests, each requiring constant attention and administration. The subtests remind one of the Army Alpha. Correlations with intelligence tests are not reported, but it seems likely that there might be a high relationship, thus eliminating the necessity for the use of such a test if a satisfactory intelligence test is used in the test battery. The timing intervals vary from 3 to 7 to 8½ minutes for each group, making it particularly difficult to administer in an employment office.

The norms are established on 143 office workers, 195 industrial workers, and 380 high school students. This number of cases hardly justifies the serious use of this test as a selecting aid in business. Information in the test manual is refined from a statistical point of view, but the refinement is hardly justified on the basis of the number of cases involved. Such a test, if carefully standardized on thousands of cases from individuals in different parts of the country and in different companies, might be of value to the personnel technician. However, its extremely complicated administration, because of irregular time intervals, makes it impractical for the typical employment office.

[631]
★Survey of Working Speed and Accuracy. Grades 9-16 and adults; 1943-44; $1.75 per 25; 35¢ per specimen set, postpaid; 20(25) minutes; Floyd Ruch; California Test Bureau.

Edward N. Hay, Personnel Officer, The Pennsylvania Company for Banking and Trusts; and President, Edward N. Hay and Associates, Inc.; Philadelphia, Pennsylvania. This test is intended for "selection, placement, upgrading, and transfer" of routine office workers and industrial checkers and inspectors who perform clerical operations.

It consists of four parts: The first part, Number Checking, includes letters and symbols and is set up with a left-margin alignment which is unusual in business situations. The second test, Code Translation, supposedly "measures the ability of the applicant to learn and apply complicated procedures." Next is a dotting test, to measure "finger dexterity as it is involved in filing and in the operation of a wide variety of office machines," and which, the author says, "is also meant to measure the ability and willingness of the applicant to work at a highly monotonous task." No one has ever proved that a so-called "dexterity test" will usefully predict success in operating office machines, and no evidence is offered that any useful information about temperament can be obtained on a test of this kind. A further drawback to the finger dexterity test is that it is printed on the same page with Code Translation, and the 5-minute time allowance may very easily lead some subjects to abandon dotting in favor of completing Test 2. The final test, Counting, requires the subject to count the vowels in each line of meaningful prose and is "intended to measure the type of ability involved in proofreading and in checking reports and statistical tables." No data are given in support of this claim.

No mention is made of validity in connection with the Counting Test, although the other three tests have been found "valid," the author says, in a study of a group of office workers in an insurance company. The fact that 88 per cent of workers rated "superior" by their supervisors had scores on each of the three tests which exceeded the median scores for those rated "inferior," is scant evidence for validity, particularly since there is no indication of the qualities on which ratings were based; of the number or type of ratings; of the sex, age, or occupation of the workers; or even of the number of individuals included in the sample.

Norms are given in percentile scores, based on a population of 400 males and 400 females, aged 16 to 50. No data about distribution of ages, education, occupation, or even the source of subjects are given, and the author has apparently overlooked the findings of Andrew and others on the sex differential in clerical operations.

The *Survey of Working Speed and Accuracy* cannot be properly evaluated until more information is given about what it measures and how efficiently it measures it.

Donald G. Paterson, Professor of Psychology, University of Minnesota, Minneapolis, Minnesota. This test, although admittedly a clerical test, is correctly labeled so as to be applicable to workers performing routine clerical operations in office or factory whether such workers are identified by a "clerical job label" or not. There are four subtests: Test 1, Number Checking, 150 pairs using numbers along with code letters, plus, minus, per cent, and dollar signs to make the test more closely resemble office and shop clerical procedures; Test 2, Code Translation or a letter-digit sub-

stitution test with 26 pairs in the key to be learned and 20 lines of about 15 numbers each to be filled in; Test 3, Finger Dexterity, consisting of 50 lines of small circles in each of which the subject is to put a pencil dot; and Test 4, counting the number of each kind of vowel in 40 lines of printed text. Time limits appear to be adequate, being 5 minutes for each subtest or 20 minutes working time. It is possible that the arrangement of the four subtests on three pages may tend to invalidate the results because of the difficulty of preventing subjects who are unusually adept at understanding directions from working ahead on a subtest while others are still listening to the examiner read or explain the directions.

A two-page, undated revised manual is provided, the first page consisting of directions for giving and scoring the test, data on validity and reliability, and standards or percentile norms and the second page giving scoring keys for each subtest.

Judged on the basis of face validity, the test appears to be most promising. Data on validity are inadequate; they show the percentage of an unknown number of life insurance office workers rated as "superior" who exceeded the median of an unknown number rated as "inferior" on each of three of the subtests and on the total score for the three subtests. No test-retest reliability correlations are given. Intercorrelations based on only 100 cases are given for the four subtests. These range from .15 to .59, code translation and number checking being 59. Correlations between each subtest and total score and standard intelligence tests for the general population classified by sex or for employed clerical workers classified by sex and occupation are not given.

Norms are given in terms of percentile ranks for a so-called true cross section of the adult population of both sexes from 16 to 50 years available for employment (N = 400 males and 400 females), but the percentile ranks are given only for N = 800 so that any sex differences that may and in all probability must exist, at least on the number checking test, are not revealed. Thus, norms for age and sex, school grade, type of curriculum, specific occupations, employed workers, unemployed workers, etc. are not given.

In the reviewer's opinion, this is a most promising test of clerical aptitude and deserves intensive research to provide the data which are essential to an adequate interpretation of the test results when used for employment or guidance purposes.

Erwin K. Taylor, Chief, Performance Evaluation and Criterion Research Unit, Personnel Research Section, The Adjutant General's Office, Washington, D. C. In the years following the first World War, the impetus given the testing movement by the use of tests in the Army resulted in the widespread publication of numerous unvalidated and poorly standardized paper-and-pencil tests about which the authors frequently made exorbitant claims. This resulted, as is too well known, in an almost complete discrediting of tests for use in industrial selection. A very real danger of a repetition of this situation exists today. If paper-and-pencil tests are to serve any useful purpose in the field of industrial psychology, a considerable amount of research must necessarily precede their publication. From all that appears in the revised manual, this test has been released prematurely. "The validity of this test," says the manual, "has been checked by a number of personnel people and through a correlation of scores with performance on the job as rated by supervisors." What sort of checks these "personnel people" obtained is not specified, nor are we informed as to the magnitude of the correlations referred to or the number of cases in each. The only data quoted are on an unspecified number of superior clerks, 88 per cent of whom exceeded the median of a so-called "inferior" group on each of three subtests.

No reliability data whatsoever are given. An intercorrelation matrix of the several subtests, based on 100 cases, is presented. Norms based on a cross section of the adult population of both sexes, age from 16 to 50 years, are presented and consist of 400 of each sex. Use of this test on anything but a purely experimental basis is not recommended.

For those who may entertain the notion of using this test, it may be interesting to note that it consists of the following parts: (*a*) a 150-item number checking test, bearing the additional "face valid" item of decimal points, fractions, percentage signs, dollar signs, asterisks, and other such symbols commonly found employed in business transactions; (*b*) a 20-line letter-substitution coding test contaminated by the employment of meaningful material; (*c*) a 2,000-item dotting test; and (*d*) a vowel cancellation test called "counting." The manual presents arguments rationalizing each of the four tasks. The validity of these arguments is not substantiated by any data.

[632]
Thurstone Examination in Clerical Work: Thurstone Employment Tests. Clerical applicants; 1922; Form A; $1.60 per 25; 35¢ per specimen set, postpaid; nontimed (60-80) minutes; L. L. Thurstone; World Book Co.

REFERENCES
1. THURSTONE, L. L. "A Standardized Test for Office Clerks." *J Appl Psychol* 3:248-51 S '19. *
2. STEDMAN, MELISSA BRANSON. "Factors Influencing School Success in Bookkeeping." *J Appl Psychol* 14:74-82 F '30. * (*PA* 4:4556)
3. JORGENSEN, C. "Analysis of Some Psychological Tests by the Spearman Factor Method." *Brit J Ed Psychol* 4:96-109 F '34. * (*PA* 8:4318)
4. DAVIDSON, CHARLES M. "Analysis of Clerical Tests." *Personnel J* 16:95-8 S '37. * (*PA* 11:5916)
5. DAVIDSON, CHARLES M. "Evaluation of Clerical Tests." *Personnel J* 16:57-64 Je '37. * (*PA* 11:4713)
6. HALES, W. M. "Clerical Tests in State Reformatory." *Personnel J* 16:316-24 Ap '38. * (*PA* 12:4278)

John M. Willits, Associate Professor of Psychology, Graduate School of Business, Stanford University, Stanford, California. In the historical background of clerical aptitude testing, this is a highly significant test. In the present-day practice of such testing, however, it is an anachronistic survival. The test and its manual bear the copyright date 1922—and evidently neither one has been revised since then. When first issued, a quarter of a century ago, this test was a tremendous forward stride in the application of psychology to personnel selection. Its author, then as now a leader in the testing field, has since moved on to other and no doubt more challenging areas of research and development—but the test remains as he left it.

The continued availability of this test through the years might be claimed as empirical evidence of its merit. Quite likely it does have numerous satisfied users, who may have (and surely should have) individually validated and standardized it. But this review is intended for prospective users rather than for past ones, and they have a right to expect in the manual of a 25-year-old test (or of *any* commercial test) far more of objective data than this one offers.

Strictly speaking, the test has no manual—only two pages of "directions" and a key. No data whatever are given on validity or reliability, beyond the statement that "it has been experimentally verified." The only guide for interpretation of scores is a set of general norms (on a wholly unmentioned population) giving 5-step adjectival ratings on "accuracy," "speed," and "combined speed-and-accuracy," with a recommendation to use only the combination ratings.

Scoring is by the now largely outmoded "time-plus-errors" method. As only the total time is recorded, there is no practical way of utilizing part-scores on the eight widely different subtests. The directions ignore the matter of part-scores, while stating that the test's purpose is to supplement the employment interview in determining "at least roughly the applicant's general intelligence as well as his accuracy and speed in doing clerical tasks."

"The several parts of the examination are sample clerical tasks," the directions continue. "The last part of the test is a generally accepted intelligence test." The last part of the test consists of *ten* proverb-matching items and one sample item. Ten items of this sort *may* have constituted "a generally accepted intelligence test" in 1922, but they would meet with no such acceptance today from anyone even slightly acquainted, for instance, with Dr. Thurstone's distinguished work on the primary mental abilities.

Most of the subtests seem to be well designed, as aptitude counterparts of clerical achievement worksamples. An exception is the one which requires the underlining of some 40 misspelled words in a reading selection of about 800 words—a literary essay of moderately high comprehension level. This subtest is a worksample of one aspect of proofreading —but not, as is sometimes assumed, a spelling test. For a poor speller, it measures an unanalyzable resultant of spelling and concentration; for a good speller, it measures concentration alone.

The scoring key is accurately spaced to fit the test blank. But in design it is as outmoded and cumbersome as the scoring method. Time-saving ideas such as fan keys were unknown in 1922, and this test is strictly a "1922 model," albeit a well-built one for its day.

E. F. Wonderlic, Vice-President, General Finance Corporation, Chicago, Illinois. This test, first published in 1922, has since been used consistently in a few business organizations with modest success. Norms and standardization material and descriptive information regarding the method of construction are not reported by the

author. The test consists of eight subtests, making it cumbersome to administer in the typical employment office. However, some of the subtests do discriminate differences in clerical ability remarkably well. Later testing techniques have perhaps surpassed this test, but the types of questions and the underlying philosophy is still the basis for many psychological and clerical tests. Careful students of testing will study this form and in spite of its being over 25 years old will find it informative and useful. However, tests developed and perfected in later years, such as the *Minnesota Clerical Test,* which are simpler to administer and have norms available on adult performance in business and industry, tend to replace this work.

INTERESTS

[633]

Basic Interest Questionnaire: For Selecting Your Vocation or Avocation. Grades 9-16 and adults; 1938–39; replaced by the *Job Qualification Inventory* (*see* 639); nontimed (75) minutes; Keith Van Allyn; National Institute of Vocational Research (now Surveys, Inc.).

Occupations 19:311–3 Ja '41. Donald E. Super. The Van Allyn Technique for Vocational Selection was developed, according to the *Manual,* to provide a sound basis for vocational guidance and selection because of the difficulties experienced by counselors in relating the results of test batteries to vocational specifications, in choosing appropriate tests from the great variety available, and in arriving at reasonably similar conclusions in making diagnoses. It consists of three items, to which a fourth is to be added, which are claimed to constitute a uniform technique which will lead to uniformity in the diagnoses made by different counselors. One might question, at the outset, the validity of a uniformity achieved by the standardization of techniques rather than by the development of more valid techniques. Validity and reliability are not, after all, synonymous. The first of these items is the *Manual,* which begins with a quotation from Emerson to the effect that each man is called to one vocation for which he is better suited than any other and in which he has no rival, a statement contradicted by all the facts of vocational psychology and to which no qualified vocational counselor would subscribe. The *Manual* is not intended "as a technical publication," but is meant for "everyone interested in guidance"; it is stated that the technique may be used by "any persons with academic background, or with special interest of a practical nature, in helping others find themselves," after "a little preparation." Near the end of the *Manual* it is stated that courses in the use of the technique conducted by Dr. Van Allyn are offered, a series of 10 two-hour lecture periods, including laboratory work. Can it be that we have all been wrong and that counselors can be made overnight regardless of previous experience and personality? To the trained counselor who examines tests critically, with their validity in mind, the *Manual* is exasperatingly ambiguous and lacking in specific data. Constant reference is made to "research" which Van Allyn has allegedly been carrying on for some years, but no data are given (with one minor exception), no reference to other publications are cited, and no other publications of this self-styled vocational psychologist (who is not a member of the American Psychological Association nor of the American Association for Applied Psychology) are listed in any issue of *Psychological Abstracts*. Several pages are devoted to a confused discussion of factors which differentiate vocations. This seems to lead to the conclusion that interests and achievement are the best indices of aptitude, that personality is so modifiable and so inconstant as to be a negligible factor, and that intelligence is relatively unimportant. Accepted methods of vocational guidance such as explanatory courses and the imparting of vocational information are surveyed and found wanting. *The Basic Interest Questionnaire* and the *Key* are then explained. The *Questionnaire* is a 12-page inventory "listing all the basic elements which constitute occupations," a "classification of 25 knowledge-fields . . . providing a means of determining the individual's dominant interests and general aptitudes." We are not told just how the basic elements of occupations were determined. Nor are we told how it was established that there are just 25 knowledge-fields ("factors" in psychology?). Each knowledge-field is "tested" by means of five questions, after which the examinee indicates by circling a 0, 1, 2, 3, 4, or 5 the extent of both his interest and aptitude in that activity. We are not told the reliability of the scores derived by the 10 responses thus obtained, although we are assured that they are consistent. The examinee is not told how to judge his "aptitude," whether this means native ability or present skill and knowledge, neither is he told how to rate his aptitude for

such activities as "preferring money for a discovery you made than fame you would receive" and "attending theatrical performances and stage shows," nor does the *Manual* show any consideration for the deficiencies of self-ratings of aptitudes and interest in this test which, its author claims, "makes it possible for one to draw a sharp conclusion as to the right vocation for each individual." *The Key to Vocational Guidance and Occupational Placement* consists of: (1) a list of "dominant interests" according to which it is claimed occupations can be classified, including classifications ranging from "Biological Sciences" through "Materials" to "Travel by Land" and "Travel by Sea and Air"; and (2) a list of occupations classified according to the supposed importance of these dominant interests, singly and in combination. Again, there are no data as to how the dominant interests were determined or as to how their role in each occupation was established; simply the statement: "All known occupations were then reviewed and were assigned representative letters. . . ." But need we continue? Perhaps the *Manual* is not meant to be technical or scientific in its presentation, and the important scientific data are, therefore, left out. But why such a manual if such evidence exists? Scientific and conscientious vocational counselors cannot use a diagnostic instrument until they are presented evidence of its validity. Let us, therefore, conclude by signifying our agreement with at least one statement in the *Manual,* emphasizing its applicability to both the Van Allyn Technique and this brief review: "If it succeeds only in raising questions in the minds of those who read it, this publication will have more than served its purpose."

[634]

★Brainard Occupational Preference Inventory. Grades 9 and over; 1945; revision of *Specific Interest Inventory* by Paul P. Brainard and Frances G. Stewart; Form A; separate record forms must be used for recording answers; 25¢ per test, postpaid; $1.35 per 25 record forms, postpaid; 60¢ per specimen set, postpaid; nontimed (30) minutes; Paul P. Brainard and Ralph T. Brainard; Psychological Corporation.

REFERENCES

1-4. *See* 40:1675.
5. SHUTTERLY, VIRGINIA. "Is the Aptitude Test a Panacea?" *Occupations* 22:260-2 Ja '44. * (*PA* 18:1904)
6. STEFFLRE, BUFORD. "The Reading Difficulty of Interest Inventories." *Occupations* 26:95-6 N '47. * (*PA* 22:1722)

Edwin W. Davis, Director of Washington Counseling Center and Associate Professor of Psychology, The George Washington University, Washington, D. C. This vocational interest inventory replaces the four forms of the *Specific*

Interest Inventory which was reviewed in earlier *Mental Measurements Yearbooks* (*see* 38:1176 and 40:1675). The new inventory is self-administering and self-scoring, but the subject would do well to have his scoring and his interpretations reviewed by a professional counselor. The subject expresses his preferences for or against 140 work situations on a self-scoring record form. Here, the subject may score his answers for 28 occupations which in turn may be combined into the 7 major occupational fields of commercial, personal service, agriculture, mechanical, professional, esthetic, and scientific. The subject records his preferences for each of the 140 questions on a five-point scale with the following numerical values: −2 dislikes greatly, −1 dislikes some, 0 neutral, 1 likes some, and 2 likes greatly. The manual lists 378 occupations classified under the 28 occupations of the inventory.

Generally the inventory is a good one. Veterans Administration Guidance Centers reported 17 per cent using it as compared to 99 per cent for Kuder, 70 per cent for Strong, 36 per cent for Lee–Thorpe and 30 per cent for Cleeton.* The author reports a reliability correlation of .81 on over 300 cases. Intercorrelations of major fields for 342 boys and girls gave a median *r* of .29 ranging from .07 to .63 with the low correlations for unrelated fields and the highest correlation between the related professional and scientific occupational fields. Norms for the 7 fields and 28 occupations were based on 335 boys, 378 girls, 95 men, and 75 women.

This test excels all others in its possibilities for self-analysis and for counselor analysis. Although its major fields do not give as good coverage as some other inventories, its 28 subfields and 378 related occupations offer better possibilities for actual analysis of occupational choices than do other interest inventories. It has the unique advantage of being keyed to hundreds of other related occupations in the USES *Dictionary of Occupational Titles, Part II.* Further validation with adults should make it a serious competitor of any other interest inventory now in use.

Herschel T. Manuel, Professor of Educational Psychology and Director of Testing and Guidance Bureau, The University of Texas, Austin, Texas. This inventory consists of 140 questions

* Baker, Gertrude, and Peatman, John Gray. "Tests Used in Veterans Administration Advisement Units." *Am Psychol* 2:99-102 Mr '47.

arranged in seven fields, each of which is further subdivided into four sections, consisting of five questions each. In the booklet containing the questions, no occupations in the sense of vocation are *named;* instead, one infers from the publisher's catalogue, each question *describes* briefly an activity characteristic of some occupation. The answer sheet provides spaces for recording scores for each field and section, which are there given names. The fields are commercial, personal service, agriculture, mechanical, professional, esthetic, and scientific. An example of the division into sections may be taken from the professional field: medicine, law and social work, education and uplift, and personnel.

According to the manual, "it is a standardized interview designed to bring to the fore the salient facts about a person with respect to his occupational interests so that he and his advisers can more intelligently and objectively discuss his occupational and educational plans." The question booklet and the answer sheet are cleverly arranged to make the administration of the inventory easy and to make it possible for the student himself to score the test, construct profiles, and make certain records preparatory to interpretation.

Preliminary "section" and "field" norms are given for the sexes separately at the high school and adult levels, and occupations are suggested for various combinations of highest scoring sections. The reliability by the Ghiselli formula is given as .81. Intercorrelations of field scores range from .07 to .63.

In the hands of qualified counselors, the Inventory can be a useful instrument. Certainly the mechanics of administration and scoring are not difficult. The publisher's term, "self-interpreting," however, implies too much. The attractive mechanics of a measuring instrument can be misleading by tending to make the process of vocational guidance appear to be a much simpler process than it can possibly be. The authors themselves recognize the complexity of vocational planning, but it needs to be emphasized over and over until the need for specially qualified counselors is fully appreciated by school and college administrators and the public.

The use of descriptive phrases representing activities of various occupations gives the inventory a degree of validity as an instrument for surveying occupational interests. Yet one cannot escape the impression that too much has been sacrificed to convenience and mechanical excellence. An inventory limited to 140 questions is entirely too brief to give adequately the variety of information attempted in the section and field summaries. Five questions can hardly be sufficient to give a very accurate picture of interests in "Law and Social Work," "Education and Uplift," or "Writing, Speaking, and Acting." In the long run, the fault may be more with the test user than the testmaker. As users of the tests, we are continually trying to oversimplify the process of dealing with human nature.

For reviews by Jack W. Dunlap, Everett B. Sackett, and M. R. Trabue of the original edition, see 38:1176 and 40:1675.

[635]
Cleeton Vocational Interest Inventory, Revised Edition. Grades 9-16 and adults; 1937–43; Form A; separate editions for men and women; IBM; separate answer sheets must be used; 10-99 tests, 7½¢ each; 4½¢ per machine-scorable answer sheet; 40¢ per set of scoring stencils; 50¢ per specimen set, postpaid; nontimed (40-50) minutes; Glen U. Cleeton; McKnight & McKnight.

REFERENCES

1. CONGDON, NORA A. "A Study of Cleeton's Vocational Interest Inventory." *Occupations* 18:347-52 F '40. * (PA 14:2594)
2. CONGDON, NORA ALVINA. *A Study of Cleeton's Vocational Interest Inventory.* Unpublished doctor's thesis, Colorado State College of Education, 1940.
3. ARSENIAN, SETH. "A Further Study of the Validity of the Cleeton Vocational Interest Inventory." *Occupations* 20:94-9 N '41. * (PA 16:744)
4. CUTLER, T. H. "The Validity of the Cleeton Vocational SR Section." *Occupations* 19:581-4 My '41. * (PA 15:3575)
5. GILGER, GEORGE A., JR. "Declaration of Vocational Interests." *Occupations* 20:276-9 Ja '42. * (PA 16:1662)
6. GORDON, HANS C., AND HERKNESS, WALTER W., JR. "Pupils Appraise Vocational Interest Blanks." *Occupations* 20:100-2 N '41. * (PA 16:757)
7. GOODMAN, CHARLES H. "A Comparison of the Interests and Personality Traits of Engineers and Liberal Arts Students." *J Appl Psychol* 26:721-37 D '42. * (PA 17:2486)
8. GORDON, HANS C., AND HERKNESS, WALTER W., JR. "Do Vocational Interest Questionnaires Yield Consistent Results?" *Occupations* 20:424-9 Mr '42. * (PA 16:2059)
9. HARTZELL, MILDRED D., AND MURPHY, FLORENCE E. "Cleeton Interest Inventory Measures Cosmetologists." *Occupations* 20:600-1 My '42. * (PA 16:3284)
10. ARSENIAN, SETH. "The Relation of Evaluative Attitudes to Vocational Interest and Social Adjustment." *J Social Psychol* 17:17-24 F '43. * (PA 17:2154)
11. BREWER, JOHN M. "Classification of Items in Interest Inventories." *Occupations* 21:448-51 F '43. * (PA 17:2159)
12. COMMINS, W. D. "The Interest Pattern of Student Nurses." *Occupations* 21:387-8 Ja '43. * (PA 17:1332)
13. SMALLENBURG, HARRY WALTER. *Teachers' Knowledge of Pupil Characteristics in a Senior High School.* Unpublished doctor's thesis, University of Southern California, 1943. (*Abstracts of Dissertations . . . 1943*, pp. 73-9.)
14. RECKTENWALD, LESTER NICHOLAS. "Grouping of Occupations in the Cleeton Vocational Interest Inventory." *Occupations* 24:162-4 D '45. *
15. RECKTENWALD, LESTER NICHOLAS. "Attitudes Toward Occupations Before and After Vocational Information." *Occupations* 24:220-3 Ja '46. * (PA 20:1695)
16. ZERFOSS, KARL P. ["Reliability of the Cleeton Vocational Interest Inventory."] *Occupations* 24:226 Ja '46. *
17. KOPP, T., AND TUSSING, L. "The Vocational Choices of High School Students as Related to Scores on Vocational Interest Inventories." *Occupations* 25:334-9 Mr '47. * (PA 21:2463)
18. RECKTENWALD, LESTER NICHOLAS. "Homogeneity of Items in Cleeton's Classification." *Occupations* 25:275-7 F '47. * (PA 21:2028)
19. STEFFLRE, BUFORD. "The Reading Difficulty of Interest Inventories." *Occupations* 26:95-6 N '47. * (PA 22:1722)

Edward B. Greene, Chief, Personnel Training, Michigan Unemployment Compensation Commission, Detroit, Michigan; and Lecturer in Psychology, University of Michigan, Ann Arbor, Michigan. Two forms are provided—one for men and one for women—each of which consists of 700 items, divided into 10 fields of work of 70 items each. The fields of work for men are: (*a*) biological sciences; (*b*) insurance, real estate and specialized selling; (*c*) physical sciences; (*d*) social sciences; (*e*) business administration; (*f*) literary occupations; (*g*) mechanical occupations; (*h*) financial and accounting; (*i*) artistic, including music, art, and public performances; and (*j*) agriculture. The fields of occupations for women are: (*a*) clerical; (*b*) retail sales; (*c*) biological sciences; (*d*) social service; (*e*) artistic creative; (*f*) grade school teacher; (*g*) high school teacher; (*h*) personal service, including actress, dancer, and singer; (*i*) household and factory mechanics; and (*j*) homemaker (child care and household economist).

According to the author, each group indicates some of the occupations, things, activities, and people that are liked by successful persons in a particular field. The scores are simply the number of plus marks for each section, although instructions asked for zeros to be placed after the items which one dislikes or thinks he would dislike.

The methods by which the fields of work were determined and the items placed in each field are not clearly indicated. The author states that the present inventories were developed from items included in forms published by Robinson, Moore, Freyd, and Ream, plus some additional items. In all of these scales the basis of selecting items has been "the extent to which people in different occupations report interest in specific items." There is no evidence, however, that the Cleeton forms have been validated by this procedure. The author states "new items appearing in the present inventories for the first time in any interest test were selected by determining the extent to which new items agreed with the basic items of known vocational significance."

The scales have been validated by applying them to 1,741 persons successfully engaged in standard occupations. The occupations, however, are not named. Among these persons the occupation actually being followed corresponded to the field of work given the highest inventory rating in 78 per cent of the cases. Figures are not given to show how much higher such ratings were than other ratings or whether or not unsuccessful persons in an occupation would show similar ratings to successful persons.

The fields of work are not intended to be mutually exclusive. Identical or nearly identical items are found in several of the sections, and a number of somewhat independent elements are found in each section. Thus, in the first section in the men's series, devoted to biological sciences and related occupations, bacteriologist, dentist, nerve specialist, optician, pharmacist, hospital laboratory technician, physician, specialist in mental diseases, public health officer, and surgeon seem to represent occupations in this field. Other related occupations are chemist and scientific research worker. In addition are included occupations which seem very little related to biological science, such as astronomer, sculptor, carpenter, explorer, cabinet maker, instrument maker, watchmaker, and ship's officer. The writer feels that this range of occupations is probably too varied to give a clear picture. It is also noted that such occupations as biologist, dental hygienist, dietician, and nurse are omitted.

Under the group of activities which indicate a liking for biological science work, we find such things as pet monkeys, cowboy movies, animal zoos, detective stories, gardening, similarity in work, operating a small business for myself, chopping wood as a recreation, men who use perfume, people who are quick tempered, people who make excuses, and repairing a clock. Other items in this list seem to be more related to the biological field of work, although many of them are rather general, such as, working for yourself instead of others, emphasis on quality of work, can you meet emergencies quickly, work which is interesting with modest income, do you drive yourself steadily, etc.

An analysis of other pages in the men's and women's forms shows more or less this same pattern. A majority of items bear directly on the field in question, but a large number of other items are of a general sort or only distantly related. It is believed that a good item analysis would yield a much shorter questionnaire which would be more reliable and valid.

The phrasing of the items leaves something to be desired. Most of them are not more than four words in length, and many of them are single words, such as golf, poker, politics, smokers, military drill, etc. Some studies have shown that many persons have difficulty in making up

their minds as to whether or not they should check items which are so vague or general. A few items stated more specifically might yield more meaningful results.

The author gives odd-even reliabilities above .82 for each subdivision of the scale. No reliabilities are given for repeated administrations of the test, although he states that on a second administration within a month of the first, 6.1 per cent of responses were changed from "0" to "plus" or from "plus" to "0."

The author provides a manual of 31 pages, of which the first 9 pages indicate the use of interest questionnaires and counseling, and pages 22 to 27 give a sample record and a discussion of handling special cases. Nine pages contain norms for men's and women's scales. Separate norms are given for 8th, 9th, 10th, 11th and 12th grades, college freshmen, upper-class college students, and adults. No indication is given of the types of school sampled, or the selection of adults. In each instance a fairly sizable sample is reported, that is, more than 700 cases.

C. A. Oakley, Lecturer in Industrial Psychology, Glasgow University, Glasgow, Scotland. Many think that vocational guidance should be based on temperament rather than on talent, but unfortunately temperament is much less, very much less, readily measured than talent. One aspect to which a good deal of attention has been given is the assessment of the subject's major interests, because of the impression that he would be happiest, even if not necessarily most successful, in an occupation which he liked very much. The distinction is, of course, to some extent artificial, since there must clearly be a positive relationship between his outstanding abilities and his chief interests. But perhaps this point should not be emphasized, since the adolescent is immature; and some of his interests, influencing considerably the way he will do his work later on, may as yet be at an early stage of formation.

The *Cleeton Vocational Interest Inventory* is well known in British laboratories, but has been given little practical application. Its purpose is to find out whether a student's interests fit in closely with the patterns of people in one (or more) of ten basic occupational groups—the assumption, based upon previous researches, being that persons in particular occupations do have common interests—although "whether this is due to training, experience or temperament is not definitely known."

So far, so good. What has tended to set some British psychologists, who have experimented along these lines, against the Cleeton inventory is the selection of the items and, incidentally, also the rather complicated way in which the students are called upon to mark their answers. They are asked how they feel towards certain occupations, school subjects, work activities, and personal traits. It would have perhaps been better to have concentrated on one—or, possibly, two—of these groups rather than to have gathered them together on one comprehensive paper. This, incidentally, would have simplified not only the administration of the inventory but also the subject's task. He must really feel a little bemused by the time he has worked his way through to section FRJ (or for women WHJ).

Each of the three groups, A, B, and C, in which the items are arranged, seems in itself to be useful. But we would have preferred to see, for instance, all of the occupations in the ten Group A's brought together to form one paper by themselves. By eliminating also some of the items in Group B, the inventory could, in our opinion, have been rendered more consistent and more suitable in length.

The general conception of the inventory is ingenious. Much imagination has been exercised in producing the individual items, particularly for the Group C's, and, if there is agreement that analyses of this kind should be dealt with as test scores, then the Cleeton inventory demonstrates how that can be done—we doubt if the possibility had occurred to British psychologists before the Cleeton test was published.

One point on which we agree wholeheartedly with Professor Cleeton is that the inventory should be used at yearly intervals for pupils in senior school classes, thus throwing light on changing inclinations as adolescence advances.

Arthur E. Traxler, Associate Director, Educational Records Bureau, New York, New York. The *Cleeton Vocational Interest Inventory* is representative of the kind of interest test in which the items are arranged in vocational groups rather than in random order. This inventory exists in two forms—one for men and one for women. These forms were first published in 1937. In that edition, each form was designed to measure interests in nine vocational groups and to yield a tenth score known as S-R, or social

adjustment. Subsequent research by Cutler (4) and others casts doubt upon the validity of the social adjustment score. A revision of both blanks was published in 1943, from which the social adjustment section was eliminated and to which a tenth interest group was added. The items in the other nine interest groups were the same as those included in the corresponding areas of the earlier edition. The men's blank yields scores for interests related to biological science, salesmanship, physical science, social science, business, legal and literary occupations, mechanical occupations, finance, public performance occupations, and agricultural occupations. The ten areas in the women's blank include office occupations, selling occupations, natural sciences, social service occupations, creative occupations, grade school teacher, high school or college teacher, performance and personal service occupations, mechanical and household occupations, and domestic interest fields.

Each interest group contains 70 items arranged in three groups—A, B, and C. Group A includes the names of 20 vocations; Group B contains 20 items pertaining to school subjects, reading materials, avocations, famous people, and the like; and Group C has 30 items concerned with activities and aspects of personality. The subject indicates each *like* or *yes* answer by means of a plus (+) and each *dislike* or *no* answer by means of a minus (−). There are no intermediate responses.

The inventory may be administered for either hand scoring or machine scoring. About 40 or 50 minutes, on the average, are required for completion of the 700 items.

It is obvious that the arrangement of the items in the Cleeton inventory greatly simplifies the scoring as compared with that of some of the other leading interest tests. This simplification comes about in three ways. In the first place, the subject has to respond with plus or minus to each item. There is no opportunity to indicate indifference or uncertainty. This procedure may be a limitation, particularly in the case of young subjects who have had little or no work experience.

In the second place, the items, as already indicated, are grouped in occupational interest fields. This arrangement has been criticized by Nelson (*see* excerpt following this review) who indicated that responses to items in random order might be significantly different from responses to items so arranged that they have an obvious relationship to interest fields and by Brewer (11) who pointed to the possible halo effect when similar items appeared in serial order. As for the correctness of the grouping, Recktenwald (14) applied the chi-square test to the grouping of the vocations in the nine categories of the 1937 edition of the men's blank and found statistical support for the grouping.

The third way in which the inventory is simplified is that only the plus items are scored, and each one is given a weight of one. The scoring procedure is so simple that in a small experiment at the Educational Records Bureau the average time to hand score the blank, record the percentile ratings, and draw the profile was 9 minutes, 35 seconds a test. This is rapid for any test containing 700 items, and far faster than the time required by most of the other interest inventories.

Spearman–Brown odd-even reliability coefficients, as given in the manual of directions, range from .822 to .910. These reliabilities are of about the same magnitude as those which have been found for Strong's *Vocational Interest Blank for Men,* the *Kuder Preference Record,* and other leading interest inventories.

Although several studies of the Cleeton inventory have been published, there is little available evidence relative to the validity of the scores. Congdon (1) found the inventory useful in guidance of students. Arsenian (3) obtained statistically significant correlations between scores on the men's blank and certain group scales on the Strong blank for men. The median of the correlations was a little below .50. Hartzell and Murphy (9) found that the PSH and NSC scores on the women's blank were useful in identifying the interests of young women entering a cosmetology training program.

A small study pertaining to the validity of the Cleeton inventory was carried on at the Educational Records Bureau in connection with the preparation of this review. Twenty-four women first ranked the ten fields subjectively in order of their interests and then filled out the women's blank. The same procedure was used by five men in connection with the men's blank. A Spearman rank-difference correlation was computed between the subjective rankings and the rank order of the test scores of each individual. The correlations for the women ranged from .13 to .87, with a median of .69; those for the men ranged from .47 to .87, with a median of .64. The median for the entire group was .68, which is fairly high but

lower than a median of .75 obtained when a similar procedure was applied to results for thirty-one members of the Bureau staff who filled out the *Kuder Preference Record.*

On the whole, this reviewer has somewhat less confidence in the Cleeton inventory than in the Strong blank or the Kuder record, but he would be inclined to use it in situations calling for a quick, easily scored measure of vocational interests.

Occupations 21:269–71 N '42. A. Gordon Nelson. [Review of the 1939 edition.] * This reviewer has found the Cleeton Inventory to be of value when used with other instruments for clinical diagnosis. The mere process of reacting to the many items of the scale appears to be a focusing experience for high school pupils who are vague regarding plans for the future. The scores on the various sections give a clue concerning the kinds of vocational information to which the counselee should be directed. Discrepancy between claimed and measured interests, and disparity between abilities and interests should be watched for. The Cleeton Inventory should be used only by persons familiar with the limitations of instruments of this type. A study of the answers to the questions on the front of the booklet and individual items throughout the Inventory may give the experienced counselor leads for interviews. The scale could be improved in validity if the items were arranged in random order rather than in easily recognizable occupational groups. This might overcome the tendency of some subjects automatically to put plus signs beside items which are obviously related to their claimed interests. The Manual contains a summary of possible uses of the Inventory, but it should give the counselor more data concerning the derivation of the norms and the results of research on reliability and validity.

For reviews by Forrest A. Kingsbury, N. W. Morton, Albert S. Thompson, M. R. Trabue, and E. G. Williamson of an earlier edition, and an excerpt from a review by Nora A. Congdon, see 38:1181 and 40:1682.

[636]

★**Gregory Academic Interest Inventory.** Grades 13-16; 1946; IBM; 1 form; scoring scales are available for 28 interest areas: agriculture, architecture, biological sciences, business administration, chemistry, civil engineering, commercial arts, electrical engineering, elementary education, English, fine arts, geology, history, home economics, journalism, languages, mathematics, mechanical engineering, military science, music, physics, physical education, psychology, public service engineering, religion, secondary education, sociology, and speech; separate answer sheets must be used; $2.50 per 25; 3¢ per machine-scorable answer sheet; 90¢ per scoring scale; 2-9 scales, 75¢ each; 10 or more scales, 65¢ each; 10¢ per manual; 2¢ per profile chart; inventories may be scored on all 28 interests for $1 each plus postage by sending to Institute for Psychological Services, 18 South Michigan Ave., Chicago 3, Ill.; nontimed (60) minutes; W. S. Gregory; Sheridan Supply Co.

REFERENCES

1. GREGORY, WILBUR S. "Data Regarding the Reliability and Validity of the Academic Interest Inventory." Ed & Psychol Meas 6:375-90 au '46. * (PA 21:891)

Paul S. Burnham, Associate Director, Student Appointment Bureau, Yale University, New Haven, Connecticut. In preparation since 1938 and copyrighted in 1946, this inventory consists of 300 academic interest items to which students respond on a 5-point scale, indicating degree of interest in each item. Scores secured make it possible to compare the student's interests with the interest profile found to be characteristic of persons majoring in each of 28 academic departments.

Approximately 165 of the 300 items start with the word "study"; for example: "Study the history of architecture." All other items start with some other action verb such as *play, repair, operate, construct, measure, make,* etc. One cannot help but wonder what effect such emphasis on the word "study" may have for the person who may be intensely interested in *doing* certain things but not much interested in *studying* them.

Scales were developed on a basis similar to that used by Strong in connection with the *Vocational Interest Blank.* Nine hundred items were administered to a freshman class at the University of Nebraska and to approximately 5,000 juniors and seniors in other colleges. Scoring weights were derived by contrasting answers given by a minimum of 100 juniors and seniors in each major with the answers of freshmen. On the basis of weights so derived, 300 items were selected for the present form.

The purpose is to provide a means of objectively measuring and comparing students' interests in various curricula in colleges and universities in the United States. The manual claims that the results are useful for educational and occupational guidance. Retest reliability (4-month interval) of the 28 scales is reported in the manual to vary from .67 to .92. Data were based on a retest of 100 students selected at random from the basic population of 1,500 University of Nebraska freshmen. Provision is made for both machine and hand scoring.

No data are given with respect to intercorrelation of scales so the user has no idea of the amount of overlapping. Apparently no factor analyses have been attempted to determine the extent to which the number of scales could be reduced. No data are given with respect to correlation with any measures of achievement or scholastic aptitude. Scores are converted into scaled scores, running from 1 through 9, with comparable percentage frequencies developed from the basic group. The author reports that it may be highly desirable for a school to develop norms for its own students. Scores are presented in the form of a profile, in an order intended to group scales which would seem to be logically related on the basis of subjective interpretation.

Much work will have to be done to provide a better description of the functional utility of this interest test. The need for such a measure is great.

Lysle W. Croft, Director of Personnel, University of Kentucky, Lexington, Kentucky. There has been a need in the counseling field for some time for such a blank as the *Gregory Academic Interest Inventory.* The inventory was developed as an aid to counselors in measuring student interests as they relate to the many curricula of colleges and universities. The author feels that the inventory is helpful in four ways: (*a*) in aiding students in their occupational planning; (*b*) in aiding students in educational planning; (*c*) in aiding students in their selection of electives; (*d*) in aiding counselors with their academic problem cases.

The administration of the inventory is simple, and it can be given in groups or individually. Although the author estimates an hour, it is rarely necessary to use over 45 minutes. The same scoring keys and norms are used for both men and women. A simplified scoring system has been developed with assigned scoring weights of +1 and −1. This is a needed improvement over the older system of weights ranging from +4 to −4. The scoring of the schedule is simple but long, tiresome, tedious, and time consuming when used individually. It is necessary for each of the 28 interests to be scored twice for each side of the answer sheet, or a total scoring of four times for each interest. This accumulates to a total of 112 scorings necessary to complete the record for one individual. The best procedure is obviously group testing and machine grading.

Gregory Academic Interest Inventory

All scores are added algebraically and recorded on the specially designed answer sheet. A special profile sheet is provided for recording the final scores. The raw scores are translated into scaled scores. Each scaled-score interval represents one-half standard deviation of an assumed normal distribution. The simplicity of the recording of the scores into scaled scores based upon a normal distribution is a good feature of the Inventory. The per cent of distribution is blocked off into the upper 22 per cent which can be used as significant, the middle 56 per cent, and the lower 22 per cent. An interesting feature, similar to the idea used on Strong's *Vocational Interest Blank,* is the grouping of the similar interests on the profile chart.

The reliability was determined by the test-retest method with the Pearson coefficients of correlation between the original and retest ranging from .92 for chemistry to .67 for physical education. The validity of the scoring method was secured by correlating scores received by the longer scoring method and the new simplified scoring method. The range of the Pearson coefficients of correlation was .95 for public service engineering and mathematics and .71 for home economics.

The author suggests, and it is certainly advisable, that norms be developed for the individual school.

As a counseling aid, the inventory has proved very satisfactory as a follow-up for the *Kuder Preference Record.* In the interpretation of the inventory, the same care should be used as is expected with other blanks.

Because of the lack of published research on this inventory, this reviewer gave the blank to a class of seventeen students (juniors, seniors, and graduate students) in psychology. The inventory definitely selected the major field of twelve students; nine subjects scored a scaled score of 9 (top 3 per cent of distribution) on their major. One student had nine fields represented in his scaled scores of eight or above. Three students seemed to be completely out of their field for their measured interest. This was confirmed for two of the students after interviews, and the third was on academic probation and undergoing conferences in the University Personnel Office.

Although it is felt that additional research is needed, particularly as to the validity, and other fields of interests, such as law (or prelaw) and accounting, should be added, the *Gregory Aca-*demic Interest Inventory is proving to be a valuable counseling tool.

Herbert A. Toops, Professor of Psychology, The Ohio State University, Columbus, Ohio. This inventory consists of 28 scales, with corresponding scoring keys (more promised later). The 28 indices are obtained from as many scorings of a 4-page, 300-item academic "interest" test. The profiled results are intended for aiding a college student in choosing, within a university, his college or curriculum; within a curriculum, his majors; within a major, specific courses; and for academic guidance generally. That is an ambitious and worthy aim.

The examinee marks one of five degrees of interest for each item, but these are telescoped, by integral combination in the scoring, to $+1$, -1, and "omit." This, according to the author's interpretation of the evidence, does little violence to the measurement and enables each scale to be fully scored with only two stencils, by hand or by IBM scoring machine, a device which unfortunately has this mechanical limitation.

It is unfortunate, too, the reviewer feels, that the response 1 means "very interested" and 5, "very disinterested," thus reversing the examinee's usual mental set where "thermometers" are concerned. The items are arranged in groups of fives, but the accompanying IBM answer sheet is not similarly sectioned; and no alignment between test sheet and answer sheet, to enable the examinee to maintain his place, is possible.

The Strong method of arriving at scoring keys was employed: concretely, it was assumed that 100 or more students in commercial arts are, in the main, interested in commercial arts. Nine hundred items were initially tried out in a number of cooperating colleges and universities, and these finally were boiled down to 300, and the simplified scoring above described was adopted. Details of the method used, it is promised, will be revealed in future articles. The reviewer wonders if, in subsequent analyses, vocationally "misplaced" persons could not be excluded as well as "bad items."

With three exceptions the test-retest reliabilities of the 28 scales, on only 99 subjects (an inadequate number), is .85 or above, and none are so high as .95, although half of them are .90 or higher. This indicates a need generally for lengthening the examination, although few present-day tests would make an equal showing. The specificity of the individual scales—which really is the issue—might better be freed, or largely freed, of attenuation before being ascertained by tryout.

Intercorrelations of the 28 scales, based on 793 men and 642 women, treated separately, indicate a very considerable specificity for at least some of the scales. These intercorrelations run from −.69 (characteristic of physics and journalism, also of speech and mechanical engineering, and also of speech and electrical engineering) to +.87 between mathematics and mechanical engineering. These would seem to prove the existence of differential academic interests. The correlations for men and women in general are of the same sign and of approximately the same magnitude, so separate scoring schemes for the sexes are not provided.

In general, the intercorrelations of scales in most instances support one's preconceived notions of the probable interdependence of the academic interests; yet a few disconcerting ones are reported: Why, for example, should mathematics correlate .70 with physical education and .80 with religion, but only .52 with physics and .37 with electrical engineering? (Mathematics, on the other hand, correlates .87 with mechanical engineering, while electrical engineering and mechanical engineering intercorrelate .81. These relations suggest possible errors in the published intercorrelations.)

No factor analysis has been made to determine how many of the scoring keys are really desirable and are minimally necessary; this would seem to be a much-needed next step.

Once dependable profiles of the 28 scores, or the suggested "factors," are obtained, one would find it useful to make transparent stencils to omit, by such means as cut-out windows, for a given occupation, the scales of the individual profile not very pertinent to a given (proposed) curriculum of a counselee. As yet experimentation has not gone so far.

The research on this test is worth watching. It has many good points. A reviewer, however, cannot help but ask, "Will not such an instrument be better for prognosis than for educational choice?" After all, one of the functions of a college education and of a college guidance program is to remove the bad effects of disabilities and inequalities of childhood environment and experience. If one "likes engineering" but "hates mathematics," or if, alternatively, he "likes medicine" but "hates dissection"—both of which curricular "requirements" it is assumed

by the author of the test are "just"—perhaps the proper action of the counselee is not to give up the objectives of engineering and medicine, respectively, but rather to seek a psychiatrist, if need be, to remove his disabling emotional impediments. The implication, too, that one's academic interests are as unchangeable, over the four years of college, as one's love for fat men or hatred of cigar smoking may or may not be borne out in practice. And the old question, "Is interest analogous to the steam in the boiler or to the recording needle on the steam gauge?" is not solved here. Another criticism, which falls particularly heavily on interest tests, applies to tests in general: A valid measuring instrument in a particular application may be used badly or well. Perhaps a testmaker is under obligation to tell us at least how *not* to use it. This our testmaker to date has not done.

J Consult Psychol 11:156 My-Je '47.

[637]

Interest Questionnaire for High School Students, 1942 Edition. High school entrants; 1930–42; IBM; $4.40 per 100 machine-scorable test-answer sheets; 60¢ per manual and stencils; 95¢ per specimen set, postpaid; nontimed (20) minutes; Oliver K. Garretson and Percival M. Symonds; Bureau of Publications, Teachers College, Columbia University.

REFERENCES

1. GARRETSON, OLIVER KELLEAM. *Relationships Between Expressed Preferences and Curricular Abilities of Ninth Grade Boys.* Columbia University, Teachers College, Contributions to Education, No. 396. New York: Bureau of Publications, the College, 1930. Pp. v, 77. Out of print. * (*PA* 4:3263)
2. SYMONDS, PERCIVAL M. *Tests and Interest Questionnaires in the Guidance of High School Boys.* New York: Bureau of Publications, Teachers College, Columbia University, 1930. Pp. 61. Paper. Out of print. (*PA* 5:2043)
3. GARRETSON, OLIVER KELLEAM. "Relationships Between the Expressed Preferences and the Curricular Abilities of Ninth Grade Boys." *J Ed Res* 23:124-32 F '31. * (*PA* 5:2537)
4. VAN EASTERN, MARY ELLEN. *A Study of the Constancy of Individuals' Responses to the Garretson-Symonds Interest Questionnaire and a Comparison of the Constancy of Responses to the Various Items of the Questionnaire.* Unpublished master's thesis, Fordham University, 1934.
5. BINGHAM, WALTER VAN DYKE. *Aptitudes and Aptitude Testing,* pp. 360-1. New York and London: Harper & Brothers, 1937. Pp. ix, 390. $3.00; 12s. 6d. * (*PA* 11:2885)
6. GORDON, HANS C., AND HERKNESS, WALTER W., JR. "Pupils Appraise Vocational Interest Blanks." *Occupations* 20:100-2 N '41. * (*PA* 16:757)

Lysle W. Croft, Director of Personnel, University of Kentucky, Lexington, Kentucky. This questionnaire is a two-page academic interest questionnaire designed to supply a counseling tool for measuring the academic interest of high school students in the academic, commercial, and technical curricula. The questionnaire consists of ten sections, a total of 234 items. The questions are answered by L (like), I (indifferent), and D (dislike).

In the interpretation of the test, the same care

is necessary that should be given to all interest blanks and they should be used only in conjunction with intelligence and aptitude tests.

The administration of the questionnaire is simple and can be given as a group test or individually. All information, including scores, is placed on the answer sheet.

Although little research has been published on the questionnaire, it should prove valuable as a counseling tool at the high school level. Counselors, when using the blank, should develop their own norms.

[638]

★Inventory of Vocational Interests: Acorn National Aptitude Tests. Grades 7-16 and adults; 1943; 1 form; $1.50 per 25; 10¢ per manual; 50¢ per specimen set; nontimed (35) minutes; Andrew Kobal, J. Wayne Wrightstone, and Karl R. Kunze; Acorn Publishing Co.

Marion A. Bills, Assistant Secretary, Aetna Life Insurance Company, Hartford, Connecticut. This test consists of 25 questions concerning various activities; for example, "What would you best like to do with a motor boat?" For each question ten choices are allowed, three of which must be marked. The blank is scored for the centering of interest in the fields of (a) mechanical, (b) academic, (c) artistic, (d) business and economics, (e) farm agricultural. Since the activities are on a rather low level of accomplishment, it is often difficult for college students to find real preferences; they find it necessary to mark the three choices disliked least. In each list the first two choices indicate mechanical interest, the second two academic, etc. This makes scoring easy, but it also allows easy bluffing.

The only relevant experimental data given are for 120 subjects apparently already employed. Their stability on the job, expressed interest, advancement on the job, and earning capacity were compared with the test scores. These showed fair relationships. No instance is quoted of applicants being tested and future progress noted. Therefore, since several studies have shown that occupational interest often changes after employment, not too much emphasis should be placed on these results for guidance purposes. The author makes the statement in his manual of instructions: "The validity of the Inventory is sufficiently high to warrant its application in individual diagnosis." The reviewer has been unable to find evidence to support this claim.

The test has the advantage of being short and easily scored. Its disadvantages are: (a) no indication of proper validation; (b) level of occupation too low for college students; (c) difficulty in interpretation unless interests are very definite, in which case the applicant probably can express them as well without a test.

Edward S. Bordin, Director, Student Counseling Center, and Associate Professor of Psychology, The State College of Washington, Pullman, Washington. The authors of this test stress the fact that it "avoids in its contents the expression of preferences for vocations which are unreal as interests." They go on to say that instead of lists of occupations to be checked, which is the standard pattern of vocational interest inventories, the test presents materials which "offer a search for the interests which are an important part of the aptitude rather than mere preferences." This inventory purports to accomplish the above-stated goal by listing 25 different questions covering as many different situations. "What would you like to do best with an automobile?" or "Which position would you prefer in a newspaper establishment?" are typical questions. Each question has ten possible responses which are arranged so as to indicate defined occupational categories. The responses are arranged so that the first two are intended to reflect mechanical interests; the next two, academic; the next two, artistic; then business and economic; and the final two, farm-agricultural.

This reviewer finds it hard to accept this test situation as significantly freer of the operation of the subject's preconceptions of himself than any of the other standard practices in vocational interest testing. The fact that the occupational types of responses always appear in the same order and two at a time seems to ensure that the subject will have every opportunity to be quite aware that by his responses he is saying, "I am the mechanical type" or "I am the academic type," and so on as the case may be. These a priori doubts are not put to rest by the meager basis for validity offered in the accompanying manual. The only data cited are: (a) a pattern of scores on the five categories which is said to be typical for a group of 60 subjects drawn from laborers, shiftless though mentally normal prison inmates, and educationally low-graded individuals (the pattern presented is an extremely depressed one); (b) a correlation between advancement on the job and interest expressed on the inventory of .65 and a correlation of .38 between recent earning capacity and the test variable, both based upon 120 subjects. No further information is given nor is the reader referred to any other source for a fuller treatment of the studies. The mere citation of validity correlations without opportunity to check the adequacy of the studies on which such validities are based is insufficient evidence to warrant acceptance of the test as a worth-while instrument. The test manual is also deficient in failing to cite any evidence on reliability or on the intercorrelation of scales. Five tables for converting raw to centile scores are presented. However, some of these are rather peculiar in that the same raw score conversion applies to as many as four different scales. Since no information is given on the method of standardization nor on the selection of the normative population, these tables must remain enigmatic.

Harold D. Carter, Associate Professor of Education, University of California, Berkeley, California. This inventory is intended for use in secondary schools, colleges, and industry. There is one form, for use with both males and females. It is in the form of a check list, with ten items under each of 25 heads. The pupils are required to check the three most liked in each group of ten items. The administration and scoring are simple and economical, requiring no scoring keys. An attempt is made to get at interests with vocational significance, by avoiding lists of occupation names as items, and by using meaningful activities. The items can be classified as indicating mechanical, academic, artistic, business and economic, and agricultural interests.

The manual indicates the purpose of the test and gives clear and adequate instructions for administration and scoring. It suggests the uses to which the test can be put in counseling. The claim is made that the tests are sufficiently valid for use in individual diagnosis, but the evidence presented is too sketchy to be convincing. There is no evidence as to the reliability of the test. The norms based upon five occupational groups seem completely inadequate as presented. The information given about the groups is vague and general. The evidence that inferior groups lack concentration of interests is interesting, but inadequate, as only sixty individuals were included. The validity coefficients of .65, .39, and .59 presented in the manual would be more meaningful if the conditions were described in more detail.

The attempt to avoid the use of lists of occupation names has not been fully successful. For example, Item 17, dealing with federal civil service, includes the following ten subitems: transportation engineer, mechanical engineer, librarian, teacher of civics, administrative clerk, custodian of art collections, draftsman, buyer for the government, agriculturist, and forester. Other items similarly contain occupation names rather than "meaningful activities" to be selected or rejected.

The attempt to eliminate the influence of the prestige hierarchy of occupations is thought provoking. One may question whether it is realistic to make such an attempt. It is not clearly desirable at present to overemphasize the element of choice among uninteresting alternatives. The fact that interests are often unrealistic in their emphasis upon ambitious striving upward does not eliminate the significance of the prestige hierarchy. Perhaps a main characteristic of the interests of some persons is the fact that they reject all activities on the dish-washing and bottle-arranging level.

One can only speculate in the absence of further data. This test seems most likely to be useful in industry and in the secondary school. It seems unlikely that it will be found adequate at the college level, especially for individuals with aims toward the professions. It seems to hold promise as a step toward fulfillment of an obvious need for measurement of interests of the masses below the professional level.

Patrick Slater, Chief Research Officer at the Social Survey and Honorary Psychometric Psychologist at St. Thomas's Hospital, London, England. This inventory serves to classify vocational interests under five main headings: mechanical, academic, artistic, business and economic, and farm-agricultural. In completing it, subjects may reveal interests concentrated in one of these classes or in a combination of two. Answers can thus be used to differentiate subjects into fifteen classes, the combinations of two main interests at a time providing an additional ten classes, viz., mechanical combined with academic, mechanical combined with artistic, etc. through to business and economic combined with farm-agricultural. Educationally low and mentally immature persons, however, tend to reveal a range of interests scattered haphazardly throughout all five classes, and the inventory is therefore not intended for application to them.

Inventory of Vocational Interests

For each of these fifteen classes a suitable list of occupations is provided.

This ground plan commends itself as reasonable. But to develop its practical usefulness an exceptionally large amount of detailed information is needed. What predominant interest or combination of interests, as defined, would you consider appropriate to the following occupations: athletic director, building superintendent, hotel manager, recreation director, radio dealer, scout leader? This is the list which the authors give as appropriate for a combination of mechanical with business and economic interests. From what detailed empirical evidence is this particular list compiled? Do these occupations really involve a homogeneous combination of interests? No detailed evidence is given. Although a total of 117 occupations is listed, the only occupational study to which the manual refers is one of the "occupational history of 120 tested subjects" in unspecified occupations.

Another question which perplexes me is what takes place in a subject's mind when he is asked, "What would you like to do best with an AIRPLANE?" The choice before him is: "(a) work on it as a mechanic; (b) pilot it; (c) study its history; (d) write about its importance in modern warfare; (e) write a poem about it; (f) make drawings or sketches of it; (g) book passengers for it; (h) advertise its uses; (i) construct a flying field for it; (j) use it on a big farm for spraying crops." For my part the three things I would genuinely like to do would be: (a) sell it; (b) if that failed, give it away; (c) if that failed, go away from it quietly, praying nobody would ever find out it was mine. I would feel more like writing a poem after I had got rid of it. But to be true to form as a psychologist what I should like best, according to the manual, should be to study its history and write about its importance in modern warfare. Regretfully I must record that this inventory leaves me sheltering behind my ignorance from the fear that I may be an occupational misfit.

[639]

★Job Qualification Inventory. Grades 9-16 and adults; 1945-47; 1 form; $3.75 per 25; $10 per copy of the manual, Job Placement Reference; 25¢ per sample copy; the Job Placement Reference and 5 blanks are obtainable on approval at a special price of $10; nontimed (30) minutes; Keith Van Allyn; Bureau of Personnel Research (now Surveys, Inc.).

REFERENCES

1. SEIBERT, EARL W. "A Comparison of Scores on the Kuder Preference Record and the Job Qualification Inventory." J Ed Res 40:178-86 N '46. * (PA 21:1295)

2. NORMAN, RALPH D. "A Comparison of Earlier and Later Success in Naval Aviation Training." J Appl Psychol 31:511-8 O '47. * (PA 22:2342)
3. SEIBERT, EARL W. "A Report of Data on the Job Qualification Inventory." J Clin Psychol 3:100-4 Ja '47. * (PA 21:2472)
4. TRIGGS, FRANCES ORALIND. "Critique of Van Allyn's System of Vocational Counseling." J Appl Psychol 31:536-44 O '47. * (PA 22:2205)
5. VAN ALLYN, B. KEITH. "Picking Good Bus Mechanics." Bus Transp 26:77-9 Ja '47. *

Ralph F. Berdie, Director, Student Counseling Bureau, and Associate Professor of Psychology, University of Minnesota, Minneapolis, Minnesota. The *Job Qualification Inventory* is a 210-item inventory summarizing self-ratings in 35 different occupational areas, and designed to be used with its accompanying manual, entitled the *Job Placement Reference*. The overly ambitious purpose of the inventory is, according to the author, to investigate "every detail of an individual's qualifications" and to present these details graphically in order of relative importance. Throughout the manual, Van Allyn states the inventory gauges ability, indicates vocational aptitude, supplies data regarding ambitions, training, experience and accomplishment, evaluates *immature* experience, investigates interest, differentiates between verified (permanent) and preference (transitory) interests, and detects malcontents and malingerers. More modestly, he maintains the inventory may be used by industry for purposes of selection and training, and by schools for purposes of guidance and counseling.

The inventory best serves as a screening device to aid in the selection of ability, attitude, and interest tests, and to provide orientation in the interview. It provides a quick and economical method of obtaining preliminary information, and may stimulate the person being tested to think in more comprehensive terms of occupational possibilities.

No mention in the manual is made of the reliability or the consistency of self-ratings obtained on the inventory, and the only statement concerning the construction of the inventory relates it is the culmination of twelve years of research. A more detailed account of this research would have been desirable, as no detailed reference to it could be found in the psychological or educational literature.

The evidence for validity consists of: (a) eight specimen profiles obtained by workers and students; (b) a composite profile based on scores of 42 industrial statisticians. The inventory was given to "a number of men and women known to be successful and happy in their work," and this data was used in preparing a composite profile of all members in each group. No information is given concerning the sizes of the specific groups, their other characteristics, nor the significance of their inventory scores. The relationships existing between the various ratings are not presented, nor are the relationships between these ratings and scores achieved on other tests, workers' output, students' grades, or ratings of satisfaction.

The manual contains three lists of a total of 1,603 occupations. The first list presents the occupations in order of the ratings so that occupations characterized by an obtained profile can be identified. The second list groups the occupations according to their basic requirements. The third list presents the occupations in alphabetical order so the profile characteristic of any given occupation can be identified. The *Job Placement Reference* contains more occupations than the *Minnesota Occupational Rating Scales,* which contains only 430, but the latter recognizes the relative independence of abilities and interests and presents ratings only for abilities, whereas the former is in terms of ratings on the inventory.

Until more data is made available regarding the *Job Qualification Inventory,* it can be used only as an informal, unproved adjunct to the employment or counseling process.

Stanley G. Dulsky, Chief of Staff, Chicago Psychological Institute, Chicago, Illinois. The job placement technique developed by Van Allyn involves the use of two tools: the *Job Qualification Inventory;* and the *Job Placement Reference,* an encyclopedia of job specifications developed specifically for use with the *Job Qualification Inventory.*

The *Job Qualification Inventory* (JQI) "provides for a detailed analysis of an individual's actual and potential job qualifications." It is concerned with vocational interest, "but performs the much broader function of verifying the expressed interests and revealing actual job qualifications—potential as well as achieved." The JQI is concerned only with *"sustained, verified* interest, and not mere expression of preference at the moment of testing."

The inventory consists of 210 questions, six questions for each of 35 areas or fields. Question 1 refers to preferences (do you enjoy such and such an activity); Question 2 refers to actual performance; Question 3 asks about education and training in that area; Question 4 determines vocational ambition for that area; Question 5 inquires about paid experience in the field; and Question 6 refers to evidence of accomplishment or recognition to suggest unusual proficiency. Each question is answered by circling NO, ?, YES. Thirty-five scores are obtained and graphed. From the graph a "key" is obtained which refers to appropriate occupations in the *Job Placement Reference.* These jobs are keyed to the *Dictionary of Occupational Titles.*

It is apparent that the JQI is a much broader instrument than an interest inventory. It is at once an interest blank (Questions 1, 2, and 4) and a personal history or application blank (Questions 3, 5, and 6). Much important information can be obtained by studying all the responses.

The integration of interest and background with specific occupations is very helpful to the counselor. The *Brainard Occupational Preference Inventory* attempts the same thing by keying the sections to the *Dictionary of Occupational Titles.* The *Job Placement Reference* goes one step further—it lists the specific occupations as well as keying them to the *Dictionary of Occupational Titles.*

This device, and the accompanying *Job Placement Reference* deserves a period of experimentation by the vocational counselor. Information obtained from it should be supplemented by tests and other pertinent data as well as the interview. Used judiciously by synthesis with other facts, it may prove to be another weapon in the battle to eliminate vocational misfits.

Mech Eng 67:864–5 D '45. Donald E. Gorseline. * the author does not give a clear-cut outline of the procedure he used in selecting, testing, and validating the contents used in the job-qualification inventory, a practice which is common procedure with most rating-scale or test builders. One has a right to ask, "Just why were the particular 35 areas of occupations used? Why not 25 areas, or 39 areas?" Likewise in the job-placement reference, the encyclopedia of jobs, what technique was used to determine the numbers and names of jobs listed on the 221 pages? Inclusion of two pages of simple description of the methods used to construct the materials used in the technique would have obviated the almost painful effort used to reassure the reader of the excellence of the system. In the second place, the manual probably would have been improved by terse staccato sentences summarizing the methods of giving and scoring the job-qualification inventory and applying the findings. This should have been done for the sake of custom, since test users expect instructions to be streamlined, if for no other reason. Constructively, much can be said for the Van Allyn procedure. The reader cannot help but feel that in spite of the almost extravagant claims made for it, the author, backed by 12 years of research, can prove his statement that this represents an important forward step in the science of properly selecting, placing, and training employees. This reviewer, who tries to keep abreast of movement and devices in the counseling field, can think of no other test or rating device that so skillfully extracts so much reliable information about interests and experiences of individuals in so brief a time. The method used to avoid falsification about qualifications of applicants is excellent, too. While the technique will be more useful to a personnel worker clinically trained in psychology than to an inexperienced counselor, yet it is simple enough to be applied by the average industrial employer. An added point in its favor is the fact that it probably has better predictive value for adults and older people; a group often neglected by test builders in the past. This reviewer is inclined to the opinion that this technique will have wide usage in industry. Unquestionably there is no other tool available that will give so much information on so wide a variety of industrial personnel problems; particularly re-employment and placement of war veterans, upgrading, downgrading, employment terminations, transfer and promotion requests, apprentice and training selection, prescreening of potential malcontents, proper placement, etc. as this one does. While it is by no means a panacea for all employment selection, it should prove to be a distinctly useful tool.

Sch R 53:433-4 S '45. Robert C. Woellner. * an excellent example of current trends in matching jobs and men, and it will serve as a counselor's reference manual for helping advisees determine the occupations in which they should be most successful and contented. This reference manual is used in conjunction with the Job Qualification Inventory—a type of questionnaire consisting of eight pages to be filled in by the advisee. The purpose of this inventory is to obtain data relating to the advisee's ambitions, training, experience, and accomplishment. On the basis of the data thus assembled, a counselor can have before him a profile of an individual's relative ratings in thirty-five general categories of traits which are supposedly basic elements and the different combinations of which are essential to success in specific occupations. The highest points in the profile serve as a letter combination for the Key Index, which in turn is used to locate the jobs which are listed in the Job Placement Reference section of the publication. In order to assist the counselor in locating specific and appropriate jobs which fit the ambitions, training, experience, and accomplishment of a given individual, this book contains a Reference Section which makes use of the Key (derived from the Job Qualification Inventory) and the code number given by the much-used *Dictionary of Occupational Titles* compiled by the United States Employment Service, along with the titles of the jobs in the particular occupational groups. * Counselors will find in this publication valuable assistance through its presentation of (1) an inventory which provides in an organized fashion the aspirations, training, experience, and accomplishment of an advisee; (2) a readily usable method for comparing the composite of these qualifications with a vast variety of jobs; and (3) a full description of the technique used. The effectiveness of the technique suggested by Van Allyn depends, to a great extent, on how the inventory is filled in. Though the questions in the inventory are chosen and phrased to encourage objectivity, there remains much opportunity for subjective evaluation by the advisee. If the individual is assisted in filling out the inventory by being supplied as much evidence as is available concerning him upon the basis of test results, objective observations of others, etc., this technique should prove useful. Counselors who deal with youth having little or no occupational experience, with veterans, and with adults vocationally disoriented by conditions of the reconversion period will find worth-while assistance in *Job Placement Reference.* It is unfortunate that, because of its price, this publication may not be given as wide use as it merits.

[640]
Kuder Preference Record. Grades 9-16 and adults; 1934-48; IBM; 1 form; 2 editions; separate answer

sheets or pads must be used; 95¢ per 25 job charts; nontimed (50) minutes; G. Frederic Kuder; Science Research Associates.

a) FORM BB: EDITION FOR SELF-SCORING. 48¢ per test; $2 per 25 answer pads; 50¢ per 25 profile sheets for either boys and girls or men and women; 75¢ per specimen set.
b) FORM BM: EDITION FOR MACHINE-SCORING. IBM; 35¢ per test; $2.35 per 100 machine-scorable answer sheets; $7.50 per set of scoring keys; 50¢ per 25 profile sheets.
c) FORM BI [A SHORT FORM FOR INDUSTRIAL USE]. 1948; IBM; separate answer sheets must be used; 45¢ per test booklet; $2.10 per 25 answer pads; $1.35 per 25 backboards; $2.35 per 100 machine-scorable answer sheets; $3 per set of machine-scoring keys; 50¢ per 25 profile sheets; 95¢ per 25 job charts; 75¢ per specimen set; (30) minutes. *This form is not reviewed below.*

REFERENCES

1-2. See 40:1671.
3. ADKINS, DOROTHY C. "The Relation of Primary Mental Abilities to Preference Scales and to Vocational Choice." Abstract. *Psychometrika* 5:316 D '40. *
4. ADKINS, DOROTHY C., AND KUDER, G. FREDERIC. "The Relation of Primary Mental Abilities to Activity Preferences." *Psychometrika* 5:251-62 D '40. * (PA 15:2259)
5. COTTINGHAM, HAROLD F. *The Value of the Kuder Preference Record in Determining the Vocational Interests of High School Seniors.* Unpublished master's thesis, State University of Iowa, 1940.
6. CROSBY, RICHARD COLLIER. *The Measurement of Interest and Its Utility in College Personnel Work.* Unpublished doctor's thesis, Cornell University, 1941. (*Abstracts of Theses . . . 1941, 1942,* pp. 95-7.)
7. CROSBY, R. C., AND WINSOR, A. L. "The Validity of Students' Estimates of Their Interests." *J Appl Psychol* 25:408-14 Ag '41. * (PA 15:5355)
8. GORDON, HANS C., AND HERKNESS, WALTER W., JR. "Pupils Appraise Vocational Interest Blanks." *Occupations* 20:100-2 N '41. * (PA 16:757)
9. TRAXLER, ARTHUR E., AND McCALL, WILLIAM C. "Some Data on the Kuder Preference Record." *Ed & Psychol Meas* 1:253-68 Jl '41. * (PA 15:5393)
10. GORDON, HANS C., AND HERKNESS, WALTER W., JR. "Do Vocational Interest Questionnaires Yield Consistent Results?" *Occupations* 20:424-9 Mr '42. * (PA 16:2059)
11. LOWRIE, KATHLEEN HARRIET. *Factors Which Relate to the Extra-Curricular Performance of College Women.* Unpublished doctor's thesis, University of Iowa, 1942.
12. PETERS, EDWIN F. "Vocational Interests as Measured by the Strong and Kuder Inventories." *Sch & Soc* 55:453-5 Ap 18 '42. * (PA 16:3299)
13. YUM, K. S. "Student Preferences in Divisional Studies and Their Preferential Activities." *J Psychol* 13:193-200 Ap '42. * (PA 16:3320)
14. BREWER, JOHN M. "Classification of Items in Interest Inventories." *Occupations* 21:448-51 F '43. * (PA 17:2159)
15. CROSBY, RICHARD C. "Scholastic Achievement and Measured Interests." *J Appl Psychol* 27:101-3 F '43. * (PA 17:2878)
16. TRAXLER, ARTHUR E. "A Note on the Reliability of the Revised Kuder Preference Record." *J Appl Psychol* 27:510-1 D '43. * (PA 18:1912)
17. TRIGGS, FRANCES ORALIND. "A Study of the Relation of Kuder Preference Record Scores to Various Other Measures." *Ed & Psychol Meas* 3:341-54 w '43. * (PA 18:2607)
18. WITTENBORN, J. R.; TRIGGS, FRANCES ORALIND; AND FEDER, DANIEL D. "A Comparison of Interest Measurement by the Kuder Preference Record and the Strong Vocational Interest Blanks for Men and Women." *Ed & Psychol Meas* 3:239-57 au '43. * (PA 18:2614)
19. BARRY, CORA MINER. "Kuder Preference Record Norms: Based on Measurements Made on High School Seniors." *Occupations* 22:487-8 My '44. * (PA 18:3275)
20. BOLANOVICH, D. J. "Selection of Female Engineering Trainees." *J Ed Psychol* 35:545-53 D '44. * (PA 19:1010)
21. BOLANOVICH, DANIEL J., AND GOODMAN, CHARLES H. "A Study of the Kuder Preference Record." *Ed & Psychol Meas* 4:315-25 w '44. * (PA 20:277)
22. FOSSELIUS, EBBA E. *A Study of the Use of and the Results of the Kuder Preference Records in the Jefferson Junior High School, Elyria, Ohio.* Unpublished master's thesis, Ohio State University, 1944. Pp. 84.
23. KUDER, G. FREDERIC. "Note on 'Classification of Items in Interest Inventories'." *Occupations* 22:484-7 My '44. * (PA 18:3294)
24. LEHMAN, RUTH T. "Interpretation of the Kuder Preference Record for College Students of Home Economics." *Ed & Psychol Meas* 4:217-23 au '44. * (PA 19:1801)
25. QUIMBY, NEAL F. "The Vocational Interests of Blind High School Students." *Outlook for Blind* 38:127-9 My '44. * (PA 18:3891)
26. THOMPSON, CLAUDE EDWARD. "Personality and Interest Factors in Dental School Success." *Ed & Psychol Meas* 4:299-306 w '44. * (PA 20:332)
27. TRIGGS, FRANCES ORALIND. "A Further Comparison of Interest Measurement by the Kuder Preference Record and the Strong Vocational Interest Blank for Men." *J Ed Res* 37:538-44 Mr '44. * (PA 18:3307)
28. TRIGGS, FRANCES ORALIND. "A Further Comparison of Interest Measurement by the Kuder Preference Record and the Strong Vocational Interest Blank for Women." *J Ed Res* 38:193-200 N '44. * (PA 19:1352)
29. TUCKMAN, JACOB. "High School Student Norms—Revised Kuder Preference Record." *Occupations* 23:26-32 O '44. * (PA 19:568)
30. WESTMORELAND, LANELLE. *An Analysis of Certain Educational Implications of Kuder Interest Scores Among High School Pupils.* Unpublished master's thesis, University of Georgia, 1944. Pp. 58.
31. WOODY, CLIFFORD. *Guidance Implications From Measurements of Achievements, Aptitudes and Interests.* University of Michigan, School of Education, Bureau of Educational Reference and Research, Bulletin No. 156. Ann Arbor, Mich.: the School, September 1, 1944. Pp. viii, 162. Paper. $1.25. * (PA 20:573)
32. HAHN, MILTON E. "Notes on the Kuder Preference Record." *Occupations* 23:467-70 My '45. * (PA 19:2751)
33. HAHN, MILTON E., AND WILLIAMS, CORNELIA T. "The Measured Interests of Marine Corps Women Reservists." *J Appl Psychol* 29:198-211 Je '45. * (PA 19:3121)
34. MEYERS, ELIZABETH S. *The Statistical Analysis of the Kuder Preference Record.* Unpublished master's thesis, University of Denver, 1945.
35. ROLLINS, REXFORD W. *A Revision of the Kuder Preference Record for the Sixth Grade.* Unpublished master's thesis, Syracuse University, 1945. Pp. 89.
36. AMERICAN NURSES' ASSOCIATION, RESEARCH DEPARTMENT. "The Kuder Preference Record in the Counseling of Nurses." *Am J Nursing* 46:312-6 My '46. * (PA 20:4249)
37. CHRISTENSEN, THOMAS E. "Some Observations With Respect to the Kuder Preference Record." *J Ed Res* 40:96-107 O '46. * (PA 21:885)
38. DETCHEN, LILY. "The Effect of a Measure of Interest Factors on the Prediction of Performance in a College Social Sciences Comprehensive Examination." *J Ed Psychol* 37:45-52 Ja '46. * (PA 21:2070)
39. EVANS, CHESTER EUGENE. *Interrelations of Evidences of Vocational Interest.* Unpublished doctor's thesis, Ohio State University, 1946. (*Abstracts of Dissertations . . . Summer Quarter 1945-46,* 1946, pp. 51-7.)
40. PATERSON, DONALD G. "Vocational Interest Inventories in Selection." *Occupations* 25:152-3 D '46. * (PA 21:1286)
41. PIOTROWSKI, ZYGMUNT A. "Difference Between Cases Giving Valid and Invalid Personality Inventory Responses." *Ann N Y Acad Sci* 46:633-38, discussion 638-40 Jl 30 '46. * (PA 20:4677)
42. SARTAIN, A. Q. "Relation Between Scores on Certain Standard Tests and Supervisory Success in an Aircraft Factory." *J Appl Psychol* 30:328-32 Ag '46. * (PA 21:250)
43. SEIBERT, EARL W. "A Comparison of Scores on the Kuder Preference Record and the Job Qualification Inventory." *J Ed Res* 40:178-86 N '46. * (PA 21:1295)
44. TOWNSEND, AGATHA. "Academic Aptitude and Interest Ratings for Independent-School Pupils," pp. 51-7. In *1945 Fall Testing Program in Independent Schools and Supplementary Studies.* Educational Records Bulletin, No. 44. New York: Educational Records Bureau, January 1946. Pp. xiii, 66. Paper, lithotyped. $1.00. * (PA 20:2105)
45. TRAXLER, ARTHUR E. "Some Results of the Kuder Preference Record in Independent Schools," pp. 37-50. In *1945 Fall Testing Program in Independent Schools and Supplementary Studies.* Educational Records Bulletin, No. 44. New York: Educational Records Bureau, January 1946. Pp. xiii, 66. Paper, lithotyped. $1.00 * (PA 20:2107)
46. WIGGINS, RUTH E. "A Report on the Use of the Kuder Preference Record." *Pittsburgh Sch* 21:1-3 S-O '46. *
47. BERG, IRWIN AUGUST. "A Study of Success and Failure Among Student Nurses." *J Appl Psychol* 31:389-96 Ag '47. * (PA 22:2384)
48. BORDIN, EDWARD S. "Relative Correspondence of Professed Interests to Kuder and Strong Interest Test Scores." Abstract. *Am Psychol* 2:293 Ag '47. * (PA 21:4610, title only)
49. DiMICHAEL, S. G., AND DABELSTEIN, D. H. "Work Satisfaction and Work Efficiency of Vocational Rehabilitation Counselors as Related to Measured Interests." Abstract. *Am Psychol* 2:342-3 Ag '47. * (PA 21:4225, title only)
50. FRANDSEN, ARDEN. "Interests and General Educational Development." *J Appl Psychol* 31:57-66 F '47. * (PA 21:2148)
51. HESTON, JOSEPH C. "College Freshmen Norms for the Kuder Preference Record." *Occupations* 26:92-4 N '47. * (PA 22:1652)
52. KOPP, T., AND TUSSING, L. "The Vocational Choices of High School Students as Related to Scores on Vocational Interest Inventories." *Occupations* 25:334-9 Mr '47. * (PA 22:2463)
53. LEWIS, JOHN A. "Kuder Preference Record and MMPI Scores for Two Occupational Groups." *J Consult Psychol* 11:194-201 Jl-Ag '47. * (PA 22:349)
54. LIPSETT, LAURENCE. "Interpreting the Kuder Preference Record in Terms of D.O.T., Part IV." *Occupations* 25:395-7 Ap '47. * (PA 21:3229)
55. ONARHEIM, JAMES. "Scientific Selection of Sales Engineers." *Personnel* 24:24-34 Jl '47. *

56. SLAYMAKER, R. R. "Admission Test Procedure." *J Eng Ed* 37:402-13 Ja '47. * (*PA* 21:1661)
57. STEFFLRE, BUFORD. "The Reading Difficulty of Interest Inventories." *Occupations* 26:95-6 N '47. * (*PA* 22:1722)
58. SPEER, GEORGE S. "The Vocational Interests of Engineering and Non-Engineering Students." Abstract. *Am Psychol* 2:341-2 Ag '47. * (*PA* 21:4612, title only)
59. SUPER, DONALD E. "The Kuder Preference Record in Vocational Diagnosis." *J Consult Psychol* 11:184-93 Jl-Ag '47. * (*PA* 22:352)
60. TRIGGS, FRANCES ORALIND. "The Measured Interests of Nurses." *J Ed Res* 41:25-34 S '47. * (*PA* 22:1723)
61. TRIGGS, FRANCES ORALIND. "A Study of the Relationship of Measured Interests to Measured Mechanical Aptitude, Personality, and Vocabulary." Abstract. *Am Psychol* 2:296-7 Ag '47. * (*PA* 21:4613, title only)
62. TYLER, F. T. "The Kuder Preference Record in a Student Veteran Counselling Programme." *Can J Psychol* 1:44-8 Mr '47. * (*PA* 21:3244)

Ralph F. Berdie, Director, Student Counseling Bureau, and Associate Professor of Psychology, University of Minnesota, Minneapolis, Minnesota. This inventory has been found clinically useful as a vocational counseling aid in secondary schools, colleges, and universities, in the Army, the Navy, and the Marine Corps, in the Veterans Administration, and in industry. It is easy to administer, only slightly monotonous to the individual tested, and convenient to score. Time for administration is usually less than one hour. Hand scoring requires about five minutes. Large groups of Form BM can be scored in even less time by running each answer sheet through the IBM test scoring machine eighteen times. Interpretation of the test is not difficult, and the classification of occupations according to major interests in the manual facilitates this.

Although the methods used in constructing the *Kuder Preference Record* were not as rigorous as those methods we would have preferred, the final judgment as to the value of the test rests not upon how the test was constructed, but rather upon how well the test serves in clinical practice and how well it predicts those occupations in which individuals will derive the most satisfaction. Since the publication of the latest edition of this test in 1942, it has become one of the two most extensively used vocational interest tests, and data are now accumulating which are relevant to this question of validity.

The 1946 revision of the manual, which contains an abundance of well presented information, summarizes the important validity studies which have appeared. In presenting the case for the validity of his test, Kuder, as Strong does with his test, places most emphasis upon the fact that people in different occupations, when tested, obtain profiles characteristic of people in those occupations. The scores are presented in tabular form, and the profiles presented graphically. Mean scores and standard deviations for each of the nine scales are given for men and women in 72 different occupations, where Strong, in his latest publication, presents data for only 56 different occupations. However, no men's occupational group studied by Strong had fewer than 147 people in it, and the sizes of the groups varied from 147 to 585. For these groups information is available concerning age, professional experience, and education.

The men's occupational groups studied by Kuder, ranged in size from 16 to 185, and no information is presented concerning these related factors. Strong has shown that in empirically constructing an interest test, criterion groups of 400 are desirable, if not necessary, and that groups of 200 may be deemed necessary. This generalization cannot be applied without experimental evidence in the validation of previously constructed scales, but evidence for validity based upon only 16 cases, or even 60, must be considered extremely tenuous. The results presented by Kuder do show, however, that each of the 72 occupational groups obtains mean scores on one or more of the nine scales which are statistically different from the mean scores on those scales for a base group of 2,667 men and another base group of 1,429 women.

Kuder also presents profiles originally obtained from a study by Barry, for groups of women students preparing to enter 24 different occupations. Here again the groups are small, ranging in size from 18 to 128, but again the obtained profiles were generally consistent with the occupation chosen.

The reliability of the test is satisfactory, with test-retest reliabilities for the 9 scales ranging from .81 to .98. These compare favorably with test-retest reliabilities, ranging from .84 to .95, reported by Burnham for 11 scales of the Strong *Vocational Interest Blank*. As the reliability of "test-interpretation" is not the same as the reliability of a test score, and as interpretations based upon profiles of test scores are different, we hope more reliable, from interpretations based upon single scores, these reliability coefficients must stand in their own frame of reference.

As with other interest tests, only low correlations have been found between the *Kuder Preference Record* and achievement tests, such as the *Cooperative English Test* and the *Iowa*

High School Content Test. None of the reported correlations exceed .59, most are much lower. Even lower correlations have been found between the *Kuder Preference Record* and ability tests. A study of the relationships between the *Tests for Primary Mental Abilities* and the *Kuder Preference Record* shows only one correlation coefficient of above .30. A similar study between the *Tests for Primary Mental Abilities* and six scales of the *Strong Vocational Interest Blank* shows only one correlation coefficient of above .30. The intercorrelations between scores on the nine scales are also low. In a group of six studies, a total of 216 intercorrelations are presented between the scales, and 36 of these are above .30, 14 above .40. As compared to other interest tests, the scales of the *Kuder Preference Record* measure relatively independent functions.

Many counselors find the specific occupational scores obtained with the Strong *Vocational Interest Blank* are more useful and that the pattern analysis introduced by Darley gives a more complete picture of the personality than can be obtained by using a limited number of scores of a more general nature. The *Kuder Preference Record,* with its more general scores, however, does provide a quick and economical point of departure in helping students select occupations and the development of regression equations that will, on the basis of the nine scales, provide scores on specific occupations, should enhance the test's clinical value.

E. G. Chambers, Assistant Director of Research in Industrial Psychology, University of Cambridge, Cambridge, England. This test is an ingenious attempt to obtain an objective score for a person's occupational preferences with the aim of helping in vocational guidance. The subject is presented with 169 groups of occupations: there are three occupations in each group and the subject is required to rank all three in order of preference. From the answers given, a score is computed for each of nine occupational spheres, including mechanical, persuasive, musical, etc.

The reviewer's small acquaintance with the use of the *Kuder Preference Record* suggests certain criticisms. Firstly, the subject often has to express a preference between activities for which he knows he has no aptitude. This puzzles some subjects since they feel sometimes that they are being asked impossibilities. Certain subjects are constrained in their answers by a knowledge of their own abilities or lack of abilities; others make an imaginative effort and give imaginative answers which may or may not have some value. Secondly, the subject is forced to make a choice in every instance. Thus, although he may dislike all three occupations in any one group, he still has to choose one as being the most preferred, and this "preference" carries equal weight with a preference which he feels positively and strongly. This counting of a dislike of varying degree as a positive preference appears to the reviewer to be unwarranted and a weakness in the test.

It is rather difficult to see exactly what is meant by the "validity" of a test of this description. Surely it is a vast assumption to take workers in a particular occupation as necessarily having strong occupational preferences for that sphere of employment? Very often it happens that individuals become experts in some career upon which they embarked through economic pressure or in some haphazard way and, though experts, their genuine preferences **may be** for something very different. Thus, a highly successful salesman may have a strong yearning to be a musician or an artist.

More important from the point of view of practical vocational guidance is that the *Kuder Preference Record* places the emphasis upon preferences rather than upon capacities. The reviewer is strongly of the opinion that capacities are much more important than preferences in vocational guidance. Many careers are wrecked for individuals who follow their preferences without having the requisite abilities. On the whole, therefore, the reviewer feels that the information obtained by the use of this test is open to some doubt and tends to overemphasise the preference factor in vocational guidance. It seems likely that a skilled interviewer could elicit important preferences more quickly and more reliably by normal interview methods than by the use of this lengthy preference record.

Donald E. Super, Associate Professor of Education, Teachers College, Columbia University, New York, New York. The simple scoring of the *Kuder Preference Record* gave it a great advantage over Strong's complex stencils when it was first published. The fact that Kuder had previously conducted research with his inventory for a period of six years seemed something of a guarantee of validity.

Unlike Strong's blank, which had been developed on occupational groups and so had vocational norms, the Kuder record had been developed on student groups, and the keys had been constructed on the basis of internal consistency and independence. For this reason its occupational significance was an open question until the inventory was administered to adults judged successful in various occupations, or students were followed up in order to ascertain the relationship between their interest scores and success in various vocations.

Data have been accumulated which now give one some basis for interpreting Kuder scores in vocational guidance. The *Kuder Preference Record* has been used in twenty-two published studies to date, and its author has accumulated scores for persons in a relatively large number of occupations. These and related material have been published in a manual which stands out because of the breadth and detail of material covered.

Enough data are on hand for the Kuder to be used with some confidence in vocational guidance, although the actual numbers in any one group are still generally small. Norms are for 2,667 adult men, classified according to 44 occupational groups, and for 1,429 women in 29 occupations. The groups range in size from 16 (men English teachers and women language teachers) to 185 (men meteorologists). The patterns of interest scores tend to differ according to expectation. Accountants, for example, are significantly high on computational, literary, and clerical interests.

Triggs compiled norms and developed an occupational scoring formula for 826 nurses, as a group and according to specialties, such as public health nursing and supervision. The close agreement of Triggs' means and standard deviations with those in Kuder's manual gives one more confidence in the validity of the data for his smaller groups. By means of such occupational indices it is possible to obtain Kuder scores which have the same type of predictive value as Strong's scales. In addition, Kuder's technique preserves the purity of traits which results from internal consistency and independence and makes the development of new occupational indices less laborious than Strong's technique. Occupational indices are now available only for nurses and for accountant-auditors, but additional occupational indices

will be developed. Kuder assumes a responsibility for the continued development of his instrument which has characterized the best tests of the past.

One of the principal weaknesses of Strong's blank has been the presence of a factor which makes scores as office worker, nurse, elementary school teacher, and housewife so common as to render impractical the use of these keys. That the Kuder does differentiate nurses and stenographers from women in general suggests that it may be more valuable for use with women than the Strong.

A survey of the literature shows that grades tend to be related to appropriately measured interests in some cases, but not in others, depending upon whether or not there is sufficient range of interest in the group in question.

No studies appear to have been made which correlated Kuder scores with achievement or continuation in a *vocation*, as Strong has done with his inventory.

Various investigators have studied the relation of Kuder scores to Strong's scores. In general the relationships were disappointingly low for those who have thought of the Kuder as a cheaper substitute for the Strong blank, for they ranged from .28 (literary-author) to .73 (scientific-chemist) for the supposedly related scales. To interpret Kuder scores on the basis of Strong validations would be quite unjustifiable. Even in the case of scales which do tend to agree, e.g., the persuasive and the business contact, the correlation is far from perfect, and one occasionally finds surprising lack of agreement.

More research needs to be done before the record can be considered a well-understood instrument, but it is already a valuable tool in the counselor's kit. More studies which will throw light on what the Kuder is measuring and how it differs from Strong's blank need to be made. At the same time the pioneering which has characterized Kuder's work should be encouraged.

Occupations 21:267–9 N '42. Arthur H. Brayfield. * Kuder attempts to identify certain generalized activity patterns which are psychologically meaningful. This approach to the measurement of interests or preference is in line with factor analysis studies of the problem as well as with clinical experience in using interest inventories. It is consistent with the "pattern analysis" interpretation of other interest inventories. A point favoring the Kuder blank is the extreme care taken in its construction and standardization. The author stresses that it is still in an experimental stage and that more studies are in progress regarding its use and validity. For example, Kuder reports in the Manual an exploratory study using the discriminant function to identify special occupational interest groups. The reviewer recommends the cautious use of the Preference Record with the feeling that, at the present time, it should be used to supplement but not to replace available interest measures which have been more adequately validated. Counselors should add to their experience with the Record before using it widely. Experience seems to indicate that significant scores on the Kuder artistic key are "easier to get" than significant ratings on the Strong artistic key. The Kuder artistic scale may make it rather easy for people with avocational interests in this area to score high. Studies quoted above show promise in the Preference Record for identifying interests which have curricular significance. Such hypotheses will be clarified with more research. Studies on the occupational significance of the test need to be made. This review applies only to the Form A series. There is little information available regarding the new Form BB. Norms for the new test are inadequate. The claims of the publishers regarding both forms should be evaluated carefully in the light of the present research.

For reviews by A. B. Crawford and Arthur E. Traxler of an earlier edition, see 40:1671.

[641]

★Motivation Indicator. Grades 10-12; 1947; IBM; 1 form; separate answer sheets must be used; $1.25 per 25; 25¢ per 25 machine-scorable answer sheets; $1 per set of scoring stencils; 25¢ per specimen set; nontimed (45) minutes; G. Bernard Baldwin; Educational Test Bureau.

Norman Frederiksen, Associate Professor of Psychology, Princeton University; Research Associate, College Entrance Examination Board; Princeton, New Jersey. The *Motivation Indicator* is an interest test designed for high school students. Its intended use is mainly to reveal to the classroom teacher the predominant curricular interests of each student in order that they may be used as a basis for motivating that student to greater effort and improved learning. It is also suggested that the test may be used, along with other information, in vocational counseling.

The test yields fourteen scores. Nine scores are related to the high school curriculum (biological sciences, physical sciences, social sciences, literary arts, graphic arts, industrial arts, agricultural arts, clerical work—verbal, and clerical work—number). Five scores are related to "the motivation of social behavior" (altruistic, promotional, administrative, distributive, and creative planning). Exactly how these interest areas were arrived at is not clear from the description given in the manual. Answers are recorded on a separate answer sheet which may be scored either by hand or by machine.

The test involves a "multiple-matched comparison technique." The part of the test involving curricular interests is a double 8½ × 11 inch page on which are printed 100 boxes in ten columns. In each box is printed a brief description of a "thing to do." The directions use the analogy of a map showing city blocks with streets. The student is directed to start in the top street and go from left to right, pausing at every second intersection. At each of these intersections he reads the four "things to do" in the four adjacent blocks, chooses the two he likes best and indicates them by blackening spaces on a separate answer sheet. When he has finished the horizontal streets, he traverses the vertical streets in the same manner. When the test is completed, each item or "thing to do" has been compared with the eight items which surround it, and it could have been chosen four times. Since there are nine items in each area of interest, the maximum score for any area is 36. The arrangement is similar for the social interest items, except that there are fewer items and the maximum score is 20. The testing method is ingenious, but one wonders how much difficulty the students find in following the rather brief directions.

Two paragraphs in the manual are devoted to a discussion of the necessity for choosing items which will serve as stimuli for "recalling to the student his own satisfying experiences." Certain of the items, such as "Study new methods of helping young people make wise vocational choices" and "Assist in a revision of the items of an aptitude test," seem rather remote from the experience of most high school students.

The reliabilities of the nine scores dealing

with curricular interests are in general satisfactory, while those for social interests are in general too low for use in individual guidance. The reliabilities were computed by the test-retest method with a six-day interval and are based on 75 high school sophomores. The nine reliability coefficients for curricular interests vary from .87 to .96, with a median of .94. The reliabilities for the five social interests vary from .64 to .87 with a median of .84.

As evidence of the validity of the *Motivation Indicator*, a study is cited which is based on a comparison of mean test scores obtained by a high-interest criterion group and a low-interest criterion group. Students were assigned to one or the other of these groups, with respect to each interest category, on the basis of criteria involving curriculum selection, hobbies and activities and achievement. About half the population could not be assigned to either the high or the low category. The critical ratios of the differences between mean interest test scores of high and low criterion groups in the various areas ranged from 9 to 13. In the absence of any report of the size of the groups used, it is impossible to evaluate such evidence of validity. If N is sufficiently large, even a small difference might be highly significant. It is stated only that junior and senior students in two high schools were used.

The test is also alleged to be valid on the basis of evidence pertaining to internal consistency. Items were selected on the basis of high intercorrelations among the items in each area. It is stated that the "median coefficient of intercorrelation between items in an area was .72," which would seem to indicate high internal consistency. The median intercorrelations for the various areas are not given, and no statistics are presented to show that items in one area have low correlations with items in other areas. It is stated that the fourteen areas were chosen because they "were most clearly differentiated from each other." The intercorrelations of scores in the various areas are not presented.

A table of norms is included, based on somewhat more than a thousand students in twenty high schools in the state of Washington. Representative sampling is said to have been secured by "proportional inclusion of agricultural, industrial, and cultural populations." Grade norms are not presented, since means vary but little from grade ten to grade twelve. Although sex 'differences are marked, no sex differentiated norms are presented.

Arthur E. Traxler, Associate Director, Educational Records Bureau, New York, New York. This new inventory is designed to measure interests in nine curricular areas and five social motivation areas. The curricular groups are biological sciences, physical sciences, social sciences, creative writing, graphic arts, industrial arts, agriculture, clerical work (verbal), and clerical work (number). The social areas are altruistic, promotional, administrative, distributive (sales), and creative (planning).

The curricular division of the inventory contains 81 items, and the social division has 25 items. Each item contains statements of four activities from which the subject is required to choose the two he likes best. Through an ingenious "block" arrangement of the booklet, each activity in the curriculum motivation division is matched with eight others surrounding it—one from each of the other eight areas. The social-motivation part is arranged in a similar manner, except for the fact that each activity is matched with activities from only four other areas. All responses are entered on separate answer sheets which may be hand scored or machine scored.

There are 212 responses in the entire inventory, of which 162 are in the first division and 50 are in the second. The Indicator is administered without a time limit. Most individuals would probably require 20 to 30 minutes to complete it.

Since each of the nine activities in each area of the curriculum section and each of the five activities in each area of the social motivation section has an opportunity to be chosen four times, the highest possible score is 36 for each curriculum area and 20 for each social area. In the manual of instructions, Baldwin reports test-retest reliabilities of the area scores based on results from high school sophomores. The reliabilities of the curriculum areas range from .873 to .957 with a median of .94; those for the social areas range from .64 to .87 with a median of .84. With the exception of the coefficient of .64 for creative initiative, these reliabilities seem definitely high for the test-retest method when applied to subtests containing only 36 and 20 responses respectively. If these coefficients are verified in subsequent studies, the *Motivation Indicator* will be among the most reliable of all tests of similar length. At the time this review was written the test was not available in quantity for use in checking this point.

In general, a good case can be made for the comparison technique employed in items in such inventories as the Baldwin's *Motivation Indicator* and the *Kuder Preference Record*. This procedure involves the comparison of each activity with a variety of other activities and thus allows the ranking of the activity among diverse experiences. Thus, the procedure probably results in a more precise indication of one's interest in a particular activity than can be obtained from an inventory which requires the subject merely to say whether he likes, dislikes, or is indifferent to the activity. On the other hand, within a given period of time, interest in a larger number of different activities can be sampled by the latter method.

One weakness in the use of the comparison type of item is that unless great care is exercised in the construction of the items, activities which are in reality not comparable will sometimes be paired. For example, the activities in one of the items of the *Motivation Indicator* are: (1) "prepare the script for an amateur radio program"; (2) "study the construction plans for an airplane"; (3) "improve livestock by careful breeding"; and (4) "illustrate the title page of the school annual." Activities 1, 2, and 4 are short-term projects requiring from a few hours to perhaps a day or two. Activity 3, however, is a long-term project calling for years, or even a lifetime, of work. An individual who had an interest in agriculture might not choose number three simply because it seems to involve such a long commitment in comparison with the other three.

Answer sheets for the *Motivation Indicator* were filled out by two members of the staff of the Educational Records Bureau. There was agreement that the setup of the booklet is rather confusing to one taking the test and that if the Indicator were administered to a group careful supervision would be required. The pattern of the area scores and percentiles agreed with subjective impressions, although it was felt that in some instances the differences between areas were exaggerated by the Indicator scores. The scoring keys definitely could be improved to facilitate speed and accuracy of scoring. The publisher has attempted to reduce the number of scoring sheets to be handled by printing the keys for two curriculum areas on each of four sheets. This arrangement is very confusing to the scorer. There should be a separate key for each curriculum area.

The *Motivation Indicator* is an interesting and novel addition to the available interest inventories, but more research data are needed on which to base a recommendation concerning the use of this new instrument in a guidance program.

J Consult Psychol 11:157 My-Je '47. * By means of an ingenious and somewhat complex system of administration, each response of an examinee is a choice among four of the items, of which two are chosen as preferred activities. *

[642]

Occupational Interest Blank for Women. 1931; 1 form; scoring scales are available for 10 occupations: bookkeepers, grade school teachers, high school teachers, office clerks, office managers, private secretaries, retail saleswomen, sales proprietors, stenographers, trained nurses; 3¢ per blank; $1 per set of scoring scales; Grace E. Manson; University of Michigan Press.

REFERENCES

1. FRYER, DOUGLAS. *The Measurement of Interests in Relation to Human Adjustments*, pp. 470-8. New York: Henry Holt and Co., Inc., 1931. Pp. xxxvi, 488. $3.60. * (PA 6:973)
2. MANSON, GRACE E. *Occupational Interests and Personality Requirements of Women in Business and the Professions*. University of Michigan, School of Business Administration, Bureau of Business Research, Michigan Business Studies, Vol. 3, No. 3. Ann Arbor, Mich.: University of Michigan Press, 1931. Pp. ix, 281-409. $1.50. Paper. * (PA 5:3503)
3. MICHELS, A. M. *Occupational Interests of Women at the College Level*. Unpublished master's thesis, University of Minnesota, 1931.
4. BERMAN, ISABEL R.; DARLEY, JOHN G.; AND PATERSON, DONALD G. *Vocational Interest Scales: An Analysis of Three Questionnaires in Relation to Occupational Classification and Employment Status*, pp. 24-8. University of Minnesota Bulletins of the Employment Stabilization Research Institute, Vol. 3, No. 5. Minneapolis, Minn.: University of Minnesota Press, August 1934. Pp. 35. Paper. $0.50. *
5. BINGHAM, WALTER VAN DYKE. *Aptitudes and Aptitude Testing*, pp. 358-9. New York and London: Harper & Brothers, 1937. Pp. ix, 390. $3.00; 12s. 6d. * (PA 11:2885)
6. LALEGER, GRACE ELIZABETH. *The Vocational Interests of High School Girls: As Inventoried by the Strong and Manson Blanks*. Columbia University, Teachers College, Contributions to Education, No. 857. Harry D. Kitson, faculty sponsor. New York: Bureau of Publications, the College, 1942. Pp. vii, 102. $1.60. * (PA 16:5023)

Gwendolen Schneidler Dickson, Chief, Educational Counseling Division, Veterans Administration, Washington, D. C. As indicated by the test author, "The present project is but another link in the long chain of investigations into the subtleties of interests and personality traits (2)." It should be recognized that the *Occupational Interest Blank for Women* represents one of the pioneer studies in the development of instruments for measuring the occupational interests of women.

Other workers, such as Strong and Kuder, however, have since produced superior and more comprehensive instruments which are available to counselors and which should be used in place of this earlier test when it is desirable to measure women's interests.

Frances Oralind Triggs, Educational Records Bureau, New York, New York. This test, copyrighted 1931, consists of 160 items, all names of occupations. The responses are made in a five-degree scale: like very much, like, no decided feeling, dislike, dislike very much. The inventory may be scored for ten occupations: private secretary, office manager, bookkeeper, stenographer, office clerk, high school teacher, grade school teacher, trained nurse, sales proprietor, retail saleswoman. The scoring is similar to that used to score Strong's *Vocational Interest Blank.* Each item has ten numerical weights differentiating the value of the score according to the ten occupations for which the inventory may be scored. These weights were arrived at by comparing the responses of 150 persons in each occupation to a group of people in general.

The study, of which this test is an outcome, was a very ambitious one. It was published in the Michigan Business Studies and will stand as a classic in the history of objective measurement of interests (2).

There have been some excellent evaluations of the results of using this test. For instance, there are data to indicate the extent of intercorrelation of scores on the test, the relationship of scores to age, the relationship of scores to general and scholastic aptitude and to other instruments purporting to measure interests, the relationship to vocational choices made by persons taking the test, the relationship to success or degree of satisfaction in a chosen educational or vocational field, and the relationship to sociological factors. Spearman–Brown reliabilities of the scores on the scales are reported by the author and range from approximately .73 to .98.

In the light of the work which has been reported in the measurement of interests of women, this test cannot be too severely criticized. However, certain comments might be made. The fact that the items on the test are based only on the names of occupations "commonly open to women" is a restricting factor from the outset. Women are not entering only occupations "commonly" open to them in our present society. The fact that the test is scored

for these occupations only does not allow the necessary breadth for a counseling tool. There is some indication in the literature that there may be a selective factor operating in the norm groups used as a basis for the present standardization of the test.

It should be said again that historically this instrument and the research based on it continue to have value in the study of interest measurement in general. Any use of this instrument as a counseling tool should be experimental only, as it has probably been replaced by others which have more value.

[643]

★Occupational Interest Inventory. Grades 7-9, 10-13 and adults; 1944–46; IBM; 1 form; 2 levels; $1.75 per 25; 25¢ per specimen set of any one level, postpaid; 7¢ per copy, machine-scoring edition; 2¢ per machine-scorable answer sheet; nontimed (30-40) minutes; Edwin A. Lee and Louis P. Thorpe; California Test Bureau.

REFERENCES

1. FAUQUIER, WILLIAM, AND SHIERSON, HARRY E. *Occupational Selection Aid: A Guidebook in Vocational and Educational Counseling (In Two Parts) For Use With the Occupational Interest Inventory,* Parts 1 and 2. Los Angeles, Calif.: California Test Bureau, 1947. Pp. 36, 32. Paper. $1.00 per part. *
2. STEFFLRE, BUFORD. "The Reading Difficulty of Interest Inventories." *Occupations* 26:95-6 N '47. * (PA 22:1722)

Edward S. Bordin, Director, Student Counseling Center, and Associate Professor of Psychology, The State College of Washington, Pullman, Washington. This is still another vocational interest test which attempts to edge into the field covered by the *Kuder Preference Record* and Strong's *Vocational Interest Blank.* Unfortunately, like so many of the other recent tests, its authors have not yet paid the price in research necessary to obtain unqualified acceptance of their instruments.

The manual accompanying the test does not even pretend to present empirical evidence of its validity. Instead its validity is argued on logical grounds, namely, that the Inventory was constructed by following admirable procedures in the selection and framing of items. Estimates of the reliability of each of the ten measures derived from the test are provided as well as percentile norms by sexes and for composite populations based upon substantial numbers of cases. One would like to know more about the composition of the norm groups for the advanced form, but the manual simply states that the sample included high school and college students, veterans, and adults, without specifying the proportions.

The format of the test and manual are reasonably effective and attractive. The descriptions of what each scale measures are clear, and the idea of using illustrative cases to aid in clarifying the interpretation is a good one. But without adequate studies to buttress them, these materials cannot be accepted. Unfortunately, the sales of such tests are too often a function of the merchandising methods of the publisher rather than of the quality of the test.

Stanley G. Dulsky, Chief of Staff, Chicago Psychological Institute, Chicago, Illinois. This inventory measures interests in six *fields:* personal-social, natural, mechanical, business, the arts, the sciences; it determines three *types* of interest: verbal, manipulative, and computational; and it reveals three *levels* of interest: low (simple, routine), medium (skilled) and high (original, creative).

The method for determining interest is the paired comparison method. The authors state, "There are no purely objective criteria for establishing the validity of an occupational interests inventory. . . . However certain factors may add or detract from the validity. . . ." They have tried to make their test valid by carefully selecting the items from the *Dictionary of Occupational Titles* so as to get a representative sample of occupations; they have designed the items to avoid reactions to occupations and to get instead reactions to groups of activities; they have tried to achieve a good balance among the items by presenting 240 groups of activities associated with six major interest fields, 40 of them in each major field. The 40 choices in each field fall into three levels so that an item in one field at a low level is compared with an item in another field at a low level; they have presented the items by the paired-choice method.

Reliability of the scale has been determined by repeating it after four weeks on 100 twelfth graders in the case of the Advanced Series and on 180 ninth grade students in the case of the Intermediate Series. Coefficients of reliability on the Advanced Series range from .88 to .93 for fields, types, and levels. In the Intermediate Series the reliability coefficients range from .84 to .93.

Percentile norms were obtained from over 1,000 twelfth grade students in a number of California high schools for the Advanced Series and from over 1,000 ninth grade students in a number of California secondary schools for the Intermediate Series. The authors claim that the norms for the Advanced Series may be used "not only for high school and junior college students but also for the general adult population." For the Intermediate Series they claim that the norms are suitable not only for high school students "but also for the general adult population, especially those who lack technical or professional training." An investigation of the norms themselves shows very little difference between the Intermediate and Advanced Series.

In the reviewer's opinion each of the six fields is too large and complex and contains too many diverse occupational activities. For example, the personal-social field contains activities such as domestic service, personal service, teaching, law and law enforcement, social service, and health and medical service. A person interested in teaching would probably score high on teaching and social service and low on the other four sections, thereby lowering the score on the field as a whole. A similar condition exists with the business field. For this reason total score might mask an important occupational preference that could be detected only by a careful analysis of the individual sections making up the field.

The analysis into types of interests—verbal, manipulative, and computational—is good and will help to overcome some of the objections mentioned above. In the reviewer's opinion the *level* of interest is the least important of the data yielded by this inventory. The level of interest at which an individual wants to work is determined primarily by intelligence. Even though a very intelligent boy who is capable of working at a professional level indicates a low level of interest, no one would guide him into a vocation that did not make full use of his mental ability. Similarly, if a dull boy expresses a high interest in creative and original work, he would still have to be guided into a skilled or semiskilled occupation. In using this inventory with a number of high school students, the reviewer has never encountered a level of interest below the medium, or skilled, level.

The authors have given no information regarding the interests of adults who are working in specific occupations. Can we assume that a high school boy interested in mechanical and scientific fields also possesses the same kind of interests as a group of mature engineers or

Occupational Interest Inventory

people entering the engineering profession? On what grounds do the authors state that the norms obtained on high school students are also suitable for the general adult population? They present no evidence to indicate that this is true. In presenting information on the norms the authors should have indicated the exact number of students on whom the test was standardized and the kind of high schools from which they were selected rather than to give a blanket statement that the norms were obtained "from over 1,000 inventories given to twelfth grade students in a number of California high schools." Certainly the norms would be affected by the type of school and the type of curriculum offered to the students used in the standardizing population.

In the reviewer's opinion the *Kuder Preference Record* is superior to this inventory for revealing broad occupational interests, not only of high school students, but also of adults.

[644]

★**Occupational Interests: Self Analysis Scale.** Applicants for employment; 1943; separate scales for men and women; $3 per introductory set including 10 tests, postpaid; 4¢ per extra test, postpaid; introductory sets may be ordered on approval; nontimed (8-12) minutes; Eugene J. Benge; Management Service Co.

Stanley G. Dulsky, Chief of Staff, Chicago Psychological Institute, Chicago, Illinois. This is one of those "quickies" that can be concocted as fast as a stenographer can type. Nothing will injure the field of interest determination so rapidly and completely as the production of armchair inventories of this kind. Any resemblance between this scale and a scientific instrument is purely coincidental. Saying any more about this scale would constitute a gross waste of space.

[645]

★**Primary Business Interests Test.** Grades 9-16 and adults; 1942; IBM; $1.65 per 25 machine-scorable test-answer sheets; 35¢ per set of hand-scoring stencils; $8 per set of machine-scoring stencils; 50¢ per specimen set; nontimed (20) minutes; Alfred J. Cardall, Jr.; Science Research Associates.

REFERENCES
1. CARDALL, ALFRED J. *A Test for Primary Business Interests Based on a Functional Occupational Classification.* Unpublished doctor's thesis, Harvard University, 1941.
2. CARDALL, ALFRED J. "A Test for Primary Business Interests Based on a Functional Occupational Classification." *Ed & Psychol Meas* 2:113-38 Ap '42. * (PA 16:3767)

George K. Bennett, President, The Psychological Corporation. New York, New York. The 75 items comprising this interest inventory are fairly specific titles descriptive of business activities. For example: "Pay bills and bring back receipts"; "Set up new system of accounts." Great emphasis is placed by the author upon the systematic selection of these items from job-analysis data. The 2,000 odd descriptive terms so obtained were then reduced to 245 items upon which a "cluster analysis" was carried out. As a result, 75 items were retained and five scoring scales constructed. The items included in each scale were selected on the basis of high mutual intercorrelation. Weights were assigned to each item in proportion to its estimated importance.

This interest check list may well be useful in guidance if the counselee has had some experience with all or most of the activities listed and where it is important to locate an area within the field of business.

Some portions of the manual are misleading, others are confusing, and at least one is clearly incorrect.

Reference is made in the manual and in the descriptive journal article (2) to the rigorous search for validity. Upon examination it appears that the author is satisfied that an item (and consequently a score) is "valid" because the item appears frequently in job analysis and also correlates positively with other similar items. No evidence is given regarding the predictive efficacy of any scale.

Since only a few items are scored for more than one scale, the number of items per scale is very small, ranging from a maximum of 23 for the accounting scale down to 6 for collecting-adjusting. Nevertheless split-half reliability coefficients of .73 to .92 are reported. These coefficients have apparently been computed on data from the same group as was used in the item selection procedure. Furthermore, several of the items within any scale are overlapping or paraphrases of each other. The propriety of this type of reliability determination is open to serious question.

In an attempt to demonstrate the discriminative power of the test, the manual cites critical ratios between commercial and academic high school seniors ranging from 1.23 to 13.15. The number of commercial seniors is 323, no number or standard deviation being given for the academic group. Aside from the dubious practice of using the critical ratio as an index of discriminating power, the interpretation of the critical ratio is in error. Referring to four CR's of 3.3 and above, the manual states,

These ratios are unusually satisfactory, indicating that there is less than one chance in ,000 that there is any likelihood of a student's core in the commercial group falling below he mean in the noncommercial group." Taking the mean scores for the academic group given on page 6 of the manual and comparing these with the percentile distributions for the ommercial group appearing on page 5, the absurdity of this high-flown statement is at once apparent. The percentage of commercial students falling below the mean of academic students becomes, for each scale, the following: accounting, over 20; collecting and adjusting, about 40; sales-office, over 40; sales-store, over 30; steno-filing, over 10.

One further defect warrants mention. Norms appear to include persons of both sexes. Since other research on vocational interest has disclosed striking sex differences (e.g., very few boys are interested in stenographic activities), the present author may be considered negligent in failing to mention this factor if, indeed, he has given it any consideration.

Glen U. Cleeton, Director, Division of Humanistic and Social Studies, Carnegie Institute of Technology, Pittsburgh, Pennsylvania. The purpose of this test according to the compiler is "to measure an individual's preference for the specific job activities which characterize beginning business jobs. These immediate and specific preferences point to the initial job, predict the individual's interest or boredom in his first activities, and determine to some extent his progress in his work. Scores indicate the relative extent of interest in five functional occupational classifications."

The five classifications are: (*a*) accounting, (*b*) collections and adjustments, (*c*) sales–office, (*d*) sales–store, (*e*) stenographic–filing. To the extent that the test measures such interests, it obviously would be useful in educational and vocational counseling and in placement in commercial employment.

In developing the test, experimental test items, selected by job analyses from work diaries of 106 individuals, were subjected to frequency study. Of 2,000 test items thus obtained, many were discarded and a residual of 115 were used to prepare an experimental edition of the test which was administered to 285 individuals. Intercorrelations were then computed, and five occupational patterns isolated. In the process the number of items was further reduced so that only 75 are included in the published edition of the test.

The usual limitations characteristic of all interest tests with reference to evidence of validity apply to this test. However, it would seem that the chief weakness of the test is the small number of items included for certain occupational patterns. There are 23 items in pattern 1, 6 items in pattern 2, 11 items in pattern 3, 30 items in pattern 4, and 9 items in pattern 5. With such a small number of items, reliability coefficients ranging from .73 to .92, computed on the basis of the split-half method, are not statistically defensible. The author argues that retention of a greater number of items to assure higher reliability "would have been at the expense of the validity of the test." This contention is, of course, likewise debatable.

Only one reference to published studies relating to this test is included in the manual.

Percentile norms based on scores of 323 high school commercial seniors and 304 business college freshmen are included in the manual of directions. Data are also included to show differences between scores of commercial high school seniors and academic high school seniors.

Several occupations, classified on the basis of the initial data used in determining the five basic patterns, are set forth in the manual as an aid to interpretation. A case study is also reported as an illustration of the procedure recommended in counseling persons to whom the test has been administered.

The test is self-administering and can be completed in 20 to 25 minutes. An answer form for use in machine scoring is provided together with a perforated stencil for hand scoring.

George A. Ferguson, Assistant Professor of Psychology, McGill University, Montreal, Canada. This test is designed to systematically appraise an individual's preferences for selected job activities or work elements which occur with greatest frequency among the lower wage level business jobs. The author recommends its use by placement officers in the allocation of employees to jobs that coincide with their specific business interests and by school administrators in the allocation of commercial students to different training programs.

Reliability coefficients calculated by the method of split-halves are reported to range from .73 to .92 for scores obtained on the different groups of items. Whether any meaning can be attached in this context to coefficients thus computed is debatable. Some exploration of the stability of the scores and resulting interest profiles over even a relatively short period of time would have proved more informative. It is not improbable that at least some of the items on this test are hypersensitive to minor occurrences in the experience of the individual and reflect transient work attitudes rather than any basic and persisting interest component.

To evaluate the use of the test in the counseling of students, the author tested a group of commercial and a group of noncommercial students. The differences between mean scores obtained by the two groups on the different interest areas may be regarded with one exception as statistically significant, the critical ratios varying from 3.3 to 13.15. The author concludes that, "These ratios are unusually satisfactory indicating that there is less than one chance in 1,000 that there is any likelihood of a student's score in a commercial group falling below the mean in the non-commercial group." This is an erroneous inference and represents an unfortunate misinterpretation of the facts. To illustrate, on collections and adjustments the mean scores obtained for the commercial and noncommercial groups are respectively 13.2 and 11.12. The difference in means is 2.08, and the critical ratio 3.3. From these data we may guess roughly that the chances are perhaps about 400 in 1,000 that a student's score in the commercial group will fall below the mean of the noncommercial group. The author is using an incorrect criterion to evaluate the discriminatory power of his test. In such cases highly significant differences between means may be obtained, and yet a test may be of very little practical value in discriminating between groups.

We may conclude that the author's claims for his test are not proved. Considerably more research data are required, and a more rigorously critical attitude applied to the interpretation of such data, before this test can be recommended for general use.

[646]

★Thurstone Interest Schedule. Ages 9-16 and adults; 1947; replaces Thurstone's *Vocational Interest Schedule;* 1 form; $1.50 per 25, postpaid; 35¢ per specimen set, postpaid; 10(15) minutes; L. L. Thurstone; Psychological Corporation.

Primary Business Interests Test

[647]

Vocational Interest Blank for Men, Revised. Age 17 and over; 1927–38; revised scoring scales are available for measuring maturity of interest, masculinity femininity, studiousness, thirty-nine occupations, an six occupational groups (I, II, V, VIII, IX, X) Group I: artist, psychologist, architect, physician dentist, osteopath; Group II: mathematician, engineer chemist, physicist; Group III: production manager Group IV: farmer, aviator, carpenter, printer, mathematics-physical science teacher, policeman, forest service man; Group V: Y.M.C.A. physical director, personnel director, public manager, Y.M.C.A. secretary, social science high school teacher; city school superintendent minister; Group VI: musician; Group VII: certified public accountant; Group VIII: accountant, office man purchasing agent, banker, mortician; Group IX: sale manager, real estate salesman, life insurance salesman Group X: advertising man, lawyer, author-journalist Group XI: president of a manufacturing concern; form; $2 per 25; 2¢ per report blank; $1 per scoring scale; 2-9 scales, 80¢ each; 10 or more scales, 70¢ each 75¢ per 25 machine-scorable answer sheets; 75¢ per 25 answer sheets for use with Hankes Scoring Machine; 15¢ per specimen set; nontimed (40) minutes; Edward K. Strong, Jr.; Stanford University Press.

REFERENCES

1-71. *See* 40:1680.
72. STEEN, F. H., AND ESTABROOKS, G. H. "Relation Between Introversion and Scholastic Interests." *Voc Guid Mag* 7:38-9 O '28. * (*PA* 3:1353)
73. DVORAK, B. *Adjustment of Pre-medical Freshmen to the University: A Study in Vocational Guidance.* Unpublished master's thesis, University of Minnesota, 1930.
74. DECKER, C. E. *An Experiment in the Use of Psychological Tests in the Selection of Life Insurance Agents.* Unpublished master's thesis, Dartmouth College, 1931.
75. FORSTER, M. C. *A Study of Father-Son Resemblances in Vocational Interest Patterns.* Unpublished master's thesis, University of Minnesota, 1931.
76. CARTER, HAROLD D. "Twin Similarities in Occupational Interests." *J Ed Psychol* 23:641-55 D '32. * (*PA* 7:1342)
77. HARTMANN, GEORGE W. *Measuring Teaching Efficiency Among College Instructors.* Archives of Psychology, No. 154. Washington, D. C.: American Psychological Association, Inc., July 1933. Pp. 45. Paper. $0.80. * (*PA* 8:5229)
78. BIDLAKE, LAURENCE A. *A Critical Analysis of the Strong Vocational Interest Blank in Its Relationship to the Selection of Lay Leaders for Activities in the Department of Physical Education in the Young Men's Christian Association.* Unpublished master's thesis, New York University, 1934. Pp. 58.
79. GLASS, CHARLES F. *An Investigational Analysis of Certain General and Specific Interests of Engineering Students.* Unpublished master's thesis, Purdue University, 1934. Pp. 102.
80. ROCK, ROBERT T., JR. "A Study of the Constancy of Responses to the Items of the Strong Vocational Interest Blank." Abstract. *Psychol B* 31:705-6 N '34. * (*PA* 9:1377, title only)
81. STRONG, EDWARD K. "Interests of Men and Women." Abstract. *Psychol B* 31:704-5 N '34. * (*PA* 9:1295, title only)
82. BURNHAM, PAUL S. *Stability of Interest Test Scores.* Unpublished doctor's thesis, Yale University, 1935.
83-4. FINCH, F. H. "Permanence of Vocational Interest." Abstract. *Psychol B* 32:682 N '35. * (*PA* 10:1134, title only)
85. TERMAN, LEWIS M., AND BUTTENWIESER, PAUL. "Personality Factors in Marital Compatibility." *J Soc Psychol* 6:143-71, 267-89 My, Ag '35. * (*PA* 10:1649, 2149)
86. SCHULTZ, RICHARD S. "Standardized Tests and Statistical Procedures in Selection of Life Insurance Sales Personnel." *J Appl Psychol* 20:553-66 O '36. * (*PA* 11:2899)
87. SHLAUDEMAN, KARL WHITMAN. *A Correlational Analysis of Idiosyncrasy of Response to Tests of Association, Interest, and Personality.* Unpublished doctor's thesis, Stanford University, 1936. (*Abstracts of Dissertations . . . 1936–37,* 1937, pp. 22-6.)
88. SATTERFIELD, ANNIE ELIZABETH. *A Comparison of Expressed Vocational Preferences With Objectively Determined Interests.* Unpublished master's thesis, University of Oklahoma, 1937. Pp. iv, 57. (*Abstracts of Theses . . . 1937,* 1939, pp. 158-9.)
89. ALTENEDER, LOUISE E. *The Value of Intelligence, Personality, and Vocational-Interest Tests in a Guidance Program.* Unpublished doctor's thesis, New York University, 1938. Pp. 130. (*Abstracts of Theses . . . [School of Education] 1938,* pp. 41-4.)
90. GILKINSON, HOWARD, AND KNOWER, FRANKLIN H. *Psychological Studies of Individual Differences Among Students of Speech.* Minneapolis, Minn.: Department of Speech, Univer-

sity of Minnesota, June 1939. Pp. iii, 196. Paper, mimeographed. Gratis. *

91. MARICLE, LeCLAIRE ROBERT. The Relationship of Certain Personality Traits to Patterns of Interest. Unpublished master's thesis, University of Oklahoma, 1939. Pp. vi, 56. (Abstracts of Theses . . . 1939, 1943, p. 132.)

92. ALTENEDER, LOUISE E. "The Value of Intelligence, Personality, and Vocational Interest Tests in a Guidance Program." J Ed Psychol 31:449-59 S '40. * (PA 15:1480)

93. BROWN, J. E. The Relationship of Personality Traits and Vocational Interest to Success in Teaching Vocational Agriculture. Unpublished master's thesis, Virginia Polytechnic Institute, 1940. Pp. 88.

94. CAMPBELL, RONALD KENNETH. The Relationships of Interests to Achievement in Engineering and Social Science Courses. Unpublished doctor's thesis, Stanford University, 1940. (Abstracts of Dissertation . . . 1940–41, 1941, pp. 212-5.)

95. DUNLAP, JACK W. "Simplification of the Scoring of the Strong Vocational Interest Blank." Abstract. Psychol B 37:550 Jl '40. * (PA 14:5701, title only)

96. HARRELL, WILLARD. "Testing Cotton Mill Supervisors." J Appl Psychol 24:31-5 F '40. * (PA 14:3709)

97. MILLER, C. W., AND GLICK, W. P. The Development of a Scale for the Strong Vocational Interest Test to Measure Basic Interests in Teaching Agriculture. Unpublished master's thesis, Virginia Polytechnic Institute, 1940. Pp. 419.

98. SKODAK, MARIE, AND CRISSEY, ORLO L. "The Relationship Between Strong Vocational Interest Scores, Stated Vocational Aims, and Intelligence of High School Senior Girls." Abstract. Psychol B 37:469 Jl '40. * (PA 14:5720, title only)

99. SUPER, DONALD E. "The Measurement of Interest in an Occupation vs. Patterns of Interests Similar to Those of Persons in That Occupation." Abstract. Psychol B 37:450-1 Jl '40. (PA 14:5724, title only)

100. TAYLOR, GEORGE JACKSON. A Comparative Study of the Vocational Interests of Ministers and Theological Students of Greater Boston as Indicated by the Strong Vocational Interest Blank. Unpublished master's thesis, Boston University, 1940. Pp. 59.

101-2. VAN DUSEN, A. C. "Permanence of Vocational Interests." J Ed Psychol 31:401-24 S '40. * (PA 15:1531)

103. BELLOWS, ROGER M., AND KAPLON, MARTIN D. "Interest Patterns of Good and Poor Dental Students: A New Scoring Key for the Strong Vocational Interest Blank." Abstract. Psychol B 38:608 Jl '41. * (PA 15:5349, title only)

104. BILLS, MARION A. "Selection of Casualty and Life Insurance Agents." J Appl Psychol 25:6-10 F '41. * (PA 15:3103)

105. CANNING, LESLIE; TAYLOR, KATHERINE VAN F.; AND CARTER, HAROLD D. "Permanence of Vocational Interests of High-School Boys." J Ed Psychol 32:481-94 O '41. * (PA 16:436)

106. CARTER, H. D.; TAYLOR, K. von F.; AND CANNING, L. B. Vocational Choices and Interest Test Scores of High School Students." J Psychol 11:297-306 Ap '41. * (PA 15:3573)

107. DARLEY, JOHN G. Clinical Aspects and Interpretaton of the Strong Vocational Interest Blank. New York: Psychological Corporation, 1941. Pp. 72. Paper. $1.20. * (PA 16:328)

108. DARLEY, JOHN G. "Counseling on the Basis of Interest Measurement." Ed & Psychol Meas 1:35-42 Ja '41. * (PA 15:74)

109. FERGUSON, LEONARD W.; HUMPHREYS, LLOYD G.; AND STRONG, FRANCES W. "A Factorial Analysis of Interests and Values." J Ed Psychol 32:197-204 Mr '41. * (PA 15:3887)

110. GILKINSON, HOWARD, AND KNOWER, FRANKLIN H. "A Study of Standardized Personality Tests and Skill in Speech." Ed Psychol 32:161-175 Mr '41. * (PA 15:3888)

111. GORDON, HANS C., AND HERKNESS, WALTER W., JR. "Pupils Appraise Vocational Interest Blanks." Occupations :100-2 N '41. * (PA 16:757)

112-3. MOORE, BRUCE V. "Analysis of Results of Tests Administered to Men in Engineering Defense Training Courses." J Appl Psychol 25:619-25 O '41. * (PA 16:1683)

114. PETERSON, BERTHA M., AND DUNLAP, JACK W. "A Simplified Method for Scoring the Strong Vocational Interest Blank." J Consult Psychol 5:269-74 N-D '41. * (PA 16:765)

115. ROBINSON, J. BEN, AND BELLOWS, ROGER M. "Characteristics of Successful Dental Students." J Am Assn Col Reg 16:309-22 Ja '41. * (PA 15:2810)

116. SUPER, DONALD E. "Avocations and Vocational Adjustment." Char & Pers 10:51-61 S '41. * (PA 16:1211)

117. TUSSING, LYLE. An Investigation of the Possibilities of Measuring Personality Traits With the Strong Vocational Interest Blank. Unpublished doctor's thesis, Purdue University, '41.

118. WALLAR, G. A. "A Practical Aid to Occupational Orientation." J Appl Psychol 25:535-57 O '41. * (PA 16:1221)

119. ACHARD, FRANCIS H. The Selection of Supervisory Employees in Business and Industry. Unpublished doctor's thesis, New York University, 1942. Pp. 337. (Abstracts of Theses . . . School of Education] 1943, pp. 1-7.)

120. BERDIE, R. F. Factors Related to Vocational Interest. Unpublished doctor's thesis, University of Minnesota, 1942.

121. BRAYFIELD, ARTHUR H. "'When Vocational-Guidance Tests Disagree'—A Reply." Sch & Soc 56:17-8 Jl 4 '42. * (PA 16:4521)

122. BURNHAM, PAUL S. "Stability of Interests." Sch & Soc 56:332-5 Mr 21 '42. * (PA 16:2845)

123. COBLENTZ, IRVING. Prognosis of Freshman Academic Achievement at the Pennsylvania State College. Unpublished doctor's thesis, Pennsylvania State College, 1942. Pp. 245. (Abstracts of Doctoral Dissertations . . . 1942, 1943, pp. 386-92.)

124. GHISELLI, EDWIN E. "1 he Use of the Strong Vocational Interest Blank and the Pressey Senior Classification Test in the Selection of Casualty Insurance Agents." J Appl Psychol 26:793-9 D '42. * (PA 17:2452)

125. GORDON, HANS C., AND HERKNESS, WALTER W., JR. "Do Vocational Interest Questionnaires Yield Consistent Results?" Occupations 20:424-9 Mr '42. * (PA 16:2059)

126. JACOBSON, CARLYLE F. "Interest Patterns and Achievement in Medical School." J Assn Am Med Col 17:153-73 My '42. * (PA 16:3782)

127. JOHNSON, A. P. The Prediction of Scholastic Achievement for Freshman Engineering Students at Purdue University. Purdue University, Division of Educational Research, Studies in Engineering Education II. Lafayette, Ind.: the Division, May 1942. Pp. 22. Paper. $0.35. * (PA 16:5020)

128. JOHNSON, A. P. The Relationship of Test Scores to Scholastic Achievement for 244 Engineering Freshmen Entering Purdue University in September, 1939. Unpublished doctor's thesis, Purdue University, 1942.

129. KOGAN, LEONARD, AND GEHLMANN, FREDERICK. "Validation of the Simplified Method for Scoring the Strong Vocational Interest Blank for Men." J Ed Psychol 33:317-20 Ap '42. * (PA 17:950)

130. LESTER, HELENE, AND TRAXLER, ARTHUR E. "Simplified Method for Scoring the Strong Vocational Interest Blank Applied to a Secondary-School Group." J Ed Psychol 33:628-31 N '42. * (PA 17:2494)

131. LOWRIE, KATHLEEN HARRIET. Factors Which Relate to the Extra-Curricular Performance of College Women. Unpublished doctor's thesis, University of Iowa, 1942.

132. MATHER, M. E. The Use of the Strong Vocational Interest Blank for Predicting Success of Students in Home Economics. Unpublished master's thesis, Pennsylvania State College, 1942. Pp. 53.

133. MOFFIE, D. J. "The Validity of Self-Estimated Interests." J Appl Psychol 26:606-13 O '42. * (PA 17:2896)

134. PARRY, DOUGLAS F. "When Vocational-Guidance Tests Disagree." Sch & Soc 55:508-11 My 2 '42. * (PA 16:3298)

135. PARRY, DOUGLAS F. "'When Vocational-Guidance Tests Disagree'—An Answer to a Reply." Sch & Soc 56:101-3 Ag 1 '42. * (PA 16:4545)

136. PETERS, EDWIN F. "Vocational Interests as Measured by the Strong and Kuder Inventories." Sch & Soc 55:453-5 Ap 18 '42. * (PA 16:3299)

137. RYAN, T. G., AND JOHNSON, BEATRICE R. "Interest Scores in the Selection of Salesmen and Servicemen: Occupational vs. Ability-Group Scoring Keys." J Appl Psychol 26:543-62 Ag '42. * (PA 17:2461)

138. SARBIN, THEODORE R., AND ANDERSON, HEDWIN C. "A Preliminary Study of the Relation of Measured Interest Patterns and Occupation Dissatisfaction." Ed & Psychol Meas 2:23-36 Ja '42. * (PA 16:2476)

139. TAYLOR, KATHERINE VAN FRIDAGH. "The Reliability and Permanence of Vocational Interests of Adolescents." J Exp Ed 11:81-7 S '42. * (PA 17:1371)

140. TUSSING, LYLE. "An Investigation of the Possibilities of Measuring Personality Traits With the Strong Vocational Interest Blank." Ed & Psychol Meas 2:59-74 Ja '42. * (PA 16:2324)

141. BARNETTE, W. LESLIE, JR. "Interests of Business College Students: An Indirect Validation of the Strong Blank." J Appl Psychol 27:93-100 F '43. * (PA 17:2874)

142. BERDIE, RALPH F. "Factors Associated With Vocational Interests." J Ed Psychol 34:257-77 My '43. * (PA 18:859)

143. BERDIE, RALPH F. "Likes, Dislikes, and Vocational Interests." J Appl Psychol 27:180-9 Ap '43. * (PA 17:3565)

144. BORDIN, EDWARD S. "A Theory of Vocational Interests as Dynamic Phenomena." Ed & Psychol Meas 3:49-65 sp '43. * (PA 17:3240)

145. BREWER, JOHN M. "Classification of Items in Interest Inventories." Occupations 21:448-51 F '43. * (PA 17:2159)

146. KLUGMAN, SAMUEL F. "Tests Scores and Graduation." Occupations 21:389-93 Ja '43. * (PA 17:1354)

147. LORIMER, MARGARET W. The Strong Vocational Interest Blank as an Aid in Vocational Prognosis. Unpublished master's thesis, Columbia University, 1943.

148. STRONG, EDWARD K., JR. Vocational Interests of Men and Women. Stanford, Calif.: Stanford University Press, 1943. Pp. xxix, 746. $6.50. * (London: Oxford University Press. 40s.) (PA 18:313)

149. WITTENBORN, J. R.; TRIGGS, FRANCES ORALIND; AND FEDER, DANIEL D. "A Comparison of Interest Measurement by the Kuder Preference Record and the Strong Vocational Interest Blanks for Men and Women." Ed & Psychol Meas 3:239-57 au '43. * (PA 18:2614)

150. BERDIE, RALPH F. "Factors Related to Vocational Interests." Psychol B 41:137-57 Mr '44. * (PA 18:2558)

151. BERDIE, RALPH F. "The Prediction of College Achievement and Satisfaction." J Appl Psychol 28:239-45 Je '44. * (PA 18:3277)

152. CARTER, HAROLD D. Vocational Interests and Job Orientation: A Ten-Year Review. Applied Psychology Monographs of the American Association for Applied Psychology, No. 2. Stanford University, Calif.: Stanford University Press, May

1944. Pp. 85. Paper, lithotyped. * (London: Oxford University Press, 1944. 9s. 6d.) (PA 18:3616)

153. DUNLAP, JACK W., AND HARPER, BERTHA P. "Profiles of Interest Scores." J Higher Ed 15:159-60 Mr '44. * (PA 18:2568)

154. KUDER, G. FREDERIC. "Note on 'Classification of Items in Interest Inventories'." Occupations 22:484-7 My '44. * (PA 18:3294)

155. TRIGGS, FRANCES ORALIND. "A Further Comparison of Interest Measurement by the Kuder Preference Record and the Strong Vocational Interest Blank for Men." J Ed Res 37: 538-44 Mr '44. * (PA 18:3307)

156. BLUETT, CHARLES G. "Vocational Interests of Vocational Rehabilitation Officers." Occupations 24:25-32 O '45. * (PA 20:533)

157. LONG, LOUIS. "Relationship Between Interests and Abilities: A Study of the Strong Vocational Interest Blank and the Zyve Scientific Aptitude Test." J Appl Psychol 29:191-7 Je '45. * (PA 19:3175)

158. SEAGOE, MAY V. "Prognostic Tests and Teaching Success." J Ed Res 38:685-90 My '45. * (PA 19:3184)

159. SHULTZ, IRVIN T., AND BARNABAS, BENTLEY. "Testing for Leadership in Industry." Trans Kan Acad Sci 48:160-4 S '45. * (PA 20:896)

160. STRONG, EDWARD K., JR. "The Interests of Forest Service Men." Ed & Psychol Meas 5:157-71 su '45. * (PA 20:1243)

161. STRONG, EDWARD K., JR. "Interests of Public Administrators." Pub Personnel R 6:166-73 Jl '45. *

162. STRONG, EDWARD K., JR. "Weighted vs. Unit Scales." J Ed Psychol 36:193-216 Ap '45. * (PA 19:2379)

163. SUPER, DONALD E. "Strong's Vocational Interests of Men and Women: A Special Review." Psychol B 42:359-70 Je '45. *

164. TOWNSEND, AGATHA. "Achievement and Interest Ratings for Independent-School Boys," pp. 49-54. In 1945 Achievement Testing Program in Independent Schools and Supplementary Studies. Educational Records Bulletin, No. 43. New York: Educational Records Bureau, June 1945. Pp. xii, 68. Paper, lithotyped. $1.50. * (PA 19:3512)

165. TYLER, LEONA E. "Relationships Between Strong Vocational Interest Scores and Other Attitude and Personality Factors." J Appl Psychol 29:58-67 F '45. * (PA 19:1729)

166. EVANS, CHESTER EUGENE. Interrelations of Evidences of Vocational Interest. Unpublished doctor's thesis, Ohio State University, 1946. (Abstracts of Dissertations . . . Summer Quarter 1945-46, 1946, pp. 51-7.)

167. FLEMMING, EDWIN G., AND FLEMMING, CECILE WHITE. "A Qualitative Approach to the Problem of Improving Selection of Salesmen by Psychological Tests." J Psychol 21:127-50 Ja '46. * (PA 20:1636)

168. PATERSON, DONALD G. "Vocational Interest Inventories in Selection." Occupations 25:152-3 D '46. * (PA 21:1286)

169. STRONG, EDWARD K., JR. "Interest of Senior and Junior Public Administrators." J Appl Psychol 30:55-71 F '46. * (PA 20:2465)

170. TOWNSEND, AGATHA. "Academic Aptitude and Interest Ratings for Independent-School Pupils," pp. 51-7. In 1945 Fall Testing Program in Independent Schools and Supplementary Studies. Educational Records Bulletin, No. 44. New York: Educational Records Bureau, January 1946. Pp. xiii, 66. Paper, lithotyped. $1.00. * (PA 20:2105)

171. BORDIN, EDWARD S. "Relative Correspondence of Professed Interests to Kuder and Strong Interest Test Scores." Abstract. Am Psychol 2:293 Ag '47. * (PA 21:4610, title only)

172. KENDALL, WILLIAM E. "The Occupational Level Scale of the Strong Vocational Interest Blank for Men." J Appl Psychol 31:283-7 Je '47. * (PA 21:4128)

173. STEFFLRE, BUFORD. "The Reading Difficulty of Interest Inventories." Occupations 26:95-6 N '47. * (PA 22:1722)

174. STRONG, EDWARD K., JR. "Differences in Interests Among Public Administrators." J Appl Psychol 31:18-38 F '47. * (PA 21:2475)

175. SUPER, DONALD E. "Vocational Interests and Vocational Choice: Present Knowledge and Future Research in Their Relationships." Ed & Psychol Meas 7:375-83 au '47. * (PA 22:3502)

For reviews by Harold D. Carter, John G. Darley, and N. W. Morton, see 38:1178 and 40:1680. For related reviews, see 648, 650, and 652.

[648]

★[Re Vocational Interest Blank for Men.] DARLEY, JOHN G. Clinical Aspects and Interpretation of the Strong Vocational Interest Blank. New York: Psychological Corporation, 1941. Pp. 72. Paper. $1.20. * (PA 16:328)

J Ed Psychol 33:556-7 O '42. Bertha Peterson Harper. * This well-written little book should serve as an informative source not only for the beginning student in this branch of psychology but also for the more experienced clinician. * Sound advice is provided those desiring to do actual counselling on vocational interest problems in a list of specific "do's" and "dont's" with helpful explanatory discussion. Darley finds that in vocational interviews it is far more effective in most cases to work "through the pattern analysis procedures and eventually arrive at the specific high letter grade, as counselling progresses." The author's suggestions are given more concrete form in the presentation of a number of well-chosen illustrative cases; he also treats the case with no primary interest pattern. * Darley's concluding contribution in this monograph is a challenging list of problems that remain to be investigated in the field. Psychologists should find this work a most worth while and useful addition to the literature on the topic of interest measurement.

Occupations 20:240–1 D '41. Donald E. Super. This is the type of book about which the reviewer wants to write, not a mere review, but another book. It says so many things which should have been said some time ago, so many of the things that one has wanted to say oneself, and it says them so well that one is tempted to say them over again in his review. * an attempt to summarize extended clinical experience with....Strong's Vocational Interest Blank * an extremely important book. Darley has taken time not only to record his clinical observations, but also to quantify his data whenever possible. Many users of Strong's Blank have made observations similar to many of Darley's, and some have made quantitative studies of specific questions; but few have organized their material so well for other workers. * four contributions will be noted. First, and perhaps most important, is the analysis of occupational scores according to occupational families. * Darley has taken this type of analysis further than other users of Strong's Blank, and has included several statistical analyses of this promising interpretive approach. A second important contribution is the chapter on the principles of counseling on the basis of Strong's Blank. All counselors, especially those with relatively little counseling experience, would do well to read and ponder these suggestions for test interpretation in the interview. The origin and development of interests are considered, the conclusion being that interests are the outgrowth of personality. Too little evidence is as yet available, but the suggestions are worth while. The clinical syndromes which Darley describes are evidence of the type which is needed and should be helpful to practical counselors. Some interesting illustrative cases are included, together with a discussion of cases with no primary interest pattern. Here, as in the discussion of other topics, Darley has pointed to challenging and important research problems and has given useful suggestions for present practice. All in all, the monograph is a valuable illustration of the contribution which can be made by the technician-counselor; it is to be hoped that soon, more and longer books of this type will be available to guide the practicing counselor in the use of his most valuable tools.

[649]
Vocational Interest Blank for Women, Revised. Women ages 17 and older; 1933–47; the 1947 revision replaces Forms WA (for women who have been out of school several years) and Form WB (for students); IBM; Form W; scoring scales are available for masculinity-femininity and 24 occupations : artist, author, buyer, dentist, dietician, housewife, lawyer, laboratory technician, librarian, life insurance saleswoman, nurse, occupational therapist, office worker, physician, psychologist, social worker, stenographer-secretary, teacher in elementary grades, teacher of English in high school, teacher of home economics in high school, teacher of mathematics and physical sciences in high school, teacher of physical education in high school, teacher of social sciences in high school, and Y.W.C.A. secretary; $2 per 25; 1¢ per report blank; $1 per scoring scale; 2 to 9 scales, 80¢ each; 10 or more scales, 70¢ each; 75¢ per 25 machine-scorable answer sheets; 75¢ per 25 answer sheets for use with Hankes Scoring Machine; 15¢ per specimen set; nontimed (30-60) minutes; Edward K. Strong, Jr.; Stanford University Press.

REFERENCES

1-9. See 40:1681.
10. BROOKS, ESTHER. "The Value of Psychological Testing." Am J Nursing 37:885-90 Ag '37. *
11. ALTENEDER, LOUISE E. The Value of Intelligence, Personality, and Vocational-Interest Tests in a Guidance Program. Unpublished doctor's thesis, New York University, 1938. Pp. 130. (Abstracts of Theses . . . [School of Education] 1938, pp. 41-4.)
12. SEDER, MARGARET. "Vocational Interest Patterns of Professional Women." Abstract. Psychol B 35:643 N '38. * (PA 13:1648, title only)
13. DUFFY, ELIZABETH, AND CRISSY, W. J. E. "Values Scores in Predicting Vocational Interest Scores and College Grades." Abstract. Psychol B 36:616-7 O '39. * (PA 14:588, title only)
14. GILKINSON, HOWARD, AND KNOWER, FRANKLIN H. Psychological Studies of Individual Differences Among Students of Speech. Minneapolis, Minn.: Department of Speech, University of Minnesota, June 1939. Pp. iii, 196. Paper, mimeographed. Gratis. *
15. HILGARD, JOSEPHINE R. "Strong Vocational Interest Scores and Completion of Training in a School of Nursing." Abstract. Psychol B 36:646 O '39. * (PA 14:505, title only)
16. ALTENEDER, LOUISE E. "The Value of Intelligence, Personality, and Vocational Interest Tests in a Guidance Program." J Ed Psychol 31:449-59 S '40. * (PA 15:1480)
17. BEDELL, RALPH. "Scoring Weighted Multiple Keyed Tests on the IBM Counting Sorter." Psychometrika 5:195-201 S '40. * (PA 15:565)
17a. BURGEMEISTER, BESSIE B. The Permanence of Interests of Women College Students: A Study in Personality Development. Archives of Psychology, No. 255. Washington, D. C.: American Psychological Association, Inc., July 1940. Pp. 59. Paper. $1.00. * (PA 15:3042)

18. GERNES, ELIZABETH. A Factorial Analysis of Selected Items of the Strong Vocational Interest Blank for Women. Unpublished doctor's thesis, University of Nebraska, 1940. (Abstracts of Doctoral Dissertations . . . , 1940, pp. 66-70.)
19. BEDELL, RALPH. "The Relationship Between Self-Estimated and Measured Vocational Interests." J Appl Psychol 25:59-66 F '41. * (PA 15:3136)
20. HIGGINBOTTOM, ARTHUR RAYMOND. A Scale for Measuring Women's Interest in a Career. Unpublished master's thesis, Clark University, 1941. (Abstracts of Dissertations . . . 1941, pp. 185-7.)
20a. PETERSON, BERTHA M., AND DUNLAP, JACK W. "Derivation and Application of a Unit Scoring System for the Strong Vocational Interest Blank for Women." Abstract. Psychol B 38:607 Jl '41. * (PA 15:5383, title only)
21. ACHAUER, M. P. The Analysis of Vocational Interests of Teachers College Freshmen and Senior Women and Relationship of Background Experiences to These Interests. Unpublished doctor's thesis, University of Nebraska, 1942.
22. ANDREWS, MARGARET E. "The Relationship Between Reading Ability and Interest Scores." J Ed Psychol 33:138-43 F '42. * (PA 16:3761)
23. COLLINS, PATRICIA J. "The Development of a Scoring Key on the Strong Vocational Interest Inventory for Women Teachers of Physical Education." Res Q 13:156-65 My '42. * (PA 17:940)
24. HARPER, BERTHA P., AND DUNLAP, JACK W. "Derivation and Application of a Unit Scoring System for the Strong Vocational Interest Blank for Women." Psychometrika 7:289-95 D '42. * (PA 17:1348)
25. LALEGER, GRACE ELIZABETH. The Vocational Interests of High School Girls: As Inventoried by the Strong and Manson Blanks. Columbia University, Teachers College, Contributions to Education, No. 857. Harry D. Kitson, faculty sponsor. New York: Bureau of Publications, the College, 1942. Pp. vii, 102. $1.60. * (PA 16:5023)
26. MERCER, MARGARET. "A Study of Interest Patterns of Succesful and Unsuccessful Home Economics Students Entering College With Similar Achievement and Aptitude." J Appl Psychol 26:738-53 D '42. * (PA 17:2497)
27. SKODAK, MARIE, AND CRISSEY, ORLO L. "Stated Vocational Aims and Strong Interest Test Scores of High School Senior Girls." J Appl Psychol 26:64-74 F '42. * (PA 16:2478)
28. TAYLOR, K. VAN F. The Reliability and Permanence of the Vocational Interests of Adolescents. Unpublished doctor's thesis, University of California, 1942.
29. TAYLOR, KATHERINE VAN FRIDAGH. "The Reliability and Permanence of Vocational Interests of Adolescents." J Exp Ed 11:81-7 S '42. * (PA 17:1371)
30. TAYLOR, KATHERINE V. F., AND CARTER, HAROLD D. "Retest Consistency of Vocational Interest Patterns of High-School Girls." J Consult Psychol 6:95-101 Mr-Ap '42. * (PA 16:2482)
31. CRIDER, BLAKE. "A School of Nursing Selection Program." J Appl Psychol 27:452-7 O '43. * (PA 18:281)
32. STRONG, EDWARD K., JR. Vocational Interests of Men and Women. Stanford University, Calif.: Stanford University Press, 1943. Pp. xxix, 746. $6.50. * (London: Oxford University Press. 40s.) (PA 18:313)
33. CARTER, HAROLD D. Vocational Interests and Job Orientation: A Ten-Year Review. Applied Psychology Monographs of the American Association for Applied Psychology, No. 2. Stanford University, Calif.: Stanford University Press, May 1944. Pp. 85. Paper, lithotyped. $1.50. * (London: Oxford University Press, 1944. 9s. 6d.) (PA 18:3616)
34. CISNEY, H. N. The Stability of Vocational Interest Scores During the High School Period. Unpublished doctor's thesis, University of Michigan, 1944.
35. KLUGMAN, SAMUEL F. "Test Scores for Clerical Aptitude and Interests Before and After a Year of Schooling." J Genetic Psychol 65:89-96 S '44. * (PA 19:550)
36. KOEPKE, HAROLD FREDERICK. A Study of the Interest Patterns of Business Education Teachers in Public Secondary Schools. Unpublished doctor's thesis, University of Iowa, 1944.
37. TRIGGS, FRANCES ORALIND. "A Further Comparison of Interest Measurement by the Kuder Preference Record and the Strong Vocational Interest Blank for Women." J Ed Res 38: 193-200 N '44. * (PA 19:1352)
38. WIGHTWICK, M. IRENE. "The Function of Interest in Vocational Choice." J Am Assn Col Reg 19:231-7 Ja '44. *
39. BARRETT, DOROTHY M. "Aptitude and Interest Patterns of Art Majors in a Liberal Arts College." J Appl Psychol 29: 483-92 D '45. * (PA 20:1248)
40. KLUGMAN, SAMUEL F. "The Effect of Schooling Upon the Relationship Between Clerical Aptitude and Interests." J Genetic Psychol 66:255-8 Je '45. * (PA 19:3499)
41. KLUGMAN, SAMUEL F. "Permanence of Clerical Interests in Relation to Age and Various Abilities." J Social Psychol 21:115-20 F '45. * (PA 19:1574)
42. SEAGOE, MAY V. "Permanence of Interest in Teaching." J Ed Res 38:678-84 My '45. * (PA 19:3183)
43. SEAGOE, MAY V. "Prognostic Tests and Teaching Success." J Ed Res 38:685-90 My '45. * (PA 19:3184)
44. WIGHTWICK, M. IRENE. Vocational Interest Patterns: A Developmental Study of a Group of College Women. Columbia University, Teachers College, Contributions to Education, No. 900. Ruth Strang, faculty sponsor. New York: Bureau of Publications, the College, 1945. Pp. vii, 231. Out of print. * (PA 19:3190)

45. CAWLEY, ANNE MARY. "A Study of the Vocational Interest Trends of Secondary School and College Women." *Genetic Psychol Monogr* 35:185-247 My '47. * (*PA* 22:450)

Gwendolen Schneidler Dickson, Chief, Educational Counseling Division, Veterans Administration, Washington, D. C. [Review of Form WA.] The ingenious technique which Dr. Strong has developed to obtain an individual's expressions of likes and dislikes and then to compare these responses with the distinctive patterns of interest which have been found to be characteristic of various occupational groups has been more effective when applied to men than to women. Whatever the reasons may be, experience with this inventory shows that many young women do not possess distinctive patterns of likes and dislikes, as measured by this test, which are characteristic of specific occupational groups of women, such as physicians, social workers, authors, librarians, artists, and lawyers. Instead, their interests are not differentiated from those of the general population of women, of housewives, and of occupational groups which do not possess distinctive interest patterns, such as stenographers, clerical workers, nurses and grade school teachers. Because of these limitations, the vocational counseling of young women with the aid of this test is sometimes more difficult than the counseling of young men. This does not mean, however, that the counselor should not attempt to use this instrument to discover the existence of such well-developed interest patterns as do occasionally appear in young women.

Despite these limitations and others which have been pointed out by the test author and previous reviewers, this test is one of the best tools available to counselors for attempting to determine objectively the vocational interests of women. It should be used with care and clinical judgment and preferably in conjunction with another test of interest such as the *Kuder Preference Record*, which, by requiring expressions of preferences for activities, yields scores on several general interest dimensions which are as distinctive and reliable for women as they are for men.

For reviews by John G. Darley and Ruth Strang, see 40:1681 and 38:1179. For related reviews, see 650 and 652.

[650]

★[*Re* Vocational Interest Blanks for Men and Women.] CARTER, HAROLD D. Vocational Interests and Job Orientation: A Ten-Year Review. Applied Psychology Monographs of the American Association for Applied Psychology, No. 2. Stanford University, Calif.: Stanford University Press, May 1944. Pp. 85. Paper, lithotyped. $1.50. * (London: Oxford University Press, 1944. 9s. 6d.) (*PA* 18:3616)

Pub Personnel R 5:247 O '44. Edward B. Greene. * by far the most readable and authoritative work of its size that has come to hand on this subject. It is entirely devoted to examining the most important pieces of research in relation to vocational interests which have been published during the last ten years. It contains no case histories or illustrative tables, but it has documented references to 262 technical articles. The author's knowledge and technical adequacy are probably second to none in this field. He and his associates have contributed important theories and facts over a period of 12 years. * divided into eight chapters of which the most important seem to be the second, "Nature of Concepts"; the fifth, "Validity and General Usefulness of Available Measures of Vocational Interests"; the seventh, "Individual Differences in Interests"; and the eighth, "The Problem of Vocational Choice" * The book is very much needed to counteract the present high-pressure sales activity of those who claim that they can contribute greatly to the selection of industrial or civil service workers, sales managers, or executives by a standard set of questions dealing with interests or emotional adjustments. At present the best interest questionnaires are about as "reliable" as the best general tests of intelligence. Interest inventories are useful "in the prediction of both educational choice and vocational choice. They are much less useful in predicting educational success or vocational success. . . . No objective definition of success seems to stand the strain of comparison of persons in various occupations."

[651]

★[*Re* Vocational Interest Blanks for Men and Women.] Hankes' Answer Sheet for Vocational Interest Blank. The answer sheets must be scored on a special scoring machine developed by E. J. Hankes and owned by Engineers Northwest; 1-49 copies, 3¢ each; 50-99, 2¾¢ each; 100-499, 2½¢ each; 500-999, 2¼¢ each; 1000 and over, 2¢ each; 70¢ for scoring one Hankes' Answer Sheet (Men are scored for 42 scales, no group scales, and women for 19 scales) plus 10¢ for each order of 5 tests or less; 90¢ for scoring directly from test booklet; 80¢ for scoring from IBM answer sheets; E. J. Hankes; Engineers Northwest.

[652]

★[*Re* Vocational Interest Blanks for Men and Women.] STRONG, EDWARD K., JR. Vocational Interests of Men and Women. Stanford University,

Calif.: Stanford University Press, 1943. Pp. xxix, 746. $6.50. * (London: Oxford University Press. 40s.) (PA 18:313)

Am J Sociol 49:378 Ja '44. Robert J. Havighurst. * Of most interest to sociologists are Strong's findings on differences of interest patterns between various social groups. *

Ed Res B 24:136 My 16 '45. William H. Stone. * The presentation is well organized to meet the needs both of those readers who want only summaries of findings and of those who are interested in the technicalities of statistical research employed. * one is not likely to overestimate the importance of this volume both to education and to guidance.

J Appl Psychol 28:532–4 D '44. John G. Darley. * [this book] is not easy reading, but it is essential reading for those who must understand the individual's motivating forces, of which interest is a significant one * While [the book's] organization seems straightforward and logical, it has occasionally led to some confusion and duplication in specific topics. For example, the topic of classifying occupations into families appears in Chapters Three, Eight, Ten, Fourteen and Twenty-two. Parallel to this, it is disconcerting to find early references to tables and discussions occurring much later in the book, as in the case of the text and many footnotes in the chapters comprising Part one. The author, by virtue of the amount and scope of his empiric data, is in the embarrassing position of having planted so many trees that he may not recognize the size and shape of his forest. The task of reporting the sheer number of researches, with the ramifications of the various studies, precludes the broad generalizations and summary hypotheses one might wish to see. This criticism, however, should not be allowed to obscure the fact that in no other source can the research worker or clinician find so much that is provocative, essential, and significant in the field of interest measurement. The task of the reviewer and reader is merely made more difficult by the close attention required to encompass all that the author has discussed. * These comments do not do full justice to the amount of material Dr. Strong has assembled, nor to the dispassionate and detached manner in which he presents it. One could almost wish he had overgeneralized his interpretations or been guilty of special pleading, so that the reviewer could denounce and defend with a fine show of critical skill. But

the book almost defies criticism first because it is a genuine and long-needed contribution to an important area of research and second because it deals almost entirely with an overwhelming mass of empirically derived data that speaks for itself over the entire range of problems in interest measurement. If the research that will follow after this volume is not significant and productive, it will be only because research workers have failed to study and understand the yeoman service Dr. Strong has performed for applied psychology.

J Consult Psychol 8:51–2 Ja-F '44. Harold D. Carter. * The presentation is such as to interest serious students of counseling, especially teachers, vocational advisors, and psychologists concerned with the problems of personality, motivation, and happiness. Strong reports penetrating research on a vital problem. * well written and attractively arranged * It lays a wealth of data before the reader, facilitating his work by means of complete, accurate, and convenient arrangements of references, index, and tables. The general style and content of the book will combine to make it attractive to a wide audience. Strong has accepted the contributions of other workers enthusiastically but critically, has assimilated them, and himself has grown in the process. Here he presents the results of research, including his own, with ready admission of limitations, with impersonal scientific emphasis upon the truth, and with a positive and constructive attitude. Stimulating suggestions for further research are numerous, and are to be found stated explicitly or contained implicitly in nearly every chapter. The reviewer accepts all the major conclusions presented by Strong in this book as true and significant. It is a pleasure to read a book in which the viewpoints are so closely in accord with the facts gathered from an imposing array of significant publications. Teachers in courses on general, developmental, social, educational, and applied psychology will find Strong's *Vocational Interests of Men and Women* a valuable reference or source book. It deserves to be read and discussed by every psychologist and guidance worker. Contributions of such importance appear but rarely.

J Ed Psychol 35:186–8 Mr '44. Stephen M. Corey. * Strong's entire argument bears upon two different problems involved in interest measurement: first, the differentiation of occupational groups; and, second, assigning individuals to one or more groups depending upon their interest scores. The author believes that his interest scale does both of these tasks reasonably satisfactorily. The reliability of the instrument, of course, has been well established, and the coefficients reported usually fall between .85 and .90. Even a reliability of this magnitude, however, leaves much to be desired when the scale is used for individual prognosis. Many questions of fundamental importance in appraising the interest inventory were answered by correlation data. * The reviewer at times was dissatisfied with the interpretation of coefficients of a certain magnitude. For example, when the author described the relationship between scores on his interest inventory and measures of intelligence as being about the magnitude of .40 (p. 49) the contention was that this represented a slight degree of association. Later on it was contended that a correlation of .73 was usually considered a high coefficient. Any criticism of this sort is not so serious as it might be in view of the fact that the author always gave the raw correlation so that a careful reader could make his own interpretation. * the evidence is clear that an adult can, if he wishes, check those interests, which will give him a high rating on a desired occupation (p. 686 f.). Strong's attitude toward this problem is expressed by the contention that "under normal conditions there is little or no apparent temptation to fudge." (sic) (p. 687). The argument behind this hope was not too convincing to the reviewer. It reminded him again of the great gap that exists between highly refined psychological tests like Strong's questionnaire and the measuring instruments that are employed by the physical scientists. The latter would have little confidence in a scale that would let a man weigh what he wanted to weigh even if under most circumstances men would want to know the truth (?) about their *avoir du pois.* The student who wants to bring himself abreast of an important area which has not been summarized since Fryer's *Measurement of Interests,* 1931, will find Strong's volume indispensable. Not only is it a 750-page storehouse of research data, but it also is full of hypotheses and questions which will be most provocative to research students in the field.

Occupational Psychol 18:148–52 Jl '44. Charles S. Myers. * Interests in occupations are, for Dr. Strong, determinable by likes, in-

differences and dislikes. He disarms criticism as to the psychological identity of "interests" with "liking" by stating that his aim has always been a practical one in the "atmosphere of applied psychology. . . . Some 'pure' psychologists," he naïvely suggests, "should investigate experimentally the nature of interests and how they develop in early life" (p. viii). Although he devotes an entire chapter to the nature of interests, perhaps his position is not so different from that of the testers of intelligence: we may not know enough to define its nature, but we may nevertheless contrive to assess it, and we may differentiate various kinds of it, with practical profit. * The candidate for guidance is required—surely unnaturally—to mark each of 100 occupations enumerated on the Blank with an L, I or D, according as he likes, is indifferent to, or dislikes each of these hundred occupations. But this Blank is by no means confined to "interests" nor to "occupations." Of the 400 items to be checked therein, only 100 relate to occupations, as such. * a large number of Dr. Strong's conclusions rest on the acceptance of the statistical manipulations to which he submits his data. Sometimes he seems to be aware of the difficulties of such acceptance. Thus in endeavouring to assess, and to establish a belief in, the permanence of late adolescent and adult interests, he obtains a correlation of 0.75 in the case of college seniors with a second scoring obtained from them ten years later. But, as Dr. Strong observes, "it must not be overlooked that these measures represent the average person—for some, permanence is much greater, and for some it is much less. We can never be certain, in the case of any one individual, that his interests will be as permanent as these figures suggest. . . ." (p. 51). Despite this caution Dr. Strong is prepared only to concede that "permanence of intelligence-test scores is somewhat greater than for interest-test scores" (p. 359). * Many would doubt the value, for any given occupation, of an average score on "interests," character and temperamental qualities thus calculated from several hundreds say of physicians (presumably including surgeons, so different in mental make-up!). They would also doubt whether interests, etc., do not notably change as, say, a medical student passes through his six or more student professional years. And they would doubt whether a college youth's "interests" inducing him to enter on a given career are associated with adequate knowledge of what will later be required of him and of what will be required of him in the other 99 listed occupations. Occasionally Dr. Strong anticipates such objections. Thus—rather surprisingly—he warns us "No one should blindly accept the guidance indicated by the interest test until he has ascertained what is required in the indicated occupation and has determined that he has the abilities and interests required for the work" (p. 55). Yet his great faith in his life's work persists unabated. For he continues—"Knowledge of one's interest score makes such a determination possible, for now one or only a few occupations need be investigated instead of all of them." * To estimate the validity of predictions....the criterion adopted by Dr. Strong is that of being still engaged in the occupation at the time of the follow-up. No attempt is made directly to ascertain either efficiency or happiness at the work. Thus the lowest criterion is chosen—that of discharge from the work in the case of inefficiency or of leaving in the case of discontent. * Dr. Strong presents an elaborate table of 703 inter-correlations between 38 occupations on the surely insecure basis of the interest scores of 285 college seniors on pairs of occupational scales. Thus he is led to classify 36 of these occupations into eleven groups, four of which, however, contain only one occupation each. One of these groups consists of artist, psychologist, architect, physician and dentist. We may well wonder why physicians "score most like artists," overlapping in scores by 37 per cent, "whereas accountants and bankers overlap with artists by only 7 and 8 per cent, respectively" (p. 110). More reasonably, mathematician, physicist, engineer and chemist form another group; and lawyer, author-journalist, and advertising man form yet another group. On the other hand, another strange group consists of aviator, farmer, carpenter, printer, mathematics-science teacher, policeman and forest service. What can there be here psychologically in common? * Enough has been said to confirm the description of its author on the paper cover as "the man who has done more than anyone else to develop [along special lines] the practical application of vocational-interest testing." But how far the lines on which he has proceeded will prove to be of permanent value must be left for the future to decide. Statistical methods, even when justified statistically, are far

from being always justified psychologically. Certainly, according to the statistical proofs of their validity adduced by Dr. Strong, his methods seem to work moderately well, *en masse*. They have the advantage of objectivity and may well have advantages for group-testing when the time available for vocational guidance and personnel selection is short, even although his scheme is a lengthy and expensive way of arriving at the information procured, and however imperfect that information may be from the psychological standpoint. The value of responses to questionnaires of this type is greatly enhanced if they are regarded as providing a basis for later discussion between the individual applicant and his vocational adviser. And the value of such questions themselves arises partly from the fact that they can hardly fail to make the applicant think.

Occupations 22:455 Ap '44. Donald E. Super. Dr. Strong's work in the measurement of vocational interests has for nearly twenty years been a landmark in the field of vocational testing, and a guidepost for vocational counselors. Any competent publication which throws light on the nature of vocational interests and on the use of Strong's Blank is therefore likely to be of considerable interest to all counselors who are alert for opportunities to improve their insight and techniques. When the publication is by Dr. Strong himself, when it deals in detail with the numerous investigations of the nature and measurement of interests which have been completed during the past twenty years, and when it is written in a clear and easily read style, it becomes a "must" book for every vocational counselor's library. * The organization of the book seems confused when the table of contents is first studied. This is primarily a typographical problem, however, resulting from the number of subheadings. These make the book more easily used, and need not discourage the reader. Although full of tables and figures, the material is clearly and interestingly presented. Any college graduate should be able to follow the argument and understand the conclusions. Certainly anyone qualified to use Strong's Interest Blank should be able to read the book with ease, and everyone who uses the test or any other interest test should read it carefully and with considerable profit. Although Dr. Strong's treatment of interest testing is broad and by no means limited to his own work, there are some important omissions. * Dr. Strong brings out some hitherto neglected facts on the nature of interests. One of these is the basic similarity of interests regardless of occupation, age, or sex; group differences are important, but limited in range. Another is the importance of occupational or socio-economic level, and the possibility of measuring vocational interests at the lower levels by taking the level into account. The author is to be congratulated on the thoroughness with which he has studied his test and the factors which it measures, and on the clarity and detail in which he presents his findings. It is a sign of maturity in vocational testing that such books are beginning to appear.

Prison World 8:35 S-O '46. * Has considerable and illuminating sections on abilities and achievement as related to interests, differentiation of occupations, guidance problems and procedures, differentiation of superior and inferior members of a group, skilled trades, etc.

Psychol B 42:359-70 Je '45. Donald E. Super. * Strong has brought together the results of nearly twenty years of work with his *Vocational Interest Blank.* Although it deals largely and at length with his work on his test, the book also brings together the results of other studies using his interest inventory and of work with the inventories to which his is related. Other instruments for the inventorying of interests are considered when work with them throws additional light on problems which Strong considers pertinent, but not otherwise: for example, the *Kuder Preference Record* is barely mentioned, the *Cleeton Inventory* not at all. Despite recent important work with information tests of interest, interest tests, as contrasted with inventories, are dismissed in less than three pages in which the approaches of Burtt, Flanagan, Super, and Wyman are briefly discussed, and the rather different approaches of R. B. Cattell and E. B. Greene are not mentioned. Even some studies with Strong's inventory are excluded, as in the case of the reviewer's investigation of the relationships of vocational and avocational interests, when they do not seem to contribute directly to the main currents of the book. * Strong has wisely devoted the first hundred pages to a review of the development, nature, and use of the test, and has reserved for the last six hundred pages the detailed discussion of matters covered more generally at first. Thus the clinician or consultant who uses the test in his regular work and who is interested only in understanding the inventory as a diagnostic or predictive instrument can, with occasional reference to later sections, quickly read the relevant part of the book: the style is clear and concise, the language not too technical, and the presentation suitable for those who have not specialized in measurement. * when, on page 414, Strong rejects the statistical combination of test scores, he is guilty of a basic inconsistency. If his inventory technique, consisting of a statistical summation of interests in specific occupations and activities, provides useful information not made available by a clinical study of responses to the specific items in the inventory, why should not a statistical summation of scores on the interest scales provide data as useful as the clinical study of those test scores? This suggestion of the reviewer's should not be taken as a suggestion that the clinical study of the scale scores is not valuable: it is, and so is the study of responses to specific items in the inventory, as Shellow has reported. Knowing the relative physicist and physician scores of an embryo psychologist, for example, could be useful in deciding between emphases in experimental and clinical psychology. But a statistical combination of these test scores could, as Strong's own arguments for the consideration of primary, secondary, and tertiary interests imply (432-448), provide an even more valid interest score for any given occupation. As Strong points out, it is dangerous to recommend an occupation on the basis of a high score in that occupation alone. This score, he states, should be supported by high scores in related occupations. Why not indicate this support by a combination of scores on related occupations? * In spite of the few defects discussed....Strong's work shows a remarkable freedom from statistical weaknesses, especially in view of the long period over which it was spread and the variety and complexity of the problems studied. * Strong and his publishers, to whom applied psychologists are becoming increasingly indebted, have done an excellent job of preparing the manuscript and putting it into print. The table of contents is well organized and very detailed, the topic headings are numerous and meaningful, the index adequate and accurate. In view of the vast amount of material that has been correctly reproduced in this lengthy volume, it seems like the act of a petty critic to point out a few errors that have been noted. * The volume is

Vocational Interest Blanks for Men and Women

a gold mine for students in search of thesis topics. But one cannot hope to deal adequately with a classic in a single review, especially when the subject of the book is twenty years of research. If some idea of the importance of the work has been conveyed, if interest has been fostered in a few problems, and if the reader has been stimulated to a thoughtful study of Strong's book, this review has accomplished its purpose.

Psychometrika 9:145–6 Je '44. G. Frederic Kuder. The *Strong Vocational Interest Blank* has made important history in the field of measurement. Since the appearance of the first form in 1927, the test has probably been the subject of more investigation and research than any other single test. And this research has been largely conducted or inspired by Strong himself. * the field of the measurement of interests through use of the Strong *Vocational Interest Blank* is covered systematically, completely, and in an interesting style. The data are reported in an impartial vein; the con's as well as the pro's bearing upon the various procedures used by Strong are reported in fine good humor. The reader may not always agree with the conclusions reached by Strong, but in any case he must recognize that the book is a model of scientific reporting. No one can consider himself abreast of the interest field if he is not familiar with the contents of this book. One fundamental point, perhaps, deserves particular mention. Thurstone's application of factor analysis to Strong's interest scales in 1931 pointed to the possibility of a new technique in obtaining scores for various occupations. Since Thurstone demonstrated that the variance of the occupational scores could be almost entirely accounted for by four factors, it followed logically that formulas could be developed by multiple correlation for obtaining occupational scores from measures of these four factors or from any set of a few selected measures which would account for the variance of all the scales. The actual scoring could then be reduced to the fundamental measures used. Later research by Strong, using more scales, increased the number of factors involved, but the implication of the findings is the same. It has been a matter of surprise to some people in the field that Strong has not followed up this lead. Strong's reasons for not doing so, as given in his book, are not convincing. The first and less important reason is that "occupational scores can be obtained by machine scoring with no less trouble than with calculations involving multiple correlations." I am inclined to doubt this assertion. Strong is comparing a streamlined scoring method done on a mass production basis with a straight computing machine job of calculating scores using regression weights. There is no reason why the application of a standard series of weights can not also be streamlined and done on a mass production basis. Strong's other reason is by far the more important, since it concerns validity. Strong cites Dwyer's data to the effect that "the multiple correlation scores will correlate '.80 or better' in only the majority of cases with the results obtained by use of occupational scales." At this point we should stop to consider the purpose of the scales. If one particular scoring method is taken as the criterion, then we are doomed to labor in vain to develop a more valid method, for we can not hope to improve on what is implicitly assumed to be perfect to begin with. A more logical basis of judgment appears to be to determine which method is more successful in differentiating those in an occupation from men-in-general. It has not been demonstrated that such differentiation is accomplished better by scoring items than by assigning multiple regression weights * to a few selected measures which account for most of the interest variance in the occupations studied. Scores obtained by the latter procedure should be more valid than those obtained by the item-scoring method. Use of the item-scoring method carried no assurance that the optimal weight is given to each factor, since the number of items representing each factor is not controlled and item intercorrelations are not allowed for in determining item weights. Theoretically, it is impossible for an occupational scale obtained by Strong's method to differentiate better than weighted selected measures, if the measures used account for all the variance of the occupational scales. There is no reason to believe that the theoretical indication will not be borne out by the evidence, when obtained.

Pub Personnel R 5:114–5 Ap '44. C. L. Shartle. * a valuable piece of work which should be read, at least in part, by persons in the personnel and vocational guidance field, and should be read in detail by those who have

---

* It should be noted that these regression weights must be developed through use of the original data from the various occupational groups, and *not* by using the occupational scale scores as criteria in developing the formulas.

Vocational Interest Blanks for Men and Women

problems in regard to the measurement of interest.

[653]

Vocational Interest Schedule. Grades 13-16; 1935–39; IBM; 1 form; replaced in 1947 by the *Thurstone Interest Schedule* (*see* 646); nontimed (10-30) minutes; L. L. Thurstone; Psychological Corporation.

REFERENCES

1-4. *See* 40:1683.
5. LENTZ, THEO. F. "The Opinionnaire Technique in Vocational Guidance." Abstract. *Psychol B* 37:451 Jl '40. * (*PA* 14:5712, title only)
6. REED, HOMER B. "The Relation of Bernreuter Personality and Thurstone Vocational Interest Scores to Each Other and to Scholastic and Mechanical Achievement." Abstract. *Psychol B* 37:449-50 Jl '40. * (*PA* 14:5716, title only)
7. WICKERT, FREDERIC. "The Interrelationships of Some General and Specific Preferences." *J Social Psychol* 11:275-302 My '40. * (*PA* 14:5149)
8. GORDON, HANS C., AND HERKNESS, WALTER W., JR. "Pupils Appraise Vocational Interest Blanks." *Occupations* 20:100-2 N '41. * (*PA* 16:757)
9. REED, HOMER B. "The Place of the Bernreuter Personality, Stenquist Mechanical Aptitude, and Thurstone Vocational Interest Tests in College Entrance Tests." *J Appl Psychol* 25:528-34 O '41. * Abstract *Psychol B* 38:711 O '41. * (*PA* 16:1205)
10. BRIGGS, LESLIE. "The Thurstone Vocational Interest Schedule and Students' Actual Vocational Choices." *Trans Kans Acad Sci* 45:272-3 '42. * (*PA* 17:1708)
11. GORDON, HANS C., AND HERKNESS, WALTER W., JR. "Do Vocational Interest Questionnaires Yield Consistent Results?" *Occupations* 20:424-9 Mr '42. * (*PA* 16:2059)
12. JENSEN, MILTON B., AND ROTTER, JULIAN B. "The Value of Thirteen Psychological Tests in Officer Candidate Screening." *J Appl Psychol* 31:312-22 Je '47. * (*PA* 21:4107)

Donald E. Super, Associate Professor of Education, Teachers College, Columbia University, New York, New York. This interest inventory has been reprinted in a new form to make possible the reproduction of the blank as a part of an IBM answer sheet. This makes it more economical in every respect than the original four-page blank with large stencils. Unfortunately this change in format represents the sum total of progress that has taken place in the development of Thurstone's *Vocational Interest Schedule* since the original work was done. At that time it was an important contribution to the field because it illustrated and stimulated the factorial approach to the study and measurement of vocational interests; as an experimental instrument for use in research it had a place in the vocational psychologist's kit.

During the 12 years that have elapsed since the first publication of the schedule, little research has been done with it. Those who were challenged by Thurstone's factorial approach apparently recognized that a reliable measure of interest would require far more items than the 72 contained in this one, and that the items would need to be less transparent than the occupational titles used exclusively by Thurstone. The scores are not reliable: changing two "likes" concerning which the writer was doubtful because of stereotyping to "dislikes" (his more considered reaction) changed his physical

science interest score from .91 (considerable interest) to .55 (slight interest). The writer has found no published studies which throw light on the validity of Thurstone's schedule in vocational guidance or selection; it is not likely that it would be found valid, when scoring keys are based on as few as nine items and the reliabilities are as low as that number of items implies.

The manual reflects this lack of occupational research with and consequent lack of knowledge about the test. It does not mention validity. It does not even mention reliability. Interpretation is discussed only in terms of factor projections: With keys based on from nine to twenty occupational items, this is tantamount to stating that people who say they would like to be physicians should consider medicine as a possible occupation.

Strong's blank, better understood now partly as a result of Thurstone's work, and Kuder's, are more reliable and less transparent. There is no possibility that so brief an instrument as this can become as useful as these two longer inventories, even if more were known about it. The publishers have therefore rendered a service to the profession by replacing this blank with a completely revised 1947 edition, the *Thurstone Interest Schedule* (*see* 646), which was received too late for review.

For reviews by Harold D. Carter, J. B. Miner, and N. W. Morton, see 38:1180 and 40:1683.

[654]

Vocational Interest Test for College Women. 1930; 1 form; $10 per 50; 25¢ per sample set; nontimed (30-40) minutes; Kathryn McHale; American Association of University Women.

REFERENCES

1. MCHALE, KATHRYN. "An Experimental Study of the Vocational Interests of a Liberal Arts College Group." *J Appl Psychol* 8:245-55 Je '24. *
2. MCHALE, KATHRYN. "An Information Test of Interests." *Psychol Clin* 19:53-8 Ap '30. * (*PA* 4:5135)

Frances Oralind Triggs, Educational Records Bureau, New York, New York. According to the author, the purpose of this information interest inventory, copyrighted in 1930, was to "formulate a working idea to guide an objective study of vocational interests . . . ; the idea being, that if one made an information test based on interests, perhaps one would arrive at something more tangible by way of a guidance tool (1)." The test consists of 246 multiple-choice items divided into seven groups: law, business, medicine and science, homemaking, costuming and sewing, agriculture and horticulture, and teaching.

This test is now only of historical interest as one type of instrument—an information test—for the measurement of vocational interests.

[655]

Vocational Inventory. Grades 8-16 and adults; 1940; 1 form; $2.50 per 25; $1.25 per 25 individual analysis reports; 25¢ per specimen set, postpaid; nontimed (150) minutes; Curtis G. Gentry; Educational Test Bureau.

REFERENCES
1. GENTRY, CURTIS G. "Knoxville's Seven-Point Vocational Guidance Program." Sch Executive 59:10-2 Ap '40. * (PA 14:5195, title only)
2. GORDON, HANS C., AND HERKNESS, WALTER W., JR. "Pupils Appraise Vocational Interest Blanks." Occupations 20:100-2 N '41. * (PA 16:757)
3. FROEHLICH, CLIFFORD. "A Study of the Gentry Vocational Inventory." Ed & Psychol Meas 2:75-82 Ja '42. * (PA 16:2449)
4. GORDON, HANS C., AND HERKNESS, WALTER W., JR. "Do Vocational Interest Questionnaires Yield Consistent Results?" Occupations 20:424-9 Mr '42. * (PA 16:2059)

Edward S. Bordin, Director, Student Counseling Center, and Associate Professor of Psychology, The State College of Washington, Pullman, Washington. Among current vocational interest inventories this one is unique in that it includes information as well as preference items in its total of over four hundred questions. Considering the fact that the former type of item was advocated, tried, and abandoned in the developmental stages of interest testing and that the author of this inventory, unlike authors of other inventories, claims that his test measures aptitudes as well as interests, one would wish to see the results of extensive research as a basis for judging the effectiveness of the instrument. The manual refers to a follow-up study of 1,000 Knoxville high school graduates which appears to have been the primary basis for the validation and standardization of the inventory. However, only fragmentary reports of the study are presented, and no references are given to sources for more complete reports. Considering the sensational claims for validity based on this study, it is a distinct disservice to the field of vocational interest testing not to make the complete report available so that critical verification would be possible.

In addition to an incomplete presentation of validity studies not expected in a test manual, the manual for the Inventory makes the glaring omission of normative tables. There are data on the distribution of highest scores for the 1,000 high school students, but nowhere can one find data on what were the average scores for this group on each scale and in what way the scores on each scale were distributed. Nat-urally, there are no tables for converting the raw scores to any form of derived scores. Without such information a test cannot be used.

In terms of format, the inventory is more cumbersome than most to score because it not only fails to provide for use of a machine scorable answer sheet but actually calls for completion or other types of write-in responses. Further, since the answers are written on the test booklet, it necessarily increases the cost of testing.

An Individual Analysis Report booklet has been prepared to accompany the inventory. It has many features which, in the hands of well-trained teacher-counselors, probably prove useful for aiding high school students to become more completely oriented in vocational terms. However, many will deplore the advocated practice of turning over test scores of this sort to the student to be kept in his permanent records and to be used or misused without supervision at some future date. Unfortunately, this is a practice which is all too common.

This reviewer finds by far the most serious offense in the publisher's statement on the folder enclosing the test materials. It follows: "Extensive knowledge of the guidance field is not necessary for deriving the benefits from and making use of the *Vocational Inventory.* The manual and accompanying accessories give necessary information for the proper use of the Inventory and the interpretation of the results." Misuse of tests and general counseling malpractice can be the only results of this type of test merchandising.

Harold D. Carter, Associate Professor of Education, University of California, Berkeley, California. This inventory is intended to supplement the usual school records as a basis for educational guidance in high school and college. It is also intended for general personal guidance and job placement and for assisting employers in personnel work.

The inventory provides an indication of one's general field of vocational interest and of likes and dislikes for activities involved in the occupations. The student's strengths and weaknesses are classified with reference to the following eight major occupational groups: social service, literary work, business, law and government, art, mechanical designing, mechanical construction, and science.

As evidence of validity, the manual presents results of a follow-up study of 1,000 high school graduates, showing that 84 per cent were at work in the occupational groups in which they rated highest on the inventory. They were found to be well adjusted vocationally, as judged by satisfaction expressed by employers and employees. The manual also presents tabled data showing the tendency of persons to succeed in courses taken in school when those courses were in agreement with measured interests. Although these data do not provide a clear quantitative indication of the degree of validity, they do show that the test has some validity.

The reliability of the test is given in terms of per cent change of returns between grades 9 and 12 for 412 students who were retested. The data indicate a marked tendency for vocational interests to remain stable, but again there is a lack of the usual evidence in correlational form. One does not know how reliable the test is in terms of the customary criteria.

For normative data, the manual presents the score frequency distributions for each of the eight vocational fields for 1,000 high school seniors. In addition, sample tabled data present the basis for profiles of interests of 16 students. The manual explains the use of the accessory materials which come with the test. It also explains how projects in homeroom guidance can be built around the use of the inventory.

The test contains a mixture of interest items and information items. It is practically self-administering and can easily be used in testing large groups. It appears likely to be useful for self-exploration of interests as a basis for occupational adjustment. Probably its other uses will be markedly restricted because about two and one half hours are required for taking the test and because the scoring is tedious. In view of the length of the test, it is probably highly reliable.

Donald E. Super, Associate Professor of Education, Teachers College, Columbia University, New York, New York. This inventory yields two types of scores, one for a number of occupational fields such as social service and business, and one for personality in terms of introversion-extraversion. This would lead one to expect a Strong- or Kuder-type inventory of vocational interests and a Bernreuter-type inventory of personality, something like the Clee-

ton before the personality section was found useless and dropped. The expectation is warranted in the case of the personality section, at least for the first 25 items, although the last 24 are a mixture of self-ratings of abilities which might be classified as introvert or extrovert and of biographical data such as the frequency of parental disciplining ("seldom corrected" by parents is weighed for introversion, on the basis of no available evidence). In the former case, however, the expectation is not warranted. Instead, one finds items of the Strong and Kuder varieties, mixed in with items which test vocational vocabulary and information, self-ratings of skill and knowledge in school subjects, and biographical questions. There are even some questions which may have been intended as information questions but which are more probably attitude items, for instance, Item 375, "Recently a factory owner retired and turned over his prosperous business to his employees. Was this wise? (Yes or No)." The answer is "yes," with credit for social service. This may be justifiable, in the light of evidence from other work, but there is no evidence in the manual or in published studies of this inventory to indicate that this is the answer given by persons engaged in social service occupations or even that people who answer "yes" to this item tend to make high scores on the other social service items (no internal consistency or item validation data are even referred to in the manual).

The use of a variety of types of items is due to the fact that Gentry has attempted to make his "inventory" not a test or inventory in the usual sense, but rather a complete inventory of the individual, including his preferences, his manifest interests (shown in specialized knowledge), aptitudes (self-rated), and personality traits. He has, in fact, attempted to make a vocational guidance test comparable to the aptitude tests used in selecting students for professional schools, but covering all the major fields. This might be an indication that Gentry has shown a high degree of sophistication in test construction, basing his work on the most promising developments in the fields of interest inventories, general information tests, specialized vocabulary tests, and personality inventories. If this were indeed the case, the instrument is one which should be widely studied and, when well understood, put to use in vocational counseling.

Vocational Inventory

Unfortunately, however, Gentry has not manifested a high level of sophistication in test construction and has not based his work on appropriate advances made by others. The *Vocational Inventory* bears the earmarks of amateurishness in many ways, some of minor importance and some quite crucial. Under the former head might be cited poor mechanics, illustrated by having the examinee actually write *yes* or *no* in the test booklet instead of marking a multiple-choice answer and by a scoring booklet which has to be matched with the test booklet so that both may be read in scoring instead of using a machine or stencil-scored answer sheet. Such a publication in 1940 reflects both on author and on publisher. Among the major defects in test construction is the lack of evidence of item analyses for either internal consistency or external validity, such as Kuder (internal consistency) and Strong (external validity) used in the construction of their interest inventories and such as work in personality and in aptitudes has repeatedly demonstrated is essential for validity. If this were in fact a soundly built aptitude battery, it would not have a separate score for the personality section: instead, these items would be weighted for various occupational fields, just as the preference, information, and other items are, except that there would be statistical evidence from item analyses to justify the weights. The grouping of items at some points in such a way as to make their relationship obvious to the examinee and thus spuriously to increase reliability and decrease validity through halo effect, as demonstrated in studies of the organization of test items, is another major defect. In a professionally ethical worker, such lack of analysis of a test is an index of technical naïveté.

In the light of the above and other similar defects, it is not surprising that Froehlich, in one of the few published studies of the Gentry inventory, concluded that "this test should be more carefully standardized and evaluated before it is used in a counseling situation" (3). This reviewer is inclined to wonder why Froehlich thought it necessary to make his study in order to demonstrate this. When such serious defects are so patent, it is certain that other less obvious defects exist. The time and effort of test users is then better spent in further validating other more promising instruments, and the energies of test constructors are better devoted to developing new instruments based on more sophisticated evaluations of current research. Gentry's basic idea is sound, but its execution is naive. This reviewer therefore considers the Gentry *Vocational Inventory* an instrument which should be withdrawn from circulation until adequate analysis of the test has been made and revision and restandardization have been completed. The norms based on 1,190 junior and 960 senior high school boys and girls which the publisher promises for the immediate future are useless without such an analysis and standardization.

Occupations 21:266–7 N '42. Arthur H. Brayfield. A thirty-page booklet containing two sections, a Vocational Inventory and a Personality Inventory. * The Personality Inventory purports to measure introversion-extroversion, but since there are other inventories for the same purpose which seem to have been better constructed and standardized, the Personality section will not be reviewed here. * appears to be an attempt to construct a single instrument which will be an over-all interest, aptitude, and information test. The author does not make a clear distinction among these three areas in his explanatory statements. The reviewer found 64 per cent of the items to be questions of information. * The author does not make clear what he is attempting to measure other than the individual's "general vocational picture." Insufficient information is given regarding the method of construction and standardization. The information which is given casts doubt upon the adequacy of the methods and techniques used. The attempts to get a measure of validity are inadequate. The reviewer is in complete sympathy with the author's attempt to provide an instrument useful in mass guidance. However, this appears to be an oversimplification. The evidence points to the desirability of adhering to certain technical considerations in test construction in order that the instrument may be *meaningful* as well as *practical.* The inventory might have some value as an *interest* measure. Obviously it is not the "all-around test" it attempts to be.

MANUAL DEXTERITY

[656]

★**Benge Han-Dexterity Test.** Adults; 1943; individual; $5 per testing outfit; worklimit (10-20) minutes; Eugene J. Benge; Management Service C⁰

C. H. Lawshe, Jr., Professor of Psychology, Purdue University, Lafayette, Indiana. This test is designed as a rough measure of the speed of eye, hand, and arm movements. It purports mainly to eliminate, for industrial positions involving rapid hand movements, those employees who have poor or slow finger and hand dexterity. Jobs involving inspection, assembly, and repetitive machine operations are indicated.

The test is of the work-limit variety, consisting of a board with ten pegs, upon each of which the applicant places ten disks, one at a time. Four trials are taken—right hand, left hand, both hands simultaneously, and both hands in alternation—total time for the four trials representing the total score on the test. Percentile norms for the complete test, based apparently upon the performance of semiautomatic machine operators, are provided.

No reliability and limited validity data are available. The test was tried on 173 employees of the Sonoco Products Company of Hartsville, S. C., manufacturers of paper specialties for the textile industry. Of 73 rated satisfactory, 78 per cent made an average score or better on the test. Of the 94 unsatisfactory workers, 72 per cent failed to attain the average score. The test was purportedly used successfully in combination with vision and intelligence tests in identifying satisfactory present and potential employees.

Administration is simple, 15 minutes being required for each test together with the scoring. Directions are, however, meager. Such details as the exact method of the alternate hands trial, what to do about dropped disks, and the voluntary or involuntary moving of the pegboard by the applicant are not sufficiently standardized. The necessary counting of the disks is a distraction to the applicant that might be eliminated by designating the upper limit for ten disks on each peg. The norms provided fail, of course, to discriminate between handedness. There is no evidence in the accompanying literature that the present length of the component parts of the test are optimum for any industrial purpose.

While the limited amount of validity data supplied by the publisher seems promising, users of the test should proceed with caution and most certainly should prepare standard directions so as not to introduce undesirable variabilities into the administration procedure.

Users should also inquire into the reliability of the test inasmuch as the publisher presents no such information.

Joseph E. Moore, Head, Department of Psychology, Georgia School of Technology, Atlanta, Georgia. "This is a short test of eye-hand coordination," to quote the test constructor. The test consists of 10 wooden pegs set into a board and a package of 100 fiber disks. The subject goes through the test four times, placing 10 fiber disks one at a time over each peg. No standard size box is provided to hold the washers or disks. The author suggests a tray approximately one inch deep by eight inches square. The test is to be taken with the subject sitting down. The board is to be placed at a height of 28 inches from the floor—no higher than 30 inches is suggested.

The test proper consists of four different operations. The subject uses his left hand, his right hand, then both hands simultaneously, and then both alternately. No penalty is indicated for errors in counting.

Decile norms are provided on the test. Neither the number nor the sex of the employees on whom the norms were secured is given. There is no reliability given for this test. The validity of the test also seems to have been overlooked. A reprint, not a part of the manual, tells how the test was applied to 173 employees in a paper manufacturing plant. These employees were previously rated either satisfactory or unsatisfactory on a formal merit rating system. The test is reported to have selected 78 per cent of the satisfactory employees, but 28 per cent of the unsatisfactory workers scored above average and 22 per cent of the satisfactory employees dropped below average on the test. The author has this to say about his test, "The HanDexterity Test has evolved over seven or eight years. We originally used a larger disk and a larger board than is now the case. Hence, our original standardizations, including validity coefficient, are not pertinent to the present board."

The data given by the testmaker are far from adequate on validity, reliability, and test norms. The information on how the norms were gathered and what the norms mean is entirely lacking. A purchaser of this test has little to go on to tell him whether or not he is getting sound value for his dollars.

Benge Han-Dexterity Test

[657]

★Benge Two Hand Coordination Test. Adults;
1943; individual; $7.50 per testing outfit; 6(15) min-
utes; Eugene J. Benge; Management Service Co.

*Milton L. Blum, Assistant Professor of Psy-
chology, The City College of New York, New
York, New York.* This is the eleventh in
a series of tests devised by the Management
Service Company. The advertising material of
the firm announces that the test is to be used
for selecting applicants with good eye-hand-arm
coordination. The applicant is to plunge a rod
held in each hand into two holes of one diameter and then into two holes of smaller diameter. A mechanical counter automatically totals
the correct thrusts.

Checking the psychological literature for the
past seven years reveals no reference to the
Benge Two Hand Coordination Test. The author in private correspondence states: "All
that we have on the tests so far are percentiles.
Administration has not been sufficiently standardized so that we get high reliability from one
situation to the other. Several validity studies
have looked promising but we also get such
high correlations between this test and our
"handexterity" test that I am coming to believe that the simple handexterity test is sufficient in most situations."

Since one does not normally expect a high
correlation between a test of finger dexterity
and an eye-hand coordination test, it would
appear that either both tests are measuring
finger dexterity, or both tests are measuring
eye-hand coordination. This is not the first instance of an author naming a test on the basis
of supposed validity and then finding that the
theoretical basis for the test is not substantiated through validation.

From the author's statement it can be seen
that the test is relatively unreliable and has
questionable validity. The claims of the author
that it can select machine operators and mechanical apprentices have not been substantiated. This test should not be used as an aid to
select employees even in jobs requiring two-
hand-eye-arm coordination.

It surely is unpleasant for the reviewer to
write this type of review but if psychological
testing in industry is not to receive a "black
eye" it would be better that unsuspecting employers and potential test users know the facts.
It may well be that further work on this test
will result in improvement and modification in
design and that the test will ultimately be accepted as a standardized test. At present, it is
not. In a brochure the claim is made that
"Benge tests . . . provide sharp instruments for
eliminating unfit candidates." This test is not
"sharp."

[658]

★Crawford Spatial Relations Test. Grades 9-16;
1942; individual; 1 form; no longer available; work-
limit (3-12) minutes; John Crawford and Dorothea
Crawford; formerly distributed by Psychological Corporation.

REFERENCES

1. CRAWFORD, JOHN EDMUND. "A Test for Tridimensional
Structural Visualization: A New Test for Mechanical Insight
Designed Primarily to Measure Ability or Aptitude in Draft-
ing." *J Appl Psychol* 24:482-92 Ag '40. (*PA* 15:82)
2. CRAWFORD, JOHN EDMUND. *Measurement of Some Factors
Upon Which Is Based Achievement in Elementary Machine De-
tail Drafting.* Unpublished doctor's thesis, University of Pitts-
burgh, 1941. (*Abstracts of Theses . . . 1941*, 1942, pp. 85-93.)
3. BENNETT, GEORGE K., AND CRUIKSHANK, RUTH M. *A
Summary of Manual and Mechanical Ability Tests,* Preliminary
Form, pp. 27-8. New York: Psychological Corporation, 1942.
Pp. v, 80. Paper, lithotyped. $0.70. *
4. CRAWFORD, JOHN EDMUND. "Spatial Perception Tests for
Determining Drafting Aptitude." *Ind Arts & Voc Ed* 31:10-2
Ja '42. *
5. ESTES, STANLEY G. "A Study of Five Tests of 'Spatial'
Ability." *J Psychol* 13:265-71 Ap '42. * (*PA* 16:3771)
6. JACOBSEN, ELDON E. "An Evaluation of Certain Tests in
Predicting Mechanic Learner Achievement." *Ed & Psychol
Meas* 3:259-67 au '43. * (*PA* 18:2537)
7. RUSMORE, JAY T. "Comparison of an 'Industrial' Problem
Solving Task and an Assembly Task." *J Appl Psychol* 28:129-31
Ap '44. * (*PA* 18:2936)

*William R. Grove, Psychologist and Director
of Child Study Service, Phoenix Elementary
Schools, Phoenix, Arizona; formerly Professor
of Psychology and Director of the Division of
Psychological Services, The University of Pittsburgh.* In the words of the test authors, "The
scheme of this test is a large tridimensional puzzle so designed that the manipulative factor is
small compared to the insight or structural visualization factor (1)." The test is indeed a cleverly designed construction puzzle consisting of
nine pieces. It fits compactly into a neat case
which is approximately ten by ten by two inches.
There are excellent photographs of the test
materials in the August 1940 issue of the *Journal
of Applied Psychology* (1).

The original test was constructed of poplar
and painted brown. Later, the Crawfords had
their test cast in aluminum. It was this equipment which is described in Bennett and Cruikshank's *A Summary of Manual and Mechanical
Ability Tests* (3). The castings are well made
and fit together neatly, but with sufficient tolerance to make them easy to manipulate. The
test materials currently available from the Psychological Corporation are somewhat less than
satisfactory. These are made of soft wood which
has been cheaply stained, permitting the grain
to show through. The pieces have been care-

lessly glued and would tend to come apart with use. These are matters that can be readily remedied by more careful gluing and by providing a more adequate paint job which should completely cover the grain of the wood. The description of the test materials in the 1946 catalog of The Psychological Corporation is *not* accurate.

When assembled, the test forms a flat round disk a little more than six inches in diameter and extending three-quarters of an inch above the base plate. In appearance it closely resembles a much older test formerly sold by the C. H. Stoelting Company. It is probable that the basic idea for this test was suggested by the older test. The test referred to was too complex to be of much practical value and never came into very general use.

That tests of this general type have a basic validity in measuring one aspect of mechanical ability has been demonstrated repeatedly. The Crawfords' data show that draftsmen and machinists exceed other workers in their performance on this test to the extent represented by mean scores which fall respectively at the 93rd and 70th percentiles of the Crawford norms.

The norms provided for the test are practically meaningless, however. They are based upon the scores of 427 men "employed in industrial and technical jobs ranging from mechanical engineers to handymen in machine shops, including designers, detailers, lay-out men, machinists, general mechanics, and other skilled and semi-skilled workers." Such norms are probably a conglomeration of accumulated records which may or may not approximate industrial norms for a particular industry or group of related industries. Normative data should be described adequately enough for other investigators to duplicate them by testing a comparable sample. Otherwise, they are of very limited usefulness.

In spite of some extremely incredible coefficients of correlation reported by the Crawfords, it is the opinion of this reviewer that this test will be found quite deficient in reliability. It is my considered judgment that a test of this type consisting of nine pieces and administered on a single-trial basis in an average of five minutes or less cannot constitute a sufficient sample to be used reliably for individual diagnosis.

In summary, I wish again to quote the test authors in a statement which seems to me to be entirely accurate and well formulated : *"Little weight should be given any score on this test in the absence of confirming evidence from other sources; but either a very high or a very low score is probably a valid basis upon which to seek such confirming data"* (1, italics mine).

[659]

★Hand-Tool Dexterity Test. Adults; 1946; individual; $16.50 per testing outfit, postpaid; worklimit (10-20) minutes; George K. Bennett; Psychological Corporation.

REFERENCES

1. BENNETT, GEORGE K., AND FEAR, RICHARD A. "Mechanical Comprehension and Dexterity." *Personnel J* 22:12-7 My '43. * (*PA* 17:2843)
2. BENNETT, GEORGE K., AND WESMAN, ALEXANDER G. "Industrial Test Norms for a Southern Plant Population." *J Appl Psychol* 31:241-6 Je '47. * (*PA* 21:4095)

C. H. Lawshe, Jr., Professor of Psychology, Purdue University, Lafayette, Indiana. Here is a test that seeks to combine measurements of achievement based on past experience in handling tools and mechanical aptitude. A wooden frame comprising two uprights attached to a horizontal baseboard is used. Twelve bolt, washer, and nut units of varying sizes are fastened securely through holes bored in the right upright. The subject is to transfer the units by means of tools (crescent wrench, end-wrenches or screwdriver) from one upright to the holes in the opposite upright. Care has been taken to standardize the procedure into an efficient motion pattern. Score is the amount of time taken by the subject to remove the nuts and bolts from the right upright and to fasten them on the left. Total time required for one administration does not normally exceed 15 minutes. Directions in the manual are precise and simple. Presumably the test could be administered to small groups, although it is primarily an individual test.

Percentile norms based on the performance of 1,123 male factory workers of the Union Bag and Paper Company, Savannah, Georgia, are available. A reliability coefficient of .91 has been computed by the retest method. A validity coefficient of .46 is reported for scores made by male machine tool operators and one of .51 for female aircraft construction riveters with foremen's ratings as a criterion. Again using the machine tool operators, a multiple correlation coefficient of .67 was obtained for the *Hand-Tool Dexterity Test*, the Bennett *Test of Mechanical Comprehension*, Form AA, and foremen's ratings. All the above test scores were obtained before hiring and the foremen's ratings were made after the subjects had had four months or more experience on the job. The relation between *specific* job experience and test scores is not reported.

The possible effect of such factors as intelligence and mechanical understanding upon the manipulative skill measured apparently is slight inasmuch as test scores are found to correlate reasonably low with both factors, .26 with the *Revised Beta Examination* and .42 with the *Test of Mechanical Comprehension,* Form AA, both for 66 machinist trainees. Later analysis gave correlations of .36 with the *Revised Beta Examination* and .28 with the *Test of Mechanical Comprehension* for 927 and 1,109 adult white male applicants respectively.

While it is apparent that the *Hand-Tool Dexterity Test* in selecting industrial tradesmen, machine operators, and industrial apprentices is best utilized in a test battery also containing a measurement of mechanical comprehension, its value would appear to be greatest in helping select workers for those industrial jobs on which speed of operation is particularly desired.

Neil D. Warren, Associate Professor of Psychology and Dean of Men, The University of Southern California, Los Angeles, California. This is a worksample test designed to measure proficiency in the use of ordinary mechanical tools such as the wrench and screwdriver. The subject is required to use these tools as well as the unaided fingers of both hands to remove a set of nuts and bolts from one upright and install them in another. It is obvious that the task demands highly complex movements involving digital dexterity, gross arm coordination, and eye-hand coordination. The very complexity of the task places a considerable burden upon the directions for administration to provide standardized procedures at all times. While the author specifically recognizes this difficulty in the manual of directions, it is believed that the instructions do not fully prevent rather great variation in the methods used by different subjects. For example, while a screwdriver is provided and may be used, there is no reference to it in the directions, nor does the task make it essential to use it at all. Three wrenches are provided which may be used in a variety of ways.

Although the specific applicability of the test would seem to be limited to occupations requir-

ing routine manipulation of hand tools, the author has implicitly extended its use in a series of studies of validity for such jobs as turret-lathe operator, precision grinder, and riveter. These studies involved the use of the *Hand-Tool Dexterity Test* as a part of a battery. The validity coefficient against foremen's ratings of machine tool operators was .46; against similar ratings of women riveters in aircraft construction it was .51. The article which reports these data fails to provide adequate information for complete interpretation of the figures.

The only norms provided in the manual are based on the performance of a large sample (N = 1,123) of male bag and paper factory workers. The nature of the group and the jobs represented are not reported. The usefulness of such norms is clearly questionable.

The reliability of the test is given in the manual as .91. This was determined by the test-retest method, but there is no indication of the nature or size of the population upon which the study was conducted.

The test has the advantage of considerable "face validity" in that the materials and tools are standard mechanic's devices and the task is much like many practical job situations. In the absence, however, of further normative information and validity data it would appear that its indiscriminate use in vocational selection is open to question. Moreover, the problem of standardization of instructions, of the nuts and bolts, and of the tools has not been fully solved by the author of the test. It is to be hoped that the results of further research on the test will soon be reported in the literature. The test is well made and, as long as the nuts turn freely on the bolts, offers few mechanical difficulties. It fills a real need for a test by which skills with tools can be measured.

[660]

Kent-Shakow Formboard: Industrial Model. Adults; 1928; 1 form; revision of the *Worcester Formboard;* $60 per testing outfit; Grace H. Kent and David Shakow; Sven G. A. Nilsson, 16 Maverick Road, Worcester, Mass.

REFERENCES

1-9. *See* 40:1401.
10. GROVE, WILLIAM R. *Modification of Kent-Shakow Formboard Series.* Unpublished doctor's thesis, University of Pittsburgh, 1937. Pp. iv, 70. (*Abstracts of Theses . . . 1937,* pp. 175-83.)
11. GROVE, WILLIAM R. "Modification of the Kent-Shakow Formboard Series." *J Psychol* 7:385-97 Ap '39. * (*PA* 13:5384)
12. BENNETT, GEORGE K., AND CRUIKSHANK, RUTH M. *A Summary of Manual and Mechanical Ability Tests,* Preliminary Form, pp. 35-6. New York: Psychological Corporation, 1942. Pp. v, 80. Paper, lithotyped. $0.70. * (*PA* 16:2432)
13. TEEGARDEN, LORENE. "Manipulative Performance of Young Adult Applicants at a Public Employment Office—Part I." *J Appl Psychol* 26:633-52 O '42. * (*PA* 17:2907)

14. TEEGARDEN, LORENE. "Manipulative Performance of Young Adult Applicants at a Public Employment Office, II." *J Appl Psychol* 26:754-69 D '42. * (PA 17:2908)

15. EBERT, ELIZABETH, AND SIMMONS, KATHERINE. *The Brush Foundation Study of Child Growth and Development: I, Psychometric Tests.* Monographs of the Society for Research in Child Development, Vol. 8, No. 2. Washington, D. C.: the Society, National Research Council, 1943. Pp. xiv, 113. Paper, lithotyped. $1.50. (PA 18:3322)

16. TEEGARDEN, LORENE. "Occupational Differences in Manipulative Performance of Applicants at a Public Employment Office." *J Appl Psychol* 27:416-37 O '43. * (PA 18:272)

17. WILSON, ALICE W. *Educational Norms for High School Boys on the Modified Kent-Shakow Formboard Series.* Unpublished doctor's thesis, University of Pittsburgh, 1944. (*Abstracts of Theses . . . , 1945, pp. 326-35.)

18. WYLIE, RUTH CAROL. *A Study of Reliability of the Modified Kent-Shakow Formboard Series.* Unpublished doctor's thesis, University of Pittsburgh, 1944.

19. NEWMAN, JOSEPH. "The Prediction of Shopwork Performance in an Adult Rehabilitation Program: The Kent-Shakow Industrial Formboard Series." *Psychol Rec* 5:343-52 Mr '45. * (PA 20:2339)

20. WYLIE, RUTH C. "Reliability of the Grove Modification of the Kent-Shakow Formboard Series." *J Appl Psychol* 31: 155-9 Ap '47. * (PA 21:2804)

Milton L. Blum, Assistant Professor of Psychology, The City College of New York, New York, New York. This test is available in two models; the larger model is the industrial form, and the smaller one, the clinical form. The formboard consists of five recesses that are quadrilaterally symmetrical. The sets of blocks furnish eight different tasks of increasing difficulty; each task involves one problem repeated five times. The repetition is intended to reduce the possibility of a chance solution. The first task, used for practice and checking the understanding of directions, consists of two blocks for each hole. The most complicated task, challenging to superior adults, requires fitting five blocks into each hole. In addition to the perception of form and position, this test in its upper levels requires resourcefulness and adaptation of procedure.

The K–S formboards have been used in a number of different situations. Shakow and Pazeien (9) have reported decile norms for the clinical formboard on groups of adults of both sexes. Teegarden (13, 14, 16) in a series of studies reports percentiles based upon large groups of adult males and females who were applicants at a public employment office. Her work on this test is interesting. She has proposed the division of the tasks into two series. The three simple tasks (2D, 3S, 4S) show no sex differences and are essentially a dexterity or speed group. The remaining tasks (3D, 4D, 4DD, 5D) might be called a capacity or adaptive group since they apparently require more than manipulative ability. This group of complex tasks shows a sex difference with males performing more rapidly, possibly because they have more experience in constructing, assembling, and putting things together. Grove (11)

has proposed a modification of the formboard and has developed percentiles on a group of delinquent adults. This test has been used also on psychotic and brain-injured cases as well as in child guidance clinics.

The test is sufficiently challenging to allow the examiner to make qualitative observations of the subject's performance. It has been suggested that an experienced examiner can observe the subject's emotional reaction to success or frustration and his adaptability and resourcefulness in varying or trying new methods.

Some of the research on this test indicates its reliability and validity. Ebert and Simmons (15) retested subjects after one or more years had intervened. They report correlations between .62 and .80. Newman (19) has used the Industrial Series for the prediction of shopwork performance in an adult rehabilitation program. A correlation of .76 is reported between shop ratings in accuracy, speed, and constructive thinking and time scores on the formboard.

However, there is a void in the research done on this test. It is unfortunate that a series of studies have not been conducted comparing test performance with job success in various types of mechanical and manipulative industrial jobs of both the simple and the complex order. Considering the use made of this and other tests, the reviewer believes that too little work has been done on this test since it first appeared in 1928. The fact that it has not disappeared from use is good. People working with tests on both the vocational guidance and vocational selection level are encouraged to use this test whenever it is possible to spend about thirty minutes in measuring performance on two-dimensional spatial relations. It has the advantage of measuring a considerable range of ability both in the simple manipulative functions and in the more complex aspects. The formboard also allows the trained examiner to make astute observations of a clinical nature.

For a review by Lorene Teegarden, see 40:1401.

[661]

MacQuarrie Test for Mechanical Ability. Ages 16 and over; 1925-43; 1 form; $1.75 per 25; 25¢ per specimen set, postpaid; Spanish edition available at same prices; 12(25) minutes; T. W. MacQuarrie; California Test Bureau.

REFERENCES

1. HORNING, S. D. "Testing Mechanical Ability by the MacQuarrie Test." *Ind Arts Mag* 15:348-50 O '26. *

2. MacQuarrie, T. W. " A Mechanical Ability Test." *J Personnel Res* 5:329-37 Ja '27. * (*PA* 1:1864)

3. Stein, Martin L. "A Trial With Criteria of the MacQuarrie Test of Mechanical Ability." *J Appl Psychol* 11:391-3 O '27. * (*PA* 2:2964)

4. Stoy, E. G. "Additional Tests for Mechanical Drawing Aptitude." *Personnel J* 6:361-6 F '28. * (*PA* 2:2660)

5. Kefauver, Grayson N. "Relationship of the Intelligence Quotient and Scores on Mechanical Tests With Success in Industrial Subjects." *Voc Guid Mag* 7:198-203+ F '29. * (*PA* 3:1637)

6. Scudder, Charles Roland, and Raubenheimer, A. S. "Are Standardized Mechanical Aptitude Tests Valid?" *J Juvenile Res* 14:120-3 Ap '30. * (*PA* 5:897)

7. Stedman, Melissa Branson. "Factors Influencing School Success in Bookkeeping." *J Appl Psychol* 14:74-82 F '30. * (*PA* 4:4556)

8. Taylor, Don H. "The Selection of Printers' Apprentices." *Voc Guid Mag* 8:281-8 Mr '30. * (*PA* 4:3624)

9. Griffitts, C. H. "A Study of Some 'Motor Ability' Tests." *J Appl Psychol* 15:109-25 Ap '31. * (*PA* 5:4086)

10. Holcomb, G. W., and Laslett, H. R. "A Prognostic Study of Engineering Aptitude." *J Appl Psychol* 16:107-15 Ap '32. * (*PA* 7:4722)

11. Burr, Mary. "The MacQuarrie Test for Mechanical Ability: An Experiment in a Nursing School." *Am J Nursing* 34:378-81 Ap '34. *

12. Jorgensen, C. "Analysis of Some Psychological Tests by the Spearman Factor Method." *Brit J Ed Psychol* 4:96-109 F '34." * (*PA* 8:4318)

13. Bingham, Walter V. "MacQuarrie Test for Mechanical Ability." *Occupations* 14:202-3 D '35. * (*PA* 10:1723)

14. Skolnik, Ruth Frances. *The Predictive Value of the MacQuarrie Test for Beauticians.* Unpublished master's thesis, Columbia University, 1936.

15. Bingham, Walter Van Dyke. *Aptitudes and Aptitude Testing*, pp. 314-8. New York and London: Harper & Brothers, 1937. Pp. ix, 390. $3.00; 12s. 6d. * (*PA* 11:2885)

16. Harrell, Willard. "The Validity of Certain Mechanical Ability Tests for Selecting Cotton Mill Machine Fixers." *J Social Psychol* 8:279-82 My '37. * (*PA* 11:5311)

17. Babcock, Harriet, and Emerson, Marion Rines. "An Analytical Study of the MacQuarrie Test for Mechanical Ability." *J Ed Psychol* 29:50-5 Ja '38. * (*PA* 12:4390)

18. Lackey, Florence Woodard. *A Study of the Prognostic Value of the MacQuarrie Test for Mechanical Ability in First-Year Typewriting Speed.* Unpublished master's thesis, Oklahoma Agricultural and Mechanical College, 1938.

19. Harrell, Willard. "A Factor Analysis of Mechanical Ability Tests." Abstract. *Psychol B* 36:524 Jl '39. * (*PA* 13:6515, title only)

20. Harrell, Willard. "A Factor Analysis of Mechanical Ability Tests." *Psychometrika* 5:17-33 Mr '40. * (*PA* 14:4285)

21. Harrell, Willard, and Faubion, Richard. "Selection Tests for Aviation Mechanics." *J Consult Psychol* 4:104-5 Jl-Ag '40. * (*PA* 14:5681)

22. Stead, William H.; Shartle, Carroll L.; Otis, Jay L.; Ward, Raymond S.; Osborne, Herbert F.; Endler, O. L.; Dvorak, Beatrice J.; Cooper, John H.; Bellows, Roger M.; and Kolbe, Laverne E. *Occupational Counseling Techniques: Their Development and Application.* Published for the Technical Board of the Occupational Research Program, United States Employment Service. New York: American Book Co., 1940. Pp. ix, 273. Out of print. * (*PA* 14:2627, title only)

23. Crawford, John Edmund. *Measurement of Some Factors Upon Which Is Based Achievement in Elementary Machine Detail Drafting.* Unpublished doctor's thesis, University of Pittsburgh, 1941. (*Abstracts of Theses . . . 1941, 1942*, pp. 85-93.)

24. Ghiselli, Edwin E. "Tests for the Selection of Inspector-Packers." Abstract. *Psychol B* 38:735 O '41. * (*PA* 16:728, title only)

25. Robinson, J. Ben, and Bellows, Roger M. "Characteristics of Successful Dental Students." *J Am Assn Col Reg* 16:109-22 Ja '41. * (*PA* 15:2810)

26. Bennett, George K., and Cruikshank, Ruth M. *A Summary of Manual and Mechanical Ability Tests*, Preliminary Form, pp. 37-8. New York: Psychological Corporation, 1942. Pp. v, 80. Paper, lithotyped. $0.70. * (*PA* 16:2432)

27. Curtis, Henry Stoddard, Jr. *A Statistical Study of the MacQuarrie Test for Mechanical Ability.* Unpublished doctor's thesis, University of Michigan, 1942.

28. Ghiselli, Edwin E. "Tests for the Selection of Inspector-Packers." *J Appl Psychol* 26:468-76 Ag '42. * (*PA* 17:2127)

29. Mitrano, Anthony J. "The Relationship Between Age and Test Performance of Applicants to a Technical-Industrial High School." *J Appl Psychol* 26:482-6 Ag '42. * (*PA* 17:2498)

30. Blum, Milton L. "Selection of Sewing Machine Operators." *J Appl Pyschol* 27:35-40 F '43. * (*PA* 17:2845)

31. Klugman, Samuel F. "Tests Scores and Graduation." *Occupations* 21:389-93 Ja '43. * (*PA* 17:1354)

32. McDaniel, J. W., and Reynolds, Wm. A. "A Study of the Use of Mechanical Aptitude Tests in the Selection of Trainees for Mechanical Occupations." *Ed & Psychol Meas* 4:191-7 au '44. * (*PA* 19:1776)

33. Morgan, W. J. "Some Remarks and Results of Aptitude Testing in Technical and Industrial Schools." *J Social Psychol* 20:19-29 Ag '44. * (*PA* 19:556)

34. Thompson, Claude Edward. "Personality and Interest Factors in Dental School Success." *Ed & Psychol Meas* 4:299-306 w '44. * (*PA* 20:332)

35. Sartain, A. Q. "The Use of Certain Standardized Tests in the Selection of Inspectors in an Aircraft Factory." *J Consult Psychol* 9:234-7 S-O '45. * (*PA* 20:1241)

36. Barrett, Dorothy M. "Prediction of Achievement in Typewriting and Stenography in a Liberal Arts College." *J Appl Psychol* 30:624-30 D '46. * (*PA* 21:1624)

37. Goodman, Charles H. "The MacQuarrie Test for Mechanical Ability: I, Selecting Radio Assembly Operators." *J Appl Psychol* 30:586-95 D '46. * (*PA* 21:1678)

38. Sartain, A. Q. "Predicting Success in a School of Nursing." *J Appl Psychol* 30:234-40 Je '46. * (*PA* 20:4350)

39. Tuckman, Jacob. "Norms for the MacQuarrie Test for Mechanical Ability for High School Students." *Occupations* 25:94-6 N '46. * (*PA* 21:914)

40. Anderson, Rose G. "Test Scores and Efficiency Ratings of Machinists." *J Appl Psychol* 31:377-88 Ag '47. * (*PA* 22-2335)

41. Goodman, Charles H. "The MacQuarrie Test for Mechanical Ability: II, Factor Analysis." *J Appl Psychol* 31:150-4 Ap '47. * (*PA* 21:2799)

42. Goodman, Charles H. "The MacQuarrie Test for Mechanical Ability: III, Follow-Up Study." *J Appl Psychol* 31:502-10 O '47. * (*PA* 22:2339)

43. Maher, Howard, and Fife, Isabelle E. "A Biological-Pharmaceutical Checker Selection Program." *J Appl Psychol* 31:469-76 O '47. * (*PA* 22:3665)

John R. Kinzer, Assistant Professor of Psychology, The Ohio State University, Columbus, Ohio. This paper-and-pencil test is widely used to furnish a rough appraisal of both manual and mechanical aptitudes. It is an easily administered group test and may be given in about a half hour. The test is in reality a battery of seven subtests which may be analyzed separately. The total score is much less valuable than the evaluation of the various subscores.

The various parts are called: tracing, tapping, dotting, copying, location, blocks, and pursuit. The *tracing* test requires the subject to draw a line through small openings in a series of vertical lines. The *tapping* test requires the subject to make pencil dots as rapidly as possible. The *dotting* test requires the subject to place one dot in each of a series of small circles spaced irregularly. The three subtests just described have the greatest manual dexterity element. The next four tests correlate highest with intelligence (in this order: blocks, pursuit, location, and copying) and are assumed to measure the ability to learn mechanical skills. The *copying* test requires the subject to copy a series of simple designs. In the *location* test the subject locates points drawn on a large scale and transposes them into an area drawn on a smaller scale. The *blocks* test requires one to visualize space by telling how many blocks in a pile touch a given block. The *pursuit* test requires the subject to follow a line in a maze, by eye alone.

MacQuarrie (2) reported reliabilities on the separate tests as follows: tracing, .80; tapping, .75; dotting, .74; copying, .86; location, .72;

blocks, .80; pursuit, .76; and a total score reliability of .90. The reviewer, in his own experience, has found some interesting correlations with other tests. The highest correlation of any test among the first three subtests and the *Minnesota Rate of Manipulation Test* is between the dotting test and the placing part of the Minnesota test. The correlation there is only .24. It, therefore, might be assumed that these three MacQuarrie tests measure a different kind of manipulatory ability than that measured by the Minnesota test. Of the last four tests (copying, location, blocks, and pursuit), blocks correlates highest with intelligence as measured by the *Otis Group Intelligence Test* (Intermediate Form). The correlation coefficient between blocks and Otis is .48 (based on 230 industrial adult males). A slight sex difference has been found by the reviewer which favors men and also the younger age groups. This probably should be taken into consideration by industrial users of this test.

The MacQuarrie test is a valuable aid in selecting trainees for mechanical occupations, particularly when it is used with other tests and with adequate application blank data.

C. H. Lawshe, Jr., Professor of Psychology, Purdue University, Lafayette, Indiana. The *MacQuarrie Test for Mechanical Ability* is a paper-and-pencil test comprised of seven parts or subtests—tracing, tapping, dotting, copying, location, blocks (tridimensional space perception), and pursuit. Certain advantages are apparent. It is adapted to group testing. Because of its brevity and simplicity of administering, the test has enjoyed widespread use in a variety of industrial selection and vocational guidance situations. Moreover, the subtests, which can be given separately, can each be correlated against a criterion. Optimum weighting of the parts as well as the whole in a test battery for specific predictive situations is thus possible.

In selecting radio assembly operators a multiple *R* of .46 (with optimum weighting) of all subtests of the MacQuarrie against a work-sample criterion was obtained. The total test score gave a simple correlation coefficient of .42, but a good time saver was achieved in obtaining a multiple *R* of .41 for the subtests of tracing, location and blocks against the criterion (37). Pursuit, tracing, and dotting "came through" in predicting probable success in typing in the case of Hunter College students, and the pursuit and blocks subtests were successful in combination with other stenographic aptitude tests in predicting superior stenographers (36). Blocks, tracing, pursuit, location, and copying selected individuals with an aptitude for mechanical drawing (4); the first four of those subtests also picked out aviation mechanics with fair success (21). The complete MacQuarrie was also instrumental in selecting aircraft inspectors in a battery including other manipulative tests and the *Otis Self-Administering Test of Mental Ability* (35). An adaptation of the tracing subtest into a sewing operation selected good experienced sewing machine operators when attempts to predict good operators from scores on the whole MacQuarrie had been unsuccessful (30). In an early report by MacQuarrie (2) validation and reliability data were established as follows: Scores on the test correlated less than .20 with an unspecified group mental test. Retest reliability for the whole test was .90. Reliability for the subtests varied from .72 for location to .86 for copying.

New norms based upon scores of 1,000 males and 1,000 females 16 years and over are supplied in the new edition for the seven subtests and the whole test. Norms for high school students aged 14 to 16 have also been worked out (39).

A working idea of the MacQuarrie's various possible uses and limitations may be obtained from careful scrutiny of the validation reports cited above. It is apparent that MacQuarrie's "mechanical ability" does not refer to the understanding of mechanical principles or familiarity with tools so much as to manipulative skills involving finger and hand dexterity, visual acuity, muscular control, and spatial relations. The test seems to merit consideration wherever measures of aptitude for jobs requiring the above worker skills and characteristics are wanted.

Alec Rodger, Senior Psychologist to the Admiralty; on leave from the National Institute of Industrial Psychology; London, England. This test is over twenty years old. It has, therefore, an old-fashioned look. We find in it a tracing test, a tapping test, a dotting test, a copying test, a location test, a blocks test, and a pursuit test—all to be performed with paper and pencil alone. But it is not to be criticised on that account. The important question is, Does the test usefully and economically add to our other means of predicting success in jobs requiring manipulative skill? So we turn hopefully to the section of the manual of directions headed "some typical experience of users," and to the separate bibliography prepared by the publishers. Do we find convincing evidence of the value of the test? Unfortunately, we do not. It has apparently been given to more than five million people, but very few of them seem to have contributed to the validation data.

But we must be cautious in our criticism even on this point. Those of us who work in the field of industrial psychology know how difficult it is, very often, to collect evidence of the usefulness of our techniques. Probably many of us use procedures which, we are certain, have value but which we would find it hard to justify to the statistician. However, this provides us with no excuse for presenting our data in the way in which it is presented in the MacQuarrie manual. What is the enquirer to make of entries of the following kind? "(6) CAN PACKERS: Dotting, .33; Tapping, .25. *Source:* Stead and Shartle. (7) ADDING MACHINE OPERATORS: Tracing, .38; Tapping, .29. *Source:* Stead and Shartle." Dr. MacQuarrie may in fact have amassed extensive and convincing evidence of the value of his test for the selection of can packers and adding machine operators, but the statements we have quoted cannot be regarded as adequate indications of this. And what is the seeker after information expected to conclude from another statement: "(10) MACHINIST AND TOOL-MAKER APPRENTICES: 80 per cent to 90 per cent of boys satisfactory if total score is 75 or better"?

[662]

★Mellenbruch Curve-Block Series. Adults; 1946; originally called *Miami-Oxford Curve-Block Series;* individual; $18 per testing outfit; 10(15) minutes; P. L. Mellenbruch; the Author, 253 Rodes Ave., Lexington, Kentucky.

REFERENCES

1. MELLENBRUCH, P. L. "A Preliminary Report on the Miami-Oxford Curve-Block Series." *J Appl Psychol* 30:129-34 Ap '46. * (*PA* 20:3334)

William R. Grove, Psychologist and Director of Child Study Service, Phoenix Elementary Schools, Phoenix, Arizona; formerly Professor of Psychology and Director of the Division of Psychological Services, The University of Pittsburgh. Those who are familiar with the O'Connor *Wiggly Block* will be interested to learn that Dr. Mellenbruch had devised a somewhat similar test prior to the appearance of the O'Connor test. This was the predecessor of his present curve-block series. The existence of this original curve-block had not been reported in the literature until recently (1) so far as this reviewer is aware. The outstanding weakness of the O'Connor *Wiggly Block* is its extreme lack of reliability, a fact which seriously limits whatever validity the test may have. The original curve-block of Mellenbruch probably had the same basic weakness. His present test is a graded series of wiggly blocks which should materially increase the reliability of the test.

In its present form the test consists of six rectangular blocks, each two and three-fourths inches square by eight inches long. Each block is cut lengthwise along wavy lines into sections. The blocks of the series are made progressively more complex by simply increasing the number of sections. The easiest block is cut into three sections, while the most difficult consists of twelve. Each block is painted a different color. A clever device that facilitates administration of the test is the numbering of each section on the end to indicate its standard position for presentation to the subject.

Although the test author has given thought and study to the structural design of the series, this reviewer believes that the test could be somewhat further improved from a structural standpoint. This should be done before an attempt is made to standardize the test. Specifically, the second block of the series should be modified so as to eliminate the possibility of an incorrect solution that is so close to the correct solution as to cause confusion for even very intelligent subjects. At other points also a careful study of the reaction of subjects would reveal that certain errors are too plausible and thus weaken the test by introducing too much of the puzzle element into its solution.

The test is as yet unstandardized. Preliminary data on 93 cases are reported, but whether these are children or adults, college students, or day laborers, is nowhere stated. Probably they represent an ill-defined accumulation of cases that have little or no meaning as normative data. It is to be emphasized that although this test series seems to have some possibilities of merit, it will require a great deal of painstaking research to develop those potentialities to the point where they will have any practical utility.

Willard A. Kerr, Associate Professor of Psychology and Education, Illinois Institute of Technology, Chicago, Illinois. This test is among the most promising of the tests which attempt to measure complex spatial ability along with the speed and accuracy of eye-finger coordination. Mellenbruch pioneered in the development of this type of three-dimensional dexterity test in 1926, antedating by two years O'Connor's somewhat similar *Wiggly Block Test.*

Mellenbruch has proceeded from his original curve-block to the production of a series of such blocks, according to these principles: (*a*) The blocks in the series should range from very simple to very difficult. (*b*) Steps of increasing difficulty from one block to the next should be approximately equal. (*c*) The total series should not be too cumbersome but should be large enough for the smallest parts to be readily perceived and easily handled. (*d*) The series should be simple enough in administration to be practically self-administering. (*e*) The test should reduce to a minimum the factor of chance success or failure.

Although the six assembled blocks are identical in shape and size, their parts are so designed that no inside surface is flat or straight —and in no instances are the sections in any one block identical or reversible, nor are the sections of different blocks interchangeable. The six curve-blocks, each of a different color, constitute an attractive series, a fact which should help elicit interest and motivation of individuals about to be tested.

Mellenbruch reports a split-half reliability coefficient of .75. No validity data are offered, but the author states a plan to run validation studies.

This spatial-manipulative test should be a useful tool in industrial research and possibly in selection of certain types of personnel.

[663]

Minnesota Rate of Manipulation. Adults; 1931–46; revision of *Minnesota Manual Dexterity Test;* individual; 1 form; $18 per testing outfit; worklimit (10-15) minutes; revision by W. A. Ziegler; Educational Test Bureau.

REFERENCES

1-4. *See* 40:1662.
5. HARRELL, WILLARD. "A Factor Analysis of Mechanical Ability Tests." *Psychometrika* 5:17-33 Mr '40. * (*PA* 14:4285)
6. STEAD, WILLIAM H.; SHARTLE, CARROLL L.; OTIS, JAY L.; WARD, RAYMOND S.; OSBORNE, HERBERT F.; ENDLER, O. L.; DVORAK, BEATRICE J.; COOPER, JOHN H.; BELLOWS, ROGER M.; AND KOLBE, LAVERNE E. *Occupational Counseling Techniques: Their Development and Application.* Published for the Technical Board of the Occupational Research Program, United States Employment Service. New York: American Book Co., 1940. Pp. ix, 273. Out of print. * (*PA* 14:2627, title only)

7. BLUM, MILTON, AND CANDEE, BEATRICE. "The Selection of Department Store Packers and Wrappers With the Aid of Certain Psychological Tests." *J Appl Psychol* 25:76-85 F '41. * (*PA* 15:3104)
8. BENNETT, GEORGE K., AND CRUIKSHANK, RUTH M. *A Summary of Manual and Mechanical Ability Tests,* Preliminary Form, pp. 45-6. New York: Psychological Corporation, 1942. Pp. v, 80. Paper, lithotyped. $0.70. * (*PA* 16:2432)
9. COOK, DAVID W., AND BARRE, MARGUERITE F. "The Effect of Specialized Industrial Norms on the Use of the Minnesota Rate of Manipulation Test as a Selective Instrument in Employment Procedure." *J Appl Psychol* 26:785-92 D '42. * (*PA* 17:2448)
10. GHISELLI, EDWIN E. "Tests for the Selection of Inspector-Packers." *J Appl Psychol* 26:468-76 Ag '42. * (*PA* 17:2127)
11. TEEGARDEN, LORENE. "Manipulative Performance of Young Adult Applicants at a Public Employment Office—Part I." *J Appl Psychol* 26:633-52 O '42. * (*PA* 17:2907)
11a. TEEGARDEN, LORENE. "Manipulative Performance of Young Adult Applicants at a Public Employment Office, II." *J Appl Psychol* 26:754-69 D '42. * (*PA* 17:2908)
12. GHISELLI, EDWIN E. "The Use of the Minnesota Rate of Manipulation and the O'Connor Finger Dexterity Tests in the Selection of Package Wrappers." *J Appl Psychol* 27:33-4 F '43. * (*PA* 17:2851)
13. JURGENSEN, CLIFFORD E. "Extension of the Minnesota Rate of Manipulation Test." *J Appl Psychol* 27:164-9 Ap '43. * (*PA* 17:3542)
14. TEEGARDEN, LORENE. "Occupational Differences in Manipulative Performance of Applicants at a Public Employment Office." *J Appl Psychol* 27:416-37 O '43. * (*PA* 18:272)
15. ROBERTS, JOHN R., AND BAUMAN, MARY K. *Motor Skills Adapted to the Blind: Minnesota Rate of Manipulation Test [and] Pennsylvania Bi-Manual Worksample.* Minneapolis, Minn.: Educational Test Bureau, 1944. Pp. 8. Paper. $0.50. *
16. TUCKMAN, JACOB. "A Comparison of Norms for the Minnesota Rate of Manipulation Test." *J Appl Psychol* 28:121-8 Ap '44. * (*PA* 18:2981)
17. TUCKMAN, JACOB. "A Study of the Reliability of the Minnesota Rate of Manipulation Test by the Split-Half and Test-Retest Methods." *J Appl Psychol* 28:388-92 O '44. * (*PA* 19:533)
18. McMURRAY, ROBERT M., AND JOHNSON, DALE L. "Development of Instruments for Selecting and Placing Factory Employees." *Adv Mgmt* 10:113-20 S '45. * (*PA* 19:3473)
19. WAR MANPOWER COMMISSION, DIVISION OF OCCUPATIONAL ANALYSIS, STAFF. "Factor Analysis of Occupational Aptitude Tests." *Ed & Psychol Meas* 5:147-55 su '45. * (*PA* 20:1242)
20. WILSON, GUY M., AND OTHERS. "Adapting the Minnesota Rate of Manipulation Test to Factory Use." *J Appl Psychol* 29:346-9 O '45. * (*PA* 20:904)
21. BAUMAN, MARY K. "Studies in the Application of Motor Skills Techniques to the Vocational Adjustment of the Blind." *J Appl Psychol* 30:144-54 Ap '46. * (*PA* 20:3267)
22. TUCKMAN, JACOB. "A Comparison of the Reliability and Performance for the Minnesota Rate of Manipulation Test for Subjects Tested Individually and in Groups of Two." *J Appl Psychol* 30:37-41 F '46. * (*PA* 20:2346)
23. OXLADE, M. N., AND WALKER, K. F. "A Note on Adapting the Minnesota Rate of Manipulation Test to Factory Use." *J Appl Psychol* 31:247-8 Je '47. * (*PA* 21:4177)
24. SURGENT, LOUIS VINCENT. *The Use of Aptitude Tests in the Selection of Radio Tube Mounters.* American Psychological Association, Psychological Monographs, Vol. 61, No. 2, Whole No. 283. Washington, D. C.: the Association, Inc., 1947. Pp. v, 40. Paper, $1.00. *
25. SEASHORE, HAROLD G. "The Improvement of Performance on the Minnesota Rate of Manipulation Test When Bonuses Are Given." *J Appl Psychol* 31:254-9 Je '47. * (*PA* 21:3915)
26. SEASHORE, HAROLD G. "The Superiority of College Students on the Minnesota Rate of Manipulation Test." *J Appl Psychol* 31:249-53 Je '47. * (*PA* 21:3916)

Edwin E. Ghiselli, Associate Professor of Psychology, University of California, Berkeley, California. This test, which in spite of some deficiencies has been accepted as standard equipment for psychometricians, has been revised by the addition of three new tasks. The original tasks of placing the blocks into the holes by one hand and turning over the blocks by both hands are retained. Following these tests the subject performs three more tests as follows: the displacing test wherein he moves each block in turn from one hole to the next hole above, the one-hand turning and placing test which is similar to the original placing test except that each block is turned over before it is inserted, and finally, the two-hand placing and turning test which involves simultaneous motions of both hands in the two tasks of turning and placing.

The reliability coefficients of the various parts of the test appear to be of the order of .90 as estimated from a single administration. This would suggest a test-retest reliability of .80 to .85. The intercorrelations among the various parts are approximately .50. Relationships of this order are too high if the different parts of the test are to be considered as measuring different functions. Under the circumstances, then, if total scores are to be used, the new additional three tests probably add very little.

It is reported that the boards and blocks are carefully constructed within close tolerances. This will certainly be a distinct gain since there has been marked variation in dimensions among various copies of the original board.

For the original test, general population norms were available from a University of Minnesota study which stood as a classic in good sampling procedure. While norms are presented for the various parts of the revised test, they cannot be evaluated since no information is given concerning the characteristics of the normative sample. The lack of breakdown of scores by age and by sex is indicative of the inadequacy of the norms.

In the use of the original test, some psychometricians have stressed the value of the qualitative data obtained by observation of the testee. The addition of the new tasks in the revised edition of the test presumably would increase its value in this respect. It has been the experience of the reviewer, however, that with normal persons the qualitative ratings are closely related to the test scores and contribute very little. On the other hand, with persons with physical handicaps which possibly might affect manual dexterity, qualitative data obtained from observations appear to be very useful. It is to be noted that the displacing and turning tests have been used with the blind and satisfactory norms are available for such persons.

A survey of the validity coefficients of the original test indicates no significant differences between the turning and placing tests. On the average, for various packing operations and jobs involving placing movements, coefficients of the order of .20 to .30 may be expected. The validity for assembly operations is disappointingly low, being of the order of .10 to .15. The manual for the revised test gives validity coefficients of .57 for one-hand placing and turning, and .33 for two-hand placing and turning, for 60 men engaged in machine operations in a paper plant. This is the only statistical evidence cited for the validity of the new test. The present publishers seem to be more impressed with incidental observations of individual correspondence between test scores and performance. It would seem that the test is a wholly adequate instrument for selecting championship heavyweight boxers and basketball teams.

The reviewer gained the impression that the publisher is much more interested in making sales to untrained and unsuspecting persons than in developing a scientifically sound instrument. In light of considerations mentioned above, the revised test would appear to have little or no advantage over the original except, perhaps, in the precision of its physical construction.

John R. Kinzer, Assistant Professor of Psychology, The Ohio State University, Columbus, Ohio. This series of tests is intended to measure rapidity of movement of the hands, fingers, and arms. The chief uses have been in the selection of both office and shop workers for occupations requiring gross manipulatory movements. The tests are all performed on a long, narrow board which contains 60 holes in four rows of 15 each, into which are fit 60 cylindrical blocks.

The revised (1946) examiner's manual describes standard procedure for administering five separate tests and gives norms for two, three, and four trials. The five tests are called: (a) Placing, (b) Turning, (c) Displacing, (d) 1-Hand Turning and Placing, (e) 2-Hand Turning and Placing. This series of five tests yields rate of manipulation scores involving a variety of manipulative movements. Arm movement predominates in the placing and displacing tests. Coordinated arm, finger, and rotating wrist movements in both right and left arms predominate in the turning test. In the 1-hand turning and placing test, coordinated finger and arm movements in the preferred hand predominate; similar movements made simultaneously by both arms are included in the 2-hand turning and placing test.

The reliability and validity data on the tests are meager. The 1946 Examiner's Manual reports certain observations of test users and a study by Clifford E. Jurgensen (13) to indicate reliability and validity. These data are extremely inadequate. A user of the tests must set up norms and critical scores for his own population. The necessity for this would be suggested also, from the reviewer's experience with the tests, because of irregularity in the construction of the boards. The manufacturer claims that the boards are constructed with "close tolerances," but in spite of that claim there is much variation in hole and block sizes. The soft material used in the boards allows the holes to become oversize quickly. Also, warping has been a prevalent source of difficulty.

In spite of certain physical variations from board to board the tests are excellent for selection and placement of workers in simple manipulatory occupations. The tests are valuable in clinical and guidance work in schools. A skillful examiner can make some very useful clinical observations of the subject's reaction to frustrating and fatiguing elements of the tests.

J Consult Psychol 11:157 My-Je '47. * summarizes in convenient form much of the work that has been done on the test since its introduction in 1933 * The "stanine," a useful 9-point standard score originated in the Air Forces, is here given what is probably its first civilian application.

For reviews by Lorene Teegarden and Morris S. Viteles, see 40:1662.

[664]
Minnesota Spatial Relations Test. Ages 11 and over; 1930; revision of H. C. Link's *Spatial Relations Test;* individual; $48 per testing outfit; worklimit (15-45) minutes; Donald G. Paterson, Richard M. Elliott, L. Dewey Anderson, Herbert A. Toops, and Edna Heidbreder; Educational Test Bureau.

REFERENCES
1-10. *See* 40:1663.
11. PAGE, MARJORIE LOU. "The Mechanical Ability of Subnormal Boys." *J Appl Psychol* 17:164-81 Ap '33. * (*PA* 7:5888)
12. STANTON, MILDRED B. *Mechanical Ability of Deaf Children.* Columbia University, Teachers College, Contributions to Education, No. 751. Rudolf Pintner, faculty sponsor. New York: Bureau of Publications, the College, 1938. Pp. ix, 65. $1.60. * (*PA* 13:144)
13. HARRELL, WILLARD. "A Factor Analysis of Mechanical Ability Tests." *Psychometrika* 5:17-33 Mr '40. * (*PA* 14:4285)
14. STEAD, WILLIAM H.; SHARTLE, CARROLL L.; OTIS, JAY L.; WARD, RAYMOND S.; OSBORNE, HERBERT F.; ENDLER, O. L.; DVORAK, BEATRICE J.; COOPER, JOHN H.; BELLOWS, ROGER M.; AND KOLBE, LAVERNE E. *Occupational Counseling Techniques: Their Development and Application.* Published for the Technical Board of the Occupational Research Program, United States Employment Service. New York: American Book Co., 1940. Pp. ix, 273. Out of print. * (*PA* 14:2627, title only)

15. BRUSH, EDWARD N. "Mechanical Ability as a Factor in Engineering Aptitude." *J Appl Psychol* 25:300-12 Je '41. * (*PA* 15:4377)
16. GHISELLI, EDWIN E. "Tests for the Selection of Inspector-Packers." Abstract. *Psychol B* 38:735 O '41. * (*PA* 16:728, title only)
17. HARMON, JANET B., AND HARMON, LINDSEY R. "Measurement of Performance-Consistency on Tests of Manual Dexterity." Abstract. *Psychol B* 38:605 Jl '41. * (*PA* 15:5322, title only)
18. MORROW, ROBERT S. "An Experimental Analysis of the Theory of Independent Abilities." *J Ed Psychol* 32:495-512 O '41. * (*PA* 16:2209)
19. BENNETT, GEORGE K., AND CRUIKSHANK, RUTH M. *A Summary of Manual and Mechanical Ability Tests,* Preliminary Form, pp. 51-2. New York: Psychological Corporation, 1942. Pp. v, 80. Paper, lithotyped. $0.70. * (*PA* 16:2432)
20. JOHNSON, A. P. *The Prediction of Scholastic Achievement for Freshman Engineering Students at Purdue University.* Purdue University, Division of Educational Research, Studies in Engineering Education II. Lafayette, Ind.: the Division, May 1942. Pp. 22. Paper. $0.35. * (*PA* 16:5020)
21. JOHNSON, A. P. *The Relationship of Test Scores to Scholastic Achievement for 255 Engineering Freshmen Entering Purdue University in September, 1939.* Unpublished doctor's thesis, Purdue University, 1942.
22. TEEGARDEN, LORENE. "Manipulative Performance of Young Adult Applicants at a Public Employment Office—Part I." *J Appl Psychol* 26:633-52 O '42. * (*PA* 17:2907)
23. TEEGARDEN, LORENE. "Manipulative Performance of Young Adult Applicants at a Public Employment Office, II." *J Appl Psychol* 26:754-69 D '42. * (*PA* 17:2908)
24. BATES, JUSTINE; WALLACE, MARJORIE; AND HENDERSON, MACK T. "A Statistical Study of Four Mechanical Ability Tests." *Proc Iowa Acad Sci* 50:299-301 '43. * (*PA* 18:3276)
25. TEEGARDEN, LORENE. "Occupational Differences in Manipulative Performance of Applicants at a Public Employment Office." *J Appl Psychol* 27:416-37 O '43. * (*PA* 18:272)
26. HALSTEAD, H., AND SLATER, PATRICK. "An Experiment in the Vocational Adjustment of Neurotic Patients." *J Mental Sci* 92:509-15 Jl '45. * (*PA* 21:281)
27. WAR MANPOWER COMMISSION, DIVISION OF OCCUPATIONAL ANALYSIS, STAFF. "Factor Analysis of Occupational Aptitude Tests." *Ed & Psychol Meas* 5:147-55 su '45. * (*PA* 20:1242)
28. MYKLEBUST, HELMER R. "A Study of the Usefulness of Objective Measures of Mechanical Aptitude in Guidance Programs for the Hypacousic." *Am Ann Deaf* 91:123-50, 205-25 Mr, My '46. * (*PA* 20:3901)

Milton L. Blum, Assistant Professor, The City College of New York, New York, New York. This test was originally part of the battery developed at the University of Minnesota under a grant to study mechanical ability (2). The forerunner of the test was Link's *Spatial Relations Test.* Reliability coefficients of about .80 and validity coefficients of about .50 are reported for the *Minnesota Spatial Relations Test.*

The test measures two-dimensional spatial relations. It does not have the element of combining and integrating as does the *Kent–Shakow Formboard.* It is therefore a test of spatial relations on a more simple level. People with rather poor ability can successfully perform the test. Speed is the most important element in this test. Accuracy is self-corrected since wrongly sized or shaped blocks do not fit.

The test consists of four boards, each containing 58 oddly shaped and differently sized spaces. Boards A and B use the same set of blocks to be placed first in Board A and then in Board B. The arrangement of the blocks prior to placement is standardized. Board B is used to place the blocks in the proper starting position for Board A. The completion of Board A makes the blocks ready for Board B. The examiner, therefore, is not troubled with arranging and rearranging the blocks. Boards C and D are slightly different and require another set of blocks; the principle is the same as in Boards A and B.

Board A is used as a practice run, and the score on the test is the time taken to complete Boards B, C, and D. The authors have published norms for men, women, and boys. The reviewer has found that it saves time to eliminate the last two boards and modify the directions slightly so as to give Boards A and B as the test. Percentile norms are available on a large group of people between the ages of 16 and 24 seeking guidance, and such will be furnished upon request.

Most of the 58 blocks come in series of three: a small, a medium, and a large block of the same shape. The blocks in each series fit relatively close to one another on the board. False size discrimination occurs more often than false shape discrimination. Some subjects gain almost immediate insight into this size relationship and proceed in methodical fashion. Most subjects begin by filling in the holes with blocks in random fashion or in a position sequence and change to the three-block procedure. Very few perform the entire test without shifting their method. If they do not shift, their scores are very poor.

The test with its large number of holes and blocks looks complicated. Actually it is not; the reviewer has never tested a person who was not able to complete the task. This serves a useful purpose when a poor subject's morale needs bolstering during a test battery. Of course there is a considerable time difference between the fastest and slowest person.

The test is simple to administer. It is self-scoring except for timetaking and is useful in a battery for vocational guidance when some indication of mechanical ability related to two-dimensional spatial relations is desired. For the measurement of tridimensional spatial relations, the *Wiggly Block Test* or *Crawford Spatial Relations Test* should be used. The test measures very little finger or hand dexterity, and O'Connor's *Finger Dexterity Test* or the Placing Test in Zeigler's *Minnesota Rate of Manipulation Test* would be better measures of these.

For a review by Lorene Teegarden, see 40:1663.

[665]

★Pennsylvania Bi-Manual Worksample. Ages 17 and over; 1943–45; individual; 1 form; $15 per testing outfit; worklimit (10-20) minutes; John R. Roberts; Educational Test Bureau.

REFERENCES
1. ROBERTS, JOHN R., AND BAUMAN, MARY K. *Motor Skills Adapted to the Blind: Minnesota Rate of Manipulation Test [and] Pennsylvania Bi-Manual Worksample.* Minneapolis, Minn.: Educational Test Bureau, 1944. Pp. 8. Paper. $0.50. *
2. BAUMAN, MARY K. "Studies in the Application of Motor Skills Techniques to the Vocational Adjustment of the Blind." *J Appl Psychol* 30:144-54 Ap '46. * (PA 20:3267)
3. MAHER, HOWARD, AND FIFE, ISABELLE E. "A Biological-Pharmaceutical Checker Selection Program." *J Appl Psychol* 31:469-76 O '47. * (PA 22:3665)

Edwin E. Ghiselli, Associate Professor of Psychology, University of California, Berkeley, California. This test departs from the usual measures of finger dexterity in that it de-emphasizes the insertion of pegs into holes and the placing of washers around pegs. The task set by the test involves the simple operations of selecting a bolt with one hand and a nut with the other, assembling the two objects and placing the assembly in a receiving hole. Upon completion of 100 such operations, the second part of the test, which consists of disassembling the nuts and bolts and returning them to their proper dishes, is administered. Two scores are obtained, one for assembly and the other for disassembly. In both cases the score is the time to complete 100 operations. For normal persons the outside time for the assembly test is about 10 minutes and for the disassembly test about 4:5 minutes, with mean times of approximately 5 and 2.6 minutes, respectively. The disassembly appears to contribute little except reduction of work for the administrator.

Reliability of the test is given as .95 by the split-half method. Particularly for speed tests of this sort the split-half method gives a spuriously high estimate of reliability. With the test-retest method, reliability undoubtedly would be of the order of .80 to .85; and, while perhaps leaving something to be desired, nevertheless, it is satisfactory in comparison with other measures of dexterity. The assembly and disassembly parts are correlated to the extent of .55. Correlations with other types of dexterity tests are of the order of .40.

Evidence relative to validity in terms of correlations with measures of job success is completely lacking. The author of the test points out that the large bulk of successfully employed industrial workers engaged in tasks demanding dexterity make scores above the median of un-selected individuals. This, however, cannot be accepted as satisfactory evidence of validity. On the other hand, the author emphasizes the qualitative observations relative to the work methods of the testee that can be gained during the administration of the test. On the surface this would seem to be true when the nature of the task is considered, and indeed, a description of work methods is given in the manual. Nevertheless many testees fail to understand or follow the standard method of work prescribed by the manual, and this fact introduces variations of unknown extent in administration. The reviewer has received favorable comments from psychometricians concerning the usefulness of the test as a means for obtaining qualitative data.

Norms are given separately for both parts of the test by age and sex. It is stated that these norms are based upon an unselected sampling. However, even though the numbers of cases for both sexes are approximately 2,000, since the classes of individuals constituting the normative sample are not given, the distribution of scores cannot be considered wholly adequate as general population norms. Useful norms are given for several hundred persons successfully engaged in manipulative industrial jobs. Of considerable significance is the fact that distributions of scores are given for blind and partially blind individuals of both sexes and broken down into those successfully employed in manipulative industrial jobs and those without such work history. While the numbers of cases on which the distributions are based are relatively small, it is important to know that there has been successful experience in administering the test to the blind.

An additional advantage of the test is that the task required is something within the experience of all testees. It has been independently reported to the reviewer that persons who are test-shy feel quite comfortable with the *Pennsylvania Bi-Manual Worksample*.

Thomas W. Harrell, Associate Professor of Psychology, University of Illinois, Urbana, Illinois. This test purports to measure a combination of "finger dexterity of both hands, gross movements of both arms, eye-hand coordination, bi-manual coordination, and some indication of the individual's ability to use both hands in cooperation."

The test objects are a board, 105 bolts, and 105 nuts. The board is 2 feet $\times$ 8 inches in which there are 100 holes and 2 trays. The holes, $\frac{1}{4}$ inch apart, are arranged in 10 equal rows. There is a tray at each end of the holes; one tray contains nuts, the other bolts. The holes are $\frac{1}{2}$ inch in diameter; the nuts are $\frac{1}{4}$ inch in diameter and the bolts are $1\frac{1}{4}$ inches long.

The task is first one of assembly and then of disassembly. In assembly, a bolt with a nut on it is placed in each of the holes. Twenty holes are used for practice, 80 for the test. Disassembly is taking nuts off the 100 bolts and putting them in the appropriate trays. Assembly and disassembly scores correlate .55.

Score is obtained in time in seconds for assembly and for disassembly separately. Norms are given for converting the time scores into percentiles and into transmuted scores based on the standard deviation.

Norms are given for an "unselected sampling" of 1,793 males and 2,186 females; for 275 high school boys and 275 high school girls; for 200 men and 200 women of an industrial group who had done manipulative tasks in industry for six months. Their jobs or occupations are not given and might be meaningful. Distributions of time scores are given for each of the above groups in comparison with 19 blind men and 3 blind women with successful employment in industry; 118 blind men and 63 blind women without industrial experience; and 23 men and 7 women who could barely see. On assembly young people are better than old and men slightly better than women.

Reliability for the whole test using the Spearman–Brown formula is .947 for assembly.

No definite validity results are given although the general statement is made in the manual that "Data . . . indicate clearly its value in differentiating the good workers on manipulative tasks, similar to the way tests of general mental ability differentiate the good student from the poor student . . . numerous small in-plant studies of successful workers on highly repetitive manual work have consistently yielded averages equal to a transmuted score of 6 or better when compared with the general population, and rarely do we find a single worker in these groups with a transmuted score of less than 5."

This seems to be a good test. The reliability is high. Satisfactory validity is recited but is not given in anything like the detail to which test users are entitled.

Albert Gibson Packard, Assistant Director in Charge of Aptitude Testing, Public Schools, Baltimore, Maryland. The manual for this worksample states that it was developed to fulfill the need in the vocational field for a test situation which would combine the basic elements inherent in a relatively simple work situation. One of the most difficult problems in test construction is that of determining content for the test. Without a systematic analysis of many simple work situations and a summarization of the basic elements that operate or function in these situations in terms of their total frequency, there is little or no assurance that these basic elements are measured as they may or may not function. This procedure is not indicated by the author.

"Moreover, observation of the individual at work will reveal certain qualitative aspects of his performance which are important over and above native speed and dexterity." This point is well taken, but the procedure requires subjective interpretation. This writer has observed qualitative aspects of performance on a number of tests but has found no way to evaluate them objectively.

"The worksample should be considered a job and, as such, needs no validation." Where the worksample duplicates or is a miniature of a specific job, there is some chance that the above statement would be justified. However, the chances are remote that any industrial or vocational psychologist would find jobs that duplicate or are miniatures of this worksample. This leaves the problem of validation of this worksample for closely related jobs and other jobs that seem to require measures of this sort in the hands of those who wish to experiment with it.

Standard scores are given for interpretation. There is no indication as to how the classifications were determined in terms of work situations. Normal or average performance on a test is usually accepted as a band between plus and minus one standard deviation or between plus and minus one-half standard deviation. The interpretation given classifies all cases on this test of 5.0 standard score and below as "probably cannot compete" or "should not be considered," and those above 5.0 standard score as "skillful" and "extremely fast and accurate."

No justification for this method of interpretation is indicated.

Reliability reported by the split-half method on 112 vocational school boys is .897 and by application of the formula for a lengthened test as .947. This reliability coefficient would justify the use of this test as an individual measure for this group. Does this reliability hold for other groups?

Correlations are given in the manual between the worksample and the *Minnesota Rate of Manipulation,* the *Revised Beta Examination* and the O'Connor *Finger Dexterity Test.* They indicate a certain degree of uniqueness in this test, for while positive they are not high (.35 to .46). The populations vary for each coefficient, which leads one to raise the question as to what they might be if all were based on the same population.

The physical make-up of the test can be classified as very good. The directions for administering are clear and adequate.

Norms are given for men and women for both aspects of the test (assembly and disassembly). The assumption must be made, however, that these groups are representative of the general male and female populations. Descriptions of these groups based on other factors would be most helpful.

Neil D. Warren, Associate Professor of Psychology and Dean of Men, The University of Southern California, Los Angeles, California. Little information about this test is available in publications other than the manual prepared by the author of the test. It is relatively new (1943), convenient, and neatly designed; hence, it would appear probable that reports of its use should begin to appear in the literature in the near future.

The test has been devised to provide a complex work situation involving both gross movements of the arms and fine coordination of the fingers. Both hands must be used to perform the task. This worksample requires the assembly and disassembly of nut and bolt units. The bolts secured from one tray and the nuts from another are assembled and placed in rows of holes before the subject. In the disassembly task the nuts and bolts are separated and returned to their respective bins. The scores are in terms of the time required to complete each of the separate tasks. It may be questioned whether such a task can be described properly as a worksample. Certainly as a standard task its applicability to specific work situations is somewhat limited.

The nature of the task as such is to require relatively long periods for both assembly and disassembly. This undoubtedly contributes to satisfactory reliability for the test. In the attractive and comprehensive manual accompanying the test reliability is given as .897 (Spearman–Brown correction: .947). The norm groups reported in the manual include a large (N = 3,979) group of "unselected adults" and adequate groups of high school students and industrial workers. The latter group is differentiated by having a history of at least six months of successful employment in manipulative tasks. The norms are listed in standard scores as well as in percentiles. Preliminary data on groups of blind subjects are also reported.

The author's evidence of validity is confined to correlational data showing the relationship of scores on the test to those on such tests as the *Minnesota Rate of Manipulation Test,* the O'Connor *Finger Dexterity Test,* and the Bennett *Test of Mechanical Comprehension.* These correlations range from .17 to .46. The data reported also provide an indication of the differences between unselected adults and industrial workers. There are, however, few published reports indicating the application of the test to specific occupations. Until the validation is expanded to include studies of the relationship of test scores to occupational criteria and the test is given further statistical elaboration, such as factor analysis, psychometrists must consider the test a promising but not yet wholly acceptable measuring instrument.

[666]

★**Purdue Pegboard.** Grades 9-12 and adults; 1941; $12.50 per testing outfit; 90¢ per 25 score sheets; 2½ (10) minutes; prepared by the Purdue Research Foundation; Science Research Associates.

REFERENCES

1. LONG, LOUIS, AND HILL, JOHN. "Additional Norms for the Purdue Pegboard." *Occupations* 26:160-1 D '47. * (*PA* 22:2154)
2. SURGENT, LOUIS VINCENT. *The Use of Aptitude Tests in the Selection of Radio Tube Mounters.* American Psychological Association, Psychological Monographs, Vol. 61, No. 2, Whole No. 283. Washington, D. C.: the Association, Inc., 1947. Pp. v, 40. Paper. $1.00. *
3. TIFFIN, JOSEPH. *Industrial Psychology,* Second Edition, pp. 126-7, 141. New York: Prentice-Hall, Inc., 1947. Pp. xxi, 553. Trade edition, $5.35; textbook edition, $4.00. * (*PA* 22:505)

Edwin E. Ghiselli, Associate Professor of Psychology, University of California, Berkeley, California. Unlike most tests of finger dexterity, the *Purdue Pegboard* is a time-limit rather than a work-limit test. This characteristic, however, appears to be its only advantage. The test consists of four parts, insertion of pegs with the right hand, the left hand, both hands simultaneously, and finally, a simple assembly involving the placing of a washer and a collar over the peg. The first three parts require a half minute each and the last part one minute, the scores on all parts being based on the number of operations completed in the time allotted.

A most unfortunate characteristic of the test is its physical construction. The base which contains the holes into which the pegs are inserted is made of wood. Insertion of the metal pegs causes sufficient wear so that after the test has been administered to a few hundred persons the holes increase in size and the test scores are significantly changed. This means that norms and data relative to reliability and validity must be considered with caution. In addition, the holes are drilled at different depths so that some testees lose time by trying to force a peg into a shallow hole. This differential depth varies from board to board and apparently is not intentional inasmuch as three or four consecutive holes may be of one depth while the following holes are of another.

The test can be administered by giving each part once, twice, or three times. For the first three parts, involving simple peg insertion, adequate reliability of about .85 is not achieved unless they are administered three times. For the assembly part this reliability can be achieved with two administrations. Norms are available for several hundred industrial workers, but the constitution of the groups is not given and therefore the distributions cannot be considered adequate.

The authors of the test state that the scores have satisfactory validity but that for reasons beyond their control they are unable to present the exact data. Under certain circumstances, correlations as low as .20 may be considered as evidence of adequate validity for a test of this sort. Since neither the coefficients nor information concerning the specific types of jobs on which the test was employed are cited, conclusions relative to validity must be held in abeyance. In light of this and other matters considered, the *Purdue Pegboard* would appear to be of doubtful value.

Thomas W. Harrell, Associate Professor of Psychology, University of Illinois, Urbana,

Illinois. No definite validity results are given in the preliminary manual or on the score sheet. The manual states that "considerable data have been accumulated as to the validity of this test in respect to a number of jobs in one of our large ordnance plants. Government regulations, however, prevent the release of these data and comparable studies are now being made elsewhere." Tiffin has written, in a letter to the reviewer, that it was impossible to obtain the ordnance data. Accompanying the Tiffin letter was a curve showing a close, but statistically undetermined relation between assembly scores and production index for approximately 30 quillers.

The score sheet states that "High scores on the *Pegboard* have been shown related to success in the majority of occupations requiring motor coordination. Such occupations include: . . ." and a list of 16 occupations follow. Data cannot be located to support this statement.

No correlation is given between insertion and assembly. Because of the lack of results it is impossible to appraise the importance of these separate scores which purportedly measure dexterities that differ in an important way.

An advantage of this test is that it has a time limit whereas many similar appearing tests have work limits; consequently the *Purdue Pegboard* can conveniently be given simultaneously to more persons per examiner. If two important different dexterities are measured, the test has the advantage of measuring them both with the same board. The disadvantage of the test is that with the exception of a small number of quillers with an undetermined validity coefficient there is no validity demonstrated.

Albert Gibson Packard, Assistant Director in Charge of Aptitude Testing, Public Schools, Baltimore, Maryland. Many tests have been designed for the measurement of motor skills. Studies indicate considerable specificity (low correlation) between them, which raises the question as to the application of such measures.

The preliminary manual for this test states that it can be applied to many job situations where the particular aspects of motor dexterity measured by the tests are required. There is no quarrel with this statement; but in order to apply a test of this type with any degree of confidence, except experimentally, it is necessary to know its predictive efficiency, an adequate description of the job situation in which it was validated, and a description of the group upon which it was established. The preliminary manual indicates that such information is not available at this time.

Psychologists have been stumbling along for many years with so-called measuring instruments which do not meet the requirements of a measuring instrument. One of the prime requisites is that of consistency. For individual test use the desirable reliability coefficient has been set at not less than .95. The coefficients reported do not meet this requirement. However, by increasing the length of the test for the first trial, it is quite likely that this reliability may be obtained.

The physical make-up, compared with some performance tests that have been placed on the market, is very good.

It would be most helpful if the manual reported intercorrelations between the right hand, left hand, both hands, and assembly administrations of the tests; also correlations between the various administrations of this test and the numerous other dexterity tests used in industrial plants. From these intercorrelations it may be possible to determine the community or the uniqueness of this test in order to match it experimentally with any particular industrial job situation or to determine the application of this test in a composite of traits for job differentiation and selection. Considerable evidence has been accumulated which indicates that job situations require a composite of characteristics which function as a pattern.

The norms for women for the one-trial administration were based on 954 applicants; for two-trial administrations they were based on 100 applicants; for the three-trial norms, on an interpolation from the two-trial norms. The assumption one must make in using these norms is that they represent the general female adult population. Are these women all of one age? Is there a significant difference between age groups? What factors other than race, previous occupation, and geographic locality were considered that would indicate that this is a representative population?

[667]

★Small Parts Dexterity Test. Adults; 1946; individual; $25 per testing outfit, postpaid; worklimit (10-25) minutes; John Crawford; Psychological Corporation.

Joseph E. Moore, Head, Department of Psychology, Georgia School of Technology, At-

lanta, Georgia. This test consists of four parts, a one-inch plywood board containing 3 circular bins for 45 metal collars, 45 pins, and 45 screws; a metal plate with 42 holes for the pins and 42 holes for the screws; and 2 metal trays, one to receive the pins, the other to receive the screws. A slot in the board serves as a receptacle for a screwdriver and a pair of tweezers, both of which are included.

The test is taken in two parts. Part 1 starts with a practice trial in which the subject, after being shown how to proceed, picks up a pin, inserts it in one of the holes, then picks up a flanged collar, and places it over the protruding end of the pin, flange down. Each pin must have a collar placed on it before the subject proceeds to the next one. He does 6 pins in the practice trial and is timed on doing 36 in the test proper. Part 2 consists of picking up a screw with the fingers, giving it "just enough of a twist to start it in the threads," and then using the screwdriver with both hands to screw it all the way through to the tray below. The practice trial for Part 2 is given over 6 screws. The test proper is the time necessary to turn 36 screws through the plate into the tray below.

The author certainly did not understate it when he put at the top of the manual the words "Preliminary Manual." It seems that everything about this test is preliminary or tentative. There are no data on reliability or validity. In the author's own words, which express a hope rather than a verified conclusion, he states that "performance on this test is expected to be related to such jobs as wiring of intricate devices, radio tube manufacture, fine inspection work, and the adjustment of motors, clocks, watches, typewriters, office machines, and other instruments." The buyer has no basis of knowing what the test measures from the manual. The author even failed to include "the small quantity of validating data obtained with a pilot set of the test." The statement that "the accumulation of really significant data waits upon the cooperation of the test's industrial users" is to the reviewer a regrettable one. Why should an industrial user have to pay a high price for an instrument that has nothing to support it except the preliminary form and a "hope" from the maker that maybe he has developed something of value?

The "tentative norms," if one wishes to use the term tentative in its loosest sense, were accumulated from "470 adult males seeking industrial employment, unselected as to education and previous experience." The norms are in three groups, high, average, and low. Separate norms for the pins and collars and those for the screws are given. The range is given. No other statistical data whatsoever are given.

This instrument and the superficial job of "validating" it and developing its wholly inadequate norms reflect adversely, and justly so, on the testmaker and the Psychological Corporation which prematurely distributed it. If the testmaker knew no better how to develop and validate a test, certainly those who passed on his material in the Psychological Corporation should have known better.

Test users should expect from a testmaker and a test distributor alike a serious and sincere effort to show what, if anything, their instrument can do that other tried tests are not doing. The failure on the part of the maker of the *Small Parts Dexterity Test* and of the distributor in meeting the foregoing standards makes a sad and regrettable episode in the field of test development.

MECHANICAL ABILITY

[668]
Detroit Mechanical Aptitudes Examination, Revised. Grades 7-16; 1928–39; Form A; $3 per 100; 15¢ per specimen set, postpaid; 31 (40) minutes; Harry J. Baker, Paul H. Voelker, and Alex C. Crockett; Public School Publishing Co.

REFERENCES
1. BAKER, HARRY J. "A Mechanical Aptitude Test." *Detroit Ed B* 12:5-6 Ja '29. *
2. BENNETT, GEORGE K., AND CRUIKSHANK, RUTH M. *A Summary of Manual and Mechanical Ability Tests*, Preliminary Form, pp. 31-2. New York: Psychological Corporation, 1942. Pp. v, 80. Paper, lithotyped. $0.70. * (*PA* 16:2432)
3. PREISCHE, WALTER A. *The Relationship of Certain Measurable Factors to Success in Secondary-School Physics.* Unpublished doctor's thesis, New York University, 1944. (Abstracts of Theses . . . [*School of Education*] 1944, pp. 217-21.)
4. PORTENIER, LILLIAN G. "Mechanical Aptitudes of University Women." *J Appl Psychol* 29:477-82 D '45. * (*PA* 20:1062)

Lloyd G. Humphreys, Supervisor of the Testing Division, University of Washington, Seattle, Washington. There is little that needs to be added to Lorge's earlier review of this test. To summarize briefly, mechanical aptitude is presumably measured by the 8 subtests of (*a*) tool recognition, (*b*) "motor" speed (marking X's in circles), (*c*) size discrimination, (*d*) arithmetic fundamentals, (*e*) disarranged pictures, (*f*) tool information, (*g*) belt and pulley motions, and (*h*) digit-letter substitution. No satisfactory explanation for this particular analysis of mechanical ability is given. The inadequate correlational data presented indicate that the parts are, as expected, quite diverse. In addition, 7 of the subtests are combined into supposedly meaningful groups as follows: motor—Tests 2 and 8; visual imagery—Tests 3, 5, and 7; mechanical information—Tests 1 and 6. Though the absence of the complete table of intercorrelations leaves this matter somewhat in doubt, it is probable that only the last of the groupings can be firmly supported empirically.

Validation data are largely lacking. Scores on an earlier form of the test were correlated with shop grades, the number of cases not specified. The resulting correlation was .64. A correlation of .65 is also reported between this test and the *Detroit Advanced Intelligence Test* for 185 twelfth grade pupils. This finding is not evaluated by the test authors. It is, of course, too high to make the test very useful. It is also needlessly high; i.e., certain sections of the mechanical test undoubtedly overlap much more with the intelligence test than do other sections. The mechanical information group—Tests 1 and 6—probably has a lower correlation than most of the other subtests with the intelligence test. Since this group also has a reasonably high degree of homogeneity and reliability, it is probable that it contributes the most useful score to be obtained from this test. This hypothesis obviously needs empirical confirmation before the counselor can proceed to use this score with confidence.

The reviewer wishes to condemn particularly the sort of validation presented on the next to the last page of the manual. A table shows the necessary levels of "mechanical ability" and "mental ability" for about seventy occupations. These levels are based on "opinions of approximately two hundred Detroit counselors and teachers." Such data are no substitute for correlation coefficients between test scores obtained before training and later criteria of success.

Dewey B. Stuit, Professor of Psychology and Dean, Student Personnel Services, The State University of Iowa, Iowa City, Iowa. This test is designed to measure mechanical aptitude. The eight subtests are as follows: (1) tool recognition, (2) motor speed, (3) size discrimination, (4) arithmetic fundamentals, (5) disarranged pictures, (6) tool information, (7) belt and pulley, (8) letter and number combinations. The titles of the first six tests are self-explanatory. Test 7 requires the examinee to determine the speed and direction of the second of two pulleys. In Test 8 the examinee places a number (taken from a key at the left of the page) under each of eight letters placed at the top of the page. The test appears to measure the speed with which this operation is performed.

The examination is easy to administer and not particularly difficult to score except that it has no separate answer sheet and, of course, is not machine scorable. There is some possibility of misinterpretation of directions in Test 7; it would have been better if the directions had stated that the arrows referred to the movement of the upper halves of the pulleys.

Validity data on the test are conspicuous by their absence. Under the heading of "validations" the authors report a correlation of .65 with the *Detroit Advanced Intelligence Test*. Evidently the authors believe that this correlation indicates that the test is not measuring the same factors as those measured by intelligence tests. Actually this correlation seems quite high, indicating considerable overlap with intelligence tests. Correlations with such criteria as shop grades are not reported in the test manual.

Considerable space is devoted in the manual to the subject of age norms. These are provided for the subtests as well as for the test as a whole. Provision is also made for converting the scores for each half-year group, ages 10 to 16, into letter ratings A, B, C+, C, C−, D, and E. Separate norms are not provided for girls and boys.

The reliability coefficient for the total test, computed by the test-retest method for 259 eighth grade pupils is .898. Reliability coefficients for the subtests range from .571 for Test 2 to .875 for Test 5. Intercorrelations are not reported except for Tests 1 and 6, the coefficient being .615.

The authors state that the test should be of value in a school's program of guidance and counseling. Some subjective data are presented indicating the level of mechanical ability (and general intelligence) required for success in various occupations. Unfortunately the authors fail to present the necessary evidence to indicate that this test *does measure* the mechanical aptitude deemed necessary for successful participation in these occupations. Until data are presented showing that this test will predict success in shop courses or in mechanical occupations it would appear that the test would prove of limited usefulness in guidance and counseling.

For a review by Irving Lorge and an excerpt from a review by J. Wayne Wrightstone, see 40:1656.

[669]

★Mechanical Aptitude Tests: Acorn National Aptitude Tests. Grades 9-16 and adults; 1943-45; 1 form; $2.00 per 25; 10¢ per manual; 50¢ per specimen set; 45(50) minutes; Andrew Kobal, J. Wayne Wrightstone, and Karl R. Kunze; Acorn Publishing Co.

Reign H. Bittner, Director of Personnel Research, Owens–Illinois Glass Company, Toledo, Ohio. The test is designed as an indicator of aptitude for a mechanical trade for pupils in the seventh to twelfth grades of school. It is also intended for industrial use in the selection of apprentices, mechanic learners, and employees in semiskilled mechanical occupations. It consists of four subtests as follows: (a) Comprehension of Mechanical Tasks; (b) Use of Tools and Materials [Verbal]; (c) Matching Tools and Operations; (d) Use of Tools and Materials [Nonverbal]. The first three subtests consist of verbal material; the last subtest is presented pictorially and, although named the same as Subtest 2, appears on inspection to measure a skill somewhat different from that tested in Subtest 2.

A well-written manual of directions is provided. Inspection of the manual indicates that the publisher has attempted to present in an unbiased manner all the known facts about the test. A class record sheet is also provided which includes directions for administration and scoring as well as a form for recording test scores. This record form is deficient in one respect; no space is provided for recording the percentile rank, only the raw score being provided for.

The test appears to be easy to administer. The format is generally satisfactory but could be improved. Answers are recorded by underlining the alternative chosen whereas a simpler and more easily scored response could be used. Because of the format of Test 3, underlining should make this especially difficult to score. The format of Test 4 presents the directions after the sample question which may be confusing to the subject.

The reliability of the test is reasonably satisfactory. An odd-even reliability coefficient of .83 is reported for the sum of the three verbal parts. A coefficient of .86 is reported for the grade 9 normative population, using the Kuder–Richardson Case IV method of computation. Presumably, this refers to the total score although it is not stated in the manual. It is the opinion of the reviewer that if the Kuder–Richardson Case II method were used to estimate the reliability a more satisfactory estimate would have resulted.

Data on the validity of the test are meager. Only one study is reported. At the Colt Firearms Company, correlations between test scores and various criteria for young employees in machine shop, sheet metal, welding, and various semiskilled machine operations were as follows: shop rating, .68; success in industrial training, .64; advancement record, .52. Details of the study are not available so that it can be properly evaluated, but these results look promising. It is regrettable that the test was not more extensively validated before publication. Whether or not this test is a valid measure of mechanical aptitude must be determined on the basis of careful empirical studies. Without further evidence of this kind, it is impossible to judge whether the test is generally applicable as a measure of mechanical aptitude.

Percentile norms are presented for separate school grades from seventh to twelfth and for mechanical and nonmechanical industrial employees. Each school grade population included about 1,000 cases. The mechanical industrial group included about 400 applicants for jobs in machine shop, metal work, and carpentry, and the nonmechanical group was composed of about 350 employees in office work, business and other nonmechanical occupations. Separate norms should probably be given for males and females since there are usually considerable sex differences on this type of test.

Directions for administration of the test do not appear complete enough to insure uniform testing procedure. In addition, the directions given in the manual differ from those printed on the class record form in important respects. Directions for scoring Part 2 of the test also differ in the manual and on the class record form: in one case *all three* required responses to an item must be correct before credit is given; in the other *each* required response marked in accordance with the key is considered correct.

An attempt has been made to simplify scoring by using a scoring key word for each sub-test. Alternatives are lettered, and the alternative which is identified by one of the letters in the key word is correct. This does away with scoring stencils, strip keys, etc. In the opinion of the reviewer this complicates rather than simplifies scoring since it makes the scoring operation a mental rather than a mechanical task. The scorer must remember the letters in the key word and compare mentally the letter of the response marked with the key letters to decide whether the item is marked correctly. It is believed that this will make scoring slow and subject to errors. Another criticism of this type of scoring key is that the key may easily be "stolen" and given wide circulation. Once the simple key word for any subtest is obtained by unauthorized persons the answers to the whole test are given away. Printing the key words on the class record form appears to be especially hazardous from this point of view.

James M. Porter, Jr., Associate Professor of Psychology, Rensselaer Polytechnic Institute, Troy, New York. This test consists of four subtests: (*a*) Comprehension of Mechanical Tasks, 15 minutes, 30 mechanical problems which require thinking along practical lines; (*b*) Use of Tools and Materials [Verbal], 12 minutes, 20 questions on the use of tools for stated jobs; (*c*) Matching Tools and Operations, 8 minutes, 40 problems requiring judgment concerning tools and mechanical devices with relation to operations; (*d*) Use of Tools and Materials [Nonverbal], 10 minutes, 20 groups of five pictures in which the examinee is to select the item out of place in each group.

Reliability and validity indices are reported only for the first three subtests. Standardization has been more adequate than is frequently the case. Study of the items leads one to doubt that the battery measures more than mere information since the testee is not required to demonstrate understanding of how mechanical devices work.

Alec Rodger, Senior Psychologist to the Admiralty; on leave from the National Institute of Industrial Psychology; London, England. The most striking feature of this test is the unsatisfactory printing. The sans-serif type is oppressive to the eye and far more suitable for advertisement display than for a 45-minute examination paper. Moreover, most pages are cramped (one very badly) and, in the reviewer's copy at least, the inking has been unevenly done. These faults are all avoidable, and they are not altogether trivial, because they may produce a strongly unfavorable impression on the potential purchaser.

The underlying notion is to gauge "mechanical aptitude" by testing everyday mechanical knowledge. Recent research lends general support to the view that this is a more profitable approach than one which makes use of tests involving such processes as tapping, tracing, and dotting, but where is the evidence that this particular test is valuable? It is certainly not offered in the manual of directions. The paragraph on validity is extremely inadequate. It gives three coefficients of correlation with vague criteria of occupational success, and one coefficient of correlation with the results of scores in other (unspecified) tests of mechanical aptitude. The numbers involved are not mentioned, nor is there any satisfactory indication of the nature of the jobs covered.

The critical student of tests, looking into the credentials of the Acorn *Mechanical Aptitude Test,* will reach a conclusion he reaches all too frequently. He will say, This *may* be a good test, but nobody seems to have shown that it is.

[670]

★Mellenbruch Mechanical Aptitude Test for Men and Women. Grades 7-16 and adults; 1944; Forms A, B; $2.85 per 25; 50¢ per specimen set; 35(40) minutes; P. L. Mellenbruch; Science Research Associates.

Lloyd G. Humphreys, Supervisor of the Testing Division, University of Washington, Seattle, Washington. The test consists of two forms of 84 items each. Items are arranged in 7 sets of 12 pictures of common mechanical objects. For each set of 12 pictures, there is a corresponding group of pictures of 14 mechanical objects, of which 12 are related to the first group. The examinee's task is to make the correct matchings.

Items were selected from an original list of 425 paired photographs. The original group of items was presented to men and women in shops and in shop-training schools. Items were discarded primarily on the basis of the relationships between individual items and ratings obtained from the foreman or teacher. Items which differed markedly in difficulty for the two sexes were also discarded. The test shows only a 6-point difference between comparable samples of men and women. Though a standard deviation is not given, this difference is probably small for a test of this type. No data are presented, however, to support this procedure; i.e., it is possible that a mechanical test should give maximum sex differences. Validity may be reduced, for both men and women, at least for most occupations, by including feminine material.

Reliability is highly satisfactory. The correlation between comparable forms, generally a conservative estimate, is .87 for 169 unselected cases.

Norms are adequately varied, but the number of cases seems to be small, particularly for the industrial groups. (I am reasoning from mean scores listed in one part of the manual with accompanying N's. The table of norms does not list the N of any group.)

Validity data are sketchy. One should not be too critical of the present test, however, since it is probably no worse than average with respect to the relative lack of validity coefficients. The correlation between test scores and teacher's rank in engineering drawing for 57 women is .59. The correlation with degree of past participation in 30 mechanical activities of 430 unselected men and women is .60. While this latter finding constitutes validity of a sort, it is not necessarily the same as predicting future success in mechanical occupations. The method of item selection indicates some degree of usefulness for the tests, but no data are presented from which a validity coefficient could be estimated.

Correlations presented indicate substantial relationships between this test and two other mechanical tests—.50 with the "Stenquist (rev.)" for 100 Air Force officers and .61 with the Air Force Mechanical Information Test, a verbal test of mechanical information, for 98 Air Force employees. Since the latter test was found to be valid for pilot selection, as well as for the more obviously mechanical occupations in the Air Corps, similar validities can be assumed for Mellenbruch's test.

For two relatively unselected samples of 131 and 127 cases, the correlations with "Army Alpha (Rev. and F.5)" are .33 and .29. The degree of relationship indicated by these data is gratifyingly low. The reviewer has the impression from taking the test, however, that this relationship could be appreciably reduced by appropriate item analysis. Several items seem to measure abstract reasoning rather than mechanical information. If the items were correlated with the Army Alpha, a considerable spread of item coefficients would probably be found. Items with high values could then be discarded. It is possible that the poor reproduction of many objects and the use of many obsolete objects also contribute to the correlation with Army Alpha. Such factors, at any rate, probably contribute unwanted variance to the total test scores and should be corrected in a revision.

C. A. Oakley, Lecturer in Industrial Psychology, Glasgow University, Glasgow, Scotland. This test is of a type which has become quite well known in recent years. It is of a pictorial character and seeks to pick out mechanically inclined people by finding whether they know what various mechanical or semi-mechanical things are used for. Drawings of these things, which are described in the manual as "common objects and devices," are set out in two columns, the person doing the test having to state for each picture in the first column which picture in the second column "goes with it best." Provision is made for 84 of these matchings.

Criticism of the general character of tests of this kind is usually concerned with two aspects: (*a*) Is the general conception sound? and (*b*) Are the articles to be paired well selected? The answer on the first point is in the affirmative. Candidates for employment are given a better opportunity in this sort of group test than in most other tests for showing whether in their everyday life they are really interested in mechanical things. In many branches of personnel selection and vocational guidance this is helpful information.

The other point raises, however, more doubt. How well have the various articles been selected? It is scarcely possible for someone from Great Britain to be specific in expressing an opinion, for some of the objects and devices are of American usage. Nevertheless, the selection does seem rather odd, for it is difficult to detect much consistency in the choices, articles of real mechanical interest appearing in the columns besides nonmechanical things such as jewelled rings and shoes. Undoubtedly something of interest has been learned when it is discovered that a candidate can differentiate, for instance, between a badminton and a tennis racket. But does it have much bearing on his *mechanical inclination?*

Although the manual does not report that the test has been tried out on large groups, some of the conclusions are interesting—particularly the low but positive correlation found with intelligence. While intelligence is unquestionably called for in doing the test, Mellenbruch seems to have been reasonably successful in keeping it to relatively small proportions.

[671]

Minnesota Assembly Test. Ages 11 and over; 1930; a revision of *Stenquist Mechanical Assembling Test* by John L. Stenquist; sometimes called *Minnesota Mechanical Assembly Test;* regular and abridged forms; $35.50 per set of testing materials; $29 per set of testing materials for abridged form; revision by Donald G. Paterson, Richard M. Elliott, L. Dewey Anderson, Herbert A. Toops, and Edna Heidbreder; C. H. Stoelting Co.

REFERENCES

1. ANDERSON, L. DEWEY. "The Minnesota Mechanical Ability Tests." *Personnel J* 6:473-8 Ap '28. * (*PA* 2:2642)
2. RILEY, G. "Stanford Binet 'Indicators' of Mechanical Ability." *Psychol Clinic* 18:128-32 My-Je '29. * (*PA* 4:1429)
3. PATERSON, DONALD G.; ELLIOTT, RICHARD M.; ANDERSON, L. DEWEY; TOOPS, HERBERT A.; AND HEIDBREDER, EDNA. *Minnesota Mechanical Ability Tests.* Minneapolis, Minn.: University of Minnesota Press, 1930. Pp. xxii, 586. $5.00. * (*PA* 5:1268)
4. HARVEY, O. L. "Mechanical 'Aptitude' or Mechanical 'Ability'?—A Study in Method." *J Ed Psychol* 22:517-22 O '31. * (*PA* 6:910)
5. FRANDSEN, ARDEN N. "Mechanical Ability of Morons." *J Appl Psychol* 19:371-8 Ag '35. * (*PA* 10:1000)
6. BINGHAM, WALTER VAN DYKE. *Aptitudes and Aptitude Testing*, pp. 294-309. New York and London: Harper & Brothers, 1937. Pp. ix, 390. $3.00; 12s. 6d. * (*PA* 11:2885)
7. STANTON, MILDRED B. *Mechanical Ability of Deaf Children.* Columbia University, Teachers College, Contributions to Education, No. 751. Rudolf Pintner, faculty sponsor. New York: Bureau of Publications, the College, 1938. Pp. ix, 65. $1.60. * (*PA* 13:144)
8. HARRELL, WILLARD. "A Factor Analysis of Mechanical Ability Tests." *Psychometrika* 5:17-33 Mr '40. * (*PA* 14:4285)
9. BRUSH, EDWARD N. "Mechanical Ability as a Factor in Engineering Aptitude." *J Appl Psychol* 25:300-12 Je '41. * (*PA* 15:4377)
10. BENNETT, GEORGE K., AND CRUIKSHANK, RUTH M. *A Summary of Manual and Mechanical Ability Tests*, Preliminary Form, pp. 43-4. New York: Psychological Corporation, 1942. Pp. v, 80. Paper, lithotyped. $0.70. * (*PA* 16:2432)
11. MYKLEBUST, HELMER R. "A Study of the Usefulness of Objective Measures of Mechanical Aptitude in Guidance Programs for the Hypacousic." *Am Ann Deaf* 91:123-50, 205-25 Mr, My '46. * (*PA* 20:3901)

William R. Grove, Psychologist and Director of Child Study Service, Phoenix Elementary Schools, Phoenix, Arizona; formerly Professor of Psychology and Director of the Division of Psychological Services, The University of Pittsburgh. This test is a revision of the *Stenquist Mechanical Assembling Test,* which it was designed to supersede. Most of what has been said in reviewing the Stenquist test is equally applicable to this one, and the reader is referred to that review (*see* 679).

The Minnesota revision of the Stenquist test increased the reliability of the latter from a raised odd-even coefficient of .72 to one of .94 in a population of junior high school boys. This increase was accomplished by lengthening the test. While the Stenquist test had consisted of 10 mechanical models in one box, the Minnesota revision consists of 33 models in three boxes. The Stenquist series could be administered in 30 minutes, but the revision requires about twice that long.

The basic validity of the method incorporated in this test for measuring the mechanical ability of junior high school boys was first established by Stenquist and fully substantiated by the Minnesota research. The principal advantage of the Minnesota test over its predecessor is the extensive research program of which this test was an important part. Not only did this research provide in this test an instrument of more adequate reliability and carefully tested validity, but it also provided data on other tests of mechanical ability validated and standardized on the same junior high school population. It was found possible by statistically combining this test with several others to predict a carefully constructed criterion of mechanical ability to the extent represented by a correlation coefficient of .65. This is a notable accomplishment when we consider the relative uniqueness of mechanical ability as contrasted with academic ability.

This test is also available in a short form which consists of twenty of the mechanical models of the long form assembled in two boxes. The short form requires about forty minutes to administer. Its raised split-half reliability coefficient is only .77, which is not too satisfactory. Because of this fact, individual scores obtained from the short form must be interpreted with extreme caution.

Research with this test has indicated that it is not a particularly suitable test for use with girls or women. It is notably less reliable when used with women and probably also less valid. Girls and women on the average obtain much poorer scores on this test than do boys and men.

Although adult male norms have been provided, the test was found to be somewhat too easy for use with mechanically inclined men. Evidence of the validity of the test for measuring an aspect of mechanical ability was obtained in the form of differential occupational norms. However, the test is much less reliable when applied to men than it is with junior high school boys.

All the weaknesses noted in discussing the

Stenquist Mechanical Assembling Test apply equally to this one. In addition, another important practical weakness should also be mentioned. It is the difficulty of keeping the materials in good working order. Parts of the several mechanical models tend to become lost or mixed up. Some parts are prone to become broken or sprung with use. Models which the test authors bought for a few cents tend to become quite expensive when ordered from a test publisher. Nor is the expense limited to the actual cost of the replacements, but it includes the time and bother of a trained person in seeing that the replacement needed is properly ordered.

Part of these criticisms could have been obviated if the test authors had provided more adequate descriptions and fuller specifications for the exact mechanical models used, together with complete pictures of each of them assembled and disassembled. It would have helped if some method of substituting alternates for outmoded models could have been provided. The test in its present form is already becoming somewhat out of date.

[672]

O'Rourke Mechanical Aptitude Test, Junior Grade. Grades 7-12; 1926-40; Forms A, B, C; $3.25 per 50, postpaid; 25¢ per specimen set, postpaid; 55(65) minutes; L. J. O'Rourke; Psychological Institute.

REFERENCES

1. SCUDDER, CHARLES ROLAND, AND RAUBENHEIMER, A. S. "Are Standardized Mechanical Aptitude Tests Valid?" *J Juvenile Res* 14:120-3 Ap '30. * (*PA* 5:897)
2. BINGHAM, WALTER VAN DYKE. *Aptitudes and Aptitude Testing*, pp. 318-20. New York and London: Harper & Brothers, 1937. Pp. ix, 390. $3.00; 12s. 6d. * (*PA* 11:2885)
3. BENNETT, GEORGE K., AND CRUIKSHANK, RUTH M. *A Summary of Manual and Mechanical Ability Tests*, Preliminary Form, pp. 53-4. New York: Psychological Corporation, 1942. Pp. v, 80. Paper, lithotyped. $0.70. * (*PA* 16:2432)
4. HANMAN, BERT. "The Performance of Adult Males on the Minnesota Paper Form Board Test and the O'Rourke Mechanical Aptitude Test." *J Appl Psychol* 26:809-11 D '42. * (*PA* 17:2887)
5. LAWSHE, C. H., JR., AND THORNTON, G. R. "A Test Battery for Identifying Potentially Successful Naval Electrical Trainees." *J Appl Psychol* 27:399-406 O '43. * (*PA* 18:265)
6. MCDANIEL, J. W., AND REYNOLDS, WM. A. "A Study of the Use of Mechanical Aptitude Tests in the Selection of Trainees for Mechanical Occupations." *Ed & Psychol Meas* 4:191-7 au '44. * (*PA* 19:1776)
7. TUCKMAN, JACOB. "The Correlations Between 'Mechanical Aptitude' and 'Mechanical Comprehension' Scores: Further Observations." *Occupations* 22:244-5 Ja '44. * (*PA* 18:1914)
8. SARTAIN, A. Q. "The Use of Certain Standardized Tests in the Selection of Inspectors in an Aircraft Factory." *J Consult Psychol* 9:234-7 S-O '45. * (*PA* 20:1241)

Jay L. Otis, Director, Personnel Research Institute and Professor of Psychology, Western Reserve University, Cleveland, Ohio. These tests were reviewed by Herbert A. Landry in *The 1940 Mental Measurements Yearbook* (*see* 40:1668) and the present writer finds himself substantially in agreement with Mr. Landry's excellent review. Apparently one form

(Form A) has been revised, since it now bears a 1940 copyright date. The forms are essentially tests of mechanical information; and, as Mr. Landry pointed out, they measure only one aspect of mechanical "aptitude." Although names may not be too important, it would help considerably if these tests were called mechanical "information" tests. This would help to minimize any possible misinterpretation on the part of persons with limited training in psychometrics.

General norms based on 9,000 out-of-school males, ages 15 to 24, are now presented with Form A. Presumably, these norms also hold for Forms B and C. Of this group, 41 per cent completed one year of high school, 31 per cent completed only elementary school, and 28 per cent had not completed elementary school. A set of norms based on 70,000 "workmen who applied for mechanical jobs" is presented for all three forms; and, in addition, average scores, standard deviations, and the range for the middle two-thirds of the scores are presented for 33 mechanical occupation groups.

Validity coefficients ranging from .64 to .84 are reported. These represent correlations between test scores and ratings in vocational training and shop courses.

It is unfortunate that Mr. Landry's constructive criticisms made in 1940 have not been heeded. What appears to be a good mechanical information test of considerable usefulness in the vocational guidance or industrial situation still contains illustrations which are much too small and sometimes confusing. Also, the reliability of the test is still unknown, except by those users who have conducted their own reliability studies.

George A. Satter, Assistant Professor of Psychology, University of Michigan, Ann Arbor, Michigan. Each of the three forms of the *O'Rourke Mechanical Aptitude Test* consists of two parts. Part I requires that line drawings of tools, parts, and materials (a nut, a threaded section of pipe, a cotter key, etc.) be matched with similar drawings of other tools, parts, and materials with which they are commonly used; in a similar fashion, in this part of the test, statements of function are to be matched with drawings of the tools and materials used in the previous matching exercise. In each of the forms, 102 matchings of the above variety sample those basic knowledges of the carpenter, the electrician, the plumber, the auto mechanic, and the machinist which the individual with the requisite interest and aptitudes might have acquired incidentally in making household repairs, in tinkering with his car, and in observing the skilled craftsman at work.

Part II of each of the forms consists of 60 five-alternative, multiple-choice items presumably designed to sample all areas of applied mechanical knowledge from carpentry and plumbing to auto mechanics and machine shop practice.

Uniformly, the items present the appearance of having been carefully constructed and of having a high degree of face validity. Several of the items in each of the forms (the old fashioned, pear-shaped incandescent bulb and the coil box and timer of the Model T, for example) definitely label the tests as products of the twenties; the content of these items does not appear to be appropriate for a test which presumably measures mechanical aptitudes by using the indirect device of measuring incidental knowledges.

The forms are printed in six-page booklets which provide, along with the conventional spaces for personal data, directions to the testee, and sample exercises, items of less commonly found subject matter—Instructions to the Examiner, a list of the "O'Rourke Series of Aids in Placement and Guidance," directions for scoring, norms, and certain data descriptive of the validity of the test. Thus, while the layout is in general good, the inclusion of subject matter, more appropriate for an accompanying manual, crowds the test materials and demands that the drawings be unnecessarily small and that special directions be given the testee concerning the irrelevant sections which appear on the first and last pages of the test booklet.

There are situations (e.g., frequently in industrial selection) where individuals must be enticed into taking tests. Face validity helps in many cases to overcome this initial prejudice; so does the appearance of the test booklet. The O'Rourke tests "score high" on the first count; "low," on the second.

The items of the two parts of the test are scored independently on a unit basis; no correction is made in scores for chance successes. Before they are summated with those of Part I, scores of Part II are multiplied by four. Whether this procedure is followed in order to equalize the dispersions on the two parts, to maximize the predictive efficiency of the parts, or for both purposes is not explained in the manual.

Percentile norms, based on the test performance of 70,000 men who applied for mechanical jobs and the average scores of workmen in 33 occupational groups, are provided. The usefulness of norms of this sort, without accompanying data descriptive of the groups from which they were compiled, is obviously quite definitely limited.

Materials which are ordinarily the subject matter of an accompanying manual are to be found in several places: (a) "Instructions to the Examiner" in administering the test appear on the first page of the test booklets; (b) "Directions for Scoring," on the final page; and (c) the scoring key, norms, and data descriptive of the test's validity appear on a separate sheet.

Other materials which the present-day test user has come to expect in manuals are conspicuous by their absence. No statement is made concerning the rationale underlying the construction of the test, the types of groups the test is intended for, and the types of jobs it can do. No word is said concerning the procedures used in standardization or in item selection. The internal characteristics of the test can only be surmised from the none-too-detailed statements of validity.

In the reviewer's opinion lack of organization in the manual materials and the apparent neglect in presenting data, which test users have come to demand, may discourage some who initially are attracted by the content of the test.

The test author reports that "Correlations . . . between test scores and shop ratings by different investigators vary considerably . . . Correlations reported between test scores and ratings in vocational training courses are as high as .84; between test scores and ratings as machinist apprentices .64; between test scores and ratings in school vocational classes .83." No information is given about the size or composition of the groups providing these coefficients.

The average scores reported for various occupational groups may be used to support the contention that the test can make valid discriminations. It is apparent from the statistics provided that the test does a reasonably good job of discriminating between apprentices and journeymen and between the highly skilled craftsman (machinist, electrician, millwright, mechanic) and the members of occupational groups which are typically less highly skilled (watchmen, timber cutters, plasterers, painters, etc.) The reviewer would doubt, however, whether the ability to make discriminations of this sort is of practical usefulness in the selection situation; standardized oral trade questions are unquestionably more appropriate.

Prospective users of the test may be a bit disturbed by the lack of statistics descriptive of the internal characteristics of the test and of the dimensions of mechanical aptitude which this test measures.

It is the reviewer's opinion that the *O'Rourke Mechanical Aptitude Test* will be found to be most useful as part of a vocational or educational guidance battery and in selecting candidates for apprenticeship training courses. Its length (the administration time is roughly one hour) may limit its usefulness in many industrial employment offices.

For a review by Herbert A. Landry, see 40:1668.

[673]

Perceptual Mechanics Test. Ages 16 and over; 1938; $3 per introductory set including 10 tests, postpaid; 5¢ per extra test, postpaid; introductory sets may be ordered on approval; (10) minutes; Eugene J. Benge; Management Service Co.

Charles M. Harsh, Associate Professor of Psychology, The University of Nebraska, Lincoln, Nebraska. This test has incomplete shaded drawings of 50 mechanical devices—auto supplies, builder's and carpenter's tools, electrical household equipment, office equipment, and plumber's tools. Performance involves recognizing an incomplete object in a group of five or ten and finding its name in a somewhat longer list of objects on the next page. This applies the clever idea that speed of recognition is related to familiarity with objects. The five-minute time limit supposedly reveals this speed of recognition, but the rather awkward scoring system puts a premium on speed of finding the appropriate name in a long list. Thus a clerical ability factor may seriously mask the mechanical familiarity factor, especially for persons whose mechanical ability is greater than their verbal or "school" ability. The manual suggests that the vocational counselor will note the subject's familiarity with the six different types of devices, but norms are available only for the total score on all devices.

The Management Service Company offers this as one of a battery of eleven selection tests. The advertisements (and the test directions) suggest that it measures mechanical aptitude for shop training. Test scores are reported to correlate .68 with a "mechanical assembly test" (assembly test and population unspecified). In view of the shortcomings of assembly tests, this is weak evidence that the test measures mechanical aptitude. Familiarity with these common devices may possibly be related to mechanical aptitude, but there is need for more convincing evidence that persons who score high in the *Perceptual Mechanics Test* turn out better in shop work than those who score lower. If such evidence could be provided, the brevity of the test would make it most attractive for screening purposes.

[674]

★**Prognostic Test of Mechanical Abilities.** Grades 7-12 and adults; 1947; IBM; Form A; $2.50 per 25; 25¢ per specimen set, postpaid; 7¢ per copy, machine-scoring edition; 2¢ per machine-scorable answer sheet; 38(45) minutes; J. Wayne Wrightstone and Charles E. O'Toole; California Test Bureau.

J Consult Psychol 11:224–5 Jl-Ag '47. This test, based on an analysis of the requirements of courses of study in mechanical trades, consists of five parts: arithmetic computation, reading drawings and blueprints, identification and use of tools, spatial relationships, and checking measurements. Total score reliabilities range from .89 to .92 for single-grade ranges; subtest reliabilities are not given. Total scores correlate .78 with systematic instructors' ratings in a course in aviation trades. Norms, based on 5,268 boys in grades 7 to 12, are given in terms of subtest and total score percentiles for each grade. Some diagnostic implications for guidance are drawn from the profile of subtest scores.

[675]

★**Purdue Industrial Training Classification Test.** Grades 9-12 and adults; 1942; preliminary manual; Forms A, B; $1.65 per 25; 50¢ per specimen set; 35(40) minutes; C. H. Lawshe and A. C. Moutoux; Science Research Associates.

REFERENCES

1. LAWSHE, C. H., JR. "The Purdue Industrial Training Classification Test." *J Appl Psychol* 26:770-6 D '42. * (PA 17: 2456)
2. LAWSHE, C. H., JR., AND THORNTON, G. R. "A Test Battery for Identifying Potentially Successful Naval Electrical Trainees." *J Appl Psychol* 27:399-406 O '43. (PA 18:265)

D. Welty Lefever, Professor of Education, The University of Southern California, Los Angeles, California. This test was developed to be used as an aid in the selection and classification of persons for admission to industrial training programs. Although originally planned for applicants completing the sophomore level of high school, further experimentation has indicated some predictive value in the selection of adults for industrial training on the pre-employment level.

The scope of the test is by no means as broad as its title might suggest. The test items consist almost entirely of elementary arithmetic exercises functioning in a setting supplied by a series of working drawings of simple objects. The ability to read dimensional data from such drawings is required. The basic computational exercises appear to have considerably greater face validity than they would possess in the usual type of arithmetic test. The use of a pictorial setting seems to represent a distinct advantage for the test but its fundamental predictive power probably lies in the close correlation between arithmetic skill (along with the prerequisite intelligence) and the ability to handle technical problems successfully.

One of the criteria employed in the construction of items is somewhat misleading: "Each item shall be of an appropriate level of difficulty to sample adequately the mechanical knowledge of individuals composing the group with which the tests will be used." The ability areas covered by items involving simple measurement, reading a drawing, and the fundamental operations of computation limited to whole numbers, fractions, and decimals would by no means measure adequately the broad field of "mechanical knowledge."

As a predictive device for selecting candidates for shop training, the validity of the test seems to be rather clearly indicated by the studies reported in the preliminary edition of the test manual. As early as possible, follow-up studies should be made in which the validation criterion will be actual trade success.

Charles I. Mosier, Director of Research, Personnel Research Section, The Adjutant General's Office, Washington, D. C. This test is designed for use as one component of a battery to select students for industrial training courses involving the use of shop mathematics. It is intended that it be supplemented with measures of other essential functions.

The 14 arithmetic operations sampled (out of an original list of 26) are listed in the manual. The items are pictorially presented with a minimum of verbal directions and in simple words. In fact, the lack of general directions may adversely affect scores of individuals who are not sophisticated in taking objective tests. The problems are in groups, each based upon a diagram. Interdependent items have been successfully avoided. Items in the final forms were selected on the basis of difficulty and item reliability. Reliability is satisfactory and relatively high for so few items. The comparability of the two forms is close, with means on the parallel forms less than one point apart. The number of items in each form is very small against usual standards, so that only a few discriminations are possible within the range. If the test is used only to determine admission to or exclusion from a training course, this is not a handicap.

The data reported in the manual show statistically significant differences between the highest and lowest rated quarters of groups of students in industrial training classes. No relationship to actual probability of success or failure is given, nor are critical scores indicated.

Norms are given for six groups, varying widely in composition and ability. The test is relatively easy and affords little discrimination for the upper quarter of such groups as high school sophomores.

Although the test has been in use since 1942, the manual, still in preliminary form, has apparently not been revised since 1944. Only two validity studies are summarized in the manual, both using instructors ratings and contrasting extreme groups. No references to technical articles are given in the manual.

The test is useful as a measure of mastery of the elementary arithmetic operations, in spatial rather than verbal content, for use as a partial predictor of success in training courses involving such mastery. Its value for either purpose, particularly prediction of job success, is unknown to the reviewer.

[676]
★Purdue Mechanical Adaptability Test. Ages 15 and over; 1945–46; Forms A (for men), T (for women); $2.50 per 25; 25¢ per specimen set, postpaid; 15(20) minutes; C. H. Lawshe, Jr., and Joseph Tiffin; Division of Applied Psychology, Purdue University.

REFERENCES
1. LAWSHE, C. H., JR.; SEMANEK, IRENE A.; AND TIFFIN, JOSEPH. "The Purdue Mechanical Adaptability Test." *J Appl Psychol* 30:442-53 O '46. * (*PA* 21:579)

Jay L. Otis, Director, Personnel Research Institute and Professor of Psychology, Western

Reserve University, Cleveland, Ohio. This test is offered as an aid in selecting men for jobs or training programs calling for mechanical interests and abilities. It is not described as an aptitude test but simply as a measure of "experiential background in mechanical, electrical, and related activities." The test consists of 60 relatively simple information items in the electrical, carpentry, machine-shop, and auto mechanics areas. It is essentially a true-false examination with provision for a "don't know" response to each item. The test is easy to administer and to score. The format and style of type used are excellent.

The authors report a correlation with intelligence of .33 with a group of 600 industrial applicants, and they feel that this is low enough to justify the conclusion that the test is sufficiently unrelated to intelligence. The reliability (stepped up from odd-even correlation) is reported as .84.

Four validity studies based upon the following are reported in the manual: 14 ice-company mechanics, 12 machine-shop apprentices, 6 time-study men in a musical instrument manufacturing plant, 46 machine operators in a screw manufacturing company. For the ice company mechanics, the rank-order correlation between supervisor's ratings and test scores was .81; for the machine-shop aprentices it was .48; and for the time-study men it was .83. A validity coefficient is not reported for the machine-operator group. However, the authors present a graph showing the per cent of machine operators rated "high" (on a standard merit rating system) when successively higher critical test scores are applied.

The norms issued with the test are based on 667 industrial applicants.

It is pleasing to note that this test is apparently the result of a rather lengthy validation study and a thorough item analysis. Originally, 400 items were administered in a series of experimental forms to high school and trade school students, and 60 items were finally selected which comprise the present form of the test. Another worth-while feature is the test manual, which, although still in "preliminary" form, presents complete information and references on reliability, validity, and derivation of the scoring method. One might quibble over the number of cases upon which a validity coefficient is based or the magnitude of a reliability coefficient, but at any rate, the authors do present this essential information forthrightly, so that those considering the test for use in the industrial or guidance situations can make a fairly accurate evaluation before purchasing in quantity.

Dewey B. Stuit, Professor of Psychology and Dean, Student Personnel Services, The State University of Iowa, Iowa City, Iowa. This test is designed to aid in identifying individuals who are mechanically inclined and who, therefore, are most likely to succeed in jobs or training programs requiring mechanical abilities and interests. The test is essentially a measure of the individual's experiential background in the mechanical and electrical fields and is based on the assumption that those persons who have been most observant of and who have profited most from past experience in these fields will make the best progress in mechanical jobs or training programs.

The sixty items comprising Form A were selected from 400 original items constructed to sample the general fields of mechanical and electrical activities. These items were arranged in four experimental forms and administered to students in grades 10, 11, and 12 in two comprehensive high schools. A test of general mental ability, the *Adaptability Test,* was administered to the same population. Items showing a high correlation with general mental ability were immediately eliminated. The 100 items which discriminated best between the upper 30 and lower 30 per cent (after eliminating items correlating highly with general mental ability) were retained as Form R. This form was administered to 250 high school students in grades 10, 11, and 12 and minor adjustments made in certain items. Experimental Form S (a slight modification of R) was then administered to a population of 462 men in industrial situations. The *Adaptability Test* was also administered to these men. Items showing high correlations with general mental ability were eliminated, and the 60 items discriminating best between the upper and lower 30 per cent of the experimental population were retained to comprise Form A.

The responses to the items are recorded in the test booklet in boxes labeled *Yes, No, Don't Know.* Scoring is done by means of a stencil. The raw score in the test is based upon a modification of the standard correction for guessing (R–W) formula, where two choices exist. Raw scores are converted to percentiles by means of a table of norms based upon the performance of 667 men in industrial situations.

The validity of the test has been studied in a variety of industrial firms. Results are reported in terms of coefficients of correlation (rank order) or in terms of percentages of high and low men (in the test) rated high or low in performance by foremen or supervisors. In general there appears to be a substantial relationship between scores in the test and success on the job. The chief criticism to be made of these studies is that they involved fairly small groups, three numbering only 6, 12, and 14 men. The largest group was made up of 46 men.

The reliability of the test, computed by the split-half method and corrected by the Spearman–Brown formula, is .84; the population used consisted of 487 men, all applicants for industrial jobs. Correlations with mental ability tests are quite low, e.g., .32 with the *Adaptability Test* for the group on which the coefficient of reliability was computed. For a group of 173 college men, using the same two tests, the correlation was .17. Correlations with the *California Capacity Questionnaire*, the *Otis Self-Administering Test of Mental Ability,* Higher Examination, and the *Minnesota Paper Formboard* were found to be low. The highest correlation was that with the Bennett *Test of Mechanical Comprehension*, .71.

The authors appear to have developed a test which is useful in the selection of men for skilled or semiskilled jobs or for training programs leading to such jobs. The test seems to measure factors largely uncorrelated with general mental ability. The selection of items was carefully done although this reviewer did find seven items containing so-called "specific determiners" such as *all, any, most,* and *always*. In each case the correct response could be determined on the basis of the "specific determiner" alone. Little evidence is presented to indicate that the test will serve a useful purpose in guidance programs; until more data are available it would seem best to recommend the use of the test in experimental selection programs.

In addition to Form A (for men) there is available Form T (for women). This test resembles Form A but contains 100 items, several of them being identical with those in Form A. Data concerning the development, validity, and standardization of Form T, comparable to those for Form A, are not available.

[677]

Revised Minnesota Paper Formboard Test. Ages 9 and over; 1934-41; Forms A, B; $1.35 per 25; 50¢ per specimen set; 20(25) minutes; Rensis Likert and William H. Quasha; Psychological Corporation.

REFERENCES

1-9. *See* 40:1673.
10. TAYLOR, DON H. "The Selection of Printers' Apprentices." *Voc Guid Mag* 8:281-8 Mr '30. * (*PA* 4:3624)
11. VITELES, M. S. "The Measurement of Motor Ability." Abstract. *Psychol B* 30:569 O '33. * (*PA* 8:1007, title only)
12. ALTENEDER, LOUISE E. *The Value of Intelligence, Personality, and Vocational-Interest Tests in a Guidance Program.* Unpublished doctor's thesis, New York University, 1938. Pp. 130. (*Abstracts of Theses . . . [School of Education] 1938*, pp. 41-4.)
13. STANTON, MILDRED B. *Mechanical Ability of Deaf Children.* Columbia University, Teachers College, Contributions to Education, No. 751. Rudolf Pintner, faculty sponsor. New York: Bureau of Publications, the College, 1938. Pp. ix, 65. $1.60. * (*PA* 13:144)
14. ERICKSON, IRVING PETER. *Number and Spatial Ability in Mathematics and Intelligence.* Unpublished master's thesis, Clark University, 1939. (*Abstracts of Dissertations . . . 1939*, pp. 151-2.)
15. THOMPSON, CLAUDE EDWARD. *A Study of Motor and Mechanical Abilities.* Unpublished doctor's thesis, Ohio State University, 1939. (*Abstracts of Dissertations . . . Autumn Quarter, Winter Quarter 1939-40*, 1940, pp. 129-34.)
16. ALTENEDER, LOUISE E. "The Value of Intelligence, Personality, and Vocational Interest Tests in a Guidance Program." *J Ed Psychol* 31:449-59 S '40. * (*PA* 15:1480)
17. STEAD, WILLIAM H.; SHARTLE, CARROLL L.; OTIS, JAY L.; WARD, RAYMOND S.; OSBORNE, HERBERT F.; ENDLER, O. L.; DVORAK, BEATRICE J.; COOPER, JOHN H.; BELLOWS, ROGER M.; AND KOLBE, LAVERNE E. *Occupational Counseling Techniques: Their Development and Application.* Published for the Technical Board of the Occupational Research Program, United States Employment Service. New York: American Book Co., 1940. Pp. ix, 273. Out of print. * (*PA* 14:2627, title only)
18. STUIT, DEWEY B. "Factors in Physics Achievement on the College Level." Abstract. *Psychol B* 37:471 Jl '40. * (*PA* 14:5723, title only)
19. BRUSH, EDWARD N. "Mechanical Ability as a Factor in Engineering Aptitude." *J Appl Psychol* 25:300-12 Je '41. * (*PA* 15:4377)
20. CRAWFORD, JOHN EDMUND. *Measurement of Some Factors Upon Which Is Based Achievement in Elementary Machine Detail Drafting.* Unpublished doctor's thesis, University of Pittsburgh, 1941. (*Abstracts of Theses . . . 1941*, 1942, pp. 85-93.)
21. GHISELLI, EDWIN E. "Tests for the Selection of Inspector-Packers." Abstract. *Psychol B* 38:735 O '41. * (*PA* 16:728, title only)
22. MOORE, BRUCE V. "Analysis of Results of Tests Administered to Men in Engineering Defense Training Courses." *J Appl Psychol* 25:619-35 D '41. * (*PA* 16:1683)
23. MORROW, ROBERT S. "An Experimental Analysis of the Theory of Independent Abilities." *J Ed Psychol* 32:495-512 O '41. * (*PA* 16:2209)
24. STUIT, D. B., AND LAPP, C. J. "Some Factors in Physics Achievement at the College Level." *J Exp Ed* 9:251-3 Mr '41. * (*PA* 15:4421)
25 WATTS, FREDERICK P. "A Comparative Clinical Study of Delinquent and Non-Delinquent Negro Boys." *J Negro Ed* 10:190-207 Ap '41. * (*PA* 15:3550)
26. BENNETT, GEORGE K., AND CRUIKSHANK, RUTH M. *A Summary of Manual and Mechanical Ability Tests,* Preliminary Form, pp. 49-50. New York: Psychological Corporation, 1942. Pp. v, 80. Paper, lithotyped. $0.70. * (*PA* 16:2432)
27. BRYAN, ALICE I. "Grades, Intelligence and Personality of Art School Freshmen." *J Ed Psychol* 33:50-64 Ja '42. * (*PA* 16:3186)
28. CRAWFORD, JOHN EDMUND. "Spatial Perception Tests for Determining Drafting Aptitude." *Ind Arts & Voc Ed* 31:10-2 Ja '42. *
29. ESTES, STANLEY G. "A Study of Five Tests of 'Spatial' Ability." *J Psychol* 13:265-71 Ap '42. * (*PA* 16:3771)
30. GHISELLI, EDWIN E. "Tests for the Selection of Inspector Packers." *J Appl Psychol* 26:468-76 Ag '42. * (*PA* 17:2127)
31. HANMAN, BERT. "The Performance of Adult Males on the Minnesota Paper Form Board Test and the O'Rourke Mechanical Aptitude Test." *J Appl Psychol* 26:809-11 D '42. * (*PA* 17:2887)
32. JOHNSON, A. P. *The Prediction of Scholastic Achievement for Freshman Engineering Students at Purdue University.* Purdue University, Division of Educational Research, Studies in Engineering Education II. Lafayette, Ind.: the Division, May 1942. Pp. 22. Paper. $0.35. * (*PA* 16:5020)
33. JOHNSON, A. P. *The Relationship of Test Scores to Scholastic Achievement for 244 Engineering Freshmen Entering Purdue University in September, 1939.* Unpublished doctor's thesis, Purdue University, 1942.

34. McGehee, William, and Moffie, D. J. "Psychological Tests in the Selection of Enrollees in Engineering, Science, Management, Defense Training Courses." *J Appl Psychol* 26: 584-6 O '42. * (*PA* 17:2186)

35. Mitrano, Anthony J. "The Relationship Between Age and Test Performance of Applicants to a Technical-Industrial High School." *J Appl Psychol* 26:482-6 Ag '42. * (*PA* 17:2498)

36. Thompson, Claude Edward. "Motor and Mechanical Abilities in Professional Schools." *J Appl Psychol* 26:24-37 F '42. * (*PA* 16:2483)

37. Bates, Justine; Wallace, Marjorie; and Henderson, Mack T. "A Statistical Study of Four Mechanical Ability Tests." *Proc Iowa Acad Sci* 50:299-301 '43. * (*PA* 18:3276)

38. Jacobsen, Eldon E. "An Evaluation of Certain Tests in Predicting Mechanic Learner Achievement." *Ed & Psychol Meas* 3:259-67 au '43. * (*PA* 18:319)

39. Klugman, Samuel F. "Test Scores and Graduation." *Occupations* 21:389-93 Ja '43. * (*PA* 17:1354)

40. Traxler, Arthur E. "Correlations Between 'Mechanical Aptitude' Scores and 'Mechanical Comprehension' Scores." *Occupations* 22:42-3 O '43. * (*PA* 18:319)

41. Baldwin, Ellsworth F., and Smith, Leo F. "The Performance of Adult Female Applicants for Factory Work on the Likert-Quasha Revision of the Minnesota Paper Form Board Test." *J Appl Psychol* 28:468-70 D '44. * (*PA* 19:1303)

42. Morgan, W. J. "The Scores on the Revised Minnesota Paper Form-Board Test at Different Grade Levels of a Technical-Industrial High School." *J Genetic Psychol* 64:159-62 Mr '44. * (*PA* 18:2263)

43. Morgan, W. J. "Some Remarks and Results of Aptitude Testing in Technical and Industrial Schools." *J Social Psychol* 20:19-29 Ag '44. * (*PA* 19:556)

44. Reichard, Suzanne. *Mental Organization and Age Level.* Archives of Psychology, No. 295. Washington, D. C.: American Psychological Association, Inc., June 1944. Pp. 30. Paper. $0.80. * (*PA* 19:1183)

45. Shuman, John T. *An Investigation Into the Value of Certain Tests in the Selection and Upgrading of Personnel in Aircraft Engine and Propeller Industries.* Unpublished doctor's thesis, Pennsylvania State College, 1944. Pp. 251. (*Abstracts of Doctoral Dissertations . . . 1944,* 1945, pp. 160-76.)

46. Tinker, Miles A. "Speed, Power, and Level in the Revised Minnesota Paper Form Board Test." *J Genetic Psychol* 64:93-7 Mr '44. * (*PA* 18:2291)

47. Tuckman, Jacob. "The Correlations Between 'Mechanical Aptitude' and 'Mechanical Comprehension' Scores: Further Observations." *Occupations* 22:244-5 Ja '44. * (*PA* 18:1914)

48. Barrett, Dorothy M. "Aptitude and Interest Patterns of Art Majors in a Liberal Arts College." *J Appl Psychol* 29:483-92 D '45. * (*PA* 20:1248)

49. Sartain, A. Q. "The Use of Certain Standardized Tests in the Selection of Inspectors in an Aircraft Factory." *J Consult Psychol* 9:234-7 S-O '45. * (*PA* 20:1241)

50. Shuman, John T. "The Value of Aptitude Tests for Factory Workers in the Aircraft Engine and Propeller Industries." *J Appl Psychol* 29:156-60 Ap '45. * (*PA* 19:2346)

51. Shuman, John T. "The Value of Aptitude Tests for Supervisory Workers in the Aircraft Engine and Propeller Industries." *J Appl Psychol* 29:185-90 Je '45. * (*PA* 19:3138)

52. Stephens, Everett W. "A Comparison of New England Norms With National Norms on the Revised Minnesota Paper Form Board Test—Series AA." *Occupations* 24:101-4 N '45. * (*PA* 20:1283)

53. War Manpower Commission, Division of Occupational Analysis, Staff. "Factor Analysis of Occupational Aptitude Tests." *Ed & Psychol Meas* 5:147-55 su '45. * (*PA* 20:1242)

54. Myklebust, Helmer R. "A Study of the Usefulness of Objective Measures of Mechanical Aptitude in Guidance Programs for the Hypacousic." *Am Ann Deaf* 91:123-50, 205-25 Mr, My '46. * (*PA* 20:3901)

55. Sartain, A. Q. "Relation Between Scores on Certain Standard Tests and Supervisory Success in an Aircraft Factory." *J Appl Psychol* 30:328-32 Ag '46. * (*PA* 21:250)

56. Anderson, Rose G. "Test Scores and Efficiency Ratings of Machinists." *J Appl Psychol* 31:377-88 Ag '47. * (*PA* 22:2335)

57. Tuckman, Jacob. "Age and Grade Norms for High School Students on the Revised Minnesota Paper Form Board Test." *Occupations* 26:97-100 N '47. * (*PA* 22:1563)

Dewey B. Stuit, Professor of Psychology and Dean, Student Personnel Services, The State University of Iowa, Iowa City, Iowa. The present revision was first published in 1934 and is a modification of the paper formboard test prepared by D. G. Paterson, R. M. Elliott, L. D. Anderson, H. A. Toops, and E. Heidbreder at the University of Minnesota in 1930.

The test consists of 64 items of the multiple-choice type which measure the examinee's ability to think spatially in two dimensions. Each item first presents the parts of a geometrical figure, cut up in various ways, followed by five "assembled" geometrical figures. The examinee is required to select the figure which represents the correct combination of the parts. Responses are recorded at the top of the page, just above the number of each item. The test is easy to administer and score; the directions to examinees are complete; and eight preliminary exercises give the examinee a good familiarity with the nature of the test exercises.

One of the most recent and welcome features of the test is the machine-scored answer sheet. Many users who had previously devised their own answer sheets will now be able to order them directly from the publisher. Norms for the machine-scored edition are presently limited to those based on a population of 548 white enlisted men in the U. S. Army. Since the machine-scored edition will be widely used, more adequate norms should soon be available.

The reliability of a single form of the test is .85. When both forms are administered, the reliability is .92. The manual does not indicate the nature of the group to which the test was administered to obtain these coefficients.

The authors indicate that the test is predictive of (*a*) ability to master descriptive geometry and mechanical drawing, (*b*) success in mechanical occupations, and (*c*) success in engineering courses. Various studies are reported in the literature indicating satisfactory experience with the test in the prediction of success in these three areas. Estes (29) reports a correlation of .27 with grades in descriptive geometry and .31 with instructor's ratings in that subject. Shuman (50) reports an average correlation of .44 with success in various skilled and semiskilled occupations. Ghiselli (30) reports a correlation of .57 between test scores and success of inspector-packers. A correlation of .49 between test scores and success in mechanical drawing is reported in the manual. It should also be stated that other investigators have found the test of less value as a predictive index (Barrett, 48; Morgan, 42).

Several studies have been made showing that scores in the test are highly correlated neither with intelligence test scores nor with other mechanical aptitude tests (Bennett and Cruikshank, 26; Morgan, 42; Traxler, 40; Tuckman, 47). Tinker (46) suggests that speed, level, and power scores be obtained for the test and their validity determined. These studies emphasize that the *Revised Minnesota Paper Formboard* should not be regarded as a complete index of mechanical promise but rather as measuring one component of mechanical and engineering aptitude. Used in that manner the test can serve a useful purpose in both guidance and personnel work. As for most other tests, the usefulness of this instrument will be greatly enhanced by the publication of more validity coefficients.

The test is presently published and distributed by Science Research Associates; it continues to be distributed by the Psychological Corporation. The manuals provided by these two organizations are practically identical except that the one published by Science Research Associates contains a table describing the major types and the conditions of mechanical work including ability requirements (academic, mechanical, social, clerical), wages, number employed (men and women), largest age group, outlook for youth, and educational or training requirements. Both manuals contain norms for various age, educational, and occupational groups. Supplementary norms have been published by Baldwin (41) and Hanman (31).

For a review by Alec Rodger, see 40:1673.

[677a]

★SRA Mechanical Aptitudes. High school and adults; 1947; Forms AH, BH; separate answer pads must be used; 43¢ per test booklet with answer pad; $1.65 per 25 answer pads; 45¢ per 25 profile sheets; 75¢ per specimen set; 35(45) minutes; prepared by Richardson, Bellows, Henry and Co., Inc.; Science Research Associates.

[678]

Stenquist Mechanical Aptitude Tests. Grades 6-12; 1921-22; 2 parts; $1.60 per 25 of either part; 35¢ per specimen set, postpaid; John L. Stenquist; World Book Co.
a) TEST 1. 45(50) minutes.
b) TEST 2. 50(60) minutes.

REFERENCES
1. STENQUIST, JOHN L. *Measurement of Mechanical Ability*. Columbia University, Teachers College, Contributions to Education, No. 130. New York: Bureau of Publications, the College, 1923. Pp. ix, 101. Paper. Out of print. *
2. TOOPS, HERBERT A. *Tests for Vocational Guidance of Children Thirteen to Sixteen.* Columbia University, Teachers College, Contributions to Education, No. 136. New York: Bureau of Publications, the College, 1923. Pp. xii, 159. Out of print. *
3. STEIN, MARTIN L. "A Trial With Criteria of the MacQuarrie Test of Mechanical Ability." *J Appl Psychol* 11:391-3 O '27. * (*PA* 2:2964)
4. KEFAUVER, GRAYSON N. "Relationship of the Intelligence Quotient and Scores on Mechanical Tests With Success in Industrial Subjects." *Voc Guid Mag* 7:198-203+ F '29. * (*PA* 3:1637)
5. PATERSON, DONALD G.; ELLIOTT, RICHARD M.; ANDERSON, L. DEWEY; TOOPS, HERBERT A.; and HEIDBREDER, EDNA. *Minnesota Mechanical Ability Tests.* Minneapolis, Minn.: University of Minnesota Press, 1930. Pp. xxii, 586. $5.00. * (*PA* 5:1268)
6. SCUDDER, CHARLES ROLAND, AND RAUBENHEIMER, A. S. "Are Standardized Mechanical Aptitude Tests Valid?" *J Juvenile Res* 14:120-3 Ap '30. * (*PA* 5:897)
7. HOLCOMB, G. W., AND LASLETT, H. R. "A Prognostic Study of Engineering Aptitude." *J Appl Psychol* 16:107-15 Ap '32. * (*PA* 7:4722)
8. SIMPSON, RAY MARS. "The Mechanical Aptitudes of 312 Prisoners." *J Appl Psychol* 16:485-96 O '32. * (*PA* 7:4011)
9. BARDEN, HAROLD E. "The Stenquist Mechanical Aptitude Test as a Measure of Mechanical Ability." *J Juvenile Res* 17:94-104 Ap '33. * (*PA* 7:4890)
10. BINGHAM, WALTER VAN DYKE. *Aptitudes and Aptitude Testing,* pp. 320-1. New York and London: Harper & Brothers, 1937. Pp. ix, 390. $3.00; 12s. 6d. * (*PA* 11:2885)
11. HARRELL, WILLARD. "The Validity of Certain Mechanical Ability Tests for Selecting Cotton Mill Machine Fixers." *J Social Psychol* 8:279-82 My '37. * (*PA* 11:5311)
12. BAURER, HERBERT T. "Some Effects of Short-Term Trade Experience Classes Upon the Stenquist Mechanical Aptitude Tests." *Ed* 61:97-100 O '40. *
13. BOYNTON, PAUL L., AND REDFEARN, LENA. "An Analysis of the Responses of Reform School Boys on the Stenquist Test of Mechanical Aptitude." *Peabody J Ed* 17:350-3 My '40. * (*PA* 14:6117)
14. DAVIS, WALLACE EARL. *Predicting Degree of Achievement in Industrial Subjects by the Use of Stenquist Mechanical Aptitude Tests.* Unpublished master's thesis, North Texas State Teachers College, 1940.
15. HARRELL, WILLARD. "A Factor Analysis of Mechanical Ability Tests." *Psychometrika* 5:17-33 Mr '40. * (*PA* 14:4285)
16. REED, HOMER B. "The Place of the Bernreuter Personality, Stenquist Mechanical Aptitude, and Thurstone Vocational Interest Tests in College Entrance Tests." *J Appl Psychol* 25:528-34 O '41. Abstract *Psychol B* 38:711 O '41. * (*PA* 16:1205)
17. BENNETT, GEORGE K., AND CRUIKSHANK, RUTH M. *A Summary of Manual and Mechanical Ability Tests, Preliminary Form,* pp. 59-60. New York: Psychological Corporation, 1942. Pp. v, 80. Paper, lithotyped. $0.70. * (*PA* 16:2432)
18. MYKLEBUST, HELMER R. "A Study of the Usefulness of Objective Measures of Mechanical Aptitude in Guidance Programs for the Hypacousic." *Am Ann Deaf* 91:123-50, 205-25 Mr, My '46. * (*PA* 20:3901)

James M. Porter, Jr., Associate Professor of Psychology, Rensselaer Polytechnic Institute, Troy, New York. Test 1 consists of 95 problem pictures, relating to common mechanical objects which require the matching of related parts. Test 2 consists in part of material similar to that employed in Test 1 and in part of cuts of machines and machine parts about which the testee has to answer questions of a general nature—no first-hand experience with the parts pictured is presupposed.

The tests do not measure manipulative abilities, but performance on Test 1 shows a median correlation of .69 with performance on the author's assembling tests; performance on Test 2 shows a median correlation of .66 with performance on the same assembling test.

A median correlation of .67 is reported between shop and science teachers' ranking for "general mechanical aptitude" and performance on Tests 1 and 2. Correlations with measures of general intelligence are reported as ranging between .2 and .4. Test 1 has been reported to correlate .146 with engineering grades, and Test 2 .428 with the same criterion.

Norms are presented in T scores and percentile ranks for 4,099 males (age 10-18) in the case of Test 1, and for 1,087 males (age 10-15) in the case of Test 2.

No measures of reliability are given. Norms

supplied by the author are based entirely on school-age boys. It would appear that more recent tests of mechanical aptitude would yield more satisfactory measures of potential ability. The principles upon which these tests were constructed have been widely copied. Portions of Test 2 probably test mechanical comprehension beyond mere information.

[679]

Stenquist Mechanical Assembling Test. Grades 3-6, 5-12 and adults; 1917-20; individual; (30) minutes; John L. Stenquist; C. H. Stoelting Co.
a) SERIES I AND II. Grades 5-12 and adults; 2 forms (Series I, II).
b) SERIES III. Grades 3-6.

REFERENCES

1. STENQUIST, JOHN L. *Measurement of Mechanical Ability.* Columbia University, Teachers College, Contributions to Education, No. 130. New York: Bureau of Publications, the College, 1923. Pp. ix, 101. Paper. Out of print. *
2. TOOPS, HERBERT A. *Tests for Vocational Guidance of Children Thirteen to Sixteen.* Columbia University, Teachers College, Contributions to Education, No. 136. New York: Bureau of Publications, the College, 1923. Pp. xii, 159. Out of print. *
3. PATERSON, DONALD G.; ELLIOTT, RICHARD M.; ANDERSON, L. DEWEY; TOOPS, HERBERT A.; AND HEIDBREDER, EDNA. *Minnesota Mechanical Ability Tests.* Minneapolis, Minn.: University of Minnesota Press, 1930. Pp. xxii, 586. $5.00. * (*PA* 5:1268)
4. SCUDDER, CHARLES ROLAND, AND RAUBENHEIMER, A. S. "Are Standardized Mechanical Aptitude Tests Valid?" *J Juvenile Res* 14:120-3 Ap '30. * (*PA* 5:897)
5. HOLCOMB, G. W., AND LASLETT, H. R. "A Prognostic Study of Engineering Aptitude." *J Appl Psychol* 16:107-15 Ap '32. * (*PA* 7:4722)
6. MCELWEE, EDNA WILLIS. "Standardization of the Stenquist Mechanical Assembling Test Series III." *J Ed Psychol* 23:451-4 S '32. * (*PA* 7:378)
7. VITELES, M. S. "The Measurement of Motor Ability." Abstract. *Psychol B* 30:569 O '33. * (*PA* 8:1007, title only)
8. LORGE, IRVING, AND METCALFE, ZAIDA F. "The Prediction of Some Measures of Vocational Adjustment on the Basis of Tests Given Eight Years Before and of the Same Tests Given Two Years After the Fact Predicted." *J Ed Psychol* 25:220-4 Mr '34. * (*PA* 8:3791)
9. FRYE, ELLIS K. "The Mechanical Abilities of Siblings." *J Genetic Psychol* 50:293-306 Je '37. * (*PA* 11:6020)
10. BENNETT, GEORGE K., AND CRUIKSHANK, RUTH M. *A Summary of Manual and Mechanical Ability Tests,* Preliminary Form, pp. 21-2. New York: Psychological Corporation, 1942. Pp. v, 80. Paper, lithotyped. $0.70. * (*PA* 16:2432)

William R. Grove, Psychologist and Director of Child Study Service, Phoenix Elementary Schools, Phoenix, Arizona; formerly Professor of Psychology and Director of the Division of Psychological Services, The University of Pittsburgh. The actual equipment developed by Stenquist for this test is now of little but historical interest, for the test has been superseded by the *Minnesota Assembly Test.* It is to be noted that the latter actually duplicates much of the Stenquist equipment and adopts the methodology developed by Stenquist almost intact. In the opinion of this reviewer, a more accurate name for the more recently developed series would have been the *Minnesota Revision of the Stenquist Mechanical Assembling Test.*

Stenquist has provided an adequate description of his test and of the steps by which it was developed (1). His monograph summarized the research data available to that time and provides an adequate manual of instructions and norms.

It is the methodology developed by Stenquist and refined by the Minnesota group that must be considered a substantial contribution rather than the actual form in which the test itself was left at the conclusion of Stenquist's research. In this sense, the more recent research of the Minnesota group has tended rather to substantiate and further document the basic nature of the contribution made. We omit a discussion of the reliability and validity of this test since this will be more appropriately considered in connection with its revision, the *Minnesota Assembly Test (see 671).*

The test is of the worksample type. The method essentially consists of presenting to the subject a series of not too complicated mechanical contrivances, easily taken apart and put together. Although nowhere explicitly stated, this reviewer is of the opinion that a further requisite is that each mechanical model shall be a standard product with which the average subject for whom the test is designed shall have had reasonable opportunity to become moderately familiar. The models are presented to the subject disassembled, and the test consists of his reassembling them. The evidence is unequivocal that this method succeeds in measuring with considerable validity one aspect of mechanical ability.

The weaknesses of this method were recognized and pointed out by Stenquist. The more obvious of these are the rather elaborate and bulky equipment required and the awkwardness of administering the test as a group test. A more subtle weakness is the tendency for certain of the mechanical models used in the standardization to become outmoded and no longer readily available. This affects adversely the basic validity of such a model as a test item and renders obsolete the standardization of which it was a part.

[680]

★**Survey of Mechanical Insight.** Grades 9-16 and adults; 1945; IBM; 1 form; $2.50 per 25; 25¢ per specimen set, postpaid; 10¢ per copy, machine-scoring edition; 2¢ per machine-scorable answer sheet; 25(35) minutes; D. R. Miller; California Test Bureau.

Reign H. Bittner, Director of Personnel Research, Owens–Illinois Glass Company, Toledo, Ohio. The test is designed to measure aptitude at the high school and adult levels for solving the types of mechanical problems involved in jobs requiring the operation, maintenance, repair, or design of various types of machinery. It is a thirty-minute test composed of 35 multiple-choice problems in the movements of gears, levers, and pulleys presented pictorially. The publishers state that this is a new approach in measuring this type of aptitude but this type of problem has been used previously in such tests as the *Test of Mechanical Comprehension* by George K. Bennett.

It is stated that an attempt has been made to rule out the effect of previous experience and special education on test scores by basing problems on machines which the average person with mechanical interest would not have seen before. Although one study is cited which found no significant difference between the scores of one group of subjects who had had one year of physics and another group who had not had the course, it seems doubtful that this objective has been achieved. The items are all based on principles of mechanics that are general in application and, if learned, should be readily applied to these problems. It is wondered how much actual training in mechanics was given to the group referred to above in the first year physics course.

The reliability of the test, reported in the manual as .88 by the split-halves method with the Spearman–Brown correction, appears to be within satisfactory limits. No data on the validity of the test are given in the manual, although one section of the manual is headed "Reliability and Validity." The publishers have provided the reviewer with the supplementary statement that the test correlated .47 with efficiency ratings of postage meter repair workers. With such meager data on validity, it is not possible to judge whether the test is a useful predictor of success in the kinds of jobs for which it is designed as a selection instrument.

Percentile norms based on 250 cases are provided for interpreting the raw scores. The normative population is described by the publisher as "a fair sample of a cross-section of the general population which included subjects from various mechanical trades, art trades, miscellaneous non-mechanical jobs, mechanical and non-mechanical night trade courses, and aircraft loftsmen and engineers." No data are given on sex, age, or education of this population. It is difficult to see how this small group as described could be representative of the general population. Percentiles derived from such a small population are usually subject to considerable unreliability. It is the opinion of the reviewer that separate norms should be provided for males and females since it is usual for the two sexes to differ markedly in performance on this type of test.

It is recommended by the publishers that subjects be separated into fast-accurate, fast-inaccurate, slow-accurate, and slow-inaccurate groups by computing for each the per cent of items attempted which are answered correctly. However, no standards are supplied to aid in the interpretation of these scores. These percentages merely give accuracy scores, and to be interpreted in terms of "fast" or "slow" one must know something about the distribution of attempts, which is not supplied.

The test is apparently easy to administer and score, although six of the items may lead to difficulties in administration. In five items no item "stem" is provided; i.e., the problem is not stated. In the other item, the stem states as a possibility a condition which is impossible. The format of the test is good. Drawings are clear and reproduction is good.

Judgment on the usefulness of this test in the kind of situations for which it was designed must be reserved until more validation data are available. It is apparently worthy of trial in such situations but should not be accepted without empirical checks on the relation of the test scores to criteria of performance.

Jay L. Otis, Director, Personnel Research Institute and Professor of Psychology, Western Reserve University, Cleveland, Ohio. This test is offered as a measure of mechanical aptitude. It consists of 35 multiple-choice items with three alternatives. The items are of the pictorial type found in many tests of mechanical comprehension which require the examinee to perceive how various parts of a mechanism will move when a given part is operated. The items are arranged in order of difficulty.

The author reports a reliability of .88, obtained for 250 cases by the split-halves method. Presumably this is the same population upon which the norms are based—"250 males and female cases selected from various occupations." It would seem that for a test of mechanical aptitude especially, the author should present separate norms for males and females. This is not done. Nor are the various occupations from

Survey of Mechanical Insight

which the cases were selected described in any manner. This makes the norms issued with the test practically useless, so that any person desiring to use the test is strongly advised to make up his own norms for specific purposes.

The author states that the test measures aptitude rather than achievement because the factors of previous experience and special education have been minimized by basing most of the items upon "machines which either are archaic or are of special design so that the probability of their having been seen by the average person with mechanical interest is remote." In support of this claim the author states that no significant difference was found between "a group" which had completed a first course in physics and a comparable group which had not had a physics course.

The *Survey of Mechanical Insight* may be a very useful measure of mechanical aptitude. Unfortunately its degree of usefulness has not yet been determined. The author presents no validity data whatsoever, and, as indicated above, the present norms are of little value. It hardly seems fair for the purchaser to have to determine the validity of the test himself and to start from scratch to accumulate data for some usable norms.

Shailer Peterson, Director of Educational Measurements, Council on Dental Education, American Dental Association; and Research Associate, The University of Chicago; Chicago, Illinois. According to the author, the purpose of the test is "to measure aptitude for solving the types of mechanical problems involved in jobs requiring the operation, maintenance, repair, or design of various types of machinery." Another statement is more specific, indicating that the "test measures the ability to predict the resultant motion of various parts of a mechanism when a given part is operated."

The test contains 35 items which appear to have been selected, at least in part, from the many systems of levers, gears, pulleys, and cams that are often found in advertisements by patent concerns. Some are relatively simple machines while others are somewhat complicated and involved. They are arranged in order of difficulty, and the author claims that those which have been selected have probably not been seen before by the average person, thereby reducing the effect of previous training and experience. Evidence that formal training does not affect these test scores is given by the fact that no significant difference in performance is found between a group having had physics and a comparable group not having had physics.

The author claims that relationships have been demonstrated between this test and both mechanical interest and aptitude. The reliability coefficient obtained by the split-halves method and corrected by the Spearman–Brown formula is .88. All of these calculations are apparently from the relatively small sample of 250 "male and female cases selected from various occupations."

The size of the sample tends to reduce the meaning of the percentile norms that are reported. The single set of norms includes all 250 cases. In an aptitude field such as this, it would seem desirable to prepare norms both on groups engaged in machine work and those not occupied in mechanical work. In addition, the percentile norms have not been prepared in as usable a fashion as one customarily finds.

From an inspection of the 35 items, one would judge that the test on the whole is very satisfactory. All the items are of the multiple-choice variety, each having three choices. On a number of items the alert student will find that if one choice is assumed correct a second must also be true, thereby leaving him with only the third alternative as long as he knows that only one response is to be made for each item.

[681]

★**Survey of Object Visualization.** Grades 9-16 and adults; 1945; 1 form; $1.50 per 25; 25¢ per specimen set, postpaid; Spanish edition available at same prices; 20(25) minutes; D. R. Miller; California Test Bureau.

Charles M. Harsh, Associate Professor of Psychology, The University of Nebraska, Lincoln, Nebraska. Like the *Thurstone Surface Development Test* and its various adaptations, this survey is a measure of three-dimensional visualization. The subject must indicate which of four objects can be formed by folding or rolling a flat pattern, such as a tinsmith might lay out. Several items in the survey may be answered correctly by merely counting sides, but the difficult items require accurate form perception and three-dimensional imagery. The manual claims that the ability measured by the test is necessary for drafting, engineering, and various mechanical and artistic occupations, but the evidence for this claim is not indicated. For a 25-minute test, the reliability of .91 seems satisfactory. Percentile norms are given for an unspecified heterogeneous sample of 250 cases. The manual suggests that speed and accuracy should be distinguished, but the diagnostic use of such information is left entirely to the ingenuity of the examiner. Since this is an interesting and apparently practical test, there is need for more evidence as to the validity of the test for predicting success in training or occupations.

A few minor faults might be remedied. Items 2, 3, 4, 26, and 35 are disconcerting to capable examinees because of perspective illusions or inaccuracies of scale. A line is omitted in the drawing for Item 16, Response A. Shading would decrease the reversible perspective which complicates such items as 33 and 34. Since increasing difficulty is desirable, Items 40, 41, and 44 should probably come before Items 29 and 33. For persons of grade school education, the test might be more valid if the figures were larger and also shaded to show the third dimension. College students are not much troubled by the perspective line drawings, but children and below-average adults often have great difficulty interpreting the drawings as three-dimensional objects. The training factor may be very important.

Hand marking and scoring is simple, but the machine-scored answer sheet introduces space discrepancies with considerable chance of error.

these occupations, nor is any mention made of effect on test scores of such factors as education, age, or sex. The author recommends that the per cent of items attempted which were answered correctly be considered in addition to the total score in order to identify the fast and accurate, fast and inaccurate, slow and accurate, and slow and inaccurate. However, no standards are given to facilitate interpretation of these four types.

No data on validity are given in the test manual. Although the test was intended for occupations such as draftsman, engineer, machinist, maintenance mechanic, commercial and fine artist, etc. and appears to be of such a nature that it might have some validity for such occupations, evidence to this effect should be included in the test manual. Lack of validity data gives rise to the suspicion that validity was not cited because it was unfavorable or that the test was published prematurely. Such suspicions do not build confidence in the test, author, or publisher.

It is to be hoped that research data will be forthcoming on validity, improved standards, relationship with other tests, etc. In the meanwhile the test should be used with extreme caution and only by those who are prepared to do basic research on the test before attaching any meaning to test scores.

Clifford E. Jurgensen, Personnel Director, Minneapolis Gas Light Company, Minneapolis, Minnesota. This test requires the examinee to predict how an object will look when its shape and position are changed. Each of the 44 items consists of a drawing of a flat pattern together with four possible shapes it may take when folded on the dotted lines or rolled together.

The test is practically self-administering. Instructions require approximately five minutes and include two examples for which the correct answer is given and two practice exercises to be worked by the examinee. The test proper has a time limit of 25 minutes. Scoring is objective, and consists of the number correct minus one-third the number incorrect.

Split-half reliability, corrected by the Spearman–Brown formula, is .91 with 266 cases. No data are given regarding the nature of the group on which reliability was computed.

Percentile norms are based on 250 male and female cases selected from various occupations. No data are given concerning the nature of

Shailer Peterson, Director of Educational Measurements, Council on Dental Education, American Dental Association; and Research Associate, The University of Chicago; Chicago, Illinois. As the catalog announcement of this test indicates, "This test measures the ability to visualize the shape a flat pattern will take when it is assembled to form a three-dimensional object." The test would appear to measure some of the same factors measured by the various paper formboard tests. The geometric forms selected have a wide range of shapes with an accompanying wide range of difficulty. The illustrations themselves are rather small, making it difficult for some students and even some proctors to distinguish easily the differences between certain multiple-choice figures. This size factor becomes noticeable in only a few of the items.

This reviewer has used this particular test on nearly six thousand cases and finds that the few items in which variations in degree of curvature are the distinguishing features seem to confuse students who have relatively little trouble with definite angles and straight folds. It would be interesting to know whether performance on the difficult items having the rolled surfaces with curved ends is related to performance on both the rolled and folded figures in which the discrimination of slope does not appear to be so confusing.

The test proves interesting to the student, which makes it easy to administer. Moreover, many of the factors that are measured by the test seem obvious to the faculty members who have occasion to refer to test data, which in turn makes the meaning and importance of the test understandable.

This reviewer has found that there is a higher correlation between performance on this test and tests measuring manual dexterity than there is with tests of mental ability. He has also found relatively high correlation between this test and grades received by students in professional schools in those courses demanding hand coordination and finger dexterity. The test publishers report that an analysis of the data indicates that the factors measured by this test are those necessary for such jobs as draftsman, engineer, loftsman, machinist, and maintenance mechanic.

The norms supplied by the publishers are very inadequate, for they are based upon only "250 male and female cases selected from various occupations." A breakdown of even these 250 cases into two or three occupational categories would be very useful. The reported reliability coefficient is .91 computed by the split-halves method and corrected by the Spearman–Brown formula.

Patrick Slater, Chief Research Officer at the Social Survey and Honorary Psychometric Psychologist at St. Thomas's Hospital, London, England. The problems presented by this test are in the form of drawings. On the left is a flat pattern. It can be visualized as rolled or folded into the shape of one of four objects shown drawn in perspective on the right. The subject must attempt to choose the correct one and record his choice.

The amount of acquired knowledge needed to solve the problems is relatively small and should not affect variations in the scores of people for whom the test is intended to any great extent. The variations observed are likely to depend mainly on differences in general intelligence and in the ability to recognize shapes

and imagine the consequences of their manipulation—i.e., the ability sometimes described as spatial judgment or practical ability. The principles involved are sound and well established, and the test undoubtedly possesses diagnostic value, as claimed, for selecting draftsmen, engineers, mechanics, commercial artists, etc. For each such specific purpose, however, supplementary selection procedures would also be needed. The test would not be (and is not claimed to be) suitable for measuring spatial judgment among young people.

Many other tests for the same abilities have already been published. In the British Isles the most notable are the form relations and space perception tests published by the National Institute of Industrial Psychology.

In the construction of such tests, attempts to represent three-dimensional objects diagrammatically give rise to serious technical problems. Right angles have to be portrayed by acute or obtuse angles according to the demands of perspective, and it is therefore difficult to indicate which are which unambiguously. It is also difficult to indicate whether an object possesses sides or angles which are not exhibited in the diagram. Still more serious is the risk of introducing reversible images. Shading may assist in solving these problems, but in my opinion no completely satisfactory solution can be reached without stereoscopic aids.

The *Survey of Object Visualization* leaves these problems unsolved and the reliability and validity of the scores must be accordingly reduced. Some items could be improved by more careful attention to these details, and the order of difficulty appears questionable in some cases. But these faults are not so grave as to prevent the test from serving its intended purposes.

The norms given are based on 250 adults, male and female together. Fuller norms would be welcome.

[682]

★**Survey of Space Relations Ability.** Grades 9-16 and adults; 1944; IBM; Form A; $2 per 25; 25¢ per specimen set, postpaid; 8¢ per copy, machine-scoring edition; 2¢ per machine-scorable answer sheet; Spanish edition available at same prices; 15(20) minutes; Harry W. Case and Floyd Ruch; California Test Bureau.

E. G. Chambers, Assistant Director of Research in Industrial Psychology, University of Cambridge, Cambridge, England. This is an interesting variant of the various forms of tests for the appreciation of spatial relations. Its basic principle is similar to that of other tests. There is a series of geometric figures, each of which is subdivided into parts of different shape, and the candidate is required in each case to pick out the constituent parts from among ten similarly shaped drawings. The chief difference from other tests lies in its resemblance to blue prints—a feature purporting to increase the motivation of test candidates. The reliability coefficient of .93 is good, but the validity coefficients, though satisfactory in magnitude, are based on very small groups. Further evidence of its validity by the "follow-up" method is desirable before it can finally be accepted as a selective test.

The test is an easy one, so much so that the speed factor enters largely into the score. The method of scoring itself is open to criticism, since omissions due to lack of time are penalized exactly equally with errors of performance. It would be worth examining the reliability and validity of the test using as score the number of correct answers only, thus avoiding the possible overemphasis of the speed factor.

The subdivision of the geometric figures makes the test purely one of recognizing different shapes, which is relatively easy. The constructive element in the appreciation of spatial relationships is entirely omitted, and the test might be improved by the inclusion of this factor. This could easily be effected by the addition (or substitution) of geometric figures which are not subdivided. The subject would then have the task of mentally building up each geometric figure from the appropriate parts. This is a harder task and one more in keeping with the usual conception of the ability to appreciate spatial relations. Making the test more difficult would tend to diminish the preponderance of the speed factor.

Clifford E. Jurgensen, Personnel Director, Minneapolis Gas Light Company, Minneapolis, Minnesota. Each of 32 items in this test consists of a design made of parts ranging in number from two to seven, and a series of ten discrete parts. Testees are instructed to select the parts which will make the specified design when fitted together, and to identify their selection by encircling corresponding numbers. Sometimes parts must be mentally turned over and rotated in order to make them fit. Lines are in white against a blue background in order to resemble a blueprint. This procedure was intended to increase the acceptability of the test to applicants and employees, and the authors are to be commended for their consideration of a much neglected but highly important problem in industrial testing. The test was designed to be useful for mechanical jobs requiring the ability to perceive rapidly and accurately the relationships among objects in space, as is important in such mechanical jobs as assembly, inspection, drafting, blueprint reading, lofting, tool and die making, etc. as well as mechanical professions such as architecture, design engineering, and mechanical engineering.

The test is practically self-administering. Instructions and practice exercises require approximately five minutes and the test itself has a fifteen-minute time limit. Scoring is completely objective.

The experimental form of the test resulted in validity coefficients ranging from .34 to .62 with five groups, the number of cases in each ranging from 17 to 52, the criteria being instructor's ratings of quality and quantity of production in various shop courses. The test manual gives no data on the correlation between course grades and subsequent job success, or between test scores and job success.

The experimental form of the test gave a reliability coefficient of .93 for the five groups (total N of 150) on which validity was determined.

Percentile norms are based on 1,000 adults including both sexes aged from 16 to 50, subjects being "selected to represent a true cross section of the adult population available to industry." No data are given regarding effect on test scores of such factors as education, age or sex, although research on other tests in the mechanical area (e.g., Bennett's *Test of Mechanical Comprehension, Revised Minnesota Paper Formboard,* etc.) have shown such factors to be quite important. No data are given on the relationship between this and other tests.

James M. Porter, Jr., Associate Professor of Psychology, Rensselaer Polytechnic Institute, Troy, New York. This test lacks adequate standardization. The total number of cases involved in the experimental validation was 150. No occupational or vocational norms are supplied. Its utility in employee selection apparently remains to be established. Its typographic makeup, white lines on blue background, is likely to prove a desirable feature.

Survey of Space Relations Ability

[683]

★Test of Mechanical Comprehension. Grades 9 and over; 1940–47; IBM; 1 form; 3 editions; separate answer sheets must be used; $3.50 per 25, postpaid; $1.50 per 50 machine-scorable answer sheets, postpaid; 35¢ per specimen set of any one edition, postpaid; nontimed (30) minutes; George K. Bennett and Dinah E. Fry; Psychological Corporation.

a) FORM AA. Men in Grades 9 and over; 1940–47.
b) FORM BB. Men in grades 13 and over; 1941.
c) FORM W-1. Women in grades 9 and over; 1942.

REFERENCES

1. MOORE, BRUCE V. "Analysis of Results of Tests Administered to Men in Engineering Defense Training Courses." *J Appl Psychol* 25:619-35 D '41. * (PA 16:1683)
2. BENNETT, GEORGE K., AND CRUIKSHANK, RUTH M. "Sex Differences in the Understanding of Mechanical Problems." *J Appl Psychol* 26:121-7 Ap '42. * (PA 16:3950)
3. BENNETT, GEORGE K., AND CRUIKSHANK, RUTH M. *A Summary of Manual and Mechanical Ability Tests,* Preliminary Form, pp. 39-42. New York: Psychological Corporation, 1942. Pp. v, 80. Paper, lithotyped. $0.70. * (PA 16:2432)
4. McGEHEE, WILLIAM, AND MOFFIE, D. J. "Psychological Tests in the Selection of Enrollees in Engineering, Science, Management, Defense Training Courses." *J Appl Psychol* 26:584-6 O '42. * (PA 17:2186)
5. BENNETT, GEORGE K., AND FEAR, RICHARD A. "Mechanical Comprehension and Dexterity." *Personnel J* 22:12-7 My '43. * (PA 17:2843)
6. JACOBSEN, ELDON E. "An Evaluation of Certain Tests in Predicting Mechanic Learner Achievement." *Ed & Psychol Meas* 3:259-67 au '43. * (PA 18:2537)
7. TRAXLER, ARTHUR E. "Correlations Between 'Mechanical Aptitude' Scores and 'Mechanical Comprehension' Scores." *Occupations* 22:42-3 O '43. * (PA 18:319)
8. McDANIEL, J. W., AND REYNOLDS, WM. A. "A Study of the Use of Mechanical Aptitude Tests in the Selection of Trainees for Mechanical Occupations." *Ed & Psychol Meas* 4:191-7 au '44. * (PA 19:1776)
9. SHUMAN, JOHN T. *An Investigation Into the Value of Certain Tests in the Selection and Upgrading of Personnel in Aircraft Engine and Propeller Industries.* Unpublished doctor's thesis, Pennsylvania State College, 1944. Pp. 251. (Abstracts of Doctoral Dissertations . . . 1944, 1945, pp. 160-76.)
10. McMURRY, ROBERT N., AND JOHNSON, DALE L. "Development of Instruments for Selecting and Placing Factory Employees." *Adv Mgmt* 10:113-20 S '45. * (PA 19:3473)
11. SARTAIN, A. Q. "The Use of Certain Standardized Tests in the Selection of Inspectors in an Aircraft Factory." *J Consult Psychol* 9:234-7 S-O '45. * (PA 20:1241)
12. SHULTZ, IRVIN T., AND BARNABAS, BENTLEY. "Testing for Leadership in Industry." *Trans Kan Acad Sci* 48:160-4 S '45. * (PA 20:896)
13. SHUMAN, JOHN T. "The Value of Aptitude Tests for Factory Workers in the Aircraft Engine and Propeller Industries." *J Appl Psychol* 29:156-60 Ap '45. * (PA 19:2346)
14. SHUMAN, JOHN T. "The Value of Aptitude Tests for Supervisory Workers in the Aircraft Engine and Propeller Industries." *J Appl Psychol* 29:185-90 Je '45. * (PA 19:3138)
15. LANE, GEORGE GORHAM. *Prediction of Success in Learning to Fly Light Aircraft.* Unpublished doctor's thesis, Ohio State University, 1946. (Abstracts of Dissertations . . . Spring Quarter 1945-46, 1947, pp. 81-8.)
16. SARTAIN, A. Q. "Relation Between Scores on Certain Standard Tests and Supervisory Success in an Aircraft Factory." *J Appl Psychol* 30:328-32 Ag '46. * (PA 21:250)
17. ANDERSON, ROSE G. "Test Scores and Efficiency Ratings of Machinists." *J Appl Psychol* 31:377-88 Ag '47. * (PA 22:2335)
18. BENNETT, GEORGE K., AND WESMAN, ALEXANDER G. "Industrial Test Norms for a Southern Plant Population." *J Appl Psychol* 31:241-6 Je '47. * (PA 21:4095)
19. JENSEN, MILTON B., AND ROTTER, JULIAN B. "The Value of Thirteen Psychological Tests in Officer Candidate Screening." *J Appl Psychol* 31:312-22 Je '47. * (PA 21:4107)

Charles M. Harsh, Associate Professor of Psychology, The University of Nebraska, Lincoln, Nebraska. The wide use of this test since the first form appeared in 1940 has made it familiar to most testers. The technique of illustrating physical principles, usually by two drawings, has appealed to many experts, as witnessed by the adaptations of the test for all of the armed forces. Forms AA, BB, and W-1 all have good format, clear type, and satisfactory drawings. The answer sheets are admirable, with arrows for page alignment. Use of the paper scoring stencil is a bit awkward, but a celluloid key (official or homemade) can easily be used. The manuals of directions are models of conciseness and honesty, including norms, references, and the available data on reliability and validity.

Form AA is suitable for males in high school or trade school; Form BB is for male applicants for engineering schools or jobs; and Form W-1 is for women. Norms are provided for school grades and for applicants for various occupations or training courses. Reliabilities from .77 to .84 are reported, with standard errors of scores from 3.7 to 4.8 points. The repeat reliability of .90 (Form BB) is of dubious significance, as it is easy to remember one's answers to most of the questions.

Despite the widespread use of the test there is no conclusive evidence as to its usefulness. The many reported correlations with other tests are only indirect evidence of validity, and (except for Form BB) it correlates as well with verbal tests as with mechanical or spatial tests. It is said to correlate from .3 to .6 with success in army engineering-type training, but the data have not yet been released to permit evaluation of their significance. If verbal and numerical tests are equally correlated with success in training, one will want to know whether the mechanical comprehension score improves on the prediction possible from the other tests. There is little doubt that the test measures comprehension of many mechanical principles, but its value for prediction has been questioned on the ground that several items involve principles or facts which one is unlikely to encounter in everyday mechanical experience, outside of a physics course. Studies reported in the manual show that persons with training in physics get scores 4 or 5 points higher, on the average, than persons without such training. The difference is large enough to be considered in interpreting a person's score. Candidates for engineering and technical courses have usually had more than average training in general science and physics, which may be sufficient to explain why their norms are considerably above the norms for average persons. But their general intelligence test scores also tend to be above average, so there is need for clearer evidence as to the specific contribution of the *Test of Me-*

chanical Comprehension. The norms for Form W-1 suggest that scores for women are more related to schooling than to mechanical interest or experience.

The uncertainty as to the test's usefulness can only be overcome by more direct studies of validity to indicate the conditions under which the test is useful for achievement screening and the conditions under which it may be useful for predicting future attainment. We hope such evidence will soon be available from the many studies in which the test has been used.

Lloyd G. Humphreys, Supervisor of the Testing Division, University of Washington, Seattle, Washington. This test is available in three forms: Form AA for men who are relatively unselected mechanically; Form BB, also for men, approximately 12 points more difficult than Form AA, for candidates to engineering schools, etc.; Form W-1 for women (for women, it is intermediate in difficulty between Forms AA and BB for men). The reviewer has pointed out elsewhere (*see* 670) that the assumption that mechanical tests which show marked male superiority should not be used for women needs empirical verification. For many occupations either Form AA or Form BB may be more valid for women than Form W-1.

Mechanical principles are pictorially represented. The examinee has three choices: result A will follow, result B will follow, or either (neither) will result. Items for Forms BB and W-1 were selected from a larger group on the basis of internal-consistency item analyses. On Form BB, the authors report a correlation of .97 between scores on the original 76 items and the final 60 items. Nothing as meaningless as this statistic, involving as it does a self-correlation of 1.00 for the 60 overlapping items, should be placed in a test manual.

Items for Form AA, on the other hand, were selected from a larger group of 75 on the basis of item correlations with a composite criterion consisting of the scores on the original items, the *MacQuarrie Test for Mechanical Ability,* the *Detroit Mechanical Aptitudes Examination,* and the *Revised Minnesota Paper Formboard.* Because of obvious deficiencies of this criterion, it is fortunate that relatively few items were discarded as a result of the analysis. If the test is good, it is the result of the author's ingenuity in the construction of the original test items and not of the statistical analysis.

Reliability is not high by older standards. Self-correlations, probably a little low since the items are not highly homogeneous, vary from .77 for Form W-1 to .84 for the other two forms. A test-retest correlation for Form BB goes as high as .90, but this is undoubtedly spuriously high because these items are relatively easily remembered. Within wide limits, reliability is not critical. The test user is interested in validity.

The reviewer is using the test quite confidently in a vocational advisement program, in spite of the relative lack of validation presented in the manual. Experience with similar tests in the selection of aircrew indicates that the present test should be exceedingly useful. These tests were among the most valid (including psycho-motor tests) for pilot and aerial gunner selection. The same tests were also related to military "occupations" more clearly mechanical. The validity for pilots is due primarily to two factors, equally valid and present in most mechanical comprehension tests in about equal amounts: a mechanical information or background factor, and a visualization factor. These factors can be described more fully as follows: All tests involving mechanical materials of any sort appear on the first of these factors. Information tests are highest on the factor. Tests involving comprehension of principles are also high. The second factor is defined by certain mechanical tests, like the present one, that involve function. Information tests have zero loadings. Also appearing on the visualization factor are such tests as the *Revised Minnesota Paper Formboard,* Thurstone's *Punched Holes and Surface Development,* and Part II of the Army's *Mechanical Aptitude Test.* To the extent that both of these factors are found in a criterion, the present tests should have good validity.

A problem that needs to be investigated for tests of this type is the effect on the function measured of training in academic physics. It would seem that the right answers could be obtained for most items on either of two bases: knowledge of theoretical physics or experience * with things mechanical, on the farm, in the shop, etc. Would these tests have different validities (and factor patterns) for two groups

* That the writer assumes that experience affects the scores made on these tests does not constitute an adverse criticism. We have reached the point where we ask if the test can be used to predict future success, not if it can be assumed to measure an innate ability.

Test of Mechanical Comprehension

differing widely in background along the lines indicated?

Norms on Form AA are varied and useful and generally based on adequate numbers of cases. Norms on the other two forms are less adequate.

The reviewer commends the inclusion in these manuals of rather generous numbers of correlations with other tests. Two tests should not be given the same name without providing the test user with data which permit him to evaluate the degree of similarity. Different names, by the same token, should not be used unless the tests are functionally different.

George A. Satter, Assistant Professor of Psychology, University of Michigan, Ann Arbor, Michigan. The three forms of this test are designed to measure understanding of a variety of mechanical and physical relationships. They may be used with high school students (and adults with comparable educational attainments), candidates for engineering schools, engineering students, and among women who are candidates for technical training or light mechanical work.

The subject matter of the 60 items which comprise each of the three forms presents the appearance of being essentially the subject matter of a high school course in physics which has been sheared of its technical jargon and placed in a work-a-day setting. Each item consists of a picture illustrating some principle of mechanics, hydraulics, etc. and a question with two or three alternatives. The pictures are drawn on an adequately large scale; they are clear and, for the most part, free from ambiguities.

The items are printed in a 16-page booklet and are prefaced with what appears to be an adequate set of directions and two sample exercises. Answers may be marked either on a separate sheet designed for easy hand-scoring or on a sheet which can be machine scored.

There is no time limit on any of the forms but the authors suggest that twenty or twenty-five minutes is adequate for most people to complete the exercises.

Scores on each of the forms represent the number of items answered correctly minus one half the number wrong (each item has three alternatives). Hand scoring is facilitated by strip keys which accompany the test.

Percentile norms are provided for a number of different types of groups which vary in size from 145 to 2,460. Form AA (the form designed for high school students and for persons of comparable educational attainment) has been administered to students at all stages of high school training, to engineering school freshmen, and to candidates for WPA mechanical courses, policeman, and fireman positions. Form BB, a form more difficult than AA, has been given to engineering school freshmen and to candidates for engineering school, merchant marine officers' training, and light mechanical work. The form designed especially for women (W-1) has been used to measure the abilities of freshmen and senior high school students, enlisted Waves, candidates for mechanical courses, and individuals employed at light mechanical work. It would seem that the test has many possibilities for use in industrial selection and placement situations; it is regrettable that the Psychological Corporation has not been able to supply data descriptive of the performance of a larger variety of industrial groups.

Manual materials accompany each of the three forms. These materials are pointed and well above the average in completeness. They cover such items as the rationale underlying the construction of the test, directions for administering and interpreting the results of the test, procedures used in construction, norms, and data descriptive of the test's reliability and validity.

While the quality of the manual materials is in general good, some might prefer that the test authors had gone into greater detail in preparing certain sections. Validity in each case is dismissed with a sentence or two; groups from which standardization data and norms were obtained are described with a word or two; and procedures used in construction and validation are presented in sketchy form.

The authors recognize the possible usefulness of an external criterion, lament their inability to obtain a suitable one, and follow the conventional, more convenient, procedure of using total test score as a criterion. In selecting items for each of the three forms of the test, the authors followed the Kelley–Wood procedure, i.e., selected items on the basis of how well they discriminated between "high" and "low" scoring groups. Internal criteria (total scores on the test) were employed in the selection of items for Forms BB and W-1; and a composite criterion made up of weighted scores on the *MacQuarrie Test for Mechanical Ability,* the

Test of Mechanical Comprehension

Detroit Mechanical Aptitudes Examination, the *Revised Minnesota Paper Formboard,* and the *Test of Mechanical Comprehension* was employed in defining the "high" and "low" groups used in selecting items for Form AA. The descriptions of the procedures presented in the test manuals do not specify the standard used in selecting items. One would presume, since no statement to the contrary is made, that in every case the authors selected 60 items with the highest discrimination values from among those (from 75 to 92) given a trial administration.

The results of the validation studies reported in the test manuals are sketchy and hardly of the sort which would be very helpful to the prospective users of the tests. No data, other than a group of correlations with other tests, are presented for Form W-1. The validity of Form BB is dismissed with the following statement, "Several studies have been made with this test as a predictor of success at engineering-type occupations with validity coefficients from .3 to .6," and a promise to release, at some time in the future, data collected from military groups. Coefficients of .5 between average grade from technical military courses and scores on Form AA and the differences in mean scores of those reporting physics training and no physics training substantiate the authors' contention that the test is useful for predicting performance in technical training.

Scores on the two forms (AA and W-1) which are designed for use with wide ability ranges correlate from .25 to .54 with paper-and-pencil measures of intelligence, with other measures of mechanical aptitude, and with achievement in physics. The use of multiple criteria (such as high correlation with total score and low correlation with measures of intelligence) in selecting items for future editions of this test might prove effective in reducing this overlap.

For selected groups (enlisted Waves, freshman engineers, and ninth-grade boys), reliabilities estimated from split-half correlations are reported as .77, .80, and .84.

The *Test of Mechanical Comprehension,* in the reviewer's opinion, should prove to be a useful tool especially to those persons engaged in educational and vocational guidance. It should also find increasing usage in the technical school and the industrial employment office. It is an attractive test; the items are intrinsically interesting; all the forms appear to have been well constructed; and they are easy to give. The range of usefulness of the test will undoubtedly increase as more validity data are made available.

MISCELLANEOUS

[684]

★**Cancellation Test.** Adults; 1946; 1 form; 75¢ per 25; 80¢ per set of scoring keys; 25¢ per specimen set, postpaid; 10(15) minutes; John R. Roberts; Educational Test Bureau.

Joseph E. King, Director, Personnel Management Consultants, Chicago, Illinois. Cancellation is an historical item type which factorial studies have labeled a measure of perceptual speed. Like items of number and word comparison, picking out the highest number, and other "proofreading" types, cancellation items measure facility in perceiving detail embedded in irrelevant material or aptitude in recognizing likenesses and differences rapidly.

The *Cancellation Test* is at present in experimental form. A study of 78 industrial workers provides preliminary norms and score ranges for six job classifications. No other statistical data are reported. The publishers indicate that the test is available "only to personnel directors known to us."

The *Cancellation Test* is an example of the almost universal fallacy in current test development and publication. A test is considered salable if a group of items have been brought together (possibly studied for internal consistency and difficulty), a reliability of .90 has been gained, and norms (and possibly validities or score ranges for given job classifications) are available. There is little concern as to (*a*) what the test measures or (*b*) whether a similar (if not identical) test is currently available. The publishers state that "basically there is nothing new or novel about a cancellation test; it is one of the oldest types." They do not speak of its factorial composition.

It seems to the writer that psychometrists and test publishers have a professional responsibility which has been infrequently realized. In the industrial field alone, about 1,000 tests are promoted to the usually nontestwise personnel director. These tests measure complex abilities, overlap from publisher to publisher, lack business and industrial orientation, and are labeled with vague titles and even vaguer definitions of what is measured and its usefulness for personnel selection and placement. Testing programs will be found in more than 5 per cent of the business world only when psychologists realize that test development is a scientific tool requiring specialized techniques and adequate research study.

[685]

Diagnostic Interviewer's Guide. Job applicants; 1937; $6 per 100; $1 per specimen set including 10 forms; E. F. Wonderlic and S. N. Stevens; E. F. Wonderlic, 750 Grove St., Glencoe, Ill.

REFERENCES

1. LAIRD, DONALD A. *The Psychology of Selecting Employees,* Third Edition, pp. 114-9. New York: McGraw-Hill Book Co., Inc., 1937. Pp. xiii, 316. $4.00. * (London: McGraw-Hill Publishing Co. Ltd. 24s.) (*PA* 9:4726)
2. HOVLAND, CARL IVER, AND WONDERLIC, E. F. "Prediction of Industrial Success From a Standardized Interview." *J Appl Psychol* 23:537-46 O '39. * (*PA* 14:1039)

Clyde H. Coombs, Assistant Professor of Psychology and Chief of the Research Division, Bureau of Psychological Services, Institute for Human Adjustment, University of Michigan, Ann Arbor, Michigan. The guide consists of a series of questions in four categories—work history, family history, social history, and personal history. An employment interviewer can use these questions as a guide and record the answers to the questions during the interview on space provided (frequently inadequate). As pointed out in the manual, the guide is designed primarily for the selection of high caliber personnel.

Each of the four main sections is followed by a series of questions, from five to twelve in number. The interviewer, on the basis of his recorded answers, is to answer the questions listed, which are scored favorably or unfavorably. A gross score is thus obtained to be used as an element in the selection of an employee.

It appears that the time of the interview would be mostly spent in writing down the answers to the questions asked during the interview. Also, the scoring procedure is rather poorly set up and would be subject to clerical error.

A particular employer might find the guide helpful if he had little knowledge of interviewing. In general, however, it would serve best as a guide for preparing an interview blank specifically designed to meet the needs of a particular situation. Much of the information to be gathered during the interview could better be gathered by a biographical inventory in an objective manner and the items eventually validated. This would also cut down a lot of writing by the interviewer during the interview.

Douglas H. Fryer, Associate Professor of Psychology, New York University, New York, New York. The *Diagnostic Interviewer's Guide* was developed for the selection of outside representatives for public contact work in the Household Finance Corporation and is recommended as a guide for a final selection interview following other screening of applicants. All major areas of the individual's life are surveyed: work history, family history, social history, and personal history. The interviewee's answers to questions about him in these areas are recorded. Following this survey, a number of yes-no questions are answered about the applicant by the interviewer; there is a total of 34 questions in the several areas, making available a score range of -34 to $+34$. The questions are largely concerned with the applicant's qualifications in contact work with people. The personnel survey provides the basis for answering the questions, but the interviewer is instructed to emphasize in his observation verbal facility, personality, attitudes, and appearance. No norms are provided for the use of the score for selection purposes, but the statement is made that "In general a negative score or a very low positive score should eliminate the applicant from serious consideration."

Reliability and validity of the *Diagnostic Interviewer's Guide,* reported elsewhere (2), are based on the interviewer's score in marking the 34 questions about the applicant. A correlation of .71 was found between different interviewers' scores on 23 cases interviewed separately. A corrected odd-even correlation of .82 is reported for 100 cases. A significant favorable difference (Cr = 4.25) is shown between 100 workers still on the job and 100 dismissed workers at the Household Finance Corporation. Scores are shown to increase relatively as workers are more likely to succeed on the job.

The *Diagnostic Interviewer's Guide* is a promising tool for estimating ability in public contact, but very little is known about what it accomplishes in personnel selection and nothing has been added to this knowledge since 1939. For example, its unbelievably high repeat reliability may be due to interviewers having common prerequisites in experience on which the answers to yes-no questions are based; the answers to the questions based on the survey of personal history may duplicate less effectively the validity of the experience record when scored; and any estimation of the goodness of the interviewee's contact behavior during the interview, while less reliably rated from this base than from the experience record, may be the only independent contribution of this interviewing procedure to the over-all measurement of the applicant's qualifications. The *Diagnostic Interviewer's Guide* is in a preliminary stage of development as a measuring device; most interviewing procedures cannot be said to have reached this stage.

[686]

★Employee Evaluation Form for Interviewers. Adults; 1943; $1 per 25, postpaid; $1.75 per manual; Richard A. Fear and Byron Jordan; Psychological Corporation.

Douglas H. Fryer, Associate Professor of Psychology, New York University, New York, New York. The *Employee Evaluation Manual for Interviewers,* by Richard A. Fear and Byron Jordan is a training manual on the use of the *Employee Evaluation Form for Interviewers,* prepared by the same authors. It is said that experienced interviewers can adapt their procedures to the use of these materials but that new and inexperienced interviewers will need training by specialists in the field.

The manual presents the philosophy and technique for the interviewing in which the goal is to consider the applicant's entire experience and personality development in relation to the requirements of a specific job. The form provides the facilities for recording. Its efficient use depends, it is said, upon complete specifications of the job for which the applicant is being interviewed. Average time of interviewing is about 22 minutes with wide variations for various levels of qualifications. The interviewer rates the applicant on the blank upon seven factors: (a) previous experience, (b) training, (c) manner and appearance, (d) sociability, (e) emotional stability, (f) maturity, and (g) leadership capacity. The first three are rated in accordance with the requirements of the job, and the latter four as phases of personality development. An over-all rating of fitness for the specific job follows. Ratings are made on a 3-point graphic scale of average, above and below average. A number of questions are to be marked on the blank under each factor, indicating satisfactory or unsatisfactory qualifications. The final task of the interviewer is to write an over-all summary statement of qualifications for the job for which the interview was given. The ratings and the marking of the questions provide the basis for this verbal summary statement from which interpretation is to be made in the hiring.

This procedure emphasizes the idea that the employer is hiring a man and not a machine and that he wants to determine how well he will fit into his organization before hiring—the old concept of a "worker-in-his-work unit" by Scott and Clothier. Here is fine practical idealism for the application of the Gestalt view in personnel work. At the higher levels of employment, e.g., in hiring a traffic manager, it would seem that this procedure could be executed in about two hours for an interview; possibly at the lower levels, e.g., in hiring a watchman, it can be accomplished in twenty-two minutes, or even less. It should satisfy personnel men that they are doing a good job of interviewing and that their judgments are based on adequate information. But it would be wise, before introducing the procedure permanently, because of its cost, for any businessman to determine for each and any type of job whether these judgments correlate higher with efficient "worker-in-his-work units" than do the "snap" judgments of personnel men from application blanks. It might turn out that long period cooperation and morale would be greatly affected by hiring from this kind of interview. Whether a battery of tests or a scored history form, taking less time of personnel men in operation, would do better or worse, with or without this interviewing procedure, is still another unanswered question. This procedure is but an idea, while beautifully worked out and with many suggestions for skillful interviewing, yet to be evaluated in any way except in opinion.

C. H. Ruedisili, Associate Dean of the College of Letters and Science and Lecturer in Psychology, The University of Wisconsin, Madison, Wisconsin. The *Employee Evaluation Form for Interviewers* is "a device for helping interviewers improve their present methods by considering the whole individual in his fitness for a job and recording this information for future use." It was designed for use in employee selection, assignment, and upgrading. The nature and purpose of the form, as well as its use and interpretation, are described in *Employee Evaluation Manual for Interviewers* by the same authors.

Based on the assumption that "the best indication of what an individual will do in the future is what he has done in the past," the interviewer rates the applicant as below average, average, or above average on each of seven factors: previous experience, training, manner and appearance, sociability (teamwork), emotional stability, maturity, and leadership capacity. Ratings on the first three factors are judged as they apply directly to the specific job, whereas those for the remaining four factors are considered as distinct phases of personality apart from any definite job requirements. Under each factor are four to eight question items to be checked (√) if the applicant's responses seem to be favorable or crossed (×) if they are unfavorable. In addition, brief facts selected from the interview to substantiate each rating are to be recorded. The interviewer then writes a summary evaluation (which, according to the authors, is the most important part of the form) of the applicant, and finally he makes an over-all rating for the specific job based on all the facts learned. Three sample cases are filled out on the forms for illustrative purposes, and indicate the kinds of facts and summaries to record. The use of the form in an aviation company indicates that the essential information needed can be obtained in about 20 to 30 minutes.

A functional outline for conducting the interview is recommended, beginning with the factor of work experience, then leading to a discussion of school or training experience, and ending with personal history. This sequence is most effective because it enables the applicant to start on a subject that he knows thoroughly and can discuss without the danger of emotional blocks. By the time the personal history section is reached, the interviewer should have effected the necessary rapport to approach this more intimate area.

The major portion of the manual (which is a brief but excellent treatise on interviewing) deals with an interpretation of the items covered on the evaluation form. Each of the 41 items is discussed with suggestions for getting the significant information relating to the individual's background. Helpful hints regarding technique and concrete tips to encourage full discussion are described. Suggestions are given for probing the various areas, with warnings and guideposts to aid the interviewer. The causes of job terminations, reasons for dropping out of school, factors leading to personality problems—these problems, and others to enable the interviewer to obtain the significant information in the different areas—are discussed clearly and succinctly. The authors readily admit, however, that the interpretation of the responses made by the applicant has only been outlined. That this depends greatly on the experience and skill of the interviewer is granted; still, it is the interpretation of the information that determines the summary evaluation and ratings.

This form has been used by the reviewer as a training tool in a class in the field of personnel psychology and proved to be more usable than such rating scales as Bingham's *Rating Form for Use of Interviewers and Oral Examiners.* Though it is more difficult to administer than Wonderlic's *Diagnostic Interviewer's Guide* (since it does not consist of very specific questions to be answered by the applicant), the additional energy spent is justified. In the hands of a competent interviewer the *Employee Evaluation Form for Interviewers* can be an effective technique to improve the interview.

Occupations 22:457 Ap '44. Martin L. Reymert. This manual, to be used in conjunction with a rating scale interview blank, gives in compact, logical form the a-b-c's of job interviewing. * The authors "do not profess to present anything profound or, in fact, new about interviewing," they have "simply gathered together some common-sense principles which have been found helpful in determining an applicant's fitness for a job and organized them in a manner suitable for industrial use." This seems an understatement, however, since this brief manual might well serve as required reading for new interviewers and, no doubt, will also prove very helpful as a reminder of pertinent items to seasoned interviewers. * The manual seems to be sound psychologically and is undoubtedly based on considerable interview experience by the two authors.

Pub Personnel R 5:244–5 O '44. Kenneth Byers. * The authors do not profess to present anything new or startling in their manual and evaluation form but they have gathered together some common sense principles which have been found helpful in determining an applicant's fitness for a job, and have organized these principles in a manner believed suitable for industrial use. The technique presented is not to be compared with a clinical interview by a trained psychologist but is to be considered as a device for helping interviewers improve their present methods by considering the whole individual in his fitness for a job and recording the information for future use. * The employee evaluation form and this manual are well worth the study of employment interviewers both in industry and government. They should prove particularly helpful in training new interviewers and in clarifying the thinking of, or opening new avenues of thought to, the experienced interviewer. Because of the employment philosophy presented, as well as the points of interest in the employee evaluation form itself, the manual should be of interest to everyone in the public personnel field.

[687]

★How Supervise? Candidates for supervisory training; 1943; Forms A, B; $1.75 per 25, postpaid; 35¢ per specimen set, postpaid; nontimed (15-40) minutes; edited by H. H. Remmers; Quentin W. File; Psychological Corporation.

REFERENCES
1. FILE, QUENTIN W. "The Measurement of Supervisory Quality in Industry." J Appl Psychol 29:323-37 O '45. * (PA 20:884)
2. FILE, QUENTIN W. "Are Management's Views of Supervision Faulty?" Discussion by Charles S. Slocombe. Personnel J 24:242-9, discussion 251-4 Ja '46. * (PA 20:1634)
3. FILE, QUENTIN W., AND REMMERS, H. H. "Studies in Supervisory Evaluation." J Appl Psychol 30:421-5 O '46. * (PA 21:572)
4. SARTAIN, A. Q. "Relation Between Scores on Certain Standard Tests and Supervisory Success in an Aircraft Factory." J Appl Psychol 30:328-32 Ag '46. * (PA 21:250)
5. SLOCOMBE, CHARLES S. "Appraisal of Mr. File's Study." Personnel J 24:251-4 Ja '46. * (PA 20:1657)

D. Welty Lefever, Professor of Education, The University of Southern California, Los Angeles, California. The measurement of skill and understanding in the area of human relationships is difficult at best. This test has been carefully and intelligently developed and seems to be sufficiently successful for use by trained workers under controlled conditions. The manual recommends the test as a "valuable aid" and not as a "cure-all" in the selection and placement of supervisors. A rather clear recognition of the limitations and precautions essential to a valid application of the test characterizes the discussion and directions contained in the manual.

The authors include in their listing of uses: the selection of candidates for training in supervision, the evaluation of the supervisory training received, the study of supervisor attitudes toward workers and toward the company, and the collection of basic data to guide the counseling and interviewing of supervisors. The test appears to be most valuable in furnishing the bases for the discussion of managerial and supervisory problems and in measuring the outcomes of training programs. This reviewer believes that considerable experimentation and careful study in a given business, industry, or civil service installation would be required before the test should be permitted to become a major factor in the actual selection of supervisory personnel.

The answers to the items are based on a modern philosophy of personnel management and were determined specifically from the replies of a group of experts from the Training Within Industry program. By keeping in mind the general principles of a democratic social philosophy and the simple precepts of mental hygiene, a very large proportion of items can be answered correctly.

Persons of superior intelligence with recent psychological study can make high scores without special course work or experience in supervisory theory or techniques. Fifty graduate students in education were given Form A of the test. The median score of the group was 54, which, according to the manual, corresponds to the 95th percentile on the table of norms based on the scores of 577 supervisors. A few items were the subject of considerable controversy. If these special items had been omitted, the median score would have reached the 99th percentile.

The manual accompanying the test is exceptionally well prepared. Much-needed cautions are given to guide in administering, scoring, and interpreting the test results. Emphasis is placed on the important principle that knowledge about the best techniques of supervision is necessary but by no means sufficient to guarantee effective practice.

Charles I. Mosier, Director of Research, Personnel Research Section, The Adjutant General's Office, Washington, D. C. The stated objective of this test is to measure understanding of supervisory principles and, by implication, ability to supervise. The authors recommend the test in selection of supervisors and selection for supervisory training, in appraising training needs and training outcomes, as well as for counseling supervisors and surveying their attitudes toward company policies.

Items were drawn from training courses and textbooks on principles of supervision, and the 70 items in each form were selected from an original 204 items on the basis of internal consistency rather than for discrimination among levels of supervisory competence. Even so, selection of the most reliable items has not resulted in a satisfactory reliability for a single form. Since both forms must be used to get satisfactorily reliable measures, the advantages of separate forms disappear.

The keyed answers were determined by the consensus of training officers and textbook writers. The items are essentially of the true-false type. (Although a third response, "?", is offered, marking it has the same effect as omitting the item.) All of the items state principles with which the candidate is to agree or disagree, or which he is to mark as desirable or undesirable. For many of these there is insufficient information to make a categorical answer satisfying. There are no items which present specific situations and call for particular solutions, although there is evidence on the validity of such items for supervisory success.* The test does, however, provide an excellent check list from which such items could be constructed. It is unfortunate that the more flexible multiple-choice form was not used, since this would not only have tended to increase reliability for the same number of items but also have permitted the presentation of problems and alternative solutions.

The only evidence of validity offered by the authors is curricular validity for a supervisory training course. The source of the items, the method of keying, and the criterion for selection of the final items support, but do not add to, the authors' finding that there is a statistically significant difference in test scores before and after a training course. None of these however, provides evidence as to the validity of the test for the prediction of supervisory success, either before or after training. Moreover, its validity for appraising the effects of training is limited to those training outcomes which are reflected in verbal statements of what should be done. Whether such outcomes alone lead to actual improvement in supervisory practice is another question.

For the more important purpose of predicting supervisory success, the only evidence offered by the authors is the postulate: Although those who do understand supervisory principles may not apply them, those who do not have the knowledge cannot apply it. This is weakened by the finding that supervisory and management officials disagree with the key (i.e., make low scores). This finding may mean, as File claims, that the sample represents unenlightened management or that the "principles of supervision" are not as directly related to supervisory success as one might suspect. The latter conclusion is supported by at least one study (4) in which there was no relationship between *How Supervise?* scores and rated success as a supervisor

* BRANSFORD, T. L.; ADKINS, D. C.; AND MANDELL, M. M. "A Study of the Validity of Written Tests for Administrative Personnel." Abstract. *Am Psychol* 1:279 '46.

(aircraft foreman). Moreover, the general soundness of the a priori logic breaks down in the case of any who, though skillful supervisors, are unable to verbalize the basis of their skill. The test does apparently provide an adequate, though relatively unreliable, measure of verbal intelligence and shows substantial correlation with tests of "intelligence." Whether it contributes more to the selection of successful supervisors is not demonstrated.

How the test is to be used to select people for supervisory training is not clear. Since the test measures course content, those with high scores are least in need of training; since the test is highly correlated with verbal intelligence, those with low scores are least able to profit from training. Neither the test nor the manual resolves this very real and very tough dilemma. Certainly the use of other tests in conjunction with this one is indicated if this particular objective is to be met.

Certain technical defects in the manual should be noted. Reliability coefficients are reported, but there is no indication of how they were determined nor of the group on which they were based. Percentile norms and standard scores are given for each form and for both combined. These norms are based on a sample of 577 supervisors, but the group is not further defined, e.g., blue-collar or white-collar, before or after training. The two forms are asserted to be equivalent, but no means or standard deviations are given in support of this. These statistics can, of course, be roughly inferred from the percentile norms, on the assumption that they are equal for both forms. Reference to technical papers on the construction or validation of the test would be helpful. The manual is written for the unsophisticated test user; this should not preclude the inclusion of the information needed by the trained test technician.

In summary, the test is limited by its item form and has inadequate single-form reliability. There is no evidence of its validity except as an achievement test of the verbal knowledge expected to result from a course on principles of supervision. Its reliability is too low to be very helpful as a diagnostic test of specific areas of training needs, and the evidence of its validity for the selection of successful supervisors is thus far unsatisfactory.

C. H. Ruedisili, Associate Dean of the College of Letters and Science, and Lecturer in Psychol-

ogy, *The University of Wisconsin, Madison, Wisconsin.* This test, of the typical inventory form, is designed to measure a person's "knowledge and insight concerning human relations in industry." Each of the two forms consists of 70 items divided into three areas: two of them, Supervisory Practices and Company Policies, pertain to specific supervisory practices and methods found in industry, and each item is to be answered as desirable, uncertain, or undesirable; the third, Supervisor Opinions, deals with the human-relations problems of handling workers, and the subject indicates his agreement, uncertainty, or disagreement with the statements.

Designed to measure supervisors' understanding of their job, the manual recommends that *How Supervise?* can be of value in selecting candidates for and measuring the results of supervisory training programs, in upgrading employees, in employee attitude studies, and in general counseling and interviewing programs. Like most manuals published by the Psychological Corporation, this one is well written and covers the topics one looks for and, too often even at the present time, fails to find in many test manuals. These are: description of test, validity and reliability, administration, scoring, norms, uses of test, precautions of use, and keys. The test is easily administered and has no time limit. Normally it should be completed in 30 minutes, but this will vary from 15 to 40 minutes depending on the reading ability of the subjects. Scoring the test, using column keys, takes from one to two minutes. Norms, for each form or for both combined, based on 577 supervisors, include both percentiles and standard scores.

Two experimental forms of 102 items each (the items were constructed after conferences with industrial supervisors and personnel men and after a careful survey of the literature in the field) were developed. "Best" or right answers were those selected by 37 members of the government's Training Within Industry supervisory staff and 8 recognized authorities in the industrial relations field. These forms were administered to 750 supervisors in 10 industries. The items chosen for the final forms were those discriminating between the high-scoring supervisors (upper 27 per cent) and the low-scoring supervisors (lower 27 per cent).

File states that two other studies indicated the improvement in test scores that results from a training program. Supervisor's scores after training were significantly higher than before; however, no statistical proof was furnished to substantiate this conclusion. Besides, these data only mean that there is an increase in knowledge of supervisory practices; there is no assurance that understanding goes with knowledge. The supervisor may know what to do in a specific situation and yet not behave in the approved pattern because of his own emotional or personality tendencies.

The reliability of one form is reported as .76, while for the combined scores on both forms it is .86.

How Supervise? is a useful measuring instrument in the field of industrial supervision, but it is not the complete answer to all the confusing questions that arise. Sartain (4), for instance, found that the experimental edition administered to 40 supervisors in an aircraft factory correlated −.18 with the criterion of success (sum of four ratings). He concluded that the test was of little or no predictive value for success in supervision in that particular plant.

File and Remmers (3) present additional evidence of validity. The average percentile scores for 46 successful supervisors and 14 non-supervisors in an office machine manufacturing company were 75 and 23; the critical ratio of the difference between the proportions above and below the 50th percentile was 5.8. A second study in a surgical supply manufacturing concern showed a difference in the mean scores for a group of superior and inferior supervisors (as rated by the testing supervisor); the critical ratio of this difference was 4.4. The last evidence deals with a group of 16 supervisors in a large laundry divided into 5 groups from "superior" to those with "most limited supervisory responsibilities." The raw scores for these groups were 54.7, 49.7, 44.7, 40, and 32. The authors, on the basis of the available evidence, frankly admit that these studies "do not constitute conclusive evidence of universal validity of *How Supervise?* as a supervisory device." Such frankness and honesty is refreshing and appreciated. They indicate that a more comprehensive investigation is now in progress, and one is definitely needed; certainly one should not accept validity on the basis of subjective evidence and mere reports of valuable results.

Though the selection value of this test has not been definitely determined, it still is a tool with interesting possibilities. When used for discussion purposes in a supervisory training program, for getting at supervisor's and employee's attitudes in this area, or as a teaching device in college courses (the reviewer uses it in a course in personnel psychology and strongly recommends it) *How Supervise?* can be of real value.

[688]

★**Interaction Chronograph.** Ages 3 and over; 1944–47; $500 per month for rental of the chronograph; the rental fee includes "instruction in giving, recording, scoring, and interpreting interviews, assistance in setting up job standards, statistical assistance in interpreting test results, machine maintenance and frequent consulting service"; Eliot D. Chapple; E. D. Chapple Co., Inc.

REFERENCES

1. CHAPPLE, ELIOT D. "The Measurement of Interpersonal Behaviour." *Trans N Y Acad Sci* 4:222-33 My '42. * (*PA* 17:223)
2. LINDEMANN, ERICH; FINESINGER, JACOB E.; AND CHAPPLE, ELIOT D. "The Measurement of Interaction During Psychiatric Examination." *Trans Am Neurol Assn* 70:174-5 '44. *
3. CHAPPLE, ELIOT D., AND DONALD, GORDON, JR. "A Method for Evaluating Supervisory Personnel." *Harvard Bus R* 24:197-214 W '46. *
4. CHAPPLE, ELIOT D., AND DONALD, GORDON, JR. "An Evaluation of Department Store Salespeople by the Interaction Chronograph." *J Marketing* 12:173-85 O '47. *
5. PIEL, GERARD. "Your Personality Sits for Its Photo." *Nation's Bus* 35:51-6 Ap '47. *

[689]

★**Minnesota Occupational Rating Scales and Counseling Profile.** Grades 9-16 and adults; 1941; the Counseling Profile is no longer available; $4 per manual; $3 per 300 record forms; earlier editions of the scales prepared by Eleanor S. Brussell, Harland N. Cisney, J. Spenser Carlson, Gwendolen G. Schneidler, and Donald G. Paterson; 1941 edition prepared by Donald G. Paterson, Clayton d'A. Gerken, and Milton E. Hahn; Science Research Associates.

REFERENCES

1. BARR, F. E. *A Scale for Measuring Mental Ability in Vocations and Some of Its Applications.* Unpublished master's thesis, Stanford University, 1918.
2. CISNEY, HARLAND N. *Classification of Occupations in Terms of Social Intelligence, Artistic Ability, and Musical Talent.* Unpublished master's thesis, University of Minnesota, 1935.
3. TRABUE, MARION R. "Functional Classification of Occupations." *Occupations* 15:127-31 N '36. * (*PA* 11:1504)
4. BINGHAM, WALTER VAN DYKE. *Aptitudes and Aptitude Testing*, pp. 365-80. New York and London: Harper & Brothers, 1937. Pp. ix, 390. $3.00; 12s. 6d. (*PA* 11:2885)
5. LOWRIE, KATHLEEN HARRIET. *Factors Which Relate to the Extra-Curricular Performance of College Women.* Unpublished doctor's thesis, University of Iowa, 1942.

M. H. Elliott, Director of Research, Public Schools, Oakland, California. These materials are intended to aid the vocational counselor. Three different items are included in the "complete unit." The *Minnesota Occupational Rating Scales* are contained in a manual of information about occupations based upon the rating scales published by Bingham (4). Occupations are rated as to level of ability required in the areas of academic ability, mechanical ability, social intelligence, clerical ability, musical talent, artistic ability. The ratings represent the "pooled judgments of vocational psychologists." The usefulness of the information is increased by inclusion of several different reclassifications such as: occupations requiring similar abilities, occupations requiring certain levels of particular abilities, etc. The Counseling Profile "is a device which facilitates use of the Occupational Rating Scales in the counseling situation." Concentric discs are set to indicate the amount of ability which the counselee is estimated to possess. There are additional settings for the stated occupational aims and for vocational interest as measured by tests. Presumably the profile will then assist in comparing the counselee's abilities with particular occupations or in reconciling stated aims with abilities. The Individual Counseling Record is a concise one-page form for use with the Profile and Rating Scales.

The authors of the manual containing the Rating Scales are very cautious in their claims. Various possible uses of the materials are described and the limitations are indicated.

The three items are not of equal value. The manual containing the Rating Scales presents some useful information about a variety of occupations in simplified and readily available form. Probably this booklet could be used in college classes in vocational guidance techniques as an introduction to the field. The information presented would also be useful as a digest which teachers of occupational information classes at the high school level could put into the hands of students. The present reviewer believes that the main usefulness of the manual containing the rating scales is at the introductory stage of counselor training and that it is of little use as a tool for the trained counselor. The danger as the authors point out is that "Many persons will feel that the techniques are so simple that anyone can use them . . . The authors have not invented a short-cut for amateurs and incompetents."

The Counseling Profile seems to be an ingenious but relatively useless "gadget."

The usefulness of the Counseling Record would depend upon the idiosyncrasies and preferences of individual vocational counselors. It appears to be a concise and adaptable form for summarizing vocational information.

[690]

★**Personnel Selection and Classification Test.** Adults; 1942–44; Forms A, B; $3.75 per 25; 50¢ per specimen set, postpaid; (80-90) minutes; Willis W. Clark, Ernest W. Tiegs, Louis P. Thorpe, T. W. MacQuarrie, and Elizabeth T. Sullivan; California Test Bureau.

Dorothy C. Adkins, Chief, Test Development Unit, U. S. Civil Service Commission, Washington, D. C. This test has the aim of meeting "a demand for a relatively short, easily administered, and dependable measure of fitness for employment in various jobs and occupations in business and industry." It is relatively short and easily administered, but most readers of the manual would fail to be satisfied, on the basis of the evidence presented, that the test provides a dependable measure of fitness for employment.

The test is composed of several subtests which yield seven scores: reading (sets of yes-no questions on several paragraphs); arithmetic (completion items on various operations); mental alertness or intelligence, also referred to as verbal intelligence (multiple-choice vocabulary items); mechanical (tapping or dotting, pursuit, and blocks tests from the *MacQuarrie Test for Mechanical Ability*); adaptability-sociability (yes-no items of the personality inventory type); dependability or persistence (yes-no items of the personality inventory type); and oral directions (25 items requiring following of oral instructions).

The poorest of these tests is the reading test. In the first place, over 90 per cent of the items can be answered correctly (aside from errors in the scoring key) by a sufficiently "intelligent" subject without access to the paragraphs on which they are supposedly based. In the second place, those subjects who do try to base their responses on the paragraphs may find the directions ambiguous. Many of the items contain specific determiners. Some individual items are poor in other respects. From the sentence, "Read all regulations carefully and observe them promptly," one is supposed to decide that "observe" means "do." From the statement that "If everyone cooperates more work is done, the business prospers, and workers are more secure," it is supposed to follow that "The more business prospers the more secure are the workers."

The arithmetic test appears to be reasonably satisfactory, although the scoring is not completely objective.

The vocabulary items, requiring choice from among four words of one that means the same as the key word, are well constructed, although the ability measured by them is probably narrower than is suggested by "mental alertness or intelligence."

The MacQuarrie test includes both a tapping test (requiring the subject to make three pencil dots in each of a series of circles) and a dotting test (requiring the subject to make one pencil dot in each of a series of smaller circles). One form of the *Personnel Selection and Classification Test* includes the tapping test and the other includes the dotting test. Question is raised as to whether the tests are really tests of the same function. The United States Employment Service has found Pearson *r*'s in the neighborhood of .55 between the two tests for five samples ranging from 99 to 591. Two tests of the same function can, of course, correlate this low because of unreliability. Data on the reliability of these individual tests, however, are reported in neither the manual accompanying the original MacQuarrie battery nor the manual for the present battery.

The tapping test presents a scoring problem. The scoring instructions call for examining the circles to see that *approximately* (italics mine) three dots are made in or near each circle. The score is "the number of circles with 3 dots in or near them divided by 2." The instructions make no mention of the hardness of lead in the pencils to be used. It is very difficult in some cases to make out whether a circle contains one, two, or three dots, especially if very soft lead is used. Dots are often made directly over other dots, so that it is difficult to arrive at a score reflecting speed of tapping very accurately.

The pursuit test consists of a maze of curved lines, each starting in a numbered square at the left and ending in a square at the right. The subject is to trace each line by eye and record its number in the proper square at the right. The drafting is definitely faulty in one place, which may mislead the subject by two score points. If the score is the number of squares correctly numbered, as apparently is intended, the scores are not directly proportional to number of correct responses.

The blocks test is satisfactory insofar as can be determined by inspection.

The tests of the personality-inventory variety, which are supposed to measure "adaptability-sociability" and "dependability-persistence," do not escape the common defect of this type of test for use in competitive situations. For almost all questions, the socially acceptable response is pretty obvious. Examples are "Do you feel that people often treat you rather badly?" and "Can you be persistent, if necessary?"

Personnel Selection and Classification Test

Inspection of the oral directions test reveals no defects.

The manual presents a Table of Minimum Desirable Specifications, indicating for 40 jobs (ranging from baker to aviator to executive) the level of performance needed on each of the seven parts of the test. Thus, an aviator needs high-average (50-80th percentile) scores on reading, arithmetic, mental alertness or intelligence, and social adaptability, and high (80-99th percentile) scores on mechanical dexterity, dependability or persistence, and understanding oral directions.

The section Notes on Selection, Placement, and Adjustment presents references to a number of researches on *such* tests as those included in this battery and a variety of statements which, although rather carefully phrased, may mislead the unwary reader into an impression that there has been considerable research on the *actual* tests in question. Such a statement as "Practically all professions, executive positions, and the higher technical callings make great demands in all of the skills and qualifications measured by the *Personnel Selection and Classification Test*" is presented without evidence. Aside from the lack of data to substantiate this statement, surely the ceilings on most of the tests are too low for them to be maximally useful for the purpose implied. And, again, "Many workers in these (inspector, bookkeeper, caterer, railway conductor, and aviator) and similar callings have failed in their positions because of a morbid, sarcastic, sensitive, antagonistic, suspicious, or lazy attitude." Surely there is an implication here that the test is going to detect such attitudes.

Under the topic Reliability and Validity, we find only that "statistical data will be furnished to users upon request" and that "the reliability coefficients of individual tests vary from .80 to .94." Data on validity might well replace some of the material provided elsewhere in the manual. One may wonder how the reliability coefficients were estimated, particularly for the speed tests included in Part 4, and how the comparability of the two forms was established. One may also be curious, when he comes to a table of Norms for General Use, as to just what constitutes a "typical adult population." This reviewer, who admittedly did not request statistical data, would take the position that such information should routinely be included in test manuals. A more recently published brochure

of the California Test Bureau, *Tests for Personnel Selection and Placement,* 1947, includes the median percentile ranks of 151 junior retail executives and 41 machinist trainees. These subjects presumably were persons already employed rather than applicants for employment in a competitive situation. If this is true, it limits the value of the results to some extent, particularly in the case of the tests of the personality inventory type. Nevertheless, such data for a variety of occupations would be very useful. From the information to which the reviewer had ready access, this test appears to warrant revision and research, but the evidence that it satisfies the purposes for which it was intended is incomplete.

George K. Bennett, President, The Psychological Corporation, New York, New York. This is a general purpose test, attempting in one booklet and in an over-all time of about 80 minutes, the measurement of seven quite disparate aspects of ability and personality. The intent is to provide the employment office or personnel department with a profile of characteristics which may be matched to the requirements of a considerable variety of jobs ranging from sales clerk to aviator. A table of Minimum Desirable Specifications in terms of broad score ranges has been included in the manual. This table "is based on personnel research at points where such research is available, and the judgments of experts in personnel work at other points." A single table of norms, "based on typical adult population," is given. (The table of norms is reported as "based on approximately 2,000 cases, mostly adult males employed in industrial and commercial concerns.") At the request of the reviewer the publisher has furnished him with tables of intercorrelations based on 200 adults and reliability coefficients (Kuder–Richardson) based on a population of 600, half of whom were secondary school students and the remainder, industrial employees.

There are several important defects in this test. For any test battery leading to a score profile, it is well established that reliabilities must be high and intercorrelations low. Data obtained through correspondence indicate that the reliabilities are relatively high (.81 to .95), and the intercorrelations are low. However, the populations used for reliability and intercorrelations are not the same, and each of the two is apparently different from the population used for the norms. The differences in populations cast considerable doubt on the adequacy of the computed statistics when the tests are used for ordinary industrial purposes. Some of the reported intercorrelations are surprisingly low: oral directions versus verbal intelligence, .41; oral directions versus arithmetic, .34; verbal intelligence versus arithmetic, .45.

A second major defect is the test content in certain sections; mechanical dexterity is measured by 5½ minutes of performance on three sections of the *MacQuarrie Test for Mechanical Ability:* tapping, pursuit, and blocks. The first of these, consuming 30 seconds, does employ some motor skill; the remaining 90 per cent of time devoted to this would seem to be occupied in perception and spatial reasoning. The two personality tests consist of 30 "yes-no" questions each. A typical "social adaptability" question is "Do you endeavor to meet new people in your community?" "Persistence-dependability" questions include "Do people often come to you for help?" and "Are you particularly successful at saving money?" In view of the mass of evidence indicating that even long and carefully constructed personality tests are ineffective as selection instruments, it seems highly improbable that brief lists of transparent questions can contribute importantly. The reading, verbal intelligence, and arithmetic tests are somewhat brief, but appear to conform to good practice.

The manual is lacking in statistical information and contains wholly inadequate norms without differentiation or identification by occupation, age, education, or even sex. Validation has not been attempted, possibly because of the great investment of time and money that would be required for a multipurpose test. However, educational and occupational group profiles of considerable value could readily have been obtained and included.

The principal objection to this test battery is that inadequate statistical procedures and dubious face validity make impossible any affirmative reaction to the usefulness of the tests.

George A. Ferguson, Assistant Professor of Psychology, McGill University, Montreal, Canada. This test is designed to explore seven areas of ability which are considered of significance in the selection of employees in business and industry.

No information on the sample of the population on which the test was standardized is provided by the authors. It is described as a typical adult population. Very few data are presented which enable an adequate appraisal of the reliability or validity of the test in different situations. Reliability coefficients of individual tests are reported to vary from .80 to .94.

The test is short, easy to administer, and covers a broad field. If the claims of its author are substantiated, it should prove a convenient instrument in certain types of industrial selection where rough and rapid appraisals are required. One comment, however, which may be warranted is that this test, in its attempt to explore a variety of different abilities and personality characteristics, appears to explore too widely and too superficially. The majority of psychologists would agree that in thorough selection work there is no easy royal road to the description of human ability and personality. More specifically the capacity of three short subtests, tapping, pursuit, and block counting, to provide an adequate measure of mechanical ability is questionable. Further it may be argued that many abilities and personality traits of marked importance in selection and classification work exist which are not measured by this test.

The conclusion is that where quick appraisals are required the test may prove of value. In the more thorough types of selection work, more comprehensive data than this test provides are usually required.

[691]

Rating Form for Use of Interviewers and Oral Examiners. Applicants for employment; 1938; IBM; $1 per 25, postpaid; 6¢ per sample copy, postpaid; W. V. Bingham; distributed by Psychological Corporation.

REFERENCES

1. BINGHAM, W. V. *Oral Examinations in Civil Service Recruitment: With Special Reference to Experiences in Pennsylvania.* Civil Service Assembly of the United States and Canada, Pamphlet No. 13. Chicago, Ill.: the Assembly, February 1939. Pp. 30. Paper. $0.50.
2. BINGHAM, WALTER VAN DYKE, AND MOORE, BRUCE VICTOR. *How to Interview,* Third Edition, pp. 112-26. New York: Harper & Brothers, 1941. Pp. xi, 263. $3.00. * (PA 16:304)

Douglas H. Fryer, Associate Professor of Psychology, New York University, New York, New York. This rating form consists of graphic rating scales of five degrees, differently described, for eight qualities—(*a*) voice and speech, (*b*) appearance, (*c*) alertness, (*d*) ability to present ideas, (*e*) judgment, (*f*) emotional stability, (*g*) self-confidence, (*h*) friendliness—and for an over-all rating of personal fitness for the position. Interviewers are instructed to observe these characteristics during the interview and to rate them in relation to the requirements of the position, not considering the applicant's experience or training.

The blank was used approximately in its present form in Pennsylvania in 1938 for the oral examination of 30,000 applicants for state civil service positions. Trained boards of 3 to 5 members interviewed the applicants in from 20 to 45 minutes, the blanks were scored by IBM scoring machines, and relative weights were assigned in summing the ratings for the different traits. The weights for the traits differed for different positions. Internal consistency was studied, and the average of the deviations from the board average for the various traits was one-ninth of the scale length of 5 points. That the interview measured something different from the written civil service examination was indicated by low correlations of .15, −.08, and .20 for three different occupations. Validity was estimated roughly by a comparison with home community opinion of 29 applicants.

The limitation in rating to what can be observed of the personality development of the applicant during the interview is unique in selection interviewing procedure. It gives an acceptable purpose to an interview, in view of its cost, when one considers that most factors upon which interviewers judge applicants can be better and more inexpensively measured otherwise. Standard conversations would assist in achieving this purpose. The possibility of scoring the interview is introduced, which, again, is unique in such personnel procedures, but the method of scoring is left to the ingenuity of the user, as is interpretation from the scoring. This procedure is undeveloped as a psychological measure, but it has the possibility of adaptation to various uses where the need is for an estimate of ability in public contact or personal relations.

For a review by Ruth Strang, see 40:1672.

[692]

★**Self-Rating Scale for Leadership Qualifications.**
Foremen and supervisors; 1942; 25¢ per copy; E. J. Benge; National Foremen's Institute, Inc.

[693]

Survey of Company Morale: Job Satisfaction Blank No. 12. Adults; 1933–43; 1 form; $2.25 per 25, postpaid; 35¢ per specimen set, postpaid; nontimed (10-20) minutes; Robert Hoppock; Psychological Corporation.

REFERENCES

1. HOPPOCK, ROBERT. "Job Satisfaction of Psychologists." *J Appl Psychol* 21:300-3 Je '37. * (PA 11:4723)

William W. Waite, Associate Professor of Industrial Engineering, Columbia University, New York, New York. This form was prepared to assist employers in surveying workers to ascertain the degree of job satisfaction present in the group. A test of this type is sorely needed in industry and business, although many employers have failed to realize the urgency of the need and continue to rely on haphazard opinion and rumor to guide them. The Hoppock survey, although copyrighted in 1943, is based largely on work done in 1933–35, and the revisions in the original form are the result of a trial of the questions on a sample of only about 300 persons. The questions in the survey originally provided for three degrees of job satisfaction, one neutral response, and three degrees of dissatisfaction. As a result of the trial, the three degrees of satisfaction were combined into a single choice and the same was done with the degrees of dissatisfaction, so that the present form has only three alternatives.

The questions in the survey are fairly simple and almost any person filling out the blank should be able to select, without undue hesitation, one of the three alternatives. However, the greatest uncertainty in any such test is the honesty with which the questions are answered. Hoppock has recognized this fact and has provided a final question, appropriately numbered 64, which reads, "In answering these questions, have you told what you honestly believe to be the truth in all cases?" It hardly seems probable that a person who had answered the preceding questions falsely would be likely to admit the fact. On the other hand, such a question appears to this reviewer to throw the veracity of all those filling out the form into question and to be likely to arouse antagonism among persons who would otherwise be cooperative and honest.

There are several questions which appear not to be significant, as they may not be related to the job and do not provide information on the basis of which specific corrective action can be taken, particularly as the survey must be anonymous. Such questions include "Do you often feel just miserable?" and "Have you been worried about anything recently?"

The "norms" given in the manual accompanying the test appear to be based on replies from 309 persons, all in one small community, taken in 1933. They can hardly be considered, therefore, as typical of postwar attitudes in vari-

Rating Form for Use of Interviewers and Oral Examiners

ously located communities of widely differing size, economic status, and degrees of industrialization. Before this survey or, for that matter, any morale survey can be considered in any way standardized, a great deal of work must be done in validation and the establishment of norms. It is to be hoped that some survey of this type will be made available shortly in a standardized form, as it is essential to the smooth and proper functioning of our industrial life.

[694]

★Test of Practical Judgment. Grades 9-16 and adults; 1942; preliminary manual; $3.75 per 25; 50¢ per specimen set; 35(40) minutes; Alfred J. Cardall; Science Research Associates.

REFERENCES

1. CARDALL, ALFRED J., JR. *A Test for Primary Business Interests Based on a Functional Occupational Classification.* Unpublished doctor's thesis, Harvard University, 1941.
2. HOGADONE, EDWINA, AND SMITH, LEO F. "Some Evidence on the Validity of the Cardall Test of Practical Judgment." *J Appl Psychol* 31:54-6 F '47. * (PA 21:2492)

Glen U. Cleeton, Director, Division of Humanistic and Social Studies, Carnegie Institute of Technology, Pittsburgh, Pennsylvania. The purpose of this test is indicated by the compiler as being the measurement of "the element of practical judgment as it operates in everyday business and social situations." This is supplemented by a statement that "practical judgment is an important consideration in the selection of executives, supervisors, salesmen, those who are working in contact occupations and those responsible for planning and supervising work." It is also suggested that the test might be used in schools as a measure of "social maturation."

It is claimed that the test measures a factor which is statistically independent. Evidence of low correlation of this test with tests of intelligence, clerical aptitude, personality, reading, and other psychological measuring devices is given to substantiate this contention. Reliability coefficients of .88 and .86 are reported.

A validity coefficient of .56 between test scores and supervisor's ratings is indicated. It is claimed also that miscellaneous applications of the test have revealed that scores can be used to discriminate between executive and clerical personnel and, furthermore, that the test "discriminates within the range of executive ability itself." Opinions of industrial users are offered as supplementary evidence of validity. The difficulty of obtaining satisfactory criteria with which to correlate test results is stressed.

The test is self-administering and is printed in such a manner as to permit answers to be indicated with a pin or special punch which perforates a circle on sealed scoring sheets. The time required for administering is approximately 35 minutes.

Percentile norms are indicated for high school seniors and adults, and means are reported for a few industrial groups.

No references to published studies are included in the manual.

In the selection of commercial and industrial personnel at the administrative and supervisory level, this test provides a measure of an important characteristic not measured by other standard instruments.

Howard R. Taylor, Professor of Psychology and Head of the Department, University of Oregon, Eugene, Oregon. Any objective method of distinguishing between "common sense" and ability to comprehend abstract verbal material such as is required for success with standard intelligence tests would be very useful and have considerable theoretical importance. Unfortunately the author seems to have published no information about the construction and validation of Cardall's *Test of Practical Judgment* except that given in the preliminary manual. The extent to which this test samples habits of thought and action unmeasured by other psychological tests is obviously crucial. Correlations between the *Test of Practical Judgment* and 24 other variables such as intelligence, clerical aptitude, arithmetic reasoning, reading comprehension, personality questionnaires and college grades are cited in the manual. All are low ranging from −.11 to +.15. Ten are negative. Neither the standard deviations of the different variables nor the number of cases involved in the computations is reported. Taken at face value, however, such negligible correlations imply that the test has nothing in common with the general intellectual factors which predominate in measures of school achievement and of clerical and scholastic aptitude.

Just why 48 questions similar to those of the practical judgment subtest in the *Army Group Examination, Alpha,* which has a high correlation with the other tests of a battery constructed to measure general intelligence, should be uncorrelated with tests known to require abstract capacity of the same sort is surprising. Such terms as nurtures, technicians, prestige, participator, mortality, feigned, etc. appear in the problem situations and various alternatives of the Cardall test. One would expect to find some correlation even in a narrow range of occupational ability. Moreover, two of the questions in the test occur also in well-known intelligence scales —one at the superior adult level in the *Revised Stanford–Binet Scale,* the other in the *Wechsler–Bellevue Intelligence Scale.* It is conceivable of course that scoring determined by a consensus of opinion from the realm of "practicality" with weightings derived by item analysis for first, second, and third choices among four alternatives could reflect chiefly "attitudes" rather than logical reasoning. Inspection of the heavy weights assigned to certain answers which seem dubious on logical grounds make this explanation plausible. The reviewer has found a correlation of .27 between scores on the Cardall test and the *Ohio State University Psychological Examination* for a group of 202 college sophomores. Hogadone and Smith (2) report a correlation of .22 between scores on the 1941 form of the ACE Psychological Examination and scores on the Cardall test made by 91 students registered in a three-year cooperative course in retailing. These students were employed by department stores in western New York for alternate four-week periods. Ratings for "practical judgment" based on a "behavior journal" and made by supervisors in close contact with the students and their employers correlated only .24 with *Test of Practical Judgment* scores. The same ratings correlated .28 with the American Council on Education Psychological Examination. Although the difference is not statistically significant, the ACE seems to be a slightly better test of practical judgment than the Cardall which was especially devised for measuring it. In so far as the ratings provide a suitable criterion of "common sense," neither test would be of much practical value.

In the manual Cardall reports a reliability coefficient of .88 estimated from self-correlation in a "homogeneous" group. The only validity coefficient cited is a correlation of .56 between scores on the test and pooled supervisory ratings in an accounting department. With independent criteria of occupational success apparently available, it should not have been necessary to use the difference between a high-scoring and a low-scoring group on the "even" scores of the test as a criterion for determination by item analysis of the weights assigned to various answers. Whatever value the criterion

of "internal consistency" may have in theoretical problems, the use of occupational success is surely preferable for practical purposes.

Possibly a detailed report of the criteria and statistical analyses used in constructing and validating the test would remove the doubts raised by the independent studies cited above. Until that happens its worth as a diagnostic instrument should be considered questionable.

[695]

Vocational Aptitude Examination, Type E-A, Revised 1946. Male high school graduates; 1935–47; 1 form; 7½¢ per copy, 10-99 copies; 50¢ per specimen set; part nontimed (65) minutes; Glen U. Cleeton and Charles W. Mason; McKnight & McKnight.

REFERENCES

1-3. *See* 40:1679.
4. CLEETON, GLEN U., AND MASON, CHARLES W. Chap. 6, "Tests of Executive Ability," pp. 171-92. In their *Executive Ability: Its Discovery and Development,* [Second Edition]. Yellow Springs, Ohio: Antioch Press, 1946. Pp. xv, 540. $4.50. * (PA 21:566)

D. Welty Lefever, Professor of Education, The University of Southern California, Los Angeles, California. The title of this battery of tests conceals rather effectively its major use in "spotting potential executive material." The examination is designed to be employed as an "aid in classifying men" into four general occupational groups: executive, sales, accounting, and technical (scientific or engineering) personnel. Such differentiation results largely from an analysis of a profile based on individual ratings from each of the eight tests forming the battery.

The examination is designed to be used in business, industry, and government in the actual selection of personnel for employment or promotion. It is assumed that all available biographical data and sources of appraisal are focused on the same problem. A well-planned personal history blank constitutes the final page of the test booklet. The authors claim greater validity when the test is applied to college graduates, and they assume the minimum of high school graduation for all testees. The examination appears, however, to be best suited for use in guiding college students in formulating vocational plans with respect to the four occupational areas concerned.

The manual states that the examination purports to measure "intellectual aptitudes." It is not easy to reconcile such a statement of limited scope with the inclusion of an interest inventory and a test of "social responsiveness." However, since there is no single summarizing score for the complete battery, these two measures may be considered as additional indicators for predicting success in the four fields rather than as parts of a unitary test of intellectual aptitude.

Interest inventories and adjustment questionnaires are subject to a certain degree of "fudging," and some allowance must be made for this factor if the subject has a personal gain at stake in a high score. This reviewer administered Test 8, Social Responsiveness, to a group of graduate students in education, first, on an unidentified, "sincere" basis and, second, on the basis of producing a score related to high executive ability. Six out of 30 made A or better on the first trial; 8 reached that level by conscious effort. The average score rose from a very low B rating on the first trial to a high B on the second trial. This gain is probably not too serious.

The major portion of the examination appears to be a modified form of scholastic aptitude test in which the verbal factor receives less than the usual emphasis and in which specialized study tends to be a handicap rather than an asset. Broad acquaintance with many areas of experience rather than systematic, academic study is required. An estimation test, for example, measures the subject's ability to guess the answers to a variety of statistical or numerical questions at a high rate of speed. The authors report high scores for the sales group and low scores for the engineers. Such differentiations indicate considerable validity for the general design of the examination. Among the four vocational areas analyzed the highest minimum score for the examination as a whole appears to be necessary for success as an executive. The evidence in general, as presented by the authors and confirmed in the observation of the reviewer, indicates that superior intelligence is necessary but not sufficient for success on the supervisorial and managerial levels.

This reviewer has often wondered why test batteries designed for use in business or industry do not include more items (such as paragraphs to be read, vocabulary to be defined, arithmetical problems to be solved, and the like) from materials with greater "face validity." This examination would have been improved if more of the subject matter possessed a greater apparent functional significance for the occupational areas concerned.

More detailed research data on validity should have been reported in the test manual or in the authors' volume, *Executive Ability: Its Discovery and Development* (4). Rather vague statements are made about "high" or "low" scores without furnishing the reader with an adequate basis for an evaluative judgment. The authors specifically deny claim to validity as measured by such criteria as earnings, continuity of employment, or other "conventional standards." The most direct evidence on validity appears to be the difference in scores made on the several tests by representatives of the occupational groups: executives, salesmen, accountants, and technical personnel. Exact quantitative statements, however, are lacking.

Benjamin Shimberg, Research Assistant, Division of Educational Reference, Purdue University, Lafayette, Indiana. This examination is offered as an aid in selecting and promoting certain types of personnel in industry and as a counseling instrument in vocational guidance. The test battery is designed to evaluate rapidly an individual with respect to (*a*) general executive aptitude; (*b*) sales aptitude; (*c*) engineering, research, and technical aptitude; and (*d*) accounting aptitude. Recommendations for the various fields are made on the basis of the pattern of scores on the eight subtests which comprise the battery.

The test battery is made up of the following subtests: Test 1, General Information; Test 2, Arithmetical Reasoning; Test 3, Judgment in Estimating; Test 4, Symbolic Relationships; Test 5, Reading Comprehension; Test 6, Vocabulary; Test 7, Interest; Test 8, Social Responsiveness. Tests 1, 2, 5, and 6, which take 40 minutes of testing time, are said to constitute an adequate measure of general intellectual ability (4, p. 176).

The reading subtest takes only six minutes and consists of five paragraphs with five questions on each paragraph. Judgment in Estimating requires the examinee to answer 30 questions calling for information such as "Estimate the average number of navy beans to the bushel." On this test, credit is granted for answers falling within a given range, with higher credit for answers which come closest to the correct figure.

The interest test consists of 100 words and phrases related to occupations and interests. The subject indicates those which he likes and those which he dislikes. Social Responsiveness is divided into five sections: dominance-submission (10 items), independence-dependence (10 items), extroversion-introversion (20 items), social responsiveness (20 items), and social knowledge (20 items). The number of items used in the various sections appears to be too few to give a reliable measure of the separate traits being investigated. As in most personality questionnaires, the questions are in a "yes" or "no" form and depend on the truthfulness of the applicant for validity. No evidence is presented to show that persons seeking employment or wishing to be considered for promotion can be depended on to reply truthfully on such questionnaires.

The 1946 revision of the examination is essentially the same as the 1935 edition. Very few items have been changed, although the information called for in the estimating subtest has been brought up to date. Scoring of the test is performed manually, with a key which is placed alongside the answers written in the test booklet. Booklets can be used only once.

A manual is provided which includes norms by which to interpret test scores for each of the occupational fields. It is necessary, however, first to convert the raw scores on each subtest into percentile equivalents and then to translate these to a seven-point scale in order to interpret the norms for each group. Two sets of norms are given. One is for use with high school graduates, college freshmen and college sophomores. The other is for use with upper-class college students and for college graduates. Persons using the test are cautioned by the authors not to interpret the test scores in absolute terms, but to weigh and judge the results in relation to other information about the individual.

The reliability coefficients reported in the manual are said to be based on 850 cases, but no description is given of the sample used. The reliabilities range between .79 and .86 for the several subtests. When the interests and the social responsiveness subtests are omitted, and the remaining six subtest scores combined into a total score, the reliability is reported to be .94. The method used to obtain reliabilities is not given.

No evidence is presented for the validity of the examination. The references cited in the manual are largely based on an investigation by one of the authors (Mason) conducted in 1930 on "The Possibilities of an Objective Executive Aptitude Test." This investigation was merely exploratory. It did not utilize criterion groups from business and industry, but relied on criterion groups made up chiefly of college students who had been *rated* by other students and by their instructors as possessing traits supposedly associated with sales, executive, and technical-research groups.

The recent book, *Executive Ability: Its Discovery and Development,* by Cleeton and Mason presents some of the background for the examination and the theory of executive ability which underlies it. However, the book fails to present any data which might be considered as validating the instrument. Most of the generalizations about the discriminating power of the test seem to have been drawn from the findings of the original study by Mr. Mason. If the authors have information which bears out their claims that the test differentiates significantly among the various groups, they have failed to give any concrete indication of their results in either the manual or in their 540-page book.

For reviews by Harold D. Carter and M. R. Trabue of an earlier edition, see 40:1679.

SPECIFIC VOCATIONS

[696]

★[American Transit Association Tests.] Selection of transit operating personnel; 1941–46; 4 tests; Glen U. Cleeton in collaboration with Merwyn A. Kraft and Robert F. Royster; American Transit Association.
a) STANDARD EXAMINATION FOR TRANSIT EMPLOYEES. 1941–46; Forms A and AA for street car operations; Forms B and BB for bus operations; 20(30) or 30(40) minutes; $5 per 100.
b) PERSONAL REACTION TEST FOR TRANSIT EMPLOYEES. 1943–46; 1 form (Series A); nontimed (30) minutes; $10 per 100.
c) AMERICAN TRANSIT MOTOR ABILITY TEST. 1946; (45) minutes; prices upon application.
d) PLACEMENT INTERVIEW FOR TRANSIT EMPLOYEES. 1946; $5 per 100.

REFERENCES
1. WAITS, J. V. "The Use of the American Transit Motor Ability Test in the Selection of Bus and Street Car Operators," pp. 340-53. In *Proceedings of the Twenty-Sixth Annual Meeting of the Highway Research Board,* December 1946.

Harold G. Seashore, Director, Test Division, The Psychological Corporation, New York, New York. The American Transit Association has prepared a manual entitled *Selection and Employment of Transit Operating Personnel.* Three stages are defined and procedures outlined for each: qualifying, testing, and evaluation. This review is concerned with the testing stage. Four testing units are prescribed: mental ability, visual skills, personal reactions (attitude and personality), motor ability. Although these tests were developed by a committee of the association and the manual contains other names, it appears that Glen U. Cleeton is the professional psychologist responsible for their development.

MENTAL ABILITY TEST. This test, entitled *Standard Examination for Transit Employees,* is an Otis-type test, with many verbal items possessing "face validity" since they involve transit terms and ideas. There are 60 items. Thirty minutes is the recommended time, but twenty minutes is permitted. Norms are in four categories of score range: normal hiring range, poor instruction risk, not likely to be satisfactory, and rapid learner who may not maintain interest. Statistical data are sparse and reference is made to an original study by Cleeton which is not published. Reliability is said to be about .90. Validity was established in the initial project, and subsequent checks are said to support the initial findings. The test is said to correlate significantly with the *Otis Self-Administering Test of Mental Ability,* but values are not given. To secure 100 "qualified operators," 150 candidates in "normal hiring range" were needed, while 280 candidates in the "unsatisfactory" category had to be screened. There are two forms, but four sets of identifying letters; A and BB are identical, and B and AA are identical except that in A and B the words "street cars" are used in one item and in BB and AA the word "buses" appears.

VISUAL SKILLS TEST. The manual recommends several of the standard visual tests and offers no special norms or procedures.

PERSONAL REACTION TEST FOR TRANSIT EMPLOYEES. This test "measures attitudes and other personality characteristics relating primarily to the qualities of stability and maturity." It is claimed that this special test is better than those commercially available because (*a*) the time requirement is shorter, (*b*) transit language is used, and (*c*) nonpsychologists can interpret the scores.

There are 50 multiple-choice items couched primarily in terms of specific transit situations or general public contacts. The reviewer encountered difficulty with the grammatical structure of the items. These are not questions with answers. The "stem" is sometimes a question, sometimes a part of a sentence which the choices will complete, and sometimes a phrase with four reactions one might make to the phrase. One of these items is reproduced.

When you have a day in which everything seems to go all wrong:
(1) I never seem to have such days
(2) Become very upset until it is all over
(3) Annoys me, but I make the best of it
(4) I seem to have more than my share of these days

It may well be that in practice such inconsistent and sometimes incorrect language makes no difference, but the reviewer feels that test items should be presented in straightforward, acceptable English.

In 26 of the 50 items of this personality test the correct answer is some minor variation of these expressions: "does not bother me," "annoys me mildly," "rarely disturbs me," or "pay no attention to it." Such responses are practically never included as wrong choices. Even though these phrases probably describe attitude and personality characteristics that are desirable in transit employees, it does seem that more imagination could have been used in getting variety and in disguising the best answer. Similarly, one would wonder what the semantic difference is between these two choices to one question: "pay little attention to it," and "does not disturb me." Both of them, it seems to the reviewer, are "well adjusted" answers to the question: "How does being observed by the examiner while taking this test affect you?"

Interpretation is in terms of accident potentialities and public relations. A score of 35 or more suggests "an excellent record with respect to accidents and public relations." A score of 25 or lower is indicative of a poor risk. The manual's statement on reliability is remarkable for its caution. It stresses the complexity of personality and the difficulty of its appraisal even with thorough clinical study. No data concerning reliability are given, only a statement to the effect that persons can misrepresent themselves and also actually do change from time to time. With respect to validity, the test is called promising. The reviewer fails to see how a test with such real difficulties can be usable by persons without the caution and psychometric sophistication of trained psychologists.

Since the test is specifically interpreted in terms of accident proneness, it seems elementary that it should not be used until a clear-cut statistical report is available concerning its ability to discriminate among transit operators with varying numbers of accidents and that, further, such data should be based upon administration of the test prior to employment of the operator. The association reports that such data may become available soon.

MOTOR ABILITY TEST. This psychomotor test is designed to measure sensori-motor coordination, ability to concentrate, ability to react speedily and accurately. It is also said to measure "teachability" and learning capacity.

The equipment is a simulated driver's station (seat, wheel, clutch, brake, and shift lever), a stimulus panel (various lights including a standard traffic signal), an examiner's control panel, and an automatic timing and recording apparatus.

The test activities are too complex for description here. They begin with simple reaction patterns involving elementary hand or leg or hand and leg movement. Later more complex decision-reaction times are involved.

The published manual of instructions does not contain the details of administration and scoring. A supplementary manual which comes with the equipment provides the details. Norms are expressed in terms of four ranges of scores.

Validity is expressed in terms of the number of candidates in several score ranges who must be selected to secure 100 qualified operators. In one study, 105 high-ranking candidates and 206 low-ranking candidates were necessary to produce 100 successful trainees from each group. It is not reported whether the other three tests were part of the screening process. If the test is as sharply discriminating as this seems to indicate, it is, first, a remarkably successful use of a motor ability test to predict later efficiency and, second, one which deserves much more complete description in the literature. During World War II, the military psychologists apparently did not secure such satisfactory predictions by means of psychomotor tests. One would also like to know to what extent scores on the motor ability test correlate with those on the mental ability test.

This series of tests is designed for use by members of the American Transit Association. It is the belief of the reviewer that the authors of a special purpose test battery are not relieved of responsibility for publishing, at least for prospective users, the statistical information usually considered essential to test evaluation. Presumably, this battery has characteristics beyond face validity which commend it. The absence of technical reports precludes an adequate appraisal at this time.

Morris S. Viteles, Professor of Psychology,

American Transit Association Tests

University of Pennsylvania, Philadelphia, Pennsylvania. The procedures for the selection and employment of transit operating personnel described in the four manuals are gratifyingly complete and balanced in general scope and disappointingly inadequate in detail. The 3-stage, 10-step program, premised on job analysis, represents an orderly approach to the selection of qualified personnel which judiciously applies what is known about good practices in employee placement. Of particular merit is the evaluation of each step in the selection program, including a delineation in terms readily understandable to the layman of the general scope and general limitations of psychological tests in relation to other selection devices.

In striking contrast are the claims made for individual procedures, especially certain of the psychological tests, in the absence of adequate supporting data. Since the manuals are written essentially for the laymen, as aids in selling the uniform selection program to the transit industry, it cannot be expected that detailed statistical data will be presented. The facts that some data on both reliability and validity are given and that reference is made to the need for further experimentation represent a refreshing note in a series of manuals which are frankly geared to a selling program. Nevertheless, the individual tests cannot be properly recommended with anything like the degree of assurance which marks their presentation in the manuals.

With respect to every test, there are questions which require answers before firm recommendations as to its usefulness can be made. For example, it is stated that the *Standard Examination for Transit Employees,* designed to "measure an applicant's capacity or ability to absorb instruction," has a reliability of .90, but no validity coefficient is given, although there is some evidence on validity in terms of the ratio of qualified employees to applicants for stated ranges of test scores.

A validity coefficient of .32 is reported between scores on the *American Transit Motor Ability Test* and "individual accident responsibility rates," and a coefficient of .39 between scores on this test and supervisory ratings, but no statement is made concerning reliability, although an earlier article reports reliabilities ranging from .76 to .82 on eight series of measures on this test. For this test, too, there are data on the percentage of men with varying scores qualifying as acceptable employees.

In the case of neither test is there any indication as to how many applicants will have to be tested in order to secure a stated number of qualified operators for each range of test scores, although from the correlations reported, it is apparent that a very large number of applicants would be required to provide a high percentage of qualified operators. Moreover, nothing is said about the correlation between the two tests although it is possible that one of the two tests may give approximately the same results as both in combination.

In general, there are inadequate data on the nature of the experimental populations, a failure to define criteria accurately, and similar important omissions. It may be that such data are available, but a review of the literature from 1935 on does not reveal sufficient supplementary data to provide the assurance needed for recommending the tests for use in the widely varying operating situations characterizing the transit industry.

In the case of the *Personal Reaction Test for Transit Employees,* specific reservations are made as to the limitations of paper-and-pencil tests in measuring personality traits and as to the use of the test as a guide rather than as a basis for final judgment of attitudes. Nevertheless, these are almost completely negated by supplementary statements, made in the complete absence of data on reliability and validity, that the test has "bearing on accident susceptibility and provides information for evaluation of prospective operators on an important phase of the job, public relations, not directly measured by other tests."

The manuals include specific recommendations as to the limits on age and other personal characteristics and scores on visual and similar examinations which should be used in selecting transit employees. At no point is there suggested the need for the experimental validation of such items, in spite of the fact that weighted application scores have shown the marked value of such an approach and also in spite of the evidence gathered, particularly during World War II, that a priori judgments concerning visual and similar requirements may be entirely untenable.

In general, the review of the manuals suggests the need for caution in accepting the recommendations and for viewing the tests as experimental instruments which require detailed verification by companies which may consider their use for the selection of operating personnel.

J. V. Waits, Personnel Psychologist, Capital Transit Company, Washington, D. C. This battery of selection tests was designed for a specific purpose and should be viewed from that perspective. The scope of its effective use is probably limited to transit, taxicab, and trucking firms. It was not the objective of the authors, nor is it general practice, to use the tests for individual prognosis, guidance, or counseling. The goal is to secure information for isolating from the general population of applicants for employment the group that will furnish the best risks as employees.

The test battery covers three of the "nine essential qualities" of the job specifications for street car and bus operators: (*a*) mental ability, (*b*) sociability, and (*c*) motor ability. These terms need no special definition.

Validation of the battery as a whole is in the very early stages. Most of the work to date has been devoted to evaluation of the technical sufficiency of the individual tests. The number of cases and the spread of use are too limited to make positive assertions about validity. Preliminary indications are promising, and extensive use of the battery in the transit industry is virtually assured.

THE STANDARD EXAMINATION. This is a disguised intelligence test. It is couched in the language of the industry, and the problems are those likely to be encountered in the day-to-day work of the operators. The language of the test is well chosen, the difficulty level is well adjusted to the population, the figures and illustrations are clear, the printing and readability are excellent. Administration, scoring, and interpretation problems are well within the capabilities of the normal employment office personnel. Individual administration of the test, a necessity for an employment office, makes it somewhat more cumbersome than some other self-administering tests. Scoring is somewhat slower because of the number of pages to be covered, making scoring errors slightly more likely.

Validity as an intelligence test is predicated on correlation with the *Otis Self-Administering Test of Mental Ability.* Correlations of .80 to .89 are reported. Validity as a selective factor of successful employees is tentative. Correlation coefficients from .20 to .30 have been found with several criteria. Use of the correlation ratio would probably increase the validity coefficients since the relationship of intelligence test scores with most criteria of the industry is curvilinear.

American Transit Association Tests

Reliability by split-half method ranges from .88 to .93 for the several forms and for varying populations. For the general use made of the test, the reliability appears satisfactory.

The test is not well adapted for use as a general employment instrument. In particular, we would hesitate to use it for clerical and office employees, although an experiment by the reviewer with a sample of about 200 indicated reliable results.

THE PERSONAL REACTION TEST. This is a multiple-choice-type test. It suffers from many of the weaknesses of tests of personality, temperament, or attitude. It has the advantage of not requiring a highly trained specialist to interpret it. The test is in a transitory stage, and results are too vague to evaluate the test at this time. Reliability coefficients of .79 to .89 are reported. Validity is far from established, although some encouraging correlations with other personality tests have been obtained.

THE MOTOR ABILITY TEST. This is a performance test which involves reaction time, attention qualities, learning ability, ability to follow directions, and motor coordination. The test involves the execution of given movements of the hands and feet with a steering wheel, gear shift lever, and two foot pedals in response to visual stimuli in the form of light patterns on a signal board in conjunction with a stand traffic signal. The test is composed of five parts, each of which is preceded by a standard practice period. Difficulty and complexity of the task increase continuously as the test progresses. Stimuli are administered automatically and responses are recorded.

Validation of the test is still in the preliminary stages. Significant correlations of test scores with subsequent accident records have been obtained. These range from .30 to .45. Biserial correlation coefficients of .48 to .63 have been obtained between test score and accident record. The mean accident record was used as the point of dichotomy. Reliability appears to be satisfactory for the general uses of the test. Split-half reliability of .82 to .88 is reported or has been obtained in experiments by the author.

The test is now in use at two companies, and some six to ten orders for test apparatus are in varying stages of process. Results to date are much more satisfactory than one would normally expect from the test. The reviewer has recently completed a two and a half year study of the test and recommended its inclusion in the Capital

Transit test battery on the basis of its predictive value.

[697]
★Detroit Retail Selling Inventory. Candidates for training in retail selling; 1940; 1 form; $4.50 per 100; 20¢ per specimen set, postpaid; part nontimed (30) minutes; Harry J. Baker and Paul H. Voelker; Public School Publishing Co.

Milton E. Hahn, Dean of Students and Professor of Psychology, University of California, Los Angeles, California. The reliability coefficients reported in the manual for this instrument are somewhat below those usually demanded for test use with individual subjects. Reliability coefficients are reported for various parts of the test as follows: personality, .86; intelligence (first half), .76; intelligence (second half), .80; checking, .98; and arithmetic, .77. The manual recommends the use of the instrument for two groups: students in (secondary?) schools being considered for retail sales training and inexperienced applicants for retail selling jobs in business. Except for the checking test, the reported reliabilities appear questionable for the first group because most modern schools can administer comparable tests and inventories with higher reliabilities. The test is defensible as a rough screen for the employment office which has insufficient professional and technical staff for a more complex screen.

In the light of the data on reliability, the use of such extremes as the top 2 to 10 per cent of the clerks for the "superior" group and the lowest 1 to 5 per cent for the "inferior" group is questionable. This maximizing of differences between extremes is not a particularly rigorous test of differentiating power. The criterion group was composed of 312 retail salesclerks "employed in seven different types of retail stores in Detroit, Michigan." The criteria of success are not stated in the manual, and no multiple regression coefficient is supplied. The familiar phenomenon of regression, or loss of efficiency, when such an instrument is used with new groups is not discussed in the manual.

The user of this instrument would have been helped somewhat in considering test validity if an optimal cut-score or percentage had been indicated. On page 11 of the manual the percentages of "superior" and "inferior" group members are given by quartiles of (total?) score distribution. Without interpolation of percentages, which is not too satisfactory a procedure when the distribution is undefined, the best estimate for the optimal cutting score is at the 50th percentile. By so cutting, 71 per cent of the "superior" and 34 per cent of the "inferior" group would have been retained.

The manual comes fairly close to being adequate. However, it implies most of the material which should have been included. For example, on page 2, it states: "Schools which already have a record of their pupils' intelligence and schools desiring to use a complete, general intelligence test, may simply omit the intelligence sections (pages 4 and 5) of this inventory." This implies that more reliable and better validated instruments could have been substituted for the shorter sections of the test having doubtful reliability. The value of nontest information about individuals is mentioned but is not sufficiently developed for the relatively naive user of the test.

The authors of the test have carefully abstained from making any sweeping claims as to its value. The general tone of the manual is reserved and cautious. With further experimentation this instrument might be demonstrated to be a real aid to the employment manager who wishes data of this type to supplement the traditional interview, letters of recommendation, and school records. If the authors revise their manual, it is suggested that they will devote more space to the problem of test score "ceilings" and "basements," particularly in regard to the sections purporting to measure "intelligence."

This inventory is a promising approach to measuring traits and qualities related to success in retail selling; it is not recommended as a substitute for longer, better standardized single instruments available in many school personnel programs. Employment managers who are untrained in psychology may find the instrument quite useful as a supplement to other techniques.

Floyd L. Ruch, Professor of Psychology, The University of Southern California, Los Angeles, California. This test was designed to test general ability to sell and contains four subtests: personality, intelligence, checking, and arithmetic. It is immediately apparent that the tests included each cover an important factor and are only slightly related.

The subtests of the inventory were originally parts of a battery of tests given to 312 sales personnel. They were included only after a statistical study proved them to be significantly important in distinguishing "good" salesmen from "poor" salesmen. Furthermore, each item of the

subtest on personality was subjected to similar statistical analysis before it was included as a part of the test.

For the most part the personality items test the personality through the element of "interests," and only a few are of the variety where a "correct" answer to get a job as a salesman is obvious. The intelligence section tests vocabulary and word analogies and gives an index of intelligence or something similar to Thurstone's verbal factor. The authors of the test point out that a full intelligence test may be included rather than this section if the tester so desires, and the standards are given for the interpretation of the inventory under this condition. The checking section of the test is a speed test in discerning whether numbers, letters or words are alike or different. It is a test of perceptual speed. The arithmetic section is not verbal, but contains sheer computation problems in addition, subtraction, multiplication, and division.

The intercorrelations of the tests run from .60 (between intelligence and arithmetic) to .05 (between personality and arithmetic).

The reliability coefficients were computed for each section by either the split-halves technique or the test-retest technique, depending upon the nature of the test; they run from .76 to .98. The reliability coefficients were established on a different group from the standardization group but the number of common cases is not given. It would seem that the reliability of the test, or the extent to which it yields the same results each time it is given, is quite acceptable.

The validity of the test, or the degree to which it selects acceptable sales personnel, was established by dividing the test scores by quartiles and giving the percentage of "inferior" salesclerks and "superior" salesclerks in each quarter of the test scores. The criterion for "inferior" or "superior" rating of the sales personnel was a purely objective one, the sales production record of each clerk. It was found that 26 per cent of the 209 superior salesclerks received a test score in the highest quarter as against 4 per cent of the 107 inferior salesclerks; while in the lowest quarter of test scores there were only 6 per cent superior clerks as against 25 per cent inferior clerks. It is not clearly stated whether this group of salesclerks is the same group as that on which the original standards were obtained; but if it is, much shrinkage may be expected when the test is applied to a new group.

The authors also give hints as to selection

when a total score may be passing although certain subtest scores are very low. Complete percentile tables are given for each subtest as well as the total test with and without intelligence.

A review of the test reveals that it seems to be worthy of the attention of persons in the business field desiring to select salesclerks as well as of persons in the vocational guidance field. However, more research is needed.

Ed Res B 21:28 Ja 14 '42. William J. Jones. * The test is very practicable, takes about 30 minutes to administer. A well-prepared Examiner's Manual contains suggestions for giving the test, tables of percentile ranks, as well as aids in interpreting the results.

J Bus Ed 17:41 Ap '42. This test does not pretend to be a basis for final prognosis of materials for success in selling occupations, but it will serve as one major aid in the selection of students for distributive occupational courses. *

[698]
★**Engineering and Physical Science Aptitude Test.** Grades 11 and over; 1943; IBM; 1 form; separate answer sheets must be used; $4.00 per 25, postpaid; 50¢ per manual and hand-scoring keys, postpaid; 50¢ per manual and machine-scoring keys, postpaid; 60¢ per specimen set, postpaid; 72(80-90) minutes; Bruce V. Moore, C. J. Lapp, and Charles H. Griffin; manual by Henry Borow; Psychological Corporation.

REFERENCES
1. GRIFFIN, CHARLES H., AND BOROW, HENRY. "An Engineering and Physical Science Aptitude Test." *J Appl Psychol* 28: 376-87 O '44. * (PA 19:543)

Norman Frederiksen, Associate Professor of Psychology, Princeton University; and Research Associate, College Entrance Examination Board; Princeton, New Jersey. This test was developed for the purpose of predicting success in engineering and science courses given by the Pennsylvania State College as part of a defense training program. The test is made up of six parts: Part 1, Mathematics (25 items); Part 2, Formulation (10 items); Part 3, Physical Science Comprehension (45 items); Part 4, Arithmetic Reasoning (10 items); Part 5, Verbal Comprehension (43 items); and Part 6, Mechanical Comprehension (22 items). Five-choice items are used in Parts 1, 2, 4, and 5; true-false items are used in Part 3; and three-choice items are used in Part 6.

The *Engineering and Physical Science Aptitude Test* was compiled from parts of previously developed tests. The selection of materials was based on their correlation with scores on the

Cooperative Physics Test for College Students: Mechanics, Form 1936 B, which was administered at the end of a course in physics. The first three parts were taken from the revised *Iowa Physics Aptitude Test.* Most of the arithmetic reasoning items were chosen from Moore's *Test of Arithmetic Reasoning* on the basis of an item analysis, using scores on the Cooperative mechanics test as the criterion. The verbal comprehension section is composed of the most technical terms in the vocabulary section of the Moore–Nell Examination for Admission which is used at the Pennsylvania State College. These items were used on the strength of the fact that many highly verbal items in the *Otis Self-Administering Test of Mental Ability* were found to have high correlations with the criterion; the actual items selected had not been previously tried out. The mechanical comprehension items were selected from Bennett's *Test of Mechanical Comprehension* on the basis of an item analysis, using the Cooperative mechanics test as the criterion.

The reliability of the total test is satisfactory, but the reliabilities of some of the part scores are too low to justify their use in individual placement or guidance. The split-half reliability of the total test, as reported in the manual, is .96, and the reliability coefficients for the part scores range from .68 to .93. The least reliable parts are Formulation (.68), Arithmetic Reasoning (.75), and Mechanical Comprehension (.82). These coefficients are based on a sample of 201 men and women students.

The intercorrelations of the parts are all below .55 except those between Mathematics and Formulation (.61) and between Physical Science Comprehension and Mechanical Comprehension (.59). The low reliability of certain of the subtests, together with their relatively high correlation with other subtests, suggests that they might be eliminated without harming the total test. The median intercorrelation of the parts is .46.

Validity coefficients are presented in the manual, based on 188 students who took a course in introductory engineering subjects. This course consisted of mathematics, chemistry, physics, drafting, and manufacturing processes. The total score on the *Engineering and Physical Science Aptitude Test* correlated with the average of the grades in all subjects to the extent of .73. The total score also had substantial correlations with mathematics (.59), chemistry (.66), and physics (.72). When the parts of the test were weighted by the multiple correlation technique, the correlation with average grade increased only to .76. Since the standard deviations of grades in the subjects are not presented, we have no way of knowing the extent to which variation in validity coefficients from subject to subject were influenced by the amount of scatter in assigned grades. No description of the group used in this validity study is given except that the students were Pennsylvania high school graduates, mostly males. As the authors rightly state, the *Engineering and Physical Science Aptitude Test* should be validated in terms of the situation in which it is to be employed.

Percentile norms for total test scores are presented for both men and women. A considerable range of talent is apparently present in the standardization groups, since 15 per cent of the group had not completed high school and a substantial proportion of the high school graduates had had some college training. The user of this test will probably find it necessary to prepare norms based on his local group.

Robert M. W. Travers, Associate Professor of Education, University of Michigan, Ann Arbor, Michigan. This test is mainly a composite of previously published tests and is vaguely described in the manual as "an aptitude test for training in work of an engineering and physical science nature." The vague nature of the suggested uses of the test makes the reviewer wonder whether the materials were gathered together after a careful analysis had been made of a well-defined selection program. It seems that the material was first put together as part of a program for testing the individuals entering a miscellaneous group of courses designated as Engineering, Science, and Management Defense Training, which were organized in the early part of the war and which provided formal instruction for more than 50,000 adults. The initial criterion of validity of the material was its effectiveness in predicting attainment in physics training. The test was found to be a fairly valid predictor of grades in introductory engineering subjects given in the Pennsylvania State College in the summer of 1942. The total test scores yielded a correlation of .73 with the average grade for the entire course of introductory engineering subjects, and the lowest correlation of .35 was with drafting.

Since several engineering schools have discovered that some form of space manipulation test predicts successfully those aspects of engineering training which require the visualization of objects in three-dimensional space, it is regrettable that the test did not include a measure of this aptitude. The percentile norms for the test were established on the basis of a group which has many unusual characteristics. Consequently, it is almost impossible to derive any satisfaction from the use of these norms. However, one is encouraged to note in the final paragraph of the manual that further investigations are in progress and that these investigations will supply more adequate data on the validity of the test.

[699]

★George Washington University Series of Nursing Tests. Prospective nurses; 1931–44; 1¢ per profile chart; 40¢ per specimen set, postpaid; (180) minutes; Thelma Hunt; Center for Psychological Service, George Washington University.
a) APTITUDE TEST FOR NURSING. 1931–40; Forms 1, 2; $10 per 100; Form 1: 45(55) minutes; Form 2: 70(80) minutes; F. A. Moss is co-author of Form 1.
b) READING COMPREHENSION TEST FOR PROSPECTIVE NURSES. 1940; Form 1; $5 per 100; 30(35) minutes.
c) ARITHMETIC TEST FOR PROSPECTIVE NURSES. 1940; Form 1; $5 per 100; 20(25) minutes.
d) GENERAL SCIENCE TEST FOR PROSPECTIVE NURSES. 1944; Form 1; $7 per 100; 30(34) minutes.
e) INTEREST-PREFERENCE TEST FOR PROSPECTIVE NURSES. 1944; Form 1; $7 per 100; nontimed (30) minutes.

REFERENCES

1. RHINEHART, JESSE BATLEY. "An Attempt to Predict the Success of Student Nurses by the Use of a Battery of Tests." J Appl Psychol 17:277-93 Je '33. * (PA 8:567)
2. MERRILL, RUTH ATHERTON. An Evaluation of Criteria for the Selection of Students in the School of Nursing of the University of Minnesota. Unpublished doctor's thesis, University of Minnesota, 1937. (Summaries of Ph.D. Theses . . . , 1939, pp. 126-31.)
3. WILLIAMSON, E. G.; STOVER, R. D.; AND FISS, C. B. "The Selection of Student Nurses." J Appl Psychol 22:119-31 Ap '38. * (PA 13:2688)
4. KRAFT, LOUISE. The Relationship Between Some Criteria Commonly Used in Selecting Nurse Applicants and Success in the School of Nursing With a Special Attempt at Validating the Moss-Hunt Aptitude Test. Unpublished master's thesis, University of Buffalo, 1940.
5. DOUGLASS, HARL R., AND MERRILL, RUTH A.; ASSISTED BY CONSTANCE M. MCCULLOUGH. "Prediction of Success in the School of Nursing," pp. 17-31. In University of Minnesota Studies in Predicting Scholastic Achievement, Part Two. Minneapolis, Minn.: University of Minnesota Press, 1942. Pp. v, 75. Paper. $1.00. * (PA 17:1342)
6. BERG, IRWIN AUGUST. "A Study of Success and Failure Among Student Nurses." J Appl Psychol 31:389-96 Ag '47. * (PA 22:2384)

[700]

Probst Service Report. Adults; 1931–46; $125 per scoring and rating device and 1000 service report forms as selected; 20-99 forms, 5¢ each; $1 per set of sample forms; J. B. Probst; Probst Rating System.
a) EDUCATIONAL FORM. "For appraising the service value of teachers, principals, supervisors and others engaged in the work of education"; 1931.
b) FIRE DEPARTMENT FORM. "For appraising the service value of fire department personnel—to be used only for those engaged in fire fighting work"; 1932–45.
c) GENERAL FORM. "For appraising the service value of employees, supervisors or any other personnel not covered by the specialized forms"; 1932–45.
d) LABOR FORM. "For appraising the service of unskilled and semi-skilled labor"; 1932.

e) PERSONAL FITNESS FORM. Also called *Probst Personal Fitness Report;* 1936–45.

f) POLICE FORM. "For appraising the service value of police personnel, guards, watchmen, and similar workers"; 1932–45.

g) PROFESSIONAL FORM. "For appraising the service value of professional personnel—library, social service, medical, engineering, and others"; 1937–46.

h) SKILLED LABOR FORM. "For appraising the service value of workers in the skilled trades and other similar employments"; 1932–45.

REFERENCES

1. PROBST, J. B. *Service Ratings.* A joint publication of the Bureau of Public Personnel Administration and the Civil Service Assembly of the United States and Canada. Chicago, Ill.: Bureau of Public Personnel Administration, 1931. Pp. 94. Out of print. *

2. PROBST, JOHN B. *Measuring and Rating Employee Value.* New York: Ronald Press Co., 1947. Pp. xi, 166. $5.00. * (PA 21:2434)

[701]

★**Purdue Test for Electricians.** Grades 9-16 and adults; 1942; preliminary manual; $3 per 25; 50¢ per specimen set; 25(30) minutes; C. W. Caldwell, H. R. Goppert, H. G. McComb, and W. B. Hill; manual by Joseph Tiffin; Science Research Associates.

John W. French, Research Associate, College Entrance Examination Board, Princeton, New Jersey. This test is completely objective and is easy to administer, requiring only thirty minutes. Its reliability of .91 for a single form is high for a test of this length. The test can be scored by machine or self-scored. Self-scoring takes less than a minute per test, but the test booklets can be used only once for self-scoring.

No validity studies have been made. The validity is said by the manual to rest on the thoroughness of the sampling of electricity and electrical operations in standard textbooks and the fact that particular industrial concepts were incorporated in the construction of the test. The sampling of the fundamentals of electricity is good, but almost the whole test is devoted to the type of material that an alert high school student can learn from a beginning course in physics. Any user of the test should realize that the test measures little more than the groundwork in electrical theory. This may well be adequate for most industrial purposes, since a person well grounded in theory can usually be expected to learn fairly rapidly on the job to use an electrician's equipment and to perform an electrician's duties. If it is desired to measure the practical knowledge which an electrician needs, a good proportion of the test, rather than just a few scattered items, should be devoted to the use and care of electricians' tools, methods of splicing wire, safety measures for wiring, standard home electrical installations, trouble shooting, the care of storage bat-

teries, and other problems which confront the electrician on the job.

[702]

★**Purdue Test for Machinists and Machine Operators.** Grades 9-16 and adults; 1942; preliminary manual; $5 per 25; 75¢ per specimen set; 50(55) minutes; H. F. Owen, C. C. Stevason, H .G. McComb, and C. D. Hume; manual by Joseph Tiffin; Science Research Associates.

William W. Waite, Associate Professor of Industrial Engineering, Columbia University, New York, New York. This test is designed to serve several purposes: (*a*) to aid industry and vocational schools in determining the amount of machine shop knowledge possessed by applicants or students; (*b*) to serve as a basic consideration for promotion or transfer or in the formation of a "utility unit"; (*c*) to serve as a terminal achievement examination in trade schools and industrial training programs.

The total score on the test reflects the testee's general achievement in machine shop practice, while separate subscores may be derived for the operation of the lathe, planer and shaper, grinder and milling machine, and for general bench work.

The reported reliability of the test is based on results obtained with 200 vocational high school students, each of whom had had at least 720 hours of practical instruction in machine shop. Coefficients of reliability were .96 for total score and ranged from .80 to .90 for the subscores.

Validity is still being established, although it is reported that a number of industrial firms have used the test with good results.

Use of the test as a selective medium in industry would provide a reasonably satisfactory substitute for a worksample test, if it were not considered feasible to administer the latter. No test of this type can indicate the extent to which an applicant possesses the various qualities of physical dexterity essential to each type of work.

For purposes of job placement, promotion, transfer, etc. this test provides an objective confirmation of the subjective opinions of employment interviewers, foremen, and others. It should prove equally valuable in trade, vocational, and apprentice schools as a final examination.

The format of the test booklet, incorporating as it does the automatic scoring feature, makes it possible to administer the test with a minimum of equipment and specialized personnel. The typographic work on the cuts illustrating the various tools and machine parts is not particularly good, however, and might, in borderline cases, impair the value of the test.

[703]

★Sales Questionnaire. Experienced sales applicants; 1936–39; $3 per introductory set including 10 tests, postpaid; 4¢ per extra test, postpaid; introductory sets may be ordered on approval; nontimed (10-20) minutes; Eugene J. Benge; Management Service Co.

REFERENCES

1. BENGE, EUGENE J. "There's a Science to Selecting Salesmen." *Adv & Sell* 37:82+ F '44. *

Robert G. Bernreuter, Professor of Psychology, The Pennsylvania State College, State College, Pennsylvania; and Technical Director, The Klein Institute for Aptitude Testing, Inc., New York, New York. This is one of the few tests available for measuring "sales background." It is a multiple-choice 25-item omnibus test which includes questions concerning judgment in sales situations, meanings of technical terms in advertising and business practice, relations between salesman and home office, and locations of manufacturing plants. The items have face validity—they are concerned with facts that experienced salesmen might reasonably be expected to know. The questionnaire is easily administered. No time limit is set, and most men will finish it in fifteen minutes.

The only norms are in terms of letter grades from A to F. Separate norms for different types of selling apparently are not available, although the author states that for lower sales jobs it is often a mistake to hire A men, for they will not be satisfied.

When administered by the reviewer to a group of 67 college men, 20 of whom had had sales experience, a reliability of .44 was obtained by the split-half, Spearman–Brown technique. It is possible that somewhat higher values would be obtained on sales applicants. The average score for the men with no experience was 15.6; the average for the men with experience was 16.7. Both of these are in the range of D scores. However, there was a wider spread of scores for the inexperienced men; 28 per cent of them got "E" scores (poor), whereas only 10 per cent of the experienced men fell in that group. None of the 67 men earned an A score (excellent).

[704]

★Steward Selection System. Sales applicants; 1940–46; revision of *Composite Inventory and Examination*

(40:1651); 1 form; 3 parts; $12.25 per 25 sets of the 3 parts; $1 per manual; 25¢ per simplified instructions and key; $1.75 per specimen set; Verne Steward; Verne Steward & Associates, P. O. Box 226, South Gate, Calif.

a) PERSONAL INVENTORY OF BASIC FACTORS, THIRD EDITION. $7.50 per 25; nontimed in part (60-80) minutes.

b) PERSONAL INVENTORY OF BACKGROUND FACTORS, THIRD EDITION. $3.50 per 25.

c) GUIDE TO HIRING DECISION. $1.25 per 25.

REFERENCES

1-3. *See* 40:1651.

4. STEWARD, VERNE. *The Use and Value of Special Tests in the Selection of Life Underwriters.* Unpublished doctor's thesis, University of Southern California, 1934.

5. STEWARD, VERNE. *Analysis of Sales Personnel Problems.* Los Angeles, Calif.: Verne Steward & Associates, 1943. Pp. iv, 128. $4.00. *

Milton E. Hahn, Dean of Students and Professor of Psychology, University of California, Los Angeles, California. The *Personal Inventory of Basic Factors* is an 8-page test booklet containing four subtests. The subtests are: (*a*) a personality inventory of 75 items "adapted from Bernreuter Personality Inventory"; (*b*) a selected series of 10 items from subtest 1, for each of which the respondent writes a short descriptive paragraph if his answer to an item was "yes"; (*c*) a 55-item test, Mental Ability, "from Otis Self-Administering Tests of Mental Ability"; and (*d*) a 44-item inventory, Vocational Interests.

The *Personal Inventory of Background Factors* is an 8-page booklet in which the respondent enters information of various kinds about himself and his past educational and vocational experiences. This booklet has many points of similarity to the *Aptitude Index for Life Insurance Salesmen* developed by the Life Insurance Sales Research Bureau of Hartford, Connecticut.

There is almost no evidence of the usual statistical treatment of data for either instrument. Some quite nebulous evidence related to the selection of life insurance salesmen is presented. The manual cites no bibliography of research efforts. On page 4 of the manual some data are supplied in Illustration 5, Validation of the Steward Appraisal System in Life Insurance. The number of cases is not given; nor are there clear clues to the experimental design followed.

The *Personal Inventory of Basic Factors* is objectively scored with the exception of subtest 2 which is highly subjective in scoring. In the absence of supporting research, this reviewer is understandably suspicious of a 165-item battery which claims to do so much. Had the battery been standardized for a particular type of salesman in a quite common working environment, the case for satisfactory validity and reliability might have been somewhat stronger. Until adequate research evidence is supplied, one must remain in doubt as to the value of the battery "in building sales organizations."

The reviewer is alarmed to think that one would attempt to select a technical salesman with a degree in engineering with the same 50-item intelligence test that he would use for the man who sells bread to a small retail store.

The manual contains some sound advice for sales managers. Unfortunately, this sound advice is too often obscured by fuzzy writing and generalizations which are so sweeping as to be almost meaningless. The best of industrial psychologists cannot come close to what Steward claims in some sections of the manual.

The *Personal Inventory of Background Factors* also falls heir to the weaknesses of generalization from the known relationship to success in a restricted occupational environment for salesmen who are homogeneous in many respects to situations which are complex, unknown, and staffed by a group which may be extremely heterogeneous relative to a number of seemingly important variables. The similarity to the *Aptitude Index for Life Insurance Salesmen* has been noted above. It is dangerous to assume that materials which have been helpful in the selection of one highly specialized type of salesman will work equally well with quite dissimilar kinds of salesmen.

The reviewer is disturbed at the attempt to "package" a Ph.D. degree for sales managers who do not have the training and experience to utilize the materials wisely. Even our highly trained and successful industrial and personnel psychologists tread cautiously with many of the concepts advocated in the manual. Perhaps the best defense for marketing these instruments is that they present an advance over present antiquated methods of selecting salesmen found in so many business organizations. For many who will use the inventories, this may be true; but for many others there is the danger that progress toward a more scientific approach to "man analysis" will be damaged. The reviewer is convinced that the sales manager who desires to use complex psychological tools and techniques will save time and money, and secure better results, if he will employ a reputable psycho-

logical consultant who is competent to tailor a program to his needs.

In summary, this battery is an interesting *experiment* which does not as yet have sufficient exposure to published research by disinterested parties to permit its recommendation for use by psychologically naive businessmen.

Floyd L. Ruch, Professor of Psychology, The University of Southern California, Los Angeles, California. The system consists of three basic parts: (a) *Personal Inventory of Basic Factors;* (b) *Personal Inventory of Background Factors;* (c) *Guide to Hiring Decision.*

The *Personal Inventory of Basic Factors* is an 8-page booklet containing 75 items adapted from Bernreuter's *Personality Inventory;* 10 trait illustrations in which testee reports actual behavior in a specific social situation; 55 items adapted from the *Otis Self-Administering Tests of Mental Ability;* and 44 vocational interest items.

The *Personal Inventory of Background Factors* is an 8-page booklet containing: 1 page of questions on physical condition; 1 page on educational background; 2 pages on experience background covering employment and military service; 1 page on financial status; ½ page on memberships and activities; ½ page on family status; ½ page on interest in product and opportunity; and ½ page on references.

The *Guide to Hiring Decision* is a 2-page leaf designed as an aid in recording and summarizing the information regarding the applicant gathered by the tests and procedures outlined above as well as from other sources. A total of 24 characteristics are rated from test and other data on a four-point scale to provide an over-all rating of quality. The author suggests that an applicant's final rating be marked unqualified, borderline, acceptable, or superior according to the number of such ratings he receives on the various factors. Thus, the key to the system is the method by which the four ratings are obtained for the 24 items.

In examining this procedure it is found that it is largely without objectivity. The first 7 of the 24 factors are determined from the *Personal Inventory of Basic Factors*. The rating given each is determined from a Table of Values, which gives the scores obtained on the tests and the appropriate rating depending upon whether the employer is using high, medium, or low employment standards on the particular factor. In turn, this employment standard is determined by using another table in which the author suggests the employment standard to be used on each factor for various types of selling positions. The data on which this table has been established are not given. Further subjectivity in this section of the system occurs in the grading of the third factor, Trait Illustrations. Here the appraiser must evaluate the illustrations given by the applicant as OK or not OK. No standards are given by the author for making this determination, yet the final rating on this factor depends upon the OK's received.

The last 17 of the 24 factors are determined from the *Personal Inventory of Background Factors,* supplemented by interview and investigation. Which of the four ratings to give to these factors is entirely up to the employer, as the author of the system states: "It is to be remembered that specific instructions for setting employment standards cannot be provided, and that the employer must assume the responsibility for getting the facts and for interpreting them according to the requirements of the work in question." As a result, the employer who is using this system must determine himself whether the age of 40 years is unqualified, borderline, acceptable or superior.

The validity of the system as a whole is indicated by the excellence of the results reported for the 1934–35 system. The number of salesmen used in the 1934–35 study is not given, nor is the important fact of whether the ratings of these salesmen were made by the author or someone applying the system blindly with only the aid of the published instructions. Corresponding figures for the new system are not given.

In summary, the success of the *Steward Selection System* depends largely upon the judgment of the employer in determining what things are important or unimportant for his particular company. No statistical studies are presented to substantiate such guidance in these decisions as is given by the author. The best description of the system would be that it is a series of tests and rating sheets to break up an interview, enabling closer scrutiny by the employer than is usually the case.

Whatever surface validity these materials may possess, the statistically trained reviewer is frustrated by the absence of the traditionally expected validation statistics.

[705]

Test for Ability to Sell: George Washington University Series. Grades 7-16 and adults; 1929; Form 1; $9 per 100, postpaid; 15¢ per specimen set, postpaid; 35(40) minutes; F. A. Moss, Herbert Wyle, William Loman, and William Middleton; Center for Psychological Service.

Floyd L. Ruch, Professor of Psychology, The University of Southern California, Los Angeles, California. This test was designed to test ability to sell, regardless of product, and contains six subtests including tests on social consciousness, arithmetical ability, memory, and ability to follow directions. The two subtests designed to measure the personality and the social consciousness factors in selling are very short and are composed of the type of item which has been proved invalid for selecting potential employees because the "correct" answer is obvious. There is no provision in the scoring for the factor of untruthful responses. On the surface, the memory tests and the following directions test would seem to have some validity. The arithmetical ability test is very short and its selective value could be questioned.

The standardization group comprised 100 persons engaged in retail selling in various departments. The criterion was a composite of objective ratings (amount of sales, number of errors, amount of merchandise returned) and subjective ratings of estimates of the examinee's ability by three supervisors.

The reliability was determined by the test-retest technique, resulting in a coefficient of .91. The validity of this coefficient is questioned because the nature of certain parts of the test (the personality and the social consciousness sections) should logically give almost perfect retest scores. Tests of this nature should be tested for reliability by the split-halves method (only possible if tests are longer than the ones included here) or by alternate equal forms (only one form available for this test). Furthermore, in the memory test it is essential to test reliability by means of alternate forms in order to exclude the "learning" factor.

The validity coefficient, or the degree to which the test selects good salesmen, was .54 on an N of 100. It was found that in some cases the "better" salesmen in one department received lower test scores than the "poorer" salesmen in another department. Obviously, some departments require lesser sales ability than others, assuming that the test selects salesmen. In view of this, the standards given for sales personnel would be difficult to interpret unless the firm using the test made their own validation studies. Standards are also given for high school and college students, but these standards are based on test scores rather than performance. Therefore, they are rather useless for predicting whether a student will be a successful salesman.

On the whole, the test has not had the benefit of rigorous statistical treatment and the results are not so clear as those for a similar test, the *Detroit Retail Selling Inventory*.

BUSINESS EDUCATION—FOURTH MMY

REVIEWS BY *Reign H. Bittner, Bertram Epstein, Leslie M. Haynes, Clifford E. Jurgensen, Harold F. Rothe, and William L. Schaaf.*

[443]

★**Bookkeeping: Achievement Examinations for Secondary Schools.** High school; 1951; 1 form; no data on reliability and validity; no manual; Minnesota norms (median and quartile deviation) available; simular norms for other regions by special arrangement with publisher; 7¢ per test, postage extra; 60(65) minutes; edited by Walter W. Cook; prepared by a curriculum committee of high school teachers for use in the Minnesota State Board Achievement Examinations Program; Educational Test Bureau, Educational Publishers, Inc. *

[444]

★**Bookkeeping I: Every Pupil Test.** High school: 1939–51; new form usually published each April; form April 1951; no data on reliability and validity; no manual; norms ('51); 2½¢ per test; 1¢ per answer key; postpaid; 40(45) minutes; Ohio Scholarship Tests, Ohio State Department of Education. *

[445]

*****Bookkeeping Test: National Business Entrance Tests.** Grades 12–16 and clerical applicants; 1938–52; this series was entitled National Clerical Ability Tests from 1938–46 and United-NOMA Business Entrance Tests in 1947; for complete battery, see 453; Form 1342 ('49); no data on reliability; general series folder ('50); series manual ('49); norms ('52); $5 per 25; $1 per test when scoring service and certificates for acceptable work are desired (tests administered only at National Business Entrance Test Centers which may be established in any community); 50¢ per

sample test; $2 per specimen set (includes all 6 tests in the series); postpaid; 120(130) minutes; prepared by the Joint Committee on Tests representing the United Business Educational Association and the National Office Management Association; Joint Committee on Tests. *

REFERENCES

Same as for 453.

For reviews by Harvey A. Andruss and Ray G. Price of the 1946 form, see 3:368; for a review by Paul S. Lomax of all 1946 tests in this series, see 3:396.

[446]

*****Business Fundamentals and General Information Test: National Business Entrance Tests.** Grades 12–16 and clerical applicants; 1938–52; this series was entitled National Clerical Ability Tests from 1938–46 and United-NOMA Business Entrance Tests in 1947; for complete battery, see 453; 3 scores: business fundamentals, general information, total; Form 1391 ('48); no data on reliability; no norms for part scores; general series folder ('50); series manual ('49); norms ('52); $5 per 25; $1 per test when scoring service and certificates for acceptable work are desired (tests administered only at National Business Entrance Test Centers which may be established in any community); available free when other tests in the series are ordered; 50¢ per sample test; $2 per specimen set (includes all 6 tests in the series); postpaid; 75(85) minutes; prepared by the Joint Committee on Tests representing the United Business Education Association and the National Office Management Association; Joint Committee on Tests. *

REFERENCES

Same as for 453.

For reviews by Vera M. Amerson and C. C. Upshall of the 1946 form, see 3:369; for a review by Paul S. Lomax of all 1946 tests in this series, see 3:396.

[447]

★**Business Relations and Occupations: Achievement Examinations for Secondary Schools.** High school; 1951; 1 form; no data on reliability and validity; no manual; Minnesota norms (median and quartile deviation) available; similar norms for other regions by special arrangement with publisher; 7¢ per test, postage extra; 60(65) minutes; edited by Walter W. Cook; prepared by a curriculum committee of high school teachers for use in the Minnesota State Board Achievement Examinations Program; Educational Test Bureau, Educational Publishers, Inc. *

[448]

*****Commercial Arithmetic Test: State High School Tests for Indiana.** High school; 1944–51; Form A ['45]; mimeographed; no data on reliability and validity; no manual; norms ['51]; 4½¢ per test; 15¢ per specimen set; postpaid; 40 (45) minutes; Charlotte Henderson and Philip Peak; State High School Testing Service for Indiana, Purdue University. *

[449]

*****Cooperative Commercial Arithmetic Test.** 1, 2 semesters high school; 1944–51; 3 scores: numerical operations, problems, total; IBM; *discontinued:* Forms U, X; no data on reliability and validity; no specific manual; general Cooperative manual ('51); norms ['47]; 40(45) minutes; Cooperative Test Division, Educational Testing Service. *

BERTRAM EPSTEIN, *Assistant Professor of Education, The City College, New York, New York.*

Form U (1944) contains a total of 80 items organized into two parts. Part I consists of 60 computation exercises with a 15-minute working time limit. These computations are of two types: (*a*) those involving the conversion, from one form to another, of common fractions, decimal fractions, and percentages, and (*b*) those involving the three cases of percentage. The items are arranged in alternate blocks of 10 items of each type. Part II consists of 20 verbal problems involving common business situations in discount, interest, profits, taxes, etc., and centering upon percentage calculations. A single sheet of percentile norms for each part and for the total score on the test is provided. These norms are based on data for 693 pupils in nine high schools at the end of one semester of study and for 376 pupils in nine high schools at the end of two semesters of study.

Form X (1947) is of the same length and type as Form U. The only apparent difference, apart

from the specific numbers employed in the exercises, is the random arrangement of the two types of items in Part I instead of their alternation in blocks of 10. Again, a single sheet of percentile norms for each part and for the total score is provided. These norms are based on data for 154 pupils in two high schools at the end of one semester of study and for 92 pupils in three high schools at the end of two semesters of study.

The single sheets of percentile norms comprise the total of explanatory and supporting material provided. No information is given concerning the nature of the normative population beyond the numbers of pupils and schools involved and the number of semesters of commercial arithmetic studied; there is no indication of the sex, age, background, type of school involved, etc. The normative data for Form X are peculiar. The median scores reported for the two parts of the test are identical for pupils completing one and two semesters of study. Also, the median total score reported for pupils completing one semester of study is actually one point higher than that reported for those completing two semesters. The norms also raise many questions concerning the weighting of the parts and the meaning of the total score. For instance, Part II (the 20 verbal problems) constitutes only about one fifth of the total score yet is given five eighths of the total working time.

There is no information given as to the sources and the validation of the test items. The items themselves seem to be in no way superior to the exercises already profusely found in any commercial arithmetic textbook.

In each part of both forms pupils are instructed to find the correct answer "by working each problem." No further instructions to the pupil or to the examiner are given concerning the material to be used for this purpose. Neither the test booklet nor the answer sheet provides working space. A testing situation in which high school pupils of the first and second years must manipulate an 8-page test pamphlet, a separate answer sheet, and several sheets of loose paper is indeed awkward.

The format of the test is poor. The size of type used calls for greater spacing between lines of print and numbers. It would probably be even better to use a larger size of type with appropriate spacing.

It is surprising to find the Cooperative Test Division imprint on a test with so many obvious faults. The most charitable comment that can be made concerning this test is to call it "disappointing."

[450]

★Gilbert Business Arithmetic. High school; 1941; Forms A, B; $1.05 per 25; 20¢ per specimen set; postpaid; 40(45) minutes; Marc D. Gilbert and Otho M. Rasmussen; Bureau of Educational Measurements, Kansas State Teachers College of Emporia. *

WILLIAM L. SCHAAF, *Associate Professor of Education, Brooklyn College, Brooklyn, New York.*

On the whole, the test seems to fulfill its purpose rather well. Its chief merit is the full and well balanced coverage of topics: simple interest, cash discount, trade discount, profit and loss, commission, bank discount, averages, depreciation, installment purchases, reconciliation of checking account, partnerships, stocks and bonds, property taxation, insurance, and mensuration are all represented. The verbal problems are, in the main, realistic from a business point of view, and a few of them require thoughtful consideration. Among possible weaknesses, the following points are to be noted: (*a*) there might have been more items involving percentage and ratio, two extremely important matters for business use; (*b*) there might have been fewer items on addition, subtraction and multiplication with denominate numbers; and (*c*) it would seem that the time allowance (40 minutes) is much too short for the 47 items. The first two are minor criticisms; the third is more pertinent, and is apparently justified by the low median scores reported. It seems unlikely that many pupils will finish the test; and since it is not intended to be a power test, its usefulness is somewhat impaired. It is also dubious whether the test will be very helpful in analyzing student and class weaknesses, as suggested by the author. However, despite these shortcomings, the test is unquestionably a sound measure of achievement, usable at the close of any typical course in high school business arithmetic, and to be recommended for that purpose.

[451]

★Hiett Simplified Shorthand Test (Gregg). 1–2 semesters high school; 1951; IBM; Forms A, B; $1.75 per 25; 35¢ per specimen set; separate answer sheets may be used; 85¢ per 25 IBM answer sheets; 25¢ per set of stencils for machine scoring of answer sheets; postpaid; (50) minutes; V. C. Hiett and H. E. Schrammel; Bureau of Educational Measurements, Kansas State Teachers College of Emporia. *

[452]

*Machine Calculation Test: National Business Entrance Tests. Grades 12–16 and clerical applicants; replaces *Key-Driven Calculating Machine Ability Test* (see 40:1487); 1941–52; this series was entitled National Clerical Ability Tests from 1938–46 and United-NOMA Business Entrance Tests in 1947; for complete battery, see 453; Form 1394 ('49); no data on reliability; general series folder ('50); series manual ('49); norms ('52); $5 per 25; $1 per test when scoring service and certificates for acceptable work are desired (tests administered• only at National Business Entrance Test Centers which may be established in any community); 50¢ per sample test; $2 per specimen set (includes all 6 tests in the series); 120 (130) minutes; prepared by the Joint Committee on Tests representing the United Business Education Association and the National Office Management Association; Joint Committee on Tests. *

REFERENCES

Same as for 453.

For a review by Elizabeth Fehrer of the 1946 form, see 3:384; for a review by Paul S. Lomax of all 1946 tests in this series, see 3:396.

[453]

*National Business Entrance Tests. Grades 12–16 and clerical applicants; 1938–52; this series was entitled National Clerical Ability Tests from 1938–46 and United-NOMA Business Entrance Tests in 1947; 6 tests (also listed separately); no data on reliability; general series folder ('50); series manual ('49); norms ('52); $5 per 25 of any one test; $1 per test when scoring service and certificates for acceptable work are desired (tests administered only at National Business Entrance Test Centers which may be established in any community); the *Business Fundamentals and General Information Test* is available free when other tests in the series are ordered; 50¢ per sample test; $2 per specimen set (includes all 6 tests in the series); postpaid; prepared by the Joint Committee on Tests representing the United Business Education Association and the National Office Management Association; Joint Committee on Tests. *

a) BOOKKEEPING TEST. Form 1392 ('49); 120(130) minutes. *For reviews by Harvey A. Andruss and Ray G. Price, of the 1946 form, see 3:368.*

b) BUSINESS FUNDAMENTALS AND GENERAL INFORMATION TEST. 3 scores: business fundamentals, general information, total; Form 1391 ('49); no norms for part scores; 75(85) minutes. *For reviews by Vera M. Amerson and C. C. Upshall of the 1946 form, see 3:369.*

c) GENERAL OFFICE CLERICAL TEST (INCLUDING FILING). Replaces *Filing Test* (see 3:379); Form 1393 ('49); 120(130) minutes.

d) MACHINE CALCULATION TEST. Form 1394 ('49); 120(130) minutes. *For a review by Elizabeth Fehrer of the 1946 form, see 3:384.*

e) STENOGRAPHIC TEST. Long Form 1395 ('49): 115 (125) minutes; Short Form ('50): 60(70) minutes. *For reviews by Ann Brewington and Elizabeth Fehrer of the 1946 Long Form, see 3:391.*

f) TYPEWRITING TEST. Formerly called *Typing Test;* Long Form 1396 ('49): 120(130) minutes; Short Form ('50): 60(70) minutes. *For reviews by E. G. Blackstone and Beatrice J. Dvorak of the 1946 Long Form, see 3:394.*

REFERENCES

1–9. See 40:1476.
10. NELSON, JOHN H. *A Study of Relationships Between Achievement of Stenographers and Typists on the National Business Entrance Tests and Their Performance in Beginning Positions.* Doctor's thesis, New York University (New York, N.Y.), 1951. Abstract: *Microfilm Abstracts* 11:938–9 no 4 '51.

For a review by Paul S. Lomax of the 1946 series, see 3:396.

[454]

SRA Dictation Skills. Grades 9–12 and adults; 1947; 2 scores: speed, accuracy; 2 parts; the Accuracy Album includes two 12-inch records (78 rpm) presenting 1 practice and 5 test letters; the Speed Album includes three 12-inch records (78 rpm) presenting 1 practice and 8 test letters; preliminary manual; 49¢ per Speed booklet and answer pad; 49¢ per Accuracy booklet and answer pad; separate answer pads must be used; $1.90 per 25 answer pads for any one part; $18.75 per set of five records; $1 per specimen set; cash orders postpaid; (40) minutes; Marion W. Richardson and Ruth A. Pedersen; Science Research Associates, Inc. *

REFERENCES

1. PEDERSEN, RUTH A. "The Development of Two Machine-Administered Scales of Stenographic Proficiency." Abstract. *Am Psychol* 2:350–1 Ag '47. * (*PA* 21:4665, title only)

HAROLD F. ROTHE, *Personnel Director, American Hospital Supply Corporation, Evanston, Illinois.*

This test may be compared with the *Seashore-Bennett Stenographic Proficiency Tests* (see 455) since they are both designed for largely the same purpose. Both tests are standardized, recorded worksamples.

In the SRA test, the examinee takes dictation by any stenographic system and then inserts the answers to questions on the answer pad which is inserted into the test booklet. The test consists of letters, printed in the test booklets, and in each letter some words are missing. The problem is to supply the missing words on the answer sheets from the notes that were taken as the records were played. The missing words are essential to meaning of the letters and hence the test questions cannot be answered by guesswork alone.

Neither the SRA nor the S-B test has a time limit. The SRA test is scored objectively, in contrast to the semisubjective scoring of the S-B test. The number of errors on each letter is counted and this number is interpreted into either work standards or norms by using several tables that are in the manual. This is true for both the speed and also the accuracy (or difficulty) sections of the SRA test.

The SRA manual describes in detail some of the research that was conducted in making this test. Word counts of the difficulty of typical business letters were made. Items in the trial form were analyzed, based on the responses of 205 high school stenography students, to select items for the final form. Performances on the two sections, speed and accuracy, were found to be only slightly related to each other (correlation of .27 for the 205 students). The reliability of the speed scale has been estimated at .80 but the manual does not specify upon what grounds this estimate is based.

There are several important aspects in which this test is weak. The most glaring technical omission is the complete lack of validation data. The test is almost bound to be valid, since it is a worksample, but proof is still necessary. Norms based on a sample of employed stenographers, not just on the 205 students, would be helpful. More information on reliability is desirable, and particularly reliability based upon a sample of employed workers.

From a practical point of view, this test suffers from being "unreal." It tests only a part of a stenographer's job. Stenographers generally expect to transcribe their notes into letters and not into answers on an answer sheet. Perhaps it is more valuable to test dictation ability and typing ability separately, and not together as in the Seashore-Bennett tests, but the value of separate testing is not demonstrated here.

The SRA test is shorter than the S-B tests, but SRA gives less information—that is, no information about typing. The SRA test is scored more objectively but involves some rather complicated tables. In general, although the preliminary research and background work is impressive for the SRA test, the end result in its present form is not very imposing.

[455]

Seashore-Bennett Stenographic Proficiency Tests: A Standard Recorded Stenographic Worksample. Adults; 1946; Forms B-1, B-2; no data on reliability and validity in manual (for data presented elsewhere by the authors, see *1*); 3 styles of vinylite recordings: standard style 78 rpm (four 12-inch records), transcription style 33⅓ rpm (one 16-inch record), "LP" microgroove style 33⅓ rpm (one 12-inch record); each record set includes manual, script, and 100 summary charts; distribution is restricted to business firms; $19.50 per standard record set; $17 per transcription record set; $13.50 per microgroove record set; $2 per 100 summary charts; 35¢ per manual; postpaid; (50–60) minutes; Harold Seashore and George K. Bennett; Psychological Corporation. *

REFERENCES

1. SEASHORE, HAROLD G., AND BENNETT, GEORGE K. "A Test of Stenography: Some Preliminary Results." *Personnel Psychol* 1:197–209 su '48. * (*PA* 22:4709)

HAROLD F. ROTHE, *Personnel Director, American Hospital Supply Corporation, Evanston, Illinois.*

This standardized worksample was designed for the use of personnel departments in selecting, training, and upgrading employees. It is used most advantageously with other types of tests and is not intended to predict all aspects of a stenographer's performance.

The test consists of five letters dictated at three levels of speed, plus a general introduction. The testee must take dictation and then transcribe the notes into "mailable" business letters. There is no fixed time limit, and the test may be stopped at any time if the testee is obviously not capable of continuing.

The ultimate scoring criterion is "mailability," and there is no single, objective scoring method. The manual suggests a way of scoring six factors: (a) neatness and cleanness of typing, (b) arrangement of the letter, (c) quality of the stroke, (d) typing errors, erasures, etc., (e) errors of English, and (f) changes in wording and meaning. The script that accompanies each test set contains a printed copy of the directions that are dictated on the record, a standard copy of each letter, and several samples of "good" and "poor" transcriptions.

Although the scoring is semisubjective, a study by the test authors (1) shows that this test can be scored fairly consistently by persons with a little training. Two clerks, scoring the papers of 52 stenographers, had reader reliability coefficients ranging from .74 to .97 on the individual letters. In the same study, scores on letters 1, 3, and 5 were compared with scores on letters 2 and 4, yielding corrected reliabilities of .80, .83, and .91 for groups numbering 39, 52, and 91 respectively. A validity coefficient of .49 was obtained with a combination of supervisors' ratings on a group of 52 employed stenographers. In addition, the test scores differentiated fairly well between this employed group and a group of 39 trainee stenographers. This is not exactly an overwhelming amount of validity data, but it does indicate that the test may be used with a reasonable expectation of valid results, at least pending further research.

These tests are valuable in that they are easy to give, there are some research data to support them, and they appear to be testing something real and practical. In this latter connection they should be compared with the *SRA Dictation Skills*, which appears "unreal" to many testees.

These tests suffer somewhat from a shortage of norms which is in turn related to the semisubjective method of scoring. It would be desirable to have more research results, especially on validity.

In the reviewer's opinion, this is a useful test and its strong points fairly well offset the weak ones. The scoring method is not bad in actual industrial practice where an exact placement of each person's abilities at one specific point in a continuum is not necessary in day-to-day work. Probably the most serious weakness is a practical one—the tests take too long. Industrial people would rather spend 10 minutes than an hour in testing. In some respects the use of records is a little inconvenient. It would probably be desirable to have ediphone or dictaphone recordings.

For a review by Ann Brewington, see 3:386.

[456]
*Shorthand I and II: Every Pupil Test. 1, 2-3 years high school; 1938-51; new form usually published each April; 2 levels; form April 1951; no data on reliability and validity; no manual; norms ('51); 2½¢ per test; 1¢ per answer key; postpaid; 25(30) minutes; Ohio Scholarship Tests, Ohio State Department of Education. *
a) SHORTHAND I. 1 year high school.
b) SHORTHAND II. 2-3 years high school; out of print.

[457]
★Simplified Shorthand Test: State High School Tests for Indiana. 1, 2, 3, 4 semesters high school; 1950-51; 4 levels; Form B ['51]; lithotyped; no data on reliability and validity; no manual; norms ['51]; 6¢ per test; 15¢ per specimen set; postpaid; 40(45) minutes; M. E. Studebaker, B. M. Swinford, Vernal H. Carmichael, Frances R. Botsford, and Russell Burkhart; State High School Testing Service for Indiana, Purdue University. *

[458]
*Stenographic Test: National Business Entrance Tests. Grades 12-16 and clerical applicants; 1938-52; this series was entitled National Clerical Ability Tests from 1938-46 and United-NOMA Business Entrance Tests in 1947; for complete battery, see 453; long, short editions; no data on reliability; general series folder ('50); series manual ('49); norms ('52); $5 per 25; $1 per test when scoring service and certificates for acceptable work are desired (tests administered only at National Business Entrance Test Centers which may be established in any community); 50¢ per sample test; $2 per specimen set (includes all 6 tests in the series); postpaid; Long Form 1395 ('49): 115 (125) minutes; Short Form ('50): 60(70) minutes; prepared by the Joint Committee on Tests representing the United Business Education Association and the National Office Management Association; Joint Committee on Tests. *

REFERENCES

Same as for 453.

For reviews by Ann Brewington and Elizabeth Fehrer of the 1946 form, see 3:391; for a review by Paul S. Lomax of all 1946 tests in this series, see 3:396.

[459]
★Test for Stenographic Skill. Applicants for stenographic positions; 1950; individual; 1 form; no data on reliability and validity; no norms; $5 per test manual ($5.50 if ordered on 10 day trial basis), postpaid; no other materials needed; nontimed (10-20) minutes; Edward N. Hay; Aptitude Test Service. *

Test for Stenographic Skill

REIGN H. BITTNER, *Assistant Director of Personnel Research, The Prudential Insurance Company of America, Newark, New Jersey.*

This test is designed to measure the ability of a stenographer to take dictation and immediately read back aloud from her shorthand notes the material dictated. Unlike most stenographic tests, the stenographer does not transcribe her notes on a typewriter. It is the author's thesis that the ability to take dictation is one thing, the ability to type is another, and that the two should not be confused in a single test but should be measured separately. There is some question, however, whether these two skills combine additively to give a measure of a stenographer's skill.

The test, which must be administered individually to each applicant, consists of a warm-up letter and 12 letters, representing three levels of difficulty, which may be read to the applicant at 40, 60, 80, 90, 100, or 120 words per minute. Difficulty was established on the bases of the number of syllables per hundred words and the sentence length. There is some evidence that these are measures of reading ease; their relation to ease of shorthand note taking is not presented, but it is reasonable to expect them to be positively correlated. The reading rate is controlled by tables giving the time in which the reader should reach the end of each line, using a sweep second watch to check his reading pace. Practice is recommended to assure the retention of the appropriate reading speeds. One may start dictating at any of the difficulty levels and at any speed between 40 and 120 words per minute. The warm-up test is designed to indicate the appropriate beginning speed for each candidate. Immediately after each letter is dictated it is read back while the examiner notes the errors made. No standard order of presenting the various letters or the number of letters to be dictated is specified.

The objective of the test is not clearly stated in the manual, but presumably it is to determine the top levels of difficulty and speed at which the applicant can perform satisfactorily. Scores on each letter are to be given in terms of "Excellent," "Good," "Fair," "Failure." The adjective ratings depend on the number of errors and the ease with which the letter is read back. Since errors are not defined and rating the ease of reading back is highly subjective, the reliability of scoring is open to question. Norms in the usual sense are not provided. The only aid provided for interpreting the test results is the adjective rating scale, but no information is given about its derivation.

No evidence of the reliability or validity of the test is given. Because of the many opportunities for variability in administration and scoring, the test's reliability should be determined. Evidence of the validity of the test—its relation to on-the-job performance—is especially needed.

CLIFFORD E. JURGENSEN, *Personnel Director, Minneapolis Gas Company, Minneapolis, Minnesota.*

The title of this test is not accurately descriptive; the test is one of shorthand skill, not of stenographic skill. An applicant can pass the test with flying colors without knowing how to insert a piece of paper into a typewriter. This objection is limited to the title of the test and is no criticism of the nature of the test. The reviewer agrees with the test author that typing ability should be measured independently of shorthand ability.

This test is a spiral bound 20-page manual consisting of 13 test items (mostly letters) together with information on the rationale of their development and instructions regarding their use. The test was developed for individual testing in situations not requiring complicated and time-consuming measures of dictation speed. The author has used various techniques to control letter difficulty and dictation speed and to keep the test simple and short. Dictated letters are read back rather than typed. This reduces testing time to a fraction of that otherwise required. A warm-up letter of 150 words is dictated at a progressively increasing rate of speed. Proficiency on this letter indicates the speed at which the first test letter should be dictated. Thus no time is wasted in starting far above or below the examinee's level of ability.

The test proper consists of 12 items, most of which are letters. Each item consists of 10 lines of 10 words each. Not all items are intended to be used with each examinee. The test is stopped whenever the examinee is unable to re-read dictated material with satisfactory fluency and accuracy. The test time is largely a function of the examiner's judgment (based on the warm-up letter) regarding the speed at which to start dictation. A vari-speed guide enables even a relatively inexperienced examiner to pace his speed quite accurately from 40 to 120 words per minute.

Test for Stenographic Skill

Test performance is scored by rating the ease and accuracy with which the examinee reads back her shorthand notes. The author recommends a four-point scale of excellent, good, fair, or failure; each of these terms is briefly defined. The rating score is one based essentially on a practical judgment, i.e., does the examinee read back her notes in such way that a satisfactorily accurate letter could be typed from the notes? No provision is made for an overall score; each dictated item must be scored separately. No data are presented on agreement in scoring by different examiners.

A careful reading of the manual together with an hour of practice should enable any competent personnel clerk to administer and score the test adequately. The same is true for line supervisors.

A major advantage of this test is the control of difficulty of dictated material by the number of syllables per hundred words. The first six letters have from 141 to 143 syllables each, the next three have 162 or 163 syllables, and the last three have 182 to 184 syllables. Based on Flesch's readability formulas these three levels are classed as fairly easy, fairly difficult, and difficult.

The author apparently believes that reliability and validity figures are irrelevant in a test of this type, for he presents no such data. Presumably such information is, or could be made, available inasmuch as development of the test started about 1935. The test appears to have been constructed with care, and one may hazard the guess that the test would be valuable in employing stenographers. However, statistical data are lacking.

In spite of the lack of validity and reliability data, the reviewer recommends the experimental tryout of this test in the employment of stenographers in situations where simplicity and brevity are important in measuring shorthand skill.

[460]
Turse Shorthand Aptitude Test. Grades 8–10; 1937–40; 8 scores: stroking, spelling, phonetic association, symbol transcription, word discrimination, dictation, word sense, total; 1 form, '40; no norms for part scores; manual ('40); $2 per 25, postage extra; 35¢ per specimen set, postpaid; (45–50) minutes; Paul L. Turse; World Book Co. *

REFERENCES
1. TURSE, PAUL L. "Problems in Shorthand Prognosis." J Bus Ed 13:17–8+ My '38. *
2. TUCKMAN, JACOB. "Study of the Turse Shorthand Aptitude Test." J Bus Ed 19:17–8 N '43. *
3. BARRETT, DOROTHY M. "Prediction of Achievement in Typewriting and Stenography in a Liberal Arts College." J Appl Psychol 30:624–30 D '46. * (PA 21:1624)
4. HOSLER, RUSSELL J. "Aptitude Testing in Shorthand." J Bus Ed 22:25 My '47. * (PA 22:834)
5. Selection and Training of Shorthand Students in Ontario Secondary Schools. A study conducted by The Shorthand Survey Committee of The Ontario Commercial Teachers' Association and The Department of Educational Research, Ontario College of Education, University of Toronto. Toronto, Canada: Sir Isaac Pitman & Sons (Canada) Ltd., 1949. Pp. vii, 68. Paper. *

LESLIE M. HAYNES, *Head, Department of Applied Psychology, Sydney Technical College, Sydney, New South Wales, Australia.*

According to the author, the abilities necessary for success in shorthand fall into two groups, those that enable the student to write shorthand from dictation and those which enable the student effectively to use the recorded shorthand matter. The author's further analysis of these abilities is fundamental to the whole test, for upon this the subtests are based. We are asked to accept the fact that "a good shorthand prognosis test should include measures of each of the following: manual dexterity; ability to write, carry matter in the mind, and listen for new matter *simultaneously;* ability to learn and combine abstract symbols; ability to associate the correct literal spelling of a word with its phonetic form; ability to discriminate between words having similar or identical shorthand outlines; spelling ability; and ability to construct entire words from the incomplete shorthand outlines." No attempt is made to justify these assumptions; some justification would seem to be necessary in view of consistent research findings that symbol writing and spelling are the principal abilities required for success in shorthand. The actual subtests are stroking (manual dexterity), spelling, phonetic association, symbol transcription, word discrimination, dictation, and word sense.

The test has been thoroughly validated against various shorthand achievement tests and, if these are accepted as adequate criteria, the figures quoted in the manual justify the inclusion of most of the subtests. The author's stated aim is to eliminate those unfit to study shorthand. The validation data seem to indicate that the test can achieve this. The stated aim is, however, not a satisfactory justification for failure to extend the validation of the test to the employment situation itself.

The manual is a well prepared document aimed at bringing about the scientific use of this measuring instrument. The directions for administering are particularly well set out, while sound advice is offered in the section dealing with the interpretation and use of the test results.

In all, this test is well worth using in the selection of students for commercial courses involving the teaching of shorthand. For this purpose it is probably best used, as the author himself indicates, with other guidance data, such as intelligence test results and teachers' marks. It would also seem to have some value as a diagnostic instrument to be used with students undergoing training.

For a review by Philip H. DuBois, see 3:393.

[461]

*Typewriting I: Every Pupil Test. High school; 1938–51; new form usually published each April; form April 1951; no data on reliability and validity; no manual; norms ('51); 2½¢ per test; 1¢ per answer key; postpaid; 45(50) minutes; Ohio Scholarship Tests, Ohio State Department of Education. *

[462]

*Typewriting Test: National Business Entrance Tests. Grades 12–16 and clerical applicants; 1938–52; formerly called *Typing Test;* this series was entitled National Clerical Ability Tests from 1938–46 and United-NOMA Business Entrance Tests in 1947; for complete battery, see 453; long, short editions; no data on reliability; general series folder ('50); series manual ('49); norms ('52); $5 per 25; $1 per test when scoring service and certificates for acceptable work are desired (tests administered only in National Business Entrance Test Centers which may be established in any community); 50¢ per sample test; $2 per specimen set (includes all 6 tests in the series); postpaid; Long Form 1396 ('49): 120(130) minutes; Short Form ('50): 60 (70) minutes; prepared by the Joint Committee on Tests representing the United Business Education Association and the National Office Management Association; Joint Committee on Tests. *

REFERENCES

Same as for 453.

For reviews by E. G. Blackstone and Beatrice J. Dvorak, see 3:394; for a review by Paul S. Lomax of all 1946 tests in this series, see 3:396.

[463]

*Typewriting Test: State High School Tests for Indiana. 1, 2 or 4, 3 semesters; 1934–51; 3 levels; mimeographed; no data on reliability and validity; no manual; norms ['51]; 4½¢ per test; 15¢ per specimen set; postpaid; Frances R. Botsford and Russell Burkhart; State High School Testing Service for Indiana, Purdue University. *
a) FIRST SEMESTER. Form B ['45]; Form A out of print; 30(35) minutes.
b) SECOND OR FOURTH SEMESTERS. Form N ['45]; second semester: 30(35) minutes; fourth semester: 40(45) minutes.
c) THIRD SEMESTER. Form B ['45]; Form A out of print; 40(45) minutes.

VOCATIONS—FOURTH MMY

REVIEWS BY *Anne Anastasi, Dwight L. Arnold, Brent Baxter, Harold Bechtoldt, George K. Bennett, Ralph F. Berdie, Reign H. Bittner, Milton L. Blum, Edward S. Bordin, Arthur H. Brayfield, Leo J. Brueckner, John B. Carroll, Harold D. Carter, E. G. Chambers, Stuart A. Courtis, Lee J. Cronbach, Edward E. Cureton, Louise Witner Cureton, Jerome E. Doppelt, George A. Ferguson, H. M. Fowler, Norman Frederiksen, Frank S. Freeman, John W. French, Clifford P. Froehlich, Edward B. Greene, Milton E. Hahn, George W. Hartmann, Edward N. Hay, Kenneth L. Heaton, Elmer D. Hinckley, Lloyd G. Humphreys, Clifford E. Jurgensen, Harry W. Karn, Raymond A. Katzell, Willard A. Kerr, Albert K. Kurtz, Charles R. Langmuir, Wilbur L. Layton, D. Welty Lefever, D. W. McElwain, Milton M. Mandell, Ross W. Matteson, Joseph E. Moore, N. W. Morton, Jay L. Otis, C. Robert Pace, Donald G. Paterson, E. A. Peel, Harry N. Rivlin, Alec Rodger, Floyd L. Ruch, G. A. Satter, Douglas G. Schultz, May V. Seagoe, I. Macfarlane Smith, Julian C. Stanley, Dewey B. Stuit, Donald E. Super, Howard R. Taylor, Albert S. Thompson, Robert L. Thorndike, Robert M. W. Travers, Arthur E. Traxler, P. E. Vernon, William W. Waite, S. Rains Wallace, Jr., Edwin Wandt, Morey J. Wantman, F. W. Warburton, A. T. Welford, Alexander G. Wesman, D. A. Worcester, and Dale Yoder.*

[710]

★**Aptitude Tests for Occupations.** Grades 9–13; 1951; IBM; 6 tests; Form A; 35¢ per specimen set of any one test, postpaid; separate answer sheets may be used; 4¢ per IBM answer sheet for any one test; 40¢ per stencil for machine scoring of answer sheets of any one test; 40¢ per stencil for hand scoring of answer sheets of any one test; 5¢ per profile chart; postage extra; 107(135) minutes; Wesley S. Roeder and Herbert B. Graham; California Test Bureau. *

a) PERSONAL-SOCIAL APTITUDE. $1.50 per 25; 20(25) minutes.
b) MECHANICAL APTITUDE. $2 per 25; 20(25) minutes.
c) GENERAL SALES APTITUDE. $1.50 per 25; 20(25) minutes.
d) CLERICAL ROUTINE APTITUDE. $1.25 per 25; 12(15) minutes.
e) COMPUTATIONAL APTITUDE. $1.25 per 25; 15(20) minutes.
f) SCIENTIFIC APTITUDE. $1.50 per 25; 20(25) minutes.

CLIFFORD P. FROEHLICH, *Associate Professor of Education, University of California, Berkeley, California.*

This battery is made up of six parts, each labeled as a test of one of the following aptitudes: personal-social, mechanical, general sales, clerical routine, computational, and scientific. The parts contain from 45 to 60 items and require from 12 to 20 minutes of testing time. The battery contains 300 items and requires 107 minutes of testing time. The length of this battery seems very short in view of its scope and the experience of such test development programs as that of the United States Air Force.

The manual states that these "tests were constructed for the purpose of obtaining a quick but valid general *vocational profile* or pictures of an individual" (italics mine). This emphasis on vocational application of the test is reiterated throughout the manual and in descriptive literature. The publisher's catalog, for example, states that these tests "are intended to serve as aids in the analysis of the individual's aptitudes in order to determine whether or not he possesses the potentialities necessary for success in a given field." The name *Aptitude Tests for Occupations* implies the vocational significance of the tests. But the manual does not report test scores obtained by persons actively engaged in any occupation. The closest it comes is to present correlation coefficients of subtests of the battery with criterion tests. For example, Clerical Routine Aptitude was correlated with the *Minnesota Clerical Test*, the clerical test of the *Differential Aptitude Tests*, and *SRA Clerical Aptitudes*. The correlations were based on groups of students in grades 9 to 13 (usually two grades together), ranging in number from 26 to 78. Of the ten coefficients reported, four are in the forties, three are in the fifties, two are in the sixties, and one is in the seventies. A comment made in the manual in connection with the intercorrelations among the subtests of the battery is pertinent here: "In evaluating these intercorrelations, it must be considered that a correlation of .50 accounts for 25 per cent of the variance, and that 75 per cent of the variance thus remains unaccounted for by the relationship between the tests." While these correlations with so called "criterion tests" yield interesting data, they provide little information about the vocational significance of the *Aptitude Tests for Occupations*.

Additional statistics concerning the test are described in the manual in these words:

The following cross-validation data were obtained by determining the raw scores at standard deviation intervals of $+2$, $+1$, 0, -1, -2 for the Aptitude Tests for Occupations and for certain criterion tests, and then converting these scores to percentiles using the norms provided for the tests. For example, for the Personal-Social Test in grade 9, the $+2$ S.D. percentiles were 98 for the Personal-Social Test and 99 for the Test of Social Comprehension; for the same grade and tests, the -1 S.D. percentiles were 10 and 10, respectively.

The two or three comparisons presented for each of the subtests indicate the school grade and sex of the group tested, the names of the tests compared, and the percentile ranks for each test at the five standard deviation points indicated above. Neither the data nor the procedures are explained further in the manual. This reviewer, in correspondence with the Director of Research and Technical Services of the California Test Bureau, raised the following questions: "What do such data reveal about the validity of the test? Could I not, by chance, find that a test of musical aptitude and Personal-Social Aptitude would yield comparable standard deviation comparisons, even though the tests were uncorrelated?" The prompt and courteous reply to this query pointed out that the data were obtained by testing "groups available in the public schools in various parts of the nation." The standard deviation points "were derived from the original plots, wherein significant correlations were found." Certainly the size of the group and the correlation coefficient obtained between a test in the battery and a criterion test should be reported in the manual if one is to make meaningful interpretations.

The reviewer was informed that the technique of standard deviation percentile rank comparisons was developed by Alice Horn "in connection with an examination of the comparability of five well-known intelligence tests * It was her feeling at the time that straight correlation would not be entirely satisfactory for her purposes. Therefore, she devised a technique which would enable her to get comparability of the data all along the scale." But, what is revealed about validity by comparing percentile ranks equivalent to certain standard deviation points? How, for example, does the fact that a group of grade 9 boys obtained a mean score equivalent to a percentile rank of 90 on General Sales Aptitude and a mean score equivalent to a percentile rank of 85 on the *George Washington University Test of Ability to Sell* reveal validity? The -2 SD equivalent percentile ranks for the same group and tests are 40 and 50 respectively. The aforementioned Director of Research and Technical Services writes, "We inserted these data

in the manual in order that the test user might see that comparability holds up even with such groups."

Perhaps a more important finding from the comparisons that are reported is the distribution of percentile ranks equivalent to the mean score in the 17 groups tested. This shows one mean equivalent to a percentile rank of 90, four to 80, three to 70, five to 60, one to 50, one to 40, and two to 30. While the reviewer recognizes that the mean score is not necessarily equivalent to a percentile rank of 50, he feels that this distribution of equivalent percentile ranks hints that the groups tested are atypical or that the published norms are inadequate.

The "occupational patterns" presented in the manual "include not only a list of occupations related to each of the six major fields of aptitude measured by the tests but also include occupations which are related to more than one field." The manual presents no information concerning the basis upon which these patterns were prepared. The basis was described, however, by the senior author of the test in a letter to this reviewer in these words:

Among the materials we found helpful in devising the list of occupational patterns were the Dictionary of Occupational Titles, Handbook of Job Facts and Occupational Monographs in "The American Job Series," and Occupational Briefs on America's Major Job Fields. We have done considerable work in collating the list with this information, and especially by observing individuals on the job. The four years spent in the army as psychologist, classification officer, and personal counselor gave unlimited opportunity to study the various individuals on their respective jobs.

The manual instructs the test user that "regardless of the nature of an individual's profile, the highest percentile ranks should be investigated"; this despite the fact that the typical standard error of measurement is 3 raw score points, which on some subtests is equivalent to a large percentile rank range. For example, the norms for Personal-Social Aptitude show that the raw scores one standard error of measurement below and one standard error of measurement above the median are equivalent to percentile ranks of 30 and 70 respectively for ninth grade girls and 20 and 80 for ninth grade boys. To this reviewer, the failure to explain the hazards of differential prediction is a grave oversight. Test users need more sophistication in interpreting the profile than the manual's statement that "the important feature of an examinee's profile is the comparison of his standing in each field with his standing in other fields." The standard error of measurement may render these comparisons meaningless.

This reviewer is of the opinion that not enough is known about this test to recommend its use for occupational guidance, selection, or classification. He recommends that the publishers correct errors and eliminate the unsupported claims in the present manual and that they collect and report sufficient data to provide a basis for judging the test's value.

J. Consult Psychol 15:515–6 D '51. *Laurance F. Shaffer.* * In the main, these tests fulfill the current expectations of psychologists for a series to measure differentiated abilities. They fall decidedly short of ultimate ideals for test development in two respects. First, there is no evidence that they measure "aptitude" as distinguished from achievement, and the magical word is likely to deceive the unwary. Second, although the tests are recommended mainly for occupational guidance, they are not accompanied by evidence to show their power to predict successful adjustment to any vocation. The latter fault can be remedied by further research.

[711]

★Differential Aptitude Tests. Grades 8–12; 1947–50; IBM; 8 tests in 7 booklets; Forms A ('47), B ('47); manual ('47); manual supplements ('48, '49, '50, '51, '51); $21.50 per 25 sets of the 7 booklets; separate answer sheets must be used; $1.85 per 50 IBM answer sheets for any one booklet; $1.25 per set of machine scoring stencils; $1.25 per set of hand scoring stencils; $2 per manual; $3 per specimen set; postpaid; 186 (240) minutes; George K. Bennett, Harold G. Seashore, and Alexander G. Wesman; Psychological Corporation. *

a) VERBAL REASONING. $3 per 25; 30(40) minutes.

b) NUMERICAL ABILITY. $2.25 per 25; 30(35) minutes.

c) ABSTRACT REASONING. $3 per 25; 25(30) minutes.

d) SPACE RELATIONS. $3.50 per 25; 30(40) minutes.

e) MECHANICAL REASONING. $3.75 per 25; 30(35) minutes.

f) CLERICAL SPEED AND ACCURACY. $3 per 25; 6(15) minutes.

g) LANGUAGE USAGE. 2 scores: spelling, sentences; $3 per 25; 35(45) minutes.

REFERENCES

1. BENNETT, GEORGE K. "The Evaluation of Pairs of Tests for Guidance Use." Abstract. *Am Psychol* 2:287 Ag '47. * (PA 21:4609, title only)

2. BENNETT, GEORGE K., AND DOPPELT, JEROME E. "The Evaluation of Pairs of Tests for Guidance Use." *Ed & Psychol Meas* 8:319–25 au '48. * (PA 23:3991)

3. BENNETT, GEORGE K., AND SEASHORE, HAROLD. "Testing for Vocational Guidance in High School," pp. 71–9. In *Exploring Individual Differences: A Report of the 1947 Invitational Conference on Testing Problems, New York City, November 1, 1947.* Henry Chauncey, Chairman. American Council on Education Studies, Vol. 12, Series 1, No. 32. Washington, D.C.: the Association, October 1948. Pp. vii, 110. Paper. *

4. BENNETT, G. K.; SEASHORE, H. G.; AND WESMAN, A. G. "The Differential Aptitude Tests: Some Comments by the Authors." *Occupations* 27:20–2 O '48. * (PA 23:1329)

5. COTTLE, WILLIAM C. "The Differential Aptitude Tests: Some Comments." *Occupations* 26:344–5 Mr '48. * (PA 22:4010)

6. BERDIE, RALPH F. "The Differential Aptitude Tests as Predictors in Engineering Training." Abstract. *Am Psychol* 4:292 Jl '49. * (PA 23:6526, title only)

7. COTTLE, WILLIAM C. "Apropos Two Recent Articles." Letter. *Occupations* 27:268–9 Ja '49. * (PA 22:4010)

8. SEASHORE, HAROLD G. "The Development of the Differential Aptitude Tests," pp. 40–50. In *The Fifth Yearbook of the National Council on Measurements Used in Education, 1947–48.* Fairmont, W.Va.: the Council, Fairmont State College, 1949. Pp. v, 56, viii. Paper, mimeographed. *

9. SUPER, DONALD E. *Appraising Vocational Fitness by Means of Psychological Tests,* pp. 368–75. New York: Harper & Brothers, 1949. Pp. xxiii, 727. * (PA 24:2130)

10. WESMAN, ALEXANDER. "Separation of Sex Groups in Test Reporting." *J Ed Psychol* 40:223–9 Ap '49. * (PA 24:2655)

11. WESMAN, ALEXANDER G., AND SEASHORE, HAROLD G. "Frequency vs. Complexity of Words in Verbal Measurement." *J Ed Psychol* 40:395–404 N '49. * (PA 24:3393)

12. COUGHLIN, GERALD J. *A Preliminary Investigation of the Differential Aptitude Tests.* Master's thesis, Fordham University (New York, N.Y.), 1950.

13. DOPPELT, JEROME EDWARD. *The Organization of Mental Abilities in the Age Range 13 to 17.* Columbia University, Teachers College. Contributions to Education, No. 962. New York: Bureau of Publications, the College, 1950. Pp. x, 86. * (PA 24:5111)

14. EMBREE, ROYAL B., JR. "A Longitudinal Study of Performance on the Henmon-Nelson Test of Mental Ability, the Differential Aptitude Tests, and the American Council on Education Psychological Examination for College Freshmen." Abstract. *Am Psychol* 5:352 Jl '50. * (PA 25:1276, title only)

15. GOLDMAN, LEO. *Relationship Between Aptitude Scores and Certain Rorschach Indices.* Doctor's thesis, Columbia University (New York, N.Y.), 1950. Abstract: *Microfilm Abstracts* 11:421–3 no 2 '51. (PA 26:2180, title only)

16. LUDLOW, HERBERT GLENN. *An Analysis of the Ability to Interpret Data and Its Relationship to Certain Other Aspects of Pupil Status.* Doctor's thesis, Indiana University (Bloomington, Ind.), 1950. (*Thesis Abstract Series....1950,* 1951, pp. 75–80.) (PA 25:7082, title only)

17. MELEIKA, LOUIS KAMEL. *The Relationship of Scores on the Differential Aptitude Tests to Achievement of Students in a Senior High School.* Master's thesis, Stanford University (Stanford, Calif.), 1950.

18. TOWNSEND, AGATHA. "The Differential Aptitude Tests: Some Data on the Reliability and Intercorrelations of the Parts," pp. 39–47. (PA 24:3897) In *1949 Fall Testing Program in Independent Schools and Supplementary Studies.* Educational Records Bulletin, No. 53. New York: Educational Records Bureau, January 1950. Pp. xiii, 70. Paper, lithotyped. *

19. "Results of the Space Relations, Mechanical Reasoning, and Clerical Speed and Accuracy Tests of the Differential Aptitude Test Battery in Six Public Schools," pp. 79–84. In *1951 Fall Testing Program in Independent Schools and Supplementary Studies.* Foreword by Ben D. Wood. Educational Records Bulletin No. 58. New York: Educational Records Bureau, February 1952. Pp. xii, 86. *

20. BENNETT, GEORGE K.; SEASHORE, HAROLD G.; AND WESMAN, ALEXANDER G. "The Differential Aptitude Tests and Success in Vocational and Educational Fields." Abstract. *Am Psychol* 6:296 Jl '51. *

21. BERDIE, RALPH F. "The Differential Aptitude Tests and Predictors in Engineering Training." *J Ed Psychol* 42:114–23 F '51. * (PA 25:8276)

22. DOPPELT, JEROME E., AND BENNETT, GEORGE K. "A Longitudinal Study of the Differential Aptitude Tests." *Ed & Psychol Meas* 11:228–37 su '51. * (PA 26:3044)

23. DOPPELT, JEROME E., AND WESMAN, ALEXANDER G. "The Differential Aptitude Tests as Predictors of Achievement Test Scores." Abstract. *Am Psychol* 6:299 Jl '51. *

24. GLASER, ROBERT. "The Application of the Concepts of Multiple-Operation Measurement to the Response Patterns on Psychological Tests." *Ed & Psychol Meas* 11:372–82 au '51. *

25. GLASER, ROBERT. "Predicting Achievement in Medical School." *J Appl Psychol* 35:272–4 Ag '51. * (PA 26:3046)

26. GLASER, ROBERT. "The Validity of Some Tests for Predicting Achievement in Medical School." Abstract. *Am Psychol* 6:298 Jl '51. *

27. GOLDMAN, LEO. "Relationships Between Aptitude Test Scores and Certain Rorschach Indices." Abstract. *Am Psychol* 6:300 Jl '51. *

28. PLUMMER, ROBERT HOWARD. *Characteristics and Needs of Selected Ninth Grade Pupils as a Basis for Curricular Changes to Meet Life Adjustment Needs.* Doctor's thesis, Indiana University (Bloomington, Ind.), 1951. (*Thesis Abstract Series....1951,* 1952, pp. 113–9.)

HAROLD BECHTOLDT, *Associate Professor of Psychology, State University of Iowa, Iowa City, Iowa.*

One of the more valuable tools for sound vocational and educational guidance available today is represented by the *Differential Aptitude*

Tests. The basic hypothesis used in the development of this battery is that the appraisal of each of several "abilities" will enable vocational and educational counselors to form realistic judgments as to the educational curricula appropriate to the skills of students and reasonable judgments as to which students should take each course.

The eight tests, presented in seven booklets, are available in two forms. Separate answer sheets are provided so that repeated use of the test booklets is possible. High editorial standards are reflected in the pleasing appearance of each booklet; the content of the items similarly reflects competent test construction work. The test items are similar in content and form to the verbal-numerical and pictorial items found in other scholastic aptitude tests. Norms, perhaps the most adequate special aptitude or ability test norms currently available, are based upon over 47,000 cases secured from nearly 100 schools selected to represent the major geographical areas of the United States and, to some extent the various socio-economic groups characteristic of urban areas. The norms are further distinguished by the reporting by sexes and by grade levels from grades 8 to 12 inclusive the major percentile points together with the means, standard deviations, and number of cases for each of the eight tests. The usual sex differences in score distributions are noted for the spatial and numerical tasks. Although the score distributions suggest somewhat inadequate discrimination at the lower 5 per cent of the eighth grade population on a few tests, the published results indicate an acceptable degree of differentiation between individuals in the populations sampled. The use of the scoring formula R-kW for all but two tests is apparently a concession to tradition. No evidence is presented to the effect that weighting the wrong responses, W, is of any value in the seven power tests. An interesting feature of the Numerical-Ability test is the use of a fifth choice, *none of these,* with each of the 40 items. A unique and very valuable adjunct of the *Differential Aptitude Tests* is the loose-leaf form of the test manual.

The test authors have not only provided the user with an extensive set of norms, but they have also included in the very extensive manual useful discursive materials and very valuable data dealing with the concepts of test reliability and validity, and of errors of estimate. The manual itself presents an interesting contrast between extreme naiveté (statements about correlation coefficients on page E-50 of the manual) and considerable sophistication in test theory (extensive tables of validity coefficients, reliability coefficients, and expectancy data). How vocational counselors can use these, or any tests, adroitly without knowing a great deal about test analysis is difficult for the reviewer to understand. Counselors administering these tests will probably acquire a "felt need" for more detailed theoretical and empirical knowledge of the relations between performance measures.

Reliability coefficients determined by a split half technique for the seven power tests are provided for each form of each test separately for the two sexes and for grades 8 to 12 inclusive. These coefficients (averages of the several grade coefficients) range from .86 to .93 for six of the tests. The coefficient for the seventh test, Mechanical Reasoning, is somewhat lower for girls. For Clerical Speed and Accuracy, an average reliability of .87 for similar groups was determined by the alternate forms method, this method being considered more appropriate for a highly speeded test. Corresponding reliability coefficients are also presented for the separate grades by form and sex. In addition, the test authors have provided in tabular form the estimates of the standard errors of measurement associated with these correlation coefficients. The use of the standard error of measurement in the evaluation of test scores is definitely recommended by the reviewer to all test publishers and consumers.

Since the several tests were designed so that each would provide a unique contribution to the counseling prediction solution, the test intercorrelations presented in detail by grade, sex, and form, together with the average correlation for similar samples, is a most admirable feature of the manual. The authors properly indicate that both high reliability and relatively independent tests are necessary for differential prediction. They might have emphasized the same requirements for efficient prediction in any one area of activity. The test intercorrelations suggest that the multiple correlation with their criteria of success may not be appreciably higher than the zero-order correlations; therefore, the magnitude of the unique contribution of some of the tests may be too small for practical use. The unique contribution required for differential prediction is analyzed in terms of Kelley's technique for estimating the proportion of differences in excess of the chance proportion for pairs of tests. The results are interpreted by the authors as evidence warranting the inclusion of all eight tests in the battery (page C-2 of the manual). The reviewer would suggest that these analyses constitute the first step in the solution of the differential prediction problem. The presentation for each academic area of study and/or each occupational job family of the linear regression equations or discriminant function weights together with their standard errors would seem to provide more relevant data as to the necessity for inclusion of all eight tests of the battery. This problem, which has not been discussed in the manual, is definitely complicated by the unsatisfactory nature of the criterion—the critical phase of the validity problem.

The relationships between the scores on the *Differential Aptitude Tests* and a variety of other tests for both men and women and for grades 9 to 13 inclusive are presented in some detail. The other tests used in the intercorrelations include the *American Council on Education Psychological Examination,* the *Primary Mental Ability Tests,* and the *General Aptitude Test Battery,* as well as objective achievement examinations in English, reading, mathematics, and social studies. These data together with the intercorrelations of the *Differential Aptitude Tests* and the intercorrelations of the other aptitude and achievement tests available to the test authors may provide eventually a practical answer as to the number of different measures (from among those studied) to be used for both selection and differential prediction problems. Correlations with the *Kuder Preference Record* covering three grades in one school system are uniformly low. Especially commendable in this connection, is the warning, on page E-85 of the manual, to vocational counselors who rely mainly upon indications of verbally expressed interest. Perhaps, from the extensive studies carried out by the authors of the *Differential Aptitude Test,* vocational counselors can be given at a later date some positive suggestions based on empirical evidence as to the recommended techniques of prediction and the associated errors of estimate. Since the test authors express concern about what the counselor can learn from the data in the manual, the reviewer would like to add the suggestion that the counselor can learn to ask himself and the test publishers, "What is the evidence for the statement or prediction?"

The manual includes rather detailed discussions of the problem of validity and of the necessity for accurate estimates of predictions. The positive correlations with school grades are consistent with the general literature on the prediction of educational success. It is very encouraging to find the authors cautioning the test user about "validity by inference" (based on similarities of test form) since the valuable and extensive data on the correlations of the eight aptitude tests with course grades often are not in line with "expectations" so frequently expressed in the vocational counseling literature. The specificity of the relationships between the predictor and criterion measures is emphasized repeatedly in the manual. The authors may be doing themselves an injustice in this case since a cursory reading of these tables of validity coefficients might lead to the conclusion that the tests are of little value.

To the reviewer, the crux of the educational guidance and differential prediction problem is the complete inadequacy of school grades as criterion measures (the problem is one of the extraneous sources of variance rather than the reliability of the school grades). The problem is one that cannot be handled in this review or in a manual aimed at a test user who has to be informed that a correlation coefficient is an index of association ranging in magnitude from −1.00 to +1.00. Briefly, the evaluation techniques currently used in our high schools are such that little, if any, differential prediction *can* be obtained. Similar unsatisfactory or inadequate definitions of "success on the job" may well lead to the conclusion that differential prediction is not attained in either educational or vocational activities with current criteria.

The reviewer would like to commend the authors of the *Differential Aptitude Tests* on their work to date, and to recommend these tests to vocational counselors for use in educational guidance or educational research programs. The results of further work by the test authors on the problem of the criterion and on the problem of differential prediction of success in educational or vocational activities will be awaited with interest. These results may indicate that the prediction (differential or simple) of the available criterion measures can be accomplished as well by composite scores based on two or three clusters or groupings on the eight tests as by the scores on the separate tests.

RALPH F. BERDIE, *Professor of Psychology, and Director, Student Counseling Bureau, University of Minnesota, Minneapolis, Minnesota.*

The adequacy of the factorial theory upon which differential aptitude testing is based determines the ultimate usefulness of differential tests. The authors of the *Differential Aptitude Tests,* after considering carefully the advantages and disadvantages of developing a differential battery of specific tests identified in factor analyses, decided instead to attempt to select tests that would fill the practical needs of personnel and guidance workers. They describe this battery as a compromise "between the desire to measure 'pure' mental abilities that emerge from factor analysis and the practical necessities continually encountered by personnel and guidance workers through the years." Several of the tests in this battery are similar to tests of "pure" abilities, as defined by factor analyses. The clerical speed and accuracy test and the language usage tests, however, purposefully present compounded pictures of two or more pure aptitudes.

Included in the battery are eight tests. With the exception of the clerical speed and accuracy tests, these are power tests with items graded in order of difficulty and with time limits that permit most people to attempt all items. For each form of the test, the authors present coefficients of correlations between each of the tests and the others, for each sex and for each grade from 8 through 12. The averages of these intercorrelations range from .06 to .67. A study conducted at the University of Minnesota found that the intercorrelations between tests for each of three groups of freshmen engineering students were no higher and in some cases lower than the intercorrelations presented by the test authors. The two language usage tests are relatively closely related both to each other and to the verbal reasoning test, but, in general, it appears that they successfully measure relatively discrete factors. It was found at Minnesota that the ceilings of the tests were too low for selected groups of college freshmen.

The test items show signs of rare ingenuity. The items in the verbal reasoning test are double analogies where the first term of the analogy is to be selected from four alternatives, and the last term of the analogy is to be selected from a second group of four alternatives. The numerical ability test ranges from simple arithmetic through more complex numerical problems involving cube root and number reasoning. The abstract reasoning test involves the detection of a principle of change occurring in four successive figures and then the selection of an appropriate fifth figure to be chosen from a group of five alternatives. The items in the space relations test involve visualizing a constructed object from a picture of a pattern of its surfaces. The authors support the choice of this type of item by saying that "the test requires mental manipulation of objects in three-dimensional space. Item forms which refer to only two dimensions are less useful since there are relatively few occasions when perception of two-dimensional space alone is important." The items in the mechanical reasoning test present pictures of mechanical situations together with simply worded questions. The clerical speed and accuracy test requires the testee to select combinations of letters and numerals marked in the test booklet and then to identify from a group of similar combinations the identical combination on the answer sheet. The first language usage test, the spelling test, requires the testee to identify from a list of words those words spelled incorrectly. The second test presents a series of sentences, each divided into five sections, and requires the testee to identify those sections containing errors.

The test items have intrinsic interest for students, and the tests are easy and convenient to administer. The printing is good, the paper stock superior, and there is sufficient white space on each page.

The most impressive feature of the *Differential Aptitude Tests* is the test manual. This is unquestionably the best test manual published, and its authors received recognition from the Council of Guidance and Personnel Associations in 1951 for the superior job they have done in presenting information about the tests. There is complete information concerning the purposes of the tests, procedures to be used in administering the tests, statistics concerning the tests and their standardization, principles to be considered in interpreting test scores, and normative frames of reference.

The manual's section on statistical information is particularly pertinent. Not only are reliability coefficients for each test presented by grade and by sex, but standard errors of measurement are also systematically presented. Too many of the tests have reliability coefficients in the .80's, the mechanical reasoning test and the clerical speed and accuracy test having somewhat lower reliabilities than the others. The reliabilities of all of these tests, however, are adequate for use in counseling individual students.

The manual contains, at present, 94 pages directly relating to the validity of these tests. Practically all of these data are in terms of correlations between test scores and course grades of high school students. Tables added to the manual summarize this mass of validity data and bear out the authors' contention that a test does not have validity but rather validities. The available information suggests that for counseling high school students the tests may have useful validities. This is a statement that, on the basis of existing data, can be made about no other existing aptitude tests.

A useful section in the manual contains eight brief case histories. These histories and ones similar to them should be useful to high school teachers and counselors attempting to gain familiarity with these tests. Another useful section describes various methods of plotting individual report forms; a convenient graphic method is also described to assist in determining the significance of differences between scores on a profile.

In summary, the *Differential Aptitude Tests* have been carefully developed and standardized by competent authors who have done an exceptionally good job in making information about these tests available to the public. The tests have some validity in predicting success in high school courses, and some evidence has appeared concerning their validity in predicting vocational success. The tests are presented primarily for use with boys and girls in grades 8 through 12, although the authors indicate that they may be useful with young adults. Because of the relatively low ceilings of the tests, young adults or college students of high ability can not be differentiated adequately by means of these tests. Finally, information concerning the relationships existing between these test scores and other types of psychologically meaningful data should be gathered as soon as possible.

LLOYD G. HUMPHREYS, *Associate Professor of Psychology, Stanford University, Stanford, California.*

The factor analysis research concerning the organization of abilities and the subsequent use of tests measuring separate abilities in industrial and military psychology led directly to the development of the *Differential Aptitude Tests*

(DAT). This battery was designed as a unit and has been standardized and validated as such. Users will normally want, therefore, to use the entire battery.

It will be noted from the list of test names that the final selection of materials represented a compromise between a straight "primary mental abilities" battery and the more familiar kinds of tests, such as clerical speed and accuracy.

The publisher has done and is continuing to do a careful professional job with these tests. There are many assets. In only one place in the manual does the desire to inform become overpowered by other motives. In presenting case reports for which IQ's and DAT scores were available, many of the cases were selected for the discrepancy between the IQ and the mean battery score. The authors must have searched for some time, for example, for the girl with an IQ of 97, supposedly the result of repeated examinations, and with superior scores on every test of the DAT. Only rarely would a discrepancy this large occur by chance if the intelligence tests were standard verbal tests and were given by trained examiners. More importantly, such cases do not illustrate the advantages to be gained from testing *separate* aptitudes.

The manual is complete and detailed and in loose-leaf form so that new material can readily be added. It is gratifying to report that new material *is* constantly being added. The reliabilities on individual tests are satisfactory and determined in a reasonably conservative fashion. If individual tests are weighted into composites, the reported reliabilities are more than adequate. Reliabilities are also reported for each grade level in which use of the test is recommended.

Many validity data, mostly follow-up, have now been reported. The publishers have presented the zero correlations along with the high ones for the schools where data were obtained and have consolidated the information obtained from many small samples, giving the test user more stable values for the various validity coefficients.

The norms are far better than those available for most tests. The numbers are large and well distributed by grade, sex, and school. Thirty different schools from several geographical sections and from communities of different sizes are represented. (Norms with a broader geographical basis are promised for the near future.) Percentile ranks are provided, but the profile form places these ranks as they would fall on a normal curve. A rule is also provided, when this profile form is used, for deciding on the probable degree of significance of differences between scores.

There are a few things to report on the liability side of the ledger. For efficiency in differential prediction, it is desirable to have a battery with low intercorrelations. While the intercorrelations among the tests in the present battery are low enough to make the battery useful, they are not as low as possible. Purer tests than several of those used here are available.

The reviewer likes to see correlations reported with other tests, particularly with competing tests. For this battery, for example, one would like to see the correlations with the Thurstone *Primary Mental Abilities*. No correlations of this type appear in the manual. (An announcement arrived as this was written concerning the early appearance of these correlations.)

A more important omission is the failure to come to grips with the problem of interpreting tests from a profile. How does the guidance worker make use of the information supplied on the significance of differences between separate scores? It is *not* obvious that with information concerning significance of differences and knowledge of validity coefficients of the individual tests the counselor can reach valid decisions from the battery as a whole. Perhaps the next step is to supply regression equations for these tests where the data permit. (A discussion of this problem has recently been announced for early publication.)

For an excerpt from a review, see 3:620.

[712]

★**Factored Aptitude Series.** Adults; 1947–50; 14 tests; battery manual ('48); norms ('50); $4.25 per 50 of any test; $2 per specimen set; $1 per specimen set of any one test; postpaid; Joseph E. King; Industrial Psychology, Inc. *
a) OFFICE TERMS. 1947–50; 1 form, '47; 5(8) minutes.
b) SALES TERMS. 1948–50; 1 form, '48; 5(8) minutes.
c) TOOLS. 1948–50; 1 form, '48; 5(8) minutes.
d) JUDGMENT. 1947–50; 1 form, '47; 5(8) minutes.
e) NUMBERS. 1947–50; 1 form, '47; 5(8) minutes.
f) PERCEPTION. 1947–50; 1 form, '47; 5(8) minutes.
g) PRECISION. 1948–50; 1 form, '48; 5(8) minutes.
h) FLUENCY. 1947–50; 1 form, '47; 6(9) minutes.
i) MEMORY. 1948–50; 1 form, '48; 5(8) minutes.
j) DIMENSION. 1948–50; 1 form, '48; 5(8) minutes.
k) PARTS. 1949–50; 1 form, '49; 5(8) minutes.
l) BLOCKS. 1949–50; 1 form, '49; 5(8) minutes.
m) DEXTERITY. 1949–50; 1 form, '49; 3(5) minutes.
n) MOTOR. 1948–50; 1 form, '48; $20 per set of testing apparatus; 6(10) minutes.

REFERENCES

1. KING, JOSEPH E. "The Perception Factor in Industrial Testing." Abstract. *Am Psychol* 5:331 Jl '50. * (*PA* 25:1300, title only)

Differential Aptitude Tests

D. WELTY LEFEVER, *Professor of Education, University of Southern California, Los Angeles, California.*

The *Factored Aptitude Series* is, as the name implies, a collection of tests based on the findings of factor analysis. With two exceptions, each test requires five minutes for administration. Eight major factors of intelligence were selected as the basic framework for the battery. These include comprehension, reasoning, systems, perception, fluency, memory, space relations, and coordination. The eight factors are sampled by means of 14 separate measures, each of which is a 2-page paper and pencil test (the Motor test requires special apparatus).

The series of tests is intended to be used in different combinations to predict success in a variety of job areas. For example, for junior clerk, the applicant takes the tests Office Terms, Numbers, and Perception; a candidate for a job as an inspector is given these "factored aptitude" tests: Tools, Precision, Parts, Blocks, and Dimension.

Raw scores are converted to stanines and are recorded on a "qualification grid" designed for each job area. The grid indicates the weights for predicting success on the job to be assigned to the several possible stanine values for each test. These weights are not always directly proportional to the test score since some applicants may show too much aptitude for the job assignment under consideration.

The author states that the aptitude series will aid management in making decisions about hiring new workers, transferring employees to job assignments for which they may be better fitted, planning the training program, assigning job duties, checking on the quality of work done in relation to aptitude or work potential, promoting employees to more complex jobs requiring greater and possibly different aptitudes, and determining staff reductions.

STRONG POINTS. (*a*) The author provides a broad base for operations by recognizing that aptitude tests must be used as "one of the many tools and sources of information for personnel planning. Aptitude tests are by no means advocated to replace the interview, personal history check, supervisor judgment, other personnel methods." (*b*) The listing of the names and publishers of other well known standardized aptitude tests indicates a less narrowly competitive attitude than characterizes some authors. (*c*) Several tests in the series employ pictorial rather than verbalized contents on the assumption that where language is not essential to job success it should not dominate the aptitude measure. Greater face validity is gained by the use of pictures of tools, photographs of personnel, and sketches of plant operations. (*d*) The need for each applicant to study his profile of test scores in relation to his own pattern of success is emphasized. Intrapersonal comparisons sometimes produce better mental hygiene and more effective vocational guidance than does the usual interpersonal analysis. (*e*) Considerable attention is given to the problem of the "overqualified" applicant whose potential may be too high for the particular job for which he is being tested. Too much ability can be the source not only of dissatisfaction but of serious inefficiency. (*f*) The design and printing of the tests and manuals are outstanding. (*g*) The general explanation of basic theory of the testing instruments and of the techniques of interpretation and use is exceptionally clear. The author has succeeded in selling his aptitude series with unusual effectiveness.

WEAK POINTS. (*a*) The manual does not present an adequate statement concerning the present limitations of aptitude tests as predictors of job success. The fact that the manual was written in a semipopular style for the administrative and personnel staff of business and industry does not excuse the author for rather vague statements implying a high order of predictive precision for the series. In the 1948 edition of the handbook he states that the study of aptitude test prediction "has quite conclusively shown that....job performance can be predicted by knowing an employee's scores on the pertinent aptitudes." Definite indications of the large errors frequently found in prediction studies should accompany such statements. It is not fair to present a few exceptionally favorable examples of aptitude test validation. This "sin of omission" is partially offset by the following quotation from the 1948 handbook: "The tools and methods of personnel measurement admittedly require a good deal of further development. They are by no means a complete answer to questions about personnel, nor will they ever be." (*b*) More direct research evidence should be presented in support of the assertions regarding the relationship of test data to the pattern of performance on the job. In the judgment of this reviewer, the general literature of industrial psychology does not support the sweeping implications of the author's discussion. For example, how were

the weights determined that were assigned to the several stanine values in the "qualification grid," and what is the order of precision involved in their use? (*c*) A strong research foundation should be offered for such broad generalizations as: "The Q_3 (well-qualified) employee pays off double (his salary and overhead) for the company." The Q_2 (average qualified) shows "productivity roughly one and one-half times his salary and overhead expense." In the absence of any supporting data, it seems highly probable to this reviewer that such ratios of productivity to cost would vary greatly with different job areas, kinds of businesses, and management policies. (*d*) The composition of the "total employed population" on which norms were established seems rather arbitrary, and the proportions of job areas represented somewhat fortuitous. (*e*) The handbook should report more specifically the data on the reliability of the tests. In the 1948 edition complete information is given for the Sales Terms test, but only one measure of reliability for each of the other tests is presented as the diagonal values of an intercorrelation matrix. Presumably, these are coefficients derived by the odd-even procedure. Since it seems quite probable (from personal observation) that most of the tests in the *Factored Aptitude Series* will show a fairly large portion of unattempted items for the average applicant, the reliability measures should consist of test-retest correlations or coefficients computed between alternate forms. Speeded tests are very likely to produce odd-even correlations that are spuriously high. The only complete data (for the Sales Terms test) show the test-retest correlation to be .81 compared with .91 for the odd-even determination.

SUMMARY. The *Factored Aptitude Series* gives evidence of careful design and thoughtful development. The test booklets, the manual, and the technical notes are exceptionally attractive and readable and produce a decided effect of face validity. Apparently, a considerable amount of thorough research has gone into the project. The general pattern of factors employed as the guiding framework for the series seems to furnish a worthwhile basis for a first class battery of aptitude measures.

In the judgment of this reviewer, the optimism of the handbook and brochures should be tempered by more definite and frequent reference to actual research and to the inherent limitations of aptitude tests for predicting job success.

Factored Aptitude Series

The few validation studies cited appear to include the more favorable examples of predictive accuracy. The aptitude series shows excellent possibilities and deserves a more complete and openly frank exposition in the manuals designed for general use.

J Consult Psychol 13:66–7 F '49. Laurance F. Shaffer. * No data on validity are given in the manual, but figures supplied by the author indicate some differentiations between jobs in a hierarchy, and between employees rated as successful and unsuccessful. * With their attractive formats and ingenious conveniences of administration and scoring, these tests will appeal to industrial clients. A critical evaluation, however, must await additional evidence of their validity.

[713]

Fife Tests of Ability. Entrants to secondary schools (England and Scotland); 1947; 4 tests (also listed separately); 1 form ['47]; no data on reliability; no data on validity in manuals (for data presented elsewhere by the author, see 1–2); manuals ['47]; 5d. per single copy of any one test; 4d. per manual of any one test; specimen set not available; postage extra; 165 (185) minutes; Frank M. Earle; University of London Press Ltd. *
a) TEST 1, ABILITY FOR ENGLISH (LANGUAGE). 6s. per 25; 30(35) minutes.
b) TEST 2, ABILITY FOR SCIENCE. 6s. per 25; 30(35) minutes.
c) TEST 3, ABILITY FOR ALGEBRA. 5s. 6d. per 25; 60(65) minutes.
d) TEST 4, ABILITY FOR GEOMETRY. 5s. 6d. per 25; 45 (50) minutes.

REFERENCES
1. EARLE, FRANK M. *Tests of Ability for Secondary School Courses.* Publications of the Scottish Council for Research in Education, No. 10. London: University of London Press, 1936. Pp. xiii, 138. *
2. EARLE, FRANK M. *Reconstruction in the Secondary School.* London: University of London Press, 1944. Pp. 188. *
3. WILSON, JAMES T. *A Consideration of the Ability for Algebra Shown by Secondary School Entrants.* Bachelor's thesis, Glasgow University (Glasgow, Scotland), 1949. Abstract: *Brit J Ed Psychol* 20:65–6 F '50. * (PA 25:570, title only)

I. MACFARLANE SMITH, *Officer-in-Charge of the Tests Division, National Foundation for Educational Research in England and Wales, London, England.*

It is now nearly twenty years since the Scottish Council for Research in Education sponsored an investigation into tests of ability for secondary school courses. Its report, by Frank M. Earle (1), published in 1936, contained four tests in an appendix. These were: Test of Ability in the Use of Words, Test of Ability in Science, Test of Ability in Algebra, and Test of Ability in Geometry. The *Fife Tests of Ability* are substantially the same as these. Some of the more difficult words have been omitted from the vocabulary section of the Test of Ability in the Use

of Words, and the test has been renamed Test of Ability for English (Language). Some minor alterations have also been made in the Test of Ability for Geometry, but the form now published is essentially the same as that printed in the 1936 report.

These tests were devised for use with pupils just commencing a secondary course, in the hope that they might help the school administrator to differentiate between those who would probably achieve a satisfactory standard of attainment in subjects cognate to the tests and those who would be unlikely to reach the required standard. It was assumed that the abilities required for the various school subjects depend not only on the presence of a general factor but also on certain group factors. In the construction of the tests, 22 draft tests were prepared from material commonly used in intelligence tests and given to about 400 children. The scores were then correlated with marks in various school subjects. The Fife tests were prepared from this material by putting together subtests which correlated most highly with individual subjects. The extent to which Dr. Earle's aim has been achieved can be gauged from the follow-up data accumulated over a period of nearly 10 years and published in an appendix to his book, *Reconstruction in the Secondary School* (2).

The tests were validated by being administered to some 1,500 Scottish pupils early in the first year of the secondary school course. Scores were also obtained for a smaller number of English pupils. The criterion adopted was the standard of attainment expected for the Junior Certificate (three years) in Scotland, and the School Certificate (four years) in England. Thus, for the Test of Ability in the Use of Words, follow-up data are given for six different years in one school in Scotland, and for 10 different schools in one year in England. From an analysis of the performance of these pupils in the Certificate Examinations, estimates were made of the probability that a pupil who gained a particular score would pass the Junior Certificate Examination in Scotland or the School Certificate Examination in England. It was also possible to find a "critical score," by means of which the number of errors made in forecasting success or failure was reduced to a minimum. The availability of extensive follow-up data is one of the great merits of the Fife tests. Few tests have been so systematically followed up over such a long period. The figures show, however, that the four tests are not of equal predictive value. When the Test of Ability for English (Language) was administered to pupils who had been selected for a secondary course and whose intention to complete the course remained unchanged, a critical score was found which, over six years, gave an average number of errors of only 10 per cent of the forecasts. For the Tests of Ability for Geometry and for Science, however, the figures showed a higher percentage of errors. Because of recent changes which have taken place in the character of the School Certificate Examinations, the tables showing probabilities of passing or failing certain examinations are now of less practical value to teachers than they were some years ago.

There are several defects which are common to all four tests. In none of them are the sections timed separately, and there is a strong probability that many pupils will not reach the later sections in the time allowed. No attempt has been made to arrange the layout of the marking keys in a form convenient for marking. Most answers are arranged closely in rows instead of in columns, and in some sections they are not even numbered to correspond with the items.

The norms for all four tests show marked irregularities in the relation between score and age. The upper and lower quartile scores of Scottish children in the Ability for Geometry Test are 87 and 60 for the age 11–6, while the corresponding figures for the age 12–9 are 68 and 42. It would appear that older children in the sample of first year pupils tested tend to be less intelligent than younger pupils. There is a similar tendency in the norms for the other tests, but it is much less marked in the norms for English children. A peculiar feature of the norms for the Ability for Geometry Test is the fact that English girls obtain very much higher scores than Scottish girls of the same age. It is difficult to account for this anomaly, except by supposing that different standards of marking have been employed. Information on the reliability coefficients of the tests would be of interest and should be included in future editions of the manuals. Apparently, the only available data on reliability are figures based on small groups, reported in Earle's first publication. Two of the tests were administered again after 16 months and the test-retest correlations were found to be: Test of Ability for Algebra, $r = .785$ (N = 48);

and Test of Ability in the Use of Words, $r = .77$ (N = 31), and $r = .72$ (N = 36).

TEST 1, ABILITY FOR ENGLISH (LANGUAGE). This test contains five sections: Vocabulary, Word Pairing, Sentence Completion, Paragraph Completion, and Sentence Construction. The possible score is 225, and the time limit is 30 minutes. The test appears to be unduly difficult, since the norms show that the upper quartile score is usually less than half the total possible score. The Word Pairing section is open to criticism on the ground that many of the items are ambiguous. For example, the pupil is required to underline the word which makes the best pair with "hazardous" from voyage, adventure, attempt, storm. The answer given is "adventure," but surely a voyage might also be hazardous. The marking of the items in the Sentence Construction section is subjective, and the manual does not give examples to help the marker to decide between satisfactory and unsatisfactory responses.

TEST 2, ABILITY FOR SCIENCE. This test is in six sections. The first involves arrangement in order of size, the second and third involve classification, the fourth consists of analogies, the fifth of multiple choice sentence completion, and the sixth of logical reasoning. The possible score is 180, and the time limit is 30 minutes. The standard of difficulty is appropriate, the median scores being somewhat above half the possible score. Most of the items are standard types used in intelligence tests, and all are objectively marked. Apart from the fact that the first section lays emphasis on a knowledge of tables (of length, capacity, etc.), it is difficult to find anything in the content of the test to lead one to expect it to have specific predictive value for courses in science.

TEST 3, ABILITY FOR ALGEBRA. This test consists of two sections: Number Series Completion and Problems involving arithmetical processes, substitution in formulae, and symbolic expression. The possible score is 120, and the time limit is one hour. The manual recommends that this test, like the others, be given between the second week and the fifth week of the first term of a grammar school course; yet many of the examples are decidedly too difficult for pupils who have only just begun the study of algebra. Some of those on substitution or symbolic representation would be more suitable for second year pupils. That the test as a whole is too difficult is evident from the norms, the upper quartile scores being considerably less than half the total possible score. Since formal knowledge of algebra is required, pupils who have received some introduction to algebra before leaving the primary school would certainly have an advantage in working the latter part of the test.

TEST 4, ABILITY FOR GEOMETRY. This test contains six sections based on diagrammatic material and originally described by Earle as tests of Form Perception and Form Analysis. The possible score is 160, and the time limit is 45 minutes. Some of the sections are what would now be termed spatial tests. The last section, for example, is a Fitting Shapes test of the creative response type and has, probably, a considerable spatial loading. The first two sections, however, probably require very little spatial ability but have the advantage that the marking is completely objective. There is considerable subjectivity in the marking of the last four sections, and the marking key gives little or no guidance to the marker. Many items require answers in the form of sketches or of lines drawn on diagrams, and most of these have alternative solutions. For three of the sections the only instructions given are that each figure is evaluated according to the conditions prescribed and that any solution which adequately satisfies the conditions is accepted. The lack of precision of these instructions is a serious weakness of the test. The provision of a key containing possible alternative solutions and showing samples of acceptable and unacceptable responses would have increased the reliability of the test as well as greatly facilitated the marking.

SUMMARY. In assessing the value of the tests as a whole, it must be borne in mind that they were originally prepared at a time when factor analysis as now understood was in its infancy, when methods of test construction were less advanced than they are now, and when many British psychologists minimised the importance of group factors. Subsequent research in the field of spatial ability has tended to justify Earle's attempt to assess aptitude for geometry at the age of 11, but there is less certainty about the existence of abilities additional to "g" for algebra or for science. Thus, the Fife tests should be regarded as the outcome of pioneering research on educational abilities. No doubt, the experience gained in the development and follow-up of the Fife tests has been fully utilised by Earle in the

preparation of his more recent *Duplex Series of Ability Tests*. The latter appear to be based on a somewhat different classification of abilities, and the results are intended to be used in a different way, but it is clear that the Duplex tests represent a very considerable advance on the Fife tests. It would be of great interest to have the results of a factor analysis of a comprehensive battery containing both the Fife and the Duplex tests.

For a review by William G. Mollenkopf of Test 3, see 380; for a review by James Maxwell, see 3:8.

[714]

★**General Aptitude Test Battery.** Ages 16 and over; 1946–47; a test battery developed in conjunction with the occupational counseling services of the United States Employment Service and released for general use in 1948; titles on test booklets are *GATB, Book I* and *GATB, Book II;* 10 scores: intelligence, verbal aptitude, numerical aptitude, spatial aptitude, form perception, clerical perception, eye-hand coordination, motor speed, finger dexterity, manual dexterity; 15 tests: 11 tests in 2 booklets and 4 performance tests; 1 form, '46; manual in 2 booklets ('47); tests available to nonprofit institutions for counseling purposes; subtests available to employers as separates in specific aptitude batteries for selection and placement of their own employees; testing services free of charge when program is conducted through the facilities of the U.S.E.S.; institutions and employers using their own facilities must purchase tests and employ testing supervisors trained by U.S.E.S.; details may be secured from local and state offices, through which all orders must be cleared; (135) minutes; United States Employment Service, Bureau of Employment Security, U.S. Department of Labor. *

a) BOOK I. $15 per 100, postpaid; U.S. Government Printing Office.
b) BOOK II. $12.50 per 100, postpaid; U.S. Government Printing Office.
c) PEGBOARD. $18.50 per set of testing materials, postage extra; distributed by Specialty Case Manufacturing Co. and Warwick Products Co.
d) FINGER DEXTERITY BOARD. $8.65 per set of testing materials, postage extra; distributed by Specialty Case Manufacturing Co. and Warwick Products Co.

REFERENCES

1. WAR MANPOWER COMMISSION, DIVISION OF OCCUPATIONAL ANALYSIS, STAFF. "Factor Analysis of Occupational Aptitude Tests." *Ed & Psychol Meas* 5:147–55 su '45. * (PA 20:1242)
2. DVORAK, BEATRICE J. "The New USES General Aptitude Test Battery." *J Appl Psychol* 31:372–6 Ag '47. * (PA 22:1939)
3. DVORAK, BEATRICE J. "The New U.S.E.S. General Aptitude Test Battery." *Occupations* 26:42–4 O '47. * (PA 22:1459)
4. ORR, BERNARD. "The General Aptitude Test Battery." *Sch & Col Place* 8:52–5 D '47. *
5. U.S. EMPLOYMENT SERVICE, DIVISION OF OCCUPATIONAL ANALYSIS AND INDUSTRIAL SERVICES DIVISION. "Aptitude Battery—No Ordinary Test." *Empl Service R* 14:14–5 Ap '47. *
6. RALPH, SALLY. *The Prediction of Success in the College of Pharmacy at the University of Utah.* Master's thesis, University of Utah (Salt Lake City, Utah), 1948.
7. RENICK, C. P. "Testing and Counseling in a Penal Institution." *Empl Security R* 15:8–9 D '48. * (PA 24:707)
8. WATSON, G. E., AND TRIPLETT, BERNICE. "Testing and Counseling for Rural Youth." *Empl Security R* 15:23 D '48. * (PA 24:672)
9. BROWN, CHARLES MANLEY. *An Evaluation of the General Aptitude Test Battery as an Instrument for Predicting Success*

in the College of Education. Master's thesis, University of Utah (Salt Lake City, Utah), 1949.

10. MOULY, GEORGE J. *A Study of the United States Employment Service General Aptitude Test Battery, B-1001 for Use on the Population of High School Seniors in the State of Minnesota.* Doctor's thesis, University of Minnesota (Minneapolis, Minn.), 1949.

11. OHIO EMPLOYMENT SERVICE, STATE TESTING STAFF. "A General Aptitude Test Battery Study With High-School Seniors." *Ed & Psychol Meas* 9:281–9 au '49. * (*PA* 26:2799)

12. PETTY, GLENN C. *A Statistical Analysis of the Predictive Efficiency of the General Aptitude Test Battery With Speech and English Students.* Master's thesis, University of Utah (Salt Lake City, Utah), 1949.

13. RALPH, RAY B. *The Predictive Efficiency of the General Aptitude Test Battery in the College of Medicine.* Master's thesis, University of Utah (Salt Lake City, Utah), 1949.

14. ROBINSON, LESLIE GEORGE M. *An Appraisal of the United States Employment Service General Aptitude Test Battery B-1001 for the Grade Ten Population of Minnesota.* Doctor's thesis, University of Minnesota (Minneapolis, Minn.), 1949.

15. SEITZ, MARGARET J. *A Follow-Up Study of the Use of the General Aptitude Test Battery of the United States Employment Service in the Placement of High School Seniors.* Master's thesis, University of Delaware (Newark, Del.), 1949. (*PA* 26:1814, title only)

16. SUPER, DONALD E. *Appraising Vocational Fitness by Means of Psychological Tests,* pp. 358–68. New York: Harper & Brothers, 1949. Pp. xxiii, 727. * (*PA* 24:2130)

17. THURMAN, C. G. *A Statistical Analysis of the Predictive Efficiency of the General Aptitude Test Battery With Biological and Physical Science Students.* Master's thesis, University of Utah (Salt Lake City, Utah), 1949.

18. WESTWOOD, DALE. *Predicting Academic Achievement of Senior Engineers With the General Aptitude Test Battery.* Master's thesis, University of Utah (Salt Lake City, Utah), 1949.

19. WOODHEAD, MARJORIE J. *The Predictive Efficiency of the General Aptitude Test Battery in Social Sciences.* Master's thesis, University of Utah (Salt Lake City, Utah), 1949.

20. BIRD, ROBERT G. *The United States Employment Service General Aptitude Test Battery as a Predictor of Academic Success in Psychology.* Master's thesis, Pennsylvania State College (State College, Pa.), 1950.

21. BISCHOF, LEDFORD JULIUS. *Relationships of General Aptitude Test Battery Scores With Scores on the ACE Psychological Examination for College Freshmen.* Doctor's thesis, Indiana University (Bloomington, Ind.), 1950. (*Thesis Abstract Series,* 1951.) (*PA* 25:7103, title only)

22. GORDAN, OAKLEY J. *A Factor Analysis of Aptitude Achievement, and Studiousness Scores of 233 University College Freshmen.* Master's thesis, University of Utah (Salt Lake City, Utah), 1950.

23. GRANT, WILLIAM VANCE, JR. *The Comparative Value of the General Aptitude Test Battery and the American Council on Education Psychological Examination in Predicting the Quality Point Averages of a Group of Florida State University Students.* Master's thesis, University of Florida (Gainesville, Fla.), 1950.

24. RALPH, RAY B., AND TAYLOR, CALVIN W. "A Comparative Evaluation of the Professional Aptitude Test and the General Aptitude Test Battery." *J Assn Am Med Col* 25:33–40 Ja '50. *

25. REITAN, HENRY MACADIE. *Predictive Value of the General Aptitude Test Battery for Student Success in Engineering.* Doctor's thesis, University of North Dakota (Grand Forks, N.D.), 1950. Review: Hermann F. Buegel. *Sch Ed Rec Univ N Dak* 36:248–51 My '51. *

26. SMITH, WILLIAM R. *The Construction of a Clerical Aptitude Test Battery for the Mountain States Telephone and Telegraph Company.* Master's thesis, University of Utah (Salt Lake City, Utah), 1950.

27. THOMPSON, JOHN W., JR. *An Evaluation of the General Aptitude Test Battery as an Aid in Selecting Architectural Students.* Master's thesis, University of Florida (Gainesville, Fla.), 1950.

28. TIZARD, J.; IN COLLABORATION WITH N. O'CONNOR AND J. M. CRAWFORD. "The Abilities of Adolescent and Adult High-Grade Male Defectives." *J Mental Sci* 96:888–907 O '50. * (*PA* 25:5421)

29. COLMEN, JOSEPH G.; FIEDLER, GOTTHELF O.; AND BLACKBURN, JAMES R. "Identification of Administrative Talent Within a Government Department." Abstract. *Am Psychol* 6:383–4 Jl '51. *

30. GIBSON, ANNE MARIE. *A Study of the Relationship of the General Aptitude Test Battery and Academic Achievement in the School of Business, Indiana University.* Doctor's thesis, Indiana University (Bloomington, Ind.), 1951. (*Thesis Abstract Series....1951,* 1952, pp. 43–9.)

31. O'CONNOR, N., AND TIZARD, J. "Predicting the Occupational Adequacy of Certified Mental Defectives." *Occupational Psychol* 25:205–11 Jl '51. * (*PA* 26:3487)

32. ODELL, C. E.; DVORAK, BEATRICE J.; AND MEIGH, CHARLES. "Role of Testing in Defense Mobilization." *Empl Security R* 18:21–3 Ap '51. *

33. TAYLOR, CALVIN W., AND OTHERS. "General Aptitude Test Battery: Patterns for College Areas." *Occupations* 29:518–26 Ap '51. * (*PA* 25:7696)

MILTON L. BLUM, *Associate Professor of Psychology, The City College, New York, New York.*

According to the United States Employment Service, the *General Aptitude Test Battery* (hereafter referred to as GATB) "is designed to measure several aptitudes which have been found important to success in many occupations." The battery is used primarily as an aid in the more effective placement of applicants who have insufficient job experiences. Various state agencies in cooperation with local school authorities have been extending the application of the battery to the counseling of high school youth.

The battery consists of 15 tests, 11 pencil and paper and 4 apparatus tests. It requires approximately 2¼ to 2½ hours for completion. The actual tests are named A, Tool Matching; B, Name Comparison; C, H Markings; D, Computation; F, Two-Dimensional Space; G, Speed; H, Three-Dimensional Space; I, Arithmetic Reason; J, Vocabulary; K, Mark Making; L, Form Matching; M, Place; N, Turn; O, Assemble; and P, Disassemble.

Most of the tests in the battery are not original. They resemble, with modifications, parts of such familiar tests as the *Minnesota Clerical Test,* the *MacQuarrie Test for Mechanical Ability,* the *Revised Minnesota Paper Formboard Test,* O'Rourke's *Survey Tests of Vocabulary,* and assorted items as usually found in group intelligence tests such as arithmetic computation and reasoning, etc.

It does appear desirable to encourage the use of test batteries in the form of a single test. This procedure has the advantage, at least, of preventing examiners from selecting inadequate single tests and also tends to prevent them from weighting intelligence too heavily in vocational considerations. A similar approach is found in the *Differential Aptitude Tests.*

The reviewer is impressed with the considerable amount of research that *must* have accompanied the development of the GATB. He is annoyed with the lack of availability of the evidence. To the best of his knowledge a complete story has never been told. The published material is spotty, sporadic, overenthusiastic, and decidedly incomplete. It may well be that a considerable portion of the research has not been reduced to reporting according to expected scientific standards. The GATB suffers as a result and compares very unfavorably with the DAT (*Differential Aptitude Tests*). The manual of the *Differential Aptitude Tests* is a masterpiece in comparison with the floundering and incomplete GATB material.

If this review encourages the USES to recognize that it has the same responsibilities as private test publishers, then it will not be in vain. That USES limits its tests to its own group is no excuse. A private counseling outfit, regardless of its reputation, would justifiably be attacked if it administered its own battery and offered little evidence of its scientific acceptability.

Another annoyance in reviewing the GATB is the matter of finding changes without any reference to why such changes occurred. For example, test booklet I contains a test, Test E, that is no longer used. The test is not mentioned in the guide or, for that matter, anywhere else. Obviously, there must have been some reason for its being dropped, but the reviewer can only guess at the reason since no explanation is offered. The test is the usual letter sequence test sometimes found among items in intelligence tests. Whether the directions were inadequate or the test too difficult, whether the test was not related to any of the factors in the GATB or found not to be important to success in any occupation is simply never mentioned.

Another irritation is reference in an early published study (*1*) to a factor "L" but to which no further reference is ever made. Apparently this factor was dropped for good and sufficient reasons, but no indication is ever offered as to why the "L" dropped out.

The GATB emerged after a factor analysis study of 59 different tests administered to 9 different groups in batteries ranging from 15–29 tests. These groups varied; the smallest consisted of 98 persons and the largest comprised 1,079. In all, 2,156 persons in 12 different geographic regions (cities) took the tests. They were all applicants or trainees in different training courses. One may immediately criticize the sample, not only because of the relatively homogeneous nature of the group (students in certain training courses) but also because no females were included.

Thurstone's factor analysis methods were applied to the test results of the above groups, and 10 factors emerged: They are G, Intelligence (measured in Tests H, J and parts of I); V, Verbal (Test J); N, Numerical (Tests D and parts of I); S, Spatial (Tests F, H); P, Form Perception (Tests L, A); Q, Clerical Perception (Test B); A, Aiming—Eye Hand Coordi-

nation (Tests C, K); T, Motor Speed (Tests K, G); F, Finger Dexterity (Tests P, O); and M, Manual Dexterity (Tests M, N).

Although the standardization process of a test battery is more difficult than that for a single test, the same rigid standards must be met. Examining the GATB for evidences of validity, reliability, and norms was not too rewarding. Answers to the most simple basic questions are not readily obtained.

The "Guide to the Use of GATB" consists of two booklets and totals 155 pages. It is really a manual describing the clerical tasks involved in administration, scoring, and interpretation of results. It presents no data on reliability and validity and does not resemble the usual test manual. It categorically states: "This battery is composed of fifteen tests selected because they are good measures of ten aptitudes that have been found to be important to successful job performance on a large number of jobs." It presents tables to convert raw scores to aptitude scores and introduces the concept of Occupational Aptitude Patterns. These OAP's are defined as "The combination or pattern of aptitudes that is required to perform satisfactorily the major tasks of the occupation identified with each pattern." For both aptitude scores and patterns, there is again no evidence either in the guide or elsewhere.

The guide appears to be written for glorified clerks who are expected to follow directions and not ask questions. Nowhere in either of the parts of the guide is there any reference to validity and reliability or even a description of the size of the sample of the population which serves as a basis for the conversion tables.

The guide or manual is merely a collection of directions, directives, and claims without evidence. This would be excusable if a supplement were available concerning the evidence of standardization, but such a compendium is not known to the reviewer and his requests for one were not successful. Furthermore, very little concerning this test battery has been published in professional publications. Apparently quite a bit has been published in mimeographed form by governmental agencies. Such reports as issued by the Bureau of Employment Security of the United States Department of Labor are often labeled "restricted" and this is puzzling to the reviewer. It does seem far fetched to assume that there is a relationship between such research studies and national defense. Insofar as a sam-

General Aptitude Test Battery

ple of such studies was furnished to the reviewer, he is assuming that no national secrets are being divulged by his reference to them. On the other hand, an hypothesis may be offered that these studies are purely experimental, and the use of these tests must be restricted until such time as much needed evidence is available. If this is true, then it does not fit at all with the very wide usage of the test within the agency and state offices, the enthusiastic claims, and the various directives issued.

The few articles published in the literature are brief and leave the reader with many gaps of knowledge. An early publication (1) describes the population from which data were obtained for the factor analysis as well as the determination of the factors. The 2,156 males in the sample were applicants or trainees enrolled in Vocational Education National Defense Training Courses. No information concerning the known occupational success and the extent of the range of occupations of these subjects is reported. A later article states that the Battery is standardized on samples of workers employed in various occupations. It is to be noted that this is quite different from the apparent standardization on the 2,156 trainees. It describes norms developed for 20 fields of work representing approximately 2,000 occupations, but not even a reference to the size of the population in any of the fields of work is presented. The norms are expressed as Occupational Aptitude Patterns and consist of "minimum aptitude scores required for occupations grouped according to the Part IV classification code structure of the *Dictionary of Occupational Titles*. It is claimed that each occupational aptitude pattern consists of minimum scores for only the most significant aptitudes required for the group of occupations covered by that pattern. Minimum scores, ranging from 85 to 130, were established to eliminate approximately the lowest third of the employed sample, but no evidence is presented that these cutoff scores are related to the lowest production group of workers. An example of a pattern is pattern 4, GNSF, with critical scores of 100 on intelligence, numerical ability, and spatial ability and 85 on finger dexterity. Occupations covered by this pattern are those on all-round metal machining and all-round mechanical repairing. Such results in such round numbers are almost too wonderful to believe.

More evidence allowing one to evaluate the establishment of any or all of the occupational ap-

titude patterns should be made available. The reviewer has seen no such evidence. The statement, "The USES Batteries are comprised of critical scores on only those aptitudes which are significant for a particular field of work" is in need of substantiation, especially with reference to the word "significant."

Test reliability is relatively easy to establish. Nevertheless the evidence of reliability of the GATB is paltry. A report based upon 156 cases establishes the test-retest reliability for each factor. The highest reported is .93 for the numerical factor, and the lowest is .81 for the finger dexterity factor. No description of the characteristics of the sample or the length of the time interval between test and retest is offered.

Another formal publication is a study reporting the use of the GATB with high school seniors (11). The battery was given to 439 high school seniors in five different schools. Senior students in commercial courses were found to be highest in P (form perception) and second highest in Q (clerical perception). Senior students in industrial arts and technical courses have S (spatial) as their highest aptitude. Seniors in academic courses are highest in G (intelligence); their V (verbal) is higher than the V of the other two groups. This study can be construed as offering indirect evidence of test battery validity. Another published study with indirect relevance to validity was the use of the GATB with 49 sophomores in a medical college (24). The verbal, spatial, and numerical factors were found to be correlated with grades. Incidentally, the intelligence factor in this study was correlated with grades to a higher degree than the others but was ruled out because it overlapped to a great extent with the other factors. Neither the statistical nor the logical reason for this is clear to the reviewer. It does, however, raise the question of the uniqueness of the factors and their contributions to the various Occupational Aptitude Patterns established.

At least 13 master's theses and 3 doctor's dissertations have been written on various aspects of the GATB. In view of the complexity of this test and much that is unknown, it is easy to predict that this test battery can become the happy hunting ground of graduate degree seekers for many years to come. According to a listing of thesis titles, most are on the predictive aspects and the evaluation of the GATB. The reviewer has read only one such study. It was written by Margaret Jane Seitz of the University of Delaware (*15*). The subjects in the study were 353 high school seniors all of whom voluntarily took the GATB. A follow-up approximately one year later determined that 212 were working. Of this number, job descriptions were available on 117. They were classified as followers if they were working in one of the fields indicated by the OAP, or nonfollowers if not working in the fields. Of this number, 87 were found to be followers and 30 were nonfollowers. The author of the thesis states, "The greater number of followers can in part be explained by the fact that the employment service counselors tried to place the graduates in follower jobs. In addition, each graduate was informed that his chances of success might be more likely in an occupational pattern shown by his GATB." The reviewer believes that this shows conclusively that if you encourage people to be "followers," they will be.

A significant contribution of the thesis indicates that the followers had higher average scores on the Hoppock *Job Satisfaction Blank* than the nonfollowers. This difference is reported as being statistically significant. The followers were also rated more highly by employers. In certain respects, this study can be regarded as evidence for the validity of the GATB as a counseling instrument.

Norms for the GATB are reported in a mimeographed leaflet of four pages. Actually, the total population consists of only 519 persons (70 males and 449 females) ; their mean age is 30.4, and their mean education is 11 years. The statement "the sample used is large and varied enough to serve as a general population" is typical of the overenthusiastic claims made in connection with the GATB. It is extremely doubtful whether this sample is large enough, and the fact that it is varied, while admittedly true, only complicates matters insofar as its projection to a general population is concerned. The 519 subjects were drawn from 22 samples. The two largest consisted of 56 "laborers, process (drug prep.)" from Berkeley, California and 47 grocery checkers from Detroit, Michigan. The two smallest samples consisted of three tabulating machine operators from Los Angeles and five electrician apprentices from Newport, Rhode Island. The median sampling size was 25. A statement is made : "The norms shown in Table II should be used as the base population for interpretation of General Aptitude Test Battery data until a more representative population can be obtained."

The criticism is obvious. This sample is totally inadequate for nationwide testing and such directives are certainly out of order. It is possible that field office interpretations based upon such inadequate norms are given too much weight. This reviewer has also seen seven technical reports all labeled "restricted." These reports have the dual purpose of developing a specific aptitude test battery and securing additional data for standardizing the GATB. Apparently employers who use the USES facilities to help them solve their selection problems are given the opportunity to have some of their employees take parts of the GATB. These studies report the relation between test results and certain job criteria and result in still another concept known as Specific Aptitude Test Batteries. These are always parts of the GATB. All reports are rather positive in their recommendations. They indicate that certain parts of GATB would have eliminated a high percentage of failures and included a high percentage of successes. Some of these technical reports can not be considered as scientific despite the statistical analysis conducted. "Feeling" apparently enters into the selection of tests. A brief quote from one of the reports is as follows : "Although D had a relatively high mean and significant correlation, it was not selected as it was felt that test I reflected numerical ability to a higher degree and also measured intelligence." There is no standardized procedure in the selection of tests for the variety of aptitude test batteries obtained. Sometimes it appears as if tests are selected on the basis of job descriptions. That is, the job analysis requirements are compared with what the test is supposedly measuring and, for example, if the clerical component is high, the clerical perception factor or name checking test is selected.

Other evidence of a statistical nature is the correlation between the test results and the job criterion ; or, sometimes, the comparison between the mean of the test results on the tested sample and the mean of the test results on the general population. These technical reports are written by people with wide differences in training and background in testing, and consequently some are rather poor. Characteristic of virtually all of these reports is an enthusiastic positivism not warranted by the evidence.

In summary, the reviewer believes that the GATB is a test battery with some promise. It must be regarded as purely in the experimental stage, and during this period the enthusiasm of

General Aptitude Test Battery

those who work with the instrument should be tempered by the understanding that there is great need for much work to be done. Efforts should be made to publish in clear and certain terms the basis for the Occupational Aptitude Patterns. A better and more realistic set of norms based upon a truly general population should be made available. Time should be taken to present adequate evidence on the reliability of this instrument. Considerable evidence is needed on the validation processes both with respect to occupational groups and with respect to the use of this battery as a counseling instrument. In all sincerity, the reviewer, adopting the enthusiasm of those who are working with this instrument, has the "feeling" that this may very well be a good test battery. However, he is certain that he has not seen the evidence.

EDWARD B. GREENE, *Educational Supervisor, Department of Supervisory Training, Chrysler Corporation, Detroit, Michigan.*

Eleven of the tests are paper and pencil tests with written and oral directions. Their range of difficulty makes them applicable to all adults who can read and understand English and handle paper and pencil situations. While no age or grade equivalents have been issued, the tests seem unsuitable for individuals with less than fifth grade accomplishment. Four of the tests require manipulation of pegs or small washers and rivets; language is a small factor in understanding the test directions. No attempt was made to have these tests look like worksamples, but they were designed to indicate the aptitudes likely to be required in successful job performance. Since all the tests are timed so that very few in a group are able to finish a test in the time allowed, speed is an important factor.

The GATB is now administered without cost to applicants who might benefit from it at the larger state employment offices throughout the country. The test forms have been made available at cost to private employers who have agreed to use only well trained examiners, to keep the test forms closely restricted, and to give the U.S. Employment Service the results of test programs. About 300 employers have already used the GATB under these conditions. A larger number of employers have requested the Employment Service to screen applicants by tests before referring them for employment.

The writer has compared the *General Aptitude Test Battery* with two other similarly prepared tests, the *Chicago Tests of Primary Mental Abilities* and the *Guilford-Zimmerman Aptitude Survey.* The three have fairly comparable sections on vocabulary, arithmetic computations, reasoning (represented by arithmetic reasoning in the GATB and the Guilford-Zimmerman), and two-dimensional space relations. The GATB and the Guilford-Zimmerman test both contain tests of form perception and three-dimensional space. Each battery has some unique parts: the PMA has word fluency and immediate memory tests, the Guilford-Zimmerman includes a measure of mechanical knowledge, and the GATB contains clerical perception, motor speed, eye-hand coordination, and dexterity tests. The overall testing time, including time for administration and practice, is about 2 hours for the PMA, $2\frac{1}{4}$ hours for the GATB, and $3\frac{1}{4}$ hours for the Guilford-Zimmerman. The Guilford-Zimmerman is thus longer than the other two and not so dependent on speed. No careful studies comparing these batteries have yet appeared, but it is probable that the similar parts will give similar results.

Only a few validation studies of the GATB have appeared. Ralph and Taylor (*24*) report correlations, based on 49 students, between total grade-point averages for five quarters of medical school work and the scores on the GATB taken near the end of the sophomore year. Four aptitudes—verbal, numerical, spatial, and form perception—were selected because the medical students had means on these tests at least one standard deviation above those for the adult sample and because these tests showed the highest correlations, about .40, with grade-point averages. Using the first three of these four tests, a multiple correlation (Wherry-Doolittle) of .55 with a standard error of .11 was found. The standard error of estimate was .4 grade points, and about 30 per cent of the variance in the criterion was accounted for by the three aptitude measures. These figures were somewhat higher than those from the *Medical College Admission Test,* given a year and a half earlier and used in part for the selection of students. The effect of the time interval here may be important.

A USES report gives validation figures for 134 survey workers (clerical) of the Bureau of Labor Statistics. The criteria were combined rank order ratings of various supervisors on quality and quantity of work and overall proficiency. Four aptitudes showed the highest tetrachoric correlations with the criteria: intelligence, verbal, numerical, and clerical perception. A total score which had a tetrachoric correlation of .56 with the criteria was secured.

Another USES report compares test scores with supervisor's ratings on a 4-point scale of overall proficiency for 81 experienced and 27 inexperienced insurance underwriters. A final battery of three tests—Name Comparison, Arithmetic Reasoning, and Vocabulary—yields a tetrachoric correlation of .57 with the criterion among experienced workers and .76 among the inexperienced.

Another USES study reports a tetrachoric correlation of .45 with a standard error of .17 between average piece-rate earnings for two weeks of 91 mounters of filaments for electric lamps and a battery of four aptitudes, Form Perception, Aiming, Finger Dexterity, and Manual Dexterity.

Several criticisms of the *General Aptitude Test Battery* can be made; all of them can be remedied by the designers or by future studies. (*a*) The test forms are expensive: at present no answer sheets are used, and each complete test requires 72 pages. (*b*) There are too many tests. Similar results would probably be secured from about 9 good tests instead of the present 11 short paper and pencil tests and 4 performance tests. The administration of so many short speed tests is expensive and leads to errors. (*c*) Some important skills, such as mechanical relations, reasoning, and fluency, as well as tests of technical knowledge, are omitted. The test of litterary vocabulary should probably be made more general. (*d*) The scoring and conversion of scores to standard scores is unreasonably time consuming. It could easily be done in profile tables. (*e*) The designation of both tests and aptitudes by capital letters is confusing; in fact, the use of both terms seems unnecessary. (*f*) The selection of test batteries for particular occupations or Occupational Aptitude Profiles seems to have been rather arbitrarily made by inspection of job analyses and rough validity correlations. It could be improved by more analytical job analyses and more adequate statistical validation. (*g*) The distribution of 2,000 job titles under 20 OAP's leaves one wondering exactly how the classification was made. The selection of workers to be used in establishing occupational norms is a persistent problem, and there is no evidence at hand to show how adequately this has been done. Specifically, evidence should be secured and published to show what proportion of the workers used in establishing norms have skills or knowledge considerably in excess of that needed for satisfactory performance of their work. For instance, the writer has found a considerable proportion of sales clerks who have vocabulary, grammar, and number skills far in excess of that needed on the job. In almost any occupational group there are persons who have skills *not* needed or used on the job. To include these persons in groups used to establish norms will raise the critical or cutoff score above a reasonable level. This seems to the writer to have occurred in quite a number of OAP's. (*h*) The use of the 33rd centile of a group as the cutoff score is questionable. Evidence should be found to show what proportion of the tested group was doing unsatisfactory work because of inability. In many instances workers are rated as unsatisfactory because of emotional or adjustment difficulties, not because of mental or physical ability. To set a cutoff score at the 33rd centile may result in eliminating the steadiest and most useful workers, particularly among routine jobs. (*i*) The use of the battery for counseling applicants or high school students is not yet supported by good norms or validation studies. Much more work is needed to show how well preemployment tests will predict success on a job a year or more later. (*j*) There should be a very determined effort to avoid the use of *overall* ratings of performance for criteria when it is obvious that quite unrelated skills and attitudes are combined in unknown quantities in such ratings. More analytical ratings can and must be secured if such an analytical battery is ever to be validated. The use of general or overall criteria will lead to excluding very important aspects in rating and in corresponding aptitude tests. (*k*) The use of the battery for selection of experienced workers has justification, particularly when the battery is pretested on a group of carefully selected, experienced workers. However, the use of the battery on inexperienced applicants is certainly justified at this time only as an experiment. The harm that can be done to applicants and employers by use of such tests for selection of inexperienced workers is probably very great, since it may result in exclusion of a variety of workers who are needed for routine work as well as for elasticity and growth of an organization.

There are several points on the credit side of the ledger: (*a*) The GATB is essentially sound in its rationale and planning, except as noted above. (*b*) It is probably as valid as most other tests now used for counseling and selection, few of which are well validated. (*c*) It has the support of a large Federal agency, and it should therefore have a continuous growth toward more accuracy and economy and better prediction. There are probably in existence today a considerable number of validation studies of the GATB and additional norms for high school and college groups which are not yet available in print.

HOWARD R. TAYLOR, *Professor of Psychology and Head of the Department, University of Oregon, Eugene, Oregon.*

To have a battery of 15 tests, various combinations of which will measure 10 basic aptitudes for 20 fields of work including approximately 2,000 of the occupations classified in the *Dictionary of Occupational Titles* (DOT), is more than most psychologists concerned with placement or vocational guidance would have dared to hope for. This does not imply, of course, that organizations using tests to hire employees will no longer need to validate these tests against their own specific criteria of success on the job. But in the general situation of searching for the best available person to fill a job as typically defined, or of finding the type of work for which an applicant is best qualified, the *General Aptitude Test Battery* (GATB) gives promise of exceptional versatility and dependability.

Occupational success in such diverse job families as creative writing; structural, mechanical, and electrical engineering; metal machining; mechanical repairing; routine recording work; plumbing; and carpentry; etc., can be forecast to advantage from a pattern of two to four aptitude scores. Predictions of grades in medical school based on the verbal, numerical, and spatial aptitudes have been shown to be more accurate than those based on the Moss *Scholastic Aptitude Test* or the new *Medical College Admission Test,* formerly called the *Professional Aptitude Test,* both of which were specifically designed for such use. The test battery and the aptitude scores derived from it are outcomes of extensive factor analysis studies. In all, 59 different tests were tried out in 9 combinations with groups of male subjects ranging in size from 98 to 1,079, in age from 17 to 39 years, and with an average of 11 years of schooling. Most of the subjects were from vocational education training courses in 12 cities located in various regions of the United States. Approximately 5 per cent were Negroes. The minimum number of factors which would explain the obtained correlations between the tests in each group were determined by the centroid (Thurstone) method. An orthogonal structure was imposed on each group; the resulting factors proved to be consistent between groups as well as with the results of previous investigations. The final selection of 10 aptitudes was made in terms of occupational validity.

By means of conversion tables in the manual, raw scores are converted to standard scores so scaled that the general population average is 100 and the standard deviation 20. Minimum scores for occupations in each of the 20 job families have been set to eliminate the lowest third of the employed sample.

All 15 tests can be administered in little over 2 hours. It is, obviously, assumed that the administration and use of the tests will be restricted to technically trained personnel. Given reasonable familiarity with the occupational classifications of the DOT they will find the manuals comprehensive, well organized and clearly written. The standardization of Occupational Aptitude Patterns in a form corresponding closely to the Entry Occupational Classifications of Part IV of the *Dictionary of Occupational Titles* has many advantages for practical use.

The test-retest reliability of the separate aptitudes has been reported by the USES with no identification of their source except that the coefficients were computed from local office applicant populations ($N = 156$). These coefficients are G, Intelligence, .89; V, Verbal, .90; N, Numerical, .93; S, Spatial, .87; P, Form Perception, .82; Q, Clerical Perception, .91; A, Aiming, .88; T, Motor Speed, .91; F, Finger Dexterity, .81; and M, Manual Dexterity, .86. Only five of the aptitudes are measured with the precision ($r = .90$) usually considered essential for appraisals of individual capacity, two are definitely lower, and the other three are perhaps borderline. Moreover, since these are test-retest correlations, they are to some extent overestimates of actual reliability; and, if there are appreciable correlations between aptitudes, the accuracy with which an individual's relative strengths and weaknesses can be diagnosed will be still further restricted.

Unfortunately, no table of the correlations between factors has been published. It might be presumed, of course, that the factor analysis on

General Aptitude Test Battery

which they were based would insure their independence; but several have such heavy factor loadings from the same tests that considerable commonality seems certain. In a study of 216 student nurses, the intercorrelations of factors G, V, N, and Q are given; they are all positive and range from .29 to .69. Hence, the assumption that the battery provides measurements of unique traits is questionable. Nevertheless, the reviewer believes that these deficiencies in the reliability of diagnostic scores on the GATB are less serious than those found in any comparable group of tests now available.

Much more significant and reassuring is the evidence of the GATB's validity in comparison with other tests similarly constructed, e.g., the *Differential Aptitude Tests* or the *Factored Aptitude Series*. Many detailed technical reports of validation studies by state and national employment services, universities, etc., have already appeared, and a continuous program of research, revision, and follow-up investigations is evidently under way. Undoubtedly there are basic occupational aptitudes which the present battery does not measure at all. It also makes no attempt to sample occupational interests or other personality characteristics. These limitations and their importance are fully recognized. It is, therefore, all the more remarkable that a single battery of this sort will do so much, so well.

[715]

The Guilford-Zimmerman Aptitude Survey. Grades 9–16 and adults; 1947–50; IBM for Parts I–II, V–VII; 7 parts; Form A ('47); 25¢ per manual ('47); 2¢ per tentative high school norm sheet ('48); 2¢ per college profile chart ('50); $1.50 per specimen set, postpaid; separate answer sheets may be used for Parts I–II, V–VII; 2¢ per IBM answer sheet for any one part; $1 per hand scoring key for any one part (*no key for Part VI*); 50¢ per stencil for machine scoring of answer sheets for any one of Parts I–II, V–VII; postage extra; 143(188) minutes; J. P. Guilford and Wayne S. Zimmerman; Sheridan Supply Co. *

a) PART I, VERBAL COMPREHENSION. IBM; $2 per 25; 25(30) minutes.
b) PART II, GENERAL REASONING. IBM; $2 per 25; 35 (40) minutes.
c) PART III, NUMERICAL OPERATIONS. $2 per 25; 8(13) minutes.
d) PART IV, PERCEPTUAL SPEED. $2 per 25; 5(10) minutes.
e) PART V, SPATIAL ORIENTATION. IBM; $3.50 per 25; 10(20) minutes.
f) PART VI, SPATIAL VISUALIZATION. IBM; $5 per 25; 30(40) minutes.
g) PART VII, MECHANICAL KNOWLEDGE. IBM; $3.50 per 25; 30(35) minutes.

REFERENCES

1. GUILFORD, J. P. "The Discovery of Aptitude and Achievement Variables." *Sci* 106:279–82 S 26 '47. * (*PA* 22:871)
2. GUILFORD, J. P., AND ZIMMERMAN, WAYNE S. "Some A.A.F. Findings Concerning Aptitude Factors." *Occupations* 26:154–9 D '47. * (*PA* 22:2198)
3. GUILFORD, J. P., AND MICHAEL, WILLIAM B. "Approaches to Univocal Factor Scores." *Psychometrika* 13:1–22 Mr '48. * (*PA* 22:3287)
4. GUILFORD, J. P., AND ZIMMERMAN, WAYNE S. "The Guilford-Zimmerman Aptitude Survey." *J Appl Psychol* 32:24–34 F '48. * (*PA* 23:453)
5. BORKO, HAROLD. *Purification of Measurement of the Spatial Visualization Factor in the Guilford-Zimmerman Aptitude Survey, Part VI.* Master's thesis, University of Southern California (Los Angeles, Calif.), 1949.
6. MICHAEL, WILLIAM B. "The Nature of Space and Visualization Abilities: Some Recent Findings Based on Factor-Analysis Studies." *Trans N Y Acad Sci* 11:275–81 Je '49. * (*PA* 24:485)
7. ZIMMERMAN, WAYNE S. *The Isolation, Definition, and Measurement of Spatial and Visualizing Abilities.* Doctor's thesis, University of Southern California (Los Angeles, Calif.), 1949. (*Abstracts of Dissertations....1949*, 1950, pp. 103–6.)
8. "Factorial Validities of the Guilford-Zimmerman Aptitude Survey." *Psychometric Notes From Sheridan Supply Company, No. 3.* Beverly Hills, Calif.: Sheridan Supply Co., September 1950. Pp. 2. Paper, lithotyped. *
9. ["Guilford-Zimmerman Aptitude Survey."] *Psychometric Notes From Sheridan Supply Company, No. 1.* Beverly Hills, Calif.: Sheridan Supply Co., May 1950. Pp. 2. Paper, lithotyped. *
10. BUCHANAN, PAUL CRAMER. *Prediction of Accident Proneness of Motorcycle Operators.* Doctor's thesis, University of Southern California (Los Angeles, Calif.), 1950. (*Abstracts of Dissertations....1950*, 1951, pp. 153–5.)
11. MICHAEL, WILLIAM B.; ZIMMERMAN, WAYNE S.; AND GUILFORD, J. P. "An Investigation of Two Hypotheses Regarding the Nature of the Spatial-Relations and Visualization Factors." *Ed & Psychol Meas* 10:187–213 su '50. * (*PA* 25:5967)
12. RAZOR, BETTY ANN LEIST. *The Relationship of the Guilford-Zimmerman Aptitude Survey to Success in Various College Courses.* Master's thesis, University of Southern California (Los Angeles, Calif.), 1950.
13. THOMPSON, PAUL O. *A Correlational Study of the Efficiency of Certain Aptitude Tests in Predicting the Success of Supervisors in an Aircraft Factory.* Master's thesis, University of Southern California (Los Angeles, Calif.), 1950.
14. BLAKEMORE, ARLINE. "Reducing Typing Costs With Aptitude Tests." *Personnel J* 30:20–4 My '51. * (*PA* 25:7749)
15. MICHAEL, WILLIAM B.; ZIMMERMAN, WAYNE S.; AND GUILFORD, J. P. "An Investigation of the Nature of the Spatial-Relations and Visualization Factors in Two High School Samples." *Ed & Psychol Meas* 11:561–77 w '51. *

ANNE ANASTASI, *Professor of Psychology, Fordham University, New York, New York.*

This test battery is an outgrowth of the research conducted by Guilford and his associates during World War II on the selection of aircraft personnel. The authors state that they plan ultimately to develop tests of approximately 20 "primary abilities." The seven parts already published, each in a separate booklet, are described as covering the leading factors in three traditional areas: abstract intelligence, clerical aptitude, and mechanical aptitude. The tests can be used according to these traditional groupings or recombined in different ways for specific purposes. For personnel classification or vocational guidance, the authors recommend the use of the entire battery which requires approximately three hours. The tests are virtually self-administering, written instructions and sample items being provided for each test. All items are of the multiple choice type, most having five alternatives. The battery is designed for use "with older children and adults," the instructions being said to require sixth grade reading ability.

Parts I and II, covering the area of abstract intelligence, include the tests Verbal Comprehension and General Reasoning. The former is a vocabulary test, in which the level of difficulty and the part of speech of all alternative responses are approximately equivalent to those of the word defined. General Reasoning is an arithmetic reasoning test in which the problems are stated in rather intricate verbal terms. In order to reduce the contribution of numerical computation in this test, items which correlated significantly with the total score on the Numerical Operations in the preliminary testing were eliminated.

Parts III and IV, designed to measure two important components of clerical aptitude, consist of the tests Numerical Operations and Perceptual Speed. The first involves addition, subtraction, and multiplication. A novel feature of this test is that six alternative responses are provided for each pair of items, thus saving space and probably reducing reading time on the part of the examinee. Part IV requires the matching of identical drawings of common objects.

For the measurement of abilities involved in mechanical pursuits, three tests are provided: Part V, Spatial Orientation; Part VI, Spatial Visualization; and Part VII, Mechanical Knowledge. The distinction between the two spatial factors measured by Parts V and VI was first made by Guilford on the basis of his Air Force research. The former refers primarily to an appreciation of the spatial relations of objects with reference to the individual's own body, an ability which proved important in learning to pilot a plane and which may be involved in many jobs requiring machine operation. The second spatial factor involves the ability to imagine movement or transformations of visual objects. All the items in Part V show two positions of the prow of a motor boat in which the examinee is supposed to be riding. The task is to determine the change in the direction in which the boat is heading from the first to the second picture. In Part VI, each item contains a drawing of a clock in an initial position, followed by verbal instructions to turn the clock in a prescribed direction over a given number of degrees. The resulting position of the clock is then to be selected from the five alternatives provided. It would seem that in both Parts V and VI the uniformity of item content might make the test monotonous for many subjects and might create a problem of sustaining interest. One wonders to what extent personality factors may be reflected in achievement on these two tests. Part

VII, like most available mechanical comprehension tests, measures knowledge of common tools or mechanical objects and their functions. The first 20 items of this test employ a combination of pictorial and verbal presentation, the remaining 35 are entirely verbal. The latter are somewhat reminiscent of the oral trade tests developed by the United States Employment Service and by the armed services. The authors point out that the mechanical knowledge test can be meaningfully applied only to adolescent or adult males in the United States culture, and should be interpreted in the light of the individual's mechanical experience.

Parts III, IV, and V are speed tests. The rest are power tests, although speed is appreciably involved in Part VI. Norms are now provided on a separate profile chart, which includes percentile, T-score, and C-score equivalents of raw scores on each part for college men and women. There is no appended explanation of these norms, nor are the sizes and other characteristics of the normative samples indicated. Preliminary estimates of reliability for each part range from .88 to .92 on groups of approximately 100 to 200 college men. These coefficients were obtained by the odd-even technique for the power tests and by separate timing of equivalent halves for the speed tests (4).

The mimeographed manual, which is almost identical with an article appearing in the *Journal of Applied Psychology* (4), includes rough estimates of the factorial validity of each part, based upon the "known factorial composition of very similar tests." In a subsequently published Psychometric Note (8), reference is made to three factor analyses of these tests, on college men, high school boys, and high school girls, in which the obtained principal factor loadings of each part were fairly close to the estimated values. Part VII was not included in these analyses, and the other parts were curtailed in length when given to the college group. As is generally found in factorially designed tests, the factorial validities indicate that the tests still fall far short of factorial purity, the loadings ranging from .52 to .89. There is also considerable overlap, the two spatial tests, for example, correlating almost as highly with each other as they do with their respective factors, and the general reasoning test having high verbal loadings in some groups. Finally, it should be remembered that factorial validity is not a substitute for empirical validity. The factorial composition of

Guilford-Zimmerman Aptitude Survey

most practical criteria is unknown. Hence only empirical validity can adequately indicate the accuracy of prediction possible with a given test. Nor is there as yet universal agreement as to the "factors" or categories to be measured. This is especially true in the areas of spatial abilities and reasoning.

Some initial effort toward empirical validation is indicated in another separately published Psychometric Note (9), which reports the correlations between grades in college courses and scores on Parts I to VI of the battery. As might be expected from earlier studies with similar tests, Verbal Comprehension tended to yield the highest correlations with grades, even in science and mathematics courses. The highest correlation in the table, however, is only .54, between Verbal Comprehension and English composition. On the whole, these correlations are no higher than, if as high as, those generally found between grades and the more crudely designed "intelligence tests." In a study on 84 supervisors in an industrial plant, the highest correlation with an index of job success was again found for Verbal Comprehension (.52), the only other significant correlation being obtained in the case of General Reasoning (.29).

All in all, this battery, although embodying many refinements and promising innovations in test construction, appears to be in a preliminary or experimental stage. There is, especially, need for more normative data and for further empirical validation. Some revision of content may be indicated as more information on different populations is accumulated. There would seem to be a real question regarding the advisability of releasing such a battery in its present stage of development without some qualifying designation such as "experimental form." It is quite likely that many test users may rely unduly on factorial labels, assuming, for example, that a student who is poor in numerical operations and in the two spatial tests should be discouraged from taking courses in geometry, trigonometry, or advanced mathematics. The lack of significant correlation between mathematics grades and scores in such tests, as found both with the present battery and with other similar tests, certainly offers no support for such a conclusion. But it is very easy for the unwary tester to slip into the habit of matching "factors" with school courses, occupations, or other practical criteria. The inclusion in the present manual of a list of "Occupations in Which the Survey Factors Are Probably Important" certainly does nothing to discourage this tendency. In a similar vein, the test authors, in a section entitled "Enlightened Selection of Batteries," state: "An inspectional job analysis made with the primary-ability categories in mind is the most effective preliminary approach to this problem * The better-known factors are so dependable that one would rarely go astray in the choice of selective tests following the approach here recommended." The available data fail to justify such optimism.

HAROLD BECHTOLDT, *Associate Professor of Psychology, State University of Iowa, Iowa City, Iowa.*

A supposedly new approach to aptitude testing is implied by the authors in their manual of instructions. This approach may be summarized as the appraisal of the several sources of variance which the authors (and nearly all other investigators in the field today) are convinced enter into the definitions of success in various activities of our society. It is the test authors' hope or conviction that the several measures of success eventually can be shown to be expressible in terms of a set of 20 performance measures or "aptitude tests."

The seven (out of 20 planned) published parts of this survey appear to be the product of a very competent test construction staff. The printing format is pleasing, the paper is heavy, and the range of difficulty on the "power" parts of the survey seems to be adequate. The complex directions utilized for Spatial Orientation (Part V) and Spatial Visualization (Part VI) may present a serious problem to students who lack considerable verbal comprehension ability. (The instructions are supposedly written for 6th grade educational level.) Marked sex differences in favor of the males exist on four parts of the survey. The distributions of test scores presented on the profile chart indicate a desirable amount of discrimination among the members of the normative group; but the absence of a definition of the standardization samples, at least in terms of geographical distribution, age ranges, educational levels, and number of cases, seems almost inexcusable in a test offered to the public for sale. The retention of the traditional scoring formulas (R − kW) for two of the so-called power tests (Parts I, II, and VII) is inconsistent with the authors' sophistication in test theory. The temporary status of these scoring formulas, however, is indicated by the authors' warning to the user to be alert for possible future changes.

The authors' report on the reliability of five of the seven parts consists of a brief paragraph giving two "internal-consistency" coefficients (formulas not stated) of .89 and .96 and three "split-half, separately timed" coefficients of .88, .92, and .92. The failure to provide more of the test score statistics precludes any more accurate evaluation of the consistency of students' behavior to these parts. Even rough estimates of reliability coefficients are lacking for Parts VI and VII; surely in the current test market, publishers assume some little technical competence on the part of the prospective buyer and provide more data than that given in the present manual and Psychometric Notes.

The problem of validity is presented to the prospective test user in two apparently unrelated topics, (a) applications of the survey and (b) factorial and practical validity. The reviewer cannot separate these two topics so conveniently; the greater number of applications would seem to be based on the "practical validities" of the tests, while the research worker or test technician would be concerned with the factorial data. The manual itself provides no "practical validity" data to support the "convictions" and "beliefs" of the test authors as to the occupations "in which the survey factors are probably important." The occupational listings reflect many similarly unsubstantiated statements in the vocational guidance literature.

The possibility of an eventual rational approach to both job analysis and test construction is accepted by many personnel psychologists today. Whether, as indicated in the manual, "an inspectional job analysis made with the primary-ability categories in mind" is, or is not, the most effective *preliminary* approach at our present stage of ignorance would seem to be debatable (for example, who is to do the inspection?). However, a point that the reviewer contends is *strictly empirical* and not debatable is the *relation* of the separate test scores singly and in combination to the criterion used to define success in each occupation.

Two master's theses are summarized briefly (9) as providing evidence of "the possibilities of differential prediction" in educational and industrial applications. The results are consistent with most such attempts to predict college grades and supervisory success (manufacturing aircraft parts); they are positive correlations of verbal and arithmetic reasoning scores with grades and with a supervisory performance criterion. The data required for the evaluation of the actuality of differential prediction in the first study was not presented. The multiple correlation between the supervisory criterion and four parts of the survey was increased from .52 to .57 for Part I alone. No indication of the expected shrinkage of this multiple correlation was presented.

The problem of factorial validity is, of course, related to that of practical validity. The eventual *empirical* analysis of sets of criterion measures with sets of test scores may provide the evidence needed for the development of efficient test batteries to be used in selection and differential prediction studies. The "factorial validities" should assist in the development of a battery covering the several factors with a minimal number of tests; the "practical validities" would indicate which of the many factors should be represented in the prediction equations.

In the vocational guidance field at present, the job family classifications of clerical and mechanical skills have considerable status. For educational counseling, academic or scholastic aptitude tests have a similar standing. The continued analysis of the criteria of success in these areas should provide the empirical evidence as to the sources of variance associated with these success measures. It is *not clear* to the reviewer, without such empirical evidence, that "the three traditional aptitude areas [verbal intelligence, clerical aptitude, and mechanical aptitude] have been broken down into their chief fundamental components" if the "breaking down" means that the common factors in the various criteria of *success on the job* have been determined.

The reviewer, in conclusion, cannot recommend these tests for use in vocational counseling or guidance at this time. The lack of evidence to support the claims presented in the manual is, unfortunately, a common characteristic of many such tests offered for sale today. The tests are recommended, on the other hand, to research workers interested in a series of relatively linearly independent measures of test behavior, although the intercorrelations among the parts are apparently higher than the test authors had expected. Eight of the 15 correlations based on a restricted (college) sample (8) are significant at the 1 per cent level. In this study these tests were curtailed in length or time of administration; the intercorrelations of the complete battery might be higher if a more heterogeneous and representative sample were used.

JOHN B. CARROLL, *Lecturer on Education, Harvard University, Cambridge, Massachusetts.*

Believing that "aptitudes of individuals can be evaluated most adequately, economically, and meaningfully by using a series of tests each of which measures a unique ability," the authors have made a very deliberate attempt to construct such tests. They plan eventually to publish tests of approximately 20 unique factors; the tests reviewed here constitute only the first installment and are intended to cover the chief abilities in three "traditional" areas—abstract intelligence, clerical aptitude, and mechanical aptitude. The basic theory is that of Thurstone's multiple factor analysis; there is no attempt to measure a general factor, even as a second-order composite of the primary abilities. The authors have attempted to build tests as factorially "pure" as possible; in some cases they have excluded items from a test because they correlate too highly with a different factor. Nevertheless, they suggest that where a perfectly pure factor test cannot be devised, "univocal factor scores" can be computed by appropriate linear combinations of raw scores.

The authors seem to have succeeded quite well in devising a series of pure factor tests. Preliminary results on rather small samples at least show that the tests have high factorial validities (i.e., have high correlations with the statistical factors they are supposed to measure). The intercorrelations of the tests are lower, in general, than in the case of Thurstone's primary mental abilities tests, although one must make such a comparison with considerable caution because of the lack of comparability of the samples. A disturbingly high correlation ($r = .55$) occurs only between Parts V and VI.

Although these tests have some technical flaws, considerable care has gone into their construction. High reliabilities are reported, but no standard errors of measurement are given. Norms are now available for college men and women (based on large groups of freshmen or sophomores at three universities), and, in a provisional form, for high school boys and girls.

As is the case with other primary mental abilities batteries, the amount of evidence on the predictive validities of these tests is disappointingly small. The few studies which have been published indicate that the tests offer some possibilities for differential prediction, but the most predictive parts of the battery are those which correspond to the usual omnibus tests of intelligence. Nevertheless, it should be remembered that tests highly similar to those of the present battery were quite useful in differential classification of aircrew personnel in the Army Air Forces during World War II. It is largely on the basis of indirect evidence—evidence which has accumulated with respect to other factor tests—that the authors have drawn up a table of occupations for which each test in the battery is "probably" important. Unfortunately, these lists go beyond existing knowledge and reflect in some cases an inadequate job analysis of the occupation in question. For example, the occupation "mathematician" is listed in connection with Part III, Numerical Operations. A mathematician, however, seldom has to make *rapid* mental computations, if he has to do them at all. While the authors' lists of occupations may have some value as a guide to hypotheses which should be tested in further research, most guidance counselors are probably wary enough to avoid taking them at face value.

The format of the tests needs improvement; in several tests (Parts IV and V) the material for each item is arranged in such a way that a right-handed examinee will continually find his hand in the way when he tries to scrutinize the choices. The scoring mechanics have not been sufficiently simplified.

Part I, Verbal Comprehension, appears to be a quite homogeneous vocabulary test; the time limit is such that it is virtually a power test. Part II, General Reasoning, could better be termed a "quantitative reasoning test"; the items have been constructed and selected so as to minimize the role of the number factor. The time limit for this test probably needs to be longer if it is to be a pure power test. Part III, Numerical Operations, is constructed along the lines of other number factor tests; one wonders, however, why the addition, subtraction, multiplication, and division sections of the test are not separately timed. Part IV, Perceptual Speed, requires the examinee to find matching pictures of various objects by comparing fine details. In addition to the defect in format mentioned earlier, the test suffers because the items are not numbered and the subject is not told in what sequence to perform them. Part V, Spatial Orientation, is an exceedingly clever test, requiring the examinee to indicate changes in the position of the prow of a motorboat with reference to a landscape in the background. A subject with a vivid sense of kinesthetic imagery will do well on this test, though he may find himself getting a trifle seasick! Part VI, Spatial Visualization, has to do with visualized rotations of an object on its three axes. Good performance on the test would possibly depend too much on the comprehension of the special instructions and definitions which are used. Part VII, Mechanical Knowledge, could be said to measure a "pure factor" only in a statistical sense; the items are a hodgepodge of facts about plumbing, auto mechanics, etc. There is only one item which concerns radio repair. The authors observe that scores on the test are valid only if the examinee has "grown up in the United States culture or a similar culture." Perhaps the same thing, of course, could be said of other subtests in the battery.

The *Guilford-Zimmerman Aptitude Survey* must therefore be evaluated as a series of research tests which succeed reasonably well in measuring, over a certain range of ability, a number of unitary traits. Guidance personnel and industrial psychologists will look forward to the extension of the battery and publication of results on its validity, for the complete battery will undoubtedly measure a somewhat different sampling of abilities from those measured by other primary mental abilities batteries.

P. E. VERNON, *Professor of Educational Psychology, Institute of Education, University of London, London, England.*

This battery is said to be suitable for high school, adult, and college populations; but norms are provided only for college men and women (numbers not stated). Most of the tests, except Perceptual Speed, will probably be too difficult for other groups, especially female, and distributions may be badly skewed.

In reviewing the *Primary Mental Abilities,* the writer has objected to the use of one test as a measure of a factor and the assumption that it will predict any educational or vocational ability that looks as though it might be related to that factor. The same criticism holds here, though to a lesser extent, because some of the tests are a good deal more thorough and because special care has been taken to purify their content. Refactorisations have yielded average loadings on the appropriate factors of .66 (variance 44 per cent) and on the largest *in*appropriate

factors of .21. Nevertheless, the first two and the last three tests tend to show considerable overlapping, and it is doubtful whether the distinction between orientation (awareness of spatial directions) and visualization (of spatial manipulations) can be maintained. The authors hope to extend the battery to cover many more of the 20 or so factors extracted in Army Air Forces researches on pilot selection. But, as the reviewer has pointed out elsewhere,[1] numerous tiny group factors are likely to emerge from investigations of populations which have been highly selected on qualifying tests—factors which fail to differentiate in more heterogeneous groups. So far the validation data against external criteria are singularly unpromising, though it is greatly to the authors' credit that they are publishing these in a series of psychometric Notes (*8, 9*), so that the user can judge for himself.

The tests are largely self-administering, though Spatial Orientation and Spatial Visualization seem likely to cause difficulties, both because of the elaborateness of the instructions and because they are none too clearly printed. Verbal Comprehension is of particular interest in that the correct answer and the distractors are all of the same level of difficulty as the word to be defined. Mechanical Knowledge has not been item analysed, and the items are clearly not arranged in order of difficulty; however, there should be sufficient time for almost all testees to try all items.

In conclusion, the battery should be of value for experimental use, particularly among male college students. The low interest correlations give promise of high multiple correlations with educational and vocational performances, but so far there is little evidence that much more is measured than the *g* and *V* abilities measured by any equally thorough verbal intelligence test. The most useful section, after Verbal Comprehension and General Reasoning, is likely to be Mechanical Knowledge.

[716]

*[Primary Mental Abilities]. Ages 5–7, 7–11, 11–17; 1938–50; 3 levels; cash orders postpaid; L. L. Thurstone and Thelma Gwinn Thurstone; Science Research Associates, Inc. *
a) SRA PRIMARY MENTAL ABILITIES: PRIMARY. Ages 5–7; 1946–48; also called PMA; formerly called *Tests of Primary Mental Abilities for Ages 5 and 6;* 6 scores: verbal-meaning, perceptual speed, motor, space, quantitative, total; 1 form, '46; manual ('48); $2.90 per 25;

1 Vernon, Philip E. *The Structure of Human Abilities.* London: Methuen & Co. Ltd., 1950. Pp. xii, 160. (New York: John Wiley & Sons, Inc., 1951.) * (*PA* 25:6026)

50¢ per specimen set; for accompanying instructional materials, see *62, 71, 84* below; (60–80) minutes.

b) SRA PRIMARY MENTAL ABILITIES: ELEMENTARY. Ages 7–11; 1948–50; also called PMA; 11 scores: words, pictures, verbal-meaning, space, word-grouping, figure-grouping, reasoning, perception, number, total non-reading, total; Form AH ('48); preliminary manual ('48); 49¢ per test and answer pad; separate answer pads must be used; $1.90 per 25 answer pads; 55¢ per 25 percentile profile sheets ('48); 55¢ per 25 age and quotient score profile sheets ('50); 75¢ per specimen set; (60) minutes.

c) SRA PRIMARY MENTAL ABILITIES: INTERMEDIATE. Ages 11–17; 1947–49; also called PMA; 6 scores: verbal meaning, space, reasoning, number, word-fluency, total; IBM; 2 editions; 1 form; revised manual ('49); separate answer pads or answer sheets must be used; 55¢ per 25 revised percentile profile sheets ('49); 75¢ per specimen set of any one edition; for an explanatory booklet, see *64* below; 26(45) minutes.

1) *Form AH (Hand Scoring Edition).* 1947; 49¢ per test and answer pad; $1.90 per 25 answer pads.
2) *Form AM (Machine Scoring Edition).* 1948; 39¢ per test; $2.90 per 100 IBM answer sheets; $2 per set of scoring stencils.

d) THE CHICAGO TESTS OF PRIMARY MENTAL ABILITIES. Ages 11–17; 1941–43; 7 scores: number, verbal meaning, space, word fluency, reasoning, memory, total; 2 editions.

1) *Six Booklets Edition.* 1938–41; originally published by the American Council on Education with the title *Tests of Primary Mental Abilities;* IBM; 6 tests in individual booklets and 5 practice booklets; 1 form, '41; manual ('41); $6 per 25 sets of 6 test-answer booklets and 5 practice booklets; $2.15 per 25 of any one of the following tests: Number, Verbal Meaning, Space, Word Fluency, and Reasoning; $1.10 per 25 of the test Memory; machine scoring stencils: Number—20¢, Verbal Meaning—30¢, Space —60¢, Reasoning—30¢, Memory—20¢, no stencil for Word Fluency; $2 per set of hand scoring stencils; $1 per set of memory cards; $3.75 per specimen set; 50¢ per specimen set of any one test; (240) minutes.
2) *Single Booklet Edition.* 1943; an abbreviated form of Six Booklets Edition; 1 form; $3.75 per 25; 75¢ per set of scoring stencils; $1 per set of memory cards; 50¢ per specimen set; (120) minutes.

REFERENCES

1–10. See 40:1427.
11–60. See 3:225.
61. HALL, WILLIAM E., AND ROBINSON, FRANCIS P. "An Analytical Approach to the Study of Reading Skills." *J Ed Psychol* 36:429–42 O '45. * (*PA* 20:1680)
62. THURSTONE, THELMA GWINN. *The Red Book: Learning to Think Series.* Chicago, Ill.: Science Research Associates, Inc., 1947. Pp. 80. Paper. * (*Teacher's Manual for The Red Book,* 1948. Pp. iii, 75. Paper. *)
63. BECKER, GEORGE J. *The Relationship Between the Thurstone SRA Primary Mental Abilities Tests and the Wechsler Bellevue Intelligence Test.* Master's thesis, Fordham University (New York, N.Y.), 1948.
64. BOUTHILET, LORRAINE, AND BYRNE, KATHARINE MANN. *You and Your Mental Abilities.* Chicago, Ill.: Science Research Associates, Inc., 1948. Pp. 48. (*PA* 23:5037) [The booklet copyrighted in 1949 is a reprinting of the 1948 edition.]
65. DAVIS, W. ALLISON, AND HAVIGHURST, ROBERT J. "The Measurement of Mental Systems: Can Intelligence Be Measured?" *Sci Mo* 66:301–16 Ap '48. * (*PA* 22:3381)
66. DELMAN, LOUIS. *The Organization of Intellectual Abilities in Psychoneurotic Veterans.* Doctor's thesis, New York University (New York, N.Y.), 1948. (*Abstracts of Theses.... [School of Education] October 1948–June 1949,* 1950, pp. 17–20.)
67. FRUCHTER, BENJAMIN. "The Nature of Verbal Fluency." *Ed & Psychol Meas* 8:33–47 sp '48. * (*PA* 22:3830)
68. JEFFRIES, LLOYD A. "The Nature of 'Primary Abilities.'" *Am J Psychol* 61:107–11 Ja '48. * (*PA* 22:3831)
69. SHAW, DUANE C. *A Study of the Relationships Between Thurstone Primary Mental Abilities and High School Achievement.* Doctor's thesis, University of Iowa (Iowa City, Iowa), 1948.
70. THURSTONE, L. L. "Primary Mental Abilities." Abstract. *Sci* 108:585 N 26 '48. * (*PA* 23:1182, title only)
71. THURSTONE, THELMA GWINN. *The Blue Book: Learning to Think Series.* Chicago, Ill.: Science Research Associates, Inc., 1948. Pp. 80. Paper. * (*Teacher's Manual for the Blue Book.* Pp. iii, 63. Paper. *)
72. CARTER, LAUNOR, AND NIXON, MARY. "Ability, Perceptual, Personality, and Interest Factors Associated With Different Criteria of Leadership." *J Psychol* 27:377–88 Ap '49. * (*PA* 23:4183)
73. CASSEL, ROBERT H., AND DANENHOWER, HAROLD S. "Mental Subnormality Developmentally Arrested: The Primary Mental Abilities Test." *Trg Sch B* 46:94–104 O '49. * (*PA* 24:2670)
74. CORTER, HAROLD M. *A Factor Analysis of Some Individually-Administered Reasoning Tests.* Doctor's thesis, Pennsylvania State College (State College, Pa.), 1949. (*Abstracts of Doctoral Dissertations....1949,* 1950, pp. 325–9.) (*PA* 24:5541, title only)
75. GIBNEY, ESTHER F. "Aptitude Tests in Relation to the Teaching of Plane Geometry." *Math Teach* 42:181–6 Ap '49. *
76. MICHAEL, WILLIAM B. "The Nature of Space and Visualization Abilities: Some Recent Findings Based on Factor-Analysis Studies." *Trans N Y Acad Sci* 11:275–81 Je '49. * (*PA* 24:485)
77. MURRAY, JOHN E. "An Analysis of Geometric Ability." *J Ed Psychol* 40:118–24 F '49. * (*PA* 24:2066)
78. SCHMIDT, LOUIS GOTTFRED. *Realism in Vocation Objectives in Terms of Performance on the Primary Mental Abilities Test.* Doctor's thesis, University of Wisconsin (Madison, Wis.), 1949. (*Summaries of Doctoral Dissertations....July 1949 to June 1950,* 1951, pp. 339–41.)
79. SHAW, DUANE C. "A Study of the Relationships Between Thurstone Primary Mental Abilities and High School Achievement." *J Ed Psychol* 40:239–50 Ap '49. * (*PA* 24:2834)
80. SMITH, ARTHUR E. *A Comparison of the SRA Primary Mental Abilities Test With the Wechsler-Bellevue Intelligence Scale.* Master's thesis, Illinois State Normal University (Normal, Ill.), 1949. (*PA* 24:382, title only)
81. SMITH, HENRY CLAY. "Psychometric Checks on Hypotheses Derived From Sheldon's Work on Physique and Temperament." *J Personality* 17:310–20 Mr '49. * (*PA* 25:2916)
82. SUPER, DONALD E. *Appraising Vocational Fitness by Means of Psychological Tests,* pp. 132–42. New York: Harper & Brothers, 1949. Pp. xxiii, 727. (*PA* 24:2130)
83. THURSTONE, L. L. "Primary Abilities." *Occupations* 27:527–9 My '49. * (*PA* 24:636)
84. THURSTONE, THELMA GWINN. *The Green Book: Learning to Think Series.* Chicago, Ill.: Science Research Associates, Inc., 1949. Pp. 80. Paper. * (*Teacher's Manual for The Green Book.* Pp. iii, 70. Paper. *)
85. WESMAN, ALEXANDER G., AND SEASHORE, HAROLD G. "Frequency vs. Complexity of Words in Verbal Measurement." *J Ed Psychol* 40:395–404 N '49. * (*PA* 24:3393)
86. ABRAMS, ELIAS NELSON. *A Comparative Factor Analytic Study of Normal and Neurotic Veterans: A Statistical Investigation of the Interrelationships of Intellectual and Emotional Factors as Disclosed in the Primary Mental Abilities Examination and the Minnesota Multiphasic Personality Inventory.* Doctor's thesis, New York University (New York, N.Y.), 1950. Abstract: *Microfilm Abstracts* 10:94–5 no 3 '50. * (*PA* 25:4555, title only)
87. BRODY, ABRAHAM BARNET. *A Factorial Study of Intellectual Functioning in Normal and Abnormal Adults.* Doctor's thesis, Columbia University (New York, N.Y.), 1950. Abstract: *Microfilm Abstracts* 11:445–6 no 2 '51. (*PA* 26:2171, title only)
88. CASSEL, ROBERT H., AND DANENHOWER, HAROLD S. "Mental Subnormality Developmentally Arrested: Social Competence." *Am J Mental Def* 54:282–9 Ja '50. * (*PA* 24:3779)
89. DEAN, DOUGLAS A. *A Factor Analysis of the Stanford-Binet and SRA Primary Mental Abilities Battery at the First Grade Level.* Doctor's thesis, Pennsylvania State College (State College, Pa.), 1950. (*Abstracts of Doctoral Dissertations.... 1950,* 1951, pp. 394–7.)
90. DEVLIN, JOHN PAUL. *An Investigation of the Tests of Primary Mental Abilities for Ages Five and Six as an Indicator of Reading Readiness and Intelligence Among a First Grade Population.* Master's thesis, Pennsylvania State College (State College, Pa.), 1950. (*PA* 24:5542, title only)
91. FORD, ALBERT H. "Prediction of Academic Success in Three Schools of Nursing." *J Appl Psychol* 34:186–9 Je '50. * (*PA* 25:4038)
92. RAMASESHAN, RUKMINI S. "A Note on the Validity of the Mental Age Concept." *J Ed Psychol* 41:56–8 Ja '50. * (*PA* 24:5112)
93. SANDERS, JOSEPH ROBERT. *Verbal Concept Formation in Relation to Personal Adjustment.* Doctor's thesis, Columbia University (New York, N.Y.), 1950. Abstract: *Microfilm Abstracts* 11:431–3 no 2 '51. (*PA* 26:2006, title only)
94. SPIVEY, GORDON MAURICE. *The Relationship Between Temperament and Achievement of a Selected Group of John Muir College Students.* Doctor's thesis, University of Southern California (Los Angeles, Calif.), 1950. (*Abstracts of Dissertations....1950,* 1951, pp. 298–300.)
95. THURSTONE, THELMA GWINN; AS TOLD TO KATHARINE MANN BYRNE. "Testing of Primary Mental Abilities." *J Nat Ed Assn* 39:346–7 My '50. *
96. ELIAS, JACK Z. *Non-Intellective Factors in Certain Intelligence and Achievement Tests: An Analysis of Factors in Addition to the Cognitive Entering Into the Intelligence and Achievement Scores of Children at the Sixth Grade Level.* Doc-

tor's thesis, New York University (New York, N.Y.), 1951. Abstract: *Microfilm Abstracts* 11:558-60 no 3 '51. (*PA 26:* 1495, title only)

97. KELLY, E. LOWELL, AND FISKE, DONALD W. *The Prediction of Performance in Clinical Psychology.* Ann Arbor, Mich.: University of Michigan, 1951. Pp. xv, 311. Lithotyped. *

98. LEVINE, SOLOMON. *The Relationship Between Personality and Efficiency in Various Hospital Occupations.* Doctor's thesis, New York University (New York, N.Y.), 1951. Abstract: *Microfilm Abstracts* 11:741–2 no 3 '51. (*PA 26:1736*, title only)

99. MEYER, HERBERT H. *Factors Related to Success in the Human Relations Aspect of Work-Group Leadership.* American Psychological Association, Psychological Monographs: General and Applied, Vol. 65, No. 3, Whole No. 320. Washington, D.C.: the Association, Inc., 1951. Pp. v, 29. Paper. * (*PA 25:7132*)

100. MICHAEL, WILLIAM B.; ZIMMERMAN, WAYNE S.; AND GUILFORD, J. P. "An Investigation of the Nature of the Spatial-Relations and Visualization Factors in Two High School Samples." *Ed & Psychol Meas* 11:561-77 w '51. *

101. THURSTONE, THELMA GWINN, AND BYRNE, KATHARINE MANN. *Mental Abilities of Children.* Chicago, Ill.: Science Research Associates, Inc., 1951. Pp. 48. Paper. * (*PA 25:7983*)

102. TYLER, LEONA E. "The Relationship of Interests to Abilities and Reputation Among First-Grade Children." *Ed & Psychol Meas* 11:255-64 su '51. * (*PA 26:2660*)

ANNE ANASTASI, *Professor of Psychology, Fordham University, New York, New York.*

Beginning in 1938 with the first experimental edition of the form for high school and college students, the Thurstone tests of primary mental abilities have undergone various metamorphoses. The original edition was the direct result of Thurstone's factorial analysis of 56 tests on a college sample, together with supplementary and corroborative studies of narrower scope on several high school samples. A subsequent factorial analysis of 60 tests on a sample of eighth grade children led to the development of the Chicago PMA tests for ages 11 to 17, which first appeared in a separate booklet edition requiring six testing sessions and, two years later, in a single booklet edition requiring two hours of testing time. The last stage in this abridgment process to date is provided by the edition called the *SRA Primary Mental Abilities* for ages 11 to 17 (Intermediate), which can be administered in from 40 to 50 minutes. This edition, available in both hand and machine scoring forms, contains only five short tests, each requiring from 4 to 6 minutes of actual working time. Another parallel development has been the extension of the series to cover still younger age levels. The *SRA Primary Mental Abilities* for ages 7 to 11 (Elementary) consists of seven tests grouped under five factors, the total testing time being approximately one hour. Finally, a form for ages 5 to 7 (Primary), also published by SRA, is approximately as long as that for ages 7 to 11 and also yields five factor scores, the number of tests for each factor varying from one to five.

The various forms, editions, and levels of this series cover different combinations of eight group factors, or "primary mental abilities," identified by Thurstone and his associates. The entire PMA list includes: Verbal-Meaning (V), Space (S), Reasoning (R), Perceptual Speed (P), Number (N), Word-Fluency (W), Memory (M), and Motor (Mo). In the original experimental form (1938), reasoning was represented by two factors, Induction and Deduction, but subsequent research failed to support such a distinction and a single R factor was substituted. Memory tests were excluded from all SRA forms, at all age levels, "because they take too long to administer" (*sic*). Word-Fluency does not appear in the two earlier age batteries, below age 11, since group tests of this ability among younger children are said to depend to a large extent upon speed of writing. Motor ability is measured only at ages 5 to 7, the test employed for this purpose being concerned primarily with the young child's ability to handle a pencil. The form for ages 5 to 7 is also characterized by the presence of a Quantitative (Q) score in place of either the N or R scores found in the older-age forms, since the two latter factors could not be clearly identified among younger children. All SRA editions yield only a single score for each factor. In the form for ages 7 to 11, however, a word and a picture test are provided for both the V and R factors, so that readers and nonreaders may be differentiated by a comparison of the two sets of scores.

In general, the format is well designed for expediency of administration and scoring. Both the 11 to 17 and 7 to 11 SRA forms employ reusable booklets with step-down pages and detachable carbonized answer pads with automatic scoring grids inside. (A machine scorable form is also available at the intermediate level.) One wonders why, in the Word-Fluency test for ages 11 to 17, the subject is directed to print his name and other personal data on the answer sheet *after* the signal to stop at the end of the test. The procedure would be better controlled if such information were requested before the specific instructions for the Word-Fluency test are given, when cheating would be impossible. The 1948 revision of the 5 to 7 year form is identical with the first edition except that all items have been printed in larger size and on a larger page, the booklet now being the same size as those for older subjects. For an unexplained reason, however, this revision is designated as the form for ages 5 to 7, while the first edition was marked for ages 5 and 6.

Norms are based on samples which, on the whole, appear satisfactory in size but which are inadequately described with reference to type of school, part of the country, proportion of urban and rural representation, national and ethnic origin, and socio-economic level. Little or no information is provided in the manuals to indicate the representativeness of the normative samples or to define the population that was sampled. No separate sex norms are reported, nor are any data on sex differences included in the manuals.

In most of the forms, percentile norms for each factor are provided at each year or half-year level. Individual profiles are constructed from these percentiles. The SRA form for ages 11 to 17 provides the most satisfactory treatment of scores, since the profiles are plotted on a sliding percentile scale in which the units are adjusted to conform to a normal distribution. Such a procedure eliminates the inequality of percentile units in the graph, but not, of course, in the numerically reported scores. The same form provides for total scores "IQ equivalents" which actually correspond to normalized standard scores with a mean of 100 and a standard deviation of 16. Despite the obvious technical advantages of the latter measure, the authors recommend the use of percentiles in preference to such an IQ "for almost all uses." It is difficult to find the justification for such a recommendation. In the form for ages 7 to 11, a sliding scale of percentiles had formerly been employed in plotting the profiles, but, in the 1950 revision of the profile sheet, a mental age unit has been substituted. This is a clear example of deterioration rather than progress in test construction. The present MA units are all treated as equal, the rise from ages 13 to 14, for example, being as large as that from 6 to 7 on the scale. Moreover, ability quotients are computed by dividing test age for each factor by CA, with no indication whether or not the SD of such quotients remains constant with age. The same quotient may thus have very different meanings at different ages or in different abilities. In the 5 to 7 year form, only MA units and quotients are provided, the scores thus being subject to the same inaccuracies as those found in the latest revision of the 7 to 11 profile sheet.

A defect common to most of the PMA tests is their undue emphasis upon speed, even in the case of such tests as Verbal Meaning and Reasoning, designed to measure power. Speed is especially prominent in all forms for ages 11 to 17, including the two longer Chicago versions

and the SRA abridgment. In the tests for ages 7 to 11, some effort was made to estimate the influence of speed, but unfortunately a very crude speed index was employed, based essentially on the proportion of individuals who attempt the last item in each test. On this basis, Perceptual Speed and Number appear to be primarily speed tests, while the remaining tests depend to a much smaller, though not negligible, degree upon speed. It would be desirable (a) to apply a more dependable and precise speed-power index, such as H^2, and (b) to reduce still further the contribution of speed to the supposedly power tests in the battery. In the form for ages 5 to 7, only the P and Mo tests are speed tests, the remaining tests being administered with no time limits.

A special weakness of the entire PMA series is the treatment of test reliability. In tests such as these, designed for intra-individual comparisons and profile analysis, the need for proper determination and reporting of reliability is particularly urgent. Yet in the various forms of the PMA tests, reliability coefficients are either inadequately reported, incorrectly computed, or completely omitted. Odd-even and Kuder-Richardson techniques have been repeatedly employed in finding the reliability of speeded tests. In several forms, no recognition is given to this problem at all, spurious and meaningless reliabilities as high as .98 being reported without comment, except to say that the reliabilities would probably be higher in more heterogeneous samples. In the manual of the form for ages 7 to 11, it is admitted that for highly speeded tests such as P and N, the usual internal consistency techniques are unsuitable. But this is followed by the astounding and erroneous conclusion that Kuder-Richardson formula 21 is applicable in such cases, and the "reliabilities" thus computed are accordingly reported for these tests! The manual of the form for ages 5 to 7 contains no reliability coefficients. In a personal communication to the present reviewer, the reliabilities of four of the five scores on this form were reported as follows: V, .77; Q, .90; P, .96; S, .87. No mention was made of the size or nature of the samples on which these reliabilities were computed nor of the techniques employed to determine reliability. In view of the suspiciously high reliability of the Perceptual Speed score, however, it appears likely that internal consistency measures were employed throughout.

It is interesting to note the implications of

test reliability for the evaluation of individual profiles. As an illustration, the Space scores on the PMA for ages 7 to 11 may be considered. With a reliability coefficient of .79, the standard error of a score on this test is .46 SD; a minimum deviation of 1.19 SD is therefore required for significance at the .01 level. Reference to the percentile profile sheet shows, however, that deviations above the 75th or below the 25th percentile on any test are interpreted as representing "high" or "low" standing, respectively, in the given ability. Such a deviation corresponds to .67 SD, not 1.19 SD. Many such deviations therefore fall well within the error of measurement of the test. In the profile sheets plotted in terms of MA units, no attempt has even been made by the authors to indicate how large a deviation from the norm is required for the meaningful interpretation of profile points.

Another important factor in the interpretation of intra-individual variations is the degree of intercorrelations among the tests. In the PMA batteries, such intercorrelations are considerable, especially at the lower age levels. At the 11 to 17 level, most of the intercorrelations among ability scores are in the .30's, those between V and R being in the .50's. At the 7 to 11 level, intercorrelations on one sample of nine-year-olds ranged from .41 to .70; at the 5 to 7 level, correlations from .46 to .67 are reported. At least some of these correlations are probably as high as the correlations between different tests designed to measure the same ability. Such a situation casts doubt upon the value of finding separate scores in these abilities for young subjects. Moreover, in the light of the probable reliability of the various tests (when reliabilities are properly computed), it would seem that a large majority of the intra-individual differences between scores on the various primary mental abilities are the result of chance errors. For example, with a mean reliability of .80 and a correlation of .50 between two tests, only about 22 per cent of the obtained differences between scores on the two tests are in excess of chance.

The validation of the PMA tests has been limited principally to an analysis of their factorial validity. In the manuals for the two forms of the Chicago PMA batteries, correlations of the composite score in each of the six abilities with each factor are reported. It may be noted that the two tables, for the six-booklet and the single-booklet edition, are identical. Obviously the original factorial validities of the longer battery were simply reproduced as though they applied to the shorter battery, without rechecking or estimating the effect which a reduction in number and variety of items would have upon the factorial validities of the tests. No factorial validities are reported for any of the SRA forms at any age level. Attempts toward the estimation of empirical validity appear to have been meager and unsystematic. A few correlations with other psychological tests, including *American Council on Education Psychological Examination, Kuhlmann-Anderson Intelligence Test, General Aptitude Test Battery, Minnesota Vocational Test for Clerical Workers,* and *Revised Minnesota Paper Formboard Test,* are reported for the 11 to 17 and 7 to 11 SRA forms. The last three tests mentioned, incidentally, are incorrectly included in a section on measures of "achievement." Correlations of the 11 to 17 form with tests of educational achievement are likewise reported. The predominant role of the V and R factors in achievement in all school subjects is suggested by these correlations.

No evidence of validity, whether factorial or empirical, is given for the 5 to 7 year form; nor is there any published report of the factor analysis from which either this battery or that for ages 7 to 11 were presumably constructed. The manual for the 5 to 7 year form contains an extensive list of references of general psychological interest, ranging from Carmichael's *Manual of Child Psychology* to Bernardine Schmidt's monograph on the rehabilitation of the feebleminded; but one searches in vain for the relevant sources giving the details of construction of the particular test. In 1948 and again in 1951, the present reviewer learned through personal communication with the publishers that the report of the factorial investigation from which the 5 to 7 year tests were developed was in preparation but delayed. It is unfortunate that it has been delayed for so many years subsequent to the publication and distribution of the tests.

It would seem that the use of the term "primary mental abilities" connotes the measurement of factors which are somewhat more basic, permanent, and universal than is warranted by the available research, whether conducted by the test authors or by other independent investigators. Moreover, both the test manuals and the profile sheets emphasize the readiness with which teachers, parents, and students may interpret the PMA profiles in terms of specific educational and vocational plans. Such recom-

Primary Mental Abilities

mendations go far beyond the available evidence for empirical validity.

In a booklet entitled *You and Your Mental Abilities,* addressed to high school students, the examinees are again urged to request and to interpret their own scores on the basis of oversimplified schemata. After a brief description of the primary mental abilities (as defined in the SRA tests), the booklet presents sample items for the student to work through, as well as hints on how to take psychological tests. The logic underlying such a booklet is puzzling. If the use of the booklet can effect an improvement in test scores, either through specific practice or through general test sophistication, then the availability of such a booklet to some individuals and not others reduces the validity of the tests. On the other hand, if scores are not appreciably raised, then it would seem that many of the statements in the booklet create misleading expectations in the reader. On the basis of what is known regarding test wiseness and the effects of practice on psychological test performance, it appears likely that the use of such a booklet would in fact influence scores.

The problem of test sophistication and specific practice is also encountered in three other booklets constituting a *Learning to Think* series and designed for kindergarten and first grade children. Covering a daily 20-minute lesson for three semesters, these booklets provide practice materials in each of the PMA areas. The similarity between these practice materials and the test items is quite close, many of the same pictures being employed, albeit in different ways. It would be helpful to know the extent to which practice on these materials leads to improvement in (*a*) scores on the PMA tests, (*b*) scores on other psychological tests, and (*c*) the child's general intellectual functioning in school work and other "criterion" situations. Only thus would it be possible to determine whether such materials provide primarily coaching, test sophistication, or education. No data bearing on any of these points, however, are cited.

In summary, the early forms of the PMA tests were the result of extensive research and represented an important and promising new step in test construction. But subsequent development, rather than providing the needed refinement and empirical validation of such an experimental instrument, has proceeded downward in the direction of abridgment and crude popularization. As for the supplementary booklets and

practice materials, perhaps their chief usefulness will be to provide problems for discussion by committees engaged in formulating codes of professional ethics for psychologists.

RALPH F. BERDIE, *Professor of Psychology, and Director, Student Counseling Bureau, University of Minnesota, Minneapolis, Minnesota.*

The original *Tests for Primary Mental Abilities* were perhaps more substantially founded on basic psychological theory than any other tests we have available today. During the past 10 years, however, these tests have been revised, renamed, and reassembled to such an extent that it is difficult to trace the present tests back to their ideational sources.

In 1938, the experimental edition of the *Tests for Primary Mental Abilities* was published by the American Council on Education. These original tests measured seven factors that provided a total of 16 separate scores. The time limit for the practice exercises and for the tests totaled 222 minutes. In 1941, the *Chicago Tests of Primary Mental Abilities* were presented by the authors. These tests provided seven scores and required 240 minutes. A single booklet edition of the *Chicago Tests of Primary Mental Abilities* was published in 1943 and required 120 minutes.

In 1946, the first of the *SRA Primary Mental Abilities* tests appeared. This series was for ages 5–7 and had originally been published under the title *Tests of Primary Mental Abilities for Ages 5 and 6.* Six scores are provided by these tests and the time required is between 60 and 80 minutes. The *SRA Primary Mental Abilities* for ages 7–11 appeared in 1947. This series provides 11 scores and requires 60 minutes. The *SRA Primary Mental Abilities* for ages 11–17 appeared in 1947 and provided six scores. The testing time was 45 minutes. Thus, the latest development of these tests requires approximately one fourth of the time required by the earlier editions. No acceptable data indicating the effect of this condensation on the reliability of the tests are available.

In light of the elaborate experimental and statistical developments of these tests, it is surprising that they are not better than they are. In fact, one can question whether there is any acceptable evidence at all to suggest that the use of these tests can be justified in an educational or guidance program.

The evidence for the reliabilities reported in

the manual is insufficient, and since these tests are, on the whole, highly speeded, the method used for determining reliability was inappropriate. Furthermore, since these tests are relatively pure factorially, any measure of reliability based on internal consistency must be high.

Little evidence concerning the validity of the test scores is presented. Tables showing correlations between the PMA and other tests are presented in the manuals. The most indicative information should come from correlations between PMA scores and achievement, but when the PMA scores are correlated with achievement test scores, it is a question whether or not the resulting correlation is due to the achievement tests being heavily loaded with the factor contained in the PMA test. Much evidence that the tests are relatively independent is presented, but nothing to show that the tests predict either scholastic success or vocational performance is available.

A minor error appears in the manual where 60 test items are reported to constitute the Number Test; actually, 70 numbers are there.

In general, one would expect these tests to be a great contribution to education and guidance. That they have not been may be due either to the test itself or to the inadequate follow-up work that the authors or others have done. It may be that in attempting to produce a test that requires relatively little time or money, the publishers have sacrificed those very things that made the tests potentially valuable. It is too bad that after such tests have been available for more than 14 years, one must still conclude that their principle uses are experimental.

JOHN B. CARROLL, *Lecturer on Education, Harvard University, Cambridge, Massachusetts.*

Administrators, teachers, and guidance personnel in both elementary and secondary schools may consider themselves fortunate in having available to them, at last, an integrated series of tests of primary mental abilities. This review is intended to appraise the major features of the series and some of its accompanying materials, to offer some thoughts about their proper use and interpretation, and to discuss the features of each of the separate batteries.

The theoretical basis for the tests is now well known: "intelligence" has been shown to be composed of a number of separate and more or less independent "abilities" or "factors." In the development of this series, an effort has been made to construct tests which are "pure" measures of the several primary (first-order) factors. Some of these tests, particularly those of the reasoning factor, correlate rather highly with a general (second-order) factor; hence, a good measure of the general intellective factor may be secured, as the authors indicate, by making appropriate combinations of scores of the primary factors. Nowhere in the test manuals is there any suggestion that regression techniques should be used to obtain measures of primary factors from which the effect of a general factor has been eliminated. The authors would probably maintain (and this reviewer would concur) that from the standpoint of pupil guidance, the elimination of the general factor from the factor scores might give rise to unnecessary difficulties in interpretation.

The authors have selected for these tests the most prominent and most often isolated factors in a long series of studies. Number, Reasoning, Verbal-Meaning, and Space are represented in all batteries reviewed here, except the primary school battery where Number and Reasoning coalesce in a single Quantitative factor, since young children have not encountered formalized instruction in number operations. The Word-Fluency (W) factor is included only in batteries designed for ages 11 to 17; the authors state that it cannot conveniently be measured earlier because the usual tests for W involve writing. Tests of M (Memory) appear only in the longer Chicago tests, for the upper age levels. Tests of P (Perceptual Speed) occur only in the SRA Primary and SRA Elementary tests. The SRA Primary battery also includes a test of "Motor Ability"; actually, this test could be better described as a measure of ability to manipulate a pencil. Apparently, it was the intention of the authors to include, at each level, tests of only those factors deemed of most importance for guidance purposes. Inclusion of other factors would have resulted in longer batteries. Most teachers would agree that measures of V (Verbal), R (Reasoning), S (Space) and N (Number) abilities should be included at all levels, but it is to be regretted that measures of P (Perceptual Speed) were omitted at the upper levels, especially if one postulates that this ability has some relevance for commercial curricula and consequently for vocational guidance. The tests of factors W (Word Fluency) and M (Memory) could easily have been dropped, because thus far we have seen little evidence of their relevance for either educational or vocational guidance. The fact that a given dimension of ability is clearly disclosed in a series of factor studies is of paramount interest in psychological research, but it does not necessarily justify the inclusion of tests of that dimension in a battery intended for practical purposes. On the other hand, with further use of the present batteries, some interesting research data pertaining to the relevance of all the various factors will undoubtedly be obtained.

In general, the tests appear to be well constructed. For any given factor, the tests used are those which have shown most factorial purity, highest factor loadings, and highest reliabilities; even in the abbreviated SRA Intermediate battery, the reliabilities of the tests are such that little accuracy of measurement or factorial validity is lost in comparison with the longer *Chicago Tests of Primary Mental Abilities* (Six Booklets Edition). The test manuals state that extensive item analysis procedures have been followed in developing the tests, but in some cases one feels that the range of item difficulty should be expanded. Furthermore, some of the tests are so short that, in spite of the high reliabilities which are reported, the standard errors of measurement must still be appreciable. This is especially true for high scores on the subtests of the SRA Primary battery, where the difference of a raw score point often corresponds to a difference of 6 or 8 months of age placement. The normative data are in most cases as adequate as can be expected at this stage of the test development program, although it is unfortunate that norms are not differentiated by sex.

The difficulties in interpreting individual scores become particularly apparent when the guidance counselor tries to decide how the scores are relevant to the individual's potential success at higher educational levels or to his choice of a career. A guidance counselor who is not familiar with the difficult technical and theoretical problems involved in making psychological interpretation of the factors can easily be misled by some of the authors' statements about the nature of the factors—statements which in the authors' research publications are offered mainly as suggestive hypotheses. For example, in the manual for the tests at the 5 to 7 year age level, the ability measured by the "motor" test is described as "the ability to coordinate hand and eye movements"; immediately following is a statement that "a high degree of motor ability

is valuable to adults." A guidance counselor, or even more likely a parent, might easily draw the erroneous conclusions that (*a*) the motor test in the 5 to 7 year battery measures the same kind of motor ability that is called for in athletics, and (*b*) this motor test predicts adult motor ability. There is a wealth of research to show that motor abilities are highly diverse and specific, and that they are probably not very predictable over long time spans. Again, the Word-Fluency factor is described as the "ability to write and talk easily." This reviewer knows of little evidence to show that W is anything more than a measure of a type of imaginative "flow" which occurs under certain experimental conditions; his own studies do not show any important relation of W with the ability to write or to talk easily. To cite one final example, the memory factor is described by the authors as "the ability to recall past experiences." Their own research has shown that a number of separate memory factors can be isolated; the usual type of memory test measures only a specific kind of immediate rote memory and thus may have little to do with the way one can recall experiences from a more remote past. There is some evidence to show that the Rote Memory factor has something to do with success in learning foreign languages where a large number of paired associations may have to be established, but this factor has not yet been shown to be of any importance in such an activity as, say, remembering the plots of novels.

The authors are undoubtedly on solid ground in their discussions of the Verbal-Meaning and Reasoning factors. In all probability, the statements which the authors make about the Number and the Space factors and their relevance to certain types of curricula and jobs will eventually be substantiated in validity studies, but this is only the reviewer's hunch. With regard to the other factors included in these batteries, the reviewer feels that it is fortunate that the tests are now available for wide use in research, but their usefulness in guidance and selection may not correspond to the usefulness one would expect from a literal interpretation of the authors' statements. The booklet, *You and Your Mental Abilities,* by Bouthilet and Byrne, is not untainted by wishful thinking, when viewed objectively, because unfortunately we simply do not know enough about the relation of the primary factors to success in school subjects and in various occupations.

Primary Mental Abilities

It is all too easy to be hypercritical of tests which have not been "validated" in the usual sense of the term. In the case of primary mental abilities tests, considerable difficulties may stand in the way of doing any conclusive validity studies. For one thing, the use of conventional types of global criteria (such as ratings of success) would be inherently inconsistent with the theory on which PMA tests are based. Success on a job or in a profession might depend upon complex combinations of abilities, with the possibility of compensation among various factors. At the present stage of research in factor analysis, it is probably more important to look for additional primary factors than to question the practical validity of the factors which have already been firmly established. There is a certain satisfaction in being able to say that a person does a certain kind of task very successfully, even when the practical importance of this task is not known. From this point of view, a careful examination of a person's profile on a number of primary factors is bound to be rewarding.

THE SRA PRIMARY BATTERY. This battery is designed for administration as a group test to children aged 5 to 7 in the first years of school. It does not require them to read. The authors have ingeniously devised a series of pencil and paper tests which seem to measure the lower levels of ability on some of the primary factors, namely, those which they call Verbal-Meaning, Perceptual Speed, Quantitative, Motor, and Space. It should be recognized that these factors are not necessarily of the same character as the corresponding factors measured in older children, although one would judge that Verbal-Meaning, Perceptual Speed, and Space are approximately on the same continuum regardless of the age level. It is interesting to see what little children can do with some of these tests; one is struck by the fact that in such an ability as Space there is remarkably little difference between what adults and children can do.

Age norms are provided, but they are not broken down by sex. They suffer from the usual difficulties of extrapolation encountered with all age norms. It is difficult to believe, for example, that a child who gets the top age placement (9 years) in Verbal-Meaning truly has the vocabulary of the average 9-year-old. The total score can be obtained by unit weighting of raw scores on V, P, Q, and S. The authors suggest also that the scores on V and P are prognostic of reading readiness, but they do not indicate exactly how the scores should be combined for this purpose.

Children find these tests interesting; the speeded parts, however, are likely to present a rather unfamiliar situation to many children who have little notion of the necessity of doing this sort of thing in a hurry. Some experience with administering the test has convinced the reviewer that it should be given at one time to as few children as possible; children should be given plenty of time in the unspeeded sections. The total test time will usually be longer than the hour suggested by the authors, who prescribe that each child should attempt all the problems in the unspeeded tests. The authors fail to say whether the child should be encouraged to guess, nor do they recommend what should be done in case the child cannot come to a decision. The reviewer heartily endorses the recommendation that the testing be divided into two sessions.

It is appropriate to comment at this point on the *Learning to Think Series,* which consists of three graded work books, one for each of the first three semesters of primary school, designed to give training and practice in eight primary mental abilities. They do not require the child to read, but provide reading readiness materials. The content is geared very closely to that of the SRA Primary battery.

According to Mrs. Thurstone, "the research that underlies this series proved clearly that young children improved markedly with training in their ability to solve problems involving the different *Primary Mental Abilities* * The use of direct training material....helps to prepare children for more efficient learning in the regular school activities of the early grades as well as in situations outside the classroom. In a real sense, increasing the child's *Primary Mental Abilities* through training is increasing his ability to think." The research of which Mrs. Thurstone speaks does not seem to have been published in detail, but it is not unreasonable to suppose that the training would have the effects described. Some will criticize the use of this series as mere "coaching" for the tests; this, in my opinion, is a shortsighted view. We cannot expect children to mature and to learn in a vacuum. Why not give them training in elementary mental operations? To the extent that the *Learning to Think Series* trains the child to perceive identities, similarities and differences; to increase his vocabulary; to reason in terms of cause and effect, genus-species, and quantity; to improve eye-hand coordination, and the like—it also will train him in the mental and motor skills which are probably basic to all complex forms of achievement. The fact that a child may possibly make a "higher score than he should" on a test after this kind of training is irrelevant. Children do not exist solely for the purpose of being tested. We may look forward to experiments designed to show whether the training afforded by this series actually transfers, as the authors hope, to the acquisition of more complex skills. One practical consideration in the use of this series is that bright children will probably lose interest unless they are given materials of a properly challenging level of difficulty. In any revision of the series it would not be out of order to include simple reading material at the upper levels.

THE SRA ELEMENTARY BATTERY. The short tests in this battery, designed for children aged 7 to 11, are probably sufficiently reliable. Many of the tests require reading ability, but the authors have fortunately made it possible to get a useful appraisal solely from the "non-reading tests." In fact, the comparison of scores on the two tests of V, one requiring reading and the other not, will probably afford a good indication of the child's visual word recognition ability independent of his vocabulary. The tests appear to be satisfactorily graded in difficulty and have adequate norms except for the lack of sex differentiation. There is considerable disparity in the length of the subtests. The Space test has only 27 items, while tests of V have 73 items altogether. It is not surprising that the reliability of the Space test is reported as only .79. The battery makes use of the SRA answer pad, which makes for efficient scoring. In the reviewer's copy, however, the answer pad could not be properly aligned with the test booklet, due to a defect in manufacture.

THE SRA INTERMEDIATE BATTERY. This battery, for ages 11 to 17, is a shortened version of the single booklet edition of the *Chicago Tests of Primary Abilities,* which in turn is a shortened version of the separate booklet edition of the same battery. The technique of shortening is simply to select, for each factor, the one test which appears to measure the factor best in terms of reliability and factor loadings. The tests have remained unchanged since originally published in 1941. In one or two cases, the test items are samples of items in the original experimental

edition published in 1938. Shortening of the test battery in such a manner does not seriously affect the reliability or factorial validity of the factor scores. The SRA version provides no measurement of the memory factor.

GENERAL EVALUATION. Viewed as a whole, the batteries in these series are an interesting application of multiple factor theory to practical test construction. In most cases, the tests for each factor have satisfactory reliabilities and factorial validities. It appears that the tests are internally quite homogeneous and, where necessary, appropriately scaled for difficulty. It is probable that some tests contain a general factor of mental speed to a greater extent than might be desirable in order to have perfectly pure factor measurements. The practical necessity of giving a wide variety of tests in a short time causes the time-limits to be somewhat too short in some cases.

The authors recognize that further research is needed before a completely adequate series of pure factor tests can be developed. They have in fact continued their research to the point of isolating a number of factors which are not represented in the batteries currently available and have indicated that new and more complete batteries will be published soon.

In the meantime, progress towards ascertaining the practical validity of primary factor tests has been disappointingly slow except in the case of such thoroughly investigated factors as Verbal-Meaning and Reasoning (to the extent that these have been measured by conventional intelligence tests). We cannot yet be sure of the practical importance the various factors may have in educational and vocational guidance. We know next to nothing about the stability of the factors over long periods of time and hence cannot make statements as to the probable long-range predictive validity of the tests administered to young children. Despite all this, if I were a school administrator, I would be eager to give the tests in all grades and compare the results with pupils' achievements after a five- or a ten-year period.

STUART A. COURTIS, *Professor Emeritus of Education, University of Michigan, Ann Arbor, Michigan.*

No tests this reviewer has ever seen or used approach the PMA tests in the care and ingenuity evident in their construction. The authors have very wisely broken away from conventional memory question-response type of items. In all tests the exercises involve mental functioning in action. The record sheet is removable so that the test booklets may be used over and over again. Percentile norms and self-interpreting profile graphs are given. There are charts and provisions for converting scores into mental ages and IQ's. Many tables and references provide reliabilities, correlations, and other background material. In other words, the tests and manuals might well serve as models for all publishers of tests to follow.

"Fifteen years of research into the nature of intelligence" have supplied the "primary mental abilities theories" upon which the tests are based. "The research projects involved the use of the statistical method called factor analysis and have revealed that intelligence is not a unitary trait." "Eight abilities have already been identified." Those "most commonly tested *are called*" (my italics) by names judged appropriate, and denoted by letters.

Every person who makes or uses tests has, of course, perfect freedom to adopt or follow any theories or methods of interpretation he pleases. For those who accept conventional mass and correlational statistics, the PMA tests can be enthusiastically accepted without criticism.

This reviewer, however, rejects as *inappropriate or totally false* both the statistical methods and the theories of primary mental abilities derived from their use. More than 40 years of educational measurement and interpretation, using mass statistics and assumptions borrowed from economic and other fields, have proved sterile in permanent contributions to educational science. There have been many changes in education since 1910, the beginning of the educational measurement movement. But philosophical theorizing led to changes in education before measurement began. While educational measurement has been a great stimulus to *speculation,* it has made no contribution to the kind of objective, verifiable, impersonal knowledge that goes by the name of science. This reviewer predicts that the PMA tests, in spite of their structural and functional excellence, will not yield laws or educational principles any more than other tests have done.

The authors have almost completely ignored the significance of individual differences and those recent advances in theory and practice that have resulted from an increasing awareness of the influence of maturation upon test scores. Many books are being published about researches in child development which prove each child's score is uniquely significant in terms of his own developmental pattern, so that his scores may not with impunity be combined with those of other children, until the scores have been established as reliable by immediate repeated retesting and then converted to comparable maturational units. This the authors of the PMA tests have not done.

The norms for the PMA tests have all the characteristics of maturation curves. From these norms 18 isochronic equations [1] have been computed, one for each test, and these equations prove the inadequacies of many of the authors' statements.

The authors appear to be well aware of the fact that tests measure performance only and that hundreds of factors contribute to every score. Yet they persistently accept single scores at their face values. No figures are given on test-retest reliability, nor is there any discussion of the causes of individual variation in score on retests.

Confronted with conflicting theories of educational measurement, the ordinary user of tests can only wait to see which theory is most productive of useful results. Today new measurement techniques, individual statistical methods, and new theories that supply competing systems against which to check the validity of this reviewer's prophecies as well as the authors' published claims are available.

P. E. VERNON, *Professor of Educational Psychology, Institute of Education, University of London, London, England.*

The *Chicago Tests of Primary Mental Abilities* (1941 and 1943) and their factorial background are so well known that the review will concentrate on the new features presented by the SRA edition.

Each of the three levels covers five factors only: (*a*) Primary (ages 5–7): V, S, Q(N + R), P, and Mo. (*b*) Elementary (ages 7–11): V, S, N, R, and P. (*c*) Intermediate (ages 11–17): V, S, N, R, and W. Me (memory) is omitted on the grounds that testing it takes too long. W (word fluency) is omitted at the two younger levels as depending too much on speed of writing, and Mo (motor) at the two higher levels because the motor coordination needed

---

[1] Those interested may secure copies of the equations and related materials by sending a 9¼″ x 12½″ self-addressed envelope plus 10¢ in stamps for postage to this reviewer at 9110 Dwight Ave., Detroit 14, Michigan.

for most scholastic purposes has largely matured by 7 years. P tests are available only in experimental form above 11 years. N and R are merged, at ages 5–7, in Q (quantitative); this is an interesting point of developmental psychology, about which one would like more information.

There is now only one test per factor, apart from certain composite tests in the Primary battery and the reading and nonreading tests of V and R in the Elementary. While this enables the testing to be reduced to between 40 and 75 minutes, depending on the level, it inevitably means that the validity of the tests (either in relation to primary trait vectors or to educational or vocational criteria) is reduced. Judging from the intercorrelations and the results of a new analysis of 10th and 12th grade scores reported in the manuals, the writer estimates that the typical factor score measures general ability, or g, to about 50 per cent and a distinctive primary ability only to about 10 per cent.

Thurstone has clearly retreated from his earlier opposition to "general" intelligence. He not only allows total scores to be calculated for each battery, but even provides for their conversion to IQ's. (Mo is omitted from the Primary total; actually its saturation with the general factor in this battery is as high as .65). Each component factor is approximately equally weighted in these totals.

That this is a wise step is indicated by the average intercorrelation of .55 at the Primary level and .50 in a 9-year-age group. The figure sinks to .34 and about .30 in grade groups 4B and 10–12. There seems to be little evidence, then, of the differentiation of abilities with age (as expounded by Garrett); the greater homogeneity within the grade groups could fully account for the reduced overlapping.

Earlier editions were criticised because all the tests were speeded. This is still true of the Intermediate battery, but not of the others, where only the P, Mo, and N tests are timed.

The V and P scores at the Primary level are claimed to be diagnostic of reading readiness, though no evidence is presented. At the Elementary level, the difference between reading and nonreading V and R scores is shown to be educationally significant; also a separate nonreading total score or IQ can be calculated by omitting the two reading tests.

You and Your Mental Abilities is a pleas-

antly written pamphlet for students in grades 9–12. It explains individual differences in intelligence and other abilities, and gives advice on taking and interpreting PMA tests. If it were true that the tests were valid predictors of educational and vocational potentialities, one could cordially recommend it.

The *Learning to Think* manuals and workbooks provide a series of daily 20-minute lessons for three half-years—kindergarten and first grade. Not having had any opportunity to try them out, the reviewer can merely record his opinion that they will be thoroughly attractive to, and suitable for, 5- to 6-year-olds. The exercises are all based on pictorial material and cover the eight factors in rotation. There is no doubt that they will improve the ability to do the SRA Primary tests. The crucial point is whether they will transfer or train any wider manifestations of these faculties. Although Mrs. Thurstone believes that they will and claims to have research evidence, the only relevant references quoted are those of the Iowa school.

As one would expect of the Thurstones and of SRA publications, the mechanics of the tests are admirable and the directions for administration and scoring clear and simple. Each test covers the specified range adequately, and the norms are based on large numbers. It is a pity that separate sex norms or at least some indication of the typical profiles of boys and girls are not provided. Reliabilities are good for the two older levels. The fact that they are not quoted for the Primary level increases one's suspicion that they are less favorable. There is no information on correlations between tests of the same factors at different levels. It is most unlikely that the Primary battery gives high predictions of scores at later ages, though the user is allowed to infer this. Still more serious is the implication that all the tests are valid educational and occupational predictors, especially since teachers, parents, and even pupils are encouraged to interpret and act on the profiles. A set of weighted scores on several tests, including suppressors, could indeed have supplied "relatively pure measures of the factors." It is most misleading to suggest that single short tests can do so. There is little enough evidence to show that pure measures of, say, W, will predict ability as "actor, stewardess, reporter, salesman, writer and advertising man." The validity of a single W test is probably much lower and is likely to derive more from its general verbal intelligence content than from its distinctive fluency component. In conclusion, the SRA tests would be valuable to a trained school psychologist who would realise their weaknesses and could supplement any diagnostic indications from the profiles by more thorough testing; but when applied and interpreted by laymen and pupils, they may often do considerable harm.

For a review by Florence L. Goodenough of the Primary test, see 3:264; for a review by Cyril Burt of the Single Booklet and the Six Booklets Editions, and a review by James R. Hobson of the Single Booklet Edition, and a review by F. L. Wells of the Six Booklets Edition, see 3:225; for reviews by Henry E. Garrett, Truman L. Kelley, C. Spearman, Godfrey H. Thomson, and Robert C. Tryon and excerpts from reviews of the Six Booklets Edition, see 40:1427; for related reviews, see 40:B1099 and 38:B503.

[717]

★[United States Employment Service Special Aptitude Tests.] Ages 16 and over; 1935–44; also called C Series; a series of tests used by the U.S.E.S. as the basis from which specific aptitude test batteries were developed for entry jobs in industrial plants; available only in batteries standardized prior to 1945, after which time they were superseded by subtests of the *General Aptitude Test Battery* (see 714) in the development of new batteries; tests C1, C2, C13–C17, C93, C100, C101 adapted from *MacQuarrie Test for Mechanical Ability* (see 759) and must be purchased from California Test Bureau, the publisher; all other tests must be purchased from U.S. Government Printing Office; 30 tests; 1 form; testing services free of charge when program is conducted through the facilities of the U.S.E.S.; institutions and employers using their own facilities must purchase tests and employ testing supervisors trained by U.S.E.S.; details may be secured from local and state offices, through which all orders must be cleared; postpaid; United States Employment Service. *

a) C1 [MOTOR SPEED]. 1942; 2.7¢ per copy; ½(5) minutes.
b) C2 [AIMING]. 1942; 2.2¢ per copy; ½(5) minutes.
c) C9 [NUMBER WRITING]. 1939; $1 per 100; 4(8) minutes.
d) C13 [EYE-HAND COORDINATION]. 1942; 2.7¢ per copy; 1(5) minutes.
e) C14 [FIGURE COPYING]. 1942; 2.2¢ per copy; 2½(7) minutes.
f) C15 [PLOTTING]. 1942; 2.7¢ per copy; 2(7) minutes.
g) C16 [SPATIAL]. 1942; 2.2¢ per copy; 4(8) minutes.
h) C17 [MAZE]. 1942; 2.2¢ per copy; 2½(7) minutes.
i) C19 [ARITHMETIC]. 1939; $1.50 per 100; 6(10) minutes.
j) C29 [NUMBER COMPARISON]. 1939; $2 per 100; 6 (10) minutes.
k) C30 [NAME COMPARISON]. 1939; $1.50 per 100; 6 (10) minutes.
l) C32 [SUBSTITUTION]. 1939; $1 per 100; 4(10) minutes.
m) C33 [PAPER FORM BOARD]. 1941; $6.75 per 100; 7 (12) minutes.
n) C43 [AUTOMOTIVE]. 1944; $2 per 100; 10(15) minutes.

o) C48 [TOOLS]. 1941; $3.50 per 100; 10(15) minutes.
p) C55 [SERIES COMPARISON]. 1941; $3.50 per 100; 4 (10) minutes.
q) C56 [SIZE AND SHAPE DISCRIMINATION]. 1941; $9 per 100; 5(10) minutes.
r) C57 [3-DIMENSIONAL SPATIAL RELATIONS]. 1941; $4.50 per 100; 4(10) minutes.
s) C61 [ARITHMETIC]. 1941; $1.50 per 100; 5(10) minutes.
t) C67 [IDENTICAL FORMS]. 1941; $3.50 per 100; 4(10) minutes.
u) C70 [SURFACE DEVELOPMENT]. 1941; $6 per 100; 6 (10) minutes.
v) C81 [REASONING PROBLEMS]. 1942; $1.50 per 100; 6(10) minutes.
w) C86 [MECHANICAL INFORMATION]. 1941; $4.50 per 100; 11(16) minutes.
x) C87 [MARKING]. 1942; $1.50 per 100; ½(5) minutes.
y) C88 [PAPER SPATIAL RELATIONS]. 1941; $1.75 per 100; 5(10) minutes.
z) C92 [MIRROR IMAGE]. 1942; $1 per 100; 3(7) minutes.
aa) C93 [BLOCK COUNTING]. 1942; 2.7¢ per copy; 3(7) minutes.
bb) C94 [DIRECTIONS]. 1942; $1.50 per 100; 5(10) minutes.
cc) C100 [3-LINE COPYING]. 1942; 2.2¢ per copy; 2½ (7) minutes.
dd) C101 [LOCATION]. 1942; 2.2¢ per copy; 2(7) minutes.

[718]

Yale Educational Aptitude Test Battery. Grades 9–16; 1946–47; 7 scores: verbal comprehension, artificial language, verbal reasoning, quantitative reasoning, mathematical aptitude, spatial relations, mechanical ingenuity; IBM; 7 tests in 2 booklets (tests 1, 2, 5, 6 in Single Booklet Edition—'46: tests 3, 4, 7 in Single Booklet Edition, Form B—'47); $1.75 per complete set of testing materials; $2.50 per complete set of testing materials including the scoring and reporting of individual results; separate answer sheets must be used; 25¢ per set of IBM answer sheets; postage extra; (45) minutes per test if practice booklets are administered previously, otherwise (60) minutes per test; Albert B. Crawford and Paul S. Burnham; distributed by Educational Records Bureau. *

REFERENCES

1. HERRMANN, WILLIAM CHARLES. *A Follow-Up Study and Evaluation of a Pre-College Program of Educational Guidance at an Engineering College.* Master's thesis, Clark University (Worcester, Mass.), 1940. (*Abstracts of Dissertations...1940*, pp. 121-3.)
2. VAUGHN, K. W. "The Yale Scholastic Aptitude Tests as Predictors of Success in the College of Engineering." *J Eng Ed* 34:572-82 Ap '44. *
3. BININGER, MARY LEE. A Study on the Prediction of Success in an Engineering College. Master's thesis, Clark University (Worcester, Mass.), 1945. (*Abstracts of Dissertations...1945*, pp. 20-21.)
4. CRAWFORD, ALBERT B., AND BURNHAM, PAUL S. *Forecasting College Achievement: A Survey of Aptitude Tests for Higher Education: Part I, General Considerations in the Measurement of Academic Promise*, pp. 134-69, 199-201, 253-71. New Haven, Conn.: Yale University Press, 1946. Pp. xxi, 291. * (London: Oxford University Press, 1946.) (*PA* 20:4331)
5. JACOBS, ROBERT. "Description of the Yale Educational Aptitude Tests," pp. 51-6. In *The Fifth Yearbook of the National Council on Measurements Used in Education, 1947-48.* Fairmont, W.Va.: the Council, Fairmont State College, 1949. Pp. v, 56, viii. Paper, mimeographed. *
6. JACOBS, ROBERT. "A Report on the Yale Educational Aptitude Test," pp. 54-62. (*PA* 23:3447) In *1948 Fall Testing Program in Independent Schools and Supplementary Studies.* Educational Records Bulletin, No. 51. New York: the Bureau, January 1949. Pp. xiii, 72. Paper, lithotyped. *
7. UHRBROCK, RICHARD STEPHEN. "Construction of a Selection Test for College Graduates." *J General Psychol* 41:153-93 O '49. * (*PA* 24:4874)

CLERICAL

[719]

★A.C.E.R. Speed and Accuracy Tests. Ages 13.5 and over; 1942; includes a "seldom used" subtest, Classification, which was not used in obtaining norms; 1 form; no data on reliability and validity; 3s. per 10; separate answer sheets must be used; 1s. 4d. per 10 answer sheets; 3d. per scoring stencil; 6d. per manual; 1s. 3d. per specimen set; cash orders postpaid within Australia; 12(20) minutes; Australian Council for Educational Research. *

D. W. McElwain, *Senior Lecturer in Psychology, University of Melbourne, Victoria, Australia.*

This booklet contains three short tests covering name checking, number checking, and classification. Responses are made on a separate answer sheet. The three tests are separately timed.

The tests were validated against the assessments of training of female students in a business college. The item types selected were found to be the best available. Subsequently it was found that the classification test was in fact only a short intelligence test, and that when a good intelligence test was already present in the battery, this test added nothing. As a result, the classification test is now seldom used. The short form, including only name checking and number checking, is thus almost identical with the *Minnesota Clerical Test.*

Studies carried out by the Australian Council for Educational Research and by the Test Construction Section of the Australian Army Psychology Service indicate that the test has a high validity for a wide variety of clerical type tasks and that it adds appreciably to the prediction given by intelligence tests for academic type learning situations.

An interesting point shown in the validity trials made by the A.C.E.R. when making the test, was that the use of the separate answer sheet seemed of itself to add to the validity of this test for clerical tasks.

These simple quasi-perceptual tests seem likely to be a source of much psychometric investigation in the future. Their performance apparently taps some orectic component of personality that is important in a variety of socially determined forms of institutionalized behaviour, such as "desire to do well at examinations."

The tests have been found generally useful; however, we may speculate about the components for their performance. They were used by all the Australian Armed Services during the war and have been used in the basic battery of the Commonwealth Vocational Guidance Service.

[720]

★Alphabetizing Test. Clerical applicants and high school; 1947; Forms A, B; manual ['47]; $2 per 25, postage extra; 50¢ per specimen set, postpaid; 6(9) minutes; David J. Chesler; Personnel Research Institute, Western Reserve University. *

[721]

★Filing Test. Clerical applicants and high school; 1947; Forms A, B; manual ['47]; $2 per 25, postage extra; 50¢ per specimen set, postpaid; 10(13) minutes; Jay L. Otis and David J. Chesler; Personnel Research Institute, Western Reserve University. *

[722]

★General Office Clerical Test (Including Filing): National Business Entrance Tests. Grades 12–16 and clerical applicants; 1948–52; replaces *Filing Test* (see 3:379); this series was entitled National Clerical Ability Tests from 1938–46 and United-NOMA Business Entrance Tests in 1947; for complete battery, see 453; Form 1393 ('49); no data on reliability; general series folder ('50); series manual ('48); norms ('52); $5 per 25; $1 per test when scoring service and certificates for acceptable work are desired (tests administered only at National Business Entrance Test Centers which may be established in any community); 50¢ per sample test; $2 per specimen set (includes all 6 tests in the series); postpaid; 12c (130) minutes; prepared by the Joint Committee on Tests representing the United Business Education Association and the National Office Management Association; Joint Committee on Tests. *

REFERENCES

Same as for 453.

[723]

★Group Test 20 [Checking]: National Institute of Industrial Psychology. Ages 15 and over; 1936; 2 scores: speed, accuracy; 1 form ['36]; no data on reliability and validity and no description of normative population in manual; data available on request; no norms for part scores; mimeographed manual ['36]; 4s. 6d. per 12; 1s. per single copy; 9d. per manual; postage extra; 12(17) minutes; National Institute of Industrial Psychology. *

REFERENCES

1. Kerr, George. "Aptitude Testing for Secondary Courses: An Essay in Control Under War-Time Difficulties." *Occupational Psychol* 16:73–8 Ap '42. *
2. Shuttleworth, Clifford W. "Tests of Technical Aptitude." *Occupational Psychol* 16:175–82 O '42. *

E. G. Chambers, *Assistant Director of Research in Industrial Psychology, University of Cambridge, Cambridge, England.*

Group Test 20 is an adaptation of the *Minnesota Clerical Test,* British names being substituted for American names in the second part. The test is very simple and consists of number checking and name checking at speed. Separate scores for speed and accuracy are obtained. Norms for these are provided in the form of percentiles based on an unspecified number of secondary school boys in the two age groups : 15 and 16 plus.

The publishers state :

This clerical test is not intended to give an indication of *general* suitability for work of an office kind. Its purpose is to provide a basis for an estimate of an individual's present speed and accuracy in straightforward clerical tasks. Any score obtained in it should always be considered in the light of the individual's intelligence test result, and in the light of his (or her) scholastic record, before a recommendation to office work is made. It should be recognized that speed and accuracy in operations of the types included in the test can to some extent be cultivated. Any score above the 70th percentile may be regarded as a favourable indication for an occupation of a clerical type ; scores below this level should not necessarily be regarded as contra-indicated.

No reliability coefficient is provided nor is there any evidence that the test has been validated. In the absence of such evidence and in view of the statement quoted, it appears to the reviewer that this test would not be very valuable by itself. The dual speed-accuracy method of scoring is a disadvantage, for in many clerical tasks accuracy alone is important. Given time, anyone above the rating of a moron should be able to do this test with perfect accuracy.

[724]

★Group Test 25 (Clerical): National Institute of Industrial Psychology. Ages 14 and over ; 1925–44 ; 7 scores : checking, classification, arithmetic, copying, filing, problems, oral instructions ; 1 form, '38 ; no data on reliability and validity in manual ; data available on request ; mimeographed manual ('44) ; 4s. 6d. per 12 ; 1s. per single copy ; 1s. 6d. per manual ; postage extra ; (35) minutes ; National Institute of Industrial Psychology. *

REFERENCES

1. VERNON, PHILIP E., AND PARRY, JOHN B. *Personnel Selection in the British Forces.* London: University of London Press Ltd., 1949. Pp. 324. * (PA 24:776)

E. G. CHAMBERS, *Assistant Director of Research in Industrial Psychology, University of Cambridge, Cambridge, England.*

This test comprises seven short subtests entitled Checking, Classification, Arithmetic, Copying, Filing, Problems, and Oral Instructions. Normally only the first five subtests are given. The Problems test is regarded as a quick intelligence test which may be given in the absence of a separate intelligence test, and the Oral Instructions test is given only when immediate memory for verbal instructions is particularly important, as in the case of telephone operators or office messengers.

Five-grade norms for tests 1–5, based on 4,509 vocational cases from secondary grammar schools, are given for the three age groups 15, 16, and 17, as are similar norms for secondary

modern school pupils aged 14 based on results of 2,168 pupils. In addition, 5-grade norms, based on 582 industrial applicants for clerical employment, are given for the three age groups 15, 16, and 17 for tests 1–5, 1–6, and 1–7 separately.

No form of reliability coefficient is provided by the publishers, and there is no evidence given that the test has been validated. However, Vernon and Parry (*1*) state that while the test was found to be useful in selection work, a test resembling it, known as the *Clerical and Instructions Test,* with a reliability of .92, was probably superior to it.

It seems very probable that Group Test 25 measures elements involved in certain types of clerical work. Whether or not the short subtests (mostly 2½ minutes each) measure these adequately is another matter and one which cannot be decided on available evidence. The method of scoring, in which one mistake counterbalances two and sometimes three correct responses, is rather arbitrary. However, among tests of this sort, where both speed and accuracy are regarded as essentials, the test should fulfil its function reasonably adequately.

[725]

★[Hay Tests for Clerical Aptitude.] Applicants for clerical positions ; 1941–50 ; 4 tests ; manuals ('50) ; $1.50 per battery manual *Tests for Clerical Aptitude: A Handbook* ('50—see *4* below) ; $2 per specimen set ; postpaid ; 13(28) minutes ; Edward N. Hay ; Aptitude Test Service. *

a) HAY TEST I: THE WARM UP. 1945–50 ; a practice exercise to precede administration of battery ; Form B ('50—a revision of the 1945 form) ; no manual ; $1.25 per 25 ; 1(3) minutes.

b) HAY NUMBER PERCEPTION TEST. 1947–50 ; Forms A ('47), B ('50—same as test copyrighted in 1947) ; $2 per 25 ; 4(7) minutes.

c) HAY NUMBER SERIES COMPLETION TEST. 1941–50 ; Forms A ('41), B ('50—same as test copyrighted in 1949) ; $1.25 per 25 ; Form A : 3(6) minutes ; Form B : 4(7) minutes.

d) HAY NAME FINDING TEST. 1941–50 ; Forms A ('41), C ('50—same as test copyrighted in 1949) ; a practice exercise, entitled Form B ('49), must precede administration of test ; $2 per 25 ; Form A : 3(10) minutes ; Form C : 4(11) minutes.

REFERENCES

1. HAY, EDWARD N. "Predicting Success in Machine Bookkeeping." *J Appl Psychol* 27:483–93 D '43. * (PA 18:1877)
2. DOUB, BETTY ALLEN. "Better Clerks Can Be Hired With Tests." *Personnel J* 29:102–3 Jl–Ag '50. * (PA 25:2074)
3. HAY, EDWARD N. "Cross-Validation of Clerical Aptitude Tests." *J Appl Psychol* 34:153–8 Je '50. * (PA 25:3991)
4. HAY, EDWARD N. *Tests for Clerical Aptitude: A Handbook.* Swarthmore, Pa.: Aptitude Test Service, 1950. Pp. iii, 26. Paper. *
5. HAY, EDWARD N. "A Warm-Up Test." *Personnel Psychol* 3:221–3 su '50. * (PA 25:2078)
6. MILLER, RICHARD B. "Reducing the Time Required for Testing Clerical Applicants." *Personnel J* 28:364–6 Mr '50. * (PA 24:4872)
7. BLAKEMORE, ARLINE. "Reducing Typing Costs With Aptitude Tests." *Personnel J* 30:20–4 My '51. * (PA 27:749)
8. HAY, EDWARD N. "Mental Ability Tests in Clerical Selection." *J Appl Psychol* 35:250–1 Ag '51. * (PA 26:3071)

REIGN H. BITTNER, *Assistant Director of Personnel Research, The Prudential Insurance Company of America, Newark, New Jersey.*

This series of tests is presented for use in selecting good clerical workers. In designing the test battery, the author apparently assumed that clerical aptitude is a composite trait, the components of which are measured by the tests in the battery, and that this composite trait is involved in success in all kinds of clerical work.

The first test in the battery, The Warm Up, is unusual, an easy one-minute test designed to help the applicant adjust to the testing situation. This may be a useful testing device, although no evidence is presented on its effectiveness. The Number Perception Test, the second test, contains common business errors and is similar to the number comparison part of the *Minnesota Clerical Test* although it is shorter and its items are less difficult. The Number Series Completion Test consists of standard items of the number series type. The Name Finding Test involves the finding of key names in a list, a variant form of name comparison.

Reliabilities of the tests are adequate with the possible exception of Number Comparison. Coefficients are .86 for Number Perception and .94 for each of the other two tests.

The validity of the test battery as a measure of general clerical aptitude cannot be assessed from the data presented. Studies are cited which indicate that certain tests in the battery predict with reasonable accuracy success on five jobs: beginning typing, machine bookkeeping, key punching, ticket press operation, and ticket inspection. This is a very limited sample of clerical jobs and seemingly atypical in that all but the last involve certain special skills. These studies do not indicate the validity of the battery as recommended for use—"passing" all three tests —since the validity of only single tests is given.

The tests are all designed for ease of administration and scoring, an objective which has been achieved. The manual is particularly good for aiding administration of the tests; as a guide for interpretation, it appears less valuable. A "passing" score is given for each test, and it is recommended that employment be limited to persons who "pass" all three tests. Presumably this requirement is recommended for applicants for all types of clerical work. It would seem that the tests in the battery might be combined in different ways to predict success in different types of clerical work, but no recognition of this possibility is given in the manual. The validation data presented, however, would seem to point to the use of various combinations of the tests for differential selection and placement rather than to a single combination of the three tests for employment for all clerical jobs.

Norms for the tests are presented in terms of the three quartiles for a number of separate groups. Generally these groups are defined only as male or female "clerical applicants." Other data defining the characteristics and aiding in the interpretation of these samples are not given. It seems likely, too, that norms presented in terms of these statistics will have little meaning to the lay user of the tests. Presumably, it is intended that the recommended "passing" scores be used as the frame of reference in interpreting the tests.

The battery of tests has certain characteristics which recommend it: it has been devised with adequate care for the technical aspects of test construction, testing time has been cut to a minimum, and ease of administration and scoring is assured. Its content emphasizes speed and perceptual factors which are generally found to be involved in clerical success. It would seem to have a good chance of proving to be a valid predictor of success in many clerical jobs, particularly if it were used along with a test of general intellectual ability.

EDWARD E. CURETON, *Professor of Psychology, The University of Tennessee, Knoxville, Tennessee.*

This battery consists of Test 1 (a warm-up test), a Number Perception Test, a Number Series Completion Test, and a Name Finding Test preceded by a special practice exercise. The tests are printed as separate sheets or booklets. Each of the tests except Test 1 has its own short manual, and there is also a 26-page handbook entitled *Tests for Clerical Aptitude* which contains most of the material in the separate manuals along with some additional data and suggestions.

Test 1 is similar to the *Wonderlic Personnel Test,* but with shortened and simplified directions. It contains 20 four-choice items and is administered with a one-minute time limit. Its use as a preliminary exercise should help set at ease examinees who are not test-wise, especially when it is followed by a group intelligence test such as the Wonderlic (5).

The Number Perception Test is essentially a

revision of the Number Comparison subtest of the *Minnesota Clerical Test*. The number pairs range in length from three to only six digits, the errors consist entirely of transpositions and substitutions, and all numbers are aligned in columns at the right. There are 200 items, and the time limit is four minutes. Though the criteria for revision appear sound, it will be difficult to demonstrate statistically that the test is any substantial improvement over the Number Comparison subtest of the *Minnesota Clerical Test*.

The first form of the Number Series Completion Test (Form A), was a reprint of a subtest of the *Army Alpha Examination: First Nebraska Edition,* with 20 items and a three-minute time limit. The later forms contain essentially similar items, but there are 30 items in each and the time limit is four minutes. Factor analysis results show that number series completion tests are typically found to be among the best tests of inductive reasoning ability.

The Name Finding Test consists of an alphabetical list of full names written in the normal order (John P. Ahern, e.g.) on one side of a sheet, and on the other side a list four times as long, including the names of the first list, but with each name consisting only of surname and initials (Ahern, J. P., e.g.). The examinee is to check in the second list those names which are also in the first list. A special Practice Exercise for the Name Finding Test (Form B), has 5 words in the first list and 20 in the second, with no time limit. Form A has 25 words in the first list, 100 in the second, and a three-minute time limit. Form C has 32 words in the first list, 128 in the second, and a four-minute time limit. From its correlations with other tests (*1*), it would appear that the Name Finding Test measures verbal ability and, to a somewhat lesser extent, reasoning and perceptual speed.

The tests of the original battery—Minnesota Number Comparison, Number Series Completion Form A, and Name Finding Form A—were selected from a trial battery of 25 tests administered to 39 bookkeeping machine operators for whom reliable production records were obtained as a criterion (*1*). Since there was a high degree of selection from among the trial tests, and the N of 39 is not large, the multiple correlation of .70 computed from the same sample is spuriously high. The battery was administered later to 82 key-punch operators (*3*), and gave a multiple correlation of .38 with a rating

criterion. Addition to this battery of the *Otis Self-Administering Test of Mental Ability* (20-minute time limit) in the first study, and of the *Wonderlic Personnel Test* in a follow-up of the second study (*8*), failed in each case to improve its predictive power to any significant degree.

The reports on reliability and validity in the manuals, the handbook, and the published papers as well, contain serious statistical errors and misinterpretations. Parallel form reliabilities (the most useful kind) are reported as test-retest reliabilities for the Number Perception Test. Odd-even reliabilities are reported for the Number Series Completion Test and the Name Finding Test despite the fact that they are both definitely speed tests. The handbook cites a study showing that the same percentages of two groups lie above —.6 SD on the Number Perception Test and the *Minnesota Clerical Test* as evidence (along with correlations of .83 and .85 between the two tests) that the four-minute Number Perception Test is essentially as good as the 15-minute *Minnesota Clerical Test* for screening clerical applicants. It is argued (*3*) that multiple cutting scores are superior to multiple regression scores because a higher percentage of a "good" criterion group is selected by the multiple cutting score technique than by the multiple regression technique *in the sample used to set the multiple cutting scores.*

Normative data cover a variety of groups but are reported only in terms of medians and quartiles. "Passing scores" are given for the three tests; these are apparently derived mainly from the multiple cutting score study with 82 key-punch operators. Equivalent Number Perception scores and Minnesota Number Comparison scores, based on 2,951 and 2,658 cases respectively (different sets of clerical applicants to the same company: 1947–49 and 1944–47), are given for every fifth percentile.

In summary, the three tests of this battery appear to be excellent four-minute tests covering some of the essential aspects of ability to perform *routine* (as distinct from highly verbal or highly numerical) clerical operations. The accompanying statistical data do not provide clear evidence concerning the reliabilities of two of the tests. The data on the validities of these tests reported so far are insufficient to support claims of general validity for clerical selection which are made in the handbook. The normative materials supplied are of little value.

Hay Tests for Clerical Aptitude

[726]

★**Martin Office Aptitude Tests.** Clerical employees and applicants for clerical positions; 1947–52; 10 tests; manual, fourth edition ('52); $1.50 per set of scoring stencils; 50¢ per scoring stencil for any one test; $1 per manual; 10–49 profile charts ('52), 10¢ each; 50–99, 9¢ each; 100 or more, 8¢ each; postage extra; Howard G. Martin; Martin Publishing Co. *

a) MARTIN NUMBER CHECKING TEST. 1947–52; Form A ('47); 10–49 test-answer sheets, 10¢ each; 50–99, 9¢ each; 100 or more, 8¢ each; 6(10) minutes.

b) MARTIN NAME CHECKING TEST. 1947–52; Form A ('47); 10–49 test-answer sheets, 10¢ each; 50–99, 9¢ each; 100 or more, 8¢ each; 5(10) minutes.

c) MARTIN NUMBER FACILITY TEST. 1947–52; Form A ('47); 10–49 test-answer sheets, 10¢ each; 50–99, 9¢ each; 100 or more, 8¢ each; 8(13) minutes.

d) MARTIN NUMERICAL OPERATIONS TEST. 1951–52; an "alternate" to *Martin Number Facility Test.* Form A ('51); 10–49 test-answer sheets, 10¢ each; 50–99, 9¢ each; 100 or more, 8¢ each; 8(13) minutes.

e) MARTIN VOCABULARY TEST. 1947–52; Forms A ('47), B ('51); 10–49 test-answer sheets, 10¢ each; 50–99, 9¢ each; 100 or more, 8¢ each; nontimed (10) minutes.

f) MARTIN ARITHMETIC REASONING TEST. 1947–52; I form, '50; 10–49 test-answer sheets, 10¢ each; 50–99, 9¢ each; 100 or more, 8¢ each; nontimed (20) minutes.

g) MARTIN ALPHABETIZING TEST. 1951–52; Form A ('51); 10–49 test-answer sheets, 10¢ each; 50–99, 9¢ each; 100 or more, 8¢ each; 6(10) minutes.

h) MARTIN NUMERICAL ORDER TEST. 1951–52; Form A ('51); 10–49 test-answer sheets, 10¢ each; 50–99, 9¢ each; 100 or more, 8¢ each; 6(10) minutes.

i) MARTIN STENOGRAPHIC TEST. 1949–52; Forms 60–70 A ['49], 80-A ['49], 90-A ['49], 100-A ['49]; $2.50 per test; 9(15) minutes.

j) MARTIN TYPING TEST. 1949–52; Form 10-A ['49]; a practice exercise must precede administration of test; $2.50 per test; 10(20) minutes.

D. WELTY LEFEVER, *Professor of Education, University of Southern California, Los Angeles, California.*

DESCRIPTION OF THE TESTS. The basic series includes the following measures: Number Checking, Name Checking, Number Facility, Vocabulary, and Arithmetic Reasoning. The first two named are very similar to the *Minnesota Clerical Tests.* Number Facility is a simple arithmetic computation test including the four basic operations for whole numbers only. The subject indicates whether the answer given is right or wrong. The Vocabulary test presents a choice of five words, one of which matches in meaning a group of words.

The basic series is supplemented by two proficiency tests: Typing, based on the customary work-sample, and Steno, requiring the typewritten transcription of four business letters dictated at 60–70, 80, 90, and 100 words per minute respectively.

Three measures of aptitude were added in 1951: Alphabetizing, Numerical Order, and Numerical Operations. The latter presents a series of arithmetic operations employing single digit numbers.

STRONG POINTS. (*a*) The aptitude tests are designed in a convenient form for administration and scoring. Each test is a single IBM answer sheet so that the items appear directly on the scoring blank. (*b*) The general appearance and design is clear and attractive. (*c*) The scoring can be effected quickly and easily with overlay stencils if mechanical scoring is not available. (*d*) The name and number comparison tests should have considerable predictive power for selecting clerical employees. Vocabulary recognition and arithmetic reasoning have long been used as measures of general intelligence. (*e*) The typing work-samples are clearly set up for easy copying and quick scoring. (*f*) The pacing of the dictation in the stenographic test appears practicable.

WEAK POINTS. (*a*) The battery offers little that is strictly new or original. No definite indication is given of fresh research evidence on validity. (*b*) In the number tests (except for Arithmetic Reasoning), the possible responses are two: the answer given is right or wrong. This restricted choice unnecessarily increases the hazard of guessing. (*c*) The directions to the test administrator and to the subject occasionally reveal a careless use of language. Examples are: "be sure and make a heavy mark," and "in order to determine if." (*d*) The basis for selecting the vocabulary words is not explained. Since the aptitude series was designed for use in business establishments, a considerably greater face validity could have been achieved by choosing words related to office work. (*e*) The most serious fault, in the judgment of this reviewer, is the dearth of information regarding reliability and validity. The argument that some test users may lack sufficient interest or training to read a more complete exposition of the basic research evidence does not excuse the author and publisher for offering the product to potential purchasers in the form of a "pig in a poke." (*f*) The manual is extremely brief. Fragments of statements from the research literature on aptitude testing in the clerical field are offered without documentation. Vague and incomplete data on validity are suggested. Such norms as "minimum aptitude requirements" are arbitrarily defined for several types of office work without indicatiing the operational basis.

SUMMARY. These tests appear to possess some definite predictive value as judged from their resemblance to more completely standardized and validated instruments. Potential users, however, should demand more complete information before purchasing.

Ross W. MATTESON, *Counselor, Michigan State College, East Lansing, Michigan.*

This is a series of relatively short tests of those abilities required for successful performance of various types of office work. The battery was designed for use both as an instrument for screening job applicants and as a guide in assigning duties to employees. As indicated in the manual of instructions, such tests measure only the ability, not the "will" to do the work.

The packaged testing program, all or part of which may be given to a particular applicant, includes tests of alphabetizing, numerical order, number checking, name checking, number facility, vocabulary, and arithmetic reasoning. There are also tests of stenographic and typing skills. Individual record charts, scoring stencils, and a manual of instructions are included.

Of these tests, Alphabetizing is designed to measure speed and accuracy in arranging names as for filing. Numerical Order presents a similar task in noting, for each of 150 pairs of numbers, which is the lower number. Number Checking and Name Checking involve the familiar task of looking at pairs of numbers or of names and indicating whether they are the same or different. These skills are considered basic for general clerical duties requiring speed and accuracy. Number Facility has 100 problems—25 each in addition, subtraction, multiplication, and division—with answers provided. Instructions are to indicate, by marking the appropriate space, whether the answers are right or wrong. No fractions or decimals are included. Vocabulary consists of 50 vocabulary problems in which the correct or best word is to be chosen to complete each statement. This test should aid in discovering capacity for assuming more responsible types of work. In Arithmetic Reasoning, 12 "story" problems are to be worked out as a measure of the applicant's ability to think logically in the quantitative area.

In addition to the above aptitude tests, Steno and Typing tests are provided for checking the applicant's basic speed in shorthand and typing.

The four letters in Steno are to be read at speeds of 60–70, 80, 90, and 100 words per minute respectively. Although each letter is marked in 15-second intervals, some practice in dictating would appear to be necessary for the test administrator.

Administration of the basic aptitude tests is relatively simple. Time limits for the alphabetizing, checking, and other speed tests range from 5 minutes to 8 minutes and must be rigidly observed. The vocabulary and arithmetic reasoning tests have no time limits.

Scoring the tests is likewise a relatively simple procedure. In the speed tests, wrongs are subtracted from rights in order to penalize for errors. The raw scores may readily be converted into a profile of comparable percentiles. As an aid to effective interpretation of the test scores, the manual of instructions gives five standard patterns of minimum requirements for typical office duties. An applicant's profile can be compared with the pattern for duties involving work with figures, for general clerical duties, for file clerks, for office machine operators, or for stenographer clerks.

Test-retest reliability of the *Martin Office Aptitude Tests* is claimed to be .90 and above. Satisfactory validity is claimed for the tests in connection with their effectiveness in predicting success on the job. Since the manual has been written primarily for the office manager or personnel director using the tests in a practical situation, it includes a minimum of statistical information.

In addition to the packaged office aptitude testing program, a numerical operations test is available. In this test, a series of numerical operations are to be performed *in the order in which they occur* in each problem. Here it would seem that the individual who might attempt to apply the basic rules presented for such operations in arithmetic and algebra textbooks would be at a complete loss. However, as indicated, the current edition of the tests does not include this particular instrument in the packaged battery.

In general, the *Martin Office Aptitude Tests* should prove of practical value in connection with the screening of job applicants and the assigning of duties to employees. Tests of skills as well as tests of aptitudes are provided. As one step in a systematic employment procedure, these tests offer the employer a readily available and easily administered means of obtaining evidence regarding applicants' qualifications for various types of office work.

Martin Office Aptitude Tests

[727]

★**Name Comparison Test for Clerical and Industrial Inspection Operations.** Clerical applicants and high school; 1945-46; Form A ('45) ; manual ['46] ; $2 per 25, postage extra; 50¢ per specimen set, postpaid; 7(10) minutes; Jay L. Otis and Louise W. Garman; Personnel Research Institute, Western Reserve University. *

[728]

★**Number Comparison Test for Clerical and Industrial Inspection Operations.** Clerical applicants and high school; 1945-46; Form A ('45); manual ['46] ; $2 per 25, postage extra; 50¢ per specimen set, postpaid; 9(12) minutes; Jay L. Otis and Louise W. Garman; Personnel Research Institute, Western Reserve University. *

[729]

★**[Personnel Research Institute Clerical Battery.]** Applicants for clerical positions; 1945-47; 8 tests (also listed separately); $2 per 25 of any one test, postage extra; 50¢ per specimen set, postpaid; Personnel Research Institute, Western Reserve University. *
a) CLASSIFICATION TEST FOR INDUSTRIAL AND OFFICE PERSONNEL. 1943-49; Forms A ('47—a revision of the 1943 form), B ('47) ; revised manual ['49] ; norms ('49); 15(20) minutes; Jay L. Otis, Evelyn Katz (A), Robert W. Henderson (A), Mary Aiken (A), David J. Chesler (B), and Gardner E. Lindzey (B). *
b) NUMBER COMPARISON TEST FOR CLERICAL AND INDUSTRIAL INSPECTION OPERATIONS. 1945-46; Form A ('45); manual ['46]; 9(12) minutes; Jay L. Otis and Louise W. Garman.
c) NAME COMPARISON TEST FOR CLERICAL AND INDUSTRIAL INSPECTION OPERATIONS. 1945-46; Form A ('45); manual ['46]; 7(10) minutes; Jay L. Otis and Louise W. Garman.
d) TABULATION TEST. 1947; Forms A, B; manual ['47]; 10(13) minutes; Jay L. Otis and David J. Chesler.
e) FILING TEST. 1947; Forms A, B; manual ['47]; 10(13) minutes; Jay L. Otis and David J. Chesler.
f) ALPHABETIZING TEST. 1947; Forms A, B; manual ['47]; 6(9) minutes; David J. Chesler.
g) ARITHMETIC REASONING TEST. 1948; Forms A, B; manual ['48]; 10(13) minutes; Jay L. Otis and David J. Chesler.
h) SPELLING TEST FOR CLERICAL WORKERS. 1947; Forms A, B; manual ['47]; nontimed (15-20) minutes; Jay L. Otis, David J. Chesler, and Irene Salmi.

LOUISE WITMER CURETON, *1814 Prospect Place, Knoxville, Tennessee.*

These tests are intended to measure most of the important aspects of office and clerical work. The Classification Test may have broader usage as a brief general intelligence test; and it, combined with the Name and the Number Comparison tests, may also be appropriate for certain industrial jobs. The tests have been prepared as separate four-page booklets. The type is clear and the format is attractive except in the case of the Classification Test, whose 100 items have been crowded in order to fit on three pages. Adequate space is provided for figuring in the Arithmetic Reasoning and the Tabulation Test book-

lets. All tests are answered on the booklets and are hand scored. Instructions to the examinees (on the face sheets of the booklets) are concise and clear except for the one ambiguous phrase, "There is no penalty for guessing," and for the omission of time limits for four of the eight tests.

The Classification Test consists of 100 multiple choice items (40 general information, 20 vocabulary, 20 arithmetic, and 20 analogy) in spiral omnibus form and resembles the familiar *Otis Self-Administering Tests of Mental Ability* without the space items. The manual states that it is a test of mental ability for the ordinary shop or office worker and a "screening test for sifting out those very superior individuals who should be tested further," and that an attempt has been made to "include items of approximately uniform difficulty....and to make the difficulty level fairly low." However, the vocabulary items range in frequency of occurrence [1] from over 49 per million running words to less than one, and the arithmetic from "How much is 41¢ and 13¢" to "Which of the following numbers is the smallest? (A) 1% (B) 0.1% (C) .01 (D) 1/100." Also the items are not arranged in order of difficulty. This would be a much better test of general mental ability if subjected to careful item analysis.

The Spelling Test is intended to measure spelling proficiency and is the result of two experimental forms and revisions. The examinee writes (instructions to print would be preferable) the correct spelling of 73 commonly misspelled business words which are each identified in the booklet by a simple phonetic spelling and a definition. This method avoids oral presentation by the examiner, and an examinee of average intelligence should have no difficulty in recognizing the intended test words.

The Name and the Number Comparison tests each have 200 items closely resembling the two parts of the *Minnesota Clerical Test* except that the duplicate items are placed on facing pages instead of in adjoining columns. This variation is probably more like the typical job task; also, it may introduce a slight memory requirement. Two scoring measures are recommended, number right for speed and number wrong for accuracy; and reliability, validity, and norms are reported for each on small samples. More data are needed before this refinement is justified.

[1] Thorndike, Edward L. and Lorge, Irving. *The Teacher's Word Book of 30,000 Words.* New York: Bureau of Publications, Teachers College, Columbia University, 1944. Pp. xiii, 274. *

The Alphabetizing Test consists of 45 sets of 5 names to be ordered. The Filing Test consists of 150 names to be matched with file folders (pictured) labeled Aa–Am, An–Az, etc.

The Tabulation Test consists of 15 short lists of persons or things to be classified and counted or multiplied, subtracted, etc., as instructed, for example, "Orders received on the first day of July were: 27 bbls., 16 boxes, 12 bales, 22 bags. Obtain the weekly sales estimate by multiplying the above figures by 6. (Ans.) Bbls.—— Boxes —— Bales—— Bags——." This is an interesting but complicated item type which has face validity for certain jobs. Without data it is impossible to judge its actual advantage over simpler items which can be used in larger quantities and hence with greater reliability.

The Arithmetic Reasoning Test contains 20 multiple choice verbal-problem items covering whole numbers, percentages, and decimals. The items vary widely in difficulty and time required and are not arranged in order of difficulty. This is a serious drawback for a sharply timed test.

The manuals (one for each test) attempt to give the reader all necessary information for using the tests. The presentations regarding the purposes of the tests, description of items, and directions for administration and for preparation and use of scoring keys are entirely adequate. However, several serious inaccuracies and confusions occur in the data. Reliability coefficients range from .89 to .99, but most of these are spuriously high because they are obtained by the odd-even method on obviously speeded tests. The test-retest method was used only for the Name and the Number Comparison tests and the reported coefficients of .90 and .95 respectively are higher than usual for this type of test; there is no information as to the amount of time intervening between the two administrations. For some tests "equivalence of forms" is reported instead of, or in addition to, reliability. These correlations between the two forms of the tests (.78 to .96) are also spuriously high because the two forms consist of items from matched pairs rather than random selections of items from the same item universe (Arithmetic Reasoning Test, Form A: "At 5 cents each what will 2 dozen pencils cost?"; Form B: "At 8 cents each, what will 3 dozen inkwells cost?"). Determination of the true reliability of these tests would be difficult, but the correlation between forms might be taken as the *upper limit* of reliability. Alternate forms are needed in the prac-

tical situation primarily so that a test may be readministered in cases where results on the first form are invalidated for some reason such as illness of the examinee, errors of administration, etc., but with such highly similar forms as these the scores on the second form might be spuriously high unless long time intervals elapse between administrations. Visual similarity between forms does not guarantee similar levels of difficulty, but similar difficulty is implied by the fact that the norms tables, showing decile equivalents for raw scores, apply to both forms for all tests having two forms. The differences in mean difficulty between forms are reported as .81 and .05 raw score points for the Spelling and Arithmetic Reasoning tests respectively. "Practice effects" are reported as −.04, 2.3, and 1.15 raw score points for the Spelling, Alphabetizing, and Arithmetic Reasoning tests respectively. Methods of determining these two sets of data are not stated, and their meaning is not clear.

Validity coefficients are reported for every test but Arithmetic Reasoning. However, the criteria are merely high school grades or other tests for all but three tests. For the Classification, Tabulation, and Alphabetizing tests, job performance criteria are used ($r = .21$ to $.49$, $.25$ to $.30$, $.29$ to $.37$, respectively). Many more studies must be made before any useful statement can be made as to the validity of these tests in the industrial or business situation. The Classification Test correlates substantially with the *California Test of Mental Maturity, American Council on Education Psychological Examination,* and *Otis Self-Administering Test of Mental Ability* (r's from .62 to .83) for several samples of examinees.

Norms (decile equivalents for raw scores) are provided for every test. The samples were those on which the validity coefficients were computed plus some employed groups for which r's are not stated. The sample size is adequate only for the Classification Test. Geographical location of the samples is seldom mentioned, although this is an important variable in studies of other similar tests. There is no separation of norms by sex. While local norms are always best, the user of these tests should be provided with many more norms from various regions to serve as preliminary guides.

The published data give no information about the relationships between these eight tests, and they are nowhere treated as component parts of a battery. Factor analysis data from other studies would suggest that (a) the Name and the Number Comparison tests are highly correlated; (b) the Name Comparison Test, the Spelling Test, and the Classification Test are correlated because they are all measures in greater or lesser degree of the verbal factor; (c) the Arithmetic Reasoning Test and the Classification Test both contain arithmetic reasoning items and hence should show considerable correlation; and (d) the Tabulation Test and the Arithmetic Reasoning Test both have loadings on the verbal and number factors. The Alphabetizing and Filing tests were developed to complement each other and may be highly correlated. However, Mosier reported on two equally face-valid alphabetizing tests which correlated .00 with each other and almost zero with supervisors' ratings.[2] If test intercorrelations or factor analysis data were available, the test user could select his experimental batteries much more efficiently.

These eight tests appear to be intrinsically good, but most of them need further editing, item analysis, and reliability data before they can be compared adequately with the better known tests which they closely resemble. Also they require many more validity and norms studies before they can be used successfully by any but the most highly trained personnel psychologist who can obtain local validation and normative data.

ALBERT K. KURTZ, *Professor of Psychology, The Pennsylvania State College, State College, Pennsylvania.*

This battery of eight clerical tests is not very useful in its present state. Most of the tests are very similar to well known types of tests that have been in use for some years; there are few really new ideas incorporated in this battery. A few items in each test would probably be criticized by most persons familiar with the characteristics of good test items. The tests are objective, and no particular difficulties in test administration or scoring are likely to be encountered. Reliability coefficients are given for each test, but in several cases these coefficients are spuriously high since they are based on odd-even correlations in which speed is a very important factor. Finally, and most important, validity is all but ignored; five of these tests have not been validated in a nonacademic situation, and the three exceptions gave low validities.

The manuals have the right headings, but the

[2] Mosier, Charles I. "A Critical Examination of the Concepts of Face Validity." *Ed & Psychol Meas* 7:191–205 su '47. *

information supplied is extremely sketchy. Nothing at all is said about any item analyses; the prospective user may well conclude that none were made.

Most of the tests have alternate forms. By looking at them we can deduce that the items were probably constructed in pairs. About half the time, we are given an indication of the size of the difference in difficulty between the two forms. In no case are we told anything about differences in variability or about differences in the shape of the distributions of scores on the two forms.

The directions for administering and scoring the tests are satisfactory. Usually the directions which the examiner reads match those on the test booklet, but there are some discrepancies here. In the manuals, one sentence is omitted from the directions for the Arithmetic Reasoning Test and two from the directions for the Alphabetizing Test.

Norms are given for all tests, but the group on which most of these norms are based is described only as "an employed clerical group." N is usually 57 for this group. For some of the tests additional norms are given.

Three important criticisms may be leveled against most of the material in the "reliability" sections of the manuals. First, all but one of these tests have a time limit which is rather short, and hence the speed element in the tests makes the usual odd-even reliability coefficient spuriously high. For example, the correlation between Forms A and B of the Filing Test is .86 or .88, but the odd-even reliability is .99. Second, the number of cases on which the reliabilities are based is sometimes extremely low (35 for the Number Comparison Test) and is not published (why?) for four of the tests. Third, these tests probably have satisfactory reliabilities, but we do not know. If we ignore the spuriously high odd-even and test-retest figures, we find stated reliabilities of .78 to .96 for the four tests (e, f, g, and h in the above list) for which data are given. We just do not know what the reliabilities of the other tests are.

Validity coefficients are conspicuous by their absence. One of the test manuals does not even mention validity; for four more of the tests, there is a section on validity which does not contain a single comparison with any industrial or business criterion; while for the other three tests there are extremely brief (never more than three lines) statements. These statements simply say that the validities "range between .25 and .30," "ranged from .29 to .37," and that the test "demonstrated low but positive validity." For none of these three tests were the groups described at all; in fact, we are not even told how many cases were involved.

CLASSIFICATION TEST. Items vary widely in difficulty, but they are not arranged in order of difficulty. Since the time limit is short (10 or 15 minutes for 100 items), people who do not skip around will not receive credit for many items that they could have easily answered. The system of classifying items into five subtests is most peculiar. For example, *"Nippon* is another name for....Japan" is a "general information" item, but "The word *Huns* is often used to refer to the....Germans" is a "vocabulary" item. In connection with norms, the following unsubstantiated and highly questionable statement is included: "The present sample is representative of factory workers found in the State of Ohio." Norms for ten different groups are supplied.

NUMBER COMPARISON AND NAME COMPARISON TESTS. These tests differ from the well known *Minnesota Clerical Test* in that it is necessary to go from one page to another in making the comparisons. In a letter to the reviewer, one of the authors, Jay L. Otis, said, "We have had some additional research on the Number and Name Checking Test which indicates that it is as good as, if not better than, typical number and name checking tests." No satisfactory data on either reliability or validity are given in the manual.

TABULATION TEST. Despite its name, several of the items in this test require that the applicant multiply by 4, by 20%, by ⅓, by 6, etc., or divide by such numbers. The manual gives only an odd-even reliability and a vague statement on validity. Norms are given for one group of 57 people.

FILING TEST. This appears to be an almost pure speed test as judged by the previously quoted spurious odd-even reliability of .99. There are no satisfactory validity figures. Norms for two groups are given.

ALPHABETIZING TEST. Data on reliability and validity are presented, but there is no description of the groups upon which the figures are based. Norms are based on two very small groups (N = 26 and 53).

ARITHMETIC REASONING TEST. This is a short test (20 items); most of the items are easy, though a few are tricky. They are obviously not in order of difficulty. The only figure given for reliability (a correlation of .78 between forms) is questioned by the authors as being too low because it is based on a highly selected group. Norms are given for one group. Validity is not even mentioned in the manual.

SPELLING TEST FOR CLERICAL WORKERS. From a purely mechanical standpoint, this test is very poorly put together. The printed directions tell the applicants to write in the wrong column, and the examiner's directions don't match those on the test booklet. It is very difficult to do a good job of phonetic spelling for a nondictated spelling test. In this test a space is inserted between syllables of the phonetic spelling and also a brief definition is given. Many people would disagree with this phonetic spelling. The use of two vowels separated by a consonant within a syllable is obviously confusing. Thus *sare* and *nare* might better be rendered as *sair* and *nair* (a method which the authors use in some other words). The final *e* in *ense, anse,* and *sorse* might well be dropped. The use of the letter *i* for the sound of the first *e* in *event* is certainly confusing. There are many other such deviations from approved pronunciations. Finally, *teri* and *eri* are printed as one but are in reality two syllables (in *notary* and *machinery*). It must in fairness be pointed out that the definitions help the applicant to understand what word is wanted. The reliability is high, but the validity is unknown. The test contains many legal and financial terms.

CONCLUSION. The reviewer cannot conscientiously recommend this battery of tests in its present state to an industrial organization that is seeking aid in the selection of better clerical employees. These tests may be useful for experimental purposes, but so are many others. If the test items are analyzed, if the tests are revised, and if they are found to be valid, the situation will be entirely different.

[730]

*Psychological Corporation General Clerical Test.** Grades 9-16 and applicants for clerical positions; 1944-50; a revision of *General Clerical Test, PCI Selection Form 20* ('42); 4 scores: clerical speed and accuracy, numerical ability, verbal facility, total; 1 form, '44; manual ('50); $3.40 per 25; 35¢ per specimen set; also available in two separate booklets (Partial Booklet A—Speed and Number, Partial Booklet B—Verbal); $2 per 25 of any one booklet; postpaid; 46(50) minutes; Psychological Corporation. *

REFERENCES

1. BARNETTE, W. LESLIE, JR. *Occupational Aptitude Patterns of Counseled Veterans.* Doctor's thesis, New York University (New York, N.Y.), 1949. Pp. viii, 385. * (PA 24:362, title only)
2. GIESE, WILLIAM JAMES. "A Tested Method for the Selec-

tion of Office Personnel." *Personnel Psychol* 2:525–45 w '49. * (*PA* 24:4278)
3. BAIR, JOHN T. "Factor Analysis of Clerical Aptitude Tests." *J Appl Psychol* 35:245–9 Ag '51. * (*PA* 26:3067)
4. BARNETTE, W. LESLIE, JR. *Occupational Aptitude Patterns of Selected Groups of Counseled Veterans.* American Psychological Association, Psychological Monographs: General and Applied, Vol. 65, No. 5, Whole No. 322. Washington, D.C.: the Association, Inc., 1951. Pp. v, 49. Paper. * (*PA* 26:2794)

EDWARD E. CURETON, *Professor of Psychology, The University of Tennessee, Knoxville, Tennessee.*

This test consists of nine parts or subtests arranged in three groups, Clerical (checking and alphabetizing), Numerical (arithmetic computation, error location, and arithmetic reasoning), and Verbal (spelling, reading comprehension, vocabulary, and grammar). It appears to test most of the abilities which have been found valid for predicting success in clerical occupations, with the exception of specific skills such as shorthand, typing, and office machine operation. The test booklet is well arranged, and the instructions for administration are clear and reasonably short. Each subtest is timed separately, the time limits ranging from 3 to 8½ minutes. The examiner must therefore be alert throughout the test period of approximately 50 minutes to be sure that every subtest is timed properly. Figures in the margin of the manual emphasize the time limits, but an unfortunate set of errors confuses the issue slightly; the sign for four minutes, e.g., is printed as 4", not as 4'.

All parts are scored number right. Part 4 (error location) is scored with a punched-hole mask, the other eight parts with a fan key. No instructions are given for folding and using the fan key, and persons unfamiliar with this device may experience some difficulty in scoring the test accurately and rapidly.

Test-retest reliabilities for the nine parts, the three subtotals, and the total score are reported in the 1950 manual, based on data from 195 commercial high school seniors retested after one month. Since the test has only one form, and several of its parts are highly speeded, the test-retest correlations will approximate equivalent form correlations more closely than will split half correlations. They will still be somewhat higher, however, than would the equivalent form correlations. The test-retest reliabilities reported for the three subtotals and the total score are .87, .82, .91, and .94 respectively. Means, standard deviations, interpart correlations, and inter-subtotal correlations, based on the first administration of the test to this group, are reported also.

The authors state, "Factorial analyses of a preliminary form....were made on two similar clerical populations of more than one hundred cases each. The first showed factors agreeing with the three divisions of the test; the second substantiated these findings." Katzell, in his review of this test in *The Third Mental Measurements Yearbook,* states that "G. K. Bennett kindly made available to the reviewer a copy of the rotated factor loadings. The results of the two analyses are not in very close accord, which is probably due in part to the relatively small number of cases in each sample (108 and 120). However, the results generally support the legitimacy of the three groupings * Parts 1 and 2 are factorially similar to each other. The same can be said of Parts 3, 4, and 5; for Parts 6 and 9; and for Parts 7 and 8." It would appear, then, that the verbal score might well be broken up into two: reading and vocabulary, and spelling and grammar. The materials in Parts 3, 4, 5, 7, and 8 would correspond quite closely to those found in typical group intelligence tests.

The manual reports a number of correlations between the *Psychological Corporation General Clerical Test* and other group intelligence tests and clerical aptitude tests ranging from .54 to .83. Both of these extreme values represent correlations with the same group intelligence test in different samples. Standard deviations are not reported along with these correlations, so that it is somewhat difficult to interpret them precisely.

Validity data from three studies are reported. The first yielded the following correlations with performance ratings: Clerical .45, Numerical .22, Verbal .42, and Total .43. Standard deviations are not given, and no reason is reported for the subscale N's ranging from 68 to 71 while the N for the total score is 73. A fourfold table shows the relation between total scores, cut at 129–130, and tenure with the firm, cut at 6 months (N = 116). The manual states, "Here again, the test could have been very useful in predicting a criterion of job tenure." The fourfold-point correlation from this table as computed by the reviewer, however, is only .24.

The second study shows the relation between total scores and supervisors' ratings of below average, average, and above average. The N's range from 64 to 121, and represent clerical personnel in seven branches of the organization. Correlations are not given. Phi coefficients computed by the reviewer from the "outside" ratings (below average and above average) range from .16 to .51, and average .32.

The third study reports the following correlations with instructors' ratings of 91 clerical trainees on completion of a four-week training course covering records and accounts: Clerical .26, Numerical .54, Verbal .42, and Total .48. Standard deviations are not reported.

The manual emphasizes the specific nature of validity by citing the low criterion correlation of the Numerical score in the first study (.22) and its high correlation in the third (.54), and recommends local validation.

The manual emphasizes the differences among the various sets of norms, stresses the advantages of local norms, and states that "Until such time as he (the test user) has collected a sufficient number of cases (preferably 100 or more) he will find the data in this manual next best for his purposes." They will certainly be better than the norms supplied with most other published clerical tests.

This test compares very favorably with most of the other general clerical tests now available. While its use makes somewhat exacting demands on the examiner, we must remember that it includes its own verbal and numerical intelligence test as well as a clerical speed and accuracy test and a spelling and grammar test.

G. A. SATTER, *Assistant Professor of Psychology, University of Michigan, Ann Arbor, Michigan.*

Four reviewers wrote evaluations of this test for *The Third Mental Measurements Yearbook.* They were consistently unenthusiastic. They thought the test was too long, that its content overlapped with that of intelligence tests, that the normative data were inadequate, and that some evidence of the predictive value of its scores should have been provided. These criticisms have, for the most part, been met and dealt with in a revision of the test's manual and in making the test available in "partial" forms.

The *Psychological Corporation General Clerical Test* consists of a battery of nine tests which are scored to yield clerical, numerical, and verbal scores. These materials are available in a single booklet edition which contains all nine tests and in a "partial booklet edition" in which the materials are divided between two booklets. In the latter form, one booklet (A) contains the clerical and numerical tests, and another (B), the verbal tests. This arrangement permits the organization which already uses an intelligence test in its clerical selection procedures to substitute it for Booklet B, and incidentally it meets the criticism that might be raised concerning overlap of the verbal test with a test of intelligence. The working time for the tests of Booklet A is 29½ minutes, for Booklet B, 16½.

The most recent edition of the manual is unusually complete. The prospective user is provided with retest reliabilities, normative data from quite a variety of sources, and with the results of a number of validity studies. There is, however, one rather conspicuous omission: the authors fail to describe the process by which the test materials were originally assembled and the process by which they were selected for final inclusion.

Reliability data and intertest correlations are reported for a group of 195 seniors in a commercial high school. The reliability data are in the form of retest coefficients. They range in value from .59 to .88 for the subtest scores and from .82 to .91 for the three part scores; these data would suggest that the user of the test probably would not want to make decisions on the basis of individual subtest scores. Intercorrelations between scores are repeated for the same group; these range from .17 to .54 for the subtest scores and from .42 to .49 for the three part scores.

Enough validity data are provided to enable one to say that this collection of tests has the potentiality for making a useful contribution to a selection battery. These data take the forms of correlation coefficients and tables which show test performances and job performances. The criteria are typically performance ratings, and the correlations are in the 40's and 50's.

Norms are presented in the form of percentile rank equivalents. They come from a variety of sources—students in business schools, applicants for clerical positions, and employed clerical personnel. A variety of business organizations is represented.

As it stands today with its revised manual, the *Psychological Corporation General Clerical Test* should be able to hold its own among the best of the clerical aptitude tests; it most certainly is worthy of consideration by every employment office in need of an instrument for selecting or placing clerical personnel. It is probably longer than it needs to be, and the separately timed tests may be an annoyance in some employment settings. Only the prospective user, however, can decide whether these characteristics are really drawbacks.

For reviews by Edward N. Hay, Thelma Hunt, Raymond A. Katzell, and E. F. Wonderlic, see 3:630.

[731]

★**Purdue Clerical Adaptability Test: Purdue Personnel Tests.** Applicants for clerical positions; 1949–50; 7 scores: spelling, memory for oral instructions, arithmetic computation, checking of names and numbers, vocabulary, copying, arithmetical reasoning; Form A ('49); preliminary manual ('50); $5 per 25, postage extra; 50¢ per specimen set, postpaid; 58(75) minutes; C. H. Lawshe, Joseph Tiffin, and Herbert Moore (test); Occupational Research Center, Purdue University. *

Edward N. Hay, *President, Edward N. Hay & Associates, Inc., Philadelphia, Pennsylvania.*

This test has been prepared with some care, and its authors are men with considerable experience in testing as applied to industry. It is surprising, therefore, to find a seven-part test, for measuring clerical aptitude, which requires nearly an hour of actual testing time. This means a total time for administration of close to an hour and a half. Public relations will not permit the employer today to ask an applicant to take so much time. In addition, the cost to the employer of administering so long a test is out of proportion to the results. It has been established that in 15 minutes or less an adequate measure of the ability to acquire speed in simple clerical tasks can be measured.

Another fault of this test is that it assumes that items such as spelling, word meaning, and computation are predictors of clerical success. They do not, however, as many experimenters have shown, predict low level clerical success as well as do tests of speed of perception.

No validities are furnished in the manual, which is very surprising. The manual states "the test consists of seven separate sections, each of which measures a skill or ability required on certain clerical jobs." Instead of submitting validity coefficients, the manual states, "a selection of the parts to be used can be made from a job analysis." All seven parts are bound together in a single booklet, which makes it expensive and inconvenient to use only those parts which may have proven validity in a given situation.

It is hard to understand why anyone should offer a test of this kind for public sale without submitting any proof of its ability to do the job for which it was designed. In the absence of such information, it is impossible to make an adequate evaluation.

In summary, the principal weaknesses of the test are that it is prohibitively long, and that no experimental evidence is given to show that it will predict clerical success.

Joseph E. Moore, *Professor of Psychology and Head of the Department, Georgia Institute of Technology, Atlanta, Georgia.*

This test includes subtests in seven areas. The spelling ability area is tested by the recognition method. Memory for oral instruction contains such items as telephone exchanges and numbers, time mail goes out, and so forth. The arithmetic computation area has 15 problems covering simple addition, subtraction, division, and percentages. The checking part has material on one page to be checked against that on another page. The word meaning section contains 35 words with multiple choice definitions after each. The copying portion requires that information be copied on particular lines, and that certain numbers and symbols be put into the proper columns and squares. The last part of the test contains typical arithmetic problems. Much of the material in this test is similar to that found in typical elementary and high school achievement tests.

The directions for administering the test are crowded together in the manual in such a way that they are both difficult to read and hard to keep separated. No information is given about the background, training, or experience of the norm group except that they were "applicants." A statement that the minimum number of 742 clerical applicants was used does appear. It would be very helpful to have had the group classified as to age, sex, and previous work experience.

The only statistical data presented other than percentile tables are split half reliability coefficients for the seven subtests. These range from .79 to .97. No data whatsoever are included on the validity of the instrument. The statistical data that are presented are incomplete, vague, and possibly misleading. This instrument needs to have an initial validity study done on it to show that it does in fact measure clerical adaptability. In its present form there is no evidence in the manual to show that the instrument can or does differentiate clerical skills or reveal clerical adaptability. The authors do not present any information to show that their test is as good as, or superior, to the numerous clerical tests already published and used.

ALEC RODGER, *Reader in Psychology, Birkbeck College, University of London; and Consulting Psychologist to the Ministry of Labour and National Service; London, England.*

Nearly 20 years ago, while on a visit to the National Institute of Industrial Psychology, Moore became enamoured of the Institute's clerical test, *Group Test 25 (Clerical)*. Later, he produced a revised version of it for use in the United States. Now, in collaboration with Lawshe and Tiffin, he has contrived yet another: it is on the whole markedly different from the original, though it retains a few of the NIIP items and instructions.

Whether it is a better clerical test is difficult to judge, for the preliminary manual (which, unlike the test booklet, bears the names of Lawshe and Tiffin only) offers no validation data. Indeed, all the potential user is given is a table of percentiles based on the scores of 742 people who are meagrely designated "clerical applicants" and a table of split half reliability coefficients. He will derive small comfort from these figures.

Nor will he be reassured by inspection of the booklet. The front page contains material that is likely to prove puzzling to many "clerical applicants": the names of the compilers, a general direction that informs the testee that "this test includes a number of sections that measure abilities that have been found to have value in identifying successful clerical employees," and a *pro forma* for raw scores and percentile positions. It could certainly not be claimed that the presence of such items on the front page is necessary; and it might well be argued that it is undesirable. Some of the instructions for the separate sections of the test appear to be similarly defective. In two of them, the testee is asked to avoid "unnecessary mistakes." What is a "necessary" mistake? The type used in the arithmetical computation section seems indefensible.

In short, although this may in fact be a good clerical test, the authors have not yet presented any evidence that this is the case. Potential users of it will have to depend mainly on their own scrutiny of the test booklet, and it is doubtful whether many of them will find it particularly attractive.

[732]
SRA Clerical Aptitudes. Grades 9–13 and adults; 1947–50; 4 scores: office vocabulary, office arithmetic, office checking, total; Form AH ('47); revised manual ('50); 49¢ per test and answer pad; separate answer pads must be used; $1.90 per 25 answer pads; 55¢ per 25 profile and norm sheets ('49); 75¢ per specimen set; cash orders postpaid; 25(35) minutes; prepared by Richardson, Bellows, Henry & Co., Inc.; Science Research Associates, Inc. *

EDWARD N. HAY, *President, Edward N. Hay & Associates, Inc., Philadelphia, Pennsylvania.*

This test has been constructed with a great deal of care and understanding. It is made up of three subtests: office vocabulary, office arithmetic, and office checking. These three subtests appear to have high face validity, but no information concerning actual validity is presented in the manual. In an effort to overcome this lack of information, *SRA Clerical Aptitudes* was administered to 21 employees in a life insurance company, along with two test batteries whose validities have been repeatedly established in various clerical situations: the *Hay Number Perception Test* and the *Hay Name Finding Tests,* and the *L.O.M.A. Clerical Test No. 2.* Although the sample was small, both batteries gave validity coefficients quite similar to those obtained in a good many other similar situations.

All of the 21 employees were engaged in performing simple clerical tasks. The measure of success as rated by two supervisors was described as "speed of working," and was intended to indicate the "volume of work of acceptable accuracy" produced by each individual. The criterion was the average of the two sets of supervisory ratings. The coefficient of reliability of the criterion as indicated by the relationship between the two sets of ratings was .91.

The validity coefficients for the *Hay Number Perception Test* and the *Hay Name Finding Test* were .64 and .60 respectively. In contrast, the arithmetic and vocabulary subtests of *SRA Clerical Aptitudes* had validity coefficients of −.05 and .08 respectively, indicating that these subtests apparently do not predict success in simple clerical tasks. The validity coefficient for the SRA checking subtest was .55, indicating that this 5-minute test is a good predictor of clerical success. Of course, the SRA arithmetic and vocabulary tests may have value in some situations, but the authors do not tell us what they are. It is hard to understand how a test of this kind could have been used for four years without information concerning its validity having been assembled.

The format of the test is good, although somewhat complex and expensive in style. Scoring is about as inconvenient as could be devised.

The 25 minutes required for administering the complete test is longer than is necessary. Most of the wasted time occurs in the office arithmetic section, which is a series of reasoning problems dealing with figures. This and the office vocabulary part are really made up of intelligence or mental ability items. Other experiments have shown repeatedly that low level clerical success is predicted more effectively by tests involving primarily speed of perception.

In summary, the serious faults of this test are: (*a*) two of the parts do not appear to be valid as claimed for predicting success in simple clerical work; (*b*) the method of scoring is cumbersome; and (*c*) the administration time is too long.

G. A. SATTER, *Assistant Professor of Psychology, University of Michigan, Ann Arbor, Michigan.*

This battery consists of three short tests which are suitable for use with high school students and industrial job applicants. The battery contains an office vocabulary test (48 items cast in same-opposites form), an office arithmetic test (24 four-alternative multiple choice items), and a checking test (144 words, keyed with numbers, which must be paired with one of five numbers). These materials are reproduced in a nonexpendable spiral binder. Answers are recorded on a self-marking answer sheet.

In the authors' words, materials for these three tests were assembled after a "critical survey of the psychological literature on measurement of clerical aptitudes." From the leads provided from the survey, experimental forms were constructed and administered to high school groups; item analyses were made and items were selected in terms of their ability to discriminate between "high" and "low" scoring groups and to yield an "even distribution of difficulty." In their assembled form, the items are scored on a unit basis, and the part and total scores may be evaluated against the percentile norms provided in the manual. Norms representing the performance of students in some 40 high schools are given separately by grade and sex; similar data are provided for industrial clerical applicants.

The materials in the manual are well organized and include data which the prospective user of the test may find useful. Subtest means, sigmas, and Kuder-Richardson reliabilities are provided for groups of boys and girls in grades 9, 10, 11, and 12. In addition, there are intercorrelations between subtest scores (these range from .30 to .50) and between subtest scores and scores on two intelligence tests and *SRA Language Skills*. The authors are not so helpful as to provide correlations with either job or training performance.

The prospective user will undoubtedly be attracted by the test layout, its high face validity, its short time limit, and the ease with which it can be scored. He will be less enthusiastic when he fails to find in the manual any statistics concerning validity; and he may look at other tests when he reads that two of this battery of three tests correlate from .49 to .75 with measures of intelligence.

[733]

★The Short Employment Tests. Applicants for clerical positions; 1951; 3 tests; Forms 1, 2, 3, 4 (distribution of Form 1 is restricted to banks which are members of the American Bankers Association; Form 4 is restricted for special uses); preliminary manual $1.60 per 25; 35¢ per specimen set; postpaid; 15(20) minutes; George K. Bennett and Marjorie Gelink; Psychological Corporation. *
a) TEST CA, CLERICAL APTITUDE.
b) TEST N, ARITHMETIC SKILL.
c) TEST V, WORD KNOWLEDGE.

[734]

★Tabulation Test. Clerical applicants and high school; 1947; Forms A, B; manual ['47]; $2 per 25, postage extra; 50¢ per specimen set, postpaid; 10(13) minutes; Jay L. Otis and David J. Chesler; Personnel Research Institute, Western Reserve University. *

[735]

★V.G.C. Clerical Indicator. High school; 1950; an adaptation of United States Employment Service's *General Aptitude Test Battery*, Part B (see 714); 1 form; preliminary manual; $1.95 per 25; separate answer sleeves must be used; 48¢ per 25 answer sleeves; 10¢ per manual; 45¢ per specimen set; postage extra; available only to Canadian schools; 10(20) minutes; Vocational Guidance Centre. *

GEORGE A. FERGUSON, *Professor of Psychology, McGill University, Montreal, Canada.*

This test is an adaptation of Part B of the United States Employment Service's *General Aptitude Test Battery*. The test material is of the name checking type. Pairs of names are presented to the subject who is required to indicate whether the names in each pair are the same or different. Speed and accuracy are important. The test material is identical in type with that contained in Test 2 of the *Minnesota Clerical Test*. The test contains 150 items, and the testee is allowed 10 minutes working time.

The distinctive features of this test are its format and method of scoring. The test forms are printed on heavy cardboard. The testee records his answers on a separate cardboard answer sheet or sleeve which is fitted over the test form. The scoring sheet is subsequently inserted in a plastic sleeve for scoring purposes. The format and method of scoring are very ingenious. Economy may be effected by using the test form many times.

Very little information on the test is presented in the manual of instructions. Rather inadequate norms are available based on a sample of 480 pupils in grades 9 and 10 in a commercial school. Scores for the grade 10 pupils are slightly higher than those for grade 9. No information on the reliability of the predictive capacity of the test in various situations is given. We may presume, however, that reliability and validity data relating to the *Minnesota Clerical Test* may have some degree of relevance to the *V.G.C. Clerical Indicator* since the test material is similar in both. The reliability and validity of this 150-item test may be expected to be somewhat lower than for the Minnesota Clerical which contains 400 items in all.

INTERESTS

[736]

*ABC Occupational Inventory. Grades 9–16 and adults; 1935–42; a checklist of over 500 occupations (classified as to work function) in 10 areas: artistic, humanistic, literary, scientific, commercial, technical, mechanical, industrial, constructional, transportational; 1 form, '42; no data on reliability and validity; no norms; 10¢ per inventory; 25¢ per specimen set; postpaid; N. A. Lufburrow; the Author, 3112 Milford Ave., Baltimore 7, Md. *

[737]

*Brainard Occupational Preference Inventory. Grades 9–12 and adults; 1945–49; a revision of *Specific Interest Inventory* (see 40:1675) by Paul P. Brainard and Frances G. Stewart; 4 occupational sections in each of 7 fields: commercial, personal service, agriculture, mechanical, professional, esthetic, scientific; Form A ('45); manual ('49); $5.50 per 25; separate answer sheets must be used; $1.60 per 25 answer sheets; 60¢ per specimen set; postpaid; nontimed (30) minutes; Paul P. Brainard and Ralph T. Brainard; Psychological Corporation. *

REFERENCES
1–4. See 40:1675.
5–6. See 3:634.
7. ROEBER, EDWARD C. "A Comparison of Seven Interest Inventories With Respect to Word Usage." *J Col Res* 42:8–17 S '48. * (PA 23:2915)

ELMER D. HINCKLEY, *Professor of Psychology and Head of the Department, University of Florida, Gainesville, Florida.*

This inventory consists of 140 items in which the subject rates on a 5-point scale different activities in terms of his disliking, liking, or neutrality toward these activities. The test is easy to administer and score and gives a profile for seven occupational fields which are broken down into 28 sections, four to each field.

This inventory is fairly new and has not been used as widely as the more popular Strong and Kuder. While the reliability coefficient of .81 quoted by the authors is acceptable for a test of this sort, no evidence of validity is offered other than logical or face validity. The test as a whole may be reliable, but the reliability of the field and section scores may be open to question. Having only 140 items, the test is too brief to yield the amount of information that the authors attempt to squeeze from it.

The norms are inadequate, but the authors state that more complete norms will be forthcoming. The norms given are for adult men, adult women, high school boys, and high school girls. Separate field and section norms are given for each of these groups with the numerical scores expressed in quintile divisions that are designated very low, low, average, high, and very high. More cases are needed in establishing norms (adult men, N = 95).

For reviews by Edwin W. Davis and Herschel T. Manuel, see 3:634; for reviews by Jack W. Dunlap and M. R. Trabue of the original edition, see 40:1675; for a review by Everett B. Sackett of the original edition, see 38:1176.

[738]

★Edmiston Inventory of Interest. Grades 11–16 and adults; 1946–48; Forms A ('46), B ('46), C ('48), D ('48); manual ['48]; 75¢ per 25; 35¢ per specimen set; postpaid; nontimed (25) minutes; R. W. Edmiston; the Author, Miami University, Oxford, Ohio. *
a) FORMS A AND B. 8 scores: business, aesthetics, science, social, journalism, mechanics, education, government.
b) FORMS C AND D. 9 scores: business, aesthetics, science, social, journalism, mechanics, biological science, numbers, clerical.

REFERENCES
1. EDMISTON, R. W., AND VORDENBERG, WESLEY. "The Relationship Between Interests and School Marks of College Freshmen." *Sch & Soc* 64:153–4 Ag 31 '46. * (PA 21:890)

ARTHUR E. TRAXLER, *Executive Director, Educational Records Bureau, New York, New York.*

Although several well known inventories of

interests have been available for a good many years, new instruments of this kind continue to be published. Perhaps in no other field do measurement instruments vary so widely in care of construction and in extent of research on the results. Years of research have been devoted to the Strong blanks. There is now a large body of data on the *Kuder Preference Record,* and several studies of the Cleeton and other interest inventories have been made available. On the other hand, certain inventories have been issued with little or no evidence that anything other than the judgment of the test author was taken into account in either the construction or tryout of the instrument.

The *Inventory of Interest* is one of the more recently published inventories on which there is not, at present, much objective information. It exists in six forms, a larger number than is available for any other instrument designed for the measurement of interests. Forms A, B, C, and D are intended to measure present interests; the other two forms, designed to measure what the test author has called "maintained interests," cover vocabularies and the names of personages connected with certain occupational fields.

The test situation presented by the forms designed to measure present interests is very simple. Each form is printed on one side of a letter-size sheet. At the top are eight lines of directions, below which are three columns, headed "Column I, WHICH MAGAZINE; Column II, WHICH COURSE; Column III, WHICH JOB." Column I contains the names of 40 magazines, either actual or fictitious, arranged in 5 groups of 8 names each. Column II contains the names of 40 courses, and Column III presents the names of 40 jobs; both lists grouped in similar fashion to Column I. The procedure in filling out the inventory is to place an X before the preferred item in each group of eight and to check two other items as the next two choices.

Forms A and B are planned to provide scores in eight fields—business, education, aesthetics, government, science, social, journalism, and mechanics. Forms C and D yield scores in nine fields—business, aesthetics, biological sciences, science, social, journalism, mechanics, clerical, and numbers. In scoring, the first choice in each of the 15 groups is given a weight of 2 and each second choice is counted as 1 point. Thus, a total of 60 points is distributed among 8 or 9 different fields. The highest possible score in any one field is 30 and the lowest is 0. The interpretation of the scores is as simple and uncomplicated as the test itself. The individual's raw scores in the eight or nine fields are simply ranked in order, and this ranking presumably indicates the relative order of one's interests. Norms are not used in the interpretation of the results; in fact, no norms appear in the manual.

At first glance, a test specialist is likely to think that this inventory is hardly worth serious consideration, especially when it is compared with certain other instruments in the field of interests which represent a considerable degree of statistical sophistication. But, notwithstanding the extreme simplicity of the scores yielded by this blank and of the procedure in interpretation, the test author presents in the manual some statistical information on reliability and validity which does not compare unfavorably with similar data on other interest inventories. Seventeen correlations between alternate forms of the inventory of present interests ranged from .66 to .92, with a median of .83. Ten reliability coefficients for the tests of maintained interests ranged from .78 to .91, with a median of .88.

In order to obtain further data on the reliability and validity of the inventory, Forms A and B were administered to 24 members of the staff of the Educational Records Bureau, 17 women and 7 men. There was an interval of 10 days between the two forms. About five days after the second form was filled out, each person was asked to rank the eight fields for which the inventory was to be scored in the order of his interests as he judged them to be. The inventories were not scored until these judgments had been obtained.

Rank order correlations were then computed for each person between Forms A and B and between each form and self-estimates of interests with respect to the eight fields. The Spearman rank-difference correlations between Forms A and B, or the reliabilities, ranged from .05 to .98, with a median of .84. Only three of the correlations were below .70. While it may be only fortuitous, it is interesting to note that the median is practically the same as the median reliability reported by the test author. This degree of reliability is not unfavorable for a measurement instrument in this field. The corresponding findings for the rank-difference correlations between each form and self-estimates of interests were as follows: Forms A, range of correlations, .10 to .99, median, .80; Form B, range of correlations, .43 to .97, median, .74. Similar brief studies of the *Kuder Preference Record* and Cleeton's *Vocational Interest Inventory* as reported by this reviewer in earlier *Mental Measurements Yearbooks* yielded median correlations of .75 for the Kuder and .68 for the Cleeton.

Obviously, it should not be inferred from these data that the Edmiston inventory is necessarily as good a measure of interests as the Kuder or the Cleeton inventories. It may be that the relatively simple test situation presented by this inventory allows a halo effect which carries over from one form to the other and from test to self-estimate. The mental process required in filling out the inventory is quite similar to the thinking which takes place when one ranks the eight fields in order of interest. Thus, the new inventory is a less sophisticated measure than an instrument such as the Kuder, which is based on comparison of activities whose relationship to the different fields may not be apparent to the subject. Nevertheless, it is noteworthy that some positive evidence of reliability and validity was obtained in this small and informal study of the Edmiston inventory. It should also be noted that this inventory was constructed for use at the school and college levels and its trial with adults may not be an entirely fair test.

Certain observations may be made about the scores and the scoring procedure. The categories are broad, and some of them are not precisely named. For example, one area is termed "social." It is not clear from this name what kinds of social activities are implied. An examination of the items contributing to the score in this field indicates that the general area of social service is sampled. Although the scoring is essentially simple, the scoring directions are the most nearly unintelligible this reviewer has seen for any measurement instrument. These directions greatly need revision and improvement. A fan key or stencil for scoring could be devised; in fact, staff members of the Educational Records Bureau formulated a scoring procedure which enabled them to score 48 inventories at an average rate of 3½ minutes an inventory. This is very rapid compared with the scoring of most other interest inventories.

Norms are needed for the interpretation of the scores on the inventory, and it may be desirable to investigate the possible need for norms differentiated according to sex.

Everything considered, this reviewer would not recommend the use of the Edmiston inventory in its present form except in an experimental way. He does, however, regard it as an interesting experiment in setting up a simple, easily administered, inexpensive instrument which may be valuable after further refinement. The fact that the inventory is not at present in the hands of a regular test publisher but is privately printed suggests that probably the test author does not regard it as a final product and that further work designed to improve it may be contemplated.

[739]

★The Guilford-Shneidman-Zimmerman Interest Survey. Grades 9–16 and adults; 1948; 18 scores: artistic-appreciative, artistic-expressive, linguistic-appreciative, linguistic-expressive, scientific-investigatory, scientific-theoretical, mechanical-manipulative, mechanical-designing, outdoor-natural, outdoor-athletic, business-political-mercantile, business-political-leadership, social activity-persuasive, social activity-gregarious, personal assistance-personal service, personal assistance-social welfare, office work-clerical, office work-numerical; Form A; no data on validity; norms ('48); $4 per 25; separate answer sheets must be used; 50¢ per 25 answer sheets; 50¢ per 25 profile sheets of high school or college norms; 25¢ per manual; postage extra; 60¢ per specimen set, postpaid; nontimed (50) minutes; J. P. Guilford, Edwin Shneidman, and Wayne S. Zimmerman; Sheridan Supply Co. *

REFERENCES
1. FOSTER, KENNETH EUGENE. *An Intercorrelational Investigation of the Guilford-Shneidman-Zimmerman Interest Survey.* Master's thesis, University of Southern California (Los Angeles, Calif.), 1949.
2. GUILFORD, J. P.; SHNEIDMAN, E. S.; AND ZIMMERMAN, W. S. "The Guilford-Shneidman-Zimmerman Interest Survey." *J Consult Psychol* 13:302–6 Ag '49. * (PA 24:875)

GEORGE K. BENNETT, *President, The Psychological Corporation, New York, New York.*

This interest inventory consists of a total of 360 items to each of which the subject responds by encircling on a separate answer sheet "D" as indicating disinterested, dislike, or don't know; "H" if the activity has appeal as a hobby; "V" if it would be acceptable as a vocation. The subject is permitted to encircle both "H" and "V" when the activity is favored in both regards. The activities are described in such terms as "Mould a statue in clay," "Write newspaper editorials," "Go to dances," and "Think out the logical deductions from a scientific discovery." The items fall into nine major categories; each of these is divided into two subcategories which are scored separately. The answer sheet is so arranged that the individual completes one cycle of the 18 subcategories to a column; this permits horizontal counting of each row to obtain the "H" and "V" scores for that classification. Thus no key is necessary.

The items used were selected from a preliminary form containing 540 activity descriptions.

The criterion for inclusion in the final form was internal consistency as determined from the data provided by 300 male college sophomores. High school normative data have been obtained from 180 boys and 176 girls entering the eleventh grade in a southern California urban school. College norms are derived from the scores of 389 men and 99 women students in a sophomore course in a southern California university. The manual states: "These norms are regarded as provisional and are to be revised as results from other parts of the country are obtained." The norms are not presented in tabular form but are incorporated into profile sheets, one for each sex and educational group. The profile sheet is prepared by encircling the individual's raw score, these scores being arranged in rows according to their positions in a normalized distribution resulting from the data of the appropriate norms group. C-score, centile, and T-score equivalents are shown at the top margin of each profile sheet. Data on reliability are provided both in the manual and in a supplementary issue of "Psychometric Notes" published in July 1950. The reliabilities are of the split half type and fall generally in the high .80's and low .90's. The supplement contains a table of tetrachoric intercorrelation coefficients based upon 300 college men. These r's range from zero to above .8. No data are given regarding validity. The authors say: "Citations of practical validity data for interest scores are typically conspicuous by their absence in connection with interest inventories. This *Survey* will be no exception to this respect." The manual (which does not report intercorrelational data) goes on to say: "Evidences of internal or factorial validity are to be found in intercorrelation data. * It is believed that the nine main category scores will intercorrelate generally low," etc. The manual, however, contains nearly two pages devoted to the vocational implications of scores. We find, for example, that the person with high outdoor-athletic interest can be expected to find some of the following vocations attractive: athlete, big game hunter, boxer, coach, golfer, gymnast, racing driver, wrestler.

This inventory contains some features which are novel and which should increase the ease of scoring and profiling. The separation of vocational and avocational interests would seem to have some advantages, and the answer sheet arrangement diminishes the time and cost of scoring to a very appreciable extent. It should be noted that each of these virtues involves attendant detriments. Some of the activities listed can hardly be considered appropriate for both hobby and vocation. This reviewer found difficulty in imagining a career based on "Going to dances" (Item 68), "Helping friends move their belongings to a new home" (Item 69), or "Helping distribute food at a picnic" (Item 105). Perhaps it is feasible to make a hobby of "Supervising a group of professional people" (Item 84) or "Being responsible for establishing policies and procedures in an industrial organization" (Item 102). The systematic arrangement of the answer sheet tends to become apparent to the examinee and the authors caution that "it is important to prepare the examinee to take the proper attitude toward the test at the start." Probably neither of these features need be a cause of serious concern.

The most serious defect in this instrument would seem to lie in the implication that a test is useful with norms obtained from small samples drawn from a single community or university. The characteristics of climate, academic opportunity, and vocational specialties in the Los Angeles area may produce interests representative of the country as a whole, but it is more likely that these are specific to an area including only a small fraction of the nation's population. It may be proper to point out that other interest inventories are lacking in validation, although this is but partially true of the Strong V.I.B.; but it does not strike the reviewer as equally justifiable to suggest that so tentative an instrument can provide useful data on the basis of which to advise an individual as to his subsequent career. The GSZ Interest Survey may well prove at some later date to have significance for educational and vocational guidance. The data so far submitted do not appear to justify its present use except as an experimental instrument.

WILBUR L. LAYTON, *Assistant Professor of Psychology, and Assistant Director, Student Counseling Bureau, University of Minnesota, Minneapolis, Minnesota.*

This survey purports to measure interests in nine general areas, each of which is then broken down into a dual classification so that 18 interest scores result. For example, in the artistic area, appreciative and expressive scores are given, distinguishing between those who like art as consumers but not as producers. In the mechani-

Guilford-Shneidman-Zimmerman Interest Survey

cal area, manipulative and design scores are given so that a distinction between the tool operator and the tool designer or engineer is possible. The same sorts of distinctions are made in each of the other areas.

Another unique feature of the survey is the dual score for each of the 18 interest fields. On the answer sheet there are three possible responses for each item: H and V stand for hobby and vocation respectively, and D represents all categories not specifically denoted by the H and V responses—dislike, disinterested, don't know, etc. The survey asks for a direct response to the type of activities listed as items, and both H and V responses may be made to a single item.

The items were selected from a preliminary form of 540 items, which was administered to 700 subjects—400 high school students, evenly divided as to sex at the beginning of the 11th grade, and 300 male college students in a sophomore course. An internal consistency item analysis was made on the data from the college group. On the basis of this analysis, the 20 most internally consistent items in each interest field were selected to comprise Form A of the survey.

In regard to validity the authors say, "Citations of practical validity data for interest scores are typically conspicuous by their absence in connection with interest inventories. This *Survey* will be no exception in this respect. Appropriate external criteria for this purpose have never been sufficiently developed." If this form of rationalization becomes widespread, we will never have appropriate criteria against which to validate interest tests. Perhaps we should spend more time developing criteria and less constructing insufficiently validated tests.

The authors present evidence for internal or factorial validity in a study of intercorrelation data. These data give some indication of how much uniqueness each score possesses. If a score shows high reliability and low intercorrelations with the other scores, it tends to measure something that none of the other scores measures. However, these data do not give one a clue as to exactly what the score does measure so uniquely, and hence are only a vague indication of validity as commonly defined.

Reliability coefficients computed on first-half versus second-half scores are given in the manual. They are based on the scores of 100 boys and 100 girls in the high school sample. The authors state that the distributions were so seriously skewed that Pearsonian correlations and standard errors of measurement would have been meaningless. Consequently, tetrachoric correlations were computed. Since the tetrachoric correlation coefficient is an estimate of the product-moment correlation coefficient in a bivariate *normal* population and not in a *nonnormal* population, the obtained coefficients are also meaningless by the authors' criterion. Nevertheless, these correlations were substituted in the Spearman-Brown formula. The resulting coefficients range from .72 for the social activity-gregarious vocational score for females to .96 for the mechanical-designing vocational score for males.

The high school norms given on the profile sheets were based on 11th grade high school students in a southern California urban school, 180 boys and 176 girls. The college norm group was composed of 389 men and 99 women students in a sophomore course in a southern California university. The manual states that these norms are provisional and are to be revised as results from other parts of the country are obtained. The test manual was copyrighted in 1948; no other normative data are available. The norms given in the manual are inadequate for general use.

As have most interest test authors recently, the authors of this test list under each scale a set of occupations which might be appropriate for people scoring high on the scale. No evidence whatsover is presented for the validity of these lists.

In summary, the survey represents a well thought out approach. The 36 scores should be very useful in counseling. However, until more adequate norms and reliability and validity data are available, the survey should be used only experimentally.

[740]

★**Henderson Analysis of Interest [Second Edition].** Grades 9–16 and adults; 1950; occupational preferences in 14 areas: business service, clerical, accounting and statistics, persuasive, managerial, social science, physical science, biological science, engineering, art and music, teaching, writing, mechanical, manual; 1 form; $9 per 100 sets of test and profile sheet; 30 day trial order: $5 per 50 sets of test and profile sheet; 40¢ per specimen set; postpaid; nontimed (25–35) minutes; Robert W. Henderson; the Author, 940 Eighth St., N.E., Massillon, Ohio. *

WILBUR L. LAYTON, *Assistant Professor of Psychology, and Assistant Director, Student Counseling Bureau, University of Minnesota, Minneapolis, Minnesota.*

The 14 scales on this test, which coincide somewhat with curricular and occupational areas, are grouped into business, professional, and active areas. Under the business area are listed the business service, clerical, accounting and statistics, persuasive, and managerial scales. Under the professional area are grouped the social science, physical science, biological science, engineering, art and music, teaching, and writing scales. Under the active area are classified the mechanical and manual scales. The label "active" for this last area seems quite inadequate to describe the items scored for the two scales.

The test items are presented in 40 groups of 7 items each. The individual is asked to select 2 items, if possible, from each group of 7. There are 20 items for each of the 14 scales. These items were taken from the author's *College Interest Inventory* and his *Work Interest Analysis* on the basis of their being "internally significant." From this, although it is not made clear in the manual, one assumes that the author conducted some form of internal-consistency item analysis.

The test author feels that "since a respondent is required to select only one or two choices from each set of seven possibilities, it is evident that his choices will be truer preferences than in such tests as the Lee-Thorpe, the new Thurstone, and Kuder where the individual is forced to select one from a choice of two or three." This, of course, assumes that there are one or two items within each group of seven that are attractive to the individual, a doubtful assumption when one looks at the items.

The items which were finally selected and included in the test are not representative of the areas which they are attempting to measure. For example, 6 of the 20 items which purport to measure interest in business service are from the occupation of beauty operator or related fields: shampoo customers' hair, hairdresser, make up expert, give facial massages, pluck eyebrows by electrolysis, massage expert, and give health baths. Five items scored for business service involve food handling: serve short orders, work behind a soda fountain, serve food in a restaurant, waiter (waitress), and serve soft drinks. In each of the other 13 areas one finds that the items are not in relative proportion to activities or occupations in the area.

Another criticism of the items can be made from the standpoint of duplication of content. For example, the "waiter (waitress)" item would be perceived by most people as identical with the item "serve food in a restaurant." This

is also true in the mechanical area where the two items "auto mechanic" and "repair automobiles" are used. Use of these items gives undue weight to that particular activity and tends to determine the factors measured by the scale. This is particularly true when an internal-consistency method of item analysis is used.

A further criticism of the items can be made in terms of their readability and understandability, particularly when the test is self-administered at the high school level. Our experience at the University of Minnesota in giving Strong's *Vocational Interest Blank* to all classes at the University High School indicates that the younger students do not have sufficient knowledge of various occupations to make intelligent choices without assistance. For such students one wonders about the suitability of many specialized items: develop aniline dyes, construct stamping dies, describe physical events with mathematics, investigate ionization problems, pluck eyebrows by electrolysis, prepare evolution charts, investigate problems of heat transfer, do research in immunology, and investigate embryo development.

Henderson gives test-retest correlation coefficients based on an N of 40 people as evidence of reliability. These coeffcents range from .80 for Business Service to .96 for Physical Science. There is no description of the group of 40 people in the manual to aid in evaluating these figures.

As partial evidence of validity Henderson reports correlations between the *Kuder Preference Record* and his test on a group of 124 high school students. The correlations range from .30 between the Henderson accounting and statistics scale and the Kuder computational scale to .77 between the two mechanical scales. This represents the doubtful procedure of validating a newly constructed inventory against an existing inventory, the validity of which is still being experimentally determined.

Henderson lists a group of representative jobs for each scale. These seem to have been classified on a speculative basis. He presents no evidence that high scores on a particular scale are related to any other measure of interest in, or satisfaction with, a particular profession.

This inventory appears to be an attempt to improve upon the *Kuder Preference Record*. If such was the intent, the author has failed. Because of poor items and the lack of adequate validity and reliability data, this inventory is not recommended for use until further research justifies it.

DONALD E. SUPER, *Professor of Education, Teachers College, Columbia University, New York, New York.*

This test consists of 40 seven-item groups, some consisting of occupational titles and some of occupational activities or duties. Thus, there are 20 items per scale. As in the case of the *Thurstone Interest Schedule* this means that one change of response can make a sizable change of score; in the case of the Business Service Scale, for example, a choice of no items puts a man at the 10th percentile (why not the 1st is not explained), a choice of one item puts him at the 30th, and a choice of three items puts him at the 70th. Despite this fact, the one-week retest reliabilities range from .80 to .96, for a group of subjects the size and heterogeneity of which is not specified.

APPLICABILITY. The test is said to be applicable to ninth grade students as well as to college students and adults, but no evidence to this effect is cited; the fact that the norms are based on high school juniors and seniors and college students suggests that there is no such evidence. Some of the vocabulary would be difficult for the average ninth grader, who probably has no idea what "ionization problems" and "geophysicists" are. Evidence as to the vocabulary level would be desirable, with the range as well as the average of the grade levels made clear.

NORMS. The manual states that "it is believed that these norms are fairly representative of young people in senior high school and in the first year of college," but no evidence is cited to show that these 90 high school juniors and seniors and 150 college students are typical. It is not stated whether they all were in one high school and one college and from one locality or whether the group is cosmopolitan. The group being as small as it is, the students are probably from one institution. It hardly seems likely that students from an academic high school in a privileged community are typical of students in a trade high school in an underprivileged neighborhood, or vice versa. Perhaps this is why the Mechanical and Manual Scales yield average raw scores of two. Obviously, a more adequate description of the norm group, and probably more adequate norms, are needed. The fact that the author cites "clinical experience" with the test as evidence of its validity is further evidence

of fuzzy thinking and, in fact, of lack of evidence concerning the appropriateness of the norms and the validity of the scales.

The norms are described as permitting the comparison of the strength of a person's interest in a field with that of other persons. Assuming that the number and representativeness of the norm group were sufficient for this, the meaning of such data would still be an open question. For they do not tell how interested a person should be, in order to have a reasonable chance of being satisfied, successful, or stable in a given occupation. Should an auto mechanic be more interested in mechanics than 25, 50, 75, or 90 per cent of high school and college students? Occupational norms are clearly needed.

A list of representative jobs for each scale is included in the manual, with no indication as to the validity of the classification of jobs. Examination of the grouping shows that it differs in certain important respects from that of the *Dictionary of Occupational Titles*,[1] Strong's research, and other empirical classifications. For example, policemen are classified as a social service occupational group and nurses as a biological science occupational group. Even "common sense" seems contradicted at certain points without supporting data: governesses are a teaching group, while nursemaids are a service group; drill press operators and weavers belong to the machine trades, while automatic machine operators are in the manual group.

VALIDITY. As in the case of many insufficiently validated tests, the author cites the nature of the items as evidence of the inventory's validity. Correlations with the *Kuder Preference Record: Vocational*, are also cited, ranging from .30 for the accounting and computational scales to .78 for the writing and literary scales, with 5 of the 11 *r*'s below .50. These low correlations are interpreted in the manual as evidence that the use of "both tests will yield a better total evaluation of interests than will either alone," but just what the Henderson is measuring that the Kuder is not measuring is not explained.

USE. At this stage, the *Henderson Analysis of Interest* can at best be described as suitable only for experimental use, in situations in which data can be gathered for the establishment of norms and for the validation of scales and in which no use is to be made of the scores for counseling or

1 War Manpower Commission, Bureau of Manpower Utilization, Division of Occupational Analysis. *Dictionary of Occupational Titles: Part IV, Entry Occupational Classification, Revised Edition.* Washington, D.C.: U.S. Government Printing Office, 1944. Pp. xiv, 242. Paper. *

Henderson Analysis of Interest

selection. When data are needed for immediate practical purposes, other inventories which are supported by far more research, and the meaning of which is at least partly understood, are available. The Henderson inventory provides further evidence that it is far easier to write seemingly good test items than it is to develop a usable test.

[741]

★Interest Check List. Adults; 1946; an interviewing aid; 8 work areas: artistic, musical, literary, entertainment, clerical and sales, service, agriculture-marine-forestry, mechanical; individual; no data on reliability and validity; $1.75 per 100; 5¢ per sample copy; remittance must accompany order; nontimed (10–30) minutes; prepared by Testing Branch, United States Employment Service; United States Government Printing Office. *

MILTON L. BLUM, *Associate Professor of Psychology, The City College, New York, New York.*

The *Interest Check List* is ostensibly an interviewer's aid. Since it is not scorable, it is not intended as an objective instrument. Accordingly, raising such questions as validity, reliability, and norms is inappropriate. A critical evaluation of the check list must, therefore, be equally as subjective as the interpretations of the counselors who use the form.

Items intended to cover eight broad work areas are included in the check list. The proportion of items to areas is an unexplained variable. For example, four of the areas have only five items each, but the other four areas have from 16 to 49 items each.

There are 25 groupings according to the code used in Part IV of the *Dictionary of Occupational Titles.*[1] These groupings also vary in the number of items; the smallest has one item and the largest has ten. Each grouping has the code reference printed alongside. One can only guess the effect that such hieroglyphics may have on the respondent. It may well serve to encourage a concentration of check marks and not be a reflection of the diversified interests of the subject who is trying to make a good (integrated) impression. A better format would be to mix the items, present them in ungrouped fashion and then provide the counselor with a templet that would mechanically reveal the occupational code classification.

The items are tasks rather than jobs. Some examples are: "Going to some trouble to make

1 War Manpower Commisson, Bureau of Manpower Utilization, Division of Occupational Analysis. *Dictionary of Occupational Titles: Part IV, Entry Occupational Classification, Revised Edition.* Washington, D.C.: U.S. Government Printing Office, 1944. Pp. xiv, 242. Paper. *

foods look attractive" (this is in cooking in the area service work); "Mixing dough for baking" (this is in the group known as processing in the mechanical work area); and "Driving an automobile" (this is in the mechanical work area). It does appear as if many of the items may be suggestive of other work areas, but no mention of such possible interpretations is made at all.

A Self-Training Handbook, in addition to a one-sheet, printed manual of instruction, accompanies the *Interest Check List.* The first paragraph of the handbook is "This is a Self-Training Handbook on the Use of the Interest Check List. You are your own instructor. The material is prepared so that you may go straight through the Handbook. For your own sake, don't look on the last page to see 'how the story ends.' "

If the authors are correct in assuming the level of the counselor, then it would appear that such a check list is inappropriate and that a simple and objectively scored check list would be safer. If, on the other hand, the authors prefer a "clinical" rather than an objective inventory and their counselors are capable of insightful clinical diagnosis, then the handbook has been written in a too indulgent and paternal manner.

This check list is not as good as the more widely known and previously published ones. Its value is limited by its format and by the extremely unknown variable of the interpretations the counselors are capable of making.

HOWARD R. TAYLOR, *Professor of Psychology and Head of the Department, University of Oregon, Eugene, Oregon.*

This questionnaire is designed to help orient people seeking employment. It is organized around the job classifications given in the *Dictionary of Occupational Titles.* Subjects check the different types of activities they "would be interested in doing even if they have never done them." Each of the 135 kinds of work is described in terms of the "action verbs" upon which the classification into job families is primarily based. As a means of securing rapport in an interview, counselors report that it is quite effective.

No attempt is made to summarize the information given in terms of a score nor to distinguish well defined interests based on experience from vague notions of what a person thinks he might like to do. The avowed purpose and chief value of the form is, therefore, to shorten the time required for interviewing and to secure a comprehensive survey of any conscious preferences an individual may have with reference to eight major fields of work which can ordinarily be entered without previous experience. There are, of course, no norms. Nor is any objective determination of reliability or validity in locating work interests possible. Since there are many research techniques which might materially enhance the usefulness of such a tool, or at least afford means of checking its adequacy, it is unfortunate that no thoroughgoing standardization seems to have been attempted.

The manual clearly explains how to present the list to subjects and to use the information obtained. There is also a handbook of typical cases which can be used as self training exercises.

As a psychological measure, however, it has all the defects of similar forms of self-report without any of the virtues which can be anticipated from multiple sampling of opinions and attitudes and their scaling to insure unity or general significance with reference to a criterion. No doubt in the hands of a skillful interviewer, the check list will provide leads for further exploration. It may also afford a client some inkling of the specific nature of job requirements. But if a person has not previously engaged in such activities, what does it mean to ask him if he likes "creating and composing musical compositions"; "doing literary research for historical publications"; "developing advertising campaigns"; "sorting, indexing, and assembling papers and other written records"; "selling insurance by pointing out advantages and disadvantages of various policies"; "studying social and economic conditions in order to help individuals or groups solve problems of general welfare"; or "mixing foods to obtain new flavor"? Verbs, like other words, derive their meaning from activities associated with them in the reader's experience.

[742]

*Kuder Preference Record—Vocational. Grades 9–16 and adults; 1934–51; IBM; 3 editions; separate answer pads or answer sheets must be used; cash orders postpaid; G. Frederic Kuder; Science Research Associates, Inc. *
a) FORM B (NINE SCALE). Grades 9–16 and adults; 1934–46; a revision of Form A; 9 scores: mechanical, computational, scientific, persuasive, artistic, literary, musical, social service, clerical; 2 editions; 1 form, '42; revised manual ('46); 55¢ per 25 profile sheets for either men and women ('46) or boys and girls ('44); 75¢ per specimen set of any one edition; nontimed (40–50) minutes.
1) Form BB (Hand Scoring Edition). 49¢ per test and answer pad; $2.15 per 25 answer pads.

2) Form BM (Machine Scoring Edition). 39¢ per test; $2.90 per 100 IBM answer sheets; $7.50 per set of scoring keys.
b) FORM BI (SHORT FORM). College and adults; 1946–48; an adaptation of Nine Scale Form for use in industrial situations; 9 scores: same as for Form B (Nine Scale); IBM; Form BI ('48); revised manual ('46—same as for Nine Scale Form); 39¢ per test; $2.90 per 100 IBM answer sheets; $3 per set of scoring stencils; 49¢ per test and answer pad; $2.15 per 25 answer pads; 55¢ per 25 profile sheets ('48); 75¢ per specimen set; nontimed (30) minutes.
c) FORM C (ELEVEN SCALE). Grades 9–16 and adults; 1948–51; 11 scores: same as for Form B (Nine Scale) plus outdoor, verification; 2 editions; 1 form, '48; second revised manual ('51); 55¢ per 25 revised profile sheets for either men and women ('51) or boys and girls ('50); 75¢ per specimen set of any one edition.
1) Form CH (Hand Scoring Edition). 49¢ per test and answer pad; $2.15 per 25 answer pads.
2) Form CM (Machine Scoring Edition). 39¢ per test; $2.90 per 100 IBM answer sheets; $7.50 per set of scoring keys.

REFERENCES

1–2. See 40:1671.
3–62. See 3:640.
63. Cox, K. J. "Aptitude Testing in Industry." B Can Psychol Assn 5:99–102 D '45. * (PA 20:2035)
64. Shierson, Harry E. "Pointing up the Occupational Interviews: Occupational Dictionary and Scores on Interest Inventory Utilized." Occupations 23:207–9 Ja '45. * (PA 19:1327)
65. Adjutant General's Office, Personnel Research and Procedures Branch, Personnel Research Section, Staff. "The Kuder Preference Scores of Successful and Unsuccessful Enlisted Men Assigned to Recruiting Functions in the United States Army." Abstract. Am Psychol 1:249 Jl '46. * (PA 20:3856, title only)
66. Berg, Irwin August. "A Study of Success and Failure Among Student Nurses." Abstract. Am Psychol 1:249–50 Jl '46. * (PA 20:3872, title only)
67. Coomb, Winifred Audrey. Word Difficulty in the Kuder Preference Record. Master's thesis, Stanford University (Stanford, Calif.), 1946.
68. Cummings, Isabelle M. The Relation Between Interest and Achievement: A Comparison of Scores of the Kuder Preference Record and Those on Co-operative Achievement Tests for College Freshmen. Master's thesis, Southern Methodist University (Dallas, Texas), 1946. (Abstracts of Theses....1946, 1947, pp. 66–7.)
69. Froehlich, Clifford P. [Letter regarding "A Comparison of Scores on the Kuder Preference Record and the Job Qualification Inventory" by Earl W. Seibert. J Ed Res 40:178–86 N '46.] J Ed Res 40:477–9 F '47. *
70. Roberts, William H. "Test Scores and Merit Ratings of Graduate Engineers." Abstract. Am Psychol 1:284 Jl '46. * (PA 20:3910, title only)
71. Baggaley, Andrew R. "The Relation Between Scores Obtained by Harvard Freshmen on the Kuder Preference Record and Their Fields of Concentration." J Ed Psychol 38:421–7 N '47. * (PA 22:2318)
72. Beamer, George Charles. The Factors of Interest in the Counseling of Adults. Doctor's thesis, University of Missouri (Columbia, Mo.), 1947. Abstract: Microfilm Abstracts 9:158–60 no 2 '49. * (PA 24:4152, title only)
73. Cerf, Arthur Z. "Kuder Preference Record, CE515A," pp. 613–6. In Printed Classification Tests. Edited by J. P. Guilford with the assistance of John I. Lacey. Army Air Forces Aviation Psychology Program Research Report, Report No. 5. Washington, D.C.: U.S. Government Printing Office, 1947. Pp. xi, 919. * (PA 22:4145)
74. Fox, William H. "The Stability of Measured Interests." J Ed Res 41:305–10 D '47. * (PA 22:2732)
75. Jackson, Joseph. "A Note on the Crystallization of Vocational Interests." J Social Psychol 26:125–30 Ag '47. * (PA 22:2644)
76. Kendall, William E., and Hahn, Milton E. "The Use of Tests in the Selection of Medical Students by the College of Medicine of Syracuse University." Abstract. Am Psychol 2:297 Ag '47. * (PA 21:4650, title only)
77. Kimber, J. A. Morris. "Interests and Personality Traits of Bible Institute Students." J Social Psychol 26:225–33 N '47. * (PA 22:4611)
78. Kutner, Mildred. The Prognosis of the Freshmen Achievement of Chemistry and Physics Students on the Basis of Interest Test Items. Master's thesis, Pennsylvania State College (State College, Pa.), 1947. Pp. iv, 113.
79. Lindgren, Henry C. "A Study of Certain Aspects of the Lee-Thorpe Occupational Interest Inventory." J Ed Psychol 38:353–62 O '47. * (PA 22:2200)
80. Monroe, Marjorie Bates. The Kuder Preference Rec-

ord as a Measure of Interest in Certain Areas of the Liberal Arts Curriculum at the University of North Carolina. Master's thesis, University of North Carolina (Chapel Hill, N.C.), 1947. (Research in Progress, October, 1945–December, 1948, 1949, p. 309.) (PA 24:6528, title only)

81. THOMPSON, CLAUDE EDWARD. "Selecting Executives by Psychological Tests." Ed & Psychol Meas 7:773–8 '47. * (PA 23:321)

82. WESLEY, S. M.; STEWART, BARBARA; AND COREY, DOUGLAS. "A Study of the Intra-Individual Relationships Between Interest and Ability." Abstract. Am Psychol 2:411 O '47. * (PA 22:1266, title only)

83. ALLEN, CHARLES L. The Development of a Battery of Psychological Tests for Determining Journalistic Interests and Aptitudes. Doctor's thesis, Northwestern University (Evanston, Ill.), 1948. (Summaries of Doctoral Dissertations....June–September 1948, 1949, pp. 204–9.)

84. BEAMER, GEORGE C.; EDMONSON, LAWRENCE D.; AND STROTHER, GEORGE B. "Improving the Selection of Linotype Trainees." J Appl Psychol 32:130–4 Ap '48. * (PA 23:965)

85. COTTLE, WILLIAM C. "A Factorial Study of Selected Instruments for Measuring Personality and Interest." Abstract. Am Psychol 3:300 Jl '48. * (PA 22:5353, title only)

86. CROSS, ORRIN H. "A Study of Faking on the Kuder Preference Record." Abstract. Am Psychol 3:293 Jl '48. * (PA 22:5422, title only)

87. DALY, JULIETTE M. Relationship of MMPI and Kuder Preference Record Scores. Master's thesis, Catholic University of America (Washington, D.C.), 1948. (PA 23:2982, title only)

88. DIAMOND, SOLOMON. "The Interpretation of Interest Profiles." J Appl Psychol 32:512–20 O '48. * (PA 23:2739)

89. EVANS, M. CATHARINE. "Differentiation of Home Economics Students According to Major Emphasis." Occupations 27:120–5 N '48. * (PA 23:4410)

90. HEADLEE, MARY KATHLEEN. The Kuder Preference Record as a Device for Differentiating Among Majors in the Division of Home Economics at Iowa State College. Master's thesis, Iowa State College (Ames, Iowa), 1948.

91. HESTON, JOSEPH C. "A Comparison of Four Masculinity-Femininity Scales." Ed & Psychol Meas 8:375–87 au '48. * (PA 23:4256)

92. KAHN, D. F. An Analysis of Factors Related to Life Insurance Selling. Doctor's thesis, Purdue University, (Lafayette, Ind.), 1948.

93. KELSO, NORMA ELAINE. The Relative Correspondence of Professed Interest to the Kuder and Strong Interest Test Scores. Master's thesis, State College of Washington (Pullman, Wash.), 1948. (PA 23:376, title only)

94. KOHN, NATHAN, JR. "Kuder Preference Record Masculinity-Femininity Scale." J Social Psychol 27:127–8 F '48. * (PA 22:4947)

95. KOHN, NATHAN, JR. An Investigation and Evaluation of the Kuder Preference, Especially in Comparison to the Strong Vocational Interest Blank. Doctor's thesis, Washington University (St. Louis, Mo.), 1948.

96. LAURO, LOUIS. "A Note on Machine Scoring the Kuder Preference Record." J Appl Psychol 32:629–30 D '48. * (PA 23:3756)

97. LONGSTAFF, HOWARD P. "Fakability of the Strong Interest Blank and the Kuder Preference Record." J Appl Psychol 32:360–9 Ag '48. * (PA 23:1332)

98–9. MALCOLM, DAVID D. The Relative Usefulness of Several Extensively Used Vocational Interest Inventories in Counseling at Various Academic Levels. Doctor's thesis, Northwestern University (Evanston, Ill.), 1948. (Summaries of Doctoral Dissertations....June–September 1948, 1949, pp. 245–50.)

100. MICHAUX, WILLIAM. "Interpreting Occupational Group Data on the Kuder Preference Record." Occupations 27:82–9 N '48. * (PA 23:4290)

101. MILES, RAY W. "A Proposed Short Form of the Kuder Preference Record." J Appl Psychol 32:282–5 Je '48. * (PA 23:1044)

102. MILLER, ALLEN DUANE. The Role of Kuder Interests in Prediction of Course Marks of Freshman Engineering Students. Master's thesis, Iowa State College (Ames, Iowa), 1948.

103. PERRY, JAMES D., AND SHUTTLEWORTH, FRANK K. "Kuder Profiles of College Freshmen by Degree Objectives." J Ed Res 41:363–5 Ja '48. * (PA 22:3204)

104. REMMERS, H. H., AND GAGE, N. L. The Abilities and Interests of Pharmacy Freshmen. The Pharmaceutical Survey, Monograph No. 1. Reprinted from The American Journal of Pharmaceutical Education Vol. 12, No. 1, January 1948. Washington, D.C.: American Council on Education, [1948]. Pp. 65 plus 13 inserts. Paper. * (PA 22:4107)

105. ROEBER, EDWARD C. "A Comparison of Seven Interest Inventories With Respect to Word Usage." J Col Res 42:8–17 S '48. * (PA 23:2915)

106. ROSE, WALLACE. "A Comparison of Relative Interest in Occupational Groupings and Activity Interests as Measured by the Kuder Preference Record." Occupations 26:302–7 F '48. * (PA 22:2648)

107. SCHEUHING, MARY A. An Analysis of the Predictive Efficiency of Certain Test Scores and Grades in the Selection of High School Students for the Industrial Auto and Electric Shop Courses. Master's thesis, Temple University (Philadelphia, Pa.), 1948.

108. SPEER, GEORGE S. "The Interest and Personality Patterns of Fire Protection Engineers." Abstract. Am Psychol 3:364 Ag '48. * (PA 23:822, title only)

109. SPEER, GEORGE S. "The Kuder Interest Test Patterns of Fire Protection Engineers." J Appl Psychol 32:521–6 O '48. * (PA 23:2744)

110. SPEER, GEORGE S. "Measuring the Social Orientation of Freshman Engineers." J Eng Ed 39:86–9 F '48. * (PA 23:1524)

111. SPEER, GEORGE S. "The Vocational Interests of Engineering and Non-Engineering Students." J Psychol 25:357–63 Ap '48. * (PA 22:4623)

112. SPEER, GEORGE S. "Vocational Interests of Fire Protection Engineers." Ill Tech Eng 13:24–5, 68–70 Mr '48. * (PA 24:4657)

113. TRIGGS, FRANCES ORALIND. "The Measured Interests of Nurses: A Second Report." J Ed Res 42:113–21 O '48. * (PA 23:3487)

114. WILSON, EARL, AND BORDIN, EDWARD S. "Instability of Interest Patterns as a Function of Shift in Curricular Orientation." Abstract. Am Psychol 3:352 Ag '48. * (PA 23:824, title only)

115. WOODS, WALTER A. "The Role of Language Handicap in the Development of Artistic Interest." J Consult Psychol 12:240–5 Jl–Ag '48. * (PA 23:595)

116. BAAS, MALCOLM L. A Study of Interest Patterns Among Professional Psychologists. Master's thesis, Purdue University (Lafayette, Ind.), 1949.

117. BARNETTE, W. LESLIE, JR. Occupational Aptitude Patterns of Counseled Veterans. Doctor's thesis, New York University (New York, N.Y.), 1949. Pp. viii, 385. * (PA 24:362, title only)

118. BATEMAN, RICHARD M. "The Effect of Work Experience on High School Students' Vocational Choice: As Revealed by the Kuder Preference Record." Occupations 27:453–6 Ap '49. * (PA 23:5010)

119. BAYLEY, NANCY. "Kuder Masculinity-Femininity Scores in Adolescent Boys and Girls Related to Their Scores in Somatic Androgyny." Abstract. Am Psychol 4:251 Jl '49. * (PA 23:6092, title only)

120. BROWN, WILLIAM E. A Study of the Elements Contributing to the Successful Selection of a Job Training Vocational Objective. Doctor's thesis, Pennsylvania State College (State College, Pa.), 1949. (Abstracts of Doctoral Dissertations....1949, 1950, pp. 318–24.) (PA 24:5539, title only)

121. CAPWELL, DORA F. Psychological Tests for Retail Store Personnel. Pittsburgh, Pa.: Research Bureau for Retail Training, University of Pittsburgh, 1949. Pp. 48. Paper. * (PA 25:3449)

122. CARTER, LAUNOR, AND NIXON, MARY. "Ability, Perceptual, Personality, and Interest Factors Associated With Different Criteria of Leadership." J Psychol 27:377–88 Ap '49. * (PA 23:4183)

123. COMER, JAMES EDWARD, JR. A Study of the Comparison of Interests of Social Science Majors With the Interests of Other Adults as Measured by the Kuder Preference Record. Master's thesis, Kansas State Teachers College (Pittsburg, Kans.), 1949.

124. COTTLE, WILLIAM C. A Factorial Study of the Multiphasic, Strong, Kuder and Bell Inventories Using a Population of Adult Males. Doctor's thesis, Syracuse University (Syracuse, N.Y.), 1949.

125. COTTLE, WILLIAM C. "Relationships Among Selected Personality and Interest Inventories." Abstract. Am Psychol 4:292–3 Jl '49. * (PA 23:6206, title only)

126. COTTLE, WM. C., AND POWELL, JACKSON O. "Relationship of Mean Scores on the Strong, Kuder and Bell Inventories With the MMPI M-F Scale as the Criterion." Trans Kans Acad Sci 52:396–8 '49. * (PA 24:2599)

127. DAY, JAMES FRANCIS. Achievement of Freshman Students at Visalia College. Doctor's thesis, Stanford University (Stanford, Calif.), 1949. (Abstracts of Dissertations....1949–50, 1950, pp. 306–10.)

128. DiMICHAEL, SALVATORE G. "The Professed and Measured Interests of Vocational Rehabilitation Counselors." Ed & Psychol Meas 9:59–72 sp '49. * (PA 23:5582)

129. DiMICHAEL, SALVATORE G. "Work Satisfaction and Work Efficiency of Vocational Counselors as Related to Measured Interests." J Appl Psychol 33:319–29 Ag '49. * (PA 24:2647)

130. EIMICKE, VICTOR W. "Kuder Preference Record Norms for Sales Trainees: With Detailed Description and Additional Psychological Test Results." Occupations 28:5–10 O '49. * (PA 24:3470)

131. EWENS, WILLIAM PRICE. Experience Patterns as Related to Vocational Preference. Doctor's thesis, Stanford University (Stanford, Calif.), 1949. (Abstracts of Dissertations....1949–50, 1950, pp. 334–41.)

132. GREEN, RUSSEL F. The Validity of Certain Psychological Tests in the Selection and Classification of Juvenile Police Officers. Master's thesis, University of Southern California (Los Angeles, Calif.), 1949.

133. HADLEY, J. M., AND KAHN, D. F. "A Comment on Wallace's Note on 'Factors Related to Life Insurance Selling.'" J Appl Psychol 33:359–62 Ag '49. * (PA 24:2882)

134. HAKE, DOROTHY TERRY, AND RUEDISILI, C. H. "Predicting Subject Grades of Liberal Arts Freshmen With the Kuder Preference Record." J Appl Psychol 33:553–8 D '49. * (PA 24:4260)

135. HANNA, JOSEPH V., AND BARNETTE, W. LESLIE, JR.

"Revised Norms for the Kuder Preference Record for Men." *Occupations* 28:168-70 D '49. * *(PA* 24:5869)

136. HARRISON, LOMA. *Application of Certain Seashore Measures of Musical Talent and the Kuder Preference Record to the Building of a Music Program in Borger High School.* Master's thesis, North Texas State College (Denton, Tex.), 1949.

137. HENRY, WALTER ORLANDO. *A Study of Two Word Tests in Relation to the Kuder Preference Record.* Master's thesis, University of Southern California (Los Angeles, Calif.), 1949.

138. JACOBS, ROBERT. "Stability of Interests at the Secondary School Level," pp. 83-7. *(PA* 24:750) In *1949 Achievement Testing Program in Independent Schools and Supplementary Studies.* Educational Records Bulletin, No. 52. New York: Educational Records Bureau, July 1949. Pp. xiii, 87. Paper, lithotyped. *

139. JENSEN, GERALD LeROY. *Relationship Between School Achievement and Scholastic Aptitude: Techniques for Ascertaining This Relationship, Their Application to Data From a Group of High School Pupils and Their Use in School Practice.* Doctor's thesis, Stanford University (Stanford, Calif.), 1949. *(Abstracts of Dissertations....1949-50,* 1950, pp. 403-8.)

140. KAHN, D. F., AND HADLEY, J. M. "Factors Related to Life Insurance Selling." *J Appl Psychol* 33:132-40 Ap '49. * *(PA* 24:357)

141. KUDER, G. FREDERIC, AND PAULSON, BLANCHE B. *Discovering Your Real Interests: For Use in Grades 9-10.* Chicago, Ill.: Science Research Associates, 1949. Pp. 48. Paper. *(PA* 23:4808) * *Instructor's Guide:* Pp. 12. Paper. *

142. MOREY, ELWYN A. "Vocational Interests and Personality Characteristics of Women Teachers." *Austral J Psychol* 1:26-37 Je '49. * *(PA* 26:1111)

143. NORTH, ROBERT D., JR. "An Analysis of the Personality Dimensions of Introversion-Extroversion." *J Personality* 17:352-67 Mr '49. * *(PA* 25:2913)

144. PERVIN, DOROTHY WILMA. *The Interests of Graduate Students in Psychology as Measured by the Kuder Preference Record.* Master's thesis, University of Pittsburgh (Pittsburgh, Pa.), 1949. *(PA* 24:379, title only)

145. PHILLIPS, W. S., AND OSBORNE, R. T. "A Note on the Relationship of the Kuder Preference Record Scales to College Marks, Scholastic Aptitude and Other Variables." *Ed & Psychol Meas* 9:311-7 au '49. * *(PA* 26:2993)

146. REMMERS, H. H., AND GAGE, N. L. "Student Personnel Studies of the Pharmaceutical Survey." *Am J Pharm Ed* 13:6-126 Ja '49. * *(PA* 23:1004)

147. ROEBER, EDWARD C. "The Relationship Between Parts of the Kuder Preference Record and Parts of the Lee-Thorpe Occupational Interest Inventory." *J Ed Res* 42:598-608 Ap '49. * *(PA* 23:5586)

148. SHAFFER, ROBERT H. "Kuder Interest Patterns of University Business School Seniors." *J Appl Psychol* 33:489-93 O '49. * *(PA* 24:3473)

149. SHAFFER, ROBERT H. "The Measured Interest of Business School Seniors." *Occupations* 27:462-5 Ap '49. * *(PA* 23:5018)

150. SILVEY, HERBERT M. *Change in Status of Iowa State Teachers College Students as Revealed by Repeating Placement Tests.* Iowa State Teachers College, Research Report No. 58. Cedar Falls, Iowa: Bureau of Research, the College, July 20, 1949. Pp. 27. Paper, lithotyped. *

151. SMITH, DOUGLAS E. "A Preliminary Study of Adjustment to Life in the North." *Can J Psychol* 3:89-97 Je '49. * *(PA* 24:775)

152. STRONG, EDWARD K., JR. "The Role of Interests in Guidance." *Occupations* 27:517-22 My '49. * *(PA* 24:671)

153. SUPER, DONALD E. *Appraising Vocational Fitness by Means of Psychological Tests,* pp. 445-65. New York: Harper & Brothers, 1949. Pp. xxiii, 727. * *(PA* 24:2130)

154. TROXEL, LEETHA LORETTA. *A Study of Three Vocational Interest Measures: Preference Record, Academic Interest Inventory, and Work Interest Analysis.* Master's thesis, University of Kentucky (Lexington, Ky.), 1949.

155. WALLACE, S. RAINS, JR. "A Note on Kahn and Hadley's 'Factors Related to Life Insurance Selling.'" *J Appl Psychol* 33:356-8 Ag '49. * *(PA* 24:2884)

156. WINN, JAMES CHARLES. *Kuder Profiles of College Freshmen by Their Expressed Fields of Concentration.* Master's thesis, University of Pittsburgh (Pittsburgh, Pa.), 1949. *(PA* 24:389, title only)

157. ZWILLING, VIRGINIA T. *The Prediction of Grades in Freshman English From a Battery of Tests of Mental Ability, Interests and Aptitudes Administered to Students Entering a Liberal Arts College.* Doctor's thesis, Fordham University (New York, N.Y.), 1949. *(Dissertations...,* 1949, pp. 62-5.)

158. ANDERSON, CLIFFORD L. *An Analysis of the Differences of the Scores Obtained by Different Cultural Groups on the Kuder Preference Record.* Master's thesis, University of Southern California (Los Angeles, Calif.), 1950.

159. BAAS, MALCOLM L. "Kuder Interest Patterns of Psychologists." *J Appl Psychol* 34:115-7 Ap '50. * *(PA* 25:1434)

160. BELMAN, H. S., AND EVANS, R. N. "Selection of Students for a Trade and Industrial Education Curriculum," pp. 9-14. In *Motives and Aptitudes in Education: Four Studies.* Edited by H. H. Remmers. Purdue University, Division of Educational Reference, Studies in Higher Education, No. 74. Lafayette, Ind.: the Division, December 1950. Pp. iii, 63. Paper. * *(PA* 26:3010)

161. BERDIE, RALPH F. "Scores on the Strong Vocational Interest Blank and the Kuder Preference Record in Relation to Self-Ratings." *J Appl Psychol* 34:42-9 F '50. * *(PA* 24:5915)

162. BORG, WALTER R. "Does a Perceptual Factor Exist in Artistic Ability?" *J Ed Res* 44:47-53 S '50. * *(PA* 25:2921)

163. BORG, WALTER R. "The Interests of Art Students." *Ed & Psychol Meas* 10:100-6 sp '50. * *(PA* 25:1243)

164. BRADFIELD, ANNE FREDERIKSEN. *Predicting the Success in Training of Graduate Students in School Administration.* Doctor's thesis, Stanford University (Stanford, Calif.), 1950. *(Abstracts of Dissertations....1949-50,* 1950, pp. 294-7.)

165. BRODY, DAVID S. "The Utilization of an Interest Inventory in a PTA Project for the Purpose of Fostering Parent-Child Understanding." *Sch & Soc* 72:311-2 N 11 '50. * *(PA* 25:6741)

166. BROWN, MANUEL N. "Client Evaluation of Kuder Ratings." *Occupations* 28:225-9 Ja '50. * *(PA* 24:3736)

167. COTTLE, WILLIAM C. "Relationships Among Selected Personality and Interest Inventories." *Occupations* 28:306-10 F '50. * *(PA* 24:4113)

168. CROSS, ORRIN H. "A Study of Faking on the Kuder Preference Record." *Ed & Psychol Meas* 10:271-7 su '50. * *(PA* 25:6420)

169. DULSKY, STANLEY G., AND KROUT, MAURICE H. "Predicting Promotion Potential on the Basis of Psychological Tests." *Personnel Psychol* 3:345-51 au '50. * *(PA* 25:3452)

170. FEATHER, DON B. "The Relation of Personality Maladjustments of 503 University of Michigan Students to Their Occupational Interests." *J Social Psychol* 32:71-8 Ag '50. * *(PA* 25:3796)

171. FORD, ALBERT H. "Prediction of Academic Success in Three Schools of Nursing." *J Appl Psychol* 34:186-9 Je '50. * *(PA* 25:4038)

172. GOSHORN, WENONAH M. *A Study of the Relationships of the Kuder Reference Record—Personal and Certain Sociometric Ratings.* Doctor's thesis, Indiana University (Bloomington, Ind.), 1950. *(PA* 25:7107, title only)

173. JOHNSON, JAMES MYRON. *Student Interests and Values and Curricular Satisfaction in Engineering.* Master's thesis, Clark University (Worcester, Mass.), 1950. *(Abstracts of Dissertations & Theses....1950,* pp. 136-8. *(PA* 25:5463, title only)

174. KLUGMAN, SAMUEL F. "Spread of Vocational Interests and General Adjustment Status." *J Appl Psychol* 34:108-14 Ap '50. * *(PA* 25:1859)

175. LATTIN, GERALD W. "Factors Associated With Success in Hotel Administration." *Occupations* 24:36-9 O '50. * *(PA* 25:3490)

176. LAWRENCE, RAY MARGARET. *An Investigation of Selected Physical, Psychological and Sociological Factors Associated With Migraine and Psychogenic Headache.* Doctor's thesis, New York University (New York, N.Y.), 1950. Abstract: *Microfilm Abstracts* 11:171-2 no 1 '51. * *(PA* 26:2355, title only)

177. MALCOLM, DAVID DONALD. "Which Interest Inventory Should I Use?" *J Ed Res* 44:91-8 O '50. * *(PA* 25:5675)

178. NORTH, ROBERT D., JR. *An Analysis of the Personality Dimensions of the Introversion-Extroversion.* Doctor's thesis, Columbia University (New York, N.Y.), 1950.

179. ROMNEY, A. KIMBALL. "The Kuder Literary Scale as Related to Achievement in College English." *J Appl Psychol* 34:40-1 F '50. * *(PA* 24:6043)

180. ROSS, GLENN R. *Changes in Interests Between 1947 to 1950 of 338 Texas A. & M. College Students as Measured by the Kuder Preference Record.* Master's thesis, Agricultural and Mechanical College of Texas (Stephenville, Tex.), 1950.

181. SPIVEY, GORDON MAURICE. *The Relationship Between Temperament and Achievement of a Selected Group of John Muir College Students.* Doctor's thesis, University of Southern California (Los Angeles, Calif.), 1950. *(Abstracts of Dissertations....1950,* 1951, pp. 298-300.)

182. STINSON, MILDRED C. *A Study of the Results of a Kuder Test Battery for Use in Vocational Guidance.* Master's thesis, Indiana State Teachers College (Terre Haute, Ind.), 1950. Abstract: *Teach Col J* 22:16 O '50. *

183. SUPER, DONALD E., AND JACK W. Sect. 16, "Interest in Work and Play," pp. 100-8. In *Handbook of Applied Psychology, Vol. I.* Edited by Douglas H. Fryer and Edwin R. Henry. New York: Rinehart & Co., Inc., 1950. Pp. xxi, 380, ix. * *(PA* 25:8309)

184. WALKER, RUTH O. *A Study of Vocational Interest Responses Leading to the Development and Evaluation of an Industrial Interest Inventory for Use in General Industrial Plant Employment Practice.* Doctor's thesis, Pennsylvania State College (State College, Pa.), 1950. *(Abstracts of Doctoral Dissertations....1950,* 1951, pp. 301-6.) *(PA* 26:2542, title only)

185. WATKINS, RICHARD WALKER. *Classification of Medical School Students by the Kuder Preference Record Using the Discriminant Function and Group Profiles.* Master's thesis, University of Pittsburgh (Pittsburgh, Pa.), 1950.

186. WESLEY, S. M.; COREY, DOUGLAS Q.; AND STEWART, BARBARA M. "The Intra-Individual Relationship Between Interest and Ability." *J Appl Psychol* 34:193-7 Je '50. * *(PA* 25:3855)

187. BARNETTE, W. LESLIE, JR. "An Occupational Aptitude Pattern for Engineers." *Ed & Psychol Meas* 11:52-66 sp '51. * *(PA* 26:2793)

188. BARNETTE, W. LESLIE, JR. *Occupational Aptitude Patterns of Selected Groups of Counseled Veterans.* American Psychological Association, Psychological Monographs: Gen-

eral and Applied, Vol. 65, No. 5, Whole No. 322. Washington, D.C.: the Association, Inc., 1951. Pp. v, 49. Paper. * (PA 26:2794)

189. BAYLEY, NANCY. "Some Psychological Correlates of Somatic Androgyny." *Child Develop* 22:47–60 Mr '51. * (PA 25:6736)

190. BELMAN, H. S., AND EVANS, R. N. "Selection of Students for a Trade and Industrial Educational Curriculum." *J Ed Psychol* 42:52–8 Ja '51. * (PA 25:6486)

191. BROWN, MANUEL N. "Evaluation of Lee-Thorpe Inventory Ratings by Veteran Patients." *Ed & Psychol Meas* 11:248–54 su '51. * (PA 26:2796)

192. BURSCH, CHARLES W., II. "The Kuder Preference Record in Selecting Vocational Agriculture Students." Abstract. *Calif J Ed Res* 2:184 S '51. *

193. EIMICKE, VICTOR WILLIAM. *A Study of the Effect of Intensive Sales Training Experience Upon the Measured Abilities and Personality Characteristics of Salesman-Candidates.* Doctor's thesis, New York University (New York, N.Y.), 1951. Abstract: *Microfilm Abstracts* 11:951–2 no 4 '51.

194. FARBER, ROBERT HOLTON. *Guidance Implications of the Freshman Testing Program at DePauw University.* Doctor's thesis, Indiana University (Bloomington, Ind.), 1951. (*Thesis Abstract Series....1951,* 1952, pp. 37–42.)

195. FORER, BERTRAM R. "Personality Dynamics and Occupational Choice." Abstract. *Am Psychol* 6:378–9 Jl '51. *

196. GREEN, RUSSEL F. "Does a Selection Situation Induce Testees to Bias Their Answers on Interest and Temperament Tests?" *Ed & Psychol Meas* 11:503–15 au '51. *

197. JACOBS, ROBERT. "A Brief Study of the Relationship Between Scores on the Lee-Thorpe Occupational Interest Inventory and Scores on the Kuder Preference Record," pp. 79–85. In *1951 Achievement Testing Program in Independent Schools and Supplementary Studies.* Foreword by Ben D. Wood. Educational Records Bulletin No. 57. New York: Educational Records Bureau, July 1951. Pp. xiii, 85. * (PA 26:984)

198. KELLY, E. LOWELL, AND FISKE, DONALD W. *The Prediction of Performance in Clinical Psychology.* Ann Arbor, Mich.: University of Michigan, 1951. Pp. xv, 311. Lithotyped. *

199. KUDER, G. FREDERIC, AND PAULSON, BLANCHE B. *Exploring Children's Interests.* Chicago, Ill.: Science Research Associates, Inc., 1951. Pp. 48. Paper. *

200. MacPHAIL, ANDREW H. "That Changing Kuder." *Occupations* 30:202–3 D '51. * (PA 26:5620)

201. NOVAK, BENJAMIN J., AND SCHEUHING, MARY A. "Predicting Success in High School Industrial Courses." *Ind Arts & Voc Ed* 40:391–4 D '51. *

202. PLUMMER, ROBERT HOWARD. *Characteristics and Needs of Selected Ninth Grade Pupils as a Basis for Curricular Changes to Meet Life Adjustment Needs.* Doctor's thesis, Indiana University (Bloomington, Ind.), 1951. (*Thesis Abstract Series....1951,* 1952, pp. 113–9.)

203. REID, JOHN W. "Stability of Measured Kuder Interests in Young Adults." Abstract. *Am Psychol* 6:378 Jl '51. *

204. REID, JOHN W. "Stability of Measured Kuder Interests in Young Adults." *J Ed Res* 45:307–12 D '51. * (PA 26:6284)

205. SILVEY, HERBERT M. "Changes in Test Scores After Two Years in College." *Ed & Psychol Meas* 11:494–502 au '51. *

206. WEBSTER, EDWARD C.; WINN, ALEXANDER; AND OLIVER, JOHN A. "Selection Tests for Engineers: Some Preliminary Findings." *Personnel Psychol* 4:339–62 w '51. * (PA 26:6572)

207. WIENER, DANIEL N. "Empirical Occupational Groupings of Kuder Preference Record Profiles." *Ed & Psychol Meas* 11:273–9 su '51. * (PA 26:2762)

208. WOLFF, W. M., AND NORTH, A. J. "Selection of Municipal Firemen." *J Appl Psychol* 35:25–9 F '51. * (PA 25:7124)

EDWARD S. BORDIN, *Associate Professor of Psychology, University of Michigan, Ann Arbor, Michigan.*

For most purposes in testing vocational interests this inventory and Strong's *Vocational Interest Blank* (VIB) are the most frequently considered choices. Since, of the most recently developed instruments, this one comes closest to meeting the standards set by Strong, it seems appropriate to evaluate this test through comparison with the VIB.

Where the Strong approaches the measurement problem by developing scales representing the constellation of preferences which distinguish one occupational group from another, the Kuder purports to isolate the important independent dimensions of vocational interests. This

is considered a gradual process: for example, the most recent edition had added a new dimension, outdoor interests. It is assumed that given these dimensions, one can then identify and derive the constellations which distinguish diverse occupational groups. This is the theoretical orientation of the factor analysis approach in psychological measurement. Though they approach the problem from opposite directions, it would appear that the two tests arrive at exactly the same point. That they are in fact transmutable has not yet been adequately demonstrated. This test identifies broad areas of vocational interest and proceeds to translate them into specific occupations (through mean profiles for occupational groups and regression equations). The Strong identifies interests of specific occupational groups and through factor analysis translates them into broad areas.

The Kuder is an instrument that went through a carefully planned and thoroughly executed developmental process. It falls short of the Strong in the thoroughness of its validation and other supporting data. One major set of validation data is the presentation in the manual of mean profiles for occupational groups largely derived from data contributed by test consumers. The author's device of soliciting validation data from test users, while a convenient way of solving a costly, time-consuming problem, is less than adequate as a rigorous demonstration that these interest scales are indeed relevant to distinguishing occupational groups in terms of interests. First, it is difficult to interpret the significance of mean test profiles for a given group without information as to the conditions under which the test was administered. Was this a study in which the subjects had no particular stake? Were they taking the test as applicants for a job? Was it for counseling? A second, and even more critical issue, is the unlikelihood that validation data obtained in this manner will represent an unbiased estimate of the validity of the test. It is hard to imagine anyone ordinarily being motivated to send to a test author data which demonstrates that it does not do what the author hopes and believes it does! A further drawback in the validation evidence is the very small number of cases on which many of the mean profiles are based. One important type of supporting data about this test that is not now available is definitive evidence about the stability of test results. Nothing approaching the long term follow-up studies on the VIB has been reported. In fact,

Kuder Preference Record—Vocational

this reviewer is not aware of any follow-up study covering a period greater than one year.

Both authors meet high standards in making available important and useful information to test users. Two important criticisms of the manual should be made. First, while data on reliability from the point of view of internal consistency are presented, there is no real consideration of the allied but different question of stability. Users need to know how rapidly, how frequently, and under what conditions changes in scores can be expected to occur. Second, the manual for Form C abandons the practice followed by preceding manuals of identifying which of the mean scores for occupational groups represent significant deviations from the means of the general population. This is the removal of a necessary safeguard against overinterpretation of the results from this test.

In summary, the Kuder can be considered an acceptable tool for the measurement of interests which has advantages over the VIB in terms of cost and time absorbed in scoring. However, it still cannot be considered as a fully developed instrument until further validation studies and evidence on stability are available.

HAROLD D. CARTER, *Professor of Education, University of California, Berkeley, California.*

This well known inventory is now available in more than one form. Form C, the new and improved product, is designed to replace the older Form B. The new inventory yields 11 scores, including the old 9, plus a new score for outdoor interests, and a verification score. The verification score is designed to help identify those who have not followed directions and those who have not answered carefully.

Another new feature is the glossary of words and phrases that may prove difficult for some students. The latest manual lists suggested occupations for each area of interests, along with appropriate references as sources of information about each occupation. New sets of norms for adult men, extended validity data, and job profiles for both men and women are also included. The *Kuder Book List,* offered by the same publishers, is a promising new development.

The claims made by the publishers are modest and reasonable. They suggest that the *Kuder Preference Record* is useful for introducing students to organized study of occupations and career selection, and for guiding them into educational and vocational activities they will find satisfying and enjoyable. In the reviewer's judgment, the *Kuder Preference Record* is the most useful available instrument for this purpose. It is especially well fitted for use with the mass of high school students, and the publishers have provided stimulating and useful auxiliary materials for teachers and counselors.

Published research has indicated that the various scores provided by the *Kuder Preference Record* are satisfactory in reliability. A digest of such studies leads to the judgment that the test is one of the best from the standpoint of validity. In the opinion of the reviewer, the Strong *Vocational Interest Blank* is often to be preferred for investigation of the vocational interests of college students. However, for use with high school students and average adults, especially those not preparing for the professions, the *Kuder Preference Record* is a practical and valuable instrument. Superior students at the seventh grade level can take this inventory with the expectation of getting valid and educationally significant results.

The provision of a glossary may be regarded as a useful practical service. The test specialist is aware, of course, that research must settle various questions as to whether the inventory is made more effective when such explanations are provided. Some studies suggest that scores are more reliable and valid when terms are not explained. Interests tend to develop along with other aspects of mentality and personality; the person who is ignorant of a thing can hardly have a well developed interest in it. Nevertheless, although glossaries and other types of explanatory material may not be very useful in the measurement of interests, they may have an important function in connection with instruction concerning interests.

In summary, the *Kuder Preference Record* is a carefully constructed and well planned instrument. While full exploration of its values and limitations remains as a field for psychological research, it is clearly one of the best available instruments of its type, especially for use with high school students. Its practical values justify extensive use by high school teachers and counselors, and by those engaged in counseling representative groups of adults.

H. M. FOWLER, *Associate Professor of Educational Research, University of Toronto, Toronto, Ontario, Canada.*

I. DEVELOPMENT AND PRESENT STATUS OF

THE KUDER PREFERENCE RECORD. Of the various interest measures now available, the *Kuder Preference Record—Vocational* is one of the two most widely used. It is estimated that in Ontario it is used, at least for high school students, more than all other interest blanks combined.

The popularity of this measure as a clinical instrument is matched by its appeal to research workers who are interested in determining its scientific value. The latest manual (March 1951) has a list of 138 bibliographic references, of which 35 are additional to those contained in the first revision of the manual in February 1950. The reported research includes studies of the reliability and validity of the record, comparative studies designed to assess the particular strengths and weaknesses of this instrument in competition with other interest inventories, and a wide variety of investigations to determine the value of the preference scores in special situations, for example, in veterans' advisory bureaus. A number of workers have supplemented the work being done by the author and his publishers by developing local norms for high school seniors, for college freshmen, for university business school seniors, and others.

One of the reasons that the *Kuder Preference Record* appeals to test users is that the author and his publishers are untiring in their efforts to improve it, to keep it up to date, and to provide necessary interpretative data. The first research was conducted during the academic year 1934–35 when the author asked 500 students at the Ohio State University to rank in order of preference five activities in each of 40 groups. Subsequently, much research has been done. Even since the publication of *The Third Mental Measurements Yearbook* in 1949, the measure has been improved and refined in a number of ways. A new scale, the tenth, in an interest area related to agricultural, naturalistic, and outdoor activities, is now available for use with the C forms. It has been called "Outdoor" by the author, and is numbered "O" in references to it in the tables of occupations. Another development has been the provision of a verification scale which was devised at the request of those who thought it necessary to identify students who had filled in the blank carelessly or without understanding. Form B1, the short form of the record, appeared in 1948 and was developed for use in industrial situations where it is not practicable to use the longer Forms BB and BM. The author recommends that, for the present,

the use of B1 be restricted to adults; later a short form may be developed for use with eighth grade or high school students.

II. COMMENTS ON THE KUDER PREFERENCE RECORD. A. THE KUDER AS A TEST. Is the Kuder really a test? According to the manual its specific uses are (*a*) to point out vocations with which the student may not be familiar but which involve activities of the type for which he has expressed preference, and (*b*) to check on whether a person's choice of an occupation is consistent with the type of thing he ordinarily prefers to do. The name, *Kuder Preference Record,* is itself suggestive. This reviewer looks upon the blank as an instrument for testing only if one considers that the student is being tested with respect to his ability to give a true and complete picture of his interests through the responses that he makes to the items.

In the administration of this blank it is extremely important to obtain the proper rapport between student and counselor. Fortunately, students are intrigued by the unusual form and appearance of the booklets and enjoy making their responses by means of the special pin-prick device. These features assist the administrator in motivating the students to be honest and thorough in choosing the responses which provide the most satisfactory self-analysis of their interests or preferences.

B. FORMAT. The format of the various forms of the *Kuder Preference Record* leaves little to be desired. The blanks are printed in clear black type. The method of marking the responses, both for hand scoring and machine scoring editions, is easily followed by most students. Some do complain about the pin recording feature, saying that the pin should have a wooden rest or that it should have a larger head. The blank can be given either individually or to groups and the administrator need give very little assistance. The directions, which are clear and not too wordy, are set up in brief paragraphs which appear on the booklets themselves. The special answer sheet system works well in general, but those who sell large quantities complain that in some runs of the booklets the pages are not lined up properly.

C. ITEMS. According to some authorities, one big disadvantage of the Kuder is the forced choice. These critics claim that to ask a student to say that he prefers one activity to another when in truth he may like the two equally well, serves only to irritate the conscientious student who would like to give accurate responses and to encourage the careless student to become even more careless. This disadvantage of the preference item may be more apparent than real. In the experience of this reviewer most students are able to make choices for most of the items without too much difficulty. A check of the blank suggests that most of the subitems are "normally competitive," to use Truman L. Kelley's expression. For example, "work mathematical puzzles" appears with "play checkers," and "study physics" appears with "study public speaking." For the few cases in which students are not able to give meaningful responses, it may be assumed that the scores for the ten scales will not be greatly affected since they depend upon the responses to large numbers of items.

Of more concern to some users is the interpretation placed by students upon some of the words and phrases used in the items. Christensen (37) completed an experiment designed to test the effect of giving systematic instruction in the meaning of the items found in the blank; he concluded that the results appear to indicate that "such instruction probably played a role in causing the subjects to change their preferences." Clearly, students' responses may vary according to what they think the items mean. The latest editions of the manual and test booklet include a glossary of terms that is intended to minimize the variation of interpretation from individual to individual. It is questionable, however, whether this has much value. It might be better to include explanatory material in the items themselves, a technique which has been used quite effectively by Lee and Thorpe in their *Occupational Interest Inventory*.

The preference item has definite advantages as well as disadvantages. This reviewer believes that to ask a student whether he prefers one activity over another provides a much more meaningful and concrete situation than merely to ask him whether he likes or dislikes certain activities. Also it makes possible choices between two activities, both of which are liked or both disliked, thus enabling the counselor to get a more complete picture of the student.

The author is to be commended, also, for avoiding in the blank the use of what might be called the "million dollar" item. Presentation of such unusual or unlikely situations is not apt to elicit the type of response that will be helpful to the counselor in the eminently matter-of-fact task of suggesting suitable vocations.

D. RELIABILITY. The *Kuder Preference Record* was constructed to yield homogeneous groups of items, and from the first, the author checked the reliability of its scoring categories. In view of this, it is rather surprising to find the following statement in the report of one study: "It is possible to obtain by chance scores on the *Kuder Preference Record* of a character which, if made by high school youngsters, might be regarded as significant." How reliable *are* the Kuder scores?

The most recent revision of the manual gives separate reliability estimates for each of the ten scoring categories for each of four different groups, labeled as follows: 1,000 men, 100 women, 100 boys, 100 girls. On the average, the reported reliabilities are approximately .90; the lowest reliability reported is .84 and the highest is .93. Some studies, such as those by Triggs, agree substantially in their estimates of reliability with those reported in the manual. Others, such as the study by Tyler (62) have given estimates which are consistently lower than those in the manual. On the whole, the evidence suggests that the Kuder scales yield scores which are at least as reliable as the average personality measure. However, it is questionable whether scores obtained from a single administration of the blank should be accepted completely at their face value. The reported reliabilities are none too high for individual differentiation, and counseling must be done on an individual basis.

The author might well provide other estimates of test reliability. Only estimates of the consistency of the scales, computed by using the Kuder-Richardson Case Four method, are given. Test-retest estimates are not given in the latest revision of the manual, although they were given in earlier editions. The test-retest reliability estimates ranged, generally, somewhat higher than the consistency estimates. Also, the author should provide more information about the groups used and the situations in which the reliability estimates were obtained. Otherwise the unsophisticated reader may think of these estimates as *the* reliability of the blank.

E. INTERPRETATION OF SCORES. The wealth of information given in the test manual includes unusually complete norms, as well as a description of the procedure to be followed in profiling the scores and relating them to suggested occupations. The high school norms are based on scores obtained on Form C by 3,418 boys and 4,466 girls in high schools well distributed over the country. Two sets of norms for male adults have been developed, and what should be considered tentative norms for female adults are provided. Two separate profile sheets, one for adult men and women and the other for boys and girls, in which raw scores are converted to percentiles, serve to center attention upon certain broad areas of interest.

A table given in the manual classifies occupations according to the profiled interest areas. However, as pointed out by Kuder, the classifications must be regarded as tentative. A number of counselors have complained about the placement of occupations. Some of the divisions and subdivisions set up to fit the ten interest areas appear to be rather fanciful. One suspects that they were developed through armchair reasoning rather than by actual study of occupational differences. However, if these listings are treated as suggestive only, as the manual directs, no serious error should result. References are provided in the tables to other sources of information about the nature of the various jobs.

In the past, one of the greatest weaknesses of the *Kuder Preference Record* has been the lack of adequate norms developed on sufficiently large groups. To some extent this has been corrected. The author has developed what might be termed national norms based on the scores of 1,296 men representative of the major occupations in the general population. Another set of norms for adult men has been obtained by inviting a group of telephone subscribers in a stratified sample of 138 cities and towns to fill out the blank. Although these two sets of norms agree fairly closely for the most part, they differ significantly for two of the scoring categories. These differences lead one to question the stability of the new norms. Because it is difficult to get a truly representative sample, genuine national norms are very difficult to obtain, but for many purposes they are not so valuable as the local norms that are now being developed by a number of workers.

More specific than the national norms are the occupational norms which are given in Tables 2 and 3 of the latest edition of the manual. These tables show the percentile ranks of average scores obtained on the ten scales by more than 15,000 individuals in various occupations. The value of the profiles for the occupational groups is limited because for most of the occupations they are based on very small numbers, and only the percentile ranks of average scores are given.

In summary, the norm groups, although greatly increased in number over those reported earlier, are still quite small (for adult women only 100 on the outdoor scale) ; in an effort to get a representative sample the author has spread his norm group very thinly over a large assortment of small groups ; and the norms cannot be employed with confidence by some users, Canadians for example, of the test.

F. VALIDITY. The occupational profiles presented in Tables 2 and 3 of the manual offer some evidence to support the hypothesis that the scores are valid. For example, accountants score very high on computational and clerical, low on persuasive and mechanical. This type of evidence, however, fails to be completely convincing. One is suspicious of any method of demonstrating validity through armchair reasoning and consequent-antecedent logic. What is needed are some genuine follow-up studies in which scores obtained by people *before* they enter occupations are compared with various measures of their vocational success. In the opinion of this reviewer, the validity of the *Kuder Preference Record* scores is still very much open to question.

Although no direct demonstration of the validity of the blank is forthcoming as yet, some information is given in the test manual which should help the user to determine how useful the scores may be in actual practice. Significant differences are reported for students in different curricula preparing for various occupations. The record scores have, in general, positive but low correlations with measures of achievement such as school grades and objective test scores, and they show only a low relationship with measures of ability, which means that counselors must consider both abilities and preferences in suggesting vocational choices. Some evidence relating to validity is available in outside studies not reported in the test manual. For example, Brown, who had a number of veterans evaluate their Kuder ratings, reports that, on the whole, the confidence in the ratings was of high statistical significance (*166*).

Of considerable concern to this reviewer is the possibility that the responder may have marked the blank insincerely or dishonestly, thus rendering the scores completely invalid. Cross has conducted a study of this possibility, and has concluded that "a subject suitably motivated may successfully fake the *Kuder Preference Record*" (*168*). Although most people will give honest responses, testers should guard against faking or dishonesty in situations, such as job applications or selection testing, in which the person being tested has something to gain by being dishonest. Under proper conditions of administration, faking becomes somewhat difficult for any but the most sophisticated, because those who are taking the blank for the first time are not familiar with the scales that are being used.

The author and his publishers present some scanty and inconclusive evidence to suggest that it may be possible to differentiate succeessful from nonsuccessful people *within* an occupation. The research done by this reviewer along similar lines has been discouraging.

G. MISCELLANEOUS. In line with the publishers' efforts to keep the test up to date and to provide interpretative data whenever possible, is the recent publication of the *Kuder Book List* and the accompanying instructor's guide. This list contains over 500 titles classified according to the ten interest areas of Form C of the record. Each book has been rated on reading difficulty. After the student has taken the preference record, his profile of scores will help him find the types of books that should interest him most. We do not yet know whether teachers will find this book list of assistance in improving reading, but it appears to be based upon the sound principle of appealing to interest to motivate the slow reader.

One reputed advantage of the *Kuder Preference Record* is that it is inexpensive and easily scored. Not all will agree. Canadian users find the test fairly expensive because they have import duties to pay over and above the ordinary costs. Guidance counselors also complain that it takes considerable time to score. Machine scoring editions are available, but these can be used only by those who have access to test scoring machines. Moreover, the test is often given to individuals or to small groups, and in such cases much of the advantage of machine scoring is lost. There would appear to be a real need to produce a shorter, less expensive form that can be scored more quickly and easily.

All editions of the manuals suggest the use of the 75th percentile in deciding which scores are significant. Although one might quarrel with the statistics presented by the author in earlier editions of the manual in defense of its use, this particular critical point appears to be as good as any other. As the manual points out, no sig-nificance point would be completely satisfactory.

III. SUMMARY AND GENERAL IMPRESSIONS. In summary, it may be said that the *Kuder Preference Record* is one of the best available measures of interests, particularly for high school students. Its preference-type items, although originally selected subjectively, have been tested by research, and it may be assumed that the scores obtained for certain wide areas of interest are reasonably objective. The reliability of the scale scores is satisfactory. The author deserves commendation for the energetic manner in which he has carried out continuous and painstaking research on the blank since its first development. The C forms, for machine and hand scoring, show refinements which make them superior to the earlier B forms: a new interest category has been added, better norms have been provided, and more occupational data are available. In many respects, the Kuder is as good an interest measure as Strong's *Vocational Interest Blank,* its chief rival; in some respects it is a better instrument.

The *Kuder Preference Record—Vocational* is recommended for use, but in the opinion of this reviewer, certain points of caution are worth stressing. In the first place, personality measurement has not yet reached the point of producing completely objective and trustworthy scores despite the very considerable progress that has been made in the past 30 years. Test score interpretation is always hazardous; the reader is advised to be particularly careful with the interpretation of interest or preference blank scores. Secondly, although the Kuder presents a worthwhile effort to describe subjects in terms of general fields of interest (in contrast with Strong's test which determines whether subjects mark the test the way successful people in various occupations mark it), it should be conceded that to a large extent the validity of the scores has yet to be demonstrated. This is not surprising in view of the way the test was constructed. The acid test of the blank, however, is whether it is clinically useful. Volume of sales, although not always a sound criterion, suggests that it is. The more conservative counselors appear to think that the administration of the Kuder blank is a good beginning point in an interview. They look upon it as a useful source of suggestive information that may be used in conjunction with data concerning ability and other personality factors in exploring the possibilities of vocational choice.

Kuder Preference Record—Vocational

For reviews by Ralph F. Berdie, E. G. Chambers and Donald E. Super and an excerpt from a review of Forms BB and BM, see 3:640; for reviews by A. B. Crawford and Arthur E. Traxler of an earlier edition, see 40:1671.

[743]

Occupational Interest Inventory. Grades 7-12 and adults, 9-16 and adults; 1943-46; 10 scores grouped in 3 categories: fields of interests (personal-social, natural, mechanical, business, the arts, the sciences), types of interests (verbal, manipulative, computational), level of interests; IBM; 2 levels; Form A ('46); lower level manual ('44), upper level manual ('43); $3 per 25 of any one level; 35¢ per specimen set of any one level, postpaid; separate answer sheets may be used; 2¢ per IBM answer sheet; 60¢ per set of stencils for machine scoring of answer sheets; 60¢ per set of stencils for hand scoring of answer sheets; postage extra; nontimed (30-40) minutes; Edwin A. Lee and Louis P. Thorpe; California Test Bureau. *

REFERENCES

1. EASTMAN, FLORENCE. *Scores of Pupils on Tests of Adjustment as Related to Teacher Ratings and Pupil Choices.* Master's thesis, Southern Methodist University (Dallas, Tex.), 1946. (*Abstracts of Theses....1946, 1947,* [no date] pp. 68-9.)
2. FAUQUIER, WILLIAM, AND SHIERSON, HARRY E. *Occupational Selection Aid: A Guidebook in Vocational and Educational Counseling (In Two Parts) for Use With the Occupational Interest Inventory, Parts 1 and 2.* Los Angeles, Calif.: California Test Bureau, 1947. Pp. 36, 32. Paper. *
3. LINDGREN, HENRY C. "A Study of Certain Aspects of the Lee-Thorpe Occupational Interest Inventory." *J Ed Psychol* 38:353-62 O '47. * (*PA* 22:2200, title only)
4. STEFFLRE, BUFORD. "The Reading Difficulty of Interest Inventories." *Occupations* 26:95-6 N '47. * (*PA* 21:1722)
5-6. MALCOLM, DAVID D. *The Relative Usefulness of Several Extensively Used Vocational Interest Inventories in Counseling at Various Academic Levels.* Doctor's thesis, Northwestern University (Evanston, Ill.), 1948. (*Summaries of Doctoral Dissertations....June-September 1948,* 1949, pp. 245-50.)
7. ROEBER, EDWARD C. "A Comparison of Seven Interest Inventories With Respect to Word Usage." *J Ed Res* 42:8-17 S '48. * (*PA* 23:2915)
8. BROWN, WILLIAM E. *A Study of the Elements Contributing to the Successful Selection of a Job Training Vocational Objective.* Doctor's thesis, Pennsylvania State College (State College, Pa.), 1949. (*Abstracts of Doctoral Dissertations....1949,* 1950, pp. 318-24.) (*PA* 24:5539, title only)
9. GLASER, ROBERT. "A Methodological Analysis of the Inconsistency of Response to Test Items." *Ed & Psychol Meas* 9:727-39 w '49. * (*PA* 26:2747)
10. ROEBER, EDWARD C. "The Relationship Between Parts of the Kuder Preference Record and Parts of the Lee-Thorpe Occupational Interest Inventory." *J Ed Res* 42:598-608 Ap '49. * (*PA* 23:5586)
11. SUPER, DONALD E. *Appraising Vocational Fitness by Means of Psychological Tests,* pp. 473-4. New York: Harper & Brothers, 1949. Pp. xxiii, 727. * (*PA* 24:2130)
12. CASSEL, RUSSELL N. *An Experimental Investigation of the "Reality-Strata" of Certain Objectively Defined Groups of Individuals by Use of the Level of Aspiration Technique.* Doctor's thesis, University of Southern California (Los Angeles, Calif.), 1950. (*Abstracts of Dissertations....1950,* 1951, pp. 288-90.)
13. IRWIN, IRL A. *Occupational Interest and the Prediction of Scholastic Success.* Master's thesis, State University of Iowa (Iowa City, Iowa), 1950.
14. IRWIN, IRL A. "Occupational Interest and the Prediction of Scholastic Success." *Psychol Service Center J* 2:34-45 Mr '50. * (*PA* 25:6469)
15. MALCOLM, DAVID DONALD. "Which Interest Inventory Should I Use?" *J Ed Res* 44:91-8 O '50. * (*PA* 25:5675)
16. MILLER, CARROLL H. *An Occupational Values Inventory for College Students.* Doctor's "Field Study No. 2," Colorado State College of Education (Greeley, Colo.), 1950. (*Abstracts of Field Studies....1950,* 1951, pp. 106-9.)
17. NAIR, RALPH KENNETH. *Predictive Value of Standardized Tests and Inventories in Industrial Arts Teacher Education.* Doctor's thesis, University of Missouri (Columbia, Mo.), 1950. Abstract: *Microfilm Abstracts* 10:77-8 no 3 '50. * (*PA* 25:4862, title only)
18. BROWN, MANUEL N. "Evaluation of Lee-Thorpe Inventory Ratings by Veteran Patients." *Ed & Psychol Meas* 11:248-54 su '51. * (*PA* 26:2796)
19. BROWN, MANUEL N. "Expressed and Inventoried Interests of Veterans." *J Appl Psychol* 35:401-2 D '51. * (*PA* 26:6354)

20. JACOBS, ROBERT. "A Brief Study of the Relationship Between Scores on the Lee-Thorpe Occupational Interest Inventory and Scores on the Kuder Preference Record," pp. 79-85. In *1951 Achievement Testing Program in Independent Schools and Supplementary Studies.* Foreword by Ben D. Wood. Educational Records Bulletin No. 57. New York: Educational Records Bureau, July 1951. Pp. xiii, 85. * (*PA* 26:984)

ARTHUR H. BRAYFIELD, *Professor of Psychology and Head of the Department, Kansas State College, Manhattan, Kansas.*

According to the authors, the major purpose of this inventory is "to aid in discovering the basic occupational interests possessed by an individual in order that he may become or remain an interested, well-adjusted, and effective person as well as a profitable employee." They stress that it is not a test of occupational abilities or skills. This seems a proper orientation to interest measurement.

The inventory purports to identify six basic fields of interest: Personal-Social, Natural, Mechanical, Business, Arts, and Sciences; to determine whether an individual is most interested in verbal, manipulative, or computational activities; and finally to identify "the levels on which an individual's basic interests exist."

The format of the inventory is good. Each section is accompanied by a manual which covers in general terms the topics usually considered essential in a test manual. Reading difficulty of the items has been checked.

To the uncritical and untrained individual the inventory should appear to be a "good buy." And it is just that—nicely packaged pieces of merchandise unaccompanied by a *caveat emptor.*

The authors furnish no information of an empirical nature which would indicate that (*a*) the interest fields identified by this instrument are basic; (*b*) the items comprising the individual scales were selected by any type of rigorous internal or external item analysis; or, (*c*) that the inventory meets any of the usual tests of validity established for interest measures by such workers as Strong, Kuder, Super, Darley, and others.

Meager data bearing on the validity of the inventory (Advanced, Form A) is furnished in a study by Lindgren (*3*). He correlated its raw scores with raw scores on the "appropriate" scales of the *Kuder Preference Record* for 50 male veterans. He found some relationships which would be significant. The highest *r*'s were Sciences vs. Scientific, .80; Business vs. Clerical, .74; Mechanical vs. Mechanical, .72; and Personal-Social vs. Social Service, .60. Business also correlated .52 with Persuasive.

Given the example of Strong and Kuder in devoting time and money to the development of their interest inventories with the objective of providing an adequate research basis for evaluation, it seems unfortunate that the authors of this inventory were content to release instruments that are primarily "arm chair" productions.

Lacking further empirical evidence appropriate to the issues enumerated above, this reviewer advises against the use of the *Occupational Interest Inventory* in any practical situation with one exception: The reviewer has used it for some years in his measurement courses to demonstrate that a well packaged, widely advertised, smartly marketed psychological test or inventory may not, on justifiable technical grounds, warrant the consumer support which it apparently receives.

For reviews by Edward S. Bordin and Stanley G. Dulsky, see 3:643.

[744]
*Self-Administering Vocational Interest Locator with Work Interest Picture. Grades 10–16 and adults; 1933–49; interest preferences in each of 10 aspects (creative, working with people, executive, lingual, mathematical, manual, medical-religious, administrative, inter-correlated, general) of 10 areas (artistic, commercial, constructional, humanistic, industrial, literary, mechanical, scientific, technical, transportational); Form 1A ('49); no data on reliability and validity; manual ('49); 25¢ per set of materials, postpaid; N. A. Lufburrow; the Author, 3112 Milford Ave., Baltimore 7, Md. *

DONALD E. SUPER, *Professor of Education, Teachers College, Columbia University, New York, New York.*

The *Vocational Interest Locator* is a collection of 100 brief descriptions of presumed types of work. These are classified in the summary Work Interest Picture (which takes the place of a scoring blank) into the areas and aspects of work named above. According to the manual, it is "not a test," it "does not present a score," and it is "not the sort of device" that needs to be accompanied by evidence of reliability or validity. Instead, the manual informs us, it is a "device for aiding in locating, analyzing and understanding the individual's work interests" (is the implication that tests do not do this?), and it "leads to a RESULT" (surely an innovation in the testing field) that "is as valid and reliable as you make it" (but are we told how valid and reliable anyone *has* made it?). The author states that "it is, in truth, a very effective interviewing aid," "certainly it can be helpful,"

"it is a fascinating device," there is "no doubt as to accuracy," and "I have used them (the classification of areas of work) constantly in guidance and placement work, without ever finding reason to alter the terminology" (presumably because no research has been done on the reliability or validity of the classification).

The above quotations should make it clear that this instrument was developed without benefit of psychological knowledge or techniques, has not been objectively evaluated, and has nothing to contribute to the armamentarium of psychologists. To describe and criticize it in more detail would be a misuse of space in a psychological publication and a waste of time for users of psychological instruments.

[745]
Thurstone Interest Schedule. Grades 9–16 and adults; 1947; replaces *Vocational Interest Schedule* (see 3:653); 10 scores: physical science, biological science, computational, business, executive, persuasive, linguistic, humanitarian, artistic, musical; 1 form; no norms; $1.50 per 25; 35¢ per specimen set; postpaid; (15) minutes; L. L. Thurstone; Psychological Corporation. *

REFERENCES
1. ZWILLING, VIRGINIA T. *The Prediction of Grades in Freshman English From a Battery of Tests of Mental Ability, Interests and Aptitudes Administered to Students Entering a Liberal Arts College.* Doctor's thesis, Fordham University (New York, N.Y.), 1949. (*Dissertations...*, 1949, pp. 62–5.)

NORMAN FREDERIKSEN, *Associate Professor of Psychology, Princeton University; and Head, Research Department, Educational Testing Service; Princeton, New Jersey.*

Replacing the older *Vocational Interest Schedule*, the *Thurstone Interest Schedule* was published in 1947. The new schedule consists of 100 pairs of occupational titles arranged in a 10 × 10 table. Each cell of the table contains two occupational titles; all of the upper left entries in any one column are related to the same interest area, and all of the lower right entries in any one row are related to the same interest area. The task of the subject is to indicate his preference for one of the two occupational titles in each cell. Each interest area is thus compared with every other interest area an equal number of times, each interest area being represented by job titles which vary from cell to cell in the row or column. As is stated clearly in the manual, the schedule is appropriate only in situations where honest and straightforward responses can be expected, since the purpose of the instrument is not disguised.

The selection of the ten interest areas was apparently not based primarily on results of factor studies; an attempt was made to include Spranger's life interests and other interest categories in common use. That the items are in general properly allocated in each field is indicated by the magnitude of the average item validities. The lowest average item validity is .64 (executive) and the highest is .85 (musical); the item validities are thus on the average considerably higher than one typically finds for most types of tests.

The intercorrelations among the ten scores (for a sample of 200 male high school graduates) ranged from .68 to −.37. The negative correlations are due at least in part to the method of measurement employed; expressing a preference for one interest area ordinarily involves withholding an expression of preference for another. The split half reliabilities ranged from .90 to .96 for a sample of 200 schedules obtained, presumably, from the same group of male high school graduates; such high reliabilities would justify use of the scores in individual guidance.

It is asserted in the manual that the schedule yields comparable scores, and a number of suggestions regarding interpretation of scores are made which assume some kind of comparability. It is stated, for example, that "the profile shows at a glance whether a man is more interested in certain fields than in other fields" and "the profile may show that he is equally interested in several fields, and not at all in certain others." One can think of several ways in which scales can be comparable; they can be comparable in the sense that corresponding scores cut off equal proportions of a population, for example, or in the sense that corresponding scores yield the same predicted performance on some criterion. The scores on the *Thurstone Interest Schedule* are certainly not intended to be comparable in either of these senses. It is difficult to specify in what sense scores must be comparable in order to justify interpretations such as those illustrated above. According to the manual, the profile scores are comparable because "each of the occupational fields is represented the same number of times in this schedule, and since every occupational field is compared with every other field." However, various job titles are used to represent each occupational field, and it is not made clear in the manual how these titles were chosen. Substituting different occupational titles, such as "drummer" for "organist," would be likely to change the mean score for a particular area, which suggests that the particular titles chosen

would not necessarily lead to comparability. No evidence is presented to show that the interest areas are represented by job titles of equal preference value or that the job titles chosen are representative of the occupations making up the interest area.

The manual states that a table of norms is not necessary because the scores are comparable. In this reviewer's opinion, even if this were so, it would still be desirable to have some sort of normative material to aid in interpretation of scores. No such materials have yet appeared in the periodical literature.

The criticisms noted above will not detract seriously from the usefulness of the schedule. The categories included in the profile cover the important interest areas, at least for clients likely to go into higher-level jobs. The schedule is unusually easy to administer and score; it may be administered in ten or fifteen minutes, and it can be scored accurately in two or three minutes. The *Thurstone Interest Schedule* should be a valuable addition to the kit of tools employed by the vocational counselor.

DONALD E. SUPER, *Professor of Education, Teachers College, Columbia University, New York, New York.*

This schedule is based on the same assumption as its predecessor was, namely, that the counselee has a good enough understanding of what occupational titles mean for the patterning of responses to, or choices of, titles to be a meaningful measure. Thus, in the new schedule the examinee indicates which of two occupational titles he prefers, or he may mark them so as to show equal liking or disliking. In responding to the choice "Judge—Tax Specialist," a delinquent adolescent boy may decide in terms of first-hand knowledge of one limited phase of the former occupation and a complete lack of knowledge of the latter occupation. Or a better informed person may feel quite lost in responding to the title "Red Cross," which he knows might mean a medical, social work, or administrative type of activity, but have a very clear idea of what is meant by the other member of the pair, "Portrait Painter." Just what effect these differences in the meanings of job titles *between* individuals and *within* individuals have on the meaning of scores on the schedule, and indeed the mere existence of such differences, has apparently not been considered by Thurstone.

Perhaps they are not as important as the

above argument suggests. Some evidence to this effect is provided by the analysis of the internal consistency of the scales, which Thurstone misleadingly calls *item validity* (misleading because the term implies validity of the item against some external criterion, such as job success, whereas the term here denotes item-test agreement, that is, agreement of the item with the total score of the scale to which it is assigned). The fact that the average correlation between musical items and the musical scale is .85 suggests that most people in the standardization group understood each musical occupational title as an occupation involving music more than anything else. But the average item-test agreement of the executive scale is .64, the range of the correlations being from .32 to .86. In this, and in some similar instances, one might ask whether a significant number of respondents did not perceive what Thurstone considered to be executive occupations as more truly humanitarian or business occupations (e.g., hospital and school superintendent, hotel manager). The low agreement between some items and the total score on the scale to which they are assigned at least suggests that this may be so in some occupational fields. And if some types of occupations are better understood in some subcultures than in others, the scores of persons in those subcultures may be consistently distorted by their inadequate perception of some occupations. Interest inventories consisting in whole or in part of items describing more familiar everyday activities, such as the Strong and the Kuder, are freer from this possible defect.

Further evidence to support Thurstone's procedure lies in the split-half reliabilities of the 20-item scales; despite the brevity of the scales, which results in one change of response substantially changing a score, the reliability coefficients range from .90 to .96.

The recommended interpretation of the schedule emphasizes the importance of intra-individual differences in scores and provides no means of comparing a person's interests with those of others. Thurstone argues with some apparent justification that it is "the ups and downs, the spread, and the shape of the individual profile that count in advising a person"; it is this, after all, that tells what a person is interested in. But satisfaction with this logic leads Thurstone to neglect altogether the question of external validity, an unwarranted neglect which seems to result from viewing differential occupational interest patterns as being nothing more than *norms,* whereas they may be evidence of validity. And it is the lack of external evidence of validity which is the most serious defect of the *Thurstone Interest Schedule.* Do people who, in high school or college, make high physical science scores tend to enter, succeed in, and be satisfied with employment in occupations such as engineering? Do men who make high humanitarian scores tend to enter occupations such as social work and teaching, do they remain in them, and do they like their work? It is questions of this type that a counselor must ask about his tests, and to which he must have answers, if they are to help him in his work. For it is only the answers to these questions that tell the counselor the practical meaning of his instruments. Thurstone has not even sought to provide the answer, as someone must before the *Thurstone Interest Schedule* can be more than a research instrument or a means of locating fields which might be explored by a student.

[746]

★**Vocational Interest Analyses: A Six-Fold Analytical Extension of the Occupational Interest Inventory.** Grades 9–16 and adults; 1951; 6 scores in each of 6 areas listed below; IBM; 6 tests; tests should be administered only in those areas in which an examinee obtains high scores on the *Occupational Interest Inventory* (see 743); 1 form; no data on reliability; no norms; $2 per 25 of any one test; 75¢ per specimen set, postpaid; separate answer sheets may be used; 8¢ per set of IBM answer sheets for use with any three tests; 60¢ per set of stencils for machine scoring of answer sheets; 60¢ per set of stencils for hand scoring of answer sheets; postage extra; nontimed (25–35) minutes per test; Edward C. Roeber and Gerald G. Prideaux in collaboration with Edwin A. Lee and Louis P. Thorpe; California Test Bureau.

a) PERSONAL-SOCIAL ANALYSIS. 6 scores: domestic service, personal service, social service, teaching and related activities, law and law enforcement, health and medical service.

b) NATURAL ANALYSIS. 6 scores: general and crop farming, animal raising and care, garden and greenhouse care, fish-game-domestic fowl, lumbering and forestry, marine work.

c) MECHANICAL ANALYSIS. 6 scores: maintenance and repairing, machine operation and tending, construction, designing, bench work and bench crafts, processing.

d) BUSINESS ANALYSIS. 6 scores: clerical, shipping and distribution, bookkeeping and accounting, buying and selling, training and supervision, management and control.

e) THE ARTS ANALYSIS. 6 scores: art crafts, painting and drawing, decorating and landscaping, drama and radio, literary activities, music.

f) THE SCIENCES ANALYSIS. 6 scores: laboratory work, mineral-petroleum products, applied chemistry, chemical research, biological research, scientific engineering.

JULIAN C. STANLEY, *Associate Professor of Educational Psychology, George Peabody College for Teachers, Nashville, Tennessee.*

In the *Third Mental Measurements Year-book* several major criticisms of the *Occupational Interest Inventory* appeared, and Stanley G. Dulsky suggested that the "total score might mask an important occupational preference that could be detected only by a careful analysis of the individual sections making up the field." In line with Dulsky's suggestion, the California Test Bureau has devised six *Vocational Interest Analyses*. Despite some indications of careful construction by Roeber and Prideaux, the Analyses seem to the reviewer severely limited in usefulness because they lack norms, internal consistency statistics, reliability coefficients, and evidence of empirical validity. In the reviewer's opinion they were released prematurely. This becomes especially obvious when the two generally unfavorable reviews of the parent instrument are considered in conjunction with the Analyses, which seem to have even more of the same flaws.

The format of each *Vocational Interest Analysis* is much like that of the *Occupational Interest Inventory*. The Analyses are less cluttered, however, and more effectively conceal from the testee the names of the categories employed. Each of the six interest areas of the Inventory is explored further with an Analysis that yields six scores by means of 120 paired-comparison couplets. Thus, for the Personal-Social Analysis 40 short statements pertain to domestic service, 40 to personal service, 40 to social service, 40 to teaching and related activities, 40 to law and law enforcement, and 40 to health and medical service. Eight of the domestic service statements are paired with eight personal service ones, eight more domestic service statements with eight social service ones, etc. Statements pertaining to simple activities are paired with other simple activity statements, and this balancing is also carried out for medium and superior level activities.

The analyses have a combination armchair and *Dictionary of Occupational Titles* origin; each statement is followed by one or more DOT code numbers. Though somewhat different from other interest inventories, they are sadly deficient in empirical support. Such statements as the following in the manual are hardly satisfying even to the measurement novice, much less to the trained tester:

Preliminary studies indicate that the reliabilities of each of the 36 categories....approximate or exceed those [for the *Occupational Interest Inventory*]. * Studies are in progress to provide additional evidences of validity. * [Not a shred of evidence for any sort of empirical validity is mentioned.] The highest interest fields for an individual are determined by the percentile ranks of the composite norms [both sexes combined] provided in the *Occupational Interest Inventory* manual. * A further justification for the use of frequency of choice in establishing a differentiation of interests [for each Analysis] is the factor of sex differences in the vocational interest fields. For example, a girl may obtain a high percentile rank (or standard score) in the Mechanical field when sex norms are used, even though she makes relatively few choices in that field. Nevertheless, the advisability of preparing percentile norms for the six *Vocational Interest Analyses* is being further investigated.

Perhaps the reviewer is missing something either subtle or obvious in this renunciation of sex norms for the Inventory and any norms at all for the Analyses, but he can find no evidence in the manual that a sheer frequency comparison is meaningful, even though, because of its counterbalanced internal structure, each Analysis must yield a mean of 20 for its six categories (120/6).

In conclusion, because of their extreme lack of an empirical foundation the reviewer cannot recommend the *Vocational Interest Analyses* at this time. He sincerely hopes that the California Test Bureau will take vigorous action to standardize these inventories before advertising them further as being reliable and valid.

[747]

*Vocational Interest Blank for Men, Revised. Ages 17 and over; 1927–51; 50 scorable categories: masculinity-femininity ('38), maturity of interest ('41), occupational level ('39), 41 occupations, 6 occupational groups (I, II, V, VIII, IX, and X); Group I: group scale ('38), artist ('38), psychologist ('49), architect ('38), physician ('38), dentist ('38), osteopath ('47), veterinarian ('49); Group II: group scale ('39), mathematician ('38), engineer ('38), chemist ('38); Group III: production manager ('38); Group IV: farmer ('38), carpenter ('38), aviator ('40), printer ('38), mathematics-physical science teacher ('38), policeman ('38), forest service man ('38); Group V: group scale ('36), Y.M.C.A. physical director ('38), personnel manager ('38), public administrator ('44), Y.M.C.A. secretary ('28), social science teacher ('38), school superintendent ('38), minister ('38); Group VI: musician ('38); Group VII: certified public accountant ('38); Group VIII: group scale ('38), senior certified public accountant ('49), accountant ('38), office man ('38), purchasing agent ('38), banker ('38), pharmacist ('49), mortician ('46); Group IX: group scale ('38), sales manager ('38), realtor ('38), life insurance salesman ('38); Group X: group scale ('38), advertising man ('38), lawyer ('38), author-journalist ('38); Group XI: president of a manufacturing concern ('38); IBM; 2 editions; 1 form, '38; manual ('51); $2 per 25; 2¢ per report blank ['38]; 2¢ per global interest chart ['43]; $1 per single scoring scale; 2–9 scales, 80¢ each; 10 or more scales, 70¢ each; 15¢ per specimen set; cash orders postpaid; nontimed (40) minutes; Edward K. Strong, Jr.; Stanford University Press. *

a) FORM M (HAND SCORING EDITION).

b) FORM MM (MACHINE SCORING EDITION). Separate answer sheets must be used; 75¢ per 25 IBM answer sheets; 75¢ per 25 Hankes answer sheets for use with Engineers Northwest scoring service (see 466).

REFERENCES

1-71. See 40:1680.

72-175. See 3:647.

176. STRONG, EDWARD K. "Relation of Interest to Ability in Terms of Life Insurance Interest Scores and Sales Production." Abstract. *Psychol B* 31:594 O '34. * (*PA* 9:911, title only)

177. ABRAMOWITZ, ELIAS. *Correlation Analysis of the Differential Weighting Technique of the Strong Vocational Interest Blank.* Master's thesis, Columbia University (New York, N.Y.), 1935.

178. PARSONS, RICHARD TORRENCE. *The Home and School Backgrounds, Measured Vocational Interests, and Vocational Choices of 869 Students Who Entered the State Teachers Colleges of Pennsylvania in the Fall of 1940.* Doctor's thesis, Pennsylvania State College (State College, Pa.), 1942. (*Abstracts of Doctoral Dissertations....1942,* 1943, pp. 220-7.)

179. ROMERO, THOMAS DANIEL. *A Comparison of Students' Scholastic Ability With the Results Obtained by a Vocational Interest Test.* Master's thesis, University of Arizona (Tucson, Ariz.), 1942. Pp. 142. (*Abstracts of Theses....1942,* 1943, p. 62.)

180. CISNEY, HARLAND N. *The Stability of Vocational-Interest Scores During the High-School Period.* Doctor's thesis, University of Michigan (Ann Arbor, Mich.), 1944.

181. OLDER, HARRY J. "An Objective Test of Vocational Interests." *J Appl Psychol* 28:99-108 Ap '44. * (*PA* 18:2972)

182. UHRBROCK, RICHARD STEPHEN. "The Expressed Interests of Employed Men," pp. 330-1, 334-6, 340-3. *Am J Psychol* 57:317-70 Jl '44. * (*PA* 18:3602)

183. ACHARD, F. H., AND CLARKE, FLORENCE H. "You *Can* Measure the Probability of Success as a Supervisor." *Personnel* 21:353-73 My '45. *

184. CISNEY, HARLAND N. "The Stability of the Vocational-Interest Profiles of High-School Students Over a Two-Year Period." *Papers Mich Acad Sci Arts & Letters* 31:309-14 '45. *

185. JACOBSEN, CARLYLE F. "Interest and Attitude as Factors in Achievement in Medical School." *J Assn Am Med Col* 21:152-9 My '46. *

186. BEAMER, GEORGE CHARLES. *The Factors of Interest in the Counseling of Adults.* Doctor's thesis, University of Missouri (Columbia, Mo.), 1947. Abstract: *Microfilm Abstracts* 9:158-60 no 2 '49. * (*PA* 24:4152, title only)

187. BLUM, LAWRENCE PHILIP. "A Comparative Study of Students Preparing for Five Selected Professions Including Teaching." *J Exp Ed* 16:31-65 S '47. * (*PA* 22:1881)

188. BURKE, HENRY R. *Personality Traits of Successful Minor Seminarians.* Doctor's thesis. Washington, D.C.: Catholic University of America Press, 1947. Pp. viii, 65. Out of print. * (*PA* 22:848)

189. CERF, ARTHUR Z. "The Strong Vocational Interest Blank for Men, CE503A." pp. 608-11. In *Printed Classification Tests.* Edited by J. P. Guilford with the assistance of John I. Lacey. Army Air Forces Aviation Psychology Program Research Reports, Report No. 5. Washington, D.C.: U.S. Government Printing Office, 1947. Pp. xi, 919. * (*PA* 22:4145)

190. DOPPELT, JEROME E. "Scoring the Strong Vocational Interest Blank on IBM Machines," pp. 84-6. In *Educational Research Forum Proceedings, Endicott, New York, August 25-29, 1947.* New York: International Business Machines Corporation, 1948. Pp. 96. Paper. *

191. KENDALL, WILLIAM E., AND HAHN, MILTON E. "The Use of Tests in the Selection of Medical Students by the College of Medicine of Syracuse University." Abstract. *Am Psychol* 2:297 Ag '47. * (*PA* 21:4650, title only)

192. KLEIST, M. E. *A Vocational Interest Scale for Music Teachers.* Master's thesis, Stanford University (Stanford, Calif.), 1947.

193. KURTZ, ALBERT K. "Selection of Managers." [*Proc*] *Annual Mtg Assn Life Agency Officers & Life Ins Sales Res Bur,* 1946 1946:106-212 '47. *

194. KUTNER, MILDRED. *The Prognosis of the Freshmen Achievement of Chemistry and Physics Students on the Basis of Interest Test Items.* Master's thesis, Pennsylvania State College (State College, Pa.), 1947. Pp. iv, 113.

195. PHELPS, HAROLD ROBERT. *Permanence of Ratings on the Strong Vocational Interest Blank.* Master's thesis, University of Nebraska (Lincoln, Neb.), 1947.

196. STRONG, E. K., JR., AND HANKES, E. J. "A Note on the Hankes Test Scoring Machine." *J Appl Psychol* 31:212-4 Ap '47. * (*PA* 21:2537)

197. TRAXLER, ARTHUR E. "Project in the Selection of Personnel for Public Accounting," pp. 51-64. (*PA* 22:3235) In *National Projects in Educational Measurement: A Report of the 1946 Invitational Conference on Testing Problems. New York City, November 2, 1946, Herschel T. Manuel, Chairman.* Edited by K. W. Vaughn. Sponsored by the Committee on Measurement and Guidance. American Council on Education Studies, Vol. 11; Series 1, Reports of Committees and Conferences, No. 28. Washington, D.C.: the Council, August 1947. Pp. vii, 80. Paper. *

198. ALLEN, CHARLES L. *The Development of a Battery of Psychological Tests for Determining Journalistic Interests and Aptitudes.* Doctor's thesis, Northwestern University (Evanston, Ill.), 1948. (*Summaries of Doctoral Dissertations....June-September 1948,* 1949, pp. 204-9.)

199. BARNABAS, BENTLEY. "Validity of Personality and Interest Tests in Selection and Placement Situations." *Trans Kans Acad Sci* 51:335-9 S '48. * (*PA* 23:2432)

200. BENTON, A. L., AND KORNHAUSER, S. I. "A Study of 'Score Faking' on a Medical Interest Test." *J Assn Am Med Col* 23:57-60 Ja '48. * (*PA* 22:4116)

201. COTTLE, WILLIAM C. "A Factorial Study of Selected Instruments for Measuring Personality and Interest." Abstract. *Am Psychol* 3:300 Jl '48. * (*PA* 22:5353, title only)

202. DREFFIN, WILLIAM B., AND WRENN, C. GILBERT. "Spatial Relations Ability and Other Characteristics of Art Laboratory Students." *J Appl Psychol* 32:601-5 D '48. * (*PA* 23:3777)

203. FEHRER, ELIZABETH; COFER, C. N.; TUTHILL, C. E.; AND GRESHAM, MARTHA. "An Exploratory Study of Relationships Between Certain Written Language Measures and Vocational Interests." *J General Psychol* 39:49-72 Jl '48. * (*PA* 23:3253)

204. FISHER, EDWARD J. *A Scoring Scale for Optometrists on the Strong Vocational Interest Blank.* Master's thesis, University of Toronto (Toronto, Canada), 1948. Pp. 46.

205. HESTON, JOSEPH C. "A Comparison of Four Masculinity-Femininity Scales." *Ed & Psychol Meas* 8:375-87 au '48. * (*PA* 23:4256)

206. HOFFMAN, E. LEE, AND STEPHENS, DEAN H. "A Comparative Study of College Freshmen With Different Interest Areas." *Proc Okla Acad Sci* 28:114-8 '48. * (*PA* 23:2401)

207. JOHNSON, GERALD KENNETH. *Personality Patterns Peculiar to Theological Students.* Master's thesis, University of North Dakota (Grand Forks, N.D.), 1947. Review: *Sch Ed Rec Univ N Dak* 33:200-3 Ap '48. *

208. KELSO, DUANE FRANCIS. *A Study of Occupational Stereotypes Reflected in the Strong Vocational Interest Test.* Master's thesis, State College of Washington (Pullman, Wash.), 1948. (*PA* 23:375, title only)

209. KELSO, DUANE F., AND BORDIN, EDWARD S. "The Ability to Manipulate Occupational Stereotypes Inherent in the Strong Vocational Interest Test." Abstract. *Am Psychol* 3:352-3 Ag '48. * (*PA* 23:816, title only)

210. KELSO, NORMA ELAINE. *The Relative Correspondence of Professed Interest to the Kuder and Strong Interest Test Scores.* Master's thesis, State College of Washington (Pullman, Wash.), 1948. (*PA* 23:376, title only)

211. KOHN, NATHAN, JR. *An Investigation and Evaluation of the Kuder Preference, Especially in Comparison to the Strong Vocational Interest Blank.* Doctor's thesis, Washington University (St. Louis, Mo.), 1948.

212. LHOTA, BRIAN. *Vocational Interests of Catholic Priests.* Catholic University of America, Studies in Psychology and Psychiatry, Vol. 7, No. 1. Washington, D.C.: Catholic University of America Press, 1948. Pp. vii, 40. Paper. * (*PA* 22:2800)

213. LONGSTAFF, HOWARD P. "Fakability of the Strong Interest Blank and the Kuder Preference Record." *J Appl Psychol* 32:360-9 Ag '48. * (*PA* 23:1332)

214. MALCOLM, DAVID D. *The Relative Usefulness of Several Extensively Used Vocational Interest Inventories in Counseling at Various Academic Levels.* Doctor's thesis, Northwestern University (Evanston, Ill.), 1948. (*Summaries of Doctoral Dissertations....June-September 1948,* 1949, pp. 245-50.)

215. OSTROM, STANLEY R. *The Relationship Between "O.L." Key of Strong Vocational Interest Blank for Men and Scholarship at Three Levels of School.* Doctor's thesis, Syracuse University (Syracuse, N.Y.), 1948.

216. ROEBER, EDWARD C. "A Comparison of Seven Interest Inventories with Respect to Word Usage." *J Ed Res* 42:8-17 S '48. * (*PA* 23:2915)

217. SHOEMAKER, H. A., AND ROHRER, J. H. "Relationship Between Success in the Study of Medicine and Certain Psychological and Personal Data." *J Assn Am Med Col* 23:190-201 My '48. * (*PA* 23:951)

218. CHAPLIN, CARYL L. "Social Class Stereotypes in Strong Vocational Interest Profiles." Abstract. *Am Psychol* 4:394 S '49. * (*PA* 24:11768, title only)

219. COTTLE, WILLIAM C. *A Factorial Study of the Multiphasic, Strong, Kuder and Bell Inventories Using a Population of Adult Males.* Doctor's thesis, Syracuse University (Syracuse, N.Y.), 1949.

220. COTTLE, WILLIAM C. "Relationships Among Selected Personality and Interest Inventories." Abstract. *Am Psychol* 4:292-3 Jl '49. * (*PA* 23:6206, title only)

221. COTTLE, WM. C., AND POWELL, JACKSON O. "Relationship of Mean Scores on the Strong, Kuder and Bell Inventories With the MMPI M-F Scale as the Criterion." *Trans Kans Acad Sci* 52:396-8 '49. * (*PA* 24:2599)

222. EICHSTEADT, ARDEN CARL. *Factors Associated With the Development and Nondevelopment of Primary Patterns on the Strong Vocational Interest Blank for Men.* Doctor's thesis, University of Wisconsin (Madison, Wis.), 1949. (*Summaries of Doctoral Dissertations....July 1949 to June 1950,* 1951, pp. 328-9.)

223. FEIL, MADELEINE HOFFMAN. *A Study of Leadership and Scholastic Achievement in Their Relation to Prediction Factors.* Doctor's thesis, Ohio State University (Columbus, Ohio), 1949. (*Abstracts of Dissertations....Summer Quarter 1948-49,* 1950, pp. 151-5.) (*PA* 24:6522, title only)

Vocational Interest Blank for Men

224. Greene, J. E.; Osborne, R. T.; and Sanders, Wilma B. "A Window-Stencil Method for Scoring the Strong Vocational Interest Blank (Men)." *J Appl Psychol* 33:141–5 Ap '49. * (*PA* 24:224)

225. Hannum, Thomas Edward. *Differential Responses of Veterinarians to the Strong Vocational Interest Blank for Men.* Master's thesis, Iowa State College (Ames, Iowa), 1949.

226. Hartshorn, Herbert Hadley. *Vocational Interest Patterns of Negro Professional Men.* Doctor's thesis, University of Minnesota (Minneapolis, Minn.), 1949.

227. Kleist, M.; Rittenhouse, C. H.; and Farnsworth, P. R. "Strong Vocational Interest Scales for Music Teachers." *Occupations* 28:100–1 N '49. * (*PA* 24:2218)

228. Kriedt, Philip H. *Differential Interest Patterns of Psychologists.* Doctor's thesis, University of Minnesota (Minneapolis, Minn.), 1949.

229. Kriedt, Philip H. "Vocational Interests of Psychologists." *J Appl Psychol* 33:482–8 O '49. * (*PA* 24:2965)

230. Marsh, James S. *Selection of Civil Engineer Corps of Officers of United States Navy.* Master's thesis, Stanford University (Stanford, Calif.), 1949.

231. Nance, R. D. "Masculinity-Femininity in Prospective Teachers." *J Ed Res* 42:658–66 My '49. * (*PA* 24:320)

232. Ostrom, Stanley R. "The OL Key of the Strong Test and Drive at the Twelfth Grade Level." *J Appl Psychol* 33:240–8 Je '49. * (*PA* 24:2094)

233. Ostrom, Stanley R. "The OL Key of the Strong Vocational Interest Blank for Men and Scholastic Success at College Freshmen Level." *J Appl Psychol* 33:51–4 F '49. * (*PA* 23:3908)

234. Rosenzweig, Saul; with the collaboration of Kate Levine Kogan. *Psychodiagnosis: An Introduction to Tests in the Clinical Practice of Psychodynamics,* pp. 87–91. New York: Grune & Stratton, Inc., 1949. Pp. xii, 380. * (*PA* 23:3761)

235. Saddler, Laurence E. *A Comparison of Students Remaining in an Engineering Curriculum and Students Transferring From Engineering to Other Curricula.* Doctor's thesis, University of Missouri (Columbia, Mo.), 1949. Abstract: *Microfilm Abstracts* 9:89–91 no 3 '50. (*PA* 24:4851, title only)

236. Strong, Edward K., Jr. "The Role of Interests in Guidance." *Occupations* 27:517–22 My '49. * (*PA* 24:671)

237. Strong, Edward K., Jr. "Vocational Interests of Accountants." *J Appl Psychol* 33:474–81 O '49. * (*PA* 24:3432)

238. Super, Donald E. *Appraising Vocational Fitness by Means of Psychological Tests,* pp. 408–44. New York: Harper & Brothers, 1949. Pp. xxiii, 727. * (*PA* 24:2130)

239. Wallace, Wimburn Leroy. *The Relationship of Certain Variables to Discrepancy Between Expressed and Inventoried Vocational Interest.* Doctor's thesis, University of Michigan (Ann Arbor, Mich.), 1949. Abstract: *Microfilm Abstracts* 9:173–4 no 2 '49. * (*PA* 24:4157, title only)

240. Barnett, Gordon James. *A Study of Satisfied and Dissatisfied Chronically Unemployed Men.* Doctor's thesis, Columbia University (New York, N.Y.), 1950. Abstract: *Microfilm Abstracts* 10:214–6 no 3 '50. *

241. Berdie, Ralph F. "Scores on the Strong Vocational Interest Blank and the Kuder Preference Record in Relation to Self-Ratings." *J Appl Psychol* 34:42–9 F '50. * (*PA* 24:5915)

242. Borg, Walter R. "Some Factors Relating to Art School Success." *J Ed Res* 43:376–84 Ja '50. * (*PA* 24:4811)

243. Bradfield, James Anne Frederiksen. *Predicting the Success in Training of Graduate Students in School Administration.* Doctor's thesis, Stanford University (Stanford, Calif.), 1950. (*Abstracts of Dissertations....1949–50,* 1950, pp. 294–7.)

244. Cottle, William C. "Relationships Among Selected Personality and Interest Inventories." *Occupations* 28:306–10 F '50. * (*PA* 24:4113)

245. Dubois, Philip H., and Watson, Robert I. "The Selection of Patrolmen." *J Appl Psychol* 34:90–5 Ap '50. * (*PA* 25:2076)

246. Fagin, William Barry. *Constitutional Factors in Vocational Interests.* Doctor's thesis, Columbia University (New York, N.Y.), 1950. Abstract: *Microfilm Abstracts* 10:218–9 no 3 '50. *

247. Fassett, Katherine K. "Interest and Personality Measures of Veteran and Non-Veteran University Freshman Men." *Ed & Psychol Meas* 10:338–41 su '50. * (*PA* 25:6212)

248. Irwin, Irl A. *Occupational Interest and the Prediction of Scholastic Success.* Master's thesis, State University of Iowa (Iowa City, Iowa), 1950.

249. Irwin, Irl A. "Occupational Interest and the Prediction of Scholastic Success." *Psychol Service Center J* 2:34–45 Mr '50. * (*PA* 25:6469)

250. Kates, Solis L. "Rorschach Responses, Strong Blank Scales, and Job Satisfaction Among Policemen." *J Appl Psychol* 34:249–54 Ag '50. * (*PA* 25:6495)

251. Kelly, E. Lowell, and Fiske, Donald W. "The Prediction of Success in the VA Training Program in Clinical Psychology." *Am Psychol* 5:395–406 Ag '50. * (*PA* 25:2183)

252. Layton, Wilbur L. "An IBM Card Profile for the Strong Vocational Interest Blank." *J Appl Psychol* 34:415–6 D '50. * (*PA* 25:4646)

253. Malcolm, David Donald. "Which Interest Inventory Should I Use?" *J Ed Res* 44:91–8 O '50. * (*PA* 25:5675)

254. Merritt, Curtis B. *The Relationship Between Interest Level and the Discrepancy Between Scholastic Aptitude and Academic Achievement.* Doctor's thesis, University of Michigan (Ann Arbor, Mich.), 1950. Pp. 129. Abstract: *Microfilm Abstracts* 10:63 no 1 '50. * (*PA* 24:6042, title only)

255. Mortensen, Donald Grant. *An Analysis of Some of the Prerequisites Essential for a Successful Career as a Life Insurance Agent.* Doctor's thesis, University of Southern California (Los Angeles, Calif.), 1950. (*Abstracts of Dissertations....1950,* 1951, pp. 306–7.)

256. Super, Donald E., and Dunlap, Jack W. Sect. 16, "Interest in Work and Play," pp. 100–8. In *Handbook of Applied Psychology, Vol. I.* Edited by Douglas H. Fryer and Edwin R. Henry. New York: Rinehart & Co., Inc., 1950. Pp. xxi, 380, ix. * (*PA* 25:8309)

257. Gustad, John W. "Vocational Interests and Q-L Scores on the A.C.E." *J Appl Psychol* 35:164–8 Je '51. * (*PA* 26:983)

258. Kelly, E. Lowell, and Fiske, Donald W. *The Prediction of Performance in Clinical Psychology.* Ann Arbor, Mich.: University of Michigan, 1951. Pp. xv, 311. Lithotyped.

259. Knauft, E. B. "Vocational Interests and Managerial Success." *J Appl Psychol* 35:160–3 Je '51. * (*PA* 26:1127)

260. Melville, S. D., and Frederiksen, Norman. "Overachievement of Freshman Engineering Students and the Strong Vocational Interest Blank." Abstract. *Am Psychol* 6:377–8 Jl '51. *

261. Murray, Stewart. *A Study of the Distortion of Responses on the Strong Interest Blank by Insurance Salesmen.* Columbia University (New York, N.Y.), 1951.

262. Rosen, Ephraim. "Differences Between Volunteers and Non-Volunteers for Psychological Studies." *J Appl Psychol* 35:185–93 Je '51. * (*PA* 26:625)

263. Ryan, Francis Joseph. *Personality Differences Between Under- and Over-Achievers in College.* Doctor's thesis, Columbia University (New York, N.Y.), 1951. Abstract: *Microfilm Abstracts* 11:967–8 no 4 '51.

264. Schweble, Milton. *The Interests of Pharmacists.* Foreword by Donald E. Super. New York: King's Crown Press, 1951. Pp. xii, 84. Paper, lithotyped. * (London: Oxford University Press.) (*PA* 26:1161)

265. Shepler, Bernard F. "A Comparison of Masculinity-Femininity Measures." *J Consult Psychol* 15:484–6 D '51. *

266. Stewart, Lawrence H. *The Relationship of Certain Social Factors to Occupational Level as Measured by Strong's Vocational Interest Blank.* Doctor's thesis, Columbia University (New York, N.Y.), 1951.

267. Stone, C. Harold, and Kriedt, Philip H. "Modified Directions for Strong Vocational Interest Blank When Used With the Hankes Answer Sheet." *J Appl Psychol* 35:169–71 Je '51. * (*PA* 26:986)

268. Strong, Edward K., Jr. "Interest Scores While in College of Occupations Engaged in 20 Years Later." *Ed & Psychol Meas* 11:335–48 au '51. *

269. Strong, Edward K., Jr. "Norms for Strong's Vocational Interest Tests." *J Appl Psychol* 35:50–6 F '51. * (*PA* 26:6922)

270. Strong, Edward K., Jr. "Permanence of Interest Scores Over 22 Years." *J Appl Psychol* 35:89–91 Ap '51. * (*PA* 25:7896)

271. Traxler, Arthur E. "Objective Testing in the Field of Accounting." *Ed & Psychol Meas* 11:427–39 au '51. *

272. Verburg, Wallace A. *A Study of the Effects of Retirement on the Interests of YMCA Secretaries as Indicated by the Vocational Interest Blank.* Doctor's thesis, Columbia University (New York, N.Y.), 1951.

273. Webster, Edward C.; Winn, Alexander; and Oliver, John A. "Selection Tests for Engineers: Some Preliminary Findings." *Personnel Psychol* 4:339–62 w '51. * (*PA* 26:6572)

Edward S. Bordin, *Associate Professor of Psychology, University of Michigan, Ann Arbor, Michigan.*

A reviewer of this interest inventory suffers from conflicting feelings. On the one hand, he feels that this test stands out among instruments of its type in terms of the thoroughness with which it was developed. From this point of view, criticism seems like perfectionism or unrealistic impractical application of standards. On the other hand, the reviewer feels that its very eminence in the field makes it more imperative that its defects be pinpointed as a vehicle for the general raising of standards in test development.

The latest edition of the test manual (1951) continues to present the basic information necessary for use of the test. In place of the results of factor studies of the occupational scales, the present edition substitutes a table of normative data showing the means and sigmas for the criterion groups and for men in general. Data on the standard score equivalent to a zero raw score and the means and sigmas obtained by dice throwing are also presented in this table. It would seem that this new table will be more useful to the average test user than the previous one. However, this reviewer feels it would have been best to include both tables, since the factor patterns involved are a very important basis for test interpretation. One obscurity in the present table arises from the fact that the standard score equivalent to a raw score of zero is presented in a column ambiguously headed "zero score." It took considerable cross checking to decipher its meaning. Other readers might not be so persistent.

As in the past, the manual fulfills all of the important functions of such a publication, summarizing information on the instrument's validity, reliability, stability of its scores, norms, directions for administration, and aid in interpreting scores. Considering the ease with which test users fall into the error of interpreting interest measures as predictions of probable success in training or in an occupation, this reviewer finds the manual quite lacking in safeguards against such interpretations.

Throughout the manual there are loopholes left for interpreting interest scores as predictors of level of achievement in training or on the job. Examples are as follows: (a) The last sentence on the title page reads, "Seemingly, also, he should be more effective there [in an occupation in which he has a high interest score] than somewhere else because he would be engaged, in the main, in work he liked"; and (b) The results of a study demonstrating a relationship between productivity and interest ratings for life insurance agents is presented as though this were a finding typical for other occupations, despite the fact that the results have been almost uniformly negative for other occupations and for prediction of achievement in training.

The VIB, despite the fact that it is one of the most time consuming and costly inventories to score and despite the shortcomings just described, remains as the interest test whose usefulness has been most carefully and thoroughly demonstrated.

ELMER D. HINCKLEY, *Professor of Psychology and Head of the Department, University of Florida, Gainesville, Florida.*

The Strong blank was the forerunner of the present-day crop of interest tests and inventories. While it has lost some of its pre-eminence to some of the newcomers, none has a more secure foundation or offers more possibilities than does the Strong. The practice of supplying new scales and revising old ones keeps the Strong up with the times.

The impressive array of statistical evidence and the methods used in constructing the various scales are too well known to need elaboration here. It is sufficient to note that the test has stood the test of time and the competition of new tests.

The major drawback of the Strong is the effort involved in a complete scoring. There are 41 vocational scales available, plus the interest maturity, MF, occupational level, and studiousness scales. The convenience of the Kuder and the thoroughness of the Strong would be a most desirable combination.

Another weakness is the ability of the testee to fake an interest score if he thinks it is desirable to do so. This is unimportant if the person is earnestly in search of vocational counseling, but where the Strong may be used as a screening device, this factor may be important. A "lie" scale would be a useful addition if such a thing were possible. This shortcoming of fakeability is shared by tests other than the Strong.

Interests should not be looked upon as a separate thing from the personality, but should be considered as a part of the total personality and judged accordingly. The Strong offers some exciting possibilities of research in the study of personality; more should be done in this line.

The Strong is a valuable instrument in the vocational counseling situation as an adjunct to other sources of information about the individual. The tedious scoring is not always a serious problem, for much valuable information can be gained from incomplete scoring.

Of all the inventories, this has been the most demanding in terms of empirical foundation and background. It is a real job to use it as it should be used, but the returns for the effort involved are good and make the use of this test well worth the while.

For excerpts from related reviews see 748, 3:648, 3:650, and 3:652; for reviews by Harold D. Carter, John G. Darley, and N. W. Morton, see 40:1680; for a review by John G. Darley of an earlier edition, see 38:1178.

Vocational Interest Blank for Men

[748]

★[*Re* Vocational Interest Blank for Men, Revised.] SCHWEBEL, MILTON. **The Interests of Pharmacists.** Foreword by Donald E. Super. New York: King's Crown Press, 1951. Pp. xii, 84. Paper, Lithotyped. $1.75. * (London: Oxford University Press. 11s. 6d.) (*PA* 26:1161)

J Consult Psychol 15:515 D '51. Laurance F. *Shaffer.* In addition to developing a pharmacist scale for the Strong Vocational Interest Blank, this study explored the relationship of job satisfaction to interest measurement. Its techniques and findings are applicable to the measurement of interest and satisfaction in other occupations.

Occupations 30:78 O '51. H. Alan Robinson. * Although much of the book may have its greatest appeal to persons who are interested in test construction and evaluation, an host of practical research and counseling procedures may be gleaned from the information presented. Dr. Schwebel is especially sensitive to the *human factor* and carries this sensitivity into his construction and evaluation of interest scales. He follows the Strong procedure but excludes all the dissatisfied from the weight and norm groups. He constructed three scales so he could isolate a number of pertinent factors and weight them against one another. In this manner he was able to add an important scale to the Strong inventories and also obtain some surprising information which should be of special concern to counselors. He found that the interests of pharmacists resemble those of office and sales workers more than they resemble the interests of physicians and dentists. Dr. Schwebel was able to make a definite distinction between apothecary pharmacists (those devoting 26 per cent or more of their time to prescription work) and business pharmacists (those devoting less than 26 per cent of their time to prescription work). When the interests of the two groups are contrasted, there is a sharp enough difference in scientific interest to select medical students successfully. Therefore, although he has shown that an occupational group has a recognizable pattern of likes and dislikes, he has also differentiated between the likes and dislikes within the specialties of the occupation. Information of this kind is important to the counselor who must often counsel on the basis of an average interest pattern when he knows the individual may not always fit that pattern. The author has gone a step ahead of usual statistical measurements; he has refined the possibilities. The same type of refinement

Vocational Interest Blank for Men

and emphasis on individual factors could be applied profitably to other fields with many specialties, such as education, farming, journalism, law, and even personnel work. * If the book has a weakness it can be likened to the new college student who complains about all his questions not being answered. He, as the reader of the book, is presented with information to stimulate thought. Practical applications of the material presented can certainly be made in the areas of test construction and evaluation, counseling and occupational advisement. Much of what is done with pharmacists, as described in this volume, can be applied to other occupations by the thoughtful practitioner. As Donald E. Super states in the foreword of the book, "Dr. Schwebel has added significantly to our knowledge of.... the relationship between inventoried interest and work satisfaction....and....the differentiations of specialties within an occupation."

MANUAL DEXTERITY

[749]

★**Martin Peg Board (Finger Dexterity Test).** High school and adults; 1947–51; 3 scores: right hand, left hand, both hands; mimeographed manual ['51]; no data on validity; $18 per testing outfit, postage extra; worklimit (5–10) minutes; Howard G. Martin; Martin Publishing Co. *

[750]

★**Moore Eye-Hand Coordination and Color-Matching Test.** Ages 2 and over; 1949; 2 scores: speed of eye-hand coordination, color-matching; individual; *discontinued;* no norms for color-matching scores of pre-school children; (10–15) minutes; Joseph E. Moore; Joseph E. Moore & Associates. * (Formerly published by California Test Bureau.)

REFERENCES

1. MOORE, JOSEPH E. "A Test of Eye-Hand Coordination." *J Appl Psychol* 21:668–72 D '37. * (*PA* 12:2919)
2. MOORE, JOSEPH E. "A Comparison of White and Negro Children on a Simple Eye-Hand Coordination Test." Abstract. *Psychol B* 37:555 O '40. * (*PA* 15:397, title only)
3. MOORE, JOSEPH E. "A Comparison of Negro and White Children in Speed of Reaction on an Eye-Hand Coordination Test." *J Genetic Psychol* 59:225–8 S '41. * (*PA* 16:1089)
4. MOORE, JOSEPH E. "A Comparison of Negro and White Preschool Children on a Vocabulary Test and Eye-Hand Coordination Test." *Child Develop* 13:247–52 D '42. * (*PA* 17:2079)
5. MOORE, JOSEPH E. "A Comparison of the Moore Eye-Hand Coordination and Color Matching Test With Other Dexterity Tests." Abstract. *Am Psychol* 2:297–8 Ag '47. * (*PA* 21:4611, title only)
6. MOORE, JOSEPH E. "The Standardization of the Moore Eye-Hand Coordination and Color Matching Test." *Ed & Psychol Meas* 10:119–27 sp '50. * (*PA* 25:669)

NORMAN FREDERIKSEN, *Associate Professor of Psychology, Princeton University; and Head, Research Department, Educational Testing Service; Princeton, New Jersey.*

The apparatus consists of a flat rectangular box; at the left end are four receptacles containing colored marbles, and extending to the right from each receptacle is a row of eight holes each of which will hold one marble. For the Eye-Hand Coordination Test, the task is to pick up marbles one at a time and place them in the holes. The test is repeated three times, and the score is the time required to place the 96 marbles. In the Color-Matching Test, a similar procedure is used with the same equipment, but each marble must be placed in a hole of similar color. The score is the time required for placing the 96 marbles plus one second for each error in matching colors. The preschool form of the test makes use of the same equipment but is half as long and does not include the color-matching portion.

The only specific purpose of the test mentioned in the manual is selection and placement of employees, although mention is made of use of the test in clinics and guidance centers. What value the preschool form might have is not specified; the supplementary manual for the preschool form merely quotes from the regular manual that "one of its major purposes is to save valuable time as well as expense in the selection and placement of employees."

With regard to reliability, the publisher's announcement states that "The test-retest method based on 187 subjects (elementary, high school, and college students, and adults) after an interval of one week, gave a coefficient of .95." Essentially the same statement is made in the manual where the coefficient is attributed to the Eye-Hand Coordination Test only, rather than to the test as a whole. High reliability certainly should be expected from a group with such an extreme range of ability. It is much more to the point to report reliabilities for groups of greater homogeneity, which is done for the Color-Matching Test in the regular manual (where a retest reliability of .82 is reported for 83 men in a college psychology class) and in the preschool manual (where a retest reliability of .95 is reported for 81 preschool children). In a later article the author again refers to the reliability of .82 and says that when corrected for restriction of range it becomes .955. The application of a formula for correction for restriction of range seems questionable in this situation, especially in view of the failure to state what amount of variability is assumed in the correction formula.

One line of evidence as to the validity of the Eye-Hand Coordination Test is that it differen-

tiates between various age groups from 2 to 16 years. A limited amount of evidence, based on very small numbers of cases, suggests that the test is predictive of success in industrial jobs; studies are reported for ice cream sandwich maker (N = 10) and loom operator (N = 23). For 62 typing students, a correlation of .81 was found between the test and speed and accuracy scores. As is true for most industrial selection tests, the validity of this test should be established for any new situation in which it is to be employed before using the scores in selection.

According to the publisher's announcement, norms are based on over 5,000 cases. This is a true statement, but it is somewhat misleading. For the preschool form, for example, percentile norms for children from 24 to 77 months of age are presented by six-month age ranges; the norms for the 24–29 month group are based on only 11 cases, while for the other eight groups the N's range from 27 to 119. Girls are said to be faster than boys in speed of eye-hand coordination, but no sex-differentiated norms are given. For adults the N's are in general much more adequate; norms for adult white men (unclassified) are based on 2,707 cases. Separate percentile norms based on white males are given for clerical and sales jobs, textile jobs, skilled mechanics, truck drivers, adult men (unclassified), and college men. Similarly, norms are presented for various groups of white women and negro men and women.

Of even more importance than the number of cases is the adequacy with which the norms group represents the population for which the norms are presented. This is of course a major problem for test publishers and is very difficult to solve adequately. However, it seems particularly dangerous to assume that men who came to the Guidance Center of the Georgia Institute of Technology "probably represent a good cross section of the general population between the ages of sixteen and sixty," as is stated in the manual.

The *Moore Eye-Hand Coordination and Color-Matching Test* is better than its manual. The test can be administered in 10 or 15 minutes, the instructions seem to be adequate, the equipment is reasonably well constructed, and provision is made for easy return of the marbles to their starting position. If one takes the precaution of performing a validity study to determine the predictive value of the test and how best to employ the scores in a selection problem, the test would seem to be well worth trying out in a situation which seems to require speed of eye-hand coordination.

JAY L. OTIS, *Professor of Psychology, and Director, Research and Service Center for Business and Industry, Western Reserve University, Cleveland, Ohio.*

This test was designed to measure the speed and accuracy with which an individual can coordinate small muscle movements involving eye-hand activity and the speed with which he can select and match four colors. The test requires the coordination of the thumb, index finger, and the eyes in a constantly changing spatial pattern. It is suggested that the test would be useful in selecting employees for work requiring speed of eye-hand coordination.

Directions for administration are clear and complete. The only criticism is that the examiner is not told how he should score the eye-hand portion of the test if the subject drops a marble on the floor and looks for it before completing the test.

Normative data are available for several groups including preschool children, college students, and occupational groups. Several thousand subjects are included and most of the groups are represented by an adequate number of cases. Most of the subjects used are from southern states. Measures of central tendency and variability from two northern colleges are similar to those from southern colleges. However, checks were not made for other groups. Nevertheless, this test should rate excellent from the standpoint of normative material.

Validity studies discussed in the manual show that the eye-hand coordination part yielded a correlation of .86 (tetrachoric) with hourly earnings of 23 textile workers, .81 with speed and accuracy of 62 typing students, and .52 with production of 10 ice cream sandwich makers. No evidence of the validity of the Color-Matching Test is given. Correlations with other dexterity tests range from .29 to .67 for the Eye-Hand Coordination Test and from .35 to .54 for Color-Matching. The validity data are encouraging. However, to one who has used dexterity tests in industry, it is surprising that all reported validity coefficients are so high. It would be useful to the industrial psychologist to know those situations, if any, in which the test has been unsuccessful, as well as those in which it has succeeded.

The *Moore Eye-Hand Coordination and Color-Matching Test* is a new test, and final judgment will be made only after more users have had an opportunity to report on its usefulness. The amount of work done on the standardization of this test is impressive. It is to be hoped that similar efforts will be made by the author and others to determine the applications in which it will have greatest validity and the possibilities for its use in individual prediction in vocational guidance work. This test merits consideration on the part of examiners who need a measure of speed of eye-hand coordination.

[751]

*Purdue Pegboard. Grades 9–16 and adults; 1941–48; 5 scores: right hand, left hand, both hands, right plus left plus both hands, assembly; 1 form, '41; manual ('48); $16.95 per testing apparatus; $1.30 per 25 profile sheets; cash orders postpaid; 2½(10) minutes; prepared by Purdue Research Foundation; Science Research Associates, Inc. *

REFERENCES

1–3. See 3:666.
4. BLUETT, C. G. "Pictures of the Mind." *J Rehabil* 13:4–10 Je '47. * (*PA* 21:3630)
5. STRANGE, J. R., AND SARTAIN, A. Q. "Veterans' Scores on the Purdue Pegboard Test." *J Appl Psychol* 32:35–40 F '48. * (*PA* 23:771)
6. TIFFIN, JOSEPH, AND ASHER, E. J. "The Purdue Pegboard: Norms and Studies of Reliability and Validity." *J Appl Psychol* 32:234–47 Je '48. * (*PA* 23:1049)
7. ALDERMAN, EVERETT. "Comparison of One-Trial and Three-Trial Purdue Pegboard Norms." *Occupations* 27:251–2 Ja '49. * (*PA* 23:3213)
8. BARNETTE, W. LESLIE, JR. *Occupational Aptitude Patterns of Counseled Veterans.* Doctor's thesis, New York University (New York, N.Y.), 1949. Pp. viii, 385. * (*PA* 24:362, title only)
9. GEIST, HAROLD. "The Performance of Amputees on Motor Dexterity Tests." *Ed & Psychol Meas* 9:765–72 w '49. * (*PA* 26:2950)
10. RINSLAND, HENRY D. "The Prediction of Veterans' Success From Test Scores at the University of Oklahoma," Part 1, pp. 59–72. In *The Sixth Yearbook of the National Council on Measurements Used in Education, 1948–1949.* Fairmont, W.Va.: the Council, Fairmont State College, 1949. Pp. v, 140 (variously numbered). Paper, mimeographed. *
11. SUPER, DONALD E. *Appraising Vocational Fitness by Means of Psychological Tests,* pp. 217–20. New York: Harper & Brothers, 1949. Pp. xxiii, 727. * (*PA* 24:2130)
12. CURTIS, JAMES W. "Administration of the Purdue Pegboard Test to Blind Individuals." *Ed & Psychol Meas* 10:329–31 su '50. * (*PA* 25:6394, 7052)
13. BARNETTE, W. LESLIE, JR. *Occupational Aptitude Patterns of Selected Groups of Counseled Veterans.* American Psychological Association, Psychological Monographs: General and Applied, Vol. 65, No. 5, Whole No. 322. Washington, D.C.: the Association, Inc., 1951. Pp. v, 49, Paper. * (*PA* 26:2794)
14. BASS, BERNARD M., AND STUCKI, RALPH E. "A Note on a Modified Purdue Pegboard." *J Appl Psychol* 35:312–3 O '51. * (*PA* 26:4003)
15. CANTOR, GORDON N., AND STACEY, CHALMERS L. "Manipulative Dexterity in Mental Defectives." *Am J Mental Def* 56:401–10 O '51. * (*PA* 26:2252)

For reviews by Edwin E. Ghiselli, Thomas W. Harrell, and Albert Gibson Packard, see 3:666.

[752]

*Small Parts Dexterity Test. High school and adults; 1946–49; individual; 2 scores: pins and collars, screws; 1 form, '46; [revised] manual ['49]; $27.50 per set of testing materials, postpaid; work-limit (10–25) minutes; John E. Crawford and Dorothea M. Crawford; Psychological Corporation. *

RAYMOND A. KATZELL, *Director and Staff Consultant, Richardson, Bellows, Henry and Company, New York, New York.*

The test consists of a metal plate in which two sets of 36 holes (6 rows and 6 columns) each are drilled. There is an additional practice row of 6 holes in each set. The holes of one set are threaded, while the holes of the other are smooth. The latter set is used for Part I of the test, which consists of placing, with the use of forceps, a pin in each hole and then a collar over the pin. Part II involves manually starting a small screw in each of the threaded holes and then screwing it down with a small screwdriver.

The score on each part is the time required to complete all 36 holes. The time required for Part I seems to range from about 3 to about 9 minutes, while that for Part II ranges from about 4 to about 16 minutes.

The test is designed as a measure of a complex of perception-dexterity coordinations such as may be involved in tasks like the assembly and adjustment of small machinery (e.g., sewing machines), or the wiring of intricate electrical apparatus.

The authors hypothesize that a composite measure, such as this test seems to furnish, is a more valid measure of the aptitudes required for jobs of the sort mentioned than tests which use the fingers or a single tool only. This conjecture gains credibility in the light of the evidence that a complex motor pattern is not closely related to the simpler movements into which it may be logically segmented. Yet this specific hypothesis remains to be empirically verified.

Thus far, evidence regarding the validity of the test is scanty. The manual cites two studies of the test's usefulness, one performed on hand engravers and etchers and the other on burlers and menders in a textile mill. But, as the authors recognize, more evidence will be required in a wider variety of situations before we can begin to generalize about the test's validity.

The reliability of the test promises to be adequate for most purposes. On four samples ranging in size from 56 to 118, the split half reliability coefficients (corrected by the Spearman-Brown formula) ranged from .80 to .94 for Part I and from .90 to .98 for Part II.

The two parts measure somewhat different functions, correlations between the two ranging from .35 to .50 in seven samples. Part I correlates about .38 with the several parts of the *Minnesota Rate of Manipulation Test,* whereas Part II correlates about .27. One wonders what the correlations would be with tests measuring finer coordinations, such as O'Connor's *Tweezer Dexterity Test* or the *Purdue Pegboard.* These tests are likely to function more nearly in the same areas as the test under review.

The manual is well written. It covers adequately the administration and scoring of the test, describes the norm groups in some detail, and pertinently discusses the available validity and reliability data. It also quite correctly emphasizes the desirability of local validation and norms. Percentile norms are furnished for four groups of adult males, three groups of high school boys, and two groups of women.

The physical construction of the test is excellent. It is convenient to carry and use, operates smoothly, and seems durable. In the latter respects, it rates somewhat higher than what is probably one of its major competitors, the *Purdue Pegboard,* but the latter is considerably less expensive and has the benefit of having seen more varied trial. The fact that the *Purdue Pegboard* is a time limit test and is somewhat shorter, is also to its advantage.

The *Small Parts Dexterity Test* has the earmarks of a promising instrument in its field, but little more can be said about it until additional evaluative data are available. Those who are in a position to experiment might do well to look into it further.

For a review by Joseph E. Moore, see 3:667.

[753]
★Spatial Test I. Ages 11–13; 1950; 1 form; 115s. per 100; 15s. per 12; 1s. 4d. per single copy; 3s. 6d. per manual; postage extra; 41 (60) minutes; I. Macfarlane Smith; National Foundation for Educational Research in England and Wales. *

REFERENCES
1. SMITH, I. MACFARLANE. "Measuring Spatial Ability in School Pupils." *Occupational Psychol* 22:150–9 Jl '48. * (PA 23:1181)

E. A. PEEL, *Professor of Education and Head of the Department, University of Birmingham, Birmingham, England.*

This test has been designed for use in conjunction with other tests to discover those children who show potential ability for such subjects as practical mathematics, technical drawing, engineering, and building. It is made up of six timed subtests: Test 1, fitting shapes; Test 2, form recognition; Test 3, pattern recognition; Test 4, shape recognition; Test 5, comparison; and Test 6, form reflection.

The items of all tests are nonverbal space

problems in two dimensions. Test 5 is composed of the familiar analogy item in space material. Presumably the object of the designer of this test was to abstract six recognisable aspects of tasks requiring spatial ability. If so, it is curious that no three-dimensional material, represented by perspective drawings or other conventions, is included. This omission may have to be remedied by applying the test with other material providing "solid" problems, particularly where interest is in the prediction of practical subjects. Albeit, the test provides suitable problems involving analytical and synthetic processes in space relations. Answers to Tests 1, 3, and 6 require very simple drawing of lines by the testee. This makes for alternative responses and requires a decision on acceptable and unacceptable answers. Provision in the key for alternative answers appears to be adequate, but their existence slows up marking to some extent.

Adequate practice items are provided, the only criticism of them being concerned with their thoroughness. Since some discussion of the items is still necessary in administering the test, this may limit the number of children who may be tested simultaneously. The manual of instructions is competent.

Norms are provided on the basis of scores standardised to a mean of 100 and standard deviation of 15 and so are roughly equivalent to IQ scores. The test is very discriminative with respect to age, as inspection of the table of norms will show. At the mean, for example, there is a rise of some 20 points of raw score between the ages of 11 and 13.9. Although the test shows significant sex differences in favour of boys, some five to six points of raw score on mean scores of about 50 points, the author has based his norms on a mixed population. This inconsistency is perhaps to be regretted, whether the test is intended for testing boys or a mixed population.

A serious criticism of the present edition of this test is that no figures for the validity of the test are provided. Possible users of the test may rightly want to know what is meant by "high correlation with assessments in technical drawing" before they commit themselves to purchase of this material. Similarly, no figures are given with regard to the correlations of the test with other tests of spatial ability and "practical" aptitude, and the reader of the test booklet must be satisfied with a brief reference to the original source of inspiration for the material in the work

of Koussy and Stephenson. Some results of factor analysis should be available to those interested, particularly as the author of the test now has available promising factorial data which show that the test compares favourably with other tests, group and individual, which are claimed to measure the gk components of intelligence.

The reliability of the test by the test-retest method is .93, and a figure of .96 has been obtained by the Kuder-Richardson method. These are very satisfactory reliabilities for spatial material.

[754]

★Spatial Test II (Three Dimensional). Ages 10–11; 1950–51; 1 form ['51]; manual ['51]; provisional norms ['51]; 115s. per 100; 15s. per 12; 1s. 4d. per single copy; 3s. 6d. per manual; postage extra; 26½ (45) minutes; A. F. Watts with the assistance of D. A. Pidgeon and M. K. B. Richards; National Foundation for Educational Research in England and Wales. *

[755]

★Stromberg Dexterity Test. Adults; 1945–51; also called SDT; individual; 1 form, '47; preliminary manual ('51); $30 per set of testing materials needed by examiner; 35¢ per manual; postpaid; nontimed (8–15) minutes; Eleroy L. Stromberg; Psychological Corporation. *

REFERENCES

1. STROMBERG, ELEROY L. "Visual Discrimination, Dexterity, and Non-Verbal Intelligence Measured by a Single, Short (8 Minute) Test." Abstract. Am Psychol 4:392 S '49. * (PA 24: 1675, title only)

JULIAN C. STANLEY, Associate Professor of Educational Psychology, George Peabody College for Teachers, Nashville, Tennessee.

This well built one-hand manipulative test gives promise of being reasonably valid for many skilled and semiskilled positions, despite several shortcomings of the preliminary (1951) manual. The rectangular wooden kit (21½ by 17¾ by 1¼ inches) opens up to reveal on one side a tricolored formboard with 6 rows and 9 columns of holes 1½ inches in diameter into which fit 54 flat, cylindrical wooden disks ¾ inches thick. Thirty disks are red on one side or the other, 6 of these being red on both sides. Likewise, 30 are yellow on one side or the other, and 30 are blue. Twenty-four are red on neither side, and similarly for yellow and blue. At the beginning of Trial 1, the testee sees in the tray on his left 6 rows of 9 blocks each, the top row being blue, the next yellow, the next red, the next blue, etc. He must transfer these as quickly as possible in a predesignated order to the formboard on his right. On Trial 2, the 9 columns in the left-hand tray are alternately red, yellow, and blue, and the directions for transferring the disks to the formboard holes are somewhat different from those for Trial 1. Trials 1 and 2 are for practice only; Trials 3 and 4 are their respective counterparts, the total number of seconds needed to complete both being the final score. Such measures range from about 2 to 4½ minutes.

The author and publisher are to be congratulated for having repeatedly cautioned against uncritical use of the test in their preliminary manual. They emphasize that "a test may have high validity for workers in one situation; but in another case, for workers with the same job title the validity of the test may be low." Yet their own validity data are not thoroughly satisfactory. For a test under trial since 1945, the evidence offered is quite meager. Their validity discussion is based upon a grand total of 69 foundry moulders in three different plants, the criterion being monthly wages dichotomized at the median separately for each plant. Thus three pairs of score distributions are shown. For each of these the "poor" (lowerpaid) workers were in general less speedy on the *Stromberg Dexterity Test*. No biserial *r*'s were computed or *t*-tests run. The reviewer finds for the plant with the *greatest* difference between the mean scores of "good and poor" workers (14 each) a biserial *r* of .56, which is significant between the 1 and 5 per cent levels. Why the author chose to dichotomize his criterion rather than use an ordinary product-moment *r* between wage and score is not stated. Certainly he was not trying merely to simplify matters for the statistically untutored, because nine *r*'s appear elsewhere in the manual. No mention is made of follow-up studies of beginning employees, even though percentiles for 77 "female assembler and welder *applicants*" (italics mine) appear in the norms.

The correlation between scores on Trials 3 and 4, stepped up with the Spearman-Brown formula, was .84 for 70 female assembler and welder job applicants, variability unspecified. For 80 male trade school students the reliability coefficient of the total SDT scores, determined in a similar fashion, was .87. Conspicuously missing are standard errors of measurement and test-retest *r*'s to reflect stability over an intervening period of time. If individual scores are to be used for selection, Trials 3 and 4 might be given twice in succession (i.e., 3, 4, 3, 4) in order to enhance reliability. With this procedure a reliability coefficient of about .92 for industrial workers similar to those reported in

the manual should be obtained with less than 15 minutes devoted to each testee.

One reliability coefficient (.90) and two thirds of the *r*'s with other tests are based upon the inevitable college students, scores for both sexes being combined. It is difficult to conceive of practical uses for the SDT with such groups, nor does the author suggest any.

The test manual does not report experimental evidence on such points as proper use with left-handed persons, relative scores with each hand, sex differences, improvement with practice, and factorial content. Concerning left-handedness it states that studies are needed but advocates the same procedure as for right-handers.

Directions for giving the test are unusually clear and adequate, except that the necessity for speed in Trials 3 and 4 is not emphasized for the subject, who may have forgotten the brief mention of speed at the start of untimed Trial 1. Some testees will be reminded of this if the stopwatch is seen and recognized, but more explicit instructions seem needed.

We are not told what to do if the subject accidentally disarranges the blocks, turns one over, forgets how to proceed, or otherwise becomes confused. Presumably, the only allowable plan is to wait until he places a block incorrectly on the formboard and then say "No, that's wrong," followed by "No, that's not the next one" if he continues to err. This might cause either an infinite score or unstandardized prompting. Starting over seems the only solution, but of course an undetermined amount of practice effect has already resulted. The examiner must watch very closely to insure that his subject does not become hopelessly enmeshed in an incorrect response pattern before a warning is given. Thus, he can hardly test more than one person at a time.

Researchers employing the SDT may want to investigate the effect of skewed time scores upon *r*'s and perhaps seek a transformation for them if curvilinear regression is found.

The noticeable chipping of paint on the disks may introduce slight progressive changes in the testing situation, though this should not be important unless large areas flake off.

The *Stromberg Dexterity Test* seems at least as complex as Stromberg (*1*) judged it to be. In addition to requiring visual discrimination, dexterity, and nonverbal intelligence, it may also have a spatial component. The manual gives little usable information on these points, however,

Stromberg Dexterity Test

since the 4 r's with related tests (*Minnesota Rate of Manipulation*, .50 for placing and .34 for turning; *Purdue Pegboard*, .30 for placing and .21 for assembly) are based upon "college men and women." The other two r's, .45 for 484 industrial workers and .39 for 90 additional industrial workers with the *Adaptability Test* (a 35-item, 15-minute measure of mental ability) are moderately high if attenuation is taken into account. Despite the statement in the manual that "the *SDT* might very possibly add to the value of a selection battery," the reviewer believes that it will perhaps be most useful as a single predictor. This is an empirical matter, though, and must be decided in terms of multiple r's rather than armchair speculation.

In summary, the *Stromberg Dexterity Test* is an attractive, sturdily constructed formboard type instrument that may *perhaps* be found to be a valid predictor of success in a rather wide range of skilled and semiskilled jobs. It is only partially standardized, so that the user will need to accumulate his own norms and to make extensive validity studies in his own situation. This must be done to some degree for almost any test, but the dearth of data in the preliminary (1951) SDT manual or in the published literature makes caution imperative.

MECHANICAL ABILITY

[756]

★A.C.E.R. Mechanical Comprehension Test. Ages 13.5 and over; 1942; 1 form; no data on reliability and validity; 3s. 10d. per 10; separate answer sheets must be used; 1s. per 10 answer sheets; 3d. per scoring stencil; 6d. per manual; 1s. 6d. per specimen set; cash orders postpaid within Australia; 30(40) minutes; Australian Council for Educational Research. *

REFERENCES

1. OXLADE, M. "An Experiment in the Use of Psychological Tests in the Selection of Women Trainee Telephone Mechanics." *B Ind Psychol & Personnel Prac* 2:26–32 Mr '46. * (*PA* 20: 4838)

D. W. McElwain, *Senior Lecturer in Psychology, University of Melbourne, Victoria, Australia.*

This test consists of 45 items. Each item is based on a drawing of some mechanical device, and usually asks what will happen to a given part when some other part is moved in a prescribed way. The diagrams are usually not of known or familiar mechanical objects but are made-up affairs which require an analysis of the particular set-up.

The test was constructed by the Australian

Council for Educational Research during the recent war for use as a selective device for choosing persons suitable for the mechanical trades (a term used in a narrower sense in Australia than in the United States to apply only to those highly skilled metal trades which work with machines, e.g., toolmaker, brass fitter, metal machinist, but not engine driver, plumber, draftsman, tinsmith). The test was used in all the Australian armed services. Probably nearly one million persons (mainly men) were given this test in the period 1942–47.

The test developed from the original work of Stenquist, as did the Bennett series in the United States and the Test N series of the Australian Institute of Industrial Psychology in Australia. The test differs, however, from the Bennett tests in that (a) four-fold selective answers are employed; (b) the items are based on drawings of unfamiliar mechanical objects; and (c) the test has a sharp difficulty gradient.

The test has a number of very good features, among them excellent photolithographic reproduction on good paper, an extended and carefully planned practice, and some useful ingenuities in matching the lettering of the diagrams to the lettering of the answers.

Several major surveys of the usefulness of the test have been made and many suggestions have been put forward for its improvement. The test has undergone a major revision by the Army Psychology Service, which has made a new test with these revisions: (a) 3-dimensional representations are used in the drawings instead of flat elevations; (b) direct validation is based on ratings on the job in the mechanical trades; and (c) items below medium difficulty for the Army have been eliminated.

While the new test is not publicly available, it is mentioned here because the revisions point up the main criticisms that can be made of the original test. The principal criticism is reflected in the change in validation criteria. The original test was validated against a combined score of the *Cox Mechanical Models Test,* and the *Cox Mechanical Diagrams Test* and its own item trial pool score.

The test has in practice given correlations of the order .3 to .7 for various populations, occupations, and vocational training facilities. It has a high *g* saturation under almost all conditions. It is easy to administer and is superior to the usual mechanical assembly test in predicting learning rate for mechanical trades.

The A.C.E.R. are presently preparing a new form of the test more suitable for adolescents in high schools and technical schools. It is planned to supplement the new form with a test on tool information.

The *A.C.E.R. Mechanical Comprehension Test* is a very good one of its kind, but like the others, has essential difficulties. The test is a composite and is certainly multidimensional; it is neither a pure factor test on the one hand, nor a job analogue on the other, but lies somewhere in between. It has, however, proved very useful. For particular selection jobs with known offering populations and within a context of a given psychometric battery, such tests are almost indispensable.

[757]

★**Form Relations Group Test.** Ages 14 and over; 1926–46; 1 form ['26]; no data on reliability and validity and no description of normative population in manual; data available on request; mimeographed manual ['46]; 6s. 9d. per 12; 1s. 6d. per single copy; 1s. per manual; postage extra; 19½(25) minutes; National Institute of Industrial Psychology. *

REFERENCES
1. LAYCOCK, S. R., AND HUTCHEON, N. B. "A Preliminary Investigation into the Problem of Measuring Engineering Aptitude." *J Ed Psychol* 30:280–8 Ap '39. * (*PA* 13:5899)
2. HOLLIDAY, FRANK. "An Investigation Into the Selection of Apprentices for the Engineering Industry." *Occupational Psychol* 14:69–81 Ap '40. * (*PA* 14:3710)
3. SLATER, PATRICK. "Some Group Tests of Spatial Judgment or Practical Ability." *Occupational Psychol* 14:40–55 Ja '40. * (*PA* 14:2644)
4. HOLLIDAY, FRANK. "A Further Investigation Into the Selection of Apprentices for the Engineering Industry." *Occupational Psychol* 15:173–84 O '41. *
5. HOLLIDAY, FRANK. "A Survey of an Investigation Into the Selection of Apprentices for the Engineering Industry." *Occupational Psychol* 16:1–19 Ja '42. *
6. KERR, GEORGE. "Aptitude Testing for Secondary Courses: An Essay in Control Under War-Time Difficulties." *Occupational Psychol* 16:73–8 Ap '42. *
7. SHUTTLEWORTH, CLIFFORD W. "Tests of Technical Aptitude." *Occupational Psychol* 16:175–82 O '42. *
8. HARDING, D. W. "Prognostic Tests for Students of Architecture." *Occupational Psychol* 17:126–31 Jl '43. * (*PA* 18:290)
9. HOLLIDAY, FRANK. "The Relation Between Psychological Test Scores and Subsequent Proficiency of Apprentices in the Engineering Industry." *Occupational Psychol* 17:168–85 O '43. * (*PA* 18:1835)
10. MOORE, B. G. R., AND PEEL, E. A. "Predicting Aptitude for Dentistry." *Occupational Psychol* 25:192–9 Jl '51. * (*PA* 26:3675)

A. T. WELFORD, *University Lecturer in Experimental Psychology, University of Cambridge, Cambridge, England.*

This is a paper and pencil test with eight sections of progressively increasing difficulty. In the easiest section the subject is required to identify one shape from among 15 to complete each of 5 incomplete squares. In the most difficult he is required to identify 2 shapes from among 12, turning them around or over if necessary, to complete each of 5 incomplete cubes drawn in perspective. There is a time limit for

each section; the whole test takes about 25 minutes to administer.

The manual supplied with the test gives the precise wording of instructions, a scoring key and norms. Statistical data on reliability, etc., are not included but are contained in articles in *Occupational Psychology* (7, 9), and are supplied on request by the National Institute of Industrial Psychology, which strictly controls the issue of the test material.

The norms are in the form of five grades: A = best 10 per cent, B = next 20 per cent, C = middle 40 per cent, D = next 20 per cent, and E = worst 10 per cent. They are given for boys and men and for girls and women of secondary grammar school (high school) education in three age ranges—16 and over, 15 to 15.11 and 14 to 14.11. Separate norms are given for a relatively unselected group of boys and men of the same age ranges and also of the range 13 to 13.11. The norms are based on the scores of 5,999 subjects, some from schools in various parts of England, and some applicants tested in the course of industrial selection work. The scatter of scores shown by the norms is satisfactorily wide and indicates that the test can discriminate at both the top and bottom ends of the scale.

The norms for the grammar school and the relatively unselected groups are surprisingly similar, indicating that performance is not closely bound up with the capacities upon which selection of pupils for grammar schools is made or upon the effects of training in these schools. It must, however, be remembered that the test was produced at a time when the selection of pupils for grammar schools on qualities likely to be measured by mental tests of this kind was less prevalent than it is today.

Scores have been found to correlate .44 with teachers' estimates of ability based on school records for a group of 109 technical school pupils, and from .22 to .54 (weighted average .35) with instructors' estimates of proficiency for nine groups of apprentices ranging in size from 91 to 16. If it is borne in mind that these are selected populations, and that the criteria must have included qualities other than those involved in performance at the test, the correlations suggest that the test is likely to form a useful component of a battery. The reliability is given as .87.

The scores, like those for almost all speeded tests, fail to distinguish between those who work slowly but accurately and those who work more quickly but with more mistakes. Research would seem to be well worth while to determine whether the value of speeded tests as a means of selection could be enhanced by taking account not only of the overall measure of achievement as represented by the usual type of score but also of the way in which this achievement is attained.

The "mental manipulation" of shapes in a form in which they are not tangible objects that can be picked up and turned around would seem to be an important feature of many practical skilled tasks. This is especially so for three-dimensional shapes as in the last two sections of the test. It is an aspect of performance upon which experimental research is desirable.

[758]

★**Group Test 81 [Space Perception Test]: National Institute of Industrial Psychology.** Ages 13–15; 1949; 1 form ['49]; no data on reliability and validity and no description of normative population in manual; data available on request; mimeographed manual ['49]; 4s. 5d. per 12; 1s. per single copy; 2s. per set of manual, key, and norms; postage extra; 15 (25) minutes; National Institute of Industrial Psychology. *

REFERENCES

1. HOLLIDAY, FRANK. "An Investigation Into the Selection of Apprentices for the Engineering Industry." *Occupational Psychol* 14:69–81 Ap '40. * (*PA* 14:3710)
2. SLATER, PATRICK. "Some Group Tests of Spatial Judgment or Practical Ability." *Occupational Psychol* 14:40–55 Ja '40. * (*PA* 14:2644)
3. HOLLIDAY, FRANK. "A Further Investigation Into the Selection of Apprentices for the Engineering Industry." *Occupational Psychol* 15:173–84 O '41. *
4. HOLLIDAY, FRANK. "A Survey of an Investigation Into the Selection of Apprentices for the Engineering Industry." *Occupational Psychol* 16:1–19 Ja '42. *
5. HOLLIDAY, FRANK. "The Relation Between Psychological Test Scores and Subsequent Proficiency of Apprentices in the Engineering Industry." *Occupational Psychol* 17:168–85 O '43. * (*PA* 18:1835)

E. G. CHAMBERS, *Assistant Director of Research in Industrial Psychology, University of Cambridge, Cambridge, England.*

This spatial perception test involves two different principles. In the first part, a small pattern formed of crosses has to be recognized and marked in a larger pattern of crosses. Fifty problems are set with a time limit of seven minutes. In the second part, five small figures, numbered 1 to 5, are given together with some larger shapes which are made up of two, three, or four of the numbered figures. The subject is required to write down the numbers of the figures composing each shape. There are 20 two-piece, 12 three-piece, and 8 four-piece problems. An overall time of eight minutes is allowed for this part. Five-grade norms (poor, fair, average, good, and very good) based on 3,061 cases from secondary modern schools are provided for ages 13.0–13.11 and 14.0–14.11.

The test covers some of the principles common to all tests which purport to measure the ability to appreciate relationships of space and form. The problems are entirely two-dimensional and the test is moderately easy, some of the more difficult elements in spatial perception not being included. It is unfortunate that an error has been made in printing the numbered figures in the second part of this test. The long sides of figures 1 and 2 do not match, so that figure 1 does not fit into either the second or the fourth of the practice examples. Whether *Group Test 81* has special excellences or deficiencies compared with other tests of a similar nature is impossible to say without validation data. It should, however, be a useful tool in the hands of the vocational adviser.

[759]

MacQuarrie Test for Mechanical Ability. Ages 7 and over; 1925–43; 8 scores: tracing, tapping, dotting, copying, location, blocks, pursuit, total; 1 form, '25; manual ('43); $2.50 per 25, postage extra; 35¢ per specimen set, postpaid; Spanish edition available at same prices; 12(25) minutes; T. W. MacQuarrie; California Test Bureau. *

REFERENCES

1–43. See 3:661.
44. STANNARD, CEDRIC. *The Prognostic Value of the MacQuarrie Test for Mechanical Ability.* Master's thesis, University of Southern California (Los Angeles, Calif.), 1930.
45. MURPHY, LAURA WHITE. "The Relation Between Mechanical Ability Tests and Verbal and Non-Verbal Intelligence Tests." *J Psychol* 2:353–66 '36. * (*PA* 11:3928)
46. MERCER, MARGARET. *An Analysis of the Factors of Scientific Aptitude as Indicated by Success in Engineering Curricula.* Doctor's thesis, Pennsylvania State College (State College, Pa.), 1938. (*Abstracts of Doctoral Dissertations…, 1938,* pp. 97–102.)
47. MOODIE, MARY. *Norms for the Hawaiian Islands on the MacQuarrie Mechanical Ability Test.* Master's thesis, University of Hawaii (Honolulu, Hawaii), 1938.
48. ANDERSON, ROSE G. "A Comparative Study of Test Scores and Supervisors' Efficiency Ratings of Machinists." Abstract. *Am Psychol* 1:243 Jl '46. * (*PA* 20:3772, title only)
49. SHULTZ, IRVIN T. "Comparison of the Scores of Design Engineering Personnel With Factory Workers on the MacQuarrie Mechanical Performance Ability Tests." *Trans Kans Acad Sci* 49:354–6 D '46. * (*PA* 21:2439)
50. BEAMER, GEORGE C.; EDMONSON, LAWRENCE D.; AND STROTHER, GEORGE B. "Improving the Selection of Linotype Trainees." *J Appl Psychol* 32:130–4 Ap '48. * (*PA* 23:965)
51. CHAPMAN, ROBERT L. "The MacQuarrie Test For Mechanical Ability." *Psychometrika* 13:175–9 S '48. * (*PA* 23:1659)
52. SUPER, DONALD E. *Appraising Vocational Fitness by Means of Psychological Tests,* pp. 260–78. New York: Harper & Brothers, 1949. Pp. xxiii, 727. * (*PA* 24:2130)
53. ZAKOLSKI, F. C. "Studies in Delinquency: I, Personality Structure of Delinquent Boys." *J Genetic Psychol* 74:109–17 Mr '49. * (*PA* 23:4925)
54. BABCOCK, HARRIET. *The MacQuarrie Test as a Clinical Instrument: Validity of Vocabulary-MacQuarrie Deviations as a Measure of Abnormal Mental Functioning When Scored in Psychological Units.* Lancaster, Pa.: Science Press, 1950. Pp. vii, 72. Paper. * (*PA* 25:5336)
55. DURAN, JUNE C. *MacQuarrie Test for Mechanical Ability.* Summary of Investigations, No. 2. Los Angeles, Calif.: California Test Bureau, 1950. Pp. 16. Paper. *
56. GOODMAN, CHARLES H. "The MacQuarrie Test for Mechanical Ability: IV, Time and Motion Analysis." *J Appl Psychol* 34:27–9 F '50. * (*PA* 24:5868)
57. TRAVERS, ROBERT M. W., AND WALLACE, WIMBURN L. "Inconsistency in the Predictive Value of a Battery of Tests." *J Appl Psychol* 34:237–9 Ag '50. * (*PA* 25:6480)
58. LANEY, ARTHUR R., JR. "Validity of Employment Tests for Gas-Appliance Service Personnel." *Personnel Psychol* 4:199–208 su '51. * (*PA* 26:1735)

For an excerpt from a related review, see 760; for reviews by John R. Kinzer, C. H. Lawshe, Jr., and Alec Rodger, see 3:661.

[760]

★[*Re* MacQuarrie Test for Mechanical Ability.] BABCOCK, HARRIET. **The MacQuarrie Test as a Clinical Instrument: Validity of Vocabulary-MacQuarrie Deviations as a Measure of Abnormal Mental Functioning When Scored in Psychological Units.** Lancaster, Pa.: Science Press, 1950. Pp. vii, 72. $2.00. * (*PA* 25:5336)

J Consult Psychol 15:263 Je '51. *Laurance F. Shaffer.* This monograph presents evidence for a new measure of efficiency of mental functioning, obtained by comparing a vocabulary age with corresponding age scores obtained from the MacQuarrie Test. The latter test is certainly as suitable as any for measuring a deteriorating mental function because of its dependence on speed, skill, and spatial perception. Although the monograph does not establish the validity of the Vocabulary-MacQuarrie difference beyond all doubt, there is considerable confirming evidence of a clinical nature. Norms are based on 1000 cases. No correction for age is provided, and the author argues against its use.

[761]

Prognostic Test of Mechanical Abilities. Grades 7–12 and adults; 1946–47; 6 scores: arithmetic computation, reading drawings and blueprints, identification and use of tools, spatial relationships, checking measurements, total; IBM; Form A ('46); manual ('47); $2 per 25; 35¢ per specimen set, postpaid; separate answer sheets may be used; 2¢ per IBM answer sheet; 20¢ per stencil for machine scoring of answer sheets; 20¢ per stencil for hand scoring of answer sheets; postage extra; 38(45) minutes; J. Wayne Wrightstone and Charles E. O'Toole; California Test Bureau. *

REFERENCES

1. MICHAEL, WILLIAM B.; ZIMMERMAN, WAYNE S.; AND GUILFORD, J. P. "An Investigation of the Nature of the Spatial-Relations and Visualization Factors in Two High School Samples." *Ed & Psychol Meas* 11:561-77 w '51. *

WILLARD A. KERR, *Associate Professor of Psychology, Illinois Institute of Technology, Chicago, Illinois.*

This test in its five sectional subscores is a shrewd and interesting compromise between the demands of factorial purity and the traditional labels of mechanical trades know-how. Its carefully prepared manual reveals sectional intercorrelations ranging from .30 to .70 and sectional correlations with total score ranging from .52 to .77. Each section seems to contribute some unique value to the test, and certainly the five sectional scores as labeled have quick and easy meaning in both educational and industrial training programs as well as in student or worker counseling. From a pure factorial standpoint, the intercorrelations reported among the five sections suggest that most of the variance in total score is accounted for by three factors: (*a*) number factor (arithmetic computation, reading drawings and blueprints, checking measurements); (*b*) functional interests factor (identification and use of tools); and (*c*) spatial factor (spatial relationships). Independent research has shown the basic importance of all three factors in predicting success in mechanical trades.

Because it recognizes the demand that a good prediction instrument should isolate to some extent the principal talents which it measures, this test represents a distinct technological advance over such competing tests as the Bennett-Fry *Test of Mechanical Comprehension* which measures but does not separate the functional interests factor and the spatial factor. Future research probably can further show its superior validity because it permits differential predictive weighting by sections (or factors) and, in addition, it measures the number factor. Evidence in the manual of its validity is unfortunately limited to sectional contingency coefficients (ranging from .60 to .71) and a total score contingency coefficient (.78) with instructors' ratings in a training course for the aviation trades. The authors write that "since this is a general type of mechanics course, it is assumed that similar coefficients would be found for other mechanical occupations or trades." The difficulty in evaluating this assumption is increased by the failure of the manual to mention the number of cases on which the study was based.

Reliability coefficients (Kuder-Richardson) range from .89 to .94 for grade levels 7–12. Extensive norms (5,268 male students in 7 states) are provided for the same grade levels. Adult norms are absent, but the authors suggest that "the norms for grade 12 be used."

Despite present modest validity data, the test seems fairly certain to yield gratifying validity coefficients in occupations such as automotive and aviation mechanics, building trades, electric installation and practice, boat building and maritime trades, art metal work, foundry work, and related metal trades not primarily emphasizing repetitive dexterity. In the latter instance, the *MacQuarrie Test for Mechanical Ability* is probably a better one.

DOUGLAS G. SCHULTZ, *Research Associate, Educational Testing Service, Princeton, New Jersey.*

Presumably this test is predictive of success in various mechanical trades and in training for those trades. The content is based on an analysis of training courses in various mechanical occupations. (The manual does not give the details of how that analysis was carried out.) Yet the only predictive validity data presented in the manual are a set of contingency coefficients relating the subtest scores and total score to "instructors' ratings which were gathered very systematically and carefully in a training course for the aviation trades." No mention is made of the number of students on whom the figures were calculated, the number of instructors who did the rating, the bases for the ratings, the level and specific characteristics of the course, etc. Such information is entirely inconclusive. This reviewer has no reason to agree (or to disagree) with the manual's contention that since the mentioned course "is a general type of mechanics course, it is assumed that similar coefficients would be found for other mechanical occupations or trades."

The Kuder-Richardson reliabilities of the total score for each of the individual grades and for the total group in grades 7-12 seem entirely satisfactory. The publisher's catalog (not the manual) mentions that the reliabilities are based on over 4,000 cases in grades 7-12. Even though use of subtest scores is stressed at several places in the manual, no reliability coefficients are given for them. The intercorrelations among the parts are moderately high, but here again the number and type of subjects used are not given.

Subtest and total score norms for individual grades and for the total group in grades 7-12 are available in the manual. Some 5,000 male students were used to establish these norms, but we are not told how many came from each grade. Generally the discrimination seems good, particularly in view of the small numbers of items in the individual subtests. In grade 12, the discrimination is somewhat poorer at the upper end of the test. This would suggest caution in the administration of the test to adults. No norms are included for adults; this reviewer would not recommend use of the grade 12 norms as suggested in the manual. The test appears to be directed toward the lower educational levels, and, while it is listed as appropriate for adults,

no material concerning its effectiveness at that level is presented.

The test parts represent the rather heterogeneous content usually found in a mechanical aptitude test. The second part has only simple drawings, and no blueprints, as the title might imply, to be read. The spatial relationships items seem to require an undue amount of fine size discrimination (up to differences $\frac{1}{16}$").

The test itself could stand a thorough editing. For example, Item 30 does not state how the circles are to be compared, and Items 39-45 on tool usage should be put in terms of "should be used" or "is used" instead of "can be used." The print is of a good size, and the arrangement is, on the whole, satisfactory. The pictures in Subtest 3 might be confusing to younger students. Option designations are not always clearly printed; "c" and "e" are likely to be misread in a number of instances. More practice items would be advisable.

The reviewer's overall impression is that this test, properly used, is one which may be of value in many situations where some kind of mechanical aptitude test is sought. The user should make his own validity studies. But the test certainly would not seem to constitute a major addition to the list of available tests.

For an excerpt from a review, see 3:674.

[762]
*Purdue Mechanical Adaptability Test: Purdue Personnel Tests.** Males ages 15 and over; 1945-50; Form A—Men ('46); Form T—Women discontinued; preliminary manual ('50); $2.50 per 25, postage extra; 25¢ per specimen set, postpaid; 15(20) minutes; C. H. Lawshe, Jr. and Joseph Tiffin; Occupational Research Center, Purdue University. *

REFERENCES

1. LAWSHE, C. H., JR.; SEMANEK, IRENE A.; AND TIFFIN, JOSEPH. "The Purdue Mechanical Adaptability Test." *J Appl Psychol* 30:442-53 O '46. * (PA 21:579)
2. LAWSHE, C. H., JR., AND TIFFIN, JOSEPH. "The Purdue Mechanical Adaptability Test." Abstract. *Am Psychol* 2:428 O '47. * (PA 22:930, title only)
3. SUPER, DONALD E. *Appraising Vocational Fitness by Means of Psychological Tests,* pp. 278-81. New York: Harper & Brothers, 1949. Pp. xxiii, 727. * (PA 24:2130)
4. BELMAN, H. S., AND EVANS, R. N. "Selection of Students for a Trade and Industrial Education Curriculum," pp. 9-14. In *Motives and Aptitudes in Education: Four Studies.* Edited by H. H. Remmers. Purdue University, Division of Educational Reference, Studies in Higher Education, No. 74. Lafayette, Ind.: the Division, December 1950. Pp. iii, 63. Paper. * (PA 26:3010)
5. ROTHE, HAROLD F. "Normative and Validity Data for the Purdue Mechanical Adaptability Test." *Personnel Psychol* 3:187-92 su '50. * (PA 25:2081)
6. WELLS, R. G. *Industrial Norms for the Purdue Mechanical Adaptability Test.* Master's thesis, Purdue University (Lafayette, Ind.), 1950.

For reviews by Jay L. Otis and Dewey B. Stuit, see 3:676.

[763]

*Revised Minnesota Paper Form Board Test.
Grades 7–12 and adults; 1930–48; IBM; 2 editions;
revised manual ('48); 35¢ per specimen set of any one
edition; postpaid; 20(25) minutes; original test by
Donald G. Paterson, Richard M. Elliott, L. Dewey
Anderson, Herbert A. Toops, and Edna Heidbreder;
revision by Rensis Likert and William H. Quasha;
Psychological Corporation. *
a) HAND SCORING EDITION. 1930–48; Forms AA ('41),
BB ('41); $1.75 per 25.
b) MACHINE SCORING EDITION. 1941–48; Forms MA
('41), MB ('41); $2.75 per 25; $1.85 per 50 IBM answer sheets.

REFERENCES

1–9. See 40:1673.
10–57. See 43:677.
58. MURPHY, LAURA WHITE. "The Relation Between Mechanical Ability Tests and Verbal and Non-Verbal Intelligence
Tests." J Psychol 2:353–66 '36. * (PA 11:3928)
59. MORRIS, CHARLES M. "An Experimental Analysis of
Certain Performance Tests." Abstract. Psychol B 34:716–7 N
'37. * (PA 12:1661, title only)
60. MERCER, MARGARET. An Analysis of the Factors of Scientific Aptitude as Indicated by Success in Engineering Curricula. Doctor's thesis, Pennsylvania State College (State College, Pa.), 1938. (Abstracts of Doctoral Dissertations..., 1938,
pp. 97–102.)
61. HACKMAN, RAY CARTER. The Differential Prediction of
Success in Two Contrasting Vocational Areas. Doctor's thesis,
University of Minnesota (Minneapolis, Minn.), 1940. (Summaries of Ph.D. Theses, 1949, pp. 100–5.) (PA 24:4154, title
only)
62. SHEPARD, EUGENE L. Measurements of Certain Non-
verbal Abilities of Urban and Rural Children. Doctor's thesis,
New York University (New York, N.Y.), 1940. (Abstracts of
Theses....[School of Education] October 1940–June 1941, 1941,
pp. 61–3.)
63. ROSS, LAWRENCE W. "Results of Testing Machine-Tool
Trainees." Personnel J 21:363–7 Ap '43. * (PA 17:2459)
64. HAVIGHURST, ROBERT J., AND JANKE, LEOTA LONG. "Relations Between Ability and Social Status in a Midwestern
Community: I, Ten-Year-Old Children." J Ed Psychol 35:357–
68 S '44. * (PA 19:476)
65. JANUS, SIDNEY. The Prediction of Learning Ability for
Certain Types of Mechanical Skill. Doctor's thesis, George
Washington University (Washington, D.C.), 1944. (Summaries of Doctoral Dissertations 1944–46, 1947, pp. 29–32.)
66. ACHARD, F. H., AND CLARKE, FLORENCE H. "You Can
Measure the Probability of Success as a Supervisor." Personnel 21:353–73 My '45. *
67. JANKE, LEOTA LONG, AND HAVIGHURST, ROBERT J. "Relations Between Ability and Social Status in a Mid-Western
Community: II, Sixteen-Year-Old Boys and Girls." J Ed
Psychol 36:499–509 N '45. * (PA 20:1999)
68. WITTENBORN, J. R. "Mechanical Ability, Its Nature and
Measurement: I, An Analysis of the Variables Employed in
the Preliminary Minnesota Experiment." Ed & Psychol Meas
5:241–60 au '45. * (PA 20:2025)
69. WITTENBORN, J. R. "Mechanical Ability, Its Nature and
Measurement: II, Manual Dexterity. Ed & Psychol Meas
5:395–409 w '45. * (PA 20:2926)
70. ANDERSON, ROSE G. "A Comparative Study of Test
Scores and Supervisors' Efficiency Ratings of Machinists."
Abstract. Am Psychol 1:243 Jl '46. * (PA 20:3772, title
only)
71. MILLER, CHARLES, AND LAUER, A. R. "The Mechanical
Aptitude of Drivers in Relation to Performance at the Wheel."
Proc Iowa Acad Sci 53:273–5 '46. * (PA 23:991)
72. WALKER, K. F., AND OXLADE, M. N. "A Tentative Battery of Tests for the Selection of Women for Cotton Textile
Spinning." B Ind Psychol & Personnel Prac 2:6–27 Je '46. *
(PA 20:4871)
73. BEAMER, GEORGE C.; EDMONSON, LAWRENCE D.; AND
STROTHER, GEORGE B. "Improving the Selection of Linotype
Trainees." J Appl Psychol 32:130–4 Ap '48. * (PA 23:965)
74. BROADHURST, JOHN C. A Differential Prediction of Success in Vocational-Technical and Vocational-Industrial Courses
in a Vocational High School. Doctor's thesis, New York University (New York, N.Y.), 1948. (Abstracts of Theses....
[School of Education] October 1948–June 1949, 1950, pp. 45–
50.)
75. DEJMEK, FRANK W. "A Study of Relationships Among
Scores on the Minnesota Paper Form Board-Revised Series AA,
the Non-Language Section of the California Test of Mental
Maturity, and Test 2 of the Non-Language Section of the California Test of Mental Maturity." J Ed Res 42:307–11 D '48. *
(PA 23:3647)
76. DREFFIN, WILLIAM B., AND WRENN, C. GILBERT. "Spatial Relations Ability and Other Characteristics of Art Laboratory Students." J Appl Psychol 32:601–5 D '48. * (PA 23:
3777)
77. HABEGGER, O. F., JR. "A Case History in Selecting
Salesmen." Mgmt Rec 10:52–4 F '48. * (PA 22:4146)
78. OXLADE, M. N. "Selection Tests for Power-Sewing Machine Operators." B Ind Psychol & Personnel Prac 4:26–36 Je
'48. * (PA 23:1486)
79. SCHEUHING, MARY A. An Analysis of the Predictive
Efficiency of Certain Test Scores and Grades in the Selection
of High School Students for the Industrial Auto and Electric
Shop Courses. Master's thesis, Temple University (Philadelphia, Pa.), 1948.
80. BARNETT, ALBERT. "A Note on Mechanical Aptitude of
West Texans." J Appl Psychol 33:316–8 Ag '49. * (PA 24:
2363)
81. BARNETTE, W. LESLIE, JR. Occupational Aptitude Patterns of Counseled Veterans. Doctor's thesis, New York University (New York, N.Y.), 1949. Pp. viii, 385. * (PA 24:362,
title only)
82. BLANCHARD, HOWARD L. A Comparison of Teachers'
Marks With an Actual Battery of Aptitude Test Percentile
Scores. Doctor's "Field Study No. 1," Colorado State College
of Education (Greeley, Colo.), 1949. (Abstracts of Field
Studies....1949, 1950, pp. 12–5.)
83. MELBERG, MERRITT E. A Comparison of Two Dimensional and Three Dimensional Representation of Items in a
Spatial Relations Test. Doctor's "Field Study No. 1," Colorado
State College of Education (Greeley, Colo.), 1949. (Abstracts
of Field Studies....1949, 1950, pp. 72–5.)
84. MURRAY, JOHN E. "An Analysis of Geometric Ability."
J Ed Psychol 40:118–24 F '49. * (PA 24:2066)
85. RINSLAND, HENRY D. "The Prediction of Veterans' Success From Test Scores at the University of Oklahoma," Part 1,
pp. 59–72. In The Sixth Yearbook of the National Council on
Measurements Used in Education, 1948–1949. Fairmont,
W.Va.: the Council, Fairmont State College, 1949. Pp. v, 140
(variously numbered). Paper, mimeographed. *
86. SUPER, DONALD E. Appraising Vocational Fitness by
Means of Psychological Tests, pp. 297–307. New York: Harper
& Brothers, 1949. Pp. xxiii, 727. * (PA 24:2130)
87. WIGHTWICK, BEATRICE. The Effect of Retesting on the
Predictive Power of Aptitude Tests. Doctor's thesis, New York
University (New York, N.Y.), 1949. (Abstracts of Theses....
[School of Education] October 1948–June 1949, 1950, pp.
141–50.)
88. BERDIE, RALPH F., AND SUTTER, NANCY A. "Predicting
Success of Engineering Students." J Ed Psychol 41:184–90 Mr
'50. * (PA 24:6056)
89. DuBois, PHILIP H., AND WATSON, ROBERT I. "The Selection of Patrolmen." J Appl Psychol 34:90–5 Ap '50. * (PA
25:2076)
90. NAIR, RALPH KENNETH. Predictive Value of Standardized
Tests and Inventories in Industrial Arts Teacher Education.
Doctor's thesis, University of Missouri (Columbia, Mo.), 1950.
Abstract: Microfilm Abstracts 10:77–8 no 3 '50. * (PA 25:
4862, title only)
91. TRAVERS, ROBERT M. W., AND WALLACE, WIMBURN L.
"Inconsistency in the Predictive Value of a Battery of Tests."
J Appl Psychol 34:237–9 Ag '50. * (PA 25:6480)
92. BARNETTE, W. LESLIE, JR. Occupational Aptitude Patterns of Selected Groups of Counseled Veterans. American Psychological Association, Psychological Monographs: General and
Applied, Vol. 65, No. 5, Whole No. 322. Washington, D.C.:
the Association, Inc., 1951. Pp. v, 49. Paper. * (PA 26:2794)
93. LANEY, ARTHUR R., JR. "Validity of Employment Tests
for Gas-Appliance Service Personnel." Personnel Psychol 4:
199–208 su '51. * (PA 26:1735)
94. NOVAK, BENJAMIN J., AND SCHEUHING, MARY A. "Predicting Success in High School Industrial Courses." Ind Arts
& Voc Ed 40:301–4 D '51. *
95. OXLADE, M. N. "Further Experience With Selection
Tests for Power-Sewing Machine Operators." B Ind Psychol
& Personnel Prac 7:27–37 Mr '51. * (PA 25:7713)

CLIFFORD E. JURGENSEN, Personnel Director,
Minneapolis Gas Company, Minneapolis, Minnesota.

The Revised Minnesota Paper Form Board
Test, first published in 1934, can be considered
a classic in measurement of mechanical aptitude. It has had a long history, has been used
widely, and still warrants high respect and frequent use.

The test is too well known to warrant a detailed description. Suffice to say that it consists
of 8 practice items and 64 test items dealing
with 2 dimensional space perception. Each test
item consists of the disarranged parts of a geometrical figure, and 5 assembled geometric fig-

ures from among which the examinee is required to pick out the one figure which is made up of the correct combination of parts.

Numerous validity studies have been made, and it is the exceptional case where the test is not sufficiently valid to warrant its use for selecting employees in mechanical type jobs such as drafting, inspection, linotype operation, machine operation, packing, and the like. Also, the test has frequently been found to be predictive of academic success in courses such as art, aviation mechanics, dentistry, drafting, engineering, and geometry. In employee selection for maintenance positions such as machinist, pipefitter, welder, and the like, this reviewer has had more favorable experience with the *Test of Mechanical Comprehension* than with the *Revised Minnesota Paper Form Board Test*. However, if time permits, he has found the Minnesota test an excellent additional test to be used.

The 16-page manual is excellent. It opens with a history of the development of the test, a description of the test materials, and a needed exhortation to follow the specified time limit. There follow simple, clear, and sufficiently detailed instructions on administering and scoring the test. Validity data are discussed on three pages, and cover many diverse studies.

Reliability is briefly discussed. For Series AA and BB reliability was found to be .85 for one form and .92 when both forms were administered to 290 high school seniors applying for admission to New York University. No reliability studies have been published for Series MA and MB. The manual states that "there is no reason to believe that it is any lower than for Series AA and BB." The reviewer concurs with this view, and also agrees with the manual that experimental evidence would be desirable.

The manual gives a large number of intercorrelations with other tests. In general, the studies show that the test is correlated only moderately with intelligence tests and with other mechanical aptitude tests. Several studies show that sex differences are small (and probably unimportant) but that males consistently excel females in score.

Extensive tables of norms are given for well-defined and large samples. Four tables are included, separate norms being given for hand and machine scored editions and for educational and industrial groups. A bibliography of 54 items (all but four being published data) is appended.

The excellence of the manual should do much

to increase further the use of this test in both vocational guidance and vocational selection.

RAYMOND A. KATZELL, *Director and Staff Consultant, Richardson, Bellows, Henry and Company, New York, New York.*

This is a familiar stand-by among tests of spatial relations ability. The current revision, published in 1934, has been competently reviewed in earlier volumes of this *Yearbook*. The present review will therefore be confined mainly to the contents of the new manual. This manual, issued in 1948, replaces a 1941 edition used for the hand scored forms of the test and a later temporary one for the machine scored series. The present edition is designed to clarify some confusions in procedures for administering and scoring the test, and to present improved and extended data on norms and validity.

DIRECTIONS. Instructions for administering both the hand and machine scored series are clearly and explicitly given in a format which can be easily read by the examiner in the testing situation.

Detailed scoring directions are also given separately for the two series. In the directions for the hand scored series, where the scoring formula is $R - W/5$, the distinction between omissions and wrong answers is not defined. There is the danger that some inexperienced scorers may follow the common school practice of regarding omissions as equivalent to wrong answers, thus arriving at erroneous scores. (Omissions occur occasionally, even though discouraged by instructions to examinees.)

VALIDITY AND RELIABILITY DATA. The extensive use of this test over a number of years has produced information on its validity in a variety of educational and industrial situations. Twenty-five studies which include validity data on the test are summarized in the manual. These studies cover the following types of personnel: engineering and technical students, art students, dental students, mechanics, sewing machine operators, packers, linotype operators, inspectors, factory supervisors, and several other types of factory jobs. The test has shown appreciable validity in most of these areas.

The manual also contains some rather scanty data on reliability as determined on groups of students, as well as a useful list of correlations with about 20 other tests of various kinds.

The information in these sections of the manual should prove most helpful in decisions on whether to use the test and its interpretations. A desirable addition would be the indication of significance levels of the validity coefficients, especially since the N is frequently not mentioned.

NORMS. When compared with most tests, this one is replete with normative data. Percentile tables are presented for 13 educational and 13 industrial groups tested with the hand scored series, and for 11 educational and 5 industrial groups tested with the machine scored series. Means and sigmas are also furnished for most of the groups. The samples are usually amply large, and represent a wide diversity of populations. A particularly commendable feature is the inclusion of a relatively detailed description of each sample.

An up-to-date bibliography of 54 entries adds to the worth of the manual, as does the fact that it is quite readable. Its otherwise good style is, however, slightly marred by the appearance, albeit rare, of such expressions as "so much.... data" (p. 3) and "unusual amount of studies" (p. 6).

Some imperfections in this revised manual have already been noted. One might also like to see more information on the rationale and construction of the test, along with more discussion of its composition as revealed by factorial studies. But, the negative comments that may be made about it are trifling in comparison with the many cogent virtues which have been mentioned.

We have here a test of demonstrated validity for various kinds of mechanical and technical work; its value is enhanced by the comprehensiveness of its new manual.

For a review by Dewey B. Stuit, see 3:677; for a review by Alec Rodger, see 40:1673.

[764]

*SRA Mechanical Aptitudes. Grades 9-12 and adults; 1947-50; 4 scores: mechanical knowledge, space relations, shop arithmetic, total; Form AH ('47); second revised manual ('50); 49¢ per test and answer pad; separate answer pads must be used; $1.90 per 25 answer pads; 55¢ per 25 profile and norm sheets ('49); 75¢ per specimen set; cash orders postpaid; 35 (45) minutes; prepared by Richardson, Bellows, Henry & Co., Inc.; Science Research Associates, Inc. *

ALEC RODGER, *Reader in Psychology, Birkbeck College, University of London; and Consulting Psychologist to the Ministry of Labour and National Service; London, England.*

This businesslike production derives chiefly from wartime experience. Among those who shared the authors' problems during that period there are not likely to be many dissentients from their conclusions about the most desirable components of a battery of mechanical aptitude tests. In fact, their decision to include tests of mechanical knowledge, space relations, and shop arithmetic would probably be echoed by almost everyone who has kept abreast of developments, in the last 12 years or so, in the selection of personnel for engineering occupations.

But they offer no validation data at all. It is true that in the manual they say "only those types of items which produced highest validities under Army research conditions were included"; and it is true that there is no reason whatever to dispute their claim. However, they should have acknowledged explicitly the fact that types of items which have high validity in certain circumstances sometimes have surprisingly low validity in apparently similar circumstances; and they should have given some indication of the steps they are taking to collect appropriate information. Until they have repaired the gap, we shall have to be cautious and take the view that this is probably a very good test for a variety of selection and guidance purposes, but that judgement on it cannot yet be passed firmly.

DOUGLAS G. SCHULTZ, *Research Associate, Educational Testing Service, Princeton, New Jersey.*

The purpose of this test is to evaluate three types of abilities usually measured in mechanical aptitude tests. The choice of the content was based on a survey of published literature, as well as on unpublished studies conducted by the armed services. Although the test is listed as appropriate for both sexes, the authors express a belief that it is not as suitable for female groups as for male groups.

The manner in which the test was constructed is well described in the manual and appears to have been very thorough. Pretesting and item analysis preceded the final selection of items, and the answer options in the shop arithmetic test grew out of free answer tallies. The general quality of the items reflects the care exercised in the test construction process.

Part-score and total-score Kuder-Richardson reliability coefficients are given for each of the grades 9-12 and for a group of described trainees (young men). The total score figures are generally acceptable except for the ninth grade girls. Only the mechanical knowledge test is reliable enough for individual counseling. The manual suggests the possibility of using extreme scores on the other two parts; it might also have mentioned that group comparisons could legitimately be made on these part scores.

Norms are available in the manual for the group of trainees mentioned above. Means and standard deviations, but not complete norm tables, are also presented for grades 9–12. The expected increases in scores with advancement in grade level are found. This reviewer's impression was that the space relations and shop arithmetic tests were a bit difficult; the data confirmed this impression. For both the trainee and high school groups the mean scores on these parts are somewhat lower than desirable. Also, for girls the mechanical knowledge scores are down toward the chance range. These facts may indicate some speededness. But, on the whole, the level and spread of scores are good.

The manual does not include any material on validity. The statement that the user will obtain maximum validity from weights developed for his own situation is a very reasonable one. But it is regrettable that results from administration of the test in some typical situations are not presented. The authors say they are developing more complete norms; let us hope they will devote some attention to validity evidence as well.

The test is well printed and bound in an attractive cover; the type size is good; and the pictures and diagrams are, with one or two minor exceptions, clear and well drawn. The SRA answer pad is very convenient but has the disadvantage (for certain purposes) that it is quite difficult to determine which specific items have been missed and which response was chosen to any item.

Sound construction and excellent presentation of materials characterize this test. It is hoped that the adequate beginning in accumulating normative data will be continued and that validity information will be added. While the test does not represent a pioneering effort in the field, it appears to be an excellent instrument to have available when a mechanical aptitude test is required.

[765]

*Survey of Space Relations Ability. Grades 9–16 and adults; 1944–49; IBM; Forms A ('44), B ('47); manual ('49); $2 per 25; 35¢ per specimen set, postpaid; separate answer sheets may be used; 2¢ per IBM answer sheet; 20¢ per stencil for machine scoring of answer sheets; 40¢ per stencil for hand scoring of answer sheets; Spanish edition available at same prices; postage extra; 15(20) minutes; Harry W. Case and Floyd Ruch; California Test Bureau. *

SRA Mechanical Aptitudes

REFERENCES

1. CASE, HARRY W. "Selection of Aircraft Engineering Draftsmen and Designers." *J Appl Psychol* 31:583–8 D '47. * (PA 22:2769)

For reviews by E. G. Chambers, Clifford E. Jurgensen, and James M. Porter, Jr., see 3:682.

[766]

*Test of Mechanical Comprehension. Grades 9 and over; 1940–51; IBM; 4 editions; $4 per 25 of any one edition; separate answer sheets must be used; $1.85 per 50 IBM answer sheets of any one edition; 35¢ per specimen set of any one edition; postpaid; nontimed (30) minutes; George K. Bennett, Dinah E. Fry (W–1), and William A. Owens (CC); Psychological Corporation. *
a) FORM AA. Men in grades 9 and over; 1940–47; 1 form, '40; manual ('47).
b) FORM BB. Men in grades 13 and over; 1941–51; 1 form, '41, revised manual ('51).
c) FORM CC. Men in engineering schools; 1949; 1 form.
d) FORM W–1. Women in grades 9 and over; 1942–47; 1 form ['47]; manual ['47].

REFERENCES

1–19. See 3:683.
20. ANDERSON, ROSE G. "A Comparative Study of Test Scores and Supervisors' Efficiency Ratings of Machinists." Abstract. *Am Psychol* 1:243 Jl '46. * (PA 20:3772, title only)
21. GREENE, RONALD RILEY. *Ability to Perceive and React Differentially to Configurational Changes as Related to the Piloting of Light Aircraft.* Doctor's thesis, Ohio State University (Columbus, Ohio), 1946. (*Abstracts of Dissertations....Autumn Quarter–Winter Quarter 1946–47*, 1947, pp. 65–72.) (PA 22:5177, title only)
22. COTTINGHAM, HAROLD F. *The Predictive Value of Certain Paper and Pencil Mechanical Aptitude Tests in Relation to Woodworking Achievement of Junior High School Boys.* Doctor's thesis, Indiana University (Bloomington, Ind.), 1947. (*Studies in Education....1945–1949*, 1950, pp. 5–10.) (PA 25:6405)
23. FISKE, DONALD W. "Validation of Naval Aviation Cadet Selection Tests Against Training Criteria." *J Appl Psychol* 31:601–14 D '47. * (PA 22:2770)
24. ONARHEIM, JAMES. "Scientific Selection of Sales Engineers." *Personnel* 24:24–34 Jl '47. *
25. COTTINGHAM, H. F. "Paper-and-Pencil Tests Given to Students in Woodworking." *Occupations* 27:95–9 N '48. * (PA 23:4408)
26. JURGENSEN, CLIFFORD E. "Norms for the Test of Mechanical Comprehension." *J Appl Psychol* 32:618–21 D '48. * (PA 23:3754)
27. BARNETTE, W. LESLIE, JR. *Occupational Aptitude Patterns of Counseled Veterans.* Doctor's thesis, New York University (New York, N.Y.), 1949. Pp. viii, 385. * (PA 24:362, title only)
28. McELHENY, W. T. "A Study of Two Techniques of Measuring 'Mechanical Comprehension.'" *J Appl Psychol* 32:611–7 D '48. * (PA 23:3757)
29. CARTER, LAUNOR, AND NIXON, MARY. "Ability, Perceptual, Personality, and Interest Factors Associated With Different Criteria of Leadership." *J Psychol* 27:377–88 Ap '49. * (PA 23:4183)
30. GORDON, THOMAS. "The Airline Pilot's Job." *J Appl Psychol* 33:122–31 Ap '49. * (PA 24:331)
31. RINSLAND, HENRY D. "The Prediction of Veterans' Success From Test Scores at the University of Oklahoma," Part I, pp. 59–72. In *The Sixth Yearbook of the National Council on Measurements Used in Education, 1948–1949.* Fairmont, W.Va.: the Council, Fairmont State College, 1949. Pp. v, 140 (variously numbered). Paper, mimeographed. *
32. SUPER, DONALD E. *Appraising Vocational Fitness by Means of Psychological Tests*, pp. 246–60. New York: Harper & Brothers, 1949. Pp. xxiii, 727. * (PA 24:2130)
33. VERNON, P. E. "The Structure of Practical Abilities." *Occupational Psychol* 23:81–96 Ap '49. * (PA 23:5313)
34. WHITLOCK, JOHN B., JR., AND CRANNELL, CLARKE W. "An Analysis of Certain Factors in Serious Accidents in a Large Steel Plant." *J Appl Psychol* 33:494–8 O '49. * (PA 24:3467)
35. BORG, WALTER R. "Does a Perceptual Factor Exist in Artistic Ability?" *J Ed Res* 44:47–53 S '50. * (PA 25:2921)
36. BORG, WALTER R. "Some Factors Relating to Art School Success." *J Ed Res* 43:376–84 Ja '50. * (PA 24:4811)
37. DuBOIS, PHILIP H., AND WATSON, ROBERT I. "The Selection of Patrolmen." *J Appl Psychol* 34:90–5 Ap '50. * (PA 25:2076)
38. HALLIDAY, ROBERT W., AND FLETCHER, FRANK M., JR. "The Relationship of Owens-Bennett Test Scores to First-Year

Achievement in an Engineering College." Abstract. *Am Psychol* 5:353 Jl '50. * (*PA* 25:1278, title only)

39. HALSTEAD, H. "Abilities of Male Mental Hospital Patients." *J Mental Sci* 96:726–33 Jl '50. * (*PA* 25:2598)

40. NAIR, RALPH KENNETH. *Predictive Value of Standardized Tests and Inventories in Industrial Arts Teacher Education.* Doctor's thesis, University of Missouri (Columbia, Mo.), 1950. Abstract: *Microfilm Abstracts* 10:77–8 no 3 '50. * (*PA* 25:4862, title only)

41. OWENS, WILLIAM A., JR. "A Difficult New Test of Mechanical Comprehension." *J Appl Psychol* 34:77–81 Ap '50. * (*PA* 25:1384)

42. TRAVERS, ROBERT M. W., AND WALLACE, WIMBURN L. "Inconsistency in the Predictive Value of a Battery of Tests." *J Appl Psychol* 34:237–9 Ag '50. * (*PA* 25:6480)

43. BARNETTE, W. LESLIE, JR. *Occupational Aptitude Patterns of Selected Groups of Counseled Veterans.* American Psychological Association, Psychological Monographs: General and Applied, Vol. 65, No. 5, Whole No. 322. Washington, D.C.: the Association, Inc., 1951. Pp. v, 49. Paper. * (*PA* 26:2794)

44. GILBERT, HARRY B. *An Evaluation of Certain Procedures in the Selection of Camp Counselors Based on Objective Test Data as Predictive of Practical Performance.* Doctor's thesis, New York University (New York, N.Y.), 1951. Abstract: *Microfilm Abstracts* 11:953–4 no 4 '51.

45. HALLIDAY, ROBERT W.; FLETCHER, FRANK M., JR.; AND COHEN, RITA M. "Validity of the Owens-Bennett Mechanical Comprehension Test." *J Appl Psychol* 35:321–4 O '51. * (*PA* 26:4199)

46. LANEY, ARTHUR R., JR. "Validity of Employment Tests for Gas-Appliance Service Personnel." *Personnel Psychol* 4:199–208 su '51. * (*PA* 26:1735)

47. WOLFF, W. M., AND NORTH, A. J. "Selection of Municipal Firemen." *J Appl Psychol* 35:25–9 F '51. * (*PA* 25:7124)

N. W. MORTON, *Director, Operational Research Group, Defense Research Board, Ottawa, Canada.*

Three forms of this test appeared about a decade ago. A fourth form was added in 1949 extending upward the range of difficulty for male subjects.

The test is intended to measure the ability of an individual to understand various kinds of everyday physical and mechanical relationships. Each form consists of 60 items. Each item includes a picture exhibiting one or more objects, physical situations, or mechanical relationships about which a question permitting a categorical answer is asked. The principles underlying these questions include leverage (perhaps the most frequently represented), force and motion, light, heat and sound, etc. Obviously, the examples used are ones arising out of most people's common experience of physical phenomena rather than coming necessarily from technical training. It is presumably for this reason that previous exposure to formal instruction in elementary physics appears to confer only a slight advantage (about 3 or 4 points).

Of the four forms, three represent different levels of difficulty for men, and one is for women (who score much lower than men even on the easiest form for men). All forms are unspeeded. Reliability (internal consistency) is of the order of .8. For purposes of individual assessment, this is not high but commonly considered as acceptable (reduction of the error by a third would presumably require an additional 20 or 25 minutes of testing time).

The illustrations are clear, well drawn, and well printed. For all but illiterate individuals the easier forms of the test would not appear to make any special demands on the subject by way of understanding the kind of performance expected of him.

Evidence of validity is given mainly by correlation with job, academic, or training course performance. These range from .3 to .6. Correlations with other tests are of the same order. For the women's form no validity data except correlations with other tests are given. A limited amount of evidence is available suggesting that this test ranks relatively high in correlating with criteria in comparison with other tests used. While its value will depend in specific situations upon the criterion predicted and the degree of correlation with other tests used, experience with the *Test of Mechanical Comprehension* would indicate generally that it is a useful addition to the stock of measuring devices available for vocational guidance and selection.

For reviews by Charles M. Harsh, Lloyd G. Humphreys, and George A. Satter, see 3:683.

[767]

★V.G.C. Object Visualization Indicator. High school; 1950; an adaptation of United States Employment Service's *General Aptitude Test Battery*, Part F (see 714); 1 form; preliminary manual; $1.95 per 25; separate answer sleeves must be used; 48¢ per 25 answer sleeves; 10¢ per manual; 45¢ per specimen set; postage extra; available only to Canadian schools; 10 (20) minutes; Vocational Guidance Centre. *

[768]

★V.G.C. Space Relations Ability Indicator. High school; 1950; an adaptation of United States Employment Service's *General Aptitude Test Battery*, Part II (see 714); 1 form; preliminary manual; $1.95 per 25; separate answer sleeves must be used; 48¢ per 25 answer sleeves; 10¢ per manual; 45¢ per specimen set; postage extra; available only to Canadian schools; 10 (20) minutes; Vocational Guidance Centre. *

[769]

★The Vincent Mechanical Models Test A (Industrial). Ages 14 and over; 1936–46; 1 form ['46—same as test copyrighted in 1936]; no data on reliability and validity and no description of normative population in manual; data available on request; mimeographed manual ['46]; norms ['46]; 18s. per 12; 1s. 6d. per single copy; 120s. per set of 8 models; separate answer sheets must be used; 1s. 6d. per 12 answer sheets; 1s. per manual; postage extra; 22(30) minutes; National Institute of Industrial Psychology. *

REFERENCES

1. HOLLIDAY, FRANK. "An Investigation Into the Selection of Apprentices for the Engineering Industry." *Occupational Psychol* 14:69–81 Ap '40. * (*PA* 14:3710)

2. SLATER, PATRICK. "Some Group Tests of Spatial Judgment or Practical Ability." *Occupational Psychol* 14:40–55 Ja '40. * (*PA* 14:2644)

3. SHUTTLEWORTH, CLIFFORD W. "Tests of Technical Aptitude." *Occupational Psychol* 16:175–82 O '42. *

4. HOLLIDAY, FRANK. "A Further Investigation Into the

Selection of Apprentices for the Engineering Industry." *Occupational Psychol* 15:173–84 O '41. *
　5. HOLLIDAY, FRANK. "A Survey of an Investigation Into the Selection of Apprentices for the Engineering Industry." *Occupational Psychol* 16:1–19 Ja '42. *
　6. HOLLIDAY, FRANK. "The Relation Between Psychological Test Scores and Subsequent Proficiency of Apprentices in the Engineering Industry." *Occupational Psychol* 17:168–85 O '43. * (PA 18:1835)
　7. LAMBERT, CONSTANCE M. "Symposium on Selection of Pupils for Different Types of Secondary Schools: VII, A Survey of Ability and Interest at the Stage of Transfer." *Brit J Ed Psychol* 19:67–81 Je '49. *

A. T. WELFORD, *University Lecturer in Experimental Psychology, University of Cambridge, Cambridge, England.*

This test is intended to assess mechanical aptitude. Eight "models" are used, each consisting of an arrangement of levers, pulleys and cords, or pinion wheels. The mechanism of each model is hidden behind a board except for two or more projecting arms or cords with a bob attached. The administrator shows the models one at a time to the subjects, works one of the projecting portions, and asks the candidates to observe the movements produced in the other projecting portions. The candidate has a booklet in which, for each model, there is a sheet showing eight diagrams of mechanisms some of which would produce movements similar to that of the model, and some of which would not. A "Yes" or "No" answer for each diagram has to be recorded on an answer sheet. A commendable refinement is that the candidates are told the correct answers to the first two diagrams (one "Yes" and one "No") of the first model which thus act as examples. A time limit of 2½ or 3 minutes is allowed for the answers about each model. Subjects are warned against guessing and told that marks will be deducted for wrong answers.

The working of the models by hand makes the test somewhat laborious to administer, but it would seem possible to arrange for the models to be worked by means of an electric motor.

The manual supplied with the test gives the precise wording of instructions, a scoring key, and norms. Statistical data on reliability, etc., are not included but are contained in articles in *Occupational Psychology,* and are supplied on request by the National Institute of Industrial Psychology, which strictly controls the issue of the test material.

The norms are in the form of five grades: A = best 10 per cent, B = next 20 per cent, C = middle 40 per cent, D = next 20 per cent and E = worst 10 per cent. They are given for a relatively unselected group of boys in three age ranges: 16 and over, 15, and 14. Separate norms,

which are substantially higher, are given for boys of secondary grammar school (high school) education. The norms are based on the scores of 3,373 subjects, some school pupils tested in the course of vocational guidance work, and some apprenticeship candidates tested in the course of industrial selection work. The scatter of scores indicated by the norms is satisfactorily wide, and indicates that the test can discriminate at both the top and bottom ends of the scale.

Correlations with instructors' estimates of proficiency have been found as follows: 91 trade apprentices (engineering), .52; 41 trade apprentices (engineering), .33; 45 apprentices (toolmakers), .60; 34 apprentices (toolmakers), .39; 71 engineering apprentices, .27; 30 engineering apprentices, .42. Bearing in mind that these are selected populations and that the criteria must have included qualities other than those involved in performance at the test, the correlations suggest that the test is likely to form a useful component of a battery. The split half reliability is given as .96.

Although the test is given with a time limit for each section, the time allowed has been found sufficient for all subjects to record an answer for each diagram if they are able to do so. It thus appears to avoid the difficulty with speeded tests that no distinction is made between the people who work quickly but inaccurately and those who work more slowly but more accurately. Further research is, however, needed to determine in just what ways performance at a task is affected by a time limit. It seems very possible that time limits exert important effects even when they appear fully adequate. The point is not advanced as a criticism of the test, but should be borne in mind when considering the validity of any test carried out with a time limit. Real life situations appear to impose speed pressures which are frequently less and occasionally more severe than those of speeded tests.

The test is almost if not quite unique, and of considerable interest in that it requires appreciation by subjects of relationships between *movements* of mechanical parts which the subjects may study directly only in an abstract, diagrammatic form. While clearly more than this is involved in mechanical aptitude defined in any realistic sense, it is a type of appreciation which is undoubtedly important, and would seem worthy of following up both as a matter of research and of practical testing. Valuable additional information from this and other tests

Vincent Mechanical Models Test A

of similar type which may be designed in the future could perhaps be gained by considering not only overall scores, but also item analyses to see whether, and in what ways, one type or complexity of mechanism is more difficult to understand than another.

MISCELLANEOUS

[770]

★**Employee Evaluation Series.** Adults; 1948; 6 tests; 1 form; $2.50 per 25 of any one test; $3 per specimen set; $1 per specimen set of any one test; postpaid; Joseph E. King; Industrial Psychology, Inc. *
a) PERFORMANCE: CLERICAL.
b) PERFORMANCE: MECHANICAL.
c) PERFORMANCE: SALES.
d) PERFORMANCE: TECHNICAL.
e) PERFORMANCE: ADMINISTRATIVE.
f) PERFORMANCE: FOREMAN.

REFERENCES
1. KING, JOSEPH E. "Multiple-Item Approach to Merit Rating." Abstract. *Am Psychologist* 4:278 Jl '49. * (PA 23:6482, title only)

BRENT BAXTER, *Director, Agencies Research Division, The Prudential Insurance Company of America, Newark, New Jersey.*

This series provides an overall package for evaluating most employees in many companies. It has many practical aspects and attempts to present a simple formula for supervisors in both reviewing and interpreting the performance of their employees.

The structure of the series is a list of statements for each of the six work areas for which a form is provided. There are 50 items for each type of work (60 in forms are to be published). The value of the forms to any given company is limited by the degree to which these general items apply to the job of the person being rated. The company might well prefer to add or subtract certain items or put a different emphasis on the job components than is included in the printed list. The instructions and language also will not be appropriate for all companies. Thus, a company which likes this multiple item approach to rating may choose between the labors of tailor-making its own form or the adoption of a carefully made form which may not fit its situation too well.

The author emphasizes that this rating approach minimizes the halo effect and lays stress on evaluating performance. But there is still ample opportunity for halo effect. Many items concern attitude rather than performance behavior, e.g., "Completely sold that this is the 'best place in town' to work." Responses to this kind of item are subject to the halo effect.

At present, there is no manual to go with the series to explain adequately its reliability and other evaluating data. The author reports one is currently being prepared. He submitted a manuscript of an APA (1949) paper indicating a corrected split half reliability for the clerical series of .92. Results from two raters correlated .81 (1). It correlated .73 with results from a man-to-standard rating scale. From the APA paper one may conclude that the clerical series has had extensive statistical analysis. Efforts have been made to weed out ambiguous items and items which correlate highly with the total score.

Considerable effort has been made to design a scale which will result in a normal distribution of scores. While this achieves a desirable spread of scores, there has been some overconcern with this aspect. Each rater is "expected" to achieve this normal distribution which may not fit his group at all.

The evaluation "system" is tied in with both percentiles and stanines. To have both of these scales may be confusing to many and is unnecessary. The stanine ranges are not calculated as is usually done (i.e., in equal class intervals).

The present series provides for the rater to check a statement if it is true about the employee and to leave it blank otherwise. Omissions thus may be counted "against" the employee. The author reports that a revised series will provide for a "not true at present" marking. Neither form allows the rater to mark the statement "not relevant" or "don't know." This may force unjust ratings to be made.

The author claims that by adding the favorable replies on the statements one achieves a total score "in which the whole is actually greater than the sum of its parts." This statement may mislead many readers into thinking that something special is added in some mysterious way. Apparently what is meant is that the items really represent a sample of the total number of statements that might be made about the employee and that conclusions may now be drawn about the total. In view of how the sample was drawn, it might be much better to limit interpretations to the specific statements.

SUMMARY. The series utilizes the multiple item rating approach to provide industry with a ready-made rating program. Although it is neatly arranged and has many practical features, it doesn't live up to some of its marketing claims, such as being a basis for "getting away from favoritism and influence." It is not a cure-all for personnel problems. It will not fit all companies; a tailor-made instrument is to be preferred.

[771]

★**Employee Merit Report.** Employees; 1949; also called *Comprehensive Plan for Rating Employees;* 13 ratings: quality of work, quantity of work, knowledge of work, dependability, attitude toward work, adaptability, cooperation, initiative, personality, judgment, supervision, safety, overall merit; no data on reliability and validity; no norms for part scores; no description of normative population; $6.25 per 100; 25¢ per specimen set; postpaid; Keith Van Allyn; Van Allyn Institute. *

[772]

★**[Employee Selection Forms.]** Job applicants; 1947; 4 parts; specimen set not available; cash orders postpaid; developed by Robert N. McMurry & Co.; Science Research Associates, Inc. *
a) APPLICATION FOR EMPLOYMENT. 1 form in 2 colors (pink for women and green for men); $1.10 per 25 of any one color.
b) APPLICATION FOR SALES POSITION. $1.70 per 25.
c) TELEPHONE CHECK WITH PREVIOUS EMPLOYERS. $4.25 per 100.
d) STANDARDIZED SELECTION INTERVIEW (SHORT FORM). $1.60 per 25.

[773]

★**[Executive, Industrial, and Sales Personnel Forms.]** Applicants for executive, office, industrial, or sales employment; 1949–50; a series of interviewing aids to facilitate selection of personnel; postage extra; developed by Robert N. McMurry & Co.; Dartnell Corporation. *
a) [EXECUTIVE PERSONNEL FORMS.]
  1) *Application for Executive Position.* Form EA-301 ('49); 1–99 copies, 10¢ each; 100–249, 8¢ each.
  2) *Patterned Interview Form—Executive Position.* Form EP-302 ('49); 1–99 copies, 30¢ each; 100–249, 25¢ each.
  3) *Telephone Check on Executive Applicant.* Form ET-303 ('50); 1–99 copies, 8¢ each; 100–249, 7¢ each.
  4) *Selection and Evaluation Summary.* Form No. ES-404 ('50); 1–99 copies, 6¢ each; 100–249, 5¢ each.
b) [INDUSTRIAL PERSONNEL FORMS.]
  1) *Application for Position.* Form No. OA-201 ('50); 1–99 copies, 7¢ each; 100–249, 6¢ each.
  2) *Application for Employment.* Form No. OC-200 ('50); 1–99 copies, 6¢ each; 100–249, 5¢ each.
  3) *Patterned Interview (Short Form).* Form No. OP-202 ('49); 1–99 copies, 10¢ each; 100–249, 8¢ each.
  4) *Telephone Check.* Form No. OT-203 ('49); 1–99 copies, 6¢ each; 100–249, 5¢ each.
  5) *Telephone Check With Schools.* Form No. OS-204 ('49); 1–99 copies, 6¢ each; 100–249, 5¢ each.
  6) *Selection and Evaluation Summary.* Same as for Executive Personnel Forms.
c) [SALES PERSONNEL FORMS.]
  1) *Application for Sales Position.* Form No. SA-101 ('50); 1–99 copies, 10¢ each; 100–249, 8¢ each.
  2) *Patterned Interview Form—Sales Position.* Form No. SP-102 ('50); 1–99 copies, 15¢ each; 100–249, 13¢ each.
  3) *Telephone Check on Sales Applicant.* Form No. ST-103 ('49); 1–99 copies, 7¢ each; 100–249, 6¢ each.

  4) *Selection and Evaluation Summary.* Same as for Executive Personnel Forms.

FLOYD L. RUCH, *Professor of Psychology, University of Southern California, Los Angeles, California.*

The use of the Patterned Interview as a predictive device is based upon the assumption that the best way to predict what a person will do in the future is to review carefully what he has done in the past. It is designed to cover systematically six major areas of information about the candidate: work history, education and training, family background, financial situation, domestic and social situations, and health record. It begins with the work history of the candidate, thus getting him "warmed up" so that the "interviewer can probe successfully into more personal matters."

The standard form on which the interviewer records the answers to the questions includes not only the questions to be asked of the candidate, but additional questions (printed in red) which are designed to help the interviewer interpret the answers to the questions. Other standard forms available for use in conjunction with the Patterned Interview are the application for position, the form for telephone check of former employers, the form for the telephone check of schools, and the selection and evaluation summary. All these forms, except the last, are available in special editions for the selection of executive personnel, industrial personnel, and sales personnel. The telephone checks are especially highly recommended by the authors, and techniques for obtaining accurate information from these are outlined in the manual, The Step-by-Step Selection Program.

After obtaining "complete information" by means of the Patterned Interview, the telephone check, and the application blank, the information which has been gathered must be interpreted. The manual lists eight character traits which are usually considered to be essential for any job. These are stability, industry, perseverance, loyalty, motivation, and maturity. In addition, two more traits, leadership and competitiveness, are listed as being important for some jobs. Each of these traits is explained in the manual as an aid to the interviewer in making the interpretation.

The overall rating is made on the basis of a 4-point scale. "This rating is *not* a mathematical summing up of points but, rather, a comparison of the applicant's qualifications with those required by the particular job." For successful use, the Patterned Interview makes a thorough knowledge of the requirements of each job mandatory on the part of the interviewer. The state of the labor market should not influence the rating. It is recommended that only the "1's" and "2's" be hired; but with a tight labor market, "3's" may be included.

According to the manual, the Patterned Interview is superior to ordinary interviewing procedures in that it provides (a) a systematic plan for the interviewer to follow; (b) a technique for getting facts; (c) a set of principles to use in interpreting the facts; and (d) a method of minimizing personal biases and prejudices.

The largest validation study made of the Patterned Interview had two criteria: length of service (from less than one week to over one year), and foreman's ratings. With an N of 587, the Pearson coefficient was .43 for length of service versus interview ratings. With an N of 407, the Pearson coefficient against the criterion of foreman's ratings was .68. These ratings were made without knowledge of interview results. In a study involving 108 truck drivers, where the criterion was length of service (on the job at the end of 11 weeks), a biserial coefficient of .61 was obtained. In still another study, in which the interview ratings were correlated against supervisor's ratings on 84 subjects, the Pearson coefficient was .61.

It should be pointed out that in all the studies above, the interviewers were well trained in psychology and/or interviewing. While these studies were certainly better controlled than the usual interview study, and while the Patterned Interview technique is no doubt an improvement over ordinary interviewing methods, the question still remains unanswered as to whether the magnitude of these validity coefficients results mainly from the use of the standard forms or from the ability of the interviewers. In the final analysis, the value of the procedure lies in the interviewer's ability to make a valid subjective rating of a comprehensive set of objective facts which the Patterned Interview has led him to accumulate.

[774]

*How Supervise? Candidates for supervisory training; 1943-48; Forms A ('43), B ('43), M ('48); Form M consists of items from Forms A and B "which proved most discriminating at higher management levels"; revised manual ('48); $2.25 per 25; 35¢ per specimen set; postpaid; nontimed (15-40) minutes; edited by H. H. Remmers; Quentin W. File; Psychological Corporation. *

REFERENCES

1-5. See 3:687.
6. KATZELL, RAYMOND A. "Testing a Training Program In Human Relations." Personnel Psychol 1:319-29 au '48. * (PA 23:1498)
7. JURGENSEN, CLIFFORD E. "Foreman Training Based on the Test 'How Supervise.'" Personnel J 28:123-7 S '49. * (PA 24:2112)
8. KARN, HARRY W. "Performance on the File-Remmers Test, How Supervise? Before and After a Course in Psychology." J Appl Psychol 33:534-9 D '49. * (PA 24:4294)
9. REMMERS, LOIS JUNE, AND REMMERS, H. H. "Studies in Industrial Empathy: I, Labor Leaders' Attitudes Toward Industrial Supervision and Their Estimate of Managements' Attitudes." Personnel Psychol 2:427-36 w '49. * (PA 24:4298)
10. BELMAN, H. S., AND EVANS, R. N. "Selection of Students for a Trade and Industrial Education Curriculum," pp. 9-14. In Motives and Aptitudes in Education: Four Studies. Edited by H. H. Remmers. Purdue University, Division of Educational Reference, Studies in Higher Education, No. 74. Lafayette, Ind.: the Division, December 1950. Pp. iii, 63. Paper. * (PA 26:3010)
11. BELMAN, H. S., AND EVANS, R. N. "Selection of Students for a Trade and Industrial Educational Curriculum." J Ed Psychol 42:52-8 Ja '51. * (PA 25:6486)
12. CANTER, RALPH R., JR. "A Human Relations Training Program." J Appl Psychol 35:38-45 F '51. * (PA 25:7152)
13. POND, BETTY BUCKINGHAM. Performance on File-Remmers' How to Supervise Test Before and After Supervisory Training. Master's thesis, Pennsylvania State College (State College, Pa.), 1951. (PA 26:4338, title only)

MILTON M. MANDELL, Chief, Administrative and Management Testing, U.S. Civil Service Commission, Washington, D.C.

Ever since 1945 there has been an awakened awareness of the need for better supervisory and executive selection programs. Every large organization in private industry and government pays at least lip service to the need for improved supervisory and executive selection methods, and in many cases fine programs in this area have actually been installed and are operating effectively. An increasing number of articles on this subject have appeared in the psychological journals during the past few years.

The test, How Supervise?, consists of two forms of 70 questions each and a third form, Form M, containing 100 questions. All of the items in Form M come from the first two forms. Form M is recommended for use in selecting higher level supervisors. For each statement the candidate is asked to indicate whether he agrees or disagrees or whether he considers the practice desirable or undesirable. The candidate can mark his answer as uncertain if he wishes to do so. In other words, the test is basically a true-false test.

The validity data available for this test indicate that it can make a moderate contribution to better supervisory selection. This contribution probably comes from both the verbal aspects of this test and the knowledge of supervisory practices involved in the questions. The test has no competitors in the sense of available tests that may be purchased from test publishers, although Richardson, Bellows, Henry and Company do market a test which measures the same information as this one and is an improvement over it. This test is a supervisory judgment test with multiple choice questions that cover the general field of supervisory practices. In addition, Professors John R. Kinzer and John E. Horrocks have published in preliminary form a test for supervisory selection called "Joe Greene: A Supervisor's Opinionnaire." This test, also in multiple choice form, seems, on the basis of internal evidence, to be a significant contribution to the supervisory selection field, although no validation data appear to be available in the literature for it.

It is probably inadvisable that *How Supervise?* should be the only part of a supervisory testing program. It is quite possible, indeed, that validation studies may indicate that this test does not contribute anything unique in a full battery of tests for supervisory selection.

As a relatively crude basis for screening first-level supervisors of relatively low educational level, this test might make a contribution, although before using it, one should first explore the greater validity that may be obtained from the use of supervisory judgment types of tests in multiple choice form and the use of aptitude tests in the field in which the supervision will take place. Pioneer efforts generally suffer by comparison with later improved versions and this seems to be the case here.

For reviews by D. Welty Lefever, Charles I. Mosier, and C. H. Ruedisili, see 3:687.

[775]

★**Interview Aids: Purdue Vocational Series.** Applicants for industrial employment; 1943; 4 interviewing aids; 1 form; no data on reliability and validity; no key; no norms; $1.70 per 25 of any one aid; 50¢ per specimen set; cash orders postpaid; (5–10) minutes per aid; edited by Joseph Tiffin; C. H. Lawshe, G. A. Satter (1), and Lawrence G. Lindahl (2); Science Research Associates, Inc. *
a) NUMBER 1: INTERVIEWER'S RATING SCALE.
b) NUMBER 2: CAN YOU READ A WORKING DRAWING?
c) NUMBER 3: CAN YOU READ A MICROMETER?
d) NUMBER 4: CAN YOU READ A SCALE?

WILLIAM W. WAITE, *Associate Professor of Industrial Engineering, Columbia University, New York, New York.*

INTERVIEWER'S RATING SCALE. This scale is designed to aid an employment interviewer in evaluating the qualifications of applicants for work. It provides a positive record instead of the rather vague notes of opinion frequently found in industry. The subject is rated on six personal characteristics: (*a*) appearance, (*b*) ability in self-expression, (*c*) friendliness and

sociability, (*d*) work record, (*e*) initiative, and (*f*) desire to work for the organization to which he has applied. Provision is also made for evaluating the subject's potentialities for each of two specific job titles, on the basis of his experience and training, as well as his information on the general occupational area involved. All the characteristics and the degree of qualification are graded in five-step scales. The degrees of each characteristic are defined clearly in terms that are easily intelligible, rather than in the often used "Good-Fair-Poor" scale or by means of single adjectives. The instructions for the use of the scale are satisfactory.

Altogether, this scale seems an excellent medium for improving interview records in employment offices by forcing interviewers to consider certain definite items with respect to each applicant and to evaluate these characteristics on a standard scale.

CAN YOU READ A WORKING DRAWING? This test consists of a single sheet with directions on one side and three views of a machine part on the other. In the blueprint, the part is rather elaborately dimensioned, and there are 23 places in which the interviewee must fill in missing figures by selecting the proper point on another view of the part and reading the dimension. While the authors do not provide any data on validity, this reviewer believes that a person with an elementary knowledge of mechanical drafting would find the test easy, but that anyone without such knowledge would find it quite difficult. The test should, therefore, prove to be fairly satisfactory.

One point which may cause difficulty if this test is used with people who are qualified machinists should be noted. The dimensions are so placed in several cases that subdimensions add up to an overall figure, which is also shown. There is a note on the drawing to the effect that tolerances are $\pm \frac{1}{64}$ of an inch. This means, for example, that, while subdimensions of $1\frac{1}{2}$ inches, $1\frac{3}{16}$ of an inch, and $2\frac{13}{16}$ inches add up to a nominal total of $5\frac{1}{8}$ inches, if the machinist making the part uses the allowed tolerance of $-\frac{1}{64}$ of an inch on each of the subdimensions, the actual total will be only $5\frac{5}{64}$ inches, or less than the required $5\frac{7}{64}$ inches which is allowed. In practice, the dimensioning of a part is carried out in such a way that tolerated deviations will not conflict, even if they are cumulative. A person who had had experience in machine work might notice this discrepancy.

CAN YOU READ A MICROMETER? This test consists of a single sheet with directions on one side and sketches of 10 micrometer readings on the other. Various standard types of micrometers for measuring outside and inside dimensions, thread diameters, depths, and the like are represented. The examples are well chosen and the figures are clear and easy to read. While the author does not state what is considered to be a satisfactory score, it is obvious that the individual who has no familiarity with the micrometer will have considerable difficulty in making a high score. The test should be of value to interviewers in identifying people who have the ability to use a micrometer.

CAN YOU READ A SCALE? This test is designed to indicate whether the interviewee is capable of reading dimensions from a standard machinist's scale or rule. It is printed on a single sheet, with simple directions on one side and 12 sketches on the other. The sketches show nuts, bolts, washers, screws, springs, and other machine parts as well as a caliper reading. The dimensions involved range down to 64ths of an inch, but the sketches are clear enough so that the dimensions can be read easily if the subject is familiar with this type of work.

The authors do not supply any information on the validity of the test or on what constitutes a satisfactory score. It is this reviewer's opinion, however, that any applicant who fails to read at least 10 of the dimensions accurately should be considered inadequately qualified in this particular field.

[776]

★Interview Rating Scale for Prospective Employees. Rating of applicants following an interview; 1948; 11 ratings: mental alertness, personal neatness, courtesy, emotional stability, self-evaluation, maturity of judgment, temperament, frankness, impressiveness, ability to persuade others, personal dominance; $1.50 per 25, cash orders postpaid; sample scale free to qualified test users; William J. Morgan and Antonia Morgan; Aptitude Associates. *

JAY L. OTIS, *Professor of Psychology, and Director, Research and Service Center for Business and Industry, Western Reserve University, Cleveland, Ohio.*

This single-page rating scale, with instructions on the reverse side, has been designed as a means of recording impressions of an applicant, either male or female. The rater is asked to enter identifying information at the top of the form, select from each of 11 groups of three trait names the one most descriptive of the applicant, answer questions concerning the applicant's liabilities and assets, and finally give his recommendations. The authors recommend the scale especially for applicants for contact occupations.

The trait names describing each characteristic to be rated are arranged from most to least desirable. However, there is no evidence that an effort has been made to select for the middle phrases terms which are equidistant from those at the extremes. In fact, the question could be raised as to whether some of the groups of three are on the same continuum. Examples of these are: "modest, complacent, boastful"; "mature, sensible, naive"; and "persuasive, responsive, taciturn."

This rating scale fails to meet the definition for standardization in several important respects. It is realized that there are many practical problems involved in determining the validity and reliability of such an instrument, but these concepts are not mentioned in the instructions. Normative data are not furnished, but the user is told that he can easily develop standards in his own situation. Trait names are not defined or discussed; nor is assistance given in determining the desirable characteristics for the various types of work. Rating each characteristic on a three-point rating scale gives only a gross description. For example, the interviewer is asked to describe the emotional stability of the applicant with one of three words: "imperturbable, steady, excitable."

Perhaps a greater inadequacy than the lack of standardization is an absence of adequate instructions accompanying this rating form. The interviewer is not aided in developing better interviewing techniques. He is not given any examples of the types of behavior which can be described by these trait names; nor is he taught to discriminate between the important and unimportant interview information.

The most important use of this rating scale would be in a screening situation in which an interviewer must see large numbers of people and make some sort of rough systematic rating of each person. However, even here it is difficult to justify its use. This rating scale, in its present stage of development, makes little contribution to industrial psychology.

S. RAINS WALLACE, JR., *Director of Research, Life Insurance Agency Management Association, Hartford, Connecticut.*

This one page interview summary is "designed

to serve as a systematic record of your impressions of a prospective employee, either male or female." It purports to cover 11 characteristics including "mental alertness," "courtesy," "self-evaluation," "impressiveness," "ability to persuade others," etc. This "coverage" is obtained by the interviewer's selection of one of three descriptive phases for each characteristic. For example, "mental alertness" is covered by indicating whether the applicant is "wide-awake, attentive, or apathetic."

The instructions state that numerical scoring is not necessary since "the ratings on the Scale speak for themselves." The reviewer, unable to hear the magical voices, wrote the publisher for information on the reliability and validity of this unscaled scale. The reply stated, "Since we regard the Scale as being of value primarily as a clinical instrument for the training of personnel interviewers, we have not made reliability and validity studies."

Also included in the instructions is the statement that "Standards vary greatly in different occupations and in different companies. Norms are, accordingly, not supplied, but your own standards can easily be developed." This reviewer can see no reason for anyone to bother.

This is an unusually blatant attempt to employ an undefined and high-sounding vocabulary in the exploitation of business men.

[777]

★Kahn Career Orientation Questionnaire: A Preliminary to Vocational or Educational Counseling, Student Form. Grades 9–16; 1948–51; 11 scores: emotional stability, unrealistic approach, lack of vocational information, lack of vocational connections, lack of job experience, unsatisfactory family adjustment, unsatisfactory school adjustment, physical limitations, defensiveness-inflexibility, intensification of defensiveness-inflexibility, anxiety; 1 form, '48; revised manual ('51); $2.50 per 25 sets of test, answer sheet, profile, and evaluation sheet; 25¢ per specimen set; postpaid; nontimed (20–30) minutes; Theodore C. Kahn; Guidance Tools. *

ARTHUR E. TRAXLER, *Executive Director, Educational Records Bureau, New York, New York.*

This questionnaire, designed for use in schools and guidance centers where professional counseling services are available, is intended to provide an introductory device to assist young people in gaining insight into their vocational preparation and plans. The questionnaire is not intended for use in clinical counseling. It is not suitable for employed adults.

The questionnaire makes up the first three pages of a four-page folder with the last page devoted to directions to permit examinees to score and interpret their own scores. The questionnaire is divided into two parts. Part I contains 50 questions concerning the personal qualifications of the subject and his vocational preparation and plans to which he responds by checking yes, no, or uncertain. Part II calls for the listing of the occupations in which the subject can earn a living, the occupations in which he will be able to start after he has completed his training, and the occupations in which he is interested.

The questionnaire is accompanied by three supplementary sheets. The "answer sheet" is actually a work sheet to be used by the student in scoring his paper and in analyzing his responses in terms of the 11 categories which are not identified for the student. The names of the categories appear on a profile and analysis sheet intended for use by the teacher or counselor. The author warns that an individual's profile is to be used in an exploratory way only and not as a basis for clinical counseling. The third sheet is used for recording miscellaneous evaluations made by the counselor.

A rather poorly edited, typewritten, five-page manual presents some information concerning the construction and use of the questionnaire. The questionnaire was designed at the Veterans Administration Guidance Center of the University of California Extension and was "standardized" on two groups of junior college students in California. Little statistical information is given. The reliability coefficients of the scores of two groups of junior college students, with periods of one month and three months between administrations, were found to be .93 and .83, respectively, figures as high as those usually found for this type of instrument. In one study of correlation of scores with counselor ratings, an r of .59 was obtained; in a second study on another group, r was .39. Although these correlations are not high, they are statistically significant and they fall within the range frequently found when interest questionnaire scores are compared with ratings. The manual also reports positive correlations between four subscores on the questionnaire and certain categories of the *Minnesota Multiphasic Personality Inventory.*

The scoring procedure, although somewhat involved and lacking in readily apparent reasons for some of its steps, should be interesting to students.

In the selection of the questionnaire which is

Interview Rating Scale for Prospective Employees

intended to help the student interpret his score, some useful advice concerning the obtaining of professional vocational counseling is given. However, in view of the author's careful warning that the questionnaire should not be used in clinical counseling, it is rather surprising to find the following printed statement to students whose scores fall within the 80–90 range: "You have an above average chance in securing and keeping a position in which you may be happy." A statement of this kind should probably be worded more cautiously.

It is difficult to form an overall judgment of the worth of an instrument for which so few research data are available as there are for this one. The present reviewer is inclined to question the value of the scores, and particularly of the subscores, which, as the author states, should be used with great caution. He feels that the questions themselves are, on the whole, well conceived. Without reference to the scores, the responses to the questions should be useful as a starting point in initial counseling interviews, although probably not more useful than those to the questions in several well known interest inventories.

[778]

★**Lawshe-Kephart Personnel Comparison System.** For rating any aspect of employee performance by the paired comparison technique; 1946–48; Form A ('46); no data on reliability and validity in manual (for data presented elsewhere by the authors see *1*); manual ('48); $2.50 per 50, postage extra; C. H. Lawshe, Jr., and N. C. Kephart; J. S. Mayer & Co. *

REFERENCES

1. LAWSHE, C. H.; KEPHART, N. C.; AND McCORMICK, E. J. "The Paired Comparison Technique for Rating Performance of Industrial Employees." *J Appl Psychol* 33:69–77 F '49. * (*PA* 23:3940)

REIGN H. BITTNER, *Assistant Director of Personnel Research, The Prudential Insurance Company of America, Newark, New Jersey.*

This system is an attempt to make the administration of paired comparisons feasible for industry. The paired comparison technique of rating requires that each employee be compared with every other employee in his work group with respect to some defined characteristic of job performance, that the pairs be presented in a random order, that the preferences be tallied, and that an index be calculated which indicates each employee's relative position in the rating group. Although it has generally been found that this technique yields quite reliable ratings, it has not been used extensively in industry because of the time required in preparing the materials, in

the rating process, and in summarizing the results. This has been particularly true when the number of employees to be rated is fairly large.

The *Lawshe-Kephart Personnel Comparison System* provides a means of systematizing the preparation of materials and the summarization of results. Perforated sheets are provided on which the pairs of names can be typed and then separated into slips on which a single pair is typed. Tables are given which enable the pairs to be arranged in random order with ease. Tally sheets for summarizing results and a table for converting preference frequencies to standard scores are provided. Thus, the work of preparing materials and summarizing results has been made a simple clerical task. The manual not only presents the process of preparing materials but also gives step-by-step instructions for obtaining the ratings.

One study (*1*) reported by the authors indicates that ratings obtained by the technique were highly reliable with respect to agreement among raters and agreement between successive ratings made on different days by the same raters. It should be noted that the reliability of any ratings is due as much or more to the raters as to the rating technique itself. Because of their recognition of this, the authors have given emphasis in their manual to the preparation of raters. No data are given on the relation of the ratings to other measures of performance as evidences of the validity of the ratings.

The authors conclude that the five to six hours required in their study to complete the entire rating process for 24 employees by one rater (including preparation of materials) is not excessive. The rater himself spent only about 30 minutes judging the 276 pairs involved. Whether the time required is excessive or not depends on the purpose and use of the ratings, the time available for obtaining ratings, and, more importantly, on whether ratings equally valid and reliable could be obtained by a less time-consuming technique. In the reviewer's judgment, it is a definite possibility that the last consideration is true. Nevertheless, the *Lawshe-Kephart Personnel Comparison System* is definitely a highly efficient method of paired comparison rating.

[779]

★**Mathematical and Technical Test.** Ages 11 and over; 1948; also called *M–T Test;* originally published 1947 in Dutch (4 forms available in Dutch and 1 form in Ghasa Indonesia); a measure of aptitude for mathematical, technical, and mechanical trades or training; 11 scores: completing pictures, copying models, calculations, completing the series, continuing patterns, filling up gaps, technical insight, figure series, geometrical figures, remembering drawings, total; Forms A, B; tentative norms; 25s. per 25; 3s. 6d. per set of figure cards for any one form; 3s. 6d. per set of keys for any one form; 3s. 6d. per booklet containing instructions, scoring key, and interpretation of the test results; 3s. 6d. per manual; 1s. 3d. per specimen set (does not include manual); purchase tax (British purchasers only) and postage extra; (75) minutes; J. Luning Prak; George G. Harrap & Co. Ltd.

CHARLES R. LANGMUIR, *Associate Professor of Education, Syracuse University, Syracuse, New York.*

This test is of interest in the United States principally as an example revealing the state of the art of test construction in Europe. The English Forms A and B are translated from the Dutch.

The 10 parts are short, speeded sections using both familiar and novel item types. By comparison with American tests constructed for similar purposes, three contrasts are striking: the M–T test contains no vocabulary section, the items seem much more difficult, and the scoring is excessively time-consuming, visually difficult and in five of the subtests is partly or wholly subjective. Even though the key, which is a test booklet overprinted in red, supplies scaled examples for two of these five tests, American consumers would find the difficulty and ambiguity of scoring unacceptable. On the other hand, these two subtests attempt the measurement of performance abilities usually neglected in American testing, i.e., spatial accuracy and draftsmanship in freehand reproduction of such geometrical designs as a repeating border or an insignia.

Completing Pictures consists of the familiar "put the missing leg on the chair" type of intelligence test item. A number of the 20 pictures would not be applicable in the diverse culture of a large region, and a number have multiple answers or are too obscure to survive careful editing. Copying Models is a graded series of nine difficult exercises similar to the copying items in the *MacQuarrie Test for Mechanical Ability.* Calculations consist of 25 arithmetic problems including five on English money. The 25 number series items are conventional. Both number tests are highly speeded, six minutes for 25 items. The continuing patterns items require freehand reproduction of a repeating geometric design. The five items are each scored one to five by comparison with keyed examples. The section Filling Up Gaps is a novel, multiple choice, paper formboard item, 17 independent

item groups yielding a maximum score of 32. Technical Insight consists of one 7-choice item, three 2-choice items, three matching items, and seven brief answer what or why questions, associated with 12 line drawings of mechanical situations. The 15 figure series items require freehand drawing of small geometric figures extending a systematically changing series. The 20 geometrical figures items combine space, number, and verbal abilities. Sub-areas defined by overlapping squares, circles, and triangles must be perceived, identified, isolated, or counted in accordance with verbal directions. In the remembering drawings section a card showing a geometric line drawing is exposed for five seconds. The candidate's reproduction from memory is scored one to five by comparison with a key. There are five items. The "time allowed for each drawing operation: reasonable enough to permit the majority to finish."

Forms A and B are structurally similar and appear to be equivalent. A reading of the 32-page manual suggests that issues of comparability of populations or of scores from alternate forms are not as well recognized in Holland as in the U.S. The statistics reported were derived from testing 3,400 Dutch students aged 11 to 15 with an "older edition," 700 pupils from large industrial and secondary schools, and 100 apprentices. No frequency distributions are reported. Evaluation of individual scores is complicated by increments and decrements for age and for errors. Various reliability coefficients are reported in the neighborhood of .8 computed from small groups otherwise unidentified. Correlation coefficients with a criterion identified as "combined results in trade schools" based on 20 to 30 cases range from .32 to .64. In general, the data describing the experimental results would be regarded as inadequate by American consumers.

F. W. WARBURTON, *Lecturer in Educational Psychology, University of Manchester, Manchester, England.*

A publisher's note in the manual describes this as a nonverbal technical test. The term "nonverbal" is used in an unusual way, since the test contains arithmetical problems, number series, and some questions which require a sentence to be written by the subjects. It is a series of intelligence, spatial, mechanical comprehension, memory, and arithmetic tests, and is said to measure technical aptitude on a practical com-

Mathematical and Technical Test

mon sense basis. Few, if any, of the factorists engaged on the analysis of ability have succeeded in isolating an aptitude peculiar to technical education or have ventured to describe a test as technical. Its claim to be called mathematical is almost as shaky. The mathematical knowledge required (except in the calculations subtest) is incidental, and does not extend beyond simple problems in percentages and the principles of leverage.

These are matters of nomenclature. This test has proved useful in industry in Holland for selecting apprentices, skilled workmen, designers, and foremen. It has also been used when children leave the elementary school and enter industrial, extension, and secondary schools.

There are 10 subtests and some of them must be difficult to score. For Continuing Patterns by drawing them freehand across the page, the marker is provided with five graded answers to each item. The Figure Series (patterns) and the Remembering Drawings tests also have to be drawn freehand and the marking cannot be completely objective. Technical Insight, a test of mechanical comprehension, is unorthodox in requiring written answers to some questions, such as "What do you think of this bow and arrow?" Four of the questions in the Geometrical Figures subtest (Form A) are mistranslated and would lead English speaking subjects to give the wrong answer; "largest figure" actually means "highest number." All in all, one would like to have figures for the correlation between different markers and for the reliability of individual markers.

Practice items are given before each subtest. The instructions are, on the whole, adequate. One agrees that a stop watch would be useful.

Raw scores are converted to a 12-point (nominally 10-point) scale, 3, 4, 5, 6−, 6, 6+, 7−, 7, 7½, 8, 9, 10, in order to accord with the practice of class teachers in Holland. This scale is offered tentatively and is based on the examination of 3,400 pupils.

No details are provided of the sample used for standardisation. The only validity quoted for a group of more than 30 pupils is satisfactory, .43 (90 pupils). Reliabilities seem satisfactory considering the selectivity of the samples and the length of the time interval. They are .74 and .79 after about two years. The two parallel forms of the test correlate .79 after 5 months and .84 after one year (100 cases).

It is puzzling to be told in the handbook that the range of application is more than that of the Binet series, particularly as the age groups given in the statistical tables range only from 11 to 15.

The author suggests that the test results be combined with those obtained from verbal intelligence tests, and provides a table for weighting scores in these two types of test according to different types of school. Whether these weights are based on multiple regression coefficients or are inspirational is not stated.

There is undoubtedly a real need for tests which will discriminate between children best suited for technical and for more academic forms of education, and which can be used within technical schools and in industry. A rather ill-defined factor of "practical ability" distinct from general intelligence and mechanical ability appears to be measured rather inefficiently by visuospatial tests. In Britain these tests have been found useful in selection for technical education and for trade apprenticeship amongst adolescents with little mechanical experience. On the whole, they seem to be superior to scholastic examination and perhaps to intelligence tests, in picking boys for "practical" careers, although how well they work as early as 11 years of age is more doubtful. Arithmetic tests, too, have often given good predictions of efficiency.

The author has clearly put in a great deal of work in trying out various types of tests, and the battery he has eventually chosen bears out experience in a similar field in Britain. No doubt the test has proved useful, particularly in conjunction with intelligence tests and mechanical dexterity tests.

The M–T test has the advantage of bringing under a single cover a wide range of tests suitable for selection for technical education and industry in Holland, where over 12,000 pupils have already been tested. Elsewhere, the same ground would probably be more efficiently, although somewhat more laboriously, covered by using well established tests such as (a) *Revised Minnesota Paper Formboard,* (b) Bennett's *Test of Mechanical Comprehension,* (c) a nonverbal intelligence test, and (d) a short test of arithmetical reasoning.

[780]

★**Miles Career Evaluation Inventory.** Job applicants; 1947; an interviewing aid for personnel directors, employers, and counselors; 5 scores: occupational, educational, personal, social, total; 1 form; no data on reliability and validity; available on royalty basis only; $25 per year, $100 for unlimited use; nontimed (45) minutes; Lester F. Miles; Mrs. Lester F. Miles, 423 East 23rd St., Brooklyn 26, N.Y. *

REFERENCES

1. MILES, LESTER F. *Brass Hat or Executive*, pp. 98–126. New York: Wilfred Funk, Inc., 1949. Pp. xvii, 269. *

[781]

★**Patterned Merit Review Form.** For rating industrial and office personnel or sales personnel; 1950; a form to be used by personnel or home office representatives for summarizing supervisors' evaluations of employee performance; 2 forms; 1–99 copies of any one form, 15¢ each; 100–249 of any one form, 13¢ each; $2 per manual; postage extra; (5–30) minutes; developed by Robert N. McMurry & Co.; Dartnell Corporation. *
a) PLANT AND OFFICE. Form No. MR-405.
b) SALES. Form No. MR-406.

HARRY W. KARN, *Professor of Psychology, Carnegie Institute of Technology, Pittsburgh, Pennsylvania.*

The Patterned Merit Review Plan is essentially an information-gathering tool for the use of management. Its primary purpose is to stimulate the supervisor's thinking about his subordinates so that he will arrive at sound evaluations on the basis of which to make decisions regarding promotions, transfers, layoffs, etc. In order to obtain evaluation data, an interview is conducted between supervisors and the representative of the company's personnel department. The representative who conducts the interview does not evaluate the employee; his primary function is to provide the supervisor with a patterned frame of reference so that the supervisor himself can do the evaluating.

The frame of reference used by the interviewer is the *Patterned Merit Review Form* on which the interviewer records notes as he talks with the supervisor about each of his employees. The form contains separate sections for job description, strong and weak points in terms of job performance, promotability, etc.

A complete patterned merit review on each employee consists of the following steps: (*a*) The supervisor's ranking of his employee in comparison with other employees on the same job. (*b*) A determination by the supervisor of the exact job duties of the employee. (*c*) The supervisor's evaluation of the employee in terms of strong and weak points. (*d*) The supervisor's statements regarding the extent to which he has helped the employee develop and to what extent he contemplates action toward future development of the employee. (*e*) A determination by the supervisor of his employee's promotability to specific jobs. (*f*) An overall supervisory rating of the employee as "outstanding," "above average," "below average," or "unsatisfactory."

These six steps are completed in sequence for one employee before discussing the next employee. After all employees up for merit rating are discussed, the supervisor is asked to repeat the first step, i.e., rerank each employee in comparison with others on the same job. The merit review procedure is next repeated on the same employees with a higher ranking supervisor. If the final ratings of the two supervisors differ considerably, the interviewer attempts to guide the supervisors into resolving their discrepancies.

Complete and detailed instructions for accomplishing the various steps in the merit review are contained in the *Manual on How to Use the Patterned Merit Review Form.* In this reviewer's opinion, thorough familiarity and adherence to the material contained in the manual should lead to a sound merit appraisal. The plan is simple and thorough. Although the interview is of the "controlled" type, the pattern or frame of reference provides for sufficient flexibility to handle most appraisal situations. The suggestive probing questions to interviewers, which are printed on the interview form, are carefully couched in concrete terms. Questions are avoided which require the supervisor to abstract out his employee's "ambitiousness" or "cooperativeness" or "initiative" rather than consider the person as a whole. The application of the principle of multiple rating in the merit review plan is obviously sound. The greatest danger in the whole procedure appears to be the probable tendency for a lower level supervisor to agree to adapt his evaluations and rankings to those of the higher level supervisor in those cases where the two supervisors are called together to resolve discrepancies. As an overall appraisal, the present reviewer feels that the Patterned Merit Review Plan is one of the most promising tools available to anyone concerned with the installation of a formalized merit rating program. Reliability and validity data are presumably not available since none are included in the manual. Any appraisal of the plan must therefore remain in the realm of opinion.

FLOYD L. RUCH, *Professor of Psychology, University of Southern California, Los Angeles, California.*

The Patterned Merit Review Plan is a combination of the forced distribution (ranking) and field review methods of merit rating. It is designed to utilize both quantitative and qualitative ratings. The interviewer fills in the form as the interview progresses. In addition to the general questions to be asked, the form contains questions (printed in red) which are designed to help the interviewer guide the interview so that specific incidents of behavior are brought out to substantiate the rating, inconsistent statements are resolved, etc.

There seem to be several advantages to this plan. It is easily adapted to the evaluation of employees on a particular job, and it is comprehensive. It circumvents the semantic problem existent in most rating forms by permitting the supervisor to talk in his own language. It aids in holding the "halo effect" to a minimum and helps the supervisor to face his human relations problems objectively and self-critically. A reported corrected reliability of .97 would indicate a great advantage for this plan over other evaluation methods.

The great disadvantage of the plan lies in the amount of time required for the operation and the resulting expense.

[782]

★Purdue Blueprint Reading Test: Purdue Vocational Test, No. 4. Grades 9–12 and adults; 1942; 1 form; mimeographed manual; $2.60 per 25; 50¢ per specimen set; cash orders postpaid; 30(35) minutes; manual by Joseph Tiffin; H. F. Owen and J. N. Arnold; Science Research Associates, Inc. *

[783]

★The Tear Ballot for Industry: General Opinions. Industrial employees; 1944–51; a job satisfaction questionnaire answered by tearing in order to conceal identity of employee; 1 form, '44; manual ('48); supplementary manual ('51); initial orders, $5 per 25; additional copies, $1 per 25; $3 per 100; postage extra; nontimed (3–5) minutes; Willard A. Kerr; Psychometric Affiliates. *

REFERENCES

1. GRIFFITH, JOHN W.; KERR, WILLARD A.; MAYO, THOMAS B., JR., AND TOPAL, JOHN R. "Changes in Subjective Fatigue and Readiness for Work During the Eight-Hour Shift." J Appl Psychol 34:163–6 Je '50. * (PA 25:4014)
2. KERR, WILLARD A.; KOPPELMEIER, GEORGE J.; AND SULLIVAN, JAMES J. "Absenteeism, Turnover and Morale in a Metals Fabrication Factory." Occupational Psychol 25:50–5 Ja '51. * (PA 25:7727)
3. VAN ZELST, RAYMOND. "Worker Popularity and Job Satisfaction." Personnel Psychol 4:405–12 w '51. * (PA 26:6586)
4. ZINTZ, F. RAYMOND, AND KERR, WILLARD A. "Hearing Loss and Worker Morale." J Appl Psychol 35:92–3 Ap '51. * (PA 25:8305)

BRENT BAXTER, *Director, Agencies Research Division, The Prudential Insurance Company of America, Newark, New Jersey.*

The *Tear Ballot* consists of 10 general items and one "special problem" item. Responses are made by tearing (ripping) the edge of the ballot at one of five arrowheads that form a continuum for each item. Similar tears are used to classify sex, age, office vs. nonoffice work, super-

visory or nonsupervisory work, and shift work.

The manual states that the ballot is a practical measure of (*a*) the job satisfaction of regular workers, (*b*) the general causes of discontent of terminating workers, and (*c*) the relationships between morale and personal characteristics, wage systems, and new company policies.

It is difficult to obtain adequate validation of this job satisfaction scale because individual scores are not ordinarily obtained and criteria of job satisfaction are either lacking or are quite indirect. The test author cites the use of criterion measures such as turnover ($r = .25$), absenteeism (.44), percentage of hearing loss (.42), popularity measures (.82), satisfaction with the union (.74), empathy (.44), and number of "serious worker-manager conversations (.76)."

You may deny the use of some or all of these criteria as adequate measures of job satisfaction. The scale author does not present his assumptions regarding the nature of job satisfaction, leaving us with only an empirical approach, that shows how the scale scores correlate with other variables. Or, taking an operational consideration of the scale, the total score is the "sum" of the answers to the 10 items making up the ballot. These deal with the kind of questions frequently found on such scales (i.e., worker feeling of job security, company interest in worker welfare, feeling toward supervision, working conditions, pay, opportunity to gripe, good intentions of management, good sense of management, and worker personal happiness). Several of these questions are very general, perhaps being deliberately vague in order to permit maximum amount of projection on the part of the employee. While the questions do tap the subjects generally considered to be related to job satisfaction, it is not likely that workers ordinarily think about their job in these broad terms.

Job satisfaction as measured by the *Tear Ballot* apparently is not the same in all groups. Factor analyses revealed matrices which "all differ in significant ways according to the workers studied and the psychological climates with which they work." "All but one of these analyses yielded three significant factors and the exception yielded two. In no two analyses were the patterns of loadings obtained similar on more than one factor."

The attempt to cover all areas of job satisfaction in 10 questions raises a question of reliability. If one assumes that job satisfaction is made up of a great many different feelings, can it be evaluated by 10 questions? If it is assumed that job satisfaction has 10 major components, is one question enough for each component? It cannot be assumed that it is one general factor since a factor analysis of just these 10 items revealed three factors. Split half reliability correlations range from .65 to .82 with a median of .75. No test retest data are available. Other job satisfaction scales having many more items have internal r's as high as .92.

Frequency distributions of raw scores and percentiles are given for many different classifications, e.g., age, sex, type of work, level of work, geographical location. These are called norms and suggested as "interesting comparative data which may help form a useful frame of reference in interpreting the results of future similar surveys." Unless much larger samples of workers are obtained, these "comparative data" are relatively useless. The fact that the "norm" group were carpenters may have been the least significant aspect of their employment as it affected job satisfaction.

The most novel part of the ballot is its method of completion. In the reviewer's opinion it is doubtful whether the method is superior to other more usual approaches such as checking points on a continuum with a pencil. While the author emphasizes the guarantee of anonymity which the ballot affords, it is difficult to see how a tear is more anonymous than a pencil check-mark. The use of pencils on questionnaires is not as "foreign" to many groups of workers as often assumed. Tearing the edges of papers is certainly a more unusual situation. In any case, it would seem that anonymity is more a function of the set of respondents, reflecting their past experience and the psychological freedom that their employers have established.

SUMMARY. The chief value of the tear ballot is its brevity, which makes administration easy. The brevity, however, is one of its major drawbacks since it is thus able to tap only in a very general way the areas of job satisfaction. It thus is unable to be particularly effective as a diagnostic instrument in determining strong and weak areas of satisfaction. It might be useful to measure group differences but not individual differences. More research data will be necessary before it can be recommended conclusively for anything beyond a very rough general measure of the answers to the 10 questions comprising the

Tear Ballot for Industry: General Opinions

ballot. In providing a scale for use in a wide variety of companies, it is less effective than a tailor-made scale.

[784]
*Test of Practical Judgment. Grades 9–16 and adults; 1942–50; Form AH ('50—same as test copyrighted in 1942); preliminary manual ('42); 49¢ per test and answer pad; separate answer pads must be used; $1.80 per 25 answer pads; 75¢ per specimen set; cash orders postpaid; 35(40) minutes; Alfred J. Cardall; Science Research Associates, Inc. *

REFERENCES
1. CARDALL, ALFRED J., JR. *A Test for Primary Business Interests Based on a Functional Occupational Classification.* Doctor's thesis, Harvard University (Cambridge, Mass.), 1941.
2. HOGADONE, EDWINA, AND SMITH, LEO F. "Some Evidence on the Validity of the Cardall Test of Practical Judgment." *J Appl Psychol* 31:54–6 F '47. * (PA 21:2492)
3. CARRINGTON, DOROTHY H. "A Study of the Validity of Cardall's Test of Practical Judgment." Abstract. *Am Psychol* 3:364 Ag '48. * (PA 23:746, title only)
4. CARRINGTON, DOROTHY H. "Note on the Cardall Practical Judgment Test." *J Appl Psychol* 33:29–30 F '49. * (PA 23:3745)
5. DULSKY, STANLEY G., AND KROUT, MAURICE H. "Predicting Promotion Potential on the Basis of Psychological Tests." *Personnel Psychol* 3:345–51 au '50. * (PA 25:3452)
6. HILL, A. M. *An Evaluation of the Cardall Test of Practical Judgment in Industrial Supervisory Selection.* Master's thesis, University of Toronto (Toronto, Canada), 1950. Pp. 25.

For reviews by Glen U. Cleeton and Howard R. Taylor, see 3:694.

SPECIFIC VOCATIONS

[785]
*Probst Rating System. Adults; 1928–47; 8 rating forms; $125 per scoring and rating device and any combination of 1,000 service report forms; 20–99 report forms, 10¢ each; 100–499, 2½¢ each; $1 per sample set of forms; postage extra; John B. Probst; Probst Rating System. *
a) PROBST SERVICE REPORT: FIRE DEPARTMENT FORM. Fire fighting personnel; 1932–47; Form F ('47).
b) PROBST SERVICE REPORT: GENERAL FORM. Clerical workers, supervisors, salesmen, salesclerks, and personnel not covered by the other forms; 1928–45; Form G ('45).
c) PROBST SERVICE REPORT: POLICE FORM. Police personnel, guards, and watchmen; 1932–46; Form PO ('46).
d) PROBST SERVICE REPORT: PROFESSIONAL FORM. Social service, library, medical, engineering, and other professions; 1932–46; [Form PR] ('46).
e) PROBST SERVICE REPORT: SKILLED LABOR FORM. Skilled trades, crafts, and special semiskilled workers; 1932–45; Form S ('45).
f) PROBST SERVICE REPORT: EDUCATIONAL FORM. Teachers, principals, and supervisors; 1931; [Form E].
g) PROBST SERVICE REPORT: LABOR FORM. Unskilled and semiskilled workers; 1932; Form L.
h) PROBST PERSONAL FITNESS REPORT: PERSONAL FITNESS FORM. Employees and applicants; 1936–45; a personality rating scale primarily used by interviewers; formerly called *Probst Personality Report: Personality Form;* [Form PF] ('45).

REFERENCES
1. PROBST, J. B. *Service Ratings.* A joint publication of the Bureau of Public Personnel Administration and the Civil Service Assembly of the United States and Canada. Chicago, Ill.: Bureau of Public Personnel Administration, 1931. Pp. 94. *
2. PROBST, JOHN B. *Measuring and Rating Employee Value.* New York: Ronald Press Co., 1947. Pp. xi, 166. * (PA 21:2434)

Milton M. Mandell, *Chief, Administrative and Management Testing, U.S. Civil Service Commission, Washington, D.C.*

The Probst rating system provides for a checking by one or more raters of those statements from a long list which describe the employee being rated. The statements can be illustrated by the following two examples: "Must generally be told what to do," and "Usually pleasant and cheerful." Statements checked are weighted on a 9-point scale from plus 2 to minus 3 with some statements being given zero weight. The overall rating is presented on a 10-point scale. Special rating forms have been prepared for some positions with the statements included in these special forms presumably being those most closely related to those groups; in addition, there is a general form for all other types of positions not covered by the special forms. The rater checks those statements which apply to the individual's work performance and which he has had a chance to observe. The summing up of the ratings is done generally by someone other than the rater.

It almost seems as if the inherent characteristics of personnel specialists require that at some time or other they become interested in performance ratings. The need for performance ratings seems so logical that anyone would seem to be an anarchist if he were to assert that repeated experience with formal rating systems seems to justify the generalization that their cost and the harm created by them outweigh the advantages that are obtained. The system under review here does not have any greater or lesser virtues than the systems included in the generalization.

The major trouble with most performance rating systems is that they start from the point of view of what system should be used rather than from the point of view of the administrative conditions in the organization where the rating system is to be installed. A second major weakness in the installation of most rating systems is that the installers are too ambitious in terms of the objectives desired. In trying to justify the installation of such a system, they claim many advantages which logically flow from the use of a performance rating system, but they forget that the inclusion of the additional objectives may interfere with the attainment of the primary objective. What this primary objective is will obviously vary from place to place, but it seems likely that the most general goal should be that of improving work performance and supervisor-employee relationships. To the extent that other goals are added, such as the use of the ratings for promotion and layoff purposes, it is highly likely that the achievement of the primary goal will be impeded and that the whole system will tend to flounder.

There are several prerequisites to the success of a rating system. There has to be a sincere interest on the part of management in having ratings before ratings can be successful. Second, management must be able and aggressive if it is going to give honest ratings. Third, the raters must be given training if their ratings are going to be successful. Fourth, the rating system must make sense in terms of simplicity and relevance to the jobs being rated. Finally, there should be no mystery as to how the final ratings are arrived at, because a mysterious system will be a suspect system that will inevitably affect the honesty of the ratings given.

The major advantage of the Probst system is that the task of the rater is relatively simple. The rater has a choice as to which statements to check for any particular employee, and the statements are relatively clear. The major disadvantages of the Probst system are that though it is quite obvious whether a given statement is favorable or unfavorable, the rater does not know what the final rating will be that results from his work; and the statements that he checks are generalizations rather than specific to any task that is performed. Technically, furthermore, it would seem unlikely that a 9-point scale for weighting each item could be justified in terms of validity or reliability and that a 10-point final overall scale could be justified in terms of the reliability of ratings. As a generalization, it is improbable that in any organization or occupational group more than a 5-point scale is justified or administratively necessary. Actually, it is highly improbable that, in order to achieve the major objective of improvement of work performance, any overall evaluation is needed. It is probably psychologically desirable not to provide for an overall evaluation.

The two most recent developments in the field of performance ratings are the Army's work on the development of the forced-choice method originally devised for the rating of officers and the critical incidents technique. The major advantage of the forced-choice method is that in one sense the raters are forced to be honest because the choices are presumably phrased in such a manner that the clues for determining positively weighted items are at a minimum and the raters do not know the scoring key. To that extent, if this is an important long-range advantage, the forced-choice method is better than the relatively unsubtle method of the Probst rating system. However, the mysterious quality of the forced-choice method constitutes a disadvantage as well, and it has been necessary in some cases to add a more customary graphic rating. The critical incidents technique has the major advantage, as compared with the Probst system, of having the statements which are to be checked based on concrete work tasks. To that extent this method is better than the general statements included in the Probst rating system. However, neither method can overcome such usual difficulties of rating systems as the lack of competence of the raters, the differences in standards used by different raters, the confusion of objectives, and the lack of desire on the part of some raters to rate honestly.

Psychometrists have learned that the obtaining of criteria for validation studies is at least as important as the preparation of predictors. It is time that devisors of rating systems learn that the administrative situation connected with the use of a rating system is as important as, if not much more important than, the system itself. In a brilliant research study, Stockford and Bissell have demonstrated the validity of this point of view.[1] Reign Bittner, in his outstanding summary of the problems of merit rating, has given in step-by-step form the essential parts of a merit-rating program.[2]

Many examples can be given of the impediment to valid ratings that results from a mixture of objectives. One of these, the inclusion of statements of personality characteristics as well as statements relating to job performance, is present in the Probst system. Approximately 20 per cent of the statements are descriptions of personality characteristics. If the primary objective is work improvement, and if one recognizes that the same personality characteristics may lead to varying levels of work performance, what is the value of the inclusion of statements on personality characteristics unrelated to specific job tasks?

If rating systems are to be continued, and it is not certain that they should be in a formal sense, then efforts will have to be made to create more propitious administrative conditions for them, to train raters, and to get their participation in the preparation of rating systems rather than emphasizing the statistical virtues or the objectivity of any particular rating method.

DALE YODER, *Director of the Industrial Relations Center, University of Minnesota, Minneapolis, Minnesota.*

These rating scales have been extensively used in the public service, and several forms are also used by private industrial and commercial organizations. Wider application in public service personnel administration is explained in part by the specialized design of several forms (police, fire department, educational, and professional) and in part by the fact that Probst has long been a public official (municipal civil service director). Many of the experiments designed to appraise and improve various forms have involved public employees in federal, state, and local agencies.

Probst's scales (except the Personal Fitness Form) consist of approximately 110 items plus provision for supplementary comments and a report on absenteeism. In the General Form, 38 of these items refer to special knowledge and skill, 22 items to accuracy, reliability, and dependability, 25 items to moods, appearance, emotional traits, and physical characteristics, and 25 items to industry and output. Probst (2) has reported that individual raters check from 20 to 25 items on an average. A distinctive feature of the Probst scales is their provision for from one to three raters to indicate their choices of items on the same rating form. The first rating is generally made by the employee's immediate supervisor. Using the same checked rating form, one or two additional supervisors may then rate the employee.

Scales may be scored by means of special stencils which facilitate tabulation of checked items. Scores are calculated as the sum of plus and minus values attached to the items. Balancing of positive and negative values is aided by an ingenious arrangement that designates plus values in black and minus values in red and records their cumulative totals on an attached "slide-rule." Calculations provide numerical scores which are usually translated into letter grades according to the distribution indicated on the "slide-rule."

Items were selected by a series of appraisals in which "experts" chose those expressions they

1 Stockford, Lee, and Bissell, H. W. "Factors Involved in Establishing a Merit-Rating Scale." *Personnel* 26:94–116 S '49. (*PA* 24:1501)
2 Bittner, Reign. "Developing an Employee Merit-Rating Procedure." *Personnel* 25:275–91 Ja '49. (*PA* 24:334) This article also describes the forced-choice method.

regarded as most effectively describing the traits generally included in rating scales. No standard definitions of qualities to be rated are included. Rather, items are expected—by their judicious use of everyday language—to indicate what qualities and standards are implied. The formula for scoring and for weighting items was developed experimentally. The final score measures the spread between total numbers of favorable items and the net score. Equivalent letter grades were established in early experiments. Experience indicates that distributions of scores are approximately normal, although no formal normalizing process has been applied.

Probst (2) has reported numerous studies indicating the reliability of ratings thus provided. Few independent studies of the system are reported. Tests of validity face the usual difficulty of establishing a satisfactory criterion. Probst dismisses output or production records for this purpose with the observation that these indicators are not sufficiently inclusive. Hence dependence is placed on comparisons of Probst ratings with informal designations by department heads or immediate supervisors. Highly significant correlations in such comparisons are reported by Probst.

For excerpts from related reviews, see 786.

[786]

[*Re* Probst Rating System.] Probst, John B. **Measuring and Rating Employee Value.** New York: Ronald Press Co., 1947. Pp. xi, 166. $5.00. * (*PA* 21:2434)

Personnel Psychol 1:111–7 sp '48. Dorothy C. Adkins. This book is really about "measuring and rating employee value" by a particular system of checking employee characteristics on one of several available check-list forms and summarizing these evaluations by means of a scoring formula. The reader who expects any orderly and thorough treatment of the basic problems of evaluating job performance will be disappointed. In fact, this reviewer emerged from two rather labored readings with only an unsatisfactory understanding of how the Probst system was developed and of the basis for some of the claims made for it. There are three parts to the book, covering twelve rather brief chapters and nine appendices. The first part, occupying 27 pages, is on "Employee Rating Plans in General." This includes a brief statement on the purposes served by service ratings and presents a somewhat over-simplified account of the dis-

advantages of various well-known methods. The reader is brought up short early in the book by the discussion of the unreliability of personal judgment ratings, under the general heading "A Critical Analysis of Rating Plans." There he finds cited a "case study" of 78 public health nurses who were rated by two supervisors. It is then stated that two nurses ranked sixth and forty-second by one supervisor were rated second and forty-fourth, respectively, by the other. One may wonder in vain how the other 76 rankings compared. Further reading brings a citation of three raters, all of whom apparently agreed that five of a group of 48 clerks, apparently not engaged in supervisory work, were of supervisory caliber. The author states that the rating officers had considerable difficulty in agreeing on the relative merits of these five. Why should this be amazing or a cause for concern? In fact, it seems surprising enough that there was agreement that all five were of supervisory caliber. This reviewer was plagued by the reading difficulty of the book which abounds in rather loose statements. For example: "They [over-all judgment ratings] also permit giving greater emphasis to the strictly personal qualifications bearing on the employee's total worth to the employer." Greater than any other rating plan? Can not the weighting of the components in other plans be adjusted to provide just as great weight? Is it not true, rather, that over-all judgments involve unknown and variable weighting of particular qualifications, including personal? At the end of the first part of the book are given several criteria against which service rating systems may be tested. Many would question the inclusion of substantial adherence to a normal distribution if, as seems probable, there is a selection factor in at least some employee groups. Another requirement that seems to this reviewer highly questionable is that the rating officer need not measure an employee as to his *relative* excellence. Are we not deluding ourselves if we believe a rating officer is not considering how other persons stand when he checks, for example, that a particular employee is "exceptionally polite and courteous"? What is the standard for exceptional behavior? Another requirement is "that the rating officer be virtually forced to report honestly, or be shown by 'internal evidence' in his own report markings that he has not done so." Elsewhere, incidentally, it is implied that the Probst system meets this requirement, and yet again it is specifically recognized that *no* rating system can force raters to be honest, although the majority of them are. Another criterion is that the rating officer be required to mark only those traits and qualities which he knows from his own knowledge will properly describe the employee. The resultant "flexibility in reporting" is later argued as an advantage of the Probst system. It is stated that, since each reporting officer checks only the items he knows fit the employee, no two reporting officers are likely to check the same items for the same person but that "yet their reports generally produce identically the same rating." A case is cited where five rating officers checked, respectively, 10, 12, 16, 21, and 27 items, yet each set of items produced precisely the same letter rating! If this finding were typical, it would forcibly raise the questions of why more than one rating officer is needed and whether or not the form could be shortened considerably. If sub-sets of items are highly correlated, their number can be reduced, although some rewording doubtless would be required. If they are not, the practice of basing different employees' ratings on different sets of items is open to serious question. It may also be noted that one of the gains to be had from requiring a supervisor to mark *all* items pertinent to a job is that he is thus forced to observe characteristics he otherwise might have ignored. The title of Part II, "An Improved Rating System," refers to the Probst system. A sample of one of the report forms is reproduced, and a so-called "scoring-rating device" is pictured. Under the heading "Selection of the Items for the Report Form," one expects to find the methods used to select the items, but he is confronted with only such statements as that "every item was carefully selected, studied, analyzed, and then experimented with in various ways." One then may remember that there is an appendix on "Item Selection." Turning to it, he finds a description of several "experiments" that had special reference to why the item "has initiative" was not included in the report forms. The supposition seems to be that everyone should respond with a pretty exact dictionary definition in defining "initiative." In one "experiment," it was found "that only 10 of the 17 had a good understanding of the true definition of initiative. The other seven were wrong." It seems to this reviewer that social sciences now have available, in the form of psychophysical scaling methods, more convincing tools to demonstrate whether a particular trait should be included and what

words should be used to describe variant degrees of it. Persons trained in the measurement field may also be dissatisfied with the description of the "scoring-rating device." This reviewer was puzzled to find that "the values and weights assigned to the individual items are relatively unimportant as compared with the scoring-rating process that must bring to a focus all the checked items on an employee's service report." But then a footnote was seen, indicating that "the formula for this evaluating process is explained in detail [in the Appendix] for the benefit of those who desire to learn more about the technical side of this work." After two or three hours with a six-page appendix on "Origin and Development of the Scoring Stencils and Formula Scales in the Probst Rating System," the reviewer was more confused than ever. At first it seemed that the author meant that, with a fairly large number of items, differential weighting had turned out to be unimportant. Actually, however, weights ranging over 6 points, from -3 to $+2$, with additional intermediate values of $-2\frac{1}{2}$, $-1\frac{1}{2}$, and $-\frac{1}{2}$, were assigned. Moreover, "the idea of a formula" and "experimenting with the spread" only added to the nonplus.[1] Nor did this reviewer find convincing the author's justification of the apparently higgeldy-piggeldy arrangement of items on the check-sheets. Turning to the statistical analysis of ratings, we find a large number of frequency distributions, which effectively demonstrate that the central tendency of ratings assigned in accordance with the scoring system is the one designated as "C." The writer seems to find in this fact corroboration of the value of the system, and comes to attach absolute rather than relative significance to particular letter designations for intervals of scores. If even a truly rectilinear distribution is normalized, however, the middle category can be called "C," and the mean score will be "C." If orders of rank used as a criterion are "normalized" by assigning letter designations of A, B, C, D, and E in a fashion such that the frequencies for each category approximate those of the normal curve, then any scoring scheme for ratings that is adjusted empirically to make the ratings cor-

[1] After trial of various multiplying factors, the final scoring formula came out to be 5 times the algebraic sum of the credits or weights for all items checked less 3 times the number of favorable items checked. This would appear to indicate that the original weights for the favorable items were relatively too low or that there were too few of them to yield optimal scoring without a corrective factor. Probst states that the multiplying factors should be 4 and 2 (instead of 5 and 3) when report sheets are checked by only one or two supervisors. This change in the formula increases still more the relative weight of the favorable items. The reviewer has been unable to rationalize this change in the scoring formula.

Probst Rating System

respond as closely as possible to the criterion categories will tend to yield a normal distribution of ratings. If the ratings and the criterion correlated fairly highly, no other result would be possible. Incidentally, however, although curves that look like normal curves are superimposed on a succession of bar graphs depicting frequency distributions, these are not the "best-fitting" normal curves. And in no case is any statistical check of normality of distribution presented. In the one case the reviewer tested, the fit of a normal curve to the distribution was clearly unacceptable. In discussing the disadvantages of various types of ratings, the writer disparages over-all judgments as highly unreliable and seriously lacking in validity. But in seeking a criterion against which to evaluate his own system, he accepts the average or consensus of such judgments made by those who best know the individuals rated. An average of two over-all judgments was used as a criterion in some instances, and the judgments often took the form of simple rankings from best to poorest. Now since the Probst system calls for separate recording by three supervisors (who presumably "best know" the individuals rated) on a form containing about 100 items and then a separate scoring process, one may question why the more easily obtainable criterion ratings should not serve as the measure of employee value. Under "Testing a Rating System," the description of the Cleveland Civil Service Commission's experiment as providing evidence of validity raises question regarding the objectivity of the methods for establishing this characteristic of the ratings. Those yielded by the Probst system were *re-submitted* to a conference of the supervisors, who reviewed the ratings and then assigned second ratings. The correlation of .92 (presumably a Pearson product-moment coefficient) between the Probst ratings and those later assigned by the conference of supervisors clearly does not show the relation between the instrument whose validity was in question and an *independent* criterion. The foregoing citation does not represent an isolated instance. It is typical of the type of finding set forth as evidence of validity. Admittedly a crucial experiment in this area is exceedingly difficult to attain. This fact does not, however, obviate need for caution in interpreting results of experiments that by their very nature can not be decisive. Part III, "The System in Practice," covers four chapters, on "Special Experimental Tests of Rating Methods," "Filling Supervisory and Key Positions," "Measuring Personal Fitness," and "Unfinished Business." The first of these cites a study comparing ranks based on production records and Probst ranks. With a rank-difference correlation coefficient in the neighborhood of .50, Probst's conclusion is that "one's faith in production records alone as an effective measure of service value is severely shaken." Granted that there are factors other than production that affect the value of an employee, however, perhaps we should not dismiss so cavalierly the possibility of measuring objectively those factors that can be so appraised. Should we not reserve more subjective judgments for those factors for which no objective measures are available? The chapters on "Filling Supervisory and Key Positions" and on "Measuring Personal Fitness" present a justification for the need of a special form to rate personal characteristics related to successful dealing with other persons, and several studies of the relation between rankings based on the Probst Personal Fitness Report and on rankings made without the form. As before, the question of independence of the "test" and the criterion, and the question of why the simpler criterion procedure does not suffice, at once arise. The last chapter, which presents fragmentary reports on studies from which the author does not feel justified in drawing definite conclusions, is followed by several appendices, some of which have been referred to above. This review should not be closed without directing attention to the fact that it should not be regarded as a critique of the Probst system. The application of the check-list idea to appraisal of employee value, as well as other features of the plan, doubtless represented definite progress at the time of the inception of the system. It can scarcely be doubted, however, that further improvements would result from application of advancements in the field of measurement— and, in particular, of the psychophysical scaling techniques developed over the last 20 years.

Pub Personnel R 8:171–2 Jl '47. Charles A. Meyer. Persons interested in the Probst service rating system and the scoring technique involved will find this text interesting. Avowedly written "to meet the needs of those who are in search of thoroughly organized and time-tested methods for correctly rating the principal capabilities and work performances of their individual employees," most of the book is devoted to the author's own service report forms. * Most of the criteria listed as goals of development of a "good" system are those commonly accepted. Some would take issue, however, with the theory that service rating scores for a select group should adhere to a normal distribution. Perhaps more disagreement would be manifested with the recommendation that the rating officer be permitted to select the traits to be checked. On this the author argues that the officer might not be sufficiently familiar with the service value of an employee to check all traits listed. Others have argued that the requirement that all traits be checked compels the officer to acquire the necessary familiarity with the employee's service. * [The] chapter headed "Development of a More Effective Rating System" . . . and subsequent chapters do not, as one might infer, deal with ways and means, but narrows down to a discussion of the Probst system. A chapter on statistical analyses of ratings, for example, consists largely of distributions of scores attained in rating various occupational groups, although some of the elementary statistical measures are defined and illustrated. * Although both text and appendices emphasize that words carry different meanings to different reporting officers, no direct explanation substantiating the use of single words or phrases is developed, except the pragmatic one that the report form as constructed works. In fact, the word "lazy" (the first item on the report) is indicated as a shock word which, as such, apparently conveys the same meaning to all reporting supervisors and accordingly leads them to consider carefully all subsequent items. Basic problems of semantics and control in terms of trait definitions and training of reporting supervisors are barely covered. In one place the statement is made that "overall judgment, unaided, is highly unreliable and seriously lacking in validity." Later on, the description of the procedures of validation includes overall ratings as the principal criterion. The author concludes that successive ratings of the same group of employees will reveal a tendency toward higher ratings because supervisors become accustomed to a higher standard of performance and thus visualize a higher type of worker as their "average" employee. More cynical observers of rating systems could attribute the phenomenon to a less ideal cause, such as lack of training of the supervisors, or perhaps lack of courage. Scattered throughout the book are conclusions borne of experience that are of general application and worth noting, but they

must be sought by the reader among the plethora of statements on the Probst system. Enough credit may never be given the author for his contribution in the initiation and development of the check-list type of rating system. Observation of the reviewer has led him to the conclusion that the check-list approach offers more than any of the other types. However, in a text entitled as this one is, more precise statistical substantiation and more thorough documentation with fewer personal inferences would reflect more credit to the rating system and add materially to the stature of this book.

ACCOUNTING

[787]

★American Institute of Accountants Testing Programs. Grades 13–16 and employees and applicants for employment in the field of accounting; 1946–51; a project to facilitate the placement of seniors and college graduates and to aid in the guidance and appraisal of undergraduates majoring in accounting; 3 tests administered in 2 programs; IBM; prepared by the Committee on Selection of Personnel, American Institute of Accountants; Ben D. Wood, Director; Arthur E. Traxler, Assistant Director; programs administered by Educational Records Bureau. *

a) COLLEGE ACCOUNTING TESTING PROGRAM. Grades 13–16; 1946–51; tests available three times annually (fall, midyear, and spring) and are rented to participating institutions; rental fee includes answer sheets, electrograph pencils, practice tests, and scoring and reporting services; individual score reports available to seniors at $2.50 per any number up to 12.

1) *Orientation Test*. Grades 13–16; 1946–51; an intelligence test weighted toward the field of business; 3 scores: verbal, quantitative, total; Forms A ('46), B ('46), C ('49); 35¢ per student; 50(70) minutes.

2) *Achievement Test: Level I*. Grades 13–15; 1946–51; Forms A ('47), B ('47), C ('51); 35¢ per student; 120(140) minutes.

3) *Achievement Test: Level II*. Grade 16; 1946–51; Forms A ('47), B ('49), C ('49), D ('50); 35¢ per student; Forms A, B: 240(280) minutes; Forms C, D: 120(140) minutes.

4) *Vocational Interest Blank for Men, Revised*. Grades 13–16; 1927–51; same edition as published by Stanford University Press; blank scored for 27 scales and plotted on an accountants profile standardized specifically for use in this program; 1–24 students, $1.70 each; 25–49, $1.50 each; 50 or more, $1.25 each; tests may be purchased at 10¢ per copy and scored locally; nontimed (40) minutes; Edward K. Strong, Jr.

b) PROFESSIONAL ACCOUNTING TESTING PROGRAM. Employees and applicants for employment in the field of accounting; 1947–51; tests available to accounting employers at any time; tests also administered at regional testing centers established by the State Societies either on dates stated by regional center or by special arrangement; details may be obtained from Educational Records Bureau; $12 per examinee for entire battery and score report.

1) *Orientation Test*. Same as *a*1 above; $2.50 per examinee if test is scored locally; $5 per examinee if test is scored by project office.

2) *Achievement Test: Level II*. Same as *a*3 above;

$2.50 per examinee if test is scored locally; $5 per examinee if test is scored by project office.

3) *Vocational Interest Blank for Men, Revised.* Same as a4 above; $2 per examinee if test is scored by project office.

REFERENCES

1. TRAXLER, ARTHUR E. "Project in the Selection of Personnel for Public Accounting," pp. 51–64. (*PA* 22:3235) In *National Projects in Educational Measurement: A Report of the 1946 Invitational Conference on Testing Problems, New York City, November 2, 1946, Herschel T. Manuel, Chairman.* Edited by K. W. Vaughn. Sponsored by the Committee on Measurement and Guidance. American Council on Education Studies, Vol. 11; Series 1, Reports of Committees and Conferences, No. 28. Washington, D.C.: the Council, August 1947. Pp. vii, 80. Paper. *
2. AMERICAN INSTITUTE OF ACCOUNTANTS, COMMITTEE ON SELECTION OF PERSONNEL. "A New Yardstick for Accounting Skills." *J Accountancy* 87:451–7 D '48. *
3. BUDD, THOMAS A. "The Selection and Educational Training of Cost Accountants." *Accounting Res* 3:183–92 Ap '48. *
4. TRAXLER, ARTHUR E. "Objective Measurement in the Accounting Field: A Second Report." *Collegiate News & Views* 2:4–7 O '48. * (*PA* 23:1001)
5. WOOD, BEN D.; TRAXLER, ARTHUR E.; AND NISSLEY, WARREN W. "College Accounting Testing Program." *Accounting R* 23:63–83 Ja '48. *
6. CAFFYN, HAROLD R. "Practical Experiences With Scientific Selection of Accounting Personnel." *J Accountancy* 88:320–5 O '49. *
7. JACOBS, ROBERT. "Measurement and Guidance in the Field of Public Accounting, Part 2," pp. 28–44. In *The Sixth Yearbook of the National Council on Measurements Used in Education, 1948–1949.* Fairmont, W.Va.: the Council, Fairmont State College, 1949. Pp. v, 140 (variously numbered). Paper, mimeographed. *
8. SCHMIDT, LEO A. "A Secondary Use for the Uniform Achievement Tests." *Accounting R* 24:88–9 Ja '49. *
9. STRONG, EDWARD K., JR. "Vocational Interests of Accountants." *J Appl Psychol* 33:474–81 O '49. * (*PA* 24:3432)
10. CAFFYN, HAROLD R., AND TRAXLER, ARTHUR E. "American Experience in Personnel Testing for Accounting Work." *Accounting Res* 1:373–84 Jl '50. *
11. JACOBS, ROBERT. "Measurement and Guidance in the Field of Public Accounting." *Accounting R* 25:27–34 Ja '50. *
12. WARD, LEWIS B., AND HASSLER, RUSSELL H. "A Critical Evaluation of the Institute Personnel and Selection Testing Program." *J Accountancy* 90:113–20 Ag '50. *
13. ANKERS, RAYMOND G. "Institute's Vocational Test Assist in Hiring and Promoting Staff Workers." *J Accountancy* 91:86–91 Ja '51. *
14. TRAXLER, ARTHUR E., "Objective Testing in the Field of Accounting." *Ed & Psychol Meas* 11:427–39 au '51. *
15. TRAXLER, ARTHUR E., AND JACOBS, ROBERT. "Validation of Professional Aptitude Batteries: Tests for Accounting," pp. 13–29. (*PA* 26:601) In *Proceedings of the 1950 Invitational Conference on Testing Problems, October 28, 1950.* Princeton, N.J.: Educational Testing Service, 1951. Pp. 117. Paper. *

DENTISTRY

[788]

★**Dental Aptitude Testing Program.** Dental school applicants; 1946–51; tests administered three times annually (May, October, March) at centers established by American Dental Association; application form and bulletin of information may be obtained from publisher; examination fee, $10; fee includes scoring service and reporting of scores to any 5 designated dental schools; scores not reported to examinees; $1 per additional report; 308(400) minutes in 3 sessions; program administered by Council on Dental Education, American Dental Association.

a) CARVING DEXTERITY TEST. 90(105) minutes; prepared by the Committee on Aptitude Testing (Bert L. Hooper, Chairman).

b) AMERICAN COUNCIL ON EDUCATION PSYCHOLOGICAL EXAMINATION FOR COLLEGE FRESHMEN. See 277; 3 scores: quantitative, linguistic, total; 38(65) minutes.

c) SURVEY OF THE NATURAL SCIENCES. 6 scores: biology, chemistry, physics, factual, application, total; 75 (80) minutes.

d) SURVEY OF OBJECT VISUALIZATION. See 3:681; 25 (35) minutes.

e) INTERPRETATION OF READING MATERIALS IN THE NATURAL SCIENCES: TESTS OF GENERAL EDUCATIONAL DEVELOPMENT: COLLEGE LEVEL, TEST 3. See 3:526; 80 (85) minutes.

REFERENCES

1. PETERSON, SHAILER. "The Dental Aptitude Testing Program Will Become Nation-Wide for the 1951 Entrants." *Col & Univ* 26:112–4 O '50. *
2. PETERSON, SHAILER. "The Dental Aptitude Testing Program Will Become Nation-Wide for the 1951 Entrants." *Sci Ed* 35:119–21 Mr '51. *

DRIVERS

[789]

★**[Driver Selection and Training Forms.]** Truck drivers; 1943–50; a part of the White Motor Co.'s *Continuing Control System of Truck Management;* individual in part; 2 parts; manual out of print; postage extra; developed for White Motor Co.; Dartnell Corporation. *

a) [DRIVER SELECTION.] 1946–50; developed by Robert N. McMurry & Co. (except for *Identical Forms*).

1) *Employment Application.* 1946; Forms No. 111 (city delivery drivers), No. 211 (over-the-road drivers), No. 311 (long distance drivers); 1–99 copies of any one form, 7¢ each; 100–249, 6¢ each.

2) *Telephone Check.* 1946–50; Form No. OT-203 ('50); 1–99 copies, 6¢ each; 100–249, 5¢ each.

3) *Patterned Interview (Short Form).* 1946–49; Form No. OP-202 ('49); 1–99 copies, 10¢ each; 100–249, 8¢ each.

4) *Serviceman Placement Interview.* A supplementary interview for servicemen; 1946; *discontinued:* Form No. 14.

5) *Identical Forms.* 1947; use is optional; also called *Visual Speed and Accuracy Test;* Form No. 15 ['47]; no data on reliability and validity; no manual; no norms; $1.35 per 25, cash orders postpaid; specimen set free; 4½(10) minutes; L. L. Thurstone; must be purchased directly from Science Research Associates, Inc., the publisher.

6) *Physical Examination Record (Drivers).* 1946; Form No. 19; 1–99 copies, 5¢ each; 100–249, 4¢ each.

b) [DRIVER TRAINING.] 1943–46.

1) *Traffic and Driver Knowledge.* 1946; Form No. 16; no data on reliability and validity; no manual; no description of normative population; 1–99 copies, 6¢ each; 100–249, 5¢ each; 6¢ per key—Form No. 17; Amos E. Neyhart and Helen L. Neyhart; also distributed by the Institute of Public Safety, Pennsylvania State College.

2) *Road Test—In Traffic: For Selecting and Training Truck Drivers.* 1943–46; 3 scores: specific driving skills, general driving habits and attitudes, total; Form No. 18 ('46); no norms for part scores; no description of normative population; manual ('45); 1–99 copies, 5¢ each; 100–249, 4¢ each; tumbling cylinder essential for administration; (30–60) minutes; Amos E. Neyhart; also distributed by American Automobile Association and Institute of Public Safety, Pennsylvania State College.

S. RAINS WALLACE, JR., *Director of Research, Life Insurance Agency Management Association, Hartford, Connecticut.*

For use in their "Continuing Control System of Truck Management," the White Motor Company asked Robert N. McMurry to develop a selection battery and procedure for truck drivers and Amos E. Neyhart to prepare tests of driving knowledge and skill. The result is a remarkable, and generally sound, program for selection and diagnosis in training.

The first screen in the selection process is a personal history blank called the Selective Application Form. The form is differently weighted for city delivery drivers, over-the-road drivers, and long distance drivers.

The form for long distance drivers includes ten significant items and is scored for three age groups in order to equate for the relation of age to the criterion—survival in the job. Validity data for 1,016 of these drivers are presented in tabular form, showing the proportion of men at eight score groups who survived for less than six months, for six months to two years, and for two years and over. No correlation coefficient is given, nor can one be obtained from the data. This will disturb some readers. It does not disturb the reviewer who believes that success tables which may be readily understood by management are usually superior to correlation coefficients, especially when the latter are computed in violation of the assumptions underlying them. In brief, 49 per cent of the applicants in the highest score category survived for two years or more compared to 6 per cent of those in the lowest. There is a regular decline in survival as the score decreases. This is very acceptable validity.

It is unfortunate that similar validity data are not presented for the other two driver types. Since the interpretation given for the score for long distance drivers in terms of norms and recommended cutoffs is much fuller than for the other two, one is led to suspect either that work has not progressed as far with them or that the validities attained are considerably lower. The suspicion is fortified (but not completely justified) by the fact that the forms for neither city delivery drivers nor over-the-road drivers are corrected for age or accompanied by norms.

The second step is a one-page blank (Telephone Check) to be used during a telephone interview with a previous employer. This is of the standard type and merits neither favorable nor unfavorable comment.

The third step is a two-page form called the Planned Interview, supplemented by a special form for the serviceman. Like all such documents, it is defended on logical rather than empirical grounds. It has the usual defect that it is based upon some common-sense stereotypes about what is good background for a position and what is bad. Since the interview is always

with us, we seem forced to prepare such documents on the assumption that an organized job of getting information and weighing it must be superior to a disorganized one. One wishes that the authors had not felt it necessary to go beyond this and state: "Interviewers quickly learn to recognize those patterns of personality adjustment traits which are most likely to lead to success in driving a truck. They learn quickly, also, to spot those patterns which mean 'danger.'" This is pious hope and nothing more and the authors know it. It is beneath the dignity of their basic approach.

However, all credit is their due for making a valiant, if ineffectual, attempt to validate their interview. They present data on 108 men, each one interviewed *after* the company had decided to hire him. Of the eight men who were scored "outstanding," 75 per cent were still on the job after an indeterminate time (minimum of eleven weeks), while 38 per cent of the 39 men rated "good," 26 per cent of the 46 men rated "questionable," and 13 per cent of the 15 men rated "poor" satisfied the criterion. Unfortunately, the failure to specify who did the interviewing makes the study meaningless. This problem of validating an intrinsically artistic device used by an unspecified but heterogeneous group is one which nobody has solved and few have dared to attack. The Planned Interview "looks" adequate to the reviewer. This, of course, means nothing.

These three steps constitute the basic selection program. For those companies which can devote additional time to processing driver applicants, four supplementary aids are offered: a test of perceptual speed and accuracy, a traffic and driver knowledge test, a road test, and a physical examination form. The first of these, Thurstone's *Identical Forms Test,* has shown some promise of adding substantially to the validity of the selection procedure. Further study of its contribution is planned. In the interim, the use of a very low cutoff score is recommended.

The Traffic and Driving Knowledge Test is composed of 57 multiple choice items mainly directed at traffic laws, efficient and safe driving practices, and engine maintenance. Examination of the test suggests the inclusion of considerable verbal component. Furthermore, the rationale underlying some of the items is quite obscure. It is easy to understand why an item on the best method for starting an empty truck on ice or for conserving gas while driving is relevant to the test purpose. But an item like "Which of these things should you think about to keep your attention on driving?" or "Which do you consider the best way to decrease accidents among commercial drivers?", suggests that the authors have attempted to get at attitudes as well as knowledge. The effectiveness of this "portmanteau" approach cannot be evaluated since no information is given concerning reliability, item consistency, or validity either for driving knowledge per se or for the survival criterion. Cutoff scores for five ratings are suggested, and the opinion is offered that a score below 45 (average) shows that the applicant needs instruction to improve his knowledge of traffic and driving and if hired with no instruction will be a poor risk as a driver.

The Road Test in Traffic represents an attempt to evaluate skill in driving with the phase-check technique. Standardization of the tasks is attempted by specifying a 5-mile route including right and left turns, stop signs, traffic lights, grades, curves, and a railroad crossing. This seems inadequate, as does the instruction to examiners to "try the test out on three drivers whose driving ability is already known....an excellent driver, an average driver, and a poor or inexperienced driver * score the tests and assign Letter Grades * The excellent driver should have a Letter Grade of A or B. The average driver should have a Letter Grade of C or possibly as high as B or as low as D. The poor driver should have a Letter Grade of D or E. If your results agree with this closely, you should be ready to start using the Road Test in Traffic for driver selection." This procedure is suggested as a check on the examiner and the standard route. It seems probable that it will, instead, increase the subjectivity of the examiner's judgments.

It is particularly unfortunate that no data on objectivity or reliability are given for this test whose validity is mainly a matter of fiat. The statement is made that applicants who score A, B, or (possibly) C have been found to be good risks as truck drivers, while those scoring E have been found to be very poor risks and should be disqualified. However, no supporting data are given. Norms are also absent.

The Physical Examination Form needs no comment.

The authors have recognized as few others have done the importance of integrating a selection system with the training which is to follow.

They present their tests of knowledge and skill as both selection instruments and diagnostic aids for determining the quantity and content of training appropriate for individuals. Unfortunately, one receives the impression that the integration broke down somewhere. The absence of selection validity data for the two dual-purpose tests is symptomatic of such a breakdown. Equally disturbing is the fact that no data are presented on the interrelations of the various instruments in the battery. The selection system is based upon a series of multiple cutoffs. This may be the most effective method but one would like to see the data which led to its preferment over the multiple correlation technique. Similarly, there is no evidence that the knowledge and skill tests have been thoroughly investigated. If the Road Test in Traffic does provide a good measure of driving skill, why should it not also be used as a criterion for the selection tests, or at least as a method of refining the survival criterion? If driving knowledge is important, why is it not also important to know more about its relation to driving skill and to survival? The failure to investigate these questions leaves the reviewer unhappy and dubious of the validities of the tests for diagnostic and training purposes.

All things considered, however, this system compares favorably with the great majority of those found in industry. With proper follow-up procedures and more careful analyses of the instruments used, it could serve as a model of the proper use of psychological techniques in selection and training.

[790]
★Road Test—In Traffic. Drivers; 1943–47; 3 scores: specific driving skills, general driving habits and attitudes, total; 2 editions; no norms for part scores; no description of normative population; 20½¢ per 25 of any one edition, postage extra; tumbling cylinder essential for administration; specimen set free to qualified test users; (30–60) minutes; Amos E. Neyhart; American Automobile Association and Institute of Public Safety, Pennsylvania State College, State College, Pa. *
a) FOR SELECTING AND TRAINING TRUCK DRIVERS. 1943–45; 1 form, '45; manual ('45).
b) FOR TESTING, RATING, AND TRAINING PASSENGER CAR DRIVERS. 1947; 1 form.

[791]
★Traffic and Driving Knowledge. Truck drivers; 1946; 1 form; no data on reliability and validity; no manual; no description of normative population; 5¢ per test and key, postage extra; nontimed (25) minutes; prepared by Amos E. Neyhart and Helen L. Neyhart for the White Motor Co.; Institute of Public Safety, Pennsylvania State College, State College, Pa. *

EDUCATION

[792]

★**Aptitude Test for Elementary School Teachers-in-Training.** Prospective elementary school teachers; 1946–51; also called ATEST; individual in part; $1.75 per 10; $1.50 per manual ('48); $2 per specimen set; postpaid; Henry Bowers; J. M. Dent & Sons (Canada) Ltd. * (American distributor: Psychometric Affiliates.)

a) PARTS I–V. 1946; 5 scores: opinions, books, occupations, interests, aspect of judgment; 1 form; nontimed (30–40) minutes.

b) PART VI, PERFORMANCE TEST, REVISED EDITION. 1946–50; a controlled interview in which the examinee delivers 3 to 5 speeches of 3 to 3½ minutes duration on different subjects; examinees also required to serve as audience for other examinees; 1 form, '50; (120–240) minutes per examinee in 4 sessions.

c) PART VII, THE HIGH SCHOOL PERCENTILE. 1946; a high school record form intended for use only in Ontario.

d) PART VII, PSYCHOMETRIC EVALUATION AND PERSONAL DATA. 1951; a high school record form intended for use outside of Ontario; available only from Psychometric Affiliates.

REFERENCES

1. BOWERS, HENRY. "The Pre-Training Selection of Teachers." *Sch* 36:490–1, 618–22+ My, Je '48. * (*PA* 22:4125)
2. BOWERS, HENRY. "New Data on the Validity of the Aptitude Test for Elementary School Teachers-in-Training." *Can J Psychol* 4:11–7 Mr '50. * (*PA* 25:593)

ROBERT M. W. TRAVERS, *Human Resources Research Center, Air Training Command, Lackland Air Force Base, San Antonio, Texas.*

It seems fair to describe this test as an attempt to do what cannot be done at the present time. The purpose of the project of which the test is a major outcome was to develop an aptitude test which would predict *"the ability to teach lessons in classrooms where the problem of control is simplified by the presence of one or two experts paid to evaluate that ability."* This statement must be carefully examined because it is based upon assumptions that do not seem tenable at the present time.

First, it implies that a so-called expert can observe a teacher and judge the extent to which desirable changes are being produced in children. This does not seem to be the case at all, for the studies by A. S. Barr and his associates show consistently low correlations between effectiveness of teaching as measured by supervisors' ratings and by objective measures of pupil growth. Those who achieve high ratings by supervisors are likely to produce just about as much and no more pupil growth than those who achieve low ratings. This fact is discouraging from an administrator's point of view but needs to be faced. It is also necessary to face the fact that measured pupil growth is a much more defensible basis for the assessment of teacher effectiveness than are supervisory ratings, and the latter cannot be accepted at the present time as a usable criterion.

Second, the statement implies that effectiveness of teaching is a concept derived from the observation of teachers; that is to say, that effective teaching is apparent when it is observed. Nothing could be further from the case. Teaching in a given situation can be considered effective if it provides changes in pupils which are considered desirable by some person. In terms of the philosophy of another individual, these same pupil changes may not seem desirable and the teaching, therefore, may not be considered effective. The effectiveness of teaching depends not only on the amount of pupil change which it produces but also on whether these changes are considered desirable.

The upshot of this discussion is that the variable which this test is designed to predict is not a meaningful one at the present time. Meaningful and valid measures of teaching effectiveness cannot be obtained. However, even if acceptable and valid measures of teacher effectiveness were available, it is doubtful whether the instrument under discussion would be particularly useful for prediction purposes.

The test consists of seven parts as follows: (*a*) Opinion (attitudes towards various social activities); (*b*) Books (attitudes towards the titles of six imaginary works); (*c*) Occupations (preference for certain occupations); (*d*) Interests (expressed interests in various activities); (*e*) An aspect of judgment (judgments of the degree of truth or falsity of several propositions); (*f*) Performance (ratings of various traits in a standardized situation); and (*g*) High school percentile (a measure of high school performance). Thus the measures derived from the test include expressions of preferences and judgment in a paper-and-pencil test situation, ratings, and a measure of previous academic achievement.

Except for the statement that the test is supposed to measure qualities which are "necessary" or "indispensable" for effective teaching, in whatever form it may occur, the rationale, if there is one, which underlies the items included in the test is not given. This implies a theory of personality which needs careful study and which can be best examined in relation to Part VI of the test, in which the student is rated for various characteristics while he delivers three, four, or five brief addresses. While the student is delivering these speeches he is "rated" for the following characteristics:

FAVORABLE DESCRIPTIONS	UNFAVORABLE DESCRIPTIONS
Businesslike	Bashful
Cheerful	Colorless
Colorful	Hesitant
Enthusiastic	Listless
Pleasing voice	Nervous
Poised	Unsatisfactory voice
Self-confident	Vague

The rater indicates those descriptions that are "highly applicable," and those that are "clearly, but not highly, applicable." In addition, ratings are made for *alertness, logical procedure, and general impression*.

Now the assumption which underlies this entire procedure is that individuals are characterized by stable traits of the kind listed, and that these traits will manifest themselves in a variety of situations which include the test situation and the teaching situation. This is largely contrary to what is known concerning the nature of personality. Characteristics of social behavior are not manifested consistently from one situation to another—it hardly seems necessary to refer to classic studies in which it was shown that most persons were not consistently honest or dishonest but varied in their behavior from one situation to another. Thus the assumptions underlying those parts of the test based on traditional trait theory are largely unacceptable in terms of a modern theory of behavior.

The author of the test has commendable courage in attempting to provide a solution for a major educational problem, but he has selected one of such complexity that the techniques needed for solving it are not available and are not likely to be available for many years to come.

EDWIN WANDT, *Statistician and Research Associate, Teacher Characteristics Study of the American Council on Education, University of California, Los Angeles, California.*

The 47-page manual provides a wealth of information regarding the validity and reliability of the various tests. Fourteen pages are devoted to discussions of validity. The test and manual obviously have resulted from a considerable amount of careful research.

Several facts appear to limit the usefulness of this test in the prediction of success in practice teaching, particularly in the United States. (*a*) The population used in the development of the test was exclusively Canadian. Use of the scoring keys on the paper and pencil sections would

be extremely risky without experimental verification of these keys with local student teacher samples. (*b*) Although five pages of the manual are devoted to detailed instructions for the performance test, no information is given regarding the scales entitled "alertness" and "logical procedure." Since these two scales contribute so heavily to the final score on the Performance Test, more detailed instructions should have been furnished. (*c*) The most important test, Test VI (Performance), depends on the availability of at least three competent raters, each of whom should have appraised the efforts of at least 500 students. There is no question that the validity coefficients for the performance test are high; however, it seems quite possible that these high correlations are due to the extensive experience of the raters involved in the validation studies rather than to any particular characteristic of the test itself.

For the above reasons it is recommended that the ATEST be used for research purposes only. Persons interested in the problems of pretraining selection of teachers will find the manual very interesting and instructive reading.

J Ed (London) 82:460–2 Ag '50. C. M. Fleming. * while specialized for Canadian conditions, is in line with recent work on interests and opinions in their relevance to teaching skill *

[793]
★Barr-Harris Teacher's Performance Record. For teacher rating and in-service training; 1943; 6 scores: understanding and use of objectives, philosophy of teaching, professional competency, personal fitness, pupil growth and achievement, general merit; 1 form; no norms; 15¢ per copy; 10¢ per manual; postage extra; A. S. Barr and A. E. Harris; Dembar Publications, Inc. *

[794]
★The Case of Mickey Murphy: A Case-Study Instrument for Evaluating Teachers' Understanding of Child Growth and Development (Second Revised Edition). Teachers in training and experienced teachers; 1942–48; 3 scores: drawing conclusions and making decisions, soundness of analysis, procedures for adjustment; 1 form, '43; no data on reliability and validity; manual ('48); $5 per 25; separate answer sheets must be used; 25¢ per specimen set (does not include manual or scoring key); postage extra; nontimed (50–80) minutes; Warren R. Baller; University of Nebraska Press. *

FRANK S. FREEMAN, *Professor of Psychology and Education, Cornell University, Ithaca, New York.*

This instrument was devised primarily as an aid to instruction rather than as a test to evaluate or measure the students' mastery of principles and procedures in dealing with problems of human development and behavior. It can be used, however, for the latter purpose in a preliminary way; but such use should be only the first step for intensive study and discussion of the problems presented in the case. Since this instrument is primarily a teaching device, the author has, apparently, not felt it necessary thus far to go through the usual statistical procedures to establish its reliability and validity. It does not seem that there is great need to be concerned with its validity as a teaching aid; but, if it is to be used as a measure of students' psychological competence, the value of the instrument will be enhanced if, as evidence of professional agreement, an analysis were made of responses given by various known groups of experts. Also, evidence of the instrument's reliability, as answered by expert persons, would be highly desirable. One study reports split half reliability coefficients (corrected with the Spearman-Brown formula) ranging from .56 to .64. But these low coefficients were based on scores of freshmen and seniors in a teachers college. A much more significant measure of reliability would be the coefficients obtained from scores of competent professional persons. With respect, by implication, to validity and reliability, the author states in the manual that the values assigned to various responses are based upon comparisons of responses by groups of persons with different degrees of training and experience. Items receiving greatest weight are those that differentiate most clearly between persons of recognized professional competence and those of little or no professional training, the latter ranging from college sophomores to graduate students who have had teaching experience. The scores of the undergraduates and of the experienced teachers are presented in separate percentile rank tables.

The materials of the case study have been arranged into separate and successive parts, each one adding more and often complicating data, and each being accompanied by its own questions, hypotheses, or interpretations—some regarded as correct or warranted, while others are not—intended to test the student's comprehension of the elements and forces operative in human behavior. The data of the case deal with the usual factors affecting behavior of all children in our society: relationships to parents, siblings, peers, teachers, and other adults; achievement in school studies, physical development,

mental development, interests, and ambitions.

The reviewer has used Baller's case study in several classes in clinical psychology at the graduate level. The instrument proved to be a very effective teaching device, in which the students took a keen interest. The case provides a wide range of materials; it deals with types of problems that are frequent and important in schools and among school children; the arrangement of materials into progressive stages is effective; and at times both students and instructor will disagree with answers, hypotheses, and interpretations offered by the author of the case, thereby providing additional material for analysis and discussion.

[795]

★Diagnostic Teacher-Rating Scale. A scale for rating teachers by children in grades 4–8; 1938; each scale has space for rating four teachers; 8 scores: liking for teacher, ability to explain, kindness-friendliness-understanding, fairness in grading, discipline, amount of work required, liking for lessons, total; Forms A, B; mimeographed; no data on reliability and validity in manual (for data presented elsewhere by the author, see *1–2*); 3¢ per scale; 15¢ per specimen set; postpaid; nontimed (30) minutes; edited by H. H. Remmers; M. Amatora Tschechtelin; Division of Educational Reference, Purdue University. *

REFERENCES
1. TSCHECHTELIN, M. AMATORA; HIPSKIND, M. JOHN FRANCES; AND REMMERS, H. H. "Measuring the Attitudes of Elementary-School Children Toward Their Teachers." *J Ed Psychol* 31:195–203 Mr '40. * (*PA* 14:4757)
2. AMATORA, S. M. "A Diagnostic Teacher-Rating Scale." *J Psychol* 30:395–9 O '50. * (*PA* 25:2740)

[796]

★Exceptional Teacher Service Record. A form for the summarization and evaluation of evidence of superior teaching; 1947; 1 form; no data on reliability and validity; no norms; manual ('47); $3 per 25, postage extra; Dwight E. Beecher; the Author, Congdon Campus School, State Teachers College, Potsdam, N.Y. *

LEO J. BRUECKNER, *Professor of Education, University of Minnesota, Minneapolis, Minnesota.*

This record form is an 8-page folder listing four groups of items that may be regarded as outstanding services rendered by a teacher. The form was developed to assist administrators to apply the system of merit rating established by the New York Legislature. The titles of each group and the number of areas included in each are as follows: (*a*) direct service to pupils, such as providing rich school experiences—15 areas; (*b*) community services, such as direct leadership of youth activities, as Boy Scouts—2 areas; (*c*) nonschool activities, such as work in public relations, research undertaken, and leadership of community organizations—11 areas; and (*d*) professional training, including advanced study, demonstration teaching, and travel—9 areas. The experimental edition of the form contained many of the items included in the Report of the Advisory Committee on Teachers' Salaries appointed by the Commissioner of Education of New York State in 1947. Consideration was also given to "research and expert judgment" in compiling the final list.

The record form assumes the maintenance of a cumulative record form for each teacher in which supervisory reports, anecdotal records, documentary evidence, and records of exceptional pupil growth are recorded. On the service record form each area is defined by concrete illustrations of typical examples. A space is provided for recording the dates on which evidence concerning each point was submitted and filed in the cumulative record, and the "number of the evidence." To arrive at a rating based on this evidence two credit points are assigned "for each area in which evidence is frequent and consistent, indicating regular practice; otherwise one credit is allowed for evidence in each area." When no evidence is recorded, no credit is given. The total number of points for each of the four parts of the form is then recorded on a summary form. This number is then converted into a "ranking score" by means of tables that are provided. Finally the results for the four areas are totalled. On the basis of this figure the individual then receives a ranking within the faculty group involved. As far as the reviewer has been able to discover, no report has as yet been made of the validity of the blank, the statistical basis of the points assigned, or of the results where the form is in use. The point rating for items appears to be quite subjective since no standards are given for assigning points. Changes in the weighting of the various items may also seem desirable to many.

There can be no doubt, however, as to the great value of the development of a systematic plan for recording outstanding services of teachers to be used as *one* basis for establishing merit ratings. The blank itself should serve as an excellent device for stimulating teachers in service to improve their contributions to the enrichment of the educational program of a community and to broaden their activities in relation to the life of the school. The service record in its present form should undoubtedly be regarded as tentative. Communities might well undertake the revision or extension of the items included in the

analysis in the light of existing conditions. Undoubtedly the extension of the list will lead to an even richer list of suggestions of the types of exceptional services teachers can render.

EDWIN WANDT, *Statistician and Research Associate, Teacher Characteristics Study of the American Council on Education, University of California, Los Angeles, California.*

The express purpose of this form is to provide "a quantitative method for the summarization of evidence of superior teaching."

The Record consists of four sections: (*a*) direct service to pupils, (*b*) community service, (*c*) nonschool activities, and (*d*) professional training. Each of these sections consists of a number of different areas in which the teacher can earn credit points. Sample types of acceptable evidence are given for each of these areas. One credit point is allowed for evidence of superior teaching in each area, and two credit points are allowed for each area in which the evidence is frequent or consistent. Additional credits (number unspecified) are allowed in cases where the evidence indicates unusually extensive benefits from the service rendered. The system assumes the maintenance of a cumulative record folder for each teacher in which evidence of exceptional service will be kept.

Scores are calculated by totaling the entries in each section separately to give a total credit on a "frequency" basis; with this, a "variety" factor may be included by adding the number of different services credited within the section.

The total of these two sums is then converted, in accordance with tables which are provided, into a "ranking score" for each section. Directions for scoring are confusing. The "variety" factor *may* be added but apparently need not be. If added, the tables for converting credit points to ranking scores are not adequate. For example, in the first section the maximum ranking score of 100 corresponds to 30 credit points. If a teacher earned 2 points in each of the 15 areas of this section, he would receive 45 credit points (30 points for "frequency" plus 15 points for "variety"); yet, there is no provision made in the ranking score for credit points of more than 30.

A single sheet serves as the manual. No evidence of reliability or validity is given.

An instrument of this type may possibly serve a useful purpose in ranking teachers according to activities engaged in and services performed;

Exceptional Teacher Service Record

however, much work is needed before it may be safely used for the judgment of superior teaching. There is a danger that school systems which use this form will be misled into thinking that their rankings of teachers are reliable and valid.

In view of the lack of evidence as to the reliability or validity of this instrument, it is suggested that it be used for research purposes only.

[797]

★**Graduate Record Examinations Advanced Education Test.** Senior year college through graduate school and candidates for graduate school; 1946–51; available only in Graduate Record Examinations programs (see 527); 180(220) minutes; prepared by the Advanced Education Test Committee appointed by Educational Testing Service: G. Lester Anderson (Chairman), R. Freeman Butts, Walter W. Cook, Harl Douglass, and Donald Durrell; Educational Testing Service. *

REFERENCES

1. SAUM, JAMES A. "The Graduate Record Examination and Its Application in the Stanford School of Education." Abstract. *Calif J Ed Res* 2:183 S '51. *
2. TREACY, JOHN P. "Interpretation of Scores on Advanced Test in Education." *Cath Ed R* 49:171–4 Mr '51. *

[798]

★**How I Counsel.** Counselors and prospective counselors; 1950; IBM; Forms A, B; preliminary norms; 2½¢ per copy; 25¢ per specimen set; separate answer sheets (IBM Form ITS 1100 A 155) may be used; IBM answer sheets must be purchased directly from the International Business Machines Corporation; postpaid; nontimed (30) minutes; Stanley C. Benz and H. H. Remmers; Personnel Evaluation Service and Research, Division of Educational Reference, Purdue University. *

REFERENCES

1. BENZ, STANLEY C. "Some Measured Dimensions of Counselors," pp. 56–62. In *Proceedings of the Thirteenth Annual Guidance Conference Held at Purdue University, November 21 and 22, 1947.* Purdue University, Division of Educational Reference, Studies in Higher Education [No.] 63. Lafayette, Ind.: the Division, November 1947. Pp. 77. Paper. *
2. BENZ, STANLEY C. *An Investigation of the Attributes and Techniques of High-School Counselors.* Edited by H. H. Remmers. Purdue University, Division of Educational Reference, Studies in Higher Education [No.] 64. Lafayette, Ind.: the Division, October 1948. Pp. 41. Paper. *
3. MCCLELLAND, WILLIAM A., AND SINAIKO, H. WALLACE. "An Investigation of a Counselor Attitude Questionnaire." Abstract. *Am Psychol* 3:363 Ag '48. * (*PA* 23:738, title only)
4. DRUCKER, A. J., AND REMMERS, H. H. "The Validity of University Counselor Self-Ratings." *J Ed Psychol* 40:168–73 Mr '49. * (*PA* 24:1485)

CLIFFORD P. FROEHLICH, *Associate Professor of Education, University of California, Berkeley, California.*

According to the manual, this test "is designed to indicate how well a person is acquainted with accepted counseling techniques, to reflect his philosophy of counseling, and to indicate his awareness of some of the basic principles of human behavior." This is a big order for a single test. From the information presented in the 4-page mimeographed manual, it is impossible to judge whether or not the test can do so much. Unfortunately, the manual does not mention that

summary data concerning the construction of this test were published in 1948 (*2*). In that year the test contained 100 items. In its 1950 format the same items are divided "on the basis of subject matter, difficulty, and the discriminating power of the items" to make up the two equated Forms A and B. Even though this means that some of the data reported in 1948 are not directly applicable to the present form of the test, the data reported in the 1948 monograph provide a better basis for understanding the test than does the manual.

Each of the two forms of this test contains 50 statements for which the testee indicates "agree," "not sure," or "disagree." The authors have classified the items under 11 "basic principles of counseling" which repeat most of the generally accepted clichés about counseling, such as, "consider the student as a whole person," or "center the interview around the problem expressed by the student." That the test does not adequately measure each of these 11 principles may be inferred from the facts that in Form A only one item is devoted to each of two of the basic principles, and that two additional principles are measured by two items each. Although it is theoretically possible to have a perfect one-item test, this reviewer does not believe that the basic principle that the counselor should "strive to be personally well adjusted" is adequately measured by the item, "a counselor should be a stable, well adjusted person." This condition should not be a serious handicap if the test user clearly recognizes the uneven distribution of items to the various principles.

The reliability coefficient is reported in the manual as .834 for the "combined scores on both forms of the test." This coefficient is comparable to the previously reported (*1*) .831 split half reliability coefficient obtained for a group of 360 composed of 306 teachers in a stratified sample of schools in Indiana, 40 teachers attending a university summer session guidance workshop, and 14 full-time veterans' counselors.

There are some indications that the test yields scores which differentiate groups in the expected manner. The mean score of 14 veterans' counselors, for example, was significantly higher than that obtained by various groups of teachers. Counselors with higher test scores were more critical of counseling services in a university than were persons with lower test scores (*4*). If it is assumed that critical evaluation is correlated with counselor competence, then the fact that counselors with higher test scores rated counseling services in a university lower than did persons who did not do as well on the test may be taken as an indication of validity. However, the validity data available to this reviewer do not seem to be substantial enough to justify the use of this test for individual selection purposes as recommended in the manual.

The test's greatest usefulness at the present is as a discussion stimulator in counselor training. For this purpose, it makes a fine companion to such tests as *Tests of Human Growth and Development*. To make the present edition of this test more useful, the authors should rewrite the inadequate manual. They should include the information which they have summarized in other publications (*1, 2*) and omit the overambitious statements regarding the test's usefulness. The authors have provided an interesting instrument. It may be that further research will demonstrate its usefulness. Persons concerned with the selection and training of counselors may find this test a useful research device.

MILTON E. HAHN, *Professor of Psychology, and Dean of Students, University of California, Los Angeles, California.*

This combination of an attitude inventory and an information test is an interesting step toward the better selection of specialized personnel in schools and colleges. After completing Forms A and B, the reviewer was of the opinion that the answers would be acceptable to the majority of competent practitioners in the field. The instrument is somewhat slanted toward *advising* rather than toward clinical or psychological *counseling*.

Validity of the instrument is based on the criterion of expert judges. While this is a standard step in final validation, it must be accepted as tentative until much more rigorous approaches are available. Acceptable validity must rest on follow-up of candidates selected on the basis of this test plus investigation of satisfied versus dissatisfied workers in relationship to the test.

The reliability coefficient for one form (50 items) is given in the manual as .73. This would not warrant great reliance on the instrument for use in individual cases, even if satisfactory validity had been established. The combined Forms A and B (100 items) are listed as having a reliability of .83, not as high as one might wish for individual application in selection.

The tentative norms in the manual are based on a sample of 346 high school teachers. This norming appears to the reviewer to be inadequate. A further norm problem with either form is that a standard deviation at the extremes is covered by a difference of not more than three raw score points. A single raw score point on both forms makes the difference between the 80th and 90th percentiles; two raw score points between the 80th and 95th percentiles.

If the present forms of the inventories are accepted as preliminary ones, the following steps are needed before they can be effectively useful in selecting candidates or measuring the outcomes of training: (*a*) Formulating a definition of counseling as contrasted to advising, psychological or clinical counseling, and psychotherapy. (*b*) Lengthening the forms to give more extensive coverage to the area described in the definition and to gain greater reliability. (*c*) Conducting research to establish reasonable validity. (*d*) Conducting research to provide adequate norms.

SUMMARY. This test appears to be the preliminary release of an instrument which may, provided the standard additional steps for sound validation are taken, be useful in selecting candidates for counseling; measuring outcomes of training; evaluating knowledge, beliefs, and techniques of counselors; and locating areas which should be emphasized in counselor training. It is not recommended in its present stage of development for other than research purposes.

[799]

How I Teach: Analysis of Teaching Practices. Teachers; 1942; also called *Purdue Teachers Examination;* IBM; Forms A, B; $2.25 per 25 IBM test-answer booklets; 75¢ per stencil for machine scoring of test booklet; $1 per manual, postage extra; $1.50 per specimen set, postpaid; nontimed (30) minutes; Ida B. Kelley and Keith J. Perkins; Educational Test Bureau, Educational Publishers, Inc. *

REFERENCES

1. KELLEY, IDA B., AND PERKINS, KEITH J. *Further Studies in Attitudes, Series IV: An Investigation of Teachers' Knowledge of and Attitudes Toward Child and Adolescent Behavior in Every day School Situations.* Purdue University, Division of Educational Reference, Studies in Higher Education, No. 42. Lafayette, Ind.: the Division, June 1941. Pp. 99. Paper. * (PA 16:344)
2. DAVENPORT, KENNETH. *An Investigation Into Pupil Rating of Certain Teaching Practices.* Foreword by Ida B. Kelley and Keith Perkins. Edited by H. H. Remmers. Purdue University, Division of Educational Reference, Studies in Higher Education, [No.] 49; Further Studies in Attitudes, Series 7. Lafayette, Ind.: the Division, January 1944. Pp. 61. Paper. * (PA 18:3282)
3. BELMAN, H. S., AND EVANS, R. N. "Selection of Students for a Trade and Industrial Education Curriculum," pp. 9–14. In *Motives and Aptitudes in Education: Four Studies.* Edited by H. H. Remmers. Purdue University, Division of Educational Reference, Studies in Higher Education, No. 74. Lafayette, Ind.: the Division, December 1950. Pp. iii, 63. Paper. * (PA 26:3010)
4. BELMAN, H. S., AND EVANS, R. N. "Selection of Students for a Trade and Industrial Educational Curriculum." *J Ed Psychol* 42:52–8 Ja '51. * (PA 25:6486)

MAY V. SEAGOE, *Professor of Education, University of California, Los Angeles, California.*

The scale is designed to measure college students' and instructors' working knowledge of mental hygiene principles as they relate to teaching and learning in college.

The experimental edition of the scale consists of 162 statements, refined from an original list of 246 items which were taken from the literature on mental health and submitted for evaluation to college instructors and college students. Later, the scale was submitted for criticism and response to nine experts in psychology and psychiatry, and 48 additional items were eliminated from scoring as a result. Answers are recorded in terms of degree of agreement on a five-point scale. "Right" answers are based on consensus of experts. Scoring is done by matching the answer sheet to the margin of each page, and the number right constitutes the total score. Norms are precentile ranks based on the scores of 314 teachers in 12 institutions of higher learning in Indiana. Norms are available in the reference cited for college students as well. Reliability (odd vs. even) is .91 on an N of 219. An abbreviated scale of 90 items based on item analysis has a reliability of .75 for men and .81 for women.

An analysis of results from 326 college men and 1,056 college women, chiefly from teacher training institutions, showed that women excel men in the insights measured; training in psychology and education are related to understanding of mental health problems; and students planning to teach older children seem to have somewhat less insight.

The test is an important pioneer contribution to the study of college mental health. It is related to rating scales for college instructors on the one hand and to college level tests of "adjustment" and certain personality measures on the other, though no studies of interrelationships were found in the literature. The original standardization procedure seems sound.

The instrument has certain mechanical defects such as hand written answers, relatively slow scoring, inclusion of nonscored items, and absence of a well organized manual. Populations covered are limited largely to a single state and represent chiefly teacher training institutions.

In conclusion, this test, though in need of refinement and improvement of mechanics and norms, is a promising instrument in a relatively undeveloped field. Until research on interrela-tionships is available, its chief uses will probably be as a research instrument and as a teaching device in college courses in education.

D. A. WORCESTER, *Professor of Educational Psychology and Measurements, University of Nebraska, Lincoln, Nebraska.*

The authors state that their problem was "to construct and evaluate an instrument to measure teachers' knowledge of the psychological nature of the children in their care." The validity of this instrument is indicated by the fact that those teachers nominated as "best" by their principals or superintendents tended to make higher scores than those rated as "worst." There were, however, many exceptions. The items of the inventory were chosen from the literature and from several practical sources such as case histories which had been prepared by teachers. The content of the test, taken mostly from the field of mental hygiene, appears to be good. However, many of the items are subject to disagreement among experts, and the opinions of 10 judges distributed among eight fields are a rather small sampling of expert judgment even though some of the judges, without doubt, were skilled in more than one field. In some instances "best" teachers disagreed with the judges, but their opinions apparently did not carry weight in the scoring.

The inventory is accompanied by a leaflet of directions which is all that is needed for the practical use of the instrument. However, the complete manual is needed to identify the three parts of the test: Teaching Practices, Opinions, and Factual Data. The manual also gives detailed reports of many statistical analyses made upon the scores of teachers of different schools, different subjects, different trainings, and so on. All of these analyses are made from a method of scoring which is different from the one recommended to test users. Because the correlation between the two methods is high (.95), the simpler one—the number of right responses—is recommended. However, the authors suggest that the more involved scoring method, which gives two points for the best answer and one point for the next best answer, has advantages when individual teachers are being studied. Since the authors recommend that the test be used for the selection of teachers—certainly individual study—norms based upon this scoring method are necessary. But only in the complete manual, which must be purchased separately,

How I Teach: Analysis of Teaching Practices

are these norms available. Also, while the research shows many significant differences (e.g., between the scores of men and women high school teachers and between teachers with longer and shorter experience on the present job), no differential norms are presented.

Forms A and B each have 75 items. In almost all cases a change in three answers changes the score by at least 10 percentiles. In Form A, for example, the score for the 10th percentile is 15.6 and for the 90th percentile is 34.7. A student getting half of the possible score stands at the 90th percentile or above. This situation probably arises from requiring exact answers to questions upon which there is so much disagreement among experts.

The reliability of the two forms is indicated by an intercorrelation of .77. The authors suggest that one form be used at the beginning of a course and the other at the end. The authors also state that care was used to check duplication as to areas: "If....one form had two items about delinquency and the other form had none, one item on delinquency was taken from one form and put into the other." An examination of the list of areas covered by items shows that of the 94 areas named, only 20 are represented in both forms; 65 areas are represented by a single item in one form only. The fairly high reliability coefficient may show, then, that a person who knows one part of his field probably knows another part, or, perhaps, the areas were not accurately identified. Apparently, the two forms do not cover the same content.

The reviewer thinks that the items of the inventory were carefully chosen and worded. He believes the instrument has value as a teaching device in some courses in education, particularly, perhaps, in a course in mental hygiene. He questions its use for the employment of teachers.

For a review by David G. Ryans, see 3:403.

[800]

★How Teach and Learn in College? Experimental Edition. College students and instructors; 1947–50; 1 form, '47; manual ('50); 8¢ per copy; 20¢ per specimen set; postpaid; nontimed (35) minutes; edited by H. H. Remmers; Jean Harvey, William R. Thompson, and R. L. Hobson; Personnel Evaluation Research Service, Division of Educational Reference, Purdue University. *

REFERENCES

1. HARVEY, LUCY JEAN. *The Mental Hygiene of Higher Learning as the Student Sees It.* Doctor's thesis, Purdue University (Lafayette, Ind.), 1945.
2. ELLIOTT, D. N. *Characteristics and Relationships of Various Criteria of Teaching.* Doctor's thesis, Purdue University (Lafayette, Ind.), 1949.
3. REMMERS, H. H., AND ELLIOTT, D. N. "The Indiana College and University Staff-Evaluation Program." *Sch & Soc* 70:168–71 S 10 '49. * (*PA* 26:2440)
4. ELLIOTT, DONALD N. "Characteristics and Relationships of Various Criteria of College and University Teaching," pp. 5–61. In *Studies in College and University Staff Evaluation.* Edited by H. H. Remmers. Purdue University, Division of Educational Reference, Studies in Higher Education [No.] 70; Further Studies in Attitudes, Series 15. Lafayette, Ind.: the Division, March 1950. Pp. 96. Paper. *

DEAN A. WORCESTER, *Professor of Educational Psychology and Measurements, University of Nebraska, Lincoln, Nebraska.*

Although this test was developed in 1943 and revised in 1947, there is little evidence as to the nature or amount of revision. The title of the test appears to be misleading; it is preponderantly a measure of one's understanding of mental hygiene, as is stated on the sheet of general information. While it perhaps should be inferred that a person who agrees with the majority of a group of experts in the field of mental hygiene is a better teacher than those who do not agree, there is no available evidence which compares the scores on this test with teaching success. It is to be noted, too, that the title is a double one, *How Teach and Learn in College,* and this implication is carried out by a student's section of a rather elaborate data sheet. No norms of any kind are given for students, nor is there any evidence that students with high scores are any more successful in their college experiences, especially those conventionally included under learning experiences, than are those with low scores.

One is also a little inclined to question the adequacy of the norms given for teachers. Scores of 36 and lower are assigned a percentile rank of 0; a score of 50, a percentile rank of 5; and scores of 104 and over, a percentile rank of 100. Since the total possible score is 159, only 68 score values lie within the range equivalent to percentile ranks of 0 to 100, and 91 score values lie outside. This suggests that a large number of disagreements with the criterion group will be found among those scoring in the high places.

It is noticeable that on many items a person will *agree* or *strongly agree* or, on the other hand, *disagree* or *strongly disagree* in the same "direction" as the key but not in the same amount. Since in most of these instances the keyed answer cannot be objectively verified but is only a matter of personal understanding, it might be wise to make allowances for these responses that are nearly correct.

The test may have value for use in a mental hygiene course, especially in a college of education, but this writer does not see how it could be recommended as a means of forecasting teaching efficiency or success in learning at the college level.

[801]

★Minnesota Teacher Attitude Inventory. Elementary and secondary school teachers and teachers in training; 1951; IBM; Form A; $3 per 25; separate answer sheets must be used; $1.85 per 50 IBM answer sheets; $15 per 500; 50¢ per set of machine scoring stencils; 60¢ per specimen set; postpaid; nontimed (20–30) minutes; Walter W. Cook, Carroll H. Leeds, and Robert Callis; Psychological Corporation. *

REFERENCES

1. LEEDS, CARROLL H. *The Construction and Differential Value of a Scale for Determining Teacher-Pupil Attitudes.* Doctor's thesis, University of Minnesota (Minneapolis, Minn.), 1946.
2. COOK, WALTER W., AND LEEDS, CARROLL H. "Measuring the Teaching Personality." *Ed & Psychol Meas* 7:399–410 au '47. * (PA 22:3652)
3. LEEDS, CARROLL H., AND COOK, WALTER W. "The Construction and Differential Value of a Scale for Determining Teacher-Pupil Attitudes." *J Exp Ed* 16:149–59 D '47. * (PA 22:2332)
4. CALLIS, ROBERT. *Change in Teacher-Pupil Attitudes Related to Training and Experience.* Doctor's thesis, University of Minnesota (Minneapolis, Minn.), 1948.
5. LEEDS, CARROLL H. "The Construction and Differential Value of a Scale for Measuring the Attitudes of Teachers Toward Pupils." Abstract. *Am Psychol* 3:296–7 Jl '48. * (PA 22:5574, title only)
6. CALLIS, ROBERT. "Change in Teacher-Pupil Attitudes Related to Training and Experience." *Ed & Psychol Meas.* 10:718–27 w '50. * (PA 25:6488)
7. LEEDS, CARROLL H. *A Scale for Measuring Teacher-Pupil Attitudes and Teacher-Pupil Rapport.* American Psychological Association, Psychological Monographs: General and Applied, Vol. 64, No. 6, Whole No. 312. Washington, D.C.: the Association, Inc., 1950. Pp. iv, 24. Paper. * (PA 25:3432)
8. FULLER, ELIZABETH M. "The Use of Teacher-Pupil Attitudes, Self Rating, and Measures of General Ability in the Preservice Selection of Nursery School-Kindergarten-Primary Teachers." *J Ed Res* 44:675–86 My '51. * (PA 26:1725)
9. GAGE, N. L., AND SUCI, GEORGE. "Social Perception and Teacher-Pupil Relationships." *J Ed Psychol* 42:144–52 Mr '51. * (PA 25:7700)

DWIGHT L. ARNOLD, *Professor of Education, and Director of Guidance Testing, Kent State University, Kent, Ohio.*

The basic approach to the MTAI seems sound and similar to Strong's very successful *Vocational Interest Blank*. The inventory consists of a series of items related to attitudes of teachers toward pupil-teacher relations. A large number of these and similar items were given to teachers who were rated by principals as successful and as unsuccessful in pupil-teacher relations. From these results, the final scale and scoring were developed. Two studies of validity were made; these studies yielded coefficients of correlation of .46 and .60 between the scores on the test and the three criteria: principal's estimate, pupil's rating, and visiting experts' rating. Consistent and thorough work has gone into construction and validation of this inventory. Clearly this represents a serious attempt on a very important and very difficult problem.

The prediction of teaching success has been found to be very difficult if not impossible. The authors of the MTAI in the first paragraph in the manual indicate "It is designed to measure those attitudes which predict how well he (the teacher) will get along with pupils." This is certainly a very laudable purpose, although research which has been done heretofore indicates that studies of this kind have not been successful in securing any significant prediction. It must be said also that none of the data presented by the authors in the manual actually involve studies of scores made by students in or before teacher training in relation to later success in teaching. Data are presented to show that persons scoring high on the test tend to be better teachers than persons scoring low on the test. This is distinctly valuable and makes the instrument worthy of publication.

Norms are presented for high school seniors, students in training, university freshmen, and experienced teachers. These norms are divided into the various levels by age of students being taught and by amount of education of the teachers. The samplings involved seem adequate for students in training and for experienced teachers in Minnesota or the Midwest. The question might be raised as to whether norms should not have been presented for the successful teacher. Although the whole inventory is based on the idea of measuring the difference in scores between successful and unsuccessful teachers, no actual data are presented as to distribution or percentiles of these successful and unsuccessful teachers.

No comment or explanation is given in the manual of the great differences in the median scores of Table I, students, and the median scores of Table II, experienced teachers. The students in education, as a group, score approximately 30 to 45 points higher than do experienced teachers. As an extreme but important example, experienced four-year academic secondary teachers make a median score of 23. Graduating education seniors from the four-year academic secondary program have a median score of 68. A student whose score is 35 stands at the 9th percentile when compared to students, and at the 60th percentile when compared with experienced secondary academic teachers. These differences are so great that the inventory will be of limited value until the following questions are answered. Which attitudes and scores are desirable, those of students or those of experienced teachers? Will these discrepancies be found in other groups? If they are confirmed, they mean that the inventory is of no value or that teacher education programs are unrealistic or that experienced teachers have undesirable attitudes. It would seem difficult to use this instrument in counseling without assuming an answer to these questions. It is entirely possible that this inventory may help force educators to face the rather unpleasant implications raised here. The MTAI will be a tool for further research on these same questions. Such research is seriously needed.

Statements in the manual are not clear as to how the inventory may be used in counseling or advising students. The following items are definitely confusing: "We have no information as to how appropriate the *Inventory* would be for use with high school seniors who plan to enter teaching"; and "Since high school....counselors will be using the *Inventory* as one of the bases for judging vocational fitness in the area of education, it seems desirable to present norms for high school seniors and university freshmen." The variation in norms makes counseling with this instrument confusing. It is difficult to know how to advise a student whose score stands at the 9th percentile for students and at the 60th percentile for experienced teachers. As is true with so many manuals, no adequate explanation is given as to just what may or may not be said to students about their scores. Every manual should include usable, defensible quotations, actual sentences which may be used in explaining results to students, instead of the usual general statements from which any of a dozen different inferences may be drawn.

From a study of the manual and norms provided, a counselor may say to the counselee as follows: "Here is an inventory which will indicate the extent to which your attitudes about pupil-teacher relations are similar to, or not similar to, those of persons who are actually teaching or are in preparation for teaching. It will also show to some extent whether your attitudes are like those of successful teachers." There is no evidence on which to say more.

The MTAI presents a new and promising approach to a difficult but important problem. It deserves considered use in counseling and extensive use in research.

LEE J. CRONBACH, *Professor of Education, Bureau of Research and Service, University of Illinois, Urbana, Illinois.*

Test development of exceptional quality lies behind this inventory. Publication was preceded by patient and careful research which is well reported in the manual. However, the research is not at this point adequate to support wide practical use of the test, but the research program is continuing.

The inventory is a device designed to predict which teachers or potential teachers will establish good relations with pupils. There are 150 opinion statements to be marked "Strongly agree," "Agree," etc. From a large trial set, items were chosen which were marked differently by criterion groups of teachers. The item selection and empirical scoring key were checked on several samples.

The central question is whether the inventory is valid for the recommended uses of teacher selection and guidance. The manual does a serious disservice by failing to make clear that the validity of the test as a predictive instrument has not been investigated. Until such studies are reported, the test should be used only on a research basis by those who are willing to conduct follow-up studies of their own. The studies reported in the manual make one optimistic that the validity of the test will prove satisfactory. The authors wisely seek to predict a particular aspect of the teaching job, success in establishing rapport with children, rather than a nebulous global criterion. Ratings of this quality by principals, observers, and pupils themselves correlate .45 to .49 with scores on the test. When the three types of rating are combined into a more reliable criterion, correlations with test score in three studies are remarkably good: .60, .63, and .46. In design, replication, and care in reporting, these studies are distinguished. There is a clear correspondence between inventory scores and teaching behavior at the time the test is given.

Split half reliability is .93. On retest, scores are only moderately stable if teachers are exposed to significant experiences. Retest reliabilities during early professional courses, and during the first months of teaching experience, are near .70. There is evidence of considerable change in mean score during the college years. It is therefore somewhat doubtful whether the test, given at the time of college entrance, would predict the attitudes and practices of a person several years later. For short term prediction, or in the hiring of experienced teachers whose attitudes have become stabilized, one can expect better results.

The norms are excellent in many respects. A stratified random sample of Minnesota teachers was used, and norms report separate percentile conversions for groups of distinct types; e.g., academic secondary teachers with five years training. The norms for students, however, are based on samples of opportunity and are stop-gaps at best. The manual should advise users to obtain their own local norms.

The inventory is probably as well designed and executed as any actuarial test can be. The reviewer nonetheless questions whether actuarial tests are the most profitable type to develop and use. The strictly empirical test is designed to allow scores to include diverse characteristics so long as they predict the criterion. A test designed to measure a psychological quality should be more homogeneous, and scores on items should have a logical meaning. While the items on the inventory are rather homogeneous, and scores reflect to some extent a child-centered, permissive attitude, the emphasis on predicting a criterion has led the authors to use weights which are sometimes illogical.

For some reason, a person who responds "Strongly disagree" persistently will tend to earn a much better score than one who expresses milder disagreement. In particular items there are scoring weights like these: Item 1, "Most children are obedient"; weights: strongly agree (1), agree (‑1), undecided or uncertain (0), disagree (−1), strongly disagree (0). Item 8, "A child's companionships can be too carefully supervised"; weights: strongly agree (0), agree (1), undecided or uncertain (0), disagree (−1), strongly disagree (−1). An agreement or disagreement on Item 1 is penalized; a suspended judgment or a *strong* agreement is rewarded. In Item 8, an agreement is good, but an emphatic agreement, which is logically identical, is not scored positively. The authors intend that any differences "with respect to faking, response set, test-taking attitude, and role-playing operate in the direction of increasing the [predictive] validity." There is evidence that scores cannot be raised by faking, and perhaps the weights which seem illogical do counteract faking.

An actuarial test permits statements to be made about probability of success. For counseling, however, the writer would prefer to use a test which describes the person's qualities so that he can gain self-understanding. Since prediction from a test almost never allows a final judgment about the individual, there is an advantage in obtaining descriptive information which can be supported or denied by supplementary evidence. Descriptive tests are also more useful for evaluating training and for research.

The *Minnesota Teacher Attitude Inventory* is a promising tool for research on teacher success. At its present stage of development, it should be employed only by people trained in research who can validate it for their purposes. It should not be used to select applicants for teacher training or beginning teachers until further validated. When so validated, it is likely to prove highly suitable for such screening. It may be used for guidance and for discussion in teacher training classes with very cautious interpretation.

[802]

★**National Teacher Examinations.** Applicants for teaching positions and teacher college seniors; 1940–51; an examination program for use in selection of teachers and the appraisal of teachers-in-training; IBM; 2 parts; tests administered annually in February at centers established by Educational Testing Service; application form and bulletin of information may be obtained from publisher; Common Examinations with or without 1 Optional Examination: $6 for full-time students, $10 for other candidates; Common Examinations with 2 Optional Examinations: $8 for full-time students, $12 for other candidates; 1 or 2 Optional Examinations: $5.50 for all candidates; fees include scoring service and reporting of scores to examinee and any 2 agencies designated at time of application; $1 per each additional report requested at that time or any time thereafter; prepared under the direction of the Staff of Educational Testing Service with the consultation of the Committee for the National Teacher Examinations; Educational Testing Service. *
a) COMMON EXAMINATIONS. 6 scores: professional information, history-literature-fine arts, science and mathematics, English expression, nonverbal reasoning, total; 185(210) minutes.
b) OPTIONAL EXAMINATIONS. Candidates may not elect more than 2 of 9 tests: Education in the Elementary School, Biological Sciences, English Language and Literature, Industrial Arts Education, Mathematics, Physical Sciences, Social Studies, French, Spanish; 80(90) minutes per test.

REFERENCES
    1. TOWNSEND, M. E. "An Experiment in the Professional Examination of Teachers." *Sch & Soc* 50:537–41 O 21 '39. * (*PA* 14:1097)
    2. COLLINS, EVAN R. "Teacher Selection by Examination." Editorial. *Harvard Ed R* 10:3–6 Ja '40. *
    3. ROWLAND, ALBERT LINDSAY. "The Proposed Teacher-Examination Service." *Harvard Ed R* 10:283–8 My '40. *
    4. RYANS, DAVID G. "The Professional Examination of Teaching Candidates: A Report of the First Annual Administration of the National Teacher Examinations." *Sch & Soc* 52:273–84 O 5 '40. * (*PA* 15:548)
    5. STODDARD, A. J. "The Selection of Teachers From the National Viewpoint." *Ed Rec* 21(sup 13):144–51 Ja '40. *
    6. WOOD, BEN D. "Making Use of the Objective Examination as a Phase of Teacher Selection." *Harvard Ed R* 10:277–82 My '40. *
    7. ANDERSON, WALTER A. "National Teacher Examinations: A Criticism." *Childh Ed* 18:179–81 D '41. *
    8. CRISSY, WILLIAM J. E. "A Reply to an Examinee's Reactions to the National Teacher Examinations." *J Higher Ed* 12:484–7 D '41. * Reply to 20. (*PA* 16:1655)
    9. CROON, CHARLOTTE W. "Performance of the Physical Science Candidates in the National Teacher Examinations." *Am J Physics* 9:45–9 F '41. *
    10. DAVIS, FREDERICK B. "The Measurement of Professional

Information Among Candidates for Teaching Positions." *Ed Adm & Sup* 27:99–106 F '41. *

11. DOUGLASS, HARL R. "National Teachers' Examinations—Menace or Answer to Prayer?" *Nation's Sch* 27:24–5 Je '41. *

12. FLANAGAN, JOHN C. "An Analysis of the Results From the First Annual Edition of the National Teacher Examinations." *J Exp Ed* 9:237–50 Mr '41. * (*PA* 15:4391)

13. FLANAGAN, JOHN C. "A Preliminary Study of the Validity of the 1940 Edition of the National Teacher Examinations." *Sch & Soc* 54:59–64 Jl 26 '41. * (*PA* 15:4791)

14. KING, HAROLD V. "The Performance of the Latin Group in the 1940 National Teacher Examinations." *Classical J* 36: 357–61 Mr '41. *

15. PILLEY, JOHN G. "The National Teacher Examination Service." *Sch R* 49:177–86 Mr '41. * (*PA* 15:2805)

16. REED, CARROLL R. "The Role of Examinations in Teacher Selection." *Ed Rec* 22(sup 14):44–53 Ja '41. *

17. RYANS, DAVID G. "The 1941 Administration of the National Teacher Examinations." *Sch & Soc* 54:361–8 O 25 '41. * (*PA* 16:767)

18. SPANEY, EMMA. "The Performance of the Mathematics Candidates in the 1940 National Teachers Examinations." *Math Teach* 34:8–10 Ja '41. * (*PA* 15:4026, title only)

19. SPAULDING, GERALDINE. "The Achievement of the Modern Language Candidates in the National Teacher Examinations." *Mod Lang J* 25:361–7 F '41. *

20. WINETROUT, KENNETH. "The National Teacher Examinations, 1941: Criticisms, Adverse and Appreciative, by a Recent Examinee." *J Higher Ed* 12:479–84 D '41. * For reply, see 8. (*PA* 16:1706)

21. WOOD, B. D. "Scores on National Committee Teachers Examinations, 1940 and 1941." *Sch & Soc* 54:625–7 D 27 '41. * (*PA* 16:1707)

22. CRISSY, WILLIAM J. E. "The National Teacher Examinations." *Phi Delta Kappan* 24:353–6 My '42. *

23. CRISSY, WILLIAM J. E., AND FLANAGAN, JOHN C. "A Plan for Using Punched Cards in Presenting Test Results in Profile Form." *J Appl Psychol* 26:94–105 F '42. * (*PA* 16: 2129)

24. NICHOLS, ALBERT S. "Laws Affecting Employment." *Phi Delta Kappan* 24:357–9 My '42. *

25. PEARSON, CARL A., AND RYANS, DAVID G. "The Performance of Science Teachers on the 1941 National Teacher Examinations." *Sci Counselor* 8:2–4+ Mr '42. *

26. WOOD, BEN D. "National Teacher Examinations: A Reply to Dr. Anderson." *Childh Ed* 18:227–30 Ja '42. *

27. RYANS, DAVID G. "New Features of the National Teacher Examination Program." *J Ed Res* 39:155 O '45. *

28. LINS, LEO JOSEPH. "The Prediction of Teaching Efficiency." *J Exp Ed* 15:2–60 S '46. * (*PA* 21:610)

29. RYANS, DAVID G. *Notes on the Selection of Classroom Teachers: The Interview.* Teacher Selection Papers and Reports, No. 6. New York: National Committee on Teacher Examinations, American Council on Education, October 9, 1946. Pp. 7. Paper, lithotyped. *

30. CROW, E. R. "Teacher Examinations and the South Carolina Certification Program." *Ed Rec* 28:454–62 O '47. *

31. EMENS, JOHN R. "National Teachers Examinations: With Suggestions for Their Improvement in Ways That Will Prevent Certain Unfavorable Results." *Nation's Schools* 39:47 F '47. * (*PA* 21:1639)

32. RYANS, DAVID G. "Appraising Teacher Personnel: A Report of Activities of the American Council on Education's Committee on Teacher Examinations and an Analysis of the Results of the Eighth Annual Teacher Examination Program." *J Exp Ed* 16:1–30 S '47. * (*PA* 22:1885)

33. RYANS, DAVID G. *Comparing the Qualifications of Teachers.* Teacher Selection Papers and Reports, No. 11. New York: National Committee on Teacher Examinations, American Council on Education, June 10, 1947. Pp. 27. Paper, lithotyped. *

34. RYANS, DAVID G. "Statistical Procedures in the Selection of Teachers." *J Ed Res* 40:695–705 My '47. (*PA* 22:469)

35. RYANS, DAVID G. *Use of the National Teacher Examinations in Colleges and Universities.* Teacher Selection Papers and Reports, No. 10. New York: National Committee on Teacher Examinations, American Council on Education, June 3, 1947. Pp. 7. Paper, lithotyped. *

36. RYANS, DAVID G. "The 1948 National Teacher Examinations: A Summary Report of Activities of the American Council on Education's Committee on Teacher Examinations Including an Analysis of the Ninth Annual Teacher Examination Program." *J Exp Ed* 17:1–25 S '48. * (*PA* 23:4441)

37. ECKELBERRY, R. H. "Higher Salaries for Superior Teachers." *Ed Res B* 28:77–8+ Mr 16 '49. *

38. RYANS, DAVID G. "An Analysis of Teacher Examination Scores of College Seniors Who Expect to Become Teachers." Abstract. *Am Psychol* 4:288 Jl '49. * (*PA* 23:6459, title only)

39. RYANS, DAVID G. "The Function of Examinations in the Selection of Teachers." *Sch Executive* 68:39–41 My '49. *

40. RYANS, DAVID G. "The Use of the National Teacher Examinations in Colleges and Universities." *J Ed Res* 42:678–89 My '49. * (*PA* 24:322)

41. RYANS, DAVID G. "The Use of National Teacher Examinations in School Systems." *Ed Adm & Sup* 35:65–88 F '49. *

42. SEAGOE, MAY V. "The Prediction of Success in a Graduate School of Education." *Sch & Soc* 69:89–93 F 5 '49. * (*PA* 25:7110)

43. RYANS, DAVID G. "The Results of Internal Consistency and External Validation Procedures Applied in the Analysis of Test Items Measuring Professional Information." *Ed & Psychol Meas* 11:549–60 W '51. *

HARRY N. RIVLIN, *Professor of Education and Chairman of the Department; and Director of Graduate Studies; Queens College, Flushing, New York.*

These examinations are objective written tests, administered under standardized conditions, which are designed to measure the relative adequacy of the preparation of candidates for teaching positions in elementary and secondary schools. New editions are prepared annually.

The examinations are available for a 30-day confidential inspection by officials of teacher education institutions and school systems whose positions give assurance that the reviewers are likely to make intelligent use of the information gained by reviewing the specific content of any one annual form of the examinations. The Educational Testing Service furnishes confidential review copies to superintendents and to examiners or personnel directors attached to their staffs. In similar fashion, the ETS seldom raises any question with regard to furnishing the president or dean of teacher education institutions with confidential review copies of the tests.

All examinees take some examinations in common and, in addition, such optional examinations as they wish to take to demonstrate their qualifications for specific types of teaching positions. The administration of the examinations was modified, beginning with the 1951 edition, so that the Common Examinations are administered in the morning session, with provision made for candidates to take one or two Optional Examinations in the afternoon session.

The Common Examination, which takes 185 minutes of testing time, includes a test of professional information (education as a social institution, child development and educational psychology, guidance and measurement in education, and general principles and methods of teaching); English expression; history, literature, and fine arts; science and mathematics; and nonverbal reasoning. The Optional Examinations, which take 80 minutes of testing time each, are offered in education in the elementary school, biological sciences, English language and literature, industrial arts education, mathematics, physical sciences, social sciences, French, and Spanish.

All scores are converted into scaled scores so that the results on one part of the examination can be compared with those on another part and the results of an examination administered one year can be compared with those of another year. At the candidate's request, the results are made available to colleges and superintendents of his choice.

Inaugurated under the auspices of the American Council on Education in 1939, these examinations have been administered annually since 1940. Few examinations have been the center of greater controversy. Within the first 10 years, more than 68 articles were published explaining, defending, and attacking them. This reviewer's analysis is based upon this published material and upon two complete sets of examinations which were made available to him for the purpose of this review.

One of the major advantages of the *National Teacher Examinations* is that it introduces an objective basis for comparing the graduates of teacher education institutions so that the student who comes from an institution that grades severely is not penalized in competing for a position with graduates of other institutions that grade more leniently.

The examinations are carefully constructed. The distribution of emphasis is sound and the items are, with few exceptions, unobjectionable. There is a definite attempt, particularly in the professional information test, to measure not only the candidate's knowledge but also his ability to apply it to classroom situations. According to ETS reports, the examinations are sufficiently reliable for the use for which they are intended. That the examinations are valid, the ETS submits, is evident from the way in which the items and the keys are reviewed by experts in the field and by the success with which they discriminate between good and poor candidates. Items which have been used are evaluated statistically and are then used in subsequent examinations as a partial basis for evaluating other examination items.

An analysis of previous examination results indicates that there is a perfect positive correlation between the average standard scores of each group and the amount of educational training the group has had. Thus, candidates with the doctorate earn a higher average standard score than do those with a master's degree; those with a master's degree have higher average standard scores than do those with only a baccalaureate degree; and college graduates have higher average standard scores than do those candidates who have had less than a four year college course.

In a recent small scale comparison, teachers in training judged by faculty members as "likely to succeed" attained significantly higher scores on the teacher examinations than did their fellow students judged "likely not to be successful teachers" (Biserial correlation coefficient .48).

The examinations admittedly measure only what the candidates know about educational theory and about their subjects. Those who construct the tests are careful to emphasize that the ability to teach is not measured. Those who are to use the results of these examinations must be equally careful not to assume that the tests measure what even the authors and editors do not claim them to do.

The subject matter tests could well be used to measure the mastery of college students who have majored in a given subject area. Though there are usually some items on each test that are directly related to the content of the secondary schools, the major source of the items is the college curriculum and not the secondary school curriculum. To be sure, the richer the prospective teacher is in his area of specialization, the more he has to share with his students. There is, however, the question of whether the person who has taken an endless number of college and university courses is really well prepared to teach the subject to junior and senior high school students if he is not thoroughly familiar with those aspects of the subject matter that play the greatest role in the lives of adolescents. It must be admitted that there are many items that test the scholarship of a graduate student but that do not indicate his ability to apply his scholarship to secondary school teaching or his familiarity with the content of the secondary school. The modern secondary school is more than a watered-down version of a college or a university. A candidate with a perfect score may not be a better equipped prospective teacher than is another candidate who misses a half dozen items. It may be that these subject matter tests would be more useful to superintendents if they drew more heavily upon the secondary school curriculum.

Everyone who has ever edited a standardized test knows how easy it is for the editor to modify questions prepared by even competent item writers. There are, therefore, bound to be a number of items on any published test to which competent people can take exception. The present examinations are no exception. There were a number of items on this test for which this re-

National Teacher Examinations

viewer would accept answers different from those given in the official answer key. While it is possible that this reviewer is in error in his answer to the items, there is also the possibility that there are situations in education where the experts will disagree in their choice of the best solution. This is particularly true where the examination, in order to measure the candidate's ability to apply his information to the classroom, presents the candidate with a classroom situation with the request that he indicate what he would do under the circumstances. The description of the situation has to be brief and, therefore, includes some data that the test authors consider to be the determining factor in the situation. Other educators, however, thinking of the circumstances under which such a situation may arise, may attach more significance to what the authors consider to be relatively trivial. While the official key may be the correct answer for most instances of the type of situation described in the item, there may be a few cases where the accepted solution may be so inadvisable that those who know schools are reluctant to offer the blanket advice suggested in the answer.

One of the difficulties in the preparation of the *National Teacher Examinations* is that we do not have a national school system. Our elementary schools, for example, vary from highly departmentalized subject matter schools to experience curriculum schools. The background which a teacher needs differs so much from one extreme of educational practice to the other that it is hard to conceive of an examination in elementary education that is equally appropriate for so wide a variety of schools. Most of the items in elementary education, for example, are still conceived in terms of a school which teaches isolated subjects and may not be most appropriate for selecting teachers for elementary schools which expect their staffs to be able to build their curriculum with the children.

How, then, should these examinations be used? Regardless of how useful these tests are as a means of measuring what a candidate knows about teaching and about the subject he teaches, they do not measure many of the most important aspects of the candidate's ability to teach. There are, for example, no ways in which these tests measure the ability to develop rapport with children, the effectiveness in communicating to children, or the candidate's own personal adjustment, to mention only some of the factors that are important in teaching success. For this

reason, those who use the *National Teacher Examinations* should supplement them with other, more personal, ones.

This reviewer has served as one of the outside consultants used by school systems to help evaluate candidates for teaching positions whose score on the *National Teacher Examinations* was known to the examining committee. In these situations, knowing the score made the interview much more efficient and effective since it was unnecessary to attempt to evaluate orally what had already been measured more objectively and more thoroughly. The examiners, therefore, were free to measure the subjective elements of the student's personal qualifications for getting along with children and with colleagues and for serving as an effective leader in a democratic classroom and school situation.

For what they are intended to serve, the examinations are undoubtedly valuable. They do measure the candidate's background of knowledge about teaching in a typical situation. For schools that are interested in knowing more about a candidate than just what he knows about teaching, these examinations should be supplemented by an examination of the candidate's college record, of his success as a teacher, and of his personal qualifications.

[803]

★The Purdue Rating Scale for Instruction. College; 1927–50; ratings on 26 characteristics of the instructor and teaching situation; formerly called *The Purdue Rating Scale for Instructors;* IBM; 1 form, '50; manual ('50); norms ('50); 3¢ per IBM scale-answer sheet; 5¢ per profile chart; 15¢ per manual; 25¢ per specimen set; postpaid; nontimed (20) minutes; H. H. Remmers, D. N. Elliott (scale), and P. C. Baker (manual); Personnel Evaluation Research Service, Division of Educational Reference, Purdue University. *

REFERENCES

1. REMMERS, H. H., AND BRANDENBURG, G. C. "Experimental Data on the Purdue Rating Scale for Instructors." *Ed Adm & Sup* 13:519–27 N '27. *
2. REMMERS, H. H., AND BRANDENBURG, G. C. "Rating Scales for Instructors." *Ed Adm & Sup* 13:399–406 S '27. *
3. REMMERS, H. H.; SHOCK, N. W.; AND KELLY, E. L. "An Empirical Study of the Validity of the Spearman-Brown Formula as Applied to the Purdue Rating Scale." *J Ed Psychol* 18:187–95 Mr '27. * (*PA* 1:1449)
4. REMMERS, H. H. "The Relationship Between Students' Marks and Student Attitude Toward Instructors." *Sch & Soc* 28:759–60 D 15 '28. * (*PA* 3:1345)
5. STALNAKER, J. M., AND REMMERS, H. H. "Can Students Discriminate Traits Associated With Success in Teaching?" *J Appl Psychol* 12:602–10 D '28. * (*PA* 3:1717)
6. REMMERS, H. H. "Departmental Difference in the Quality of Instruction as Seen by Students." *Sch & Soc* 30:332–4 S '29. * (*PA* 3:4649)
7. REMMERS, H. H., AND WYKOFF, G. S. "Student Rating of College Teaching—a Reply." *Sch & Soc* 30:232–4 Ag '29. * (*PA* 3:4293)
8. REMMERS, H. H. "The Measurement of Teaching Personality and Its Relation to the Learning Process." *Ed* 51:27–35 S '30. *
9. REMMERS, H. H. "To What Extent Do Grades Influence Student Ratings of Instructors?" *J Ed Res* 21:314–6 Ap '30. * (*PA* 4:3293)
10. REMMERS, H. H. "The Equivalence of Judgments to

Test Items in the Sense of the Spearman-Brown Formula."
J Ed Psychol 22:66–71 Ja '31. * (PA 5:2591)

11. REMMERS, H. H. "Reliability and Halo Effect of High
School and College Students' Judgments of Their Teachers."
J Appl Psychol 18:619–30 O '34. * (PA 9:2984)

12. HOSHAW, LOYAL D. "The Construction and Evaluation
of a Scale for Measuring Attitude Toward Any Teacher," pp.
238–51. (PA 11:3415) In *Further Studies in Attitudes, Series
II.* Edited by H. H. Remmers. Bulletin of Purdue University,
Vol. 37, No. 4; Studies in Higher Education, No. 31. Lafayette,
Ind.: Division of Educational Reference, Purdue University,
December 1936. Pp. 298. Paper. *

13. WARD, WILLIAM D.; REMMERS, H. H.; AND SCHMALZRIED,
N. T. "The Training of Teaching-Personality by Means of
Student-Ratings." *Sch & Soc* 53:189–92 F 8 '41. *

14. SCHMALZRIED, N. T., AND REMMERS, H. H. "A Factor
Analysis of the Purdue Rating Scale for Instructors." *J Ed
Psychol* 34:363–7 S '43. * (PA 18:897)

15. REMMERS, H. H.; DAVENPORT, K. S.; AND POTTER, A. A.
"The Best and Worst Teachers of Engineering." *J Eng Ed*
36:296–8 D '45. *

16. REMMERS, H. H.; DAVENPORT, K. S.; AND POTTER, A. A.
The Best and the Worst Teachers of Engineering. Purdue Uni-
versity, Division of Educational Reference, Studies in Higher
Education [No.] 57; Studies in Engineering Education [No.]
3. Lafayette, Ind.: the Division, October 1946. Pp. 17. Paper. *
(PA 21:2029)

17. ELLIOTT, D. N. *Characteristics and Relationships of Various Criteria of Teaching.* Doctor's thesis, Purdue University
(Lafayette, Ind.), 1949.

18. REMMERS, H. H., AND ELLIOTT, D. N. "The Indiana
College and University Staff-Evaluation Program." *Sch & Soc*
70:168–71 S 10 '49. * (PA 26:2440)

19. REMMERS, H. H.; MARTIN, F. D.; AND ELLIOTT, D. N.
"Are Students' Ratings of Instructors Related to Their Grades?"
pp. 17–26. (PA 25:2679) In *Student Achievement and Instructor Evaluation in Chemistry.* Edited by H. H. Remmers. Purdue
University, Division of Educational Reference, Studies in
Higher Education [No.] 66. Lafayette, Ind.: the Division, July
1949. Pp. 29. Paper. *

20. CREAGER, JOHN A. "A Multiple-Factor Analysis of the
Purdue Rating Scale for Instructors," pp. 75–96. (PA 24:4909)
In *Studies in College and University Staff Evaluation.* Edited
by H. H. Remmers. Purdue University, Division of Educa-
tional Reference, Studies in Higher Education [No.] 70;
Further Studies in Attitudes, Series 15. Lafayette, Ind.: the
Division, March 1950. Pp. 96. Paper. *

21. CREAGER, JOHN ALDEN. *A Multiple Factor Analysis of
the Purdue Rating Scale for Instructors.* Master's thesis, Purdue University, (Lafayette, Ind.), 1950. (PA 24:4909, title
only)

22. DRUCKER, A. J., AND REMMERS, H. H. "Do Alumni and
Students Differ in Their Attitudes Toward Instructors?" pp.
62–74. In *Studies in College and University Staff Evaluation.*
Edited by H. H. Remmers. Purdue University, Division of
Educational Reference, Studies in Higher Education [No.]
70; Further Studies in Attitudes, Series 15. Lafayette, Ind.: the
Division, March 1950. Pp. 96. Paper. *

23. ELLIOTT, DONALD N. "Characteristics and Relationships
of Various Criteria of College and University Teaching," pp.
5–61. In *Studies in College and University Staff Evaluation.*
Edited by H. H. Remmers. Purdue University, Division of
Educational Reference, Studies in Higher Education [No.]
70; Further Studies in Attitudes, Series 15. Lafayette, Ind.:
the Division, March 1950. Pp. 96. Paper. *

24. BAKER, P. C., AND REMMERS, H. H. "Progress in Research on Personnel Evaluation." *J Teacher Ed* 2:143–6 Je '51. *

25. CARTER, GERALD C. "A Factor Analysis of Student Personality Traits." *J Ed Res* 44:381–85 Ja '51. * (PA 25:8264)

26. DRUCKER, A. J., AND REMMERS, H. H. "Do Alumni and
Students Differ in Their Attitudes Toward Instructors?" *J
Ed Psychol* 42:129–43 Mr '51. * (PA 25:7698)

KENNETH L. HEATON, *Richardson, Bellows,
Henry and Company, Inc., Philadelphia, Pennsylvania.*

The 1950 edition of this scale presents the 10
instructor traits included in the original 1927
scale together with 16 characteristics which describe the teaching situation ("Suitability of the
method or methods by which the subject matter
is presented," "Suitability of the size of the
class," "Degree to which the objectives of the
course were clarified and discussed," etc.).

No effort has been made to validate the instrument as a " 'true' measure of the instructor's
ability." The authors present the instrument as

"primarily a device for ascertaining student
judgments concerning the traits in question"
but have not validated it on this basis. The manual includes a report of findings from experimental use of previous forms. These reports indicate that such instruments have motivated instructors to make needed improvements. The
manual also includes a discussion of the instrument and factors to be considered in its use, so
presented as to be reassuring to the instructor
who is not used to the technical details involved
or who is reluctant to encourage an expression
of student criticism.

The rating form itself is designed for either
IBM scoring or for hand scoring. The mechanics seem unnecessarily complex in that the first
10 items are to be marked and scored on one
basis and the last 16 items on another. There is
no apparent reason for the difference in format.

The scale can be useful as an encouragement
to criticism. The need for supplementary exchanges of more analytical and specific suggestions for improvement, and the need for criticism from those who are more expert than
students in judging the educational process, is
obvious.

[804]

★**Scale for Rating Effective Teacher Behavior.**
Teachers; 1947; 38 behavior items grouped under 6
categories: fairness, cheerfulness, sympathetic understanding, control, ability to stimulate response, knowledge; 1 form; no description of normative population;
manual ('47); norms ('50); $2 per 25, postage extra;
Dwight E. Beecher; the Author, Congdon Campus
School, State Teachers College, Potsdam, N.Y. *

REFERENCES

1. BEECHER, DWIGHT F. *The Evaluation of Teaching: Backgrounds and Concepts.* Introduction by Maurice E. Troyer.
New York: Syracuse University Press, 1949. Pp. xi, 105. Paper. (PA 24:3901)

LEO J. BRUECKNER, *Professor of Education,
University of Minnesota, Minneapolis, Minnesota.*

The items in this scale consist of "those qualities which available evidence indicates are universally apparent to pupils" when they are asked
to appraise the work of teachers. Each item is
expressed as observable teacher "reaction behaviors" which can be noted by an observer of
the activities of a teacher in a classroom situation.

In stating the items an unfortunate use is
made of such "universal" expressions as "no
pets," "all pupils," "every opportunity," and
"never disregarded." The observer is required
to make an appraisal on an either-or basis.
Either the item as stated in the list was observed,
in which case a plus rating is given, or the re-

verse type of behavior was observed, in which case a minus rating is given. Space is provided on the blank for "anecdotal records of behavior." When the item is not observed, as the author indicates is often the case, no rating is given. There is no differentiation in the weighting given to the various items in the scale. The score on which a rating is based is the percentage of items observed for which the rating was plus.

The dichotomy used in appraising the items in the scale is obviously open to question. For example, a rating of Item 12, "friendly in manner and tone of voice to all pupils," would be an expression of a judgment and would be complicated by the word "all." How would an observer rate the item if the manner was friendly but the voice did not appear to be friendly? How would the item be rated if the teacher for even an instant betrayed irritation with some single pupil in the class who raised a disturbance? Technically the rating would have to be minus because of the word all, whereas otherwise the rating might have been a plus, as judged by the general impression given. Universals should not be included in a rating device. Nor should ratings be either plus or minus, since degrees exist in the extent to which any observable behavior may be present. The use of some sort of profile chart might make possible some expression of the degree to which any item of behavior was present.

EDWIN WANDT, *Statistician and Research Associate, Teacher Characteristics Study of the American Council on Education, University of California, Los Angeles, California.*

This rating scale consists of 38 items of observable teacher behavior which are reacted to most frequently and intensely by pupils. The basic assumption of the author is "that pupil-teacher relationships are a vital, if not the most important, factor in effective teaching."

The 38 items are grouped into 6 categories: indications of fairness (6 items), indications of cheerfulness (5 items), indications of sympathetic understanding (7 items), business-like procedure in controlled situations (8 items), ability to get pupil response (6 items), and knowledge and technique (6 items).

The scale is filled out by an observer who sees the teacher in the classroom. Each item of behavior which the teacher exhibits is marked plus, and each item which is noticeably lacking, in the face of opportunity for its occurrence, is marked minus. Sufficient observation time is allowed for the checking of approximately 25 items. Two or more classroom visits will usually be necessary for one "complete observation." The author recommends that two such "complete observations" be made at intervals of several weeks or months, and that the results be averaged. The score on the scale is the percentage which the plus items are of all items checked. For example, a teacher who received 20 plus items and 5 minus items would receive a score of 80.

Scores on the scale correspond fairly well with estimates of teaching efficiency obtained from administrators. A contingency coefficient of .72 was obtained between judges' ratings and scores on the scale based on a sample of 50 teachers. (The coefficient .88 reported in the manual is not a contingency coefficient but rather a questionable estimate of the product moment correlation coefficient.)

The reliability of the total scale of 38 items, as reported for two small samples, seems to be adequate. A correlation coefficient of .90 was obtained between two sets of observations made by Beecher ($N = 50$). A correlation coefficient of .79 was obtained between the observations made by two independent judges ($N = 50$).

The norms consist of the nine deciles. Although the median should equal the fifth decile, different values are reported. Because the number of teachers, the kinds of teachers, and the schools from which the teachers came are not reported, the norms are meaningless. If norms are desired, users of the scale are advised to ignore those furnished norms and to develop their own local ones.

The one-page manual furnished with the scale is inadequate. Persons using the scale will probably wish to read Beecher's monograph (*1*), which contains an account of the development of the scale. (Some of the data reported in this review were obtained from this monograph.)

The choice of items ("observable teacher behaviors to which....pupils react most frequently and intensely") has produced a scale made up of teacher behaviors which many educators feel are associated with effective teaching. The scale is easy to use, and, if the method suggested by the author (two or more "complete observations," each consisting of two or more classroom visits) is followed, it would seem that a sample of important teacher behaviors can be obtained.

Scale for Rating Effective Teacher Behavior

[805]
★Teacher Opinionaire on Democracy. Teachers;
1949; democratic aspects of teacher philosophy; Forms
G, H; manual ['49]; $1 per 25; $1.50 per 25 booklets
containing both forms; 35¢ per specimen set; postpaid;
nontimed (20) minutes; Enola Ledbetter and Theo. F.
Lentz (manual); Character Research Association. *

George W. Hartmann, *Professor of Psychology and Chairman of the Department, Roosevelt College, Chicago, Illinois.*

Two forms, G and H, each containing 65 attitude statements, attempt to measure the degree of "democraticness" manifested by teachers in dealing with educational situations by means of expressed agreement with such items as "Children in a teacher-controlled classroom are no better than slaves," "Loyalty to authorized subject-matter is one of the greatest enemies of democratic living in the classroom," etc. The instructions declare the purpose of the instrument to be a determination of "how teachers feel about what is and is not wise in our treatment of children in school." The context suggests that that variant of the progressive outlook championing maximal pupil freedom of purposing in the *elementary* years is taken as normative by the key. That ethically we can be free only to do the right, that in the long run, a humane, kindly, friendly temper prevents the acceptance of every goal on an equal basis, is a neglected or rejected position.

In principle, there is no question that instructional procedures, as well as personalities, vary from more to less democratic in spirit; but some segmented responses can be dangerously misleading when treated in isolation or mechanically. Thus, the AAUP would officially affirm, in the honored name of hard-won academic freedom, that "Pupils' wishes should have nothing to do with promotion or dismissal of teachers," yet the key considers that an undemocratic position. Certainly it is arguable whether a democratic commitment means the elimination of all compulsory courses, permitting gum-chewing in school, that a principal is unnecessary, simplified spelling, and opposition to systematically organized subject matter per se—all as decreed "authoritatively" by the six harmonizing judges employed in the validation process! The Achilles' heel is right here.

Reliability is given as .87, and percentile norms derived from 400 teachers appear in the manual which sketches, in readable essay fashion, some of the philosophic, social, and professional complications encountered in the development of this device.

The chief merits of the test seem to be in its pioneer novelty, bold willingness to see what can be done to formulate an operative consensus of values, adaptability to a variety of in-service training conditions, and utility as an agency for promoting insight via conceptual analysis into the "logic" of one's instructional practices. But as its authors somewhat apologetically recognize, despite their evangelical motivation, there is some peril that an unofficial supreme court will try to freeze in impressive test form both its sound and unsound decisions as to what is or is not truly democratic conduct. It would seem more in accord not only with field theory but with the very nature of democracy itself that there can be no tenable restricted, local, absolute, authoritative, or "final" determination of either its universal essence or specific pedagogical manifestations.

C. Robert Pace, *Chairman, Department of Psychology, Syracuse University, Syracuse, New York.*

One of the most commendable things about this test is the clear and concise manual: it presents specifically the basic assumptions underlying the Opinionaire; it describes the Opinionaire as a tentative and research instrument; it gives extensive item analysis and reliability data; it suggests uses for the test; it is written in a spirit of humility and as an invitation for others to try the Opinionaire, criticize it, and share in its improvement.

The Opinionaire consists of two forms, each containing 65 statements which the subject is asked to mark plus or minus, indicating general agreement or disagreement. Both forms are printed in the same four-page booklet.

Specific criticisms follow: First, and of most importance, is the choice of basic assumptions underlying the construction of the Opinionaire —that is, the definitions of democracy. Lentz and collaborators recognize this when they say in the manual, "The acceptance of the instrument and the key will vary from one educationist to another * it seemed impossible to the authors to get the test entirely outside the realm of controversy." Yet the basic structure of the test is so important that one wishes the authors had sought a wider range of scholars, especially scholars outside the field of education, before arriving at the design of the instrument. The key was devised by the authors with a check by six outside judges.

Second, the total score is simply the number of statements marked which agree with the key; yet the statements themselves include quite a variety of topics—from racial equalitarianism to the method of making administrative decisions to the desirability of pupils' asking permission before going to the toilet. Presumably, the statements can be grouped about various subtopics, but we do not know what relationship exists among these subtopics or whether, statistically, they should be combined to arrive at a total score. Using the score as a criterion for item analysis or for other statistical study will produce little improvement in the instrument; for, as Davis has so aptly said, "By the time the tryout forms for a test have been constructed, much of the opportunity for selecting items has already passed." [1]

Third, some of the statements in the test lack clarity and simplicity as a consequence of the authors' tendency to be epigrammatic. Here are two examples: "Teachers don't want to encourage pupils to want what they (pupils) want, because they (teachers) are afraid the pupils won't want what the teachers want them to want" and " 'Living cannot take place without learning' is truer than the phrase 'learning cannot take place without living.' " Other statements are difficult to respond to because they contain two concepts which are not necessarily related (e.g., "In a democratic school the principal is unnecessary. Decisions concerning the school life should be made by pupils and teachers jointly.") or because they contain prejudicial words which the authors define in a special way (e.g., "When a child dares to question the teacher's authority or opinion, i.e., when he begins to think for himself, then democracy is working").

Beyond these specific criticisms, most of which are of the sort one could frequently make about test materials still in the rather early stages of development, it seems reasonable to ask whether authors and publishers should print and sell tests for the chief purpose of inviting others to experiment with their materials. The intent of the *Teacher Opinionaire on Democracy* is most admirable and important. If purchasers buy it with the idea of using it to promote discussion about democracy, rather than with the

idea of using it as a measuring instrument, its publication will have been worthwhile.

[806]

Teaching Aptitude Test: George Washington University Series. Grades 12–16; 1927; Form 1; no data on reliability and validity; mimeographed manual; $3 per 25; 30¢ per specimen set; postpaid; 37(45) minutes; F. A. Moss, J. Hunt, and F. C. Wallace; Center for Psychological Service, George Washington University. *

REFERENCES

1–8. See 3:405.

MAY V. SEAGOE, *Professor of Education, University of California, Los Angeles, California.*

An important contribution of the test is its attempt to get away from entirely verbal and remote abstractions and to devise practical situations requiring the application of judgment and professional information. Correlations with grades in student teaching, teacher ratings, and supervisor's ratings are low, in part because of the low reliability of such ratings.

The test has, however, certain limitations. The date of publication (1927) means inevitably that some of the terminology is now obsolete (as "mischievous pupils are usually vicious pupils"), the pictures are noticeably crude, and the typography a little difficult. More important, the sections on "observation and recall" and "recognition of mental states from facial expressions" seem based on assumptions current psychological thought might question.

In conclusion, this reviewer considers the test useful chiefly as a research instrument. Revision might improve its predictive value.

For a review by A. S. Barr, see 3:405.

[807]

★**Wilson Teacher-Appraisal Scale.** Rating of instructors by students in grades 9–16; 1948; 19 ratings: knowledge of subject, sense of humor, presentation, student teacher relationship, self confidence, attitude toward students, interest in students, answering questions, explanations, attitude toward differences, assignments, examinations, examination questions, fairness of examinations, fairness in grading, course, home work, enjoyment, overall; 1 form; no data on reliability and validity; no manual; no norms; $1.50 per 50, postpaid; sample scale free; Howard Wilson; Economic Institute. *

ENGINEERING

[808]

★**College Entrance Examination Board Special Aptitude Test in Spatial Relations.** Candidates for college entrance; 1939–51; available only in College Entrance Examination Board Admissions Testing Program (see 526); 60(70) minutes; prepared by the Staff of Educational Testing Service; program admin-

1 Davis, Frederick B. Chap. 9, "Item Selection Techniques," p. 266. In *Educational Measurement.* Edited by E. F. Lindquist. Washington, D.C.: American Council on Education, 1951. Pp. xix, 819. $6.00. *

istered by Educational Testing Service for the College Entrance Examination Board. *

ROBERT L. THORNDIKE, *Professor of Education, Teachers College, Columbia University, New York, New York.* [Review of Forms VAC2, WAC2, XAC, YAC, and ZAC.]

This test, which is taken by a rather small fraction of CEEB examinees, is designed primarily as an aptitude measure for candidates for engineering and technical schools. As in all CEEB examinations, a new form is assembled for each testing based largely on the existing pool of items for which an accumulation of item analysis data is available. During the academic year 1950–51, the several editions of the test included two or three of the following six item types: (*a*) block counting, (*b*) surface development, (*c*) intersections (of a plane and a 3-dimensional form), (*d*) identical blocks, (*e*) relation of solid forms, and (*f*) number decorated cubes. All of the item types deal with static 3-dimensional forms, and appear to require in varying proportions abilities to visualize, to manipulate mentally and translate in space, to reason deductively, and to be careful and systematic in analysis of a problem.

Inspection of the test items indicates that they are generally well conceived and adequately drawn, though in isolated instances the visual cues seem rather meager. From the internal statistics reported for the various forms of the test, one may conclude that the test (*a*) has an appropriate level and spread of difficulty for the group tested; (*b*) is primarily a power test, though somewhat speeded; and (*c*) has high reliability, represented by odd-even coefficients over .90.

Reported validity data are limited to one set of correlations with freshman grades at Cooper Union School of Engineering for a group of 87 students. The highest correlations were with grades in descriptive geometry (.40 and .49) and physics (.40 and .34). The correlation with freshman grade-point average was .33, and the test appeared to make a small addition to the composite prediction resulting from other College Board tests and high school grades.

In general, this appears to be a workmanlike test in a somewhat specialized aptitude area. However, further evidence would be desirable on the range and level of the test's validity as a predictor of different phases of college achievement.

[809]

★College Entrance Examination Board Test in Pre-Engineering Science Comprehension. Candidates for college entrance; 1949–51; available only in College Entrance Examination Board Admissions Testing Program (see 526); 60(70) minutes; prepared by the Staff of Educational Testing Service; program administered by Educational Testing Service for the College Entrance Examination Board. *

[810]

*Engineering and Physical Science Aptitude Test. Grade 12 and technical school entrants; 1943–51; 7 scores: mathematics, formulation, physical science comprehension, arithmetic reasoning, verbal comprehension, mechanical comprehension, total; IBM; 1 form, '43; revised manual ['51]; $4.25 per 25; separate answer sheets must be used; $2.10 per 50 IBM answer sheets; 50¢ per set of manual and machine scoring stencils; 50¢ per set of manual and hand scoring stencils; 60¢ per specimen set; postpaid; 72(80–90) minutes; manual by Henry Borow; Bruce V. Moore, C. J. Lapp, and Charles H. Griffin; Psychological Corporation. *

REFERENCES
1. GRIFFIN, CHARLES H., AND BOROW, HENRY. "An Engineering and Physical Science Aptitude Test." *J Appl Psychol* 28:376–87 O '44. * (*PA* 19:543)
2. COOPRIDER, H. A., AND LASLETT, H. R. "Predictive Values of the Stanford Scientific and the Engineering and Physical Science Aptitude Tests." *Ed & Psychol Meas* 8:683–7 w '48. * (*PA* 24:1488)
3. BARNETTE, W. LESLIE, JR. *Occupational Aptitude Patterns of Counseled Veterans.* Doctor's thesis, New York University (New York, N.Y.), 1949. Pp. viii, 385. *
4. TREUMANN, MILDRED JENKINS, AND SULLIVAN, BEN A. "Use of the Engineering and Physical Science Aptitude Test as a Predictor of Academic Achievement of Freshman Engineering Students." *J Ed Res* 43:129–33 O '49. * (*PA* 24:2804)
5. BARNETTE, W. LESLIE, JR. *Occupational Aptitude Patterns of Selected Groups of Counseled Veterans.* American Psychological Association, Psychological Monographs: General and Applied, Vol. 65, No. 5, Whole No. 322. Washington, D.C.: the Association, Inc., 1951. Pp. v, 49. Paper. * (*PA* 26:2794)
6. GREGG, GEORGE W. "An Investigation of the Reliability and Validity of the Engineering and Physical Science Aptitude Test." *J Ed Res* 45:299–305 D '51. * (*PA* 26:6546)

JOHN W. FRENCH, *Research Associate, Educational Testing Service, Princeton, New Jersey.*

The materials for this test were compiled from earlier standardized tests with the purpose of measuring aptitude for training in work of an engineering and physical science nature. To point out that a test contains nothing new might be taken as an adverse comment. However, in the area of physical science and engineering prediction, we have gotten beyond the notion that the best test is the one containing the newest and most ingenious mind twisters. The method of test construction used here can be depended upon to result in a highly satisfactory test battery, since selection of materials can be based on a history of good performance.

Selection of the subtests and some of the items was based on correlation with Form 1936B of the *Cooperative Physics Test for College Students: Mechanics* given at the end of a physics course. Although this is an excellent selection technique, several different tests should have been used as criteria since the EPSAT is supposed to predict various aspects of physics and engineering as well as mechanics. For example, the use of such a criterion as end-of-course proficiency in engineering drawing would probably have led to the inclusion of a test of spatial ability, a well known predictor of success in graphic work.

Although the range of materials may have been limited in some degree by the narrow nature of the criterion used for their selection, the quality of the materials is very high, as are the tests from which they were selected. The mathematics part is varied and appropriately independent of specific knowledge; the formulation part is a highly ingenious measure of the ability to put verbal expression into quantitative form; the part on physical science comprehension has a wide coverage and includes information that an alert high school student can pick up outside of specific courses, although a course in physics would certainly help; the arithmetic reasoning part is good but is probably too short to be adequately reliable; the verbal comprehension part covers information that, although technical, can be learned outside of specific courses; and the mechanical comprehension part reflects the high quality of Bennett's original instrument.

The manual as revised in 1951 is considerably above most test manuals in both comprehension and understandability. There are included a fair discussion of purpose, excellent directions for administration, satisfactory directions for scoring, a good explanation of the construction of the battery, and detailed discussions of its validity and reliability. The discussion of test validity, although based on small numbers (53 to 296), includes descriptions of five different studies. For one of these a very unusual table gives the validity of the battery for each of the eight semesters of work at an engineering college. The discussion of reliability recognizes that reliability computed by the split half technique is spuriously high. The figure of .96 is given as the split half reliability for the battery. As a lower limit for the true reliability the figure .84 is given as the reliability of the battery estimated by correlating Parts I, III, and IV with Parts II, V, and VI. No mention is made of a Spearman-Brown correction. A table of intercorrelations among the parts of the battery and one with other tests are included. Percentile norms are given for six groups of students, one group of

applicants for engineering training at an airplane plant, and two employee groups. The numbers in these groups range from 113 to 6,695. Very appropriately no national norming is attempted. The norms for the nine groups mentioned are all presented in one table and give a very clear picture of the meaning of the test scores.

This test is a very good composite of earlier test materials designed to measure physics and engineering aptitude. With some limitations resulting from the use of a test of mechanics as a criterion for selecting subtests, the choice of materials is wise and the resulting test is of wide coverage and good validity. The nature of the test and the excellence of the manual will result in unusual ease of administration and clarity of interpretation.

For reviews by Norman Fredericksen and Robert M. W. Travers, see 3:698.

[811]

★Graduate Record Examinations Advanced Engineering Test. Senior year college through graduate school and candidates for graduate school; 1939–51; available only in Graduate Record Examinations programs (see 527); 180(220) minutes; prepared by the Advanced Engineering Test Committee appointed by Educational Testing Service: Ernst Weber (Chairman), Ovid W. Eshbach, Frederic T. Mavis, William E. Reaser, and John Henry Rushton; Educational Testing Service. *

[812]

★Pre-Engineering Ability Test. Engineering school entrants; 1951–52; an abbreviated adaptation of *Pre-Engineering Inventory* ('43); IBM; Form ZPA ('51); [revised] manual ('52); $10 per 25; separate answer sheets must be used; 80¢ per 25 IBM answer sheets; 25¢ per stencil for scoring answer sheets; cash orders postpaid; $1 per specimen set, postpaid; 80(90) minutes; Educational Testing Service. *

REFERENCES

1. VAUGHN, KENNETH W. "Pre-Engineering Inventory." *J Eng Ed* 34:615–25 My '44. *
2. VAUGHN, K. W. "The Measurement and Guidance Project in Engineering Education—A Report of Progress and Plans." *J Eng Ed* 36:676–84 Je '46. * (*PA* 21:297)
3. JEX, FRANK BIRD. *The Predictive Value of the Pre-Engineering Inventory.* Master's thesis, University of Utah (Salt Lake City, Utah), 1947.
4. LONG, LOUIS, AND PERRY, JAMES D. "Entrance Examinations at the City College of New York." *Ed & Psychol Meas* 7:765–72 w '47. * (*PA* 23:310)
5. SLAYMAKER, R. R. "Admission Test Procedure." *J Eng Ed* 37:402–13 Ja '47. * (*PA* 21:1661)
6. VAUGHN, K. W. "The Projects of the Graduate Record Office," pp. 41–50. (*PA* 22:3216) In *National Projects in Educational Measurement: A Report of the 1946 Invitational Conference on Testing Problems, New York City, November 2, 1946*, Herschel T. Manuel, Chairman. Edited by K. W. Vaughn. Sponsored by the Committee on Measurement and Guidance. American Council on Education Studies, Vol. 11; Series 1, Reports of Committees and Conferences, No. 28. Washington, D.C.: the Council, August 1947. Pp. vii, 80. Paper. *
7. SWEENEY, J. W. *The Value of Pre-Engineering Tests in Predicting Scholastic Success in an Engineering Curriculum.* Master's thesis, Georgia Institute of Technology (Atlanta, Ga.), 1948.
8. WREN, HAROLD A. "Alice in Testingland." *Occupations* 27:34–7 O '48. * (*PA* 23:1335)
9. JOHNSON, A. PEMBERTON. "College Board Mathematical Tests and the Pre-Engineering Inventory Predict Scholastic Success in Colleges of Engineering." Abstract. *Am Psychol* 5:353 Jl '50. * (*PA* 25:1279, title only)

10. LORD, FREDERIC; COWLES, JOHN T.; AND CYNAMON, MANUEL. "The Pre-Engineering Inventory as a Predictor of Success in Engineering Colleges." *J Appl Psychol* 34:30-9 F '50. * (PA 24:6061)
11. PIERSON, GEORGE A., AND JEX, FRANK B. "Using the Cooperative General Achievement Tests to Predict Success in Engineering." *Ed & Psychol Meas* 11:397-402 au '51. *

JEROME E. DOPPELT, *Assistant Director, Test Division, The Psychological Corporation, New York, New York.*

This test was made by selecting items from two tests of the *Pre-Engineering Inventory*. The purpose was to produce an instrument which would be cheaper, shorter and easier to administer than the Inventory and, at the same time, would yield a score approximating the validity of the Inventory composite score. This composite score, which is based on three of the seven Inventory tests, had been found to be an effective predictor of general engineering aptitude. The new test is composed of 85 items divided into two parts: Comprehension of Scientific Materials and General Mathematical Ability. Each part is separately timed but only a single overall score is obtained.

The comprehension section requires the reading of scientific selections, tables and graphs and answering questions based on the readings. The point is made that no specific factual knowledge is needed to answer the questions because the passages supply all of the needed information. There are, however, several items which definitely require knowledge beyond that imparted by the passages. There is also one item on the number of chemical elements which does not have a correct response, if we recognize recent developments in chemistry and physics.

The mathematics part of the test consists of problems in arithmetic, algebra, and geometry. One group of four items is based on a very long passage from analytic geometry. It might have been more advisable to reduce the amount of reading and to substitute additional items. Space for computation is provided in the booklet. This is an advantage to the student but it means that the booklets are not reusable. It would certainly be cheaper for the test purchaser if provision were made for separate scratch paper.

The manual gives .90 as the estimated reliability coefficient for a group entering the freshman class of an engineering college. The validity is approximated by a series of statistical steps from data for the two parent tests in the *Pre-Engineering Inventory*. The estimated validity coefficient against a criterion of average first-term grades is reported as .57. It should be noted, however, that the data used in the various steps leading up to the validity coefficient are average values (medians) taken from a study of the *Pre-Engineering Inventory* with 14 school groups and the coefficient of .57 is a summarizing value. The test user will still want to study carefully the validity of the instrument in more specific situations.

The norms consist of a table equating raw scores on the *Pre-Engineering Ability Test* with composite scores on the *Pre-Engineering Inventory,* based on a study at one engineering college. This table also includes three columns of data for the Inventory (not the ability test) which show percentile ranks for various composite scores. Unfortunately, there is a misprint in the number of cases for one of these columns: the N should be 2,043, not 7,043. Another table shows comparable scores on the *Pre-Engineering Ability Test* and three other tests. However, the use of such a table is limited to comparisons of students' scores on the four selected tests.

In general, this test reflects a competent job of extracting the essence of two other tests. It has face validity and will probably be found as useful as the longer Inventory in the selection of engineering candidates. Additional norms tables and reliability and validity data for specific situations would be very desirable.[1]

DEWEY B. STUIT, *Dean, College of Liberal Arts, State University of Iowa, Iowa City, Iowa.*

This test is an abbreviated form of the *Pre-Engineering Inventory* developed in 1943 by the Graduate Record Office of the Carnegie Foundation as a joint project of the American Society for Engineering Education, the Engineers' Council for Professional Development, and the Foundation. The Long Form of the original Inventory required six hours for administration and the Short Form, four hours. The engineering colleges felt that a shorter, less expensive test would serve their needs better; hence work was started on the *Pre-Engineering Ability Test* which consists of only two parts and requires only 80 minutes of working time.

The two parts of the test are Comprehension of Scientific Materials and General Mathematical Ability, these two subtests being the ones which contributed most to the validity of the composite score of the *Pre-Engineering Inven-*

[1] Since the writing of this review (a copy of which was sent to the publisher), the publisher has issued a slightly revised copy of the manual and test which is not subject to some of the specific criticisms noted in this review. Re-use of the test booklet is now possible if scratch paper is supplied to the examinees, the typographical error in one of the norms tables has been corrected and one of the items has been slightly changed.

tory. The 90 best comprehension items and the 80 best general mathematical ability items were first selected and one half of the selected test items for each part were chosen for the 80-minute *Pre-Engineering Ability Test*. While only a single overall score is obtained, the two parts are timed separately, 45 minutes for Comprehension of Scientific Materials and 35 for General Mathematical Ability.

Since the *Pre-Engineering Ability Test* is in essence a revision of the *Pre-Engineering Inventory* it was possible to use the normative and validity data of the latter test (*10*) in estimating similar data for the new test. The composite scores of the two tests were first equated and norms were then provided for engineering freshmen from public colleges, private colleges, and the two groups combined. The estimated validity of the test is .57 and the reliability .90. Data are also given showing the correlation of the test with the *American Council on Education Psychological Examination* (.77), the mathematics section of the *College Entrance Examination Board Scholastic Aptitude Test* (.71), and the *College Entrance Examination Board Achievement Test in Physics* (.69). The test manual conforms to the standards now usually expected for tests of this type. The purposes of the test (selection, placement, guidance) are discussed, the construction of the test described, normative data provided, and information given on validity and reliability. The directions for administration and scoring are clear.

The *Pre-Engineering Ability Test* promises to be an effective instrument for the prediction of scholastic success in engineering. It has a good background and should appeal to engineering colleges as an easily administered test. The fact that it is published by an organization with a reputation for sound and efficient work will enhance its prestige. Whether it will be superior to subject matter tests in science and mathematics or other aptitude tests in the field as a predictor of success in engineering remains to be seen. One may rest assured, however, that the Educational Testing Service will make appropriate studies as the test becomes widely used in the field.

[813]

Stanford Scientific Aptitude Test. Entrants to schools of engineering and science; 1929-30; 1 form, '30; manual ('30); examiner's direction booklet and scoring key ('30); $4 per 25; 25¢ per specimen set; cash orders postpaid; nontimed (60-120) minutes; D. L. Zyve; Stanford University Press. *

REFERENCES

1-3. See 40:1676.
4. BENTON, ARTHUR L., AND PERRY, JAMES D. "A Study of the Predictive Value of the Stanford Scientific Aptitude Test (Zyve)." *J Psychol* 10:309-12 O '40. * (*PA* 15:1085)
5. LONG, LOUIS. "Relationship Between Interests and Abilities: A Study of the Strong Vocational Interest Blank and the Zyve Scientific Aptitude Test." *J Appl Psychol* 29:191-7 Je '45. * (*PA* 19:3175)
6. COOPRIDER, H. A., AND LASLETT, H. R. "Predictive Values of the Stanford Scientific and the Engineering and Physical Science Aptitude Tests." *Ed & Psychol Meas* 8:683-7 w '48. * (*PA* 24:1488)
7. UHRBROCK, RICHARD STEPHEN. "Construction of a Selection Test for College Graduates." *J General Psychol* 41:153-93 O '49. * (*PA* 24:4874)

JOSEPH E. MOORE, *Professor of Psychology and Head of the Department, Georgia Institute of Technology, Atlanta, Georgia.*

This test purports to measure a conglomerate of 11 mental and character traits considered to be components of scientific aptitude. These traits are as follows: experimental bent; clarity of definitions; suspended versus snap judgment; reasoning; inconsistencies; fallacies; induction, deduction, and generalization; caution and thoroughness; discrimination of values in selecting and arranging experimental data; accuracy of interpretation; and accuracy of observation. A separate exercise is devoted to each trait and each exercise is weighted, the assigned weights ranging from two to seven points. No time limit is set for taking the test but an overall working time of two hours is suggested.

According to the author, scientific aptitude rather than specific ability is stressed because "'capacities' or 'aptitude' are controlled by laws inherent in the organism and are very loosely dependent upon the individual's achievement whereas the abilities of an individual are chiefly determined by his experiences and achievement." For this reason the test is constructed so that it is not dependent upon any information beyond that usually acquired in the elementary school; and, even so, whatever specific information is needed is provided right in the test.

The test itself is an excellently printed job; the material is well spaced and is very legible. A combined manual and scoring key contains general instructions for giving and scoring the test. The scoring is needlessly cumbersome and very time consuming. A separate information booklet explains the rationale of the test, describes the different exercises and discusses their significance, and summarizes the research conducted by the author 22 years ago to establish the validity and reliability of the test. A validity of .82 and a reliability of .93 are reported.

The criterion group on which the original

data were obtained consisted of 50 research students at Stanford University, of whom 21 were from the chemistry department, 10 from the physics department, and 19 from the electrical engineering department. Correlations between the estimates of faculty members of the scientific aptitude of these students and scores obtained by the students on the test ranged from .74 for the whole criterion group to .95 for the physics group. The reviewer ran a test of significance of difference between the mean scores for the different groups making up the criterion group, and found that none of the differences was statistically significant.

The author also tested several other groups, including 246 unselected freshmen, 79 science freshmen, 14 non-science faculty, 21 science faculty, and 47 non-science seniors and graduates of Stanford University. Only the scores of the latter two groups were substantially different, being, as one might expect, much lower than those of the other groups. In testing the difference between the mean scores of the two freshman groups, the reviewer obtained a critical ratio of 2.29. Although the obtained difference favored the science group, it was not statistically significant.

The author rests his claim for the validity of the test mainly on the results of the research reported above. The reviewer considers the author's data almost entirely inadequate. Face validity is not enough; facts are needed which show how well this instrument can predict or forecast performance in science subjects and scientific achievement. No data of this kind are presented. The reviewer suggests a follow-up study of the actual performance in science courses of a large number of students who take the test during their freshman year.

In summary: This test contains many unusual types of material. It is well printed and attractively arranged. It is easy to administer but tedious to score. It was developed over 22 years ago and, unfortunately, has had little research done on it since. The validity data are based on scores obtained by student and faculty groups at Stanford University and a comparison of the scores obtained by individual students in some of these groups and faculty estimates of the scientific aptitude of individual students in the groups. While the data indicate that the test probably has high face validity, they do not answer the fundamental question of whether students who perform best on the *Stanford Scientific Aptitude Test* also perform best in science courses.

DEWEY B. STUIT, *Dean, College of Liberal Arts, State University of Iowa, Iowa City, Iowa.*

This test is one of the earliest attempts to construct a predictive instrument for a subject matter professional field. In keeping with much of the early test construction practice the test is based largely upon hunches and guesses as to the type of exercise which will work in a given situation. The test attempts to measure a considerable variety of factors believed to be associated with success in the study and practice of science. In the words of the author, the test "is concerned with detecting a conglomerate of basic traits which enter into what may be called aptitude for science or engineering."

The test consists of 11 exercises or parts as follows: Experimental Bent; Clarity of Definition; Suspended versus Snap Judgment; Reasoning; Inconsistencies; Fallacies; Induction, Deduction and Generalization; Caution and Thoroughness; Discrimination of Values in Selecting and Arranging Experimental Data; Accuracy of Interpretation; Accuracy of Observation. Each of the exercises consists of relatively few items and is weighted in accordance with its capacity to discriminate between groups of science and non-science students. The weights vary from 2 to 7 and the maximum weighted scores from 10 to 28. The total maximum score in the test is 203. It requires two hours for administration.

The validity data supplied by Zyve are limited. For a group of 50 science students Zyve (2) found a correlation of .50 between aptitude scores and scholarship and a correlation of .74 between aptitude scores and ratings of these students by a group of judges, the judges being asked to rank the students on aptitude for science. For this same group the *Thorndike Intelligence Examination* correlated .27 with scholarship. Correlations of .13 to .50 were found between group intelligence test scores and scores on the test. Benton and Perry (4) found a correlation of .45 between the *American Council on Education Psychological Examination* and the aptitude test scores. These investigators found correlations of .30 and .37 between aptitude scores and scholarship based upon four years of work.

Cooprider and Laslett (6) studied the predictive value of the Stanford test along with the

Engineering and Physical Science Aptitude Test, the *American Council on Education Psychological Examination,* and the *Ohio State University Psychological Examination.* Scores on the Stanford test were found to correlate no better with grades in engineering and science courses than the scholastic aptitude tests. The test also failed to differentiate between scientific and general scholastic ability. Long (5) reported significant correlations with scores in the appropriate scales of Strong's *Vocational Interest Blank.*

The format of the test and the manual reflect the early vintage of the test. The directions are scanty, norms are limited to means for three different groups, reliability data are not discussed except in passing, and the interpretation of the scores is left almost entirely to the user. Actually the manual gives only the general directions for giving the test and the scoring key. The test is described and factual data are presented in the explanatory booklet which accompanies the test. There is no separate answer sheet.

This reviewer would agree with A. B. Crawford, writing in *The 1940 Mental Measurements Yearbook,* that the test as it stands cannot be recommended for use in the measurement of scientific aptitude. While the Stanford University Press reports that "the demand for the test has remained steady for several years," the small number of published articles would make it appear that the test is not used in research studies which are brought to the attention of professional counselors and test constructors. The test does have some interesting exercises deserving of further study and research. As a finished instrument for use in 1951, however, it falls below the standards now generally required for tests in the aptitude field.

For a review by A. B. Crawford, see 40:1676.

LAW

[814]

★**Iowa Legal Aptitude Test: 1946 Revision.** Law school applicants; 1946–48; 8 scores: analogies, reasoning, opposites, relevancy, mixed relations, memory, information, total; the test may be shortened to include only the subtests in reasoning, relevancy, and information; 1 form, '46; no norms for part scores; manual ('48); $13 per 100 sets of test and answer sheet; separate answer sheets must be used; $3 per 100 answer sheets; postage extra; 40¢ per specimen set, postpaid; 170(190) minutes or 90(110) minutes; Michael Adams, L. K. Funks, and D. B. Stuit; Bureau of Edu-

cational Research and Service, State University of Iowa. *

REFERENCES

1. ADAMS, MICHAEL. *An Experimental Study of the Prediction of Scholastic Success in Colleges of Law.* Doctor's thesis, University of Iowa (Iowa City, Iowa), 1942.
2. ADAMS, WM. MICHAEL. "Prediction of Scholastic Success in Colleges of Law: I, The Experimental Edition of the Iowa Legal Aptitude Test." *Ed & Psychol Meas* 3:291-305 w '43. * (*PA* 18:2520)
3. ADAMS, WILLIAM MICHAEL. "Prediction of Scholastic Success in Colleges of Law: II, An Investigation of Pre-Law Grades and Other Indices of Law School Aptitude." *Ed & Psychol Meas* 4:13-9 sp '44. * (*PA* 18:3271)
4. ADAMS, MICHAEL, AND STUIT, DEWEY B. "The Predictive Efficiency of the 1946 Revision of the Iowa Legal Aptitude Test." *Ed & Psychol Meas* 9:23-7 sp '49. * (*PA* 23:5779)
5. FEENEY, BERNARD J. "How Good Are Legal Aptitude Tests?" *J Legal Ed* 4:69-85 au '51. *

ALEXANDER G. WESMAN, *Associate Director, Test Division, The Psychological Corporation, New York, New York.*

This test was constructed through the cooperation of a number of law schools and is intended for general use by law schools and college personnel counselors.

Part 1, Analogies, requires the examinee to select from a group of six words a pair of words which bear the same relationship to each other as do words in the stimulus pair. Part 2, Reasoning, calls for a judgment of the truth or falsity of a conclusion drawn from postulated major and minor premises. Part 3, Opposites, requires the selection of an opposite with changes in the part of speech, for example, an adverb which is most nearly opposite in meaning to a given adjective. In Part 4, Relevancy, a long summary of a legal controversy is presented, together with 35 postulated propositions of law; the examinee is to indicate whether the proposition favors the plaintiff, or the defendant, or is irrelevant to the cases of both. Each item in Part 5, Mixed Relations, presents 6 words, 3 of which are to be identified as somehow related to one another. Part 6, Memory, contains 25 questions based on a 23-line legal case report which the examinee had studied for 8 minutes at the beginning of the examination (a little more than 2 hours earlier). Part 7, Information, contains 80 true-false items concerned with more or less common facts of law.

The test will be acceptable to many potential users because of its "face validity." The reasoning, relevancy, memory, and information tests have content appealing to teachers and practitioners in law; even the other three parts will share in this appeal, since they deal with word skill, a talent generally deemed desirable in budding lawyers and jurists. No doubt the students will also be favorably affected by the reasonableness of the content. One suspects that the face validity is based on a somewhat stereotyped notion of what the law profession is all about; but if teachers and students share the stereotype, the sought effect is accomplished.

There may be some question as to whether an aptitude test should sample knowledge in the field. The reviewer believes that it may properly do so. It is reasonable to expect that those who have learned relevant information and developed relevant skills will learn more effectively in that same area than those who have not. Since the principal purpose of this test is to predict which students are most likely to succeed in law schools, the inclusion of information content is defensible in so far as it aids in that prediction.

The manual contains generally good directions for administering the test; unfortunately, that is its best feature. A single paragraph provides the only information with respect to reliability and validity of the test. The long form "has yielded coefficients of correlation between total test scores and measures of first-year law school achievement in four law schools of .44, .49, .52, and .53, respectively. At the latter two schools, the total scores in Parts 2, 4, and 7 were also correlated with first-year grades and correlation coefficients of .56 and .60 were obtained." Comparison of these coefficients with those obtained at the University of Iowa Law School using prelaw grade-point averages as predictors results in some disappointment in the tests. The undergraduate record yielded validity coefficients ranging from .45, in colleges other than Iowa, to .67 for Iowa undergraduates (4). It may be that the authors of the test can present evidence that the test can augment the predictive power of prelaw grades appreciably; unfortunately, the manual does not offer such evidence.

The reliability of the long form is cited as being .93; for the short form (Parts 2, 4 and 7) it is given as .80. No information is offered in the manual as to the extent to which speed is a factor in the test. This is an important omission since the aforementioned reliability coefficients were estimated by the Kuder-Richardson method; if speed plays a significant role in the test, these coefficients may be overestimates of the real reliability of the instrument. On the other hand, the combination of somewhat heterogeneous content in the several parts would presumably result in underestimates of the real reliability. One wishes that the authors had provided information with respect to the speeded-

ness of the test parts and estimated reliability by means of split half techniques if the test is unspeeded. Since only one form of the test is available, alternate form estimates of reliability could not be attempted; a test-retest estimate would have been welcome.[1]

Norms are presented for the long form in terms of percentile equivalents of total scores achieved by 1,280 students in the first year of law at 6 schools. Norms for the short form are based on only 986 students. Since the 1,280 students must obviously have taken the three parts which comprise the short form, it is unfortunate that all were not included. The authors' belief that the norms are "fairly typical" is based on the fact that the law schools included were "all fully accredited and at the same time none of them exercised particularly stringent entrance requirements" may be typical; the reviewer does not know whether or not this is the case. In any event, law schools which do have stringent requirements will probably find these norms too low.

It should be noted that the above criticism is addressed to failure of the manual to provide adequate information rather than to positive deficiencies in the test itself. Law schools which are willing to investigate the validity and reliability of the test in their own local situations, and to develop local norms—steps which would be recommended even if the manual *had* provided better information—may find the *Iowa Legal Aptitude Test* a useful adjunct to their admission procedures.

[815]

★**Law School Admission Test.** Law school applicants; 1948; test administered four times annually (November, February, April, and August) at centers established in each state by Educational Testing Service; application form and bulletin of information may be obtained from publisher; examination fee, $10; fee includes scoring service and reporting of score to examinee and to any 3 law schools designated at time of application; $1 per each additional report requested at that time or any time thereafter; 210(270) minutes; prior to November 1951, 360(450) minutes in 2 sessions; prepared by the Staff of Educational Testing Service under the direction of the Law School Admission Test Policy Committee; Educational Testing Service. *

REFERENCES

1. OLSEN, MARJORIE A. "Validity of the Law School Admission Test for Predicting First-Year Law School Grades." Abstract. *Am Psychol* 5:283–4 Jl '50. * (*PA* 25:1280, title only)
2. BRADEN, GEORGE D. "Use of the Law School Admission Test at the Yale Law School." *J Legal Ed* 3:202–6 w '50. *
3. JOHNSON, A. PEMBERTON. "The Development and Use of Law Aptitude Tests." *J Legal Ed* 3:192–201 w '50. *

1 One of the authors (Dewey B. Stuit) has indicated that the tests have been so generously timed as to be almost pure power tests. If so, the quoted reliability coefficients may be accepted as reasonable estimates.

4. SCHRADER, WILLIAM B., AND OLSEN, MARJORIE. *The Law School Admission Test as a Predictor of Law School Grades.* Princeton, N.J.: Educational Testing Service, September 1950. Pp. 10. Paper, lithotyped. *
5. FEENEY, BERNARD J. "How Good Are Legal Aptitude Tests?" *J Legal Ed* 4:69–85 au '51. *
6. JOHNSON, A. PEMBERTON. "Validation of Professional Aptitude Batteries: Tests for Law," pp. 30–4. (*PA* 26:592) In *Proceedings of the 1950 Invitational Conference on Testing Problems, October 28, 1950.* Princeton, N.J.: Educational Testing Service, 1951. Pp. 117. Paper. *

ALEXANDER G. WESMAN, *Associate Director, Test Division, The Psychological Corporation, New York, New York.* [Review of Form YLS2.]

The *Law School Admission Test* is actually a program rather than a test and must be evaluated as such. The most recent form available for review, YLS2, is an outgrowth of earlier forms developed by the testing organization since 1947. At present, the test consists of two booklets which contain six tests. Book 1 consists of a Principles and Cases section (46 items, 45 minutes) in which the applicant judges the relevance of stated principles to the described cases; a Data Interpretation section (35 items, 60 minutes) intended to measure mathematical reasoning; and a Reading Comprehension section (46 items, 60 minutes) containing eight passages with rather general content. Book 2 contains a section called Debates (60 items, 20 minutes) in which the applicant indicates whether a statement supports, refutes, or is irrelevant to the resolution it follows; a Best Arguments section (32 items, 45 minutes) which requires the evaluation of arguments which are offered in described disputes; and a somewhat speeded paragraph reading section (30 items, 10 minutes) in which a word is to be located which spoils the meaning of each of the paragraphs.

No direct estimate of the test-retest reliability of the current form is available. This fact is perhaps not especially surprising since the test is part of a continuous program in which new forms are to be prepared each year. Evidence presented for a previous form (WLS) indicates that it was very reliable. A coefficient of .91 was obtained for a group of 72 applicants who were retested at their own request; since they had been low scorers originally (thus being restricted in range) and claimed illness or other conditions predisposing to an underestimate of their real ability (which would also result in important score changes), the coefficient of .91 may be accepted as probably an absolute minimum of the reliability of Form WLS. It is regrettable that test-retest coefficients have not been presented for the present form since there

are some sharp differences in content between the previous and present forms; in a program as extensive as this, into which so much experimental and statistical work has gone, one would expect some opportunities to have arisen for obtaining such reliability estimates.[1] However, the nature of the tests and the data for previous forms would lead to confidence that the present total test scores are unquestionably highly reliable.

Validity studies of the present form must naturally await the completion of a year's academic work by the students. Extensive studies have been reported for form WLS; a summary reported by Schrader and Olsen (*4*) presents validity coefficients for 21 groups of students for the *Law School Admission Test* and validity data for prelaw grades, both alone and combined, for 14 of these groups. The 21 LSAT coefficients ranged from .18 to .65; the average *r* was .44. To the extent that LSAT scores were considered in the admission process, these coefficients are underestimates. Validity coefficients for the prelaw grades alone against average first year law school grades ranged from −.04 to .50; LSAT score and prelaw grades combined yielded coefficients from .34 to .68. The poorest of these coefficients are discouraging (if one forgets the unreliability of the criterion grades and similar considerations); the best of them are heartening. It is a welcome sight to see so many studies reported, and perhaps the variation in success of prediction will indicate to the cooperating law schools how specific validity is. Certainly the differences found from school to school emphasize the inadequacy of tests and programs which cite validity data in only one or two institutions.

The content of the present form seems to have been selected for face validity as well as empirical validity. In keeping with the view set forth by the Policy Committee of the participating law schools, no specific legal information has been included, although an applicant may find it easier to read many of the items if he has previously encountered such legal terms as "warranty," "title certificate," "statutory grant," etc., or is familiar with stilted legal phraseology. The absence of questions on specific information is explained by Schrader and Olsen: "A systematic effort has been made to minimize the role of specific subject-matter preparation in the test and to focus attention on basic abilities. This

---

[1] The reviewer is informed that a retest study similar to the one described above for Form WLS will have been done by the time this volume is published.

emphasis should be kept in mind in comparing the validity coefficients (cited above) with those summarized in reviews of other law school tests by Kandel, Adams and Stuit." (*4*) The reviewer questions that this proposition can stand on its own feet. If it can be demonstrated that an information test does not predict law school grades, or that it adds nothing to a prediction from prelaw grades, then the proposition is acceptable. If, on the other hand, an information test is a valuable member of a predicting team, it has a rightful place in a prediction program which cannot be gainsaid by such a phrase as "basic abilities." The reviewer would prefer empirical demonstrations of ineffectiveness of good general legal information tests to having such tests summarily read out of court.

The instructions sent to supervisors and the attractive pamphlet which each applicant receives are well prepared and contain much useful information. Of particular merit are the provision of a set of sample questions to prepare the student for the kind of examination he will face and a detailed statement informing him of such regulations as apply to the use of slide rules and other devices, the value of a watch for pacing himself, etc. Although the instructions to the student are generally clear and concise, one statement is simply silly. The student is informed that there will be no correction for guessing and advised to use shrewd guesses but to "omit questions about which you have absolutely no knowledge, since you can use your time more profitably in other parts of the test." It is obvious that a student who has necessarily already spent time reading a question can far more profitably immediately record a guess which *might* do him some good and does not penalize him than omit the guess and lose whatever possibilities reside in chance guesses. This admonition may well impair the applicant's confidence in other information given him.

A highly desirable aspect of the program is the preparation of analyses of test results by undergraduate college. This kind of report provides information concerning the caliber of students coming from individual prelaw schools which could not be gathered by most law schools except over a considerable period of time. Activities such as these are potent advantages of a service program over the simple outright purchase of tests. The cost is, of course, much greater, but proper cost accounting of student failure should persuade administrators that having a service program is less expensive than not having one. Another excellent feature is the availability of two parallel forms of the test each year; this is valuable both for security and for retesting if the occasion demands it.

Perhaps just because the organization which runs this program has so much experienced talent available to it, the reviewer takes exception to certain flaws which do not, for the most part, affect the quality of the tests or program as such. For example, reliability coefficients based on odd-even and Kuder-Richardson techniques are reported for tests which are admittedly speeded. This is improper. As another example, a column of validity coefficients is corrected for range on the assumption that each of the schools would have an applicant population as heterogeneous as the total population, and on the further assumption that all such applicants would have been admitted if the tests had not been used to select them. It is doubtful that these assumptions are warranted.

The format of the test booklets is reasonably good and the type face (reduced typewriting) one of the clearer of its species. This last is fortunate, for the size of the type is, in the reviewer's judgment, much too small when it is remembered that the applicant spends several hours reading it. The applicant may not mind very much when there is enough space between the lines, but the longer paragraphs are quite formidable and might well contribute to the reading difficulty of the passages.

In evaluating the program as a whole, certain considerations arise. There seems to be little doubt that the program can contribute to better selection of students in those law schools which do not have their own programs. It seems equally clear that the services performed by the program are real contributions to the cooperating institutions, especially if those institutions do not have skilled measurement people on their staffs. The existence of a program, permitting joint effort and economies, is a good thing. However, are these the best tests for the purpose—the prediction of law school success? We have mentioned above the lack of evidence with regard to the possibilities of an information test. Can validity equal to that now being attained be achieved by more efficient tests in less time, or is four hours really necessary? It would be interesting, for example, to see comparative predictions from the same organization's Verbal Factor and Profile Mathematics sections of the

Graduate Record Examination, or some similar test of general academic aptitude.

If the separate parts of the *Law School Admission Test* were shown to be differentially predictive of specific law school courses, the length of the present examination could be justified. If the law schools were interested in the broad cultural backgrounds of their applicants, a long multipart test which accomplished that purpose could be justified. That a single-score test with a single purpose needs to be four hours long seems less credible—however, both the law schools and their candidates may believe that a long examination is *ipso facto* a fairer one than a shorter test of equal reliability and validity. Although a number of studies of various item types, some time-consuming and others less so, have been done, one wonders if shorter item types could not be found to compete with the present series.

MACHINISTS

[816]

*Purdue Test for Machinists and Machine Operators: Purdue Vocational Test, No. 2. Grades 9–12 and adults; 1942–49; 6 scores: lathe, planer and shaper, grinder, milling machine, general bench operations, total; Form BH ('49—same as test copyrighted in 1942); preliminary manual ['49]; 49¢ per test and answer pad; separate answer pads must be used; $1.90 per 25 answer pads; 75¢ per specimen set; cash orders postpaid; 50(55) minutes; manual by Joseph Tiffin; H. F. Owen, C. C. Stevason, H. G. McComb, and C. D. Hume; Science Research Associates, Inc. *

For a review by William W. Waite, see 3:702.

MEDICINE

[817]

★Medical College Admission Test. Candidates for medical school; 1946–51; formerly called *Professional Aptitude Test;* 4 scores: verbal, quantitative, understanding of modern society, science; test administered twice annually (May and November) at centers established by Educational Testing Service; application form and bulletin of information may be obtained from Educational Testing Service; examination fee, $10; fee includes scoring service and reporting of scores to any 3 recognized medical schools designated at time of application; $1 per each additional report requested at that time or any time thereafter; 360(390) minutes in 2 sessions; prepared by the Staff of Educational Testing Service for the Association of American Medical Colleges; distributed by Educational Testing Service. *

REFERENCES

1. VAUGHN, K. W. *The Interpretation and Use of the Professional Aptitude Test: A Manual for Committees on Admission in Colleges of Medicine.* New York: Graduate Record Office, January 1947. Pp. i, 19. Paper, lithotyped. *
2. SHOEMAKER, H. A., AND ROHRER, J. H. "Relationship Between Success in the Study of Medicine and Certain Psychological and Personal Data." *J Assn Am Med Col* 23:190–201 My '48. * (PA 23:951)
3. YOUNG, RICHARD H., AND PIERSON, GEORGE A. "The Professional Aptitude Test, 1947: A Preliminary Evaluation." *J Assn Am Med Col* 23:176–9 My '48. * (PA 23:954)
4. HURD, ARCHER W. *Factors Influencing Student Success in Medical Education, exhibits 614–7.* Richmond, Va.: Bureau of Educational Research and Service, Medical College of Virginia, August 1950. Pages not numbered. Paper, mimeographed. *
5. RALPH, RAY B., AND TAYLOR, CALVIN W. "A Comparative Evaluation of the Professional Aptitude Test and the General Aptitude Test Battery." *J Assn Am Med Col* 25:33–40 Ja '50. *
6. STALNAKER, JOHN M. "Medical College Admission Test." *J Assn Am Med Col* 25:428–34 N '50. *
7. TAYLOR, CALVIN W. "Check Studies on the Predictive Value of the Medical College Admission Test." *J Assn Am Med Col* 25:269–71 Jl '50. *
8. GLASER, ROBERT. "Predicting Achievement in Medical School." *J Appl Psychol* 35:272–4 Ag '51. * (PA 26:3046)
9. MORRIS, W. W. "Validity of the Professional Aptitude Test in Medicine." *J Med Ed* 26:56–8 Ja '51. *
10. SCHULTZ, DOUGLAS G. "The Relationship Between Scores on the Science Test of the Medical College Admission Test and Amount of Training in Biology, Chemistry, and Physics." *Ed & Psychol Meas* 11:138–50 sp '51. * (PA 26:2979)
11. STALNAKER, JOHN M. "Validation of Professional Aptitude Batteries: Tests for Medicine," pp. 46–51. (PA 26:599) In *Proceedings of the 1950 Invitational Conference on Testing Problems, October 28, 1950.* Princeton, N.J.: Educational Testing Service, 1951. Pp. 117. Paper. *

MOREY J. WANTMAN, *Associate Professor of Education, and Director, Bureau of Educational Statistics, The University of Rochester, Rochester, New York.*

This test is intended as an aid to admissions officers of members of the Association of American Medical Colleges and of "certain other professional schools." Scores of all applicants are reported to all members of the Association of American Medical Colleges. The scores are reported in intervals of 10 on a standard scale with a mean of 500 and a standard deviation of 100; the range is 200 to 800. The group on which the 1950 scale is based consisted of approximately 5,000 candidates who took the examination in May. Percentile ranks reported for specific standard scores imply that the distribution of each test is normal. The actual distributions deviate from the normal slightly.

This test comes up to the usual high standards of test construction characteristic of the Educational Testing Service. The format of the test booklets is excellent, the bulletin of information to applicants is clearly written, and the well organized instructions to examiners are as complete as possible.

A close examination of the 1951 Bulletin of Information suggests, however, that it can stand some revision. On page 18, the section on "Advice to Candidates," the bulletin instructs the candidates as follows: "Do not cram. A general review of science may be of value, but intensive last-minute cramming will not be helpful. The test is to be taken in stride." This reviewer has been asked many times by applicants to interpret these instructions, and has been forced to advise them to spend as much time as they can afford in reviewing their elementary college course work. Now that this reviewer has had an opportunity to examine the contents of the test of Understanding Modern Society, he will probably find himself advising applicants to re-read the Constitution of the United States, copies of *Time* and *Newsweek* for the last two years, and so on.

The bulletin goes on to mislead the applicant by stating that "there is no reason to become worried or disturbed if you find that you are unable to answer a number of questions in the test or if you are unable to finish. The test is so designed that the average person taking it will answer correctly only about fifty per cent of the questions." This same type of misleading statement appears on the directions for each test booklet. These statements give some of the applicants a mistaken confidence in a cautious, methodical pace. Actually, at least 79 per cent of a random sample of 500 applicants finished 75 per cent of each of the sections of the 1950 test, and as great a percentage as 89 of this sample finished at least one section of the test.

Again, the directions on page 19 of the 1951 Bulletin of Information, are somewhat ambiguous. The bulletin's statement with respect to guessing is as follows:

Many candidates wonder whether or not to guess the answers to questions about which they are not certain. In general, it is best to answer all questions about which you have any knowledge at all, because a shrewd guess is more often right than wrong. On the other hand, it is best to skip questions about which you have absolutely no knowledge, since you can use your time more profitably in other parts of the test. If you complete a section of the test before time is called, it is wise to go back and reconsider any questions about which you were not certain at first.

The directions on the test booklets are no clearer in view of the fact that there is "no correction for wrong answers." The applicant who is testwise, either through experience or coaching, may proceed to answer at random all remaining questions in a section as he observes the time limit for the section approaching.

Another question may be raised regarding the policy with respect to the reporting of scores. It is not clear why the applicant who submits himself to almost six hours of examination time and pays a $10 fee is not entitled to a report of his scores. The Graduate Record Examination reports scores to applicants who are applying for admission to graduate schools of arts and science. The reasons for failing to do so in the case of applicants to medical schools is not clear.

The Bulletin of Information reflects fairly accurately the content of the various sections of the test. However, two points might well be made in connection with the test content: (*a*) A review of algebra might aid an applicant on the Quantitative section; and (*b*) Some of the questions on Understanding Modern Society call for answers which could be judged to be matters of opinion. This situation has led some applicants to report to this reviewer their mistaken judgment that this particular section is a test of "Conservatism—Radicalism."

The statistical data supplied by the Educational Testing Service for the 1950 test give further information about the contents of the test. The correlation between the Verbal score and the score on Understanding Modern Society is reported as .77. In general, the intercorrelations between the reported scores are high. They range from a high of .77 to a low of .58. The latter correlation is between the Quantitative and Understanding Modern Society scores. The intercorrelations involving the Verbal, Science, and Understanding Modern Society scores are all higher than .67, suggesting that these three sections are heavily loaded with a "verbal factor."

The Science section is claimed to sample only "concepts and problems taken from the basic college courses in biology, chemistry, and physics." Schultz's study (*10*) of the Science section indicates that the claim is justified. His evidence led him to the conclusion that:

The results of this study would appear to offer no support for the hypothesis that taking additional courses in biology, chemistry, and physics beyond a certain minimal number leads to better scores on the Medical College Admission Test science section. This is a general conclusion, of course, and may very well not apply to any specific individual or in any given situation.

The reliability data reported for the 1950 tests cannot be judged to be more than "satisfactory." The reliability coefficients, computed by means of the Kuder-Richardson formula 20 are .93, .89, .91, and .94 for the Verbal, Quantitative, Science, and Understanding Modern Society scores respectively. The corresponding standard errors of measurement are 4.1, 2.8, 4.9, and 4.7 for raw scores. For standard scores these are 26.7, 33.2, 30.7, and 25.4. Thus the 95 per cent confidence interval for a Quantitative score extends over approximately 130 points. Such a large zone of approximation for a "true score," coupled with the fact that the Kuder-Richardson technique for estimating reliability may be overestimating the reliability since speed is a factor in the test, prevents one from concluding that the reliability of the test scores is more than "satisfactory."

In the last analysis, any test must stand or fall on its demonstrated validity for a specific purpose. The validity of the *Medical College Admission Test* for aiding in the selection problem for medical schools has not yet been demonstrated. The justification of its use together with the other evidence in the selective procedures is based on faith that it has "intrinsic validity." This view has been expressed by Stalnaker (*11*). In this same reference, Stalnaker examines the criterion data which might be used to evaluate the test and finds the limitations of these data so great that he does not see any reason for waiting for the completion of validity studies before taking the test out of the experimental category.

This attitude on the part of the director of the project is somewhat disturbing in view of the fact that the published evidence up to 1951, admittedly meager, is on the negative side. Two studies (*3, 5*) carried out at the University of Utah Medical School used first quarter medical school grades as the criterion. Stuit and Schlicher [1] and Young and Pierson (*3*) have reported that first year medical school grades are indicative of later success in medical school. In neither of the studies could the evidence be used to defend the use of the test scores to predict the criterion. In fact, in the Young and Pierson study, where the now discarded *Moss Scholastic Aptitude Test for Medical Students* (testing for science achievement only) was also administered, the Moss test was the best predictor of the criterion; the correlation reported was .44. This finding raises the question as to why the Moss test was dropped as a selective device before the *Medical College Admission Test* had been demonstrated to be superior to it.

In a study reported by Morris (*9*), premedical science college grades correlated .55 with first year medical grades at the University of Iowa Medical School. The best predictor among the scores of the *Medical College Admission Test* was the science achievement test score; the correlation was .48.

The limitations of criterion data in the form of grades must be admitted. Nevertheless, from the practical point of view, the test constructors must face the fact that at the present time these data constitute the criterion they are trying to predict. Until the criterion has been revised, the test scores must be required to correlate as highly as possible with it. If this requirement is not insisted upon, then the *Medical College Admission Test* must be considered an additional criterion of success in medical schools. If the American Association of Medical Colleges maintains the latter, then one cannot question the intrinsic validity of the test unless he wishes to question the judgment of the Association regarding the criteria by which they characterize medical school success.

Even though Stalnaker expresses the view cited above, he reports (*11*) that the study of the present criterion and its prediction is being pursued. The staff of the *Medical College Admission Test* and the American Association of Medical Colleges are working in the following areas: medical school drop-outs, tests of interests, devices to detect serious emotional instability, the interview as a predictor, study along psychiatric lines of the nature of students entering medical school, and routine correlational studies.

It would be interesting to know the value of a multiple correlation which could be obtained from some of the variables in the above list, when applied in combination with the currently used predictors. As one aspect of this, a multiple correlation between the separate scores of the *Medical College Admission Test* and medical school success should be investigated. One would not expect this correlation to be much higher than the highest zero-order r's in view of the high intercorrelations among these scores. On the other hand, a multiple correlation based on the previous college record and the *Medical College Admission Test* may be appreciably higher than the zero-order r's. Stuit and Schlicher's summary of correlations between the quality of premedical college work and medical school grades indicates that there is a positive useful relationship between these two variables.[1] Jacobsen similarly concludes: "I believe that there was uniform agreement that the academic record, for all of its weaknesses, was still the best single criterion and the best single guide that we might have in the choice of a competent student." [2]

Morris' (*9*) study confirms Jacobsen's conclusions. Furthermore, when Morris used premedical science test scores in combination with the premedical science college grades to predict

[1] Stuit, Dewey B., and Schlicher, Raymond J. *Handbook for Advisers to Students Planning to Enter Medicine.* Chicago, Ill.: Association of American Medical Colleges, [1950]. Pp. iv, 34. *

[2] Jacobsen, Carlyle. "Student Selection Problems." *J Assn Med Col* 25:7-11 Ja '50.

first year medical school grades, the zero-order *r* was increased only to a multiple correlation of .60. Thus, the relationship between the *Medical College Admission Test* science score and previous scholastic science record is high enough so that the *Medical College Admission Test* does not improve the prediction to any great extent.

In summary, this reviewer would rate the *Medical College Admission Test* as technically among the best of the available standardized tests. Its reliability is satisfactory but its validity for aiding in the selection of medical students remains to be demonstrated.

NURSING

[818]

*George Washington University Series of Nursing Tests. Prospective nurses; 1931–50; 4 parts; [revised] mimeographed manual ('50); 2¢ per profile chart ['44]; 60¢ per specimen set; postpaid; (180) minutes; Thelma Hunt; Center for Psychological Service, George Washington University. *

a) APTITUDE TEST FOR NURSING. 1931–40; Forms I ('31), 2 ('40); $2.75 per 25; Form I: 45(55) minutes; Form 2: 70(80) minutes; F. A. Moss is co-author of Form I.

b) ARITHMETIC TEST FOR PROSPECTIVE NURSES. 1940–49; Form 2 ('49—a revision of Form I); $2 per 25; 20(25) minutes.

c) READING COMPREHENSION TEST FOR PROSPECTIVE NURSES. 1940; Form I; $2.50 per 25; 30(35) minutes.

d) GENERAL SCIENCE TEST FOR PROSPECTIVE NURSES. 1944; Form I; $2.50 per 25; 30(35) minutes.

e) INTEREST-PREFERENCE TEST FOR PROSPECTIVE NURSES. 1944; Form I; $2.50 per 25; nontimed (30) minutes.

REFERENCES

1–6. See 3:699.
7. BERG, IRWIN AUGUST. "A Study of Success and Failure Among Student Nurses." Abstract. *Am Psychol* 1:249–50 Jl '46. * (*PA* 20:3872, title only)
8. FORD, ALBERT H. "Prediction of Academic Success in Three Schools of Nursing." *J Appl Psychol* 34:186–9 Je '50. * (*PA* 25:4038)

[819]

★NLNE Achievement Tests for Basic Professional Nursing Program. Students in state approved schools of professional nursing; 1943–51; to be administered at or near completion of instructional period in subject-matter area; IBM; 14 tests; examination fee, 50¢ per test per student tested; fee includes all test materials, scoring test papers, and reporting results; nontimed (90) minutes per test; prepared by the Department of Measurement and Guidance of the National League of Nursing Education, Inc. in cooperation with nurse educators; National League of Nursing Education, Inc.

a) ANATOMY AND PHYSIOLOGY. 1943–49; Form 149 ('49).

b) CHEMISTRY. 1943–49; Form 149 ('49).

c) MICROBIOLOGY. 1943–49; Form 149 ('49).

d) FUNDAMENTALS OF NURSING. 1945–50; Form 750 ('50).

e) NUTRITION AND DIET THERAPY. 1946–49; Form 149 ('49).

f) PHARMACOLOGY AND THERAPEUTICS. 1944–49; Form 149 ('49).

g) MEDICAL NURSING. 1944–49; Form 149 ('49).

h) SURGICAL NURSING. 1944–49; Form 149 ('49).

i) OBSTETRIC NURSING. 1945–49; Form 149 ('49).

j) NURSING OF CHILDREN. 1945–49; Form 149 ('49).

k) COMMUNICABLE DISEASE NURSING. 1946–49; Form 149 ('49).

l) PSYCHIATRIC NURSING. 1945–49; Form 149 ('49).

m) SOCIAL FOUNDATIONS OF NURSING. 1945–50; Form 750 ('50).

n) TUBERCULOSIS NURSING. 1946–50; Form 750 ('50).

[820]

★NLNE Graduate Nurse Qualifying Examination. Registered professional nurses who are candidates for advanced college training or are entering merit systems; 1945–51; IBM; test dates determined by test user; application form must be obtained from the school or merit system to which the candidate has applied; 8 tests; Plan A: A.C.E. Psychological Examination, Reading Comprehension, and NLNE Graduate Nurse Examinations, $6 per examinee; Plan B: NLNE Graduate Nurse Examinations and a choice of either A.C.E. Psychological Examination or Reading Comprehension, $5 per examinee; Plan C: NLNE Graduate Nurse Examinations only, $4 per examinee; fee includes all test materials, scoring test papers, reporting results to the school to which examinee has applied, and an examiner to supervise testing if Plan A or B is used for 15 examinees or more; if test taken individually or with smaller group, the test user or candidate must make arrangements with individual examiner; $1 per additional report. Plan C prepared by the Department of Measurement and Guidance of the National League of Nursing Education, Inc. in cooperation with nurse educators; National League of Nursing Education, Inc.

a) AMERICAN COUNCIL ON EDUCATION PSYCHOLOGICAL EXAMINATION FOR COLLEGE FRESHMEN. See 277; 3 scores: quantitative, linguistic, total; 1948 Edition; 38 (65) minutes.

b) READING COMPREHENSION: COOPERATIVE ENGLISH TEST: HIGHER LEVEL, TEST C2. See 547; 3 scores: vocabulary, speed, level; Form T ('43); 40(45) minutes.

c) NLNE GRADUATE NURSE EXAMINATIONS. 6 tests; Form 149A ('49); nontimed (60) minutes per test.

   1) *Medical Nursing.*
   2) *Surgical Nursing.*
   3) *Obstetric Nursing.*
   4) *Nursing of Children.*
   5) *Communicable Disease Nursing.*
   6) *Psychiatric Nursing.*

[821]

★NLNE Practical Nurse Achievement Examinations. Students completing program in approved schools of practical nursing; 1950–51; an end-of-program examination; IBM; Form 150 ('50); examination fee, 50¢ per student tested; fee includes all test materials, scoring test papers and reporting results; nontimed (120) minutes; prepared by the Department of Measurement and Guidance of the National League of Nursing Education, Inc. with the assistance of representatives from the field of practical nurse education; National League of Nursing Education, Inc.

[822]

★NLNE [Practical Nurse] Pre-Admission and Classification Examination. Candidates for admission to approved schools of practical nursing; 1950–51; an examination program administered by individual schools for use in the selection and guidance of applicants and students; IBM; 3 tests; examination fee, $4 per candidate; fee includes all test materials, scoring test papers, and reporting results to any one approved school of practical nursing; nontimed (210) minutes; tests *b* and *c* prepared by the Department of Measurement and Guidance of the National League of Nursing Education, Inc.; National League of Nursing Education, Inc. *

a) GENERAL ABILITY EXAMINATION. An adaptation of *Army General Classification Test* (see 280); Form 650 ('50).

b) GENERAL INFORMATION AND JUDGMENT EXAMINATION. 4 scores: information, judgment, arithmetic, total; Form 650 ('50).

c) VOCABULARY EXAMINATION. Form 650 ('50).

[823]

★**NLNE Pre-Nursing and Guidance Test Battery.** Candidates for admission to state-approved schools of nursing; 1941-51; examination program for use in the selection and guidance of student nurses; IBM; tests administered on specified dates throughout the year at centers established by the National League of Nursing Education, Inc.; application form and schedule of examinations may be obtained from the League or the director of any state-approved school of nursing; application form must be signed by the authorized head of the school to which the candidate has applied; 5 tests; examination fee, $5 per candidate tested if taken with group of 15 or more; less than 15, candidate or school must also assume administration costs; fee includes all test materials, test administration (for groups of 15 or more), scoring test papers, and reporting results to any 1 state-approved school of nursing; $1 per additional report; 190(220) minutes; National League of Nursing Education, Inc.

a) AMERICAN COUNCIL ON EDUCATION PSYCHOLOGICAL EXAMINATION FOR COLLEGE FRESHMEN. See 277; 3 scores: quantitative, linguistic, total; 1948 Edition.

b) READING COMPREHENSION: COOPERATIVE ENGLISH TEST: HIGHER LEVEL, TEST C2. See 547; 2 scores: speed, level; Form T ('43).

c) MATHEMATICS. An adaptation of *Cooperative Mathematics Test for Grades 7, 8, and 9* (see 370); Form Q ('40).

d) A TEST OF GENERAL PROFICIENCY IN THE FIELD OF NATURAL SCIENCES: COOPERATIVE GENERAL ACHIEVEMENT TEST, REVISED SERIES, TEST II. See 595; Form T ('42).

e) COOPERATIVE GENERAL CULTURE TEST, PART II: HISTORY AND SOCIAL STUDIES. See 6; Form T ('43).

REFERENCES

1. SHAYCOFT, MARION F. "A Validation Study of the Pre-Nursing and Guidance Test Battery." *Am J Nursing* 51:201-5 Mr '51. *

SALESMEN

[824]

★**Aptitude Associates Test of Sales Aptitude: a Test for Measuring Knowledge of Basic Principles of Selling.** Sales applicants; 1947-50; Form A ('47); manual ('50); 10¢ per test; 20¢ per scoring key; 75¢ per manual; 75¢ per specimen set; cash orders postpaid; nontimed (20-30) minutes; Martin M. Bruce; the Author, Apt. 6A, 624 East 20th St., New York 9, N.Y. *

REFERENCES

1. McCORNACK, R. L. *An Investigation of "A Test of Sales Aptitude."* Master's project, University of Minnesota (Minneapolis, Minn.), 1951. Pp. 54.

MILTON E. HAHN, *Professor of Psychology, and Dean of Students, University of California, Los Angeles, California.*

The manual states: "This test can be of value

as an aid in appraising sales aptitude for selecting sales personnel and for vocational guidance purposes. *However, it should be emphasized that it is an aid only.* Many other factors are important. Interest, intelligence, motivation, appearance, health and the like must be taken into account."

The preliminary work done in developing the test is better than that of many tools offered for sale prematurely. The norms appear to be accumulating satisfactorily, since the test has a copyright of 1947. If attention is paid to further accumulation of norms for specific sales groups as well as more comprehensive data for men and women in general, the author is meeting his ethical obligations in this regard. As the norms now stand, they are inadequate for maximal usefulness.

The manual presents as evidence of validity, in distinguishing salesmen from nonsalesmen, chi square and critical ratio values which are significant at or beyond the 1 per cent level of significance when the two distributions are compared. Representativeness of the original and subsequent samples was also investigated, according to the manual.

"The test has an estimated test-retest reliability of .74." The reviewer questions whether the instrument should be used for predictions with individual cases, because sound forecasts cannot be made when the coefficient of reliability is this low. The method of determining the reliability coefficient is not given.

The reviewer raises a question regarding use of the word "aptitude" in naming this test. The low *r* of .02 with an intelligence test plus the learned and specific nature of some items, such as 7, 18, 22, 28, 36, 37, 43, and 49, indicate that this instrument has a loading of learned specifics which do not appear related to insights accrued from usual experiences. May it be that the test is as closely related to trade as to aptitude tests? Paterson, Strong, Kuder, Bills, and others have contributed research which permits the hypothesis that an appropriate measured interest pattern is the best single indication of sales aptitude. The low correlation of .08 cited in the manual between this instrument and the persuasive interest scores on the *Kuder Preference Record* runs counter to this hypothesis unless the test taps a new and unique factor in general selling. A more tenable assumption may be that this test is a form of trade test for general sales.

The reviewer questions the value of this instrument for vocational guidance in educational institutions with clients who have had no sales experience or training. The first objection is an ethical one—the correct answers to some items such as 36 and 37 are lies to outwit lower echelon employees (receptionists). The second objection is that the specific learning involved for answering some items is not part of the students' experience.

In summary, this is an instrument which will be useful in selecting general sales personnel from applicants with sales experience and training. The author properly cautions the user against its use as a single criterion of selection. The "estimated" reliability coefficient of .74 is lower than the acceptable minimum for use with individuals. Additions to norms are needed, particularly some evidence of discrimination between successful and unsuccessful sales persons in a variety of sales areas. If the test is revised, the reviewer would recommend that the trade test aspects be emphasized and that the title be changed to conform better with the usual concepts of aptitude.

DONALD G. PATERSON, *Professor of Psychology, and Member of Staff of Industrial Relations Center, University of Minnesota, Minneapolis, Minnesota.*

This 4-page test contains 50 items (most of them describing hypothetical sales situations) each followed by four possible answers, one of which is to be checked as be.ng the best of the four. A 9-page mimeographed manual and a single page scoring key are provided.

Test-retest reliability is reported to be .74 for a heterogeneous group of 658 "men, women, and salesmen." In view of the reported sex difference and the sales-nonsales differences, this *r* is decidedly suspect. Correlation between test score and total score on the *Otis Self-Administering Test of Mental Ability* is .02 for 145 college students and .08 for a heterogeneous group of 178 "men, women, and salesmen." Correlation between test score and persuasive interest score on *Kuder Preference Record*, Form BB, is .08 for 88 "individuals."

Validity is based on the extent to which test scores differentiate between salesmen and individuals in other occupations. Weights (from +5 to −5) for scoring each of the possible responses to each item were derived on the basis of obtained differences between sales and nonsales groups. Naturally, distributions of total

test scores for sales and nonsales groups given in the norms show large differences. It is claimed that these differences hold up in cross-validation and distributions of scores of additional special groups of salesmen bear out this claim.

Should independent validations confirm the author's claims, this test would represent an important contribution to the problem of sales selection. One such independent validation by McCornack (*1*), however, casts serious doubt upon the universal validity of this test. He found that design engineers and accountants were not sharply differentiated from "successful" life insurance salesmen. He also found the split half reliability to be in the neighborhood of only .29. It is probable that the complicated weighted scoring system developed for this test maximizes chance differences. For this and other reasons personnel psychologists would be loathe to recommend this test for practical sales selection work at the present time.

[825]

*Aptitude Index. Prospective life insurance agents; 1938–50; 1 score, combining an evaluation of personal background, interests, and attitudes; [revised] Form 4 ('50) ; manual ('48) ; separate scoring keys for United States and Canada ; distribution is restricted to life insurance companies which are members of Life Insurance Agency Management Association ; (30) minutes ; Life Insurance Agency Management Association. *

REFERENCES

1–5. See 40:1646.
6. KURTZ, ALBERT K. "Selecting Salesmen by Personal History Items: Methods and Results." Abstract. *Psychol B* 36:528 Jl '39. * (*PA* 13:6431, title only)
7. HAVILAND, F. H. "Progress in Selection of Agents." [*Proc*] *Annual Mtg Assn Life Agency Officers & Life Ins Sales Res Bur*, 1940 1940:88–95 '40. *
8. KURTZ, ALBERT K. "Recent Research in the Selection of Life Insurance Salesmen." *J Appl Psychol* 25:11–7 F '41. * (*PA* 15:3115)
9. KURTZ, ALBERT K. "Scoring Rating Scales After the Responses Are Punched on IBM Cards," pp. 28–34. In *Proceedings of the Research Forum, Endicott, New York, August 26–30, 1946*. New York: International Business Machines Corporation, 1947. Pp. 94. Paper. *
10. WALLACE, S. RAINS, JR. "The Basis of Decision." [*Proc*] *Annual Mtg Life Ins Agency Mgmt Assn*, 1947. 1947:141–64 '48. *
11. KAHN, D. F. *An Analysis of Factors Related to Life Insurance Selling*. Doctor's thesis, Purdue University (Lafayette, Ind.), 1948.
12. KURTZ, ALBERT K. "The Weighted Application Blank." *Mgmt Rec* 10:2–4 Ja '48. *
13. HADLEY, J. M., AND KAHN, D. F. "A Comment on Wallace's Note on 'Factors Related to Life Insurance Selling.'" *J Appl Psychol* 33:359–62 Ag '49. * (*PA* 24:2882)
14. KAHN, D. F., AND HADLEY, J. M. "Factors Related to Life Insurance Selling." *J Appl Psychol* 33:132–40 Ap '49. * (*PA* 24:357)
15. WALLACE, S. RAINS, JR. "How Association Research Can Help the Agency Officer." [*Proc*] *Annual Mtg Life Ins Agency Mgmt Assn*, 1948. 1948:56–71 '49. *
16. WALLACE, S. RAINS, JR. "A Note on Kahn and Hadley's 'Factors Related to Life Insurance Selling.'" *J Appl Psychol* 33:356–8 Ag '49. * (*PA* 24:2884)
17. WALLACE, S. RAINS, JR. "The Revised Index." [*Proc*] *Annual Mtg Life Ins Agency Mgmt Assn*, 1948. 1948:97–102, discussion 102–8 '49. *
18. WALLACE, S. RAINS, JR.. AND TWICHELL, CONSTANCE M. "Managerial Procedures and Test Validities." *Personnel Psychol* 2:277–92 au '49. * (*PA* 24:2131)
19. FERGUSON, LEONARD W.; ASSISTED BY JOHN J. HOPKINS. "Management Quality and Its Effect on Selection Test Validity." *Personnel Psychol* 4:141–50 su '51. * (*PA* 26:1734)

DONALD G. PATERSON, *Professor of Psychology, and Member of Staff of Industrial Relations Center, University of Minnesota, Minneapolis, Minnesota.*

Part I is a personal history blank covering the following ten items: age, prior experience in life insurance selling, number of dependents, recent civilian occupation, education, employment status, organizations belonged to and offices now held, net worth, minimum current living expenses, and amount of insurance carried. Part II contains three subtests: (*a*) 21 Yes-No-? questions pertaining to interests and attitudes; (*b*) self-ratings of 18 personal characteristics on a 1 to 6 point scale; and (*c*) forced choice tetrads regarding attitudes toward 12 situations and activities. Both parts are scored by hand. Item weights (item analysis against external criterion of "success") are assigned, and total weighted score for Parts I and II constitute the *Aptitude Index*. These scores are then divided into a 5-step (A, B, C, D, and E) rating.

Research on both parts of this selection device was begun in 1932–33. The first edition of the *Aptitude Index* appeared in 1938. Form 4, the latest revision, appeared in 1948. Continuous research is being carried on.

Extensive validity studies have been made and published. Two criteria have generally been employed, namely, survival rate during first year and production during first year equal to or greater than the median production for one-year survivors in a given agency. Survival rate and production level for A, B, C, and D or E ratings on the *Aptitude Index* for United States companies and for Canadian companies clearly show the value of the device, especially for rejection of applicants. Validity coefficients are not computed because of statistical difficulties inherent in the fact that it is easier to predict failure than to predict success. The predictive value of the ratings is also shown to be dependent upon the efficiency of agency management. This latter fact is considered to be so important that future revisions of the *Aptitude Index* will undoubtedly take it into account with a probable further increase in validity. Cross-validation studies of item weights have been found to hold up in a satisfactory manner. It is unfortunate that validities are not reported separately for Parts I and II. The personnel psychologist would like to know the relative validity of personal history versus personality and interest measurement.

No estimates of the reliability of the *Aptitude Index* as a whole or of its parts have been obtained, except for corrected Spearman-Brown *r*'s of .64 and .54 computed for two subtests of Part II with the original validation sample. The association which finances the Index research has offered the opinion that evidence concerning reliability is not essential to test users so long as sound evidence of validity can be presented. However, since the Index is used with individuals in selection (especially rejection), it would seem reasonable to expect that test users should be provided with data concerning the reliability of the test for use in individual diagnosis.

Comparative studies of the reliabilities and validities of Part I and Part II, and of Strong's *Vocational Interest Blank* should be undertaken. It is possible that the Strong test is actually superior to the *Aptitude Index*. Marian Bills' work at the Aetna Life Insurance Company with both the Index and the Strong test shows clearly that agencies relying on the *Aptitude Index* alone are not doing as good a job as could be done.

Even though the *Aptitude Index* is confidential and distributed exclusively for use by participating agencies, it would seem to be in the interest of the life insurance business to make it available to bona fide guidance agencies with proper security provisions. Since guidance and counseling agencies in schools, colleges, government agencies, and social agencies are here to stay and are being manned with professionally trained personnel psychologists, it would seem that enlightened self-interest would lead the Life Insurance Agency Management Association to cooperate directly with such agencies.

ALBERT S. THOMPSON, *Associate Professor of Education, Teachers College, Columbia University, New York, New York.*

The *Aptitude Index* is one of the few tests which has had a long history of continuous development, cross-validation, trial-by-fire under field conditions, and a research-oriented agency behind it. It is a pleasure to review it since, although it is available only to members of the Life Insurance Agency Management Association, the association has provided the necessary information from which an evaluation may logically be made. Would that publishers of some commercially available tests were as open and above board.

The first edition appeared in 1938 and the

latest form was developed in 1950. Part I consists of personal history items, such as previous occupation, number of dependents, education, financial status, etc. Part II consists of Bernreuter-type personality inventory questions, self-ratings according to short personality descriptions, and questions concerning motivations and interests. Detailed instructions for administering, scoring, and translating into a letter-grade rating (A, Excellent, to E, Poor) are given in an accompanying manual for use by field-office managers. The Index is designed for use only with applicants having no previous life insurance selling experience.

The rationale for the Index is that success in selling ordinary life insurance is predictable from personal history data and self-ratings when these are empirically validated and weighted. That the rationale is, in general, a sound one is evidenced by the results of periodic validation studies which rather consistently show a positive relationship between Index scores and criterion data such as survival rate and production level.

The rationale has certain limitations, however, which the research group responsible for the test are aware of and attempt to alleviate. The predictive value of personal history items varies with such factors as time, locality, age of testee, etc. Periodic revisions are necessary to maintain correct item weights, a separate scoring key has been devised for use in Canadian companies, and total scores are given different letter ratings according to the testee's age and sex. Research data indicate that the Index has differential validity depending upon the age, marital status, and educational level of the applicant and upon the financing arrangement (commission vs. salary) and quality of management of the employing agency. Fortunately, those applicants obtaining low ratings have poor chances of success regardless of the variables mentioned above.

Probably the basic limitation is the attempt to develop an industry-wide selection test based on items as subject to variable influences as are personal history and self-rating items. To insure predictive efficiency in a specific agency will require not only continuous checking and research (such as the LIAMA has done and will continue to do) but also local validation studies. Many insurance companies are research-oriented and the combination of vigorous industry-wide research and local research efforts bodes well for the continued improvement of this selection tool.

Aptitude Index

[826]

★[Bigelow] Hiring Kit. Sales applicants; 1944-48; a series of 8 hiring aids to facilitate the selection of sales personnel; manual ('48); distribution is restricted to business firms employing the consultant services of publisher; Edwin G. Flemming and Burton Bigelow; Division for Sales Personnel Selection, Burton Bigelow Organization. *
a) PRELIMINARY EXPLORATORY INTERVIEW QUESTIONS. 1947; (6) minutes.
b) RESULTS OF PRELIMINARY EXPLORATORY INTERVIEW. 1947; a checklist to aid in the evaluation of the preliminary interview; (10) minutes.
c) PERSONAL HISTORY RECORD. 1944; title on test booklet is *Application for Employment;* (20-30) minutes.
d) EVALUATION OF PERSONAL HISTORY RECORD. 1946; (10-15) minutes.
e) QUESTIONS TO ASK PREVIOUS EMPLOYERS. 1947; (10-30) minutes per employer.
f) PATTERNED ANALYTICAL INTERVIEW: PART I, INTERVIEW GUIDE. 1947; (30-45) minutes.
g) PATTERNED ANALYTICAL INTERVIEW: PART II, INTERVIEWER'S JUDGMENTS BLANK. 1947; (20-30) minutes.
h) QUESTIONS FOR MEDICAL EXAMINER. 1947.

[827]

★Sales Situation Test. Prospective salesmen; 1951; Form A; no data on reliability; mimeographed manual ['51]; $2.50 per 25; 35¢ per specimen set; postpaid; nontimed (30-40) minutes; Milton L. Rock; Aptitude Test Service. *

REFERENCES
1. ROCK, MILTON L. "A Sales Situation Test." *J Appl Psychol* 35:331-2 O '51. * (PA 26:4228)

[828]

*Steward Selection System, 1951 Edition. Sales applicants; 1934-51; a revision of *Composite Inventory and Examination* (see 40:1651); 20 scores: mental ability, dominance, stability, vocational interests, maturity, appearance-grooming-speech, health-vitality-strength, education, occupational experience, financial status, memberships and activities, family status, miscellaneous factors, caliber level, aptitude for selling, mental health, interest in selling activities, probable effort in job, capacity to survive, total; 3 parts; $1.75 per manual ('51) and keys; $2.50 per specimen set; postage extra; Verne Steward; Verne Steward & Associates. *
a) PERSONAL INVENTORY OF BASIC FACTORS. 1934-51; testing materials include the *Otis Self-Administering Tests of Mental Ability* and an adaptation of *Bernreuter's Personality Inventory;* 1 form, '48; $8 per 25; nontimed in part (60-80) minutes.
b) PERSONAL INVENTORY OF BACKGROUND FACTORS. 1934-51; 1 form, '51; $5.75 per 25.
c) GUIDE TO EMPLOYMENT DECISION: FOR SALES PERSONNEL ONLY. 1945-51; 1 form, '51; $3.25 per 25.

REFERENCES
1-3. See 40:1651.
4-5. See 3:704.
6. MORTENSEN, DONALD GRANT. *An Analysis of Some of the Prerequisites Essential for a Successful Career as a Life Insurance Agent.* Doctor's thesis, University of Southern California (Los Angeles, Calif.), 1950. (*Abstracts of Dissertations ....1950, 1951, pp. 306-7.)*
7. STEWARD, VERNE. [Steward Selection System], pp. 66-73. In *A Survey of 195 Companies on the Use of Tests in Selecting Salesmen.* By Donald G. Paterson. Released for use of subscribers to the Dartnell Sales Service. Dartnell Research Report No. 598. Chicago, Ill.: Dartnell Corporation, [1950]. Pp. 106, 17 inserts. Loose-Leaf binder, mimeographed. *

DONALD G. PATERSON, *Professor of Psychology, and Member of Staff of Industrial Relations*

Center, University of Minnesota, Minneapolis, Minnesota.

One is in a quandary as to what to do about reviewing Verne Steward's *Sales Selection System.* It is not a test but a whole personnel selection system, and it is almost impossible to put your finger on the reliability and validity of any part of the system or even on the reliability and validity of the system as a whole. In the reviewer's opinion, in spite of Steward's attempts to clothe his System with an aura of science by means of testimonial statements from two psychologists, enough scientific evidence has not been provided by him or by anyone else to permit an objective and searching appraisal of its reliability and validity. The reader is, therefore, referred to the two unfavorable reviews which apeared in the *Third Mental Measurements Yearbook,* one by Milton E. Hahn and the other by Floyd M. Ruch. The unpublished Mortensen doctoral thesis which has been completed since the previous reviews were written and which is supposed to have evaluated this System is so defective in design that its findings are of little value, even if the findings were to be published in detail which they have not been.

ALBERT S. THOMPSON, *Associate Professor of Education, Teachers College, Columbia University, New York, New York.*

The 1951 edition, like the edition described fully in the previous *Yearbook,* consists of a mental ability test, a personality inventory, vocational interest items, self-analysis questions, and a detailed personal information blank. These data, plus those obtained in personal interview and from references, form the basis for ratings made through the use of the *Guide to Employment Decision.* The end result is a set of ratings on 19 factors on a four-point scale (unqualified, borderline, acceptable, superior) and a "Final Rating for Person as a Whole." An accompanying manual gives detailed instructions for administering and scoring the tests and presents "favorable cues" and "danger signs" to be considered in rating the applicant on the Personal History factors and Key to Success factors.

What we have here is not a battery of selection tests, objectively scored and weighted to predict success in a given occupation, but rather a selection *procedure* providing guides and tools for acquiring information about the applicant which can then be compared judgmentally with employment standards so that a final employment decision may be made. Steward recommends that these employment standards be set by job and analysis, with adjustments made as the result of experience. Whether the selection procedure will work depends, therefore, upon the adequacy of the applicant data obtained and the validity of the employment standards for the specific situation involved. The Steward materials per se do not insure that these two requirements will be met.

It is a rather trying experience to attempt to evaluate the Steward materials in the usual way, i.e., by studying technical data on the reliability and validity of the instruments involved. An August 1950 statement by the author, entitled *Development and Validation of the Steward Sales Personnel Selection Materials,* describes eight research studies; but the descriptions deal merely with the subjects, instruments, and criteria, and do not include the results of comparisons between the selection instruments and the criteria. From descriptive data provided by the author, the reviewer was able to find two studies which approached validation in the usual sense: a follow-up study of 51 agents hired with the Steward system; and a comparison of 21 "successful" and 11 "marginal" agents employed by a company with its own selection system but on whom Steward ratings were obtained. In both studies a positive relationship was found between ratings, using the Steward materials, and the criterion.

It would appear that the author has recently been making a sincere attempt to obtain and present research data necessary for evaluating his materials. Those presented so far, however, do not cause this reviewer to disagree with the overall evaluations made by the reviewers in *The Third Yearbook.* As a "battery of selection tests," they need further validation (as do most tests). As a "system of selection procedures," they would appear to depend upon the good judgment and occupational acumen of the user and thus require empirical validation in the specific situation.

The most disturbing thing to the present reviewer is the test author's assumption that the materials, developed on *life insurance agents,* apply equally well to other sales personnel. The author states that "the materials can be used with success in any field of selling as soon as suitable employment standards have been established." No evidence to support this statement is presented.

For reviews by Milton E. Hahn and Floyd L. Ruch, see 3:704.

[829]
*Test for Ability to Sell: George Washington University Series. Grades 7–16 and adults; 1929–50; Form 2 ('50—a revision of Form 1); manual ('50); $3 per 25; 30¢ per specimen set; postpaid; 45(50) minutes; original test: F. A. Moss, Herbert Wyle, William Loman, and William Middleton; revised test: Thelma Hunt, Robert George, and William Schnell; Center for Psychological Service, George Washington University. *

For a review by Floyd L. Ruch, see 3:705.

[830]
★Test of Sales Judgment. Sales applicants; 1946; 1 form; distribution is restricted to business firms employing the consultant services of publisher; nontimed (15–20) minutes; Edwin G. Flemming and Cecile W. Flemming; Division for Sales Personnel Selection, Burton Bigelow Organization. *

BUSINESS EDUCATION – FIFTH MMY

REVIEWS BY *Dorothy C. Adkins, Gale W. Clark, Edward B. Greene, Edward N. Hay, Clifford E. Jurgensen, James Lumsden, Bernadine Meyer, Jacob S. Orleans, I. David Satlow, and Wimburn L. Wallace.*

[502]

*Bookkeeping: Achievement Examinations for Secondary Schools. High school; 1951–53; Forms 1 ('51), 3 ('53); no specific manual; no data on reliability; norms: Forms 1 ['52], 3 ('53); 10¢ per test, postage extra; [60–90] minutes; Helen L. Haberman;

Educational Test Bureau. *

[503]

*Bookkeeping: Every Pupil Scholarship Test. High school; 1926–58; new form usually issued each January and April; norms available following testing program; no data on reliability; 4¢ per test; 4¢ per

scoring key; postage extra; 50(55) minutes; Bureau of Educational Measurements. *

[504]

★**Bookkeeping: Midwest High School Achievement Examinations.** High school; 1952–55; Forms A ('55), B ('52, identical with Form 2 of *Bookkeeping: Achievement Examinations for Secondary Schools*); no specific manual; no data on reliability; norms: [A, '55; B, '57]; 10¢ per test, postage extra; 60(65) minutes; Lois E. Hastings (A); Educational Test Bureau. *

I. DAVID SATLOW, *Chairman, Department of Accounting and Distributive Education, Thomas Jefferson High School, Brooklyn, New York.*

The test is fairly representative of the theory covered in the first year of bookkeeping. The arithmetic phase, unfortunately, is not sufficiently representative either in scope or weight; only 4 of the 164 items deal with arithmetic.

There is no evidence of any attempt at validation, a step that would have eliminated much of the vagueness, ambiguity, and inaccuracy that characterizes the test in its present form. A significant number of questions are not sufficiently clear. A number of the questions are susceptible to several responses. Items 2, 52, and 56 are answerable by *all* choices. Items 95, 98, 100, and 137 are answerable in ways that are at variance with the key. Items 15, 88, 90, 120, 147, and 148 contain inaccuracies. In the absence of scoring directions, the rater does not know whether any penality is to be imposed for guessing or whether any deviation from the language of the scoring key is acceptable.

The editing is somewhat haphazard. Ordinary rules of English grammar are overlooked. In Section 1, the student is asked to "choose the word or words which best completes [sic] the statements below." Question 4 likewise ignores the rule governing the agreement of subject and predicate, "Assets which the average American family possess." The language employed might be improved so that the test would measure the acquistion of bookkeeping knowledge and skill more reliably. The terms "payment" in Item 139, "merchandise" in Item 142, and "charged" in Item 52 tend to mislead the student.

There appears to be a decided lack of uniformity in the construction of the multiple choice questions in Section 1. Twenty-four questions offer three possible responses, 11 offer four choices, 2 present five choices, and one double question calls for two responses out of four choices. Section 2 omits all question numbers from the answer column, thus making it difficult to answer 25 questions that span across seven inches of printed line space. In Section 4, column 2 appears underneath column 1, which in turn is broken up into two columns. For *each* of the 25 items in column 2, the student is compelled to refer to column 1 and to select *one* of *nine* classifications. Even the systematic student will find it necessary to spend an inordinate amount of time identifying each of the 25 items. Notably lacking are sample questions—an element that is taken for granted as a *sine qua non* of test construction.

The test may serve the purpose of a specific teacher in a specific classroom; in its present form it is not recommended for usage on a mass scale. At best the test is based solely on the acquisition of specific knowledges and skills. It does not attempt to measure the ability to interpret the learning outcomes of the study of bookkeeping. Several questions aim at breadth of coverage, but none aims at depth. No records and reports are presented for interpretation, nor are materials presented in increasing order of difficulty. Thus, the test fails to measure the attainment of some important objectives of bookkeeping instruction, and measures quantity and not quality of what it does seek to ascertain.

[505]

*****Bookkeeping I: Every Pupil Test.** 1 year high school; 1939–58; new form usually issued each April; norms available following testing program; 3¢ per test; 1¢ per scoring key; cash orders postpaid; 40(45) minutes; Ohio Scholarship Tests. *

[506]

*****Bookkeeping Test: National Business Entrance Tests.** Grades 12–16 and adults; 1938–57; for complete battery, see 515; 1 form; 2 editions; general information ['56]; no data on reliability; postpaid; 120(130) minutes; Joint Committee on Tests of the United Business Education Association and the National Office Management Association; United Business Education Association. *
a) [GENERAL TESTING SERIES.] Form 19-52 ('55); manual ('55); correction manual ['55]; no adult norms; 50¢ per test.
b) [OFFICIAL TESTING SERIES.] Administered only at NBET Centers which may be established in any community; Form 18-42 ('54); manual ('54); norms ['57]; examination fee, $1; specimen set not available.

For reviews by Harvey A. Andruss and Ray G. Price of the 1946 Form, see 3:368. For reviews by Edward N. Hay, Jacob S. Orleans, and Wimburn L. Wallace of the entire series, see 515; for a review by Paul S. Lomax of the 1946 Form, see 3:396.

[507]

★**Business Education: National Teacher Examinations.** College seniors and teachers; 1956–58; for more complete information, see 538; IBM; 80(90) minutes; Educational Testing Service. *

For reviews by William A. Brownell, Walter W. Cook, and Lawrence G. Derthick of the entire series, see 538; for a review by Harry N. Rivlin of an earlier edition, see 4:802.

[508]

*****Business Fundamentals and General Information Test: National Business Entrance Tests.** Grades 12–16 and adults; 1938–57; for complete battery, see 515; 1 form; 2 editions; general information ['56]; no data on reliability; postpaid; 45(55) minutes; Joint Committee on Tests of the United Business Education Association and the National Office Management Association; United Business Education Association. *
a) [GENERAL TESTING SERIES.] Form 19-51 ('55); manual ('55); correction manual ['55]; no adult norms; 50¢ per test.
b) [OFFICIAL TESTING SERIES.] Administered only at NBET Centers which may be established in any community; Form 18-41 ('54); manual ('54); norms ['57]; available free when any one of the tests in the series is ordered.

For reviews by Vera M. Amerson and C. C. Upshall of the 1946 Form, see 3:369. For reviews by Edward N. Hay, Jacob S. Orleans, and Wimburn L. Wallace of the entire series, see 515; for a review by Paul S. Lomax of the 1946 Form, see 3:396.

[509]

*****Business Relations and Occupations: Achievement Examinations for Secondary Schools.** High school; 1951–53; Forms 1 ['51], 3 ('53); no specific manual; no data on reliability; norms: Forms 1 ['52], 3 ('53) 10¢ per test, postage extra; [60–90] minutes; A. Donald Beattie (3); Educational Test Bureau. *

[510]

★**Business Relations and Occupations: Midwest High School Achievement Examinations.** High school; 1952–55; Forms A ('55), B ('52, identical with Form 2 of *Business Relations and Occupations: Achievement Examinations for Secondary Schools*); no specific manual; no data on reliability; norms: [A, '55; B, '57]; 10¢ per test, postage extra; 60(65) minutes; A. Donald Beattie (A); Educational Test Bureau. *

[511]

*****General Office Clerical Test (Including Filing): National Business Entrance Tests.** Grades 12–16 and adults 1948–57; for complete battery, see 515; 1 form; 2 editions; general information ['56]; no data on reliability; postpaid; 120(130) minutes; Joint Committee on Tests of the United Business Education Association and the National Office Management Association; United Business Education Association. *
a) [GENERAL TESTING SERIES.] Form 19-53 ('55); manual ('55); correction manual ['55]; no adult norms; 50¢ per test.
b) [OFFICIAL TESTING SERIES.] Administered only at NBET Centers which may be established in any com-

munity; Form 18-43 ('54); manual ('54); examination fee, $1.25; norms ['57]; specimen set not available.

For reviews by Arnold E. Schneider and C. C. Upshall of the 1946 Form, see 3:379. For reviews by Edward N. Hay, Jacob S. Orleans, and Wimburn L. Wallace of the entire series, see 515; for a review by Paul S. Lomax of the 1946 Form, see 3:396.

[512]

Hiett Simplified Shorthand Test (Gregg). 1–2 semesters high school; 1951; IBM; Forms A, B; mimeographed; $1.95 per 25 tests; separate answer sheets may be used; 85¢ per 25 IBM answer sheets; 30¢ per hand scoring stencil; postage extra; 45¢ per specimen set, postpaid; (50) minutes; Victor C. Hiett and H. E. Schrammel; Bureau of Educational Measurements. *

GALE W. CLARK, *Instructor in Business, Western Michigan University, Kalamazoo, Michigan.*

The two forms of the test are substantially alike, the only differences being in content and dictation rate. There are some errors on Form A, but they are adequately indicated on the scoring key for that form of the test.

Each form has four parts, the first consisting of the dictation of material to be used in answering questions presented in the final part of the test. Here the student is required to "take" dictation for five minutes at approximately 80 words per minute on Form B and approximately 60 words per minute on Form A. The second activity consists of a series of longhand and shorthand presentations of statements. For each statement the student must select the incorrectly written shorthand character (if any), or indicate that the sentence is correctly written. The third part of the test is divided into three sections. Section A presents a shorthand character for which four longhand transcripts are provided; the student selects the correct longhand equivalent. Section B is a reverse pattern of Section A in that a longhand word is presented and four shorthand characters are given from which the student selects the appropriate character. The small changes in characters in this section will be very confusing to many excellent shorthand students, especially those who have been taught to improvise characters when in doubt. Section C consists of 20 incomplete statements in shorthand from which the final characters are omitted. In each case the final character must be chosen from a selection of four endings. The fourth part is a group of 25 true-false questions based on the original dictation and requiring the student to determine from the dictation whether each statement presented is true or false. Questions in this part of the test could be answered by an attentive student even though he has no knowledge of shorthand. It is not necessary to quote the material exactly and many students could remember enough details to answer the questions.

The dictation at the beginning is too rapid for most first semester students and for many second semester students. Of course, this may be in interpretation of progress, but such progress depends upon teaching methods designed to build speed. This reviewer believes that the test would not be a fair examination for first semester students on the secondary school level, but that it would be quite satisfactory for students on the college level. Unfortunately, the norms provided are based entirely on the performance of high school students.

In taking the test, the student may record his answers either on the test blank or on a separate answer sheet. Because directions for both methods are presented on the test blank, careful explanation on the part of the administrator is necessary to insure that the examinee understands exactly which directions are to be followed and which are to be disregarded.

A good feature is the possibility of using the same test copies several times if separate answer sheets are used. However, there may be discrepancies between scores when different answering methods are used, especially since the test is timed.

Because of the rate discrepancy between Form A and Form B, the two forms cannot be used interchangeably. Actually, the two forms are at different levels. Teachers should select the form to be used depending on the progress of the class. The author suggests the use of Form A for first semester students and Form B for second semester students. There are no end-of-year norms for Form A.

Properly administered, the test is easily scored with a minimum of error. Scores may be interpreted in terms of percentile ratings and letter grade equivalents. Provision for the latter is unusual but helpful, especially to beginning teachers. The specific interpretation of such grades must, of course, serve only as a guide; the grade equivalents should not be considered an austere grading scale. With the qualifications noted, the test should be fairly

good for two of its stated purposes, determining achievement and checking instruction. It is probable that college teachers will find it much more reliable than secondary teachers. The test should be used only as a general guide for assigning marks. The reviewer doubts its motivational characteristics.

[513]

Kimberly-Clark Typing Ability Analysis. Grade 12 and adults; 1942; 3 scores: speed, accuracy, total; 1 form; $3.75 per 25 tests, postage extra; 25¢ per specimen set, postpaid; administration time not reported; Clifford E. Jurgensen; [the Author], 6101 Oliver Ave. South, Minneapolis 19, Minn. *

REFERENCES

1. JURGENSEN, CLIFFORD E. "A Test for Selecting and Training Industrial Typists." *Ed & Psychol Meas* 2:409–25 O '42. * (*PA* 17:1350)
2. GIESE, WILLIAM JAMES. "A Tested Method for the Selection of Office Personnel." *Personnel Psychol* 2:525–45 W '49. * (*PA* 24:4278)

For a review by E. G. Blackstone, see 3:383.

[514]

***Machine Calculation Test: National Business Entrance Tests.** Grades 12–16 and adults; 1941–57; for complete battery, see 515; 1 form; 2 editions; general information ['56]; no data on reliability; postpaid; 120(130) minutes; Joint Committee on Tests of the United Business Education Association and the National Office Management Association; United Business Education Association. *
a) [GENERAL TESTING SERIES.] Form 19-54('55); manual ('55); correction manual ['55]; no adult norms; 50¢ per test.
b) [OFFICIAL TESTING SERIES.] Administered only at NBET Centers which may be established in any community; Form 18-44 ('54); manual ('54); norms ['57]; $1 per examinee; specimen set not available.

DOROTHY C. ADKINS, *Professor of Psychology and Chairman of the Department, University of North Carolina, Chapel Hill, North Carolina.*

The test is intended for key-driven machine operators, but the use of any machine, electric or hand operated, is permitted. The order in which the parts are taken varies with the kind of machine used. The examinee is directed to note on the test booklet the kind of machine used, but it is not clear who does what with the information. It seems to have no bearing on the norms presented by the authors, a situation which is particularly strange because, although the test is said not to be a "speed-spurt" test, a bonus of one point is given for each minute saved in the 2-hour time period.

The test must be scored by hand. In an effort to present problems that will appear practical (such as those involving adding sales figures vertically and horizontally to obtain branch totals and monthly totals or those requiring

Hiett Simplified Shorthand Test

computation of total time worked for each of several employees from weekly time cards), scoring convenience is sacrificed. Although the service sold with the official series includes scoring, inconvenient, time-consuming scoring is expensive no matter where it is done. The scoring instructions for some of the problems also imply dual penalties for errors in certain problems such as those requiring the extension of invoice items and addition of the extensions. An incorrect extension entails, say, a 1-point penalty and then an additional 4-point penalty for the wrong total.

Percentile norms for secondary school and college students are available. For the general series edition, the total n's were 486 and 142, respectively; the table for the official series tests omits the n's.

In a sales brochure on the National Business Entrance Tests entitled "What About Reliability and Validity?" it is variously noted that the tests are "prepared by specialists and reviewed by qualified office executives," that "originally, such tests were validated by administering them to experimental and control groups in offices and schools," that "since then the general form of the tests has been retained, in order to perpetuate the qualities which make them reliable and valid," that every step is taken to insure having tests which *are* valid and reliable, and that the Joint Committee on Tests "employs, as consultant, a nationally recognized expert in test construction and measurement." It is to be regretted that more specific reference to empirical evidence of reliability and validity was not presented in the bulletins available for review.

For a review by Elizabeth Fehrer of the 1946 Form, see 3:384. For reviews by Edward N. Hay, Jacob S. Orleans, and Wimburn L. Wallace of the entire series, see 515; for a review by Paul S. Lomax of the 1946 Form, see 3:396.

[515]
*National Business Entrance Tests. Grades 12–16 and adults 1938–57; 1 form; 3 editions; 6 tests (also listed separately); general information ['56]; no data on reliability; postpaid; Joint Committee on Tests of the United Business Education Association and the National Office Management Association; United Business Education Association. *
a) [GENERAL TESTING SERIES.] 1 form; 6 tests; manual ('55); correction manual ['55]; no adult norms; 50¢ per test.
1) *Machine Calculation Test.* 1941–56; Form 19-54 ('55); 120(130) minutes.

2) *Typewriting Test.* 1941–56; Form 19-56 ('55); 120(130) minutes.
3) *Business Fundamentals and General Information Test.* 1938–56; Form 19-51 ('55); 45(55) minutes.
4) *Bookkeeping Test.* 1938–56; Form 19-52 ('55); 120(130) minutes.
5) *General Office Clerical Test (Including Filing).* 1948–56; Form 19-53 ('55); 120(130) minutes.
6) *Stenographic Test.* 1938–56; Form 19-55 ('55); 120(130) minutes.
b) [SHORT FORM SERIES.] 1 form; no data on reliability; no norms; 50¢ per test.
1) *Typewriting Test.* 1 form ('55); 45(55) minutes.
2) *Stenographic Test.* 1 form ('55); directions sheet ('55); (60) minutes.
c) [OFFICIAL TESTING SERIES.] Administered only at NBET Centers which may be established in any community; 1 form; 6 tests; manual ('54); norms ['57]; specimen set not available.
1) *Machine Calculation Test.* 1941–57; Form 18-44 ('54); examination fee, $1; 120(130) minutes.
2) *Typewriting Test.* 1941–57; Form 18-46 ('54); examination fee, $1; 120(130) minutes.
3) *Business Fundamentals and General Information Test.* 1938–57; Form 18-41 ('54); available free when any one of the tests in the series is ordered; 45(55) minutes.
4) *Bookkeeping Test.* 1938–57; Form 18-42 ('54); examination fee, $1; 120(130) minutes.
5) *General Office Clerical Test (Including Filing).* 1948–57; Form 18-43 ('54); examination fee, $1.25; 120(130) minutes.
6) *Stenographic Test.* 1938–57; Form 18-45 ('54); correction manual ('54); examination fee, $1.25; (125–135) minutes.

REFERENCES

1–9. See 40:1476.
10. See 4:453.

EDWARD N. HAY, *Chairman of the Board, Edward N. Hay and Associates, Inc., Philadelphia, Pennsylvania.*

These tests have been designed to evaluate skills necessary to five basic office jobs—stenography, typewriting, machine calculation, bookkeeping, and general office work (including filing). The committee states that these measurements of achievement can be utilized in (*a*) evaluating the status of high school or college business students compared with the performance of students in other schools; (*b*) evaluating the effectiveness of teachers; (*c*) screening prospective employees; and (*d*) granting proficiency certificates to examinees who have passed one or more of the tests satisfactorily.

Although there are no alternative forms available, there are two similar series of tests. The General Testing Series for which no proficiency certificates are given is intended for school and office use. The Official Testing Series is available only for administration at National Business Entrance Test Centers. These test centers can be set up by interested individuals with the only apparent qualification being that of an established minimum of five examinees for each center. In 1955, there existed 92 such centers in the United States and Canada.

If the Official Testing Series is administered by a recognized testing center, then a grading service is provided. On this basis, it might be wise to use only this series, for the scoring appears time-consuming and somewhat complicated for a rapid evaluation of the measured skills. The criterion for passing these tests appears to be somewhat tenuous for, according to the Committee, it rests primarily on the discretion of the administrator or the needs of the local business population. It seems that this is proficiency measured only by the qualifications demanded by schools, employers, etc., rather than a true delineation of proficiency in the basic skills evaluated. Perhaps, with more research, the criticism will become unwarranted.

The Committee states that the validity and reliability of the tests have been established by research workers and competent authorities. Statistical data are not reported; therefore, people who contemplate using this service should request the information to evaluate the tests properly. Although three doctoral dissertations which are said to have evolved around the predictive validity of different tests in the series are mentioned, no implications of these findings are reported. Validity and reliability coefficients would be a sound background on which to base the Committee's plea for better business education.

In the explanatory manual, there is a suggestion that users clinically appraise scores obtained on the various tests as they relate to one another, and specifically as they relate to those on the *Business Fundamentals and General Information Test*. The implication is that this latter test is a basic measure of intellectual capacity and that achievement on it should be used in making judgments regarding quality of instruction, motivation of examinees, and examinees' efficiency in use of capacities. It would appear that such an interpretative approach should be used with utmost caution—if at all.

JACOB S. ORLEANS, *Lecturer in Psychology, Southern Regional Division, University of Nevada, Las Vegas, Nevada.*

The prospective user of such a series of tests, or of any one of the separate tests, looks first for evidence of predictive validity. The validity of these tests rests on the accuracy with which they predict the success of the examinee on the job, if not in merely securing a job. There is no "manual of directions" in the usual sense of the term. The administrator's manual contains the instructions for administering all but the stenography test. There is a separate manual for administering that test. A correction manual contains scoring keys and instructions for scoring. There is also a set of stapled sheets with such headings as "Origin of the Tests," "Who Benefits From These Tests?," "Your Testing Center," "What Are the NBETests?," "General Information About the Tests," "Percentile Norms," "Growth and Trends of NBET," "What About Reliability and Validity?," a list of 92 testing centers at which "official" testing has taken place, and registration and order forms.

All the information furnished on both validity and reliability is contained in this short paragraph:

National Business Entrance Tests are prepared by specialists and reviewed by qualified office executives. Originally, such tests were validated by administering them to experimental and control groups in offices and schools. Since then the general form of the tests has been retained, in order to perpetuate the qualities which make them reliable and valid. The Joint Committee on Tests is aware of the importance of these factors and takes every step to insure having tests which *are* valid and reliable. It employs, as consultant, a nationally recognized expert in test construction and measurement.

The users of the tests are asked to accept on faith the claim that the persons who prepared the first series of the tests were "specialists" and that the office executives who reviewed them were "qualified"; that the first series of tests was found to have adequate predictive validity; that retaining the general form of the tests has maintained their validity and reliability over the years; that "every step [taken] to insure having tests which *are* valid and reliable" has actually resulted in predictive validity; and that the efforts of the nationally recognized expert who serves as a consultant maintain the predictive validity of the tests. In short, the test user is asked to take the predictive validity of the tests on faith. No information is given concerning the sources of the types of tasks or other content in the tests other than such general statements as that "the calculating machine operator must be able to handle a variety of computations rapidly and accurately as well as to maintain a satisfactory, sustained pace. Hence the test is made up of samplings of computational work common to many offices." The fact that the content of the tests is extensive and appears to be representative of office tasks is not very helpful to the user who should be given evidence—for instance, in the form of the frequency of occurrence of certain tasks and their importance for job success.

The announcement leaflet for the tests lists the following purposes and values of the series: "For improving educational programs in the schools; for upgrading vocational business education; for in-service training of younger teachers; for more effective evaluation of school business curricula; give evaluation device with national norms; give uniform grading of tests; give Certificates of Proficiency to those who qualify; give reliable criteria for measuring vocational training outcomes." It may well be that the tests can be used validly and reliably to perform these functions, but in nothing accompanying the tests do the publishers present any evidence to show that this is so. Nor is the test user told how the tests can be employed to serve these purposes.

The customary manuals accompanying published tests present information about the tests and the purposes they are intended to serve, and evidence to show that they can serve these purposes; descriptions of the tests, the source of the content, and the method of preparation; norms, the sources of the norms, and the interpretation of scores; and suggestions for using the test results. There is no such manual available for the NBET tests. Instead, the prospective user is presented with some 16 pages of what is essentially advertising matter—except for a 1-page table of percentile norms and a page on the interpretation of scores. The norms are based on 7,875 secondary school skill tests and 1,278 college tests. It is not clear whether this means 7,875 secondary school graduates and 1,278 college graduates, or whether the numbers include those who have not yet been graduated from these levels. No information is given concerning the geographical distribution of the examinees on whom the norms are based, nor the types of schools from which they come —public or private, general or commercial. Since suggestions are given concerning the interpretation of group averages, it would be helpful to have differential norms for different types of schools. The number of examinees on whose scores the norms are based varies for the college group from 115 on the *General Office Clerical Test* to 652 on the *Business Fundamentals and General Information Test*. For the secondary group the numbers vary from 486 on the *Machine Calculation Test* to 6,661 on the *Business Fundamentals and General Information Test*. There is no evidence that, despite the differences in the groups on whom the norms are based, the norms are comparable. The suggestions for interpreting the test scores obviously assume such comparability.

It is suggested that the score on the *Business Fundamentals and General Information Test* be used as a criterion for the evaluation of scores on the other tests—something like using an individual's mental test status to evaluate his achievement status: "A student scoring at only the 30th percentile in a skill test and at about the same in the Business Fundamentals and General Information Test is scoring in skill up to our expectation for her (or him)." No argument and no data are offered to explain this criterion or to support the validity of it.

The *Business Fundamentals and General Information Test* consists of 100 multiple choice questions. The scoring is quite objective. Each item is allowed 1 point, and the total score is 100 points. With the exception of parts of the *General Office Clerical Test,* the other tests, being performance tests, are of necessity liable to some subjectivity of scoring. Detailed instructions for scoring are given which should go a long way to make the scoring objective. Specified amounts of score are allowed for the various parts of each task. There may be some rationale for the total score allowed for each test; if so, it is not explained. There is apparently no reason that the total possible score on the *Bookkeeping Test,* for instance, should not be 120 points or 180 points or 360 points, rather than the 240 actually allowed. Except for the *Stenographic Test* and the *Business Fundamentals and General Information Test,* the total score is the same for all the tests, 240 points.

Despite the apparent attempt at comparability reflected in having the maximum score the same for four of the tests, the 50th percentile scores differ by large amounts from test to test. The table of percentile norms lists a "passing score" for each of the five skill tests. No mention is made, nor any explanation given, of the reason for the "passing score," or of how it was derived. The table also contains a row of figures showing the "per cent passed" for each test—the per cents varying for the secondary group from 77 per cent on the *General Office Clerical Test* to 44 per cent on the *Machine Calculation Test,* and, for the college group, from 94 per cent on the *General Office Clerical Test* to 40 per cent on the *Machine Calculation Test.*

For lack of information it is difficult, if at all possible, for the prospective user of any of these tests to judge their value for him. That is most unfortunate. It is likely that the tests are good ones and that they can serve important purposes in a valid manner and with high reliability. When a large amount of time and effort has gone into the preparation of tests, as has apparently been true of the NBET tests, it is unfortunate that the information is lacking which the prospective user needs to satisfy himself that they are good tests.

WIMBURN L. WALLACE, *Director, Professional Examinations Division, The Psychological Corporation, New York, New York.*

The National Business Entrance Tests (NBET) comprise a battery of six tests intended to assess the proficiency of students in high schools and colleges in clerical areas. Five are skill tests and one covers general information and fundamentals. Original forms issued in 1937 were called the *National Clerical Ability Tests.* In 1947 the program was taken over by the joint sponsorship of the United Business Education Association and the National Office Management Association.

Two parallel series of tests, the official and the general, are available. The official series (currently the "1800 series") is restricted to program use in established testing centers. Students may take any number of the six tests but must include the Business Fundamentals and General Information Test. For a modest fee the central agency provides all materials, instructions, scoring services, and proficiency certificates for the official series. Schools or employers may purchase the general series (currently the "1900 series") for practice or screening testing; no scoring service or certificates are provided with it.

The test booklets and materials for both series are well designed and attractively printed. Directions for administration are meticulously

clear and precise. Procedures for conducting the official series are described in adequate detail. In other words, the mechanics of the testing program are very well conceived and executed. Literature describing the program is somewhat overly promotional to be consistent with the dignity it should reflect. The user of the general series might be somewhat handicapped by the complex, awkward, time-consuming, arduous system of scoring.

Percentile norms are provided for each series. Separate norms are shown for secondary schools and for colleges on each test. The population for the norms for the official series is described only as "all participants in the National Business Entrance Testing program who have used the 1800 series tests." Numbers of cases, mean scores, and standard deviations are not reported. Suggested passing scores for the five skill tests are given, but there is no indication of the basis for the selection of these cutoff points. This is a serious omission of information. Until recently, proficiency certificates were granted or withheld depending upon attainment of the passing score, but the current procedure is to report raw scores to the local test center administrator who issues the certificates in the light of local situations.

Norms for the general series are based on all the candidates tested in NBET centers in 1955. The table shows number of cases and passing score for each category as well as the percentile equivalents of the raw scores. Although explanation and illustrations are provided for the interpretation of percentile scores, little or nothing is said about the interpretation of the test results themselves. Apparently one has to be somewhat familiar with the contents of the tests in order to understand the significance of particular scores on them.

The fact that the manual provides no data at all on reliability, validity, form equivalence, or score consistency is the greatest deficiency in this battery of tests. While content validity might be claimed as most appropriate for this type of instrument, the opportunities for studies of concurrent validity with grades in appropriate courses and of predictive validity with employment records should not be neglected. Mention is made in the manual of the existence of doctoral dissertations involving such research, but none of the results are reported. There is no excuse for failure to supply other statistics. Data must be readily available for estimations of reliability, and the existence of the parallel series makes the investigation of interform consistency and reliability feasible.

In summary, the NBET is a well designed battery of tests in clerical areas. The testing program uses a restricted series of the tests and is excellently organized in its mechanical aspects. The alternate series is available for purchase and has the same high standards of clarity in format and procedures, but the scoring method is complex and difficult. The most serious defect in the battery is the lack of any data in the manual concerning the reliability, validity, or interform consistency of the tests. This omission prevents a complete evaluation of the psychometric quality of the instruments.

For a review by Paul S. Lomax of the 1946 edition, see 3:396. For reviews of individual tests, see 506, 508, 511, 514, 522, 526, 3:368–9, 3:379, 3:384, 3:391, and 3:394.

[516]

★**Office Worker Test 30-A.** Office workers; 1956–58; 11 scores: reading, vocabulary, reasoning, arithmetic, checking, filing, spelling, punctuation, usage, information, total; 1 form ('56); preliminary mimeographed manual ('56); norms ('58); separate answer sheets must be used; PPA member agency: 10–49 tests, 38¢ each; others, 46¢ each; $2 per specimen set; postpaid; 90(100) minutes; Public Personnel Association. *

[517]

★**Personnel Research Institute Test of Shorthand Skills.** Stenographers; 1951–54; title on test is *Otis and Laurent Test of Shorthand Skills;* 2 scores: transliteration, transcription; Forms A, B ('51); tentative norms; $3.75 per 25 tests; 50¢ per set of scoring key and manual ('54); $1 per specimen set; cash orders postpaid; (20–35) minutes; [Jay L. Otis and Harry Laurent]; Personnel Research Institute. *

[518]

★**SRA Typing Adaptability Test.** High school and adults; 1954–56; formerly called *Columbia-Southern Typing Test;* 3 scores: time, error, total; 1 form ('56); manual ('56); no data on reliability; tentative norms; $2 per 20 tests; $2 per 20 typing forms; 75¢ per specimen set; postage extra; (45) minutes; Mary Tydlaska and Clem White; Science Research Associates. *

GALE W. CLARK, *Instructor in Business, Western Michigan University, Kalamazoo, Michigan.*

This test is designed to measure the adaptability of the typist in using a variety of typing skills to perform competently on the job. The test is presented in a 4-page folder of general directions given to the typist. The typing is done in a second 4-page folder. A third 4-page folder describes the test and gives directions for administering and scoring it and interpreting test results.

Test 1 requires the reproduction of a rough draft into an acceptable manuscript. The directions are given on the first page of the instructions while the test is presented on the second page. Although the test is very adequate insofar as testing the ability of the typist to type a corrected manuscript is concerned, it is inconvenient to use because of the necessity of turning from page 1 to page 2 to be sure that directions are being followed. Test 2 requires the student to transfer tabular material from page 3 of the test folder to page 3 of the typing forms folder, following directions printed on page 1 of the former. Again, considerable manipulating of pages is required. The job required by this test may be presented differently in various training programs; the directions do not take this into account. Test 3 requires the writing of five names and addresses in alphabetical order according to an example provided.

The typist is carefully instructed that the individual tests are not timed, but that a record will be made of the amount of time needed to complete the whole test. This procedure is good; however, some typists might work faster if they knew that time is considered in the scoring.

Not all phases of typing skill are tested, but this is a good measure of performance ability except in straight copy work. The chief criticism of the test is that of organization. Directions are difficult to follow when they are placed elsewhere than with the problem. This is an especially important consideration when one of the aims of the test is to test "the ability to follow directions."

EDWARD B. GREENE, *Supervisor of Personnel Testing, Chrysler Corporation, Detroit, Michigan.*

The test measures ability to follow directions and type quickly and accurately. The examinee is asked (*a*) to make a corrected copy of a fairly difficult letter with corrections shown in longhand, (*b*) to copy material containing dates and costs on a printed form with lined columns, and (*c*) to rearrange five names and addresses and type them in alphabetical order. The examinee is told to erase all errors and advised that he will be penalized 1 point for each corrected error and 2 points for each uncorrected error. He is told that the total amount of time spent will be included in the score, but no time limits are set. Ten minutes are allowed for the silent reading of directions. After reasonable questions are answered, the starting time is recorded. In large groups each examinee may record his own finishing time; with individuals or small groups the recording is done by the examiner.

Detailed directions for finding the error score are given in the manual. Time and error scores are added for a total score. For example, a person who makes 4 errors and finishes the work in 12 minutes has a total score of 16, a very superior score. Average scores, based on a group which is not described as to number or characteristics, range from 28 to 37. Scores of 48 and over are very inferior. Another table gives mean scores and standard deviations for groups of 50 students, applicants, and employees. The students took almost twice as long to complete the test and made almost twice as many errors as the employees. No indications are given of the practice effects of this test. The writer suspects that the scores might go up a great deal for some examinees on a retest.

This test appears to be very useful as a short screening test which is easy to administer and can be scored by a careful clerk in about two minutes. The emphasis on speed in determining the total score is probably not realized by most examinees, and one's speed often varies with the time of day and the amount of coffee recently drunk.

[519]

*The Seashore-Bennett Stenographic Proficiency Tests: A Standard Recorded Stenographic Work-sample. Adults; 1946–56; Forms B-1, B-2 ('46); revised manual ('56); 3 types of recordings: 4 standard 12-inch records (78 rpm), LP microgroove 12-inch record (33⅓ rpm), 2 tapes (3.75" per sec.); distribution is restricted to business firms; $19.50 per set of script, manual, 100 summary charts, and standard records; $13.50 per set of script, manual, 100 summary sheets, and either the microgroove record or a set of tape recordings; $2 per 100 summary charts; 35¢ per manual; postpaid; (65–70) minutes; Harold Seashore and George K. Bennett; Psychological Corporation. *

REFERENCES

1. See 4:455.
2. "Comparative Performances of Different Groups on the Seashore-Bennett Stenographic Proficiency Test." *Test Service B* (50):6 Je '56. *
3. McCarty, John J. "Normative Data Information Exchange, No. 10-41." *Personnel Psychol* 10:533 w '57. *

For a review by Harold F. Rothe, see 4:455; for a review by Ann Brewington, see 3:386.

SRA Typing Adaptability Test

[520]

*Shorthand Aptitude Test. High school; 1953–54; 1 form ['53]; mimeographed manual ['54]; 5s. per 10 tests; 3s. per manual; 3s. 6d. per specimen set; postpaid within Australia; 31(45) minutes; manual by V. Brownless and S. Dunn; Queensland Department of Public Instruction; Australian Council for Educational Research. *

James Lumsden, *Lecturer in Psychology, University of Western Australia, Nedlands, Australia.*

The test consists of material similar to the first four subtests of the *Turse Shorthand Aptitude Test*. There is a saving in testing time of approximately 25 per cent.

Reliability data are not reported in the manual. Since the test is recommended only for prediction of a single criterion which is unambiguously assessed, this is not serious, though researchers may be interested in the extent to which failure of prediction arises from random error or systematic bias.

Validity was determined by a follow-up study of 239 Queensland girls given the test on entry to a shorthand course. Test results were correlated with shorthand examination marks obtained after three terms ($n = 200$) and after five terms ($n = 155$). This test yielded slightly higher correlations than the Turse. The validity coefficients (.54 and .69) indicate that the test has sufficient predictive power to be of considerable assistance in selection for shorthand courses. It was notable that Test 3, phonetic association, gave correlations almost as high as the total test on both occasions. It would seem that this subtest, requiring less than one third of the time, could be substituted for the total test, particularly if considered alongside other data routinely available, e.g., group intelligence test scores. The manual very sensibly recommends that users develop expectancy tables based on a follow-up of their own cases and gives an example which clearly reveals the predictive power of the test.

Centile norms are provided based on the results of a sample of about 500 Queensland girls with an average age of approximately 13 years, 3 months. Such norms would be of little use to the user and the adoption of the recommendation concerning local expectancy tables should make it unnecessary ever to use them.

The test gives every appearance of being soundly constructed. No extravagant claims are made in the manual which, apart from the lack of reliability data, is adequate. Its use by those willing to develop expectancy tables is recommended. Further work on the test should produce further savings in testing time without reducing validity.

[521]

*Shorthand I: Every Pupil Test. 1 year high school; 1938–58; new form usually issued each April; norms available following testing program; no data on reliability; 25¢ per set of teacher's dictation sheets, cash orders postpaid; 36(45) minutes; Ohio Scholarship Tests. *

[522]

*Stenographic Test: National Business Entrance Tests. Grades 12–16 and adults; 1938–57; for complete battery, see 515; 1 form; 3 editions; general information ['56], no data on reliability; postpaid; Joint Committee on Tests of the United Business Education Association and the National Office Management Association; United Business Education Association. *
a) [GENERAL TESTING SERIES.] Form 19-55('55); manual ('55); correction manual ['55]; no adult norms; 50¢ per test; 120(130) minutes.
b) [SHORT FORM SERIES.] 1 form ('55); directions sheet ('55); no data on reliability; no norms; 50¢ per test; (60) minutes.
c) [OFFICIAL TESTING SERIES.] Administered only at NBET Centers which may be established in any community; Form 18-45 ('54); manual ('54); norms ['57]; examination fee, $1.25; specimen set not available (125–135) minutes.

EDWARD B. GREENE, *Supervisor of Personnel Testing, Chrysler Corporation, Detroit, Michigan.*

The authors state that the purpose of this test is to measure "ability to take dictation and transcribe it under office conditions." Although these are two quite separate operations, the test yields only one overall score. One cannot tell, therefore, whether a candidate is deficient in both ability to take notes and ability to type, or only in one of these abilities. The reviewer has found that separate scores are highly desirable both for selection and training.

There are two long forms and one short form of the *Stenographic Test.* The two long forms appear to be similar but no data are furnished to show their reliability or comparability. Each form consists of 13 letters. The shortest letter contains about 80 words, and the longest about 190 words. Numbers are very rare in these letters. The short form was not received. It contains only five letters and allows 10 minutes for dictation and 45 minutes for transcription. No data are given to show its reliability or relation to the long forms.

All the letters are to be read aloud by an examiner at a rate of just 80 words a minute. The results would doubtless be more significant if the rate were varied from 60 to 100 words

per minute, and if a phonograph record or other sound device were used for dictation. The test is preceded by a short practice dictation, after which the examinee is allowed to check her notes with a printed copy of the material.

The text from which the examiner dictates indicates the amount to be read each 15 seconds, the words to be spelled out, and the punctuations and capitals to be dictated. The total dictation time is 20 minutes. However, after each group of three or four letters, two minutes are allowed for rest, answering questions, and redictation "of any reasonable request." Variations among examiners on what are reasonable requests will occur. Some examiners will probably be much more lenient than others even after considerable training.

After the last letter has been dictated, there is a 5-minute rest period. Then the examinees are furnished with printed names and addresses to go with the letters they have taken. Dictionaries are made available. Ninety minutes are allowed to type an original and one or two carbons of each letter. This requires a typing rate of only about 19–20 words per minute.

In scoring, errors are deducted from the maximum points for each letter. The shortest letters have 9 points maximum and the longest, 22. The total is 180. If the total deductions for a letter exceed its maximum, the item is given a zero. Sixteen correctable types of errors are listed with penalties ranging from 1 to 3 points; 13 noncorrectable types of errors cause rejection of the whole letter. There are a considerable number of situations where the scorer must use judgment, such as: "Transcripts must make the sense intended by the test administrator, but the words dictated and those transcribed need not be identical in all cases," and "Be especially lenient with commas, avoiding penalties on them if possible."

In the 1955 use of Series 19-50, 2,501 secondary school students and 407 college students took the *Stenographic Test.* Resulting percentile norms indicate median scores of 78 for the secondary school students and 102 for the college students. Norms for 1957 show medians of 83 and 106. In both cases, a cutoff score of 75 is recommended for determining the recipients of proficiency certificates. This would allow one to be certified even when half the letters were rejected or 105 points were deducted. This seems to be a rather low standard.

The test is not recommended for either business schools or personnel offices because there are excellent separate typing and stenographic tests already available. In spite of these many criticisms, the *Stenographic Test* is probably as good as any of the tests on the market which use this combined testing procedure. However, the reviewer believes that test accuracy has been sacrificed in the attempt to simulate office conditions.

For reviews by Ann Brewington and Eliza-beth Fehrer of the 1946 Form, see 3:391. For reviews by Edward N. Hay, Jacob S. Orleans, and Wimburn L. Wallace of the entire series, see 515; for a review by Paul S. Lomax of the 1946 Form, see 3:396.

[523]
★**Test for Typing Skill.** Typists; 1952; Forms A, B; no data on reliability; $1.50 per set of each form, manual, directions sheet, and norms, postage extra; 8(20) minutes; Edward N. Hay; Aptitude Test Service. *

BERNADINE MEYER, *Assistant Professor, School of Business Administration, Duquesne University, Pittsburgh, Pennsylvania.*

Entitled a *Test for Typing Skill,* this is actually nothing more than an 8-minute timed writing from straight copy. The typist copies the material line for line, making no changes and no erasures.

The test is designed for use in selecting typists for office work, particularly beginners. The test user should bear in mind that the test is only a measure of speed and accuracy in copying from typed material; it does not measure ability to do such things as type from rough drafts or arrange tabular reports or business letters, and it is not intended for use with applicants for positions where such skills are necessary.

The test has other limitations. It does not test an applicant's ability to type numbers or the special characters on the keyboard, such as the "$" or the "%." The ability to type numbers and special characters is generally less well developed, particularly in beginning typists, than the ability to type the letters of the alphabet.

The typist's speed is reported in net words per minute (after 10 words have been deducted for each error). An accuracy ratio is determined by dividing by total strokes typed the total strokes typed less a penalty of 50 strokes (10 words) for each error. It seems to this re-

viewer that the use of net words per minute with the error penalty, along with an accuracy ratio, measures accuracy twice and does not really measure speed. A better measure of speed would result from the use of either gross words per minute with no penalty for errors or correct words per minute with one word deducted for each error.

Directions for taking the test are simple and clear; so are the directions for administering and scoring it. The reviewer would add a suggestion that the typist might be given two 8-minute writings, one from each form, and the better of the two writings scored. Some time could be saved in the scoring process if the test copy showed the word count instead of the stroke count.

The suggestions for interpreting the test results are less satisfactory. Norms are provided for speed and accuracy scores, but they are based upon the performance of only 132 unselected women clerical applicants on the West Coast in 1952. A larger normative group spread over a wider geographic area is needed. Thirty words per minute is suggested as the minimum speed for hiring. This speed seems low; one must remember, however, that it is in terms of net words per minute and that it covers a writing time of eight minutes.

In summary, the reviewer feels that this test will serve its purpose if the test user will bear in mind its limitations and the fact that its results are reported in terms of net words per minute.

[524]
★**Typewriting I and II: Every Pupil Scholarship Test.** 1 or 2 years high school; 1928–58; new form usually issued each January and April; norms available following testing program; no data on reliability; 4¢ per test; 4¢ per scoring key; postage extra; 42(50) minutes; Bureau of Educational Measurements. *

[525]
*Typewriting I: Every Pupil Test.** 1 year high school; 1938–58; 2 scores: speed, performance; new form usually issued each April; norms available following testing program; no data on reliability; 3¢ per test; 1¢ per scoring key; cash orders postpaid; 35(40) minutes; Ohio Scholarship Tests. *

[526]
*Typewriting Test: National Business Entrance Tests.** Grades 12–16 and adults; 1941–57; for complete battery, see 515; 1 form; 3 editions; general information ['56]; no data on reliability; postpaid; Joint Committee on Tests of the United Business Education Association and the National Office Management Association; United Business Education Association. *
a) [GENERAL TESTING SERIES.] Form 19-56 ('55); manual ['55]; no adult norms; 50¢ per test; 120(130) minutes.

b) [SHORT FORM SERIES.] I form ('55); no manual; no data on reliability; no norms; 50¢ per test; 45(55) minutes.

c) [OFFICIAL TESTING SERIES.] Administered only at NBET Centers which may be established in any community. Form 18-46 ('54); manual ('54); norms ['57]; examination fee, $1; specimen set not available; 120(130) minutes.

CLIFFORD E. JURGENSEN, *Assistant Vice President in Charge of Personnel, Minneapolis Gas Company, Minneapolis, Minnesota.*

This is a work sample test simulating common office jobs such as typing letters and memos (albeit from running printed copy), filling in form letters, setting up and typing tabulated material, and typing from corrected handwritten draft. It requires typing envelopes, making carbon copies, using letterheads and other printed forms, and the like. The test is scored on form and arrangement of typed material, accuracy, speed, and ability to follow instructions. A total score is obtained by summing the various part scores.

The manual states that the test was prepared by specialists and reviewed by qualified office executives, that it was originally validated with experimental and control groups in offices and schools, and that the general form of the test has been retained in subsequent editions "in order to perpetuate the qualities which make them reliable and valid." No statistics or other pertinent evaluative data are given. In fact, the entire discussion of reliability and validity requires only eight lines in the manual. Inasmuch as forms of this test have been available since 1937, the reader may well raise an eyebrow regarding this lack of basic information.

Although evaluative data are absent, the tests do create a generally favorable impression. The nature of the typing tasks is likely to make sense to the typical office manager because they closely approximate jobs being done daily by office typists. Scoring procedures are also likely to make sense to persons not technically trained in test procedures. Variable penalties are assigned to different types of errors, the size of penalty appearing to correlate with the difficulty in correcting the error and the seriousness of the error from usual office standards. Test parts which would not be usable in an office situation are given a penalty equal to the total point value assigned to the item. This type of scoring raises a question of reliability. For example, a word omitted at the end of a line is penalized

I point whereas that same omission from the middle of a line is penalized up to 40 points. Thus, chance exerts considerable influence on the score.

Although detailed instructions are given for penalizing different types of errors, it nevertheless appears that scoring may be highly subjective. For example, different scorers may differ in their opinion as to what is messy appearance or poor form. Also, how is the examiner to know whether carbon smudges are due to carelessness of the testee or to factors not controllable by the testee such as improper handling of materials by packers, shippers, test monitors, and others?

In former years certificates of proficiency were issued by the official scoring staff for those examinees who passed the test. Henceforth, such certificates will be issued to examinees whose tests are graded by the scoring staff, but each school will determine which of its examinees have passed. This procedure makes possession of a certificate of proficiency meaningless, for a certificate will henceforth indicate unspecified achievement on a typing test for which validity and reliability are unknown.

In summary, this test is likely to appear highly practical to persons untrained in testing, but evidence is lacking to indicate whether this impression is right or wrong. The publishers should immediately replace the informational (and sales) manual with one which gives at least a minimum of statistical data useful for evaluative purposes. Whatever the reason for absence of statistical data, a test which has been available as many years as this, and is as widely used as this, should be considered suspect in the absence of any information on validity and reliability.

For reviews by E. G. Blackstone and Beatrice J. Dvorak of the 1946 Form, see 3:394. For reviews by Edward N. Hay, Jacob S. Orleans, and Wimburn L. Wallace of the entire series, see 515; for a review by Paul S. Lomax of the 1946 Form, see 3:396.

[527]

★United Students Typewriting Tests, Volume 14. 1, 2, 3, 4 semesters; 1932–58; 1 form ('58); 4 levels; directions sheet ['58] for each level; no data on reliability; $2.10 per 30 tests; $1.50 per specimen set; postpaid; 35–36(40) minutes; Committee on Tests, UBEA Research Foundation; United Business Education Association. ★

MULTI-APTITUDE BATTERIES—FIFTH MMY

REVIEWS BY *Dorothy C. Adkins, Anne Anastasi, Harold P. Bechtoldt, Ralph F. Berdie, John B. Carroll, Ruth Churchill, Andrew L. Comrey, Norman Frederiksen, Clifford P. Froehlich, Benjamin Fruchter, Lloyd G. Humphreys, Albert K. Kurtz, E. A. Peel, H. H. Remmers, Donald E. Super, Philip E. Vernon, and S. Rains Wallace.*

[602]

*****[Aptitude-Intelligence Tests.]** Adults; 1947–57; former title, *Factored Aptitude Series,* still on test booklets; *a–n:* 1 form ('56); 15 tests; supplement ('57); 20¢ per test; $10 per manual ('56); postage extra; French edition available for tests *a–n,* Spanish edition available for tests *c–d, f–h, j–m;* Joseph E. King; Industrial Psychology. *

a) OFFICE TERMS. 5(10) minutes.
b) SALES TERMS. 5(10) minutes.
c) TOOLS. 5(10) minutes.
d) NUMBERS. 5(10) minutes.
e) PERCEPTION. 5(10) minutes.
f) JUDGMENT. 5(10) minutes.
g) PRECISION. 5(10) minutes.
h) FLUENCY. 6(10) minutes.
i) MEMORY. 5(10) minutes.
j) PARTS. 5(10) minutes.
k) BLOCKS. 5(10) minutes.
l) DIMENSION. 5(10) minutes.
m) DEXTERITY. 3(5) minutes.
n) MOTOR. $15 per motor apparatus ['47]; 6(10) minutes.
o) FACTORY TERMS. 1957; 10(15) minutes.

HAROLD P. BECHTOLDT, *Associate Professor of Psychology, State University of Iowa, Iowa City, Iowa.*

The previous review of this aptitude series in 1953 by D. W. Lefever (see 4:712) covers the background and the composition of the tests very well. This reviewer wishes to state his opinion that the 15 separate measures defin-ing the 8 "factors" appear to be well designed, to be printed nicely on good stock, and to be arranged so as to be reasonably interesting to young adults. The content is such that some "face validity" might be expected.

The tests, and especially the manual, are designed for industrial applications, and only passing references are made to the use of these materials for vocational counseling and guidance in the high schools or colleges. Accompanying the publisher's notes on the development and use of the tests are a series of "company research studies" in which "emphasis is placed on the cost reduction implications, achieved by scientific personnel evaluations." In this connection the authors present, in four separate studies, examples of their comments and recommendations to the company for which the study was carried out. The four studies involve chemical engineers, file clerks, route salesmen, and women assemblers, with a range of 50 to 82 cases per study.

STRONG POINTS. The strongest point of the *Factored Aptitude Series* is the generally adequate test construction procedures. As indicated in a 1953 report entitled Development of

Job-Tests Program, the development of the items involved careful consideration of the distribution of difficulty indices, measures of internal consistency, magnitude of the item-score correlations, and the relative effectiveness of the four alternatives for the separate items. The reliabilities as reported seem reasonably adequate for short 5-minute tests. The ranges of the distributions of scores are such as to permit fairly effective discrimination between individuals from an industrial viewpoint.

A second important consideration is the extremely simple format of the test scoring, recording, and weighting devices. In terms of simplicity, the "hiring summary worksheets" represent the closest approximation this reviewer has yet seen to a "cookbook" for industrial personnel clerks. In view of our general ignorance as to the variables important to the prediction of behavior, a third point might be the emphasis upon a combination of testing and interviewing procedures for the selection, placement, promotion, and transfer of employees.

WEAK POINTS. The most conspicuous weak point in this program is the entirely inadequate evidence supporting the claims made by the publisher. Evidence as to the accuracy of these claims surely would be found in the manual if such evidence were available. The few items of data offered neither justify the statements made nor indicate any superiority of this program over that of competing testing programs.

In the 1953 publisher's notes, the intercorrelations among the tests are reported as having an average value of .35 with specific tests showing intercorrelations from .05 to .50. Correlations between the tests and certain other tests are listed with the numbers of cases. The results, in general, are consistent with the correlations among similar tests in various journals. Selected correlations, termed "Validation Statistics," are also reported by job-test areas in the 1953 notes. These "validity" correlations for tests retained in the "job area" batteries range from .56 for the numbers test against a criterion of rated job performance as a numbers clerk to .26 for the test of perception against rated performance as an instructor. The numbers of cases shown for the "validation" data range from 1,465 semiskilled workers to 113 writers. Since these correlations apparently were computed on groups combined from different companies in different jobs, the variables influencing these indices include every source of variance in an industrial installation. The absence of data in the manual as to the intercorrelations of these tests on these same subjects precludes an accurate evaluation of the differences between validity coefficients.

The lack of statistical tests of significance, together with a surprising faith in the stability of the means of the arrays of these bivariate distributions, represents a situation which the reviewer thought was disappearing in industrial psychology. Nonlinear correlations indicated in a 1957 report entitled How to Tailor Personnel Tests to Your Company Operation could be based upon samples of as few as 40 cases. As any psychologist can determine in a few minutes, tests of nonlinearity (using the F distribution) are not very sensitive with samples of this size. It is also simple to demonstrate that the direction as well as the magnitude of any nonlinearity index found in one sample can be expected to vary markedly from that in another sample of 40 cases. There are several indications that the weights used to determine the "qualification grades" represent the "expert guesses or hypotheses" of a group of two or more industrial psychologists. Such hypotheses are, of course, understandable and necessary in the initial stages of theoretical or empirical formulations. However, presenting these "guesses" as established relations with no more evidence than is contained in the manual is hard to justify.

Besides the absence of acceptable statistical support for the general statements, a further serious limitation is the lack of evidence as to the cross validation of these tests and test batteries. On three of the four company research studies, the "correlations, score classifications, and weights" are not released. Instead, scatterplots of four to seven qualification levels with 9-point job efficiency ratings are offered. However, even these data are not acceptable because, as an accompanying statement in the manual indicates for one group, "since this is the group of engineers on whom the tests are validated, the plot is somewhat biased." Most psychologists would probably say with Cureton that such data are more aptly described as "baloney." [1] The only study for which cross validation data are provided is a 1956 report made by the Transformer Engineers Company,

[1] CURETON, EDWARD E. "Validity, Reliability, and Baloney." Ed & Psychol Meas 10:94–6 '50.

Aptitude-Intelligence Tests

Pasadena, California, and furnished to the publisher. This report indicates the correlations between merit ratings and the tools, precision, and motor tests of .42, .23, and .44, respectively. The means and standard deviations are also shown. "The correlation between the weighted score and merit rating was .30." For a sample of 57 cases, the correlation of .30 is significant at the 5 per cent level. However, the publisher, for some unknown reason, recommends that this company use the weighted score, which has a correlation of .30 with the criterion, instead of the tools or motor tests alone, which show correlation coefficients with the criterion of .42 and .44. The contrast is great between the elaborate set of guesses reflected in this program and Meehl's demonstration of how empirical data can be used to provide a "good cookbook" approach even in the more difficult area of prediction in clinical psychology.[2]

It is to be hoped that, in the future, additional studies will be reported in which the data provide acceptable evidence as to the usefulness of the weighting and testing procedures which have been recommended so confidently.

A further serious weakness, in the opinion of this reviewer, is the level of psychological sophistication indicated by the emphasis in developing tests on a "present employee" basis and applying the results to applicants with the justification that "the psychological traits are a constant (are matured by the age of 20 and remain fairly static after that time)." It seems strange in 1957–58 to find industrial psychologists confusing "trade test" procedures with "predictive test" procedures. Surely the available evidence as to the effects of training or experience on the job upon test performance is such that the statements in the manual can be considered hard to explain.

In summary, the tests themselves are well designed. Furthermore, the publisher has an appreciation of the low order of skill and knowledge to be expected of clerical help in a personnel department. The materials are written in a beautifully simple fashion. The vocabulary and stylistic form of the manual represents the journalistic "fourth grade education" approach carried to an extreme. An industrial concern might well use these tests in their own long term *research* program, but this re-

2 MEEHL, PAUL. "Wanted—a Good Cookbook." *Am Psychol* 11:263-72 '56.

Aptitude-Intelligence Tests

viewer cannot recommend the tests for the selection or classification of job applicants.

For a review by D. Welty Lefever of an earlier edition, see 4:712 (1 excerpt).

[603]

*Detroit General Aptitudes Examination. Grades 6–12; 1938–54; assembled from *Detroit Mechanical Aptitudes Test, Detroit Clerical Aptitudes Test,* and *Detroit Advanced Intelligence Test;* 20 scores: intelligence, mechanical, clerical, total, and 16 subtest scores; Form A ('38); revised manual ('54, identical with manual copyrighted in 1941 except for minor changes); $3.40 per 25 tests; 35¢ per copy of *Ayres Measuring Scale for Handwriting;* 40¢ per manual; 65¢ per specimen set; postpaid; 60(90) minutes; Harry J. Baker, Alex C. Crockett, and Paul H. Voelker; Public School Publishing Co. *

For reviews by G. Frederic Kuder, Irving Lorge, and John Gray Peatman, see 40:1654.

[604]

★Differential Ability Tests. Ages 10–17 (standards 5–10); 1951; 9 tests; mimeographed manual ['51]; separate answer sheets must be used for *b, c,* and *d;* 5s. per 100 answer sheets; postage extra; specimen set not available; Afrikaans edition available; 201 (470) minutes in 4 sessions 1 day apart; National Bureau of Educational and Social Research. *
a) [LANGUAGE TESTS.] 3 forms; 3 tests; 16s. 9d. per 100 tests except Form B of the *Silent Reading Test (Paragraphs: Senior)* which is 15s. 8d. per 100 tests; 58(75) minutes.
  1. *Silent Reading Test (Paragraphs: Senior).* Forms A, B, C ['51]; 18(25) minutes.
  2. *Silent Reading Test (Vocabulary: Senior).* Forms A, B, C ['51]; 10(15) minutes.
  3. *English Usage Test (Senior).* Forms A, B, C ['51]; 30(35) minutes.
b) [GENERAL ABILITY TESTS.] 2 forms; 2 tests; 48(60) minutes.
  1. *Verbal Reasoning Test.* Forms A, B ['51]; 13s. 3d. per 100 copies of Form A; 17s. 3d. per 100 copies of Form B; 20(25) minutes.
  2. *Non-Verbal Reasoning.* Forms A, B ['51]; 18s. 9d. per 100 copies of Form A; 17s. 4d. per 100 copies of Form B; 28(35) minutes.
c) ARITHMETIC TEST. 2 scores: mechanical arithmetic, problems; Forms A, B ['51]; 16s. 7d. per 100 copies of Form A; 16s. 1d. per 100 copies of Form B; 30(35) minutes.
d) [TESTS OF SPECIFIC ABILITIES.] Form A; 3 tests; 65(100) minutes.
  1. *Memory Test.* Form A ['51]; 21(35) minutes.
  2. *Space Perception.* Form A ['51]; 26(40) minutes.
  3. *Mechanical Comprehension Test.* Form A ['51]; 18(25) minutes.

[605]

*Differential Aptitude Tests. Grades 8–12; 1947–58; IBM; Forms A, B ('47); 8 tests in 7 booklets; manual, second edition ('52); supplement ('58); directions for administration ['52, reprinted from manual]; separate answer sheets must be used; $1.90 per 50 IBM answer sheets; $1.25 per set of hand scoring stencils; $1.40 per set of machine scoring stencils; $1.25 per 50 profiles ['53]; $2 per manual; $3 per specimen set; $1.75 per casebook ('51, see 29 below); postpaid; 186(240) minutes; George K. Bennett, Harold

G. Seashore, and Alexander G. Wesman; Psychological Corporation. *

a) VERBAL REASONING. $3 per 25 tests; 30(40) minutes.

b) NUMERICAL ABILITY. $2.25 per 25 tests; 30(35) minutes.

c) ABSTRACT REASONING. $3 per 25 tests; 25(30) minutes.

d) SPACE RELATIONS. $3.50 per 25 tests; 30(40) minutes.

e) MECHANICAL REASONING. $3.75 per 25 tests; 30(35) minutes.

f) CLERICAL SPEED AND ACCURACY. $3 per 25 tests; 6(15) minutes.

g) LANGUAGE USAGE. 2 scores: spelling, sentences; $3 per 25 tests; 35(45) minutes.

REFERENCES

1–28. See 4:711.
29. BENNETT, GEORGE K.; SEASHORE, HAROLD G.; AND WESMAN, ALEXANDER G. Counseling From Profiles: A Casebook for the Differential Aptitude Tests. New York: Psychological Corporation, 1951. Pp. 95. * (PA 26:3399)
30. KERMEEN, BARBARA G. A Factor Analysis of the Differential Aptitude Tests and a Factor Analysis of the Kuder Preference Record, Vocational. Master's thesis, University of California (Berkeley, Calif.), 1951.
31. SHELDON, F. A. Validation of the Differential Aptitude Tests in a Selected High School Population. Master's thesis, Stanford University (Stanford, Calif.), 1951.
32. "Results of the Space Relations, Mechanical Reasoning, and Clerical Speed and Accuracy Tests of the Differential Aptitude Test Battery in Six Public Schools." Ed Rec B 58:79–84 F '52. * (PA 26:7240)
33. BENNETT, GEORGE K.; SEASHORE, HAROLD G.; AND WESMAN, ALEXANDER G. "Aptitude Testing: Does It 'Prove Out' in Counseling Practice?" Occupations 30:584–93 My '52. * (PA 27:1240)
34. DOPPELT, JEROME E., AND WESMAN, ALEXANDER G. "The Differential Aptitude Tests as Predictors of Achievement Test Scores." J Ed Psychol 43:210–7 Ap '52. * (PA 27:3784)
35. FRUCHTER, BENJAMIN. "Orthogonal and Oblique Solutions of a Battery of Aptitude, Achievement and Background Variables." Ed & Psychol Meas 12:20–38 sp '52. * (PA 27:6180)
36. GLASER, ROBERT. "The Reliability of Inconsistency." Ed & Psychol Meas 12:60–4 sp '52. * (PA 27:5523)
37. HODGES, JOHN M. Primary Mental Abilities vs. Differential Aptitude Tests. Master's thesis, Illinois State Normal University (Normal, Ill.), 1952.
38. MELEIKA, LOUIS K. Intra-Individual Variability in Relation to Achievement, Interest, and Personality. Doctor's thesis, Stanford University (Stanford, Calif.), 1952.
39. STINSON, PAIRLEE J. A Statistical Analysis of the Differential Aptitude Tests for the Purpose of Predicting First Semester Grade Averages of a Freshman High School Group. Master's thesis, Oklahoma A. & M. College (Stillwater, Okla.), 1952.
40. WESMAN, ALEXANDER G. "The Differential Aptitude Tests." Personnel & Guid J 31:167–70 D '52. * (PA 27:6201)
41. WILLIAMS, NANCY. "A Study of the Validity of the Verbal Reasoning Subtest and the Abstract Reasoning Subtest of the Differential Aptitude Tests." Ed & Psychol Meas 12:129–31 sp '52. * (PA 27:5914)
42. BEAMER, GEORGE C.; PENDER, FRANCES RUSSELL; AND PARTON, NORMA WEST. "Selection of Teachers of Homemaking." J Home Econ 45:98–100 F '53. * (PA 27:7412)
43. CROUCH, MILDRED S. The Relative Value of the Differential Aptitude Tests and the Otis Quick-Scoring Mental Ability Test for Predicting Scholastic Success. Master's thesis, Tennessee Agricultural and Industrial University (Nashville, Tenn.), 1953.
44. SEASHORE, HAROLD G. "Tests in the Tenth Grade as Predictors of Graduating Status and Status on College Entrance Tests." Abstract. Am Psychol 8:431–2 Ag '53. *
45. YOUNG, DOROTHY M. The Use of the Differential Aptitude Scores in Predicting Success in Certain School Subjects in Schools in New Castle, Pennsylvania. Master's thesis, Kent State University (Kent, Ohio), 1953.
46. "Validity Information Exchange, No. 7-065: D.O.T. Code 5-92.411, Foreman II." Personnel Psychol 7:301 su '54. *
47. "Validity Information Exchange, No. 7-094: D.O.T. Code 7-80.120, Beginner Mechanics." Personnel Psychol 7:572 w '54. *
48. "Validity Information Exchange, No. 7-095: D.O.T. Code 7-94.112 and 7-94.100, Tool and Die and Machinist Apprentice." Personnel Psychol 7:573 w '54. *
49. "Validity Information Exchange, No. 7-096: D.O.T. Code 9-03.01, Riveter Assistants (Rivet-Buckers)." Personnel Psychol 7:574 w '54. *
50. FROEHLICH, C. P., AND MOSER, W. E. "Do Counselees Remember Test Scores?" J Counsel Psychol 1:149–52 fall '54. * (PA 29:6245)
51. GLASER, ROBERT, AND JACOBS, OWEN. "Predicting Achieve-

ment in Medical School: A Comparison of Preclinical and Clinical Criteria." J Appl Psychol 38:245–7 Ag '54. * (PA 29:6271)
52. HALL, ROBERT C. A Study of the Relationships Among Certain Occupational Groups in Performance on the Differential Aptitude Test Battery. Doctor's thesis, University of Connecticut (Storrs, Conn.), 1954. (DA 15:84)
53. SEASHORE, HAROLD. "Tenth Grade Tests as Predictors of Twelfth Grade Scholarship and College Entrance Status." Comment by David V. Tiedeman. J Counsel Psychol 1:106–15 su '54. * (PA 29:3054)
54. BENNETT, GEORGE K. "The D.A.T.—A Seven-Year Follow-Up." Test Service B (49):1–4 N '55. * (PA 30:7751)
55. HARRISON, ROSS; HUNT, WINSLOW; AND JACKSON, THEODORE A. "Profile of the Mechanical Engineer: 1, Ability." Personnel Psychol 8:219–34 su '55. * (PA 30:5414)
56. JENSON, RALPH E. "Using Multiple Aptitude Measures to Improve Guidance in a Secondary School System," pp. 29–50. In Fourth Annual Western Regional Conference on Testing Problems, March 4, 1955. Princeton, N.J.: Educational Testing Service, [1955]. Pp. iv, 87. * (PA 30:1617)
57. PAUK, WALTER J. An Analysis of Certain Characteristics of Above-Average and Below-Average Male and Female Readers at the Ninth-Grade Level. Doctor's thesis, Cornell University (Ithaca, N.Y.), 1955. (DA 16:285)
58. PERRINE, MERVYN WILLIAM. "The Selection of Drafting Trainees." J Appl Psychol 39:57–61 F '55. * (PA 30:1725)
59. SCHULMAN, J. A Comparison Between 9th and 12th Grade Students on Self-Estimates of Abilities and Objective Scores on the Differential Aptitude Tests. Doctor's thesis, New York University (New York, N.Y.), 1955.
60. SEASHORE, HAROLD. "Cross-Validation of Equations for Predicting CEEB-SAT Scores From DAT Scores." J Counsel Psychol 2:229–30 fall '55. *
61. STOUGHTON, ROBERT W. The Differential Predictive Values of the Differential Aptitude Tests in the Connecticut Technical Schools. Doctor's thesis, University of Connecticut (Storrs, Conn.), 1955. (DA 15:1355)
62. VINEYARD, E. E. A Longitudinal Study of the Relationship of Differential Aptitude Test Scores With College Success. Doctor's thesis, Oklahoma A. & M. College (Stillwater, Okla.), 1955.
63. WOLKING, WILLIAM D. "Predicting Academic Achievement With the Differential Aptitude and the Primary Mental Abilities Tests." J Appl Psychol 39:115–8 Ap '55. * (PA 30:1636)
64. "Predicting CEEB-SAT Status From Grade 10 Scores on the Differential Aptitude Tests." Test Service B (50):4 Je '56. *
65. BENNETT, GEORGE K.; SEASHORE, HAROLD G.; AND WESMAN, ALEXANDER G. "The Differential Aptitude Tests: An Overview." Comments by Donald E. Super. Personnel & Guid J 35: 81–93 O '56. * (PA 31:8809)
66. ELTON, CHARLES F., AND MORRIS, DONALD. "The Use of the D.A.T. in a Small Liberal Arts College." J Ed Res 50: 139–43 O '56. * (PA 32:941)
67. HALSEY, HUGH. The Predictive Value of Certain Measures Used in Selecting Freshmen for the Technical Curricula in a Community College. Doctor's thesis, New York University (New York, N.Y.), 1956. (DA 17:542)
68. McCLINTIC, STANLEY A. The Prognostic Value of Selected Sub-Tests of the Differential Aptitude Test for Programming Students in 9th Grade Foreign Language Classes. Master's thesis, Claremont College (Claremont, Calif.), 1956.
69. BRAYFIELD, ARTHUR H., AND MARSH, MARY MARKLEY. "Aptitudes, Interests, and Personality Characteristics of Farmers." J Appl Psychol 41:98–103 Ap '57. *
70. HALL, ROBERT C. "Occupational Group Contrasts in Terms of the Differential Aptitude Tests: An Application of Multiple Discriminant Analysis." Ed & Psychol Meas 17:556–67 w '57. *
71. STEWART, LAWRENCE H. "Does Knowledge of Performance on an Aptitude Test Change Scores on the Kuder?" J Counsel Psychol 4:161–4 su '57. *
72. DUNNETTE, MARVIN D., AND KIRCHNER, WAYNE K. "Validation of Psychological Tests in Industry." Personnel Adm 21: 20–7 My–Je '58. *
73. LAYTON, WILBUR L., AND SWANSON, EDWARD O. "Relationship of Ninth Grade Differential Aptitude Test Scores to Eleventh Grade Test Scores and High School Rank." J Ed Psychol 49:153–5 Je '58. *
74. MARTENS, W. LEON. "Normative Data Information Exchange, No. 11-3." Personnel Psychol 11:131–2 sp '58. *
75. MENDICINO, LORENZO. "Mechanical Reasoning and Space Perception: Native Capacity or Experience." Personnel & Guid J 36:335–8 Ja '58. *
76. SMITH, D. D. "Abilities and Interests: I, A Factorial Study." Can J Psychol 12:191–201 S '58. *
77. VINEYARD, EDWIN E. "A Longitudinal Study of the Relationship of Differential Aptitude Test Scores With College Success." Personnel & Guid J 36:413–6 F '58. *

JOHN B. CARROLL, *Professor of Education, Harvard University, Cambridge, Massachusetts.*

The *Differential Aptitude Tests* represent an attempt to measure a number of relatively distinct abilities thought to be of prime importance in assessing the potentialities of high school students. While each test has satisfactory reliability and validity in its own right, the tests are intended ordinarily to be administered as a total battery—not all on one day, but at least within a relatively short span of time. (Several possible testing schedules are suggested in the manual.) The tests are completely objective. Reusable test booklets are utilized, all answers being recorded on separate IBM answer sheets.

The term "differential" implies not only that the tests measure *different* abilities but also that differences in score level within a single individual's profile are likely to be significant and interpretable. In constructing the battery, the authors banked heavily upon the results of the various researches which have been done on the dimensions of human ability, that is, researches utilizing the statistical techniques of factor analysis. Nevertheless, they were not as intent upon constructing "pure" tests of the various dimensions as they were upon constructing highly reliable, valid, and useful tests. In some cases, therefore, the separate tests measure a combination of factors of ability; the counselor needs to be aware of what each test measures. The following paragraphs describe the tests and indicate the *probable* factorial composition of each, based largely upon Fruchter's (*35*) study.

Verbal Reasoning presents a series of verbal analogies items which probably measure a combination of the "verbal ability" and "deductive reasoning" factors. In any event it is a good measure of the student's ability to handle complex logical relationships which can be stated in verbal terms, and, in this sense, it is largely a measure of "intelligence" as this is ordinarily conceived.

Numerical Ability presents a series of relatively simple numerical problems requiring a minimum of arithmetic reasoning. It is thus chiefly a measure of mental computational skill (or, in factor analysis jargon, the "number" ability), but it also may measure specific educational achievement in simple mathematics because it contains some problems involving square and cube roots, solving proportions, and evaluation of fractions.

Abstract Reasoning requires the student to indicate which of a series of choices properly carries out the logical development exhibited

by a sequence of figures. It was intended to be a nonverbal measure of reasoning ability. This intention was well realized in the test, but factorial studies show that to some extent it is also a measure of the student's ability to visualize spatial patterns and shapes; this undoubtedly explains some of its correlation with another test, Space Relations.

Space Relations utilizes the familiar "unfolded paper boxes" technique and measures chiefly the ability to visualize objects and forms in two or three dimensions.

Mechanical Reasoning asks the subject to answer simple questions in what someone has called "barnyard physics," based on pictures showing thrown balls, gears, levers, propellers, etc. It probably measures a combination of "mechanical experience" and ability to visualize in two or three dimensions.

Clerical Speed and Accuracy requires the subject to make quick comparisons of arbitrary patterns of letters and numbers; it measures what has usually been called the "perceptual" factor—more specifically, the ability to scan visual materials rapidly and locate designated items.

The spelling subtest of Language Usage requires the subject to indicate whether each of 100 words is spelled right or wrong. In addition to a component of verbal knowledge, this subtest probably contains a highly specific component of spelling ability. The second subtest of Language Usage asks the student to find "errors" (grammar, punctuation, or spelling) in a series of English sentences. Like the spelling subtest, this subtest measures both general verbal knowledge and a specific factor, knowledge of "correct" English usage.

Super, in his review of multifactor guidance tests (*65*), considers only two of the currently available batteries "ready for use in counseling": the *Differential Aptitude Tests* and the United States Employment Service's *General Aptitude Test Battery*. If this accolade is justified, and the reviewer thinks it is, the DAT battery merits serious consideration for use in high school testing programs. Super's implicit assumption—a correct one—is that a test is not merely the test booklet, the answer sheet, the scoring key, and the other paraphernalia one has to purchase in order to use the test, but something more: the product of careful, scientific research in test construction, norming, and validation. One purchases a great deal of

Differential Aptitude Tests

this in the DAT; in fact, Super warns that the counselor is likely to feel overwhelmed by the literally hundreds—even thousands—of validity coefficients and other statistics which are available to the user of this test if he wants to go to the trouble of collecting them all. The DAT is probably one of the few tests the data on which are so voluminous that they have had to be deposited in the American Documentation Institute. But the publishers of the DAT can hardly be criticized for making too *much* data available, and they cannot be criticized for failing to offer materials to help the counselor learn how to use the test, for they have indeed done this illuminatingly in their 1951 *Counseling From Profiles: A Casebook for the Differential Aptitude Tests* (29.) Even with respect to making the available validity data digestible, they have done an admirable job of summarization and presentation in their manual, which is a model of organization, comprehensiveness, and clarity. They have even presented a full bibliography of relevant research publications by others who have studied the DAT; one is struck by the fact, however, that the text of their manual makes no direct reference to any research not done "in the house."

The authors have done such a thorough and technically satisfactory job that a reviewer finds it hard to make himself appear sufficiently critical. With one or two possible exceptions, the tests are excellent in format, item construction, standardization, validation, and just about every other aspect which is regarded as important in the testing fraternity. Just as an example of the fine points to which the authors have attended, note the completeness with which validity data are reported: date test taken, date and grade in which course marks reported, number of cases, correlation coefficients for each test. No question here about whether the validities are "concurrent" or "predictive"! Most are clearly predictive, that is, derived in a situation where the test was given a considerable number of months before the course grades were collected and thus having a bearing on the guidance decisions that might have been taken at the time the tests were given.

Since the tests, manuals, and associated data so clearly meet high standards of technical excellence, the reviewer shall utilize the remaining space to raise some questions—some of them possibly quibbling, others dead serious.

He is intrigued first by problems of test construction and test content. One would suppose that item analysis techniques had been used in the original construction of the tests or at least in the construction of equivalent forms, but no statement to this effect can be found. We have no assurance that there are no "dead-wood" items nor items with debatable answers. As a matter of fact, the reviewer is already on record [1] as having raised serious questions about the sentence subtest of Language Usage, which appears to him to be based on obsolete norms of English usage. For example, Item 13 of that test (Form A) is keyed so as to require that the sentence "Is it I whom they are calling?" be regarded as correct, and, in Item 5, "It is me" is keyed as wrong. But in *Teaching English Usage,* Pooley points out that "it is me" has been accepted usage for hundreds of years and deserves no class time. When the reviewer filled out the test in the light of Pooley's standards, his raw score was 66 out of a possible 90, which is equivalent to a percentile of 94. It is probable that many students with excellent grasp of language usage are getting a number of items wrong because their standards are several decades in advance of those on which the test was apparently based.

There has been debate as to whether the DAT is truly *differential,* i.e., do the tests really measure different abilities? To be sure, the intercorrelations are only low to moderate, and the authors have computed statistics to show "the proportion of differences between the standardized test scores on any pair of tests which are in excess of the chance proportion." These proportions range, for boys, from .29 to .52, and for girls, from .20 to .48. For both sexes combined and for all pairs of tests, it works out that only about 37 per cent of all possible differences are beyond those expected by chance. We can put a favorable light on this result by saying that in the long run we can expect about 10 of the 28 possible differences between pairs of test scores for one individual case to be significant. Thus, a *typical* profile can be expected to be "flat" except for 1 or 2 deviant scores (1 deviant score producing 7 significant differences, 2 deviant scores producing 12 or 13 significant differences depending upon whether the 2 deviant scores them-

1 CARROLL, JOHN B. "An Evaluation of Language Tests From the Standpoint of the Psychology of Language," pp. 75–80. *Ninth Yearbook of the National Council on Measurements Used in Education,* 1952.

Differential Aptitude Tests

selves are significantly different from each other). Even this amount of difference is enough to provide some leverage in differential counseling; the differences, of course, are more or less equally likely to occur in different parts of the profile. But is this not less than we have a right to expect from so long a test battery? Is there not still an undue amount of overlap and high correlation between tests? Although meaningful comparisons are impossible to make because of the lack of readily available data, it would seem that the *General Aptitude Test Battery* or even the *Flanagan Aptitude Classification Tests* offer more in the way of differential diagnosis *as such*. Many of the DAT tests, incidentally, correlate well with their opposite numbers in the *General Aptitude Test Battery*. The overlap of abilities apparently measured by the subtests of the DAT is sometimes disturbing, and it will take experience and training on the part of the counselor to use the profiles wisely.

Of course, any multifactor battery like the DAT tends to be handicapped by the fact that even if truly independent aptitudes exist, the differences between them are obscured by common educational experiences and by degrees of motivation for school learning and for test taking which more or less uniformly make for a high, medium, or low level of performance on a series of tests. There is not much chance that *any* set of differential tests designed chiefly for general educational guidance, as the DAT is, would not be substantially affected by these influences.

The authors make much of the fact that the DAT battery is a group of tests, each of which is valid and useful in itself; they appear to advise against the combination of weighted scores. In the notable controversy about "clinical" versus "statistical" prediction they are on the side of "clinical" prediction. Paradoxically, this position prevents them from displaying some of the undoubted powers of the test in affording statistical prediction from weighted combinations of scores. In the whole array of validity coefficients presented there is not a single multiple correlation. The authors hesitate to get the counselor into what might appear to be needless complexities, but in view of the high importance to the individual of such decisions as whether to plan emphasis on liberal or on technical studies, would it not be possible to provide the counselor with simple ways of combining scores in order to make predictions of superior accuracy? At all events, it is hoped that the authors' remarks about score combinations will not deter the development of prediction equations in local situations.

At the present time, it can be said that, considering the tests themselves and all the supporting data, the DAT constitutes the best available foundation battery for measuring the chief intellectual abilities and learned skills which one needs to take account of in high school counseling.

NORMAN FREDERIKSEN, *Director of Research, Educational Testing Service, Princeton, New Jersey.*

At the time the *Differential Aptitude Tests* were introduced, the multidimensional nature of mental ability was well recognized. Tests were appearing which measured the "primary" mental abilities. The authors of the DAT recognized the need for aptitude tests which produced scores for separate abilities, but they rejected the pure factor test idea. Instead they sought test types which were not necessarily pure in a factorial sense but which had demonstrated their usefulness in a variety of situations and which could readily be interpreted by teachers and counselors.

Eight tests, printed in seven reusable test booklets, are included in the battery. All are power tests except Clerical Speed and Accuracy. Answers are recorded on IBM answer sheets which may be scored by hand or by machine. The time allowances permit all eight tests to be administered in six class periods. Alternate forms of all tests are available.

The 50 items of Verbal Reasoning are analogies, but they are unusual in that both the first and the last elements of the analogy are omitted. The task is to choose the appropriate words, from options provided, to complete the analogy. The items are probably more complex, factorially, than the usual analogy item. The particular item type would seem to require verbal ability and reasoning; in addition, some of the items depend on a background of information. Still other items seem to require flexibility, since they contain words which are homonyms spelled alike, and it may be necessary to reject one meaning of a word in order to find another which permits an interpretation consistent with a correct answer.

There are 40 multiple choice arithmetic items

in Numerical Ability. The option "none of these" is employed each time, which decreases the likelihood that an estimating technique or some other short cut method can be employed in taking the test. Factorially, the test probably measures both number and reasoning factors. Some of the items are straight computation items involving the adding, subtracting, multiplying, and dividing of whole numbers, decimals, and fractions. Other problems seem to require reasoning, although the form of the items resembles the purely computational type.

The 50 items in Abstract Reasoning all employ abstract figures. The operation of a principle is portrayed in a sequence of four figures and the task is to choose from five additional figures the one which logically follows in the sequence. The drawings are reasonably large and are clearly printed. Size estimations or other difficult visual discriminations are not required in order to solve the problems.

The items employed in Space Relations are of the type called surface development, but with the added feature that the solid figures which comprise the options may be rotated to various positions in space. The task is to indicate all the solid figures which can be made from the pattern. All items involve three- rather than two-dimensional space. Drawings are large, and finding the correct answers does not depend upon visual discrimination.

Mechanical Reasoning is a new form of the Bennett *Test of Mechanical Comprehension*. Each item depicts the operation of a physical principle by means of a drawing, and is accompanied by a question such as, "Which man must pull harder to lift the weight?" Three choices are presented: A, B, and a third option such as, "If either, mark C." (C is the correct answer only 11 times for the 68 items in Form A.) This type of test has been widely used in military classification work and has been shown to be of value for predicting a variety of occupational and training criteria. Factorially, the test is probably quite complex.

Clerical Speed and Accuracy is the only test in the battery which is speeded. Each item in the booklet presents five pairs of symbols such as 2y, 5y, 57, 37, and y3; one of the pairs is underlined. The same pairs are printed above the answer spaces on the answer sheet, but in a different order. The task is to find the pair which was underlined and to mark the answer space below it. There are two separately timed

parts, each containing 100 items. The test is supposed to measure speed of response in a simple perceptual task.

The spelling subtest of Language Usage includes 100 words; the task is to indicate whether each word is spelled right or wrong. The choice of words and incorrect spellings is based on Gates' work on spelling difficulties. In order to minimize the effects of a possible acquiescent response set, the correctly spelled words were carefully selected to be effective items when presented in the correct form.

In the sentences subtest of Language Usage 50 sentences are included, each of which is broken into five parts by slant lines. The task for each sentence is to mark the answer positions corresponding to those parts which contain errors in grammar, punctuation, or spelling. The number of errors per sentence may vary from 0 to 5. Thus the test contains the equivalent of 250 2-choice items of a "correct- incorrect" sort; the operation of an acquiescent response set on this test is therefore a distinct possibility.

For each form of the DAT, norms are presented for boys and girls separately at each grade level from 8 through 12. There are thus 20 norms tables in all. The norms table is entered with the raw score for a particular test, and the corresponding percentile rank for the grade and sex group is found.

The number of cases on which each norms table is based ranges from 2,100 to 7,400 for Form A and from 350 to 1,075 for Form B. Over 100 school systems, from all the major geographic regions of the country, are involved. The manual does not go into details about size of communities and types of schools, but detailed tables may be obtained from the American Documentation Institute.

Profile sheets are provided for plotting the eight scores for each person. Scores are to be plotted on the basis of percentiles. The percentile values are positioned to correspond to a standard score scale, and such a scale is printed on the profile sheet, for those who wish to convert to standard scores.

The profile chart is set up so that one inch of vertical distance is equal to 10 standard score units, or one standard deviation. The arrangement makes possible a simple rule for evaluating approximately the significance of the difference between two scores earned by a student. If the vertical distance between two scores is one inch or more, it is reasonable to assume that the student is really better in one of the abilities than the other; but if the distance is less than half an inch, it is highly probable that the abilities do not really differ. This is a very simple device which helps the counselor to make cautious interpretations.

When the DAT was first released in 1947, the manual was printed in looseleaf format so that pages could be added as the results of validity studies became available. Reports of such studies were issued in such numbers that when the manual was revised in 1952 it was necessary to present validity data in summary form. The current manual therefore contains frequency distributions of validity coefficients for the most common educational criteria and summary tables which contain the correlations (but not means and standard deviations) for all the studies completed so far. The original tables may be obtained from the American Documentation Institute.

All the validity coefficients are apparently reported: none is omitted because it happened to be low. The results strikingly verify the statement in the manual that there is no "validity of a test" but there are many validities describing the relation between test scores and various more fallible or less fallible criteria. The user of the test is encouraged to use local data for the development of expectancy tables in order to find out how the test works in his own situation. Examples of expectancy tables and how they can be constructed and used are included.

Validity studies summarized in the manual employ as criteria high school grades (including courses taken up to four years after testing), achievement test scores, college grades, and educational and vocational placement after graduation from high school. All studies reported as predictive validity studies are strictly that; that is, the tests were administered prior to the time when the criterion measures were earned.

It is impossible to summarize the wealth of validity studies within the scope of this review. There is ample evidence of the usefulness of DAT scores in a wide variety of situations. Course grades are predictable, and achievement test scores even more so (presumably because of their greater reliability). DAT scores appear to differentiate groups tested in high school who went on to various educational and voca-

tional careers (although measures of dispersion of score distributions are not presented). There is even evidence that the tests might be useful at the college freshman level, in certain institutions, for predicting freshman grades.

The question might legitimately be raised as to how "differential" the tests are, especially for predicting academic criteria. The distributions of validity coefficients are quite similar for high school courses, whether English, mathematics, science, or social studies. The three best predictors for all four of these course areas are Verbal Reasoning, Numerical Ability, and the sentences part of Language Usage. Since the summary tables do not present means, it is impossible to tell how well one could discriminate on the basis of level; but with relatively minor variations the same abilities are involved in all four course areas. For such courses as shorthand and typing the clerical and spelling tests show predictive value, and for industrial arts and mechanical drawing the spatial and mechanical reasoning tests may be related to grades. But even in such courses as bookkeeping, business arithmetic, physical education, health, home economics, and music the sentences test often shows high predictive value. High school teachers can apparently recognize ability to write grammatically correct sentences on an examination, regardless of the name of the course!

Reliability was determined by the split-half method for all tests except the highly speeded Clerical Speed and Accuracy; the reliability of this test was determined by the use of alternate forms. Reliabilities were separately computed for boys and for girls at each grade level from 8–12. The reliabilities are predominantly quite satisfactory: in the high .80's and low .90's. One test, Mechanical Reasoning, is apparently less suitable for girls than for boys; its reliability for girls ranges from .69 to .73. So far as reliability is concerned, the tests are equally good at grades 8 through 12. Standard errors of measurement are presented for each test by grade and by sex.

As might be expected with a test battery of this sort, the intercorrelations are not as low as one might desire. For boys, the mean intercorrelation coefficients range from .06 to .62, and for girls, from .12 to .67. (Some test batteries claimed to measure pure factors have intercorrelations about as high.) A table of the "proportion of differences in excess of the chance proportion" of differences between scores on pairs of tests is included. For boys, these proportions range from .29 (the verbal reasoning and sentences tests) to .52 (the space relations and spelling tests). For girls, the proportions range from .20 to .48. The proportions involving the mechanical reasoning test are all low (.20 to .24), presumably because this test is relatively unreliable for girls. As described above, the instructions for using profile charts provide a rule of thumb for deciding which differences are the ones which are large enough to be considered "in excess of chance."

Evidence from validity studies and from intercorrelations suggests that fewer than eight variables could be used without loss in predictive value, and with some increase in ease of interpretation.

Correlations of DAT with a great variety of other tests are presented. Correlations with tests of general intelligence are high enough to suggest that administration of such a test is unnecessary if DAT scores are available. Scores on the *Kuder Preference Record* are for the most part unrelated to the DAT ability measures—evidence that interest measures should not be used in lieu of ability measures (and vice versa). The information given should be useful to those who are considering the choice of a test battery; more generally, it throws light on the nature of the abilities measured by DAT.

The DAT manual is a model which other test publishers might well emulate. It presents a great deal of information clearly and without the annoying omissions which so often make it difficult or impossible to interpret statistical data in test manuals. One cannot help feeling that this is an honest and complete description of all the relevant findings, both favorable and unfavorable, which resulted from a great deal of research. Much of this work has been done by Psychological Corporation staff members, but the bibliography of 91 references also includes work by many other workers.

The authors do not hesitate to take space in the manual to instruct when they consider it desirable, and the result is a manual which is not only useful in understanding the DAT but also might well be used as supplementary reading for courses in measurement.

Some publishers of multifactor test batteries advocate use of combinations of certain scores for specific purposes. For example, methods may be recommended for weighting and combining scores to yield IQ equivalents or measures of scholastic aptitude. The DAT authors do not advocate such a procedure; instead they strongly urge the practice of counseling from profiles. They have prepared a booklet, *A Casebook for the Differential Aptitude Tests* (29), which presents DAT profiles and other information about a variety of student problems and which shows how counseling from profiles can be done. Such a clinical approach has merit, and the clinical approach, in fact, must be used in many situations. But in order to take full advantage of a multitest battery, one should also employ statistical methods to discover how best to combine scores for use in certain important and recurring problem situations. Some reference in the manual to multiple regression methods would have been desirable.

The tests are technically of very high quality, and there is ample evidence that they can be usefully employed in a wide variety of educational selection, placement, and guidance areas. This reviewer does not hesitate to recommend the *Differential Aptitude Tests* for use in testing programs at the secondary school level.

For reviews by Harold Bechtoldt, Ralph F. Berdie, and Lloyd G. Humphreys, see 4:711; see 3:620 (1 excerpt).

[606]

★**Differential Test Battery.** Ages 11 to "top university level" (range for Test 1 extends downward to age 7); 1955; 1 form; 12 tests in 7 booklets; no data on validity; 6s. 5d. per battery manual; 69s. 9d. per specimen set; postpaid in the U.K.; 136.5(200) minutes; J. R. Morrisby; distributed by the National Foundation for Educational Research in England and Wales. *

a) TEST I, COMPOUND SERIES TEST. Ages 7 and over; "mental work power"; separate answer sheets must be used; 32s. 3d. per test; 5s. 7d. per 25 answer sheets; 3s. 6d. per set of scoring key and manual; 30(40) minutes.

b) GENERAL ABILITY TESTS. Ages 11 and over; 3 tests; 32s. 3d. per 25 tests; 11s. 9d. per set of scoring stencils and manual for all 3 tests.

   1) *Test 2, General Ability Tests: Verbal.* 12(20) minutes.

   2) *Test 3, General Ability Tests: Numerical.* 29(40) minutes.

   3) *Test 4, General Ability Tests: Perceptual.* 23 (35) minutes.

c) TEST 5, SHAPES TEST. Ages 11 and over; spatial ability; separate answer sheets must be used; 7s. 6d. per test; 6s. 4d. per 25 answer sheets; 5s. 10d. per set of scoring stencil and manual; 10(15) minutes.

d) TEST 6, MECHANICAL ABILITY TEST. Ages 11 and over; separate answer sheets must be used; 5s. 7d. per test; 6s. 4d. per 25 answer sheets; 3s. 10d. per set of scoring key and manual; 15(20) minutes.

e) SPEED TESTS. Ages 11 and over; 6 tests in a single booklet; no specific manual; no data on reliability; provisional norms; 48s. 6d. per 25 tests; 17.5(30) minutes.

1) *Test 7 (Speed Test 1), Routine Number and Name Checking.*
2) *Test 8 (Speed Test 2), Perseveration.*
3) *Test 9 (Speed Test 3), Word Fluency.*
4) *Test 10 (Speed Test 4), Ideational Fluency.*
5) *Test 11 (Speed Test 5), Motor Speed.*
6) *Test 12 (Speed Test 6), Motor Skill.*

E. A. PEEL, *Professor of Education, University of Birmingham, Birmingham, England.*

According to the author, this battery represents an attempt to assess mental ability by a method that will "enable the more subtle differences between persons to be readily observed, and....show the nature of a person's mental ability structure in perspective, in the round." The tools chosen for this purpose indicate Morrisby's views about the structure of intelligence. First there is a general intelligence test which reminds one a little of a matrices test. Then there are three general ability tests dealing, respectively, with verbal, numerical, and perceptual material; a shapes test, whose purpose is to measure the spatial element; a mechanical ability test, which deals with more *km* abilities; and, finally, six speed tests of number and name checking, perseveration along the lines of the traditional copying of *s*'s and reversed *s*'s, word and ideational fluency, and motor speed and skill. The tests themselves are well produced. The manuals for the battery and for each of the several tests give adequate instructions for administering and scoring and percentile norms for appropriate age groups.

In spite of the abundance of information provided so far, however, Morrisby has failed to produce the kind of information that is essential in guiding pupils into different kinds of educational programs and into different types of vocations. For example, he reports no correlations between the tests and relevant criteria. Here he might do well to look at the technical supplement produced by the Thurstones for the *SRA Tests of Educational Ability*, in which correlations between the tests and criteria for many schools and subjects are provided so that the would-be user can judge for himself the validity of any claim that the tests differentiate as suggested. Furthermore, Morrisby does not give any data about the reliability of his test or about the standard deviations of the scores at the various age levels—statis-

tics which should certainly be provided with such a battery.

The reviewer cannot conceive of the use of these tests at the moment except in experimental and research situations. When information now lacking is forthcoming, then one can judge how useful the battery will be in school and vocational guidance.

DONALD E. SUPER, *Professor of Education, Teachers College, Columbia University, New York, New York.*

This English battery, first published in 1955, is based on the factorial structure of mental and other abilities as revealed by psychological research, particularly in Great Britain, but also in America. Thus, the American test user will encounter familiar types of tests of verbal, numerical, abstract (perceptual), and mechanical reasoning, of spatial visualization, perceptual speed and accuracy (number and name checking), and even of manual speed and dexterity (dotting and tracing); he will also find tests of types more often used in Britain than here, namely, perseveration, word fluency, and ideational fluency. As the latter types have been more useful in laboratory studies than in educational and vocational prediction, one may be inclined to question their value in a battery designed for school and college use, but that is a question to be answered by validity data.

The first test, the Compound Series Test, is a nonverbal intelligence test designed to cover the age range 7 to 22, a wider range than the other tests in the battery. It is essentially an ingenious paper and pencil version of the familiar bead stringing performance test. Morrisby suggests that it measures "mental workpower," i.e., persistence and concentration in the performance of an intellectual task, but whether or not the test measures anything other than what performance tests of intelligence generally measure is apparently a matter of conjecture. Time limits vary with age, being 20, 25, or 30 minutes, and the test is said to be a power test, but examination of the norms shows increasing scores with increasing time, which suggests that speed does play a part. It is noteworthy that the correlations between scores on this test and school grades are, on the whole, about as high as those between the more typical verbal and numerical intelligence tests and school grades. This may prove to be a most useful nonverbal test.

The General Ability Tests are three in number: Verbal, Numerical, and Perceptual. Each has three parts, the first in each case stressing speed and the last stressing comprehension; the total score weights the parts in such a way as to deemphasize speed somewhat. The perceptual test is comparable to some American abstract reasoning tests, but in each test there is evidence of ingenuity in item construction. This test is designed for use with, and standardized on, students from age 11 to age 22, as are all the tests which follow.

The Shapes Test is intended to measure spatial visualization, the "K" factor in Britain, defined as mental manipulation of perceptual figures. The items are unusual, and, although designed to minimize the use of adventitious clues, seem to this reviewer to depend upon a principle the seeing of which is a matter of intelligence, and which, if seen, changes the nature of the trait measured from complex mental manipulation to a very simple form. The trick seems to be to imagine a pin placed in the white dot occurring in each of the three shapes and mentally to let the shape rotate or fall into position around that point: the answer is then immediately obvious. But whether or not the trick is discovered is left up to the subject. Morrisby states that the ability measured by this test is not developed before about age 11, about half of that age group making zero scores; this is perhaps a defect arising from depending entirely upon one type of item with no apparent item gradient.

The Mechanical Ability Test is based on the now familiar Bennett-type item. Among the speed tests, the routine number and name checking tests, combined to give one score, otherwise resemble American tests of this type. Perseveration, Word Fluency, Ideational Fluency, Motor Speed, and Motor Skill are made up of familiar types of items and need no additional comment.

The general manual points out that the psychological interpretation of the test results must at present be limited since there is little information on which to base it. But the author proceeds, injudiciously in this reviewer's judgment, to suggest that "a great deal can be done by considering subjectively the nature of the functions measured by the various tests and judging a priori their likely interrelationships with other variables such as those we need to predict." He goes on to state, quite properly,

that "the test variables do not always behave in the way we might expect." Obviously, normative and validity data are needed.

Reliability data, it may be noted, seem adequate. The author has taken speed into account in determining reliability, and the coefficients are up to standard.

Norms leave a great deal to be desired, which may be understandable in a new test and can be excused if the author is proceeding apace to collect better norms. All the tests in the battery have "general," "grammar school," and "university" norms. At present the general norms for the Compound Series Test are based on what is "considered to be a representative sample" of nearly 3,000 boys and girls aged 7 to 15, extrapolated to provide norms for ages 6 and 16. The reasons for so thinking regarding representativeness are not given, leaving the potential user to accept the norms on faith or to reject them on the basis of sad experience. The general norms for the bulk of the battery are based on "about 800 boys and girls from secondary modern and grammar schools," essentially junior and senior high school students of all types. The grammar school (or, in American terms, junior and senior high school, college preparatory only) norms are based on "771 boys and a few girls"; it is not claimed that they are a representative sample, and the possibility of sex differences is noted but not examined. The university norms are based on 214 apparently assorted but undescribed students of both sexes, with no account taken of sex differences or of sampling.

Obviously, the norms leave a great deal to be desired before a British user can use them with any confidence, and they are of no value to a possible American user (for whom they are not intended). There is no way of knowing how representative the samples are, and sex differences, always noted on tests of mechanical reasoning and generally on tests of verbal, numerical, spatial, and perceptual abilities, are not taken into account. It is no exaggeration to say that the norming of the battery still remains to be done.

Validity has been considered in only two ways: the logic of the item writing and construction, and correlation with grades. There has been, as yet, no attempt to check the adequacy of Morrisby's spatial items, for example, by ascertaining their correlation with other, thoroughly studied tests of spatial visualiza-

Differential Test Battery

tion. It is this reviewer's expectation that this spatial test will not correlate as highly with existing spatial tests as they do among themselves, while the verbal and several of the other tests will probably yield the usual interform reliabilities. Hence one cannot simply accept Morrisby's recommended use of a priori judgment.

The predictive validity data are still very limited, but they are rather encouraging so far as they go. Correlations with school grades are available for what we would call 115 10th grade and 79 11th grade college preparatory high school boys, for the compound series, verbal, numerical, perceptual, shapes, and mechanical tests, and, in the case of the 11th graders, for the ideational fluency test as well. The first four tests are reasonably good predictors of grades in all subjects, the median r for the first test, for example, being .38 and all but two r's being .30 or higher. English grades are predicted best by the verbal and numerical tests, mathematics grades by the compound series and perceptual tests, and physics by the mechanical, shapes, and perceptual tests, these highest r's ranging from .36 to .80. It is noteworthy that the ideational fluency test is unrelated to any of the three subjects for which validity coefficients were obtained (English, French, and mathematics). This raises again the question of just what use a counselor or admissions officer will make of the scores on this and the other laboratory, or typically unvalidated, tests.

Manufacture of the tests, manuals, and scoring keys is quite uneven. Test booklets and answer sheets (hand scoring) are generally well printed and on suitable stock. But the holes in the scoring stencils are often imperfectly spaced and alignment in scoring is difficult to verify, no aids being provided in the form of guide lines or guide holes. The administrators' manuals are well printed but weakly bound; the use of red and black inks to differentiate explanatory material from oral directions is a helpful innovation. Mimeographed supplementary manuals and a variety of binding devices, including one with a frustrating plastic string tie-binder, give one the impression of an ill thought out profusion of materials which is not entirely justified but persists nevertheless. As one who has often decried the expenditure of more energy on merchandising than on validation by some test publishers, this reviewer hesitates to recommend more attention to packaging, but this battery would benefit by it.

In summary: this is an interestingly conceived and at points ingeniously devised multifactor battery which builds on both British and American factor analysis and test construction work. British in origin and designed for use in Britain, it has not been standardized in a way which makes it usable for practical purposes in North America, but it includes some well designed tests which may recommend it to persons conducting certain types of research in this country. The Compound Series Test, in particular, might well be exploited in America. The manual makes some unwarranted assumptions, and neither standardization nor validation has progressed far enough in Great Britain for effective use to be possible there as yet. However, the battery looks promising, and it is to be hoped that more adequate norms, studies of the relationships between these tests and others whose meaning and validity are better established, and studies of the predictive value of the tests for larger numbers of individuals in a greater variety of criterion situations (including academic subjects and occupations) will in due course be forthcoming.

PHILIP E. VERNON, *Professor of Educational Psychology, University of London, Institute of Education, London, England.*

This battery, though the first of its type to be published in England, is similar to the *General Aptitude Test Battery* or, since it disclaims factorial purity, the Psychological Corporation *Differential Aptitude Tests.* Insufficient information is available wherewith to judge the reliabilities, validities, adequacy of norming, or usefulness of the tests for any purpose. The present manual merely contains the administration and scoring instructions and norms. While a more extensive manual is promised for the future, more than two years have already gone by since the original publication. A duplicated "Preliminary Notice" by the author does little more than describe the tests and give some correlations between the first half dozen tests and grammar school examination grades of 15- and 16-year-old boys. On the basis of these figures, there would appear to be slightly better differential prediction of different school subject grades than is generally obtained by the DAT or *SRA Primary Mental Abilities.*

The battery consists of tests in 7 areas and yields 12 scores. It occupies 139 minutes of working time, but probably takes over 3 hours to administer, since the oral instructions are rather elaborate. The various types of tests may be described as follows:

a) Compound Series Test—a nonverbal reasoning test based on the completion of bead patterns. This is novel and ingenious, though its use of colored patterns possibly handicaps the color defective.

b) General verbal ability tests: three subtests—identification of synonyms and antonyms, classification of similar words, and construction of analogies.

c) Number ability tests: three subtests—checking additions and multiplications, completion of number series, and completion of number matrices. No reason is given for combining N and I tests in the same total score.

d) Perceptual ability tests: three subtests—identification of identical shapes, classification of similar figures, and selection of analogous figures. Again, the combination of perceptual speed and nonverbal reasoning tests seems curious.

e) Shape judging test—identification of reversed shapes. This is probably a sound test of S factor, but it is too difficult for younger and duller children.

f) Mechanical comprehension test—a test similar to the Bennett *Test of Mechanical Comprehension,* but with four- and five-choice items. This test, too is somewhat lacking in discrimination at the lower end.

g) Speed tests: a series of six separately scored tests—number and name checking (clerical speed); perseveration in letter writing; word completion; ideational fluency revealed through words and drawing; motor speed (similar to a dotting test); and motor coordination in drawing lines along narrow paths. No reason is given for expecting motor perseveration to be predictive of anything.

A somewhat irritating feature is the frequent alternation between black and red pencils, presumably with the object of preventing testees from working outside the time limits. This should hardly be necessary with good invigilation. Otherwise, administrative instructions and preliminary practice material are good, and the tests are well printed throughout. Tests 1, 5, and 6 employ booklets which can be reused with fresh answer sheets. Scoring, by means of stencils, appears reasonably convenient, but might well take 15 minutes per testee. Tables are provided for converting raw scores to scaled scores (0–20) and scaled scores into equivalent T scores, percentiles, or standard IQ's, for each age group from 11 plus to 16 plus. There are also scaled score norms for grammar school and college students.

In conclusion, the tests seem to be generally well constructed, and they may be of considerable potential value in educational and vocational guidance. But no overall evaluation is possible in the absence of a proper manual.

[607]

★**Employee Aptitude Survey.** Ages 16 and over; 1952–58; IBM; 10 tests; battery manual ('58); Lockheed manual ('57); manual ['58] for each test; $2.50 per 25 test-answer sheets; postage extra; $2.50 per complete specimen set; 50¢ per specimen set of any one test; postpaid; G. Grimsley (*a–h*), F. L. Ruch (*a–g, i, j*), N. D. Warren (*a–g*), J. S. Ford (*a, c, e–g, j*); Psychological Services, Inc. *

a) TEST 1, VERBAL COMPREHENSION. 1952–58; IBM; Forms A, B ('56); 5(10) minutes.
b) TEST 2, NUMERICAL ABILITY. 1952–58; IBM; Forms A ('52), B ('56); 10(15) minutes.
c) TEST 3, VISUAL PURSUIT. 1956–58; IBM; Forms A ('56), B ('57); 5(10) minutes.
d) TEST 4, VISUAL SPEED AND ACCURACY. 1952–58; IBM; Forms A ('52), B ('56); 5(10) minutes.
e) TEST 5, SPACE VISUALIZATION. 1952–58; IBM; Forms A, B ('57); 5(10) minutes.
f) TEST 6, NUMERICAL REASONING. 1952–58; IBM; Forms A, B ('57); 5(10) minutes.
g) TEST 7, VERBAL REASONING. 1952–58; IBM; Forms A, B ('57); 5(10) minutes.
h) TEST 8, WORD FLUENCY. 1953–58; Forms A, B ('53); 5(10) minutes.
i) TEST 9, MANUAL SPEED AND ACCURACY. 1953–58; 1 form ('53); 5(10) minutes.
j) TEST 10, SYMBOLIC REASONING. 1956–58; IBM; Forms A, B ('57); 5(10) minutes.

DOROTHY C. ADKINS, *Professor of Psychology and Chairman of the Department, University of North Carolina, Chapel Hill, North Carolina.*

The *Employee Aptitude Survey* is comprised of nine 5-minute tests and one 10-minute test. This series has many convenient features: each test is on a single 8½ by 11 inch sheet; the time required is very short; scoring, in most cases possible by IBM scoring machine, is facilitated by stencils for right and wrong responses; norms for various job categories for each test as well as for a cross-section of the working population are provided; alternate forms, together with special retest norms, are available; separate manuals for each test report validation studies.

The general manual states that the series was

withheld from general industrial use for several years until the tests' validities against job performance could be established. To this end, it acknowledges the support of the United States Air Force, Lockheed Aircraft Corporation, Northrop Aviation, AiResearch Manufacturing Company, University of Southern California School of Engineering, and Los Angeles City College Department of Engineering.

The authors have developed this battery on the principle that "maximum validity per minute of testing time is achieved through a battery of short, mutually independent tests." The tests in the battery, together with some reference variables, were given to 90 high school boys and factor analyzed. Little information about the analysis is given in the materials accompanying the tests, but the two to four highest loadings of each of nine tests on nine factors are tabulated. The 10th test (Test 9), Manual Speed and Accuracy, correlated so low with the others that it was excluded from the analysis.

In general, alternate-forms reliability coefficients are presented, in several cases for two groups. The reporting of reliability indices as well seems unnecessary for the sophisticated and possibly misleading for the naive.

For several of the tests correlations with other standardized tests, including the *Otis Employment Test,* the *California Test of Mental Maturity,* and Bennett's *Test of Mechanical Comprehension,* are given. Unwarranted inferences are drawn from some of these correlations; e.g., the conclusion that, because the new test called Numerical Ability correlates .53 with the Bennett test, numerical ability has been shown to be an important ingredient of mechanical aptitude.

The separate examiner's manuals accompanying the different tests summarize validity data, which, altogether, form a rather impressive array. A number of the 50-odd correlations with measures other than standardized tests represent relationships with measures of success in training courses—proficiency tests, teacher evaluations, or pass-fail criteria—rather than measures of success in job performance as such. Nevertheless, a few studies were based upon job performance criteria, and information on the predictability of indices of success in training programs is distinctly better than no validity data at all.

Also provided for each test are raw score equivalents for the following centile points: 90,

75, 60, 55, 50, 45, 40, 25, 10. These norms are based on groups of subjects that differ somewhat from test to test. In all cases, norms for the "general population" are reported. Several of the tests have norms for such groups as general college students, general graduate engineers, accountants, high school students, and so on. Charts presenting norms for several additional groups for the six tests used by Lockheed Aircraft Corporation (Tests 1, 2, 4, 5, 6, and 7) are contained in a Manual for Interpreting the Employee Aptitude Survey published by that company. The authors are careful to urge each user of the tests to explore their validity in his own situation.

The bulletin How to Use the Employee Aptitude Survey contains a table of suggested cutting scores on tests recommended for various occupations. This covers 29 occupational titles, several of which do not seem to correspond to the jobs for which validity or normative data are provided elsewhere. This table is presented immediately after mention of the validation of the various tests against actual job performance criteria, and it is said that "the table of recommended tests and minimum acceptable scores....is based on the results of this long-range research program." One is at first led to believe that all of the recommendations concerning which tests to use and what cutting points are appropriate are based upon empirical validation research specific to the occupation in question and against measures of actual job success. While the authors doubtless have in their files some additional unreported research results, one can scarcely avoid the thought that, in at least some instances, they were applying the "rule of thumb" that they recommend at the end of this bulletin. Here they note that "it is common practice to set the cutting score at some raw score value between the 10th and 25th centiles for the particular occupational group in question." They further remark that, when a battery of tests is used, cutting scores between the 10th and 15th centiles are "usually most realistic." It may be reasonable to suppose, then, that where they lacked validity data but had occupational norms they applied the foregoing rule. It could even be that where they lacked both validity data and norms for a particular occupation they used their best judgment, based upon performance of similar occupational groups. Such procedures may be quite

Employee Aptitude Survey

defensible and helpful, but in any case the methods followed should be clearly indicated.

Among other materials presented are tables of the coefficients of independence among the tests in the battery for four samples. These are in keeping with the authors' emphasis on unique tests.

The reviewer was disappointed to see a bulletin entitled Estimating Otis IQ from Employee Aptitude Survey Tests. Why anyone would want to administer an aptitude battery and then attempt to estimate such a defective index as the IQ for adults is incomprehensible.

A brief description and critique of each test follows.

Test 1, Verbal Comprehension, consists of 30 four-choice vocabulary items, with a ceiling that appears undesirably low. The authors will doubtless improve or replace some of the items. In a few cases, a good one-word answer does not seem possible. Thus "magnitude" does *not* mean the same as "minuend," since the latter is a particular kind of magnitude. Nor, except archaically, can "soil" be regarded as equivalent to "loam." "Rancorous" and "indignant" also have quite different connotations. The alternate-forms reliability coefficient of .83 seems unnecessarily low, especially since it was based on a wide range sample of 535 job applicants. With the 90th centile falling at 27 or above for 8 of the 15 groups for which norms are provided, it is clear that the test difficulty could well be increased.

Test 2, Numerical Ability, contains three separately timed parts: 25 items based on fundamental arithmetic operations with no larger than 3-digit numbers; 25 items involving operations with decimals and percentages; and 25 items involving simple fractions. The one-page arrangement of three parts intended to have separate time limits may well prove faulty. A "cycle omnibus" arrangement of the items with one time limit might be preferable. The reliability coefficients for the total and the three parts are not stated but can be computed from the indices of reliability that are given (.96 for the total score). The test probably could be improved if the answers followed the common plan of arranging numerical answers in ascending or descending numerical order.

Test 3, Visual Pursuit, contains 30 items patterned after the well known visual maze form. Several validation studies against training course grades are reported, along with one study against a pass-fail criterion for engineering students at the end of their first year. These studies, together with norms for "a general population," industrial leadmen, high school seniors, and freshman engineering students, do not clearly substantiate such a statement as, "The test is also useful in the selection of personnel for certain very specific clerical positions such as card-punch operators and similar jobs in which a major task component involves the scanning of paper-work." Either the substantiating data should be reported or the statement should be more cautious.

Test 4, Visual Speed and Accuracy, is a 150-item test modeled after the *Minnesota Clerical Test,* with which it correlated to the extent of .82 for a heterogeneous group of 89 job applicants. It uses various admixtures of digits, letters, and other familiar typewriter symbols (such as $, #, %, ., *, -, 1), and an occasional fraction. Alternate-forms and test-retest coefficients of from .84 to .87 are reported, along with several empirical validity studies. From a table of median scores for different occupational groups, the authors conclude that persons in job categories requiring heavy, detailed paper work obtained relatively high scores on this test. It is then curious to note that a "top management" group has scores rather similar to those of "employed stenographers" and that "college students" exceed both these groups as well as two engineering groups. It would seem that this test could bear further study.

Test 5, Space Visualization, is a 50-item block counting test with reported alternate-forms reliabilities of .87 and .89. Surprisingly enough, freshman engineering students and college students in general show almost identical norms.

Test 6, Numerical Reasoning, contains 20 number series items. A large proportion of the items that the reviewer tested were defective in that the rule for the progression that the test constructor intended could not be established until after the available answers had been inspected. Thus in the series 5 4 3 6 9 8 7 ?, the answer could be 14 (as keyed) or 10. To be sure, 10 is not among the answers presented, but this is no excuse for including annoyingly ambiguous items. The general principle, is, of course, that the rule of progression should be inducible by the time the end of the series is reached. This defect in the items may indeed account for the rather low reliability

Employee Aptitude Survey

figures reported for this test: .76 (test-retest) for 90 high school males, and .60 (alternate-forms) for 335 freshman engineering students.

Test 7, Verbal Reasoning, contains six sets of five items each, each set consisting of conclusions to be judged as true, false, or uncertain upon the basis of four or five simple factual statements. One might suppose that errors within each set would be substantially correlated, thus lowering the reliability per item. Alternate-forms coefficients of .79 for 90 high school males and .70 for 335 freshman engineering students were obtained.

Test 8, Word Fluency, is of the familiar form with 75 spaces for words beginning with a designated letter. Alternate-forms reliability for the 335 engineering students was .75. No predictive validity data are given for this test.

Test 9, Manual Speed and Accuracy, involves the familiar task of placing a pencil dot in as many as possible of a series of O's within the time allowed. Reported retest reliability for 335 engineering students is .79. Only "general population" norms (for an unspecified n) are presented.

Test 10, Symbolic Reasoning, is a 30-item test containing items of the sort "$X < Y < Z$, therefore $X < Z$." The subject marks them true, false, or uncertain. Reported reliability coefficients are .68 and .69. The authors state that repeated studies have shown that mean scores of engineers and engineering students are distinctly superior to the general population mean. Norms for these three groups and for general college students and high school seniors are presented. With the 90th centile for graduate engineers at 21 (maximum score being 30) and the distribution for the general population positively skewed (as evidenced by the mean falling at the 61st centile), the test probably could be improved by adjustment of the item difficulties.

S. RAINS WALLACE, *Director of Research, Life Insurance Agency Management Association, Hartford, Connecticut.*

This is a battery of 10 short (nine have 5-minute time limits and one has a 10-minute limit) paper and pencil tests. It represents an attempt to achieve "maximum validity per minute" by taking advantage of findings which indicate that the addition to a battery of many tests having relatively unique variance enhances predictive validity to a much greater extent than the shortening of tests (with concomitant reduction in reliability) reduces it. The intercorrelations among the tests and a factor analysis (the latter, unfortunately, based on only 90 cases) support the contention that the tests are substantially independent. They have been standardized for a variety of occupational groups.

The authors provide an examiner's manual for the battery and a brochure entitled How to Use the Employee Aptitude Survey. In both of these documents there is a refreshing insistence on the importance of establishing predictive validity before using a test as a selection device. Recognition is also explicitly made of the fact that "the validity of a particular test for a particular job depends upon the specific requirements for that job in a specific organization," and potential users are urged to validate the component tests against job performance in their own organizations. However, in describing procedures for such validation, the major emphasis is placed on concurrent validities, although it is admitted that predictive validation "permits more accurate validation in the long run."

Furthermore, validity data given for each of the tests are based upon very small samples. The criteria employed are typically not measures of job performance but, instead, ratings, course or test grades, etc., which are notoriously (and spuriously) predictable. The populations are only too often freshman engineers, drafting students, or commerce students. When actual workers are studied, the validities are concurrent rather than predictive. In the case of one test (Word Fluency) no validities are reported, yet cutoff scores are recommended for three occupations.

In general, both the battery manual and the brochure represent excellent jobs of describing the test battery and its construction, and of providing a sound basis for its use and interpretation. Unfortunately, one has the feeling that the authors have violated some of their own tenets in their eagerness to establish a basis for the battery's wide and varied use. For example, the brochure presents a table of suggested cutting scores for 29 different occupations, including electrical engineers, junior executives, sales persons, inspectors, etc. A closer examination of this table in conjunction with the separate manuals for each of the tests raises some doubts about the manner in which the cutoff scores were derived. One thing which immediately strikes the eye is that the tests and cutoff scores suggested for electrical engineers, mechanical engineers, and aeronautic engineers are practically identical. One must wonder why, in this case, the heading "engineers" would not have sufficed, particularly since the individual test manuals indicate that the basic validity data were derived from the performance of some 90 freshman engineering students in their first year. Examination of the cutoff scores in conjunction with the normative tables given for each test for 251 "general graduate engineers" reveals that the recommendation is (with some very minor deviations) to cut off the bottom 25 per cent on each of the six tests recommended for engineering occupations. These tests are named, Verbal Comprehension, Numerical Ability, Visual Pursuit, Visual Speed and Accuracy, Space Visualization, and Symbolic Reasoning. Since the intercorrelations of these tests are demonstrably low, it seems surprising that cutoffs for maximum efficiency would be so similar. Also, while a recommended cutoff at the 25th centile might appear conservative, its use for each of six relatively independent tests might well produce a prohibitively low selection ratio, even in a period of recession. This could produce a very bad effect unless the validity of the suggested battery is much higher than any evidence presented would suggest. The authors give no warnings about this point.

For selecting sales persons, five tests are recommended. None of the appropriate manuals provides validity data for such occupations, but examination of the norms for 253 security salesmen and 302 sales representatives reveals that the suggested cutoff scores fall at about the 10th centile for each of the tests recommended (Verbal Comprehension, Numerical Ability, Visual Speed and Accuracy, Verbal Reasoning, and Word Fluency). One is led to the conclusion that the recommendations regarding tests and cutoff scores for the various occupations were reached through a process of arbitrary rules coupled with the authors' professional judgment about which of the occupations lend themselves most readily to prediction.

In summary, this is an outstandingly well thought out and well constructed battery of tests based upon unusually competent analysis. The format, instructions, and scoring keys are uniformly excellent. It deserves the attention of anyone who has a selection problem, particularly for a wide variety of occupations. The warnings of the authors concerning the importance of specific predictive validation of each test and the development, accordingly, of cutoff scores also deserve attention—more attention than they have received from the authors themselves.

[608]

★**Flanagan Aptitude Classification Tests.** Grades 12–16 and adults; 1951–56; also called FACT; 14 tests; manual ('53); $2.55 per 20 tests; 60¢ per 20 classification sheets ('53); 30¢ per examiner's manual ('53); 30¢ per technical supplement ('54); 40¢ per counselor's booklet ('53); 25¢ per manual for interpreting scores ('56); 25¢ per student's booklet for interpreting scores ('53); 50¢ per personnel director's booklet ('53); $3 per educational specimen set; $5.75 per industrial specimen set; postage extra; 210(328) minutes in 2 sessions; John C. Flanagan; Science Research Associates. *

a) FACT 1A, INSPECTION. Form A ('53); 6(12) minutes.
b) FACT 2A AND 2B, CODING. Forms A ('53), B ('54); 10(30) minutes.
c) FACT 3A AND 3B, MEMORY. Forms A ('53), B ('54); 4(5) minutes.
d) FACT 4A, PRECISION. Form A ('53); 8(15) minutes.
e) FACT 5A, ASSEMBLY. Form A ('53); 12(18) minutes.
f) FACT 6A, SCALES. Form A ('53); 16(28) minutes.
g) FACT 7A, COORDINATION. Form A ('53); $2\frac{2}{3}(8)$ minutes.
h) FACT 8A, JUDGMENT AND COMPREHENSION. Form A ('53); (35–40) minutes.
i) FACT 9A, ARITHMETIC. Form A ('53); 10(20) minutes.
j) FACT 10A, PATTERNS. Form A ('53); 20(28) minutes.
k) FACT 11A, COMPONENTS. Form A ('53); 20(24) minutes.
l) FACT 12A, TABLES. Form A ('53); 10(15) minutes.
m) FACT 13A AND 13B, MECHANICS. Forms A ('53), B ('54); 20(25) minutes.
n) FACT 14A, EXPRESSION. Form A ('53); (35–45) minutes.

REFERENCES

1. LATHAM, ALBERT J. *Job Appropriateness: A One-Year Follow-up of High School Graduates.* Doctor's thesis, University of Pittsburgh (Pittsburgh, Pa.), 1948.
2. VOLKIN, LEONARD. *A Validation Study of Selected Test Batteries Applied to Fields of Work.* Doctor's thesis, University of Pittsburgh (Pittsburgh, Pa.), 1951.

HAROLD P. BECHTOLDT, *Associate Professor of Psychology, State University of Iowa, Iowa City, Iowa.*

The *Flanagan Aptitude Classification Tests* (FACT) is one of the newest and most elaborately organized of the aptitude batteries. Fourteen tests are available in Form A, and three tests in Form B. According to the manual, additional tests are being prepared to increase the accuracy of coverage of the job elements in a number of occupations.

Each test is prepared in a separate booklet

of the self-scoring (carbon transfer) type which requires the responses to be made in the test booklet. There are extensive practice materials, to be presented by the examiner, which should reduce the possibility of misunderstanding the test instructions. The test items are obviously the product of a very competent test construction staff. Accompanying the several test booklets is a series of rather extensive pamphlets for examiners, counselors, personnel directors, and students, together with a Technical Supplement summarizing the available data. The separate printing of these materials allows the test purchaser considerable flexibility in planning an order.

The Examiner Manual indicates that the battery "has been developed in an effort to establish a standard classification system for describing those aptitudes that are important for successful performance of particular occupational tasks." The two suggested uses, for vocational counseling and for the selection and placement of employees, are discussed in detail in the Counselor's Booklet and the Personnel Director's Booklet. The "aptitude" feature of these tests is emphasized in striking fashion by the omission, in the suggested procedures, of any trade or achievement tests for occupational placement and of any academic performance measures for counseling high school or college students. In view of the uniformly high correlations regularly reported between past performance and future performance in both of these areas, such omissions would seem serious in terms of "predicting successful performance."

The instructions to the examiner are quite detailed and very clearly prepared. Time limits and suggested schedules for the complete battery and for portions of the battery are provided. The use of several timed practice trials in the tests Precision and Coordination is an interesting innovation as well as a possible motivating device. A few specific suggestions to the examiner as a result of the reviewer's trial of the instructions are as follows: (a) More emphasis should be given to the unusual procedure for circling, rather than erasing, a response to be changed. (b) The omission of a question by marking a vertical line should also be emphasized, when appropriate. (c) In Coordination, the instructions to try to control both speed and accuracy might well be emphasized more. The time (40 seconds) allowed on

the second and third trials is twice as long as the time for the first practice trial. (d) In the Patterns Test, the example for Part 2 contains both an upsidedown (flopping) movement and a rotation of 90 degrees, although the instructions refer only to the upsidedown movement.

The scoring formulas and procedures are sufficiently simple to justify having the examinees exchange booklets and score them. For most tests the score is the total number of correct responses; for three tests there is a correction. Differential weighting of separate performances is required for two of the tests. Convenient conversion tables for translating raw scores to stanine scores are provided. In addition, an "answer grid" for the determination of occupational stanine scores (minus and plus values are shown for many of the occupations) provides a very convenient summary sheet for scores on the several tests.

The number of tests in the individual occupational "batteries" varies from two (usually Tests 8 and 14) to seven. The frequency with which a given test enters into the prediction equations for 30 occupations is indicated on the Aptitude Classification Sheet. Test 2, Coding, is used in only two occupational equations while Test 14, Expression, is involved in 15 occupational equations and Test 8, Judgment and Comprehension, in 22. Since Coding must precede Test 3, Memory, its use is actually required for 10 occupations.

Although the authors point out correctly that differential weighting does not markedly increase the validity of a composite score when the number of tests combined is large, the application of the principle of equal weights to small batteries of two to seven tests seems hardly appropriate. In fact, the authors repeatedly use multiple correlation coefficients (with differential weights, not unit weights) as evidence of the usefulness of the batteries.

The rationale offered for the aptitude battery involves an implicit rejection of the miniature job sample approach and the primary mental factor approaches. The authors prefer an intermediate procedure, said to start from a job element approach based on "a comprehensive list of critical behaviors involved in the job or jobs being studied." In the Technical Supplement, these critical behaviors are stated to be the ones that "really make a difference with respect to on-the-job success and failure." The selection of these behaviors, however, seems to be based on the opinions of a few industrial psychologists. The classifications of these behaviors into job elements are then "tested" in some unspecified way. It is also claimed, without supporting evidence, that this "very practical origin" of the job element approach makes possible a type of generalization and application which is excluded by the more strictly empirical approach of the job sample and primary factor procedures. (This is the first time this reviewer has seen the factor approach *criticized* for its "almost exclusive reliance on empirical validation studies.") The authors further claim that using the job element approach tends to make the personnel research worker more of a "professional worker" than a "technician."

At a time when clinical testing seems to be becoming more objective and empirical, the established emphasis on "demonstrated empirical relations" in industrial personnel work apparently is here being modified toward more emphasis on so-called professional or clinical judgment and opinion. Further evidence of such a shift can be seen in the discussion of the data offered in support of claims of prediction of "successful performance" reviewed below.

The data provided in the Technical Supplement and in the booklets for counselors and personnel directors are chiefly summaries of three large scale testing programs carried out in the Pittsburgh public high schools in 1947, 1951, and 1952, involving 1,500, 500, and 1,563 seniors, respectively. The first two of these studies provided evidence as to the adequacy of the test materials and furnished data for two follow-up studies, one by Latham (*1*) and the other by Volkin (*2*). The third provided the data for the calculation of standard scores, and intercorrelations among the 14 tests. The median intercorrelation coefficient is .29, with three tests (Assembly, Scales, and Patterns) accounting for all but one of the intercorrelations of .50 or higher. The highest intercorrelation, .69, is between Coding and Memory, which essentially are 2-response measures from different trials of the same general task.

Reliability coefficients, as well as standard errors for three stanine ranges, are provided for both Form A and Form B tests, with test-retest procedures used for the speeded tasks. The authors carefully point out that the standard errors of measurement on some of the tests are fairly substantial and that the sample sizes in several cases are not large. The lowest reliability coefficient is for Mechanics, Form A, which contains only four mechanical problems with a total of 20 questions. Since Form B of this test has been made longer and less difficult, the two forms are not parallel. The claims as to comparability of the Form A and Form B series, with the exception of the mechanics test, seem reasonable. No explicit statement is made as to the computation of the reliability coefficients for "representative combined scores," but the slight increase in the coefficient over the most reliable of the several components suggests that the generalized Kuder-Richardson formulation for the reliability of a composite was used. In general, the separate reliability coefficients seem high enough to warrant serious consideration of stanine score differences of about 2.0.

Although the authors apparently question placing much reliance on empirical validation studies, they do mention the data regarding the predictive value of test scores for various types of performance. Volkin (*2*) in his 3-year follow-up of the 1947 testing program obtained positive correlations significant at the 1 per cent level for 6 out of 10 comparisons, the number of cases in the several comparisons ranging from 15 to 275. The validity coefficients using the unit nominal weights of the aptitude classification sheet are in every case considerably lower than the multiple correlation coefficients computed with optimum (beta) weights. Since the occupational combinations of Volkin were based on "tests selected at the time of initial testing as likely to be most important for the work fields," it is interesting that the authors, in the Personnel Director's Booklet, suggest that the currently recommended (but somewhat different) sets of tests will result in more accurate predictions than those reported by Volkin. If this point is sound, would it not seem reasonable for the publishers to have recomputed the validity coefficients using the currently recommended tests and weights?

During World War II, Flanagan pioneered the classic personnel research study in which nearly 1,100 airmen were given a complete aptitude battery and then sent without restriction into pilot training. The justification for this drastic action was that in no other way could the usefulness of the tests for pilot selection be unambiguously determined. It would seem nearly as important to provide similarly unequivocal data when predictions are to be

Flanagan Aptitude Classification Tests

made in 30 occupations. If the students had been tested on the complete battery and then followed up for three to five years, we could determine which of the many possible combinations would give the greatest likelihood of successful prediction. It would then not be necessary to use "educated guesses" concerning the similarities of the FACT tests to other published tests and the comparability of criterion measures in a variety of studies in formulating the recommended batteries for different occupations.

Probably most personnel psychologists would like also to obtain unbiased estimates of the predictive usefulness, if any, added to a set of tests by guidance and counseling procedures. Such unbiased estimates should be obtained after the test "validities" are determined and in such a way that the test and counseling contributions to "successful prediction" can be evaluated. Yet, in the Counselor's Booklet we find discussions of counseling failures on the one-year follow-up study written as though the tests were used prior to the "validity" determinations in suggesting occupational goals to the Pittsburgh high school students. Such discussions are indeed relevant to the evaluation of statements justifying current counseling procedures. However, the data so obtained cannot provide unbiased estimates of the accuracy of predictions determined from the tests alone or from the combination of tests and interviews.

In summary, the *Flanagan Aptitude Classification Tests* constitute a well designed series worthy of serious consideration for a guidance program. The test battery is judged as comparable to other available batteries for such a purpose. Although the data are considered by this reviewer as inadequate justification for many of the claims made, no other battery of tests currently available is free of this fault.

RALPH F. BERDIE, *Professor of Psychology, and Director, Student Counseling Bureau, University of Minnesota, Minneapolis, Minnesota.*

The concepts underlying the development of this battery of tests and the vast amount of relevant psychometric experience of the author suggest that the FACT battery should be of use to vocational counselors. The results of two studies, cited in the manual, involving approximately 1,000 Pittsburgh high school students, suggest that the scores derived from the tests are related to subsequent educational and vocational history. The published information, however, is only suggestive and, although promising, provides a rather tenuous basis for using the battery.

The battery itself is based upon the work of Flanagan and his colleagues in the United States Army Air Force during World War II. Different tests were given to half a million persons and the scores compared to performance and achievement in a variety of military occupations. The tests included in the FACT battery can be considered as lineal descendants of the Air Force tests.

Many of the tests are quite different from those used in similar batteries. In the inspection test, for instance, each item consists of 15 different pictures of the same object; the examinee must respond to the imperfections in some of the pictures. The coding test presents brief codes to be learned and simple words or phrases to be translated into code. The memory test consists of items which measure the subject's ability to remember the codes previously learned. The precision test requires the subject to draw a line in the narrow area between two concentric circles without crossing either circle; this is done first with one hand, and then with both hands at the same time. The assembly test consists of pictures of the component parts of an object, and the subject is required to select from five objects pictured that one which consists of the components presented.

In the scales test the subject answers questions based on two graphs. In the coordination test he must draw a pencil line in the areas lying between rather large incomplete concentric circles without touching the figures; this test requires both hand and arm movement. The judgment and comprehension test items consist of a paragraph followed by multiple choice questions based in part upon the content of the paragraph. The arithmetic test includes simple and combined addition and subtraction items involving both numbers and less meaningful abstract symbols (x's), and multiplication and division of numbers. The pattern test requires the subject to reproduce simple pattern outlines and to reproduce the outlines with the figures reversed.

The components test consists of items, each of which presents a set of simple figures and a number of more complicated figures; the subject is required to determine which simple figure is contained within each complex figure.

The tables test requires the subject to answer questions, making use of first, a numerical table, and secondly, an alphabetical table. The mechanics test presents pictures of relatively simple mechanical components and the subject must answer questions pertaining to possible uses and functions of the components. The expressions test is a true and false type English examination of both grammatical usage and sentence structure.

Although only 4 of the 14 tests have items that appear to be of a verbal nature, these 4 tests (Coding, Memory, Judgment and Comprehension, and Expression) use about 37 per cent of the entire testing time. Conspicuously absent are some of the more traditional verbal items, particularly relatively simple vocabulary items, same-opposite items, and items of the analogy type. As these missing item types have in the past frequently proved to be the best predictors of academic achievement, particularly at the college level, one might suspect that the FACT battery may not prove to be useful for this purpose. Flanagan reports that seven additional tests are being prepared for publication and that these will include more tests of interest to persons concerned with predicting college success.

The items included in the FACT battery tend to be similar in type to the work sample test items which bear a direct relationship to many skilled and semiskilled jobs. The job orientation of the author is well illustrated by his attempt to make the test scores meaningful through the use of the concept of job elements. Flanagan studied a number of occupations making use of the critical incident technique and defined 21 job elements which provide information on the tasks which he thinks determine success and failure in the occupations most frequently encountered by high school graduates. These job elements were used in selecting the tests to be included in the battery as well as in arriving at estimates as to the test score patterns appropriate for most jobs.

The author and the publishers have made available a profusion of manuals for test users, but the content of each manual tends to be pretty much the same as that of the other manuals. The Examiner Manual provides a brief description of the tests and instructions for administering and scoring them. Another manual, Interpreting Test Scores, presents the results of follow-up studies with mean scores

for specific groups. A Technical Supplement describes the concepts underlying the development of the battery and the job element approach used in constructing the tests, and summarizes the information about validity, reliability, and norms. The Counselor's Booklet contains job descriptions of 30 occupations, recommendations regarding the tests to be used for each of the different occupations, and suggestions for the interpretation and use of the tests. The Personnel Director's Booklet contains essentially the same information but changed somewhat from an educational orientation to a business orientation. Finally, a bulletin for students, entitled Your FACT Scores and What They Mean, presents much of the same information, including the occupational descriptions. This bulletin cannot be substituted for the counseling provided by a qualified counselor.

The validity of the battery is suggested by the study done on 1,000 Pittsburgh high school students, which shows that students following different educational and vocational paths have different profiles. Other than this study, no additional validity data have been presented by the author, and no other published studies regarding this battery of tests have been found. Quite relevant, however, is the information about the parent Air Force battery of tests and a study by Thorndike and Hagen provides quite conclusive evidence that the scores on tests identical to or very similar to those used in the FACT battery do differentiate among persons upon the basis of occupational careers. The Thorndike-Hagen study, soon to be published in full, suggests also that test scores are not related to success on a job, as shown either by salary or self-ratings, but only to differentiations among persons in different jobs. One must conclude that as much evidence regarding the validity of these scores is available as is true for other tests at comparable stages of developments; nevertheless, the validity evidence now available warrants only cautious counseling guidance and counseling use of these tests.

The tests are relatively elaborate and complex in terms of administration and timing. When all 21 tests are finally available, they will require at least 7 hours of testing time. For many of the tests, as much time is involved in preparing the person to do the test exercises as in taking the items themselves. Whether or not

Flanagan Aptitude Classification Tests

this is the best use of testing time is a question.

The scoring of the tests will present a real problem if they are used in large groups. Machine scoring is not yet available. Machine scorable answer sheets are being prepared, along with single booklet editions. The present test booklets are not reusable; compared to similar tests they are relatively expensive. In those schools where counselors are reluctant to have students score their own tests—and there is much justification for this attitude—the difficulty of mass scoring now presents an almost insoluble problem.

The author's adaption of the stanine concept from his work in the Army Air Force requires more justification than he provides. Most teachers, and many counselors, are only now grasping the meaning of percentiles and standard scores. To confuse this problem now by introducing stanines may be statistically and psychologically sound, but in terms of practical problems of in-service training in test use, some real problems may be encountered.

The tests were standardized on a group of Pittsburgh public high school seniors and the norms are based on scores of these pupils. Nothing in the manual indicates how representative this group of Pittsburgh students is of United States students in general, and no attempt is made to provide norms on a nationwide sample. Whether one uses percentiles or stanines, one should know much about the nature of the group from which these scores were derived. It is hoped that more normative information will soon be available, as the author has promised.

The intercorrelations of the tests are low. Only 7 of the 91 coefficients are as high as .50 and the median coefficient is .29. The tests seem to be reasonably independent. The reliability coefficients of the 14 tests vary from .26 to .86. Standard errors of measurement are provided to help the more sophisticated counselor interpret the test scores. In general, the reliabilities of the tests in the FACT battery appear to be somewhat lower than reliabilities of tests in comparable batteries. The median reliability coefficient for the *Differential Aptitude Tests* as presented in its manual is .89. For FACT, reliability coefficients are presented not only for the individual tests but also for the combined occupational stanine scores. These coefficients range from .83 to .93.

In summary, this battery of tests is relatively long, difficult to administer and to handle, and expensive. These characteristics are unimportant if the validity and usefulness of the tests warrant the expenditure of time, effort, and money. The present evidence suggests that eventually this battery may be proved of satisfactory validity, but at the present time, as with so many other tests, one must warn the test user to approach these scores with somewhat more than the usual amount of skepticism, and with the hope that during the next few years the author will be able to present information that will reduce the need for such doubt.

JOHN B. CARROLL, *Professor of Education, Harvard University, Cambridge, Massachusetts.*

The *Flanagan Aptitude Classification Tests* comprise a group of tests, each with its own separate booklet, intended to measure a number of independent abilities which its author thinks likely, on the basis of professional judgment and previous research, to be relevant to various jobs, vocations, and professions. Materials accompanying the tests offer ingenious and easily used procedures for obtaining special scores that are supposed to be predictive of success in 30 different occupations or job fields. The orientation is distinctly towards vocational counseling and personnel selection at the high school senior level and above. On the whole, the intercorrelations among the tests are quite low.

The tests are designed to measure what the author calls "critical job elements," i.e., elements in jobs which "really make a difference with respect to on-the-job success and failure." In this way, the author feels he has been able to strike a happy balance between the miniature job sample approach and the "primary mental factor" approach. The former of these approaches he regards as impractical because it would require work samples for a very large number of jobs, while the latter approach, he believes, relies too heavily on "empirical validation studies," to the extent that "the personnel research worker becomes almost entirely a technician rather than a professional worker." In Flanagan's opinion, the testmaker or the personnel worker who uses the "job element" approach has the opportunity to call upon all his powers of observation and understanding of the abilities and performances that make for success in work. It is difficult, however, to see just how this view differs from that of the factor analyst, who is just as anxious as Flanagan to understand the nature of the abilities required in different jobs and to learn the extent to which they are relevant. If the job element approach discloses abilities which the factor analyst had not envisaged, it is the fault only of the factor analyst's creative imagination or perception, not of his analytic model. Flanagan's "critical job element" approach is factor-analytic thinking in a slightly new guise, and it does not in any way preclude the need for careful and extensive validation studies, however tiresome such studies may seem.

Flanagan's total program calls for the publication of 21 FACT tests in all, but at this writing only 14 are available, 3 of them with alternate forms. Planned for later publication are tests of vocabulary, reasoning, planning, ingenuity, alertness, tapping, and carving. No explanation is given for delaying the publication of these tests, some of which might conceivably be more generally useful than some of the first 14 tests; the battery is short on purely intellectual tests.

One is inclined to feel that the author would have been well advised to delay the publication of some of the tests until they had been subjected to considerable revision or validation. There is no evidence that the items in the various tests were selected through analyses of item difficulty and item validity. We are told that a 27-test battery was developed and experimentally administered in 1947, and that 11 revised tests underwent preliminary tryouts with about 500 high school senior boys in 1951; thereafter, we find only that the 14 tests currently available were administered in their "final" form to a sample "representative of all Pittsburgh Public High School seniors" in December 1952. The published stanine norms are based on this latter sample, but the results sometimes belie the author's claim that the tests produce "a satisfactory spread among those tested." For example, the raw scores on the 120-item Test 6, Scales, have a mean of 17.9 and a standard deviation of 12.0! The distribution is highly skewed, and the test is highly speeded. As another example, it appears that scores on Test 13, Mechanics, are largely chance (mean score is 6.5; each of the 20 items has 5 alternatives). This test involves questions on drawings of fairly complicated pieces of mechanical equipment which would be generally unfamiliar to most examinees—even those with a mechanical bent. Test 13, in fact, has a split-half reliability of only .26 and an alternate-form reliability of .59, despite its 20-minute time limit. The fact that this test has low intercorrelations with other tests in the battery is hardly spectacular.

The reported reliabilities of the subtests seldom exceed .80, but these are excused on the ground that the subtest scores are intended to be combined in teams of from two to seven scores in accordance with the scheme worked out for this purpose (the Aptitude Classification Sheet). Since some of the resulting "vocational aptitude scores" are shown to have high reliabilities and useful validity coefficients, we may tentatively accept the author's judgment, but with the reservation that the reliabilities could probably have been improved in many of the subtests by standard test construction techniques.

Solely on the basis of careful perusal of the tests themselves, this reviewer judges that the currently available subtests are extremely uneven in quality. Test 1, Inspection, is highly speeded and might be a reasonably good measure of some sort of perceptual ability involved in factory inspection tasks and the like, except that the "inspection" of a parade of little pictures on a piece of paper is a far cry from the real task in a factory. It correlates only .22 with the DAT clerical speed and accuracy test, at least in one sample. Test 2, Coding, suffers from the fact that its task is ambiguous: subjects can succeed either by quickly memorizing the codes or by being nimble in referring to them. Most subjects will probably be lazy and try to rely on looking them up; thus they will be ill prepared for Test 3, Memory, which, unheralded, asks the examinee to demonstrate his memory for the codes. The reliability of .55 does not speak well for the test. Test 4, Precision, is a paper and pencil performance test of fine coordination ability; what has to be demonstrated, however, is that this kind of task is really similar to the finger and tweezer precision tasks actually encountered in industry. On the surface, Test 5, Assembly, looks as if it would measure the so-called spatial visualization factor, and perhaps it really does ($r =$ .59 with Space Relations, DAT); the task of matching up pictured 3-dimensional forms in terms of alphabetical symbols seems overly distracting, however. Even the practice items are at a high level of difficulty.

We have already mentioned the poor score spread on Test 6, Scales. For the individual without special training, the task of reading values from 2-dimensional graphs and from a chart of polar coordinates will be very difficult; the situation is not helped by very fine, close printing and excessive photographic reduction. For those who know how to read graphs and scales, the test is really a measure of "carefulness." Test 7, Coordination, is another paper and pencil performance test, this time measuring a grosser kind of hand-arm coordination than Test 4, with which it intercorrelates .39 (in the 1952 standardization sample). Test 8, Judgment and Comprehension, seems to be a combined reading comprehension and practical judgment test. It has poor score spread (mean 15.2, SD 3.8, 24 items) and poor reliability (.65), and seems not to be worth the investment of 35 minutes or more of testing time. Its factorial complexity would probably make score interpretations problematical; many of the items are ambiguous and open to question. Test 9, Arithmetic, is similar to number ability tests found in other batteries; it displays reasonably good test characteristics in view of its 10-minute working time. Test 10, Patterns, is a paper and pencil performance test probably measuring a combination of spatial ability and carefulness; it is reminiscent of the copying test in the *MacQuarrie Test for Mechanical Ability* but requires closer visual attention. Test 11, Components, is reminiscent of the Gottschaldt figures test, but again, it is quite difficult and taxing; furthermore, one would be hard pressed to conceive a job in which the ability to detect a specified visual pattern within a larger field would be critical (except perhaps in detecting military camouflage!). Test 12, Tables, would be a good measure of the perceptual speed factor if its reliability were more satisfactory; it correlates .40 with the DAT clerical speed and accuracy test. Test 13, Mechanics, has already been commented on as being too difficult and specialized for the ordinary test taking population. Test 14, Expression, is a reasonably satisfactory test of knowledge of grammatical "rules" and sensitivity to the more superficial aspects of good English writing; it correlates .68 with DAT Language Usage—Part II (Sentences).

So much for the tests themselves. There is not so much to say about the validation of the tests because this is up to now more in the realm of plan than of reality. The author has adopted the strategy of making the test widely available at the outset and planning extensive periodic follow-up studies. The results of the one validity study reported in the Technical Supplement are of moderate promise, however, even if we restrict our attention to the coefficients based on "equal weights." Success in sales, electrical work, structural work, and mechanical work can be predicted with validity coefficients of .45 to .65. The validities for college work are low, however, and probably reflect the fact that the battery contains few tests of the conventional college aptitude type. It will take a major effort over a period of years to provide adequate validation data for the FACT tests. But the basic material to be validated is of such dubious quality, on the whole, that one wonders whether the author might not better serve the cause of multifactor testing by stopping to make judicious revisions of the tests before undue amounts of time and money are expended in standardizing the current series.

In this light, it is hard to understand the air of assurance which seems to be adopted by the author (or his publishers or editors) in setting forth elaborate procedures for combining scores, interpreting score profiles, and using the tests in personnel selection. The extensive studies made by Super and by Ghiselli of the general problem of predicting occupational success cannot make one overwhelmingly confident that occupational guidance is a simple matter of making judicious mixtures of "critical job elements" whereby to match men and jobs. For all of Flanagan's earnest exhortations to personnel workers to seek to apply superior wisdom and psychological insight to the understanding of the behavior of men working on tasks, one is faced with the fact that Flanagan's own insight has its dim moments. Consider the test in the present series called Memory (Test 3), which figures in the vocational aptitude scores for accountant, businessman, office clerk, humanities professor, lawyer, nurse, physician, salesperson, secretary, and writer. According to the description provided, "This test measures ability to remember the codes learned in Test 2." And what are those codes? A series of arbitrary alphabetical and numeral symbols which might represent "office room numbers of departments," "delivery truck routes," etc. While we might grant that such a kind of memory could be useful to an accountant, a nurse, or a physician, it would hardly be regarded as "critical" to them—and certainly not to a "humanities professor" or a "writer."

One may go so far as to characterize the FACT tests as sleek and even handsome in format and appearance. The scoring device involving a carbon insert is ingenious and will have many advantages, although it was noticed that on some of the tests the carbon was not heavy enough to produce a clear carbon impression on the scoring grid.

Because of the somewhat undeveloped state of some of the tests and the rather weak validation data available to date, the *Flanagan Aptitude Classification Tests* should be regarded as constituting an interesting research instrument which may potentially develop into a useful counseling tool.

[609]

*General Aptitude Test Battery. Ages 16 and over; 1946–58; test battery developed for use in the occupational counseling program of the United States Employment Service and released in 1947 for use by State Employment Services; titles on tests are *GATB Book 1, GATB Book 2, GATB Part 8;* 9 scores (12 tests): intelligence, verbal, numerical, spatial, form perception, clerical perception, motor coordination, finger dexterity, manual dexterity; IBM except Part 8 and apparatus tests; Forms A ['52], B ['53]; manual ('58) in 3 sections; directions for administering ['52] apparatus tests; mimeographed record blank ['52] for apparatus tests; profile ['56]; aptitude pattern card ['57]; tests available to nonprofit institutions for counseling purposes; testing services free of charge when program is conducted through the facilities of State Employment Service offices; institutions using their own facilities must purchase tests and employ testing supervisors trained by U.S.E.S.; details may be secured from local and state offices, through which all orders must be cleared; separate answer sheets must be used; $9.50 per 500 IBM answer sheets; specimen set not available; 49(135) minutes; United States Employment Service.
a) BOOK 1. 4 tests: name comparison, computation, three-dimensional space, vocabulary; $14 per 100 copies of Form A; $15 per 100 copies of Form B; postpaid; Government Printing Office.
b) BOOK 2. 3 tests: tool matching, arithmetic reasoning, form matching; $10 per 100 copies of Form A; $12 per 100 copies of Form B; postpaid; Government Printing Office.
c) PART 8. 1 test: mark making; $2.75 per 100 tests, postpaid; Government Printing Office.
d) PEGBOARD. 2 tests: place, turn; $20.50 per set of test materials; postpaid; distributed by Specialty Case Manufacturing Co. and Warwick Products Co.
e) FINGER DEXTERITY BOARD. 2 tests: assemble, disassemble; $9.65 per set of test materials; postpaid; distributed by Specialty Case Manufacturing Co. and Warwick Products Co.

REFERENCES

1–33. See 4:714.
34. ODELL, CHARLES E. "Cooperative Research in Aptitude Test Development." *Ed & Psychol Meas* 9:396–400 au '49. * (*PA* 26:3050)
35. BIERBAUM, WILLIAM B. *The Prediction of Scholastic Success of Graduate Students in Psychology by Means of the United States Employment Service General Aptitude Test Battery.* Master's thesis, University of Florida (Gainesville, Fla.), 1951.
36. MORGAN, MARCELLUS. *An Evaluation of the United States Employment Service General Aptitude Test Battery for the Field of Forestry.* Master's thesis, University of Florida (Gainesville, Fla.), 1951.
37. ASHE, MARGARET R. *Predicting Scholastic Success at Texas State College for Women Through the Use of the General Aptitude Test Battery: An Inquiry Based on a One Year's Study.* Master's thesis, Texas State College for Women (Denton, Tex.), 1952.
38. BOULGER, JOHN R. *The Generalized Distance Function and Differential Aptitude Testing.* Doctor's thesis, University of Minnesota (Minneapolis, Minn.), 1952. (*DA* 13:254)
39. DVORAK, BEATRICE J.; FOX, FRANCES C.; AND MEIGH, CHARLES. "Tests for Field Survey Interviewers." *J Marketing Res* 16:301–6 Ja '52. *
40. ISAACSON, LEE E. "Predictors of Success for Cooperative Occupational Education Classes in Kansas City, Missouri, High Schools." Abstract. *Am Psychol* 7:379 Jl '52. *
41. O'CONNOR, N. "The Prediction of Psychological Stability and Anxiety-Agressiveness From a Battery of Tests Administered to a Group of High Grade Male Mental Defectives." *J General Psychol* 46:3–17 Ja '52. * (*PA* 27:2055)
42. RALPH, RAY B., AND TAYLOR, CALVIN W. "The Role of Tests in the Medical Selection Program." *J Appl Psychol* 36:107–11 Ap '52. * (*PA* 27:674)
43. STORRS, SIBYLL V. *An Evaluative Comparison of the United States Employment Service General Aptitude Test Battery and the Wechsler Bellevue Intelligence Scale.* Master's thesis, University of Florida (Gainesville, Fla.), 1952.
44. STORRS, SIBYLL. "Evaluative Data on the G.A.T.B." *Personnel & Guid J* 31:87–90 N '52. * (*PA* 27:6164)
45. TAYLOR, EDWIN S. *The Prediction of Scholastic Success of Engineering Seniors With the General Aptitude Test Battery.* Master's thesis, University of Florida (Gainesville, Fla.), 1952.
46. BOULGER, JOHN R. "The Generalized Distance Function and Differential Aptitude Testing." Abstract. *Am Psychol* 8:324 Ag '53. *
47. GERBER, VERNON R. *Prediction of College Success From the General Aptitude Testing Battery.* Master's thesis, University of Toledo (Toledo, Ohio), 1953.
48. JEX, FRANK B., AND SORENSON, A. GARTH. "G.A.T.B. Scores as Predictors of College Grades." *Personnel & Guid J* 31:295–7 F '53. * (*PA* 28:1565)
49. MALECKI, HENRY R. *An Investigation of the Validity of the General Aptitude Test Battery for the Vocational Guidance of High School Graduates.* Doctor's thesis, Purdue University (Lafayette, Ind.), 1953.
50. MAPOU, ALBERT. "Development of General Working Population Norms for the USES General Aptitude Test Battery." Abstract. *Am Psychol* 8:401–2 Ag '53. *
51. MORGAN, JOSEPH P. *Investigation Into the Use at Senior High School Level of the U.S. Employment Service General Aptitude Test Battery.* Master's thesis, Boston College (Chestnut Hill, Mass.), 1953.
52. SCHENKEL, KENNETH F. *Tabulator Operator Selection, Emphasizing Relationships Among Aptitudes, Interests, Proficiency, Job- and Vocational-Satisfaction.* Doctor's thesis, University of Minnesota (Minneapolis, Minn.), 1953. (*DA* 13:1251)
53. "Validity Information Exchange, No. 7-050: D.O.T. Code 0-98.07, Manager, Insurance Office." *Personnel Psychol* 7:285 su '54. *
54. ANDERSON, MARY R. "Standardization of the General Aptitude Test Battery for Three Certification Areas at Stephens College." *Trans Kans Acad Sci* 57:354–65 S '54. *
55. MINNESOTA STATE EMPLOYMENT SERVICE. "Validity Information Exchange, No. 7-052:D.O.T. Code 1-25.64, Tabulating-Machine Operator." *Personnel Psychol* 7:287–8 su '54. *
56. MINNESOTA STATE EMPLOYMENT SERVICE. "Standardization of the GATB for the Occupation of Tabulating Machine Operator." *J Appl Psychol* 38:297–8 O '54. * (*PA* 29:6358)
57. UNITED STATES EMPLOYMENT SERVICE. "Validity Information Exchange, No. 7-001:D.O.T. Code 0-13.10, Dentist." *Personnel Psychol* 7:125 sp '54. *
58. UNITED STATES EMPLOYMENT SERVICE. "Validity Information Exchange, No. 7-002:D.O.T. Code 0-33.27, Nurse." *Personnel Psychol* 7:126 sp '54. *
59. UNITED STATES EMPLOYMENT SERVICE. "Validity Information Exchange, No. 7-003:D.O.T. Code 0-50.22, Chemist Assistant." *Personnel Psychol* 7:127 sp '54. *
60. UNITED STATES EMPLOYMENT SERVICE. "Validity Information Exchange, No. 7-006:D.O.T. Code 1-02.01, Bookkeeping-Machine Operator I." *Personnel Psychol* 7:132 sp '54. *
61. UNITED STATES EMPLOYMENT SERVICE. "Validity Information Exchange, No. 7-008:D.O.T. Code 1-06.02, Teller." *Personnel Psychol* 7:135 sp '54. *
62. UNITED STATES EMPLOYMENT SERVICE. "Validity Information Exchange, No. 7-013:D.O.T. Code 1-36.04, Survey Worker." *Personnel Psychol* 7:143 sp '54. *

63. UNITED STATES EMPLOYMENT SERVICE. "Validity Information Exchange, No. 7-015:D.O.T. Code 1-37.12, Stenographer; 1-37.32, Typist." *Personnel Psychol* 7:146 sp '54. *

64. UNITED STATES EMPLOYMENT SERVICE. "Validity Information Exchange, No. 7-020:D.O.T. Code 1-42.01, Central-Office Operator." *Personnel Psychol* 7:155 sp '54. *

65. UNITED STATES EMPLOYMENT SERVICE. "Validity Information Exchange, No. 7-025:D.O.T. Code 4-52.760, Pilot-Control Operator." *Personnel Psychol* 7:161 sp '54. *

66. UNITED STATES EMPLOYMENT SERVICE. "Validity Information Exchange, No. 7-026:D.O.T. Code 4-75.010, Machinist." *Personnel Psychol* 7:162 sp '54. *

67. UNITED STATES EMPLOYMENT SERVICE. "Validity Information Exchange, No. 7-027:D.O.T. Code 4-97.010, Electrician." *Personnel Psychol* 7:163 sp '54. *

68. UNITED STATES EMPLOYMENT SERVICE. "Validity Information Exchange, No. 7-028:D.O.T. Code 4-97.910, Electrician, Airplane." *Personnel Psychol* 7:164 sp '54. *

69. UNITED STATES EMPLOYMENT SERVICE. "Validity Information Exchange, No. 7-029:D.O.T. Code 5-25.110, Carpenter." *Personnel Psychol* 7:165 sp '54. *

70. UNITED STATES EMPLOYMENT SERVICE. "Validity Information Exchange, No. 7-030:D.O.T. Code 5-30.210, Plumber." *Personnel Psychol* 7:166 sp '54. *

71. UNITED STATES EMPLOYMENT SERVICE. "Validity Information Exchange, No. 7-031:D.O.T. Code 6-06.450, Cheese Wrapper." *Personnel Psychol* 7:167 sp '54. *

72. UNITED STATES EMPLOYMENT SERVICE. "Validity Information Exchange, No. 7-032:D.O.T. Code 6-12.341, Wrapper Layer and Examiner, Soft Work; 6-12.351, Wrapper Layer." *Personnel Psychol* 7:168 sp '54. *

73. UNITED STATES EMPLOYMENT SERVICE. "Validity Information Exchange, No. 7-033:D.O.T. Code 6-27.560 Through 6-27.589, Special Sewing Machine Operators, Garment; 6-27.530 Through 6-27.539, Standard Sewing Machine Operators, Garment." *Personnel Psychol* 7:169 sp '54. *

74. UNITED STATES EMPLOYMENT SERVICE. "Validity Information Exchange, No. 7-034:D.O.T. Code 6-54.052, Bomb-Fuse-Parts Assembler." *Personnel Psychol* 7:170 sp '54. *

75. UNITED STATES EMPLOYMENT SERVICE. "Validity Information Exchange, No. 7-035:D.O.T. Code 6-99.166, Electric-Motor Assembler." *Personnel Psychol* 7:171 sp '54. *

76. UNITED STATES EMPLOYMENT SERVICE. "Validity Information Exchange, No. 7-036:D.O.T. Code 7-00.020, Mounter; 7-00.016, Mounter I." *Personnel Psychol* 7:172 sp '54. *

77. UNITED STATES EMPLOYMENT SERVICE. "Validity Information Exchange, No. 7-037:D.O.T. Code 7-05.901, Outboard-Motor Assembler III." *Personnel Psychol* 7:173 sp '54. *

78. UNITED STATES EMPLOYMENT SERVICE. "Validity Information Exchange, No. 7-038:D.O.T. Code 7-16.900, Decorator, Hand." *Personnel Psychol* 7:174 sp '54. *

79. UNITED STATES EMPLOYMENT SERVICE. "Validity Information Exchange, No. 7-039:D.O.T. Code 8-04.10, Fruit Sorter." *Personnel Psychol* 7:175 sp '54. *

80. UNITED STATES EMPLOYMENT SERVICE. "Validity Information Exchange, No. 7-040:D.O.T. Code 8-09.01, Laborer, Poultry." *Personnel Psychol* 7:176 sp '54. *

81. UNITED STATES EMPLOYMENT SERVICE. "Validity Information Exchange, No. 7-041:D.O.T. Code 8-09.11, Slaughtering and Meat Packing Workers." *Personnel Psychol* 7:177 sp '54. *

82. UNITED STATES EMPLOYMENT SERVICE. "Validity Information Exchange, No. 7-042:D.O.T. Code 8-49.01, Bindery Workers." *Personnel Psychol* 7:178 sp '54. *

83. UNITED STATES EMPLOYMENT SERVICE. "Validity Information Exchange, No. 7-043:D.O.T. Code 8-53.01, Table Worker." *Personnel Psychol* 7:179 sp '54. *

84. UNITED STATES EMPLOYMENT SERVICE. "Validity Information Exchange, No. 7-044:D.O.T. Code 9-68.01, Packer, Tea Bag." *Personnel Psychol* 7:180 sp '54. *

85. UNITED STATES EMPLOYMENT SERVICE. "Validity Information Exchange, No. 7-046:D.O.T. Code 0-15.01, 0-16.01, 0-17.01, 0-19.01, Engineer." *Personnel Psychol* 7:280–1 su '54. *

86. UNITED STATES EMPLOYMENT SERVICE. "Validity Information Exchange, No. 7-047:D.O.T. Code 0-25.10, Pharmacist." *Personnel Psychol* 7:282 su '54. *

87. UNITED STATES EMPLOYMENT SERVICE. "Validity Information Exchange, No. 7-048:D.O.T. Code 0-26.10, Physician." *Personnel Psychol* 7:283 su '54. *

88. UNITED STATES EMPLOYMENT SERVICE. "Validity Information Exchange, No. 7-049:D.O.T. Code 0-30.02, Teacher, Nursery School." *Personnel Psychol* 7:284 su '54. *

89. UNITED STATES EMPLOYMENT SERVICE. "Validity Information Exchange, No. 7-051:D.O.T. Code 1-17.02, File Clerk II." *Personnel Psychol* 7:286 su '54. *

90. UNITED STATES EMPLOYMENT SERVICE. "Validity Information Exchange, No. 7-054:D.O.T. Code 1-44.12, Ticket Agent (Reservation Clerk)." *Personnel Psychol* 7:290 su '54. *

91. UNITED STATES EMPLOYMENT SERVICE. "Validity Information Exchange, No. 7-056:D.O.T. Code 2-38.20, Nurse, Practical." *Personnel Psychol* 7:292 su '54. *

92. UNITED STATES EMPLOYMENT SERVICE. "Validity Information Exchange, No. 7-057:D.O.T. Code 4-35.720, Upholsterer II." *Personnel Psychol* 7:293 su '54. *

93. UNITED STATES EMPLOYMENT SERVICE. "Validity Information Exchange, No. 7-058:D.O.T. Code 4-44.010, Compositor, Hand." *Personnel Psychol* 7:294 su '54. *

94. UNITED STATES EMPLOYMENT SERVICE. "Validity Information Exchange, No. 7-059:D.O.T. Code 4-48.010, Cylinder-Press Man; 4-48.030, Web-Press Man." *Personnel Psychol* 7:295 su '54. *

95. UNITED STATES EMPLOYMENT SERVICE. "Validity Information Exchange, No. 7-060:D.O.T. Code 4-84.012, Shipfitter." *Personnel Psychol* 7:296 su '54. *

96. UNITED STATES EMPLOYMENT SERVICE. "Validity Information Exchange, No. 7-061:D.O.T. Code 4-88.622, Sheet Metal Worker." *Personnel Psychol* 7:297 su '54. *

97. UNITED STATES EMPLOYMENT SERVICE. "Validity Information Exchange, No. 7-062:D.O.T. Code 5-81.010, Automobile Mechanic." *Personnel Psychol* 7:298 su '54. *

98. UNITED STATES EMPLOYMENT SERVICE. "Validity Information Exchange, No. 7-063:D.O.T. Code 5-83.123, Calculating-Machine Serviceman." *Personnel Psychol* 7:299 su '54. *

99. UNITED STATES EMPLOYMENT SERVICE. "Validity Information Exchange, No. 7-066:D.O.T. Code 6-14.171, Boarder II; 6-14.173, Boarding-Machine Operator." *Personnel Psychol* 7:302 su '54. *

100. UNITED STATES EMPLOYMENT SERVICE. "Validity Information Exchange, No. 7-067:D.O.T. Code 6-88.627, Forming-Press Operator." *Personnel Psychol* 7:303 su '54. *

101. UNITED STATES EMPLOYMENT SERVICE. "Validity Information Exchange, No. 7-068:D.O.T. Code 8-98.71, Record Pressman." *Personnel Psychol* 7:304 su '54. *

102. UNITED STATES EMPLOYMENT SERVICE. "Validity Information Exchange, No. 7-072:D.O.T. Code 1-18.33, Claims Taker; 0-68.71, Employment Interviewer." *Personnel Psychol* 7:409–10 au '54. *

103. UNITED STATES EMPLOYMENT SERVICE. "Validity Information Exchange, No. 7-080:D.O.T. Code 8-27.77, Carding Machine Operator." *Personnel Psychol* 7:427 au '54. *

104. UNITED STATES EMPLOYMENT SERVICE. "Validity Information Exchange, No. 7-081:D.O.T. Code 8-53.51, Laborer (Fireworks)." *Personnel Psychol* 7:428 au '54. *

105. UNITED STATES EMPLOYMENT SERVICE. "Validity Information Exchange, No. 7-083:D.O.T. Code 0-39.93, Dietitian." *Personnel Psychol* 7:555 w '54. *

106. UNITED STATES EMPLOYMENT SERVICE. "Validity Information Exchange, No. 7-088:D.O.T. Code 5-83.411, Radio Repairman I." *Personnel Psychol* 7:563–4 w '54. *

107. UNITED STATES EMPLOYMENT SERVICE. "Validity Information Exchange, No. 7-092:D.O.T. Code 6-19.041, Spinner, Ring Frame." *Personnel Psychol* 7:570 w '54. *

108. UNITED STATES EMPLOYMENT SERVICE. "Validity Information Exchange, No. 7-093:D.O.T. Code 7-00.070, Light-Bulb Assembler." *Personnel Psychol* 7:571 w '54. *

109. WISE, ROBERTA M. *The Educational Significance of the General Aptitude Test Battery for Howard University School of Pharmacy.* Master's thesis, Howard University (Washington, D.C.), 1954.

110. BLACKBURN, JESSIE B. *The Use of the General Aptitude Test Battery Recorded Interviews in Vocational Counseling.* Master's thesis, Oregon State College (Corvallis, Ore.), 1955.

111. DVORAK, BEATRICE J. "New G.A.T.B. Occupational Aptitude Pattern: Norm Structure." *Voc Guid Q* 3:110–2 su '55. *

112. GJERNES, OSCAR. *The Use of the General Aptitude Test Battery to Predict Success for Students in Professional Courses in Agriculture and Chemical Technology.* Master's thesis, North Dakota Agricultural College (Fargo, N.D.), 1955.

113. MADDEN, GORDON J. *The Standardization of the General Aptitude Test Battery and Development of Selection Aptitude Test Battery for Student Nurse.* Master's thesis, Marquette University (Milwaukee, Wis.), 1955.

114. MAPOU, ALBERT. "Development of General Working Population Norms for the USES General Aptitude Test Battery." *J Appl Psychol* 39:130–3 Ap '55. * (PA 30:1720)

115. SORENSON, GARTH, AND SENIOR, NOEL. "Changes in GATB Scores With College Training." *Calif J Ed Res* 6:170–3 S '55. * (PA 30:6340)

116. TRAEGER, CARL. *Effectiveness of the United States Employment Service General Aptitude Test Battery in Employment Counseling of High-School Seniors.* Doctor's thesis, University of Wisconsin (Madison, Wis.), 1955.

117. UNITED STATES EMPLOYMENT SERVICE. "Validity Information Exchange, No. 8-01:D.O.T. Code 0-13.10. Dentist." *Personnel Psychol* 8:105–6 sp '55. *

118. UNITED STATES EMPLOYMENT SERVICE. "Validity Information Exchange, No. 8-02:D.O.T. Code 0-34.10, Veterinarian." *Personnel Psychol* 8:107–8 sp '55. *

119. UNITED STATES EMPLOYMENT SERVICE. "Validity Information Exchange, No. 8-05:D.O.T. Code 1-38.01, Stock Clerk II." *Personnel Psychol* 8:113 sp '55. *

120. UNITED STATES EMPLOYMENT SERVICE. "Validity Information Exchange, No. 8-06:D.O.T. Code 2-42.20, Nurse Aide." *Personnel Psychol* 8:114 sp '55. *

121. UNITED STATES EMPLOYMENT SERVICE. "Validity Information Exchange, No. 8-07:D.O.T. Code 4-25.030, Dressmaker." *Personnel Psychol* 8:115 sp '55. *

122. UNITED STATES EMPLOYMENT SERVICE. "Validity Information Exchange, No. 8-08:D.O.T. Code 4-44.010, Compositor, Hand and Machine." *Personnel Psychol* 8:116–7 sp '55. *

123. UNITED STATES EMPLOYMENT SERVICE. "Validity Information Exchange, No. 8-10:D.O.T. Code 6-27.513, Seamer." *Personnel Psychol* 8:120 sp '55. *

124. UNITED STATES EMPLOYMENT SERVICE. "Validity Information Exchange, No. 8-11:D.O.T. Code 6-57.174, Pressman." *Personnel Psychol* 8:121 sp '55. *

General Aptitude Test Battery

125. UNITED STATES EMPLOYMENT SERVICE. "Validity Information Exchange, No. 8-12:D.O.T. Code 8-53.01, Laborer; 7-68.015, Filling-Machine Operator II; 9-68.20, Labeler, Hand; 9-68.10, Laborer, Container Capping; 9-68.30, Packer II; 9-68.20, Stamper II." *Personnel Psychol* 8:122–3 sp '55. *

126. UNITED STATES EMPLOYMENT SERVICE. "Validity Information Exchange, No. 8-15:D.O.T. Code 5-30.010, Pipe Fitter; 5-30.210, Plumber." *Personnel Psychol* 8:264–6 su '55. *

127. UNITED STATES EMPLOYMENT SERVICE. "Validity Information Exchange, No. 8-18:D.O.T. Code 6-14.341, Pairer (Hosiery)." *Personnel Psychol* 8:269 su '55. *

128. UNITED STATES EMPLOYMENT SERVICE. "Validity Information Exchange, No. 8-20:D.O.T. Code 8-12.10, Stripper, Hand (Tobacco)." *Personnel Psychol* 8:271 su '55. *

129. UNITED STATES EMPLOYMENT SERVICE. "Validity Information Exchange, No. 8-21:D.O.T. Code 1-04.01, Clerk, General; 1-05.01, Clerk, General Office; 1-25.02, Billing Machine Operator; 1-25.13, Comptometer Operator." *Personnel Psychol* 8:375–6 au '55. *

130. UNITED STATES EMPLOYMENT SERVICE. "Validity Information Exchange, No. 8-22:D.O.T. Code 1-18.65, Stock Chaser II." *Personnel Psychol* 8:377 au '55. *

131. UNITED STATES EMPLOYMENT SERVICE. "Validity Information Exchange, No. 8-24:D.O.T. Code 4-35.720, Upholsterer II." *Personnel Psychol* 8:379–80 au '55. *

132. UNITED STATES EMPLOYMENT SERVICE. "Validity Information Exchange, No. 8-25:D.O.T. Code 6-24.234, Decorator." *Personnel Psychol* 8:381 au '55. *

133. UNITED STATES EMPLOYMENT SERVICE. "Validity Information Exchange, No. 8-28:D.O.T. Code 0-97.61, Manager, City District." *Personnel Psychol* 8:493 w '55. *

134. UNITED STATES EMPLOYMENT SERVICE. "Validity Information Exchange, No. 8-29:D.O.T. Code 6-14.235, Stocking Inspector I." *Personnel Psychol* 8:494 w '55. *

135. UNITED STATES EMPLOYMENT SERVICE. "Validity Information Exchange, No. 8-30:D.O.T. Code 6-24.235, Straw Hat Sewing Machine Operator I; 6-27.530 through 6-27.539, Standard Sewing Machine Operators, Garment; 6-27.560 through 6-27.589, Special Sewing Machine Operators, Garment." *Personnel Psychol* 8:495–6 w '55. *

136. UNITED STATES EMPLOYMENT SERVICE. "Validity Information Exchange, No. 8-31:D.O.T. Code 6-66.361, Paster." *Personnel Psychol* 8:497 w '55. *

137. UNITED STATES EMPLOYMENT SERVICE. "Validity Information Exchange, No. 8-32:D.O.T. Code 7-35.100, Routeman." *Personnel Psychol* 8:498 w '55. *

138. UNITED STATES EMPLOYMENT SERVICE. "Validity Information Exchange, No. 8-33:D.O.T. Code 8-66.01, Fettler." *Personnel Psychol* 8:499 w '55. *

139. UNITED STATES EMPLOYMENT SERVICE. "Validity Information Exchange, No. 8-34:D.O.T. Code 9-00.91, Assembler, Dry Cell Battery." *Personnel Psychol* 8:500 w '55. *

140. DVORAK, BEATRICE J. "Advantages of the Multiple Cut-Off Method." *Personnel Psychol* 9:45–7 sp '56. * (*PA* 31:5188)

141. DVORAK, BEATRICE J. "GATB in Foreign Countries." *J Appl Psychol* 40:197–200 Je '56. * (*PA* 31:6726)

142. DVORAK, BEATRICE J. "The General Aptitude Test Battery." Comments by Donald E. Super. *Personnel & Guid J* 35:145–54 N '56. *

143. SAMUELSON, CECIL O. "The General Aptitude Test Battery in Predicting Success of Vocational School Students." *J Ed Res* 50:175–82 N '56. * (*PA* 32:958)

144. UNITED STATES EMPLOYMENT SERVICE. "Validity Information Exchange, No. 9-3:D.O.T. Code 0-30.11, Teacher." *Personnel Psychol* 9:106 sp '56. *

145. UNITED STATES EMPLOYMENT SERVICE. "Validity Information Exchange, No. 9-6:D.O.T. Code 1-57.40, Claims Examiner." *Personnel Psychol* 9:111 sp '56. *

146. UNITED STATES EMPLOYMENT SERVICE. "Validity Information Exchange, No. 9-8:D.O.T. Code 2-32.15, Beauty Operator." *Personnel Psychol* 9:113–4 sp '56. *

147. UNITED STATES EMPLOYMENT SERVICE. "Validity Information Exchange, No. 9-9:D.O.T. Code 3-48.94, Artificial-Breeding Technician." *Personnel Psychol* 9:115 sp '56. *

148. UNITED STATES EMPLOYMENT SERVICE. "Validity Information Exchange, No. 9-10:D.O.T. Code 4-19.332, Mender; 6-19.331, Burler." *Personnel Psychol* 9:116 sp '56. *

149. UNITED STATES EMPLOYMENT SERVICE. "Validity Information Exchange, No. 9-11:D.O.T. Code 4-55.030, Stillman." *Personnel Psychol* 9:117 sp '56. *

150. UNITED STATES EMPLOYMENT SERVICE. "Validity Information Exchange, No. 9-12:D.O.T. Code 4-97.010, Electrician." *Personnel Psychol* 9:118–9 sp '56. *

151. UNITED STATES EMPLOYMENT SERVICE. "Validity Information Exchange, No. 9-13:D.O.T. Code 4-97.910, Electrician, Airplane." *Personnel Psychol* 9:121–2 sp '56. *

152. UNITED STATES EMPLOYMENT SERVICE. "Validity Information Exchange, No. 9-15:D.O.T. Code 5-53.235, Central-Office Repairman." *Personnel Psychol* 9:124 sp '56. *

153. UNITED STATES EMPLOYMENT SERVICE. "Validity Information Exchange, No. 9-16:D.O.T. Code 5-80.100, Airplane Mechanic." *Personnel Psychol* 9:125 sp '56. *

154. UNITED STATES EMPLOYMENT SERVICE. "Validity Information Exchange, No. 9-17:D.O.T. Code 6-12.043, Stemmer, Machine (Tobacco)." *Personnel Psychol* 9:126–7 sp '56. *

155. UNITED STATES EMPLOYMENT SERVICE. "Validity Information Exchange, No. 9-18:D.O.T. Code 7-57.501, Presser, Hand." *Personnel Psychol* 9:128 sp '56.

156. UNITED STATES EMPLOYMENT SERVICE. "Validity Information Exchange, No. 9-20:D.O.T. Code 9-57.21, Continuous Towel Roller; 9-57.21, Flatwork Catcher; 9-57.21, Flatwork Feeder; 9-57.21, Flatwork Folder." *Personnel Psychol* 9:130 sp '56. *

157. UNITED STATES EMPLOYMENT SERVICE. "Validity Information Exchange, No. 9-22:D.O.T. Code 0-50.04, X-Ray Technician." *Personnel Psychol* 9:248 su '56. *

158. UNITED STATES EMPLOYMENT SERVICE. "Validity Information Exchange, No. 9-23:D.O.T. Code 2-42.20, Nurse Aide." *Personnel Psychol* 9:249–50 su '56. *

159. UNITED STATES EMPLOYMENT SERVICE. "Validity Information Exchange, No. 9-24:D.O.T. Code 4-80.010, Sheet-Metal Worker." *Personnel Psychol* 9:251 su '56. *

160. UNITED STATES EMPLOYMENT SERVICE. "Validity Information Exchange, No. 9-25:D.O.T. Code 5-03.552, Assemblyman I; 5-03.562, Plumber, Aircraft; 5-03.572, Engine-Installation Assembler; 5-03.572, Rigger I." *Personnel Psychol* 9:252 su '56. *

161. UNITED STATES EMPLOYMENT SERVICE. "Validity Information Exchange, No. 9-27:D.O.T. Code 6-27.513, Seamer." *Personnel Psychol* 9:255–6 su '56. *

162. UNITED STATES EMPLOYMENT SERVICE. "Validity Information Exchange, No. 9-28:D.O.T. Code 7-00.904, Assembler, Electrical Accessories II." *Personnel Psychol* 9:257 su '56. *

163. UNITED STATES EMPLOYMENT SERVICE. "Validity Information Exchange, No. 9-29:D.O.T. Code 7-13.043, Fishing-Rod Assembler." *Personnel Psychol* 9:258 su '56. *

164. UNITED STATES EMPLOYMENT SERVICE. "Validity Information Exchange, No. 9-30:D.O.T. Code 8-04.10, Peeler, Hand." *Personnel Psychol* 9:259 su '56. *

165. UNITED STATES EMPLOYMENT SERVICE. "Validity Information Exchange, No. 9-37:D.O.T. Code 4-01.100, Baker (Bake. Prod.); 4-01.400, Baker (Hotel & Rest.)." *Personnel Psychol* 9:383 au '56. *

166. UNITED STATES EMPLOYMENT SERVICE. "Validity Information Exchange, No. 9-38:D.O.T. Code 5-86.514, Multiple-Photographic-Printer Operator." *Personnel Psychol* 9:384 au '56. *

167. UNITED STATES EMPLOYMENT SERVICE. "Validity Information Exchange, No. 9-39:D.O.T. Code 8-42.01, Take-Off Man (Paper Goods)." *Personnel Psychol* 9:385 au '56. *

168. UNITED STATES EMPLOYMENT SERVICE. "Validity Information Exchange, No. 9-40:D.O.T. Code 8-42.01, Scrapper (Paper Goods)." *Personnel Psychol* 9:386 au '56. *

169. UNITED STATES EMPLOYMENT SERVICE. "Validity Information Exchange, No. 9-42:D.O.T. Code 0-30.11, Teacher, Grade or Grammar School; 0-31.01, Teacher, High School." *Personnel Psychol* 9:518–9 w '56. *

170. UNITED STATES EMPLOYMENT SERVICE. "Validity Information Exchange, No. 9-43:D.O.T. Code 0-46.01, Clothes Designer." *Personnel Psychol* 9:520–1 w '56. *

171. UNITED STATES EMPLOYMENT SERVICE. "Validity Information Exchange, No. 9-48:D.O.T. Code 6-66.311, Tile Sorter; 6-66.361, Paster." *Personnel Psychol* 9:528–9 w '56. *

172. UNITED STATES EMPLOYMENT SERVICE. "Validity Information Exchange, No. 9-49:D.O.T. Code 6-85.060, Welder, Spot." *Personnel Psychol* 9:530 w '56. *

173. NICKSICK, THEODORE, JR. *Relationship Between Aptitudes and Major Fields of Study.* Doctor's thesis, North Texas State College (Denton, Tex.), 1957. (*DA* 17:1030)

174. UNITED STATES EMPLOYMENT SERVICE. "Validity Information Exchange, No. 10-1:D.O.T. Code 0-65.20, Director, Funeral; 0-65.10, Embalmer." *Personnel Psychol* 10:73–4 sp '57. *

175. UNITED STATES EMPLOYMENT SERVICE. "Validity Information Exchange, No. 10-2:D.O.T. Code 1-25.13, Comptometer Operator." *Personnel Psychol* 10:75–6 sp '57. *

176. UNITED STATES EMPLOYMENT SERVICE. "Validity Information Exchange, No. 10-4:D.O.T. Code 2-26.32, Cook (Hotel & Rest.)." *Personnel Psychol* 10:79 sp '57. *

177. UNITED STATES EMPLOYMENT SERVICE. "Validity Information Exchange, No. 10-6:D.O.T. Code: 5-83.322, Knitting-Machine Fixer." *Personnel Psychol* 10:81 sp '57. *

178. UNITED STATES EMPLOYMENT SERVICE. "Validity Information Exchange, No. 10-7:D.O.T. Code 7-00.971, Toy Train Assembler; 9-13.01, Assembler (Toys and Games)." *Personnel Psychol* 10:82–3 sp '57. *

179. UNITED STATES EMPLOYMENT SERVICE. "Validity Information Exchange, No. 10-8:D.O.T. Code 8-04.10, Laborer; 8-04.10, Vegetable Picker." *Personnel Psychol* 10:84–5 sp '57. *

180. UNITED STATES EMPLOYMENT SERVICE. "Validity Information Exchange, No. 10-9:D.O.T. Code 8-04.10, Corn-Husking Machine Operator; 8-04.10, Corn-Cutting Machine Operator." *Personnel Psychol* 10:86–7 sp '57. *

181. UNITED STATES EMPLOYMENT SERVICE. "Validity Information Exchange, No. 10-10:D.O.T. Code 8-04.10, Peeling-and-Coring-Machine Operator." *Personnel Psychol* 10:88 sp '57. *

182. UNITED STATES EMPLOYMENT SERVICE. "Validity Information Exchange, No. 10-11:D.O.T. Code 8-57.51, Cementer." *Personnel Psychol* 10:89 sp '57. *

183. UNITED STATES EMPLOYMENT SERVICE. "Validity Information Exchange, No. 10-18:D.O.T. Code 4-48.010, Cylinder-Press Man; 4-48.040, Embossing-Press Operator; 4-48.041, Engraving-Press Operator; 4-48.050, Offset-Press Man; 4-48.011, Overlay Cutter; 4-48.020, Platen-Press Man; 4-48.030, Web-Press Man." *Personnel Psychol* 10:209–12 su '57. *

184. UNITED STATES EMPLOYMENT SERVICE. "Validity Information Exchange, No. 10-19:D.O.T. Code 4-88.018, Cold Mill

General Aptitude Test Battery

Operator; 4-88.018, Hot Mill Operator; 6-94.821, Payoff Operator; 6-94.822, Rewind Operator; 6-94.205, Slitting-Machine Operator II." *Personnel Psychol* 10:213-4 su '57. *

185. UNITED STATES EMPLOYMENT SERVICE. "Validity Information Exchange, No. 10-20:D.O.T. Code 6-88.807, Crusher Inspector; 6-88.808, Mill-End Inspector; 6-88.801, Mill Inspector; 6-88.806, Pipe & Coupling Sizer; 6-88.804, Pipe Walker; 6-88.808, Thread Inspector." *Personnel Psychol* 10:215-7 su '57. *

186. UNITED STATES EMPLOYMENT SERVICE. "Validity Information Exchange, No. 10-21:D.O.T. Code 8-10.25, Nut Sorter I." *Personnel Psychol* 10:218 su '57. *

187. UNITED STATES EMPLOYMENT SERVICE. "Validity Information Exchange, No. 10-22:D.O.T. Code 9-68.01, Bagger II; 9-68.30, Bag Sealer; 9-68.30, Packer II; 9-68.01, Weigher II." *Personnel Psychol* 10:219-21 su '57. *

188. UNITED STATES EMPLOYMENT SERVICE. "Validity Information Exchange, No. 10-23:D.O.T. Code 9-68.35, Packer (Agric.)." *Personnel Psychol* 10:222-4 su '57. *

189. UNITED STATES EMPLOYMENT SERVICE. "Validity Information Exchange, No. 10-26:D.O.T. Code 4-32.100, Cabinetmaker I." *Personnel Psychol* 10:345 au '57. *

190. UNITED STATES EMPLOYMENT SERVICE. "Validity Information Exchange, No. 10-27:D.O.T. Code 5-83.444, Electronics Technician." *Personnel Psychol* 10:346 au '57. *

191. UNITED STATES EMPLOYMENT SERVICE. "Validity Information Exchange, No. 10-28:D.O.T. Code 6-19.635, Weaver." *Personnel Psychol* 10:347-8 au '57. *

192. UNITED STATES EMPLOYMENT SERVICE. "Validity Information Exchange, No. 10-29:D.O.T. Code 6-41.940, Paper Sorter and Counter." *Personnel Psychol* 10:349-50 au '57. *

193. UNITED STATES EMPLOYMENT SERVICE. "Validity Information Exchange, No. 10-30:D.O.T. Code 6-94.515, Coil Assembler; 8-93.41, Unit Assembler; 8-94.51, Unit Assembler." *Personnel Psychol* 10:351 au '57. *

194. UNITED STATES EMPLOYMENT SERVICE. "Validity Information Exchange, No. 10-32:D.O.T. Code 7-68.831, Candy-Wrapping Machine Operator II." *Personnel Psychol* 10:354 au '57. *

195. UNITED STATES EMPLOYMENT SERVICE. "Validity Information Exchange, No. 10-45:D.O.T. Code 1-04.01, Copy Holder; 1-10.07, Proofreader; 1-10.07, Reader, First II." *Personnel Psychol* 10:494-5 w '57. *

196. UNITED STATES EMPLOYMENT SERVICE. "Validity Information Exchange, No. 10-48:D.O.T. Code 1-18.31, Employment Clerk." *Personnel Psychol* 10:500-1 w '57. *

197. UNITED STATES EMPLOYMENT SERVICE. "Validity Information Exchange, No. 10-55:D.O.T. Code 4-73.520, Pantographer." *Personnel Psychol* 10:516 w '57. *

198. UNITED STATES EMPLOYMENT SERVICE. "Validity Information Exchange, No. 10-56:D.O.T. Code 5-17.010, Patternmaker, Metal; 5-17.020, Patternmaker, Wood." *Personnel Psychol* 10:517 w '57. *

199. UNITED STATES EMPLOYMENT SERVICE. "Validity Information Exchange, No. 10-57:D.O.T. Code 5-24.010, Bricklayer." *Personnel Psychol* 10:518 w '57. *

200. UNITED STATES EMPLOYMENT SERVICE. "Validity Information Exchange, No. 10-58:D.O.T. Code 5-51.010, Powerhouse Engineer I." *Personnel Psychol* 10:519 w '57. *

201. UNITED STATES EMPLOYMENT SERVICE. "Validity Information Exchange, No. 10-59:D.O.T. Code 6-27.512, Glove Sewer." *Personnel Psychol* 10:520 w '57. *

202. UNITED STATES EMPLOYMENT SERVICE. "Validity Information Exchange, No. 10-60:D.O.T. Code 7-03.040, Insulation-Blanket Maker." *Personnel Psychol* 10:521-2 w '57. *

203. HAY, JOHN E. "The GATB at Work in Vocational Counseling." *Voc Guid Q* 6:174-6 su '58. *

204. UNITED STATES EMPLOYMENT SERVICE. "Validity Information Exchange, No. 11-1:D.O.T. Code 0-50.01, Medical Technologist." *Personnel Psychol* 11:97-8 sp '58. *

205. UNITED STATES EMPLOYMENT SERVICE. "Validity Information Exchange, No. 11-4:D.O.T. Code 5-80.100, Airplane Mechanic." *Personnel Psychol* 11:105 sp '58. *

206. UNITED STATES EMPLOYMENT SERVICE. "Validity Information Exchange, No. 11-10:D.O.T. Code 6-66.311, Tile Sorter; 8-66.01, Tile Placer; 6-66.361, Paster." *Personnel Psychol* 11:121-3 sp '58. *

207. UNITED STATES EMPLOYMENT SERVICE. "Validity Information Exchange, No. 11-11:D.O.T. Code 0-01.20, Accountant, General; 0-01.60, Auditor." *Personnel Psychol* 11:237-9 su '58. *

208. UNITED STATES EMPLOYMENT SERVICE. "Validity Information Exchange, No. 11-12:D.O.T. Code 4-76.040, Tool-and-Die Maker." *Personnel Psychol* 11:240-1 su '58. *

209. UNITED STATES EMPLOYMENT SERVICE. "Validity Information Exchange, No. 11-19:D.O.T. Code 5-83.411, Radio Repairman; 5-83.416, Television Service and Repairman." *Personnel Psychol* 11:260-2 su '58. *

ANDREW L. COMREY, *Associate Professor of Psychology, University of California, Los Angeles, California.*

The *General Aptitude Test Battery* (Form B-1001) was reviewed in *The Fourth Mental Measurements Yearbook.* Forms B-1002A and B-1002B constitute a revised battery in which separate answer sheets have been introduced for paper and pencil tests 1–7. The revised battery consists of 12 separately timed objective tests: (1) Name Comparison, 6 minutes; subject compares two names which may or may not differ slightly, and judges them to be identical or different; similar to traditional clerical speed and accuracy tests. (2) Computation, 6 minutes; subject does addition, subtraction, multiplication, and division; similar to the common numerical ability test. (3) Three-Dimensional Space, 6 minutes; a three-dimensional figure is shown flattened into two dimensions; subject chooses among several drawings the one which shows how the figure would look in three dimensions. (4) Vocabulary, 6 minutes; four words are given; subject picks two that are synonyms or two that are antonyms, whichever is available. (5) Tool Matching, 5 minutes; a test drawing of a tool is accompanied by several similar drawings and one identical drawing, which the subject must identify; similar to the traditional perceptual speed test. (6) Arithmetic Reasoning, 7 minutes; subject solves the usual thought problem in arithmetic. (7) Form Matching, 6 minutes; subject must find a figure in a second group which is identical to each test figure in the first group. (8) Mark Making, paper and pencil, 10 seconds; the subject makes an underlined quotation mark in each square. (9) Place, apparatus, 15 seconds; using both hands, subject transfers pegs from one set of holes to another; three trials. (10) Turn, apparatus, 30 seconds; using the preferred hand, subject inverts and replaces pegs. (11) Assemble, apparatus, 90 seconds; subject picks up a rivet with the preferred hand, puts a washer on it with the other hand, and places the assembly in a preassigned hole. (12) Disassemble, apparatus, 60 seconds; subject does the reverse of what he did in Part 11.

Tests C and G of the original Form B-1001 have been dropped in the new edition because they apparently did not add to what was accomplished alone by Part K of Form B-1001, identical to Part 8 in the new editions. Part F in the old edition was dropped also, because Part H, or Part 3 in the new edition, could do about as well alone. Otherwise, the 12 tests in the two-form new edition are virtually alternate forms of corresponding tests in the old edition, being identical for Parts 8–12.

Factor studies of Form B-1001 provided the basis for isolation of nine factors for which scores are derived from the 12 test scores. These factors, and the equally weighted parts used to measure them are: (G) intelligence, 3, 4, 6; (V) verbal aptitude, 4; (N) numerical aptitude, 2, 6; (S) spatial aptitude, 3; (P) form perception, 5, 7; (Q) clerical perception, 1; (K) motor coordination, 8; (F) finger dexterity, 11, 12; and (M) manual dexterity, 9, 10. Factor, or aptitude, scores, are expressed for each subject in scaled form.

Reliability data, unfortunately, are given only for the factor aptitude scores, rather than for the individual tests. Reliabilities based on combined test-retest data from several studies totaling about 500 males and 500 females are in the .80's for G, V, N, and S; in the .70's for P, Q, K, and M; and in the .60's for F. Alternate-form reliabilities for Parts 1–7 are generally in the .80's. Most of the reliability studies cited are based upon student rather than working groups. It is to be expected that reliabilities for individual tests would be lower than reliabilities for composite aptitude scores. Those for Parts 11 and 12 particularly are too low.

Normative data have been collected on 4,000 workers, typical of the general working population, according to the 1940 census, with respect to age, sex, educational, occupational, and geographical distribution. These excellent data are for Form B-1001, however, rather than for the revised forms. Extrapolations for B-1002 have been made upon the basis of administering B-1001 and B-1002A to smaller student groups. Norms for B-1002B are in turn extrapolated from the extrapolated results for B-1001A by giving both forms to other student groups. With the vast data collection facilities of the United States Employment Service, it would seem reasonable to expect direct norms on the B-1002 forms themselves, although probably no great differences would be found. A very considerable amount of valuable data is given on the test performance of different occupational groups.

Data on validity are being continuously collected for this battery of tests. The various state employment offices collaborate with the USES in validating the test battery in local work situations. As far as possible, the validation procedure for each new situation is to carry out an aptitude oriented job analysis followed by the development of a suitable criterion of proficiency. Production records, earnings, work samples, and ratings may be used. The test battery is administered. Validity data are obtained in the form of a tetrachoric correlation between criterion and aptitude scores. Concurrent and longitudinal designs are utilized, although the latter type is relatively uncommon, except with student groups. On the basis of the statistical finding and other considerations, critical aptitudes are selected for the occupation and cutting scores determined for each aptitude. This is done in such a way as to eliminate about one third of the individuals. Where possible, cross validation is undertaken, although this has not been common so far. An attempt is made to fit the occupation into an already established occupational aptitude pattern (a set of two to four aptitudes with cutting scores) of which there are 22 at present. Thus, if the occupation in question shares two of three, or three of four critical aptitudes with an established occupational aptitude pattern, with cutting scores within 10 points, it is grouped with that particular pattern. If not, it is held out for later grouping with a new pattern, and may be used singly in the meantime.

These procedures represent a very rough compromise with practical realities and are probably justified with the amount of information now available. More precise procedures should be adopted eventually. For example, the cutting score approach should be replaced except where minimum aptitude levels are shown to exist and compensatory effects in other aptitudes are shown to be lacking. At present, cutting scores are established too arbitrarily. Such coarse grouping of occupations should be stopped and more aptitudes should be considered in making an evaluation.

Over 50 per cent of the occupations considered in counseling are placed in one of the 22 established occupational aptitude patterns merely on the basis of job analysis and armchair thinking, although the entire structure is being placed more and more upon an empirical basis as additional validation data are collected. Unfortunately, the reporting of validity studies is not complete, being confined to tabular summarization of validity coefficients and a few other data. Studies are carried out by local office personnel under conditions which

General Aptitude Test Battery

probably fail to meet scientific standards in many instances. Tetrachoric coefficients are used with small samples, in spite of the large sampling error. It seems safe to conclude, however, that validation has reached the point where these tests can definitely be said to have considerable value in many work situations. The amount of information now available is only a fraction of what is needed; nevertheless it is extensive in comparison with what is available for other tests.

The foundation of factorial studies upon which this multiple factor battery is based leaves much to be desired. Several exploratory studies using relatively small numbers of variables and trainee groups were carried out about 1942, yielding 11 factors of which only 9 are presently used. Many more carefully designed factorial studies on a larger scale, including a wide variety of variables, are needed to verify the basic factorial structure. These studies should attempt particularly to clarify the nature of the GATB general intelligence factor. This factor is defined by three tests which are also used to define other factors, introducing artificial dependence between aptitude scores. More evidence is needed to be certain that a system of correlated ability factors would not be superior.

The factorial coverage of this battery is not great enough. While Guilford has recently pointed to the existence of at least 40 ability factors, only about 9 are covered here. Furthermore, all the tests are speeded, every paper and pencil test correlating over .4 with the perceptual speed test. The apparatus tests have lower correlations, but their reliabilities are also lower. Although the manual emphasizes the importance of personality factors in job success and the necessity of taking them into account in counseling, no thought of developing tests in these areas seems contemplated. In fact, the tendency has been to narrow the factor content of the battery rather than to enlarge it. The reviewer would recommend, therefore, *continuing* factorial analyses of the GATB tests together with newer experimental tests with the constant objective of increasing the technical excellence and the factorial coverage of the battery.

In summary, one can scarcely help but be impressed with the tremendous amount of effort and thought which has gone into the development and validation of these tests. The manual is generally very complete, giving extremely meticulous directions for the use of the tests, validity information, reliability information, test development information, correlations between tests and with other tests, and instructions for administration which even list errors commonly made by subjects and what to do about them. Although the GATB is somewhat short on factor analytic foundation and too narrow factorially at present, certainly in the vast test program of the USES we have one of the main hopes for developing a legitimate and effective empirical science of selection and guidance by means of psychological tests.

CLIFFORD P. FROEHLICH, *Professor of Education, University of California, Berkeley, California.*

It is a unique experience to prepare a review of a test about which so many data are available. Dvorak and her associates in the United States Employment Service have shown considerable sophistication in the standardization of this battery and in gathering validity data, both concurrent and predictive.

The comprehensive looseleaf manual has the advantage that new data have been added as they have been acquired. Unfortunately, the constant addition of data and subsections has resulted in a conglomerate for which no adequate index is available. It is not an easy document to use.

The outstanding characteristic of this multifactored aptitude test is that a person's scores can be compared with 23 occupational aptitude patterns. These patterns are believed to be pertinent to about 500 occupations. In nearly 250 of them the patterns were empirically established; the others were included upon the basis of judgments made from job analysis data. If the developers continue their present practices, additional data bearing on the relationship of occupational aptitude patterns to specific occupations will be made available from time to time.

The occupational norms are designed on the assumption that about one third of the employees in a given job are regarded as unsatisfactory. This may be a valid assumption, but this reviewer believes that the Minnesota Employment Stabilization Research Institute data indicate that the percentage would vary with labor market conditions. There is the possibility that this test could be used to deter some persons from entering occupations in which they could compete successfully in certain labor markets.

The USES has wisely established the policy that the GATB is a "controlled" test, i.e., not available except with approval of the Service or its affiliated state employment services. However, in some instances known to this reviewer, the control has interfered with the battery's most efficient and effective use by schools. The USES has prepared excellent materials to train counselors in the proper use of the battery and has fostered institutes for the training of counselors. There is, however, much room for improvement in the procedures for making this battery available to qualified counselors working in agencies other than public employment services.

A summary evaluation of this battery must include these points: (a) the test developers have made only modest and fair claims regarding its reliability and validity; (b) adequate data are now available to support its use in vocational counseling; and (c) as usual, further research is recommended. At this writing, the battery can be recommended for use in counseling and selection of persons 16 years and older.

LLOYD G. HUMPHREYS, *Professor of Psychology, University of Illinois, Urbana, Illinois.*

The *General Aptitude Test Battery* (GATB) of the United States Employment Service (USES) constitutes one of the best known of the factored aptitude test batteries, even though it is not available for general use. There are 12 tests in the battery which are combined to measure the following factors: intelligence (G), verbal aptitude (V), numerical aptitude (N), spatial aptitude (S), form perception (P), clerical perception (Q), motor coordination (K), finger dexterity (F), and manual dexterity (M).

There are many desirable features of this battery. The tests are generally well selected and constructed. The most important feature is the mass of data which have been accumulated concerning the use of GATB. Such data are of primary importance for selection or guidance purposes. As long as the battery covers the major functions or factors, the manner in which this is accomplished is relatively unimportant. Distributions of item difficulties and correlations of items with total

score, within rather wide limits, contribute relatively little to the effectiveness of the tests in use. The location of the test vectors in the battery is of even less importance. If adequate data on reliability, stability, and validity are available on factor scores obtained from the unrotated principal components of an aptitude battery, these "arbitrary" scores will be completely satisfactory for personnel selection or vocational guidance purposes.

FACTOR SCORE DEFICIENCIES. Thus there is little profit in speculating about the selection of item type "A" rather than "B." Of substantially greater importance is the omission of an important function or factor from the battery. An error of the latter type in GATB is the lack of any measure of mechanical information or comprehension. A great deal of data are available concerning the importance of this function in vocational predictions. The argument that mechanical information is not an aptitude is not convincing. One can rest the case for mechanical information in the statement "It works." In addition, the position that general vocabulary measures aptitude while specialized vocabulary measures achievement is logically unsound.

The inclusion of a general factor in GATB, and the way in which it is measured, is also worthy of note. The introduction of a general factor measure is somewhat rare in the post-Thurstone era. The present use of both a general factor and group factor measures in the same battery is unfortunate. The reviewer has no objection to a measure of "g" as such. As a matter of fact, a general factor is clearly indicated in aptitude test data. Since "g" is always composed of the group factors which define it, however, it is statistically superfluous to measure both.

The decision to measure the general factor may have been dictated by the reluctance of users to give up the intelligence test to which they had become accustomed. The present measure of "g" is close to the centroid of intelligence tests—components are vocabulary, spatial relations, and arithmetic reasoning—and is technically sound in itself. But this does not make the procedure as a whole desirable. The first two components of the measure of intelligence also appear as separate factor measures, and the third is used with numerical operations to measure the number factor. The part-whole correlations involving intelligence and these three group factor measures are very high and together almost completely determine the variance of the intelligence test. The only information furnished by the measure of the general factor is the difference between the functions measured by arithmetic reasoning and numerical operations. This is ordinarily a useful distinction to make, but the procedure used to make it here is certainly awkward. A desire for psychological realism might suggest the use of a general factor measure in future aptitude batteries, but some other solution is required.

DEFICIENCIES IN ANALYSIS. There is a high level of professional competence involved in the development of GATB. The reviewer has selected certain practices for adverse criticism, but this does not detract from an overall favorable evaluation.

For most problems of prediction, the multiple regression model is preferable statistically to the multiple cutoff procedure for combining two or more tests. Nevertheless, to predict many criteria from a single battery and to minimize computational difficulties for relatively untrained people, multiple cuts can easily be defended. One cannot defend, however, the publication of unshrunken validities. If the cuts are made after inspecting the joint distributions of tests and criteria the multiple cutoff procedure will produce substantially more shrinkage than will multiple regression. The reviewer is willing to state dogmatically that the only sample too small for the use of cross validation is one in which there would be zero degrees of freedom available in the split samples. In all other cases and particularly for small n's cross validate!

Interpretation of published validation data is also complicated by the choice of the statistic used to relate pass-fail on the multiple cutoff to the criterion. The test analyst in the USES typically uses a dichotomous criterion, even if continuous data are available, and describes the relationship between tests and criterion with the tetrachoric correlation. This statistic is not acceptable. It tells one what the product-moment correlation would be if both variables were continuously and normally distributed. Since the multiple cutoff procedure results inevitably in a dichotomous predictor variable, depending on the nature of the criterion variable, the analyst has available only two correlation coefficients from which to choose. Neither is the tetrachoric. If he wishes to predict a dichotomous criterion, he should report a phi coefficient; if he wishes to predict a continuous criterion, he should report a point biserial.

The combination of the two errors discussed above, use of unshrunken tetrachoric validity coefficients, has produced some remarkably high values. One's feeling that they are too high to be true is probably correct. On the other hand, relatively high correlations can be expected when one is working in the full range of human talent.

It was mentioned earlier that a substantial amount of both concurrent and predictive validation had been accomplished. The only possible reason for obtaining concurrent validity on a selection and guidance battery is a need for quick results. Concurrent validity can and should be replaced as quickly as possible by predictive validity. At one point a USES publication implies that concurrent can be substituted for predictive because, empirically, the former coefficients are on the average no higher than the latter. This is insufficient empirical justification. In addition to differences in size, pattern of validities could differ in the two cases, i.e., concurrent validation may select the wrong variables for predictive use. On a priori grounds one might expect this error to be more serious with motivational and personality variables than with ability variables, but empirical demonstration is lacking. The USES research program may well have the relevant data. It would be useful to analyze those data from this point of view.

THE MANUALS. The mass of data referred to, including both concurrent and predictive validation results, does not appear in the manuals, but much has been published in the professional literature. The reviewer has no quarrel with these practices. The authors of this battery have different practical and ethical problems than the authors of commercial tests. On the practical side the tests are used by interviewers to refer job applicants to potential employers. It is debatable whether adding the "why" to the "how" would help this function. On the ethical side, they are responsible primarily to their organization for their products, not to a diffuse consuming public. There is then an acceptable double standard for writing test manuals, though only a single standard for professional competence.

There may be objections in certain quarters

to the cut and dried instructions for use of the battery contained in the manuals. There are two aspects to this question. One, the job to be done, has already been alluded to. On this score, since the function of the battery is as much selection as guidance, rigidity is desirable. The second has to do with what the counselor can add to the information furnished by the tests. The weight of the evidence here is that the counselor is more apt to degrade than to improve test information unless his area of decision making is sharply circumscribed. Thus, a military type standardized operating procedure, though politically unrealistic for other batteries, would probably improve their effectiveness in use.

CONCLUSIONS. For purposes of summary, three conclusions have been drawn about the GATB. These are worded conservatively, though with no intent to damn with faint praise. The frame of reference is other similar batteries. (*a*) The tests of the GATB were selected and constructed as well as most. (*b*) The GATB has been validated and otherwise analyzed as well as or better than most. (*c*) If interviewers follow instructions, the GATB battery is used more effectively than most.

For reviews by Milton L. Blum, Edward B. Greene, and Howard R. Taylor, see 4:714.

[610]

★**Holzinger-Crowder Uni-Factor Tests.** Grades 7–12; 1952–55; 5 scores: verbal, spatial, numerical, reasoning, scholastic aptitude; IBM; Forms AM ('52), BM ('53); manual ('55); separate answer sheets must be used; $6.40 per 35 tests; $3.90 per 35 sets of IBM answer sheets; 50¢ per set of right keys for hand or machine scoring; 30¢ per set of item elimination keys for machine scoring; postage extra; 50¢ per specimen set, postpaid; 40.5(90) minutes in 2 sessions; Karl J. Holzinger and Norman A. Crowder; World Book Co. *

REFERENCES
1. MITCHELL, BLYTHE C. "The Relation of High School Achievement to the Abilities Measured by the Holzinger-Crowder Uni-Factor Tests." *Ed & Psychol Meas* 15:487–90 w '55. * (PA 30:7771)
2. CROWDER, NORMAN A. "The Holzinger-Crowder Uni-Factor Tests." Comments by Donald E. Super. *Personnel & Guid J* 35:281–8 Ja '57. * (PA 32:2103)
3. NORTH, ROBERT D. "The Holzinger-Crowder Uni-Factor Tests: Profile, Reliability, and Correlation Data Based on Independent School Results." *Ed Rec B* 69:53–9 F '57. * (PA 32:2121)

ANNE ANASTASI, *Professor of Psychology, Fordham University, New York, New York.*

The four factor scores yielded by this battery are derived from nine tests. The verbal score is based on Word Meaning and Odd Words, both tests requiring the discrimination of word meanings. The spatial factor is meas-

ured by two tests, Boots and Hatchets, in which the subject must determine whether the two boots or hatchets, respectively, in each item are viewed from the same side or different sides. The two tests measuring numerical ability, Mixed Arithmetic and Remainders, call for simple computational skills. The reasoning score is based on three tests utilizing verbal, numerical, and spatial content. These tests include: Mixed Series, consisting of number-letter series completions; Figure Changes, composed of figure analogies items; and Teams, presenting a series of syllogisms concerned with overlapping membership on different athletic teams. The spatial and numerical tests are highly speeded; the verbal and reasoning tests measure predominantly power. Answers on the nine tests are recorded on two answer sheets, each used in a different testing session. An individual profile chart is provided on the reverse side of one of the answer sheets.

Norms for each of the four factor scores are in the form of end-of-year percentiles for each of grades 7–12. The normative sample was obtained from 38 schools located in 28 communities in 7 states, the number of cases in each grade varying from 827 to 2,562. December norms derived by linear interpolation from the June standardization data are available on request from the publisher, as are separate sex norms. In the derivation of the latter, significant but slight mean differences in favor of girls were found in the verbal factor; larger significant differences favoring the boys were obtained on the spatial factor. Sex differences in the numerical and reasoning factors were small and inconsistent but tended to favor girls.

Percentile scores are plotted on a normalized percentile chart, in which a half inch is approximately equal to the standard error of a score. Similarly, the standard error of the difference between scores on any two factors corresponds to a little less than three fourths of an inch. The manual recommends that these distances be used in interpreting scores. Being based on ± 1 SE, however, these values correspond to a rather low confidence level. It might be noted that, with the scale employed, 1 inch designates a significant deviation at the .03 level within a single factor, and 1½ inches a significant difference at the .02 level between factors. Since these significance levels are closer to the usual standards and correspond to easily measured distances on the graph, they would appear preferable to the limits suggested in the manual.

Alternate-form reliabilities for the four factor scores, computed on single-grade groups, ranged from .758 to .951. Split-half reliabilities of verbal and reasoning scores (neither of which depends appreciably on speed) are all above .90 except for a single value of .88. Validity was investigated through correlations with achievement tests and teachers' grades in a variety of courses. Most of the coefficients are based on concurrent validity, although a few measure predictive validity. With few exceptions, the verbal factor yielded the highest correlations and the spatial factor the lowest, regardless of the nature of the course—a finding indicative of little differential validity. Moreover, the correlations of any one factor tended to vary more among schools or communities than among criteria. With regard to absolute size, the correlations with the verbal factor compare favorably with corresponding correlations obtained with common group intelligence tests. With numerical and reasoning factors, the median correlations are generally in the .40's and .50's. The spatial factor yields few correlations at this level, except in predominantly manual vocational courses.

On the basis of a large number of available validity coefficients, a regression equation was derived for a scholastic aptitude score, in which the largest weight is given to the verbal score, progressively smaller weights are given to reasoning and numerical scores, and the spatial factor is omitted. This composite score, for which percentile norms are also provided, yields somewhat higher validities than generally found with intelligence tests. At the same time, the correlations of the scholastic aptitude score with each of several common group intelligence tests are about as high as the correlations ordinarily found between any two intelligence tests. Similar regression equations have been worked out for predicting achievement in mathematics, science, social studies, and English.

That the four factor scores do not represent independent measures is indicated by the substantial intercorrelations among them. The medians of these correlations in 36 single-grade groups range from .31 to .53. Nevertheless, in view of the high reliability of the factor scores, it is estimated that approximately 40 per cent of intra-individual score differences are in excess of chance. On this basis, the use of profiles would seem justified, although the meager evidence for differential validity makes the diagnostic interpretation of such profiles doubtful.

The battery was evidently developed by means of factorial analyses, although the procedure and findings are not clear. A table of factor loadings, based on earlier forms of the nine tests, seems to show a remarkably close approximation to simple structure. Each test has virtually zero loadings (none above .11) on three of the factors, while loadings on the fourth are all over .78 and two are over 1.00! Without information regarding the method of factor analysis employed and what other tests (if any) were factorized in the battery, it is difficult to evaluate these factor loadings. It would probably have been better not to try to cover the relevant factorial research in the manual, but rather to insert a reference to a published source where the detailed data should be made available.

On the whole, however, the manual provides a well organized, effective presentation of essential facts. It is clear, helpful, and intelligible to the unsophisticated test user, and yet sufficiently informative for the technically oriented reader. The construction and evaluation of this test reveal the characteristic thoroughness and soundness which we have come to expect from its publisher. These qualities are evident in the careful choice of appropriate statistical techniques, the full presentation of data, and the objective and cautious interpretation of results. Special mention should be made of the use of regression equations to find composite scores, a procedure which represents the most effective way of predicting complex criteria from multiple aptitude batteries.

Despite their technical merits, in actual operation the *Holzinger-Crowder Uni-Factor Tests* do not appear to be substantially superior to other available multiple factor batteries or intelligence tests. The lack of convincing evidence of differential validity highlights the principal shortcoming of the battery. Nor does the derivation of composite scores raise the validity much above that obtained with other instruments. The chief difficulty probably stems from the limited nature of the test content. Although a variety of item types and materials is included, it would seem that the battery leaves untapped intellectual functions which may be important in academic achievement. The tests concentrate unduly on relatively simple processes and routine intellectual skills. Even the three reasoning tests demand little complex or original thought. It is also noteworthy that, in the regression equation for the composite science score, the numerical factor does not appear. Apparently the type of quantitative thinking required in science is not covered by those tests.

The original formulation of items would have profited from a more imaginative approach. The authors' rather compulsive justification for the inclusion of the spatial tests reveals a fundamental weakness in their choice of test content. Thus they write that "inclusion of spatial tests stems more from the repeated emergence of a spatial component in factor-analysis studies of mental measures than from any evidences of substantial utility of the spatial factor, as measured by the Holzinger-Crowder or other tests, for predicting success in various educational or occupational endeavors." Of course the reason such a spatial factor emerged in the early factorial research of Holzinger, Thurstone, and others is that spatial tests were included in the batteries. More recent research with other types of tests, as cited for example in Guilford's "The Structure of Intellect," [1] has revealed many other more promising factors. The present battery exemplifies the all-too-common practice of *ex post facto* validation, in which tests are chosen without adequate reference to the behavior domain to be measured, and validity coefficients are subsequently computed against criteria within that domain. A more productive approach would be to begin with a "job analysis" of the area to be investigated and then develop tests to predict the most important behavior functions within that area.

BENJAMIN FRUCHTER, *Associate Professor of Educational Psychology, The University of Texas, Austin, Texas.*

This battery of nine general aptitude tests yields scores in four aspects of mental ability useful for educational and ultimately vocational guidance. The verbal factor is represented by Word Meaning and Odd Words; the spatial factor by Boots and Hatchets; the numerical factor by Mixed Arithmetic and Remainders; and the reasoning factor by tests

1 GUILFORD, J. P. "The Structure of Intellect." *Psychol B* 53:267–93 Je '56. *

called Mixed Series, Figure Changes, and Teams.

Considering the wide variety of item types that have been developed in recent years to measure spatial abilities, the tests used to measure the spatial factor are rather limited in structure and scope. The task they set is to determine whether the two members of a pair of pictured boots or hatchets are viewed from the same or different sides. From the point of view of validity, the correlations of the factor scores derived from these tests with academic grades and achievement tests are as high as or higher than those obtained with other spatial scores. Teams, a test in syllogistic form, is likely to be difficult for some students in the lower grades, but it probably gives needed "top" to the reasoning scores for some of the brighter students in the upper grades.

The manual is unusually complete and has much useful information. There are, however, almost no data concerning the individual tests, the norms, reliability, validity, and other data being reported for the factor scores only. The norms furnished in the manual are end-of-year percentile ranks by grades for the four factor scores and the total scholastic aptitude score. They are based on approximately 10,000 cases from 28 communities in 7 states. Since neither the communities and states nor the basis for selecting them are specified, one suspects that some sections of the country may not be represented. A table for converting percentile ranks to stanine scores is furnished.

A formula is provided for weighting the verbal, numerical, and reasoning scores to yield a scholastic aptitude score, intended to be comparable to the single score derived from a general intelligence test. Norms are provided for this general score and a table is furnished for estimating Terman-McNemar IQ's from them. Weights are given for predicting achievement in science, social studies, English, and mathematics. Only for the last named subject are the weights much different than for the general scholastic aptitude score, in which the verbal score receives the highest weight, followed by the reasoning and numerical scores, with the spatial score not being weighted since it does not contribute significantly. The validities of the factor scores for teachers' marks and achievement test scores follow a similar pattern. The prescribed weights are derived from averages and it is suggested that each school develop its own regression weights.

Validity information is reported in the form of correlations between factor scores and teachers' marks for a number of subjects, as well as correlations with other standardized tests. While the degree of independence between factors is good relative to most batteries of this type, the correlation between factors is still appreciable. The reported median correlation of the verbal score with the other three scores is .44, the spatial .37, the numerical .45, and the reasoning .50.

In a relatively short testing time (two class periods) this battery yields four reliable factor scores useful for educational guidance at the secondary level. The scores are as independent as any derived from this type of scholastic aptitude battery. Preliminary results show good validity for the verbal, spatial, numerical, and reasoning scores. The tests can be efficiently administered and scored. A score for predicting general scholastic aptitude can be derived from the factor scores and corresponding IQ's can be estimated. Additional work needs to be done in gathering normative and validity data for educational and vocational guidance.

PHILIP E. VERNON, *Professor of Educational Psychology, Institute of Education, University of London, London, England.*

This battery raises afresh the question of the superiority of differential aptitude or factor-based tests over the general scholastic aptitude or intelligence test. As one would expect from the senior author, the subtests have been chosen after extensive research, not merely for their high saturations with their own factor, but also for their low overlap with other factors. The nine subtests are combined to yield separate scores for verbal, spatial, numerical, and reasoning factors. Each of the tests shows good reliability, the mean parallel-form coefficient being .86. The median factor score intercorrelation for several one-grade populations is .44. The authors calculate that 40 per cent of the differences between paired factor scores should exceed chance expectation, so that the battery should be adequate for differential predictive or counseling purposes.

However, the manual also summarizes the results of 90 comparisons between factor scores and tests or teachers' marks in a variety of school subjects, and these show a disappointing lack of differentiation. In almost all subjects, V has the highest correlations, followed closely by R; N shows lower correlations, though these rise somewhat with mathematics courses and, curiously enough, with foreign languages; while S seldom makes any useful contribution, except possibly to geometry and to some vocational courses. Thus it is found that a scholastic aptitude total score, based on $5V + N + 3R$, gives almost as good predictions of achievement in any area as do differentially weighted combinations. Likewise, the median correlations of the four factors with a number of intelligence tests are .79 (V), .35 (S), .55 (N) and .63 (R), and there appear to be no marked variations in these figures at different age levels. The logical inference would seem to be that it is the verbal intelligence component of the tests $(g + v)$ which alone contributes to educational prediction, and that the 40 per cent of significant score differences derive almost wholly from the specific variance of the tests (s factors), which is educationally irrelevant.

As against this interpretation, it may be noted that standard intelligence tests seldom yield as high correlations with any achievement criterion as do one or the other of the factor scores, though this may be due merely to chance variations. However, the authors further point out that the patterns of correlations with any one school subject vary markedly, and often significantly, in different school groups, and suggest that the educational counselor should work out for himself the most appropriate profiles, or weighted combinations, of scores for his own local criteria. In the present writer's view it has still to be demonstrated whether regression equations based on specific courses are sufficiently stable or consistent to yield better predictions than a single equation for all courses (or maybe two equations—one for linguistic, and one for quantitative courses). It is only when very much more varied batteries are used, incorporating tests of previous attainment and of interest in particular subjects, that any real gain in differential prediction is achieved.

Except in the reasoning tests, the content is rather narrow; i.e., the tests cannot claim to provide representative samplings of the factors concerned. Nevertheless the battery is superior to those which provide only one test per factor or aptitude. It will be apparent that the fairly low factor intercorrelations may have arisen less because these are pure factor tests than because there are differences in speed conditions and form of response, and because the reasoning tests use predominantly symbolic or non-verbal materials.

Within the limitations noted, this battery may be accepted as a well constructed and thoroughly standardized and validated instrument, one of the good ones of its kind. The manual is one of the most informative the writer has met.

[611]

★**The Jastak Test of Potential Ability and Behavior Stability.** Grades 7–9; 1958; 10 scores: coding, picture reasoning, arithmetic, vocabulary, space series, social concept, verbal reasoning, number series, space completion, and spelling; 6 derived scores: language, reality, motivation, psychomotor, intelligence, capacity; 1 form; $4.25 per 25 tests; $1.50 per manual; $1 per set of scoring keys; postage extra; $1.50 per specimen set, postpaid; 65(90) minutes; J. F. Jastak; Educational Test Bureau. *

[612]

★**The Multi-Aptitude Test.** College courses in testing; 1955; miniature battery of 10 tests for instructional use; Forms A, B; $1.25 per study kit; 10 or more study kits, 90¢ each; postpaid; 35(50–60) minutes; Edward E. Cureton, Louise Witmer Cureton, and students; Psychological Corporation. *

REFERENCE

1. WESMAN, ALEXANDER G. "A Test Battery for Teaching Tests and Measurements." *Yearb Nat Council Meas Used Ed* 13:76–8 '56. *

H. H. REMMERS, *Professor of Psychology and Education, Purdue University, Lafayette, Indiana.*

This test battery is admirably designed to serve its intended purpose—to provide an instructional device "which can be used both to familiarize students and laymen with the more usual kinds of ability measures and to provide material for practice in test administration, scoring, and analysis."

The 10 tests, which range in length from 8 to 30 items, cover vocabulary, general information, arithmetic, number series, figure classification, mechanical comprehension, word recognition, scrambled letters, checking, and paper formboard. Testing time ranges from 1 to 5 minutes per test. A variety of scoring devices have purposely been included.

The authors suggest that the test may be used to supplement instruction in a variety of courses in statistics, measurement, and evaluation and to serve as illustration for lectures to lay groups. So far as cognitive functions are concerned, the battery can admirably serve these purposes.

The manual is usefully detailed and relevant. The rationale of construction and the scoring, standardization, and psychological meaning of the tests are clearly explained. Tables of illustrative statistical data give information on mean scores, standard deviations, interform reliability coefficients, comparative difficulties of the two forms, practice effects, sex differences, and illustrative centile and standard score norms, all based on a group of 113 college students.

The battery represents a very useful idea competently and carefully implemented with psychological and statistical sophistication of a high order. It is an excellent instructional tool to teach the measurement of cognitive functions.

[613]

★**Multiple Aptitude Tests.** Grades 7–13; 1955; 13 scores: 9 tests plus combinations of tests *a, b,* and *c* (verbal comprehension), *d* and *e* (perceptual speed), *f* and *g* (numerical reasoning), *h, i,* and *j* (spatial visualization); IBM; 1 form; $24.50 per 35 sets of 9 tests; separate answer sheets may be used; 8¢ per set of IBM answer sheets; 60¢ per set of either hand or machine scoring stencils; postage extra; $1.75 per complete specimen set, postpaid; 175.5(220) minutes in 3 sessions for complete battery; David Segel and Evelyn Raskin; California Test Bureau. *

a) WORD MEANING. $2.45 per 35 tests; 12(20) minutes.

b) PARAGRAPH MEANING. $3.50 per 35 tests; 30(35) minutes.

c) LANGUAGE USAGE. $2.45 per 35 tests; 25(30) minutes.

d) ROUTINE CLERICAL FACILITY. $2.45 per 35 tests; 6.5 (10) minutes.

e) ARITHMETIC REASONING. $2.45 per 35 tests; 30(35) minutes.

f) ARITHMETIC COMPUTATION. $2.45 per 35 tests; 22 (35) minutes.

g) APPLIED SCIENCE AND MECHANICS. $4.55 per 35 tests; 30(35) minutes.

h) SPATIAL RELATIONS—TWO DIMENSIONS. $3.50 per 35 tests; 8(10) minutes.

i) SPATIAL RELATIONS—THREE DIMENSIONS. $3.50 per 35 tests; 12(15) minutes.

REFERENCES

1. MENDENHALL, GEORGE V. *A Statistical Investigation of the Interrelationships in the Multiple Aptitude Tests.* Master's project, University of Southern California (Los Angeles, Calif.), 1952.
2. SEGEL, DAVID. "The Multiple Aptitude Tests." Comments by Donald E. Super. *Personnel & Guid J* 35:424–34 Mr '57. * (PA 32:1645)

RALPH F. BERDIE, *Professor of Psychology and Director of Student Counseling Bureau, University of Minnesota, Minneapolis, Minnesota.*

This battery consists of nine tests which provide nine separate scores, which in turn yield scores on four basic factors. The tests are designed primarily for secondary school students, and the authors state the strategic time for testing is in grade 8 or 9, with further possibilities for testing during the latter half of grade 10 and in grades 11 and 12. The absence of an alternate form presents a retesting problem. The tests have been designed mainly as tools to be used by school counselors who assist students with problems involving educational and vocational decisions. The tests and the standardization process appear to be as well conceived as for similar batteries, but because of their relative youth, they have not been subjected to the same kind of examination through research and use as have older batteries. The item types in the tests are identical with item types in traditional tests.

The word meaning test consists of a 60-item simple multiple choice vocabulary test, with the student instructed to select the one of four alternatives which is synonymous with the key word. The paragraph meaning test consists of eight paragraphs, each of about 100 words and each followed by from four to nine brief multiple choice questions based upon the content of the preceding paragraph. The language usage test consists of 60 discrete brief sentences, each divided into four parts. Some of these parts contain errors in spelling, grammar, punctuation, or capitalization, and the student is to identify sections in which errors are found.

The routine clerical facility test consists of 90 pairs of names and numbers, among which the student is to identify the pairs which are similar and different. The arithmetic reasoning test consists of 35 arithmetic problems presented verbally and involving simple arithmetic computations. The arithmetic computation test consists of 35 brief problems presented numerically and involving addition, subtraction, multiplication, division, and percentage.

The applied science and mechanics test consists of drawings of 52 simple mechanical arrangements or practical situations, each accompanied by one or more sets of questions of the multiple choice type. The two spatial relations tests present 25 simple drawings each. The first test consists of 2-dimensional drawings of completed figures accompanied by sets of segments of figures, and the student is instructed to select that set of segments which will form the completed figure; the second test presents 3-dimensional drawings of completed figures accompanied by sets of "unfolded" patterns, and the student is required to select that pattern which when properly assembled will form the 3-dimensional figure.

Each of these item types has appeared in earlier tests, and the authors of the *Multiple Aptitude Tests* use for evidence of validity for their tests the assumed or demonstrated validity of the earlier tests. Certainly they are justified to some extent in doing this, and the many substantial correlations between the *Multiple Aptitude Tests* and the earlier tests suggest that the new tests tend to measure much the same things measured by the earlier tests. For instance, correlations between the word meaning test and other tests of verbal ability extend from .48 through .96. One correlation between the paragraph meaning test and the reading vocabulary score of the *California Achievement Test* is .99. A correlation between the *Barrett-Ryan-Schrammel English Test* and the language usage test is .81. The clerical scores on the *Multiple Aptitude Tests* and the *Minnesota Clerical Test* correlate between .53 and .99. One correlation between the arithmetic reasoning score and the numerical score of the *Differential Aptitude Tests* is .96. A correlation between the applied science and mechanics score and the score on the *Test of Mechanical Comprehension* is .93 (in fairness, it should be stated that for another group this correlation is .26). The correlations between scores on the spatial relations test and on other tests are somewhat lower, however, ranging from −.07 to .70. Thus, the correlations between scores on the *Multiple Aptitude Tests* and on tests that tend to have similar kinds of items confirm the similarity of the tests, and the evidence for validity of the earlier tests suggests, but certainly does not demonstrate, that the new tests have comparable validity.

Reliability coefficients and standard errors of measurement for each of the nine *Multiple Aptitude Tests* are presented for each sex by grade, from grade 7 through grade 13. Thus, for each test 14 reliability coefficients are available. All of these coefficients, except for the routine clerical facility test, were calculated by Kuder-Richardson formula 21; those for the clerical score were based on test-retest. The coefficients for the word meaning test range from .81 to .92, with a median of .90. Coefficients for the paragraph meaning test range from .74 to .85, with a median coefficient of .81. The range of coefficients for the language usage test is from .86 to .91, with a median of

.89, and for the routine clerical facility test the correlations range from .75 to .94, with a median of .87. The coefficients for the arithmetic reasoning test range from .84 to .90, with a median coefficient of .87, and the range of coefficients for arithmetic computation is from .88 to .98. The range of coefficients for the applied science and mechanics test is from .66 to .88, with a median coefficient of .76; for the 2-dimension spatial relations test, from .83 to .89, with a median coefficient of .88; and for the 3-dimension spatial relations test, from .71 to .82, with a median of .77. Thus, it appears that the word meaning, language usage, and arithmetic computation tests have very good reliability; but that reliability for paragraph meaning, arithmetic reasoning, applied science and mechanics, and spatial relations is not as good.

The paragraph meaning test is a short test when one considers the length of test needed to get a reliable reading score. It well might be that for some of these tests with lower than desired reliabilities an extension in the length of the test might be warranted.

The authors are to be commended for including the standard errors of measurement for raw scores for each of the tests by sex and by grade. The careful test user will find this information useful in making more careful interpretations of the score.

The intercorrelations of some of the tests are quite high. More important than the intercorrelations of the tests, however, are the intercorrelations of the four factor scores: verbal comprehension, based upon scores on the tests for word meaning, paragraph meaning, and language usage; perceptual speed, based upon the language usage score and the routine clerical facility score; numerical reasoning, based upon the scores on tests of arithmetic reasoning and arithmetic computation; and spatial visualization, based upon scores on the test for applied science and mechanics and the two spatial relations tests. Reliability coefficients and standard errors of measurement are provided for these factor scores, the former ranging from .91 to .95. Since these coefficients were based upon large groups of students drawn from grades 7 through 13, and thus were derived from a much more heterogeneous group than were the reliability scores for individual tests, the two cannot be directly compared.

The correlations between factor scores range from −.10 to .73. Some interesting and confusing sex differences are apparent here. For instance, for the males the correlation between factor one and factor two is −.10; for the females it is .70. When information regarding the relationships between tests is summarized, it is obvious that the tests are far from independent from one another and that some of them to a large extent measure overlapping abilities. The factor structure of the battery is complex, and factor analysis information perhaps will be of less help in determining what the validity of the battery is than will information derived from prediction studies.

The authors base much of their evidence for validity of these tests upon correlations between test scores and school grades. An abundance of these data is presented in the manual, and an effective profile method of presenting the information is used. For instance, the correlations between grades in algebra and each of the nine tests for boys range from .06 to .39, the highest correlation being with score on the arithmetic computation test. The correlations between physics grades and test scores for boys range from .21 to .47, the highest correlation being with the paragraph meaning test. As is true with all such correlations for tests similar to these, the correlation between grades and scores is disappointingly low, being hardly ever higher than .50 and usually no higher than .40. In most cases, the patterns of correlations are in the expected differences, but in some cases they are not.

Unfortunately, one cannot tell from the information presented in the manual whether the tests were given at the beginning or at the end of the school year. Thus, one does not know whether the information presented here pertains to predictive validity or concurrent validity.

Although no information is presented in the manual concerning the validity of these tests as determined by a vocational criterion, the authors have made available to the reviewer a study done in one large company where test scores were related to ratings of success made by supervisors for a great variety of occupations in that company. Although these scores appear to have little, if any, relationship with rated success, the mean scores of persons doing different kinds of work tended to vary in the expected direction. In other words, again we have evidence that tests such as these perhaps cannot predict how successful men will be on a job, but rather can serve to differentiate among persons who enter in and are minimally successful in different occupations.

The authors have done much to assist the school counselor as he uses the tests. An extended profile facilitates the visual presentation of the test scores and, more importantly, a convenient means is provided for determining the statistical significance of differences between scores. Counselors frequently work with students who have, for example, a percentile score of 40 on word meaning and 60 on arithmetic reasoning, and they must help the student decide whether his word meaning ability really is superior to his arithmetic reasoning ability, or whether this is a chance fluctuation. Segel has been concerned with this problem for many years, and in the *Multiple Aptitude Tests* he and Raskin have presented a convenient means for the counselor to make inferences concerning the meaning of test score discrepancies.

Another counseling aid, this one of more questionable usefulness, is the transparent profile provided for the tests. This profile allows the student's scores to be plotted on a semitransparent chart and then compared with the profiles of groups of students who have done well and who have done poorly in various subjects. Segel was one of the earliest psychologists to see the counseling use of expectancy tables, and a comprehensive series of these is presented in the manual. Counselors cannot assume, however, that the data in the manual will necessarily be useful for predicting success or failure in their schools; each school will probably find that it must use its own data in deriving its expectancy tables and success and failure profiles. For those counselors who have enough ambition and energy to construct similar devices based upon their local information, the methods suggested in the manual will be most helpful.

In summary, the *Multiple Aptitude Tests* are a very new series of tests that have as yet been subjected to little careful scrutiny through research and use. The authors have done a careful job of test construction and standardization, and the finished tests do not look inferior to the similar tests that are available. Unfortunately, the tests themselves seem to have nothing that other tests do not have. Inevitably, one will want to compare these tests with the *Differential Aptitude Tests,* which, as of this date, have the advantage because of the greater amount of research data accumulated during recent years. The authors of the *Multiple Aptitude Tests* have some interesting ideas regarding the counseling use of these tests, and their work has been carefully and rigorously done.

BENJAMIN FRUCHTER, *Associate Professor of Educational Psychology, The University of Texas, Austin, Texas.*

This battery of differential aptitude tests is designed for use with secondary level students to aid in counseling them concerning the choice of appropriate school curricula, to give them some information concerning their relative strengths and weaknesses in four scholastic aptitude areas, and to yield information on how they compare with other students in these areas. It is based, as are a number of other differential aptitude test batteries, on the results of the extensive factor analytic studies of intellectual abilities and aptitudes that have been carried out during the past 20 years.

The authors have done a professional job of developing the test battery and providing the materials necessary for its efficient use and interpretation. The principal limitation is that only one form is so far available. The tests come in nine separate booklets; if desired, parts of the battery can be selected for administration. Fall norms, based on approximately 11,000 cases widely distributed over the country, are provided. These are given in percentiles and T scores, by sex, for each grade. In addition, differential percentile norms, by sex, for grades 7–9 and 10–12, are furnished for comparing a given examinee's aptitude scores with the scores of others of similar intelligence.

Several types of validation data are furnished in the manual. The correlations of each test in the battery with a number of other widely used intelligence and scholastic aptitude tests are reported. The usefulness of this type of validity data for most test users is very limited and often open to misinterpretation. Its location in an appendix rather than its present prominent position would probably be preferable.

A more direct type of validation data is represented by the correlation of the test scores with teachers' grades. The correlations of scores on the separate tests with school marks for males in 16 school subjects and for females in 15 school subjects are given in tabular and graphical form. These correlations are overall values with no indication given of how much they would fluctuate from time to time or place to place. The mean standard scores on the nine tests for the highest and lowest 10 per cent of the students in each subject, and the significance of the differences between them, are reported. The profiles for these mean scores are presented in graphical form for the various school subjects. An ingenious transparent profile, on which may be entered the scores for a given student, is placed over the graphs to determine the school subjects for which his aptitude score profile is in accord with averages of the top 10 per cent or the bottom 10 per cent of the validation group.

One advantage of this type of test battery over the more conventional intelligence test is that it yields differential information in several areas of ability. Inspection of the factor intercorrelation matrix given in the manual indicates that there is considerable relationship among performances on the verbal comprehension, numerical reasoning, and spatial visualization factors. The authors explain this, in part, by pointing out that "items were selected on the basis of the highest possible correlation with the test in which they were placed, without regard to whether or not they were incidentally measuring some other ability." In other words, the emphasis in construction was on internal consistency of the tests rather than on purity of factors. The reviewer factor analyzed the corrected intercorrelation matrix for males by the centroid method. After rotation of axes his results agreed closely with factor analysis results reported by the authors.

With the exception of Routine Clerical Facility, all of the tests are power tests and their reported reliabilities were appropriately computed by Kuder-Richardson formula 21. The reliability of the speeded clerical test was computed by the test re-test method on scores obtained one week apart. The average reliabilities of the separate tests, for grades 7 through 13, range from .72 to .92. In addition to the reliability coefficients, the standard errors of measurement both for raw scores and for standard scores (T scores) are provided for each sex at each grade level. The reliabilities for the four factor scores, derived by combining appropriate test scores, range from .91 to .95.

In summary, this is a battery of differential aptitude tests for counseling at the secondary

level. The mechanics for administration, scoring, and interpretation are well worked out and the necessary auxiliary materials are provided. The test and factor scores have satisfactory reliability for use in individual counseling. Some information is furnished concerning the validity of the scores for several school subjects. These data should be regarded as suggestive rather than definitive since no indication is given concerning how much these values may be expected to fluctuate under varying conditions. The results of the factor analysis, the correlation profiles for various school subjects, and the reliability of differences between scores for tests of different factors indicate that the differential approach upon which the battery is based is a sound one.

This promising battery is not as far along in its development as some of its competitors since only one form is available, end-of-year norms are not furnished, and validation data are not extensive or detailed.

[614]
*SRA Primary Mental Abilities. Grades kgn-2, 3-6, 7-12; 1946-58; IBM for ages 11-17; 3 levels; postage extra; L. L. Thurstone and Thelma Gwinn Thurstone; Science Research Associates. *
a) FOR AGES 5 TO 7. Grades kgn-2; 1946-53; formerly called *Tests of Primary Mental Abilities for Ages 5 and 6;* 6 scores: verbal, perception, quantitative, motor, space, total; 1 form ('53); manual, third edition ('53); supplement ('53); $3 per 20 tests; 50¢ per specimen set; (60-80) minutes in 2 sessions 1 day apart.
b) ELEMENTARY: AGES 7 TO 11. Grades 3-6; 1948-56; 5 factor scores (verbal, space, reasoning, perception, number), IQ, nonreading IQ, reading aptitude, arithmetic aptitude, and 4 part scores; Form AH ('48); manual, second edition ('54); supplement ('54); profile ('54); separate answer pads must be used; $9.80 per 20 tests; $2.15 per 20 answer pads; 90¢ per 20 interpretation folders ('54); 90¢ per 20 short form interpretation folders ('54); 75¢ per specimen set; 39(60) minutes in 2 sessions.
c) INTERMEDIATE: AGES 11 TO 17. Grades 7-12; 1947-58; 6 scores: verbal, spatial, reasoning, number, word-fluency (optional), total; IBM; Forms AH ('47, hand scored), AM ('48, machine scored); manual, third edition ('58); separate answer pads or answer sheets must be used; $9.80 per 20 tests; $5 per 100 IBM answer sheets; $2.15 per 20 answer pads; $3 per set of machine scoring stencils; 60¢ per 20 profiles; 75¢ per specimen set; 21(35-45) or 26(40-50) minutes.

REFERENCES
1-10. See 40:1427.
11-60. See 3:225.
61-102. See 4:716.
103. WHEATLEY, MABEL M. *Primary Mental Abilities of Deaf Children.* Doctor's thesis, University of Maryland (College Park, Md.), 1947.
104. AVAKIAN, SONIA A. *An Investigation of Trait Relationships Among Six-Year-Old Children.* Doctor's thesis, Fordham University (New York, N.Y.), 1951.
105. OLSON, DONALD J. *A Study of the Iowa Tests of Educational Development and the SRA Primary Mental Abilities in the Montana State Wide Cooperative Testing Program.* Master's thesis, Montana State University (Missoula, Mont.), 1951.
106. ANSBACHER, H. L. "The Goodenough Draw-A-Man Test

and Primary Mental Abilities." *J Consult Psychol* 16:176–80 Je '52. * (*PA* 27:5141)

107. BECHTEL, RAYMOND. *A Study of Thurstone's Primary Mental Abilities Test.* Doctor's thesis, St. John's University (Brooklyn, N.Y.), 1952.

108. CORTER, HAROLD M. "Factor Analysis of Some Reasoning Tests." *Psychol Monogr* 66(8):1–31 '52. * (*PA* 27:4995)

109. HODGES, JOHN M. *Primary Mental Abilities vs. Differential Aptitude Tests.* Master's thesis, Illinois State Normal University (Normal, Ill.), 1952.

110. HUTCHEON, JAMES F. *The Application of the Primary Mental Abilities Test to Mental Defectives.* Doctor's thesis, State University of Iowa (Iowa City, Iowa), 1952. (*DA* 12:587)

111. JOHNSON, RALPH W. *SRA Primary Mental Abilities vs. Algebra Aptitude: A Study.* Master's thesis, Illinois State Normal University (Normal, Ill.), 1952.

112. McKEE, JOHN P. "The Tests of Primary Mental Abilities Applied to Superior Children." *J Ed Psychol* 43:45–56 Ja '52. * (*PA* 26:7235)

113. MARQUIS, FRANCIS N. *A Study of Reading Ability in Its Relation to the SRA Primary Mental Abilities Test.* Doctor's thesis, University of Missouri (Columbia, Mo.), 1952. (*DA* 12:518)

114. MICHELI, GENE S. *The Relationship Between Speed of Concept Formation and Five "Primary Mental Abilities."* Master's thesis, Fordham University (New York, N.Y.), 1952.

115. MOODY, CAESAR B., JR. *The SRA Primary Mental Abilities Test in Relation to School Marks and Other Tests.* Doctor's thesis, University of North Carolina (Chapel Hill, N.C.), 1952.

116. ROBERTS, S. OLIVER, AND ROBINSON, JAMES M., SR. "Intercorrelations of the Primary Mental Abilities Tests for Ten-Year-Olds by Socioeconomic Status, Sex, and Race." Abstract. *Am Psychol* 7:304–5 Jl '52. *

117. ROCHLIN, ISAIAH. "The Investigation, Through the Use of Projective Techniques, of Nonintellectual Factors in the Learning of Mathematics." Abstract. *Am Psychol* 7:368 Jl '52. *

118. TOWNSEND, AGATHA, AND SPAULDING, GERALDINE. "The SRA Primary Mental Abilities Tests in the Independent-School Testing Program." *Ed Rec B* 58:58–70 F '52. * (*PA* 26:7237)

119. BURRALL, LUCILLE. *A Study of Internal or Trait Variability in Achievement of Pupils at the Fifth Grade Level.* Doctor's thesis, Pennsylvania State College (State College, Pa.), 1953.

120. CHAMBERS, JAMES R. *A Study of the Use of the Primary Mental Abilities Test With Negro Students in Mining, Rural, Urban, and Industrial Areas of West Virginia.* Master's thesis, West Virginia University (Morgantown, W.Va.), 1953.

121. DRAKE, JOHN D. *An Investigation of the Reliability of the SRA Primary Mental Abilities Test for Ages Eleven to Seventeen.* Master's thesis, Fordham University (New York, N.Y.), 1953.

122–3. HOLLOWAY, HAROLD D. *Effects of Training Upon, and Relationships Between, Two Standard Child Intelligence Tests.* Doctor's thesis, State University of Iowa (Iowa City, Iowa), 1953. (*DA* 13:884)

124. SCHAIE, K. WARNER; ROSENTHAL, FRED; AND PERLMAN, ROBERT M. "Differential Mental Deterioration of Factorially 'Pure' Functions in Later Maturity." *J Gerontol* 8:191–6 Ap '53. * (*PA* 28:2376)

125. SCHMIDT, LOUIS G. "Primary Mental Abilities and Occupational Choices." *J Ed Res* 47:297–300 D '53. * (*PA* 28:6174)

126. STEMPEL, ELLEN FLAUM. "The WISC and the SRA Primary Mental Abilities Test." *Child Develop* 24:257–61 S–D '53. * (*PA* 29:4089)

127. TRUMBULL, RICHARD. "A Study of Relationships Between Factors of Personality and Intelligence." *J Social Psychol* 38:161–73 N '53. * (*PA* 28:5589)

128. TYLER, LEONA E. "Changes in Children's Scores on Primary Mental Abilities Tests Over a Three-Year Period." Abstract. *Am Psychol* 8:448–9 Ag '53. *

129. ZIMMERMAN, WAYNE S. "A Revised Orthogonal Rotational Solution for Thurstone's Original Primary Mental Abilities Test Battery." *Psychometrika* 18:77–93 Mr '53. *

130. ALLEBACH, NANCY L. *Raven's Colored Matrices and Tests of Primary Mental Abilities With Young Children.* Master's thesis, Pennsylvania State University (University Park, Pa.), 1954.

131. ANASTASI, ANNE, AND DRAKE, JOHN D. "An Empirical Comparison of Certain Techniques for Estimating the Reliability of Speeded Tests." *Ed & Psychol Meas* 14:529–40 au '54. *

132. BAKER, EMILY H. *An Analysis of Four Aspects of Elementary School Geography.* Doctor's thesis, St. Louis University (St. Louis, Mo.), 1954.

133. BLEWETT, D. B. "An Experimental Study of the Inheritance of Intelligence." *J Mental Sci* 100:922–33 O '54. * (*PA* 29:6909)

134. BURRALL, LUCILLE. "Variability in Achievement of Pupils at the Fifth Grade Level." *Calif J Ed Res* 5:68–73 Mr '54. * (*PA* 28:9038)

135. DELANCY, ELMER O. *A Study of Three Psychological Tests as Related to Reading Achievement in Grade One American School Reading Readiness Test, Form A: SRA Primary Mental Abilities, Primary Form: Otis Quick-Scoring Mental Ability Tests, Alpha Test: Form A.* Doctor's thesis, Pennsylvania State University (University Park, Pa.), 1954.

136. HERZBERG, FREDERICK, AND LEPKIN, MILTON. "A Study of Sex Differences on the Primary Mental Abilities Test." *Ed & Psychol Meas* 14:687–9 w '54. * (*PA* 29:7283)

137. HOLLOWAY, HAROLD D. "Effects of Training on the SRA Primary Mental Abilities (Primary) and the WISC." *Child Develop* 25:253–63 D '54. * (*PA* 29:7284)

138. KOCH, HELEN L. "The Relation of 'Primary Mental Abilities' in Five- and Six-Year-Olds to Sex of Child and Characteristics of His Sibling." *Child Develop* 25:209–23 S '54. * (*PA* 29:6913)

139. KOLSTOE, OLIVER P. "A Comparison of Mental Abilities of Bright and Dull Children of Comparable Mental Ages." *J Ed Psychol* 45:161–8 Mr '54. * (*PA* 29:2270)

140. SCHMIDT, LOUIS G., AND ROTHNEY, J. W. M. "Relationship of Primary Abilities Scores and Occupational Choices." *J Ed Res* 47:637–40 Ap '54. * (*PA* 29:3004)

141. SHALLOE, M. PARACLETA. *A Study of the S.R.A. Primary Mental Abilities Battery as a Means of Educational Guidance in Selected Schools.* Doctor's thesis, Fordham University (New York, N.Y.), 1954.

142. BERDIE, RALPH F. "Aptitude, Achievement, Interest, and Personality Tests: A Longitudinal Comparison." *J Appl Psychol* 39:103–14 Ap '55. * (*PA* 30:1498)

143. BOND, GUY L., AND CLYMER, THEODORE W. "Interrelationship of the SRA Primary Mental Abilities, Other Mental Characteristics, and Reading Ability." *J Ed Res* 49:131–6 O '55. * (*PA* 30:7752)

144. MEREDITH, PHILIP. *The Thurstone Primary Mental Abilities and Academic Achievement in the Junior Forms of an English Grammar School.* Master's thesis, University of Manchester (Manchester, England), 1955. (Abstract: *Brit J Ed Psychol* 27:222)

145. MILL, CYRIL R., AND TURNER, CHARLES J. "The Measurement of Primary Mental Abilities by the Columbia Mental Maturity Scale." Abstract. *J Consult Psychol* 19:472 D '55. *

146. POOLER, MARY H. "Prediction of School Success Through the Use of the SRA Test of Primary Mental Abilities for Ages 5 to 7 Administered at the Kindergarten or First Grade Level." *Yearb Nat Council Meas Used Ed* 12(pt 2):76–81 '55. *

147. SATTER, GEORGE. "Psychometric Scatter Among Mentally Retarded and Normal Children." *Training Sch B* 52:63–8 Je '55. * (*PA* 30:3078)

148. SCHAIE, K. WARNER, AND STROTHER, CHARLES R. "Age Changes in the Primary Mental Abilities in a Group of Superior Older People." Abstract. *Am Psychol* 10:339 Ag '55. *

149. WELLINGTON, JOHN A. *Factors Related to the Academic Success of Resident Freshman Men at a Midwestern Liberal Arts College During the Academic Year 1952–1953.* Doctor's thesis, Northwestern University (Evanston, Ill.), 1955. (*DA* 16:69)

150. WOLKING, WILLIAM D. "Predicting Academic Achievement With the Differential Aptitude and the Primary Mental Abilities Tests." *J Appl Psychol* 39:115–8 Ap '55. * (*PA* 30:1636)

151. BRUCE, MARTIN M. "Normative Data Information Exchange, No. 4." *Personnel Psychol* 9:268–70 su '56. *

152. FRYE, U. CASSIAN. *The Relevancy of the SRA Primary Mental Abilities Test and the SRA Reading Record to Ninth Grade Achievement in a Catholic Boys' High School.* Master's thesis, St. Louis University (St. Louis, Mo.), 1956.

153. MITCHELL, JAMES V., JR. "A Comparison of the Factorial Structure of Cognitive Functions for a High and Low Status Group." *J Ed Psychol* 47:397–414 N '56. *

154. ROGERS, CARL A. *Measuring Intelligence in New Zealand: A Re-standardisation of Thurstone's Primary Mental Abilities (or Intermediate Test) for Ages 11 to 17 Years.* Auckland University College, Monograph Series No. 2. Auckland, New Zealand: Pilgrim Press, 1956. Pp. 127. * (*PA* 32:2658)

155. SHINN, EDMOND O. "Interest and Intelligence as Related to Achievement in Tenth Grade." *Calif J Ed Res* 7:217–20 N '56. * (*PA* 31:8844)

156. KAMIN, LEON J. "Differential Changes in Mental Abilities in Old Age." *J Gerontol* 12:66–70 Ja '57. * (*PA* 32:4021)

157. LONG, JAMES R. *Academic Forecasting in the Technical-Vocational High School Subjects at West Seattle High School.* Doctor's thesis, University of Washington (Seattle, Wash.), 1957. (*DA* 17:1951)

158. WELLMAN, F. E. "Differential Prediction of High School Achievement Using Single Score and Multiple Factor Tests of Mental Maturity." *Personnel & Guid J* 35:512–7 Ap '57. * (*PA* 32:4631)

159. THURSTONE, THELMA GWINN. "The Tests of Primary Mental Abilities." Comments by Donald E. Super. *Personnel & Guid J* 35:569–78 My '57. * (*PA* 32:3909)

160. SMITH, D. D. "Abilities and Interests: I, A Factorial Study." *Can J Psychol* 12:191–201 S '58. *

161. WALTERS, RICHARD H. "The Intelligence Test Performance of Maori Children: A Cross-Cultural Study." *J Abn & Social Psychol* 57:107–14 Jl '58. *

NORMAN FREDERIKSEN, *Director of Research, Educational Testing Service, Princeton, New Jersey.*

The tests of *SRA Primary Mental Abilities*

are direct descendants of the tests used in the factor studies performed with high school and college students by L. L. Thurstone at the University of Chicago in the 1930's. An experimental edition called *Tests for Primary Mental Abilities,* published in 1938, provided measures of seven factors and required 222 minutes to administer; another edition, published in 1941, required 240 minutes. A shorter version, requiring 120 minutes, was published in 1943. The present high school level tests represent a further abbreviation of the test battery and require 40 to 50 minutes to administer. Other test batteries for lower age groups have appeared which are also intended to measure separate mental abilities.

ITEM TYPES. In the present battery, five factors are measured at each level. Only two of these factors, however, are common to all three levels—verbal meaning and space. The 7–11 and 11–17 tests measure in common two additional factors—reasoning and number. The fifth factor at the 11–17 level is word fluency. The two lower level batteries measure in common the perceptual speed factor (in addition to verbal meaning and space). Factors measured only at the 5–7 level are motor and quantitative factors. The latter is thought to differentiate into the reasoning and number factors at higher ages.

Tests bearing the same name at different levels do not necessarily involve the same types of items. The verbal meaning factor is measured at the 5–7 level by requiring the child to choose the picture corresponding to a word or idea stated orally. At the 7–11 level, the same factor is measured partly by a printed synonyms test and partly by a picture choosing test. At the 11–17 level, the factor is measured entirely by a printed synonyms test.

The space factor is measured at the 5–7 level by two subtests, one which requires finding "the rest of the square" and one which requires the child to complete a simple line drawing to make it like another drawing. At the 7–11 level, only the "find the rest of the square" type of item is used, while at the 11–17 level the task is to identify all the figures like the first figure in the row, when some of the figures are mirror images and all have been rotated into positions unlike the first.

Reasoning at 7–11 is measured by two subtests: which word does not belong? and which

picture does not belong? At 11–17, reasoning is measured by a letter series test.

The number factor is measured at both the 7–11 and 11–17 levels by addition tests. At 7–11, numbers are to be added and the answer written down. At 11–17, the task is to indicate whether the answer given is right or wrong.

Perceptual ability is measured at both levels (5–7 and 7–11) by similar tasks: find the picture exactly like the first picture.

The quantitative factor, measured only at the 5–7 level, involves marking pictures to show understanding of quantitative relationships, e.g., "mark the largest dog" and "Bobby and Billy want to dig. How many shovels do they need?" The motor ability factor, also measured only at the 5–7 level, is based on a test of how many lines the child can draw in the time allowed.

Word fluency, which occurs only at the 11–17 level, requires the examinee to write as many words beginning with a designated letter as he can in five minutes.

TIMING. The 5–7 test requires a little over an hour, preferably in two sessions on successive days. From 60 to 75 minutes are required for the 7–11 tests; again two sessions are recommended. The 11–17 tests require only 26 minutes of actual working time for the 5 scores, the overall testing time being 40 to 50 minutes. At the 5–7 level, only the perceptual speed and motor tests are timed (1½ and 1 minute, respectively, are allowed); the other tests are not speeded. At 7–11, the perception and number tests are speeded tests, and at 11–17 all tests are speeded. Thus scores at different levels which bear the same name may be measured not only by different types of items but also under different conditions with regard to speededness.

FORMAT. The test booklets are generally attractive and the arrangement convenient. The 5–7 booklet makes use of small pictures at the tops of pages and opposite certain items to assist the children in locating the proper place in the booklet. The cover of this particular test booklet is used as a profile chart, which makes a rather uninteresting cover for a six-year old.

The 7–11 booklet has a plastic ring binding and step-down pages so that an answer sheet can be inserted in the back in such a way as to align the answer spaces with the items. The answer sheet spacing does not permit the alignment to be made very accurately, although the lack of coincidence is probably not great enough to disturb a child seriously. The number test is printed on the answer sheet itself. The answer sheet may be opened to reveal a scoring stencil which is automatically marked by means of carbon paper. This method should result in quicker and more accurate scoring than would be possible by using a separate stencil.

The 11–17 booklet employs an IBM answer sheet whose columns correspond to the items on the pages of the test booklet and which can be aligned with the items quite accurately. Item numbers on booklet and answer sheet are adjacent when positioned properly, which should reduce errors resulting from putting answer marks in the wrong place.

The tests are obviously the work of competent people. The items appear to be good and the instructions clear. From the standpoint of test construction one can find little fault with the tests of *SRA Primary Mental Abilities*.

THE MANUALS. The examiners' manuals and technical supplements at the 5–7 and 7–11 levels were last revised in 1954. A new manual, dated May 1958, has just appeared for the 11–17 tests, the previous manual having been issued in 1949. A number of improvements characterize the 1958 manual which the publishers might well emulate in revisions of the lower level test manuals. In the new manual, references to pertinent research accompany claims which are made, and the list of references at the end is reduced from 91 to 21 references—references which are really appropriate. More statistical information about the 11–17 test has been added, especially validity data.

DESCRIPTIONS OF ABILITIES MEASURED. In the 5–7 and 7–11 manuals the description of each test includes a sample item and gives an interpretation in terms of school subjects or of occupations in which one is likely to do well if he is high in the ability measured. In describing verbal meaning at the 5–7 level, for example, the manual states that older children high in this ability usually do well in English, history, and foreign languages, and, as adults, are likely to succeed as secretaries, librarians, teachers, and executives. No evidence is presented to support such statements, and, in the case of executives at least, the statement vastly oversimplifies the problem. The vocational guidance implications of such statements are

disturbing, especially in view of the absence of any evidence that a high verbal score earned at age 5 to 7 on the PMA is associated with a high verbal score on an acceptable measure of verbal ability at college age.

The description of the verbal meaning factor in the 5–7 manual also states that "young children high in V should....learn to read easily, to communicate their ideas well, and to comprehend oral directions." One would not think of quarreling with this statement but for the data presented in the accompanying technical supplement. Correlations and beta weights are given for the prediction of scores on the *Chicago Reading Tests* in the second grade from PMA scores in the first grade. The correlations are .35 for V and .49 for Q, and the beta weights are .085 and .358 respectively. The text attributes the low weight for V to restriction in range of ability, but this interpretation is not borne out by data presented in the technical manual.

In the new 1958 manual for the 11–17 age level, such overenthusiastic descriptions of the traits measured do not occur. In revising the manual's description of word fluency, for example, the description was changed from "the ability to write and talk easily" to "the ability to produce words easily," which, in view of the nature of the test, is much more defensible. The more objective descriptions of abilities, without implication that high scores are associated with success in specific jobs, are to be preferred.

RELIABILITY. The reliabilities reported in the 5–7 technical supplement are split-half reliabilities, even for the highly speeded perceptual speed test. The reliabilities range from .77 for verbal meaning to .96 for perceptual speed. Reliability of the motor test is not reported. The reliabilities reported for the 7–11 level tests are based on Kuder-Richardson formula 20 (or 21 for the speeded perception and number tests). The correlations range from .79 to .95. The 1949 manual for 11–17 reported "Spearman-Brown" reliabilities ranging from .87 to .96. In the revised manual, these reliabilities are again reported (except that the reliability for word fluency is omitted); in addition, reliabilities obtained by Anastasi and Drake (*131*) by correlating separately timed halves are reported. These later correlations, based on a method which is more appropriate for speeded tests, yielded somewhat lower reliabilities ranging from .72 to .90. Anastasi, in reviewing the PMA in *The Fourth Mental Measurements Yearbook,* criticized the manual for using internal consistency methods for estimating reliability of speeded tests. The reliability data she and Drake provided are presented in the new manual; the 10-year-old split-half data are, however, still included.

INTERCORRELATIONS. At the 5–7 level, the intercorrelations among the five scores range from .51 to .73, and are described as "low to moderate." The .73 correlation is between verbal and quantitative scores. One might question whether the scores should be referred to as measures of "separate mental abilities." At the 7–11 level the intercorrelations among the main subtests are lower, ranging from .10 to .63. The question of how separate the abilities are is still pertinent, however. One of the two parts of the test of verbal ability, for example, correlates higher with one of the reasoning subtests than with the other verbal subtest. The two parts of the reasoning test correlate .46 with each other; this is lower than the correlation of .63 reported between verbal and reasoning abilities.

The new 11–17 manual reports six intercorrelation studies, including four from the 1949 manual. The median values range from .13 to .50; the correlation between verbal and reasoning abilities remains fairly high even at this age level. A table of "proportion of differences in excess of chance" which is included in the new manual helps in the interpretation of reliabilities and intercorrelations. The entries in the table represent the proportion of differences between scores on two tests which are so large that they cannot reasonably be attributed to chance. The median intercorrelations and the Anastasi-Drake reliabilities were used in computing the values. The proportions range from .27 (for number-word fluency) to .37 (for verbal-number). Tables such as this might well be added to the manuals at the other two levels whenever revisions are made.

If only a quarter to a third of the differences between pairs of scores are great enough to be attributable to something other than chance, it would be wise to provide the test user with appropriate information as to how big a difference must be before he should pay attention to it. In the manuals much is made of the usefulness of scores on the separate mental abilities in guidance and placement, but nowhere is there a word of advice about a difference being so small that it should be ignored.

NORMS. The norms are based on fairly large numbers of cases, but the manuals leave much to be desired as to descriptions of the groups. The 5–7 technical supplement states that the PMA 5–7 was administered to 1,200 children whose ages ranged from 5 to 8; no further description of the children is given. Another table of means and standard deviations of raw scores for 263 first graders is given, again with no description of the group beyond the age range. Similarly, the technical supplement for the 7–11 tests states the age range of the 4,744 children used in the standardization, but gives no other description.

The revised 11–17 manual gives considerably more information than the 1949 manual it replaces. The old manual indicates that 18,000 students, a "random sampling" of junior and senior public high school students, were used. In the new manual, the 18,000 students are identified as Chicago students, and several other groups which contributed to revision of the norms are mentioned. The groups are predominantly from large cities, although the West Virginia sample presumably includes schools from small communities.

The revised norms are substantially different from those of 1949. Verbal meaning scores which would have been at the 50th percentile on the old norms place a student below the 35th percentile for most age groups on the 1958 norms. For reasoning and number scores, the differences are in the same direction but not quite as great. The correction for the space score is of comparable magnitude but in the opposite direction. Only for word fluency are the differences between the old and new norms tables minor.

Sex differences are not discussed in the technical supplements for levels 5–7 and 7–11. The new 11–17 manual reports data from a 1954 study by Herzberg and Lepkin (*136*) dealing with sex differences. The study showed that at age 17 there were significant sex differences on four of the five tests, differences between means which were separated by 10 or more percentile points in the region of the scale where they occurred. A study of 14-year olds done by Rogers (*154*) in 1956 also showed significant differences between sexes. No sex differentiated norms are presented however.

The profile sheet for 5–7 permits a profile

to be drawn on the basis of the five raw scores earned. The side entries permit translation to mental age, and directions are given for computing quotient scores, analogous to IQ's, for each score and for a total score. The weights used for determining the total quotient score provide an estimate of a Stanford-Binet IQ. At the 7–11 level the profile sheet is similarly interpreted in terms of mental age and quotient scores. A computation form is provided for weighting certain scores properly to get estimates of IQ for children who can read and for children who cannot, and also for reading aptitude and arithmetic aptitude quotients. At the 11–17 level, the profiles may be translated into either percentiles or quotients, although the former is recommended.

None of the profiles or manuals gives any indication of how big a difference should be before it can reasonably be attributed to something other than chance, although teachers, parents, and students are encouraged to use differences in scores as a basis for decisions on educational or occupational problems.

VALIDITY. Validity data of various sorts are presented in the three manuals. Correlations with intelligence tests such as the Stanford-Binet and Kuhlmann-Anderson are high. At the 5–7 levels, single tests such as those for verbal and reasoning ability correlate as high as .75 with Binet IQ's, with multiple correlations in the .80's. When the Binet is given a year after the PMA, the correlation is almost as large. Correlations with reading readiness tests are above .50. At the 7–11 level the correlations with IQ's are slightly lower. High correlations with reading and arithmetic tests are also reported. Both the technical supplements present regression equations for predicting Stanford-Binet IQ's. At the 7–11 level, regression equations are included for predicting reading age and arithmetic grade equivalent. This use of regression equations is an excellent way to take advantage of the fact that several abilities are measured in the battery. The inclusion in the 7–11 interpretation folder of convenient computing forms capitalizes more fully on the advantages of the multifactor test battery.

Validity data at the 11–17 level include correlations with the United States Employment Service *General Aptitude Test Battery*, the *Iowa Tests of Educational Development*, the Otis test, the ACE examination, the Kuhlmann-Anderson, and with grades in a variety of courses. Multiple correlations with tests of general intelligence or scholastic aptitude are high. On the basis of results found in the literature, the formula $2V + R$ is suggested as a measure of scholastic aptitude.

CHANCE SCORES. In general the raw scores which are likely to occur are well out of the chance score level, but there are a few exceptions. The 5–7 perception test has 30 four-choice items. If a child answered the items randomly he would be expected by chance to get about seven right. A raw score of seven is equivalent to a mental age of five, according to the information on the profile sheet. The 7–11 verbal test contains 73 four-choice items, so that a child who responded entirely by guessing might be expected to get 18 right. This raw score is equivalent to an MA of eight years, four months.

On the profile sheet for the 11–17 tests, percentiles are presented for each age from 11 to 17. Some of the tests are apparently too difficult for 11-year-olds; chance scores are quite high—above the 50th percentile for verbal scores and the 25th for reasoning scores. A correction for guessing is employed for the 11–17 space and number tests but not for the verbal and reasoning tests.

LONGITUDINAL STUDIES. In view of the long history of the Primary Mental Abilities, one might expect to find in a recent manual information on the correlations among levels. Such longitudinal studies apparently have not been made. The descriptions of the abilities strongly imply that an ability with a particular name is the same whether measured at 5 or at 17 years of age. The fact that item types and conditions of testing, particularly speededness, may vary considerably with test level suggests, on the other hand, that the abilities may not be the same. Longitudinal studies which result in correlations across levels are needed to answer questions of this sort.

SUMMARY. The PMA tests are sound and well constructed, and, if the scores are properly used, the tests could be of considerable value to teachers and school administrators. The outstanding needs, in this reviewer's opinion, are for (a) words of caution about insignificant differences between scores on a profile chart, and some graphic means of calling the user's attention to this problem; and (b) longitudinal studies to help determine to what extent the same ability is measured at different levels by tests bearing the same name.

ALBERT K. KURTZ, *Professor of Psychology, University of Florida, Gainesville, Florida.*

EFFECT OF PREVIOUS REVIEWS. Previous reviewers of *SRA Primary Mental Abilities* listed a number of highly specific criticisms (some major, some minor) of the tests. They did not all agree on all of these criticisms, nor does the present reviewer, although he feels that the great majority of them are justified. Since the appearance of *The Fourth Mental Measurements Yearbook,* the manuals and profiles have all been revised. (So have some of the test booklets and technical supplements.) Thus, there has been opportunity to make changes. The present reviewer's analysis leads him to conclude that some action has been (or already had been) taken with respect to the following earlier criticisms:

a) Reliability coefficients are inadequately reported, incorrectly computed, or omitted. This is still true for the two younger age groups, but the manual for ages 11–17 also cites recent figures based on separately timed halves.

b) Little evidence concerning validity is given and the recommendations for interpretation go far beyond available evidence for empirical validity. At the two lower levels, the only validity figures are correlations with other tests. At the 11–17 level, correlations with high school and college grades and ratings are also reported. No correlations with vocational success are reported. Discussions of the importance of certain factors in various occupations continue. It seems doubtful that the earlier reviewers would regard the present validity data as justifying these discussions.

c) No separate sex norms are given nor are data on sex differences included. Two tables in the age 11–17 manual show 10 of the 20 reported sex differences to be significant at the 1 per cent level, yet separate norms are not given at any age.

d) The authors have almost completely ignored the significance of individual differences and recent advances regarding influence of maturation. It is a matter of opinion as to whether or not this remains true.

e) Guidance counselors and parents may easily draw erroneous conclusions from some of the statements made. The definition of W has been changed from "the ability to write and talk easily" to "the ability to produce words easily," but the other allegedly misleading statements remain.

f) All editions yield only a single score for each factor. This is true (and the present reviewer feels properly so) for most subtests, although two part scores are available for V and for R at ages 7–11.

g) The authors indicate that V and P are prognostic of reading readiness, but they do not give evidence to support the claim or indicate how the scores should be combined. The manual cites two studies, each showing that V, P, and Q are related to subsequent reading achievement. Combination of scores is now explained and illustrated, using scores on V, P, and Q.

h) The motor test at ages 5–7 could better be described as a test of ability to manipulate a pencil. The manual says it "is important in learning to use a pencil properly."

i) The subject should print his name and other data before taking the word fluency test for ages 11–17 in order to eliminate cheating. This printing is now inconsistently done *before* the test on Form AM, but *after* it on Form AH. (May 1958 Manual.)

j) The manual says there are 60 number items; actually, there are 70. The manual now omits this statement.

The present reviewer may have overlooked something, but, as far as he could tell, the following additional criticisms have been rejected or ignored in revising the PMA materials.

k) No figures are given on test-retest reliability. This is still true.

l) There is no information on correlations between tests of the same factors at different levels. This is still true.

m) It is most misleading to suggest that single short tests can supply relatively pure measures of the factors. This is still implied.

n) The norm samples are inadequately described and insufficient information is given to determine their representativeness. This is still true.

o) Tests of W should be dropped because of little evidence for relevance in educational or vocational guidance. This test is still used.

p) Tests of perceptual speed should have been added at the upper levels. This has not been done.

q) Memory tests were excluded "because they take too long to administer." They are still excluded.

r) The authors recommend percentiles instead of (normalized) IQ. They still do in the two advanced levels.

s) The change from the earlier sliding scale of percentiles to 1950 MA units (all treated as equal) represents a deterioration in test construction. The MA units are still used.

t) Profile sheets should indicate how large a deviation must be to be meaningful. This has not been done, although a table showing the proportion of differences in excess of chance for pairs of PMA subtests is included in the manual for ages 11–17.

u) The authors fail to say whether the child should be encouraged to guess and to recommend what should be done if he cannot come to a decision. These points have not been clarified.

v) Speed is too prominent in the tests. The tests are unchanged.

w) A better method should be used to evaluate effect of speed on the tests. The same method is used.

x) The manuals do not suggest that regression techniques be used to obtain measures from which the effect of a general factor has been eliminated. This is still true.

y) No report is given of factorial investigation from which the tests at the 5–7 level were developed. This report is still delayed.

Enough of earlier reviews; it is time for the present review to begin.

GENERAL. The test items are well written. The directions are almost always clear. The tables of quotients (IQ's) and precomputed weights are excellent. Testing time is short—

probably too short. Most of the cited reliability coefficients are faulty (see *a* above), the best current estimates of the reliabilities of five subtests being .72, .75, .83, .87, and .90—obviously far lower than most test specialists would desire. With respect to the most important single characteristic of any test, we simply do not yet know much about the validities of these tests. Norms are not separated by sex and norm groups are inadequately described. Statements in the manuals and on the profiles tend to foster misinterpretations.

AGES 5–7. The 24-page test booklet and the directions for administering the test are very nicely coordinated. With the possible exception of lack of guessing instructions, everything connected with the mechanics of administering the tests seems well designed to get the child to respond as well as he is able. It is only after the child has recorded all his answers that we encounter any trouble. While technically correct, the directions for scoring are unnecessarily confusing. The neophyte (and all users start out as such) cannot tell at a glance which pages are to be scored, nor is he told what a perfect score is on any subtest. It would be simple to give the latter information (which would result in both faster and more accurate scoring of good papers) and to put some circles, squares, and other designs around the numbers of the pages to be scored, tying these symbols in to the spaces where the raw scores are recorded.

After the five raw scores are obtained, recorded, and plotted as a profile, "weights" for four of the scores are copied, added, and used in obtaining a mental age. Here arises the mystery of why the motor score vanishes. The motor score has no "weights" beside it and is not used further. The user may wonder why he should bother testing for motor if it isn't good enough to put in the total. Perhaps he should be told.

Most unfortunately, there still are remarkably few figures on the really important characteristics of the tests. Their reliabilities are unknown, the only set of figures being subject to the criticism in *a* above.

As to validity, these subtests can be so weighted as to give a multiple *r* of around .70 to .80 with Stanford-Binet. They can also be weighted to give a multiple *r* of around .50 with scores on reading tests. Further, the quantitative score correlates around .77 with arithmetic achievement of 75 children measured three

months later. More validity data should be available for a widely used test first copyrighted in 1946, even if the manual did come out in 1953.

Norms (the same for both sexes) are given in MA units only. (See *c* and *s* above.)

The manual helpfully provides and discusses a full-page sample interpretation. Unfortunately, the present reviewer believes that both he and some of the earlier reviewers will feel that the criticism in *e* above still applies. The interpretations should be much more conservative—at least until we have data to justify them.

The *Learning to Think Series,* by the same author and publisher, which was so thoroughly criticized in earlier reviews of this test, is still recommended in the manual.

AGES 7–11. At this level, there is a test booklet and separate answer sheet, readily scorable in "about three minutes." The selection of abilities to be tested is good, and there should be no problems connected with giving or scoring the tests.

Again, we encounter trouble with respect to test statistics. Only one set of reliability coefficients is given. Most were computed by Kuder-Richardson formula 20, but for some peculiar reason K-R 21 was used for two "tests in which speed is of major importance." This is highly inappropriate since *all* K-R formulas are inapplicable to speed tests. It is too bad we know so little about the reliabilities of these tests.

The validity data consist solely of correlations with other tests. As was true at ages 5–7, these subtests can be so weighted as to give a multiple *r* of around .70 to .80 with Stanford-Binet or Kuhlmann-Anderson IQ. The verbal score based on words (Vw) also correlates around .75 with reading tests; and a regression equation gives a multiple *r* of around .60 with an arithmetic test. Most, if not all, of these figures are concurrent validities. It seems that nothing is known about how well these tests will *predict* anything at some future time. This statement has important implications concerning the use of the tests in counseling and guidance. (See *b* and *e* above.)

In one of the two tables of intercorrelations, after we exclude the part scores, the correlations run from .10 to .63 with a median of .34. In the other, no total scores are given for V and R, so after we eliminate the correlations between Vw and Vp and between Rw and Rf, the other 19 correlations run from .34 to .73 with a median of .46. Both these sets of correlations seem far too high for tests which are supposed to measure relatively independent factors. (Remember that if we could correct these correlations for attenuation, they would be higher by an unknown amount.)

Norms (the same for both sexes) are given in MA units only, just as was true at the 5–7 year level. As was true at the younger ages, the recommended interpretations frequently do not seem justified by the available data. Because both the verbal and reasoning scores are divided into two parts, as well as a total, the five factors yield nine separate scores to be plotted on profiles. This is, indeed, a large superstructure to be erected on a foundation about which so little is known.

AGES 11–17. The same test booklet can be used with either hand scored or machine scored answer sheets. The two sets of directions for giving the tests are very conveniently presented in two parallel columns. The only criticism, and it is a minor one, centers on the statement, "If necessary, explain....that once a word has been used, it is incorrect to...." The optional nature of this may result in slightly different scores on the word fluency test. This subtest is hand scored on both answer sheets. The scoring directions for all subtests are simple and clear.

Whereas the other manuals were revised in 1953 and 1954, the one for ages 11–17 was revised in 1958. It is well prepared, starting with "an overview" and a very complete table of contents and ending, not with a 64-item, largely unused bibliography (as was true at the earlier ages) but with one of 21 recent items, every one of which is referred to in the text.

One of the earlier reviewers, Anastasi, is responsible for the only correct reliabilities that have yet been reported for these tests. She and Drake computed the reliabilities and got much lower figures [1] than the incorrectly computed figures previously reported. In the case of the space subtest, the effect was catastrophic, the figure changing from .96 to .75. The manual concedes the correctness of these lower figures. It would be even better if something were done to raise them. Specifically, the application of the general form of the Spearman-Brown

formula for lengthening tests shows that the reliabilities of V and R could be raised to .95 and those of S, N, and W to .90 by nearly tripling the present working time of 26 minutes while only doubling the present overall testing time of 40 to 50 minutes. If these scores are to be used for guidance or any other worthwhile purpose, it is imperative that some such steps be taken to make them reliable.

It is, of course, even more important that the scores be valid. Several hundred correlations between PMA subtests and other test scores are given. Usually V and R, the most reliable subtests, show the highest correlations. The reader may be interested in knowing that an arithmetic reason test correlates negligibly higher with V than with either N or R. There are about six studies in which school grades are correlated with PMA scores. In one of them, the PMA tests were taken about two years *after* the grades were given. Since the usual purpose is prediction of achievement rather than of PMA scores, such correlations are not very helpful. In at least one other study, the tests were given first, as they should be. Let us temporarily define validity as the correlation between the high school grades and whatever PMA subtest shows the highest correlation with the grades. So defined, the 13 high school validities run from .22 to .66, the median being .48. In four instances, the correlation with V was not computed; in six of the other nine, V gave the highest correlation. Stated differently, this PMA correlates reasonably well with high school grades; the verbal test, alone, would do nearly as well.

There are only two validity studies not relating to test scores or to ordinary high school grades. One used multiple correlation to predict ratings of progress in three vocational high school courses (auto mechanics, electric wiring, and woodworking). The validities were only .31, .38, and .17, respectively. The other study attempted to predict college grades from PMA tests administered in the 12th grade. "Correlations with grades in a variety of college courses were inconsistent and low." Reasons are given for both these failures to predict.

There are six sets of intercorrelations of the subtests. These correlations run from .10 to .55 with a median of .31. Thus, they are a little, but not much, lower than those for the preceding age group.

Sex differences are clearly revealed in two

1 Even these figures are perhaps not so low as they should be. Anastasi and Drake used boys in the 11th and 12th grades. Reliabilities within a single grade would almost certainly be lower.

tables and in the text. Ten of the 20 differences are significant at the 1 per cent level of confidence, the significant differences running from about 2 to 6 points. This largest difference means that the average boy has a percentile of about 45, while the average girl has one of 65. Separate sex norms are needed, but still not provided. (See *c* above.)

The May 1958 "Profile" is a single sheet with no directions or explanations on it and not much in the manual. It gives "Percentiles" at one side and "Quotients" at the other, the former being recommended as more meaningful for almost all uses. The present reviewer would disagree, but this is a matter on which there are differences of opinion. (See *r* and *s* above.) By omitting the directions and explanations which were printed on earlier editions of the profile, the authors have left the teacher, parent, or student somewhat bewildered, but they have eliminated some of the force of criticisms *b, e, m,* and *r* above.

OVERALL EVALUATION. This is not an excellent test battery, but it is a good one. Most of its defects were pointed out in earlier *Mental Measurements Yearbooks*. It is objective, easy to administer, and has high face validity. But its reliability is low at ages 11–17 and unknown, and probably very low, at the younger ages. Its validity is no better than that of many other tests. It correlates fairly well with achievement test scores and some high school grades; it does not correlate with vocational training ratings or with college grades. (The test may be much better or worse than this sentence implies; the chief defect is that there are so few studies of its predictive value.)

The theoretical rationale underlying the test is sound. It may well be that an excellent test can be developed upon this foundation. Until the reliabilities are improved and satisfactory validity data are available, the potential user should investigate other possibilities also. The present reviewer is not familiar with competing tests at ages 5–7. At ages 7–11, almost any reliable intelligence (or other) test with a large verbal component should do as well as the PMA in predicting school achievement. At ages 11–17, this simple procedure would also work, but a better procedure would be to use a competing battery about which more information is available, such as the *Differential Aptitude Tests*. Although these require more time for administration and have higher average in-

tercorrelations, the latter is in part due to their much higher reliability. They also have validities which are known and which are much higher than the few available for the *SRA Primary Mental Abilities* test batteries.

[615]

*Yale Educational Aptitude Test Battery. Grades 9–16; 1946–53; 7 scores: verbal comprehension, artificial language, verbal reasoning, quantitative reasoning, mathematical aptitude, spatial relations, mechanical ingenuity; IBM in part; 1 form; 7 tests in 3 booklets (tests 3, 4, and 7 in booklet entitled "Single Booklet Edition," '46; tests 1, 2, 5, and 6 in booklet entitled "Second Single Booklet Edition," '47; practice booklet, '47); mimeographed directions ('47); descriptive bulletin ('53); profile ('47); norms ('47); separate answer sheets must be used; $1.75 per set of test booklets, answer sheets, and profile; $2.50 per set of scoring stencils; $2.50 per battery with scoring service; postage extra; (60–70) minutes per test; Albert B. Crawford and Paul S. Burnham; distributed by Educational Records Bureau. *

REFERENCES

1–7. See 4:718.
8. CRAWFORD, ALBERT B., AND BURNHAM, PAUL S. "Freshman Aptitude Tests: How Yale Predicts Undergraduate Scholastic Performance." *Yale Scientific Mag* 23:9–10+ O '48.
9. McCARTHY, MARY VITERBO. *An Empirical Study of the Personality Profiles Characterizing Differential Quantitative and Linguistic Ability.* Catholic University of America, Studies in Psychology and Psychiatry, Vol. 8, No. 4. Washington, D.C.: Catholic University of America Press, 1953. Pp. viii, 45. * (PA 28:4043)
10. SKARD, ØYVIND; AURSAND, INGER MARIE; AND BRAATEN, LEIF J. "Development and Application of Tests for University Students in Norway: A Report on Parts of a Research Project." *Psychol Monogr* 68(12):1–24 '54. * (PA 29:7971)
11. BURNHAM, PAUL S. *Entrance to a University College: An Exploratory Study.* Christchurch, New Zealand: Canterbury University College, 1955.

ANNE ANASTASI, *Professor of Psychology, Fordham University, New York, New York.*

Originally developed as an integrated series of aptitude tests for use in the educational counseling of Yale freshmen, this battery has recently been made available for wider distribution. The current form has evolved through some 15 years of systematic research with both Yale students and secondary school boys. It consists of seven tests, grouped into two booklets (but labeled "single booklet edition"!), to be administered in separate testing sessions. The tests are:

Test 1, Verbal Comprehension, requiring the identification of synonyms, antonyms, and inappropriate words; Test 2, Artificial Language, calling for a demonstration of linguistic facility; Test 3, Verbal Reasoning, comprising logical inference, deductive judgment, and similar functions; Test 4, Quantitative Reasoning, calling for the manipulation of hypothetical data and the derivation of principles analogous to but different from those met in the natural sciences; Test 5, Mathematical

Aptitude, requiring the performance of various tasks with equations; Test 6, Spatial Relations, including block counting, projections, and other item types that utilize two-dimensional representations of three-dimensional figures; and Test 7, Mechanical Ingenuity, requiring the solution of problems in gear or pulley movements, structural stability, and other mechanical operations.

Raw scores on each of the seven tests can be converted into standard scores with mean 50 and SD 10, as well as into percentile equivalents. The norms provided for these conversions were obtained on approximately 2,000 students tested in 13 secondary schools. Most of these subjects were in eastern private preparatory schools. No information regarding sex or grade level of the normative sample is given, although personal communication with the test distributors revealed that most of the subjects were 10th grade boys. Percentile norms on Yale freshmen may be obtained on request. These norms are offered only as suggestive data, test users being urged by the authors to develop their own local norms. It is stated (4, 8) that, with appropriate modifications in norms, the battery can be used effectively from the 10th grade to the college freshman level. In general, amount of previous education exerts maximum influence on the two tests (Verbal Comprehension and Mathematical Aptitude) which, in some respects, are similar to the CEEB *Scholastic Aptitude Test*. At the other extreme, grade means exhibit the least change in Tests 6 and 7, Spatial Relations and Mechanical Ingenuity, although relevant job experience (as in the course of military service) is reflected in superior performance on these tests (4, 8).

It is reported that split-half reliability coefficients of .92 to .96 have been found for each of the seven tests with different populations and educational levels, although detailed data are not given. Kuder-Richardson coefficients on two samples in grades 10–12 fell between .75 and .97 (6). Retests over a two-year interval (some involving closely similar but not identical tests) yielded stability coefficients of .56 to .82, most being in the .60's (4). Intercorrelations of the seven tests in a Yale freshman class of approximately 850 students ranged from .19 to .64, with a mean of .41 (4). Very similar patterns of correlations were obtained in other Yale freshman classes and among secondary school students, although the

correlations tended to run higher in the latter population.

Differential validity of each part of the Yale battery has been checked principally against grades in appropriate college courses. The large majority of these validity coefficients fall between .45 and .65, while correlations with inappropriate courses (for example, scores on Mathematical Aptitude with English grades) are reported as generally under .20, many being statistically insignificant. For purposes of educational counseling, the authors recommend a classification of the tests into three overlapping groups: Tests 1, 2, and 3 indicating aptitude for the liberal arts; Tests 3, 4, and 5 for pure science and mathematics; and Tests 5, 6, and 7 for technological studies such as engineering.

Certain limitations of the test in its present form obviously stem from its having been designed for restricted use. There is, for example, no manual in the usual sense, the necessary information being provided in a 4-page descriptive booklet and another leaflet containing general directions, time limits, and norms. Although the descriptive booklet presents a concise, objective, and well balanced picture of the technical characteristics of the battery, the reader must consult Chapter 5 of *Forecasting College Achievement* (4) for supporting data. Even this source omits much relevant material; reference is made repeatedly to a projected second volume which has not appeared. Two recent publications concerned with the use of these tests in other countries are of some interest. Burnham (11) has described the application of parts of the battery to a small group of secondary school boys in New Zealand. Data on differential validity, intercorrelations, and factorial analysis of a Norwegian adaptation of the battery are reported by Skard and others (10).

In appearance, the test booklets fall short of the "deluxe" standards attained by some commercial tests, although the reproduction of test items is sufficiently clear. Another minor detail concerns the numbering of test parts which is now quite confusing, especially since Arabic and Roman numerals are used inconsistently to refer to the same parts. Finally, the preparation of a unified and fuller manual would be of considerable assistance to the potential general user of the battery.

With regard to the more basic requirements of test construction, the Yale battery represents an outstanding achievement. Available data on its reliability and validity indicate unusual promise for differential prediction of academic performance in broad curricular areas. In its objectives, this battery falls between traditional achievement tests and such multiple factor batteries as the *SRA Primary Mental Abilities,* but it appears to be closer to the latter than to the former. Although the research leading to its development was initiated more than two decades ago, the Yale battery reflects important current trends in test development in its use of a multiple aptitude profile and in its emphasis on the measurement of reasoning. Closely allied to the latter characteristic is the relatively extensive coverage of aptitudes relevant to science. And of special interest in this connection is the content of the quantitative reasoning test which requires the analysis of imaginary scientific data.

RUTH CHURCHILL, *Professor of Education and Psychology, Antioch College, Yellow Springs, Ohio.*

The *Yale Educational Aptitude Battery,* developed in the 1940's by Crawford and Burnham at Yale University, is one of the small number of aptitude batteries available. The distinctive characteristic of these batteries is the attempt to sample a range of abilities significant for educational and vocational guidance by means of a group of tests all standardized on the same population. Most of the aptitude batteries, however, such as the *Flanagan Aptitude Classification Tests* are designed for general vocational guidance and sample abilities widely. They include many perceptual, manual, and motor tests, so that skills needed for a wide variety of jobs, clerical and skilled as well as professional, are tapped. The Yale battery is the only one specifically designed with the question of educational, rather than vocational, guidance at both the high school and the college levels clearly in mind.

In the descriptive bulletin, the following statements made concerning the aim of the Yale tests clearly illustrate the concentration on educational guidance:

The purpose of this battery may....be defined as the provision of a series of differential measures severally pointing towards comparative *learning capacity in one direction or another.* * Tests I, II, and III appraise scholastic promise for the Liberal Arts—English, languages, history, economics and related (Verbal) subjects. Tests III, IV, and V point towards comparative

ability, or lack of it, for the physical (Quantitative) sciences and mathematics. Tests V, VI and VII measure aptitude for technological studies, such as engineering.

From the practical standpoint, the major problem in the use of this battery is that of time. The practice booklet takes 2 hours, and the typical time limit for each of the seven tests is 45 minutes. When time is allowed for distribution and collection of materials for each test, the total time for the battery is about eight hours, including the practice booklet but exclusive of rest periods. Conceivably the test can be given in one day, but three half-day testing sessions would be better, or students can be requested to complete the practice booklet before the day of testing. It is also possible to give the test without the use of the practice booklet and with longer time limits (about one hour) for each individual test. Again a full day is necessary. In a letter to the reviewer, Arthur Traxler gives some indication of the amount of use of the test in the past few years. Each year about 15 to 18 schools and colleges have used the test. He feels that its limited use has been the result of the amount of time needed to give the battery.

Over and above practical considerations involved in using a test or battery of tests, one of the first major considerations is the reliability of the various tests. The explanatory materials available indicate that split-half correlations adjusted by the Spearman-Brown formula range from .92 to .96 for the various tests, with a median of .94. These are for an unnamed sample of unknown size. In a study by Jacobs (6), Kuder-Richardson reliability coefficients for two groups of high school students (grades 10–12) ranged from .91 to .97 for all the tests except Test 5 for which the coefficients were .87 to .88 and Test 7 for which they ranged from .75 to .85. This reviewer obtained Kuder-Richardson formula 21 reliability coefficients ranging from .87 to .95 for Tests 1–7 (Test 2 omitted) for a group of 319 students entering Antioch College in September 1957. The two reliability coefficients below .90 for this group were .87 for Test 5 and .89 for Test 7. Thus, the reliability of the battery, with the possible exception of Test 7, seems adequate then in both high school and college populations.

The questions linked to the suitability of the battery for various groups are the difficulty level of the various tests and the availability of norms based on known groups. The test is recommended for use throughout the high school and college years. Jacobs presents data which indicate that the tests are somewhat difficult for an independent school 10th grade group (median percentage right on any one test is 25 per cent), but that they are not too difficult (median percentage right, 37 per cent) for a 12th grade group. For the group of 319 students entering Antioch College in 1957 the median percentage right on any one test was 44 per cent. Four of the six tests were close to 50 per cent in difficulty for this group while two, Mathematical Aptitude and Mechanical Ingenuity, were difficult for it. While the high difficulty level of the test may be a disadvantage at the high school level, it is one of the test's greatest advantages at the college level. The tests of the battery are sufficiently difficult to permit distinguishing differences among superior college students; the reviewer has found few other aptitude tests which do so.

The norms furnished are based on "some 2000 students in 13 secondary schools. These were mostly eastern private preparatory institutions which as a group ranked at approximately the sixty-third percentile on the independent-school norms for general scholastic aptitude prepared by the Educational Records Bureau." Other norms referred to in the descriptive bulletin as being available are based on Yale freshmen. These norm groups have two serious shortcomings. First, they include no women. Both the Jacobs study and Antioch data indicate that women do better than the men in the verbal tests but poorer in the quantitative and technical tests. Second, the norm group of secondary school students (and that for college students, for that matter) is a highly selected one. Independent school norms in general run higher than public high school norms, and the students upon whom the reported norms are based were selected even for an independent school group. Norms based on both sexes (or given separately by sex) and on more typical high school and college groups would be desirable. Of course, the ideal solution is the development of local norms; for even when norms based on a range of groups are available, it is difficult to find the exact set most appropriate to each particular situation.

Crawford and Burnham (4) point out that they have compromised between a battery which attempts to measure factors in as pure

a form as possible and one which stresses relevance to needs for prediction in educational guidance. The intercorrelations among the Yale tests are evidence of this compromise between factorial purity and everyday relevance in complex situations. In most cases, the intercorrelations are low enough to suggest that the various tests of the battery do measure somewhat independent variables. Although each test is a composite of several subtests and thus can scarcely be pure factorially, as Crawford and Burnham point out, factor analyses by them did indicate three factors in addition to a residual factor labeled "general scholastic ability": verbal-linguistic facility, quantitative-mathematical reasoning, and spatial-mechanical aptitude.

Data on the validity or usefulness of such a test battery as the Yale can be of many kinds. What are the relationships of these tests to other tests and to relevant course grades? What studies are there of the usefulness of the test profile in educational guidance? What discussion is there of these profiles in counseling? Again, it is clear that *Forecasting College Achievement* rather than the materials provided with the battery must be considered the manual for the test. The descriptive bulletin summarizes validation studies in one paragraph, emphasizing correlations between test scores and appropriate and inappropriate college grades. It states, "Coefficients in general ranged from about .45 to .65 or higher, between test scores and *appropriate* criteria of subsequent academic grades; from .10 or less to about .20 with *inappropriate* criteria." The paragraph concludes with a reference to the cumulative validation studies in *Forecasting College Achievement*.

In this work, the validation studies are amplified, but the above statement from the manual is a good summary of the studies dealing with the prediction of course grades. Unfortunately the only material presented on the usefulness of the *profile* of test scores consists of a comparison of profiles for groups of 1944 Yale freshmen entering the liberal arts and the engineering curricula and the presentation of a few individual profiles together with relevant material on their later academic performance at Yale.

Over the course of 10 years' use, this reviewer has collected data on the usefulness of the Yale battery. Some of this is formal data of the sort to be hoped for in manuals; some of it is informal data based on acquaintance with the test. The net result of this long acquaintance has been a decided impression that the test is useful for the purposes for which it was designed.

In summary, the *Yale Educational Aptitude Test Battery* is a well constructed, carefully standardized, thorough, difficult battery which is well designed for use at the college level. At a time when everyone is concerned about our best college students, such a test should be extremely useful. If norms for the test and studies of the test are scanty, these shortcomings can be traced to the fact that the test has had far too few users, which can in turn be traced to the length of administration time required. Unfortunately, a thorough, comprehensive job of differential testing cannot be done in an hour or so. Although the requirement that the tests be used as a complete battery is a wise one (otherwise the essential value of a battery is lost), one possible compromise might shorten the length of the battery without weakening it. Test 1, Verbal Comprehension, and Test 5, Mathematical Aptitude, are very similar to the two parts of the *Scholastic Aptitude Test* of the College Entrance Examination Board. In fact, in some of the research on the Yale battery they have been used interchangeably. In colleges which use the *Scholastic Aptitude Test,* why could not the SAT be substituted for Tests 1 and 5 of the Yale battery, thus shortening the battery by an hour and a half to two hours? Perhaps, this compromise should be considered by the Educational Records Bureau.

In a way it is a sad commentary on guidance programs when one day's time cannot be found for gathering information which may improve decisions for four or more years of education. With the latest Office of Education figures reporting that only 40 per cent of entering freshmen graduate at the end of four years, surely there is room for improving educational guidance at the college level. Everything about the *Yale Educational Aptitude Test Battery* indicates that it is an excellent instrument for this task.

VOCATIONS—FIFTH MMY

REVIEWS BY *Brent Baxter, Edward S. Bordin, Arthur H. Brayfield, E. G. Chambers, J. F. Clark, Andrew L. Comrey, William C. Cottle, Jerome E. Doppelt, Henry S. Dyer, John W. French, Clifford P. Froehlich, Edward B. Greene, John W. Gustad, Lloyd G. Humphreys, John R. Jennings, A. Pemberton Johnson, Robert A. Jones, Clifford E. Jurgensen, Martin Katz, Raymond A. Katzell, Albert K. Kurtz, Wilbur L. Layton, John Liggett, D. W. McElwain, I. G. Meddleton, P. L. Mellenbruch, William J. Micheels, John B. Morris, Charles T. Myers, Mary Ellen Oliverio, John Pierce-Jones, Arthur B. Royce, William B. Schrader, Donald Spearritt, Donald E. Super, Erwin K. Taylor, Albert S. Thompson, Herbert A. Tonne, Arthur E. Traxler, S. Rains Wallace, Neil D. Warren, Alexander G. Wesman, Haydn S. Williams, and Alfred Yates.*

CLERICAL

[845]

★**A.C.E.R. Short Clerical Test.** Ages 13 and over; 1953–57; Forms A ('53), B ('56); no manual; mimeographed directions sheet ['57]; no data on reliability and validity; no norms; distribution of Form A restricted; 6s. per 10 tests; 1s. 6d. per set of directions and scoring key; 2s. per specimen set; postpaid within Australia; 10(15) minutes; Australian Council for Educational Research. *

[846]

***A.C.E.R. Speed and Accuracy Tests.** Ages 13.6 and over; 1942–57; 1 form ['57]; 2 tests: number checking, name checking; revised mimeographed manual ['53]; no data on reliability; separate answer sheet must be used; 5s. per 10 tests; 1s. 9d. per 10 answer sheets; 2s. per manual; 2s. 6d. per scoring key; 5s. per specimen set; postpaid within Australia; 12(20) minutes; Australian Council for Educational Research. *

REFERENCES
1. HOHNE, H. H. *Success and Failure in Scientific Faculties of the University of Melbourne.* Melbourne, Australia: Australian Council for Educational Research, 1955. Pp. vii, 129. * (*PA* 31:3787)
2. BUCKLOW, MAXINE, AND DOUGHTY, PATRICIA. "The Use of Aptitude Tests in Clerical Employment: The Selection of Accounting Machinists." *Personnel Pract B* 13:35–44 S '57. *

For a review by D. W. McElwain of an earlier form, see 4:719.

[847]

***Clerical Aptitude Test: Acorn National Aptitude Tests.** Grades 7–16 and adults; 1943–50; 4 scores: business practice, number checking, date-name-address checking, total; 1 form ('50, identical with test copyrighted in 1943); manual ('50, identical with manual copyrighted in 1943); directions sheet ('50, identical with sheet copyrighted in 1943); no norms for part scores; $3 per 25 tests; 25¢ per manual; 50¢ per specimen set; postage extra; 40(45) minutes; Andrew Kobal, J. Wayne Wrightstone, and Karl R. Kunze; Acorn Publishing Co. *

REFERENCE
1. BAIR, JOHN THEODORE. *Factor Analysis of Tests Purporting to Measure Clerical Aptitudes.* Doctor's thesis, Ohio State University (Columbus, Ohio), 1949.

For reviews by Marion A. Bills, Donald G. Paterson, Henry Weitz, and E. F. Wonderlic, see 3:623.

[848]

★**Clerical Tests 1 and 2.** Ages 12–14.0; 1952–54; 1 form; 2 tests; no data on reliability and validity; distribution restricted to directors of education; 4s. 6d. per 12 tests; 5d. per single copy; 1s. 6d. per manual; postage extra; published for the National Foundation for Educational Research in England and Wales; Newnes Educational Publishing Co. Ltd. *
a) CLERICAL TEST 1. 1952–53; 1 form ['52]; manual ['52]; norms ['53]; 40(60) minutes; M. K. B. Richards.
b) CLERICAL TEST 2. 1953–54; 1 form ['53]; manual ['53]; norms ['54]; 43(75) minutes; G. A. V. Morgan.

[849]

*[Hay Tests for Clerical Aptitude.]** Applicants for clerical positions; 1941–55; 4 tests; manual ('50); 75¢ per battery manual ('50); $1 per specimen set; postage extra; 13(28) minutes; Edward N. Hay; Aptitude Test Service. *
a) TEST 1: THE WARM UP. 1945–55; practice exercise to precede administration of battery; Form B ('50, revision of the 1945 form); directions sheet ('55); $1.25 per 25 tests; 1(3) minutes.
b) NUMBER PERCEPTION TEST. 1947–50; Forms A ('47), B ('50, same as test copyrighted in 1947); $2 per 25 tests; 4(7) minutes.
c) NUMBER SERIES COMPLETION TEST. 1941–55; Forms B ('50, same as test copyrighted in 1949), C ('55); no norms for Form C; $1.25 per 25 tests; 4(7) minutes.
d) HAY NAME FINDING TEST. 1941–55; Forms C ('50, same as test copyrighted in 1949), D ('55); practice exercise, Form B ('49); $2 per 25 tests; 4(11) minutes.

REFERENCES
1–8. See 4:725.
9. SEASHORE, HAROLD G. "Validation of Clerical Testing in Banks." *Personnel Psychol* 6:45–56 sp '53. * (*PA* 28:1670)
10. HAY, EDWARD N. "Comparative Validities in Clerical Testing." *J Appl Psychol* 38:299–301 O '54. * (*PA* 29:6351)

For reviews by Reign H. Bittner and Edward E. Cureton, see 4:725.

[850]

Minnesota Clerical Test. Grades 8–12 and adults; 1933–46; formerly called *Minnesota Vocational Test for Clerical Workers* (see 40:1664); 2 scores: number comparison, name comparison; 1 form ('33); revised manual ('46); $1.80 per 25 tests; 35¢ per specimen set; postpaid; 15(20) minutes; Dorothy M. Andrew, Donald G. Paterson, and Howard P. Longstaff; Psychological Corporation. *

REFERENCES

1–18. See 40:1664.
19–40. See 3:627.
41. HACKMAN, RAY CARTER. *The Differential Prediction of Success in Two Contrasting Vocational Areas.* Doctor's thesis, University of Minnesota (Minneapolis, Minn.), 1940.
42. STEAD, WILLIAM H.; SHARTLE, CARROLL L.; OTIS, JAY L.; WARD, RAYMOND S.; OSBORNE, HERBERT F.; ENDLER, O. L.; DVORAK, BEATRICE J.; COOPER, JOHN H.; BELLOWS, ROGER M.; AND KOLBE, LAVERNE E. *Occupational Counseling Techniques: Their Development and Application.* Published for the Technical Board of the Occupational Research Program, United States Employment Service. New York: American Book Co., 1940. Pp. ix, 273. *
43. CRISSEY, ORLO L. "Test Predictive of Success in Occupation of Job-Setter." Abstract. *Psychol B* 39:436 Jl '42. *
44. ACHARD, F. H., AND CLARKE, FLORENCE H. "You Can Measure the Probability of Success as a Supervisor." *Personnel* 21:353–73 My '45. *
45. COX, K. J. "Aptitude Testing in Industry." *B Can Psychol Assn* 5:99–102 D '45. * (PA 20:2035)
46. CARPENTER, EDWIN KENNETH. *The Effect of Ego-Involved Attitudes on Aptitude Test Performance.* Doctor's thesis, Clark University (Worcester, Mass.), 1947.
47. KENDALL, WILLIAM E., AND HAHN, MILTON E. "The Use of Tests in the Selection of Medical Students by the College of Medicine of Syracuse University." Abstract. *Am Psychol* 2:297 Ag '47. *
48. STRONG, EDWARD K., JR. "Norms for Graduate School Business Students on the Minnesota Vocational Test for Clerical Workers." *J Appl Psychol* 31:594–600 D '47. * (PA 22:2775)
49. BEAMER, GEORGE C.; EDMONSON, LAWRENCE D.; AND STROTHER, GEORGE B. "Improving the Selection of Linotype Trainees." *J Appl Psychol* 32:130–4 Ap '48. * (PA 23:965)
50. BAIR, JOHN THEODORE. *Factor Analysis of Tests Purporting to Measure Clerical Aptitudes.* Doctor's thesis, Ohio State University (Columbus, Ohio), 1949.
51. BLACK, MARGARET H. *An Evaluation of the Differences Obtained by White and Negro Veterans on the Minnesota Clerical Test.* Master's thesis, University of Delaware (Newark, Del.), 1949.
52. BLANCHARD, HOWARD L. *A Comparison of Teachers' Marks With an Actual Battery of Aptitude Test Percentile Scores.* Doctor's "Field Study No. 1," Colorado State College of Education (Greeley, Colo.), 1949.
53. CAPWELL, DORA F. *Psychological Tests for Retail Store Personnel.* Pittsburgh, Pa.: Research Bureau for Retail Training, University of Pittsburgh, 1949. Pp. 48. * (PA 25:3449)
54. CARTER, LAUNOR, AND NIXON, MARY. "Ability, Perceptual, Personality, and Interest Factors Associated With Different Criteria of Leadership." *J Psychol* 27:377–88 Ap '49. * (PA 23:4183)
55. JACKSON, JOSEPH. "An Analysis of the Minnesota Vocational Test for Clerical Workers in a High School Situation." *J Social Psychol* 30:149–53 Ag '49. * (PA 24:2652)
56. SUPER, DONALD E. *Appraising Vocational Fitness by Means of Psychological Tests,* pp. 164–83. New York: Harper & Brothers, 1949. Pp. xxiii, 727. * (PA 24:2130)
57. WIGHTWICK, BEATRICE. *The Effect of Retesting on the Predictive Power of Aptitude Tests.* Doctor's thesis, New York University (New York, N.Y.), 1949.
58. BERKSHIRE, ROGER, AND FLEET, DONALD. "College Junior Norms for 1947 A.C.E. and Minnesota Clerical Tests." *Occupations* 29:30–1 O '50. * (PA 25:3417)
59. BORG, WALTER R. "Does a Perceptual Factor Exist in Artistic Ability?" *J Ed Res* 44:47–53 S '50. * (PA 25:2921)
60. ENGELHARDT, OLGA E. DE CILLIS. "The Minnesota Clerical Test: Sex Differences and Norms for College Groups." *J Appl Psychol* 34:412–4 D '50. * (PA 25:4878)
61. HAY, EDWARD N. "Cross-Validation of Clerical Aptitude Tests." *J Appl Psychol* 34:153–8 Je '50. * (PA 25:3991)
62. JOHNSON, RALPH H., AND BOND, GUY L. "Reading Ease of Commonly Used Tests." *J Appl Psychol* 34:319–24 O '50. * (PA 26:299)
63. LEE, MARILYN C. *Relationship of Masculinity-Femininity to Tests of Mechanical and Clerical Abilities.* Master's thesis, University of Minnesota (Minneapolis, Minn.), 1950.
64. MILLER, RICHARD B. "Reducing the Time Required for Testing Clerical Applicants." *Personnel J* 28:364–6 Mr '50. * (PA 24:4872)
65. BAIR, JOHN T. "Factor Analysis of Clerical Aptitude Tests." *J Appl Psychol* 35:245–9 Ag '51. * (PA 26:3067)
66. BLAKEMORE, ARLINE. "Reducing Typing Costs With Aptitude Tests." *Personnel J* 30:20–4 My '51. * (PA 25:7749)
67. HAY, EDWARD N. "Mental Ability Tests in Clerical Selection." *J Appl Psychol* 35:250–1 Ag '51. * (PA 26:3071)
68. PETRIE, ASENATH, AND POWELL, MURIEL B. "The Selection of Nurses in England." *J Appl Psychol* 35:281–6 Ag '51. * (PA 26:3090)

69. PURDY, BENJAMIN FRANK. *A Study of Certain Tests and Personal History Factors as Predictors of Job Success for a Group of Clerical Workers.* Master's thesis, Southern Methodist University (Dallas, Tex.), 1951.
70. AMERICAN GAS ASSOCIATION, PERSONNEL COMMITTEE. *Personnel Testing in the Gas Industry.* New York: the Association, January 1952. Pp. 10. *
71. LEE, MARILYN C. "Relationship of Masculinity-Femininity to Tests of Mechanical and Clerical Abilities." *J Appl Psychol* 36:377–80 D '52. * (PA 27:6431)
72. ANDERSON, ROSE G. "Do Aptitudes Support Interests?" *Personnel & Guid J* 32:14–7 S '53. * (PA 28:4495)
73. BRAYFIELD, ARTHUR H. "Clerical Interest and Clerical Aptitude." *Personnel & Guid J* 31:304–6 F '53. * (PA 28:1616)
74. JENKINS, JAMES J. "Some Measured Characteristics of Air Force Weather Forecasters and Success in Forecasting." *J Appl Psychol* 37:440–4 D '53. * (PA 29:1642)
75. SEASHORE, HAROLD G. "Validation of Clerical Testing in Banks." *Personnel Psychol* 6:45–56 sp '53. * (PA 28:1670)
76. COYLE, FRANCIS P. *The Effect of Perceptual Training Upon Minnesota Clerical Speed Test Performance.* Master's thesis, Utah State Agricultural College (Logan, Utah), 1954.
77. GRAHAM, WARREN R. "Identification and Prediction of Two Training Criterion Factors." *J Appl Psychol* 38:96–9 Ap '54. * (PA 29:1798)
78. LEE, PHYLLIS JEANNE. *The Effectiveness of a Test Battery in Predicting Chemistry Grades.* Master's thesis, Alabama Polytechnic Institute (Auburn, Ala.), 1954.
79. LONGSTAFF, HOWARD P. "Practice Effects on the Minnesota Vocational Test for Clerical Workers." *J Appl Psychol* 38:18–20 F '54. * (PA 29:1645)
80. LOWE, LEWIS M. *The Effects of Drill on the Numerical Aspects of the Minnesota Clerical Test.* Master's thesis, Atlanta University (Atlanta, Ga.), 1954.
81. RUSMORE, JAY, AND MARTIN, FRED. "Validity Information Exchange, No. 7-053: D.O.T. Code 1-37.34, Clerk-Typist." *Personnel Psychol* 7:289 su '54. *
82. YOUNG, MARY B. *The Predictive Value of the Wonderlic Personnel Test and the Minnesota Clerical Test in the Selection of Clerical and Telephone Sales Workers.* Master's thesis, Boston University (Boston, Mass.), 1954.
83. FORSTER, CECIL R. *The Relationship Between Test Achievement and Success in Training of a Selected Group of Tuberculosis Patients.* Doctor's thesis, New York University (New York, N.Y.), 1955. (DA 15:1201)
84. KIRKPATRICK, DONALD L. "The Minnesota Clerical Test." *Personnel Psychol* 10:53–4 sp '57. *
85. SAWYER, JACK. "Validity Information Exchange, No. 10-12: D.O.T. Code 9-88.40, Order-Filler." *Personnel Psychol* 10:90 sp '57. *
86. LONGSTAFF, HOWARD P., AND BELDO, LESLIE A. "Practice Effect on the Minnesota Clerical Test When Alternate Forms Are Used." *J Appl Psychol* 42:109–11 Ap '58. *

DONALD E. SUPER, *Professor of Education, Teachers College, Columbia University, New York, New York.*

The *Minnesota Clerical Test,* first published in 1933, has become something of a fixture, almost an institution, among American test batteries. More thoroughly studied as a new test than are most such devices, supported by nearly a score of studies before it was much more than five years old, and with a manual which was revised according to contemporary ideas of what a manual should be immediately after World War II, this test was virtually a model test in a field surprisingly short of models. But now a dozen years have passed since the revised manual was published, and it is time to take another look at the test.

This reviewer examined seven studies published within the past 12 years. One (65) is a factor analysis of 18 clerical aptitude tests which isolated three factors, all of which are found to have heavy loadings in the MCT, making it one of the best in the group. The factors (perceptual analysis, speed, and comprehension of verbal relationships) are thus broken down further than they were in the earlier studies which used less refined batteries of tests. A second paper (*84*) reports a defect in the construction of the numbers test which seems not to have been noticed before. The others are minor normative studies, summaries of validities, and a study of the relationship between aptitude and interest.

Does the *Minnesota Clerical Test* need further studying, a new manual? Are validity, standards, and meaning permanent and immutable? Have new questions been raised? Are there any unanswered questions? It may be helpful to review the issues here. They fall under three headings: technical refinements, norms, and criteria.

TECHNICAL REFINEMENTS. Kirkpatrick has pointed out that, whereas in the names test the dissimilar elements in nonidentical pairs are evenly distributed throughout the names, in the numbers test 77 per cent of the differences are to be found in the last half of the numbers, 14 per cent in the first half, and 9 per cent in the middle. This means that an alert examinee can save time by reading each pair backwards, and that he and those who read backwards anyhow are favored in this subtest. Since the correlation between numbers and intelligence is negligible, not many alert persons can have noticed this fact, but the defect should be corrected.

NORMS. More significant than the ordering of the items is the matter of norms, for either these are old, based on very small numbers, and local in nature (Tables 4–5, 8–9), or, if more up to date, they are based on a single company in a single community (Tables 6–7) or on samples which are selected in undefined ways which make them not very meaningful (Tables 10–12). When these norms were first published, and even when the 1946 manual appeared, they were so much better than the norms available for most civilian vocational tests that they were widely welcomed. But what was good in 1946 is not good now, in the light of higher standards and of time in which to improve. Let me be specific.

The "Norms for Employed Clerical Workers" (Table 4) are presumably the crucial norms for a test of aptitude for clerical work when the aptitude has been shown not to be influenced by training or experience. Although it is not so stated, these appear to be norms

collected by the Minnesota Employment Stabilization Research Institute early in the 1930's, and, as stated, they include 284 women and 120 male clerical workers, presumably those used to provide the more specific occupational norms in Table 8. How adequate today are clerical norms based on 120 men in Minneapolis and St. Paul a quarter century ago? How representative now are the 17 bank tellers, 29 accountants and bookkeepers, 44 general clerical workers, and 30 routine clerical workers?

The educational norms can be criticized in the same way. The increase in scores with age and grade shown in Tables 10–11 may be due to selection, or it may be due to maturation. If the latter, then conversion tables are needed, based on age changes, so that adolescents may be compared with the adult occupational groups with which they will in due course compete. (Contrary to the statement made on page 6 of the manual, and by one of the reviewers in *The Third Yearbook,* one is not primarily interested in making age- or grade-group comparisons in vocational counseling; instead, one needs to compare the individual with those with whom he will compete, and his competitors are other entrants into the occupation he is considering, not his classmates.) The New England norms are not, as suggested, a "cross-section sampling of 6,262 pupils from 76 representative high schools from Maine to Rhode Island." Unless the reviewer was misinformed while working in that same area when those data were gathered, the boys and girls who took those tests were students in schools which *happened* to cooperate in Boston University's high school testing program, a program conducted more for public relations and recruiting purposes than for any other reason; furthermore, they were the boys and girls in those schools who wanted to take the Boston University tests. That hardly makes them a "cross-section sampling" from "representative high schools." We know how to do better than this now.

CRITERIA. The treatment of validity in the manual was, in 1946, unusually good. The results of studies are reported according to criterion type: ratings, grades in accounting, speed of typing, occupational differentiation, success (with training and work oddly confused), and other clerical tests. But reliance is, for today, too heavily on excellent original work, and, as one reviewer in *The Third*

Yearbook pointed out, the occupations have not been well enough defined. No use was made of studies cited by Ghiselli (*25*) and Copeland (*7, 12*), nor of the varied USES data reported by Stead and Shartle (*42*). Furthermore, we have learned a great deal about validation since World War II, so that during the ensuing decade many more studies should have been made of the criteria of success in various types of clerical jobs, and this test should have been validated against well defined criteria of success in specific clerical occupations. Hay's study (*31*) of success in machine bookkeeping is one such study that is cited in the manual: the criterion, number of entries per hour, was well studied and the job well defined, but the manual does not reveal this nor has any apparent effort been made to obtain more such data for other clerical jobs and to incorporate them in the manual.

In summary, the *Minnesota Clerical Test* is as good a test as it ever was, and still probably has no effective rival. But it has not kept up with the times, either in the studies which have been published concerning it or in the manual which guides its use by vocational counselors and personnel men. It is time for the authors and publishers to protect their investment in this test by investing in it again, to make a minor technical improvement, to collect current and representative age and occupational norms, and to validate it against well defined criteria of success in specific clerical occupations.

For reviews by Thelma Hunt, R. B. Selover, Erwin K. Taylor, and E. F. Wonderlic, see 3:627; for a review by W. D. Commins, see 40:1664.

[851]

*O'Rourke Clerical Aptitude Test, Junior Grade. Applicants for clerical positions; 1926–58; 2 parts; no manual; no data on reliability and validity; $1.95 per 50 copies of either part, postage extra; 25¢ per specimen set, postpaid; L. J. O'Rourke; Psychological Institute. *

a) CLERICAL PROBLEMS. 1926–35; Form 1 ('35); 25(30) minutes.
b) REASONING TEST. 1926–58; Form A ('58, essentially the same as Form A copyrighted in 1936 except for changes in a few items); 20(25) minutes.

REFERENCES

1–3. See 3:629.
4. BAIR, JOHN T. "Factor Analysis of Clerical Aptitude Tests." *J Appl Psychol* 35:245–9 Ag '51. * (*PA* 26:3067)

For a review by Raymond A. Katzell, see 3:629.

[852]

★Personnel Institute Clerical Tests. Applicants for office positions; 1957–58; manual ('58) for both batteries; no data on reliability and validity; $4.50 per 5 sets of tests of either battery; $3 per manual; $12 per kit of manual and 5 copies of each battery; postage extra; Personnel Institute, Inc. *
a) BATTERY A: FOR TYPIST-STENOGRAPHERS. 1957–58; 1 form ('57); 35.5(80) minutes.
  1) *EM-AY Inventory.* Reprint under new title of *Otis Employment Tests,* Test 2, Form A ('22); intelligence; 20(30) minutes.
  2) *Grammar Test.* 3(8) minutes.
  3) *Spelling Test.* 2.5(7) minutes.
  4) *Test of Typewriting Ability.* 10(20) minutes.
  5) *Personal History Inventory.*
b) BATTERY B: FOR CLERICAL PERSONNEL. 1957–58; 1 form ('57); 26(75) minutes.
  1) *EM-AY Inventory.* Same as *a*(1).
  2) *Comparing Names Test.* 1.5(6) minutes.
  3) *Copying Numbers Test.* 3(8) minutes.
  4) *Arithmetic Test.* 1.5(6) minutes.
  5) *Personal History Inventory.*

[853]

*Purdue Clerical Adaptability Test, Revised Edition: Purdue Personnel Tests. Applicants for clerical positions; 1949–56; 6 scores: spelling, computation, checking, word meaning, copying, reasoning; Form A ('56); manual ('56); $5 per 25 tests, postage extra; 50¢ per specimen set, postpaid; 47.5(60) minutes; C. H. Lawshe, Joseph Tiffin (test), and Herbert Moore (test); distributed by University Bookstore. *

REFERENCES

1. SINCLAIR, GORDON ROGERS. *Standardization of the Purdue Clerical Adaptability Test.* Master's thesis, Purdue University (Lafayette, Ind.), 1950.
2. LAWSHE, C. H., AND STEINBERG, MARTIN D. "Studies in Synthetic Validity: I, An Exploratory Investigation of Clerical Jobs." *Personnel Psychol* 8:291–301 au '55. * (*PA* 30:7381)

MARY ELLEN OLIVERIO, *Associate Professor of Education, Teachers College, Columbia University, New York, New York.*

The traditionally measured abilities of prospective clerical workers are included in the six subsections of this test.

Section 3, Checking, would have been more appropriately set up if the lines on the two pages matched. In this section, the subject should be instructed to mark the errors and then count them for recording the number in the blank at the end of the line. In the actual clerical situation, the worker marks copy where errors are to be corrected.

The manual contains a brief but clear description of the manner in which the test was constructed and of the reliability and validity measures used. The authors caution the test user as to the interpretations of the various measures used. The cautions are appropriate. For example, although norms are provided, the statement is made that the "safest and best way is for each user to develop his own norms." This caution is exceedingly important since the reader is given no information concerning the 3,970 applicants for clerical positions at Purdue University and the 650 applicants in eight companies whose scores were used for the establishment of the norms. Inasmuch as the test, during the experimental stages, was found to be far too difficult for girls just leaving high school and was revised, some question might be raised about the use of the norms given for large groups of young workers entering their first jobs. The user is not given the age, level of education, or previous experience of the groups used for the establishment of norms. It would be helpful to know if these 4,620 applicants are representative of the group entering clerical occupations each year.

This test should prove helpful to those organizations that must choose large numbers of clerical workers and that have clearly identified that the job skills needed are those measured in this test.

DONALD SPEARRITT, *Senior Research Assistant, Australian Council for Educational Research, Melbourne, Australia.*

Measurement of clerical aptitude appears to have reached the stage where the most useful item types are reasonably well established. As a result, most tests of clerical aptitude now exhibit a fairly common pattern, and the Purdue test is no exception. Clerical tasks differ among themselves, however, and it is satisfying to note that the authors of this test suggest that the results of a job analysis should guide the test user in deciding which subtest scores are worth using in his own situation.

The test itself leaves nothing to be desired in the way of layout or typography, but a number of criticisms can be made of the content and form of presentation of some subtests. Testees are warned against making "unnecessary" mistakes in two of the subtests. In the vocabulary test, "proper" is taken to mean the same as "propriety," while obscure words like ture, spodumene, naroud, and lyrate are included among the distractors.

The lowest one per cent of the norming sample made a score of 23 on the spelling test, so it appears that the number of items in this test could be greatly reduced, with a consequent saving in testing time. The procedure of counting as well as finding mistakes in the checking test does not seem to reflect the actual clerical task which usually requires only the identification of errors. Testees are given no indication of the approach they should adopt in working the copying test; a candidate who was under the impression that neatness or accuracy at all costs was the chief aim of this test would be penalised. For additional information on accuracy in a speeded task, the test user would do well to note the number of items attempted in the checking test, as the correlation between the speed test (checking) and the accuracy test (copying) is not high (.35).

In this revision of the test, the authors have incorporated the concepts of reliability and validity set out by the American Psychological Association in 1954. Although the difficulties involved in obtaining test-retest coefficients of reliability with applicant groups are formidable, it is essential to obtain such reliabilities for speed tests if no equivalent form of the test is available. High school groups in the last year of their course and with prospects of employment in sight should be sufficiently motivated to make a genuine attempt at the test early and late in the school year. The authors recognize that the split-half reliability coefficients are likely to be spuriously high for the speed tests. If the only reliability coefficients available for speed tests are split-half coefficients, it is debatable whether they should be presented at all. There is no mention of a standard error of measurement and no indication of the standard deviation of the scores of the group used for estimating reliabilities.

The brief note on content validity could be profitably expanded by making some analysis of common clerical tasks and showing how the subtest areas were related to these. The authors are right in emphasizing that the test user should build up his own evidence of predictive validity in his particular situation. Expectancy charts based on a very small number of cases suggest that the subtests have satisfactory predictive validity for later job performance. Extensive evidence of the test's concurrent validity for distinguishing between different types of clerical workers is presented in the form of group profiles. The concept of synthetic validity is also introduced. In requiring a more detailed statement of the operations involved in the criterion, it draws on the notion of content validity to some extent, but is mainly a variation of predictive validity. It would seem preferable to present validity data in terms of established concepts, rather than to introduce new concepts with which few test users would be familiar.

Despite the criticisms leveled at the test, the validity data suggest that it would be a useful aid in the selection and placement of clerical personnel. Its value could be better assessed if further evidence of predictive validity were collected, and if the characteristics of the norming sample were described in more detail. The inclusion of a reasoning subtest is likely to give it an advantage over tests such as the *Turse Clerical Aptitudes Test* for selecting higher level clerical personnel. But the extensive time required for its administration inevitably places it at a marked disadvantage with shorter tests such as the *Short Employment Tests*.

For reviews by Edward N. Hay, Joseph E. Moore, and Alec Rodger of the previous edition, see 4:731.

[854]

*The Short Employment Tests. Applicants for clerical positions; 1951–56; Forms 1 ('51), 2 ('51), 3 ('51), 4 ('51); 3 tests: CA ('51, clerical), N ('51, numerical), V ('51, verbal); revised manual ('56); distribution of Form 1 restricted to banks which are members of the American Bankers Association; Form 4 is restricted for special uses; $1.80 per 25 tests; 35¢ per specimen set; postpaid; 15(20) minutes; George K. Bennett and Marjorie Gelink; Psychological Corporation. *

REFERENCES

1. BENNETT, GEORGE K., AND GELINK, MARJORIE. "The Short Employment Tests." *Personnel Psychol* 6:151–7 su '53. * (PA 28:3339)
2. WILKINSON, BRYAN. "Validity of Short Employment Tests." *Personnel Psychol* 6:419–25 w '53. * (PA 28:8194)
3. RUSMORE, JAY, AND MARTIN, FRED. "Validity Information Exchange, No. 7-053:D.O.T. Code 1-37.34, Clerk-Typist." *Personnel Psychol* 7:289 su '54. *
4. WESTBERG, WILLIAM C.; FITZPATRICK, EUGENE D.; AND McCARTY, JOHN J. "Validity Information Exchange, No. 7-073: D.O.T. Code 1-37.32, Typist." *Personnel Psychol* 7:411–2 au '54. *
5. WESTBERG, WILLIAM C.; FITZPATRICK, EUGENE D.; AND McCARTY, JOHN J. "Validity Information Exchange, No. 7-074: D.O.T. Code 1-37.32, Typist." *Personnel Psychol* 7:413 au '54. *
6. WESTBERG, WILLIAM C.; FITZPATRICK, EUGENE D.; AND McCARTY, JOHN J. "Validity Information Exchange, No. 7-087: D.O.T. Code 1-37.32, Typist." *Personnel Psychol* 7:561–2 w '54. *
7. FITZPATRICK, EUGENE D., AND McCARTY, JOHN J. "Validity Information Exchange, No. 8-35:D.O.T. Code 9-00.91, Assembler VII (Electrical Equipment)." *Personnel Psychol* 8: 501–4 w '55. *
8. HUGHES, J. L., AND McNAMARA, W. J. "Relationship of Short Employment Tests and General Clerical Tests." *Personnel Psychol* 8:331–7 au '55. * (PA 30:7828)
9. BENNETT, GEORGE K., AND DOPPELT, JEROME E. "Item Difficulty and Speed of Response." *Ed & Psychol Meas* 16: 494–6 w '56. *
10. McCARTY, JOHN J., AND FITZPATRICK, EUGENE D. "Validity Information Exchange, No. 9-26:D.O.T. Code 5-92.621, (Foreman II)." *Personnel Psychol* 9:253 su '56. *
11. WALKER, FRANCIS C. "Normative Data Information Exchange, Nos. 5–6." *Personnel Psychol* 9:271–2 su '56. *
12. McCARTY, JOHN J. "Validity Information Exchange, No. 10-14:D.O.T. Code 1-33.01, Secretary." *Personnel Psychol* 10: 202–3 su '57. *
13. McCARTY, JOHN J. "Validity Information Exchange, No. 10-15:D.O.T. Code 1-33.01, Secretary." *Personnel Psychol* 10: 204–5 su '57. *
14. McCARTY, JOHN J. "Normative Data Information Exchange, Nos. 10-20, 10-21, 10-22." *Personnel Psychol* 10:242–4 su '57. *
15. McCARTY, JOHN J. "Normative Data Information Exchange, No. 10-30." *Personnel Psychol* 10:364 au '57. *
16. DUNNETTE, MARVIN D., AND KIRCHNER, WAYNE K. "Validation of Psychological Tests in Industry." *Personnel Adm* 21: 20–7 My–Je '58. *

P. L. MELLENBRUCH, *Professor of Psychology, University of Kentucky, Lexington, Kentucky.*

The *Short Employment Tests* were developed to supplement tests being used by member banks of the American Bankers Association for the selection of clerical workers. The Personnel Testing Committee of the ABA participated in the outlining of general specifications for the series, and recommends the SET as one of a group of tests suitable for use by member banks. The recommendation specifies that the tests are regarded as "suitable for use with candidates for clerical employment, but not for administrative trainees nor for maintenance employees." Further, it is suggested that banks administer all three tests—verbal, numerical, and clerical—to each such applicant, "rather than omitting a test which seems not to be closely related to the contemplated job."

The results of tests N and CA are said to be particularly important for general clerical jobs, while V score and the total score are to be stressed for stenographers and applicants for "positions involving much writing or oral communication." "Pending completion of local studies," the authors recommend cutoff scores corresponding to the 25th percentiles (for stenographers, the 50th percentile for the verbal score). No evidence is presented to show that these cutoff points were arrived at empirically.

The working time for each test is five minutes and the instructions are not too time-consuming, so the specification that the entire series not consume over 20 minutes has been met. A second specification was that test-retest reliabilities should exceed .80. Reliabilities seem fairly satisfactory for successive administrations of alternate forms. Reliabilities for V and N range from .83 to .91, and CA reliabilities range from .77 to .85. A third specification, that the directions and scoring be simple, is met easily for test N. Directions for V are clear though somewhat more complex than for N. Directions for CA are rather complex and probably quite foreboding to the type of person who will take the test. There is too much massed print in these directions and there are too many cases in the sample problem.

The final specification for the series was that "content should encompass verbal, numerical, and clerical skills." Herein lies the chief problem. Two of the three areas are not *encompassed*. There is a coverage of the various usual numerical operations involved in lower level clerical work; however, only one narrow segment or slice is measured in each of the verbal and clerical skills areas. Only word meaning is sampled in the V area and only classifying or filing is sampled in CA. If V and CA need no broader sampling than this, then perhaps N might well be made up of items involving but one single arithmetic operation, e.g., simple addition. No evidence is offered to show that the single ability sampled in V and in CA was arrived at empirically and that this sampling gives validity as good as or better than what would be given by a more *encompassing* array of items. As a matter of fact, if but a single kind of item is to be used, there is good reason to believe that a test composed of only the very best of the items which are provided would give as reliable and valid results as the total number employed in these tests, unless, of course, the test is also a test of fatigue and perhaps boredom.

Considerable attention has been given to the validation of this series. Nineteen studies, all based on female subjects, are reported in the manual. Generally speaking, the validity coefficients are not very impressive.

Of course, the reviewer is quite sure that the reported validity coefficients are spuriously low as is true for most reported test validities. First of all, the criteria are of questionable value. Supervisors' ratings, which were the chief criteria, are notoriously subjective. Furthermore, correlation rests upon an unsound principle with respect to most employment situations. This is true whether we use linear, biserial, or some other of the usual forms of correlation. The fallacy lies in the assumption that the higher the score on a particular test the greater the expectancy of success. For most jobs this is not true. Instead, for almost any job, there is an optimum range within the total span of scores for any differentiating trait which should serve as the most appropriate prediction of success. Scores outside the cutoff points used would indicate a greater probability of failure. Were cutoff points used, it would doubtless be possible to show that for various clerical jobs a particular candidate would most probably be a successful employee if his score fell within a predetermined range of scores on any one or more of the tests. Optimum cutoff points for each of these tests should, therefore, be established empirically for each class of clerical positions. If this were done, a satisfactory validity would be more probable.

Correlations with other tests as reported in the manual are about what might be expected. Each test shows a fair correlation with other tests which have face validity, but these figures are hardly sufficiently high to justify substituting one for the other.

Altogether, it might be more appropriate to identify the tests as V-vocabulary, N-numerical, and C-classifying, because there is no evidence that the verbal factor in office jobs can be satisfactorily measured by testing vocabulary only, or that CA (skills? aptitude?) can be adequately sampled by the single activity of classifying.

[855]

★**Turse Clerical Aptitudes Test.** Grades 8–12 and adults; 1955, c1953–55; 7 scores: verbal, number, written directions, learning ability, clerical speed, clerical aptitude, accuracy; 1 form ('55); manual ('55); no adult norms; no norms for accuracy; $3.35 per 35 tests, postage extra; 35¢ per specimen set, postpaid; 28(40) minutes; Paul L. Turse; World Book Co. *

REFERENCE
1. PRESCOTT, GEORGE A. "Prediction of Achievement in Commercial Subjects." *Ed & Psychol Meas* 15:491–2 w '55. * (PA 30:7772)

ROBERT A. JONES, *Assistant Director, Testing Bureau, University of Southern California, Los Angeles, California.*

This test consists of six subtests: Verbal Skills, Number Skills, Written Directions, Checking Speed, Classifying-Sorting, and Alphabetizing. Scores on the first three subtests are combined to give a measure of "learning ability," while the last three yield a clerical speed score and, optionally, a clerical accuracy score. All six in weighted combination yield the "general clerical aptitude" score.

The test booklets are not reusable. Since separate answer sheets cannot be used because the first three parts are, in general, made up of completion type items, the test must be hand scored. While care was exercised in designing the scoring keys to make scoring as simple as possible, scoring is not a rapid process. The method of scoring specified, i.e., no penalty for wrong answers even on the sections of 2-choice, highly speeded items, perhaps represents a compromise to shorten scoring time.

Turse Clerical Aptitude Test

This seems rather undesirable to the reviewer. There is no objection to number right scoring on the first three parts.

The format of the test booklet, especially the cover page, seems a little cluttered. The practice items for Number Skills are not separated from the body of the subtest. Since the part is admitted to contain an element of speed, this seems to be inappropriate. Also, there are no practice items for Written Directions, which seems (to the reviewer) to need practice material. Perhaps practice material for Verbal Skills, Number Skills, and Written Directions could all be placed on a revised cover sheet.

The section of the manual covering instructions for test administration seems clear and explicit. The time required for test administration (less than the usual class period) seems reasonable for high school use, but the test probably requires too much time for business use as a pre-employment test.

The manual states that the general clerical aptitude score (the weighted total score) is a combination of twice the learning ability score plus the clerical speed score. In many clerical tasks accuracy is more important than speed. For this reason the author's decision to place emphasis on speed while making accuracy minor (optional) seems regrettable.

Except for norms for girls in a 12th grade commercial course and mean scores for boys and girls, separate norms by sex are not provided. Even though the author feels that such norms are not very useful in the high school, the differences between the total population norms and the norms for 12th grade girls and the mean scores by sex are large enough to be statistically significant. The test user should have available to him norms by sex in addition to those presently included. No adult norms are provided. Standard deviations are not presented so completely as means. More specific information about the composition of the norm group is needed.

Verbal Skills is more difficult than it should be for maximally efficient measurement for all groups included in the norms. The difficulty level may be acceptable for adults, but no data are presented for adults. While not intended to be the usual verbal measure, Verbal Skills includes, in addition to vocabulary items, items of spelling, word sense, and phonetic association. The subtest correlates highly (.68) with total scores on Form OM of the *Cooperative*

English Test. One type of item used sometimes seemed slightly obtuse to the reviewer. For example, a word written as it is pronounced (tox) is given and the examinee is to supply the correct spelling (talks).

In addition to test-retest values, corrected split-half reliabilities for the first three subtests (the least speeded parts) and the learning ability total are given. The manual states that these values for Written Directions differ appreciably. Standard errors of measurement are given for both test-retest and corrected split-half coefficients and, while notice is taken of the differences, those based on corrected split-half scores are not firmly disclaimed. The split-half correlation would better be left out entirely.

There are some other objections to the content of the manual. With regard to use of the test in making educational and vocational plans, the manual is a little expansive. The statement is made that "the student's profile of TCAT strengths and weaknesses will be helpful in determining the kind of clerical job that should be sought"; however, most of the facts needed for such counseling would have to be supplied by the user to supplement those in the manual. While, in general terms, the manual cautions the user in general about interpretation of test results, the possible relationship of response set to poor performance is not noted. No validation data on Written Directions are given.

In one study reported, the learning ability score correlated .72 with Terman-McNemar IQ's. Although the manual cautions that the learning ability score is a "rather restricted" measure of intelligence, the statement needs clarification in the absence of any other statistical evidence.

On the whole, the workmanship on this test is competent. While the existence of the test on the market is in no sense decried, the reviewer feels that the test does not meet uniquely any need which other tests do not fulfill just as well.

DONALD SPEARRITT, *Senior Research Assistant, Australian Council for Educational Research, Melbourne, Australia.*

The title of this test is sufficient to indicate its purpose to most test users. With the possible exception of the written directions test, the subtest item types are characteristic of those usually included in tests of clerical aptitudes. The test of verbal skills departs from the general practice in presenting phonetic association and word sense items in cyclic form with spelling and vocabulary items. A realistic coverage of the number skills involved in clerical work is attempted in the test of number skills, which covers cross-addition, cancellation, and negative balances, as well as the four basic arithmetic processes. These efforts to improve the content validity of the tests are commendable, but, at the same time, some comparison of their predictive validity for a given criterion with that of a single item type verbal or number test would have been desirable. The test of written directions takes the form of a test of attention; more realistic content, based on sets of instructions actually used in clerical situations, could have been devised. The three speed tests, which involve checking, classifying and sorting, and alphabetizing, all measure important aspects of clerical jobs. In selecting applicants for particular clerical positions, a personnel officer may find it necessary in some cases to look beyond the single clerical speed score obtained for these three tests.

The format and layout of the tests are adequate, and the folded strip and stencil scoring keys are simple and effective. The profile chart on the front page of the test enables the user to obtain a quick graphical picture of a candidate's performance and, equally important, some idea of the likely one standard error range for true scores on various subtests.

The manual contains most of the technical information that would normally be asked for by a test user. The provision in the general directions for the use of erasers seems to be unwise in the case of speed tests; blocking out wrongly marked answers would be preferable. Other minor faults in the manual concern the absence of information about the criterion used in the item analysis in the preliminary tryouts of the items and about the method or groups used to determine the weights for arriving at the general clerical aptitude score.

Correlations with various achievement measures are provided for all subtests except Written Directions. Most of these predictive validities attain a very satisfactory level. The amount of attention given to the collection of adequate validity data is praiseworthy, especially the preparation of work sample tests to assess the validity of the clerical speed tests. The discussion of validity could be improved, however, by

the introduction of the concepts of content and construct validity. Reliability coefficients are satisfactory, except perhaps for Written Directions. The provision of test-retest reliability coefficients for all normed subscores and of standard errors of measurement based on these coefficients meets accepted technical standards for speed tests. The only criticisms that can be made in this connection concern the absence of clear data to indicate whether the standard errors of measurement differ at different points of the score range, and the need for additional interpretative material illustrating the actual use of the standard errors of the differences in subtest percentile ranks.

The problems involved in presenting both accuracy and speed scores in a meaningful way for the clerical speed tests may justify the author's decision not to present accuracy norms. But his statement that "it is necessary to determine the *number attempted* only if a Clerical Accuracy score is to be derived" does not seem appropriate to the use of the clerical speed tests in selection situations. It is often as important to know how many items a candidate marks wrongly in these tests as it is to know the number he marks correctly.

This test shows evidence of a highly competent and realistic approach to the task of measuring the important skills and abilities involved in clerical work. The technical information provided in the manual is of a high standard and indicates that the various subtests will give reliable predictions of success in relevant achievement and job performance areas. The test's most important deficiency is the absence of adult norms. For assessing aptitude for most clerical tasks, the test would seem to be superior to tests such as the *Purdue Clerical Adaptability Test* because of its higher content validity and shorter administration time.

INTERESTS

[856]

*Brainard Occupational Preference Inventory. Grades 8–12, adults; 1945–56; 6 scores: commercial, mechanical, professional, esthetic, scientific, personal service (girls), agriculture (boys); IBM; Form R ('45); revised manual ('56); no adult norms; separate answer sheets must be used; $3.25 per 25 tests; $1.90 per 50 IBM answer sheets; 25¢ per machine scoring stencil; 35¢ per specimen set; postpaid; (30) minutes; Paul P. Brainard and Ralph T. Brainard; Psychological Corporation. *

REFERENCES
1–4. See 40:1675.
5–6. See 3:634.
7. See 4:737.
8. Torr, Donald V. "A Factor Analysis of Selected Interest Inventories." Abstract. *Am Psychol* 7:296 Jl '52. *
9. Anderson, Rose G. "Do Aptitudes Support Interests?" *Personnel & Guid J* 32:14–7 S '53. * (*PA* 28:4495)

William C. Cottle, *Professor of Education, The University of Kansas, Lawrence, Kansas.*

This inventory covers six broad occupational fields, with 20 items each in commercial, mechanical, professional, esthetic, and scientific areas. For the sixth field, changes were made in the current revision to allow for sex differences, males now answering 20 items for an agricultural score, and females answering 20 items for a personal service score. Each field has four occupational sections with five items devoted to each section. For example, the 20 items in the commercial field have five items each devoted to accounting, clerical work, selling, and business management. One wonders how much validity and reliability can be attached to a score secured from only 20 items and what the effect of mixing four kinds of items within a field has had upon the reported reliabilities of each field.

Normative data have been developed on 9,695 pupils in 14 school systems. Means and standard deviations by grade for boys and for girls in grades 8–12 are also reported. Since not enough differences were found among grades, percentile norms reported are based on total groups by sex, undifferentiated by grade.

Correlations with the *Kuder Preference Record—Vocational* are reported. Although the manual points out that these correlations seem to indicate little relationship between the Brainard and Kuder interest inventories, the positive and negative relationships that one might logically expect between the scales of the two inventories are demonstrated. For example, the correlation between mechanical scales was .58 for boys and .51 for girls; that between scientific scales was .53 for boys and .58 for girls. The publishers claim that the Brainard has an advantage over the Kuder because it does not contain forced choice items. No other evidence of validity is reported and this is a major weakness at present. The counselor must develop validity in his local situation through experience in using the test and through local research.

The section on interpretation of scores points out that the raw scores show variations in an individual's interest among the six fields and the percentile ranks show strength of interest according to the norms groups. The user will need to verify any interpretations by personal experience.

The authors and publisher are to be commended for the improvements they have made in the test and in the new manual. Since the references above do not show as widespread use or as much research for this inventory as for the Strong or the Kuder, evidence of validity is quite limited. This means that the inventory must be used with considerable caution. However, with the addition of norms for grades 8–12, a simplified scoring procedure, and evidence of limited overlap with the Kuder, the Brainard inventory could possibly serve a useful function in high school counseling and placement.

For a review by Elmer D. Hinckley, see 4:737; for reviews by Edwin W. Davis and Herschel T. Manuel, see 3:634; for reviews by Jack W. Dunlap and M. R. Trabue of the original edition, see 40:1675; for a review by Everett B. Sackett, see 38:1176.

[857]

★Devon Interest Test. Ages 11–13; 1955; 2 scores: practical, academic; separate forms for boys and girls; 100 or more tests, 5d. each; 7d. per single copy; 2s. per manual ['55]; postage extra; administration time not reported; Stephen Wiseman and T. F. Fitzpatrick; Oliver & Boyd Ltd. *

REFERENCES
1. Fitzpatrick, T. F. "Summaries of Researches Reported in Degree Theses: The Construction of a Test of Practical Ability With Special Reference to Woodwork." *Brit J Ed Psychol* 23:133–5 Je '53. *
2. Fitzpatrick, T. F., and Wiseman, Stephen. "An Interest Test for Use in Selection for Technical Education." *Brit J Ed Psychol* 24:99–105 Je '54. * (*PA* 29:3038)
3. Wiseman, Stephen. "The Use of an Interest Test in 11 Plus Selection." *Brit J Ed Psychol* 25:92–8 Je '55. * (*PA* 30:3469)

Arthur B. Royse, *Lecturer in Psychology, University of Hull, Hull, England.*

This new test is not a measure of general interests. It attempts only to determine whether, irrespective of strength of other interests, a child's practical interests are stronger or weaker than his academic interests. Devised to improve predictability of whether a child of 11 plus is better suited to a technical rather than an academic education, the test is intended to be used solely as an addition to customary selection procedures. In this very specific field it promises to be a useful addition if and when its predictive validity is established.

The child is required to indicate his like or

dislike for doing certain things by reacting to a series of statements, e.g., "learning history." The statements are grouped in 16 blocks, each block containing items reflecting practical, academic, social, and "distractor" activities. The child must also indicate which activity in each block he likes best and which he likes next best. Only practical and academic items chosen as best or next best liked are scored, thus yielding a practical (P) interest score and an academic (A) interest score.

Although the test can be given as a group test, some individual supervision is necessary to ensure that it is completed satisfactorily. Scoring is simple but its objectivity is a little marred by the authors' failure to give specific instructions for every possible scoring contingency. Illustrative norms are given but it is necessary for users to establish their own norms in relation to the number and type of school places available.

Reliability is good, split-half coefficients for the two scores varying from .85 to .91 on one 11 plus sample and two 13 plus samples. Self-consistency of P scores and A scores and their independence from the remaining items have been determined by an item analysis.

No predictive validity for the test has yet been established. The test has been published at this stage in the hope that follow-up experiments can be more widely based. The authors have tried to show from their available evidence, however, that follow-up studies now in progress can reasonably be expected to demonstrate some predictive validity, although whether this will be higher than that of existing selection procedures is by no means certain. This evidence (1–3) comprises demonstration of (a) very low correlations of P scores with intelligence, arithmetic, and English test results; (b) significant differences among the P scores and A scores of children at grammar, technical, and modern schools; (c) similar factor patterns between P scores and teacher estimates of practical interests and abilities; and (d) presence of an interest factor with loadings of .53 (P score) and −.92 (A score) which shows a higher variance than the k factor measured by those space tests customarily used for technical selection.

Although these results are only tentative, particularly the two factor analyses which are based on relatively few tests and children, the fact that the evidence is all in the same direction suggests that the hope that reasonably high predictive validity will be established is not unrealistic.

In short, the test shows some promise of becoming a useful addition to test batteries used for educational selection but whether this promise will be realised must await future experimentation.

ALFRED YATES, *Senior Research Officer, National Foundation for Educational Research, London, England.*

This test was designed for a strictly limited and utilitarian purpose—that of improving the methods of selection employed by education authorities in England and Wales. These authorities are required to allocate primary school leavers (children between 10 and 11 years of age) to courses of secondary education that are suited to their abilities and aptitudes. One important decision that has to be made is whether an able child shall proceed to an academic course or to a technical course. The aim of the *Devon Interest Test* is to furnish information that will improve the validity of this kind of discrimination.

The test is in the form of a questionnaire, requiring the testee to indicate his likes and dislikes from a wide area of activities and experiences. It yields two separate scores: a P-score (practical interest) and an A-score (academic interest). The authors outline a procedure, involving the use of this test along with tests of verbal intelligence, English, arithmetic, and spatial ability, whereby children may be assigned to a number of groups: those clearly suitable for an academic course, usually provided in grammar schools; those better fitted for a technical course; those between whose aptitudes it is not possible clearly to discriminate but who appear to be capable of succeeding in either type of course; those whose level of ability is such that they should be assigned to secondary modern schools, which, in most parts of England and Wales, cater to the least gifted pupils who lack the intellectual stamina to embark on courses that are designed to lead to further education in universities, technical colleges, and the like.

The procedure advocated by the authors has been tried out on a sample of 175 11-year-old boys and found to result in a positive classification in almost 60 per cent of the cases. Split-half reliabilities have been calculated for this sample and for a sample of 417 13-year-old boys and girls, the values ranging from .85 (A-score for boys of 11+) to .91 (P-score for boys of 13+). The authors emphasise that no predictive validity has yet been secured although there is research evidence to show that the inclusion of the test in a battery tends to improve the validity of selection for technical courses.

The authors make no claims for the usefulness of their test outside the limited context for which it was specifically prepared. Nevertheless, it could well be a useful instrument for other purposes and in other circumstances. It would accord well with the authors' intentions, however, if those who employ the test for purposes other than those for which it was designed do so on a strictly empirical basis. The authors warn that the norms supplied in the manual are tentative only.

[858]

★G. C. Self-Scoring Interest Record, Second Experimental Edition. Grades 9 and over; 1958; 12 scores: outdoor, managerial, social service, verbal, operative, skilled mechanical, scientific, persuasive, clerical, artistic, numerical, musical; Form 1 ('58); manual ['58]; tentative norms; $2.50 per 25 tests; 90¢ per 25 punch pins; 85¢ per 25 backing boards; 47¢ per 50 profiles ['58]; 30¢ per specimen set (must be purchased to obtain manual); postage extra; (30–40) minutes; H. M. Fowler and M. D. Parmenter; Guidance Centre. *

[859]

★How Well Do You Know Your Interests. Grades 13–16, adults; 1957; 54 scores: numerical, clerical, retail selling, outside selling, selling real estate, one-order selling, sales complaints, selling intangibles, buyer, labor management, production supervision, business management, machine operation, repair and construction, machine design, farm or ranch, gardening, hunting, adventure, social service, teaching service, medical service, nursing service, applied chemistry, basic chemical problems, basic biological problems, basic physical problems, basic psychological problems, philosophical, visual art appreciative, visual art productive, visual art decorative, amusement appreciative, amusement productive, amusement managerial, literary appreciative, literary productive, musical appreciative, musical performing, musical composing, sports appreciative, sports participative, domestic service, unskilled labor, disciplinary, power seeking, propaganda, self-aggrandizing, supervisory initiative, bargaining, arbitrative, persuasive, disputatious, masculinity-femininity; Form B-22; 2 editions (profiles only differ): college, personnel; $7.50 per 30 tests, postage extra; $2.74 per specimen set of any one level, postpaid; (20–30) minutes; Thomas N. Jenkins; Executive Analysis Corporation. *

Jerome E. Doppelt, *Assistant Director, Test Division, The Psychological Corporation, New York, New York.*

Devon Interest Test

This interest inventory consists of 120 statements of activities related to various kinds of occupations, use of leisure time, dealings with people, etc. The examinee indicates on a 6-point scale the extent to which he likes or dislikes each activity. The inventory booklet has been cleverly designed to permit the transcription of scores for 53 scales, and a score for either masculinity or femininity, directly on a profile sheet. The scales are grouped in interest domains such as "outdoor vocational interest domain" and "mechanical vocational interest domain."

It is rather startling to find that 53 scores are obtained from 120 items. Examination of the scoring templates reveals that each of 46 scales is based on two items and each of the remaining 7 scales contains four items. The scoring weights for an item range from 0 to 5, corresponding to the six possible responses. For a two-item scale, this gives possible scores of 0 to 10. For the scales containing four items, the scoring weights count only half and the range of possible scores remains 0 to 10. The manual points out that the raw score on a scale is meaningful in itself since scores below the neutral point of 5 indicate an overall negative attitude to the job functions, whereas scores above 5 tend to indicate positive interests. With two items in a scale it is, of course, possible to have a tremendous liking for one activity and an equally hearty dislike for the other activity. The corresponding responses would yield a score of 5 for the scale. It is difficult to think of such a score, obtained from two extreme feelings, as indicative of indifference or neutrality. Although one may not often encounter situations in which the subject gives such disparate responses, the user of the inventory should be aware of the possibility.

Percentile norms are available for composite groups of office and factory employees, college students, and a group of 200 young, unmarried men from 29 states. There is evidently recognition of the need for norms based on specific occupational, educational, and age groups since it is mentioned that such norms will be "published as they are completed."

The discussion of the factorial nature of the inventory does little to explain the structure of the instrument. It is emphasized that an objective in the development of the test was the selection of items which would yield pure and reliable measures of interest factors. What is meant by the purity of measurement is not made clear. The issue is further confused by the existence of higher order factors leading to "interest domains," a situation which would imply lack of purity among scales. The manual mentions that a considerable amount of research work was done in the process of developing the inventory but, unfortunately, no bibliography is given. Some issues might be clarified by reading the complete research reports. Conspicuously absent are data showing the relationships between this inventory and other measures of interest, information which would justify the titles and descriptions of the 53 scales, and evidence of validity in counseling or personnel selection.

The reviewer feels that the extraction of 53 scores from 120 items is an attempt to obtain an excessive amount of information from the specific activities listed in the inventory. The assumption that interest areas can be effectively measured or even identified by two items seems too hazardous to accept.

HENRY S. DYER, *Vice President in Charge of Research, Educational Testing Service, Princeton, New Jersey.*

The author of this interest inventory claims that it has five principal advantages over other similar instruments:

a) It is convenient to give and score. This is a valid claim. The directions and the wording of the items are so clear and simple that an average high school student should have little trouble doing the test under his own steam, though one may wonder whether such students are likely to have genuine familiarity with many of the activities to which they are expected to react. The format of the test itself and the ingenious hand scoring system make it possible to get the results much more quickly than is the case with other interest inventories known to this reviewer.

b) It is applicable to a wide variety of work and jobs. True. In the opinion of this reviewer, the test comes close to exhausting the vocational interest domain.

c) It gives information related to specific job tasks and duties. Also true. The test yields scores on 44 types of vocational activity and on 9 types of vocationally related behavioral tendencies, as well as on either masculinity or femininity depending on the sex of the examinee.

Each of the 55 rubrics is briefly and simply defined in the manual.

d) It utilizes a scoring method which permits a direct reading of an individual's dislikes or aversions as well as his interests. This claim rests not only on the scoring system but also on the type of response the examinee is required to make to each item. He has six options ranging from "like tremendously" to "dislike tremendously." The scoring system is such that a 10 automatically means extreme interest, a zero extreme aversion, and a 5 indifference. However, no evidence is given to show whether a given score, say 7, stands for the same *amount* of interest from scale to scale. An investigation is needed to determine to what extent the psychological distance between any two scale points is, as the scoring system implies, actually the same from scale to scale. Furthermore, the information on the test-retest reliability of the individual scales is insufficient to indicate how much of a difference between any two scale scores can be trusted.

e) The manual illustrates basic uses of different profiles of scores by means of a set of actual cases. Four actual cases of job applicants are analyzed in the manual. Four additional cases of students seeking vocational guidance are in preparation. In the opinion of this reviewer, these cases are well done and should be useful in showing personnel managers and guidance counselors how to make effective use of the scores.

The norms for this instrument are inadequate and not well defined. The fact that they are built into the profile chart seems to make the latter more confusing than helpful in the interpretation of the scores. A profile based on the raw scores only, with percentile norms furnished in separate tables as they accumulate, would make for easier, and probably safer, interpretation of the results.

Although the author reports "factorial validities" for the individual scales in terms of factor loadings which are comfortably high, he leaves this reviewer wondering just how valid the test is in terms of the degree to which it gives results which actually correspond to an individual's interests. The factorial validities are in a sense not much more than indicators of the internal consistency of each scale. Since most of the scales are based on only *two items each,* one can hardly escape the impression that the sampling of the subject's response to any

How Well Do You Know Your Interests

one area of activity is too narrow to be representative. For each scale, the two—occasionally four—items were chosen on the basis of their factor loadings from an original set consisting of 7 to 12 items. In other words, the two (or four) were taken as most representative of the total set. From this it can be argued that the sampling in each scale is more representative than it seems on the surface; it means that the responses to the items selected are highly predictive of the responses to the items not selected. But no solid evidence is given on how well responses to the items selected predict responses to innumerable aspects of the actual job situation.

It should be obvious that this reviewer has some misgivings about resting the case on factorial validity alone. On the other hand, he gave the test to himself and was amazed at the accuracy with which the raw scores reflected his own interests and aversions. Perhaps there is more to this 120-item test than meets the eye. Perhaps in the hands of a wise clinician it will prove to be helpful.

[860]

*Interest Check List. Grades 9 and over; 1946–57; interviewing aid; 1 form ['57]; no data on reliability; no norms; $2.50 per 100 copies; 5¢ per single copy; 5¢ per directions sheet ['57]; postpaid; (20) minutes; prepared by United States Employment Service; United States Government Printing Office. *

For reviews by Milton L. Blum and Howard R. Taylor of the original edition, see 4:741.

[861]

*Inventory of Vocational Interests: Acorn National Aptitude Tests. Grades 7–16 and adults; 1943–57; interest in five areas: mechanical, academic, artistic, business and economic, farm-agricultural; 1 form ('43); manual ('57, identical with manual copyrighted in 1943); directions sheet ('56); no data on reliability; $2 per 25 tests; 25¢ per manual; 50¢ per specimen set; postage extra; (35) minutes; Andrew Kobal, J. Wayne Wrightstone, and Karl R. Kunze; Acorn Publishing Co. *

For reviews by Marion A. Bills, Edward S. Bordin, Harold D. Carter, and Patrick Slater, see 3:638.

[862]

★Kuder Preference Record—Occupational. Grades 9–16 and adults; 1956–58; 39 scores: verification, county agricultural agent, farmer, forester, minister, newspaper editor, physician [revised], clinical psychologist, industrial psychologist, YMCA secretary, school superintendent, accountant, meteorologist, personnel manager, department store salesman, psychology professor, mechanical engineer, counseling psychologist, journalist, architect ['57]; electrical engineer (revised), civil engineer, lawyer, retail clothier,

insurance agent, dentist, veterinarian, industrial engineer, pediatrician, psychiatrist, radio station manager, interior decorator, high school counselor, high school science teacher, high school mathematics teacher, chemist, mining and metallurgial engineer, druggist, job printer ['58]; IBM; Form D ('56); manual, second edition ('57); research handbook, second edition ('57); separate answer sheets must be used; $9.80 per 20 tests; $6.25 per 100 IBM answer sheets; $1 per scoring stencil for any one score; $2.50 per book of computational sheets ('56) for developing local occupational keys; $2.50 per research handbook; $2 per specimen set; postage extra; (25–35) minutes; G. Frederic Kuder; Science Research Associates. *

EDWARD S. BORDIN, *Professor of Psychology, University of Michigan, Ann Arbor, Michigan.*

The *Kuder Preference Record* is second only to Strong's *Vocational Interest Blank* in length of service as one of the leading interest inventories. This latest version, Form D (Occupational), is intended to give direct evidence of how closely a subject's responses typify each of 22 different occupational groups.

The format and contents follow the patterns laid down in the other forms (Vocational and Personal), in that the subject is asked to choose which one of three activities he would like the most and which one he would like the least. Many of the groups of items are drawn from previous forms.

One of the hallmarks of this test has always been ingenuity in the choice of items and soundness in the methods of item analysis utilized. This form is no exception. The manual and the Research Handbook, which are available for those who wish to construct additional scales, discuss and describe very thoroughly what considerations guided the accumulation of the pool of items and the statistical criteria applied for selecting the final set. The author proves in analytical terms his contention that it is more efficient to sacrifice internal consistency reliability for validity where one or more relatively independent variables are required to account for a criterion. Therefore, he argues, it is a matter of no great concern that the Kuder-Richardson reliabilities for the scales range from .42 to .82, with a median of .62. The median test-retest reliabilities are .79 and .86, respectively, for high school and college student populations. Unfortunately, we are not told the length of the time interval between testings.

This reviewer finds convincing Kuder's arguments regarding reliability as internal consistency, but contends that the equally important question of stability still remains. The user needs to know how much the interests tapped by this inventory may be expected to change with the passage of time for different age groups and what effects, if any, different types of intervening experiences may have. No evidence bearing on this question is presented. Nowhere, either in the manual or in the Research Handbook is this question ever discussed.

The occupational keys have been developed by selecting items which discriminate the selected occupational group from a norm group. The norm group, composed of 1,000 men selected among telephone subscribers in 138 cities and towns, defies identification. Approximately 70 per cent are from three major occupational classifications: professional and semiprofessional workers; proprietors, managers, and officials; and clerical, sales, and kindred workers. The test cannot be faulted on this because there is certainly no clear answer as to what is the most important base group to use for developing scales. However, the author and publisher are to be criticized for failing to offer any information about the expected distribution of scores among the relevant populations, e.g., high school or college students, the adult population at large. This lack is acknowledged and users are encouraged to develop their own norms.

Though its validity is to be the main index of its worth, there is remarkably sparse evidence offered. In fact, the only evidence is contained in tables that demonstrate that considerable success was attained in discriminating occupational groups from the norm group and that the degree of discrimination was fairly well maintained in cross validation samples. One may argue that not enough time has elapsed to permit the completion of the many other types of studies necessary to establish construct validity. Since interest inventories are rarely used to predict discrete behavioral criteria, e.g., level of academic achievement or job performance, the basis for their use rests most clearly on construct validity. Yet, such easily obtained basic information as the intercorrelation of the occupational scales is not made available. There is no sign or promise of the follow-up studies, lack of which has long been criticized in the vocational form. Perhaps it is assumed that data accumulated in connection with the vocational form can provide some

of this validational underpinning. Nowhere is this assumption explicitly stated; however, even if this assumption is made, then we need evidence that the relationship between the vocational and occupational forms is such as to make reasonable such a transfer of validity.

To summarize, this inventory is well developed and looks promising. However, at the present time it lacks most of the further data necessary for operational use.

JOHN W. GUSTAD, *Professor of Psychology and Director, University Counseling Center, University of Maryland, College Park, Maryland.*

According to its author, this form of the *Kuder Preference Record* was produced to provide "a relatively short interest inventory suitable for use in the development of interest keys for specific occupations." It is to be used, Kuder indicates, by counselors trying to help vocationally undecided clients and by personnel directors in selection, placement, and classification. How successful it will be in these functions remains to be seen. On the whole, it looks promising.

Those familiar with the earlier vocational forms will recall that they contained 9 or 10 scales, each reflecting an area or cluster of activity such as mechanical, social service, or outdoor. These scales were developed by inbreeding items until a high degree of homogeneity was attained among the items of a scale. This method is in marked contrast to the approach taken by Strong in the development of his *Vocational Interest Blank*. Here, criterion groups of successfully employed men in a variety of occupations were compared with respect to their item responses to a presumably representative group of men in general. The aim was to develop keys—clusters of items—which would indicate whether the person taking the test resembled the successful men or not.

In this version of the Preference Record, Kuder has abandoned his earlier approach and taken the road blazed by Strong. In many ways, this revision resembles Strong's inventory more than it does earlier forms of the Preference Record. Although it is too early to tell whether it will be as useful as the Strong, the information provided in the manual suggests that it will receive much well deserved attention. The reviewer is inclined to feel that it will be used more in research than in practice, at least for some time. Considering the number of unanswered questions, this seems highly desirable.

The Kuder Occupational contains 100 triadic items very much like those used in earlier forms. Many items were, in fact, taken from the earlier forms, with some of them modified for clarity and readability. Items were selected by a modification of the criterion vector method which is described in some detail in the handbook accompanying the test. The reduction to 100 items reduces total testing time to about 30 minutes on the average, although there is no formal time limit applied in administration.

Of most interest in this form are the various occupational keys or scales. These were developed by locating a representative norm population, then contrasting their responses with those of certain occupational groups. The norm group contained a thousand cases, approximately 85 per cent of which came from professional through craft levels. It is thus a sample with considerable upward bias, but, as Kuder indicates, "The best reference group for any specific situation is ordinarily the group from which the subjects are to be distinguished."

Occupational groups were then selected in 22 fields or subfields. Item analysis methods were employed to identify items which differentiated the occupational group from the norm group. These item pools were then cross validated to see whether the differentiation held up. It seemed to do so quite well.

Only one kind of validity—concurrent—is dealt with. Using the approach indicated, concurrent validity is the kind which must be dealt with first. Concurrent validity is indicated by the extent to which the test corresponds to current criterion status. That is, it must be shown that the occupational keys do in fact yield different distributions for men in the occupations and for men in the norm group.

Concurrent validity is not enough, however. Predictive validity must be dealt with some time, and there is no evidence cited to show that the Kuder Occupational has predictive validity. Work of the sort done with the Strong must be done before the general utility of this form can be accepted for counseling or personnel work.

The reliability of the instrument appears to be satisfactory, at least with respect to its con-current validity. Kuder-Richardson reliabilities range from .42 to .93. Test-retest reliabilities tend to be somewhat higher. The period between testings is not indicated, but it certainly does not approach the 18-year period discussed in Strong's latest book.

Interpretation of the scores is based on the differentiation ratio (DR). Percentiles of the norm and occupational groups are also available, but Kuder prefers the DR approach. This DR is the ratio of the proportion of the two groups, occupational and norm, exceeding a given score. The suggested meanings for these DR's lead one to many of the interpretive problems encountered in using the Strong.

Administration of the test appears to be at least as simple as with earlier forms. Scoring may be done by hand or on IBM machines. Raw scores are readily converted into DR's by means of tables printed on the scoring keys. A verification key, designed to assess the attitude and understanding of the test taker, is also included. The data cited seem to indicate that the test works well in screening out people who fail to understand the directions or who try to distort their answers.

In addition to the test and the manual, Kuder has developed a Research Handbook and a booklet of computation sheets. The first is of special interest since it contains detailed discussion of the theory and practice of interest inventory development and will enable even those without high level statistical skills to undertake the development of keys for special purposes. The Research Handbook is an intriguing and welcome addition to the test package.

This instrument is not ready yet for widespread use by counselors and personnel directors. It looks very promising for cautious experimental work by highly skilled and experienced psychologists. Until a great deal of research and clinical experience has been accumulated, however, it should not be considered on a par with the Strong or even with the earlier forms of Kuder's inventories. Its simplicity, the obvious care in its construction, its brief administration time, its easy scoring, and especially its potential as a source of new keys tailor-made to specific situations makes it a very promising instrument, one which should receive a great deal of attention in the near future.

Kuder Preference Record—Occupational

[863]

*Kuder Preference Record—Vocational. Grades
9–16 and adults; 1934–56; IBM; 2 forms; 2 editions;
separate answer sheets or pads must be used; $9.80
per 20 tests; 75¢ per specimen set of any one edition;
postage extra; (40–50) minutes; G. Frederic Kuder;
Science Research Associates. *
a) FORM B [NINE SCALE]. 1934–46; 9 scores: mechanical, computational, scientific, persuasive, artistic, literary, musical, social service, clerical; masulinity-femi-
ninity score also obtainable; 1 form; 2 editions; revised
manual ('46); 60¢ per 20 profile sheets for adults ('46)
or for children ('44).
1) [*Hand Scoring Edition.*] Form BB ('42); $2.35
per 20 answer pads.
2) [*Machine Scoring Edition.*] IBM; Form BM
('42); $4.50 per 100 IBM answer sheets; $7.50 per
set of scoring stencils.
b) FORM C [ELEVEN SCALE]. 1934–56; revision and expansion of Form B; 11 scores: same as for Form B
plus outdoor, verification; 1 form; 2 editions; manual,
sixth edition ('56); 60¢ per 20 profile sheets for adults
('51) or for children ('50); 90¢ per 20 profile leaflets
for adults ('54) or for children ('53) for comparing
vocational and personal (see 80) scores.
1) [*Hand Scoring Edition.*] Form CH ('48); $2.35
per 20 answer pads
2) [*Machine Scoring Edition.*] IBM; Form CM
('48); $4.50 per 100 IBM answer sheets; $7.50 per
set of scoring stencils.

REFERENCES

1–2. See 40:1671.
3–62. See 3:640.
63–208. See 4:742.
209. HAHN, MILTON E. *An Investigation of Measured Aspects of Social Intelligence in a Distributive Occupation.* Doctor's thesis, University of Minnesota (Minneapolis, Minn.),
1942.
210. LESHNER, SAUL S. *Interrelations Between the Vocational
Interest Areas of the Gentry, Kuder and Thurstone Interest
Inventories.* Master's thesis, Temple University (Philadelphia,
Pa.), 1942.
211. TRIGGS, FRANCES O. "Kuder Preference Record in the
Counseling of Nurses." *Am J Nursing* 46:312–16 '46. *
212. BILLING, PATRICIA S. *Voluntary Selection as Corroborated by the Kuder Preference Record: To Test the Value of
Music as a Universal Outlet for Extracurricular Activity.* Master's thesis, University of North Dakota (University, N.D.),
1948.
213. BURDETTE, WALTER E., JR. *Norms for the Occupation of
Industrial Arts Teachers in Conjunction With the Kuder Preference Record.* Master's thesis, Kansas State Teachers College
(Pittsburg, Kan.), 1948.
214. REDLENER, J. *A Comparative Study of the Efficiency of
the Kuder Preference Record and the Strong Vocational Interest
Blank in the Prediction of Job Satisfaction.* Master's thesis,
University of Southern California (Los Angeles, Calif.), 1948.
215. WILSON, EARL H. *Stability of Interest Patterns as Reflected in the Kuder Preference Record.* Master's thesis, State
College of Washington (Pullman, Wash.), 1948.
216. BATH, JOHN A. "Differential Interests of Agricultural
College Students as Measured by the Kuder Preference Record."
Proc Iowa Acad Sci 57:347–51 '50. *
217. CARSE, DOROTHY. *A Study of the Relationships Between
the Wechsler-Bellevue Intelligence Scale and the Kuder Preference Record-Personal.* Master's thesis, North Texas State College (Denton, Tex.), 1950.
218. CASNER, DANIEL. *Certain Factors Associated With Success and Failure in Personal-Adjustment Counseling.* Doctor's
thesis, New York University (New York, N.Y.), 1950.
219. CHASE, JOHN B., JR. *An Analysis of the Change of Interest of One Hundred and Fifty Secondary School Pupils.* Master's thesis, University of North Carolina (Chapel Hill, N.C.),
1950.
220. JOHNSON, RALPH H., AND BOND, GUY L. "Reading Ease
of Commonly Used Tests." *J Appl Psychol* 34:319–24 O '50. *
(*PA* 26:299)
221. NEUMANN, THOMAS M. *A Study of the Relation of Occupational Interests to Certain Aspects of Personality.* Master's
thesis, Illinois State Normal University (Normal, Ill.), 1950.
222. VAUGHAN, GEORGE E., JR. *Interest and Personality Patterns of Experienced Teachers.* Master's thesis, North Texas
State College (Denton, Tex.), 1950.
223. WEYNAND, ROBERT S. *A Study of the Relationship Between Interest Preferences and Academic Success for 622 A. &
M. College Students.* Master's thesis, Agricultural and Mechanical College of Texas (College Station, Tex.), 1950.

224. WISDOM, JESSIE R. *A Study of the Interest Patterns of
Premedical Students as Revealed by the Kuder Preference Record and the Strong Vocational Interest Inventory.* Master's
thesis, North Texas State College (Denton, Tex.), 1950.
225. BROWN, MANUEL N. *Clinical Status of Veteran Patients
Related to Six Interest Variables.* Doctor's thesis, University of
Portland (Portland, Ore.), 1951.
226. DALY, JOAN M. *A Comparison of the Relation of the
Thurstone Interest Schedule to the Kuder Preference Record
and to Self-Estimated Interests.* Master's thesis, Fordham University (New York, N.Y.), 1951.
227. HILLMAN, CAROL. *An Empirical Validation of a Sales
Personnel Selection Program.* Master's thesis, Vanderbilt University (Nashville, Tenn.), 1951.
228. HUFFMAN, WARREN J. *Personality Variations Among
Men Preparing to Teach Physical Education.* Doctor's thesis,
University of Illinois (Urbana, Ill.), 1951. (*DA* 12:28)
229. KERMEEN, BARBARA G. *A Factor Analysis of the Differential Aptitude Tests and a Factor Analysis of the Kuder Preference Record, Vocational.* Master's thesis, University of California (Berkeley, Calif.), 1951.
230. KUDER, G. FREDERIC, AND CRAWFORD, LURA E. *Kuder
Book List.* Chicago, Ill.: Science Research Associates, Inc., 1951.
Pp. 8. (*Instructor's Guide,* 1951. Pp. 4.) *
231. MANZANO, ILUMINADO B. *The Relation of Personality
Adjustment to Occupational Interests.* Doctor's thesis, University of Southern California (Los Angeles, Calif.), 1951.
232. MARTIN, GLENN C. "Test Batteries for Trainees in Auto
Mechanics and Apparel Design." *J Appl Psychol* 35:20–2 F
'51. * (*PA* 25:7123)
233. PEMBERTON, CAROL L. "Personality Inventory Data Related to ACE Subscores." *J Consult Psychol* 15:160–2 Ap '51. *
(*PA* 26:6569)
234. REID, JOHN W. "Stability of Measured Kuder Interests
in Young Adults." *J Ed Res* 45:307–12 D '51. * (*PA* 26:6284)
235. SCHNEBLY, LOUIS M. *A Comparison of the Scores Made
by Teachers on the Kuder Preference Record and the California Test of Personality.* Master's thesis, Montana State University (Missoula, Mont.), 1951.
236. SHERMAN, E. C. *Relationship of Kuder Scores to Differential College Achievement.* Master's thesis, Iowa State College (Ames, Iowa), 1951.
237. BARRETT, RUTH E. *The Relation Between Strength of
Kuder Preferences and Aptitude, Temperament, and Academic
Achievement.* Doctor's thesis, University of Pittsburgh (Pittsburgh, Pa.), 1952.
238. BOUTON, ARTHUR G. *The Stability of Kuder Vocational
Interest Patterns During Late Adolescence and Early Adult
Life.* Doctor's thesis, University of Pittsburgh (Pittsburgh, Pa.),
1952.
239. BUEGEL, HERMANN F., AND BILLING, PATRICIA STRATTE.
"Inventoried Interests of Participants in Music Groups." *J Ed
Res* 46:141–6 O '52. *
240. BURSCH, CHARLES W., II. "Certain Relationships Between the Kuder Preference Record and the Minnesota Multiphasic Personality Inventory." *Calif J Ed Res* 3:224–7+ N
'52. * (*PA* 27:5144)
241. CARTER, GERALD C. "Measurement of Supervisory Ability." *J Appl Psychol* 36:393–5 D '52. * (*PA* 27:6801)
242. CASE, HARRY W. "The Relationship of Certain Tests to
Grades Achieved in an Industrial Class in Aircraft Design."
Ed & Psychol Meas 12:90–5 sp '52. * (*PA* 27:6106)
243. COCKRUM, LOGAN V. "Personality Traits and Interests
of Theological Students." *Relig Ed* 47:28–32 Ja–F '52. * (*PA*
26:4229)
244. DRESSEL, PAUL L., AND MATTESON, ROSS W. "The Relationship Between Experience and Interest as Measured by the
Kuder Preference Record." *Ed & Psychol Meas* 12:109–16 sp
'52. * (*PA* 27:5957)
245. FRANDSEN, ARDEN N. "A Note on Wiener's Coding of
Kuder Preference Record Profiles." *Ed & Psychol Meas* 12:
137–9 sp '52. * (*PA* 27:5871)
246. FREEHILL, MAURICE F. "Student Self-Estimates as Guidance in Selecting Courses." *Col & Univ* 27:233–42 Ja '52. *
247. GUILFORD, J. P. "When Not to Factor Analyze." *Psychol B* 49:26–37 Ja '52. * (*PA* 27:33)
248. HALE, PETER PAUL. "A Comparison of Kuder Teachers'
Interest Patterns With Those of Veteran Teacher Trainees."
Ed Adm & Sup 38:412–20 N '52. * (*PA* 27:6172)
249. HARMON, LINDSEY R. *Inter-Relations of Patterns on the
Kuder Preference Record and the Minnesota Multiphasic Personality Inventory.* Doctor's thesis, University of Minnesota
(Minneapolis, Minn.), 1952. (*DA* 13:257)
250. ISAACSON, LEE E. "Predictors of Success for Cooperative Occupational Education Classes in Kansas City, Missouri,
High Schools." *Am Psychol* 7:379 Jl '52. *
251. KERNS, ROBERT DENEILLE. *The Relation of Interests as
Measured by the Kuder Preference Record to Level of Attainment in Engineering School.* Master's thesis, University of Pittsburgh (Pittsburgh, Pa.), 1952.
252. KRUMM, RICHARD L. *Inter-Relationships of Measured
Interests and Personality Traits of Introductory Psychology Instructors and Their Students as Related to Student Achievement.* Doctor's thesis, University of Pittsburgh (Pittsburgh,
Pa.), 1952.
253. MAGILL, JOHN W. *A Validation of the Kuder Preference Record Against Functional Criteria of Campus Activity.*

Doctor's thesis, University of Pittsburgh (Pittsburgh, Pa.), 1952.

254. MALLINSON, GEORGE GREISEN, AND CRUMRINE, WILLIAM M. "An Investigation of the Stability of Interests of High School Students." *J Ed Res* 45:369–83 Ja '52. * (*PA* 27:2977)

255. MELEIKA, LOUIS K. *Intra-Individual Variability in Relation to Achievement, Interest, and Personality.* Doctor's thesis, Stanford University (Stanford, Calif.), 1952.

256. MOSER, WILBUR E. "The Influence of Certain Cultural Factors Upon the Selection of Vocational Preferences by High School Students." *J Ed Res* 45:523–6 Mr '52. * (*PA* 27:2038)

257. MUGAAS, HENDRIK D., AND HESTER, RUPORT. "The Development of an Equation for Identifying the Interests of Carpenters." *Ed & Psychol Meas* 12:408–14 au '52. * (*PA* 27:6184)

258. RENKE, WILFERD W. *Discrimination of the Kuder Preference Record.* Doctor's thesis, University of North Dakota (Grand Forks, N.D.), 1952.

259. ROGGE, HAROLD J. *A Statistical Study of Certain Personality Factors Among Pupils in a Selected High School.* Master's thesis, Ohio University (Athens, Ohio), 1952.

260. ROSENBERG, PHYLLIS. *The Predictive Value of the Kuder Preference Record.* Master's thesis, Western Reserve University (Cleveland, Ohio), 1952.

261. RUSSELL, DIANA. *The Effect of Experience and Change of Occupational Choice on the Kuder Preference Record.* Master's thesis, University of Pittsburgh (Pittsburgh, Pa.), 1952.

262. RUSSELL, DIANA, AND HERZBERG, FREDERICK. "Kuder Occupational Interest Patterns in Vocational Counseling." Abstract. *Am Psychol* 7:383 Jl '52. *

263. STANLEY, JULIAN C., AND WALDROP, ROBERT S. "Intercorrelations of Study of Values and Kuder Preference Record Scores." *Ed & Psychol Meas* 12:707–19 w '52. * (*PA* 27:5906)

264. STEINBERG, ARTHUR. "The Relation of Vocational Preference to Emotional Adjustment." *Ed & Psychol Meas* 12:96–104 sp '52. * (*PA* 27:5965)

265. UECKER, ALBERT E. *A Comparative Study of the Vocational Interests, Aspirations, and Achievements of Selected Groups of Veteran Psychiatric Patients.* Doctor's thesis, University of Minnesota (Minneapolis, Minn.), 1952. (*DA* 12:392)

266. WOODWARD, C. L. "A Critical Analysis of Certain Interest Tests." *Yearb Nat Council Meas Used Ed* 9:101–8 '52. *

267. ANDERSON, ROSE G. "Do Aptitudes Support Interests?" *Personnel & Guid J* 32:14–7 S '53. * (*PA* 28:4495)

268. AUSUBEL, DAVID P.; SCHIFF, HERBERT M.; AND ZELENY, MARJORIE P. " 'Real-Life' Measures of Level of Academic and Vocational Aspiration in Adolescents: Relation to Laboratory Measures and to Adjustment." *Child Develop* 24:155–68 S–D '53. * (*PA* 29:3700)

269. BAER, BARBARA S. *Interest Patterns for Four Occupations: Kuder Preference Record.* Master's thesis, Utah State Agricultural College (Logan, Utah), 1953

270. BEAMER, GEORGE C.; PENDER, FRANCES RUSSELL; AND PARTON, NORMA WEST. "Selection of Teachers of Homemaking." *J Home Econ* 45:98–100 F '53. * (*PA* 27:7412)

271. BEAVER, ALMA PERRY. "Kuder Interest Patterns of Student Nurses." *J Appl Psychol* 37:370–3 O '53. * (*PA* 29:1483)

272. BORDIN, EDWARD S., AND WILSON, EARL H. "Change of Interest as a Function of Shift in Curricular Orientation." *Ed & Psychol Meas* 13:297–307 su '53. * (*PA* 28:4875)

273. BRAYFIELD, ARTHUR H. "Clerical Interest and Clerical Aptitude." *Personnel & Guid J* 31:304–6 F '53. * (*PA* 28:1616)

274. BROGDEN, H. E.; BAIER, D. E.; AND TAYLOR, E. K. "Experimental Design: Utilization of an Unreliable and a Biased Criterion." *Ed & Psychol Meas* 13:27–33 sp '53. * (*PA* 28:112)

275. CANFIELD, A. A. "Administering Form BB of the Kuder Preference Record, Half Length." *J Appl Psychol* 37:197–200 Je '53. * (*PA* 28:3342)

276. FARROW, EDWARD G. *The Development of a Masculinity-Femininity Scale for the Kuder Preference Record-Personal.* Master's thesis, North Carolina State College of Agriculture and Engineering (Raleigh, N.C.), 1953.

277. FRANDSEN, ARDEN N., AND SESSIONS, ALWYN D. "Interests and School Achievement." *Ed & Psychol Meas* 13:94–101 sp '53. * (*PA* 28:1560)

278. FREEHILL, MAURICE F. "Interest Scores in Selection of Freshman Courses." *Col & Univ* 28:197–203 Ja '53. *

279. GIVENS, PAUL R. "Kuder Patterns of Interest as Related to Ac¹ievement in College Science Courses." *J Ed Res* 46:627–30 A₁' '53. * (*PA* 28:3234)

280. HASELHORN, HARRY. *The Vocational Interests of a Group of Homosexuals.* Doctor's thesis, New York University (New York, N.Y.), 1953. (*DA* 13:582)

281. HEALY, IRENE, AND BORG, WALTER R. "The Vocational Interests of Nurses and Nursing Students." *J Ed Res* 46:347–52 Ja '53. * (*PA* 28:1679)

282. HERZBERG, FREDERICK, AND RUSSELL, DIANA. "The Effects of Experience and Change of Job Interest on the Kuder Preference Record." *J Appl Psychol* 37:478–81 D '53. * (*PA* 29:1615)

283. HOLLAND, JOHN L.; KRAUSE, ALLEN H.; NIXON, M. ELOISE; AND TREMBATH, MARY F. "The Classification of Occupations by Means of Kuder Interest Profiles: I, The Development of Interest Groups." *J Appl Psychol* 37:263–9 Ag '53. * (*PA* 28:6172)

284. KERN, DONALD W. *The Prediction of Academic Success*

of Freshmen in a Community College. Doctor's thesis, New York University (New York, N.Y.), 1953. (*DA* 15:85)

285. LIVINGSTON, EUGEÑIA. *A Comparison of the Results of the Kuder Preference Record Given to One Hundred and Four Students as Freshmen and Again as Juniors in the Helena High School.* Master's thesis, Montana State University (Missoula, Mont.), 1953.

286. LONG, LOUIS, AND PERRY, JAMES D. "Academic Achievement in Engineering Related to Selection Procedures and Interests." *J Appl Psychol* 37:468–71 D '53. * (*PA* 29:1571)

287. PARKER, JAMES W., JR. "Psychological and Personal History Data Related to Accident Records of Commercial Truck Drivers." *J Appl Psychol* 37:317–20 Ag '53. * (*PA* 28:6695)

288. ROBB, GEORGE P. *Relationships Between Interests and Student Teaching Achievement.* Doctor's thesis, Indiana University (Bloomington, Ind.), 1953. (*DA* 14:1050)

289. ROBBINS, ARTHUR. *An Experimental Study of the Relationship Between Needs as Manifested on the Thematic Apperception Test and Kuder Preference Record Scales of Adolescent Boys.* Doctor's thesis, Columbia University (New York, N.Y.), 1953.

290. ROSENBERG, NATHAN. "Stability and Maturation of Kuder Interest Patterns During High School." *Ed & Psychol Meas* 13:449–58 au '53. * (*PA* 28:4891)

291. SHAFFER, ROBERT H., AND KUDER, G. FREDERIC. "Kuder Interest Patterns of Medical, Law, and Business School Alumni." *J Appl Psychol* 37:367–9 O '53. * (*PA* 29:1716)

292. STERNBERG, CARL. "Differences in Measured Interest, Values, and Personality Among College Students Majoring in Nine Subject Areas." Abstract. *Am Psychol* 8:442–3 Ag '53. *

293. STERNBERG, CARL. *The Relation of Interests, Values and Personality to the Major Field of Study in College.* Doctor's thesis, New York University (New York, N.Y.), 1953. (*DA* 13:1095)

294. STOOPS, JOHN A. "Stability of the Measured Interests of High School Pupils Between Grades Nine and Eleven." *Ed Outlook* 27:116–8 Mr '53. *

295. TIFFIN, JOSEPH, AND PHELAN, R. F. "Use of the Kuder Preference Record to Predict Turnover in an Industrial Plant." *Personnel Psychol* 6:195–204 su '53. * (*PA* 28:3385)

296. TRIGGS, FRANCES ORALIND. "Kuder Preference Record," pp. 782–8. (*PA* 27:7799) In *Contributions Toward Medical Psychology: Theory and Psychodiagnostic Methods, Vol. II.* Edited by Arthur Weider. New York: Ronald Press Co., 1953. Pp. xi, 459–885. *

297. WAY, HARRISON H. *The Relationship Between Forced Choice Scores and Differentiated Response Scores on the Kuder Preference Record-Vocational.* Doctor's thesis, Indiana University (Bloomington, Ind.), 1953. (*DA* 13:1097)

298. BENDIG, A. W., AND HUGHES, J. B., III. "Student Attitude and Achievement in a Course in Introductory Statistics." *J Ed Psychol* 45:268–76 My '54. * (*PA* 29:2952)

299. BERNARD, JACK. *Selection of Technical School Students: An Investigation of the Relationship Between Certain Personality Characteristics, Interests and Abilities, and Success in a Radio and Television Curriculum.* Doctor's thesis, New York University (New York, N.Y.), 1954. (*DA* 15:631)

300. BOURDO, ERIC A., JR. "The Interests of Forestry Students." *Ed & Psychol Meas* 14:680–6 w '54. * (*PA* 29:8150)

301. BROOKS, MELVIN S., AND WEYNAND, ROBERT S. "Interest Preferences and Their Effect Upon Academic Success." *Social Forces* 32:281–5 Mr '54. *

302. BRUCE, MARTIN M. "Validity Information Exchange, No. 7-079:D.O.T. Code 7-83.058, Electrical Appliance Serviceman." *Personnel Psychol* 7:425–6 au '54. *

303. BRYAN, JOHN L. *The Kuder Interest Test Patterns of the Students and the Graduates of the Fire Protection School at Oklahoma A. & M. College.* Doctor's thesis, Oklahoma Agricultural and Mechanical College (Stillwater, Okla.), 1954.

304. BURSCH, CHARLES W. *Utility of the Kuder Preference Record in Selection of Students for Vocational Agriculture.* Doctor's thesis, Stanford University (Stanford, Calif.), 1954. (*DA* 14:2275)

305. CALLIS, ROBERT; ENGRAM, WILLIAM C.; AND McGOWAN, JOHN F. "Coding the Kuder Preference Record—Vocational." *J Appl Psychol* 38:359–63 O '54. * (*PA* 29:6347)

306. CARTER, GERALD C. "Kuder Preference Record Scores and Success in Engineering College." *J Counsel Psychol* 1:196 ᵀall '54. *

307. CONNER, HAROLD T. *An Investigation of Certain Factors for the Selection and Guidance of Prospective Students Entering a School of Public Health.* Doctor's thesis, University of North Carolina (Chapel Hill, N.C.), 1954.

308. CURRAN, JAMES P. *A Study of the Effectiveness of the Kuder Preference Record-Vocational in Private Secondary School for Girls.* Master's thesis, Catholic University of America (Washington, D.C.), 1954

309. DAVIS, SANDFORD S. *The Relationship Between School Superintendents' Ratings of Elementary Teachers and the Kuder Preference Record-Personal and Other Measured and Rated Teacher Characteristics.* Doctor's thesis, University of Colorado (Boulder, Colo.), 1954.

310. DURNALL, EDWARD J., JR. "Falsification of Interest Patterns on the Kuder Preference Record." *J Ed Psychol* 45:240–3 Ap '54. * (*PA* 29:3122)

311. GOCHE, L. N. *Relationship of Interests and Temperament Traits to Attrition and Survival of Engineering Students.* Master's thesis, Iowa State College (Ames, Iowa), 1954.

312. GOWAN, JOHN CURTIS. "The Interest Patterns of Student Leaders." *Ed & Psychol Meas* 14:151–5 sp '54. * (*PA* 28: 8019)

313. GRANT, DONALD L. "Validity Information Exchange, No. 7-085:D.O.T. Code 1-01.05, Budget Clerk." *Personnel Psychol* 7:557–8 w '54. *

314. GRANT, DONALD L. "Validity Information Exchange, No. 7-086:D.O.T. Code 1-01.05, Budget Clerk." *Personnel Psychol* 7:559–60 w '54. *

315. GUAZZO, EUGENE J., JR. *Predicting Academic Success of Architecture Students.* Master's thesis, Alabama Polytechnic Institute (Auburn, Ala.), 1954.

316. GUILFORD, J. P.; CHRISTENSEN, PAUL R.; BOND, NICHOLAS, A., JR.; AND SUTTON, MARCELLA A. "A Factor Analysis Study of Human Interests." *Psychol Monogr* 68(4):1–38 '54. *

317. HAMMILL, DAMIEN. *An Analysis of the Interest Patterns of High School Seniors on Form CH of the Kuder Preference Record.* Master's thesis, Fordham University (New York, N.Y.), 1954.

318. HERZBERG, FREDERICK, AND BOUTON, ARTHUR. "A Further Study of the Stability of the Kuder Preference Record." *Ed & Psychol Meas* 14:326–31 su '54. * (*PA* 29:2605)

319. HERZBERG, FREDERICK; BOUTON, ARTHUR; AND STEINER, BETTY JO. "Studies of the Stability of the Kuder Preference Record." *Ed & Psychol Meas* 14:90–100 sp '54. * (*PA* 28:8114)

320. JACOBS, ROBERT, AND TRAXLER, ARTHUR E. "Use of the Kuder in Counseling With Regard to Accounting as a Career." *J Counsel Psychol* 1:153–8 fall '54. * (*PA* 29:5835)

321. KEGAN, ESTHER O. "Interests of Women Lawyers Shown on the Kuder Preference Record." *Personnel Psychol* 7:499–507 w '54. * (*PA* 29:8157)

322. KELLY, JAMES G. *Feelings of Dominance and Judgments of Humor as Measured by a Non-Projective Preference Scale and a Selected Population of Jokes.* Master's thesis, Bowling Green State University (Bowling Green, Ohio), 1954.

323. KRIEDT, PHILIP H., AND GADEL, MARGUERITE S. "Use of the Kuder Preference Record in Selecting Clerical Employees." Abstract. *Am Psychol* 9:409–10 Ag '54. *

324. LEACH, KENT W. "Intelligence Levels and Corresponding Interest Area Choices of Ninth Grade Pupils in Thirteen Michigan Schools." *J Exp Ed* 22:369–83 Je '54. * (*PA* 29:4651)

325. LEE, PHYLLIS J. *The Effectiveness of a Test Battery in Predicting Chemistry Grades.* Master's thesis, Alabama Polytechnic Institute (Auburn, Ala.), 1954.

326. LEVINE, PHYLLIS ROSENBERG, AND WALLEN, RICHARD. "Adolescent Vocational Interests and Later Occupation." *J Appl Psychol* 38:428–31 D '54. * (*PA* 29:5837)

327. LIPSETT, LAURENCE, AND WILSON, JAMES W. "Do 'Suitable' Interests and Mental Ability Lead to Job Satisfaction?" *Ed & Psychol Meas* 14:373–80 su '54. * (*PA* 29:2607)

328. McCARTY, JOHN J. "Validity Information Exchange, No. 7-077:D.O.T. Code 5-92.621, (Foreman II)." *Personnel Psychol* 7:420–1 au '54. *

329. McCARTY, JOHN J.; WESTBERG, WILLIAM C.; AND FITZPATRICK, EUGENE D. "Validity Information Exchange, No. 7-091:D.O.T. Code 5-92.621, (Foreman II)." *Personnel Psychol* 7:568–9 w '54. *

330. McCOY, RAYMOND A. *Stability and Change of Measured Vocational Interests of High School Students.* Doctor's thesis, University of Missouri (Columbia, Mo.), 1954. (*DA* 15:85)

331. McCULLY, CYRUS H. *The Validity of the Kuder Preference Record.* Doctor's thesis, George Washington University (Washington, D.C.), 1954

332. MEEK, CLINTON R. *The Effect of Knowledge of Aptitude Upon Interest Scores.* Doctor's thesis, George Peabody College for Teachers (Nashville, Tenn.), 1954.

333. PIERCE-JONES, JOHN. "The Readability of Certain Standard Tests." *Calif J Ed Res* 5:80–2 Mr '54. * (*PA* 28:8729)

334. PIERCE-JONES, JOHN, AND CARTER, H. D. "Vocational Interest Measurement Using a Photographic Inventory." *Ed & Psychol Meas* 14:671–9 w '54. * (*PA* 29:7438)

335. ROBERTS, S. OLIVER, AND GUNTER, LAURIE MARTIN. "An Evaluation of the Kuder Interest Patterns of Negro Nurses." Abstract. *Am Psychol* 9:456 Ag '54. *

336. ROSENBERG, NATHAN, AND IZARD, CARROLL E. "Vocational Interests of Naval Aviation Cadets." *J Appl Psychol* 38:354–8 O '54. * (*PA* 29:6363)

337. SHAW, CARL E. *An Investigation of the Validity of the Kuder Preference Record-Vocational for Educational Guidance.* Doctor's thesis, Purdue University (Lafayette, Ind.), 1954. (*DA* 14:1622)

338. SWEENEY, FRANCIS J. "Intelligence, Vocational Interests and Reading Speed of Senior Boys in Catholic High Schools of Los Angeles." *Calif J Ed Res* 5:159–65 S '54. * (*PA* 29:4656)

339. TAYLOR, ERWIN K., AND SCHNEIDER, DOROTHY E. "Validity Information Exchange, No. 7-023:D.O.T. Code 1-86.11, Salesman, Commercial Equipment and Supplies." *Personnel Psychol* 7:158 sp '54. *

340. TIEDEMAN, DAVID V., AND BRYAN, JOSEPH G. "Prediction of College Field of Concentration." *Harvard Ed R* 24:122–39 sp '54. * (*PA* 29:3058)

341. TRAXLER, ARTHUR E. "The Stability of Profiles on the Kuder Preference Records—Vocational and Personal—for Different Groups of Public Accountants." *Yearb Nat Council Meas Used Ed* 11:9–14+ '54. *

342. WESTBERG, WILLIAM C.; FITZPATRICK, EUGENE D.; AND McCARTY, JOHN J. "Validity Information Exchange, No. 7-073:

D.O.T. Code 1-37.32, Typist." *Personnel Psychol* 7:411–2 au '54. *

343. WESTBERG, WILLIAM C.; FITZPATRICK, EUGENE D.; AND McCARTY, JOHN J. "Validity Information Exchange, No. 7-087: D.O.T. Code 1-37.32, Typist." *Personnel Psychol* 7:561–2 w '54. *

344. WRIGHT, RUTH L. *Comparison of Mental Ability and Interest Preferences of a Group of High School Students as Measured by the Terman-McNemar Test of Mental Ability and the Kuder Preference Record.* Master's thesis, Southwest State Teachers College (San Marcos, Tex.), 1954.

345. ATKINSON, EDITH, AND BARON, SAMUEL. "Exploring Vocational Interests in the Ninth Year." *High Points* 37:46–8 Ja '55. *

346. COMREY, ANDREW L., AND HIGH, WALLACE S. "Validity of Some Ability and Interest Scores." *J Appl Psychol* 39:247–8 Ag '55. * (*PA* 30:5278)

347. COOPER, MATTHEW N. *To Determine the Nature and Significance, If Any, of Certain Differences in the Social and Personal Adjustment of Fifty-One Successful and Fifty-One Non-Successful College Students at Texas Southern University.* Doctor's thesis, New York University (New York, N.Y.), 1955. (*DA* 16:497)

348. FOLEY, A. W. "Adjustment Through Interest Changes." *J Counsel Psychol* 2:66–7 sp '55. *

349. FORCE, RONALD C., AND THOMAS, PAUL L. "Development of a Covert Test for the Detection of Alcohol Addiction by a Keying of the Kuder Preference Record." Abstract. *Am Psychol* 10:449 Ag '55. *

350. FORER, BERTRAM R. "The Stability of Kuder Scores in a Disabled Population." *Ed & Psychol Meas* 15:166–9 su '55. * (*PA* 30:3020)

351. FORSTER, CECIL R. *The Relationship Between Test Achievement and Success in Training of a Selected Group of Tuberculosis Patients.* Doctor's thesis, New York University (New York, N.Y.), 1955. (*DA* 15:1201)

352. KELLEY, ELVAN P. *An Investigation Into the Value of Selected Tests and Techniques for Guidance of Prospective Teachers Enrolled in Community Experiences Course.* Doctor's thesis, University of Houston (Houston, Tex.), 1955. (*DA* 15: 1209)

353. KLUGMAN, SAMUEL F. "A Study of the Interest Profile of a Psychotic Group and Its Bearing on Interest-Personality Theory." Abstract. *Am Psychol* 10:366 Ag '55. *

354. McCULLY, C. HAROLD. "A Longitudinal Study of the Validity of the Kuder Preference Record." Abstract. *Am Psychol* 10:374 Ag '55. *

355. MAGILL, JOHN W. "Interest Profiles of College Activity Groups: Kuder Preference Record Validation." *J Appl Psychol* 39:53–6 F '55. * (*PA* 30:1564)

356. NEWMAN, JOSEPH. "The Kuder Preference Record and Personal Adjustment: A Study of Tuberculous Patients." *Ed & Psychol Meas* 15:274–80 au '55. * (*PA* 30:5059)

357. PATTERSON, CECIL H. *Test and Background Factors Related to Drop-Outs in an Industrial Institute.* Doctor's thesis, University of Minnesota (Minneapolis, Minn.), 1955. (*DA* 15: 1024)

358. PERRINE, MERVYN WILLIAM. "The Selection of Drafting Trainees." *J Appl Psychol* 39:57–61 F '55. * (*PA* 30:1725)

359. SHOEMAKER, WILFRED L. *Rejection of Measured Vocational Interest Areas by High School Students.* Doctor's thesis, University of Missouri (Columbia, Mo.), 1955. (*DA* 16:499)

360. STERNBERG, CARL. "Personality Trait Patterns of College Students Majoring in Different Fields." *Psychol Monogr* 69(18):1–21 '55. * (*PA* 31:1705)

361. STEWART, LAWRENCE H., AND ROBERTS, JOSEPH P. "The Relationship of Kuder Profiles to Remaining in a Teachers' College and to Occupational Choice." *Ed & Psychol Meas* 15:416–21 w '55. * (*PA* 30:7792)

362. STOWE, EDWARD W. *The Relation of the Kuder Vocational Preference Record to Ammons' Appreception Test.* Master's thesis, Illinois State Normal University (Normal, Ill.), 1955.

363. TUTTON, MARIE E. "Stability of Adolescent Vocational Interest." *Voc Guid Q* 3:78–80 sp '55. *

364. ARBUCKLE, DUGALD S. "Client Perception of Counselor Personality." *J Counsel Psychol* 3:93–6 su '56. * (*PA* 31:4639)

365. BEAVER, ALMA P. "Psychometric Data and Survival in a College of Nursing." *Psychol Rep* 2:223–6 Je '56. * (*PA* 31: 1738)

366. DOWNIE, N. M. "The Vocational Interest Patterns of Students Who Stay in Engineering Compared With Those Who Leave the Engineering Curriculum." Abstract. *Ind Acad Sci Proc* 66:324 '56. *

367. EWENS, WILLIAM PRICE. "Experience Patterns as Related to Vocational Preference." *Ed & Psychol Meas* 16:223–31 su '56. * (*PA* 31:4803)

368. GEHMAN, W. SCOTT, AND SOUTHERN, J. ALBERT. "The Kuder Electrical Engineering Scale for Counseling College Students." *J Counsel Psychol* 3:17–20 sp '56. * (*PA* 31:3749)

369. GOLDSTEIN, ARNOLD P. *The Fakability of the Kuder Preference Record and the Vocational Apperception Test.* Master's thesis, City College of New York (New York, N.Y.), 1956.

370. GOWAN, J. C. "Achievement and Personality Test Scores of Gifted College Students." *Calif J Ed Res* 7:105–9 My '56. * (*PA* 31:3783)

371. GUBA, E. G., AND GETZELS, J. W. "Interest and Value

Patterns of Air Force Officers." *Ed & Psychol Meas* 16:465–70 w '56. * (*PA* 32:977)

372. HALE, PETER P., AND LEONARD, REGIS J. "The Kuder Preference Record and the Professional Curriculum." *J Ed Res* 50:71–4 S '56. * (*PA* 31:6222)

373. HASELKORN, HARRY. "The Vocational Interests of a Group of Male Homosexuals." *J Counsel Psychol* 3:8–11 sp '56. * (*PA* 31:3211)

374. HENDERSON, ERWIN C. *The Kuder-Preference Record-Vocational in Appraising the Apparent Suitability of Vocational Choices of High School Students.* Master's thesis, Utah State Agricultural College (Logan, Utah), 1956.

375. HOLE, RICHARD M. *A Comparison of Students' Vocational Interests With Parental Judgments of Students' Interests.* Master's thesis, Ohio University (Athens, Ohio), 1956.

376. HOOVER, KENNETH H., AND MICKA, HELEN K. "Student-Parent Interest Comparisons in Counseling High School Students." *Personnel & Guid J* 34:292–4 Ja '56. * (*PA* 30:7735)

377. HYMAN, BERNARD. "The Relationship of Social Status and Vocational Interests." *J Counsel Psychol* 3:12–6 sp '56. * (*PA* 31:3212)

378. KINGSTON, ALBERT J.; GEORGE, CLAY E.; AND EWENS, W. PRICE. "Determining the Relationship Between Individual Interest Profiles and Occupational Forms." *J Ed Psychol* 47:310–6 My '56. * (*PA* 32:2043)

379. KLINE, MILTON V., AND CUMINGS, RUTH. "A Study of the Learning Characteristics of Public Health Nurses in Relation to Mental Health Education and Consultation: IV, Kuder Vocational Interest Patterns." *J Genetic Psychol* 88:37–59 Mr '56. * (*PA* 31:4805)

380. LANGE, HERBERT M. *An Analysis of the Kuder Preference Record Results at Hardin-Simmons University.* Master's thesis, Hardin-Simmons University (Abilene, Tex.), 1956.

381. LIVINGSTON, CHARLES D. *The Personality Correlates of High and Low Identification With the Father Figure.* Doctor's thesis, University of Houston (Houston, Tex.), 1956. (*DA* 16:2525)

382. SAMUELSON, CECIL O., AND PEARSON, DAVID T. "Interest Scores in Identifying the Potential Trade School Dropout." *J Appl Psychol* 40:386–8 D '56. * (*PA* 32:2126)

383. SHINN, EDMOND O. "Interest and Achievement as Related to Achievement in Tenth Grade." *Calif J Ed Res* 7:217–20 N '56. * (*PA* 31:8844)

384. SINNETT, E. ROBERT. "Some Determinants of Agreement Between Measured and Expressed Interests." *Ed & Psychol Meas* 16:110–8 sp '56. * (*PA* 31:6226)

385. STERNBERG, CARL. "Interests and Tendencies Toward Maladjustment in a Normal Population." *Personnel & Guid J* 35:94–9 O '56. * (*PA* 31:7975)

386. THARPE, FRANK D. *Usefulness of the Kuder Preference Record for Predicting Shop Achievement of Senior High School Students in Industrial Arts.* Master's thesis, Iowa State College (Ames, Iowa), 1956.

387. VOPATEK, S. H. "Normative Data Information Exchange, No. 32." *Personnel Psychol* 9:544 w '56. *

388. ZENTI, RICO N. *A Comparison of the Results Obtained by the Mitchell and Kuder Interest Measures When Administered to Male Freshmen at the University of Michigan.* Doctor's thesis, University of Michigan (Ann Arbor, Mich.), 1956. (*DA* 17:1265)

389. ADAMS, FRANK J. *A Study of the Stability of Broad Vocational Interests at the High School Level.* Doctor's thesis, New York University (New York, N.Y.), 1957. (*DA* 19:270)

390. BEAMER, GEORGE C., AND LEDBETTER, ELAINE W. "The Relation Between Teacher Attitudes and the Social Service Interest." *J Ed Res* 50:655–66 My '57. *

391. BENDIG, A. W. "Validity of Kuder Differences Among Honors Majors." *Ed & Psychol Meas* 17:593–8 w '57. *

392. BONE, JOHN H. *A Statistical Analysis of Interest Patterns of High School Students and Their Relationship to Intelligence and Achievement.* Doctor's thesis, Pennsylvania State University (State College, Pa.), 1957. (*DA* 18:115)

393. BRAYFIELD, ARTHUR H., AND MARSH, MARY MARKLEY. "Aptitudes, Interests, and Personality Characteristics of Farmers." *J Appl Psychol* 41:98–103 Ap '57. *

394. BRODY, DAVID S. "Kuder Interest Patterns of Professional Forest Service Men." *Ed & Psychol Meas* 17:599–605 w '57. *

395. BRUCE, MARTIN M. "Normative Data Information Exchange, No. 10-42." *Personnel Psychol* 10:534–5 w '57. *

396. DAY, MERLE E. *Kuder Preference Record Responses of a Selected Group of Schizophrenics (Counseling Referrals) as a Function of Personality Traits.* Doctor's thesis, New York University (New York, N.Y.), 1957. (*DA* 18:654)

397. GOWAN, J. C. "Intelligence, Interests, and Reading Ability in Relation to Scholastic Achievement." *Psychol Newsl* 8:85–7 Mr–Ap '57. * (*PA* 32:3346)

398. GOWAN, J. C., AND SEAGOE, MAY. "The Relation Between Interest and Aptitude Tests in Art and Music." *Calif J Ed Res* 8:43–5 Ja '57. *

399. KLUGMAN, SAMUEL F. "A Study of the Interest Profile of a Psychotic Group and Its Bearing on Interest-Personality Theory." *Ed & Psychol Meas* 17:55–64 sp '57. *

400. KUDER, G. FREDERIC. "A Comparative Study of Some Methods of Developing Occupational Keys." *Ed & Psychol Meas* 17:105–14 sp '57. *

401. LAIRD, J. T. "A Note on the Scoring Rationale of the Kuder Preference Record." *Can J Psychol* 11:133–5 Je '57. *

402. McCARTY, JOHN J. "Normative Data Information Exchange, No. 10-37." *Personnel Psychol* 10:527–8 w '57. *

403. MAIER, GLEN E. *The Contribution of Interest Test Scores to Differential Academic Prediction.* Doctor's thesis, University of Washington (Seattle, Wash.), 1957. (*DA* 18:150)

404. SHAH, SALEEM A. *An Investigation of Predictive Ability in Hospital Personnel and University Students.* Doctor's thesis, Pennsylvania State University (State College, Pa.), 1957. (*DA* 18:288)

405. STEWART, LAWRENCE H. "Does Knowledge of Performance on an Aptitude Test Change Scores on the Kuder?" *J Counsel Psychol* 4:161–4 su '57. *

406. STONE, SOLOMON. *The Contribution of Intelligence, Interests, Temperament and Certain Personality Variables to Academic Achievement in a Physical Science and Mathematics Curriculum.* Doctor's thesis, New York University (New York, N.Y.), 1957. (*DA* 18:669)

407. TOPETZES, NICK JOHN. "A Program for the Selection of Trainees in Physical Medicine." *J Exp Ed* 25:263–311 Je '57. *

408. ARNOLD, DWIGHT L. "Student Reaction to the Kuder." *Personnel & Guid J* 37:40–4 S '58. *

409. BARRETT, RICHARD S. "The Process of Predicting Job Performance." *Personnel Psychol* 11:39–57 sp '58. *

410. CRAVEN, ETHEL C. *Social Concomitants of Interest.* Doctor's thesis, Columbia University (New York, N.Y.), 1958. (*DA* 19:353)

411. FORCE, RONALD C. "Development of a Covert Test for the Detection of Alcoholism by a Keying of the Kuder Preference Record." *Q J Studies Alcohol* 19:72–8 Mr '58. *

412. FRENCH, JOSEPH L. "Interests of the Gifted." *Voc Guid Q* 7:14–6 au '58. *

413. GLAZER, STANFORD H. "Educational Attainment and Interest Patterns." *Voc Guid Q* 6:183–6 su '58. *

414. HILL, GEORGE E., AND HOLE, RICHARD M. "Comparison of the Vocational Interests of Tenth Grade Students With Their Parents' Judgments of These Interests." *Ed & Psychol Meas* 18:173–87 sp '58. *

415. HILL, GEORGE E., AND ROGGE, HAROLD. "The Relation of Kuder Preference Record Scores to Mental Maturity Scores in High School." *J Ed Res* 51:545–8 Mr '58. *

416. MOORE, CHARLES W. *Some Relationships Between Standardized Test Scores and Academic Performance in the College of Business Administration of the University of Houston.* Doctor's thesis, University of Houston (Houston, Tex.), 1958. (*DA* 19:356)

417. SAMUELSON, CECIL O. "Interest Scores in Predicting Success of Trade School Students." *Personnel & Guid J* 36:538–41 Ap '58. *

418. SMITH, D. D. "Abilities and Interests: I, A Factorial Study." *Can J Psychol* 12:191–201 S '58. *

419. WRIGHT, JOHN C., AND SCARBOROUGH, BARRON B. "Relationship of the Interests of College Freshmen to Their Interests as Sophomores and as Seniors." *Ed & Psychol Meas* 18:153–8 sp '58. *

CLIFFORD P. FROEHLICH, *Professor of Education, University of California, Berkeley, California.*

The principal differences between the earlier Form B (1942) and the later Form C (1948) are the addition of verification and outdoor scores and new normative data for adolescent and adult profiles. Since these changes represent substantial improvements in the instrument, this reviewer sees no reason for anyone to continue using the older Form B. Because that form is now obsolete no further reference will be made to it in these comments.

Form C follows the long established pattern of the *Kuder Preference Record* with claims for being "self-administering," and having "self-interpreting profiles." More accurate claims would be that the test is relatively easy to administer and that most persons are able to score it and prepare a profile of their scores. Interpreting the profile requires all the acumen a skillful counselor can bring to the task.

This reviewer's greatest dissatisfaction with

this instrument lies in the author's implication that the scores have *established* relevance to occupations. The latest manual (1956) again presents fragmentary percentile ranks of the median scores of a variety of occupations. Except in the instances where data were reported by other investigators, accurate descriptions of the occupational groups are lacking. What, for example, is the denominational affiliation of the 43 clergymen for whom median scores are reported? Or what positions are held by the 65 school administrators whose scores are reported?

Further lack of confidence in the occupational significance of the scores stems from the fact that many were contributed by test users. Whether these tests were administered to persons as a part of a counseling relationship or to persons seeking employment is unknown.

There is a need for the author to develop data which would facilitate the interpretation of the profile. The current manual suggests that scores above the 75th percentile indicate occupational areas which should be considered by the testee, and that those below the 25th percentile give clues to occupations which should be eliminated from consideration. Interpretation of the test in this manner neglects the pattern of scores. Work with the *Strong Vocational Interest Blank* indicates pattern analysis is a fruitful approach in understanding the meaning of an interest profile. This reviewer's opinion is that Kuder's halfhearted invitation for users to develop specific occupational keys by means of Fisher's discriminant function is no substitute for data which would assist the counselor in interpreting the profile as a whole.

The opinions expressed above should not be construed as meaning that this reviewer does not recommend this inventory. Among those available, it is his choice when the use of Strong's blank is inappropriate or not feasible. Perhaps his opinions are reinforced by impatience because the author and publisher have not made more data available for interpreting a test which has been so widely used and highly respected for almost 20 years.

JOHN PIERCE-JONES, *Associate Professor of Educational Psychology, The University of Texas, Austin, Texas.*

The Fourth Mental Measurements Yearbook presented three reviews of the *Kuder Prefer-* ence *Record—Vocational* (KPR-V) based mainly on the 1951 manual for Form C. Those discussions should be consulted by KPR-V users. This review considers the inventory in relation to various strengths and weaknesses pointed up in the earlier discussions.

The KPR-V is an attractive, popular inventory useful in vocational counseling with high school youth and many adults. It is easily administered and conveniently scored by hand or by machine. Appropriate answer sheets, scoring stencils, and profile sheets are available for Forms B and C. Examinees find the KPR-V an interesting inventory, although some have difficulty choosing among seemingly equally attractive, or unattractive, alternatives in the triadic forced choice items. It can still be said correctly that the KPR-V, among interest inventories, is a carefully planned, well constructed instrument approaching, without attaining, the standard of technical thoroughness set by the *Strong Vocational Interest Blank*.

In the past, an outstanding feature of the Kuder has been the conscientious provision by the author and the publisher of current interpretive data, research summaries, and improved norms. The 1956 manual is, however, essentially identical with the 1951 edition albeit 91 titles have been added to the list of references, and a slightly revised job chart (Table 1) appears. The published norms do not appear to have changed in five years. There seem to have been no additions to old reliability data; information concerning the temporal stability of scores is still missing. No important additional evidence regarding KPR-V validity has been summarized. Therefore, this reviewer thinks it important to sample some recent research bearing on these considerations.

Work with the SVIB has shown that its interest scores are remarkably stable over rather long periods. Does this hold also for the KPR-V? Certainly there is less evidence regarding the stability of Kuder scores, but what exists does point to relatively high stability. Rosenberg (*290*) examined high school pupils in ninth grade and, later, in twelfth grade obtaining test-retest correlations ranging between .47 and .75, a result corroborated by Herzberg and Bouton (*318*). Reid's (*234*) work with college level subjects resulted in a median retest correlation of .77 over a 15-month interval.

Validity, a complicated consideration in respect of any psychometric device, is an exceptionally complex matter in considering interest inventories. In the present KPR-V manual, as in earlier ones, mean profiles for small, not demonstrably representative occupational groups constitute the main evidence of validity. Meteorologists, for example, average high in scientific and low in persuasive interest. This is attractive but unconvincing material. The needed research using the KPR-V with specific criterion groups has appeared infrequently, but the present manual lags behind what exists. For example, Stewart and Roberts (*361*) have shown that female teacher trainees leaving a training college after two years had different profiles from those remaining to graduate. Kline and Cumings (*379*) found public health nurses different from other nurses, physicians, and laboratory technicians. Samuelson and Pearson (*382*) found no differences between successful trade school students and dropouts. Arbuckle (*364*) reported KPR-V differences between counselor trainees perceived by peers as those to whom clients would be most and least likely to go for help. Newman (*203*) and Forer (*350*) found evidence of relationships between Kuder scores and physical and emotional disabilities. Haselkorn (*373*) found differences between male homosexuals and matched controls. Klugman (*399*) reported that profiles for psychotics in remission do not differ significantly from Kuder's base groups. Pierce-Jones [1] has developed KPR-V scales which predicted an objective criterion of socio-economic status in cross validation groups. Still other recent research (*326, 334, 346, 372*) bears on the validity of this inventory.

In summary, a fair current appraisal of the KPR-V would seem to be that it is an excellent inventory for preliminary surveys of interests in counseling and in school guidance and occupational instruction. Immediate attention ought to be devoted to providing more representative occupational group norms and a more comprehensive edition of the manual including newer data on the stability of scores and on validity in terms of particular criteria. Perhaps, in view of the very extensive use that is made of the Kuder in clinical and educational settings, a volume dealing with the

1 PIERCE-JONES, JOHN. "Vocational Interest Correlates of Socio-Economic Status in Adolescence." *Ed & Psychol Meas,* in press.

Kuder Preference Record—Vocational

KPR-V in the same way in which Strong treated the SVIB in *Vocational Interests of Men and Women* should be considered.

For reviews by Edward S. Bordin, Harold D. Carter, and H. M. Fowler, see 4:742; for reviews by Ralph F. Berdie, E. G. Chambers, and Donald E. Super of Forms BB and BM, see 3:640 (1 excerpt); for reviews by A. B. Crawford and Arthur E. Traxler of an earlier edition, see 40:1617.

[864]

*Occupational Interest Inventory, 1956 Revision. Grades 7–16 and adults, 9–16 and adults; 1943–56; 10 scores grouped in 3 categories: fields of interests (personal-social, natural, mechanical, business, the arts, the sciences), types of interests (verbal, manipulative, computational), level of interests; IBM; 1 form ('56); 2 levels: intermediate, advanced; intermediate manual ('56); advanced manual ('56); intermediate norms based upon norms for advanced form; $4.90 per 35 tests; separate answer sheets may be used; 4¢ per IBM answer sheet; 7¢ per Scoreze answer sheet; 60¢ per set of either hand or machine scoring stencils; postage extra; 50¢ per specimen set of either level, postpaid; (30–40) minutes; Edwin A. Lee and Louis P. Thorpe; California Test Bureau. *

REFERENCES

1–20. See 4:743.
21. BARKSDALE, ANNE. *Comparison of Achievement in Typewriting and Interest as Measured by an Occupational Interest Inventory.* Master's thesis, University of North Carolina (Chapel Hill, N.C.), 1947.
22. PRIDEAUX, GERALD G. *The Development of Diagnostic Aids for the Lee-Thorpe Occupational Interest Inventory.* Master's thesis, Kansas State Teachers College (Pittsburg, Kan.), 1949.
23. JOHNSON, RALPH H., AND BOND, GUY L. "Reading Ease of Commonly Used Tests." *J Appl Psychol* 34:319–24 O '50. * (PA 26:299)
24. BROWN, MANUEL N. *Clinical Status of Veteran Patients Related to Six Interest Variables.* Doctor's thesis, University of Portland (Portland, Ore.), 1951.
25. FERSON, REGIS F. *The Probabilities of Success in Trade Training as Estimated by Standardized Tests.* Doctor's thesis, University of Pittsburgh (Pittsburgh, Pa.), 1951.
26. VACCARO, JOSEPH J. *A Study of Psychological Factors That Contrast the Most and Least Efficient Psychiatric Aids in a Mental Hospital.* Doctor's thesis, Fordham University (New York, N.Y.), 1951.
27. LIEN, ARNOLD JUEL. "A Comparative-Predictive Study of Students in the Four Curricula of a Teacher Education Institution." *J Exp Ed* 21:81–219 D '52.
28. MACPHAIL, ANDREW H., AND THOMPSON, GEORGE R. "Interest Patterns for Certain Occupational Groups: Occupational Interest Inventory (Lee-Thorpe)." *Ed & Psychol Meas* 12:79–89 sp '52. * (PA 27:5960)
29. MASTEN, FRANK D. *The Personality Development and Occupational Interests of the Sixth, Seventh, and Eighth Grade Pupils at Father Flanagan's Boys' Home, Boys Town, Nebraska.* Doctor's field study, Colorado State College of Education (Greeley, Colo.), 1952.
30. TORR, DONALD V. "A Factor Analysis of Selected Interest Inventories." Abstract. *Am Psychol* 7:296 Jl '52. *
31. WOODWARD, C. L. "A Critical Analysis of Certain Interest Tests." *Yearb Nat Council Meas Used Ed* 9:101–8 '52. *
32. AUSUBEL, DAVID P.; SCHIFF, HERBERT M.; AND ZELENY, MARJORIE P. " 'Real-Life' Measures of Level of Academic and Vocational Aspiration in Adolescents: Relation to Laboratory Measures and to Adjustment." *Child Develop* 24:155–68 S–D '53. * (PA 29:3700)
33. BRIDGE, LEOPOLD, AND MORSON, MEYER. "Item Validity of the Lee-Thorpe Occupational Interest Inventory." *J Appl Psychol* 37:380–3 O '53. * (PA 29:1042)
34. MACPHAIL, ANDREW H. "Interest Patterns for Certain Degree Groups on the Lee-Thorpe Occupational Interest Inventory." *J Appl Psychol* 38:164–6 Je '54. * (PA 29:4691)
35. SINGER, STANLEY L., AND STEFFLRE, BUFORD. "The Relationship of Job Values and Desires to Vocational Aspiration of Adolescents." *J Appl Psychol* 38:419–22 D '54. * (PA 29:5843)

36. GEORGE, CLAY E., AND KINGSTON, ALBERT J. "The Stability of Interest Scores of College Freshmen." *J Ed Psychol* 46: 243-6 Ap '55. * (*PA* 30:1557)
37. LINDGREN, HENRY CLAY, AND GILBERG, RICHARD L. "Interpreting Occupational Interest: The Relationships Between the Lee-Thorpe Occupational Interest Inventory and the Strong Vocational Interest Test for Men." *Calif J Ed Res* 6:15-21 Ja '55. * (*PA* 29:7430)
38. STEFFLRE, BUFORD. "Vocational Aspiration and Level of Interest Scores on the Lee-Thorpe Occupational Interest Inventory." *Personnel & Guid J* 33:385-8 Mr '55. * (*PA* 30:3031)
39. RAMEY, WALTER S. *Usefulness of the Lee-Thorpe Occupational Interest Inventory for Predicting Achievement and Choice of Core Areas in Des Moines Technical School.* Master's thesis, Iowa State College (Ames, Iowa), 1956.
40. CONGDON, ROBERT G., AND JERVIS, FREDERICK M. "A Different Approach to Interest Profiles." Comment by Paul Dressel. *J Counsel Psychol* 5:50-7 sp '58. *

MARTIN KATZ, *Assistant Director, Evaluation and Advisory Service, Educational Testing Service, Princeton, New Jersey.*

The manual for the *Occupational Interest Inventory* makes much of the fact that the scores for the six "fields of interests" are based on forced choices between paired statements. In discussing interpretation of scores, the manual recommends that after identification of the "one or two highest" interest fields, "the next step is a study of the 3 Types," which further refine the areas of major interest: "For example, a high score in the Personal-Social Field combined with a high score in the Manipulative Type would result in examination of a different group of occupations than would be the case if a high score in the Personal-Social Field were supported by a high score in the Computational or Verbal Types." This, on the face of it, might seem quite reasonable.

However, it should be noted that the type scores are not independently derived from forced choices between pairings of statements purporting to represent the different types. Instead, 90 of the 240 field statements are also designated as representing interest types (30 for each type). Thus, each tally for a type score rides in on the coattails of a forced choice for a field statement.

The manual recognizes that "several of these combinations [between field and type] are much more frequently found than are others," implying that such combinations reflect actual relationships which are significant for occupational focus. It neglects to point out that field-type score combinations are largely artifacts of the inventory. For example, of the 30 verbal type statements on the advanced inventory, 14 are designated also as personal-social field statements, 7 are business field, and 9 are arts field (on the intermediate inventory, the corresponding numbers are 13, 9, and 8).

Thus, it is not at all surprising to find in the intercorrelation matrices relatively high coefficients of correlation between verbal type and personal-social field scores (.64 to .74) and lower but still positive coefficients of correlation between verbal type and business field scores (.33 to .57) and verbal type and arts field scores (.19 to .40). Since not a single scientific field statement is classified as a verbal type statement, it is not surprising to find negative coefficients of correlation between verbal type and scientific field scores (−.33 to −.49). Thus, the inventory, *by the nature of its construction,* would tend to give a high verbal type score for people with high personal-social field scores but would rarely give a high verbal type score in conjunction with a high scientific field score.

To carry this demonstration further, on the intermediate inventory 15 of the 30 manipulative type statements are also arts field statements; only 2 of the 30 are mechanical field statements. Therefore, one must not be surprised to find on the intermediate battery correlation coefficients of .59 (for females) and .69 (for males) between manipulative type and arts field scores, along with correlation coefficients of −.39 and −.24 between manipulative type and mechanical field scores. However, in the advanced inventory only 8 of the 30 manipulative type statements are also arts field statements, while 7 of the 30 are mechanical field. Consequently, on the advanced inventory the correlation coefficients between manipulative type and arts field scores are −.07 and .06; but between manipulative type and mechanical field, .18 and .32.

Similarly, computational type statements are tied almost exclusively to business and scientific fields (respectively, 17 and 10 of 30 on the advanced inventory, 15 and 10 of 30 on the intermediate). Thus, the correlation coefficients between mechanical field and computational type scores range from −.21 to −.47, and a high mechanical field-computational type combination would tend to be rare.

It does not seem likely that the foregoing coefficients are offered as representative of hypothesized relationships between the various fields and types of interests. If so, some of them would be rather startling and provocative —for example, even allowing for idiosyncrasies of nomenclature, one would not ordinarily expect a negative relationship between categories labeled "Mechanical" and "Manipulative." On the other hand, to recognize the apparent relationships merely as artifacts of the inventory is to weaken seriously the publisher's case for interpretation of scores.

Unfortunately, this case is already quite weak. Normative and validity data presented in the manual are such that useful interpretation of scores must be, for the most part, arbitrary or intuitive. The previous edition of the inventory was soundly spanked (see 3:643 and 4:743) for two major deficiencies: failure to describe the composition of the norms group and lack of research on validity. It must be reported that the manual for the 1956 Revision still falls short of full disclosure. Here is the complete passage describing "The Normative Population" in the manual for the advanced inventory:

> The percentile norms presented in this Manual were obtained from over 25,000 Inventories given to high school and college students, veterans, and other adults. They are based on cases reported from New England, Tennessee, California, Utah, and Idaho. The norms are suitable not only for high school pupils and college students but also for the general adult population. This is particularly true because the instrument requires a comparison and choice between 120 pairs of activities in which the distribution of choices rather than a total score provides the significant data.
> Norms for the *Occupational Interest Inventory, Advanced* reflect the performance of examinees who are representative of the population nationally on interest inventory items which have been carefully selected and validated.

The glib array of nonsequiturs provided by the last three sentences is certainly no substitute for more specific information about the norms group. Lumping together these "over 25,000....high school and college students, veterans, and other adults" in unspecified proportions, with no hint of stratification, to provide omnibus or all-purpose norms, might be justified on the grounds that these subgroups were virtually indistinguishable from each other. Such a condition not only is contrary to logic; it is contrary to the few specific score summaries actually reported for different groups. Thus, the catch-as-catch-can "normative population" certainly cannot be said to provide an intrinsically meaningful comparison group for any individual's scores. There is no evidence that it is "representative of the population nationally," or that it is suitable for use with *any* of the groups mentioned (high school pupils, college students, general adult population), let alone all of them. In short, it is not

a norms group; it is merely an agglomeration of cases.

The manual for the intermediate inventory maintains that the intermediate norms are suitable "not only for junior high school pupils but also for the general adult population." In fact, the norms for the intermediate inventory were not independently derived, but were linked to the norms for the advanced inventory. Advanced and intermediate inventories were both administered to 118 male and 118 female 10th graders (no further characterization of this group is given):

> The two tests were equated on the basis of the raw scores. The raw scores of the Intermediate Inventory were then given the percentile rankings of the corresponding raw scores of the Advanced Inventory. The norms that resulted....were compared with norms based on cases reported for 5,470 male and 4,870 female students enrolled in grades seven to nine. The two sets of norms were encouragingly comparable.

In the absence of more precise data (and why so bashful about presenting "encouraging" data?), this reviewer cannot share the publisher's feeling of encouragement. He can derive no feeling of security from the knowledge that the intermediate norms are anchored in the amorphous jelly of the advanced norms. Even if the advanced norms were of firmer substance there would remain a need to state and reason about some of the assumptions involved in using this common anchorage.

Of course even well defined and coherent norms groups would not in themselves solve the many problems of meaningful interpretation of scores. They would, however, be more likely to lead to fruitful hypotheses and research on validity. At present, the manual stresses use of score patterns for guidance. But to what purpose should the counselor ascertain that Joe Smith, confronted with a series of forced choices, preferred more descriptive statements of a certain category than did 90 per cent—or 50 per cent—or 10 per cent—of an appropriate comparison group? First, he needs to know what, if any, significance Joe's relative preference for this and other categories of statements has for educational and occupational decisions. Thus, suppose Joe's scientific field score placed him at the 70th percentile of a normative population of 10th grade boys. What does this mean about his potential interest in a high school physics course? in a college engineering program? in medical studies? in the occupation of nuclear physicist? According to

Occupational Interest Inventory

the manual, scores at the 70th percentile or higher in any category are to be regarded as significant for choices assumed to involve a substantial amount of activity corresponding to that interest category. Then, presumably, if Joe ranked at the 50th percentile in the mechanical field and at the 70th percentile in the scientific field, he would be described as having "more" interest in scientific than in mechanical fields and would probably be encouraged (ability data and other circumstances permitting) to consider educational and occupational choices characterized more heavily by "scientific" than by "mechanical" activities.

But even if we assumed the categories to be accurate and the norms unexceptionable, where is the evidence that preferences resulting in a 70th percentile on the scientific field are likely to lead to satisfaction or interest in high school physics, engineering college, medical school, or a career as a nuclear physicist? One might be equally justified in asserting that a 50th percentile in the mechanical field is more conducive to interest and satisfaction in a high school industrial arts course and the occupation of carpenter than a 70th percentile in the scientific field is to interest and satisfaction in a high school physics course and a career as a nuclear physicist. In the absence of the most elementary empirical validation, perhaps it is supererogatory to fuss about norms at all.

Certainly the validation of an interest inventory is a knotty problem. In the manual for the 1956 Revision of the *Occupational Interest Inventory* will be found no sword of Alexander to cut this Gordian knot. At best, there have been a few routine hacks at it with blunt scissors. Thus, phi coefficients for the statements in each category are furnished; correlation studies with *Kuder Preference Record* scales and with *Strong Vocational Interest Blank* scales are charted; there is some crowing about a factor analysis of six interest inventories including the *Occupational Interest Inventory*. (The manual does not name the other five inventories—among which, it turns out, was neither the Kuder nor the Strong. Analyses which have included these instruments have turned up factors less similar to the *Occupational Interest Inventory* rubrics.)

The correlation study with the Strong involved only 60 cases. Although the manual calls attention to the positive correlations which might have been expected a priori between some *Occupational Interest Inventory* fields and Strong scales, there is no attempt to account for the following correlation coefficients: between Strong physician scale and inventory personal-social field (which includes, as one of its subcategories, "Health and Medical Service"), −.03; between Strong policeman scale and inventory personal-social field (which includes "Law and Law Enforcement" as one of its subcategories), −.16; between inventory "level of interests" score and Strong scales for president (manufacturing concern), physician, mathematician, and physicist, −.07, −.23, −.14, and −.03, respectively.

Nevertheless, publication of such data is a step in the right direction. With more (and more ambitious) validity studies, the *Occupational Interest Inventory* may yet become useful. Meanwhile, it is a shame to have to describe it again, after the number of years in which it has been marketed and used, as a "promising instrument."

WILBUR L. LAYTON, *Professor of Psychology, and Assistant Director, Student Counseling Bureau, University of Minnesota, Minneapolis, Minnesota.*

It is very frustrating to this reviewer, in considering the possible impact of this review, to find that an inventory which received very unfavorable reviews in both the third and fourth *Mental Measurements Yearbooks* is still in existence, has been researched and revised so little, and is still being offered for sale as a valid instrument. The revision has consisted of the replacement of a few items and an increase in the number of items contributing to the type scores. In addition, some changes have been made in the manual. At present, the manual is written so that it breathes an air of respectability which close and critical scrutiny reveals is rather thin. Most of the research presented is based on the unrevised inventory, and attempts have been made to adjust these data to reflect changes in the inventory. There is no indication of how these adjustments were made or, for that matter, of the appropriateness of making such changes.

It is in the area of validity that the manual is perhaps most misleading. A great deal of weight is placed by the test authors on content validity, but, as the research of Strong has indicated, content validity is not a *sine qua non* to discriminating occupational groups on the basis of interest. There is little further evidence of validity, although the intercorrelation study by Torr (*30*) is presented as one demonstration of validity. In addition, correlations between the unrevised *Occupational Interest Inventory,* the *Strong Vocational Interest Blank,* and the *Kuder Preference Record* are presented as evidence of validity. Patterns of mean scores for several college and high school groups are also presented. These data are, however, very meager. The authors still have not collected data on occupational groups, although certainly this is most desirable. As the *Technical Recommendations for Psychological Tests and Diagnostic Techniques* points out, most interest inventories are used for prediction purposes. The interpretation of an interest inventory to a counseling client implies some predictive validity. Thus, it is particularly important that such inventories have evidence of predictive validity. Although the authors present the inventory as useful in counseling high school and college students, there has been no attempt to do a long-range longitudinal study which would provide meaningful data concerning the validity in predicting occupational criteria.

The only reliability data given are of the test-retest variety. There is no indication in the manual as to whether these data are based upon the revised or original form. It is to the credit of the authors that they present standard errors of measurement, but some of these are disturbingly large compared to the standard deviations listed. This means, of course, that the reliabilities for the scales involved are not good enough to justify their use in individual counseling. This conclusion is supported by the research of George and Kingston (*36*).

The norms are also inadequate; they are based on the unrevised advanced form. The authors state they are suitable, not only for high school pupils and college students, but also for the general adult population. But, there is no indication of the representativeness of these norms for any well defined population. The authors state the norms were adjusted to take into account the revision of the inventory. No details of this adjustment are given. The authors suggest that when the inventory is being used for selection and placement in business and industry the composite population norms should be used. This, of course, would obscure the relationship of sex

to score and, according to data presented, there is such a relationship. What justification the authors have for making this suggestion to business and industry is beyond this reviewer's comprehension.

On the basis of the limited amount of information available about the *Occupational Interest Inventory,* this reviewer recommends that it be considered an experimental inventory at best and that it be so labeled so that the unwary prospective user will not be led astray. He further recommends that it not be used in counseling individual students and that its use be restricted to experimental and research purposes until it has been properly standardized.

For reviews by Arthur H. Brayfield of the original edition, see 4:743; for reviews by Edward S. Bordin and Stanley G. Dulsky, see 3:643.

[865]

★**Picture Interest Inventory.** Grades 7 and over; 1958; 9 scores: interpersonal service, natural, mechanical, business, esthetic, scientific, verbal, computational, time perspective; IBM; 1 form; separate answer sheets must be used; $5.25 per 35 tests; 5¢ per IBM answer sheet; $1 per set of hand or machine scoring stencils; postage extra; 50¢ per specimen set, postpaid; scoring service available; (20–30) minutes; Kurt P. Weingarten; California Test Bureau. *

[866]

★**Qualifications Record.** Sales personnel; 1958; 45 interests in 7 areas: arts, biology, computation, literary, physical, social, technology; Form A; no data on reliability and validity; $23.75 per 100 tests; $1 per specimen set; $12.50 per individual job qualifications report; postpaid; (45) minutes; Keith Van Allyn; Bureau of Personnel Research, Inc. *

[867]

★**Rothwell Interest Blank, Miller Revision.** Ages 13 and over; 1958; Forms M, F ('58) ; manual ('58) ; 3s. per 10 blanks; 12s. 6d. per manual; postpaid within Australia; (20–30) minutes; Kenneth M. Miller and J. W. Rothwell; Australian Council for Educational Research. *

[868]

*****Strong Vocational Interest Blank for Men, Revised.** Ages 17 and over; 1927–59; 57 scoring scales (47 occupations, 6 occupational group scales, and 4 nonvocational scales): Group I: group scale ('38), artist ('38), psychologist ('28–49) by P. H. Kriedt, architect ('38), physician ('38–52), psychiatrist ('52), osteopath ('47), dentist ('38), veterinarian ('49) by T. E. Hannum; Group II: group scale ('39), physicist ('52), chemist ('38), mathematician ('38), engineer ('38) ; Group III: production manager ('38) ; Group IV: farmer ('38), carpenter ('38), printer ('38), mathematics-physical science teacher ('38), policeman ('38), forest service man ('38), army officer ('52), aviator ('40) ; Group V: group scale ('38), Y.M.C.A. physical director ('38), personnel manager ('38), public administrator ('44), vocational counselor ('52) by Clements D. Brown, Y.M.C.A. secretary ('38), social science high school teacher ('38), city school superintendent ('38), minister ('38), social worker ('54); Group VI: music performer ('54), music teacher ('54); Group VII: C.P.A. owner ('38); Group VIII: group scale ('38), senior C.P.A. ('49), junior accountant ('38) [designation on scoring scale is accountant], office worker ('38), purchasing agent ('38), banker ('38), mortician ('46), pharmacist ('49) by Milton Schwebel; Group IX: group scale ('38), sales manager ('38), real estate salesman ('38), life insurance salesman ('38); Group X: group scale ('38), advertising man ('38), lawyer ('38), author-journalist ('38); Group XI: president of manufacturing concern ('38); nonvocational scales: occupational level ('39), masculinity-femininity ('38), specialization level ('52) by Milton G. Holmen, interest maturity ('41); IBM; Form M('46); manual ('59); $4 per 25 tests; $1.15 per 25 individual report blanks ('59); 75¢ per 25 interest global charts ('43); hand scoring stencils: $1.25 per single scale, $10 per set of any 10 scales, $46 per complete set; separate answer sheets may be used; $2.25 per 50 IBM answer sheets; $2.25 per 50 Hankes' answer sheets ('47) for use with the scoring service of Testscor (see 529); machine scoring stencils: $2.50 per single scale, $20 per set of any 10 scales, $95 per complete set; postage extra; $1 per specimen set (does not include scoring stencils) of SVIB for men and for women, cash orders postpaid; (30–60) minutes; Edward K. Strong, Jr.; Consulting Psychologists Press. *

REFERENCES

1–71. See 40:1680.
72–175. See 3:647.
176–273. See 4:747.
274. HAHN, MILTON E. An Investigation of Measured Aspects of Social Intelligence in a Distributive Occupation. Doctor's thesis, University of Minnesota (Minneapolis, Minn.), 1942.
275. REDLENER, J. A Comparative Study of the Efficiency of the Kuder Preference Record and the Strong Vocational Interest Blank in the Prediction of Job Satisfaction. Master's thesis, University of Southern California (Los Angeles, Calif.), 1948.
276. DALEY, ROLLAND F. A Determination of the Relationship Between Vocational Preference as Measured by the Method of Paired-Comparisons and the Strong Vocational Interest Test. Master's thesis, Pennsylvania State College (State College, Pa.), 1950.
277. HANNUM, THOMAS E. "Response of Veterinarians to the Strong Vocational Interest Blank for Men." Proc Iowa Acad Sci 57:381–4 '50. *
278. JOHNSON, RALPH H., AND BOND, GUY L. "Reading Ease of Commonly Used Tests." J Appl Psychol 34:319–24 O '50. * (PA 26:299)
279. MITCHELL, WALTER M. An Analysis of the Relationship Between Performance on the MF Scale of the Minnesota Multiphasic Personality Inventory and the Strong Vocational Interest Blank for Men. Master's thesis, Montana State University (Missoula, Mont.), 1950.
280. WISDOM, JESSIE R. A Study of the Interest Patterns of Premedical Students as Revealed by the Kuder Preference Record and the Strong Vocational Interest Inventory. Master's thesis, North Texas State College (Denton, Tex.), 1950.
281. BROWN, MANUEL N. Clinical Status of Veteran Patients Related to Six Interest Variables. Doctor's thesis, University of Portland (Portland, Ore.), 1951.
282. GARRY, RALPH J. Individual Differences in Ability to Fake Vocational Interests. Doctor's thesis, Stanford University (Stanford, Calif.), 1951.
283. HILLIS, DONALD J. Biographical Information Blank Responses as Related to Selected Areas of the Strong Vocational Interest Blank. Master's thesis, Western Reserve University (Cleveland, Ohio), 1951.
284. MORGAN, HENRY H. An Analysis of Certain Structured and Unstructured Test Results of Achieving and Nonachieving High Ability College Students. Doctor's thesis, University of Minnesota (Minneapolis, Minn.), 1951. (DA 12:335)
285. PIERSON, ROWLAND R. Vocational Interests of Agricultural Extension Workers as Related to Selected Aspects of Work Adjustment. Doctor's thesis, Michigan State College (East Lansing, Mich.), 1951. (DA 12:274)
286. SIMES, FRANK J. The Development of a Basis for the Selection of Resident Advisers at the Pennsylvania State College. Doctor's thesis, Pennsylvania State College (State College, Pa.), 1951.
287. STRONG, EDWARD K., JR. "Vocational Interests and Occupation Twenty Years Later." Abstract. Am Psychol 6:497 S '51. *
288. TYLER, LEONA E. "The Differential Significance of 'Like' and 'Dislike' Responses on the Strong Vocational Interest Blank." Abstract. Am Psychol 6:497 S '51. *
289. ANDERSON, MARY R. A Descriptive Study of Values and Interests of Four Groups of Graduate Women at the University of Minnesota. Doctor's thesis, University of Minnesota (Minneapolis, Minn.), 1952. (DA 12:851)
290. BARNETT, GORDON J.; HANDELSMAN, IRVING; STEWART, LAWRENCE H.; AND SUPER, DONALD E. "The Occupational Level Scale as a Measure of Drive." Psychol Monogr 66(10):1–37 '52. * (PA 27:5778)
291. BILLS, MARION A. Chap. 8, "A Tool for Selection That Has Stood the Test of Time," pp. 131–7. In Applications of Psychology: Essays to Honor Walter V. Bingham. Edited by L. L. Thurstone. New York: Harper & Brothers, 1952. Pp. xi, 209. *
292. CLARK, PATRICIA N. A Study of the Relationship Between the Interest Level on the Strong Vocational Interest Blank and Separation From College of a Selected Group of Students. Master's thesis, Kansas State College of Agriculture and Applied Arts (Manhattan, Kan.), 1952.
293. ESTENSON, LYLE O. An Investigation of the Relationship Between Personality as Measured by the Minnesota Multiphasic Personality Inventory and Occupational Interests as Measured by Strong's Vocational Interest Blanks. Doctor's thesis, University of Minnesota (Minneapolis, Minn.), 1952.
294. FREDERIKSEN, NORMAN, AND MELVILLE, S. D. "Improving the Predictive Value of an Interest Test." Abstract. Am Psychol 7:285–6 Jl '52. *
295. GUILFORD, J. P. "When Not to Factor Analyze." Psychol B 49:26–37 Ja '52. * (PA 27:33)
296. GUSTAD, JOHN W. "Academic Achievement and Strong Occupational Level Scores." J Appl Psychol 36:75–8 Ap '52. * (PA 27:492)
297. HOLMEN, MILTON G. Vocational Interest Patterns of Professional Specialists. Doctor's thesis, Stanford University (Stanford, Calif.), 1952.
298. HOLT, ROBERT R., AND LUBORSKY, LESTER. "Research in the Selection of Psychiatrists: A Second Interim Report." B Menninger Clinic 16:125–35 Jl '52. *
299. KRIEDT, PHILIP H.; STONE, C. HAROLD; AND PATERSON, DONALD G. "Vocational Interests of Industrial Relations Personnel." J Appl Psychol 36:174–9 Je '52. *
300. LAWSHE, C. H., AND DEUTSCH, STANLEY. "The Interests of Industrial Psychology Students." J Appl Psychol 36:180–1 Je '52. *
301. LAYTON, WILBUR L. "Predicting Success of Students in Veterinary Medicine." J Appl Psychol 36:312–5 O '52. * (PA 27:5418)
302. MELVILLE, S. D., AND FREDERIKSEN, NORMAN. "Achievement of Freshman Engineering Students and the Strong Vocational Interest Blank." J Appl Psychol 36:169–73 Je '52. *
303. MOFFIE, DANNIE J., AND MILTON, CHARLES R. "The Relationship of Certain Psychological Test Scores to Academic Success in Chemical Engineering." Abstract. Am Psychol 7:379–80 Jl '52. *
304. MORGAN, HENRY H. "A Psychometric Comparison of Achieving and Nonachieving College Students of High Ability." J Consult Psychol 16:292–8 Ag '52. * (PA 27:4570)
305. NELSON, KENNETH G. The Interests of Teachers of Vocational Agriculture as Related to Vocational Satisfaction. Doctor's thesis, University of Minnesota (Minneapolis, Minn.), 1952. (DA 13:125)
306. POE, WESLEY A., AND BERG, IRWIN A. "Psychological Test Performance of Steel Industry Production Supervisors." J Appl Psychol 36:234–7 Ag '52. * (PA 27:3794)
307. STRONG, EDWARD K., JR. "Amount of Change in Occupational Choice of College Freshmen." Ed & Psychol Meas 12:677–91 w '52. * (PA 27:6760)
308. STRONG, EDWARD K., JR. "Interests of Negroes and Whites." J Social Psychol 35:139–50 My '52. * (PA 27:3479)
309. STRONG, EDWARD K., JR. "Nineteen-Year Followup of Engineer Interests." J Appl Psychol 36:65–74 Ap '52. * (PA 27:497)
310. STRONG, EDWARD K., JR. Chap. 7, "Twenty Year Follow-up of Medical Interests," pp. 111–30. In Applications of Psychology: Essays to Honor Walter V. Bingham. Edited by L. L. Thurstone. New York: Harper & Brothers, 1952. Pp. xi, 209. *
311. STRONG, EDWARD K., JR., AND TUCKER, ANTHONY C. "The Use of Vocational Interest Scales in Planning a Medical Center." Psychol Monogr 66(9):1–61 '52. * (PA 27:5483)
312. SUNDBERG, NORMAN D. The Relationship of Psychotherapeutic Skill and Experience to Knowledge of Other People. Doctor's thesis, University of Minnesota (Minneapolis, Minn.), 1952. (DA 12:390)
313. TORR, DONALD V. "A Factor Analysis of Selected Interest Inventories." Abstract. Am Psychol 7:296 Jl '52. *
314. TRAPHAGEN, ARTHUR L. "Interest Patterns and Retention and Rejection of Vocational Choice." J Appl Psychol 36:182–5 Je '52. *
315. TRUEBLOOD, GERALD E. Predicting Achievement in Algebra From the Iowa Tests of Educational Development. Master's thesis, Iowa State College (Ames, Iowa), 1952.

316. VERBURG, WALLACE A. "Vocational Interests of Retired YMCA Secretaries." *J Appl Psychol* 36:254-6 Ag '52. * (*PA* 27:3404)

317. WOODWARD, C. L. "A Critical Analysis of Certain Interest Tests." *Yearb Nat Council Meas Used Ed* 9:101-8 '52. *

318. BARNETT, GORDON J.; STEWART, LAWRENCE H.; AND SUPER, DONALD E. "Level of Occupational Interest: Deadweight or Dynamism?" *Ed & Psychol Meas* 13:193-208 su '53. * (*PA* 28:4496)

319. BERNSTEIN, ALVIN J. *Absence of Primary Interest Patterns in Adolescent Boys.* Doctor's thesis, Columbia University (New York, N.Y.), 1953. (*DA* 14:181)

320. BILLS, MARION A., AND TAYLOR, JEAN G. "Over and Under Achievement in a Sales School in Relation to Future Production." *J Appl Psychol* 37:21-3 F '53. * (*PA* 28:1664)

321. BURGESS, ELVA. *Personality Factors in Over- and Under-Achievers in Engineering.* Doctor's thesis, Pennsylvania State College (State College, Pa.), 1953.

322. COOPER, CHARLES E., JR. *Vocational Interests of Industrial Arts Teachers.* Doctor's thesis, University of Missouri (Columbia, Mo.), 1953. (*DA* 13:1099)

323. ERLANDSON, FORREST L. *Socio-Economic Factors Related to Vocational Interests as Measured by the Strong Vocational Interest Blank for Men.* Doctor's thesis, University of Minnesota (Minneapolis, Minn.), 1953. (*DA* 13:1256)

324. GARRY, RALPH. "Individual Differences in Ability to Fake Vocational Interests." *J Appl Psychol* 37:33-7 F '53. * (*PA* 28:1621)

325. HAGENAH, THEDA. *A Normative Study of the Revised Strong Vocational Interest Blank for Men.* Doctor's thesis, University of Minnesota (Minneapolis, Minn.), 1953. (*DA* 14:498)

326. HAMPTON, PETER JAN. "The Development of a Personality Questionnaire for Drinkers." *Genetic Psychol Monogr* 48:55-115 Ag '53. * (*PA* 28:4571)

327. HASELKORN, HARRY. *The Vocational Interests of a Group of Homosexuals.* Doctor's thesis, New York University (New York, N.Y.), 1953. (*DA* 13:58)

328. HELPER, MALCOLM M., AND McQUITTY, LOUIS L. "Some Relations of Personality Integration to Occupational Interests." *J Social Psychol* 38:219-31 N '53. * (*PA* 28:6171)

329. HENDRIX, O. R. "Predicting Success in Elementary Accounting." *J Appl Psychol* 37:75-7 Ap '53. * (*PA* 28:1479)

330. LONG, LOUIS, AND PERRY, JAMES D. "Academic Achievement in Engineering Related to Selection Procedures and Interests." *J Appl Psychol* 37:468-71 D '53. * (*PA* 29:1571)

331. MacINTOSH, ARCHIBALD. *A Study of Factors Associated With the Stability of Vocational Goals in College Students.* Doctor's thesis, University of Pennsylvania (Philadelphia, Pa.), 1953. (*DA* 13:262)

332. NELSON, KENNETH G. "The Interests of Teachers of Vocational Agriculture as Related to Vocational Satisfaction." Abstract. *Am Psychol* 8:408-9 Ag '53. *

333. PERRY, DALLIS K. *Forced-Choice vs. L-I-D Response Items in Vocational Interest Measurement.* Doctor's thesis, University of Minnesota (Minneapolis, Minn.), 1953. (*DA* 14:552)

334. STORDAHL, KALMER E. *The Stability of Strong Vocational Interest Blank Patterns for Pre-College Males.* Doctor's thesis, University of Minnesota (Minneapolis, Minn.), 1953. (*DA* 13:1265)

335. STRONG, EDWARD K., JR. "Validity of Occupational Choice." *Ed & Psychol Meas* 13:110-21 sp '53. * (*PA* 28:1121)

336. STRONG, EDWARD K., JR. "Vocational Interest Test for Men and Women," pp. 789-96. *In Contributions Toward Medical Psychology: Theory and Psychodiagnostic Methods, Vol. II.* Edited by Arthur Weider. New York: Ronald Press Co., 1953. Pp. xi, 459-885. *

337. BRAASCH, WILLIAM F., JR. *Regional Differences in Occupational Interests.* Doctor's thesis, Columbia University (New York, N.Y.), 1954. (*DA* 14:1254)

338. BROWN, MANUEL N. "An Interest Inventory as a Measure of Personality." *J Counsel Psychol* 1:9-11 F '54. * (*PA* 28:7510)

339. CHILLE, RALPH A. *The Use of the OL Key of the Strong Vocational Interest Blank as a Predictor of Scholastic Success for Students in the School of Business at Niagara University.* Master's thesis, Niagara University (Niagara Falls, N.Y.), 1954.

340. CLARK, KENNETH E., AND GEE, HELEN H. "Selecting Items for Interest Inventory Keys." *J Appl Psychol* 38:12-7 F '54. * (*PA* 29:1044)

341. COLLISTER, E. GORDON. "A Comparison of Scoring the Strong Vocational Interest Blank for High School Senior Boys Using Group and Occupational Scoring Keys." Abstract. *Am Psychol* 9:350 Ag '54. *

342. COOPER, ALVA C. *A Study of the Group Scales of the Strong Vocational Interest Blank as Predictors of Academic Achievement and of the Relationship of the Group Scales to Primary Interest Patterns.* Doctor's thesis, Columbia University (New York, N.Y.), 1954. (*DA* 14:1176)

343. COTTLE, WILLIAM C. "Interest and Personality Inventories." *Personnel & Guid J* 33:162-7 N '54. * (*PA* 29:5695)

344. DuBOIS, PHILIP H., AND WATSON, ROBERT I. "Validity Information Exchange, No. 7-075:D.O.T. Code 2-66.23, Policeman." *Personnel Psychol* 7:414-7 au '54. *

345. FIELD, LEWIS W. *Personality Correlates of College Achievement and Major Areas of Study.* Doctor's thesis, University of Houston (Houston, Tex.), 1954. (*DA* 14:1344)

346. FREDERIKSEN, NORMAN, AND MELVILLE, S. DONALD.

"Differential Predictability in the Use of Test Scores." *Ed & Psychol Meas* 14:647-56 w '54. * (*PA* 29:7961)

347. GARMAN, GLEN D. *The Strong Vocational Interest Inventory as a Measure of Manifest Anxiety.* Doctor's thesis, University of Michigan (Ann Arbor, Mich.), 1954. (*DA* 14:711)

348. GUSTAD, JOHN W. "Vocational Interests and Socio-Economic Status." *J Appl Psychol* 38:336-8 O '54. * (*PA* 29:6196)

349. HANNUM, T. E., AND THRALL, JOHN R. "Stability and Validity of the Strong Vocational Interest Blank in the Prediction of Success in Veterinary Medicine Curriculum." *Proc Iowa Acad Sci* 61:361-6 '54. * (*PA* 30:3461)

350. HEWER, VIVIAN H. *Vocational Interest-Achievement-Ability: Interrelationships at the College Level.* Doctor's thesis, University of Minnesota (Minneapolis, Minn.), 1954. (*DA* 14:1257)

351. HOLMEN, MILTON G. "The Specialization Level Scale for the Strong Vocational Interest Blank." *J Appl Psychol* 38:159-63 Je '54. * (*PA* 29:4752)

352. McARTHUR, CHARLES. "Long-Term Validity of the Strong Interest Test in Two Subcultures." *J Appl Psychol* 38:346-53 O '54. * (*PA* 29:6355)

353. McCOLLUM, ERNEST L. *A Study of the Vocational Interest Profiles of USAF Personnel Officers With and Without Formal Personnel Training.* Doctor's thesis, University of Minnesota (Minneapolis, Minn.), 1954. (*DA* 14:2120)

354. McCORNACK, ROBERT L. *Sex Differences in the Vocational Interests of a Professional Group.* Doctor's thesis, University of Minnesota (Minneapolis, Minn.), 1954. (*DA* 14:1252)

355. MILAM, ALBERT T., AND SUMNER, F. C. "Spread and Intensity of Vocational Interests and Evaluative Attitudes in First-Year Negro Medical Students." *J Psychol* 37:31-8 Ja '54. * (*PA* 28:8027)

356. POWERS, MABEL K. *A Longitudinal Study of Vocational Interests During the Depression Years.* Doctor's thesis, University of Minnesota (Minneapolis, Minn.), 1954.

357. RUST, RALPH M., AND RYAN, F. J. "The Strong Vocational Interest Blank and College Achievement." *J Appl Psychol* 38:341-5 O '54. * (*PA* 29:6204)

358. STORDAHL, KALMER E. "Permanence of Interests and Interest Maturity." *J Appl Psychol* 38:339-40 O '54. * (*PA* 29:5844)

359. STORDAHL, KALMER E. "Permanence of Strong Vocational Interest Blank Scores." *J Appl Psychol* 38:423-7 D '54. * (*PA* 29:5845)

360. STRONG, EDWARD K., JR. "Validity Versus Reliability." *J Appl Psychol* 38:103-4 Ap '54. * (*PA* 29:2618)

361. TRINKAUS, WILLIAM K. "The Permanence of Vocational Interests of College Freshmen." *Ed & Psychol Meas* 14:641-6 w '54. * (*PA* 29:7440)

362. WILKINSON, MARGARET A., AND JACOBS, ROBERT. "A Brief Study of the Relationships Between Personality Adjustment and Vocational Interests as Measured by the Multiple-Choice Rorschach and the Strong Vocational Interest Blank." *J Ed Res* 48:269-78 D '54. * (*PA* 29:7335)

363. BERDIE, RALPH F. "Aptitude, Achievement, Interest, and Personality Tests: A Longitudinal Comparison." *J Appl Psychol* 39:103-14 Ap '55. * (*PA* 30:1498)

364. COLLINS, CHARLES C. *The Relationship of Breadth of Academic Interest to Academic Achievement and Academic Aptitude.* Doctor's thesis, Stanford University (Stanford, Calif.), 1955. (*DA* 15:1782)

365. DARLEY, JOHN G., AND HAGENAH, THEDA. *Vocational Interest Measurement: Theory and Practice.* Minneapolis, Minn.: University of Minnesota Press, 1955. Pp. xvii, 279. * (*PA* 30:4726)

366. ENRIGHT, JOHN B., AND PINNEAU, SAMUEL R. "Predictive Value of Subjective Choice of Occupation and of the Strong Vocational Interest Blank Over Fifteen Years." Abstract. *Am Psychol* 10:424-5 Ag '55. *

367. HANNUM, T. E., AND THRALL, JOHN B. "Use of the Strong Vocational Interest Blank for Prediction in Veterinary Medicine." *J Appl Psychol* 39:249-52 Ag '55. * (*PA* 30:5413)

368. HARRISON, ROSS; HUNT, WINSLOW; AND JACKSON, THEODORE A. "Profile of the Mechanical Engineer: II, Interests." *Personnel Psychol* 8:315-30 au '55. * (*PA* 30:7890)

369. JENSON, PAUL G. *A Normative Study of the Strong Vocational Interest Blank for Male Adult Workers.* Doctor's thesis, University of Minnesota (Minneapolis, Minn.), 1955. (*DA* 15:2289)

370. KELLY, E. LOWELL. "Consistency of the Adult Personality." *Am Psychol* 10:659-81 N '55. * (*PA* 30:6915)

371. LAYTON, WILBUR L. "Theory and Research on the Strong Vocational Interest Blank: A Conference Report." *J Counsel Psychol* 2:10-2 sp '55. * (*PA* 30:1035)

372. LINDGREN, HENRY CLAY, AND GILBERG, RICHARD L. "Interpreting Occupational Interest: The Relationships Between the Lee-Thorpe Occupational Interest Inventory and the Strong Vocational Interest Test for Men." *Calif J Ed Res* 6:15-21 Ja '55. * (*PA* 29:7430)

373. McARTHUR, CHARLES. "Predictive Power of Pattern Analysis and of Job Scale Analysis of the Strong." *J Counsel Psychol* 2:205-6 fall '55. * (*PA* 30:4731)

374. McARTHUR, CHARLES, AND STEVENS, LUCIA BETH. "The Validation of Expressed Interests as Compared With Inventoried Interests: A Fourteen-Year Follow-Up." *J Appl Psychol* 39:184-9 Je '55. * (*PA* 30:3024)

375. MELTON, RICHARD S. "Differentiation of Successful and

Strong Vocational Interest Blank for Men

Unsuccessful Premedical Students." *J Appl Psychol* 39:397–400 D '55. * (*PA* 30:7769)

376. PERRY, DALLIS K. "Validities of Three Vocational Interest Keys for U. S. Navy Yeomen." *J Appl Psychol* 39:134–8 Ap '55. * (*PA* 30:1726)

377. POWELL, FRANK V. *A Comparison Between the Vocational Interest Patterns of Students in Five Colleges of a State University.* Doctor's thesis, University of Wisconsin (Madison, Wis.), 1955. (*DA* 15:2471)

378. SCHULTZ, RAYMOND E., AND OHLSEN, MERLE M. "Interest Patterns of Best and Poorest Student Teachers." *J Ed Sociol* 29:108–12 N '55. * (*PA* 30:7790)

379. SEGAL, STANLEY J. "The Role of Personality Factors in Vocational Choice." Abstract. *Am Psychol* 10:365–6 Ag '55. * (*PA* 30:5310)

380. STRONG, EDWARD K., JR. "Are Medical Specialist Interest Scales Applicable to Negroes?" *J Appl Psychol* 39:62–4 F '55. * (*PA* 30:892)

381. STRONG, EDWARD K., JR. "Predictive Validity of Interest Scores." Abstract. *Am Psychol* 10:375 Ag '55. *

382. STRONG, EDWARD K., JR. *Vocational Interests 18 Years After College.* Minneapolis, Minn.: University of Minnesota Press, 1955. Pp. xiv, 207. * (*PA* 30:4738)

383. THOMAS, ROSS R. "Permanence of Measured Interests of Women Over Fifteen Years." Abstract. *Am Psychol* 10:375 Ag '55. *

384. TUCKER, ANTHONY C. "Vocational Interests of Medical Administrative Officers." *US Armed Forces Med J* 6:685–90 My '55. * (*PA* 30:5310)

385. WOEHR, HARRY J. *The Relationship of Masculinity-Femininity Scores to Temperament and Interest Profiles.* Doctor's thesis, Temple University (Philadelphia, Pa.), 1955. (*DA* 16:388)

386. WOOLF, MAURICE D., AND WOOLF, JEANNE A. "Is Interest Maturity Related to Linguistic Development?" *J Appl Psychol* 39:413–5 D '55. * (*PA* 30:7711)

387. BARTHOL, RICHARD P., AND KIRK, BARBARA A. "The Selection of Graduate Students in Public Health Education." *J Appl Psychol* 40:159–63 Je '56. * (*PA* 31:6666)

388. BURGESS, ELVA. "Personality Factors of Over- and Under-Achievers in Engineering." *J Ed Psychol* 47:89–99 F '56. * (*PA* 31:8811)

389. DRAKE, JOHN D. *An Empirical Investigation of the Vocational Interest Blank for Men for Principles Governing the Construction of Valid Interest Inventory Items.* Doctor's thesis, Western Reserve University (Cleveland, Ohio), 1956.

390. DUNNETTE, MARVIN D., AND MERRIAM S. "Validity Information Exchange, No. 9-21: D.O.T. Code, Design and Development Engineers." *Personnel Psychol* 9:245–7 su '56. *

391. ENGLAND, GEORGE W. *The Interest Factor in Undergraduate Engineering Achievement.* Doctor's thesis, University of Minnesota (Minneapolis, Minn.), 1956. (*DA* 17:902)

392. GOODLING, RICHARD A. ["Relationship Between the IM Scale of the SVIB and Scales of the Guilford-Zimmerman Temperament Survey."] *J Counsel Psychol* 3:146+ su '56. *

393. HASELKORN, HARRY. "The Vocational Interests of a Group of Male Homosexuals." *J Counsel Psychol* 3:8–11 sp '56. * (*PA* 31:3211)

394. HEWER, VIVIAN H. "A Comparison of Successful and Unsuccessful Students in the Medical School at the University of Minnesota." *J Appl Psychol* 40:164–8 Je '56. * (*PA* 31:6675)

395. KLOSTER, CLAIR G. *The Relation Between Measured Vocational Interests and Job Satisfaction.* Doctor's thesis, University of Minnesota (Minneapolis, Minn.), 1956. (*DA* 16:1104)

396. McCORNACK, ROBERT L. "Vocational Interests of Male and Female Social Workers." *J Appl Psychol* 40:11–3 F '56. * (*PA* 31:3216)

397. POWERS, MABEL K. "Permanence of Measured Vocational Interests of Adult Males." *J Appl Psychol* 40:69–72 Ap '56. * (*PA* 31:6225)

398. RHODES, GEORGE S. *An Investigation of Response Sets in the Strong Vocational Interest Blank for Men and Response Set Effects on Scores of Selected SVIB Scales.* Doctor's thesis, University of Kansas (Lawrence, Kan.), 1956.

399. SAUNDERS, DAVID R. "Moderator Variables in Prediction." *Ed & Psychol Meas* 16:209–22 su '56. * (*PA* 31:5101)

400. SINNETT, E. ROBERT. "Some Determinants of Agreement Between Measured and Expressed Interests." *Ed & Psychol Meas* 16:110–8 sp '56. * (*PA* 31:6226)

401. THOMPSON, JORGEN S. *A Study of the Relationships Between Certain Measured Psychological Variables and Achievement in the First Year of Theological Seminary Work.* Doctor's thesis, University of Minnesota (Minneapolis, Minn.), 1956. (*DA* 16:1846)

402. WITKIN, ARTHUR A. "Differential Interest Patterns in Salesmen." *J Appl Psychol* 40:338–40 O '56. * (*PA* 31:9058)

403. WITKIN, ARTHUR A. *The Prediction of Potentials for Effectiveness in Certain Occupations Within the Sales Field.* Doctor's thesis, New York University (New York, N.Y.), 1956. (*DA* 16:1718)

404. BRAMS, JEROME M. *The Relationship Between Personal Characteristics of Counseling Trainees and Effective Communication in Counseling.* Doctor's thesis, University of Missouri (Columbia, Mo.), 1957. (*DA* 17:1510)

405. DUNNETTE, MARVIN D. "Vocational Interest Differences Among Engineers Employed in Different Functions." *J Appl Psychol* 41:273–8 O '57. *

406. FREDERICK, MARVIN L. "Testing the Tests." *J Account* 103:42–7 Ap '57. *

407. GEHMAN, W. SCOTT. "A Study of Ability to Fake Scores on the Strong Vocational Interest Blank for Men." *Ed & Psychol Meas* 17:65–70 sp '57. *

408. GRAFF, FRANKLYN A. *Occupational Choice Factors in Normally Achieving and Underachieving Intellectually Superior Twelfth Grade Boys.* Doctor's thesis, University of Connecticut (Storrs, Conn.), 1957. (*DA* 17:2207)

409. HARKER, JOHN B. "A Comparison of Personality and Interest Patterns." Abstract. *Am Psychol* 12:408 Jl '57. *

410. HEWER, VIVIAN H. "Vocational Interest-Achievement-Ability Interrelationships at the College Level." *J Counsel Psychol* 4:234–8 fall '57. *

411. KING, LESLIE A. "Stability Measures of Strong Vocational Interest Blank Profiles." *J Appl Psychol* 41:143–7 Je '57. *

412. LYERLY, SAMUEL B. "'Chance' Scores on the Strong Vocational Interest Blank for Men." *J Appl Psychol* 41:141–2 Je '57. *

413. MAIER, GLEN E. *The Contribution of Interest Test Scores to Differential Academic Prediction.* Doctor's thesis, University of Washington (Seattle, Wash.), 1957. (*DA* 18:150)

414. STRONG, EDWARD K., JR. "Interests of Fathers and Sons." *J Appl Psychol* 41:284–92 O '57. *

415. COOPER, ALVA C. "The Strong Group Scales and Primary Interest Patterns." *Personnel & Guid J* 36:461–4 Mr '58. *

416. DUNNETTE, MARVIN D., AND KIRCHNER, WAYNE K. "Validation of Psychological Tests in Industry." *Personnel Adm* 21:20–7 My–Je '58. *

417. DUNNETTE, MARVIN D.; KIRCHNER, WAYNE K.; AND DeGIDIO, JoANNE. "Relations Among Scores on Edwards Personal Preference Schedule, California Psychological Inventory, and Strong Vocational Interest Blank for an Industrial Sample." *J Appl Psychol* 42:178–81 Je '58. *

418. ENGLAND, GEORGE W., AND PATERSON, DONALD G. "Relationship Between Measured Interest Patterns and Satisfactory Vocational Adjustment for Air Force Officers in the Comptroller and Personnel Fields." *J Appl Psychol* 42:85–8 Ap '58. *

419. GARMAN, GLEN D., AND UHR, LEONARD. "An Anxiety Scale for the Strong Vocational Interest Inventory: Development, Cross-Validation, and Subsequent Tests of Validity." *J Appl Psychol* 42:241–6 Ag '58. *

420. HUGHES, J. L., AND McNAMARA, W. J. "Limitations on the Use of Strong Sales Keys for Selection and Counseling." *J Appl Psychol* 42:93–6 Ap '58. *

421. JENSON, PAUL G. "Relationship Between Stated and Measured Interests of Two Groups of United States Air Force Officers." *J Appl Psychol* 42:33–5 F '58. *

422. KING, LESLIE A. "Factors Associated With Vocational Interest Profile Stability." *J Appl Psychol* 42:261–3 Ag '58. *

423. LASCH, HENRY A. *A Comparison of the Results Obtained by the Mitchell and Strong Interest Measures When Administered to Male Freshmen at the University of Michigan.* Doctor's thesis, University of Michigan (Ann Arbor, Mich.), 1958. (*DA* 19:1286)

424. LAYTON, WILBUR L. *Counseling Use of the Strong Vocational Interest Blank.* Minnesota Studies in Student Personnel Work, No. 8. Minneapolis, Minn.: University of Minnesota Press, 1958. Pp. 40. *

425. RABINOWITZ, WILLIAM, AND ROSENBAUM, IRA. "A Failure in the Prediction of Pupil-Teacher Rapport." *J Ed Psychol* 49:93–8 Ap '58. *

426. WILLIAMS, RAYMOND E. *The Measurement and Prediction of Cooperating Teacher Effectiveness in Music Teacher Education.* Doctor's thesis, University of Illinois (Urbana, Ill.), 1958. (*DA* 19:1023)

For reviews by Edward S. Bordin and Elmer D. Hinckley, see 4:747; for reviews by Harold D. Carter, John G. Darley, and N. W. Morton, see 40:1680; for a review by John G. Darley of an earlier edition, see 38:1178; for related reviews, see B115, B414, 4:748, 3:648, 3:650, and 3:652.

[869]

Strong Vocational Interest Blank for Women, Revised. Ages 17 and over; 1933–59; 29 scoring scales (28 occupational scales and 1 nonvocational scale): artist ('46), author ('46), librarian ('46), English teacher ('46), social worker ('46–54), psychologist ('46), social science teacher ('46), Y.W.C.A. secretary ('46), lawyer ('46), life insurance saleswoman ('46), buyer ('46), business education teacher ('48) by H. F. Koepke, office worker ('47), stenographer-secretary ('47), housewife ('46), elementary teacher ('46) by Ralph Bedell, music performer ('54), music teacher ('54), home economics teacher ('46), dietitian ('46), college physical education teacher ('55) by Rosena M. Wilson, high school physical education teacher ('46) by Patricia Collins, occupational therapist ('46), nurse ('46), mathematics-science teacher ('46), dentist ('46), laboratory technician ('46), physician ('46), femininity-masculinity ('47) ; IBM ; Form W ('46) ; manual ('59) ; $4 per 25 tests; $1.15 per 25 individual report blanks ['59] ; hand scoring stencils : $1.25 per single scale, $10 per set of any 10 scales, $25 per complete set; separate answer sheets may be used ; $2.25 per 50 IBM answer sheets; $2.25 per 50 Hankes' answer sheets for use with the scoring service of Testscor (see 529) ; machine scoring stencils : $2.50 per single scale, $20 per set of any 10 scales, $48 per complete set; postage extra; $1 per specimen set (does not include scoring stencils) of SVIB for women and for men, cash orders postpaid; (30–60) minutes; Edward K. Strong, Jr.; Consulting Psychologists Press. *

REFERENCES

1–9. See 40:1681.
10–45. See 3:649.
46. PARSONS, RICHARD T. *The Home and School Backgrounds, Measured Vocational Interests, and Vocational Choices of 869 Students Who Entered the State Teachers Colleges of Pennsylvania in the Fall of 1940.* Doctor's thesis, Pennsylvania State College (State College, Pa.), 1942.
47. KUTNER, MILDRED. *The Prognosis of the Freshmen Achievement of Chemistry and Physics Students on the Basis of Interest Test Items.* Master's thesis, Pennsylvania State College (State College, Pa.), 1947. Pp. iv, 113.
48. MYDELLE, ELLA KLEIST. *A Vocational Interest Scale for Music Teachers.* Master's thesis, Stanford University (Stanford, Calif.), 1947.
49. ALLEN, CHARLES L. *The Development of a Battery of Psychological Tests for Determining Journalistic Interests and Aptitudes.* Doctor's thesis, Northwestern University (Evanston, Ill.), 1948.
50. DREFFIN, WILLIAM B., AND WRENN, C. GILBERT. "Spatial Relations Ability and Other Characteristics of Art Laboratory Students." *J Appl Psychol* 32:601–5 D '48. * (PA 23:3777)
51. ESPENSCHADE, ANNA. "Selection of Women Major Students in Physical Education." *Res Q* 19:70–6 My '48. * (PA 22:4635)
52. LINNICK, IDA. *Effect of Instructions and Resulting Vocational Classifications on a Vocational Interest Inventory as Related to Response Patterns of College Women.* Doctor's thesis, New York University (New York, N.Y.), 1948.
53. KLEIST, M.; RITTENHOUSE, C. H.; AND FARNSWORTH, P. R. "Strong Vocational Interest Scales for Music Teachers." *Occupations* 28:100–1 N '49. * (PA 24:2218)
54. MOREY, ELWYN A. "Vocational Interests and Personality Characteristics of Women Teachers." *Austral J Psychol* 1:26–37 Je '49. *
55. RITTENHOUSE, C. H. *Vocational Interests of Women Music Teachers.* Master's thesis, Stanford University (Stanford, Calif.), 1949.
56. SHEPLER, BERNARD F. "A Comparison of Masculinity-Femininity Measures." *J Consult Psychol* 15:484–6 D '51. * (PA 26:7011)
57. VERNSON, ELIZABETH E. *An Interpretation of the Housewife Scale of the Strong Vocational Interest Blank for Women as Applied to Women Who Have Expressed an Interest in Marriage.* Master's thesis, Pennsylvania State College (State College, Pa.), 1951.
58. ANDERSON, MARY R. *A Descriptive Study of Values and Interests of Four Groups of Graduate Women at the University of Minnesota.* Doctor's thesis, University of Minnesota (Minneapolis, Minn.), 1952. (DA 12:851)
59. MITZEL, HAROLD E. *Interest Factors Predictive of Teachers' Rapport With Pupils.* Doctor's thesis, University of Minnesota (Minneapolis, Minn.), 1952. (DA 12:712)
60. NAVRAN, LESLIE. "Validity of the Strong Vocational Interest Blank Nursing Key." *J Appl Psychol* 37:31–2 F '53. * (PA 28:1626)
61. TOMEDY, FRANCIS J. *The Relationship of Personality Characteristics to Measured Interests of Women Teachers of English, Social Science, Mathematics, and Physical Science in Certain Senior High Schools.* Doctor's thesis, New York University (New York, N.Y.), 1952. (DA 12:540)
62. SNYDER, DOROTHY F. *A Study of Relationships Between Certain Socio-Economic Factors and the Strong Vocational Interest Blank for Women.* Doctor's thesis, University of Minnesota (Minneapolis, Minn.), 1953. (DA 13:868)
63. GUNNELL, DOROTHY C., AND NUTTING, RUTH E. "Prediction of Achievement in Schools of Nursing." *Calif J Ed Res* 8:184–91 S '57. *
64. HOYT, DONALD P., AND KENNEDY, CARROLL E. "Interest and Personality Correlates of Career-Motivated and Homemaking-Motivated College Women." Comment by Charles McArthur. *J Counsel Psychol* 5:44–9 sp '58. *

For a review by Gwendolen Schneidler Dickson, see 3:649; for a review by Ruth Strang of an earlier edition, see 40:1681; for a review by John G. Darley, see 38:1179; for related reviews, see 3:650 and 3:652.

[870]

Vocational Interest Analyses: A Six-Fold Analytical Extension of the Occupational Interest Inventory. Grades 9–16 and adults; 1951; 6 scores in each of 6 areas; IBM; 1 form; 6 tests; tests administered only in those areas in which an examinee obtains high scores on the *Occupational Interest Inventory* (see 864) ; no data on reliability ; no norms ; $3.50 per 35 copies of any one test ; separate answer sheets may be used ; 6¢ per IBM answer sheet for use with any three tests ; 60¢ per set of either hand or machine scoring stencils ; postage extra ; 75¢ per complete specimen set, postpaid ; (25–35) minutes per test ; Edward C. Roeber and Gerald G. Prideaux in collaboration with Edwin A. Lee and Louis P. Thorpe ; California Test Bureau. *

a) PERSONAL-SOCIAL ANAYLSIS. 6 scores: domestic service, personal service, social service, teaching and related activities, law and law enforcement, health and medical service.

b) NATURAL ANALYSIS. 6 scores: general and crop farming, animal raising and care, garden and greenhouse care, fish-game-domestic fowl, lumbering and forestry, marine work.

c) MECHANICAL ANALYSIS. 6 scores: maintenance and repairing, machine operation and tending, construction, designing, bench work and bench crafts, processing.

d) BUSINESS ANALYSIS. 6 scores: clerical, shipping and distribution, bookkeeping and accounting, buying and selling, training and supervision, management and control.

e) THE ARTS ANALYSIS. 6 scores: art crafts, painting and drawing, decorating and landscaping, drama and radio, literary activities, music.

f) THE SCIENCES ANALYSIS. 6 scores: laboratory work, mineral-petroleum products, applied chemistry, chemical research, biological research, scientific engineering.

REFERENCE

1. MELTON, WILLIAM R., JR. "An Investigation of the Relationship Between Personality and Vocational Interest." *J Ed Psychol* 47:163–74 Mr '56. * (PA 31:8791)

WILBUR L. LAYTON, *Professor of Psychology and Assistant Director, Student Counseling Bureau, University of Minnesota, Minneapolis, Minnesota.*

Julian C. Stanley, in his review of the six *Vocational Interest Analyses* in the *Fourth Mental Measurements Yearbook* (see 4:747), stated, "Despite some indications of careful construction by Roeber and Prideaux, the Analyses seem to the reviewer severely limited in usefulness because they lack norms, internal consistency statistics, reliability coefficients, and evidence of empirical validity. In the reviewer's opinion, they were released prematurely. This becomes especially obvious when the two generally unfavorable reviews [see 3:643] of the parent instrument are considered in conjunction with the Analyses, which seem to have even more of the same flaws."

As far as the present reviewer can determine, only one research report has been published on the Analyses since Stanley's review, even though, in the 1951 manual, promises were made that reliability and validity data would be made available when the extensive studies, then in process, were completed. One can only conclude that these studies were never completed, or that they were completed and never published.

The authors also promised, in the 1951 manual, to investigate further the advisability of preparing percentile norms for the six Analyses. Evidently, this further investigation has resulted in the authors' conclusion not to provide percentile norms, although, to this reviewer, such norms would be highly desirable.

The approach to interest measurement offered by the combination of the *Occupational Interest Inventory* and the *Vocational Interest Analyses* is very seductive. One administers first an inventory to determine which of six broad areas incorporate the individual's interests. Then one administers the appropriate Analyses to subdivide the broad areas of interests into more specific interest areas. This approach is seductive because most counselors find it difficult to talk about specific occupations when faced with a high score in a broad interest area. The Analyses promise a solution to this problem. Of course, a more adequately standardized interest inventory, the *Strong Vocational Interest Blank,* has the solution to this problem built into the inventory. At any rate the authors have still presented no evidence that scores resulting from the Analyses provide for adequate further differentiation of individuals classified within a broad interest area.

This reviewer cannot recommend the *Vocational Interest Analyses* for counseling use. If the publisher wants to make these inventories available, they should be clearly labeled experimental and the prospective user should be warned against using them in individual counseling. It would be extremely desirable for the publisher to withdraw these Analyses from the market except for experimental use and present them for general sale again only after they have been adequately standardized.

For a review by Julian C. Stanley, see 4:746.

MANUAL DEXTERITY

[871]

*Crawford Small Parts Dexterity Test. High school and adults; 1946–56; individual; 2 scores: pins and collars, screws; 1 form; apparatus ('46); revised manual ('56); tentative timelimit norms; $29.50 per set of test materials, postpaid; worklimit (10–25) minutes or timelimit 8(15–20) minutes; John E. Crawford and Dorothea M. Crawford; Psychological Corporation. *

REFERENCES

1. BRUCE, MARTIN M. "Validity Information Exchange, No. 7-079: D.O.T. Code 7-83.058, Electrical Appliance Serviceman." *Personnel Psychol* 7:425–6 au '54. *
2. FITZPATRICK, EUGENE D., AND McCARTY, JOHN J. "Validity Information Exchange, No. 8-35: D.O.T. Code 9-00.91, Assembler VII (Electrical Equipment)." *Personnel Psychol* 8:501–4 w '55. *
3. BRUCE, MARTIN M. "Normative Data Information Exchange, Nos. 15, 33-5." *Personnel Psychol* 9:390–1, 545–50 au, w '56. *
4. BRUCE, MARTIN M. "Normative Data Information Exchange, No. 33." *Personnel Psychol* 9:545–6 w '56. *
5. OSBORNE, R. TRAVIS, AND SANDERS, WILMA B. "The Crawford Small Parts Dexterity Test as a Time-Limit Test." *Personnel Psychol* 9:177–80 su '56. * (*PA* 31:8973)
6. WALKER, FRANCIS C. "Normative Data Information Exchange, No. 9." *Personnel Psychol* 9:275 su '56. *
7. SPEER, GEORGE S. "Validity Information Exchange, No. 10-5: D.O.T. Code 5-00.933, (Relay Adjustors)." *Personnel Psychol* 10:80 sp '57. *
8. BAUMAN, MARY K. *A Manual of Norms for Tests Used in Counseling Blind Persons.* AFB Publications, Research Series, No. 6. New York: American Foundation for the Blind, 1958. Pp. 40. * (*PA* 32:1949)

NEIL D. WARREN, *Professor of Psychology and Head of the Department, University of Southern California, Los Angeles, California.*

This is a neat, well constructed test designed to measure "fine eye-hand coordination" of the sort involved in assembly and adjustment of such devices as electric clocks and hearing aids, and in manipulation of small hand tools.

All components of the test are contained in a 10-inch square board. There are three round wells for the parts to be manipulated, i.e., pins, collars, and screws; a metal plate containing 42 unthreaded and 42 threaded holes; two metal trays beneath the plate to receive the pins and screws; a tweezers; and a small screwdriver.

The test is administered in two separately scored parts. Part 1 requires the examinee to use the tweezers to pick up a pin, insert it in the small hole in the metal plate, and place a collar over it. The preferred hand is used. Part 2 requires him to pick up a screw, start it in a threaded hole with the fingers, and then screw it through the metal plate with the screwdriver. Both hands are used in the last operation. After 6 practice trials in each part, the remaining 36 holes constitute the test.

The test has been used mostly on a work limit basis, with the scores being the time required to complete the 36 operations in each

part. The average time for Part 1 is approximately 5 minutes in addition to time for instructions and practice. The scores in various
normative groups range from 3 to 10 minutes.
The time for Part 2 averages about 10 minutes with a range of 4 to 18 minutes. It would
appear that total testing time could be as much
as 35 or 40 minutes in the case of very slow
individuals.

The use of time limits of 3 minutes for Part
1 and 5 minutes for Part 2 is suggested by the
manual. Timelimit norms are published for one
group of 177 female applicants for assembly
jobs. This procedure would reduce overall testing time and permit simultaneous testing of
more than one examinee. There is no significant loss in reliability.

Split-half reliability coefficients for four
samples range from .80 to .91 for Part 1 and
from .90 to .95 for Part 2 using worklimit
scores. Reliabilities for timelimit scores are
reported as .90 and .89 for Parts 1 and 2, respectively.

The correlation between Parts 1 and 2 is
relatively low, ranging from .10 to .50 for nine
samples, with the median correlation being .42.
This degree of independence is, of course, typical of dexterity tests. It is probable that correlations of about the same level would be found
between either part of this test and such similar
tests as the *Finger Dexterity Test,* the *Tweezer
Dexterity Test,* and the *Purdue Pegboard.* No
data concerning such relationships are given
in the manuals, however. Correlations between
the *Small Parts Dexterity Test* and various
scores on the *Minnesota Rate of Manipulation
Test* vary from .23 to .39 for one small sample.
Correlations with measures of intelligence are
low.

Considering the fact that this test was on
the market for 10 years prior to the publication
of the revised manual in 1956, the amount of
validation data is disappointingly small. Four
studies are reported, one of which involved six
employees of an engraving firm, hired because
they had exceeded critical scores on both parts
of the test. The production of these employees
is reported to have been "300% of former output." The reviewer agrees with the authors
that, in such a study, "conclusions must be
drawn with caution."

In a study of 56 female burlers and menders
of woolen goods, the manual reports a tetrachoric correlation of .76 between "passing" or

"failing" both parts of the test and high versus
low piece rate earnings. A correlation of such
magnitude needs confirmation from other studies. Moreover, one wonders what established
"high" or "low" earnings since the group was
not split at the median.

The other validation figures involved female
electronic assembly workers. Two groups of 80
and 70 employees were used. Correlations between the test and supervisors' ratings varied
from .17 to .49.

In general, it appears that the test stands
most on face validity. Norms are provided for
several groups, including students, job applicants, and employees. Differences in median
scores of applicants and employees indicate a
somewhat better test performance by employees. This, too, must be interpreted with caution
since there are many unknown variables. The
test could be used as part of a selection battery
if validity correlations for specific jobs were
determined and appropriate weights assigned
to the test scores. Its use as an independent
selection test or for vocational guidance purposes is not justified by the data provided in
the manual.

The manual itself is attractive in format and
clear in its instructions for using the test. It is
unfortunate that it does not have more data
on the test's usefulness.

*For a review by Raymond A. Katzell, see
4:752; for a review by Joseph E. Moore, see
3:667.*

[872]

*Moore Eye-Hand Coordination and Color-
Matching Test. Ages 2–6, 7 and over; 1949–55; individual; 1 form; 2 levels; mimeographed supplementary data sheet ['55]; $1 per 100 score sheets ['49];
postpaid; Joseph E. Moore; Joseph E. Moore and
Associates. *

a) THE MOORE EYE-HAND COORDINATION TEST: PRE-
SCHOOL FORM. Ages 2–6; 1 form; 16-hole test apparatus
['55]; $10 per set of test materials; 50¢ per supple-
mentary manual ['49]; (5–10) minutes.

b) MOORE EYE-HAND COORDINATION AND COLOR-MATCH-
ING TEST. Ages 7 and over; 2 scores: eye-hand coordination, color matching; 1 form; 32-hole apparatus
['49]; $20 per set of test materials; 50¢ per manual
['49]; (10–15) minutes.

REFERENCES

1–6. See 4:750.
7. WILLIAMS, WILBUR ALLEN. *Relationship of Eye-Hand Coordination in Children to Total Development.* Doctor's thesis,
University of Michigan (Ann Arbor, Mich.), 1952. (DA 12:
530)

*For reviews by Norman Frederiksen and Jay
L. Otis, see 4:750.*

[873]

Purdue Pegboard. Grades 9–16 and adults; 1941–48; 5 scores: right hand, left hand, both hands, right plus left plus both hands, assembly; 1 form ('41); $18.95 per testing apparatus; 95¢ per 20 profiles ('48); 25¢ per manual ('48); postage extra; 2.5(10) or 7.5(20) minutes; Purdue Research Foundation under the direction of Joseph Tiffin; Science Research Associates. *

REFERENCES

1–3. See 3:666.
4–15. See 4:751.
16. COMREY, ANDREW L. "Group Performance in a Manual Dexterity Task." *J Appl Psychol* 37:207–10 Je '53. * (*PA* 28:3345)
17. RADLEY, SHIRLEY. *A Statistical Study Based on a Short Experimental Music Test, Purdue Pegboard Scores, and General Intelligence.* Master's thesis, Syracuse University (Syracuse, N.Y.), 1953.
18. SOPER, MERWIN E. *The Value of the ACE Psychological Examination and the Purdue Pegboard Test of Manual Dexterity in Predicting High School Typewriting Grades.* Master's thesis, Drake University (Des Moines, Iowa), 1953.
19. BRUCE, MARTIN M. "Validity Information Exchange, No. 7-079: D.O.T. Code 7-83.058, Electrical Appliance Serviceman." *Personnel Psychol* 7:425–6 au '54. *
20. COMREY, ANDREW L., AND DESKIN, GERALD. "Further Results on Group Manual Dexterity in Men." *J Appl Psychol* 38:116–8 Ap '54. * (*PA* 29:2053)
21. COMREY, ANDREW L., AND DESKIN, GERALD. "Group Manual Dexterity in Women." *J Appl Psychol* 38:178–80 Je '54. * (*PA* 29:3529)
22. FLEISHMAN, EDWIN A., AND HEMPEL, WALTER E. "A Factor Analysis of Dexterity Tests." *Personnel Psychol* 7:15–32 sp '54. * (*PA* 29:2061)
23. ALBRIGHT, LEWIS EDWIN. *The Development of a Selection Process for an Inspection Task.* Doctor's thesis, Purdue University (Lafayette, Ind.), 1956. (*DA* 16:2201)
24. ALBRIGHT, LEWIS E. "Validity Information Exchange, No. 9-44: D.O.T. Code 0-66.93, Seed Analyst." *Personnel Psychol* 9:522–3 w '56. *
25. SHIMOTA, HELEN EMMA. *The Relation of Psychomotor Performance to Clinical Status and Improvement in Schizophrenic Patients.* Doctor's thesis, University of Minnesota (Minneapolis, Minn.), 1956. (*DA* 16:2530)
26. SIEGEL, MAX, AND HIRSCHHORN, BORIS. "Adolescent Norms for the Purdue Pegboard Test." *Personnel & Guid J* 36:563–5 Ap '58. *

NEIL D. WARREN, *Professor of Psychology and Head of the Department, University of Southern California, Los Angeles, California.*

The purpose of this test is to aid in selecting employees for industrial jobs requiring manipulative dexterity. It is intended to measure both gross movements of arms, hands, and fingers, and "tip of the finger" dexterity.

The pegboard is made of wood and contains two rows of 25 holes into which pins are to be inserted. At the top of the board are four cups containing pins, washers, and collars to be assembled. No tools are employed.

The test involves two types of operations. One requires rapid placing of pins in the holes. It is scored for each hand separately, for the sum of right and left hand scores, and for alternating right and left hand movements. There is a time limit of 30 seconds for each trial. The other operation requires assembly of pins, washers, and collars using both hands. The score is the number of components assembled in each 1-minute trial.

A profile sheet provides spaces for recording scores and norms for converting scores to percentiles. Norms are given for male industrial applicants and for a group of veterans and college students. Norms for women are based on combined groups of college students and industrial applicants except for the assembly task where differences between the groups were found. No information is given in the manual concerning the composition of these groups as relates to industry or job involved, age, or other variable. Norms are available for one-trial and for three-trial totals. The three-trial norms are extrapolations from the one-trial figures. They were computed to take into account the improvement resulting from practice. The only data on such improvement are based on performance of 484 college students. Whether or not the same rate of improvement applies to other groups should be determined and not assumed.

The reliability data reported in the manual indicates that test-retest correlations for the one-trial administration range from .60 to .76 with a median of .68. The authors argue that this is adequate in view of the relatively low validity to be expected of such tests. This argument is not convincing. Stepping up the reliability coefficient to the three-trial length raises the median to .86. In view of the low reliability of the one-trial procedure there is a serious question about the recommendation of the manual that it be used for hiring purposes. Even at the three-trial level the reliability coefficient is about as low as usually considered acceptable.

The manual recommends that validation studies be conducted on the population for which the test is to be used. Essential as such a procedure is, it would limit the test's usefulness to relatively large industrial organizations and exclude it entirely from use for vocational guidance. If the advice has been taken and more validity studies have been done in industry, the data should be summarized in the manual for the guidance of the potential user. As it is, he has little to go on except the face validity.

All but one of the validity coefficients reported are based on various one-trial scores and involve such small samples as to be virtually meaningless. If, as the manual reports, the test has been experimentally administered "in numerous plants which involved the testing of several thousand employees in a wide variety of industrial jobs," validity coefficients based on as few as 15 cases seem inexcusable. Moreover, the data are reported for four jobs only. For one sample of 233 radio tube mounters, given three trials of the assembly task, the correlation of scores with ratings was .64. It is not possible to determine how meaningful this criterion is, but if it has practical meaning, it is the kind of evidence which would justify use of the test as part of industrial selection batteries.

The manual points out the well known specificity of manipulative and dexterity tasks. However, no correlations are given with other frequently used tests in this area. Nor are there correlations among the scores on the various parts of the test.

In summary, the *Purdue Pegboard* is a widely used device measuring a variety of manual manipulations. The manual presents very limited evidence to justify its use as a selective device in industry or for vocational guidance. A more up-to-date manual containing more significant information is needed.

For reviews by Edwin E. Ghiselli, Thomas W. Harrell, and Albert Gibson Packard, see 3:666.

MECHANICAL ABILITY

[874]

*A.C.E.R. Mechanical Comprehension Test. Ages 13-6 and over; 1942–53; 1 form ['42]; revised mimeographed manual ['53]; no data on reliability; separate answer sheets must be used; 15s. per 10 tests; 1s. 6d. per 10 answer sheets; 2s. 6d. per manual; 6d. per scoring key; 4s. 6d. per specimen set; postpaid within Australia; 30(40) minutes; Australian Council for Educational Research. *

REFERENCES

1. OXLADE, M. "An Experiment in the Use of Psychological Tests in the Selection of Women Trainee Telephone Mechanics." *B Ind Psychol & Personnel Prac* 2:26–32 Mr '46. * (PA 20: 4838)
2. HOHNE, H. H. *Success and Failure in Scientific Faculties of the University of Melbourne.* Melbourne, Australia: Australian Council for Educational Research, 1955. Pp. vii, 129. * (PA 31:3787)

JOHN R. JENNINGS, *Research and Testing Officer, New Zealand Department of Education, Wellington, New Zealand.*

The test of 45 items has been in use since 1943. The standardization for children was carried out in Tasmania in 1947; the numbers tested are not given. Norms for adults, obtained in 1943, are based on 2,000 male recruits and 1,000 females. In addition, mean scores and standard deviations are reported for 715 first year students at Melbourne University, grouped according to faculty and sex. Similar data are reported for 277 male students in first, second, and third year classes at Melbourne College. Where separate norms for males and females are given, there are wide differences between them, with consistently superior performance being evident among the males. In the norming, an unfortunate complication was introduced by the use of two time limits, 30 and 40 minutes. The university group was given the longer time limit.

The diagrams in the test booklet are reasonably well reproduced. The mechanisms shown in the diagrams are not parts of standard machines, but have been specially drawn to illustrate various mechanical principles and mechanisms. Mechanisms illustrated include levers and pivots, wheels and connecting rods, pulleys and belts or cables, cog and gear wheels, cams and camrods, and the like.

Compared with Bennett's *Test of Mechanical Comprehension,* this test covers fewer theoretical principles and places more emphasis on mechanisms, some of them fairly complicated. The Bennett test includes questions on a wide range of topics not covered by this test, a good many of them outside what is usually understood as "mechanical," e.g., electricity, specific gravity, heat conduction, speed of sound and light, illumination.

The Bennett test, an excellent production, has been so widely used that it is useful to have an alternative test available. The *A.C.E.R. Mechanical Comprehension Test* is a reasonably satisfactory alternative. Though it does not tap nearly such a large range of theoretical knowledge, it does seem to give a reasonable measure of a subject's understanding of straight mechanical principles and of how mechanisms work. It may be regarded as particularly useful for the selection of apprentices to mechanical trades and for candidates for foremanship or junior management in positions where mechanical comprehension is required.

HAYDN S. WILLIAMS, *Assistant Superintendent of Technical Education, Education Department, Perth, Australia.*

This is a paper and pencil test of 45 items similar in kind to Bennett's *Test of Mechanical Comprehension,* but also reflecting the influence of the work of Cox in Great Britain in that the emphasis is on problems involving levers, gears, and pulleys. These are mainly connected in systems not likely to be familiar to persons taking the test. The test is attractively produced with good, clear diagrams. Separate answer sheets are used and marking is by means of a transparent sheet. The general format of the test and the adequate instructions and practice exercises suggest careful preparation.

The manual gives no information concerning the development of the test; it was, however, initially prepared for use in the Australian Armed Services during World War II. The aim, as given in the introductory section for test subjects, is "to see how well you understand mechanical ideas." In practice the test is widely used in vocational guidance organisations throughout the Commonwealth of Australia, and, in conjunction with a space form relation test of the *Minnesota Paper Form Board Test* variety, is used to predict success in practical type occupations mainly at the skilled trade and higher levels.

Although the manual does not report any direct occupational validity data, correlations of .36 and .51 are reported between scores on the test and average marks on woodwork, metalwork, and trade drawing for a group of industrial high school pupils. Evidence is also reported to suggest that, among university students, science and engineering students tend to score higher on the test than arts, law, and commerce students, and that there are higher mean scores produced by the more successful as compared with the less successful engineering students. It is understood that investigations of this test made by the services but not reported in the manual tend to support its value.

No reliability data are reported in the manual nor is any information provided on the test's factorial content, which is clearly complex. The form of the questions and the multiple choice answers suggests a considerable general verbal factor. A correlation of .39 is reported with the Higher Examination of the *Otis Self-Administering Tests of Mental Ability* for the group of high school boys previously referred to. Correlations of .5 between a derivative of this test and the Intermediate Examination of the Otis were obtained by the reviewer using representative samples of 13- and 14-year-old boys. As one might expect,

substantial correlations up to .47 are reported with the *Minnesota Paper Form Board Test*. It therefore appears likely that the test has also a substantial space factor component.

Norms in the form of percentile ranks and standard deviation units are provided for children aged 13.6 to 14.6 and male army recruits aged 18 to 19. The norming appears to have been carefully done on well defined and substantial populations.

To sum up, this test appears to be a well prepared one which warrants further investigation to establish its validity in a much wider range of situations. The manual could have given much more positive guidance to users as to the derivation of the test, its significance, and its uses, as well as the additional validity data which the manual suggests will be added as it becomes available. On the basis of the data so far presented, considerable caution needs to be exercised in the use of the test for individual prediction, where it should only be used as a supplement to other data. This limitation is apparently recognised by the publishers who will only supply copies of the test to persons who are graduates in psychology.

For a review by D. W. McElwain, see 4:756.

[875]
★A.C.E.R. Mechanical Reasoning Test. Ages 14-9 and over; 1951–54; abbreviated adaptation of *A.C.E.R. Mechanical Comprehension Test;* 1 form ['51]; mimeographed manual ['54]; separate answer sheets must be used; 7s. 6d. per 10 tests; 1s. 6d. per 10 answer sheets; 1s. per scoring stencil; 3s. per manual; 4s. 9d. per specimen set; postpaid within Australia; 20(30) minutes; manual by D. Spearritt; Research and Guidance Branch, Queensland Department of Public Instruction and the publisher; Australian Council for Educational Research. *

JOHN R. JENNINGS, *Research and Testing Officer, New Zealand Department of Education, Wellington, New Zealand.*

This test of 24 items is a shortened version of the *A.C.E.R. Mechanical Comprehension Test.* There are three new items, the remainder being reprinted, with some revision, from the parent test.

The question booklet is adequately produced, with diagrams that are larger and clearer than those in the longer test. The answer sheet and scoring key are neat and workmanlike. Mechanisms illustrated include levers and pivots, wheels and connecting rods, pulleys and belts or cables, cog and gear wheels, cams and camrods, and so on. Compared with Bennett's

Test of Mechanical Comprehension, this test covers fewer theoretical principles and places more emphasis on mechanisms.

So far as standard of production is concerned, this test is an improvement over the *A.C.E.R. Mechanical Comprehension Test.* However, it is difficult to be entirely happy about a test of this kind that contains only 24 items, particularly in the absence of any data on validity except the rather sketchy occupational norms. The longer test of 45 items seems well worth the extra 10 minutes of working time.

HAYDN S. WILLIAMS, *Assistant Superintendent of Technical Education, Education Department, Perth, Australia.*

This is a modified and shortened version of the *A.C.E.R. Mechanical Comprehension Test,* which is separately reviewed. It consists of 24 items in place of the original 45; three of the items are not in the parent test. There are five alternative answers to each question in place of four; there is some effort to reduce verbal content by replacing words with direction arrows; and more effective "three dimensional" diagrams are used for some items. Format and printing are clear and attractive. The manual which accompanies the test is an improvement over that for the parent test in format, printing, and content.

The test is "designed to assess a person's aptitude for solving problems involving the understanding of mechanical ideas." It is aimed at adolescents and is suitable for use with unselected male adults but is not sufficiently discriminating among university students and others taking technical courses at an advanced level. There is evidence of careful tryout of the items.

The only information which might be considered as validity data is a series of norms in deciles relating to six major occupational groups drawn from the army recruit population. From these it appears that fitters and mechanics of various kinds score higher on the test than constructional tradesmen, that clerks score nearly as high as constructional tradesmen, and that university students score higher than all other groups. The manual sounds a very proper note of warning concerning the tentative nature of these data in view of the small numbers involved, and the possibility that they are not representative of the occupational groups concerned.

Reliability coefficients obtained by the split-half method and by the Kuder-Richardson formula 20 are of the order of .8, using a sample of 100 of the army recruits. A commendable feature is that this reliability is interpreted for the test user in terms of the probable error of measurement. The reliability is somewhat low compared with that normally considered as satisfactory for individual prediction. When this low reliability is taken into account with correlations of the order of .6 with a word knowledge test, verbal and nonverbal intelligence tests, and a spatial relations test, it appears that scores on the *A.C.E.R. Mechanical Reasoning Test* can be very largely accounted for by general verbal and spatial factors.

This is a carefully prepared test which deserves further tryout by qualified psychologists. The manual provides a satisfactory range of information concerning the test insofar as such information is available. However, the evidence at present available is not adequate enough to justify the use of the test for individual prediction at this stage. Since the test has been produced collaboratively by the A.C.E.R. and the Research and Guidance Branch of the Queensland Education Department, both of which are noted in Australia for sound scientific work in the field of test research, one can reasonably hope that further data on the test will be obtained and published.

[876]

★Chriswell Structural Dexterity Test. Grades 8–9; 1953–54; individual; Form B ('53, revision of unpublished Form A) hectographed manual ('53); $30 per set of test materials, 50 record blanks, and manual; $2.50 per 50 record blanks ['54]; $1 per manual; postage extra; 6.5(15) minutes; M. Irving Chriswell; C. H. Stoelting Co. *

REFERENCE

1. CHRISWELL, M. IRVING. "Validity of a Structural Dexterity Test." *J Appl Psychol* 37:13–5 F '53. * (PA 28:1618)

A. PEMBERTON JOHNSON, *Assistant Director, Counseling Center, Newark College of Engineering, Newark, New Jersey.*

The manual states that "structural dexterity may be defined as the ability to translate the visualization of structures into specific motor responses. It is probably closely related to the 'on-the-job' skill of interpreting blue prints through appropriate manual work on bench and machine."

This ingenious test will undoubtedly interest boys with the inclination to take machine shop courses. The product-moment correlation coefficient of .41 for 100 9th and 10th grade students between scores on this test and averaged ratings by two independent judges of layout, precision, and quality of work in making a small "c" clamp suggests a promising validity. Test-retest reliability is estimated at .86. Criterion reliability is estimated at .87 for ratings by two judges of the 100 students. A product-moment correlation coefficient of .51 between scores and the machine shop instructor's single rating is also promising ($r = .55$ with age partialled out).

The reference, "Validity of a Structural Dexterity Test" (1), gives evidence of careful experimental work on validity and on reliability, particularly the reliability of the criterion. Although reference to this article appears in the manual, the article presents the experimental results far more crisply and effectively than does the manual. The directions for administering the test could be improved. For example, in leading from the practice session into the beginning of Part 1, on which a 1-minute time limit is used, about 30 seconds of instructions appear after the wording "now you are ready to begin the test proper." A wording such as "now let me give you the instructions for the test proper" might result in more reliable scores. Test administration and scoring are time consuming.

Unfortunately, validity data for the *Revised Minnesota Paper Form Board* and the *MacQuarrie Test of Mechanical Ability* are not available on a comparative basis. One wonders whether one of these might not be as valid as the *Chriswell Structural Dexterity Test* in many technical and vocational high school situations and, at the same time, be far less costly to administer and score. (The manual appears to be overoptimistic in suggesting that as many as five examinees may be tested at one time by one examiner.) Perhaps other tests of ability to visualize and of dexterity might also be studied.

[877]

★**Group Test 80A.** Ages 15 and over; 1943-51; 1 form ['51]; no data on reliability and validity; mimeographed manual ['51]; separate answer sheets must be used; 27s. per 12 tests; 2s. 3d. per single copy; 1s. 6d. per 12 answer sheets; 2s. 3d. per manual; postage extra; 20(30) minutes; National Institute of Industrial Psychology. *

E. G. CHAMBERS, *Assistant Director of Research in Industrial Psychology, Psychological Laboratory, Cambridge, England.*

This test contains four subtests of spatial perception with practice examples for each. The first two subtests are called Turning Shapes Over; the third, Turning Shapes Round; and the fourth, Turning Shapes Over and Round. In each item a given shape has to be turned mentally and compared with four similar shapes, only one of which is the given shape turned over or round. Each subtest includes 20 items to be completed in 5 minutes, so that the overall time of the complete test is about 30 minutes. The score for the whole test is the number of correct answers less one third of the number of wrong answers to the nearest whole number. Norms from samples of unspecified size are given for boys in the general population for the ages 15-0 to 15-11 and 16+, and also for boys and girls of similar age in secondary grammar schools. No reliability or validation evidence is given.

The principle underlying the test is the recognition of shapes presented from different points of view, a principle common to most tests of spatial perception. The test is of moderate difficulty; the grading of difficulty in the subtests is obtained by making the four possible answers very similar in shape and size. This involves judgments of length of lines and size of angles which must be very close to the perceptual threshold in some instances since actual measurement is not allowed.

The test should be a useful one in the battery of the vocational adviser, but the reviewer feels that the rather arbitrary scoring system needs justification.

JOHN LIGGETT, *Lecturer in Applied Psychology, University of Durham, Newcastle, England.*

Group Test 80A consists of four sets of 20 spatial problems. In the first two tests, called Turning Shapes Over, the subject is required to select from four alternatives the shape which would be produced by laterally reversing the problem figures or, as the instructions say, by turning them over "sideways like a page of a book." The shapes employed range from simple parallelograms to complex irregular and overlapping figures. In the third test, Turning Shapes Round, the subject has to select from four alternatives the shape which represents an angular rotation in the same plane of the problem figure. Again a wide variety of shapes are employed, from triangles to irregular polygons. There appears to be no consistent principle underlying the selection of figures employed. The fourth set of problems, Turning Shapes Over and Round, requires the subject to imagine the problem figures both rotated and laterally reversed. The participation of the test administrator is limited to starting and timing the test and giving instructions to turn over pages at appropriate intervals. Detailed printed instructions are given to the subject on a separate printed page preceding each set of 20 problems and there are worked examples.

Norms issued with the test relate to (a) boys in the general population and (b) boys and girls from secondary grammar schools. Each group is subdivided into those above 16 years and those between 15 and 16 years. The manual gives no other information about the groups. The test publisher reports that the norms were obtained by giving a group both *Group Test 80A* and the *Form Relations Group Test*. Equivalent scores of the two tests were calculated from these data and norms for Test 80A were obtained from the *Form Relations Group Test* norms. The publisher indicates that Test 80A has been used mainly for industrial work, but that data from 1,738 school children have become available to check the norms.

The split-half reliability of the test, also reported by the publisher but not in the manual, is .86.

Though the aim and purpose of the test designer is nowhere stated, the main interest of the test presumably resides in its sensitivity to "spatial ability." The publisher, however, is unable to report any factorial or other studies which bear on this problem. The utility of the test as a cognitive measure is clearly limited by the scantiness of the normative data. It is possible, however, that the material may prove useful in original empirical studies (for example, in studies of brain damage), since the material is conveniently arranged and scoring is relatively simple. The investigator would no doubt want to consider very carefully the propriety, in relation to his special problem, of employing the verbal instructions as they stand. To use them would be to make serious assumptions about the verbal capacity of his subjects —assumptions which would render the test

much less a measure of "spatial ability" and much more a measure of other, including verbal, abilities.

[878]
*Mechanical Aptitude Test: Acorn National Aptitude Tests. Grades 7–16 and adults; 1943–52; 5 scores: comprehension of mechanical tasks, use of tools and materials (verbal), matching tools and operations, use of tools and materials (non-verbal), total; 1 form ('52, identical with test copyrighted in 1943); directions sheet ('43); no norms for part scores; $3 per 25 tests; 25¢ per manual ('45); 50¢ per specimen set; postage extra; 45(50) minutes; Andrew Kobal, J. Wayne Wrightstone, and Karl R. Kunze; Acorn Publishing Co. *

For reviews by Reign H. Bittner, James M. Porter, Jr., and Alec Rodger, see 3:669.

[879]
★Mellenbruch Mechanical Motivation Test. Grades 6–16 and adults; 1956–57; Forms A, B ('57); no norms for grades 14–16; $1.95 per 20 tests; $1 per specimen set (must be purchased to obtain manual) including 10 tests, manual ('56), and scoring key; postage extra; 35(40) minutes; P. L. Mellenbruch; Psychometric Affiliates. *

ARTHUR H. BRAYFIELD, *Professor of Psychology and Head of the Department, Pennsylvania State University, University Park, Pennsylvania.*

The antecedents of the present measure are to be found in the work of Rice, Toops, O'Rourke, and Stenquist who, almost 40 years ago, devised or developed picture recognition tests of mechanical information. Historically, such tests have had no clear rationale. They have been discussed by Fryer and Super in the context of interest measures; they also are components of tests labeled aptitude (Stenquist, O'Rourke). Actually, there has been so little empirical investigation of the nature of mechanical information tests of a picture recognition nature that it is difficult to appraise them with respect to a given rubric.

The brief manual for the *Mellenbruch Mechanical Motivation Test* explicitly states the fundamental assumption underlying the test: "Persons who are mechanically inclined are actively interested in all sorts of objects, machines and devices, and they are so definitely interested in these 'things' that they give attention to their uses, parts, and relationships. An adequate and proper sampling of one's 'recognition' of common objects and devices should therefore give us an index of one's mechanical inclination and hence his or her trainability." Apparently, the author attempted to measure a condition predictive of a person's ability to profit from training. It is clear that he was not interested in the conventional interest measure criterion of job satisfaction or continuance in an occupation.

The test consists of 84 pairs of items representing objects commonly seen and used (lamp, curling iron, skate key, bottle capper, hose coupling, etc.). The task is to match pairs of objects such as a faucet and its missing handle or an ice tong and an ice chopper. An item analysis of the responses of approximately 1,000 men and women was the basis for item selection. There are two forms available and the intercorrelation is given as .87, group unspecified. The test is easy to administer and score.

The print job is rather poor and the shading of some of the representations of objects affords cues for correct discriminations. Items which are not easily related on the basis of relative size or shape are included. This probably increases the difficulty level of a number of otherwise fairly obvious items.

Odd-even and alternate-form reliabilty coefficients are of the order of .87. The groups studied are not described and the existence of sex differences may have inflated these results if they are for combined groups. More data are needed.

Correlations with intelligence test scores are low but positive. Among a group of Air Force officers, the correlation with a test described only as "Stenquist (Rev.)" is .50. For a group of Air Force employees, the correlation with an Air Force mechanical information test is .61.

Among 57 women engineering drawing students, the test correlates .59 with a criterion described only as teacher estimates or teacher rank. The only other "validation" study reported is for 430 general population members whose test scores correlated .60 with "mechanical activities." This criterion appears to be an index (self-report) of the level of complexity of mechanical skill attained by the respondent through choice or necessity. Its significance as a criterion is problematical. Validation data for the test are inadequate.

There is an increase in mean scores by grade and therefore by age level among the groups sampled. Persons in selected mechanical pursuits (i.e., graduate mechanical engineers and aircraft shop men) make higher mean scores than does the general public. These findings are so inadequately reported that it is impossible to gain much information from them. There are significant (reviewer's estimate) sex differences.

Separate sex norms are available. The most extensive norms are by school grade groups. The general public norm groups are undescribed; there are norms for one male and two female occupational groups. The norms are inadequate.

This is an experimental edition (although not so labeled by the publisher) of a measure of one type of mechanical information about which very little useful data are reported in the limited one-sheet (printed on both sides) manual. There is little or no evidence stemming from the operations involved in developing the test which would justify its designation as a test of mechanical motivation. The test is sufficiently ingenious in conception and execution to merit inclusion in research projects concerned both with practical prediction problems and the theoretical problems involved in untangling the relationships among interest, aptitude, achievement, and satisfaction. Perhaps the test author's primary contribution has been to keep alive the historic *prospect* that interest *may* be appraised through the assessment of informational backgrounds.

JOHN B. MORRIS, *Associate Professor of Psychology, and Director of Institutional Research, The University of Mississippi, University, Mississippi.*

The rationale for this test is that persons who are mechanically inclined are actively interested in all sorts of objects, machines, and devices and attend to their uses, parts, and relationships. The author believes that one's recognition of a sample of common objects and devices should yield an index of one's mechanical inclination and hence his mechanical trainability. The assumption that this technique measures motivation to the extent implied by the name given the test seems somewhat tenuous to this reviewer. In fact, the word "motivation" does not occur at any place in the manual except in the title, and the test is discussed in terms of its ability to measure "mechanical inclination" and "mechanical aptitude."

The task involved in the test consists of matching a mechanical object in the stimulus column with the object most closely related to it in an adjacent column. To reduce chance success, extra objects are included in each response group. The item quality appears to be good throughout the test, but the reproductions on tests furnished for review were, in many cases, of very poor quality.

There are 84 items on each form of the test, and they are so arranged that the same scoring key may be used on either form. The two forms are structurally similar and appear to be equivalent. A correlation of .87 is reported between the two forms, but no indication of the group used to obtain this figure is given.

In general, the test statistics reported leave something to be desired. For example, the odd-even reliability is reported as .88, but no indication is given as to whether this is a corrected figure or not. Moreover, there is some doubt as to the applicability of this technique for determining reliability anyway, inasmuch as the test is timed and no information is furnished to indicate the adequacy of the time allowed.

The validities reported for the test appear to be relatively high for specific cases. The correlation between test scores and teacher rank for women in engineering drawing classes was .59; between test scores and rank on a mechanical activities scale for the general public, .60. The test also correlated fairly well with other tests of mechanical aptitude; with tests of general intelligence the correlation was positive but low.

Percentile norms for several vocational groups, for men and women of the general public, and for boys and girls in grades 7 through 12 are supplied in the manual. In addition, mean scores are given for several selected groups. The manual states that these indicate that the test differentiates between the various groups. While there is a difference of about 4 points between the means of most groups, no indication of the amount of variability present in each group is given, making it difficult to assess the significance of the differences.

That this test has promise is evidenced by the relatively high validity coefficients reported. At the present time, however, some of the author's recommendations for use of it in employment and placement seem unjustified in the light of the scarcity of evidence. A more comprehensive and straightforward manual and a more descriptive title would do much to overcome some of this reviewer's objections.

[880]

★N.I.I.P. Squares Test. Grades 9 and over; 1944–51; formerly published by National Institute of Industrial Psychology; title on test is *Squares Test;* 1 form ['44]; mimeographed directions sheet ['51]; no data on reliability and validity; norms ['58] for first year university students only; 2s. 6d. per 10 tests; 6d. per scoring key; 6d. per directions and norms sheet; 1s. 3d. per specimen set; postpaid within Australia; 10(15) minutes; National Institute of Industrial Psychology; Australian Council for Educational Research. *

REFERENCES

1. HOLLIDAY, FRANK. "An Investigation Into the Selection of Apprentices for the Engineering Industry." *Occupational Psychol* 14:69–81 Ap '40. * (*PA* 14:3710)
2. SLATER, PATRICK. "Some Group Tests of Spatial Judgment or Practical Ability." *Occupational Psychol* 14:40–55 Ja '40. * (*PA* 14:2644)
3. HOLLIDAY, FRANK. "A Further Investigation Into the Selection of Apprentices for the Engineering Industry." *Occupational Psychol* 15:173–84 O '41. * (*PA* 16:732)
4. SLATER, PATRICK. "Tests for Selecting Secondary and Technical School Children." *Occupational Psychol* 15:10–25 Ja '41. * (*PA* 15:3177)
5. SHUTTLEWORTH, CLIFFORD W. "Tests of Technical Aptitude." *Occupational Psychol* 16:175–82 O '42. *
6. SLATER, PATRICK, AND BENNETT, ELIZABETH. "The Development of Spatial Judgment and Its Relation to Some Educational Problems." *Occupational Psychol* 17:139–55 Jl '43. *
7. LINGWOOD, JOAN. "Test Performances of ATS Recruits From Certain Civilian Occupations." *Occupational Psychol* 26:35–46 Ja '52. * (*PA* 26:6567)
8. HOHNE, H. H. *Success and Failure in Scientific Faculties of the University of Melbourne.* Melbourne, Australia: Australian Council for Educational Research, 1955. Pp. vii, 129. * (*PA* 31:3787)
9. KRATHWOHL, DAVID R., AND CRONBACH, LEE J. "Suggestions Regarding a Possible Measure of Personality: The Squares Test." *Ed & Psychol Meas* 16:305–16 au '56. *

J. F. CLARK, *Professor of Applied Psychology, New South Wales University of Technology, Kensington, New South Wales, Australia.*

This test was prepared as a spatial test by the National Institute of Industrial Psychology in London almost two decades ago. It has been reprinted without alteration by the Australian Council for Educational Research.

The test consists of 54 items of increasing difficulty, each of which is completed by drawing a straight line to divide an irregular two-dimensional figure into two smaller figures which when fitted together make a square. Thus it requires the person taking the test to be constructive, differing in this respect from those tests requiring simply a choice between a series of possible answers.

First impressions are that this is a promising test, but experience by psychologists using it over the years in Britain and Australia has shown that the test has only limited usefulness.

There are no norms, reliability, or validation data supplied by either of the distributors so the value of the test can be established only by using it. Those who have developed their own norms and validation data find that the test assists them only in a limited way for very specific purposes. It cannot, therefore, be recommended for general use.

[881]

★**Newcastle Spatial Test.** Ages 10-0 to 11-11; 1958–59; selection of students for technical schools or courses; 1 form ('58); mimeographed manual of instructions ['58]; provisional norms ['59]; no data on reliability and validity; 203s. 6d. per 100 tests; 3s. 6d. per manual; 3s. per single copy; postage extra; 39(60–70) minutes; I. Macfarlane Smith and J. S. Lawes; distributed by Department of Education, King's College, University of Durham, Newcastle upon Tyne, England. *

[882]

★**O'Rourke Mechanical Aptitude Test.** Adults; 1939–57; Forms A ('57), B ('39), C ('39); key-manual sheets (no dates); no data on reliability; $4.50 per 50 tests of Form A; $3.25 per 50 tests of Forms B or C; postage extra; 25¢ per specimen set, postpaid; 55(65) minutes; L. J. O'Rourke; Psychological Institute. *

[883]

★**Purdue Mechanical Performance Test.** Ages 17 and over; 1957; 4 scores: transfer boards, spatial relations, hub assemblies, total; individual; 1 form ['57]; manual ['57]; record sheet, Form A ['57]; $175 per set of test materials; postage extra; (20) minutes; Ernest J. McCormick and Robert L. Brown; Lafayette Instrument Co. *

REFERENCE

1. BROWN, ROBERT LEE. *The Development and Validation of a Mechanical Performance Test.* Doctor's thesis, Purdue University (Lafayette, Ind.), 1957. *(DA 17:1583)*

[884]

Revised Minnesota Paper Form Board Test. Grades 9–16 and adults; 1930–48; IBM; 2 forms, 2 editions; manual ('48); 35¢ per specimen set; postpaid; 20(25) minutes; original test by Donald G. Paterson, Richard M. Elliott, L. Dewey Anderson, Herbert A. Toops, and Edna Heidbreder; revision by Rensis Likert and William H. Quasha; Psychological Corporation. *
a) [HAND SCORING EDITION.] 1930–48; Forms AA ('41), BB ('41); $2.10 per 25 tests; French edition (Forms AA-FE, BB-FE, '55) available.
b) [MACHINE SCORING EDITION.] 1941–48; IBM; Forms MA ('41), MB ('41); $3 per 25 tests; $1.90 per 50 IBM answer sheets.

REFERENCES

1–9. See 40:1673.
10–57. See 3:677.
58–95. See 4:763.
96. EDWARDS, KARL D. *Work-Limit vs Time-Limit Scores on the Minnesota Paper Form Board Test.* Master's thesis, Kansas State College (Manhattan, Kan.), 1945.
97. FERSON, REGIS F. *The Probabilities of Success in Trade Training as Estimated by Standardized Tests.* Doctor's thesis, University of Pittsburgh (Pittsburgh, Pa.), 1951.
98. LITTLETON, ISAAC T. "Prediction in Auto Trade Courses." *J Appl Psychol* 36:15–9 F '52. * *(PA 26:7256)*
99. MOFFIE, DANNIE J., AND MILTON, CHARLES R. "The Relationship of Certain Psychological Test Scores to Academic Success in Chemical Engineering." Abstract. *Am Psychol* 7:379–80 Jl '52. *
100. NEWMAN, SIDNEY H.; FRENCH, JOHN W.; AND BOBBITT, JOSEPH M. "Analysis of Criteria for the Validation of Selection Measures at the United States Coast Guard Academy." *Ed & Psychol Meas* 12:394–407 au '52. * *(PA 27:6159)*
101. BODLEY, E. A. "Selection Tests for Women Packers." *B Ind Psychol & Personnel Prac* 9:24–32 Mr '53. *
102. COLEMAN, WILLIAM. "An Economical Test Battery for Predicting Freshman Engineering Course Grades." *J Appl Psychol* 37:465–7 D '53. * *(PA 29:1562)*
103. JENKINS, JAMES J. "Some Measured Characteristics of Air Force Weather Forecasters and Success in Forecasting." *J Appl Psychol* 37:440–4 D '53. * *(PA 29:1642)*
104. "Validity Information Exchange. No. 7-095: D.O.T. Code 7-94.112 and 7-94.100, Tool and Die and Machinist Apprentice." *Personnel Psychol* 7:573 w '54. *
105. BALINSKY, BENJAMIN, AND HUJSA, CHARLES. "Performance of College Students on a Mechanical Knowledge Test." *J Appl Psychol* 38:111–2 Ap '54. * *(PA 29:3028)*

106. DuBOIS, PHILLIP H., AND WATSON, ROBERT I. "Validity Information Exchange, No. 7-075: D.O.T. Code 2-66.23, Policeman." *Personnel Psychol* 7:414–7 au '54. *
107. GUAZZO, EUGENE J., JR. *Predicting Academic Success of Architecture Students.* Master's thesis, Alabama Polytechnic Institute (Auburn, Ala.), 1954.
108. HUEBER, JOANNE. "Validity Information Exchange, No. 7-089: D.O.T. Code 5-83.641, Maintenance Mechanic II." *Personnel Psychol* 7:565–6 w '54. *
109. SCHMITZ, ROY M., AND HOLMES, JOHN L. "Relationship of Certain Measured Abilities to Freshman Engineering Achievement," pp. 32–42. *(PA 29:1584)* In *Selection and Counseling of Students in Engineering.* Edited by Wilbur L. Layton. Minnesota Studies in Student Personnel Work, No. 4. Minneapolis, Minn.: University of Minnesota Press, 1954. Pp. iv, 89. *
110. CANTONI, LOUIS J. "High School Tests and Measurements as Predictors of Occupational Status." *J Appl Psychol* 39:253–5 Ag '55. * *(PA 30:4722)*
111. CUOMO, SYLVIA, AND MEYER, HERBERT H. "Validity Information Exchange, No. 8-19: D.O.T. Code 6-78.632, Floor Assembler." *Personnel Psychol* 8:270 su '55. *
112. HOHNE, H. H. *Success and Failure in Scientific Faculties of the University of Melbourne.* Melbourne, Australia: Australian Council for Educational Research, 1955. Pp. vii, 129. * *(PA 31:3787)*
113. MALLOY, JOHN P.; WYSOCKI, BOLESLAW; AND GRAHAM, LEO F. "Predicting Attrition-Survival in First Year Engineering." *J Ed Psychol* 46:217–21 Ap '55. * *(PA 30:1624)*
114. PATTERSON, CECIL H. *Test and Background Factors Related to Drop-Outs in an Industrial Institute.* Doctor's thesis, University of Minnesota (Minneapolis, Minn.), 1955. *(DA 15:1024)*
115. PERRINE, MERVYN WILLIAM. "The Selection of Drafting Trainees." *J Appl Psychol* 39:57–61 F '55. * *(PA 30:1725)*
116. POIDEVIN, B. "A Test Battery to Select Knitting Machine Operators." *Personnel Pract B* 11:22–6 Mr '55. * *(PA 30:3577)*
117. SMITH, OTTO B. *Predicting Grade Success of High School Students in Radio and Drafting.* Master's thesis, Alabama Polytechnic Institute (Auburn, Ala.), 1955.
118. BRUCE, MARTIN M. "Normative Data Information Exchange, No. 16." *Personnel Psychol* 9:392 au '56. *
119. OTTERNESS, WILLIAM B.; PATTERSON, C. H.; JOHNSON, R. H.; AND PETERSON, LENNIS R. "Trade School Norms for Some Commonly Used Tests." *J Appl Psychol* 40:57–60 F '56. * *(PA 31:3803)*
120. PATTERSON, C. H. "The Prediction of Attrition in Trade School Courses." *J Appl Psychol* 40:154–8 Je '56. * *(PA 31:6680)*
121. BRUCE, MARTIN M. "Normative Data Information Exchange, No. 10-5." *Personnel Psychol* 10:99–100 sp '57. *
122. BRUCE, MARTIN M. "Normative Data Information Exchange, No. 10-6." *Personnel Psychol* 10:101–2 sp '57. *
123. SPEER, GEORGE S. "Validity Information Exchange, No. 10-13: D.O.T. Code 0-88.31, Ship Pilot." *Personnel Psychol* 10:201 su '57. *
124. BARRETT, RICHARD S. "The Process of Predicting Job Performance." *Personnel Psychol* 11:39–57 sp '58. *

D. W. McELWAIN, *Professor of Psychology, The University of Queensland, Brisbane, Australia.*

The "form board" setting of problems was established in the earliest days of mental testing. Edouard Seguin developed what was probably the first set before 1850, and the use of such tests was well known before Binet began his work in Paris. The test was thought to be what we would now call a nonverbal measure of general cognitive capacity.

Spearman as early as 1905 conceived cognitive capacity to have a single underlying factor which he termed *g*. The first breakdown of this position came from the work of El Koussy, who showed that it was reasonable to posit a "space" factor to account for the intercorrelations of certain tests which could not be accounted for solely in terms of general capacity. The Minnesota researches of Paterson and others about 1930 into mechanical ability confirmed the existence of this special capacity to handle spatial relations. The *Minnesota Paper Form Board Test* arose from these studies. This test was later revised by Likert and Quasha to produce the present test.

The test has had many "pirate" forms, and although these may offend its originators, they are a tribute to the appeal of the test. The pirated forms are amazingly diverse in layout but maintain an extraordinary fidelity in the reproduction of the specific test items.

One of the most vexatious problems about the test has been the time provided. Some have preferred to emphasize the power function and to give a "long time" of 20 minutes or more. No one doubts that the late items in the test are difficult. Others have argued that there is no demonstrable increase in validity after 15 minutes' testing. The result has been a confused literature on the test. The authors plead for a fixed time of 20 minutes. A definitive investigation on the effects of time for testing on various validities would be welcomed.

There are many convincing studies on the usefulness of the test, especially where "spatial imagery" is a requirement, such as in engineering, architecture, military tactical exercises, drafting, fitting, and so forth. The predictions however are generally of the same order as are given by intelligence tests.

The factor loading of the test is not wholly clear, and in any case appears to alter with age and with sex.

The test appears to serve usefully even if regarded merely as a general test of cognitive capacity in a nonverbal medium.

Some recent investigations which have been undertaken with very primitive preliterates in the Territory of Papua and New Guinea show that the test if presented more concretely with moveable parts is a good predictor of "educable potential."

The five years since the *Mental Measurements Yearbook* last reviewed this test have provided no essentially new material but have confirmed that the test has a very useful place in the battery of the psychometrician.

For reviews by Clifford E. Jurgensen and Raymond A. Katzell, see 4:763; for a review by Dewey B. Stuit, see 3:677; for a review by Alec Rodger, see 40:1673.

[885]

Spatial Tests I and II. Ages 11-0 to 13-11, 10-7 to 13-11; 1950–56; 1 form; 2 tests; distribution is restricted to directors of education; 13s. 6d. per 12 tests; 1s. 3d. per single copy; 3s. 6d. per manual; postage extra; National Foundation for Educational Research in England and Wales. *

a) SPATIAL TEST I. Ages 11-0 to 13-11; 1950; 1 form ['50]; manual ['50]; 41(60) minutes; I. Macfarlane Smith.

b) SPATIAL TEST II. Ages 10-7 to 13-11; 1950–56; 1 form ['51]; manual ['51]; provisional norms ['56]; no data on reliability and validity; 26.5(45) minutes; A. F. Watts with the assistance of D. A. Pidgeon and M. K. B. Richards.

REFERENCE

1. SMITH, I. MACFARLANE. "Measuring Spatial Ability in School Pupils." *Occupational Psychol* 22:150–9 Jl '48. * (PA 23:1181)

E. G. CHAMBERS, *Assistant Director of Research in Industrial Psychology, Psychological Laboratory, Cambridge, England.*

Test I, designed for use in allocating children to technical courses, has six subtests: Fitting Shapes, Form Recognition, Pattern Recognition, Shape Recognition, Comparisons, and Form Reflections. These all deal with two-dimensional figures and patterns. According to the manual, the test has been shown to have a high loading in the spatial factor as well as in the general factor, and it "has been found to give high correlations with assessments in technical drawing."

Test II has five subtests: Match Box Corners, Shapes and Models, Square Completion, Paper Folding, and Block Building. All except the third of these involve three-dimensional representations.

These tests embody a number of principles involved in spatial perception, some of which are not commonly found in spatial tests. Although rather lengthy, the subtests are of sufficient variety to maintain interest and endeavour. They should be useful instruments in the hands of those responsible for allocating children to further training in technical disciplines, although no direct evidence of validation is given.

CHARLES T. MYERS, *Associate in Test Development, Educational Testing Service, Princeton, New Jersey.*

These tests have a very important advantage over most spatial tests in that they each use a variety of item types in separately timed parts. In general the directions for each type are clear and effective. The printing is good. The tests appear to be easy to administer. The item difficulty is well suited to the groups for which the tests are intended. The whole of the possible score range was effectively used by the norms sample. In these respects it would be hard to find a better spatial test. Unfortunately, the effect of these good qualities is mitigated by the serious lack of information in the manual about the reliability and validity of these tests and the norms for them.

Test I begins with Fitting Shapes, a test made up of items of the familiar paper form-board type. The next part, Form Recognition, is a multiple choice test of the Gottschaldt figures shown by Thurstone to be a measure of what he called the second closure factor. The other four item types, which are less familiar, call for matching or comparison of simple shapes. The total number of items is 100.

Test II, also a 100-item test, begins with Match Box Corners, a test which presumably measures Thurstone's first spatial factor. The second and fourth tests are Shapes and Models, which is a variety of surface development problem, and Paper Folding. Both of these tests are probably measures of Thurstone's second spatial factor, which has generally proved to be more valid than the first for most of the purposes for which spatial tests are used. Until more research has been done, however, it is probably wise to use somewhat heterogeneous measures to be on the safe side. It is too easy for a test taker to get off the track on a single spatial item type. The Shapes and Models item type has the same complication that seems to be present in the original *Minnesota Spatial Relations Test*—that a good deal of effort is required to find the figures you are looking for and that observation and memory have a large influence on test variance.

The selection of the item types used in these tests was in part based on research conducted in 1934 and reported in 1948 by I. Macfarlane Smith (1). Unfortunately, two of the six item types used in Test I and four of the five item types used in Test II were not included in this research and no information is given about these other item types. It may well be as ridiculous to assume that a test is a valid spatial test merely because it is presented pictorially as it would be to assume that a test is a valid vocabulary test merely because it is presented verbally. Tests of history, science, or music appreciation can be presented verbally. The United States Air Force research has demonstrated

that there are many different factors that can be measured by graphic tests. Even the above mentioned article demonstrated that several graphic item types failed to have any loadings on the spatial, or *k,* factor. All the item types used in these tests appear to be appropriate to the purpose of the test, but it would be sounder to have some better criterion than subjective judgment. Incidentally, several of the item types would probably be inappropriate for spatial testing at a higher level.

British and American psychologists generally have tended to disagree about the number and significance of the different factors that can be found in different graphic tests. The evidence on both sides of the argument still seems to be inconclusive, although, in general, the British point of view that there is only one spatial factor seems better borne out in studies of children and the American concept of several spatial factors is supported largely by studies of adults. One's judgment of the quality of these tests is, therefore, likely to depend in part on a judgment about this controversy.

Strangely enough in view of this, Test II has been designated "three dimensional." This reviewer is unaware of any research that shows a significant difference between so-called two-dimensional tests and three-dimensional tests. Further, a subjective examination of the item types used in Test II casts serious doubt about the fact that these item types are really three-dimensional. Three of the five item types do use drawings of three-dimensional objects, but the problems can always be solved in terms of successive two-dimensional steps. It is true that these item types can be distinguished from those in Test I in terms of complexity and this complexity seems in these three item types to be a by-product of the use of three-dimensional figures. In the reviewer's judgment, the complexity of the problems, the amount of inference required in their solution, the effect of time limits, and the degree of perceptual discrimination needed are all far more important than the number of dimensions in the objects represented in the drawings.

A further judgment, supported to some extent by United States Air Force research, is that the element of perceptual discrimination is likely to decrease the validity of a spatial test for most important criteria. Scales, dividers, and measuring tapes are easily bought and applied, thus minimizing the importance of perceptual discrimination, but the ability to solve spatial problems is not so easily obtained. A number of spatial tests, such as the famous *Revised Minnesota Paper Form Board Test,* seem to be measuring in part a trivial skill since in so many problems the difference between a right and a wrong answer is only a very small difference in the length of a line. Tests I and II have this characteristic to only a small extent, but in a number of problems it is difficult for the test taker to know how careful his discrimination must be. This unintended problem is likely to have the effect of distracting him from the problem that he is supposed to solve. This ambiguity also leads to some difficulty in scoring. Since there are so many possible ways of presenting spatial problems, it seems unfortunate that item types should be used where this is a problem. However, there seems to be no general consensus among testmakers, nor any clear statements, as to what type of mental activity they are trying to elicit with spatial tests and a testmaker may be justified in using his own judgment in this regard.

With tests that are intended for a purpose as abstruse as these, it would be well for the author to make a clear statement in the manual of what he thought his test would measure, taking more than a phrase to say whether it was spatial reasoning, visual imagery, ability to read drawings, adaptability to unfamiliar and nonverbal problems, mechanical intelligence, or something else. There are a number of less general comments that might be made about the tests and manuals. We would like to know how similar these tests are to the tests that were validated in Smith's study. We would also like more information about the sample on which the reliability estimate was based and about the conditions of the test-retest administrations. The norms sample should be more fully described in terms of age distribution, class in school, and sex. This reviewer would prefer norms based exclusively on boys since in most tasks in which this ability is pertinent a girl is likely to be competing mostly with boys. Some information should always be given about the speededness of tests. Although these tests do not appear to be speeded, this does not prove that speed of work is irrelevant. If used in America, the directions for administration would

need some slight revisions to clarify some British expressions for American children.

The norms of these tests are somewhat like IQ's since they have a mean of 100 and a standard deviation of 15. It is interesting to note that they have a smaller change with age than do intelligence quotients. Is this the result of some peculiarity of the norms sample or some lack of representativeness at each age level, or is it because this ability matures earlier and has nearly reached a peak by the age of 13?

In summary, then, these tests appear to have more good qualities than undesirable ones. Their variety of item types and their simple and effective directions particularly commend their use. They deserve further study and a more complete manual.

For a review by E. A. Peel of Spatial Test I, *see 4:753.*

[886]
*Survey of Mechanical Insight. Grades 9–16 and adults; 1945–55; IBM; 1 form ('55); manual ('55); no college norms; $4.20 per 35 tests; separate answer sheets may be used; 3¢ per IBM answer sheet; 20¢ per machine scoring stencil; 50¢ per specimen set; postage extra; 30(40) minutes; Daniel R. Miller; California Test Bureau. *

REFERENCES

1. MARTIN, GLENN C. "Test Batteries for Trainees in Auto Mechanics and Apparel Design." *J Appl Psychol* 35:20–2 F '51. * (*PA* 25:7123)
2. POE, WESLEY A., AND BERG, IRWIN A. "Psychological Test Performance of Steel Industry Production Supervisors." *J Appl Psychol* 36:234–7 Ag '52. * (*PA* 27:3794)
3. WORPELL, DONALD FREDERICK. *A Study of Selection Factors and the Development of Objective Criteria for Measuring Success in a Co-operative General Machine Shop Training Program.* Doctor's thesis, University of Michigan (Ann Arbor, Mich.), 1956. (*DA* 17:1270)

ARTHUR H. BRAYFIELD, *Professor of Psychology and Head of the Department, Pennsylvania State University, University Park, Pennsylvania.*

As stated in the manual, "the test is made up of thirty-five three-response multiple-choice items. Each item includes a drawing of a mechanical device. To the right of the drawing is a statement concerning some aspect of the machine's operation. Beneath this statement are three possible responses from which the examinee must choose the one that is most correct." The items appear to be based on general principles of mechanics.

This is a revision of the 1945 edition. According to the manual, "the figures in the test have been redrawn and the items have been arranged in order of difficulty." The directions for administration have been revised and the materials have been arranged in a new format.

The manual makes the claim that previous experience "operates minimally in this test, since the pictures do not depict machines that are currently being used." No data are presented to bolster this assertion.

Reliability data are inadequate. For a sample of 250 male and female trade and industrial personnel, the split-half corrected coefficient is .88; this probably is inflated due to sex differences. A second sample of 297 male applicants for laborer jobs with a large oil company gives a Kuder-Richardson formula 20 coefficient of .87.

Validity data are presented for four occupational groups. The test has been found to discriminate between "high" and "low" rated supervisors ($n = 33$) in a steel manufacturing plant. The publisher also presents data for 50 postage meter repairmen, 45 lathe operator trainees, and 45 auto mechanic trainees, using the criteria, respectively, of supervisor's merit ratings, instructor's ratings, and instructor's ratings of classroom work. The correlations are in the .40's. No reference is made to the nature of the ratings, their reliability, or the circumstances under which they were obtained.

The SMI has been correlated with scores on three other mechanical tests with r's generally in the .60's. The most informative is the correlation of .66 with Mechanical Reasoning of the *Differential Aptitude Tests* for 40 oil company construction department applicants. Apparently the same sample was used in an appraisal of the relationship between SMI scores and educational level; the correlation was .21. However, no grade distribution is given so that it is difficult to judge the results. The reviewer rank-ordered eight occupational norm groups on the basis of his judgment of general ability level requirements and correlated these rankings with the median SMI scores reported for the samples. The rank-order correlation was .9 which suggests that general ability *may* be significantly related to SMI scores. However, this is merely suggestive of further investigation of the relationship.

In short, there is some "loose" evidence for the validity of the test in predicting performance in a few mechanically related occupations, especially during the training period. However, the manual does not explicitly state that the validity data and the intertest correlations refer to the revised 1955 edition and, in fact, two of the validation studies almost surely were done with the original 1945 edition. The correlation between the two editions is not reported.

Nine additional norm groups are furnished in the revised manual for a total of 10. Obviously these samples were obtained on a fortuitous basis; seven are job applicant samples. The norms are not particularly helpful. Separate sex norms are not provided, although there is some evidence in one of the tables that, at least at the 10th grade level, there may be significant sex differences.

The publisher suggests that the per cent of items attempted be used for diagnostic purposes to classify four types of examinees. This is a dubious procedure and no evidence is given to back up the recommendation.

The manual itself is, in the reviewer's judgment, marked by ambiguity and a certain amount of indirection which amounts to overselling. For one example, there is overemphasis upon the use of a "short, single instrument" for selection purposes. This caters to an unfortunate trend in industrial testing which already is too prevalent.

In summary, the *Survey of Mechanical Insight* is a perhaps "promising" instrument for specific selection validation research although it should be "pitted" against other tests such as the Bennett *Test of Mechanical Comprehension,* which has a much more substantial history of test development. Its present utility for counseling is minimal. Research on the influence of previous experience and training is a very real need, particularly in view of "come on" statements in the manual.

For reviews by Reign H. Bittner, Jay L. Otis, and Shailer Peterson of the original edition, see 3:680.

[887]

*Survey of Object Visualization. Grades 9–16 and adults; 1945–55; IBM; 1 form ('55); manual ('55); $3.50 per 35 tests; separate answer sheets may be used; 3¢ per IBM answer sheet; 20¢ per scoring stencil; postage extra; 50¢ per specimen set, postpaid; Spanish edition available; 25(30) minutes; Daniel R. Miller; California Test Bureau. *

REFERENCES

1. WEISS, IRVING. "Prediction of Academic Success in Dental School." *J Appl Psychol* 36:11–4 F '52. * (PA 26:7296)
2. LAYTON, WILBUR L. "Predicting Success in Dental School." *J Appl Psychol* 37:251–5 Ag '53. * (PA 28:6712)
3. LYNCH, BENJAMIN L. *The Miller Object Visualization Test as a Prognostic Aid in Dental Education.* Master's thesis, Creighton University (Omaha, Neb.), 1953.
4. WEBB, SAM C. "The Prediction of Achievement for First Year Dental Students." *Ed & Psychol Meas* 16:543–8 w '56. * (PA 32:962)

5. WORPELL, DONALD FREDERICK. *A Study of Selection Factors and the Development of Objective Criteria for Measuring Success in a Co-operative General Machine Shop Training Program.* Doctor's thesis, University of Michigan (Ann Arbor, Mich.), 1956. (*DA* 17:1270)

WILLIAM J. MICHEELS, *Professor of Industrial Education and Chairman of the Department, University of Minnesota, Minneapolis, Minnesota.*

This test is designed "to measure aptitude for solving problems in perceptual recognition of an object's appearance in altered position or shape." The instrument is intended to be useful in identifying the ability to perceive spatial relationships.

Each of the 44 multiple choice problems consists of a flat pattern which, if folded on the dotted lines or rolled together correctly, would take the shape of one of the four objects pictured as options. To select the correct response, the examinee must be able to visualize the three-dimensional shape that the pattern would assume.

In the 1955 revision the items have been rearranged "in order of difficulty." Apparently this was done on the basis of an item analysis, although the technique is not mentioned. The major improvement of the new edition is in the test manual which now contains more validation and normative data. Directions for administration have been revised in order to insure more uniform administration of the test.

The 10 norm groups include a sample of 250 males and females in what is called the "general population"; worker groups in aircraft, petroleum refining, and drafting; and college students or applicants in dentistry (the largest group), engineering, clothing construction, and general college students. A catalog description of the survey states that it is appropriate for grade 9 through the adult level. The manual mentions young people and school students, but no meaningful data are included with respect to uses of the test at these lower levels. One wonders about the sampling adequacy in obtaining data for several of the norm groups. Most of the reported experiences in using the test refer to applicants for dental schools.

Reliability coefficients of .91 (split-half) and .92 (Kuder-Richardson formula 21) are reported for two different populations—a sample ($n = 266$) of male and female trade and industrial personnel and a sample ($n = 188$) of general helpers in the petroleum refining industry. Validity is indicated by a correlation coefficient of .44 between scores on the survey and freshmen technic grades in a dental school.

It would be interesting to see some data on survey test scores in relation to previous experiences with layout work or elementary drafting. The manual states that the test is "so designed that aptitude rather than experience is sampled." This is a moot question. More information is needed on the rationale and construction of the test.

The reviewer gave the test to an advanced graduate student with an engineering background. He reported that after working several items he stopped trying to visualize the total pattern and adopted a logical analysis approach wherein he identified the shape of a base, which usually eliminated one or two answer choices, and then counted sides or parts. With the aid of a few handy rules known to most persons familiar with layout work, it became rather easy to pick out the right selections without any conscious effort at visualizing the whole object. This is reported as an observation rather than a criticism since it may be that logical analysis is an important part of the visualization process. This leads the reviewer to suggest that the survey might serve a useful purpose as a pretest for courses in engineering graphics or mechanical drafting.

For those occupations that require this type of visualization ability, the test can serve a useful purpose. It can be quickly administered and easily scored. The new manual contains information on the several ways in which the test results might be used.

For reviews by Charles M. Harsh, Clifford E. Jurgensen, Shailer Peterson, and Patrick Slater of the original edition, see 3:681.

[888]
Survey of Space Relations Ability. Grades 9–16 and adults; 1944–49; IBM; Forms A ('44), B ('47); manual ('49); $4.20 per 35 tests; separate answer sheets may be used; 3¢ per IBM answer sheet; 20¢ per scoring stencil; postage extra; 25¢ per specimen set, postpaid; Spanish edition available; 15(20) minutes; Harry W. Case and Floyd Ruch; California Test Bureau. *

REFERENCES

1. CASE, HARRY W. "Selection of Aircraft Engineering Draftsmen and Designers." *J Appl Psychol* 31:583–8 D '47. * (*PA* 22:2769)
2. AMERICAN GAS ASSOCIATION, PERSONNEL COMMITTEE. *Personnel Testing in the Gas Industry.* New York: the Association, January 1952. Pp. 10. *
3. CASE, HARRY W. "The Relationship of Certain Tests to Grades Achieved in an Industrial Class in Aircraft Design." *Ed & Psychol Meas* 12:90–5 sp '52. * (*PA* 27:6106)

Survey of Object Visualization

4. Poe, Wesley A., and Berg, Irwin A. "Psychological Test Performance of Steel Industry Production Supervisors." *J Appl Psychol* '36:234–7 Ag '52. * (*PA* 27:3794)

D. W. McElwain, *Professor of Psychology, University of Queensland, Brisbane, Australia.*

This is a so-called space relations test. It is clearly a derivative of the *Minnesota Paper Form Board Test* which in turn comes from El Koussy's studies under Spearman on the "space" group factor done about 1928. In the Minnesota test the testee is given some "parts" and asked which of 5 wholes could be made from the parts, but in this test he is given a whole and asked which parts from 10 given would make up the whole. The tests are otherwise similar—both being group, pencil and paper, two-dimensional, machine scorable tests scored with a correction for wrong answers.

The test has a "gimmick" in that the problems are presented in coarse white lines on a blue background, instead of fine black lines on a white background as in the Minnesota test. The blue printing is supposed to give the subject the impression that the test is fair and practical, since the test simulates blueprints. Since there are now better methods of reproduction of plans than blueprinting, the typography has no other virtue than novelty, or perhaps historical interest.

The standardization of the test is adequate. There are two parallel forms, though no direct data other than a bald assertion that they are alternate forms are presented concerning the equality of the forms. Relatively high reliability is reported.

The test has a practice section with but two items. Tests of this kind usually show large short-term practice effects which, unless diminished by longer fore-practice, decrease the validity of the test. This is particularly true if the subjects are nonacademic, as we might expect them to be if they are candidates for selection for training in skilled manual trades.

The format of the test is attractive. The directions for administering and scoring are clear. The scoring provides for what is in effect a rights minus wrongs formula (where the wrongs include omissions). It would be surprising if this formula rather than rights minus an empirically determined fraction of wrongs is optimal for validity.

The validity coefficients reported (correlations with supervisors' ratings and teachers' grades) are such as one would expect, generally ranging from the .30's to the .60's. They are probably of the same order as would obtain for any group, cognitive capacity, pencil and paper, nonverbal test, using the criteria selected. This type of validity evidence is often useful, but one looks for any significant increase in predictive or selective capacity that a test of this kind can provide over and above that of the "ordinary" intelligence test. No such evidence is provided.

In short, the original features of this test (requiring the selection of parts to make a given whole and using white lines and blue background) are probably insignificant changes. The test is seemingly no better and probably no worse than the several dozen other available "space" tests of its kind.

For reviews by E. G. Chambers, Clifford E. Jurgensen, and James M. Porter, Jr., see 3:682.

[889]

***Test of Mechanical Comprehension.** Grades 9 and over; 1940–54, c1940–57; IBM; 4 editions (labeled forms); separate answer sheets must be used; $4.25 per 25 tests; $1.90 per 50 IBM answer sheets; 35¢ per specimen set; postpaid; (25–45) minutes; George K. Bennett, Dinah E. Fry (BB, test only; W1), and William A. Owens (CC); Psychological Corporation. *
a) FORM AA. Grades 9 and over; 1940–54, c1940–55; 1 form ('40); manual ['47]; supplement ('54); French and Spanish editions available.
b) FORM BB. Men in grades 13 and over; 1941–51; 1 form ('41); revised manual ('51); Spanish edition available.
c) FORM CC. Men in engineering schools; 1949; 1 form; manual ['49].
d) FORM W1. Women in grades 9 and over; 1942–47; 1 form ('42); manual ['47].

REFERENCES

1–19. See 3:683.
20–47. See 4:766.
48. Johnson, Ralph H., and Bond, Guy L. "Reading Ease of Commonly Used Tests." *J Appl Psychol* 34:319–24 O '50. * (*PA* 26:299)
49. Lee, Marilyn C. *Relationship of Masculinity-Femininity to Tests of Mechanical and Clerical Abilities.* Master's thesis, University of Minnesota (Minneapolis, Minn.), 1950.
50. Ferson, Regis F. *The Probabilities of Success in Trade Training as Estimated by Standardized Tests.* Doctor's thesis, University of Pittsburgh (Pittsburgh, Pa.), 1951.
51. Miller, Gilbert E. "Some Components of Mechanical Composition." *Proc Iowa Acad Sci* 58:385–9 '51. *
52. Carter, Gerald C. "Measurement of Supervisory Ability." *J Appl Psychol* 36:393–5 D '52. * (*PA* 27:6801)
53. Case, Harry W. "The Relationship of Certain Tests to Grades Achieved in an Industrial Class in Aircraft Design." *Ed & Psychol Meas* 12:90–5 sp '52. * (*PA* 27:6106)
54. Gilbert, Harry B. "The Use of Tests and Other Objective Data in the Selection of Camp Counselors." Abstract. *Am Psychol* 7:369 Jl '52. *
55. Krathwohl, David R.; Ewing, T. N.; Gilbert, W. M.; and Cronbach, Lee J. "Prediction of Success in Architecture Courses." Abstract. *Am Psychol* 7:288–9 Jl '52. *
56. Lee, Marilyn C. "Relationship of Masculinity-Femininity to Tests of Mechanical and Clerical Abilities." *J Appl Psychol* 36:377–80 D '52. * (*PA* 27:6431)
57. Lingwood, Joan. "Test Performances of ATS Recruits From Certain Civilian Occupations." *Occupational Psychol* 26: 35–46 Ja '52. * (*PA* 26:6567)
58. Littleton, Isaac T. "Prediction in Auto Trade Courses." *J Appl Psychol* 36:15–9 F '52. * (*PA* 26:7256)
59. Poe, Wesley A., and Berg, Irwin A. "Psychological Test Performance of Steel Industry Production Supervisors." *J Appl Psychol* 36:234–7 Ag '52. * (*PA* 27:3794)

60. BRUCE, MARTIN M. "The Prediction of Effectiveness as a Factory Foreman." *Psychol Monogr* 67(12) 1–17 '53. * (*PA* 28: 5019)

61. COLEMAN, WILLIAM. "An Economical Test Battery for Predicting Freshman Engineering Course Grades." *J Appl Psychol* 37:465–7 D '53. * (*PA* 29:1562)

62. "Validity Information Exchange, No. 7-064: D.O.T. Code 5-92.411, Foreman I." *Personnel Psychol* 7:300 su '54. *

63. "Validity Information Exchange, No. 7-065: D.O.T. Code 5-92.411, Foreman II." *Personnel Psychol* 7:301 su '54. *

64. BRUCE, MARTIN M. "Validity Information Exchange, No. 7-076: D.O.T. Code 5-91.101, Foreman II." *Personnel Psychol* 7:418–9 au '54. *

65. BRUCE, MARTIN M. "Validity Information Exchange, No. 7-079: D.O.T. Code 7-83.058, Electrical Appliance Serviceman." *Personnel Psychol* 7:425–6 au '54. *

66. DuBois, PHILLIP H., AND WATSON, ROBERT I. "Validity Information Exchange, No. 7-075: D.O.T. Code 2-66.23, Policeman." *Personnel Psychol* 7:414–7 au '54. *

67. GROHSMEYER, FREDERICK A., JR. *Validation of Personnel Tests for a Paper Mill.* Doctor's thesis, Purdue University (Lafayette, Ind.), 1954. (*DA* 14:1796)

68. HUEBER, JOANNE. "Validity Information Exchange, No. 7-089: D.O.T. Code 5-83.641, Maintenance Mechanic II." *Personnel Psychol* 7:565–6 w '54. *

69. McCARTY, JOHN J. "Validity Information Exchange, No. 7-077: D.O.T. Code 5-92.621, (Foreman II)." *Personnel Psychol* 7:420–1 au '54. *

70. McCARTY, JOHN J.; WESTBERG, WILLIAM C.; AND FITZPATRICK, EUGENE D. "Validity Information Exchange, No. 7-091: D.O.T. Code 5-92.621, (Foreman II)." *Personnel Psychol* 7:568–9 w '54. *

71. SCHMITZ, ROY M., AND HOLMES, JOHN L. "Relationship of Certain Measured Abilities to Freshman Engineering Achievement," pp. 32–42. (*PA* 29:1584) In *Selection and Counseling of Students in Engineering.* Edited by Wilbur L. Layton. Minnesota Studies in Student Personnel Work, No. 4. Minneapolis, Minn.: University of Minnesota Press, 1954. Pp. iv, 89. *

72. CUOMO, SYLVIA. "Validity Information Exchange, No. 8-17: D.O.T. Code 5-92.601, Foreman II." *Personnel Psychol* 8: 268 su '55. *

73. CUOMO, SYLVIA, AND MEYER, HERBERT H. "Validity Information Exchange, No. 8-16: D.O.T. Code 5-92.601, Foreman II." *Personnel Psychol* 8:267 su '55. *

74. CUOMO, SYLVIA, AND MEYER, HERBERT H. "Validity Information Exchange, No. 8-19: D.O.T. Code 6-78.632, Floor Assembler." *Personnel Psychol* 8:270 su '55. *

75. FITZPATRICK, EUGENE D., AND McCARTY, JOHN J. "Validity Information Exchange, No. 8-35: D.O.T. Code 9-00.91, Assembler VII (Electrical Equipment)." *Personnel Psychol* 8: 501–4 w '55. *

76. FORSTER, CECIL R. *The Relationship Between Test Achievement and Success in Training of a Selected Group of Tuberculosis Patients.* Doctor's thesis, New York University (New York, N.Y.), 1955. (*DA* 15:1201)

77. HARRISON, ROSS; HUNT, WINSLOW; AND JACKSON, THEODORE A. "Profile of the Mechanical Engineer: 1, Ability." *Personnel Psychol* 8:219–34 su '55. * (*PA* 30:5414)

78. PATTERSON, CECIL H. *Test and Background Factors Related to Drop-Outs in an Industrial Institute.* Doctor's thesis, University of Minnesota (Minneapolis, Minn.), 1955. (*DA* 15: 1024)

79. SMITH, OTTO B. *Predicting Grade Success of High School Students in Radio and Drafting.* Master's thesis, Alabama Polytechnic Institute (Auburn, Ala.), 1955.

80. "Reducing Turnover in a Steel Company by Means of the Mechanical Comprehension Test." *Test Service B* (50):5 Je '56. *

81. BRUCE, MARTIN M. "Normative Data Information Exchange, No. 17." *Personnel Psychol* 9:393 au '56. *

82. BRUCE, MARTIN M. "Normative Data Information Exchange, Nos. 18, 37." *Personnel Psychol* 9:394, 552–3 au, w '56. *

83. McCARTY, JOHN J., AND FITZPATRICK, EUGENE D. "Validity Information Exchange, No. 9-26: D.O.T. Code 5-92.621, (Foreman II)." *Personnel Psychol* 9:253 su '56. *

84. OTTERNESS, WILLIAM B.; PATTERSON, C. H.; JOHNSON, R. H.; AND PETERSON, LENNIS R. "Trade School Norms for Some Commonly Used Tests." *J Appl Psychol* 40:57–60 F '56. * (*PA* 31:3803)

85. PATTERSON, C. H. "The Prediction of Attrition in Trade School Courses." *J Appl Psychol* 40:154–8 Je '56. * (*PA* 31: 6680)

86. WALKER, FRANCIS C. "Normative Data Information Exchange, No. 10." *Personnel Psychol* 9:276 su '56. *

87. McCARTY, JOHN J. "Normative Data Information Exchange, No. 10-31." *Personnel Psychol* 10:365 au '57. *

88. MOLLENKOPF, WILLIAM G. "An Easier 'Male' Mechanical Test for Use With Women." *J Appl Psychol* 41:340–3 O '57. *

89. SAUNDERS, WM. J., JR. "Normative Data Information Exchange, No. 10-32." *Personnel Psychol* 10:366 au '57. *

90. TOPETZES, NICK JOHN. "A Program for the Selection of Trainees in Physical Medicine." *J Exp Ed* 25:263–311 Je '57. *

91. BARRETT, RICHARD S. "The Process of Predicting Job Performance." *Personnel Psychol* 11:39–57 sp '58. *

92. DECKER, ROBERT L. "A Study of the Value of the Owens-Bennett Mechanical Comprehension Test (Form CC) as a Measure of the Qualities Contributing to Successful Performance as a Supervisor of Technical Operations in an Industrial Organization." *J Appl Psychol* 42:50–3 F '58. *

93. RILAND, LANE H., AND UPSHALL, CHARLES C. "Normative Data Information Exchange, No. 11-10." *Personnel Psychol* 11:275 su '58. *

For a review by N. W. Morton, see 4:766; for reviews by Charles M. Harsh, Lloyd G. Humphreys, and George A. Satter, see 3:683.

[890]

★**Tool Knowledge Test.** Ages 13 and over; 1951–54; 1 form ['51]; mimeographed manual ['54]; separate answer sheets must be used; 5s. per 10 tests; 1s. 6d. per 10 answer sheets; 9d. per scoring stencil; 2s. 6d. per manual; 3s. 9d. per specimen set; postpaid within Australia; 10(20) minutes; manual by D. Spearritt; Research and Guidance Branch, Queensland Department of Public Instruction; Australian Council for Educational Research. *

J. F. CLARK, *Professor of Applied Psychology, New South Wales University of Technology, Kensington, New South Wales, Australia.*

This test was devised to measure the interest in practical activities of 13-year-old boys faced with the problem of choosing between a technical and an academic course of further study. It is based on the hypothesis that tests of the tool information type are valid indicators of practical interest in boys who have had no formal experience with skilled trades work.

The test consists of a 4-page booklet containing 24 pictures of commonly used trade tools taken from an engineering catalogue. Each tool is accompanied by a question relating either to its name or its function or to the workman who would normally use it. The boys choose an answer from among five alternatives. Scores are interpreted in the light of a boy's home background and experience.

The test was prepared by the Research and Guidance Branch of the Queensland (Australia) Department of Public Instruction to assist guidance officers counseling youths at the time of choosing the nature of advanced secondary schooling. The manner in which the test was constructed appears to have been thorough. Pretesting and item analysis preceded the final selection of items and the determination of order of difficulty of the items in the final test. The test is well printed and the presentation of the photographs is clear.

The test has been used widely with school populations in Queensland, and norms are available for groups of average age 13-7 and 14-3. There are also norms on a Tasmanian population aged 14-9 to 15-3 and on a group of Victorian National Service trainees aged 18 years. From the Victorian group occupational norms have been computed for each of six general occupational classifications, viz., farmers, mechanics, carpenters, salesmen, clerks, and university students. In general, the level and spread of scores are satisfactory.

A split-half reliability of .72 and a Kuder-Richardson (formula 20) reliability of .82 have been obtained on each of 100 cases of Victorian National Service trainees.

For 783 trainees the test gave the following correlations with other tests: *A.C.E.R. Word Knowledge*, .39; Raven's *Progressive Matrices*, .45; Higher Examination of the *Otis Self-Administering Tests of Mental Ability*, .39; *A.C.E.R. Mechanical Reasoning Test*, .57; *Minnesota Paper Form Board*, .49. Thus, at least with older groups it seems to be testing abilities common to the so-called group intelligence and mechanical reasoning tests.

Apart from the so-called occupational norms which are based on broad occupational categories of 18-year-old youths, no data regarding predictive validity are presented. Tests of tool knowledge have been found useful in combination with mechanical appreciation, space form, and arithmetical tests for the prediction of success in engineering occupations. Whether this test, either alone or in combination with others, is useful for this purpose or valid in predicting future success in technical courses cannot be determined from the information presented in the manual. Until more information is available, this reviewer doubts its usefulness as a psychometric instrument but is willing to grant that it may be of some help when used as a counseling aid in the educational guidance of adolescent males.

I. G. MEDDLETON, *Deputy Head, Research Department, University of Queensland, Brisbane, Australia.*

The purpose of this test is to assess a boy's knowledge of trade tools—their names, their purposes, and by whom they are used. It acts as a measure of interest in rather than aptitude for practical activities. The manual cautions that scores are to be interpreted in the light of a boy's home background and experience.

The 24 items are based on pictures of commonly used tools, which the boy is required to identify by selecting the appropriate answer from among five alternatives. The pictures are excellent likenesses of the tools portrayed and

the quality of the paper on which they are produced is good. Separate answer sheets are used. The time limit of 10 minutes is apparently ample, the manual showing that 96 per cent of an 18-year-old group of 100 servicemen completed the test within the time allowed.

The manual clearly sets out a description of the test, together with directions for administering and scoring it. The manual claims that the extent of a boy's interest in tools can best be assessed by comparing his score on the test with the scores of a group of boys living in similar environmental conditions. However, in assessing interest from test score, much is left to the examiner's interpretation and to experience gained by him in testing other boys.

Percentile norms are given in the manual for such groups as Queensland boys aged approximately 13-7 and 14-3, Tasmanian boys aged 14-9 and girls aged 15-3, and, despite the fact that the test was actually constructed for 13- and 14-year-old boys with little trade experience, for Victorian National Servicemen aged 18+ years. Further norms are given for male occupational groups within Australia, but the manual emphasises that these can be looked upon as a rough guide only. Unfortunately, the norms were obtained on an earlier printed version of the test. Since the present form has been slightly changed, it would appear that new norms are needed.

With 100 cases selected at random from among 783 trainees in the National Service group, a split-half coefficient of .79 was obtained for the earlier form of the test. For the same group, product-moment correlations of .45, .39, .57, and .49 were obtained between tool knowledge scores and scores on Raven's *Progressive Matrices,* the Higher Examination of the *Otis Self-Administering Tests of Mental Ability,* the *A.C.E.R. Mechanical Reasoning Test,* and the *Minnesota Paper Form Board Test,* respectively. The manual is not clear as to whether the earlier or the final form of the test was used in obtaining the product-moment coefficients.

In summary: the photo lithographics of the trade tools are excellently produced on paper of good quality. The directions and practice exercises are adequate. The norms are unsatisfactory; any extensive user of the test would do well to accumulate his own. Until further evidence is available regarding the prognostic

Tool Knowledge Test

value of the test, scores should be interpreted with caution.

MISCELLANEOUS

[891]

Aptitude Tests for Occupations. Grades 9–13 and adults; 1951; IBM; Form A; 6 tests; $14.35 per 35 sets of the 6 tests; separate answer sheets may be used; 4¢ per IBM answer sheet; 40¢ per either hand or machine scoring stencil; $1.05 per 35 profiles (free upon request with orders for all 6 tests); postage extra; 75¢ per complete specimen set, postpaid; 107 (135) minutes; Wesley S. Roeder and Herbert B. Graham; California Test Bureau. *
a) PERSONAL-SOCIAL APTITUDE. $2.80 per 35 tests; 20-(25) minutes.
b) MECHANICAL APTITUDE. $3.50 per 35 tests; 20(25) minutes.
c) GENERAL SALES APTITUDE. $2.80 per 35 tests; 20(25) minutes.
d) CLERICAL ROUTINE APTITUDE. $2.10 per 35 tests; 12(15) minutes.
e) COMPUTATIONAL APTITUDE. $2.10 per 35 tests; 15-(20) minutes.
f) SCIENTIFIC APTITUDE. $2.80 per 35 tests; 20(25) minutes.

LLOYD G. HUMPHREYS, *Professor of Psychology, University of Illinois, Urbana, Illinois.*

The *Aptitude Tests for Occupations*, six in number, have the following labels: Personal-Social, Mechanical, General Sales, Clerical Routine, Computational, and Scientific. There is ample precedent in the aptitude test literature for certain of the item types and names selected, e.g., Mechanical and Clerical Routine. For others, e.g., Personal-Social and General Sales, there is no adequate precedent, and the authors have not provided data in the manual to justify their selection. It is possible that interest measurement categories suggested these particular aptitude designations. A certain amount of parallelism between interest and aptitude tests might well promote the sales of both.

The battery is introduced as a differential aptitude battery early in the manual and in one way or another this theme recurs many times. The manual stresses the merits of the several tests for this purpose and neglects potential uses of separate tests for guidance or selection. The mechanical test, for example, has a promising selection of item types and might, with appropriate item difficulty levels and adequate timing, be quite useful.

The battery was adequately and fairly reviewed by Froehlich in *The Fourth Mental Measurements Yearbook*. He recommended that the publishers correct the errors in the manual, eliminate unsupported claims, and report sufficient data to provide a basis for judging the value of the tests. Also, since the date of publication of the tests, the test standards of the American Psychological Association have become available. Whereas Froehlich might have concluded in 1953 that the publisher had been careless and the authors uninformed concerning good psychometric practices, today one cannot be that generous. By offering these tests with the current manual for sale to the public in 1958 the authors and publisher flaunt their disregard for minimum technical standards for their product. "Careless" becomes "calculated" and "uninformed" becomes "contemptuous."

The bill of particulars is a lengthy one. Errors of commission or omission occur in every part. There are both known statistical errors and suspected errors of fact. The crystal ball is used generously. Since the reviewer's judgment is harsh, these errors are discussed in more than ordinary detail in the following paragraphs.

RELIABILITY. With the exception of one test-retest estimate on the acknowledged speed test of clerical routine, estimates of reliability are Kuder-Richardson coefficients. The claim is made that such estimates are conservative and that "true reliabilities are probably much higher than those indicated below." This statement would be undesirable under the best of circumstances, and present circumstances are hardly the best. Since the computational test is also described by the authors as a speed test, at least one of these Kuder-Richardson estimates is admittedly not applicable. The remaining tests are also somewhat speeded although the manual states otherwise. Experience with judgment items indicates that the 45 personal-social items covering most of seven pages cannot be answered by high school students in 20 minutes. As another example, the 60 generally complex mechanical items are also given a time limit of 20 minutes. The distribution of raw scores on the latter test is also very low. Even with moderate speeding, Kuder-Richardson reliability estimates are no longer conservative.

A second factor makes Kuder-Richardson estimates too high for several of these tests. Groups of sequentially dependent items are used rather frequently. This is particularly descriptive of the personal-social and scientific tests. This technique substantially increases the size of interitem correlations, but the increase is spurious from the standpoint of reliability estimation. A proper reliability estimate can be obtained by a split-half technique only if care is taken to place each homogeneous sequency entirely in one half or the other.

The mistakes discussed in the preceding paragraphs are the merest of quibbles, relatively speaking, when the implications of this completely undocumented statement, which appears later in the same section, are grasped. "All coefficients have been corrected for range." What were the standard deviations in the samples used for reliability estimation? What were the assumed standard deviations to which correction was made? What was the basis for concluding that the latter would be more representative than the former of the distributions of examinees to whom the test would usually be given? These gaps in the discussion make the reliabilities reported meaningless.

As one looks into this matter further, there is some ground for believing that no such corrections were made after all! The reliability estimates in the grades 9–13 column of the summary table can be reproduced almost perfectly from the use of the average means and standard deviations given in adjoining columns. But these values are presumably based upon the formula scores and would erroneously inflate Kuder-Richardson estimates! The only thing certain is that the manual is seriously defective. There are several bases for inferring that the reliabilities are overestimates, but the amount of error cannot be guessed.

VALIDITY. The first validity data presented in the manual are the intercorrelations of the six tests. The manual suggests to the reader that these correlations be squared in order to estimate the amount of variance unaccounted for between pairs of tests. This practice is highly undesirable. It is significant that this is the only table of correlations in this section not corrected for attenuation. Even with the reliabilities presented in the manual, there would be a lot less unaccounted variance after taking errors of measurement into account. In several instances adequate reliabilities would leave very little indeed.

Next, correlations are presented between each of the *Aptitude Tests for Occupations* and various other tests. Unfortunately, this pairing is not systematic although adequate data must have been available. For example, the reader is informed concerning the correlation between the scientific score and the Q score of the *American Council on Education Psychological Examination*, but the correlation of the latter with the computational score is not reported. Systematic data here would provide a basis for judging the possibilities of differential prediction from the battery. The data actually reported are useless in judging the battery as a whole, and even for purposes of evaluating individual tests most of the *n*'s are inadequate (median = 47).

The predictive validity correlations are erroneously corrected for attenuation. Again only partial data are presented. Since selected tests were paired with grades in certain high school courses, information about differential prediction is therefore lacking. Would these predictions be just as good if some other test were used? Would they be even better if combinations of tests were used? Again the *n*'s are mostly so small (median = 54) that adequate answers to such questions could not be obtained.

The last tables presented in the validity section are inexplicable except as hocus-pocus. Certain of the aptitude tests are paired with other commonly used tests, five standard score points are selected (one assumes in a particular sample, but this is not clear), and the percentile ranks from the published norms of these standard score points are presented. In some cases the mean corresponds to the 50th percentile, in others it does not. For some of the paired tests the percentile ranks of the same standard scores are comparable, for others they are not. The first finding describes the extent to which a particular sample differs from published norms. The second finding describes the extent to which published norms for different tests correspond in a particular sample. These data could be useful if properly documented, but they are in no sense validation data.

OCCUPATIONAL PATTERNS. All too little is known about differential occupational patterns for standard aptitude batteries. Even less is known concerning some of the nonstandard tests used in the battery under discussion. The unsophisticated reader would not learn this from the manual. He is told that tests and occupations are related, but not that the relationship was determined from a cloudy crystal ball. Almost three pages of occupations are listed under each of the several tests and under combinations of the tests taken two at a time. There is a certain amount of hedging in this listing, since the same occupation frequently appears several times. Physicist, in one form or another, occurs four times and "research worker" is found in five categories. There are also some rather odd choices as seen in a different crystal ball. Mathematician is grouped under computational along with bookkeeper and accountant. College or university teacher is found under personal-social. An operator of statistical machines is placed under clerical routine. The specific grouping should not be overemphasized, however, since it is the encouragement to make use of a lot of chance differences between test scores that is most undesirable.

The emphasis here is clearly on differences. The section concludes as follows: "Regardless of where an individual's profile falls, the jobs of the occupational pattern list in which he has the highest aptitude should be considered." Rolling dice would be cheaper, and in an all too large proportion of the cases would be equally effective. The battery could, on the other hand, be used to detect across the board differences in profile level, and the importance of this is pointed out in the manual, but no standards for level are provided for any occupation.

DIRECTIONS FOR ADMINISTRATION. This section is generally straightforward. With a minor exception—the reviewer recommends that "time allotments" should not be modified by "suggested"—the directions are clearly written. The introductory statement to this section of the manual contains a curious statement, however. "This series is primarily diagnostic but it also yields percentile ranks and standard scores of examinees." One wonders how diagnostic information would be obtained from raw scores of tests of different lengths and unequal difficulties.

NORMS. At first glance the sampling design for obtaining norms looks good. Thus we find the following statements: "the United States was divided into eight regions for sampling purposes * Samples representative of large and small school districts and colleges were first drawn at random from each of these regions * the norms for the Aptitude Tests for Occupations have been based on a controlled (stratified) sampling." A closer look reveals that these fine words conceal something more aptly titled "catch as catch can" sampling. One clue is that California is listed as one of the eight

regions. Another is that so-called random sampling in New England and the deep South produced schools only in Maine and in Louisiana, respectively. It should also be noted that if school districts were sampled at random, the important *n* to be reported is the number of districts, not the number of students.

Other minor matters briefly noted are that the intelligence test used in stratifying is not named and that normalcy of the distributions was checked without giving the results. With respect to the first, intelligence tests are not sufficiently standardized in content or norming so that just any one could be used. With respect to the second, characteristics of the tables of percentile equivalents of raw scores indicate that some of the distributions may be normal, but others are certainly not. Normalcy is not really important in the raw score distribution, but the unsophisticated reader does not know this. The mention of normalcy in this context is apparently an attempt to propagandize the reader without imparting information.

CONCLUSION. Only one conclusion to a review of this sort is possible: it is recommended that the publisher remove the *Aptitude Tests for Occupations* from the test market. Test users should encourage the publisher in this course of action by refusing to buy the inadequate product.

For a review by Clifford P. Froehlich, see 4:710 (1 excerpt).

[892]

★[Biography Forms]: Application-Interview Series. Industry; 1948–56; 5 forms ('56): clerical, mechanical, sales, technical, supervisor; no specific manual; directions sheet ('56); 20¢ per single copy; postage extra; administration time not reported; Joseph E. King; Industrial Psychology, Inc. *

[893]

★Business Judgment Test. Adults; 1953–56; 1 form ('53); supplement ('56); norms ['56]; 15¢ per test; 25¢ per scoring key; 50¢ per manual ('53); 75¢ per specimen set; cash orders postpaid; (10–20) minutes; Martin M. Bruce; the Author. *

REFERENCES
1. BRUCE, MARTIN M. "Normative Data Information Exchange, No. 25." *Personnel Psychol* 9:404–5 au '56. *
2. BRUCE, MARTIN M., AND FRIESEN, EDWARD P. "Validity Information Exchange, No. 9-35: D.O.T. Code 1-55.10, Salesman, House-to-House." *Personnel Psychol* 9:380 au '56. *

EDWARD B. GREENE, *Supervisor of Personnel Research, Chrysler Corporation, Detroit, Michigan.*

Each of the 25 four-choice items consists of a short statement of a stress situation, followed by four actions which might be taken in the situation. The first person is used throughout. For instance, Item 16 reads:

> If I overheard a co-worker lie about his work to the supervisor, I would
> _____point out the error to my co-worker.
> _____explain the situation to the supervisor.
> _____overlook the matter altogether.
> _____tell the supervisor the truth in a letter.

Two keys are distributed with the test. On one, a single correct choice is indicated for each item and one point credit allowed for each item so marked. The other, marked "Revised Scoring Key," gives weighted credit to each choice, credit ranging from zero to three points. Although the weighted scoring system reflected in the revised key is intended to replace the original right-wrong approach, the author indicates that both keys are still distributed since some users prefer to continue using the original scoring method. There are, however, marked discrepancies between the two keys, particularly on Items 4, 7, 10, 13, 15, 16, and 19. On some of these items the preferred choice on the original key is either given little or no credit on the revised key or less credit than some other choice on the revised key. In the case of four items, the choice given three points credit on the revised key is given no credit on the original key. The two keys cannot be used interchangeably.

These discrepancies point to the problem of determining which choices are to be given credit in scoring. Two of the criteria used in selecting the test items were that men rated high in business judgment should tend to choose the designated "right" choices, and that men rated low should not select these choices. There is no indication as to what standards were used by the raters in assigning men to these high and low categories. It would be interesting to know whether the qualities or behaviors considered by the raters were the same as those which the test is intended to measure.

Since the author does not explain what he means by business judgment, the reviewer attempted to determine this through a subjective analysis of the response choices. It is possible to name, at least roughly, the attitude which could lead to making each choice. For instance, in Item 16 above, the first choice (given three points credit on the revised scoring key) seems to indicate an aggressive or dominating attitude. The second and fourth choices (for which no credit is allowed) might indicate willingness to help management and also some independence in willingness to tell on a co-worker. (These second and fourth choices would reflect good business judgment if the lie were serious or a lot of people were involved.) The third choice (given two points) seems to indicate withdrawal. If the foregoing analysis of motivating attitudes is correct, good business judgment depends, as far as this item is concerned, on attitudes either of domination or withdrawal but not on cooperating with the management if it involves tattling. Similar subjective analysis of the remaining 44 choices which are assigned some credit on the revised key shows 19 choices which could indicate withdrawal and 14 an initiating or dominating attitude.

To ascertain the fakability of the test, the reviewer asked three men and three women to mark it so as to please an employer who wanted aggressive employees. The average score (weighted scoring key) for the dominating choices was 30.4 and for the submissive choices, 4.6. Another group of office clerks was asked to mark the test to imitate people who are meek and mind their own business. The average scores were 12.2 for dominating choices and 27.0 for submissive choices. Similar results were obtained with a third group of factory employees. It appears that this test can be faked by unsophisticated employees to a very significant degree.

The test title is misleading, since, to many businessmen, business judgment refers to familiarity and wisdom in merchandising, finance procedures, and related fields. The test is primarily concerned with attitudes about tact, initiative, submission, and getting facts in a variety of situations, some of which are not business situations. There is considerable evidence that many people behave somewhat differently in nonbusiness situations than in work-stress situations.

In view of the probability of persons obtaining the same score with very different attitudes, the fakability, the lack of analysis of what is being measured, and the inadequacy of validation data reported, this test is NOT recommended.

[894]

Cancellation Test. Adults; 1946; perceptual speed; Form J; no data on reliability and validity; $1.10 per 25 tests, postage extra; 10¢ per specimen set, postpaid; 10(15) minutes; John R. Roberts; Educational Test Bureau. *

HERBERT A. TONNE, *Professor of Education, New York University, New York, New York.*

This test consists of a jumbled sequence of letters in which every "A" and every "B" are to be crossed out. The raw score is simply the number of letters correctly marked. Raw scores are converted to standard scores, the nature of the scores not specified. The only normative data are means and standard deviations based on the scores of 79 factory workers, distributed in six different job classifications.

The directions say: "This test seems to measure speed in the visual perception of minute details * It may be useful in the selection of visual inspectors, proofreaders, and the like." The caution is very much justified for the likelihood of meaningful validity seems slight. Visual inspectors are so varied in their work that almost nothing can be said about their specific assignment except that they use their eyes. Proofreaders have numerous elements to look for in their tasks, among which the correction of misplaced letters seems to be quite a minor activity. An automobile driver's test which limited itself to a check on whether the prospective driver knew how to use the brake when the car was not running would probably be worse than no test at all because it would give some the notion that successful completion was evidence of the ability to drive. That seems to be the status of this test.

The test seems useless. If a proofreader is to be hired, why not give him a job of proofreading? If a parts inspector is to be hired, why not give him a trial in inspecting a typical segment of the parts he is to inspect?

For a review by Joseph E. King, see 3:684.

[895]
*[Employee Rating and Development Forms.] Executive, industrial, office, and sales personnel; 1950–58; $2 per manual ('50) for a(2–3); postage extra; (5–30) minutes; Robert N. McMurry and associates; Dartnell Corporation. *
a) [PATTERNED MERIT REVIEW FORMS.] 1950–56.
 1) *Patterned Merit Review—Executive.* Form No. MR-407 ('55); 15¢ per copy.
 2) *Patterned Merit Review Form—Plant and Office.* Form No. MR-405 ('50); 15¢ per copy.
 3) *Patterned Merit Review—Sales.* 1950–55; Form No. MR-406R ('55); 10¢ per copy.
 4) *Patterned Merit Review—Technical Office, Special Skills.* Form No. MR-408 ('56); 10¢ per copy.
b) PATTERNED EXIT INTERVIEW. Form No. EX-501 ('53); 10¢ per copy; $2 per manual ('53).
c) PERSONAL HISTORY REVIEW FORM. I form ['57]; 10¢ per copy.
d) PHYSICAL RECORD. Form No. PX-701 ('58); 15¢ per copy.

Cancellation Test

For reviews by Harry W. Karn and Floyd L. Ruch of a(2–3), see 4:781.

[896]
*[Executive, Industrial, and Sales Personnel Forms.] Applicants for executive, office, industrial, or sales positions; 1949–56; interviewing aids for personnel selection; postage extra; Robert N. McMurry and associates; Dartnell Corporation. *
a) [EXECUTIVE PERSONNEL FORMS.]
 1) *Application for Executive Position.* 1949–53; Form No. EA-301 ('53); 10¢ per copy.
 2) *Patterned Interview Form—Executive Position.* Applicants for management positions; 1949–53; Form No. EP-302 ('53); 30¢ per copy.
 3) *Patterned Interview Form.* Applicants for positions of supervisor, foreman, engineer; 1955; Form No. EP-312; 15¢ per copy.
 4) *Telephone Check on Executive Applicant.* 1950–53; Form No. ET-303 ('53); 7¢ per copy.
 5) *Selection and Evaluation Summary.* 1950–55; Form No. ES-404R ('55); 6¢ per copy.
 6) *Position Analysis.* 1956; Form No. JA-601; 7¢ per copy.
b) [INDUSTRIAL PERSONNEL FORMS.]
 1) *Application for Position.* 1950–52; Form No. OA-201 ('52); 7¢ per copy.
 2) *Application for Employment.* 1950–53; Form No. OC-200 ('53); 6¢ per copy.
 3) *Application for Office Position.* 1953; Form No. OA-205; 7¢ per copy.
 4) *Patterned Interview (Short Form).* 1949–53; Form No. OP-202 ('53); 10¢ per copy.
 5) *Patterned Interview Form.* Same as a(3) above.
 6) *Telephone Check [With Previous Employers.]* 1949–53; Form No. OT-203 ('53); 6¢ per copy.
 7) *Telephone Check With Schools.* 1949–53; Form No. OS-204 ('53); 7¢ per copy.
 8) *Selection and Evaluation Summary.* Same as a(5) above.
 9) *Position Analysis.* Same as a(6) above.
c) [SALES PERSONNEL FORMS.]
 1) *Application for Sales Position.* 1950–53; Form No. SA-101 ('53); 10¢ per copy.
 2) *Patterned Interview Form—Sales Position.* 1950–52; Form No. SP-102 ('52); 15¢ per copy.
 3) *Telephone Check on Sales Applicant.* 1949–53; Form No. ST-103 ('53); 7¢ per copy.
 4) *Sales Application Verification.* 1953; Form No. SV-104; 6¢ per copy.
 5) *Home Interview Report Form.* 1954–55; Form No. SH-114R ('55); 7¢ per copy.
 6) *Selection and Evaluation Summary.* Same as a(5) above.
 7) *Position Analysis.* Same as a(6) above.

For a review by Floyd L. Ruch, see 4:773.

[897]
★**The Fiesenheiser Test of Ability to Read Drawings.** Trade school and adults; 1955; 1 form; hectographed manual; $4 per 50 tests; $1 per specimen set (must be purchased to obtain manual); postage extra; 30(35) minutes; Elmer I. Fiesenheiser; Psychometric Affiliates. *

[898]
★**Hiring Summary Worksheet.** Industry; 1956; forms for summarizing scores obtained on tests and biographical forms published or distributed by the publisher relevant to each of 24 positions; 1 form; 24 worksheets; no specific manual; 10¢ per single copy,

postage extra; directions sheet by Joseph E. King; Industrial Psychology, Inc. *

[899]

*Identical Forms. College and adults; 1958, c1947; perceptual speed; Research Form IF47; mimeographed directions sheet ['58]; no data on reliability and validity; tentative norms; $1.30 per 20 tests; 15¢ per specimen set; postage extra; 3(10) or 5(10) minutes; L. L. Thurstone; Science Research Associates. *

[900]

*Merit Rating Series. Industry; 1948–57; formerly called *Employee Evaluation Series;* 1 form; 5 scales; 20¢ per scale; 20¢ per normal curve summary ('53); $3 per complete specimen set; postage extra; (10–20) minutes; Joseph E. King and Judith W. Wingert (*b, c, d, e,* and descriptive material); Industrial Psychology, Inc. *
a) PERFORMANCE: CLERICAL. 1957.
b) PERFORMANCE: MECHANICAL. 1953.
c) PERFORMANCE: SALES. 1953.
d) PERFORMANCE: TECHNICAL. 1957.
e) PERFORMANCE: SUPERVISOR. 1953.

For a review by Brent Baxter of the original series, see 4:770.

[901]

★Per-Flu-Dex Tests. College and industry; 1955; 7 tests: symbol number substitution, letter perception and counting, number counting and perception, word completion and verbal fluency, arithmetic computation, manual speed of movement, aiming accuracy and speed; 1 form; $2 per 50 tests; $2 per 50 profiles; $1 per specimen set (must be purchased to obtain manual); postage extra; 7(25) minutes, 1(5) minutes for any one test; Frank J. Holmes; Psychometric Affiliates. *
a) PER-SYMB TEST.
b) PER-VERB TEST.
c) PER-NUMB TEST.
d) FLU-VERB TEST.
e) FLU-NUMB TEST.
f) THE DEX-MAN SCALE.
g) DEX-AIM TEST.

ANDREW L. COMREY, *Associate Professor of Psychology, University of California, Los Angeles, California.*

These seven 1-minute tests require the following activities: (*a*) labeling figures with numbers according to a code given at the top of the test page; (*b*) counting the number of K's in rows of interspersed letters K and H; (*c*) counting the number of 6's in rows of interspersed numbers 6 and 8; (*d*) adding letters to make words; (*e*) performing simple addition, subtraction, multiplication, and division; (*f*) marking X's in small squares on a zigzagging line of small squares; and (*g*) marking X's in large squares in several rows of squares.

There is a discrepancy between the standardization sample sizes given in the manual and those alluded to on the norm tables provided with each test key. In fact, the manual does not describe any norms sample as such, referring to sample sizes only in connection with various investigations concerning reliability and validity. Since the norm tables refer to sample sizes (150 college students and a business and industrial group of 38 for some tests and 74 for others) having no corresponding numbers in the manual, one may infer that standardization data other than those mentioned in the manual were used in preparing the norms. No mention of any "business" group could be found in the manual despite the fact that "business-industrial" norms are presented. Test-retest reliabilities based on only 95 students range from .71 to .95. Test intercorrelations based upon combined college student and assembly worker groups range from zero to .56.

Various bits of data are put forth as evidence of validity. Median scores on each test are compared for 12 female assembly workers rated high on job performance by their foremen and for 12 rated low. Four of the tests are said to reveal significant differences, although no variability data are reported. Median scores on each test for the top 25 and bottom 75 per cent of students in a college general psychology class are reported. Six of the tests are said to give significant differences. Unaccountably, the numbers of cases for these two groups are given as 25 and 83, respectively. Median scores for 10 students rated by deans as "leaders" and 30 rated as "non-leaders" are listed. No significance data are given. Finally, median scores for students pursuing different major fields are compared. Where given, the numbers of cases for these groups range from 11 to 23. No significance data are given.

The *Per-Flu-Dex Tests* are not recommended by this reviewer for the following reasons: (*a*) The rationale, if it exists, is not sufficiently elaborated in the sketchy manual. (*b*) The standardization samples are unrepresentative, too small, and inadequately described. (*c*) Virtually no evidence is given to show what these tests are measuring. No factorial investigations are reported relating these tests to one another or to other tests. No evidence is offered to show in what way these tests actually supplement other standardized tests, as they are supposed to do. (*d*) The validity data reported are based upon insufficient numbers of cases and fail to provide information upon test score variability in the groups compared. (*e*) Carelessness is evident in the preparation of the tests and the test manual. The manual is dittoed from stencils which contain visible strike-over typing errors, crossed out words, and poorly aligned columns. Numbers and kinds of cases fail to agree between the manual and test norms. Percentages and numbers of cases lack consistency at one point. (*f*) Lastly, although the reliabilities reported are high for 1-minute tests, in several instances they are not adequate for careful psychometric work.

JOHN W. FRENCH, *Research Associate, Educational Testing Service, Princeton, New Jersey.*

One-minute tests of this kind are quite feasible. The reviewer has found many to have reliabilities at least as high as the range of .71 to .85 reported for these. As suggested in the manual, their usefulness will be in supplementing batteries of intelligence, clerical, or mechanical ability tests. Despite their possible usefulness, it is not easy to find anything to commend in the way these tests have been selected, set up, or described in the manual.

The manual says that the testing literature indicated these seven different measures of perception, fluency, and dexterity to be suitable for administration in groups. The tests selected are suggestive, but only suggestive, of the factors established by the United States Employment Service in the course of the thorough studies leading to the development of the *General Aptitude Test Battery.*

Examination of the probable factorial content of the seven tests indicates that there is some unnecessary overlapping and confusion of what is being measured. Per-Symb, Per-Verb, and Per-Numb all seem to test a perceptual speed factor that may be called speed of symbol discrimination. In addition to this factor, Per-Symb probably measures speed in making associations between symbols and numbers, an ability of possible use, but one tested here only in an indirect way. Per-Verb and Per-Numb are more direct measures but may suffer from the distraction produced by the counting requirement. The other perceptual speed factor found useful in measuring clerical competence, that best exemplified by tests requiring the rapid comparison of such things as numbers or addresses, is not tested here.

Flu-Verb probably measures what Thurstone called "word fluency," a semantic habit not as yet having any proven validity. Flu-

Numb seems to be a quite reasonable test of number facility. Dex-Man is much the same as other standard paper and pencil manual or motor dexterity tests. Dex-Aim probably measures much the same thing as Dex-Man. To measure factors of aiming or eye-hand coordination, the drawing of an X should not be required, and the degree of precision should be increased by making the squares on the response sheet smaller.

In general, the tests and manual are set up in a manner that is acceptable for practical purposes. However, some sloppy typing and freehand supplements to the typing are not conducive to whetting a reviewer's admiration. Art work on a test should, perhaps, be considered irrelevant, but that displayed here deserves special notice for its unspeakable ugliness.

The directions in the manual for administering the tests, the directions appearing on the test copies, and the scoring directions printed on the keys are all adequate. The manual's overall attitude of caution and suggestion that the tests be used only as supplementary instruments are commendable. However, the tables of figures shown, particularly those concerned with validity, are misleading. Appropriate discrimination by some of these tests between levels of excellence in clerical and mechanical jobs may be expected, but the large relationships found with academic work in various fields and with campus leadership seem only to reveal biased or lucky samples. The very small number of cases for many of the groups may have led to the astonishing relationships reported. Judging from the behavior of similar tests in other academic and industrial situations, the reviewer has no alternative but to disbelieve that the figures can be generalized.

[902]
★The Performance Record. Industry; 1955; form for recording behavior incidents; 1 form; 3 editions: hourly employees, nonsupervisory salaried employees, foremen and supervisors; $3 per 20 record booklets of any one edition; 35¢ per administrator's manual; $3.45 per 20 employee handbooks; 50¢ per supervisor's handbook for any one edition; postage extra; John C. Flanagan and Robert B. Miller; Science Research Associates. *

REFERENCE
1. FLANAGAN, JOHN C., AND BURNS, ROBERT K. "The Employee Performance Record: A New Appraisal and Development Tool." *Harvard Bus R* 33:95-102 S-O '55. *

ALBERT K. KURTZ, *Professor of Psychology, University of Florida, Gainesville, Florida.*

The *Performance Record* is not a test. It is not a criterion either, although it might have been if its authors had desired to make it so. Rather, it is a procedure for classifying and recording critical incidents, for conferring with employees concerning their progress, and, in short, for doing most of the other things commonly associated with merit rating.

From the viewpoint of the worker, the *Performance Record* is a sheet on which his foreman or supervisor records good (blue) and bad (red) things that he does. From the viewpoint of the supervisor, it is a procedure for recording and evaluating the actions of his men. From the viewpoint of the administrator, it is "a standardized personnel program for getting and using the facts of job performance." From the viewpoint of its authors, it is "a procedure for collecting the significant *facts* about employe performance * It is not simply a new form, but *a new approach.*" (Italics as in original.) From the viewpoint of this reviewer, it is a method of classifying items of good or bad behavior under 10 to 16 headings, adding these up under each heading (but never getting a grand total), and then using these 20 to 32 subtotals along with the blank in talking to the employee and in making personnel decisions.

There are different record forms for hourly employees, nonsupervisory salaried employees, and foremen and supervisors. There are three corresponding handbooks for the foremen, supervisors, and superintendents who keep and use the three types of records designed for these three types of employees.

The *Performance Record* form for hourly employees, for instance, contains 16 topics:

Physical and Mental Qualifications
  1. Physical Condition
  2. Coordination
  3. Checking and Inspecting
  4. Arithmetic Computations
  5. Learning and Remembering Procedures and Instructions
  6. Judgment and Comprehension
  7. Understanding and Repairing Mechanical Devices
  8. Improving Equipment and Showing Inventiveness
Work Habits and Attitudes
  9. Productivity
  10. Dependability
  11. Accepting Supervision and Organizational Procedures
  12. Accuracy of Reporting
  13. Response to Departmental Needs
  14. Getting Along with Others
  15. Initiative
  16. Responsibility

Each of these topics is divided into two parts with from 2 to 10 subdivisions for classifying good or bad critical incidents. When an incident occurs, the supervisor classifies it (e.g., 14 A blue = getting along with others—remained calm under stress—good) and enters at the appropriate place on the form the date, the designation of the subdivision, and two or three key words to help him remember it later. It is said that it took less than 5 minutes a day to record all critical incidents in a department of 30 people when records were kept daily. (Even if it should take twice this long, it is still fast.)

All the printed materials are written for production people. Hence, it is difficult and perhaps unfair to evaluate them in terms of the standards usually applied in this *Yearbook*. Even so, it is a bit distressing to note the cavalier fashion in which "old-fashioned merit rating" is dismissed as being "necessarily biased and unfair" and requiring nearly impossible tasks, while the *Performance Record* "is based on established fact." No figures are cited to back up such claims as "The 'halo effect' is eliminated" or "A single outstanding characteristic cannot bias his [the supervisor's] judgment."

Supervisors are told to get red and blue totals, which are counts of the numbers of critical incidents under each of the 2 by 16 headings, but they are told not to regard these totals as scores and not to add them together to get a single overall score or rating. This, of course, means that there can be no possible quantitative comparison of this procedure with any (other) merit rating. For people who like to look at a configuration of subtotals and individual incidents, this is fine; for those who like to have an objective procedure that can be evaluated quantitatively, it leaves much to be desired. This is reminiscent of the perennial arguments between advocates of projective techniques and advocates of objective tests.

The reviewer has attempted to evaluate the *Performance Record* in terms of some relatively common objective standards, realizing that there may be intangible values not readily susceptible to measurement: *reliability,* unknown—no data; *validity or relevance,* unknown—no data; *face validity,* high; *objectivity,* dubious—"what you might consider a 'blue' incident of effective performance could actually be a 'red' incident of ineffective per-

formance in another department"; *practicality,*
high; and *norms or other standards,* none.

To summarize: The *Performance Record*
may well be a good method of evaluating employees; it probably is, but it is unfortunate that
its very nature makes it well nigh impossible
to ascertain objectively whether or not this is
so. It is even more difficult to find out how it
stacks up against competing procedures.

ALBERT S. THOMPSON, *Professor of Education, Teachers College, Columbia University,
New York, New York.*

The *Performance Record,* a standardized
personnel program for getting and using facts
of job performance, is based on research and development in a variety of military and civilian
situations. This research utilized the critical incident technique to derive a series of behavior
descriptions symptomatic of successful or unsuccessful job performance. The *Performance
Record* for nonsupervisory salaried employees,
for example, includes 15 sections with headings
such as Carrying Out Instructions, Accuracy,
Productivity, and Response to Need for Extra
Effort. Under each section are specific behaviors representing desirable or undesirable
job performance. Record forms have been developed for three broad categories of jobs:
hourly employees, nonsupervisory salaried employees, and foremen and supervisors.

The *Performance Record* is not a rating
scale or measuring instrument per se. It is a
program, consisting of record forms and procedures designed to help supervisors analyze
and evaluate the performance of their employees. The "incident sheet" helps supervisors
to direct their observations, to record critical
incidents accurately and systematically, to classify behaviors, and to review employee performance (with the employee) from time to
time.

As a personnel form, the *Performance Record* is admirably suited to practical use. The
form is attractively printed with red and blue
sections to identify unsatisfactory and satisfactory behavior. For each form, there is a handbook for use by the person filling out the form.
This contains clear explanations of the rationale underlying the procedure, guides for its use,
and sample exercises to develop familiarity
with its content and procedures. If used conscientiously and systematically, there is little
doubt that personnel evaluations will be fairer,

personnel decisions will be based more on facts,
and supervisors will be more alert to careful
observation and evaluation of their supervisees'
behavior.

In a review for a measurements yearbook,
one is tempted to evaluate it as a measuring
device. This cannot be done, at least from the
information made available by the publisher,
since the usual data on reliability, validity,
norms, etc. are not provided. They are not provided presumably because they are irrelevant;
the *Performance Record* is a program for recording and analyzing behaviors, not a scale
for measuring human characteristics. As the
manual states, "Supervisors are not asked to
rate the people with whom they are in intimate
daily contact. They merely record the facts of
what employees do or fail to do. Individual differences show up in the recorded facts."

There is an implicit assumption, of course,
that the critical behaviors included on this
form will be similarly critical in a wide variety
of settings. The items were initially derived
from research and have high logical and face
validity, but whether they will really separate
the sheep from the goats on a particular job
in a particular company is a matter for local
research by the user. It is hoped that the publisher will provide help in such research as well
as in the installation of *Performance Record*
programs.

[903]

*Personal Data Blank. Counselees of ages 15 and
over; 1934–52; 1 form ('52); $3.50 per 25 sets of rec-
ord blanks and summary sheets; 25¢ per manual ('52);
50¢ per specimen set; cash orders postpaid; J. Gustav
White; Consulting Psychologists Press. *

ARTHUR E. TRAXLER, *Executive Director,
Educational Records Bureau, New York, New
York.*

This instrument is not a test but a blank for
obtaining detailed information from counselees.
The blank was first prepared more than 20
years ago, but the present version was copyrighted in 1952, the same year that a 16-page
manual for the blank was issued.

The blank includes 93 items, most of which
are open-end questions, grouped under the following headings: (*a*) personal history, (*b*)
your problems, (*c*) your interests and traits,
(*d*) your education, and (*e*) your occupation.
There is a sixth section called "Your Story,"
in which the counselee is asked to write anything about his life that he feels is important.

The blank can be used with anyone from the age of 15 on, but it appears to be best suited to vocational counseling with college students and young adults.

After filling out most of the questions in the blank, the present reviewer estimates that an hour or more would be required for doing the blank completely, including the free writing section, "Your Story." This amount of time may seem excessive to some counselees, but the information obtained should be of considerable help in counseling interviews.

Three items on the first page having to do with race, religion, and church affiliation may be objectionable to some counselees, and it would be contrary to law to ask these questions in certain states. The author frankly recognizes these possible objections and comments upon them in the manual. This reviewer agrees with the author's position that information on these items is useful in counseling, but it may be preferable to infer these kinds of information from observations made during interviews rather than to run the risk of antagonizing some counselees by asking for this information directly in the blank. The other questions in the blank seem well designed to obtain the co-operation of the counselee in supplying the needed data.

The last page of the blank provides for a summary and discussion of the counseling data followed by general recommendations. A facsimile of this page is printed on a separate sheet so that it may be filled out in duplicate and one copy turned over to the counselee, if desired.

In the upper portion of the summary page, a table for use in summarizing the results of the tests is printed. The results are to be entered on a graphic percentile or letter grade scale. This reviewer does not find that table very satisfactory, and he would not be inclined to use it. The general areas of measurement provided for in the table are mental classification, aptitudes, personality, and vocational interests. The printed designations under these general headings seem too restricted. No provision is made for recording results on achievement tests, and only one space is allowed for a score on a personality inventory. Space is provided for the recording of six areas of vocational interests in order of preference; a profile allowing for the showing of contrasts in interests would be likely to be more useful in counseling than the listing of the more pronounced

interests with percentile ratings. In fairness to the author, however, it should be stated that he indicates that additional special reports on the test results should be carefully noted.

A column headed "Norm" in the table for test results is ambiguous. There is no indication as to whether the kind of norm group, such as public school grade 10 or independent school grade 9, should be entered in the column or whether the mean or average score, which is sometimes referred to as a norm, should be shown there.

In the manual the author explains the purpose and structure of the blank, gives directions for administering and suggestions for interpreting, reviews general counseling tools, and provides a list of references. The manual is addressed directly to the counselor; everyday language rather than technical terminology is used; and the style is simple and clear.

This reviewer's assessment of the *Personal Data Blank* and the accompanying manual is generally favorable, but he suggests that another revision designed to correct several weaknesses, particularly in the summary page, would be desirable.

For reviews by Edward S. Jones and Donald G. Paterson of an earlier edition, see 40:1669.

[904]

★**Personnel Institute Hiring Kit.** Business and industry (applicants for sales positions); 1954–57; individual in part; manual ('56); no data on reliability and validity; $10 per kit of manual and 10 copies each of *a–d*; postage extra; scoring service available; $15 per applicant when *e* is used, $30 per applicant when *f* is used; fee includes scoring, interpretation, and report of results; Personnel Institute, Inc. *

a) PRELIMINARY SCREENING INTERVIEW. 1 form ('57); individual; $1 per 10 copies; 10 minutes.

b) PERSONAL HISTORY INVENTORY. 1 form ('57); $1.50 per 10 copies; 30(45) minutes.

c) DIAGNOSTIC INTERVIEWER'S GUIDE. 1 form ('56); individual; $2 per 10 copies; 30 minutes.

d) WORK REFERENCE INVESTIGATION. 1 form ('57); individual; $1 per 10 copies; 10 minutes.

e) SELECTOR TEST BATTERY. Applicants for routine selling jobs; 1955–56; directions sheet ('56); scoring by publisher only; (85–100) minutes.

1) *EM-AY Inventory.* Reprint under new title of *Otis Employment Tests*, Test 2, Form A ('22); test of mental alertness; 30(35) minutes.

2) *ESS-AY Inventory.* 1 form ('55); test of sales aptitude; (40–45) minutes.

3) *The Personality Inventory.* 1 form ('35); (15–20) minutes.

f) COMPREHENSIVE TEST BATTERY. Applicants for complex selling jobs; 1955–57; directions sheet ('57); scoring by publisher only; (195–220) minutes.

1) Same as *e*(1) above.

2) Same as *e*(2) above.

3) Same as $e(3)$ above.

4) *Vocabulary Inventory*. 1 form ('56); (30) minutes.

5) *Social Intelligence Test*. 1 form; 3 scores: tact and diplomacy, understanding of human nature, total; (40) minutes.

6) *B-B-ESS Inventory*. 1 form ('56); test of business skills; 8 scores: comparing, computation, reading, spelling, vocabulary, arithmetical reasoning, English, total; 40(50) minutes.

[905]

★**SRA Employee Inventory.** Employees; 1951–58; attitudes toward job; 1 form; 2 editions; manual, third edition ('52); directions for administering, second edition ('52); profiles and report forms ['51–52]; preliminary norms ('52); typed norms supplement ['58]; (10–25) minutes; Robert K. Burns, L. L. Thurstone, David G. Moore, and Melany E. Baehr; Science Research Associates. *

a) REGULAR EDITION. Form A ('51); separate answer pads must be used; 85¢ per test; $3 per 20 answer pads; 75¢ per manual; 25¢ per directions for administering; $1 per specimen set; postage extra.

b) GOVERNMENT EDITION. Form GX ('51); test materials rented only; details may be obtained from publisher.

REFERENCES

1. ASH, PHILIP. "The SRA Employee Inventory—A Statistical Analysis." *Personnel Psychol* 7:337–64 au '54. * (PA 29:4762)

2. BAEHR, MELANY E. "A Factorial Study of the SRA Employee Inventory." *Personnel Psychol* 7:319–36 au '54. * (PA 29:4763)

3. WHERRY, ROBERT J. "An Orthogonal Re-Rotation of the Baehr and Ash Studies of the SRA Employee Inventory." *Personnel Psychol* 7:365–80 au '54. * (PA 29:4788)

4. DABAS, ZILE SINGH. *The Dimensions of Morale: An Item Factorization of the SRA Employee Inventory.* Doctor's thesis, Ohio State University (Columbus, Ohio), 1955. (DA 16:798)

5. MOORE, DAVID G., AND RENCK, RICHARD. "The Professional Employee in Industry." *J Bus* 28:58–66 Ja '55. *

6. BAEHR, MELANY E. "A Reply to Robert J. Wherry Concerning 'An Orthogonal Re-Rotation of the Baehr and Ash Studies of the SRA Employee Inventory.'" *Personnel Psychol* 9:81–91 sp '56. * (PA 31:4017)

7. WHERRY, ROBERT J. "A Rejoinder to Baehr's Reply on Rotation of the SRA Employee Inventory Studies." *Personnel Psychol* 9:93–9 sp '56. * (PA 31:4017)

8. BRAYFIELD, ARTHUR H.; WELLS, RICHARD V.; AND STRATE, MARVIN W. "Interrelationships Among Measures of Job Satisfaction and General Satisfaction." *J Appl Psychol* 41:201–5 Ag '57. *

9. BRUCE, MARTIN M. "Normative Data Information Exchange, No. 10–35." *Personnel Psychol* 10:370 au '57. *

10. DABAS, ZILE S. "The Dimensions of Morale: An Item Factorization of the SRA Inventory." *Personnel Psychol* 11:217–34 su '58. *

ERWIN K. TAYLOR, *President, Personnel Research and Development Corporation, Cleveland, Ohio.*

Broadly viewed, there are three major approaches to the measurement of employee attitudes: (*a*) the polling approach, in which the percentages of responses to alternatives of individual questions are tabulated; (*b*) the clinical approach, usually based on "depth" interviews which are interpreted in the light of the interviewer's background; and (*c*) the mental test approach, in which attitudinal domains are empirically identified and groups of items measuring each incorporated in an objective instrument.

Most employee attitude surveys are of the

political poll type. In smaller surveys the clinical approach is often used. The *SRA Employee Inventory* is, to the best of this reviewer's knowledge, the first attempt to apply the mental test approach to attitude measurement on a commercial scale. The inventory consists of 78 short statements such as "The people I work with are very friendly." Subjects respond to each statement by indicating one of the following three alternatives: (1) agree, (2)?, (3) disagree. The test booklet is reusable, answers being marked on a snapout carbon form which is prekeyed on the back for easy scoring.

The inventory purports to measure 15 a priori attitudinal areas with from two to seven items in each. Factor analyses of the scales (omitting the total) by Ash (*1*) and Baehr (*2, 6*) and the integration of these by Wherry (*3, 7*) strongly indicate that the areas suggested by the publisher have no independent reality. This is reinforced by the factor analysis for the 78 items in the scale reported by Dabas (*10*). On the basis of these findings, it would seem that the original areas should now be abandoned and new scoring keys developed on the basis of the factor analysis results.

From a study of the General Manual and Directions for Administering and Scoring the SRA Employee Inventory, it would appear that this instrument was developed primarily for use by amateurs whose knowledge of the appropriateness of conducting an attitude survey and of how to interpret and use the results effectively is questionable. This reviewer is concerned with the availability of psychological devices to individuals not adequately trained to evaluate the appropriateness of their application in a given situation, their limitations, or the proper interpretation of results. The *SRA Employee Inventory* appears to have been intentionally designed to appeal to the untrained "do-it-yourself" market. Recent advertising by the publisher claims that "high morale almost invariably means: high productivity, low absenteeism and turnover, confidence in management, a harmonious and creative atmosphere." No research of which the reviewer is aware justifies so broad a generalization.

The manual makes no mention of norms as such. These are taken care of by plotting raw scores on the profile sheet. It is implied that the 1952 norms were based on "approximately 25,000 inventories." The fourth edition of the Report of Survey Results (February 1953) shows some substantial differences (particularly at the low end of the scales) from the second (January 1952) edition. The first percentile for the "inventory as a whole" was 33.70 in 1952 and 27.00 in 1953. The median for this scale changed from 49.40 to 50.75 and the 99th percentile from 65.22 to 69.00. Whether this is a function of changing times or of the broader sample of the normative population, we do not know. In any event, the user should be certain to be consistent in his use of the forms or he may find shifts taking place that are purely a function of the edition of the report form used.

A January 1958 norms supplement not generally distributed gives a population breakdown of the general norms based on 35,000 cases and compares it with the Department of Commerce percentages for the total work force. In May 1958, the publisher announced (but did not supply) separate norms for four industries and production workers and supervisors. Separation of male and female norms groups has evidently not been made.

In summary, the *SRA Employee Inventory* appears to be the first attempt by a commercial test publisher to employ the test construction approach in attitude measurement. Its a priori scoring has been demonstrated to be unsound, and available norms are somewhat questionable. It has been too highly touted as supplying pat answers to involved questions and as being effectively usable on a "do-it-yourself" basis. Nevertheless, it is probably a better device than the average, homemade questionnaire. Scored in accordance with the factor analysis findings, separately standardized by sex, occupation, and level, and used by professionals qualified to interpret its results in a psychologically meaningful manner, the *SRA Employee Inventory* would constitute a valuable psychological tool.

ALBERT S. THOMPSON, *Professor of Education, Teachers College, Columbia University, New York, New York.*

An "ideal" instrument to determine the attitudes of employees toward their work has to meet a variety of requirements. It should be short and easily read and answered. It should be easily scored and yield a measure of overall level of morale as well as of attitudes toward specific aspects of the work situation. It should be reliable and should stimulate a desire to answer truthfully and completely. It should permit comparisons of individuals with groups, subgroups with each other, and local groups with national groups. It should permit study of factors peculiar to the specific setting.

The *SRA Employee Inventory* meets most of these requirements. Its 78 items can be answered in 10 to 20 minutes and are phrased in language understandable to employees with fourth grade education or better (according to the manual). It yields a total inventory score and 14 profile category scores, such as Job Demands, Pay, Confidence in Management, Adequacy of Communication, etc. To the 78 standard items printed in the published form can be added up to 12 tailor-made items. A special edition adapted for use with employees of government agencies has been devised. Test-retest reliability coefficients from several studies range in the .60's and .70's for category scores of individuals and in the high .90's when used as a group instrument.

It is designed to be answered anonymously, but it has space to record desired group identifications, such as department, length of service, etc. The printed answer sheet has space for free comments.

The instrument was originally prepared at the Industrial Relations Center of the University of Chicago and resulted from careful construction and pretesting of the items. The publisher has further developed it, particularly with respect to format, administration, and profiling of results. A confidential test used by the consulting division of SRA, it is made available to clients for attitude surveys of their employees. In addition to purchasing arrangements, SRA provides the materials, scoring and analysis of group results at a charge (as of April 1958) of $1.65 per employee surveyed.

So far, so good. As a device to elicit responses to the 78 job related statements listed, it is certainly better than the potpourri of items frequently thrown together by hurried personnel workers faced with an order from above to make an attitude survey. The procedures for administering, scoring, and analyzing the results are well worked out and designed to yield quickly information of value to management.

On the matter of its value as a scientific measure of employee morale or as a systematic survey of the basic attitudes of employees, however, one must reserve judgment until more data are available. There is little or no information as to the relationship between the category scores and criterion measures of these categories. Factor analysis studies were used in the original grouping of items into the 14 categories, but subsequent studies have yielded fewer factors and one investigator has questioned the factor method used and presented evidence of a large general factor.

The manual and catalog descriptions refer to national norms based on over 1,000 companies with industrial and occupational breakdowns, but the latest manual, dated 1952, does not present or describe these norms.

In summary, as a device for obtaining employee attitudes toward the 78 items involved, the *SRA Employee Inventory* and the related consulting services of the publisher should provide a useful personnel tool. Considered as an instrument to measure morale and its basic components, it needs further research and development, a comment which can be made about most attitude survey questionnaires.

[906]

★A Self-Rating Scale for Leadership Qualifications. Adults; 1942–48; 1 form ('48); profile ('48); no manual; no data on reliability and validity, no norms; 25¢ per single copy, postage extra; administration time not reported; E. J. Benge; National Foremen's Institute, Inc. *

SPECIFIC VOCATIONS

[907]

★Accounting Orientation Test: High School Level. Grades 11–12; 1953–56; 4 scores: vocabulary, arithmetic reasoning, accounting problems, total; IBM; Forms S, T ('53); manual ('56); preliminary norms; $2.50 per 25 tests; separate answer sheets may be used; 2¢ per IBM answer sheet; postage extra; 25¢ per specimen set, postpaid; 40(50) minutes; Committee on Personnel Testing, American Institute of Certified Public Accountants. *

REFERENCES

1. JACOBS, ROBERT, AND TRAXLER, ARTHUR E. "A Professional Aptitude Test for High School." *Clearing House* 28:266–8 Ja '54. *
2. MORICI, ANTHONY R. "Relation Between the Scores on the A.I.A. Orientation Test With the A.I.A. Elementary, Advanced Accounting Tests and Accounting Grades." *J Ed Res* 51:549–52 Mr '58. *

[908]

★Achievement Tests in Nursing. Nurses: 1952–58; IBM; 1 form; 12 tests; directions sheet ['57]; norms ['58] for each test; no charge to schools requiring Entrance Examinations for Schools of Practical Nursing; 35¢ per test per student for other schools, postpaid; (40) minutes per test; Psychological Corporation. *
a) ANATOMY AND PHYSIOLOGY. 1953–58; 1 form ['53].
b) CHEMISTRY. 1954–58; 1 form ['54].
c) COMMUNICABLE DISEASES. 1953–58; 1 form ['53].
d) MEDICAL NURSING. 1952–58; 1 form ['52].
e) MICROBIOLOGY. 1952–58; 1 form ['58].

f) NUTRITION AND DIET THERAPY. 1952–58; 1 form ('57).
g) OBSTETRICAL NURSING. 1952–58; 1 form ['52].
h) PEDIATRIC NURSING. 1952–58; 1 form ['52].
i) PHARMACOLOGY. 1952–58; 1 form ('57).
j) PSYCHIATRIC NURSING. 1952–58; 1 form ('57).
k) PSYCHOLOGY AND SOCIOLOGY. 1958; 1 form ['58]; no data on reliability; no norms.
l) SURGICAL NURSING. 1952–58; 1 form ('57).

[909]

★Achievement Tests in Practical Nursing. Practical nursing students; 1957; 2 scores: medical and surgical nursing, nutrition-pediatric-obstetrical nursing; IBM; 2 parts; directions sheet ['57]; no charge to schools requiring Entrance Examinations for Schools of Practical Nursing; 35¢ per student for other schools, postpaid; (100) minutes; Psychological Corporation. *

[910]

★Admission Test for Graduate Study in Business. Business graduate students; 1954–58; test administered 4 times annually (November, February, April, July) at centers established by the publisher; 3 scores: quantitative, verbal, total; IBM; examination fee, $10; fee includes reporting of scores to any 3 schools designated at time of application; $1 per additional report; 200(230) or 205(235) minutes; Educational Testing Service. *

[911]

*American Institute of Certified Public Accountants Testing Programs. Grades 13–16 and accountants; 1946–57; IBM; 2 programs; $2.50 for 1 to 12 transcripts; American Institute of Certified Public Accountants. *
a) COLLEGE ACCOUNTING TESTING PROGRAM. Grades 13–16; 1946–57; tests available 3 times annually (fall, midyear, spring); manual ['57]; postage extra.
   1) *Orientation Test*. Grades 13–16; 1946–49; 3 scores: verbal, quantitative, total; Forms A ('46), B ('46), C ('49); 50¢ per student; 50(70) minutes.
   2) *Achievement Test: Level 1.* Grades 13–15; 1946–57; 3 long forms: Forms A ('57), B ('47), C ('51), 120(140) minutes; 3 short forms: Forms A-S ('55), B-S ('56), C-S ('57), 50(70) minutes; 50¢ per student.
   3) *Achievement Test: Level 2.* Grade 16; 1946–51; 2 long forms: Forms A ('47), B ('49), 240(260) minutes; 2 short forms: Forms C ('51), D ('50), 120(140) minutes; 50¢ per student.
   4) *Strong Vocational Interest Blank for Men, Revised.* See 868; grades 13–16; 1927–50; Form M ('38); blank scored for 27 scales and plotted on an accountant's profile ['50]; 1–24 students, $1.80 each; tests not distributed for local scoring; (40) minutes.
b) PROFESSIONAL ACCOUNTING TESTING PROGRAM. Accountants; 1947–57; tests available to accounting employers at any time; tests also administered at regional testing centers throughout the year; 4 tests; revised manual ('51); norms ('54); $2.50 per examinee if test is scored locally; $5 per examinee if test is scored by publisher; 3 transcripts available free; postpaid.
   1) *Orientation Test.* 1946; Form A; same as *a*(1) above.
   2) *Achievement Test: Level 1.* 1946–57; Form A ('57); same as *a*(2) above.
   3) *Achievement Test: Level 2.* 1946–51; Forms A ('47), C ('51); same as *a*(3) above.
   4) *Strong Vocational Interest Blank For Men, Revised.* Same as *a*(4) above; tests not distributed for local scoring; $2 per examinee.

REFERENCES

1-15. See 4:787.
16. HENDRIX, O. R. "Predicting Success in Elementary Accounting." *J Appl Psychol* 37:75-7 Ap '53. * (*PA* 28:1479)
17. HENDRIX, O. R. " 'A Note' Acknowledged." *J Appl Psychol* 38:9 F '54. * (*PA* 29:1451)
18. JACOBS, ROBERT. "A Note on 'Predicting Success in Elementary Accounting.' " *J Appl Psychol* 38:7-8 F '54. * (*PA* 29:1456)
19. FREDERICK, MARVIN L. "Testing the Tests." *J Account* 103:42-7 Ap '57. *
20. MORICI, ANTHONY R. "Relation Between the Scores on the A.I.A. Orientation Test With the A.I.A. Elementary, Advanced Accounting Tests and Accounting Grades." *J Ed Res* 51:549-52 Mr '58. *
21. NORTH, ROBERT D. "Tests for the Accounting Profession." *Ed & Psychol Meas* 18:691-713 W '58. *

[912]

*[American Transit Association Tests.] Transit operating personnel; 1941-51; 4 tests; $3.50 per battery manual ('46); postpaid; Glen U. Cleeton, Merwyn A. Kraft, and Robert F. Royster; American Transit Association. *

a) STANDARD EXAMINATION FOR TRANSIT EMPLOYEES. 1941-46; intelligence; Forms A ('41), AA ('43) for street car operators; Forms B ('41), BB ('43) for bus operators; manual ('46); $7.50 per 100 tests; 20(30) or 30(40) minutes.

b) PERSONAL REACTION TEST FOR TRANSIT EMPLOYEES. 1943-46; personality; Series A ('46) ; manual ('46); no data on reliability; $10 per 100 tests; (30) minutes.

c) THE PLACEMENT INTERVIEW FOR TRANSIT EMPLOYEES. 1946; 9 ratings (moral character, mental ability, motor ability, health, motivation, stability, maturity, sociability, manner and appearance) in 3 areas (work experience, schooling and childhood, personal history) ; 1 form; $5 per 100 interview forms.

d) A STANDARDIZED ROAD TEST FOR BUS OPERATORS. 1951 ; 1 form; $2 per 100 checklists; 50¢ per manual.

For reviews by Harold G. Seashore, Morris S. Viteles, and J. V. Waits, see 3:696.

[913]

*Aptitude Index. Prospective male life insurance agents; 1938-56; 1 score combining an evaluation of personal background, interests, and attitudes; Forms 5 ['54], 6 ['56]; forms differ in experimental items only; manual ['54]; separate scoring keys for United States and Canada; no data on reliability; separate answer booklets must be used; distribution restricted to home offices of member life insurance companies; details may be obtained from publisher; cash orders postpaid; French edition available; (60) minutes; Life Insurance Agency Management Association. *

REFERENCES

1-5. See 40:1646.
6-19. See 4:825.
20. BILLS, MARION A., AND TAYLOR, JEAN G. "Over and Under Achievement in a Sales School in Relation to Future Production." *J Appl Psychol* 37:21-3 F '53. * (*PA* 28:1664)

For reviews by Donald G. Paterson and Albert S. Thompson of an earlier form, see 4: 825.

[914]

*Aptitude Associates Test of Sales Aptitude: A Test for Measuring Knowledge of Basic Principles of Selling. Sales applicants; 1947-58; Form A ('47); hectographed manual, 16th edition ('58); 15¢ per test; 25¢ per scoring key; 75¢ per manual; $1 per specimen set; cash orders postpaid; (20-30) minutes; Martin M. Bruce; the Author. *

For reviews by Milton E. Hahn and Donald G. Paterson, see 4:824.

[915]

★A Chart For the Rating of a Foreman. Ratings of foremen by supervisors; 1941-48; 1 form ('48) ; no data on reliability; no norms; 50¢ per single copy, postage extra; administration time not reported; R. D. Bundy; National Foremen's Institute, Inc. *

[916]

*Dental Aptitude Testing Program. Dental school applicants; 1946-58; tests administered 3 times annually (January, April, October) at centers established by the publisher; IBM except *a;* 5 tests; examination fee, $15; fee includes reporting of scores to any 5 schools designated at time of application; $1 per additional report; postpaid; scores not reported to examinees; 323(415) minutes in 2 sessions; Division of Educational Measurements, Council on Dental Education, American Dental Association. *

a) CARVING DEXTERITY TEST. 1946-58; 90(110) minutes; Committee on Aptitude Testing.

b) AMERICAN COUNCIL ON EDUCATION PSYCHOLOGICAL EXAMINATION FOR COLLEGE FRESHMEN. See 308; 1924-54; 3 scores: linguistic, quantitative, total; IBM; 1954 Edition; 38(75) minutes.

c) READING COMPREHENSION IN THE NATURAL SCIENCES. 1953-55; IBM; Forms 54 ('53), 55 ('54) ; 80(85) minutes; Committee on Aptitude Testing.

d) SPACE RELATIONS TEST. See 605; 1947; IBM; Forms A, B ('47); 40(45) minutes.

e) SURVEY OF THE NATURAL SCIENCES. 1951-58; 5 scores: biology, chemistry, factual, application, total; IBM; 1 form ('58); 75(80) minutes; Committee on Aptitude Testing.

REFERENCES

1-2. See 4:788.
3. MARLES, LESLIE. *A Study of the Relationship of Academic Achievement to Aptitude Scores of the American Dental Association's Experimental Testing Program.* Master's thesis, Temple University (Philadelphia, Pa.), 1948.
4. PETERSON, SHAILER. "Validation of Professional Aptitude Batteries: Tests for Dentistry," pp. 35-45. (*PA* 26:595) In *Proceedings of the 1950 Invitational Conference on Testing Problems, October 28, 1950.* Princeton, N.J.: Educational Testing Service, 1951. Pp. 117. *
5. ANDERSON, ADOLPH V., AND FRIEDMAN, SIDNEY. "Prediction of Performance in a Navy Dental Prosthetic Technician Training Course." Abstract. *Am Psychol* 7:288 Jl '52. *
6. WEISS, IRVING. "Prediction of Academic Success in Dental School." *J Appl Psychol* 36:11-4 F '52. * (*PA* 26:7296)
7. LAYTON, WILBUR L. "Predicting Success in Dental School." *J Appl Psychol* 37:251-5 Ag '53. * (*PA* 28:6712)
8. WEBB, SAM C. "The Prediction of Achievement for First Year Dental Students." *Ed & Psychol Meas* 16:543-8 W '56. *

[917]

★Dental Hygiene Aptitude Testing Program. Dental hygiene school applicants; 1947-57; tests administered 3 times annually (October, February, May) at centers established by the American Dental Hygienists' Association; IBM; 1 form; 4 tests; manual ['57]; examination fee, $9; fee includes reporting of scores to 3 schools designated at time of application; $1 per additional report; scores not reported to examinees; postpaid; 98(175) minutes; Psychological Corporation. *

a) STUDY-READING TEST. 1955; Form S; 20(25) minutes.

b) DENTAL HYGIENE APTITUDE TESTING PROGRAM, PARTS 1 AND 2. 1947-57; IBM; 1 form ['57]; 48(55) minutes.

c) COLLEGE QUALIFICATION TEST, TEST 1. See 320; 1955-56; IBM; Form A ('56) ; 30(35) minutes.

d) THE PERSONAL PREFERENCE SCHEDULE. 1953-55; adaptation of *Edwards Personal Preference Schedule* (see 47) ; 1 form ('55) ; (40-60) minutes.

[918]

*[Driver Selection Forms and Tests.] Truck drivers; 1943–55; part of White Motor Co.'s *Continuing Control System of Truck Management;* individual in part; manual out of print; 25¢ per specimen set; postage extra; Dartnell Corporation. *
a) [DRIVER SELECTION FORMS.] 1946–55.
   1) *Employment Application.* 1946; Form Nos. 111 (city delivery drivers), 211 (over-the-road drivers), 311 (long distance drivers); 7¢ per copy.
   2) *Telephone Check.* 1946–53; Form No. OT-203 ('53); 6¢ per copy.
   3) *Driver Interview.* 1946; Form No. 13 ['46]; 10¢ per copy.
   4) *Physical Examination Record.* 1946–54; Form No. 19 ('54); 5¢ per copy.
   5) *Selection and Evaluation Summary.* 1950–55; Form No. ES-404R ('55); 6¢ per copy.
b) [DRIVER SELECTION AND TRAINING TESTS.] 1943–54.
   1) *Traffic and Driving Knowledge.* 1946–54; Form No. 16 ('46); no manual; no data on reliability; 6¢ per test; 6¢ per directions sheet-scoring key ('54, Form No. 17); administration time not reported; Amos E. Neyhart and Helen L. Neyhart; also distributed by Institute of Public Safety, Pennsylvania State University.
   2) *Road Test in Traffic.* 1943–46; 3 scores: specific driving skills, general driving habits and attitudes, total; individual; 1 form [45]; instruction sheet ('45); score sheet ('46, Form No. 18); 5¢ per copy; (30–60) minutes; Amos E. Neyhart; also distributed by American Automobile Association and Institute of Public Safety, Pennsylvania State University.

For a review by S. Rains Wallace, Jr., see 4:789.

[919]

★Engineering Aide Test 50-A. Engineering aides; 1957; Form 50-A; preliminary mimeographed manual; no norms; separate answer sheets must be used; PPA member agency: 10–49 tests, 96¢ each; others, $1.20 each; $2 per specimen set; postpaid; 90(100) minutes; Public Personnel Association. *

[920]

★Entrance Examinations for Schools of Practical Nursing. Practical nursing school applicants; 1942–57; tests administered at regional testing centers established by the publisher; IBM; 1 form; 3 tests; manual ['57]; examination fee, $6; fee includes reporting of scores to one school designated at time of application; $2 per additional report; scores not reported to examinees; postpaid; 95(210) minutes; Psychological Corporation. *
a) ENTRANCE EXAMINATION FOR SCHOOLS OF PRACTICAL NURSING. 1957; 5 scores: verbal ability, numerical ability, academic ability, household information, arithmetic; Form A ('57); 65(75) minutes.
b) TEST OF MECHANICAL COMPREHENSION. See 889; 1942; Form WI ('42); 30(35) minutes.
c) THE PERSONAL PREFERENCE SCHEDULE FOR STUDENT NURSES. 1953–55; adaptation of *Edwards Personal Preference Schedule* (see 47); 6 scores: achievement, orderliness, persistence, congeniality, altruism, respectfulness; 1 form; (45) minutes.

[921]

★Firefighter Test. Firemen; 1954–58; title on Form 20-A is *Test for Firefighter;* IBM; Forms 20-A ('54), 20-B ('57); revised mimeographed manual ('57); norms ('58); no data on reliability and validity; separate answer sheets must be used; PPA member agency:

10–49 tests, $1.20 each; others, $1.60 each; $2 per specimen set; postpaid; 105(115) minutes; Public Personnel Association. *

[922]

★General Test on Traffic and Driving Knowledge. Drivers; 1949–50; 1 form (50); directions sheet ('49); no data on reliability; no norms; 47¢ per 25 tests, postage extra; specimen set free; administration time not reported; Traffic Engineering and Safety Department, American Automobile Association; published jointly by American Automobile Association and Institute of Public Safety, Pennsylvania State University. *

[923]

*The Graduate Record Examinations Advanced Tests: Engineering. College seniors and graduate students; 1939–57; for more complete information, see 601; IBM; 180(200) minutes; Educational Testing Service. *

For a review by Harold Seashore of the entire series, see 601.

[924]

★Hall Salespower Inventory. Salesmen; 1946–57; title on test is *Salespower Inventory;* 10 scores: background, intelligence, aggressiveness, dominance, sales temperament, sales interest, introversion-extroversion, motivation, emotional, total; Form A ('46); no data on reliability and validity; norms ('53); distribution restricted to industries; 1–10 tests, $2.50 each; $5 per set of scoring keys and manual ('57); postpaid; (60) minutes; Clifton W. Hall and Richard M. Page; Hall & Liles. *

[925]

★Hanes Sales Selection Inventory, Revised Edition. Insurance and printing salesmen; 1954–55; 3 scores: verbal, personality, drive; 1 form ('55); manual ('55); no data on reliability and validity of drive score; $3 per 20 tests; $1 per specimen set (must be purchased to obtain manual); postage extra; (30–40) minutes; Bernard Hanes; Psychometric Affiliates. *

[926]

How Supervise? Supervisors; 1943–48; Forms A ('43), B ('43), M ('48, consists of items from Forms A and B); revised manual ('48); $2.45 per 25 tests; 35¢ per specimen set; postpaid; administration time not reported; Quentin W. File and H. H. Remmers (manual); Psychological Corporation. *

REFERENCES

1–5. See 3:687.
6–13. See 4:774.
14. HOLMES, FRANK J. "Validity of Tests for Insurance Office Personnel." *Personnel Psychol* 3:57–69 sp '50. * (*PA* 24:5490)
15. MILLER, FRANK G., AND REMMERS, H. H. "Studies in Industrial Empathy: II, Managements' Attitudes Toward Industrial Supervision and Their Estimates of Labor Attitudes." *Personnel Psychol* 3:33–40 sp '50. * (*PA* 24:5504)
16. CARTER, GERALD C. "Measurement of Supervisory Ability." *J Appl Psychol* 36:393–5 D '52. * (*PA* 27:6801)
17. MALONEY, PAUL W. "Reading Ease Scores for File's *How Supervise?*" *J Appl Psychol* 36:225–7 Ag '52. * (*PA* 27:3804)
18. MILLARD, KENNETH A. "Is *How Supervise?* an Intelligence Test?" *J Appl Psychol* 36:221–4 Ag '52. * (*PA* 27:3805)
19. WICKERT, FREDERIC R. "*How Supervise?* Scores Before and After Courses in Psychology." *J Appl Psychol* 36:388–92 D '52. * (*PA* 26:6822)
20. WICKERT, FREDERIC R. "Relation Between *How Supervise?*, Intelligence and Education for a Group of Supervisory Candidates in Industry." *J Appl Psychol* 36:301–3 O '52. * (*PA* 27:5453)
21. WEITZ, JOSEPH, AND NUCKOLS, ROBERT C. "A Validation Study of 'How Supervise?'" *J Appl Psychol* 37:7–8 F '53. * (*PA* 28:1672)
22. "Validity Information Exchange, No. 7-065: D.O.T. Code 5-92.411, Foreman II." *Personnel Psychol* 7:301 su '54. *

23. JOHNSON, ROSSALL J. "Validity Information Exchange, No. 7-090: D.O.T. Code 5-91, Foreman II." *Personnel Psychol* 7:567 w '54. *
24. PATTON, WENDELL M., JR. "Studies in Industrial Empathy: III, A Study of Supervisory Empathy in the Textile Industry." *J Appl Psychol* 38:285-8 O '54. * (PA 29:6378)
25. BARTHOL, RICHARD P., AND ZEIGLER, MARTIN. "Evaluation of a Supervisory Training Program With *How Supervise?*" *J Appl Psychol* 40:403-5 D '56. * (PA 32:2189)
26. DECKER, ROBERT L. "An Item Analysis of *How Supervise?* Using Both Internal and External Criteria." *J Appl Psychol* 40:406-11 D '56. * (PA 32:2190)
27. McCORMICK, ERNEST J., AND MIDDAUGH, RICHARD W. "The Development of a Tailor-Made Scoring Key for the How Supervise? Test." *Personnel Psychol* 9:27-37 sp '56. * (PA 31:5203)
28. FARBRO, PATRICK C., AND COOK, JOHN M. "Normative Data Information Exchange, No. 10-7." *Personnel Psychol* 10:103 sp '57. *
29. MOWRY, HARLEY W. "A Measure of Supervisory Quality." *J Appl Psychol* 41:405-8 D '57. *
30. SAUNDERS, WM. J., JR. "Normative Data Information Exchange, No. 10-33." *Personnel Psychol* 10:367-8 au '57. *
31. DUNNETTE, MARVIN D., AND KIRCHNER, WAYNE K. "Validation of Psychological Tests in Industry." *Personnel Adm* 21:20-7 My-Je '58. *

For a review by Milton M. Mandell, see 4: 774; for reviews by D. Welty Lefever, Charles I. Mosier, and C. H. Ruedisili, see 3:687.

[927]

★**Information Index.** Life insurance agents; 1951-58; Forms A, B ('57); manual ('57); directions sheet ['57]; norms supplement ['58]; separate answer sheets must be used; distribution restricted to home offices of member life insurance companies; details may be obtained from publisher; cash orders postpaid; Canadian edition available; 60(70) minutes; Life Insurance Agency Management Association. *

REFERENCES

1. GUEST, THEODORE A. *The Construction and Analysis of a Test of Life Insurance Information.* Master's thesis, Trinity College (Hartford, Conn.), 1952.
2. BAIER, DONALD E., AND DUGAN, ROBERT D. "Tests and Performance in a Sales Organization." *Personnel Psychol* 9:17-26 sp '56. * (PA 31:5169)
3. BAIER, DONALD E., AND DUGAN, ROBERT D. "Factors in Sales Success." *J Appl Psychol* 41:37-40 F '57. *

[928]

*Law School Admission Test.** Law school entrants; 1948-58; test administered 4 times annually (November, February, April, August) at centers established by the publisher; IBM; examination fee, $10; fee includes reporting of score to any 3 law schools designated at time of application; $1 per additional report; 215(245) minutes; Educational Testing Service. *

REFERENCES

1-6. See 4:815.
7. JOHNSON, A. PEMBERTON, AND OLSEN, MARJORIE A. "Comparative Three-Year and One-Year Validities of the Law School Admission Test at Two Law Schools." Abstract. *Am Psychol* 7:288 Jl '52. *
8. OLSEN, MARJORIE A., AND SCHRADER, WILLIAM B. "An Empirical Comparison of Five Methods of Shortening a Test." Abstract. *Am Psychol* 7:286-7 Jl '52. *
9. BUCKTON, LaVERNE, AND DOPPELT, JEROME E. "Freshman Tests as Predictors of Scores on Graduate and Professional School Examinations." *J Counsel Psychol* 2:146-9 su '55. * (PA 30:3453)
10. JOHNSON, A. PEMBERTON. "The Development of Shorter and More Useful Selection Tests." *J Ed Psychol* 46:402-7 N '55. * (PA 31:3790)
11. JOHNSON, A. PEMBERTON; OLSEN, MARJORIE A.; AND WINTERBOTTOM, JOHN A. *The Law School Admission Test and Suggestions for Its Use: A Handbook for Law School Deans and Admission Officers.* Princeton, N.J.: Educational Testing Service, April 1955. Pp. 148. * (PA 31:6677)
12. OLSEN, MARJORIE. *The Law School Admission Test as a Predictor of Law School Grades, 1948-53.* Statistical Report SR-55-9. Princeton, N.J.: Educational Testing Service, March 1955. Pp. i, 17. *
13. BRESLOW, EVELYN. "The Predictive Efficiency of the Law School Admission Test at the New York University School of Law." *Psychol Newsl* 9:13-22 S-O '57. * (PA 32:4586)

For a review by Alexander G. Wesman of Form YLS2, see 4:815.

[929]

★**LIAMA Inventory of Job Attitudes.** Life insurance agents; 1956; job satisfaction scores in 17 areas; 1 form ['56]; no data on reliability; no norms; distribution restricted to home offices of member life insurance companies; details may be obtained from publisher; cash orders postpaid; [20-30] minutes; Life Insurance Agency Management Association. *

[930]

★**Managerial Scale for Enterprise Improvement.** Supervisors; 1955; job satisfaction; 1 form; hectographed manual; $3 per 50 tests; $1 per specimen set (must be purchased to obtain manual) including 10 tests, manual, and scoring key; postage extra; (12) minutes; Herbert A. Kaufman, Jr.; Psychometric Affiliates. *

BRENT BAXTER, *Director of Agencies Research, Prudential Insurance Company, Newark, New Jersey.*

This scale is a list of 34 conditions which might affect morale in a business enterprise. The respondents, supposedly only management personnel, indicate where they perceive the current status of each condition in the range from "very good" to "very poor." The total score is supposed to reveal "management morale."

The manual reports a corrected odd-even reliability of .89 for 213 management people, presumably from one company's department heads, supervisors, and foremen. For this same group a tetrachoric correlation of .47 between score and length of management experience is reported, the author claiming that this reveals validity. Percentile norms for the group are given.

The only unusual feature about this instrument is that the respondent is oriented toward evaluating conditions in the company that need improvement. This may be contrasted to the more direct morale survey approach which frankly asks the respondent to tell how he feels about his job. There is no evidence to suggest that this new approach is superior to the direct approach.

This instrument is not likely to find widespread use. The list of job conditions is not unique, but is drawn from conventional sources. Evidence demonstrating validity is not convincing. The directions for administration are incomplete. The norms are limited and inadequately described. This is not an instrument especially adapted to management personnel. A homemade instrument would probably be preferred since it could be adapted to local terminology and problems.

EDWARD B. GREENE, *Supervisor of Personnel Research, Chrysler Corporation, Detroit, Michigan.*

This is a 34-item rating sheet to be filled out anonymously by supervisors. Each item is a short statement such as, "Fair allocation of work force." The statements are printed in a column on the left side of a sheet. On the right hand side are five blank columns with the words "very good," "good," "average," "poor," and "very poor" printed across the column tops. Over the column of statements is boldly printed the one word "REQUIRE-MENTS." The significance of this word is not explained, nor is it clear to the reviewer.

Although no specific instructions are given, one is cautioned in the manual *not* to tell the respondent that the scale is a measure of morale, but rather to indicate that it is for the purpose of enterprise improvement.

Although most of the items seem fairly clear, some are not. For instance the statements "Administrative encouragement of fundamental supervisory achievement" and "Effectiveness of supervisory voice in policy making" seem ambiguous. No analysis is given of the areas covered by the form.

The form requests the respondent to indicate whether he is a department manager, a supervisor, or a foreman. This also need clarification because, in many offices and plants, the word supervisor is a general term which includes both department managers and foremen.

To score the form one simply adds the checks in each column and allows 5 points for "very good," 4 for "good," 3 for "average," and so on. Omitted items are all scored 3. The percentile norms indicate a 50th percentile of 106 points for 213 supervisors. On the assumption that managers with more than 90 days experience were "more successful in meeting the goals which make for managerial satisfaction" than managers with less than 90 days experience, the author computed a tetrachoric correlation between performances of the two groups. He found this to be .47 and concluded that this indicated the tendency for "individuals with greater experience to have higher management morale." An odd-even reliability coefficient of .89 (stepped up by the Spearman-Brown formula) is reported.

Managerial Scale for Enterprise Improvement

The reviewer is *not* happily impressed with this form because of its appearance, its vagueness, and the lack of analysis of what it covers.

[931]

★**Measure of Consociative Tendency.** Applicants for sales and supervisory positions; 1951; personal history blank; 1 form; mimeographed directions sheet; $2.50 per 100 blanks, postage extra; specimen set not available; (10–20) minutes; Doncaster G. Humm and Kathryn A. Humm; Humm Personnel Consultants. *

[932]

***Medical College Admission Test.** Medical school entrants; 1946–56; 4 scores: verbal, quantitative, modern society, science; test administered 2 times annually (May, October) at centers established by the publisher; IBM; examination fee, $10; fee includes reporting of scores to any 3 schools designated at time of application; $1 per additional report; scores not reported to examinees; 245(275) minutes; Educational Testing Service. *

REFERENCES

1–11. See 4:817.
12. RALPH, RAY B., AND TAYLOR, CALVIN W. "The Role of Tests in the Medical Selection Program." *J Appl Psychol* 36:107–11 Ap '52. * (*PA* 27:674)
13. STALNAKER, JOHN M. "Medical College Admission Test," pp. 797–805. (*PA* 27:8040) In *Contributions Toward Medical Psychology: Theory and Psychodiagnostic Methods, Vol. II.* Edited by Arthur Weider. New York: Ronald Press Co., 1953. Pp. xi, 459–885. *
14. BUCKTON, LAVERNE, AND DOPPELT, JEROME E. "Freshman Tests as Predictors of Scores on Graduate and Professional School Examinations." *J Counsel Psychol* 2:146–9 su '55. * (*PA* 30:3453)
15. DAVIS, JOHN ROBERT. *Predicting Students' Performance in a General Medical Clinic.* Doctor's thesis, University of Colorado (Boulder, Colo.), 1955. (*DA* 16:1182)

ALEXANDER G. WESMAN, *Associate Director, Test Division, The Psychological Corporation, New York, New York.*

In *The Fourth Mental Measurements Yearbook,* the *Medical College Admission Test* was reviewed by Morey Wantman. The reader would do well to acquaint himself with that review. Most of the statements in the earlier review, both favorable and critical, apply as fully to the succeeding Forms CMC1, CMC2, DMC, and EMC as they did to the 1950 form discussed by Wantman. The high standards of test construction, the clear writing of the bulletin of information sent to applicants, and the well organized, complete directions to examiners are again very much in evidence. The format of the booklets remains excellent. The Educational Testing Service is to be commended for maintaining this quality.

Unfortunately, too little attention has been paid to the adverse criticisms directed at the instrument and accompanying materials. The applicant is better informed concerning the profitability of guessing; but he is still being misled with regard to the desirability of intensive review of science and social studies materials. In the absence of evidence to the contrary, one must assume that with the kind of content in the test, intensive review may quite likely prove a good investment. Similarly, the reassurance of the applicant that "there is no reason to become disturbed if you....are unable to finish" is still unwarranted; the examinee should be informed of the advantages of finishing the test. (The publisher reports that the forthcoming bulletin of information will correct these impressions.)

The reliability coefficients reported for the new forms are not as high as those for the 1950 form; for the verbal and science sections the decrease is negligible—from .93 and .91, respectively, in the older form, to .91 and .89 in the succeeding editions. The quantitative and understanding world affairs sections do not fare as well. The former drops from .89 to .82 in Form EMC; the latter drops from .94 to .84 in Form CMC2. Partly because the coefficients are computed by the Kuder-Richardson technique, which may be overestimating reliability because of the speededness of the tests, Wantman said, "The reliability data reported for the 1950 tests cannot be judged to be more than 'satisfactory.'" The lower coefficients reported for later forms offer less reason for satisfaction.

Coefficients of intercorrelation among the tests are a little lower, and therefore better, for all the later forms. They average about .60; this is probably as low as one may expect in view of the verbal saturation of three of the tests.

The tests are obviously shorter than those of the 1950 edition. Working time for the four tests is approximately three hours; another 30 to 60 minutes is devoted to pretesting experimental material for which no score is reported. The total administration is accomplished in a testing session of approximately four and a half hours—a single sitting, but a long one.

The earlier review of MCAT took issue with the policy of withholding scores from applicants. The present reviewer agrees with the policy, rather than with his predecessor. A rejected student who knew his score was higher than that of an accepted student might draw a number of unpleasant, and probably unwarranted, conclusions about admission practices of a particular institution. The potential harm of revealing scores to students outweighs the probable benefits.

The crucial question concerning any test or battery is that of validity. In the case of the MCAT, one may expect two broad goals to be sought: the prediction of success in medical school, and the selection of those applicants who will be the kind of people the medical schools believe the profession wants or needs. There is evidence that the AAMC has been preoccupied with the latter criterion and that the content of the test battery (e.g., inclusion of the section on understanding modern society) has been at least partly determined by these considerations. Whether or not the tests do actually select the kind of people the profession wants is a matter of subjective judgment—no data are available, so far as the reviewer is aware.

Data are becoming available (at long last) with respect to success in medical school. The reviewer has been permitted to see coefficients of correlation between MCAT test scores and rank in class, scores on tests of the National Board of Medical Examiners, and grades in courses. The data were prepared separately for each of 16 medical schools.

Since only admitted students are included in the research populations, the prediction is probably better than the validity coefficients seem to indicate. Nevertheless, the reviewer finds the results of the studies disappointing. For example, in half the institutions, the highest coefficient between any of the four parts of MCAT and freshman rank is below .40; when senior rank is the criterion, the best coefficient in 14 of the 16 institutions is below .30. The prediction of scores on the Medical Board tests is somewhat better, as one might expect.

The overall picture of validity provokes one to question whether the individual medical schools are (or should be) satisfied with the program. If, as is possible, the schools accept indifferent validity in the tests because of believed defects in the grades, perhaps further research efforts might better be devoted to improving those grades rather than to experimenting with more esoteric item types. In any event, if medical schools are willing to settle for validity of the order thus far demonstrated, the applicant might well be spared at least half the time and money he now expends; a shorter, more efficient test is very likely to do as well. The reviewer's hope is that the Association of American Medical Colleges, which sponsors the MCAT program, will somehow persuade medical schools to reappraise their grading methods with a view to clarifying the criterion, and will instruct the test constructors to concern themselves with efficient measurement of the improved criteria. The selection of students who will be the kind of people the schools think the profession wants or needs might well be left to the subjective judgment of admissions committees.

For a review by Morey J. Wantman, see 4:817.

[933]

★Minnesota Engineering Analogies Test. Candidates for graduate school and industry; 1954–55; Forms E, F ('54); preliminary manual ('55); distribution restricted to specified licensed testing centers; details may be obtained from the publisher; (45–60) minutes; Marvin D. Dunnette; Psychological Corporation. *

REFERENCES
1. DUNNETTE, MARVIN D. "The Minnesota Engineering Analogies Test." *J Appl Psychol* 37:170–5 Je '53. * (PA 28:1847)
2. DUNNETTE, MARVIN D. "The Minnesota Engineering Analogies Test—A New Measure of Engineering Ability." *J Personnel Adm & Ind Rel* 1:1–10 Ja '54. * (PA 29:3224)
3. DUNNETTE, MARVIN DALE. *A Special Analogies Test for the Evaluation of Graduate Engineers.* Doctor's thesis, University of Minnesota (Minneapolis, Minn.), 1954. (DA 14:1250)
4. DUNNETTE, MARVIN D. "Tests for Guidance and Counseling." *J Eng Ed* 46:434–40 Ja '56. *
5. DUNNETTE, MARVIN D., AND AYLWARD, MERRIAM S. "Validity Information Exchange, No. 9-21: D.O.T. Code, Design and Development Engineers." *Personnel Psychol* 9:245–7 su '56. *
6. OWEN, MARJORIE L. "Validation of a Test Battery for Engineers." Abstract. *Am Psychol* 12:450 Jl '57. *

A. PEMBERTON JOHNSON, *Assistant Director, Counseling Center, Newark College of Engineering, Newark, New Jersey.*

The items in this test, like those in the *Miller Analogies Test,* are concisely stated analogies with, however, a heavy mathematical and scientific content. In this test, familiarly known as the MEAT, the conceptual analogies may be wholly verbal, wholly mathematical, or mixed verbal and mathematical. They frequently cross subject matter boundaries. The concepts of the 50 items in each form are taken largely from the first two years of "core" courses for all engineering students, in inorganic chemistry and physics (about 37 per cent), mathematics through integral calculus (about 37 per cent), mechanics—including statics, dynamics, and hydraulics—and strength of materials (19 per cent), and thermodynamics and basic electrical engineering (7 per cent).

Estimates of reliability indicate that although use of a single form is probably adequate for group survey comparisons (where Hoyt reliability coefficients of .75 to .87 were obtained for groups of 44 to 488 cases), average or summed scores for both forms are preferred in evaluating individuals.

Content validity, which one would infer from the manual to be reasonably high, is most difficult to insure with 50 items in any one form. This is true also because engineering curricula are undergoing critical reevaluation and change in many parts of the United States. The severe restriction of the item type precludes use of items which evaluate functional understanding of many important basic principles and laws. The author has, however, largely avoided items which require the memorization of minutiae. All any test in this field can do is to sample some basic areas. The manual does not mention the setting of content objectives or the review of content by an expert committee.

Information on concurrent validity consists of correlations of MEAT scores with undergraduate and graduate grades. One study (6) reports a low predictive validity ($r = .30$) against salary for 156 development engineers. Some construct validity is indicated by higher mean scores for research engineers than for supervisory, production, and design engineers; and median scores 3 to 6 points higher for engineers with the doctor's degree than for holders of bachelor's degrees.

Normative data are inadequate for employed engineers 0–2 years after graduation and particularly for graduate students. Apparently several companies have begun to accumulate data for sizeable groups which, it is hoped, can soon be made available.

The MEAT is a potentially useful measure of that limited aspect of engineering ability to reason by analogy using one's knowledge of basic science and mathematics. It does not purport to measure knowledge of the scientific method, creativity, managerial ability, practical know-how, cost mindedness, ability to use experimental data, ability to report findings in simple, effective language, or other important traits of engineering graduates. Engineers in many of the special fields of engineering will, by the very nature of the design of this test, find little of especial interest to them.

The average score of both forms should be used in ranking individuals. For work placement of engineering graduates the test should only be used along with interview data, interest and personality test data, and preferably at least brief experience with the functional types of engineering work involved.

In general, the separate items are excellently fashioned although the same concepts underlie parts of several different items in the same form. Unpublished data at one company for a group of about 130 young engineers show the dual verbal-mathematical content of the test: there is a .67 correlation coefficient between MEAT scores and scores on the highly verbal *Miller Analogies Test,* and a .71 correlation coefficient between MEAT scores and *Doppelt Mathematical Reasoning Test* scores.

Better normative data for engineering graduates, either those newly employed in industry or those applying for graduate work, are needed if the test is to have wider use. Further validity studies involving larger clearly specified groups are also needed. It is hoped that somehow the publishers of the MEAT and of the *Graduate Record Examinations Advanced Tests: Engineering* might cooperatively seek, from appropriate employed and graduate student populations, comparative normative, validity, and reliability data on these two tests.

WILLIAM B. SCHRADER, *Director, Statistical Analysis, Educational Testing Service, Princeton, New Jersey.*

This is a relatively brief, easily administered, power test designed to measure abstract reasoning and engineering achievement at a difficulty level appropriate to graduate engineers. Presumably, its most frequent use would be in predicting success in graduate study or in engineering work. The items are set in the form of analogies, but they draw heavily on information and concepts learned during the first two years of study in an engineering college. About two fifths of the items are mathematical. The test yields a single overall score.

The mechanics of the testing process have been competently handled. Instructions are explicit, brief, and complete. The booklet is a convenient 8½ by 11 inch size and is well printed, except that exponents, especially fractional exponents (Item 37 of Form E and Item 19 of Form F) are printed in such small type as to place unnecessary demands on visual discrimination. Adequate space for scratch work is provided on the answer sheet. The preliminary manual is well written and attractively printed. The interpretive materials provide some information on virtually all the points which the user needs to know.

A serious weakness is the inadequate description of test development procedures. The manual says nothing about the item analysis work

which was done. Moreover, no evidence is given that qualified persons, other than the author, participated in writing or reviewing the items or in establishing content specifications. It is true that an effort was made to distribute the emphasis by areas of instruction to correspond to the proportion of time given to these basic areas in a typical engineering curriculum, and the author has succeeded well enough in avoiding trivial or esoteric items. Nevertheless, a test which is as clearly concerned with achievement as this one is should draw on the experience of a number of teachers if a balanced instrument is desired. In the reviewer's opinion, there is an undue emphasis on terminology, factual matters, and relatively simple skills, and too little emphasis on problem solving of a relatively complex kind, on application of knowledge, and on reading comprehension. This underemphasis probably resulted in part from the decision to use analogies items only.

The reliability of either of the two forms of this test is somewhat below customary standards. Indeed, for engineering school seniors, the reliability coefficients, as determined by the Hoyt method, are about .75. For graduate students, they are less than .80. These results lend weight to the author's suggestion that both forms be administered where higher reliability is needed. A reliability higher than .75 would surely be needed if appreciable importance is to be given to scores in making decisions about individuals. Hoyt coefficients for employed engineers were about .85. Alternate-forms reliability coefficients for five small groups of employed engineers ranged from .71 to .88.

With respect to norms, the author properly stresses their tentative character and urges the development of local norms. The norms given are broken down according to academic level for engineering students and according to years of experience for employed engineers. It may be noted that the data presented indicate that the test was appropriate in difficulty for the available norms groups. Unfortunately, no useful description of the norms groups is provided with respect to such matters as the universities and companies from which the sample was drawn, the relative proportion of different types of engineers included, and the motivating conditions under which the examinees took the test. Moreover, there is no indication that a systematic norms program which would go beyond data submitted by users is under way.

Minnesota Engineering Analogies Test

A number of validity coefficients are reported. All of the empirical studies described in the manual are concerned with concurrent validity, a fact which complicates the interpretation of the results. The test shows reasonably high correlation coefficients with success in graduate school, but the findings regarding relationships with ratings of employed engineers must be regarded as inconclusive.

The test is based on a reasonable approach to obtaining an overall measure of promise in graduate study or engineering work. In spite of certain limitations in the test and in the interpretive materials provided, it should provide useful and pertinent information about the ability level of students who have completed an engineering program.

[934]

*NLN Achievement Tests for Basic Professional Nursing Program. Students in state-approved schools of professional nursing; 1943–58; IBM; 1 form; 16 tests; manual ['58]; interpretive manual ('58, see *1* below); norms ['58]; *a–n*: 75¢ per test per student; *o–p*: $1 per test per student; $1.25 per interpretive manual; postpaid one way; (90–120) minutes per test; National League for Nursing, Inc.
a) ANATOMY AND PHYSIOLOGY. 1943–55; Form 155 ('55).
b) CHEMISTRY. 1943–55; Form 155 ('55).
c) MICROBIOLOGY. 1943–55; Form 155 ('55).
d) NUTRITION AND DIET THERAPY. 1946–57; Form 757 ('57).
e) PHARMACOLOGY AND THERAPEUTICS. 1944–55; Form 155 ('55).
f) MEDICAL NURSING. 1944–49; Form 149 ('49).
g) SURGICAL NURSING. 1944–49; Form 149 ('49).
h) NURSING OF CHILDREN. 1945–55; Form 155 ('55).
i) COMMUNICABLE DISEASE NURSING. 1946–55; Form 155 ('55).
j) PSYCHIATRIC NURSING. 1945–55; Form 155 ('55).
k) SOCIAL SCIENCES IN NURSING. 1956; Form 156 ('56).
l) MEDICAL-SURGICAL NURSING. 1956; Form 156 ('56).
m) OBSTETRIC NURSING. 1945–56; Form 156 ('56).
n) PUBLIC HEALTH NURSING. 1956; Form 956 ('56).
o) NATURAL SCIENCES IN NURSING. 1957; Form 957 ('57); 3 scores: facts and principles (knowledge, application), total.
p) MATERNAL AND CHILD HEALTH NURSING. 1958; Form 658 ('58): 3 scores: psychological aspects, nonpsychological aspects, total.

REFERENCE

1. NATIONAL LEAGUE FOR NURSING. *The NLN Achievement Test, Second Edition.* The Use of Tests in Schools of Nursing Pamphlet No. 2. New York: National League for Nursing, Inc., 1958. Pp. iii, 44. *

[935]

*NLN Graduate Nurse Qualifying Examination. Registered professional nurses; 1945–56; tests administered throughout the year at centers established by NLN; IBM; 1 form; 3 tests; norms ('57); manual ['54]; interpretive manual ('54, see *1* below); Plan A, all tests: examination fee, $10; Plan B, *Clinical Test* and one other: examination fee, $9; Plan C, *Clinical Test* only: examination fee, $8; fees include reporting scores to one college and examiner's fee if taken with group of 10 or more; less than 10,

applicant or college assumes administration costs; $2 per additional report; $1.25 per interpretive manual; postpaid one way; National League for Nursing, Inc.
a) AMERICAN COUNCIL ON EDUCATION PSYCHOLOGICAL EXAMINATION FOR COLLEGE FRESHMEN. See 308; 3 scores: quantitative, linguistic, total; 1954 Edition; 38(65) minutes.
b) READING COMPREHENSION: COOPERATIVE ENGLISH TEST: HIGHER LEVEL, TEST C2. See 179; 2 scores: speed, level; Form Z ('53); 25(35) minutes.
c) CLINICAL TEST. 4 scores: medical-surgical nursing, maternal and child health nursing, psychiatric nursing, total; Form 1253 ('53); 3 booklets; 295(325) minutes.

REFERENCE

1. NATIONAL LEAGUE OF NURSING. *The NLN Graduate Nurse Qualifying Examination.* The Use of Tests in Schools of Nursing Pamphlet No. 3. New York: National League of Nursing, Inc., 1954. Pp. v, 39. *

[936]

*NLN Practical Nurse Achievement Tests. Students in approved schools of practical nursing; 1950–58; IBM; 1 form; 2 tests; no manual; mimeographed norms ('58); postpaid one way; National League for Nursing, Inc.
a) PRACTICAL NURSE BASIC ACHIEVEMENT TEST. 1957–58; 4 scores: body structure and function, basic nursing procedures, nutrition and diet therapy, total; Form 857 ('57); mimeographed directions sheet ('58); examination fee, $1; (90) minutes.
b) PRACTICAL NURSE ACHIEVEMENT TEST. 1950–56; Form 856 ('56); mimeographed directions ['57]; examination fee, 75¢; (120) minutes.

[937]

*NLN Pre-Admission and Classification Examination. Practical nursing school entrants; 1950–58; IBM; 1 form ('50); 2 tests; directions booklet ['54]; norms ['58]; examination fee, $3 per student; fee includes scoring service and reporting scores to any one school of practical nursing; National League for Nursing, Inc.
a) GENERAL INFORMATION AND JUDGMENT EXAMINATION. 3 scores: information and judgment, arithmetic, total; Form 650 ('50); 75(85) minutes.
b) VOCABULARY EXAMINATION. Form 650 ('50); 30 (35) minutes.

[938]

*NLN Pre-Nursing and Guidance Examination. Applicants for admission to state-approved schools of professional nursing; 1941–57; tests administered throughout the year at centers established by the NLN; 1 form; 5 tests; manual ['57]; interpretive manual ('57, see *2* below); examination fee, $10 if taken with group of 10 or more; less than 10, applicant or college assumes administration costs; fee includes reporting scores to one school of nursing; $2 per additional report; $1.25 per interpretive manual; postpaid one way; 168(230) minutes in 2 sessions; National League for Nursing, Inc.
a) AMERICAN COUNCIL ON EDUCATION PSYCHOLOGICAL EXAMINATION FOR COLLEGE FRESHMEN. See 308; 3 scores: quantitative, linguistic, total; 1954 Edition; 38(65) minutes.
b) READING COMPREHENSION: COOPERATIVE ENGLISH TEST: HIGHER LEVEL, TEST C2. See 179; 2 scores: speed, level; Form Z ('53); 25(35) minutes.
c) MATHEMATICS. Adaptation of *Cooperative Mathematics Test for Grades 7, 8, and 9* (see 421); Form Q ('40); 35(40) minutes.
d) COOPERATIVE GENERAL ACHIEVEMENT TESTS: TEST II, NATURAL SCIENCE. See 703; Form T ('42); 40(50) minutes.

e) COOPERATIVE GENERAL CULTURE TEST, PART II, HISTORY AND SOCIAL STUDIES. See 7; Form XX ('51); 30 (40) minutes.

REFERENCES

1. SHAYCOFT, MARION F. "A Validation Study of the Pre-Nursing and Guidance Test Battery." *Am J Nursing* 51:201–5 Mr '51. *
2. NATIONAL LEAGUE FOR NURSING. *The NLN Pre-Nursing and Guidance Examination, Second Edition.* The Use of Tests in Schools of Nursing Pamphlet No. 1. New York: National League for Nursing, Inc., 1957. Pp. v, 42. *

[939]

★**Personnel Service Rating Report.** Library personnel; 1948; 1 form ['48]; no manual; no data on reliability; no norms; $1.25 per 25 scales, postage extra; specimen set not available; administration time not reported; Subcommittee on Service Ratings of the ALA Board on Personnel Administration; American Library Association. *

[940]

★**Policeman Test.** Policemen; 1953–57; Forms 10-A ('53), 10-B ('56); revised mimeographed manual ('57); norms ('56); no data on reliability and validity; separate answer sheets must be used; PPA member agency: 10–49 tests, $1.20 each; others, $1.60 each; $2 per specimen set; postpaid; 95(105) minutes; Public Personnel Association. *

[941]

★**Punched Card Machine Operator Aptitude Test.** Prospective IBM punched card equipment operators; 1952–55; 1 form ('52); revised manual ('55); separate answer sheets must be used; no charge; 32(40) minutes; Walter J. McNamara; distributed by International Business Machines Corporation. *

[942]

★**Purdue Trade Information Test for Sheetmetal Workers: Purdue Personnel Tests.** Sheetmetal workers; 1958; 1 form; preliminary manual; reliability data based on preliminary form; $4 per 25 tests, postage extra; 50¢ per specimen set, postpaid; (30–45) minutes; Joseph Tiffin, B. R. Modisette, and Warren B. Griffin; distributed by University Book Store. *

[943]

★**Purdue Trade Information Test in Carpentry: Purdue Personnel Tests.** Vocational school and adults; 1952; 1 form; preliminary manual; $4 per 25 tests, postage extra; 50¢ per specimen set, postpaid; (35–50) minutes; Joseph Tiffin and Robert F. Mengelkoch; distributed by University Book Store. *

REFERENCE

1. MENGELKOCH, ROBERT F. *A Trade Information Test for Carpenters.* Master's thesis, Purdue University (Lafayette, Ind.), 1953.

P. L. MELLENBRUCH, *Professor of Psychology, University of Kentucky, Lexington, Kentucky.*

This carpenter's test represents another instance in which a test is put on sale before it is ready. Information about the test is limited and the evidence as to its value is meager.

The authors state in the preliminary manual that the test is designed "to aid industry and vocational schools in determining the amount of information in this field that is possessed by applicants or students. The test is particularly useful as an aid in the selection of new carpenters from applicants who claim to have had training and/or experience in this trade." The test is also suggested as a "terminal achievement examination" for vocational schools.

No data are presented to indicate whether the test actually is suitable for carpenters who are applying for jobs. In fact, there is no evidence that the test has ever been tried out on carpenters presently employed as such, and, consequently, no attempt has been made to obtain cutoff scores or norms for those who are now doing carpentry work. It would seem better under the circumstances to make no reference to the use of this test for selection purposes.

The test was developed apparently in a Smith-Hughes trade school atmosphere and all of the testing of the test confined to such vocational school students. The original items were "submitted to an expert [one?] tradesman" to be checked for "aptness of the subject matter, plausibility of the incorrect answers, and correctness of the right answer."

The reviewer attempted to get some additional information respecting the test by administering it to members of the carpenters' union at Lexington, Kentucky. Out of a group of some 60 persons attending the union meeting he succeeded in getting 22 to complete the test. Some half dozen or so who had volunteered turned in their booklets when they saw the length of the test. The general reaction was that it might be a good test for home construction carpenters but it had little in it related to commercial carpentering.

Though the number of cases is small, three very broad concluding observations might be made: (*a*) Amount of schooling seemingly does not affect one's score appreciably. (*b*) There are too few difficult items. (*c*) This test represents an excellent problem on the MA degree level but was published prematurely.

[944]

★**Purdue Trade Information Test in Engine Lathe Operation: Purdue Personnel Tests.** Vocational school and adults; 1955; 1 form; preliminary manual; $4 per 25 tests, postage extra; 50¢ per specimen set, postpaid; (50–65) minutes; Robert Cochran and Joseph Tiffin; distributed by University Book Store. *

WILLIAM J. MICHEELS, *Professor of Industrial Education and Chairman of the Department, University of Minnesota, Minneapolis, Minnesota.*

This test is intended to "aid industry and vocational schools in determining the amount of information....possessed by applicants or students" on engine lathe operation.

It is a test of what a person knows about engine lathe operation rather than what the person can do on an engine lathe. The 74 items measure primarily a knowledge of specifics. There are very few questions that call for application of knowledge or problem solving abilities related to engine lathe operation. A large majority of the items are of a highly factual nature.

If this test is to have wide use, considerably more attention must be given to preparing a more informative manual. The test can serve a useful purpose in quickly screening out people who have had little or no experience with engine lathe operation. It is doubtful, however, whether the test should be used alone as "a terminal achievement examination."

[945]

★Purdue Trade Information Test in Welding, Revised Edition: Purdue Personnel Tests. Vocational school and adults; 1951–52; 1 form ('52); preliminary manual; $4 per 25 tests, postage extra; 50¢ per specimen set, postpaid; (65–80) minutes; Joseph Tiffin and Warren B. Griffin; distributed by University Book Store. *

[946]

★Road Test Check List for Testing, Selecting, Rating, and Training Coach Operators. Coach operators; 1958; 1 form; no data on reliability; 48¢ per set of 25 score sheets and manual, postage extra; specimen set free; driving jerk recorder essential for administration; Amos E. Neyhart; published jointly by American Automobile Association and Institute of Public Safety, Pennsylvania State University. *

[947]

*Sales Comprehension Test. Sales applicants; 1953–57; revision of *Aptitudes Associates Test of Sales Aptitude;* Form M ('53); supplement ('57); 20¢ per test; 25¢ per scoring key; 75¢ per manual ('53); $1 per specimen set; cash orders postpaid; (15–20) minutes; Martin M. Bruce; the Author. *

REFERENCES

1. BRUCE, MARTIN M. "A Sales Comprehension Test." *J Appl Psychol* 38:302–4 O '54. * (PA 29:6346)
2. BRUCE, MARTIN M. "Normative Data Information Exchange, Nos. 19–22." *Personnel Psychol* 9:395–9 au '56. *
3. BRUCE, MARTIN M. "Validity Information Exchange, No. 9-45: D.O.T. Code 0-97.61, Manager, Sales." *Personnel Psychol* 9:524 w '56. *
4. BRUCE, MARTIN M., AND FRIESEN, EDWARD P. "Validity Information Exchange, No. 9-35: D.O.T. Code 1-55.10, Salesman, House-to-House." *Personnel Psychol* 9:380 au '56. *
5. BRUCE, MARTIN M. "Normative Data Information Exchange, No. 10-23." *Personnel Psychol* 10:245 su '57. *
6. HECHT, ROBERT, AND BRUCE, MARTIN M. "Normative Data Information Exchange, No. 10-43." *Personnel Psychol* 10:536 w '57. *
7. MURRAY, L. E., AND BRUCE, MARTIN E. "Normative Data Information Exchange, No. 10-9." *Personnel Psychol* 10:105–6 sp '57. *
8. ALBRIGHT, LEWIS E.; GLENNON, J. R.; AND SMITH, WALLACE J. "Normative Data Information Exchange, No. 11-12." *Personnel Psychol* 11:277 su '58. *
9. BRUCE, MARTIN M. "Normative Data Information Exchange, No. 11-4." *Personnel Psychol* 11:133–4 sp '58. *
10. SMITH, WALLACE J.; ALBRIGHT, LEWIS E.; AND GLEN-

NON, J. R. "Normative Data Information Exchange, No. 11-11." *Personnel Psychol* 11:276 su '58. *

RAYMOND A. KATZELL, *Professor of Psychology and Management Engineering, New York University, New York, New York.*

The present revision consists of 30 items drawn, on the basis of item analysis, from the 50 constituting the earlier form of the test. The selected items were those which continued to discriminate between salesmen and nonsalesmen, and which showed some degree of consistency in distributions of responses in three successive item analysis samples. New scoring weights have been computed for the selected items, proportional to their power in differentiating between salesmen and nonsalesmen.

This abbreviation, while having the obvious virtue of reduced administration time, seems to have done the test no harm. In one study where scores were obtained by both keys, the two had nearly equal validity, exhibiting correlations of about .3 with performance ratings of sales personnel ($n = 86$). Test-retest reliability was also approximately the same for both editions, being in the .70's. A correlation coefficient of .65 was obtained between the scores yielded by the old keys and the new keys in a large heterogeneous sample.

VALIDITY. By way of cross validating the scoring key for the revised edition, the mean score of 334 salesmen was compared with that of 661 nonsalesmen. Both samples appear to have been rather heterogeneous with respect to employing agency and geographical distribution, but no data are provided regarding their comparability with respect to age, education, test variance, or other pertinent factors. In any event, the difference between their means was significant at beyond the 1 per cent level of confidence (presumably the mean for the sales group was higher, although this is not stated). Several validation studies have recently been reported in the Validity Information Exchange of *Personnel Psychology* (2-10). The *Sales Comprehension Test* exhibited statistically significant validity (concurrent) in three of these studies, in which the samples comprised, respectively, house to house salesmen, wholesale steel warehouse salesmen, and a group consisting mainly of wholesale salesmen. The test clearly lacked validity in one study utilizing six samples of salesmen of foodstuffs; on the other hand, it fared no worse than did a variety of 14 other psychometric scales which were used. In a fifth study, based on 82 sales managers in the cosmetics industry, the t-ratio between the test means of "good" and "poor" criterion groups turned out to be 1.9, which falls slightly short of the 5 per cent level of confidence.

RELIABILITY. Test-retest reliability was .71 in a sample of 103 college students. The interval between tests is not reported, although this would be useful in interpreting the result. Using this *r*, the reliability of the test was estimated for a heterogeneous sample comprising salesmen, nonsalesmen, and women. The resulting estimate was .79. The more restricted range of scores that would probably characterize the applicants of a given company would lead one to guess that the unaugmented figure of .71 is closer to what would obtain for such samples.

NORMS. Percentile equivalents are provided in the manual for a sample of 397 miscellaneous salesmen, heterogeneous samples of 872 men and 132 women, 55 supply salesmen, 86 electronics salesmen, 360 college students of salesmanship, plus a few additional small samples of special sales groups. In addition, the author has been conscientiously reporting supplementary tables in the Normative Data Information Exchange of *Personnel Psychology*.

OTHER CORRELATIONS. The *Sales Comprehension Test* appears to measure something other than tested intelligence. Its correlation with the total score of *SRA Primary Mental Abilities* is essentially zero, and that with the *Otis Self-Administering Tests of Mental Ability* is slightly negative. There is a significantly positive correlation (.39) with the persuasive score of the *Kuder Preference Record*.

GENERAL COMMENTS. The test's content, together with its correlations with other tests, support the author's contention that it is a measure of "understanding and appreciation of basic principles of selling." That such a measure may be of use in selecting sales personnel is supported by the positive results of several validation studies. That this utility is not universal is indicated by other studies, employing either the revised or original edition.

It is one of the hopes of the editor and reviewers of *The Mental Measurements Yearbooks* that their efforts may lead to the improvement of tests. Without inferring direct cause and effect, this reviewer was gratified to find ameliorations in the revised edition of this test that correspond to several of those recommended in the reviews of the original edition.

Among them are the retitling of the test as a comprehension rather than an aptitude test, the compilation of additional norms for specific sales groups, and the accumulation of more studies of the test's correlation with sales performance. It is hoped that further progress in this last regard will result in better understanding of the situations in which this type of measure is likely to be valid or not; studies of predictive validity would be particularly welcome. Also desirable would be information on how test performance is related to such background factors as education and job experience. In the meantime, the test merits experimental use for purposes of sales personnel selection.

For reviews by Milton E. Hahn and Donald G. Paterson of the original edition, see 4:824.

[948]

★**Sales Motivation Inventory.** Sales applicants; 1953; Form A; 20¢ per test; 25¢ per scoring key; 50¢ per manual; $1 per specimen set; cash orders postpaid; (25–30) minutes; Martin M. Bruce; the Author. *

REFERENCES

1. BRUCE, MARTIN M. "Normative Data Information Exchange, Nos. 23–4." *Personnel Psychol* 9:400–3 au '56. *
2. MURRAY, L. E., AND BRUCE, MARTIN M. "Normative Data Information Exchange, No. 10-10." *Personnel Psychol* 10:107–9 sp '57. *

S. RAINS WALLACE, *Director of Research, Life Insurance Agency Management Association, Hartford, Connecticut.*

This test is "designed to aid in the appraisal of interest in or motivation for sales work." Sales work is defined as a type of job for which compensation takes the form of commissions or bonuses based on amount of sales. The test score is claimed to provide an objective measure of one aspect of sales aptitude for the use of the tester in industry as well as the vocational counselor.

There are 75 items, each consisting of a group of four activities from which the subject picks one. The format is simple and clear, although the instructions seem somewhat inadequate. The scoring procedure and stencil appear to lend themselves to considerable error.

The test was "validated" by showing a statistically significant differentiation between 210 salesmen (type unspecified) and 521 nonsalesmen (334 men and 187 women). No cross validation data are provided in the Examiner's Manual but subsequent publications in the Normative Data Information Exchange of *Personnel Psychology* tend to support the conclusions obtained from the original study. Norms are presented for the various groups and show acceptable consistency. The odd-even reliability is estimated from the original sample as .90. No test-retest reliabilities are available.

While the test is a workmanlike job and supporting data have been carefully obtained, there are three negative features. The absence of any predictive validity for actual sales performance leaves the test in an experimental status so far as the tester in industry is concerned. For the vocational counselor, the assumption of a general sales aptitude is troublesome. Validities for similar predictors against performance in different sales fields indicate that the assumption is subject to considerable doubt.[1] Furthermore, the high correlations between this test and the three sales keys of the *Strong Vocational Interest Blank* (.71 to .83) might lead the counselor to prefer the older test for which predictive validity in some fields has been demonstrated.

Finally, as is true with most self-report tests, the possibility of faking seems great.

[949]

★**Sales Personnel Description Form.** Salesmen; 1953–55; forced-choice rating scale; 1 form ('53); mimeographed manual ['55]; no data on reliability and validity; no norms; 50¢ per form including scoring service; 25¢ per specimen set; cash orders postpaid; [10] minutes; Personnel Research Institute. *

[950]

★**Steward Life Insurance Knowledge Test.** Applicants for life insurance agent or supervisory positions; 1956; 5 scores: arithmetic, vocabulary, principles, functions, total; 1 form ('56); manual ('56); no data on reliability and validity; tentative norms for total score only; $1.50 per 5 tests; $1.50 per manual; postage extra; specimen set not available; administration time not reported; Verne Steward; Verne Steward & Associates. *

[951]

★**Steward Occupational Objectives Inventory.** Applicants for supervisory positions in life insurance companies or agencies; 1956–57; ratings in 8 areas: caliber level, life insurance knowledge, selling skills, leadership ability, supervisory skills, personal adjustment, survival on job, supplementary items; 1 form ('57); $3.75 per 5 tests; $3 per manual ('57); postage extra; specimen set not available; (90–105) minutes; Verne Steward; Verne Steward & Associates. *

[952]

★**Steward Personal Background Inventory.** Salesman applicants; 1949–57; ratings in 7 areas: health, education, experience, financial status, activities, family status, miscellaneous; 1 form ('57); manual ('57); $2 per 5 tests; $2.25 per manual; postage extra; specimen set not available; (60–70) minutes; Verne Steward; Verne Steward & Associates. *

1 HUGHES, J. L., AND McNAMARA, W. J. "Limitations on the Use of Strong Sales Keys for Selection and Counseling." *J Appl Psychol* 42:93–6 Ap '58. *

[953]

★**Steward Sales Aptitude Inventory.** Applicants for sales positions; 1957–58; 5 scores: business knowledge, arithmetic skill, selling aptitude, vocational interest in selling, freedom from personal handicaps; 1 form ('58); $2 per 5 tests; $1.25 per manual ('58); postage extra; specimen set not available; (60–80) minutes; Verne Steward; Verne Steward & Associates. *

[954]

★**The Store Personnel Test.** Food store employees; 1946–51; 2 scores: checking, problems; Form FS ('46); manual ('51); tentative norms ('50); distribution restricted to food stores; $11 per 100 tests; specimen set available upon request; postpaid; 20(25) minutes; Harold G. Seashore and Charles E. Orbach; Psychological Corporation. *

REFERENCE

1. DOPPELT, JEROME E., AND BENNETT, GEORGE K. "Reducing the Cost of Training Satisfactory Workers by Using Tests." *Personnel Psychol* 6:1–8 sp '53. * (*PA* 28:1601)

RAYMOND A. KATZELL, *Professor of Psychology and Management Engineering, New York University, New York, New York.*

As stated in the manual, the *Store Personnel Test* "was developed to meet the need for a single test measuring mental alertness and speed and accuracy" and having face validity for food store personnel. These objectives were achieved by constructing a test comprising a 3-minute checking subtest and a 20-minute "mental ability" subtest. The latter consists of reasoning, vocabulary, information, and computation items, in cycle omnibus arrangement. Most items in both subtests are couched in terms manifestly related to the food industry. The format is such that the test answers must be marked on the booklet and scored by hand; a slotted key is provided.

VALIDITY. Correlation coefficients are reported between each subtest and ratings of initiative, adaptability, and performance on the job, plus the sum of the three ratings. In a sample of 215 male produce workers, the correlations of the checking and mental ability subtests with the sum ratings were, respectively, .21 and .42. The comparable correlations in a sample of 109 male checkers were .16 and .36; in a sample of 248 female checkers they were .37 and .35. Commendably, all the foregoing coefficients represent predictive, rather than merely concurrent, validity. In one organization, a sample of 50 managers was divided into upper and lower halves on the basis of overall job success; statistically significant mean differences were found between the groups on both subtests. The direction of these differences is not indicated, but we hope for the best.

RELIABILITY. Test-retest reliability coefficients were .82 and .87, respectively, for the two parts of the test in a sample of high school students. The corrected odd-even reliability coefficient for the mental ability part was .92 for the sample of students, and .94 for a sample of employees.

NORMS. Percentile equivalents are given for scores on each part of the test for each of the following normative samples: 93 male managers and supervisors in a single food chain; 469 applicants (male and female combined) who were hired by a single chain; 162 male checkers, 261 female checkers, and 229 male produce department employees, tested at the time of application and hired by another single chain; 101 commercial students (both male and female) in a single high school. The manual points out the bias introduced in the norms by the representation of hired applicants only. Another limitation is that the norms are by now at least seven or eight years old.

OTHER CORRELATIONS. The correlation of the two parts is fairly high (about .6) suggesting that performance on the checking part may more heavily reflect its verbal than its numerical content. The mental ability part was found to correlate .67 with the *Wonderlic Personnel Test,* in a sample of 328 employed workers; the latter test seems to have had a rather restricted range, suggesting that the former may have a more appropriate distribution of difficulty for this type of population.

GENERAL COMMENTS. The *Store Personnel Test* has adequate reliability, and shows moderate validity for the selection of food store clerks. While the test probably measures essentially what would be measured by any standard checking test and low-level test of mental ability, its face validity may be of some advantage for use with food store personnel. The manual is complete and explicit. Indeed, a deliberate effort has been made to pitch the presentation at such a level that the test can be applied and interpreted by nonpsychologists. But there remain technical problems that transcend a simplified procedure and lucid manual. For what classes of personnel is the test appropriate? (The manual mentions not only store clerks, but also supervisors and managers; one doubts that the test is ideal for the latter group, but would the central office of a food chain know this?) What are the effects of time, and a changing labor market, on the test's norms and validity? Should not age differences enter into interpretation of the test results? Is it sufficient to set selection standards on the basis of norms, or should there not be some effort to ascertain functional critical scores? And so forth. It would seem that the use of competent psychological consultation or supervision, even in such a program, is not only a matter of saving "time and money," as the manual advises, but more crucially a question of sound practice. Should not the "do-it-yourself" movement be stopped short of professional psychology?

JOHN B. MORRIS, *Associate Professor of Psychology, and Director of Institutional Research, The University of Mississippi, University, Mississippi.*

The authors of this test state that it was developed "to meet the need for a single test measuring mental alertness and speed and accuracy" for retail food stores. The test is a good example of an instrument developed for a specific industry, a practice that was not so popular when this test was issued in 1951, but that seems to be growing at the present time.

The specifications for this test were suggested by advisers from the retail food industry. The advisers stipulated that the test must have "face validity" and that it must be simple enough to administer, score, and interpret that company personnel could be trained to use it efficiently. The copy of the test submitted for review, Form FS, represents a good effort at meeting the foregoing criteria.

Part 1, Checking, is a 3-minute test of speed and accuracy in inspecting two lists of food store merchandise. The task consists of inspecting successive pairs of items to determine if each member of the pair under the "merchandise billed" heading is identical to that in the "merchandise delivered" column. The testee records his response by making a check if the items are in agreement and a cross if they are dissimilar. This section of the test consists of 75 items.

Part 2, Problems, is a 17-minute mental ability test that is similar in content to several popular tests of this type that are currently on the market. It contains 80 reasoning, vocabulary, information, and simple numerical computation items.

The entire test is scored for the number of correct responses by use of a single scoring key. In order to use the key, some maneuvering on the part of the scorer is necessary, but, in the opinion of this reviewer, this difficulty is outweighed by the convenience of having a single template.

The test is attractively arranged, and item quality appears good throughout the test. Only one item appeared to be ambiguous to the reviewer.

The manual is attractive, well written, and should be understood easily, even by personnel managers who are not well versed in test statistics. While test technicians might wish for information that is not included, it is doubtful that those for whom the manual was prepared (it is restricted in sale to food store organizations) will find it deficient. The general quality of the technical data supplied is good if somewhat sparse. The authors recognize some of the deficiencies and urge that companies using the test conduct experimentation before attempting to set definite cutoff points for employment. They cite an example of what was done by one company as a possible guide.

The only estimate of reliability available for Part 1 is based upon two administrations of the test to 101 commercial department students in the 10th, 11th, and 12th grades. The coefficient of correlation between the tests, repeated after an interval of one week, was .82. The same technique and students yielded a reliability of .87 for Part 2.

Further evidence of reliability for Part 2 is reported from a study based upon a random sample of 100 cases drawn from a population of newly hired employees of a food store chain in Texas. The corrected odd-even coefficient was .94. The odd-even technique could not be used appropriately for Part 1 as it is a highly speeded test.

Correlations between Part 1 and Part 2 are given for three separate samples. The values reported for these studies are .55, .61, and .56. The authors state that these values are "quite typical of correlations generally found between checking tests and intelligence tests."

The test was validated against criteria selected by food store personnel. Each worker who took the test and was subsequently employed was rated on initiative, adaptability, and performance by his supervisors. The ratings were accomplished independently of knowledge of test performance. The validity coefficients obtained varied with the position held, the factor rated, and the part of the test used. For

male produce workers and female checkers the tests were reasonably predictive. For males rated as checkers the tests had lower predictability. In general, judicious use of the different parts of the test in selecting workers for various positions should make use of the tests advantageous in the selection of successful workers.

In summary, this is a test for a specific purpose that quite frankly recognizes regional differences in norms and refuses to generalize from a small sample in one geographic region to an industry that is national in scope. The fact that its usefulness to an organization is partially dependent upon the ability of someone in that organization to run further studies of reliability and validity and to construct local norms may account in part for an apparent lack of acceptance by the food distribution industry. It may be that industry still wants test constructors to supply them with *the* reliability and *the* validity of a test whether or not they are appropriate for the local situation.

[955]

★**Supervisory Practices Test.** Supervisors; 1957; 1 form; 20¢ per test; 25¢ per scoring key; 75¢ per manual; $1 per specimen set; cash orders postpaid; (20-30) minutes; Martin M. Bruce; the Author. *

REFERENCE
1. BRUCE, MARTIN M., AND LEARNER, DAVID B. "A Supervisory Practices Test." *Personnel Psychol* 11:207-16 su '58. *

CLIFFORD E. JURGENSEN, *Assistant Vice President in Charge of Personnel, Minneapolis Gas Company, Minneapolis, Minnesota.*

This test consists of 50 completion type items dealing with attitudes and opinions toward supervisory actions involving people. Its purpose is to aid in appraising supervisory ability and potential.

The test is self-administering, has no time limit, and is scored with a strip key. Percentile norms, mean, standard deviation, and standard error of measurement are reported for each of three groups: 52 executives, 239 managers, and 598 nonsupervisors. The test correlates .27 with total score on the *SRA Primary Mental Abilities* and .56 with Form M of *How Supervise?*

Two status validity studies showed a significant difference between means of supervisors and nonsupervisors at the 1 per cent level. Two studies are reported on concurrent validity: a rank correlation of .81 was found between SPT scores and the ratings of 15 foremen; a product-moment *r* of .38 was found between SPT scores of 16 foremen and the mean attitude scores on the *SRA Employee Inventory* of the employees under their supervision. Two testimonial cases are cited: a manufacturing manager who scored within the top 5 per cent of supervisors was rated by subordinates as the best supervisor they had had in 14 years, and a vice president who scored at the 12th percentile before being hired was fired at the end of six months for inability to gain acceptance and cooperation from his department heads.

Item weights were determined by the ability of the item to differentiate between nonsupervisors and supervisors, and the degree to which supervisory as well as nonsupervisory personnel agree. The second of these criteria is based on the rationale that the perspective of the majority, whether supervisors or nonsupervisors, is important. This emphasis on communality will be disputed by some persons and in some companies.

The manual is more complete than usual; it was prepared using the recommendations of the APA Committee on Test Standards and of the Committee on Ethical Standards on Psychology. It fairly and wisely points out that "the responses given by a person in an artificial or test situation are no guarantee of the person's acting in that fashion when he is faced with the actual situation," and that the person using this test in a business or industry should be oriented to the organization because "the generalizations concerning desirable supervisory practices may not always be applicable in a specific organization." The author is to be commended for mentioning these points which decrease test validity for selection purposes.

A test-retest correlation of .77 is reported for 112 supervisors. Split-half biserial reliability for 177 supervisors and nonsupervisors is .82. The manual states that "this appears sufficiently high for group situations to warrant confidence in its consistency of measurement." The word *group* in the previous sentence is important. The author does not claim that the test is sufficiently reliable to warrant confidence in the score of an individual.

Reliability is probably reduced because item stems do not (and cannot) always give all relevant and necessary information. The "best" answer sometimes depends on factors not mentioned. If the respondent makes the same assumptions as the test author, he is likely to get a higher score than if he makes other assumptions. In some tests, of course, such differences

in assumptions account for test validity, but this does not seem to be the case here. Low reliability is not surprising if item weights are analyzed in relation to norms. A change in response to a single item—whether resulting from carelessness, absence of relevant data, item ambiguity, or what have you—can change the raw score as much as 10 points and the percentile rank on executive norms as much as 37 points.

Because of the unreliability of scores for individual predictions, differing "best" answers in various companies, and absence of information necessary to determine the best answer in some items, this reviewer recommends the test not be used in situations where total scores are obtained. Nevertheless, there is one type of situation where the test is recommended. This is in supervisory training conferences and classes. Thoughtful and profitable discussion can result if members of the group fill in the test and then discuss answers to each item. The weaknesses of the test for selection purposes become strong points when the test is used for training. Discussion brings out differing viewpoints, approaches, and assumptions. These differences can be used to emphasize the importance of looking at supervisory problems thoroughly and from all angles rather than jumping to conclusions without considering all relevant factors.

Mary Ellen Oliverio, *Associate Professor of Education, Teachers College, Columbia University, New York, New York.*

This test claims to provide a measure of only one aspect of supervisory ability: the ability to function effectively in situations which require decisions involving people. The test consists of 50 items written in the first person. The subject is to assume that he is the supervisor faced with the problems identified in the items. He is asked to choose the solution he feels is the best in each instance.

The test is simple to administer and can be taken individually as well as in a group. Some question might be raised about the test's being untimed. Deliberation on the items might well lead to more frequent selection of the BEST solution, since the best solution tends to become more obvious with rereading. There would be some merit in getting the immediate response of the subject.

The procedure used in developing the items,

analyzing them, weighting them, and checking the validity and reliability of the final form of the test appears to be generally sound. The author states that predictive validity is suggested by several case histories, but only two are cited. It is not clear whether or not these cited are representative of the case histories.

Norms are based on the scores of 52 executives, 239 managers, and 598 nonsupervisors. No information is given concerning the source of the samples or their representativeness of the total groups. The executives appear more homogeneous than the nonsupervisors, for example. This difference could reflect the fact that executives are more alike than are nonsupervisors in the variable under study. At the same time, there is no way of knowing what a larger sample of executives would reveal.

This test might have value in those situations where the evaluator has had no opportunity to learn how a prospective supervisor makes decisions involving people. Many such situations occur when people in a company are being considered for promotions.

[956]
★**Truck Driver Test 60-A.** Drivers of light and medium trucks; 1957–58; 1 form ('57); preliminary mimeographed manual ('58); general PPA mimeographed directions ['57]; no norms; separate answer sheets must be used; PPA member agency: 10–49 tests, 80¢ each; others, $1 each; $2 per specimen set; postpaid; 90(100) minutes; Public Personnel Association. *

[957]
★**Veterinary Aptitude Testing Program.** Veterinary school applicants; 1951; tests administered at centers established by the publisher; 4 scores: reading comprehension, science information, verbal memory, total; IBM; 1 form; 4 tests; manual ['51]; examination fee, $6; fee includes reporting of scores to any 2 schools designated at time of application; $1 per additional report; postpaid; scores not reported to examinees; 145(180) minutes; Loyal C. Payne and William A. Owens; Psychological Corporation. *
a) VETERINARY APTITUDE TEST, PARTS I, 3, 4. 1 form ['51]; 105(115) minutes.
b) VETERINARY ACHIEVEMENT TEST, PART 2. 1 form ['51]; 40(50) minutes.

REFERENCES
1. OWENS, WILLIAM A. "Development of a Test of Aptitude for Veterinary Medicine." *Proc Iowa Acad Sci* 57:417–23 '50. *
2. LAYTON, WILBUR L. "Predicting Success of Students in Veterinary Medicine." *J Appl Psychol* 36:312–5 O '52. * (*PA* 27:5418)
3. PAYNE, LOYAL C. *Development and Validation of a Veterinary Medical Aptitude Test.* Doctor's thesis, Iowa State College (Ames, Iowa), 1954.

REPRINTED FROM *The Sixth Mental Measurements Yearbook*

BUSINESS EDUCATION – SIXTH MMY

REVIEWS BY *Irol Whitmore Balsley, Lawrence W. Erickson, Melvin R. Marks, Jacob S. Orleans, Ray G. Price, Harold L. Royer, Edward O. Swanson, and Henry Weitz.*

[28]

*Business Education: National Teacher Examinations.** College seniors and teachers; 1956-63; for more complete information, see 700; IBM; 80(90) minutes; Educational Testing Service. *

For reviews of the testing program, see 700; 5:538, and 4:802.

[29]

★**Business Education: Teacher Education Examination Program.** College seniors preparing to teach secondary school; 1957; an inactive form of *Business Education: National Teacher Examinations;* for more

complete information, see 709; IBM; 80(95) minutes; Educational Testing Service. *

For a review of the testing program, see 5:543. For reviews of the National Teacher Examinations, see 700, 5:538, and 4:802.

[30]

*Business Fundamentals and General Information Test: National Business Entrance Tests.** Grades 11–16 and adults; 1938–62; 4 forms: General Testing Series Form 19-51 ('55), Official Testing Series Forms 18-41 ('54), 20-61 ('59), 21-71 ('60); for further information, see the battery entry, 33;

Joint Committee on Tests of the United Business Education Association and the National Office Management Association (Forms 19-51 and 18-41 only) ; National Business Education Association. *

For reviews by Vera M. Amerson and C. C. Upshall of the 1946 form, see 3:369. For reviews of the complete battery, see 33, 5:515, and 3:396.

[31]

★**General Business: Every Pupil Scholarship Test.** High school; 1959-61; 3 forms: April '59, January '61, April '61, (2–4 pages) ; general directions sheet ['63, 2 pages] ; no data on reliability ; 4¢ per test; 4¢ per scoring key; postage extra ; 40(45) minutes; Bureau of Educational Measurements. *

RAY G. PRICE, *Professor of Business Education, University of Minnesota, Minneapolis, Minnesota.*

The Every Pupil Scholarship Test is a series of tests used to determine levels of achievement for students in Kansas but also available to out-of-state users. *General Business* is one of the tests in this series. The April 1959 form consists of 100 items; Part 1 has 45 true-false items; Part 2, 25 multiple choice items; and Part 3, 30 matching items. The January 1961 and April 1961 forms each contain 75 multiple choice items. The scoring is quite easy and objective. Each item is worth one point.

Unfortunately, no data on reliability or validity was reported for any form of the test. Lacking this information, it is difficult, if at all possible, for the prospective user to judge its value as a measuring instrument.

Also missing was the manual that usually accompanies a published test and which contains such information as (a) the purpose of the test; (b) source of content and method of preparation; (c) statistical evidence of validity and reliability; and (d) suggestions for using the test results.

Supposedly, each of the three test forms covers the essential material presented in a general business course. The basis used for selecting the content, however, is not clear. For example, in the April 1959 form only two items out of 100 pertain to insurance. The January 1961 form, on the other hand, contains 23 items on insurance out of a total of 75. This seems to indicate a lack of balance in covering the content of the general business course. In addition, the test items tend to emphasize specific details and a knowledge of facts rather than general understanding, reasoning ability,

and critical discrimination. But perhaps, it is only fair to say that the test may be a reflection of the way the average general business course is taught.

Nevertheless, the test *General Business* is a worthy effort. Furthermore, the two later forms (January and April, 1961) are a vast improvement over the earlier form. Properly revised, the test could be developed into a useful measuring instrument that is greatly needed.

[32]

*General Office Clerical Test (Including Filing): National Business Entrance Tests.** Grades 11–16 and adults; 1948-62; 4 forms (8–10 pages plus accessories) ; General Testing Series Form 19-53 ('55), Official Testing Series Forms 18-43 ('54), 20-63 ('59), 21-73 ('60) ; for further information, see the battery entry, 33; Joint Committee on Tests of the United Business Education Association and the National Office Management Association (Forms 19-53 and 18-43 only) ; National Business Education Association. *

REFERENCES

1. HAMILTON, HERBERT A. *Relationship of Success in Beginning General Clerical Occupations to Achievement in the Information and Skill Aspects of General Office Clerical Division of the National Business Entrance Tests Series.* Doctor's thesis, New York University (New York, N.Y.), 1951.

For reviews by Arnold E. Schneider and C. C. Upshall of the 1946 form, see 3:379. For reviews of the complete battery, see 33, 5:515, and 3:396.

[33]

*National Business Entrance Tests.** Grades 11–16 and adults; 1938-62; formerly called *National Clerical Ability Tests* and *United-NOMA Business Entrance Tests;* 3 series; 6 tests (also listed separately) ; no data on reliability; no adult norms; Joint Committee on Tests of the United Business Education Association and the National Office Management Association (for 1800, 1900, and short forms only) ; National Business Education Association. *
a) [GENERAL TESTING SERIES.] 1938-59; 1 form; 6 tests; directions for administering ('55, 4 pages) ; correction manual ['55, 15 pages] ; norms ['59, 1 page] ; 50¢ per test; 50¢ per set of directions for administering and correction manual (free with orders of $3 or more) ; $3 per specimen set; cash orders postpaid.
　1) *Machine Calculation Test.* 1941-59; Form 19-54 ('55, 7 pages) ; 120(130) minutes.
　2) *Typewriting Test.* 1941-59; Form 19-56 ('55, 4 pages plus accessories) ; 120(130) minutes.
　3) *Business Fundamentals and General Information Test.* 1938-59; Form 19-51 ('55, 8 pages) ; separate answer sheets must be used; 45(55) minutes.
　4) *Bookkeeping Test.* 1938-59; Form 19-52 ('55, 7 pages plus accessories) ; 120(130) minutes.
　5) *General Office Clerical Test (Including Filing).* 1948-59; Form 19-53 ('55, 10 pages plus accessories) ; 120(130) minutes.
　6) *Stenographic Test.* 1938-59; Form 19-55 ('55, 2 pages plus accessories) ; manual ('55, 11 pages) ; 90(130) minutes.
b) [SHORT FORM SERIES.] 1938-55; 1 form ('55) ; 2 tests; no norms; 50¢ per test, cash orders postpaid.

1) *Stenographic Test*. 1938–55; 1 form (2 pages plus accessories); directions sheet ('55, 2 pages); 45(65) minutes.
2) *Typewriting Test*. 1941–55; 1 form (4 pages); no manual; 45(55) minutes.
c) [OFFICIAL TESTING SERIES.] 1938–62; administered only at NBET Centers which may be established in any community; 3 forms; 6 tests; directions for administering 1800 forms ('54), 2000 forms ('59), 2100 forms ('60), (4 pages); norms for 1800 forms ['56, 1 page], 2000 forms ['62, 2 pages], 2100 forms ['62, 1 page]; postpaid; fee includes scoring, reporting, and consultation services.
1) *Machine Calculation Test*. 1941–62; Forms 18-44 ('54, 7 pages), 20-64 ('59, 4 pages), 21-74 ('60, 7 pages); examination fee, $1; 60(70) minutes for Form 20-64, 120(130) minutes for Forms 18-44 and 21-74.
2) *Typewriting Test*. 1941–62; Forms 18-46 ('54), 20-66 ('55), 21-76 ('60), (4 pages plus accessories); examination fee, $1; 60(70) minutes for Form 20-66, 120(130) minutes for Forms 18-46 and 21-76.
3) *Business Fundamentals and General Information Test*. 1938–62; Forms 18-41 ('54), 20-61 ('59), 21-71 ('60), (8 pages); separate answer sheets must be used; available free when one or more of the tests in the series are ordered; 40(50) minutes for Form 20-61, 45(55) minutes for Forms 18-41 and 21-71.
4) *Bookkeeping Test*. 1938–62; Forms 18-42 ('54), 20-62 ('59), 21-72 ('60); examination fee, $1; 60(70) minutes for Form 20-62, 120(130) minutes for Forms 18-42 and 21-72.
5) *General Office Clerical Test (Including Filing)*. 1948–62; Forms 18-43 ('54, 10 pages plus accessories), 20-63 ('59, 8 pages plus accessories), 21-73 ('60, 10 pages plus accessories); examination fee, $1.25; 60(70) minutes for Form 20-63, 120(130) minutes for Forms 18-43 and 21-73.
6) *Stenographic Test*. 1938–62; Forms 18-45 ('54), 20-65 ('59), 21-75 ('60), (11 pages); manual for Forms 18-45 ('54, 11 pages), 20-65 ('59, 8 pages), 21-75 ('60, 11 pages), examination fee, $1.25; 60(90) minutes for Form 20-65, 90(130) minutes for Forms 18-45 and 21-75.

REFERENCES

1–9. See 40:1476.
10. See 4:453.
11. CRISSY, WILLIAM J., AND WANTMAN, M. J. "Measurement Aspects of the National Clerical Ability Testing Program." *Ed & Psychol Meas* 2:37–46 Ja '42. * (*PA* 16:2441)
12. NELSON, JOHN HOWARD. *A Study of the Relationships Between Achievement on the National Business Entrance Tests and the Job Performance of Beginning Stenographers and Typists.* Doctor's thesis, New York University (New York, N.Y.), 1951.
13. LILES, PARKER. "National Business Entrance Tests Motivate Business Students." *Bus Ed Forum* 14:22+ F '60. *
14. SLAUGHTER, ROBERT E. "The National Business Entrance Tests," pp. 338–46. In *Evaluation of Pupil Progress in Business Education.* The American Business Education Yearbook, Vol. 17, 1960. New York: New York University Bookstore, 1960. Pp. x, 399. *
15. BAIRD, MARGARET W. "National Business Entrance Tests: Personal Experience." *J Bus Ed* 36:287–8 Ap '61. *
16. NATALE, GLORIA MARIE. *Measurement Aspects of the National Business Entrance Tests.* Doctor's thesis, Columbia University (New York, N.Y.), 1963. (*DA* 24:1887)

MELVIN R. MARKS, *Professor of Business Administration, The University of Rochester, Rochester, New York.* [Review of Series 1900, 2000, and 2100.]

The NBE tests are offered in a General Testing Series and an Official Testing Series. Each series includes six tests: bookkeeping, general office clerical, machine calculation, stenography, typewriting, and "business fundamentals and general information." On the positive side the five specific tests appear to have adequate face validity for their subject matter. Unfortunately, no other positive points can be made by this reviewer. The format and number of items in the tests of the General Testing Series and the long forms of the Official Testing Series are identical, and the item content is highly similar. Thus, in appearance, they seem to be parallel forms. However, the publisher says that they have different purposes and that "careful consideration should be made of the purpose intended when ordering these tests." What are these purposes? "Tests in the Official Testing Series are available solely for administration at National Business Entrance Testing Centers * Included at no extra charge are the scoring, reporting, and consultation services * The General Testing Series is used in schools for grading purposes and in preparing students for the Official Testing Series. Business also makes use of the General Testing Series for employment and placement purposes." This distinction in purpose does not appear to be one which would be accepted by most sophisticated users of tests. It is not a distinction which in any way bears upon the content, reliability, validity, or usefulness of the tests. Thus, as far as the reviewer is concerned the Official Series represents only an additional service, not a different kind of test, and the implication that the Official Series is "better" is not warranted.

The adverse comments on the NBET appearing in *The Fifth Yearbook* could well stand as written for the current presentation of the tests. Additionally, the publishers furnished a copy of an exhaustive critique by Alexander Wesman made for the Joint Committee on Tests. Except for some favorable comments on face validity, the critique is almost wholly adverse (although, admittedly, the review is said to have deliberately concentrated on negative criticisms). Presumably this critique was available to the NBEA before the current versions of the NBET were released. The less than enthusiastic response of the reviewers to the almost complete lack of data on reliability and predictive validity has not persuaded the test publisher to remedy the deficiencies. A leaflet describing the tests offers the following under the heading "What about reliability and validity?": (*a*) that the tests are "prepared by testing specialists and business educators.... [and] reviewed by qualified office executives"; (*b*) that "several graduate research studies have been made relating to the tests and their effectiveness in predicting successful employment and adjustments in office occupations"; and (*c*) that "Persons interested in further evaluations of the NBETests are referred to recent editions of the 'Mental Measurements Yearbook.'" None of these "data" are useful answers to the questions on reliability and validity. This reviewer wrote to the publishers, pointing out the deficiencies. The reply referred again to the dissertations, but did not quote figures. The Wesman review referred to above was critical of the dissertation findings as to both technique and interpretation.

The point has been made that the General and Official Testing Series appear to contain parallel forms. The normative data bear out this assumption with respect to each of the six subtests, although the Official Testing Series appears to be slightly more difficult. It may be that in the process of revision (the Official Testing Series forms are said to be "revisions and improved versions" of General Testing Series forms) the Official Series has unintentionally been made more difficult. In any case, since new forms are introduced without any accompanying statement on the degree to which difficulty, parallelism, reliability, and validity have been held constant, the use of the word "improved" is not warranted.

Some additional adverse comments are in order. (*a*) There is no rationale for the complicated scoring procedure. (*b*) There is no rationale for the differential weighting of items within subtests or the differential weights of the subtests. (*c*) There is no indication that the intended weights have been realized by compensating for varying standard deviations of the tests or for their contributions to prediction of job performance. (*d*) There is frequent duplication of content areas between subtests; for example, numerical skills are required in several subtests. (*e*) Some subtests are so short (20 items) that their reliabilities may be seriously questioned.

Percentile rank on the Business Fundamentals and General Information Test seems to be regarded as a criterion for evaluating performance on the other tests. The user is told that if the examinee achieves a higher per-

centile rank on a skill test than on the fundamentals test "the quality of instruction, and level of achievement would be judged better than average," and conversely. This attribution of what may be random variation, or genuine intraindividual differences (for example, test specificity) to the inferred relationship between a general and a specific measure displays considerable naïveté.

In summary, while it may be true that the NBET could be useful in the evaluation of achievement in business education or for the prediction of office performance, the verdict of this reviewer is *not proven,* and thus the tests cannot be recommended for these purposes.

For reviews by Edward N. Hay, Jacob S. Orleans, and Wimburn L. Wallace, see 5:515; for a review by Paul S. Lomax of the 1946 forms, see 3:396. For reviews of individual tests, see 55, 5:506, 5:508, 5:511, 5:514, 5:522, 5:526, 3:368–9, 3:379, 3:384, 3:391, and 3:394.

[Other Tests]

For tests not listed above, see the following entries in *Tests in Print:* 48 and 52; out of print: 49.

BOOKKEEPING

[34]

*Bookkeeping: Every Pupil Scholarship Test. High school; 1926–64; new form (2–4 pages) usually issued each January and April; forms from previous testing programs also available; general directions sheet ['63, 2 pages]; no data on reliability; norms for new forms available following testing program; 4¢ per test; 4¢ per scoring key; postage extra; 40(45) minutes; Bureau of Educational Measurements. *

[35]

*Bookkeeping: Minnesota High School Achievement Examinations. High school; 1952–63; series formerly called *Midwest High School Achievement Examinations;* new form issued each May; norms available in June following release of new form; Form F ('63, 6 pages) used in 1963 testing; no specific manual; series manual ('63, 4 pages); series norms ['63, 4 pages]; series cumulative profile ('62, 2 pages); no data on reliability; no description of normative population; 12¢ per test; $2.50 per 100 profiles; postage extra; 20¢ per specimen set, postpaid; 60(65) minutes; American Guidance Service, Inc. *

HAROLD L. ROYER, *Associate Professor of Accounting, University of Miami, Coral Gables, Florida.* [Review of Form F.]

The coverage of this bookkeeping examination is fairly representative of the theory in first year high school bookkeeping. However, the examination could certainly be improved upon by including some questions or problems about the worksheet, computation of inventories, bank reconciliation, and petty cash, and by having several problems on the computation of depreciation. Several questions aim at breadth of coverage, but none aims at depth.

The examination is composed of 118 questions divided into 13 units as follows: general principles (32 questions); statements (12 questions); adjusting and closing entries (7 questions); special journals (8 questions); problems relating to sales and purchases (5 questions); payroll and taxes (6 questions); depreciation (6 questions); bad debts (6 questions); notes and interest (6 questions); accrued expense and income (5 questions); partnerships, corporations, and cooperatives (10 questions); banking services (5 questions); and "Problems" (10 questions). The problem section is not sufficiently representative either in scope or weight.

There is very little evidence of any attempt to work on validity. A number of the questions have several responses; items 4, 8, and 28 have more than one answer. Item 29 is answerable in a way which is at variance with the scoring key. Items 39 and 41 should have better accounting terminology for their answers. Neither at the beginning nor at any point throughout the examination is there a sample question.

The percentile norms are worked out for each new form of the examination, but we do not know how many examinations were given to base the norms upon. No information is given concerning the geographical distribution of the examinees on whom the norms are based, nor the types of schools from which they come—public or private, general or commercial.

The examination may serve the purpose of the teacher who wants a very general test at the end of the semester or at the end of the school year. There are not enough questions or problems in a single unit to obtain detailed information and to diagnose a student's ability to work the worksheet and make the statements.

For a review by I. David Satlow of earlier forms, see 5:504.

[36]

*Bookkeeping Test: National Business Entrance Tests.** Grades 11–16 and adults; 1938–62; 4 forms: General Testing Series Form 19-52 ('55), Official

Testing Series Forms 18-42 ('54), 20-62 ('59), 21-72 ('60); for further information, see the battery entry, 33; Joint Committee on Tests of the United Business Education Association and the National Office Management Association (Forms 19-52 and 18-42 only); National Business Education Association. *

For reviews by Harvey A. Andruss and Ray G. Price of the 1946 form, see 3:368. For reviews of the complete battery, see 33, 5:515, and 3:396.

[37]

*First-Year Bookkeeping: Every Pupil Test.** 1 year high school; 1939–64; new form (4 pages) usually issued each April; forms from previous testing programs also available; general directions sheet ('63, 2 pages); no data on reliability; Ohio norms for new forms available following testing program; 5¢ per test; 3¢ per scoring key; postpaid; 40(45) minutes; Ohio Scholarship Tests. *

[Other Tests]

For tests not listed above, see the following entries in *Tests in Print:* 55, 58–9, and 61–2; out of print: 63.

MISCELLANEOUS

[38]

★**Commercial Law: Every Pupil Scholarship Test.** High school; 1951; 1 form (2 pages); general directions sheet ['63, 2 pages]; no data on reliability; 4¢ per test; 4¢ per scoring key; postage extra; 40(45) minutes; Bureau of Educational Measurements. *

[39]

*Machine Calculation Test: National Business Entrance Tests.** Grades 11–16 and adults; 1941–62; earlier tests called *Key-Driven Calculating Machine Ability Test;* 4 forms: General Testing Series Form 19-54 ('55), Official Testing Series Forms 18-44 ('54), 20-64 ('59), 21-74 ('60); for further information see the battery entry, 33; Joint Committee on Tests of the United Business Education Association and the National Office Management Association (Forms 19-54 and 18-44 only); National Business Education Association. *

For a review by Dorothy C. Adkins, see 5:514; for a review by Elizabeth Fehrer of the 1946 form, see 3:384. For reviews of the complete battery, see 33, 5:515, and 3:396.

[Other Tests]

For tests not listed above, see the following entry in *Tests in Print:* 66.

SHORTHAND

[40]

★**APT Dictation Test.** Stenographers; 1955; 1 form (33⅓ rpm record); comparison script (1 page); no data on reliability; no norms; distribution restricted to clients; $12.50 per set of testing materials, postage extra; 4[10] minutes; Associated Personnel Technicians, Inc. *

[41]

★Byers' First-Year Shorthand Aptitude Tests. First year students in grades 9–13 and business school; 1959; 6 scores: total and 5 scores listed below; 1 form; 2 parts; manual (13 pages); no data on reliability; no norms for college or business school students; 50¢ per set of both parts; 50¢ per manual (free with 10 or more sets of both parts); postage extra; Edward E. Byers; Allied Publishers, Inc. *
a) PART 1. 2 scores: phonetic perception, retention ability; orally administered in part; 1 form (3 pages); 35(40) minutes.
b) PART 2. 3 scores: observation aptitude, pattern from parts, hand dexterity; 1 form (13 pages); 35(40) minutes.

REFERENCES

1. BYERS, EDWARD ELMER. *Construction of Tests Predictive of Success in First-Year Shorthand.* Doctor's thesis, Boston University (Boston, Mass.), 1958. (*DA* 19:1610)

EDWARD O. SWANSON, *Assistant Professor, and Senior Student Personnel Worker, University of Minnesota, Minneapolis, Minnesota.*

Shorthand is "a rapid method of writing by substituting characters or symbols for letters, words, etc." (*Webster's New Collegiate Dictionary*) and is synonymous with "stenography." The Byers' test purports to measure aptitude for utilizing this method and "to predict success in first-year shorthand." The tests "were constructed for use as prognostic testing instruments that would assist in the (1) placement of beginning shorthand students, (2) early identification of unqualified students, and (3) improvement of effective classroom instruction." No effort was made "to measure functional factors concerned with transcription or vocational success."

The test consists of five subtests entitled Phonetic Perception (writing, in regular spelling, words listed by phonetic spelling), Retention Ability (a digit to letter substitution task when a string of digits are read orally to the examinees), Observation Aptitude (choosing a given pattern of symbols from five patterns when curves and straight lines in the pattern are reversed), Pattern From Parts (marking a diagonal for missing letters from a paragraph with the letters strung out equally spaced), and Hand Dexterity (marking as many as possible of prescribed patterns on a dotted field in a 20-second time period). The five tests are divided into two parts, each requiring about 35 minutes to administer.

The tasks were arrived at by observation of processes of shorthand, interviews with short-

hand teachers and students, reviews of other shorthand tests, and surveys of writing and research on shorthand prognosis.

These shorthand tests appear to be overelaborate attempts to match armchair-derived component functions of the shorthand process with similarly derived tasks that will supposedly measure these functions. Each test author has the prerogative of defining what domain is to be measured, but he is also bound to present validation data for his approach. The manual presents no reliability data and the most meager of validity data. Even necessary descriptive data are lacking (sample sizes, means, and standard deviations).

Validity information consists of three multiple correlation coefficients between the test and "shorthand accomplishment tests (partial transcription of seven dictated letters, each requiring 2½ minutes to dictate, with dictation rates ranging from 45 to 75 words a minute) administered at the end of one year of shorthand study." No sample sizes are given, and the groups are *not* described. Presumably the multiple correlation coefficients are each obtained by combining the five subtests in optional statistical fashion but the manual does not make this clear, simply stating the subtest scores are weighted in order to produce the highest possible multiple correlations. Neither a table of zero order intercorrelations nor of beta weights is presented; consequently, the reader cannot decide which subtests carry what weights in the regression equations. Outside of the sentence quoted, the reader will learn nothing about the criterion measure. No concurrent validities are shown. Though the author presumably derived his ideas in part by reference to other shorthand tests, he did not see fit to relate results of his tests to results of other shorthand tests or to factor tests of a similar nature.

A norms table for a high school group is presented for an averaged "Z" score of the five subtests. No description of the high school sample is given, neither its size nor its representativeness. How the "Z" scores (ranging from 86 to 928) were derived is totally unexplained. No suggested cutting points for selecting or possibly sectioning shorthand students are given.

Because of the nature of the tasks presented, two of the tests appear difficult to administer and score. Retention Ability requires 56 timed intervals ranging from 6 seconds to 11 seconds and Hand Dexterity requires 16 intervals of 20 seconds each. This hardly recommends these tests for easy administration particularly since speed is an important part of the task involved. Retention Ability requires each substituted letter to be correct for the item to be counted as correct, while Hand Dexterity requires a scorer's judgment as to whether a pattern drawn is accurate enough to be counted correctly.

The symbols for Observation Aptitude are poorly printed, the lines appearing blurred, the squares not quite square, and the circles not quite circular. A reasonably good draftsman and use of the photo-offset process would have permitted a considerably better printing job. Directions in the manual do not have clearly differentiated breaks between the finish of one subtest and the start of another.

The reviewer cannot recommend this test. No descriptive statistics, poor validity data, no information about intercorrelations of the subtests, no description of the criterion group and the criterion measure, no evidence on test reliability, and insufficient norm information all combine to make a flat non-recommendation necessary.

[42]

*First-Year Shorthand: Every Pupil Test. 1 year high school; 1938–64; test booklet titles vary; new form (4 pages) usually issued each April; forms from previous testing programs also available; general directions sheet ('63, 2 pages); no data on reliability; Ohio norms for new forms available following testing program; 25¢ per set of teacher's dictation sheets, postpaid; 30(45) minutes; Ohio Scholarship Tests. *

[43]

Personnel Research Institute Test of Shorthand Skills. Stenographers; 1951–54; title on test is Otis and Laurent Test of Shorthand Skills; 2 scores: transliteration, transcription; Forms A, B, ('51, 2 pages); manual ('54, 6 pages); tentative norms; 15¢ per test; 50¢ per set of scoring key and manual; $1 per specimen set; postage extra; (20–35) minutes; [Jay L. Otis and Harry Laurent]; Personnel Research Institute. *

IROL WHITMORE BALSLEY, *Professor of Office Administration and Head of the Department, Louisiana Polytechnic Institute, Ruston, Louisiana.*

The authors recommend in the manual, published in 1954, that this test be used only for preliminary screening, since a "minimum of data is available with respect to its validity, and norms are based on relatively small sam-

ples." Apparently, no further attempt at validation has been made in the past nine years.

Since Forms A and B are of the same design, specific comments will be made regarding Form A only.

The first part of the test consists of a business letter presented in printed form with space under each line of copy for the testee to write the shorthand outlines for the words. There is no explanation in the manual of the procedure used to select the vocabulary for the letter or to decide upon the length of it.

The testee is timed on his writing of the shorthand notes, and his time is recorded in minutes and seconds. No maximum amount of time to be allowed is stated. In scoring the first part, only the time taken to write the shorthand is considered. The completeness or accuracy of the shorthand notes is disregarded. The material consists of 332 actual words, or 384 words using the Gregg 1.4 syllable standard word.

The second part of the test requires the testee to supply 60 selected words or phrases (70 actual words) in a partially completed printed transcript of the letter, using his own shorthand notes previously written from print. In Form A, this partial transcript contains approximately 52 per cent of the letter. The 21 per cent of the transcript to be filled in by the testee is indicated by single-line markings; the remaining 27 per cent, indicated by double-line markings, is not to be filled in.

In speaking of the suitability of this type of test, the authors state that "In an analysis of shorthand skills preparatory to actual test construction, it was found that the primary difference distinguishing the skilled from the mediocre stenographer appeared to be not so much in speed of taking down the shorthand (transliteration) as in accuracy in reading the notes after they had been taken (transcription) * It was found, however, that the speed of transliteration of printed material was related to the rate of transliteration of orally presented material." No explanation of the nature of the analysis that led to these conclusions is given.

Teachers of shorthand would be likely to challenge such conclusions for at least two reasons. First, in the writing-shorthand-from-print test, a basic element is missing that is present in the writing-shorthand-from-dictation test. The shorthand writer is not required to carry in his memory the dictated message as he writes the outlines. Second, he has the opportunity to go back over the printed copy several times if need be to fill in outlines that he could not think of in the first writing.

In taking dictation in an office situation, the rate at which a stenographer can take dictation and transcribe the notes accurately is of importance. This test provides no measure of dictation rate the testee can take. If the assumption is made that the testee can take dictation at the rate at which he is able to write the message from the printed copy, the rates indicated by the times recorded in the manual for the validation groups would be vastly different from what they are.

For in the decile norms for Form A, the time required by employed stenographers in the 1st tenth was 4 minutes, 20 seconds or less; in the 10th tenth, more than 8 minutes, 50 seconds. The time required by the advanced students in the 1st tenth was 5 minutes, 45 seconds or less; in the 10th tenth, more than 8 minutes, 45 seconds. According to these figures, only the testees in the 1st tenth of the advanced students would be taking dictation in excess of 70 words a minute and only testees in the 1st tenth of employed stenographers would be taking dictation in excess of 75 words a minute. The mean rate in each group would be less than 60 words a minute. It must be remembered, also, that these recorded times give no indication of the completeness or accuracy of the shorthand written. A testee could be very weak, quit trying in a few minutes, and have a high score on this aspect of the test.

The second part of the test is designed to measure the testee's ability to transcribe his shorthand notes. The real measure of the adequacy of a person's shorthand skill is, of course, his ability to transcribe completely and accurately. This process involves skill not only in reading shorthand notes but also in applying rules of grammar and punctuation, in spelling, in word usage, and in typing the transcript. Skill in typing the transcript is not, of course, measured in any way. Skill in reading shorthand notes is measured on the basis of transcribing less than 20 per cent of the dictation. The scorer of a test paper is directed to consider as an error any mistake in spelling or in hyphenation. There are four hyphenated words in Form A. No measure of ability to apply

rules of grammar and punctuation is provided. Thus, it is evident that much of the transcription process is not measured by this test.

The authors state that since Forms A and B differ in difficulty, they have provided separate norms for the two forms. They explain that the norms given are not based on large samples and are not representative of a wide variety of training institutions or stenographic employers.

In establishing the correlation between scores on the various aspects of the test and final grades of advanced stenographic students, the authors used small numbers of cases, between 36 and 45. In no instance was the absolute correlation greater than .63 for the second part of the test or .53 for the first part.

In establishing the correlation between scores on the various aspects of the test and words-per-minute rate for employed stenographers, the authors used a total of 50 cases. The highest absolute correlation with accuracy of transcription was .25; and with speed of transliteration, .56. These figures arouse suspicion concerning the statement of the authors that the correlations between test scores and final grades "indicate satisfactory validity for both the rights and the time scores."

In summary, this test is of little value for its stated purpose. The customary dictation test used in the classroom would be a more valid test; and, incidentally, it (like this test) can be administered by a person who does not know any shorthand system.

[44]

★**Revised Standard Graded Tests for Stenographers.** High school and business school; 1958–59, c1956–59; 4 scores: mailability, speed of transcription, accuracy of transcription, accuracy of typing; Form A ('59); instructions and script ('59, 14 pages); no data on reliability; no norms; instructions and script free; [45] minutes; H. M. Overley; the Author. * (Test withdrawn.)

[45]

★**Shorthand Test: Individual Placement Series (Area IV).** Adults; 1960; Forms A, B, (2 pages); also available on 33⅓ rpm record; no manual; no data on reliability; no description of normative population; $10 per 25 tests; $10 per record containing both forms; $2 per specimen set without record; $12 per specimen set with record; postpaid; (20–25) minutes; J. H. Norman; the Author. *

[46]

★**Stenographic Dictation Test.** Applicants for stenographic positions; 1962–64; 6 forms ['62, 2 mimeographed pages]; forms 60A and 60B (60 wpm), 80A and 80B (80 wpm), 100A and 100B (100 wpm); practice sheet (1 page); manual ('64, 8 pages); no data on reliability; $35 per 25 tests; specimen set loaned for rental fee of $5, which may be applied to purchase price; postpaid; (20–30) minutes for test; McCann Associates. *

[47]

*Stenographic Test: National Business Entrance Tests. Grades 11–16 and adults; 1938–62; earlier tests called *Stenographic Ability Tests;* 5 forms (2 pages plus accessories): General Testing Series Form 19-55 ('55), Official Testing Series Forms 18-45 ('54), 20-65 ('59), and 21-75 ('60), Short Form ('55); for further information, see the battery entry, 33; Joint Committee on Tests of the United Business Education Association and the National Office Management Association (except Forms 20-65 and 21-75); National Business Education Association. *

REFERENCES

1. NELSON, JOHN HOWARD. *A Study of the Relationships Between Achievement on the National Business Entrance Tests and the Job Performance of Beginning Stenographers and Typists.* Doctor's thesis, New York University (New York, N.Y.), 1951.

For a review by Edward B. Greene, see 5:522; for reviews by Ann Brewington and Elizabeth Fehrer of the 1946 form, see 3:391. For reviews of the complete battery, see 33, 5:515, and 3:396.

[48]

★Test of Dictation Speed. Stenographers; 1958; 1 form ('58, 4 pages); no manual; directions sheet ['58, 1 page]; no data on reliability; no norms; $3 per 25 tests, postage extra; 50¢ per specimen set, postpaid; (5) minutes; Richardson, Bellows, Henry & Co., Inc. *

[Other Tests]

For tests not listed above, see the following entries in *Tests in Print:* 70–1, 74–5, 78, 80, 82, and 84; out of print: 69 and 83; status unknown: 79.

TYPEWRITING

[49]

*First-Year Typewriting: Every Pupil Test. High school; 1938–64; 2 scores: speed, performance; new form (4 pages) usually issued each April; forms from previous testing programs also available; general directions sheet ('63, 2 pages); no data on reliability; Ohio norms for new forms available following testing program; 5¢ per test; 3¢ per scoring key; postpaid; 35(40) minutes; Ohio Scholarship Tests. *

[50]

★[McCann Typing Tests.] Applicants for typing positions; 1961–64; 3 scores: speed, accuracy, total; Form A, B, C, ('61, 2 pages); mimeographed manual ('64, 14 pages); no data on reliability; no norms for part scores; $35 per 10 tests; specimen set loaned for rental fee of $5, which may be applied to purchase price; postpaid; 5(10) minutes for practice test, 10(25) minutes for test; McCann Associates. *

[51]

SRA Typing Skills. Grades 9–12 and adults; 1947; 2 scores: speed, accuracy; Forms A, B, (4 pages); preliminary manual (4 pages); no data on reliability; $2.45 per 20 tests; 50¢ per specimen set; postage extra; 10(15) minutes; Marion W. Richardson and Ruth A. Pedersen; Science Research Associates, Inc. *

REFERENCES

1. SKULA, MARY, AND SPILLANE, ROBERT F. "Validity Information Exchange, No. 7-016: D.O.T. Code 1-37.32, Typist." *Personnel Psychol* 7:147–8 sp '54. *
2. ASH, PHILIP. "Validity Information Exchange, No. 13-07, Stenographers, Typists, General Clerks, and Secretaries." *Personnel Psychol* 13:456 w '60. *

LAWRENCE W. ERICKSON, *Associate Professor of Education, University of California, Los Angeles, California.*

The *SRA Typing Skills* test is described in the manual as consisting of "a business letter, approximately 225 words long, which is copied by the examinee as often as possible in a 10-minute period." The test, however, is little more than a 10-minute straight-copy test with only a salutation and a complimentary close included with the body of the letter. The typist is confronted with none of the placement problems involved in typing letters. The work sheet includes a lined box within which the salutation is to be typed. The body of the letter starts two spaces below this point. The typist is directed to copy the material line for line, with no changes and no erasures. Other lined boxes, appropriately placed on the work sheet, are provided for any repetition of the material.

There are other limitations of the test. It does not measure such essential attributes of a good typist as the abilities to make decisions in placement of material on the page, to type from rough-draft copy, to arrange material in tabulated or tabular form, and to proofread typed copy.

The typist's speed is scored in terms of net words per minute, with a 10-word (50 stroke) penalty for each error. Research has shown that such a penalty is unrealistic—it does not adequately express the "true" cost of an error. The manual gives some helpful suggestions for interpreting speed scores in relation to the accuracy ratio, which is determined by dividing the net stroking rate by the gross stroking rate.

No information is given in the manual as to the validity of the test other than to say, "It yields results which are closely related to those obtained on mutilated [*sic*] copy, tabular materials, hand-written drafts, etc." No evidence is provided for this statement. To the best knowledge of this reviewer, there is no research which would indicate that straight-copy skill automatically transfers to problem-and-production typing situations which characterize office work. As stated in the manual, "much research needs to be done in this field, particularly in determining standards on tests given for actual employment purposes."

The manual also states that the test is available in two equated forms. This statement seems to be true only to the extent that Form A and Form B of the test include similar copy (a so-called business letter). No evidence is given as to the method used to equate the copy. The usual procedure followed by authors of typewriting materials is to determine the syllabic intensity of the material. A syllabic intensity study of the copy on both forms was made by this reviewer. The copy of Form A has the following syllabic intensity: paragraph 1, 1.64; paragraph 2, 1.66; paragraph 3, 1.77; paragraph 4, 1.80. The syllabic intensity of the copy of Form B is as follows: paragraph 1, 1.61; paragraph 2, 1.58; paragraph 3, 1.57; paragraph 4, 1.60. To the extent that syllabic intensity is a measure of the difficulty of copy, the two forms of this test are not of the same difficulty. The examinees would, in all probability, make somewhat higher speed scores on Form B.

The chief attribute of the test is that the directions for the examinee are simple and clear; so are the directions for administering and scoring.

In summary, it is the judgment of this reviewer that this test measures straight-copy copying skill only. To the extent that this type of skill transfers to office typing situations, the test may be a helpful selection device. As an initial screening device, the test has merit since it is easy to administer and it can be given in a minimum of time. However, the same results could be obtained by having the examinee type from regular straight-copy material which can be secured at a lower cost. If this test is used, this reviewer recommends that examinees be allowed to erase. Such practice is realistic in terms of office work and provides evidence as to the proofreading ability and erasing skill of the examinee. The words-a-minute rate, obtained under these conditions, would be more nearly a measure of the typist's skill.

JACOB S. ORLEANS, *Professor of Psychology, University of Nevada, Southern Regional Division, Las Vegas, Nevada.*

DESCRIPTION. Each form consists of (*a*) a practice exercise in which the examinee types some 165 words of the instructions; and (*b*) a letter for the typing of which 10 minutes are allowed, the examinee to type the letter over if time is still available. The letter has about 260 "words," a word being defined as 5 strokes (including one space).

The test is in the form of a long sheet accordion folded into eight pages, the backs of the pages being blank. The instructions and the letter to be typed take a little more than one and one half pages. The rest is a work sheet on which the examinee is to type the letter line for line, starting with the salutation in a box provided for that purpose. Margins are furnished for both elite and pica type. Space is designated for as many as three typings of the letter.

ADMINISTRATION AND SCORING. Examinees competent to take this test should have no difficulty carrying out the instructions properly under an experienced examiner. Detailed instructions and suggestions are given concerning the testing room, lighting, materials needed, and timing. The scoring is simple and is in accord with standard techniques for determining number of words per minute and number of errors. The instructions for scoring are detailed and clear. The scoring method produces for each examinee the following three measures: total number of strokes; net speed (number of words a minute); and accuracy ratio. The authors furnish nomographs for finding both net speed score and accuracy ratio.

NORMS. The test is designed "for the proper selection and placement of stenographic personnel." The prospective employer should know what typing speed and accuracy level the job demands. The test scores will tell whether the applicant meets the demands of the job. It would seem helpful to have available distributions of scores, both speed and accuracy, for typical groups of applicants for specified levels of typing jobs.

EVALUATION. No data are furnished on validity or reliability. No information is provided on how the test was prepared. There is no evidence that the letters used in the two forms are satisfactory for the purpose and no information as to how the letters were selected. It would seem to be a simple matter to administer Forms A and B, or the same form again after an interval of a week or two, to the same group of examinees and to compute a reliability coefficient. To publish and distribute the test without such readily obtainable information means that the authors and publisher regard such information as unnecessary or irrelevant.

The examinee who completes the standard letter before the time is up types it over again. No evidence is offered that this procedure is more valid or produces more reliable measures than typing new context throughout the 10 minutes. It might be noted that provision is made on the work sheet for a maximum of not quite 80 words a minute (with perfect accuracy).

SRA Typing Skills has all the earmarks of a clever usable test, concerning which almost no data are made available to the prospective user. Apparently the user is expected to accept the test on faith as a valid and reliable instrument.

[52]

★The Tapping Test: A Predictor of Typing and Other Tapping Operations. High school; 1959–63; 1 form ('59, 12 pages); manual ('63, 24 pages); $5.50 per 25 tests; $2.50 per 25 sets of color tablets; postage extra; $1.50 per specimen set, postpaid; (30) minutes; John C. Flanagan, Grace Fivars (manual), Shirley A. Tuska (manual), and Carol F. Hershey (manual); Psychometric Techniques Associates. *

REFERENCES

1. FLANAGAN, JOHN C.; FIVARS, GRACE; AND TUSKA, SHIRLEY A. "Predicting Success in Typing and Keyboard Operation." *Personnel & Guid J* 37:353–7 Ja '59. * (PA 35:1319)
2. KIRCHNER, WAYNE K., AND BANAS, PAUL. "Prediction of Key-Punch Operator Performance." *Personnel Adm* 24: 23–6 Ja–F '61. *

RAY G. PRICE, *Professor of Business Education, University of Minnesota, Minneapolis, Minnesota.*

This rather elaborate aptitude test was developed "to predict ability to operate a typewriter or other keyboard machines." Specifically, the test is designed to measure two of the aptitudes needed in learning to type, "the ability to tap quickly and accurately with one finger at a time by controlling each finger separately and independently" and the ability "to learn to respond with a particular finger on perceiving a letter, number, or other type of symbol."

The 12-page test booklet contains 3 pages of instructions and practice exercises and 9 pages of timed test material. In preparation for the test, the examinee attaches felt pads to the tips of eight fingers (thumbs are not used). Each pad is then moistened with a different color so that when the fingers are tapped on a piece of paper, colored dots are produced. A letter is assigned to each finger, beginning with A

for the little finger of the left hand and ending with H for the right hand little finger.

The first aptitude is measured by having the examinee tap "as fast as possible making dots in a series of circles, using each of the four fingers of each hand in succession." The second aptitude, the ability to associate a particular finger with a symbol, is measured by having the examinee "tap the appropriate finger to spell out simple words in short performance exercises." The dots are to be within a circle. In fact, tapping inside a circle is an important element of the test. A dot more than half outside the circle is considered an error.

The test requires approximately 30 minutes to administer. Two thirds of this time is devoted to instructions and preparations such as applying dots and color. Actual testing time is only about 10 minutes. Each page of the test consists of either a separately timed section or an example problem. The nine timed pages are arranged in order of increasing difficulty. A complete manual of instructions accompanies the test. Reliability coefficients indicate that the test conforms to accepted standards as a measuring instrument.

As a screening instrument for use in selecting students for typewriting instruction, the *Tapping Test* has merit. Its greatest potential use, however, is in the selection of trainees to be prepared as typists in government, business, and the armed services. In the secondary schools, where it is generally accepted that typewriting should be available to all students, the chief value of the test would be to aid in grouping students according to ability. But on the basis of evidence indicating a high relationship between initial key striking ability and success in typewriting as measured by straight copy tests or teachers' grades in typewriting, one might justifiably question the need for this intricate procedure involving felt pads, paint tablets, and tapping dots inside circles rather than having examinees tap the actual keys of a typewriter.

Certainly one could seriously question whether an instrument prepared to predict ability to operate a typewriter would also predict ability to operate "other keyboard machines" since no evidence is cited to confirm that such a relationship actually exists. This is not to say that the *Tapping Test* lacks validity as a predictor of ability to operate keyboard machines other than the typewriter but neither can its predictive value for this purpose be assumed. Even though some teachers of typewriting believe that a positive relationship exists between playing the piano and operating the typewriter, research evidence does not bear this out.

HENRY WEITZ, *Associate Professor of Education, and Director, Bureau of Testing and Guidance, Duke University, Durham, North Carolina.*

This test is designed to provide a basis for estimating a student's chances of developing, through training, skill in typing or other keyboard machine operations. The data reported in the manual and elsewhere seem to suggest that this purpose can be achieved.

The test requires the examinee to tap in coded sequences with four fingers of each hand in small circles printed on the test booklet. By covering the fingers with color-coded inked pads, the taps are recorded in scorable form on the booklet. This rather ingenious method of recording tapping responses is explained fully in the manual and in some detail in an article by Flanagan, Fivars, and Tuska (*1*).

Predictive validity coefficients with typing course grades and words per minute as criteria range from .05 to .73 with average validity coefficients for a number of studies hovering in the area .35 to .40. This suggests that the use of the test score would make some contribution to predicting performance and might aid in the selection of students. Charts are provided relating test performance to typing course achievement. These might provide suggestions for tentative cutoff scores for selection. Users of the test, however, would be well advised to establish local criteria.

Reliability data, based on groups of students at various levels of training in typing classes, suggest that the instrument is sufficiently reliable for individual prediction. Corrected split-half coefficients for fairly homogeneous groups range from .84 to .95 with an average of .90. Evidence is presented to indicate that the score on this test is relatively independent of intelligence and that typing skill is also independent of intelligence. It is probable, therefore, that the test may be a useful independent measure of unique job elements.

This seems to be a very promising test of the ability to learn to type. It appears to be relatively easy to administer and score. The instructions for administration, scoring, and interpreting the scores are well written and should make these psychometric chores as painless as possible. With further standardization, the test should be especially effective when candidates for a typing course in a school exceed the available facilities. By logical extension, it would seem that the test would be useful in estimating the trainability of key-punch operators and other personnel for similar keyboard operating tasks. If this turns out to be true, the test would have considerable value as part of an employment test battery.

[53]

★**Test of Typing Speed.** Applicants for clerical positions; 1958–63; 2 scores: net speed, accuracy; forms A, B, ('58, 5 pages, forms not differentiated on test booklets); manual ['63, 3 unnumbered pages]; no data on reliability; tentative norms; $3 per 25 tests, postage extra; 50¢ per specimen set, postpaid; 5(10) minutes; Richardson, Bellows, Henry & Co., Inc. *

[54]

Typewriting I and II: Every Pupil Scholarship Test. 1 or 2 years high school; 1928–64; new form (4 pages) usually issued each January and April; forms from previous testing programs also available; general directions sheet ['63, 2 pages]; no data on reliability; norms for new forms available following testing program; 4¢ per test; 4¢ per scoring key; postage extra; 36(40) minutes; Bureau of Educational Measurements. *

[55]

Typewriting Test: National Business Entrance Tests. Grades 11–16 and adults; 1941–62; earlier tests called *Typing Ability Test;* 5 forms: General Testing Series Form 19-56 ('55), Official Testing Series Forms 18-46 ('54), 20-66 ('55), and 21-76 ('60), Short Form ('55); for further information see the battery entry, 33; Joint Committee on Tests of the United Business Education Association and the National Office Management Association (except Forms 20-66 and 21-76); National Business Education Association. *

REFERENCES

1. NELSON, JOHN HOWARD. *A Study of the Relationships Between Achievement on the National Business Entrance Tests and the Job Performance of Beginning Stenographers and Typists.* Doctor's thesis, New York University (New York, N.Y.), 1951.

LAWRENCE W. ERICKSON, *Associate Professor of Education, University of California, Los Angeles, California.* [Review of Forms 19-56, 20-66, 21-76, and the Short Form.]

This problem-and-production typing skill test covers such typical office typing tasks as typing letters, filling in forms, arranging statistical material in tabular form, addressing envelopes, typing from rough draft copy, and other related activities. To the extent that such activities are a measure of the kind of work that the typist will be expected to do in the office, these are good tests for use in the final selection process after applicants have been screened initially by a test which is more easily administered and scored, such as a straight-copy, timed typing test.

The tests are realistic, in terms of office typing work, in that the examinee is called upon to solve placement problems, to follow various directions, to erase and correct errors, to divide words correctly at the ends of lines, and to make other decisions relating to work of the kind found in an on-the-job situation. Since typing errors are to be corrected by erasing, an evaluation can be made of the erasing skill and proofreading ability of the examinee. This is a far more realistic testing practice than that of penalizing the examinee 10 words (50 strokes) for each error made in the copy and determining speed in terms of net words per minute.

The directions are clear and concise, and they are of a kind that test the skill and problem solving ability of the examinee. The directions in the Administrator's Manual are also easy to follow. Probably the greatest limitation of Forms 19-56 and 21-76 is that either test takes two hours to administer. However, on the basis of such a test, the examiner would have information which would enable him to make an intelligent evaluation of the examinee's production typing skill. A typist selected by this testing procedure could be expected to succeed on the job, all other things being equal. Form 20-66, however, can be administered in 60 minutes. A short form is also available which can be administered in 45 minutes.

An excellent Correction Manual is furnished for each of the tests. Despite this fact, another limitation of the tests is the time it would take to score the completed work properly. However, this would be time well spent in terms of improved selection of qualified office typists.

The publisher states that several graduate research studies have been made on the effectiveness in predicting successful employment and adjustment in office occupations. However, no data on the correlation of the test results with job success are cited. Such statistical data would be welcomed by test users, if indeed job success can be predicted from a single test such as this. A battery of tests covering various aspects of office work would, in all probability, be a better indicator of job success.

The greatest shortcomings of these tests are the time it takes to administer them and the subjectivity which may occur in the evaluation and scoring. The latter problem may be partially solved by careful training of persons who do the scoring. The directions for the examinees would be improved if more emphasis were given to the fact that copy containing uncorrectable errors will be considered as unacceptable, with no points being allowed for it in the scoring. This may lead the examinee to exercise greater care and caution and thereby increase the reliability of the test. Similarly, the tests might yield the same results if the test materials were shortened somewhat so that a production timed typing sample of, say, 30 minutes could be used. This would enable the examiner to give and score a test in less than an hour. Production rates could be determined which would be somewhat more objective than the point-scoring system now used with these tests.

In summary, these tests of typing production skill are much better indicators of the typing skill needed in an office situation than is the straight-copy test which is frequently used as a selection device. As indicated above, a straight-copy test may well be used as an initial screening device, with one of the typing tests of the *National Business Entrance Tests* being used as a final selection device.

For a review by Clifford E. Jurgensen, see 5:526; for reviews by E. G. Blackstone and Beatrice J. Dvorak of the 1946 form, see 3:394. For reviews of the complete battery, see 33, 5:515, and 3:396.

[56]
★Typing Test: Individual Placement Series (Area IV). Adults; 1959; Forms C, D, (2 pages); scoring instructions-norms (2 pages) for each form; no data on reliability; no description of normative population; $10 per 25 tests; 50¢ per scoring instructions-key; $2 per specimen set; postpaid; 5(15) minutes; J. H. Norman; the Author. *

[Other Tests]
For tests not listed above, see the following entries in *Tests in Print*: 86, 89, 92, 96, and 98: out of print: 85 and 87–8.

MULTI-APTITUDE BATTERIES – SIXTH MMY

REVIEWS BY *Dorothy C. Adkins, Anne Anastasi, Harold P. Bechtoldt, John B. Carroll, S. S. Dunn, Norman Frederiksen, Leo Goldman, William H. Helme, Lloyd G. Humphreys, J. A. Keats, Benjamin Kleinmuntz, William B. Michael, John E. Milholland, Joseph E. Moore, Paul F. Ross, Stanley I. Rubin, Richard E. Schutz, Julian C. Stanley, Erwin K. Taylor, William W. Turnbull, and Leroy Wolins.*

[766]

★**Academic Promise Tests.** Grades 6–9; 1961–62, c1959–62; 7 scores: abstract reasoning, numerical, nonverbal total, language usage, verbal, verbal total, total; IBM; Forms A, B, ('61, 20 pages); manual ('62, 54 pages); separate answer sheets must be used; $4.50 per 25 tests; $3.75 per 50 IBM answer sheets; $1.10 per 50 student report forms; 50¢ per set of manual and scoring stencil; 90¢ per specimen set; postpaid; 90(120) minutes; George K. Bennett, Marjorie G. Bennett, Dorothy M. Clendenen, Jerome E. Doppelt, James H. Ricks, Jr., Harold G. Seashore, and Alexander G. Wesman; Psychological Corporation. *

JULIAN C. STANLEY, *Professor of Educational Psychology, and Director, Laboratory of Experimental Design, University of Wisconsin, Madison, Wisconsin.*

Three subtests, Abstract Reasoning (AR), Numerical (N), and Verbal (V), of the *Academic Promise Tests* (APT) represent a welcome downward extension of the *Differential Aptitude Tests.* This reviewer wonders whether the 60-item fourth subtest, Language Usage (LU), containing 24 grammar items, 23 spelling items, 8 capitalization and punctuation items, and 5 correct sentences items in Form A,

is as good from the standpoint of content, even though its correlation with school marks is relatively high. In particular, the misspelled words seem to test clerical ability for minor details of a sentence. Ten of the 23 are as follows, in order of their appearance in Form A: shoping, efect, strugle, comunicate, apeal, compeled, acompany, arive, generaly, and posibility. The authors do not tell why they chose these words and the other 13 [allways, clamed, telagram, reseption, regester, hight, greif, compaired, insurence, anyway (for "any way"), when ever, celler, and talant], except to mention "careful editorial scrutiny," difficulty, and discrimination of more able from less able students. Some explicit content validity rationale for choosing the items themselves seems needed.

One also would like to know the basis for including at least 15 verb items among the 24 grammatically faulty sentences. Were content specifications drawn up initially and adhered to throughout the tryout phase? Without such information, and on the basis of my content analysis of the Form A language usage items, I would prefer to substitute a reading comprehension test for LU.

The content of the other three subtests (AR, N, and V) seems considerably better. Abstract Reasoning consists of 60 ingenious plane geometry items, for each of which the examinee must decide which one of four "answer figures" goes with the three "problem figures." Inductive reasoning and spatial relations ability both seem to play a considerable part in these.

One fourth of the N items in Form A are number series. The remaining 45 are straightforward arithmetical computation or arithmetical reasoning items of the same sort as that pioneered by A. S. Otis and E. L. Thorndike, as contrasted with the various new-type quantitative reasoning items in the mathematical subtest of the *College Entrance Examination Board Scholastic Aptitude Test*. Only five items are accompanied by figures, perhaps in an attempt to keep overlap with AR minimal.

For each of the 60 N items, the last option is "D. None of these." On Form A, D is the keyed option for items 2, 7, 10, 14, and 19 of the N subtest—only 5 times instead of 60/4 = 15. LU has exactly the same arrangement: 21 keyed A's, 19 B's, 15 C's, and 5 D's. Thus, response biases of examinees may affect their N and LU scores considerably. The keyed A, B, C, D option positions for AR and V are much better balanced: 13, 17, 15, and 15.

While generally good, the 60 V items in Form A, all analogies, could have benefited from more careful editing. Items 11 and 37 have as the first part of their stems "HAMMER is to NAIL" and "HOUSE is to NAILS," respectively. "Mississippi" appears in the stem of item 9 and as an option in item 26. "Wilson" (the president) appears in the stem of item 23 and as an option in item 52.

Item 23, "WORLD WAR I is to WORLD WAR II as WILSON is to (A) Lincoln, (B) Roosevelt, (C) Grant, (D) Eisenhower," may become more difficult as time goes by. Item 52, "JOHNSON is to LINCOLN as ARTHUR is to (A) Adams, (B) Tyler, (C) Wilson, (D) Garfield," may now be confusing.

Item 54 can be answered correctly without knowing who Allen is if the examinee remembers that Marion was called the "Swamp Fox": "MOUNTAIN is to SWAMP as ALLEN is to (A) Wolfe, (B) Marion, (C) Burgoyne, (D) Sheridan."

Because no correction for chance is employed ("If you are not sure of an answer, select the choice which is your best guess"), a sixth grade student who guesses at all 240 items with the expected degree of success (15 marked according to the key for each subtest) would obtain higher percentile ranks on AR, N, V, and LU than if he marked nothing: 20, 30, 15, and 20 versus 1, 1, 1, and 1.

The comprehensive APT manual provides excellent information on predictive validity for school marks, comparable forms reliability for single grade groups, standard errors of measurement, practice effects, and APT-WISC equivalence. The detailed validity data for schools of various types all over the country occupy 18 large pages of the manual. Percentile norms for each of the four grades are given for AR, N, AR + N, V, LU, V + LU, and AR + N + V + LU.

The *Academic Promise Tests* resemble the analogous grade levels of the *Cooperative School and College Ability Tests,* but offer in addition the nonverbal AR subtest, which to this reviewer appears greatly superior to the nonverbal material of the *California Test of Mental Maturity*. APT's LU portion seems rather out of date and out of place among AR, N, and V, but it certainly does correlate well with school grades—particularly in English, where the median r's are .60 for LU, .50 for N, .45 for V, and .31 for AR. Even for mathematics it is excelled only by N (.41 versus .58).

Everything considered, this excellent new battery offers schools convenient, attractive, predictively valid, reliable measurement in four areas.

WILLIAM W. TURNBULL, *Executive Vice President, Educational Testing Service, Princeton, New Jersey.*

The new *Academic Promise Tests* should prove to be a quick and economical way to identify talented students and those who need remedial help. They are well designed and produced. Instructions are clear, the format is attractive, and several features have been introduced to simplify giving, scoring, and interpreting the tests.

Four separate scores are derived: Abstract Reasoning (AR), Numerical (N), Verbal (V), and Language Usage (LU). In addition, the first two scores (AR + N) are summed to provide a measure of nonverbal reasoning ability and the last two (V + LU) to afford a measure of competence with verbal materials. Finally, a total score is derived from all four parts. Although the time limits are short, the reliabilities are acceptably high, even on the individual sections where a rigorous test of reliability (parallel forms correlated within a single school grade) is employed. The validity data given are extensive and the correlations with school grades are very satisfactory. It should be noted that predictions over more than a few months have not yet been undertaken but presumably will be consistent with the short-run predictions now available.

While the tests are generally well made, the logic underlying the composition of the battery and the derivation of its two subtotal scores seems open to some question. To begin with, the purposes for which the tests are recommended include sectioning and grouping for instructional purposes. For this use, it would seem important to tap at least the student's mathematical achievement (whether "new" or "traditional") and his attainments in science and social studies. These are not separately represented in this battery. Thus for sectioning and placement, the user will need to supplement the *Academic Promise Tests* with more specific measures of academic achievement.

A real problem concerns the inclusion of Abstract Reasoning in the battery. This is a well constructed and edited test of figure classification. The manual states: "Then, there are students whose educational background has been such as to arouse doubt that verbal or numerical tests are adequate measures of their potential learning ability, or whose strengths are better represented by nonverbal performance tasks. To provide description of nonverbal, non-numerical competence, the Abstract Reasoning test has been designed." In principle, this seems reasonable. The manual provides no evidence about the usefulness of the test for students with unusual educational backgrounds, however. Instead, it includes coefficients of correlation between each score (including Abstract Reasoning) and school grades achieved by regular students in regular classes, grades 6 through 9. Here the evidence is that the AR score is not particularly useful: it yields correlations whose median is about .30 in contrast to about .45 for the other three

scores taken singly. Moreover, this pattern seems to hold quite consistently over the major subject areas where the data are extensive enough to permit conclusions. It is possible that later research will justify retention of this section, but unfortunately the disappointing results reported in the manual are fairly typical of what has usually been found in attempts to measure academic potential by abstract reasoning tests of the nonverbal and non-numerical variety. On the evidence at hand, it is hard to escape the conclusion that inclusion of Abstract Reasoning represents a triumph of hope over experience and that the testing time could have been better utilized for other purposes.

The second section, Numerical, is a well made test with good variety in its items. From the validity data, moreover, it appears to be performing just as one would hope a good quantitative test would perform. When the scores are lumped together with those from the AR section to provide a nonverbal subtotal, however, both their meaning and a degree of their utility is lost. The data in the manual show that invariably the combined score is less valid than the score of the numerical section taken alone. As suggested in the previous paragraph, one way to prevent this erosion of validity would be to drop the AR section entirely.

The verbal test is composed of well written analogies. As the manual states, "The analogy process *per se* is a kind of reasoning; the content to which the reasoning is applied may be as varied as desired." Capitalizing on this feature, the authors have drawn upon the materials of science, mathematics, history, and geography as well as upon everyday word relationships for their verbal test items. One consequence is that the test appears to stress general verbal reasoning and general information rather than word relationships more narrowly defined. The validity coefficients show that the resulting composite is indeed predictive of school grades. Whether or not the scores from this widecoverage test should be combined with LU to yield an overall "verbal" score is, however, debatable. It should be noted that the single V score correlates more highly with N ($r = .69$) than with LU ($r = .63$). This fact points up the question of whether or not a combination of V and LU is especially appropriate and reinforces the observation that V is more a test of reasoning than of word understanding per se.

Academic Promise Tests

The test of "Language Usage" combines items on spelling, grammar, and punctuation. Generally, it is a competently written test, although more careful editing might have improved an ambiguous item here and there. Both reliability and validity coefficients are satisfactory, however, and the test scores should be helpful for the purposes stated for the battery —including, in this instance, pupil sectioning.

The manual accompanying the battery is unusually good in several respects; notably, in the completeness of the data given (e.g., on practice effect, reliability of differences between pairs of scores, and relations with scores on other tests) and in its clear discussion of such points as the contruction of expectancy tables. The techniques of reporting and profiling scores are efficient and clearly described. Inclusion of instructions for the use of score bands (within which the true score is likely to lie) rather than exact score points is a welcome feature.

In summary, the *Academic Promise Tests* are well prepared and produced with a professional touch. Validity data involving predictions over three to four months are encouraging. Generally, the individual scores may be found more revealing than their sums. The usefulness of Abstract Reasoning is questioned and the view is presented that the APT would be improved by its omission. Overall, however, the tests should have real utility as relatively brief measures of general academic development and promise and should be of supplementary help in sectioning and placement.

[767]

*Differential Aptitude Tests. Grades 8–13 and adults; 1947–63; 9 scores: verbal reasoning, numerical ability, total (scholastic aptitude), abstract reasoning, space relations, mechanical reasoning, clerical speed and accuracy, language usage (spelling, sentences); IBM and (Form L only) MRC; Forms A ('47), B ('47), L ('62, c1947–62), M ('62, c1947–62); Forms L and M are revisions of Forms A and B, respectively; manual, third edition ('59, c1947–59, 98 pages, based on Forms A and B but also used with Forms L and M); individual report forms (2 pages): for Forms A and B ('61), for Forms L and M ('63, c1961–63); individual report folder ('61, 6 pages) for Forms A and B; casebook ('51, 93 pages, see 29 below); separate answer sheets must be used; $1.25 per 50 individual report forms; $3 per 50 individual report folders; $1.75 per casebook; $2 per manual; postpaid; George K. Bennett, Harold G. Seashore, and Alexander G. Wesman; Psychological Corporation. *

a) FORMS A AND B. 1947–61; IBM; 2 editions; directions for administration and scoring, third edition ('59, 23 pages, reprinted from manual); $3 per specimen set; Spanish edition available; 186(240–270) minutes in 2–6 sessions.

1) *Combined Booklet Edition*. 3 booklets; 50¢ per set of either hand or machine scoring stencils for any one booklet; $1 per set of hand scoring stencils for all 3 booklets; $1.10 per set of machine scoring stencils for all 3 booklets.
(*a*) Combination 1—VN. 3 scores: verbal reasoning, numerical ability, total (scholastic aptitude); 9 pages; $4 per 25 tests; $2.85 per 50 IBM answer sheets; 60(85) minutes.
(*b*) Combination 2—MR-LU-SR. 4 scores: mechanical reasoning, space relations, language usage (spelling, sentences); 34 pages; $7.50 per 25 tests; $4.45 per 50 IBM answer sheets; 95(135) minutes.
(*c*) Combination 3—CSA-AR. 2 scores: clerical speed and accuracy, abstract reasoning; 12 pages; $4.50 per 25 tests; $4 per 50 sets of IBM answer sheets; 31(50) minutes.
2) *Separate Booklet Edition*. 7 booklets; $2 per 50 IBM answer sheets for any one booklet; 50¢ per hand or machine scoring stencil for any one booklet; $1.25 per complete set of hand scoring stencils; $1.40 per complete set of machine scoring stencils; 50¢ per specimen set of any one booklet (includes directions but not manual).
(*a*) Verbal Reasoning. 6 pages; $3 per 25 tests; 30(40) minutes.
(*b*) Numerical Ability. 3 pages; $2.25 per 25 tests; 30(35) minutes.
(*c*) Abstract Reasoning. 7 pages; $3 per 25 tests; 25(30) minutes.
(*d*) Space Relations. 11 pages; $3.50 per 25 tests; 30(40) minutes.
(*e*) Mechanical Reasoning. 19 pages; $3.75 per 25 tests; 30(35) minutes.
(*f*) Clerical Speed and Accuracy. 6 pages; $3 per 25 tests; 6(15) minutes.
(*g*) Language Usage. 2 scores: spelling, sentences; 7 pages; $3 per 25 tests; 35(45) minutes.
b) FORMS L AND M. 1947–63; also called *Two-Booklet Edition* and *Differential Aptitude Tests, 1963 Edition;* IBM and (Form L only) MRC; 2 booklets (a separate booklet combination of verbal reasoning and numerical ability subtests is also available); directions and norms ('63, c1947–63, 34 pages); directions ('63, 4 pages) for use of MRC answer sheets with Form L; no data on reliability; norms for grades 8–12 only; $7.75 per 25 tests of either booklet; 60¢ per set of scoring stencils for IBM answer sheets; $8 per 50 MRC answer sheets; $1 per set of stencils for hand scoring MRC answer sheets (machine scoring service, by Measurement Research Center, Inc., may be arranged through the publisher); $3 per specimen set with manual for *a;* $1.50 per specimen set without manual; 181(235–245) minutes in 2–6 sessions.
1) *Booklet 1*. 1961, c1947–61, 21 pages; 4 scores: verbal reasoning, numerical ability, abstract reasoning, clerical speed and accuracy; $5.50 per 50 IBM answer sheets; 91(120) minutes.
2) *Booklet 2*. 1962, c1947–62, 38 pages; 4 scores: mechanical reasoning, space relations, language usage (spelling, grammar); $4.50 per 50 IBM answer sheets; 90(115) minutes.

REFERENCES

1–28. See 4:711.
29–77. See 5:605.
78. CHOTHIA, F. S. "Predicting Success in Multi-Purpose Schools." *Indian J Psychol* 31:139–40 Jl–D '56. *
79. CURETON, EDWARD E. "Service Tests of Multiple Aptitudes." *Proc Inv Conf Testing Probl* 1955:22–39 '56. * (*PA* 31:3017)
80. JACOBS, JAMES NAJEEB. *An Evaluation of Certain Measures of Aptitude and Achievement in the Prediction of Scholastic Success.* Doctor's thesis, Michigan State University (East Lansing, Mich.), 1957. (*DA* 22:4268)

81. SININGER, ROLLIN ALBERT. *Development and Evaluation of Visual Aids for Interpreting the Differential Aptitude Test and Kuder Preference Record.* Master's thesis, University of Texas (Austin, Tex.), 1957.

82. VINEYARD, EDWIN E., AND MASSEY, HAROLD W. "The Interrelationship of Certain Linguistic Skills and Their Relationship With Scholastic Achievement When Intelligence Is Ruled Constant." *J Ed Psychol* 48:279–86 My '57. * (*PA* 33:2200)

83. WEEKS, WILLIAM R. *A Study of the Predictability of High School Grades and the Differential Aptitude Tests for Predicting Success in a Two-Year Terminal Program at Western Michigan University.* Master's thesis, Western Michigan University (Kalamazoo, Mich.), 1957.

84. CATTELL, RAYMOND B., AND SCHEIER, IVAN H. "The Objective Test Measurement of Neuroticism, U.I. 23 (—)." *Indian J Psychol* 33:217–36 pt 4 '58. *

85. MYERS, MAURICE. *A Comparison of Differential Aptitude Test Patterns of Junior College Students in Five Semi-Professional Fields.* Doctor's thesis, New York University (New York, N.Y.), 1958. (*DA* 19:3218)

86. SMITH, D. D. "Abilities and Interests: 2, Validation of Factors." *Can J Psychol* 12:253–8 D '58. * (*PA* 33:9347)

87. CALIA, VINCENT FRANK. *The Use of Discriminant Analysis in the Prediction of Performance of Junior College Students in a Program of General Education at Boston University Junior College.* Doctor's thesis, Boston University (Boston, Mass.), 1959. (*DA* 20:3190)

88. DOPPELT, JEROME E., AND SEASHORE, HAROLD G. "Psychological Testing in Correctional Institutions." *J Counsel Psychol* 6:81–92 sp '59. * (*PA* 34:6012)

89. DOPPELT, JEROME E.; SEASHORE, HAROLD G.; AND ODGERS, JOHN G. "Validation of the Differential Aptitude Tests for Auto Mechanics and Machine Shop Students." *Personnel & Guid J* 37:648–55 My '59. * (*PA* 35:2775)

90. FRIESEN, DAVID. *The Differential Aptitude Tests as Predictors in Education I at the University of Manitoba.* Master's thesis, University of Manitoba (Winnipeg, Man., Canada), 1959.

91. HASCALL, EDWARD ORSON, JR. *Predicting Success in High School Foreign Language Study.* Doctor's thesis, University of Michigan (Ann Arbor, Mich.), 1959. (*DA* 19:3245)

92. JACOBS, JAMES N. "Aptitude and Achievement Measures in Predicting High School Academic Success." *Personnel & Guid J* 37:334–41 Ja '59. * (*PA* 35:1263)

93. JAYALAKSHMI, G. "Correlation of Tests of Psychomotor Ability With Intelligence and Non-motor Tests." *J Psychol Res* 3:78–84 S '59. *

94. MOSHIN, S. M. "Plea for a Scientific Aptitude Test and a Preliminary Report of the Development of Such Test." *Indian J Psychol* 34:36–42 pt 1 '59. *

95. NORTON, DANIEL P. "The Relationship of Study Habits and Other Measures to Achievement in Ninth-Grade General Science." *J Exp Ed* 27:211–7 Mr '59. * (*PA* 35:1283)

96. OAKES, FREDERICK, JR. *The Contribution of Certain Variables to the Academic Achievement of Gifted Seventh Grade Students in an Accelerated General Science Curriculum.* Doctor's thesis, New York University (New York, N.Y.), 1959. (*DA* 20:4002)

97. SMITH, D. D. "Traits and College Achievement." *Can J Psychol* 13:93–101 Je '59. * (*PA* 34:4780)

98. STINSON, PAIRLEE J., AND MORRISON, MILDRED M. "Sex Differences Among High School Seniors." *J Ed Res* 53:103–8 N '59. *

99. STOCKSTILL, KIAH, JR.; FRYE, ROLAND L.; AND STRITCH, THOMAS M. "Comparison of Differential Aptitude Test Scores for Junior High School Students." *Psychol Rep* 5:765–8 D '59. * (*PA* 34:6174)

100. BOURNE, ROBERT K., AND ROTHNEY, JOHN W. M. "Assessments of Counselees Writing Skills by Tests and Essays." *Voc Guid Q* 9:21–4 au '60. *

101. CALIA, VINCENT F. "The Use of Discriminant Analysis in the Prediction of Scholastic Performance." Comments by David V. Tiedeman. *Personnel & Guid J* 39:184–92 N '60. * (*PA* 35:3949)

102. CASSEL, RUSSELL N., AND STANCIK, EDWARD J. "Factorial Content of the Iowa Tests of Educational Development and Other Tests." *J Exp Ed* 29:193–6 D '60. *

103. FILELLA, JAMES F. "Educational and Sex Differences in the Organization of Abilities in Technical and Academic Students in Colombia, South America." *Genetic Psychol Monogr* 61:115–63 F '60. * (*PA* 34:7630)

104. FOOTE, RICHARD PAUL. *The Prediction of Success in Automotive Mechanics in a Vocational-Industrial Curriculum on the Secondary School Level.* Doctor's thesis, New York University (New York, N.Y.), 1960. (*DA* 21:3014)

105. HARRIS, YEUELL Y., AND DOLE, ARTHUR A. "A Pilot Study in Local Research With the Differential Aptitude Test Battery." *Personnel & Guid J* 39:128–32 O '60. * (*PA* 35:5366)

106. HUGHES, HERBERT HOWARD. *Expectancy, Reward, and Differential Aptitude Tests Performance of Low and High Achievers With High Ability.* Doctor's thesis, Florida State University (Tallahassee, Fla.), 1960. (*DA* 21:2358)

107. MILTON, OHMER. "Primitive Thinking and Reasoning Among College Students." *J Higher Ed* 31:218–20 Ap '60. *

108. ROSINSKI, EDWIN F. "Must All Tests Be Multi-Factor Batteries?" *J Exp Ed* 28:235–40 Mr '60. *

109. BRIM, CHARLES WILLIAM. *Inter-High School Variability and Its Effect on the Prediction of College Achievement.* Doctor's thesis, University of Illinois (Urbana, Ill.), 1961. (*DA* 22:3466)

110. EELLS, KENNETH. "How Effective Is Differential Prediction in Three Types of College Curricula?" *Ed & Psychol Meas* 21:459–71 su '61. * (*PA* 36:2KJ59E)

111. EWALD, HATTIE HOFF. *The Relationship of Scores on the Differential Aptitude Tests to Scholarship in High School and Freshman College.* Doctor's thesis, University of South Dakota (Vermillion, S.D.), 1961. (*DA* 22:800)

112. HAGER, CHARLES WILLIAM. *Correlation of Personality and Character Traits With Differential Achievement in High School.* Doctor's thesis, University of Texas (Austin, Tex.), 1961. (*DA* 22:3520)

113. HASCALL, EDWARD O. "Predicting Success in High School Foreign Language Study." *Personnel & Guid J* 40:361–7 D '61. * (*PA* 36:4KL61H)

114. McGUIRE, CARSON. "The Prediction of Talented Behavior in the Junior High School." *Proc Inv Conf Testing Probl* 1960:46–67 '61. *

115. NUGENT, FRANK A. "The Relationship of Discrepancies Between Interest and Aptitude Scores to Other Selected Personality Variables." *Personnel & Guid J* 39:388–95 Ja '61. * (*PA* 35:6212)

116. BROMER, JOHN A.; JOHNSON, J. MYRON; AND SEVRANSKY, PAUL. "Validity Information Exchange, No. 15-02: D.O.T. Code 4-97.010, 4-75.120, 4-85.040, Craft Foremen Correspond to Foremen I; 5-91.875, 5-91.088, 5-91.091, 5-91.831, 5-91.812, Process, Production, and Warehouse Foremen Correspond to Foremen II." *Personnel Psychol* 15:107–9 sp '62. *

117. COBB, BART B. "Problems in Air Traffic Management: 2, Prediction of Success in Air Traffic Controller School." *Aerospace Med* 33:702–13 Je '62. *

118. MERENDA, PETER F.; HALL, CHARLES E.; CLARKE, WALTER V.; AND PASCALE, ALFRED C. "Relative Predictive Efficiency of the DAT and a Short Multifactor Battery of Tests." *Psychol Rep* 11:71–81 Ag '62. * (*PA* 37:5665)

119. MUKHERJEE, B. N. "The Factorial Structure of Aptitude Tests at Successive Grade Levels." *Brit J Stat Psychol* 15:59–65 My '62. * (*PA* 37:7182)

120. RUDD, JOHN PAUL. *A Study of the Validity of Selected Predictors for Placement in Three-Rail Curricula.* Doctor's research study No. 1, Colorado State College (Greelev, Colo.), 1962. (*DA* 24:184)

121. SPRINGOB, H. KARL, AND JACKSON, CLIFTON W. "Measured Abilities and Inventoried Interests of Ninth Grade Boys." *Voc Guid Q* 11:37–40 au '62. * (*PA* 37:8279)

122. SUPER, DONALD E., AND CRITES, JOHN O. *Appraising Vocational Fitness by Means of Psychological Tests, Revised Edition,* pp. 339–49. New York: Harper & Brothers, 1962. Pp. xv, 688. * (*PA* 37:2038)

123. YOUNG, CHARLES RAY. *Factors Associated With Achievement and Underachievement Among Intellectually Superior Boys.* Doctor's thesis, University of Missouri (Columbia, Mo.), 1962. (*DA* 23:2406)

124. AIJAZ, SAIYID MOHAMMAD. *Predictive Validity of the Three Versions of the "Verbal Reasoning" and the "Numerical Ability" Subtests of the Differential Aptitude Tests for East Pakistan.* Doctor's research study No. 1, Colorado State College (Greeley, Colo.), 1963. (*DA* 24:1068)

125. ALVI, SABIR ALI. *Traditional and "Culture Fair" Aptitude Test Performance of College Students From Different Academic and Cultural Backgrounds.* Doctor's thesis, Indiana University (Bloomington, Ind.), 1963. (*DA* 24:2775)

126. BLOSSER, GEORGE H. "Group Intelligence Tests as Screening Devices in Locating Gifted and Superior Students in the Ninth Grade." *Excep Child* 29:282–6 F '63. * (*PA* 38:2434)

127. CHENEY, TRUMAN M., AND GOODISH, NAOMI. "Analysis —Between Certain Variables and Achievement in Beginning Shorthand." *J Bus Ed* 38:317–9 My '63. *

128. LUNDY, CHARLES T., AND SHERTZER, BRUCE. "Making Test Data Useful." *Personnel & Guid J* 42:62–3 S '63. *

129. OSBURN, H. G., AND MELTON, R. S. "Prediction of Proficiency in a Modern and Traditional Course in Beginning Algebra." *Ed & Psychol Meas* 23:277–87 su '63. * (*PA* 38:1386)

J. A. KEATS, *Reader in Psychology, University of Queensland, Brisbane, Queensland, Australia.*

The revised forms of the *Differential Aptitude Tests* contain only minor changes in the tests themselves. Possibly the major change which necessitated the production of the revised forms was the decision to change from a score "corrected" for guessing to a score equal to the number of correct responses for all tests. Such a change necessitated extensive changes in norms and these alone would have required a revised edition. The content of four of the eight tests is unchanged—these are Numerical Ability, Abstract Reasoning, Mechanical Reasoning, and Language Usage 1: Spelling. Verbal Reasoning still consists of double ended analogies of the form "? : word 1 :: word 2 : ?" but the alternatives are now listed as five pairs of words, the first of each pair corresponding to a possible first word of the analogy and the second word of the pair corresponding to a possible last word in the analogy. In the previous edition the subject had to seek two words from 16 options. Language Usage 2: Grammar (formerly entitled Sentences) and Space Relations have more items with only one correct response per item (instead of a varying number). Clerical Speed and Accuracy has been reset in clearer type. Norms for the new edition, based on over 50,000 cases from 195 schools in 43 states are presented with the new forms but the necessary revisions to the manual were not available at the time this review was written.

In this review it is not proposed to restate the many advantages of a battery of tests based on research results and on which research is continuing. The *Differential Aptitude Tests* have been in use for more than 16 years and many reviewers in these yearbooks and elsewhere have stressed the value of the contribution made by this battery. This reviewer agrees with most of the advantages claimed, but rather than restate these, he wishes to make suggestions for further research and development.

The practice of using "corrected" scores rather than simply the number of correct responses has been commented on by other reviewers in this series and elsewhere. It is gratifying to see a change to the latter procedure in the revised edition. The change in the analogies items of Verbal Reasoning also follows a questioning of the possible factorial complexity of the earlier items by a previous reviewer in this series. However, no evidence has been given to show that this present change goes far enough in the direction of reducing possible factorial complexity. Perhaps this evidence is given in the new manual but, unless results of research are available on this point, there is always the question as to whether the change is simply one towards the conventional rather than one resulting from scientific findings. The changes in Spatial Relationships and Language Usage 2: Grammar do follow the important point made by a previous reviewer that in the original form each *option* became a true-false item and could be scored as such. The value of continuous research and review of a soundly based test battery is well illustrated by these changes. A further example was noted in the provision of correlations with *SRA Primary Mental Abilities* following the suggestion of an MMY reviewer.

There are, however, a number of points made by previous reviewers which have not been met by this revision. The criticism that Language Usage 2: Grammar tends to accept out-of-date standards of usage does not seem to have been met. Indeed, the item used by an earlier reviewer as an example of this tendency still appears in the revised form. There are, of course, difficulties of changes in usage inherent in testing grammar, but surely these can be avoided by experienced item writers. A second point concerns the possibility of an acquiescence response set in both parts of Language Usage. It would be of considerable interest to know the correlation between the two parts of the spelling test obtained by separating items for which R (right) is the correct response from those for which W (wrong) is the correct response. Do these two sets of items combine to produce a homogeneous test? A similar question arises for the grammar items, since the "no error" option is sometimes correct.

Earlier comments have raised the question of the homogeneity of the items in the tests. Superficial homogeneity obtained by having all items of the same type in each of the eight tests does not necessarily guarantee homogeneity (or unidimensionality) in the sense of Lazarsfeld's definition,[1] which requires that pairs of items should be essentially zero correlated for persons at the same ability level. This property may be checked experimentally by methods used by Lord,[2] which are essentially factor analytic in form. If this check has not been made for the revised form—and there is no evidence that it has—then this is a further task in the improvement of this already important battery. It is

1 LAZARSFELD, PAUL F. Chap. 10, "The Logical and Mathematical Foundation of Latent Structure Analysis," pp. 362–412. In *Measurement and Prediction*. By Samuel A. Stouffer and others. Princeton, N.J.: Princeton University Press, 1950. Pp. x, 756. *
2 LORD, FREDERIC. "A Theory of Test Scores." *Psychometric Monographs*, No. 7. Princeton, N.J.: Psychometric Society, 1953. Pp. x, 84. *

not intended to imply that all, or even any, of the tests are not homogeneous but merely to stress the point that it is the responsibility of the test constructor to investigate the question and so be able to assure users that the test scores have an unambiguous meaning—at least in this sense. The research required is certainly not beyond present methods of analysis, either theoretically or computationally.

A feature of the present manual is the presentation of standard errors of measurement as well as reliability coefficients for each test (Forms A and B) at each of the grade levels tested. This feature has drawn favourable comment from previous reviewers which this reviewer echoes as far as the presentation of standard errors of measurement is concerned. There is, however, evidence that the standard error of measurement depends on the particular score obtained and that these variations would be greater than the variation in standard error between grade groups. If there is variation in standard error with score value of the kind found in experimental studies, this would account—in part at least—for variations in standard error between grades and so would be a more basic measure to report for at least some different score levels. This practice has already been adopted by at least one test publisher and is recommended for this battery, particularly in view of the stress placed on profile interpretation.

A further feature of the present manual that has attracted favourable comment is that continuous up-to-date information is provided from validity studies. This acknowledgment of responsibility to keep users informed of current results is commendable and the criticism that virtually all of the studies are carried out by the publisher's staff is not entirely valid. There is always the rebuttal that only in this way can the publisher be sure of the soundness of the research he is reporting. However, there is an obligation in this situation for the publisher to ensure that all relevant research methods are tried and at least a representative sample of the results reported. Previous reviewers in this series have commented on the absence of multiple correlations in the validity data presented. The use of discriminant function analysis seems also to be pertinent, but published results of such analyses are absent from the manual. The availability of these data would greatly assist the sophisticated user in establishing the guid-

ance programme most efficient for his particular situation. Considerations such as testing time available might cause him to reject the full battery for a particular purpose, whereas a selection of the tests, based on multiple correlation data, might indicate that a sub-battery would prove to be just as efficient. Perhaps the new manual will remedy this deficiency. A further advantage of using these more advanced techniques is that they may help to condense the enormous amount of validity data presently published for this battery and so assist the user in gaining a clearer impression of the established usefulness of the programme. Of course, no user can complain at having too much validity data, but the more sophisticated user is well aware that first order correlations are not necessarily a true indication of the relative contributions of the tests to the information provided by the battery as a whole.

The need to explore and report applications of modern research methods arises also in connection with establishing the percentiles which form the basis of the norms presented. Presumably, these have been estimated from the cumulative frequency distribution of the observed data. An overall standardisation sample of more than 50,000 cases seems very substantial indeed but when it is subdivided by grade, sex, and time of testing it is found that each set of norms is based on little more than 2,000 cases. Even these samples are quite adequate and probably larger than those used by most other agencies. However, in the reviewer's experience even distributions of this size show many irregularities and the raw percentiles, particularly those at the extremes, are likely to be somewhat unstable and possibly biased. This problem has received too little attention from theorists. Some theoretical distributions have been proposed [3] but until more work is done in theory and application, the problem of the stability of norms will remain. It is by large organisations using well established tests that the necessary applied work must be carried out.

In summary, the *Differential Aptitude Tests* were founded on the findings of research up to 1947 and most of the minor changes in the revised battery are based on research. The re-

3 KEATS, J. A. *A Statistical Theory of Objective Test Scores.* Melbourne, Australia: Australian Council for Educational Research, 1951. Pp. viii, 48. *

KEATS, J. A., AND LORD, FREDERIC M. "A Theoretical Distribution for Mental Test Scores." *Psychometrika* 27:59–72 Mr '62. *

viewer is of the opinion that more changes and more evidence for the changes made, as well as for retaining old forms, are called for to enable the battery to represent the standard to which others should aspire. Much of the material required could well appear in the revised manual which was, of course, not available to the reviewer. In any case, the battery will be widely used and the extensive preparation and renorming of the revised forms justify this choice.

RICHARD E. SCHUTZ, *Professor of Education, and Director, Testing Service, Arizona State University, Tempe, Arizona.*

The additions to the DAT which have appeared since the battery was reviewed in *The Fifth Mental Measurements Yearbook* simply add to the thickness of the frosting on an already well frosted cake. Revised Forms L and M have been produced, a revised manual was published in 1959 with another promised in 1964, and a new pamphlet for use in reporting and interpreting scores to students, parents, and teachers has appeared.

The revisions incorporated into the revised Forms L and M serve to increase the practical usability of the tests. The single booklet edition has given way completely to a two-booklet edition, although a VR-NA combination is still available as a separate. The responses to the entire battery are recorded on both sides of two answer sheets.

The new Form L is based on the content of the original Form A, while Form M is based on Form B. Content modification varies from test to test. In Verbal Reasoning, the stems of the double-ended analogies have been retained intact, but the 16 options previously available in the combinations of the 4 choices for opening and 4 for closing the analogy have been reduced to 5 fixed pairs.

The content of Numerical Ability and Abstract Reasoning is unchanged, but the layout of NA has been improved to increase the amount of white space on each page.

The items in Space Relations have been completely reworked to convert them to single-keyed responses, and the number of items has been increased from 40 to 60. Mechanical Reasoning is reproduced intact. The content of Clerical Speed and Accuracy remains unchanged but the items have been reset in a smaller non-serifed type face and printed on one page rather than two. No change has been made in the spelling subtest of Language Usage. The sentences subtest has been retitled "Grammar." In addition, the multiple-keyed items have been converted to single-keyed responses and the number of items increased from 50 to 60.

The new forms have been standardized with even greater care than was exercised in the 1952 standardization. More than 50,000 students from 195 schools in 95 communities representing 43 states were tested. Tables are presented demonstrating that the standardization sample is representative of the U.S. population with respect to geographic distribution and community size. Almost all of the tests were administered in October, November, and December rather than throughout the year as in 1952. Thus the norms are most relevant for fall testing programs. Tables of spring norms, also provided, were obtained by interpolating between successive grades tested in the fall. Although only interpolations, the spring norms are probably more accurate than were previous "windage" allowances. As in the original edition, percentile norms are presented for boys and girls separately.

Previous reviewers have been hard pressed to find valid criticisms of the DAT. The new DAT materials appear to eliminate some of these criticisms including the following:

a) No evidence is presented to demonstrate that subtracting wrong responses is of any value in scoring the power tests. Apparently, there was no such evidence to be presented. All eight tests of Forms L and M are scored rights only.

b) Few correlations with other tests are presented. The 1959 manual presents four full-page tables reporting the correlations of Forms A and B with a wide variety of intelligence, aptitude, achievement, and interest tests.

c) The authors fail to come to grips with operational problems in interpreting the test results. The new six-page student report folder represents an important step towards overcoming this criticism. The folder is evaluated more fully later in the review.

The following criticisms made by previous reviewers are still judged to be relevant:

d) No information is given concerning item analysis techniques used in constructing the tests. Although the 1959 manual includes a brief section on "Principles Governing the Test

Construction," it remains silent concerning the details of item analysis procedures and criteria. Possibly the 1964 manual will include additional information in this area.

e) *There is an undue amount of overlap and high correlation between tests.* This is a criticism which is not likely to be overcome, since it is inherent in the overall structure of the battery. The criticism is, of course, a relative one. Since one has no control over the obtained correlations after the test content has been definitely established, the criticism can best be avoided by demonstrating that the tests have adequate validity despite the overlap and correlation. This in turn involves attending to the next listed criticism.

f) *No use has been made of multiple regression and discriminant analysis procedures in establishing the validity of the various tests.* Although the 1959 manual presents numerous impressive arrays of predictive validity coefficients, only a single set of multiple regression equations is included. The equations involve the use of the DAT given in grade 10 as predictors of scores on the *College Entrance Examination Board Scholastic Aptitude Test* taken in grade 12. Two equations based on the performance of 85 boys are given and another two based on the performance of 60 girls from a single school. Optimal weighting of Verbal Reasoning, Spelling, and Sentences produced a multiple correlation coefficient of .79 between predicted and actual SAT Verbal scores. Weighting Numerical Ability, Verbal Reasoning, and Space Relations produced a multiple correlation of .85 with SAT Mathematics scores. These are quite respectable correlations. Unfortunately, no information is given concerning the first-order correlations between the DAT and SAT for the two groups so that it is impossible to evaluate the increased efficiency provided by using the multiple tests. Nor is it possible to even guess what the multiple correlations might look like for criteria other than a scholastic aptitude test.

Thus, despite the extensive predictive validity coefficients for separate DAT subtests, the *differential* validity of the tests in predicting various criteria is still without substantiation. Moreover, visual inspection of the patterns of correlations that are presented in the 1959 manual casts doubt that the battery does provide the differential utility implied in its title.

The 1959 manual steers the user in the direction of expectancy charts rather than regression equations. Although only illustrative samples of such charts are included in the manual, users are encouraged to prepare charts based on local data and references for the construction of such charts are given. While expectancy charts are unquestionably more feasible than regression equations for school people working by hand, the increasingly widespread availability of electronic data processing equipment in even the smaller school districts makes more sophisticated statistical procedures a thoroughly reasonable possibility. It is hoped that the DAT authors and publisher will help reduce the technological lag by continuing to exercise professional leadership in encouraging DAT users to utilize the best available resources for analyzing test results. The kind of operationally useful suggestions included in previous supplements and other auxiliary materials are most commendable.

g) *Adequate occupational validity and normative data are lacking.* The DAT was born and has been reared in an educational context. No occupational validity data are reported in the 1959 manual. The only occupational normative data presented are of a follow-back variety. These were obtained from a 5-year questionnaire follow-up of 2,900 juniors and seniors in 6 cities, and a 7-year follow-up on 2,386 of the same students in 5 of the cities. A return of about 60 per cent was obtained in each study. Since no criterion measures were available, the study yielded only descriptive characteristics of various subsamples in terms of their high school DAT scores. With the huge number of DAT's that have been administered by school districts in continuous testing programs for more than 15 years, data are certainly available for more definitive occupational validity studies.

So much for the current status of the DAT. Probably the most important innovation in DAT usage as far as the individual examinee is concerned will be found in the simple little six-page student report folder. Teachers, parents, and students are usually left cold by impressive psychometric characteristics of a test. They want to know what the results mean for them personally. All other data are of secondary importance. Although one can only speculate about the nature of the conclusions that users draw from the DAT, the new individual report folder provides some clear clues concerning the authors' philosophy and practice in interpreting DAT results.

I am frankly ambivalent concerning the contents of the folder. When one explicitly outlines the specific inferences he derives from test results, he reveals the nude consequences of the test. I feel the authors are to be commended for being forthright and specific in their generalizations, but nudity is a vulnerable form. The following statements are illustrative: "A student who wants to major in such fields as mathematics, physics, chemistry, or any branch of engineering, may expect to encounter some difficulty if his NA score is not in the top third or top quarter." "Students who do well on SR should have an advantage in work such as drafting, dress designing, architecture, mechanical engineering, die-making, building construction, and some branches of art and decoration." "If you do well on both these tests [Language Usage] and on VR, you should be able to do almost any kind of practical writing provided you have a knowledge of your topic and a desire to write about it."

Although the folder is sprinkled with almost as many disclaimers and cautions as a typical stock market advice sheet, I have an uneasy feeling that students and parents, who are certain to be highly involved emotionally and completely naïve statistically, run a high probability of making unjustified decisions on the basis of the material included in the folder. Optimally, of course, an expert counselor should be available to assist in the interpretation. But will he be available, and can he be expected to be as accurate in his inferences or as effective in communicating them as the report folder? Although I would not argue the soundness of any of the inferences included in the folder, I cannot find data in the 1959 manual to support many of them directly. This adds to my ambivalence, since undeniably I, along with every other DAT user, have drawn much wilder inferences on the basis of less substantial evidence.

I am able to resolve this ambiguity only by exercising both an absolute and a relative evaluation criterion, a discrimination which extends to my evaluation of the DAT in general. From a relative point of view, this is the best we can currently offer; no alternative procedures of any sort which possess greater utility can be suggested at the present time. From an absolute point of view, we have a long way to go to achieve optimal effectiveness. Fortunately, the road toward improvement appears to be sufficiently well defined to permit a few additional steps.

For reviews by John B. Carroll and Norman Frederiksen, see 5:605; for reviews by Harold Bechtoldt, Ralph F. Berdie, and Lloyd G. Humphreys, see 4:711; see also 3:620 (1 excerpt).

[768]

*Differential Test Battery. Ages 11 to "top university level" (range for Test 1 extends downward to age 7); 1955–59; 12 tests in 7 booklets; battery manual ('55, 53 pages, including 12 pages of provisional norms for the Speed Tests which are now superseded by the norms in the separate manual); no data on validity; 8s. per battery manual; 86s. per specimen set; prices include purchase tax; postpaid within U.K.; 136.5(200) minutes; J. R. Morrisby; distributed by the National Foundation for Educational Research in England and Wales. *

a) TEST 1, COMPOUND SERIES TEST. Ages 7 and over; "mental work power"; 1955; 1 form ('55, 68 pages); manual ('55, 22 pages); separate answer sheets must be used; 39s. per test; 7s. per 25 answer sheets; 4s. per set of key and manual; 30(40) minutes.

b) GENERAL ABILITY TESTS. Ages 11 and over; 1955; 3 tests; manual ('55, 32 pages); 39s. per 25 tests; 15s. per set of scoring stencils and manual for all 3 tests.

1) *Test 2, General Ability Tests: Verbal.* 1 form ('55, 9 pages); 12(20) minutes.

2) *Test 3, General Ability Tests: Numerical.* 1 form ('55, 8 pages); 29(40) minutes.

3) *Test 4, General Ability Tests: Perceptual.* 1 form ('55, 9 pages); 23(35) minutes.

c) TEST 5, SHAPES TEST. Ages 11 and over; 1955; spatial ability; 1 form ('55, 13 pages); manual ('55, 13 pages); separate answer sheets must be used; 9s. per test; 8s. per 25 answer sheets; 10s. per set of scoring stencil and manual; 10(15) minutes.

d) TEST 6, MECHANICAL ABILITY TEST. Ages 11 and over; 1955; 1 form ('55, 10 pages); manual ('55, 11 pages); separate answer sheets must be used; 7s. per test; 8s. per 25 answer sheets; 6s. per set of key and manual; 15(20) minutes.

e) SPEED TESTS. Ages 11 and over; 1955–59; 6 tests in a single booklet ('55, 16 pages); manual ('55, 32 pages); no data on reliability; 59s. per 25 tests; 8s. per set of manual and key for Test 7 (no keys necessary for other tests); 17.5(30) minutes.

1) *Test 7 (Speed Test 1), Routine Number and Name Checking.*

2) *Test 8 (Speed Test 2), Perseveration.*

3) *Test 9 (Speed Test 3), Word Fluency.*

4) *Test 10 (Speed Test 4), Ideational Fluency.*

5) *Test 11 (Speed Test 5), Motor Speed.*

6) *Test 12 (Speed Test 6), Motor Skill.*

For reviews by E. A. Peel, Donald E. Super, and Philip E. Vernon, see 5:606.

[769]

*Employee Aptitude Survey. Ages 16 and over; 1952–63; IBM; 10 tests (2 pages); battery manual ['63, 25 pages]; technical report ('63, 81 pages);

$2.50 per 25 test-answer sheets; 40¢ per set of scoring stencils for any one test; 50¢ per manual; $2 per technical report; $3 per specimen set of all tests (without technical report); postage extra; G. Grimsley (*a–h*), F. L. Ruch (*a–g, i, j*), N. D. Warren (*a–g*), and J. S. Ford (*a, c, e–g, j*); Psychological Services, Inc. *

a) TEST 1, VERBAL COMPREHENSION. 1952–63; IBM; Forms A Revised, B Revised, ('56); 5(10) minutes.
b) TEST 2, NUMERICAL ABILITY. 1952–63; IBM; Forms A ('52), B ('56); 10(15) minutes.
c) TEST 3, VISUAL PURSUIT. 1956–63; IBM; Forms A ('56), B ('57); 5(10) minutes.
d) TEST 4, VISUAL SPEED AND ACCURACY. 1952–63; IBM; Forms A ('52), B ('56); 5(10) minutes.
e) TEST 5, SPACE VISUALIZATION. 1952–63; IBM; Forms A Revised, B Revised, ('57); 5(10) minutes.
f) TEST 6, NUMERICAL REASONING. 1952–63; IBM; Forms A Revised, B Revised, ('57); 5(10) minutes.
g) TEST 7, VERBAL REASONING. 1952–63; IBM; Forms A Revised, B Revised, ('57); 5(10) minutes.
h) TEST 8, WORD FLUENCY. 1953–63; 3 forms; the same test blank ('53) is used with all 3 forms; 5(10) minutes.
i) TEST 9, MANUAL SPEED AND ACCURACY. 1953–63; 1 form ('56); 5(10) minutes.
j) TEST 10, SYMBOLIC REASONING. 1956–63; IBM; Forms A, B, ('57); 5(10) minutes.

REFERENCES

1. RUCH, FLOYD L. "Validity Information Exchange, No. 13-02: D.O.T. Code 0-48.18, Engineering Draftsman (Trainee)." *Personnel Psychol* 13:448 w '60. *
2. RUCH, FLOYD L., AND RUCH, WILLIAM W. "Predicting Success in Draftsman Training With Short Time Limit Aptitude Tests." *Ed & Psychol Meas* 20:827–33 w '60. * (*PA* 35:4068)
3. HANEY, RUSSELL; MICHAEL, WILLIAM B.; AND GERSHON, ARTHUR. "Achievement, Aptitude, and Personality Measures as Predictors of Success in Nursing Training." *Ed & Psychol Meas* 22:389–92 su '62. * (*PA* 37:3869)
4. MICHAEL, WILLIAM B.; HANEY, RUSSELL; AND GERSHON, ARTHUR. "Intellective and Non-Intellective Predictors of Success in Nursing Training." *Ed & Psychol Meas* 23:817–21 w '63. *

PAUL F. ROSS, *Industrial Psychologist, Imperial Oil Limited, Toronto, Ontario, Canada.*

The *Employee Aptitude Survey* (EAS) multitest battery was reviewed in *The Fifth Mental Measurements Yearbook* by Dorothy C. Adkins and by S. Rains Wallace. Since those reviews, the original 10 examiner's manuals, one for each test, have been combined into one Examiner's Manual describing test administration and scoring, and the technical information about the tests has been published in a Technical Report. The test battery itself remains unchanged except for one test, Word Fluency (Test 8), which has been standardized using a third letter of the alphabet as the starting, or stimulus, letter. Thus the battery contains eight tests with two forms each, one test with three forms (Word Fluency, Test 8), and one test (Manual Speed and Accuracy, or dotting, Test 9) with one form. This review was prepared after examining the 10 tests in their several forms, the Examiner's Manual (no date of publication), the Technical Report (1963), the Manual for Interpreting the Employee Apti-

tude Survey (Lockheed Aircraft Corporation, 1957), and the 1963–64 test catalog describing the EAS battery.

The Examiner's Manual is easy to read, presenting instructions for the administration of a test on one side of a page and scoring instructions on the back side of the same page. General instructions describe such practical matters as writing down start and stop times when a watch with a sweep second hand is used for timing and having two pencils for each examinee. Calculating raw scores from rights and wrongs using scoring formulae with fractions is made easy by a fold-out table on the inside back cover; raw scores for all but three tests can be read directly from the table. The 78-page Technical Report contains five chapters and a list of 13 references. Chapters present the rationale for the test battery, its reliability and factorial content, norms by occupation and educational level, validity data, and correlations with other tests. Alternate form correlations (reliability estimates) vary from .75 to .91 for the 10 tests, these correlations coming from samples of 853 to 1,885 examinees. The alternate form correlations are higher than those previously reported, with two relatively unimportant exceptions. The "50-odd correlations with measures other than standardized tests," which Adkins called "a rather impressive array" of validity data, have increased at least five-fold (see comments about validity data below). Most impressive of all, norms covering 45 jobs and 7 educational and industrial groups and "based on over 100,000 test scores" are presented. The jobs are described with a job code from the *Dictionary of Occupational Titles* and a short, one or two sentence job description. The sexes are kept separate in reporting norm data.

Adkins remarked about the many convenient features for using the EAS battery, and Wallace summarized his comments by saying: "This is an outstandingly well thought out and well constructed battery of tests based upon unusually competent analysis. The format, instructions, and scoring keys are uniformly excellent. It deserves the attention of anyone who has a selection problem, particularly for a wide variety of occupations." This reviewer agrees.

But no review is complete without criticisms, and important criticisms can be made of the technical data about this test battery. A summary of the criticisms by Adkins and Wallace can serve as a starting place. They found the battery could be criticized because (*a*) criteria for judging validity of the tests were frequently training criteria rather than on-the-job measures of performance, (*b*) minimum hiring scores, or cutting scores, were recommended for occupations for which no validity data were reported, (*c*) one test (Word Fluency, Test 8) had no validity data reported for it, (*d*) the factor analysis reported was something less than satisfying to the reviewers, and (*e*) general college students do as well as engineers in Space Visualization (Test 5) when Adkins' guesses seem to be that the engineers should do better than general college students. Adkins goes on to say that (*f*) Verbal Comprehension (Test 1) is too easy, (*g*) Symbolic Reasoning (Test 10) "could be improved by adjustment of the item difficulties," which must mean that the test is too difficult, (*h*) the three separately timed parts of the numerical ability test (Test 2) probably should not be printed side by side on an answer sheet, but rather should be in cyclic omnibus order under one time limit, and (*i*) some correct answers for the number series items (Numerical Reasoning, Test 6) are not shown among the answer alternatives.

The test authors appear to have responded to these criticisms. They have increased the amount of validity data reported, and on-the-job ratings of performance are included as criteria. A few validity coefficients are reported for Word Fluency (Test 8). *Suggested cutting scores have been dropped altogether.* The authors discuss why some of the right answers to the number series items are not among the alternatives; the discussion is presented in the Technical Report. But, in this reviewer's opinion, a number of the Adkins-Wallace observations and criticisms can still be made. Validity data based on on-the-job performance measures are still quite thin; the factor analysis may be misleading; Verbal Comprehension is quite easy and Symbolic Reasoning quite difficult (for example, office managers get a mean Verbal Comprehension score of 24 out of a maximum of 30 points, and a mean Symbolic Reasoning score of 9 out of 30 points); Numerical Ability would be easier to administer and perhaps could be shortened to five minutes if it were administered under one time limit with the item types (integers, decimals, fractions) in cyclic omnibus form; engineers, design engineers, and draftsmen now have Space Visualization (Test

5) mean scores which are approximately half a standard deviation higher than the mean scores for male college students and top and middle management.

The factor analysis reported in the Technical Report is the same factor analysis reported in earlier manuals for the EAS battery. The new report seems to be somewhat more complete. But the factor matrix, as reported, could be misleading. The authors omit reporting whether the "factors" are independent (orthogonal) or correlated (oblique) after rotation. The reported factor loadings convey the impression that the tests are virtually factor pure; only three out of nine tests have loadings on more than one factor. If the factors are assumed to be orthogonal, the reader could conclude from the factor matrix that the test intercorrelations are virtually zero. Yet in examining the intercorrelations among the 10 tests, particularly when based on samples of industrial leadmen or utility clerks, it is quite clear that there is a "general factor" present in most of the tests as attested by the moderate, all positive, intercorrelations among most tests in the battery. The modestly high test intercorrelations observed with industrial leadmen are reduced appreciably when the test intercorrelations are based upon persons like General Motors Institute engineering students; that is, the effects of the "general factor" are substantially reduced. Do these tests have enough "ceiling" for the GMI students and other persons with high general ability? Further examination of several sets of intercorrelations among the EAS battery suggests that Test 3 has loadings on two or more common factors just as Tests 2, 4, and 7 have already been found to be factorially complex. The authors need to consider doing additional factor analytic studies of their test battery.

The validity data are contained in 270 correlation coefficients. On-the-job criteria of job performance have been used to estimate 83 of the 270 validity coefficients; 187 coefficients are based on training criteria such as course grades and instructor's ratings. Of the 83 validity coefficients based upon on-the-job criteria, 10 are based on "large" samples of 80 or more people, 18 come from samples of 40 to 79 people, 27 come from samples of 21 to 39 people, and 28 "validity coefficients" come from samples of 20 or fewer people! It seems fair to conclude that there is rather little validity data based upon on-the-job measures of job performance with samples of reasonable size.

Criticism of validity data is not ended with a criticism of the overuse of training criteria or the small samples. The statistical significance of validity coefficients is not called to the reader's attention, thus making it quite possible to examine a "validity" coefficient of .68 based upon a sample of nine people without realizing that the coefficient is not significantly different from zero. Often ratings of job performance were obtained by asking the supervisor to place subordinates in upper and lower groups based on overall job performance, or classroom performance. Using this dichotomized criterion, biserial and tetrachoric correlation coefficients are calculated to report 109 of the 270 validity coefficients. It would seem that there would be little extra work in obtaining ratings on a graphic scale, or ranks, thus improving somewhat on the criterion measurement and making possible the use of the Pearson product-moment or the Spearman rank-order correlation coefficients. One of the reasons why test batteries of this kind are attractive is that the multiple, independent dimensions of human abilities measured by the battery hold the promise of increased validities through the combination of scores from several tests. It is of interest to the reviewer that no validity data are reported for cross-validated combinations of test scores. Not even multiple correlation coefficients are reported among the validity data. The authors present the validity data in such a way that it is impossible to tell which work was done under their own supervision and which was done under the supervision of other researchers. It is very difficult to tell which is new validity information and which has appeared in previous editions of the test manuals. It would seem that the methods of research report writing and citation of bibliographic references common to publication in scientific journals could be used to better advantage in the Technical Report. Validation studies are reported in outlines describing the job, sample, criterion, and validity. The resulting reports can be scanned quickly, and are convenient in that sense. But criteria described as "supervisor's ratings based on over-all job proficiency" or "instructor's ratings" are vaguely described at best and are impossible to reproduce in another study.

Extensive use of references to a much enlarged list of sources is desirable.

The normative information supplied in the Technical Report is the most valuable part of the new information contained in the report. Few test publishers have assembled so much norm data for a test or test battery. The norms by occupation and sex make the data particularly valuable. To continue in the role of the critic, however, this reviewer thinks that norm data showing the relationship of test scores to age should be provided; no data of this kind are presented. The addition of a report of the mean and standard deviation of age, educational level, and job service for persons included in a norm group, reporting sex and occupation as already provided, would make an individual's scores even more interpretable. (The norms by educational level have not been overlooked; information obtained by examining them supports the notion of reporting the mean and standard deviation of educational level for all occupational norm groups.) For example, if test data are included in specific occupational norms only after individuals have survived several years in the occupation, it may be possible for vocational counselors and employers to use the norm data as guidelines and thereby add operational definition to the idea of being "over qualified" or "under qualified" for a job. Test users would be fortunate if the test authors have some of the age, educational level, and occupational service information available for the large amount of occupational norm data already published.

Several miscellaneous criticisms can be made. The catalog suggests that certain tests should be used as a battery for certain occupations, 21 occupations altogether being named in this way, but too many of the suggestions are not supported with *validity* data based on either training or on-the-job performance criteria. The third form of Word Fluency (Test 8), which has been added since the last review of this test in the MMY, is not described in terms of either reliability or validity in the Technical Report. The qualifications of the test administrator are not described, nor are the qualifications of the tests' interpreter described. The catalog states: "All orders from recognized business firms (other than employment agencies) and from members of the American Psychological Association will be filled immediately." Is this ade-

Employee Aptitude Survey

quate control over the qualifications of the test purchaser, particularly when any "recognized business firm" can order tests? Is the investment that private (industrial) users make in norming and validating the tests for their own use adequately protected by this sales policy? It may be that the sales policy is appropriate; the reviewer would like to point out that the sales policy cannot be adequately assessed by an examination of the test catalog.

Potential purchasers of the EAS battery will want to compare it with competing test batteries in terms of administration time, administration convenience, apparent factorial content, normative data, validity data, cost, and publisher's sales policy. The long and venerable genealogy of useful tests from which this test battery has descended cannot be overlooked when considering the validity data (which are given a bit of knocking about in this review). The technical data are an improved product over what they were when last reviewed in the MMY, and the test battery itself was appropriately described at that time as "an outstandingly well thought out and well constructed battery of tests based upon unusually competent analysis." The authors and publisher appear to have responded constructively to a few of the criticisms previously offered, thereby improving the technical data and promising, by their behavior, more improvement for the future. The criticisms contained in this review are offered for the attention of the potential purchaser of the tests, who is assumed to be technically qualified to evaluate tests and criticism of tests. The criticisms should not be taken by the casual reader as indicating an overall negative opinion of this battery nor as reflecting doubt about the practical usefulness of the tests.

Erwin K. Taylor, *President, Personnel Research and Development Corporation, Cleveland, Ohio.*

This battery of 10 short tests (nine have a 5-minute time limit and one a 10-minute limit) was comprehensively and quite analytically reviewed in *The Fifth Mental Measurements Yearbook.* It is being reconsidered at this time because of the publication of a 78-page technical manual for which a nominal charge of two dollars per copy is made. Since the reviewer would have nothing of significance to add to what the previous MMY reviewers of this bat-

tery said, he will confine his remarks to the technical manual.

The manual consists of five chapters covering the following areas: Rationale of the *Employee Aptitude Survey,* Test Battery Statistics, Occupational and Educational Norms, Validity, and Correlations with Other Tests.

The first chapter, after devoting a page to ease of administration and scoring, availability of alternate forms, face validity, and the existence of short time limits, goes into a rather elaborate rationale for the use of short tests of low intertest correlation. It demonstrates the well documented, but infrequently considered, fact that increases in reliability beyond the value of .70 add very little to a test's potential validity. The manual goes on to demonstrate that by the use of short tests with low intertest correlations, higher validity can be obtained through multiple correlation than through the use of more reliable tests of greater length. This point is—in part, at least—denied by the manual's authors in that they say in the same section that in vocational guidance, which they refer to as "usually a leisurely process," "it is often advisable to use two forms of each EAS test to gain the advantage of greater reliability." It is also noted that in the fourth chapter, which reports a variety of validation studies, only zero order validities, rather than multiple correlations, are reported. The remainder of the first chapter is devoted to a description of the rationale and content of each of the 10 tests in the battery.

The second chapter is devoted to reliability, intercorrelations, and factorial content. Alternate form reliability information is provided for 9 of the 10 tests and test-retest data for the tenth. Based on samples ranging from 853 to 1,885, reliabilities range from .75 to .91. The means and standard deviations of the reliability sample, as well as the standard error of measurement, are given for each. Considering that the tests were apparently administered on a time rather than a power basis these reliabilities may be somewhat inflated by the speed factor. In any event, it would appear that the tests are sufficiently reliable to support substantial validity.

To provide information on the intercorrelations among the tests, the manual contains the equivalent of seven intercorrelation matrices. These are conveniently arranged to give the seven sets of correlations of each test with all the others. Samples range in size from a group of 138 security sales applicants to 335 engineering students. It is interesting to note the wide variability of the intercorrelations in these seven populations. For example, the correlation of Test 1 with Test 2 ranges from .12 to .49, the correlation of Test 3 with Test 10 ranges from .04 to .45, and the correlation of Test 1 with Test 5 ranges from −.01 to .41. Unfortunately, since the manual does not provide the means and standard deviations for these seven groups, there is no opportunity to determine the extent to which the instability of the intertest correlations is a function of the level and homogeneity of the group tested. Nevertheless, it is noteworthy that the manual does provide the reader with a basis for reaching the valid conclusion that the intercorrelations of the tests are not as fixed and final as most test manuals would lead us to believe.

The intercorrelations among the tests are summarized in a single matrix in which the entries are z transformed averages of the equivalent entries from the seven individual matrices.

In the light of the instability of the test intercorrelations demonstrated in the preceding section, one might question the stability of a single factor analysis based on only 90 cases in what is apparently a homogeneous population. It does not appear unlikely that additional factor analysis with larger, different populations might yield considerably different results from the evidence given in the manual.

Both forms of the nine tests for which alternate forms are available were administered to 330 junior college students, half taking each form first. For Test 1 there was no significant difference between the means. For each of the other tests, however, highly significant differences were found. This finding was attributed to a practice or warm-up effect which apparently operated differently at various score levels. It might be noted parenthetically at this point that to the extent that a practice effect existed, the manual's claims with respect to the relationship of reliability and validity to the length of testing time may not be wholly true. A rather extensive table is given for each test, enabling the user to equate the two forms where both are given. Apparently, this difference is purely a function of order of administration, rather than of any lack of equivalence of the two forms.

Chapter 3, "Occupational and Educational Norms," presents 47 sets of norms on employed personnel and 5 on various categories of students. Norms are conveniently arranged by major groupings and are listed in a table of contents at the beginning of the chapter. Accompanying each set of norms is the job title, its DOT code, the sex of the population, and a brief job description. The variability in the n for the several tests for each group suggests that some of the norms groups are apparently composites of smaller populations. The n's vary from a low of 40 "test pilots—jet aircraft" to a high of 2,739 employees of the Denver Division of the Martin-Marietta Corporation. Not all tests were administered to all populations and the number of tests on which norms are available vary from only 3 for telephone operators and electric truck operators up to 9 or 10 for many occupations. It is apparent that a number of the tests, even with their fairly rigid time limits, are somewhat on the easy side and do not provide adequate ceiling for higher level jobs. Thus, the tests appear more appropriate for clerical, semiskilled, skilled, technical, and some sales jobs than for positions at higher levels of technical, managerial, and executive responsibility.

Chapter 4 presents the validity of various tests within the battery for 31 samples from a wide variety of occupational situations. Samples vary from as few as 9 programmers to as many as 474 students at a Texas state college. Most of the validities are against supervisors' ratings or actions of some sort. Many of the correlations reported are biserials. A few are tetrachorics and some are product-moments. Each study names the job, describes the size and nature of the population, and indicates whether the validity is of a concurrent or follow-up nature. Unfortunately, either no other predictors than the EAS tests were incorporated in any of the studies or, if they were, the authors neglected to report them, so that the validity of the EAS tests cannot be compared with that of other instruments which might have been used along with it. In each case only zero order validities are reported and, as previously noted, in spite of the author's earlier plug for multiple correlations, none is presented in the validity chapter.

Validities are quite variable, ranging in one study of 44 male computer programmers from

−.24 for Test 5, Space Visualization, to .41 for Test 6, Numerical Reasoning. Since no credits are given anywhere in this chapter to other researchers, all of the validity data presented were apparently collected by the authors; the claim is made that "more than 2,000,000 EAS tests have been administered since the publication of the 1958 Manuals," and that "many of the results have been made available to the publishers." It would seem logical to assume that additional validity research has been accomplished; it is surprising that so little independent research has been reported in the literature. It seems rather unfortunate that in preparing the manual, and particularly the chapter on validity, the authors did not track down the results obtained by others who may have performed validity studies of these tests.

The final section of the manual deals with the correlational relation of the EAS with such other tests as the *SRA Primary Mental Abilities* and the *California Tests of Mental Maturity* as used on the factor analysis population, as well as scattered reports on Bennett's *Tests of Mechanical Comprehension,* the *Otis Employment Tests,* the *Minnesota Clerical Test,* and the DAT Clerical Speed and Accuracy. The relationships are about what would be expected.

While in reviewing this manual I have found occasion here and there to criticize negatively, my overall impression is highly favorable. The manual certainly does not achieve perfection; however, it presents more industrial data in a more honest and straightforward fashion than does the manual for any other general aptitude battery prepared for industrial use. The authors are to be congratulated for not endeavoring to group similar sounding job titles into so-called "job families" on an armchair basis and then arbitrarily assuming specified tests in their battery to have ubiquitous validity for any position, regardless of level or complexity, that happens to carry the title of one of the jobs in one of the families.

This manual could well serve as a model that publishers of other tests intended for industrial selection use would do well to copy.

J Counsel Psychol 10:407–8 w '63. John O. Crites. [Review of 1963 Technical Report.] * The Technical Report....is a well-organized and well-written manual which presents data on the EAS in a straightforward and professional manner. Unlike some test manuals, its shortcomings are more the result of omission than commission * The reliability estimates are.... quite acceptable, being in the .80's and .90's for all but two of the tests. Data on the interrelationships of the tests are equally favorable, in that they support their independence. Only three tests correlate with each other as high as .40, in contrast to a median r of .50 for the entire DAT battery, and these are ones which might be expected to be interrelated (e.g., Verbal Comprehension and Verbal Reasoning). The factor loadings of the EAS battery on appropriate reference variables are generally impressive and further substantiate the essential statistical purity of the tests. * contains norm tables for various occupational groups * Each table includes a job description and DOT code for the occupation, along with centile norms, N's, means, and standard deviations for the EAS tests which are most relevant to the occupation. How the tests were selected, however, and how the norms should be used are not clear, since there is no discussion of them in the report. The implication is that a comparison of an examinee's score with an occupational norm group is in some way meaningful. Actually, about the only information this procedure gives is the relative standing of the examinee in the group: he may rank at the top, in the middle, or at the bottom. How successful he might be in the occupation is not indicated by the normative data, since the groups were not selected on some criterion of success. Even if they had been, there would be the problem of deciding what cut-off scores to use and whether to weight scores on some tests more than others. In short, occupational norms for a multifactor aptitude battery such as the EAS not only have little or no practical utility but they mislead some test users into interpreting them as validity data. * chapter [4] summarizes the relationships of the EAS tests to job performance criteria in clerical, sales, management and supervisory, skilled and semiskilled, and technical occupations. The intent of the chapter is to establish the validity of the battery as a predictor of success in a variety of jobs, but unfortunately the evidence which is presented is not very convincing, for three reasons. First, the N's for the validation samples are, in most cases, very small. Throughout the chapter, the test authors report r's based upon samples with as few subjects as 9, 10, 18, 19, 20, 29, 30, 31, 35, and 36. Not only are r's computed on such N's very unstable, but they often tend to be spuriously high. Second, no significance levels for the r's are reported, and no indication is given that the biserial r's derived from a comparison of more and less successful workers are for extreme groups. If they are not, then they are inflated. Third, and most important, no multiple correlations are reported for the EAS tests, despite the rationale for the battery that less reliable measures should be combined for optimal predictive efficiency. * The EAS is based upon a sound rationale and consists of tests which have proven validity when used separately. As a battery, however, much remains to be demonstrated as far as its usefulness is concerned. In particular, multiple correlations of the tests with job success criteria in large samples need to be conducted and then replicated to establish the magnitude of the R's and the stability of the Beta's for predictive purposes. Until such data are available, personnel workers and counselors should use the EAS as a battery with caution.

For reviews by Dorothy C. Adkins and S. Rains Wallace, see 5:607.

[770]

*Flanagan Aptitude Classification Tests. Grades 9–12, 10–12 and adults; 1951–60; also called FACT; 2 editions; postage extra; John C. Flanagan; Science Research Associates, Inc. *
a) [SEPARATE BOOKLET 16-TEST EDITION.] Grades 10–12 and adults; 1951–60; 16 tests; examiner's manual ('53, 27 pages); technical supplement ('54, 16 pages); supplementary manuals, preliminary editions ('60, 6 pages) for Tests 15 and 16; counselor's booklet ('53, 35 pages); personnel director's booklet ('53, 27 pages); manual for interpreting scores ('56, 12 pages); aptitude classification sheet ('53, 1 page); student's booklet for interpreting scores ('53, 20 pages); $2.55 per 20 self-marking tests; 60¢ per 20 classification sheets; 30¢ per technical supplement; 25¢ per supplementary manual for either 15 or 16; 40¢ per counselor's booklet; 25¢ per manual for interpreting scores; 25¢ per student's booklet; 50¢ per personnel director's booklet; $3 per educational specimen set; $5.75 per industrial specimen set; 258(388) minutes in 2 sessions.
1) *FACT 1A, Inspection.* 1953–56; form A ('53, 6 pages); 6(12) minutes.
2) *FACT 2A and 2B, Coding.* 1953–56; forms A ('53), B ('54), (6 pages); 10(30) minutes.
3) *FACT 3A and 3B, Memory.* 1953–56; forms A ('53), B ('54), (3 pages); 4(5) minutes.
4) *FACT 4A, Precision.* 1953–56; form A ('53, 4 pages); 8(15) minutes.

5) *FACT 5A, Assembly.* 1953–56; form A ('53, 6 pages); 12(18) minutes.
6) *FACT 6A, Scales.* 1953–56; form A ('53, 6 pages); 16(28) minutes.
7) *FACT 7A, Coordination.* 1953–56; form A ('53, 8 pages); 2⅔(8) minutes.
8) *FACT 8A, Judgment and Comprehension.* 1953–56; form A ('53, 7 pages); (35–40) minutes.
9) *FACT 9A, Arithmetic.* 1953–56; form A ('53, 6 pages); 10(20) minutes.
10) *FACT 10A, Patterns.* 1953–56; form A ('53, 6 pages); 20(28) minutes.
11) *FACT 11A, Components.* 1953–56; form A ('53, 6 pages); 20(24) minutes.
12) *FACT 12A, Tables.* 1953–56; form A ('53, 6 pages); 10(15) minutes.
13) *FACT 13A and 13B, Mechanics.* 1953–56; forms A ('53), B ('54), (6 pages); 20(25) minutes.
14) *FACT 14A, Expression.* 1953–56; form A ('53, 6 pages); (35–45) minutes.
15) *FACT 15A, Reasoning.* 1957–60; form A ('57, 6 pages); 24(30) minutes.
16) *FACT 16A, Ingenuity.* 1957–60; form A ('57, 7 pages); 24(30) minutes.
b) [19-TEST EDITION.] Grades 9–12; 1957–60; MRC; 19 tests (same as for *a* plus vocabulary, planning, alertness) in 2 booklets: gray book ('57, 64 pages), blue book ('57, 24 pages); examiner's manual ('58, 70 pages); mimeographed norms ['58, 23 pages]; administrator's manual ('58, 17 pages); technical report, first edition ('59, 65 pages); mimeographed manual for planning short batteries ('60, 10 pages); student's booklet for interpreting scores ('58, 25 pages); separate answer sheets must be used with gray book (blue book, containing Tests 14–19, is scored by students); 60¢ per gray book; 20¢ per blue book; 8¢ per MRC answer sheet; $1.03 per set of stencils for hand scoring MRC answer sheets (machine scoring through the publisher only; fees: $1 per student including copy of student's booklet for each student, 70¢ per student without student's booklet); 35¢ per student's booklet; 50¢ per examiner's manual; 35¢ per administrator's manual; $2 per technical report; $3 per specimen set; manual for planning short batteries free; (630) minutes in 3 sessions.

REFERENCES

1. LATHAM, ALBERT J. *Job Appropriateness: A One-Year Follow-Up of High School Graduates.* Doctor's thesis, University of Pittsburgh (Pittsburgh, Pa.), 1948.
2. VOLKIN, LEONARD. *A Validation Study of Selected Test Batteries Applied to Fields of Work.* Doctor's thesis, University of Pittsburgh (Pittsburgh, Pa.), 1951.
3. FLANAGAN, JOHN C. "Job Element Aptitude Classification Tests." *Personnel Psychol* 7:1–14 sp '54. * (PA 29:3127)
4. CURETON, EDWARD E. "Service Tests of Multiple Aptitudes." *Proc Inv Conf Testing Probl* 1955:22–39 '56. * (PA 31:3017)
5. FLANAGAN, JOHN C. "The Flanagan Aptitude Classification Tests." Comments by Donald E. Super. *Personnel & Guid J* 35:495–507 Ap '57. *
6. WHITE, ARDEN JUNIOR. *A Comparison of the Flanagan Aptitude Classification Tests With the Wechsler Adult Intelligence Scale, the School and College Ability Test, and Three Other Measures of Mental Variables at the High School Level.* Doctor's research study No. 1, Colorado State College (Greeley, Colo.), 1959.
7. BOLTON, FLOYD B. "Value of a Vocational Aptitude Test Battery for Predicting High School Achievement." *Personnel & Guid J* 42:280–4 N '63. *

NORMAN FREDERIKSEN, *Director of Research, Educational Testing Service, Princeton, New Jersey.* [Review of the 19-Test Edition.]

FACT (the *Flanagan Aptitude Classification Tests*) is a battery of tests intended for use in counseling high school students with respect to educational and vocational plans. Guidance materials have been prepared that lead to specific predictions of success in 37 occupational areas, 20 of which require college preparation and 17 of which do not. The earlier (1953) edition of FACT contained 14 tests [1] and was somewhat lacking in predictors of academic achievement. The 1958 version contains 19 tests. The added tests, which bear the titles Reasoning, Vocabulary, Planning, Ingenuity, and Alertness, appear to make up this deficiency. Most, but not all, FACT tests are multiple choice tests with five options. The time required for administration is about 10½ hours. The suggested procedure is to give the tests in three 3½-hour sessions.

Each FACT test corresponds to an aptitude, or job element. According to the Technical Report, job elements are identified by a method that includes (a) listing the critical behaviors in a job, (b) translating the critical behaviors into hypotheses about the nature of the aptitudes involved, and (c) testing the hypothesis that variations in job performance are correlated with measures of the related aptitude. Since it is not usually possible to test hypotheses about the relationships between aptitude and job performance with a high degree of rigor (because satisfactory criteria of job performance are lacking), and since the identification of "critical" behaviors and the generation of hypotheses about the relevant aptitudes are both rather subjective procedures, the test selection does not have a strong empirical foundation. The author regards this as an advantage and is inclined to disparage heavy dependence on empirical studies. Whether or not one agrees with the rationale of the procedure described, the test selection in general seems sensible. Indirectly it does have considerable empirical foundation through the author's extensive experience in Air Force selection during World War II.

Test 1, Inspection, is supposed to measure ability to spot flaws in articles quickly and accurately. The 80 items consist of small pictures —120 to a page—of objects such as safety pins, screws, and buckles. The task is to identify the one in each set of five that is not like the model. Test 2, Mechanics, consists of four-choice items about diagrams depicting devices such as an electric motor and a pressure gauge. The test is rather difficult; according to the norms, ninth graders get 9 of the 30 items right, on the average, while twelfth graders get 11 right. Test 3, Tables, requires the student to look up cell entries in tables. Test 4, Reasoning, requires the student to translate problems stated in words into mathematical notation. It contains 24 five-choice items. Ninth graders on the average get 6 items right and twelfth graders get 9 right. Test 5, Vocabulary, is a conventional synonyms test of 60 five-choice items. This test is also rather difficult for high school students, the median raw score for ninth graders being 13 and for twelfth graders 20. Each item of Test 6, Assembly, requires the student to choose the one of five pictures that represents how several solid parts would look when properly assembled. Drawings are reasonably clear and accurate, but with 10 items per page they are quite small. Test 7, Judgment and Comprehension, is a reading comprehension test, with 4 items based on each of 6 paragraphs. Test 8, Components, is a variation of a hidden figures test. It contains 40 five-choice items and is rather difficult, the figures being hidden in rather complex drawings. The mean is 17 for ninth graders and 22 for twelfth graders. Test 9, Planning, requires the student to rearrange steps in the execution of a task, such as making a cake or building a patio, into a good order. Test 10, Arithmetic, measures speed and accuracy in adding, subtracting, multiplying, and dividing. Test 11, Ingenuity, is supposed to measure ability to devise ingenious solutions to problems presented in short paragraphs. The solution to each problem must be expressed in a word or so, and the multiple choice answer is selected on the basis of first and last letters of the words. Test 12, Scales, requires the student to read values from graphs. The median raw scores for ninth and twelfth graders on the 72 items are 19 and 25, respectively. Test 13, Expression, measures knowledge of English grammar, usage, and sentence structure. Items consist of sentences; some are to be evaluated as right or wrong from the standpoint of grammar, and some are to be ranked in sets of three in terms of clarity and smoothness. All the above 13 tests are printed in one test booklet for use with a separate answer sheet.

[1] The 16-Test Edition referred to in the entry preceding the review contains two additional tests which were added in 1957.—Editor.

Flanagan Aptitude Classification Tests

A second booklet contains tests that do not require a separate answer sheet. Test 14, Precision, is supposed to measure ability to do precision work with small objects. The task is to draw lines rapidly between guide lines in small circular and square patterns. Test 15, Alertness, consists of 36 pictures, each of which depicts a potentially dangerous situation, such as a frayed electric cord, in a complex setting. The task is to identify the dangerous object in each picture. Test 16, Coordination, is another tracing task, this one requiring hand and arm movements. Test 17, Patterns, is a test in which the student reproduces geometrical designs, some of them upside down, on a grid. The instructions for Test 18, Coding, tell the student to mark the correct code numbers for sales districts, paint colors, etc., memorizing them as he goes along. It is possible, and perhaps more efficient, to perform the task without memorizing. The last test, Memory, demands that the student use the correct code numbers from the previous test without the possibility of looking them up. Performance on Memory thus depends in part upon how the student chose to do the coding in the previous test.

No information is given about item difficulties or item validities; in fact, there is nothing in the Technical Report to suggest that item analyses were made. Information from the norms tables suggests that a number of the tests are rather difficult even for high school seniors and that a selection of items that are less difficult might have improved the reliability of some of the tests. Nevertheless the test construction job in general appears to have been well done. The directions to supervisors seem clear and complete, and instructions to students seem satisfactory.

National norms tables are presented for ninth, tenth, eleventh, and twelfth grades, from which raw scores on each test may be converted to percentiles and stanines. These "general national norms" were based on a standardization group said to be "as typical as possible of ninth-, tenth-, eleventh-, and twelfth-grade students throughout the country." The group is described as including almost 11,000 students from 11 states—1 in the East, 5 in the South, 3 in the Middle West, and 2 in the West. From a statement in the Acknowledgments it is possible to deduce that the East is

represented by West Virginia; the South by Mississippi, Kentucky, Oklahoma, Georgia, and South Carolina; the Middle West by Illinois, Michigan, and Wisconsin; and the West by Utah and California. Some of these states contributed very few cases, the smallest number being 59. Two school systems in two states contributed almost 7,000 of the 11,000 cases. Labeling these data as "national" norms is questionable.

Most of the reliabilities that are reported are based on correlations between separately timed parts, which is appropriate in view of the fact that most of the tests are speeded. Odd-even correlations are used in the case of two unspeeded tests—Judgment and Comprehension, and Expression. Alternate form reliabilities from an earlier study of twelfth graders are reported for Coding and Memory. The median of the 17 reliability coefficients reported for ninth graders is .75, with a range from .52 (for Mechanics) to .86 (for Coordination). The comparable values for the 19 tests for the twelfth grade (including the earlier data for Coding and Memory) are .75, .55 (for Memory), and .91 (for Vocabulary). The reliabilities tend to be rather low for tests intended for use in counseling. The author states, however, that the tests are not intended for use separately but rather in combinations selected for various occupational fields. Reliabilities for several combinations are presented. The reliability (for twelfth grade students) of the combination of seven tests for chemist is reported to be .93, of the four tests for office clerk .87, and of the six tests for mechanic .91, to cite a few.

Intercorrelations of the 19 tests are reported separately for ninth and twelfth grades, based on about 1,000 students in each grade from the two school systems that contributed most of the norms data. Intercorrelations are in general fairly low; the median correlations are .20 and .31 for ninth and twelfth grades, respectively. Pairs of tests such as Arithmetic and Tables ($r = .60$), Ingenuity and Vocabulary ($r = .62$), and Reasoning and Judgment and Comprehension ($r = .58$) have correlations that are relatively high. Among the less academic tests, correlations of Patterns with Scales ($r = .49$) and Coding with Memory ($r = .51$) are fairly high, the latter partly because of

Flanagan Aptitude Classification Tests

experimental dependence. (The r's reported above are for twelfth grade students.)

The information on reliability and intercorrelations is summarized in a meaningful way by dividing the variance of each test into three parts: error variance, overlapping variance, and unique variance. Inspection of the table for ninth graders reveals, for example, that 48 per cent of the variance of Mechanics is attributable to error, 27 per cent is overlapping variance (i.e., can be predicted by other tests in the battery), and 25 per cent is unique variance (variance potentially useful for prediction and not found in other parts of the battery). We find in the twelfth grade table that 10 per cent of the variance for Expression is error variance, 39 per cent is overlapping variance, and 51 per cent is unique; while for Reasoning 26 per cent is error variance, 65 per cent is overlapping, and 9 per cent is unique. The usefulness of such information in test battery construction is apparent. The information about FACT tests might logically have led to a battery with fewer than 19 tests.

FACT tests are intended to be used in combination, and recommendations are made as to how the tests are to be combined into occupational aptitude scores. The recommendations are based on a survey of follow-up studies, concurrent validity studies, and job analysis findings. According to the Technical Report, the recommendations are to be viewed as working hypotheses that are subject to revision as the results of validity studies accumulate. The recommendations seem sensible. For the occupational area engineer, for example, the recommended tests are Mechanics, Reasoning, Assembly, Judgment and Comprehension, Components, Scales, and Patterns. For clergyman, the tests are Vocabulary, Judgment and Comprehension, Expression, and Memory; and for printer they are Inspection, Mechanics, Scales, and Precision. Although the recommendations viewed one at a time seem eminently reasonable, comparisons of recommendations for similar occupations yield a few surprises. For example, it seems strange that Planning is judged to be important for physicist but not for engineer, that Ingenuity is required for psychologist but not for lawyer, and that Precision is important for electrician but not for draftsman. It appears that some effort was made to reduce overlap in the recommen-

dations; the more overlap, the less differential prediction is possible.

The intercorrelations of the composite occupational aptitude scores are very high for occupations requiring college training, largely because of similarities in the test recommendations. In one case (for humanities teacher and clergyman) the tests recommended are exactly the same and the correlation is of course 1.00. Of the 210 correlations in the twelfth graders' table for college occupations, 74 are .90 or greater and 149 are .80 or greater. The correlation between composites for teacher and business administrator is .97; between physician and artist, .96; and between physicist and lawyer, .95. The student seeking some basis for a choice between such pairs of occupations will get little help from FACT. Intercorrelations of composites for non-college jobs are much lower; they range from .34 to .98, with a median of .70, for twelfth grade data.

Predictive validity studies have been conducted, using data from students tested in 1952 with the earlier version of FACT. For college-level occupations, the criteria used combined measures of progress in the field and performance as measured by college grades. College achievement must have accounted for most of the variation in the criteria, since, for the period of time covered, progress in the field is largely progress in academic training. The number of cases is usually small because the 1,200 students studied entered a large number of different occupations. With n's ranging from 24 to 133, the nine correlations between the criterion and occupational stanine scores ranged from .04 to .65. An attempt was also made to build criteria based on salary and promotion for non-college occupations. Correlations with occupational stanines for five business and clerical fields approximated zero, but somewhat better luck was obtained with three technical fields. A large number of concurrent validity studies, mostly with grade criteria, are also described, as well as correlations with other tests. The report of all these studies leaves one with two impressions: (a) that academic criteria can be predicted with certain FACT tests about as well as with conventional scholastic aptitude tests; and (b) that better solutions to criterion problems in occupational areas will have to be found before the results of validity studies will be very useful in guiding aptitude test development.

The Student's Booklet provides the student with a simple procedure for interpreting his test scores in terms of predicted success and satisfaction in the 37 occupational areas. The cover of the booklet extends an inch above the inside pages, and in this space the student places a gummed strip containing a report of his percentile scores. The scores are thus visible no matter where the booklet is opened. The pages contain sections corresponding to the occupational areas. The section for each area includes a short job description, a list of related job titles, and a list of the FACT tests that have been chosen to form the occupational test composite. The student copies his scores in spaces opposite the names of the tests. Then he rearranges the percentiles in rank order and finds the median, which is his occupational score. Finally, he compares the median percentile with the cutting score given for that occupation.

The method of combining test scores to form occupational composites that was used in obtaining reliabilities, intercorrelations, and validities is not specified in the Technical Report, but it seems unlikely that medians were used. Judging from the method used for the earlier version of FACT, it is more likely that occupational scores were formed by combining stanine scores with equal weights. If this assumption is true, the reliabilities, intercorrelations, and validities would all be slightly lower for scores produced by the method described in the Student's Booklet, since the median has a larger error than a mean.

The Administrator's Manual describes the cutting scores by saying that "of those students who entered and succeeded in the occupation, 80 percent exceeded the cut-off score; 20 percent did not." This statement implies the existence of data supporting the choice of each cutting score; but one looks in vain to find it. Score distributions are shown for "students subsequently identified as satisfied and successful members of certain occupational groups," but the data obviously do not justify the "80 percent" interpretation of the cutting scores for most areas. For example, one table presents score distributions for students subsequently identified as satisfied and successful engineers and scientists. The table is based on only 22

cases—17 engineers, 4 chemists, and 1 biologist. But separate cutting scores are given in the Student's Booklet for engineers, chemists, and biologists (to say nothing of physicists, for whom no data are reported). Predictive validity data for single specific occupations, with n's varying from 1 to 312, are presented for fewer than half of the 37 occupations for which cutting scores are recommended. Even when concurrent validity studies and studies reported in a section called "Validity Exchange" are considered, there are still a substantial number of occupations for which recommended cutting scores are included in the Student's Booklet but no validity data are reported. A statement in the Technical Report that many of the recommendations are based only on job analyses, and not on validity studies, seems to be more accurate than the statement in the Administrator's Manual.

From many points of view, the FACT battery is of high quality. There is a defensible rationale for the tests, they are for the most part good tests, the accessory materials are well planned, and the statistical analyses are competent. But there is less empirical justification for using FACT as the basis for a counseling program than seems at first glance to be supplied by the Technical Report. The informed judgment of an experienced psychologist is the real basis for the FACT tests and the recommendations for their use.

WILLIAM B. MICHAEL, *Professor of Education and Psychology, University of California, Santa Barbara, California.* [Review of the 19-Test Edition.]

In comparison with the 1953 edition of the *Flanagan Aptitude Classification Tests* (FACT), which consisted of 14 tests printed in separate booklets, the 1958 edition is composed of 19 tests which have been issued in two booklets. The "gray book" includes the first 13 tests, which may be completed on separate answer sheets designed for machine scoring. These tests may be reused many times. The "blue book" includes the remaining six tests, which are not reusable and which are to be hand scored by the examinees themselves.

The five new tests include Reasoning (Test 4), Vocabulary (Test 5), Planning (Test 9), Ingenuity (Test 11), and Alertness (Test 15). That Tests 4 and 5, and possibly Tests 9 and 11, reflect academic aptitudes should serve substantially to correct a major weakness of the first edition as a predictor of success in college work—a shortcoming that Carroll pointed out in his review of the 1953 edition of the FACT battery in *The Fifth Mental Measurements Yearbook*. Although Flanagan's total testing program called for the coverage of 21 job elements, two measures, Carving and Tapping, have not been included in the present battery, since they are not pencil and paper tests.

There are many commendable features in the 1958 edition—especially the elegant format of both the test materials and manuals and the mechanics of administration, scoring, reporting, and interpretation. Both the Administrator's Manual and the Examiner's Manual are comprehensive and clear. Whether or not one agrees with Flanagan's rationale concerning the construction of tests and the interpretation of their scores around critical job requirements, the Student's Booklet offers a straightforward and stimulating appraisal of the meaning of scores on sub-batteries—typically three to seven tests—considered to be pertinent to 37 different job families (the activities of which are lucidly described in operational terms in the Student's Booklet). The examinee simply places in rank order the centiles he has earned on each test of the sub-battery and determines whether his median centile is above or below a value that is recommended for success in the occupation cited. Although serious questions may be raised concerning the accuracy of the recommended cutting score, examinees are taking an active part in determining their own potentialities and in discovering their own relative strengths or weaknesses on each of the tests of the battery, in the general college aptitude composite, and in each of 37 occupational composites. Despite the fact that students are warned in their own manual that the scores are not absolute, it appears that the emphasis has not been strong enough. Of course, if the teachers and counselors utilize the group counseling sessions in terms of the specific directions and cautions cited and follow other suggestions in the Administrator's Manual, the risk of misinterpretation should be minimized.

The major weaknesses in the program of FACT lie in the inadequacy of the norms, in the degree of reliability of several of the subtests, and particularly in the *evidence* presented concerning the validity both of the job element approach and of the tests themselves. In fairness it should be emphasized that there have been substantial improvements—especially in the new normative data.

In the Technical Report the data for a national standardization of the test on a group of 10,972 students from 17 schools representing 11 school systems and 11 states are reported for ninth, tenth, eleventh, and twelfth grades. The attempt was made to select this norm group in order that at the eleventh grade level it would be nearly equivalent to a much larger national sample on which the *Iowa Tests of Educational Development* had been standardized. Normative data are presented in terms of both centile and stanine values. (Most of the individuals in the original normative samples, which included a group of approximately 1,400 Pittsburgh students tested in December 1952, participated in one-year and five-year follow-up studies of occupational success. The resulting data are reported in the validity section of the Technical Report.)

From an inspection of the normative data for each test it appears that most of the tests yield for each grade level in high school a substantial range of scores, an adequate basis for differentiation among individuals, and relatively symmetrical distributions of scores. There are exceptions. Tests 5 and 18, Vocabulary and Coding, furnish, respectively, positively and negatively skewed distribution of scores. With only 30 four-response items, the normative data for Mechanics reveal the 50th and 99th percentiles of raw scores to be 9 and 20, respectively, for ninth graders, and 11 and 25, respectively, for twelfth graders. Reliability estimates of only .52 and .67 for ninth and twelfth graders, respectively, are reported. (The reviewer was unable to find any information concerning the nature of the scoring formula used.) Similar comments might also be made concerning the 24-item Test 4, Reasoning. Serious doubt is cast on the usefulness of either one of these tests as a separate unit for assessment purposes.

A comparison of the estimates of reliability furnished for the 1953 and 1958 editions reveals similar values. For ninth graders and twelfth graders, respectively, the range of the 17 estimated reliabilities in the 1958 normative group (no 1958 figures are reported for Coding and Memory) was from .52 to .86 and from .61 to .91, median values being .75 and .77, respectively. Flanagan has proposed using composites of three or more tests for the purpose of occupational classification; the reliabilities of the composites are probably adequate. Lacking information concerning either item analysis statistics or any revisions of items in light of preliminary tryouts of test material, one wonders how much the estimates of reliability of individual tests might have been improved through additional efforts in test construction.

The greatest potential weakness of the FACT program may well rest on its validity, although admittedly differences in theoretical position or philosophical orientation concerning what is meant by the term validity will not permit a definitive conclusion. The reliance in both the 1953 and 1958 editions on development of test items that can be matched against descriptions of hypothesized psychological activities in a given occupation will be challenged by many who prefer either empirical studies or the utilization of the factor analytic model. Since in *The Fifth Mental Measurements Yearbook* both Bechtoldt and Carroll presented detailed critiques of Flanagan's job element position, further comment seems superfluous.

Those who favor empirical procedures will take some measure of satisfaction from a limited amount of empirical data in the Technical Report, which, as mentioned previously, consisted of one-year and five-year follow-up studies. A numerical code for progress was developed and applied to several different occupational areas, and predictive validities of occupational stanines relative to the constructed criterion measures were obtained for many relatively small groups of individuals taken from the 1952 Pittsburgh standardization sample. These predictive validities showed about as much promise as those indices one may find for competing test batteries. Reported in a separate section of the Technical Report are validity studies in which concurrent criteria such as grades in various high school courses were correlated with scores on individual test units. An extensive collection of concurrent validity coefficients of the FACT scales with test measures from other batteries is also presented. Again the results seem to compare favorably with those revealed by competing publishers for their tests.

Somewhat less satisfactory to many measurement specialists as evidence of validity are

the data in the Technical Report concerning the proportion of *unique variance* and *error variance* in each test. The application of a correction for attenuation of the multiple correlation coefficient of each composite of 18 tests with the single test not in the composite was made to allow for errors of measurement in the composite. The unique variance is equal to the difference between the reliability estimate for a single test and the ratio of the coefficient of multiple determination to the reliability of the composite. Since corrections for attenuation can be deceptive, there is considerable doubt in the reviewer's mind concerning the helpfulness to the test consumer of this approach. Additional evidence for the uniqueness of each of the 19 tests is furnished by the relatively low intercorrelations which, to a considerable extent, were probably facilitated by the relatively low reliabilities of certain test units.

Finally, the validity of these tests may be viewed in terms of whether other test specialists agree with Flanagan and his associates concerning the job elements these tests measure. No such evidence has been presented. Careful reading of Carroll's detailed analysis in *The Fifth Mental Measurements Yearbook* of the content in each of the 14 tests in the 1953 edition of FACT would indicate that there may be room for considerable disagreement. As nearly as the reviewer can determine, relatively few changes have been made in the content of the items in the tests common to the 1953 and 1958 editions. Apparently Carroll's criticisms of Coding have not been given serious study, and certainly the carry-over of Coding's defects to the Memory test, in which the examinee must respond in terms of the codes, has not been remedied.

What may be said of the content of the five new tests in the 1958 edition? Reasoning and Vocabulary appear to be similar to those that bear the same names in competing batteries, although the reliability of the former test is relatively low, probably because of its containing only 30 items. Planning, which requires the examinee's placing in an appropriate order the steps involved in designing or carrying out a certain project, suggests alternatives that may not necessarily have a single best sequence. In this test the four problem situations associated with only 32 items have yielded scores with reliability estimates of only .73 and .66 for ninth and twelfth graders, respectively. To the reviewer the test titled Ingenuity, which appears to be highly complex factorially, demands of the examinee a high level of reading comprehension, a substantial vocabulary, possession of considerable general information, and a fluency with words. The reviewer would be at a loss to match the items of this test with the hypothesized psychological processes underlying elements of particular job families, although the instrument might be expected to display substantial predictive validity in certain college curricula. In the fifth new test, Alertness, 36 pictures are presented; in each, the task is to pick the one of five lettered objects which presents a potential danger or detrimental influence. The low estimates of reliability of .63 and .61 for ninth and twelfth graders, respectively, may be a function of the exceedingly short time limit of three minutes, although the range of scores is substantial.

In summary, the 19 FACT tests cover a variety of different aptitudes, the measurement of which has been anchored to a rationale for the construction of items around critical job activities. The detailed and explicit manuals for the examiner, administrator, and student, as well as careful application of information in the Technical Report, may be expected to result in a program which is highly efficient in the mechanics not only of administering and scoring tests, but also of reporting and interpreting their results. Although under adequate supervision the instructional and guidance value of the FACT program for the high school student should be substantial, several of the individual tests could be improved from the standpoint of revamping certain blocks of items, furnishing up-to-date normative information, increasing the level of reliability of the scales, and obtaining additional estimates of their predictive validities. Despite the limitations cited, the FACT battery compares favorably with other batteries that are being marketed by competing test publishers.

For reviews by Harold P. Bechtoldt, Ralph F. Berdie, and John B. Carroll of a, see 5:608.

[771]

***General Aptitude Test Battery.** Ages 16 and over, grades 9–12 and adults; 1946–63; developed for use in the occupational counseling program of the United States Employment Service and released in 1947 (*a*)

and 1952 (*b*) for use by State Employment Services; IBM, NCS, and DocuTran for *b*; 2 editions; manual in 3 sections: section 1, administration and scoring ('63, 63 pages for *a*; '62, 68 pages for *b*) and sections 2, norms-occupational aptitude pattern structure ('62, 113 pages) and 3, development ('62, 237 pages) for *b* but also used with *a*; record blank ['61, 2 pages] for apparatus tests of both editions; tests (except for separate booklet edition of *b*) available to nonprofit institutions for counseling purposes; no testing fee for applicants tested through the facilities of State Employment Service offices; institutions using their own facilities must purchase tests and employ trained testing supervisors; manual available for unrestricted sale at 45¢ for either edition of section 1, 70¢ for section 2, and $2 for section 3; orders for tests and all other accessories must be cleared through State Employment Service offices, from which details may be secured; postpaid; specimen set not available; 51(135) minutes; United States Employment Service; test materials except for performance tests distributed for the Service by United States Government Printing Office. *

a) GATB, B-1001, [EXPENDABLE BOOKLET EDITION]. Ages 16 and over; 1947–63; 10 scores: intelligence, verbal, numerical, spatial, form perception, clerical perception, aiming, motor speed, finger dexterity, manual dexterity; 1 form ('46); 15 tests: 11 tests in 2 booklets plus 4 performance tests; revised profile card ('61, 2 pages); revised adult aptitude pattern card ('61, 2 pages).

1) *Book 1.* 1 form (34 pages); 5 tests: tool matching, name comparison, H markings, computation, two-dimensional space; $18.75 per 100 tests.
2) *Book 2.* 1 form (27 pages); 6 tests: speed, three-dimensional space, arithmetic reasoning, vocabulary, mark making, form matching; $15 per 100 tests.
3) *Pegboard.* 2 tests: place, turn; $18.50 per set of testing materials; distributed by Specialty Case Manufacturing Co. Test Equipment and Warwick Products Co.
4) *Finger Dexterity Board.* 2 tests: assemble, disassemble; $8.65 per set of testing materials; distributed by Specialty Case Manufacturing Co. Test Equipment and Warwick Products Co.

b) GATB, B-1002, [SEPARATE ANSWER SHEET EDITION]. Grades 9–12 and adults; 1952–63; 9 scores: same as for *a* above except for omission of aiming and motor speed; IBM, NCS, and DocuTran except for part 8 and performance tests; Forms A ('52), B ('53) of paper and pencil tests; 12 tests: 8 tests in 3 booklets plus 4 performance tests; paper and pencil tests also available in 8 separate booklets for restricted use by State Employment Services in testing adults; supplement to section 1 ['62, 30 pages] of the manual, for use when DocuTran scoring service is employed; supplement to section 1 ['63, 38 pages] of the manual, for use with NCS answer sheets; revised profile card ('61, 2 pages); revised aptitude pattern cards ('61, 2 pages) for grades 9, 10, adults (only the card for adults is used with the separate booklet edition); separate IBM, NCS, or (combined booklet edition only) DocuTran answer sheets must be used; $9.50 per 500 IBM answer sheets; (NCS accessories and scoring service available through National Computer Systems: fee, 25¢ per examinee, plus $3 per 100 NCS answer sheets, $2 per 100 test center identification sheets, 50¢ per optional hand scoring stencil, 25¢ per NCS supplement to section 1 of the manual, postage extra; DocuTran accessories and scoring service available through Science Research Associates, Inc.: fee, 25¢ per examinee, plus $2 per 100 DocuTran answer sheets, 60¢ per 20 test center identification sheets, 50¢ per set of optional hand scoring keys, 25¢ per DocuTran supplement to section 1 of the manual, postage extra) ; *separate booklet edition prices:* $4.25 ($5.50) per 100 tests of Form A (Form B) name perception, computation, or arithmetic reasoning, $2.50 ($2.75) per 100 tests of Form A (Form B) vocabulary or form matching, $7.50 ($8.75) per 100 tests of Form A (Form B) three-dimensional space or tool matching, $2.75 per 100 tests of part 8.

1) *Book 1.* 2 forms (24 pages) ; 4 tests : name perception, computation, three-dimensional space, vocabulary ; $14 per 100 tests of Form A ; $15 per 100 tests of Form B.

2) *Book 2.* 2 forms (17 pages) ; 3 tests : tool matching, arithmetic reasoning, form matching ; $10 per 100 tests of Form A ; $12 per 100 tests of Form B.

3) *Part 8* [*Mark Making*]. 1 form (4 pages) ; $2.75 per 100 tests.

4) *Pegboard.* Same as a3 above.

5) *Finger Dexterity Board.* Same as a4 above.

REFERENCES

1-33. See 4:714.

34-209. See 5:609.

210. SENIOR, NOËL. *An Analysis of the Effect of Four Years of College Training on General Aptitude Test Battery Scores.* Master's thesis, University of Utah (Salt Lake City, Utah), 1952.

211. BEAMER, GEORGE C., AND ROSE, TOM. "The Use of the GATB and the AIA Tests in Predicting Success in Accounting." *Acctg R* 30:533-5 Jl '55. *

212. ANDERSON, PAULINE K. "The Use of the General Aptitude Test Battery in the Employment Service." *Proc Inv Conf Testing Probl* 1955:16-21 '56. * (*PA* 31:3202)

213. CURETON, EDWARD E. "Service Tests of Multiple Aptitudes." *Proc Inv Conf Testing Probl* 1955:22-39 '56. * (*PA* 31:3017)

214. JEX, FRANK B. *University of Utah Studies in the Prediction of Academic Success.* University of Utah Research Monographs in Education, Vol. 1, No. 1. Salt Lake City, Utah: the University, July 1957. Pp. ix, 51. *

215. HIRT, MICHAEL LEONARD. *Use of the General Aptitude Test Battery to Determine Aptitude Changes With Age and to Predict Job Performance.* Doctor's thesis, University of Nebraska (Lincoln, Neb.), 1958. (*DA* 19:1436)

216. PICKETT, LOUIS M. *The General Aptitude Test Battery as a Predictor of College Success.* Master's thesis, Utah State University (Logan, Utah), 1958.

217. UNITED STATES EMPLOYMENT SERVICE. "Validity Information Exchange, No. 11-25: D.O.T. Code 4-15.020, Weaver; 6-19.635, Weaver." *Personnel Psychol* 11:440-1 au '58. *

218. UNITED STATES EMPLOYMENT SERVICE. "Validity Information Exchange, No. 11-26: D.O.T. Code 6-14.420, Looper." *Personnel Psychol* 11:581-2 w '58. *

219. UNITED STATES EMPLOYMENT SERVICE. "Validity Information Exchange, No. 11-27: D.O.T. Code 6-98.251, Grid Operator." *Personnel Psychol* 11:583-4 w '58. *

220. UNITED STATES EMPLOYMENT SERVICE. "Validity Information Exchange, No. 11-28: D.O.T. Code 7-76.110, Egg Candler." *Personnel Psychol* 11:585 w '58. *

221. UNITED STATES EMPLOYMENT SERVICE. "Validity Information Exchange, No. 11-30: D.O.T. Code 9-68.60, Fruit Sorter; 9-68.60, Olive Sorter; 9-68.35, Packer (Agric.)." *Personnel Psychol* 11:587-90 w '58. *

222. HIRT, MICHAEL. "Another Look at the Relationship Between Interests and Aptitudes." *Voc Guid Q* 7:171-3 sp '59. *

223. HIRT, MICHAEL. "Use of the General Aptitude Test Battery to Determine Aptitude Changes With Age and to Predict Job Performance." *J Appl Psychol* 43:36-9 F '59. * (*PA* 34:4828)

224. NICKSICK, THEODORE, JR., AND BEAMER, GEORGE C. "Aptitude Patterns for Selected Major Fields of Study." *Personnel & Guid J* 38:43-5 S '59. *

225. SHARP, H. C., AND PICKETT, L. M. "The General Aptitude Test Battery as a Predictor of College Success." *Ed & Psychol Meas* 19:617-23 w '59. * (*PA* 34:6573)

226. UNITED STATES EMPLOYMENT SERVICE. "Validity Information Exchange, No. 12-8: D.O.T. Code 2-63.10, Fireman II." *Personnel Psychol* 12:313-4 su '59. *

227. UNITED STATES EMPLOYMENT SERVICE. "Validity Information Exchange, No. 12-9: D.O.T. Code 4-44.110, Linotype Operator." *Personnel Psychol* 12:315 su '59. *

228. UNITED STATES EMPLOYMENT SERVICE. "Validity Information Exchange, No. 12-10: D.O.T. Code 5-83.641, Packaging-Machine Mechanic." *Personnel Psychol* 12:316 su '59. *

229. UNITED STATES EMPLOYMENT SERVICE. "Validity Information Exchange, No. 12-11: D.O.T. Code 6-14.063, Transfer Knitter." *Personnel Psychol* 12:317 su '59. *

230. UNITED STATES EMPLOYMENT SERVICE. "Validity Information Exchange, No. 12-12: D.O.T. Code 6-14.064, Seamless-Hosiery Knitter." *Personnel Psychol* 12:318-9 su '59. *

231. UNITED STATES EMPLOYMENT SERVICE. "Validity Information Exchange, No. 12-13: D.O.T. Code 6-62.055, Clicking-Machine Operator." *Personnel Psychol* 12:320-1 su '59. *

232. UNITED STATES EMPLOYMENT SERVICE. "Validity Information Exchange, No. 12-14: D.O.T. Code 6-94.682, Production Assembler." *Personnel Psychol* 12:322 su '59. *

233. UNITED STATES EMPLOYMENT SERVICE. "Validity Information Exchange, No. 12-15: D.O.T. Code 7-36.240, Petroleum Transport Driver." *Personnel Psychol* 12:323 su '59. *

234. UNITED STATES EMPLOYMENT SERVICE. "Validity Information Exchange, No. 12-16: D.O.T. Code 7-88.414, Fork-Lift Truck Operator." *Personnel Psychol* 12:324 su '59. *

235. UNITED STATES EMPLOYMENT SERVICE. "Validity Information Exchange, No. 12-17: D.O.T. Code 9-68.30, Cereal Packer." *Personnel Psychol* 12:325 su '59. *

236. UNITED STATES EMPLOYMENT SERVICE. "Validity Information Exchange, No. 12-20: D.O.T. Code 4-85.040, Welder, Combination." *Personnel Psychol* 12:484-5 au '59. *

237. UNITED STATES EMPLOYMENT SERVICE. "Validity Information Exchange, No. 12-21: D.O.T. Code 5-00.020, Units Mechanic." *Personnel Psychol* 12:486 au '59. *

238. UNITED STATES EMPLOYMENT SERVICE. "Validity Information Exchange, No. 12-22: D.O.T. Code 5-17.010, Patternmaker, Metal; 5-17.020, Patternmaker, Wood." *Personnel Psychol* 12:487-8 au '59. *

239. UNITED STATES EMPLOYMENT SERVICE. "Validity Information Exchange, No. 12-23: D.O.T. Code 6-78.905, Machine Operator, General." *Personnel Psychol* 12:489 au '59. *

240. UNITED STATES EMPLOYMENT SERVICE. "Validity Information Exchange, No. 12-24: D.O.T. Code 8-04.10, Corn-Cutting-Machine Operator; 8-04.10, Corn-Husking-Machine Operator; 8-04.10, Cutter, Machine." *Personnel Psychol* 12:490-1 au '59. *

241. UNITED STATES EMPLOYMENT SERVICE. "Validity Information Exchange, No. 12-25: D.O.T. Code 8-04.10, Cutter, Hand; 9-68.60, Inspector, Belt; 9-68.60, Sorter, Food Products; 8-04.10, Trimmer; 8-04.10, Vegetable Packer; 9-68.01, Weight Checker." *Personnel Psychol* 12:492-4 au '59. *

242. UNITED STATES EMPLOYMENT SERVICE. "Validity Information Exchange, No. 12-26: D.O.T. Code 9-13.01, Assembler (Toys and Games); 9-13.01, Model Airplane Assembler; 7-00.971, Toy Train Assembler." *Personnel Psychol* 12:495-6 au '59. *

243. UNITED STATES EMPLOYMENT SERVICE. "Validity Information Exchange, No. 12-27: D.O.T. Code 1-05.01, Clerk, General Office." *Personnel Psychol* 12:629 w '59. *

244. UNITED STATES EMPLOYMENT SERVICE. "Validity Information Exchange, No. 12-28: D.O.T. Code 4-46.205, Stripper (Print. & Pub.) II." *Personnel Psychol* 12:630 w '59. *

245. UNITED STATES EMPLOYMENT SERVICE. "Validity Information Exchange, No. 12-29: D.O.T. Codes 5-27.010 and 5-28.100, Painter-Decorator." *Personnel Psychol* 12:631 w '59. *

246. UNITED STATES EMPLOYMENT SERVICE. "Validity Information Exchange, No. 12-30: D.O.T. Code 6-42.420, Bag-Making-Machine Operator; 4-42.400, Cellophane-Bag-Machine Operator; 4-42.400, Waxed-Bag-Machine Operator." *Personnel Psychol* 12:632-3 w '59. *

247. UNITED STATES EMPLOYMENT SERVICE. "Validity Information Exchange, No. 12-31: D.O.T. Code 6-72.333, Jewelry Assembler." *Personnel Psychol* 12:634 w '59. *

248. UNITED STATES EMPLOYMENT SERVICE. "Validity Information Exchange, No. 12-32: D.O.T. Code 6-93.404, Luggage-Hardware Assembler." *Personnel Psychol* 12:635 w '59. *

249. UNITED STATES EMPLOYMENT SERVICE. "Validity Information Exchange, No. 12-33: D.O.T. Code 6-94.352, Power Lawn Mower Assembler." *Personnel Psychol* 12:636-7 w '59. *

250. UNITED STATES EMPLOYMENT SERVICE. "Validity Information Exchange, No. 12-34: D.O.T. Code 6-95.001, Solderer I." *Personnel Psychol* 12:638 w '59. *

251. UNITED STATES EMPLOYMENT SERVICE. "Validity Information Exchange, No. 12-35: D.O.T. Code 7-54.621, Water Filterer." *Personnel Psychol* 12:639 w '59. *

252. UNITED STATES EMPLOYMENT SERVICE. "Validity Information Exchange, No. 12-36: D.O.T. Code 7-57.501, Presser, Hand; 7-57.501, Silk Finisher, Hand." *Personnel Psychol* 12:640-1 w '59. *

253. DROEGE, ROBERT C. "G.A.T.B. Norms for Lower High School Grades." Comments by Albert S. Thompson. *Personnel & Guid J* 39:30-6 S '60. * (*PA* 35:3969)

254. McDANIEL, ERNEST D., AND STEPHENSON, HOWARD W. "Prediction of Scholastic Achievement in Pharmacy at the University of Kentucky." *Am J Pharm Ed* 24:162-9 sp '60. *

255. SOUEIF, M. I., AND METWALLY, A. "Testing for Organicity in Egyptian Psychiatric Patients." *Acta Psychologica* 18(4):285-96 '61. * (*PA* 36:5JG85S)

256. McNAMARA, THOMAS A. "Identification of Vocational Aptitudes," pp. 330-7. In *Education and National Purpose: Forty-Ninth Annual Schoolmen's Week Proceedings.* Edited

by Helen Hus. Philadelphia, Pa.: University of Pennsylvania Press, 1962. Pp. 358. *

257. RUSSO, J. ROBERT. "Two Governmental Sources for Aptitude Testing." *Sch Counselor* 9:140–1 My '62. *

258. STEIN, CARROLL I. "The GATB: The Effect of Age on Intersample Variations." Comments by Robert C. Droege. *Personnel & Guid J* 40:779–85 My '62. * (PA 37:2964)

259. SUPER, DONALD E., AND CRITES, JOHN O. *Appraising Vocational Fitness by Means of Psychological Tests, Revised Edition,* pp. 330–9. New York: Harper & Brothers, 1962. Pp. xv, 688. * (PA 37:2038)

260. BELL, FOREST O.; HOFF, ALVIN L.; AND HOYT, KEN-NETH B. "A Comparison of Three Approaches to Criterion Measurement." *J Appl Psychol* 47:416–8 D '63. * (PA 38:6737)

261. BURT, SAMUEL M. "Aptitude Test for Selection of Vocational-Technical School Printing Students." *Am Voc J* 38:23 N '63. *

262. DROEGE, ROBERT C.; CRAMBERT, ALBERT C.; AND HENKIN, JAMES B. "Relationship Between G.A.T.B. Aptitude Scores and Age for Adults." *Personnel & Guid J* 41:502–8 F '63. * (PA 39:1384)

263. GAVURIN, EDWARD, AND POCKELL, NORMAN E. "Comparison of Bare-Handed and Glove-Handed Finger Dexterity." Abstract. *Percept & Motor Skills* 16:246 F '63. *

264. TAYLOR, FRED R. "The General Aptitude Test Battery as Predictor of Vocational Readjustment by Psychiatric Patients." *J Clin Psychol* 19:130 Ja '63. * (PA 39:2368)

HAROLD P. BECHTOLDT, *Professor of Psychology, University of Iowa, Iowa City, Iowa.* [Review of Edition B-1002.]

The *General Aptitude Test Battery* (GATB) of the United States Employment Service (USES) represents the outcome of one of the longest programs of test battery development in existence. The change from battery B-1001 to the revised one, B-1002, was reviewed in *The Fifth Mental Measurements Yearbook* by Humphreys, Comrey, and Froehlich. Since available information listed in the three sections of the Guide to the Use of the General Aptitude Test Battery, dated January and October 1962, indicate little, if any, further change from the material of the earlier reviews, the present set of comments will cover the few additional data and amplify the more crucial points of the previous reviews. This restatement seems desirable since the current manuals and recent studies are still open to serious criticism.

The relationships of the GATB test scores to scores of a variety of other tests, to educational level, to sex, and to age are treated briefly in the Guide, but with incomplete data reporting. The discussions generally are considered and cautious. The serious problems associated with attempting to conduct acceptable research studies in a variety of field units with field personnel are recognized. Studies of test stability and of equivalence of forms indicate values comparable to those found in other test batteries. The successive-step procedure, however, introduces untested assumptions. Changes in means and variances are noted with respect to practice effects but the discussion of the effect of heterogeneity on "reliability" coefficients is inadequate. Reports of the standard errors of measurement are needed. A brief, but inadequate, discussion deals with the possible influence both of experience on the job and of specific academic courses on GATB scores. The positive relationship of educational level to GATB scores is noted at several points, but this point is not pursued. A longitudinal follow-up study of job placement of high school students was started in 1958, but the results are not yet available. The use of minimum qualifying scores for each occupational group simplifies the clerical use of the test results to the greatest possible extent; these qualifying norms are said to include only "the most significant aptitudes" that are required by the occupation. The Guide points out that "a deficiency in one significant aptitude cannot be compensated for by a superabundance of another." All available data other than GATB scores are to be integrated or interpreted by the counselor; large scale studies have regularly shown such judgments to be a serious source of error in a prediction situation.

The more important comments deal primarily with certain procedures and points of view in the three parts of the Guide available to the user. These comments are made possible by the extensive report of the work which has been done by the USES organization on the development of the GATB.

PURPOSE. The present manual indicates that a change in objective has developed since 1940. Whereas the task of the Employment Service was previously stated "to promote the satisfactory placement of work seekers in jobs,"[1] the Guide indicates the USES is now interested "not only in establishing test norms for a single occupation, but also in relating a given set of occupational norms to the norm structure for groups of occupations." The test norms purport to involve job performance by expressing minimum levels on essential aptitudes for each of a large number of occupations. However, no acceptable evidence is presented to indicate that these values define *minimum* levels of *essential* aptitudes. The USES aptitude tests "are designed to measure capacities to learn various jobs," yet only a few of the many studies attempt to predict performance on the

1 STEAD, WILLIAM H., AND ASSOCIATES. *Occupational Counseling Techniques.* New York: American Book Co., Inc., 1940. Pp. ix, 273. *

job after training. The presentation of validity data indicates a primary objective of the USES is the empirical prediction of a criterion defined mainly by ratings of supervisors. The use of such inadequate criteria of worker "job performance" probably is responsible in part for the failure to use predictors other than GATB scores. The evidence offered of the success with which the predictions are achieved consists of sets of tetrachoric correlations summarized in Tables 34 to 37, Section 3 of the Guide. Other data appear in a technical report *Selecting Employees for Developmental Opportunities.*[2] The previous cogent criticism of the use of tetrachoric correlations in this connection has led to statements that the more appropriate phi coefficients are currently being used. The use of point-biserial or other product-moment correlations with multiple-level criteria would be even more informative.

CONCEPTUAL FRAMEWORK. A preliminary comment is needed regarding the term aptitude. A discussion in the manuals and in the most recent study of the battery is characteristic of the "hypothetical underlying trait" approach found in the writings of some factor analysts. The empirically untenable positions of postulated innate abilities and of a distinction between ability and performance are presented. One current dictionary of psychological terms [3] points out that the words aptitude, capacity, and ability have many referents; the preferred position, consistent with an APA definition of a test,[4] is that these terms are referring either to observed or to predicted (and observable) performance. This view is represented by the USES selection of one, two, or three test scores to define the aptitudes. The aptitudes so defined may be named as response-defined or behavioral variables. In the GATB B-1002, nine aptitudes are defined by linear functions of a set of 12 test scores. The overriding commitment to the older notion of aptitudes is evident, however, in the restrictions as to predictor variables to be used. No historical, biographical, or situational variables are used in any of the prediction functions.

2 UNITED STATES ARMY ORDNANCE CORPS. *Selecting Employees for Developmental Opportunities.* Technical Report. Rock Island, Ill.: Rock Island Arsenal, July 1962.
3 ENGLISH, HORACE B., AND ENGLISH, AVA CHAMPNEY. *A Comprehensive Dictionary of Psychological and Psychoanalytic Terms.* New York: Longmans, Green & Co., Inc., 1958. Pp. xiv, 594. *
4 AMERICAN PSYCHOLOGICAL ASSOCIATION. "Report of Testimony at a Congressional Hearing." *Am Psychologist* 13:217–23 My '58. *

The hunches or guesses of an investigator about relationships of defined behavioral variables to environmental or training concepts and to other behavioral concepts (called criteria) defined by performance on the job are examples of hypotheses about relationships involving two or more empirical and observed variables. As noted by Humphreys, once the definitions of any set of predictors are provided, the hunches or procedures leading to the definitions are of little, if any, concern. What is of concern then is the usefulness of these definitions; for the USES problems, usefulness is primarily accuracy of prediction of the criterion variable. However, too little consideration is given to the acceptability of ratings as criterion variables.

The reduction of nearly 100 tests (of the pre-1940 era) to a set of 15 (B-1001) and then to 12 (B-1002) represents a simplification which potentially is of value for theoretical purposes as well as for the pragmatic objectives of absolute and differential prediction. The adequacy of this formulation is not, however, indicated by an internal analysis using some factor analysis technique. The factor analysis results may provide hypotheses (as to possibly useful sets of variables) that are subsequently confirmed, but these factor analysis results are *not* substitutes for appropriate empirical evidence of criterion prediction.

It seems clear that if linear or nonlinear regression procedures were to be used, the cogency of the previous criticisms of the USES formulations would be evident. For example, Humphreys points out that no definition of mechanical information or comprehension is included; such test defined concepts have been found useful for the USES type of problem by other investigators. This and other possibly serious omissions are clearly indicated in the study reported in Section 3 (Wherry and Black) and by the work of other investigators. A second problem, also noted by Humphreys, is the "experimental dependence" resulting from the definition of G (intelligence) as a linear combination of scores also used to define F (finger dexterity), N (numerical aptitude), and S (spatial aptitude). This dependence precludes the use of efficient regression procedures and introduces into the system the problem of correlated errors and of linear constraints. One solution is to develop a new test to define "G." A third problem is the use of "multiple cut-off" scores instead of linear or nonlinear continuous functions of the predictors to develop the estimated (or predicted) criterion variable. The criterion variable is also dichotomized. As a result, only predictions of high or of low standing are provided. The available data indicate that more than two levels of job performance may be consistently and usefully observed. In addition, the usefulness of defining an ability by performance on a single task or test situation could also be evaluated by empirical data in the suggested regression framework.

RESTRICTION OF VARIABLES TO APTITUDES. Prior to 1940, the USES used a combination of aptitude tests and trade tests in their counseling activities. Aptitude tests were used to define properties of performance of individuals who had not had relevant job experiences. Trade tests defined behavioral variables which were involved in specific job experiences. The orientation since 1945, as indicated by the statements in Section 3, is on aptitudes whose high relationship to job success is to be independent of variations in amount or kind of job training. It is assumed that the GATB scores are such aptitudes. If so, then the usefulness or "validity" of the aptitude test scores can be evaluated by testing workers already on the job in the "concurrent validity" type of design. The substitution of concurrent validation studies (using relatively homogeneous groups of workers on the job) for longitudinal or actual prediction studies is justified in the Guide by reference to a similar statement by Ghiselli and Brown. If the assumed invariance of linear relationships tends to hold, then the correlation coefficients will increase when more heterogeneous groups of applicants are used.

Three comments are indicated with respect to this assumption: First, this reviewer knows of no acceptable evidence tending to support this assumption of relationships being independent of experience *in general*. Skills required for learning a job are not necessarily those skills which differentiate between job performances after a period of time on the job. Such differences are often indicated when performance, rather than rating criteria, are used. Second, skills required to learn a job would be observed prior to being on the job. The evaluation would be in terms of performance change during a period of training on the job. Third, both laboratory and industrial studies indicate that experience or practice on one task will influence performance on some other tasks. The criterion used is important in such studies. That this assumption is also considered questionable by the USES is indicated in several statements in which the greater cogency of "longitudinal validity" paradigms, as opposed to the concurrent validation designs, is recognized.

In specific cases, there may be some test performances relevant to either rate of acquisition or rate of skilled performance, which are not strongly influenced by specific or general skills acquired on the job. The data of Table 34, however, suggest that both educational level and experience on the job will change the mean values, as well as the standard deviations and possibly the relationships involving performances on some of these GATB scores. Furthermore, the relationships of age and education to test performance shown in the Ordnance Corps technical report suggest that some of these aptitude performances can be replaced by the simple and gross variable "number of years of education." Partial correlations with education held constant then would indicate any additional relationships attributable to these tests as such.

If the desired levels of absolute and differential prediction of adjustment to the job, of tenure in the job, or of actual performance on the job are to be achieved, it is likely that variables in addition to the nine currently used will be required. The simplest of these additional variables will be the educational level and present technical skill and previous experience (on the job). It may be necessary to define these technical and job-acquired skills by several trade or information tests and by biographical (historical) data.

USE OF MULTIPLE CUTOFF SCORES. A serious question can be raised regarding the appropriateness of the wholesale application of the technique of multiple cutoff scores for the problem of predicting "job success" by specifying a set of occupational norms. One reason offered for this technique is the simplification of the advising procedure in the several field offices of the USES. The clerks have only to compare the several aptitude scores, which require at most the addition of two or three values, with the GATB B-1002 cutoff values. A more important reason is the notion that

General Aptitude Test Battery

noncompensatory sets of skills are characteristic of *all* occupations; minimum levels on a set of essential skills are implied for all jobs. This reviewer knows of no evidence involving test scores such as those of the GATB, which supports this assumption even for *one* occupation. The published evidence indicates that linear and nonlinear functions of test scores in a compensatory combination are as useful as or more useful than the multiple cutoff procedures. For some prediction problems, nonlinear functions are more useful than linear ones.

References are made in the Guide to articles from 1950 to 1953 in support of the use of multiple cutoff procedures. Since 1953, psychologists generally have become aware of several useful alternative procedures, such as nonlinear transformation of scores and nonlinear functions involving the use of powers and products of variables in a regression equation. The details of these procedures are given by statisticians such as Rao [5] and Williams. [6] Computer programs are available. Examples also have been provided by Horst [7] and by other psychologists. Horst [8] and his associates have also considered the linear prediction problem at some length. More recently, Lord [9] has pointed out the theoretical inadequacy of the cutting score techniques for the case of such "fallible" variables as test scores and job performances. Since the entire GATB was administered to all subjects used in the several validity studies, a systematic reanalysis of the better of these studies by more adequate techniques would appear to be indicated. Simplification of the regression equation for office use by clerks might then be developed so that the effected loss in accuracy would be tolerable and known.

The combination of a large number of variables in a multiple linear or nonlinear regression function developed on small samples will often lead to marked shrinkage of the correlation coefficient in subsequent cross validation trials in

part from the effects of correlated errors. Humphrey's point that shrinkage can also be expected in the multiple cutoff values in the small USES samples seems sound; selection of a subset of variables from a larger set is involved. However, at least three cross validation studies are reported in Section 3 of the manual. These studies, as presented, indicate either no shrinkage or a significant increase in accuracy of prediction on the subsequent studies. The use of judgmental (logical) criteria in the battery selection may have reduced the effects of correlated errors in the data. Section 3, however, discusses what has been called "double cross-validation." It is, therefore, not clear whether the cutoff values determined in the first study were actually retained for use in the subsequent studies. One possibility is that adjustments were made on the two or more successive studies, to obtain the best separation of the "high" and "low" workers. The point is that the cross validation data and the validity values reported in Table 34 are simply not consistent with those of other comparable investigations. The use of small samples and of the multiple cutoff procedures by other organizations does not lead to such favorable results even when the inappropriate tetrachoric correlation coefficient is used.

SELECTION OF SUBSETS OF APTITUDES. For the purpose of simplifying the advising procedures, cutoff scores are proposed only for subsets of two to four of the nine aptitudes. The procedures used in this selection of a subset, as detailed both in the Guide (Section 3) and in the Ordnance Corps technical report, involve the application of four criteria. These include a relatively high mean test score, a relatively low test score standard deviation, a significant correlation of the test score with the criteria, and a logical judgment of importance of an aptitude (test score) on the basis of job analysis description. The first three of these criteria might be justified. Relatively high scores for workers on the job may arise either from the effect of job experience on the test or from a level of pre-job performance that is indicative of success on the job. However, low scores may also provide useful predictions. A relatively low standard deviation implies reduced variability which might be expected in certain job skills; such reduced variability could then also appear in the test data. Such reduced variability may be achieved

5 Rao, C. Radhakrishna. *Advanced Statistical Methods in Biometric Research.* New York: John Wiley & Sons, Inc., 1952. Pp. xvii, 390. *
6 Williams, E. J. *Regression Analysis.* New York: John Wiley & Sons, Inc., 1959. Pp. ix, 214. *
7 Horst, Paul. "Pattern Analysis and Configural Scoring." *J Clin Psychol* 10:1–11 Ja '54. *
8 Horst, Paul. "A Technique for the Development of a Differential Prediction Battery." *Psychol Monogr* 68(9):1–31 '54. *
Horst, Paul, and MacEwan, Charlotte. "Predictor Elimination Techniques for Determining Multiple Prediction Batteries." *Psychol Rep* 7:19–50 Ag '60. *
9 Lord, Frederic M. "Cutting Scores and Errors of Measurement." *Psychometrika* 27:19–30 Mr '62. *
Lord, Frederic M. "Cutting Scores and Errors of Measurement—A Second Case." *Ed & Psychol Meas* 23:63–8 sp '63. *

by eliminating cases from either end (or both ends) of a test distribution directly or indirectly through some selective process involving attributes characteristic of the job. In terms of the variation in job and test performances actually observed, significant linear (correlation) or nonlinear (correlation ratio) coefficients are useful indices of the desired empirical relationships.

Variation in job skills, however, does not mean that any of the workers on the job are "unsatisfactory." Changes in the classification of given workers (as high or satisfactory and low or unsatisfactory) may develop from changes in the job market, in the job (by simplification and by automation), and in the interpersonal aspects (by labor relations). There is no indication in these manuals that the influence of such changes is considered relevant to evaluating the prediction of success on the job.

The questionable criterion for selecting subsets of variables is the introduction of a rating of logical appropriateness by a job analyst. Such judgments restrict the set of possible empirical relationships to those in line with preconceptions of fallible individuals having vested interests in certain job analysis and ability-performance formulations. It is generally accepted that it is human to err; job analysts are human. The effects of these restrictive (armchair) analyses are clearly shown both in the Guide and in the Ordnance Corps technical report. Additional inadequate criteria used in the Ordnance study also involve the wrong regression line; pass and fail test score categories are "predicted" (fitted to the sample data) *from* concurrent high and low supervisory ratings.

SUMMARY. The present reviewer concurs in general with the earlier reviews by Humphreys and Comrey (5:609) with respect both to the strengths and weaknesses of the test battery. The tests provided are fairly well constructed; the empirical data are as complete as, or more complete than, those for any other available test battery. The results to be expected from using the tests, either as recommended or as they might be used, are probably as good as those from the use of any other existing test battery.

JOHN B. CARROLL, *Professor of Educational Psychology, Harvard University, Cambridge, Massachusetts.* [Review of Edition B-1002.]
The *General Aptitude Test Battery* was

rather completely described, and reviewed in generally favorable terms, in both *The Fourth* and *The Fifth Mental Measurements Yearbooks.* The chief complaint of the reviewers was that the research data on reliability, validity, occupational aptitude patterns, and so forth were either too scanty or too widely scattered. The publication, in October 1962, of Section 3 of the Guide to the Use of the General Aptitude Test Battery, with the title Development, certainly goes far in satisfying these complaints. This publication of 217 pages plus numerous fold-out tables is a rich source of information about all aspects of the GATB, including history, methods of construction, item analysis and factor analysis studies, development of norms, intercorrelations of tests, validity studies for numerous occupations, reliability and effects of practice, effect of training, effect of aging, and use of the test. It is, in fact, to be highly recommended as outside reading in courses in tests and measurement and in individual differences. One of the major faults of Section 3 of the Guide is that it lacks an index.

From this manual it will be abundantly evident that even though the GATB is widely operational in United States Employment Service offices and cooperating institutions, it is also regarded as a research test by its makers. New validity data are being collected continually, in both concurrent and longitudinal designs. In the light of these studies, the Occupational Aptitude Pattern structure is revised periodically; the most recent revision, according to this manual, was made in 1961. A major longitudinal study involving 36,000 high school students is now under way in order to secure data on the long-term validity of the GATB given in high school as a predictor of occupational success. Various interesting questions about the battery are being pursued by the research staff in the USES and also by numerous independent investigators throughout the country. In fact, the GATB seems to be a very popular object of study in master's and doctor's theses. Of particular interest are the data presented in the Guide on the effects of aging: it is shown that even when educational level is controlled, there are significant decrements in nearly all the factors measured by the GATB. Only Verbal Aptitude (V) seems to be impervious to the effects of aging, a finding which squares with those obtained elsewhere.

Likewise, interesting data on reliability and the effects of practice are presented. The authors continue to offer reliability data only on aptitude scores and not on individual tests from which the aptitude scores are derived; I would defend their position on this point on the ground that publication of reliability data on individual tests might tend to encourage the possibly ill-advised use of such tests singly. Actually, four factors (V, S, Q, and K) are defined by single tests, and their reliabilities are satisfactory. The authors are to be applauded for presenting most of their reliability data in the form of coefficients of stability, i.e., test-retest coefficients for periods from a week to a year. The fact that nearly all these coefficients are in the range of .80 to .90 speaks well for the measurement characteristics of the tests. On the other hand, these coefficients are generally derived from very heterogeneous samples, and I cannot find a single mention of a standard error of measurement; there is some question in my mind about the possible imprecision of the scores and its consequences for the assignment of people to Occupational Aptitude Patterns.

It is reported that a practice effect was consistently observed for all aptitudes. Such practice effects can hardly be avoided and it is a good thing that the magnitudes of the practice effects are reported here so that they can be taken into account by counselors in interpreting retest scores.

It is unfortunate that so little could be reported concerning the effects of training on GATB scores. The authors apparently had to rely on the meager research on the problem conducted outside the government.

With a degree of immodesty that is only partly excused by the inclusion of supporting references to the comments of favorable independent reviewers, the Guide (Section 3, p. 176) makes the following statement: "The GATB probably comes closer than any other multi-factor test battery to meeting the requirement of validity for success in a variety of occupations." The information contained in the Guide now makes it possible to assess the claims of the GATB itself; the Guide does not pretend to present comparative validity data for other multifactor test batteries, although it devotes a chapter to the presentation and discussion of correlations between the GATB and other tests. Extensive validity data are reported for 198 specific occupations or clusters of highly similar occupations. These data are reported in two forms: (a) tetrachoric r's resulting from the cross classification of a dichotomous criterion with qualification versus nonqualification in terms of an individual's meeting a series of cut-off scores; and (b) Pearsonian r's for aptitude scores against a continuum-measured criterion (ratings, work sample, production record, etc.). Reviewers of the GATB in previous yearbooks have already complained about the inexactitude of the multiple cutoff procedure, but the authors of the Guide defend it in terms of practicality, and they have a point. Counselors probably have enough trouble with the relatively simple procedures whereby a profile of scores is matched against Occupational Aptitude Patterns, without getting into the computation of multiple regression equations even in a simplified form. Nevertheless, with the era of the computer already well under way one would think that the facilities of the USES could include means of feeding GATB data into an electronic processing system to yield something more informative and precise than the occupational classifications yielded by the present system. In fact, it is now possible to have GATB tests scored by Science Research Associates' DocuTran or by National Computer Systems' machines, either of which surely could be geared to produce classifications based upon multiple regressions.

For the moment, however, we must be satisfied with the tetrachoric correlations listed in the voluminous tables of the Guide. In all, Table 34 presents 317 tetrachoric correlations with values ranging from .24 to .96 and with a median of about .65. Taken at face value, these results are truly impressive. One could have thought that a great many more low validity coefficients would have been obtained; actually only 11 out of the 317 coefficients are less than .40. Nearly all the correlations are based on concurrent validity designs; the median of the 39 coefficients listed as "predictive" validities based on longitudinal designs is .71, somewhat higher than the median of the concurrent validities. But one is justified in harboring certain misgivings about all these results. Each tetrachoric r listed in Table 34 is matched by a series of Pearsonian correlations in Table 36. Examination of these data reveals that the tetrachoric r may often be spuriously high, due to capitalization on error. Consider, for example, the tetrachoric r of .96 given as the predictive validity of the GATB "norms" (cutting scores) for laborer (fireworks) against supervisory ratings. In Table 36, however, the criterion correlations for the two aptitude scores involved in the norms for this occupation are .69 and .57, respectively; even if these two scores (F and M) were correlated zero, which is unlikely, the multiple correlation could not be higher than about .89. An even stranger contrast is afforded by the data for stenographer, where for a sample labeled Cross-Validation II the tetrachoric r is given as .62, but the Pearsonian r's for the aptitude scores are for the most part significantly *negative!* (These are only examples of a number of cases that could be cited.)

Previous reviewers have pointed out that the tetrachoric r is not the best statistic to characterize prediction in a 2 by 2 table; although the authors of the Guide state that in recent studies they have been using the phi coefficient, they do not present any such coefficients in their statistical tables.

All in all, the data now available on the GATB support the claim that it is indeed comprehensive in the sense that it measures most of the ability traits that are important in predicting success in a substantial sample of occupations that can be identified. Further, the subtests have been demonstrated to be reliable and valid enough to yield highly significant and useful results in the hands of the employment or guidance counselor who knows how to use and interpret them. Whether the battery could be improved by the inclusion of measurements of further factors (e.g., rote memory, mechanical knowledge) is uncertain. One hopes that the USES test construction staff will continue to maintain this test by providing additional alternate forms and further validity results. In particular, they need to give attention to the problem of identifying the skills of workers technologically unemployed by automation. Although validity coefficients are given for certain occupations catering to the new leisure (e.g., fishing rod assembler) there are no data on how to select computing machine operators or programmers.

One hopes also that the USES will make provision for the test results to be used with more discrimination; if, as the authors claim, the test results predict a dichotomous criterion so well, they could surely be even better used in predicting a continuous criterion. In this way a counselor could make better estimates of the probabilities of success in an occupation or occupational group than he can with the present system.

For reviews by Andrew L. Comrey, Clifford P. Froehlich, and Lloyd G. Humphreys of b, see 5:609; for reviews by Milton L. Blum, Edward B. Greene, and Howard R. Taylor of a, see 4:714.

[772]

*The Guilford-Zimmerman Aptitude Survey. Grades 9–16 and adults; 1947–56; IBM except for parts 3 and 4; 7 parts; manual, second edition ('56, 7 pages); separate answer sheets may be used except for parts 3 and 4; 4¢ per IBM answer sheet for any one part; 75¢ per scoring stencil for any one part except parts 3 and 4 ($1); 40¢ per manual; $2.35 per complete specimen set; postage extra; J. P. Guilford and Wayne S. Zimmerman; Sheridan Supply Co. *
a) PART 1, VERBAL COMPREHENSION. IBM; Form A ('47, 4 pages); $2.50 per 25 tests; 75¢ per specimen set; 25(30) minutes.
b) PART 2, GENERAL REASONING. IBM; Form A ('47, 4 pages); $2.50 per 25 tests; 65¢ per specimen set; 35(40) minutes.
c) PART 3, NUMERICAL OPERATIONS. Form A ('47, 4 pages); $2.50 per 25 tests; 60¢ per specimen set; 8(13) minutes.
d) PART 4, PERCEPTUAL SPEED. Form A ('47, 4 pages); $2.50 per 25 tests; 60¢ per specimen set; 5(10) minutes.
e) PART 5, SPATIAL ORIENTATION. IBM; Form A ('47, 8 pages); $4 per 25 tests; 75¢ per specimen set; 10(20) minutes.
f) PART 6, SPATIAL VISUALIZATION. IBM; Form B ('53, 7 pages); $4 per 25 tests; 75¢ per specimen set; 10(15) minutes.
g) PART 7, MECHANICAL KNOWLEDGE. IBM; Form A ('47, 8 pages); $4 per 25 tests; 75¢ per specimen set; 30(35) minutes.

REFERENCES

1–15. See 4:715.
16. BALL, JOE M. *An Experimental Study of the Relationship Between the Ability to Impart Information Orally and the Primary Mental Abilities, Verbal Comprehension and General Reasoning.* Doctor's thesis, University of Southern California (Los Angeles, Calif.), 1951.
17. MARTIN, GLENN C. "Test Batteries for Trainees in Auto Mechanics and Apparel Design." *J Appl Psychol* 35:20–2 F '51. * (*PA* 25:7123)
18. TOMKINS, SILVAN S. Chap. 6, "Personality and Intelligence: Integration and Psychometric Technics," pp. 87–95. (*PA* 27:445) Discussion by Joseph Zubin (pp. 103–4). In *Relation of Psychological Tests to Psychiatry.* Edited by Paul H. Hoch and Joseph Zubin. New York: Grune & Stratton, Inc., 1952. Pp. viii, 301. *
19. CURETON, EDWARD E. "Service Tests of Multiple Aptitudes." *Proc Inv Conf Testing Probl* 1955:22–39 '56. * (*PA* 31:3017)
20. GUILFORD, J. P. "The Guilford-Zimmerman Aptitude Survey." Comments by Donald E. Super. *Personnel & Guid J* 35:219–24 D '56. * (*PA* 31:7919)
21. BERGER, R. M.; GUILFORD, J. P.; AND CHRISTENSEN, P. R. "A Factor-Analytic Study of Planning Abilities." *Psychol Monogr* 71(6):1–31 '57. * (*PA* 33:6967)
22. HILLS, JOHN R. "Factor-Analyzed Abilities and Success in College Mathematics." *Ed & Psychol Meas* 17:615–22 w '57. * (*PA* 33:4696)
23. MILLER, ROBERT S., AND COTTLE, WILLIAM C. "Relationships Between MMPI Scales and GZTS Scales: An Adult Female Sample." *Univ Kans B Ed* 11:54–9 F '57. *
24. BALL, JOE M. "The Relationship Between the Ability

to Speak Effectively and the Primary Mental Abilities, Verbal Comprehension and General Reasoning." *Speech Monogr* 25: 285–90 N '58. * (*PA* 33:9492)

25. STINSON, PAIRLEE J. "A Method for Counseling Engineering Students." *Personnel & Guid J* 37:294–5 D '58. * (*PA* 36:2KI94S)

26. GUILFORD, J. P. *Personality.* New York: McGraw-Hill Book Co., Inc., 1959. Pp. xiii, 562. *

27. HANEY, RUSSELL; MICHAEL, WILLIAM B.; AND JONES, ROBERT A. "Identification of Aptitude and Achievement Factors in the Prediction of the Success of Nursing Trainees." *Ed & Psychol Meas* 19:645–7 w '59. * (*PA* 34:6164)

28. MICHAEL, WILLIAM B.; JONES, ROBERT A.; AND HANEY, RUSSELL. "The Development and Validation of a Test Battery for Selection of Student Nurses." *Ed & Psychol Meas* 19: 641–3 w '59. * (*PA* 34:6171)

29. WILSON, JOHN E. "Evaluating a Four Year Sales Selection Program." *Personnel Psychol* 12:97–104 sp '59. * (*PA* 34:3533)

30. LONG, JOHN MARSHALL. *The Prediction of College Success From a Battery of Tests and From High School Achievement.* Doctor's thesis, University of Virginia (Charlottesville, Va.), 1960. (*DA* 21:1100)

31. MERRIFIELD, P. R.; GUILFORD, J. P.; CHRISTENSEN, P. R.; AND FRICK, J. W. "The Role of Intellectual Factors in Problem Solving." *Psychol Monogr* 76(10):1–21 '62. *

32. *Normative Information: Manager and Executive Testing.* New York: Richardson, Bellows, Henry & Co., Inc., May 1963. Pp. 45. *

For reviews by Anne Anastasi, Harold Bechtoldt, John B. Carroll, and P. E. Vernon, see 4:715.

[773]
*The Jastak Test of Potential Ability and Behavior Stability. Ages 11.5–14.5; 1958–59; test booklet title is *The Jastak Test;* 16 scores: 10 direct scores (vocabulary, number series, coding, picture reasoning, space series, verbal reasoning, social concept, arithmetic, space completion, spelling) and 6 derived scores (language, reality, motivation, psychomotor, intelligence, capacity); 1 form ('59, 14 pages, called short form, all items selected from the original 1958 long form); manual ('59, 59 pages); three fourths of the technical data reported (excluding norms) relate to the long form; $4 per 25 tests; $1 per set of keys; $1.50 per manual; postage extra; $1.50 per specimen set, postpaid; 35(50) minutes; J. F. Jastak; Educational Test Bureau. *

REFERENCES

1. STRETCH, LORENA B. "The Jastak Test." *Peabody J Ed* 36:268–71 Mr '59. *

2. CONDELL, JAMES F. "Comparison of Henmon-Nelson and Jastak Scores of Seventh Graders." *Psychol Rep* 9:622 D '61. *

3. O'BLOCK, FRANCIS R. *Reality Scores on the Jastak Test of Potential Ability and Behavior Stability as Associated With Teachers' Judgment of Social and Personal Adjustment.* Master's thesis, Bowling Green State University (Bowling Green, Ohio), 1962.

ANNE ANASTASI, *Professor of Psychology, Fordham University, New York, New York.*

The item types employed in the Jastak test are quite similar to those encountered in intelligence tests, although the scores are treated and interpreted in some unusual ways. The scores from the 10 subtests are first reduced to standard scores with mean 10 and standard deviation 2.5 and then further manipulated to yield three types of measures designated as intelligence, capacity, and stability scores. Intelligence is measured by a deviation IQ based on the sum of the 10 subtest standard scores. Although

these IQ's are not simply the sum of the 10 scores, but are found from a conversion table, it is not clear what their SD is. The manual reports 16.61 (a strange value to choose if it refers to the converted scale) and elsewhere gives SD's ranging from 16.25 to 17.97 for different age and sex groups. Which, if any, of these values refer to deviation IQ's and which to sums of scores cannot be determined from the manual.

Even more puzzling are the procedures employed in computing capacity and stability scores. "Capacity" is estimated through a comparative analysis of the subject's performance on the 10 subtests, which differ widely in the intellectual functions covered. Quite apart from the dubious rationale of such intertest comparisons and the theoretically questionable concept of potentiality itself, the specific procedure followed in computing the capacity score makes its meaning highly suspect. The individual's standard scores on the 10 subtests are first ranked from highest to lowest and each score is then converted to an equivalent score in terms of normative values for the 10 ranks. The individual's highest equivalent score is taken as his capacity score (regardless of which subtest he obtained it on). If this score is appreciably higher than his other equivalent scores, the conclusion is that he is performing below capacity. According to this procedure, an individual will appear to be functioning below capacity if his 10 scores cover a wide range (when his top score will therefore be relatively high), or if they cover a narrow range (when his bottom score will be relatively high), or if he has a run of equal scores in any rank position (when the lowest of the scores in this run will be relatively high). It is difficult to see what a "capacity score" so derived could possibly mean. Yet the manual asserts categorically: "A large discrepancy between the intelligence score and the capacity score is always indicative of adjustment problems."

The procedures followed in computing stability scores are more complex and still more obscure. Their underlying rationale seems to be that profile irregularities indicate emotional instability. It is well known that scatter analysis as an approach to personality diagnosis has not proved fruitful when applied to other instruments, such as the Wechsler scales. As applied to the Jastak test, it seems totally without foundation. Elaborate interpretations of low or high performance in different groups of subtests are offered, with no supporting evidence. Although the manual includes one table giving the results of a factor analysis, the group-factor loadings required to justify the combination of subtests into groups to obtain stability scores are missing. Yet by different groupings of the 10 subtests, the author derives what he terms "language," "reality," "motivation," and "psychomotor" scores. And the individual's relative standing in these four stability scores provides the basis for detailed personality descriptions.

All norms are based on a national sample of 3,000 school children, chosen so as to approximate the 1955 census distribution with regard to geographical areas. The sample consists of 500 boys and 500 girls at each year of age from 12 to 14. Although schools were selected so as to represent high, average, and low socioeconomic levels, no data on parental occupation or other socioeconomic indices are provided.

Split-half subtest reliabilities within single age groups are all in the .80's, but these coefficients are difficult to interpret because of a number of questionable procedures. In fact, if reliability was actually computed by the procedures described in the manual (p. 54), then the coefficients must be incorrect for all but 3 of the 10 subtests. It might also be added that all reliabilities were computed with a longer form of the test, about which nothing is reported other than that it correlated .97 with the present form. No information is given about the relative length of the two forms, how the short form was developed, or the conditions under which the correlation of .97 was obtained. The manual contains no mention of validity, nor any data permitting an evaluation of the test's validity. It ends with a chronological list of the author's publications, but there is no indication of which of these publications (if any) provide material relevant to the test.

While this test offers some ingenious adaptations of intelligence test items that may be of interest to research workers and test constructors, it does not appear to be ready for general use. The manual is quite unclear regarding technical aspects of test construction and evaluating; and it abounds in loose statements and unsupported interpretations. Some of the numerical juggling of subtest scores appears to yield meaningless results. Several statistical procedures are either incorrectly reported or simply incorrect. There is a conspicuous lack of validity data. Yet the tone of the manual makes it evident that the test is being offered, not as a research instrument, but for immediate operational use in the schools. Much of the discussion is addressed to teachers and guidance counselors, who are presumably regarded as the test's chief users. In a personal communication, the test author states that he plans to publish a major study in the future, explaining the complete test construction procedures he followed. It is unfortunate that publication of the test for general use was not delayed until this technical report became available.

BENJAMIN KLEINMUNTZ, *Associate Professor of Psychology, Carnegie Institute of Technology, Pittsburgh, Pennsylvania.*

The Jastak test is in the tradition of multiple aptitude batteries and consists of 10 tests which provide 10 separate scores which in turn yield 6 derived scores. The tests are intended for youngsters between the ages of 11.5 and 14.5. A longer version of essentially the same test was published in 1958; the present form can be administered in about one half the time of the earlier test (35 versus 65 minutes). Most of the statistical data reported in the 1959 manual are relevant to the earlier version, and this reviewer could find no explanation in the manual for the abridgment of the long form. It seems that the time spent in abridging the 1958 form might have been more profitably put to use had the test author worked in the direction of furnishing the potential test user with data on the validation of the earlier batteries and perhaps in providing an alternate form of the earlier version of the test.

The 10 direct scores are gotten from tests of vocabulary, number series, coding, picture reasoning, space series, verbal reasoning, social concept, arithmetic, space completion, and spelling; and the derived scores consist of intelligence, capacity, language, reality, motivation, and psychomotor factors. The standard score equivalents for each of the subtest raw scores can be obtained by consulting the appropriate tables, and the intelligence score is obtained by totaling these standard scores and consulting another table. The capacity score is derived by rank ordering the standard scores and finding the capacity score equivalents in a table prepared for that purpose. The correlation between intelligence and capacity scores is reported as .93, and presumably the capacity score, which on the average is 9.68 higher than the intelligence score, is "a measure of optimum potential." A large discrepancy between the intelligence and the capacity scores, according to the manual, is "always indicative of adjustment problems." No empirical evidence is offered to substantiate this interpretation.

Four other derived scores—language, reality, motivation, and psychomotor—are referred to as stability factors. The manual is not at all clear as to the origin of these "factors," but the one thing that seems certain about these scores is that they were not obtained from any of the conventional forms of factor analysis. Here the manual would have one believe that linear transformations of standard scores to regressed scores, which in turn yield "range" scores, are equivalent to extracting factors. To make the illusion of factor analysis complete, there is a statement that the "quartimax method" of factor analysis was made and that factor variances "were obtained from the 'psycho-logical' method of successive score transformations." If a factor analysis was performed by the quartimax method, which is really nothing more than a variation on Thurstone's simple structure in which the sum of *fourth* powers of elements in the rotated matrix is maximized, the test author has certainly done a good job of obscuring this fact in the test manual.

Each of the 10 subtests, except the spelling test, is timed for either 2, 3, or 4 minutes. The directions for administering the test are carefully prepared and clearly presented in the manual. The test booklet is a 15-page expendable form which the examinee will find quite readable and on which his summary statistics can be conveniently entered. Of questionable usefulness is the visual aid provided in the form of a circular graph which allows for the plotting of test scores. This circular graph has 10 radii, one for each of the subtests, which fan out from the middle and which are marked off numerically in accordance with the standard scores 6, 10, and 14. The number 10 circle represents average ability, and the number 6 and 14 circles represent mental retardation and superiority, respectively. These test profiles are inappropriately referred to as "personality profiles" by the test author. Most of the subtests have appeared

elsewhere before, and no rationale for their present appearance in the form of the Jastak test is presented in the manual.

The vocabulary test consists of six pictures and a list of 21 words underneath. The student is required to identify the meaning of each word by correctly specifying the picture in which it occurs. For example, the word "instruction" is correctly identified in the picture in which an instructor is lecturing about geography. Unfortunately, due to a combination of poor artistic workmanship, unclear reproduction, and oversight, matters are not always that unambiguous. For instance there are four pictures in which the word "peruse" could plausibly be identified, but only one of these pictures is considered the correct answer. In one of these pictures a man is standing near a newstand with a newspaper, and his eyes seem to be on the reading matter; however, one learns from a subsequent answer that he is apparently reaching in his pocket for money, and the newspaper is under his arm. "Remuneration" seems to be the correct identification here. In two other pictures possibly relevant to the word "peruse," a nurse is reading a patient's chart, and a group of men is looking at a map of the United States. None of these identifications is correct, and the appropriate picture is one in which a man is reading a newspaper while sitting on the train. The reproduction of the picture has blotted out his eyes, however, and it is not obvious that he is not sleeping behind that paper and therefore a candidate for a subsequent word, "indolent."

The number series test consists of 15 rows of four numbers arranged according to some order. In order for the student to furnish numbers for two blank lines following the four number series, he must discover the principle that accounts for the ordering of the series. The coding test consists of a key with nine pairs of nonsense marks, and the task requires the student to consult this key in order to respond with the correct symbol when given one of the symbols in a pair. This is an interesting and more difficult version of the digit-symbol coding task.

The picture reasoning subtest consists of 10 series of five pictures each. The pictures within each of the 10 items can be arranged in some logical order, and ranked from 1 to 5. In this test as well as in the social concept test, none of the objections which were raised earlier concerning the quality of the artistic workmanship and reproduction are valid. The drawings and the format are quite clear and errors are strictly a function of the individual's abilities. A series of 13 rows of 10 geometric figures make up the space series test. The first five figures in each row change in some consistent order, and the examinee has to identify two of the remaining five figures that fit in with the changing pattern. The verbal reasoning test has 14 items and for each of these words the student has to select from among five words one that is the same and one that is opposite to the meaning of the first word on each line.

The social concept test is comprised of 11 rows of four pictures. Each row of pictures deals with some form of human action, attitude, or convention and the examinee has to identify the one picture out of four which does not fit the social concept pictured in the other three. The arithmetic test is a straight computation exercise in which 22 problems are arranged in order of complexity. Two other tests complete the batteries and these are the space completion and spelling tests. The former test consists of 11 problems in which the student has to find the two or more parts which go together to make up the stimulus figure. In the spelling test 22 words are dictated to the students to be written in their correct spelling on the lines provided for them.

In view of the fact that all except one (spelling) of the above are speeded tests, the test author's use of odd-even reliability coefficients is a questionable procedure. To the extent that individual differences in the obtained test scores depend upon speed of performance, the reliability coefficients found by this method will be spuriously high. The use of an equivalent forms reliability estimate would, of course, have been the method of choice; however, since no alternate form has been devised, the author could have split the test into times rather than into odd and even items. There are two ways to accomplish this. One way is to split each of the subtests into two half tests and to observe separate time limits. Each form would then be half the length of the complete test and therefore a Spearman-Brown or some such other correction formula could be used to estimate the reliability of the complete test. An alternative to this procedure would be to divide the total time into quarters, and to find the score for each

of the four quarters. Both methods require some planning, and it would seem almost as easy to develop an equivalent form. The absence of the latter, however, does not serve as a license to use an inappropriate procedure. Having said this, it is important to point out that the odd-even reliability coefficients reported in this manual are not relevant to the present test, and therefore no stability data for any of the scores are available.

The principal weakness of the Jastak test is the lack of convincing evidence for the validity of either the individual subtest scores or any of the composite or derived scores. Unless this reviewer has missed something in the manual, the only evidence presented for the validity of the present battery is its correlation with two other tests and with the long form of this test. Correlations are reported of .87 between the short form of the Jastak test and the *California Test of Mental Maturity,* and .89 between the Jastak test (short form?) and the *Kuhlmann-Finch Tests.* The long form and the short form intelligence scores of the Jastak test yielded a coefficient of .97. In the Statistical Appendix of the manual, the latter correlation gave rise to this statement: "Except where indicated the statistical data here presented apply to the long form of the Jastak Test. Since the two forms are highly correlated ($r = .97$), the results are similar for both tests." There is no trace of either concurrent or predictive validity evidence; to the extent that factor analysis could be considered construct validity evidence, a gesture in the direction of providing construct validity is made in the form of correlation matrices which report the intercorrelation coefficients of the various subtests. No factor loadings are reported and there were probably no matrix rotations. Neither these incomplete factorial data nor the correlations between the Jastak and other tests are offered as validity evidence. As a matter of fact, except in the very loosest sense, the word validity is not mentioned in the manual.

In this light it is difficult to understand the test author's rather extensive 15-page section on the interpretation of test results. In the introductory remarks to that section, Jastak promises the reader that "if these pages are diligently studied and properly understood, considerable benefits will accrue to the examiner and the examined child." And for his efforts, the reader is rewarded with such incredibly muddled information as the following:

> The primary purpose of psychological testing is to know the child as well as possible and to help him improve his learning behavior.
>
> A disturbed individual will be more intelligently disturbed if he is bright than if he is dull. Intelligence enhances the symptoms of mental illness. It is of little value in overcoming them.
>
> We favor a definition of intelligence in ethically neutral terms. Biologically, intelligence represents the quantity, variety, and speed of responses and their manifold relationships available to the individual.
>
> Ability and personality adjustments are nearly identical. Personality differences are known to us only through the study of behavior reactions in response to many different tasks and situations.

On the other hand, the section which describes the collection of normative data and the standardization procedure itself are in the best tradition of psychological test development. The student population upon which this test was standardized consisted of boys and girls between the ages of 11.5 and 14.5. In order "to obtain the desired sampling, the United States was divided into nine population regions * A representative cross section within each region was selected," and care was exercised to consult the appropriate sources (e.g., U.S. Census Bureau and state census agencies) in order to divide the sample into high, middle, and low socioeconomic standing. A total of 8,500 tests were completed and from this sample, 3,000 records were randomly chosen for the derivation of the norms. The selection was designed to furnish 1,000 students (500 boys and 500 girls) for each of three age levels. An additional 600 children (200 for each age) "were selected to represent all levels of intelligence," and the statistical tables presenting the total normative sample of 3,600 cases are conveniently arranged so that the test user can easily obtain standard score equivalents for raw scores.

In summary then, it may be said that the Jastak test has technical faults which it shares with many of the multiple aptitude batteries that have evolved from the pioneer studies of L. L. Thurstone. True to the direction of the evolution of the subsequent versions of the primary mental abilities tests, the present edition of the Jastak test offers an abridgment and simplification of its own earlier form rather than providing the much needed empirical validation and technical refinements. Some of the shortcomings of the Jastak test are improper procedures for computing reliability of speeded

tests (actually no reliability data are reported for the short form), meager validity data, and unsupported interpretations. The format of the test booklet and manual and the collection and presentation of the normative data are the battery's chief assets.

Am J Mental Def 65:300 S '60. Earl C. Butterfield. In issuing this shorter, group form of his intelligence test, Jastak reaffirms his faith that people, including the retarded, possess an intellectual potential which is greater than that which they reveal on the standard intelligence measure. Unfortunately, Jastak's test manual does little to convince us that his faith is founded in fact. He offers no evidence of the empirical validity of the capacity scores which his test yields. His test must therefore be considered an *experimental instrument* which has yet to be put to a telling test. Although the test's ten subscales are all composed of academic or intelligence test type items, Jastak purports to derive personality measures from them. He does demonstrate that these personality scores (Reality, Motivation, and Psychomotor) are relatively independent of or uncorrelated with the intellectual indices. Again, however, he does not offer any empirical evidence for the validity of these scores. In considering the probability of such validity demonstrations, it should be pointed out that Jastak, in proposing to measure personality from intelligence test subscale scatter (or stability as he calls it), is launching himself upon the same flight from which Wechsler and Rappaport have so recently and frequently been shot down. Is Jastak's flight also one of fantasy? Only *future* research will tell. The test's manual is written to educators. Whether by intent or not, it seems ideally suited to the seduction of the psychometrically unsophisticated teacher. It is a frightening, if ingenious, piece of propaganda for the "mental measurement movement" in general, and this test in particular. It timidly tackles the educator's coveted concept of the "whole child" in an effort to convince the conservative that the whole is not greater than the sum of its parts, but rather that the whole (child) can best be understood as parts and their inter-relationships. It reaches unparalleled heights in making complex statistical procedures such as factor analysis *seem* comprehensible to the unbaptised. It speaks to the teacher in her own idiom, that of the indi-

Jastak Test of Potential Ability and Behavior Stability

vidual child, by presenting both pathetic and inspiring case studies in which the Jastak test is always "right." By virtue of its very effectiveness in tapping teachers' beliefs in "diagnosis," "individual pupil planning," and the "whole child," the manual becomes unfit for distribution to *unsuspecting* teachers. This is because it is highly likely that the manual will leave such teachers with the impression that this test has some demonstrated practical utility, while, in fact, it has no such thing. Being an experimental instrument, the most that can be said for it is that it has "potential" utility. Among the test's ten subscales are some ingenious modifications of item types which have heretofore been used almost exclusively in individual rather than group tests. The group test constructor would do well to examine Jastak's Vocabulary, Picture Reasoning and Social Concept subscales. They reflect a real originality. It should be noted that this test is of limited utility to those people interested primarily in mental retardation. It is built for just the age range of 11½ to 14½ and is a group test intended primarily for use in normal populations. Those investigators interested in the relationships of functional and potential intellectual levels and personality variables might well view this test as a welcome aid, however.

J Consult Psychol 24:466 O '60. Edward S. Bordin. This briefer form of the 1958 edition ....is reported to correlate .97 with its parent. This correlation and the extremely high reliability coefficients reported are fallaciously high estimates because they were computed on the same sample that provided the data for item analysis on the basis of which the items to be included in this form were selected. The manual is essentially unchanged. I must repeat my conclusion regarding the long form: without further validation data, the *Jastak Test* cannot be accepted as a way of obtaining inferences other than general level of ability.

[774]

*Job-Tests Program. Adults; 1947–60; battery of aptitude tests, personality tests, and biographical forms used in various combinations in different jobs in business and industry; 1 form; 3 series; manual ('56, 8 looseleaf pages); directions for administering ('60, 4 looseleaf pages); hiring summary worksheets ('60, 1 page) for 24 job fields: numbers clerk, junior clerk, office machine operator, contact clerk, senior clerk, secretary, unskilled worker, semiskilled worker, factory machine operator, vehicle operator, inspector, skilled worker, sales clerk, salesman, sales engineer.

scientist, engineer, office technical, writer, designer, instructor, office supervisor, sales supervisor, factory supervisor; no data on reliability presented in manual; $15 per complete set of aptitude tests, personality tests, biographical forms, hiring summary worksheets, scoring stencils, manual, and rating forms from the *Merit Rating Series;* $5 per set of aptitude tests, personality tests, biographical form, hiring summary worksheet, scoring stencil, and manual for a particular job field; $3 per set of aptitude tests, hiring summary worksheet, scoring stencil, and manual for a particular job field; postage extra; Industrial Psychology, Inc. *

a) FACTORED APTITUDE SERIES. Formerly listed as [*Aptitude Intelligence Tests*]; 15 tests; $5 per 20 tests; French and Spanish editions available; Joseph E. King (1–2, 4–15) and H. B. Osborn, Jr. (3).

  1) *Office Terms.* 1947–56; 1 form ('56, 3 pages); 5(10) minutes.
  2) *Sales Terms.* 1948–56; 1 form ('56, 3 pages); 5(10) minutes.
  3) *Factory Terms.* 1957; 1 form (3 pages); 10(15) minutes.
  4) *Tools.* 1948–56; 1 form ('56, 3 pages); 5(10) minutes.
  5) *Numbers.* 1947–56; 1 form ('56, 3 pages); 5(10) minutes.
  6) *Perception.* 1948–56; 1 form ('56, 3 pages); 5(10) minutes.
  7) *Judgment.* 1947–56; 1 form ('56, 3 pages); 5(10) minutes.
  8) *Precision.* 1947–56; 1 form ('56, 3 pages); 5(10) minutes.
  9) *Fluency.* 1947–56; 2 scores: words ending in tion and jobs, or words beginning with pre and equipment; 1 form ('56, 3 pages, contains 4 parts of which examinee takes only 2); 6(10) minutes.
  10) *Memory.* 1948–56; 1 form ('56, 4 pages); 5(10) minutes.
  11) *Parts.* 1949–56; 1 form ('56, 3 pages); 5(10) minutes.
  12) *Blocks.* 1948–56; 1 form ('56, 3 pages, adapted from *Army General Classification Test*); 5(10) minutes.
  13) *Dimension.* 1947–56; 1 form ('56, 3 pages); 5(10) minutes.
  14) *Dexterity.* 1949–56; 3 scores: maze, checks, dots; 1 form ('56, 4 pages); 3(10) minutes.
  15) *Motor.* 1948–56; 1 form ('56, 4 pages, plus motor apparatus); $20 per set of motor apparatus; 6(10) minutes.

b) EMPLOYEE ATTITUDE SERIES. 3 tests; $5 per 20 tests of CPF or NPF; $10 per 20 tests of 16 PF; French and Spanish editions available; R. B. Cattell, J. E. King (1–2), and A. K. Schuettler (1–2).

  1) *CPF.* 1954; 1 form ('54, 3 pages, published also by Institute for Personality and Ability Testing as Form A of *IPAT Contact Personality Factor Test*); combined interpretation sheet for CPF and NPF [no date, 2 pages]; (4–10) minutes.
  2) *NPF.* 1954; 1 form ('54, 3 pages, published also by Institute for Personality and Ability Testing as *IPAT Neurotic Personality Factor Test* bearing 1955 copyright); combined interpretation sheet for CPF and NPF [no date, 2 pages]; (4–15) minutes.
  3) *16 PF.* 1956–60; special printing with new item format, labeled Industrial Edition A, of *Sixteen Personality Factor Questionnaire,* Form C; revised interpretation sheets ('60, 4 pages); (20–30) minutes.

c) APPLICATION-INTERVIEW SERIES. 1948–56; questions in 8 areas: job stability, job experience, education, financial maturity, health-physical condition, family, domestic, activities; 1 form ('56, 4 pages); 5 biography booklets; descriptive sheets ('56, 3 pages); no norms for part scores; $5 per 20 biography booklets; (15–20) minutes; Joseph E. King.

1) *Biography-Clerical.*
2) *Biography-Mechanical.*
3) *Biography-Sales.*
4) *Biography-Technical.*
5) *Biography-Supervisor.*

WILLIAM H. HELME, *Supervisory Research Psychologist, United States Army Personnel Research Office, Washington, D.C.*

In the *Job-Tests Program* the authors have assembled a comprehensive set of ability measures, personality-attitude questionnaires, and background-experience questionnaires for use in selection for a wide variety of business and industrial jobs. Many of the instruments have been adapted from earlier tests on which originators conducted extensive reliability and factor analysis studies. Some, such as Cattell's personality measures, have been incorporated without further change. All are carefully constructed and presented with clear and concise instructions for administration and scoring. Moreover, these sets of measures are reported by the present authors to have been used in some 5,000 industrial concerns. In short, the stage appears all set for presentation of an impressive, well documented battery with clear guidelines for wide industrial application.

But the presentation never comes off. The reason is the absence of adequate validation. Seventeen research bulletins on validation for particular jobs are presented. Sample sizes in the studies range from 16 to 106. Validity coefficients are reported for only a small number of measures for each sample. Several of the samples are of relatively routine clerical jobs; other studies are concerned with electrical assemblers, salesmen, sales managers, printing estimators, policemen, and engineering supervisors. In each sample a few unbiased zero-order coefficients of correlation with performance ratings are reported. These findings can perhaps be characterized as "promising" individual instances of validity, but scarcely as a basis for supporting or recommending wide use.

The research bulletins also present both nonlinear correlations and validity coefficients of weighted test composites. Since there is likelihood of substantial shrinkage in the correlation ratio for a single test validity or in the validity of a weighted composite on samples of this size, these validity estimates should be discounted. This error is perpetuated in the manual, in a section entitled "How to Tailor Personnel Tests to Your Company Operation." This section recommends the practice of obtaining "tailored" weights on samples of 40 or more cases, and also illustrates the use of nonlinear correlations, without mention of the shrinkage in validity to be expected when the weights are applied to new samples. There is a statement that the statistical correlations and derivation of weights is "best carried out by a trained industrial psychologist or psychometrician"—but the best trained psychologist can scarcely make up for the inadequate data or design.

The reviewer feels that little purpose would be served by more detailed discussion of the *Job-Tests Program* at this time. As pointed out in earlier reviews in the *Mental Measurements Yearbook,* what is needed is thorough and conscientious validation if this set of measures is to be put on a sound scientific basis for industrial use. With all the participating companies, and with use of other research resources, it is hard to see why a really comprehensive validation program has not already been carried out in the more than 15 years since these tests were released "for general use in business and industry." Until this is done, industrial users would be well advised to be wary of applying these measures without application of standard statistical methods for their evaluation, or, as an alternative, utilizing one of the other industrial batteries such as the *Flanagan Aptitude Classification Tests* or other selection battery for which more adequate information is available.

STANLEY I. RUBIN, *Coordinator, Assessment Services, Personnel Research and Development Corporation, Cleveland, Ohio.*

The "Complete" *Job-Tests Program* offers a series of tests for each of 24 job fields which are broadly categorized as Clerical, Mechanical, Sales, Technical, and Supervisory. In all, there are 23 tests and forms which are used in different combinations and which include aptitude, intelligence, and personality tests, and biographical forms.

The fundamental rationale for the various tests is based upon the theory of factor analysis. Thus, for the aptitude-intelligence portion of the series, the tests attempt to measure eight essentials which "are very important tests for every job field, since they indicate if the applicant has the basic brainpower to learn and perform the assignments in that job field."

The personality measures are predicated on the factorial studies conducted by R. B. Cattell, and are designed to "find out if the applicant is personally adjusted and how he gets along and deals with poeple." Three different personality "tests" are offered: the CPF test measuring extroversion-introversion, the NPF test measuring stability-neuroticism, and the 16 PF test measuring 16 different personality factors. The latter test also offers a distortion or "lie" factor as well as six "complex" personality scores which "tap broader areas of personality significant at certain job assignments."

Finally, there are five biographical forms, one for each of the job categories mentioned above. The data obtained from these forms (each item is weighted) are designed to reveal information relative to a person's job stability, job experience, educational background, financial maturity, health and physical condition, family background, domestic situation, and outside activities. This in turn is used to determine the adequacy of an applicant's background for a particular job field.

The tests in the "Program" are geared primarily for use in business and industry. The publisher appeals to the cost conscious personnel manager and advises that the various combinations of tests will assist management in making better initial selections by utilizing "scientific methods for psychological testing and interviewing." In addition to suggesting tests to be used in determining an applicant's suitability for a particular job field, the publisher presents some interesting notions and tips for personnel clerks on such topics as recruiting, hiring, test administration, and follow-up procedures.

With few exceptions, the tests offer the advantage of little administration time since only five minutes is required for each measure. In addition, for each job area there is a "Hiring Summary Worksheet" complete with a qualification grid on which an applicant's raw scores are quickly weighted and converted to stanine scores. Once they have been obtained, a simple technique is followed for determining whether the applicant is under-qualified, minimum-qualified, well-qualified, best-qualified, or over-qualified for the field in which he is being tested. According to the manual, the "qualification level" provides an easy method for determining the extent to which an applicant measures up to successful workers in a particular field, as well as comparing him with other applicants.

STRONG POINTS. The major advantage that the "Complete" *Job-Tests Program* has to offer is its typography. All of the materials are attractive, easy to read, and presented in a well written style. The publisher has apparently taken great pains to develop clear "how to do it" procedures designed to appeal to personnel clerks in industry. The tests are simple to administer and score, and any individual taking them will find the instructions easy to understand. Similarly, the inclusion of a Hiring Summary Worksheet enables the personnel clerk to obtain a "quick fix" on an applicant's suitability for a particular position, and to determine whether further testing is justified. Furthermore, companies utilizing the program are encouraged to establish individual standards specifically tailored for their own organizations. In fact, the various steps necessary to carry out such a project are presented in concise form.

The tests in the program offer the advantage of providing a certain amount of face validity. That is, most of the items in the aptitude-intelligence portion of the series give the appearance of appropriateness.

It is the opinion of this reviewer that the major strong point about the program is that it is a clearly written, easily administered "do it yourself" testing program that requires a minimum of sophistication on the part of its users.

WEAK POINTS. Two previous reviews of the aptitude series portion of the program, one in 1953 by D. Welty Lefever and another in 1959 by Harold P. Bechtoldt, criticized the authors for making too many claims about the predictive value of the instruments in the absence of supportive evidence. Once again this criticism is justified in view of the sparsity of data and published studies about the series in recognized professional journals. In the manual, the phrase "validation studies" appears time and time again, but no statement is made as to where these are published in the professional literature.

Second, there is the question of the job test fields themselves. The manual lists a number of job titles, 800 to be exact, that exist in industry. Then, on an a priori basis, these 800 titles are assigned to the 24 job test fields. The assumption made is that the job test fields are sufficiently basic to be used in such a manner. Furthermore, it is assumed that the various tests suggested for each of these fields is appropriate. For example, users are advised that they can use the tests in the job area labeled Sales Engineer to test a man being considered for a job as an underwriter, as well as for such divergent positions as lawyer, jobber, industrial engineer, manuscript reader, optometrist, purchasing agent, securities broker, and others. Such a broad claim requires much more substantiating evidence than is provided in the manual.

The manual also fails to take into consideration the fact that within each field of work there exist various levels of complexity. For example, in suggesting tests to be used for selecting secretaries, no attempt is made to account for the differences in complexity of duties to be performed or in the caliber of person required under differing employment conditions or work environments. Surely one would expect more from a secretary to the president of a large corporation than a secretary who works for one of the salesmen.

Third, there is the matter of claiming purity of items by the technique of name similarity. While the manual does admit that this series "was not developed from a full scale factor analysis," the publisher implies that it was by calling it a "Factored Aptitude Series." It would appear that an effort was made to approximate "purity" by developing "item-types." What this apparently means is that in lieu of a factor analysis on this series, the publisher has settled for second best in the hope that the items created for a particular aptitude would closely approximate those emerging from other factorial studies. The authors fail to realize, however, that items and not types are factorially pure. In the opinion of this reviewer, it is misleading to label the series "Factored Aptitude Series" when the items in the tests have not been subjected to a factor analysis.

In the discussion of the intercorrelations between the various tests in the aptitude series the manual reports that the "average intercorrelation between the factors is in the neighborhood of .35." Reporting this statistic is of little value unless one has an opportunity to examine the intercorrelation matrix for the eight so-called "factors" involved. Once again no mention is made of any publication, in professional literature, where this matrix can be examined.

In an effort to make the personnel man's job easier, the publisher offers "pre-set" weights and standards established on the series of tests for each of 24 job fields. Again in the absence of published studies, the authors claim to have differentiated successful from unsuccessful employees in each of these job fields. What they suggest is that in the absence of a validation study within a company, the personnel man should utilize the pre-set standards which they have "researched out." This "Procrustean Bed" is nothing more than an inappropriate generalization when one considers that the standards used in selecting industrial salesmen operating out of a large metropolitan office in New York City can be expected to differ significantly from those utilized in selecting industrial salesmen working out of a small city in Mississippi.

Finally, there is the matter of the 16 PF test or, as the manual states, "sixteen unitary, independent, and source traits of personality." Not only are many of the items in this test of Lilliputian stature when considering the complex nature of an individual's personality, but they are downright insulting to the intelligence of most individuals capable of coping with even the simplest of problems in logic. One of the items in this test is as follows: "Are you always a sound sleeper, who does not walk or talk in his sleep?" The respondent is then asked to answer (A) Yes; (B) In between; (C) No.

This reviewer believes that the authors are guilty of gross over simplification in the technique they suggest for measuring the complex dimensions of an individual's personality. They would have us believe that all an untrained person has to do to determine the complexities of a personality is to add up the rank scores on four variables, compute the total, obtain the combined rank, then make an interpretation. For example, to determine a person's stability, add Factors C (mature), L (trustful), E (dominant), and O (self-confident). If a high rank is obtained, by means of simple addition, then the individual has a "non-neurotic personality." This same method is suggested for measuring extroversion, anxiety level, leadership, research creativity, and initiative-drive.

The authors make the error of assuming that a person's personality is a static entity unaffected by a multitude of needs and environmental conditions. Furthermore, little appreciation is offered for the commonly accepted notion among professionals that "the whole is greater than the sum of its parts." Kenneth S. Nickerson [1] commenting on the 16 PF has aptly stated, "a significant aspect of complex human behavior cannot be measured by six abstruse items, and sixteen such measures do not make a personality." This reviewer is in full agreement.

SUMMARY. The "Complete" *Job-Tests Program* offers a well written, easy to administer, and simple to score group of tests that are presented in stylish fashion. It has been developed with great concern for the problems of the personnel man in industry. In fact, the series is probably the most attractive one on the market today. It has a great deal of face validity, but the authors have failed to make available, in sufficient quantity and in recognized professional journals, the kind of data that one must submit for professional scrutiny before claims of validity can be voiced. Indeed, it is unfortunate that the authors, talented writers who have taken the time, effort, and pains to communicate so much to personnel clerks on how to administer and score the *Job-Tests Program*, have failed to make available evidence of validity.

In the opinion of this reviewer, the program does have something to offer for a personnel man interested in conducting a validity study within his plant on current employees. However, until further evidence is submitted to substantiate the numerous claims about the predictive value of the series, it cannot be recommended as a selection device for general use in industry.

For a review by Harold P. Bechtoldt of the Factored Aptitude Series, *see 5:602; for a review by D. Welty Lefever of an earlier edition of this series, see 4:712 (1 excerpt); for reviews of the personality tests, see 174, 5:71, 5:74, 5:112, and 4:87.*

[775]

★Measurement of Skill: A Battery of Placement Tests for Business, Industrial and Educational Use. Adults; 1958–62, c1956–62; 8 tests (3 pages except for *g*); manual ('62, c1960–62, 42 looseleaf pages); revised profile card ('62, c1960, 1 page); Skillsort cards ('62, 54 cards) and manual ('62, 9

1 NICKERSON, KENNETH S. "Comments on the Brain Watchers." Letter. *Am Psychologist* 18:529–31 Ag '63. *

pages) for job profile determination; $3.75 per 25 tests; $20 per set of scoring stencils for all tests; $8 per 100 profiles; $7.50 per set of Skillsort cards; $5 per manual (including any supplements issued during year following purchase); $1 per specimen set of tests only; $25 per specimen set of tests, manual, and stencils; postpaid; 5(10) minutes per test (except for *g*); Walter V. Clarke Associates, Inc.; AVA Publications, Inc. *

a) SKILL WITH VOCABULARY. Form MOS-1 ('59, c1956–59).
b) SKILL WITH NUMBERS. Form MOS-2 ('59, c1956–59).
c) SKILL WITH SHAPE. Form MOS-3 ('59, c1956–59).
d) SPEED AND ACCURACY. Form MOS-4 ('59, c1956–59).
e) SKILL IN ORIENTATION. Form MOS-5 ('59, c1958–59).
f) SKILL IN THINKING. Form MOS-6 ('58, c1957–58).
g) SKILL WITH MEMORY. Form MOS-7 revised ('61, c1960, 5 pages); 7(12) minutes.
h) SKILL WITH FINGERS. Form MOS-8 ('59, c1956–59).

REFERENCES

1. MERENDA, PETER F. "Relative Predictive Efficiency of a Short Versus a Long Test Battery for High School Students." *Psychol Rep* 8:62 F '61. * (*PA* 36:1KJ62M)
2. MERENDA, PETER F.; HALL, CHARLES E.; CLARKE, WALTER V.; AND PASCALE, ALFRED C. "Relative Predictive Efficiency of the DAT and a Short Multifactor Battery of Tests." *Psychol Rep* 11:71–81 Ag '62. * (*PA* 37:5665)

DOROTHY C. ADKINS, *Professor of Psychology, The University of North Carolina, Chapel Hill, North Carolina.*

That the *Measurement of Skill* battery has been prematurely made available to prospective purchasers and submitted for review in this compendium is unfortunate. It consists of eight short subtests, for five of which the only estimate of reliability is based upon test-retest correlation, with a four-week interval, for 36 summer-school college students! For one test an additional test-retest estimate is given for 30 college students and a five-week interval. For the memory test, three test-retest estimates (for 56 undescribed cases after four weeks, 26 undescribed cases after five weeks, and 71 salesmen after a two-day memory course) are offered. For the eighth test, a six-month interval and 102 high school students were used. Whether or not the college students are representative of the job applicants for which the test is presumably designed may also be questioned.

In the reviewer's opinion, the test-retest method is useful principally as a device for introducing the meaning of the concept of reliability to undergraduate students. With brief tests as simple and economical to develop and reproduce as the ones under consideration, no reasonable excuse occurs to one for failure to determine estimates of reliability from correlations between different forms of the tests.

The manual states that the tests were designed "primarily as aids in the proper selection, classification, and assignment of business and industrial employees at *all levels* of the occupational hierarchy" (reviewer's italics) and that "in addition they show promise for use in predicting high school achievement." Centile norms are provided for each test for from five to nine groups, in each case including a group designated "General Industrial and Business Employees," which evidently contains the individuals in other employee groups classified as professional, executives and managerial, general office, and skilled and semiskilled. For six tests, the total group n is at least 759, while the other two n's are 176 and 589. Means and standard deviations of each test for each group are also given.

The individual using a table of norms for a test is instructed to read off the "percentile" score in the column for the group with which the subject is being compared. Following the description of the norms appear four pages that are marked "Restricted to AVA Analysts Only." These discuss ipsative profile interpretation and observe that the mean score "has been found to be related to intelligence as a general concept $(r = .55)$"—whatever that means! Before the scores are averaged, they are converted to a scale of numbers ranging from 0 to 100 by means of the MOS Record Summary Card. The reviewer was unable to determine exactly what kind of "standard score equivalents" these converted scores represent. The converted score of 50, for example, uniformly corresponds to neither the mean score nor the 50th centile point.

These same pages present a table from which an approximation of IQ score as measured by the Otis can be found at the intersection of the column containing an individual's mean MOS score and the row containing his AVA Resultant Activity Score. Elsewhere it is mentioned that the multiple correlation of these two scores with the *Wonderlic Personnel Test* was .59 for 244 cases. In any case, the suggestion that what is ordinarily meant by the symbol IQ can be inferred from the mean MOS score and the AVA Resultant Activity Score is unfounded.

Arguing that the usefulness of a battery of tests is a function of the differences among them, the authors present a table of "coefficients of independence," based upon the average intercorrelations from four samples. The coefficients given range from 0 to 100 for perfect independence or maximum possible difference. The coefficient may be simply $100(1 - r)$ but it is more likely to equal $100(1 - r^2)$, what is sometimes called the coefficient of nondetermination. This would mean that the intercorrelation coefficients corresponding to the tabled values 78 to 99 range from about .10 to about .47. The original correlation coefficients and the method used for averaging them might well have been presented.

As to validity, the manual first states that the tests have been carefully designed to insure face validity, claiming that the nature of the tasks is consistent with the test titles and is homogeneous within each test. In the case of certain tests, however, the tasks do not represent what psychologists would expect from the title or even from the manual's descriptions of the tests. The "Skill With Vocabulary" test is referred to as a test of verbal fluency. Each item consists of definitions of a word, with the first letter and the number of letters given. Unlike the usual vocabulary test, this test does indeed seem to draw upon fluency, not to mention spelling ability. The "Speed and Accuracy" test calls for identifying the number of X's embedded in rows of letters of the alphabet. A better name for this test might connote its perceptual or visual character—Perceptual Speed, for example. The "Skill With Fingers" test, intended to test finger dexterity, requires the subject to write in blank squares as many figure 4's as he can in the allotted time.

But, as the authors recognize, mere face validity (however defined) is not sufficient. Hence they report that "empirical statistical validity studies against well defined criteria are being made." Except in the case of predicting high school scholarship (see below), these important studies were not yet available when the manual was released. In the meantime, it is argued that the validity of the series and of parts of it is attested to by combinations of MOS tests correlated with other single tests. For various subtests, correlations are reported with such tests as the *Wonderlic Personnel Test,* Bennett's *Tests of Mechanical Comprehension, Revised Minnesota Paper Form Board*

Test, and *Minnesota Clerical Test,* with *n*'s ranging from 25 to 175. Multiple correlations for composites of various tests of the MOS series with other tests are presented. The value of such coefficients (based upon as few as 25 cases, with the zero-order coefficients corrected for restriction in range) is highly questionable. Estimating the standard deviations on MOS tests for an *n* of 8,597 cases (a composite of normative samples for the *Revised Minnesota Paper Form Board Test*) from data for 25 cases and then using these estimates in reaching a multiple correlation is attempting to squeeze too much out of a limited amount of raw information.

Also reported in the manual is what purports to be a comparative study of the validity of the MOS battery and the substantially longer *Differential Aptitude Tests.* The MOS battery was administered in the spring of 1960 to the eleventh graders of a large city high school. The tests were correlated with marks in different courses achieved by these students in the tenth, eleventh, and twelfth grades. The manual states that the class had previously taken the DAT battery of eight tests, which also could be correlated with course marks. The two sets of zero-order and multiple correlations are of about the same order. Only upon reference to two articles in *Psychological Reports (1–2)* does one learn that the DAT was administered when the subjects were in the eighth grade!

In the 1962 article (*2*) the authors make much of their finding that the coefficients of independence (see above) for the MOS tests are greater than for the DAT tests. Perhaps it will be sufficient to observe that the anticipated coefficients of independence for a battery of tests all of zero reliability would be 100. The 1962 article also observes from factor analyses that the uniqueness values for the tests in the DAT battery are substantially lower than the communalities, whereas the converse is generally true for the tests in the MOS series. Since the uniqueness of a test consists not only of any factors specific to it but also of a variable error factor, a finding that less reliable tests have greater U^2 values is exactly what should be expected, other things being equal.

We turn to a few features of the tests as gleaned from inspection. Skill With Vocabulary, first copyrighted in 1956, still contains what appear to be serious errors. In one item,

for example, the answer "renegade" is to be given for a definition that includes "turncoat." In the very next item, "turncoat" is to be given for a definition that includes "renegade." In general, the items contain many specific determiners. Some of these are so obvious that one wonders whether for some subtle reason they were intentional.

In the case of Skill With Numbers, an improved test design could produce many more than a maximum of 48 responses in the five-minute time limit. Moreover, the suggestion that part scores be obtained for sets of 12 simple items on the four basic arithmetic operations is unwise.

The figures in Skill With Shape are unduly small; and the drafting is far from perfect, so that the sizes of areas that are supposed to be the same are not. One also wonders about the variance introduced by having the subject indicate the answer by shading the areas within the complex figures that correspond to black areas shown at their right. Some will make a few rough lines, others do meticulous shading.

The perceptual ability required for MOS-4, Speed and Accuracy, may be confounded with a numerical factor, since the subject must count the number of X's in each row. The number of separate items in the "Orientation" test (10) is too small. The test should be redesigned or another format substituted to yield more responses per unit of time. Skill in Thinking probably involves a specific algebraic skill. The scoring of Skill With Memory could be simplified by casting it in multiple choice form. The number "4" seems a poor choice for Skill With Fingers since it can be written in two ways.

Accompanying the MOS test battery is a set of 54 Skillsort cards and a sorting tray. The cards contain statements like "Operates a variety of machines," "Compiles statistical data," and so on. On the back of each card are three numbers that apparently represent the tests in the MOS battery that have been judged to test the ability to perform the duty described on the face of the card. According to the "Instructions for Skillsort Profile Determination," one decides for each card whether it does or does not describe some aspect of a job under consideration and then tallies the test numbers on the backs of the selected cards. Each of the frequencies is multiplied by one of a set of weights that range from .03 to .13 and that appear to be inversely but not linearly related to the frequency of occurrence of the test numbers on the backs of the cards. The weighted frequencies are converted by means of a table to "C scores" that range from 31 through 78. These possibly represent some form of normalized scores with a mean of 50 and a standard deviation of 10. The sum of the C scores is multiplied by .125 (although the directions say .0125), and the resulting average C score is indicated by a line on a profile form that contains a scale ranging from 20 to 80. The C scores for the eight separate tests are plotted and the points connected by lines. Presumably this profile is supposed to suggest which MOS tests should be used or weighted most heavily for the job under consideration.

The design and physical quality of all these materials are exceptionally good.

LLOYD G. HUMPHREYS, *Professor of Psychology and Head of the Department, University of Illinois, Urbana, Illinois.*

The *Measurement of Skill* test battery has as a subtitle "A Battery of Placement Tests for Business, Industrial and Educational Use." There are eight subtests of varying numbers of items, each of which requires five minutes for administration. The manual recommends these tests as substitutes for longer test batteries, such as the DAT. The adjectives "short" and "practical" are used liberally in the manual. Data of a sort are presented under headings drawn from the APA's test standards, and the claim is made that these tests perform at least as well if not better than longer and more complex instruments. There is ample sales appeal for the unwary personnel manager or school administrator. Unfortunately, however, the MOS battery represents a poor professional job of test construction, validation, standardization, and manual writing.

Reliabilities are test-retest, interval is typically about four weeks, *n* is typically 36. Most item types are easily remembered, and the number of items to remember is frequently small. Reliabilities reported vary from .44 to .82, but this reviewer strongly suspects that larger *n*'s and parallel forms coefficients would result in values *much* lower than these in any reasonable sort of population.

The validation section is in each case woefully weak. Apparently, the *Measurement of Skill* tests were correlated with whatever ability tests happened to be available. The Wonderlic is used frequently and appears to be as satisfactory a reference test for Skill With Shape or Skill in Orientation as it is for Skill With Vocabulary.

Intercorrelations of the tests in the battery are low because the reliabilities of the tests are low, though the authors report coefficients of independence in place of the usual correlation coefficients. The root of the quantity $(1 - r^2)$ has the very satisfying property, from the point of view of the salesman, of approaching unity quite closely even for moderate values of r.

The authors discuss the values in the use of a battery of tests. One of these is the possibility of using differential weights for the prediction of different criteria. Unfortunately, the tests are so short and reliabilities are presumably so low that stable differential weighting cannot be accomplished on samples of the size typically found in business and in education. The authors also state, in one place, that short tests with low reliabilities should not be used in isolation. However, norms are presented for each of the tests individually; a section is devoted to the ipsative interpretation of test profiles; and the user is even encouraged to obtain part scores on Skill With Numbers.

One study of the comparative validity of the DAT and the MOS batteries has been accomplished. School grades were used as criteria. The study is discussed in the manual and is also to be found in *Psychological Reports* (*1–2*). Unfortunately, there is a major flaw in the design. The DAT was administered during the eighth grade; the *Measurement of Skill* was administered during the spring semester of the eleventh grade; criteria used were grades at the end of the tenth, eleventh, and twelfth grades. The difference in time interval between the two test administrations and the criterion performances makes the data basically worthless. Furthermore, in the tenth grade, where the time interval difference is smallest, comparisons are between correlations computed on overlapping but nonidentical samples.

In summary, the *Measurement of Skill* should not be used; it should not have been published; it should not be sold.

Measurement of Skill

JOSEPH E. MOORE, *Regents Professor of Psychology, Georgia Institute of Technology, Atlanta, Georgia.*

According to the manual, these tests were developed "primarily as aids in the proper selection, classification and assignment of business and industrial employees at all levels of the occupational hierarchy. In addition they show promise for use in predicting high school achievement." The claim of face validity is made for all of the tests and concurrent validity data are presented for several of them. However, predictive validity data based on business or industrial use do not appear for any of the tests. The authors state that "since face validity alone is not sufficient evidence that the series will perform as expected, empirical statistical validity studies against well defined criteria are being made." It is most unfortunate that the manual does not contain at least one such study. A rather loosely designed study of predictive validity is presented for one high school in Rhode Island. In this, scores from the MOS and the *Differential Aptitude Tests* were compared with later success in certain subject matter areas. No cross validation is reported on any of these tests.

For the authors to administer a series of tests to so many hundreds of workers and publish business and industrial norms without reporting a single study against job performance criteria is unfortunate, if not inexcusable. To say that such studies are being made and will be published later does not excuse these authors. The claim that the eight separate tests measure separate skills of some kind should have been verified on different jobs against meaningful performance criteria. Evidence of predictive validity in the business and industrial area is, at this time, entirely lacking.

A rather ingenious procedure for rating job characteristics is also available for use in conjunction with the MOS. The material consists of 54 cards containing descriptive phrases. The rater sorts these cards into seven boxes representing his judgment of the significance or importance to the job of each descriptive phrase. Each card also has on its back side a code for the particular MOS test which seems to be required by the particular characteristic. These codes are tallied and the resultant frequencies are given C score ratings from which a "Skillsort profile" is drawn for all eight tests. It is

unfortunate that no rationale is given for the Skillsort technique. No data are given showing the reliability of the ratings by such a method. Furthermore, no data are presented to show that the MOS coded characteristics differentiate between jobs in the expected direction. The general description of the Skillsort method and the use of terms are remarkably close to the old United States Employment Service job analysis procedure. This similarity should make the Skillsort somewhat more understandable and meaningful to many users.

The general instructions for each of the MOS tests are clear and concise. The exact statements the tester is to say are presented in boldface type that is easy to read. The instructions for scoring are clearly given and the use of plastic stencils that fit over the test sheets makes scoring very rapid.

It very well could be that the authors might have made a strong case for the MOS and the Skillsort procedures if they had shown that such instruments and C score ratings clearly differentiate performance ratings of superior and inferior personnel on specific jobs. Since they have not done so, however, use of the MOS and the Skillsort procedure by business or industry *cannot* be recommended. There are no data to show that these instruments differentiate at all between jobs. Certainly one should not use these instruments until the authors have made good their promise to furnish "empirical statistical validity studies against well defined criteria."

[776]

*Multiple Aptitude Tests, 1959 Edition. Grades 7–13; 1955–60; tests identical with those of 1955 edition except for booklet organization; 14 scores: scholastic potential plus 13 scores listed below; IBM and Grade-O-Mat; 1 form ('59); 9 tests in 4 booklets; administration and scoring manual ('59, 24 pages); interpretation manual ('60, 55 pages); technical report ['60, 79 pages]; extended profile ('59, 1 page); student report ('60, 4 pages); separate answer sheets or cards may be used; 10¢ per set of IBM answer sheets; 10¢ per set of Cal-Cards; 75¢ per set of either hand or machine scoring stencils for answer sheets; 75¢ per set of hand scoring stencils for Cal-Cards; 14¢ per set of Grade-O-Mat scorable punch-out cards; 6¢ per stylus; 6¢ per backing pad; 2¢ per extended profile (free on request with all 4 booklets); 2¢ per transparent profile (no date); 3¢ per student's report; 50¢ per interpretation manual; postage extra; $1.25 per complete specimen set, postpaid; technical report free; 175.5–177 (220–222) minutes in 2–3 sessions; David Segel and Evelyn Raskin; California Test Bureau. *

a) FACTOR I, VERBAL COMPREHENSION. 3 scores: word meaning, paragraph meaning, total; 1 form (12 pages); $4.20 per 35 tests; 42(52) minutes.

b) FACTOR 2, PERCEPTUAL SPEED. 3 scores: language usage, routine clerical facility, total; 1 form (12 pages); $4.20 per 35 tests; 33(43) minutes.

c) FACTOR 3, NUMERICAL REASONING. 3 scores: arithmetic reasoning, arithmetic computation, total; 1 form (12 pages); $4.20 per 35 tests; 52(62) minutes.

d) FACTOR 4, SPATIAL VISUALIZATION. 4 scores: applied science and mechanics, 2-dimensional spatial relations, 3-dimensional spatial relations, total; 1 form (32 pages); $8.40 per 35 tests; 50(65) minutes.

REFERENCES

1. MENDENHALL, GEORGE V. *A Statistical Investigation of Interrelationships in the Multiple Aptitude Tests.* Master's thesis, University of Southern California (Los Angeles, Calif.), 1952.

2. CURETON, EDWARD E. "Service Tests of Multiple Aptitudes." *Proc Inv Conf Testing Probl* 1955:22–39 '56. * (*PA* 31:3017)

3. SEGEL, DAVID. "The Multiple Aptitude Tests." Comments by Donald E. Super. *Personnel & Guid J* 35:424–34 Mr '57. * (*PA* 32:1645)

4. D'AMICO, LOUIS A.; BRYANT, J. HOWARD; AND PRAHL, MARIE R. "The Relationship Between MAT Scores and Achievement in Junior College Subjects." *Ed & Psychol Meas* 19:611–6 w '59. * (*PA* 34:6564)

5. KHAN, LILIAN. *Factor Analysis of Certain Aptitude and Personality Variables.* Doctor's thesis, University of Southern California (Los Angeles, Calif.), 1959. (*DA* 20:2889)

6. MINER, JOHN B. "The Concurrent Validity of the PAT in the Selection of Tabulating Machine Operators." *J Proj Tech* 24:409–18 D '60. * (*PA* 35:5391)

7. KHAN, LILIAN. "Factor Analysis of Certain Aptitude and Personality Variables." *Indian J Psychol* 37:27–38 Mr '62. * (*PA* 37:6716)

8. CAPLAN, STANLEY W.; RUBLE, RONALD A.; AND SEGEL, DAVID. "A Theory of Educational and Vocational Choice in Junior High School." *Personnel & Guid J* 42:129–35 O '63. *

S. S. DUNN, *Assistant Director, Australian Council for Educational Research, Hawthorn, Victoria, Australia.*

The tests in the 1959 edition are identical with those used in 1955 but are now published in four booklets each containing the tests for one factor. Test 3, Language Usage, is dropped from Factor 1 and with Test 4, Routine Clerical Facility, provides the basis for Factor 2, Perceptual Speed.

The material about the tests now appears in three parts—a manual, a guide to interpretation, and a technical report. The manual, which sets out very carefully the directions for administration and scoring, lists 10 changes in the 1959 edition, and it can be assumed that these represent an improvement or additional data since the 1955 printing.

The appearance of the material is pleasant. A glance at the technical report reveals no less than three chapters on validity—construct, concurrent, predictive—and 63 tables. One might be pardoned for thinking that the report has been prepared with an eye on *The Mental Measurements Yearbook*. Undoubtedly the reviewers of the 1955 edition will find that attempts have been made to remedy most of their criticisms, except the need for two forms of the tests.

Nevertheless, the reviewer was frankly worried by the vast superstructure of statistics and the small amount of space devoted to discussing the nature of the "aptitudes" measured and the extent to which they are affected by good teaching or superior environment.

The word aptitude is subject to a good deal of misunderstanding by lay people, and probably by many professionals. From certain incidental references one can guess that the authors probably intend to use it in the sense that any test used to predict is an "aptitude" test. However, although they do not clearly say this and follow up the implications, other references give the impression that they believe the factors have been responsible for *determining* school performance.

The verbal comprehension factor has two tests, Word Meaning and Paragraph Meaning. The same two item types are the basis of most reading achievement tests. Because success in most school subjects will depend in part on reading skills, such tests are useful predictors of later success. However, differences in reading scores are due to multiple influences and for many pupils scores can be changed significantly under appropriate conditions. Thus children from culturally impoverished homes or from a school where the teaching has been poor can be helped. The MAT report does not give attention to this problem.

Likewise, the Factor 3 tests—Arithmetic Reasoning and Arithmetic Computation—are typical of tests a teacher would use in assessing arithmetic achievement. In discussing a case a reference is made to the possibility of improvement in computation. Now, there is no reason why tests of achievement in reading and arithmetic should not be given and used to predict future success. The English have been doing it for years with children at 11+ and obtaining validity coefficients higher than the typical figures quoted for these tests. But if the tests are referred to as aptitude tests rather than achievement tests, it would not be surprising if teachers and pupils *act in different ways* about what is in fact an identical score.

There are certain advantages to be gained by separating the technical report from the rest of the material on the test, but one doubts the value of separating the manual and the guide to interpretation. Users of the test surely need both of these.

A mass of correlation data is given in the

technical report. In fact, with 63 tables and 42 graphs for occupational groups, it is doubtful if anybody other than a reviewer would be willing to tackle it at a sitting. Evaluation of these data by the authors, however, is not adequate. There is no satisfactory discussion of the relationship of scores to performance in school subjects and the probable reasons for the figures discovered. Thus, Test 3, Language Usage, is likely to predict English grades to the extent that the criterion test emphasizes usage.

The dangers in using the occupational data are not sufficiently stressed. A paragraph in the technical report states that since the samples used come from the same geographical locale they are not representative samples. This information is not repeated in the interpretive guide. The occupational information is valuable but more discussion and evaluation of it is warranted. The authors should be able to do this more competently than the vast majority of users.

The quality of the tests is undoubtedly as good as most of their kind; the correlation data are exceeded by those of few tests. The psychometrics are impressive. In fact, the burden of the reviewer's complaint is that the psychometric erudition is not matched by an equivalent understanding of the educational process.

Leroy Wolins, *Associate Professor of Psychology and Statistics, Iowa State University, Ames, Iowa.*

The improvements brought about by the revision are apparently relevant to criticisms made by the users of this battery as well as reviewers. The user will find the test easier to administer since directions for each subtest are printed on the test booklet. The user also will find scoring facilitated by allowing the subjects to respond on either IBM cards or the conventional answer sheets. Responding on cards may also facilitate research, since it potentially makes the expensive process of key punching of test scores and item responses unnecessary.

In the technical report is included substantial evidence for the various kinds of validity and reliability required of a good test battery. Of special interest is the new information on predictive validity using grades in individual courses and the grade-point average as criteria. The data presented for predictive validity are based on many samples, each of which came from a single school and some of which apparently came from a single classroom. Only the zero-order correlations with the criterion are presented for each part of the battery. It is highly appropriate that such samples as these be used in validating a test since the user of this test is interested in distinguishing among individuals within such samples. However, since such samples of necessity are often small, the wide fluctuations that might be anticipated are observed in the reported validities.

Although no new normative data were ostensibly collected, the original samples of males and females were combined and norms based on both sexes are reported. Also, for each sample used in the validity study, means and standard deviations are reported; the user of this test may find useful normative information by examining these statistics from homogeneous samples.

Multiple correlations are not reported but they should be. A major justification for deriving several scores rather than one is that the proper weighting of several scores will result in better prediction than a single score. It is true that multiple correlations would be subject to even greater fluctuations than the zero-order correlations. However, not all the samples were small; several involved over 100 individuals and two involved over 300 individuals. Despite this, evidence for incremental validity of the separate parts of the test comes from two sources: a study (4) involving this battery at a junior college where individual course grades were predicted and multiple correlations were computed, and inspection of the relative values of the zero-order coefficients reported using various criteria and noting that they generally make sense.

Also included in the technical report are many figures depicting the relative performance of various occupational groups on the parts of the battery. It is stated that this presentation shows that occupational differences and differences in performance on the several parts of the battery within any one occupation make sense relative to the traits being measured. Since these data are not derived from random samples, the authors and publisher deserve commendation for not presenting them in tabular form and for presenting a minimum amount of scale information. Thereby they avoid inviting the user of the battery to use this information normatively.

Multiple Aptitude Tests

The guide to interpretation is excellent. It contains several case studies in which scores are interpreted in the context of other information. It contains abacs for testing significance of differences between points on a profile and discussion of procedures for using ancillary materials. Throughout this guide the reader is explicitly reminded of the fallibility of test scores and warned against common errors of interpretation.

Thus, in terms of content, analyses, and supplementary materials, this reviewer judges this battery to be excellent. Its utility is limited, however, in that only one form of the test is available. It would seem that scores in the numerical reasoning factor, in particular, would increase as a function of practice.

J Counsel Psychol 8:92 sp '61. Laurence Siegel. * The battery in its present form is the culmination of research by the senior author spanning a twenty-five year period. The fact that MAT was developed with extreme care rather than in haste is apparent throughout, and particularly in the excellent Technical Report. * Demonstrations of the validity of this battery are impressive. * may be used for studies of inter-individual or intra-individual differences. Analyses of the latter type should prove to be particularly valuable for counseling at the high school and early college levels. Users of the battery are provided with a separate publication concerning the interpretation of MAT scores. This helpful supplement to the Technical Report and Manual contains discussions and illustrations of the ways in which factor and test scores may be interpreted. There is always the danger that such a supplement may be used by unqualified persons who come to regard themselves as expert counselors by virtue of this short course in test interpretation. A kind of internal safeguard against this is provided by the level at which this supplement is written. It will seem like gibberish to persons who are only slightly familiar with test theory. Furthermore, it contains a discussion of the necessity for supplementing aptitude data with other kinds of evidence before attempting to counsel individual students.

For reviews by Ralph F. Berdie and Benjamin Fruchter of the original edition, see 5:613.

[777]

★**N.B. Aptitude Tests (Junior).** Standards 4–8; 1961–62; 12 scores: reasoning, classification, computations, spare parts, synonyms, squares, name comparison, figure perception, memory for names and faces, word fluency, coordination, writing speed; 1 form ['62, 32 pages, Afrikaans and English in 1 booklet]; manual ['62, 53 pages, 26 pages in Afrikaans and 26 in English]; separate answer sheets must be used; R8.21 per 100 tests; 14c per manual; postpaid; specimen set not available; 104(135) minutes in 3 sessions; National Bureau of Educational and Social Research. *

[778]

★**National Institute for Personnel Research High Level Battery.** Adults with at least 12 years of education; 1960–62; 4 tests in a single booklet: mental alertness, arithmetical problems, reading comprehension, vocabulary; 1 form ('60, 28 pages); no manual; mimeographed norms ('61–62, 7 pages); separate answer sheets must be used; R200 per 100 tests; R5 per 100 answer sheets; R2.25 per specimen set; postpaid; 117(130) minutes; National Institute for Personnel Research. *

REFERENCES

1. SCHEPERS, J. M. "A Components Analysis of a Complex Psychomotor Learning Task." *Psychologia Africana* 9:294–329 '62. * (*PA* 37:4314)

[779]

★**National Institute for Personnel Research Normal Battery.** Standards 6–10 and job applicants with 8–11 years of education; 1960–62; 5 tests in a single booklet: mental alertness, comprehension, vocabulary, spelling, computation; 1 form ['60, 30 pages]; no manual; mimeographed norms ('62, 5 pages); separate answer sheets must be used; R130 per 100 tests; R5 per 100 answer sheets; R1.50 per specimen set; postpaid; Afrikaans edition available; 115(140) minutes; National Institute for Personnel Research. *

[780]

*****SRA Primary Mental Abilities, Revised.** Grades kgn–1, 2–4, 4–6, 6–9, 9–12; 1946–63; previous edition (see 5:614) still available; earlier editions titled *Tests for Primary Mental Abilities* and *Chicago Tests of Primary Mental Abilities;* IBM for grades 4–12; 5 levels; no data on reliability and validity of present edition; postage extra; L. L. Thurstone (earlier editions) and Thelma Gwinn Thurstone; Science Research Associates, Inc. *

a) GRADES K–1. 5 scores: verbal meaning, perceptual speed, number facility, spatial relations, total; 1 form ('62, c1946–62, 24 pages); manual ('63, 31 pages); $3 per 20 tests; 50¢ per specimen set; (65–75) minutes in 2 sessions.

b) GRADES 2–4. 5 scores: same as for grades kgn–1; 1 form ('62, c1946–62, 32 pages); manual ('63, 39 pages); prices and time same as for grades kgn–1.

c) GRADES 4–6. 1946–63; 6 scores: same as for grades kgn–1 plus reasoning; IBM; 1 form ['63, 41 pages]; manual ('63, 46 pages); profile ('63, 2 pages); separate answer sheets must be used; $11 per 20 tests; $5 per 100 IBM scorable answer sheets; $1 per set of scoring stencils; 70¢ per 20 profiles; $1 per specimen set; 52(107) minutes.

d) GRADES 6–9. 5 scores: verbal meaning, number facility, reasoning, spatial relations, total; IBM; 1 form ('62, c1946–62, 24 pages); manual ('63, 40 pages); profile ('63, 2 pages); prices same as for grades 4–6; 35(75) minutes.

e) GRADES 9–12. 5 scores: same as for grades 6–9; IBM; 1 form ('62, c1946–62, 24 pages); manual ('63, 40 pages); profile ('63, 2 pages); prices same as for grades 4–6; 34(74) minutes.

REFERENCES

1–10. See 40:1427.
11–60. See 3:225.
61–102. See 4:716.
103–161. See 5:614.
162. CURETON, EDWARD E. "Service Tests of Multiple Aptitudes." *Proc Inv Conf Testing Probl* 1955:22–39 '56. * (*PA* 31:3017)
163. TAYLOR, PRESTON L. *A Study of the Relationship Between Intelligence as Measured by SRA Primary Mental Abilities Tests and Validity Scores on the Kuder Vocational Preference Record.* Master's thesis, Texas Southern University (Houston, Tex.), 1956.
164. ROWAN, T. C. "Psychological Tests and Selection of Computer Programmers." *J Assn Comput Mach* 4:348–53 Jl '57. *
165. STROTHER, CHARLES R.; SCHAIE, K. WARNER; AND HORST, PAUL. "The Relationship Between Advanced Age and Mental Abilities." *J Abn & Social Psychol* 55:166–70 S '57. * (*PA* 33:3294)
166. HUTTNER, LUDWIG, AND STENE, D. MIRIAM. "Foremen Selection in Light of a Theory of Supervision." *Personnel Psychol* 11:403–9 au '58. * (*PA* 33:11090)
167. KACZKOWSKI, HENRY R., AND CONNERY, THOMAS F. "PMA Factors as Predictors of High School Workshop Performance." *Psychol Newsl* 9:232–3 Jl–Ag '58. * (*PA* 33:4811)
168. LLOYD, CLAUDE J. *The Relationship Between the Scores Made by Pupils on the Primary Mental Abilities Test, the Metropolitan Achievement Reading Test, and the Kuhlmann-Anderson Intelligence Test.* Master's thesis, University of Southern California (Los Angeles, Calif.), 1958.
169. SCHAIE, K. WARNER. "Occupational Level and the Primary Mental Abilities." *J Ed Psychol* 49:299–303 D '58. * (*PA* 36:2LB99S)
170. SCHAIE, K. WARNER. "Rigidity-Flexibility and Intelligence: A Cross-Sectional Study of the Adult Life Span From 20 to 70 Years." *Psychol Monogr* 72(9):1–26 '58. * (*PA* 33:9923)
171. SMITH, D. D. "Abilities and Interests: 2, Validation of Factors." *Can J Psychol* 12:253–8 D '58. * (*PA* 33:9347)
172. TYLER, LEONA E. "The Stability of Patterns of Primary Mental Abilities Among Grade School Children." *Ed & Psychol Meas* 18:769–74 w '58. * (*PA* 34:2122)
173. WILSON, JOHN A. R. "Differences in Achievement Attributable to Different Educational Environments." *J Ed Res* 52:83–93 N '58. * (*PA* 33:10949)
174. CHAMBERS, JACK A. "Preliminary Screening Methods in the Identification of Intellectually Superior Children." *Excep Child* 26:145–50 N '59. * (*PA* 35:3249)
175. COLEMAN, JAMES C. "Perceptual Retardation in Reading Disability." *Percept & Motor Skills* 9:117 Je '59. *
176. EMM, M. ELOISE. *A Factorial Study of the Problem-Solving Ability of Fifth Grade Boys.* Catholic University of America, Educational Research Monograph, Vol. 22, No. 1. Washington, D.C.: Catholic University of America Press, April 1959. Pp. vi, 57. * (*PA* 35:672)
177. HARRIS, DALE B. "A Note on Some Ability Correlates of the Raven Progressive Matrices (1947) in the Kindergarten." *J Ed Psychol* 50:228–9 O '59. * (*PA* 36:1FE28H)
178. KELLY, E. LOWELL, AND GOLDBERG, LEWIS R. "Correlates of Later Performance and Specialization in Psychology: A Follow-Up Study of the Trainees Assessed in the VA Selection Research Project." *Psychol Monogr* 73(12):1–32 '59. * (*PA* 34:7952)
179. LORANGER, ARMAND W., AND MISIAK, HENRYK. "Critical Flicker Frequency and Some Intellectual Functions in Old Age." *J Gerontol* 14:323–7 Jl '59. * (*PA* 34:4153)
180. McTAGGART, HELEN PATRICIA. *A Factorial Study of the Problem-Solving Ability of Fifth-Grade Girls.* Washington, D.C.: Catholic University of America Press, 1959. Pp. viii, 27. *
181. RACKY, DONALD J. "Predictions of Ninth Grade Woodshop Performance From Aptitude and Interest Measures." *Ed & Psychol Meas* 19:629–36 w '59. * (*PA* 34:6572)
182. SCHAIE, K. WARNER. "Cross-Sectional Methods in the Study of Psychological Aspects of Aging." *J Gerontol* 14:208–15 Ap '59. * (*PA* 34:1144)
183. VANDENBERG, STEVEN G. "The Primary Mental Abilities of Chinese Students: A Comparative Study of the Stability of a Factor Structure." *Ann N Y Acad Sci* 79:257–304 O 31 '59. * (*PA* 35:3420; 36:3HD57V)
184. WILKINS, MURIEL F. *Is There a Schizophrenic Pattern on the PMA?* Master's thesis, University of Ottawa (Ottawa, Ont., Canada), 1959.
185. CHASE, CLINTON I. "The Position of Certain Variables in the Prediction of Problem-Solving in Arithmetic." *J Ed Res* 54:9–14 S '60. *
186. DURKIN, DOLORES. "A Case-Study Approach Toward an Identification of Factors Associated With Success and Failure in Learning to Read." *Calif J Ed Res* 11:26–33 Ja '60. * (*PA* 34:8336)
187. HARBILAS, JOHN N. *The Iowa Tests of Basic Skills and the SRA Primary Mental Abilities as Predictors of Success in Seventh Grade Science.* Master's thesis, Stetson University (DeLand, Fla.), 1960.
188. JACOBS, RONALD E. "A Comparison of Tests: The Primary Mental Abilities: The Pintner Mental Abilities: The California Test of Mental Abilities." *Sch Counselor* 8:12–8 O '60. *
189. LORANGER, ARMAND W., AND MISIAK, HENRYK. "The Performance of Aged Females on Five Non-Language Tests of Intellectual Functions." *J Clin Psychol* 16:189–91 Ap '60. * (*PA* 36:2FI89L)
190. MEYER, WILLIAM J. "The Stability of Patterns of Primary Mental Abilities Among Junior High and Senior High School Students." *Ed & Psychol Meas* 20:795–800 w '60. * (*PA* 35:3278)
191. SARASON, SEYMOUR B.; DAVIDSON, KENNETH S.; LIGHTHALL, FREDERICK K.; WAITE, RICHARD R.; AND RUEBUSH, BRITTON K. *Anxiety in Elementary School Children: A Report of Research*, pp. 136–47, 313–9. New York: John Wiley & Sons, Inc., 1960. Pp. viii, 351. * (*PA* 34:7494)
192. AVAKIAN, SONIA ASTRID. "An Investigation of Trait Relationships Among Six-Year-Old Children." *Genetic Psychol Monogr* 63:339–94 My '61. * (*PA* 36:1FF39A)
193. BURGESS, THOMAS C. "Retest Reliability of the Primary Mental Abilities Tests." *Psychol Rep* 9:678 D '61. *
194. CLARK, PHILIP J.; VANDENBERG, STEVEN G.; AND PROCTOR, CHARLES H. "On the Relationship of Scores on Certain Psychological Tests With a Number of Anthropometric Characters and Birth Order in Twins." *Hum Biol* 33:163–80 My '61. * (*PA* 36:3DP63C)
195. MEYER, WILLIAM J., AND BENDIG, A. W. "A Longitudinal Study of the Primary Mental Abilities Test." *J Ed Psychol* 52:50–60 F '61. * (*PA* 36:2HD50M)
196. SILVERSTEIN, A. B. "Test Anxiety and the Primary Mental Abilities." *Psychol Rep* 8:415–7 Je '61. * (*PA* 36:2HK15S)
197. CANISIA, M. "Mathematical Ability as Related to Reasoning and Use of Symbols." *Ed & Psychol Meas* 22:105–27 sp '62. * (*PA* 37:1212)
198. CLELAND, DONALD L., AND TOUSSAINT, ISABELLA H. "The Interrelationships of Reading, Listening, Arithmetic Computation and Intelligence." *Reading Teach* 15:228–31 Ja '62. *
199. DERRICK, MURIEL W., AND GODIN, MALCOLM A. "A Cross-Validation Study of a Diagnostic Pattern on the P.M.A." *Ont Hosp Psychol B* 8:13–5 D '62. *
200. DONALD, MERLIN W., AND LAGAN, ANTHONY E. "A Study of the Diagnostic Efficiency of a Schizophrenic Pattern on the PMA." *Ont Hosp Psychol B* 7:5–7 Ap '62. *
201. McFARLAND, ROBERT L.; NELSON, CHARLES L.; AND ROSSI, ASCANIO M. "Prediction of Participation in Group Psychotherapy From Measures of Intelligence and Verbal Behavior." *Psychol Rep* 11:291–8 Ag '62. * (*PA* 37:5190)
202. MEYERS, E.; ORPET, R. E.; ATTWELL, A. A.; AND DINGMAN, H. F. *Primary Abilities at Mental Age Six.* Monographs of the Society for Research in Child Development, Vol. 27, No. 1, Serial No. 82. Lafayette, Ind.: Child Development Publications, 1962. Pp. 40. * (*PA* 38:8462)
203. SUPER, DONALD E., AND CRITES, JOHN O. *Appraising Vocational Fitness by Means of Psychological Tests, Revised Edition*, pp. 129–38. New York: Harper & Brothers, 1962. Pp. xv, 688. * (*PA* 37:2038)
204. WAGNER, ROSE M. *A Study of the Long Range Predictive Value of Various Factors of the Primary Mental Abilities Test Given in Grade Five.* Master's thesis, University of Washington (Seattle, Wash.), 1962.
205. WILSON, JOHN A. R., AND STIER, LEALAND D. "Instability of Sub-Scores on Forms of SRA Primary Mental Ability Tests: Significance for Guidance." *Personnel & Guid J* 40:708–11 Ap '62. * (*PA* 37:1984)
206. BENDIG, A. W., AND MEYER, WILLIAM J. "The Factorial Structure of the Scales of the Primary Mental Abilities, Guilford Zimmerman Temperament Survey, and Kuder Preference Record." *J General Psychol* 68:195–201 Ap '63. * (*PA* 38:53)
207. CATTELL, RAYMOND B. "Theory of Fluid and Crystallized Intelligence: A Critical Experiment." *J Ed Psychol* 54:1–22 F '63. * (*PA* 37:7991)
208. CENTER, WILLIAM RUSSELL. *A Factor Analysis of Three Language and Communication Batteries.* Doctor's thesis, University of Georgia (Athens, Ga.), 1963. (*DA* 24:1918)
209. OSBURN, H. G., AND MELTON, R. S. "Prediction of Proficiency in a Modern and Traditional Course in Beginning Algebra." *Ed & Psychol Meas* 23:277–87 su '63. * (*PA* 38:1386)
210. SANDERS, RICHARD M. "The Use of Intelligence Tests." *J Ed Res* 56:500 My–Je '63. *
211. WHITE, HORTENSE G. "Typing Performance as Related to Mental Abilities and Interests: A Preliminary Study." *J Ed Res* 56:535–9 Jl–Ag '63. *

JOHN E. MILHOLLAND, *Professor of Psychology, The University of Michigan, Ann Arbor, Michigan.*

The 1953–54 edition of these tests had three levels: ages 5–7, 7–11, and 11–17. The 1962–63 edition has five levels identified by school grades rather than by age: K–1, 2–4, 4–6, 6–9, and 9–12. "The motor test has been dropped from the lowest level and the verbal fluency test from the highest. Verbal, number, and spatial scores are now provided for every level." There is a perceptual speed test in each of the K–1, 2–4, and 4–6 levels, and a reasoning test in the 4–6, 6–9, and 9–12 levels. Tests for the upper three levels are printed in reusable booklets suitable for use with separate answer sheets; the tests for the K–1 and 2–4 levels are printed in consumable booklets.

Five "primary mental abilities" labels are used to designate the subtests. The presence of and emphasis given to each of the abilities in the various levels reflect the judgment of the authors with respect to the relative importance of these abilities at the indicated grade levels.

Claims are still made for the differential utilities of the subtest scores. All of the examiners' manuals contain the statement "The profile of five primary mental abilities helps counselors and teachers to evaluate, understand, and interpret the often puzzling individual differences in behavior and performance among children who appear to be of comparable intelligence." The manual for the lowest level also contains the statement that "individual subtest scores provide a helpful index of [a child's] readiness for certain kinds of school tasks such as reading, writing, and arithmetic; they indicate the areas where he has the ability to learn most easily and those where he may need help." A similar statement is included in the manual for grades 2–4. In the case of the three upper level tests, the claims are made in a profile interpretation sheet that is intended to be given to pupils who take the test: "Looking at your high scores can give you an idea of the kind of school subjects you'll probably do best in. Verbal Meaning (V), for example, is particularly important in English, foreign languages, and social studies. Number Facility (N) is important in math." The advice is also given that a pupil making a total stanine score of 7 or above has an indication that he has "the mental ability to do well on college entrance examinations and to do good college work." Those with stanine scores of 5 or 6 may find it "difficult to gain admission to a highly selective college." Those with stanine scores below 4, however, and with school grades and other test scores generally low are advised that "it is somewhat doubtful that other factors could compensate sufficiently to enable you to do college-level work successfully."

There are two bases on which claims such as these may be substantiated. One is logical, that the verbal meaning factor *ought* to be important in English, foreign language, and social studies, the numerical factor important in math, etc. In this case the focus would be on how well the subtests were measuring the factors whose labels they carried. The only assurance we have that they are doing this is the similarity of the items to those originally used by Thurstone and the fact that an item was included in the tests only when three judges agreed on its appropriateness. A more convincing procedure would be a factor analysis of current PMA subtests along with the original ones.

The second basis for justification of the claims is empirical—the demonstration that persons with particular kinds of profiles do in fact perform better in the areas characterized by their high scores. Practically all the data here merely show that persons high in V, for example, do better in English than persons low in it, or that those high in N do better than those low in it in math. Such studies as these, even, are relatively rare, and their results are often inconclusive. None of them is described in the manuals.

In all the manuals the promise is made that a technical supplement will be available shortly, but as of this writing (January 1964) it has not been issued. Through the courtesy of the publishers I have, however, seen a preliminary draft of portions of it. In a section on how to use the test results, the following statement appears: "The validity studies make it possible to form some judgments about the newly revised PMA scores in factors that most affect achievement in various courses." The discussion goes on to point out that verbal meaning is necessary to almost all school subjects and has generally been found most highly related to achievement in almost all academic courses. Reasoning is also highly related to achievement. The relationship of spatial relations to drafting, geometry, and trigonometry is probably significant and number facility appears to be most useful in predicting arithmetic grades. Perceptual speed is considered to be important in the early grades in areas where a child is beginning to learn symbols such as letters, words, and numbers. The support for this conclusion is found in the validity studies in the lower grades, where perceptual speed correlates about as well with reading grades as verbal meaning does. Some appropriate cautions are given about the likelihood of different results under different situations and the danger of relying too much on a single test score. The only data presented in this section are from a study of reading readiness carried out on a sample of 377 pupils who took the PMA K–1 and who 13 months later were given the *SRA Achievement Series: Reading.* The results show a satisfactory but, of course, not unexpected relationship between total PMA scores and the reading test scores. There is no treatment whatever of subtest validities.

There is, however, a separate section of the technical supplement devoted to validity. Here the same reading readiness study is referred to and subtest correlations are given. The conclusion is "the single PMA total score was an effective predictor of reading scores." An inspection of the correlations themselves confirms the lack of differential validity for the separate PMA scores.

Data are also presented showing the correlation between PMA subtest and total scores and elementary and high school grades in various subjects. Three elementary schools and one high school were used. In the elementary schools there were only two exceptions (Reasoning versus reading and Reasoning versus language arts —both in the same school) to the superiority of total score over any subtest for predicting grades in the separate subjects. The median subtest–subject grade correlation was .45; the median total score-grade correlation was .59. In the high school, the subtests showed up a little better, although the validities were generally too low (−.18 to .39, median .22) to be of much use in prediction. It makes some sense, however, that the numerical and reasoning subtests should correlate highest of the five subtests with grades in college preparatory mathematics (.30 and .29) and in science (.23 and .24) and that the reasoning and verbal subtests should be the best predictors of English (.37 and .39) and of social studies (.35 and .27).

The median correlation of total scores with high school subject grades was .22.

It does not seem to me that the correlations of subtests with grades in various subjects shed much light on the soundness of the rationale for saying that different primary mental abilities are required for different subjects. The research that would demonstrate the utility of PMA profiles for counseling has not been done yet. In the meantime, counselors would be well advised to follow leads furnished by such things as interest and background in advising students to enter certain lines of work. Scores on the PMA subtests might provide only some inkling of areas that might be worthwhile to explore. The evidence in the preliminary draft of the technical supplement (and other studies done in the past) provides no justification for reporting separate PMA scores in elementary school. If the correlation is taken as a measure, the total score gives more information about any subject than the primary mental ability score supposedly most relevant for it. Probably the most useful kind of multiscore test for elementary school is one that provides just a verbal and a nonverbal measure.

The draft of the technical supplement also contains a section on reliability. Data presented there meet the criticism of earlier reviewers of the tests, that because of speededness internal consistency estimates of reliability were too high and should be replaced by test-retest estimates. A test-retest study was done in the public schools of Goldsboro, North Carolina. The verbal subtest showed up best, with reliabilities varying from .73 to .93 in the different grades and IQ standard errors of measurement for the different test *levels* going from 4.14 to 6.01. The perceptual speed subtest was poorest, with reliabilities from .51 to .81 and standard errors from 5.29 to 9.42, the latter in the K–1 level, where perceptual speed is thought to be particularly important. Total score single grade reliabilities go from .84 to .94; level standard errors from 3.65 to 4.56. Total score reliability, at least, is satisfactory.

Although the supplement is sprinkled with admonitions urging caution, the following statement also appears: "The subtests are often used for differential diagnostic and predictive purposes." In furtherance of this practice, tables of reliabilities and standard errors of difference scores are given. An interesting feature is a set of tables which are supposed to give the probabilities that differences of 10 or 20 IQ points are due to true score differences rather than to error. The technique for determining the probabilities is not explained, and I suspect a faulty rationale. It is true that the probabilities of differences of 10 or 20 points due to error can be calculated, but the complements of these are the probabilities that errors will be less than 10 or 20 points, not that the 10 or 20 point differences are due to true score differences.

If even as rudimentary a technical supplement as I examined is published, it will represent at least a small step toward psychometric respectability on the part of those responsible for PMA. They still have a long way to go before they come up to levels already reached by a number of the better test producers on the scene today. Carrying out the research and development necessary to meet technical standards is a costly process, and the producers of PMA may regard it as prohibitively expensive.

For reviews by Norman Frederiksen and Albert K. Kurtz of the previous edition, see 5:614; for reviews by Anne Anastasi, Ralph F. Berdie, John B. Carroll, Stuart A. Courtis, and P. E. Vernon, see 4:716; for reviews by Cyril Burt, Florence L. Goodenough, James R. Hobson, and F. L. Wells of an earlier edition, see 3:225 and 3:264; for reviews by Henry E. Garrett, Truman L. Kelley, C. Spearman, Godfrey H. Thomson, and Robert C. Tryon, see 40:1427 (3 excerpts); for excerpts from related book reviews, see 40:B1099 and 38:B503.

[781]

★**Vocational Guidance Program.** Grades 10–16; 1947–62; a battery of aptitude and personality tests; except for modification noted in *a* below, two title changes, and directions for all tests, tests *a–h* are identical with corresponding tests of the *Factored Aptitude Series* (1947–57) which are also used in the *Job-Tests Program;* tests *i* and *j* are identical, except for directions, with two other tests of the *Job-Tests Program;* 1 form; 10 tests ('62, 3 pages except *h*, 4 pages) used in various combinations for different job areas; 4 bulletins serve as manual and interpretive materials: bulletin 1 ['62, 4 pages], how program operates, bulletin 2 ['62, 4 pages], job fields checklist for students, bulletin 3 ['62, 2 pages], directions for administering and scoring, bulletin 4 ('62, 4 pages), job qualification profiles; no data on reliability and validity presented with tests (data based on use of the corresponding tests in the *Job-Tests Program* available on request); norms, based on employees, the same as those reported with the *Job-Tests Program;* separate answer sheets must be used (except with *h*); $2 per 20 copies of any one test except *h*; $1 per 20 copies of *h*; $2 per 20 self-mark-ing answer sheets; 75¢ per 20 copies of either bulletin 2 or bulletin 4; $2 per "manual" consisting of all 4 bulletins, single copies of each test, and 4 answer sheets; postage extra; 7(10) minutes per test except for *h–j*; Joseph E. King; Industrial Psychology, Inc. *

a) BUSINESS TERMS. A combination of items (two-thirds of them with revised option order) from *Sales Terms* and *Office Terms* of the *Factored Aptitude Series.*

b) SYSTEMS. Identical with *Numbers* test of the *Factored Aptitude Series.*

c) PERCEPTION.

d) JUDGMENT.

e) TOOLS.

f) PRECISION.

g) PARTS.

h) DEXTERITY. 3(10) minutes.

i) CPF. A special printing of *IPAT Contact Personality Factor Test* (see 123); (5–10) minutes.

j) NPF. A special printing of *IPAT Neurotic Personality Factor Test* (see 5:74); (5–10) minutes.

LEO GOLDMAN, *Associate Professor of Education, Brooklyn College, Brooklyn, New York.*

Except for directions, title changes, and a modification of one test, this battery of tests is identical to those in the *Job-Tests Program*, a battery developed for industrial selection. The tests themselves seem, like their predecessors, to be for the most part well constructed, both in their items and in the mechanics of administration and scoring. Since the parent tests have been used in industry for some 16 years, they could provide a good foundation for vocational guidance testing in high schools.

There is, however, almost none of the evidence that one would require before using these adult selection tests in counseling with high school students. There are, for example, no high school norms; there is only the statement in Bulletin 1 that "The psychological factors measured by the tests mature by age 16 or 17, and rarely change after that. Thus, what the student ranks when you test him at 16, is what he will be for the rest of his life." Anyone who has taken even a first measurement course should be able to recognize the illogic of that statement and the absurdity of its conclusion.

Furthermore, one might ask for validity studies based on a follow-up of high school students into jobs. These would be especially necessary with those tests, such as Business Terms and Perception, which are most sensitive to experience on related jobs. All that is offered is a group of reprints and summaries of validity studies done in industry. These do not suffice. These earlier studies bear little enough evidence of the usefulness for industrial selection of the parent series. There is even less evidence to support the vocational guidance interpretations which are now suggested. The Job Qualification tables, for example, show desirable profiles for each of 24 job fields but nowhere does one find either a rationale or documentary evidence to support these tables.

One would expect information about the reliability of these tests with high school students. Nothing is presented except a summary of the earlier reliability studies, presumably done with adults during the initial standardization of these tests. Even those data are inadequately reported (lacking description of the samples used). For what they are worth, the retest correlations range from .79 to .91, with the median being .83. Although these are impressive reliability correlations for seven-minute tests, they are below the level expected for counseling use.

We can guess that one of the adaptations which the author made for the application of these tests to vocational guidance students is a table (Bulletin 3) which tells how to obtain an IQ for Business Terms and Judgment (one IQ for each), and a nonlanguage IQ for Parts. This is quite a tour de force when one realizes that Business Terms is merely a business vocabulary test, Judgment a letter and number series reasoning test, and Parts a spatial visualization test. There is no explanation of the derivation of these IQ's, nor any rationale for their use. And, oh yes, the IQ table classifies IQ's of 130 and up as genius!

The sparsity of research on norms, reliability, validity, and all the other standardization topics has not prevented the author and publisher from making some of the most naïve and unfounded claims this reviewer has seen in a long time. They report, for example, that "Averaging the Judgment and Parts test ranks gives an index of the student's creative thinking or research ability." These, remember, are a test of letter and number series reasoning, and a test of spatial visualization, respectively!

Elsewhere one is told that validity correlations of .26 to .39 permit a "definite prediction of job performance, and thus [the] test can differentiate applicants who will become good vs. poor performers." Furthermore, validity coefficients from .40 to .55 permit "excellent prediction of job performance." Although recognizing with the author that validity correlations higher than .55 are rare, one doesn't conclude that therefore the best coefficients available provide "excellent predictions."

One could cite many more such unwarranted claims, oversimplifications, and violations of basic principles of measurement. The flaws of the original tests have been multiplied in this so-called adaptation for guidance use. The "manual" for the *Vocational Guidance Program* is not a manual at all, but a grab-bag: except for the instructions for test selection, administration, scoring, and interpretation, there is only a collection of unbound summaries and reprints of studies done with the parent series.

These tests were judged by earlier reviewers to be inadequate for industrial selection applications. They are even less adequate for guidance use. Practically all of the modern multifactor batteries are far superior to this one. This battery is not ready for guidance use in schools, or anyplace else, for that matter.

For reviews by William H. Helme and Stanley I. Rubin of the Job-Tests Program, *see 774; for a review by Harold P. Bechtoldt of the* Factored Aptitude Series, *see 5:602; for a review by D. Welty Lefever of an earlier edition of the* Factored Aptitude Series, *see 4:712 (one excerpt); for reviews of the personality tests, see 174, 5:71, 5:74, 5:112, and 4:87.*

[Other Tests]

For tests not listed above, see the following entries in *Tests in Print:* 1368–9, 1378, and 1380; out of print: 1370, 1374, and 1385–6.

VOCATIONS — SIXTH MMY

REVIEWS BY *E. Anstey, Alexander W. Astin, Richard S. Barrett, Ralph F. Berdie, Arthur H. Brayfield, David P. Campbell, Joel T. Campbell, John O. Crites, Jerome E. Doppelt, Philip H. DuBois, Marvin D. Dunnette, Robert L. Ebel, Leonard W. Ferguson, John P. Foley, Jr., John W. French, Edward J. Furst, Leo Goldman, L. V. Gordon, Milton E. Hahn, John K. Hemphill, David O. Herman, John R. Hills, Kenneth B. Hoyt, Stephen Hunka, C. E. Jurgensen, Martin Katz, Raymond A. Katzell, William E. Kendall, Willard A. Kerr, Wayne K. Kirchner, Philip H. Kriedt, Albert K. Kurtz, Seymour Levy, Arthur C. MacKinney, Samuel T. Mayo, Richard S. Melton, Philip R. Merrifield, Joseph E. Moore, Warren T. Norman, William A. Owens, Jean Maier Palormo, Lyman W. Porter, Ray G. Price, Paul F. Ross, Douglas G. Schultz, D. H. Schuster, Benjamin Shimberg, I. Macfarlane Smith, Harry L. Stein, Donald E. Super, Paul W. Thayer, Albert S. Thompson, Leona E. Tyler, and Charles F. Warnath.*

[1023]

★**Airman Qualifying Examination.** Grade 12 (including girls); 1946–63; successor to *Airman Classification Battery;* test administered at high schools by United States Air Force personnel at any time (arrangements for test administration may be made through local United States Air Force Recruiting Office); 4 aptitude scores: electronic, mechanic, general, administrative; IBM; Form AF PRT 15 ('63, 36 pages); supervisor's manual ('62, 18 pages); descriptive booklet ['63, 13 pages]; comparison chart ['63, 1 sheet]; no charge for testing and reporting of scores to high school counselors; postpaid; 120(150) minutes; Air Force Personnel Research Laboratory; Headquarters, United States Air Force Recruiting Service (ATC). *

REFERENCES

1. RUSSO, J. ROBERT. "Two Governmental Sources for Aptitude Testing." *Sch Counselor* 9:140–1 My '62. *

[1024]

★**[Aptitude Inventory.]** Employee applicants; 1957–63; 1 test ('57, 4 pages) published in the same form under 3 titles; 4 scores for each test: intelligent job performance, leadership behavior, proper job attitudes, relations with others; manual ('61, 11 pages); no data on reliability based on present scoring keys; $35 per 100 tests; $1 per specimen set; postpaid; [15–20] minutes; John C. Denton; Psychological Business Research. *

a) MANAGEMENT APTITUDE INVENTORY. Applicants for management and supervisory positions; 1957–61.
b) EMPLOYMENT APTITUDE INVENTORY. Applicants for office and factory positions; 1957–61.
c) SALES APTITUDE INVENTORY. Applicants for sales positions; 1957–63; supplementary norms ['63, 1 page].

REFERENCES

1. DENTON, J. C. "Validity Information Exchange, No. 16-05: D.O.T. Code: Business Forms Salesman." *Personnel Psychol* 16:283–8 au '63. *

LEONARD W. FERGUSON, *Program Director, Research Division, Life Insurance Agency Management Association, Hartford, Connecticut.*

This test consists of 98 items. Fifty of them are in Section 1: "Which phrase [out of two] is more like you?" Twenty-five items are in Section 2: "Which phrase [out of two] would you like better?" Twenty-three items are in Section 3: "Mark 'Y' (Yes) if the phrase describes you; Mark 'N' (No) if it does *not*."

According to the author, items in the test were derived from merit rating studies and, except for the fact that they are worded in the first person singular, are almost "verbatim" descriptions of good and poor performance as described by top management personnel in several companies. Under each of the three titles in which the test appears (*Employment Aptitude Inventory, Sales Aptitude Inventory,* and *Management Aptitude Inventory*), the purpose is to measure "four factors important to success on the job." According to the author, these four factors are: (*a*) Intelligent Job Performance, "the degree to which the individual's job behavior is alert, open-minded, mature in judgment, and analytical"; (*b*) Leadership Behavior, "the ability to gain respect, motivate associates and lead a group"; (*c*) Proper Job Attitudes, "willingness to work hard to get ahead; ambition and determination"; and (*d*) Relations with Others, "getting along well, tolerant, not critical." In the order just named, the number of items in each factor scale is 25, 28, 24, and 24. Only three items are utilized in more than one scale. Two of these items are common to the last two scales; the other item is common to the first two scales. On each scale, the score is the number of "right" answers. A table permits the conversion of each score into a percentile rank.

Validity data supplied in the manual are as follows: (*a*) Correlations with "a combined ranking from judgments made independently by the company president and executive vice president" for 31 managers and executives in a midwestern plastics manufacturing company. The coefficients reported are .03, .51, .28, and −.22 for each of the scales in the order named above. (*b*) Correlations with "an overall ranking obtained from the Sales Personnel Manager," for 27 men who had entered a training program two years before the ranking was ob-

tained. The coefficients obtained were −.36, .43, .44, and −.06. (*c*) Correlations with an initial two-way classification of "potential for success" at the start of the training program mentioned above. Coefficients (biserial, apparently) were −.08, .20, .33, and .10. According to the author, "the 'true' validities" lie somewhere between the second and third sets of coefficients. Accepting the author at his word, and splitting the difference, this would make the "true" validities −.22, .32, .38, and .02.

At best, these validites have dubious meaning. The two highest coefficients, .32 and .38, *may* indicate that the scales concerned have a useful, practical, predictive validity in the sense that the scores yield results in the same direction as a supervisor's more general observation and rating. But, even if this be the case, in no sense do the coefficients validate the claim that the variables in question are, in fact, Leadership Behavior and Proper Job Attitudes. Conversely, the negative correlation of −.22 and the near-zero correlation of .02 do not indicate that the corresponding scales do *not* measure Intelligent Job Performance and Relations With Others. They merely indicate *lack* of relation between whatever variables are involved and overall ratings of job success as these overall ratings were secured in the author's studies.

On the basis of a factor analysis of the intercorrelations among merit rating items for 216 sales managers and salesmen, the author found the following intercorrelations among the four factors that his later scales were designed to measure: Between *a* and *b*, .69; *a* and *c*, .70; *a* and *d*, .55; *b* and *c*, .68; *b* and *d*, .64; *c* and *d*, .50. On a "pre-publication model" of the aptitude inventory, when "approximately" 400 individuals rated themselves, the corresponding correlations were as follows: .21, −.14, −.23, −.06, −.03, and −.40. In order "to change....the generally negative matrix of intercorrelations....to more positive values," the author conducted item analyses on two samples of 100 "typical professional and managerial people." He also increased the number of items in each scale and modified the scoring keys. He then obtained corresponding intercorrelations as follows: .13, −.14, −.26, .17, .02, and −.23. In view of these results, it is difficult to accept the author's implied claim that the factors measured by his inventory are the same as those isolated by his factor analysis of intercorrelations among merit items utilized by supervisory personnel.

For five groups of workers (one group of salesmen, three groups of factory workers, and one group of factory foremen), the author reports 20 validity coefficients. These range from −.44 to .38, and have a median value of .07. Cases in each group ranged from 22 to 38. For Intelligent Job Performance, these coefficients range from −.44 to .25 and have a median value of +.10. For Leadership Behavior, the coefficients range from −.24 to .37 and have a median value of +.20. For Proper Job Attitudes, the coefficients range from −.17 to .38 and have a median value of .03. For Relations With Others, the coefficients range from −.27 to .13 and have a median value of −.14. From the standpoint of correlations with overall job success, the most satisfactory scales are Leadership Behavior and Proper Job Attitudes. But, whether these scales measure that which their respective names imply, is an open question, as was indicated above. In a release dated April 5, 1963, the author states that "enough data are available for the *Sales Aptitude Inventory* that one would not begin with the hypothesis that the true population validities are zero." In view of the data presented by the author, one wonders: "Why not?"

C. E. JURGENSEN, *Assistant Vice President, Personnel, Minneapolis Gas Company, Minneapolis, Minnesota.*

The test consists of 98 items: 50 pairs in forced-choice format in which the applicant is to indicate which item in each pair is more like him, 25 pairs to be responded to on the basis of which item in each pair is preferred, and 23 phrases to be checked as self-descriptive or nondescriptive. These self ratings are scored on four dimensions similar to those found by other investigators to emerge from factor analyses of supervisory descriptions of good and poor employees.

Most of the data in the manual on validity and reliability come from background research studies and a prepublication model of the inventory. Such data, of course, are of little value in evaluating the present test form which was changed from the prepublication model by increasing the number of items in each of the four keys, editing the questions, changing pair-

ing of phrases, and revising the scoring keys. These changes were based on item analyses conducted on two samples of 100 cases. This is an exceedingly small *n* for item analyses of this type, and it is possible that the revised test is actually inferior to the earlier form.

Although four years elapsed between publication of the test (1957) and the mimeographed manual (1961), evidence of the effectiveness of the published test is meager. Although the author states that citing specific information concerning the many studies on the inventory would be prohibitive, the selected evidence he gives is based on five situations wherein the *n*'s ranged from 22 to 38 and validity coefficients ranged from −.44 to +.38. Validities of this magnitude and based on *n*'s of this size cannot seriously be taken as evidence of test effectiveness. The manual also includes testimonial-type statements such as business managers expressing considerable confidence in the inventory, a sales manager refusing to hire a salesman unless he exceeds an established minimum score, and the management team of a manufacturing company being strengthened successfully and materially largely by the use of the inventories. As is well known, testimonials of this type frequently are not supported by objective evidence.

Test-retest reliabilities for 113 college students over a two-week period ranged from .61 to .66. Many test experts will not agree with the author that reliabilities of this magnitude are acceptable. The author points out that a composite score based on the sum of the scores on two of the scales has reliability of .80 for the students, and suggests use of a composite score in practical situations. However, this is inconsistent with norms, which are limited to the four single scales. It is also inconsistent with the author's emphasis on the *pattern* of abilities, and with his emphasis on the scale Proper Job Attitudes as the best single predictor of future sales volume.

One reason for low reliability is the narrow range of obtained scores. A difference of a single point can raise the score as much as 20 percentile points, and a change in 10 raw score points is enough or more than enough to raise the score from the 5th to the 95th percentile in each of the four dimensions.

In addition to data given in the manual, the test author supplied the reviewer with a mimeographed report of a study conducted by the test author in 1963. It is based on 68 salesmen and 35 sales trainees, and includes a total of 24 validity coefficients ranging from −.11 to .47, nine of the coefficients being negative. Instead of giving data on their significance, the author states: "A significance test for these validities is an irrelevant procedure. Enough data are available for the *Sales Aptitude Inventory* that one would not begin with the hypothesis that the true population validities are zero." Statisticians are likely to raise their eyebrows and smile, for such coefficients are typical of those obtained when the true validity is zero.

In summary, there appears to be little reason to recommend this test. Sales-like generalities regarding the value of the test are neither relevant nor backed up by data given in the manual or in a supplementary study. Sophisticated test users are not likely even to consider seriously use of a test for which so little and so unfavorable data are available so many years after publication.

J Counsel Psychol 6:319–20 w '59. Laurence Siegel. * This is, at its present stage of development, an inadequate instrument accompanied by a somewhat irksome manual [the 1958 preliminary manual]. The reviewer offers this opinion with full realization of the necessity for phrasing manuals for potential industrial clients in an abbreviated fashion and with a minimum of statistical jargon. There is, however, no excuse for misleading generalizations like the following: "Psychology has....run into some confusion factors in the study of leadership. * A systematic approach to most problems is conspicuously absent." * Specific validities for the published MAI are not given in the manual. Two multiple correlations supportive of predictive validity using the two most valid subscales as predictors of managerial ratings are cited, however, for the prepublication version of the test. It is a moot question whether these coefficients indicate anything about the validity of the MAI as a measure of managerial aptitude. This validation procedure seems merely to indicate that it is possible for persons to describe themselves in a way that corresponds with the descriptions of them made by managerial raters. There is an element of circularity in this type of vali-

dation. Perhaps the gravest deficiency of the MAI is inadequate norming. * The....Inventory is supposed to predict success of managerial and sales applicants. Perhaps it does. The presently available normative and validity data, however, prohibit its use without extensive research within each company wishing to try it out. It is, at its present stage of development, valueless as an instrument for use by high school and college counselors.

[1025]

★**ETSA Tests.** Job applicants; 1960, c1957–60; formerly called *Aptitests;* Form A ('60, c1957–59); 8 tests (4 pages except Test 1A, 3 pages); manual ['60, 23 pages]; norms booklet ('60, 19 pages); publisher recommends use of Tests 1A, 8A, and one other; $20 per 10 copies of Tests 1A, 8A, and any one other; $7 per 10 copies of any one tests; $2 per manual; $5 per specimen set; 50¢ per norms booklet; $1.50 per 12 application-record folders ('60); 15¢ per single copy; postpaid; S. Trevor Hadley, George A. W. Stouffer, Jr., and the Psychological Services Bureau of Indiana, Pa.; Educators'-Employers' Tests & Services Associates. *

a) ETSA TEST 1A, GENERAL MENTAL ABILITY TEST. (45) minutes.

b) ETSA TEST 2A, OFFICE ARITHMETIC TEST. 40(45) minutes.

c) ETSA TEST 3A, GENERAL CLERICAL ABILITY TEST. 20(25) minutes.

d) ETSA TEST 4A, STENOGRAPHIC SKILLS TEST. (45) minutes.

e) ETSA TEST 5A, MECHANICAL FAMILIARITY TEST Validity data for males only; (60) minutes.

f) ETSA TEST 6A, MECHANICAL KNOWLEDGE TEST. Validity data and norms for males only; (90) minutes.

g) ETSA TEST 7A, SALES APTITUDE TEST. 8 scores: sales judgment, interest in selling, personality factors, occupational identification, level of aspiration, insight into human nature, awareness of sales approach, total; no data on reliability of part scores; (60) minutes.

h) ETSA TEST 8A, PERSONAL ADJUSTABILITY TEST. 8 scores: community spirit, attitude toward cooperation, attitude toward health, attitude toward authority, nervous tendencies, leadership, job stability, total; no data on reliability of part scores; (60) minutes.

MARVIN D. DUNNETTE, *Professor of Psychology, University of Minnesota, Minneapolis, Minnesota.*

According to the manual, the *ETSA Tests* are classified as Level A instruments, available to any company official in charge of a personnel function. It seems unwise to include the Sales Aptitude Test and the Personal Adjustability Test in the A classification. They are obviously intended to assess interest and personality factors and their proper interpretation probably requires a greater amount of professional knowledge than would be possessed by the typical company personnel officer.

The tests are rather lengthy, requiring administration times ranging from 20 minutes for the General Clerical Ability Test to 90 minutes for the Mechanical Knowledge Test. According to the manual, however, "To measure all the important factors which indicate capable or incapable personnel, ETSA recommends that each testee be given test 1-A and the appropriate test or tests selected from 2-A through 7-A, depending on the requirements of the job under consideration. Test 8-A should also be given when the person's personality is important in your consideration."

The manual is primarily an administrator's manual as well as a sales package apparently designed to convince the typical businessman that the tests will solve many of his firm's personnel ills and that they are easily administered and readily interpreted by following the simple guidelines offered by the authors. Although no norms are offered in the manual, the score distributions for each of the tests are grouped into ranges and assigned the descriptive labels (from low to high) of poor, questionable, average, good, and excellent. For each of the categories, brief descriptive paragraphs are provided to facilitate easy interpretation of an examinee's scores. This grouping of scores for interpretation seems wise for it should help to overcome the common tendency among unsophisticated users to overinterpret the seemingly fine gradations among examinees shown by the raw score distributions. The manual offers *no* information concerning reliability or validity and gives *no* descriptions of the development of the tests nor of the groups on which they were normed. Thus, if one were to judge the relative merits of the *ETSA Tests* solely on the basis of evidence from the manual, one's conclusions would be unalterably negative.

Fortunately, however, the authors have published a comprehensive technical supplement to the manual entitled "The ETSA Tests Hand Book of Norms." In marked contrast to the test manual, the handbook does *not* give the reader the feeling that the authors are trying to pull the wool over his eyes. Quite to the contrary—one learns that the item content of the tests is based on careful content analyses of standard textbooks in a variety of fields and on interviewing experience with a large number of applicants. The tests have been extensively item analyzed, and reliabilities and validities have been estimated in a variety of situations and on many different groups of subjects. Although an impressive number of validity studies is reported for each of the tests, for the most part the studies have not been done in industrial settings; instead, the groups consist rather often of students enrolled in business courses and the criteria are instructor ratings. Even so, the validity coefficients are generally rather good (ranging in the .40's and .50's) and a sufficient number of industrial validations are reported to give the user confidence in the potential utility of the tests as aids in making industrial personnel decisions.

The Handbook of Norms serves most importantly, however, as a demonstration of the competence and research mindedness of the test authors. The tests appear to have been systematically and seriously constructed, and a continuing program of research appears to be underway. From this laudatory pattern of past behavior, a continuing accumulation of research studies and additional validity information can be expected in future editions of the technical supplement to the manual.

In summary, the *ETSA Tests* appear to have a good deal of merit for industrial use. Ideally, however, the buyer and user should be one who has the training to conduct individual validity studies in his own firm. I personally believe that the sales pitch of the test manual should be "toned down" and that the technical information from the supplement should be incorporated into it. On the other hand, the authors have developed what appear to be rather good tests and they have done more thorough research on them than is typical. Thus, their sins of omission in the test manual may be more excusable than would usually be the case.

RAYMOND A. KATZELL, *Professor of Psychology and Head of the Department, New York University, New York, New York.*

These eight tests are printed clearly on paper of good quality, and possess reasonably high reported reliability and face validity. This reviewer finds little else to commend them.

CONTENT. The manual advises that a battery be selected for each job, composed of the Personal Adjustability Test, the General Mental Ability Test, and one or more others corresponding to the type of job, i.e., clerical, mechanical, or sales. Why the first should be universally recommended is not clear, since it is a specimen of personality inventory which, as a class, has not been found predictive of job performance, save possibly in the sales category.

There is little evidence that psychometrically rigorous procedures were followed in the construction of the individual tests. In content, each is mostly a rehash of the kinds of items in one or more preexisting tests. For example, the General Mental Ability Test comprises vocabulary, number progressions, and general information; the General Clerical Ability Test contains short sections on alphabetizing, number matching, name matching, spelling, office vocabulary and mailing information; and so on for the other tests. Among the few out of the ordinary parts is one in the Personal Adjustability Test purporting to measure "attitude toward cooperation." Typical of the 15 items in this section is: "The government should promise everyone a decent job." A response of agreement to such an item counts toward being considered a "poor risk" for employment. Grave questions exist concerning the use to which such information might be put by a psychometrically and morally obtuse employment official.

VALIDITY. The foregoing observations might be considered as cavil were there substantial evidence of concurrent or predictive validity for the battery or its individual tests. However, only a few validity data are reported, and these are often on students rather than on employed samples such as those for which the tests are intended. In several instances, the major evidence for validity of the aptitude tests rests on the tenuous basis of a difference in the distributions of scores of an occupationally experienced and an inexperienced sample; this type of evidence is further weakened by the absence of indications that the contrasted samples were otherwise comparable. In other instances, the only evidence of validity lies in the correlation of ETSA tests with well known ones; examples include the correlations of the General Mental Abilities Test with the *American Council on Education Psychological Examination* $(r = .68)$ and with the *Otis Employment Test* $(r = .78)$, and the correlation of the Personal Adjustability Test with the *California Test of Personality* $(r = .72)$. This type of validity evidence inevitably raises the question of why we are supposed to use the new test rather than the other, but no answer is suggested in the present case.

Only for the Sales Aptitude Test are data furnished comparing the test with an external criterion of success in employed samples. In two small samples, correlations between the test and employers' rankings turned out to be .71 and .82; in two other samples, the test correlated with salesmen's salaries to the extent of .72 and .61. These concurrent validity coefficients are surprisingly high, considering both the results of other test research on salesmen and the fact that these coefficients are in the neighborhood of the test's reliability (the corrected split-half correlation in a sample of salesmen is reported as .77). Indeed, so amazing are these results that it behooves us to suspend judgment on their generality until other investigations have been reported.

In view of the nature and extent of the evidence reported, this reviewer remains unconvinced of the validity of these tests in terms of their power to correlate appreciably with criteria of job performance.

MANUAL AND NORMS. What is usually contained in a single manual is here organized into two pamphlets. The test manual briefly introduces the nature of the battery, gives instructions on administration and scoring, and outlines a cookbook guide to interpreting the test results. The Handbook of Norms furnishes rather sketchy information on the construction and standardization of the tests. Reactions to its reports of construction, reliability, and validity have already been noted. There remains the need to comment on its normative and interpretative sections.

The only statistical norms provided for each test are the mean and standard deviation of a vaguely defined sample of between 200 and 400 adults ($n = 860$, and is better defined, in the case of Test 8A). The reason for this, we are told, is that "norms are unimportant" for the kinds of tests and uses offered. This curious position seems to be based on two arguments. One is that norms (e.g., percentile ranks) which permit an interpretation of the relative status of an individual score are statistically more fallible than those (e.g., fifths) which produce grosser categorizations. The other is that general norms are not useful when one is mainly interested in selecting the better candidates from a local pool of job applicants.

ETSA Tests

Each of these arguments is, of course, erroneous. Therefore so is the failure to develop and report adequate normative data. The manual proceeds to subdivide the range of raw scores on each test into five categories, ranging from "Poor" to "Excellent," apparently quite oblivious to its own argument that local experience should supersede general guidelines. To make matters worse, if any empirical foundations exist for this categorization, they are not made explicit. We are in effect expected to take on faith the assertion that a person, say, who scores below 66 on the Personal Adjustability Test is a "poor risk" for employment, whereas one who scores above 96 is an "excellent risk."

In addition to technical deficiencies, the manual and handbook are equivocal about the value and utility of these tests. On the one hand, we are reminded every so often that they have yet to be thoroughly investigated and tested. But at other points the prospective consumer is also assured that the "ETSA Tests are a proven series of aptitude tests" which "provide scientifically accurate facts on which to base your hiring, placing, and promoting decisions." The mailing piece and order form addressed to personnel managers further expostulates: "Reduce Hiring Costs—Stop Expensive Personnel Turnover—Wasted Training—Don't Guess—Test!!" This is surely a tone more in keeping with the huckstering of nostrums than with the dissemination of scientific devices.

SUMMARY. *Caveat emptor!*

[1026]

★**General Adaptability Battery.** Illiterate and semiliterate job applicants; 1949–58; tests administered at centers established by firms employing the publisher's consulting and training services; 2 batteries; manual ('58, 166 pages, largely mimeographed); no data on reliability and validity in manual; instructions provided in several languages; test materials may be constructed locally or purchased from the publisher at a cost of R40–R50 per set of materials for testing one candidate; R2 per manual; training courses, assistance in setting up testing centers, and local norms service available; details available from the publisher; National Institute for Personnel Research. *
a) GENERAL CLASSIFICATION BATTERY. Illiterate and semiliterate applicants for semiskilled and laboring jobs; 8 tests: *Nuts and Bolts, Sorting Test 1 (Mechanical Parts), Sorting Test 2 (Letters and Numbers)*, [*N.I.P.R.*] *Cube Construction Test, Tripod Assembly Test, Formboards Test*, 2 modifications of Kohs' *Block-Design Test;* R40 per 16 mm. silent film; projector necessary for administration; [20] minutes.
b) [BOSSBOY SELECTION TESTS]. Illiterate and semiliterate applicants for bossboy and supervisory jobs who score in top category of *a* above; supervisory ability; 3 tests, called *Leaderless Group Test;* [30] minutes per test.

REFERENCES
1. GOTSMAN, E. "A Sequential Procedure for Selecting and Classifying African Industrial Workers and Labourers." *J Nat Inst Personnel Res* 8:117–21 D '60. * (*PA* 35:5388)

[1027]

★**Individual Placement Series.** Adults; 1957–61; 8 tests; profile ['61, 1 page]; record card ['61, 2 pages]; no description of normative population; separate answer sheets must be used (except with *c, e*, and *f*); $1 per 25 answer sheets; 75¢ per 25 profiles; $1.50 per 25 record cards; $1 per 25 tabulation sheets; $18 per complete specimen set (including 10 answer sheets for each test); postpaid; J. H. Norman; the Author. *
a) ACADEMIC ALERTNESS "AA." 1957–59; 7 scores: general knowledge, arithmetic, vocabulary, reasoning ability, logical sequence, accuracy, total; Forms A, B, ('57, 6 pages); preliminary manual ('59, 15 pages); no data on reliability; $20 per 25 tests; 50¢ per key; $2.50 per specimen set; 20(25) minutes.
b) PERFORMANCE ALERTNESS "PA" (WITH PICTURES). 1961; Form C ('61, 4 pages); no manual; no data on reliability and validity; $12.50 per 25 tests; $1 per key; $2.50 per specimen set; 12(17) minutes.
c) READING ADEQUACY "READ" TEST. 1961; 3 scores: reading rate, per cent of comprehension, corrected rate; Form C ('61, 4 pages); no manual; no data on reliability; $4 per 25 tests; $1 per key; $2.25 per specimen set; [10–15] minutes.
d) SURVEY OF CLERICAL SKILLS (SOCS). 1959; 5 scores: spelling, office math, office terms, filing, grammar; Form C ('59, 8 pages); no manual; no data on reliability; no norms; $20 per 25 tests; $1 per key; $3 per specimen set; 40(45) minutes.
e) TYPING TEST. 1959; Forms C, D, ('59, 2 pages); scoring instructions-norms ('59, 2 pages) for each form; no data on reliability; $10 per 25 tests; 50¢ per scoring instructions-norms; $2 per specimen set; 5(15) minutes;
f) SHORTHAND TEST. 1960; Forms A, B, ('60, 2 pages); also available on 33⅓ rpm records; no manual; no data on reliability; $10 per 25 tests; 50¢ per key; $10 per record containing both forms; $2 per specimen set without record; $12 per specimen set with record; (20–25) minutes.
g) SURVEY OF PERSONAL ATTITUDE "SPA" (WITH PICTURES). 1960; 3 scores: social attitude, personal frankness, aggressiveness; Form A ('60, 14 pages); no manual; no data on reliability and validity; $32.50 per 25 tests; $1 per key; $3.50 per specimen set; [20–25] minutes.
h) OCCUPATIONAL INTEREST SURVEY (WITH PICTURES). 1959; 9 scores: scientific, social service, literary, agricultural, business, mechanical, musical, clerical, artistic; Form A ('59, 14 pages); preliminary manual ['59, 8 pages]; $27.50 per 25 tests; $2.25 per specimen set; (15–20) minutes.

[1028]

★**Screening Tests for Apprentices.** Standards 5–10 (ages 14–20); 1957–60; 8 scores: arithmetic (computations, problems), form relations (form perception, two dimensions, three dimensions), synonyms (Afrikaans, English), mechanical aptitude; 1 form ['57, 34 pages, Afrikaans and English in 1 booklet]; mimeographed preliminary manual ['60, 28 pages, 14 pages each in Afrikaans and English]; no data on validity; separate answer sheets must be used; R10.52 per 100 tests and answer sheets, postage extra; manual free; specimen set not available; 81(120) minutes; National Bureau of Educational and Social Research. *

[1029]

★**Steward Personnel Tests (Short Form), 1958 Edition.** Applicants for sales and office positions;

1957–58; abbreviated version of *Steward Sales Aptitude Inventory* and *Steward Vocational Fitness Inventory;* 10 scores: business knowledge, arithmetic, occupational interests (clerical, artistic, supervisory, accounting, writing, selling, mechanical, selling activities); 1 form ('58, 4 pages); manual ('58, 4 pages); no data on reliability and validity; tentative norms for business knowledge part score; $3 per set of 5 tests and manual; $1.50 per manual; postage extra; (35–60) minutes; Verne Steward; Steward-Mortensen & Associates. *

LEONARD V. GORDON, *Chief, Behavioral Evaluation Research Laboratory, U.S. Army Personnel Research Office, Washington, D.C.*

The *Steward Personnel Tests (Short Form)* constitute essentially an abridged version of the *Steward Sales Aptitude Inventory* and the *Steward Basic Factors Inventory,* which was originally called the *Steward Vocational Fitness Inventory.* The battery measures (*a*) business knowledge, (*b*) arithmetic, and (*c*) occupational interests, and is intended for use in the selection of sales or office personnel.

The recommended procedures for using the battery are similar to those for the *Steward Basic Factors Inventory.* The caliber of the individual required for a given job is determined by the employer. Raw scores on the business knowledge and arithmetic tests are converted by means of a prepared chart into ratings of unqualified, borderline, acceptable, superior, or "more than needed." The occupational interest section is scored for seven interest areas, and standards are provided for rating the applicant's interest in selling, which is the total of his scores for "selling" and "supervisory." No standards are provided for evaluating interest in different types of office jobs. The scores for each of the seven fields of interest are to be examined, and ratings are to be assigned by the "direct judgment method." Several illustrations of the method are given.

The *Steward Personnel Tests (Short Form)* suffer from the same general deficiencies noted in the reviewer's evaluation of the *Steward Basic Factors Inventory* (see 1182). Directions for establishing the job level are inadequate; no validity or reliability data are presented in the manual for the short form; the validity section in the manual for the *Steward Sales Aptitude Inventory* (this manual was included in the materials supplied for review) does not include a single validity coefficient; descriptive statistics are lacking; and no information is provided regarding the development

of the table for converting raw scores into ratings.

In view of the availability of a number of standardized and better documented short personnel tests, the reviewer cannot recommend use of the *Steward Personnel Tests (Short Form).*

LYMAN W. PORTER, *Associate Professor of Psychology, University of California, Berkeley, California.*

These tests consist of 35 items pertaining to "business knowledge"; 15 "practical business arithmetic computation" items; and 49 "job activity" interest items designed to measure vocational interests in seven areas. The business knowledge items are in multiple choice format, and the interest items require a "yes" or "no" response.

The four-page manual provides "values" for converting scores on each part of the test into one of five possible ratings: unqualified, borderline, acceptable, superior, and "more than needed" (a possible rating for the first two parts of the test only). Each of these values is adjusted for three different "caliber levels" of sales and office personnel. Thus, a score that might produce a rating of unqualified for a high level sales job such as "wholesale merchant" might produce a rating of acceptable for a "house-to-house route salesman." The interesting thing about these conversion tables is that nowhere in the manual do the authors provide information as to how the "conversion values" were developed. In fact, nothing is given in the manual itself pertaining to the development of the three subtests, let alone data on why a particular score should be given a rating of "acceptable" or any other specific rating. In short, there are no norms given in the manual.

In a 1958 manual for the *Steward Sales Aptitude Inventory* which was made available to this reviewer, some scanty norms are given for the business knowledge subtest. These norms provide median scores on five groups (total *n* for the five groups is 420), including eighth grade students, high school students, college students majoring in nonbusiness courses, college students majoring in business, and life insurance agents preparing for CLU examinations. Median scores increase from the first-mentioned group to the last-mentioned.

According to the authors, the scores made on this subtest are "estimated to have more than 50 per cent higher correlation with the degree of success achieved in sales work (determined by squares of correlation coefficients) than the scores made on a standard mental ability test." This might possibly be true, but there is certainly no way to determine the accuracy of such a statement from the data presented in this manual. This is because the manual gives no coefficients concerning the predictive ability of the business knowledge subtest, nor is it even clear from the quoted statement which specific mental ability test, if any, is being referred to. The 1958 manual fails to provide any norms on either of the other two subtests of the *Steward Personnel Tests (Short Form)*.

In summary, based on both the four-page manual accompanying the *Steward Personnel Tests (Short Form)* and the previous (but relevant) 1958 manual, there are simply insufficient reliability data, validity data, and norms to justify the use of these tests in selection.

[Other Tests]

For tests not listed above, see the following entries in *Tests in Print:* 1819, 1824, and 1826–7.

CLERICAL

[1030]

*A.C.E.R. Short Clerical Test. Ages 13 and over; 1953–60; 2 scores: checking, arithmetic; Forms A ('53), B ('56), (4 pages); mimeographed manual ('60, 20 pages); no data on validity; distribution of Form A restricted; 8s. per 10 tests of Form A; 6s. per 10 tests of Form B; 1s. per key; 7s. 6d. per manual; 8s. 6d. per specimen set; postpaid within Australia; 10(15) minutes; Australian Council for Educational Research. *

[1031]

*A.C.E.R. Speed and Accuracy Tests. Ages 13.5 and over; 1942–62; 2 scores: number checking, name checking; Forms A ['57], B ['61], (5 pages); revised mimeographed manual ('62, 25 pages); no norms for subscores; separate answer sheets must be used; 10s. per 10 tests; 2s. 3d. per 10 answer sheets; 2s. per scoring stencil; 5s. 6d. per specimen set; postpaid within Australia; 12(20) minutes; T. M. Whitford (revised manual) and the Australian Council for Educational Research; the Council. *

REFERENCES

1. HOHNE, H. H. *Success and Failure in Scientific Faculties of the University of Melbourne.* Melbourne, Australia: Australian Council for Educational Research, 1955. Pp. vii, 129. * (PA 31:3787)
2. BUCKLOW, MAXINE, AND DOUGHTY, PATRICIA. "The Use of Aptitude Tests in Clerical Employment: The Selection of Accounting Machinists." *Personnel Prac B* 13:35–44 S '57. *

For a review by D. W. McElwain of an earlier form, see 4:719.

Steward Personnel Tests

[1032]

★Beginner's Clerical Test. Applicants for clerical positions; 1958; abbreviated adaptation of *Group Test 25 (Clerical)* (see 4:724); 1 form (4 pages); manual (3 pages); no data on reliability; $1 per 25 tests; 20¢ per specimen set; postage extra; 10(15) minutes; Herbert Moore; Guidance Centre. *

STEPHEN HUNKA, *Assistant Professor of Educational Psychology, University of Alberta, Edmonton, Alberta, Canada.*

The *Beginner's Clerical Test*, "an abbreviated version of the N.I.I.P. Clerical Test," is described by its author as an experimental test to be used as the first test in a two stage testing program for selecting clerical workers. The test contains eight subtests to which the reviewer has given the following names: number selection, number operations A, coding, proofreading, copying, number operations B, alphabetic arrangement, and message checking. The author claims that the test measures "general intelligence," "speed and accuracy with which elementary clerical operations are made," the ability to grasp the meaning of directions, and ability to "give simultaneous attention to a number of details." Since unit weighting is used in scoring the responses, the total test score tends to reflect to a great extent the candidate's ability to work with numbers. Because of the nature of certain subtests, scoring must be carried out manually.

The author has suggested that a raw score below 50 out of a maximum score of 71 is unsatisfactory and should indicate rejection of the candidate and therefore termination of any further data collection. If, however, the raw score is above this value, further data should be collected, using the N.I.I.P. clerical test, an interest inventory, an intelligence test, a personality questionnaire, and an interview by the office manager. Although this strategy may be a reasonable one, the decision rules are not specifically formulated beyond the first stage.

The efficacy of this instrument as a screening device is lacking. The user does not know what proportion of the candidates from a specific population can be expected to be missed and thus excluded from the second phase of testing. Similarly, there is no indication of the extent to which candidates who do well on this test do not do well on the N.I.I.P. or on other test variables at stage two and thus should have been excluded. Since the author suggests a pre-reject procedure, some evidence must be given concerning the two types of errors that might be incurred. These should be stated as probabilities of error for various groups that might be tested in order that the user may take these probabilities into account while attempting to maximize a specific utility function for his institution.

Information on technical characteristics is also lacking. Norms provided have been based on "the first thousand" cases. No information concerning the norming sample is given, even though it would be reasonable to expect norms for both sexes. Validity data, reliability data, the correlation between this test and the N.I.I.P., and directions to guide the final decision to accept or reject on the basis of the complete strategy are also lacking. In addition, means and standard deviations of the total test and its subtests are not reported. To state that this test has proven value because some companies have released low scoring candidates while other companies have reported early promotion for high scoring candidates is totally inadequate.

The reviewer suspects that unless this test and the strategy within which it is used are reconsidered in the light of institutional decision theory, in order to provide evidence which indicates that the test can be expected to cut selection and training costs and thus to show that it is possible to approach maximization of some institutional utility index, the test will continue to be of an "experimental nature." The test is worthy of further study since it does attempt to measure a variety of basic clerical skills. In light of the fact that this test is designed as a screening device in a specific pre-reject strategy, no other test can be suggested as preferable.

HARRY L. STEIN, *Professor of Education, and Director of Graduate Studies in Education, University of British Columbia, Vancouver, British Columbia, Canada.*

This clerical "quickie" is, according to the publisher's catalog, designed for applicants in the education range grade 8 and up. The norms in the manual, however, are based upon applicants and employees with secondary school graduation. In Canada, secondary school graduation can have almost a limitless variety of interpretations, not only from one province to another but within a single province. In British Columbia, for example, there are at least five different types of secondary schools or programs.

The very skimpy manual suggests that the test "has been used in an experimental form.... chiefly as an elimination tool rather than directly as a selection tool." The manual also reports that the "correlation between this Test and the Otis is 65 [no decimal point]," and that there is thus "some indication that the Test may measure level of intelligence." Little evidence is presented that it does, in fact, measure clerical ability or aptitude. The only evidence of validity is given in the statement that "as a measure of promise for elementary types of clerical work, it has *proven* [italics mine] value; companies have reported hiring students who did poorly on the Test and later being obliged to release them; and companies finding students with high scores report promoting them in less than average time."

The manual provides a table showing how to convert raw scores into percentages. This table is titled "Norms." The maximum possible raw score is 71. A raw score, for example, between 60 and 70 is equivalent to a percentage score of 91–100. However, these are not norms in the sense that they indicate typical performance at any given level. They are merely the result of "statistical checking of the first thousand cases," which were apparently secondary school graduates. Just what statistics were used in the checking is not indicated. Interpretation of scores of candidates in the early secondary grades would be quite difficult.

There are nine *apparent* subtests covering recognition of the size of numbers; simple arithmetic operations including two column additions, and one each of subtraction, multiplication, and division; an attempt at simple filing; checking of names; copying; alphabetizing; and checking errors in coded material. The time allotment is 10 minutes. Scoring is by no means simple and may be subject to many errors because of the format of the test and the scoring key.

As a quick, rough and ready screening test of clerical ability, the *Beginner's Clerical Test* does not compare favorably with a highly standardized instrument such as the *Minnesota Clerical Test*. The publisher is hardly justified in placing a test of this kind on the market until

Beginner's Clerical Test

he can satisfy potential users more effectively than he does at present.

[1033]

★**Cardall Test of Clerical Perception.** Applicants for clerical positions; 1960; 2 scores: checking names and addresses, checking numbers; 1 form (4 pages); no manual; no data on reliability; norms-key ['60, 2 pages]; $8.50 per 100 tests; 25¢ per norms-key; 75¢ per specimen set; postage extra; 6(10) minutes; Alfred J. Cardall; Cardall Associates. *

[1034]

★**Checking Test.** Applicants for clerical and stenographic positions; 1948–63; 1 form ['48, 4 pages]; manual ['63, 7 unnumbered pages]; no data on reliability; $3 per 25 tests; 10¢ per key; 75¢ per manual; postage extra; $1 per specimen set, postpaid; 5(10) minutes; Richardson, Bellows, Henry & Co., Inc. *

[1035]

★**Classifying Test.** Business and industry; 1950–63; 3 scores; speed, accuracy, total; Forms 1 ('50), 2 ('57), (5 pages); manual ['63, 22 unnumbered pages]; no data on reliability of total score; $3.50 per 25 tests; 10¢ per key; $1.50 per manual; postage extra; $1 per specimen set, postpaid; 10(15) minutes; Richardson, Bellows, Henry & Co., Inc. *

[1036]

★**Clerical Tests, Series N.** Applicants for clerical positions not involving frequent use of typewriter or verbal skill; 1940–59; 5 tests and 1 application form; 5 scores: comparing names and numbers, copying names, copying numbers, addition and multiplication, mental ability; manual ['59, 8 pages, same as for *Clerical Tests, Series V*]; profile ('51, 1 page); norms ['51, 1 sheet]; no data on reliability; $8.50 per set of 10 copies of each test and application form; $1 per set of manual and keys; postage extra; specimen set not available; Stevens, Thurow & Associates Inc. *
a) INVENTORY E, COMPARING NAMES AND NUMBERS. 1951; 1 form (4 pages); 5(10) minutes.
b) INVENTORY F, COPYING NUMBERS. 1951; 1 form (3 pages); 3(5) minutes.
c) INVENTORY G, ADDITION AND MULTIPLICATION. 1951; 1 form (2 pages); 6(10) minutes.
d) INVENTORY H, COPYING NAMES. 1951; 1 form (3 pages); 4(10) minutes.
e) INVENTORY NO. 2. 1956; mental ability; 1 form ['56, 4 pages]; 15(20) minutes. See 463.
f) APPLICATION FOR POSITION. 1951; 1 form ['51, 2 pages]. See 1129.

[1037]

★**Clerical Tests, Series V.** Applicants for typing and stenographic positions; 1940–59; 5 tests and 1 application form; 5 scores: grammar, spelling, vocabulary, typing (words per minutes), mental ability; manual ['59, 8 pages, same as for *Clerical Tests, Series N*]; profile ('51, 1 page); norms ['51, 1 sheet]; no data on reliability; $8.50 per set of 10 copies of each test and application form; $1 per set of manual and keys; postage extra; specimen set not available; Stevens, Thurow & Associates Inc. *
a) INVENTORY A, GRAMMAR. 1951; 1 form (2 pages); 3(5) minutes.
b) INVENTORY B, SPELLING. 1951; 1 form (2 pages); 5(10) minutes.
c) INVENTORY C, VOCABULARY. 1951; 1 form (4 pages); [10–15] minutes.

d) TEST OF TYPEWRITING ABILITY. 1951; 1 form (2 pages); 10(20) minutes.
e) INVENTORY NO. 2. 1956; mental ability; 1 form ['56, 4 pages]; 15(20) minutes. See 463.
f) APPLICATION FOR POSITION. 1951; 1 form ['51, 2 pages]. See 1129.

[1038]

★**Clerical Worker Examination.** Clerical workers; 1962–63; test booklet title is *Clerical Worker*; 5 scores: clerical speed and accuracy, verbal ability, quantitative ability, total ability, total; IBM; 1 form; 2 parts (6 pages): booklet 1, clerical ('63), booklet 2, ability ('62); practice test for booklet 1 ['62, 1 page]; manual ['62, 23 pages]; candidate identification sheet ('62, 1 page); no data on reliability and validity; no norms for verbal and quantitative part scores; distribution restricted to municipalities, employers, and agencies for use in selection of personnel; separate IBM scorable answer sheets must be used; 10–49 tests, $1 each; specimen set loaned free; postpaid; 5(10) minutes for practice test for booklet 1, 10(15) minutes for booklet 1, 50(60) minutes for booklet 2; McCann Associates. *

[1039]

★**Cross Reference Test.** Clerical job applicants; 1959; 1 form (3 pages); manual (4 pages); $3 per 25 tests; $2 per specimen set of 10 tests and manual; cash orders postpaid; 5(10) minutes; James W. Curtis; Psychometric Affiliates. *

PHILIP H. KRIEDT, *Associate Director of Personnel Research, The Prudential Insurance Company, Newark, New Jersey.*

This test is intended for use with applicants for clerical and shop or warehouse positions. The author claims that the test has a Gestalt-like quality, that it measures the ability "to synthesize an emergent function—simultaneous combination of simple checking and arithmetical skill." As a consequence, according to the author, the test will supplement most existing clerical aptitude tests. This may or may not be so. No evidence of any kind is given in the test manual to support this claim. No correlations with other clerical tests are furnished.

The manual is brief and unimpressive in content. A test-retest reliability of .90 is reported. Norms are given for clerical applicants, unselected nonclerical applicants, and "employed and unemployed adults." The norms are presented as evidence of validity because the clerical applicants scored higher than the nonclerical applicants.

In a tryout of the test with a small group, the reviewer found that several subjects had difficulty in understanding the directions quickly. The task to be done is rather complicated and may cause problems even with fairly sophisticated subjects. Several of the subjects developed a set as they went along of obtaining only approximate answers in doing the simple mental arithmetic that is required. In most instances, this is all that is necessary to get the correct answer. The test appears to be most suitable as an indication of aptitude for work requiring fast but not necessarily precise mental arithmetic. As a selection device for jobs of this kind, the *Cross Reference Test* may prove useful. It will probably have little value for selecting employees to perform noncomputational clerical work.

[1040]

*Minnesota Clerical Test. Grades 8–12 and adults; 1933–59; formerly called *Minnesota Vocational Test for Clerical Workers;* 2 scores: number comparison, name comparison; 1 form ('33, 5 pages); revised manual ('59, 11 pages); $2.15 per 25 tests; 50¢ per specimen set; postpaid; 15(20) minutes; Dorothy M. Andrew, Donald G. Paterson, and Howard P. Longstaff (test); Psychological Corporation. *

REFERENCES

1–18. See 40:1664.
19–4d. See 3:627.
41–86. See 5:850.
87. Petro, Peter K. *Student Aptitudes and Abilities Correlated With Achievement in First Semester High School Bookkeeping.* Master's thesis, Iowa State Teachers College (Cedar Falls, Iowa), 1957.
88. Bender, W. R. G., and Loveless, H. E. "Validation Studies Involving Successive Classes of Trainee Stenographers." *Personnel Psychol* 11:491–508 w '58. * (*PA* 34:2143)
89. Champion, John Mills. *A Method For Predicting Success of Commerce Students.* Doctor's thesis, Purdue University (Lafayette, Ind.), 1958. (*DA* 19:2134)
90. Shore, Richard P. "Validity Information Exchange, No. 11-22: D.O.T. Code 1-02.01, Bookkeeping-Machine Operator (Banking)." *Personnel Psychol* 11:435–6 au '58. *
91. Shore, Richard P. "Validity Information Exchange, No. 11-23: D.O.T. Code 1-06.02, Teller." *Personnel Psychol* 11:437–9 au '58. *
92. Shore, Richard P. "Validity Information Exchange, No. 11-24: D.O.T. Code 1-25.68, Proof-Machine Operator." *Personnel Psychol* 11:438–9 au '58. *
93. Cass, John C., and Tiedeman, David V. "Vocational Development and the Election of a High School Curriculum." *Personnel & Guid J* 38:538–45 Mr '60. *
94. Garrett, Wiley S. "Prediction of Academic Success in a School of Nursing." *Personnel & Guid J* 38:500–3 F '60. * (*PA* 35:3954)
95. Crane, William J. "Screening Devices for Occupational Therapy Majors." *Am J Occup Ther* 16:131–2 My-Je '62. * (*PA* 37:4078)
96. Super, Donald E., and Crites, John O. *Appraising Vocational Fitness by Means of Psychological Tests, Revised Edition,* pp. 162–79. New York: Harper & Brothers, 1962. Pp. xv, 688. * (*PA* 37:2038)

For a review by Donald E. Super, see 5:850; for reviews by Thelma Hunt, R. B. Selover, Erwin K. Taylor, and E. F. Wonderlic, see 3:627; for a review by W. D. Commins, see 40:1664.

[1041]

*National Institute of Industrial Psychology Clerical Test (North American Revision). Ages 16 and over; 1934–60; 8 scores: oral instructions, classification, arithmetic, copying, checking, filing, problems, total; 1 form ['60, identical—except for minor changes in item order—with *N.I.I.P. Clerical Test: American Revision* which was published in the United States in 1934 and which was a revision of an earlier form of *Group Test 25 (Clerical),* see 4:724]; manual ['60, 11 pages]; no data on reliability; norms

the same as those reported in the 1934 United States manual; $2.25 per 25 tests; 30¢ per specimen set; postage extra; (30) minutes; J. H. Moore; Guidance Centre. *

REFERENCES

1–2. See 40:1665.
3–6. See 3:628.

Harry L. Stein, *Professor of Education, and Director of Graduate Studies in Education, University of British Columbia, Vancouver, British Columbia, Canada.*

This test appears, on the surface, to have those qualities required of a good clerical test if a superficial comparison is made of its content with that of similar tests which have received considerable approbation either through wide acceptance and use or through satisfactory reviews in the literature of testing.

This is the North American revision of the long established British edition. There are, however, a few elements in the test where the revision appears to have fallen a little short for North American use. For example, in item 2 of Test 1, Oral Instructions, the use of the term "post" is not usual, even for Canada. In item 4, the use of the term "Messrs." may confuse the listener. Also, the uniformity of administration is questionable; different accents and different emphases might have an effect upon the norms for this subtest. In Test 2, a term like "Victrola Records" might date the item.

This revision of the N.I.I.P. clerical test has many of the earmarks of *Group Test 25 (Clerical)* first published in 1925. The order of presentation of the subtests has been changed. In reviewing this test in *The Fourth Yearbook,* E. G. Chambers says, "It seems very probable that Group Test 25 measures elements involved in certain types of clerical work. Whether or not short subtests (mostly 2½ minutes each) measure these adequately is another matter and one which cannot be decided on available evidence." Nothing has been seriously changed in the most recent revision to alter what Chambers has said. The manual is entirely inadequate from the standards set up by the APA. Users of tests are entitled to this much consideration. Validity, reliability, and norms reporting are practically nonexistent, or so limited as to be of little value to users.

The manual supplies a few norms in deciles for normal high school students. It does not say whether or not they are graduates. It is assumed that "normal" means that they are without business training. It would seem that high school students with business training would be the most likely applicants for clerical positions. The only information supplied for students of this kind is that their median score was 77. The highest and lowest scores attained are given, but the manual does not say from what group these scores were obtained. Frequencies upon which the meager norms are based are not given.

The last page of the manual makes the claim, on the basis of about 100 cases, that the test makes a "fairly definite distinction between.... satisfactory secretarial workers" and "fair" office workers, or those not regarded as secretarial material. This conclusion is based upon the results of two or three of the very short subtests whose reliability may be questioned seriously, because of their short time allotment. This is the extent of the validation information supplied in the manual.

The test may be useful on an experimental basis only if local norms are developed and if the user can satisfy himself as to the validity and reliability of the test.

For a review by R. B. Selover of the American revision, see 3:628; for a review by Donald G. Paterson, see 40:1665.

[1042]

★**Number Checking Test.** Business and industry; 1957–63; 2 scores: checking forward, checking backward; 1 form ('57, 5 pages); manual ['63, 13 unnumbered pages]; no data on reliability; $3.50 per 25 tests; 10¢ per key; $1 per manual; postage extra; $1 per specimen set, postpaid; 6(16) minutes; Richardson, Bellows, Henry & Co., Inc. *

[1043]

★**Office Skills Achievement Test.** Employees; 1962–63; 7 scores: business letter, grammar, checking, filing, arithmetic, written directions, total; Form A ('63, 8 pages); manual ('62, 4 pages); no data on reliability of part scores; $3 per 25 tests; $1 per specimen set; cash orders postpaid; 20(25) minutes; Paul L. Mellenbruch; Psychometric Affiliates. *

DOUGLAS G. SCHULTZ, *Associate Professor of Psychology, Western Reserve University, Cleveland, Ohio.*

This test is intended for use in the employment of general clerical workers, although the manual contains no explicit statement of the test's purpose or uses or of the basis for content selection. The parts cover subject matter that can reasonably be expected to be predictive of competence in general office work. Office

machine skills (typewriter, adding machine, etc.) are not directly assessed.

The published test is the third revision of an original which contained more items and two additional sections that were later dropped. Some kind of item analysis was performed at each stage but the details are not clear from the manual. The two forms (only Form A was available at the time this review was prepared) "were matched with regard to form, content and difficulty" on the basis of the pretest data. The little evidence in the manual raises some doubt as to how well equivalence was achieved.[1]

The manual makes an attempt to present empirical data to support the test, but a careful reading raises many questions. Apparently most of the statistical data described in the manual are based on the pretest samples, even though a few items were substituted and the timing of two parts was changed in the published version. The various groups and test forms used are not clearly defined.

All the parts are highly speeded, which is appropriate for this kind of test. For the reliability of a speeded test it is proper to administer the test twice, using one form each time. But it is not clear what one can conclude about an office skills test from statistics based on nursing trainees and college students. As a result, only one of the four groups for whom reliability data are presented is appropriate. This group consisted of only 35 cases and they apparently took a pretest form. The resultant correlation of .76 between administrations of the two forms 10 weeks apart would seem to be marginally acceptable, at best, if the test is to be used for the evaluation of individuals. Three validity coefficients are reported against supervisors' ratings, but the groups are small and the data again are apparently derived from administration of a pretest form. Percentile norms, based on the same pretest group, are given for each part score and the total, although no reliability figures are given for the part scores; one would not expect the part reliabilities to meet acceptable levels in view of the small numbers of items and the very short time limits.

Many of the items are of poor quality. For example, the classification of errors required in answering the first part (Business Letter) in-

---

1 No second form is mentioned in the publisher's 1965 catalog received in October 1964.—Editor.

troduces an unnecessary element; the important office skill is the ability to detect (and correct), not to classify, errors. In Part 3 (Checking) the directions do not say how certain differences, like written versus printed copy and small versus capital letters, are to be handled. Other items involve ambiguous examples of the principle being tested and many are presented in a confusing manner. The items and answer spaces are poorly arranged on the page in several instances. The materials are frequently crowded or placed in such a way as to induce errors in marking answers. The directions are inadequate and the print is unclear.

The scoring formulas used are strange; the manual states that they were devised to produce equal weightings for the test parts. There are a few errors in the scoring key.

This is a good example of a test that should not have been published. If it is to be used at all, additional and better items need to be constructed, more and sounder analytical data developed, and a better designed test booklet and much more complete and explicit manual prepared. For the present, several other available tests, e.g., the *Short Employment Tests* or a combination of something like the *Minnesota Clerical Test* and the *Wonderlic Personnel Test,* do everything this test might do in approximately the same time and do it much better.

PAUL W. THAYER, *Director of Human Resources Research, Life Insurance Agency Management Association, Hartford, Connecticut.*

According to the manual, "This 1962 instrument overcomes deficiencies of many previous clerical tests by broadening the base of task challenge to include business letter writing, English usage, checking, filing, simple arithmetic, and following written directions." By "broadening the base," Mellenbruch seems to have taken his own advice in *The Fifth Mental Measurements Yearbook,* that a broad slice of the verbal and clerical skills areas should be sampled.

The first impression upon examining the test is negative simply because of extremely inadequate reproduction. The test resembles a poor mimeographing job. It hardly sets a standard for an examinee taking an "Office Skills Achievement Test." The overlay scoring template should be made of more durable material.

Correct responses are indicated by heavy black dots which apparently must be punched out by the test administrator before the template can be used. One gets the impression that every attempt was made to cut reproduction costs.

Although reference is made to Form B in the manual and alternate form reliabilities are reported involving Forms A and B, only Form A was available to the reviewer. Form B is "to be printed in 1963–64." Intercorrelations among the subtests for a sample of 132 office and industrial employees are reported, but it is not clear whether they apply to Form A or B. The intercorrelations are generally low, although some are in the low .40's. Part 2 (Grammar) correlations "may not now be altogether correct due to the fact that one half minute has been added to the administration time" so that almost 10 per cent could finish all items. Although the author feels that this change should not affect the intercorrelations to any great extent, it may increase the subtest-test correlation above its reported .49.

Alternate form reliabilities seem quite adequate. Correlations with Form A of the *Henmon-Nelson Tests of Mental Ability* are reported at .51 (Form A) and .54 (Form B), based on the scores of 42 psychology students. One wishes that data on the range of the mental ability test scores were given to permit assessment of their appropriateness for a population of clerical applicants. Assuming some range restriction and considering the subtest intercorrelations, it is possible that these two correlations are underestimates of the relation to mental ability and that the battery has a high verbal loading.

The only validity data presented are for 80 clerical employees broken into three groups according to job level and rated by their supervisors. The correlations are .46 (routine), .29 (semi-routine), and .37 (high level) and are "distressingly low." Evidence for restriction of the range of ratings is presented and the author also offers the "proper test score cut-off" argument to account for these correlations. The fact remains that the samples are too small (19, 45, and 16, respectively). In addition, they are concurrent validity data despite the recommendation that the test be used predictively.

Although subtest reliabilities are lacking, normative data are based on only 132 office employees, and validity data are deficient, the

Office Skills Achievement Test

test author makes cautious recommendations as to approximate scoring patterns considered desirable for the three levels of clerical workers. The publisher's catalog is more extravagant: "Excellent for high school guidance, school and employment, vocational placement, upgrading clerical personnel, and as a check on clerical training." No evidence is offered to support the bulk of these claims.

The test author requests reports from test users, especially validity and reliability data so that they can be included in future manuals. In this reviewer's opinion, considerably more such data should have been gathered prior to publication. The author should also study the relationships of the subtests and battery with other tests to determine the unique contribution made, if any. This test seems somewhat broader than many clerical tests in use today and *may* be quite useful. Considerably greater use under research conditions is needed before any definite conclusions can be reached.

[1044]

*Office Worker Test. Office workers; 1956–60; 11 scores: reading, vocabulary, reasoning, arithmetic, checking, filing, spelling, punctuation, usage, information, total; forms 30-A ('56), 30-B ('59), 30-C ('60), (19 pages plus foldout answer sheet); mimeographed manual ['56, 23 pages, formerly called preliminary manual]; mimeographed general PPA directions ['57, 7 pages]; norms ('58, 1 page, based on form 30-A); no data on reliability of current forms; 10–49 tests, 46¢ each; $2 per specimen set; postpaid; 90(100) minutes; Public Personnel Association. *

RAY G. PRICE, *Professor of Business Education, University of Minnesota, Minneapolis, Minnesota.*

The purpose of the *Office Worker Test* is to *assist* in the selection of office workers at the entrance level. As defined in the manual, office workers include "office clerks, typists, stenographers, and other miscellaneous office classes, e.g., receptionists, messengers, etc."

The test contains 100 multiple choice items divided into 10 subtests of 10 items each. In each subtest the items are arranged in ascending order of difficulty, from those answered correctly by 75 per cent of applicants tested to items answered correctly by only 50 per cent of applicants. The working time allowed for the actual test is 90 minutes. The emphasis is on level of performance rather than speed.

Construction of the test began with an analysis of tests for office workers developed by a selected group of 25 public personnel agencies.

A tabulation was made of the amount and kinds of subject matter included in these tests. A tryout form of the test, containing 200 items covering the 10 topics measured by a majority of the agencies, was then reviewed by experts in each of the subject matter fields. Using item analysis, only the 100 most discriminating items were selected for the final test.

Content validity was established by submitting the tryout form to "authorities" for their judgment regarding whether or not the items did measure those knowledges and abilities important for successful office work. Unfortunately, no follow-up of individuals tested has been undertaken to determine their subsequent performance in the office. There is no evidence that those who make high scores will be better able to do office work than those who do less well on the test. Neither is evidence provided with respect to correlations between test scores and intelligence test scores. This reviewer is of the opinion that the correlation might be rather high. In addition, the *Office Worker Test* does not emphasize the speed factor.

The total information given on reliability follows: "Using the Kuder-Richardson formula, the median (eight samples) reliability coefficient for the total score on the try-out form of the test was .92, with a range from .87 (N = 35) to .96 (N = 97)." Although the test being reviewed is only half as long as the tryout form, the authors "estimate" the final form has higher reliability since only the "most discriminating items" were used. This should not have been left to conjecture. The evidence should have been provided.

Each of the three forms has the same number of items within each subgroup. But evidence of the extent to which the tests are "equivalent" forms is lacking. The limited evidence of validity and reliability that is provided applies only to one form of the test. Yet it is a well known fact that preparing equivalent test forms to measure equally the same thing is extremely difficult.

The manual contains detailed and complete directions for administering and scoring the test. Some information usually found in test manuals, however, is missing. For example, as indicated above, adequate statistical evidence of validity and reliability is not provided, nor is evidence of form equivalence and test norms cited.

Office Skills Achievement Test

The *Office Worker Test* has numerous limitations. This is not to say that the test has no merit. It is to say that its sphere of helpfulness is restricted, even as stated in its announced purpose, "to *assist* in the selection of office workers at the entrance level." For those wanting evidence of knowledge in areas covered by the test, it may be an adequate measuring instrument. For anyone wanting a more complete measure of the actual or potential competence of office workers, on the other hand, such information as the test provides will need to be supplemented with data from other sources—interviews, references, performance tests, etc.

DOUGLAS G. SCHULTZ, *Associate Professor of Psychology, Western Reserve University, Cleveland, Ohio.*

This test is one of a series offered for use by public personnel agencies and "qualified officials who are responsible for the selection of personnel." The purchaser signs a statement that he will use the test "exclusively for the official purposes of this agency" and that he will protect its security. The *Office Worker Test* is designed to assist in the selection of clerks, typists, stenographers, receptionists, etc. The selection of subject matter was based on a study of office worker tests developed by 25 public personnel agencies. The test's 10 parts measure such basic variables as general intelligence, clerical ability, knowledge of English, and simple office information. Specialized office skills, like typewriting and shorthand, are not included.

The test booklet is attractive but not fancy; the print is satisfactory. The answer sheet for form 30-A is a little crowded but the IBM format introduced in the other forms is a considerable improvement. The items are sound and appear to be well written, with generally good options. The time limits are ample, even for the parts like arithmetic reasoning, arithmetic computation, checking, and filing, which are usually speeded. The explanation for the de-emphasis of speed sounds sensible but would be more compelling if backed up with some empirical evidence.

Although the manual (undated) is designated as applying to all three forms, it seems apparent that the description of the test's development applies only to the first form (30-A). The original items were well prepared and pretested on a large sample of appropriate subjects. The publisher told this reviewer that no pretesting or item analysis was carried out on the items in forms 30-B and 30-C but that the items were written to parallel those of form 30-A. The purpose of the test is well presented in the manual and the features and parts well described. Elaborate, excellent directions are included for administering the test.

The great weakness of the test is the lack of adequate statistical analysis. The manual sections on using the test results, validity, and reliability do essentially nothing to help a potential user or a reviewer evaluate the test. No validity data are reported; only reasons why validity is difficult to establish are given, along with some poor statements about "content" validity. The only reliability figure given is a median Kuder-Richardson coefficient (formula number not specified) of .92 derived from eight agency samples for the total score on the *pretest* form, which was twice the length of the published test. This coefficient drops to .85 for a test half as long and it is likely the figure appropriate to the published test is nearer to that level than, as the manual "confidently" states, "even greater than that of the tryout form." No other reliability information is available, e.g., for forms 30-B and 30-C or for the part scores of any of the forms. This reviewer would consider it inadvisable to use part scores in any way whatsoever in spite of statements in the manual that they may be suggestive.

The only normative data that are available are contained in a "Test Service Memo" dated June 1958. This leaflet presents a distribution of 986 total scores on form 30-A, apparently reported by the users of the test. The sample is not specified beyond that. From this distribution it appears that the test discrimination is very good and the mean score about where it should be, with few scores in the chance range. Part score means and standard deviations were also computed and they look reasonable from the standpoint of the utilization of the score range; the sample size for the part score calculations is not given. The publisher told this reviewer that no further analyses of any of the tests are currently available, although data are still being received from the client agencies

Office Worker Test

and plans are being made for additional analyses.

Public personnel agencies must operate within a legal, political, and ethical framework that militates against the collection of empirical data to support a test. The need for utmost security prior to test administration, the requirement that candidates be allowed to see the test after they have taken it, and other aspects of their field of operation make it difficult to accumulate the kinds of data which have come to be expected of good tests. Yet other groups who depend upon tests as much as merit system personnel (e.g., workers in college admission) face many of the same problems but have made valiant and successful efforts to overcome them. The public personnel field must provide the energy, time, and funds to produce empirical support for the tests they use. The publisher of this test is in an excellent position to demonstrate leadership in this respect.

In summary, this test appears to be sound to the editorial eye. But there are essentially no empirical data to support its acceptance or utility. For a test that has been on the market for seven years, statistical evidence to help users evaluate and interpret the scores is long overdue. This is clearly not a standardized or proven instrument.

[1045]

The Short Employment Tests. Applicants for clerical positions; 1951–56; Forms 1, 2, 3, 4, ('51); 3 tests: CA (clerical, 3 pages), N (numerical, 4 pages), V (verbal, 3 pages); revised manual ('56, 11 pages); distribution of Form 1 restricted to banks which are members of the American Bankers Association; $2.10 per 25 tests; 50¢ per specimen set; postpaid; 15(20) minutes; George K. Bennett and Marjorie Gelink; Psychological Corporation. *

REFERENCES

1–16. See 5:854.
17. SHORE, RICHARD P. "Normative Data Information Exchange, Nos. 11-33, 11-34." *Personnel Psychol* 11:599–600 w '58. *
18. SHORE, RICHARD P. "Validity Information Exchange, No. 11-22: D.O.T. Code 1-02.01, Bookkeeping-Machine Operator (Banking)." *Personnel Psychol* 11:435–6 au '58. *
19. SHORE, RICHARD P. "Validity Information Exchange, No. 11-23: D.O.T. Code 1-06.02, Teller." *Personnel Psychol* 11:437–9 au '58. *
20. SHORE, RICHARD P. "Validity Information Exchange, No. 11-24: D.O.T. Code 1-25.68, Proof-Machine Operator." *Personnel Psychol* 11:438–9 au '58. *
21. BUEL, WILLIAM D., AND STEVENS, SAMUEL N., JR. "Normative Data Information Exchange, Nos. 12-28, 12-29, 12-30." *Personnel Psychol* 12:647–9 w '59. *
22. SHORE, RICHARD P. "Normative Data Information Exchange, Nos. 12-5, 12-6, 12-7, 12-8." *Personnel Psychol* 12:148–51 sp '59. *
23. ASH, PHILIP. "Validity Information Exchange, No. 13-07, Stenographers, Typists, General Clerks, and Secretaries." *Personnel Psychol* 13:456 w '60. *
24. HARKER, JOHN B. "Cross-Validation of an IBM Proof Machine Test Battery." *J Appl Psychol* 44:237–40 Ag '60. * (PA 35:4055)
25. KIRCHNER, WAYNE K., AND BANAS, PAUL. "Prediction of Key-Punch Operator Performance." *Personnel Adm* 24:23–6 Ja–F '61. *

LEONARD W. FERGUSON, *Program Director, Research Division, Life Insurance Agency Management Association, Hartford, Connecticut.*

According to the manual, the purpose of the *Short Employment Tests* is to "provide the economy of short time limits without sacrificing accuracy of measurement." This purpose was accomplished, state the authors, "by selection of highly efficient item types, by very careful test construction, and by aiming the tests at a well-defined population—applicants for clerical jobs."

The authors had four objectives: (a) "that the entire battery should consume not over twenty minutes"; (b) "that the test-retest reliabilities should exceed .80"; (c) "that instructions and scoring should be simple"; and (d) "that content should encompass verbal, numerical and clerical skills."

To meet the fourth objective, the authors prepared test V (a verbal test) of 50 "items in which the applicant is asked to choose from among four words the one which means most nearly the same as the problem word"; test N (a numerical test) of 90 "simple computations involving the fundamental skills of addition, subtraction, multiplication, and short division"; and test CA (a clerical aptitude test) of 60 items, each of which "requires the subject to locate and verify a name in an alphabetic list, and to read and code the amount entered opposite that name." Four forms of each of these three tests were constructed, but the use of one of these forms is restricted to members of the American Bankers Association.

From the data presented in the manual, it would appear that the *Short Employment Tests* meet the objectives stated by the authors. Each test takes only 5 minutes to give, and each can be scored in about 30 seconds. The reliabilities (alternate forms) vary from .77 to .91, and average .88, .87, and .81 for the V, N, and CA tests, respectively. Test-retest reliabilities for a two year interval are reported as .84, .75, and .71 for the V, N, and CA tests, respectively.

The authors supply three types of data relative to the value of the tests in employment. These are (a) correlations with various criteria, (b) correlations with other well known tests, and (c) intercorrelations among the *Short Employment Tests*. Based on records secured in four groups, each with more than 200 cases, intercorrelations range from .08 to .51 and have a median value of .34. Least intercorrelated are the N and V tests (.08 to .34), next least intercorrelated are the V and CA tests (.13 to .36), and most highly intercorrelated are the N and CA tests (.37 to .51). "These coefficients," state the authors, "are sufficiently small to indicate that each test measures a relatively *independent aspect* [italics added] of clerical aptitude." If this really be the case, then one might wonder why correlations of apparently comparable magnitude are cited to show that the tests are *"effective* [italics mine] for the separation of good from poor individuals." But as soon as one recalls that the frame of reference for the interpretation of test intercorrelations is different from the frame of reference in terms of which validity coefficients must be interpreted, it can be seen that the validity coefficients are comparatively high, and that the test intercorrelations are comparatively low, even if not as independent as this word seems to suggest. In fact, the *Short Employment Tests* intercorrelate about as well as do typical groups of items in practically all short mental alertness (or intelligence) tests. Otherwise, they would not correlate as well as they do with scores on the *Wonderlic Personnel Test, Minnesota Clerical Test* (names and numbers), and the *Psychological Corporation General Clerical Test* (verbal, numerical, and total). These correlations, based on groups which vary in size from 100 to over 1,000, range from .53 to .91 and have a median value of .70.

The manual gives 72 validity coefficients, 24 for each of the three tests. Only one of these coefficients is negative (−.03), and only one is exactly .00. Thus, 70 of the coefficients are positive, with the highest value reported being .65. For the V test, the coefficients range from −.03 to .53; for the N test, they range from .08 to .65; and for the CA test, they range from .00 to .55. In this same order, the median coefficients are .27 (V), .36 (N), and .32 (CA).

Twelve of the 72 validity coefficients reported are based upon test scores secured before employment and upon criterion data secured after employment; 15 are based upon test scores secured subsequent to employment and upon criterion data secured at a later time;

24 are based on test scores of employees for whom criterion data were obtained concurrently; 18 are coefficients "appearing in the literature"; and 3 show the correlation between test scores and the certification of a group of secretarial students.

The most telling of these coefficients are, of course, the 12 first mentioned. Based upon four groups of applicants, with sample sizes varying from 40 to 131, these coefficients range from .08 to .45 and have median values of .24 (V), .28 (N), and .34 (CA). Roughly, these average coefficients can be said to be significant at about the .05 (two-tailed) level, based on an *n* of 50.

When employees were tested, but time was allowed to elapse before criterion data were secured, coefficients ranged from .00 to .55 and had median values of .33 (V), .35 (N), and .25 (CA). Concurrent validity coefficients range from .09 to .65 and have median values of .30 (V), .38 (N), and .42 (CA). Coefficients "appearing in the literature" range from −.03 to .49 and have median values of .12 (V), .35 (N), and .26 (CA).

In the table from which the above values were taken, the authors indicate that four types of criteria were employed. These were (*a*) certification at completion of training in a secretarial school, (*b*) job level and job grade, (*c*) a production index, and (*d*) supervisory ratings. Supervisory ratings were secured in the form of a checklist or overall appraisal or merit rating, as well from ratings of job performance, general aptitude, mental efficiency, quality and quantity of work, and "employability."

As generally has been found to be the case with mental alertness tests, correlations with job level or job grade tend to be among the highest: .33 and .53 for V, .49 and .60 for N, and .30 and .46 for CA. Thus, the *Short Employment Tests* would appear to be useful indicators of promotability. With a production index, correlations were .10, .26, and .34, and with a checklist score they were .24, .33, and .45 for the V, N, and CA tests, respectively. With certification status, the correlations were .15, .48, and .47. When the criterion consisted of some form of overall supervisory or merit rating, validity coefficients for V ranged from −.03 to .48 and had a median value of .27. For N, they ranged from .08 to .65 and had a median of .35. And for CA, they ranged from .00 to .55 and had a median of .29.

To many individuals (too many), these validity coefficients may not seem particularly high. Be that as it may, they are certainly large enough to command respect and in fact, on the average, are much larger than those of many tests now used in industry. As is well known, a correlation coefficient is a rather severe (too severe) index of test validity for most employment tests. It is to be regretted, therefore, that the authors did not provide an expectancy table, or a series of expectancy tables, to show what percentage of various test score groups could be expected to pass and fail critical levels in each of several criteria.

It is not surprising that the authors found, and reported, that a sum of the scores on all three tests yielded higher validity coefficients than did the separate tests. Thirteen such coefficients are reported. They range from .31 to .60 and have a median value of .46. Thus, the most accurate predictions come, not from the separate tests but from the composite score based on all three tests. In view of this fact, most employers (but not all employers) will be well advised to give all three tests and to utilize the score based on all three tests as a basis for employment.

For a review by P. L. Mellenbruch, see 5:854.

[1046]

★**Short Tests of Clerical Ability.** Applicants for office positions; 1959-60; Form A ('59); 7 tests; preliminary manual ('60, 12 pages); norms for female office workers only; $1.95 per 20 tests (except *d*, $2.50 per 20 tests); 25¢ per scoring template for any one test; 25¢ per manual; $1 per specimen set; postage extra; Jean Maier; Science Research Associates, Inc. *

a) CODING. 2 pages; 5(10) minutes.
b) CHECKING. 2 pages; 5(10) minutes.
c) FILING. 2 pages; 5(10) minutes.
d) DIRECTIONS—ORAL AND WRITTEN. 3 pages; 5(10) minutes.
e) ARITHMETIC. 3 scores: computation, business arithmetic, total; 2 pages; no data on reliability of total score; 9(14) minutes.
f) BUSINESS VOCABULARY. 2 pages; reliability data and norms based on experimental form; 5(10) minutes.
g) LANGUAGE. 2 pages; reliability data and norms based on experimental form; 5(10) minutes.

PHILIP H. KRIEDT, *Associate Director of Personnel Research, The Prudential Insurance Company, Newark, New Jersey.*

Tobacco companies have learned that it is profitable to offer a variety of cigarette brands to the public. Although the brands differ only slightly, they will attract different customers for one reason or another. Test publishers have apparently arrived at the same conclusion, and, as a result, they are turning out an ever-increasing number of tests which differ only slightly from those already on the market. The *Short Tests of Clerical Ability* are a good illustration. Five of the seven tests in this battery are much like other published tests, and they will provide a real contribution only if they prove to be superior to other tests measuring the same abilities.

The test manual is well prepared. It strikes a reasonable compromise between meeting the demands of commercial salesmanship and the standards suggested in the American Psychological Association publication, *Technical Recommendations for Psychological Tests and Diagnostic Techniques.* Considering the shortness of the tests, the reliability coefficients that are reported seem satisfactory. The reliability coefficients for Business Vocabulary and Language are based on preliminary forms, however. The results of an assortment of validity studies based on numbers varying from 17 to 54 are fairly typical for tests of this kind. No intercorrelations among these tests are given although such information is planned for the next manual. Norms are given for all tests based on groups of from 133 to 368 employed office personnel. Here also the Business Vocabulary and Language results are based on preliminary forms.

Transparent plastic keys are furnished for all tests. These keys are somewhat unsatisfactory as correct answers are circled but no holes are cut. Because of this, the test scorer cannot check correct items but must keep a count of them some other way. The plastic material also has an undesirable glare which interferes with scoring.

This reviewer first read through the tests and administrative material and was favorably impressed by them. The tests are attractive in appearance and format and on casual inspection seem to be well constructed and ready for use. After trying them out with a small group of subjects, however, a number of flaws came to light which had not been apparent previously. Several of the tests proved to be much more difficult to administer than was expected.

The most useful test in the battery in the opinion of this reviewer is Language. It fills the need for a short separately administered test measuring a combination of spelling, punctuation, and the grammar skills. It should be useful in screening candidates for stenographic jobs and other positions requiring language skills. The test cannot, of course, be used for diagnostic purposes to indicate specific language skill deficiencies. Two other tests, Business Vocabulary and Arithmetic, appear to be satisfactory tests. The arithmetic test, however, is somewhat awkward in that the computation and arithmetic reasoning sections, which have separate time limits, are presented on the same page.

Three tests in the battery can be classified as clerical speed and accuracy measures. These are Checking, Coding, and Filing. All three are more complicated and confusing than is desirable. The *Minnesota Clerical Test* and the clerical subtest of the *Short Employment Tests* are recommended as more easily administered measures of the clerical speed factor.

Directions—Oral and Written, the most original test in the group, is unfortunately the least ready for use. The administrator reads an orientation lecture on a company's office procedures and policies while the subject takes notes. Then the subject is given an objective test on the information. The instructions say that the lecture should be read in about seven minutes allowing about one second for each dash indicating a pause. In trying out this test the administrator found it impossible to follow the time standards suggested. A word count revealed that if a second were allowed for each dash indicating a pause one would have to read at a rate of 480 words per minute to finish this material in seven minutes! This is, of course, unreasonable, and one wonders how rapidly the material was dictated in obtaining the norm group results. One also wonders whether a person who can take shorthand will have an advantage over others. The test given on the lecture material is confusing and the time limit is restrictive. All in all, this is a frustrating test to administer and a frustrating test to take.

This battery of tests is promising in some ways, but it has been placed on the market before it is really ready. Bennett and Gelink's *Short Employment Tests* can be used with greater confidence in selecting employees for most clerical positions.

PAUL W. THAYER, *Director of Human Resources Research, Life Insurance Agency Management Association, Hartford, Connecticut.*

This battery is an attempt to broaden the sampling of abilities to be tested for clerical jobs and includes tests of business vocabulary, arithmetic, name and number checking, filing, oral and written directions, coding, and language usage. Norms are based only on samples of female employees ranging in number from 133 to 368, and those given for Business Vocabulary and Language are estimates based on the administration of experimental forms. Subtest reliabilities appear to be adequate with the exception of Part 2 of Arithmetic. The test-retest reliability of .68 is much too low for accurate interpretation of an individual score.

Concurrent validity data for supervisory ratings are reported for all subtests (except Business Vocabulary and Language) in the form of biserial correlations for office personnel in two manufacturing concerns. The samples consist of approximately 50 in each case. In addition, the manual clearly points out that the moderate validities reported would change under predictive conditions.

The manual, tests, and scoring stencils are reproduced well. Subtests are printed separately for flexibility of administration. The tone of the manual is conservative and deficiencies in the available data are clearly indicated, making the job of the reviewer and potential user considerably easier than with many other tests.

As noted above, the manual is a preliminary edition. Unfortunately, three to four years have passed and data promised in the manual are still not available on intercorrelations of subtest scores, normative data on applicants and additional employee groups of different job levels, validity data showing appropriate combinations of tests for various job classes, and correlations of the battery with other tests.

Such data would be extremely valuable in assessing the contribution of this battery to the solution of clerical selection problems. Predictive validities also are needed. This reviewer hopes that enough research will be done in the near future to determine whether this attempt to increase the variety of abilities sampled has been successful and whether such an increase does aid in the selection of clerical personnel of various types.

Short Tests of Clerical Ability

[1047]

★Survey of Clerical Skills (SOCS): Individual Placement Series (Area IV). Adults; 1959; 5 scores: spelling, office math, office terms, filing, grammar; Form C (8 pages); no manual; no data on reliability; no norms; separate answer sheets must be used; $20 per 25 tests; $1 per 25 answer sheets; $1 per key; $3 per specimen set; postpaid; 40(45) minutes; J. H. Norman; the Author. *

[Other Tests]

For tests not listed above, see the following entries in *Tests in Print*: 1831, 1834, 1836-9, 1844-9, and 1853-4; out of print: 1832; status unknown: 1833 and 1840.

INTERESTS

[1048]

★Burke Inventory of Vocational Development. Grades 9-16 and adults; 1958; unscored checklist of occupational titles for use prior to vocational counseling interview; 1 form (3 pages); directions (1 page); no data on reliability; 6¢ per copy with directions; 25¢ per specimen set; postpaid; (15-30) minutes; Charles Burke; the Author. *

[1049]

★Career Finder. Grades 9-16 and adults; 1960; a short adaptation of the *Qualifications Record;* self-administered checklist of interests, activities, and experiences; 45 scores classified under 7 headings: arts (music, art, dramatics, dancing, graphic arts, crafts), biology (physiology, zoology, botany, foods, sports), computation (accounting, mathematics, drafting, purchasing, records, dexterity), literary (journalism, language, transcription, advertising, research), physical (tools, machinery, transportation, strength, hazards), social (management, instruction, public contacts, sales, consulting, religion, services, investigation, discipline), technology (chemistry, astronomy, electricity, mechanics, construction, geology, physics, aeronautics, standards); 1 form (4 pages in a 2-page sleeve); instruction leaflet (2 pages); no data on reliability and validity; $14 per 12 copies; $2 per copy; cash orders (postpaid) only; (60) minutes; Keith Van Allyn; Personnel Research, Inc. *

ARTHUR C. MacKINNEY, *Associate Professor of Psychology, Iowa State University, Ames, Iowa.*

Since the *Career Finder* is a shortened version of the *Qualifications Record* (see 1068 for my review), and since there is even less information available on the *Career Finder* than on the parent test, an extensive review does not seem required or even possible. Since the *Qualifications Record* is inadequately researched and standardized, it is safest to assume that all its limitations are also present in the *Career Finder*. Some no doubt have been exaggerated by the shortening process. As a result, this reviewer recommends against using this test.

CHARLES F. WARNATH, *Associate Professor of Psychology, and Director, Counseling Center, Oregon State University, Corvallis, Oregon.*

This is the self-administering, self-scoring form of the *Qualifications Record* reviewed under 1068. Except for the deletion of the achievement factor from the seven factors used to obtain scores on the so-called "45 basic vocational elements of the Qualifications Record," the content of this instrument is essentially the same as that of the Q/R.

The *Career Finder* is pretty much the "poor man's Q/R." A simple slide-through sleeve format turns up on one horizontal row the six factor questions related to 1 of the 45 basic vocational elements. The respondent places a check mark in the appropriate box if he can answer "yes" to the question. He then adds up the number of checked boxes for each of the six factors and indicates the score on a profile of the 45 elements printed on the sleeve.

On the inside of the two-page slide-through sheets on which the questions are asked is a listing of about 500 occupations, each followed by four numbers corresponding to 4 of the 45 basic vocational elements considered necessary for success in that occupation. The respondent circles any element number for which he has received a factor score of 4, 5, or 6 on the profile. He then lists those occupations on the interpretation leaflet for which he has checked all four of the elements and, in another column, those for which he has checked three. The scoring and interpretation leaflet states at this point: "The occupations you have listed above are suggested fields of endeavor which tend to meet with your basic patterns of knowledge and skills."

On the sleeve are presented questions related to education and employment records, military record, dependents, etc. What relevance this information has to the *Career Finder* results is not clear, as its use is not mentioned in any of the materials furnished the respondent. The instruction leaflet suggests that the respondent may wish to contact a vocational counselor or psychologist or to write to Personnel Research "for more specific information concerning your situation." It goes on to say: "This is necessary because of the influence [of] your personal finances, sex, age, education, experience and other factors which may affect your vocational objectives."

This last sentence is, perhaps, the most telling argument against the types of vocational guidance typified by this instrument. The job seeker is led to believe on the basis of the description furnished by the publisher that this instrument will give definite answers to questions related to finding an occupation. However, it is only in the last sentence of the information folder which comes with his purchase of the instrument that he discovers that finding a job in which he can be "successful" may involve more than this instrument can accomplish. Nothing is said in the informational materials about the cost of a more extensive analysis of the *Career Finder* results by the publisher.

As with its parent instrument, the *Qualifications Record*, there is no evidence offered that this instrument has any reliability. In fact, the statement at the top of the *Career Finder* sleeve can be quite misleading in its implications regarding the "analysis of over 281,000 case studies of traits in 3,000 key occupations," since no effort is made to relate this work to the occupations for which the *Career Finder* is keyed.

The conclusions reached in my review of the Q/R would also be relevant to the *Career Finder*: Until detailed, scientifically verifiable information related to reliability and validity is presented, it is impossible to support the publicity claims for this instrument.

[1050]

★Chatterji's Non-Language Preference Record. Ages 11–16; 1962; 10 scores: fine arts, literary, scientific, medical, agricultural, mechanical, crafts, outdoor, sports, household work; Form 962 ['62, 16 pages]; mimeographed tentative manual ['62, 24 pages]; profile ['62, 2 pages]; reliability and validity data and most norms based on an earlier form (author recommends use of local norms); separate answer sheets must be used; Rs. 25 per 25 tests; Rs. 5 per 100 answer sheets; Rs. 12.50 per set of scoring stencils; Rs. 4.50 per pad of 100 profiles; Rs. 6 per manual; Rs. 22.50 per specimen set with scoring stencils, Rs. 9.50 per specimen set without stencils; postage extra; (45–55) minutes; S. Chatterji; distributed by Manasayan. *

[1051]

★College Planning Inventory, Senior College Edition. High school seniors seeking counseling on choice of college; 1959; unscored checklist of college names and fields of study for use prior to educational counseling interview; 1 form (5 pages); directions (2 pages); no data on reliability; 10¢ per copy with directions; 25¢ per specimen set; postpaid; (15) minutes; Franklyn Graff and Charles Burke; Charles Burke. *

[1052]

★Curtis Interest Scale. Grades 9–16 and adults; 1959; 10 scores (business, mechanics, applied arts, direct sales, production, science, entertainment, interpersonal, computation, farming) and 1 rating (desire for responsibility); 1 form (4 pages); manual (4 pages); $3 per 25 tests; $1 per 25 profiles; $1 per specimen set of 7 tests, 7 profiles, and manual; cash orders postpaid; (10–15) minutes; James W. Curtis; Psychometric Affiliates. *

WARREN T. NORMAN, *Associate Professor of Psychology, The University of Michigan, Ann Arbor, Michigan.*

Based on information presented in the very brief manual and profile sheet, the only published sources available at present, the most that can be said for this device is that it takes very little time to administer, is easy to score, and is probably capable of discriminating between *group averages* for samples drawn from dissimilar occupations. By way of contrast, the manual asserts that this instrument is "a means of providing insight into the vocational interest patterns of *individuals* [italics mine]." The published sources, however, provide no data whatever on interindividual variability for the scales and no measures of relationship reflecting covariation among individual scores either among the scales or between them and any external criteria. Indeed, the only direct support offered for the asserted interpretability of individual scores is the statement that test-retest reliabilities over a six-week interval range between .81 and .88 for the various occupational keys.

In support of validity, the manual reports only averages of raw scores for groups of persons in mixed occupations superficially related to the name of each key. For example, a mixed group of 275 "bookkeepers," "numbers clerks," and "bank tellers" has a reported average raw score of 37.40 on the computation scale and 32.33 on the business scale. But, in the absence of any general normative data, the only possible interpretational basis for these data derives from the item format and scoring procedures employed. The exhaustive scoring of rank-order responses to the 10 stems, one presumably reflective of each occupational field, in each of 5 blocks produces raw scores for which the *profile elevation* for each respondent is a constant—22.5. But the fact that the average *across the 10 keys* is a constant for any respondent in no way implies that *each (or any) scale* has an average value of 22.5 *over people* in any normative sample. However, the headnote to the table in the manual which presents these group averages asserts that a raw score of 22.5 indicates "average interest." The unwary reader is thus led to confuse these two senses of "average" and consequently is apt to misinterpret even that scanty bit of validity information which is presented.

On the profile sheet are presented mean profiles for 11 small occupational samples (numbers range from 17 to 56). But the absence of any data on the variability of scores on the several scales, the limited number of occupations included, the minimal sample sizes employed, and the complete absence of any information concerning the sources of these data, the demographic characteristics of the respondents or the method of their selection, together make these profiles very nearly worthless as an aid to score interpretation.

The manual alludes to additional validity studies in progress. In response to a request for data from these studies, the reviewer was sent four sets of validity coefficients against various criteria for samples of sales engineers in a large electronics firm and a table of correlations between the occupational keys and the scales of the ACE, the three Guilford-Martin inventories, the *Study of Values,* and Kuder-Vocational based on 31 personnel executives in a large mail order company. In the former studies the interpersonal scale appears to have a validity of about .20 against a criterion of "average annual increase in income since entering full-time employment" while no other scale appears to have any consistent validity against this or any other criterion employed. In the latter study, a fair degree of correspondence appears to exist between similarly labeled scales on the Curtis and Kuder inventories although absence of intra-inventory correlations and the small sample employed make judgments of convergent and discriminant relationships more than a bit hazardous.

The "Desire for Responsibility" scale is supported by no data presented in the manual save for a vague allusion to "a high coefficient of correlation between level so marked and actual willingness to assume responsibility, as determined by ratings of supervisors, foremen and other administrative superiors." Similarly, there are no data presented to support the statements that "experience has shown that scores above 30 may be considered as designating 'primary interests,' and those ranging from 24 through 29 as identifying 'secondary interests' " or that "scores below 15 frequently reflect an emotional rejection of the associated work area."

In short, there is very little firm evidence to support the routine use of this device in either guidance or personnel selection contexts at the present time. The *Kuder Preference Record—Vocational* and the *Strong Vocational Interest Blank* both provide far better sources of information on occupational interest patterns of individuals or groups than does the Curtis scale. Unfortunately, the brevity of the Curtis scale, the ease with which it can be scored, the superficial appearance of relevance of the item content to the names of the scales, and the oversimplified presentation of the "validity" data are apt to lead to its use in situations where its utility is as yet unknown but likely to be minute. As he reviews this instrument, one remembers with renewed anguish Stagner's classic paper [1] on "The Gullibility of Personnel Managers." The release of this device for other than research use appears to have been, at the very least, premature.

LEONA E. TYLER, *Professor of Psychology, University of Oregon, Eugene, Oregon.*

This very brief test consists of five sets of 10 items each plus a supplementary set of 5 items designed to indicate the level of responsibility at which the subject prefers to work. In the 10-item sets, each item refers to an activity required by one of the main occupational fields: applied arts, business, computation, direct sales, entertainment, farming, interpersonal, mechanics, production, and science. The subject is instructed to rank the 10 items in each of these sets. The sum of the ranks he gives each type of activity constitutes the score for the occupational field.

The brief manual gives very little technical information. The selection of these particular 10 fields is said to have "resulted from a careful study of job placements of several thousands of clients of a vocational rehabilitation agency in the state of Illinois during an eight year period. The fields selected accounted for over 95% of employer requests for trainees or employees."

[1] STAGNER, ROSS. "The Gullibility of Personnel Managers." *Personnel Psychol* 11:347-52 au '58. *

Reliability and validity evidence is scanty and not very precise. Test-retest coefficients for "140 individuals who could be retested at a six week interval" (age, sex, educational level, and other characteristics not specified) are reported to be from .81 to .88 for the individual occupational fields. Preliminary data suggest that persons employed in occupations the author classifies as belonging to the 10 major fields show the kinds of average scores and profiles one would expect of them. But these data are deficient in many ways. Each average is based on a mixture of specific occupational groups apparently combined on the basis of the author's judgment alone. (For example, the interpersonal group includes ministers, psychologists, school teachers, physicians, and nurses. Strong's extensive studies would suggest that the interests of these groups are not much alike.) Furthermore, there is no way of judging the amount of overlapping between the various interest groups. Only mean scores are presented.

There are other deficiencies as well. The author gives no norms of any kind except for a set of comparison profiles. There is no indication that he has considered the possible influence of response sets, including outright faking, on a subject's performance. There is no attempt to link this instrument up with the extensive body of knowledge about interests that has accumulated around the Strong and Kuder blanks.

However, when a reviewer asks himself whether a test like this one, technically deficient in all respects, should be used for any purpose whatever, the answer is not quite an unqualified "No." Used strictly as an interview aid in a counseling situation, these questions might stimulate some constructive thinking about occupational goals. The trouble with the test, as things now stand, is that inadequately trained counselors and naïve clients may be tempted to attach more importance to these scores and profiles than they deserve.

[1053]

★Fowler-Parmenter Self-Scoring Interest Record. Grades 9 and over; 1958-61; formerly called *G.C. Self-Scoring Interest Record;* 12 scores: outdoor, managerial, social service, verbal, operative, skilled mechanical, scientific, persuasive, clerical, artistic, numerical, musical; Form 1 ('60, c1958, 20 pages including profile); manual ('60, 25 pages); supplementary interest-occupation chart ['61, 7 pages]; separate profile ('60, 2 pages); $3.10 per 25 tests; $1.25 per 25 punch pins; 95¢ per 25 backing boards; 47¢ per pad of 50 profiles; 30¢ per manual; 30¢ per specimen set; postage extra; (30-40) minutes; H. M. Fowler and M. D. Parmenter; distributed by Guidance Centre. *

REFERENCES
1. FOWLER, H. M. "Interests of Grade 9 Boys as Measured by the G.C. Self-Scoring Interest Record in the University of Toronto Schools and the Central Technical School." *Sch Guid Worker* 14:32-40 Je '59. *
2. FOWLER, H. M. "More About the G.C. Interest Record." *Sch Guid Worker* 15:27-32 My '60. *

DAVID P. CAMPBELL, *Associate Professor of Psychology, and Director, Center for Interest Measurement Research, University of Minnesota, Minneapolis, Minnesota.*

In past editions of *The Mental Measurements Yearbook,* reviewers have often fallen back on the label "promising" for those instruments that have little of proven value to recommend them. This reviewer would like to make it clear at the outset that he feels this is too complimentary a term to be applied to this inventory. This is not a case of an instrument being published prematurely before adequate psychometric data are available; rather the authors seem to believe that sort of information is not essential. Not only have they published a manual without it, but, from their statements, it seems unlikely that they will ever furnish it. Their viewpoint is expressed in the following quotes:

> Although the authors have no strong desire to provide comprehensive norms for the Record, they recognize that [they would be useful].

> The validity of any evaluative instrument may be determined either by procedures involving judgment or by estimates obtained from empirical evidence.

> It may be argued that, in the case of an interest test, a rational judgment of validity may be just as valuable as a coefficient obtained by using numerical evidence.

> In the final analysis, the validity of the Record may best be judged by those who use it.

This inventory consists of 238 statements of specific activities that the authors have assigned to the 12 scales listed above by arbitrarily deciding which interest they feel a given item is measuring. The student completes the record by using a pin punch to indicate whether he likes or dislikes each activity, punching twice to indicate a strong like or dislike. The same items and scales are used for both men and women. The booklet is cleverly arranged and the student can score his blank in a matter of minutes. Whether the scores are worth obtaining is another matter.

Two profiles are generated, one called the "Like Profile," the other the "Dislike Profile." Just why two profiles are used is not clear as they are virtual mirror images, varying from this only if the student punches twice for dislikes and once for likes, or vice versa. The profiles are based on norms, not of any specific criterion group, but simply on ninth grade students, a high score indicating that the student selected more of the items that the authors felt belonged in the scale than most other ninth grade students.

Norms for adults are available, based on 179 men and 134 women. Although the authors point out in a parenthetical comment in the text that these adults were "mostly teachers," the treatment of the results in the tables and profiles implies that these are men and women in general. To advise an adult man scoring high on the skilled mechanical scale that he has more mechanical interests than the average man when he, in fact, really only has more mechanical interests than the average teacher would be grossly misleading, but this is only one example of the errors that would be made routinely by anyone using this record.

Once the profile is constructed, the manual and other interpretive aids give the student or counselor some clues as to which occupations the student might enjoy. Again, it is an armchair approach with no research to buttress it. For example, if a student has high scores on the social service and scientific scales, some of the recommended occupations for him to consider are: chiropractor, clinical psychologist, detective, doctor, economist, pharmacist, secret service man, and social worker. This is a unique grouping of occupations by interests and, based on what is known about the organization of interests as shown by the Strong blank, it is very likely inaccurate.

The only validity data presented are tables showing that boys and girls differ in the expected way on the scales, e.g., boys score higher on the skilled mechanical scale and lower on the artistic scale than girls. Of these tables the authors say, "The results shown in Tables 3, 5 and 6 can hardly be considered completely legitimate norms," and go on to point out that they are based on small numbers that were not collected systematically. Yet a page or two later they say, "Tables 3, 5 and 6 provide presumptive evidence of validity."

No correlations between scales are given, although the authors' expressed intention was to build "reasonably independent" scales. Nor are there any correlations provided between the record and other interest inventories, or achievement and ability tests, or any other behavioral indices. The median K-R 21 reliability for the 12 scales is roughly .90. No indication of stability over time is provided.

The 1960 manual lists four "further improvements" that "have been made in recent months." One of those improvements was putting in a "kink" in the punch pin to prevent too enthusiastic punching; another was reducing the size of the backing board (placed under the record to protect desk tops) so that it could be stored in a file drawer. That the authors list these sorts of things as improvements is a far more eloquent evaluation of this inventory than anything the reviewer could say.

Clearly, either the *Strong Vocational Interest Blank* or the *Kuder Preference Record* would be a far wiser choice than this instrument for almost any situation. Even though this inventory was developed for Canadian use, this reviewer feels its weaknesses are so glaring that a user would be better off risking cultural differences in norms on the established inventories.

In summary, this instrument has been developed almost entirely by subjective methods and has all the flaws guaranteed by such an approach. Not only are the basic psychometric data missing, the authors—based on what they say in the manual—are not particularly concerned with providing them. In its present state, this instrument is of little value to any practitioner in any situation, particularly as far better blanks are available.

JOHN W. FRENCH, *Professor of Psychology, and College Examiner, New College, Sarasota, Florida.*

The authors of this inventory have written a manual that is exceptionally clear and honest. Because research on the inventory has not yet provided representative norms or predictive validity data, it is not possible to use the instrument for accurately comparing a student's interests with those of students in any standard groups, and it is not possible to advise students with regard to their expectancies for success or satisfaction in certain jobs. However, the manual does not claim these things for the instrument. It states a modest but very useful goal: to suggest occupations, courses, subjects, and leisure time pursuits worthy of special consideration in planning for the future and to provide useful pre-interview information for the counselor. While the interpretation of inventory scores should always be done with the aid of an experienced counselor, the manual for this instrument is written in such a way that even relatively naïve persons should be able to use it properly. The rules of testing ethics are well observed in the manual by repeatedly reminding the reader of the modest goals of the inventory and the need to consider aptitudes as well as interests in vocational planning.

Each of the 238 items briefly describes a vocational activity or a course leading up to a vocational activity. Since names of obscure vocations are avoided, students should have little trouble understanding what the activity is, even though most of the jobs described will be unfamiliar to them. The responses are made by pricking a hole through one or two circles marked "like" to indicate degree of liking, pricking through one or two circles marked "dislike" to indicate degree of disliking, or failing to prick through any circle to indicate a lack of decision. The inventory has 12 "like" scores and 12 "dislike" scores determined conveniently by counting pricks in chains of rectangles or ovals. Each of the 12 scores is derived from either 29 or 30 items. Thus, some items are used in two of the scores and a few are used in three. This multiple use of items, though perhaps not serious, seems contradictory to the goal of independent scores stated in the manual. No intercorrelations of scores are presented to show how independent the scores actually turned out to be.

The instructions for interpretation are well presented. Several examples of score profiles are given and sample case histories are discussed. The manual also makes clear the nature and limitations of the reliability and norming data that are provided. A warning is sounded in the manual that interest scores have relative, rather than absolute, meaning. Ipsatively scored instruments such as the *Kuder Preference Record* have scores that are entirely relative, for, in those instruments, the scores in one area of interest are depressed by high interest, or raised by meager interest, in other fields. In this instrument, on the other hand, the scores are relative only insofar as the subject himself compares his intensity of liking from field to field. It is at least possible for a subject to show a liking for all fields. To this extent the Fowler-Parmenter inventory provides a good compromise between the extremes of relative and absolute scores. The manual explains this situation carefully and provides sample case histories that show how to avoid misleading interpretations.

An unusual example of lucid instruction for interpretation of scores is presented with a table of means and standard deviations. The positively skewed nature of the score distributions, probably characteristic for this kind of inventory, is described, and the consequent greater significance of deviations above the mean as compared to deviations below the mean is pointed out.

While the content and presentation of the Fowler-Parmenter inventory look good to this reviewer, and the manual is thorough and honest, it is nevertheless true that the stated limitations do exist. It is to be hoped that validity data, in particular, will be supplied at some future time. It is true that some amount of content validity may be assured by examining the items. However, even when a counselor merely suggests that his client consider certain vocations, there is implied a prediction that the client is more likely to succeed at these vocations or to find them more satisfying than he would find other vocations. To fully justify such implications as this, a validity study, using success and satisfaction criteria, ought to be carried out in such a way that the part played by the interest scores and the part played by appropriate aptitude test scores can be determined empirically.

[1054]

★The Geist Picture Interest Inventory, [1964 Revision]. Grades 8–16 and adults; 1959–64; 18 (males) or 19 (females) scores: 11 or 12 interest scores (persuasive, clerical, mechanical, musical, scientific, outdoor, literary, computational, artistic, social service, dramatic, personal service—females only) and 7 motivation scores (family, prestige, financial, intrinsic and personality, environmental, past experience, could not say); 1 form ('64); separate editions for males (11 pages) and females (9 pages); manual ('64, 56 pages); no data on reliability and validity of motivation scores; $12 per set of 10 tests of each edition and manual; $5 per 10 tests; $4 per manual; postpaid; specimen set not available; (40–65) minutes; Harold Geist; Western Psychological Services. * (Spanish edition published by Psychological Test Specialists.)

REFERENCES

1. ABDEL-MEGUID, SAAD GALAL MOHAMED. *The Reliability of an Experimental Picture Interest Inventory of Vocational Interests.* Master's thesis, Stanford University (Stanford, Calif.), 1951.
2. GEIST, HAROLD, AND McDANIEL, H. B. "Construction and Validation of a Picture Vocational Interest Inventory." Abstract. *Am Psychologist* 7:383–4 Jl '52. *
3. CLARKE, CARL TELLES. *A Comparative Study of the Geist Pictorial Vocational Interest Test and the Kuder Preference Record.* Master's thesis, University of Hawaii (Honolulu, Hawaii), 1959.
4. GEIST, HAROLD. "The Geist Picture Interest Inventory: General Form: Male." *Psychol Rep* 5:413–38 S '59. * (PA 38:4265)
5. GEIST, HAROLD. "Research Implications of a Pictorial Interest Test." *Calif J Ed Res* 10:25–8 Ja '59. * (PA 34:2036)
6. GEIST, HAROLD. "A Comparison of Observations of Parents of Their Children's Interests and Scores on a Picture Interest Inventory." *Calif J Ed Res* 11:207–12 N '60. * (PA 35: 4730)
7. MAGARY, JAMES FREDERICK. *An Analysis of the Vocational Interests of Educable Mentally Retarded Adolescent Boys From Three Occupational Classes.* Doctor's thesis, Indiana University (Bloomington, Ind.), 1960. (DA 21:3703)
8. GEIST, HAROLD. "An Exploratory Study of the Relationship Between Grades and a Pictorial Interest Test." *Calif J Ed Res* 12:91–6 Mr '61. * (PA 36:1KI91G)
9. GEIST, HAROLD. "A Five Year Follow-Up of the Geist Picture Interest Inventory." *Calif J Ed Res* 13:195–208 N '62. * (PA 37:7223)
10. GEIST, HAROLD. "An Occupational Validation of a Pictorial Interest Test." *Calif J Ed Res* 13:32–8 Ja '62. * (PA 36:5LB32G)
11. GEIST, HAROLD. "An 81-Variable Cluster Analysis of a Picture Interest Inventory." Abstract. *Psychol Rep* 12:40 F '63. * (PA 38:2474)
12. GEIST, HAROLD. "Work Satisfaction and Scores on a Picture Interest Inventory." *J Appl Psychol* 47:369–73 D '63. * (PA 38:6693)

MILTON E. HAHN, *Professor of Psychology, University of California, Los Angeles, California.* [Review of the 1959 edition published by Psychological Test Specialists and now withdrawn.]

The inventory is a test booklet containing 132 drawings organized into 44 triads. Although the inventory appears nonverbal, there are verbal directions which provide differing sets in which to make choices. Selection of one choice from a triad is to be indicated on an answer sheet which can be hand or machine scored. Areas in which the items are scored are the familiar ones employed by the *Kuder Preference Record:* Persuasive, Clerical, Mechanical, Musical, Scientific, Outdoor, Literary, Computational, Artistic, and Social Service. To these Geist adds Dramatic.

Items carry unit weights for the appropriate scales. The scores which one can obtain on the scales vary from 11 for Clerical and Social Service, to 20 for Computational.

A large 18 by 18 inch sheet is provided for the subject to indicate why he made a response. The motivational areas selected by Geist for reflecting these explanations are: Could Not Say, Family, Prestige, Financial, Intrinsic and Personality, Environment, and Past Experience. Although the manual makes suggestions that the qualitative checklist scores be inter-

preted by percentage of responses in the category, no norms are provided. Selection of the motivational areas reflects no theoretical position regarding the dimensions or structure of motivation, nor are there references in the manual to sources from which a structure for the selected areas can be inferred.

RELIABILITY. Reliability of the inventory is presented in terms of test-retest scores (six-month interval); the statements that "Consistency of response is likely to be much higher where the examinee is responding to stimuli which are closer to those he experiences in real life" and that "A good impression of a test's reliability in use can be obtained by computing the percentages of same responses given on retesting" need qualification. The first basis for reliability may lie in the distances between and among choices presented by some of the very ambiguous pictures. Although the manual states that "the author eliminated all photographs in which the occupation or hobby was not recognized correctly by at least 90% of those taking the inventory," he goes on to say: "Since many photographs were still ambiguous, it was decided to use drawings rather than photographs, retaining those which met the identification criterion, and substituting new drawings for those that did not." In taking the inventory, the reviewer was forced to resort to Table 1, Identifications of Drawings in the GPII, 29 times. This is far from a 90 per cent recognition rate, although the sample on which the recognition rate was determined might have reached the figure given. There are no data in the manual which deal with item analysis, either in terms of discriminating power or difficulty.

No proof is offered that the drawings represent "stimuli which are closer to those he experiences in real life." A simple test of this assumption would have been to offer a verbal form of the test with the items being the names of the occupations, or activities, represented by the drawings.

The third criterion of reliability, that the percentage of the respondents selecting the same items on retest is high, could suffer from the same difficulty which plagues the first—distances among and between choices are so great in some triads that it would be difficult *not* to reselect the original choice, e.g., potter, dentist, and musician.

VALIDITY. The case for validity is made by use of three criteria: (a) "Just as use of drawings should increase the reliability of the GPII by providing stimuli which are less ambiguous than those in typical all-verbal inventories, such use should contribute to the validity of the GPII"; (b) "since 10 of the 11 interest area scores provided by the GPII are similar to the scores for the 10 Kuder scales, it is possible roughly to evaluate the validity of the GPII by correlating the two sets of scores"; and (c) "examinees with reading problems will give more valid responses to the GPII than to highly verbal inventories."

The untested assumptions regarding the superiority of the particular drawings in the GPII, or drawings in general, are not confirmed by evidence presented in the manual. Moreover, that the scores correlate with scores with the same scale names on the *Kuder Preference Record* assumes that if A correlates highly with B, then C, which correlates with B, must also correlate highly with A. This does not hold in all cases. The validities of the Kuder and SVIB reside in establishing patterns based on scores from members of vocational, or avocational, groups. No evidence is presented that there are characteristic occupational patterns represented by patterns of scale scores on the GPII. Some evidence of this type might have been obtained by samples from those boys successful and satisfied in academic, general, clerical, and vocational curricula, as well as those from trade school and remedial reading groups.

Unless a clearer description is made available regarding the remedial reading sample, it is difficult to judge whether or not acceptable validity exists, even for a special group. The relationship between reading and general adjustment problems is such that this does not appear as a strong bit of evidence for general validity. The question here, too, is: "Validity for what?"

GENERAL EVALUATION. The *Geist Picture Interest Inventory* does not justify the statement in the manual, "The GPII has shown itself to be quite adequate in research as well as in counseling and guidance work, providing a quick and satisfactorily reliable and valid estimate of interest in 11 areas." (a) The hypothesis that drawings, or pictures, are closer to an undefined real life situation than are verbal cues is not tested. No supporting evidence is included in the manual, nor is any research from the literature cited to establish acceptance. (b) Reliabilities are not convincing. As high, or higher, correlations may be obtained by within-triad choices which are not scaled for distance in terms of general social desirability. Some scales are of too few items. Samples do not appear adequate in size or method of selection. (c) Validity is questionable if the inventory is intended for use in the vocational, avocational, or educational counseling or guidance of youth. It has been demonstrated that the scales will separate some secondary school males on the dimensions used, but the meaning of the differential scale patterns has not been established. Content validity is questionable; concurrent validity is not clearly demonstrated; construct validity is assumed; no predictive validity has been established in terms of environmental criteria. (d) No systematic approach is presented in the manual regarding the composition or size of standardization samples. The 615 mainland cases for grades 9–12 may be from a single school or school system. The mainland trade school sample has but 60 cases. Only 75 University of California freshmen and sophomores comprise the university sample. The remedial reading sample is from grades 8 and 10, with but 50 cases in each grade. Puerto Rican students number 340 cases, which provide norms for grades 8, 11, and 12, a trade school, and the University of Puerto Rico. The Hawaiian sample is from unnamed schools, grades 11 and 12, and has but 99 cases. (e) Statistical treatment reported in the manual is not impressive. There is no evidence as to the factor composition of the scales. No evidence is presented to demonstrate that a nonverbal, or essentially nonverbal, test measures the same dimensions or factors as does a verbal test. Rigorous research methodology is missing. (f) The references at the end of the manual do not include Bordin, Clark, Darley, Fryer, Holland, Strong, Super, Tyler, and other major contributors to the field of interest measurement. No mention is made of Weingarten's *Picture Interest Inventory,* a competitor in the field. No theoretical position is stated regarding the nature of interests. No important hypotheses are stated and accepted or rejected by the presentation of research.

SUMMARY OPINION. An experimental instrument in the first stages of development, this inventory is not ready for distribution for other than research uses.

BENJAMIN SHIMBERG, *Director of Educational Relations, Cooperative Test Division, Educational Testing Service, Princeton, New Jersey.* [Review of 1964 revision.]

DESCRIPTION. The *Geist Picture Interest Inventory* (GPII) is presented as an antidote to most of the existing inventories which require considerable verbal proficiency on the part of examinees. The author suggests that "disconcerting discrepancies often arise between real interests manifested by life behavior and 'interests' estimated from highly verbal interest inventories." Such inventories, he states, "are often used with children and adults who may have *limited verbal facility or who may be almost illiterate*" (italics mine).

Geist has approached interest measurement via occupationally oriented drawings. It is his belief that picture items are "less ambiguous with respect to life referents than most verbal items."

The 1964 edition of GPII comes in the form of two consumable booklets, one for men and another for women. Pictures are arranged in triads: 44 for men and 27 for women. The respondent is required to make a "forced choice" among the pictures in each triad by circling one of the pictures. Beneath each triad are captions such as: "If you had the ability, which would you rather do?" "Which man [or woman] would you rather be?" "Which picture is most interesting to you?" "About which would you rather study?" The author states that the questions have been varied to reduce task monotony and to avoid response repetition. There is no indication that the influence of question wording on response has been studied in a systematic fashion.

The scoring is in terms of broad fields of interest using Kuder's nomenclature. Geist has added two scales: Dramatic and Personal Service (for females only).

EVALUATION. Bauernfeind [1] has recently suggested some things to look for in reviewing an interest inventory. This reviewer has decided to follow Bauernfeind's suggestions with respect to the Geist inventory.

What are the intended purposes of the in-

1 BAUERNFEIND, ROBERT H. "What to Look for in a Review of an Interest Inventory." *Personnel & Guid J* 42:925–7 My '64. *

strument as viewed by the author and publisher? The author stresses the advantages of the pictorial approach for young people and adults who have difficulty understanding highly verbal materials. One would, therefore, conclude that this is the special audience toward which the GPII is directed and that its purpose is to facilitate interest measurement where highly verbal instruments are inappropriate. However, the manual stakes out a larger domain. It states that GPII "is a highly reliable and valid instrument in the quantitative determination of occupational and avocational interests of male and female populations, ranging from the eighth grade, through high school and college, and with adult groups."

How well are the actual test questions aligned with the stated purpose? The drawings permit an individual to identify with people at work (man welding, sawing, fixing TV set, etc.). It is in this realm that the GPII shows considerable promise. However, in an effort to make the instrument applicable to a broad population group, the author has included many drawings (over 30 per cent in the form for males) depicting people engaged in activities which require a high degree of verbal facility or advanced professional training. These are not activities likely to appeal to those with verbal handicaps. Indeed, they would appear to narrow the range of meaningful choice for those in this group whose interests are being probed.

What are the score areas and what does each score really mean? The score areas are the same as those used by Kuder with two additions. Space does not permit a detailed analysis of what each scale score means, but a close look at one area may be indicative of the problems that are likely to arise in the interpretation of scores. The manual defines the outdoor scale as indicating a preference for "outdoor or open air activities." The pictures contributing to a high outdoor score include those of a tree surgeon, a door-to-door salesman, a recreation director, a commercial fisherman, a farmer, a surveyor, a telephone lineman, a baseball player, a track runner, a dog trainer, some botanical specimens, and a man receiving a set of Air Force wings. True, all of these have an out-of-doors referent, but one might well ask whether the outdoors interest depicted by a tree surgeon represents the same set of values as those of the athlete or the Air Force pilot. This reviewer's skepticism is compounded when he notes that the author selected physical education teachers to represent the "outdoor" category in his norming and validation studies.

Are the scores derived from forced choice items such that all students tend to attain a balance of "high" or "low" scores? The forced choice technique may have certain advantages when every item is paired with every other item or combination of items. However, it is difficult to follow the logic of forced choice when there does not appear to be any systematic pairing or rotation. The various areas are unevenly represented. In the form for men, the clerical area is represented by 12 pictures, the persuasive area by 22. In the form for women, the mechanical area is represented by 24 pictures, the literary area by 4.

Are general norms provided or is it expected that scores will be interpreted using local norms? The author provides T score norms for students in grades 8–12, for two remedial reading groups, for a trade school sample, and for a university group. These are referred to as "the U.S. Mainland sample," meaning students from schools and colleges located in California. There are also norms for similar groups of students in Puerto Rico and Hawaii. In addition, T score tables are provided to show how members of various occupational groups scored on the various scales.

In transforming raw scores into T scores, the author assumes that the interests he is measuring are normally distributed in the specific norms populations he has established. This is a highly questionable assumption, and it throws serious doubt on the usefulness of the norms that are provided.

Since the number of cases represented in the various norms groups is not stated explicitly, one is left with the impression that they were established on a representative sample of lawyers, librarians, engineers, scientists, etc. One discovers, after some digging, that these norms were probably based on responses from not more than 12 lawyers, 24 librarians, 31 engineers, and 57 scientists. The median *n* for these occupational groups is 38 cases—an extremely small sample when one considers the great amount of variability *within* the various groups.

Are various scale scores reliable? Test-retest reliabilities for each interest area after a six-month interval for males in the mainland sample fluctuate between .13 and .94. Agreement

was highest for a sample of 75 university students and lowest for samples of trade school and remedial reading students. Median reliability was in the .60's. No reliability data are presented for female groups.

What types of follow-up validity studies have been reported? The author has attempted to demonstrate validity of GPII through the use of various criteria in five studies. (*a*) Manifest interest of children as reported by their parents. (*b*) GPII scores of individuals in occupations related to each interest area. (*c*) A five year follow-up of students tested in high school to determine (by questionnaire) the occupations in which they were currently engaged. (*d*) Correlation between GPII and Kuder scores. (*e*) Comparison of GPII scores and scores on a job satisfaction scale. The small number of cases used in each of these studies, problems of sampling, and other methodological questions make it difficult to interpret or place much credence in the results.

In the manifest interest study, for example, the author reports relatively high correlations on three scales: Persuasive (.71), Social Service (.62), and Musical (.42). He reports low correlations on Artistic (.17), Mechanical (.19), Clerical (.20), and Outdoor (.22). However, these results are based on only 101 cases which had to be further subdivided into 11 interest categories. The *n* for each category is not given.

The five year follow-up study was based on replies from 289 students out of a total group of 1,522 to whom questionnaires were sent. The author concludes that five of his scales are "highly valid," while two are "not at all valid." The reviewer does not feel that any meaningful conclusions can be reached on the basis of the very small, self-selected sample.

The occupational validation also suffers from inadequate sampling (see section on norms). Moreover, conclusions regarding validity seem to rest on relatively small differences in T scores. There is no indication that the standard error of measurement of the T scores has been taken into consideration in drawing conclusions regarding the significance of the differences under discussion.

Correlations between Kuder and GPII scores for men range from .24 to .38 for three groups of U.S. high school students, and between .49 and .65 for five groups of Hawaiian high school students. The author regards these positive

Geist Picture Interest Inventory

correlations as evidence of validity. One might ask what merit there may be in attempting to predict Kuder scores when the meanings of such scores are themselves open to serious question.[2]

The author attaches special significance to the fact that his remedial reading groups in the U.S. ($n = 70$) and in Hawaii ($n = 76$) showed somewhat lower correlations with Kuder scores than did other groups. He concludes, "GPII scores are more valid than Kuder scores for individuals with reading handicaps." This statement may be true, but this reviewer fails to see how the author can make it on the basis of the evidence he has presented.

CONCLUSION. The author has devised two experimental instruments which may be useful in situations where individuals suffer from reading disabilities. However, he has not yet demonstrated their usefulness for this special purpose, nor has he demonstrated that they produce useful or meaningful results when used with a more general population.

This reviewer can see possibilities in using the GPII as a clinical tool with the poor readers. Any attempt to provide guidance on the basis of normative information currently available would be a serious mistake.

Personnel & Guid J 38:506-7 F '60. David V. Tiedeman. * Although I find that the *Inventory* has faults, both logical and technical, the set of picture stimuli intelligently used either clinically or more formally might: (1) assess interest in a fuller context than usual and hence predict choice better than we can now do; (2) help us separate interest and capacity; and (3) identify interests in occupations besides the professions if the picture repertoire were expanded. Because of this potential, I have directed your attention to this *Inventory*. Perhaps some of you may have opportunity to test some of this potential and to let others know about it. I think it may be profitable to orient investigations of occupational motivations to pictures of work situations. [See original review for critical comments not excerpted.]

2 BAUERNFEIND, ROBERT H. "The Matter of 'Ipsative Scores.'" *Personnel & Guid J* 41:210-7 N '62. * (PA 37:6919)
KATZ, MARTIN. "Interpreting Kuder Preference Record—Vocational Scores: Ipsative or Normative." *Voc Guid Q* 10:96-100 w '62. (PA 37:1972)

Personnel & Guid J 39:59 S '60. Harold Geist. [An unexcerpted criticism of the above review by David V. Tiedeman. Also an unexcerpted reply by David V. Tiedeman.]

[1055]

★**Geist Picture Interest Inventory: Deaf Form: Male.** Deaf and hard of hearing males (grades 7-16 and adults); 1962; adaptation of *Geist Picture Interest Inventory;* 10 scores: persuasive, clerical, mechanical, scientific, outdoor, literary, computational, artistic, social service, dramatic; 1 form (29 pages); optional card form (81 cards) for determining occupation most preferred; record booklet-answer sheet (4 pages); manual (41 pages); no data on reliability of card form; separate answer sheets must be used; $2 per test (booklet form); $6.50 per 25 record booklet-answer sheets; $2.50 per set of keys; $6.50 per set of cards; $3 per manual; postpaid; [30-50] minutes; Harold Geist; Western Psychological Services. *

REFERENCES

I. GEIST, HAROLD. "Occupational Interest Profiles of the Deaf." *Personnel & Guid J* 41:50-5 S '62. * (PA 37:5340)

[1056]

★**Gordon Occupational Check List.** High school students not planning to enter college; 1961-63; 5 or 11 scores: business, outdoor, arts, technology, service, and 6 optional response summarization scores (preceding 5 areas and total); 1 form ('63, 6 pages); manual ('63, 15 pages); no norms; $4 per 35 tests; 40¢ per specimen set; postage extra; (20-25) minutes; Leonard V. Gordon; Harcourt, Brace & World, Inc. *

JOHN O. CRITES, *Associate Professor of Psychology, University of Iowa, Iowa City, Iowa.*

Designed specifically for use with individuals who have a high school education or less, the *Gordon Occupational Check List* (OCL) is an interest inventory which contains 240 statements of job duties and tasks, such as "install or repair plumbing in houses" and "fire and tend a large commercial furnace," found in occupations at the middle and lower levels of skill and responsibility. The statements are classified into five broad occupational groupings (Business, Outdoor, Arts, Technology, and Service) which roughly correspond to the groups in Roe's occupational classification scheme. Rather than Roe's six levels of skill and responsibility being represented in OCL, however, it includes only the lower levels, 3 through 6, which means that the top level professional and managerial occupations are not included. Within each of the OCL groupings further clusterings of statements have been made on the basis of common factorial structure, level of performance required, and the worker characteristics required for performance of the tasks. The groupings of items are not made explicit to the examinee, who is instructed simply to underline the statements of activities he would like to do and then to go back and circle the numbers of statements he would like to do the most. These responses are summarized for interpretative purposes in boxes provided at the end of a row of statements. In this respect, as in several others, the OCL is patterned after the *Mooney Problem Check List.*

Several kinds of reliability data are reported in the manual, most of which indicate that responses are reasonably stable over time. The total test-retest reliabilities for 52 male and 45 female twelfth graders, for example, were .81 and .82, respectively, with a month's interval, the data being percentage of items underlined identically on the two occasions. As the manual points out, these reliability estimates are attenuated by two factors: they do not take into consideration either the items not marked by the examinee or changes in response between highly similar items. When the first factor is accounted for by including a count of identical responses which were both underlined and not underlined, the reliabilities increase appreciably to .97 for males and .97 for females. Again, however, these coefficients are somewhat spurious because only a relatively small proportion of items is usually underlined. Probably the best conclusion which can be drawn is that the reliability of the OCL is in the middle or high .80's and should be sufficient for most counseling and research purposes.

Evidence for the validity of the OCL is less extensive and convincing than that for its reliability, consisting primarily of logical arguments for the instrument's comprehensiveness, response selectivity, and acceptance by examinees. About the best that can be said is that the OCL samples a fairly wide range of occupations which are commonly entered, it elicits responses to about one third of the items, and it appears to be considered worthwhile by those who take it. The relationships of the OCL to other variables, such as intelligence, inventoried interests, curricular choice, and occupational entry, have not been studied, and consequently its validity and usefulness is largely unknown.

The concepts and purposes which guided the construction of the OCL are sound: there is definitely a need for an inventory of lower level interests which can be used with high school age students as well as with older individuals

seen in rehabilitation centers and employment agencies. If the OCL is used as a checklist, which is its unique feature, it should have considerable value as an aid to interview discussions of specific job duties and tasks and their relative desirability to individuals who are headed for lower level occupations.

KENNETH B. HOYT, *Professor of Education, University of Iowa, Iowa City, Iowa.*

This inventory represents an attempt to construct, through logical means, an instrument which can be used to assess occupational interests of high school students not planning to enter college. The logic consisted of selecting 240 occupations, using Roe's group and level schema of occupational classification, which: "(1) could be successfully pursued by an individual with no more than a high school or equivalent education; (2) were relatively widespread geographically; (3) existed in some reasonable number; and (4) would not be considered objectionable by young people." Activity items representing critical job duties for each occupation were then written for each of the 240 occupations using the 1949 *Dictionary of Occupational Titles* and the 1961 *Occupational Outlook Handbook* as guides. These items constitute the prime content of the inventory.

While not stated in the manual, it appears that one must also assume, as part of the logic underlying construction of this inventory, that: (a) the concept of occupational interest is appropriate as a reason for choosing one of these occupations; (b) high school students will be familiar with the occupational tasks comprising the items and will be able to read the items as they appear; and (c) the manner in which high school students respond to these items bears some relationship to their occupational future. The manual reports no tests of these additional assumptions.

The 240 items are unevenly distributed among five areas of occupational interest. Technology (with 96 items) is most heavily represented. Both Business and Service have half as many items as Technology, while Outdoor and Arts each have one fourth as many. Items are clustered both by area and by level in the inventory. Four questions requiring varying amounts of writing from the student are placed at the end. There are no time limits.

A preliminary form of the checklist was administered to more than 6,000 high school students. The final form was constructed on the basis of analyses of responses of these students. Seventeen item substitutions were made in the final form. All statistical data reported in the manual are based on results obtained using the preliminary form. Information gleaned from reliability data presented indicate that: (*a*) the total number of items underlined in a test-retest situation is about the same; (*b*) in a test-retest situation, about two thirds of the items underlined by the same individuals are identical; (*c*) there is a substantial relationship between the specific items to which samples of boys and girls respond in a test-retest situation; and (*d*) there is a high relationship between the individual items responded to by two samples of boys and a similarly high relationship for girls. The numbers of students represented here range from 45 to 100. All were twelfth graders.

There are no norms reported. Means and standard deviations of numbers of responses by area and for the entire checklist are presented for 161 boys and 133 girls in the twelfth grade. The standard deviations are almost as large, and in several cases considerably larger, than the means, indicating a markedly skewed distribution. Evidently, a few students must have underlined a great many items and many students must have underlined very few.

The manual states the criterion of response selectivity as one to be used in assessing validity of the checklist. These means and standards are presented as evidence that this criterion has been met. I would interpret them as meaning that this criterion was not met well.

A second claim for validity is made on the basis of comprehensiveness by showing that, when one sample of 172 high school students were given an opportunity to list other occupations in which they were interested, very few did so. In the third place, when students in another sample were asked to write at the end of the checklist the life work they would choose for themselves, their responses were "closely related" to the occupations students had just underlined in the checklist. Finally, a claim for validity is made on the basis of the fact that a majority of students reported they enjoyed answering the checklist. No evidence is presented with respect to such factors as relationships between responses on the checklist and entry or persistence in an occupation

nor satisfaction with occupations. Those looking for these kinds of evidence of validity will conclude that, to date, there is no reason to believe the checklist to be a valid instrument.

The 240 occupations represented in the checklist are presented as ones which could be successfully pursued with no more than a high school or equivalent education. Many will question whether such occupations as occupational therapist, X-ray technician, literary writer, watchmaker, public relations man, clergyman, or hotel manager could really be so classified. It would seem that some distinctions might have been made between what is *possible* with no more than a high school education and what is likely to be attainable. Certainly, some distinction should be made between occupations requiring further specialty training (albeit, not at the college level) and those requiring only a high school education. Likewise, it would seem that consideration might be given to distinguishing between entry occupations and non-entry occupations in selection of items for the checklist. These are serious weakneses.

The manual states that "much of this same information could be elicited during the course of an interview." This would seem to be an honest representation of the value of the checklist at present.

[1057]

★The Guilford-Zimmerman Interest Inventory. Grades 10–16 and adults; 1962–63; 10 scores: mechanical, natural, aesthetic, service, clerical, mercantile, leadership, literary, scientific, creative; 1 form ('63, 4 pages); manual ('63, 5 pages, called preliminary in text); profile ('62, 1 page); reliability and validity data based on an earlier longer form; norms for college freshmen only; separate answer sheets must be used; $3.50 per 25 tests; 20¢ per single copy; 5¢ per IBM scorable answer sheet; $2.50 per set of scoring stencils; 5¢ per profile; 35¢ per manual; postage extra; (20–30) minutes; Joan S. Guilford and Wayne S. Zimmerman; Sheridan Supply Co. *

KENNETH B. HOYT, *Professor of Education, University of Iowa, Iowa City, Iowa.*

This is an interest inventory which, if used at present, must be largely accepted on faith. Such faith must encompass many dimensions. First, one must have faith that the 10 interest categories in which scores may be obtained are inclusive for the range of occupational interests. The authors present no evidence showing this to be the case.

Second, one must accept the authors' contention that the 150 items (15 for each of the 10 scales) are accurate representations of the interest each stands for. Certainly, there is no intuitive way of establishing this to be the case and, again, no evidence is presented by the authors. Items were selected for inclusion on the basis of those which discriminated best among a sample of approximately 800 college freshmen who were administered a "preliminary experimental form" consisting of 450 items.

Third, in seeking answers regarding reliability of the scales, one must accept the authors' contention that the intra-scale correlations will be high. The authors base this claim on their report of average intra-scale correlations in the preliminary experimental form ranging "from .68 to .88." No reliability data for the present published form are presented.

Fourth, one must accept the authors' statement that "useful external criteria have not been sufficiently developed for the establishment of validity data." Those conversant with the literature reported with reference to validity of the SVIB may have some difficulty here.

Fifth, one is asked to accept the authors' statement with respect to their norm group of about 800 college freshmen that "students in the two Southern California colleges....have, in previous testing, proved to be fairly representative of liberal arts college students throughout the United States." The authors do note that further standardization is in progress and its results will be reported later.

One major feature of this instrument is that it is a non-ipsative measure. Examinees are asked to mark one of four responses to each item. These responses are assigned constant weights. A "Definite Dislike" response is scored 0; a "No Interest or Mild Dislike" is scored 1; a "Some Interest or Slight Like" is scored 2; and a "Definite Like" is scored 3. With 15 items per scale, the possible range of scores for each scale runs from 0 to 45. No data are reported relative to the appropriateness of these assigned weights.

Another feature is the presence of a "Creative" scale. Some may find themselves wondering whether it is possible to build such items independent of other interests. For example, could not a highly creative person with no mechanical interests mark "Build a unique structure out of unconventional materials" as a "Definite Dislike," not because he is without creative interests, but simply because he has no interest in things mechanical? Other examples

of items from this scale which could be similarly questioned include "Invent a new 'gadget'" and "Experiment with materials to produce a unique art object."

Other claims made in the manual include the fact that administration time is short, scoring is quick and easy, and the scales are built using factor analysis procedures. Each of these claims appears justified. Those who are satisfied with such claims may find this inventory acceptable.

The manual suggests that the inventory be used in grades 10 through college age groups. Why the authors feel this instrument to be appropriate at grade 10 in spite of the fact the norms are for college freshmen is not explained.

By and large, it would seem that this inventory may be intended to compete with the SVIB. However, before it can sensibly be expected to do so, it is in need of much further development.

[1058]

★Hackman-Gaither Vocational Interest Inventory, Revised Edition. Grades 9–12 and adults; 1962–64; 8 scores: business contact, artistic, scientific-technical, health and welfare, business clerical, mechanical, service, outdoor; IBM; 1 form ('64, 12 pages); manual ('63, c1962–63, 22 pages); scoring instructions ('64, 2 pages); technical report ('63, 40 pages); profile ('62, 2 pages); student summary—curricular group means chart ('64, 4 pages); job preference indicator ('62, 2 pages) for each score field; separate answer sheets must be used; $7 per 20 tests; $1.60 per 20 IBM scorable answer sheets; $1.20 per 20 profiles; 10¢ per student summary—curricular group means chart; $1 per 20 job preference indicators for any one score field; 30¢ per manual; 60¢ per technical report; postage extra; $1.75 per specimen set, postpaid; (25–30) minutes; Roy B. Hackman and James W. Gaither; Palmer Associates. *

REFERENCES

1. ARNS, JOSEPHINE. *A Factorial Analysis of the Vocational Interests of Two Hundred Adult Female Students.* Doctor's thesis, Temple University (Philadelphia, Pa.), 1958. (*DA* 19:562)
2. BERRIER, JOHN G. *A Factorial Analysis of the Occupational Interests of Two Hundred Vocationally Experienced Adult Male Students.* Doctor's thesis, Temple University (Philadelphia, Pa.), 1958. (*DA* 19:1645)
3. GAITHER, JAMES WALLACE. *A Factorial Analysis of the Occupational Interests of Two Hundred Vocationally Inexperienced Adult Male Students.* Doctor's thesis, Temple University (Philadelphia, Pa.), 1958. (*DA* 19:868)
4. COHEN, LEONARD MARLIN. *The Relationship Between Certain Personality Variables and Prior Occupational Stability of Prison Inmates.* Doctor's thesis, Temple University (Philadelphia, Pa.), 1959. (*DA* 20:3375)

[1059]

*How Well Do You Know Your Interests. High school, college, adults; 1957–62; 54 scores: numerical, clerical, retail selling, outside selling, selling real estate, one-order selling, sales complaints, selling intangibles, buyer, labor management, production supervision, business management, machine operation, repair and construction, machine design, farm or ranch, gardening, hunting, adventure, social service, teaching service, medical service, nursing service, applied chemistry, basic chemical problems, basic biological problems, basic physical problems, basic psychological problems, philosophical, visual art appreciative, visual art productive, visual art decorative, amusement appreciative, amusement productive, amusement managerial, literary appreciative, literary productive, musical appreciative, musical performing, musical composing, sports appreciative, sports participative, domestic service, unskilled labor, disciplinary, power seeking, propaganda, self-aggrandizing, supervisory initiative, bargaining, arbitrative, persuasive, disputatious, masculinity (for males only) or femininity (for females only); Form B-22 (6 pages); 3 editions (identical except for profiles): secondary school ('58), college ('57), personnel ('57); manual ('57, 24 pages); educational guidance supplement ('58, 12 pages); technical summary ('62, 4 pages); no description of normative population for personnel edition; $7.50 per 30 tests; $2.50 per specimen set of any one edition; postage extra; (20–30) minutes; Thomas N. Jenkins; Executive Analysis Corporation. *

REFERENCES

1. MENDELSON, MARTIN A. *Personality and Interests of Air Force Personnel.* Doctor's thesis, New York University (New York, N.Y.), 1957. (*DA* 21:3844)

JOHN R. HILLS, *Director, Testing and Guidance, The University System of Georgia, Atlanta, Georgia.*

HWDYKYI purports to be an interest inventory based on the principles and application of factor analysis. The Manual of Instructions mentions "over 1,000 factor analyses," "about 3,000,000 correlations," and "a fifteen year investigation of personality and personality appraisal." However, in the manual, the Educational Guidance Supplement, and the Technical Summary, only one research report which appears to include this inventory is mentioned, that one being a 1957 doctoral thesis (*1*) with no indication that it was ever published. Query to the publisher resulted in reprints concerning factor analyses of personality, but not of interests.

The idea behind the instrument apparently was factor analyzing interest items into homogeneous groups and using two to four of the most highly loaded items on each factor to represent that factor in the inventory. This should be a route to efficient measurement of a wide variety of independent variables. The inventory provides 53 scores from 120 items, each used only once, except that an item may be reused to measure masculinity-femininity, the 54th score.

The basic idea is good. Why is the reviewer unenthusiastic? First, the manual, the Educational Guidance Supplement, and the Technical Summary don't agree in detail with each other, even though long sections duplicate each other.

They are poorly edited, e.g., Table 5 is referred to in the Technical Summary but appears only in the manual; the Educational Guidance Supplement shows that 513 secondary school students were used to develop test-retest reliability coefficients, but the Technical Summary implies that 2,603 students participated in the reliability study. Other examples of this type could be cited.

Beside poor editing, other signs of carelessness appear in annoying numbers. The manual says, "A random sample of at least 200 employees is necessary for establishing an accurate set of local norms." Yet it states, "For those who prefer a more representative sample of young men throughout the United States, Table 3 has been included. These norms are based on a sample of 200 unmarried men from 29 states." Apparently, local norms require a random sample, but a representative sample of young men throughout the United States need not be random, nor even stratified by geographical region. The same casual approach appears in the case of secondary school norms. The Educational Guidance Supplement indicates that those norms are based on students from 8 western, 2 midwestern, 17 northeastern, and 1 southern secondary schools. Eight of the 28 schools were in New York City!

The Technical Summary and the Manual of Instructions both state, "The median value of the 53 mean validities is 79.5." This is mathematical nonsense in terms of factorial validities, the kind of validity coefficient stressed for this test. It apparently is an error in decimal placement, but occurs in two documents published over a five-year interval.

One could go on at length, but why must one bother with such tangential evidence of inadequacy? Why not discuss the factor analyses, the content of the items which were used in the "over 1,000 factor analyses," the interpretation of the factors, the appropriateness of the communality estimates, the method of extraction, the method of rotation, the criteria for stopping extraction, etc., as they apply to this inventory? These data would reveal what the test measures factorially. The reason is that one can't examine these basic issues. The data specific to this interest test are not presented nor given bibliographic citation in standard publications or otherwise, and cannot be obtained upon query of the organization responsible for the instrument. Since a reviewer or a potential user cannot examine the basic data, he must study what is available to him, and in this case it is grossly inadequate. Until this is remedied, it is of no consequence that the test may be clever, easy to use, comprehensive, economical, or otherwise superior.

A test is of no value unless one can ascertain reasonably clearly what its scores measure. For a factored test with little or no published empirical evidence of validity, the definition of score meaning comes from study of items and factor loadings. In this case, only two items and their loadings are given for most of the scores. The ordinary user cannot readily find out what sets of items these were chosen to represent, what sets were included in the factor analyses on which the inventory is based, or what the factor loadings were of the items on various factors. Correspondence with the publisher leaves one sympathetic with his problems, i.e., the cost of publishing all these data and the fact that others will "borrow" good items once they are published. While solutions to these problems would be welcomed, recognition of them is no help to the potential user. He must decide whether to use this unknown device with a client. The ethical decision can only be to use it only for experimental purposes until more information is released by the publisher or until the user's own research reveals the value of the instrument. The reviewer is left disappointed that such a good effort toward improved, modern measurement of interests was left incomplete by the death of the author!

J Counsel Psychol 7:154 su '60. Gordon V. Anderson. This interest inventory has been designed to give reliable information about vocational interests over the widest possible range of occupational possibilities with greatest convenience possible and maximum saving of time. It appears to have achieved this remarkably well. * perhaps we do here have a useful contribution to interest measurement * The vocabulary level does not appear to be above that of the secondary school level, and the activities described are easily understood and unambiguous. The directions for responding to the inventory are simple * when all factors are considered, the cost of an interest profile obtained from this inventory is probably as low as from any other comparable standard inventory. The manual is well written, and a high professional standard is set in the recommen-

dations which are made in it. Information about the development of the inventory and the procedures used for its standardization is somewhat skimpy. * Regardless of the inventory used, counselors are not likely to accept the results obtained at face value. The very nature of attitudes makes us reluctant to generalize readily from a quantitative result. The score or the profile is useful primarily as a starting point for counseling. The Jenkins vocational interest inventory holds out attractive clinical promise, with studies of patterning, both within the principal interest domains and among them, offering interesting possibilities. It would seem likely that an insightful counselor would find the profile very helpful in working with students to help them understand themselves better. Its very complexity should serve to discourage overgeneralizations and unsound predictions.

For reviews by Jerome E. Doppelt and Henry S. Dyer, see 5:859.

[1060]
*Inventory of Vocational Interests: Acorn National Aptitude Tests. Grades 7–16 and adults; 1943–60; 5 scores: mechanical, academic, artistic, business and economic, farm-agricultural; 1 form ('57, c1943–57, 4 pages, identical with test copyrighted 1943); manual ('60, c1943–60, 6 pages, identical with manual copyrighted in 1943); directions sheet ('60, c1943–60, 1 page, identical with sheet copyrighted in 1943); no data on reliability; $2.50 per 25 tests; 25¢ per manual; $1 per specimen set; postage extra; (35) minutes; Andrew Kobal, J. Wayne Wrightstone, and Karl R. Kunze; [Psychometric Affiliates]. *

JOHN W. FRENCH, *Professor of Psychology, and College Examiner, New College, Sarasota, Florida.*

Each of the 25 items of this inventory asks the subject to check the nature of his interest with respect to some very general piece of equipment, organization, or situation. In each item he is to check exactly 3 out of 10 activities, labeled *a* through *j*. These options are worded differently as appropriate for each item, but their nature and sequence are fixed: *a* and *b* are mechanical activities, *c* and *d* are academic, *e* and *f* are artistic, *g* and *h* are business and economic, and *i* and *j* are farm-agricultural. The scores are then simply the number of checks recorded in each of these five areas of interest. The highest possible score is 50, resulting, for example, from checking both *a* and *b* in every item. The manual considers a score of 35 in one field to indicate "an outstanding quantity of interest." When no score for a field reaches this amount, the two fields with the highest scores are to be considered. Vocational counseling is then done on the basis of a one-page "Index of Basic Occupations" that lists occupations for each of the five fields and for every combination of two fields. For example, "carpenter" is one of 17 occupations listed for mechanical; "psychologist" is one of 14 listed for academic; and chemist is one of 13 listed for the combination of these two fields.

Compared to other vocational interest inventories this one has some advantages and some important shortcomings. Its advantages are: (*a*) The time it takes to complete is relatively short. (*b*) The scoring is so simple that the students can be asked to score their own tests. (*c*) The items are written about activities that are familiar to students rather than written in terms of occupational titles. (*d*) The activities among which the subjects must choose are well balanced for their social or prestige appeal.

The disadvantages of this inventory include: (*a*) The scores are ipsative, that is, the scores in the five areas may be compared only within a subject; the scores are not such that the intensity of interest can be compared from subject to subject, because relative interest in one field causes a depressed score in another field. Conversely, very meager interest in four fields will make a very modest interest in the fifth field seem to be intense. (*b*) The fixed sequence for the 10 options in each item makes the subject very much aware at all times what interests he is revealing. At best this is distracting; at worst it leads the subject unconsciously to mold his interest scores to a preconceived pattern or allows him consciously to fake in order to attain some practical goal. (*c*) Reliability and validity data are inadequate. The manual claims that "validity" of the inventory is sufficiently high to warrant its application in individual diagnosis. This sounds more like a claim of reliability, and it is not supported by data. Validity is claimed on the basis of rather interesting data for 60 cases showing a flat interest pattern or lack of interest in educationally low graded individuals. Data on 120 subjects is used to show a correlation of .65 between test scores and previous job advancement and a correlation of .38 with wages. More cases, more different groups, predictive rather than concurrent validity, and more information about the subjects is required before validity of the

test can be considered to be established. (*d*) In their present form and with their present description in the manual, the "norms" tables are misleading. They do not, as might be expected, indicate an individual's percentile with respect to the intensity of his interest in a given field as compared to the interest of other individuals in the same field. Because of the ipsative nature of the scoring, the norms tables indicate merely an individual's percentile with respect to the amount of imbalance among his own interests as compared to the amount of imbalance displayed by other individuals.

This is an interest inventory that is simple and pleasant to use. It should be an interesting candidate for trial in a vocational testing situation. However, a user should not put reliance on the scores until they have been shown to predict future job behavior in the situation for which the test is to be used.

For reviews by Marion A. Bills, Edward S. Bordin, Harold D. Carter, and Patrick Slater, see 3:638.

[1061]
★**Job Choice Inventory.** Male job applicants and employees in oil and chemical industries; 1951–63; 5 scores: general mechanical, electrical and precision, construction and handiwork, process and laboratory, vehicle operation; Form O-C ('51, 3 pages); manual ['63, 17 unnumbered pages]; $3 per 25 tests; $2.50 per set of keys; $1.25 per manual; postage extra; $3 per specimen set, postpaid; (25–30) minutes; Richardson, Bellows, Henry & Co., Inc. *

[1061a]
*★**Kuder General Interest Survey.** Grades 6–12; 1934–64; revision and downward extension of *Kuder Preference Record—Vocational,* Form C; 11 scores: outdoor, mechanical, computational, scientific, persuasive, artistic, literary, musical, social service, clerical, verification; form E ('63, 15 pages); manual ('64, 52 pages); separate profiles ('63, 4 pages) for grades 6–8, 9–12; separate answer pads must be used; $11 per 20 tests; $2.60 per 20 self-marking answer pads; 70¢ per 20 profiles; 75¢ per specimen set; postage extra; (45–60) minutes; G. Frederic Kuder; Science Research Associates, Inc. *

[1062]
*★**Kuder Preference Record — Occupational.** Grades 9–16 and adults; 1956–63; 51 scores: verification, county agricultural agent, farmer, forester, minister, newspaper editor, physician [revised], clinical psychologist, industrial psychologist, YMCA secretary, school superintendent, accountant, meteorologist, personnel manager, department store salesman, psychology professor, mechanical engineer, counseling psychologist, journalist, architect ['57], electrical engineer (revised), civil engineer, retail clothier, insurance agent, dentist, veterinarian, industrial engineer, pediatrician, psychiatrist, radio station manager, interior decorator, high school counselor, high school science teacher, high school mathematics

teacher, chemist, mining and metallurgical engineer, druggist, job printer ['58], bank cashier ('59), male librarian ('59), pharmaceutical salesman ('59), X-ray technician ('59), podiatrist ('61), florist ('61), heating and air conditioning engineer ('61), heating and air conditioning sales engineer ('61), auto mechanic ('61), long distance truck driver ('61), teaching sister ('63), teaching brother ('63); IBM; Form D ('56, 12 pages); manual, fourth edition ('61, c1956–59, 17 pages); special accessories for use in developing occupational keys: computation sheet booklet ('56, 26 pages), research handbook, second edition ('57, c1956, 47 pages); separate answer sheets must be used; $11 per 20 tests; $6.25 per 100 IBM answer sheets; $1 per scoring stencil for any one score; $2.50 per computation sheet booklet; $2.50 per research handbook; $2 per counseling specimen set; $6 per research specimen set; postage extra; (25–35) minutes; G. Frederic Kuder; Science Research Associates, Inc. *

REFERENCES

1. JONES, CHARLES W. *Kuder Preference Record Occupational Form D: Scoring for Secondary Teachers.* Master's thesis, Iowa State College of Agriculture and Mechanic Arts (Ames, Iowa), 1957.
2. BARTON, ERVIN M. *Development of a Kuder Preference Record Occupational Form D, Scoring Key for Secondary School Counselors.* Master's thesis, Iowa State University (Ames, Iowa), 1958.
3. BLANCHARD, ROBERT EUGENE. *The Development and Validation of Instruments for Selecting Farm Operators for Farm Management Services.* Doctor's thesis, Purdue University (Lafayette, Ind.), 1959. *(DA* 20:2884)
4. JAMES, FLEMING. *The Stability of the Civil, Electrical, and Mechanical Engineering Scales of the Kuder Preference Record Occupational, Form D, and Some Implications for Counseling.* Master's thesis, Duke University (Durham, N.C.), 1959.
5. JOSEPH, MICHAEL P. "The Strong Vocational Interest Blank and the Kuder Preference Record—Occupational (Form D): A Comparative Study of Eight Same-Named Scales." *Yearb Nat Council Meas Ed* 18:145–54 '61. *
6. WARD, GLEN R. *Interest Patterns of the Kuder Preference Record Occupational Form D.* Master's thesis, Utah State University (Logan, Utah), 1961.
7. BOYCE, RICHARD W. "The Construction and Validity of an Interest Key for Medical Technologists." *Am J Med Tech* 28:349–51 N–D '62. *
8. CAMPBELL, JOEL T.; OTIS, JAY L.; LISKE, RALPH E.; AND PRIEN, ERICH P. "Assessments of Higher-Level Personnel: 2, Validity of the Over-All Assessment Process." *Personnel Psychol* 15:63–74 sp '62. * *(PA* 37:3908)
9. SCHUTZ, RICHARD E., AND BAKER, ROBERT L. "A Comparison of the Factor Structure of the Kuder Occupational, Form D for Males and Females." *Ed & Psychol Meas* 22:485–92 au '62. * *(PA* 37:5696)
10. SCHUTZ, RICHARD E., AND BAKER, ROBERT L. "A Factor Analysis of the Kuder Preference Record—Occupational, Form D." *Ed & Psychol Meas* 22:97–104 sp '62. * *(PA* 37:1265)
11. WALKER, ROBERT WILLIAM. *Development of a Vocational Agriculture Interest Inventory for Guidance of Eighth Grade Students.* Doctor's thesis, Pennsylvania State University (University Park, Pa.), 1962. *(DA* 23:3702)
12. KUDER, G. FREDERIC. "A Rationale for Evaluating Interests." *Ed & Psychol Meas* 23:3–12 sp '63. * *(PA* 38:3242)
13. TERWILLIGER, JAMES S. "Dimensions of Occupational Preference." *Ed & Psychol Meas* 23:525–42 au '63. * *(PA* 38:6698)

DAVID P. CAMPBELL, *Associate Professor of Psychology, and Director, Center for Interest Measurement Research, University of Minnesota, Minneapolis, Minnesota.*

The Kuder-Occupational is a 100 triad inventory requiring the respondent to choose one item in each triad as liked most and one as liked least. It is a derivative of earlier forms of the *Kuder Preference Record,* and, as in those earlier forms, the author has done a careful job of selecting items and developing scales.

Unlike earlier forms of the Kuder, and like the *Strong Vocational Interest Blank,* it is scored on occupational keys developed by comparing answers of men in specific occupations with a group of men in general. Thus it competes directly with the SVIB, and most of this review will be devoted to comparing these two instruments.

Only concurrent validity results are reported in the manual and these are quite satisfactory. The scales do separate occupational groups from men in general, and they hold up well on cross validation. No data are furnished on the predictive validity, an area well researched with positive results for the Strong. And, regrettably, there are no data useful in the construct validity sense; no scale intercorrelations are presented; there are no groupings of occupations into larger, more meaningful categories, a technique very useful in interpreting the Strong; there are no indications of sex or age differences.

There are bound to be differences in the validity of these two instruments since the correlations between scales with the same name are only moderately high; they are measuring different things. In one study (5) using 45 students, the median correlation between eight like-named Kuder and Strong scales was .50. Another study, reported in the same paper, using 164 students on 10 scales, reported a median correlation of .45. There is no way of knowing from these studies which scale is best. The Kuder has the advantage of being developed more recently and thus should capitalize on any changes in the makeup of the occupations, while the Strong has an overwhelming amount of research to show that its scales are valid.

Kuder argues clearly and cogently in his manual that reliability as measured by internal consistency measures is not important when the intent is to separate occupations, and neither he nor this reviewer is particularly uncomfortable that these reliabilities are somewhat low (median K-R 20 = .81). But reliability over time, test-retest stability, is another matter. In advising a student about his future plans, test users need to have some assurance that the qualities being measured are stable. The Strong blank has good data on this point for periods up to 18 years. The only data presented in the Kuder manual are for a one month interval, where the median test-retest correlation for college students is .85, slightly lower than comparable figures for the Strong. The Kuder has yet to be proven over a lengthy time span, and, from this one indication, its stability may be less than the Strong.

Kuder has done considerable thinking about how to assure that the individual's answers are honest and careful, and, to this end, he has developed a verification scale to identify careless or dishonest answers. From the data presented, this scale works well. This is a worthwhile feature, although its importance is exaggerated in the manual; more space is devoted to this topic than to either reliability or validity. No such detection key has been developed for the Strong.

In ease of administration and scoring the Kuder definitely has an edge over the Strong. It is shorter, and scoring is much simpler. Other features of the Kuder include a Research Handbook and computational sheets which should be quite helpful to anyone wishing to develop his own scales.

In summary, this inventory has been developed with careful attention to item selection and scale development and it has some useful features not found in other interest inventories. However, in the bread-and-butter areas of reliability, validity, and ease of interpretation, it is still not well established and falls far behind the *Strong Vocational Interest Blank*. Practitioners are advised to continue with the Strong until more developmental research eliminates some of the unanswered questions about this inventory.

For reviews by Edward S. Bordin and John W. Gustad, see 5:862.

[1063]

*Kuder Preference Record—Vocational. Grades 9–16 and adults; 1934–62; IBM; 2 forms; 2 editions of each; separate answer sheets or pads must be used; $11 per 20 tests; 70¢ per 20 profiles; 75¢ per specimen set of any one edition; postage extra; (40–50) minutes; G. Frederic Kuder; Science Research Associates, Inc. *

a) FORM B [NINE SCALE EDITION]. 1934–60; 9 scores: mechanical, computational, scientific, persuasive, artistic, literary, musical, social service, clerical; masculinity-femininity score also obtainable; 1 form; 2 editions; revised manual ('60, 25 pages); profile for adults ('46, 2 pages); profile for children ('44, 2 pages).

1) [*Hand Scoring Edition.*] Form BB ('42, 15 pages, called Form BH in publisher's catalog); $2.60 per 20 self-marking answer pads; 75¢ per 20 punch pins; $1.65 per 20 backing cardboards.

2) [*Machine Scoring Edition.*] IBM; Form BM ('42, 19 pages); $5 per 100 IBM answer sheets; $7.50 per set of scoring stencils.

b) FORM C [ELEVEN SCALE EDITION]. 1934–62; revision and expansion of Form B; 11 scores: same as for Form B plus outdoor, verification; 1 form; 2 editions; revised manual ('60, 27 pages); profile for adults ('51, 2 pages); profile for children ('50, 2 pages); profile leaflets (4 pages) for adults ('54) and for children ('53) for comparing vocational and personal (see 132) scores.

1) [*Hand or DocuTran Scoring Edition.*] Form CH ('48, 15 pages); supplementary manual ('62, 15 pages) for use with DocuTran scoring service; $2.60 per 20 self-marking answer pads; fee for DocuTran scoring service: 25¢ per student; fee includes answer sheet, supplementary manual, and 3 copies of profile report of scores.

2) [*Machine Scoring Edition.*] IBM; Form CM ('48, 20 pages); $5 per 100 IBM answer sheets; $7.50 per set of scoring stencils; scoring service available.

REFERENCES

1–2. See 40:1671.
3–62. See 3:640.
63–208. See 4:742.
209–419. See 5:863.
420. McCARTHY, THOMAS N. *The Relationship of Vocational Interests to Personality Traits.* Master's thesis, Catholic University of America (Washington, D.C.), 1952.
421. D'ARCY, PAUL F. *Constancy of Interest Factor Patterns Within the Specific Vocation of Foreign Missioner.* Catholic University of America, Studies in Psychology and Psychiatry, Vol. 9, No. 1. Washington, D.C.: Catholic University of America Press, 1954. Pp. ix, 54. * (PA 29:6444)
422. JACOBS, ROBERT, AND TRAXLER, ARTHUR E. "What Manner of Man Is the Average Accountant." *J Accountancy* 97:465–9 Ap '54. *
423. MOFFETT, CHARLES R. *Operational Characteristics of Beginning Master's Students in Educational Administration and Supervision.* Doctor's thesis, University of Tennessee (Knoxville, Tenn.), 1954.
424. LUTON, JAMES N. *A Study of the Use of Standardized Tests in the Selection of Potential Educational Administrators.* Doctor's thesis, University of Tennessee (Knoxville, Tenn.), 1955.
425. WOMER, FRANK B., AND FURST, EDWARD J. "Interest Profiles of Student Nurses." *Nursing Res* 3:125–6 F '55. *
426. FURST, EDWARD J., AND FRICKE, BENNO G. "Development and Applications of Structured Tests of Personality." *R Ed Res* 26:26–55 F '56. * (PA 31:6081)
427. GARRETT, GENE A. *A Study of the Causes of Unsatisfactory Verification Scores on the Kuder Preference Record Vocational.* Master's thesis, University of Missouri (Columbia, Mo.), 1956.
428. TAYLOR, PRESTON L. *A Study of the Relationship Between Intelligence as Measured by SRA Primary Mental Abilities Tests and Validity Scores on the Kuder Vocational Preference Record.* Master's thesis, Texas Southern University (Houston, Tex.), 1956.
429. URSCHALITZ, M. ODELIA. *Measurement of General Interests and Interests Relevant to Vocation Aim Among Religious Women.* Master's thesis, Fordham University (New York, N.Y.), 1956.
430. WAUCK, LE ROY. *An Investigation of the Usefulness of Psychological Tests in the Selection of Candidates for the Diocesan Priesthood.* Doctor's thesis, Loyola University (Chicago, Ill.), 1956.
431. BOOTH, MARY D. "A Study of the Relationship Between Certain Personality Factors and Success in Clinical Training of Occupational Therapy Students." *Am J Occup Ther* 11:93–6+ Mr–Ap '57. * (PA 32:4585)
432. GOWAN, J. C. "A Summary of the Intensive Study of Twenty Highly Selected Elementary Women Teachers." *J Exp Ed* 26:115–24 D '57. * (PA 33:4731)
433. LUCIO, WILLIAM H., AND RISCH, FRANK. "Relationships Among Tests of Intelligence, Vocational Interest and Aptitude." *Calif J Ed Res* 8:198–203 N '57. * (PA 33:7005)
434. PETRO, PETER K. *Student Aptitudes and Abilities Correlated With Achievement in First Semester High School Bookkeeping.* Master's thesis, Iowa State Teachers College (Cedar Falls, Iowa), 1957.
435. SININGER, ROLLIN ALBERT. *Development and Evaluation of Visual Aids for Interpreting the Differential Aptitude Test and Kuder Preference Record.* Master's thesis, University of Texas (Austin, Tex.), 1957.
436. ANIKEEFF, ALEXIS M., AND BRYAN, JOHN L. "Kuder Interest Pattern Analysis of Fire Protection Students and Graduates." *J Social Psychol* 48:195–8 N '58. * (PA 34:6157)
437. CHAMPION, JOHN MILLS. *A Method For Predicting Success of Commerce Students.* Doctor's thesis, Purdue University (Lafayette, Ind.), 1958. (DA 19:2134)

438. COULSON, ROGER WAYNE. *Relationships Among Personality Traits, Ability and Academic Efficiency of College Seniors.* Doctor's thesis, State University of Iowa (Iowa City, Iowa), 1958. (*DA* 19:1647)

439. GITLIN, SIDNEY. *A Study of the Interrelationships of Parents' Measured Interest Patterns and Those of Their Children.* Doctor's thesis, Temple University (Philadelphia, Pa.), 1958. (*DA* 19:3352)

440. HALE, PETER P. "Profiling the Kuder." *Voc Guid Q* 7:76 w '58. *

441. KENNEDY, EUGENE C. *A Comparison of the Personality Traits of Successful and Unsuccessful Seminarians in a Foreign Mission Seminary.* Master's thesis, Catholic University of America (Washington, D.C.), 1958.

442. NAMANI, ABDEL-KADER. *Factors Associated With High and Low Correlations Between Individuals' Scores on Two Interest Inventories.* Doctor's thesis, Cornell University (Ithaca, N.Y.), 1958. (*DA* 19:2538)

443. OSTLUND, LEONARD A. "Kuder Interest Patterns of Outstanding Science Teachers." *Peabody J Ed* 36:101–8 S '58. *

444. RISHER, CHARITY CONRAD. *Some Characteristics Which Differentiate Between Academically Successful and Unsuccessful College Business Students.* Doctor's thesis, University of Missouri (Columbia, Mo.), 1958. (*DA* 19:2006)

445. SMITH, D. D. "Abilities and Interests: 2, Validation of Factors." *Can J Psychol* 12:253–8 D '58. * (*PA* 33:9347)

446. STINSON, PAIRLEE J. "A Method for Counseling Engineering Students." *Personnel & Guid J* 37:294–5 D '58. * (*PA* 36:2KI94S)

447. THOMAS, PAUL L. *The Development of a Covert Test for the Detection of Alcoholism by a Keying of the Kuder Preference Record.* Master's thesis, West Texas State College (Canyon, Tex.), 1958.

448. WHITE, ROBERT MARSHALL. *The Predictive Relationship of Selected Variables to the Vocational Interest Stability of High School Students.* Doctor's thesis, University of Minnesota (Minneapolis, Minn.), 1958. (*DA* 19:2141)

449. BENDIG, A. W. "Kuder Differences Between Honors and Pass Majors in Psychology." *J Ed Res* 52:199–202 Ja '59. * (*PA* 34:283)

450. BUDD, WILLIAM C. "Prediction of Interests Between Husband and Wife." *J Ed Sociol* 33:37–9 S '59. * (*PA* 36:1IQ37B)

451. CALIA, VINCENT FRANK. *The Use of Discriminant Analysis in the Prediction of Performance of Junior College Students in a Program of General Education at Boston University Junior College.* Doctor's thesis, Boston University (Boston, Mass.), 1959. (*DA* 20:3190)

452. CANNON, WILLIAM M. *A Study of the Responses of Blind and Sighted Individuals to the Kuder Preference Record.* Doctor's thesis, Duke University (Durham, N.C.), 1959. (*DA* 20:3815)

453. COHEN, LEONARD MARLIN. *The Relationship Between Certain Personality Variables and Prior Occupational Stability of Prison Inmates.* Doctor's thesis, Temple University (Philadelphia, Pa.), 1959. (*DA* 20:3375)

454. FLEMING, W. G. *The Kuder Preference Record—Vocational as a Predictor of Post-High School Educational and Occupational Choices.* Atkinson Study of Utilization of Student Resources, Supplementary Report No. 2. Toronto, Canada: Department of Educational Research, Ontario College of Education, University of Toronto, 1959. Pp. vii, 49. *

455. GEHMAN, W. SCOTT. "Validity Generalization and Cross-Validation of the Kuder Electrical Engineering Scale for Counseling College Students." *Ed & Psychol Meas* 19:589–97 w '59. * (*PA* 34:6163)

456. GEHMAN, W. SCOTT; KRAYBILL, EDWARD K.; AND KATZENMEYER, WM. G. "Application of New Kuder Engineering Scales for Counseling University Students." *J Eng Ed* 50:166–9 N '59. *

457. GUILFORD, J. P. *Personality,* pp. 213–20. New York: McGraw-Hill Book Co., Inc., 1959. Pp. xiii, 562. *

458. HASCALL, EDWARD ORSON, JR. *Predicting Success in High School Foreign Language Study.* Doctor's thesis, University of Michigan (Ann Arbor, Mich.), 1959. (*DA* 19:3245)

459. HIRT, MICHAEL. "Another Look at the Relationship Between Interests and Aptitudes." *Voc Guid Q* 7:171–3 sp '59. *

460. KENNEY, CHARLES E. *Differential Vocational Interest Patterns of Successful and Unsuccessful Foreign Mission Seminarians.* Doctor's thesis, Loyola University (Chicago, Ill.), 1959.

461. KING, PAUL; NORRELL, GWEN; AND ERLANDSON, F. L. "The Prediction of Academic Success in a Police Administration Curriculum." *Ed & Psychol Meas* 19:649–51 w '59. * (*PA* 34:6166)

462. KLUGMAN, SAMUEL F. "A Profile Coding System for the Kuder Preference Record—Vocational." *Ed & Psychol Meas* 19:569–76 w '59. * (*PA* 34:6167)

463. KRAUSE, ALLEN H., AND BAXTER, JAMES L. "A Scale Ranking Method for Profiling the Kuder." *Voc Guid Q* 8:19 au '59. *

464. LANE, PAUL ANTHONY. *The Relationship Among Some Measures of Preferred Interest, Vocational Objectives and Academic Performance.* Doctor's thesis, University of Connecticut (Storrs, Conn.), 1959. (*DA* 20:1431)

465. LESSING, ELISE ELKINS. "Mother-Daughter Similarity on the Kuder Vocational Interest Scales." *Ed & Psychol Meas* 19:395–400 au '59. * (*PA* 34:6170)

466. McRAE, GLENN G. *The Relationship of Job Satisfaction and Earlier Measured Interests.* Doctor's thesis, University of Florida (Gainesville, Fla.), 1959. (*DA* 24:631)

467. MOTTO, JOSEPH J. "Interest Scores in Predicting Success in Vocational School Programs." *Personnel & Guid J* 37:674–6 My '59. * (*PA* 35:2766)

468. MUNSON, HOWARD ROGER. *Comparison of Interest and Attitude Patterns of Three Selected Groups of Teacher Candidates.* Doctor's thesis, State College of Washington (Pullman, Wash.), 1959. (*DA* 19:323?)

469. NUNNERY, MICHAEL Y. "How Useful Are Standardized Psychological Tests in the Selection of School Administrators." *Ed Adm & Sup* 45:349–56 N '59. * (*PA* 35:7092)

470. OAKES, FREDRICK, JR. *The Contribution of Certain Variables to the Academic Achievement of Gifted Seventh Grade Students in an Accelerated General Science Curriculum.* Doctor's thesis, New York University (New York, N.Y.), 1959. (*DA* 20:4002)

471. PATTERSON, C. H. "Kuder Patterns of Industrial Institute Students." *Personnel Psychol* 12:561–71 w '59. * (*PA* 34:6172)

472. PETERSON, MARTHA ELIZABETH. *An Evaluation of Relationships Between Test Data and Success as a Residence Hall Counselor.* Doctor's thesis, University of Kansas (Lawrence, Kan.), 1959. (*DA* 21:3364)

473. PIERCE-JONES, JOHN. "Socio-Economic Status and Adolescents' Interests." *Psychol Rep* 5:683 D '59. * (*PA* 34:5854)

474. PIERCE-JONES, JOHN. "Vocational Interest Correlates of Socio-Economic Status in Adolescence." *Ed & Psychol Meas* 19:65–71 sp '59. * (*PA* 34:2051)

475. RACKY, DONALD J. "Predictions of Ninth Grade Woodshop Performance From Aptitude and Interest Measures." *Ed & Psychol Meas* 19:629–36 w '59. * (*PA* 34:6572)

476. SHOEMAKER, WILFRED L. "Rejection of Vocational Interest Areas by High School Students." *Voc Guid Q* 8:72–4 w '59–60. *

477. SMITH, D. D. "Traits and College Achievement." *Can J Psychol* 13:93–101 Je '59. * (*PA* 34:4780)

478. STAUFFACHER, JAMES C., AND ANDERSON, CLIFFORD L. "The Performance of Schizophrenics on the Kuder Preference Record." *Ed & Psychol Meas* 19:253–7 su '59. * (*PA* 34:4701)

479. TAVRIS, EDWARD C. *D² as a Profile Similarity Measure of Kuder Scales.* Doctor's thesis, Illinois Institute of Technology (Chicago, Ill.), 1959.

480. THRASH, PATRICIA ANN. *Women Student Leaders at Northwestern University: Their Characteristics, Self-Concepts, and Attitudes Toward the University.* Doctor's thesis, Northwestern University (Evanston, Ill.), 1959. (*DA* 20:3638)

481. VAUGHAN, LAWRENCE E. *Relationship of Values to Leadership, Scholarship, and Vocational Choice.* Doctor's thesis, University of Nebraska (Lincoln, Neb.), 1959. (*DA* 20:209)

482. VOAS, ROBERT B. "Vocational Interests of Naval Aviation Cadets: Final Results." *J Appl Psychol* 43:70–3 F '59. * (*PA* 34:4845)

483. WAGNER, EDWIN ERIC. *Predicting Success for Young Executives From Objective Test Scores and Personal Data.* Doctor's thesis, Temple University (Philadelphia, Pa.), 1959. (*DA* 20:3371)

484. CALIA, VINCENT F. "The Use of Discriminant Analysis in the Prediction of Scholastic Performance." Comments by David V. Tiedeman. *Personnel & Guid J* 39:184–92 N '60. * (*PA* 35:3949)

485. CASS, JOHN C., AND TIEDEMAN, DAVID V. "Vocational Development and the Election of a High School Curriculum." *Personnel & Guid J* 38:538–45 Mr '60. *

486. CLARK, KENNETH E. "Problems of Method in Interest Measurement," pp. 146–62. In *The Strong Vocational Interest Blank: Research and Uses.* Edited by Wilbur L. Layton. Minnesota Studies in Student Personnel Work, No. 10. Minneapolis, Minn.: University of Minnesota Press, 1960. Pp. viii, 191. * (*PA* 36:1LC91L)

487. COSTELLO, CHARLES G., AND ANDERSON, MARIAN E. "The Vocational and Personal Preferences of Psychiatric and General Nurses." *Nursing Res* 9:155–6 su '60. *

488. DIENER, CHARLES L. "Similarities and Differences Between Over-Achieving and Under-Achieving Students." *Personnel & Guid J* 38:396–400 Ja '60. *

489. FOOTE, RICHARD PAUL. *The Prediction of Success in Automotive Mechanics in a Vocational-Industrial Curriculum on the Secondary School Level.* Doctor's thesis, New York University (New York, N.Y.), 1960. (*DA* 21:3014)

490. GIBLETTE, JOHN FRANKLIN. *Differences Among Above Average, Average, and Below Average Secondary School Counselors.* Doctor's thesis, University of Pennsylvania (Philadelphia, Pa.), 1960. (*DA* 21:812)

491. GOLBURGH, STEPHEN JON. *A Study of the Vocational Interests of Four Types of Psychotic Subjects.* Doctor's thesis, Boston University (Boston, Mass.), 1960. (*DA* 21:3851)

Kuder Preference Record—Vocational

492. GOLDSTEIN, ARNOLD P. "The Fakability of the Kuder Preference Record and the Vocational Apperception Test." *J Proj Tech* 24:133–6 Je '60. * (*PA* 35:1321)

493. KIMBELL, FONTELLA THOMPSON. *The Use of Selected Standardized Tests as Predictors of Academic Success at Oklahoma College for Women.* Doctor's thesis, University of Oklahoma (Norman, Okla.), 1960. (*DA* 20:4335)

494. KLUGMAN, SAMUEL F. "Comparison of Total Interest Profiles of a Psychotic and a Normal Group." *J Counsel Psychol* 7:283–8 w '60. * (*PA* 36:1JQ38K)

495. LEBLANC, CLIFFORD R. "Vocational Interests of Ninth Grade and Twelfth Grade Students." *Sch Counselor* 7:60–4 Mr '60. *

496. MINER, JOHN B. "The Kuder Preference Record in Management Appraisal." *Personnel Psychol* 13:187–96 su '60. * (*PA* 36:2LD87M)

497. REED, WOODROW W.; LEWIS, EDWIN C.; AND WOLINS, LEROY. "Differential Interest Patterns of Engineering Graduates." *Personnel & Guid J* 38:571–3 Mr '60. * (*PA* 35:1221)

498. STERNE, DAVID M. "Use of the Kuder Preference Record, Personal, With Police Officers." *J Appl Psychol* 44:323–4 O '60. * (*PA* 35:3444)

499. WAGNER, EDWIN E. "Differences Between Old and Young Executives on Objective Psychological Test Variables." *J Gerontol* 15:296–9 Jl '60. * (*PA* 35:1328)

500. WELNA, CECILIA THERESA. *A Study of Reasons for Success or Failure in College Mathematics Courses.* Doctor's thesis, University of Connecticut (Storrs, Conn.), 1960. (*DA* 21:1811)

501. ALLEN, ROSCOE JACKSON. *An Analysis of the Relationship Between Selected Prognostic Measures and Achievement in the Freshman Program for Secretarial Majors at the Woman's College of the University of North Carolina.* Doctor's thesis, Pennsylvania State University (University Park, Pa.), 1961. (*DA* 23:122)

502. ANASTASI, ANNE. *Psychological Testing, Second Edition*, pp. 536–9. New York: Mamillan Co., 1961. Pp. xiii, 657. * (*PA* 36:1HA57A)

503. BARRILLEAUX, LOUIS E. "High School Science Achievement as Related to Interest and I.Q." *Ed & Psychol Meas* 21:929–36 w '61. * (*PA* 36:5KJ29B)

504. BRIDGMAN, C. S., AND HOLLENBECK, G. P. "Effect of Simulated Applicant Status on Kuder Form D Occupational Interest Scores." *J Appl Psychol* 45:237–9 Ag '61. * (*PA* 36:4LB37B)

505. BROWN, THELMA E. "Factors Relating to Turnover Among Veterans Administration Nursing Assistants." *J Clin & Exp Psychopathol* 22:226–34 D '61. *

506. BUEL, WILLIAM D., AND BACHNER, VIRGINIA M. "The Assessment of Creativity in a Research Setting." *J Appl Psychol* 45:353–8 D '61. * (*PA* 37:1211)

507. COATS, J. E.; WITH THE ASSISTANCE OF R. G. GARNER. *A Study of the Nature of the Chemical Operator's Occupation and the Personal Qualities That Contribute to Successful Operator Performance.* Midland, Mich.: Dow Chemical Co., March 1961. Pp. iv, 112. *

508. CRAVEN, ETHEL CASE. *The Use of Interest Inventories in Counseling.* Chicago, Ill.: Science Research Associates, Inc., 1961. Pp. iv, 44. *

509. GARRETT, GENE AUBREY. *A Comparison of the Predictive Power of the Kuder Preference Record and the Strong Vocational Interest Blank in a Counseling Setting.* Doctor's thesis, University of Missouri (Columbia, Mo.), 1961. (*DA* 22:1506)

510. GORMAN, JOHN R. *A Study of Adjustment and Interests for Fourth Year Minor Seminarians Studying for the Diocesan Priesthood.* Master's thesis, Loyola University (Chicago, Ill.), 1961.

511. HASCALL, EDWARD O. "Predicting Success in High School Foreign Language Study." *Personnel & Guid J* 40:361–7 D '61. * (*PA* 36:4KL61H)

512. HORNADAY, JOHN A., AND KUDER, G. FREDERIC. "A Study of Male Occupational Interest Scales Applied to Women." *Ed & Psychol Meas* 21:859–64 w '61. * (*PA* 36:5LE59H)

513. HOSFORD, PRENTISS MCINTYRE. *Characteristics of Science-Talented and Language-Talented Secondary School Students.* Doctor's thesis, University of Georgia (Athens, Ga.), 1961. (*DA* 22:2687)

514. LEVINSON, BORIS M. "The Vocational Interests of Yeshiva College Freshmen." *J Genetic Psychol* 99:235–44 D '61. * (*PA* 36:3KD35L)

515. LEWIS, EDWIN C., AND MACKINNEY, ARTHUR C. "Counselor vs. Statistical Predictions of Job Satisfaction in Engineering." *J Counsel Psychol* 8:224–30 f '61. * (*PA* 36:5KI24L)

516. MCDONAGH, ANDREW J. *A Study of Adjustments and Interests of First-Year College Seminarians for the Diocesan Priesthood.* Master's thesis, Loyola University (Chicago, Ill.), 1961.

517. MCMILLEN, DANIEL MORRIS. *A Study of the Effectiveness of the Kuder Preference Record-Vocational in Discriminating Among Purdue Engineering Graduates.* Doctor's thesis, Purdue University (Lafayette, Ind.), 1961. (*DA* 22:162)

518. MINK, OSCAR GORTON. *A Study of Certain Cognitive and Conative Factors Affecting Academic Progress in Chemi-*

cal and Metallurgical Engineering at Cornell University. Doctor's thesis, Cornell University (Ithaca, N.Y.), 1961. (*DA* 22:2695)

519. NOVAK, DANIEL F. "A Comparison of Delinquent and Nondelinquent Vocational Interests." *Excep Child* 28:63–6 S '61. *

520. NUGENT, FRANK A. "The Relationship of Discrepancies Between Interest and Aptitude Scores to Other Selected Personality Variables." *Personnel & Guid J* 39:388–95 Ja '61. * (*PA* 35: 6212)

521. O'LOUGHLIN, DANIEL R. "Helping Students Understand the Kuder." *Sch Counselor* 9:60–1 D '61. *

522. PIERCE-JONES, JOHN. "Social Mobility Orientations and Interests of Adolescents." *J Counsel Psychol* 8:75–8 sp '61. * (*PA* 36:3FH75P)

523. ROBBINS, JAMES E., AND KING, DONALD C. "Validity Information Exchange, No. 14-02: D.O.T. Code 0-97.61, Manager, Sales." *Personnel Psychol* 14:217–9 su '61. * (*PA* 37:1221)

524. SILVER, REUBEN J., AND CASEY, E. W. "Stability of the Kuder Vocational Preference Record in Psychiatric Patients." *Ed & Psychol Meas* 21:879–82 w '61. * (*PA* 36:5JP79S)

525. SUTTER, CYRIL ROBERT. *A Comparative Study of the Interest and Personality Patterns of Major Seminarians.* Doctor's thesis, Fordham University (New York, N.Y.), 1961. (*DA* 22:328)

526. WITHERSPOON, ROBERT PAUL. *A Comparison of the Temperament Trait, Interest, Achievement, and Scholastic Aptitude Test Score Patterns of College Seniors Majoring in Different Fields at the Arkansas State Teachers College.* Doctor's thesis, University of Arkansas (Fayetteville, Ark.), 1961. (*DA* 22:1091)

527. WOLINS, LEROY; MACKINNEY, A. C.; AND STEPHANS, PAUL. "Factor Analyses of High School Science Achievement Measures." *J Ed Res* 54:173–7 Ja '61. * (*PA* 35:7129)

528. ATKINSON, JOHN ALLEN. *Factors Related to the Prediction of Academic Success for Disabled Veterans in a Four Year College Engineering Program.* Doctor's thesis, University of Denver (Denver, Colo.), 1962. (*DA* 23:2786)

529. BAUERNFEIND, ROBERT H. "The Matter of 'Ipsative Scores.'" *Personnel & Guid J* 41:210–7 N '62. * (*PA* 37:6919)

530. BUCKALEW, ROBERT J. *An Investigation of the Interrelationships Among Measures of Interests, Intelligence, and Personality for a Sample of One Hundred Sixty-Two Eighth Grade Boys.* Doctor's thesis, Temple University (Philadelphia, Pa.), 1962. (*DA* 23:3232)

531. CAMPBELL, ROBERT E. "Counselor Personality and Background and His Interview Subrole Behavior." *J Counsel Psychol* 9:329–34 w '62. * (*PA* 39:2294)

532. CHATTERJEE, S., AND MUKERJEE, MANJULA. "Relation Between Kuder Preference Record and a Non-Verbal Interest Inventory Modelled After It to Suit Indian Condition." *J Psychol Res* 6:115–7 S '62. * (*PA* 38:8406)

533. CHRISTENSEN, C. M. "Dimensions and Correlates of Texture Preferences." *J Consult Psychol* 26:498–504 D '62. * (*PA* 39:1723)

534. COUTTS, ROBERT LAROY. *Selected Characteristics of Counselor-Candidates in Relation to Levels and Types of Competency in the Counseling Practicum.* Doctor's thesis, Florida State University (Tallahassee, Fla.), 1962. (*DA* 23:1601)

535. CRANE, WILLIAM J. "Screening Devices for Occupational Therapy Majors." *Am J Occup Ther* 16:131–2 My–Je '62. * (*PA* 37:4078)

536. D'ARCY, PAUL F. "Review of Research on the Vocational Interests of Priests, Brothers and Sisters," pp. 149–200. In *Screening Candidates for the Priesthood and Religious Life.* By Magda B. Arnold and others. Chicago, Ill.: Loyola University Press, 1962. Pp. x, 205. *

537. DREW, ALFRED STANISLAUS. *The Relationship of General Reading Ability and Other Factors to School and Job Performance of Machinist Apprentices.* Doctor's thesis, University of Wisconsin (Madison, Wis.), 1962. (*DA* 23:1261)

538. FREEMAN, FRANK S. *Theory and Practice of Psychological Testing, Third Edition*, pp. 581–4, 588–96. New York: Holt, Rinehart & Winston, Inc., 1962. Pp. xix, 697. *

539. KATZ, MARTIN. "Interpreting Kuder Preference Record Scores: Ipsative or Normative." *Voc Guid Q* 10:96–100 w '62. * (*PA* 37:1972)

540. LANNA, MATTHEW GEORGE. *Vocational Interests in Relation to Some Aspects of Personality and Adjustment.* Doctor's thesis, Columbia University (New York, N.Y.), 1962. (*DA* 23:4421)

541. O'HARA, ROBERT P. "Acceptance of Vocational Interest Areas by High School Students." *Voc Guid Q* 10:101–5 w '62. * (*PA* 37:1976)

542. REID, JOHN W.; JOHNSON, A. PEMBERTON; ENTWISLE, FRANK N.; AND ANGERS, WILLIAM P. "A Four-Year Study of the Characteristics of Engineering Students." *Personnel & Guid J* 41:38–43 S '62. * (*PA* 37:5655)

543. ROHRS, DENNIS KERLIN. *Predicting Academic Success in a Liberal Arts College Music Education Program.* Doctor's thesis, State University of Iowa (Iowa City, Iowa), 1962. (*DA* 23:2937)

544. RUPIPER, OMER JOHN. "A Psychometric Evaluation of Experienced Teachers." *J Ed Res* 55:368–71 My '62. *

545. SPRINGOB, H. KARL, AND JACKSON, CLIFTON W. "Meas-

ured Abilities and Inventoried Interests of Ninth Grade Boys." *Voc Guid Q* 11:37–40 au '62. * (*PA* 37:8279)

546. SUPER, DONALD E., AND CRITES, JOHN O. *Appraising Vocational Fitness by Means of Psychological Tests, Revised Edition*, pp. 461–92. New York: Harper & Brothers, 1962. Pp. xv, 688. * (*PA* 37:2038)

547. *Normative Information: Manager and Executive Testing*. New York: Richardson, Bellows, Henry & Co., Inc., May 1963. Pp. 45. *

548. BAUERNFEIND, ROBERT H. *Building a School Testing Program*, pp. 212–31. Boston, Mass.: Houghton Mifflin Co., 1963. Pp. xvii, 343. *

549. BECKER, JAMES A. "An Exploratory Factor Analytic Study of Interests, Intelligence, and Personality." *Psychol Rep* 13:847–51 D '63. * (*PA* 38:8399)

550. BENDIG, A. W., AND MEYER, WILLIAM J. "The Factorial Structure of the Scales of the Primary Mental Abilities, Guilford Zimmerman Temperament Survey, and Kuder Preference Record." *J General Psychol* 68:195–201 Ap '63. * (*PA* 38:53)

551. CASSEL, RUSSELL N. "Comparing IBM Card and Hand Scoring Pad Administration of the Kuder Vocational Preference Record." *Calif J Ed Res* 14:31–5 Ja '63. * (*PA* 37:8259)

552. EWENS, WILLIAM P. "Relationship of Interest to Aptitude by Profiles and by Interest Areas." *Personnel & Guid J* 42:359–63 D '63. * (*PA* 39:1660)

553. GILBERT, JOSEPH. "Vocational Archetypes: A Proposal for Clinical Integration of Interests and Values in Vocational Counseling and Selection." *Psychol Rep* 13:351–6 O '63. *

554. HORNADAY, JOHN A. "Interest Patterns of Dietitians." *J Am Dietetic Assn* 43:99–103 Ag '63. *

555. IVEY, ALLEN E. "Interests and Work Values." *Voc Guid Q* 11:121–4 w '63. * (*PA* 38:1441)

556. JONES, KENNETH J. "Predicting Achievement in Chemistry: A Model." *J Res Sci Teach* 1:226–31 S '63. *

557. KING, PAUL; NORRELL, GWENDOLYN; AND POWERS, G. PAT. "Relationships Between Twin Scales on the SVIB and the Kuder." *J Counsel Psychol* 10:395–401 w '63. * (*PA* 38:9342)

558. MILLER, WILLIAM G., AND HANNUM, THOMAS E. "Characteristics of Homosexually Involved Incarcerated Females." Abstract. *J Consult Psychol* 27:277 Je '63. *

559. MOORMAN, JANE DOUGLAS. *A Study of the Meaning of High and Low Social Service and Persuasive Scores on the Kuder Preference Record as Measured by the Semantic Differential*. Doctor's thesis, University of Kansas (Lawrence, Kan.), 1963.

560. OVERALL, JOHN E. "A Masculinity-Femininity Scale for the Kuder Preference Record." *J General Psychol* 69:209–16 O '63. * (*PA* 39:1817)

561. PERRY, MARIAN LOUISE. *The Relationship of Selected Variables to the Success of Camp Counselors*. Doctor's thesis, University of Southern California (Los Angeles, Calif.), 1963. (*DA* 24:613)

562. RADCLIFFE, J. A. "Some Properties of Ipsative Score Matrices and Their Relevance for Some Current Interest Tests." *Austral J Psychol* 15:1–11 Ap '63. *

563. SASSENRATH, JULIUS M., AND FATTU, NICHOLAS A. *Relationships Among Factors Obtained for Elementary and Secondary Student Teachers*. Bulletin of the School of Education, Indiana University, Vol. 39, No. 5. Bloomington, Ind.: Bureau of Educational Studies and Testing, the School, September 1963. Pp. vii, 34. * (*PA* 38:6666)

564. SPRINGOB, H. KARL. "Relationship of Interests as Measured by the Kuder Preference Record to Personality as Measured by the California Psychological Inventory Scales." *Personnel & Guid J* 41:624–8 Mr '63. * (*PA* 39:1760)

565. WARBURTON, F. W.; BUTCHER, H. J.; AND FORREST, G. M. "Predicting Student Performance in a University Department of Education." *Brit J Ed Psychol* 33:68–79 F '63. * (*PA* 38:1416)

566. WHITE, HORTENSE G. "Typing Performance as Related to Mental Abilities and Interests: A Preliminary Study." *J Ed Res* 56:535–9 Jl–Ag '63. *

567. ZIMMERER, ANN MORGAN. *A Study of Selected Variables for Predicting Success in a College of Engineering*. Doctor's thesis, University of Houston (Houston, Tex.), 1963. (*DA* 24:842)

MARTIN KATZ, *Assistant Director, Evaluation and Advisory Service, Educational Testing Service, Princeton, New Jersey.*

Since a number of comprehensive reviews of the *Kuder Preference Record—Vocational* (KPR-V) are already available in previous editions of *The Mental Measurements Yearbooks* (as indicated below), this reviewer will

focus on an important aspect of score interpretation that seems to have been overlooked.

Like most other inventories and tests, the KPR-V produces raw scores that are not regarded as meaningful in themselves. That is to say, the tally of preferences (in response to forced-choice triads) is not taken at simple face value as representing "how much" interest an individual has in each of the 9 or 10 "areas." Instead, the profile sheet provides for a conversion of the raw sums to percentile ranks in the norms sample. It then directs that scores above the 75th percentile be regarded as high, scores below the 25th percentile be regarded as low, and those in between be regarded as average. High, low, and average are, the reviewer recognizes, comparative rather than absolute terms. For interpretation, it is of course crucial to know the nature of the comparison being made.

The publisher tells us that "Scores may be profiled so that the student can see how his interests compare with each other as well as with the norm group." (1963–64 catalog; similar statements appear in promotional materials and on the profile sheet for Form C.) In other words, the user is invited to make two kinds of comparison.

One kind involves comparing an individual with other people. This is the familiar normative comparison that seems to be inherent in the very process of converting raw scores to percentiles. It would appear to answer such relevant questions as, "Does Joe have more or less scientific interest than Fred?" "How does he stand in relation to other high school boys generally?" "How does he stand in relation to a representative sample of physicists?" (In view of the age of this instrument and its extensive use—over 2,000,000 students tested in 10,000 schools each year, says the publisher—one might also be justified in asking, "How does Fred stand in relation to high school boys who later became physicists?")

The other kind of comparison is intraindividual—when we compare one person's interest in something with his interest in something else. For example, "Does Joe have more scientific than literary interest?" Cattell has dubbed this kind of comparison *ipsative*.

NORMATIVE INTERPRETATION. For interpretation of normative scores, knowledge of the nature of the reference group is crucial. Ideally, the information we would like to derive from an interest inventory used for guidance is whether the individual has "enough" potential interest in a given occupation, vocational area, school subject, major field, or whatever other variables the inventory scales presumably pertain to. For example, if he should enter such-and-such an occupation, will he derive "enough" satisfaction from the job activities themselves to stay in that occupation (unless another occupation offers superior extrinsic rewards)? Will he be attentive "enough" to his work (assuming sufficient ability) to satisfy his employer, customers, or clients? Or, conversely, will lack of interest tend to make him unhappy, ineffective, unstable in that occupation? These are "payoff" questions in educational and occupational choice. To answer such questions, validity studies of considerable scope and careful design are needed. Not to belabor the point here, this reviewer has previously commented on the inadequacy for this purpose of the catch-as-catch-can "occupational norms" provided in the manual (*539*).

In fact, empirical evidence often fails to substantiate the notion that a score above the 75th percentile promises satisfaction or success in a given occupation or school subject. Thus Diamond (*88*) points out that a score at the 75th percentile of the KPR-V Musical scale is more than two standard deviations below the mean of an occupational group of musicians. Conversely, in our culture a high school boy might have a low percentile rank on Mechanical and still have *enough* mechanical interest for success and satisfaction in occupations generally labeled mechanical. Bauernfeind (*529*), in a summary of studies relating KPR-V scores to subsequent academic performance or to job tenure and reports of job satisfaction, found that the scores "at best yield only anemic predictions." (For example, he cites Kuder's study —reported in the old Form B manual—showing virtually no significant differences in KPR-V scores between "satisfied" and "dissatisfied" workers in five occupational fields.)

To go an important step farther, even a more general normative interpretation is questionable. An individual's percentile rank on a KPR-V scale does not even indicate how strong an interest he has in comparison with the general population of his peers (high school stu-

dents or adults of the same sex). For example, if Joe scores at the 85th percentile on Scientific, we cannot infer that his interest in whatever the Scientific items represent is necessarily higher than or as high as that of 85 per cent of the boys in the high school norms group. This rather elementary inference will often be incorrect simply because the KPR-V places certain artificial limits on the number of areas in which a student's interests may be high or low.

On the surface, the conversion of raw scores to percentile ranks and the subsequent interpretation of these derived percentile ranks as "high" or "low" seems quite analogous to the similar conversion and interpretation of achievement and aptitude test scores in respect to "national" norms. However, it is obvious that an individual's raw score on one test of an achievement battery is experimentally independent of his raw scores on the other tests of the battery. Thus, an individual might be high —say above the 95th percentile—in all the tests of an achievement battery.

KPR-V raw scores, on the other hand, are not independent. These scores, it will be remembered, are derived from a tally of preference responses when a statement representing one "area" is compared with a statement representing another "area," the statements being presented in triads. In the great majority of the triads a preference tallied for one "area" precludes a tally for another "area" represented by another statement. Thus, each raw score tally may be said to be made at the expense of another scale. Therefore, total raw score in each "area" is not experimentally independent of raw scores in other "areas."

For example, Joe's 85th percentile rank on the Scientific scale does not necessarily denote that he has "more" interest in the activities represented by that scale than Fred, who ranks at the 65th percentile. The more statements representing other areas Fred likes, the lower his Scientific raw score and percentile rank tend to be. In general, then, a person with many strong interests might be lower on a given scale than another person who has only mild interest in that "area" but even less in others. Thus, KPR-V scores would fail to reflect a generally high or low level of interest (in the sense of intensity or salience); for example, the evidence that high ability students tend to be characterized by many high interests [1] could not be properly reflected by KPR-V scores.

IPSATIVE INTERPRETATION. But, it may be claimed, the absolute height of the percentile ranks is not important, and interpersonal comparisons are not required: for individual guidance, only the relative heights among scores obtained by a single student should be used. In other words, this argument runs, interpretation should be ipsative, not normative; the individual need know only in what "areas" he is highest and lowest—not whether he is high "enough" or as high as some other person. This argument assumes a closed system in which all choices are encompassed and one of those choices must be made. It does not permit a remark like Samuel Johnson's when Boswell asked him whether he preferred Rousseau or Voltaire: "Sir," rumbled Johnson, "it is impossible to settle the proportion of iniquity between them!"

The forced choice response process is clearly ipsative. But the resulting raw scores for each "area" defy direct interpretation. Raw score comparisons are obscured by different numbers of statements representing the various "areas" and by considerable range in the frequency with which the various "areas" are pitted against each other in the triads. Nevertheless, it may be illuminating to consider two scales, the Outdoor and the Persuasive, for which identical maximum raw scores of 80 appear at the top of the "Male" columns on the profile sheet. Here we may see an interesting reversal between raw score and percentile rank. A raw score of 56 on Outdoor places a boy at the 70th percentile, while a raw score of 54 on Persuasive places him at the 90th percentile. Similar reversals can be found in other pairings. A striking example appears in a comparison between Literary and Mechanical. Converting raw scores to per cents of maximum possible raw scores in order to take into account differences in the number of statements representing each "area," we find that 40 per cent of the highest possible raw score for Lit-

1 FRYER, DOUGLAS. The Measurement of Interests: In Relation to Human Adjustment. New York: Henry Holt & Co., 1931. Pp. xxxvi, 488. *
STRONG, EDWARD K., JR. "Nineteen-Year Followup of Engineer Interests." J Appl Psychol 36:65–74 Ap '52. *
TERMAN, LEWIS M., EDITOR. Genetic Studies of Genius: 1, Mental and Physical Traits of a Thousand Gifted Children. Stanford, Calif.: Stanford University Press, 1925. Pp. xv, 648. *
WIEGERSMA, S., AND BARR, FRANK. "Interest Testing in Educational and Vocational Guidance." Ed Res 2:39–64 N '59. *

erary would rank Joe at the 50th percentile on high school norms, while 50 per cent of the highest possible raw score for Mechanical would place him at only the 20th percentile. To say on the basis of the percentile ranks that Joe has "more" interest in Literary than in Mechanical activities flies in the face of the ipsative raw score comparison.

In the same way, if Mary obtains 50 per cent of the maximum possible raw score on both Mechanical and Social Service, she will be at the 89th percentile in Mechanical interest and at the 24th percentile in Social Service interest on the norms for high school girls. Does this mean that she is "high" in one and "low" in the other? The counselor who makes this interpretation will want to be sure-footed about what he means by "high" and "low."

Joe's and Mary's percentile ranks simply reflect a *general* tendency of American high school boys to prefer Mechanical over Literary activities and high school girls to prefer Social Service over Mechanical activities. The fact that Joe deviates more from the centroid of the norms group on Mechanical than on Literary does not mean that he has—in this case—less Mechanical than Literary interest. Joe might like ice cream less than most people do, but still clearly prefer it to spinach. So the normative conversion spoils ipsative interpretation.

At the same time, the fact that raw scores are derived from solipsistic forced choice preferences tends to block meaningful normative inferences. Fred, whose general appetite level is lustier than Joe's, might like both ice cream *and* spinach more than Joe does (according to such criteria as amount consumed, gusto with which eaten, etc.), and yet rank lower than Joe on an "ice cream" scale derived from forced choice preferences.

UTILITY OF THE INSTRUMENT. In brief, then, the KPR-V percentile scores are derived from an alternation of ipsative and normative procedures. Close scrutiny of attempts to interpret the scales in either ipsative or normative terms suggests that these procedures tend to nullify each other, making either type of comparison dubious.

One further point. Severe criticisms of the KPR-V sometimes seem to prompt the rather naïve defense that the scores are interpreted only tentatively, that the primary purpose in administering the inventory is exploratory—to stimulate students to think constructively about interests in relation to vocational development.

Let us grant immediately that the young student's experience is often too limited for informed and rational decision making. Many activities are outside his range and ken. Tryout—enlarged experience—is the logical remedy for this limitation. Thus, we might echo Emerson's urging to "eat of every apple."

However, interest inventories are rather ineffectual as tryouts. Some of the KPR-V statements, for example, may baffle the young student, especially when they do not describe specific activities which lend themselves to ready visualization but instead represent complex combinations that are virtually occupational titles. Consider as an illustration the following triad:

> Be the director of a group conducting research
>   on propaganda methods
> Be a dean in a university
> Be an expert in color photography.

There are many similar "Be a...." items (e.g., "Be a chemist," "Be a salesman," "Be a bookkeeper"). Scores obtained from responses to such items seem redundant. The student can be forgiven if he says, "But that's why I'm taking the inventory—to predict whether I'd like this or that occupation." He is asked to invest the very coin he hopes to earn. Most of us want the payoff on our investments transmuted into something of greater utility than what we pay in.

If exploration is the primary objective, it seems possible to expose the student to more active and enlightening tryouts either of "the real thing" or of vivid simulations. Even straightforward verbal presentations, as in most occupational information materials, can offer the student better opportunities to visualize himself in specific educational or occupational activities and roles, to "taste" them, and judge whether he likes or dislikes what he has tasted. The point here is that inventories often provide a formal designation and classification of interests before the student has been exposed to a range and variety of experiences appropriate for making realistic, valid, and stable judgments of preference. Decisions based in large part on such premature judgments may serve to foreclose the opportunity for further experience in the very areas where it is most deficient.

If opportunities for a wide range of experiences were equally available to all, the very se-

lectivity implicit in a person's narrow range would in itself be revealing of interests. This is the basis of "informational" interest tests: given fairly equal accessibility to different kinds of information, the individual will know more about topics which interest him. But despite the exploratory activities offered by schools, many students do not have much access to certain kinds of relevant experience, activity, or information. Evidence that inventoried interests have not stabilized in the early secondary school years is probably a consequence not so much of genetic immaturity as of insufficient exploration.

Use of an inventory like the KPR-V tends to assume that such exploration has already taken place—at least to a sufficient extent for meaningful comparisons between statements. The inventory items themselves do not contribute to discovery, do not tell the person "what his interests are." On the contrary, their hope of stability depends on his having already developed a firm consciousness of likes and dislikes among a wide range of activities. But there would be no need to give a student who had just completed courses in woodwork and French an interest inventory to find out which he liked better. Just ask him.

The rationale for use of the KPR-V assumes, however, that the student is unable on his own to classify his discrete likes and dislikes, to organize them, make sense out of them, and relate them to alternatives for choice (occupational or educational).

But, to recapitulate, how can the scores be interpreted when we see that (a) a student with a distinctly *higher* percentile rank than another student on a KPR-V scale may have distinctly *less* interest than the other student has in that area, and (b) a student may have *more* interest in an area represented by a scale on which his percentile rank is *low* than in another area represented by a scale on which his percentile rank is *high?* Bauernfeind (548) has tried manfully to indicate the kind of language a counselor must use in interpreting, say, a high school student's 90th percentile rank on Artistic: "Your interests in artistic activities are higher (we don't know how much higher) than your own average of interests (whatever that is) relative to the interests of other boys in the national norms group." This bit of gobbledygook represents, adds Bauernfeind, "a conscientious effort to interpret the

Kuder profile honestly; and it is guaranteed to chill the counseling session."

Finally, then, if scores are interpreted at all properly, the KPR-V does not stand up well for tentative exploration and stimulation. The problems involved in the derivation and interpretation of scores must rank it well below such other vocational interest inventories as the *Strong Vocational Interest Blank* and the *Kuder Preference Record—Occupational* in usefulness.

For reviews by Clifford P. Froehlich and John Pierce-Jones, see 5:863; for reviews by Edward S. Bordin, Harold D. Carter, and H. M. Fowler, see 4:742; for reviews by Ralph F. Berdie, E. G. Chambers, and Donald E. Super of a, see 3:640 (1 excerpt); for reviews by A. B. Crawford and Arthur E. Traxler of an earlier edition, see 40:1671.

[1064]

*Occupational Interest Inventory, 1956 Revision. Grades 7-16 and adults, 9-16 and adults; 1943-58; 10 scores grouped in 3 categories: fields of interests (personal-social, natural, mechanical, business, the arts, the sciences), types of interests (verbal, manipulative, computational), level of interests; IBM; 1 form ('56, 14 pages); 2 levels: intermediate, advanced; manuals ('56): intermediate (28 pages), advanced (36 pages); interest analysis report ['58, 4 pages] for both levels; intermediate norms based upon norms for advanced form; $5.25 per 35 tests; separate answer sheets may be used; 5¢ per IBM answer sheet; 9¢ per Scoreze answer sheet; 75¢ per set of hand scoring stencils; 90¢ per set of machine scoring stencils; postage extra; 50¢ per specimen set of either level, postpaid; (30-40) minutes; Edwin A. Lee and Louis P. Thorpe; California Test Bureau. *

REFERENCES

1-20. See 4:743.
21-40. See 5:864.
41. SMITH, JOHN ALLAN, AND NASH, PHILIP G. "Differences in Interest Patterns According to High School Major Sequences." *Calif J Ed Res* 9:179-85 S '58. * (PA 34:2053)
42. BOYKIN, LEANDER L., AND BRAZZIEL, WILLIAM F., JR. "Occupational Interests of 1741 Teacher Education Students as Revealed on the Lee-Thorpe Inventory." *J Negro Ed* 28: 42-8 w '59. * (PA 36:3KD42B)
43. WEAVER, SAMPSON JOSEPH. *Interests of Graduates of Eighteen Liberal Arts Concentration Fields as Indicated by the Lee-Thorpe Occupational Interest Inventory.* Master's thesis, Brown University (Providence, R.I.), 1959.
44. MACKINNEY, ARTHUR C., AND WOLINS, LEROY. "Validity Information Exchange, No. 13-01, Foreman II, Home Appliance Manufacturing." *Personnel Psychol* 13:443-7 w '60. *
45. CASSEL, RUSSELL N., AND HENDSCH, GENE. "A Comparative Analysis of Occupational Interest Scores Between Gifted and Typical 5th Grade Pupils." *J Psychol* 54:241-4 Jl '62. * (PA 37:3856)
46. DUNN, FRANCES E. "Interest Patterns of College Majors." *J Col Student Personnel* 4:79-85+ D '62. *

For reviews by Martin Katz and Wilbur L. Layton, see 5:864; for a review by Arthur H. Brayfield of the original edition, see 4:743; for reviews by Edward S. Bordin and Stanley G. Dulsky, see 3:643.

[1065]

★Occupational Interest Survey (With Pictures): Individual Placement Series (Area II). High school and adults; 1959; subtest of *Individual Placement Series;* 9 scores: scientific, social service, literary, agricultural, business, mechanical, musical, clerical, artistic; Form A ('59, 14 pages); preliminary manual ['59, 8 pages]; no description of normative population; separate answer sheets must be used; $27.50 per 25 tests; $1.10 per 25 answer sheets; $2.25 per specimen set; postpaid; (15-20) minutes; J. H. Norman; the Author. *

[1066]

Picture Interest Inventory. Grades 7 and over; 1958; 9 scores: interpersonal service, natural, mechanical, business, esthetic, scientific, verbal, computational, time perspective; IBM; 1 form (23 pages); manual (24 pages); separate answer sheets must be used; $5.25 per 35 tests; 5¢ per IBM answer sheet; $1 per set of either hand or machine scoring stencils; postage extra; 50¢ per specimen set, postpaid; (30-40) minutes; Kurt P. Weingarten; California Test Bureau. *

REFERENCES

1. WEINGARTEN, KURT P. *The Measurement of Interests in Non-Professional Vocations by Means of a Pictorial Inventory.* Doctor's thesis, University of Southern California (Los Angeles, Calif.), 1953.
2. WEINGARTEN, KURT P. "The Measurement of Interests in Nonprofessional Vocations by Means of a Pictorial Inventory." *Calif J Ed Res* 5:7-10 Ja '54. * (PA 28:7657)
3. CASSEL, RUSSELL N., AND HENDSCH, GENE. "A Comparative Analysis of Occupational Interest Scores Between Gifted and Typical 5th Grade Pupils." *J Psychol* 54:241-4 Jl '62. * (PA 37:3856)
4. HOUSTON, LAWRENCE NATHANIEL. *An Investigation of the Relationship Between the Vocational Interests and Homosexual Behavior of Institutionalized Youthful Offenders.* Doctor's thesis, Temple University (Philadelphia, Pa.), 1963. (DA 24:2984)

RALPH F. BERDIE, *Professor of Psychology, and Director, Student Counseling Bureau, University of Minnesota, Minneapolis, Minnesota.*

The publication of Meehl's paper, "The Dynamics of 'Structured' Personality Tests," in the *Journal of Clinical Psychology* in 1945, gave explicit recognition to the principle that the apparent meaning or content of personality and interest inventory items are of minor importance compared to the empirical validity of the items and the derived scales. Only two interest inventories, the Strong and the Kuder, have several decades of research providing evidence of validity and the proved items in these blanks are verbal. In contrast, the inventory reviewed here, the *Picture Interest Inventory,* is almost completely nonverbal. The manual states, "One of the outstanding features of the *Picture Interest Inventory* is its completely non-verbal character. The examinee has no verbal symbols to interpret."

The use of any practical item type is justified if it serves the desired purpose. If items consisting of pictures do as well as or better than verbal items, their use is justified. A long history of research has demonstrated the validity of verbal items, however, and one wishing to introduce a different interest item has a responsibility to show that it is at least as effective as the proven verbal item.

Very little short term and no long term research has demonstrated that the pictorial items used in this inventory, or in the similar *Geist Picture Interest Inventory,* have validity comparable to that of verbal items. Authors of picture interest inventories should not be discouraged from exploring the potential of this approach, but they must be careful in statements concerning the validity of nonverbal items without such evidence.

Weingarten's inventory is based on his doctoral dissertation done at the University of Southern California in 1953 (*1*). Knowing this, one is not surprised that the *Picture Interest Inventory* is closely related to the *Occupational Interest Inventory,* a verbal inventory, or that the development and standardization of the *Picture Interest Inventory* were closely tied to the other publication from the California Test Bureau. The reviewer would feel more comfortable with the validity of the *Picture Interest Inventory* if he had greater confidence in the validity of the *Occupational Interest Inventory.*

The *Picture Interest Inventory* provides scores in six occupational interest fields. The manual does not specify how the decision was made to include activities in these fields. Questions can be raised concerning how unitary these fields are, particularly when one observes grouped in the business field activities related to "operating an adding machine, selling produce, typing, making a ledger entry, wrapping a shirt, selling an automobile, filing, sorting mail, showing real estate, and court reporting." Similarly, one can question how much reality the occupational interest field of interpersonal service has when this includes "teaching arithmetic, directing traffic, addressing a jury, cutting hair, giving room service, examining a patient, waiting on tables, umpiring a playground game, carrying luggage on a ship, and delivering a sermon." Groupings of occupational activities should have an empirical basis. Here they do not.

The tables presenting statistics concerning the reliability of the inventory are more impressive than some of the statements in the manual which more properly belong in a salespiece

than in a test manual. For example, under reliability and validity appears the statement, "The data in these sections indicate the considerable confidence with which one may employ the scales of this instrument." The test author should present the supporting evidence and allow the reader to make his own inferences concerning its acceptability. The manual again reads more like a sales publication because of the generous use of the word "very" when statistics are described. For example, statements such as this appear frequently: "The time perspective scale has a very significant relationship with the Occupational Level key of the Strong Blank." (This correlation, based on 52 college freshmen, is .51.)

Test-retest correlations obtained after a one-week interval range from .69 to .92, somewhat lower than the correlations reported for the Kuder Vocational and about the same as those reported for the Strong blank over a two year period. The reliabilities of the *Picture Interest Inventory* are no higher and perhaps in some cases are lower than similar reliabilities of other interest inventories.

Available information concerning the validity of the inventory is limited to that contained in the manual as no publications reporting such information could be located in the literature and the publishers of the test, who reported some research in progress, could provide information on only one study using 41 subjects. Most of the discussion in the manual concerning validity refers to content validity, with some weight placed on concurrent validity as shown by correlations with other inventories.

One item analysis involved the comparison of responses of persons scoring high and low on relevant scales of the *Occupational Interest Inventory,* a heavy load to place on the questionable validity of this older test.

The manual presents selected correlation coefficients between scores on the *Picture Interest Inventory* and SVIB. Although most of these are in the expected direction and most of them of a size that could be anticipated, there are some exceptions. For example, the correlation between the score on the interpersonal service scale and the social worker scale is .61, though the correlation between the interpersonal service scale and the physician's scale is −.03. The correlation between the business scale and the accountant's scale is .49, but that between business scale and the real estate salesman's scale is .26. The correlations between the es-thetic scale and the artist's and architect's scale are, respectively, .28 and .13.

Reported correlations between the *Picture Interest Inventory* and the Kuder range be-tween .13 and .68. The computational scale on the first inventory and the clerical scale on the second correlate .67, but the interpersonal service and social service scales correlate only .44. The business and computational scales cor-relate .28, whereas the business and persuasive scales correlate .51. These correlations all tend to be lower than the correlations between the *Picture Interest Inventory* and the *Occupa-tional Interest Inventory*, where the correla-tions range from .56 to .77.

The method used in pretesting items, assign-ing items to scales, and standardizing the test appears satisfactory although the descriptions of these procedures in the manual are unneces-sarily cumbersome.

Table 13 in the manual presents statistics which reveal a marked sex difference on eight of the nine scales. Norms are presented for girls but no profile or report form is available for this sex.

Information is not reported concerning the scores or profiles characteristic of students in different curricula or different schools, or men or women in different occupations. No validity data are reported concerning the predictive efficiency of the scores.

In summary, the *Picture Interest Inventory* is an intriguing experiment in interest measure-ment and provides a promising research instru-ment. The information in the manual on the validity of the inventory and the lack of sys-tematic clinical experiences with the instrument do not justify the use of the scales for counsel-ing purposes.

DONALD E. SUPER, *Professor of Psychology and Education, Teachers College, Columbia University, New York, New York.*

This inventory relies on pictures of voca-tional activities to parallel the verbal *Occupa-tional Interest Inventory* developed by Lee and Thorpe. The line drawings are large and clear. The answer sheet is easy to use and quickly scored by hand or machine.

The PII manual claims distinction on the ground that the inventory avoids problems of vocabulary (once directions are understood) by using pictures. This goal is generally but not quite achieved: for example, picture 13a re-quires that the subject understand what the terms "Set No. 1, Cafe" mean when seen on what could be a crate or a bit of stage scenery, and picture 24b demands that he know, or guess with the help of a picture of a gadget for which this reviewer does not know the name, the meaning of the term "Tensile Test." Furthermore, independence of vocabulary does not mean independence of the vocabulary-pro-ducing experience or of the knowledge nor-mally expressed in words: for example, one must know that materials are tested for strength, and that stages have movable sets. But even relative independence of vocabulary should make the inventory more widely usable than existing verbal inventories.

The interests assessed by the PII are classi-fied as in the Lee-Thorpe inventory. Lumped together in one category are business detail and business contact interests, in another are bio-logical and physical sciences, and in another social and personal service are combined. No data are given to justify disregarding the evi-dence from occupational scales such as Strong's which show that differentiation rather than combination is desirable.

The interpersonal service field includes min-isters, physicians, barbers, and janitors, all "concerned primarily" with "serving others" by preaching, examining eyes, cutting hair, and checking doors and windows. The grouping of these items is based on logic and on item analy-sis which showed that they differentiated be-tween high and low scores on the appropriate a priori scales of the PII and of the OII. This empirical check is important, but item-scale correlation does not guarantee scale purity.

Time perspective is a new scale, using teacher ratings to supplement an a priori scale in the item analysis; it is described as preference for occupations involving extensive training and as related to level of vocational aspiration. Is it perhaps prestige need?

Reliability data (retest after one week) are quite satisfactory. But no data are given on stability over time, which has been shown to vary with age and with the method of measure-ment.

Validity receives a total of eight pages, a re-freshing development in manuals. Content and concurrent types dominate, understandable in a recently published instrument. Construct va-lidity arguments include a Chinese proverb and the claim that pictures avoid the halo effect associated with occupational titles, this without evidence despite the probability that a man in a white coat is a man in white.

Content validity data include the fact of item-scale correlation, the classification of pictures by occupational levels to avoid social desirability effects, and trial of both forced choice and like-dislike methods. Item-scale correlations are insufficient evidence of what a scale measures, but a good beginning has been made.

One predictive validity study is reported: the time perspective scale shows a promising correlation of .40 with teacher ratings 11 months after testing.

Concurrent validity data include correlations with SVIB, with the Kuder Vocational, and with the Lee-Thorpe. The sampling in the SVIB study is odd, for it consists of 52 male freshmen in two universities. Unfortunately, the only correlations which were computed were those which looked sizable or which corresponded logically. This last procedure appears to have been inadequate, for physicians were classified as interpersonal service despite the evidence of Strong's work, and the interpersonal service scale correlates only −.03 with the SVIB physician key, with which the scientific scale correlates .63.

However, the expected relationships tend to occur. The interpersonal service scale correlates .61 with the social worker and .59 with social science teacher scales; the scientific scale correlates .63 with physician and .63 with engineer; and time perspective correlates .51 with occupational level.

The Kuder Vocational has similar relationships. The Lee-Thorpe (intermediate level) correlations for similarly named scales range from .56 for the interpersonal service field to .77 for the natural field (median = .68), surprisingly low in view of the conceptual and empirical anchoring of the PII to the OII. For the advanced level of the OII the correlations are somewhat higher (median .71).

Intercorrelations of the various PII scales are also reported here, although this is content, not concurrent, validity. The mechanical and interpersonal service fields and the business and natural fields have substantial negative correlations, other field intercorrelations being negligible, but that of −.01 between mechanical and natural interests is surprising. Verbal and computational interests correlate .59, perhaps because of an intelligence factor.

Norms consist of data on 1,000 persons in secondary schools and colleges. The vague claim that there are no grade differences is surprising in view of Strong and Kuder data. A nationwide scattering of normative cases is noted, but that this is actually a sample rather than a scattering is not made evident.

Scores which exceed the 70th percentile are to be considered first "because of their direct significance," along with fields below the 30th. But their occupational significance is not demonstrated. No consideration is shown for the fact, frequently pointed out by critics of the Kuder, that elevation in relation to occupational groups is as important as ipsative or general normative elevation. The counselor is instructed to use his knowledge of occupations in using the verbal, computational, and time perspective scales to obtain "further information regarding occupational interest," but no help is given him in knowing what these scales can tell him.

Norms for 140 girls are available. The items depict only men, but administration to girls "has suggested" to the author that the inventory is usable with both sexes. Girls' means do differ in expected ways (interpersonal service is higher, mechanical lower, etc.), but whether the mechanical or scientific interests of girls are well tested by items selected for boys is a question.

No norms are given for persons from non-English-speaking cultures, nor for cultural groups which differ in other respects from the dominant American culture. Taken alone, this is an acceptable limitation. But the inventory is recommended in the manual as "ideally suitable" "wherever the examinee has little or no knowledge of English or wherever low reading ability may seriously interfere with assessment," disregarding the fact that these conditions may accompany lack of knowledge of other artifacts such as tensile strength tests or chemists' balances. The test is, as an occupational interest inventory must be, culture-laden.

In conclusion, the *Picture Interest Inventory* could be a promising beginning in the measurement of vocational interests by nonverbal methods. It would benefit from factor analysis and from the needed purification of the scales which this would make possible. It deserves to be used in research to throw further light on its concurrent validity. In addition, much research is needed on the stability of such interests at various age levels and on its predictive validity for various curricula and occupations. As a good deal is known about these aspects of interests as measured by Strong's blank and by the Kuder, it is incumbent upon the author and publishers of *this* instrument to conduct such research and to make the results available. The PII is not yet ready for use in counseling, despite the attractiveness of its content, its simple scoring, its retest reliability, and the persuasive (business contact but not social service!) approach of its manual.

J Counsel Psychol 6:166–7 su '59. Laurence Siegel. * an attempt to develop a nonverbal measure of occupational interest. As such, it is a good idea. Much remains to be done with it, however, before it can take a place along side such well-developed inventories as the Strong and the Kuder. The manual conveys the impression that the PII was published somewhat prematurely. The evidence now available does, to be sure, substantiate the potential utility of the instrument. The problem is that there is not yet enough evidence. Perhaps the most serious objections to this inventory stem from the fact that assertions are incautiously made in the manual and that deficiencies are not properly spotlighted. This is not yet the polished instrument that the author and publisher would have us believe it is.

[1067]

Primary Business Interests Test. Grades 9–16 and adults; 1941–42; 5 scores: accounting, collections and adjustments, sales-office, sales-store, stenographic-filing; 1 form ('41, 1 page); manual ('42, 4 pages); norms for grades 12–13 only; $2.75 per 25 tests; $1 per specimen set; postage extra; (20–25) minutes; Alfred J. Cardall; Cardall Associates. *

REFERENCES

1. CARDALL, ALFRED J. *A Test for Primary Business Interests Based on a Functional Occupational Classification.* Doctor's thesis, Harvard University (Cambridge, Mass.), 1941.
2. CARDALL, ALFRED J. "A Test for Primary Business Interests Based on a Functional Occupational Classification." *Ed & Psychol Meas* 2:113–38 Ap '42. * (PA 16:3767)

For reviews by George K. Bennett, Glen U. Cleeton, and George A. Ferguson, see 3:645.

[1068]

*Qualifications Record, 1961 Revision. Job applicants and employees; 1958–61; includes *Job Qualification Inventory* ('47); 45 scores classified under 7 headings: computation (accounting, mathematics, drafting, purchasing, records, dexterity), social (management, instruction, public contacts, sales, consulting, religion, services, investigation, discipline), literary

(journalism, language, transcription, advertising, research), arts (music, art, dramatics, dancing, graphic arts, crafts), biology (physiology, zoology, botany, foods, sports), physical (tools, machinery, transportation, strength, hazards), technology (chemistry, astronomy, electricity, mechanics, construction, geology, physics, aeronautics, standards); Comprehensive Form XL8 ('61, c1957–61, 8 pages); scoring instructions ['61, 4 pages]; scoring form ('61, 1 page); no data on reliability; 3 procedures of use available: (*a*) completed records are sent to the publisher for scoring and interpretation, (*b*) publisher is commissioned to develop tailored job standards for particular jobs within an organization and records of future applicants are scored and interpreted locally using these standards, (*c*) records are scored and interpreted locally using published "industry-wide" job standards based on data accumulated by the publisher; 4 "industry-wide" job standard portfolios (45 pages, 28 of which are common to all portfolios) available: securities salesman ('61), department manager-industrial ('60), life insurance salesman ('61), electronic sales engineer ('61); $7.50 per 25 tests; 75¢ per 25 scoring forms; $1 per specimen set; $15–$100 per applicant for procedure *a*, depending on type of report requested; $250 per job standard portfolio; postpaid; fees for procedure *b* available from the publisher; (60) minutes; Keith Van Allyn; Personnel Research, Inc. * [As of July 1964, the "industry-wide" job standards which are referred to under procedure *c* and which are evaluated in the following reviews have been withdrawn from sale according to the publisher.]

ARTHUR C. MACKINNEY, *Associate Professor of Psychology, Iowa State University, Ames, Iowa.*

It must be that the publisher of the *Qualifications Record* has never heard of the APA *Technical Recommendations for Psychological Tests and Diagnostic Techniques.* Virtually none of the information labeled as "essential" in the Technical Recommendations is provided in the instruction leaflets or the "Job Standard portfolios."

The claims made for the Q/R, both in publicity pamphlets and in the Job Standards are outlandish. For example (from a publicity pamphlet): "It [the Q/R] exposes each person's interests, activities, ambitions, training, achievements and experience, and the four behaviour traits: social, emotional, mental and physical, in relation to the 45 vocational elements found in *all* occupations. By this means, it brings into focus all significant facts concerning a man's capabilities, limitations and potentialities." And elsewhere: "Why is the Q/R different from any and all other instruments of measurement? It is dramatically different because it exposes the individual to the full spectrum of traits, skills and knowledge found in *all* occupations in a single, all-inclusive examination." Many other similar examples could be cited.

The Q/R is extremely difficult to describe. It consists of 315 "items," roughly resembling life history and vocational interest items, providing scores on 45 "elements" classified under seven headings. The "elements" are profiled. But one interesting feature is the attempt to make the seven "items" scored under each "element" represent levels of response, from interest—representing wishful thinking—at the lowest level to relevant work experience at the highest. Unfortunately, however, the "items" do not appear to represent a hierarchy of levels, and no evidence is offered to support the contention. In some instances the keyed item content for a given element is *not* the same as what the manual says is keyed.

The word "items" is in quotes because they frequently are not items in the conventional sense. Some are standard interest-type items but the large majority have several, and occasionally many, components. For example, "Sports" (classified under "Biology") lists 57 sports activities and if the respondent has acquired "valid skills and knowledge through intensive effort" in any one he answers "yes" and receives a point on that "item" and "element."

This is unquestionably one of the slickest promotion and format jobs around. The promotional brochures have already been noted. Furthermore, these brochures are handsome and, because they contain unsupported generalities (e.g., the published material repeatedly insists that the Q/R is "readily verifiable"), they might sound very impressive to the lay user. The Job Standard books are beautifully bound in heavy, blue plastic with gold imprinting, and the norms are provided on acetate overlays.

In spite of the publisher's claim that the Q/R is "dramatically different," and "nothing comparable to it is available anywhere," I don't see anything new here. It is basically a series of complex stimuli, presumed to be arranged in spiral form, which are in turn somehow grouped into categories or "elements." The use of norms within occupational or job groups dates at least from the early 1930's. And the promotion is reminiscent of P. T. Barnum's approach.

VALIDITY. The claims for validity take generally three forms: (*a*) The norms are based on "superior" employees. Unfortunately, no mention is made of what use, if any, is made of the other-than-superior employees in the validation process. (*b*) The order of progression of the items up the hierarchy, mentioned earlier, is assumed to be a logical order (questionable) and, from this, validity is inferred (even more questionable). (*c*) The improvement that comes whenever the Q/R is used.

None of these presumed bases for validity are helpful. There is no evidence cited that this test is a valid predictor of any criterion, nor does this reviewer see any content or construct validity. Thus, neither empirical evidence nor theory provides bases for interpreting the meaning of scores from this test.

RELIABILITY. One of the advertising brochures claims "a reliability factor of better than 86%." There is no sure way of knowing what this statement means. Reliability is not appropriately reported this way. One clue from the manual says, "when Qualifications Record forms are submitted to a group of 'superior' employees in a given job classification, better than 86 per cent of these employees will consistently respond in the same manner to the same questions." Subsequent correspondence with the publisher verified that this statement *is* the basis for the reliability figure. Since items such as "How many heads do you have?" would evoke complete consistency of response from one administration to another, the proportion of consistent responses is irrelevant to reliability. On the other hand, the writer's correspondence with the publisher gives the reliability as .86 (test-retest), but fails to say of what this is the reliability. This gives no assurance that profiling 45 separate scores is justifiable.

LOGICAL DIFFICULTIES. (*a*) The clustering in the Q/R, both of elements and items, apparently has no firm basis. Certainly no data are presented for any empirical clustering attempts. (*b*) The degrees within each element, wherein the seven items represent levels of whatever is being measured, are not supported by evidence, and they do not appear to be levels of the same thing. (*c*) There are a very large number of stimuli included in most of the "items." The respondent does not have a reasonable task set for him by such complex items, and a score so derived is not interpretable. (*d*) The manual, publicity brochures, and other written materials tend to be loaded with word magic. The verbal footwork may sound impressive but it is short of meaning. (*e*) A one-hour sample from a lifetime of behavior is supposed to do almost everything: measure intelligence, interest, accident proneness, personality, and training needs.

SUMMARY. The basic questions concerning any measuring instrument are, of course, what is measured and how well. For the Q/R the flat statement can be made that there is no definitive information on what is being measured, nor on how well it is being measured. Furthermore, the test is loaded with logical inconsistencies. Since most other tests and inventories are virtually certain to be better than this one, the use of the Q/R is not indicated.

CHARLES F. WARNATH, *Associate Professor of Psychology, and Director, Counseling Center, Oregon State University, Corvallis, Oregon.*

The authors of the materials accompanying this instrument state: "The Qualifications Record is *not* a test but a complete inventory of the individual's qualifications." The Job Standard Profile, which is the profile developed from the answers given to the *Qualifications Record,* is described as: "a composite study of significant traits, knowledge and skills of personnel engaged in this occupation and rated 'superior' in performance by their employers."

The responses given to the 315 questions of the Q/R are designed to compare the answers of the person taking the inventory with the answers given by "superior" workers in various occupations. The method of determining "superior" workers is not described. Seven factors (interest, activity, ambition, training or education, experience, achievement, and work behavior) are related to "45 basic vocational elements." These 45 basic vocational elements fall into the seven major categories itemized in the above entry.

By summing the "yes" responses to the appropriate questions on the Q/R, the administrator gets an 0 to 7 score for each of the 45 elements. These are plotted on a Job Standard Profile and then a plastic sheet is dropped over the profile. Imprinted on the sheet are colored bars covering several contiguous numbers for each of the elements. If a score falls under the bar for an element, it is considered acceptable for that element on the basis of its similarity to the score for "superior" workers in the occupation for which the Job Standard was

developed. Low scores outside the acceptable are reported to "indicate that the person lacks basic traits essential for the job and training may be the answer to build up the responses. Positive deviations indicate the person is overqualified in the element or trait designated."

As a replacement for the employment screening interview, the Q/R can probably do an adequate job, for its range of questions is broad and it is likely to be no less subject to error or distortion than an interview. However, the major problems connected to the Q/R other than the price (as indicated above) are those related to the lack of evaluation studies offered to the purchaser or reviewer. The approach is one of slickness and surface logic. The plastic covered "industry-wide" Job Standards give one the feel of solid accomplishment. But one will look in vain for reliability or validity figures except for a nonsupported "86% reliability" figure mentioned in some of the promotional material.

The materials have undoubtedly been developed with an eye toward the businessman who may not have a personnel director trained to develop his own testing program. At several points in the "Personnel Screening and Evaluation" section of the Job Standards, comments are made which indicate that nonacademic definitions are used (for intelligence and personality, for instance), because the more academic definitions are inappropriate in the area of vocations. Words seem to be defined to fit the inventory questions. However, as is usual with these materials, no evidence is presented to support such contentions as: Intelligence "is the sum total of the basic factors of Interest, Activity, Ambition, Training, Experience, Work Behavior and Achievement, reliably evidenced by performance."

It is commendable that the publisher encourages the purchaser to develop local job standards, but then the purchaser must pay Personnel Research, Inc. to analyze the Q/R's for superior employees of the company and to develop the local job standards for the company. If the company depends on the "industrywide" Job Standards, it must take much on faith. The Job Standard for "Department Managers" indicates that it "represents a survey of 166 managers of departments in 11 industrial plants," but does not elaborate. The Job Standards for "Sales Engineer-Electronics" and "Salesman, Insurance" do not mention even the number or distribution of the norm groups.

This may be a good instrument, but in the absence of information related to its validity and reliability, it is impossible to support the publicity claims for the instrument. Tests and inventories purporting to do some job for the purchaser need to present more than simply layman logic and paraphrased summaries of "satisfied customer" statements as evidence for effectiveness.

[1069]

★Safran Vocational Interest Test. Grades 10–13; 1960–62; test booklet title is "S" Interest Scale; 11 scores: 7 interest scores (economic, technical, outdoor, service, humane, artistic, scientific) and 4 ability self-ratings (academic, mechanical, social, clerical); 1 form ('60, 8 mimeographed pages); mimeographed manual ['62, 6 pages, reprint of 1 below]; mimeographed occupations manual ('60, 4 pages); norms ('61, 8 pages) for college freshmen; norms ['62, 3 pages] for technology students; no norms for ability self-ratings; $10 per 100 tests with accessories; 10¢ per test without accessories; postage extra; (30) minutes; C. Safran; the Author. *

REFERENCES

1. STEWART, JAMES A., AND SAFRAN, CARL. "An Introduction to the Safran Vocational Interest Test and a Report of Its Administration to University of Alberta, Calgary, Freshmen (1961–62 Class)." Alberta J Ed Res 7:185–95 D '61. * (PA 36:5HB85S)

[1070]

*Strong Vocational Interest Blank for Men, Revised. Ages 17 and over; 1927–63; 64 scoring scales (54 occupations, 6 occupational group scales, and 4 nonvocational scales): group 1: group scale ('38), artist ('38), psychologist ('28–'49) by P. H. Kriedt, architect ('38), physician ('38–'52), psychiatrist ('52), osteopath ('47), dentist ('38), veterinarian ('49) by T. E. Hannum, biologist ('62) by Carl A. Lindsay, Louis M. Herman, and Martin L. Zeigler; group 2: group scale ('39), physicist ('52), chemist ('38), mathematician ('38), engineer ('38); group 3: production manager ('38); group 4: farmer ('38), carpenter ('38), printer ('38), mathematics-science teacher ('38), policeman ('38), forest service man ('38), army officer ('52), aviator ('40); group 5: group scale ('38), Y.M.C.A. physical director ('38), personnel manager ('38), physical therapist ('58), public administrator ('44), vocational counselor ('52) by Clements D. Brown, Y.M.C.A. secretary ('38), social science high school teacher ('38), business education teacher ('59) by Robert V. Bacon, city school superintendent ('38), minister ('38), social worker ('54), rehabilitation counselor ('62) by Nathan E. Acree; group 6: music performer ('54), music teacher ('54); group 7: C.P.A. owner ('38); group 8: group scale ('38), senior C.P.A. ('49), junior accountant ('38), office worker ('38), purchasing agent ('38), banker ('38), mortician ('46), pharmacist ('49) by Milton Schwebel, credit manager ('50); group 9: group scale ('38), sales manager ('38), real estate salesman ('38), life insurance salesman ('38), association of chamber of commerce executive ('62) by the Clifton Corporation and the author; group 10: group scale ('38), advertising man ('38), lawyer ('38), author-journalist ('38), librarian ('63); group 11: president of manufacturing concern ('38); non-

vocational scales: occupational level ('39), masculinity-femininity ('38), specialization level ('52) by Milton G. Holmen, interest maturity ('41); IBM, Hankes, MRC, NCS, and FAST; Form M; 2 editions: hand scored edition ('46, 8 pages), machine scored edition ('45, c1938–45, 7 pages); combined manual ('59, 40 pages) for this test and test 1071; profile ('45, c1938–45, 2 pages); interest global chart ('45, 2 pages); student's guide to profile interpretation ('62, 4 pages); separate answer sheets or cards must be used with machine scored edition; $4 per 25 expendable tests; $6 per 25 reusable tests; $2.50 per 50 IBM answer sheets; $3.25 per 50 NCS answer sheets (scored by National Computer Systems only, see 671); $4 per 50 sets of FAST answer cards; see 667 for prices of Hankes answer sheets and scoring services; see 670 for prices of MRC answer sheets and scoring services; hand scoring stencils: $1.25 per single scale, $10 per set of any 10 scales, $55 per complete set; IBM scoring stencils (IBM scoring of a large number of scales is not recommended): $3 per single scale, $28 per set of any 10 scales, $150 per complete set; $1.25 per 25 profiles; 85¢ per 25 interest global charts; $3.50 per 50 student's profile guides; $2.50 per manual; $1.50 per combined specimen set (includes description and student's profile guide but not manual or scoring stencils) of SVIB for men and for women; postage extra: special service available for end-of-year testing of high school juniors: fee, 75¢ per student (fee includes loan of tests, scoring service, profile report the following September, and copy of student's guide); (30–60) minutes; Edward K. Strong, Jr.; Consulting Psychologists Press, Inc. *

REFERENCES

1–71. See 40:1680.
72–175. See 3:647.
176–273. See 4:747.
274–426. See 5:868.
427. FARNSWORTH, PAUL R. "Rating Scales for Musical Interests." J Psychol 28:245–53 Jl '49. * (PA 24:528)
428. FISHER, SEYMOUR, AND HINDS, EDITH. "The Organization of Hostility Controls in Various Personality Structures." Genetic Psychol Monogr 44:3–68 Ag '51. * (PA 26:2889)
429. FRIEDL, FRANCIS P. Vocational Interests of Successful and Unsuccessful Seminarians in a Foreign Mission Society. Master's thesis, Catholic University of America (Washington, D.C.), 1952.
430. KOLB, ALFRED. Vocational Interests of the Brothers of the Sacred Heart. Master's thesis, Catholic University of America (Washington, D.C.), 1952.
431. MCCARTHY, THOMAS N. The Relationship of Vocational Interests to Personality Traits. Master's thesis, Catholic University of America (Washington, D.C.), 1952.
432. D'ARCY, PAUL F. Constancy of Interest Factor Patterns Within the Specific Vocation of Foreign Missioner. Catholic University of America, Studies in Psychology and Psychiatry, Vol. 9, No. 1. Washington, D.C.: Catholic University of America Press, 1954. Pp. ix, 54. * (PA 29:6444)
432a. HILTON, ANDREW C.; BOLIN, STANLEY F.; PARKER, JAMES W., JR.; TAYLOR, ERWIN K.; AND WALKER, WILLIAM B. "The Validity of Personnel Assessments by Professional Psychologists." J Appl Psychol 39:287–93 Ag '55. * (PA 30:5294)
433. CRITES, J. O. Ability and Adjustment as Determinants of Vocational Interest Patterning in Late Adolescence. Doctor's thesis, Columbia University (New York, N.Y.), 1957. (DA 17:1593)
434. MURRAY, JOHN B. Training for the Priesthood and Personality Interest Test Manifestations. Doctor's thesis, Fordham University (New York, N.Y.), 1957.
435. SCHOLL, CHARLES ELMER, JR. The Development and Evaluation of Methods for Isolating Factors That Differentiate Between Successful and Unsuccessful Executive Trainees in a Large, Multibranch Bank. Doctor's thesis, University of Michigan (Ann Arbor, Mich.), 1957. (DA 18:2034)
436. BACON, ROBERT V. A Study of the Interest Patterns of Men Business Teachers in Public Secondary Schools. Doctor's thesis, University of California (Los Angeles, Calif.), 1958.
437. CARNES, GILES DERWOOD. The Relations of Chronicity, Morbidity, and Social Class to the Vocational Interests of Psychiatric Patients. Doctor's thesis, University of Missouri (Columbia, Mo.), 1958. (DA 19:2142)
438. FERGUSON, LEONARD W. "Life Insurance Interest, Abil-

ity and Termination of Employment." *Personnel Psychol* 11: 189–93 su '58. *

439. FORMICA, LOUIS ANTHONY. *A Comparative Study of Selected Factors in the Vocational Development of Intellectually Superior College Girls From the Working and Upper-Class Levels.* Doctor's thesis, University of Connecticut (Storrs, Conn.), 1958. *(DA* 19:1012)

440. HENDERSON, HAROLD L. *The Relationship Between Interests of Fathers and Sons and Sons' Identification With Fathers: The Relationship of the Adolescent Son's Identification With his Father to Father-Son Interest Similarity as Measured by the Strong Vocational Interest Blank.* Doctor's thesis, Columbia University (New York, N.Y.), 1958. *(DA* 19:361)

441. HOLT, ROBERT R., AND LUBORSKY, LESTER; WITH THE COLLABORATION OF WILLIAM R. MORROW, DAVID RAPAPORT, AND SIBYLLE K. ESCALONA. *Personality Patterns of Psychiatrists: A Study of Methods for Selecting Residents, Vol. 1.* New York: Basic Books, Inc., 1958. Pp. xiv, 386. * *(PA* 33: 5751)

442. HUTTNER, LUDWIG, AND STENE, D. MIRIAM. "Foremen Selection in Light of a Theory of Supervision." *Personnel Psychol* 11:403–9 au '58. * *(PA* 33:11090)

443. KENNEDY, EUGENE C. *A Comparison of the Personality Traits of Successful and Unsuccessful Seminarians in a Foreign Mission Seminary.* Master's thesis, Catholic University of America (Washington, D.C.), 1958.

444. KNOWLES, REX HANNA. *Differential Characteristics of Successful and Unsuccessful Seminary Students.* Doctor's thesis, University of Nebraska (Lincoln, Neb.), 1958. *(DA* 19: 1655)

445. MALONE, ROBERT LINCOLN. *A Configural Versus the Standard Method of Scoring the Strong Vocational Interest Blank.* Doctor's thesis, University of Illinois (Urbana, Ill.), 1958. *(DA* 19:1110)

446. METZGER, PAUL LYMAN. *An Investigation of Some Correlates of Vocational Interest Similarity Between Fathers and Sons.* Doctor's thesis, University of Oregon (Eugene, Ore.), 1958. *(DA* 19:1116)

447. NAMANI, ABDEL-KADER. *Factors Associated With High and Low Correlations Between Individuals' Scores on Two Interest Inventories.* Doctor's thesis, Cornell University (Ithaca, N.Y.), 1958. *(DA* 19:2538)

448. STEIMEL, RAYMOND J. *A Study of the Relationship of Recalled Childhood Identification and Association to Masculinity-Femininity of Interest Scores on the MMPI and SVIB Among Scholarship Finalists.* Doctor's thesis, University of Kansas (Lawrence, Kan.), 1958.

449. STEWART, LAWRENCE H. "Non-Occupation Scales of the Strong Vocational Interest Blank and Amount of College Education." *Calif J Ed Res* 9:137–40 My '58. * *(PA* 33:9028)

450. THOMAS, EDWIN RUSSELL. *The Relationship Between the Strong Vocational Interest Blank and the Guilford-Martin Personality Inventory Among Salesmen.* Doctor's thesis, Syracuse University (Syracuse, N.Y.), 1958. *(DA* 19:2139)

451. WEBB, SAM C., AND GOODLING, RICHARD A. "Test Validity in a Methodist Theology School." *Ed & Psychol Meas* 18:859–66 w '58. * *(PA* 34:2123)

452. WEISSMAN, MARTIN P. *An Approach to the Assessment of Intellectual Disposition Among Selected High Ability Students.* Doctor's thesis, University of California (Berkeley, Calif.), 1958.

453. WRIGHT, ROBERT MATTHEW. *The Development and Use of an Occupational Factors Rating Scale in College Counseling.* Doctor's thesis, University of Missouri (Columbia, Mo.), 1958. *(DA* 19:2141)

454. ARMATAS, JAMES PHILIP. *An Investigation of Personality Effects Related in L-I-D Response Patterns on the Strong Vocational Interest Blank.* Doctor's thesis, University of Kansas (Lawrence, Kan.), 1959.

455. CRITES, JOHN O. "A Coding System for Total Profile Analysis of the Strong Vocational Interest Blank." *J Appl Psychol* 43:176–9 Je '59. * *(PA* 34:5931)

456. CROFTCHIK, VICTOR PAUL. *A Study to Establish a Scoring Key for Male Elementary and Secondary Art Teachers to Be Used With the Strong Vocational Interest Blank.* Doctor's thesis, Michigan State University (East Lansing, Mich.), 1959. *(DA* 20:4593)

457. CROWDER, DOLORES GARCIA. "Prediction of First-Year Grades in a Medical College." *Ed & Psychol Meas* 19:637–9 w '59. * *(PA* 34:6563)

458. FILBECK, ROBERT WORTH. *The Differentiation of Freshman Curricular Groups by Means of Empirically Derived Academic Interest Scales.* Doctor's thesis, University of Missouri (Columbia, Mo.), 1959. *(DA* 20:2675)

459. GRAY, CLIFTON WELLINGTON. *Detection of Faking in Vocational Interest Measurement.* Doctor's thesis, University of Minnesota (Minneapolis, Minn.), 1959. *(DA* 20:1429)

460. GUILFORD, J. P. *Personality,* pp. 206–12. New York: McGraw-Hill Book Co., Inc., 1959. Pp. xiii, 562. *

461. GUTEKUNST, JOSEF GRANT. *The Prediction of Art Achievement of Art Education Students by Means of Standardized Tests.* Doctor's thesis, Temple University (Philadelphia, Pa.), 1959. *(DA* 20:3202)

462. KELLY, E. LOWELL, AND GOLDBERG, LEWIS R. "Correlates of Later Performance and Specialization in Psychology: A Follow-Up Study of the Trainees Assessed in the VA Se-

lection Research Project." *Psychol Monogr* 73(12):1–32 '59. * *(PA* 34:7952)

463. KENNEY, CHARLES E. *Differential Vocational Interest Patterns of Successful and Unsuccessful Foreign Mission Seminarians.* Doctor's thesis, Loyola University (Chicago, Ill.), 1959.

464. KIRK, DANIEL. *A Study of the Interests of Brother Candidates and Professed Brothers, on the Strong Minister and Clerical Interest Scales.* Doctor's thesis, St. John's University (Brooklyn, N.Y.), 1959.

465. McCORNACK, ROBERT L. "An Evaluation of Two Methods of Cross-Validation." *Psychol Rep* 5:127–30 Mr '59. * *(PA* 34:147)

466. NICKELS, JAMES BRADLEY. *Inventoried and Expressed Vocational Interests: Their Intra-Group Consistency and Inter-Predictability.* Doctor's thesis, University of Missouri (Columbia, Mo.), 1959. *(DA* 20:3820)

467. NOLAN, EDWARD GILLIGAN. *Uniqueness in Monozygotic Twins.* Doctor's thesis, Princeton University (Princeton, N.J.), 1959. *(DA* 21:247)

468. RODGERS, FRANK P. *A Psychometric Study of Certain Interest and Personality Variables Associated With Academic Achievement in a College Level Printing Curriculum.* Doctor's thesis, University of Buffalo (Buffalo, N.Y.), 1959. *(DA* 19:3219)

469. SCHUTZ, RICHARD ARLEN. *The Relationship of Self-Satisfaction to Stated Vocational Preferences.* Doctor's thesis, University of Minnesota (Minneapolis, Minn.), 1959. *(DA* 20:2148)

470. STEPHENSON, RICHARD RYLE. *A Comparison of the Strong VIB Profiles of High Ability Male S. L. A. Freshmen Who Change Expressed Vocational Choice With Those Who Do Not Change Such Expressions.* Doctor's thesis, University of Minnesota (Minneapolis, Minn.), 1959. *(DA* 20: 4166)

471. STEWART, LAWRENCE H. "Interest Patterns of a Group of High-Ability, High-Achieving Students." *J Counsel Psychol* 6:132–9 su '59. * *(PA* 34:4799)

472. STEWART, LAWRENCE H. "Mother-Son Identification and Vocational Interest." *Genetic Psychol Monogr* 60:31–63 Ag '59. * *(PA* 34:4542)

473. STRUNK, ORLO, JR. "Interest and Personality Patterns of Preministerial Students." *Psychol Rep* 5:740 D '59. * *(PA* 34:5635)

474. TYLER, LEONA E. "Distinctive Patterns of Likes and Dislikes Over a Twenty-Two Year Period." *J Counsel Psychol* 6:234–7 f '59. * *(PA* 35:4037)

475. WHITLOCK, GLENN EVERETT. *The Relationship Between Passivity of Personality and Personal Factors Related to the Choice of the Ministry as a Vocation.* Doctor's thesis, University of Southern California (Los Angeles, Calif.), 1959. *(DA* 20:2392)

476. BARROWS, GORDON A., AND ZUCKERMAN, MARVIN. "Construct Validity of Three Masculinity-Femininity Tests." *J Consult Psychol* 24:441–5 O '60. * *(PA* 35:4891)

477. BERDIE, RALPH F. "Strong Vocational Interest Blank Scores of High School Seniors and Their Later Occupational Entry." *J Appl Psychol* 44:161–5 Je '60. * *(PA* 35:3920)

478. BERDIE, RALPH F. "Validities of the Strong Vocational Interest Blank," pp. 18–61. In *The Strong Vocational Interest Blank: Research and Uses.* Edited by Wilbur L. Layton. Minnesota Studies in Student Personnel Work, No. 10. Minneapolis, Minn.: University of Minnesota Press, 1960. Pp. viii, 191. * *(PA* 36:1LC91L)

479. BROWN, DONALD JAMES. *An Investigation of the Relationships Between Certain Personal Characteristics of Guidance Counselors and Performance in Supervised Counseling Interviews.* Doctor's thesis, Ohio State University (Columbus, Ohio), 1960. *(DA* 21:810)

480. BURDOCK, E. I.; CHEEK, FRANCES; AND ZUBIN, JOSEPH. "Predicting Success in Psychoanalytic Training," pp. 176–91. In *Current Approaches to Psychoanalysis.* Proceedings of the 48th Annual Meeting of the American Psychopathological Association Held in New York City, February 1958. Edited by Paul H. Hoch and Joseph Zubin. New York: Grune & Stratton, Inc., 1960. Pp. 207. * *(PA* 36:4IE07H)

481. CLARK, KENNETH E. "Problems of Method in Interest Measurement," pp. 146–62. In *The Strong Vocational Interest Blank: Research and Uses.* Edited by Wilbur L. Layton. Minnesota Studies in Student Personnel Work, No. 10. Minneapolis, Minn.: University of Minnesota Press, 1960. Pp. viii, 191. * *(PA* 36:1LC91L)

482. CRITES, JOHN O. "Ego-Strength in Relation to Vocational Interest Development." *J Counsel Psychol* 7:137–43 su '60. * *(PA* 35:4012)

483. DARLEY, JOHN G. "The Theoretical Basis of Interests," pp. 118–45. In *The Strong Vocational Interest Blank: Research and Uses.* Edited by Wilbur L. Layton. Minnesota Studies in Student Personnel Work, No. 10. Minneapolis, Minn.: University of Minnesota Press, 1960. Pp. viii, 191. * *(PA* 36: 1LC91L)

484. DUNNETTE, MARVIN D., AND KIRCHNER, WAYNE K. "Psychological Test Differences Between Industrial Salesmen and Retail Salesmen." *J Appl Psychol* 44:121–5 Ap '60. * *(PA* 35:4029)

485. EDDY, RAYMOND T. "Interest Patterns of Rehabilitation

Counselors." *J Counsel Psychol* 7:202–8 f '60. * (*PA* 36:1IPo2E)

486. ENGLAND, GEORGE W. "The Interest Factor in Undergraduate Engineering Achievement." *Personnel & Guid J* 38:401–5 Ja '60. *

487. FREDERIKSEN, NORMAN, AND GILBERT, ARTHUR C. F. "Replication of a Study of Differential Predictability." *Ed & Psychol Meas* 20:759–67 w '60. * (*PA* 35:7953)

488. HAGENAH, THEDA. "Normative Data, Patterning, and Use of the Strong Vocational Interest Blank," pp. 104–17. In *The Strong Vocational Interest Blank: Research and Uses.* Edited by Wilbur L. Layton. Minnesota Studies in Student Personnel Work, No. 10. Minneapolis, Minn.: University of Minnesota Press, 1960. Pp. viii, 191. * (*PA* 36:1LC91L)

489. HARRELL, THOMAS W. "The Relation of Test Scores to Sales Criteria." *Personnel Psychol* 13:65–9 sp '60. * (*PA* 35:7192)

490. HEIST, PAUL. "Personality Characteristics of Dental Students." *Ed Rec* 41:240–52 Jl '60. * (*PA* 35:7081)

491. HOYT, DONALD P. "Measurement and Prediction of the Permanence of Interests," pp. 93–103. In *The Strong Vocational Interest Blank: Research and Uses.* Edited by Wilbur L. Layton. Minnesota Studies in Student Personnel Work, No. 10. Minneapolis, Minn.: University of Minnesota Press, 1960. Pp. viii, 191. * (*PA* 36:1LC91L)

492. KIRCHNER, WAYNE; HANSON, RICHARD; AND BENSON, DALE. "Selecting Foremen With Psychological Tests." *Personnel Adm* 23:27–30 N–D '60. *

493. KNAPP, ROBERT H., AND GREEN, SAMUEL. "Preferences for Styles of Abstract Art and Their Personality Correlates." *J Proj Tech* 24:396–402 D '60. * (*PA* 35:4841)

494. KULBERG, GORDON E., AND OWENS, WILLIAM A. "Some Life History Antecedents of Engineering Interests." *J Ed Psychol* 51:26–31 F '60. * (*PA* 34:7954; 35:2738)

495. LAYTON, WILBUR L., EDITOR. *The Strong Vocational Interest Blank: Research and Uses: Papers From the Institute on the Strong Vocational Interest Blank Held at the University of Minnesota in February 1955.* Minnesota Studies in Student Personnel Work, No. 10. Minneapolis, Minn.: University of Minnesota Press, 1960. Pp. viii, 191. * (*PA* 36:1LC91L)

496. MacKINNEY, ARTHUR C., AND WOLINS, LEROY. "Validity Information Exchange, No. 13-01, Foreman II, Home Appliance Manufacturing." *Personnel Psychol* 13:443–7 w '60. *

497. MARKWARDT, FREDERICK CHARLES, JR. *Pattern Analysis Techniques in the Prediction of College Success.* Doctor's thesis, University of Minnesota (Minneapolis, Minn.), 1960. (*DA* 21:2990)

498. MAYFIELD, EUGENE CUNLIFFE. *Interests as a Predictor of Graduation in Engineering.* Doctor's thesis, Purdue University (Lafayette, Ind.), 1960. (*DA* 21:1248)

499. NORRELL, GWEN, AND GRATER, HARRY. "Interest Awareness as an Aspect of Self-Awareness." *J Counsel Psychol* 7:289–92 w '60. * (*PA* 36:1HF89N)

500. PAPPAS, ANGELINE J., AND GYSBERS, NORMAN C. "A Worksheet for Interpreting the Strong Vocational Interest Blank." *Voc Guid Q* 8:129–31 sp '60. *

501. PERRY, DALLIS. "Problems of Item Form and Criterion Group Definition," pp. 163–77. In *The Strong Vocational Interest Blank: Research and Uses.* Edited by Wilbur L. Layton. Minnesota Studies in Student Personnel Work, No. 10. Minneapolis, Minn.: University of Minnesota Press, 1960. Pp. viii, 191. * (*PA* 36:1LC91L)

502. RALEY, COLEMAN LAVAN. *Personality Traits of High-Academic Achievers at Oklahoma Baptist University, 1958–1959.* Doctor's thesis, University of Oklahoma (Norman, Okla.), 1960. (*DA* 20:2680)

503. SHIRLEY, JACK HAROLD. *A Comparative Study of the Academic Achievements, Interests, and Personality Traits of Athletes and Non-Athletes.* Doctor's thesis, University of Oklahoma (Norman, Okla.), 1960. (*DA* 20:4005)

504. SMITH, STUART ELWOOD. *The Relationship Between Scores on the Strong Vocational Interest Blank and Academic Performance at the State University of New York College of Medicine at Syracuse.* Doctor's thesis, Syracuse University (Syracuse, N.Y.), 1960. (*DA* 22:166)

505. STEIMEL, RAYMOND J. "Childhood Experiences and Masculinity-Femininity Scores." *J Counsel Psychol* 7:212–7 f '60. * (*PA* 36:1HF12S)

506. STEWART, LAWRENCE H. "Modes of Response on the Strong Blank and Selected Personality Variables." *J Counsel Psychol* 7:127–31 su '60. * (*PA* 35:3461)

507. STONE, VERNON W. "Measured Vocational Interests in Relation to Intraoccupational Proficiency." *J Appl Psychol* 44:78–82 Ap '60. * (*PA* 35:4102)

508. STRONG, EDWARD K., JR. "An Eighteen-Year Longitudinal Report on Interests," pp. 3–17. In *The Strong Vocational Interest Blank: Research and Uses.* Edited by Wilbur L. Layton. Minnesota Studies in Student Personnel Work, No. 10. Minneapolis, Minn.: University of Minnesota Press, 1960. Pp. viii, 191. * (*PA* 36:1LC91L)

509. STRONG, EDWARD K., JR. "Use of the Strong Vocational Interest Blank in Counseling," pp. 178–91. In *The Strong Vocational Interest Blank: Research and Uses.* Edited by Wilbur L. Layton. Minnesota Studies in Student Personnel Work,

No. 10. Minneapolis, Minn.: University of Minnesota Press, 1960. Pp. viii, 191. * (*PA* 36:1LC91L)

510. SUPER, DONALD E., AND MOSER, HELEN P. "Some Correlates of Interest Maturity in Early Adolescence," pp. 76–92. In *The Strong Vocational Interest Blank: Research and Uses.* Edited by Wilbur L. Layton. Minnesota Studies in Student Personnel Work, No. 10. Minneapolis, Minn.: University of Minnesota Press, 1960. Pp. viii, 191. * (*PA* 36:1LC91L)

511. WHITEHORN, JOHN C., AND BETZ, BARBARA J. "Further Studies of the Doctor as a Crucial Variable in the Outcome of Treatment With Schizophrenic Patients." *Am J Psychiatry* 117:215–23 S '60. *

512. ANASTASI, ANNE. *Psychological Testing, Second Edition,* pp. 529–36. New York: Macmillan Co., 1961. Pp. xiii, 657. * (*PA* 36:1HA57A)

513. BOYD, J. B. "Interests of Engineers Related to Turnover, Selection, and Management." *J Appl Psychol* 45:143–9 Je '61. * (*PA* 36: 4LI43B)

514. BROWN, FRED G. "A Note on Expectancy Ratios, Base Rates, and the SVIB." *J Counsel Psychol* 8:368–9 w '61. * (*PA* 37:3894)

515. BURACK, BENJAMIN. "Have You Checked Machine-Scoring Error Lately?" *Voc Guid Q* 9:191–3 sp '61. * (*PA* 36:1KI91B)

516. DUDA, WALTER BOLESLAV. *The Prediction of Three Major Dimensions of Teacher Behavior for Student Teachers in Music Education.* Doctor's thesis, University of Illinois (Urbana, Ill.), 1961. (*DA* 22:1518)

517. DUNKLEBERGER, CLARENCE J., AND TYLER, LEONA E. "Interest Stability and Personality Traits." *J Counsel Psychol* 8:70–4 sp '61. * (*PA* 36:3FF70D)

518. FILBECK, ROBERT W., AND CALLIS, ROBERT. "A Verification Scale for the Strong Vocational Interest Blank, Men's Form." *J Appl Psychol* 45:318–24 O '61. * (*PA* 36: 5LB18F)

519. FORER, BERTRAM R. "The Case of E1: Vocational Choice." *J Proj Tech* 25:371–4 D '61. *

520. GARRETT, GENE AUBREY. *A Comparison of the Predictive Power of the Kuder Preference Record and the Strong Vocational Interest Blank in a Counseling Setting.* Doctor's thesis, University of Missouri (Columbia, Mo.), 1961. (*DA* 22:1506)

521. GOODSTEIN, LEONARD D., AND KIRK, BARBARA A. "A Six-Year Follow-up Study of Graduate Students in Public Health Education." *J Appl Psychol* 45:240–3 Ag '61. * (*PA* 36:4LB40B)

522. HEIST, PAUL; McCONNELL, T. R.; MATZLER, FRANK; AND WILLIAMS, PHOEBE. "Personality and Scholarship." *Sci* 133:362–7 F 10 '61. * (*PA* 36:2KD62H)

523. HEIST, PAUL A., AND WILLIAMS, PHOEBE A. "Variation in Achievement Within a Select and Homogeneous Student Body." *J Col Student Personnel* 3:50–9 D '61. *

524. JOHNSON, RICHARD WILBUR. *The Relationship Between Measured Interests and Differential Academic Achievement.* Doctor's thesis, University of Minnesota (Minneapolis, Minn.), 1961. (*DA* 22:3923)

525. JOSEPH, MICHAEL P. "The Strong Vocational Interest Blank and the Kuder Preference Record—Occupational (Form D): A Comparative Study of Eight Same-Named Scales." *Yearb Nat Council Meas Ed* 18:145–54 '61. *

526. KIRCHNER, WAYNE K. " 'Real-Life' Faking on the Strong Vocational Interest Blank by Sales Applicants." *J Appl Psychol* 45:273–6 Ag '61. * (*PA* 36:4LB73K)

527. KIRK, BARBARA A.; GOODSTEIN, LEONARD D.; AND CUMMINGS, ROGER W. "The Strong Vocational Interest Blank and Collegiate Nursing Education." *Personnel & Guid J* 40:160–3 O '61. * (*PA* 36:4KJ60K)

528. LEWIS, EDWIN C., AND MacKINNEY, ARTHUR C. "Counselor vs. Statistical Predictions of Job Satisfaction in Engineering." *J Counsel Psychol* 8:224–30 f '61. * (*PA* 36:5KI24L)

529. MacKINNON, DONALD W. "Fostering Creativity in Students of Engineering." *J Eng Ed* 52:129–42 D '61. * (*PA* 36:4HD29M)

530. MAHONEY, THOMAS A.; JERDEE, THOMAS H.; AND NASH, ALLAN N. *The Identification of Management Potential: A Research Approach to Management Development.* Dubuque, Iowa: Wm. C. Brown Co., 1961. Pp. xiii, 79. *

531. MUSSEN, PAUL. "Some Antecedents and Consequents of Masculine Sex-Typing in Adolescent Boys." *Psychol Monogr* 75(2):1–24 '61. * (*PA* 36:3FH24M)

532. PALUBINSKAS, ALICE L., AND EYDE, LORRAINE D. "SVIB Patterns of Medical School Applicants." *J Counsel Psychol* 8:159–63 su '61. * (*PA* 36:3KL59P)

533. PORTER, ALBERT. *Predictors of Organizational Leadership.* Doctor's thesis, Stanford University (Stanford, Calif.), 1961. (*DA* 22:457)

534. RAJU, NAMBURY SITARAMA. *Vocational Interests of Chamber of Commerce and Trade Association Executives as Measured by the Strong Vocational Interest Blank.* Master's thesis, Purdue University (Lafayette, Ind.), 1961.

535. SCHUTZ, RICHARD A., AND BLOCHER, DONALD H. "Self-Satisfaction and Level of Occupational Choice." *Personnel & Guid J* 39:595–8 Mr '61. * (*PA* 35:6308)

536. SPRINKLE, RONALD LEO. *Permanence of Measured Vocational Interests and Socio-Economic Background.* Doctor's

thesis, University of Missouri (Columbia, Mo.), 1961. (DA 22:3527)

537. STEPHENSON, RICHARD R. "Chance Versus Nonchance Scores on the SVIB." *J Appl Psychol* 45:415–9 D '61. * (PA 37:2037)

538. STEPHENSON, RICHARD R. "A New Pattern Analysis Technique for the SVIB." *J Counsel Psychol* 8:355–62 w '61. * (PA 37:3896)

539. STEPHENSON, RICHARD R. "Predicting S.V.I.B. Profiles of High Ability Male Arts College Freshmen." *Personnel & Guid J* 39:650–3 Ap '61. * (PA 36:1KD50S)

540. STONE, VERNON W. "The Strong Vocational Interest Blank and Occupational Proficiency." *J Ed Res* 55:138–40 N '61. * (PA 36:5LC38S)

541. WATLEY, DONIVAN JASON. *Prediction of Academic Success in a College of Business Administration.* Doctor's thesis, University of Denver (Denver, Colo.), 1961. (DA 22:3527)

542. WEGNER, KENNETH WALTER. *An Analysis of Interest Patterns and Psychological Need Structures Related to L-I-D Response Patterns on the Strong Vocational Interest Blank for Women.* Doctor's thesis, University of Kansas (Lawrence, Kan.), 1961. (DA 22:3931)

543. ARMATAS, JAMES P., AND COLLISTER, E. GORDON. "Personality Correlates of SVIB Patterns." *J Counsel Psychol* 9:149–54 su '62. * (PA 37:3910)

544. BEDROSIAN, HRACH. *An Analysis of Vocational Interests at Two Levels of Management.* Doctor's thesis, Columbia University (New York, N.Y.), 1962. (DA 23:1067)

545. BURK, KENNETH WINFIELD. *Biographic, Interest, and Personality Characteristics of Purdue Speech and Hearing Graduates.* Doctor's thesis, Purdue University (Lafayette, Ind.), 1962. (DA 23:3021)

546. CRITES, JOHN O. "Parental Identification in Relation to Vocational Interest Development." *J Ed Psychol* 53:262–70 D '62. * (PA 37:4744)

547. CUMMINGS, ROGER WESLEY. *The Relationship Between Authoritarianism and the Strong Vocational Interest Blanks.* Doctor's thesis, University of California (Berkeley, Calif.), 1962. (DA 24:1071)

548. D'ARCY, PAUL F. "Review of Research on the Vocational Interests of Priests, Brothers and Sisters," pp. 149–200. In *Screening Candidates for the Priesthood and Religious Life.* By Magda B. Arnold and others. Chicago, Ill.: Loyola University Press, 1962. Pp. x, 205. *

549. EADDY, MORRIS LEE. *An Investigation of the Cannot Say Scale of the Group Minnesota Multiphasic Personality Inventory.* Doctor's thesis, University of Florida (Gainesville, Fla.), 1962. (DA 23: 1070)

550. ENGEL, ILONA MARIA. *A Factor Analytic Study of Items From Five Masculinity-Femininity Tests.* Doctor's thesis, University of Michigan (Ann Arbor, Mich.), 1962. (DA 23:307)

551. FREEMAN, FRANK S. *Theory and Practice of Psychological Testing, Third Edition,* pp. 584–96. New York: Holt, Rinehart & Winston, Inc., 1962. Pp. xix, 697. *

552. HEMPHILL, JOHN K.; GRIFFITHS, DANIEL E.; AND FREDERIKSEN, NORMAN; WITH THE ASSISTANCE OF GLEN STICE, LAURENCE IANNACCONE, WILLIAM COFFIELD, AND SYDELL CARLTON. *Administrative Performance and Personality: A Study of the Principal in a Simulated Elementary School.* New York: Bureau of Publications, Teachers College, Columbia University, 1962. Pp. xix, 432. *

553. HERMAN, LOUIS M.; LINDSAY, CARL A.; AND ZEIGLER, MARTIN L. "A Vocational Interest Scale for Biologists." *J Appl Psychol* 46:170–4 Je '62. * (PA 37:2104)

554. HOLLAND, JOHN L., AND ASTIN, ALEXANDER W. "The Prediction of the Academic, Artistic, Scientific, and Social Achievement of Undergraduates of Superior Scholastic Aptitude." *J Ed Psychol* 53:132–43 Je '62. * (PA 37:2010)

555. KINNANE, JOHN F., AND SUZIEDELIS, ANTANAS. "Work Value Orientation and Inventoried Interests." *J Counsel Psychol* 9:144–8 su '62. * (PA 37:7226)

556. KLEIN, FREDERICK L.; MCNAIR, DOUGLAS M.; AND LORR, MAURICE. "SVIB Scores of Clinical Psychologists, Psychiatrists, and Social Workers." *J Counsel Psychol* 9:176–9 su '62. * (PA 37:5960)

557. KNAPP, ROBERT H.; GEWIRTZ, HERBERT; AND HOLZBERG, JULES D. "Some Personality Correlates of Styles of Interpersonal Thought." *J Proj Tech* 26:398–403 D '62. * (PA 37:6717)

558. KORN, HAROLD A. "Differences Between Majors in Engineering and Physical Sciences on CPI and SVIB Scores." *J Counsel Psychol* 9:306–12 w '62. * (PA 39:2870)

559. KORN, HAROLD A., AND PARKER, EDWIN B. "A Normative Study of the S.V.I.B. Using an Objective Method of Pattern Analysis." *Personnel & Guid J* 41:222–8 N '62. * (PA 37:7172)

560. LANNA, MATTHEW GEORGE. *Vocational Interests in Relation to Some Aspects of Personality and Adjustment.* Doctor's thesis, Columbia University (New York, N.Y.), 1962. (DA 23:4421)

561. MCNAIR, DOUGLAS M.; CALLAHAN, DANIEL M.; AND LORR, MAURICE. "Therapist 'Type' and Patient Response to Psychotherapy." *J Consult Psychol* 26:425–9 O '62. * (PA 39:2070)

562. MARTIN, ANN MILDRED. *The Development and Cross-Validation of an Academic Interest Scale for the Strong Vocational Interest Blank.* Doctor's thesis, University of Pittsburgh (Pittsburgh, Pa.), 1962. (DA 24:384)

563. MORSE, PAUL KENNETH. *The Strong Vocational Interest Blank and Minnesota Multiphasic Personality Inventory as Measures of Persistence Toward the Ministry as a Vocational Goal.* Doctor's thesis, University of Michigan (Ann Arbor, Mich.), 1962. (DA 23:3239)

564. OLHEISER, MARY DAVID. *Development of a Sister Teacher Interest Scale for the Strong Vocational Interest Blank for Women.* Doctor's thesis, Boston College (Chestnut Hill, Mass.), 1962.

565. PATERSON, DONALD G. "Values and Interests in Vocational Guidance," pp. 118–25. (PA 37:5694) In *Industrial and Business Psychology.* Proceedings of the XIV International Congress of Applied Psychology, Vol. 5. Copenhagen, Denmark: Munksgaard, Ltd., 1962. Pp. 229. *

566. PATTERSON, C. H. "Test Characteristics of Rehabilitation Counselor Trainees." *J Rehabil* 28:15–6 S–O '62. * (PA 37:6953)

567. PORTER, ALBERT. "Effect of Organization Size on Validity of Masculinity-Femininity Score." *J Appl Psychol* 46:228–9 Je '62. * (PA 37:2135)

568. RUPIPER, OMER JOHN. "A Psychometric Evaluation of Experienced Teachers." *J Ed Res* 55:368–71 My '62. *

569. SCHUTZ, RICHARD E.; STAATS, ARTHUR W.; AND STAATS, CAROLYN K. "Conditionability of Responses to Occupational Scale Items of the Strong Vocational Interest Blank for Men." *Psychol Rep* 10:447–50 Ap '62. * (PA 37:3846)

570. SEEMAN, WILLIAM, AND MARKS, PHILIP A. "A Study of Some 'Test Dimensions' Conceptions." *J Proj Tech* 26:469–73 D '62. * (PA 37:6678)

571. SLIFE, WAYNE GORDON. *The Measurement of Identification and Its Relationship to Behavioral Indices of Personality Organization.* Doctor's thesis, University of Houston (Houston, Tex.), 1962. (DA 23:3505)

572. STEFFLRE, BUFORD; KING, PAUL; AND LEAFGREN, FRED. "Characteristics of Counselors Judged Effective by Their Peers." *J Counsel Psychol* 9:335–40 w '62. * (PA 39:2312)

573. STEPHENSON, RICHARD R. "Faking 'Chance' on the SVIB." *J Appl Psychol* 46:252–6 Ag '62. * (PA 37:3899)

574. STEWART, LAWRENCE H. "Relationship of Two Indices of Interest Stability to Self-Satisfaction and to Mother-Son Identification." *Calif J Ed Res* 13:51–6 Mr '62. * (PA 37:897)

575. STRONG, EDWARD K., JR. "Good and Poor Interest Items." *J Appl Psychol* 46:269–75 Ag '62. * (PA 37:3900)

576. SUPER, DONALD E., AND CRITES, JOHN O. *Appraising Vocational Fitness by Means of Psychological Tests, Revised Edition,* pp. 418–56. New York: Harper & Brothers, 1962. Pp. xv, 688. * (PA 37:2038)

577. TUCKER, ANTHONY C., AND STRONG, EDWARD K., JR. "Ten-Year Follow-Up of Vocational Interest Scores of 1950 Medical College Seniors." *J Appl Psychol* 46:81–6 Ap '62. *

578. WATLEY, DONIVAN J., AND MARTIN, H. T. "Prediction of Academic Success in a College of Business Administration." *Personnel & Guid J* 41:147–54 O '62. * (PA 37:5656)

579. WHITLOCK, GLENN E. "Passivity of Personality and Role Concepts in Vocational Choice." *J Counsel Psychol* 9:88–90 sp '62. * (PA 38:3249)

580. WINTERS, JOSEPH STEPHEN. *The Inventoried Interests of Male Librarians.* Doctor's thesis, New York University (New York, N.Y.), 1962. (DA 24:1484)

581. WOODS, JAMES EDWARD. *Strong Vocational Interest Blank Profiles of Vocational Rehabilitation Counselor Trainees.* Doctor's thesis, University of Illinois (Urbana, Ill.), 1962. (DA 23:4235)

582. ANKER, JAMES M.; TOWNSEND, JOHN C.; AND O'CONNOR, JAMES P. "A Multivariate Analysis of Decision Making and Related Measures." *J Psychol* 55:211–21 Ja '63. * (PA 37:6186)

583. BENDIG, A. W. "The Relation of Temperament Traits of Social Extraversion and Emotionality to Vocational Interests." *J General Psychol* 69:311–8 O '63. * (PA 39:1800)

584. BROWN, FREDERICK G. "Further Evidence on Strong V.I.B. Response Tendencies and Personality Characteristics." *J Counsel Psychol* 10:199–200 su '63. *

585. CAMPBELL, DAVID. "Chance on SVIB: Dice or Men?" *J Appl Psychol* 47:127–9 Ap '63. * (PA 37:8297)

586. CARKHUFF, ROBERT R., AND DRASGOW, JAMES. "The Confusing Literature on the OL Scale of the SVIB." *J Counsel Psychol* 10:283–8 f '63. * (PA 38:4742)

587. COOLEY, WILLIAM W. "Predicting Choice of a Career in Scientific Research." *Personnel & Guid J* 42:21–8 S '63. *

588. CRITES, JOHN O. "Vocational Interest in Relation to Vocational Motivation." *J Ed Psychol* 54:277–85 O '63. * (PA 38:4744)

589. DE SENA, PAUL AMBROSE. *Identification of Non-Intellectual Characteristics of Consistent Over-, Under-, and Normal-Achievers Enrolled in Science Curriculums at the Pennsylvania State University.* Doctor's thesis, Pennsylvania State University (University Park, Pa.), 1963. (DA 24:3144)

590. DUNNETTE, MARVIN D. "A Note on *The* Criterion." *J Appl Psychol* 47:251–4 Ag '63. * (PA 38:3219)

591. DURFLINGER, GLENN W. "Academic and Personality Differences Between Women Students Who Do Complete the

Elementary Teaching Credential Program and Those Who Do Not." *Ed & Psychol Meas* 23:775–83 w '63. *

592. FEIN, ARTHUR; LIPTON, LEONARD; AND ELTON, CHARLES F. "Comparison of Strong Vocational Interest Patterns of Schizophrenics and Normals." *Psychol Rep* 13:887–94 D '63. * (*PA* 38:9044)

593. FUNKENSTEIN, DANIEL H. "Mathematics, Quantitative Aptitudes and the Masculine Role." *Dis Nerv System* 24(Sect 2):140–6 Ap '63. *

594. GUTHRIE, GEORGE M., AND McKENDRY, MARGARET S. "Interest Patterns of Peace Corps Volunteers in a Teaching Project." *J Ed Psychol* 54:261–7 O '63. * (*PA* 38:4126)

595. HOLLAND, JOHN L. "Explorations of a Theory of Vocational Choice and Achievement: 2, A Four-Year Prediction Study." *Psychol Rep* 12:547–94 Ap '63. * (*PA* 38:4747)

596. KING, PAUL; NORRELL, GWENDOLYN; AND POWERS, G. PAT. "Relationships Between Twin Scales on the SVIB and the Kuder." *J Counsel Psychol* 10:395–401 w '63. * (*PA* 38:9342)

597. KIRK, BARBARA A.; CUMMINGS, ROGER W.; AND HACKETT, HERBERT R. "Personal and Vocational Characteristics of Dental Students." *Personnel & Guid J* 41:522–7 F '63. *

598. KOLE, DELBERT M., AND MATARAZZO, J. D. "Intellectual and Personality Characteristics of Medical Students." Abstract. *J Med Ed* 38:138–9 F '63. *

599. LAIME, BARBARA F., AND ZYTOWSKI, DONALD G. "Women's Scores on the M and F Forms of the SVIB." *Voc Guid Q* 12:116–8 w '63–64. * (*PA* 38:9344)

600. LAUNER, PHILIP T. *The Relationship of Given Interest-Patterns to Certain Aspects of Personality.* Doctor's thesis, New York University (New York, N.Y.), 1963. (*DA* 24:2564)

601. LEE, EUGENE C. "Career Development of Science Teachers." *J Res Sci Teach* 1:54–63 Mr '63. *

602. LESTER, ROBERT ANDREW. *The Relationship of SVIB and ACT Scores to Differential Academic Achievement.* Doctor's thesis, University of Minnesota (Minneapolis, Minn.), 1963. (*DA* 24:1076)

603. LIND, AMY. "Measured Personality Characteristics of Occupational Therapy Graduates and Undergraduates at the University of North Dakota." *Univ N Dak Col Ed Rec* 48:69–73 F '63. *

604. POLLACK, IRWIN W., AND KIEV, ARI. "Spatial Orientation and Psychotherapy: An Experimental Study of Perception." *J Nerv & Mental Dis* 137:93–7 Jl '63. *

605. PORTER, ALBERT. "Effect of Organization Size on Validity of Occupational-Level Score." *Personnel & Guid J* 41:547–8 F '63. *

606. SCHUMACHER, CHARLES F. "Interest and Personality Factors as Related to Choice of Medical Career." *J Med Ed* 38:932–42 N '63. *

607. SHERRY, NANCY MARIE. *Inconsistency Between Measured Interest and Choice of College Major.* Doctor's thesis, University of California (Berkeley, Calif.), 1963. (*DA* 24:2368)

608. SMITH, LOUIS M., AND WIENTGE, KINGSLEY M. "Some Observations on the Vocational Interests of Gifted Adolescents in an Intensive Summer Academic Experience." *Personnel & Guid J* 42:15–20 S '63. *

609. STEIMEL, RAYMOND J., AND SUZIEDELIS, ANTANAS. "Perceived Parental Influence and Inventoried Interests." *J Counsel Psychol* 10:289–95 f '63. * (*PA* 38:4751)

610. STRONG, EDWARD K., JR. "Reworded Versus New Interest Items." *J Appl Psychol* 47:111–6 Ap '63. * (*PA* 37:8300)

611. SUZIEDELIS, ANTANAS, AND STEIMEL, RAYMOND J. "The Relationship of Need Hierarchies to Inventoried Interests." *Personnel & Guid J* 42:393–6 D '63. * (*PA* 39:1761)

612. TAYLOR, DONALD W. Chap. 19, "Variables Related to Creativity and Productivity Among Men in Two Research Laboratories," pp. 228–50. In *Scientific Creativity: Its Recognition and Development.* Edited by Calvin W. Taylor and Frank Barron. New York: John Wiley & Sons, Inc., 1963. Pp. xxiv, 419. * (*PA* 38:2689)

613. WHITLOCK, GLENN E. "Role and Self Concepts in the Choice of the Ministry as a Vocation." *J Pastoral Care* 17:208–12 w '63. * (*PA* 38:9350)

614. CALLIS, ROBERT; WEST, DORAL N.; AND RICKSECKER, E. L. *The Counselor's Handbook: Profile Interpretation of the Strong Vocational Interest Blanks.* Urbana, Ill.: R. W. Parkinson & Associates, 1964. Pp. 100. Paper. *

ALEXANDER W. ASTIN, *Director of Research, American Council on Education, Washington, D.C.*

The latest (1959) manual for the *Strong Vocational Interest Blank* is well organized and provides detailed information on the rationale, construction, reliability, and validity of the SVIB, as well as an informative section on use and interpretation of the test in counseling and personnel work. Recent major research studies (*365, 382, 495*), which are summarized only briefly in the manual, now make it clear that the SVIB is useful for predicting membership in given occupations over long periods of time, and of moderate value for predicting success within a few selected occupations.

The manual does contain a somewhat misleading interpretation of Strong's 18-year follow-up study (*382*): "the chances are 50-50 that a man will enter an occupation on which he has a B rating. The chances become greater as he obtains higher scores....and....less as he obtains lower scores." The reader should have been told that these conclusions assume a 50-50 base rate in the population (which is, of course, seldom the case for a single occupation in any population). In future editions of the manual, the publisher might also consider presenting these longitudinal data in expectancy tables showing the probabilities of entering and remaining in some of the more common occupations or occupational groups as a function of the relevant scale or group keys. In particular, knowledge of the extremely low probabilities associated with scale scores of "C" should be valuable to the user.

The SVIB has for many years been a popular instrument among personnel workers in colleges and universities; there now appear to be increased efforts by the publisher to promote the use of the blank in counseling at the secondary school level. Apparently, it is assumed that knowledge of the information contained in the SVIB blank and knowledge of the vast and impressive body of relevant research will somehow enable the student and his counselor to work out a better vocational plan for the student than would be possible without such knowledge. As far as this reviewer knows, however, there is no convincing evidence to support this assumption. While this lack of evidence applies to any other test which has been recommended for use in counseling, it is hoped that the advocates of the SVIB will continue their tradition of pioneering empirical research by initiating studies to evaluate the usefulness of the SVIB in counseling and guidance.

A criticism frequently made of the SVIB is that scoring is a tedious and costly procedure. However, there are now in existence several commercial firms which provide rapid and accurate scoring at a cost of approximately 65 cents per blank. Slightly lower rates are available if large numbers of blanks are scored at one time.

In comparison with competing tests, the major liability of the SVIB would seem to be the complex problem of interpreting a profile based on such a large number of scales, although the extensive work which has recently been done with group keys (365) has alleviated much of this difficulty. In any case, there is still little doubt that the SVIB remains as the best constructed and most thoroughly validated instrument of its kind.

EDWARD J. FURST, *Associate Professor of Psychology, The Ohio State University, Columbus, Ohio.*

During the 10-year period since the previous review, the vitality of this inventory has continued undiminished. Important publications include the author's *Vocational Interests 18 Years After College (382)*, Darley and Hagenah's *Vocational Interest Measurement (365)*, and a new manual. To these should be added such further interpretive aids as Layton's monograph (495), substantial treatments in testing books, such as that by Super and Crites (576), and upwards of a hundred research studies in periodicals and dissertations. Moreover, in 1958 a national committee was established to provide a clearing house and depository to facilitate research on the blank and to insure continuing evaluation of it; and, in 1962, Strong announced that a revised blank was to be published in the near future.

With a revision forthcoming, it may seem unnecessary to review the current form. There are, however, at least a few good reasons for doing so. One is that purposes, theory, and technique remain essentially the same. Strong still holds to his original position that the objective is not to measure interests as such, but to differentiate men engaged in different occupations and thus to aid young persons to find the occupation best suited to them. Another reason is that the current form may well be in use yet for some years. (Disregarding 43 items to be reworded only and scored as before, about 102 of the 400 items will be new. Existing scales, based upon the 298 carryover items, will continue in use until gradually replaced by new scales based upon the entire new form. Preliminary results on certain of the scales have shown that the elimination of the 102 items does not lower the validity.)

The current blank bears the copyright date 1946 but, except for minor changes on the score page, it is the same as the 1938 revision. The score page is even more up to date than the manual, as it now provides spaces for scores on 50 specific occupational scales. Prospective users of the inventory should appreciate that it is more than a survey of interests. An inspection of the 400 items, the vast majority of which are answered Like, Indifferent, or Dislike, reveals that most of them elicit attitudes about a great variety of stimuli not primarily vocational in content. The items are of a kind that could just as well appear on a "personality" inventory. It is not at all surprising, then, that the scores show high retest consistency in late adolescence and adulthood, nor that high and low scores on many scales correlate with outside ratings of personality.

The revised manual, running to 40 pages, impresses the reviewer as being comprehensive yet concise and functional. It combines the separate men's and women's manuals, and includes much more helpful material on interpretation than the earlier edition. The author was especially careful to indicate the limitations of the four nonoccupational scales—Interest Maturity, Occupational Level, Masculinity-Femininity, and Specialization Level, scales which, because of their ambiguity, could just as well have been dropped. Despite its thoroughness, the manual necessarily leaves out a great deal of background material which the professional user can best get from books and monographs on the inventory. On the interpretation of scores in the so-called chance range, the manual and the profile report form are not now up to date. Current research has shown that such scores are not random scores in the sense that tosses of dice are random (537, 585).

The basic merit of the Strong is that it gives scores on specific occupational scales through a comprehensive inventory. At the same time, this feature invites an overemphasis upon occupational labels in counseling. Fortunately, modern counseling theory can forestall that tendency. There is also the problem of broadening the usefulness of the results beyond the specific occupational scales. To some extent, the use of "pattern analysis," the grouping of scales into clusters, and the provision of group keys will meet this need. But these refinements place a

Strong Vocational Interest Blank for Men

heavy demand upon the user, so that the Strong is not a suitable device for the untrained. Also, the present interest clusters are somewhat tentative and incomplete; they need to be clarified and their number increased. The proposed revision, through the substitution of 102 new items, should help realize these changes as well as provide for additional specific scales.

Scoring of the Strong is inherently laborious, even with the prospect of unit weights in lieu of the present −4 to +4 weights. However, the availability of fast and inexpensive electronic scoring services minimizes this handicap and, in fact, will permit a vastly greater exploitation of the instrument's possibilities. Users should be able to look forward to scoring keys that not only differentiate men in a given occupation from men in general, but also distinguish men in a given occupation from men in other specific occupations—a comparison which, as Kuder has recently argued, almost always reflects the kind of vocational decision the person must make. To be a truly multistage instrument, then, the Strong must provide these additional scales which permit finer differentiation of interests. With its 400 items, as against 100 in the Kuder Occupational (Form D), it would seem to have a splendid potential for this.

All in all, the Strong remains a solidly based but rather complex inventory suitable mainly for older adolescents and adults considering higher level occupations. It may be used with mature adolescents as young as 14 or 15 but is most widely used with college students. For such uses, the Strong is probably still preferable to its leading rival, the Kuder Vocational, but the latter has its own special advantages and uses. In any case, the two instruments differ enough as to justify using both in some cases. It is perhaps still too early to compare the Strong and the Kuder Occupational (Form D), as the latter is relatively new.

For reviews by Edward S. Bordin and Elmer D. Hinckley, see 4:747; for reviews by Harold D. Carter, John G. Darley, and N. W. Morton, see 40:1680; for a review by John G. Darley of an earlier edition, see 38:1178; for excerpts from related book reviews, see B304-5, 5:B115, 5:B414, 4:748, 3:648, 3:650, and 3:652.

[1071]

*Strong Vocational Interest Blank for Women, Revised.** Ages 17 and over; 1933-62; 31 scoring

scales (30 occupational scales and 1 nonvocational scale): artist ('46), author ('46), librarian ('46), English teacher ('46), social worker ('46-'54), psychologist ('46), lawyer ('46), social science teacher ('46), Y.W.C.A. secretary ('46), life insurance saleswoman ('46), buyer ('46), housewife ('46), elementary teacher ('46) by Ralph Bedell, music performer ('54), music teacher ('54), office worker ('47), stenographer-secretary ('47), home economics teacher ('46), dietitian ('46), college physical education teacher ('55) by Rosena M. Wilson, high school physical education teacher ('46) by Patricia Collins, occupational therapist ('46), nurse ('46), mathematics-science teacher ('46), dentist ('46), laboratory technician ('46), physician ('46), business education teacher ('48) by H. F. Koepke, engineer ('54), physical therapist ('58), femininity-masculinity ('47); IBM, NCS, MRC, Hankes, and FAST; Form W ('46, c1933-46); 2 editions: hand scored edition (8 pages); machine scored edition (7 pages); combined manual ('59, 40 pages) for this test and 1070; profile ('46, 2 pages); student's guide to profile interpretation ('62, 4 pages); separate answer sheets or cards must be used with machine scored edition; $4 per 25 expendable tests; $6 per 25 reusable tests; $2.50 per 50 IBM answer sheets; $3.25 per 50 NCS answer sheets (scored by National Computer Systems only, see 671); $4 per 50 sets of FAST answer cards: see 667 for prices of Hankes answer sheets and scoring services; see 670 for prices of MRC answer sheets and scoring services; hand scoring stencils: $1.25 per single scale, $10 per set of any 10 scales, $25 per complete set; IBM scoring stencils (IBM scoring of a large number of scales is not recommended): $3 per single scale, $28 per set of any 10 scales, $75 per complete set; $1.25 per 25 profiles; $3.50 per 50 student's profile guides; $2.50 per manual; $1.50 per combined specimen set (includes description and student's profile guide but not manual or scoring stencils) of SVIB for men and for women; postage extra; special service available for end-of-year testing of high school juniors: fee, 75¢ per student (fee includes loan of tests, scoring service, profile report the following September, and copy of student's guide); (30-60) minutes; Edward K. Strong, Jr.; Consulting Psychologists Press, Inc. *

REFERENCES

1-9. See 40:1681.
10-45. See 3:649.
46-64. See 5:869.
65. BIRD, DOROTHY JEAN. *An Analysis of Psychological Needs of Groups of College Freshmen Women by SVIB-W Patterns.* Doctor's thesis, University of Kansas (Lawrence, Kan.), 1958.
66. HALL, OLIVE A. "Factors Related to Achievement of Home Economics Majors in Chemistry." *J Home Econ* 50:767-8 D '58. *
67. ISENBERGER, WILMA. "Self-Attitudes of Women Physical Education Major Students as Related to Measures of Interest and Success." *Res Q* 30:167-78 My '59. *
68. OBST, FRANCES. "A Study of Selected Psychometric Characteristics of Home Economics and Non-Home Economics Women at the University of California, Los Angeles." *Calif J Ed Res* 10:180-4+ S '59. * (*PA* 34:7957)
69. PETERSON, MARTHA ELIZABETH. *An Evaluation of Relationships Between Test Data and Success as a Residence Hall Counselor.* Doctor's thesis, University of Kansas (Lawrence, Kan.), 1959. (*DA* 21:3364)
70. WARREN, PHYLLIS ANN. "Vocational Interests and the Occupational Adjustment of College Women." *J Counsel Psychol* 6:140-7 su '59. * (*PA* 34:4543)
71. WHITE, BECKY J. "The Relationship of Self Concept and Parental Identification to Women's Vocational Interests." *J Counsel Psychol* 6:202-6 f '59. * (*PA* 35:3945)
72. PARKER, AILEEN WEBBER. *A Comparative Study of Selected Factors in the Vocational Development of College Women.* Doctor's thesis, Indiana University (Bloomington, Ind.), 1961. (*DA* 22:1087)
73. WEGNER, KENNETH WALTER. *An Analysis of Interest Patterns and Psychological Need Structures Related to L-I-D Response Patterns on the Strong Vocational Interest Blank for*

Women. Doctor's thesis, University of Kansas (Lawrence, Kan.), 1961. (*DA* 22:3931)

74. McCarthy, M. Kieran, and McCall, Raymond J. "Masculinity Faking on the FM Scale of an Interest Inventory." *Personnel & Guid J* 41:346–9 D '62. * (*PA* 37:7228)

75. Durflinger, Glenn W. "Personality Correlates of Success in Student-Teaching." *Ed & Psychol Meas* 23:383–90 su '63. * (*PA* 38:1427)

76. Laime, Barbara F., and Zytowski, Donald G. "Women's Scores on the M and F Forms of the SVIB." *Voc Guid Q* 12:116–8 w '63–64. * (*PA* 38:9344)

For a review by Gwendolen Schneidler Dickson, see 3:649; for a review by Ruth Strang of an earlier edition, see 40:1681; for a review by John G. Darley, see 38:1179; for excerpts from related book reviews, see B304-5, 3:650, and 3:652.

[1072]

★**VALCAN Vocational Interest Profile (VIP).** Ages 15 and over; 1960–61; title on manual and profile is *PSYCAN Vocational Interest Profile;* formerly called *WIPCO Vocational Interest Profile;* 9 scores: numerical, mechanical, scientific, clerical, persuasive, musical, literary, artistic, service; 1 form ('61, 4 pages, essentially the same as 1960 research edition); preliminary users' guide ('60, 8 pages); profile (2 pages); $3 per 35 tests; 3¢ per profile; 50¢ per specimen set; postage extra; (20–25) minutes; R. N. Smith and J. R. McIntosh; [Evaluation Institute of Canada (VALCAN)]. *

[1073]

★**Vocational Sentence Completion Blank, Experimental Edition.** High school and college; 1952–60; 28 scores: general self concern (problem, achievement, independence, satisfaction, material, obligation, effectiveness), general emphasis (intellectual, active, other people, recreational), specific preference area (outdoor, mechanical, computational, scientific, persuasive, artistic, literary, musical, social service, clerical, domestic, academic, negative academic), miscellaneous (other, negative, neutral, omit); Form D ('52, 4 pages); 6-part mimeographed manual ('59 except for 1 part copyrighted 1958, 139 pages); mimeographed norms supplement ('60, 2 pages); mimeographed profiles ['59, 1 page] for men, women; no data on reliability and validity in manual; no norms for high school; 5¢ per test; 1¢ per profile; postage extra; manual free; (40–55) minutes; Arthur A. Dole; test and profiles distributed by University of Hawaii Bookstore; manual distributed by the Author.

REFERENCES

1. Dole, Arthur A. *An Investigation of Sentence Completion as a Method of Measuring Certain Dimensions of the Normal Personality and as Applied to Prospective Teachers.* Doctor's thesis, Ohio State University (Columbus, Ohio), 1951.

2. Souza, S. P. *The Interests and Goals of Lower Division Women in Teachers College and the College of Business Administration at the University of Hawaii as Measured by the Vocational Sentence Completion Blank.* Master's thesis, University of Hawaii (Honolulu, Hawaii), 1953.

3. Dole, Arthur A., and Fletcher, Frank M., Jr. "Some Principles in the Construction of Incomplete Sentences." *Ed & Psychol Meas* 15:101–10 su '55. * (*PA* 30:2869)

4. Dole, Arthur A. "The Vocational Sentence Completion Blank in Counseling." *J Counsel Psychol* 5:200–5 f '58. * (*PA* 34:3147)

[1074]

★**William, Lynde & Williams Analysis of Interest.** Male adults; 1956–62; 8 scores: management, accounting, engineering, mechanical, sales, service, teaching, writing; 1 form ('60, 4 pages); mimeographed combined manual ('62, 8 pages) for this test and test

199; no data on reliability of present edition; $4 per 25 tests, postpaid; [15] minutes; R. W. Henderson; William, Lynde & Williams. *

[1075]

★**Your Educational Plans.** Grades 6–9, 9–12; 1958–61, c1956–61; for analysis of biographical data and environmental factors related to educational and vocational goals; 2 levels; no data on reliability; separate answer sheets must be used; examination fee: 65¢ per student; fee includes purchase of test materials and reporting of coded responses on counselor's worksheets; $1 per counselor's kit (kits for additional counselors in participating schools free); postage extra; Samuel A. Stouffer with the assistance of Paul D. Shea (counselor's manual for *b*); Science Research Associates, Inc. *

a) [JUNIOR HIGH SCHOOL EDITION.] Grades 6–9; 1959; also part of *Pupil Record of Educational Progress;* 1 form, second edition ('59, 8 pages); counselor's worksheet ('59, 4 carbon-interleafed pages); no data on validity; (30–35) minutes.

b) HIGH SCHOOL EDITION. Grades 9–12; 1958–61; 1 form ('58, 7 pages); counselor's version ('58, 8 pages); counselor's manual ('59, 43 pages); counselor's workbook ('59, 44 pages of sample worksheets and answer sheets); counselor's worksheet ('61, 4 carbon-interleafed pages); (40–45) minutes.

REFERENCES

1. Gikas, Athena M. *An Evaluative Study of the "Your Educational Plans Inventory."* Master's thesis, Chico State College (Chico, Calif.), 1959.

Leo Goldman, *Associate Professor of Education, Brooklyn College, Brooklyn, New York.* [Review of the High School Edition.]

This questionnaire attempts to reveal the degree of realism of a high school pupil's aspirations regarding college and to identify factors which may contribute toward unrealism. The authors and editors seem to have in mind those schools in which counselors do not have enough time to interview and be well acquainted with all their counselees. For such counselors, YEP is offered as an aid in organizing the counselor's limited time, locating students with problems regarding college orientation, and determining the counselor's strategy in counseling. In addition, the inventory can provide information about the college orientation of an entire class or school, for the guidance of curriculum specialists and administrators.

The pupil answers 31 multiple choice questions regarding his educational and occupational goals, his academic success in the past, and the attitudes of his parents regarding the student's educational future. Other questions seek information about the parents' education and occupations, siblings and their educational experiences, and the family's financial condition in relation to college attendance. The questions are well constructed and soundly reflect many of the insights which have come from psychological and sociological research. There is explicit attention given, for example, to the distinction between a family's ability to finance a college education and its attitudes regarding the importance of attending college. Other important variables which have been found to influence college going are also tapped, e.g., availability of a college within commuting distance, parental occupation, and the attitudes of close friends.

A carbon copy of the answer sheet is returned to the publisher, along with an IQ, or an achievement test percentile, for each pupil. The publisher prepares a Counselor's Worksheet via IBM equipment. The worksheet contains a tabulation of all pupils, first by grade, then within each grade by high school curriculum (college preparatory or not) and whether planning to attend college, and finally in decreasing order of IQ or achievement percentile. Each pupil's responses to 22 of the YEP items are given in tabular form, a single digit being used to represent each response. In general, the coding is such that the lowest numbers are those most favorable to college entrance.

The Counselor's Manual and Workbook contain a wealth of excellent illustrative material and suggestions for interpretation of individual and class data. Many counselors would find these materials instructive and sensitizing, even without using the inventory and the tabulating service.

In effect, then, YEP is a convenient service to overloaded counselors. It asks vital questions and tabulates the answers in functional form. The counselor can quickly spot those pupils who are most likely to be thinking and acting unrealistically regarding college. The preliminary edition of YEP for the junior high school aims at an even more vital target —the realism of choice of high school course of study.

But asking good questions and tabulating the responses are only parts of the project. The part that is not yet available will hopefully provide information regarding the reliability and validity of the responses. And here we have only the publisher's promise that "statistical norms" will be reported in revised editions of the manual when available. Illustrative data from a few high schools whet the appetite, but they also suggest that all we may ever get

from the publisher are predictive validity data which show the relation between responses to specific items and actual college attendance, and tables which show the interrelationship between items of the questionnaire. There is no suggestion of plans to provide construct and concurrent validity data. There is an occasional indication in the manual that the authors collected much more data during the standardization period, but it is not clear why these have not been reported in the present manual.

For the rather high cost of the limited information provided in the YEP program, users are entitled to some assurance that the answers are dependable. Otherwise YEP has little more to offer at this time than convenience. Each school can easily enough make up its own questions about college orientation and tabulate the answers. In fact, there may, for some schools at least, be an advantage in using a local form: it can address itself more specifically to the facts and attitudes which are of particular importance and concern in that school and community.

YEP is, in summary, a well conceived and well designed questionnaire to get at the realism of a pupil's orientation toward college. The scoring and tabulating service appears to be well organized and to provide a great deal of important information in usable form. There is, however, almost no evidence regarding the reliability and validity of the instrument. Until such evidence is reported, this questionnaire must be considered tentative and should be interpreted with great caution.

Personnel & Guid J 38:754–8 My '60. Henry Borow and Donald E. Super. * The reviewers do not intend the foregoing catalogue of reservations [see original review for critical comments not excerpted] to convey general disapproval of Your Educational Plans or to imply that this instrument cannot be made useful to the working counselor. They believe it possesses considerable potential merit. The kinds of events and attitudes it draws upon to build its picture of the student are not new or of unknown validity. Experimental work with weighted application blanks, standardized interviews, and autobiographical records has been known to the literature for a quarter of a century or more. But while these approaches to the diagnosis and prediction of behavior have had some visible impact upon industrial and military personnel psychology, they have had peculiarly little influence upon the systematic practices of guidance counselors. And now comes this new tool which implicitly recognizes the restricted value of conventional psychometric devices as unilateral predictors of the major social choices and actions of youth and which attempts to do something about it. Your Educational Plans draws upon crucial social variables which bear upon college intentions and decisions and provides the counselor with one method of fusing the data they yield with findings derived from tests and grades. Judiciously used, such an in-gathering and summarizing procedure permits the counselor to correct and enlarge his image of the student as an academic person and, consequently, to make sounder inferences about his educational prospects. Still, if it is to serve school counselors with maximum effectiveness, Your Educational Plans will have to undergo many of the modifications which the reviewers have proposed. The professional eminence of those associated with the development of this instrument, the impressive philanthropic foundation support from which it has benefited, the provisions which have been farsightedly evolved for insuring continuing work with it —all these produce bright expectations which the actual product, as it now stands, falls far short of fulfilling. Yet, these same conditions of strength make wholly possible and, indeed, even likely the refinement and expanding usefulness of Your Educational Plans which the reviewers are urging.

[Other Tests]

For tests not listed above, see the following entries in Tests in Print: 1856, 1859, 1862, 1864, 1867-9, 1871, 1877, 1881-3, 1886, and 1889-91; out of print: 1863, 1872, and 1876; status unknown: 1855 and 1880.

MANUAL DEXTERITY

[1076]

★APT Manual Dexterity Test. Automobile and truck mechanics and mechanics' helpers; 1960; 1 form; manual (4 pages); no data on reliability; distribution restricted to clients; $19.50 per set of testing materials, postage extra; (10–20) minutes; Associated Personnel Technicians, Inc. *

[1077]

*Minnesota Rate of Manipulation Test, [1946 Edition]. Adults; 1931-57; revision of the 1933 edition of the same title which is still available and which is a revision of Minnesota Manual Dexterity Test ('31); 5 scores: placing, turning, displacing, 1-

hand turning and placing, 2-hand turning and placing; individual; 1 form ('33); manual ('57, 18 pages, identical with manual copyrighted in 1946 except for new norms for placing and turning); $34 per set of testing materials including manual; 75¢ per manual purchased separately; postage extra; (10–15) minutes; Gilbert L. Betts (manual) and W. A. Ziegler; Educational Test Bureau. *

REFERENCES

1-4. See 40:1662.
5-26. See 3:663.
27. MOORE, JOSEPH E. "A Test of Eye-Hand Coordination." J Appl Psychol 21:668-72 D '37. * (PA 12:2919)
28. HACKMAN, RAY CARTER. The Differential Prediction of Success in Two Contrasting Vocational Areas. Doctor's thesis, University of Minnesota (Minneapolis, Minn.), 1940.
29. TIFFIN, JOSEPH, AND ROGERS, H. B. "The Selection and Training of Inspectors." Personnel 18:14-31 Jl '41. *
30. WALKER, K. F., AND OXLADE, M. N. "A Tentative Battery of Tests for the Selection of Women for Cotton Textile Spinning." B Ind Psychol & Personnel Prac 2:6-27 Je '46. * (PA 20:4871)
31. STRANGE, J. R., AND SARTAIN, A. Q. "Veterans' Scores on the Purdue Pegboard Test." J Appl Psychol 32:35-40 F '48. * (PA 23:771)
32. GEIST, HAROLD. "The Performance of Amputees on Motor Dexterity Tests." Ed & Psychol Meas 9:765-72 w '49. * (PA 26:2950)
33. SUPER, DONALD E. Appraising Vocational Fitness by Means of Psychological Tests, pp. 187-203. New York: Harper & Brothers, 1949. Pp. xxiii, 727. * (PA 24:2130)
34. BAUMAN, MARY K. Chap. 8, "Mechanical and Manual Ability Tests for Use With the Blind," pp. 97-113. (PA 26:487) In Psychological Diagnosis and Counseling of the Adult Blind: Selected Papers From the Proceedings of the University of Michigan Conference for the Blind, 1947. Edited by Wilma Donahue and Donald Dabelstein. New York: American Foundation for the Blind, Inc., 1950. Pp. vii, 173. *
35. WYNDHAM, A. J. "Selection Tests for Machine-Shop Operators." B Ind Psychol & Personnel Prac 8:12-21 S '52. * (PA 27:5454)
36. BODLEY, E. A. "Selection Tests for Women Packers." B Ind Psychol & Personnel Prac 9:24-32 Mr '53. *
37. FLEISHMAN, EDWIN A. "A Note on the Minnesota Rate of Manipulation Test as a Time Limit Test." Ed & Psychol Meas 14:156-60 sp '54. * (PA 28:7520)
38. FLEISHMAN, EDWIN A., AND HEMPEL, WALTER E. "A Factor Analysis of Dexterity Tests." Personnel Psychol 7:15-32 sp '54. * (PA 29:2061)
39. TOPETZES, NICK JOHN. "A Program for the Selection of Trainees in Physical Medicine." J Exp Ed 25:263-311 Je '57. * (PA 33:7024)
40. BAUMAN, MARY K. A Manual of Norms for Tests Used in Counseling Blind Persons. AFB Publications, Research Series, No. 6. New York: American Foundation for the Blind, 1958. Pp. 40. * (PA 32:1949)
41. DISTEFANO, MICHAEL K., JR.; ELLIS, NORMAN R.; AND SLOAN, WILLIAM. "Motor Proficiency in Mental Defectives." Percept & Motor Skills 8:231-4 S '58. * (PA 33:5438)
42. SHORE, RICHARD P. "Validity Information Exchange, No. 11-24: D.O.T. Code 1-25.68, Proof-Machine Operator." Personnel Psychol 11:438-9 au '58. *
43. BOURASSA, G. LEE, AND GUION, ROBERT M. "A Factorial Study of Dexterity Tests." J Appl Psychol 43:199-204 Je '59. * (PA 34:6585)
44. DRUSELL, RUTH D. "Relationship of Minnesota Rate of Manipulation Test With the Industrial Work Performance of the Adult Cerebral Palsied." Am J Occup Ther 13:93-6+ Mr-Ap '59. * (PA 34:1869)
45. JAVALAKSHMI, G. "Correlation of Tests of Psychomotor Ability With Intelligence and Non-motor Tests." J Psychol Res 3:78-84 S '59. *
46. JAVALAKSHMI, G. "Studies in Psychomotor Abilities." J Psychol Res 3:13-20 Ja '59. *
47. PARKER, JAMES F., JR., AND FLEISHMAN, EDWIN A. "Ability Factors and Component Performance Measures as Predictors of Complex Tracking Behavior." Psychol Monogr 74(16):1-36 '60. * (PA 36:2CD36P)
48. FLEISHMAN, EDWIN A., AND ELLISON, GAYLORD D. "A Factor Analysis of Fine Manipulative Tests." J Appl Psychol 46:96-105 Ap '62. *
49. SUPER, DONALD E., AND CRITES, JOHN O. Appraising Vocational Fitness by Means of Psychological Tests, Revised Edition, pp. 185-200. New York: Harper & Brothers, 1962. Pp. xv, 688. * (PA 37:2038)
50. WOLINS, LEROY, AND MACKINNEY, ARTHUR C. "Validity Information Exchange, No. 15-04: D.O.T. Code 9-68.30, Packer II." Personnel Psychol 15:227-9 su '62. *

For reviews by Edwin E. Ghiselli and John R. Kinzer, see 3:663 (1 excerpt); for reviews

*by Lorene Teegarden and Morris S. Viteles,
see 40:1662.*

[1078]

O'Connor Finger Dexterity Test. Ages 14 and over; 1920–26(?); individual; 1 form ['26?]; mimeographed manual ['26?, 4 pages, includes a 1940 reference]; no data on reliability; $20 per set of testing materials, postage extra; (8–16) minutes; Johnson O'Connor; C. H. Stoelting Co. *

REFERENCES

1–15. See 40:1659.
16. McCULLOUGH, CONSTANCE M. *Prediction of Success in the School of Dentistry at the University of Minnesota by Means of Tests and Certain Other Factors.* Doctor's thesis, University of Minnesota (Minneapolis, Minn.), 1938.
17. THOMPSON, CLAUDE EDWARD. *A Study of Motor and Mechanical Abilities.* Doctor's thesis, Ohio State University (Columbus, Ohio), 1939.
18. HACKMAN, RAY CARTER. *The Differential Prediction of Success in Two Contrasting Vocational Areas.* Doctor's thesis, University of Minnesota (Minneapolis, Minn.), 1940.
19. O'CONNOR, JOHNSON. *Unsolved Business Problems,* pp. 85–6. Boston, Mass.: Human Engineering Laboratory, Inc., 1940. Pp. x, 159. *
20. STEAD, WILLIAM H.; SHARTLE, CARROLL L.; OTIS, JAY L.; WARD, RAYMOND S.; OSBORNE, HERBERT F.; ENDLER, O. L.; DVORAK, BEATRICE J.; COOPER, JOHN H.; BELLOWS, ROGER M.; AND KOLBE, LAVERNE E. *Occupational Counseling Techniques: Their Development and Application.* Published for the Technical Board of the Occupational Research Program, United States Employment Service. New York: American Book Co., 1940. Pp. ix, 273. *
21. BLUM, MILTON, AND CANDEE, BEATRICE. "The Selection of Department Store Packers and Wrappers With the Aid of Certain Psychological Tests." *J Appl Psychol* 25:76–85 F '41. * *(PA* 15:3104)
22. BLUM, MILTON L., AND CANDEE, BEATRICE. "The Selection of Department Store Packers and Wrappers With the Aid of Certain Psychological Tests: Study 2." *J Appl Psychol* 25:291–9 Je '41. * *(PA* 15:4336)
23. MORROW, ROBERT S. "An Experimental Analysis of the Theory of Independent Abilities." *J Ed Psychol* 32:495–512 O '41. * *(PA* 16:2209)
24. O'CONNOR, JOHNSON. *The Too Many Aptitude Woman,* pp. 47–53, passim. Boston, Mass.: Human Engineering Laboratory, Inc., 1941. Pp. xii, 185. *
25. BENNETT, GEORGE K., AND CRUIKSHANK, RUTH M. *A Summary of Manual and Mechanical Ability Tests, Preliminary Form,* pp. 59–60. New York: Psychological Corporation, 1942. Pp. v, 74. *
26. GHISELLI, EDWIN E. "Estimating the Minimal Reliability of a Total Test From the Intercorrelations Among, and the Standard Deviations of, the Component Parts." *J Appl Psychol* 26:332–7 Je '42. * *(PA* 16:3863)
27. THOMPSON, CLAUDE EDWARD. "Motor and Mechanical Abilities in Professional Schools." *J Appl Psychol* 26:24–37 F '42. * *(PA* 16:2483)
28. GHISELLI, EDWIN E. "The Use of the Minnesota Rate of Manipulation and the O'Connor Finger Dexterity Tests in the Selection of Package Wrappers." *J Appl Psychol* 27:33–4 F '43. * *(PA* 17:2851)
29. JACOBSEN, ELDON E. "An Evaluation of Certain Tests in Predicting Mechanic Learner Achievement." *Ed & Psychol Meas* 3:259–67 au '43. * *(PA* 18:2537)
30. O'CONNOR, JOHNSON. *Structural Visualization,* pp. 51–5, passim. Boston, Mass.: Human Engineering Laboratory, Inc., 1943. Pp. xiv, 182. *
31. ROSS, LAWRENCE W. "Results of Testing Machine-Tool Trainees." *Personnel J* 21:363–7 Ap '43. * *(PA* 17:2459)
32. SURGENT, LOUIS VINCENT. "The Use of Aptitude Tests in the Selection of Radio Tube Mounters." *Psychol Monogr* 61(2):1–40 '47. *
33. TIFFIN, JOSEPH. *Industrial Psychology, Second Edition,* pp. 122–5, 131–44. New York: Prentice-Hall, Inc., 1947. Pp. xxi, 553. *
34. RINSLAND, HENRY D. "The Prediction of Veterans' Success From Test Scores at the University of Oklahoma." *Yearb Nat Council Meas Used Ed* 6:59–72 pt 1 '49. *
35. SUPER, DONALD E. *Appraising Vocational Fitness by Means of Psychological Tests,* pp. 203–17. New York: Harper & Brothers, 1949. Pp. xxiii, 727. * *(PA* 24:2130)
36. LANEY, ARTHUR R., JR. "Validity of Employment Tests for Gas-Appliance Service Personnel." *Personnel Psychol* 4:199–208 su '51. * *(PA* 26:1735)
37. BODLEY, E. A. "Selection Tests for Women Packers." *B Ind Psychol & Personnel Prac* 9:24–32 Mr '53. * *(PA* 29:1633)
38. FLEISHMAN, EDWIN A. "A Modified Administration Procedure for the O'Connor Finger Dexterity Test." *J Appl Psychol* 37:191–4 Je '53. * *(PA* 28:3349)

39. FLEISHMAN, EDWIN A., AND HEMPEL, WALTER E. "A Factor Analysis of Dexterity Tests." *Personnel Psychol* 7:15–32 sp '54. * *(PA* 29:2061)
40. PRAKASH, J. C. "Standardised Norms for Selected Psychological Tests." *Indian J Psychol* 31:147–8 Jl–D '56. * *(PA* 35:3975)
41. BOURASSA, G. LEE, AND GUION, ROBERT M. "A Factorial Study of Dexterity Tests." *J Appl Psychol* 43:199–204 Je '59. * *(PA* 34:6585)
42. JAYALAKSHMI, G. "Correlation of Tests of Psychomotor Ability With Intelligence and Non-motor Tests." *J Psychol Res* 3:78–84 S '59. *
43. JAYALAKSHMI, G. "Studies in Psychomotor Abilities." *J Psychol Res* 3:13–20 Ja '59. *
44. PARKER, JAMES F., JR., AND FLEISHMAN, EDWIN A. "Ability Factors and Component Performance Measures as Predictors of Complex Tracking Behavior." *Psychol Monogr* 74(16):1–36 '60. * *(PA* 36:2CD36P)
45. FLEISHMAN, EDWIN A., AND ELLISON, GAYLORD D. "A Factor Analysis of Fine Manipulative Tests." *J Appl Psychol* 46:96–105 Ap '62. *
46. RIM, Y. "The Predictive Validity of Seven Manual Dexterity Tests." *Psychologia* 5:52–5 Mr '62. * *(PA* 38:1417)
47. SUPER, DONALD E., AND CRITES, JOHN O. *Appraising Vocational Fitness by Means of Psychological Tests, Revised Edition,* pp. 200–13. New York: Harper & Brothers, 1962. Pp. xv, 688. * *(PA* 37:2038)

For a review by Morris S. Viteles, see 40: 1659.

[1079]

O'Connor Tweezer Dexterity Test. Ages 14 and over; 1920–28(?); individual; 1 form ['28?]; mimeographed manual ['28(?), 4 pages, includes a 1937 reference]; no data on reliability; $21 per set of testing materials, postage extra; (8–10) minutes; Johnson O'Connor; C. H. Stoelting Co. *

REFERENCES

1–13. See 40:1678.
14. McCULLOUGH, CONSTANCE M. *Prediction of Success in the School of Dentistry at the University of Minnesota by Means of Tests and Certain Other Factors.* Doctor's thesis, University of Minnesota (Minneapolis, Minn.), 1938.
15. THOMPSON, CLAUDE EDWARD. *A Study of Motor and Mechanical Abilities.* Doctor's thesis, Ohio State University (Columbus, Ohio), 1939.
16. HACKMAN, RAY CARTER. *The Differential Prediction of Success in Two Contrasting Vocational Areas.* Doctor's thesis, University of Minnesota (Minneapolis, Minn.), 1940.
17. O'CONNOR, JOHNSON. *Unsolved Business Problems,* pp. 87–9. Boston, Mass.: Human Engineering Laboratory, Inc., 1940. Pp. x, 159. *
18. STEAD, WILLIAM H.; SHARTLE, CARROLL L.; OTIS, JAY L.; WARD, RAYMOND S.; OSBORNE, HERBERT F.; ENDLER, O. L.; DVORAK, BEATRICE J.; COOPER, JOHN H.; BELLOWS, ROGER M.; AND KOLBE, LAVERNE E. *Occupational Counseling Techniques: Their Development and Application.* Published for the Technical Board of the Occupational Research Program, United States Employment Service. New York: American Book Co., 1940. Pp. ix, 273. *
19. MORROW, ROBERT S. "An Experimental Analysis of the Theory of Independent Abilities." *J Ed Psychol* 32:495–512 O '41. * *(PA* 16:2209)
20. O'CONNOR, JOHNSON. *The Too Many Aptitude Woman,* pp. 53–4, passim. Boston, Mass.: Human Engineering Laboratory, Inc., 1941. Pp. xii, 185. *
21. BENNETT, GEORGE K., AND CRUIKSHANK, RUTH M. *A Summary of Manual and Mechanical Ability Tests, Preliminary Form,* pp. 59–60. New York: Psychological Corporation, 1942. Pp. v, 74. *
22. CRISSEY, ORLO L. "Test Predictive of Success in Occupation of Job-Setter." Abstract. *Psychol B* 39:436 Jl '42. *
23. THOMPSON, CLAUDE EDWARD. "Motor and Mechanical Abilities in Professional Schools." *J Appl Psychol* 26:24–37 F '42. * *(PA* 16:2483)
24. JACOBSEN, ELDON E. "An Evaluation of Certain Tests in Predicting Mechanic Learner Achievement." *Ed & Psychol Meas* 3:259–67 au '43. * *(PA* 18:2537)
25. O'CONNOR, JOHNSON. *Structural Visualization,* pp. 51–5, passim. Boston, Mass.: Human Engineering Laboratory, Inc., 1943. Pp. xiv, 182. *
26. SURGENT, LOUIS VINCENT. "The Use of Aptitude Tests in the Selection of Radio Tube Mounters." *Psychol Monogr* 61(2):1–40 '47. *
27. BEAMER, GEORGE C.; EDMONSON, LAWRENCE D.; AND STROTHER, GEORGE B. "Improving the Selection of Linotype Trainees." *J Appl Psychol* 32:130–4 Ap '48. * *(PA* 23:965)

28. SUPER, DONALD E. *Appraising Vocational Fitness by Means of Psychological Tests*, pp. 203–17. New York: Harper & Brothers, 1949. Pp. xxiii, 727. * (*PA* 24:2130)

29. PETRIE, ASENATH, AND POWELL, MURIEL B. "The Selection of Nurses in England." *J Appl Psychol* 35:281–6 Ag '51. * (*PA* 26:3090)

30. ALBRIGHT, LEWIS E. "Validity Information Exchange, No. 9-44: D.O.T. Code 0-66.93, Seed Analyst." *Personnel Psychol* 9:522–3 w '56. *

31. ALBRIGHT, LEWIS EDWIN. *The Development of a Selection Process for an Inspection Task.* Doctor's thesis, Purdue University (Lafayette, Ind.), 1956. (*DA* 16:2201)

32. PRAKASH, J. C. "Standardised Norms for Selected Psychological Tests." *Indian J Psychol* 31:147–8 Jl–D '56. * (*PA* 35:3975)

33. BOURASSA, G. LEE, AND GUION, ROBERT M. "A Factorial Study of Dexterity Tests." *J Appl Psychol* 43:199–204 Je '59. * (*PA* 34:6585)

34. LEE, TERENCE. "The Selection of Student Nurses: A Revised Procedure." *Occup Psychol* 33:209–16 O '59. *

35. RIM, Y. "The Predictive Validity of Seven Manual Dexterity Tests." *Psychologia* 5:52–5 Mr '62. * (*PA* 38:1417)

36. SUPER, DONALD E., AND CRITES, JOHN O. *Appraising Vocational Fitness by Means of Psychological Tests, Revised Edition*, pp. 200–13. New York: Harper & Brothers, 1962. Pp. xv, 688. * (*PA* 37:2038)

For a review by Morris S. Viteles, see 40: 1678.

[1080]

★**Purdue Hand Precision Test.** Ages 17 and over; 1941; 3 scores: attempts, correct responses, error time; individual; apparatus ['41]; no manual; typewritten instructions (2 pages); no data on reliability; no norms; administration time not reported; $115 per instrument, postage extra; [Joseph Tiffin]; [Lafayette Instrument Co.]. *

REFERENCES

1. TIFFIN, JOSEPH, AND ROGERS, H. B. "The Selection and Training of Inspectors." *Personnel* 18:14–31 Jl '41. *

2. TIFFIN, JOSEPH. *Industrial Psychology, Second Edition*, pp. 76, 78, 128–9, 304–8. New York: Prentice-Hall, Inc., 1947. Pp. xxi, 553. * (*PA* 22:505)

[1081]

Purdue Pegboard. Grades 9–16 and adults; 1941–48; 5 scores: right hand, left hand, both hands, right plus left plus both hands, assembly; 1 form ('41); manual ('48, 8 pages); profile ('48, 2 pages); $18.95 per set of testing apparatus and manual; 95¢ per 20 profiles; postage extra; 2.5(10) or 7.5(20) minutes; Purdue Research Foundation under the direction of Joseph Tiffin; Science Research Associates, Inc. *

REFERENCES

1–3. See 3:666.
4–15. See 4:751.
16–26. See 5:873.

27. SHORE, RICHARD P. "Validity Information Exchange, No. 11-24: D.O.T. Code 1-25.68, Proof-Machine Operator." *Personnel Psychol* 11:438–9 au '58. *

28. BOURASSA, G. LEE, AND GUION, ROBERT M. "A Factorial Study of Dexterity Tests." *J Appl Psychol* 43:199–204 Je '59. * (*PA* 34:6585)

29. EYMAN, RICHARD K.; DINGMAN, HARVEY F.; AND WINDLE, CHARLES. "Manipulative Dexterity and Movement History of Mental Defectives." *Percept & Motor Skills* 9:291–4 S '59. * (*PA* 34:6216)

30. MAXFIELD, KATHRYN E., AND PERRY, JAMES D. "Performance of Blind Vocational Rehabilitation Clients on the Purdue Pegboard." *Percept & Motor Skills* 11:139–46 O '60. * (*PA* 35:2495)

31. PARKER, JAMES F., JR., AND FLEISHMAN, EDWIN A. "Ability Factors and Component Performance Measures as Predictors of Complex Tracking Behavior." *Psychol Monogr* 74(16):1–36 '60. * (*PA* 36:2CD36P)

32. TOBIAS, JACK, AND GORELICK, JACK. "The Effectiveness of the Purdue Pegboard in Evaluating Work Potential of Retarded Adults." *Training Sch B* 57:94–104 N '60. * (*PA* 35:3791)

33. HOAG, RALPH LYNN. *A Comparative Study of Certain Motor Skills of Deaf and Hearing Mentally Retarded Children.* Doctor's thesis, University of Arizona (Tucson, Ariz.), 1961. (*DA* 22:488)

34. MOFFIE, D. J. "The Selection of Employees in Industry." *Arch Environ Health* 3:94–9 Jl '61. *

35. ZUBIN, JOSEPH; SUTTON, SAMUEL; SALZINGER, KURT; SALZINGER, SUZANNE; BURDOCK, E. I.; AND PERETZ, DAVID. Chap. 10, "A Biometric Approach to Prognosis in Schizophrenia," pp. 143–203. In *Comparative Epidemiology of the Mental Disorders.* The Proceedings of the Forty-Ninth Annual Meeting of the American Psychopathological Association, Held in New York City, February 1959. Edited by Paul H. Hoch and Joseph Zubin. New York: Grune & Stratton, Inc., 1961. Pp. xvi, 290. * (*PA* 36:2JV90H)

36. FLEISHMAN, EDWIN A., AND ELLISON, GAYLORD D. "A Factor Analysis of Fine Manipulative Tests." *J Appl Psychol* 46:96–105 Ap '62. *

37. RIM, Y. "The Predictive Validity of Seven Manual Dexterity Tests." *Psychologia* 5:52–5 Mr '62. * (*PA* 38:1417)

38. SUPER, DONALD E., AND CRITES, JOHN O. *Appraising Vocational Fitness by Means of Psychological Tests, Revised Edition*, pp. 213–7. New York: Harper & Brothers, 1962. Pp. xv, 688. * (*PA* 37:2038)

39. VAUGHAN, HERBERT G., JR., AND COSTA, LOUIS D. "Performance of Patients With Lateralized Cerebral Lesions: 2, Sensory and Motor Tests." *J Nerv & Mental Dis* 134:237–43 Mr '62. * (*PA* 37:1664)

40. WOLINS, LEROY, AND MACKINNEY, ARTHUR C. "Validity Information Exchange, No. 15-04: D.O.T. Code 9-68.30, Packer II." *Personnel Psychol* 15:227–9 su '62. *

41. COSTA, LOUIS D.; VAUGHAN, HERBERT G., JR.; LEVITA, ERIC; AND FARBER, NORMAN. "Purdue Pegboard as a Predictor of the Presence and Laterality of Cerebral Lesions." *J Consult Psychol* 27:133–7 Ap '63. * (*PA* 37:8141)

For a review by Neil D. Warren, see 5:873; for reviews by Edwin E. Ghiselli, Thomas W. Harrell, and Albert Gibson Packard, see 3:666.

[Other Tests]

For tests not listed above, see the following entries in *Tests in Print*: 1898–9, 1902–3, 1905, 1908, and 1911; status unknown: 1897 and 1900–1.

MECHANICAL ABILITY

[1082]

★**A.C.E.R. Mechanical Reasoning Test.** Ages 13-9 and over; 1951–62; abbreviated adaptation of *A.C.E.R. Mechanical Comprehension Test;* 1 form ['51, 4 pages]; revised manual ('62, 15 pages); separate answer sheets must be used; 6s. per 10 tests; 2s. per 10 answer sheets; 1s. per scoring stencil; 3s. per manual; 4s. 9d. per specimen set; postpaid within Australia; 20(30) minutes; T. M. Whitford (revised manual), Research and Guidance Branch, Queensland Department of Public Instruction (test), and the Australian Council for Educational Research; Australian Council for Educational Research. *

For reviews by John R. Jennings and Hayden S. Williams, see 5:875.

[1083]

★**Chriswell Structural Dexterity Test, 1963 Revision.** Grades 7–9; 1953–63; identical with 1953 edition except for additional norms and technical data in manual; title on manual is *Structural Dexterity Test of Mechanical Ability;* individual; Form B ('53, revision of unpublished Form A); revised manual ('63, c1953–63, 12 pages); record card ['53, 1 page]; $30 per set of testing materials, 50 record cards, and manual; $2.50 per 50 record cards; $1 per manual; postage extra; 6.5(15) minutes; M. Irving Chriswell; Vocational Guidance Service. *

REFERENCES

1. CHRISWELL, M. IRVING. "Validity of a Structural Dexterity Test." *J Appl Psychol* 37:13–5 F '53. * (*PA* 28:1618)

For a review by A. Pemberton Johnson of the 1953 edition, see 5:876.

[1084]

★**College Entrance Examination Board Placement Tests: Spatial Relations Test.** Entering college freshmen; 1962–63, c1954–63; tests are reprints of 1954–55 forms of *College Entrance Examination Board Special Aptitude Test in Spatial Relations;* IBM; Forms KPL1, KPL2 in a single booklet (c1954–55, 27 pages) ; for more complete information, see 759; 60(70) minutes; program administered for the College Entrance Examination Board by Educational Testing Service. *

REFERENCES

1. NEWMAN, SIDNEY H.; FRENCH, JOHN W.; AND BOBBITT, JOSEPH M. "Analysis of Criteria for the Validation of Selection Measures at the United States Coast Guard Academy." *Ed & Psychol Meas* 12:394–407 au '52. * (*PA* 27:6159)
2. MYERS, CHARLES T. "A Note on a Spatial Relations Pretest and Posttest." *Ed & Psychol Meas* 13:596–600 w '53. * (*PA* 28:5656)
3. BLADE, MARY F., AND WATSON, WALTER S. "Increase in Spatial Relations Test Scores During Engineering Study." *Yearb Nat Council Meas Used Ed* 11:23–9 '54. *
4. BLADE, MARY F., AND WATSON, WALTER S. "Increase in Spatial Visualization Test Scores During Engineering Study." *Psychol Monogr* 69(12):1–13 '55. * (*PA* 30:5226)

For a review of the College Entrance Examination Board Special Aptitude Test in Spatial Relations, *see 4:808.*

[1085]

★**[Curtis Object Completion and Space Form Tests.]** Applicants for mechanical and technical jobs; 1960–61; 1 form ('60, 1 page) ; 2 tests; manual ('61, 4 pages) ; $3 per 50 tests; $1 per specimen set (must be purchased to obtain manual) ; cash orders postpaid; 1(5) minutes per test; James W. Curtis; Psychometric Affiliates. *
a) OBJECT-COMPLETION TEST.
b) SPACE FORM TEST.

RICHARD S. MELTON, *Assistant Director, Test Development Division, Educational Testing Service, Princeton, New Jersey.*

These two tests are intended to provide estimates of ability to visualize separated parts of two-dimensional figures as a whole figure and to relate three-dimensional figures to their two-dimensional patterns or "unfolded designs." Each test consists of a single page of drawings (items), 24 such items in the Object-Completion Test and 16 in the Space Form Test. Each test is administered with a one-minute time limit. No data on speededness are given in the manual, but it is evident that what is being tested is the speed with which an individual can perform these tasks. However, the subjects are not told that speed of performance is important, nor are they told that only one minute will be allowed.

The first item on each test is a trial item with the correct answer given. Provision is made for the examiner to assure himself at this point that all subjects understand why this is the correct answer and to explain the task further, if necessary. This provision is obviously intended to reduce errors of measurement due to failure to understand the task, but it can also lead to the opposite kind of error for an applicant who understands the task and uses the extra explanation time to study the remainder of the items for several minutes, possibly, before the examiner gives the signal to begin. (The wisdom of printing the answer keys to the two tests in large letters on the first and last pages of the manual may also be questioned, because if the examiner were ever to pick up the manual and refer to it while administering the test, an alert examinee sitting near him could easily read off the correct answers to the test.)

Test-retest reliability coefficients, based on one sample of 150 persons, are reported as 91 for the Object-Completion Test and .86 for the Space Form Test. However, the time intervals between testings are not reported; one week would seem to be a minimum interval for tests of this kind. The correlation between the two tests could also have been obtained from these data, as well as information on practice effects, which would be substantial on tests of this type. However, no such information is reported in the manual.

No validity data of the usual kind are reported, but the manual states that sizable percentages of those who scored above the 23rd percentile on both tests and were subsequently hired were considered by their superiors to be satisfactory (or better) employees, whereas the majority of the few who scored below the 23rd percentile and were subsequently hired were reported as having significant difficulties in adapting to the requirements of their jobs. Why the 23rd percentile was chosen for a cutoff, what number of workers was involved, what the nature of their jobs was, and how many companies were represented is not indicated; thus the significance of these statements, and hence the validity of the tests, cannot be evaluated.

The primary norm table for the Object-Completion Test is based on a general unselected group of 418 male and 82 female applicants for jobs or vocational training in mechanical fields. A second table of norms is described as based on 200 skilled applicants, although the manual text says that the group was of the general unselected type described above. Two norm tables are also given for the Space Form Test, one based on 450 unselected applicants and one based on 200 skilled applicants. The latter group is described in the manual as job applicants or potential trainees for skilled work; no description of the sample of 450 is given. The final paragraph in the interpretation section of the manual recommends the establishment of local norms by each organization using the test, a recommendation heartily to be endorsed. (Lacking local norms, most users would probably do best to use the norm tables based on the larger numbers of cases, as the minor differences between these and the tables based on 200 cases may represent little more than chance departures from the values in the primary norm tables.)

EVALUATION. On the basis of the data presented in the manual, there are no grounds for recommending these tests over other tests on which there are more data. The two reliability coefficients reported are of satisfactory magnitude, but the conditions under which they were obtained are not described. It would be desirable to have additional estimates based on other samples, particularly when the tests are as short as these. The primary norm tables are based on samples of reasonable size, but the description of the composition of the samples is quite meager. It might be surmised that the majority of the individuals were tested in connection with the test author's consulting practice, and that they therefore represent a limited geographical area. Most seriously, there is no quantified evidence of either the predictive or concurrent validity of the tests. Finally, there is good reason to believe that the mode of administration of the tests is such that sizable errors of measurement could easily occur as a result of a small lapse in alertness on the part of the examiner. For these reasons, these tests are not to be recommended for use in selection until they are more adequately standardized and validated.

I. MACFARLANE SMITH, *Principal Lecturer (Research), Garnett College for Training Technical Teachers, London, England.*

The test consists of two parts. The Space Form Test presents five drawings of "unfolded" boxes. Below these there are 16 representations of three-dimensional boxes, viewed from varying angles. The subject is given one minute to match as many boxes as he can with the "unfolded" patterns printed above. The Object-Completion Test presents eight simple closed figures differing from one another in shape. Below these are 24 drawings of incomplete circles or squares, each of which may be completed by fitting one of the eight figures given above. The subject is given one minute to identify the figure required to complete each of the 24 incomplete drawings.

Each subtest consists of one sheet, printed on one side, and the total time required to work both parts is only two minutes. The material is of a kind which has long been known to provide measures of a factor named Visualization (Vz) in America and Spatial (k) in Britain. The first subtest involves thinking about objects in three dimensions and the second involves two-dimensional thinking only. The long-standing argument as to whether these two types of test material should be regarded as providing measures of two distinct factors or simply of one factor does not appear to be settled as yet. The manual states that "these two tests have been devised to provide estimates of....competence in two basic areas of mechanical aptitude and pattern visualization, with a minimal demand upon the time of the examiner and examinee."

The aims of speed and simplicity of administration seem to have been achieved, however, by ignoring most of the precautions usually taken to ensure complete understanding of the instructions and adequate sampling of the abilities tested. In the reviewer's opinion, the tests are much too short to ensure adequate standards of reliability and validity. It is well known that particular care should be taken in constructing spatial tests of these types since they are very susceptible to disturbances caused by misunderstanding of instructions or by inadequate time allowances.

At the beginning of each test, there is one worked item and one practice item, the latter misleadingly referred to in the instructions as "the first item." The manual states that if the subject answers the practice item incorrectly, the examiner should assist him to decide the correct response and only then should give the starting signal. Obviously, when the test is being given to a group of subjects, it may be difficult to prevent work being done on the test proper before the starting signal is given. Thus the time actually taken to work the test may be somewhat imprecise, and a difference of a second or two may be important when the time allowance is only one minute.

The tests comprise 22 and 14 items, respectively. Since the number of items is so small one might expect that the figures would be carefully drawn; but in fact many have been drawn very badly indeed. Lines intended to be parallel are frequently not parallel and triangles intended to be isosceles are sometimes scalene. The sector of a circle shown in the top line of one test is obviously less than a quadrant, yet in line 3, the missing corresponding part is just as obviously greater than a quadrant. The isosceles triangle shown in the top line is only about half the area of the corresponding triangle which is missing from the square in line 4. A subject gifted with high spatial ability might well be handicapped in performing this test because there are no given figures which exactly fill the gaps in some of the drawings.

In view of the shortness of the tests and the limited provision for preliminary practice, it is astonishing that the reliability coefficients are as high as those reported (.86 and .91 by the test-retest method). No reference is made in the manual to standardized scores and it is presumed that the figures for reliability are based on raw scores only. Separate tables of percentile norms for two different groups are provided. One of these tables is based on the scores obtained by a "general unselected group" of 500 applicants for jobs in the fields of mechanics, assembly work, etc. The other table is based on the scores obtained by a group of 200 "skilled applicants." These groups were composed of both men and women. It is desirable that separate tables be provided for each sex, since tests of spatial ability almost invariably show highly significant differences in mean score as between men and women.

The evidence of validity given in the manual can scarcely be regarded as satisfactory. Making every allowance for the fact that sufficient time has not yet elapsed for the collection of data from follow-up studies, the information provided is distinctly meagre. Given cutoff scores are said to discriminate between workers considered "satisfactory" and those who had "difficulty in adapting to some performance phases of the job." We should like to know how these tests compare with other tests of this type or of other types. Data from studies involving correlational, factorial, or regression analysis would have been helpful in evaluating the tests.

Until such evidence is made available, the tests cannot be recommended in their present form. Their only advantages would appear to be ease of administration and scoring and the shortness of the time required to apply them. It is difficult to think of any situation in which these advantages would offset the tests' disadvantages.

[1086]

★Flags: A Test of Space Thinking. Industrial employees; 1959, c1956–59; Form A ('56, 6 pages); manual ('59, 9 pages); no data on reliability; no data on validity of current form; norms for males only; $4 per 20 tests, postage extra; $1 per specimen set, postpaid; 5(10) minutes; L. L. Thurstone (test), T. E. Jeffrey (test), and Measurement Research Division, Industrial Relations Center, University of Chicago (manual); Education-Industry Service. *

I. MACFARLANE SMITH, *Principal Lecturer (Research), Garnett College for Training Technical Teachers, London, England.*

This test is intended to measure one of the primary mental abilities concerned with visual orientation in space, viz., the first space factor identified by Thurstone in several factor analytic studies.

The test consists of 21 items, each calling for six responses, and yields a maximum raw score of 126. The time allowed for working the test is five minutes. Each of the 21 items presents a flag on the left. There are six other flags on the right and these represent either the same or the opposite side of the flag given on the left. All six flags are in different positions, and the subject has to decide which side, the same or opposite, is represented by each of these six flags and to record his answer by crossing out either "S" or "O" underneath each flag.

The instructions are clear and well set out. The difference between the two sides of a flag is illustrated by the device of printing two sides of a flag on the front and back of the first page. This device is certainly helpful for impressing on the examinees the difference in the appearance of the flag when it has been turned over. Practice exercises are provided with the stipulation that explanation be given if examinees make mistakes on these. Thus every opportunity is given to the subject to understand the task before he is expected to begin.

The manual has some other features for

which the authors must be commended. The provision of templates markedly facilitates scoring. Guessing is allowed for by basing the final raw score on the number of correct answers less the number of wrong answers. There is a table for converting raw scores to normalized standard scores with a mean of 50 and a standard deviation of 10. The norms are based on the scores made by 278 male industrial employees.

The manual contains no information regarding reliability and validity, though no doubt data could have been supplied for the older form of the test. The present form differs from the earlier in that a different flag design is used for each item. This innovation was intended to make the test more interesting and there is no reason to suppose that either the reliability or validity will have been affected by the change. Wisely, however, the authors have not quoted figures obtained from earlier studies, pending empirical confirmation that the present version does not differ essentially from the older one. At the date of publication of the manual (1959) there were no validation studies of the present version. It is unlikely that anyone who studies the form and content of the test will seriously question its reliability.

There might, however, be some difference of opinion regarding its validity. It is intended to measure Thurstone's first space factor, which was described by him as the ability to visualize a rigid configuration when it is moved into different positions. This factor was one of five which Thurstone claimed to have identified clearly in his research on mechanical aptitude. *Flags* was not included in this research, although several other tests of the first space factor were included. The authors of the new version of *Flags* state that though measurement of the first space factor "is not essential to the measurement of mechanical aptitude, tests of [this] factor did differentiate between the high and low mechanical interest and experience groups." This was shown in Thurstone's study, though tests of the second space factor S_2 (probably the same as Vz or k) provided the better differentiation. There have been subsequent studies, however, in which the spatial orientation factor, believed to be the same as the first space factor measured by *Flags,* has been shown to have substantial validity for various courses, e.g., in engineering and mathematics at college level. Thus, there

is little reason to doubt that the test under review will be shown to have validity for certain types of courses and occupations.

The reviewer would support the authors' claim that this test is likely to be useful for selecting those with high mechanical interest and aptitude. He would add, however—and the authors would probably agree—that it should be used in conjunction with other tests, particularly of the second space factor, called by Thurstone S_2 and sometimes designated in America as Vz and in Britain as k.

[1087]

★Hazlehurst Primary Mechanical Ability Tests. Applicants for positions requiring mechanical ability; 1940–50; 5 scores: crosses, bolts, tools, missing lines, total; 1 form ('50, 4 pages); 4 tests; manual ('50, 20 pages); no data on reliability; $10 per set of 25 copies of each test; $1 per set of manual and keys; postage extra; specimen set not available; J. H. Hazlehurst; Stevens, Thurow & Associates Inc. *
a) TEST 1, CROSSES. 3(5) minutes.
b) TEST 2, BOLTS. 4.5(10) minutes.
c) TEST 3, TOOLS. 9(15) minutes.
d) TEST 4, MISSING LINES. 5(10) minutes.

[1088]

★Mechanical Information Questionnaire. Employee applicants; 1944–57; 11 scores: automotive information, bench work, building construction, electrical, foundry practice, industrial engineering, maintenance, metal working, pipe fitting, woodworking, total; Forms A ('44), B revised ('57), (4 pages); mimeographed instructions ['44, 2 pages]; no data on reliability and validity; no description of normative population; $4 per 10 tests, cash orders postpaid; specimen set not available; (30) minutes; Eugene J. Benge; [Management Service Co.]. *

[1089]

★Mechanical Movements: A Test of Mechanical Comprehension. Industrial employees; 1959–63, c1956–63; abbreviated version of a Thurstone test developed about 1918; Form A ('56, 4 pages); manual ('63, 14 pages); norms for males only; $3 per 20 tests, postage extra; $1 per specimen set, postpaid; 14(19) minutes; L. L. Thurstone (test), T. E. Jeffrey (test), and Measurement Research Division, Industrial Relations Center, University of Chicago (manual); Education-Industry Service. *

WILLIAM A. OWENS, *Professor of Psychology, Purdue University, Lafayette, Indiana.*

Mechanical Movements is a paper and pencil test designed specifically to measure mechanical comprehension. The test booklet contains one page of instructions and three pages of test items. Each of the 37 items has two, four, or six response options, and all are based upon a total of 11 drawings of mechanical types of apparatus. A subject responds by drawing a black line, on the test booklet, under a number representing the option of his choice. The test is timed and is alleged to be "a measure of both speed and ease of mechanical comprehension."

There are no obvious flaws in the test format. The directions for administration are clear and the two sample problems are appropriate. No special sophistication is required of the examiner. Testing time is 14 minutes and total time for administration is estimated at 17 minutes. The scoring key consists of three columns of answers each of which can be matched against a corresponding column on the test booklet.

Mechanical Movements was originally developed by Thurstone in 1918 as a test of visualization. It has been modified by subsequent research and the present form is about half as long as the original. This change may be unfortunate, since the authors report a split-half reliability of .85 in a study of engineering freshmen. Such an estimate is, of course, inflated to an unknown, but probably substantial, extent by speeding. In the absence of other evidence, it must be concluded that the intrinsic reliability of *Mechanical Movements* is unknown and is probably unsatisfactory. If this is indeed the case, several factors may be responsible. First, the test is relatively brief at 37 items and 14 minutes. Second, since as many as seven questions are sometimes based upon a single drawing, a failure to comprehend one of these could cause the subject to make not one, but seven, incorrect responses. The correlation of item errors thus introduced may be regarded either as decreasing the effective number of items or as increasing the error variance, per se. According to either conception it has the effect of reducing test reliability.

Relationships with representative measures of other psychological functions are not reported, although it is noted that *Mechanical Movements* has failed to load substantially on a verbal factor in five analyses and that scores may therefore be presumed to be relatively independent of verbal ability.

With respect to the all important requirement of validity, *Mechanical Movements* is difficult to evaluate because adequate evidence is not presented. The test undoubtedly has some construct validity since it is reported to have "high" loadings on Thurstone's second space factor, defined as the ability to visualize internal movement or displacement of parts within a flexible configuration. On the other hand, no correlations with external criteria of mechanical aptitude are provided. The closest

approach is a statement indicating a probability less than .001 that groups with high versus low degrees of mechanical interest and experience would not be discriminated. Clearly, a statement of probability is not an estimate of magnitude, and a P-value of .001 really tells the reader nothing about differences between means, or the correlation of the test with the experience-interest criterion (which sounds truncated).

The only other evidence regarding validity comes from a norm table which indicates mean scores for professionals and managers, foremen, and hourly workers as being 20.32, 14.46, and 15.02, respectively. In evaluating these, it is somewhat disturbing to note that foremen do not outscore hourly employees, but that professionals and managers substantially outscore both groups. Since an unstated number of the professionals are engineers, some members of this top group may actually have a high degree of mechanical aptitude. Unhappily, it could equally well be that scores are fairly substantially related to some more general cognitive ability. It is hoped that further research with *Mechanical Movements* will clarify the extent of its relationship with both other representative tests and selected external criteria of mechanical ability.

The norms themselves are based upon the combined scores of the three occupational groups priorly identified. Since the groups are combined, the frame of reference for a particular score is rather fuzzy. As more data are gathered separate norms for various subgroups will hopefully be developed.

In summary, certain vital questions regarding the reliability and validity of *Mechanical Movements* remain to be answered. Until this is done the test must necessarily be granted a less enthusiastic endorsement than can be accorded such well documented devices as Bennett's *Tests of Mechanical Comprehension*.

[1090]

★**Moray House Space Test 2.** Ages 10.0–12.0; 1951–61; 1 form ['61, 11 pages]; manual ['61, 12 pages]; distribution restricted to education authorities; 56s. per 100 tests; 1s. 9d. per manual; purchase tax extra; postpaid; 49(55) minutes; Department of Education, University of Edinburgh; University of London Press Ltd. *

REFERENCES

1. EMMETT, W. C. "Evidence of a Space Factor at 11+ and Earlier." *Brit J Psychol, Stat Sect* 2:3–16 Mr '49. * (*PA* 23:4509)
2. SWANSON, Z. "Further Investigation of the Moray House Space Test." Abstract. *Adv Sci* 7:95 My '50. *

Mechanical Movements: A Test of Mechanical Comprehension

3. WRIGLEY, JACK. "The Factorial Nature of Ability in Elementary Mathematics." *Brit J Ed Psychol* 28:61–78 F '58. * (PA 33:6845)
4. SMITH, I. MACFARLANE. "The Validity of Tests of Spatial Ability as Predictors of Success on Technical Courses." *Brit J Ed Psychol* 30:138–45 Je '60. *

E. ANSTEY, *Chief Psychologist, Civil Service Commission, London, England.*

The test is intended to form one of a battery of selection tests in an 11+ examination for allocation to secondary schools. These tests often consist entirely of verbal reasoning, English, and arithmetic items, which are highly predictive of the degree of suitability for an academic type of education, but give no particular indication of suitability for a technical type of education. The *Moray House Space Test 2* was designed to meet this need, to identify among boys and girls aged between 10.0 and 12.0 those likely to be successful at scientific and technical subjects such as technical drawing, woodwork, and metal work.

Throughout the test the subject is required to appreciate shapes and the relationship between them. On 4 of the 10 pages the diagrams are in three dimensions, presented so that the subject has to visualise parts of a simple structure that are hidden from him or to imagine how pieces might fit together. Apart from the written instructions, there is little use of words, but on four pages counting is required. The test might therefore be expected to have a high spatial and some numerical content, but less verbal-educational content than most 11+ tests. Some evidence to this effect is quoted in the manual, in the form of rather lower correlations with other standard tests than these tests have with each other. As all the correlations exceed .75, however, it would be wrong to regard the test, on its own, as more than a pointer towards a child's particular bent. Combined with information about the child's performance in other tests, his interests, and his aspirations, it might well be a useful pointer.

One would like to see more research into the progress of children at different types of secondary schools, grammar, technical, and modern, or in the corresponding streams within comprehensive schools, and to assess the predictive value, for instance, of an index contrasting performance in a space test with that in a clerical test.

Technically, the test is excellent. The layout is attractive, the instructions and examples clear, and the answers totally free from ambiguity. One minor criticism relates to page 9 of the test. Although there are six shapes to choose from in answering any question, the effective choice, for any subject who has grasped what to do, is between the two shapes which are mirror images of each other, i.e., there might be nearly a 50 per cent chance of getting the answer right by guessing. This is not to say that in practice the children do guess, but the design of this page could easily be altered to eliminate this minor technical flaw.

The test has a split-half reliability coefficient of .97, and in the course of preparation it was found to correlate about .94 with a parallel form of test.[1] One would not want higher reliability coefficients than these. Indeed the test could probably be reduced in length and still remain a reliable indicator.

Trials with 5,719 boys and 5,528 girls established a highly significant difference in performance between the sexes of 5 raw score points in favour of boys, equivalent to about a sixth of the standard deviation of the standardised scores. In view of the superior performance of boys, it is unfortunate that separate norms are not provided for boys and girls.

The *Moray House Space Test 2* is of excellent design and carefully standardised. For the intended purpose of helping to identify among children aged between 10.0 and 12.0 those likely to be successful at scientific and technical subjects, it would make a reliable measuring instrument. But full account should be taken of all other information available about a child before making any decisions about his or her future education.

[1091]

O'Connor Wiggly Block. Ages 16 and over; 1928–51; individual; 1 form ['28]; mimeographed manual ['28(?), 3 pages]; record blank ('51, 1 page); no data on reliability; $25.25 per set of blocks, 50 record blanks, and manual; $1.50 per 50 record blanks; postage extra; [15–30] minutes; Johnson O'Connor; C. H. Stoelting Co. *

REFERENCES

1. KEANE, FRANCIS L., AND O'CONNOR, JOHNSON. "A Measure of Mechanical Aptitude." *Personnel J* 6:15–24 Je '27. * (PA 1:2090)
2. STOY, E. G. "Additional Tests for Mechanical Drawing Aptitude." *Personnel J* 6:361–6 F '28. * (PA 2:2660)
3. REMMERS, H. H., AND SCHELL, J. W. "Testing the O'Connor Wiggly Block Test." *Personnel J* 12:155–9 O '33. * (PA 8:1800)
4. VITELES, M. S. "The Measurement of Motor Ability." Abstract. *Psychol B* 30:569 O '33. *
5. O'CONNOR, JOHNSON. *Psychometrics: A Study of Psychological Measurements.* Cambridge, Mass.: Harvard University Press, 1934. Pp. xxxiv, 292. *
6. PHILIP, B. R. "A Comparison of an Electric Circuit Tracing Test With the O'Connor Wiggly Block Test." *J Appl Psychol* 19:148–65 Ap '35. * (PA 9:5365)

1 The reliability coefficient based upon alternate forms was reported to the writer by A. E. G. Pilliner.

7. REMMERS, H. H., AND SMITH, J. M. "Reliability and Practice Effect in the O'Connor Wiggly Block Test." *J Appl Psychol* 20:591–8 O '36. * (*PA* 11:2981)

8. FRYE, ELLIS K. "The Mechanical Abilities of Siblings." *J Genetic Psychol* 50:293–306 Je '37. * (*PA* 11:6020)

9. HARRELL, WILLARD. "The Validity of Certain Mechanical Ability Tests for Selecting Cotton Mill Machine Fixers." *J Social Psychol* 8:279–82 My '37. * (*PA* 11:5311)

10. HARRIS, ALBERT J. "The Relative Significance of Measures of Mechanical Aptitude, Intelligence, and Previous Scholarship for Predicting Achievement in Dental School." *J Appl Psychol* 21:513–21 O '37. * (*PA* 12:2113)

11. HARRELL, WILLARD. "A Factor Analysis of Mechanical Ability Tests." *Psychometrika* 5:17–33 Mr '40. * (*PA* 14:4285) (Abstract: *Psychol B* 36:524)

12. BRUSH, EDWARD N. "Mechanical Ability as a Factor in Engineering Aptitude." *J Appl Psychol* 25:300–12 Je '41. * (*PA* 15:4377)

13. GIESE, WILLIAM JAMES. "A New Method for Scoring the Wiggly Block." Abstract. *Psychol B* 38:721 O '41. *

14. BENNETT, GEORGE K., and CRUIKSHANK, RUTH M. *A Summary of Manual and Mechanical Ability Tests, Preliminary Form,* pp. 57–8. New York: Psychological Corporation, 1942. Pp. v, 74. *

15. ESTES, STANLEY G. "A Study of Five Tests of 'Spatial' Ability." *J Psychol* 13:265–71 Ap '42. * (*PA* 16:3771)

16. BATES, JUSTINE; WALLACE, MARJORIE; and HENDERSON, MACK T. "A Statistical Study of Four Mechanical Ability Tests." *Proc Iowa Acad Sci* 50:299–301 '43. * (*PA* 18:3276)

17. O'CONNOR, JOHNSON. *Structural Visualization,* pp. 1–46. Boston, Mass.: Human Engineering Laboratory, Inc., 1943. Pp. xiv, 182. *

18. LICHT, MARIE. *The Relation of Wiggly Block to Black Cube.* Human Engineering Laboratory, Inc., Technical Report No. 194. Boston, Mass.: the Laboratory, December 1945. Pp. 4. *

19. LICHT, MARIE. *The Relationship of Vocabulary and Wiggly Block Scores of Seven Test Administrators.* Human Engineering Laboratory, Inc., Technical Report No. 177. Boston, Mass.: the Laboratory, October 1945. Pp. 7. *

20. KHAN, HAKIM I. A. "The Correlation Between Wiggley Block Test and School Achievement." Abstract. *Proc 34th Indian Sci Congr, Delhi, 1947* 34:3 '46. *

21. MILLER, CHARLES, AND LAUER, A. R. "The Mechanical Aptitude of Drivers in Relation to Performance at the Wheel." *Proc Iowa Acad Sci* 53:273–5 '46. * (*PA* 23:991)

22. BITTEL, JANE. *Standard Error on Worksample No. Three.* Human Engineering Laboratory, Inc., Technical Report No. 367. Boston, Mass.: the Laboratory, February 1947. Pp. 27. *

23. FOLEY, JEANNE. *A Description of a New Technique in Obtaining Practice and Conversion Factors for All Trials of Wiggly Block Beginning With Worksample 3: The Preliminary Factors.* Human Engineering Laboratory, Inc., Technical Report No. 364. Boston, Mass.: the Laboratory, January 1947. Pp. i, 25. *

24. MCINTOSH, W. JOHN. "Use of Manual Dexterity and Mechanical Aptitude Tests in Shop Counseling of Mentally Retarded Adolescent Boys." *J Excep Child* 14:81–4 D '47. * (*PA* 22:4481)

25. BUNCH, RICHARD H.; KJERLAND, R. N.; AND LAUER, A. R. "Reliability of the O'Connor Block Test." *Proc Iowa Acad Sci* 57:353–6 '50. *

26. KJERLAND, R. N. "Age and Sex Difference in Performance in the O'Connor Blocks." *Proc Iowa Acad Sci* 58:371–4 '51. *

27. PHILLIPS, J. J.; GREEN, M. C.; AND KJERLAND, R. N. "The Validity of a Pencil and Paper Version of the O'Connor Block Test." Abstract. *Proc Iowa Acad Sci* 59:392 '52. *

[1092]

Revised Minnesota Paper Form Board Test. Grades 9–16 and adults; 1930–48; IBM; 2 forms; 2 editions; manual ('48, 16 pages); 75¢ per specimen set of both editions; postpaid; 20(25) minutes; original test by Donald G. Paterson, Richard M. Elliott, L. Dewey Anderson, Herbert A. Toops, and Edna Heidbreder; revision by Rensis Likert and William H. Quasha; Psychological Corporation. * (Australian edition: Australian Council for Educational Research.)
a) [HAND SCORING EDITION.] 1930–48; Forms AA ('41), BB ('41), (6 pages); French-Canadian edition (Forms AA-FE, BB-FE, '55) available; $2.50 per 25 tests.
b) [MACHINE SCORABLE EDITION.] 1941–48; IBM; Forms MA ('41), MB ('41), (6 pages); separate answer sheets must be used; $3.50 per 25 tests; $2 per 50 IBM answer sheets; 40¢ per set of manual and scoring stencils.

REFERENCES

1–9. See 40:1673.
10–57. See 3:677.
58–95. See 4:763.
96–124. See 5:884.

125. CHOTHIA, F. S. "Predicting Success in Multi-Purpose Schools." *Indian J Psychol* 31:139–40 Jl–D '56. *

126. NEWALL, K. "Selection Testing of Sewing Machinists." *Personnel Prac B* 14:36–8 D '58. * (*PA* 34:2164)

127. SKOLNICKI, JOHN. "Normative Data Information Exchange, Nos. 11-23, 11-24." *Personnel Psychol* 11:453–4 au '58. *

128. ALBRIGHT, LEWIS E.; SMITH, WALLACE J.; AND GLENNON, J. R. "A Follow-Up on Some 'Invalid' Tests for Selecting Salesmen." *Personnel Psychol* 12:105–12 sp '59. * (*PA* 34:3463)

129. SMITH, WALLACE J.; GLENNON, J. R.; AND ALBRIGHT, LEWIS E. "Normative Data Information Exchange, Nos. 12-9, 12-10." *Personnel Psychol* 12:152–3 sp '59. *

130. ASH, PHILIP. "Validity Information Exchange, No. 13-06: D.O.T. Code 5-83.127, Typewriter Serviceman." *Personnel Psychol* 13:455 w '60. *

131. CASS, JOHN C., AND TIEDEMAN, DAVID V. "Vocational Development and the Election of a High School Curriculum." *Personnel & Guid J* 38:538–45 Mr '60. *

132. HAKKINEN, SAULI, AND TOIVAINEN, YRJO. "Psychological Factors Causing Labour Turnover Among Underground Workers." *Occup Psychol* 34:15–30 Ja '60. * (*PA* 35:7162)

133. MACKINNEY, ARTHUR C., AND WOLINS, LEROY. "Validity Information Exchange, No. 13-01, Foreman II, Home Appliance Manufacturing." *Personnel Psychol* 13:443–7 w '60. *

134. MASON, P. L., AND CASEY, D. L. "The Use of Psychological Tests for Selecting Tabulating Machine Operators." *Personnel Prac B* 16:39–41 S '60. * (*PA* 35:4063)

135. TYLER, DONALD J. *An Experimental Investigation of the Effects of a Course in Mechanical Drawing on the Interform Reliability of the Revised Minnesota Paper Form Board Test.* Master's thesis, Western Illinois University (Macomb, Ill.), 1960.

136. WATLEY, DONIVAN JASON. *Prediction of Academic Success in a College of Business Administration.* Doctor's thesis, University of Denver (Denver, Colo.), 1961. (*DA* 22:3527)

137. REID, JOHN W.; JOHNSON, A. PEMBERTON; ENTWISLE, FRANK N.; AND ANGERS, WILLIAM P. "A Four-Year Study of the Characteristics of Engineering Students." *Personnel & Guid J* 41:38–43 S '62. * (*PA* 37:5655)

138. SAXENA, K. N. "Predictive Efficiency of Revised Minnesota Paper Form Board Test (AA Series) for Achievement in Science for Delta Class Students." *Manas* 9:55–6 '62. * (*PA* 38:4702)

139. SUPER, DONALD E., AND CRITES, JOHN O. *Appraising Vocational Fitness by Means of Psychological Tests, Revised Edition,* pp. 290–300. New York: Harper & Brothers, 1962. Pp. xv, 688. * (*PA* 37:2038)

140. WATLEY, DONIVAN J., AND MARTIN, H. T. "Prediction of Academic Success in a College of Business Administration." *Personnel & Guid J* 41:147–54 O '62. * (*PA* 37:5656)

For a review by D. W. McElwain, see 5:884; for reviews by Clifford E. Jurgensen and Raymond A. Katzell, see 4:763; for a review by Dewey B. Stuit, see 3:677; for a review by Alec Rodger, see 40:1673.

[1093]

*Spatial Tests 1, 2, and 3. Ages 11-0 to 13-11, 10-7 to 13-11, 10-0 to 11-11; 1950–59; 1 form; 3 tests; distribution restricted to directors of education; prices include purchase tax; postage extra; published for the National Foundation for Educational Research in England and Wales; Newnes Educational Publishing Co. Ltd. *
a) SPATIAL TEST 1. Ages 11-0 to 13-11; 1950–59; 1 form ['50, 23 pages]; revised manual ('59, 24 pages); 17s. 6d. per 12 tests; 1s. 9d. per single copy; 3s. per manual; 41(60) minutes; I. Macfarlane Smith.
b) SPATIAL TEST 2 (THREE-DIMENSIONAL). Ages 10-7 to 13-11; 1950–56; 1 form ['51, 20 pages]; manual ['51, 13 pages]; provisional norms ['56] for ages 10-7 to 11-6; norms ['55] for ages 13-0 to 13-11; no data on reliability and validity; no norms for ages 11-7 to 12-11; 15s. per 12 tests; 1s. 6d. per single copy; 1s. 6d. per manual; 26.5(45) minutes; A. F. Watts with

the assistance of D. A. Pidgeon and M. K. B. Richards.

c) SPATIAL TEST 3 (NEWCASTLE SPATIAL TEST). Ages 10-0 to 11-11; 1958–59; 1 form ['58, 23 pages]; manual ('59, 11 pages); no norms for ages 11-4 to 11-11; 17s. 6d. per 12 tests; 1s. 9d. per single copy; 1s. 3d. per manual; 39(60) minutes; I. Macfarlane Smith and J. S. Lawes.

REFERENCES

1. SMITH, I. MACFARLANE. "Measuring Spatial Ability in School Pupils." *Occup Psychol* 22:150–9 Jl '48. * (*PA* 23:1181)
2. SMITH, I. MACFARLANE. "The Validity of Tests of Spatial Ability as Predictors of Success on Technical Courses." *Brit J Ed Psychol* 30:138–45 Je '60. *
3. TAYLOR, C. COLIN. "A Study of the Nature of Spatial Ability and Its Relationship to Attainment in Geography." Abstract of master's thesis. *Brit J Ed Psychol* 30:266–70 N '60. *
4. LAWES, J. S. "The Construction and Validation of a Spatial Test." Abstract of master's thesis. *Brit J Ed Psychol* 31:297–9 N '61. *

For reviews by E. G. Chambers and Charles T. Myers of tests 1 and 2, see 5:885; for a review by E. A. Peel of test 1, see 4:753.

[1094]

Tests of Mechanical Comprehension. Grades 9 and over; 1940–54; IBM; 4 editions; separate answer sheets must be used; $4.75 per 25 tests; $2 per 50 IBM answer sheets; 40¢ per set of manual and scoring stencils; 50¢ per specimen set; postpaid; (25–45) minutes; George K. Bennett, Dinah E. Fry (*b*, test only; *d*), and William A. Owens (*c*); Psychological Corporation. *

a) FORM AA. Grades 9 and over; 1940–54; 1 form ('40, 16 pages); manual ('47, 8 pages); supplement ('54, 1 page); Spanish edition and bilingual French-English edition available.

b) FORM BB. Men in grades 13 and over; 1941–51; 1 form ('41, 16 pages); revised manual ('51, 8 pages); Spanish edition available.

c) FORM CC. Men in engineering schools; 1949; 1 form (15 pages); manual ('49, 4 pages).

d) FORM W-1. Women in grades 9 and over; 1942–47; 1 form ('42, 16 pages); manual ('47, 4 pages).

REFERENCES

1–19. See 3:683.
20–47. See 4:766.
48–93. See 5:889.
94. GLENNON, J. R.; SMITH, WALLACE J.; AND ALBRIGHT, LEWIS E. "Normative Data Information Exchange, Nos. 11-35, 11-36." *Personnel Psychol* 11:601–2 w '58. *
95. JUERGENSON, ELWOOD M. *The Relationship Between Success in Teaching Vocational Agriculture and Ability to Make Sound Judgments as Measured by Selected Instruments.* Doctor's thesis, Pennsylvania State University (University Park, Pa.), 1958. (*DA* 19:96)
96. KAZMIER, LEONARD J. "Normative Data Information Exchange, No. 12-23." *Personnel Psychol* 12:505 au '59. *
97. OWENS, W. A. "A Comment on the Recent Study of the Mechanical Comprehension Test (CC) by R. L. Decker." *J Appl Psychol* 43:31 F '59. * (*PA* 34:4842)
98. ASH, PHILIP. "Validity Information Exchange, No. 13-06: D.O.T. Code 5-83.127, Typewriter Serviceman." *Personnel Psychol* 13:455 w '60. *
99. CASS, JOHN C., AND TIEDEMAN, DAVID V. "Vocational Development and the Election of a High School Curriculum." *Personnel & Guid J* 38:538–45 Mr '60. *
100. MACKINNEY, ARTHUR C., AND WOLINS, LEROY. "Validity Information Exchange, No. 13-01, Foreman II, Home Appliance Manufacturing." *Personnel Psychol* 13:443–7 w '60. *
101. DURRETT, HAROLD L. "Validity Information Exchange, No. 14-03: D.O.T. Code 5-21.010, Continuous Miner Operator (Bituminous Coal Industry)." *Personnel Psychol* 14:453–5 w '61. *
102. CLEGG, HERMAN D., AND DECKER, ROBERT L. "The Evaluation of a Psychological Test Battery as a Selective Device for Foremen in the Mining Industry." *Proc W Va Acad Sci* 34:178–82 N '62. *
103. CRANE, WILLIAM J. "Screening Devices for Occupational Therapy Majors." *Am J Occup Ther* 16:131–2 My-Je '62. * (*PA* 37:4078)

104. DREW, ALFRED STANISLAUS. *The Relationship of General Reading Ability and Other Factors to School and Job Performance of Machinist Apprentices.* Doctor's thesis, University of Wisconsin (Madison, Wis.), 1962. (*DA* 23:1261)
105. SUPER, DONALD E., AND CRITES, JOHN O. *Appraising Vocational Fitness by Means of Psychological Tests,* Revised Edition, pp. 242–56. New York: Harper & Brothers, 1962. Pp. xv, 688. * (*PA* 37:2038)
106. *Normative Information: Manager and Executive Testing.* New York: Richardson, Bellows, Henry & Co., Inc., May 1963. Pp. 45. *
107. CAMPBELL, JOEL T. "Validity Information Exchange, No. 16-04: D.O.T. Code 7-36.250, Gas Deliveryman." *Personnel Psychol* 16:181–3 su '63. *
108. TAYLOR, DONALD W. Chap. 19, "Variables Related to Creativity and Productivity Among Men in Two Research Laboratories," pp. 228–50. In *Scientific Creativity: Its Recognition and Development.* Edited by Calvin W. Taylor and Frank Barron. New York: John Wiley & Sons, Inc., 1963. Pp. xxiv, 419. * (*PA* 38:2689)

For a review by N. W. Morton, see 4:766; for reviews by Charles M. Harsh, Lloyd G. Humphreys, and George A. Satter, see 3:683.

[1095]

★**Three-Dimensional Space Test.** Industrial workers in mechanical fields; 1950–63; 1 form ('50, 6 pages); manual ['63, 4 unnumbered pages]; no data on reliability; $4.25 per 25 tests; 10¢ per key; 75¢ per manual; postage extra; $1 per specimen set, postpaid; 10(15) minutes; Richardson, Bellows, Henry & Co., Inc. *

[1096]

★**Tool Knowledge Test.** Industry; 1951–63; 1 form ('51, 12 pages); manual ['63, 4 unnumbered pages]; $7.25 per 25 tests; 10¢ per key; 75¢ per manual; postage extra; $1.25 per specimen set, postpaid; (20–25) minutes; Richardson, Bellows, Henry & Co., Inc. *

[1097]

★**Two-Dimensional Space Test.** Business and industry; 1948–63; 1 form ('48, 5 pages); manual ['63, 5 unnumbered pages]; norms for males only; $3.50 per 25 tests; 10¢ per key; 75¢ per manual; postage extra; $1 per specimen set, postpaid; Spanish edition available; 10(15) minutes; Richardson, Bellows, Henry & Co., Inc. *

[1098]

★**Weights and Pulleys: A Test of Intuitive Mechanics.** Engineering students and industrial employees; 1959, c1956–59; Form A ('56, 3 pages); manual ('59, 10 pages); no data on reliability of current form; norms for male industrial employees only; $3 per 20 tests, postage extra; $1 per specimen set, postpaid; 3(8) minutes; L. L. Thurstone (test), T. E. Jeffrey (test), and Measurement Research Division, Industrial Relations Center, University of Chicago (manual); Education-Industry Service. *

WILLIAM A. OWENS, *Professor of Psychology, Purdue University, Lafayette, Indiana.*

As the manual states, "The test consists of one page of instructions and practice exercises and two pages of test items. There are 32 items in the test proper. Each item shows a diagram of a system of weights and pulleys. The subject decides whether the system is 'stable' or 'unstable' * The test is timed, and thus is a measure of the speed and ease with which the subject can visualize stability or change in the diagrams."

In format the test is simple and well arranged, and the items are clear and intelligible line drawings. Instructions for administration and sample problems, of which there are three, are adequate, and should require a minimum of examiner sophistication. Testing time, per se, is three minutes, and estimated total time for administration is six minutes. Since no answer sheet is utilized, scoring involves the use of two simple lay-over stencils which are provided.

The background of basic research which sired *Weights and Pulleys* is impressive; it was specifically developed as a measure of the second space factor identified by Thurstone in his analysis of mechanical aptitude. However, the test itself seems to have been marketed prior to the provision of several very critical types of interpretative data. Norms are based upon the scores of 285 industrial employees from five categories: professional, executive, junior executive, foreman, and hourly. The smallest group is 28 and the largest 103. If the groups are combined, the standard of comparison is very vague; if they are not combined, the *n*'s are inadequate.

For reliabilities of two shorter forms of the test Thurstone earlier reported estimates of .60 and .85 among engineering freshmen. It is implied that the present form is more reliable because it is twice as long. Correcting the lower figure for length still yields only .75, which is relatively unsatisfactory and completely speculative in view of the fact that *no direct estimate is reported*. Similarly, no correlations with cognitive measures are reported, although reference is made to a correlation of .40 with *Mechanical Movements* in a sample of 112 "industrial men."

Evidence as to the validity of *Weights and Pulleys* is somewhat scattered. Inferentially, it has construct validity, since tests with comparable items load highly on Thurstone's second space factor, defined as the ability to visualize movement or displacement within a flexible configuration. On the other hand, the manual states that there has been no industrial validation; and no direct evidence to the effect that the test will discriminate groups known or presumed to differ in mechanical aptitude is provided. A relevant examination of the hierarchy of means of the norm subgroups is disturbing,

since it shows foremen only slightly more than 1 point above hourly workers and nearly 3 points below junior executives. It may be, as suggested by the publisher, that this sample of executives which was drawn largely from among chemical engineers has a high level of mechanical aptitude. Or, alternatively, it is equally possible that the test is relatively heavily saturated with a more general, intellective ability. In any event, the mean differences are small and their implication is dubious.

As things stand, the greatest weakness of *Weights and Pulleys* is that experience with it has apparently not been adequate to permit the answering of vital questions regarding its reliability and validity. Hopefully, time and the collection of further data will provide answers to these questions, pro or con. In the meantime it is not possible to recommend the use of this test as alternative to the use of an instrument of such well documented merit as Bennett's *Tests of Mechanical Comprehension*.

[Other Tests]

For tests not listed above, see the following entries in *Tests in Print*: 1912, 1915, 1917, 1919–23, 1925, 1927, 1929–30, 1932, 1934, 1936–7, 1940, 1943–5, 1947, and 1950; out of print: 1928, 1935, 1938, 1942, and 1948–9.

MISCELLANEOUS

[1099]

★**The Biographical Index.** College and industry; 1961–62; 5 scores: drive to excel, financial status, human relations orientation, personal adjustment, stability; 1 form ('61, 8 pages); manual ('61, 8 pages, including 1962 norms); separate answer sheets must be used; $10 per 25 tests; $2 per 25 answer sheets; $2 per specimen set (must be purchased to obtain manual); cash orders postpaid; (10–20) minutes; Willard A. Kerr; William James Press. *

JOHN K. HEMPHILL, *Director, Developmental Research Division, Educational Testing Service, Princeton, New Jersey.*

The *Biographical Index* is a collection of 79 biographical items, the responses to which are keyed to yield scores on five index areas: Drive to Excel, Financial Status, Human Relations Orientation, Personal Adjustment, and Stability, but none of these scores is further described or adequately defined. A total or composite score, made up of the sum of the five index scores is also suggested.

The index was developed by "reworking" a pool of biographical items that had been assembled by a search of the research literature for items that had, at one time or another, been shown to be correlated with some criterion of job success. A preliminary edition was administered to 38 executives and 62 students. Responses to each item were correlated with six hypothesized basic scores (the above five plus Energy Level) and items were then reassigned if "misplaced."

It is extremely difficult to determine the meaning of any one of the five scores, either by resort to reasoning from the title given to the index area or by examination of the item area correlation data for the preliminary form given in an appendix to the manual. For example, we find that having held a full time job before is keyed toward a high score in Human Relations Orientation, as is living in the same general community as the present job location, or the ability to list all past immediate supervisors and how they might still be reached. These items would not define a high human relations score for most reasonable people and indeed appear to be extremely strange bedfellows. If, then, we abandon reason for dust bowl empiricism and look at the item versus area index score correlation statistics we find, for example, that getting a master's degree within one year after the bachelor's degree has a .05 correlation with Drive to Excel, for which it is keyed in the present form, but also a .10 correlation with Financial Status, for which it is not; or that having reached the age of 30 or over is keyed for Stability, with which it correlates .64, but not for Financial Status, with which it correlates .95. The author's statements, "On the basis of the size of these correlations of items with basic area, items were re-assigned objectively to their quantitatively appropriate area" and "A few items correlating equally well with two or more basic areas were assigned on the basis of face validity" seem difficult to interpret.

The manual contains a review of studies of the validity of biographical items against job success criteria, presumably for the purpose of establishing the reasonableness of the procedure used to develop the index. About two pages of the eight-page manual are devoted to this review, contrasting sharply with less than a third of a column on reliability, and about two thirds of a column giving the results of two validity studies (using one sample of 36 executives and another of 26 executives). The norms provided are also quite inadequate. One norm group is simply described as 85 sales and executive personnel, and another as 93 college upperclassmen. The 1962 supplementary norms are based on 501 cases described as "managerial personnel" ($n = 107$) and "candidates for important sales positions." These later norms are organized by 41 specific age groups, but without note of the number of cases contained within each group.

Split-half reliability coefficients ($n = 100$) reported for the five scores range from .42 for Personal Adjustment to .74 for Stability and Drive to Excel. (The reliability for the combined five scores is reported as .88.) Intercorrelations among the scores are not provided. Validity coefficients for a criterion described as "the average annual increment to monthly salary of executives during their entire full-time working careers" range from −.10 to .50 for 36 executives from the Chicago area, and from −.15 to .60 for 26 executives from "all over the country." The highest coefficients for both groups (.50 and .60) were obtained for Personal Adjustment, but this score also has the lowest estimated reliability. These data leave much to be desired when presented as evidence of the potential usefulness of the test.

There is little that this reviewer can find in the description of the way the index was developed, or in the other information provided in the manual, that would support a recommendation for its use as a means of indicating individuals who "tend to be good job risks with superior probability of winning unusual merit increases and accumulating steady years of faithful service."

RICHARD S. MELTON, *Assistant Director, Test Development Division, Educational Testing Service, Princeton, New Jersey.*[1]

This inventory provides, as the manual states, "an objective quantification of background data." It consists of five scales which were originally formed on an a priori basis but modified subsequently in the light of item-scale correlations. Split-half reliability coefficients for the five scales, based on 100 cases, range from .42 to .74. In view of the diversity of the items and of the weights assigned to different items, the use of the split-half technique is questionable, and the absence of any other re-

[1] At the time this review was requested the reviewer was Assistant Director, Professional Examinations Division, The Psychological Corporation, New York, New York.

liability data raises a serious question about the use of the index in making personnel decisions. The reliability of a composite score, which is presumably based on a sum of the five scale scores, is reported as .88, but no validity data or norms are given for this composite.

The validity data for the five scales consist of two sets of correlations with a criterion measure obtained on the answer sheet, the individual's annual increment to monthly salary. One set of correlations was based on 36 Chicago executives, and the other set was based on a "national" sample of 26 executives; both groups were participants in a management development seminar. The 10 correlations ranged from −.15 to .60, four being statistically significant. However, only one scale, Personal Adjustment, showed consistent significant results in both samples.

Three sets of norms are provided, one based on 85 sales and executive personnel, one on 93 college upperclassmen, and the third, a set of age norms, based on 501 "upper level sales applicants," including 107 managerial personnel. The third table, which shows that scores on all five scales increase with age, is clearly the best of the three. However, inasmuch as it includes ages 18 to 58, the average number of cases at each age is less than 13. (A personal communication from the test author indicates that the entries in the table were obtained by a moving average curve fitting technique.) The table also indicates that in many age brackets the score variability is frequently less than would be desired; in one extreme case a 1-point increment in raw score increases the percentile rank by 50 points. Clearly an age norm table based on more substantial numbers of cases is a necessity for the proper interpretation of scores on these scales.

No intercorrelations among the five scales are reported; means, standard deviations, and standard errors of measurement must be estimated by the user from the norm tables and the reliability coefficients reported. The "background research" summarized in the manual consists of brief reviews of research done on biographical inventories as far back as 1925; the purpose of including this extended review appears to be that of convincing potential users of the index that there is a long history of positive results with biographical data. More convincing evidence of the value of the present instrument would be much more welcome.

While the authors are to be commended for including a complete table of item-scale correlations ($n = 100$) and item-criterion correlations ($n = 38$), it would also have been desirable to include the percentages of responses to each of the keyed options. Such data would, among other things, help describe the nature of the sample. For example, it can be inferred from the correlations reported that at least one of the 38 executives earned a Ph.D. in three years. It would be of interest to know how many reported this (and other) achievements.

A review of the items in the index indicates a number of problems, including ambiguities which should not be left to the discretion of the individual or the examiner. One of these arises in connection with those items to which multiple responses are permissible and the score consists of the number of response categories checked. Not all such items make it clear that multiple responses are permissible. Some items call for comparisons with brothers or sisters. The individual having no siblings is presumably not to respond to such items, but the inclusion of items which are obviously not applicable to certain individuals raises obvious questions about the meaning of the scores.

The use of multiple response items also creates other problems. In one scale having a mean of approximately 11, 9 points can be obtained from a single item by checking every response category.

The naming of the scales was apparently done by inspection of the item content. This procedure is not without its defense, but when it leads to a 16-item scale measuring Personal Adjustment, the procedure must be questioned.

In summary, there is good reason to believe that an objective quantification of background data can be useful in the selection of certain classes of employees, but the suggestion on page 1 of the *Biographical Index* manual that "individuals who score high" on this instrument "tend to be good job risks with superior probability of winning unusual merit increases and accumulating steady years of faithful service" is not substantiated by the data reported on the following pages. The reliability data reported are such as to raise a serious question about the use of the instrument with individuals, the validation evidence is extremely meager, the norms are inadequate, and the nature of some of the items and of the scoring weights is such as to lead to some uncertainty about the meaning of the scores obtained. The index should be considered as a research instrument only, and this should be clearly designated in the manual and in any auxiliary publications.

[1100]

★**Breadth of Information.** Business and industry; 1957–63; "practical intelligence and attention to the ordinary happenings of the world"; 1 form ('57, 5 pages); manual ['63, 12 unnumbered pages]; $3.50 per 25 tests; 10¢ per key; $1 per manual; postage extra; $1 per specimen set, postpaid; (20–25) minutes; Richardson, Bellows, Henry & Co., Inc. *

[1101]

*Business Judgment Test. Adults; 1953–65; 1 form ('53, 4 pages); revised manual ('65, 12 pages); $5 per 25 tests; 25¢ per revised scoring key ['56]; $1.75 per manual; $2.50 per specimen set; cash orders postpaid; Portuguese edition available; (10–20) minutes; Martin M. Bruce; the Author. *

REFERENCES

1. BRUCE, MARTIN M. "Normative Data Information Exchange, No. 25." *Personnel Psychol* 9:404–5 au '56. *
2. BRUCE, MARTIN M., AND FRIESEN, EDWARD P. "Validity Information Exchange, No. 9-35: D.O.T. Code 1-55.10, Salesman, House-to-House." *Personnel Psychol* 9:380 au '56. *
3. WATLEY, DONIVAN JASON. *Prediction of Academic Success in a College of Business Administration.* Doctor's thesis, University of Denver (Denver, Colo.), 1961. *(DA* 22:3527)
4. WATLEY, DONIVAN J., AND MARTIN, H. T. "Prediction of Academic Success in a College of Business Administration." *Personnel & Guid J* 41:147–54 O '62. * *(PA* 37:5656)

For a review by Edward B. Greene, see 5: 893.

[1102]

*Cardall Test of Practical Judgment. Adults in business and industry; 1942–62; 3 scores: factual, empathic, total; Form 62 ('62, 4 pages); manual ('61, 4 pages); $12 per 100 tests; $1.50 per specimen set; postage extra; (30–40) minutes; Alfred J. Cardall; Cardall Associates. *

REFERENCES

1–6. See 4:784.
7. GLADSTONE, ROY. "A Note on Certain Test Score Relationships and Their Implications for Research in Teacher Selection." *J Ed Psychol* 43:116–8 F '52. * *(PA* 26:7242)
8. RUSMORE, JAY T. "Validity Information Exchange, No. 8-04: D.O.T. Code 1-18.68, Service-Order Dispatcher." *Personnel Psychol* 8:112 sp '55. *
9. TOPETZES, NICK JOHN. "A Program for the Selection of Trainees in Physical Medicine." *J Exp Ed* 25:263–311 Je '57. * *(PA* 33:7024)
10. RUSMORE, JAY T. "A Note on the 'Test of Practical Judgment.'" *Personnel Psychol* 11:37 sp '58. * *(PA* 33:9101)

For reviews by Glen U. Cleeton and Howard R. Taylor of an earlier edition, see 3:694.

[1103]

★**Conference Meeting Rating Scale.** Conference leaders and participants; 1959; 1 form (2 pages); manual (2 pages); no data on reliability; $3 per 50 scales; $1 per specimen set of 10 scales and manual; cash orders postpaid; (10) minutes; B. J. Speroff; Psychometric Affiliates. *

[1104]

★**Dartnell Self-Administered Employee Opinion Unit.** Industry; 1955–58; attitudes toward job; 2 edi-

tions; administration manual ('58, 8 pages); handbook, *Planning and Conducting Employee Opinion Surveys* ('57, 218 pages); no data on reliability; 50¢ per set of scoring stencils; 50¢ per administration manual; $24 per handbook; postage extra; (35–60) minutes; Central Surveys, Inc. (questionnaire) and Charles Parker and staff (handbook); Dartnell Corporation. *

a) EMPLOYEE QUESTIONNAIRE. 1 form ('55, 4 pages); 1–99 copies, 15¢ each.

b) SUPERVISOR'S QUESTIONNAIRE. 1 form ('55, 5 pages, same as *a* above except for 11 additional items); 1–99 copies, 30¢ each.

RAYMOND A. KATZELL, *Professor of Psychology and Head of the Department, New York University, New York, New York.*

There are two separable features in this kit: a "do-it-yourself" handbook on the conduct of questionnaire surveys of employee attitudes, and a specific set of questionnaires for such purposes. The handbook or manual is devoted to the subjects of survey goals, planning, questionaires, procedures, tabulating and reporting, and follow-up implementation. It is the most detailed procedural guide on this subject that the reviewer has encountered, and should serve as a useful *vade mecum* even to the experienced professional. Its emphasis on the hows of its subject rather than the whys makes it essentially a cookbook, to be used only with great caution by the amateur unless bolstered with expert advice. As with all cookbooks, the greatest weakness lies in the domain of inference and interpretation.

The handbook contains specimens of the two Dartnell attitude questionnaires, one for supervisory and the other for nonsupervisory employees. The latter comprises 36 questions, most of which are multiple choice and several of which elicit opinions on more than one issue. The former has the same questions, plus 11 more which deal specifically with concerns of supervisors, particularly low level ones. Items may be scored by a key which allots points to each alternative on a scale of favorability from 0 to 4. By summing the results of a scant two to five items, a score may be obtained for each of 16 areas or categories of attitude; these categories are grouped under three main rubrics, Supervision, Company Policies and Practices, and Job Attitude (e.g., advancement, security, teamwork, etc.).

The handbook, so complete on survey procedures, is unfortunately quite devoid of psychometric data on the questionnaires. Among the missing are facts about the method of item construction and selection, the basis of the weights used for scoring each response as to favorability, the method of arriving at the 16 attitude categories and the allocation of items to them, reliability, and correlations with other variables. About the only data which the technically oriented reader can find in the manual are "national averages" of questionnaire responses, but even for these there are no indices of variability or information about the size and composition of the normative sample.

In the absence of technical data to the contrary, the questionnaires give the appearance of being rather superficial and amateurish instruments for assessing job attitudes. The procedures manual, on the other hand, is a useful distillation of practical experience in the conduct of employee attitude surveys. Fortunately, the latter can be purchased and used without the former, although its price may repel many individuals.

[1105]

★**Employee Opinion Survey.** Business and industry; 1956; opinions in 5 areas: management and the company, supervision, work conditions, pay and benefits, general; 1 form ['56, 6 pages]; no manual or other accessories; no data on reliability and validity; distribution restricted to clients; $7 per 25 surveys, postpaid; analysis and reporting fees vary and are additional; [20] minutes; R. W. Henderson; William, Lynde & Williams. *

[1106]

★**The Jenkins Job Attitudes Survey.** Industrial employees; 1959; derived from an unpublished form of *How Well Do You Know Yourself?*; identification of accident-prone individuals; Form AR-11 (6 pages); manual (6 pages); no data on reliability; $1 per test, postage extra; price includes scoring service; (25–40) minutes; Thomas N. Jenkins, Harold T. Fagin (manual), and John H. Coleman (manual); Executive Analysis Corporation. *

REFERENCES
1. JENKINS, THOMAS N. "The Accident-Prone Personality: A Preliminary Study." *Personnel* 33:29–32 Jl '56. * (PA 31: 6752)

[1107]

★**The Organization Survey.** Employees in industry; 1958–61; formerly called *Organization Attitude Survey;* administered by the publisher's representatives; 11 scores: work organization, work efficiency, administrative effectiveness, leadership practices, communication effectiveness, personnel development, pay and benefits, immediate supervision, work associates, job satisfaction, organization identification, reactions to the survey; 1 form ('61, 4 pages, identical with form copyrighted in 1958 except for format); program description manual ('61, 25 pages); planning manual ('61, 37 pages); sample survey report ('61, 31 pages); survey analyzer ('61, 60 pages); manager's guide ('61, 23 pages); no data on reliability; distribution restricted to companies using the publisher's survey services; price information available from the publisher; specimen set not available; [30–40] minutes; [Richard Renck, Robert K. Burns, Melany E.

Baehr, and Robert H. Waechter]; Industrial Relations Center. *

[1108]

*The Tear Ballot for Industry.** Employees in industry; 1944–62; job satisfaction questionnaire; 1 form ('44, 2 pages); revised manual ('62, 21 pages, hectographed); profile ('56, 1 page); $4 per 50 tests; $3 per 50 profiles; $5 per examiner's kit of 50 tests, profile, and manual; specimen set not available; cash orders postpaid; (3–5) minutes; Willard A. Kerr; Psychometric Affiliates. *

REFERENCES
1–4. See 4:783.
5. KERR, WILLARD A. "On the Validity and Reliability of the Job Satisfaction Tear Ballot." *J Appl Psychol* 32:275–81 Je '48. * (PA 23:1499)
6. TOPAL, J. R. *The Factorial Analysis of Job Satisfaction.* Master's thesis, Illinois Institute of Technology (Chicago, Ill.), 1950.
7. PRESSEL, G. L. *Pattern Analysis of Job Satisfaction Attitudes of Hospital Nurses.* Master's thesis, Illinois Institute of Technology (Chicago, Ill.), 1951.
8. KERR, WILLARD A. "Summary of Validity Studies of the Tear Ballot." *Personnel Psychol* 5:105–13 su '52. * (PA 27:4630)
9. SPEROFF, B. J. "Job Satisfaction Study of Two Small Unorganized Plants." *J Appl Psychol* 43:315 O '59. * (PA 34:6628)

RAYMOND A. KATZELL, *Professor of Psychology and Head of the Department, New York University, New York, New York.*

The core of this questionnaire consists of 10 five-alternative multiple choice items intended to elicit expressions of attitude toward major features of one's job, such as security, ability of supervisors, working conditions, and income. The item alternatives are arbitrarily scaled from 1 (least satisfied) to 5 (most satisfied). A total score may be obtained by adding the scores of the 10 items.

Split-half reliability coefficients have been calculated for the total score in a dozen small samples. The obtained coefficients range from .65 to .88, and average about .83. This is quite satisfactory for the determination of job satisfaction of groups, the use for which the questionnaire is intended.

The manual cites 10 sets of studies in support of the instrument's validity. These studies typically involved correlating the total score with some other variable. Without being labeled as such, the spirit in which these results are offered is in the nature of establishing the construct validity of the questionnaire. Some of these other variables (e.g., turnover or absenteeism) appear to be closer to the construct, "job satisfaction," than do others (e.g., empathic ability or hearing loss). Nevertheless, the general picture does suggest that the questionnaire reflects the construct of job satisfaction in most of the samples studied. This is hardly surprising since the questionnaire is essentially asking people 10 times how well they like their jobs. One important limitation should be noted: the samples all consisted of non-managerial, nonprofessional workers. It may be doubted that a questionnaire covering these particular topics would correlate as well with other indications of job satisfaction in a sample, say, of executives or of chemists.

In addition to summarizing the development of the instrument and available validity and reliability data, the manual furnishes several sets of percentile norms. The individual samples are too small and specialized to be of much use. However, the consolidated results, organized by sex and geographical region, may provide a helpful frame of reference. A table of item results is also provided, together with normative charts for profiling them; however, interpretation of the results of single items might be hazardous because of low reliability.

The author and publisher are to be commended for setting modest prices for the materials. However, the reviewer's copy of the hectographed manual was indistinct in places, and its stapled binding came apart promptly. It seems likely that most users of the manual would prefer to pay an extra 25 or 50 cents for higher quality production.

In summary, *The Tear Ballot for Industry* provides a quick and inexpensive way of obtaining a gross indication of general job satisfaction of workers in lower level occupations. The evidence is that the instrument possesses degrees of reliability and construct validity which are reasonably adequate for this purpose. Anyone interested in such an instrument may wish to compare this one with the Brayfield-Rothe Index of Job Satisfaction.[1]

For a review by Brent Baxter, see 4:783.

[1109]

★[Tests A/9 and A/10.] Applicants for technical and apprentice jobs; 1955–57; interest in scientific fields; 2 parts (English and Afrikaans editions in the same booklet); no manual; mimeographed norms ['57, 1 page]; separate answer sheets must be used; R40 per 100 sets of both parts; R5 per 100 answer sheets; 60c per specimen set; postpaid; National Institute for Personnel Research. *
a) TEST A/9: [TECHNICAL AND SCIENTIFIC KNOWLEDGE]. 1 form ['55, 7 pages]; 15(20) minutes.
b) TEST A/10: [TECHNICAL READING COMPREHENSION]. 1 form ['55, 7 pages]; 10(15) minutes.

1 BRAYFIELD, ARTHUR H., AND ROTHE, HAROLD F. "An Index of Job Satisfaction." *J Appl Psychol* 35:307–11 O '51. *

[1110]

★Whisler Strategy Test. Business and industry; 1959–61, c1955–61; "intelligent action"; 6 scores: 4 direct scores (number circled-boldness, number attempted-speed, number right-accuracy, net strategy) and 2 derived scores (caution, hypercaution); 1 form ('59, 8 pages); manual ('59, 4 pages); profile-supplementary norms ('61, 1 page); reliability data for net strategy score only; separate answer sheets must be used; $3 per 20 tests; $1 per 20 answer sheets; $1 per specimen set (must be purchased to obtain manual); cash orders postpaid; 25(30) minutes; Laurence D. Whisler; Psychometric Affiliates. *

REFERENCES
1. KERR, WILLARD A., AND ABRAMS, PETER. "Halstead Brain Impairment, Boldness, Creativity and Group Intelligence Measures." *J Clin Psychol* 18:115–8 Ap '62. * (PA 38:8458)

JEAN MAIER PALORMO, *Head, Industrial Test Research, Science Research Associates, Inc., Chicago, Illinois.*

To quote the test manual: "There is within the business community an explicit philosophy of intelligent action. There has been, however, no measurement technique directed to the measurement of intelligent action as so defined. The Strategy Test is presented as a venture in such measurement." The author distinguishes between the meaning of the term "intelligence" as used in the practical business setting, for example, and the meaning of the term when used by psychologists to describe mental capacity. The business man is judged as "intelligent" by his superiors and peers when "he makes wise use of the resources available to him at the moment."

This test contains 126 items of various types —vocabulary, general information, specific subject information, reasoning, checking, space, etc. Approximately 70 items are typical of those commonly found in traditional intelligence tests. The examinee's task is clearly stated in the instructions: he is to try for the highest possible score in the 25 minutes allotted by skipping about and answering the easiest blocks of questions first. If he is very certain of an answer, he should circle it; if it is right he receives a bonus point to reward him for his conviction, but if it is wrong he is heavily penalized.

The author reports a split-half reliability on college students and graduates of .56, which appears to be uncorrected. Two validity studies are cited. The first yielded a coefficient of .60 for 43 high school seniors, but the nature of the dependent variable is not given in the manual. The second study involved 63 university students who made self-ratings of their past success in 10 different decision or behavior areas. The summation of these ratings gave a "past strategy score," which when correlated with the Whisler test scores resulted in a Pearsonian coefficient of .29.

The norms published in the manual are based on 204 college students and graduates, most of whom "were in their twenties." This table presents percentile equivalents for four direct scores. A later supplement provides norms on 273 additional cases, described by the author as "key management and sales personnel." In addition to the four direct scores, percentile equivalents are given for the two derived scores, Caution and Hypercaution.

The information about the test presented in the manual is minimal at best, and the statistics that are given raise grave questions as to the adequacy of this "test" as a measurement device.

The reported reliability for *one score* only does not meet the accepted standard for an instrument to be used in individual classification. The method used in dividing the test is not given, but if alternate items were used to obtain the part scores, the coefficient is probably an overestimate because of the block arrangement of item types. The examinee does not have time (and perhaps knowledge) to answer all the items; his instructions are to *choose* those blocks of items which he thinks he can do best; and the items included represent only a small sampling of the universe of intelligent actions and knowledges. If an instrument is to yield a measure of an individual's strategy in utilizing his resources, the reliability of that measure should be based upon alternate test forms, each containing different samples of items from the universe. Such reliability studies should be extended to include *all* scores presented to the user in the norms tables.

The norms are not extensive, but manuals for new instruments frequently provide only minimum norms tables. The normative samples are not described as adequately as is desirable. A more serious problem, however, is the failure of the author to describe the rationale and the experimental operations which led to the presentation of a six-score profile. Without these, the user is at a loss to evaluate the scoring system or interpret test results.

Nor does the user receive help in his understanding of the test from the validity section of the manual. Again, few test manuals provide sufficient predictive validity information to meet the needs of all users. In the case of the Whisler test, the need for predictive validity data is perhaps secondary to the need for evidence of construct validity. The name of the test and the opening paragraphs of the manual in which the author describes "intelligent action" in the business situation are very appealing to the unsophisticated test user. Since every personnel man would welcome a measure of "practical judgment," it is imperative that the author who implies this measurement from his set of items provide evidence to substantiate his inferences.

Finally, it is necessary to question the appropriateness of the collection of items. About 40 per cent of the items are in the multiple choice format, calling for specific bits of information, and can be answered very quickly by the person who knows these facts. The remaining items, requiring reasoning and problem solving abilities, are much more time consuming. Thus, the examinee who happens to possess factual knowledge in the limited fields of specialization represented by items in the test has a tremendous advantage over the examinee whose factual knowledges are in other fields. The manual does not describe the research and results that led to the collection of this set of items to measure "strategy." The final paragraph of the manual recognizes that problems exist: "There are 'item-difficulty' problems. There are 'equivalent forms' problems. There are problems of factor analysis of kinds of items attempted. And there are problems of optimum composition."

It would seem to this reviewer that these are problems to be solved *prior* to the publication of a "test," and until they are solved no reliable and valid measurement of "intelligent action" can be achieved.

In summary, the *Whisler Strategy Test* cannot be recommended for operational use. It presents an interesting and unique measurement hypothesis which should be of interest to research people. However, the first research efforts might better be aimed at the investigation of test composition, rather than toward establishing validity of the collection of items presented in the current edition of the test.

PAUL F. ROSS, *Industrial Psychologist, Imperial Oil Limited, Toronto, Ontario, Canada.*

The *Whisler Strategy Test* is a 126-item, 25-

minute time limit test. Each item has two answers from which the respondent chooses the right one. The manual states that "three groups of vocabulary items and twenty-six other types of items are used in the Strategy Test." The reviewer finds vocabulary items, including a few in Spanish, French, and German; spatial relations items of puzzle parts, line length, map reading, and maze tracing types; general information items testing knowledge that does not go out of date; clerical skills items which seem related to checking and coding; and a few items which could be called number series and word series. There is little arithmetic and numerical content in the test. The respondent is instructed to "Try for the highest possible score; when you start the test, look it over. * See what kinds of questions seem easiest. * Start any place you wish, and skip around as much as you want to. Remember the time is only 25 minutes." The respondent marks his answers on an answer sheet, indicating his confidence in the correctness of his answer by circling the answers he is very sure are correct. Scores consist of (a) the number of items attempted, (b) the number of right answers, (c) the number of circled answers, and (d) a "net strategy" score which adds points for confidence in the correctness of right answers and subtracts points when the respondent is very sure a wrong answer is right. Two discrepancy scores—(e) items attempted minus circled answers, and (f) right answers minus circled answers—are computed and recorded on the answer sheet.

The manual does not say in a short, quotable statement what it is that the scores measure. The reader of one part of the manual understands that the test measures some aspect of intelligence. In another part, the discrepancy scores are referred to as a "plunger index," although "Experience will be needed to discover which discrepancy [score] will best serve as an index of style of performance." The manual reports reliability, validity, mean, and standard deviation *for only one of the six scores*. No information, other than norm tables, is reported for the other five scores. The net strategy score is reported to have a "split half reliability" of .56 when estimated from a sample of 204 college students. One of the two validity coefficients for the net strategy score is reported without any description whatsoever of the criterion. The other validity co-efficient, based upon self-ratings of past success in a variety of activities, is reported as .29 when estimated from a sample of 63 university students. No intercorrelations of the six scores are reported. No mention of the use of item analysis techniques is made. No correlations of the scores from the test with scores from intelligence tests or personality tests are reported. In the reviewer's opinion, the net strategy score has a reliability adequate for only the crudest of test uses, and the evidence given as validity data amounts to *no* evidence for the valid use of this test for any purpose.

The manual is poorly organized and discouragingly incomplete. Instructions for administering the test are not adequate for accurate timing of the respondent's performance. The instructions are broken into two widely separated locations in the manual. No description is given of the qualifications of the test administrator or of the test interpreter. The manual cites no references to published research using the *Whisler Strategy Test*. Normative data for 204 people, "162 men and 42 women," are presented. By making an inference, the user of the manual can guess that these people were "college students or college graduates," but the guess may be wrong. Additional normative data published in 1961 are based on 273 "key management and sales personnel." The user does not know the ages, the educational level, or the occupation of the people in the norms groups. Test performance by men and by women is combined into one norm, in spite of the fact that the general information items in the test ask questions about metal working, plumbing, carpentry, mining, chemistry, and physics!

The reviewer wonders whether the publishers had an editorial review of this material before they undertook its publication. This test is an arresting example of poor practice in test design, test construction, and manual writing. Publication probably is not justified. The test should not be used, even for experimental purposes, until the instructions for administering it and perhaps the printed presentation of items and materials related to items are improved. The test is not ready for any practical use.

[1111]
★**Work Information Inventory.** Employee groups in industry; 1958; morale; 1 form (4 pages); manual (4 pages); mean score norms only; $3 per 50 tests; $1 per specimen set (must be purchased to obtain

manual); cash orders postpaid; (15) minutes; Raymond E. Bernberg; Psychometric Affiliates. *

[Other Tests]

For tests not listed above, see the following entries in *Tests in Print:* 1952, 1960–1, 1963–4, 1966, and 1971; out of print: 1954, 1957, 1959, 1962, 1967–8; status unknown: 1969.

SELECTION & RATING FORMS

[1112]

★**APT Controlled Interview.** Applicants for employment; 1945–56; revision of *APT Quick-Screening Interview;* 19 ratings: job experience (2 ratings), work history, financial status (2 ratings), marital status, voice (3 ratings), appearance (4 ratings), health (2 ratings), family background, relations with the law, social history, total; 1 form ['56, 1 interview-rating card]; manual ['56, 24 pages]; no data on reliability; distribution restricted to clients; $2.50 per 50 interview-rating cards; $3 per manual; postage extra; [12–30] minutes; Associated Personnel Technicians, Inc. *

[1113]

★**Career Counseling Personal Data Form.** Vocational counselees; 1962; 1 form (11 pages); no manual or other accessories; no data on reliability and validity; $10 per 25 forms; $5.50 per specimen set of 10 forms; cash orders postpaid; [45–60] minutes; John B. Ahrens; Martin M. Bruce. *

[1114]

★**[Cardall Interviewing Aids.]** Adults; 1958–61; 3 record forms; no manual; no data on reliability and validity; specimen set free; postage extra; administration time not reported; Alfred J. Cardall; Cardall Associates. *
a) APPLICATION BLANK. 1958; 1 form (2 pages); $2.50 per 100 forms.
b) INTERVIEWING GUIDE. 1958; 1 form (2 pages); $2.50 per 100 forms.
c) CURRENT ACTIVITIES AND BACKGROUND INVENTORY. 1961; 1 form (2 pages); $3.50 per 100 forms.

[1115]

*Diagnostic Interviewer's Guide.** Applicants for employment; 1935–42; 1 form ('42, 4 pages, identical with form copyrighted in 1937); manual ('42, 4 pages); no data on reliability and validity; $8 per 100 forms; $1 per specimen set of 10 forms and manual; postage extra; E. F. Wonderlic; E. F. Wonderlic & Associates. *

REFERENCES

1. LAIRD, DONALD A. *The Psychology of Selecting Employees, Third Edition,* pp. 114–9. New York: McGraw-Hill Book Co., Inc., 1937. Pp. xiii, 316. * (*PA* 11:4726)
2. HOVLAND, CARL IVER, AND WONDERLIC, E. F. "Prediction of Industrial Success From a Standardized Interview." *J Appl Psychol* 23:537–46 O '39. * (*PA* 14:1039)

ALBERT K. KURTZ, *Fulbright Lecturer, Ein Shams University, Cairo, United Arab Republic.*

It is difficult to evaluate this interviewing guide in an objective manner. It shouldn't be. It came out in a revised edition in 1937 which

was apparently copyrighted both in 1937 and in 1942. It provides for an objective score ranging between possible extremes of −34 and +34. A naïve reviewer might think that by now there would be many studies telling how well these scores correlate with some subsequently determined criterion of success. There is only one, published in 1939, which is somewhat out of date 25 years later. That report (*2*) gave reliability coefficients and validity information, but not a validity coefficient.

This lack of evidence does not mean that we should wait longer for it to appear. When 25 years have passed without any further data being made available, it is high time that potential users tried a competing device for which reliability and validity figures are available. Regrettably, this is sometimes easier said than done, but in the present case there are satisfactory alternatives. Perhaps the first choice, because validity figures are known and fairly high, is the set of patterned interview forms by Robert N. McMurry & Co. (see 1119).

Although validity is the most important single characteristic of a measuring device, let us consider some other aspects of this interviewer's guide, assuming that we may still wish to use it rather than its competitors.

This blank has four pages, each containing 6 to 14 questions for the interviewer to ask the job applicant about his work history, family history, social history, and personal history. At the bottom of each page, there are 5 to 12 yes-no questions (a total of 34) for the interviewer to answer about the applicant. These give the score.

Most of the questions seem relevant and well worded, although research on claims of various pseudo-sciences would not provide much justification for retaining the anachronistic "Can this applicant look you in the eye?"

The 4-page manual clarifies the use of the interviewer's guide and also gives a number of pertinent suggestions regarding the conduct of the interview, including references to some good, but now somewhat out-of-date, books and articles on the subject.

In conclusion, this is a form that was reasonably well constructed and well explained. It once had what was then a satisfactory reliability coefficient and a positive validity of unknown size in one company. If the author or anyone else had compiled more recent data on its validity, the form might have proved valid, thus justifying its continued use. Since this has not been done, but has been done for at least one competing device, there seems to be no reason for recommending the use of this somewhat aging form of unknown value.

For reviews by Clyde H. Coombs and Douglas H. Fryer, see 3:685.

[1116]

★**Employee Performance Appraisal.** Business and industry; 1962; 7 merit ratings by supervisors: quantity of work, quality of work, job knowledge, initiative, inter-personal relationships, dependability, potential; 1 form (4 pages); no manual or other accessories; no data on reliability and validity; $5 per 25 forms; $2.75 per specimen set of 10 forms; cash orders postpaid; [10–20] minutes; Martin M. Bruce; the Author. *

Jean Maier Palormo, *Head, Industrial Test Research, Science Research Associates, Inc., Chicago, Illinois.*

This form is presented as an aid to " 'force' the evaluator into being more critical, more analytical, more objective, and more of a thinker." While these are worthy aims, there is no evidence to show that the *Employee Performance Appraisal* achieves them. In view of the claims made by the author, one would expect that he would provide the user with at least a brief manual reporting intra- and inter-rater reliabilities and some evidence on scale intercorrelations. However, such is not the case.

Ratings are made on seven "factors" which have resulted from a "systematic outline of factors important in practically all jobs." What is meant by "systematic outline" is not known. These factors would certainly place high in a survey of popular use, for they are essentially those that have been used on hundreds of company-developed rating forms over the past 20 years. Some of these factors, or traits, have been shown to be highly susceptible to the constant errors of ratings. For example, Symonds demonstrated that the "halo effect" is most prevalent in rating traits of character and factors involving reactions with other people. Four of the seven factors on the form can be so classified.

The author has taken some steps to minimize rating errors. He has combined the numerical and graphic scales; the line is extended to include seven cue positions; most of the range is given to degrees of favorable report, which tends to counteract the leniency error. However, most investigators agree that the cues along the trait continuums contribute most to the control of rating errors, and the author appears to have neglected these in his developmental research.

The development of adequate rating forms involves a considerable amount of experimental work in the selection and placement of cues. There should be no doubt among raters as to the rank position of a cue among other cues. On the *Employee Performance Appraisal,* this reviewer finds many of these more confusing than helpful. For example, consider three adjacent cues on the factor "Quantity of Work":

Turns out a little more than most people in similar jobs.
Can be counted on to turn out more than most people. Does not need much supervision.
A superior employee. *Almost always can be counted on to do more than a full share.*

The italicized statements (italics the reviewer's) bear directly on the question of quantity. The other phrases in the second and third statements are not necessarily relevant, and certainly not unique, to the factor of "quantity," thus encouraging the rater to introduce errors of rating. If the rater ignores these phrases and considers only the statements relevant to the factor of quantity, he may be even more confused. There seems to be little difference between the first and second statements except in the words "more" and "little more"; both statements imply that this performance occurs 100 per cent of the time. Now, in the third statement the employee does "more," as he does in the first and second statements, but "almost always" instead of 100 per cent of the time. Yet, on the form these statements cover a numerical range of 19 through 35, with *the third statement being the highest!*

Similar confusions, at least for this reviewer, occur somewhere among the cues listed for every factor on the form. This leads one to wonder, particularly since no manual describing the form's development is available, about the method by which the scale positions for the cues were established.

In addition to careful experimental work in scale development, investigators have found the training of raters to be a very important factor in reducing errors of rating. The author of this form attempts to cover this in 10 points under "Directions." If, indeed, the raters follow the rules given in these brief statements, the author's claims for the form might be somewhat justified. However, it is doubtful whether a short direction telling the rater to "be fair, honest, impartial, and objective" will make him so.

The above paragraphs discuss technical inadequacies of the form. Perhaps the most important criticism, however, is the implication that the form can be used successfully for all employees in all jobs. In recent years many competent personnel research workers have reported studies pointing to the specificity of criterion factors. It is disturbing that this relatively new form, published in 1962, ignores so much of the research that has been done on performance evaluation and criterion development.

[1117]
*[Employee Rating and Development Forms.] Executive, industrial, office, and sales personnel; 1950–59; manual for *b* only; no data on reliability and validity in manual; postage extra; [5–30] minutes; Robert N. McMurry; Dartnell Corporation. *
a) [PATTERNED MERIT REVIEW FORMS.] 1950–59.
  1) *Patterned Merit Review—Executive.* 1955–59; Form No. MR-407 ('59, 4 pages, identical with form copyrighted in 1955); 1–99 copies, 15¢ each.
  2) *Patterned Merit Review Form—Plant and Office.* 1950–59; Form No. MR-405 ('59, 4 pages, identical with form copyrighted in 1950); 1–99 copies, 15¢ each.
  3) *Patterned Merit Review—Sales.* 1955–59; Form No. MR-406R ('59, 2 pages, identical with form copyrighted in 1955); 1–99 copies, 10¢ each.
  4) *Patterned Merit Review—Technical, Office, Special Skills.* 1956–57; Form No. MR-408 ('57, 2 pages, identical with form copyrighted in 1956); 1–99 copies, 10¢ each.
  5) *Statement of Supervisory Expectancies.* 1958; Form No. ER-602 (2 pages); 1–99 copies, 10¢ each.
b) PATTERNED EXIT INTERVIEW. 1953–59; Form No. EX-501 ('59, 2 pages, identical with form copyrighted in 1953); manual ('53, 12 pages); 1–99 copies, 10¢ each; $2 per manual.
c) PERSONAL HISTORY REVIEW FORM. 1957; 1 form ['57, 4 pages]; 1–99 copies, 10¢ each.

RICHARD S. BARRETT, *Associate Professor of Management Engineering and Psychology, New York University, New York, New York.*

Since the forms and manuals discussed in this review represent about one fifth of the forms and manuals which are listed in the current catalogue of the Dartnell Corporation as having been prepared by Robert N. McMurry, they may be considered as a sample of his "Patterned" approach to personnel selection, appraisal, rating, and development.

Most of the forms are attractively printed in two colors. Black is used for the questions which are to be answered by an interviewer, a job incumbent, or an applicant. Colored ink is used to ask questions or to give instructions to the person who is interpreting the information to help him to get the most out of the material collected by the forms.

The Merit Review Forms, designed for use in the evaluation of employees on different types of positions, differ considerably from each other to reflect specific job duties and performance standards. They range in size from a single sheet used in sales and some office positions to a 4-page form for reviewing executive performance. The *Patterned Merit Review Form—Plant and Office* states, "A special manual on the 'Patterned Merit Review Plan' has been prepared"; yet the current (1961) order form lists no such manual, nor are manuals for the other Merit Review Forms listed.

In this reviewer's eyes, the questions on the most extensive form, *Patterned Merit Review —Executive,* start out in a sensible fashion but deteriorate toward the end of the form. In the beginning, the questions ask about functions of the executive's position, basic responsibilities, authority, and so forth. Specific questions are asked about his education, training, and experience, his demonstrated ability in such activities as analyzing work loads and market costs, holding meetings, speaking in public, and his attitudes toward the company and its supervisory and management policies. Then the questions become less specific, asking about leadership qualities, such as the ability to make decisions or to empathize. The last section asks questions which only the most sophisticated psychologist could be expected to answer adequately, and even he would be hard pressed to show how the answers would be related to a person's job performance. The rater is asked, for instance, to report on insecurity, defensiveness, impulsiveness, pleasure-mindedness, and other personality traits of dubious significance.

The *Patterned Exit Interview* is a single sheet which provides for identifying information, and for notes of an interview with the employee who is leaving, and of a related interview with his supervisor. A 16-page manual describes the benefits of the exit interview and provides suggestions for conducting the interview. There is illustrative material on how to chart an analysis of reasons for termination, but there is no explanation of how this material is prepared. There are no data from research studies which would support the claims in the manual that the use of the *Patterned Exit Interview* will help to salvage good employees, improve vertical communication, provide for catharsis on the part of the employee or his supervisor, or provide a continuing audit of personnel policies and practices.

The *Personal History Review Form* is a 4-page sheet which, in addition to identifying information, provides space for a report on the employee's performance with the company by which he is currently employed; previous employment, including part-time and school jobs; education; home and finances; domestic and social status; and health. There is no manual for the *Personal History Review Form* and no indication on the form itself of how the information is to be used. The reviewer assumes that the data are to be collected and up-dated periodically to help in planning each individual's career with the company. But just how the information is to be used is not clear.

These forms may provide a useful service to a personnel department by helping to record relevant information in a systematic way. Each follows a logical sequence, starting with adequate identifying information, followed with questions which the personnel specialist can ask directly or paraphrase. The additional questions and statements on interpretation give him some clues as to what can be gained from the answers to the questions and what areas should be probed if the original response is not completely informative. Some questions, as noted, require considerable psychological sophistication of the personnel specialist and may well provide information which is not relevant, even if it is correct.

An attempt to review forms which are designed to be placed in the hands of staff members in personnel departments or of supervisors who may not have any special personnel training highlights the inherent difficulty in evaluating personnel forms without knowing how they are used. These forms are well thought out and could provide a useful guide for systematic report by an astute observer. But, they could equally be used to report ill-considered prejudices of an inadequately trained observer who did not understand what he was looking for. Manuals are not available for several of the instruments being reviewed. Those which are available present instructions that could be useful if elaborated in an adequate training program but which may other-

wise be no more useful than a collection of homilies.

The value of the forms is inherently researchable but there is no report in the manuals that any research has been performed on any of the forms since 1947. The lack of evidence makes it unfortunate that one manual so forthrightly states "actually the Patterned Exit Interview is a multi-purpose tool; it can make significant contributions in all of the following areas." The areas listed are important; it remains to be seen whether the form makes significant contributions toward them.

For reviews by Harry W. Karn and Floyd L. Ruch of a (2 and 3), see 4:781.

[1118]

★[**Employee Rating Forms.**] Employees; 1946–63; supervisors' ratings in 3 areas; human factor, work history, developmental factor; 3 rating forms; no manual; no data on reliability and validity; $8.75 per 25 forms, postage extra; specimen set not available; administration time not reported; Personnel Institute, Inc. *

a) EMPLOYEE RATING REPORT. 1950–62; 1 form ('62, 4 pages, identical with form copyrighted in 1950 except for format).

b) MANAGER RATING REPORT. 1946–63; 1 form ('63, 4 pages, identical with form copyrighted in 1946 except for format).

c) SALESMAN RATING REPORT. 1947–63; 1 form ('63, 4 pages, identical with form copyrighted in 1947 except for format).

[1119]

*[**Executive, Industrial, and Sales Personnel Forms.**] Applicants for executive, office, industrial, or sales positions; 1949–62; most current forms are essentially the same as or identical with earlier forms; postage extra; Robert N. McMurry; Dartnell Corporation. *

a) [EXECUTIVE PERSONNEL FORMS.]

1) *Application for Executive Position.* 1949–59; Form No. EA-301 ('59, 4 pages); 1–99 copies, 10¢ each.

2) *Patterned Interview Form—Executive Position.* Applicants for management positions; 1949–62; Form No. EP-302 ('62, 6 pages); 1–99 copies, 30¢ each.

3) *Patterned Interview Form.* Applicants for positions of supervisor, foreman, engineer; 1955–59; Form No. EP-312 ('59, 4 pages); 1–99 copies, 15¢ each.

4) *Telephone Check on Executive Applicant.* 1950–59; Form No. ET-303 ('59, 1 page); 1–99 copies, 7¢ each.

5) *Selection and Evaluation Summary.* 1950–59; Form No. ES-404R ('59, 1 page, revision of form copyrighted 1955); 1–99 copies, 6¢ each.

6) *Position Analysis.* 1956–58; Form No. JA-601 ('58, 2 pages); 1–99 copies, 7¢ each.

7) *Physical Record.* 1958; Form No. PX-701 (4 pages); 1–99 copies, 15¢ each.

b) [INDUSTRIAL PERSONNEL FORMS.]

1) *Application for Position.* 1950–59; Form No. OA-201 ('59, 2 pages); 1–99 copies, 7¢ each.

2) *Application for Employment.* 1950–59; Form No. OC-200 ('59, 1 card); 1–99 copies, 6¢ each.
3) *Application for Office Position.* 1953–59; Form No. OA-205 ('59, 2 pages); 1–99 copies, 7¢ each.
4) *Patterned Interview (Short Form).* 1949–59; Form No. OP-202 ('59, 2 pages); 1–99 copies, 10¢ each.
5) *Patterned Interview Form.* Same as a(3) above.
6) *Telephone Check [With Previous Employers].* 1949–59; Form No. OT-203 ('59, 1 page); 1–99 copies, 6¢ each.
7) *Telephone Check With Schools.* 1949–57; Form No. OS-204 ('57, 1 page); 1–99 copies, 7¢ each.
8) *Selection and Evaluation Summary.* Same as a(5) above.
9) *Position Analysis.* Same as a(6) above.
10) *Physical Record.* Same as a(7) above.
c) [SALES PERSONNEL FORMS.]
1) *Application for Sales Position.* 1950–59; Form No. SA-101 ('59, 4 pages); 1–99 copies, 10¢ each.
2) *Patterned Interview Form—Sales Position.* 1950–58; Form No. SP-102 ('58, 4 pages); 1–99 copies, 15¢ each.
3) *Telephone Check on Sales Applicant.* 1949–59; Form No. ST-103 ('59, 1 page); 1–99 copies, 7¢ each.
4) *Sales Application Verification.* 1953–59; Form No. SV-104 ('59, 1 page); 1–99 copies, 6¢ each.
5) *Home Interview Report Form.* 1954–59; Form No. SH-114R ('59, 1 page); 1–99 copies, 7¢ each.
6) *Selection and Evaluation Summary.* Same as a(5) above.
7) *Sales Position Analysis.* 1962; 1 form (2 pages); 1–99 copies, 7¢ each.
8) *Physical Record.* Same as a(7) above.

REFERENCES

1. McMURRY, ROBERT N. *Tested Techniques of Personnel Selection.* Chicago, Ill.: Dartnell Corporation, 1961. Variously paged. *

JOHN P. FOLEY, JR., *President, J. P. Foley and Company, Inc., New York, New York.*

Prepared by the staff of the McMurry Company, the multilithed, looseleaf manual (*1*) covering this series of forms is divided into 12 sections, separated by appropriate index-tabbed dividers. Pages are numbered consecutively within each section. In addition to text material, the manual contains lists of tests, samples of charts, and other exhibits such as simple recruiting ads and diagrams of recommended space layouts for an efficient personnel department. The various selection forms—including position analysis, application, telephone and school check, physical record, patterned interview, as well as selection and evaluation summary forms—are classified into three types or groups for use with factory or office, sales, and executive personnel, respectively.

The purpose of the manual is to describe a comprehensive step-by-step selection program, to provide a practical reference source for personnel workers, and to furnish a text for the training of those engaged in the hiring process. Following a brief introduction highlighting the costly nature of selection errors, the manual presents a logical sequence of steps to be followed in the processing of job candidates. This sequence, as well as the essential content of the manual itself, can be best described by listing the consecutive sections: Why every business needs a planned selection program; Whom to hire, where to find them, how to screen them; What psychological tests contribute; Getting all the facts from and about the applicant; The patterned interview and how to use it; Interpreting the patterned interview; Motivation and emotional maturity in job placement; Matching the applicant and the job; Applying the step-by-step program to selecting plant and office employees; Applying the step-by-step program to selecting salesmen; Applying the step-by-step program to selecting executives and supervisors; and Using the step-by-step program effectively.

Three sections of the manual (9, 10, and 11) include a few briefly reported case histories of companies using the recommended program in the selection of different types of personnel. These are essentially *promotional testimonials,* however, and *cannot be accepted as validity data.* In fact, the reviewer finds in the manual no reported evidence of validity in the rigorous sense of the term.

Within the limitations necessarily imposed by a selection manual of this type, a number of *favorable features* deserve special notice. The need for extensive and effective recruiting is emphasized. Recognition is also given to the basic role of job specifications, the interviewer and others involved in the selection process being cautioned to think in terms of specific jobs and correlated requirements. Moreover, the tremendous diversity within the specifications for "selling" and other jobs bearing the same verbal tag is fully recognized.

Both the advantages and limitations of psychological tests are discussed. The reviewer was also impressed by the obvious, though all too frequently overlooked, distinction between the validities of personality tests applied in clinical or vocational counseling on the one hand, and personnel evaluation or selection situations on the other. Lip service is likewise given to the need for test validation.

In discussing the patterned interview, the authors commendably attempt to encourage the interviewer to dig beneath the surface facts, i.e., those reported by the applicant, in order to get at implications and other clues which are often the most significant findings of all. To this end, use is made of a "forcing technique" in which questions to be asked of the applicant are printed in black ink on the left hand side of the Interview Form, with space at the right of each question for the interviewer to record the applicant's answer—and with questions in red ink under each line which will force the interviewer to interpret (literally, to "question himself about") the applicant's answer. Use is also made of transparent overlays, each of which is geared to a key trait to which possible clues may be obtained from information supplied on different sections of the Interview Form. As indicated above, the purpose of such "forcing techniques" is commendable. And the techniques may—and undoubtedly do—work to a degree in some cases. But in the reviewer's opinion it is doubtful that such "canned procedures" represent the most effective approach to the depth interview.

Also commendable is the recognition of the fact that, irrespective of the accuracy and completeness of the applicant's rating on relevant job specifications, the final selection decision *cannot* be reached by summating or averaging the factor ratings. Thus, at the bottom of the Selection and Evaluation Summary the rater is cautioned: "Do not add or average these factors in making the over-all rating. Match the qualifications of the applicant against the requirements of the *particular position* for which he is being considered, and consider the importance of each mismatch." Although the manual omits much that could be said about compensating and other significant relationships within the makeup of an individual, there is at least some attempt to come to grips with the applicant's clinical makeup. The distinction between "can do" and "will do" factors represents an additional effort in the same desirable direction.

The techniques described in the manual are, of course, not limited to psychological tests. Rather, they encompass a variety of procedures to be followed in a comprehensive selection program. Most of these techniques have been utilized by companies for many years, although it is undoubtedly true that in many instances their application can be improved. It is precisely this role that the current selection manual is designed to serve. However, the pur-

ist might well question the use of the word "tested" in the manual's title.

One may also question the occasional loose or inconsistent use of terminology, as well as the confusion of degrees of abstraction. For example, the following are designated and discussed as "character traits": stability, industry, perseverance, ability to get along with others, loyalty, self-reliance, and leadership. With the possible exception of some aspects of "loyalty," one finds no reference to character as such. Rather, most of these traits fall within the motivational and personality spheres. Moreover, such a trait as "leadership" would seem to represent more of a composite trait than do others. One might likewise question why "manner" is listed under "can do" as opposed to "will do" factors. The reviewer would tend to feel that the latter distinction is essentially between "ability" and "motivational" considerations, in which case "manner" would fall within a very different category. Still another illustration of questionable terminology is found in the use of the term "empirical" in the following sentence: "Here the standards used are empirical —that is, by common sense analysis and judgment." As a matter of fact, psychologists use the term in exactly the opposite way, "empirical standards" being those established by experimentation rather than by a priori judgment and opinion.

"Diagnostic screening"—a technique employed in "go—no-go screening"—is described as being based upon careful scrutiny of the application form and any other written biographical material supplied by the candidate. With this in mind, it is difficult to see how "fine screens enable the rater to consider and weigh both favorable and unfavorable characteristics in the prospective employee." In the reviewer's opinion, such clinical-type judgments cannot—and should not—be made in the early screening stages of selection. Rather, they should be reserved for the final step of selection, viz., the intensive interview.

The "patterned interview" advocated by McMurry is little more than an orally administered questionnaire. True, certain "forcing techniques" are employed to encourage true evaluation, as noted above. However, the recommended technique is much too mechanical. Hence it loses many of the advantages of the true depth interview. Although one can certainly not criticize efforts to encourage the in-

Executive, Industrial, and Sales Personnel Forms

terviewer to penetrate beneath superficial information, one wonders if the procedures advocated provide the most effective answer to the problem. In the reviewer's opinion, the suggested technique is not sufficiently fluid or penetrating. Moreover, the impression is created that the "getting" and the "evaluating" of pertinent information are discrete temporal processes—an impression which is further accentuated by the use of the transparent overlays in interpreting information recorded in response to questions on the Interview Form.

When viewed overall, the selection program described in the present manual has much to commend it, providing the advocated procedures are utilized with both common sense and real skill. The manual fails to emphasize, however, that even careful study of such a printed program will not guarantee efficient selection. The real danger lies in blind application without understanding or skill. Certainly, no selection program will be any more effective than the way in which it is practiced.

For a review by Floyd L. Ruch, see 4:773.

[1120]

★Individual Background Survey. Business and industry; 1949–63; personal history and personality characteristics; 2 editions; no data on reliability; (25) minutes; Richardson, Bellows, Henry & Co., Inc. *
a) FORM S. 2 scores: part 1 (background), part 2 (self-description); 1 form ('49, 5 pages); manual ['63, 13 unnumbered pages]; $3.50 per 25 tests; 50¢ per key; $1 per manual; postage extra; $1 per specimen set, postpaid.
b) FORM T. 4 scoring scales: female clerical applicants and employees, male industrial applicants and employees, male clerical applicants and employees, male sales-supervisory-professional applicants and employees; 1 form ('52, 5 pages); manual ['63, 13 unnumbered pages]; $3.50 per 25 tests; 50¢ per set of keys; $1.25 per manual; postage extra; $1.50 per specimen set, postpaid.

[1121]

★Job Description Questionnaire. Employees; 1947–60; 1 form ('60, 8 pages, identical with form copyrighted in 1947 except for format); no manual; $8.75 per 25 forms, postage extra; specimen set not available; administration time not reported; Personnel Institute, Inc. *

[1122]

★The McQuaig Manpower Selection Series. Male applicants for office and sales positions; 1957; 4 parts in 2 booklets; no manual; 1–25 sets of a and b, 60¢ each; 1–25 copies of either a or b, 30¢ each; cash orders postpaid; Jack H. McQuaig; McQuaig Institute of Executive Training. *
a) [PARTS 1–3.] 1 form (6 pages).
   1) *Part 1, The McQuaig Telephone Reference Check List.* [5–10] minutes.

2) *Part 2, The McQuaig Screening Interview Guide.* [30] minutes.
3) *Part 3, Personal History and Experience Record.* [20] minutes.
b) PART 4, THE MCQUAIG OCCUPATIONAL TEST. 1 form (6 pages); no data on reliability and validity; 15(20) minutes.

[1123]

*Merit Rating Series. Industry; 1948–59; formerly called *Employee Evaluation Series;* 4–5 scores; 1 form (4 pages); 5 scales; manual ('53, 20 pages); mimeographed supplement ['59, 2 pages]; normal curve summary ('53, 4 pages); $5 per 20 forms; $5 per 20 normal curve summaries; postage extra; specimen set not available (forms and manual included in the complete set of the *Job-Tests Program*); (10–20) minutes; Joseph E. King; Industrial Psychology, Inc. *
a) PERFORMANCE: CLERICAL. 1956; 5 scores: quantity, accuracy, job knowledge, personal-work habits, overall; 1 form (some printings copyrighted in 1957).
b) PERFORMANCE: MECHANICAL. 1953–57; 5 scores: production, quality, job knowledge, personal-work habits, overall; 1 form ('57, identical with form copyrighted in 1953).
c) PERFORMANCE: SALES. 1953–57; 5 scores: volume, accuracy, job knowledge, personal-work habits, overall; 1 form ('57, identical with form copyrighted in 1953).
d) PERFORMANCE: TECHNICAL. 1953–57; 5 scores: same as for b; 1 form ('57, identical with form copyrighted in 1953).
e) PERFORMANCE: SUPERVISOR. 1953–57; 4 scores: department operation, employee relations, job knowledge, personal-work habits; 1 form ('57, identical with form copyrighted in 1953).

SEYMOUR LEVY, *Manager, Personnel Research and Manpower Development, The Pillsbury Company, Minneapolis, Minnesota.*

The *Merit Rating Series* is an elaborately designed and constructed set of instruments to measure job performance in five major job classifications. These measurement devices are part of an overall merit rating program that is described in a 20-page manual.

Materials fall into three categories: (*a*) a general description of a merit rating program as part of an overall personnel system, (*b*) the individual merit rating forms with scoring keys, and (*c*) a special form called the "Normal Curve Summary," to be used in providing some personnel controls on the evaluation process.

Rating forms have been developed for five major job families—clerical, mechanical, sales, technical, and supervisor. Each form is composed of 60 specific behavior statements to be answered either "yes" or "not true at present." The manual reports extensive data dealing with the item selection of each of these forms. For example, the frequency of endorsement of the item as listed for each of the five forms and phi coefficients are also presented for relating each item to the total score. The difficulty values have a mean of about .61 and the phi coefficients of .57. Items are given scoring weights based on the magnitude of the correlation with the total score. Each form consists of a number of specific statements that have been categorized into different performance areas. For example, the technical form includes items judged related to production, quality, job knowledge, personal work habits, and overall performance. Separate scores are provided for these subcategories.

Each merit rating scale contains three "bias" items that are comparable to the L scale items in the MMPI. In addition, there are several pairs of items of similar content with different phrasing designed to determine if the rater is consistent in his reporting on the subordinate. The bias items appear to be a very worthwhile contribution in the design of a measuring instrument. It is unfortunate that no specific data are reported relevant to their validity in screening out possible faking tendencies. Similarly, no data are reported with respect to the frequency of conflicting responses—the second control device.

There is considerable evidence with respect to the reliability of the different instruments and all the reliabilities appear to be quite satisfactory. Studies reporting satisfactory external validation are recorded for the clerical and for the mechanical scales. No validation data are made available for the other forms.

The Normal Curve Summary sheet is an elaborate control device to permit an overall evaluation of the ratings done by an individual supervisor and is a basis for a review of his personnel management practices. The scoring of the reports allows for a variety of different kinds of feedback to be made available to the rater, including such things as a tendency for his average rating to be too high or too low, insufficient variability, rating jobs rather than individuals, rating new employees too high or too low, salaries in relation to ratings, ratings out of line with aptitudes or with other personal records. This appears to be a possible and imaginative use of such kinds of data, but no information is provided to show what actually occurs when the material is used in this way.

The major value of these instruments is that they would appear to give some numerical esti-

mate of the effectiveness of individuals. They represent, however, a point of view with respect to the merit rating process; namely, that it aims at defining individuals' behavior along specific kinds of traits or specific aspects of behavior. The difficulty with this concept is that it seems to be inconsistent with or in contradiction to the more recent thinking with respect to performance reviews, which emphasizes the goals for the future and the individual's development in his performance on the job, rather than measurement of his current performance level.

The test developer is to be congratulated on the intensiveness and care with which he has developed these instruments. From a technical design point of view, he has exhibited great care in developing this set of instruments; there has been care to insure that equal numbers of positive and negative statements appear in each of the performance reviews. It is unfortunate that he does not have more validation data. From his Normal Curve Summary sheet he should be able to develop, for example, some validation data with a salary criterion.

There is an increasing amount of research that raises some questions about this kind of instrument. In a series of recent studies conducted by the writer, as well as others, it has become clear that there are significant differences in the way that more and less effective managers describe the behavior of their subordinates on a series of specific behavior statements. It is evident that different kinds of behavior are valued and are elicited by different kinds of supervisors. These differences in supervisory style may limit the validity of specific statement rating forms and if these differences are ignored, they give greater weight and significance to these numerical scores than might be deserved.

For a review by Brent Baxter of the original series, see 4:770.

[1124]

★**The Nagel Personnel Interviewing and Screening Forms.** Job applicants; 1963; 4 forms; manual (12 pages plus sample copies of each form); no data on reliability and validity; $5 per 25 copies of *a* or *d*; $6.50 per 25 copies of *b* or *c*; $2.50 per manual; postpaid; Jerome H. Nagel Associates; Western Psychological Services. *

a) THE NAGEL INITIAL INTERVIEW FORM. 10 ratings: first impression, physical appearance, voice and speech, educational background, poise and self-confidence, ambition-motivation, intelligence, knowledge of

company, maturity, total impression; 1 form (2 pages); (15) minutes.
b) THE NAGEL PERSONAL HISTORY INVENTORY. 1 form (4 pages); [20–30] minutes.
c) THE NAGEL DEPTH INTERVIEW. Ratings in 8 areas: work factors, social and educational factors, economic factors and goals, personal factors, ability to do job, motivation to do job, likelihood to remain on job, suitability of personality; 1 form (4 pages); (30) minutes.
d) THE NAGEL EMPLOYMENT REFERENCE CHECK. 1 form (2 pages); [15–30] minutes.

[1125]

★**[Performance Review Forms.]** Employees, managers; 1960–61; 2 forms; no data on reliability or validity; cash orders postpaid; Seymour Levy; Martin M. Bruce. *
a) COUNSELING INTERVIEW SUMMARY. Employees, managers; 1960; for summarizing a performance review interview; 1 form (2 pages); 2 editions; counselor's manual (24 pages); preparatory manual for counselees (14 pages); form for employees: $2.50 per 25 forms, $1.50 per specimen set of 10 copies; form for managers: $3.00 per 25 forms, $1.75 per specimen set of 10 copies; $2.25 per counselee's manual; $2.50 per counselor's manual.
b) MANAGERIAL PERFORMANCE REVIEW. Managers; 1961; ratings by supervisors preparatory to performance review interview; 1 form (9 pages); $10 per 25 forms; $5.50 per specimen set of 10 forms.

[1126]

★**Personal History Record.** Applicants for executive and managerial positions; 1953; 1 form (9 pages); no manual; $5.50 per 25 copies, postage extra; 50¢ per specimen set, postpaid; Richardson, Bellows, Henry & Co., Inc. *

[1127]

★**[Personnel Interviewing Forms.]** Business and industry; 1956; no manual or other accessories; no data on reliability and validity; cash orders postpaid; Judd-Safian Associates; Martin M. Bruce. *
a) INITIAL INTERVIEW TABULATION. For recording ratings in 10 areas: appearance, voice and speech, poise, health, education, manner, responsiveness, experience, job stability, motivation; 1 form (1 page); $2.50 per 25 forms; $1.50 per specimen set.
b) PERSONAL HISTORY AUDIT. Job applicants; 1 form (4 pages); $5 per 25 forms; $2.75 per specimen set.
c) DEPTH INTERVIEW PATTERN. For interviewing in 5 areas: work evaluation, educational and social evaluation, economic evaluation, personality evaluation, ambitions evaluation; 1 form (4 pages); $6.25 per 25 forms; $3.50 per specimen set.
d) EMPLOYMENT REFERENCE INQUIRY. For securing employee evaluation from previous employers; 1 form (1 page); $2.50 per 25 forms; $1.50 per specimen set.

[1128]

★**[Selection Interview Forms.]** Business and industry; 1962; 2 parts; no data on reliability and validity; cash orders postpaid; Benjamin Balinsky; Martin M. Bruce. *
a) SELECTION INTERVIEW FORM. 1 form (6 pages); $6.25 per 25 forms; $3.50 per specimen set of 10 forms; [60–90] minutes.
b) INTERVIEW RATING FORM. 1 form (4 pages); $5 per 25 forms; $2.75 per specimen set of 10 forms; [15] minutes.

[1129]

★**[Stevens-Thurow Personnel Forms.]** Business and industry; 1951–64; 12 record and rating forms; postage extra; specimen sets not available; $7.50 per *Handbook on How to Hire* ('60, 121 pages) which contains copies of many of the forms and manuals listed below; Stevens, Thurow & Associates Inc. *
a) PERSONAL HISTORY RECORD. Applicants, employees; 1951–64; 2 forms: form for applicants ('64), form for employees ('62), (4 pages); manual ['51, 12 pages]; $3 per 25 forms; 50¢ per manual.
b) APPLICATION FOR POSITION. Applicants for clerical positions; 1951; 1 form ['51, 2 pages]; $1.50 per 25 forms.
c) APPLICATION FOR EMPLOYMENT. Applicants for shop or plant positions; 1951; 1 form (2 pages); $1.50 per 25 forms.
d) PRELIMINARY INTERVIEW. Prospective employees; 1954; 1 form (1 page); manual ['54, 3 pages]; $1.50 per 25 forms; (15) minutes.
e) INTERVIEWER'S GUIDE AND RATING FORM FOR PROSPECTIVE EMPLOYEES. Prospective employees; 1956–63; 1 form ('63, 4 pages, essentially the same as form published in 1956); manual ('62, 19 pages); $3 per 25 forms; $1 per manual.
f) EMPLOYMENT INTERVIEW SCHEDULE. Prospective employees; 1956; 1 form ('56, 2 pages); $1.50 per 25 forms.
g) WORK REFERENCE INVESTIGATION. 1951–63; 1 form ('63, 1 page); instructions ['63, 2 pages]; $1.50 per 25 forms.
h) JOB DESCRIPTION, [SHORT FORM]. 1956; 1 form (4 pages); $3 per 25 forms.
i) JOB DESCRIPTION QUESTIONNAIRE, [LONG FORM]. 1952; 1 form (8 pages); $6.25 per 25 forms.
j) APPRAISAL REPORT FOR MANAGEMENT PERSONNEL. Managers' rating of employees; 1959; 1 form ['59, 12 pages]; $6 per 25 forms.
k) APPRAISAL REPORT FOR MANAGEMENT PERSONNEL (SUPPLEMENTARY FORM FOR SALES MANAGERS). 1959; 1 form ['59, 4 pages]; $3 per 25 forms.
l) WORK BEHAVIOR INVENTORY. Supervisor's rating of employees; 1951–63; 2 forms ('63, 4 pages): *Employee Rating Report, Salesman Rating Report;* $3 per 25 forms.

[Other Tests]

For tests not listed above, see the following entries in *Tests in Print:* 1978, 1982, 1985, 1988–9, and 1991; out of print: 1979 and 1983.

SPECIFIC VOCATIONS

[Other Tests]

For tests not listed above, see the following entry in *Tests in Print:* 1993.

ACCOUNTING

[Other Tests]

For tests not listed above, see the following entries in *Tests in Print:* 1994–5.

DENTISTRY

[Other Tests]

For tests not listed above, see the following entries in *Tests in Print:* 1996–7.

ENGINEERING

[1130]

★AC Test of Creative Ability. Engineers and supervisors; 1953–60; 9 scores: quantity (parts 1, 2, 5), uniqueness (parts 1, 2, 3, 5), quality (part 4), total; parts 1, 2, and 5 may be administered alone for quantity scores only; Forms A ('53), B ('54), (12 pages); manual ('60, 25 pages); no data on reliability of subscores; norms for quantity scores only; scoring keys for uniqueness and quality scores must be developed locally; $6 per 20 tests; $1.25 per manual; postage extra; $1 per specimen set, postpaid; 80(90) minutes for full test, 45(50) minutes for parts 1, 2, and 5 alone; Richard H. Harris (test), A. L. Simberg (test), and Measurement Research Division, Industrial Relations Center, University of Chicago (manual); Education-Industry Service. *

REFERENCES

1. PARNES, SIDNEY J., AND MEADOW, ARNOLD. "Evaluation of Persistence of Effects Produced by a Creative Problem-Solving Course." *Psychol Rep* 7:357–61 O '60. * (PA 35:2700)

SAMUEL T. MAYO, *Associate Professor of Education, Loyola University, Chicago, Illinois.*

From an experimental sample of 14 short tests, the present test consists of 5 which held up under validation. Each of the original tests was based upon some facet of creativity as it was being discussed in 1953. Most of the hypotheses existing at that time had stemmed from Guilford's work, although the authors did not have access to his experimental tests. The above information was revealed in a private communication from one of the authors.

The scoring rationale was based upon the assumption that "more creative" persons would produce higher quantities of ideas, more unique ideas, and ideas of better quality. Unlike the *Owens' Creativity Test* and the *Purdue Creativity Test,* this test consists of verbal material rather than pictorial material. It is undoubtedly contaminated by a verbal fluency factor, judging from the correlations of .41 of the total score with the *Wonderlic Personnel Test* and .33 with the Kuder literary scale. Some of the specific content of Part 3 in both forms seems open to criticism as harboring potential biases associated with differing past experiences of individuals. For example, "Lawn Mower (Not motor driven)" is listed as one of several common machines or appliances. This device was much more common in 1953 than in 1963. Other devices which might be subject to bias would be "Gas Furnace" and "Electric Razor" (both in Form A), and "Table-model Radio" and "Gas Stove" (both in Form B).

The manual reports an unidentified Kuder-Richardson reliability coefficient of .92 for the total score without specifying the number of cases. An alternate form reliability coefficient of .75 is reported for 39 cases. The reliability estimates would seem to indicate that errors of measurement are larger than one would wish them to be for personnel selection or classification, especially on an individual basis.

Evidence of validity is presented in the manual in several sets of data, all of them based upon rather small samples which range in size from 35 to 56. It was disappointing to find that all the sets of data were in the form of tests of significance among means or medians or expectancy tables, to the exclusion of validity coefficients. Some of the mean or median scores on various subtests and total scores show significant differences between criterion groups judged as relatively high or low in creativity. In private communication with the author and some of his colleagues, it was reported that the test shows low to moderate correlations with two other tests associated with creative ability —*Word Fluency* and the *Cree Questionnaire.* It may also be revealing that the test correlates only .18 with Bennett's *Tests of Mechanical Comprehension* and shows predominantly non-significant correlations with a number of non-cognitive measures. Taken as a whole, the statistical evidence in the manual is not very convincing.

In view of the disappointing statistical evidence for reliability and validity and also of the fact that the test has been administered to over 5,000 engineers and technical and supervisory personnel in industry, it seems unfortunate that correlational evidence of validity based upon much larger samples could not have been garnered.

When content validity is considered rationally, parts other than Part 3 seem satisfactory as stimuli to evoke divergent responses. The relevance of the item content to criteria seems intermediate between that of the *Owens' Creativity Test for Machine Design* and the *Purdue Creativity Test.*

This test cannot be recommended for application in predicting success in "tool design, gauge design, engineering, manufacturing, or process development," as the authors intended. The only kind of validity available in the manual is concurrent, while predictive validity studies are needed to support claims for generalizations from the test to the above work areas. Some doubt is also raised by unproved relevance of the highly semantic content of the test for the figural and symbolic content in the work areas. One hopes that the forthcoming revised manual promised by the publisher in a communication with the reviewer will report better norms and substantial statistical evidence on the adequacy of the test, as well as updated test content.

PHILIP R. MERRIFIELD, *Director, Bureau of Educational Research, Kent State University, Kent, Ohio.*

This test requires the examinee to write consequences of a described situation, explanations of statements assumed to be true, improvements of common appliances, solutions to situational problems, and uses of common objects. The similarity of these tasks to those used by other researchers in factor analytic studies is great; no reference to such research is made, nor is other factor analytic evidence adduced for the authors' interpretation of the results of their items and scoring procedures. The parts of this test do not appear to be measures of the same factor, although combining them into a composite called "creativity" is not illogical.

The procedures for scoring are, except for Part 4, quite mechanical. The quantity, or "Q," score is the total number of relevant responses, no guidelines being given in the manual as to relevance. The uniqueness, or "U," score is based on weights assigned inversely to frequency with which a response occurs. No guidelines are given to categorizing responses, so that a different verbalization of essentially the same idea would not necessarily count as a replication of that idea; further, the weighting procedure as described is quite sensitive both to size of sample used in establishing the weights and to the quantity of responses in that sample. This procedure induces experimental dependence of Q and U scores, and this accounts in part for the large correlation, .80 or greater, of the two scores from the same part. In the manual, this outcome is submitted as evidence for the "efficiency" of the Q scores at measuring U-performance, the latter apparently having some validity for the authors. Little information is lost using Q for U because so little was added in the measurement of U.

A reliability of .92 is claimed for the total test scores, based on Q and U scores from three of the five parts, U only from Part 3

and quality score from Part 4, all from a sample of size 36. Clearly this estimate is too high, due to the experimental dependence of Q and U scores from the same responses; it is unfortunate that the claim concludes a paragraph, apparently intended as tutorial, on the tendency of internal consistency estimates of reliability to be conservatively low. When the interpart correlations for Q are averaged and extended by Spearman-Brown procedures, the reliability estimate is .68; for the U scores, .74 seems a better estimate based on interpart correlations. As noted, the only reliabilities cited are based, apparently, on an early sample of AC Spark Plug Division engineers; other studies are cited, without additional reliability estimates reported. Perhaps the greatest question arises when one notes that the norms are based on 333 examinees; surely some estimate of reliability is available from so large a pool.

Validity is asserted on the basis of five studies, four from AC Spark Plug Division and one from Massachusetts Institute of Technology. Means of high and low criterion groups in two of the AC studies are, for every part, higher than the 99th percentile in the norms included in the manual. Unless the AC employees are indeed that much superior to the rest of the norms group, or the norms themselves are in error, the discrepancy requires explanation. In the MIT study, of 51 students with grades as a criterion, medians of the scores of A and B students are said to be significantly different, but no statistical test is named as being applied; the correlation between four grades—A, B, C, D—and rankings by quarters on the test is nearly zero; instructor's comments are referred to for 45 students in a table, but for 51 in a graph; quartiles for this graph differ from those used in the comparison of grades, although the examinees, and their scores, are presumably the same.

The only evidence of correlation between Form A and Form B, as published, is the report of a correlation of .75 between alternate forms before and after training.

In summary, the test items are ingenious and stimulating; they should educe interesting results in situations where semantic, not figural or symbolic, fluency is considered an appropriate measure. The uniqueness score adds little, partly because it is so mechanically derived; the user might consider developing a weighting scheme along more psychological lines, as in the recommended score for quality. However, he should not expect much help from the manual. Evidently the authors and publisher were aiming at an APA Level A test; with the present scoring procedures the test can be used as that, but with a sizable waste of potential information. Better tests for the factors implicit in these items are those by Guilford and his associates—*Consequences, Alternate Uses,* and *Christensen-Guilford Fluency Tests,* to name three. Norms for most of those tests are based on high school and college samples; the tests are factor analyzed; unfortunately, validation data are not extensive. The reviewer is involved as co-author of several of these tests, a fact the reader may wish to consider. Tests of other than semantic aspects of creativity, developed by Owens and by Lawshe and Harris, are reviewed elsewhere in this volume.

ALBERT S. THOMPSON, *Professor of Psychology and Education, Teachers College, Columbia University, New York, New York.*

This paper and pencil test of creative ability "is designed to give a measure of the quantity and the uniqueness of the ideas an individual can produce in a given situation." Each of the two parallel forms consists of five parts, requiring (a) listing possible consequences to problem situations as described, (b) giving reasons for a statement assumed to be true, (c) describing desirable improvements in common appliances, (d) giving solutions to specified problem situations, (e) listing possible uses of specified objects. Quantity scores are derived from Parts 1, 2, and 5, a "uniqueness" score from four of the parts, and a quality score from one.

The test materials are well printed and the instructions clear. Group administration is possible. Parts 1, 2, and 5 taken alone yield the quantity score based on 45 minutes of testing. The quantity score (Q) is standard and norms are provided based on 333 engineering and supervisory personnel. It is recommended in the manual that scoring keys and norms for the uniqueness and quality scores be developed for the specific situations and step-by-step procedures for developing such keys and norms are given.

This test was developed in the AC Spark Plug Division of General Motors Corporation for use in situations involving research, design, and development work. The data concerning the test are based on studies in this setting with various technical and engineering groups.

Although the test materials are oriented toward use in engineering-type situations, the items are sufficiently common in nature to be usable with a variety of groups. The procedures for developing scoring keys for the uniqueness and quality scores are designed to facilitate widespread use without danger of misinterpretation.

In summary, this test appears to be soundly constructed to yield a sample of the individual's productive behavior, for which quantity and quality scores can be derived. Except for the quantity score with engineering groups, norming and validation are required for other uses.

The reported research gives little insight into the nature of the characteristic being measured, except by a content analysis of the items and by noting the correlation with other tests and among the parts. No clear rationale as to the basic dimensions of creative behavior is presented or inferrable from the research data. In contrast to the Guilford and Purdue studies, the purpose is pragmatic prediction rather than analytic study. Further research and validation are necessary for the test to be useful in any ongoing employee appraisal program.

[1131]

*Engineering Aide Test. Engineering aides; 1957–60; form 50-A ('57, 22 pages plus fold-out answer sheet); preliminary mimeographed manual ('57, 11 pages); general PPA mimeographed manual ['57, 7 pages]; norms ('60, 1 page); 10–49 tests, $1.20 each; $2 per specimen set; postpaid; 90(100) minutes; Public Personnel Association. *

[1132]

*The Graduate Record Examinations Advanced Tests: Engineering. Grades 16–17; 1939–62; for more complete information, see 762; 180(200) minutes; Educational Testing Service. *

For a review of the testing program, see 5:601.

[1133]

*Minnesota Engineering Analogies Test. Candidates for graduate school and industry; 1954–63; IBM; Forms E, F, ('54, 4 pages); preliminary manual ('55, 11 pages); bulletin of information ('63, 36 pages); revised procedures for testing center operation ('63, 8 pages); distribution restricted and test administered at specified licensed university centers; scoring and reporting handled by the local center; examination fee to centers: $1 per examinee; fees to examinees are determined locally and include reporting of scores to the examinee and to 3 institutions or companies designated at the time of testing; additional score reports may be secured from the publisher at a fee of $1 each; (45–60) minutes; Marvin D. Dunnette; Psychological Corporation. *

REFERENCES

1–6. See 5:933.
7. MacKinnon, Donald W. "Fostering Creativity in Students of Engineering." *J Eng Ed* 52:129–42 D '61. * (*PA* 36:4HD29M)
8. Spencer, George M., and Reynolds, Harlan J. "Validity Information Exchange, No. 14-04: D.O.T. Code 0-17, 0-19, Electrical and Mechanical Engineers." *Personnel Psychol* 14:456–8 w '61. *

For reviews by A. Pemberton Johnson and William B. Schrader, see 5:933.

[1134]

★**National Engineering Aptitude Search Test: The Junior Engineering Technical Society.** Grades 7–12; 1963, c1947–62; tests administered each spring at Junior Engineering Technical Society chapter centers; 5 scores: verbal reasoning, numerical ability, total, mechanical reasoning, space relations; IBM; 1 form ['63, c1947–62, 34 pages, special reprint of corresponding parts of *Differential Aptitude Tests,* Form M]; mimeographed directions for administering ['63, 2 pages]; information bulletin ['63, 5 pages]; score reports based on regular DAT norms; examination fee, $2 per student; postage extra; 115(130) minutes; Psychological Corporation. *

[1135]

★**The Owens' Creativity Test for Machine Design.** Engineers and engineering students; 1960; 4 scores: power source apparatus designs (workable solutions, total solutions), applications of mechanisms, weighted total; Form CT-1 (31 pages); manual (31 pages); no norms; publisher recommends use of local norms; $7.50 per 20 tests; 75¢ per manual; $1.25 per specimen set; cash orders postpaid; 160(170) minutes; William A. Owens; Iowa State University Press. *

REFERENCES

1. Owens, W. A.; Schumacher, C. F.; and Clark, J. B. "The Measurement of Creativity in Machine Design." *J Appl Psychol* 41:297–302 O '57. *

Samuel T. Mayo, *Associate Professor of Education, Loyola University, Chicago, Illinois.*

The present test consists of 15 problems of two kinds. Ten minutes are allowed for each problem. In Part 1 the task in each problem is to design as many mechanisms to connect two types of given motions as one can in the time allowed. In Part 2 the task in each problem is to list as many different devices in which each given connecting mechanism might function. Content of problems is specific to machine design and was chosen upon the advice of a panel of mechanical engineers at a university.

Actual construction of the test is not described either in the manual or in the one published article on the test (*1*). The article describes a study to determine the effectiveness of nine instruments in discriminating creative from noncreative design engineers. The present test, or "battery" as the author calls it, consists of two of the four instruments to survive

item analysis and cross validation, and, it must be noted, the only cognitive instruments to survive. According to the article, the impetus behind the study, which culminated in the present test, was the critical shortage of creative machine designers during World War II and the fact that "an alarmingly small proportion of those present were either native born or the products of American Schools of Engineering."

Ease of scoring varies among the three component scores. Two of the scores—"total solutions" and "applications of mechanisms"—are arrived at quite easily and objectively by simple classification and counting processes guided by directions largely free of ambiguity. The "workable solutions" score of the Power Source Apparatus Test involves a considerable degree of subjectivity. The manual gives drawings for a number of more frequently occurring solutions. For drawings not shown, the examiner must use the instructions in the manual and his own best judgment. This would seem at first glance to be a decided disadvantage. However, the evidence on the reliability of the "workable solutions" score seems quite satisfactory. Furthermore, in spite of the high intercorrelation between the total and "workable" scores of the Power Source Apparatus Test for combined data for all companies (.89), the author seems justified in keeping both scores, in view of the evidence in the article from both simple and multiple biserial correlation coefficients and from discriminant analysis.

Only indices of equivalence are provided, and, according to the author, evidence as to the stability of test scores over time was not available at the time the manual was written.

Concurrent validity is reported but not predictive or construct validity. Content validity appears to be claimed on the basis of (*a*) the author's cautious statement that no validity for the battery is claimed outside the machine design field and (*b*) the fact that a panel of mechanical engineers screened the test content. In his article, however, the author did promise a predictive validity study with 1,500 students at 24 colleges and universities and in private communication with the reviewer he reported that the study was in progress at the time of the review. The author summarizes his quantitative evidence for validity in the following statement from the manual:

Let us assume two equal groups of engineers employed by a particular firm and matched for age, education, and relevant experience; let us further assume that one of the groups would be rated as "creative" by its immediate superiors and that the other would be rated as "non-creative." Based upon past experience, test scores obtained from the present battery would coincide with the posited ratings of creativity or noncreativity in about three-fourths of the cases.

No correlations with any outside tests are reported. However, some evidence is available, in the article and in personal correspondence with the author, against the hypothesis that relations between the scores and the criterion could be explained by common mental ability factors. In the study reported in the article, three aptitude tests—Space Relations, Figure Matrices, and Number Series—failed to discriminate the criterion groups. Furthermore, the author reported to the reviewer in private communication that engineers rated as creative were found to have had college averages typically of about C+.

The author is to be commended for his excellent reporting of evidence for concurrent validity, for his detailed and clear directions for scoring the more objective parts of the test, for his brave attempt at describing a scoring system for the more subjective parts, and for his clear operational definitions of the two criterion groups of creative and noncreative designers. Adversely, there seems to be much information which could well have been included in the manual, some of which is known by the reviewer to have been available at the time the manual was written. Examples of such information include a description of how the test problems themselves were constructed and tried out, more of the statistical results which are reported in the article, correlations with other tests, and evidence to discount the hypothesis that the test is heavily loaded with mental ability factors. The author also seems open to criticism in his use of the word "development" as indicating noncreative design work since the term is used to indicate creativity (the opposite) in two other tests, the *AC Test of Creative Ability* and the *Purdue Creativity Test*.

In summary, this appears to be a psychometrically good test. It has demonstrated its usefulness in differentiating creative from noncreative among experienced machine designers. When the results are available from the study of predictive validity, its usefulness as a pre-dictor will be better known. Of the tests of creativity in engineering which are known to the reviewer, this would clearly be the best for use in machine design. It is not recommended for use outside machine design at the present time.

PHILIP R. MERRIFIELD, *Director, Bureau of Educational Research, Kent State University, Kent, Ohio.*

The author states that his intention is to differentiate "creative designers in the machine design field from those better suited for development work." Within this specific area, his test should do a good job; however, it does require a certain amount of ability to sketch machine parts and to visualize spatial changes in the relations of objects. Presumably the level needed would have been attained by employed engineers in the course of their training, and thus differences in these abilities would not contribute much to the differences in scores on this test. Another source of unwanted differentiation, not emphasized by the author, is the tendency of scorers to reward neat, precise drawings which may be little better, in terms of creative solutions, than less skillful products. On the other hand, perhaps that difference is related to the value of the employee in terms of how well he can communicate his ideas in a hasty sketch.

The instructions for scoring the Power Source Apparatus Test (Part 1) items as "unworkable," "common and workable," or "unique and workable" are detailed and explicit, with sketches for each item. Nevertheless, as the author recommends, the scorer will need some knowledge of machine design terminology as a basis for judgment.

The item format for the Applications of Mechanisms Test (Part 2) could be improved by adding lines to guide the examinee's written responses. Perhaps more space would be enjoyed by the examinee and by the scorer, who must decide how many separate applications are suggested. The mechanisms might be more easily visualized were the sketches three-dimensional views instead of elevations.

Reliabilities were computed from odd-even scores, as the test appeared to be not speeded; the values given are .85 for PSA total, .83 for PSA workable, and .91 for the Applications of Mechanisms Test; AMT scores correlate about .40 with PSA workable and .50 with

PSA total; but there is a correlation of nearly .90 between the PSA total and PSA workable, induced at least in part by their mutual experimental dependence. Using both scores in a multiple regression problem, as the author did, may result in an inflated value for the multiple correlation, or, as in the present case, in a negative weight for one of the scores in the regression equation.

The validity studies are summarized by the author by combining the results from several (number not stated) companies for a total of 159 employed design engineers tested in 1953 and 1954. Validities are described in terms of per cent of correct predictions, assuming 50 per cent to be creative in computing the selection ratios. The validity for all examinees pooled was 66 per cent, compared to an average of 86 per cent for the within-company predictions. These data support the author's advice that each user should develop his own norms.

In summary, this is an interesting test, possessing both high face validity and some concurrent validity against supervisor's rating of creativity. The manual is excellent; the author categorizes the test as Level C in terms of APA standards, and the reviewer agrees.

[1136]

★Purdue Creativity Test. Applicants for engineering positions; 1960, c1957–60; test booklet title is *Creativity Test*; 3 scores: fluency, flexibility, total; Forms G, H, ('60, c1957, 21 pages); manual ('60, 10 pages); $7.50 per 25 tests, postage extra; 50¢ per specimen set, postpaid; 40(50) minutes; C. H. Lawshe and D. H. Harris; distributed by University Book Store. *

REFERENCES

1. HARRIS, DOUGLAS HERSHEL, JR. *The Development of a Test of Creativity in Engineering.* Doctor's thesis, Purdue University (Lafayette, Ind.), 1959. (*DA* 20:2374)
2. HARRIS, DOUGLAS. "The Development and Validation of a Test of Creativity in Engineering." *J Appl Psychol* 44: 254–7 Ag 60. * (*PA* 35:4032)

SAMUEL T. MAYO, *Associate Professor of Education, Loyola University, Chicago, Illinois.*

The stated purpose of this test is to find out how "fluent, flexible, and original" engineering personnel are in their thinking. According to the publisher's catalog, it is recommended for identifying design engineers who "have the capacity to be really creative in the designs they produce" and research and development engineers "whose success depends upon the production of new ideas." Furthermore, the catalog states, "This test measures creativity in engineering." The 20 items, each requiring two minutes, are of three kinds. In the first 8,

one is asked to list as many possible uses as he can for each object alone as shown in a three-dimensional drawing; in the next 4 items one is asked to list as many uses as he can for two objects when used together as shown in a three-dimensional drawing; in the last 8 items one is asked to look at a line drawing and answer the question, "What is this?" and to "List as many possibilities as you can." Neither items nor pages are numbered. In administering the test the only oral instruction given when going on to the next item is the word, "Time," every two minutes. The flexibility score is obtained from the first 12 items by counting and summing the number of different categories of uses represented by responses, while the fluency score is obtained from the last 8 items by counting and summing the number of responses to each item. The total score is obtained by adding the flexibility subscore to one half of the fluency subscore. The manual does not explain the origin of the formula.

The authors recommend that each user accumulate his own applicant norms. The only norms reported in the manual are a set based upon 106 professional engineers. Norms are ostensibly given for fluency, flexibility, and total scores. Any test user would intuitively expect the total scores in the norms table to be based upon application of the formula for combining the two subscores. However, it is obvious that the norms for total score have not been derived from the formula. As an example, if we assume that a person places at the 95th percentile in both Fluency and Flexibility, he would place at only the 67th percentile on the published norms. Furthermore, a person at the median on both subtests would place at the 20th percentile on total score.

The reliability data reported are based upon a sample of only 64 professional engineers and leave much to be desired. The authors say that the two forms were "considered" to be comparable, although they do not report any empirical data on comparability. The split-half coefficients reported are .86 for Flexibility, .93 for Fluency, and .95 for total score. The two forms were used "interchangeably" in obtaining these coefficients, so that one does not know upon which form each coefficient was based. Separate coefficients should have been reported for the two forms. The second kind of reliability reported is that of interscorer agreement for two scorers; these coefficients are .87 for Flexibility and .97 for total score. Again, the authors' language is ambiguous. It is not clear whether the same form or alternate forms were used. The kind of coefficient which should have been reported is alternate form (once with same graders and again with different graders).

The only kind of validity reported for the published test is in the form of expectancy tables. From an earlier, experimental form of the test, cross validation on 29 machine design students, according to the manual, yielded validities of .16 for Fluency and .73 for Flexibility with a criterion of instructors' rating on the ability to produce original ideas for the development of machines to perform certain unusual functions. In view of the insignificant validity of the fluency score, the statement of the authors that "These correlations indicated....that the Creativity Scores showed considerable promise in the measurement of creativity" seems incredible. A series of expectancy tables in bar graph form is presented. Their effectiveness is weakened by the small samples involved. The samples range from 29 to 42 cases for three separate samples, with 104 cases for the samples combined. It would have been helpful if the manual had indicated that the intervals given under the column labeled "Test Scores" include equal numbers of persons. This information was reported in correspondence with one of the authors but does not appear in the manual. It is not at all clear how the two samples with odd numbers of cases (29 and 33) could have been split into two equal sized groups. Also, when percentages are computed from subgroups of around 15 cases each, a change of 1 case makes a change of nearly 7 per cent. Since the norms for total score were based upon scores which are not in accordance with the recommended scoring formula, one is led to suspect that the expectancy tables are also based upon such inappropriate scores.

Correlations with two other tests are reported, the *Wonderlic Personnel Test* and the *Tests of Mechanical Comprehension*. The coefficients for subtests and total score are all nonsignificant. Thus, this test appears to be measuring something different from general mental ability or mechanical aptitude. Correlations of creativity scores with age, education, and experience are not clearly demonstrated, but the wording of the manual suggests that

these factors may not have been significantly related. One is left in the peculiar position of knowing some of the variables with which the test is not related but knowing little about what the test is actually measuring.

In summary, this test cannot be recommended for its intended purposes on the basis of the presently available data. It may very well be potentially an effective test for its stated purposes, but the manual does not adequately support these claims. It is to be hoped that the authors and publisher will see fit to gather some acceptable statistical evidence on the test's characteristics and will clarify the manual so that the user will know how and why he is using a particular score in a particular manner.

PHILIP R. MERRIFIELD, *Director, Bureau of Educational Research, Kent State University, Kent, Ohio.*

The tasks in this test are three, all based on three-dimensional drawings of objects: list possible uses for a single object; list possible uses for two objects together; and list possible identifications for an object. There are 20 items in each form; each item is to be answered in two minutes. Close proctoring may be necessary to maintain time limits on items presented on facing pages.

Somewhat surprisingly, the authors obtain only two subscores from the three item types; perhaps a third score would add sensitivity to the test. More importantly, the fluency and flexibility scores are derived from disjoint sets of items, so there is no experimental dependence. Flexibility scores are based on items 1–12, eight of the first type noted above, and four of the second. The score for an item is the number of categories, specified in the manual, into which the examinee's responses fall; the flexibility score for the test is the sum of item scores; all items are scored using the same categories. This kind of scoring can verge on being a fluency score, if the examinee spreads his responses widely over the structure imposed by the scorer. In the reviewer's opinion, this procedure leads to a measure better called "sensitivity to dimensions of a problem" than the traditional "flexibility." However, it is a component of the composite behavior called "creative." The fluency score is the number of responses from items 13–20, all of the third type, after duplicate ideas have been eliminated. Examples of duplicates are given in the manual. Total score is defined as the score for flexibility plus one half the score for fluency; however, when used to combine the fluency and flexibility scores for given centiles in the "norms" in the manual, this formula gives results inconsistent with the given centiles for total score. It would appear that the score entry under Fluency is in fact the fluency component, i.e., one half the raw score for fluency. Under this assumption, the reviewer estimates the correlation between Fluency and Flexibility to be about .40; a value for this correlation is not reported in the manual. It is to be hoped that the authors will clarify this confusion in the next edition of the manual. In the meantime the user is well advised to follow their suggestion to develop his own norms.

Two kinds of reliability estimates are given for the flexibility score: an interscorer correlation of .87 and a split-half reliability coefficient of .86. Split-half reliabilities of .93 and .95 are reported for the fluency and total scores, respectively. The interscorer correlation for total score was .97. These values would be of greater use were the standard deviations of the scores presented; the standard error of estimate is more indicative of practical utility than is an average index of a relationship. No means or standard deviations are reported.

Concurrent validity is reported for total score only, using a group of 104 product, process, and project engineers rated by their supervisor on a criterion of creativity, defined as the ability to develop new solutions for problems. Better predictions were obtained in the product and process engineer groups than in the project engineer group; the criterion was applied in the first two by a paired-comparison technique, and in the third by a nomination technique, so there may be some confounding of procedure of criterion evaluation and the results. Users should, of course, investigate procedures for making criterion assessment both reliable and valid. The results are presented in bar graphs labeled "chances in a hundred of being superior." No statistical probabilities of the outcomes are given. In the composite graph for all three groups, five bars represent chances of groups which are separated approximately into fifths according to the norms in the manual; for the three kinds of engineers separately, the dichotomy point for scores varies. Perhaps it is the median for each group.

In summary, this test appears to have been soundly developed, with reliability adequate for use with group averages and perhaps with individuals, and with concurrent validity of some significance. Except for the matter of the norms discussed above, the manual appears to be carefully done, and contains references. One might wish for a more elaborate statistical treatment of the results of validation studies, and for some attempt by the authors to provide factorial validity for the constructs they claim to measure. However, in general, this test should be quite useful.

[Other Tests]

For tests not listed above, see the following entries in *Tests in Print:* 2001–2 and 2006–8.

LAW

[Other Tests]

For tests not listed above, see the following entries in *Tests in Print:* 2009–10.

MEDICINE

[1137]

*Medical College Admission Test. Applicants for admission to member colleges of the Association of American Medical Colleges; 1946–64; 4 scores: verbal, quantitative, general information, science; administered 2 times annually (spring, fall) at centers established by the publisher; IBM; examiner's manual ('63, 11 pages); announcement ('64, 23 pages); examination fee, $15; fee includes reporting of scores to 1–6 schools designated at time of application; $1 per additional report; scores not reported to examinees; 210(255)minutes; Psychological Corporation. *

REFERENCES

1–11. See 4:817.
12–15. See 5:932.
16. SCOTT, J. ALLEN, AND BRENKUS, PEGGY M. "Medical College Admission Test Scores as an Aid in Teaching Medical Statistics." *J Med Ed* 29:39–43 Ap '54. * (*PA* 29:4644)
17. STALNAKER, JOHN M. "Report of the Director of Studies." *J Med Ed* 29:42–6 D '54. *
18. STALNAKER, JOHN M. "The Study of Applicants, 1954–1955." *J Med Ed* 30:625–36 N '55. * (*PA* 30:5243)
19. WATSON, ROBERT I. "Predicting Academic Success Through Achievement and Aptitude Tests." *J Med Ed* 30:383–90 Jl '55. * (*PA* 30:5248)
20. GEE, HELEN HOFER. "The Study of Applicants, 1955–56." *J Med Ed* 31:863–9 D '56. *
21. GLASER, ROBERT J. "Appraising Intellectual Characteristics." *J Med Ed* 32:31–43 O pt 2 '57. *
22. JACKSON, GEORGE GEE, AND KELLOW, WILLIAM F. "An Experiment With the Group Interview in the Selection of Medical Students." *J Med Ed* 33:491–500 Je '58. *
23. CROWDER, DOLORES GARCIA. "Prediction of First-Year Grades in a Medical College." *Ed & Psychol Meas* 19:637–9 w '59. * (*PA* 34:6563)
24. HILL, JOSEPH K. "Assessment of Intellectual Promise for Medical School." *J Med Ed* 34:959–64 O '59. *
25. KLINGER, ERIC, AND GEE, HELEN HOFER. "The Study of Applicants, 1957–58." *J Med Ed* 34:424–35 Ap '59. *
26. "Medical College Admission Test Data for 1959–60 Applicants." *J Med Ed* 35:1037–9 N '60. *
27. JOHNSON, DAVIS G. "An 'Actuarial' Approach to Medical Student Selection." *J Med Ed* 35:158–63 F '60. *
28. KLINGER, ERIC, AND GEE, HELEN HOFER. "The Study of Applicants, 1958–59." *J Med Ed* 35:120–33 F '60. *
29. LITTLE, J. MAXWELL; GEE, HELEN HOFER; AND NOVICK, MELVIN R. "A Study of the Medical College Admission Test in Relation to Academic Difficulties in Medical School." *J Med Ed* 35:264–72 Mr '60. *

30. "Application Activity and MCAT Data of Applicants to the Class of 1960–61." *J Med Ed* 36:1619–20 N '61. *

31. GARFIELD, SOL L., AND WOLPIN, MILTON. "MCAT Scores and Continuation in Medical School." *J Med Ed* 36:888–91 Ag '61. *

32. HUTCHINS, EDWIN B., AND GEE, HELEN HOFER. "The Study of Applicants, 1959–60." *J Med Ed* 36:289–304 Ap '61. *

33. RICHARDS, JAMES M., JR., AND TAYLOR, CALVIN W. "Predicting Academic Achievement in a College of Medicine From Grades, Test Scores, Interviews, and Ratings." *Ed & Psychol Meas* 21:987–94 w '61. *

34. SCHUMACHER, CHARLES F., AND GEE, HELEN HOFER. "The Relationship Between Initial and Retest Scores on the Medical College Admission Test." *J Med Ed* 36:129–33 F '61. *

35. SCHWARTZMAN, A. E.; HUNTER, R. C. A.; AND PRINCE, R. H. "Intellectual Factors and Academic Performance in Medical Undergraduates." *J Med Ed* 36:353–8 Ap '61. *

36. "MCAT Data of Applicants to the Class of 1961–62." *J Med Ed* 37:1130–1 O '62. *

37. BUEHLER, JOHN A., AND TRAINER, JOSEPH B. "Prediction of Medical School Performance and Its Relationship to Achievement." *J Med Ed* 37:10–8 Ja '62. *

38. CEITHAML, JOSEPH. "Student Selection in United States Medical Schools." *J Med Ed* 37:171–6 Mr '62. *

39. GEE, HELEN HOFER, AND SCHUMACHER, CHARLES F. "Reply to a Note on the Validity of the Medical College Admission Test." *J Med Ed* 37:787–9 Ag '62. *

40. GROFF, MORRIS, AND GRUBER, EDWARD C. *How to Score High on the Medical College Admission Test, Revised Edition.* New York: Arco Publishing Co., 1962. Pp. 278. *

41. HUTCHINS, EDWIN B. "The Student and His Environment." *J Med Ed* 37:67–82 D '62. *

42. HUTCHINS, EDWIN B., AND GEE, HELEN HOFER. "The Study of Applicants, 1960–61." *J Med Ed* 37:1203–12 N '62. *

43. JOHNSON, DAVIS G. "A Multifactor Method of Evaluating Medical School Applicants." *J Med Ed* 37:656–65 Jl '62. *

44. LEVITT, EUGENE E., AND TYLER, EDWARD A. "A Note on the Validity of the Medical College Admission Test." *J Med Ed* 37:395–6 Ap '62. *

45. MOORE, ROBERT A. "The Use of Objective Tests in the Selection of Medical Students." *J Med Ed* 37:455–62 My '62. *

46. RICHARDS, JAMES M., JR.; TAYLOR, CALVIN W.; AND PRICE, PHILIP B. "The Prediction of Medical Intern Performance." *J Appl Psychol* 46:142–6 Ap '62. *

47. SCHWARTZMAN, A. E.; HUNTER, R. C. A.; AND LOHRENZ, J. G. "Factors Related to Medical School Achievement." *J Med Ed* 37:749–59 Ag '62. *

48. SCHWARTZMAN, A. E.; HUNTER, R. C. A.; AND LOHRENZ, J. G. "Factors Related to Student Withdrawals From Medical Schools." *J Med Ed* 37:1114–20 O '62. *

49. WORK, HENRY H. "A Rationale for Grouping of Medical Students." *J Med Ed* 37:130–2 F '62. *

50. "Application Activity and MCAT Data of Applicants to the Class of 1962–63." *J Med Ed* 38:774–5 S '63. *

51. CONGER, JOHN J., AND FITZ, REGINALD H. "Prediction of Success in Medical School." *J Med Ed* 38:943–8 N '63. *

52. GOUGH, HARRISON G.; HALL, WALLACE B.; AND HARRIS, ROBERT E. "Admissions Procedures as Forecasters of Performance in Medical School." *J Med Ed* 38:983–98 D '63. *

53. HOFFMAN, E. LEE; WING, CLIFF W., JR.; AND LIEF, HAROLD I. "Short and Long-Term Predictions About Medical Students." *J Med Ed* 38:852–7 O '63. *

54. HUTCHINS, EDWIN B. "The Study of Applicants, 1961–62." *J Med Ed* 38:707–17 S '63. *

55. HUTCHINS, EDWIN B. "The Study of Applicants, 1962–63." *J Med Ed* 38:999–1003 D '63. *

56. HUTCHINS, EDWIN B., AND MORRIS, WOODROW W. "A Follow-Up Study of Non-Entrants and High Ability Rejected Applicants to the 1958–59 Entering Class of U.S. Medical Schools." *J Med Ed* 38:1023–8 D '63. *

57. RUDMAN, JACK. *How to Pass Medical College Admission Test: Questions and Answers, Second Edition.* Brooklyn, N.Y.: College Publishing Corporation, 1963. Pp. 298. *

58. SANAZARO, PAUL J., AND HUTCHINS, EDWIN B. "The Origin and Rationale of the Medical College Admission Test." *J Med Ed* 38:1044–50 D '63. *

ROBERT L. EBEL, *Professor of Education, Michigan State University, East Lansing, Michigan.* [Review of Forms Q and R.]

TEST CONTENT. The content of these forms is essentially the same as that of recent earlier forms. Items testing verbal and mathematical skills and knowledge in the areas of science and general culture are included. An outline of the current forms shows this composition: Part 1, Verbal (75 items, 20 minutes), Part 2, Science (86 items, 60 minutes), Part 3, Quantitative (50 items, 45 minutes), Part 4, General Information (75 items, 25 minutes), and Part 5, Experimental (86 items, 60 minutes). The fifth part does not contribute to the examinee's reported score.

For a test intended to assess aptitude for the study of medicine, this type of content seems quite appropriate. Verbal and mathematical skills are essential tools of learning, and items testing for these skills have established their value in tests of scholastic aptitude at all educational levels. A good foundation of knowledge of the sciences of biology, chemistry, and physics is clearly essential to the study of medicine. While a test of general culture, composed of items on history, literature, art, music, philosophy, economics, government, etc., may not have the highest relevance to success in the study of medicine, it can provide important information on the cultural backgrounds and prospects of future physicians. In the judgment of this reviewer, such a test is entirely appropriate in a battery intended to select medical students.

From time to time the *Medical College Admission Test* has been criticized for its emphasis on such conventional educational outcomes as knowledge and skills, presumably to the neglect of complex, higher mental abilities such as flexibility in thinking, balanced judgment, critical perception, and synthesizing ability. But these abilities are seldom defined in terms of operations that might be used to measure them. Further, the psychological soundness of speculations concerning their nature and functions often seems open to question. Until better evidence is available that such "higher" abilities do in fact exist as definite, significant, measurable factors of success in the study or practice of medicine, this test should not be criticized for seeming to neglect them.

ITEM STYLE. While the content of the current forms resembles that of earlier forms quite closely, there are perceptible differences in item style. The current items tend to be shorter, and perhaps simpler and more direct in statement. When an estimate of the total number of words in the test was divided by the number of items, a quotient of approximately 20 words per item was obtained for the current forms. The corresponding figure for earlier forms was 38 words per item. This verbal brevity is reflected in the size of the test booklet, currently 32 pages contrasted with 52 pages earlier. More of the shorter items (372) are included in the current 210-minute test than of the previous longer items (316) in a 215-minute test.

The increase in number of items obviously is not proportional to the reduction in number of words per item. Shortening the items probably reduces the time required for reading but may not reduce correspondingly the time required to choose a best answer. It is also possible that current forms have even more generous time limits than earlier forms. Limited data available to the reviewer tend to support this hypothesis. (Unfortunately, since there is little agreement among test specialists on a common, valid, easily interpretable measure of speededness, a common basis for comparing the speededness of two tests is not often available.)

Briefly stated items are likely to be regarded as more purely factual and, hence, less intellectually respectable than items based on more complex problems. But in spite of the current preference for test items which look nonfactual, there have been few cogent arguments, and there is surprisingly little experimental evidence, to support the view that such items measure something different from, or more useful than, that which factual items measure. The current forms of the test do require the examinee to use the factual knowledge he possesses to solve reasonably significant problems. This reviewer is not inclined to criticize the test on the ground that its items are excessively factual.

METRIC PROPERTIES. Analysis of the scores on Form R of the test, obtained from 2,960 applicants tested in May 1963 yielded these statistics.

Subtest	Items	Mean	SD	Reliability
Verbal	75	47 (47)	13 (9)	.91
Science	86	54 (54)	12 (11)	.89
Quantitative	50	32 (31)	8 (6)	.90
General Information	75	41 (47)	9 (9)	.79

The numbers in parentheses after the subtest means express hypothetical optimum values for the means, defined as scores midway between the maximum possible score and the expected chance score. It is apparent that, except for the general information test, the obtained means are very close to these hypothetical optima.

The numbers in parentheses after the subtest standard deviations express hypothetical minimum values for the standard deviations, defined as one sixth of the range between the maximum possible score and the expected chance score. Again, except for the general information test, the obtained standard deviations all exceed these minima.

Part of the reason for the somewhat high difficulty and the somewhat low reliability (K-R 20) of the general information subtest may be the heterogeneity and specificity of the item content. These characteristics are inherent in a test which asks for specific information over a broad area of knowledge. But it is also probable that more stringent selection of the best items from a larger pool of tryout items would result in a somewhat better test. In Form R of this test, 41 of the 75 items showed reasonably good item statistics (r of .20 or higher, and p between .35 and .80). But, 27 of the 75 items were below .20 in discrimination, and 8 more were either very easy (p above .80) or very difficult (p below .35). If these 34 weak items were replaced by items higher in discrimination and more appropriate in difficulty, this subtest would show somewhat better metric properties. Incidentally, the general information subtest of Form Q yielded a better spread of scores, and more reliable scores, than that of Form R.

Intercorrelations of the subtest scores, ranked from high to low, are as follows: .68, Verbal and General Information; .58, Science and Quantitative; .53, Verbal and Science; .48, Science and General Information; .34, Verbal and Quantitative; .31, Quantitative and General Information. In view of the content of the various subtests and their generally high reliabilities, these values are about what would be expected. None is high enough to cast serious doubt on the usefulness of separate subtest scores. There is no reason to believe that the intercorrelations have been inflated by test form factors or that any changes in the type of items used in the subtests would result in a useful reduction of the intercorrelations.

Since 1951, the reported scores on each subtest have been standard scores with a mean of 500 and a standard deviation of 100, with all standard scores for each new form presumably equivalent in meaning to those issued in 1951. Statistics of the distributions of standard scores actually issued since 1951 show a high degree of consistency. Scores from the May administrations tend to be higher than those from the October administrations, but the score levels from year to year show no appreciable change.

There are good reasons for equating scores on different forms of a test when students who have taken those different forms may be competing for admission to the same medical school class. If the job is done competently and carefully, as it has undoubtedly been done in the case of these tests, the equating is likely to be reasonably precise and dependable, in the short run. But it would be dangerous to claim, and there is really no need to claim, that the standard scores can retain identical meanings perpetually. Successive forms of the *Medical College Admission Test* change from year to year, as they must if they are to improve. The demands of medical schools on students also change, as they also must if they are to improve. So also must premedical education change. Many other changes may affect indirectly the kinds of students the medical schools need and are likely to get. In the face of all these complications, the question, "Did medical schools get better students in 1963 than they got in 1951?" becomes an essentially unanswerable question. About the only thing that can be said with reasonable certainty is that they probably did get, and probably should have gotten, a somewhat different kind of student.

VALIDITY. The tests comprising the *Medical College Admission Test* were selected and designed rationally and on the basis of considerable prior experience with similar tests intended to serve the same or closely related purposes. These tests thus possss the same kind of validity as do the curricula offered by medical schools in their efforts to develop the medical competence of their students. The best claim to validity that this or any similar test can have rests on the informed judgments of the experts selected to design and construct it. Their judgments, of course, are not infallible. If those who make higher scores on the test do not succeed in the study of medicine better than those of their classmates who made lower scores, the judgments may be called into serious question. But the essential validity of these tests is built into them. It is not something on which judgment must be completely suspended until after the test has been given, the students have earned some grades, and correlations between test scores and grades have been computed. Nor is it something simple enough to be adequately reported by a single coefficient of correlation between some composite of the test scores and some single set of imperfect criterion measures.

The content and form of this test battery seem well chosen in view of the purposes it is intended to serve. Various kinds of data from various sources confirm the expectation that students who receive high scores on the test succeed better in medical schools than those who receive lower scores. Some of these data are reported in a preliminary version of an MCAT handbook. Other data have been reported from time to time in various journals and newsletters. The medical school which cannot improve its selection of students by taking scores on these tests (or similar tests) into consideration will be a rare exception.

Some types of aptitude tests, particularly those composed of a few types of novel, unusual tasks, have proved to be subject to seriously invalidating influences of special coaching. But tests like the MCAT, which use more conventional types of test items and which sample more extensively in the fields of knowledge relevant to a broad area of professional study such as medicine, are less likely to be injured by special coaching. Students who repeat the test without special intervening study may expect to gain from 20 to 40 points on the standard score scale. Students who have not been studying science or mathematics just prior to taking the test will undoubtedly benefit from some careful reviewing in these areas. But the gain in score even on these tests is not likely to be spectacular. On the other tests, which measure verbal skills and general information, the amount of material to be reviewed is so large and diffuse that a very considerable effort in review would be likely to yield only a very small gain in score. On the whole, the test appears to be satisfactorily resistant to the invalidating effects of special coaching.

GENERAL EVALUATION. No doubt it is apparent that the reviewer looked for weaknesses in these tests where he thought they might be found, but that he found few of any degree and none that seemed serious. It should also be apparent that he was generously supplied by the publisher with descriptions and statistics on which to base his evaluations.

The *Medical College Admission Test* is a well

designed, expertly constructed test that serves its intended purposes admirably. Those who make the test and those who direct its use have recognized their responsibilities and discharged them competently. Better selections of students for admission to medical schools are being made with the help of this test than could possibly be made without it (or some test closely resembling it). All those who have been responsible for the development of these tests and of the supporting statistical data deserve high praise.

PHILIP H. DuBois, *Professsor of Psychology, Washington University, St. Louis, Missouri.* [Review of Forms Q and R.]

The *Medical College Admission Test,* produced by the Psychological Corporation under contract with the Association of American Medical Colleges, is only for the eyes of bona fide applicants for admission to medical training, who, on an appointed day, are exposed to 286 functional items for exactly 2 hours, 30 minutes. For reasons of security, the test is not copyrighted, but rather controlled by an exact accounting for every copy. Two forms were seen; other forms exist or will be made.

In the present state of the art of psychometrics it is not difficult to produce a test of useful validity for any curriculum involving lectures and assigned readings. Reading comprehension will work; vocabulary (especially vocabulary close to the technical area) will work; a reasonably germane information test will work. Accordingly, it is not surprising that predictive validity against classroom success is considered to be satisfactory for a test having the following content: 75 verbal items (analogies, antonyms, synonyms), 86 science items (biology, chemistry, physics), 50 quantitative items (algebra, arithmetic, geometry), and 75 general information items (humanities, social science).

There is no doubt that the MCAT is competently prepared. The patina is right: precise instructions; carefully phrased item stems; four choices for each item; attractive decoys for the unknowing. The timing has been adjusted so that few candidates fail to finish, and the scoring formula is simply the number right. Such characteristics denote workmanship.

Statistical data rate the five stars awarded only to the best: a scaled score system (with expected mean of 500 and standard deviation

of 100, which relate the present forms to their predecessors); norms in terms of percentages of applicants scoring below selected scaled scores by subtest, by sex, by college status, by undergraduate major, and by region; internal consistency reliabilities within subtests ranging from .79 to .93; consistent subtest intercorrelation patterns from administration to administration. (Correlations of the quantitative score with the verbal and general information scores are in the .30's; correlations of the science subtest are in the .50's; while the verbal and general information scores correlate in the .70's. The overall factor pattern is complex, just as the science subtest is reported to be internally.)

MCAT is the product of group planning and group evaluation. An impressive vector of talent—psychologists and medical educators from the Association of American Medical Colleges, and outside psychological and subject matter consultants—have advised the administrative and technical staff of the contractor in formal and informal conferences. Plans exist for the construction, refinement, and standardization of further alternate forms; for determining relationships with other high level tests; for finding predictive validities in medical education, school by school and course by course, and in the clinical years; and for modifications as premedical and medical curricula are changed and as new measurement approaches are conceived and perfected.

The MCAT handbook, seen by this reviewer in draft form, is intended for the use of members of admission committees of participating medical colleges. It discusses the use of selection devices currently available to medical schools, including the application form, letters of recommendation, interviews, interest and personality schedules, and college grades, all in relation to the MCAT, which is represented as the most objective, but not necessarily the most revealing, source of information about the applicant. The test is stated to be a uniform measure of aptitude and achievement, which makes possible direct comparisons of applicants with widely varying backgrounds. These claims are modest, and are well supported by validity data.

An important social problem is the recruitment and selection of doctors, just as it is of scientists, government administrators, military leaders, industrial executives, and hundreds of other varieties of top level personnel. Those who write selection tests and who sit on admission committees determine an appreciable portion of future variance within an occupation. Of course, with medicine we are dealing with an enlarging cluster of occupations—for which the common prerequisites have been judged by the MCAT makers to center around general intelligence and scientific knowledge.

Measurement techniques and the overall frame of reference being what they are, we can expect little better than the present MCAT. As criteria become better defined, and as selection materials are refined, validities may go up a bit, but no reviewer is likely to suggest changes that will radically improve the instrument.

He can, however, express surprise that the instrument has only three types of symbols: verbal, mathematical, and chemical-physical. In an instrument to select for occupations involving people and their health he had expected more pictorial content and graphical representation and more items reflecting knowledge of and interest in human beings. If doctors are to be physical scientists, the MCAT will pick them. On the other hand, if the bedside manner is worth conserving, the MCAT won't conserve it—that is left to the admission committees.

For a review by Alexander G. Wesman of forms previously published by Educational Testing Service, see 5:932; for a review by Morey J. Wantman, see 4:817.

[1138]

★Medical School Instructor Attitude Inventory. Medical school faculty members; 1961; 6 scores: democratic-autocratic attitude toward teaching, critical-complimentary attitude toward medical schools, liberal-traditional attitude toward medical education, appreciative-depreciative attitude toward medical students, favorable-unfavorable attitude toward full-time teachers, favorable-unfavorable attitude toward part-time teachers; 1 form (120 cards); manual (19 pages); 75¢ per set of cards; $2.50 per 100 sets of record sheets; manual free; $1 per specimen set; postpaid; (75) minutes; Edwin F. Rosinski; the Author. *

REFERENCES
1. ROSINSKI, EDWIN F. "Changing the Attitudes of Medical School Instructors." *J Ed Res* 55:128-31 N '61. *

[1139]

*Veterinary Aptitude Test. Veterinary school applicants; 1951-58; tests administered at centers established by the publisher; 4 scores: reading comprehension, science information, verbal memory, total; IBM; 1 form ('58); 4 parts in 3 booklets: Parts 1 (14 pages), 2 and 3 (11 pages, formerly called *Veterinary Achievement Test*), 4 (6 pages); directions for

administering ['58, 8 pages, mimeographed]; examination fee, $10; fee includes reporting of scores to any 3 schools designated at time of application; $2 per additional report; postpaid; scores not reported to examinees; 135(165) minutes; Loyal C. Payne and William A. Owens; Psychological Corporation. *

REFERENCES
1-3. See 5:957.
4. OWENS, WILLIAM A. "An Aptitude Test for Veterinary Medicine." *J Appl Psychol* 34:295-9 O '50. * (PA 26:594)
5. BROWN, FREDERICK G. "Predicting Success in the Clinical and Preclinical Years of Veterinary Medical School." *J Am Vet Med Assn* 137:428-9 O 1 '60. *
6. RAY, D. K. *A Validation Study of the Revised Veterinary Aptitude Test.* Master's thesis, Purdue University (Lafayette, Ind.), 1961.

[Other Tests]
For tests not listed above, see the following entry in *Tests in Print:* 2012.

MISCELLANEOUS

[1140]

★Card Punch Operator Aptitude Test. Prospective trainees on IBM card punch equipment; 1952-60; formerly called *Card Punch Aptitude Test;* 1 form ('52, 9 pages); revised manual ('60, 7 pages); no data on reliability; "reasonable quantities" and specimen sets free; 12(20) minutes; W. J. McNamara; distributed by International Business Machines Corporation. *

REFERENCES
1. MCNAMARA, W. J., AND HUGHES, J. L. "The Selection of Card Punch Operators." *Personnel Psychol* 8:417-27 w '55. * (PA 31:1835)
2. SHOTT, GERALD L.; ALBRIGHT, LEWIS E.; AND GLENNON, J. R. "Predicting Turnover in an Automated Office Situation." *Personnel Psychol* 16:213-9 au '63. * (PA 38:6714)

[1141]

★Chemical Operators Selection Test, Revised Edition. Male high school students and applicants for positions of chemical operator; 1958-63; 6 scores: physical principles, tables, graphs, judgment, flow sheet, total; IBM; Forms [A] ('59, 21 pages, mimeographed), B ('63, 12 pages); no manual; no data on reliability; norms ['59, 9 pages] for total score only; separate answer sheets must be used; 30¢ per test; 50¢ per 25 answer sheets; 50¢ per scoring stencil; 25¢ per set of norms; postage extra; 60[70] minutes; M. A. Storr, J. H. McPherson, P. A. Maschino, and R. G. Garner (norms and Form B); Dow Chemical Co. *

REFERENCES
1. COATS, J. E.; WITH THE ASSISTANCE OF R. G. GARNER. *A Study of the Nature of the Chemical Operator's Occupation and the Personal Qualities That Contribute to Successful Operator Performance.* Midland, Mich.: Dow Chemical Co., March 1961. Pp. iv, 112. *

[1142]

★The Diebold Personnel Tests. Programmers and systems analysts for automatic data processing and computing installations; 1959; 5 tests; manual (19 pages); no data on reliability; no norms; scoring by the publisher only; $35 per set of tests (including scoring service); postpaid; John Diebold & Associates. *
a) SYMBOLS BLOCK DIAGRAM TEST. 1 form (16 pages); 60(85) minutes.
b) CODE INDEX TEST. 1 form (4 pages); 5(10) minutes.
c) RELATIONS IN NUMBERS TEST. 1 form (10 pages); 60(90) minutes.
d) CODE MATCHING TEST. 1 form (10 pages); 30(50) minutes.

e) WORD SEQUENCE TEST. 1 form (6 pages); 15(25) minutes.

[1143]

*Firefighter Test. Prospective firemen; 1954–61; title on form 20-A is *Test for Firefighter;* forms 20-A ('54, 31 pages plus fold-out answer sheet), 20-B ('57, 26 pages plus fold-out answer sheet), 20-C ('61, 26 pages plus fold-out answer sheet); revised mimeographed manual ('61, 10 pages); general PPA mimeographed directions ['57, 7 pages]; no data on reliability of form 20-C; no data on validity; no norms for form 20-C; 10–49 tests, $1.60 each; $2 per specimen set; postpaid; 105(115) minutes; Public Personnel Association. *

[1144]

*[Firefighting Promotion Tests.] Prospective firemen promotees; 1960–63; IBM; 3 tests; manual ('63, 17 pages); no data on reliability; rental fee: 5 or fewer examinees, $25; specimen set of any one test loaned for fee of $5, which may be applied to rental fee; 210(225) minutes; McCann Associates. *
a) ASSISTANT FIRE CHIEF. 1961–63; 4 scores: firefighting knowledge, fire supervision, fire administration, total; 1 form ('61, 20 pages).
b) CAPTAIN. 1962–63; 5 scores: pre-fire practices, extinguishment practices, overhaul-salvage-rescue, fire supervision, total; 1 form ('62, 22 pages).
c) LIEUTENANT. 1962–63; 4 scores: pre-fire practices, extinguishment practices, fire supervision, total; 1 form ('62, 18 pages).

[1145]

*Fireman Examination. Prospective firemen; 1961–62; 8–9 scores: learning ability (verbal, quantitative, total), fireman aptitude (interest, common sense, mechanical, total), easy verbal learning (form 70 only), total; IBM; forms 62, 70; form 70, which is identical with form 62 except for easy verbal learning subtest, is recommended when a fixed passing score of 70 or 75 per cent is required; 2 parts: booklet 1 ('61, 7 pages, learning ability), booklet 2 ('61, 9–11 pages, fireman aptitude); separate manuals ('61, 17–19 mimeographed pages) for forms 62 and 70; candidate identification sheet ('62, 1 page); distribution restricted to civil service commissions and municipal officials; no data on reliability and validity; norms for subtotal and total scores only; separate IBM scoreable answer sheets must be used; 10–49 tests, $1.50 each; specimen set loaned free; postpaid; 50(60) minutes for booklet 1, 90(100) minutes for booklet 2 of form 62, 120(130) minutes for booklet 2 of form 70; McCann Associates. *

[1146]

*Memory and Observation Tests for Policeman. Prospective policemen; 1962; for use with *Police Examination;* IBM; 1 form; 2 tests; manual (8 pages); candidate identification sheet (1 page); no data on reliability; no description of normative population; distribution restricted to civil service commissions and municipal officials; separate IBM scorable answer sheets must be used; specimen set loaned free; postpaid; McCann Associates. *
a) MEMORY TEST FOR POLICEMAN. 1 form (5 pages); memory sheet (1 page); 1–49 tests, 25¢ each; 10(15) minutes for memory sheet, 10(15) minutes for test booklet.
b) OBSERVATION TEST FOR POLICEMAN. 1 form (6 pages); observation sheet (2 pages); 10–49 tests, 50¢ each; 10(15) minutes for observation sheet, 30(35) minutes for test booklet.

Diebold Personnel Tests

[1147]

*[NCR Test Battery for Prospective Check-Out Cashiers.] Prospective checkstand operators; 1961; 2 tests; battery manual (19 pages); $3 per set of 10 tests of *a* and 10 answer-scoring sheets for *b*; 30¢ per single copy of *a*; 75¢ per single copy of *b*; $1 per manual; postpaid; Ward J. Jenssen, Inc.; National Cash Register Co. *
a) PERSONNEL TEST FOR PROSPECTIVE CHECK-OUT CASHIERS. 3 scores: register tape checking, non-verbal reasoning, register key X-ing; 1 form (18 pages); 20(30) minutes.
b) PERSONAL OPINION BALLOT FOR PROSPECTIVE CHECK-OUT CASHIERS. Attitude and temperament survey; 1 form (9 pages); separate answer-scoring sheets must be used; (30) minutes.

DAVID O. HERMAN, *Staff Psychologist, The Psychological Corporation, New York, New York.*

This battery of four subtests has been designed for a specific employment situation, the selection of checkout cashiers. The first three tests measure perceptual and cognitive abilities in one booklet, called the Personnel Test. The fourth section is a single-purpose, single-score, personality device, entitled the Personal Opinion Ballot.

The manual and the reusable booklet of questions for the personality device are printed on durable stock. The manual is well written and organized, and the directions for administration and scoring are clear. On the other hand, the manual's omissions are unusual by current publishing standards, and make a full evaluation of the battery impossible.

Part 1, Register Tape Checking, of the Personnel Test reproduces pairs of cash register tapes which are to be compared, line by line. Part 2, Non-Verbal Reasoning, contains a variety of abstract and numerical problems of several types, such as series completion, analogy completion, and identifying which of several decimal numbers is the largest. Each item in Part 3, Register Key X-ing, consists of a printed representation of two columns of keys on a cash register, above which a price is written. The examinee marks the keys he would punch in ringing up the given price. These three tests are scored directly in the test booklet by means of strip keys.

The Personal Opinion Ballot consists of nine groups of 14 items each. For each block of items the examinee must check the seven which are more true of him and the seven which are less so. About two thirds of the items are keyed, each one adding from 1 to 5 points to an individual's score. The items' scoring weights were derived empirically by contrasting responses to individual items made by employed cashiers who were rated high in interpersonal relations, with the responses of those rated low in this area. Reading through the keyed items, one gathers that high scorers could be described as self-effacing, noncompetitive, uncomplaining, and inclined to mind their own business. To be sure, one is unlikely to locate managerial talent with this test, and the author's claim that it measures qualities shared by successful checkout cashiers has some face validity. Unfortunately, empirical evidence is not offered.

To score the Personal Opinion Ballot, the semitransparent answer sheet is laid over the key, which is essentially a replica of the working part of the answer sheet with scoring weights written into the answer spaces for the keyed responses. These weights are summed over all of the keyed responses which the examinee has checked to give the raw score. Instead of summing all item scores in one step, the raw score is obtained by summing nine subtotals (one for each item block) which are obtained and recorded separately, presumably to help minimize scoring errors. The scoring could be greatly simplified if item weights of only 0 or 1 were used instead of weights of 0 through 5. The manual mentions no study of the effect which unit weighting has on reliability and validity; since the effect has often been found negligible, the author should investigate this simplified procedure.

Percentile norms are presented for each of the three parts of the Personnel Test, and another table gives short verbal descriptions of people scoring at four levels on the Personal Opinion Ballot. In addition, the manual describes a single weighted composite of raw scores on all four parts, which was derived through multiple regression analysis. This combined score may be conveniently computed using a table printed on the cover of the Personnel Test booklet. The regression coefficients are not presented, nor can they be reconstructed, since the tests' standard deviations are also not given. Furthermore, the regression weights used for the total weighted composite appear not to have been cross validated, and "freezing" them at this point may be premature.

Since each test's influence on the battery composite is unknown, it may be that the three sections of the Personnel Test alone predict job performance nearly as well as they do in combination with the Personal Opinion Ballot. This issue is important because it appears that the item scoring weights for the Ballot were derived using one criterion—ratings of success in store-related interpersonal relations—while the Ballot's regression weight, which is used in computing the total weighted score for the entire battery, was derived using another criterion—a single score which may or may not have reflected interpersonal relations. Briefly, when a test is valid for one purpose, it may not be valid for another.

Although norms are not given for the composite predictor, the manual discusses the issues involved in setting a cutting score, such as personnel needs in relation to labor market conditions, the quality of current employees, and so on. An illustrative expectancy table is presented, which shows the chances of job success for those scoring in various ranges on the battery composite. The source of this table is not specified, however, and its entries, which are per cents, have apparently been rounded, for they are all multiples of 10 per cent.

Retest reliability coefficients for the four part scores of the battery, computed on a sample of 207 checkout cashiers, are said to range from .79 to .86. Surprisingly, the reliability of the recommended composite of these scores is not given.

The manual presents no evidence of the battery's validity, except for the questionable expectancy table mentioned above. One section of the manual does claim validity for each part of the battery; for instance it is said of Register Tape Checking that it "correlates extremely well with both accuracy of work and with speed of performance as a check-out cashier." Similar claims made for the other sections are at least consistent with what one would expect after examining the tests' content, but no supporting statistics whatever are offered to help the reader reach his own conclusions.

SUMMARY. This battery is an interesting example of a collection of tests constructed for a specific task. Its success in fulfilling its purpose cannot be evaluated, since not enough pertinent information is provided by the manual. Although the tests comprising the battery do have apparent face validity, until more detailed information, such as from a local validity study or an adequately revised manual, is available the battery must be considered experimental.

[1148]

★**Police Performance Rating System.** Policemen; 1964; ratings by immediate supervisors on 100 traits yielding 7 factor ratings (quality of work, interpersonal relationship traits, quantity of work, personality traits, character traits, quality of supervision given, quality of administrative work) and an overall rating; individual trait rating sheet (2 pages); summary form (1 page); manual (18 pages); no data on reliability and validity; $2 per 50 rating sheets; $2 per 100 summary forms; 50¢ per manual; specimen set loaned for rental fee of $2; postpaid; "more than an hour"; McCann Associates. *

[1149]

★**Police Promotion Examinations.** Prospective policemen promotees; 1960–63; IBM; 5 tests; manual ('63, 17 pages); no data on reliability; separate answer sheets must be used; rental fee: 5 or fewer examinees, $25; specimen set of any one test loaned for a fee of $5, which may be applied to rental fee; postpaid; 210(235) minutes; McCann Associates. *
a) CHIEF OF POLICE. 1960–63; 6 scores: police supervision, police administration, crime investigation, other police knowledges, law, total; 1 form ('60, 20 pages).
b) CAPTAIN. 1962–63; 6 scores: same as for a; 1 form ('62, 23 pages).
c) DETECTIVE. 1962–63; 4 scores: investigative judgment, crime investigation, law, total; 1 form ('62, 24 pages).
d) LIEUTENANT. 1962–63; 6 scores: patrol, other police knowledges, crime investigation, law, police supervision, total; 1 form ('62, 23 pages).
e) SERGEANT. 1962–63; 6 scores: same as for d; 1 form ('62, 23 pages).

[1150]

★**Policeman Examination.** Prospective policemen; 1960–62; IBM; 8–9 scores: learning ability (verbal, quantitative, total), police aptitude (interest, common sense, public relations, total), easy verbal learning (forms 70 only), total; forms 62A, 62B, 70A, 70B; forms 70A and 70B, which are identical with the corresponding forms 62A and 62B except for the easy verbal learning subtest, are recommended when a fixed passing score of 70 or 75 per cent is required; 2 parts: booklet 1 ('62, 7 pages, learning ability, common to forms 62 and 70), booklet 2 ('62, 11–14 pages, police aptitude); separate manuals ('60, 17–19 pages) for forms 62 and 70; candidate identification sheet ('62, 1 page); distribution restricted to civil service commissions and municipal officials; no data on reliability and validity; norms for subtotal and total scores only; separate IBM scorable answer sheets must be used; 10–49 tests, $1.50 each; specimen set loaned free; postpaid; 50(60) minutes for booklet 1, 90(100) minutes for booklet 2 of forms 62A and 62B, 120(130) minutes for booklet 2 of forms 70A and 70B; McCann Associates. *

[1151]

***Policeman Test.** Policemen and prospective policemen; 1953–60; forms 10-A ('53), 10-B, ('56), 10-C ('60), (30 pages plus fold-out answer sheet); mimeographed manual ['60, 12 pages]; general PPA mimeographed directions ['57, 7 pages]; no data on reliability and validity; 10–49 tests, $1.60 each; $2 per specimen set; postpaid; 95(105) minutes; Public Personnel Association. *

[1152]

★**The Potter-Nash Aptitude Test for Lumber Inspectors and Other General Personnel Who Handle Lumber.** Employees in woodworking industries; 1958; title on test is *The P-N Test;* arithmetic; 1 form ['58, 1 mimeographed page]; mimeographed description ('58, 2 pages); no data on reliability; no description of normative population; $2.50 per 4 tests, postpaid; specimen set not available; (30) minutes; F. T. Potter and N. Nash; N. Nash. *

[1153]

★**Revised Programmer Aptitude Test.** Applicants for programming training on IBM electronic computers; 1955–59; revision of *Programmers Aptitude Test;* IBM; 1 form ('59, 15 pages); manual ('59, 7 pages); "reasonable quantities" and specimen sets free; 60(75) minutes; J. L. Hughes and W. J. McNamara; distributed by International Business Machines Corporation. *

REFERENCES
1. McNamara, W. J., and Hughes, J. L. "A Review of Research on the Selection of Computer Programmers." *Personnel Psychol* 14:39–51 sp '61. * (*PA* 36: 4LD39M)
2. Oliver, Thomas C., and Willis, Warren K. "A Study of the Validity of the Programmer Aptitude Test." *Ed & Psychol Meas* 23:823–5 w '63. *

[1154]

★**Visual Comprehension Test for Detective.** Prospective police detectives; 1963; IBM; 1 form (7 pages); stimulus material presented by 16 mm. film; no manual; no data on reliability and validity; rental fee: 10 or fewer examinees, $50; specimen set (including film) loaned for fee of $35, which may be applied to rental fee; postpaid; (25) minutes for film, 45(50) minutes for test; McCann Associates. *

[Other Tests]

For tests not listed above, see the following entries in *Tests in Print:* 2014–5, 2017, 2019, 2021–2, and 2025–7.

NURSING

[1155]

***Achievement Tests in Nursing.** Nursing school students; 1952–63; tests administered at any time by individual schools; IBM; 12 tests; directions sheet ['57, 1 page]; technical data sheet ('63, 1 page); no charge to schools requiring *Entrance Examination for Schools of Nursing;* 35¢ per test per student for other schools; postpaid; fee includes scoring and reporting service; (40) minutes per test; Psychological Corporation. *
a) ANATOMY AND PHYSIOLOGY. 1953–63; 1 form ('60, 8 pages).
b) CHEMISTRY. 1954–63; 1 form ['54, 13 pages].
c) COMMUNICABLE DISEASES. 1953–63; 1 form ('61, 10 pages).
d) MEDICAL NURSING. 1952–63; 1 form ('61, 12 pages).
e) MICROBIOLOGY. 1952–63; 1 form ('61, 11 pages).
f) NUTRITION AND DIET THERAPY. 1952–63; 1 form ('57, 8 pages).
g) OBSTETRICAL NURSING. 1952–63; 1 form ('61, 12 pages).
h) PEDIATRIC NURSING. 1952–63; 1 form ('63, 11 pages).
i) PHARMACOLOGY. 1952–63; 1 form ('57, 10 pages).
j) PSYCHIATRIC NURSING. 1952–63; 1 form ('57, 11 pages).

k) PSYCHOLOGY AND SOCIOLOGY. 1957–63; 1 form ('57, 8 pages).

l) SURGICAL NURSING. 1952–63; 1 form ('57, 10 pages).

[1156]

★**Entrance Examination for Schools of Nursing.** Nursing school applicants; 1938–63; tests administered at centers established by the publisher; 13 scores: 7 ability scores (verbal, numerical, science, reading comprehension, arithmetic processes, general information, scholastic aptitude total) and 6 personality scores (achievement, orderliness, persistence, congeniality, altruism, respectfulness); IBM; Forms 1 ('62), 2 ('63), (30 pages); part 6, Personal Preference Schedule (formerly printed separately as *The Personal Preference Schedule for Student Nurses*) is an adaptation of *Edwards Personal Preference Schedule* and is common to both forms; manual ['62, 9 pages]; norms ['63, 1 page] for each form; interpretation leaflet ['62, 4 pages]; examination fee: $8 for initial testing, $10 for reexamination; fee includes reporting of scores to the school of nursing through which application for examination was made; $2 per additional report; postpaid; scores not reported to examinees; 155(210) minutes; Psychological Corporation. *

REFERENCES

1. CARRUTH, MARGARET SCRUGGS. *Predictive Value of Nursing School Tests.* Master's thesis, Southern Methodist University (Dallas, Tex.), 1944.
2. SARTAIN, A. Q. "Predicting Success in a School of Nursing." *J Appl Psychol* 30:234–40 Je '46. * (*PA* 20:4350)

[1157]

*NLN Achievement Tests for Basic Professional Nursing.** Students in state-approved schools of professional nursing; 1943–64; tests loaned to schools for their own use; IBM; 1 form; 2 levels; mimeographed manual ('63, 20 pages); directions for administering [no date, 4 pages]; interpretive manual for schools ('64, 45 pages, see *1* below); mimeographed norms ('61–63, 1–2 pages) for each test; examination fees: 75¢ per test where total score reported only, $1 where part scores reported; postpaid one way; [90–120] per test; National League for Nursing, Inc. *

a) [REGULAR ACHIEVEMENT TESTS.] Undergraduates completing courses in the subjects specified; 1943–63; 10 tests.

1) *Anatomy and Physiology.* 1943–55; Form 155 ('55, 19 pages).
2) *Chemistry.* 1943–63; Form 963 ('63, 24 pages).
3) *Microbiology.* 1943–61; Form 761 ('61, 21 pages).
4) *Normal Nutrition.* 1946–62; formerly called *Nutrition and Diet Therapy;* Form 662 ('62, 23 pages).
5) *Basic Pharmacology.* 1944–60; formerly called *Pharmacology and Therapeutics;* Form 960 ('60, 22 pages).
6) *Medical-Surgical Nursing.* 1956–62; 4 scores: medical nursing, surgical nursing, medical-surgical nursing, total; Form 862 ('62, 28 pages).
7) *Public Health Nursing.* 1956–61; for degree programs only; 4 scores: nursing practice and service, public health nursing, science and general information, total; Form 661 ('61, 36 pages).
8) *Obstetric Nursing.* 1945–61; 4 scores: antepartal care, partal and post-partal care of mothers, care of newborn, total; Form 361 ('61, 29 pages).
9) *Nursing of Children.* 1945–61; 4 scores: normal growth and development, pediatric nursing (psychosocial aspects, other aspects), total; Form 461 ('61, 29 pages).

10) *Psychiatric Nursing.* 1945–59; 3 scores: psychiatric nursing practices, facts and principles, total; Form 359 ('59, 34 pages).

b) [COMPREHENSIVE ACHIEVEMENT TESTS.] Seniors about to graduate; 1957–63; 8 tests.

1) *Diet Therapy and Applied Nutrition.* 1962; Form 762 ('62, 27 pages).
2) *Pharmacology in Clinical Nursing (Facts and Principles and Their Application).* 1960; Form 860 (29 pages).
3) *Natural Sciences in Nursing.* 1957; 3 scores: facts and principles (knowledge, application, total); Form 957 (28 pages).
4) *Maternal and Child Health Nursing.* 1958; 3 scores: psychological aspects, non-psychological aspects, total; Form 658 (34 pages).
5) *Disaster Nursing.* 1961; 3 scores: general nursing applied to disasters, facts and principles of disasters and disaster nursing, total; Form 261 (38 pages).
6) *Medical-Surgical Nursing, Part 1.* 1961; 4 scores: orthopedic nursing, neurological-neurosurgical nursing, eye-ear-nose-and-throat nursing, total; Form 262 (31 pages).
7) *Medical-Surgical Nursing, Part 2.* 1962; 3 scores: medical nursing, surgical nursing, total; Form 962 (35 pages).
8) *Communicable Disease Nursing.* 1946–63; 3 scores: prevention and transmission, disease manifestations and other aspects, total; Form 863 ('63, 31 pages).

REFERENCES

1. NATIONAL LEAGUE FOR NURSING. *The NLN Achievement Test, Third Edition.* The Use of Tests in Schools of Nursing Pamphlet No. 2. New York: National League for Nursing, Inc., 1964. Pp. iv, 41. *

[1158]

★**NLN Achievement Tests for Psychiatric Aides.** Hospital psychiatric aides and attendants; 1958–63; tests loaned to hospitals; either or both tests may be used; IBM; 1 form (22 pages); 2 tests; mimeographed manual ('63, 6 pages); guide for interpretation of score reports ('58, 2 pages); fee includes reporting results to hospitals; postpaid one way; (90) minutes per test; National League for Nursing, Inc. *

a) ELEMENTARY PSYCHIATRIC NURSING. Form 858; examination fee, 75¢.

b) BASIC NURSING PROCEDURES AND ELEMENTARY NUTRITION. 3 scores: basic nursing procedures, elementary nutrition, total; Form 958; examination fee, $1.

[1159]

*NLN Graduate Nurse Examination.** Registered professional nurses; 1945–62; formerly called *NLN Graduate Nurse Qualifying Examination;* tests administered throughout the year at centers established by the NLN; IBM; 1 form; 6 tests; manual ('60, 30 pages]; interpretive manual for schools ('62, 29 pages, see *4* below); mimeographed norms ('61, 11 pages); profile ['60, 1 page]; Plan A, all tests: examination fee, $10; Plan B, Nursing Tests and one other: examination fee, $9; Plan C, Nursing Tests only: examination fee, $8; Plan D, *NLN Test of Academic Aptitude* and *NLN Reading Comprehension Test:* examination fee, $4; fees include reporting results to 1 college; $2 per additional report; $1 per interpretive manual; postpaid; scores not reported to examinees; National League for Nursing, Inc. *

a) NLN TEST OF ACADEMIC APTITUDE. Special printing of level 1 (for grades 12–14) of *Cooperative School and College Ability Tests;* 3 scores: quantitative, verbal, total; Form B ('55, 12 pages): 70(85) minutes.

b) NLN READING COMPREHENSION TEST. Special printing of higher level (for grades 13–14) of *Reading Comprehension: Cooperative English Tests,* [*1960 Revision*] ; 2 scores: speed, level; Form B ('60, 8 pages) ; 25(35) minutes.

c) [NURSING TESTS.] Earlier test called *Clinical Test;* 5 scores: total and 4 scores of tests listed below; 4 tests.

   1) *Medical-Surgical Nursing Section.* Form 360 ('60, 31 pages) ; 105(115) minutes.
   2) *Psychiatric Nursing Section.* Form 360 ('60, 21 pages) ; 60(70) minutes.
   3) *Maternal and Child Nursing Section.* Form 360 ('60, 27 pages) ; 75(85) minutes.
   4) *Science Section (Selected Areas of the Natural Sciences and Applications).* Form 360 ('60, 17 pages) ; 60(70) minutes.

REFERENCES

1. "The NLN Graduate Nurse Qualifying Examination." *Nursing Res* 3:21–5 Jl '54. *
2. NATIONAL LEAGUE FOR NURSING. *The NLN Graduate Nurse Qualifying Examination.* The Use of Tests in Schools of Nursing Pamphlet No. 3. New York: National League for Nursing, Inc., 1954. Pp. v, 39. *
3. CLELAND, VIRGINIA. "A Critical Inquiry Into the Use of the Graduate Nurse Qualifying Examination Clinical Test by One Institution." *Nursing Res* 8:202–6 f '59. *
4. NATIONAL LEAGUE FOR NURSING. *The NLN Graduate Nurse Examination, Second Edition.* The Use of Tests in Schools of Nursing Pamphlet No. 3. New York: the League Inc., 1962. Pp. iii, 27. *

[1160]

*NLN Practical Nurse Achievement Tests. Students in approved schools of practical nursing; 1950–63; IBM; tests loaned to approved schools of practical nursing for their use; 1 form ('57) ; 2 tests; mimeographed manual ('63, 10 pages) for these tests and test 1161; directions for administering ['63, 4 pages] ; examination fee, $1 for each test; postpaid one way; fees include reporting results to schools; National League for Nursing, Inc. *

a) PRACTICAL NURSE BASIC ACHIEVEMENT TEST. 1957–63 ; 4 scores: body structure and function, basic nursing procedures, nutrition and diet therapy, total; Form 857 (28 pages) ; mimeographed norms ('63, 2 pages) ; (90) minutes.

b) PRACTICAL NURSE ACHIEVEMENT TEST. 1950–63 ; 3 scores: medical-surgical, maternal-child, total; Form 856 (29 pages) ; mimeographed norms ('63, 1 page) ; (120) minutes.

[1161]

*NLN Pre-Admission and Classification Examination. Practical nursing school entrants; 1950–63; tests administered throughout the year at centers established by the NLN; 8 scores: total and 7 scores listed below; IBM; 1 form ('58) ; 2 tests; mimeographed manual ('63, 10 pages) for this test and test 1160; norms ('63, 5 pages) ; profile ['58, 1 page] ; examination fee, $6; fee includes reporting results to 1 school of nursing; $2 per additional report; postpaid; scores not reported to examinees; National League for Nursing, Inc. *

a) GENERAL INFORMATION AND JUDGMENT TEST. 4 scores: science and health, general information, arithmetic, total; Form 458 (24 pages) ; 90(95) minutes.

b) VOCABULARY AND READING TEST. 3 scores: vocabulary, reading, total; Form 458 (25 pages) ; 105(115) minutes.

REFERENCES

1. HESLIN, PHYLIS, AND KATZELL, MILDRED. "A Validation Study of the NLN Pre-Admission and Classification Examination." *Nursing Res* 11:26–9 w '62. *

[1162]

*NLN Pre-Nursing and Guidance Examination. Applicants for admission to state-approved schools of professional nursing; 1941–63; tests administered throughout the year at centers established by the NLN; IBM; 1 form; 5 tests; manual ['61, 27 pages] ; interpretive manual for schools ('61, see 7 below); report form ['63, 2 pages] ; mimeographed norms ('63, 11 pages) ; examination fee, $10; fee includes reporting results to 1 school of nursing; $2 per additional report; $1.25 per interpretive manual; postpaid; scores not reported to examinees; 210(300) minutes in 2 sessions; National League for Nursing, Inc. *

a) NLN TEST OF ACADEMIC APTITUDE. Special printing of level 1 (for grades 12–14) of *Cooperative School and College Ability Tests;* 3 scores: quantitative, verbal, total; Form B ('55, 12 pages) ; 70(85) minutes.

b) NLN READING COMPREHENSION TEST. Special printing of higher level (for grades 13–14) of *Reading Comprehension: Cooperative English Test,* [*1960 Revision*] ; 2 scores: speed, level; Form B ('60, 8 pages) ; 25(35) minutes.

c) NLN MATHEMATICS TEST. Abbreviated edition of an earlier form of *Cooperative Mathematics Test for Grades 7, 8, and 9;* Form B ('40, 7 pages) ; 35(40) minutes.

d) NLN NATURAL SCIENCE ACHIEVEMENT TEST. Special printing of *Cooperative General Achievement Tests: Test 2, Natural Science;* Form YZ ('51, 7 pages) ; 40(50) minutes.

e) NLN SOCIAL STUDIES ACHIEVEMENT TEST. Special printing of *Cooperative General Achievement Tests: Test 1, Social Studies;* Form YZ ('55, 8 pages) ; 40(50) minutes.

REFERENCES

1. SHAYCOFT, MARION F. "A Validation Study of the Pre-Nursing and Guidance Test Battery." *Am J Nursing* 51:201–5 Mr '51. *
2. BRUTON, FLORRIE ERB. "Some Implications of National Pre-Nursing Tests for the Selection of Students for Alabama Hospital Schools of Nursing." *Nursing Res* 3:60–73 O '54. *
3. NATIONAL LEAGUE FOR NURSING. *The NLN Pre-Nursing and Guidance Examination, Second Edition.* The Use of Tests in Schools of Nursing Pamphlet No. 1. New York: National League for Nursing, Inc., 1957. Pp. v, 42. *
4. MEYER, BURTON. "An Analysis of the Results of Pre-Nursing and Guidance, Achievement, and State Board Test Pool Examinations." *Nursing Outlook* 7:538–41 S '59. *
5. FERGUSON, RUTH H. *Predictive Study of Academic Success in the Freshman Term at a Selected Three-Year Hospital School of Nursing From Scores on the National Test for Nursing, Pre-Nursing and Guidance Test Battery.* Master's thesis, De Paul University (Chicago, Ill.), 1960.
6. HEYWARD, ROSALIND W. *Study of the Results of the National League for Nursing Pre-Nursing and Guidance Test in Relation to Performance in College and on the National State Board Test Pool Examination for a Selected Group of Students.* Master's thesis, Teachers College, Columbia University (New York, N.Y.), 1960.
7. NATIONAL LEAGUE FOR NURSING. *The NLN Pre-Nursing and Guidance Examination, Third Edition.* The Use of Tests in Schools of Nursing Pamphlet No. 1. New York: the League, Inc., 1961. Pp. v, 34. *
8. ROWE, HAROLD R. "Requirements for Admission to Basic Programs of Professional Nursing." *Personnel & Guid J* 42: 155–9 O '63. *

[1163]

★PSB-Entrance Examination for Schools of Practical Nursing. Applicants for admission to practical nursing schools; 1961; test booklet title is *PSB-Aptitude for Practical Nursing Examination;* 5 scores: general mental ability, spelling, natural sciences, judgment in practical nursing situations, personal adjustment index; IBM; 1 form (22 pages) ; manual (29 pages) ; separate answer sheets must be used; $1 per test; $1 per manual (free with 25 tests) ; $1 per set of IBM answer sheets including scoring service; $1.50 per specimen set; postage extra;

180(190) minutes; Anna S. Evans, [George A. W. Stouffer, Jr.], and the Psychological Services Bureau of Indiana, Pa.; Educators'-Employers' Tests & Services Associates. *

[Other Tests]

For tests not listed above, see the following entries in *Tests in Print*: 2029 and 2031–2.

RESEARCH

[1164]

★**Research Personnel Review Form.** Research and engineering and scientific firms; 1959-60; for supervisor's evaluation of research personnel in preparation for a performance review interview; 1 form ('59, 6 pages); manual ('60, 13 pages); $4.95 per 20 forms; $1 per manual; $1.50 per specimen set; postage extra; tabulating service available; Morris I. Stein; [Morris I. Stein & Associates, Inc.]. *

[1165]

★**Supervisor's Evaluation of Research Personnel.** Research personnel; 1960; ratings by supervisors; 1 form (2 pages); manual (9 pages); $2.25 per 20 test-answer sheets; 25¢ per scoring stencil; 50¢ per manual; $1 per specimen set; postage extra; (15) minutes; William D. Buel; Science Research Associates, Inc. *

REFERENCES

1. BUEL, W. D. "Stability of Preference Indices in Forced-Choice Rating Scale Items." *Eng & Ind Psychol* 1:134-7 W '59. * (*PA* 35:4046)
2. BUEL, WILLIAM D. "The Validity of Behavioral Rating Scale Items for the Assessment of Individual Creativity." *J Appl Psychol* 44:407-12 D '60. * (*PA* 35:3403)
3. BUEL, WILLIAM D., AND BACHNER, VIRGINIA M. "The Assessment of Creativity in a Research Setting." *J Appl Psychol* 45:353-8 D '61. * (*PA* 37:1211)

JOHN W. FRENCH, *Professor of Psychology, and College Examiner, New College, Sarasota, Florida.*

The *Supervisor's Evaluation of Research Personnel* (SERP) calls for the ranking of four statements in each of 13 tetrads of statements according to their descriptiveness of the ratee. These forced-choice items, according to the manual, were constructed by matching two statements "on high preference value and two [statements] on low preference value, one statement in each pair having significant discriminative ability and the other having little or none." This is the correct way to develop forced-choice items. The manual notes that the statements were also matched on standard deviation of preferences and on length. This is commendable. The idea behind the construction of SERP is good. However, this reviewer feels that more varied items would be desirable and some more convincing evidence of validity is required before the scale should be recommended for operational use. It seems desirable also that the manual not describe SERP as "a means of *objectively* comparing the research

competence of staff members." This is a *subjective* instrument.

The 13-item scale requires about 15 minutes to complete. While this brevity has obvious administrative advantages, it is asking too much to expect 13 items to cover all important qualities in a research worker in any one field, much less the qualities that should be considered in evaluating research personnel in general, as this instrument claims to do. A few seemingly important characteristics of the researcher not covered by SERP are ability to write clearly, ability to make oral presentations of research results, and ingenuity in initiating ideas for research. This limitation in the scope of research activities covered by SERP occurs despite development activities which included the listing of 900 descriptive statements made by 20 research supervisors and the selection of statements from among these by means of cluster analysis including McQuitty's linkage analysis. Since the research supervisors were all on the staff of a single oil company, it seems likely that some kinds of research activities were insufficiently represented.

More data should be collected to establish validity, reliability, and norming statistics for the instrument. Until that is done, some of the statements made in the manual do not seem to be fully justified. Odd-even reliabilities, corrected by the Spearman-Brown formula, of .92 and .95 represent only that part of the measurement error resulting from item sampling. Even this source of error is not fully represented, because "halo" in the ratings made by a single rater tends to elevate reliability coefficients spuriously. A different and still greater source of error that should be considered when presenting evidence of reliability is the disagreement among raters. The manual quite rightly recommends that a research worker be rated by more than one rater whenever possible.

The validity data are limited to two rather small groups. Correlations between SERP and objective criteria concerned with patents are only in the low .20's. However, with some justification, the manual questions whether patents define a good criterion. Other validity coefficients given in the manual range from .61 to .72. These coefficients use other ratings as criteria. Unfortunately, the other ratings may not have any more "true" validity than the instrument itself. In addition, the manual does not make it clear whether the criterion ratings and SERP ratings were made by different people. Some further suspicion about what is actually being measured is aroused by the fact that the highest validity coefficient, .72, was found with the criterion "rating of mental qualifications," evidently a rating of general intelligence having no particular connection with research ability. Correlations between SERP and some personality and interest measures are presented in the manual and are found to be desirably low. It would be helpful, however, to see the correlation between SERP and scores on some general intelligence or aptitude tests.

J Counsel Psychol 10:100–1 sp '63. Laurence Siegel. This device was not really intended for counseling purposes. It was developed for those industrial applications wherein it is desirable to obtain objectively scored assessments of research competence. The *Supervisor's Evaluation of Research Personnel* (SERP) is briefly described here because of its possible implications for counseling graduate students and assessing their research competence. SERP is a forced-choice inventory completed by a supervisor (or faculty member) who is describing the ratee's research behavior. It contains thirteen tetrads and can be completed within 10 or 15 minutes. * Correlations between SERP and several personality, interest and values inventories tend not to be statistically significant. Also, SERP scores do not correlate either with age or length of service. SERP norms are exceedingly weak. Percentile conversions are presented for a total of only 149 cases. The failure to call attention to this deficiency in the Manual is extremely unfortunate. The inventory could use considerably more work before it can confidently be used in industry for the suggested applications of personnel evaluation and selection. However, the idea is an intriguing one. Without making a brief for its use as an operational tool, either in or out of industry, it should be interesting to use SERP on a *research* basis for attempting to improve our assessments of graduate students.

[1166]

★**Surveys of Research Administration and Environment.** Research and engineering and scientific firms; 1959–60; 2 forms for gathering information and opinions on the company and its research activities; manual ('60, 21 pages); no data on reliability and validity; no description of normative population;

$1.50 per manual; $3 per specimen set; postage extra; tabulating service available; Morris I. Stein; [Morris I. Stein & Associates, Inc.].
a) STEIN SURVEY FOR ADMINISTRATORS. Supervisors and administrators; also part of *Technical Personnel Recruiting Inventory;* 1 form ('59, 12 pages); $9 per 20 forms; (30–40) minutes.
b) STEIN RESEARCH ENVIRONMENT SURVEY. Research and technical personnel; 1 form ('59, 12 pages); $9 per 20 forms; (90–120) minutes.

[1167]

★**Technical Personnel Recruiting Inventory.** Research and engineering and scientific firms; 1959–60; 3 parts; manual ('60, 20 pages); no data on reliability and validity; no norms; $1.50 per manual; $2.50 per specimen set; postage extra; (30–60) minutes per form; tabulating service available; Morris I. Stein; [Morris I. Stein & Associates, Inc.]. *
a) INDIVIDUAL QUALIFICATION FORM. Supervisors; description of an available research position; 1 form ('59, 4 pages); $2.75 per 20 forms.
b) PERSONAL DATA FORM FOR SCIENTIFIC, ENGINEERING, AND TECHNICAL PERSONNEL. Job applicants; 1 form ('59, 6 pages); $9 per 20 forms.
c) STEIN SURVEY FOR ADMINISTRATORS. Administrators; description of company's research environment; also part of *Surveys of Research Administration and Environment;* 1 form ('59, 12 pages); $9 per 20 forms.

SELLING

[1168]

*Aptitude Index Selection Procedure.** Prospective male ordinary life insurance agents; 1938–60; 2 tests; manual ['60, 4 pages]; recruiting diagnosis profile ['59, 2 pages] for maintaining records on candidates tested; separate scoring keys for United States and Canada; distribution restricted to home offices of member life insurance companies; details may be obtained from publisher; Life Insurance Agency Management Association. *
a) BIOGRAPHICAL PROFILE. 1960; preliminary screening test scored locally; 1 form ('60, 2 pages, also serves as mailing envelope for returning answer booklet for *b* for scoring); [5] minutes.
b) APTITUDE INDEX. 1938–60; 1 score combining an evaluation of life insurance information, personal background, interests, and attitudes; Form 7 ('60, 25 pages); scored by the publisher only; separate answer booklets ('60, 15 pages including information test, answer cards for remaining tests, and score report cards) must be used; French edition available; (60–90) minutes.

REFERENCES

1–5. See 40:1646.
6–19. See 4:825.
20. See 5:913.
21. FERGUSON, LEONARD W. "Ability, Interest, and Aptitude." *J Appl Psychol* 44:126–31 Ap '60. * (*PA* 35:4048)

For reviews by Donald G. Paterson and Albert S. Thompson of an earlier form of b, *see 4:825.*

[1169]

*Aptitudes Associates Test of Sales Aptitude: A Test for Measuring Knowledge of Basic Principles of Selling.** Applicants for sales positions; 1947–60; for a revision, see 1178; Form A ('47, 4 pages); revised manual ('60, 8 pages, identical with 1958 manual except for format, modification in some normative tables, and extension of bibliography); $5 per 25 tests; 25¢ per key; 75¢ per manual; $1 per specimen set; cash orders postpaid; (20–30) minutes; Martin M. Bruce; the Author. *

REFERENCES

1. BRUCE, MARTIN M. "Validity Information Exchange, No. 7-022: D.O.T. Code 1-86.11, Salesman, Commercial Equipment and Supplies." *Personnel Psychol* 7:157 sp '54. *
2. UNITED STATES EMPLOYMENT SERVICE. "Validity Information Exchange, No. 7-021: D.O.T. Code 1-57.30, Underwriter." *Personnel Psychol* 7:156 sp '54. *
3. GRAY, EDWARD J., AND ROSEN, JOHN C. "Validity Information Exchange, No. 9-7: D.O.T. Code 1-80.02, Salesman." *Personnel Psychol* 9:112 sp '56. *
4. HARLESS, BYRON B., AND BRUCE, MARTIN M. "Normative Data Information Exchange, No. 10-8." *Personnel Psychol* 10:104 sp '57. *
5. SPEER, GEORGE S. "Validity Information Exchange, No. 10-16: D.O.T. Code 1-86.01, Salesman, Wholesale (Steel Warehouse)." *Personnel Psychol* 10:206 su '57. *
6. *Normative Information: Manager and Executive Testing.* New York: Richardson, Bellows, Henry & Co., Inc., May 1963. Pp. 45. *

For reviews by Milton E. Hahn and Donald G. Paterson, see 4:824.

[1170]

★**Combination Inventory.** Prospective debit life insurance salesmen; 1954–59; 5 parts: arithmetic, mental alertness (items in parts 1 and 2 selected from tests developed by the Life Office Management Association), vocational interest (items selected from *Strong Vocational Interest Blank for Men, Revised*), personality (social desirability), personal history (economic maturity, same for both forms); Forms 1A, 1B, ('54, 14 pages); no manual; mimeographed scoring rules ['54, 5 pages] for each form; mimeographed scoring standards ('59, 7 pages) for personal history section; no data on reliability; separate answer booklets (which also contain personal history section) must be used; distribution restricted to home offices of member life insurance companies; details may be obtained from publisher; [90–120] minutes; Life Insurance Agency Management Association. *

REFERENCES

1. FERGUSON, LEONARD W. "Ability, Interest, and Aptitude." *J Appl Psychol* 44:126–31 Ap '60. * (PA 35:4048)

[1171]

★**The Dealer Inventory.** Manufacturers' distributors; 1956–58; attitudes and opinions about company represented; 11 scores: company relations, administrative services, company products, product services, sales promotion, distribution system, pricing policies, credit policies, administrative ability of company representative, technical competence of the company representative, reactions to survey; 1 form ('56, 8 pages); manual of general information ('56, 61 pages); program description manual ('56, 18 pages); survey analyzer ('56, 51 pages); profile ('58, 1 page); no data on reliability; distribution restricted to companies using the publisher's survey services; price information available from publisher; specimen set not available; [30–40] minutes; Richard Renck, George Y. Ogawa, David N. Larson, and Robert K. Burns; Industrial Relations Center. *

[1172]

★**The Evaluation Record.** Prospective life insurance agency managers; 1947–63; combination of evaluation procedures yielding a composite score; 3 parts; manual ('63, 4 pages); instructions-record folder ('55); revised scoring kit ('62, c1947); profile ('55, 1 page); rating form ('55, 1 page); no data on relia-

bility; distribution restricted to home offices of member life insurance companies; details may be obtained from publisher; Life Insurance Agency Management Association. *

a) EXPERIENCE FORM. Completed by candidates; Form A ('58, 2 pages); [30] minutes.

b) STRONG VOCATIONAL INTEREST BLANK FOR MEN, REVISED. See 1070; scored for production manager only; special answer sheets must be used; (30) minutes.

c) HOME OFFICE RATING CHART. Ratings of personal qualities by 1–3 supervisors; Form B ('55, 2 pages); [10] minutes.

[1173]

Hanes Sales Selection Inventory, Revised Edition. Insurance and printing salesmen; 1954–55; 3 scores: verbal, personality, drive; 1 form ('55, 4 pages); manual ('55, 2 pages); no data on reliability and validity of drive score; $3 per 25 tests; $1 per specimen set (must be purchased to obtain manual); cash orders postpaid; (30–40) minutes; Bernard Hanes; Psychometric Affiliates. *

WILLIAM E. KENDALL, *Director, Personnel and Marketing Research Division, The Psychological Corporation, New York, New York.*

The *Hanes Sales Selection Inventory* is described as "designed to help select potentially successful insurance, printing and closely allied salesmen from the general run of applicants for such positions." Having made this statement, there is no further mention of printing and closely allied salesmen. The inventory is said to have been "constructed by an item analysis aimed at maximizing the differences between applicants and successful salesmen. The present edition is based upon a two-year follow up of successful salesmen." Since there is no indication of the criteria employed to measure success in sales positions, the reviewer has no basis for judging the degree to which the inventory does succeed in separating successful salesmen from among the applicants.

Part 1 of the inventory is a personal history form which resembles many application blanks commonly used in business. The responses to 10 of the items are scored as either favorable or unfavorable. The manual states, "In general, the author has found that three unfavorable responses indicate a poor risk regardless of other scores." In the light of the author's earlier statement about Part 1 that "what the man did in the past is one indication of his future performance," it is of interest to examine the seven responses which are rated as unfavorable. These are: age between 20 and 25; not now employed; employed on present job less than one year; started but did not finish college; single; no children; wife works. Of these responses only "started but did not finish college" appears to describe past behavior which may be an indication of future performance and even this response may require qualification. The remaining unfavorable responses are dependent to a significant degree on the age of the respondent, a fact which may account for their appearance in the course of doing an item analysis which failed to consider item interrelationships. Eight responses, e.g., married, member of two or more organizations, are considered favorable to the applicant, but there is no suggested use for this information.

Part 2 is described as "an excellent short yardstick of verbal knowledge." It consists of 18 items of which 3 are verbal analogies, 2 are simple verbal arithmetic items, and 13 require the respondent to pick a synonym for the stimulus word. Correct responses are given weights of 3, 2, or 1 so that a score of 33 is possible on this part of the inventory. Scores on Part 2 are converted into percentile ranks.

Norms are given for insurance salesmen ($n = 154$) and steel salesmen ($n = 30$). In a paragraph headed "Inventory Validity and Reliability" it is stated that Part 2 "was found to correlate .39 (Rho) with total PMA Intelligence on 30 college graduates applying for sales positions with a steel company." In the absence of evidence to the contrary, it seems reasonable to assume that the 30 college graduates referred to are the same 30 individuals whose scores appear in the Part 2 norm table.

The author states that "The best minimum qualifying score from the point of view of maximum selection of successful applicants and maximum rejection of poor bets" is the 55th percentile for Part 2. "Approximately 71 percent of the potentially successful salesmen will score 55 or better on Part 2." Split-half reliability for Part 2 is given as .84. No other data are presented.

Part 3, according to the manual, "provides some of the important personality variables. Successful salesmen are more similar in their personality than men in general and unsuccessful salesmen. The Drive Score (Items 25 through 30) of Part III is a good predictor of sales success—and its norms in Table 1 are based on 140 salesmen—seventy successful and seventy failures—within a year period."

Part 3 consists of 37 statements to which the respondent checks "yes" or "no" according to whether the statement is most often true or not. Only the "yes" answers are scored.

Responses are differentially weighted; e.g., "Usually become a leader in social activities" is +3, "Most executives dodge the tough work" is +2, "Stop and think of consequences before acting" is −2, "Think out complicated problems" is −3, and "Depressed when criticized" is −4. The user is left to infer what the "important personality variables" are that are being measured in Part 3.

The weighting scheme produces negative scores in the normative groups for Part 3 (195 insurance and 31 steel salesmen) with a score of 0 being at the 95th percentile. A percentile rank of 65 is suggested as a minimum qualifying score. Approximately 65 per cent of the potentially successful salesmen will be at or above the 65th percentile on Part 3. The split-half reliability of Part 3 is reported to be .89.

The six items which constitute the Drive Score are so weighted that the range of possible scores is from −1 to +9. Norms based on 140 cases are given for this score. There is no comment on the Drive Score other than the statement that it "detects those few individuals in a hundred who receive a good score on Part 3 because they answer only a few questions in the affirmative."

In a personal communication the author reports that while he is using the inventory continuously, he has not had the occasion to compute other normative data.

Both the inventory and the manual are carelessly prepared. Copies of the forms appear to have been set in several type faces and printed, then after additional data had been gathered, to have been overprinted and rerun by offset. Thus, the appearance is not to the credit of either the author or the publisher.

In summary, whatever the basis on which one chooses tests, be it attractiveness of the layout, face validity of the items, or completeness of reporting of cross-validation studies, the prospective user will not find what he wants when he examines this product.

ALBERT K. KURTZ, *Fulbright Lecturer, Ein Shams University, Cairo, United Arab Republic.*

This sloppy test may have some validity and then again it may not. The entire validity information for Part 1 is presented in one sentence: "In general, the author has found that three unfavorable responses indicate a poor risk regardless of other scores." A 2 by 2 table gives the percentage of high and of low scores for "general applicants" and for "successful salesmen" on each of the other two parts. The sample sizes are given as 154 and 195, but on the other side of the single sheet manual, norms are given that may refer to 154 insurance salesmen for Part 2 and 195 such for Part 3. Where, or if, the "general applicants" come in is a minor puzzle that may not matter since the point that should be at issue is not the comparison referred to but rather whether the test will differentiate *at the time of hiring* between "successful salesmen" and *unsuccessful salesmen*. No information bearing in any way on either of these italicized requirements is supplied.

The two tables do show some differences which are not overly large (tetrachoric *r* cannot be computed because neither the cell frequencies nor the cell proportions are available), but it is neither surprising nor unusual that a test can differentiate between successful salesmen and general applicants. To be useful, the test must differentiate *in advance* between those who will later become successful and those who will later become *unsuccessful*. Such tests are not impossible to make; the reviewer was coauthor of one (4:825) for differentiating between potentially successful and unsuccessful life insurance salesmen as long ago as 1938.

In teaching testing courses, the reviewer has never placed much emphasis on face validity. Perhaps this was wrong. Maybe I should at least have mentioned that when changes are made, neither the test nor the manual should look so much like the patched up jobs they actually are. This test appears to have been set in type and used for some time, then a typist who didn't bother to clean the type (especially the letter a) added some material so that boxes (crudely drawn) could be inserted for answers to some of the items, and this altered test was reproduced by a photographic process.

The manual appears to have been patched up by the same typist, who included two uncorrected strikeovers. The directions for scoring are strewn around under "Administration and Scoring," "Scoring Interpretation," and "Mechanics of Scoring." One of these places rightly says to record the sectional scores, but it doesn't say where—possibly because there is no place on the test to record them. There is

what appears to be a percentile grid on page 1 of the test, but it is not referred to anywhere.

The key for Part 1 counts age 20–25 as unfavorable, but the typed limits on the test are 18–25. This key also counts less than 1 year on the job as unfavorable, but the typed boxes correspond to 1, 2, 3, and 4 or more, with no way for the applicant to indicate anything less than 1 year.

In describing Part 2, the manual says, "Having a good vocabulary and being able to solve some simple problems is vital for success." If one believes this, will he be happy with only two mathematics problems? Some of the other items have dubious answers. How, for instance, would you answer item 5? It reads, "Sun is to Moon as Light bulb is to (a) lamp, (b) mirror, (c) light, (d) glass." The key gives (b), but the relation "is brighter than" seems fairly reasonable and yields a different answer.

Norms are given for "Insurance" and "Steel." Whether "Insurance" means successful insurance salesmen, applicants, or both is not clear. "Steel" probably means 30 college graduates applying for sales positions with a steel company.

In conclusion, this test has a poor appearance, appears to have been prepared carelessly, and has not yet been shown to be valid for picking successful rather than unsuccessful men in any selling field.

[1174]

Information Index. Life insurance agents; 1951–63; life insurance information; Forms A ('57), B ('61), (15 pages); revised manual ('63, 6 pages); directions sheet ['57, 2 pages]; separate answer sheets must be used; distribution restricted to home offices of member life insurance companies; details may be obtained from publisher; postage extra; Canadian edition available; 60(80) minutes; Life Insurance Agency Management Association. *

REFERENCES

1–3. See 5:927.
4. BAIER, DONALD E., AND DUGAN, ROBERT D. "Normative Data Information Exchange, Nos. 11-3." *Personnel Psychol* 9:277–82 su '56. *

[1175]

★*Interviewer's Impressions—Sales Applicants.* Adults; 1956; ratings following an interview; 6 scores: persuasiveness, industriousness, confidence, knowledge, social development, total; 1 form ['56, 1 page]; instructions-norms ['56, 2 pages]; no data on reliability; $4 per 10 forms, cash orders postpaid; specimen set not available; (5) minutes; [Eugene J. Benge]; [Management Service Co.]. *

[1176]

Personnel Institute Hiring Kit. Applicants for sales positions; 1954–62; manual ('57, 24 pages, same as manual copyrighted in 1956 except for one minor change); no data on reliability and validity; $15 per kit of manual and 10 copies each of *a–d*; postage extra; scoring service available: $15 per applicant when *e* is used, $45 per applicant when *f* is used; fee includes scoring, interpretation, and report of results; Personnel Institute, Inc. *

a) PRELIMINARY SCREENING INTERVIEW. 1 form ('57, 1 page); $1.50 per 10 copies; (10) minutes.

b) PERSONAL HISTORY INVENTORY. 1 form ('62, 6 pages, same forms also copyrighted in 1957); $2.50 per 10 copies; (30–45) minutes.

c) DIAGNOSTIC INTERVIEWER'S GUIDE. 1 form ('56, 4 pages); $3.50 per 10 copies; (30) minutes.

d) PERSONAL OR TELEPHONE WORK REFERENCE INVESTIGATION. Formerly called *Work Reference Investigation;* 1 form ('59, 1 page); $1.50 per 10 copies; (10) minutes.

e) SELECTOR TEST BATTERY. Applicants for routine selling jobs; 1955–57; directions sheet ('56, 2 pages); scoring by publisher only; (85–100) minutes.

　1) *EM-AY Inventory.* Reprint of *Otis Employment Tests,* Test 2, Form A ('22), see 4:310; mental alertness; 1 form ('22, 4 pages); 30(35) minutes.

　2) *ESS-AY Inventory.* Sales aptitude; 1 form ('57, 11 pages, same as test copyrighted in 1955); (40–45) minutes.

　3) *The Personality Inventory.* See 157; 4 scores: extroversion, dominance, self-confidence, social dependence; 1 form ('35, 4 pages); (15–20) minutes.

f) COMPREHENSIVE TEST BATTERY. Applicants for complex selling jobs; 1955–62; directions sheet ('57, 2 pages); profile ('62, 2 pages); scoring by publisher only; (195–220) minutes.

　1) Same as *e*(1) above.

　2) Same as *e*(2) above.

　3) Same as *e*(3) above.

　4) *Vocabulary Inventory.* 1 form ('56, 4 pages, same as test copyrighted in 1954); (30) minutes.

　5) *ESS-EYE Inventory.* Reprint of the SP (Special) Edition of the *Social Intelligence Test: George Washington University Series, Revised Form* ('47), see 176; 3 scores: social judgment, social observation, total; no norms for part scores; 1 form ('62, 8 pages); (40) minutes.

　6) *B-B-ESS Inventory.* Business skills; 8 scores: comparing, computation, reading, spelling, vocabulary, arithmetical reasoning, English, total; no norms for part scores; 1 form ('56, 8 pages, same as test copyrighted in 1954); 40(50) minutes.

REFERENCES

1. BRUCE, MARTIN M. "The Prediction of Effectiveness as a Factory Foreman." *Psychol Monogr* 67(12):1–17 '53. * (*PA* 28:5019)

2. BRUCE, MARTIN M. "Validity Information Exchange, No. 7-004: D.O.T. Code 0-97.61, Manager, Sales." *Personnel Psychol* 7:128–9 sp '54. *

3. BRUCE, MARTIN M. "Validity Information Exchange, No. 7-076: D.O.T. Code 5-91.101, Foreman II." *Personnel Psychol* 7:418–9 au '54. *

[1177]

★**SRA Sales Attitudes Check List.** Applicants for sales positions; 1960; extension of *Sales Personnel Description Form;* 1 form (4 pages); preliminary manual (11 pages); no data on reliability; $4.95 per 20 tests; 25¢ per manual; 50¢ per specimen set; postage extra; (10–15) minutes; Erwin K. Taylor and the Personnel Research & Development Corporation; Science Research Associates, Inc. *

JOHN P. FOLEY, JR., *President, J. P. Foley and Company, Inc., New York, New York.*

A modification of the original *Sales Personnel Description Form,* which was designed to be used by sales supervisors or managers in rating their sales personnel, the present form is a self-description checklist intended to aid in salesman selection. The form consists of 31 forced-choice items, each comprising a tetrad of self-descriptive statements. From each set of four statements the examinee is to select the one statement he believes is most descriptive of his own behavior, as well as the one statement least descriptive. The test, given without time limit, is said to require from 5 to 15 minutes for completion. It can be administered individually or in groups. Utilizing a carbon insert sheet, the form is self-scoring.

Although it is recognized that sales positions vary widely in their requirements—and although emphasis is placed on the desirability of item analysis as a basis for maximizing validity within the local organization—it is maintained that the present instrument can contribute to the prediction of sales success when used as part of a sales selection test battery. In such a case, use is made of the established a priori key, which was developed on the basis of item analysis of the earlier form (*Sales Personnel Description Form*). However, users are encouraged to develop their own keys, reflecting the specifics of their sales situations, when justified by the size of their sales forces.

No evidence of reliability is provided in the manual, although it is claimed that "the repeated evidences of validity in various sales situations....indicate that the reliability is sufficiently high to make the *Check List* useful in predicting sales success."

Although it is recognized that the validity of the instrument has not been established for a wide variety of sales jobs, preliminary or suggestive indications of validity are reported in three instances, although the reader is cautioned against generalizing, even to seemingly similar situations. In one study, based on scores made by 197 new car automobile salesmen from four divergent geographical locations throughout the United States, checklist scores yielded a biserial correlation of .31 with average monthly earnings (corrected for locale) for a 12-month period, this correlation being significant at the .01 level of significance. In a second study, scores correlated .23 with average monthly sales for a group of 23 office equipment salesmen from widely different sales territories, but correlated only .04 with the average *number* of orders written monthly by the same group. In a third study based on the scores of several groups of railroad traffic salesmen, the criterion consisted of a rating of "over-all performance" by each man's superior. In the case of five separate subgroups, distinguished from each other on the basis of age and technical specialization, the correlation coefficients were .15, .44, .11, .37, and .02, respectively. It might be added that in all three of the studies cited the validities were concurrent, i.e., determined by testing current employees whose pretest performance was rated. Hence it is possible that "restriction of range" may have unduly lowered the validity coefficients obtained.

Based on the "a priori scoring" noted above, norms are presented in the manual on the following five groups: 197 automobile salesmen, 54 utility salesmen, 141 office equipment salesmen, 95 freight traffic salesmen, and 180 applicants for "sales and sales managerial positions." The variability among and within these groups illustrates the need for the empirical development of local norms as well as validation data.

Format of the test and manual is good. The self-scoring technique is very efficient. The reviewer is even more impressed by the emphasis on the a priori nature of the scoring key, the tentativeness of the reported norms, and the desirability of local validation whenever possible. Apart from the restrictions imposed by the relatively small number of groups on which normative data are currently available, the chief limitations of the present instrument are those inherent in any forced-choice test. Chief among these are the question of the degree to which distortion, faking, or falsification has actually been minimized or eliminated, the considerable cost and effort involved in local standardization or revalidation, and the lack of "face validity" evidenced by frustration and other negative reactions on the part of applicants tested. Moreover, in the present instrument, several of the items are awkwardly worded. A few involve the use of the "double negative." Lastly, one could question the appropriateness of the test's title. Although one might argue that the test is attitudinal in that each item necessarily involves a determination of salesman behavior as seen through the eyes of the salesman himself, it is nevertheless true that the test is not designed to measure salesman attitude, as the title implies, but rather, it attempts to measure different aspects of the salesman's on-the-job behavior.

[1178]

*Sales Comprehension Test. Sales applicants; 1947–63; revision of the still-in-print *Aptitudes Associates Test of Sales Aptitude;* Form M ('53, 4 pages); revised manual ('63, 20 pages); profile ('62, 1 page); $5 per 25 tests; 25¢ per key; $2.75 per 25 profiles; $1.75 per manual; $2.50 per specimen set; cash orders postpaid; (15–20) minutes; Martin M. Bruce; the Author. *

REFERENCES

1–10. See 5:947.
11. HECHT, ROBERT, AND ARON, JOEL. "Normative Data Information Exchange, No. 12-16." *Personnel Psychol* 12:332 su '59. *
12. MURRAY, L. E., AND BRUCE, MARTIN M. "Normative Data Information Exchange, No. 12-17." *Personnel Psychol* 12:333 su '59. *
13. MURRAY, LESTER E., AND BRUCE, MARTIN M. "A Study of the Validity of the Sales Comprehension Test and Sales Motivation Inventory in Differentiating High and Low Production in Life Insurance Selling." *J Appl Psychol* 43:246-8 Ag '59. * (*PA* 34:6609)
14. ASH, PHILIP. "Validity Information Exchange, No. 13-05: D.O.T. Code 1-86.12, Salesman, Typewriters." *Personnel Psychol* 13:454 w '60. *
15. ASH, PHILIP. "Validity Information Exchange, No. 13-06: D.O.T. Code 5-83.127, Typewriter Serviceman." *Personnel Psychol* 13:455 w '60. *
16. DUGAN, ROBERT D. "Validity Information Exchange, No. 14-01: D.O.T. Code 0-98.07, Manager, Insurance Office." *Personnel Psychol* 14:213-6 su '61. *
17. BASS, BERNARD M. "Further Evidence on the Dynamic Character of Criteria." *Personnel Psychol* 15:93-7 sp '62. * (*PA* 37:3906)

For a review by Raymond A. Katzell, see 5:947; for reviews by Milton E. Hahn and Donald G. Paterson of the original edition, see 4:824.

[1179]

★Sales Employee Inventory. Outside salesmen; 1958; attitudes and opinions about company represented; 14 scores: the company, management, supervisory administrative skills, supervisory communication skills, company products, pricing and credit, customer service, advertising, sales training, work goals, job satisfaction, pay, benefits, reactions to the survey; 1 form (8 pages); manual of general information (59 pages); program description manual (19 pages); survey analyzer (62 pages); supervisor's guide (20 pages); profile (1 page); no data on reliability; distribution restricted to companies using the publisher's survey services; price information available from publisher; specimen set not available; [30–40] minutes; Richard Renck, George Y. Ogawa, and David N. Larson; Industrial Relations Center. *

[1180]

*Sales Personnel Description Form. Salesmen; 1953-60; forced-choice rating scale; 1 form ('53, 4 pages); manual ['60, 10 pages]; scoring by the publisher only; 50¢ per form including scoring service; 25¢ per specimen set; cash orders postpaid; [10] minutes; Personnel Research Institute. *

REFERENCES

1. TAYLOR, ERWIN K.; SCHNEIDER, DOROTHY E.; AND SYMONS, NANCY A. "A Short Forced-Choice Evaluation Form for Salesmen." *Personnel Psychol* 6:393-401 w '53. * (*PA* 28:8152)
2. TAYLOR, ERWIN K., AND HILTON, ANDREW C. "Sales Personnel Description Form: Summary of Validities." *Personnel Psychol* 13:173-9 su '60. * (*PA* 36:2LD73T)

WAYNE K. KIRCHNER, *Manager, Personnel Research, Minnesota Mining and Manufacturing Company, St. Paul, Minnesota.*

This is not a test, but is a form for rating the performance of salesmen. It consists of three parts: one forced-choice rating of performance on 12 tetrads of sales behavior, and two graphic rating scales—one on present value to company and one on future potential as a salesman. It is not lengthy; even a slow reader would be hard pressed to spend more than 10 minutes on this form.

Operationally, the user must send the form to the publisher for scoring. This is supposed to be an advantage, according to the manual, but the reviewer suspects that it is more of a disadvantage. In any case, the graphic rating scales on the form do not seem particularly significant in value or different from any other graphic rating scale that might be made up. From the norms that were available to the reviewer (but not to the user of the form), it was evident that the two graphic rating scales produced two extremely skewed distributions. It appears that most salesmen are rated high on these two scales and that an average score is quite near the top end of the scale in both cases. The score obtained on the forced-choice section, however, is more normally distributed.

As far as reliability goes, the manual cites one test-retest study done on a group of 104 salesmen with an r of .71. This does not seem too bad for this kind of instrument. Validity, however, is another matter. Nine studies are cited in the manual with correlation coefficients listed which show the relationship between the scores on the SPDF and various other criteria of sales performance. Unfortunately, the reviewer is unable to tell from the table which of the three scores obtained on this form correlated with the particular criterion in question, so the table serves no particular useful purpose. Since correlations as high as .58 between this form and various criteria of sales performance are reported, however, it is reasonable to assume that the scores probably do correlate positively with most criteria of sales performance. From that standpoint, then, this would appear to be a valid instrument. The validity itself cannot be determined to any great extent by the information provided in the manual, however.

In summary, this is a sales performance rating form which cannot be scored by the user.

It provides three separate scores: one from the forced-choice rating section, and two from graphic rating scales which produce extremely skewed distributions on the normative data that was provided. Whether or not this particular form is of any great value to any one in the sales field is markedly open to question. It is at best a substitute for any other measure of sales performance that might be available. It might be useful to check on present appraisal methods, for example, but this reviewer questions seriously whether or not this form actually produces much better information than might be obtained by a simple ranking of sales job performance.

[1181]

★The Sales Sentence Completion Blank. Applicants for sales positions; 1961; 1 form (3 pages); manual (25 pages); $5 per 25 tests; $1.75 per manual; $2.50 per specimen set; cash orders postpaid; (20–35) minutes; Norman Gekoski; Martin M. Bruce. *

WILLIAM E. KENDALL, *Director, Personnel and Marketing Research Division, The Psychological Corporation, New York, New York.*

The *Sales Sentence Completion Blank* consists of 40 sentence fragments constructed so as to elicit sales-oriented responses.

After a series of interviews with insurance salesmen and their supervisors, a preliminary form containing 54 sentence fragments was administered to 82 life insurance salesmen working in the Philadelphia area. The men were employees of three different insurance organizations. An unspecified number of the men were agency supervisors who, presumably, also sold insurance.

Of the 82 men, usable data were available on 60. These men were divided into high and low criterion groups. Average income of the 30 men in the high criterion group was $13,500 (sales experience averaged nine years, two months) while that of the 30 men in the low criterion group was $5,000 (average sales experience was two years, six months). In the manual, no mention is made of the relative proportion, in the two groups, of salesmen and supervisors. Supervisors, it must be assumed, have more service and higher incomes.

Responses to each sentence fragment were categorized and scoring values from 1 to 7 assigned, based upon the relative frequencies among high and low criterion cases. Scores of 7 are assigned to responses most typical of highly successful salesmen, while responses weighted 1 are typical of men found to be poorer salesmen. It should be noted that of the 40 items, 18 have a range of possible scores from 2 to 6. On only 4 items is it possible to obtain a score of 7. In order to score the blank, one must match completions against principles listed for each item. A total score is obtained by summing score values over all items.

Test-retest reliability (total score) based on administration to 30 college students is .84. The standard error of the total score based on the college student sample is 2.5 points.

The manual reports under the heading "Statistical Analysis" that the blank was validated against a group of 37 men for whom criterion data were obtained after the blanks had been scored. Product moment coefficients of .64 and .53 are reported between sales sentence blank total scores and actual earnings and sales index, respectively.

Percentiles are given for 37 life insurance salesmen, 64 auto insurance salesmen, 45 real estate salesmen, and 33 electrical parts salesmen, but there is no other mention in the manual of the source of these data or the use of the blank with these men.

The test catalog describes the blank as "valuable as an aid in evaluating applicants and employed sales personnel." There is no evidence of any kind presented in the manual to support the use of the blank in evaluating applicants. And, as is apparent from the preceding paragraphs, the fragments of data presented on the standardization group of employed sales personnel raise more questions than they answer.

The catalog also describes the *Sales Sentence Completion Blank* as a "projective form," "amenable to quantified, objective scoring as well as clinical interpretation," and says that it "combines the probing advantages of projective methods with scoring objectivity." If these claims are to be believed, it is clear, by APA standards, that the blank is a "Level C" instrument to be used only by qualified psychologists.

The reviewer tried, unsucccessfully, to obtain additional information from both author and publisher. Thus, based on the published data, this reviewer must conclude that in its present form, publication of the *Sales Sentence Completion Blank* is premature. It should be treated as an instrument suitable only for limited, experimental use by competent professionals.

J Counsel Psychol 8:374 w '61. John O. Crites. * The sentence stems....were developed primarily from interviews with a group of 82 life insurance salesmen from Philadelphia. There are 40 incomplete sentences in the Blank which were selected from 54 trial items because they seemed to elicit "sales-oriented responses." The Manual outlines fairly detailed scoring principles, with sample completions, for obtaining an over-all "sales achievement" score. Provision is also made for scoring omissions, simple responses of fact or opinion, stereotyped answers, ambiguous completions, multiple statements, and qualified responses. No data are reported, however, on inter-scorer agreement in using the scoring principles. The incomplete sentence stems which resulted from the initial standardization are generally adequate and provocative, although some of them are too long and introduce overly complex thought. The major question which the early work with the Blank raises concerns the validity of the scoring system. The scoring principles were developed from comparing the responses of the most and the least successful salesmen in the original sample, each group numbering 30 Ss. The criteria of success were (1) income and (2) the ratio of the number of personal contacts made by the salesmen to the number of policies sold. The high criterion group had an average income of $13,500, with an average experience in selling life insurance of nine years and two months, whereas the low criterion group had a mean salary of $5,000, with an average of *only* two years and six months selling experience. Since income in life insurance sales is partly a function of the number of years in the occupation, due to the contribution of renewals, experience and ability were confounded in the success criteria. The high and low salesmen should have been matched on number of years in the field. Less serious, but still notable shortcomings of the Blank's development have to do with its reliability and norms. Although a test-retest reliability coefficient of .84 was obtained for a one-week period, the Ss were a very small (and presumably statistically unstable) group of 30 college students of unknown characteristics (age, sex, college major, etc., were not specified). Norms are given for Auto Insurance Salesmen, Life Insurance Salesmen, Real Estate Salesmen, Electrical Parts Salesmen, and all groups combined, but the numbers in each are quite small, ranging from 33 to 64 for the occupational samples, with the general norms based upon 179 cases. The *Sales Sentence Completion Blank* represents a novel approach to the measurement of sales aptitude and has promise for further research, but at present it is not ready for practical use by counselors and personnel workers. Additional study of its validity is badly needed, with particular emphasis upon its correlation with criteria of sales success in a sample which is homogeneous in years of selling experience. Also, the objectivity of the scoring system has not been established, and the stability of scores in sales samples has not been determined. Finally, since one of the reasons for using incomplete sentences was to reduce the social (or "selection") response set, it seems important to gather some empirical evidence on how effectively this was done.

[1182]

*Steward Basic Factors Inventory (1960 Edition). Applicants for sales and office positions; 1957–63; revision of *Steward Sales Aptitude Inventory*; originally called *Steward Vocational Fitness Inventory*; 14 scores: business knowledge (vocabulary, arithmetic, total), dominance, personal adjustment, occupational interests (clerical, artistic, supervisory, accounting, writing, selling, mechanical, total), total; 1 form ('60, 8 pages) ; manual, second edition ('60, 8 pages) ; technical report ['60, 8 pages, typewritten in part] ; supplementary data ('63, 4 pages) ; no data on reliability ; no norms for separate occupational interest scores ; $4.35 per set of 5 tests and manual ; $2.25 per manual ; postage extra ; (60–70) minutes ; Verne Steward ; Steward-Mortensen & Associates. *

LEONARD V. GORDON, *Chief, Behavioral Evaluation Research Laboratory, U.S. Army Personnel Research Office, Washington, D.C.*

The *Steward Basic Factors Inventory* is the latest in a series of instruments devised by the author for the selection of salesmen and office personnel. No particular background in personnel work or in the use of employment tests is specified as required of the user of the inventory. The author claims that the manual provides the necessary instructions for application of the inventory for selection purposes, and that skill in using the materials may be achieved by carefully reading the manual and by tryout appraisal of two or three persons well known to the user.

The Steward "system" involves, as a first step, the determination by the employer of the caliber of individual required for a given job (levels A through D). After the applicant has been administered the inventory, the vocabulary and arithmetic tests are used as a first test hurdle, cutoff scores being provided in the manual for each job level. Next, the employer checks, with the applicant's former employers, references, spouse, and with credit agencies, those personal data responses which he considers to be questionable. The remainder of the inventory is then scored, and raw scores on each test are converted into ratings of unqualified, borderline, acceptable, or superior, using tables provided in the manual. A final overall rating is then given the applicant. While standards are provided for giving "unqualified" final ratings, the employer is asked to use the "direct judgment method" in the assigning of acceptable, superior, or over-qualified ratings. The manual recommends that a standard personal data blank also be used in making the final employment decision, since applicants who are acceptable on the inventory may have other disqualifying weaknesses.

While the items in the tests appear to be relevant to their intended use, it is difficult to appraise the technical adequacy of the tests themselves because of the lack of statistical information in the manual. No reliability data are presented for tests in the present form. The standard errors of the means, which appear in the reliability section of the supplement, have no bearing on the stability of the tests for individual use.

The manual also is deficient in providing validity information. No validity data are presented for office jobs. Fragmentary concurrent validity data, obtained from 1934 through 1938 on the first form of the inventory, are reported for insurance salesmen, with tetrachoric coefficients ranging from .44 to .75. While group comparisons are presented for the 1960 form, these essentially show that insurance salesmen can be differentiated from college education majors on the basis of "dominance" and "selling interest." The authors estimate, on page 3 of the validity supplement, "that this Inventory with its Manual has 75 percent more value as a selection tool than their first 4-page Inventory." In the light of the validities reported for the first form, this is a most extravagant statement.

In view of the fact that the inventory is reported as having been administered in its present and earlier forms to more than a million persons for employment purposes, it would be expected that some longitudinal validity information, together with a range of descriptive statistics, would have been available for reporting in the manual. None is presented.

The manual as a whole is poorly written, and is deficient in a number of respects. For example, in the introduction, it states that "the materials have many features never before incorporated in sales personnel selection systems," citing as two of the six more important novel features, the use of objective scoring (scoring by keys), and the inclusion of instructions for administering, scoring, and interpreting the forms in one manual. Such a statement may have had some validity several decades ago.

The guidelines provided for deciding on the caliber of individual required for a given job are inadequate and, in places, appear not to have been carefully thought out. For example, the same level of arithmetic ability is prescribed for a typist and a bookkeeper; and the job of sales clerk is evaluated at one level in the text and at another level in the chart. Clear, objective guidelines for establishing job levels are important for the proper use of the system, since cutoff scores on which employment decisions are based differ for different levels of jobs.

No information is provided as to the basis on which the table for converting raw scores to categorical ratings was developed. It would be important to know, for example, the nature of the samples used in developing the tables, the number of cases, the nature of the jobs involved, the types of companies involved, whether the subjects were tested as applicants or as employees, and the criteria used in development of the table. The user of the inventory must accept, on blind faith, the universal applicability and universal validity of the conversion table.

In evaluating the interest test scores, the user is told that only the interest area relevant to the job under consideration need be scored. It would seem important to obtain scores on all interest areas, since the applicant may report a stronger interest in areas unrelated to the job under consideration, or even a strong interest in all areas.

A minor error in interpretation may be noted in the validity section. Business knowledge items were interpreted as being more valid than mental ability items, with respective coefficients of .59 and .44, where the lower quarter of the criterion group was not included in the latter analysis.

In the opinion of the reviewer, the *Steward Basic Factors Inventory* is inappropriate for industrial application in the manner outlined in the manual. It is entirely conceivable that the items comprising the inventory may be valid for certain selection purposes. However, it is incumbent on the author to prepare a manual which will provide the prospective user with sufficient statistical information to enable him to estimate the probable utility of the inventory for his employment purposes, and to restrict distribution of the materials to those individuals who have sufficient training to properly evaluate and apply them.

LYMAN W. PORTER, *Associate Professor of Psychology, University of California, Berkeley, California.*

This 8-page inventory contains three basic parts: Part 1, 55 "business knowledge" items, including 33 vocabulary and 22 business arithmetic computation items; Part 2, 70 "personality" items (answered "yes" or "no"); and Part 3, 98 "occupational interest" items (answered "like" or "dislike").

An 8-page manual is provided, which contains instructions on the administration and use of the test, scoring keys, and tables for converting scores on each part of the test into one of four possible ratings (unqualified, borderline, acceptable, superior). On the front page of the manual, the following statement is made: "These materials [the inventory plus the manual] have many features never before incorporated in sales personnel selection systems." Some of these features are, to quote the manual: (a) "This manual contains instructions for the objective scoring....[of] the tests." (b) "The Inventory contains one personality test which measures two factors, dominance and adjustment. The test is based upon personal data and cannot be 'fudged' by applicants without detection by alert employers." (c) "The Inventory's parts are published in one 8-page booklet; the instructions for administering, scoring and interpreting the form are included in one Manual." To say that these are features which have "never before been incorporated in sales personnel selection systems" is misleading at best and false at worst.

The manual turns out to be completely inadequate. Information is lacking on the following: the development of the test; how the items were obtained; how the tables for conversion of scores to ratings were developed; norms; reliability; and validity.

Two supplementary documents—one partly printed and partly typewritten—were made available to the reviewer. These documents supposedly supply information not contained in the manual itself concerning the "development and validation of the *Steward Basic Factors Inventory*." An opening statement on one of these documents makes the following claims:

> The present *Inventory* and its predecessors has [*sic*] been the subject of research, revision and application for approximately forty years. * During these periods, the Steward tests have been the subject of continual experimental study and revision, offering present users objectively scored, concise, reliable and valid instruments for evaluating probable success in the insurance business.

Let us examine each of these claims in the light of the evidence presented:

a) Objective scoring: This is an accurate claim.

b) Conciseness: Since the authors state that the average time required to complete the inventory is about 60 minutes, the adjective "concise" is probably appropriate.

c) Reliability: The authors state, "The only meaningful estimate of reliability for a heterogeneous test such as the *Basic Factors Inventory* is a test-retest estimate." Ignored are the possibilities of obtaining reliability estimates for the supposedly homogeneous subparts of the test by either the comparable-half or Kuder-Richardson methods. At any rate, the authors imply that although test-retest reliability data would be most desirable, they were unable to obtain any sample which they could retest at a later date. Therefore, they make their reliability claims on the following basis:

> To overcome this common problem in industrial test construction [the "problem" of not being able to retest particular samples], stability of sub-scores of the Inventory were [*sic*] examined with respect to their expected variability on retesting of the same or similar populations. Mean scores, standard deviations, and standard errors of the mean were computed on a sample of 100 successful life insurance salesmen. [The results, in terms of standard scores] show that mean scores obtained on the same or similar populations should vary very little. * This range of values [of standard errors of means for different subparts of the test for this sample of 100 life insurance salesmen]

....is well within acceptable limits of reliability and it can be assumed that on retesting, average scores of a similar sample population would vary very little from the obtained scores.

All of this ignores (*a*) the fact that the size of the standard error of a mean is partly a function of *n;* and (*b*) the fact that the size of a standard error of a mean says nothing at all directly about reliability. A test composed of items that produced completely random responses on the part of the individuals taking the test might produce consistent mean scores from sample to sample, and yet be a completely unreliable test instrument. It is obvious, therefore, that no acceptable data are provided concerning reliability.

d) Validity: The authors present mean scores for a sample of 63 life insurance salesmen and 26 college students on each of the various parts of the test. The college students scored significantly lower on all but one of the subparts of the test. From these results the authors conclude that there is "concurrent validity," even though there are no data presented on test scores in relation to differential sales performance on the job for any sample of life insurance salesmen or any other group of salesmen. Furthermore, even as "concurrent validity" data, a sample of 63 life insurance salesmen and 26 college students is not only small but hardly representative of either category of individuals (especially when no information is given as to where or how these two samples were obtained). The only conclusion possible is that adequate validity of the *Steward Basic Factors Inventory* has in no way been demonstrated.

In summary, this test is not recommended for use at the present time.

[1183]

*Steward Personal Background Inventory (1960 Revised Edition). Applicants for sales positions; 1949–60; revision of *Personal Inventory of Background Factors;* ratings of 5 factors (caliber, aptitude, adjustment, survival, supplementary) in 7 areas (health, education, experience, financial status, activities, family status, miscellaneous); 1 form ('60, 8 pages); manual ('60, c1957, 11 pages, same as 1957 manual except for minor changes); no data on reliability and validity; $4.20 per 25 forms, postage extra; specimen set not available; [60–70] minutes; Verne Steward; [Steward-Mortensen & Associates]. *

LEONARD V. GORDON, *Chief, Behavioral Evaluation Research Laboratory, U.S. Army Personnel Research Office, Washington, D.C.*

The *Steward Personal Background Inven-*

tory is an information blank intended primarily for use, either by itself or as part of a battery, in the selection of salesmen. The inventory is reported to have been developed over a period of nearly 25 years. No particular level of training is specified for its use. According to the author, skill in using the materials is acquired by reading the inventory and manual, and by trying out the inventory on several persons well known to the prospective user.

The inventory elicits the type of information characteristically obtained on standard application forms and background data blanks. The 112 personal history items, which are of the completion type, are organized into seven content areas and are also examined by means of five "key to success" factors which cut across content areas. Fifty-four of the items, which are asterisked, reflect possible "danger signs."

Steps in evaluating the inventory include, in order: examining the completed form; going over questionable items with the applicant; checking the information with the applicant's former employer, references, wife (or parents); and finally, scoring the inventory itself. Scoring consists of marking favorable responses with a dash and unfavorable responses to each asterisked item with a double x (a danger sign). Responses that are neither favorable nor unfavorable are unmarked. The employer then is to "appraise the evidence" and assign a rating of unqualified, borderline, acceptable, superior, or over-qualified for each area and factor. No standards are provided for making the ratings.

The employer then evaluates each item marked with a danger sign "to determine whether a single weakness or handicap is sufficient for rejection." Applicants are rejected if they have six or more danger signs, if they have any rating of unqualified, or if certain combinations of borderline ratings are obtained. The employer is then to make hire or reject decisions for the survivors. "Here the decision will obviously be one in which the judgment of the employer plays the most important part." No guidelines for making the decision are provided.

The manual gives the impression of providing more guidance than it actually does. For example, objective scoring is claimed as a special feature of the system. Scoring of many of the items, however, is not objective, being based on the scorer's judgment. Further-more, no scores are obtained for either the areas or the factors. The final ratings are for the most part arrived at judgmentally. The manual also purports to provide instructions for "appraising the evidence by section of the completed Inventory" and "rating the evidence for 'key to success' factors." However, these "instructions" are little more than statements that individuals differ in various respects.

An oddity appears in the ordering of the steps for using the inventory. The manual recommends that a personal investigation of the applicant be conducted *prior* to scoring his inventory. Since applicants are later eliminated on the basis of certain negative information obtained from the inventory, it would be preferable, as a first step, to "score" the inventory and eliminate those who are unqualified, with personal investigations being conducted for the survivors.

Information regarding the validity of the inventory is covered by the statement, "for our research groups [the system] has rejected more than half of unqualified and marginal persons without eliminating those of superior qualifications." No supporting data or references are provided. No information is given as to how the recommended standards for rating applicants as being "unqualified" were arrived at, and no statistical data are provided regarding their validity in application.

The *Steward Personal Background Inventory* is, in a sense, a hybrid of the keyed background information blank and the patterned interview form, but unfortunately lacks the primary advantage of each. It does not yield area or "factor" scores, nor does it provide the user with an indication of the significance of each response and guides for further probing. As an employment blank, the inventory does have the potential for providing the employer with useful information about the applicant. However, the utility of the inventory for selection purposes will depend entirely upon the skill of the user in developing techniques for assessing the significance of the applicant's responses for success or tenure in a particular type of job.

LYMAN W. PORTER, *Associate Professor of Psychology, University of California, Berkeley, California.*

This inventory, to quote from the manual, is "an 8-page form containing 112 personal history items which is to be completed by applicants for work and/or other persons whose qualifications are desired." Apparently, as one reads through the manual, the phrase "applicants for work" really means prospective salesmen, at least as far as the inventory authors are concerned.

The inventory attempts to gather data in seven areas of personal history (health, education, etc.) and five aspects of personal history (adjustment, aptitude for selling). In other words, each of the 112 items is cross-classified into one of the seven areas and one of the five factors.

Before discussing the data provided in the manual, it is necessary to say a few words concerning the nature of the 112 items. Some of them ask for objective and easily verifiable information (e.g., number of dependent children, number of college courses completed in economics, etc.) and others ask for semi-subjective responses which would be difficult to verify (e.g., "Have you ever spoken out in a group of adults on important business problems?"; "Are you enthusiastic with respect to the worth of the products or services to be sold?"). Although the applicant is supposed to be able to complete the form in 60 to 70 minutes, one wonders if this is realistic when one of the 112 questions asks the applicant to make out a budget allotment of monthly salary among 24 different items! It is clear, of course, that many of a respondent's answers are open to distortion on his part. This factor is recognized by the authors since they emphasize the importance of verifying the obtained data by use of interview, checking with former employers, checking with the applicant's wife, etc. However, since so many of the items are subject to easy falsification, it is doubtful that really adequate checking can be undertaken without a great deal of time and effort on the employer's part.

The manual provides scoring instructions for each item. The scorer is to give a "—" for a response indicating a "favorable clue," an "✕✕" for a "danger sign," and no mark if the response is intermediate (neither a "favorable clue" nor a "danger sign").

Other than the instructions for scoring each item, the so-called manual was found by this reviewer to be highly inadequate. No information is given as to how the items were constructed. No information is given as to

how the scoring procedures were developed (i.e., information as to why a particular response to a given item should be scored "✕✕"). No method for calculating total scores on the inventory is provided other than the statement that if more than six items receive "✕✕" scores the applicant is to be considered disqualified. (From looking back over the scored responses in a given section of the test, the administrator of the inventory is supposed to make a subjective rating from 1 to 4 as to the applicant's qualifications in that section of the test.) Since total scores are not possible to calculate, no norms are given in the manual. Finally, no reliability or validity data are supplied in the manual.

About all that can be said in a positive way about this inventory is that many of the items appear to tap useful areas of personal background information. But, until the authors can provide norms and adequate reliability and validity information, its use is not advocated by the reviewer.

[1184]
★Word Check Forms. Applicants for sales and managerial positions; 1952-62; series of sentence completion and checklist forms yielding a "motivational" profile of 49 scores in 5 categories: wants, working media, pattern of behavior, level of activity, occupational tie-in; author recommends use of *Cardall Test of Practical Judgment* as a check on wants score and for obtaining additional information on level of activity score; 12 parts: 4 occupational preference checklists (Forms 1, 4, 7, 10, '62, 1 page), 4 self-description checklists (Forms 2, 5, 8, 11, '58, 1 page), and 4 sentence completion forms (Forms 3, 6, 9, 12, '59, 1 hectographed page); Forms 13 ('58), 14 ('59), 15 ('62), (1 page) also available for checking purposes; hectographed directions for administering ('58, 6 pages); hectographed norms booklet ('58, 7 pages); profile explanation booklet ('59, 14 pages); hectographed scoring stencil booklet ('60, 23 pages); profile ('59, 1 page); no data on reliability and validity; no description of normative population; no norms for Forms 3, 6-9, and 12; distribution restricted to clients; $5 per set of all 12 parts (arrangements can be made with author for local reproduction), postpaid; [120-210] minutes; V. J. Swanson; the Author. *

[Other Tests]
For tests not listed above, see the following entries in *Tests in Print*: 2046, 2050, 2052, 2056-7, 2063-4, 2066, 2068-9, 2073, and 2075-6; out of print: 2053, 2059, 2072, and 2074.

SKILLED TRADES

[1185]
★Automotive Mechanic Test. Prospective automotive mechanics (especially master mechanics and journeymen); 1962-63; 9 scores: motor, transmission, rear end, brakes, front end, electrical system, tune-up, carburetor, total; IBM; 1 form ('62, 16 pages); man-

ual ('63, 16 pages); no data on reliability and validity; separate IBM scorable answer sheets must be used; $25 per 10 tests; specimen set loaned for rental fee of $5; postpaid; 180(200) minutes; McCann Associates. *

[1186]

The Fiesenheiser Test of Ability to Read Drawings. Trade school and adults; 1955; 1 form (4 pages); hectographed manual (3 pages); $5 per 50 tests; $1 per specimen set (must be purchased to obtain manual); cash orders postpaid; 30(35) minutes; Elmer I. Fiesenheiser; Psychometric Affiliates. *

JOSEPH E. MOORE, *Regents Professor of Psychology, Georgia Institute of Technology, Atlanta, Georgia.*

The author states that this test was constructed "with the intent of sampling knowledge that might be obtained in both formal instruction and in shop experience." Four areas of information (information on the multiview projection method of drawing, reading of drawings, practice problems in drawing, and definitions) are sampled by 12 multiple choice questions, 3 drawings of different views of objects, 13 matching definitions for commonly used terms, and 22 written definitions of commonly used symbols.

The type and printing of the test material is clear; that is, it is bold and black and is easy to read. However, the section on definitions of commonly used terms appears to be unnecessarily crowded together. It would have helped the testee if one line had been skipped between the questions and the answers. The weakness here is in the arrangement of the material, rather than in the content. It might be better to say that this is a criticism more of the typist (the test is offset from typewritten copy) than of the author. The scoring key is certainly poorly prepared and in many places difficult to read. The drawings to be used as guides for scoring are very carelessly done and do not reflect credit on the author.

This is primarily a speed test with 50 items to be completed within 30 minutes. The statistical data on the test are rather skimpy. The split-half reliability of .88 for 139 cases is not very high but reasonably satisfactory. However, the basis for the validity data is not at all clear. The validity data were based on 32 mechanical engineers, 58 civil engineers, 9 individuals from other engineering disciplines, and 39 "liberal studies college students." The total is given as 136. This total is in error. It should read 138. The author also confuses the reader by stating that only "62 of these subjects had had no experience using prints and only 22 had never had a course in technical or engineering drawing in either high school or college," but he does not specify who these individuals are, whether the majority of them are students in the liberal studies college or whether they are engineers.

The normative group was composed of 32 mechanical engineers, 58 civil engineers, 39 nonengineers, and 136 who are called "total college." It would have been helpful to know whether the total college group included any engineering students or whether it is a composite group of individuals from many different college majors. The percentile table does not appear to warrant separating the two engineering groups. No data are presented to show the means and standard deviations of the two groups and the scores appear to be very similar.

In summary, one should not have much confidence in the value of this test to separate men with various degrees of experience in reading engineering drawings until its validity is established further. However, the test does appear to have sufficient value to be used as a rough screening device in selecting those who have as their task the reading of various kinds of architectural and engineering drawings.

[1187]

★**Technical Tests.** Standards 6–8 (ages 13–15); 1962; 5 scores: arithmetic, mechanical insight, spatial relations (2 scores), tool test; 1 form ['62, 36 pages, in Afrikaans and English]; mimeographed manual ['62, 22 pages, 11 pages each in Afrikaans and English]; separate answer sheets must be used; R7.66 per 100 tests; R0.50 per 100 answer sheets; R6.66 per 100 scoring keys; postpaid; manual free; specimen set not available; 72(92) minutes; National Bureau of Educational and Social Research. *

[1188]

★**Written Trade Tests.** Plumbers, electricians, carpenters, maintenance mechanics; 1962–63; IBM; tests designed primarily for master mechanics and journeymen; 4 scores: blueprint reading, identification of tools, trade practices and materials, total; 1 form ('62, 14 pages); 4 tests: Plumber, Electrician, Carpenter, Maintenance Mechanic; manual ('63, 18 pages); candidate identification sheet ('62, 1 page); no data on reliability; no description of normative population; separate IBM scorable answer sheets must be used; 10–49 tests, $2.50 each; $2 per 50 extra answer sheets; specimen set of any one test loaned for rental fee of $5, which may be applied to purchase price; postpaid; 150(165) minutes; McCann Associates. *

[Other Tests]

For tests not listed above, see the following entries in *Tests in Print*: 2080–8; out of print: 2079.

SUPERVISION

[1189]

How Supervise? Supervisors; 1943–48; Forms A ('43), B ('43), M ('48, consists of items from Forms A and B), (4 pages); revised manual ('48, 8 pages); $2.90 per 25 tests; 50¢ per specimen set; postpaid; administration time not reported; Quentin W. File and H. H. Remmers (manual); Psychological Corporation. * (Australian edition: Australian Council for Educational Research.)

REFERENCES

1–5. See 3:687.
6–13. See 4:774.
14–31. See 5:926.
32. HILTON, ANDREW C.; BOLIN, STANLEY F.; PARKER, JAMES W., JR.; TAYLOR, ERWIN K.; AND WALKER, WILLIAM B. "The Validity of Personnel Assessments by Professional Psychologists." *J Appl Psychol* 39:207–93 Ag '55. * (PA 30:5294)
33. MEYER, HERBERT H. "An Evaluation of a Supervisory Selection Program." *Personnel Psychol* 9:499–513 w '56. * (PA 32:3394)
34. ALBRIGHT, LEWIS E.; SMITH, WALLACE J.; AND GLENNON, J. R. "A Follow-Up on Some 'Invalid' Tests for Selecting Salesmen." *Personnel Psychol* 12:105–12 sp '59. * (PA 34:3463)
35. ALBRIGHT, LEWIS E.; SMITH, WALLACE J.; AND GLENNON, J. R. "Normative Data Information Exchange, Nos. 12-11, 12-12." *Personnel Psychol* 12:154–5 sp '59. *
36. DECKER, ROBERT L. "A Cross-Validation Study of a Test of Supervisory Ability." *Proc W Va Acad Sci* 29:105–9 My '59. * (PA 34:3496)
37. NEEL, ROBERT G., AND DUNN, ROBERT E. "Predicting Success in Supervisory Training Programs by the Use of Psychological Tests." *J Appl Psychol* 44:358–60 O '60. * (PA 35:4081)
38. ROSEN, NED ARNOLD. *The Revision and Validation of the How Supervise? Test—1960.* Doctor's thesis, Purdue University (Lafayette, Ind.), 1960. (DA 21:364)
39. ROSEN, NED A. "How Supervise?—1943–1960." *Personnel Psychol* 14:87–99 sp '61. * (PA 36:4LD87R)
40. WIENER, DANIEL N. "Evaluation of Selection Procedures for a Management Development Program." *J Counsel Psychol* 8:121–8 su '61. * (PA 36:3LD21W)

JOEL T. CAMPBELL, *Research Psychologist, Educational Testing Service, Princeton, New Jersey.*

This test is designed to measure the supervisor's "knowledge and insight concerning human relations in industry." It is available in three forms, A, B, and M. Forms A and B each consist of 70 items, divided into the three areas of supervisory practices, company policies, and supervisor opinions. For supervisory practices and company policies, the person indicates whether he considers the item "desirable," "uncertain," or "undesirable." For supervisor opinions, the response is "agree," "uncertain," and "disagree." Form M, designed for higher levels of management, is composed of 100 items selected from the other two forms, and contains the same three sections.

Forms A and B were equated in construction. For Forms A and B, percentile and standard score equivalents of total raw scores on a single form and the two forms combined are reported. Comparison groups are (a) "higher level supervisors," defined as "top management, office supervisor, and producton supervisors

above foreman level," and (b) "lower level supervisors," defined as "operating supervisors, foremen and below." For Form M, percentile and standard score equivalents are given for two comparison groups: "top management supervisors" and "office and middle management supervisors." The groups are large enough to provide stable comparisons. Since the manual was last revised in 1948, it is possible that there has been a change in "supervisory climate" since that time, with accompanying shift in percentile and standard scores. However, use of the norms table, even if it is outdated, probably does little damage in individual cases.

The single form reliability of Forms A and B is reported as .77, and the two forms combined have a reliability of .87. For Form M, the reported reliability is .87. These would appear to be adequate to warrant the use of the test.

Three different approaches were used to establish validity. First, mean scores on Forms A and B combined were compared for three different levels of supervisors. All critical ratios were significant at the 1 per cent level. Second, pre-training scores on one form were compared with post-training scores on the alternate form for the three management levels. These comparisons were uniformly significant. Third, for two small groups comparisons of test scores and executive ratings produced correlations between .50 and .60.

In addition to the material reported in the manual, a substantial body of research results has been reported in the psychological literature over the years. A number of aspects of the test have been controversial. One of these was the extent to which it was a disguised measure of verbal ability. Wickert (*20*) appears to have established fairly definitely that for those below high school level, the test measures largely verbal ability. For those above high school level, *How Supervise?* scores have little relationship with intelligence test scores.

A second aspect of controversy has been over whether the knowledge as measured by the test is reflected in supervisory behavior on the job. The published research on this point is contradictory. Rosen (*39*), who reviewed this literature, concludes: "On balance the literature contains more positive evidence supporting the proposition that *How Supervise?* scores are related to supervisory success than negative results."

A less controversial use has been to measure effectiveness of training programs. Here also a fairly large volume of research results is available in the literature, and, in general, results obtained are in the predicted direction. Scores after human relation or leadership training average higher than pre-training scores (*6, 12, 25*) while scores for control groups do not increase (*12*) or do not increase as much as the training group (*8*).

This reviewer was struck by the fact that he could not locate any study in the literature where the items were factor analyzed or the total score included in a factor analysis.

When this test was developed it was keyed by opinion of two groups of experts in the field of supervisory training and industrial relations or mental hygiene. Thus it was intended to measure knowledge of accepted supervisory practices as taught by supervisor training courses. It probably is not unfair to say that *How Supervise?* espouses the "democratic" leadership of the Lewin studies. Since that time the Ohio State leadership studies and others have emphasized a multifactor approach to supervision. This reviewer would hypothesize that *How Supervise?* measures the aspect of leadership Halpin and Winer [1] defined as "consideration" and fails to measure their "initiating structure" factor. At any rate, it would be interesting to see the items or scores from this test factor analyzed along with such measures as the social service score of the *Study of Values* and the nurturance score of the *Edwards Personal Preference Schedule,* as well as the consideration and initiating structure measures.

To summarize, the following points may be made: (*a*) The test probably should not be used for those with less than twelfth grade education. (*b*) The test probably measures knowledge of one aspect of supervisory behavior. (*c*) The test can be useful in evaluating results of a human relations type of supervisor training course.

1 HALPIN, ANDREW W., AND WINER, B. JAMES. Chap. 3, "A Factorial Study of the Leader Behavior Descriptions," pp. 39–51. In *Leader Behavior: Its Description and Measurement.* Edited by Ralph M. Stogdill and Alvin E. Coons. Ohio State University, Bureau of Business Research, Research Monograph No. 88. Columbus, Ohio: the Bureau, 1957. Pp. xv, 168. *

For a review by Milton M. Mandell, see 4:774; for reviews by D. Welty Lefever, Charles I. Mosier, and C. H. Ruedisili, see 3:687.

[1190]

★**Leadership Opinion Questionnaire.** Supervisors and prospective supervisors; 1960; 2 scores: structure, consideration; 1 form (4 pages); preliminary manual (12 pages); $4.95 per 20 tests; 35¢ per manual; 60¢ per specimen set; postage extra; (15–20) minutes; Edwin A. Fleishman; Science Research Associates, Inc. *

REFERENCES

1. FLEISHMAN, EDWIN A. "Leadership Climate, Human Relations Training, and Supervisory Behavior." *Personnel Psychol* 6:205–22 su '53. * (*PA* 27:3376)
2. FLEISHMAN, EDWIN A. "The Measurement of Leadership Attitudes in Industry." *J Appl Psychol* 37:153–8 Je '53. * (*PA* 28:3324)
3. FLEISHMAN, EDWIN A. Chap. 10, "The Leadership Opinion Questionnaire," pp. 120–33. In *Leader Behavior: Its Description and Measurement.* Edited by Ralph M. Stogdill and Alvin E. Coons. Ohio State University, Bureau of Business Research, Research Monograph No. 88. Columbus, Ohio: the Bureau, 1957. Pp. xv, 168. * (*PA* 32:1466)
4. BASS, BERNARD M. "Leadership Opinions as Forecasts of Supervisory Success: A Replication." *Personnel Psychol* 11:515–8 w '58. * (*PA* 34:2185)
5. STANTON, ERWIN S. "Company Policies and Supervisors' Attitudes Toward Supervision." *J Appl Psychol* 44:22–6 F 60. * (*PA* 34:8464)
6. FLEISHMAN, EDWIN A., AND PETERS, DAVID R. "Interpersonal Values, Leadership Attitudes, and Managerial 'Success.'" *Personnel Psychol* 15:127–43 su '62. * (*PA* 37:7321)

JEROME E. DOPPELT, *Assistant Director, Test Division, The Psychological Corporation, New York, New York.*

This questionnaire provides measures of two independent dimensions of supervisory leadership: structure and consideration. Structure (S) is defined as the extent to which an individual is likely to structure his own role and those of his subordinates toward goal attainment, and consideration (C) is the extent to which an individual is likely to have job relationships characterized by mutual trust, a certain warmth between supervisor and subordinates, and the like. The question booklet contains 40 short statements to which the examinee responds by expressing his opinion on how frequently he *should* do what is described, e.g., "Criticize poor work." For each item, scoring weights of 0 to 4 correspond to the five choices. Scores on the S and C scales, each based on 20 items, are readily obtained from an answer sheet cleverly embedded in the booklet.

The claim that the S and C scales are independent is based, in part, on the background of the questionnaire. Factor analysis studies revealed these two patterns as independent. Further evidence is offered in a table of correlations between S and C, reported in the manual. For 13 groups, the correlation coefficients varied between −.23 and .08. Low correlations are also reported between scores on the questionnaire and several measures of mental ability and of personality. It is unfortunate that the tables of correlation data suffer from poor description of the groups of subjects. The table relating questionnaire scores to personality measures does not identify the groups at all. Two tables include such incomplete descriptions as "22 Top Executives," "394 Industrial Employees," and "145 ROTC Cadets." None of the correlation tables shows means and standard deviations of, questionnaire scores or of the other variables. The reader who is interested in determining the similarity between any of the reported groups and his own group, either in terms of description or of score distributions, will find it difficult to do so.

Reliability estimates, computed by the split-half method for four groups, vary between .79 and .88 for the S scale and between .62 and .89 for the C scale. Test-retest coefficients for two small groups (31 first-line employees who are not otherwise described and 24 Air Force noncommissioned officers) were .74 and .67 for S and .80 and .77 for C. The test-retest coefficients are low for the assessment of individuals although the odd-even coefficients are higher than would be expected of such short scales. It is possible the odd-even reliability estimates are increased by the inclusion of some items which are essentially alike. For example, "Be willing to make changes," and "Reject suggestions for changes," appear to be the same item with a change in polarity. (Again, the failure to show means and standard deviations for the reliability samples hinders generalization of the findings.)

Percentile norms for each scale are given for a group of 780 "General Supervisory Personnel" and for six "Special Manager Groups" which include foremen, college seniors majoring in engineering and industrial administration, executives, etc. Except for the college seniors, the sources of the norms groups are not made clear and it would be advisable to heed the manual's suggestion: "These may be used as guidelines for interpreting the LOQ scale scores until local normative and validity data are accumulated."

The author of the LOQ feels that the factor analysis and item selection procedures used to develop the consideration and structure measures support the construct validity of the instrument. Perhaps so, but even more important is this sentence in the same paragraph: "It is urged that validity studies, relating these dimensions to independent critera of effectiveness, be carried out in particular organizations." Two of the three studies reported in the manual are of interest: In one, 53 supervisors in a petrochemical plant were rated on performance two years after testing; in the second, 42 sales supervisors were rated three years after testing. The S scale showed no relationship to the criterion in either study. The C scale correlated .29 and .32 with the criteria of the two studies.

Supplementary unpublished materials sent to the reviewer summarized several additional studies of the questionnaire. One of these was a further follow-up of the second study noted above. Five years after the administraton of the questionnaire, ratings and C scores correlated .37 for the 26 people who remained in the group. The relationships between C and S scores and various types of ratings were studied in a pharmaceutical company, a shoe manufacturing company, and in three hospitals. Some of the findings were encouraging and some possible uses of the questionnaire were suggested.

In summary, the *Leadership Opinion Questionnaire* is a short, easily administered instrument which yields two scores. It is important to heed the author's caution, "If used for selection purposes, individual validity studies should be carried out first." The questionnaire may be useful as an aid in management training programs which want to concentrate on the encouragement or suppression of the attitudes exemplified by the items. The current manual is labeled "Preliminary Edition"; future editions would be improved by more generous description of the data.

WAYNE K. KIRCHNER, *Manager, Personnel Research, Minnesota Mining and Manufacturing Company, St. Paul, Minnesota.*

This questionnaire consists of 40 items related to supervisory or managerial behavior. It is scored on two dimensions or factors: structure and consideration. Essentially, structure characterizes the extent to which a person likes to direct group activities and, in a sense, is directed toward getting out the work. Consideration reflects the extent to which a supervisor is human relations oriented or how warm he is in dealings with subordinates. The basic use' of the questionnaire is to determine an individual's leadership "style" in terms of the two dimensions. The two dimensions of supervisory behavior were identified in the well known Ohio State leadership studies of a few years ago and were derived through factor analytic techniques. Past research in this area is impressive.

Statistically, the instrument appears to be fairly reliable. Correlations are cited for a variety of groups for both the split-half and test-retest methods. Correlations range from .62 to .89 for the two scales. It seems likely, therefore, that this is a reasonably reliable instrument.

Several validity studies are cited. There is good evidence that consideration scores, for example, correlate with successful ratings of supervisory performance in a variety of different activities. It appears, therefore, that this questionnaire has some validity in determining leadership style or supervisory behavior.

Norms are available for several different groups. They encompass the range from the perennial college senior to such groups as educational supervisors. In addition, they contain norms for a sizable ($n = 780$) group of general supervisory personnel.

Does the questionnaire have defects? Certainly, one question that comes to mind is the degree of fakability of the questionnaire. Could a supervisor completing this questionnaire make himself appear much higher in consideration than he normally is? This is highly possible. In using the questionnaire with a group of people from his own company, the reviewer found some people, who by all external criteria were quite hard hearted and non-human relations minded, who scored high on consideration. Informal interviews with these people and a review of the items on the scoring key suggest that this might be a somewhat fakable instrument.

Its particular value ought to be in terms of use within the structure of a supervisory or managerial training program. Where persons fill out the questionnaire honestly, one can estimate how they stack up against other supervisors and managers. This should have some beneficial effect. Data relevant to this question are presented in the manual and in related material.

Overall, this is not a bad instrument. It has been developed through careful research and careful statistical techniques. It appears to be reliable, presents good evidence of validity, and presents reasonably good norms. It seems well suited for research activities and training activities, although it is probably not the best thing to use as an evaluative instrument of supervisory performance.

[1191]

★Personal Development Record. Supervisors; 1957–63; 5 parts: self-evaluation of abilities, self-evaluation of job performance, strengths and weaknesses, plans for improvement, summary; Form S ('57, 9 pages) ; manual ['63, 4 unnumbered pages] ; no data on reliability; norms for males and for first three parts only; $6.75 per 25 records; 10¢ per key; postage extra; $1 per specimen set, postpaid; (30) minutes; Richardson, Bellows, Henry & Co., Inc. *

[1192]

★Supervisory Index. Supervisors; 1960; 5 attitude scores: management, supervision, employees, human relations practices, total; 1 form (4 pages) ; preliminary manual (11 pages) ; $4.95 per 20 tests; 25¢ per manual; 50¢ per specimen set; postage extra; (10–20) minutes; Norman Gekoski and S. L. Schwartz; Science Research Associates, Inc. *

REFERENCES

1. SCHWARTZ, SOLOMON L., AND GEKOSKI, NORMAN. "The Supervisory Inventory: A Forced-Choice Measure of Human Relations Attitude and Technique." J Appl Psychol 44:233–6 Ag '60. * (PA 35:4130)

ARTHUR H. BRAYFIELD, *Executive Officer, American Psychological Association, Washington, D.C.*

The *Supervisory Index* poses a neglected ethical problem.

The instructions to the testee say : "Remember, this is NOT a test; there are no right or wrong answers. You should mark those statements which best describe how you feel about these things."

In the manual, there is a section on suggested uses of the index which includes selection, placement, and training. Thus: "The scores on the *Index* may be used, in conjunction with other appropriate instruments, for selecting from the pool of supervisory candidates those most likely to be 'successful.' In some companies the total score may be a significant predictor of success; in other company environments a composite score obtained by applying appropriate weights to the area scores may yield the best results." In short, personnel actions based on scores derived from the index are suggested.

In the light of the instructions on the front page of the index, these suggestions embrace a form of deception. I recommend that the index be withdrawn from the market pending clarification of this question.

ALBERT K. KURTZ, *Fulbright Lecturer, Ein Shams University, Cairo, United Arab Republic.*

This is a very carefully constructed test which has been shown to correlate with two somewhat different criteria of the success of 73 men already employed as supervisors. If it can show similar validity coefficients when given to new (and preferably larger) groups who are tested when appointed as supervisors and evaluated later, it will have shown itself to be a very worthwhile test.

Except for a few places where minor objections might be raised, the bulk of the manual is well written and sufficiently detailed to give the prospective test user an excellent description of the steps taken in constructing and validating the test. Further, the work appears to have been done well.

The *Supervisory Index* was cross validated against ratings made by plant psychologists on two criteria: (*a*) attitudinal characteristics and (*b*) administrative and production skills. The reviewer's work as an industrial psychologist may be responsible for his marked preference for the second criterion against which the total score gave a validity of .33 as opposed to .61 for the first criterion. Even though .33 does not appear to be very high, it is difficult to achieve high validities in industry, especially on supervisory jobs. (Besides, for people who prefer the other criterion, that validity of .61 is indeed high.) As hinted above, the crucial issue is whether or not these figures on concurrent validity are typical of the at present unknown predictive validity of the test.

The directions for giving the test are too casual. The test administrator is supposed to read the directions to "large groups," implying that this is not to be done for individuals tested singly or in small groups. He is to "emphasize" some points, "warn" the people taking the test, and check to see that each person "has filled in the information requested in the box on the cover of the booklet completely." The latter may be a bit difficult, both because the directions say nothing about filling in these blanks and because as soon as anyone starts answering the test, the box (completed or ignored) is no longer visible. In brief, the direc-

tions need to be clarified and standardized. This will necessitate changes both in the manual and on the test blank.

The difficulty which Science Research Associates had for years in getting the printer to so align his pages that the pinholes in the *Kuder Preference Record* would register properly for scoring is here again, even though no pinholes are used. This test is answered by blackening small circles. In 5 of the 24 forced-choice items, the answer circles for two of the alternatives are so close together (because some of the alternatives are only one instead of several lines long) that a tiny printer's error in alignment could (and on my copy of the test would) lead to errors in scoring. This is minor because it would be so easy to correct, but it is also a major criticism because it may lead to erroneous scores.

Another criticism, applying to this and several hundred other tests, is that the four part scores are not reliable enough to justify their use for differential diagnosis. The total score alone should be used.

The *Supervisory Index* is a well constructed and validated test. If it can be shown to have predictive validity as well as the concurrent validity it possesses, it will be a good test for selecting supervisors in industry. The test is badly in need of improved directions for administering it. Other aspects of the test could also be improved if the authors and publisher have the desire to do so.

[1193]

★**Supervisory Inventory on Human Relations.** Supervisors and prospective supervisors; 1960; 1 form (3 pages); revised manual (9 pages); $4.95 per 20 self-marking tests; 25¢ per manual; 50¢ per specimen set; postage extra; (15) minutes; Donald L. Kirkpatrick and Earl Planty; Science Research Associates, Inc. *

REFERENCES

1. KIRCHNER, WAYNE; HANSON, RICHARD; AND BENSON, DALE. "Selecting Foremen With Psychological Tests." *Personnel Adm* 23:27–30 N–D '60. *

SEYMOUR LEVY, *Manager, Personnel Research and Manpower Development, The Pillsbury Company, Minneapolis, Minnesota.*

This test asks the subject to indicate his agreement or disagreement with 80 items reflecting various principles and practices and attitudes related to supervisory behavior. Item content reflects concepts dealing with understanding and motivating employees, the supervisor's role in management, developing positive employee attitudes, some awareness of principles of learning and training, and, lastly, five items on problem solving techniques. The test is presented in an attractive format. It is easily readable and probably does not pose any technical difficulties in completion of the instrument. The language of the items is clear and the statements are short and should not pose undue difficulties in interpreting their meaning.

The inventory was originally developed as a measuring tool for evaluating institutes on human relations for foremen and supervisors at the Management Institute of the University of Wisconsin. The items thus reflect the course content of this program. Item scoring was developed by obtaining agreement of the instructors who presented the course.

The authors suggest this instrument may be used: (a) to determine needs for human relations training, (b) to provide information for on-the-job coaching, (c) as a device for conference discussions, (d) to determine the effectiveness of a human relations course, and (e) to assist in the selection of supervisors. Very few data are provided on the validity of the inventory in these different situations. The norms that are provided are clearly inadequate. While it is stated that the norm table includes scores of foremen, office supervisors, and middle and top management groups, no measures of standard deviation and no percentiles are provided. This leaves real ambiguity with respect to variability. The publisher reports that percentiles will be made available in a future manual.

A split-half reliability of .94 is reported. No data, however, are provided with respect to the number of persons involved in this sample and the nature of their backgrounds.

The validity and significance of this inventory is still to be determined. The instrument raises more questions than it answers. For example: Are there differences in scores at different job levels of supervisory responsibility? What is the correlation with intelligence and with experience? Are there differences among supervisors in different industries? Does change in score through teaching reflect itself in improved performance on the job?

[1194]

*Supervisory Practices Test. Supervisors; 1957-64; 1 form ('57, 4 pages); revised manual ('64, 12 pages); $5 per 25 tests; 25¢ per key; $1.75 per manual; $2.50 per specimen set; cash orders postpaid;

French, Portuguese, and Belgian editions available; (20-30) minutes; Martin M. Bruce; the Author. *

REFERENCES
1. BRUCE, MARTIN M. "Normative Data Information Exchange, No. 10-34." *Personnel Psychol* 10:369 au '57. * (*PA* 33:80)
2. BRUCE, MARTIN M., AND LEARNER, DAVID B. "A Supervisory Practices Test." *Personnel Psychol* 11:207-16 su '58. *
3. WATLEY, DONIVAN JASON. *Prediction of Academic Success in a College of Business Administration.* Doctor's thesis, University of Denver (Denver, Colo.), 1961. (*DA* 22:3527)
4. WATLEY, DONIVAN J., AND MARTIN, H. T. "Prediction of Academic Success in a College of Business Administration." *Personnel & Guid J* 41:147-54 O '62. * (*PA* 37:5656)

For reviews by Clifford E. Jurgensen and Mary Ellen Oliverio, see 5:955.

[1195]

★Test of Supervisory Judgment. Business and industry; 1949-63; Forms S ('49), T ('53), (9 pages); Form T is a revision of Form S (with 60 per cent of the items the same) rather than a parallel form; separate manuals for Forms S ['63, 13 unnumbered pages], T ['63, 6 unnumbered pages]; $5.50 per 25 tests; $1 per set of keys; $1.25 per manual for Form S; $1 per manual for Form T; postage extra; $2 per specimen set, postpaid; (30-35) minutes; Richardson, Bellows, Henry & Co., Inc. *

[1196]

★WLW Supervisor Survey. Supervisors; 1956-62; 2 scores: considerate attitudes, initiative; Form 3 ('62, 8 mimeographed pages); mimeographed manual ('62, 3 pages); mimeographed teaching manual ('57, 14 pages) for an earlier form; no data on reliability and validity; 15¢ per test, postpaid; teaching manual free; [35] minutes; R. W. Henderson; William, Lynde & Williams. *

[Other Tests]

For tests not listed above, see the following entries in *Tests in Print:* 2092 and 2098; out of print: 2093; status unknown: 2089.

TRANSPORTATION

[1197]

[Driver Selection Forms and Tests.] Truck drivers; 1943-55; part of White Motor Company's *Continuing Control System of Truck Management;* individual in part; no manual; postage extra; Dartnell Corporation. *

a) EMPLOYMENT APPLICATION. 1946; 3 editions: Form Nos. 111 (city delivery drivers), 211 (over-the-road drivers), 311 (long distance drivers), ['46, 2 pages]; 1-99 copies, 7¢ each.

b) TELEPHONE CHECK. 1946-53; Form No. OT-203 ('53, 1 page); 1-99 copies, 6¢ each; Robert N. McMurry.

c) DRIVER INTERVIEW. 1946; Form No. 13 ['46, 2 pages]; 1-99 copies, 10¢ each.

d) PHYSICAL EXAMINATION RECORD. 1946-54; Form No. 19 ('54, 1 page); 1-99 copies, 6¢ each.

e) SELECTION AND EVALUATION SUMMARY. 1950-55; Form No. ES-404R ('55, 1 page); 1-99 copies, 6¢ each; Robert N. McMurry.

f) STANDARDIZED TEST: TRAFFIC AND DRIVING KNOWLEDGE FOR DRIVERS OF MOTOR TRUCKS. 1946-54; Form No. 16 ['46, 4 pages]; directions sheet-scoring key ['46, 2 pages]; no data on reliability; 1-99 copies, 10¢ each; 7¢ per directions sheet-scoring key; administration time not reported; Amos E. Neyhart and

Helen L. Neyhart; also distributed by Institute of Public Safety, Pennsylvania State University.

g) ROAD TEST IN TRAFFIC FOR TESTING, SELECTING, RATING, AND TRAINING TRUCK DRIVERS. 1943–46; 3 scores: specific driving skills, general driving habits and attitudes, total; individual; 1 form ['45]; score sheet ['46, Form No. 18, 2 pages]; no manual; no data on reliability; no norms; 1–99 copies, 7¢ each; [30–60] minutes; Amos E. Neyhart.

JOSEPH E. MOORE, *Regents Professor of Psychology, Georgia Institute of Technology, Atlanta, Georgia.*

There are 10 forms in this series. The three employment application forms are identical except for the color of the paper. Form OT-203, Telephone Check, asks only one question concerning driving, "What accidents has he had?" Form 13, Driver Interview, is the typical patterned interview form with six specific questions concerning accidents. On the basis of replies to such questions as "What was the worst driving accident you ever had?" the interviewer is asked "Is he careless?" On the response to the question "How did it happen?" the interviewer is asked, "Does this indicate 'accident proneness'?" It is doubtful if many or perhaps any interviewer could ascertain significant behavior from such short questions. These forms are for interviewing and evaluating applicants but, as in using all such forms, the significant value comes from the skill, training, and clinical insight possessed by the interviewer. However, the patterned interview forms could very well suggest questions that the average interviewer is not competent to evaluate and thus do a disservice, if not a rank injustice, to the applicant.

Form 16 claims to be a standardized test of traffic and driver knowledge for drivers of motor trucks. This test is composed of 57 multiple choice questions, each containing four choices. Form 17 is the scoring key. There is no manual or other information pertaining to validity or reliability of the test. Form 18 is the road test. This is merely a checklist and score sheet for 16 areas of performance covering such things as starting the engine through signaling and positioning of the vehicle on the roadway.

Form 19 is a typical physical examination record for drivers.

Form ES-404R, the Selection and Evaluation Summary, contains certain items grouped under background, character traits, motivation, and emotional maturity. The rater assigns values from 1 through 4 and tries to match the applicant's qualities against the requirement for a particular position.

The forms are printed in clear legible type. The arrangement of items is, for the most part, logical and sequential. The users of these forms should be alerted to the fact that they will not, in and of themselves, improve selection procedures. The unsubstantiated claims set forth in the general booklet entitled *Developing a Better Personnel Selection Program* should be taken as just that. For example, the exaggerated statements "Even the addition of a telephone check plan may double the effectiveness of personnel selection in many organizations," and "the patterned interview has been designed to overcome the limitations and faults of ordinary interviewing" have no data whatsoever supporting them.

For a review by S. Rains Wallace, Jr., see 4:789.

[1198]

★[McGuire Safe Driver Scale and Interview Guide]. Prospective motor vehicle operators; 1961–62; 2 parts; driver selection guide ('62, 26 pages including copies of both parts and manual for *a*); $15 per set of 25 copies of *a*, manual for *a*, and 25 copies of *b*; $5 per driver selection guide; postpaid; Frederick L. McGuire; Western Psychological Services. *
a) THE MCGUIRE SAFE DRIVER SCALE. Title on test is *The McGuire S D Scale;* items selected in part from *Kuder Preference Record-Personal* and *Minnesota Multiphasic Personality Inventory;* 1 form ('61, 4 pages); manual ('62, 8 pages); reliability data for part 1 only; $6.50 per 25 tests; $3 per manual; (10–20) minutes.
b) THE MCGUIRE SAFE DRIVER INTERVIEW GUIDE. 1 form ('61, 4 pages); no specific manual; instructions contained in driver selection guide; no data on reliability and validity; $6.50 per 25 forms; [30–60] minutes.

REFERENCES

1. MCGUIRE, FREDERICK L. "The Safe-Driver Inventory: A Test for Selecting the Safe Automobile Driver." *U S Armed Forces Med J* 7:1249–64 S '56. * (PA 31:3052)

WILLARD A. KERR, *Professor of Psychology, Illinois Institute of Technology, Chicago, Illinois.*

This well printed 4-page test of 78 temperament, value, and interest items is outwardly labeled simply *The McGuire S D Scale.* All items are objectively stated and scored, and the scoring process is simple.

The McGuire kit also contains a 4-page "Safe Driver Interview Guide," which is a conventional guide for making and recording one's impressions of the driver job applicant. The eight areas of guided discussion with an observation of the applicant are work history, school history, military record, health history, family history, marital history, social level, and aspiration level. The guide is concluded by a total summation rating of risk. The manual provides no supportive evidence of validity or even of specific research derivation.

The purpose of the test is to help detect the safe driver. Items employed have been found to discriminate between driver groups with good safety records and driver groups with weaker safety records. All items are of the voluntary commitment type, such as temperament test and interest test items. Content of the accompanying manual suggests a thoughtful and competent approach to the psychology of this difficult problem, including a provocative summary of characteristics of drivers with superior safety records. An odd-even reliability of .88 on 153 Navy personnel is reported.

The six validity studies which are briefly reported convince the reviewer that the test can discriminate between better and poorer drivers *when both are tested after already being hired*. Under this limited condition, using a raw cutting score of 46, the efficiency of prediction is reported to range between 61 and 88 per cent. Although some of these studies are referred to as cross validations and, in a sense, are, none of them seems to be based on pre-employment testing and later follow-up in service which is the crucial test of validity of all voluntary commitment devices.

The manual is weak specifically in that (*a*) no validity coefficients are given, and (*b*) although there is implication that the test is useful in selecting safe drivers, none of the validity evidence appears to be from pre-employment evaluation situations. Therefore, one can only speculate whether or not the test will predict driver safety when it is administered as part of the pre-employment evaluation. The motivation to "look good" to the prospective employer will probably reduce the test's usefulness substantially, as it does in current temperament and interest measures in pre-employment testing; nevertheless, the test shows ingenuity and deserves a fair trial in the pre-employment selection of taxi and truck drivers.

D. H. Schuster, *Staff Psychologist, Collins Radio Company, Cedar Rapids, Iowa.*

MC GUIRE SAFE DRIVER SCALE. According to the manual, the MSDS "is a paper-and-pencil test for use in selecting safe motor-vehicle drivers." In the test derivation, two assumptions were made about predicting motor vehicle accidents. The first was that "the largest and most important factor operating to produce motor-vehicle accidents is the attitude and personality pattern of the individual driver." The second was that "it is more productive and efficient to identify and select the safe driver than to identify the accident producer." The first assumption is subject to question, since the reviewer has found that motor vehicle accidents can be predicted at least as well on the basis of risks taken while driving (i.e., amount of night driving or annual mileage driven) as on the basis of the driver's attitude. The second assumption is justified in the context of the intended use of this test, that is, selection of the safe driver for commercial transportation organizations.

Many of the items in the MSDS were selected by item analysis from standard tests cited in the manual. Items retained were those which differentiated an accident group from an accident-free group at the 5 per cent level of significance. The accident group consisted of drivers (U.S. Marines) who reported that they had been involved within the previous two years in an accident and also had received a moving violation citation at the time of the accident. The tacit assumption is that the driver was, accordingly, responsible for the accident. The accident-free group consisted of drivers who claimed that they had never been involved in any accidents while driving, nor had they ever incurred any moving violation citations. Thus a considerable number of drivers with intermediate records were omitted from the item analysis; how many is not stated. This process conceivably could select just the more extreme problem drivers. It should be noted that the criterion for assigning drivers to the groups was a dual one, involving both accidents and moving violation citations. No information on the correlation between these two variables is reported in the manual, but, from unpublished studies made by this reviewer, the correlation would appear to be about .20 to .30. In the original sample used for item analysis, drivers reportedly could be assigned to the correct driver group with an accuracy of 88 per cent.

In one cross validation, the efficiency of correct assignment was 65 per cent versus a

chance level of 50 per cent. In other cross validations with Marine Corps drivers, the accuracy varied from 61 to 70 per cent correct.
These results are statistically significant at or
beyond the 1 per cent level. Thus, in several
cross validations, the MSDS appears to have
some predictive validity for current accident
records of drivers. It should be noted that the
"prediction" was really postdiction, not prediction as would be obtained from a follow-up
study after testing of the drivers.

The cutoff score is not reported in all cases
for the cross validation studies. In a number
of studies a raw cutoff score of 46 was used,
corresponding to a centile score of 69 for
"Private Operators," reasonably close to the
percentage of accident-free drivers in a three-
year period. A raw cutoff score of 54 should
be used for professional drivers, as this corresponds to a centile score of 71. The cutoff
score should be adjusted by the user, depending on the supply of applicants and on how
confident he wishes to be about the future
accident record of the applicants.

Norms for three groups are given in the
manual, and these will be quite useful to the
test user. The user is well advised to collect
data and develop his own norms as soon as
possible.

In two of the three studies in which accident and nonaccident groups were compared,
there was an equal number of drivers in each
of the groups; this is far from the accident
distribution found in practice. Most drivers
in a given one- or even three-year period have
not had any accidents. Thus the prediction
problem is particularly bad, since the aim of
the MSDS is to weed out the rare driver with
a poor record. The usefulness of the test can
be judged by seeing how much improvement it
produces above chance or existing selection
procedures. In selecting civilian professional
drivers in a transit company, the MSDS was
able to produce an improvement of 16 percentage points (86 per cent correct selection compared to 70 per cent) over the established
hiring procedure of the company. Thus the
scale appears to have some merit for improving the chances of hiring a safe driver.

Reliability of Part 1 appears to be satisfactory (.88); no reliability data are given for
Part 2. No figures are given for validity in
terms of correlation coefficients.

MC GUIRE SAFE DRIVER INTERVIEW GUIDE.
The manual for the interview guide (MSDIG)
presents the background of the research in
greater detail than the manual for the MSDS.
The temperament and personality traits which
have been found to be related to moving violation and accident-incurring drivers are reviewed. The MSDIG incorporates the MSDS
as an important factor in the employment interview. In addition, an interview guide is provided to direct the questions asked of the applicant by the interviewer. The following areas
are covered: work history, school history, military record, health, family history, marital history, social history, and aspiration level. In
general, the interview guide is designed to
elicit information of positive and negative
factors with respect to hiring a good employee,
as well as hiring a good and safe driver. The
approach in using the MSDIG is clinical or
global, and no validity data for the guide by
itself are presented. Its use is justified by the
important negative finding (such as a very
poor attitude) it may uncover occasionally.

SUMMARY. The interview guide and MSDS
appear to be worthwhile instruments in the
selection of safe drivers. Actual data on predictive validity of the two instruments are not
yet available. The test does offer some validity
for locating accident-having drivers. The prospective user also should consider tests of
driving performance, driving information, and
driving aptitude in the selection of drivers. No
data are given in the test manual, or are available anywhere—at least not to the reviewer's
knowledge—that support this specific recommendation. The recommendation for using
other tests is based on the general consideration that predictive validity is increased in general by sampling as many different relevant
factors as possible.

[1199]

Truck Driver Test. Drivers of light and medium
trucks; 1957–58; form 60-A ('57, 15 pages plus fold-
out answer sheet); preliminary mimeographed manual
('58, 5 pages); general PPA mimeographed directions ['57, 7 pages]; no norms; 10–49 tests, $1 each;
$2 per specimen set; postpaid; 90(100) minutes;
Public Personnel Association. *

WILLARD A. KERR, *Professor of Psychology,
Illinois Institute of Technology, Chicago, Illinois.*

A 14-page reusable test booklet with separable answer sheet is accompanied by a brief

normless manual which states that the test is intended "to assist in the selection of light and medium truck drivers for the public service."

The test, which contains 75 multiple choice items arranged in ascending order of difficulty within each subject matter field, is primarily an information test. Most items have high face validity for light truck driving, but the manual is devoid of actual validity evidence. The items are relevant (safe driving practices, maintenance service and repairs, traffic regulations, mechanical aptitude and ability to understand written orders) and it is reasonable to believe that the test has validity for selecting individuals with appropriate knowledge for truck driving. It does not pretend to be a test of skill in actual driving.

D. H. SCHUSTER, *Staff Psychologist, Collins Radio Company, Cedar Rapids, Iowa.*

The items in the test were developed on the basis of task analysis of the typical duties and responsibilities for the job of truck driver. Many public personnel agencies were polled and only the items rated by two or more agencies as involved in the job of truck driver were retained. The trial form reflected the common core of subject matter included by most agencies in their own test for the truck driver class. The trial form of the test was administered to more than 800 applicants by eight public agencies throughout the United States and Canada. An item analysis was employed with the criterion apparently (not so stated) the total item score. Items retained were correlated at least .30 with the criterion. The validity of the test is essentially that of content validity plus face validity. The test, by agreement among the agencies originally polled, does measure the knowledge and abilities important in the selection of truck drivers. No predictive validity checks with an external criterion have been made. The reason given is that there is no global criterion or suitable yardstick to measure the success of truck drivers. Thus the validity of the test is qualitatively that agreed upon by personnel agencies and has no quantitative figure. In the opinion of the reviewer, a suitable external criterion might be merit ratings or driving record of violations and accidents.

The reliability, as estimated by the split-half technique, is "greater than 0.90." The develop-

ment of the *Truck Driver Test* is yet to be completed. Although the manual is dated January 1958, no further validity or evaluation data have yet appeared.

In summary, the test appears to be valid for testing what a truck driver needs to know in terms of operating rules, procedures, and practices. It is not a driving performance test. The most notable lack is quantitative validity information. In addition, it seems the test could well be supplemented by tests involving personality variables or aptitudes pertinent to driver selection.

[1200 [1]]

★**Wilson Driver Selection Test.** Prospective motor vehicle operators; 1961; 6 scores (visual attention, depth visualization, recognition of simple detail, recognition of complex detail, eye-hand coordination, steadiness) and safety aptitude rating (based on number of subtests passed); 1 form (15 pages); manual (28 pages); $10 per 25 tests; 25¢ per key; $1.75 per manual; $2.50 per specimen set; cash orders postpaid; 26(50) minutes; Clark L. Wilson; Martin M. Bruce. *

WILLARD A. KERR, *Professor of Psychology, Illinois Institute of Technology, Chicago, Illinois.*

This test consists of a well printed 16-page booklet containing six chiefly nonverbal aptitude tests plus an unscored page of biographical information. It is intended to measure ability to operate vehicles with minimal risk. The six subtests are Visual Attention (5 minutes), Depth Visualization (5 minutes), Recognition of Simple Detail (4 minutes), Recognition of Complex Detail (5 minutes), Eye-Hand Coordination (2 minutes), and Steadiness (5 minutes). Reliabilities reported are, respectively, .59, .75, .79, .81, .84, and .93.

Perceptual speed and spatial relations form the central aptitude bases of this test, the rationale excluding personality variables. The specific measures have good face validity and seem well constructed.

The author notes consistent lack of predictive validity of paper and pencil tests for driver accident prevention published up to 1961. Why the present test content would perform better is not clear. Nevertheless, crude (null hypothesis rejection statistics) evidence is presented showing validity trends favoring the test for 71 bus drivers, 88 milk truck drivers in one group, 899 other milk truck drivers,

---

[1] Because of the insertion of additional tests (8a, 74a, 74b, 84a, 146a, 230a, 307a, 313a, 342a, 716a, 844a, 867a, 872a, 887a, 909a, 931a, 951a, 1013a, and 1061a), the total number of test entries is 1219.

206 salesmen, and 85 police motorcycle officers. Without validity coefficients, however, the strength of these relations is unclear.

The manual makes deferential reference to the APA standards for test manuals and then proceeds to display seven pages of validity data without reporting a single validity coefficient. Nevertheless, this test apparently has *some* validity for screening low aptitude people away from driving jobs; a communicable validity study on it is needed.

D. H. Schuster, *Staff Psychologist, Collins Radio Company, Cedar Rapids, Iowa.*

This is a battery of six short timed tests measuring four visual aptitudes listed above and two psychomotor tests. A cutoff score, established on the basis of a pass-fail dichotomy for the accident records of bus drivers, was established for each test. The battery score is simply the number of tests out of six that the driver passed (number of tests on which the driver's score was at or above the test cutoff score).

A number of validity studies were made with different types of drivers—bus drivers, milk delivery drivers, field salesmen, passenger car drivers, and motorcycle drivers. While most of the studies were concerned with postdiction, or the prediction of accident records of drivers in the immediate past, two of the validity studies were concerned with predicting the accident records of drivers subsequent to testing. Using at-fault accidents as the criterion, most of the studies showed that the final test battery score (0 to 6) does discriminate between drivers with and without accidents. The level of significance in these studies varied from close to the 5 per cent level to well beyond it. Even when the criterion was somewhat weaker, merely accident involvements, the test also provided significant discrimination. Since the battery score was not dichotomized, accuracy of prediction figures are not given. The reviewer took the liberty of establishing a cutoff score for one of the validity studies and determined that the battery score discriminated with an accuracy of 59 per cent between motorcylists with and without accident involvements, versus the 47 per cent discrimination expected by chance in this case.

The reliability for the battery as a whole is a satisfactory .84. The reliabilities for the six individual tests are lower but range from .59 to .93.

Missing from the manual are data that show the correlation between the battery score and number of accidents, or information about the factor structure of the six tests. Also missing is any information on the reliability of the accident criterion. In the experience of the reviewer, the reliability of accidents is fairly low, ranging from approximately .3 to .4, based upon communality estimates. While the prediction obtained with this test is thus likely close to the maximum attainable, the user ought to consider driver attitude, driving information, and performance tests in his selection battery.

In summary, the validity studies show that the *Wilson Driver Selection Test* does have a low but useful validity in discriminating between drivers with and those without accidents.

[Other Tests]

For tests not listed above, see the following entries in *Tests in Print:* 2100 and 2102–3.

REPRINTED FROM *The Seventh Mental Measurements Yearbook*

BUSINESS EDUCATION — SEVENTH MMY

REVIEWS BY *Lawrence W. Erickson, Bernard H. Newman, Mary Ellen Oliverio, Ray G. Price, Leonard J. West, and William L. Winnett.*

[552]
★Bookkeeping Achievement Test: Business Edu-

cation Achievement Test Series. 1, 2 semesters high school; 1967; 2 forms; 2 levels; manual (6

pages) ; 35(45) minutes; developed by the Psychological Corporation; Gregg Division, McGraw-Hill Book Co., Inc. * (*Out of print.*)
a) FIRST SEMESTER. Forms A (14 pages), B (12 pages).
b) FIRST YEAR. Forms C, D, (15 pages).

BERNARD H. NEWMAN, *Professor of Business and Business Division Director, Essex County College, Newark, New Jersey.*

This test has been developed to test achievement in bookkeeping on the secondary level after the first semester and after the first year. Each level has two equivalent forms and all tests are objective. The test is described as having been designed to include material generally covered in bookkeeping classes and is appropriate for classes using any of the common textbooks. In order to make the test even more generally applicable, synonymous accounting terms are listed on the cover page of the test where the student may refer to them during the test.

The objective questions make the test easy to grade, but the student is never asked to perform operationally. Thus, he does not journalize, post, prepare work sheets, or prepare statements. The questions, even on the forms of the test which are designed to be taken after the completion of one year of bookkeeping, are not as difficult to answer as the preparation of worksheets, statements and closing entries would be. It is also questionable whether operational performance ability and objective question answering ability always coincide. The American Institute of Certified Public Accountants has always felt that it was necessary to ask operational performance questions in order to test the knowledge of accountants.

In addition to the absence of performance questions this test does not even faintly touch on any matters relating to accounting theory. In this instance the defense might be made that high school textbooks are sadly deficient in this area as it could *not* be made in the case of performance questions. However, it must be presumed that teachers deal with the concept of matching expenses and revenue in order to teach entry adjustment. Essay questions might be more appropriate for ascertaining student achievement in this area. Nevertheless, there is little excuse for the almost total void of bookkeeping theory questions. A development of the understanding of accounting terminology in bookkeeping is important; the practice of including synonomous terms in the test rather than requiring students to know them might also be questioned.

The questions are generally simple and clear. There are a few instances in which they are poorly worded or ambiguous. For example, "What happens when merchandise is sold at a price above its cost?" The correct answer is "Liabilities remain unchanged." Although this answer is "correct," it does not respond to the question directly. An appropriate answer might be "a gross profit on sales is achieved." In another instance, an answer is "Closing entries are recorded in the general ledger." In another form of the test an answer is "Adjusting entries are recorded in the general journal." Both answers should be consistent as to the correct answer, and the latter is preferable to the former.

The ultimate measure of the validity of the test is whether it covers what it should in the course work. The reservations in this regard have been previously stated. Using the equivalent halves method and a randomly selected 200 cases for each form of the test, the reliability reported (.89 and .92) is satisfactory.

This test might be used by bookkeeping teachers in lieu of their own objective test. However, if it is desired that the student's total achievement be measured, it would be well also to test operational performance and understanding of accounting theory and terminology.

WILLIAM L. WINNETT, *Professor of Business Education, San Francisco State College, San Francisco, California.*

The two forms of the *Bookkeeping Achievement Test* for use at each of the two stated levels of instruction are essentially equivalent, and they may be used alternately as desired. For the most part, the usual multiple choice type of question is employed with a possible score of 65 for each form. However, the multiple points allotted for analyzing the debit and credit elements of a transaction and designating the appropriate special journal reduces the number of separate question stems to 57 each in Forms A and B, and to 46 in each of Forms C and D. This raises serious questions concerning the scope and depth of the test, particularly for a first year test.

The test is designed for use with any textbook. The problem of varying terminology among the different textbooks is recognized by including on the cover page of each test booklet a list of six bookkeeping terms together with synonymous terms often used. For other unfamiliar terms, the student is requested to do his best. Also, varying sequence of topics presents a minor problem. For example, the first semester edition contains one question each concerning petty cash, cash short and over, and promissory notes; but some textbooks do not introduce these topics until well into the second semester.

Performance testing in standardized bookkeeping examinations is much too rare. It is commendable that such testing is introduced by requiring the examinee to adjust entries on the work sheet. Hopefully, later revisions will extend this type of testing to other segments of bookkeeping work.

Norms for the test are given in percentile form. According to the test manual, the norms were developed on the basis of over 2,000 public secondary school students at 35 high schools in 16 states (34 schools in 17 states for the first-semester edition). The name and location of each school is given. Except for the statement that both urban and rural schools were invited to participate, no further information is given concerning the type and size of the schools or the grade level of the students.

Reliability of the test seems to be quite adequate, .89 for the first semester and .92 for the first year. These coefficients were computed by the split-half method.

This test goes no further than other tests in this field to establish a measure of validity using an objective, performance criterion. According to the test manual, validity was achieved by selecting items according to the content of widely used bookkeeping textbooks, then submitting these items to subject matter experts for review. This method is similar to practices commonly followed in the field; however, it is hoped that test developers will soon discover more objective measures of validity for bookkeeping examinations.

Teachers are invited to compare the test coverage with the objectives of their own courses. To facilitate such comparisons, the manual contains a table of subject matter coverage for each form according to number of points of score as well as percent of total points. For example, the distribution of score points for Form C is given as follows: general information, 10 points (15%); recording transactions, 24 points (37%); preparation of finan-cial reports, 16 points (25%); closing the books, 9 points (14%); banking and handling cash, 1 point (2%); purchases and sales, 3 points (4%); payrolls and taxes, 2 points (3%). Two factors, however, limit the value of these tables for determining the subject matter scope and depth: first, multiple responses reduce the number of separate questions in some categories; and, second, operational classifications, such as general information, recording transactions, and preparing financial reports, do not indicate the nature and/or difficulty of the topics involved. Prospective users of the test must perform an item by item analysis in order to obtain much usable information concerning topic scope and depth. The manual points out this deficiency of information provided. It would seem that such an analysis could have been included in the manual with very little additional effort.

All forms of the test show especially skillful construction. The questions are well organized and stated with a minimum of ambiguity. Simple, easy-to-understand directions combine with a liberal use of sample questions to insure a smooth movement of students through the examination. In addition to items mentioned earlier, the manual contains very explicit directions for administering and scoring, a table for easy conversion of raw scores to percentile norms, and considerable assistance with interpreting the results.

The *Bookkeeping Achievement Test* rates among the better tests of its type currently available in standardized form. It can serve very well to indicate relative position of a class or a student with respect to many others across the country. However, the small number of question stems, particularly in the first year edition, limits the power to show *total* achievement at respective levels. It is hoped that later revisions will employ the same high quality of item construction and format to increase both depth and scope as well as to extend the use of performance testing.

[553]

*Bookkeeping: Minnesota High School Achievement Examinations.** High school; 1952-71; new or revised form issued each May; Form EH Rev. ['71, c1968, 6 pages]; no specific manual; series manual ('71, 16 pages); no data on reliability; 15¢ per test; separate answer sheets (IBM 1230) may be used; 10¢ per answer sheet including scoring service; $1 per series manual; postage extra; $1.10 per specimen set, postpaid; 60(65) minutes; edited by V. L. Lohmann; American Guidance Service, Inc. *

For a review by Harold L. Royer of an earlier form, see 6:35; for a review by I. David Satlow, see 5:504.

[554]

★**General Business Achievement Test: Business Education Achievement Test Series.** High school; 1967; Forms A, B, (13 pages); manual (4 pages); 35(45) minutes; developed by the Psychological Corporation; Gregg Division, McGraw-Hill Book Co., Inc. * (*Out of print.*)

MARY ELLEN OLIVERIO, *Professor of Economic Education, Teachers College, Columbia University, New York, New York.*

This test is designed for use at the conclusion of a year of study of general business. While the test is not tied to a specific high school text, the content is closely related to the topics included in the commonly used 9th grade textbooks in general business. The percentage distribution of items by topics for Form A follows: American business system, 8; money and banking services, 10; consumer buying and credit, 20; savings and investments, 10; budget and recordkeeping, 3; insurance, 10; transportation and communication services, 17; labor, management, government activities, 13; occupational planning, 8.

There are 60 multiple choice items and 35 minutes are allowed for the completion of the test. The two forms of the test were evaluated for comparability of content and of difficulty. In both forms, approximately one-third of the items are simple definition questions. Illustrations of such are "The type of insurance which covers an employee who suffers a job connected injury is called" (four alternatives follow) and "The payment which an insured person makes to an insurance company is called the" (four alternatives follow). Simple rote memorization of information would appear sufficient to enable one to do well on such a test. The items are comparable to those one is likely to find on a test prepared by a teacher with no experience in teaching or no knowledge of test construction. This test is at best a *limited* measure of achievement. Teachers who have been critical of their teaching during recent years would have moved far beyond the teaching of mere facts, particularly in a practical, realistic subject such as general business. A general business test that reflected the range of understandings sought in today's teaching would have been extremely valuable.

The test is simple to administer. Students re-spond by checking the correct answer in the test booklet. Tests, therefore, must be hand scored. The test manual provides discussion of norms, validity, and reliability. The standardization process was not an impressive one; however, the quality of the test hardly deserved a comprehensive process. Norms were based on scores of 1,967 students who were completing a one-year course in general business in the spring of 1966 in public secondary schools in 26 schools in 15 states. Geographic and type of community (rural/urban) seem to be the only two variables that were given consideration in determining representativeness. No information is provided concerning the students or the level of the course. Who were the students who took general business? How many of them were in courses required for *all* students in the school? (There are some schools in the United States that require general business of all students.) How many of them were in the first course for those in a business curriculum? Were students in 9th grade only? (There are schools where the class rolls in general business have students from all four classes.) A single set of norms based on an undescribed school population is not a useful item of information. The one set of norms is given in percentile ranks in relation to raw scores on either form of the test.

Validity was determined by comparing content with that of commonly used texts and a reliability coefficient was computed by use of the split-half method. Standard error of measurement was also computed. The test manual explains each of the technical terms and aids the teacher unfamiliar with standarized testing in the interpretation of scores.

There is little use for this test except for the teacher who does not want to construct the simplest of tests—that which tests recognition of definitions or descriptions. Could we not leave to the classroom teacher the task of writing tests to determine this order of knowledge and expect a test developed by experts with facilities for standardization to provide measures of the extent to which critical understandings, interpretations, applications of new information have been achieved in a course?

RAY G. PRICE, *Professor of Business Education, University of Minnesota, Minneapolis, Minnesota.*

This test "has been developed....for the measurement of achievement at the end of a one-year course in general business in secondary schools." The course is usually taught at the ninth or tenth grade. Each form of the test consists of 60 multiple choice items.

The test is easily administered. Instructions for the proctors are uncomplicated and easy to follow. Directions to the student are presented in a clear, direct manner. The tests are designed for direct marking of the booklets. A scoring key is provided for each of the two forms.

Percentile rank equivalents of a raw score are given. "Norms....are based on scores obtained from public secondary school students completing a one-year course in general business in the spring of 1966."

According to the test publishers, validity was achieved by surveying "the contents of general business textbooks in widespread....use." Unfortunately for the test publishers, they surveyed the textbooks published before 1966. Therefore, even though their test may support the course content in general business before 1966, it is not appropriate for the course after 1966. This test is appropriate for the traditional content of general business courses of the 1950's and early 1960's. Since this test was developed, the emphasis in general business has been in the area of the development of economic understandings. Yet, in this test, only 12 (20 percent) of the 60 items measure economic understanding.

The weakness of the *General Business Achievement Test* is typical of many commercially prepared tests. The emphasis is on recall of specific details. It does not conform with what is taught now, but rather with what was taught in the past. Those who are interested in testing deeper economic understandings and the application of principles would be well advised to select the tests that accompany a modern textbook in general business.

The test needs to be revised to cover the current course content and to include more items that will measure higher levels of learning than the mere recall of specific facts. Properly revised, the test could provide a useful measuring instrument for general business.

[555]
*Hiett Simplified Shorthand Test (Gregg). 1, 2 semesters high school; 1951–63; Forms A, B, ('51, 8 pages); manual ('51, 6 pages); $2.40 per 25 tests; separate answer sheets may be used; 50¢ per key; postage extra; 75¢ per specimen set, postpaid; an identical edition except for use of Diamond Jubilee shorthand is available without manual under the title

Hiett Diamond Jubilee Shorthand Test ('63); (50) minutes; Victor C. Hiett and H. E. Schrammel (manual only); Data Processing and Educational Measurement Center. *

For a review by Gale W. Clark, see 5:512.

[556]
*National Teacher Examinations: Business Education. College seniors and teachers; 1956–70; Forms K-ONT ('69, 20 pages), RNT ('69, 19 pages), SNT1 ('70, 23 pages), SNT2 ('70, 20 pages); descriptive booklet ('70, 8 pages); for more complete information, see 582; 120(165) minutes; Educational Testing Service. *

RAY G. PRICE, *Professor of Business Education, University of Minnesota, Minneapolis, Minnesota.* [Review of Form SNT2.]

Four forms of the examination (Form K-ONT 1966, 1969; Form RNT, 1969; Form SNT1, 1970; Form SNT2, 1970) were presented for review. This review, however, will cover only Form SNT2 because of its more recent publication. A cursory review of the other forms indicated that this review is applicable to the other forms. All of the forms consist of 160 multiple choice items with five "plausible" answers. From the five answers, the test taker is instructed to choose the one he considers to be best, except in the last section, constituting approximately six percent of the test, where all answers but one are considered desirable and the candidate is asked to choose the least plausible.

As with all of the National Teacher Examinations, the Business Education test is well prepared. The test makers used a competent advisory committee of business educators. The test analysis is thorough and the statistical data are impressive and acceptable in the areas of reliability, standard deviation, skewness, and mean item difficulty. The clear directions for taking the test can be followed easily by the administrator and the test taker.

In general, the NTE in Business Education is well-constructed, with most items of good quality. All things considered, this test should provide prospective employers with one bit of information of use in evaluating business teacher candidates.

Obviously, a score on an objective test in business is only one clue to the qualifications of a successful business teacher. It is generally accepted that a "good" business teacher is one who understands content and methodology. The test does not, nor is any claim made that it does, measure other important qualities of a successful business teacher. Many of these other qualities have not been clearly identified, nor are they susceptible to objective measurement. These qualifications must be determined by less objective means such as interviews, observations, and other types of examinations. This acceptance of the limited assessment of teacher qualifications by the NTE in business may account for the lack of any reported attempt to establish the validity of the test by means of success on the job.

The limitation that confines the test taker to five alternative answers may cause some frustration. In some instances the offered choices may not fit at all the thoughtful student's concept of what the answer should be. With a number of items, none of the proposed answers may seem plausible. The student may wish to offer an entirely different, but acceptable, point of view than is suggested by the alternative choices. Yet, no such opportunity is provided. Or, as found by this reviewer, more than one alternative may seem to be an appropriate answer. These comments point up the difficulty of preparing multiple choice questions with five plausible answers, only one of which would be accepted as the best answer by most business educators.

It follows, therefore, that this test mostly tends to measure facts rather than attempting to assess the quality of the test taker's thinking and judgment. Yet on page 11 of the publisher's booklet, *ETS Builds a Test,* it states that:

It is erroneously believed in some quarters that objective items, although satisfactory for assessing knowledge of specific facts and information, cannot get at the quality of the test-taker's thinking and judgment—e.g., his ability to interpret, analyze, synthesize, evaluate. However, competent test writers have developed skill in writing objective test items that tap not just recall of facts but also highly complex intellectual functions and abilities.

This reviewer found very few questions, less than 10 percent, that do a respectable job of measuring the test taker's "ability to interpret, analyze, synthesize, and evaluate." Some questions are irrelevant in that they do not represent information a business teacher needs to know.

One of the concerns of this reviewer is the use of terminology. In some test items, the questions are concerned with "learning experiences for a first course in accounting at the high school level," while other items raise questions about the high school bookkeeping course. Even within a restricted area such as "practice

sets" some questions refer to "practice sets in bookkeeping," while others mention "accounting practice sets." Another confusing use of terminology involves the terms "office practice," "office procedures," and "clerical practice." Many test takers would be concerned with the use of terminology that may be used interchangeably but may differentiate between courses. For example, high school accounting may be a vastly different course from one in bookkeeping. Is an "office procedures" course different from one titled "office practice?" It would seem that standardization of terminology in a test of this kind would be desirable. If there is intended to be a difference, then this should be made clear.

In general, the test covered most of the major areas of secondary business teaching: typewriting, shorthand, accounting, data processing, office procedures, marketing, general business, business law, and economics. From 10 to 18 questions are devoted to each of the subjects identified above. The reviewer feels that two important areas, consumer education and cooperative education in office and distributive occupations, were inadequately represented, with only two items in each.

Many users of this test might consider the content rather traditional and shallow. Little in the way of new challenges to the business teacher is evident in content areas such as career development, consumer information, and labor-management relations. Recent developments involving block scheduling, business education for the disadvantaged, the advanced basic business course, and use of multi-media techniques are only a few examples of new trends that are not incorporated in this test.

One serious limitation is that the test attempts to measure the preparation needed by a teacher to teach all of the business subjects. That is, the test covers the content and methodology needed by the teacher in each of the following subject matter areas: accounting and data processing, economics and basic business, secretarial, clerical, and marketing and distributive education. This represents the situation of the past, when business teachers started in small schools which required that business teachers be able to teach all of the business subjects. There is a growing belief among business teacher educators that because of the increasing breadth of the field and because of school consolidation, a new concept of business teacher preparation is needed. Increasingly, teacher-education institutions are preparing students to teach only one or two phases of business rather than all phases. Several states are responding to this point of view by changing their business certification requirements. Emphasis is placed on a broad background of business courses, with specialization and certification in one or two phases of business, such as accounting and data processing, economics and basic business, secretarial, clerical, or marketing and distributive education.

Since the future preparation of business teachers is likely to continue in the direction of greater depth in more limited areas than at present, the current teacher examination in the field of business is not appropriate. For example, the student prepared to teach only in the special area of economics and basic business would be at a disadvantage in taking the NTE Business Education test, since more than one-third of the questions deal with the skill areas of typewriting, shorthand, and office procedures. Also, the student who was prepared to teach the secretarial and clerical phases of business would likely have difficulty with the questions in the marketing and distributive education phase of business. One solution for this deficiency would be to prepare a common business teacher examination accompanied by a series of specialized tests designed to cover, in greater depth than now, the five separate phases of business teacher preparation and certification.

For reviews of the testing program, see 582 (2 reviews), 6:700 (1 review), 5:538 (3 reviews), and 4:802 (1 review).

[557]

Reicherter-Sanders Typewriting I and II. 1, 2 semesters high school; 1962–64; first published 1962–63 in the Every Pupil Scholarship Test series; Forms A, B, ('64, 4 pages); 2 levels labeled Tests 1, 2; manual ('64, 3 pages); $1.75 per 25 tests, postage extra; 75¢ per specimen set, postpaid; (40–50) minutes; Richard F. Reicherter and M. W. Sanders; Data Processing and Educational Measurement Center. *

LAWRENCE W. ERICKSON, *Professor of Education and Assistant Dean, Graduate School of Education, University of California, Los Angeles, California.*

Forms A and B of Test I are designed for administration at the end of the first semester (one-half year) of typewriting instruction; and Forms A and B of Test II, at the end of the

second semester (one year) of typewriting instruction. The coefficient of reliability of these tests, as determined by the split-half method, ranges from .89 to .93. No information is given if the norms were derived from test results with high school or college students. According to the authors, the test results may be used for (*a*) determining pupil achievement; (*b*) checking the efficiency of instruction; (*c*) assigning school marks; (*d*) analyzing pupil and class weaknesses; and (*e*) motivating pupil effort.

Since the same format is used for all these tests, they are reviewed according to the parts making up the tests. Each test is made up of five parts as follows:

PART 1. This part consists of a series of paragraphs, primarily of a straight-copy nature; however, Test I, Form A, and Test II, Form B, contain some figures and symbols. All directions are the same for this part: The copy is to be typed with a 60-space line for four minutes. The first paragraph is to be typed without error before advancing to the second, etc. Apparently points are given for each correctly typed paragraph, but neither the manual nor the test directions give any indication of the number of points to be given.

This was the first confusing element of Part 1 of both Forms A and B. The second confusing element, and this seems to be far more serious, is that the paragraphs making up the copy are not graded by any commonly recognized measure of copy difficulty, such as syllable intensity, word length, or percentage of high frequency words. A quick check of the paragraphs by this reviewer reveals that they do indeed vary in difficulty. This fact may cause the students taking the tests to make more errors on the more difficult paragraphs. Furthermore, it seems to this reviewer to be entirely unrealistic to expect first-year typewriting students to type paragraphs without error. Even for the experienced typist, this is a frustrating direction. A much better procedure, and more nearly realistic, would be to have the errors erased and corrected.

PART 2. This part consists again of a series of paragraphs to be copied by the typist; however, he is now directed to correct his errors in an "appropriate manner." Just what this appropriate manner is, is not specified. One wonders if the typist could use such corrective devices as correction tape or fluid, or even if the errors might be "x'd" out. The latter procedure is an entirely "appropriate manner" in producing rough-draft materials in the business office.

In each of the tests, six minutes is allowed for the typing called for in the section. (There is considerable discrepancy in the length of the copy given for Tests I and II, of Form A.) No directions are given for the student who might finish the copy before time is called. Does he just stop typing and sit quietly, or does he start over? It would be helpful to have this question answered. Again, no plan for scoring the test is given, except that the manual does say that "All material should be graded according to International Contest Rules." This directive would be rather difficult to follow since no word count is given for the paragraphs. Do the authors intend that "errors" are to be marked according to the International Contest Rules? If so, this information should be given to avoid confusion. Also, the test directions say "This is not a speed test but instead a challenge to produce usable copy." No indication is given of the meaning of "usable copy." Furthermore, the question might be asked, "Are all students to be evaluated in the same way regardless of the amount of copy they produce?" Such an evaluation would be grossly unfair to the fast typists; yet no directions are given of how such students are to be evaluated.

Also, the directions for this part read, "You should proofread your work carefully so as to avoid heavy penalty for uncorrected errors." Again, no statement is given as to what exactly this "heavy penalty" really is.

PART 3. This part consists of business-letter copy which is to be typed in the style specified in the directions. The maximum time allowance is seven minutes. For first-semester students, the letter style is the so-called "Box Style"— a rarely-used style in actual business correspondence. Additionally, few if any beginning typewriting students would have had previous experience with this style. This part in Form A therefore violates one of the cardinal principles of education, for the student is tested on a letter style with which he has had no previous experience. Again, the directions given are confusing. The student is directed to "proofread carefully and correct all errors." Since errors can be corrected in a variety of ways, we cannot assume that the student will know the way intended by the authors. Finally, no scoring system is given for the part. Just how it is to

be graded remains a mystery. The copy given in all four tests shows great variation in its difficulty.

PART 4. This part consists of material which contains numerous errors of various kinds (spelling, punctuation, and the like). The student is directed to "locate the errors and make a correct copy of the article." The student is directed to use an eraser to correct errors, and he is admonished to make the copy mailable, but no criteria as to what constitutes mailability is given. Again, no directions for scoring the material is given.

PART 5. This part consists of copy to be arranged in table form. Errors are to be corrected by the use of an eraser. The student is given 12 minutes to complete the assignment which varies as to difficulty and length on each of the tests. No directions for scoring this part are given.

The Reicherter-Sanders tests may have merit for some kinds of evaluation, but to this reviewer they seemed to have too many inconsistencies. The copy varied as to difficulty, directions were vague, and no method of scoring the test results was given, at least in the material seen by this reviewer which consisted of the manual prepared by the authors, and the tests themselves. Furthermore, some of the directions such as "typing paragraphs" without error seem unrealistic at least for first-semester students who still make many errors which are primarily of the "chance" type. To direct them to type without error is a frustrating if not impossible direction. Finally, this reviewer would hope that the authors of these tests would devote the time and energy needed to improve these tests if they are to be used for evaluating first-year typewriting students. In their present form, they leave much to be desired.

*Russell-Sanders Bookkeeping Test. 1, 2 semesters high school; 1962–64; first published 1962–63 in the Every Pupil Scholarship Test series; Forms A, B, ('64); 2 levels labeled Tests 1 (2 pages), 2 (4 pages); manual ('64, 3 pages); $1.75 per 25 tests, postage extra; 75¢ per specimen set, postpaid; 40(45) minutes; Raymond B. Russell and M. W. Sanders; Data Processing and Educational Measurement Center. *

BERNARD H. NEWMAN, *Professor of Business and Business Division Director, Essex County College, Newark, New Jersey.*

This test was designed to evaluate achievement in first year bookkeeping and accounting.

Although the manual makes no statement about the level for which it has been prepared, it is clearly on the high school level. Much more disconcerting is the statement that the test is produced in "Four equivalent forms, I-A, I-B, II-A, and II-B." No evidence for equivalence or comparability of difficulty is cited. Forms II-A and II-B appear to test more advanced subject matter than is tested by Forms I-A and I-B. Topics which are not covered or are treated in a more limited manner in Form I-A and I-B are depreciation, notes, and freight charges.

Each test is divided into parts and in the course of the four forms a variety of objective questions are given. A number of proofreading errors have been made, one of which would be quite confusing to a student taking Form I-A of the test. The directions for Part I of Form I-A state, "If the statement is false, place a minus (−) in the parentheses." An example is then given below, which indicates that a zero (o) is to be placed in the parentheses for an incorrect statement. Other examples of the inconsistencies caused by inadequate proofreading are that the keys refer to the pages of the test forms, but the test form pages are not numbered and the keys refer to columns but the test is divided into parts.

In Forms I-A and I-B of the test many of the questions are definitions in which the correct answer permits the student to think only in terms of a traditional hand-bookkeeping system. An example of this type of question and then the correct answer is:

If an error is discovered in a book of original entry **before** the item has been posted, it is preferable to correct the error by....drawing a line through the error and writing the correction immediately above.

However, in a bookkeeping machine system or a hand system with strong internal control features in this area it *would* be necessary to make a correcting journal entry.

The use of objective questions as the only type of questions in a bookkeeping/accounting examination creates some difficulties. For one, it rewards reading and objective question answering ability over operational ability. The student is never asked to make journal entries, post, or prepare financial statements and worksheets. Secondly, it is impossible for the student to explain his views fully or to deal with accounting theory as he might in essay questions.

The great difficulty in dealing with accounting theory in this type of examination makes it all the more important that questions be worded correctly and that they reflect current trends and developments in the practice of accounting. The test, however, can only be rated as average at best in this regard.

An example of the kind of outdated theory, slipshod terminology, and even incorrect theory which is found in some of the questions and correct answers is "Prepaid insurance is listed as a deferred charge on the balance sheet," a statement keyed as true. A deferred charge is a long-term prepaid asset. The American Institute of Certified Public Accountants has suggested that this classification is not well understood and its use should be limited. Prepaid insurance is almost invariably listed as a current asset. Another example, keyed as true, is "Each adjustment of the ledger should first be authorized by an entry in the journal." Accountants do not think of entries in the journal as authorization for "adjustments" in the ledger. Once the entry is made in the journal the posting to the ledger *must* be made. Therefore, authorization is obtained prior to the entry being made in the journal. A number of additional examples might be cited.

The split-half reliability of each form is satisfactory, ranging from .88 to .91. Norms as computed from the results made by students in "schools in many different states" are provided in the manual. There is insufficient description of the student population to make comparisons meaningful.

This test in its various forms might be used by bookkeeping teachers if they do not have the time to prepare an objective test themselves. However, prior to their use the forms should be carefully reviewed by the teacher for inaccurate instructions and for level. Also, after the test is given the teacher should provide some time to explain poorly worded questions.

[559]

★Stanford Achievement Test: High School Business and Economics Test. Grades 9–12; 1965–66; catalog uses the title *Stanford High School Business and Economics Test;* Forms W, X, ('65, 6 pages); no specific manual; battery manual ('65, 48 pages); supplementary directions ('66, 4 pages) for each type of answer sheet; separate answer sheets (IBM 805, IBM 1230) must be used; $8.20 per 35 tests; $2.30 per 35 IBM 805 answer sheets; $2.80 per 35 IBM 1230 answer sheets; 70¢ per scoring stencil; $1.20 per battery manual; $2 per specimen set; postage extra; scoring service, 19¢ and over per test; 40(45) minutes; Eric F. Gardner, Jack C. Merwin, Robert

Callis, and Richard Madden; Harcourt Brace Jovanovich, Inc. *

MARY ELLEN OLIVERIO, *Professor of Economic Education, Teachers College, Columbia University, New York, New York.*

This test is one of the newest additions to the High School Battery of the *Stanford Achievement Tests.* This is a wise addition, since it provides for a more extensive testing of the high school population.

There are 65 multiple choice items and the time allowed is 40 minutes. The test is considered a power test and not a speed test inasmuch as most high school students will be able to complete the test in the 40-minute period.

The manual states that "this test is designed to serve two functions: (1) as a general test in the field of business education and (2) as a measure of business and economics for the educated citizen."

A review of the items raises some questions about the extent to which these functions are actually achieved by the test. Content includes 5 items on proofreading, 10 on business arithmetic, 10 on bookkeeping, 17 on general business, 5 on business law, and 18 on clerical and secretarial. This content reflects relatively accurately the content of traditional business education courses in American high schools. Content validity was determined through "examining appropriate courses of study and textbooks in common use and by consulting with experts" in the field. Such analysis does seem appropriate inasmuch as a testing program must have close relevance to what is being taught. However, the ultimate validity of the test as a measure of an individual's business behavior is indeterminable inasmuch as the materials have yet to be rigorously tested for validity. Therefore, we cannot conclude that here is a measure of the "field of business education" or of "business and economics for the educated citizen."

Furthermore, the content is tested at a relatively low level of understanding. Facts, such as what type of mail can be mailed through a special rate or the meaning of A. B. A. numbers, are sufficient to answer the major portion of the test. In fact, approximately 15 percent of the test might be classified as testing understanding. While it is indeed appropriate to test for mastery of facts, should not an achievement test strive to measure the higher-level learnings

that have been receiving particular emphasis in the past decade? An "educated citizen" needs to read and interpret information about consumer goods or rights contained in a contract. Why not include some items that provide a measure of such skill? This test suffers from the same weakness as many teacher prepared tests—the testing of that which is easiest to test and failure to test that which is most significant to test.

The standardization groups for each of the grades 10, 11, and 12 included a special "semester" group, which consisted of students who had studied business subjects continuously since the beginning of the ninth grade. Since statistics are provided for this group as well as for the college preparatory group and the total group, some interesting comparisons are possible. Standard scores, percentile ranks, stanines, and item difficulty values are all presented with lucid discussions that make possible interpretations by those who have had no professional study in tests and measurements.

If the test user remembers that he is testing facts *primarily* and if he is interested in seeing how the scores of a particular group of students compare with nationally established norms, there may be limited value to the use of this test. Inasmuch as no items deal with economics, possibly a more accurate title should be selected. Maybe the word "consumer" before economics would be sufficient to identify the content more precisely.

[559A]

★Typewriting Achievement Test: Business Education Achievement Test Series. 1, 2 years high school; 1967; 2 forms; 2 levels; developed by the Psychological Corporation; Gregg Division, McGraw-Hill Book Co., Inc. * (*Out of print.*)
a) YEAR 1. 7 scores: basic information, straight copy (speed, accuracy), production (letter, revised manuscript, tabulation, total); Forms A, B, (24 pages in 5 parts); manual (27 pages); 51(80) minutes.
b) YEAR 2. 7 scores: straight copy (speed, accuracy), production (form letters, revised manuscript, tabulation, invoices, total); Forms R, S, (24 pages in 5 parts); manual (31 pages); 45(70–80) minutes.

LAWRENCE W. ERICKSON, *Professor of Education and Assistant Dean, Graduate School of Education, University of California, Los Angeles, California.*

The two levels of the *Typewriting Achievement Test* were designed to provide an objectively scorable measure of achievement in typewriting at the end of the first and second years of instruction. Both levels of the test present an adequate sampling of the skills and knowledge expected of students who have had the relevant instruction in typewriting. The norms are based on a seemingly adequate sample of first and second year students. The manual for each level is unusually comprehensive.

YEAR 1. This test consists of five parts: Basic Information, Straight-Copy Typing, Business Letter Typing, Revised Manuscript Typing, and Tabulation Typing.

Part 1. Basic Information. Generally speaking, the content of the 60 multiple choice items is good; a few items, however, are either debatable or the answers are not based on generally acceptable modern practice. For example, a letter with 250 words in the body can now, for placement purposes, be classified as either long or average, depending on the textbook used in the typewriting course. Other items call for responses in terms of 5-inch or 6-inch line lengths, when modern business practice uses neither; rather, placement of material is in terms of outside margins of 1 inch, 1½ inches, or 2 inches. Despite these criticisms, this subtest measures much pertinent and relevant information.

Part 2. Straight-Copy Typing. The copy in this 5-minute subtest has a syllabic intensity of 1.4, which is a commonly accepted measure of copy difficulty. Recent research indicates that student rates do vary according to the difficulty of the copy, and a more nearly uniform control of copy difficulty may well incorporate such controls as syllabic intensity, percentage of high-frequency words, and average word length.

The straight-copy timed writing is scored in terms of gross words typed as a speed score, and the number of errors as an accuracy score. Most authorities in the typewriting field favor this practice when erasing is not permitted.

Because of the increase in both statistical copy and rough-draft copy typing in the business office, a comprehensive test battery should also measure these basic skills. As is true for straight-copy measurements, a timed writing of five minutes' duration is adequate for measurement purposes. It would increase the time needed for administering the test, but it would be time well spent.

Parts 3–5. Production Units. These three subtests measure business letter typing, revised manuscript typing, and tabulation typing. The manual describes the tests as "open-ended" by which is meant that the time allowed is less than that needed by the average student. The "raw score" for each subtest is determined by subtracting the total number of errors from the gross words typed; the sum of these three scores is the Total Production score.

The time allowed—6, 7, and 8 minutes, respectively, for Parts 3, 4, and 5—appears adequate. The tasks measured in these subtests are appropriate. Erasing, however, should be permitted to make the tasks in line with business office practice.

YEAR 2. The second year test also consists of five parts (Straight-Copy Typing, Invoice Typing, Tabulation Typing, Form Letter Typing, and Revised Manuscript Typing) yielding seven scores.

Part 1. Straight-Copy Typing. Since the tasks in this subtest are of the same kind as those in Test 1, the same comments apply.

Parts 2–5. Production Units. These subtests measure four of the common typing tasks required of typists: invoice typing, tabulation typing, form letter typing, and revised manuscript typing. In administering the subtests, each of the four parts is to be timed for 10 minutes. Reading and following directions and determining typewriting adjustments are included in the timed portions of each test. Scores are obtained as for the first year test. The common tasks included for measurement are appropriate. Again, erasing should be permitted. No typist in the business office counts his errors and subtracts them from the gross words typed; rather he erases and corrects his errors as he makes them, or as he discovers them as he proofreads the completed work.

SUMMARY. Both levels of this test should be rated as good to excellent. Tests 1 and 2 adequately cover the kinds of tasks performed and the knowledge needed by first and second year students in typing courses.

LEONARD J. WEST, *Professor of Education, The City University of New York, New York, New York.*

The TAT is intended for nationwide use to assess achievement after one and two years of typing instruction in the secondary schools. As such, it was developed and standardized on a large number of students in a sizable number of high schools across the country. Its content is reportedly based on the content of typewriting textbooks and the judgment of specialists. Indeed, the major test components (letters, tables,

Typewriting Achievement Test

revised manuscripts) are the prominent classes of tasks among employed typists and, to slightly lesser extent, in personal typing activities. The test manual contains full technical details supporting the satisfactory reliability of the tests, well developed norms, and other statistical data —accompanied by lucid explanations that cannot but contribute to the understandings of teachers about the measurement of typewriting proficiency. The scoring directions are explicit and generally acceptable. Scoring for errors is necessarily detailed and time consuming, whereas scoring keys make scoring for speed rapid and easy.

Differences between the Year 1 and Year 2 tests make it convenient to discuss the two levels separately. However, there are three questionable features applicable to the tests at both levels : seriously reduced validity resulting from prohibiting error correction by examinees, the use of composite scoring of uncertain interpretability, and straight copy materials well below average difficulty. Details on these three features, given in my review of the *Typing Test for Business* (1007), are also applicable here.

The Year 1 Test includes a test of Basic Information that covers much content in little time, even though nearly all the items could be directly measured in actual typing performance, as some were. This reviewer takes exception to a number of items whose model answers do not represent, variously, best or sole correct practice (Items 7, 48, 50, 54 in Form A; Items 10, 36, 47 in Form B). Furthermore, the scoring key is not sufficiently durable for extended use; scoring stencils on heavier stock would have been preferable.

The Letter subtest consists of typing one letter from printed copy, whose length (in words) is given to the typist, but whose vertical and horizontal margins must be determined by the examinee, using a specified letter style shown in a model. The norms for this subtest show that 15 percent of examinees were able to begin the letter a second time, while 60 percent of examinees did not get beyond the body of the letter to the closing elements. It would have been preferable to provide two letters, the first quite short.

The Tables subtest requires the student to type two 2-column tables : the first without column headings, the second with. Again, 15 percent of the norms group were able to begin

the tables a second time, whereas more than half the examinees did not get as far as the first data row in the table with column headings. Reversing the order of the two tables and the addition of a third table would have been preferable.

The Revised Manuscript requires the student to type from typed copy with longhand corrections, using nine different proofreader's marks. Although 15 percent of examinees completed the manuscript and began it again—so that the addition of about another 100 words to it would have been preferable—this subtest is judged to be very adequate for its purposes. One mild reservation, however, given in my review of the *Typing Test for Business* (see 1007), is also applicable here.

The Year 2 Test substitutes for the Basic Information measure an Invoices subtest, providing 10 minutes for 4 invoices. This subtest is perfectly adequate for its purposes. However, in view of the need for more letter-typing time (see below), the invoices subtest might well have been reduced by one or two invoices and by 3 or 5 minutes, hopefully with little adverse effect on reliability.

The Letter subtest consists of typing one long form letter, requiring eight insertions. The length of the letter (in words) is given to the examinee, but he must select his own margins. More than 40 percent of the norms group were able to begin the letter a second time, whereas at least one-fourth of the examinees did not get beyond the body of the letter to the closing elements. Although this subtest is very good for its purposes, it would have been preferable either to use two letters (the first quite short) or to borrow additional time from the unnecessarily long invoice test.

The four 3-column items in the Tables subtest provide (redundantly) for variations in three features (with and without subhead, 1- and 2-line column heads, column heads longer and shorter than the items beneath). It might have been preferable to substitute other features for the redundant ones (e.g., four or more columns, braced heads, footnotes). As in the first year test, the examinee makes his own decisions on intercolumn space. However, the scoring procedure for that aspect is worded puzzlingly and appears to accept unequal intercolumn space in tables whose content requires the same spacing between all columns.

The Revised Manuscript parallels that for

Year 1 in form, but uses 12 different proof-reader's marks. Although it is a good subtest for its purposes, the reservation referred to for the Year 1 subtest also applies here.

In summary, the TAT is distinguished by test items generally appropriate to their purposes, satisfactory reliability, ease of administration, convenience for in-school use, completeness of scoring instructions and rapidity of scoring for speed, well developed norms, established equivalency of forms, and, not least, pertinent technical data accompanied by lucid explanations that may be expected to enhance the understandings of teachers who use the test. However, the no-error-correction rule for the production subtests is judged to have important adverse effects on validity, and the scoring procedures are judged to give excessive weight to speed in relation to quality of work. Lastly, the distribution of norms for some subtests makes those subtests applicable mainly to examinees in the middle range of proficiency; they are somewhat weaker for those at the extremes.

MULTI-APTITUDE BATTERIES— SEVENTH MMY

REVIEWS BY *M. Y. Quereshi, Richard E. Schutz, and David J. Weiss.*

[672]

*Academic Promise Tests. Grades 6–9; 1959–69; APT; 7 scores: abstract reasoning, numerical, non-verbal total, language usage, verbal, verbal total, total; Forms A, B, ('61, 20 pages); revised manual ('65, 75 pages); student report forms ('61, 1 page, hand prepared; '69, 1 page, computer prepared); separate answer sheets (Digitek, Digitek precoded, IBM 805, IBM 1230, MRC, NCS) must be used; $4.50 per 25 tests; $3.75 per 50 IBM 805 answer sheets; $4 per 50 IBM 1230 or Digitek answer sheets; $4.60 per 50 Digitek precoded answer sheets; $3.50 per 50 MRC answer sheets; $12.50 per 250 NCS answer sheets; $1.10 per 50 student report forms; 50¢ per set of Digitek or IBM scoring stencils; 80¢ per set of MRC hand scoring stencils; 75¢ per manual; 90¢ per specimen set; postage extra; IBM 805 and Digitek precoded scoring service, 35¢ and over per test ($10 minimum); MRC scoring service, 25¢ and over per test ($12.50 minimum); 90(120) minutes; George K. Bennett, Marjorie G. Bennett, Dorothy M. Clendenen, Jerome E. Doppelt, James H. Ricks, Jr., Harold G. Seashore, and Alexander G. Wesman; Psychological Corporation. *

REFERENCES

1. BEYMER, CHARLES LAWRENCE. *A Study of the Effects of Group Interpretation of Aptitude Test Results Upon the Estimates of Abilities and the Estimates of Test Performance of a Group of Seventh Grade Pupils.* Doctor's thesis, Michigan State University (East Lansing, Mich.), 1963. (*DA* 25:283)
2. JOHNSON, HALVIN SHERWOOD. *The Relationship of Scores on Aptitude and Achievement Tests Taken at Late Elementary and Junior High School Levels to Scholarship in Ninth Grade.* Doctor's thesis, University of South Dakota (Vermillion, S.D.), 1965. (*DA* 26:4449)
3. WILLARD, LOUISA A. "A Comparison of Culture Fair Test Scores With Group and Individual Intelligence Test Scores of Disadvantaged Negro Children." *J Learn Dis* 1:584–9 O '68. * (*PA* 45:3968)
4. CHURCH, JOHN J. *An Investigation of the Distribution on the Abstract Reasoning Subtest of the Academic Promise Test in Year Six.* Master's thesis, University of New Brunswick (Fredericton, N.B., Canada), 1970.
5. MANN, LESTER; TAYLOR, RAYMOND G., JR.; PROGER, BARTON B.; DUNGAN, ROY H.; AND TIDEY, WILLIAM J. "The Effect of Serial Retesting on the Relative Performance of High- and Low-Test Anxious Seventh Grade Students." *J Ed Meas* 7(2):97–104 su '70. * (*PA* 44:19362)
6. MORSE, JOHN L. *The Adaptation of a Non-Verbal Abstract Reasoning Test for Use With the Blind.* Doctor's thesis, Boston University (Boston, Mass.), 1970. (*DAI* 31:2113A)

For reviews by Julian C. Stanley and William W. Turnbull, see 6:766.

[673]

*Differential Aptitude Tests. Grades 8–12 and adults; 1947–69; DAT; 9 scores: Booklet 1 (verbal reasoning, numerical ability, total, abstract reasoning, clerical speed and accuracy), Booklet 2 (mechanical reasoning, space relations, spelling, grammar); 2 forms; original Forms A and B still available (see 6:767); manual, fourth edition ('66, 184 pages); directions and norms ('66, 60 pages, reprinted from manual); casebook ('51, 95 pages, see 29 below); directions ('66–67, 4 pages) for each type of answer sheet; student report forms ('63, 6 pages; '63, 2 pages, hand prepared; '69, 2 pages, computer prepared); no adult norms; separate answer sheets (Digitek, IBM 805, IBM 1230, IBM Mark-Sense Cards, MRC, NCS) must be used; $17.60 per 25 copies of the battery; $10 per 50 MRC answer sheets; $11.25 per 50 Digitek answer sheets; $11.25 per 50 sets of IBM answer sheets; $47.50 per 250 NCS answer sheets; $1.40 per 50 2-page report forms; $3.25 per 50 6-page report forms; 80¢ per set of IBM 805 scoring stencils; $1 per set of Digitek hand scoring stencils; $1.50 per set of IBM 1230 hand scoring stencils; $1.75 per casebook; $2.50 per manual; $3 per specimen set; postage extra; MRC scoring service, 25¢ and over per student ($12.50 minimum); IBM 805 scoring service, 50¢ and over per student ($10 minimum); 181(235) minutes in 2 or more sessions; George K. Bennett, Harold G. Seashore, and Alexander G. Wesman; Psychological Corporation. *

a) BOOKLET 1. Forms L, M, ('61, 21 pages, except for the reduction in the number of response options in 1 test, the 4 tests are identical with Forms A and B copyrighted in 1947); verbal reasoning and numerical ability also available in a single booklet ('61, 11 pages); $8.80 per 25 tests; 91(120) minutes.

b) BOOKLET 2. Forms L, M, ('62, 38 pages, 2 of the 4 subtests are identical with Forms A and B copyrighted in 1947); $8.80 per 25 tests; 90(115) minutes.

REFERENCES

1–28. See 4:711.
29–77. See 5:605.
78–129. See 6:767.
130. RECTOR, ALICE PHILLIPS. *A Study of the Need for Vocational Education for High School Graduates in Southern Illinois.* Doctor's thesis, Washington University (St. Louis, Mo.), 1953. (*DA* 14:1038)
131. LUNDQUIST, JUSTIN NELS. *The Use of Selected Subtests of the Differential Aptitude Tests for Programming Ninth Grade Students at Grossmont High School.* Master's thesis, San Diego State College (San Diego, Calif.), 1954.

---

132. ZUCKMAN, LEONARD. *The Relationship Between Sex Differences in Certain Mental Abilities and Masculine-Feminine Sex Identification: An Analysis and Evaluation of Test Measures on Eighth Grade New York City Public School Students Equated as to Age, Intelligence, Health, Parent Rearage and Socio-Economic Status.* Doctor's thesis, New York University (New York, N.Y.), 1955. (*DA* 15:1251)

133. GWYDIR, ROBERT R., JR. *Predicting the Success of Students in the Construction Technology Curriculum at the New York City Community College of Applied Arts and Sciences.* Doctor's thesis, New York University (New York, N.Y.), 1957. (*DA* 18:1684)

134. LEBOLD, WILLIAM KERNS. *A Longitudinal Study of Purdue Engineering Students.* Doctor's thesis, Purdue University (Lafayette, Ind.), 1957. (*DA* 17:2057)

135. LITTRELL, ROBERT THOMAS. *Differential Characteristics Among Students Graduating From Various Curricular Patterns.* Doctor's thesis, University of Nebraska (Lincoln, Neb.), 1957. (*DA* 17:2208)

136. FRANKEL, EDWARD. *A Comparative Study of Achieving and Underachieving High School Boys of High Intellectual Ability.* Doctor's thesis, Yeshiva University (New York, N.Y.), 1958. (*DA* 20:956)

137. SHUKLA, N. N. "The Relation of Intelligence and Ability to Scholastic Achievement of Pupils in the S.S.C. Class." *J Ed & Voc Guid* 5:38–44 Ag '58. *

138. HORN, FERN MAY. *A Study of the Relationships Between Certain Aspects of Clothing and the Ability to Handle Selected Clothing Construction Tools With the Developmental Levels of Early Adolescent Girls.* Doctor's thesis, Michigan State University (East Lansing, Mich.), 1959. (*DA* 20:3278)

139. O'HARA, ROBERT P., AND TIEDEMAN, DAVID V. "The Vocational Self-Concept in Adolescence." *J Counsel Psychol* 6:292–301 w '59. * (*PA* 35:3279)

140. PIPPERT, RALPH REINHARD. *The Prediction of the Correctness of Post-High School Written Language Performance.* Doctor's thesis, University of Wisconsin (Madison, Wis.), 1959. (*DA* 20:2104)

141. HAROOTUNIAN, BERJ, AND TATE, MERLE W. "The Relationship of Certain Selected Variables to Problem Solving Ability." *J Ed Psychol* 51:326–33 D '60. * (*PA* 36:1KK26H)

142. JENKINS, THOMAS VINNEDGE. *A Study of the Relationship Between Music Aptitudes and Mental Ability, Science Aptitudes, and Mathematics Aptitudes Among Secondary School Pupils in Texas.* Doctor's thesis, University of Texas (Austin, Tex.), 1960. (*DA* 21:2592)

143. CARMICAL, LaVERNE LATHROP. *The Identification of Certain Characteristics of Selected Achievers and Underachievers of Bellaire Senior High School.* Doctor's thesis, University of Houston (Houston, Tex.), 1961. (*DA* 22:2244)

144. EDINGTON, EVERETT D. *Abilities and Characteristics of Young Adult Dairy Farmers in Pennsylvania Which Are Associated With Successful Farm Management.* Doctor's thesis, Pennsylvania State University (University Park, Pa.), 1961. (*DA* 22:3791)

145. McGUIRE, CARSON; HINDSMAN, EDWIN; KING, F. J.; AND JENNINGS, EARL. "Dimensions of Talented Behavior." *Ed & Psychol Meas* 21:3–38 sp '61. * (*PA* 36:1KH03M)

146. RUBIN, ROSALYN AARON. *Social Comparison Processes of Superior Ninth Grade Pupils.* Doctor's thesis, University of Minnesota (Minneapolis, Minn.), 1961. (*DA* 22:2698)

147. SKELLY, CLYDE G. *Some Variables Which Differentiate the Highly Intelligent and Highly Divergent Thinking Adolescent.* Doctor's thesis, University of Connecticut (Storrs, Conn.), 1961. (*DA* 22:2699)

148. FINK, DONALD D. *The Efficiency of Certain Criteria in Predicting School Dropout.* Doctor's thesis, Michigan State University (East Lansing, Mich.), 1962. (*DA* 23:1555)

149. NASH, MARION J. *Relationship Between Scores on the Clerical Portion of the Differential Aptitude Tests and Ability to Attain High Speeds in Typewriting.* Master's thesis, Drake University (Des Moines, Iowa), 1963.

150. PASRICHA, P. "A Try-out of Abstract Reasoning Test With Children of Baroda." *J Voc & Ed Guid* 9:118–21 Ag '63. * (*PA* 38:6571)

151. ROBEY, DALE LEWIS. *A Differential Diagnosis of Low-Academic Ninth Grade Male Students as Compared With Average-Academic Ninth Grade Male Students.* Doctor's thesis, Indiana University (Bloomington, Ind.), 1963. (*DA* 24:5252)

152. TREMEL, JEROME GEORGE. *A Study of the Relationships Among Basic Ability Factors and the Learning of Selected Operations on the Set of Integers.* Doctor's thesis, Purdue University (Lafayette, Ind.), 1963. (*DA* 24:5259)

153. BLANTON, WINCIE L., AND PECK, ROBERT F. "College Student Motivation and Academic Performance." *Ed & Psychol Meas* 24:897–912 w '64. * (*PA* 39:8695)

154. BONEY, JEW DON. *A Study of the Use of Intelligence, Aptitude, and Mental Ability Measures in Predicting the Academic Achievement of Negro Students in Secondary School.* Doctor's thesis, University of Texas (Austin, Tex.), 1964. (*DA* 25:5726)

155. CAIN, RALPH WINSTON. *An Analysis of the Achievement of Students in Selected High School Biology Programs in Relation to Their Mathematical Aptitude and Achievement.* Doctor's thesis, University of Texas (Austin, Tex.), 1964. (*DA* 25:5149)

156. CARMICAL, LAVERNE. "Characteristics of Achievers and Under-achievers of a Large Senior High School." *Personnel & Guid J* 43:390–5 D '64. * (*PA* 39:10711)

157. CHASE, CLINTON I.; LUDLOW, H. GLENN; AND PUGH, RICHARD C. *Predicting Success for Master's Degree Students in Education.* Indiana Studies in Prediction No. 5. Bloomington, Ind.: Bureau of Educational Studies and Testing, 1964. Pp. v, 25. *

158. CHASE, CLINTON I.; LUDLOW, H. GLENN; PUGH, RICHARD C.; AND POMEROY, MARTHA C. *Predicting Success for Advanced Graduate Students in Education.* Indiana Studies in Prediction No. 4. Lafayette, Ind.: Bureau of Educational Studies and Testing, January 1964. Pp. v, 18. *

159. COBB, BART B. "Problems in Air Traffic Management: 5, Identification and Potential of Aptitude Test Measures for Selection of Tower Air Traffic Controller Trainees." *Aerospace Med* 35:1019–27 N '64. * (*PA* 39:16518)

160. DAYAL, P. "Study of the Relationship Between a Verbal Intelligence Test (B.P.T. 15) and Verbal Reasoning Plus Numerical Ability Test Scores of the D.A.T." *J Voc & Ed Guid* 10:83–9 Ag '64. * (*PA* 39:5114)

161. FANGMAN, ELMER G. *A Comparison of Kuder Preference Record-Vocational Scores for Groups of Ninth Grade Boys and Girls Who Differ in Aptitude on Two Scales of the Differential Aptitude Tests.* Master's thesis, University of Kansas (Lawrence, Kan.), 1964.

162. GILES, GEORGE C., JR. "Predictive Validity of Progressive Matrices and Two Other Nonlanguage Tests of Mental Ability." *J Ed Meas* 1:65–7 Je '64. * (*PA* 39:7757)

163. IRWIN, JOHN T. *Prediction of Grade Point Average for Senior High School by Means of the Differential Aptitude Tests.* Master's thesis, Northern Illinois University (DeKalb, Ill.), 1964.

164. KORNHAUS, DONALD C. *The Relationship Between Physical Ability, Differential Aptitude, and Academic Achievement.* Master's thesis, University of Kansas (Lawrence, Kan.), 1964.

165. McNEMAR, QUINN. "Lost: Our Intelligence? Why?" *Am Psychologist* 19:871–82 D '64. * (*PA* 39:7823)

166. MEARIG, JUDITH SUZANNE. *Fluency and Dependency as Predictors of Sex Differences in Ability and Achievement.* Doctor's thesis, University of Michigan (Ann Arbor, Mich.), 1964. (*DA* 25:3401)

167. MUELLER, DANIEL EUGENE. *An Analysis of the Results of the Differential Aptitude Test and the General Aptitude Test Battery Administered at the Juvenile Diagnostic Center, Columbus, Ohio.* Master's thesis, Ohio State University (Columbus, Ohio), 1964.

168. QUIDWAI, ANIS AHMED. *Evaluation of Criteria for Selection of Students in the Master of Education Program at the Institute of Education and Research, Dacca, East Pakistan.* Doctor's research study No. 1, Colorado State College (Greeley, Colo.), 1964. (*DA* 25:6414)

169. SCHRECK, THOMAS C. "Selected Factors Related to Academic Success in College." *Ed & Psychol R* 4:71–6 Ap '64. *

170. TRITES, DAVID K. "Problems in Air Traffic Management: 6, Interaction of Training-Entry Age With Intellectual and Personality Characteristics of Air Traffic Control Specialists." *Aerospace Med* 35:1184–94 D '64. * (*PA* 39:16533)

171. UNRUH, LEROY DAVID. *An Inquiry Into the Relationship Between Certain Differential Aptitude Test Scores and Grades Earned in Junior and Senior High School Industrial Arts.* Master's thesis, Kansas State Teachers College (Emporia, Kan.), 1964.

172. WAKELAND, WILLIAM FLOYD. *A Study of the Teaching of Sightsinging of Melodic Configurations to a Group of Secondary-School Students by Means of a Teaching Machine.* Doctor's thesis, Southern Illinois University (Carbondale, Ill.), 1964. (*DA* 25:5165)

173. ZIMMER, JOSEPH H. *Predicting High School Success From the Differential Aptitude Tests and the Iowa Tests of Educational Development.* Master's thesis, Catholic University of America (Washington, D.C.), 1964.

174. BAE, AGNES YOUNG-OK. *The Prediction of the Learning of Chemistry Among Eleventh Grade Girls.* Doctor's thesis, Catholic University of America (Washington, D.C.), 1965. (*DA* 28:487A)

175. BERG, ORRIN DONALD. *Prediction of College Achievement on the Basis of Ninth Grade Differential Aptitude Test Scores.* Doctor's thesis, University of Denver (Denver, Colo.), 1965. (*DA* 26:3147)

176. BLOOM, THOMAS K. *Differential Aptitude Test and Success in Drafting I.* Master's thesis, California State College (Long Beach, Calif.), 1965.

177. BUSBY, WALTER ALVIN. *A Multivariate Analysis of the Relationship of Academic Motivation, Aptitude, Socio-Economic Status, and Age to Persistence in Adult Evening School.* Doctor's thesis, Michigan State University (East Lansing, Mich.), 1965. (*DA* 26:4414)

178. COOLEY, DONALD B. *The Relationship Between Eighth Grade Differential Aptitude Test Scores and Marks Assigned for Ninth Grade Courses in Knox County High School.* Master's thesis, University of Tennessee (Knoxville, Tenn.), 1965.

179. COOLEY, WILLIAM W., AND MILLER, JUDY D. "The

Project TALENT Tests as a National Standard." *Personnel & Guid J* 43:1038–44 Je '65. *

180. DAYAL, P. "Applicability of D.A.T. Battery at Higher Secondary Stage for Hindi Speaking Students." *J Voc & Ed Guid* 11:136–9 N '65. *

181. GRAY, BERNARD. "The Differential Aptitude Tests in a Military Academic Setting." *J Ed Res* 58:352–4 Ap '65. * (*PA* 39:16449)

182. GROBMAN, HULDA. "Identifying the 'Slow Learner' in BSCS High School Biology." *J Res Sci Teach* 3(1):3–11 '65. *

183. GUILFORD, J. P.; HOEFFNER, RALPH; AND PETERSEN, HUGH. "Predicting Achievement in Ninth-Grade Mathematics From Measures of Intellectual-Aptitude Factors." *Ed & Psychol Meas* 25:659–82 au '65. * (*PA* 40:3376)

184. JOHNSON, HALVIN SHERWOOD. *The Relationship of Scores on Aptitude and Achievement Tests Taken at Late Elementary and Junior High School Levels to Scholarship in Ninth Grade.* Doctor's thesis, University of South Dakota (Vermillion, S.D.), 1965. (*DA* 26:4449)

185. JONES, CHARLES W., AND McMILLEN, DAN. "Engineering Freshman Norms for the D.A.T. Mechanical Reasoning and Space Relations Tests Utilizing Fifteen-Minute Time Limits." *Ed & Psychol Meas* 25:459–64 su '65. * (*PA* 39:16507)

186. KEBBON, LARS. *The Structure of Abilities at Lower Levels of Intelligence: A Factor-Analytical Study.* Stockholm, Sweden: Skandinaviska Testförlaget AB, 1965. Pp. 112. *

187. MERENDA, PETER F.; CLARKE, WALTER V.; AND JACOBSEN, GWENDOLYN. "Relative Predictive Validities of MOS and DAT Batteries for Junior High School Students." *Psychol Rep* 16:151–5 F '65. * (*PA* 39:8688)

188. MERWIN, JACK C. "A Study of the Inter-Form Reliability of DAT Tests Over a Four-Month Period." *Personnel & Guid J* 43:910–1 My '65. *

189. MILHOLLAND, JOHN E., AND WOMER, FRANK B. "The Relation of Ninth and Tenth Grade Differential Aptitude Test Scores to Choices of Academic Majors at the University of Michigan." *J Ed Meas* 2:65–8 Je '65. *

190. OTA, YOSHIKO KAY. *Prediction of the Learning of Chemistry Among Eleventh Grade Boys.* Doctor's thesis, Catholic University of America (Washington, D.C.), 1965. (*DA* 26:4455)

191. PEDERSEN, EDWARD C. *A Longitudinal Study of Differential Aptitude Test Scores of the Same Students at the Eighth and Tenth Grade Levels in the Franklin Pierce School District.* Master's thesis, Pacific Lutheran University (Tacoma, Wash.), 1965.

192. PEEL, RUTH A. *Predicting Academic Success or Failure in Major Subjects at the Sophomore Level From the Differential Aptitude Test Given at the Freshman Level.* Master's thesis, Southern Connecticut State College (New Haven, Conn.), 1965.

193. RICHMAN, JAY T. *A Comparison of the Phonetic Structure of a Basal Vocabulary List and the Spelling Section of the Differential Aptitude Test.* Master's thesis, Utah State University (Logan, Utah), 1965.

194. RIDDLE, C. W. "Non-Verbal Aptitude Testing Among Punjabi Students." *Indian Psychol R* 1:126–35 Ja '65. * (*PA* 39:10213)

195. ROBINSON, FRANCES K. *An Investigation of the Value of the ACT Battery, the College Board Scholastic Aptitude Test, the Differential Aptitude Test Battery, and the University of Kansas Placement Battery as Predictors of University of Kansas Freshmen Grades.* Master's thesis, University of Kansas (Lawrence, Kan.), 1965.

196. BAROYA, GEORGE MANORANJAN. *Reliability, Validity, and Comparability of Forms L and M of the "Verbal Reasoning" and the "Numerical Ability" Subtests of the Differential Aptitude Tests for Use in East Pakistan.* Doctor's research study No. 1, Colorado State College (Greeley, Colo.), 1966. (*DA* 27:2865A)

197. BARRY, JOHN R., AND FULKERSON, SAMUEL C. "Chronicity and the Prediction of Duration and Outcome of Hospitalization From Capacity Measures." *Psychiatric Q* 40:104–21 Ja '66. * (*PA* 40:6764)

198. BHATT, L. J., AND OJHA, J. M. "A Hindi Revision of the Differential Aptitude Tests." *Manas* 13(2):63–77 '66. *

199. BONEY, J. DON. "Predicting the Academic Achievement of Secondary School Negro Students." *Personnel & Guid J* 44:700–3 Mr '66. * (*PA* 40:8064)

200. CAIN, RALPH W. "Relationships of Verbal Reasoning and Numerical Ability to Achievement in First-Year Algebra." *Sch Sci & Math* 66:131–4 F '66. *

201. DAYAL, P. "Applicability of D.A.T. Battery for Hindi Speaking Students." *Indian Psychol R* 2:135–8 Ja '66. * (*PA* 40:9430)

202. DIRR, PIERRE MARIE. *Intellectual Variables in Achievement in Modern Algebra.* Doctor's thesis, Catholic University of America (Washington, D.C.), 1966. (*DA* 27:2873A)

203. GILLAM, ELIZABETH SPECHT. *An Analysis of Performance on the Differential Aptitude Test of Bingham High School Students.* Master's thesis, University of Utah (Salt Lake City, Utah), 1966.

204. HASHMI, SHAMIM AHMAD. *Effect of Previous Academic Achievement on the Performance of First-Year College Students of East Pakistan on the "Verbal Reasoning" and the "Numeri-

cal Ability" Subtests of the Differential Aptitude Tests.* Doctor's research study No. 1, Colorado State College (Greeley, Colo.), 1966. (*DA* 27:2391A)

205. JEX, FRANK B. *Predicting Academic Success Beyond High School.* Salt Lake City, Utah: University of Utah Bookstore, 1966. Pp. vi, 41. *

206. KARP, ROBERT EUGENE. *An Analysis of Aptitudes, Abilities, and High School Class Rank and Their Relation to the Academic Success of First-Year Private Business School Students.* Doctor's thesis, Northern Illinois University (DeKalb, Ill.), 1966. (*DA* 27:3289A)

207. LOPEZ, FELIX M., JR. "The Industrial Psychologist: Selection and Equal Employment Opportunity (A Symposium): 3, Current Problems in Test Performance of Job Applicants: 1." *Personnel Psychol* 19:10–8 sp '66. * (*PA* 40:9282)

208. LOUGHRIDGE, ROBERT E. *The D.A.T. as a Predicator in Woodworking.* Master's thesis, California State College (Long Beach, Calif.), 1966.

209. MARTIN, BERNARD LOYAL. *Spatial Visualization Abilities of Central Washington State College Prospective Elementary and Secondary Teachers of Mathematics.* Doctor's thesis, Oregon State University (Corvallis, Ore.), 1966. (*DA* 27:2427A)

210. MERENDA, PETER F.; JACOBSEN, GWENDOLYN; AND CLARKE, WALTER V. "Cross-Validities of the MOS and DAT Batteries." *Psychol Rep* 19:341–2 O '66. * (*PA* 41:789)

211. PARMENTER, WILLIAM H. *An Investigation of the Predictive Validity of the Spatial and Mechanical Tests of the Differential Aptitude Tests in Regard to Success in Industrial Arts.* Master's thesis, California State College (Long Beach, Calif.), 1966.

212. SCHUSLER, MARIAN M. "Prediction of Grades by Computer for High School Students: A Cross-Validation and Experimental Placement Study." *J Ed Data Processing* 3:97–110 su '66. *

213. STAFFORD, RICHARD E. "Bimodal Distribution of 'True Scores' by Twins on the Differential Aptitude Tests." *Percept & Motor Skills* 23:470 O '66. * (*PA* 41:572)

214. BAE, AGNES Y. "The Prediction of the Learning of Chemistry Among Eleventh Grade Girls Through the Use of the Stepwise and Doolittle Techniques." *Ed & Psychol Meas* 27:1131–6 w '67. * (*PA* 42:9494)

215. BINGMAN, RICHARD MARVIN. *Aptitude and Interest Profiles of Tenth Grade Biology Students Participating in the Montgomery County, Pennsylvania Science Fairs (1962–1966).* Doctor's thesis, Temple University (Philadelphia, Pa.), 1967. (*DA* 28:4039A)

216. CLARKE, ROBERT B., AND GELATT, H. B. "Predicting Units Needed for College Entrance." *Personnel & Guid J* 46:275–82 N '67. * (*PA* 42:4512)

217. GARLAND, KENNETH EDWARD. *An Investigation of the Academic Achievement of Ninth Graders, With Varying Elementary School Backgrounds, From Selected Minnesota School Districts.* Doctor's thesis, University of Minnesota (Minneapolis, Minn.), 1967. (*DA* 28:2894A)

218. GAVURIN, EDWARD I. "The Relationship of Mental Ability to Anagram Solving." *J Psychol* 66:227–30 Jl '67. * (*PA* 41:13594)

219. HAHN, MARSHALL STERLING. *The Influence of Creativity on the Effectiveness of Two Methods of Instruction.* Doctor's thesis, University of Minnesota (Minneapolis, Minn.), 1967. (*DA* 28:2895A)

220. HANNA, GERALD S. "The Use of Students' Predictions of Success in Geometry and Year of High School to Augment Predictions Made From Test Scores and Past Grades." *J Ed Meas* 4:137–41 f '67. *

221. HAWKES, NORMA JEANNE. *Analysis of Channel Selection by Junior Secondary School Students on the Reorganized Curriculum in British Columbia Schools.* Doctor's thesis, University of Oregon (Eugene, Ore.), 1967. (*DA* 28:3463A)

222. HELM, CHRISTOPHER R. *Watson-Glaser-DAT Graduate Norms.* Master's thesis, University of Toledo (Toledo, Ohio), 1967.

223. HERIOT, MARY R. *The Differential Aptitude Test as an Indicator of Success in the Engineering Technologies at Richland Technical Education Center.* Master's thesis, University of South Carolina (Columbia, S.C.), 1967.

224. HOLLENBECK, GEORGE P. "Predicting High School Biology Achievement With the Differential Aptitude Tests and the Davis Reading Test." *Ed & Psychol Meas* 27:439–42 su '67. * (*PA* 41:14218)

225. KING, CHARLES EULLE. *An Investigation of Curricular Loads Which Tend to Promote Maximum Achievement by Eighth Grade Pupils.* Doctor's thesis, American University (Washington, D.C.), 1967. (*DA* 28:1211A)

226. MARTIN, WILLIAM T. "Analysis of the Abstracting Function in Reasoning Using an Experimental Test." *Psychol Rep* 21:593–8 O '67. * (*PA* 42:4815)

227. O'HARA, ROBERT P. "Vocational Self Concepts of Boys Choosing Science and Non-Science Careers." *Ed & Psychol Meas* 27:139–49 sp '67. * (*PA* 41:9476)

228. RICE, VICTOR. *An Appraisal of the Predictive Value of Patterns of Subtest Scores in Achievement Test Batteries.* Doctor's thesis, American University (Washington, D.C.), 1967. (*DA* 28:1267A)

229. ROBERTSON, GARY JEROME. *Relationships Among Verbal*

Differential Aptitude Tests

Meaning and Fluency Tasks. Doctor's thesis, Columbia University (New York, N.Y.), 1967. *(DA* 28:506A)

230. Ross, DONALD RUFUS. *Test Performance of Deaf Adults Under Two Modes of Test Administration.* Doctor's thesis, University of Arizona (Tucson, Ariz.), 1967. *(DA* 28:2992A)

231. SCHROTH, MARVIN L. "Spatial Aptitude and Its Relationship to Art Judgment." *Percept & Motor Skills* 24:746 Je '67. *

232. STILGEBAUER, LARRY K. *A Study of Selected Data in Predicting Success in Ninth Grade Mathematics at Jefferson Junior High School, Mattoon, Illinois.* Master's thesis, Eastern Illinois University (Charleston, Ill.), 1967.

233. TRITES, DAVID K.; KUREK, ADOLPH; AND COBB, BART B. "Personality and Achievement of Air Traffic Controllers." *Aerospace Med* 38:1145-50 N '67. *

234. TUCKER, WILLIAM FRANCIS. *The Prediction of Achievement in Selected High School Subjects From Junior High School Data.* Doctor's thesis, New York University (New York, N.Y.), 1967. *(DA* 28:1317A)

235. WILKERSON, CAROLYN DOWNEY. *The Effects of Four Methods of Test Score Presentation to Eighth Grade Students.* Doctor's thesis, Arizona State University (Tempe, Ariz.), 1967. *(DA* 28:1318A)

236. ANANT, SANTOKH S. "Relative Effectiveness of Aptitude Tests." *Alberta J Ed Res* 14:43-7 Mr '68. * *(PA* 44:4165)

237. BINGMAN, RICHARD MARVIN. "Aptitude and Interest Profiles of Biology Participants in Montgomery County (Pennsylvania) Science Fairs." *J Res Sci Teach* 5(2):245-52 '67-68. *

238. BOWEN, COLLIN WELDON. *The Use of Self-Estimates of Ability and Measures of Ability in the Prediction of Academic Performance.* Doctor's thesis, Oklahoma State University (Stillwater, Okla.), 1968. *(DAI* 30:978A)

239. DOSAJH, N. L. "Extracting DAT Factors." *Indian Psychol R* 4:114-9 Ja '68. * *(PA* 43:11820)

240. HUNTER, NORMAN W. *A Study of Factors Which May Affect a Student's Success in Quantitative Analysis.* Doctor's thesis, University of Toledo (Toledo, Ohio), 1968. *(DA* 29:2437A)

241. IRVINE, FLEET RAYMOND. *A Study of Creative Thinking Ability, and Its Relationship to Psychomotor Ability, Mechanical Reasoning Ability, and Vocational Aptitude of Selected High School Industrial Arts Students.* Doctor's thesis, Utah State University (Logan, Utah), 1968. *(DA* 29:1768A)

242. KIRKPATRICK, JAMES J.; EWEN, ROBERT B.; BARRETT, RICHARD S.; AND KATZELL, RAYMOND A. *Testing and Fair Employment: Fairness and Validity of Personnel Tests for Different Ethnic Groups,* pp. 17-21, 25-7, 51-69, 71-93. New York: New York University Press, 1968. Pp. x, 145. *

243. KOHLI, PAUL EUGENE. *An Analysis of Differential Aptitude Test Scores and Prediction of High School Academic Performance.* Doctor's thesis, University of Toledo (Toledo, Ohio), 1968. *(DA* 29:2528A)

244. NAUGHTON, JACK. "A Modest Experiment on Test Motivation." Letter. *Personnel & Guid J* 46:606 F '68. *

245. NELSON, LEONARD THEODORE, JR. *The Relationship Between Verbal, Visual-Spatial, and Numerical Abilities and the Learning of the Mathematical Concept of Function.* Doctor's thesis, University of Michigan (Ann Arbor, Mich.), 1968. *(DAI* 30:218A)

246. WOOD, DONALD A., AND LEBOLD, WILLIAM K. "Differential and Overall Prediction of Academic Success in Engineering: The Complementary Role of DAT, SAT and HSR." *Ed & Psychol Meas* 28:1223-8 w '68. * *(PA* 44:7339)

247. ARMBRUST, ROBERT. *An Investigation of the Role of Selected Non-Verbal Intelligence Factors in Beginning Drafting Success.* Doctor's thesis, Southern Illinois University (Carbondale, Ill.), 1969. *(DAI* 30:2895A)

248. DIXON, ANNIE SYLVIA. *A Use of Differential Aptitude Test Scores in Counseling in Three High School Programs.* Master's thesis, University of Alberta (Edmonton, Alta., Canada), 1969.

249. DUTT, KARL FREDERICK. *The Comparative Effects of General and Specific Aptitude Test Interpretative Materials on the Vocational Choice-Related Decisions, Attitudes, and Preparedness of Ninth-Grade Boys.* Doctor's thesis, Lehigh University (Bethlehem, Pa.), 1969. *(DAI* 30:5231A)

250. FRANDSEN, ARDEN N., AND HOLDER, JAMES R. "Spatial Visualization in Solving Complex Verbal Problems." *J Psychol* 73(2):229-33 N '69. * *(PA* 44:7705)

251. GARNER, GLENN LAMAR. *High School Freshmen DAT Clerical Speed and Accuracy Scores and English Grades as Predictors of Success in Business Courses.* Master's thesis, Millersville State College (Millersville, Pa.), 1969.

252. GOOLSBY, THOMAS M., JR.; FRARY, ROBERT B.; AND LASCO, RICHARD A. "Selecting and Supplementing an Appropriate Achievement Battery for an Experimental School—A Factor Analytic Approach." *Ed & Psychol Meas* 29(2):403-8 su '69. * *(PA* 44:17319)

253. HALL, LUCIEN TALMAGE, JR. *The Prediction of Success in Each of Six Four-Year Selections of Secondary Mathematics Courses.* Doctor's thesis, University of Virginia (Charlottesville, Va.), 1969. *(DAI* 30:4141A)

254. HARTLAGE, LAWRENCE C. "Nonvisual Test of Spatial Ability." Abstract. *Proc 77th Ann Conv Am Psychol Assn* 4(1):163-4 '69. * *(PA* 43:16635)

255. HEWICK, WALTER ELTON. *A Study to Compare the Effectiveness of the Differential Aptitude Tests and the Adapted Guyanese Tests for Identifying Aptitudes Among Students in Guyanese Secondary Schools.* Doctor's thesis, American University (Washington, D.C.), 1969. *(DAI* 30:3635A)

256. JENKINS, FARRELL TERRY. *Predicting Academic Success at Utah Technical College at Salt Lake.* Doctor's thesis, University of Utah (Salt Lake City, Utah), 1969. *(DAI* 30:2421B)

257. MERENDA, PETER F.; JACOBSEN, GWENDOLYN; AND CLARKE, WALTER V. "Further Cross-Validities of the MOS and DAT Batteries." *Psychol Rep* 24(2):541-2 Ap '69. * *(PA* 43:15013)

258. PARMON, ROYCE E. *Validation of the Differential Aptitude Tests for Predicting Freshman Performance at the University of Tennessee.* Master's thesis, East Tennessee State University (Johnson City, Tenn.), 1969.

259. SHAPPELL, DEAN LEROY. *The Relationship of Socio-Economic Status to School Motivation and Occupational Orientation.* Doctor's thesis, Ohio State University (Columbus, Ohio), 1969. *(DAI* 30:2345A)

260. SUTHERLAND, KELLEY. *The Predictive Value of School and College Ability Test, Sequential Test of Educational Progress, Differential Aptitude Test, Iowa Silent Reading Test, and California Test of Mental Maturity Scores at Clintwood High School, Clintwood, Virginia.* Master's thesis, East Tennessee State University (Johnson City, Tenn.), 1969.

261. THOMSON, WILLIAM D. *Predicting Practical Nursing Course Grades From the California Psychological Inventory and the Differential Aptitude Test.* Master's thesis, Brigham Young University (Provo, Utah), 1969.

262. CHEONG, GEORGE S. C. "Relations Among Age, Schooling, Differential Aptitude Test, and the ACER Test." *Ed & Psychol Meas* 30(2):479-82 su '70. *

263. CRONBACH, LEE J. *Essentials of Psychological Testing, Third Edition,* pp. 353-75. New York: Harper & Row, Publishers, Inc., 1970. Pp. xxxix, 752. *

264. DWORKIN, SAMUEL F. "Further Correlational and Factor Analyses of the DAT as a Predictor of Informance: Conclusions and Summary." *J Dental Ed* 34(4):44-50 D '70. *

265. GRANT, DONALD L., AND BRAY, DOUGLAS W. "Validation of Employment Tests for Telephone Company Installation and Repair Occupations." *J Appl Psychol* 54(1):7-14 F '70. *

266. KINSEY, DON R., AND SMITH, GEOFFREY. "Predicting Success in Shorthand." *Sch & Commun* 57(3):23 N '70. *

267. REINHART, WILLIAM C. *An Expectancy Table Based on the Differential Aptitude Tests for the Purpose of Predicting Success in First Year Bookkeeping.* Master's thesis, Glassboro State College (Glassboro, N.J.), 1970.

268. SAKALOSKY, JOSEPH C. *A Study of the Relationship Between the Differential Aptitude Test Battery and the General Aptitude Test Battery Scores of Ninth Graders.* Master's thesis, Millersville State College (Millersville, Pa.), 1970.

M. Y. QURESHI, *Professor of Psychology, Marquette University, Milwaukee, Wisconsin.*

The second edition of the *Differential Aptitude Tests,* published in 1962, consists of two forms, L and M, respectively replacing Forms A and B of the 1947 edition. The publication of the fourth edition of the technical manual in 1966 has made available to the user a wealth of pertinent information.

Reviewers in the past have justifiably dubbed the DAT as the "best" available instrument of its kind. However, they have also indicated the improvements which are still needed to make it an even more effective tool for educational and vocational guidance. Some of these past suggestions have been implemented in the current version of the DAT, but others have received little attention. The battery still consists of eight tests bearing the same names as in the first edition: Verbal Reasoning (VR), Numerical Ability (NA), Abstract Reasoning (AR), Clerical

Speed and Accuracy (CSA), Mechanical Reasoning (MR), Space Relations (SR), Language Usage I: Spelling (LU-I), and Language Usage II: Grammar (LU-II). LU-I and LU-II are achievement tests, but are included in the battery because of their presumed curricular or vocational relevance. Scoring has been simplified for NA, AR, MR, and LU-I by the elimination of the correction for guessing. The items in CSA have been set in new type and condensed to two pages instead of four without any change in the number or content of the items. VR, SR, and LU-II have been changed in length or in item format. The following evaluation seems to be justified on the basis of the available evidence.

NORMATIVE DATA. The norms are based on a sample of 50,510 boys and girls, representing a cross section of the U.S. public school population in grades 8 through 12 in 43 states. Tables 2 and 3 in the manual present the percentages of the total public school population in various geographical regions and communities relative to the percentages of boys and girls in grades 8 through 12 actually included in the sample; however, these tables do not present the overall percentages which could be readily compared with the overall "desired" percentages given in column 2 of either table. The actual overall percentages, which the reviewer computed from the data in Table 2, indicate that whereas the Northeast and the North Central regions are approximately proportionately represented, the South is grossly under-represented and the West is grossly over-represented. Similar indices computed from the data in Table 3 indicate that communities of 5,000 to 99,999 are seriously under-represented and the "urban fringes" are clearly over-represented. In addition, no information is available regarding the relative representation of various ethnic or socioeconomic groups.

There is ample justification for presenting separate norms for males and females, since differences between the sexes on some tests are quite substantial. Norms are available in raw scores, centiles, and stanines, but not in normalized standard scores such as T scores. The centile interpretation of scores is very popular and easily understood, but it is doubtful that many high school counselors use stanines. The size of the sample, even when broken down by grade and sex, is adequate, but whether it is representative of the U.S. public school population in grades 8–12 depends on the tenability of the assumptions that the selected sample includes a proportionate number of ethnic minorities and that under- or over-representation of certain geographical regions is irrelevant to the measurement of cognitive and psychomotor characteristics as sampled by the DAT.

RELIABILITY DATA. The reliability coefficients for all tests except CSA are split-half correlations corrected by the Spearman-Brown formula. All these coefficients are reported separately for Forms L and M, for each test, "for each sex in each grade, for a sample of students drawn from the standardization population." Since CSA is speeded, its reliability represents the correlation between Forms L and M concurrently administered to students in grades 8–12 in a particular high school and corrected for the range of the norms group. These coefficients attest to the high degree of short-term consistency of the DAT scores. Parallel-form coefficients involving Forms A and M are also available, though they are reported in the chapter on Equivalence of Forms and not with the rest of reliability data. Long-term consistency of the DAT measures is supported by reprinting the test-retest (over a 3-year period) coefficients for Form A from the second edition (1952) of the DAT manual.

EQUIVALENCE OF FORMS. The authors of DAT appropriately emphasize the need for demonstrating the equivalence of Forms L and M with Forms A and B. Since Form A has been frequently employed in research and service, they chose to demonstrate the "educational and psychological" equivalence of Forms A and M. They also report means and standard deviations for Forms A and L, as well as for Forms L and M, for comparative purposes. Thus, data are available for comparing two forms at a time. This piecemeal approach is unsatisfactory on two counts: (a) It does not readily provide the user adequate information for the comparability of Forms A, L, and M. (b) It rejects the appropriate and exact statistical procedures which should be employed when three or more forms are involved. Although Form L includes four tests which are identical with their namesakes in Form A, the changes in the remaining four tests are substantial enough to require that the equivalence of Forms A, L, and M be judged simultaneously. The appropriate statistical techniques

Differential Aptitude Tests

for this purpose are available in the literature.[1] These procedures test for the equality of means, variances, and covariances together, but they can be applied partially to variances and covariances alone if the equality of raw score means is considered unimportant.

The authors present the intercorrelations of tests in Form A and of those in Form M for various age groups, by sex, separately in Tables 4–8. On the basis of inspection, they arrive at the conclusion that "the basic measurement inherent in these tests is largely unchanged." An appropriate procedure for ascertaining whether such is the case would be to apply a test for the homogeneity of dispersions[2] instead of relying on subjective estimates.

VALIDITY DATA. The section on validity is the longest in the manual and presents correlations of DAT scores with course grades in all sorts of areas and with scores on a variety of achievement tests. Correlations with other standardized aptitude (including PMA and GATB), achievement, and interest measures are reported in a separate chapter and should adequately meet an earlier criticism along these lines. These are all (with one exception) zero-order coefficients representing the predictive value of the DAT scores over a period of a few weeks to several years. However, there is only one study, based on 1,700 respondents to a questionnaire, which compares the DAT scores with post high school educational and vocational careers. This study was later extended to cover a seven-year period from the date of testing with DAT to the time of securing criterion measures. The results indicate that the groups of persons in various occupational fields can be effectively differentiated from each other on the basis of their *level* of performance on the DAT. However, this is hardly an evidence of differential validity of a multiple aptitude battery, since similar discriminations can be made on the basis of VR+NA scores alone or on the basis of global scores on group mental ability tests. The proper evidence of the differential value of DAT should present (*a*) the appropriate combination of scores which sets one occupational group apart from another, and (*b*) the contribution that a par-

ticular test makes to the discriminant function identifying people in a particular occupation. Similarly, for predicting achievement in certain curricular fields, one would like to know the contribution to multiple R of the test(s) presumably predictive of success in certain special areas over and above that of a global measure such as VR+NA. No such information is presented anywhere in the manual. The only data bearing on the differential validity of the DAT scores covers about one page in Section 7 of the manual and represents the results of the application of a procedure developed by T. L. Kelley.[3] Although Kelley's index provides some useful information, as applied to DAT it may not be accepted as an adequate test of the differential validity for the following reasons: (*a*) To this reviewer's knowledge, the standard errors of the "percentages of differences in excess of chance" have never been determined. (*b*) Pairwise comparisons without considering all the tests in the battery capitalize on chance deviations. (*c*) The percentages are based on the data for five grades combined and not for separate grades. (*d*) According to the arbitrary 25 percent criterion, even the *Stanford Achievement Test* of the 1920 vintage (used by Kelley to illustrate his procedure) turns out to be a satisfactory differential instrument.

There is adequate evidence to indicate that, except for CSA, tests in the DAT are factorially complex. This reviewer conducted a factor analysis, employing the principal axis method with varimax rotation, of the data in Tables 4, 69, and 70 in the manual in order to catch a glimpse of the factorial complexity of each test as well as to ascertain the maximum possible numbers of factors measured reliably by the total battery. The results indicate that CSA is factorially the purest, followed by LU-I and MR in that order. However, only CSA and LU-I may be treated as factorially pure since MR and the other five tests have substantial loadings on two or more factors. If three factors are extracted, the percents of accountable reliable variance range between 84 and 94; if four are extracted, the percents range between 88 and 97; and if five factors are extracted, the percents range from 92 to 99. However, when five factors are obtained, one of them invariably turns out to be a "garbage" factor, totally un-

1 WILKS, S. S. "Sample Criteria for Testing Equality of Means, Equality of Variances, and Equality of Covariances in a Normal Multivariate Distribution." *Ann Math Stat* 17:257–81 S '46. *

VOTAW, DAVID F., JR. "Testing Compound Symmetry in a Normal Multivariate Distribution." *Ann Math Stat* 19:447–73 D '48. *

2 BOX, G. E. P. "A General Distribution Theory for a Class of Likelihood Criteria." *Biometrika* 36:317–46 D '49. *

3 KELLEY, TRUMAN L. "A New Method for Determining the Significance of Differences in Intelligence and Achievement Scores." *J Ed Psychol* 14:321–43 S '23. *

Differential Aptitude Tests

interpretable. Three factors generally account for about 90 percent of the reliable variance, indicating that the battery probably encompasses three factors, but definitely no more than four. A number of tests (e.g., VR, LU-I, and LU-II) have equally high loadings on the same factor, evidencing undue redundancy in measurement. A judicious selection (e.g., VR, NA, CSA, MR, and SR) from the current conglomerate can do the job as effectively as the whole battery. The DAT, despite its technical superiority over its competitors, represents a substantial degree of inessential duplication of time, effort, and expense.

CONCLUDING REMARKS. The effectiveness of DAT is enhanced by such supportive data as given in *Counseling from Profiles (29)* and the recurring pedagogic emphasis in the technical manual. It has so far not lived up to the promise of a differential instrument, but no other instrument for the given age range has yet succeeded in this respect. However, the DAT, if certain steps are taken, has better chances of attaining an acceptable level of differential efficiency than any other comparative battery.

Personnel & Guid J 43:396–401 D '64. Jack C. Merwin. * the changes from the earlier edition to the new edition are desirable but leave the two editions enough alike so that the findings of the extensive research that has been conducted on the earlier edition will be generally applicable to interpretation of scores from....the 1963 edition * The reliability of the tests appears adequate on the basis of coefficients obtained by a variety of procedures. * An earlier reviewer commented that "....evaluation techniques currently used in our high schools are such that little, if any, differential prediction can be obtained" (Bechtoldt, 1953). It is interesting to note that if a group has a relatively high correlation between scores on one of the tests and grades in a given subject, the coefficients of the other tests with this criterion also tend to be higher than the coefficients for other groups and their grades in this subject area. This points up the need to consider carefully the characteristics of the criterion measure used and the limitations it places on prediction with any test. * Aids to interpretation provided by the publisher and the results of validity studies in numerous settings can be helpful in a general consideration of the value of this battery. However, for a specific

school setting there is need to look beyond these data. The validity data provided by the authors indicate that these tests can be of value for counseling in grades 8–12. However, the value of the test for a particular use in a school system needs independent study. The results of these tests, as well as of any test used in a counseling program of a school, should not continue in use without evaluation. The way in which the test results can best be used in an individual school system can only be assessed using validity evidence obtained in the local setting. The way in which individual tests might be selected to aid in specific decisions, how they can be used jointly to maximize prediction, and how test scores can be combined with other information available in the school should be matters of concern to counselors using this battery. * For the school system considering the use of a test battery covering a variety of aptitudes, the *Differential Aptitude Test* battery provides a series of relatively independent tests which are easily administered and simple to score (particularly the 1963 edition). An abundance of material has been prepared to aid in the interpretation of scores that can be readily profiled. Many examples of the use of DAT results as predictive indices for course grades as well as illustrative interpretations of profiles from the battery are available. In addition to scores from eight different tests the battery yields a single measure which is probably as good a measure of general academic ability as any test they may now have in use. Any school using the *Differential Aptitude Tests* for the first time is encouraged to use Form L or M rather than A or B. The changes in the new edition are highly desirable but are not radical enough to suggest an urgent need for schools now using Forms A and B to change.

For reviews by J. A. Keats and Richard E. Schutz, see 6:767; for reviews by John B. Carroll and Norman Frederiksen, see 5:605; for reviews by Harold Bechtoldt, Ralph F. Berdie, and Lloyd G. Humphreys, see 4:711; see also 3:620 (1 excerpt).

[674]

★**Experimental Comparative Prediction Batteries.** Grades 9–12, 13–16; 1963–64; ECPB; for research use only; guidance and counseling; 2 levels; manual ('64, 57 pages); expectancy chart ('63, 1 page); no data on reliability; no norms; 10¢ per expectancy chart; 30¢ per supervisor's manual; $2 per manual; $4.50 per specimen set; cash orders postpaid; John W. French (manual); Educational Testing Service. *

a) HIGH SCHOOL LEVEL. Grades 9–12; 3 tests; supervisor's manual ('63, 14 pages).

1) *Book A-1.* 3 scores: induction, integration, visualization; 1 form ('63, 14 pages); separate answer sheets (SCRIBE) must be used; 30¢ per test; scoring service, 50¢ per test ($25 minimum); (90–95) minutes.

2) *Book B.* 3 scores: meaningful memory, spatial orientation, number facility; 1 form ('63, 16 pages); 35¢ per test; (30–35) minutes.

3) *Book C.* Revision of *Cooperative Interest Index* (see 2:1225–6); 12 scores: biological sciences, English, art, mathematics, social sciences, secretarial, physical sciences, foreign languages, music, engineering, home economics, executive; 1 form ('63, 10 pages); separate answer sheets (SCRIBE) must be used; 30¢ per test; scoring service, $1.25 per test ($62.50 minimum); (45–50) minutes.

b) COLLEGE LEVEL. Grades 13–16; 3 tests; supervisor's manual ('63, 8 pages).

1) *Book A-2.* 3 scores: same as for *a1*; 1 form ('63, 16 pages); separate answer sheets (SCRIBE) must be used; 30¢ per test; scoring service and time same as for *a1*.

2) *Book B.* Same as for *a2*.

3) *Book C.* Same as for *a3*.

REFERENCES

1. FRENCH, JOHN W. "Comparative Prediction of College Major-Field Grades by Pure-Factor Aptitude, Interest, and Personality Measures." *Ed & Psychol Meas* 23:767–74 w '63. *
2. FRENCH, JOHN W. "Comparative Prediction of High-School Grades by Pure-Factor Aptitude, Information, and Personality Measures." *Ed & Psychol Meas* 24:321–9 su '64. * (*PA* 39:3162)
3. FRENCH, JOHN W. "New Tests for Predicting the Performance of College Students With High-Level Aptitude." *J Ed Psychol* 55:185–94 Ag '64. * (*PA* 39:5979)

[675]

Flanagan Aptitude Classification Tests. Grades 9–12, 10–12 and adults; 1951–60; FACT; 2 editions; postage extra; John C. Flanagan; Science Research Associates, Inc. *

a) SEPARATE BOOKLET 16-TEST EDITION. Grades 10–12 and adults; 1951–60; 16 tests; examiner's manual ('53, 27 pages); technical supplement ('54, 16 pages); personnel director's booklet ('53, 27 pages); manual for interpreting scores ('56, 12 pages); $5.10 per 25 self-marking tests; 40¢ per technical supplement; 55¢ per manual for interpreting scores; 80¢ per personnel director's booklet; $6.10 per specimen set; 258(388) minutes in 2 sessions.

1) *FACT 1A, Inspection.* 1953–56; form A ('53, 6 pages); 6(12) minutes.

2) *FACT 2A and 2B, Coding.* 1953–56; forms A ('53, 6 pages), B ('54, 6 pages); 10(30) minutes.

3) *FACT 3A and 3B, Memory.* 1953–56; forms A ('53, 3 pages), B ('54, 3 pages); 4(5) minutes.

4) *FACT 4A, Precision.* 1953–56; form A ('53, 4 pages); 8(15) minutes.

5) *FACT 5A, Assembly.* 1953–56; form A ('53, 6 pages); 12(18) minutes.

6) *FACT 6A, Scales.* 1953–56; form A ('53, 6 pages); 16(28) minutes.

7) *FACT 7A, Coordination.* 1953–56; form A ('53, 8 pages); 2⅔(8) minutes.

8) *FACT 8A, Judgment and Comprehension.* 1953–56; form A ('53, 7 pages); (35–40) minutes.

9) *FACT 9A, Arithmetic.* 1953–56; form A ('53, 6 pages); 10(20) minutes.

10) *FACT 10A, Patterns.* 1953–56; form A ('53, 6 pages); 20(28) minutes.

11) *FACT 11A, Components.* 1953–56; form A ('53, 6 pages); 20(24) minutes.

12) *FACT 12A, Tables.* 1953–56; form A ('53, 6 pages); 10(15) minutes.

13) *FACT 13A and 13B, Mechanics.* 1953–56; forms A ('53, 6 pages), B ('54, 6 pages); 20(25) minutes.

14) *FACT 14A, Expression.* 1953–56; form A ('53, 6 pages); (35–45) minutes.

15) *FACT 15A, Reasoning.* 1957–60; form A ('57, 6 pages); supplementary manual ('60, 6 pages); 40¢ per supplementary manual; 24(30) minutes.

16) *FACT 16A, Ingenuity.* 1957–60; form A ('57, 7 pages); supplementary manual ('60, 6 pages); 40¢ per supplementary manual; 24(30) minutes.

b) 19-TEST EDITION. Grades 9–12; 1957–60; 19 tests (same as for *a* plus vocabulary, planning, alertness) in 2 booklets: gray book ('57, 64 pages), blue book ('57, 24 pages); examiner's manual ('58, 70 pages); mimeographed norms ['58, 23 pages]; administrator's manual ('58, 17 pages); technical report ('59, 65 pages); mimeographed manual for planning short batteries ('60, 10 pages); score interpretation booklet for students ('58, 25 pages); separate answer sheets (MRC) must be used with gray book (blue book is scored by students); $3.25 per specimen set; (630) minutes in 3 sessions.

1) *SRA Scored.* Scoring service available only for MRC answer sheets used with gray books.

(*a*) Complete Rental Plan. Rental and scoring service, $1.60 per student.

(*b*) Scoring Only Plan. $8.50 per 25 blue books; $25 per 25 gray books; scoring service, $1.36 per student.

2) *School Scored.* $8.50 per 25 blue books; $25 per 25 gray books; $11.25 per 100 MRC answer sheets and 3 examiner's manuals; $2 per set of MRC hand scoring stencils for gray books; $10.75 per 25 score interpretation booklets; $3.25 per set of interpretive materials (administrator's manual, technical report, norms, and manual for planning).

REFERENCES

1–7. See 6:770.
8. ALTMAN, JAMES WILLIAM. *Measuring Technician Performance.* Doctor's thesis, University of Pittsburgh (Pittsburgh, Pa.), 1954. (*DA* 14:1452)
9. FLANAGAN, JOHN C. "The Relation of a New Ingenuity Measure to Other Variables." *Univ Utah Res Conf Identif Creat Sci Talent* 3:104–23 '59. *
10. JEX, FRANK B. "Negative Validities for Two Different Ingenuity Tests." *Univ Utah Res Conf Identif Creat Sci Talent* 3:124–7 '59. *
11. ALFORD, MARY LEE. *Teacher Judgments as Related to Certain Predictors of Artistic Creativity in Senior High-School Students.* Doctor's thesis, North Texas State University (Denton, Tex.), 1964. (*DA* 25:1039)
12. COOLEY, WILLIAM W. "Further Relationships With the TALENT Battery." *Personnel & Guid J* 44:295–303 N '65. *
13. SCOTT, RUSSELL H.; PHIPPS, GRANT T.; AND MORGART, HELEN S. "Prediction of Success in a Dental Assisting Course." *J Dental Ed* 29:348–57 D '65. *
14. ANDERSON, ROGER CLARE. *A Study of Academic and Biographical Variables for Predicting Achievement in Technical Programs at the North Dakota State School of Science.* Doctor's thesis, University of North Dakota (Grand Forks, N.D.), 1966. (*DA* 27:2046A)
15. GUILLIAMS, CLARK IRVIN. *Predicting Creative Productivity in College Classes Where Creative Thinking Is Emphasized.* Doctor's thesis, University of Arkansas (Fayetteville, Ark.), 1966. (*DA* 27:675A)
16. LITTLE, ELLIS BEECHER. "Creativity and the Correction-for-Chance-Success Formula: Flanagan Test of Ingenuity." *Sch Sci & Math* 67:3–8 Ja '67. *
17. FLANAGAN, JOHN C. "Ingenuity Test." *J Creative Behav* 2:215–6 f '68. * (*PA* 43:5360)

Personnel & Guid J 43:607–11 F '65. Harold D. Murphy and John P. McQuary. * In most instances the directions for administering the various tests are detailed and explicit. However, the most experienced teacher or counselor will often have trouble mastering the skills necessary for proper administration even when directions are followed closely. There are several requirements that make the administration of the test difficult at times. Among these are: (1) the necessity for the same test booklet to be returned to each student at each of three testing sessions; (2) the extreme variation in time limits imposed on each test, ranging from eight seconds on practice items in test 14 (precision) to unlimited time for tests 7 (judgment and comprehension) and 13 (expression); (3) the necessity for students to transfer answers from the Blue Books to the answer sheets on test 9 (planning); and (4) the necessity for timing separately two sets of practice problems such as those in test 12 (scales). It would seem that some confusion might be avoided by eliminating separate time limits for practice problems. On this particular test (scales), it would also facilitate administration if practice problems for each part immediately preceded that part rather than being arranged together before part one. The current arrangement causes the student to turn back in the booklet in order to work the practice problems. Some typical comments from counselors who use the test are: (1) The test is too long; students tire before they finish. (2) On the parts with short time limits, such as test 14, 15, and 16, the slower students become discouraged and create a problem in maintaining the proper test atmosphere. (3) The use of different types of pencils complicates the administration for large groups. * It should be noted that reliability estimates for individual tests fall short of that necessary for individual prediction. However, the tests are not intended to be used separately. They are intended to be used in combination for predictions in broad occupational fields. When this criterion is met, the reliability coefficients range considerably higher and are adequate for individual prediction. * Correlation coefficients for occupational stanines with criteria of progress and performance in college fields are relatively good, with the exception of a .04 coefficient for clergyman, missionary, and social worker. * No evidence is presented that the coefficients are any higher than those which might have been obtained by the use of other predictors such as high school grades, mental ability, or achievement-test scores. The validity coefficients for occupational stanines with criteria of progress and performance in business and clerical fields were uniformly low, the range being from +.10 for

secretary, stenographer, typist, to a −.17 for sales clerk. In other samples, referred to in the technical report, validity data for business and clerical occupations are somewhat better. However, validity is still not as high as one would expect from a battery of this length and scope. * One's reaction to all FACT materials is ambivalent. There is no question that these represent a definite strength. At the same time, it would be less than honest to say that when one looks at the gray book for FACT (containing the first 13 tests), the blue book (containing tests 14–19), the *Technical Report,* the *Examiner's Manual,* the *Administrator's Manual,* and the *Student's Booklet* (for interpretation), there are feelings of being overwhelmed by test materials and of wonder if somehow the client as an individual will be forgotten by counselors since there are so many other measurement things to remember. Both the *Administrator's Manual* and the *Examiner's Manual* are well written in a logical, concise arrangement. These require the type of study one is *expected* to give to the administration of any standardized test. The section in the *Administrator's Manual* on "How the FACT Program Works" is excellent. * The material in the *Student's Booklet* anticipates trouble spots, such as on page 4 where an explanation is given for the meaning of each test, or on page 6 where "cut off" scores are indicated as not being absolute. However, one wonders how well these explanations are given to students. After examining the test booklets and all other aids, it can be concluded that, despite expected use of the FACT in group testing, it is more apt to achieve the results that Flanagan intended if it is administered and interpreted individually. Interpretation of the FACT is accomplished through the use of the *Student's Booklet* in which the student works out median percentile scores for 37 occupational fields and for general college aptitude. * From the comments of a sample of school counselors ....the reviewers have found both positive and negative attitudes toward the *Student's Booklet* as a device for interpretation. Most of the school counselors surveyed feel that the *Student's Booklet* stimulates interest in occupations. They also agree that this device fosters the idea that a cluster of aptitudes is necessary for each vocation. While all agree that individual interpretation is desirable, it is not always possible where the student-counselor ratio is extremely high. In such cases, they feel that the *Student's Booklet* provides a better interpretation than might be possible through other group-interpretation methods. The same group of school counselors indicates that there is the danger of mechanization and assembly-line counseling when using the *Student's Booklet* in groups. A frequent criticism of the *Student's Booklet* arises from the fact that students of superior ability exceed the cut-off score in most every instance while students of low ability often fall below the cut-off on practically all occupational fields. This lack of discrimination on either end of the scale still leaves unsolved the selection of vocations suitable to these ability levels; states of confusion may be compounded. The cut-off scores are derived from group performance. When these scores are then used for individual prediction or selection, there is a danger of placing too much trust in the precision of a particular score. The impression left with the student is that the prediction of occupational success is a simple yes or no process. The booklet fails to stress the importance of nonintellectual factors. * many of the negative comments concerning interpretation may reflect more on the use of the test than on the test itself. SUMMARY. There are several features that recommend this test to the counselor for use in vocational counseling. Foremost among these is the continued research aimed at validating the claim of the importance of matching job elements with aptitude clusters. Secondly, the quality of the testing materials and the aids to counselors are superior. On the other hand, counselors should be alert to the limitations of the test. Among these are its length and its difficulty of administration. In addition, this test would appear to be more useful when individual testing and interpretation are employed than when used in group situations. The seeming simplicity of the *Student's Booklet* may leave the impression that vocational choice is an easy process. This could lead to an assembly-line approach to vocational counseling which overlooks the importance of nonintellectual factors to occupational success. In summary, the reviewers feel that this is a well-designed battery of tests and that the novel approach used by the test constructor warrants its continued use. It is hoped that Flanagan will continue his validation studies so that this instrument will be of more benefit to vocational counseling.

For reviews by Norman Frederiksen and William B. Michael, see 6:770; for reviews by Harold P. Bechtoldt, Ralph F. Berdie, and John B. Carroll, see 5:608.

[676]

*General Aptitude Test Battery.** Ages 16 and over, grades 9-12 and adults; 1946-70; GATB; for a nonreading adaptation, see the *Nonreading Aptitude Test Battery;* developed for use in the occupational counseling program of the United States Training and Employment Service and released for use by State Employment Services; 2 editions; manual in 4 sections: section 1—administration and scoring ('66, 54 pages for *b*; '70, 127 pages for *c*), section 2—norms for counseling ('70, 139 pages), section 3—development ('70, 388 pages), section 4—norms for specific occupations ('70, 77 pages); record blank ('70, 1 page) for apparatus tests; profile-record card ('70, 2 pages) for *b* and *c*; no testing fee for applicants tested through State Employment Service offices; tests available to nonprofit institutions for counseling purposes; $1.50 per 100 record blanks; $3.75 per 100 profile-record cards; manual available for unrestricted sale: 40¢ per copy of section 1 for *b*, $1.50 per copy of section 1 for *c*, $2 per copy of section 2 or 4, $3 per copy of section 3; postpaid; specimen set not available; orders for tests and all other accessories must be cleared through a State Employment Service office; United States Training and Employment Service; test booklets and manuals distributed by United States Government Printing Office. *

a) SCREENING AND PRETESTING EXERCISES. 1966-68.

1) *GATB Screening Exercises.* 1966; to identify examinees who are deficient in reading skills and should be tested with nonreading adaptation of battery; 1 form (2 pages); counselor's guide (11 pages); demonstration card (2 pages); $5 per 100 tests; $5 per 100 demonstration cards; 25¢ per guide; (5-10) minutes.

2) *USTES Pretesting Orientation Exercises.* 1968; test-taking practice for disadvantaged persons; 1 form (18 pages); manual (26 pages); practice booklet (14 pages); marking exercise (2 pages); separate answer sheets (NCS) must be used; 30¢ per test; $10 per 250 answer sheets; 15¢ per practice booklet; $1.25 per 100 marking exercises; 30¢ per manual; (90) minutes.

b) GATB, B-1001, [EXPENDABLE BOOKLET EDITION]. Ages 16 and over; 1947-70; 9 scores: intelligence, verbal, numerical, spatial, form perception, clerical perception, motor coordination, finger dexterity, manual dexterity; 1 form; 12 tests: 8 paper and pencil tests plus 4 performance tests; 39(150) minutes.

1) *Book 1.* 1 form ('66, 16 pages); 3 tests: tool matching, name comparison, computation; $11.25 per 100 tests.

2) *Book 2.* 1 form ('66, 24 pages); 4 tests: three-dimensional space, arithmetic reasoning, vocabulary, form matching; $15 per 100 tests.

3) *Part K [Mark Making].* 1965; revised form (2 pages); $1 per 100 tests.

4) *Pegboard.* 2 tests: place, turn; set of wooden testing materials: $18.25 (K & W Products Co., Inc.), $18.50 (Warwick Products Co.); $16.25 per set of plastic testing materials (Specialty Case Manufacturing Co.).

5) *Finger Dexterity Board.* 2 tests: assemble, disassemble; set of testing materials: $7.50 (Specialty Case Manufacturing Co.), $8.65 (Warwick Products Co.), $12.25 (K & W Products Co., Inc.).

c) GATB, B-1002, [SEPARATE ANSWER SHEET EDITION].

Grades 9–12 and adults; 1952–70; scores same as for *b*; 12 tests: same as for *b*; separate answer sheets (Digitek, IBM 805, IBM 1230, NCS) must be used with Books 1 and 2; $10 per 250 NCS answer sheets; $12.60 per 100 sets of Digitek answer sheets; $23.26 per 500 sets of IBM 805 answer sheets; $94.50 per 500 sets of IBM 1230 answer sheets; 50¢ per NCS hand scoring stencil; $1.50 per Digitek hand scoring stencil; $57 per 100 sets of IBM 805 hand scoring stencils; $55 per 20 sets of IBM 1230 hand scoring stencils; NCS scoring service, 25¢ and over per student; Spanish edition available; 48(150) minutes.

1) *Book 1.* Forms A ('65, 24 pages, identical with test published in 1952), B ('53, 24 pages); 4 tests: name comparison, computation, three-dimensional space, vocabulary; $18.75 per 100 tests.

2) *Book 2.* Forms A ('52, 17 pages), B ('53, 17 pages); 3 tests: tool matching, arithmetic reasoning, form matching; $15 per 100 tests.

3) *Part 8 [Mark Making].* 1965; revised form (2 pages); $1 per 100 tests.

4) *Pegboard.* Same as *b*4 above.

5) *Finger Dexterity Board.* Same as *b*5 above.

REFERENCES

1–33. See 4:714.
34–209. See 5:609.
210–264. See 6:771.
265. ENNEIS, WILLIAM HOWARD, JR. *Prediction of Academic Achievement With the General Aptitude Test Battery in the College of Engineering at the University of Tennessee.* Master's thesis, University of Tennessee (Knoxville, Tenn.), 1952.
266. RAWLINGS, TRAVIS DEAN. *Mental Organization as a Function of Brightness.* Doctor's thesis, University of Kentucky (Lexington, Ky.), 1956. (*DA* 21:2778)
267. CURRIE, CAROLINE. *The Relationship of Certain Selected Factors to Achievement in Freshman Composition.* Doctor's thesis, Northwestern University (Evanston, Ill.), 1957. (*DA* 18:884)
268. SADNAVITCH, JOSEPH MATTHEW. *Assessment of Vocational Rehabilitation Potential of Mentally Sub-Normal Institutionalized Individuals.* Doctor's thesis, University of Nebraska (Lincoln, Neb.), 1958. (*DA* 19:1658)
269. ROSEN, MORTON HAROLD. *The Relationship Between Unevenness of Cognitive Functioning as Derived From Verbal-Spatial Discrepancy Scores and Measures of Personality Functioning.* Doctor's thesis, New York University (New York, N.Y.), 1960. (*DA* 20:4724)
270. STEFFEN, HANS HERMANN JULIUS. *Relationship Between Self-Estimates of Occupational Competence and Achievement of High School Students.* Doctor's thesis, University of Nebraska (Lincoln, Neb.), 1960. (*DA* 21:1860)
271. MULLEN, ROBERT A. *An Analysis of the Relationship of the Scores Made by Students on Aptitudes of the General Aptitude Test Battery and First Year Marks Made on Technical Subjects in Three North Carolina Industrial Education Centers.* Master's thesis, North Carolina State College (Raleigh, N.C.), 1963.
272. ROTMAN, CHARLES B. *A Study of the Effect of Practice Upon Motor Skills of the Mentally Retarded.* Doctor's thesis, Boston University (Boston, Mass.), 1963. (*DA* 25:1755)
273. WEINER, MURRAY. *The Organization of Mental Abilities From Ages 14 to 54.* Doctor's thesis, Columbia University (New York, N.Y.), 1963. (*DA* 25:4254)
274. BANAS, PAUL ANTHONY. *An Investigation of Trans-situational Moderators.* Doctor's thesis, University of Minnesota (Minneapolis, Minn.), 1964. (*DA* 26:1158)
275. BELL, FOREST O.; HOFF, ALVIN L.; AND HOYT, KENNETH B. "Answer Sheets *Do* Make a Difference." *Personnel Psychol* 17:65–71 sp '64. * (*PA* 39:1714)
276. CULHANE, MARGARET M. "The General Aptitude Test Battery: Its Availability and Use." *Voc Guid Q* 13:63–5 au '64. *
277. EISEN, IRVING, AND FEINGOLD, WINIFRED. "Using Multiple Cut-Off Criteria for Interpreting Aptitude Test Scores." *Voc Guid Q* 12:197–201 sp '64. * (*PA* 39:5978)
278. FLOYD, WILLIAM A. "Aptitude Testing With Mental Patients." *Voc Guid Q* 12:203–6 sp '64. *
279. HIRT, MICHAEL L. "Aptitude Changes as a Function of Age." *Personnel & Guid J* 43:174–7 O '64. * (*PA* 39:10870)
280. INGERSOLL, RALPH WALTER, JR. *The Predictive Abilities of the GATB in Grades Nine and Ten in Vocational and Academic Courses of Study in Selected Ohio High Schools.* Doctor's thesis, Ohio State University (Columbus, Ohio), 1964. (*DA* 25:4542)
281. KLUGMAN, S. F. "Comparisons Between Scores on the GATB and Related Tests of Intelligence and Aptitude in a
Neuropsychiatric Population." *Newsl Res Psychol* 6:23 N '64. *
282. LOUDERMILK, KENNETH MELVIN. *The Relationship Between Aptitude, Personality, Physical Fitness, and Personal Data, and Job Performance in a Combined Lumber and Paper Mill.* Doctor's thesis, University of Idaho (Moscow, Idaho), 1964. (*DA* 25:5405)
283. MEADOW, LLOYD. "Assessment of Students for Schools of Practical Nursing." *Nursing Res* 13:222–9 su '64. *
284. MUELLER, DANIEL EUGENE. *An Analysis of the Results of the Differential Aptitude Test and the General Aptitude Test Battery Administered at the Juvenile Diagnostic Center, Columbus, Ohio.* Master's thesis, Ohio State University (Columbus, Ohio), 1964.
285. PERRONE, PHILIP A. "Technicians: Somewhere in Between." *Voc Guid Q* 13:137–41 w '64–65. * (*PA* 39:8783)
286. WEINER, MURRAY. "Organization of Mental Abilities From Ages 14 to 54." *Ed & Psychol Meas* 24:573–87 f '64. * (*PA* 39:3205)
287. BIGGERS, ALMA F. *A Study of the GATB Performance of 52 High School Pupils With Implications for Counseling.* Master's thesis, North Carolina College (Durham, N.C.), 1965.
288. CARLSON, ROBERT E. *An Empirical Evaluation of Selected Hypotheses From a Theory of Work Adjustment.* Doctor's thesis, University of Minnesota (Minneapolis, Minn.), 1965. (*DA* 27:4548B)
289. COOLEY, WILLIAM W. "Further Relationships With the TALENT Battery." *Personnel & Guid J* 44:295–303 N '65. *
290. CULLUM, FELDER WILSON. *The Isolation of GATB Aptitude Patterns for Six Major Fields of Study.* Doctor's thesis, North Texas State University (Denton, Tex.), 1965. (*DA* 26:5223)
291. DROEGE, ROBERT C. "Validity Extension Data on the General Aptitude Test Battery." *Voc Guid Q* 14:56–8 au '65. * (*PA* 40:4760)
292. DVORAK, BEATRICE J.; DROEGE, ROBERT C.; AND SEILER, JOSEPH. "New Directions in U.S. Employment Service Aptitude Test Research." *Personnel & Guid J* 44:136–41 O '65. * (*PA* 40:3427)
293. KEBBON, LARS. *The Structure of Abilities at Lower Levels of Intelligence: A Factor-Analytical Study.* Stockholm, Sweden: Skandinaviska Testförlaget AB, 1965. Pp. 112. *
294. KUNTZ, ROBERT H., AND EDINGTON, EVERETT D. "Tests Can Predict Success of ARA Enrollees." *Ag Ed Mag* 37:197–8 F '65. *
295. SUMMERS, MILDRED D. *Academic Patterns Depicted by the General Aptitude Test Battery, Putnam County Schools, 1960–1963.* Master's thesis, Tennessee Technological University (Cookeville, Tenn.), 1965.
296. TATE, FOREST EARLY. *The Relationship Between the General Aptitude Test Battery and Achievement of Eleventh Grade Students in Selected Vocational and Technical Courses.* Doctor's thesis, University of Missouri (Columbia, Mo.), 1965. (*DA* 27:1162A)
297. TELLEGEN, AUKE. "The Performance of Chronic Seizure Patients on the General Aptitude Test Battery." *J Clin Psychol* 21:180–4 Ap '65. * (*PA* 39:12312)
298. WYSONG, H. EUGENE. "The Use of the General Aptitude Test Battery in Grades Nine and Ten." *Personnel & Guid J* 43:508–12 Ja '65. * (*PA* 39:10828)
299. AYERS, LONNIE DOUGLAS. *An Evaluation of the Iowa Tests of Educational Development and the General Aptitude Test Battery for Predicting Academic Success at Cedar City High School.* Master's thesis, University of Utah (Salt Lake City, Utah), 1966.
300. BANAS, PAUL A., AND NASH, ALLAN N. "Differential Predictability: Selection of Handicapped and Non-Handicapped." *Personnel & Guid J* 45:227–30 N '66. *
301. BRIGGS, PETER F., AND YATER, ALLAN C. "Counseling and Psychometric Signs as Determinants in the Vocational Success of Discharged Psychiatric Patients." *J Clin Psychol* 22:100–4 Ja '66. * (*PA* 40:4472)
302. DROEGE, ROBERT C. "Effects of Practice on Aptitude Scores." *J Appl Psychol* 50:306–10 Ag '66. * (*PA* 40:11518)
303. DROEGE, ROBERT C. "GATB Longitudinal Maturation Study." *Personnel & Guid J* 44:919–30 My '66. * (*PA* 40:10471)
304. GOLDEN, JAMES FRANKLIN. *Aspirations and Capabilities of Rural Youth in Selected Areas of Arkansas in Relation to Present and Projected Labor Market Requirements.* Doctor's thesis, University of Arkansas (Fayetteville, Ark.), 1966. (*DA* 27:1199A)
305. GRANT, G. V. "Levels of Reasoning in African Mineworkers." *Psygram* 9:43–56 S '66. *
306. GRIESS, JERALD ALFRED. *Selection of Trainees for a Twelve-Week Pre-Occupational Basic Education Program.* Doctor's thesis, Pennsylvania State University (University Park, Pa.), 1966. (*DA* 27:3704A)
307. INGERSOLL, RALPH W., AND PETERS, HERMAN J. "Predictive Indices of the GATB." *Personnel & Guid J* 44:931–7 My '66. * (*PA* 40:10474)
308. JEREMIAS, HERMINE IRMA. *An Examination of Discrepancy Indices Between Self-Descriptions and Vocational Preferences and Their Relationship to Selected Personality Characteristics.* Doctor's thesis, Temple University (Philadelphia, Pa.), 1966. (*DA* 27:956A)

General Aptitude Test Battery

309. JEX, FRANK B. *Predicting Academic Success Beyond High School.* Salt Lake City, Utah: University of Utah Bookstore, 1966. Pp. vi, 41. *

310. LEWIS, HARRY JACKSON. *The Relationship Between Aptitudes and Success in Vocational and Educational Pursuits.* Doctor's thesis, North Texas State University (Denton, Tex.), 1966. (*DA* 27:2890A)

311. LOUDERMILK, KENNETH M. "Prediction of Efficiency of Lumber and Paper Mill Employees." *Personnel Psychol* 19: 301–10 au '66. * (*PA* 41:865)

312. TRAXLER, HOWARD WESLEY. *Determining the Usefulness of the General Aptitude Test Battery in Predicting Student Success in a Technical Vocational High School.* Doctor's thesis, University of Denver (Denver, Colo.), 1966. (*DA* 27: 970A)

313. WEISS, DAVID J.; DAWIS, RENE V.; LOFQUIST, LLOYD H.; AND ENGLAND, GEORGE W. *Instrumentation for the Theory of Work Adjustment.* University of Minnesota, Industrial Relations Center Bulletin 44; Minnesota Studies in Vocational Rehabilitation 21. Minneapolis, Minn.: the Center, December 1966. Pp. viii, 85. *

314. WOOLINGTON, JAMES MURVIN. *An Exploration of the Vocational Potential of Institutionalized Mental Retardates.* Doctor's thesis, University of Southern Mississippi (Hattiesburg, Miss.), 1966. (*DA* 28:355B)

315. AKERMAN, RICHARD H. *The Prediction of Student Achievement in High School English and Social Science by the Use of the General Aptitude Test Battery.* Master's thesis, Drake University (Des Moines, Iowa), 1967.

316. DEABLER, HERDIS L., AND WILLIS, C. H. "Correlation Between Factor B of the 16 PF Test and the G Score of the GATB." *Newsl Res Psychol* 9:14–5 F '67. *

317. DENSLEY, KENNETH GORDON. *Determining Discrepancies That Might Exist Between Aptitude Self-Concept and Measured Aptitude.* Doctor's thesis, Utah State University (Logan, Utah), 1967. (*DA* 28:2981A)

318. DREILING, THOMAS L. *An Experimental Study Toward the Development of a Non-Reading Version of the General Aptitude Test Battery.* Doctor's thesis, University of Oklahoma (Norman, Okla.), 1967. (*DA* 28:2089A)

319. DROEGE, ROBERT C. "Effects of Aptitude-Score Adjustments by Age Curves on Prediction of Job Performance." *J Appl Psychol* 51:181–6 Ap '67. * (*PA* 41:7992)

320. DROEGE, ROBERT C. "Sex Differences in Aptitude Maturation During High School." *J Counsel Psychol* 14:407–11 S '67. * (*PA* 41:15817)

321. EISEN, IRVING, AND HASLER, KERMIT R. "Estimation of GATB Occupational Aptitude Patterns With the Measurement of Skill Series." *Fla J Ed Res* 9:11–20 Ja '67. *

322. HARFORD, THOMAS C.; WILLIS, CONSTANCE H.; AND DEABLER, HERDIS L. "Personality Correlates of Masculinity-Femininity." *Psychol Rep* 21:881–4 D '67. * (*PA* 42:7316)

323. HARFORD, THOMAS C.; WILLIS, CONSTANCE H.; AND DEABLER, HERDIS L. "Personality, Values, and Intellectual Correlates of Masculinity-Femininity." *Newsl Res Psychol* 9:17–8 Ag '67. *

324. HOWELL, MARGARET A.; VINCENT, JOHN W.; AND GAY, RICHARD A. "Testing Aptitude for Computer Programming." *Psychol Rep* 20:1251–6 Je '67. * (*PA* 41:15911)

325. KISH, GEORGE B., AND BUSSE, WILLIAM. "Intelligence, Aptitudes, and Sensation-Seeking." *Newsl Res Psychol* 9:11–3 N '67. *

326. LUCAS, DONALD HERBERT. *Personality Correlates of Agreement and Nonagreement Between Measures of Ability and Interest for Two Groups of Institutionalized Males.* Doctor's thesis, University of Kansas (Lawrence, Kan.), 1967. (*DA* 28:2986A)

327. LUNNEBORG, CLIFFORD E., AND LUNNEBORG, PATRICIA W. "Uniqueness of Selected Employment Aptitude Tests to a General Aptitude Guidance Battery." *Ed & Psychol Meas* 27:953–60 w '67. * (*PA* 42:9425)

328. PETERSON, MARVIN ANHILM. *Correlates of Size of Course Offerings in California's Public Junior Colleges.* Doctor's thesis, Stanford University (Stanford, Calif.), 1967. (*DA* 29:518A)

329. PUGH, RICHARD C. "Predicting Job Corpsmen's Performance on the Tests of General Education Development." *Sch & Soc* 95:268–9 Ap 15 '67. *

330. SHOWLER, WILLIAM K., AND DROEGE, ROBERT C. "Adjusting Aptitude Retest Scores for the Effects of Exposure to Initial Testing." Abstract. *Proc 75th Ann Conv Am Psychol Assn* 2:263–4 '67. * (*PA* 41:12839)

331. SOMMERFELD, DONALD, AND FATZINGER, FRANK A. "The Prediction of Trainee Success in a Manpower Development and Training Program." *Ed & Psychol Meas* 27:1155–61 w '67. * (*PA* 42:9550)

332. SULLIVAN, THOMAS WILLIAM. *Predicting Success in Vocational-Technical Programs in Community Colleges Using the General Aptitude Test Battery.* Doctor's thesis, Colorado State College (Greeley, Colo.), 1967. (*DA* 28:2502A)

333. TATE, JAMES R. "The Retiring Military Non-Commissioned Officer: A Challenge to Counselors." *Adult Lead* 16: 85–6+ S '67. *

334. BEMIS, STEPHEN E. "Occupational Validity of the General Aptitude Test Battery." *J Appl Psychol* 52:240–4 Je '68. * (*PA* 42:11398)

335. DROEGE, ROBERT C. "GATB Aptitude Intercorrelations of Ninth and Twelfth Graders—A Study in Organization of Mental Abilities." *Personnel & Guid J* 46:668–72 Mr '68. * (*PA* 42:16012)

336. DROEGE, ROBERT C. "GATB Longitudinal Validation Study." *J Counsel Psychol* 15:41–7 Ja '68. * (*PA* 42:6136)

337. DROEGE, ROBERT C. "Occupational Aptitudes of High School Dropouts." *Voc Guid Q* 16:185–7 Mr '68. *

338. DROEGE, ROBERT C. "Validity of USES Aptitude Test Batteries for Predicting MDTA Training Success." *Personnel & Guid J* 46:984–9 Je '68. * (*PA* 43:3166)

339. FINCH, CURTIS R. "Predicting Mathematics Achievement in Technical Training." *Voc Guid Q* 16:193–7 Mr '68. *

340. GAGNI, ARSENIO OREVILLO. *The Differential Prediction of Selected Measurements in Ornamental Horticulture.* Doctor's thesis, Cornell University (Ithaca, N.Y.), 1968. (*DA* 29: 4181A)

341. GOBLE, ROSS LAWRENCE. *Psychological Determinants of Consumer Credit Behavior.* Doctor's thesis, University of Utah (Salt Lake City, Utah), 1968. (*DA* 29:4139A)

342. HEGGEN, JAMES RICHARD. *A Study of Aptitudes and Achievement of Students Confined at the Utah State Industrial School for the Purpose of Determining Occupational Aptitude Patterns to Be Used as Guidelines for Formulating a Vocational Education Curriculum.* Doctor's thesis, Utah State University (Logan, Utah), 1968. (*DA* 29:2543A)

343. HOUNTRAS, PETER T., AND THIEL, PETER G. "The Effects of Prevocational MDTA Training on Selected Aptitudes as Measured by the GATB: A Pilot Study." *Col Ed Rec* 54: 47–51 D '68. *

344. HUDDY, JAMES ANTHONY, JR. *An Analysis of Occupational Aptitudes of Educable Mentally Retarded and Slow Learning Pupils in Relation to the General Aptitude Test Battery.* Doctor's thesis, Syracuse University (Syracuse, N.Y.), 1968. (*DA* 30:584A)

345. HUNTER, NORMAN W. *A Study of Factors Which May Affect a Student's Success in Quantitative Analysis.* Doctor's thesis, University of Toledo (Toledo, Ohio), 1968. (*DA* 29: 2437A)

346. KISH, GEORGE B., AND CHENEY, TRUMAN M. "Impaired Abilities in Chronic Alcoholism as Measured by the General Aptitude Test Battery." *Newsl Res Psychol* 10:16–9 Ag '68. *

347. LOFGREEN, JOHN C. *An Analysis of the Use of the Information Derived From the Finger and Manual Dexterity Aptitudes of the General Aptitude Test Battery With High School Students.* Master's thesis, Brigham Young University (Provo, Utah), 1968.

348. MATHIS, HAROLD I. "Relating Environmental Factors to Aptitude and Race." *J Counsel Psychol* 15:563–8 N '68. * (*PA* 43:727)

349. SHERR, RICHARD DANNER. *The Interrelationships of Measured and Estimated Interests and Aptitudes Among Non-Academic High School Students.* Doctor's thesis, Temple University (Philadelphia, Pa.), 1968. (*DAI* 30:1828A)

350. SPENCER, SAMUEL JUNIUS. *Personal Correlates of Success of High School Dropouts in a Manpower Development Training Act Program.* Doctor's thesis, Ohio University (Athens, Ohio), 1968. (*DA* 29:2971A)

351. SPERGEL, PHILIP. *The Relationship Between Vocational Interest, Aptitude and Personality Integration With Disadvantaged Youth.* Doctor's thesis, Temple University (Philadelphia, Pa.), 1968. (*DA* 29:1760A)

352. WALLNER, CAROL A. *The General Aptitude Test Battery and Disadvantaged Youth.* Master's thesis, California State College (Hayward, Calif.), 1968.

353. BIDWELL, GLORIA P. "Ego Strength, Self-Knowledge, and Vocational Planning of Schizophrenics." *J Counsel Psychol* 16(1):45–9 Ja '69. * (*PA* 43:5726)

354. BOOKOUT, DWAYNE V. T., AND HOSFORD, RAY E. "Administration Effects of the S-329 of the GATB Using Three Experimental Treatments." *J Employ Counsel* 6(3):124–33 S '69. *

355. BOTTERBUSCH, KARL F.; DROEGE, ROBERT C.; HAWK, JOHN A.; AND BEMIS, STEPHEN E. "Development of a Nonreading Edition of the General Aptitude Test Battery." Abstract. *Proc 77th Ann Conv Am Psychol Assn* 4(1):159–60 '69. * (*PA* 43:16632)

356. BRENNA, DAVID W. "Use of the GATB in Predicting Success on the Tests of General Educational Development." *J Employ Counsel* 6(4):181–5 D '69. *

357. CARLSON, ROBERT E.; DAWIS, RENE V.; AND WEISS, DAVID J. "The Effect of Satisfaction on the Relationship Between Abilities and Satisfactoriness." *Occup Psychol* 43(1): 39–46 '69. * (*PA* 44:17573)

358. COOK, GRANT L. *Prediction of Scholastic Achievement in an Electronics Technician Training Program With the General Aptitude Test Battery.* Master's thesis, Brigham Young University (Provo, Utah), 1969.

359. DUTT, KARL FREDERICK. *The Comparative Effects of General and Specific Aptitude Test Interpretative Materials on the Vocational Choice-Related Decisions, Attitudes, and Preparedness of Ninth-Grade Boys.* Doctor's thesis, Lehigh University (Bethlehem, Pa.), 1969. (*DAI* 30:5231A)

360. FLANAGAN, JOHN, AND LEWIS, GEORGE. "Comparison of Negro and White Lower Class Men on the General Aptitude

Test Battery and the Minnesota Multiphasic Personality Inventory." *J Social Psychol* 78(2):289–91 Ag '69. * (*PA* 44:6578)

361. HARMON, JAMES STEPHEN. *Effects of a Multi-Media Environment in College Level Electronics.* Doctor's thesis, Colorado State College (Greeley, Colo.), 1969. (*DAI* 30:2250A)

362. HOLLENDER, JOHN W., AND BROMAN, HARVEY J. "Intellectual Assessment in a Disadvantaged Population." *Meas & Eval Guid* 2(1):19–24 sp '69. *

363. IMPELLITTERI, JOSEPH T., AND KAPES, JEROME T. "Using the GATB With Vocational or Technical Bound Ninth Grade Boys." *Voc Guid Q* 18(1):59–64 S '69. *

364. JONES, RICHARD DENNIS. *A Study on the Relationship Among Ego-Strength, Persistence, and Degree of Success in Rehabilitation Activity.* Doctor's thesis, University of California (Los Angeles, Calif.), 1969. (*DAI* 30:1868A)

365. KAUPPI, DWIGHT R., AND WEISS, DAVID J. "Efficiency of Commonly Used Measures in Predicting Inventory Validity." Abstract. *Proc 77th Ann Conv Am Psychol Assn* 4(2):691–2 '69. * (*PA* 44:675)

366. KISH, GEORGE B. "GATB and Shipley Profiles of 71 Male Alcoholics." *Newsl Res Psychol* 11(4):16–7 N '69. *

367. KISH, GEORGE B. "Obscure Figures Test (OFT): 2, Relationships With Intelligence and Aptitudes." *Newsl Res Psychol* 11(2):15–6 My '69. *

368. KISH, GEORGE B. "Relationships Between the Shipley and the GATB in a Group of Male Alcoholics." *Newsl Res Psychol* 11(4):18–9 N '69. *

369. KISH, GEORGE B., AND CHENEY, TRUMAN M. "Impaired Abilities in Alcoholism: Measured by the General Aptitude Test Battery." *Q J Studies Alcohol* 30(2A):384–8 Je '69. * (*PA* 44:884)

370. KLEIN, FREDA. *Use of the General Aptitude Test Battery "G" Score for Predicting Achievement on the General Educational Development Test.* Master's thesis, University of Nevada (Las Vegas, Nev.), 1969.

371. KOOKER, EARL W., AND BELLAMY, ROY Q. "Some Psychometric Differences Between Graduates and Dropouts." *Psychol* 6(2):65–70 My '69. * (*PA* 43:14868)

372. McDONALD, KAROLD L. *Value of the General Aptitude Test Battery in Predicting Success in Manpower Development and Training Act Courses.* Master's thesis, Iowa State University (Ames, Iowa), 1969.

373. MEHRENS, WILLIAM A., AND LEHMANN, IRVIN J. *Standardized Tests in Education*, pp. 107–15. New York: Holt, Rinehart & Winston, Inc., 1969. Pp. xi, 323. *

374. NESBITT, JULIAN D. *Environmental Influences on Psycho-Motor Factors on General Aptitude Test Battery.* Master's thesis, East Texas State University (Commerce, Tex.), 1969.

375. NITARDY, JUDITH R.; PETERSON, COURTNEY D.; AND WEISS, DAVID J. "Differential Influence of Test Format Variables on Ability Test Performance." Abstract. *Proc 77th Ann Conv Am Psychol Assn* 4(1):139–40 '69. * (*PA* 43:16629)

376. SANDMANN, CHARLES WILLIAM. *An Evaluation of the General Aptitude Test Battery in Predicting Success in Area Vocational-Technical Centers.* Doctor's thesis, University of Oklahoma (Norman, Okla.), 1969. (*DAI* 30:1792A)

377. SHOWLER, WILLIAM K., AND DROEGE, ROBERT C. "Stability of Aptitude Scores for Adults." *Ed & Psychol Meas* 29(3):681–6 au '69. * (*PA* 44:18734)

378. STONE, THOMAS CARL. *A Case Study: Predictors of Success in Post-High School Vocational Trade, Industrial, and Technical Programs.* Doctor's thesis, Colorado State University (Ft. Collins, Colo.), 1969. (*DAI* 30:4348A)

379. STROWIG, R. WRAY, AND ALEXAKOS, C. E. "Overlap Between Achievement and Aptitude Scores." *Meas & Eval Guid* 2(3):157–67 f '69. * (*PA* 44:11609)

380. WOODS, NORMAN JAMES. *A Comparative Study of the Manual Dexterity of Selected Undergraduates and Freshmen Dental Students.* Doctor's thesis, University of Oregon (Eugene, Ore.), 1969. (*DAI* 31:1045A)

381. AUCKER, JOHN ROBERT. *The Prediction of Success in Vocational Education From Student Characteristics.* Doctor's thesis, University of Northern Colorado (Greeley, Colo.), 1970. (*DAI* 31:3864A)

382. BELLUCCI, JOSEPH T. *The Contribution of Values in Predicting Success in Practical Nursing Training Programs.* Doctor's thesis, Lehigh University (Bethlehem, Pa.), 1970. (*DAI* 31:2731A)

383. CARBUHN, WAYNE M. "Predicting General Education Development (GED) Test Performance of Urban Job Corpsmen." *Ed & Psychol Meas* 30(4):993–8 w '70. *

384. COBB, KENNETH C. *The General Aptitude Test Battery Used in the Prediction of Probable Success of Automotive Trade Students in the Flint Hills Area Vocational-Technical School Emporia, Kansas.* Doctor's thesis, Kansas State Teachers College (Emporia, Kan.), 1970.

385. CRONBACH, LEE J. *Essentials of Psychological Testing*, Third Edition, pp. 353–75. New York: Harper & Row, Publishers, Inc., 1970. Pp. xxxix, 752. *

386. DESMOND, RICHARD E., AND WEISS, DAVID J. "Measurement of Ability Requirements of Occupations." Abstract. *Proc 78th Ann Conv Am Psychol Assn* 5(1):149–50 '70. * (*PA* 44:19624)

387. DROEGE, ROBERT C., AND HAWK, JOHN. "A Factorial

Investigation of Nonreading Aptitude Tests." Abstract. *Proc 78th Ann Conv Am Psychol Assn* 5(1):113–4 '70. * (*PA* 44:17768)

388. DROEGE, ROBERT C.; SHOWLER, WILLIAM; BEMIS, STEPHEN; AND HAWK, JOHN. "Development of a Nonreading Edition of the General Aptitude Test Battery." *Meas & Eval Guid* 3(1):45–53 sp '70. * (*PA* 45:1505)

389. FLEMING, SHARON V. *Predictive Validity of the General Aptitude Test Battery for Manpower Development Training Outcome When Used With Disadvantaged Youth.* Master's thesis, Sacramento State College (Sacramento, Calif.), 1970.

390. FOZARD, JAMES L., AND NUTTALL, RONALD L. "Age and Socioeconomic Status Influences on Performance on Ability Tests." Abstract. *Proc 78th Ann Conv Am Psychol Assn* 5(2):687–8 '70. * (*PA* 44:18409)

391. HAWK, JOHN A. "Linearity of Criterion—GATB Aptitude Relationships." *Meas & Eval Guid* 2(4):249–51 w '70. *

392. KISH, GEORGE B. "Alcoholics' GATB and Shipley Profiles and Their Interrelationships." *J Clin Psychol* 26(4):482–4 O '70. * (*PA* 45:4569)

393. KISH, GEORGE B. "Cognitive Innovation and Stimulus-Seeking: A Study of the Correlates of the Obscure Figures Test." *Percept & Motor Skills* 30(1):95–101 F '70. *

394. KISH, GEORGE B. "Oral Passivity, Interests, and Aptitudes." *Newsl Res Psychol* 12(1):22–3 F '70. *

395. KLEIN, FREDA, AND TRIONE, VERDUN. "Use of the GATB 'G' Score for Predicting Achievement on the GED." *J Employ Counsel* 7(3):93–7 Ag '70. *

396. NINEMEIER, JACK D.; McKINLEY, MARJORIE M.; AND MONTAG, GERALDINE M. "Aptitudes in Selection and Training of Food Service Personnel." *J Am Dietetic Assn* 57(4):341–4 O '70. *

397. NUTTALL, RONALD L., AND FOZARD, JAMES L. "Age, Socioeconomic Status and Human Abilities." *Aging & Hum Develop* 1(2):161–9 My '70. *

398. ROSS, JANE E. "Simplification of Human Abilities With Age in Four Social Class Groups." Abstract. *Proc 78th Ann Conv Am Psychol Assn* 5(2):685–6 '70. * (*PA* 44:18417)

399. SAKALOSKY, JOSEPH C. *A Study of the Relationship Between the Differential Aptitude Test Battery and the General Aptitude Test Battery Scores of Ninth Graders.* Master's thesis, Millersville State College (Millersville, Pa.), 1970.

400. SHIPMAN, VESTAL C. *An Analysis of the Relationship Between Instructor's Ratings for Students Enrolled in High School Automobile Mechanics and Scores on the General Aptitude Test Battery.* Master's thesis, University of Alabama (University, Ala.), 1970.

401. SHORE, THOMAS CLINARD, JR. *A Study of Relationships Between the General Aptitude Test Battery Scores and Achievement in Selected Industrial Cooperative Training Programs in North Carolina.* Doctor's thesis, University of Maryland (College Park, Md.), 1970. (*DAI* 31:2720A)

402. WARMAN, ROY E., AND MYERS, RICHARD W. "A Comparison of GATB Results Between Hospitalized Neuropsychiatric Patient and Uses Clients." *Newsl Res Psychol* 12(1):23–5 F '70. *

DAVID J. WEISS, *Associate Professor of Psychology, University of Minnesota, Minneapolis, Minnesota.*

According to its authors, the GATB is the "best validated multiple aptitude test battery in existence for use in vocational guidance." On a relative basis this may well be true, but the GATB leaves much to be desired if it is to be adequately used for vocational guidance.

The often-criticized multiple cutoff method for determining whether an individual "passes" or "fails" the minimum qualifying scores (Occupational Aptitude Patterns, or OAP's) for a job or group of jobs severely limits its use in guidance. The OAP approach, as operationalized by the United States Training and Employment Service (USTES), fails to give any indication of the relative probabilities of success if the individual qualifies for more than one OAP. At a minimum, USTES should provide the counselor with tables of "hit rates" for predictions of "success" and "non-success" for each validity coefficient it reports. But USTES has failed to provide empirical evidence to show the superiority of the multiple cutoff approach over alternative prediction models. USTES continues to argue that its approach is superior because it can be easily applied. With the current availability of computers, problems of applying alternative methods of prediction have disappeared; a simple computer program can be written to compute predicted scores for an individual on the OAP's, determine whether he "qualifies" (if USTES insists on adhering rigidly to this inappropriate dichotomous criterion), and interpret the results to the user in his natural language. If the GATB is to be used in guidance, scoring and interpretation by computer should be mandatory; there is simply too much data for the counselor to integrate meaningfully.

The argument of the "noncompensatory" character of the multiple cutoff method also has not been subject to empirical test by USTES. It has yet to document statistically the "common observation that if an aptitude is truly important to a job, a lack of that aptitude places a limit on the worker's achievement." Some of the data in the manual seem to suggest that this, too, is a pseudo-argument in the case of the GATB. The use of a compensary prediction technique is inappropriate only if the predictor variables are independent of (uncorrelated with) each other. To the extent that the predictors are correlated, they have common underlying factors which might permit a lack of one ability to be substituted for by a higher score on another. If USTES continues to apply the noncompensatory model, it should at least strive to develop truly uni-factor tests that represent uniquely uncorrelated factors; then the multiple cutoff model might be appropriate, but its appropriateness should still rest on empirical evidence.

USTES also defends multiple cutoffs on the basis of: (a) stability of results from sample to sample; (b) the problem of non-linearity; and (c) the inclusion of rational as well as empirical evidence in the development of OAP's. The stability of multiple cutoff predictions has not been systematically compared to that of other prediction techniques; USTES has the data in its files—it should permit others to see how it makes its selection of techniques.

Nonlinearity is a pseudo-problem; USTES makes dichotomous predictions, and non-linearity of predictor-criterion relationships cannot exist against a dichotomous criterion. By its own methods of OAP development, USTES further denies the existence of nonlinearity. The requirement that an ability have a high mean (relative to other means in the occupational profile) and a low standard deviation, as a partial criterion for that ability's inclusion in the OAP, is a denial of the likelihood that nonlinearity may occur—or an acceptance of the linear model. Suppose that the bivariate relationship between a continuous aptitude score and the continuous criterion resulted in a perfect inverted-U relationship with a high correlation ratio and zero correlation coefficient. The mean aptitude score for this significant aptitude would not likely be relatively high; the standard deviation would not likely be low. Curvilinear regression, or other prediction methods, would identify that ability as a significant one; the linear model which USTES uses (but says it does not use) would yield no predictability.

Other prediction techniques, in addition to multiple cutoff methods, can include "rational as well as empirical evidence on the importance of an aptitude." There is no reason why a given ability cannot be eliminated from a regression or other kind of prediction equation on the basis of information from a job analysis. However, USTES has not demonstrated that the inclusion of such "rational" information in the development of OAP's improves the predictability of job success; perhaps validity coefficients are lowered by this approach.

If the GATB is a tool for vocational guidance, USTES should take a close look at the range and nature of the "aptitudes" that it measures. According to the manual, the GATB "was designed to provide a separate measure for each of the....aptitude factors that had been definitely established." The data presented in the manual, however, do not permit others to determine what factors were "definitely established." The manual does not include one complete factor matrix; only high loadings on factors are summarized; yet a factor is best established and interpreted in the total context of the factor loading matrix.

More important, though, while the manual professes "separate factors," the methodology does not meet the objectives. Factor G is deliberately composed of a linear combination of scores from three other "factors," which in turn are not very independently measured. A careful reading of the manual gives the feeling that the developers of the GATB were not really sure why G is there, measured the way it is. Sometimes G is called "general intelligence"; later on it is referred to as "general learning ability." It is described as being "related to doing well in school." Yet this conflicts with an interpretation of "general" ability for an aptitude battery that is designed for vocational placement or counseling; success in school by no means implies success in occupations. The data on G show that it does nothing more for prediction than a statistical combination of V, N, and S does; it could not be expected to do more. Previous reviews have pointed out some of these problems with G; USTES, however, has failed to provide any data that indicate any *differential* utility for the G "factor."

GATB tests "are designed to measure capacities to learn various jobs." This kind of thinking has pervaded the ability measurement field for generations. Based on the lack of evidence to support the "capacity to learn" assumption, ability test constructors should accept the fact of what their tests really measure. USTES has presented no direct evidence to indicate that individuals with high scores on a given test can *learn* to do any job better than individuals with low scores. In the absence of evidence to the contrary, the GATB subtests must be interpreted as measures of *current status* and not ability to learn. The data from the GATB longitudinal follow-up study support this interpretation. GATB scores of individuals change with time; exposure to environmental experiences results in changes in *current status* on abilities measured. Interpretation of GATB scores as "capacity to learn" would imply that simply as a result of maturation or experience, in a year or two an individual's "capacity to learn" changes, sometimes substantially. Such an interpretation is inappropriate. GATB validity data indicate that individuals high on an ability today are also likely to be rated high in ability to perform related tasks tomorrow (or even the same day). Nothing need be assumed about "capacity to learn" until some data show that interpretation to be a legitimate one.

It has been said before, but it bears continual repetition, that the GATB tests are too highly speeded. The data presented in the manual on the decline of "aptitude" scores with age show that the most highly speeded tests decline in average scores most quickly (in cross-sectional groups) as a function of age. But all aptitudes, except V, show a general decline with age. Yet it is unreasonable to assume that older people have less "ability to learn" many of the functions measured in the GATB. Rather, it is a more reasonable assumption that speed of response declines with age, maybe a function of physiological decline, but also possibly a function of test-taking skill and motivation as well as other factors. Yet the speeded tests continue to penalize the older individual. Time limits for ability tests are purely an administrative convenience (except, of course, when only speed of response is being measured); however, when an administrative convenience serves to complicate the measurement of a variable for some individuals, it is time to reexamine its desirability.

At the time the GATB was developed, many of the jobs available were in the blue-collar category. The GATB norms, which are badly in need of revision, also reflect the "blue-collar" impetus for its development. However, the labor market has changed importantly in the quarter century since the GATB was developed. The kinds of abilities identified in factor analyses over 20 years ago do not represent all important vocational abilities for jobs today, nor are they likely to represent abilities important in jobs that will be available in the future. Most jobs now are in white-collar, service, and professional areas. But the GATB has not changed with the times. The end result is that the GATB, as it currently stands, will be of decreasing utility for vocational planning for a large portion of the labor force. USTES should immediately embark on a program to greatly expand the number and kinds of abilities measured by the GATB if the test battery is to have more than minor utility in the next decade. Rather than measuring "verbal ability" it should measure many kinds or components of verbal ability; the same holds true for the other cognitive and perceptual abilities.

USTES has a communications problem with individuals using the GATB on contract. There appears to be no systematic distribution list to inform GATB users of new developments and new ways of using the battery. For example, within the last year or two, comparison of GATB scores with OAP's began to take into account the standard error of measurement. However, this practice was not systematically communicated to GATB users, since this reviewer, who has been using the GATB for over 10 years, discovered it only in the process of preparing this review. If USTES is concerned with proper use of the GATB, it should improve its communications with users outside of the state employment services.

SUMMARY. The GATB is certainly the best researched of the multiple aptitude batteries. Because of its large amount of validity data, it should be useful to vocational counselors; but it suffers from a stagnation which limits its usefulness in many situations. Rather than continue the same old kinds of research and methods it has pursued for the past 25 years, USTES should carefully reexamine its data and methods and proceed in some of the new directions outlined above so that the GATB will continue to be useful to the vocational counselor.

For reviews by Harold P. Bechtoldt and John B. Carroll of earlier forms, see 6:771; for reviews by Andrew L. Comrey, Clifford P. Froehlich, and Lloyd G. Humphreys, see 5:609; for reviews by Milton L. Blum, Edward B. Greene, and Howard R. Taylor, see 4:714.

[677]

*Measurement of Skill: A Battery of Placement Tests for Business, Industrial and Educational Use. Adults; 1956-67; MOS; 8 tests (3 pages except for *e, g*); manual ('64, 76 looseleaf pages plus tests and reprints of *1, 2, 5*, and 6 below); revised profile card ('67, 1 page); $4.50 per 25 tests; $25 per set of scoring stencils for all tests; $9.25 per 100 profiles; $15 per manual (including any supplements issued during year following purchase); $1.25 per specimen set of tests only; $62.50 per kit of 25 copies of each test, set of stencils, and manual; postpaid; Italian and Portuguese editions available; 5(10) minutes per test (except for *g*); Walter V. Clarke Associates, Inc.; AVA Publications, Inc. *
a) SKILL WITH VOCABULARY. Form MOS-1 ('59).
b) SKILL WITH NUMBERS. Form MOS-2 ('59).
c) SKILL WITH SHAPE. Form MOS-3 ('59).
d) SPEED AND ACCURACY. Form MOS-4 ('59).
e) SKILL IN ORIENTATION. Form MOS-5 ('66, 4 pages).
f) SKILL IN THINKING. Form MOS-6 ('58).
g) SKILL WITH MEMORY. Form MOS-7 revised ('66, 4 pages, identical with test copyrighted in 1960 except for format); 7(12) minutes.
h) SKILL WITH FINGERS. Form MOS-8 ('59).

REFERENCES

1-2. See 6:775.
3. MERENDA, PETER F.; CLARKE, WALTER V.; AND JACOBSEN, GWENDOLYN. "Relative Predictive Validities of MOS and DAT Batteries for Junior High School Students." *Psychol Rep* 16: 151-5 F '65. * (*PA* 39:8688)
4. BAILEY, WANITA MAE BURRIS. *Some Factors Related to Success in Industrial Apprenticeship.* Doctor's thesis, Indiana University (Bloomington, Ind.), 1966. (*DA* 27:1644A)
5. MERENDA, PETER F.; JACOBSEN, GWENDOLYN; AND CLARKE, WALTER V. "Cross-Validities of the MOS and DAT Batteries." *Psychol Rep* 19:341-2 O '66. * (*PA* 41:789)
6. MERENDA, PETER F.; JACOBSEN, GWENDOLYN; AND CLARKE, WALTER V. "Further Cross-Validities of the MOS and DAT Batteries." *Psychol Rep* 24(2):541-2 Ap '69. * (*PA* 43:15013)

For reviews by Dorothy C. Adkins, Lloyd G. Humphreys, and Joseph E. Moore, see 6:775.

[678]

★National Institute for Personnel Research Intermediate Battery. Standards 7-10 and job applicants with 9-12 years of education; 1964-69; 7 tests in a single booklet: mental alertness, arithmetical problems, computation, spot-the-error (speed, accuracy), reading comprehension, vocabulary, spelling; spot-the-error subtest available as separate (see 1005); Forms A, B, ('64, 51 pages); manual ('69, 93 pages); no data on reliability for spot-the-error speed test; no data on validity; separate answer sheets must be used; R83.10 per 25 tests; R3.50 per single copy; 75c per 25 answer sheets; 50c per set of scoring stencils; R5 per manual; postpaid within South Africa; Afrikaans edition available; 165(210) minutes; Anne-Marie Wilcocks (manual); National Institute for Personnel Research. *

[679]

★Nonreading Aptitude Test Battery, 1969 Edition. Disadvantaged grades 9-12 and adults; 1965-70; NATB; nonreading adaptation of the *General Aptitude Test Battery;* 9 scores: intelligence, verbal, numerical, spatial, form perception, clerical perception, motor coordination, finger dexterity, manual dexterity; 1 form (NCS test-answer booklet for *a-h*); 14 tests: 10 paper and pencil tests plus 4 performance tests; manual in 2 sections: section 1—administration, scoring, and interpretation ('70, 108 pages), section 2—development ('70, 27 pages); GATB norms manuals (sections 2 and 4) must also be obtained; record blank ('70, 1 page) for apparatus tests; profile-record card ('70, 2 pages); for screening exercise materials, see 676a1; tentative use of GATB norms suggested; $1.85 per set of 8 tests (*a-h*); $1.50 per 100 record blanks; $3.75 per 100 profile-record cards; $4 per set of NCS hand scoring stencils; manual: $1 per copy of section 1, 35¢ per copy of section 2 (available for unrestricted sale); postpaid; specimen set not available; NCS scoring service (Books 1-8), $1.95 per examinee; (190) minutes; United States Training and Employment Service; orders for test materials must be cleared through a State Employment Service office; manuals, accessories, and GATB Part 8 distributed by United States Government Printing Office; Books 1-8 and scoring keys distributed by National Computer Systems, Inc. *
a) BOOK 1, PICTURE WORD MATCHING. Form A ('69, 11 pages); 2 tests: picture word matching, oral vocabulary; $10.40 per 100 tests.
b) BOOK 2, COIN MATCHING. Form A ('69, 14 pages); $13.40 per 100 tests.
c) BOOK 3, MATRICES. Form A ('69, 11 pages); $10.40 per 100 tests.
d) BOOK 4, TOOL MATCHING. Form A ('69, 11 pages); $10.40 per 100 tests.
e) BOOK 5, THREE-DIMENSIONAL SPACE. Form A ('69, 11 pages); $10.40 per 100 tests; 20¢ per set of cut outs.
f) BOOK 6, FORM MATCHING. Form A ('69, 9 pages); $10.40 per 100 tests.
g) BOOK 7, COIN SERIES. Form A ('69, 27 pages); $23.70 per 100 tests.
h) BOOK 8, NAME COMPARISON. Form A ('69, 4 pages); $3.65 per 100 tests.
i) GATB PART 8 [MARK MAKING]. 1 form ('65, 2 pages); $1 per 100 tests.
j) PEGBOARD. 2 tests: place, turn; set of wooden testing materials: $18.25 (K & W Products Co., Inc.), $18.50 (Warwick Products Co.); $16.25 per set of

plastic testing materials (Specialty Case Manufacturing Co.).

k) FINGER DEXTERITY BOARD. 2 tests: assemble, disassemble; set of testing materials: $7.50 (Specialty Case Manufacturing Co.), $8.65 (Warwick Products Co.), $12.25 (K & W Products Co., Inc.).

REFERENCES

1. DVORAK, BEATRICE J.; DROEGE, ROBERT C.; AND SEILER, JOSEPH. "New Directions in U.S. Employment Service Aptitude Test Research." *Personnel & Guid J* 44:136–41 O '65. * (*PA* 40:3427)
2. DROEGE, ROBERT C., AND HAWK, JOHN. "A Factorial Investigation of Nonreading Aptitude Tests." Abstract. *Proc 78th Ann Conv Am Psychol Assn* 5(1):113–4 '70. * (*PA* 44:17768)
3. DROEGE, ROBERT C.; SHOWLER, WILLIAM; BEMIS, STEPHEN; AND HAWK, JOHN. "Development of a Nonreading Edition of the General Aptitude Test Battery." *Meas & Eval Guid* 3(1):45–53 sp '70. * (*PA* 45:1505)

[680]

*SRA Primary Mental Abilities, 1962 Edition.
Grades kgn–1, 2–4, 4–6, 6–9, 9–12, adults; 1946–69; PMA; earlier editions titled *Tests of Primary Mental Abilities* and *Chicago Tests of Primary Mental Abilities;* separate answer sheets (DocuTran, IBM 805, IBM 1230) must be used in grades 4 and over; 6 levels; technical report ('65, 30 pages); $1 per technical report; $1 per specimen set of any one level; postage extra; L. L. Thurstone (earlier editions) and Thelma Gwinn Thurstone; Science Research Associates, Inc. *

a) GRADES K–1. 1946–65; 5 scores: verbal meaning, perceptual speed, number facility, spatial relations, total; 1 form ('62, 24 pages); manual ('63, 31 pages); $4.15 per 20 tests; (65–75) minutes in 2 sessions.

b) GRADES 2–4. 1946–65; 5 scores: same as for grades kgn–1; 1 form ('62, 32 pages); manual ('63, 43 pages); prices and time same as for grades kgn–1.

c) GRADES 4–6. 1946–69; 6 scores: same as for grades kgn–1 plus reasoning; 1 form ('62, 42 pages); IBM 805 manual ('63, 46 pages); DocuTran manual ('65, 55 pages); IBM 1230 directions ('69, 5 pages); profile ('63, 2 pages); 52(107) minutes.

1) *SRA Scored.*
  (*a*) Complete Rental Plan. Rental and DocuTran scoring service, 50¢ and over per student.
  (*b*) Scoring Only Plan. $11.55 per 20 tests; DocuTran answer sheet and scoring service, 38¢ and over per test.

2) *School Scored.* $11.55 per 20 tests; $6.60 per 100 IBM 805 answer sheets; $7.70 per 100 IBM 1230 answer sheets; $12.50 per 250 NCS answer sheets; 75¢ per 20 profiles; $1 per set of IBM scoring stencils; 50¢ per DocuTran manual; 50¢ per IBM 1230 directions.

d) GRADES 6–9. 1946–69; 5 scores: verbal meaning, number facility, reasoning, spatial relations, total; 1 form ('62, 24 pages); IBM 805 manual ('63, 40 pages); DocuTran manual ('65, 48 pages); IBM 1230 directions ('69, 5 pages); profile ('63, 2 pages); 35(75) minutes.

1) *SRA Scored.* Prices same as for grades 4–6.
  (*a*) Complete Rental Plan.
  (*b*) Scoring Only Plan.

2) *School Scored.* Prices same as for grades 4–6 except: $1.50 per set of IBM scoring stencils.

e) GRADES 9–12. 1946–69; 5 scores: same as for grades 6–9; 1 form ('62, 24 pages); IBM 805 manual ('63, 40 pages); DocuTran manual ('65, 48 pages); IBM 1230 directions ('69, 5 pages); profile ('63, 2 pages); prices same as for grades 6–9; 34(74) minutes.

f) ADULT. 1946–69; 5 scores: same as for grades 6–9; 1 form ('65, identical with test for grades 9–12 except for title); IBM 805 manual ('63, 40 pages); no norms for adults; $11.55 per 20 tests; $1.30 per 20

IBM 805 answer sheets; $1.50 per set of scoring stencils; 34(74) minutes.

REFERENCES

1–10. See 2:1427.
11–60. See 3:225.
61–102. See 4:716.
103–161. See 5:614.
162–211. See 6:780.
212. KOLSTOE, OLIVER PAUL. *A Comparison of Mental Abilities of Bright and Dull Children Having the Same Mental Ages.* Doctor's thesis, State University of Iowa (Iowa City, Iowa), 1952. (*DA* 12:707)
213. BINDER, ARNOLD. *An Investigation of Differential Decrement in the Intell.gence of Schizophrenics.* Doctor's thesis, Stanford University (Stanford, Calif.), 1953. (*DA* 14:392)
214. DREVDAHL, JOHN E. *An Exploratory Study of Creativity in Terms of Its Relationships to Various Personality and Intellectual Factors.* Doctor's thesis, University of Nebraska (Lincoln, Neb.), 1954. (*DA* 14:1256)
215. POUNCEY, ANTHONY TRUMAN. *Psychological Correlates of Journalism Training Completion.* Doctor's thesis, University of Minnesota (Minneapolis, Minn.), 1954. (*DA* 14:1180)
216. SUTHERLAND, THOMAS ESTILL. *The Effect of School Departmentalization on the Organization of Certain Mental Abilities.* Doctor's thesis, University of Kentucky (Lexington, Ky.), 1954. (*DA* 20:4167)
217. VANDENBERG, STEVEN GERRITJAN. *A Comparative Study of the Stability of a Factor Structure.* Doctor's thesis, University of Michigan (Ann Arbor, Mich.), 1955. (*DA* 15:1649)
218. RAWLINGS, TRAVIS DEAN. *Mental Organization as a Function of Brightness.* Doctor's thesis, University of Kentucky (Lexington, Ky.), 1956. (*DA* 21:2778)
219. STONESIFER, FRED A. *Intellectual and Perceptual Performance of Defective Idiopathic Epileptics and Familial Mental Defectives.* Doctor's thesis, Pennsylvania State University (University Park, Pa.), 1956. (*DA* 17:400)
220. KAPLAN, HENRY KAY. *A Study of Relationships Between Handwriting Legibility and Perception Adjustment and Personality Factors.* Doctor's thesis, University of Wisconsin (Madison, Wis.), 1957. (*DA* 17:1950)
221. MANGAN, GORDON L., AND CLARK, JAMES W. "Rigidity Factors in the Testing of Middle-Aged Subjects." *J Gerontol* 13:422–5 O '58. * (*PA* 33:10073)
222. NOVACK, HARRY SAMUEL. *A Longitudinal Study of Mental Traits in Elementary School Children.* Doctor's thesis, Syracuse University (Syracuse, N.Y.), 1958. (*DA* 19:1954)
223. WILSON, RICHARD CARLTON. *The Relationship of Primary Mental Abilities to Reading and Spelling Achievement of Phonetically Deficient Fourth Grade Students With Normal or High Intelligence.* Doctor's thesis, University of North Carolina (Raleigh, N.C.), 1958. (*DA* 19:2298)
224. BECK, ISABEL HOLDERMAN HANDLEY. *A Study of Criteria of Social Perception and Some Related Variables.* Doctor's thesis, University of Southern California (Los Angeles, Calif.), 1959. (*DA* 20:2372)
225. SMITH, GARY RICHARD. *An Examination of Selected Measures of Achievement and Aptitude for Use in Normative Grade Placement of Science Concepts on Light.* Doctor's thesis, Northwestern University (Evanston, Ill.), 1960. (*DA* 21:2952)
226. AURIA, CARL. *Differences in Specific Intellectual Functioning Among Children of the Same General Intellectual Ability but of Different Chronological Ages.* Doctor's thesis, University of Buffalo (Buffalo, N.Y.), 1961. (*DA* 22:2679)
227. TOUSSAINT, ISABELLA HASTIE. *Interrelationships of Reading, Listening, Arithmetic, and Intelligence and Their Implications.* Doctor's thesis, University of Pittsburgh (Pittsburgh, Pa.), 1961. (*DA* 22:819)
228. WILSON, RICHARD C. "The Relationship Between Reading Comprehension and Intellectual Factors for Phonetically Deficient Fourth Grade Students." *Fla J Ed Res* 3:25–8 Ja '61. *
229. PERRY, JAMES OLDEN. *A Study of a Selective Set of Criteria for Determining Success in Secondary Student Teaching at Texas Southern University.* Doctor's thesis, University of Texas (Austin, Tex.), 1962. (*DA* 23:1617)
230. VANDENBERG, STEVEN G. "The Hereditary Abilities Study: Heredity Components in a Psychological Test Battery." *Am J Hum Genetics* 14:220–7 Je '62. * (*PA* 37:2665)
231. ANANT, SANTOKH SINGH. *Physical Maturation as a Moderator Variable in Predicting High School Achievement From Primary Mental Abilities.* Doctor's thesis, University of Michigan (Ann Arbor, Mich.), 1963. (*DA* 24:616)
232. BLUMENFELD, WARREN S., AND BLUMENFELD, ESTHER R. "An Empirical Evaluation of Grade-Point-Average as a Predictive Index." *J Psychol Studies* 14:191–3 D '63. *
233. KASHIWAGI, SHIGEO. "A New Objective Procedure for the Orthogonal Rotation in Factor Analysis (2)." *Jap Psychol Res* 5:109–11 S '63. * (*PA* 39:181)
234. McCORMICK, JAMES HAROLD. *Differences in the Relationship Between Achievement and Selected Measures of Aptitude Under Programmed and Non-Programmed Instruction.* Doctor's thesis, University of Pittsburgh (Pittsburgh, Pa.), 1963. (*DA* 25:6438)
235. ZAIDI, SAIYID WIQAR HUSAIN. *The Influence of Age and Social Status on Individual Differences in Primary Mental*

Abilities. Doctor's thesis, Stanford University (Stanford, Calif.), 1963. (*DA* 25:305)

236. AMUNDSON, GORDON J. *A Study of the Correlation Between the California Achievement Test and the SRA Primary Mental Abilities Test.* Master's thesis, Northern Illinois University (DeKalb, Ill.), 1964.

237. ANANT, SANTOKH S., AND KETCHAM, WARREN A. "Physical Maturation as a Moderator Variable in Predicting High School Achievement From Primary Mental Abilities." *Manas* 11(1):11–9 '64. * (*PA* 39:2874)

238. BROVERMAN, DONALD M. "Generality and Behavioral Correlates of Cognitive Styles." *J Consult Psychol* 28:487–500 D '64. * (*PA* 39:7680)

239. FARRANT, ROLAND H. "The Intellective Abilities of Deaf and Hearing Children Compared by Factor Analyses." *Am Ann Deaf* 109:306–25 My '64. * (*PA* 39:2442)

240. FINLEY, PETER J. "Performance of Male Juvenile Delinquents on Four Psychological Tests." *Training Sch B* 60:175–83 F '64. * (*PA* 39:5704)

241. KINGSLEY, RONALD FRANCIS. *The Relationship of the Primary Mental Abilities, Sex, and Social Class to Associative Learning Ability in Educable Mentally Handicapped Children.* Doctor's thesis, Syracuse University (Syracuse, N.Y.), 1964. (*DA* 25:324)

242. LEWIS, D. G. "The Factorial Nature of Attainment in Elementary Science." *Brit J Ed Psychol* 34:1–9 F '64. * (*PA* 38:9173)

243. MEARIG, JUDITH SUZANNE. *Fluency and Dependency as Predictors of Sex Differences in Ability and Achievement.* Doctor's thesis, University of Michigan (Ann Arbor, Mich.), 1964. (*DA* 25:3401)

244. RONAN, W. W. "Evaluation of Skilled Trades Performance Predictors." *Ed & Psychol Meas* 24:601–8 f '64. * (*PA* 39:6074)

245. TUTT, MARY L. *A Comparison of the Wechsler Intelligence Scale for Children and the SRA Primary Mental Abilities Test.* Master's thesis, Northern Illinois University (DeKalb, Ill.), 1964.

246. CLAUSEN, JOHS. "PMA Subscores in Retardates and Normals: Pattern, Scatter, Correlations, and Relation to Etiology." *Am J Mental Def* 70:232–47 S '65. * (*PA* 40:716)

247. COHEN, S. ALAN. *A Study of the Relationships Among Measurements of Reading, Intelligence and Vision Development, Using a Dynamic Theory of Vision, in Socially Disadvantaged Junior High School Children.* Doctor's thesis, Boston University (Boston, Mass.), 1965. (*DA* 26:5222)

248. CONRY, ROBERT, AND PLANT, WALTER T. "WAIS and Group Test Predictions of an Academic Success Criterion: High School and College." *Ed & Psychol Meas* 25:493–500 su '65. * (*PA* 39:15216)

249. GARDNER, R. C., AND LAMBERT, W. E. "Language Aptitude, Intelligence, and Second-Language Achievement." *J Ed Psychol* 56:191–9 Ag '65. * (*PA* 39:15290)

250. JUNKALA, JOHN BURGESS. *An Investigation Into the Possibility of a Qualitative Difference in Intelligence Between Normal and Mongoloid Individuals.* Doctor's thesis, Syracuse University (Syracuse, N.Y.), 1965. (*DA* 27:114A)

251. KEBBON, LARS. *The Structure of Abilities at Lower Levels of Intelligence: A Factor-Analytical Study.* Stockholm, Sweden: Skandinaviska Testförlaget AB, 1965. Pp. 112. *

252. MUELLER, MAX W. *A Comparison of the Empirical Validity of Six Tests of Ability With Young Educable Retardates.* Institute of Mental Retardation and Intellectual Development, IMRID Behavioral Science Monograph No. 1. Nashville, Tenn.: Peabody College Bookstore, 1965. Pp. vii, 130. *

253. MUELLER, MAX WILLIAM. *A Comparison of the Empirical Validity of Six Tests of Ability With Educable Mental Retardates.* Doctor's thesis, George Peabody College for Teachers (Nashville, Tenn.), 1965. (*DA* 26:6853)

254. MUKHERJEE, BISHWA NATH. "The Prediction of Grades in Introductory Psychology From Tests of Primary Mental Abilities." *Ed & Psychol Meas* 25:557–64 su '65. * (*PA* 39:15251)

255. RAINEY, ROBERT G. "A Study of Four School-Ability Tests." *J Exp Ed* 33:305–19 su '65. * (*PA* 39:12306)

256. REDDIG, GARY L. *A Study of the Prognostic Validity of the SRA Primary Mental Abilities Test.* Master's thesis, Millersville State College (Millersville, Pa.), 1965.

257. WEISE, PHILLIP; MEYERS, C. E.; AND TUEL, JOHN K. "PMA Factors, Sex, and Teacher Nomination in Screening Kindergarten Gifted." *Ed & Psychol Meas* 25:597–603 su '65. * (*PA* 39:14718)

258. BRENNAN, JOSEPH T., JR. *Estimating Expected Reading Achievement in the Junior High School.* Doctor's thesis, University of Pittsburgh (Pittsburgh, Pa.), 1966. (*DA* 27:4033A)

259. CHANSKY, NORMAN M. "Anxiety, Intelligence and Achievement in Algebra." *J Ed Res* 60:90–1 O '66. *

260. FERGUSON, LUCY RAU, AND MACCOBY, ELEANOR E. "Interpersonal Correlates of Differential Abilities." *Child Develop* 37:549–71 S '66. * (*PA* 40:12147)

261. JUNKALA, JOHN B. "Changes in PMA Relationships in Noninstitutionalized Mongoloids." *Am J Mental Def* 71:460–4 N '66. * (*PA* 41:1841)

262. KERR, WILLIAM D., AND WILLIS, WARREN K. "Interest and Ability: Are They Related?" *Voc Guid Q* 14:197–200 sp '66. * (*PA* 40:10493)

263. LARSON, ANNE A. *A Study to Determine the Correlation Between a Set of Scores Received on the SRA Primary Mental Abilities Test Given in Kindergarten and a Set of Scores Received on the Kuhlmann-Finch Group Intelligence Test in Third Grade.* Master's thesis, Moorehead State College (Moorehead, Minn.), 1966.

264. MONEY, JOHN, AND ALEXANDER, DUANE. "Turner's Syndrome: Further Demonstration of the Presence of Specific Cognitional Deficiencies." *J Med Genetics* 3:47–8 Mr '66. *

265. BRENDEMUEHL, FRANK LOUIS. *The Influence of Reading Ability on the Validity of Group Non-Verbal Intelligence Tests.* Doctor's thesis, University of Minnesota (Minneapolis, Minn.), 1967. (*DA* 28:2088A)

266. FREEMAN, JOHN A. "Sex Differences, Target Arrangement, and Primary Mental Abilities." *J Parapsychol* 31:271–9 'D '67. * (*PA* 42:4700)

267. GALE, DARWIN FRED. *A Comparison of Reading Readiness Skills of Mentally Retarded and Normal Children.* Doctor's thesis, Brigham Young University (Provo, Utah), 1967. (*DA* 28:2090A)

268. HUMPHREYS, LLOYD G. "Critique of Cattell's 'Theory of Fluid and Crystallized Intelligence: A Critical Experiment.'" *J Ed Psychol* 58:129–36 Je '67. * (*PA* 41:10447)

269. NICHOLLS, J. G. "Anxiety, Defensiveness, Self-Esteem, and Responsibility for Intellectual Achievement: Their Relation to Intelligence and Reading Achievement Test Score." *N Zeal J Ed Studies* 2:125–35 N '67. *

270. STAVELEY, BRYAN. *The Abilities and Interests of Craft and Technician Students of Mechanical Engineering.* Master's thesis, University of Manchester (Manchester, England), 1967. (Abstract: *Brit J Ed Psychol* 38:324)

271. VANDENBERG, STEVEN G. "The Primary Mental Abilities of South American Students: A Second Comparative Study of the Generality of a Cognitive Factor Structure." *Multiv Behav Res* 2:175–98 Ap '67. * (*PA* 41:11813)

272. WERNER, EMMY E.; SIMONIAN, KEN; AND SMITH, RUTH S. "Reading Achievement, Language Functioning and Perceptual-Motor Development of 10- and 11-Year-Olds." *Percept & Motor Skills* 25:409–20 O '67. * (*PA* 42:5403)

273. YATES, LOUISE GRAHAM. *Comparative Intelligence of Negro and White Children From a Rural-Southern Culture.* Doctor's thesis, University of North Carolina (Chapel Hill, N.C.), 1967. (*DA* 28:4768B)

274. ANANT, SANTOKH S. "Relative Effectiveness of Aptitude Tests." *Alberta J Ed Res* 14:43–7 Mr '68. * (*PA* 44:4165)

275. BAUGHMAN, E. EARL, AND DAHLSTROM, W. GRANT. *Negro and White Children: A Psychological Study in the Rural South,* pp. 48–60, passim. New York: Academic Press Inc., 1968. Pp. xx, 572. *

276. BEERY, KEITH E. "Geometric Form Reproduction: Relationship to Chronological and Mental Age." *Percept & Motor Skills* 26:247–50 F '68. * (*PA* 42:9853)

277. BONFIELD, JOHN RONALD. *Predictors of Achievement for Educable Mentally Retarded Children.* Doctor's thesis, Pennsylvania State University (University Park, Pa.), 1968. (*DAI* 30:1009A)

278. BUSSE, THOMAS V. "Establishment of the Flexible Thinking Factor in Fifth-Grade Boys." *J Psychol* 69:93–100 My '68. * (*PA* 42:11690)

279. CATTELL, RAYMOND B., AND BUTCHER, H. J. *The Prediction of Achievement and Creativity,* pp. 161–79, passim. Indianapolis, Ind.: Bobbs-Merrill Co., Inc., 1968. Pp. xiv, 386. *

280. CAWLEY, JOHN F., AND GOODMAN, JOHN O. "Interrelationships Among Mental Abilities, Reading, Language Arts, and Arithmetic With the Mentally Handicapped." *Arith Teach* 15:631–6 N '68. *

281. CRONHOLM, BÖRJE, AND SCHALLING, DAISY. "Cognitive Test Performances in Cerebrally Palsied Adults Without Mental Retardation." *Acta Psychiatrica Scandinavica* 44(1):37–50 '68. * (*PA* 43:2937)

282. DAVIS, MILTON R. *A Study of the Relationship Between the Full Scale IQ's and Number Facility Scores From the Primary Mental Abilities Test and the Achievement Level of Seventh Grade Students.* Master's thesis, Mississippi State University (State College, Miss.), 1968.

283. FREEMAN, JOHN A. "Sex Differences and Primary Mental Abilities in a Group Precognition Test." *J Parapsychol* 32:176–82 S '68. * (*PA* 43:13488)

284. HUNDLEBY, JOHN D. "The Trait of Anxiety, as Defined by Objective Performance Measures, and Indices of Emotional Disturbance in Middle Childhood," pp. 7–14. In *Progress in Clinical Psychology Through Multivariate Experimental Designs.* Edited by Raymond B. Cattell. Ft. Worth, Tex.: Society of Multivariate Experimental Psychology, Inc., 1968. Pp. 168. *

285. LEWIS, LAURA H. "Acquiescence Response Set: Construct or Artifact?" *J Proj Tech & Pers Assess* 32:578–84 D '68. * (*PA* 43:9763)

286. MEYERS, C. EDWARD; ATTWELL, ARTHUR A.; AND ORPET, RUSSELL E. "Prediction of Fifth Grade Achievement From Kindergarten Test and Rating Data." *Ed & Psychol Meas* 28:457–63 su '68. * (*PA* 42:19423)

287. MUELLER, MAX W. "Validity of Six Tests of Ability With Educable Mental Retardates." *J Sch Psychol* 6:136–46 w '68. * (*PA* 42:11152)

288. Schaie, K. Warner, and Strother, Charles R. "A Cross-Sequential Study of Age Changes in Cognitive Behavior." *Psychol B* 70:671–80 D '68. * (*PA* 43:6779)

289. Schaie, K. Warner, and Strother, Charles R. "The Effect of Time and Cohort Differences on the Interpretation of Age Changes in Cognitive Behavior." *Multiv Behav Res* 3:259–93 Jl '68. * (*PA* 43:3834)

290. Werner, Emmy E.; Simonian, Kenneth; and Smith, Ruth S. "Ethnic and Socioeconomic Status Differences in Abilities and Achievement Among Preschool and School-Age Children in Hawaii." *J Social Psychol* 75:43–59 Je '68. * (*PA* 42:13553)

291. Weston, Leslie Donald. *An Exploration of the Interrelationships Among Children's Arithmetic Achievement, Their Styles of Learning, Their Responsibility for Intellectual Academic Achievement, and Their Parents' Attitudes.* Doctor's thesis, Wayne State University (Detroit, Mich.), 1968. (*DAI* 30:1087A)

292. Asbury, Charles Alexander. *Factors Associated With Discrepant Achievement in Rural Economically Deprived White and Negro First Graders.* Doctor's thesis, University of North Carolina (Chapel Hill, N.C.), 1969. (*DAI* 31:208A)

293. Bruininks, Robert H. "Auditory and Visual Perceptual Skills Related to the Reading Performance of Disadvantaged Boys." *Percept & Motor Skills* 29(1):179–86 Ag '69. * (*PA* 44:2835)

294. Butcher, H. J. "The Structure of Abilities, Interests and Personality in 1,000 Scottish School Children." *Brit J Ed Psychol* 39(2):154–65 Je '69. * (*PA* 44:7217)

295. Butcher, H. J., and Pont, H. B. "Predicting Arts and Science Specialisation in a Group of Scottish Secondary School Children: Some Preliminary Results." *Scottish Ed Studies* 1(3):3–10 Je '69. *

296. Cropley, A. J., and Maslany, G. W. "Reliability and Factorial Validity of the Wallach-Kogan Creativity Tests." *Brit J Psychol* 60(3):395–8 Ag '69. * (*PA* 44:2349)

297. Ertl, John P., and Schafer, Edward W. P. "Brain Response Correlates of Psychometric Intelligence." *Nature* 223(5204):421–2 Jl 26 '69. *

298. Frank, Harry, and Fiedler, Edna R. "A Multifactor Behavioral Approach to the Genetic-Etiological Diagnosis of Mental Retardation." *Multiv Behav Res* 4(2):131–45 Ap '69. * (*PA* 43:16258)

299. Gaspar, Mary A. *A Descriptive Study of the Characteristics of Students Who Show a High Discrepancy Between Scores in the S.R.A. Primary Mental Ability Test and the Stanford Achievement Test in Reading.* Master's thesis, Chapman College (Orange, Calif.), 1969.

300. Kanderian, Suad Sirop. *Study of the Relationship Between School Achievement and Measures of Intelligence and Creativity for Students in Iraq.* Doctor's thesis, University of Southern California (Los Angeles, Calif.), 1969. (*DAI* 31:644A)

301. Kilman, Marvin Dyer. *Some Factors Related to Map-Reading Ability of Fourth Grade Pupils.* Doctor's thesis, University of Southern California (Los Angeles, Calif.), 1969. (*DAI* 30:1751A)

302. Krebs, Eleonore Goodlin. *The Wechsler Preschool and Primary Scale of Intelligence and Prediction of Reading Achievement in First Grade.* Doctor's thesis, Rutgers—The State University (New Brunswick, N.J.), 1969. (*DAI* 30:4279A)

303. Martin, William A. "Word Fluency: A Comparative Study." *J Genetic Psychol* 114(2):253–62 Je '69. * (*PA* 43:17282)

304. Mueller, Max W. "Prediction of Achievement of Educable Mentally Retarded Children." *Am J Mental Def* 73(4):590–6 Ja '69. * (*PA* 43:8703)

305. Schaffer, Marilyn Cercone. *Parent-Child Similarity in Psychological Differentiation.* Doctor's thesis, Purdue University (Lafayette, Ind.), 1969. (*DAI* 30:1888B)

306. Asbury, Charles A. "Some Effects on Training on Verbal Mental Functioning in Negro Pre-School Children." *J Negro Ed* 39(1):100–3 w '70. * (*PA* 46:5717)

307. Crandall, Virginia C., and Battle, Esther S. "The Antecedents and Adult Correlates of Academic and Intellectual Achievement." *Minn Symposia Child Psychol* 4:36–93 '70. *

308. Freeman, John A. "Sex Differences in ESP Response as Shown by the Freeman Picture-Figure Test." *J Parapsychol* 34(1):37–46 Mr '70. * (*PA* 44:11552)

309. Poteet, James Allen. *Identification Classification and Characteristics of First Grade Students With Learning Disabilities in Reading, Writing and Mathematics.* Doctor's thesis, Purdue University (Lafayette, Ind.), 1970. (*DAI* 31:3994A)

M. Y. Quereshi, *Professor of Psychology, Marquette University, Milwaukee, Wisconsin.*

Except for the DocuTran edition of the manuals and the addition of IBM 1230 directions for grades 4–6, 6–9, and 9–12, the PMA

tests remain the same as reviewed in *The Sixth Mental Measurements Yearbook*. Although there are now six levels (K–1, 2–4, 4–6, 6–9, 9–12, and adult), the test for adults is identical to that for grades 9–12, except for its title on the cover page. The batteries provide scores on five factors: Verbal Meaning (V), Number Facility (N), Reasoning (R), Spatial Relations (S), and Perceptual Speed (P). However, only one battery (grades 4–6) includes all five factors; P is omitted from levels 6–9 and 9–12 and R is excluded from K–1 and 2–4.

The 1962 PMA descends from the previous editions, beginning with the downward extension of the original PMA tests to the 5-year level between 1946 and 1948. The original series, published between 1938 and 1941, were based on extensive factor analytic work and represented a major contribution to test construction at that time. However, the changes effected since 1941, culminating in the 1962 revision, are so extensive that the present series must be evaluated on its own. Previous reviews, beginning with *The Third Mental Measurements Yearbook* and including *The Sixth Mental Measurements Yearbook,* have pointed out a number of deficiencies of the past editions as well as those of the 1962 revision. The present review will not necessarily enumerate the past criticisms, but will concentrate on those aspects which represent major improvements in the PMA tests between 1946 and 1962 and the deficiencies that still exist as of August 1970.

IMPROVEMENTS. Several changes have been made which meet a number of the past criticisms. Some of these changes are omissions of (*a*) statements from the manuals or profile charts which lacked empirical justification, (*b*) tests which had little educational relevance, and (*c*) psychometric data which represented inaccurate use of certain statistical techniques. Other changes embody a positive approach of either providing essential data which were previously nonexistent or substituting improper procedures with appropriate ones.

Normative Data. The standardization sample consisted of 32,393 children between the ages of 4 and 20 taken from certain public schools in five different regions of the U.S. The description of the sampling procedure is satisfactory enough to permit an evaluation of some of the biases, but no information is provided regarding the representation of either the ethnic minorities or the financial fringes of the society. In addition, the data regarding sex distribution in various age groups are not reported. Even if one disregards the aforementioned deficiencies, the sample is definitely biased, since various regions (i.e., Northeast, Great Lakes, and West) are disproportionately represented in the sample. Only for the Southeast and the Plains do the percentages of pupils in the sample closely approximate those in the total public secondary school population. Thus, despite obvious improvements, normative data still fall short of the optimum standards for such a battery. Probably the most glaring fact about the norms is the consistent disregard of the PMA producers for presenting data by sexes or demonstrating the insignificance of sex differences on the abilities involved.

The use of deviation IQ's for representing scores on each factor as well as the total is a step in the right direction, but even here the progress is marred by the retention of ratio IQ's for K–1 and 2–4 levels—for the latter though both deviation and ratio IQ's are presented—due to the users' demand for mental ages at the lower grade levels. A more defensible procedure would have been to provide mental ages as a supplementary index without changing the standard deviation unit for the IQ's at the lowest end, a procedure employed with the WISC and WPPSI for meeting the practical need for mental ages. In addition to IQ's, scores can also be expressed as centiles and stanines from the fourth grade up.

Reliability Data. Reliability coefficients represent the correlation between two testings on the same form administered to small homogeneous groups in separate grades either one week or four weeks apart. The indices for the total scores range between .83 and .95 and may be deemed satisfactory, but for individual factor scores they vary considerably from one grade to another and, in many cases, are too low to inspire much confidence in individual factor scores. Large sampling errors due to small sample sizes (ranging from 14 to 34) are probably responsible for some unusual fluctuations in the stability coefficients (e.g., the S scores in the ninth grade yielded a coefficient of .53 for 1-week and .89 for the 4-week retest). In general, P and S scores are much more unstable than any other factor scores, with the median retest reliabilities being .78 and .67, respectively.

Validity Data. Empirical evidence for the usefulness of PMA scores consists of correlations between PMA scores and (*a*) overall grade point average, (*b*) grades in various subject matter areas, (*c*) *Kuhlmann-Anderson Intelligence Tests* scores, and (*d*) *Iowa Tests of Basic Skills* composite scores. The data on grades were secured from one or more of the four high schools selected from four different states. The correlations of total scores with grade point average are substantial for grades 2 to 8, but are rather low in grades 9 to 12. V and N often have correlations with grade point average as high as the total score, but P and S fare very poorly. Correlations between PMA scores and grades in various subject matter areas are inflated, since children were pooled across four or more grades in computing correlations. In any case, there is little evidence supporting differential validity of factor scores at any level. In general, one could take verbal meaning and number facility (and reasoning at the upper grades) and predict performance in various subject matter areas with about the same level of accuracy.

Intercorrelations of the subtests are presented for each grade in the five batteries on the basis of the data obtained from the same four schools mentioned above. There are two points that need to be made here: first, some of the samples are too small to provide dependable data (e.g., 25 children in the kindergarten group) and second, there is no indication in the technical report whether correlations of individual factor scores with the total scores were corrected for part-whole spuriousness. The correlations, however, are usually too homogeneous to lend support to any claims of differential measurement such as those implied in the very first paragraph of the technical report and repeated continuously in the introductory remarks to each of the five examiner's manuals.

The claim that PMA K–1 is a good predictor of reading readiness is based on the data of a study correlating the PMA scores of 377 first graders with their scores on the *SRA Achievement Series: Reading.* The correlations indicate that either PMA K–1 is a poor measure of vocabulary or the SRA Vocabulary is a poor test, or both the PMA K–1 and the SRA reading test are poor measures of vocabulary or, as the technical report concludes, the PMA total score is "an efficient predictor of reading performance" provided that vocabulary is excluded from reading performance.

SRA Primary Mental Abilities

Interpretation of Data. The technical report exhibits an increasing degree of restraint in interpreting some of the data. For example, it is stated that "the need for verbal understanding is less in the early years and increases as the child advances; on the other hand, the relative importance of perceptual speed decreases from one year to the next." However, the same degree of caution is not apparent in the examiner's manual for level 4–6. The first part of the same statement is changed to "the importance of verbal meaning, for instance, increases in school work as a child advances through school." Factually, whether one judges the importance of a particular measure V or P either in terms of its correlation with total PMA scores or with grade point averages, the second part of the said statement is not borne out at all by the data and the first part is only partially corroborated (in the data from school C).

The technical report's interpretation of differences, despite the adequate quota of admonitions, misleads the test users into employing an incorrect procedure by suggesting that "if the difference between two test scores exceeds the sum of the respective standard errors [of measurement], one can be fairly confident that a true difference exists." One wonders whether the "rule of thumb" presented in the same section deserves any credence considering the faulty rationale that precedes it and in view of the absence of any data bearing on the frequency with which differences of 13 IQ points or more are actually encountered in normal children. Data on the reliability of the difference scores should be presented before any attempt is made to indulge in estimating "true" intra-individual differences.

DEFICIENCIES LEFT UNATTENDED. The foregoing evaluation concerns those aspects which presumably reflect some degree of improvement over previous editions. There are, however, several points which have not received any attention: (*a*) No information is provided regarding correlations between tests of the same factors at different levels. Whether tests bearing identical names measure "identical" abilities at different levels cannot be judged without such data. (*b*) No factorial investigation has been reported concerning the tests at the K–1 level. (*c*) Speed has substantial effect on performance; it is still not clear why such emphasis continues to exist. (*d*) Tests of perceptual speed should be included at the upper levels. (*e*) The

technical report and the examiner's manuals continue to make the misleading suggestion that single short tests can provide relatively adequate and pure measures of the said factors. (*f*) Addition of the so-called adult level, without any separate adult norms or standardization data, represents a definite deterioration in standards for test construction and standardization as represented by the PMA.

OVERALL EVALUATION. The PMA producers have had the benefit of competent critiques for almost a whole generation. Yet the response to these criticisms has resulted in improvements which can best be described as too little and too late. If the current trends in the U.S. are any indication of the future demands, then the emphasis on the quality of life rather than the quantity of production may relegate all ability tests, regardless of their technical adequacy, to the testing archives or, at least, change their function drastically. Since traditions die hard, there may yet be a transitional period during which "classical" batteries of ability and aptitude tests may continue to sell and survive. Whatever the future of ability testing, the PMA tests do not seem to offer much competition to the technical superiority of several other instruments covering the same "waterfront." This reviewer would recommend that for grades 8 through 12 the *Differential Aptitude Tests* be used instead of the PMA, and for grades 3 through 7, a general intelligence test (e.g., The *Lorge-Thorndike Intelligence Tests*) be employed. Since differential measurement by means of the PMA, especially at the elementary school levels, is simply a will-o'-the-wisp, it is justified to use a general intelligence test which has more adequate standardization data and employs more defensible test construction procedures. The PMA tests served an important purpose as research tools in the advancement of the multiple factor notion of ability but have not fulfilled the practical promise of differential educational or vocational measurement. Since they have also failed to keep up with several competing batteries in a number of technical aspects, their future may depend chiefly on the consumer's nostalgia for a product which had an auspicious beginning but could never realize its potential.

RICHARD E. SCHUTZ, *Director, Southwest Regional Laboratory for Educational Research and Development, Los Alamitos, California.*

SRA Primary Mental Abilities

Historians have as yet devoted little attention to the field of educational measurement, and educational measurement specialists have devoted little attention to the history of their field. When at some time in the future a systematic interest in the history of educational measurement arises, the *SRA Primary Mental Abilities* battery could well provide a significant marker variable for the 50-year era circa 1930–1980. While extrapolation into the future is speculative, the past trend and current status of PMA provide a stronger basis for alarm than for celebration.

From nearly every perspective, the history of PMA is much more disappointing than its larger embedding professional-technical context. When originally issued, PMA was the pride and joy of the psychometric world. The high aspirations for the battery reflected in early reviews were never realized within PMA; the modest psychometric revolution which PMA heralded occurred outside the PMA battery. While the PMA authors continued to contribute to both multifactor science and technology after PMA was made commercially available, very little of their knowledge and know-how found its way back into PMA. Thus, at an early stage PMA was outstripped by competing tests in terms of technical quality and functional utility.

While the history of PMA as a test has been one of steady decline, the history of primary mental abilities as a paradigm has been one of steady growth. The undergirding conceptual framework of PMA provided a common paradigm which not only generated competing multifactor instruments but also structured the "normal science" within which such tests are still being viewed and used. Although rumblings of revolt against this paradigm are increasing in frequency and intensity, PMA thought is likely to remain the most prevalent view in mental abilities measurement long after the time that the popularity of PMA as an operational exemplification of that view has declined.

The changes in PMA since the tests were reviewed in *The Sixth Mental Measurements Yearbook* are minuscule and indicative of the senescent state of the battery. An adult form has appeared. Ordinarily, the extension of a test battery into the adult years constitutes a major development. However, in this instance, the effort was limited to verbal magic. The adult tests are identical to the grade 9–12 tests; only the title has been changed to dupe the innocent. Not even a pass was made at preparing adult norms, and no additional psychometric characteristics at the adult level are included in the documentation.

Answer sheets for the modern test scoring machines have been issued, and standard forms for preparing automated printed score listings and individual gummed labels have also been made available. No steps, however, have been taken to modernize the test substance or to update the test norms. A Technical Report, pertaining to the 1962 revision, was issued in 1965. This was available in draft form for the review appearing in *The Sixth Mental Measurements Yearbook*. However, nothing has been done to remove the deficiencies noted in that review.

How does one account for the opposite growth trends of a field and an instrument which opened the field? The recent history of the PMA, consistent with its earlier past, appears to have been more influenced by commercial expediency than by a full exploitation of the psychometric art. In the early 1940's, reviewers pointed out that the tests constituted a compromise between "test tube" instruments derived from and contributing to scientific knowledge and engineered instruments with established utility for educational and vocational decision making. While minor technical flaws that characterized the early battery were patched up during the 1950's and 1960's, the major structural deficiencies were never eliminated.

Meanwhile, the rest of the mental measurement world was progressing. Further factor analytic work, exemplified by the programmatic efforts of Guilford and Cattell, showed clearly that the factors represented in PMA account for only fragmentary and arbitrary facets of cognitive space. Concurrently, further test construction, exemplified by the *Differential Aptitude Tests* and the *General Aptitude Test Battery,* was creating multiple-test batteries with demonstrated educational and counseling utility.

Consequently, the PMA is currently analogous to the Ford Model A. Neither a modern researcher nor a practitioner is likely to find it an attractive new buy, considering the other models available to him. At the same time, the user who has continued to nurture and maintain the battery through personal use will find the diminishing benefit of procuring replacement parts to be a function of his personal attachment and of the magnitude of his accrued investment.

For a review by John E. Milholland, see 6:780; for reviews by Norman Frederiksen and Albert K. Kurtz of an earlier edition, see 5:614; for reviews by Anne Anastasi, Ralph F. Berdie, John B. Carroll, Stuart A. Courtis, and P. E. Vernon, see 4:716; for reviews by Cyril Burt, Florence L. Goodenough, James R. Hobson, and F. L. Wells, see 3:225 and 3:264; for reviews by Henry E. Garrett, Truman L. Kelley, C. Spearman, Godfrey H. Thomson, and Robert C. Tryon, see 2:1427 (3 excerpts).

[681]

★**Senior Aptitude Tests.** Standards 8–10 and college and adults; 1969–70; SAT; 12 scores: verbal comprehension, numerical fluency, word fluency, visual perception speed, reasoning (deductive, inductive), spatial visualization (2 dimensional, 3 dimensional), memory (paragraphs, symbols), psychomotor coordination, writing speed; 1 form ('69, 72 pages, English and Afrikaans); preliminary manual ('70, 27 pages, English and Afrikaans); no data on validity; norms for standard 10 only; separate answer sheets (IBM 1230 and hand scored) must be used; R5.50 per 10 tests; R15 per 100 sets of answer sheets; R1 per set of scoring stencils; 80c per manual; postpaid within South Africa; specimen set not available; 88(120) minutes; F. A. Fouche and N. F. Alberts; Human Sciences Research Council. *

VOCATIONS—SEVENTH MMY

REVIEWS BY *C. J. Adcock, Lewis E. Albright, Thomas S. Baldwin, Harold P. Bechtoldt, Ralph F. Berdie, Jack L. Bodden, David P. Campbell, Dorothy M. Clendenen, Nancy S. Cole, John O. Crites, Robert H. Dolliver, Jerome E. Doppelt, Robert C. Droege, Robert Fitzpatrick, John P. Foley, Jr., Thomas T. Frantz, Norman Frederiksen, John W. French, Edward J. Furst, Cecil A. Gibb, Gary R. Hanson, Mary T. Harrison, David G. Hawkridge, A. W. Heim, John K. Hemphill, David O. Herman, Richard T. Johnson, Clive Jones, Martin R. Katz, Barbara A. Kirk, Charles J. Krauskopf, Paul R. Lohnes, John N. McCall, Arthur C. MacKinney, Leo A. Munday, David A. Payne, Hugh F. Priest, James M. Richards, Jr., A. Oscar H. Roberts, John W. M. Rothney, Lyle F. Schoenfeldt, Douglas G. Schultz, Benjamin Shimberg, David V. Tiedeman, Donald J. Veldman, W. Bruce Walsh, Charles F. Ward, William C. Ward, Richard W. Watkins, Henry Weitz, Leonard J. West, Bert W. Westbrook, Emory E. Wiseman, and Donald G. Zytowski.*

[975]

★**Alpha Biographical Inventory.** Grades 9–12; 1968, c1966–68; ABI; earlier experimental editions called *Biographical Inventory, Forms A, B, C, C-1, J, K, L, M, N, O;* 2 scores: creativity, academic performance in college; 1 form ('68, 23 pages); a separate booklet, *College Academic Performance Biographical Inventory* (CAPBI), is available for obtaining only the academic performance score; manual ('68, 18 pages); separate answer sheets (NCS) must be used; data on reliability and validity are for earlier editions only; $8.75 per 25 tests; $2.25 per 25 answer sheets; postage extra; $2.50 per manual, postpaid; scoring service, 85¢ or less per test; scoring keys not available; (90–120) minutes; Prediction Press. *

REFERENCES

1. ELLISON, R. LOREN. *The Relationship of Certain Biographical Information to Success in Science.* Master's thesis, University of Utah (Salt Lake City, Utah), 1960.
2. CLINE, VICTOR B.; RICHARDS, JAMES M., JR.; AND ABE, CLIFFORD. "Predicting Achievement in High School Science With a Biographical Information Blank." *J Exp Ed* 32:395–9 su '64. * (*PA* 39:5968)
3. ELLISON, R. L. *The Development of Scoring Procedures for a Biographical Inventory to Predict Various Criteria of Success in Science.* Doctor's thesis, University of Utah (Salt Lake City, Utah), 1964. (*DA* 25:3674)
4. CLINE, VICTOR B.; TUCKER, MICHAEL F.; AND MULAIK, STANLEY A. "Predicting Factored Criteria of Performance Measures of Pharmaceutical Scientists." *J Indus Psychol* 4(1):7–15 '65. *
5. TAYLOR, CALVIN W.; ELLISON, ROBERT L.; AND TUCKER, MICHAEL F. *Biographical Information and the Prediction of Multiple Criteria of Success in Science.* Greensboro, N.C.: Creativity Research Institute of The Richardson Foundation, February 1966. Pp. vi, 114. *
6. HINMAN, SUSAN LEE. *A Predictive Validity Study of Creative Managerial Performance.* Greensboro, N.C.: Creativity Research Institute of The Richardson Foundation, Inc., November 1967. Pp. vi, 124. *
7. MOFFIE, D. J., AND GOODNER, SUSAN. *A Predictive Validity Study of Creative and Effective Managerial Performance.* Greensboro, N.C.: Creativity Research Institute of The Richardson Foundation, Inc., December 1967. Pp. 80. *
8. TAYLOR, CALVIN W., AND ELLISON, ROBERT L. "Biographical Predictors of Scientific Performance." *Sci* 155:1075–80 Mr 3 '67. * (*PA* 41:6228)
9. TUCKER, MICHAEL F.; CLINE, VICTOR B.; AND SCHMITT, JAMES R. "Prediction of Creativity and Other Performance Measures From Biographical Information Among Pharmaceutical Scientists." *J Appl Psychol* 51:131–8 Ap '67. * (*PA* 41:7348)
10. JAMES, LAWRENCE R.; ELLISON, ROBERT L.; McDONALD, BLAIR W.; AND TAYLOR, CALVIN W. "Effectiveness of Biographical Information in Predicting Teacher Assessments of Creativity and Leadership." Abstract. *Proc 76th Ann Conv Am Psychol Assn* 3:231–2 '68. *
11. HARRINGTON, CHARLES. "Forecasting College Performance From Biographical Data." *J Col Stud Personnel* 10(3):156–60 My '69. *
12. PRICE, JOSEPH S. *The Effectiveness of the Alpha Biographical Inventory in Prediction of First Semester Grades of Wake Forest University Freshmen.* Master's thesis, Wake Forest University (Winston-Salem, N.C.), 1969.
13. ABE, CLIFFORD. *The Prediction of Academic Achievement of Mexican-American Students.* Doctor's thesis, University of Arizona (Tucson, Ariz.), 1970. (*DAI* 31:4535A)

14. DAMM, VERNON J. "Creativity and Intelligence: Research Implications for Equal Emphasis in High School." *Excep Children* 36(8):565–9 Ap '70. * (PA 46:1754)

15. ELLISON, ROBERT L.; JAMES, LAWRENCE R.; AND CARRON, THEODORE J. "Prediction of R & D Performance Criteria With Biographical Information." *J Indus Psychol* 5(2): 37–57 Je '70. *

16. ELLISON, ROBERT L.; JAMES, LAWRENCE R.; FOX, DAVID G.; AND TAYLOR, CALVIN W. *The Identification of Talent Among Negro and White Students From Biographical Data.* An unpublished report to the U.S. Office of Education, Research Project No. 9-H-033, Institute for Behavioral Research in Creativity, 1970. Pp. iv, 71. *

JOHN K. HEMPHILL, *Laboratory Director, Far West Laboratory for Educational Research and Development, Berkeley, California.*

The *Alpha Biographical Inventory* consists of 300 multiple choice items. Approximately one-third of them refer to directly school-related topics, including several self-estimates of quality of school performance. Many more items refer to factors that are known to correlate with academic success (e.g., socioeconomic status and school achievement of parents). Other items tap aspirations, interests, and motivations with respect to education. Several items ask for self-reports about originality, creativity, and curiosity. It is important that the item content of the inventory be carefully noted by the potential user, since the interpretation of the scores it yields must depend for a considerable part upon "content" validity. None of the items included among the 300 should raise serious questions about social bias or invasion of privacy.

The inventory provides scores for creativity and academic performance, the latter for males and females separately. The scores result from weighting one or more of the alternatives to an item either +1 or −1, summing the item weights, and adding a constant to achieve a raw score which is then transformed into a reported score. The user is spared the difficulty of engaging in these scoring gymnastics, since all scoring must be carried out by National Computer Systems. The scoring keys are not made available. This procedure, of course, protects the test but also makes it difficult to examine the logical content of the score critically. This reviewer does not know which items are scored or which weight is given to which responses, and despite the need to rely heavily upon the "content" of the instrument in evaluating it, he can only guess about what responses enter into these scores.

A well-organized 15-page manual gives a concise summary of an extensive research program on the prediction of creativity, from which the inventory has grown. This program is now being carried forward through the Institute of Behavioral Research in Creativity. The manual contains a wealth of interesting data but leaves much to be desired as a tool for interpreting scores. Although the inventory is recommended for counseling and guidance, academic selection, and occupational selection, as well as for research, it is this reviewer's opinion that at this time it can properly be used for research only. For other than research use, one must rely upon content validity (a difficult assignment, as noted above), since no evidence is provided of the predictive validity of scores. All evidence provided for validity of the ABI stems from one extensive study with a prior form of the instrument on a large number of high school students from North Carolina. This evidence is entirely concurrent (not predictive) and does not include information about college student performance, which it is designed to predict. Although the background data in the manual would provide some basis for confidence in a possible construct validity for the creativity score, the manual itself warns the reader of risks in this area.

In summary, it seems to this reviewer that the publication of the *Alpha Biographical Inventory* was somewhat premature. It is to be hoped and expected, on the basis of the careful work that characterizes the basic research program from which this instrument springs, that within a short time the evidence needed to use it with confidence will become available. In the meantime, it would seem prudent for anyone tempted to employ this inventory as a tool for selecting students for admission to college to resist the urge until he can satisfy himself that its scores have a predictive significance superior to that of the more readily available, nonfakable, and traditional rank-in-class or grade-point-average information.

WILLIAM C. WARD, *Research Psychologist, Educational Testing Service, Princeton, New Jersey.*

The *Alpha Biographical Inventory* was designed to predict grade point average and creativity of students in grades 9 through 12. The instrument consists of 300 multiple choice items and can be self-administered in a period of one and one-half to two hours.

The items are diverse in content. Areas emphasized include present and childhood interests and activities, plans and expectations for the future, and self-assessment of dimensions of personality and intellectual competence. No explicit theory appears to have guided item selection; rather, empirical keys were developed and crossvalidated within each sample tested. Evaluation of reliability and validity is made somewhat uncertain by changes in items and in scoring keys from study to study, since the present version of the inventory differs somewhat from all those versions on which this information is given by the test manual.

Normative data are given on a sample of approximately 11,000 high school students, drawn from schools in North Carolina. Norms are given for creativity, male academic performance, and female academic performance keys. No justification is supplied for the use of separate scoring keys for the two sexes, nor is it stated explicitly how much change was made in the instrument between the present form and the slightly different versions used in the normative study, one for the ninth grade and one for the twelfth.

One minor reliability study has been performed on an earlier form of the inventory. With 224 ninth graders retested after a two and one-half month interval, test-retest reliabilities ranging from .82 to .88 were obtained for the three scores, and no substantial changes in means were found over this period.

Validity was demonstrated for the academic performance scores by a crossvalidation study in which still another earlier form of the inventory was given to a sample of over 1,400 students of each sex who were entering Ohio University. Within that sample, with first semester grade point average as the criterion, empirically derived scoring keys yielded "cross validities of .60 for females and .58 for males."

Less direct and less adequate validity evidence is available for the creativity score. In studies with scientists and engineers at NASA and in several industrial settings, seven earlier versions of the inventory were used to predict a number of creativity criteria. An overall creativity rating by the individual's supervisor was common to all studies, and was predicted with crossvalidities in the .40's by the creativity index in these various studies. Moreover, the creativity key derived from the first of the NASA studies also predicted the creativity criterion in the remaining two NASA studies with correlations in the .40's, and a key derived from all the NASA work correlated with the empirical keys from the industrial studies from .83 to .91. Thus, the basis for discrimination seems to have remained relatively constant across studies.

This evidence is only suggestive so far as validity of the creativity score for high school students is concerned. Not only were the items and scoring keys changed from the previous studies, but the population in question was younger and less highly selected on ability and interests. It is also uncertain whether prediction can be made for domains of production other than the scientific and technical, and even within this domain whether a rating of creativity is a better criterion than, for example, number of publications or other recognized products. Follow-up studies of individuals tested while in school are needed to resolve the validity question. However, despite the severity of these problems, no other published test of creativity offers even this much evidence for predictive validity.

Construct validity for the academic performance scores is provided by correlations on the order of .4 with IQ scores from the school records for the normative sample. A finding in need of explanation is that while the IQ and achievement tests showed large race differences, with correlations on the order of .4, the academic and creativity scores were virtually unrelated to race. The academic scores predicted grade point average and rank in class less well for Negroes than for whites, but still significantly (average correlation was .66 for whites, .45 for Negroes). Also of interest for research purposes was the negligible relationship of extracurricular activities to the creativity score, since several of the tests used as creativity measures by other investigators have shown positive relations with such activities.

Especially with the creativity score, further validity and reliability evidence, based on the current form of the inventory, is needed before decisions affecting individuals should be based on this inventory. Several questions germane to self-report instruments—such as the degree to which favorable profiles can be faked, and the influence of personality or response styles on scores—also must be investigated. Despite these reservations, it appears likely that the *Alpha Biographical Inventory* can provide meaningful variance that is not identical to the variance captured by more standard instruments in the creativity and academic performance domains, and that it is deserving of attention now as a research instrument, and eventually as a possible aid in academic and occupational selection.

[976]

★The Dailey Vocational Tests. Grades 8–12 and adults; 1964–65; DVT; 3 tests; examiner's manual ('65, 35 pages) ; profile ('65, 2 pages) ; no data on predictive validity; separate answer sheets (MRC) must be used; $8.55 per 100 MRC answer sheets for any one test; $1.50 per 35 profiles; 60¢ per manual; $3 per specimen set; postage extra; scoring service, 57¢ for set of 3 tests; John T. Dailey and Kenneth B. Hoyt (manual) ; Houghton Mifflin Co. *

a) TECHNICAL AND SCHOLASTIC TEST. TST; 3 scores for males in grades 8–10 and for females : technical, scholastic, total; 11 scores for others: technical (electricity, electronics, mechanics, science, total), scholastic (arithmetic, algebra, vocabulary, total), total, mechanical (mechanics and arithmetic) ; 1 form ('64, 19 pages) ; the manual states that—except for the technical, scholastic, mechanical, and composite scores—the reliabilities of the 7 subtest scores "are almost consistently lower than would be needed for use of these subtests as separate scores with individual examinees"; $6.60 per 35 tests; $2.16 per set of keys; scoring service, 27¢ per test; 65(75) minutes.

b) SPATIAL VISUALIZATION TEST. SVT; 1 form ('64, 10 pages) ; no norms for females; $4.80 per 35 tests; 60¢ per key; scoring service, 21¢ per test; 20(30) minutes.

c) BUSINESS ENGLISH TEST. BET; 1 form ('64, 6 pages) ; no norms for males; $3.90 per 35 tests; 60¢ per key; scoring service, 21¢ per test; 30(40) minutes.

REFERENCES

1. MALONE, FRANCIS EDWARD, JR. A Study of Students Enrolled in Post-High School Public Vocational Education Programs in Iowa During the 1964–1965 School Year. Doctor's thesis, University of Iowa (Iowa City, Iowa), 1966. (DA 27:678A)
2. DOERR, JOHN JOSEPH. Application of the Discriminant Function to the Classification of Trade and Industrial Education Students. Doctor's thesis, University of Missouri (Columbia, Mo.), 1967. (DA 28:2516A)
3. COX, STEVEN GRAHN. A Study of Relationships Between Student Scores on Various Predictor Measures and Vocational Success of Students Who Were Followed Up One and Five Years Following Training in Selected Private Trade, Technical, and Business Schools. Doctor's thesis, University of Iowa (Iowa City, Iowa), 1968. (DA 29:3827A)
4. PASSMORE, JAMES LAURENCE. Validation of a Discriminant Analysis of Eight Vocational-Technical Curricular Groups. Doctor's thesis, University of Missouri (Columbia, Mo.), 1968. (DA 29:4292A)
5. STONE, THOMAS CARL. A Case Study: Predictors of Success in Post-High School Vocational Trade, Industrial, and Technical Programs. Doctor's thesis, Colorado State University (Ft. Collins, Colo.), 1969. (DAI 30:4348A)

THOMAS S. BALDWIN, Associate Professor of Education, University of North Carolina, Chapel Hill, North Carolina.

The Spatial Visualization Test is a 30-item test similar to other spatial visualization tests. The Business English Test contains 111 items measuring knowledge of spelling, punctuation, capitalization, and use of correct grammar and is obviously designed to have applicability to the field of secretarial or business occupations. The Technical and Scholastic Test, in addition to a total score, yields both technical and scholastic composite scores. The technical score

can be broken down further into electrical and mechanical subscores. The two major subscales, technical and scholastic, can also be broken down into seven types of items which yield seven different scores.

The most disconcerting feature of the series is the implication that these tests can be all things to all people. The manual suggests that the tests are appropriate for academic guidance in junior high schools; for both academic and vocational guidance in senior high schools; "for screening, selection, and evaluation" in "post-high school trade, technical, and business training institutions"; and "for selection, placement, and evaluation of training" by "personnel departments in business and industry." It is hard to conceive of any test battery that could fulfill all of these basic needs. While extensive norms are provided at each level for which the test is suggested for use, it is hard to imagine how the same instrument could be used for personnel selection in industry as well as for evaluation and training at the end of an industrial training program, as is suggested in the manual. Through the use of the extensive norms provided, the tests probably do have utility across a broad range of age levels for some purposes; but their use in evalution of training programs is highly questionable, since instruments with this purpose would normally have to be designed for the specific educational objectives of the program.

The norms provided for this test are indeed extensive and are based on very respectable numbers of students at various age levels. Much care is devoted to the appropriate use of the norm tables, including such matters as sex differences and the time of year at which the normative tests were administered.

The author is careful to point out that detailed validity studies need to be conducted, particularly in the industrial situation.

The manual claims that the best evidence for validity of these tests is concurrent validity or "the relation of scores to current success in either training programs or in performance on the job." While this is generally the accepted definition of concurrent validity, the data provided to support this do not conform to the usual types of statistical analysis. For example, the manual presents means and standard deviations for each of the SVT tests for groups of subjects by area of specialization (e.g., drafting). This is scant evidence for validity and most certainly does not conform to the usually accepted definition of concurrent validity. The manual does point out that differences in means for different occupational groups should be interpreted only as gross differences between groups and that the validity for individual use should be evaluated in terms of the correlation between test scores and an external criterion of performance. Evidence of this sort is presented for certain occupational groups and is quite respectable in terms of the multiple correlation between test scores and instructors' ratings. The implication that a test is valid because two occupational groups have different means is nevertheless present and may lead to unwarranted conclusions regarding the validity of the test for those who are not famiilar with the concept of statistical validity.

The well-prepared manual contains a good discussion of reliability and the appropriateness of various estimates of reliability. Very respectable reliabilities are reported for total scores on the SVT (.84 to .93), TST (.84 to .96), and BET (.90 to .95). In addition, the reliabilities (.81 to .97) for the scholastic subtest are quite adequate for individual use. Since the reliabilities for electrical (.58 to .93) and mechanical (.65 to .90) scores are somewhat lower, their adequacy for use in making decisions regarding individual students should be judged with respect to the particular type of examinee in question. The seven subscores on the TST, as the author points out, "are almost consistently lower [in reliability] than would be needed for use....as separate scores with individual examinees."

Intercorrelations among the various scores derived from the battery are presented and are generally low to moderate. The table contains some part-whole correlations, and a note that these are high is provided, although a further explanation of the concept of part-whole correlation would be desirable.

It is unfortunate that the longest of the three subtests, the Technical and Scholastic Test, which covers a wide variety of technical, scientific, arithmetic, and verbal material must be administered in its entirety in order to derive the subscores that are possible. The testing time of 65 minutes is not practicable in many instances. More flexibility and economy in testing time would have been realized had this test been published as a series of several tests with homogeneous subject matter.

In general, the *Dailey Vocational Tests* appear to have considerable potential for use with students who expect to go into a vocational or technical field at the undergraduate level. One gets the feeling in reading the manual, however, that the publisher has attempted to expand the applicability of the test into areas for which it is not well suited: for example, junior high school academic guidance, or evaluation of training in industry. The tests do not appear to be appropriate for these groups.

Benjamin Shimberg, *Senior Program Director, Vocational-Technical Education Projects, Educational Testing Service, Princeton, New Jersey.*

The *Dailey Vocational Tests* "are designed particularly for use with those who plan to enter occupations at the skilled level in trade, technical, and business fields." Contrary to an assertion by the authors, the tests do not "measure the potential of young people for a wide range of occupations." There is no mention of such skilled trades as plumbing, carpentry, or sheet metal work or the graphic arts; no reference to health occupations or service occupations; and only passing mention of jobs related to computers and data processing.

There are three tests in the series: (*a*) *Technical and Scholastic Test.* The manual suggests that the technical score "measures the subject's background for undertaking technical training in the broad band of occupations requiring knowledge and skills involving mechanical devices, electrical wiring, and electronics." The scholastic score is characterized as "closely related to current measures of general intelligence." It is suggested that this score is indicative of *"level* of potentiality." (*b*) *Spatial Visualization Test.* This test is a 30-item measure of the "ability to visualize objects presented in two-dimensional drawings as they would appear in three-dimensional space." It consists of nine pairs of figures with several questions based on each figure. (*c*) *Business English Test.* Each of the 111 items in this test consists of a sentence in which may appear an error of spelling, punctuation, capitalization, grammar.

RELIABILITY. The K-R 21 reliabilities are reported for nine groups, and split-half reliabilities for five other groups. Reliabilities for total scores on the three tests are generally high, ranging from .84 to .96. Those for the scholastic composite also tend to be high. Lower reliabilities are reported for an electrical (.58 to .93) and a mechanical composite (.65 to .90), especially for female groups. As the manual notes, the reliabilities for the seven subtests of the TST are "consistently lower than would be needed for use of these subtests as separate scores with individual examinees."

NORMS. Percentile rank norms are presented for each of "the three general uses of the tests." (a) For "guiding students in academic and vocational choices at the Junior and Senior High School levels," the manual presents within-grade percentile norms separately by sex for each of grades 8–12. Subtest norms for the *Technical and Scholastic Test,* however, are given only for males in grades 11–12. (b) For "screening students in trade, technical, and business schools," percentile norms within specialties are reported for "predominantly male" groups specializing in auto-diesel repair, body and fender repair, machinist trade, drafting, electronics, or business administration, and for "predominantly female" groups specializing in secretarial training or clerical training. (c) For "selecting personnel for certain jobs in business and industry" percentile norms are presented for about 100 "Applicants to a Midwest Manufacturing Corporation." No further information about these applicants or the positions for which they were applying is reported.

The usefulness of these norms is questionable in the light of the validity data—or lack thereof —as discussed below.

VALIDITY. The manual presents means and standard deviations for students enrolled in college preparatory and various vocational programs. It also provides zero-order correlations for total scores, component scores, and individual TST subtest scores with instructor ratings in various programs. Finally, multiple correlations are given between test scores and instructor ratings of students pursuing specified occupational programs in certain institutions.

These data do not constitute adequate evidence of validity. With respect to the first stated purpose (academic and vocational guidance), there are tables which show that the college preparatory students tend to make higher scores on the TST than do students in the vocational, commercial, or general curriculum. But this information should hardly come as a surprise, since similar tests of in-

telligence or academic ability were probably used in channeling students into the college preparatory curriculum in the first place. The manual does not provide any evidence that students with high scores on the various tests are more likely to succeed in specified academic or occupational programs than are students with low scores. In the absence of such data, the norms can be used to make descriptive statements about students, but they would be of little value in guiding academic or vocational decisions.

The second stated purpose is "screening students in trade, technical, and business schools." Here one does find some correlational data between TST scores and instructors' ratings in nine occupational programs. However, the number of cases on which these correlations are based tends to be small (N = 56 for office machine repair students; N = 114 for body and fender students; N = 167 for tool and die students; N = 210 for drafting students). Apart from the fact that the correlations are based on a very limited sample of students in a very small number of schools, there is no evidence provided as to the ultimate success of the students in completing the program in question. This reviewer would hesitate to use these scores to "screen students" without better evidence that there was indeed a meaningful relationship between test performance and success in training. Why use a test to make a rather poor estimate of an instructor's rating?

As for the use of these tests for "selecting personnel for certain jobs in business and industry," there are no data to show that any of the scores are related to job success. Thus, any claim of potential usefulness in this sphere must be regarded as wholly unsupported by evidence.

SUMMARY. There is a great need for dependable tools to aid in the guidance and placement of students, especially in occupational programs. Regretfully, the *Dailey Vocational Tests* offer little hope of meeting this need. Neither the test manual nor correspondence with the author and publisher has provided any convincing evidence that these instruments can accomplish any of the purposes stated. Until such time as meaningful validation data are presented, this reviewer would not recommend use of the DVT for guidance, screening, or employment purposes.

Dailey Vocational Tests

J Counsel Psychol 13:498–500 w '66. Jack C. Merwin. The three tests in this series....are said to meet a part of the need for greater emphasis on guidance in schools on post-school training, and on job selection. Whether these tests can meet these laudatory goals must at this time rest on the care with which they have been developed and the research underlying their final publication. Crucial empirical data to make this judgment is not provided in the current manual. * In general, the coefficients are sufficiently high for the uses proposed by the author. He quite appropriately points out that the coefficients for the subtests of the TST are "consistently lower than would be needed for use of these subtests as separate scores for individual examinees." He also calls attention to the need for the user to ascertain the reliability of subscores for his own group, since the degree of reliability seems to be heavily dependent on the amount of training of the individuals tested. For example, the coefficient reported for the Electricity subscores of a group of secretarial students is .18; for "Industrial applicants" it is .80. The potential user would do well to carefully study the brief but important statement on reliability in the manual prior to making a judgment about the potential adequacy of the test for his purposes. * The validity evidence provided....is concurrent validity information. * all scores from this test series are significantly loaded with general academic ability, including the subscores from the TST * Zero-order correlations with instructors' ratings of students with various speciality school majors are quite low except for electronics majors. All except the BET scores correlate higher with instructors' ratings for electronics majors than for any other group. Coefficients range from .32 to .44 for this group. This raises questions as to whether the variance of ratings, and/or general academic ability of this group is significantly greater than for the other groups. Such information is not reported in the manual. It is proposed that multiple correlations provide a more useful way of looking at the value of these tests. Multiple correlation coefficients using instructors' ratings (apparently collected at the time of testing) as the criterion are reported. For the nine groups of speciality school majors these coefficients range from .27 to .56. Taken school by school, the multiple correlation coefficients are in some cases quite high. From a practical standpoint, however, the importance of these coefficients is not obvious for several reasons; the coefficients had been corrected for attenuation in the criterion and no information on the variance and reliability of the criterion is provided, the higher coefficients reported are based on very small numbers of students, no cross-validation information is provided and these are apparently concurrent, rather than predictive validity coefficients. A "proof of the pudding" approach to a test series proposed for use in academic and vocational guidance, screening, placement and selection procedures is the extent to which it increases predictions for these purposes. The only validity evidence provided in the current manual is concurrent validity evidence. Thus, crucial questions concerning validity are not answered by the data provided. * While 11 sets of norms based on speciality school groups are presented, the author appropriately notes that some of these are based on small numbers of students from a single school and that these schools were not selected to be representative of all specialities. * A unique device, the value of which is not readily apparent, is presented as an aid to interpretation of the TST total score. Based on a joint administration of the TST and Project Talent Information Test to a group of twelfth grade boys, "estimated" TST percentiles corresponding to Information Test percentiles were derived ($r = .825$). The mean scores for students tested on the Information Test in 1960 and reported membership in various educational or occupational groups obtained from a follow-up in 1961 are shown on the equated percentile scales. Before attempting to use this chart as a basis for guidance, the counselor should have firmly in mind the fact that these are reported occupational and educational areas of involvement and not levels of success in those occupations or at those educational levels. It is proposed in the manual that in interpreting the scores with junior and senior high school students the total score is to be considered a measure of "engineering and scientific ability at the sub-professional level." This is an interesting proposal in light of the data showing that students in college preparatory programs had the highest total score mean of the academic specialization groups. It is also proposed that for high school students the total score can be used in conjunction with the listed mean percentiles for various occupational and educational groups through the equating procedure mentioned above. Again,

Dailey Vocational Tests

the reader is reminded that these groups were established on the basis of membership, not success. SUMMARY. This test "series" presents an interesting approach in a very complex area. It is not a test battery; the tests in the series not being normed and proposed for administration to the same groups. On the other hand it is more than a set of tests. That there is need for good guidance materials specifically designed for academic and vocational guidance in professional and vocational courses is unquestionable. The present status of this series with nearly 20 years of development behind it and the involvement of some of the most knowledgeable and experienced people in this field argues for the complexity of this task. The care with which this series of tests has been developed and the data that is provided indicate that they may well have the potential of being a useful tool for academic guidance and selection for trade and technical schools. In its present state of development, however, it is proposed that the series would most appropriately be used in experimental studies designed to evaluate predictive validity.

J Ed Meas 3:65–70 sp '66. Betty W. Ellis. * The internal consistency *r*'s for the seven subtests....are too low to permit the use of separate subtest scores with individuals, although it is suggested in the Manual that they may be used appropriately with individuals "who have considerable knowledge of the subject." * Test-retest stability coefficients would be desirable, in view of the fact that scores appear to change as individuals grow older. * *The Dailey Vocational Tests* series represents an approach to the measurement of vocational potential as a combination of scholastic ability, technical knowledge, and aptitude. The intended purposes have merit. Students should demonstrate appropriate aptitude and interest in a field before entering an educational program designed to develop occupational competencies; and it would be helpful if they could be identified prior to entry. Whether it is feasible or desirable at junior high level to separate students into two groups to attend two kinds of schools is debatable. It has been pointed out in this review that little is known about the stability of these tests over time nor their usefulness in prediction. Present data indicate that the tests should be used only with special groups, with considerable caution, and with full understanding of the limitations involved. *

Dailey Vocational Tests

[977]

★**Flanagan Industrial Tests.** Business and industry; 1960–65; FIT; adaptation for business use of the *Flanagan Aptitude Classification Tests;* 2 series; $3.15 per 25 tests; $1.50 per scoring stencil; 80¢ per manual; $4 per specimen set; postage extra; John C. Flanagan; Science Research Associates, Inc. *
a) FORM A SERIES. 1960–65; job applicants and employees; 18 tests; 1 form (4 pages); manual ('65, 23 pages); no data on validity for industrial selection and placement; norms for grade 12 and college entrants only; 165(218) minutes.
  1) *Arithmetic.* Form A ('60); 5(7) minutes.
  2) *Assembly.* Form A ('60); 5(8) minutes.
  3) *Components.* Form A ('60); 5(7) minutes.
  4) *Coordination.* Form A ('60); 5(7) minutes.
  5) *Electronics.* Form A ('60); 15(17) minutes.
  6) *Expression.* Form A ('60); 5(8) minutes.
  7) *Ingenuity.* Form A ('60); 15(18) minutes.
  8) *Inspection.* Form A ('60); 5(9) minutes.
  9) *Judgment and Comprehension.* Form A ('62); 15(17) minutes.
  10) *Mathematics and Reasoning.* Form A ('60); 15(18) minutes.
  11) *Mechanics.* Form A ('60); 15(18) minutes.
  12) *Memory.* Form A ('63); 10(19) minutes.
  13) *Patterns.* Form A ('60); 5(7) minutes.
  14) *Planning.* Form A ('62); 15(18) minutes.
  15) *Precision.* Form A ('60); 5(8) minutes.
  16) *Scales.* Form A ('60); 5(7) minutes.
  17) *Tables.* Form A ('60); 5(8) minutes.
  18) *Vocabulary.* Form A ('60); 15(17) minutes.
b) FORM AA SERIES. Entry level job applicants; 1960–63; this revision of the Form A series involves changes in time limits and directions and the rewording, rearrangement, and omission of items to make the tests more suitable for entry level job applicants; 1 form (4 pages); no manual; no data on reliability and validity; 70(105) minutes.
  1) *Assembly.* Form AA ('60, rearrangement of same 20 items of Form A); 10(15) minutes.
  2) *Components.* Form AA ('60, identical with Form A); 10(14) minutes.
  3) *Electronics.* Form AA ('60); 15(17) minutes.
  4) *Ingenuity.* Form AA ('60); 15(18) minutes.
  5) *Inspection.* Form AA ('60); 5(10) minutes.
  6) *Memory.* Form AA ('63); 10(19) minutes.
  7) *Scales.* Form AA ('60); 5(10) minutes.

REFERENCE

1. PENFIELD, ROBERT VERDON. *The Psychological Characteristics of Effective First-Line Managers.* Doctor's thesis, Cornell University (Ithaca, N.Y.), 1966. (DA 27:1610B)

C. J. ADCOCK, *Retired Professor of Psychology, Victoria University of Wellington, Wellington, New Zealand.*

This is a shorter form of the FACT battery which required about 630 minutes to administer in full. The present form has 18 tests with a total administration time estimated at 218 minutes. Coding and Alertness have been dropped and Electronics added. The coding test was the basis of the memory test in FACT and confounded the results of the latter, but the new memory test is self-contained. Alertness has probably been eliminated because of its low reliability and Electronics added because of the increasing importance of this area. Inspection and Planning use new kinds of items and are not comparable with the FACT form.

The choice of tests is based on aptitudes hypothesised from studies of critical behaviours involved in jobs. This can lead to test overlap. Twelve intercorrelations exceed .200 and in some cases are so high as to raise doubts about the usefulness of the separate measures. For example, FIT Vocabulary correlates .619 with FIT Judgment and Comprehension and only .751 with the corresponding FACT test which doubtless has a higher reliability. One can conclude that the correlations between these two tests are dangerously near the limits of their reliabilities. In the case of Precision and Coordination, the correlations between forms are .552 and .506, respectively, while the intercorrelation between the two scales is .510. The implication of this is underlined when we note that FIT Coordination correlates .505 with FACT Precision, only .001 less than its correlation with FACT Coordination. Even more striking is the finding that FIT Judgment and Comprehension correlates only .525 with the FACT counterpart but .672 with FACT Vocabulary.

Considerations such as these suggest that users of the FIT should regard it as a reservoir from which to select rather than as a battery to be used as a whole. Indeed, this is indicated by the manual but without any specific advice. For this the user must go to the Counsellor's Manual for the FACT.

Five of the tests have just been revised. The memory test has been reduced in size and presumably the 10 items eliminated from the original 50 are the least reliable. The electronics test has been completely revamped, with more stress on theoretical concepts and an updating of content (e.g., transistors substituted for valves in a circuit diagram). The revised ingenuity test has the directions considerably simplified, some examples reworded, the order of presentation changed, and half a dozen completely new items. Scales has its items reduced from 60 to 32 and the instructions amplified. For Inspections a similar change is made, items being reduced from 36 to 30. For Components a new direction page has been supplied. This should eliminate some undesirable sources of error.

No reliability coefficients are given, but the correlations between the new FIT and the old FACT scales, where applicable (three tests have no equivalent), give some indication. Users not familiar with the FACT data will be rather frustrated by this approach, however. The same data have to serve also as a guide to validity. The manual provides tables for the conversion of FIT scores into corresponding FACT scores so that the research done with regard to the significance of the latter scores can be used while FIT data are being accumulated. Intending users will therefore need to consult reviews of the earlier test before deciding whether the new one will meet their requirements. In general, however, the new form seems to be an improvement for many purposes, since it provides comparable data with a tremendous time economy and without any undue sacrifice of reliability or validity. For vocational selection it will probably find increasing use. For vocational guidance the position is somewhat different, since one may require a comprehensive coverage of aptitudes, which is not exactly what the tests have aimed at. This may throw one back on using the full battery, but it should be noted that the tests can be divided into two broad categories: those which are largely measuring natural abilities and those which are quite obviously measuring special acquired skills. In the latter group one finds the tests Mechanics, Electronics, Mathematics and Reasoning, Planning, and Scales. These are all very much dependent upon a particular form of sophistication and would be wasted in a guidance situation where it was already known that the client lacked such sophistication.

The former group includes measures of a number of well-known aptitudes, such as spatial (Patterns and Assembly), number (Arithmetic), flexibility of perceptual closure (Components), perceptual speed (Tables), memory, and two related forms of manual dexterity (Precision and Coordination). To this group could be added Vocabulary as a measure of verbal intelligence and, related to this, Expression, which measures knowledge of grammatical usage and sentence structure, and Judgment and Comprehension, which measures the capacity to understand printed information. Ingenuity probably taps an aspect of creativity, but despite indications of good reliability, this test seems to have little relation to college performance, possibly because the test items are rather practical in nature, possibly because measures of ingenuity depend so much on familiarity with the data involved and this may vary very much from person to person. One wonders, too, how much the method of answering by selection among phrases indicated by first and last letters complicates the factorial content of the measure.

The inclusion of the perceptual flexibility test (Components) seems of doubtful value. Wand [1] found no evidence for a general flexibility factor, and Adcock and Martin [2] found that the Gottschaldt-type tests loaded on the speed-of-closure factor. Carroll (5:608) queried the usefulness of this test in the FACT battery, and the validation data for FIT show uniformly negligible correlations with college grades. Probably this test has rather restricted application and can frequently be dispensed with.

One would expect Inspection to involve perceptual speed but the FACT form had only a very small correlation with the DAT test of this ability. In the light of his own studies, the present reviewer suspects that the usual measures of perceptual speed involve very familiar symbols whose recognition makes rather different demands from those made by relatively unfamiliar forms. If this is so, the predictive value of such a test as the present one could be very doubtful, since the actual inspection situation would involve very well learned material. A further complication would arise from the difference between concrete objects as compared with small diagrams. Careful validation studies seem necessary here.

The two measures of spatial ability appear to relate to the two usual forms of this aptitude but in both cases appear to be considerably contaminated by other factors. Patterns demands considerable care, while Assembly involves continual checking of letter references which might call upon some aspect of perceptual span or speed. Information as to the factorial content of tests such as these could add appreciably to their general usefulness.

In conclusion, one may welcome this test as a very useful addition to the tools available for vocational selection but regret that a more determined attempt has not been made to isolate basic nonoverlapping aptitudes which could provide a comprehensive basis for vocational guidance. When more direct validity data have been collected, the test should become very useful and a better knowledge of its factorial

1 WAND, BARBARA. *Flexibility in Intellectual Performance.* Unpublished doctor's thesis, University of Toronto (Toronto, Canada), 1958. Pp. vii, 141. *
2 ADCOCK, C. J., AND MARTIN, W. A. "Flexibility and Creativity." *J General Psychol* 85(1):71–6 Jl '71. *

content may permit broader applications. In the meantime, sophisticated users will find much of value in it.

ROBERT C. DROEGE, *Research Psychologist, Manpower Administration, United States Department of Labor, Washington, D.C.*

The *Flanagan Industrial Tests* are a set of 18 short aptitude tests designed for use in personnel selection and placement programs for a wide variety of jobs. Twelve of the tests have verbal or arithmetic item content, making them unsuitable for use with individuals who have limited education. The directions for administration for all of the tests assume that the examinee has at least some literacy and test-taking skills. Modification of the recommended procedure will be required if the tests are to be administered to educationally disadvantaged applicants. Ordinarily, not all of the 18 tests would be administered to an individual or a group. Rather, those tests appropriate for the job or jobs being considered would be selected for administration. The tests are printed in separate booklets to allow that flexibility in the testing program which the author encourages.

The FIT is an adaptation of the longer *Flanagan Aptitude Classification Tests.* Both batteries provide measures of job elements identified from job analysis studies as important requirements common to a number of jobs. This job-element approach to test development has much to recommend it. A systematic study of jobs is a solid basis for the construction of tests to measure the job elements involved. The FIT test battery, constructed on this basis, provides a wide range of tests from which preliminary selections can be made for specific jobs. But these must be regarded as only tentative selections subject to occupational validation. Unfortunately, the manual does not emphasize this need for the empirical validation that is so essential to establish the approach recommended: "The personnel administrator can select the specific set of job elements required in each position and use the best combination of tests to select personnel for each job." At this stage of development of FIT, there is no evidence to support such a recommendation. The only validity data provided in the manual are correlations with college freshmen grades. These correlations may be of interest to some users of the battery, but they are not much help to the company personnel man, for whose

Flanagan Industrial Tests

use the tests were designed. There is a need for validation studies, but they should be done on occupational samples. Only through such studies can the job-element approach, which the reviewer regards as promising, be validated.

Only indirect evidence of reliability is available. Correlations were obtained between corresponding tests in the FIT and FACT batteries administered to several high school and college groups. These correlations were all below .80 and eight of them were only in the .50's. The correlations for three of the tests (Inspection, Memory, and Planning) were less than .50, but for these tests the item content of the FIT tests was somewhat different from that of their FACT counterparts. The correlations between the FIT and FACT batteries are disappointingly low, even allowing for the fact that the difficulty levels of some of the tests are somewhat different. Other attempts to provide indirect evidence of reliability are included in the manual, but they are not persuasive. One of these consists of Spearman-Brown and Kuder-Richardson estimates, which the author concedes are inappropriate for speeded tests. It seems clear from the data presented that some of the tests have questionable reliability. Certainly there is a need for more adequate studies.

The manual includes a table of intercorrelations of the tests for a group of college freshman men. The intercorrelations tend to be quite low, indicating that, to the extent that the low correlations are not simply a reflection of low reliability, the tests are measuring different abilities.

It takes a careful reading of the manual to realize that the table of FIT percentile norms for high school seniors is based on students tested on the FACT battery. The tests of FIT were "equated" to the corresponding tests of FACT to provide these preliminary norms. Such "equating" is a questionable procedure because of the low correlations between many of the FIT tests and their FACT counterparts.

There is a problem with the scoring instructions for the arithmetic and inspection tests. According to the manual, a combination of correct answers and errors is used to derive a "combined performance score" for these tests, but the instructions on the scoring keys for how to derive these scores do not correspond to those in the manual. On the arithmetic key no mention is made of obtaining an error count; on the Inspection key the instructions on how

to count errors differ from those in the manual.

The review set contained modified forms (designated as Form AA) of seven of the tests. The modifications—consisting of extended time limits, expanded directions, and in some cases different item content—were intended to make the tests more suitable for applicants for entry jobs. No mention is made of these forms in the manual, but in promotional literature they are listed as available alternatives to the Form A series. They should not be used operationally without appropriate conversion tables. (A representative of the publisher has indicated to the reviewer that such tables are available and are being sent to those ordering the new forms.)

Because FIT is relatively new, data on its reliability, validity, and standardization are not extensive. However, additional research is being done by the publisher to obtain normative and validity data for entry-level jobs. This is encouraging, because increasingly our society is demanding proof of adequacy in job selection procedures to ensure that minority groups are not discriminated against unfairly. The job-element approach, which forms the basis for the *Flanagan Industrial Tests,* is promising, but empirical verification is required. Hopefully, research will be done that will show the extent to which the author's recommended application of task analysis and critical incident techniques can be used to identify FIT tests that do predict success on the job.

J Ed Meas 3:191–6 su '66. John L. Horn. * an offspring of FACT * FIT probably is a worthy addition to the world's population of tests * Certainly there are some interesting and worthwhile features about its development. * The general approach characterizing this work derives more remotely from Truman Kelley's attempts in the 1920's and 1930's to define and classify abilities according to occupations wherein they are particularly needed. In Professor Flanagan's refinements, this is called the *job-element* approach. A job element is defined in terms of "critical behaviors" involved in a number of jobs or occupations. * Flanagan has not used factor analytic procedures (or the like) in his test construction, he has been much more careful than most test constructors to ensure that his 18 tests represent truly independent attributes. Moreover—and this is indeed refreshing—the Manual provides data

Flanagan Industrial Tests

bearing pointedly on this question: the multiple correlation of each test with the 17 other tests in the battery. These range from .30 to .67 and all are low enough (relative to the assumed reliabilities—see below) to suggest that each test is reliably measuring something that is not measured by the other tests. Would that more test manuals contained this kind of information! But in some important respects the promise of the FIT battery is only that—a promise. The evidence which could indicate its true validity simply has not been gathered. With respect to this lack of evidence, there are several things which the wary potential user should consider. The Manual tells us that the FIT tests "like the FACT series....are based on the identified job elements....," but the Manual is not at all clear in indicating the source research in which these job elements were identified. It appears that this research is essentially that upon which the FACT was based and that this was mainly the research conducted under Flanagan's direction during WW II. This being the impression, one wonders if the job-elements thus far identified are important elements of today's occupations. In a sense, of course, this argument is specious, for the tests refer to fairly general abilities, not specific elements of jobs that would have changed since WW II. In this respect the tests assess attributes like the primary mental abilities isolated by means of factor analyses; indeed, it is evident that the FACT and FIT batteries contain measures of many of the ability factors so far identified * The FIT Manual makes no reference to this line of research, however. But the principal virtue of the job-element approach would seem to be that it promises to identify features of job performance not identified by other means and, in particular, features of today's jobs as they are performed today. One might expect, for example, that this approach would lead to the identification of interesting new abilities related to performance in computer programming, a very important occupation in today's world but one which has come into being only in the last 15 or 20 years (i.e., since WW II). Yet there is no reference in the FIT Manual to research showing which—if any—elements of such jobs have been identified. In fact, the FIT Manual does not clearly direct the reader to the sections of the FACT Manuals wherein the relationships between FACT scores and job performances are indicated * A closely related point has to

do with the norms and practical validities (i.e., relevancies) available for use with FIT. These are of two kinds: (1) those derived by administering the FIT tests to persons in different academic programs and determining percentile norms and relationships between test scores and academic performance in these groupings, and (2) those obtained by "equating" scores on a given FIT test with scores on a comparable FACT test and using this as a basis for treating the information available on the FACT as applicable to the FIT. In either case, as concerns the author's intent to provide a battery for use with adults in personnel selection programs, the information presently available leaves much to be desired. Percentile norms are provided on a sample of 3,359 twelfth-grade students and a sample of 701 entering freshmen at a select men's university. Neither of these samples would appear to be representative of adults encountered "....in personnel selection programs for a wide variety of jobs." * Correlations and step-wise multiple correlations and regression equations are given for fall and spring grades in four of the five university programs. The samples in a few of these analyses are small (e.g., N = 69). Several of the reported regression coefficients are very likely unstable and somewhat misleading. Nevertheless, the results, overall, indicate that some of the tests have relevance for predictions of academic performance. But, of course, it doesn't follow from these results that the tests have relevance for predictions of occupational success, even in fields seemingly related to the college programs, much less in a "variety of jobs." * the main difference between FIT and FACT is that the difficulty levels for the former have been increased. The correlations between corresponding FIT and FACT tests are in some cases very low. For example, FIT Inspection correlates only .28 with FACT Inspection. This could result because of a difference in difficulty level for the two tests. But even so, it makes use of the results from equating FIT and FACT scores a dubious procedure. Also, some FIT tests correlate rather high with non-corresponding FACT tests or with other FIT tests —i.e., high relative to the correlation between corresponding FIT and FACT tests. For example, although FIT Planning correlates .38 with FACT Planning, it correlates .43 with FACT Ingenuity. Explanation of this kind of outcome in terms of differences in difficulty levels is not at all compelling. To use FACT norms as applicable to a FIT test in a case like this would seem to be a very dubious procedure indeed. For at least three FIT tests—Inspection, Memory and Planning—the above-mentioned problems are very real. * in these cases, particularly, and with respect to other tests to a lesser degree, the user should be cautious in attempting to interpret FIT tests in terms of practical validities, etc., found for FACT tests. If tests are intended for use with "....adults in personnel selection programs for a wide variety of jobs" it would seem desirable to have data indicating the relationships between test performances and such variables as age, speediness and education. * to use tests in personnel selection for a wide variety of jobs, one should nevertheless know about these matters, for it is certain that speediness is not essential to performance in some jobs where an ability like that measured in a speeded test would seem to be involved and, likewise, there are situations where one would want to make an adjustment to remove age differences found on the test but not relevant for predicting job success. Yet the Manual provides no information of the kind here specified. * the FIT reliabilities are surely non-zero, almost certainly all above .3, some perhaps not appreciably lower than for corresponding FACT tests, and perhaps most in a range of from about .50 to .85. It would seem, therefore, that the reliabilities are adequate for many uses for which the test is intended (viz., institutional decisions). One should, of course, be cautious about using the test for purposes for which it was not intended—viz., for individual decisions. There are a few other rather minor points which, however, may be worth mentioning. For example, this reviewer objects to a description of a test as "self-administering" when, in fact, administration requires that one adhere closely to time limits set for various subtests, as in the FIT battery. * The test certainly is not self-administering in the sense that a secretary can hand it to a job applicant with instructions to take it into the next room and return with it in X minutes. This....would seem to be the implicit meaning of the term self-administering. The manual provides suggestions for combining tests, or using tests singly, to give estimates of "general ability," but no good rationale for these procedures is given. It so happens that the suggested composite—"Judgment and Comprehension, Mathematics and Reasoning, and

Vocabulary"—is similar to the crystallized dimension defined in recent research * This is no doubt a good predictor of academic performance, as is pointed out in the Manual, but it is questionable whether it is the best general ability measure to use in personnel selection with adults having widely different academic backgrounds. The other tests said to have "....broad usefulness in screening for general intellectual ability...."—viz., "Ingenuity, Expression and Scales"—have not been identified as representative (on their own) of "general ability" in any research of which this reviewer is aware. Rather such tests represent abilities at a lower order than "general ability" in hierarchical organizations of abilities (e.g. Vernon, 1950) or they represent primary (not general) abilities in single-level theories * The test author may mean that these three tests in combination with others (not specified) may define a general ability dimension, but no research is cited to support this suggestion. In fact, assuming that the term "general ability" is not completely equivocal, the Manual provides no evidence to support a contention that the three tests, either singly or in combination, measure a distinct "general ability." While some of the statements made here are critical, they should not be interpreted to mean that the FIT tests are of low quality or that the Manual grossly misleads. In fact, the tests seem to be exceedingly well put together, the claims for the FIT are not generally over-stated and much information desired in a Manual is found in this one. Several of the cautions noted above are at least adumbrated in the Manual, for example. Probably the most damning thing that can be said about the test is that not enough data have been accumulated to show that it is highly useful in the kinds of situations for which it is intended. This should give caution to potential users who would jump from face validity or relevancy in other situations to a belief in the test's relevancy for use in the potential user's situation, but it should not discourage use of the test. As is pointed out in the manual, "For personnel selection purposes each company needs to determine its own local standards." The test seems to be well-suited for research aimed in this direction.

[978]

★**Fundamental Achievement Series.** Semiliterate job applicants and employees; 1968-69, c1965-69; FAS; research edition; 3 scores: numerical, verbal, total; 2 tests; 2 forms; manual ('68, 16 pages); supplement ('69, 4 pages); tape (3¾ ips, 5 inch reel) administered; data on reliability for Form A only; no data on validity; distribution of Form A restricted to personnel departments; $21 per 25 sets of each test, tapes, scoring keys, and manual; $3.25 per 25 tests; 50¢ per set of scoring keys; 40¢ per manual; $7.50 per tape; $1 per specimen set (without tape); postage extra; George K. Bennett and Jerome E. Doppelt; Psychological Corporation. *

a) NUMERICAL. Forms A ('66, 7 pages), B ('69, 7 pages); (30) minutes.

b) VERBAL. Forms A ('66, 8 pages), B ('69, 8 pages); (30) minutes.

NORMAN FREDERIKSEN, *Director, Division of Psychological Studies, Educational Testing Service, Princeton, New Jersey.*

The *Fundamental Achievement Series,* consisting of a Verbal test and a Numerical test, is intended for use with disadvantaged individuals for employment or training programs. They are said to cover "a range of ability from basic literacy to somewhat above the eighth-grade level." Each test requires about 30 minutes of testing time. Administration and timing are accomplished in a standardized manner merely by playing a tape. Answers are recorded in the test booklet. Scoring is done by hand; three scores are reported: V, N, and V + N.

The easiest items in the Verbal test require the examinee to demonstrate elementary reading ability. The voice on the tape asks him to find the sign that "means the same as No Parking" (Answer: Parking Prohibited), to find the picture of the bus that would take him to "Cliff St.," to find in an apartment house listing the apartment number of Mr. Joseph A. Bailey and then write it down, and to find in a telephone book listing the telephone number of Wm. Corwin and write it down. He is also asked by the voice on the tape to answer questions based on a menu, such as, "What must you pay for a dinner of onion soup, a roast chicken platter and coffee?" Some of these items may be tricky because the price of the platter includes soup and coffee or tea. Although this is a verbal test, addition is required for several items. The examinee is required next to copy three sentences in longhand. There are also 24 printed spelling items (right-wrong), 18 four-choice picture vocabulary items, and 24 conventional four-choice synonyms items. Ten items are based on three aurally-presented announcements of events that involve names, dates, times, and places. The tape-recorded instructions forbid taking notes, but close proctoring would be required to prevent it.

The Numerical test also begins at the level of basic literacy. The first item requires finding and marking raffle ticket number "fourteen-twenty"; other items have to do with telling time, counting, writing numbers, adding the values of pictured coins, and identifying values involving percent signs, dollar signs, Roman numerals, fractions, and percentages. An item showing a picture of a hex-head machine screw and a ruler might cause some difficulty for a person with some machine shop experience; the question has to do with the length of the screw, and the keyed answer assumes that the screw head is included in its length. Other items require the examinee to add sales slips, fill in the dollar amount on checks, use a calendar, interpret a bar graph, look up values in tables of postal rates and mileages, and identify on a diagram the radius of a circle. Finally, there are 20 conventional computation items and 10 conventional arithmetic "word" problems. The computation items range from addition of two-digit numbers to division of fractions, and the word problems involve such concepts as negative values (below-zero temperatures), percentages, area of a rectangle, and addition of pounds and ounces.

As the manual points out, there are many easy questions, both in the Verbal and in the Numerical tests. The reason is to permit even poorly informed candidates an opportunity to get many items right. If most examinees do indeed get most easy items right, it follows that much of the variance in test scores is attributable to the harder items. One might judge that the hard items for the Verbal test are those based on memory of announcements, the spelling items, and the synonym items. If this is true, the functioning part of the test is not much different from the conventional paper-and-pencil test of verbal ability (except for the 10 items based on memory of announcements). Variance on the Numerical test, similarly, may be due mainly to the harder items, which appear to be the 30 more conventional arithmetic items at the end. FAS may not really be very different from conventional tests in the extent to which it reflects school achievement in verbal and quantitative areas.

The results of an item analysis would make the answer to this question less speculative. Unfortunately, no item analysis information is presented. With the variety of unusual item types that have been put together in FAS, one would think that item data would be essential in selecting items for tests "based on experiences thought to be familiar to both advantaged and disadvantaged persons." If such an analysis was performed, it is not reported.

Another kind of relevant information is available: correlations with a number of well-known mental ability tests. Correlations of V and N with the *Wonderlic Personnel Test,* for example, are .63 and .73, respectively, for 89 white job applicants in the South. The correlation of V with the DAT Verbal Reasoning score is .56 and that of N with DAT Numerical Ability is .79 for 55 male white 8th grade students in the South; the corresponding correlations are .44 and .40 for 71 male Negro 8th graders in the same school system. The V score correlates .94 with the *Gates-MacGinitie Reading Tests* for 43 truckdriver trainees. N's are small for most of the correlations reported, but the general impression is that the FAS behaves about like most conventional aptitude tests of verbal and arithmetical abilities.

Percentile norms are given for 6th, 8th, 10th, and 12th grade white and Negro students from a "southern city school system" and for 6th, 8th, and 10th grade white and Negro students from a "northern city school system." There are also norms for 111 applicants and 105 employees at a southern food processing plant. For the latter two groups, the mean scores are 78 and 76 for the 100-item Verbal test—better than the 6th grade students but, generally speaking, not as good as the 8th graders.

Reliability coefficients for each norm group are also presented, but for some reason they are (in most instances) based on subsamples of only 50 cases. Reliabilities are highest for 6th graders (.92 and .90 for V and N, respectively); the lowest is .75 for the Verbal test for white 12th graders. It is interesting that the standard error of measurement is consistently smaller for white than for Negro students. Reliabilities are in the .90's for the southern food plant applicants. Test-retest reliabilities reported are based on very small N's and are generally .90 or higher.

There are two forms of FAS. Form A was published in 1968 and was designated as a Research Edition because of the absence of validity data. The test is nevertheless offered for sale. Users of the test are invited to participate in validity studies. A manual supplement (published in 1969) announces that "Form B is available to governmental and social agencies, business and industrial firms, and to educators." It is not designated as a research edition, although it is very similar to Form A in content and format, and, like Form A, it has no validity data.

The manual supplement presents data showing that Forms A and B are similar with respect to means and standard deviations for three groups: 27 trainees in an antipoverty program, 55 and 67 applicants to schools of practical nursing, and 32 Puerto Rican trainees in an antipoverty program. Additional norms tables are presented for various groups of trainee and employed groups, and they are labeled as appropriate for both Form A and Form B, although the correlation between the two forms is not reported and the evidence that the score distributions are similar is pretty skimpy.

Test users have come to expect from the Psychological Corporation the very highest standards not only in the development of tests but also in providing information about the psychometric properties of the test. The FAS manual is well below their usual standards in this regard. The tests themselves, including the tape-recorded instructions as well as the test items, appear to be competently prepared. If one decides to use FAS for testing applicants from disadvantaged backgrounds, he will have to make the choice in the absence of information he would normally expect the Psychological Corporation to provide—particularly information about predictive validities of the tests.

J Ed Meas 7(2):134-6 su '70. Lewis R. Aiken, Jr. * the FAS should prove motivating to examinees of low literacy * Clearly, performance on the FAS depends greatly on reading ability, an observation substantiated by a correlation of .94 between FAS Verbal and scores on the Gates-MacGinitie Reading Test, obtained on a group of 43 truckdriver trainees. * nowhere is there a reliability coefficient for Form B or a Form A–Form B equivalence coefficient of any sort. It would seem that such important information could have been obtained easily enough and included in the supplement. Very little validity information is reported in the 1968 manual, but this is consistent with the authors' suggestion that local prediction studies be conducted with this "research edition" of the test. * The authors cite some evidence that Negro groups perform over a wider range on the FAS than on other tests, and consequently it may be a more useful measure of their "fundamental achievement." But this remains to be seen, and what is needed now are studies comparing the predictive validities of the FAS and its competitors, both traditional and modern, for various groups and criteria. * a well designed test of verbal and numerical abilities at the eighth grade level and below, with more "practical" content and perhaps having more "floor" than conventional tests of general intelligence or scholastic ability, but certainly quite similar to them in factor composition. Because of its content, however, the FAS may be more motivating to certain groups of examinees than scholastically oriented tests. The internal consistency and test-retest reliabilities of Form A of the test are satisfactory, but no data concerning its predictive validity are given. The FAS, like the Adult Basic Learning Examination, is a promising tool for educational and vocational placement of the disadvantaged, but at present it must be regarded as only a research instrument.

[979]

*Individual Placement Series. Adults (*a–g*), high school and adults (*h*); 1957–66; 8 tests; series manual ('66, 107 pages); profile B ['66, 1 page] for *a–g*; record card ['66, 2 pages]; vari-o-graph ['66, 1 page]; tabulation sheets ['66, 1 page] for 0–3 intervals; separate answer sheets must be used (except with *c, e,* and *f*); $4 per 100 answer sheets; $4 per 100 profiles; $5 per 100 record cards; $4 per 100 vari-o-graphs; $4 per 100 tabulation sheets; $2.50 per series manual; $20 per complete specimen set ($30 with 33⅓ rpm record); cash orders postpaid; J. H. Norman; Personnel Research Associates, Inc. *

a) ACADEMIC ALERTNESS "AA." 1957–66; 7 scores: general knowledge, arithmetic, vocabulary, reasoning ability, logical sequence, accuracy, total; Forms A, B, ('57, 6 pages); $25 per 20 tests; 50¢ per key; $1.95 per specimen set (without manual); 20(25) minutes.

b) PERFORMANCE ALERTNESS "PA" (WITH PICTURES). 1961–66; Form C ('61, 4 pages); $12 per 20 tests; 50¢ per scoring stencil; $1.25 per specimen set (without manual); 12(17) minutes.

c) READING ADEQUACY "READ" TEST. 1961–66; 3 scores: reading rate, comprehension, corrected reading rate; Form C ('61, 4 pages); $3.70 per 20 tests; 50¢ per key; 70¢ per specimen set (without manual); [13–20] minutes.

d) SURVEY OF CLERICAL SKILLS (SOCS). 1959–66; 5 scores: spelling, office math, office terms, filing, grammar; Form C ('59, 8 pages); $25 per 20 tests; 50¢ per scoring stencil; $1.95 per specimen set (without manual); 40(45) minutes.

e) TYPING TEST. 1959–66; Forms C, D, ('59, 2 pages); $8 per 20 tests; 50¢ per key; $1 per specimen set (without manual); 5(15) minutes.

f) SHORTHAND TEST. 1960–66; Forms A, B, ('60, 2 pages); also available on 33⅓ rpm record and 7½ ips tape recording; $8 per 20 tests; $10 per record or tape containing both forms; $3 per specimen set without

record or tape; $13 per specimen set with record or tape; (20–25) minutes.

g) SURVEY OF PERSONAL ATTITUDE "SPA" (WITH PICTURES). 1960–66; 3 scores: social attitude, personal frankness, aggressiveness; Form A ('60, 14 pages); $30 per 20 tests; $1 per scoring stencil; $2.65 per specimen set (without manual); [20–25] minutes.

h) OCCUPATIONAL INTEREST SURVEY "OIS" (WITH PICTURES). High school and adults; 1959–66; 9 scores: scientific, social service, literary, agricultural, business, mechanical, musical, clerical, artistic; Form A ('59, 14 pages); profile C ['66, 1 page]; $28 per 20 tests; $4 per 100 profiles; $1.55 per specimen set (without manual); (15–20) minutes.

[980]

★Job Attitude Analysis. Production and clerical workers; 1961–65; JAA; an inventory for employment interviewing and vocational counseling; 1 form ('65, 3 pages); manual ('65, 4 pages); job key ('65, 1 page) prepared locally; no data on reliability; no norms; $2.50 per 25 tests; 5¢ per job key; 50¢ per specimen set; postage extra; [20] minutes; P. L. Mellenbruch; the Author. *

REFERENCE

1. MELLENBRUCH, P. L. "Recognizing Worker Attitudes in Job Assignments." *Personnel J* 43:607–9 D '64. * (*PA* 39:8856)

[981]

★Personal History Index. Job applicants; 1963–67; PHI; for research use only; 8 scores: school achievement, higher educational achievement, drive, leadership and group participation, financial responsibility, early family responsibility, parental family adjustment, stability; 1 form ('65, 12 pages); manual ('65, 33 pages); supplementary age group norms ['67, 5 pages]; $8 per 20 tests, postage extra; $2 per specimen set, postpaid; (10–20) minutes; Melany E. Baehr, Robert K. Burns, and Robert N. McMurry; Industrial Relations Center, University of Chicago. *

REFERENCES

1. BAEHR, MELANY E., AND WILLIAMS, GLENN B. "Underlying Dimensions of Personal Background Data and Their Relationship to Occupational Classification." *J Appl Psychol* 51:481–90 D '67. * (*PA* 42:3010)
2. BAEHR, MELANY E., AND WILLIAMS, GLENN B. "Prediction of Sales Success From Factorially Determined Dimensions of Personal Background Data." *J Appl Psychol* 52:98–103 Ap '68. * (*PA* 42:8085)
3. BAEHR, MELANY E.; FURCON, JOHN E.; AND FROEMEL, ERNEST C. *Psychological Assessment of Patrolman Qualifications in Relation to Field Performance.* Washington, D.C.: United States Government Printing Office, 1969. Pp. vii, 246. *
4. HUBER, NORMAN ANDREW. *Superior-Subordinate Similarity, Performance Evaluation, and Job Satisfaction.* Doctor's thesis, Wayne State University (Detroit, Mich.), 1970. (*DAI* 31:4380B)
5. MARKS, LEONARD GEORGE, JR. *An Exploratory Study of Behavioral Characteristics of Certain Selected Municipal Firefighters Utilizing the Personal History Index.* Doctor's thesis, University of Southern California (Los Angeles, Calif.), 1970. (*DAI* 31:3625A)

JOHN K. HEMPHILL, *Laboratory Director, Far West Laboratory for Educational Research and Development, Berkeley, California.*

The PHI is an 87-item employment information questionnaire. It is organized into six sections: Work Experience, Present Family Information, Parental Family Information, Educational Experience, Activities and Interests, and Health. The number of items per section ranges from 5 (for Health) to 33 (for Work

Experience). The content of the items varies from what one might expect to find on the usual employment application form (e.g., "How many years of selling experience have you had?") to that which might be included in a personality quiz (e.g., "At what age did you start dating girls as a fairly regular part of your social life?"). The index contains an unusually large number of questions concerning personal financial responsibilities. Generally the questions are acceptable, since they are within reasonable limits with regard to "invasion into privacy" and are free from obvious racial or ethnic bias. Despite provision of a space on the front page for the applicant to record his sex, the index is rather obviously *for men only.*

An informative technical manual is available for the PHI. It contains instructions for administration, scoring, interpretation; very limited norms; and technical data. The scoring system for the index is based upon the results of a factor analysis of 150 carefully selected items. Eight of the 15 factors identified were retained for the scoring system; these eight factors, or scores, are listed above. Scoring is accomplished by counting specific responses to designated items. Sometimes the same items and the same responses are keyed in the same manner for different scores. The rationale for selecting responses for scoring is not made explicit, but one can infer that it is based upon the loading of the item upon the factors. It should be noted, however, that 27 of the 87 items in the index are not scored for any factor but are retained "to maintain continuity in the overt structure of the Index" and "to allow interested persons or organizations to score the remaining seven factors for continuing research purposes."

Validity evidence for the factor scores is to be presented in the form of analyses of differences between occupational groups. According to the 1965 manual, "These research results will shortly be available in a technical paper." Reliability is reported for each of the 15 factor scores: the K-R 20's ranging from .43 to .76 with median .60 and the K-R 21's ranging from .34 to .72 with median .55. Norms are provided for ten populations: professionals (N = 95), middle and upper executives (N = 74), junior executives (N = 26), district sales managers (N = 39), sales (N = 128), foremen (N = 51), hourly (N = 79), community school directors (N = 45), school administrators (N =

82), and internal revenue auditors (N = 61).

The manual places great emphasis upon the need to interpret scores in terms of profiles and recommends using the index with a Personal History Interview not yet published. In view of the perhaps premature publication of the index, this reviewer would recommend a careful research and validation study of the *Personal History Index* within the setting for which it is to be used, before it becomes a part of a regular employee selection procedure. The items in the index have been selected upon the basis of a huge amount of industrial employment experience and can provide a solid point of departure, but the index as it now exists should not be used without due caution.

[982]

★**RBH Industrial Questionnaire.** Unskilled male applicants; 1953–63; formerly titled *Personnel Questionnaire PM-1A;* reading comprehension, chemical comprehension, and arithmetical reasoning; 1 form ('57, 13 pages); manual ['63, 7 pages]; directions (no date, 2 pages); all norms and statistical data based upon oil refinery employees; separate answer sheets must be used; $4.50 per 10 tests; 9¢ per answer sheet; $1 per key; $1.50 per manual; $2 per specimen set; postage extra; (60) minutes; Richardson, Bellows, Henry & Co., Inc. *

[983]

★**TAV Selection System.** Adults; 1963–68; TAV; vocational selection and counseling; 7 tests; manual ('68, 65 pages); norms consist of means and standard deviations for 8 occupational groups (state traffic officers, municipal patrolmen, female high school teachers, male high school teachers, life insurance claims adjusters, life insurance salesmen, deputy sheriff cadets, and female probation counselors); 1–50 sets of test-answer sheets (IBM 805 scorable) for the battery, $1.10 per set; $4.25 per set of scoring stencils for the battery; $3.25 per manual; $8.10 per specimen set; postage extra; (180) minutes for the battery, (15–20) minutes for any one test; R. R. Morman; TAV Selection System. *

a) TAV ADJECTIVE CHECKLIST. 1963–68; 3 scores: toward people (T), away from people (A), versus people (V); 1 form ('63, 2 pages); 1–50 test-answer sheets, 15¢ each.

b) TAV JUDGMENTS. 1964–68; 3 scores as in *a;* 1 form ('64, 4 pages on 2 sheets); 1–50 sets of the 2 test-answer sheets, 18¢ per set.

c) TAV PERSONAL DATA. 1964–68; 3 scores as in *a;* 1 form ('64, 4 pages on 2 sheets); 1–50 sets of the 2 test-answer sheets, 18¢ per set.

d) TAV PREFERENCES. 1963–68; 3 scores as in *a;* 1 form ('63, 2 pages); 1–50 tests, 15¢ each.

e) TAV PROVERBS AND SAYINGS. 1966–68; 3 scores as in *a;* 1 form ('66, 3 pages on 2 sheets); 1–50 sets of the 2 test-answer sheets, 18¢ per set.

f) TAV SALESMAN REACTIONS. 1967–68; 3 scores as in *a;* 1 form ('67, 4 pages on 2 sheets); 1–50 sets of the 2 test-answer sheets, 18¢ per set.

g) TAV MENTAL AGILITY. 1965–68; 3 scores: follow directions and carefulness, weights and balances, verbal comprehension; 1 form ('65, 3 pages on 2 sheets); 1–50 sets of the 2 test-answer sheets, 18¢ per set.

REFERENCES

1–11. See P:263A.
12. HANKEY, RICHARD O.; MORMAN, R. R.; HEYWOOD, H. C.; AND KENNEDY, P. K. "Evaluating Patrolmen Performance: A New Test Method." *Police Chief* 34:33–5 Ja '67. *

J Counsel Psychol 16(2):181–4 Mr '69. John O. Crites. * Unique in its conception and item content, this battery of checklists and tests derives its name from the theory which was used to develop it. The letters T, A, V stand, respectively, for the three interpersonal orientations of (*a*) moving *toward* people, (*b*) moving *away* from people, and (*c*) moving *versus* (against) people which were delineated by Horney (1945) in her book *Our Inner Conflicts.* To measure these modes of relating to others, several different item types were chosen and assembled into the following tests: Adjective Check List (self-descriptive adjectives, e.g., funloving, talkative, independent); Personal Data ("Parents rewarded you for good grades"); Proverbs and Sayings ("A rolling stone gathers no moss"); Preferences (liking for various kinds of job functions and occupational titles); Sales Reactions (endorsement of "good" salesman behaviors, e.g., "Do not have customers for friends"); Judgments (selection of statements which show "good" judgment, e.g., "Most people are unaware of their potential"); and, Mental Agility (three subtests—Follow Directions and Carefulness, Verbal Comprehension, and Weights and Balance). If some of these names seem unfamiliar, even unusual, it is because the author of TAV has attempted to write subtle personality items which might be less subject to response biases. Apparently, he has achieved some success in this effort, since he observes that "no one has 'seen through' the TAV Selection System's basic theory of construction [Manual, p. 1–5]." He does not report any evidence, however, which would empirically support this contention. If the entire TAV battery is administered, it takes about $3\frac{1}{2}$ hours, which may be a drawback to its use in counseling settings although not necessarily so in personnel selection. The tests differ in their reading difficulty levels, as determined by Flesch formulae, with the Adjective Check List, Preferences, and Weights and Balances the hardest to read and Proverbs and Sayings, Sales Reactions, and Verbal Comprehension the easiest. The average difficulty of the System is at approximately the ninth-grade level. No standardization data on such breakdowns as age, educational level, and sex are reported in the Manual, however, so that the applicability of the TAV to groups other than those used in its validation, which were comprised largely of employed adults, is unknown. Similarly, no test-retest data on reliability are presented (one study is in progress), but most of the Kuder-Richardson (which formula is not specified) estimates of internal consistency are acceptable. The least homogeneous tests were Personal Data, Following Directions and Carefulness, and Verbal Comprehension. The T, A, and V scales within the several tests intercorrelated fairly highly, indicating that they may not have as great divergent validity as would be desired. Data on the convergent validity of the scales across tests were more encouraging, with cognates correlating highest with each other (*r*'s ranged from .28 to .69). Some of the tests were closely related, such as Adjective Check List, Preferences, and Proverbs and Sayings, but generally they appear to be contributing unique variance to the system. It is important that they are relatively independent, since the multiple correlational model has been used in validating them against on-the-job criteria of performance, and, other things being equal, R is higher when the predictors are less highly related. The Manual reports in detail the results of 13 such studies, most of which indicate that, in various combinations, the TAV tests are highly correlated with job success in such different occupations as law enforcement and life insurance sales. The Rs ranged from .53 to .90 for these groups, and test efficiency indices, for example, successes with and without tests, percentage correct predictions, utility cost ratios, etc., provided favorable evidence of TAV's usefulness for selection purposes as compared to base rates of success and failure. It should be noted, however, that most of the samples used in the multiple correlational research were quite small, the Ns varying from 26 to 62 cases. In other words, the expectation would be that, upon replication with other Ss, the Rs would shrink considerably and the betas might change enough that another subset of tests would constitute a better battery of predictors than the original one. The author of TAV is aware of this possibility, as he notes in the Manual, and is currently collecting additional data to check the initial validity findings. * the TAV System....represents an ingenious approach to the measurement of personality which appears to have....promise. The TAV needs further refinement of the individual tests, with the possible elimination of the less internally consistent and valid ones, and additional research on its relationship to more explicitly defined criteria of the variables it was designed to measure. To the counseling psychologist, for example, it would be of considerable interest to know whether the Adjective Check List, which seems to be the most appropriate for working with adolescents and adults, correlates with behavioral and self-ratings (for other nontest indices) of movement toward, away from, and versus people. If it can be shown that it does, it would be a most useful inventory for the appraisal of client personalities.

[984]

★**Vocational Planning Inventory.** Vocational students in grades 8–10, 11–12 and grade 13 entrants; 1968–70, c1954–70; VPI; the battery consists of the *SRA Arithmetic Index, SRA Pictorial Reasoning Test, SRA Verbal Form, Survey of Interpersonal Values, Survey of Personal Values,* Mechanics subtest of the *Flanagan Aptitude Classification Test,* and the following subtests of the *Flanagan Industrial Tests:* Arithmetic, Assembly (*a*), Expression (*a*), Memory (*a*), Scales (*b*), and Tables (*b*); tests cannot be locally scored; the student's copy of his test report presents predicted grades in 9 or 10 areas: agriculture (*a* only), business, construction trades, drafting and design, electronics and electrical trades, home economics and health, mechanics and mechanical maintenance, metal trades, general academic, general vocational; the counselor's copy of an individual test report also presents national percentile rank norms for the component tests: single scores for the 7 (or 8) nonpersonality tests and 12 value scores (practical mindedness, achievement, variety, decisiveness, orderliness, goal orientation, support, conformity, recognition, independence, benevolence, leadership) on the 2 personality tests; 1 form; 2 levels; manual ('68, 37 pages); report forms ('68, 1 page) for counselor, student, and files; student interpretive leaflet ('68, 12 pages); no information is presented on intercorrelations, means, variances, and multiple regression equations; separate answer sheets (MRC) must be used; $2.20 per specimen set of either level, postage extra; Science Research Associates, Inc. *

a) HIGH SCHOOL PREDICTION PROGRAM. Vocational students in grades 8–10; 1968–70, c1954–70; for predicting success in grades 9–12 in areas listed above; regression equations based upon testing and course grades in grade 12 only; 1 form ('68, 33 pages); examiner's manual ('68, 11 pages); interpretive supplement ('70, 9 pages); 130(200) minutes in 3 sessions.

1) *Complete Rental Plan.* Rental and scoring service, $1.20 per student.

2) *Scoring Only Plan.* $10.95 per 25 tests; scoring service, $1.10 per student.

b) POST-HIGH SCHOOL PREDICTION PROGRAM. Vocational students in grades 11–12 and grade 13 entrants; 1968, c1954–68; for predicting success in grade 13 in areas listed above; regression equations based upon testing and course grades in grade 13 only; 1 form ('68, 27 pages); examiner's manual ('68, 10 pages); scoring service and prices same as for *a;* 120(166) minutes in 2 sessions.

[985]

★**WLW Employment Inventory, Short Form.** Adults; 1957–64; 4 scores: general knowledge, emotional stability, humility, friendliness; 1 form ('64, 4 pages); mimeographed manual ('57, 5 pages); no data on reliability; $17 per 100 tests, postpaid; specimen set free to industrial firms; (25–50) minutes; Robert W. Henderson (manual); William, Lynde & Williams. *

CLERICAL

[986]

*★**ACER Short Clerical Test—Form C.** Ages 13 and over; 1953–67; 2 scores: checking, arithmetic; 1 form ('66, 4 pages, essentially the same as Form B copyrighted in 1956 except for conversion to decimal currency); mimeographed interim manual ('67, 22 pages); Aus 65¢ per 10 tests; 50¢ per key; 75¢ per manual; $1.35 per specimen set; postpaid within Australia; 10(15) minutes; Australian Council for Educational Research. *

[987]

★**Business Career Aptitude Test.** Prospective business and clerical employees; 1962–64, c1947–64; BCAT; 1 form; 2 booklets; manual for administration and interpretation ('63, 69 pages); supplement ('64, 9 pages); technical appendix on validity ('64, 13 pages); manual of interpretation ('63, 46 pages plus technical appendix); profile ('63, 4 pages); no data on reliability; administered at testing centers established by the publisher; examination fees, $5 or less per examinee; data analysis, correlational analyses for local validity studies, and local norms may be requested from SRA for an additional fee; (120) minutes; tests prepared and previously published by Science Research Associates, Inc.; program administered by ITT Educational Services, Inc. *

a) PART 1. All subtests identical with tests also published by SRA as part of either a clerical battery for applicants for office positions or a stenographic aptitude test for grades 9 and over; 11 scores: checking, coding, arithmetic (computation, business arithmetic), filing, business vocabulary, language, directions–oral and written, speed of writing, phonetic spelling, word discrimination; 1 form ('62, c1947–62, 24 pages); examiner's script for oral directions subtest ('59, 2 pages); [previously published tests by Jean Maier and Walter L. Deemer, Jr.].

b) PART 2. 3 scores: linguistic, problem solving, total; 1 form ('62, c1952, 4 pages, identical with *Thurstone Test of Mental Alertness*).

For reviews of the originally published versions of the subtests in Part 1, see 6:1046 and 3:372; for reviews of the originally published version of Part 2, see 5:391 and 3:265.

[988]

★**Clerical Skills Series.** Clerical workers and applicants; 1966–69; CSS; 10 tests; manual ('66, 18 pages); profile ('66, 1 page); $3.25 per 20 profiles; 35¢ per key (keys not needed for *e* and *j*); $2 per manual; $6.50 per specimen set of series; cash orders postpaid, 10% extra on charge orders; Martin M. Bruce; Martin M. Bruce, Ph.D., Publishers. *

a) ALPHABETIZING-FILING. 1966; 1 form (4 pages); $5 per 20 tests; $2.50 per specimen set; 8(13) minutes.

b) ARITHMETIC. 1966–69; 1 form ('69, 3 pages, identical with test copyrighted in 1966); $5 per 20 tests; $2.50 per specimen set; 8(13) minutes.

c) CLERICAL SPEED AND ACCURACY. 1966; 1 form (4 pages); $5 per 20 tests; $2.50 per specimen set; 3(8) minutes.

d) CODING. 1966; 1 form (2 pages); $4 per 20 tests; $2.25 per specimen set; 2(7) minutes.

e) EYE-HAND ACCURACY. 1966; 1 form (4 pages); $5 per 20 tests; $2.50 per specimen set; 5(10) minutes.

f) GRAMMAR AND PUNCTUATION. 1966; 1 form (2 pages); $4 per 20 tests; $2.25 per specimen set; (5–10) minutes.

g) SPELLING. 1966–69; 1 form ('69, 2 pages, identical with test copyrighted in 1966); $4 per 20 tests; $2.25 per specimen set; (15–20) minutes.

h) SPELLING-VOCABULARY. 1966; 1 form (3 pages); $5 per 20 tests; $2.50 per specimen set; (15–20) minutes.

i) VOCABULARY. 1966; 1 form (3 pages); $5 per 20 tests; $2.50 per specimen set; (10–15) minutes.

j) WORD FLUENCY. 1966; 1 form (2 pages); $4 per 20 tests; $2.25 per specimen set; 5(10) minutes.

ROBERT FITZPATRICK, *Principal Research Scientist, American Institutes for Research, Pittsburgh, Pennsylvania.*

The development of the tests in this series was based in part on analyses of clerical jobs, on study of previously published clerical tests, and on review of literature such as Bair's factorial study[1] of clerical tests. These matters are discussed only in very general terms in the manual. There is an extensive listing of job titles, but little description of the analysis method or of the rationales or procedures by which the job analyses influenced item construction.

The tests, though legibly and neatly printed, show signs of careless construction:

Alphabetizing-Filing is arranged so that a testwise examinee could start Part 2 while others are still reading the directions for that part. Some of the items may function as "trick" questions, such as the inclusion in a set to be alphabetized of *LaBoheme* [sic] to be filed under *B*. Also, there is an error in the key: Sweets Philately Co. should be filed in space 42 and not, as the key says, in 24.

The Arithmetic test presents some problems in ambiguous form, e.g., $12 + 2 \div 7 = ?$ The test starts with a series of progressively more difficult addition and subtraction problems, then presents a similar series involving multiplication and division, and finally a mixed series. The testwise examinee could skip from one series to another with profit.

Clerical Speed and Accuracy contains at least one unspecified rule. The task is to determine if two items are "identical"; apparently this

1 BAIR, JOHN T. "Factor Analysis of Clerical Aptitude Tests." *J Appl Psychol* 35:245–9 Ag '51. *

means only the letters and numbers involved, since in at least two cases the sets are spaced differently but are keyed as identical.

In the Grammar and Punctuation test, some keyed answers are questionable. For example, one item is scored as correct only if the examinee indicates that the word *data* takes a plural verb, although current usage allows the singular.

In Spelling, the key gives *raisin* as the corrected spelling for *raisen,* but an equally plausible answer is *raised. Ukelele,* a spelling accepted by current dictionaries, is shown as a misspelling. The stimulus *escalter* was quite a puzzle to this reviewer until he saw the keyed correction of *escalator.*

In Spelling-Vocabulary, the key does not accept *sombre* as a correct spelling, though current dictionaries do.

Vocabulary consists of the odd-numbered items of the *Bruce Vocabulary Inventory.* The reader is referred to the reviews of the latter test; most of the comments are applicable to this truncated version. In addition, for item 19, the intended correct choice of *joy* is misprinted *job.*

Six of the tests are speeded. One of these, Clerical Speed and Accuracy, is scored rights minus wrongs. The others, as well as the unspeeded tests, are scored rights only. No rationale is given for the scoring. Examinees are to be told the time limits by the examiner for all speeded tests except Eye-Hand Accuracy. In most cases, the directions suggest that the examinee "work quickly and accurately"; he is not told the scoring formula. The written and oral directions differ within tests and from test to test in minor ways, for reasons that are not clear.

Eye-Hand Accuracy would appear to require careful monitoring to insure that examinees are following directions, but the instructions for administration ignore this problem. Part 1 of this test is to be done with the right hand and Part 2 with the left, but the directions do not prepare the left-hander for this sequence in advance. No evidence is given that the sequence is fair to all or that a sequence of "preferred" and then "non-preferred" hand might not be better.

Reliabilities given are test-retest at an interval of eight weeks (N = 62) and split-half (N = 150). The author states that the coefficients are "typical of those found with other instruments of this sort," but some of them appear to be on the low side (e.g., Grammar and Punctuation, .70 test-retest and .78 split-half). The numbers of subjects are, in any case, too small for a stable determination of reliability.

Separate norms are provided for male and female groups, though there are not wide differences on most tests. Most of the norm sample were currently employed clerical workers; all had at least one year of experience on some kind of clerical job. The numbers in the female group ranged from 367 to 376 and in the male, from 239 to 252.

The author argues that he achieved a degree of content validity through the procedures used in item construction. Specifically, he states that spelling, arithmetic, grammar, and punctuation "items were chosen from part of the universe of such specific material in the business and industrial world." A worthy concept, but since the method of choice and the selection of the part of the universe are not described in any detail, it is not possible to verify the claim.

What the author calls *concurrent* validity data are really a weak form of *construct* validity data: correlations with other tests. These data suggest that the tests are measuring approximately the intended abilities but also raise questions as to whether they are measuring anything unique. Several criterion-oriented validity studies, mostly of the concurrent type and using small numbers of cases, are reported. These tend to suggest moderately good validities but are quite inadequate as more than suggestions.

The inadequacy of the validity and other data and the preliminary nature of the tests are frankly acknowledged in the manual. The author makes almost all of the appropriate qualifications and points out limitations. An attempt is made to describe examinee groups; the attempt is laudable and should be extended in further editions of the manual.

A major fault in the manual is the suggestion that profiling the scores on the various tests for an individual examinee "will provide the test user with considerable information at a glance." No warning is provided the unwary test user about the many dangers and difficulties of interpretation of test profiles. On the contrary, a profile form is provided to make the process easy.

The *Clerical Skills Series* contains some interesting test concepts. Although the tests do not differ radically from others already available, it is possible that they could contribute a modest increment of benefit in measuring clerical abilities. Unfortunately, the potential for gain seems, at least at this time, to be outweighed by the paucity of validity data and careless construction of the tests.

[989]

★Clerical Tests. Applicants for clerical positions; 1951–66; 6 tests; no manual; norms ['66, 2 pages]; no data on reliability; $3 per 25 tests, postage extra; specimen set not available; Stevens, Thurow and Associates, Inc. *
a) INVENTORY J, ARITHMETICAL REASONING. 1966; 1 form (3 pages); 7(10) minutes.
b) INVENTORY K, ARITHMETICAL PROFICIENCY. 1951–66; 1 form ('51, 3 pages); 7(10) minutes.
c) INVENTORY M, INTERPRETATION OF TABULATED MATERIAL. 1951–66; 1 form ('51, 3 pages); 3(7) minutes.
d) INVENTORY R, INTERPRETATION OF TABULATED MATERIAL. 1951–66; 1 form ('51, 3 pages); 7(10) minutes.
e) INVENTORY S, ALPHABETICAL FILING. 1951–66; 1 form ('51, 2 pages); 3(7) minutes.
f) INVENTORY Y, GRAMMAR. 1951–66; 1 form ('51, 2 pages); 7(10) minutes.

[990]

★Curtis Verbal-Clerical Skills Tests. Applicants for clerical positions; 1963–65; CVCST; 4 tests: computation, checking, comprehension, logical reasoning ability; manual ('64, 4 pages); supplement ('65, 2 pages); $3 per 50 tests; $1 per specimen set (must be purchased to obtain manual); cash orders postpaid; 8(10) minutes; James W. Curtis; Psychometric Affiliates. *

[991]

★Group Tests 61, 64, and 66. Clerical applicants; 1956–69; 3 tests; mimeographed manual ['69, 11 pages]; instructions ('69, 1–2 pages) for each test; publisher recommends use of local norms; 7p per instructions; 17p per manual; postpaid within U.K.; National Institute of Industrial Psychology. *
a) GROUP TEST 61. 1956–69; filing, classification, and checking; 2 scores: speed, accuracy; 1 form ['56, 12 pages]; no data on reliability of accuracy score; 60p per 10 tests; 12p per single copy; 12p per key; 20(35) minutes.
b) GROUP TEST 64. 1957–69; spelling; 1 form ['57, 1 page]; 20p per 10 tests; 4p per single copy; 10p per key; (15) minutes.
c) GROUP TEST 66. 1957–69; arithmetic; 2 scores: basic operations, problems; 1 form ['57, 3 pages]; no data on reliability; 30p per 10 tests; 6p per single copy; 5p per key; 15(20) minutes.

[992]

★[L & L Clerical Tests.] Applicants for office positions; 1964–70; 6 tests; no manual; statistical data ['70, 4 pages]; no data on reliability; distribution restricted to business firms; $4.50 per 20 tests (a–e); $6 per specimen set (without f); postpaid; L & L Associates. *
a) ARITHMETIC REVIEW. 1964; 1 form (2 pages); 5(10) minutes.
b) CHECK LIST REVIEW. 1964; 1 form (3 pages); 5(10) minutes.
c) GENERAL EMPLOYMENT REVIEW. 1964–70; 4 scores: vocabulary, mathematics, perception-general knowledge, total; 1 form ('70, 4 pages); (40–50) minutes.

d) OFFICE ABILITY REVIEW. 1964; 6 scores: spelling, grammar and punctuation, arithmetic, filing, business terms, total; 1 form (4 pages); (35–40) minutes.

e) SPELLING REVIEW. 1964; 1 form (3 pages); 10(15) minutes.

f) TYPING REVIEW. 1964; 1 form (2 pages); no norms; $1.30 per test; 5(10) minutes.

[993]

*[Personnel Institute Clerical Tests.] Clerical personnel and typists-stenographers-secretaries; 1922–67; manual ('67, 171 pages, plus keys); separate profile charts ('67, 1 page) for clerical personnel and for typists-stenographers-secretaries; no data on reliability; no description of normative populations; $12.50 per 5 sets of tests (*a–i*) and profile chart for clerical personnel; $12.50 per 5 sets of tests (*a–f, j–l*) and profile chart for typists-stenographers-secretaries; $6.25 per 25 profiles; $17.50 per manual (includes keys and reproductions of all tests); Personnel Institute, Inc. *

a) PRELIMINARY SCREENING INTERVIEW. 1957–67; 1 form ('67, 3 pages); $6.25 per 25 forms; (10) minutes.

b) CONFIDENTIAL PERSONAL HISTORY INVENTORY. 1957–67; 1 form ('67, 4 pages); $6.25 per 25 forms; (40) minutes.

c) DIAGNOSTIC INTERVIEWER'S GUIDE. 1956–67; 1 form ('67, 4 pages); $6.25 per 25 forms; (20) minutes.

d) WORK REFERENCE INVESTIGATION. 1957–67; 1 form ('63, 3 pages); $6.25 per 25 forms; (10) minutes.

e) MENTAL ALERTNESS TEST. 1922; formerly called *EM-AY Inventory;* reprint of the *Otis Employment Test;* 1 form ('22, 4 pages); $8.75 per 25 tests; 20(25) minutes.

f) VOCABULARY TEST. 1954–67; 1 form ('67, 4 pages, identical with forms copyrighted in 1954 and 1956); $8.75 per 25 tests; (20–25) minutes.

g) COMPARING NAMES TEST. 1957–67; 1 form ('67, 2 pages, identical with test copyrighted in 1957); $6.25 per 25 tests; 1.5(6) minutes.

h) COPYING NUMBERS TEST. 1957–67; 1 form ('67, 3 pages, identical with forms copyrighted in 1957 and 1962); $8.75 per 25 tests; 3(8) minutes.

i) ARITHMETIC TEST. 1957–67; 1 form ('67, 3 pages, identical with forms copyrighted in 1957 and 1963); $8.75 per 25 tests; 1.5(6) minutes.

j) GRAMMAR TEST. 1957–67; 1 form ('67, 2 pages, identical with forms copyrighted in 1957 and 1960); $6.25 per 25 tests; 3(8) minutes.

k) SPELLING TEST. 1957–67; 1 form ('67, 2 pages, identical with forms copyrighted in 1957 and 1963); $6.25 per 25 tests; 2.5(7) minutes.

l) TYPING TEST. 1957–67; 1 form ('67, 2 pages, identical with forms copyrighted in 1957 and 1960); $6.25 per 25 tests; 10(20) minutes.

[994]

RBH Checking Test. Applicants for clerical and stenographic positions; 1948–63; catalog uses the title *The RBH Coding Test;* 1 form ['48, 4 pages, booklet title is *Coding Test*]; manual ['63, 8 pages]; directions (no date, 2 pages); no data on reliability; $3.50 per 25 tests; 50¢ per key; $1.50 per manual; $1.50 per specimen set; postage extra; 5(10) minutes; Richardson, Bellows, Henry & Co., Inc. *

DOUGLAS G. SCHULTZ, *Associate Professor of Psychology, Case Western Reserve University, Cleveland, Ohio.*

The *RBH Checking Test* is a multiple choice version of the code substitution test, the key in this case pairing three-letter words with two-digit numbers. A widely used code substitution test, digit symbol, appears in the Wechsler intelligence scales, a fact which suggests that more than a very simple clerical or perceptual speed skill is being tested by the *RBH Checking Test*. The manual says the test is "designed to measure the ability of the individual to perceive simple relationships, to retain these relationships mentally and to make decisions based upon the several relationships quickly and accurately." In view of this, it is not surprising that the manual indicates that the test correlates almost as highly with a learning ability test and a test of nonverbal reasoning as it does with other clerical tests (contrary to a statement in the introductory section of the manual).

The test booklet is generally well designed and printed. Answers are to be placed in the test booklet. The items could be spread out a little more to minimize the possibility of marking the wrong line. The directions on the booklet are satisfactory, although no comment is made about the fact that in the example the 6 key words are not alphabetized, while in the test proper the 16 key words are. Recognition of this should increase reaction time significantly.

The manual is almost useless. The introductory paragraphs include some statements not justified by the data presented later. Reliability is not even mentioned. Of course, since this is a speeded test, an alternate form is needed to judge reliability adequately, but none is available.

The validity data reported are very inadequate. Six of the seven studies were done in one oil company and all used small numbers of subjects. The three studies involving men all produced low *negative* correlations. The poorest of these (validity of −.19), based on 42 office boys, is dismissed with the statement that "the first year job was not likely to challenge a group such as this." If so, this study should not have been included. It is then stated that "studies of similar young men after promotion to high levels give substantially different results," but no further evidence is presented. The median validity for the four studies predicting first-year performance of women clerks and office girls is .34, a respectable figure. In all seven validity studies the test was used as part of the selection battery, thus restricting the test score range and underestimating validity to an unknown extent.

Norms are included for formidable numbers

of men (1,102) and women (2,707). The groups are poorly described. They seem to come from a limited number of companies. Clerical applicants and employees are thrown together in the male norms. One male subgroup consists of 147 sales trainee applicants. The significance of the sales group for a clerical test is not clear, but it is interesting that its mean score is slightly higher than that of the clerks. The female sample is separated into clerical applicants and employees. It is a curious fact that the mean score for the applicants is about a third of a standard deviation higher than that of the employees. These groups are so variable that they provide no basis for the generalization that "men tend to score somewhat lower on the average."

The distributions seem to make good use of the available score range, and the test difficulty appears about right for the subjects examined for norm purposes (typical clerks?). The administrative directions are acceptable and scoring is straightforward, although a little difficult with the fan key.

This test was originally copyrighted in 1948, and the manual is dated 1963. The publisher has a clear obligation to produce a sounder base of empirical support if he continues to sell it. For the present, its potential is unknown. It is obviously not a proven instrument. Its contribution to a battery of clerical tests, especially a battery including measures of verbal and number skills, might be worth exploring. Any purchaser should do his own evaluative studies before using the test for practical purposes. With a battery such as the Short Employment Tests available and supported by a considerable accumulation of empirical data, only unusual circumstances would warrant anyone working with the *RBH Checking Test*.

[995]

RBH Classifying Test. Business and industry; 1950–63; 3 scores: speed, accuracy, rights minus wrongs; Forms 1 ('61, 4 pages, identical with test copyrighted in 1950 except for cover, booklet title is *Sorting and Classifying Test*), 2 ('57, 4 pages, booklet title is *Classifying Test*); manual ['63, 18 pages]; directions (no date, 2 pages); no data on reliability for women or for rights minus wrongs score; no norms for rights minus wrongs score; $4 per 25 tests; 50¢ per key; $1.50 per manual; $1.50 per specimen set; postage extra; 10(15) minutes; Richardson, Bellows, Henry & Co., Inc. *

DOUGLAS G. SCHULTZ, *Associate Professor of Psychology, Case Western Reserve University, Cleveland, Ohio.*

The manual describes this test as "a unique instrument in the clerical aptitude field." The task involved, calling for the identification of items according to multiple specifications, does appear to be rather novel. Precisely what is being measured and why it is important is not clear, however. Beyond the description of the test as "unique" and the statement that it "has proved particularly valuable in situations where decisions must be made quickly on multiple variables," there is no discussion in the manual of the purpose of the test. There is even some confusion over its name since "Classifying Test" is used on most of the materials but "Sorting and Classifying" is the title on the Form 1 booklet.

Some insight into the nature of the test and its purpose might be gained from details of its construction. But the manual contains no such description; presumably no pretesting or item analysis was done.

Factorially, the test would appear to involve a complicated blend of memory and perceptual speed, varying to some extent with how one goes about the task presented. The presence of the memory factor suggests the involvement of general intelligence and may help to explain the rather high correlations, reported in the manual, of this test with the *RBH Test of Learning Ability* and with the *Watson-Glaser Critical Thinking Appraisal*.

Reading the manual is a frustrating experience. Although it is 18 pages long and contains considerable data, there are many inadequacies and omissions and much of the information is not especially helpful. For example, the only reliability figures given, one for the speed score and one for the accuracy score, are based on a study of only 23 men (full-time students or employed, part-time students?) studying personnel management in a southern university. The same data show a difference of a quarter of a standard deviation between the means of the two forms, but, in spite of this, the statement is made that "the forms were demonstrably equivalent," and only one overall set of norms is presented, for use with either form. The rather limited validity data, mostly concurrent, are only briefly described. The studies appear to be concentrated in one or more oil companies, and the coefficients are generally low and even negative in some instances. The administrative directions are fair but they could be clarified and corrected.

The greatest part of the manual is devoted to norms for the speed and accuracy scores derived from a variety of industrial samples, male and female. Complete distributions are given for generally large groups and means and standard deviations for additional groups. Only the briefest descriptions of the samples are given, e.g., "managers and executives." The largest group of men (1,453) is simply described as "general." Although it looks impressive, such information can be no more than suggestive and could be misleading. The publisher urges development of local norms, a commendable view, and the reporting of scores to the publisher, a step which "will enable us to give you increasingly valuable information on the meaning of test scores." Yet nothing new has been produced since 1963.

The speed score would seem to be most useful of the three proposed. Its distribution is symmetrical and the skimpy data indicate that it may be more reliable and valid than the accuracy score. The accuracy score should probably be avoided because its distribution is badly skewed and because it is a ratio. The rights-minus-wrongs score, used in most of the reported validity studies, is mentioned on the first page of the manual as one of three scores obtained from the test but is not referred to in the scoring directions and no norms are given for it.

The idea of this test may be worth salvaging. The scores probably have some validity for certain kinds of clerical and managerial positions which involve rapid recognition of items which meet complex requirements, i.e., clerical checking skill with a major memory component. But the publisher should start all over again, carefully review the test content and directions, and develop sound supporting data and materials.

[996]
★RBH Language Skills and Dictation Test. Secretaries and stenographers; 1957–63; formerly called *RBH Stenographic Proficiency Tests;* 7 scores: language skills, dictation (85 wpm, 105 wpm), typing (speed, accuracy, format), total; Form 1 ('57, 17 pages and 33⅓ rpm record); mimeographed manual ['63, 8 pages]; directions ['63, 7 pages]; no data on reliability; no norms for typing format score; no norms for males; $8 per 20 test booklets; $9 per record; $1.50 per key; $1.50 per manual; $2 per specimen set without record; postage extra; (90–100) minutes; Richardson, Bellows, Henry & Co., Inc. *

[997]
RBH Number Checking Test. Business and industry; 1957–63; 2 scores: checking forward, checking backward; 1 form ('57, 5 pages); manual ['63, 13 pages]; directions (no date, 1 page); no data on re-

liability; $4 per 25 tests; 50¢ per key; $1.50 per manual; $1.50 per specimen set; postage extra; 6(12) minutes; Richardson, Bellows, Henry & Co., Inc. *

Douglas G. Schultz, *Associate Professor of Psychology, Case Western Reserve University, Cleveland, Ohio.*

The *RBH Number Checking Test* is another modification of the number comparison test that first appeared in 1933 as one part of the *Minnesota Clerical Test* and that has been included in various forms in several other clerical tests. The number comparison test is a good measure of perceptual speed. Here, the format is a little different from that of the Minnesota test. Furthermore, a second, separately timed section, in which the comparison is between a number and that number reversed, is included.

The test booklet is attractively prepared, and the instructions on the booklet are clear. The directions for the second part are presented on the page facing the test proper for the first test; it might have been preferable to insert a blank page between the parts. The administrative directions in the manual are not specific enough with respect to the multiple-page arrangement of the test booklet but are generally satisfactory. The answer format (crossing out S or D) does not lend itself to accurate scoring with a fan key.

Although the manual is 13 pages long, it provides almost no basis for evaluating the test. There is no presentation of test construction details. Except for a few vague introductory remarks, there is no discussion at all of some 10 pages of data. The data are mostly related to norms. There is no indication of reliability and no mention of validity, although long lists of intercorrelations with a variety of other tests are included. The general impression one gets is that the Number Checking scores have low to moderate positive correlations with a wide variety of tests ranging from language perception to arithmetic reasoning. But the tests are so varied and the results so variable that it is difficult to reach any firm or meaningful conclusions from them.

Great emphasis is placed on the two parts of the test—forward and backward checking. The manual states that "this test is actually two separate tests bound in one cover," and the scoring directions warn the user that "the two scores are not to be combined in any way, and each of the scores is to be interpreted separately." Norms are given separately for forward and backward checking. No justification is produced for this arrangement. Since these are very short tests (three minutes for each part), the reliabilities of the part scores are undoubtedly somewhat limited. Furthermore, the reported intercorrelations between the two scores for several groups, male and female, average about .50 to .60. If the reliabilities are limited to any degree, the parts are measuring much the same thing. In view of these considerations, this reviewer would strongly favor use of only a total score on the two parts.

The norms that are presented in the manual are based on large numbers of cases, for the most part. However, the groups are poorly described and are not likely to be representative of the populations suggested by the descriptions. For example, 86 percent of the male "clerical applicant" group (N = 273) was drawn from an oil refinery in the Philippines. There is no explanation of why one should assume these men to be representative of clerical applicants in the U.S. Two odd subgroups of men, financial managers (N = 10) and technical and professional employees (N = 76), are included in the norms tables. Employees and applicants are combined in the women's group, almost all of which is drawn from one oil company. Such norms can hardly be of much help to the general test user.

The *RBH Number Checking Test* itself seems quite acceptable, in spite of a few administrative and scoring deficiencies mentioned previously. But, in view of the fact that it is essentially an unknown entity, there would seem to be little reason to use it in preference to any of the other number comparison tests available. If it is selected, the user should thoroughly evaluate its characteristics in his situation before applying it for any purpose.

[998]
★Secretarial Performance Analysis. Employees; 1969; SPA; ratings by supervisors; 4 scores: basic skills, executive skills, personal attributes, total; 1 form (4 pages); instruction card (2 pages); no data on reliability; no description of normative population; $5.50 per 25 forms; $1 per instruction card; $1 per specimen set; cash orders postpaid; [10–20] minutes; William T. Martin; Psychologists and Educators Press. *

[999]
★Selection Tests for Office Personnel. Insurance office workers and applicants; 1962–64; STOP; 10 tests; 1 form ('62, 3 pages except *i*, self-marking except *h* and *j*); manual ('64, 15 pages); no data on reliability; $12.50 per 10 copies of each test (except 2 copies each of coding, stenography, and typing), 10

application blanks, and manual; 15¢ per single copy; postpaid; specimen set not available; 5(10) minutes per test (except *f* and *h*); Walter A. Eggert and Albert H. Malo; distributed by National Association of Mutual Insurance Agents. *
a) LANGUAGE SKILLS 1A.
b) DATA PERCEPTION 2A.
c) ARITHMETIC 3A.
d) CODING 4A.
e) RATING 5A.
f) PERSONALITY 6A. (5–10) minutes.
g) FILING 7A.
h) STENOGRAPHY 8A. [5–10] minutes.
i) SPELLING 9A. 1 form (2 pages)
j) TYPING 10A.

[1000]
★Short Occupational Knowledge Test for Bookkeepers. Job applicants; 1970; score is pass, fail, or unclassifiable; 1 form (2 pages, self-marking); series manual (15 pages); $5.30 per 25 tests; 75¢ per manual; $3.30 per specimen set of the 12 tests in the series; postage extra; (10–15) minutes; Bruce A. Campbell and Suellen O. Johnson; Science Research Associates, Inc. *

[1001]
★Short Occupational Knowledge Test for Office Machine Operators. Job applicants; 1970; score is pass, fail, or unclassifiable; 1 form (2 pages, self-marking); series manual (15 pages); $5.30 per 25 tests; 75¢ per manual; $3.30 per specimen set of the 12 tests in the series; postage extra; (10–15) minutes; Bruce A. Campbell and Suellen O. Johnson; Science Research Associates, Inc. *

[1002]
★Short Occupational Knowledge Test for Secretaries. Job applicants; 1969–70; score is pass, fail, or unclassifiable; 1 form ('69, 2 pages, self-marking); series manual ('70, 15 pages); $5.30 per 25 tests; 75¢ per manual; $3.30 per specimen set of the 12 tests in the series; postage extra; (10–15) minutes; Bruce A. Campbell and Suellen O. Johnson; Science Research Associates, Inc. *

[1003]
*Shorthand Test: Individual Placement Series. Adults; 1960–66; Forms A, B, ('60, 2 pages); also available on 33⅓ rpm record and 7½ ips tape recording; no specific manual; series manual ('66, 107 pages); $8 per 20 tests; $10 per record or tape containing both forms; $2.50 per series manual; $3 per specimen set without record or tape; $13 per specimen set with record or tape; cash orders postpaid; (20–25) minutes; J. H. Norman; Personnel Research Associates, Inc. *

[1004]
★Skill in Typing: Measurement of Skills Test 9. Job applicants; 1966–68; MOS 9; individual; 1 form ('67, 7 pages); manual ['68, 8 pages]; no data on reliability; $12.50 per 25 tests, postpaid; specimen set free; 15(25) minutes; Walter V. Clarke Associates, Inc.; AVA Publications, Inc. *

[1005]
★Spot-the-Error Test. Clerical workers with 9–12 years of education; 1964–69; subtest of *National Institute for Personnel Research Intermediate Battery*; 2 scores: speed, accuracy; Forms A, B, ('64, 7 pages); manual ('69, 35 pages); no data on validity; separate answer sheets must be used; R9.20 per 25 tests; 50c

per single copy; 75c per 25 answer sheets; 40c per scoring stencil; R3 per manual; postpaid within South Africa; Afrikaans edition available; 10(20) minutes; Anne-Marie Wilcocks (manual); National Institute for Personnel Research. *

[1006]

*Survey of Clerical Skills: Individual Placement Series. Adults; 1959–66; SOCS; 5 scores: spelling, office math, office terms, filing, grammar; Form C ('59, 8 pages); no specific manual; series manual ('66, 107 pages); separate answer sheets must be used; $25 per 20 tests; $4 per 100 answer sheets; 50¢ per scoring stencil; $2.50 per series manual; $4.45 per specimen set; cash orders postpaid; 40(45) minutes; J. H. Norman; Personnel Research Associates, Inc. *

[1007]

★Typing Test for Business. Applicants for typing positions; 1967–68; TTB; 6 scores: straight copy (speed, accuracy), letters, revised manuscript, numbers, tables; 5 tests plus practice test; manual ('68, 23 pages); distribution restricted to personnel departments; $2.75 per 25 tests of b–f; $1 per set of keys; 50¢ per manual; $2 per specimen set of both forms; postage extra; Psychological Corporation (test), Jerome E. Doppelt (manual), Arthur D. Hartman (manual), and Fay B. Krawchick (manual); Psychological Corporation. *
a) PRACTICE COPY. Forms A, B, ('67, 4 pages); 80¢ per 25 tests; 2(5) minutes.
b) STRAIGHT COPY. 2 scores: speed, accuracy; Forms A, B, ('67, 4 pages); 5(10) minutes.
c) LETTERS. Forms A, B, ('67, 8 pages); 10(15) minutes.
d) REVISED MANUSCRIPT. Forms A, B, ('67, 4 pages); 10(15) minutes.
e) NUMBERS. Forms A, B, ('67, 3 pages); 3(5) minutes.
f) TABLES. Forms A, B, ('67, 5 pages); 10(15) minutes.

MARY T. HARRISON, *Supervisor, Personnel Services Division 3255, Sandia Laboratories, Albuquerque, New Mexico.*

The *Typing Test for Business* was designed as a multi-unit test comprised of sections measuring skill in typing straight copy, letters, revised manuscript, numbers, and tables, any or all of which may be administered. Difficulty level of the material is average (1.4 syllabic intensity) for the units on Letters and Straight Copy and somewhat more difficult for the Revised Manuscript (1.6 syllabic intensity), which seems appropriate.

Regardless of which units are administered, directions call for administration of the Practice Copy, timed for two minutes. Its administration is intended to serve as a warm-up for the typist and to familiarize him with the machine he will be using and with the testing procedure. This reviewer would like to have the Practice Copy lengthened, especially for use with job applicants.

The manual contains complete, specific, and

clearly written instructions for scoring the units. No scoring errors should occur as a result of varying assumptions on the part of scorers.

Reliability coefficients are based on correlations between first and second testings, regardless of form. The coefficients, based on an N of 125, range from .67 for Tables to .87 for Speed and Letters. The standard error of measurement for Letters, Revised Manuscript and Tables is somewhat larger than one might wish but these are also the units on which one might expect learning to be reflected on the retest score.

The only claim of validity is for face validity. The authors have presented a worksample measuring different aspects of typing skill. The difficulty of the tasks presented appears appropriate for the time allowance.

Three norms tables are provided, one based on students and trainees, one on an applicant population, and one on an employed population. It would be helpful if the populations were described in more detail. Gross words per minute for the straight copy units are reported in percentiles, followed by the accuracy scores reported in quartiles. This procedure seems less valuable than reporting net typing scores in percentile form. An individual who types 65 wpm with 9 errors (net 56) is at the 90th percentile; an individual who types 56 wpm with no errors is at the 50th. From a production point of view, the individual at the 50th percentile might be more efficient than the individual at the 90th. The manual recommends that local norms be developed but that in the interim the norms in Tables 1–4 may be helpful. Since typing is a vocational skill, the most valuable norms table is Table 3, based on 126 employed typists at a public utility company.

The TTB provides a useful and needed assessment of a typist's ability and does so with a minimum of testing time, which is an important consideration in an industrial setting. No extravagant claims are made in either the manual or the catalog; however, the order form brochure states that the test provides "a comprehensive assessment of typing skills for high-level secretaries." The units are not difficult enough to justify such a description, and there is insufficient sampling on which to select a secretary with the highest degree of typing knowledge and skill. It is a good screening test. If an organization tests large numbers of individuals it might become annoying to have to dispose of so much paper in a secure fashion; it would be helpful to have at least some of the test material presented in reusable form. The manual does not caution the user regarding destruction of test copy.

LEONARD J. WEST, *Professor of Education, Office of Teacher Education, The City University of New York, New York, New York.*

The TTB is an alternate-form, worksample test intended primarily for use in screening applicants for typing positions. The subtests are individually purchasable, and a test manual of exceptional clarity includes percentile norms for each subtest for each of three groups of "entry level" typists. Closely comparable means and standard deviations for the two forms of the test support the interchangeability of the forms and their use (pre and post) for such purposes as assessing the effects of training programs. Test-retest and alternate-form reliability coefficients (for 125 examinees) range between .67 (for Tables) and .87 (for Straight Copy speed). The former value is uncomfortably low, reflecting, in part, the shortness of a 10-minute sample of table typing and, in part, the variability in the prior training of examinees for the variety of features built into the four tables that make up this subtest.

Content validity is claimed for the test; indeed, surveys reveal the prominence of letters, tables, and manuscripts in the nontrivial work of employed typists. Although the test publisher recommends that user companies undertake studies of predictive validity of the test for their own employees and mentions the difficulties of such studies, it is hoped that the publisher will also undertake such studies.

The scoring rules detailed in the test manual are gratifyingly clear; the accompanying scoring keys permit rapid speed scoring and are printed on durable, heavy stock. The 40 minutes of actual typing in the total test (including a 2-minute, unscored practice test) can be administered in about an hour.

The foregoing virtues of the TTB notwithstanding, one general feature of the test is judged to be a compelling weakness, and another general feature is felt to be questionable. The compelling weakness lies in the adverse effects on validity of "do *not* stop to correct errors" as a rule for the examinee. Awareness of errors and their correction are such central features of a typist's work as to call into

question the usability of any test that does not provide for error correction. Granting occasional scoring ambiguity in assessing the acceptability (neatness) of a correction, the TTB rule ignores the notorious variability in proofreading skills among typists. Also, speed scores are inflated in relation to those that would result were errors to be corrected.

A second questionable feature arises from scoring rules "simplified as much as is consistent with reliable measurement." Each subtest score (except for Straight Copy) is defined as number of words typed minus the number of errors. The need for an eventual single score representing both speed and quality is obvious. However, any given composite score can represent innumerable combinations of gross output and errors. An output of 242 words with 2 errors and one of 252 words with 12 errors both lead to a score of 240—but the two typists are clearly not of equivalent skill. Furthermore, such scoring gives very large weight to speed in relation to quality of work. Means and reliability data for separate speed and error scores would be most informative, and inquiry into the effects on reliability (and eventually on validity) of differential weighting of errors according to their seriousness is also recommended to the publisher.

A number of the more consequential reservations about each of the subtests follow:

STRAIGHT COPY. The materials purport to be of "average" difficulty at a syllabic intensity (average number of speech syllables per dictionary word) of 1.40. The mean syllabic intensity of "the vocabulary of written business communication" is, in fact, 1.54.[1] Accordingly, this subtest overestimates copying skills. Also, the line-for-line copy does not include a single divided word (i.e., an opportunity to use the hyphen key).

LETTERS. For three letters of substantially different lengths, the examinee is instructed to use identical side margins. Thus the test fails to provide a measure of the trainee's ability to vary horizontal placement with letter length. More important, each of the three "unarranged" letters is preceded by a model form that shows not only the vertical spacing between letter parts but also very nearly the exact vertical placement of the entire letter on the page. Even

1 WEST, LEONARD J. *Acquisition of Typewriting Skills,* pp. 534–6. New York: Pitman Publishing Corporation, 1969. Pp. xxvi, 635.

so, the scoring instruction for vertical placement is unnecessarily vague: "neither excessively high nor excessively low." In contradistinction to the precision of the other scoring rules, no definition of "excessive" is given. Little of consequence is measured by this subtest, and it is judged to be deficient for its purposes. Validity has been sacrificed to ease and reliability of scoring, and the resulting scores are probably inflated in relation to those that would result from a more valid measure.

TABLES. The four tables that make up this subtest are admirably conceived: they are stripped down to essentials and provide, in turn, a variety of features (varied number of columns, with and without subheads, 1- and 2-line column heads, braced heads). The test copy, however, specifies the vertical spacing between components and the number of spaces to be used between columns in all tables. Ease and reliability of scoring are thereby enhanced, but validity suffers by removing such decisions from the examinee's activities. The table subtest reduces itself to a measure of the ability to follow directions, to center column headings in relation to their columns, and to center the entire table horizontally on the page. Objection might also be taken to the underscoring of both lines of a 2-line column head; it is more elegant to underscore only the bottom line (across the width of the longer line).

REVISED MANUSCRIPT. The 500-word manuscript in each form consists of typed copy with a lavish number of longhand changes involving 13 different proofreader's marks, each used a number of times. The content is judged to be very good for its purposes. However, the frequency of longhand or mixed typed-and-longhand copy among typists in general—not merely among those who work for employers who know and use formal proofreader's marks—suggests that this subtest would be more widely applicable to more typists if the more recondite proof marks had been avoided. Most of the corrections can easily be indicated in less formal ways. In an undeterminable number of instances, what should be a measure of the ability to follow changes in copy becomes, in part, a measure of knowledge of formal proofreader's marks.

NUMBERS. This subtest consists of typing 4-digit numbers arrayed in 5 columns (for which the appropriate tabular stops are preset). The extent to which the task represents the context in which heavy number typing is done

by typists is not known to this reviewer, nor does the test manual speak to that point.

SUMMARY. The TTB reflects ingenuity in the design and format of a typing employment test for easy and speedy administration and scoring. Its content seems generally appropriate. It has demonstrated reliability, and the amount of pertinent test data in the manual is commendable. However, important aspects of validity (especially the "no error correction" rule) appear to have been sacrificed to considerations of ease of administration and scoring. That feature aside, the Letters test is very weak; the Revised Manuscript is very good, as is the Tables test if more time is provided for it or if the first of the four tables is discarded. The Straight Copy test is adequate for those who (mistakenly) think that straight copy proficiency matters. The Numbers test probably applies to a relatively small proportion of typists.

[1008]

*Typing Test: Individual Placement Series. Adults; 1959–66; Forms C, D, ('59, 2 pages); no specific manual; series manual ('66, 107 pages); $8 per 20 tests; 50¢ per key; $2.50 per series manual; $3.50 per specimen set; cash orders postpaid; 5(15) minutes; J. H. Norman; Personnel Research Associates, Inc. *

MARY T. HARRISON, *Supervisor, Personnel Services Division 3255, Sandia Laboratories, Albuquerque, New Mexico.*

Two forms of a five-minute straight copy test have been provided. The test is reusable, being printed on lightweight cardboard. The test is preceded by a five-minute practice exercise which is printed on the other side of the test copy. The test copy's being single spaced could contribute to additional errors on the part of the test candidate. It would be helpful to have the copy double-spaced for easier reading. The instructions direct that the test candidate also single space when taking the test, making scoring more difficult. The intent of the publisher may have been to avoid the need for the more rapid typists to insert another sheet of paper. If so, it could be suggested that the test candidate be provided with legal size paper.

The manual states that the scoring of this test has been streamlined without affecting the accuracy. The directions for counting the total number of errors are so brief that many things are left to the discretion of the scorer. For example, if the test candidate loses home position, is he charged one error for the loss of position or one error for each word he typed this way? Is he to be charged an error for poor touch which results in uneven spacing? If more than one individual were responsible for scoring, a job applicant could have an advantage or disadvantage if there were inconsistencies among scorers.

The norms are based on corrected scores for which a penalty of two for each actual error is subtracted from the gross words per minute. The manual suggests that the user may prefer to use the actual performance gross and error scores (only one penalty point per error), and for industry this method is preferred by the reviewer.

Reliability coefficients on retest of same form and retest on alternate forms are .871 and .846 respectively. These appear sufficiently high, although the N's were small—27 and 41—and reporting the coefficient to three figures does not seem justified with such a small sample.

Three validity coefficients, ranging from .241 for 19 department clerks to .457 for 24 secretaries, are provided in the manual but it is impossible to interpret their meaning as the criterion used was job performance rating. Presumably this was an overall rating rather than a specific rating on typing abilities.

The norms population was 692 females who were assigned to or hired into clerical positions. The table also includes percentiles for secretaries, steno-clerks, typists, and filing clerks.

The statement of difficulty level provided in the manual seems somewhat ambiguous: "the level of language used in the test corresponds to that of a typical business letter." Both forms approach 1.4 syllabic intensity (number of syllables divided by number of standard words), which is considered average difficulty level.

The greatest advantage of this test is its reusability. The difficulty level is appropriate. Scoring instructions are incomplete and could lead to inconsistencies. The single spaced format makes the test more difficult both for test candidate and scorer. I would prefer using the timed writing provided by the *Typing Test for Business*.

[1009]

★USES Clerical Skills Tests. Applicants for clerical positions; 1968; 6 tests; manual (58 pages); distribution restricted to State Employment Services affiliated with the United States Employment Service; no testing fee for applicants tested through the facilities of State Employment Service offices; 40¢ per manual (available for unrestricted sale), postpaid; specimen set not available; United States Training and Employment Service; test materials distributed for the Service by United States Government Printing Office. *

a) TYPING TEST. 2 scores: speed, accuracy; Forms A, B, C, D, E, F, (1 page, mimeographed); practice test (1 page, mimeographed); 5(10) minutes for practice test, 5(10) minutes for test.

b) DICTATION TEST. Administered orally or by tape recording in part; Forms A, B, C, D, E, F, (2 pages, mimeographed) for dictation at 60, 80, and 100 wpm; separate NCS test-answer sheets (2 pages) must also be used; practice test (1 page, mimeographed) for each speed; 2(5) minutes for practice test, 25(30) minutes for test.

c) SPELLING TEST. Forms A, B, (2 pages, NCS scorable); 10(15) minutes.

d) STATISTICAL TYPING TEST. 2 scores: speed, accuracy; Form A (2 pages, mimeographed); 10(15) minutes plus untimed practice test.

e) MEDICAL SPELLING TEST. Dictation list (1 page, mimeographed); separate answer sheets must be used; (10–15) minutes.

f) LEGAL SPELLING TEST. Details same as *e* above.

REFERENCE

1. CRAMBERT, ALBERT C. "National Norms for a Separate-Answer-Sheet Dictation Test." *Personnel J* 48(6):434-9 Je '69. * (*PA* 44:2909)

INTERESTS

[1010]

★The ACT Guidance Profile, Two-Year College Edition. Junior college; 1965-69; GP; the occupational interests section is the same as the *Vocational Preference Inventory;* self-administered inventory in 5 areas of which the following 3 are profiled: occupational interests, potentials, competencies; 1 form ('67, 10 pages); revised manual ('69, c1968, 43 pages); profile ['69, 2 pages]; $8.75 per 25 sets of tests and profile sheets, postpaid; specimen set free on request; (30–45) minutes; Research and Development Division, American College Testing Program; the Program. *

a) AMBITIONS AND PLANS.

b) SELF-ESTIMATES.

c) OCCUPATIONAL INTERESTS. 7 scores: technical-realistic, scientific-intellectual, artistic, social, enterprising, clerical-conventional, infrequency.

d) POTENTIALS. 8 scores: technical, scientific, artistic, musical, literary, dramatic, social-enterprising, clerical.

e) COMPETENCIES. 10 scores: skilled trades (technical), home economics (technical), scientific, artistic, social (community service), business (enterprising), leadership (enterprising), clerical, sports, language; no norms for sports score.

REFERENCES

1. LUTZ, SANDRA W. "Do They Do What They Say They Will Do?" *ACT Res Rep* 24:1-31 Mr '68. * (*PA* 42:16016)
2. KEE, BYRON EUGENE. *Differences in Selected Characteristics Between Students Enrolled in Occupational Curriculums and Students Enrolled in Baccalaureate Curriculums at Thorton Community College.* Doctor's thesis, Ball State University (Muncie, Ind.), 1970. (*DAI* 31:2706A)

RICHARD W. WATKINS, *Associate Laboratory Director for Programs, Far West Laboratory for Educational Research and Development, Berkeley, California.*

The general purpose of the *ACT Guidance Profile* is to organize in one comprehensive form some of the information a counselor might obtain in a counseling interview and a testing session. Three specific kinds of uses are proposed : individual guidance, group guidance, and research. Responses to questions about ambitions and plans, and a self-estimate on 26 traits are to be considered individually. Responses to questions about vocational preferences and activities that the student has participated in (Potentials) or can do well (Competencies) are cumulated to yield a number of scores. The user of the GP is urged, however, to give attention to the individual questions as well as to the scores.

The *ACT Guidance Profile* was published even though still in the process of development because the authors felt that "being helpful now seemed preferable to waiting for perfection." The profile includes a number of items that are not scored and yields two scores for which no interpretive information is yet available. Thus, as with a number of instruments of this type, it will be useful in individual counseling primarily as a basis for focusing counseling sessions. Additionally, the counselee has to give some thought to questions relevant to educational and occupational choices that he might otherwise have overlooked. For this latter purpose, the profile may be particularly useful, since it draws attention to a variety of kinds of relevant questions : plans, occupational preferences, self-estimates of abilities, and accomplishments. It provides a useful vehicle for a counselor to help a student consider all of these factors in follow-up interviews. The fact that the counselee's responses on parts of the instrument can be cumulated in various ways may also be of some value, but the obvious possibilities for misinterpretation or overinterpretation of the scores suggest very strongly that the profile should not be used unless a counselor can check for and correct misinterpretations by each individual student.

Because the developers have pulled together a number of different factors with considerable imagination and sophistication, the profile may also be quite useful as a research device. Its usefulness for this purpose will be a function, however, of the sophistication of the person doing the research. Using it simply to collect and summarize descriptive statistics for various local groups will probably not be very rewarding to the user, nor will such use take advantage of the potential offered by the profile.

There are two major weaknesses in this instrument in its present form : the lack of adequate reliability for its use with individual students, particularly if scores are profiled, and the inadequacy of the normative data, which appear to be little more than a description of a relevant but fortuitous sample of two-year college students. The low reliabilities result from the developers' laudable efforts to obtain quite a lot of information in a brief period of time. However, it appears that if the instrument is to yield scores to be interpreted by conversion to percentile ranks, too much has been sacrificed in the interests of brevity. The internal consistency reliability estimates for the Vocational Preference Inventory part of the profile are generally in the mid-eighties for what appears to be a quite heterogeneous sample. However, the internal consistency coefficients for the Potential ("record of how a student says he spends his time") and Competency ("achievements that fall between the lower-level Potential scales and the higher-level Nonacademic scales in the Student Profile Section") scales range generally from the low seventies to the low eighties, with a few even below .70. Some of the scores are derived from as few as five responses ; none is based on more than 20 responses, although a greater score range is obtained since some responses are weighted. The effect of the limited number of responses on which scores are based is particularly crucial, because the score distributions for the norming sample are markedly skewed. For example, on 6 of the 24 scales, giving just one positive response places a student above the 33rd percentile.

As measures, the scores to be profiled at best indicate with some accuracy whether a student scores high on the various attributes. Unfortunately, encouraging students to profile the scores to the nearest even percentile implies much more than this. The information presented in the manual and its organization is such that even a sophisticated counselor would find it difficult or impossible to help the counselee avoid overinterpretation of the information in the GP.

To return to some of the more positive aspects of the profile, the instrument is based on what seems to be a sound premise—that the best way to get good information for educational and occupational planning is to ask straightforward questions. The questions are probably accepted by most students as reasonable ones, particularly for terminal two-year college students. Where responses are to be scored, this can be done fairly quickly by the student, although the interspersing of some unscored responses could introduce some small amount of error.

The section of the instrument on ambitions and plans asks for first and second choices; a useful method for classifying the similarity or disparity of these choices is presented. There is some evidence that similarity-disparity is related to the stability of these choices, and this suggests some worthwhile questions to pursue in the research use of the profile. However, the manual seems deficient because of the lack of detail on exactly how similar and dissimilar occupations have been classified. There are also some useful ideas and suggestions for relating plans, self-estimates, preferences, and accomplishments as a student thinks about future planning.

Overall, the *ACT Guidance Profile* is potentially a very useful instrument. Presently, it is probably useful as a device to get students to give thought to some important issues in educational-occupational decision making, while making sure that they do not overlook important factors. It may also be useful for guidance research. But more and better information about the meaning and use of the scores must be available before it can be said to justify all the uses suggested in the manual. In its present form, the scores it yields are not very satisfactory for profiling for use in guidance and should be used only if individual counseling is possible. As long as the developer's goal is to obtain information in such a wide range of areas in a relatively limited amount of time, increased technical development is not likely to improve this particular deficiency.

[1011]

★A.P.U. Occupational Interests Guide: Intermediate Version. Ages 14–18; 1966–69; OIG; 8 scores: scientific, social service, clerical/sales, literary, artistic, computational, practical, outdoor; separate forms for males, females, ('69, 8 pages) ; manual ('69, 62 pages) ; validity data based on experimental version; separate answer sheets (IBM 1230) must be used; £1 per 20 tests ; 50p per 20 answer sheets; 80p per set of scoring stencils ; 70p per manual ; £1.50 per specimen set; postage extra; (20–40) minutes; S. J. Closs, W. T. G. Bates (manual), M. C. Killcross (manual), and D. McMahon (manual) ; University of London Press Ltd. *

REFERENCE

1. KILLCROSS, M. C., AND BATES, W. T. G. "The APU Occupational Interests Guide: A Progress Report." *Occup Psychol* 42:119–22 Ap-Jl '68. * (PA 43:13345)

DAVID P. CAMPBELL, *Professor of Psychology and Director, Center for Interest Measurement Research, University of Minnesota, Minneapolis, Minnesota.*

This inventory has been developed with careful thought, and considerable research has been done with the instrument. The decisions made during the development appear to have been based on this research, and consequently the inventory has a firmer foundation than most new instruments.

The booklet contains 224 job activity statements arranged in 112 pairs; the individual is asked to indicate which one of each pair he prefers. There are actually two forms of the booklet—one for men, one for women. The 224 items were drawn from eight areas consistently appearing as important dimensions in factor analytic studies of vocational interests. There are 28 items for each of the eight areas.

The items have been carefully selected and submitted to a variety of tryouts. They seem quite reasonable for an inventory of this nature. They are easy to read and should be within the level of comprehension of most 15- and 16-year-olds. None of the items are controversial or likely to offend anyone. The item selection for this instrument has been done uncommonly well.

The authors exhibit great concern for issues such as balancing the order of the items, position sets, response sets, good impression biases, and the like; they have taken many steps to guard against such problems and, in fact, they have been so concerned about these issues that they may have substantially weakened the power of their inventory. For example, to guard against response set, they used the paired-comparison item format. This means, of course, that they are using a forced-choice technique, which means that their scores are ipsative, i.e., having a forced relationship with each other.

The advantage of this method is obvious; it allows one to look at the relative strengths of the individual's interests in the eight areas. However, there are some significant disadvantages: first, hardly any sense can be made out of normative data ; second, comparisons between groups are difficult, if they should even be made at all; third, relationships between the scales are almost impossible to interpret.

Probably the power of the inventory to discriminate between highly diverse groups has been weakened also. Thus, the information in the manual indicates that the scales show only one standard deviation between extreme groups on any given scale; this is disturbing, as good inventories almost always show at least two standard deviations between groups and some— such as the Strong, which is set up to maximize differences—show up to four or five. Because the item content of this inventory, which is excellent, should be capable of eliciting such differences between groups, one can only conclude that the scoring system is not taking full advantage of the power of the items. The same problem appears in the reliability data, where the correlations are about 10 points lower than one would expect. Only limited comparative data are included in the manual, so further sweeping generalizations about the psychometric strengths or weaknesses cannot yet be made.

The emphasis in interpreting the scores is on the two highest and two lowest scores, and this is quite sensible for a system that emphasizes the rank order of the scales. In general, all of the administrative and interpretive comments reflect common sense and experience in working with the inventory.

In summary, this inventory has been constructed with great care by a group of investigators who have paid attention to both their data and their common sense. The inventory is probably not as powerful as it could be, because they may have made a poor strategic choice in the scoring techniques. Still, it appears to be useful in its present form for its intended purpose—to help students ascertain the relative strengths of their interests in eight important areas—and the authors' demonstrated concern for using research findings to constantly improve their system augurs well for an even better instrument in the future.

DAVID G. HAWKRIDGE, *Director, Institute of Educational Technology, The Open University, Bletchley, Bucks, England.*

The first point that should be stressed about the OIG is that it is still experimental. While considerable work went into both the initial experimental version and the Intermediate Version now published, the authors feel that they have but yielded to public pressure in releasing the Guide before developmental work ends in 1971. The wisdom of their action might be judged against both the experience of users and the opinion of critics, but counseling is often loose-jointed enough to take the mild shock of inadequate instrumentation, and it is

difficult to see what improvements are likely to be suggested by users. Critics, on the other hand, comment all too often without having actually used the Guide for counseling.

The general impression given by both the Guide and its manual is very good. The team that prepared the manual worked with great thoroughness on instructions for administration, score interpretation, and so on. Considerable statistical analysis was undertaken and the main results are presented in the manual, along with nonstatistical explanations of the implications of the analysis. There is certainly no lack of detailed information on how the test was constructed or on its reliability.

There are several points that should be raised in the minds of potential users, however, including two important ones related to validity: the definition of interests and the predictive power of the Guide.

INTERESTS. The authors of the manual are at pains to define *interest*. They point out that there are many definitions of the term in the general literature of occupational psychology but choose as their definition, "interest is the satisfaction which a person derives from indulging in certain types of activities." They emphasize that *satisfaction* is central to their concept of interest. The Guide is designed to yield scores showing the relative strengths of interest in eight areas.

This definition of interest seems contradicted, however, when the authors point out that "error would occur if the counsellor assumed that high scores in any category of the Guide always meant that the subject liked that type of activity." They say that in most cases the counselor can make this assumption. In some, he should not, but they do not indicate which cases are the exceptions.

The definition of interest becomes even more vital when we examine individual items (which are paired statements). The authors of the manual point out the very real problem of persuading children to say what they would like to do when they do not know enough about the world of work, but the Guide has not overcome this problem. The items list tasks that are clearly occupational, such as: "serve meals in a restaurant." Since the Guide is intended for ages 14–18, the subjects have to make imaginative leaps to choose one of each pair of statements. It is true that the Guide aims at relative scores of interest, not absolute ones. This fact allows the authors to be less than concise in their conceptualization of interest because the woolliness of the children's thinking about each statement is spread about equally over all the categories.

PREDICTIVE POWER. No studies of the predictive power of the published Intermediate Version have been reported yet. The validity data quoted in the manual refer to the Experimental Version, which was substantially different in two categories. The authors conclude that "the Guide does give a valid indication of a person's occupational interests," but this conclusion scarcely seems justified from the evidence they present.

To begin with, there is no indication of how many adults were questioned about their job satisfaction, although 548 replies were received. Those who answered may have been a biased sample. Moreover, most of them could have been in employment only a very short time, or possibly were pursuing further education. It seems likely that their answers would reflect test-retest reliability rather than the predictive power of the Guide.

There seems a good deal of room for improvement here. The validity of the Guide does not appear to be truly established yet, and the authors' conclusion is unwarranted in the light of the evidence they offer.

GENERALIZABILITY. A further note of warning should be sounded concerning the population on which the Guide was developed, and hence the Guide's generalizability. The population employed was restricted to Edinburgh schools. Although it numbered several thousands, there is no indication in the manual of its representativeness of the area, let alone of British society. Cultural bias in the Guide may be too slight to influence the *relative* scores, of course, but if the Guide were to be used in another country, such as the United States, many of the items would need to be altered. To quote a few: "Write a summary or précis of a novel," "Draw and paint coats of arms," "Work with a horse to drag timber from a forest," and "Straighten a buckled bicycle wheel." These may be all right for Scotland, or even for England, but they would be unsuitable in many other countries.

TRAINING FOR USERS. In the foreword to the manual it is stated that the Guide will not be supplied to any counselor before he or she attends a short training course. Apart from the fact that no details are offered in the manual or by the publishers about such a course, the completeness of the manual apparently leaves little room for further training. The only clue to the possible content of training is the comment that interpretation of scores on the Guide in relation to other data available is a skilled job. This comment makes one wonder what in-group mystique is to be preached and whether the Guide's effectiveness depends on the user's having been initiated. Surely not.

AUTOMATED SCORING. Although the manual says that arrangements were being made for a scoring service (and IBM 1230 forms are supplied for answers), no such service is in fact available. At four minutes per subject, manual scoring could be quite tedious. Probably the provision of a scoring service will come only when many copies per year are used. The embryonic counseling services in British schools do not yet generate high demands.

SUMMARY. The Guide is the best yet developed in Britain, although its development is incomplete. For British secondary school children, it can be recommended over imported materials such as the Kuder and SVIB, in spite of the fact that these two are far longer established. The Guide is better than the *Connolly Occupational Interests Questionnaire;* it appears to have been prepared and tried out with more care and is more suitable for school children.

[1012]

★**California Occupational Preference Survey.** Grades 9–16 and adults; 1966–70; COPS; 14 scores: science professional, science skilled, technical professional, technical skilled, outdoor, business professional, business skilled, clerical, linguistic professional, linguistic skilled, aesthetic professional, aesthetic skilled, service professional, service skilled; 1 form; 2 editions; excerpts from manual of interpretation ('70, 22 pages, only manual available); 75¢ per manual; $2.25 per specimen set; postage extra; (30–40) minutes; Robert R. Knapp, Bruce Grant, and George D. Demos; Educational and Industrial Testing Service. *

a) CONSUMABLE EDITION. 1 form ('66, 5 pages); self interpreting profile ('66, 4 pages); $5 per 25 tests; $4.25 per 50 profiles.

b) REUSABLE EDITION. 1 form ('66, 4 pages); profile ('66, 1 page) for high school; profile ('68, 1 page) for college; separate answer sheets (Digitek, IBM 1230) must be used; $4.25 per 25 tests; $4 per 50 answer sheets; $3.50 per 50 profiles; $7 per set of IBM hand scoring stencils; scoring service, 85¢ or less per test.

REFERENCE

1. FREEBERG, NORMAN E. "Assessment of Disadvantaged Adolescents: A Different Approach to Research and Evaluation Measures." *J Ed Psychol* 61(3):229–40 Je '70. *

JACK L. BODDEN, *Assistant Professor of Psychology, Texas Tech University, Lubbock, Texas.*

While there are some minor variations, the COPS is basically quite similar in its construction to the *Kuder Preference Record—Vocational.* Both instruments involve homogeneous keying. Scales on the COPS were derived from a factor analysis of items written to reflect differences in occupational activity and differences in occupational levels (i.e., professional vs. skilled).

The COPS has certain novel and commendable features. One example is that it is designed to be equally useful with college students, high school students who are planning to attend college, and those who are not. It accomplishes this objective by breaking six of its interest groupings into professional and skilled categories. In so doing, the COPS tends to avoid being a predominantly professional, college-oriented instrument, such as the *Strong Vocational Interest Blank.*

Another virtue of the COPS is that it does not employ a forced-choice format, which many subjects find offensive. Instead, it allows the subject to choose from four alternatives in order to indicate whether and to what degree he likes or dislikes a given activity. There may also be some advantages to the fact that items are composed almost entirely of *activities* rather than a mixture of activities and occupational titles. This arrangement would appear to help free the scores of contamination resulting from occupational ignorance and status considerations.

Finally, the test authors have tried to construct the manual in such a manner as to facilitate the acquisition of occupational information relevant to a subject's measured interests. The manual is keyed to the *Dictionary of Occupational Titles* (DOT). For example, under each interest dimension, the manual lists representative occupations, along with DOT codes and page numbers. Hopefully, such a feature might encourage counselors and clients to pursue the additional information to be found in the DOT.

While possessing certain desirable attributes, the COPS has its share of flaws. To begin with, specific information about the nature of the norm groups is not to be found. In fact, the only statement about norms is that there are high school and college norms and that percentiles are printed on the profile sheets.

Another, more serious weakness is the dearth of validity information presented in the manual. For instance, no correlations between the COPS and existing interest inventories, such as the Kuder or Strong, are given. The manual does make some vague reference to studies presumably carried out by the authors on "small samples from a variety of occupations." These studies were reported to show that persons working in a given occupation generally obtained their highest COPS score on the logical or expected scale (e.g., radiomen had their highest score on the Technical-Skilled scale). Obviously it is a difficult and time-consuming task to collect convincing validity data, but it seems that the authors of the COPS have not expended enough effort in this regard.

Another annoying omission is the manual's failure to report reliability and stability data obtained from a college population. The manual does report reliability and stability information obtained with high school students, and, in general, the reliability coefficients are satisfactory. Stability coefficients obtained over one- and two-year periods are less satisfactory (e.g., median coefficient for one year was .66 and for a two-year interval was .63). These lower-than-wished-for coefficients obtained with 10th–12th graders are not really surprising. What is surprising is that the authors did not attempt (or at least report) stability data based on college students, since it is generally known that vocational interests are more stable at the college level than they are during high school.

There are a few other problems with the manual, such as its failure to report scale intercorrelations, but most stem from its skimpiness.

One final caution for potential users should be noted. The COPS (like the Kuder, Form C) is an example of homogeneous keying, and, therefore, high scale scores do not always correspond to the interests of persons actually working in the "logical" or "expected" occupation. This caution is especially important when no empirical evidence is available.

In conclusion, there seems to be little reason for potential users to select the *California Occupational Preference Survey* over established inventories such as the Kuder, Forms C, D, or DD, or the *Strong Vocational Interest Blank.* The COPS suffers from most of the same general limitations found in the other inventories but does not receive any of the benefit from the research data which have accumulated around these more established inventories. Also, such inventories as the Kuder, Form DD, and the newest revision of the Strong are more versatile than the COPS, in that they utilize both empirical keying and homogeneous keying. Perhaps if some of the weaknesses described above are remedied, the COPS could be considered as a viable alternative to the KPR-V.

JOHN W. FRENCH, *Research Consultant, Sarasota, Florida.*

This is a free-response inventory of activities. That simple statement indicates how the author of this instrument has settled some of the difficult issues that bear upon the measurement of interests.

First, there must be a justification for measuring interests at all. Why not simply ask a person which occupations do in fact interest him the most? For most people there is a good answer to this. They do not know of the existence of many occupations, and, even for the ones they know, they are very vague about what activities are important in performing them. The *Strong Vocational Interest Blank,* for example, lists a multitude of occupational titles or job names. If the student can understand many of these names, he may be usefully reminded of the many possibilities available to him. However, it takes an activities inventory like this one to supply the needed connection between actual kind of work and job title.

The reading materials for the *California Occupational Preference Survey* illustrate the usefulness of this kind of instrument by emphasizing the idea of broadening the student's vocational knowledge. To this end the test is set up so that a student can learn much about vocations from the process of taking the test, scoring it, and interpreting the scores. The manual urges that he be helped to use this knowledge to explore further the occupations that are most likely to form his career. Particular stress is placed on the student's choice between professional and skilled employment. Contrasting college level jobs with vocational school or noncollege jobs is of obvious importance to counseling in high schools. Even within college it is important to keep a student's attention on the occupational goals to which he is reasonably able to aspire by maintaining certain

kinds of academic progress. Further confidence in this inventory can come from the fact that the major distinction between skills and professions, as well as the division of a comprehensive list of interests into 14 occupational families, was suggested by a careful factor-analytic research approach.

The authors of this inventory have chosen to score the 14 scales by simply adding up points of credit on each one: three points for liking a related activity very much, two points for liking it moderately, one point for disliking it moderately, and nothing for disliking it very much. This is a much criticized psychometric technique, because subjects have no clear standard for what is meant by *liking.* On a mere whim, some subjects could respond that they like nearly everything, while others with equally high interests might indicate a strong liking only on rare occasions. For this reason, comparisons across subjects are not accurate, even though internal consistency or test-retest reliability is adequate. Perhaps a warning about this would have been appropriate in the manual. Actually the norms presented in the manual have to do less with interest than with the average subject's interpretation of the word *like.* Nevertheless, it is quite proper to present a table of norms for whatever use it may have. The table presented here is clear, although more information about the subjects would give it more meaning.

In order to circumvent the problem that arises because of the varying standards of response to the word *like,* some interest tests employ forced choices between the members of pairs of alternatives, rather than free responses. This solves the standardization problem, but a new problem arises, because the selection of one member of a pair not only enhances the score for one interest but also depresses the score for another. In consequence, there appear spuriously low or negative intercorrelations between interest scores. Free responses, on the other hand, lead to spuriously high scores on all interests for subjects who indicate a liking too freely, while they lead to spuriously low scores for subjects who take a strict interpretation of the word *like.* As a result, the intercorrelations of free-response interest scores tend to be quite high. Indeed the intercorrelations among the scales of this inventory are all positive, and they run upwards into the .80's. The authors express satisfaction that this situation contrasts with the low or negative intercorrelations found for forced-choice inventories. However, the high intercorrelations are just as false but in the opposite direction. It is probable that improved measurement would result from a compromise between the two methods of testing. Some restriction of response could be balanced by some degree of response freedom, as illustrated by the *College Interest Inventory*. Other combinations of the two methods should be tried.

The authors claim that their free responses produce honest scores. Indeed it can be said that free responses have an advantage over forced-choice responses, because subjects find them far more agreeable to make, and so rapport between subject and experimenter is better. At the same time, however, free responses have a disadvantage in that they make it easier to fake a desired score. It seems to follow, therefore, that where subjects can be counted on as willing counselees who desire the truth about themselves, this free-response instrument will be liked by the subjects and will produce honest scores. On the other hand, where subjects are required to take the test, the most honest scores may well be those that are obtained from a forced-choice test that cannot easily be faked.

Two studies of reliability show satisfactory figures, although more information about the groups tested in the studies is required for evaluation. A good study demonstrating satisfactory stability of scores over two years is reported. Construct validity, as demonstrated by a factor analysis, seems to be quite good. Concurrent validity studies with people already in several occupations are mentioned. There is no mention of any check on predictive validity.

COPS suffers, along with other free-response inventories, by being rather easily fakable and by being subject to variability of individual standards as to what is meant by *liked* or *disliked*. In addition, too little research is reported on concurrent validity and none is reported on predictive validity. Nevertheless, it seems likely to this reviewer that the instrument will be useful to students who desire to learn about their own interests. Construction of the scales was carried out competently; coverage of both professions and skills is excellent; and the test and manual are set up so as to be highly instructive to the student.

J Ed Meas 6(1):56–8 sp '69. Robert H. Bauernfeind. The "in" thing these days is to criticize all self-report inventories as being sterile, fakable, inane. Although I lean toward that view myself, I also find many positive features in the California Occupational Preference Survey (COPS). But first we need a context for this review. The COPS instrument, like other self-report inventories, is clearly fakable, and it thus has no place in employment work. But if we think of high school students, and if we assume that most of these students would not care to fake their responses, the instrument begins to come to life—for five quite independent reasons: (1) The COPS instrument has a solid rationale, developed and checked through multiple-factor analysis studies. The area scores make sense. (2) The questionnaire items are written in good clear English. A few items involve technical terms that may hamper a poor reader—terms like "psychotherapy," "alleviate," "corrosive," "interpersonal." But perhaps there are no suitable synonyms for these terms. In any event, it is not possible to develop a printed questionnaire that can accommodate all of the reading problems one finds in high schools. (3) The COPS instrument uses the free response (graduated response) format, such that a student can show *how* he feels about each activity presented. Each item is marked: L = Like very much, l = like moderately, d = dislike moderately, D = Dislike very much. Unlike the Kuder, Edwards, and Lee-Thorpe instruments, COPS is an "honest" questionnaire, designed to help the student to say how he really feels. (And, wonder of wonders, the correlations among the COPS area scores are positive: Some students are just plain more interested in everything than others. These intercorrelation data contrast beautifully with the dull negative intercorrelations one usually obtains after shoving children through a Kuder-type forced-choice instrument.) (4) Twelve of the scores represent six couplets—Science-Professional and Science-Skilled, for example. By contrasting these pairs of scores, the counselor can judge whether the student's interest would or would not require post-high school education. The counselor can then check the student's "college aptitude" from other tests to see whether the student may have overaspirations or underaspirations for his possible future careers. (5) The Self-Scoring Booklet is very easy for the student to mark, and very easy for the counselor to study. Each response is lined up directly with the stimulus item. Thus, the counselor can quickly circle all of the student's "L" (Like very much) responses; and, by turning the pages back and forth he can quickly note the actual items that evoked the "L" responses. Because this is not an ipsative forced-choice questionnaire, the item responses have straight-forward meanings, and each item response can be studied as a useful piece of information. Our ninth-grade son completed the inventory in about 30 minutes' time—a fact that supports the authors' contention that most students will finish the instrument in one class period. I quickly noted that he had marked "L" on three items; I looked up the three items, and thought about them as they related to his area-scores profile—all in about two minutes' time. Thus, the instrument seems manageable in the real-life setting of busy counselors preparing for student interviews. A thought keeps recurring that is difficult to communicate, but that should be tried: The authors of the COPS instrument seem to have been more concerned with youngsters than with standard deviations—more concerned with helping busy counselors than with straining for minute increases in scale reliabilities. We need more test authors like these who are people oriented. * The authors....report not only split-halves estimates but also stability coefficients for 1-week, 1-year, and 2-year intervals. The median coefficient for the 2-year study was .63, which seems quite satisfactory for so straightforward a questionnaire. * As noted earlier, the authors cleverly rejected the ipsative forced-choice format, and they consistently report positive correlations among the scales, which makes sense psychologically. In one study of high school girls, the intercorrelations ranged from +.12 to +.85. In a similar study of high school boys, the intercorrelations ranged from +.16 to +.87. The scores are interpreted as percentile ranks on general norms; but the "general norms" are not defined, and it is not clear what populations they represent. This is probably not a serious shortcoming, however, since many larger schools will prefer to develop their own local norms anyway. The one really bad thing about the authors' work to date is an error of commission: They have printed "typical profiles" (group means, apparently) for very small occupational groups, with no accompanying information about who was involved, when, where, and under what testing conditions. Thus, the typical profile for 39 cosmetology students, and the typical profile

for 25 men in skilled trades—these "typical profiles" are a menace; some counselor somewhere just might be silly enough to use them in a counseling interview. The authors should eliminate all of these profiles from their publishing program immediately! They should then adopt one of two policies: *Do it right, or forget it!* "Do it right" means doing a comprehensive job of testing workmen from all over the country, replicating a couple of times, and then publishing "typical profiles" along with detailed reports of how the data were compiled.

SUMMARY. The California Occupational Preference Survey was developed with professional skill and with human sensitivity. It was designed to confirm the occupational areas of major interest to a student, and to help his counselor to judge whether or not his present interests would require a college education. It is an honest questionnaire, with straightforward items—easy to mark, easy to score, and maybe sometimes easy to interpret. Finally there is the question of the value of these kinds of instruments at all. Many counselors say they do not need these kinds of questionnaires to confirm a student's interests, and they are probably right—for themselves. Other counselors insist that such questionnaires often help with the counseling interview. For the latter group, the COPS instrument can be strongly recommended as the best this reviewer has seen.

[1013]

★California Pre-Counseling Self-Analysis Protocol Booklet. Student counselees; 1965; unscored survey of information and interests to be completed by student prior to counseling; 1 form (4 pages); no manual; no data on reliability; $5.50 per 25 booklets, postpaid; (5–20) minutes; George D. Demos and Bruce Grant; Western Psychological Services. *

[1014]

★College Interest Inventory. Grades 11–16; 1967; CII; 16 scores: agriculture, home economics, literature and journalism, fine arts, social science, physical science, biological science, foreign language, business administration, accounting, teaching, civil engineering, electrical engineering, mechanical engineering, law, total; 1 form (9 pages); manual (12 pages); profile (1 page); separate answer sheets (IBM 805) must be used; $20 per 25 tests; $1 per single copy; $9 per 100 answer sheets; $6 per 100 profiles; $2.50 per set of scoring stencils; $1 per manual; cash orders only; (30) minutes; Robert W. Henderson; Personal Growth Press. *

JOHN W. FRENCH, *Research Consultant, Sarasota, Florida.*

This inventory makes a contribution by offering a rather simple and reasonable compromise in the controversy between the two principal interest-measuring instruments. On the one hand, the *Strong Vocational Interest Blank* permits expression of all degrees of interest, "strongly like" to "strongly dislike," on every item. This results in independently made measurements in each separate interest area, and the freedom of response is agreeable to test takers. However, different standards of like and dislike or different whims can cause wide variation in individual test results and spuriously high correlations between interest scores. On the other hand, the *Kuder Preference Record—Vocational* presents a forced choice between two activities with every item. This results in spurious negative correlations between interest scores, and it is notably annoying to test takers. Nevertheless, this system entails an automatic ipsative standard that produces stability in the scores and also forces the test taker to think hard as he makes his responses. For a long time psychologists have been aware that both of these techniques have serious disadvantages.

The *College Interest Inventory* represents a clearly understandable compromise between these two. Each of the 45 main items offers some restriction but much freedom of response. Within each of these items there are 15 subitems consisting of occupations, areas of study, or activities. The task is to mark the most interesting one, two, three, four, or five of the subitems in each main item. This technique partially supplies the ipsative standard yet provides some leeway for expressing varying degrees of total interest.

The compromise results in intercorrelations among the scores that seem reasonably balanced: similar interests are highly correlated, while dissimilar interests have low or negative relationships. Also, there is a moderately agreeable task for the test taker. For each item, he is not forced to mark "yes" for one activity and "no" for the other as he is in the Kuder, but he must mark positively at least one item out of 15 even if he dislikes them all, and he may not mark more than 5 even if he likes them all. This sounds very good, but it occurs to this reviewer that, for some test takers, it may be quite an effort, maybe an impossible one, to consider 15 subitems all at once in order to make careful discriminations among them.

The construction, the interpretation, and the presentation of data for this inventory in its manual are pleasingly simple and straightforward for busy users. However, such simple

treatment of a new instrument can never be justified, because decisions as to what instrument to use and how it should be interpreted can be complex and should be aided by a full understanding of the details of construction and research in conjunction with the individual user's full comprehension of the use he has in mind. A summary of some of the missing details follows:

We are told that 675 most discriminative subitems were retained and 825 less discriminative ones were eliminated from the "original....inventory." In a private communication, the author has indicated something of this discrimination and it seems fairly satisfactory. However, we need to know something of the purpose, scope, and construction of the original items.

Standardization of the inventory is based on "junior and senior college students who have indicated that they intend to follow the occupation relevant to the college curriculum." Also through private communication, the author elaborated that these were 537 University of Kentucky students representing the colleges of arts and sciences, commerce, engineering, education, and agriculture. Supplemental information for students at Baldwin-Wallace College is helpful. This population is probably not too bad for use in item selection, but it is wholly inadequate for constructing a table of norms, except for use at the University of Kentucky or at Baldwin-Wallace College. Norms for a generalizable published test should be based on results from a distribution of colleges. When they are based on a restricted population like this one, the manual should present other data to describe peculiarities in the population that was used and should tell the user quite precisely what kind of differences to expect at colleges that are of different types and located in other regions.

Characteristically, validity data take longer to acquire than norming or reliability data. Since this is a new instrument, the validity data are correspondingly thin. Evidence for validity is introduced in the manual as "preliminary validity." Indeed there is mention of ongoing studies to correlate interest scores with appropriate grades in college. There is some encouraging evidence that a high total score on the test is associated with a high grade point average. It can be argued very readily that a test should not be placed on the market until some direct validity data and some correlations with other tests are available. Two claims to validity are made in the present manual. One of these consists of significant differences between inventory scores appropriate for subjects and made by subjects planning to enter certain occupations as compared to scores made by the entire group of subjects. The other evidence of validity is the fact that the intercorrelations among the interest scores are reasonable: high correlations between similar occupations and low or negative ones between dissimilar ones. It must be pointed out, however, that even these claims for validity may be spurious, since the significance tests and intercorrelations were evidently performed with the same population that was used for item selection and the separation of items into scales. Crossvalidation is urgently needed.

In summary, this is an attractive, simple, and direct interest inventory for college students, which embodies a compromise between the problems that are inherent in the forced choice and in the free response technique. At the present stage in the development of the instrument, however, we cannot be sure of its validity or of the proper interpretation of its norms at colleges other than the one where the norms tables were constructed. At present only highly experienced persons should attempt to make safe judgments and interpretations from the scores.

DAVID A. PAYNE, *Professor of Educational Psychology and Curriculum and Supervision, University of Georgia, Athens, Georgia.*

This inventory, proposed as a tool useful in academic counseling aimed at exploring occupationally-related curricular choices, is based on an interesting implicit premise. This premise is that a combination of forced and free-choice methodology should yield the most valid interest measurement. Data supplied by the author and publisher are suggestive but far from conclusive.

This inventory is virtually self-administering. Directions lead the respondent to select "at least one but not more than five choices" from each group of 15 items. There are 45 such blocks, each being concerned with (*a*) a course of study, (*b*) an occupation, or (*c*) a behavior activity or task associated with a course of study or occupation.

Validity of the CII relates to the question, "Do the scores on this instrument in fact reflect the interests they purport to measure?" A tentative "probably" must be the answer to this question at this stage of development. Basically, validity was established by use of contrasted groups criterion-keying methodology. Items which discriminated those students who indicated an intent to follow a vocation closely connected with a particular curriculum (e.g., C.P.A. with Accounting) from students in general were selected from an original pool of 100 items. This is surely an acceptable practice. Its application here, however, may be open to question on two counts. First, there is a question of voiced intent versus actual entry into the particular occupations or even successful completion of the course of study. Second, the criterion group sample sizes were severely restricted in size, some being as small as 16.

Interscale correlations support the relative independence of the 15 curricular groupings. These, about half between −.20 and .20, can partially be accounted for as an artifact of the forced-choice methodology.

Obviously, more validity data are needed. One would be interested in data on academically successful high scorers, for example, or follow-up data related to professed interest and field of entry.

Internal consistency (corrected split-half) within curriculum groupings is excellent. The lack of stability reliability data is unfortunate.

Test interpretation is facilitated by the use of a profile sheet which contains the means of the criterion groups as well as a shaded area corresponding to the score range for the middle 70 percent of each of those groups, and the mean scores for the "students in general" on a particular scale. Percentile ranks can be approximated from the profile chart. However, only 11 to 13 percentiles per curriculum are provided for guidance in making the approximations.

The counselor is more or less left to his own devices with regard to using the test information with clients. Some general suggestions are made and some probing questions presented. The test undoubtedly can provide a valuable function by serving as a springboard in initiating student self-appraisal and establishing a counseling relationship. It would be extremely helpful if a kind of casebook were provided potential users. Such a reference could suggest ways in which CII data may be used with particular types of students.

College Interest Inventory

The CII in its present form should probably be considered a preliminary, or experimental, edition. As new data are incorporated into a new manual and the essential recommendations of the *Standards for Educational and Psychological Tests and Manuals* are emphasized, concern about the psychometric properties of the CII will lessen. The basic problem with the CII during its current infancy is lack of validity data. If for no other reason than this, its many competitors, chiefly the *Strong Vocational Interest Blank,* must be preferred.

[1015]

★Connolly Occupational Interests Questionnaire. Ages 15 and over; 1967–70; COIQ; 7 scores: scientific, social welfare, persuasive, literary, artistic, clerical-computational, practical; 1 form ('67, 4 pages); manual ('68, 38 pages); supplementary manual ('70, 19 pages); no data on reliability; £3.75 per 100 tests; 42½p per set of scoring stencils; 52½p per manual; 30p per supplementary manual; £1.25 per specimen set; postpaid within U.K.; [15–20] minutes; T. G. Connolly and Joshua Fox (supplementary manual); Careers Research and Advisory Centre. *

REFERENCES

1. CONNOLLY, THOMAS GERARD. *A Contribution to the Measurement of Occupational Interests.* Doctor's thesis, Birkbeck College, University of London (London, England), 1955.
2. MOREA, P. C. "Interests in Relation to Student Success." *Occup Psychol* 43(2):145–50 '69. * (PA 44:17553)

DAVID G. HAWKRIDGE, *Director, Institute of Educational Technology, The Open University, Bletchley, Bucks, England.*

The *Connolly Occupational Interests Questionnaire* should have been published as an experimental version. The depth and extent of work behind the COIQ leave much to be desired.

CONSTRUCTION. The seven fields of interest included in the questionnaire were derived from earlier studies by others, with acknowledgements to both the *Kuder Preference Record— Vocational* and the *Strong Vocational Interest Blank.* The manual states that "the interest factors that these studies had revealed were examined by the use of such statistical techniques as factor analysis and items [*sic*] analysis," but no bibliographical reference is provided for these studies nor is it stated who carried them out. The author also states that the choice of occupations within each field of interest was initially arbitrary to some extent and that "subsequent statistical analysis has indicated a high degree of validity." He offers no details or data in support of this statement.

The selection of occupations was followed by the selection of statements to describe one activity within each occupation. There is no indica-

tion in the manual of how the statements were generated or finally selected to become (in pairs) the items in the questionnaire.

Having constructed the set of items, the author apparently decided to provide a base profile of interests, for comparison purposes. A random sample of 300 adults in the general population completed the questionnaire. Again, the manual provides no details of how the sample was drawn or what precautions were taken against sampling bias in this risky area.

Two histograms show the base profiles from Parts 1 and 2 of the questionnaire. The means and standard deviations are given, but the author irritatingly tells one that "even without any statistical analysis it is immediately apparent that there is a striking similarity between [the parts]." He does not present the analysis at all, leaving it to the reader to confirm the pictorial representation for himself.

Other histograms show the profiles for samples drawn from three occupational groups. Again there is no information on how the samples were selected, although the sample characteristics are at least stated clearly, and the statistical results of analysis of differences are quoted for these profiles.

VALIDITY. There is no statement in the manual about the validity of the Connolly. The three small studies of occupational groups were intended to increase the user's confidence in the instrument, perhaps. Certainly, the existence of some kind of construct validity could be inferred, say, from the fact that people interested in words, such as authors, journalists, and so on, scored highly on Group H (e.g., "write articles or special reports for magazines").

Unfortunately, no such firm pattern emerges. The 85 structural engineering draughtsmen, all professionally qualified and in the occupation for at least five years, showed only average interest in Group K, a mixture of clerical and computational tasks. The author says that item analysis here showed that they may have liked the computational tasks but not the clerical ones. The same draughtsmen showed themselves quite interested in Group E, a range of scientific research interests, and highly interested in Group L, mechanical and manipulative tasks.

A study of 200 department store sales staff shows that Group G (persuasive) interests were high, but, surprisingly, Group H (artistic) interests were also relatively high. For 260 post office clerks, Group K interests were high, but this fact is difficult to interpret, since the actual clerical and computational tasks listed in the Connolly are only slightly more closely related to post office clerking than they are to engineering draughtsmanship. Group L (mechanical/manipulative) interests were almost as high as those for Group K.

RELIABILITY. No studies of reliability are quoted, not even the usual test-retest type using groups of schoolchildren. There seems to have been no attempt to assess the internal consistency of the questionnaire.

INSTRUCTIONS. The instructions for administering the Connolly are given in a manual published in 1968, after the 1967 edition of the questionnaire itself and presumably after some considerable experience with the questionnaire. From data quoted later in the manual, over 800 *adults* had completed the questionnaire. Additional notes issued in 1970 following use of the Connolly in classrooms of secondary schools are quite contradictory. Perhaps *children* do require different testing conditions, but one is left wondering whether the different instructions are more a function of the teachers' authoritarian views than anything essential for successful use of the Connolly. No attempt is made by the author to reconcile the glaring differences.

SCORING. Scoring of the questionnaire is a tedious business. No automated service is available. Scoring templates are provided, but the 1970 additional notes suggest that two persons work together to do the scoring, since the templates do not help the scorer to pick out quickly all the answers belonging to a particular group. A tally system has to be used instead.

INTERPRETATION. The interpretation of scores on the Connolly is intended to yield data that are only part of the data available for counselling the individual. The author is on safe ground in pointing out that many other factors should be taken into consideration in the counselling process. The user has to be taught how to speculate on what the questionnaire data mean, however, and the manual suggests that he consider scores above the 75th or below the 25th percentile. The author says that "these percentiles lie between the 1% and 5% levels of significance for tests having a reliability of 0.9." It is hard to interpret this statement when the Connolly has no quoted reliability coefficient. It is sufficient to note that on the three profiles given in the manual, scarcely any of the percentile ranks lie beyond the limits just quoted; one might say that the scores reflected random variations in most cases.

SUMMARY. Norms for the Connolly were first gathered in 1954. It is incredible that so little has been done to refine the questionnaire or to provide statistical support for it. What is even more surprising is that it should be sponsored and published by an independent nonprofit research and advisory centre with a panel of distinguished advisers.

There seem to be no grounds for claiming that the Connolly should be used, in Britain or elsewhere. It is not a proven instrument, psychologically speaking. Use of the *A.P.U. Occupational Interests Guide,* or the American instruments mentioned earlier, would be much preferred.

[1016]

★Crowley Occupational Interests Blank. Ages 13 and over of average ability or less; 1970; COIB; 10 scores: 5 interest areas (active-outdoor, office, social, practical, artistic) and 5 sources of job satisfaction (financial gain, stability-security, companionship, working conditions, interest); separate forms for boys, girls, (2 pages); manual (52 pages); no data on reliability; registration fee for administrator: £1 (includes manual and scoring stencil); £3.50 per 100 tests; postpaid within U.K.; specimen copy of blanks available to schools; (20–30) minutes; A. D. Crowley; Careers Research and Advisory Centre. *

[1017]

★Educational Interest Inventory. Grades 11–13; 1962–70; EII; 18 or 19 scores: literature, music, art, communication, education, business administration (men), engineering (men), industrial arts (men), agriculture (men), secretarial arts (women), nursing (women), library arts (women), home economics (women), botany, zoology, physics, chemistry, earth science (men), history and political science, sociology, psychology, economics, mathematics; Forms A ('64, 13 pages, for men), B ('64, 12 pages, for women); manual ('62, 4 pages); profile ('62, 2 pages); validity report ['65, 4 pages] by Thomas C. Oliver and Warren K. Willis; norms ['70, 5 pages] for grade 13 only; separate answer sheets must be used; 50¢ per test; 10–99 answer sheets, 10¢ each; 5¢ per profile; 50¢ per manual and validity report; $2 per specimen set; postage extra; [40–45] minutes; James E. Oliver; Educational Guidance, Inc. *

REFERENCES

1. RISHEL, DARRELL FRED. The Development and Validation of Instruments and Techniques for the Selective Admission of Applicants for Graduate Studies in Counselor Education. Doctor's thesis, Pennsylvania State University (University Park, Pa.), 1961. (DA 22:2271)
2. MEISGEIER, CHARLES HENRY. Variables Which May Identify Successful Student Teachers of Mentally or Physically Handicapped Children. Doctor's thesis, Pennsylvania State University (University Park, Pa.), 1962. (DA 23:3803)
3. WEISER, JOHN CONRAD. A Study of College of Education Students Divided According to Creative Ability. Doctor's thesis, University of Missouri (Columbia, Mo.), 1962. (DA 23:4611)
4. MILLER, C. DEAN, AND THOMAS, DONALD L. "Relationships Between Educational and Vocational Interests." Voc Guid Q 15:113–8 D '66. * (PA 41:12640)

5. MORRILL, WESTON H.; MILLER, C. DEAN; AND THOMAS, LUCINDA E. "Educational and Vocational Interests of College Women." *Voc Guid Q* 19(2):85–9 D '70. *

6. THOMAS, LUCINDA E.; MORRILL, WESTON H.; AND MILLER, C. DEAN. "Educational Interests and Achievements." *Voc Guid Q* 18(3):199–202 Mr '70. *

[1018]

★**The Factorial Interest Blank.** Ages 11–16; 1967; FIB; 8 scores: rural-practical, sociable, humanitarian, entertainment, physical, literate, aesthetic, scientific-mechanical; 1 form ['67, 4 pages]; manual ['67, 23 pages]; profile ['67, 2 pages]; separate answer sheets must be used; 65p per 25 tests; 50p per 25 answer sheets; 50p per 25 profiles; 20p per set of scoring stencils; £1 per manual; £1.42 per specimen set; postage extra; (20–60) minutes; P. H. Sandall; distributed by NFER Publishing Co. Ltd. *

REFERENCE

1. SANDALL, P. H. *An Analysis of the Interests of Secondary School Pupils.* Doctor's thesis, University of London (London, England), 1960.

DAVID P. CAMPBELL, *Professor of Psychology and Director, Center for Interest Measurement Research, University of Minnesota, Minneapolis, Minnesota.*

This is a short inventory, easy to administer and fairly easy to score; that about exhausts its favorable points.

The booklet has 120 paired comparison items: "Spend a wet afternoon weaving a scarf OR playing the gramophone." The items are generally straightforward and unambiguous, with considerable face validity. But there is no rationale given for why they should be forced-choice rather than free-response.

The inventory has eight scales, generated from a factor analysis study that was apparently part of the author's doctoral dissertation at the University of London. Some, but not all, of his scales have appeared in most other factor analyses of interests. And some factors which turn up in virtually everybody's studies are absent here, such as sales interests or general business interests. Although the author takes pains in the manual to demonstrate how his scales fit into the results from other factor analytic studies (presumably to coattail on their validity results), the similarities are forced and overdone.

The eight scales were built to be internally consistent—but the mean corrected split-half reliability coefficient was only .78 for boys, .74 for girls, scarcely high enough to generate much confidence in the integrity of the factors. The mean test-retest reliability coefficient over a one month period is .90, which is adequate short-term stability.

The validity statistics are horribly shoddy. Two studies are reported. In the first, the distribution of scores on the Scientific-Mechanical scale for 81 secondary school boys who "chose a course with a definite scientific bias" were compared with a chance distribution; when the chi-square came out significant, the author concluded that "Category Sci. is highly significant as a predictor." There is no mention of the other high scores that these boys might have had or of the possibility that other boys might have had equally high scores on this scale. The author was apparently not even aware that these might be potential problems.

The second validity study reports a follow-up study of 600 boys and girls; the entire account takes only four sentences and two pages of tables. This is totally inadequate and it is a disservice to the testing profession to pretend that this is useful information.

In summary, this is a fourth- or fifth-rate inventory. Because it has fairly adequate face validity and two or three scales that always carry a lot of variance in interest measurement, such as Scientific-Mechanical and Aesthetic, there is a certain air of reasonableness to it. Conceivably it could serve as a stimulus for classroom discussions of occupations. But to use it in any sense as a predictive instrument, or as one to advise students in career decisions, or in research studies where one needs some decent measures of occupational interests, is not warranted. The author and publisher should withdraw this inventory from use until much more developmental research is done.

HUGH F. PRIEST, *Senior Lecturer in Psychology, University of Canterbury, Christchurch, New Zealand.*

The *Factorial Interest Blank* gives ipsative measures of eight interest categories: Rural-Practical, Social-Display, Humanitarian, Entertainment, Physical Activity, Literate, Aesthetic, and Scientific-Mechanical. Norms are presented for each year for each sex in terms of five grades (very low, low, average, high, very high) formed by using percentile cutoff scores of 10, 30, 70, and 90.

The format is paired comparison, forced choice, and the subject is asked to choose one from each of 120 pairs of descriptions of activities. A curious feature of the scoring system is that only two-thirds of the possible choices contribute to the scores. The other 80 choices, if made, are ignored in scoring. This comes about because for each interest category there are, to use the author's terminology, 10 "dual" and 10 "single" items. If either statement of a "dual" item is chosen this increases the score on one of two scales, but with the "single" items only one statement of each pair, if chosen, can contribute to the scoring. This does not mean, apparently, that unscored choices are irrelevant to the eight interest categories. To choose to play cards with a friend (item 74) increases the Entertainment score, but to choose to play draughts with him (item 1) is not scored. The dual pairings seem to have been made at random, in that two interest categories may be paired (in scoring) often or not at all.

The eight categories of interests are stated to have been derived from a factor analytic procedure and contain some curious bedfellows. The merging of Rural and Practical might seem odd to some. Humanitarian not only includes religion but is to a large extent equated with formal Christianity. Literate includes clerical work and politics.

A look at some of the items and the scores arising from them shows how these linkages operate. Taking the Humanitarian category first: to prefer to "Take a leading part in a Christian group" adds one unit to the Humanitarian score, as does preferring to be given a book of prayers rather than a book of poems. Surprisingly, to opt for the Red Cross or to run a charity adds nothing to the Humanitarian score, while to choose to volunteer to help in a citizens' advice bureau increases the Literate score only. In all, about half of the 20 possible choices which can contribute to the Humanitarian score are directly tied to religion, so that it is impossible to score highly unless one is religious.

Another close linkage is a negative one between Sociable and Scientific. Six of the "dual" items involve direct choice between these categories, and a further 6 of the 10 "singles" contributing to Sociable force a choice between sociability and some intellectual or practical scientific activity. The result is that it is impossible to score very high or very low on both these categories. While all the eight measures are ipsative in some degree, these two have an especially close ipsative relationship within the larger framework. The construction of the test forces them to be opposites.

However, the manual states that the interest categories were derived from a factor analysis and that, following this, the items were chosen from a larger pool by means of an item analysis

which was also dependent on the factor analysis. Hence, this attempt at the measurement of interests really stands or falls on the technical aspects of its construction. If the construction was sound, then the foregoing criticisms must be largely irrelevant. On the other hand, if the construction was faulty, then this might explain the origin of these strange groupings and scores.

The author began by classifying 500 interest items into 28 categories. It is not specified by what means this was done. He states, "Tests were constructed to measure the proportion of interest in each of these for every individual tested, and the correlations between them were then subjected to factorial analysis in order to reveal any underlying common factors." It is clear from this that the 28 interest categories were ipsatively measured. It is a very basic error to intercorrelate such scores. Ipsative data matrices give rise to ipsative correlations and these are quite meaningless in the ordinary sense, as Guilford[1] has repeatedly pointed out. As noted by the present reviewer,[2] the usual ipsative data matrix is subject to two tendencies. The format of the ipsative test, usually a forced choice ranking procedure, forces maximum differentiation between measures within persons. At the same time the aim of the test maker, to measure individual differences, tends towards maximizing the differentiation between persons within measures. These two tendencies force the matrix towards having a negative mean intercorrelation of $-1/(n-1)$, with n the number of variables. Since intercorrelations among the scores of FIB are not presented in the manual, there is no way to determine whether the mean intercorrelation is, in fact, $-.14$.

This step in the construction of the *Factorial Interest Blank,* namely, the intercorrelation of ipsative measures, would have produced, then, a matrix of meaningless correlations. To be precise, the matrix would have a certain specialised mathematical meaning, but the obtained ipsative correlations need bear absolutely no relationship in sign or size to the correlations which would have been obtained had the variables been measured independently. To factor

1 GUILFORD, J. P. "When Not to Factor Analyse." *Psychol B* 49:26–37 Ja '52. *
   GUILFORD, J. P. *Psychometric Methods, Second Edition.* New York: McGraw-Hill Book Co., Inc., 1954. Pp. ix, 597. *
   GUILFORD, J. P. "Psychological Measurement: A Hundred and Twenty-Five Years Later." *Psychometrika* 26:109–27 Mr '61. *
2 PRIEST, HUGH F. "Range of Correlation Coefficients." *Psychol Rep* 22:168–70 F '68. *

Factorial Interest Blank

analyse such a matrix is to pile absurdity on absurdity. To then use the resulting factors as a basis for grouping interests in categories can only be called a nonsensical procedure.

In summary, this attempt to measure interests has been built on a foundation of methodological error. Its faults are many and obvious.

[1019]

*Gordon Occupational Check List. High school students not planning to enter college; 1961–67; GOCL; 5 or 11 scores: business, outdoor, arts, technology, service, and 6 optional response summarization scores (preceding 5 areas and total); 1 form ('63, 6 pages); revised manual ('67, 16 pages); no norms; $5.90 per 35 tests; $1.50 per specimen set; postage extra; (20–25) minutes; Leonard V. Gordon; Harcourt Brace Jovanovich, Inc. *

JOHN N. MCCALL, *Associate Professor of Psychology, Southern Illinois University, Edwardsville, Illinois.*

This instrument was designed to be used with noncollege-bound high school students who are ready to discuss vocational plans, primarily in a counseling situation. It contains 240 statements of job activities found in occupations with middle and lower degrees of skill and responsibility. Students are asked to underline those which describe activities they would like to do as full-time work and to circle those which they would especially like. They may also write down which one job they want for a life's work and why. And they may add interests not already listed, report present educational plans, and predict the work they will be doing five years hence.

The revised manual fairly well reports methods used to construct and organize items and the logic, plus some facts, which justify the use of the checklist. Roe's occupational classification scheme was used to define five main occupational areas which include middle and lower level occupations. Consideration was also given to reading comprehension, abilities required, and expected range of popularity. Activity statements are grouped on the checklist in accordance with the five theoretical areas, apparently with little notice on the part of twelfth graders who were asked. Such grouping aids the counselor, who must rely principally on inspection to evaluate responses. Important to him also is the manual, which lists the occupational code and page number of the most closely related occupation in the *Dictionary of Occupational Titles*. The revised manual was so produced that these codes and page numbers would be up-to-date. Such cross references are useful for more detailed information on abilities required for the job and other facts. Apparently, no new facts about reliability and validity are included in the revised manual. Deficiencies identified by Crites and Hoyt in the 6th MMY —those concerning norms, information about entry and non-entry occupations, and comparisons with other interest measures—have gone unheeded.

Do checklists really measure interests? In a trivial, but also useful, sense of the word *measure,* they do. At least the observer gets some indication of relative frequency of responses in designated categories. Surely, this checklist can be accepted as a means by which students may communicate some of their aspirations. Perhaps they could do so orally with a few well-placed questions, but at least the written record facilitates systematic thinking, preparation for an interview, and provides some useful forms of indirect survey over large groups.

To claim measurement in a more fundamental sense implies intrinsic scaling properties and evidence of validity for the construct "interest." Since the 240 items are very unevenly distributed over the five occupational areas, the response summary boxes printed on the checklist can be grossly misleading. Corrective weights could be applied in serious research work and, to Gordon's credit, he indicates that actual responses should be the primary working data.

It seems pointless to consider the checklist's merits for assessing interests in a serious theoretical sense. Far more psychometric work would be required to generate scalable properties, and evidence of concurrent and predictive validity is needed. So long as the GOCL is claimed to merely facilitate client-counselor communication about work, evaluation might be directed to that point. Hard evidence of this kind is lacking, so one must rely upon appearances.

BERT W. WESTBROOK, *Associate Professor of Psychology, North Carolina State University, Raleigh, North Carolina.*

The GOCL was reviewed in *The Sixth Yearbook.* No changes have been made in the instrument itself since it was reviewed earlier, and the only basic modification of the manual is a revision of the former appendix (now

Factorial Interest Blank

Table 7) to incorporate occupational title changes in the most recent edition of the *Dictionary of Occupational Titles* (DOT). Inasmuch as no new data have been reported in the revised manual (1967), the previous criticisms are as relevant today as when they were written.

An additional criticism of the GOCL can be made at this time: it has failed to show progress over the years in collecting new data which meet the criteria set forth in *Standards for Educational and Psychological Tests and Manuals*. Although the GOCL has been criticized for relying strictly upon comprehensiveness, response selectivity, and acceptance by examinees as evidence of its validity, the revised manual does not present data in support of its predictive validity for different curricula and occupations. A serious effort has been made to demonstrate that the inventory contains items which sample occupations in levels 3 through 6 of Roe's occupational classification scheme, but the manual does not present evidence that a student's score predicts his satisfaction in a given job.

The manual reports reliability data which suggest that the inventory is reasonably stable over a period of one month. Nevertheless, appropriate research on its stability at various age levels has not been reported. Since some schools administer interest inventories only at intervals of two or three years, the manual should have reported correlations and changes in means and standard deviations for the GOCL when it is administered at such intervals. Without this information, the user does not know how rapidly the inventory scores become obsolete with the passage of time.

The inventory can be used to help students become familiar with occupations associated with activities in which they have expressed an interest. Since each item (activity statement) in the GOCL is related to a different job, student responses can be interpreted in terms of actual job characteristics as described in the DOT. Each activity statement describes the essential characteristic of a job which is coded in the DOT. The DOT code indicates "the group to which the occupation belongs....and the level of performance required with respect to data, people, and things." The manual refers to the appropriate page in the DOT for the occupation referred to by each item. Thus, the GOCL and the DOT serve complementary

functions which should facilitate the occupational exploration process.

In summary, the absence of overdue research on the GOCL is discouraging. The use of the occupational area scores is limited by the lack of evidence on long-term stability and predictive validity. The best use of the checklist is to direct students to DOT descriptions of occupations which they might enjoy. Counselors using the GOCL for this purpose must become thoroughly acquainted with the DOT and how it may enhance the value of the GOCL.

For reviews by John O. Crites and Kenneth B. Hoyt, see 6:1056.

[1020]

*Hackman-Gaither Vocational Interest Inventory: Standard Edition.** Grades 9–12 and adults; 1962–68; HGVII; positive (like), negative (dislike), and total scores for each of 8 areas: business contact, artistic, scientific-technical, health and welfare, business-clerical, mechanical, service, outdoor; 1 form ('68, 12 pages, identical with form copyrighted 1965); manual ('68, 30 pages); technical bulletins ('63, 39 pages; '66, 40 pages) are out of print; profile ('68, 2 pages, identical to profile copyrighted in 1962); student summary ('68, 2 pages); curricular group comparison chart ('68, 4 pages, identical to chart copyrighted in 1964); reliability data are for earlier editions and are for positive scores only; no norms for grades 9–10; no norms for positive and negative scores; total score norms for grades 11–12 are based on original 1962 edition; separate answer sheets must be used; $7 per 20 tests; $1.20 per 20 answer sheets; $1.20 per 20 profiles; $1.20 per 20 summary sheets; $1.20 per 20 comparison charts; $1 per manual; $1.25 per specimen set; postage extra; (25–30) minutes; Roy B. Hackman and James W. Gaither; Psychological Service Center of Philadelphia. *

REFERENCES

1–4. See 6:1058.
5. BUCKALEW, ROBERT J. *An Investigation of the Interrelationships Among Measures of Interests, Intelligence, and Personality for a Sample of One Hundred Sixty-Two Eighth Grade Boys.* Doctor's thesis, Temple University (Philadelphia, Pa.), 1962. (*DA* 23:3232)
6. EDDINS, EDGAR LEE. *A Factor Analytic Study of Interest Patterns and Their Relationship to Personality for Two Hundred High Achieving High School Seniors.* Doctor's thesis, Temple University (Philadelphia, Pa.), 1962. (*DA* 23:3464)
7. LUBETKIN, ARVIN IRA. *The Relationship Between Response Consistency on a Vocational Interest Inventory and Certain Personality Attributes.* Doctor's thesis, Temple University (Philadelphia, Pa.), 1964. (*DA* 25:4817)
8. MILLER, JERRY. *An Investigation of the Rate and Degree of Vocational Interest Maturity of Adolescent Males.* Doctor's thesis, Temple University (Philadelphia, Pa.), 1964. (*DA* 25:5744)
9. SILVERMAN, EDWARD HENRY. *An Investigation of Certain Occupational Interests of 1600 Students Enrolled in Eight Selected Vocational and Technical Training Programs Not Requiring a College Degree.* Doctor's thesis, Temple University (Philadelphia, Pa.), 1964. (*DA* 25:4253)
10. HESS, ALFRED WILLIAM. *A Study of Relationships Between Vocational Interests and Work Values.* Doctor's thesis, Temple University (Philadelphia, Pa.), 1965. (*DA* 26:4447)
11. KLINE, GUY RALPH. *A Study of the Stability of the Vocational Interest Patterns of a Sample of High School Students.* Doctor's thesis, Temple University (Philadelphia, Pa.), 1965. (*DA* 26:1482)
12. LLANA, ANDRESS, JR. "Automation of the Hackman-Gaither Interest Inventory." *J Ed Data Processing* 2:15–21 w '64–65. *
13. REITFR, ROBERT GRAYSON. *A Quantitative Scaling of the Occupational Preferences of Eleventh Grade Girls and Boys*

and a Comparison of Two Methods of Ascertaining Such Preferences. Doctor's thesis, Temple University (Philadelphia, Pa.), 1965. (DA 26:1485)

14. DeCencio, Dominic V. Relationship Between Certain Interest and Personality Variables in a Sample of College Women. Doctor's thesis, Temple University (Philadelphia, Pa.), 1966. (DA 27:1288B)

15. Gash, Ira Arnold. The Stability of Measured Interests as Related to the Clinical Improvement of Hospitalized Psychiatric Patients. Doctor's thesis, Temple University (Philadelphia, Pa.), 1966. (DA 27:1290B)

16. Jeremias, Hermine Irma. An Examination of Discrepancy Indices Between Self-Descriptions and Vocational Preferences and Their Relationship to Selected Personality Characteristics. Doctor's thesis, Temple University (Philadelphia, Pa.), 1966. (DA 27:956A)

17. Logue, John Joseph. A Comparison of Interest and Personality Variables in Two Job Categories. Doctor's thesis, Temple University (Philadelphia, Pa.), 1966. (DA 27:1282B)

18. Creamer, Wilma. An Analysis of the Readability of the Standard Edition of the Hackman-Gaither Interest Inventory. Master's thesis, Glassboro State College (Glassboro, N.J.), 1967.

19. Smith, John Alexander. The Relationship of Measured Interest and Student Orientation to Achievement, Satisfaction, and Persistence in College. Doctor's thesis, Temple University (Philadelphia, Pa.), 1967. (DA 28:975A)

20. Cook, Kenneth Leon. The Development of an Occupational Semantic Differential and Its Application to Occupational Stereotypes of High School Students. Doctor's thesis, Temple University (Philadelphia, Pa.), 1968. (DA 29:1100A)

21. Dressler, Richard M. Relationships Among Needs, Interests, and Curricular Choice in a Sample of College Men. Doctor's thesis, Temple University (Philadelphia, Pa.), 1968. (DAI 30:1356B)

22. Sherr, Richard Danner. The Interrelationships of Measured and Estimated Interests and Aptitudes Among Non-Academic High School Students. Doctor's thesis, Temple University (Philadelphia, Pa.), 1968. (DAI 30:1828A)

23. Spergel, Philip. The Relationship Between Vocational Interest, Aptitude and Personality Integration With Disadvantaged Youth. Doctor's thesis, Temple University (Philadelphia, Pa.), 1968. (DA 29:1760A)

24. Sullivan, James William. The Development of a Vocational Interest Maturity Key and Its Relationship to Intelligence in Adolescent Boys and Girls. Doctor's thesis, Temple University (Philadelphia, Pa.), 1969. (DAI 31:1027A)

25. Ziegler, Daniel J. "Self-Concept, Occupational Member Concept, and Occupational Interest Area Relationships in Male College Students." J Counsel Psychol 17(2):133-6 Mr '70. * (PA 44:9412)

Henry Weitz, *Professor of Education and Director, Counseling Center, Duke University, Durham, North Carolina.*

The Hackman-Gaither Standard Edition is an instrument designed for use in educational and vocational counseling and guidance. * The ultimate test of a [vocational interest] measuring instrument is the extent to which the counselor is assisted in meeting the multitude of practical pressures stemming from the varied needs of individuals, groups, and institutions. It is the hope of the authors that the Inventories, the graphic aids, and the counseling notes, together with the Technical Bulletins, will assist counselors to lead students toward further understanding and motivated action.

Thus the authors describe their inventory and their hopes for it. These hopes do not appear to have been realized in the Standard Edition of the inventory, the three accompanying profile systems, or the examiner's manual.

Moreover, the two technical bulletins are reported to be out of print, although they were made available to this reviewer. Yet the manual makes repeated reference to these bulletins. Descriptions of the standardization populations, inadequate though they are; descriptions of the "occupational analysis of the structure of the

Dictionary of Occupational Titles," which served as one basis of item selection, superficial though it seems; reports of the factorial analyses that resulted in the present item selection and vocational area keys development; and reports of crossvalidation studies—all these, and more, are tucked away in the out-of-print technical bulletins and hence are unavailable to the counselor who wishes some of the basic knowledge he needs before he tries to assist a client in avoiding what the authors call one of "the most crippling conditions observed in man....characterized by the impairment of the ability to choose between alternatives with some degree of consistency." Before the hopes for this inventory can be realized, it will be necessary to include in the manual these and other matters alluded to below that are presently available only in the technical bulletins.

Some of the technical information reported in the manual appears to support the use of the instrument. Split-half reliabilities for separate scales range from .76 to .96, with 35 of the 40 coefficients above .85. Test-retest reliabilities range from .37 (after 24 months) to .92 (after 4 months). The reader is left with some feelings of uneasiness, for the populations and procedures are inadequately described, and in several instances there are indications that the reported coefficients were derived from a rescoring of earlier and different versions of the inventory with the Standard Edition keys, but through use of populations on which the keys were developed.

Content ("logical") validity is supported on the grounds that "the items are all directly related to the world of work, since they were taken from the *Dictionary of Occupational Titles."* Face validity is defended on the grounds that "it is obvious [because of the methods used in item selection] to the respondent that he is evincing his *vocational* interests—rather than having his privacy invaded by being asked to answer so-called personality items which often deal with rather intimate aspects of a person's life." It seems to this reviewer that issues of content and face validity are, at best, insignificant arguments in support of an interest inventory. What the counselor wants to know about a vocational interest inventory is whether or not it will tell him anything useful about how a client's vocational motivation is structured now and, more important, how this motivation is likely to be structured in the future.

In this context the manual reports, "Evidence was found for meaningful differentiation between high school curricular groups on the various keys. This represented a first approximation to the determination of *concurrent* validity in terms of educational choices and commitments, which, of course, are directly related to vocational choices." Unfortunately, the reader is incorrectly referred for the evidence to pages 16–17 of the manual, in which he finds (on pages 17–18) a curricular profile with no indication of the population sizes, means, or standard deviations that would permit him to check the "evidence," or to the first technical bulletin, which, as indicated, is out of print. (Incidentally, the information provided in the technical bulletin is similarly meager.)

The report on "factorial validity" of the keys suggests that the items in each of the eight areas measured appear to hang together rather well, with average communality at .70 and average factor loadings, for all keys combined, at .58–.59. However, this tells us very little about what the instrument is measuring that is external to the test itself.

Thus, as is the case with most interest inventories, validity data are hard to come by.

The inventory itself (there is only one inventory, the Standard Edition, although the manual refers to *inventories* several times) comprises 100 job titles and 100 "brief job descriptions or job elements" drawn from the DOT. Respondents are afforded four options in recording their interests in these vocational stimuli: "like-sure, like-not sure, dislike-not sure, dislike-sure," which, in scoring, are weighted +2, +1, −1, and −2, respectively, to yield the eight occupational area scores shown in the entry above. There are 20 items included in each area score and 40 items for which responses are recorded but not scored. No adequate explanation is given for this unused 20 percent of the inventory items.

The inventory is essentially self-administering. Respondents can quickly and easily score their own inventories with little assistance from the examiner. The instructions for transferring scores to the three profiles and to the Individual Summary Worksheet appear to be adequate for the respondent to manage the mechanics of the processes himself, again with only minor supervision from an examiner. What he has when he is finished is more paper than the typical adolescent or young adult (for whom the inventory is presumably intended) can cope with effectively, several profiles based on confusing if not questionable statistical procedures, and some preachment by way of interpretation, an example of which, drawn from the Individual Summary Worksheet, follows:

> What you have underlined above may be things that could be mastered by hand [*sic*] work, by the learning of special methods, or by self-discipline. If a vocational field is important to you, talk to those people for whom you have respect about the sort of person you want to become. Read occupational material about jobs and their educational requirements. Analyze the results and use this information when you select courses at school. Act in accord with your goals in searching for part-time or summer jobs, selecting hobbies, and in extracurricular participation.

TALK   READ   ANALYZE   ACT

Three profiles make up the "graphic aids" referred to in the hope quoted above: a Self-Comparison Profile, a Group Comparison Profile, and a Curricular Profile.

The Self-Comparison Profile is completed by recording the respondent's plus and minus scores separately on a bar graph for each scale and blackening the space between. Precisely what this blackened area of the bar represents is never made clear, although the upper ends (the plus scores) of the profile are identified as interests and the lower ends (the minus scores) as avoidance. The profile of these scores is claimed to provide an ipsative interest profile in which the relative strengths of interest (and avoidance) within the individual are shown without regard to the relationship of the individual's responses to the responses of a normative population. The authors claim, "In many instances scores that have little normative significance may prove, when considered from an ipsative viewpoint, to be thought-provoking and meaningful. Essentially, the ipsative scores are measures of personal inclination apart from the competitive measure of the norm." The issue here is not whether this system of profiling converts an essentially nonipsative measuring instrument into an ipsative one—which it does not, for a truly ipsative measure requires that the selection of one alternative automatically rejects another alternative—but rather whether or not the Self-Comparison Profile as presently designed tells one what the authors claim it tells.

Each of the eight scales on the Self-Comparison Profile has a possible score of +40 points measuring interest. (It also provides for

−40 points measuring avoidance, but the following discussion will concern itself only with the positive scores.) Each point on each scale is shown as representing the same distance on the profile; hence, it carries with it the assumption that a like-sure ($+2$) or like-not sure ($+1$) response on any scale represents the same amount of vocational interest as the same response on another scale. An examination of the group norms suggests that this assumption may not be valid. For example, a male who has a score of $+21$ on the service scale would be at the 99+ percentile on that scale relative to his group, but the same score, $+21$, on the mechanical scale would place him at the 82nd percentile. Thus, for males in the norm population, at least, the units on these two scales differ. It therefore seems reasonable to suppose that for any individual, similar differences in unit size from scale to scale would be found. If this is the case, then, simply adding score units on a scale and comparing the sums from scale to scale tells us very little about the relative vocational motivations within the individual and may produce not only a self-fulfilling prophecy but also a misleading one. No adequate solution to this problem is known to this reviewer—certainly a standard score profile would only partially solve the problem—but it is clear that the use of the Self-Comparison Profile, far from giving a clear picture of the motivational structure within the individual, may be obscuring the picture.

The Group Comparison Profile purports to provide a graphic description of the respondent's interests relative to his sex group. If the instructions for completing this profile given on page 9 and repeated on page 11 of the manual are followed, only plus scores are recorded. Only the male profile is reproduced in the manual. A separate sheet, entitled Extension of Scoring Methods for the Hackman-Gaither Vocational Interest Inventory, explains the method of getting scores appropriate to the Group Comparison Profile that accompanies the test supplies submitted for review. The appropriate scores for this profile are the algebraic sums of the plus and minus scores of the individual scales. From the information supplied in the manual, it is impossible to determine the characteristics of the comparison groups, beyond sex, for either the profile in the manual or the separate and different profile. Presumably, both sets of group comparison profiles are based on the same groups and only the scoring systems differ.

The Curricular Comparison Chart shows the approximate mean scores of 17 curricular groups including "college bound," art, professional nursing, practical nursing, cosmetology, carpentry, etc. The only description given of these groups is found in the out-of-print technical bulletins, one of which says that they comprise "a sample of 460 11th and 12th grade students, including those in the norm samples." Precisely what data were used for the profile included in the Standard Edition is not clear.

Finally, the authors' hopes for this inventory's usefulness are related to the "Counseling Notes" provided in the manual. The three brief paragraphs of notes are either comments on the obvious things a moderately well trained counselor should already know (for example, that interests and abilities are not necessarily highly correlated and therefore both should be considered in guidance, or that large negative scores may reflect an emotional repudiation of parental, sibling, or environmental patterns) or are based on "clinical evidence" unsupported by research (for example, that certain scales reflect an interest in high-level academic training, while others suggest a rejection of learning). The profile interpretation suggestions are similarly obvious or undocumented.

In summary, then, the *Hackman-Gaither Vocational Interest Inventory* may well be a useful accessory to counseling and guidance, but the incomplete, badly written, and badly edited manual; the inadequately documented profiles; and the superficial interpretive guides do nothing to recommend its use for any purpose at this time. The *Kuder Preference Record—Vocational,* for example, used in conjunction with the well written and well documented manuals, provides more useful information for counseling than the inventory under review. Other inventories, especially the SVIB, with the new keys and profiles, are more useful, if considerably more costly in time and money.

[1021]

★**Hall Occupational Orientation Inventory.** Grades 9–16 and adults; 1968, c1965–68; HOOI; 23 scales: creativity-independence, risk, information-understanding, belongingness, security, aspiration, esteem, self-actualization, personal satisfaction, data orientation, routine-dependence, object orientation, people orientation, location concern, aptitude concern, monetary concern, physical abilities concern, environment concern, co-worker concern, qualifications concern, time concern, extremism, defensiveness; 1 form ('68, c1965, 16 pages); manual ('68, 46 pages); profile ('68, 4 pages) for ages 14–20, profile ('68, 4 pages) for ages 18–27; parents' folder ('68, 4 pages); high school norms same for all grades; separate answer sheets (hand scored, IBM 1230) must be used; $10.50 per 20 tests; $3 per 20 hand scored answer sheets; $9.90 per 100 IBM 1230 answer sheets; $3 per 20 profiles; $1.20 per manual; postage extra; specimen set free to counselors; scoring service, 30¢ and over per test (100 or more tests); [40–60] minutes; L. G. Hall; Follett Educational Corporation. *

REFERENCES

1. HALL, LACY GILBERT. *An Occupational Orientation Inventory: A Preliminary Investigation.* Doctor's thesis, University of North Carolina (Chapel Hill, N.C.), 1966. (*DA* 27:4126A)
2. TARRIER, RANDOLPH BRENAN. *Vocational Counseling: A Comparative Study of Different Methods.* Doctor's thesis, Case Western Reserve University (Cleveland, Ohio), 1968. (*DAI* 30:938A)
3. SHAPPELL, DEAN LEROY. *The Relationship of Socio-Economic Status to School Motivation and Occupational Orientation.* Doctor's thesis, Ohio State University (Columbus, Ohio), 1969. (*DAI* 30:2345A)
4. SHAPPELL, DEAN L.; HALL, LACY G.; AND TARRIER, RANDOLPH B. "School Motivation and Occupational Orientation." *Voc Guid Q* 19(2):97–103 D '70. *

DONALD G. ZYTOWSKI, *Associate Professor of Psychology and Assistant Director, Student Counseling Service, Iowa State University, Ames, Iowa.*

Since the publication of the last MMY, a new form of interest inventory has begun to emerge. The *Hall Occupational Orientation Inventory* is one example of this: an inventory which purports to measure "on a level beyond that of superficial interests" and at the level of "psychological needs and value fulfillment, worker traits, and job characteristics." That is, the new approach is to assess the attractiveness or relative importance to the person of a number of factors or attributes of work. It is congruent with a trend in occupational behavior theories to use need or value constructs as determinants. Interests are not enough; a reliable forecast of what a person is most likely to be satisfied with is better made from a broader set of predictors.

Hall has developed items for his inventory with an exemplary rationale. They are designed to tap components of work, which are descriptive to some degree of every job but not of any specific job.

Twenty-three scales were evolved from 46 content areas and 345 items by a method which is not described. Thirteen of the scales are directional, designed to measure the person's orientation toward or away from the areas which the scales describe. They are the first 13 listed above, from creativity-independence to people orientation. The next 8 are degree scales, indicating the degree to which each factor named is important to the person. The last 2 scales are verification scales, reflecting bias in the responses of the inventory taker.

The answer format is free choice, allowing every item to be answered through a 5-point scale ranging from "essential" to "intolerable." The author believes that the opportunity to make an emphatic, as opposed to ordinary, response offers valuable additional information. The inventory taker is encouraged to hand score and profile his inventory as a part of his learning-about-self. A machine scoring service, offering also group summaries and item frequency data, is available.

Norming of raw scores is achieved by profiling them on the appropriate interpretive folder. The stanine is the standard score employed. Since many inventories with homogeneous scales use percentiles as standard scores, some description of the attributes of stanine scores for the counselor would seem appropriate for the manual. None is given.

The norms for different ages and educational groups rarely differ by more than 2 raw score points. If raw scores are converted to a 9-point standard scale, differences of 2 raw score points or less would not seem to call for separate norms. At least this conclusion could be justified from the lack of separate norms for women, who show differences from the mean scores of men as great as 5 raw scores, statistically significant on 17 of 23 scales.

The interpretive folders give brief descriptions of the content of each scale, plus some rationale for relating the conceptual framework of the inventory to planning one's work or career. Instructions are also given for profiling obtained scores and two paragraphs are devoted to a beginning interpretation of scores. Another folder is available to explain the inventory to parents.

Data reflecting the reliability and validity of the HOOI are minimal and are presented in a fashion which is unlikely to tax a high school guidance worker. Tests of statistical significance are not visible; enough details about samples or experimental conditions are omitted that findings could not be replicated by an independent worker; and only one reference is given in support of any of the findings reported.

The only report of reliability shows a median correlation of .84 for the 23 scales over a three-week interval for 1,400 subjects of various ages.

Validity data are given both for items and for scales, mainly in the form of discrimination between different age, educational, or sex groups. For a number of occupational samples, with N's varying between 40 and 125, the scales that significantly differentiate between them are presented. Usually 8 to 10 scales are listed for each of the 13 occupational groups, and all 23 scales appear, suggesting that they are all carrying some load.

Finally, a matrix of intercorrelations of scales is presented. A number of values are higher than the likely scale homogeneities: Esteem and Personal Satisfaction correlate .87 and Information-Understanding correlates .79 with Data Orientation. Of the 253 correlations, 195 are significant at the .05 level, which suggests that the scales are not as independent as might be desired.

The author disavows extensive psychometric analysis in favor of instruction on the "varied and productive counseling uses of the inventory." But, unless it is shown that the inventory rests on some firmly demonstrated, valid foundations, no counseling with it can be validly productive, for the dimensions of a person's self-concept which are generated or clarified could be completely spurious in relation to the real world, or the inventory's scales could be unrelated to job or work satisfaction. That existing relationships might not be reflected by the HOOI is a serious consideration.

The manual does give good coverage of suggested counseling uses, but their value is dependent on whether or not the validity of the inventory is established. In addition, tapes are being prepared to demonstrate interpretive approaches to the neophyte. This is an innovation which any test or inventory publisher would do well to imitate.

Any publisher of an instrument which is designed to predict into future time can rightfully plead costs in defense of limitations on psychometric information. But the HOOI, I believe, falls below the minimum acceptable level of this kind of information for any confident use at this time. This is true despite the attractiveness of its face, or content, validity for the items and the scales. Perhaps it will attract additional tests of its validity. Hopefully, the author will be interested in incorporating additional data of this kind into the manual. Until then, the reviewer advises circumspect use.

Hall Occupational Orientation Inventory

[1022]

*How Well Do You Know Your Interests. High school, college, adults; 1957–70; 54 scores: numerical, clerical, retail selling, outside selling, selling real estate, one-order selling, sales complaints, selling intangibles, buyer, labor management, production supervision, business management, machine operation, repair and construction, machine design, farm or ranch, gardening, hunting, adventure, social service, teaching service, medical service, nursing service, applied chemistry, basic chemical problems, basic biological problems, basic physical problems, basic psychological problems, philosophical, visual art appreciative, visual art productive, visual art decorative, amusement appreciative, amusement productive, amusement managerial, literary appreciative, literary productive, musical appreciative, musical performing, musical composing, sports appreciative, sports participative, domestic service, unskilled labor, disciplinary, power seeking, propaganda, self-aggrandizing, supervisory initiative, bargaining, arbitrative, persuasive, disputatious, masculinity (for males only) or femininity (for females only); Form B-22 (6 pages); 3 editions (identical except for profiles): secondary school ('58), college ('57), personnel ('57); manual ('70, 24 pages); $7.50 per 30 tests; $2 per set of scoring keys; $1.25 per manual; $3.50 per specimen set of all 3 editions; postage extra; (20–30) minutes; Thomas N. Jenkins, John H. Coleman (manual), and Harold T. Fagin (manual); Executive Analysis Corporation. *

REFERENCES

1. See 6:1059.
2. SCHWARTZ, MILTON M., AND LEVINE, HERBERT. "Union and Management Leaders: A Comparison." *Personnel Adm* 28:44–7 Ja–F '65. *
3. GRIGGS, SHIRLEY ANN. *A Study of the Life Plans of Culturally Disadvantaged Negro Adolescent Girls With Father-Absence in the Home.* Doctor's thesis. Columbia University (New York, N.Y.), 1967. (*DA* 28:4950A)

For a review by John R. Hills, see 6:1059 (1 excerpt); for reviews by Jerome E. Doppelt and Henry S. Dyer, see 5:859.

[1023]

★An Inventory of Religious Activities and Interests. High school and college students considering church-related occupations and theological school students; 1967–68; IRAI; for research use only; 11 scales: counselor, administrator, teacher, scholar, evangelist, spiritual guide, preacher, reformer, priest, musician, check scale; Form 67 ('67, 10 pages); mimeographed preliminary manual ('68, 77 pages); profile ('67, 2 pages); no norms for female high school students; separate answer sheets must be used; 30¢ per test; 5¢ per answer sheet; 65¢ per 25 profiles; $5 per set of scoring stencils; $2.50 per manual; $2.50 per specimen set; cash orders postpaid; (40–45) minutes; Sam C. Webb; Educational Testing Service. *

DONALD G. ZYTOWSKI, *Associate Professor of Psychology and Assistant Director, Student Counseling Service, Iowa State University, Ames, Iowa.*

The IRAI is, according to the manual, "designed to measure interest in activities performed by persons employed in a variety of church-related occupations." It does not measure degree of religiousness, and it is intended to be "primarily descriptive and only secondarily predictive."

The claim of descriptiveness is based on the fact that the items were derived from activities actually performed in church-related occupations, clustered by several successive factor analyses into 10 scales representing roles or role-segments which characterize church-related occupations. Inspection of the scale names will reveal that they are oriented around fairly traditional church roles, such as evangelist, reformer, priest, spiritual guide, as compared with the more pure factor scales of the *Theological School Inventory.*

The review which follows is based on materials which are to be added to the manual in an imminent revision. It is assumed that this edition (probably 1971) will be available to purchasers by the time the present MMY is published.

Responses to items are free choice, on a 5-point scale ranging from "Do not like it" to "Indifferent" and on through three levels of liking. The user should realize that a raw score of 20 equals disliking, and that half of the total possible score on a scale is midway between indifference and mild liking.

A check scale has been composed of items of low popularity. A score of 60 is suggested as the level indicating a carelessly answered inventory, but this score appears in the norm tables at a high percentile among groups who could have been expected to take the inventory quite seriously.

Reliability is reflected in temporal stability coefficients for 29 theology students over a two-week interval and by correlations between scores on Parts A and B, of 10 items each, which the author calls homogeneity. This seems a rather weak index of scale homogeneity. Test-retest reliabilities are all in the .80's, while those for alternate forms range from .69 to .92. The manual suggests that either part of the inventory may be given alone, but it does not give data on the effects of such a practice on reliability or validity.

The manual comes through most strongly in giving evidence of the inventory's validity. There are sections devoted to scale intercorrelations, median scores of occupational specialities on the scales, consistency of factor structure, overlap of score distributions in each scale for various groups, correlations with other measures, and the like.

Intercorrelations between scales obtained from the responses of a group of 772 theology students average about .39, but evangelist, spiritual guide, and preacher have an average correlation of about .63. Students who are in church-related colleges and in high school show scale intercorrelations much higher, those for the latter group averaging about .75. This suggests considerable homogeneity of response among nontheology students, a situation which makes the test's use with this group questionable. These students apparently will tend to get much flatter profiles—whatever one scale score is, the rest will be similar. The manual does not remark on this.

Considerable space is given to showing that the rank ordering of median scores on each scale for persons in different church occupations is different. Thus counselors tend to score higher on the counselor scale than do groups with other employment, etc. But close examination of the tables reveals that the Spiritual Guide scale is typically higher than or the same as the occupationally relevant scale in nearly every group. For guidance purposes, it would be necessary to realize this precedence of the Spiritual Guide over the role-relevant scale.

Rank ordering of scales on groups employed in different roles shows that a fourth of the 28 comparisons possible for males and two-thirds of those for females are not reliably distinctive in terms of their scale profiles. It would be desirable if all groups had unique profiles, but no inventory succeeds in meeting this ideal. Nor is there any general agreement as to what degree makes an inventory defective. Impressionistically, it does seem that the IRAI is lacking in this regard. Data on percent of overlap of the score distributions of scales are also presented; the same failing seems apparent.

Tables of correlations are given of IRAI scales with the scales of the *Theological School Inventory,* two personality inventories, and the venerable SVIB. It is impossible to summarize these many correlations, except to say that the IRAI seems to be tapping different domains by and large, but the expected relationships seem to be present.

Although one line of the manual implies that the IRAI may be used with high school students, the author does not state explicitly whether it should be or not, and no data are offered to support this use. Nothing is known about whether responses given by high school-

Inventory of Religious Activities and Interests

ers are stable until they enter theological school, or whether they predict eventual intended role in theology school. This, plus the homogeneity of scales noted previously, surely should limit the user's confidence in this inventory with any person of high school age.

In sum, the IRAI appears to be a fairly well constructed, moderately valid inventory for a limited purpose: assisting Protestant theology students in their choice of traditional occupational roles after graduation. No utility has been shown in secular colleges or in church-related colleges or high schools for persons intending to enter the ministry. For them, the IRAI can function only as a checklist of occupational activities through which the person can explore the range of his own interests in church-related work. It seems a shame that so much expertise and energy have been devoted to an inventory with so narrow an application.

[1024]

Kuder General Interest Survey. Grades 6–12; 1934–70; KGIS; revision and downward extension of *Kuder Preference Record—Vocational,* Form C; 11 scores: outdoor, mechanical, computational, scientific, persuasive, artistic, literary, musical, social service, clerical, verification; 1 form; 2 editions; $1.65 per specimen set of either edition, postage extra; (45–60) minutes; G. Frederic Kuder; Science Research Associates, Inc. *

a) SELF-SCORING CONSUMABLE EDITION. 1934–70; Form E ('63, 25 pages, format changed in 1970); manual ('64, 52 pages); instructions ('70, 4 pages); $8.45 per 25 tests.

b) MACHINE SCORING EDITION. 1934–63; Form E ('63, 19 pages); DocuTran manual ('63, 15 pages); profile ('63, 1 page); separate answer sheets (DocuTran) must be used; $16.30 per 25 tests; scoring service, 75¢ and over per student; fee includes answer sheet, manual, and profile.

REFERENCES

1. PLOTKIN, ALAN LEONARD. *The Effect of Occupational Information Classes Upon the Vocational Interest Patterns of Below Average, Adolescent Males.* Doctor's thesis, Catholic University of America (Washington, D.C.), 1966. (*DA* 27: 2895A)
2. MOONEY, ROBERT FRANCIS. *A Multiple Discriminant Analysis of the Interest Patterns of High School Girls.* Doctor's thesis, Boston College (Chestnut Hill, Mass.), 1968. (*DAI* 30:216A)
3. REPLOGLE, JAMES ROBERT. *The Relation of Teacher-Pupil Profile Pattern Similarities on Measures of Interest and Personality to Grades and Perceived Compatibility.* Doctor's thesis, Lehigh University (Bethlehem, Pa.), 1968. (*DA* 29:1426A)
4. SCHNEIDER, DAVID LEE. *Perceptions of Family Atmosphere and the Vocational Interests of Physically Handicapped Adolescents: An Application of Anne Roe's Theory.* Doctor's thesis, New York University (New York, N.Y.), 1968. (*DA* 29:2574A)
5. MOONEY, ROBERT F. "Categorizing High School Girls Into Occupational Preference Groups on the Basis of Discriminant-Function Analysis of Interests." *Meas & Eval Guid* 2(3):178–90 f '69. * (*PA* 44:13325)
6. SHANN, MARY HALLIGAN. *Multiple Discriminant Prediction of Occupational Choice of Vocational High School Boys Based on Inventoried and Self-Rated Interest Patterns.* Doctor's thesis, Boston College (Chestnut Hill, Mass.), 1969. (*DAI* 31:315A)
7. TILLINGHAST, B. S., JR.; SHAPIRO, RONALD M.; AND CARRETT, PAULINE. "Experimental Use of the Kuder General Interest Survey, Form E, With Sixth Grade Pupils." *Meas & Eval Guid* 2(3):174–7 f '69. * (*PA* 44:13301)

8. CRONBACH, LEE J. *Essentials of Psychological Testing, Third Edition,* pp. 457–86. New York: Harper & Row, Publishers, Inc., 1970. Pp. xxx, 752. *

BARBARA A. KIRK, *Director, Counseling Center, University of California, Berkeley, California.*

The *Kuder General Interest Survey* is a revision of the familiar *Kuder Preference Record—Vocational,* Form C, and is very similar to it in item and inventory format, score profiles, and suggested interpretation. In the manual's words, the KGIS "was developed in response to a need for such an instrument for use with younger people, particularly at the junior high level." New and reworked items and a 6th grade reading level appear to be its major features. Its 10 occupational scales and Verification scale are identical in name and similar in psychometric characteristics to the Form C scales, and the brief, formal scale descriptions are to all intents and purposes the same. The two interpretive profile leaflets to be given to those completing the inventory, one for grades 6–8 and the other for grades 9–12, are identical except for their norms, which are further separated for boys and girls.

Since the KGIS and its manual were published in 1963 and 1964, respectively, it is somewhat surprising that by 1970 it still appears to be a relatively unresearched and unreviewed instrument. This is perhaps because it is so seemingly similar to the Kuder Form C, about which just the opposite is true. However, the KGIS is appropriately to be considered a completely new instrument, especially for the purposes for which it was developed and for which the publisher recommends it.

One of the most striking things about earlier, similar forms of the Kuder is the controversy which has existed over a period of more than 25 years as to how the scores are to be understood and appropriately interpreted to people completing the inventory. There are *some* straightforward and helpful interpretations that can be made; there are, however, many others which are susceptible to the impression that they are restatements, logical extensions, or general expectations of any test score but which are, in fact, not so. For example, a person who gets a higher percentile score on the Scientific than on the Social Service scale *cannot* confidently conclude that he has more of a Scientific interest than a Social Service interest or that he has more Scientific interest than a friend whose Scientific score is lower.

As recently as *The Sixth Yearbook* Katz discussed the Form C scores extensively, while Husek, writing elsewhere (see excerpted review below) raised some of the same points in connection with the KGIS. Interpretation is the central concern of the present reviewer. The overriding issue is whether this instrument can be adequately or soundly interpreted in the way in which the publisher recommends or in which it will probably be used, and thus whether, on balance, the young people who complete the KGIS will benefit from the experience, rather than being harmed. Without any possibility of being able to resolve these issues here or even to discuss them adequately, it is essential to repeat the fact that a given individual's results are *far* more complicated than the apparently simple and straightforward scales and percentile values suggest.

As a further example of what may be considered questionable practice in regard to the test's impact on the individual, no special qualifications for administrators or users of the KGIS are suggested. The manual says, "Administration of the *Survey* should be followed by group interpretation of the results. Particular reference should be made to the interpretive section of the profile leaflet, which describes the ten interest areas covered by the Survey. Students may fill out the small profile on page 4 and take home the interpretive part of the leaflet to discuss with their parents and keep for future reference." This reviewer feels that despite some new psychometric materials, the manual is less helpful than Form C's and that it and the profile leaflet are generally inadequate for appropriate interpretation, and would be even if the scores themselves could be considered to have absolutely clear meaning. For example, since separate norms are necessary for boys and girls, thus giving as many girls as boys high scores on the Mechanical scale, how might a young girl or even her teacher be expected to make appropriate sense from the leaflet description: "Mechanical interest means preference for working with machines and tools. If you like to tinker with old clocks, repair broken objects, or watch a garage mechanic at work, you might enjoy shop courses in school. Aviator, toolmaker, machinist, plumber, automobile repairman, and engineer are among the many jobs involving high mechanical interest." *No interpretive scale descriptions whatever appear in the manual,* and neither it nor the profile leaflet provide any demonstration of how the complex world of work is reflected in all of the scales considered together, i.e., in patterns.

The manual also presents no predictive validity data specific to the KGIS and, aside from face and content validity, rests its case on job satisfaction studies based on the *Kuder Preference Record—Vocational.* The temporal stability of the Form E scores is modest, and the fact that this stability is positively related to intelligence raises additional complex questions. Many technically good procedures were used in developing and standardizing the KGIS, but not enough is yet known about the developmental structure of interests in people of high school age and their relationship to adult vocational behavior to warrant more than proceeding with great caution.

In many ways, even if the interpretive materials available were extensive, the test's most appropriate use would seem to be in research rather than in individual or group counseling. Whether the KGIS is really necessary in junior high school as an aid in exploratory vocational reading or in the choice of electives is a moot question, and many educators and psychologists may feel uncomfortable with the manual's suggestion that the KGIS will "help him [the student] determine the kind of high school curriculum to choose—academic or college preparatory, vocational, business or commercial, or general."

This reviewer shares Husek's opinion that there is a definite middle class bias to the items, some of it offensive, and that in trying to develop items that would be acceptable for 6th graders as well as adults, the author has not accommodated either group very well. These are larger topics than can be pursued in this review. The KGIS scales were constructed to be generally independent of one another, but there is reason for some concern that these objectives have been too successfully attained; interest dimensions which we assume may be associated to some degree in real life (e.g., Computational and Scientific; Literary, Artistic, and Musical) are here assessed as being unrelated. The Form E scales are shown, in the manual, to be about as highly correlated with like-named Form C scales as they are with themselves on retest, but we are not told if the score *levels* and *patterns* on the two forms are comparable, e.g., whether a student in the 10th grade taking both forms could be expected to have scores of essentially the same magnitude and profiles of the same shape. The importance of this information for counseling is obvious, especially since the two forms are being linked for validity. The manual says that Form E is usually completed in 45 to 60 minutes, but the publisher's catalog lists the testing time as 30 to 40 minutes.

According to the manual, the KGIS is usable at the 6th grade level, but on the basis of a study of the Verification scores for 6th, 7th, and 8th graders, it is not recommended for general use in the 6th grade. Reassuringly, a study by Tillinghast, Shapiro, and Carrett (7) found that 6th graders had fewer Verification scores in the unacceptable range than the manual suggests. Also in an affirmative vein, Mooney (5) found that statistically the KGIS gave significantly different interest patterns for college-oriented 10th, 11th, and 12th grade girls with different occupational aspirations.

In summary, the KGIS is the latest complete revision of the original *Kuder Preference Record—Vocational* and in particular shares many of the assets and liabilities of Form C, which it closely resembles. Important problems concern its use with junior high school students, who, along with students in grades 9 through 12, constitute the population for which it is intended. Most serious are the inadequacies of the interpretive materials, which combine with the inherent complexities of the scores to make it seem probable that a considerable amount of serious misunderstanding of the results will exist among students who take the inventory, their parents, and their teachers and school counselors. Its use for research seems more promising. Six years after publication there is a remarkable dearth of validity data for the instrument, but for the early high school years it may be about as good an instrument as exists. For some 10th graders and for students in the 11th and 12th grades who may be considering going on to college, the new forms of the *Strong Vocational Interest Blank* appear to be clearly superior.

PAUL R. LOHNES, *Professor of Education, State University of New York at Buffalo, Buffalo, New York.*

It is obligatory that the user of the *Kuder General Interest Survey* study the review by Katz (6:1063) of the *Kuder Preference Record—Vocational* as well as the KGIS manual, which contains a substantial, point-by-point re-

buttal [1] or accommodation to each of the Katz points. This edifying exchange of incisive criticism and intelligent, constructive reaction honors the critic, the test author, and the profession. Katz shows exactly how the interest survey can be misinterpreted in schools. The manual replies with a sophisticated, facilitative view of guidance. Unfortunately, the manual cannot guarantee against primitive behavior by counselors. The user has to be informed about the Katz-Kuder dialogue. There need be no great worry about the technical adequacy of the *Kuder General Interest Survey.* We do need to worry about the adequacy of guidance programs that incorporate this interest survey, or any interest survey. This review concentrates on limitations of the manual that might contribute to bad guidance practices. The manual's 1964 copyright is the rub, for significant research findings made available by Project TALENT in the last five years contradict major assumptions of the guidance philosophy Kuder expresses in the manual.

How stable are interests during adolescence? How do inventoried interests interact with and compare to explicitly expressed career goals as predictors? How do interests interact with and compare to abilities as predictors? Cooley's 1967 monograph [2] gives the most definitive answers available. Cooley had previously shown that the career goals stated by TALENT subjects one year beyond high school were related to their measured interests in 9th grade only to the extent that career plans were stable between 9th grade and the year after graduation, and that follow-up career plans did not change to be more consistent with 9th grade interests. In his 1967 monograph, Cooley showed that a simple statement of a career goal made in the 9th grade was as good a predictor of career goals years later as an entire 9th grade interest inventory score vector with 17 elements. He also found about 25 percent variance overlap between 9th and 12th grade interest measures, which is consistent with results cited in the manual. However, this needs to be compared with 54 percent stability of a six-category goals variable over the same period. Kuder's manual

1 Since Katz's review was published in 1965, the "rebuttal" in the 1964 manual must have been to an earlier, but very similar, critique: KATZ, MARTIN. "Interpreting Kuder Preference Record Scores: Ipsative or Normative." *Voc Guid Q* 10: 96–100 w '62. *—The Editor.
2 COOLEY, WILLIAM W. "Interactions Among Interests, Abilities, and Career Plans." *J Appl Psychol Monogr* 51(5, pt 2): 1–16 O '67. *

Kuder General Interest Survey

misses the point that simple career goals are more stable than inventoried interests and are just as valid predictors of later goals.

Cooley's most ingenious and informative analyses involve partial canonical correlations between 9th grade abilities and 12th grade interests with 9th grade interests partialled out, and between 9th grade interests and 12th grade abilities with 9th grade abilities partialled out. This is an effort to discover whether early abilities predict subsequent changes in interests, and whether early interests predict subsequent change in abilities. The results show that both phenomena exist, and to about the same modest extent. The details of the canonical variates, which are predictable change factors of interests and abilities, describe how interests change in accordance with abilities and vice versa. The relations among abilities, plans, and interests, which counselor and client need to understand, are far more complex than the manual suggests.

Lohnes [3] factor analyzed the 17 TALENT interest inventory scales, along with 21 other typical performance scales, for over 16,000 subjects. Since the items were not ipsatively scaled, the intercorrelations were meaningful. He found that only four interest factors could be supported: Business, Outdoor and Shop, Cultural, and Science. The possibility exists that Kuder's ipsative scoring masks the small number of really different interest traits.

Cooley and Lohnes [4] researched the predictive validities of 12th grade measurement traits for career criteria up to five years beyond high school. They lend support to Kuder's general faith that interests have predictive validities, but they show the manual to be incorrect in two major assumptions. The manual states that "interests are even more important determinants of field or type of education or occupation than are other indicators such as aptitudes, social status, temperament, or personality," yet the TALENT studies show that the abilities factors of Verbal Knowledges (a *g* measure) and Mathematics outperform the interest factors consistently. The manual claims that "interests may be viewed as determinants of *direction* of effort and activity, whereas aptitudes play a more important part in determining the *level* of attainment," but the TALENT studies show beyond a shadow of a doubt that both abilities and interests, in partnership, are required to effectively discriminate career groups in either the fields or level dimension. One of the most striking findings of the Project TALENT studies is that approximately the same plane in the measurement space of 11 abilities factors and 11 motives factors provides the best two discriminant functions for 14 different career criteria, including career goal changes over five years. The first function of this plane, named Science-oriented Scholasticism, has highest loadings on factors of Verbal Knowledges, Mathematics, Scholasticism, and Science Interests, and governs level of aspiration or achievement. The other function, called Technical versus Sociocultural, has highest loadings on Mathematics, Visual Reasoning, Outdoor and Shop Interests, Science Interests, and Cultural Interests. Interests do not work separately from abilities and they should not be considered separately.

The lack of information in the manual about recent research is accompanied by a lack of attention to the need for computer generated interpretations of abilities and interests in guidance programs. Along lines suggested by Cooley [5] and Lohnes,[6] interest inventories will make their best contributions in guidance programs that provide for complex statistical transformations of score vectors into relevant information. The biggest problem with the *Kuder General Interest Survey* is that the manual is not able to provide objective follow-up validities of the sort required if guidance is to encourage intelligent, analytical decision making. Longitudinal research is imperative.

The Kuder interest inventories have made a monumental contribution to psychometrics and trait psychology. This reviewer, however, would urge prospective users to consider the different look in interest profiles (which this reviewer considers advantageous for both research and counseling) of the *Vocational Preference Inventory* before bowing to tradition, honorable as it is.

3 LOHNES, PAUL R. *Measuring Adolescent Personality.* Project TALENT Five-Year Follow-Up Studies, Interim Report 1. U.S. Office of Education Project No. 3051. Pittsburgh, Pa.: American Institutes for Research, 1966. Pp. iv, 226. *
4 COOLEY, WILLIAM W., AND LOHNES, PAUL R. *Predicting Development of Young Adults.* Project TALENT Five-Year Follow-Up Studies, Interim Report 5. Palo Alto, Calif.: Project TALENT Office, 1968. Pp. ix, 224. *
5 COOLEY, WILLIAM W. "A Computer-Measurement System for Guidance." *Harvard Ed R* 34:559–72 f '64. *
6 LOHNES, PAUL R. "Reformation Through Measurement in Secondary Education." *Proc Inv Conf Testing Probl* 67:102–21 '68. *

Kuder General Interest Survey

JOHN N. MCCALL, *Associate Professor of Psychology, Southern Illinois University, Edwardsville, Illinois.*

This most recent form of the Kuder series of preference records parallels the *Kuder Preference Record—Vocational* (Forms B and C) in construction and use. Thus, experience with earlier forms has good transfer value. The *Kuder General Interest Survey* (Form E) differs mostly in that it was devised for junior high school students. Claims that it may also serve senior high students and adults seem reasonable.

As before, Kuder's manual of directions and technical information sets a high standard and it is must reading for the counselor or researcher who uses the inventory. Readers are properly cautioned against using Form E as a sole basis for choosing occupations. Counselors, depending upon their own persuasions, may find the discussion of counseling uses for Form E to their liking. Interpreting the meaning of similar scores for different students, or different scores for the same student, is forthrightly discussed. But it seems simpler to conclude that one has at best a vaguely relative comparison of preferences taken from a common pool. Kuder is far more masterful when discussing the implications of ipsative, or interlocking, scores and when justifying his construction of a special Verification scale. This scale is important for identifying students who misunderstand directions or who, for several other reasons, mark items in the wrong way. The fact that 11 to 21 percent of the sixth graders tested by Kuder earned questionable Verification scores led him to recommend that Form E not be used with most sixth graders. Such caution is commendable.

We should wonder how a single inventory can adequately survey the interests of a wide-ranging population, from seventh grade through adulthood. A deliberate effort was made to keep the vocabulary and reading demands down to the sixth grade level; and occupational titles were avoided. Inspection of the items suggests they are still meaningful to adults. The answer partly lies in what one is specifically trying to measure. As long as one is satisfied to survey the relative strengths of broadly defined interest areas, as provided in Kuder Forms C and E, the instrument may prove useful. Where comparisons with adults in given occupations are needed, the *Kuder Preference Record—Oc-*

cupational or the *Strong Vocational Interest Blank* should be used.

KGIS reflects Kuder's special expertise in the construction of homogeneous interest scales. The K-R reliabilities for all scales are above .70. And most of the scale intercorrelations are "close to zero." Typical of the underlying manipulations to get these results is the compensation for the less reliable answers of younger children by increasing the number of scorable items per scale.

The fact that comparable Form E and C scales all correlated at or above .65 for a sample of tenth graders suggests that the newer scales measure similar interest traits. But there is dissimilarity also. More studies are needed to establish the stability and the precise meaning of these scores, particularly in relation to developmental experiences which characterize most children at different school levels. In this direction, the manual reports studies which established coefficients of stability obtained by retesting students after a six-week period and after a four-year period. The former study, based on sixth through twelfth graders, produced high correlations in the .70's and .80's for most students. Results for the sixth graders were somewhat lower, as expected. The latter study, based on sixth and seventh graders, showed distinctly lower correlations. Also, score stability proved to be a function of intelligence.

Form E is thus a psychometrically polished instrument with apparently good potential for assessing momentary interests. Definite cautions must be taken with respect to testing the immature student, interpreting scores, and making long-term predictions. Like previous Kuder inventories, the KGIS should be a marketable product for professionals with limited testing or service needs. Its value to vocational science would be enhanced by a more systematic program of research and evaluation.

J Counsel Psychol 18(2):190–1 Mr '71. Robert F. Stahmann. * Instructions are provided so that with supervision the testee can score his own test and plot the score profile on a Profile Leaflet * The inference is....that students in junior high school can score and profile the GIS accurately; however, no evidence supporting this is presented * In the Kuder GIS, items have been revised and increased in number in order to enhance the reliability of the instrument with younger students. However, because the test is both ipsative and normative, problems in interpreting the test results remain for the counselor. For example, if a student had a percentile score of 90 on the Mechanical scale of the GIS and a percentile score of 70 on the Artistic scale, does this mean that he had more interest in mechanical activities than in artistic activities? No! All that can be said is that when responding to the alternatives presented in the test items triads, the student chose mechanical activities more frequently than 90% of the norm group and artistic activities more frequently than 70% of the group. Another question common to counseling situations results when two individuals' scores on the same scale are compared. Assume that one boy had a percentile score of 90 and another boy a percentile score of 70, both on the Mechanical scale. Is it correct to conclude that the boy with the 90 was more interested in mechanical activities than the boy with the 70? No, again! The correct interpretation would be that the boy with the 90, when responding to the alternatives presented in the test triads, indicated a preference for mechanical activities more frequently than the boy with the 70. Further research must be done with the GIS for the counselor to be able to conclude, as was done in the Manual that, "other things being equal, the boy with the 90 is more likely to select mechanical activities from among the choices available to him in real life than is the boy with the 70 [p. 7]."

J Ed Meas 2:231–3 D '65. T. R. Husek. * Used in conjunction with tests of ability and achievement, and interpreted with the assistance of a sensible and sensitive counselor, the GIS could be useful in a junior high school counseling situation. But the reviewer has grave doubts that the GIS will be of value if given and interpreted in a group setting, as is suggested in the manual. As with previous forms of the Kuder vocational inventories, the scores reported to the subject are the percentile ranks for that subject for each interest area. As in the past, this means that the reported score may be high when the subject has little interest in the area. A subject may obtain a higher percentile rank on the clerical scale than on the scientific scale and nevertheless be much more interested in scientific materials than in clerical affairs. * Stability data are presented in the manual for 328 girls and 311 boys who were given a prepublication form of the GIS in the sixth or seventh grade and then retested four years later in 1963. Correlation coefficients are presented between scale raw scores on the two occasions. The average correlation for all scales for the boys is .50. The average for the girls is .43. These coefficients do not support the use of the instrument for counseling purposes if the counseling assumes that the scores are stable. Furthermore, the coefficients are not the appropriate statistics to present in any case. The profile of the ten scores is the interpreted result of the instrument, and data on the stability of the profile is necessary. It is important to know whether the higher scale scores remain high over time and the lower scale scores remain low; these high and low scales provide the information which is most often used in counseling. * the ambitious attempt to write items appropriate for adults as well as children may have created more problems. The inclusion of activities which should be sensible to youngsters and written at the level that the sixth grader can understand means that many of the items seem silly to the adult. * Can a junior high student be expected to meaningfully respond to such alternatives as "Join a club that discusses problems of modern life" or "Cash checks for people in a bank" or "Earn part of your expenses in college by helping in a laboratory" or "Manage a well-planned village for factory workers" or "Do research to improve television" or "Be an authority on outdoor advertising" or "Explain to children how the buying value of the dollar changes"? The inventory carries a middle class flavor to it. There are a number of items involving activities with which economically disadvantaged subjects may have little opportunity to be acquainted. The eight references to activities with "poor people" were a little irritating to the reviewer and may also produce unknown effects on "poor" people, who presumably will be able to attend schools that might use the GIS. * It is obvious that it is undesirable to have spurious correlations between the scales resulting from items being keyed on more than one scale, but it is not clear why some of the interest area scales should not otherwise be related, e.g., musical and artistic positively, and outdoor and computational negatively. * The profile leaflet given to the subject defines the interest areas in a manner which is incorrect at this stage of the development of the GIS and is mildly disturbing. Various occupational categories are used as examples of people who possess a particular interest. There is no evidence in the manual that any data have been collected to support such statements. Until the data are collected the reviewer feels that there is a mite too much of the "hard sell" associated with the claims made. In spite of its limitations, the GIS is easy to take and simple to score. The items appear to be understandable for the moderately bright sixth grader and most of them are probably meaningful. Research on the development and change of children's interests is important * a good instrument for younger children would be useful. The GIS may become a valuable instrument for this research purpose, and its value for research should not be underestimated. In conclusion, the reviewer feels that the GIS has many problems as an instrument for group counseling with junior high school students. They include the lack of stability of results, the difficulty of interpretation of the profile, and the content of many of the items. Some of these problems are also pertinent to high school students, but the GIS is as good as anything currently available for high school students and considerably better than most. The most pressing need is some way of obtaining data which can be reported to subjects in a clear, easily interpretable form. Until this is done the reviewer feels that individual counseling is necessary to adequately interpret the results, and as long as individual counseling is necessary, the reviewer wonders whether a directed interview might not be an adequate or superior substitute for the more formal instrument.

[1025]

*Kuder Occupational Interest Survey. Grades 11–16 and adults; 1956–70; KOIS; items same as those in *Kuder Preference Record—Occupational* but differently scored; 106 scales for men: 77 occupational, 29 college major; 84 scales for women: 57 occupational, 27 college major; Form DD ('64, NCS test-answer sheet); manual ('68, 67 pages); instructions ('70, 4 pages); interpretive leaflet ('70, 6 pages); $30 per 20 tests; purchase price includes scoring of tests which may be submitted in any quantity; $2.50 per specimen set (includes scoring); postage extra; (30–40) minutes; G. Frederic Kuder; Science Research Associates, Inc. *

REFERENCES

1. VISWANATHAN, KAMAKSHI. *Interest Measurement With Particular Reference to the Kuder Preference Record and Its Use in the Selection of Student Teachers.* Master's thesis, University of McGill (Montreal, Que., Canada), 1965.
2. KUDER, G. FREDERIC. "The Occupational Interest Survey." *Personnel & Guid J* 45:72–7 S '66. *
3. DAUW, DEAN C. "Vocational Interests of Highly Creative Computer Personnel." *Personnel J* 46:653–9 N '67. * (*PA* 42:4632)
4. WILSON, ROBERT NICHOLI. *A Comparison of Similar Scales on the Strong Vocational Interest Blank and the Kuder Occupational Interest Survey, Form DD.* Master's thesis, Kansas State University (Manhattan, Kan.), 1967.
5. ANDERSON, THOMAS EDWIN, JR. *The Effect of Reading Skill on the Comparability of the Kuder Preference Record and the Occupational Interest Survey.* Master's thesis, University of Texas (Austin, Tex.), 1968.
6. CLEMANS, WILLIAM V. "Interest Measurement and the Concept of Ipsativity." *Meas & Eval Guid* 1:50–5 sp '68. * (*PA* 44:7280)
7. DIAMOND, ESTHER E. "Occupational Level Versus Sex Group as a System of Classification." Abstract. *Proc 76th Ann Conv Am Psychol Assn* 3:199–200 '68. *
8. RICHARD, JAMES THOMAS. *A Study of the Relationship of Certain Background Factors and the Choice of Police Work as a Career.* Doctor's thesis, Temple University (Philadelphia, Pa.), 1968. (*DAI* 30:1028A)
9. RITCHIE, CLINTON MCCAY. *Vocational Interests as a Factor in the Academic Achievement of Male Students in a Teacher Education Institution.* Doctor's thesis, Rutgers—The State University (New Brunswick, N.J.), 1968. (*DA* 29:3026A)
10. WILSON, ROBERT N., AND KAISER, HERBERT E. "A Comparison of Similar Scales on the SVIB and the Kuder, Form DD." *J Counsel Psychol* 15:468–70 S '68. * (*PA* 42:19287)
11. ZYTOWSKI, DONALD G. "Relationships of Equivalent Scales on Three Interest Inventories." *Personnel & Guid J* 47:44–9 S '68. * (*PA* 43:5936)
12. CAIN, ENOCH THOMAS, II. *Factors Operative in Curricular and/or Occupational Choice: A Study of Super's Theory.* Doctor's thesis, University of Idaho (Moscow, Idaho), 1969. (*DAI* 31:949A)
13. DRUM, DAVID JOHN. *A Study of the Relationships Between Level of Development of Educational Interests and Academic Performance in First-Year College Students.* Doctor's thesis, American University (Washington, D.C.), 1969. (*DAI* 30:3317A)
14. KUDER, FREDERIC. "A Note on the Comparability of Occupational Scores From Different Interest Inventories." *Meas & Eval Guid* 2(2):94–100 su '69. * (*PA* 44:13462)
15. ZYTOWSKI, DONALD G. "A Test of Criterion Group Sampling Error in Two Comparable Interest Inventories." *Meas & Eval Guid* 2(1):37–40 sp '69. * (*PA* 44:11612)
16. DIAMOND, ESTHER E. "Relationship Between Occupational Level and Masculine and Feminine Interests." Abstract. *Proc 78th Ann Conv Am Psychol Assn* 5(1):177–8 '70. * (*PA* 44:18655)
17. HORNADAY, JOHN A., AND BUNKER, CHARLES S. "The Nature of the Entrepreneur." *Personnel Psychol* 23(1):47–54 sp '70. * (*PA* 44:17555)
18. LEFKOWITZ, DAVID M. "Comparison of the Strong Vocational Interest Blank and the Kuder Occupational Interest Survey Scoring Procedures." *J Counsel Psychol* 17(4):357–63 Jl '70. * (*PA* 44:19776)
19. O'SHEA, ARTHUR J., AND HARRINGTON, THOMAS F., JR. "Using the Strong Vocational Interest Blank and the Kuder Occupational Interest Survey, Form DD, With the Same Clients." *J Counsel Psychol* 18(1):44–50 Ja '71. * (*PA* 45:8952)

ROBERT H. DOLLIVER, *Associate Professor and Counseling Psychologist, University of Missouri, Columbia, Missouri.*

There are two major difficulties in accurately viewing this test. First, it is necessary to understand exactly which of the several Kuder tests and revisions we are talking about. Second, it is important to overcome the tendency to view the *Strong Vocational Interest Blank* as an ultimate model of a vocational interest test. This tendency leads to a bias against the Kuder and interferes with an accurate appraisal of it.

Regarding the first of the points, Stahmann (see excerpted review below) has done an admirable job of differentiating between the various Kuder tests, along with providing a review of their development. Reference may also be made to Kuder's introductory article (2) on this test as well as to his paper [1] presenting his general thinking about interest measurement.

[1] KUDER, FREDERIC. "Some Principles of Interest Measurement." *Ed & Psychol Meas* 30(2):205–26 su '70. *

The *Kuder Occupational Interest Survey* (Form DD) is the elaboration of the *Kuder Preference Record—Occupational* (Form D). The items are in the same triad format as in Form D; the subject picks his most and his least preferred activity from the three alternatives. Kuder comments that this format keeps potential response bias from operating. Each item can have any of six possible combinations of response. Thus, the 100 test triads become 600 potential patterns of item response.

The major change noticeable to the test user is the addition of scales for college majors (like similar scales which make up the *College Interest Inventory*). The number of occupational scales has been increased since Form D. New scales have been normed on women for 37 occupations and for 19 college majors. In addition, women receive scores on 20 occupational scales and 8 college major scales which were normed on men. The Verification scale remains the same as on Form D. Experimental scales (printed on only one of the test report forms) reflect a combination of the factors of sex, age, and the attempt to make a best impression. The scores for each scale are reported as correlation coefficients. And the highest 10 occupational and the 10 top college major correlations are rank ordered at the bottom of the test report. The rank ordering, a very helpful practice, appears to have been inaugurated since the manual was printed.

The major departure which this test makes from other interest tests (including the Kuder Form D) is that there is no general reference group used in developing the scales. In this departure from the men-in-general concept, Kuder believes that he has made a breakthrough. (Finding the right group of men from which to differentiate individual occupations is a vexing problem.) Note, however, that the same rationale, shared with other interest tests, continues in effect: resemblance to those already in the occupation means that the test subject ought to consider entering that occupation. The Kuder DD makes a direct comparison between the scores of the individual test taker and the modal responses of those in each occupation and in each college major. Employing a procedure suggested by Clemans, Kuder reports lambda correlation coefficients (a statistic similar in concept to the biserial correlation). Kuder did comparative studies with his test items and found that lambda scores greatly improved

concurrent prediction over the differentiation method.

The rank order of scores, rather than their absolute level, is stressed. But test reports with no scores higher than .31 "should be regarded with caution," and "if there are no scores over .39 and only a few scores in the .32 through .39 range, any interpretation must be highly tentative." The manual reports that, in 30 of the criterion groups which were studied, 80 percent of the subjects obtained scores of .45 or over on their own occupational scale and many scored above .60. (Theoretically, of course, it is possible to score as high as 1.00.) Scores which fall within .06 of the highest score are recommended for primary consideration. It appears that frequently six or eight scale scores would be within that range. Test users may be confused by the seeming frequently limited overall range of the correlations. In the two test reports shown in the test manual, the ranges for the 77 male and the 57 female occupations were .21 to .51 and .24 to .48, respectively. And for the 29 male and 27 female college majors the ranges shown were .29 to .53 and .27 to .64, respectively. The sample test in the interpretive leaflet shows a similarly restricted range.

Several correlational studies compare the Kuder DD with the SVIB (*10, 11, 19*). They have clearly established that the two tests do not give the same results for same and similar scales. What is needed, as Kuder comments (*14*), are studies which compare the predictive efficiency of the tests. Two studies of this sort were identified. The first study (*18*) reported on the concurrent validity of the Kuder DD and the SVIB scoring systems using SVIB items with 600 engineers. The Kuder DD had 80% correct classification, while the SVIB had 70% correct classification. However, when tied scores were considered as an incorrect classification, the Kuder DD had 53% correct classifications and the SVIB had 67%. In the second study (*19*), the Kuder DD and the SVIB were compared for 72 engineering students, testing the predictive validity over two years. In relation to the total group of subjects, the Kuder DD produced more valid positives (26% vs. 6%) but also more false positives (33% vs. 14%) than the SVIB. The SVIB produced more valid negatives (54% vs. 35%) but also more false negatives (26% vs. 6%). When the valid predictions are added, each instrument was accurate about 60 percent of the time. The results in both studies were apparently influenced by the fact that more subjects had high engineering scale scores on the Kuder DD than on the SVIB.

The test manual is attractive and informative. The short section on where to obtain occupational information seems useful. Much effort has been directed toward reporting the intensive study of 3,000 subjects on 30 "core" scales (23 men's and 7 women's scales, both occupational and college major scales). The manual acknowledges that it is an assumption that results from the other 132 scales would be similar in that the same method was used to develop them. Research on the other scales is promised, and this is needed. Reports of reliability are unnecessarily ambiguous regarding time lapse and number of scales used. Earlier reviews (6:1062 and 5:862) of the Kuder D mention this problem regarding unspecified time lapses which could easily be corrected. One reliability study illustrated with eight bar graphs consisted of 100 subjects (males and females from high school and college) and did identify the time lapse as a two-week period for comparisons of 25 to 28 scales. Another study tested 92 high school males and 50 college females on 142 scales, but no time lapse is specified. Results reported for perhaps the same 92 high school males compare the "repeat reliabilities of differences between pairs of lambda scores on 4 scales." A final study involved 93 engineering students over a 3-year period on an unspecified number of scales. These data probably come from a reanalysis of work published by Gehman [2] which dealt with the reliability of the *Kuder Preference Record—Occupational*. If so, it would seem that some reference to that source would be appropriate. Results reported earlier in this review (*19*) suggest that studies which do not include false positives tend to inflate the apparent accuracy of the Kuder DD. (The 93 engineering students remained in engineering over the 3-year period.) Reports of validity revolve around the 3,000 "core" subjects and the 30 "core" scales. All of these data are based on concurrent validity, and an undisclosed number of the subjects were among those used to develop the scales. Reading and interpreting the validity information presented in Tables 5–7 would be aided by summary statements regarding means and modes for the tabular data. The information provided in the manual gives some assurance that this is a very good test. But more reliability and validity data are needed from more groups over longer time periods before the test can be used with confidence in individual counseling. Since the Kuder DD items are the same as the Kuder D items, the process of accumulating reliability and validity data ought to be speeded through the rescoring of answer sheets in Kuder's files. There is enough evidence now to support that this is useful as a heuristic device to suggest possible occupations and college majors for thoughtful consideration.

Inevitably, a comparison must be made between the Kuder DD and the SVIB. The DD has these advantages: (*a*) scoring of college major interests, (*b*) having a broader range of occupations (more technical and trade level occupations), (*c*) using the same test for males and females, (*d*) providing scores for female test takers on selected male occupational and college major scales, and (*e*) having norm groups which were more recently tested. But because the SVIB has accumulated more supporting reliability and validity data, the SVIB remains the better test, in this reviewer's opinion.

The Kuder DD is a great improvement over the Kuder D. Present evidence supports Kuder's contention that the lambda correlation scoring will be shown to be highly accurate. But this has not yet been sufficiently demonstrated.

W. BRUCE WALSH, *Associate Professor of Psychology, The Ohio State University, Columbus, Ohio.*

The *Kuder Occupational Interest Survey* (Form DD) is a 100-triad inventory requiring the respondent to choose the one activity in each triad he prefers most and the one activity in each triad he likes least. It is a derivative of the *Kuder Preference Record—Occupational* (Form D), with items at approximately the 6th grade vocabulary level. As in other Kuder inventories, a Verification scale is included along with eight experimental scales for research purposes. Scores on the KOIS attempt to show how an individual's preferences are like those typical of people in various occupations and fields of study. The Interpretive Leaf-

2 GEHMAN, W. SCOTT, AND GEHMAN, ILA H. "Stability of Engineering Interests Over a Period of Four Years." *Ed & Psychol Meas* 28:367–76 su '68. * (*PA* 42:19551)

let indicates that the person who has an interest pattern similar to that of people in a particular occupation is likely to find satisfaction in that occupation.

Kuder (*1*) reports that the KOIS was developed to be used when a person is about to commit himself to preparing for or entering a specific line of work. Other uses suggested by the manual include identifying potential occupations for probable 10th grade school dropouts, aiding 11th and 12th grade students to make vocational decisions, helping college freshmen select a major field of study, and working with adults in employment and placement counseling.

The scores for the KOIS express the correlation (lambda coefficients) between an individual's responses and those of the members of a defined criterion group. The coefficients express the extent to which an individual's pattern of interests resembles that of various occupational and college major groups. The upper limit of the lambda is 1.00 for all groups. Lefkowitz (*18*) compared the effects on interest scores of the scoring systems of the *Strong Vocational Interest Blank* and the KOIS. For the sample of engineers used in the study, the KOIS did not differentiate between and within individuals as well as the SVIB scoring system. Essentially, the findings reveal that the two scoring systems produce different interest scores. However, this study used only engineers.

On the profile sheet the highest KOIS scores (usually 10) for the occupational and college major scales are reported separately by sex. The report of scores for women includes selected scales developed from the male criterion groups. Scores for men include only the scales developed from the male criterion groups. The manual should be read extensively before one attempts to interpret the scores.

In regard to validity, only concurrent validity studies are cited in the manual. The findings indicate that the KOIS is able to discriminate between various existing criterion groups. However, no data are available on the predictive validity of the KOIS. Furthermore, related occupational and college major scales are not grouped into meaningful categories. Such categories have been useful in interpreting the SVIB.

Three recent studies of similarly named scales on the SVIB and the KOIS have shown mostly low positive correlations between the two inventories. Wilson and Kaiser (*10*) found a mean correlation coefficient of .32 for 27 same-named scales on the two inventories. Zytowski (*11*) obtained a median correlation coefficient of .25 for 57 equivalent scales. Most recently O'Shea and Harrington (*19*) found a median correlation coefficient of .39 for 51 similar-named scales on the two instruments. They further compared the correlation coefficients among all occupational scales of the two inventories. The results show that an occupational scale on one of the inventories often correlates more highly with a dissimilar scale on the other inventory than with a similar-named scale. Thus, it seems that the two inventories may be designed to measure different aspects of the interest domain. However, in making a choice of inventories for use in counseling, the SVIB is difficult to reject because of the large number of supportive validity studies, particularly in the area of predictive validity.

The manual refers to two types of reliability for the KOIS. One type is test-retest; the other refers to the consistency of the differences between scores on selected pairs of scales for two administrations. Test-retest stability coefficients for a two-week time period were quite stable for 12th grade and college students. Each group was composed of 25 students. The median reliability for all cases was .90. In another test-retest study, a median reliability of .93 was reported for 92 male high school seniors and a median reliability of .96 was found for 50 female college seniors. However, the manual does not report the test-retest time interval for these two samples. The manual also reports a three-year test-retest for three groups of college students (N = 93) majoring in engineering. The median reliability for the total group was .89. Essentially, the above findings are encouraging but additional test-retest reliability studies need to be completed using larger sample size.

In order to explore the second type of reliability, differences between scores in each possible pair on four scales were correlated for 92 high school seniors in two administrations. The correlation coefficients ranged from .84 to .92. The findings suggest a high degree of consistency for the scales involved. However, only four scales were used.

In summary, the KOIS has been developed with careful attention to rationale, construction, and scoring procedure. The inventory also includes college major scales, a feature not available on the SVIB. However, in the areas of validity, reliability, and ease of interpretation the KOIS falls short of the SVIB. Basically, the SVIB shows evidence of predictive validity, which the KOIS does not. Predictive validity studies using the KOIS need to be completed. The reliability evidence for the KOIS is supportive, but there is a need for additional evidence using a larger sample size. In regard to interpretation, the scales are not grouped into categories. Furthermore, the meaning of low and middle scores is not discussed (see Stahmann's excerpted review below). One research study also suggests that the KOIS scoring system does not differentiate between and within individuals as well as the SVIB scoring system. Thus, until additional validity and reliability data are accumulated for the KOIS, practitioners will probably be assuming less risk by using the more soundly researched SVIB.

J Counsel Psychol 18(2):191–2 Mr '71. Robert F. Stahmann. * Scores on the OIS over a 2-week time span were quite stable. For both male and female high school seniors ($N = 25$ each) the median reliability was .90. Slightly higher reliabilities were obtained for two other samples; however, the test-retest time was not indicated. One long-term study, using three samples of engineering students at one university tested and retested "over a period of approximately three years," has been reported * Median reliability for the three groups combined was .89, but it can be argued that engineering is a particularly stable and unique field of study. Additional reliability studies must be completed specifying the exact time interval between testing and using samples in which the N is larger. The effect of age at testing must also be examined. For example, it has been found when the Strong Vocational Interest Blank (SVIB) was used with those below the age of 21, age when first tested was the major factor influencing the size of test-retest correlations * Judging from the data presented....the concurrent validity....is satisfactory. However, the real use of an interest inventory is in connection with predictive validity, generally for predicting future occupation. Such data for the OIS are lacking. *Conclusions.* The Kuder OIS is a well-constructed instrument which offers promise of becoming a useful tool for the counselor. However, this reviewer believes that the OIS will be slow in

replacing or supplementing the popular SVIB. In the first place, an interest inventory must have demonstrated predictive validity: the OIS has not, the SVIB has. Secondly, because of the simple alphabetical listing of scores on the OIS without regard to grouping, considerable time must be spent by the counselor in retrieving the test data, that is, in finding the high and low scores from among the many listed. The ranking of the 10 highest scores at the bottom of the report sheet is of some help. What about the low and middle scores? Should the counselor ignore them? In summary, the profile report sheet for the OIS is a handicap to use in counseling when compared with profile reports available with the SVIB and Minnesota Vocational Interest Inventory.

Meas & Eval Guid 4(2):122–5 Jl '71. Frederick G. Brown. * Although the manual suggests that the OIS may be used as early as 10th grade, no evidence is presented regarding the stability of interests at this age. * Rather surprisingly, the manual includes no data relating to the reliability of individual scales; evidence of neither stability nor homogeneity (internal consistency) is given. Some data are presented that indicate that profiles are quite stable (r's > .90) over short time periods (two weeks), but no data are available on stability over longer periods. Although long-term test-retest data obviously cannot be available for a new test, data for periods of greater than two weeks surely could be collected. Also, one would hope (demand?) that the publishers systematically collect data on the long-term stability of OIS scores and profiles, for, without demonstrated stability, use of an interest measure is unwarranted. * the more important validity test will be the ability of the OIS scales to predict occupational choice and satisfaction over the long haul. Here again one would hope for a systematic attempt by the publishers to collect relevant data. I encountered one puzzlement in the validity data—the practice of combining data from occupational scales and educational major scales in the same analysis. One consequence is to make the test's validity look poorer than it is. For example, when studying errors in classification, if an electrical engineer scored higher on the electrical engineering major scale than on the electrical engineer occupational scale, an error would be counted. But surely this is not an error of any substance. Separate analyses of the two types of scales would provide more meaningful and less cumbersome analyses. * No attempt has been made to group scales into clusters, and this fact, coupled with the nature of the score printout, makes the patterning of scores less obvious than on most multiscale inventories. Finally, we will consider what is perhaps the most important question regarding any empirically derived interest inventory—the composition of the criterion groups. The OIS groups were selected on the basis of criteria similar to those used with the SVIB (workers between the ages of 25 and 65 who had been employed in the occupation for at least three years and who met certain job satisfaction criteria). Samples were obtained from professional organizations and from nationwide sampling. College major scales were developed from samples of college seniors from a wide variety of schools. The exact composition of each group is given in the manual. While it appears that Kuder did a reasonably good job of sampling, an ugly fact occurs: A recent spate of studies has indicated that various interest inventories do not agree with each other, even when considering persons in the same occupation. This does not mean that Strong's physicians are a better sample than Kuder's, or vice versa. It does suggest that the composition of and requirements for criterion groups need to be studied further. Until we can be certain that our criterion groups are representative of an occupation or a particular segment of an occupation, use of scores based on such possibly nonrepresentative groups will only result in poor occupational choices.

[1026]

★Minnesota Vocational Interest Inventory. Males age 15 and over not planning to attend college; 1965–66; MVII; 30 scores: 21 occupational scales (baker, food service manager, milk wagon driver, retail sales clerk, stock clerk, printer, tabulating machine operator, warehouseman, hospital attendant, pressman, carpenter, painter, plasterer, truck driver, truck mechanic, industrial education teacher, sheet metal worker, plumber, machinist, electrician, radio-TV repairman) and 9 area scales (mechanical, health service, office work, electronics, food service, carpentry, sales-office, clean hands, outdoors); 1 form; 2 editions; manual ('65, 31 pages); 75¢ per manual; $1 per specimen set; postage extra; (45–50) minutes; Kenneth E. Clark and David P. Campbell (manual); Psychological Corporation. *
a) NCS EDITION. 1965; test-answer sheet (6 pages); $4.50 per 25 test-answer sheets; scoring service: 85¢ to 50¢ per test (daily service), 45¢ to 33¢ per test (weekly service, $11.25 minimum).
b) MRC EDITION. 1965–66; 1 form ('65, 7 pages); profile ('65, 2 pages); directions ('66, 6 pages); separate answer sheets (MRC) must be used; $5.50 per 25

tests; $4.50 per 50 answer sheets; $2 per 50 profiles; $7 per set of hand scoring stencils and directions; scoring service, 45¢ to 33¢ per test ($12.50 minimum).

REFERENCES

1. CLARK, KENNETH E. "A Vocational Interest Test at the Skilled Trades Level." J Appl Psychol 33:291–303 Ag '49. * (PA 24:2846)
2. SCHENKEL, KENNETH FRANCIS. Tabulator Operator Selection, Emphasizing Relationships Among Aptitudes, Interests, Proficiency, Job- and Vocational-Satisfaction. Doctor's thesis, University of Minnesota (Minneapolis, Minn.), 1953. (DA 13: 1251)
3. GEE, HELEN HOFER. Empirical vs. Homogeneous Scoring Keys in Interest Measurement. Doctor's thesis, University of Minnesota (Minneapolis, Minn.), 1955. (DA 16:798)
4. PERRY, DALLIS K. "Forced-Choice vs. L-I-D Response Items in Vocational Interest Measurement." J Appl Psychol 39:256–62 Ag '55. * (PA 30:4734)
5. PERRY, DALLIS K. "Validities of Three Vocational Interest Keys for U.S. Navy Yeomen." J Appl Psychol 39:134–8 Ap '55. * (PA 30:1726)
6. NORMAN, WARREN THEODORE. A Dispersion Analysis of the Interests of 115 Occupational and Reference Groups. Doctor's thesis, University of Minnesota (Minneapolis, Minn.), 1957. (DA 18:1485)
7. BRADLEY, ARTHUR DICKINSON. Estimating Success in Technical and Skilled Trade Courses Using a Multivariate Statistical Analysis. Doctor's thesis, University of Minnesota (Minneapolis, Minn.), 1958. (DA 21:313)
8. CHRISTIANSEN, HARLEY DUANE. The Relationship of Several Self-Other Indices to Claimed and Measured Interests of Vocational High School Seniors. Doctor's thesis, University of Minnesota (Minneapolis, Minn.), 1959. (DA 20:4032)
9. GHEI, SOMNATH. The Relationship Between Classification Keys and Predictor Keys in Interest Measurement. Doctor's thesis, University of Minnesota (Minneapolis, Minn.), 1959. (DA 20:368)
10. CAMPBELL, DAVID PHILLIP. Psychometric Analysis of Response Patterns to Interest Inventory Items. Doctor's thesis, University of Minnesota (Minneapolis, Minn.), 1960. (DA 21: 3156)
11. GHEI, SOMNATH. "Vocational Interests, Achievement, and Satisfaction." J Counsel Psychol 7:132–6 su '60. * (PA 35: 4014)
12. NORMAN, WARREN T. "A Spatial Analysis of an Interest Domain." Ed & Psychol Meas 20:347–61 su '60. * (PA 35: 7248)
13. CLARK, KENNETH E. The Vocational Interests of Nonprofessional Men. Minneapolis, Minn.: University of Minnesota Press, 1961. Pp. xi, 129. * (PA 36:5LB29C)
14. MAHLMAN, RICHARD WILLIAM. Assessing Vocational Interests of Mental Patients. Doctor's thesis, University of Minnesota (Minneapolis, Minn.), 1961. (DA 22:2876)
15. SCOTT, THOMAS BLYTHE, JR. Counseling Interpretations for the Minnesota Vocational Interest Inventory Based on Comparisons With the Strong Vocational Interest Blank. Doctor's thesis, University of Minnesota (Minneapolis, Minn.), 1961. (DA 22:634)
16. CAMPBELL, DAVID. "The Use of Response Patterns to Improve Item Scoring." J Appl Psychol 46:194–7 Je '62. * (PA 37:2097)
17. NELSON, HOWARD F. "Selection of Students." Yearb Am Council Indus Arts Teach Ed 11:139–67 '62. *
18. CAMPBELL, DAVID. "Another Attempt at Configural Scoring." Ed & Psychol Meas 23:721–7 w '63. * (PA 38:8405)
19. CAMPBELL, DAVID P., AND SORENSON, WAYNE W. "Response Set on Interest Inventory Triads." Ed & Psychol Meas 23:145–52 sp '63. * (PA 38:2707)
20. CAMPBELL, DAVID P., AND TROCKMAN, RACHEL W. "A Verification Scale for the Minnesota Vocational Interest Inventory." J Appl Psychol 47:276–9 Ag '63. * (PA 38:3236)
21. MESSMAN, WARREN BROWN. Interest Patterns of Freshmen Industrial Arts Majors in Comparison With Personality Traits. Doctor's research study No. 1, Colorado State College (Greeley, Colo.), 1963. (DA 25:314)
22. BARNETTE, W. LESLIE, JR., AND McCALL, JOHN N. "Validation of the Minnesota Vocational Interest Inventory for Vocational High School Boys." J Appl Psychol 48:378–82 D '64. * (PA 39:8775)
23. CAMPBELL, DAVID P. "The Center for Interest Measurement Research." J Counsel Psychol 11:395–9 w '64. *
24. McCALL, JOHN N. "'Masculine Striving' as a Clue to Skilled-Trade Interests." J Appl Psychol 49:106–9 Ap '65. * (PA 39:10205)
25. CAMPBELL, DAVID P. "The Minnesota Vocational Interest Inventory." Personnel & Guid J 44:854–8 Ap '66. *
26. BARCLAY, JAMES R. "Approach to the Measurement of Teacher 'Press' in the Secondary Curriculum." J Counsel Psychol 14:552–67 N '67. * (PA 42:4525)
27. DOERR, JOHN JOSEPH. Application of the Discriminant Function to the Classification of Trade and Industrial Education Students. Doctor's thesis, University of Missouri (Columbia, Mo.), 1967. (DA 28:2516A)

28. LOWMAN, CLARENCE LUDWELL. *The Relationships Between Certain Characteristics of Enrollees and Measures of Their Success in Selected Manpower Development and Training Act Curriculums.* Doctor's thesis, Florida State University (Tallahassee, Fla.), 1967. (*DA* 28:879A)

29. SILVER, HARVEY ALLAN. *A Longitudinal Validation Study of the Minnesota Vocational Interest Inventory Utilizing Vocational High School Boys.* Doctor's thesis, State University of New York (Buffalo, N.Y.), 1967. (*DA* 28:3067B)

30. VANDENBERG, STEVEN G., AND STAFFORD, RICHARD E. "Hereditary Influences on Vocational Preferences as Shown by Scores of Twins on the Minnesota Vocational Interest Inventory." *J Appl Psychol* 51:17–9 F '67. * (*PA* 41:4610)

31. BONFIELD, JOHN. "Development and Validation of an Identification Scale for High Ability Dropouts." *Voc Guid Q* 16:177–80 Mr '68. *

32. FRENCH, JOSEPH L., AND CARDON, BARTELL W. "Characteristics of High Mental Ability School Dropouts." *Voc Guid Q* 16:162–8 Mr '68. *

33. MARTIN, GLEN RAY. *Job Satisfaction in Practical Nursing as a Function of Measured and Expressed Interests.* Doctor's thesis, University of Illinois (Urbana, Ill.), 1968. (*DAI* 30:266B)

34. MICHIE, JACK. *Dominant Factors Influencing the Employment Success of a Selected Group of Disadvantaged Youth.* Doctor's thesis, University of California (Los Angeles, Calif.), 1968. (*DA* 28:4825A)

35. OLSON, DENNIS W., AND JOHNSON, RICHARD W. "Reliability of Measured Interests of Hospitalized Psychiatric Patients." *Meas & Eval Guid* 1:115–21 su '68. * (*PA* 44:8519)

36. PASSMORE, JAMES LAURENCE. *Validation of a Discriminant Analysis of Eight Vocational-Technical Curricular Groups.* Doctor's thesis, University of Missouri (Columbia, Mo.), 1968. (*DA* 29:4292A)

37. THORNDIKE, ROBERT M.; WEISS, DAVID J.; AND DAWIS, RENÉ V. "Multivariate Relationships Between a Measure of Vocational Interests and a Measure of Vocational Needs." *J Appl Psychol* 52:491–6 D '68. * (*PA* 42:3161)

38. ZYTOWSKI, DONALD G. "Relationships of Equivalent Scales on Three Interest Inventories." *Personnel & Guid J* 47:44–9 S '68. * (*PA* 43:5936)

39. HALE, PETER P., AND BEAL, LANCE E. "MVII Occupational Interest Profile for Hospital Housekeeping Aides." *Voc Guid Q* 17(3):218–20 Mr '69. *

40. KAUPPI, DWIGHT R., AND WEISS, DAVID J. "Comparison of Single Item and Triad Verification Keys for the MVII." Abstract. *Proc 77th Ann Conv Am Psychol Assn* 4(1):149–50 '69. * (*PA* 43:16628)

41. KAUPPI, DWIGHT R., AND WEISS, DAVID J. "Efficiency of Commonly Used Measures in Predicting Inventory Validity." Abstract. *Proc 77th Ann Conv Am Psychol Assn* 4(2):691–2 '69. * (*PA* 44:675)

42. RAVENSBORG, MILTON R. "Psychiatric Technicians' Ranking of Five Potential Employment Screening Tests." *Personnel J* 48(1):39–41 Ja '69. * (*PA* 44:2910)

43. BLANK, PATRICIA M. *The Use of the Minnesota Vocational Interest Inventory by a Select Psychiatric Population.* Master's thesis, Springfield College (Springfield, Mass.), 1970.

44. JOHNSON, RICHARD W., AND ST. JOHN, DAVID E. "Use of the MVII in Educational Planning With Community College 'Career' Students." *Voc Guid Q* 19(2):90–6 D '70. *

45. SILVER, HARVEY A., AND BARNETTE, W. LESLIE, JR. "Predictive and Concurrent Validity of the Minnesota Vocational Interest Inventory for Vocational High School Boys." *J Appl Psychol* 54(5):436–40 O '70. * (*PA* 45:3133)

JOHN O. CRITES, *Professor of Psychology, University of Maryland, College Park, Maryland.*

Constructed to measure the vocational interests of nonprofessional men, for which there has been no generally appropriate assessment device, the MVII was developed from work originally done by Clark (*13*) for the Navy in classifying personnel at the skilled (petty officer) level. The civilian version of the instrument is shorter than its military predecessor, consisting of 158 triads about occupationally relevant activities, as contrasted with 190 triads in the original. An illustrative item from the MVII is:

Minnesota Vocational Interest Inventory

a. Be a master mechanic.
b. Be a chemist.
c. Be a recreation director.

The respondent is instructed to indicate which of these he likes the most and which he dislikes the most (or likes the least). In other words, he endorses two of the three foils, leaving the third blank. There are, therefore, six possible response patterns: Like a—Dislike b; Like a—Dislike c; Like b—Dislike a; etc. Thus, the response format is of the "forced choice" type.

Scoring keys for the MVII were developed empirically by comparing the responses of 21 nonprofessional occupational groups, ranging in N's from 72 to 519, with a tradesmen-in-general group of 240. Plus and minus keys for each occupation reflect whether the criterion group or tradesmen-in-general endorsed an item more frequently. Following this procedure, 21 occupational scales have been constructed; in addition, 9 so-called "homogeneous" scales have been developed from items which are highly intercorrelated. Scores from both sets of scales are displayed on a profile sheet in standard score form, with a mean of 50 and a standard deviation of 10. The occupational scales are grouped into clusters according to their intercorrelations, the two largest ones being "white-collar, clerical" and "blue-collar, mechanical." The median correlation between these two clusters is $-.72$, which suggests that they "represent opposite ends of the same dimension." It might also be concluded from this finding that, given the high within-cluster correlations, any one scale would yield as much information as all of the scales taken together. That is, a high score on the Retail Sales Clerk scale, which is in the "white-collar, clerical" cluster, would indicate that an examinee has interests similar to those of men in this occupation, as well as all others in the cluster, and that he does not have interests similar to those of men in the "blue-collar, mechanical" cluster. Whether it would be more economical to score just one of the 10 scales in these two clusters rather than all of them, assuming that essentially the same information can be obtained, is a decision the test user will have to make.

One reason for the high positive and negative correlations within and between the white- and blue-collar clusters may be their ipsative construction, which would tend to yield such interrelationships. Clark (*13*) argues to the contrary, however, pointing out that:

This *may* [italics in original] be the case when triads are scored; it is not the case for this inventory, since responses are forced, but scoring is not. That is, the individual who completes the inventory must make precisely 190 "like" responses, and 190 "dislike" responses [military edition]. His choice of responses in a mechanical domain will not, however, place any direct limitation on the magnitude of his score in another domain except in the small number of instances where a given response is scored on both keys, but in the opposite direction. This effect occurs just as easily with free-choice procedures as it does with forced-choice ones.

What Clark is saying is that, because the scoring keys for the MVII were constructed empirically, rather than on a priori grounds, the forced choice format does not necessarily make the scales ipsative. For example, that an examinee marks Like for the statement "Be a master mechanic" does not automatically lower his score on any other scale, except those keyed Dislike to this response.

It can be shown both logically and empirically, however, that Clark's argument is not valid and that the MVII scales have ipsative attributes. Consider first the possible patterns of response to item 41 given above. When a subject endorses any foil as Like, then he does not endorse the other two foils as Like and therefore does not receive a plus for any scales which are so keyed to them. To illustrate, foil "a" of item 41 is keyed plus to Truck Mechanic whereas foil "c" is keyed plus to Retail Sales Clerk. A Like endorsement of "a" would add one point to the Truck Mechanic scale score but none to the Retail Sales Clerk scale score. In a free choice response format a subject might endorse both as Like and receive points on both occupational scales. Similarly, when a subject marks any foil as Dislike, then he may not indicate Dislike for the other two foils and thus is not credited with minuses for scales so keyed to them. An example is Machinist, for which a Dislike to foil "b" is scored a minus, and Milk Wagon Driver, for which a Dislike to foil "c" is scored a minus. With free-response options, a subject might endorse both as Dislike. Ipsativeness is further introduced into the MVII, as Clark notes, when the same response is scored differently for two scales. Thus, foil "a" in item 41 is keyed as minus for Retail Sales Clerk as well as plus for Truck Mechanic. The correlation between these two scales, incidentally, is −.89.

In fact, an analysis of the intercorrelation matrix for the occupational scales of the MVII empirically substantiates their logically-deduced ipsative characteristics. In general, the average intercorrelation of ipsative scales is given by the formula $-1/(n-1)$, where n is the number of scales. For the 21 scales of the MVII, the expected value is −.05; the obtained value from data given in the manual is −.03. The difference between the two coefficients is probably due to rounding errors in converting r to z for averaging, since r's were carried to only two places in the manual. In short, the intercorrelations of the MVII scales closely resemble those which would be expected among ipsative measures. Unfortunately, data for further testing this conclusion by analyzing the correlations of the MVII scales to other variables are not available in the literature. If they are ipsative, then the r's between them and any other variable should average to approximately zero.[1] Incomplete evidence on this issue has been reported by Zytowski (*38*), who intercorrelated same- or similar-named scales from the *Kuder Occupational Interest Survey, Strong Vocational Interest Blank,* and MVII. The median correlations and number of scales involved were as follows: KOIS–MVII, .19 (14 scales) and SVIB–MVII, .08 (3 scales). Further research utilizing all of the MVII scales needs to be done, but it appears from these findings that the MVII is not highly related to other interest inventories, most likely because of its ipsative construction.

To the extent that the MVII *is* ipsative, it is subject to all of the shortcomings of such instruments, the principal one of which is difficulty in interpreting scores to clients. With regard to the *Kuder General Interest Survey,* Bauernfeind[2] concludes that the most accurate interpretation of a scale which might be made —although, as he observes, it is "a classic case of communication invalidity"—is as follows: "Your interests in Artistic activities are higher —we don't know how much higher—than your own average interests—whatever that is—relative to the interests of other boys in the national norms group." Much of the same kind of interpretation of MVII scores must be formulated in relating them to clients, and hence their psychological meaningfulness is considerably restricted. About the best which can be said of MVII scores, pending further research, is

1 RADCLIFFE, J. A. "Some Properties of Ipsative Score Matrices and Their Relevance for Some Current Interest Tests." *Austral J Psychol* 15:1–11 Ap '63. *
2 BAUERNFEIND, ROBERT H. "The Matter of 'Ipsative Scores.'" *Personnel & Guid J* 41:210–7 N '62. *

that they provide indices of intraindividual similarity of interests in relation to 21 non-professional occupational groups.

BERT W. WESTBROOK, *Associate Professor of Psychology, North Carolina State University, Raleigh, North Carolina.*

The *Minnesota Vocational Interest Inventory* is probably the only commercially available instrument for measuring the similarity between an examinee's interests and the interest patterns of men in a variety of nonprofessional occupations. Based upon extensive research with Navy enlisted men (*13*), the MVII incorporates several modifications in construction which stem from a careful reexamination of some of the methodological assumptions underlying the *Strong Vocational Interest Blank*. Although it employs a forced choice format, like the *Kuder Preference Record—Vocational*, the scoring keys were developed empirically, as in the SVIB, by differentiating the responses of an occupational group from those of tradesmen-in-general.

The MVII was prepared by reducing the number of items in an original research form of the inventory. The manual, however, does not specify clearly how much new evidence has been obtained for the shorter form or what methods were employed to determine the comparability of the published version and the original version of the inventory.

The manual effectively warns against serious errors of interpretation that arise when some users of interest inventories think of scores as capacities rather than motivation. It stresses that interest does not necessarily imply ability and is only one factor to be considered in choosing among occupations.

Unfortunately, the validity of the inventory has not been determined on subjects who are at the age of persons for whom the inventory is recommended in practice. While the manual states that the inventory "should be suitable for students in the ninth grade or higher," data are not reported for high school or college samples. The validity of the occupational scales is based on groups of workers in nonprofessional civilian occupations, Navy enlisted men, and industrial education teachers. Two validity studies are based on students in a Navy Electronics Technician school and a group of Navy Yeomen. Since the MVII is intended largely for the guidance of high school pupils, validity

should be determined on subjects tested prior to or near the time when they are making educational and vocational choices.

The manual reports detailed statistics which indicate the efficiency with which the inventory separates men in various occupations (criterion groups) from tradesmen-in-general (reference group). The "percentage of overlap" with tradesmen-in-general ranges from 27 for the Industrial Education Teacher scale and the Radio-TV Repairman scale to 63 for the Stock Clerk scale. The ability of the occupational scales to differentiate between occupational groups and tradesmen-in-general does not, in and of itself, warrant using the inventory in the counseling of high school and college students. Better evidence could be obtained by administering the inventory to students, determining the nature of their later employment, and then establishing the relation between pre-occupational score and later occupation.

The tradesmen-in-general group is inadequately described in the manual. We are told only that it consists of a group of "workers from 16 different civilian occupations with no single group contributing more than 10 percent of the total number of two hundred and forty." The manual does not indicate which specific occupations were included. Thus, the user cannot evaluate the statement in the manual that the tradesmen-in-general group represents "a cross-section of all adult men in the skilled trades."

Test-retest reliability coefficients for all but one of the occupational scales are in the .70's and .80's, but they are based on an interval of only 30 days, and on subjects (N = 98) enrolled in an industrial institute rather than on high school pupils. Scores on the MVII would probably be retained in a high school pupil's record, to be consulted as new questions about him arise. Therefore, the manual should have reported data which indicate the length of time following the test during which the score could continue to be used effectively for counseling purposes.

The procedures for scoring the inventory are described in sufficient detail and clarity. When the answer sheets are hand scored, however, some errors are likely to occur because of the difficulty in seeing answer marks through the scoring stencils. Machine scoring services for both the reusable booklet format and the expendable booklet format represent a decided advantage, particularly in large-scale testing.

The norms reported in the manual are quite restrictive in terms of geographical representation. Seventeen of the occupational scales were validated on workers from the St. Paul-Minneapolis area, with the samples ranging from a minimum of 72 plasterers to a maximum of 349 electricians in a crossvalidation sample. Three of the occupational scales are based on men who held occupational "rates" and were selected "from the ten thousand men passing through Naval Receiving Stations in 1951." The remaining occupational scale was validated on a sample of 105 industrial education teachers (with two crossvalidation samples of 94 and 103) from four Midwestern universities.

Performance on the inventory is appropriately reported in terms of standard scores having a mean of 50 and a standard deviation of 10 for each of the occupational scales. Interpretation of scores is facilitated through use of a profile sheet which includes a shaded area depicting the range of scores for the middle third of a group of tradesmen. The profile shows that a person who has a high degree of interest in an occupation when compared to tradesmen-in-general will have a lower degree of interest when compared with persons actually engaged in that field.

In conclusion, the MVII represents a promising beginning in the measurement of interests of men in nonprofessional occupations. It should be used in research with high school pupils to shed further light on its validity. In addition, much research is needed on its stability at various age levels and on its predictive validity for different curricula and occupations. Despite its uniqueness and its extensive research with Navy enlisted men, the MVII should be used cautiously in educational and vocational guidance at the secondary level because its reliability and validity with high school pupils have not yet been established.

J Ed Meas 3:337–41 w '66. Donald W. Hall. * There is no other inventory on the market which measures the similarity between the examinee's expressed interests and those of men employed in a variety of non-professional occupations. * The quality of paper, clarity of printing and other physical characteristics of the majority of test materials are excellent. However, the format and size of print on the Measurement Research Center separate answer sheet for the reusable booklet format does not measure up to the quality of the other materials. * hand-scoring of the Occupational Scales MVII would not be a practical undertaking. The work activity Area Scales, or Homogeneous Scales as they are also labeled in the manual, were derived by identifying clusters of items that had a high positive correlation with each other. Names were assigned to the scales *after* inspection of the items falling into each cluster. No specific definition of what constituted a high positive inter-item correlation is provided by the manual. * The sample on which the norms are based for each of the 21 Occupational Scales is given in suitable appendix form in the manual. It is unfortunate that for 17 of the 21 scales, the samples were made up entirely of workers from the Minneapolis-St. Paul area. The assumption has apparently been made by the test author that truck drivers—as well as 16 other occupational groups included in the inventory—in Minneapolis have essentially similar interests to truck drivers in other parts of the United States for which he deems the test useful in vocational counseling. This is possibly the greatest single weakness of the inventory at this stage of its development. * In general....the major weaknesses of the norms appear to be in the selection of the standardization sample for many of the occupational scales due to very restricted geographical representation, a lack of definitive description of the Tradesmen-in-General group, and a failure to cross-validate 14 of the 21 Occupational Scales. For those seven scales for which there was at least one cross-validation group, however, the raw score means and standard deviations were quite comparable to those of the original sample. * Unfortunately, the only description of the reliability sample declares that it is "based on 98 students from the Dunwoody Industrial Institute, Minneapolis, Minnesota." Some estimate of the inventory's reliability for the high school levels by grade would seem particularly desirable over a much longer period than the thirty-day interval utilized in the one study reported. * Each of the 158 item triads were constructed to describe work related activities and do not include items characteristic of personality or biographical type inventories. Although it is claimed that an attempt has thus been made to provide scores which are relatively independent of such measures, it is unfortunate that the manual does not provide information on representative intercorrelations of the Occupational and Homogeneous Area Scales with, for example, such inventories as the validity and clinical scales of the MMPI, the scales of the Edwards Personal Preference Schedule, the Adjective Check List, and the Kuder Preference Record-Personal. * The statement in the manual that point-biserial correlations from .40 to .80 would be obtained from this type of data seems potentially misleading, and fails to point out that such a coefficient would merely indicate the tendency of the occupational group on whom the scale was developed to score in the appropriately higher direction on the scale than the Tradesmen-in-General group. Some notation is also made of "errors of classification," with the general guide-line presented to the reader that the percentage of overlap is roughly twice the per cent of individuals who would be misclassified if individuals were assigned to either the Occupational or Tradesmen-in-General groups on the basis of a particular scale score alone. This statement assumes equal numbers in the various Occupational as compared to the Tradesmen-in-General group, which is not the case in the sample N's indicated in the manual, and equal variability of raw scores, which appears fairly well substantiated by inspection of the relevant tables provided. For the Homogeneous Area Scales, the only evidence for validity noted is the procedure by which they were derived (i.e., high intercorrelations among the items of a particular scale and the subjective identification of the central core of each scale by inspection of the items), and the "meaningful information about the characteristics of the scales" provided by the occupational groups that score high on each of the scales. This is referred to in the manual as evidence for "construct validity," but, as such, is too self-contained within the framework of the MVII to lend much support to the instrument. It is indeed unfortunate that practically no information is given on the empirical relationship of the MVII scales to other interest inventories such as the Kuder Preference Record-Vocational (KPR-V) and the SVIB. Although the references given in the manual cite a doctoral dissertation entitled "Counseling Interpretations for the MVII Based on the SVIB," almost all of the discussion relating to other interest measures is of a speculative rather than empirical nature. * At the present time, too much

of the validity argument for *the MVII in particular* rests on what is known of *interest measurement in general,* with many references being made to research utilizing the SVIB. The only direct empirical comparison between the two inventories which is cited in the manual, however, concerns words of caution about interpretation of the Printer Scale, common in name only to the two instruments. *Summary.* Although the MVII is plagued by several potentially serious inadequacies in the standardization sampling procedure and the conduct and reporting of reliability and validity studies, it appears to the reviewer to be an inventory of sufficient promise to merit its use in a variety of settings for vocational counseling and classification purposes. It is definitely not as transparent as the KPR-V, but probably more so than the SVIB. Hence, its use in employment selection programs is probably questionable as indicated by the manual. The MVII should find its greatest utility in counseling and guidance activities for non-college bound males of average intellectual ability in the general U.S. population who are likely to be motivated to seek employment in skilled-non-professional occupations. Use of the instrument with minority groups is also questionable, however, until more adequate norming procedures for that purpose have been completed. A fine array of interpretive suggestions are provided in the manual for use by the counselor. The reviewer has serious questions, however, about the desirability of providing the examinee with a profile sheet for self-interpretation of the MVII, even though the intent and scales of the inventory are described with due clarity and caution. Experience indicates that such "tear sheets," no matter how carefully designed for examinee interpretation, provide opportunity for considerable distortion of the valuable information which an inventory such as the MVII may provide.

J Counsel Psychol 14:189–91 Mr '67. *John W. M. Rothney.* * Used in this inventory are 158 triads said to describe tasks or activities involved in a variety of trades and nonprofessional occupations. A subject indicates his preferences for the tasks in each triad by choosing the activity most liked and the activity most disliked. The third task is not marked. Number 91 of the triads, for example, is: "A. take still-life pictures; B. take news photographs; C. practice golf shots." Number 81 is: "A. build a fire in a fireplace; B. fix a noisy radiator; C.

Minnesota Vocational Interest Inventory

make half quantity of a recipe." The author gives as an example in the manual this triad: "A. putter around in the garden; B. take part in an amateur contest; C. cook spaghetti." Can such items *really* measure interest in nonprofessional occupations? Any man in any occupation could be enthusiastic about any of them, and we are not told at any time how men in professional occupations respond to such items. Scores on nine area (homogeneous) scales are said to show the examinee's likes and dislikes for certain general kinds of work common to several occupations. Scores on 21 occupational scales purport to show the extent of similarity between the examinee's expressed interests and those of men employed in vocations ranging from baker to industrial education teacher (nonprofessional?). The area scales are interesting. They are christened mechanical, health service, office work, electronics, food service, carpentry, sales-office, clean hands, and outdoors. (Some wag wants to know why there is no subterranean scale for miners and subways workers.) The occupation of milk-wagon (*not* truck) driver is used to illustrate how the area scores are useful in understanding the patterns of an individual's interests and they, in turn, are said to be helpful in understanding the interests of men in a single occupation. After presentation of correlations of scores of 400 Navy men-in-general on the milk-wagon driver and the nine area scales it is concluded, *with all seriousness,* that milk-wagon drivers are really sales clerks operating from vehicles. * But does percentage of overlap provide data that can be useful in counseling? A completely satisfactory TIG group can probably never be found, and certainly not if it is limited to Navy men (even if they have as much freedom of choice of ratings as is suggested) and workers limited to the twin cities area. Those who think they might use this inventory should consider carefully how they would answer a counselee who really wanted to know why he was compared with TIG, who was represented in TIG, and how the comparison would help him in his choice of an occupation. The authors turn to the concept of construct validity to indicate the value of the area scales. It is said that, "For most of the scales the common theme running through the items is fairly apparent, though there are exceptions." An attempt to "identify subjectively" the central core of the *clean hands* scale reads as follows: "There seems to be no easily interpretable common theme indicated by these items, although it appears that high scores reflect preference for clean hands kinds of activities." The correlation of scores on the clean hands classification and the hospital attendant scale is .02! * "Test-retest" reliability over 30-day intervals on 98 students in an industrial institute in Minneapolis (not tradesmen in general) are said to be high enough to meet "usual standards." Of the 21 coefficients 13 are in the .80 to .89 category, 7 are in the .70 to .79 group, and 1 (pressman) is .64. * Four and one-half pages of the manual are presented under the general heading of Use of the Minnesota Vocational Interest Inventory * Much of the discussion is repetitious of what has many times been said in hortatory fashion about the use of inventories in counseling. What is considered positive by the authors is emphasized; what is negative is rationalized, considered to be relatively unimportant, or it is simply stated that the reasons for the findings are not clear. Much of....[my] criticism of the Strong [see 1036] applies to this inventory and to all such devices. Fakeability, forcing of choices, vocabulary problems (in the sense of in-depth understanding of what is involved), lack of opportunity to indicate real enthusiasm or the opposite, and many other problems have been ignored. One is forced then to look at the data to see if, despite these difficulties, the inventory offers more than that which a good counselor can get from the other techniques in his kit. No comparative data are offered and the descriptive data presented do not inspire confidence. This reviewer can see no good reason why a counselor should use this instrument. The Minnesota Inventory seems to be the Psychological Corporation's bid to cut into the area in which the Kuder is commonly used. Bad as the Kuder is, this one is not likely to offer it serious competition. * [See original review for additional critical comments not excerpted.]

J Counsel Psychol 14:192 Mr '67. David P. Campbell. "Reaction to Rothney's Review." Rothney's comments on the MVII are of the same general caliber as those....[listed in my reply to his review of the *Strong Vocational Interest Blank* (see 1036)], and rebuttal of each point would be frustrating, useless, and sometimes difficult, for occasionally he is right. *

[1027]

★19 **Field Interest Inventory.** Standards 8–10 and college and adults; 1970; 19FII; 21 scores: fine arts, performing arts, language, historical, service, social work, sociability, public speaking, law, creative thought, science, practical-male, practical-female, americal, business, clerical, travel, nature, sport, v rk-hobby, active-passive; 1 form (11 pages, Englis' and Afrikaans) ; preliminary manual (31 pages, English and Afrikaans) ; no data on validity; norms for Standard 10 only; separate answer sheets (IBM 1230) must be used; R2.50 per 10 tests; R12 per 100 sets of answer sheets; 80c per manual; postpaid within South Africa; specimen set not available; (35–45) minutes; F. A. Fouché and N. F. Alberts; Human Sciences Research Council. *

[1028]

*Occupational Interest Survey (With Pictures): Individual Placement Series. Industrial applicants and employees; 1959–66; OIS; 9 scores: scientific, social service, literary, agricultural, business, mechanical, musical, clerical, artistic; Form A ('59, 14 pages) ; no specific manual; series manual ('66, 107 pages) ; profile ['66, 1 page] ; separate answer sheets must be used; $28 per 20 tests; $4 per 100 answer sheets; $4 per 100 profiles; $2.50 per series manual; $4.05 per specimen set; cash orders postpaid; (15–20) minutes ; J. H. Norman; Personnel Research Associates, Inc. *

ROBERT H. DOLLIVER, *Associate Professor of Psychology and Counseling Psychologist, University of Missouri, Columbia, Missouri.*

This is an untimed test designed for group administration. There are 12 pages, each containing nine pictures. Each picture reflects one of the nine occupational areas covered by the test. The pictures show people performing different job activities. On each page the test-taker simply identifies the picture that reflects his first choice as an occupation, then his second choice, and then his third choice. The instructions read that the choice is one that "you would make if you had the necessary training to do any of the jobs pictured." The same test is used with both men and women.

The scoring is simply a tally of the number of times pictures reflecting each occupational area were selected. However, each picture reflects one of the areas primarily and another secondarily. For example: a picture of a physician looking through a microscope is scored primarily as scientific and secondarily as social service. Thus on each page of nine pictures there are six scores to be tallied (the primary and secondary occupational areas reflected on each of three choices). The use of secondary interests appears to be an attempt to give a more sophisticated appearance, since it adds a scoring dimension and makes the test less fully transparent. The number of opportunities for secondary scoring varies on the different scales from 2 to 19, thus making the raw score potential between interest areas vary from 52 to 82.

The secondary scores are consistently tied to certain of the primary interest areas, e.g., science is tied to mechanical and to agriculture but not to business. Many of the secondary interest connections are overly obscure, e.g., a girl painting a ceramic pot is scored as secondarily scientific. Because of the cited difficulties, the scoring of secondary interests is of doubtful value.

Validity and reliability data are inadequate due to the small numbers of subjects used. The only direct validity data reported are concurrent validity based on 23 persons. Additionally, the mean correlation of .61 is reported between the OIS and the *Kuder Preference Record—Vocational* for 179 people. Test-retest reliabilities are presented for two groups of subjects, 33 in one group (time lapse unspecified) and 57 in another group (six months). In the seven years between the copyright of the test and the copyright of the series manual, it would seem that more validity and reliability data should have been generated. A table of intercorrelations between the nine OIS areas is reported for 52 subjects. Norms presented are based on 682 adults working in industry. Those norms are based on a general group and do not reflect the scores attained by people working in each of these areas.

The designation of the nine interest areas appears to closely follow those in the *Kuder Preference Record—Vocational.* The identification of representative jobs in the areas is somewhat confusing. For example, teaching is representative of six of the areas, and draftsman is representative of both the artistic and the mechanical areas.

The use of pictures to register vocational interest is innovative, but it is questionable whether anything more is gained in giving the survey than by simply asking the person what he is interested in. Unless the test-taker is nonverbal, illiterate, or highly unsophisticated, it does not appear that the test would be beneficial. The potential benefit of this approach would appear to be to gain information about job qualities desired by the test-taker rather than job area desired. For instance, pictures already included could be scored in relation to working alone versus working with others, supervising versus being supervised, but these aspects are irrelevant in the present test.

The OIS provides an interesting approach to reflecting vocational interests. But because of the directness and transparency, it is not likely to produce any information beyond what would be gained by simply asking the test-taker what he is interested in. And because the reliability and validity data are so limited, the survey is best regarded as appropriate for experimental use only.

DAVID O. HERMAN, *Assistant Director, Test Division, The Psychological Corporation, New York, New York.*

The *Occupational Interest Survey* provides scores in nine general vocational areas. The manual presents no rationale for choosing these particular areas.

The test presents 108 pictures of people engaged in various activities, arranged 9 to a page, with each picture on a page representing a different one of the nine occupational fields, together with one allied field. For example, one picture shows a man behind a counter in what appears to be a grocery store, showing a carton of eggs to a woman. The major occupational field for this picture is given as Business, and the allied field is Clerical. From each page the examinee chooses the three pictures that would be his first, second, and third choices as occupations and records these choices on a separate answer sheet.

Scoring is rather simple in concept. Each of the examinee's choices is scored twice, once for the major occupational field reflected by the picture and once for the allied field. Four, three, and two points are added to the major-field score, depending on whether the picture was the first, second, or third choice, respectively. The allied field represented by each choice is always given two points of score.

Scoring must be carried out by hand. For each choice made, the scorer plots the proper number of points to be given for the major and allied fields directly on a profile chart that is printed on the answer sheet. This process turns out to be lengthy and tedious, and presents considerable opportunity for scoring error. Although the manual does not recommend an independent scoring check, this reviewer suggests that it is essential.

Two validity studies are reported in the manual. Correlations with other measures of the same basic variables can provide evidence of the convergent validity of a scale, and to this end the manual presents, for a sample of 179 unidentified cases, correlations between the scales of the OIS and the matching ones of the *Kuder Preference Record—Vocational* (OIS Agricultural is paired with Kuder Outdoor; OIS Business is paired with Kuder Persuasive). These coefficients range from .50 to .83, with a median of .62. To complete this portion of the validity picture, there should be evidence that the OIS scales correlate less well with the nonmatching than with the matching Kuder scales. This check cannot be made, however, since the correlations among nonmatching pairs of OIS and Kuder scales are not given.

In the second validity study, a correlation of .93 is reported between the occupations in which 23 people were employed and the occupational fields suggested from their scores on the OIS. How this coefficient was computed is unclear, and therefore so is its meaning.

Thus, the statistical validity of the instrument may fairly be described as not yet determined, and the reviewer must turn to other evidence, such as its face validity, as reflected by the apparent congruence of the pictures and their keyed occupational scales. In this reviewer's opinion, most of the pictures match reasonably well their major occupational fields as indicated by the key. However, why is a picture of a man repairing a crack in a wall with plaster scored for Artistic?

On the other hand, the identification of allied fields is often peculiar. The plasterer mentioned above has Agricultural given as his allied field. For a picture of a woman in a laboratory setting, pouring liquid from one test tube to another, the major field is Scientific, while the allied field is Agricultural. A picture of two men in another laboratory setting, one of them inspecting the contents of a test tube, is scored first for Scientific and second for Literary! A picture of a woman seated at a typewriter is scored first for Clerical, and second for Artistic. And so on. Of course, scoring each picture on two separate scales is an efficient technique for increasing the possible range of scores on the scales, providing that the double keying can be justified. In the case of the OIS, however, it seems likely that the keying procedure has added irrelevant variance to some of the scores. In any case, the validity of the instrument must be called undetermined.

Test-retest reliability coefficients with an interval of six months range from .85 to .93 for a group of 57 high school seniors. The supporting means and standard deviations are not given.

Occupational Interest Survey

The entire description of the other available reliability study is quoted here verbatim : "Test-retest reliability in one group of 33 subjects was .892." It is fair to call this information incomplete.

Intercorrelations of the OIS scales are given for 52 unidentified cases and range from a negative .59 to a positive .61, with median − .13. These coefficients are hard to interpret, first because the strangeness of the allied-field scoring calls into question the meaning of the basic variables. Furthermore, the correlations between pairs of the scales are in part spurious, being "forced" by the scoring method which awards points to two different scales for each picture chosen by the examinee.

The published norms for the OIS, which consist of the percentile conversions given graphically on the profile chart, are based on the scores of "682 adults from all levels of jobs in industry," primarily males. No other description of the norms sample is given, and the author properly urges the reader to gather his own local normative information. Incidentally, the percentage points shown on the profile are spaced in an unusual and irregular manner. Test users who have worked with similar profile forms are familiar with charts that plot percentiles unevenly, with greater distance between adjacent percentile points at the ends of the scale (say, between the first and fifth percentiles) than in the middle of the scale (as between the 50th and 55th percentiles). The spacing of the OIS profile form is idiosyncratic, with a large distance between the 60th and 70th percentiles, a smaller distance between the 70th and 80th percentiles, and then back to large intervals between the 80th and 90th, and the 90th and 100th percentiles. Just why the implied discrimination among adjacent deciles should be so discontinuous is anyone's guess.

So much for specifics. The publisher of any new interest inventory should offer evidence that it is at least the equal of its nearest or most similar competition—in this case the Kuder Vocational—or that it measures new types of variables or new interest domains. No such evidence is available for the OIS, and the use of pictorial rather than written stimuli receives no explanation in the manual other than a statement that picures were used "for more accurate communication and for quicker administration," with no support offered for this claim.

The face validity of the instrument, as revealed by the keying of the items, is not impressive. Though administering the inventory is simple, scoring is a bleak task, and one with many possibilities for error. In their present form, the OIS materials suggest an instrument lacking adequate rationale, meaningful supporting research, and an informative manual. This reviewer suggests that no one should adopt the OIS for any nonexperimental purpose without some compelling excuse, such as an acceptable demonstration of local validity.

[1029]

★Ohio Vocational Interest Survey. Grades 8–12; 1969–70; OVIS; tests cannot be locally scored; 24 scores: manual work, machine work, personal services, caring for people or animals, clerical work, inspecting and testing, crafts and precise operations, customer services, nursing and related technical services, skilled personal services, training, literary, numerical, appraisal, agriculture, applied technology, promotion and communication, management and supervision, artistic, sales representative, music, entertainment and performing arts, teaching-counseling-social work, medical; 1 form ('70, 16 pages) ; directions for administering ('70, 14 pages) ; manual for interpreting ('70, 74 pages) ; norms consist of means and standard deviations; separate answer sheets (MRC) must be used; $9.50 per 35 tests ; $4 per 35 answer sheets ; $2.50 per manual; $1.75 per specimen set; postage extra; scoring service, 60¢ and over per test ; (60–90) minutes ; Ayres G. D'Costa, David W. Winefordner, John G. Odgers, and Paul B. Koons, Jr.; Harcourt Brace Jovanovich, Inc. *

REFERENCES

1. D'COSTA, AYRES G. J. E. *The Differentiation of High School Students in Vocational Education Areas by the Ohio Vocational Interest Survey.* Doctor's thesis, Ohio University (Athens, Ohio), 1968. (*DA* 29:1161A)
2. D'COSTA, AYRES, AND WINEFORDNER, DAVID. "A Cubistic Model of Vocational Interests." *Voc Guid Q* 17(4):242–9 Je '69. *
3. MORRISON, JESSIE SYKES. *Characteristics of Students in Two-Year Post-High School Occupational Education Programs.* Doctor's thesis, Ohio State University (Columbus, Ohio), 1969. (*DAI* 30:4228A)
4. WINEFORDNER, DAVID W. "Interest Measurement in Vocational Decision Making: The Use of the Ohio Vocational Interest Survey." *Am Voc J* 44(2):56–7 F '69. *

THOMAS T. FRANTZ, *Associate Professor of Counselor Education, State University of New York at Buffalo, Buffalo, New York.*

For the counselor looking for a good, current, well standardized vocational interest inventory to use with high school pupils, the *Ohio Vocational Interest Survey* is worth considering, and in a few more years it may well be the best choice.

There are, however, some indications that it might have been published prematurely. Some paragraphs appear in more than one place in the manual. Twenty-one of its 280 items were retained despite their failure to meet the authors' criteria for inclusion in the inventory.

Comments about the instrument's structure and item content from many examiners who administered the inventory were not used in its construction, but "will be taken into account in future revisions of the instrument." The need for internal consistency scale reliabilities is acknowledged by the authors but none are provided in the manual. In fact, the manual misleadingly states that "test-retest reliabilities are estimates of the internal consistency reliabilities for the first administration of OVIS."

Such problems can and probably will be corrected. Test-retest reliability coefficients hovering around .80, each based on approximately 500 subjects, are reported for each sex for samples of eighth and tenth graders on all 24 scales. Normative data including means, standard deviations, and scores at five different percentile points are reported for each scale by sex, grade, and geographical region. Each student's raw scores, percentiles, stanines, and clarity indices are available to him in a personalized student report folder.

A scale clarity index reflects whether, on a given scale, the student is consistent, moderately consistent, or inconsistent in his preferences for the eleven job activities on that scale. A low score would indicate that a student very much likes some of the job activities on the scale but dislikes others, while a high score is indicative of constant liking or disliking of the activities on the scale.

The inventory itself and the machine-scored answer sheet are thorough and well designed; easily followed directions are provided in an examiner's manual. Six preliminary questions about vocational plans and high school program precede the actual inventory, as does space for up to eight questions of local interest which may be added by an individual counselor or school system. The inventory must be machine scored by the publisher, a fact which leads to the first of three difficulties with the OVIS.

Though OVIS is intended as a guidance tool and the manual implies that counselors should explore inconsistent clarity indices to determine which items are liked and which are disliked, no method of hand scoring or local scoring is available and it is seemingly impossible to determine how a specific student responded to a given item once the inventory is sent away for scoring. Such information might be helpful to both student and counselor. The impossibility of hand scoring reduces flexibility in using the instrument. Given the simple scoring key, the inventory could be hand scored quite easily.

A second problem with the OVIS is the lack of validity data. No concurrent, or predictive, or any kind of criterion-related validity information is offered. The scales have apparently not been correlated with any other inventories. The authors' feelings on validity are made clear in the manual:

The primary purpose of the *Ohio Vocational Interest Survey* is to help students to understand their interests and to relate them to the world of work. In this respect, use of the results in predicting future behavior is not considered to be as important as their immediate use in career orientation and vocational exploration. The validity and reliability of the instrument should be assessed in terms of how well it helps students, parents, and counselors to develop realistic plans for the future.

If we accept the authors' position that validity is to be determined by assessing the extent to which realistic plans for the student's future are developed, then the manual ought to contain data to this effect—a difficult chore, to be sure.

Finally and most importantly, there are too many unanswered questions about the rationale for construction of the inventory. We are told that the instrument is based on a cubistic model of vocational interests derived from data-people-things categorization in the *Dictionary of Occupational Titles* (DOT). This model is neither theoretical nor empirical and no rationale or explanation of it is offered.

In the DOT model there are seven levels of involvement with data and eight levels with people and things. These levels are combined in the OVIS to yield three levels on each dimension—a 3 x 3 x 3 matrix of 27 cells. This cubistic model is used to generate the OVIS scales. Seemingly, such a procedure would result in 27 scales, but there are only 24 scales on the inventory. Furthermore, nine of the 27 cells have no scales to represent them and five cells are represented by two or more often-unrelated scales. For example, the high data, low people, low things cells in the model contains both the numerical and literary scales, which intercorrelate .39 for men and .29 for women. For both men and women there are 16 scales that correlate higher with the literary scale than does the numerical scale. Why, if the cubistic model is useful, was it abandoned? On what grounds were one third of the cells in the data-people-things matrix omitted? What rationale led to putting two and, in one case, three often unrelated scales in one cell?

In a number of instances the authors mention 114 worker-trait groups from the DOT that were "plotted in the data-things-people cube" to form OVIS scales. Plotted how? What is the relationship of such clusters to the levels of data, people, and things? Factor analytic studies are alluded to but not presented in the manual. In looking up one such study, the reviewer found that the 24 scales were factored into five factors, each including various combinations of data, people, and things, and thus not really supporting the model.

Despite the above problems, I am optimistic about the future of the OVIS. The authors have clearly made a major effort to construct an appealing and useful vocational instrument. A number of problems are present; but most—including the lack of validity data—can, if the authors maintain their ambition, be remedied. The major problem lies in the questions surrounding the rationale and implementation of the data-people-things model.

JOHN W. M. ROTHNEY, *Professor of Counseling and Guidance, University of Wisconsin, Madison, Wisconsin.*

This inventory was advertised for sale in the publisher's 1969–70 catalog but the manual was not made available to potential users until early 1971. This reviewer was provided with a Xerox copy of the manual, which the editor indicated was still in the developmental stage. The practice of encouraging persons to buy and use instruments without reading the manual violates standards for educational and psychological tests and measurements set up jointly by APA, AERA, and NCME.

In construction of the inventory, the authors adopted the *Dictionary of Occupational Titles* concept that jobs can be best described in terms of activities performed and the worker traits associated with such activities. They have also accepted the DOT idea that job description can be done most effectively by classifying activities in terms of level of involvement with data, people, and things. The 24 inventory scores indicated in the entry above are said to represent the 114 worker trait groups presented in the DOT. Thus the manual work scale is said to require low involvement with data and people, and average involvement with things. The teaching, counseling, and social work scale is said to represent high involvement with data and people, but low involvement with things. The DOT

concepts were developed for use in the placement and classification of adults and the authors have simply assumed that it would be suitable for use with students in junior and senior high schools. No justification for the assumption is presented other than the authors' opinion that it is useful. It may or may not be so.

The 280 items in the interest inventory are those finally selected after an initial pool of 640 items had been examined by judges and tried out on various groups of students. A student responds to each of the items by marking one of five choices ranging from like very much, through neutral, to dislike very much. It is unlikely that a high school student would be equally familiar with all 280 items, including such activities as "Train riding horses to jump," "Write stories for popular magazines," "Examine children and diagnose their illnesses," "Analyze traffic studies to determine the need for new highways," "Inform people of their legal rights," "Translate foreign books into English," and "Give eye examinations and prescribe glasses." In view of this lack of familiarity and the unevenness of familiarity with such activities, as well as the training required for them, one must wonder how useful such a response as "I am *neutral,* I would *neither like nor dislike* the activity" can be.

The "I would *like* this activity *very much*" response to an item is given a value of 5 and an "I would *dislike* this activity *very much*" reply is scored as 1. Thus, for each of the 24 areas, the highest possible score on 11 items is 55 and the lowest is 11. Assigning such numerical values to responses so that by simple arithmetic the *like very much* response is five times as favorable as the *dislike very much* response is the kind of witchcraft which has become standard practice in this area of measurement.

Raw scores on each of the scales (unfortunately labeled as scale scores) may be translated into local or national percentiles or stanines. The authors do not come to grips with problems of ipsative and normative interpretations of the percentiles. With 24 percentiles, which in the sample presented in the student report folder range from 96 to 27, there will be many possible interpretations, and a counselor may have difficulty with counselees who ask pertinent questions about what the figures mean. Of course, there is the possibility of avoiding the issues by resorting to the superficial response indicated by the authors, that "you have shown more interest in the job activities that make up the scales at the top of the list than you have in the job activities that make up the scales at the lower end of the list." But what will the counselor answer when the counselee asks, "So what?"

The student information questionnaire section of the survey requires junior and senior high school students to make a first and second choice of statements which "best [describe] the kind of work you would like to do" from 27 items which include such statements as "Legal work as a judge or lawyer" and "Promotional activities, as in publicity work, recruiting, or advertising." Since high school students have not experienced such activities, it seems likely that glamour and ignorance may determine choices. And one must wonder how selection of 2 from 27 options can have real meaning. The other items in the information questionnaire simply ask the student what subjects he likes best, what high school program he is taking, his plans for education beyond high school, and his choice among business and vocational training programs if several were offered. These kinds of questions are commonly asked on locally-constructed questionnaires and there seems to be no need to spend school funds to get a printed form.

The authors do not discuss such matters as transparency of the items, deliberate or unintentional faking, arbitrary assignment of numbers to responses, elaboration of the obvious, superficiality of items, vocabulary difficulties, variability in moods and sets, forcing of choices when there is no genuine choice, and many other criticisms of the inventory approach that have appeared in the literature. The bibliography in the manual omits any mention of books, articles, and reviews in which critiques of the inventory techniques are presented.

It is stated in the manual that "validity and reliability....should be assessed in terms of how well [the OVIS] helps students, parents, and counselors to develop realistic plans for the future." The discussion which follows then ignores that statement and presents elaborate statistics on item-scale correlations, stability of scores over a two-week period, and descriptions of the care that was taken to see that "the 24 scales were providing meaningful information about students' interests in the jobs chosen to represent the world of work." In all the data there is no evidence that the reliability and va-

lidity have been assessed in the manner indicated in the quotation from the manual which appears in the first sentence of this paragraph. (The word "parents" used in the quotation is the only mention of them that this reviewer could find in the manual.)

If one has faith in the inventory procedure despite its many limitations (and one must act on faith, since the evidence is scanty) the OVIS may prove to be as useful as other inventories of its kind. What it needs now is a thorough tryout with some students over an extended period of time. Statistical manipulation of scores will not substitute for longitudinal studies to see if a test does what it purports to do, and it is unfortunate that the OVIS has been offered for sale without such studies. The authors and publishers of similar instruments have shown, however, that such scales can be sold in great quantities without evidence that they can do what they purport to do. Hopefully, that period in the development of the guidance movement is past. Knowledgeable counselors will not spend public funds for the purchase of this new instrument until it has been tried out in longitudinal studies and the results have been evaluated by persons who do not have a conflict of interest.

[1030]

★Phillips Occupational Preference Scale. Ages 14 and over; 1959–65; POPS; 10 scores: clerical, computational, practical, scientific, mechanical (males), medical (females), persuasive, social service, literary, artistic, outdoor; Forms F, M, ['60, 12 pages] for females, males; manual ('65, 33 pages); no norms for males age 14; separate answer sheets must be used; Aus $4.50 per 10 tests; 45¢ per 10 profile-answer sheets; $5 per set of scoring stencils; $1.25 per manual; $7.20 per specimen set; postpaid within Australia; (20–30) minutes; G. R. Phillips; Australian Council for Educational Research. *

[1031]

★Preference Analysis. Standards 8 and over; 1968–69; PA; 11–13 scores: adventurous, outdoors, clerical, domestic-decorative (females only), domestic routine (females only), fine arts and music, natural sciences, persuasion, social sciences, technical, altruistic, verbal, mathematical interest; separate forms for males, females, ('68, 11 pages); manual ('69, 207 pages); no data on validity; separate answer sheets (IBM 1230) must be used; R5.25 per 25 tests; 25c per single copy; R1.25 per 25 answer sheets; R7 per set of scoring stencils for males, R8.30 for females; R5 per manual; postpaid within South Africa; Afrikaans edition available; (25–45) minutes; P. Lourens; National Institute for Personnel Research. *

[1032]

RBH Job Choice Inventory. Male job applicants and employees in oil and chemical industries; 1951–63; 5 scores: general mechanical, electrical and precision, construction and handiwork, process and laboratory, vehicle operation; Form O-C ('51, 3 pages); manual ['63, 17 pages]; directions (no date, 1 page); $4 per 25 tests; $1.50 per set of keys; $1.50 per manual; $2.50 per specimen set; postage extra; (25–30) minutes; Richardson, Bellows, Henry & Co., Inc. *

DAVID P. CAMPBELL, *Professor of Psychology and Director, Center for Interest Measurement Research, University of Minnesota, Minneapolis, Minnesota.*

This is a short (two pages) inventory developed, apparently, for in-house use. While it might conceivably be of some value to a personnel man who worked with it constantly and thus had accumulated some informal information on its characteristics, no general use is warranted.

The entire discussion of the purpose of the test, description of scale construction, and suggestions for use are on one mimeographed page. (That page also contains statements such as, "it has been conclusively proven" and "any validity obtained is almost certain to add to prediction of success on the job.")

Following this are 16 pages of statistics supposedly related to scale validity and reliability. They are simply tables, poorly laid out with unlabelled columns and unspecified variables, and no discussion. What information can be gleaned from them is not particularly reassuring; frequently differences between extreme groups do not exceed one standard deviation, and sometimes not that. There is no empirical comfort here.

In other vague, hard-to-specify ways, the test smacks of shoddiness. For example, the items are not numbered. Anyone who has done any research on inventories knows that the first thing that must be done is to identify the items numerically so that they can be studied. Clearly this has not happened here.

Even for an in-house instrument, this inventory seems inadequate. Certainly it is of no use for anything else.

DAVID O. HERMAN, *Assistant Director, Test Division, The Psychological Corporation, New York, New York.*

The *RBH Job Choice Inventory* is an interest inventory that provides measures of interest in five general fields of work in refineries and chemical plants. It is probably intended as an aid in the selection and placement of men in certain blue-collar jobs within these industries—but the manual makes no direct suggestions for

using the scores. The inventory is of the forced choice variety and consists of 56 items, each one a triad of three tasks. For each item, the examinee chooses the one activity he would like most to do and the one that he would like least to do. His answers are marked directly on the test booklet and are scored—a bit clumsily—with five cardboard stencils, one for each scale. The manual provides norms based on several groups of applicants and employees in various companies, chiefly oil refineries and chemical plants.

Although the names of the five scores suggest applicability to many blue-collar occupations, some of the tasks included in the items appear specific to chemical and oil work. For example, two of the choices are "Change and clean screens used to eliminate trash in cooling towers" and "Take a sample of a hot catalyst from a line through a hand opened valve." The inventory seems unlikely to find use outside these industries.

The manual is a curiously spotty affair, with some sections vague, others interpretable only with supplementary materials, and still others quite complete. As noted above, statements of purpose and suggestions for field use are entirely lacking. The description of the construction of the inventory is incomplete. It is clear that the instrument was developed empirically through several stages of tryout, using a basic item pool that reflected tasks from many jobs in refineries and chemical plants. The tryout samples consisted of experienced chemical and refinery personnel. Beyond this, not much information is given.

For each scale, percentile norms are given for several well-defined groups of male applicants and employees, mostly from chemical plants and oil refineries, plus a "general" sample consisting of all groups combined. The composition of these normative samples is described in detail. For instance, percentile norms for the General Mechanical score are presented for a general sample of 1,439 cases and for the four relatively homogeneous groups making up this sample. An accompanying table gives a further breakdown of these latter groups to show certain data concerning the subsamples that are included: a brief verbal description, the number of cases, and the mean and standard deviation of the score in question. The publishers should be commended for this practice.

Unhappily, study of these details raises questions that the manual does not answer. For example, there are four groups (not counting the general sample) that show up in the norms tables for all of the scales, but not always with the same numbers of cases. In one instance the table of percentile norms and the accompanying table showing the composition of the norms groups are inconsistent with regard to the counts for two of the samples. Incidentally, one of the four basic norms groups consists of 25 truck drivers employed by a packing company. The reader is left wondering why larger samples of vehicle drivers from chemical and oil companies could not have been found for norming the inventory.

It will be recalled that the "general" norms for each of the five scores reflect the performance of all normative samples used for that score. For some reason two samples of examinees are found in the norms for only one of the scales. Thus the general norms are based on shifting samples from scale to scale and, in fact, only two of the scales share the same general sample. The manual offers no justification of these floating N's, and this reviewer questions why the extra samples reported for some scales were excluded from the norms for the others.

Evidence of the validity of the inventory is limited to two concurrent studies of the correlation of the five scores with a performance criterion—presumably an overall work evaluation. For 99 "process" employees, the coefficients ranged from −.20 to .26, with the highest coefficient for the Process and Laboratory score. For 85 mechanical employees, the coefficients ranged from −.14 to .17, with the highest coefficient for the General Mechanical score. These correlations do not offer adequate validity evidence, and more validation studies should certainly be pursued.

Correlations with other tests are reported but are hard to interpret. The other tests are not adequately described, and most test users will not be familiar with them and what they measure. No correlations with other measures of vocational interest are given. The fact that the available correlations are low may or may not indicate, as the manual states, that "any validity obtained is almost certain to add to prediction of success on the job."

Intercorrelations of the five scores are also presented for two samples. Some of these correlations are quite high and negative, particularly those between the General Mechanical

and the Process and Laboratory scales, which exceed −.85. At first glance, one might suspect that there is little point in deriving separate measures for these two interest areas, but to some extent this high negative coefficient may be "forced" by the ipsative nature of the inventory and the method of keying—by the reviewer's count, of the 56 triads on the inventory, 25 have at least one task that is keyed in opposite directions on these two scales. To a lesser degree the same situation holds for the other pairs of scales with high negative correlations.

In summary, there is not much to say about the inventory. It may be adequate for its intended purposes, and then again it may not. The contents of the manual make it plain that quite a lot of developmental work has been completed on the inventory, but because this work is poorly described and other important work remains to be done, the instrument is hard to evaluate.

It is unlikely that other publishers will undertake to construct a similar instrument. This reviewer suggests that any oil refining or chemical firm give consideration to the *RBH Job Choice Inventory,* providing it has funds available for local experimentation to determine the usefulness of the instrument.

[1033]

★Rating Scales of Vocational Values, Vocational Interests and Vocational Aptitudes. Grades 8–16 and adults; 1966; VIA; 3 scales for obtaining self-ratings of aptitudes, interests, and values with regard to various vocational activities; 20 scores for each of the 3 scales: administrative, animal, artistic, athletic, clerical, commercial, computational, creative, dramatic, executive, literary, manual, mechanical, musical, organizing, plant, scholastic, scientific, service, socializing; 1 form (2 pages); 3 parts; manual (8 pages); profile (1 page); no data on reliability and validity; norms based upon "high school and college students" not otherwise described; no adult norms; $3.50 per 25 tests; $3 per 25 profile sheets; 50¢ per manual; $2.25 per specimen set; postage extra; scoring service, 45¢ or less per scale; (45–50) minutes; George D. Demos and Bruce Grant; Educational and Industrial Testing Service. *
a) RATING SCALE OF VOCATIONAL VALUES.
b) RATING SCALE OF VOCATIONAL INTERESTS.
c) RATING SCALE OF VOCATIONAL APTITUDES.

EDWARD J. FURST, *Professor of Education, University of Arkansas, Fayetteville, Arkansas.*

It is asserted by the authors of the VIA that there is a need for integrating self-assessments of vocational values and of aptitudes with measures of interests, to aid an individual in evolving a wise career plan; and further, that their devices provide a useful integrated source of such information.

Three essentially self-administering forms carry the burden. Each is a single sheet having instructions on one side and all have the same 60 activity-items on the other. The student works down the three columns, rating each activity on a scale of 5-4-3-2-1-0 or marking "U" if uncertain. Either he or someone else may score the 20 scales by visually summing the weights across the rows, since the three items in each row comprise one of the 20 "vocational areas." Thus the format is simple and compact, the scoring easy, and the desired integration partly achieved by the use of common stimuli.

The manual moves this integration ahead functionally with suggestions for using the results. One first converts raw scores into percentiles, then studies the profiles to identify areas of greatest value and interest and to check for level of aptitude, and lastly considers appropriate occupations from a classified list.

This overall procedure seems straightforward, but it rests squarely upon the information provided by the scales and the manual. How sound are this base and its underlying assumptions?

Content is crucial here and yet the authors have not given their specifications for selecting it. The 20 areas do represent a comprehensive list of major common-sense categories. They are not uniformly alike, however. In some, like Animal, Plant, and Musical, it is the content more than the activity that seems to define the area; in several others, the opposite.

The specific items also imply sampling on a logical basis—chosen because they seem important activities of the given area. This is a working assumption only, as the authors have not reported empirical data such as intercorrelation of items. Such data would have brought to light ambiguous or nondefinitive items as, for example, the activities in the Clerical scale—Perceiving rapidly, Being accurate, and Giving attention to detail. On the basis of inspection and a small tryout, this reviewer believes that as many as a fifth of the 60 items are so general, ambiguous, or sophisticated as to make interpretation difficult. The manual gives no evidence that these brief phrases are interpreted as intended.

Intercorrelations among the 20 scales support the conclusion that a majority of the scales on each form are relatively independent. On both Values and Interests, however, seven scales showed enough intercorrelation to support the existence of a strong group or second-order factor that could be called "general mental work." These seven are Clerical, Computational, Creative, Executive, Organizing, Scholastic, and Scientific. Inspection of items on these scales revealed that most of the activities are general and often devoid of vocational content—e.g., Developing facts, Acquiring information, Solving problems.

The manual does not report reliability or stability of scores. The omission of the first seems more serious, as one is inclined to reject the assumption that three items can adequately sample an important vocational area.

Many of the scales yield a negatively skewed distribution, so that there is no good discrimination in the higher segment. The possible range of 15 points (0–15) does not look wide when one considers this fact and the likelihood of an error of measurement of a point or more. Systematic tendencies for persons to rate too high or too low will further add to the inaccuracy of measurement.

Most persons will find the rating relatively easy. On Values and Interests some will find the distinction between 5 and 4, "very much" and "strongly," and between 3 and 2, "moderately" and "mildly," too slight. The directions are otherwise clear and adequate.

Granted that the student will find meaning in most of the items and will be able to use the rating scale, the validity of these self-assessments will depend largely upon self-understanding. It seems that this last assumption will be most true on Interests and least true on Aptitudes. One questions whether the ratings on Aptitudes can signify anything accurate, since the typical student will lack an adequate tryout in many activities. Taking beliefs about aptitudes at face value is a big assumption.

The careful reader may find himself asking of some activities, "for what purpose?" On Values he judges each activity as its own end; so this question is by-passed. But one may still ask why values of vocational significance have been omitted: advancement, security vs. risk-taking, etc.

There is also the matter of overlap between Values and Interests. It hardly seems a distinction to judge an activity as to how "worthwhile" it is and then on the other form as to how much one "likes" it. Some blurring occurs, too, because certain activities carry an implicit value. Item 25, "Being accurate," is not so much an activity as a goal. Items 20, 40, and 60, "Getting along with men," etc., imply the value of good human relations. It is no surprise that the authors have found scale-by-scale correlations for Values and Interests ranging from .56 to .79, median of .65. For a small sample this reviewer found correlations from .76 to .92, median of .88, basing each correlation upon one person's paired V-I scores on the 20 vocational scales. These data lead him to conclude that either values and interests develop to comparable levels or that the method of measurement has failed to separate the two.

Viewed as a whole, the VIA will yield some useful self-assessments. But the scales are far from adequately tested. How they will aid integration of vocational values, interests, and aptitudes in the forming of a wise career plan, and whether they will improve upon established inventories, are all-important questions still to be answered. This reviewer would prefer established inventories until these questions have been satisfactorily answered.

DAVID V. TIEDEMAN, *Professor of Education, Harvard University, Cambridge, Massachusetts.*

The VIA consists of three identical sets of 60 activities, 3 in each row for each of the 20 areas listed above. The subject rates each of the identical items according to (a) their value to him (their worthwhileness), (b) their interest for him (the degree to which he likes to do the activity), and (c) his aptitude for the activity (his perception of his aptitude relative to the aptitude which he attributes to "most people"). He indicates the degree to which each item applies to his values, interests, and aptitudes on a seven-point scale which essentially consists of only six points ranging from none to high applicability. The user is permitted to mark a seventh point when he is uncertain about the applicability of the activity and this is later scored as absence.

Percentile ranks permit comparison of the summed scores in any of the 20 areas on each of the three scales. "Norms for the VIA are based on responses of [645] high school and college students." An area of high value and interest can be only approximately identified by this procedure, since the norms are not adequately described. Occupations which a subject might look into may subsequently be located for each of the 20 areas by means of a table in the manual. The occupations suggested for an area are somewhat graded according to the level of required aptitude.

The manual gives no indication of how the 60 activities were selected and classified or of how the suggested occupations in each area were picked and graded according to required aptitude. In addition, no reliability data are reported. Almost as many factors as there are scales appear in a reported factor analysis, but even so, the reported data do not permit determination of whether the scales were the factors.

The Rating Scales are obviously not highly polished psychometric instruments. If they are used at all, they might be used for their possible heuristic effect. The 20 areas in each rating scale probably have a fairly understandable general meaning. Each point on the values rating scale has a fairly obvious correspondence with its parallel point on the interest rating scale. The subject can therefore know whether he places as much value on the activities of an area as he attributes interest to them.

The tricky part of extending this procedure rests in the subject's interpreting his rating of aptitude in each area. First, the aptitude rating is the subject's own statement of his aptitude, not his position as determined by an aptitude test. Furthermore, the reference for the aptitude ratings is to people in general, not to personal potential known in substantive terms by the subject himself. Therefore, it will remain a moot point with my suggested alternative procedure as to whether aptitude ratings will mean anything to the subject or not. However, if the subject believes that he can lend his own meaning to his aptitude ratings, he will have achieved a rather quick survey of his values and interests, which he can also compare with his perception of his aptitude in each interesting area held of value to him. Furthermore, the suggested occupational linkages in the manual may provide leads to possible work which the subject has not yet investigated.

The substitute procedure I suggest is a far cry from a test procedure. However, it might well help a person under guidance of a counselor to learn how linkages may be created in his mind between daily activities and occupations by carefully considering what he likes, what he wants to do, and whether or not he thinks he does well what he likes and wants.

[1034]

★Rothwell-Miller Interest Blank [British Edition]. Ages 11 and over; 1958–68; RMIB; British adaptation of original Australian edition; 12 scores: outdoor, mechanical, computational, scientific, persuasive, aesthetic, literary, musical, social service, clerical, practical, medical; Forms M, F, ('68, 4 pages) for males, females; manual ('68, 111 pages); 75p per 25 blanks; £1.75 per manual; £2.05 per specimen set; postage extra; (20–30) minutes; original test by J. W. Rothwell; 1958 and 1968 revisions by Kenneth M. Miller; NFER Publishing Co. Ltd. *

REFERENCES

1. MILLER, KENNETH M. "The Measurement of Vocational Interests by a Stereotype Ranking Method." *J Appl Psychol* 44:169–71 Je '60. * (*PA* 35:4093)
2. NELSON, D. M. "The Predictive Value of the Rothwell-Miller Interest Blank." *Occup Psychol* 42:123–31 Ap–Jl '68. *

A. W. HEIM, *The Psychological Laboratory, University of Cambridge, Cambridge, England.*

The *Rothwell-Miller Interest Blank* is an ipsative measure, consisting of nine sets of occupational titles, each set comprising 12 jobs, the same types of job occurring in each set. The titles are as follows: Outdoor (e.g., forester, transport driver), Mechanical (e.g., welder, civil engineer), Computational (e.g., income tax assessor, mathematics teacher), Scientific (e.g., astronomer, laboratory assistant), Persuasive (e.g., auctioneer, advertising agent), Aesthetic (e.g., window dresser, photographer), Literary (e.g., historian, librarian), Musical (e.g., dance band leader, composer), Social Service (e.g., minister of religion, youth club worker), Clerical (e.g., town clerk, office worker), Practical (e.g., shoe repairer, plumber) and Medical (e.g., veterinary surgeon, pharmacist).

These examples are drawn from the male blank. The blank for females is similar except for the omission of a few occupations which were thought to be inapplicable to women. Thus, for instance, "forester" is replaced by "physical education teacher" and "income tax assessor" is replaced by "accounting machine operator."

The subject is instructed to rank the members of each group from 1 (his most preferred job) to 12 (the occupation he would like least in each group). He is asked to disregard questions of salary and of ability. He ranks the jobs simply in accordance with how he would like the kind of work. Thus, the *interest* in the title of the test is deduced from the *job-preferences* of the subject. It is stressed, in the manual, that many people "hold stereotyped conceptions about the nature of occupations" and that "a

stereotype may be fairly accurate or almost completely false." This fact, however, is not thought by Miller to detract from the validity of the RMIB, since (*a*) he writes that "the important point is not the accuracy of the stereotype but the fact that it does exist" and (*b*) the completed blank is designed for use primarily as a basis for career-interviewing. It is intended that the testing be followed up by a vocational interview.

The examples of occupations given above illustrate three points. First, they show the very considerable range of status and pay to be found within each job-group, with the exception of the nine jobs in the Practical category, all of which denote modest manual occupations. Secondly, the groups overlap substantially with one another. "Welder" could as well have been placed in the Practical as in the Mechanical category; "librarian" could as well have represented the Clerical as the Literary category; "astronomer" is as Computational as "mathematics teacher"; teaching (in any subject) could well be regarded as more Social Service oriented than "minister of religion." Indeed, "primary teacher" and "headmaster (headmistress)" are actually listed under Social Service, in both the male and the female blanks.

Linked with the second point is a third, namely, the arbitrariness of the choice of jobs and of occupational categories. Persuasive, for instance, is intended to mean personal contact: "An interest in talking to people, in persuading and discussing, arguing, mixing with others. Confidence in making personal contacts of all kinds." But seven out of the nine male Persuasive jobs (and six of the female) are very strongly flavoured with finance and money-making, e.g., salesman, commercial traveller, sales manager, insurance salesman.

The validity of the RMIB does, however, compare quite favourably with that of other tests of interests and job-preferences. The validation evidence is described as being of three main types: content validity, construct validity, and criterion-related information. The comment is made in the manual that "with interest blanks and similar measures, content validity is not easily separable from construct validity." This reviewer would warmly agree; indeed this applies to all psychological tests.

The test's content validity is assessed by means of matrices of intercorrelations between the scales. Several are quoted from the Australian standardisation, but another matrix is shown for 15-year-olds. The lowness of most of the intercorrelations is thought by Miller to establish the independence of the scales. There are, however, several which are over .40, e.g., Outdoor with Practical for boys (.45), Mechanical with Practical for both sexes (.61 and .58), Computational with Clerical for both sexes (.59 and .67), Medical with Scientific for both sexes (.50 and .42). The fact is, of course, that job contents (like interests) do overlap and also that people are influenced in occupational preference by such mundane questions as status and salary. Any test which successfully ignored such matters would probably lose more than it gained.

Certain artifacts are inherent in ipsative scoring. One is that the mean of the intercorrelations of ipsative variables is necessarily $-1/(n-1)$, n being the number of variables. In the case of the 12-variable Rothwell-Miller test, this value is $-.09$. Both the matrices presented in Table 10(1) conform exactly to this value. Another related artifact is that sets of correlations such as those presented in Tables 10(3) and 10(4) will have zero means. In fact, the overall mean of Tables 10(3) and 10(4) is $-.0007$. This implies that any conclusions from these correlations should be drawn very tentatively.

The "construct validity" consists of comparisons between the relevant scales of the RMIB and those of other tests. The results are for the most part strongly positive, as is to be expected. The "criterion-related" validity data are based on differences between academic faculties, both school and university, and yield reasonably satisfactory results.

The section on reliability is brief and consists mainly of test-retest coefficients obtained over periods ranging from three weeks to five months. Some of these are unimpressive, in particular those gained from a group of 179 engineering apprentices whose coefficients sink as low as .37 (for Persuasive) and .42 (for Clerical). A few data on split-half correlations are given: these (corrected) coefficients range from .56 to .91.

In general, the manual is intelligibly written, though the author evidently uses the word "juxtaposition" in a somewhat esoteric way (to mean "interchange") and he is guilty of an occasional unfortunate sentence such as the following: "The item analysis of the Australian form showed that each category as a whole was satisfactory in that the total of ranks for occupations in the category was lower for those respondents whose interest was in a category than was the total for any other category."

Miller has a tendency to blame those of his examinees who yield internally inconsistent test results for "carelessness," "lack of insight," "unrealistic attitudes," and "opposition to the testing." As suggested above, however, such results may well be due to the design of test, especially for subjects with individualistic patterns of job preferences. The Rothwell-Miller seems to be rather a dubious sledgehammer to use for cracking the nut of vocational interviewing.

CLIVE JONES, *Consultant, Management Selection Ltd., London, England.*

According to the manual, "The basic rationale for the Blank is that many persons hold stereotyped conceptions about the nature of occupations and base their choice of occupation on them." Of the 12 occupational categories making up this scale, 10 are the same as those found in the *Kuder Preference Record—Vocational.* The two new categories are Practical (working with one's hands) and Medical.

The RMIB consists of nine lists of 12 occupations, each category represented by one occupation. The subject ranks the 12 occupations in order of preference. Some of the less familiar occupations are described in a glossary printed on the back of the blank. The blank is scored by adding the assigned rank for each stereotype across the nine blocks. The instructions and the scoring procedure are clear and straightforward.

The manual presents percentile norms for a wide variety of school populations, as well as some norms based on higher levels of education and on adult populations.

Test-retest reliabilities, over a period of three months, for individual categories ranged from .33 to .84, with median .63. The median of the four test-retest reliabilities reported for each of the 12 categories follows: .70, Scientific; .70, Practical; .67, Medical; .67, Musical; .64, Mechanical; .64, Literary; .60, Outdoor; .60, Computational; .57, Social Service; .52, Aesthetic; .50, Clerical; and .48, Persuasive. Split-half reliabilities are reported as ranging from .56 to .91, with median .78. These reliabilities are discouragingly low for individual measurement.

Although the information presented on validity is very limited, it is reassuring that some evidence has been presented. The most meaningful comparisons are correlations between corresponding scores on the Kuder Vocational and the RMIB. Unfortunately, the results reported are for the Australian edition of the RMIB. The medians of the correlations reported for 10 groups follow: .79, Musical; .73, Outdoor; .72, Scientific; .69, Aesthetic; .67, Literary; .65, Persuasive; .65, Clerical; .60, Computational; .55, Social Service; and .52, Mechanical. These correlations, of course, do not give any information about the correspondence of the profiled peaks and valleys.

The main objective of this interest blank is to suggest inferences or hypotheses which career counsellors may use in the interview situation. The reviewer has no hesitation in recommending the blank for this purpose. Because of its origin, it is more appropriate for use in the United Kingdom than either the SVIB or the Kuder-V, and since the experimental evidence presented in the manual is promising, it should also find preference in the United Kingdom over its major competitor, the *Connolly Occupational Interests Questionnaire.*

[1035]
Safran Student's Interest Inventory. Grades 8–12; 1960–69; SSII; revision of *Safran Vocational Interest Test;* 11 scores: 7 interest scores (economic, technical, outdoor, service, humane, artistic, scientific) and 4 ability self-ratings (academic, mechanical, social, clerical); 1 form ('69, 12 pages); counsellor's manual ('69, 30 pages); student's manual ('69, 8 pages); reliability data based on shorter original edition; no norms for ability self-ratings; Can $7 per 35 tests; $2.50 per 35 student's manuals; $1.20 per counsellor's manual; $1.49 per specimen set; postage extra; [60–70] minutes; Carl Safran and Edgar N. Wright; Thomas Nelson & Sons (Canada) Ltd. *

REFERENCE

1. See 6:1069.

THOMAS T. FRANTZ, *Associate Professor of Counselor Education, State University of New York at Buffalo, Buffalo, New York.*

Developed in Canada for use with Canadians, the easily self-scored non-reusable *Safran Student's Interest Inventory* is designed to measure vocational interests of high school students, and as such it represents the sloppy implementation of some interesting ideas.

In their brief manual, the authors emphasize that the inventory is designed to be a learning, rather than a decision making, device and must be woven into the guidance program to be effective. The inventory was not meant to be nor should it be used for research purposes. To enhance the SSII's use as a guidance tool, the manual discusses ipsative (paired comparison) scores; differences in manifest, expressed, and inventoried interests; the relationship of abilities and aptitudes to interests. It also lists possible occupations corresponding to each of the seven interest scales.

Normative data are based on an ambitiously chosen sample of 3,055 ninth graders and 2,277 twelfth graders from all over Canada. (The manual misleadingly implies that the norms are based on 5,553 ninth and 3,388 twelfth graders, neglecting to make clear that approximately 45 and 33 percent, respectively, of the ninth and twelfth grade inventories were discarded as invalid.) The inventory is alleged to be suitable for grades 8 through 12; however, no norms are given for grade 10 and the very incomplete norms for grades 8 and 11 are based on only six schools in one province.

A unique feature of the inventory is the method for assessing the consistency of a student's interest hierarchy. Each of the eight pages of the inventory is composed of 7 activities (one from each of the interest areas) paired with each other in all possible ways to produce 21 items. Since for a given set of seven activities each activity is compared with all six others, a consistent or inconsistent interest hierarchy can be established. For example, if a student prefers activity A over B and B over C and A over C, he is consistent; but if he prefers activity A over B and B over C and C over A, he is inconsistent. Subjects may be checked for consistency on each of the eight pages. The authors state that "where four or more pages display inconsistencies the pattern of interests should be ignored because the pattern has little, if any, validity." Approximately one-third of the subjects return inventories which are invalid for this reason.

Unfortunately, the price paid to accomplish the consistency check seems quite high. The major loss is in the reduced number of occupations per scale. Though the inventory consists of 168 items, there are actually only 56 stimuli to respond to and only eight per scale. Eight diverse stimuli (e.g., "studying the science of computers" and "preparing special diets for hospital patients" are both supposed to be indicative of scientific interests) are probably not enough to accurately assess interest in a vocational area.

The SSII also includes a section for students to rate themselves in four areas of ability: academic, mechanical, clerical, and social. Each occupation listed in the student's and counsellor's manuals is followed by the authors' opinion of the minimum ability level, in the four ability areas, needed to be successful in the occupation. The key used by the authors to rate occupational ability levels is not explained in either the student's or the counsellor's manual. Furthermore, these subjective ability ratings are quite arbitrary in some cases; e.g., the authors state that to be a painter, sports writer, nurse, or actor one must have at least a university degree.

Yet to be mentioned are the most serious problems with this inventory. No reliability data are reported. The manual does give Kuder-Richardson and test-retest data on another Safran inventory constructed in 1960; but even these data are virtually worthless, since the relationship between 1960 and 1969 versions is never discussed, except to say that the 1960 version is much shorter and that 60 percent of the subjects used were college freshmen and not high school students, for whom the inventory is intended.

Validity data are reported on only 183 college students in the fields of nursing, electrical, creative arts, and business administration, indicating that each group scores highest on the anticipated scale. About the best that can be said, considering that no validity data on high school students are given, is that the validity of the inventory is unknown.

Response sets could artificially increase reliability and decrease validity, a problem the authors could easily have solved but were seemingly unaware of, since on each of the eight pages of the inventory the order of the activities listed is the same; e.g., the first item is from the economic scale, the second from the technical scale, the third from the outdoor scale, and so on through all 21 items on the page.

The choice of scales and items on the inventory is unexplained and confusing. Seven interest scales are used with no rationale or data supplied to support them. Four ability scales which do not correspond to the interest scales are used, likewise with no theoretical or empirical justification. The choice of occupa-

tions and their classification into interest scales in both the inventory and the manual were evidently accomplished without benefit of data, using only the authors' opinion. The occupational categories in the counsellor's manual are inconsistent and incomplete. Additionally, the inventory requests students to rank 12 school subjects, but the counsellor's manual discusses only 11. Another minor but irritating problem is that the items are not numbered.

Despite discussing the differences between ipsative and normative data, the authors state that scores on their forced choice inventory can be interpreted in a normative fashion and fail to explain the problems inherent in doing so. Worse, they claim that it is simply a matter of preference whether scores are interpreted on a normative or ipsative basis.

In summary, the instrument cannot begin to compete with other vocational interest inventories such as the *Strong Vocational Interest Blank,* the Kuder inventories, the *Vocational Preference Inventory*—either as a guidance tool or as a research device. It was constructed entirely by subjective methods of unexplained rationale. Its reliability is unknown and its validity has yet to be established. Its various scales and items appear haphazard, it is vulnerable to response set biases, and the actual numbers of stimuli on the inventory and subjects in the norm group are much fewer than the manual implies.

[1036]

*Strong Vocational Interest Blank for Men.** Ages 16 and over; 1927–71; SVIB; 84 scoring scales (22 basic interests, 54 occupational, 8 nonoccupational) and 6 administrative indices; BASIC INTERESTS: adventure ('69), agriculture ('69), art ('69), business management ('69), law/politics ('69), mathematics ('69), mechanical ('69), medical service ('69), merchandising ('69), military activities ('69), music ('69), nature ('69), office practices ('69), public speaking ('69), recreational leadership ('69), religious activities ('69), sales ('69), science ('69), social service ('69), teaching ('69), technical supervision ('69), writing ('69); OCCUPATIONAL: *group 1, biological science:* dentist ('32–66), osteopath ('47–66), veterinarian ('49–66, original scale by T. E. Hannum), physician ('28–66), psychiatrist ('52–66), psychologist ('28–66, original scale by P. H. Kriedt), biologist ('62–66, original scale by Carl A. Lindsay, Louis M. Herman, and Martin L. Zeigler); *group 2, physical science:* architect ('28–66), mathematician ('30–66), physicist ('30–66), chemist ('28–66), engineer ('28–66); *group 3, technical supervision:* production manager ('38–66), army officer ('52–66), air force officer ('66); *group 4, technical and skilled trades:* carpenter ('33–66), forest service man ('38–66), farmer ('28–66), math-science teacher ('38–66), printer ('38–66), policeman ('34–66); *group 5, social service:* personnel director ('28–66), public administrator ('44–66), rehabilitation counselor ('50–

66, original scale titled vocational counselor by Nathan E. Acree), YMCA secretary ('28–66), social worker ('54–66), social science teacher ('38–66), school superintendent ('30–66), minister ('28–66); *group 6, aesthetic-cultural:* librarian ('63–66), artist ('33–66), musician performer ('33–66), music teacher ('54–66); *group 7, CPA owner:* CPA owner ('49–66); *group 8, business and accounting:* senior CPA ('49–66), accountant ('32–66), office worker ('30–66), purchasing agent ('28–66), banker ('38–66), pharmacist ('49–66, original scale by Milton Schwebel), mortician ('46–66); *group 9, sales:* sales manager ('38–66), real estate salesman ('28–66), life insurance salesman ('28–66); *group 10, verbal-linguistic:* advertising man ('28–66), lawyer ('28–66), author-journalist ('28–66); *group 11, president, manufacturing concern:* president, manufacturing ('38–66); *group 12, supplementary occupational:* credit manager ('59–66), chamber of commerce executive ('62–66), physical therapist ('58–66), computer programmer ('66), business education teacher ('59–66, original scale by Robert V. Bacon), community recreation administrator ('66); NONOCCUPATIONAL SCALES: academic achievement ('66), age related interests ('69), diversity of interests ('69), masculinity-femininity II ('34–69), managerial orientation ('69), occupational introversion-extroversion ('69), occupational level ('39–66), specialization level ('52–66, original scale by Milton G. Holmen); ADMINISTRATIVE INDICES: total responses ('69), unpopular responses ('69), form check ('69), like percentage ('69), indifferent percentage ('69), dislike percentage ('69); Form T399 ('66, 8 pages); combined manual ('66, 79 pages) and supplement ('69, 25 pages) for tests for men and women; handbook ('71, 551 pages, see *1099* below); item weights for each basic interest scale ('69, 2 pages) and for each of the other scales ('66, 2 pages); separate answer sheets (Hankes, MRC, NCS, hand scored) must be used; $6 per 25 tests; $1.75 per 25 hand scored answer sheets; $100 per set of hand scoring stencils (not available for 1969 scales); $10 per set of 59 item weights tables; $1.50 per 25 profiles; $3 per manual; $1.75 per supplement; $6 per specimen set of tests for men and women; postage extra; a test booklet, Form T399R, in which responses are recorded and later transferred to answer sheets is available for research use; for special scoring services, see below; (30–60) minutes; Edward K. Strong, Jr. (except 1969 supplement), David P. Campbell, Ralph F. Berdie (1966 test), and Kenneth E. Clark (1966 test); Stanford University Press. *

a) HANKES (TESTSCOR) SCORING SERVICE. Hankes answer sheets: $2.25 per 50, $8.50 per 250; scoring service (duplicate profile report): first 10 tests within a month, $1.20 each; thereafter, $1.10 each or an 80¢ coupon ($40 per 50 coupons); telephone service available; cash and coupon orders postpaid; 1 day service on up to 50 tests; Testscor, Inc. *

b) MRC SCORING SERVICE. MRC answer sheets: $1.50 per 25, $4 per 100; scoring service (duplicate profile report): 1–25 tests, 75¢ each; 26–100 tests, 65¢ each; 101–1000 tests, 60¢ each; $1.50 handling charge; postage extra; 48 hour service; Measurement Research Center. *

c) NCS SCORING SERVICE. NCS answer sheets: $2 per 25, $7 per 100; scoring service (duplicate profile report): 1 day service (1–5 tests, $1.25 each; 6–24 tests, $1 each; 25 or more tests, 90¢ each); prepaid scoring certificates may be used for scoring tests in any quantity; 1 week service (25–99 tests, 80¢ each); optional statistical services also available; postage extra; National Computer Systems. *

REFERENCES

1–71. See 2:1680.
72–175. See 3:647.
176–273. See 4:747.
274–426. See 5:868.
427–614. See 6:1070.
615. LUCAS, JOSEPH R. *An Evaluation of Strong's Minister Scale Applied to the Roman Catholic Clergy.* Master's thesis, University of Ottawa (Ottawa, Ont., Canada), 1946.
616. WEIR, JOHN R. *An Attempt to Identify Vocational Interest Profiles Within a Neuropsychiatric Population.* Doctor's thesis, University of California (Los Angeles, Calif.), 1951.
617. WHITTOCK, JOHN MELVILLE, JR. *Study of the Interests of the Female Students Enrolled in the School of Library Science, Drexel Institute of Technology, as Measured by the Strong Vocational Interest Blank and the Kuder Preference Record.* Master's thesis, Drexel Institute of Technology (Philadelphia, Pa.), 1952.
618. LABUE, ANTHONY CHARLES. *An Analysis of Some Factors Associated With Persistence of Interest in Teaching as a Vocational Choice.* Doctor's thesis, Syracuse University (Syracuse, N.Y.), 1954. (*DA* 14:2001)
619. MAFFIA, L. A. *Measured Interests of Priests, Seminarians, and Former Seminarians in the Selection of Seminary Applicants.* Doctor's thesis, University of Oregon (Eugene, Ore.), 1954.
620. MEHENTI, PERIN MUNCHERSHAW. *Agreement Between Vocational Preference and Inventoried Interest in Relation to Some Presumed Indices of Vocational Maturity.* Doctor's thesis, Columbia University (New York, N.Y.), 1954. (*DA* 14:1454)
621. ROADMAN, HARRY EDWARD. *Relationship of Measured Interests to Career Data for Air Force Officers in the Comptroller Field.* Doctor's thesis, University of Minnesota (Minneapolis, Minn.), 1954. (*DA* 14:1253)
622. SEGAL, STANLEY JACOB. *The Role of Personality Factors in Vocational Choice: A Study of Accountants and Creative Writers.* Doctor's thesis, University of Michigan (Ann Arbor, Mich.), 1954. (*DA* 14:714)
623. TANNER, WILLIAM C., JR. "Personality Bases in Teacher Selection." *Phi Delta Kappan* 35:271–4+ Ap '54. *
624. TERMAN, LEWIS M. "Scientists and Nonscientists in a Group of 800 Gifted Men." *Psychol Monogr* 68(7):1–44 '54. * (*PA* 29:4848)
625. BERTNESS, HENRY J. *An Analysis of the Interests of Lutheran Ministers as Measured by the Strong Vocational Interest Blank.* Doctor's thesis, University of Minnesota (Minneapolis, Minn.), 1955. (*DA* 15:2094)
626. TAYLOR, GERRY MAILAND. *Vocational Interests of Male Librarians in the United States.* Master's thesis, University of Texas (Austin, Tex.), 1955.
627. BOYCE, ERNEST MARSHALL. *A Comparative Study of Overachieving and Underachieving College Students on Factors Other Than Scholastic Aptitude.* Doctor's thesis, University of Wisconsin (Madison, Wis.), 1956. (*DA* 16:2088)
628. DEAN, JAMES W. *The Curriculum and Vocational Choices of 250 Entering Freshman Engineers at the Pennsylvania State University, 1954–1955.* Doctor's thesis, Pennsylvania State University (University Park, Pa.), 1956. (*DA* 16:1369)
629. KING, LESLIE ALBERT. *Factors Associated With the Stability of Vocational Interests of General College Freshmen.* Doctor's thesis, University of Minnesota (Minneapolis, Minn.), 1956. (*DA* 16:1840)
630. KEMP, CLARENCE GRATTON. *Changes in Patterns of Personal Values in Relation to Open-Closed Belief Systems.* Doctor's thesis, Michigan State University (East Lansing, Mich.), 1957. (*DA* 19:271)
631. PATTERSON, C. H. "Interest Tests and the Emotionally Disturbed Client." *Ed & Psychol Meas* 17:264–80 su '57. * (*PA* 32:5620)
632. SIROTA, LEON MICHAEL. *A Factor Analysis of Selected Personality Domains.* Doctor's thesis, University of Michigan (Ann Arbor, Mich.), 1957. (*DA* 18:1503)
633. COHEN, DAVID. *The Relation of Independence of Work Experience to General Adolescent Independence and Certain Indices of Vocational Maturity.* Doctor's thesis, Columbia University (New York, N.Y.), 1958. (*DA* 19:164)
634. DUBIN, WILLIAM. *Toward a Definition of Effective Functioning.* Doctor's thesis, Columbia University (New York, N.Y.), 1958. (*DA* 18:1858)
635. HENNESSY, THOMAS, AND BLUHM, HAROLD. "Using Interest Inventories in Religious and Sacerdotal Counseling." *Cath Counselor* 2:46–9 w '58. *
636. REDMOND, JOHN FRANCIS. *A Study of the Relationship Between Problem-Solving Rigidity and Selected Areas of Vocational Interests.* Doctor's thesis, University of Washington (Seattle, Wash.), 1958. (*DA* 19:1658)
637. STRONG, EDWARD K., JR. "Satisfactions and Interests." *Am Psychologist* 13:449–56 Ag '58. * (*PA* 34:731)
638. WARMAN, ROY ELTON, JR. *Differential Perceptions of the Counseling Role of a University Counseling Center.* Doctor's thesis, Ohio State University (Columbus, Ohio), 1958. (*DA* 19:874)
639. DUBROW, MAX. *Factors Related to the Vocational Readiness of Adolescent Boys.* Doctor's thesis, Columbia University (New York, N.Y.), 1959. (*DA* 20:1068)
640. GARDNER, PAUL LEON. *Academic Failure, Reinstatement, and Follow-Up.* Doctor's thesis, Ohio State University (Columbus, Ohio), 1959. (*DA* 20:3627)

641. GOLDBERG, LEWIS ROBERT. *Personality Development and Vocational Choice: A Study of Therapists, Academicians, and Administrators in Clinical Psychology.* Doctor's thesis, University of Michigan (Ann Arbor, Mich.), 1959. (*DA* 19:3363)

642. GORDON, BARBARA JANE ARTHUR. *The Determination and Study of Academic Underachievement in the New York State College of Home Economics at Cornell University With Implications for Counseling and Admissions.* Doctor's thesis, Cornell University (Ithaca, N.Y.), 1959. (*DA* 20:1675)

643. KIRK, J. P. *A Study of the Interests of Brother Candidates and Professed Brothers on the Strong Minister and Clerical Interest Scales.* Doctor's thesis, St. Johns University (Jamaica, N.Y.), 1959.

644. LYON, JAMES BURKE. *A Study of Experiential, Motivational, and Personality Factors Related to Vocational Decision Versus Indecision.* Doctor's thesis, University of Minnesota (Minneapolis, Minn.), 1959. (*DA* 20:1269)

645. MURRAY, JOHN B. "Personality Study of Priests and Seminarians." *Homiletic & Pastoral R* 59:443–7 F '59. *

646. SAGUIGUIT, GIL FRANCO. *The Maximum Separation of Students Into Two Programs of Course Work in a College of Agriculture by Discriminant Analysis Involving Certain Selected Measurements.* Doctor's thesis, Pennsylvania State University (University Park, Pa.), 1959. (*DA* 20:2986)

647. BOND, PATRICIA JANE. *The Relationship Between Selected Nonintellective Factors and "Concealed Failure" Among College Students of Superior Scholastic Ability.* Doctor's thesis, Purdue University (Lafayette, Ind.), 1960. (*DA* 21:121)

648. MAHONEY, T. A.; JERDEE, T. H.; AND NASH, A. N. "Predicting Managerial Effectiveness." *Personnel Psychol* 13:147–63 su '60. * (*PA* 36:2LI47M)

649. MURPHY, RAYMOND ORIN. *Non-Intellectual Factors in Early Discontinuances of the 1959–1960 Freshman Class in Engineering of the Pennsylvania State University.* Doctor's thesis, Pennsylvania State University (University Park, Pa.), 1960. (*DA* 21:2536)

650. NAUSS, ALLEN HENRY. *Scholastic Ability, Self-Concept and Occupational Plans.* Doctor's thesis, University of Missouri (Columbia, Mo.), 1960. (DA 21:2596)

651. WILLIAMS, FRANK JEFFERSON, JR. *Predicting Success in Business.* Doctor's thesis, Stanford University (Stanford, Calif.), 1960. (*DA* 20:4304)

652. WOO-SAM, JAMES MCDOWELL. *A Study of Selected Factors Related to Teaching Effectiveness of Mathematics Instructors at the College Level.* Doctor's thesis, Purdue University (Lafayette, Ind.), 1960. (*DA* 21:237)

653. MARTUCCI, LEO GEORGE. *Some Correlates of Responses to a Standard Interview Among High School Boys.* Doctor's thesis, Rutgers University (New Brunswick, N.J.), 1961. (*DA* 22:3266)

654. RISHEL, DARRELL FRED. *The Development and Validation of Instruments and Techniques for the Selective Admission of Applicants for Graduate Studies in Counselor Education.* Doctor's thesis, Pennsylvania State University (University Park, Pa.), 1961. (*DA* 22:2271)

655. SCOTT, THOMAS BLYTHE, JR. *Counseling Interpretations for the Minnesota Vocational Interest Inventory Based on Comparisons With the Strong Vocational Interest Blank.* Doctor's thesis, University of Minnesota (Minneapolis, Minn.), 1961. (*DA* 22:634)

656. CHANEY, FREDERICK BENNETT. *The Life History Antecedents of Selected Vocational Interests.* Doctor's thesis, Purdue University (Lafayette, Ind.), 1962. (*DA* 23:2974)

657. FRINSKO, WILLIAM. *Experimental Post-Degree Program at Wayne State University—An Analysis of the Selective and Predictive Factors in Student Teaching.* Doctor's thesis, Wayne State University (Detroit, Mich.), 1962. (*DA* 24:1901)

658. KODAMA, HABUKU. "Study of Interests of Japanese Men With Special Reference to Developmental Aspect." *Jap Psychol Res* 4(3):119–28 '62. * (*PA* 39:1271)

659. KOLE, DELBERT MERRILL. *A Study of Intellectual and Personality Characteristics of Medical Students.* Master's thesis, University of Oregon Medical School (Portland, Ore.), 1962.

660. KOPROWSKI, EUGENE J. *Ego Strength and Realism in Curriculum Choice.* Doctor's thesis, University of Denver (Denver, Colo.), 1962. (*DA* 24:4286)

661. MASIH, LALIT KUMAR. *Career Saliency and Its Relation to Certain Personality and Environmental Variables.* Doctor's thesis, Syracuse University (Syracuse, N.Y.), 1962. (*DA* 24:181)

662. MORRISON, JACK SHERMAN. *Four Hundred New Students in Theater Arts: An Experimental Study of Those Who Dropped Out and Those Who Achieved the B.A. Degree at UCLA.* Doctor's thesis, University of Southern California (Los Angeles, Calif.), 1962. (*DA* 23:3239)

663. BATES, CHARLES O. *A Study of Creative Potential as Found in Elementary Student Teachers.* Doctor's thesis, Ball State Teachers College (Muncie, Ind.), 1963. (*DA* 24:4561)

664. BECHTEL, ROBERT DARYL. *An Analytic Study of Selected Freshmen Students Assumed to Possess Creative Mathematical Ability.* Doctor's thesis, Purdue University (Lafayette, Ind.), 1963. (*DA* 24:5187)

665. BOHN, MARTIN J., AND STEPHENSON, RICHARD R. "Vocational Interests and Self-Concept." *Newsl Res Psychol* 5:21–2 Ag '63. * (*PA* 38:9336)

666. FOREMAN, MILTON EDWARD. *Some Empirical Correlates of Positive Mental Health.* Doctor's thesis, Ohio State University (Columbus, Ohio), 1963. (*DA* 24:4831)

667. GAREIS, FRITZIE EMMA. *Differential Interest Patterns of a Selected Group of College and University Administrators.* Doctor's thesis, University of Michigan (Ann Arbor, Mich.), 1963. (*DA* 25:229)

668. HALL, WILLIAM JOSEPH. *College Women's Identifications With Their Fathers in Relation to Vocational Interest Patterns.* Doctor's thesis, University of Texas (Austin, Tex.), 1963. (*DA* 24:5192)

669. NASH, ALLAN NYLIN. *Development and Evaluation of a Strong Vocational Interest Blank Key for Differentiating Between Potentially Effective and Less Effective Business Managers.* Doctor's thesis, University of Minnesota (Minneapolis, Minn.), 1963. (*DA* 25:2606)

670. NORTON, EARL DOUGLAS, JR. *An Investigation of Interest, Aptitude, and Performance Measures as They Relate to Degree Objective-Changing Behavior of Selected Counselees.* Doctor's thesis, Purdue University (Lafayette, Ind.), 1963. (*DA* 24:5092)

671. SCHLETZER, VERA MYERS. *A Study of the Predictive Effectiveness of the Strong Vocational Interest Blank for Job Satisfaction.* Doctor's thesis, University of Minnesota (Minneapolis, Minn.), 1963. (*DA* 27:4567B)

672. URAY, RICHARD MARTIN. *An Analysis of Scores Made by a Group of Radio Announcers in Texas on Selected Psychological Tests.* Doctor's thesis, University of Houston (Houston, Tex.), 1963. (*DA* 25:950)

673. WILLIAMS, CECIL LEE. *A Study of the Strong Vocational Interest Blank and Scores From a Factor Analysis of the Minnesota Multiphasic Personality Inventory.* Doctor's thesis, University of Kansas (Lawrence, Kan.), 1963. (*DA* 25:1764)

674. WINTER, FRANK. *Development of a USAF Officer's Interest Scale.* Master's thesis, University of California (Los Angeles, Calif.), 1963.

675. ANDERSON, WAYNE, AND ANKER, JAMES. "Factor Analysis of MMPI and SVIB Scores for a Psychiatric Population." *Psychol Rep* 15:715–9 D '64. * (*PA* 39:7831)

676. BANAS, PAUL ANTHONY. *An Investigation of Trans-situational Moderators.* Doctor's thesis, University of Minnesota (Minneapolis, Minn.), 1964. (*DA* 26:1158)

677. BEDROSIAN, HRACH. "An Analysis of Vocational Interests at Two Levels of Management." *J Appl Psychol* 48:325–8 O '64. * (*PA* 39:6109)

678. CAMPBELL, DAVID P. "The Center for Interest Measurement Research." *J Counsel Psychol* 11:395–9 w '64. *

679. CARNES, G. DERWOOD. "Vocational Interest Characteristics of Abnormal Personalities." *J Counsel Psychol* 11:272–9 f '64. * (*PA* 39:5170)

680. CHANEY, FREDERICK B., AND OWENS, WILLIAM A. "Life History Antecedents of Sales, Research, and General Engineering Interest." *J Appl Psychol* 48:101–5 Ap '64. * (*PA* 39:6039)

681. CLARK, ARTHUR B., III. "Development of an Occupational Interest Scoring Scale for College Student Personnel." *Personnel & Guid J* 42:801–2 Ap '64. * (*PA* 39:5016)

682. DAYLEY, ALAN JAY. *The Strong Vocational Interest Blank: A Fifteen Year Follow-Up.* Doctor's thesis, University of Utah (Salt Lake City, Utah), 1964. (*DA* 25:5107)

683. DEKKER, JAMES HERMAN. *A Comparative Study of the Interests, Values, and Personality of Activity Leaders and Non-Participating Students at Purdue University.* Doctor's thesis, Purdue University (Lafayette, Ind.), 1964. (*DA* 25:998)

684. DeSENA, PAUL A. "The Non-Occupational Scales of the SVIB and Achievement in College." *Voc Guid Q* 13:58–62 au '64. *

685. DICK, WILLIAM W. *Vocational Self-Concept in Terms of the Vocational Interests and Values of Seminarians and Ministers.* Master's thesis, University of Ottawa (Ottawa, Ont., Canada), 1964.

686. DUNNETTE, MARVIN D.; WERNIMONT, PAUL; AND ABRAHAMS, NORMAN. "Further Research on Vocational Interest Differences Among Several Types of Engineers." *Personnel & Guid J* 42:484–93 Ja '64. * (*PA* 39:6040)

687. ERICKSON, PAUL. *Selection Factors Relating to Success in a Counselor Education Program.* Doctor's thesis, University of Southern California (Los Angeles, Calif.), 1964. (*DA* 25:3391)

688. FAIR, DONALD CLARENCE. *Life History Correlates of Selected Vocational Interests.* Doctor's thesis, University of Minnesota (Minneapolis, Minn.), 1964. (*DA* 25:5383)

689. FEIST, JESS. *A Study of the Relationship Between SVIB Profiles of High School Boys and Their Occupations Six to Ten Years Later.* Doctor's thesis, University of Kansas (Lawrence, Kan.), 1964. (*DA* 26:198)

690. FIELDER, DANIEL WILLIAM. *A Nomothetic Study of the Southern California School of Theology Seminarian.* Doctor's thesis, Southern California School of Theology (Claremont, Calif.), 1964. (*DA* 26:1192)

691. GIESZ, WILLIAM GEORGE. *Psychosexual Categories as Associated With Vocational Experience.* Doctor's thesis, University of Maryland (College Park, Md.), 1964. (*DA* 25:4816)

Strong Vocational Interest Blank for Men

692. HAYES, ALBERTINE BRANNUM. *Personal, Social and Academic Characteristics of Southern Education Foundation Fellows in Participating Colleges and Universities.* Doctor's thesis, University of Oklahoma (Norman, Okla.), 1964. (*DA* 25:3323)

693. HODGE, STEPHEN ERNEST. *Differentiation of Prospective and In-Service Elementary, Secondary and College Teachers on an Extroversion-Introversion Scale and the Strong Vocational Interest Blanks.* Doctor's thesis, University of Missouri (Columbia, Mo.), 1964. (*DA* 25:5736)

694. HORSMAN, VIRGINIA GLENN. *Critical Factors in Differentiating Between Effective and Ineffective Counselors.* Doctor's thesis, Texas Technological College (Lubbock, Tex.), 1964. (*DA* 26:1170)

695. HOWLAND, RICHARD HENRY. *A Study of Successful and Unsuccessful Freshman Pharmacy Students as Related to Their Occupational Group Scores on the Strong Vocational Interest Blank.* Doctor's thesis, University of Michigan (Ann Arbor, Mich.), 1964. (*DA* 25:3324)

696. HUTCHINS, EDWIN B. "The AAMC Longitudinal Study: Implications for Medical Education." *J Med Ed* 39:265-77 Mr '64. *

697. JOHNSON, DOROTHY ETHEL. *A Study of Interests and Personality Characteristics of Counselor Trainees and Counseling Effectiveness.* Doctor's thesis, Purdue University (Lafayette, Ind.), 1964. (*DA* 26:2051)

698. KELLY, E. LOWELL. "Alternate Criteria in Medical Education and Their Correlates." *Proc Inv Conf Testing Probl* 1963:64-85 '64. *

699. KNAPP, ROBERT H., AND GREEN, HELEN B. "Personality Correlates of Success Imagery." *J Social Psychol* 62:93-9 F '64. * (*PA* 39:1807)

700. KNAPP, ROBERT H., AND HOFFMAN, EDWARD G. "Vocational Interest Scores and Patterns of Aesthetic Preference." *J Social Psychol* 64:299-306 D '64. * (*PA* 39:7844)

701. KRAUSKOPF, C. J.; ELDER, DOROTHY; AND MAPELI, DELIA. "Some Characteristics of Students Who Transfer From Engineering to Arts and Sciences." *Voc Guid Q* 12:187-91 sp '64. * (*PA* 39:5981)

702. KUNCE, JOSEPH, AND BREWER, BLAYNE. "Response Set of Neuropsychiatric Patients to the Strong Interest Inventory." *J Clin Psychol* 20:247-50 Ap '64. * (*PA* 39:7866)

703. MARTIN, ANN MILDRED. "The Development and Successive Refinement of an Academic Interest Scale for the Strong Vocational Interest Blank." *Ed & Psychol Meas* 24:841-52 w '64. * (*PA* 39:7780)

704. MATARAZZO, JOSEPH D.; ALLEN, BERNADENE V.; SASLOW, GEORGE; AND WIENS, ARTHUR N. "Characteristics of Successful Policemen and Firemen Applicants." *J Appl Psychol* 48:123-33 Ap '64. * (*PA* 39:6047)

705. MERRILL, KEITH ELMER. *The Relationship of Certain Non-Intellective Factors to Lack of Persistence of Higher-Ability Students and Persistence of Lower-Ability Students at the University of California, Berkeley.* Doctor's thesis, University of California (Berkeley, Calif.), 1964. (*DA* 25:3939)

706. PALUBINSKAS, ALICE L. "Sophisticated Faking on the Strong Vocational Interest Blank." Abstract. *J Med Ed* 39:887 S '64. *

707. PETERSEN, DWAIN FRANKLIN. *Factors Common to Interest, Value, and Personality Scales.* Doctor's thesis, University of Nebraska (Lincoln, Neb.), 1964. (*DA* 25:5747)

708. POOL, DONALD A., AND BROWN, ROBERT A. "Kuder-Strong Discrepancies and Personality Adjustment." *J Counsel Psychol* 11:63-6 sp '64. Supplementary letter to the editor. 11:298 f '64. * (*PA* 38:8596)

709. REINSTEDT, ROBERT N.; HAMMIDI, BEAULAH C.; PERES, SHERWOOD H.; AND RICARD, EVELYN L. *Computer Personnel Research Group Programmer Performance Prediction Study.* Memorandum RM-4033-PR. Santa Monica, Calif.: Rand Corporation, 1964. Pp. vii, 64. *

710. SCHUMACHER, CHARLES F. "Personal Characteristics of Students Choosing Different Types of Medical Careers." *J Med Ed* 39:278-88 Mr '64. *

711. SIESS, THOMAS FREDERICK. *Personal History Factors and Their Relation to Vocational Preferences.* Doctor's thesis, University of Minnesota (Minneapolis, Minn.), 1964. (*DA* 25:4552)

712. STEWART, LAWRENCE H. "Change in Personality Test Scores During College." Comment by David V. Tiedeman. *J Counsel Psychol* 11:211-20 f '64. * (*PA* 39:5184)

713. STEWART, LAWRENCE H. "Factor Analysis of Nonoccupational Scales of the Strong Blank, Selected Personality Scales and the School and College Ability Test." *Calif J Ed Res* 15:136-41 My '64. * (*PA* 39:3201)

714. STEWART, LAWRENCE H. "Selected Correlates of the Specialization Level Scale of the Strong Vocational Interest Blank." *Personnel & Guid J* 42:867-73 My '64. * (*PA* 39:6054)

715. STRICKER, LAWRENCE J., AND ROSS, JOHN. "Some Correlates of a Jungian Personality Inventory." *Psychol Rep* 14:623-43 Ap '64. * (*PA* 39:1848)

716. STRONG, E. K., JR.; CAMPBELL, DAVID P.; BERDIE, RALPH F.; AND CLARK, KENNETH E. "Proposed Scoring Changes for the Strong Vocational Interest Blank." *J Appl Psychol* 48:75-80 Ap '64. * (*PA* 39:5101)

717. THOMSON, ROBERT WILLIAM. *A Factor Analysis of the Life History Correlates of Engineering Interests.* Doctor's thesis, Purdue University (Lafayette, Ind.), 1964. (*DA* 25:1325)

718. THRUSH, RANDOLPH S., AND KING, PAUL T. "Differential Interests Among Medical Students." *Voc Guid Q* 13:120-3 w '64-65. * (*PA* 39:8785)

719. TYLER, LEONA E. "The Antecedents of Two Varieties of Vocational Interests." *Genetic Psychol Monogr* 70:177-227 N '64. * (*PA* 39:10878)

720. VANDENBERG, STEVEN G., AND KELLY, LILLIAN. "Hereditary Components in Vocational Preferences." *Acta Geneticae Medicae et Gemellologiae* 13:266-77 Jl '64. * (*PA* 39:6056)

721. VERDA, MARTHA MALIK. *A Comparison of Certain Characteristics of Undergraduate Women at Eastern Michigan University Who Remain in or Voluntarily Withdraw From the Physical Education Curriculum.* Doctor's thesis, University of Michigan (Ann Arbor, Mich.), 1964. (*DA* 25:7068)

722. WILLIAMS, FRANK J., AND HARRELL, THOMAS W. "Predicting Success in Business." *J Appl Psychol* 48:164-7 Je '64. * (*PA* 39:6076)

723. WILLIAMS, PHOEBE ANN. *The Relationship Between Certain Scores on the Strong Vocational Interest Blank and Intellectual Disposition.* Doctor's thesis, University of California (Berkeley, Calif.), 1964. (*DA* 26:2863)

724. ABRAHAMS, NORMAN MYRON. *The Effect of Key Length and Item Validity on Overall Validity, Cross-Validation Shrinkage, and Test-Retest Reliability of Interest Keys.* Doctor's thesis, University of Minnesota (Minneapolis, Minn.), 1965. (*DA* 27:954B)

725. ACKERMAN, BERNARD R. *The Relationship of Certain Personality Variables to the Executive Role in the Funeral Service Industry: An Evaluation of the Personality Variables of Rigidity, Lability, Self-Concept and Interests in Executive and Technical Personnel in the Funeral Service Industry.* Doctor's thesis, New York University (New York, N.Y.), 1965. (*DA* 27:606B)

726. ADAMS, JAMES F. "The Reliability and Accuracy of Commercial Machine Scoring of the Strong Vocational Interest Blank." *J Ed Meas* 2:85-90 Je '65. *

727. ANDERSON, HARRY E., JR., AND BARRY, JOHN R. "Occupational Choices in Selected Health Professions." *Personnel & Guid J* 44:177-84 O '65. * (*PA* 40:3419)

728. BERDIE, RALPH F. "Strong Vocational Interest Blank Scores of High School Seniors and Their Later Occupational Entry II." *J Appl Psychol* 49:188-93 Je '65. * (*PA* 39:13064)

729. BOYD, JOSEPH D. "Vocational Interest Measurement in High School: What Do the Findings Mean?" *J Assn Col Adm Officers* 10:9-14 w '65. *

730. CAMERON, ALEXANDER ROBERT. *An Analysis of the Interests, Educational Preparation and Vocational Background of Student Personnel Deans.* Doctor's thesis, University of Michigan (Ann Arbor, Mich.), 1965. (*DA* 28:1226A)

731. CAMPBELL, DAVID P. "Note: A Comparison of the Performance of Four SVIB Scoring Services." *J Ed Meas* 2:218-9 D '65. *

732. CAMPBELL, DAVID P. "The Vocational Interests of American Psychological Association Presidents." *Am Psychologist* 20:636-44 Ag '65. *

733. CORDREY, LEROY JAY. *Characteristics of Curricularly Committed and Uncommitted Students.* Doctor's thesis, University of California (Berkeley, Calif.), 1965. (*DA* 26:7153)

734. DICKEN, CHARLES F., AND BLACK, JOHN D. "Predictive Validity of Psychometric Evaluations of Supervisors." *J Appl Psychol* 49:34-47 F '65. * (*PA* 39:8793)

735. FAIR, DONALD C. "Life-History Correlates of Selected Vocational Interests." Abstract. *Proc Ann Conv Am Psychol Assn* 73:335-6 '65. * (*PA* 39:16505)

736. GOLDSCHMID, MARCEL LUCIEN. *The Prediction of College Major in the Sciences and the Humanities by Means of Personality Tests.* Doctor's thesis, University of California (Berkeley, Calif.), 1965. (*DA* 26:4073)

737. HAVLICEK, LARRY L. *An Investigation of the Correlations Between Scales on the Strong Vocational Interest Blank.* Doctor's thesis, University of Kansas (Lawrence, Kan.), 1965. (*DA* 26:3153)

738. HEWER, VIVIAN H. "Vocational Interests of College Freshmen and Their Social Origins." *J Appl Psychol* 49:407-11 D '65. * (*PA* 40:3417)

739. HOOD, ALBERT B. "Prediction of Medical School Attendance From College Freshman SVIBs." *J Appl Psychol* 49:110-1 Ap '65. * (*PA* 39:10236)

740. HOWARD, LORRAINE HARRIS. *A Comparison of Freshmen Attending Selected Oregon Community Colleges and Oregon State University in Terms of Interests, Values, and Manifest Needs.* Doctor's thesis, Oregon State University (Corvallis, Ore.), 1965. (*DA* 25:5738)

741. HUMMEL, RAYMOND, AND SPRINTHALL, NORMAN. "Underachievement Related to Interests, Attitudes and Values." *Personnel & Guid J* 44:388-95 D '65. * (*PA* 40:4101)

742. JOHNSON, RICHARD W. "Are SVIB Interests Correlated With Differential Academic Achievement?" *J Appl Psychol* 49:302-9 Ag '65. * (*PA* 39:15357)

Strong Vocational Interest Blank for Men

743. KASSARJIAN, WALTRAUD M., AND KASSARJIAN, HAROLD H. "Occupational Interests, Social Values and Social Character." *J Counsel Psychol* 12:48–54 sp '65. * (*PA* 39:10055)

744. KOLE, DELBERT M., AND MATARAZZO, JOSEPH D. "Intellectual and Personality Characteristics of Two Classes of Medical Students." *J Med Ed* 40:1130–44 D '65. *

745. LEE, ROBERT JULIAN. *Correlates of Interest Maturity.* Doctor's thesis, Western Reserve University (Cleveland, Ohio), 1965. (*DA* 26:6840)

746. LEWIS, EDWIN C.; WOLINS, LEROY; AND HOGAN, JOHN. "Interest and Ability Correlates of Graduation and Attrition in a College of Engineering." *Am Ed Res J* 2:63–74 Mr '65. *

747. LIEF, VICTOR F.; LIEF, HAROLD I.; AND YOUNG, KATHLEEN M. "Academic Success: Intelligence and Personality." *J Med Ed* 40:114–24 F '65. *

748. MCARTHUR, CHARLES. "The Validity of the Yale Strong Scales at Harvard." *J Counsel Psychol* 12:35–8 sp '65. * (*PA* 39:10138)

749. MCIFF, LYLE HATCH. *The Relationship of Certain Selected Factors to the Success or Failure of Second-Quarter Accounting Students at Utah State University.* Doctor's thesis, University of Southern California (Los Angeles, Calif.), 1965. (*DA* 26:5767)

750. MERWIN, JACK C.; BRADLEY, ARTHUR D.; JOHNSON, RALPH H.; AND JOHN, ELMER R. "S.V.I.B. Machine Scoring Provided by a Test Scoring Agency." *Personnel & Guid J* 43:665–8 Mr '65. *

751. NASH, ALLAN N. "A Study of Item Weights and Scale Lengths for the SVIB." *J Appl Psychol* 49:264–9 Ag '65. * (*PA* 39:15253)

752. NASH, ALLAN N. "Vocational Interests of Effective Managers: A Review of the Literature." *Personnel Psychol* 18:21–37 sp '65. * (*PA* 39:16589)

753. OGDEN, WILLIAM EUGENE. *Field Dependency in a Sample of University Counseling Center Clients.* Doctor's thesis, University of Kansas (Lawrence, Kan.), 1965. (*DA* 27:679A)

754. ORTENZI, ANGELO. *Establishment and Cross-Validation of Selection Criteria for Resident Counselors at the Pennsylvania State University.* Doctor's thesis, Pennsylvania State University (University Park, Pa.), 1965. (*DA* 26:6451)

755. PERRY, DALLIS K., AND CANNON, WILLIAM M. *Project Summary: Vocational Interests of Computer Programmers.* Technical Memorandum TM-2655/001/00. Santa Monica, Calif.: System Development Corporation, 1965. Pp. 8. *

756. PERRY, DALLIS K., AND CANNON, WILLIAM M. *SVIB Scores and Programmer Key: Vocational Interests of Computer Programmers.* Technical Memorandum TM-2655/002/00. Santa Monica, Calif.: System Development Corporation, 1965. Pp. 55. *

757. PETRIK, NORMAN DALE. *Socio-Economic Status, Vocational Interests and Persistence in Selected Curricula.* Doctor's thesis, University of Nebraska (Lincoln, Neb.), 1965. (*DA* 26:5242)

758. PIERSON, JEROME SANDERS. *Cognitive Styles and Measured Vocational Interests of College Men.* Doctor's thesis, University of Texas (Austin, Tex.), 1965. (*DA* 26:875)

759. RICHMOND, ALLEN M. *The Relationship Between Achievement Status and Inventoried Interests of Speech Pathology and Audiology Majors.* Doctor's thesis, Ohio University (Athens, Ohio), 1965. (*DA* 26:5879)

760. ROCK, DONALD ALAN. *Improving the Prediction of Academic Achievement by Population Moderators.* Doctor's thesis, Purdue University (Lafayette, Ind.), 1965. (*DA* 26:1801)

761. ROSS, SHERMAN; DENENBERG, V. H.; AND CHAMBERS, R. M. "SVIB Scores of High School and College Biological Science Research Students." *Voc Guid Q* 13:187–92 sp '65. * (*PA* 40:1973)

762. ROYS, KEITH BENJAMIN. *Differential Interests of Male Administrators in Community Recreation as Compared to Other Occupations Described by the Strong Vocational Interest Approach.* Doctor's thesis, University of Illinois (Urbana, Ill.), 1965. (*DA* 26:7147)

763. SHAZO, DEL DE. *Vocational Interest Development as a Function of Parental Attitudes.* Doctor's thesis, University of Kansas (Lawrence, Kan.), 1965. (*DA* 27:957B)

764. STUFFLEBEAM, DANIEL LEROY. *Investigation of Individual Characteristics Associated With Guidance Competence Versus Individual Characteristics Associated With Counseling Competence.* Doctor's thesis, Purdue University (Lafayette, Ind.), 1965. (*DA* 26:1490)

765. SURETTE, RALPH FRANCIS. *The Relationship of Personal and Work-Value Orientations to Career Versus Homemaking Preference Among Twelfth Grade Girls.* Doctor's thesis, Catholic University of America (Washington, D.C.), 1965. (*DA* 26:4462)

766. TAYLOR, RONALD G., AND BONDY, STEPHEN. "Interest Patterns of Male Technical and Commerce Graduates." *Voc Guid Q* 13:279–82 su '65. * (*PA* 40:1952)

767. TOEWS, JAY M. *Predicting Degree of Interest Patterning From Measures of Ego-Strength, Intelligence, and Choice-Making.* Doctor's thesis, Washington State University (Pullman, Wash.), 1965. (*DA* 26:3158)

768. TOLLEFSON, NONA FALMLEN. *Relationship of Counselor Need Orientation to Counselor Effectiveness and Counselor Per-*

sonality. Doctor's thesis, Purdue University (Lafayette, Ind.), 1965. (*DA* 27:122A)

769. TRIMBLE, JOHN THOMAS. *A Ten-Year Longitudinal Follow-Up Study of Inventoried Interests of Selected High School Students.* Doctor's thesis, University of Missouri (Columbia, Mo.), 1965. (*DA* 26:5252)

770. WALKER, THOMAS HOWARD. *An Analysis of Ten Strong Vocational Interest Blank Scores as Related to Choice of College Curricula and Scholastic Success at Indiana University.* Doctor's thesis, Indiana University (Bloomington, Ind.), 1965. (*DA* 26:5255)

771. WEIGEL, RICHARD; ROEHLKE, ART; AND POE, CHARLES. "Re-evaluating Machine Scoring Consistency." *Voc Guid Q* 13:209–11 sp '65. *

772. ZYTOWSKI, DONALD G. "Characteristics of Male University Students With Weak Occupational Similarity on the Strong Vocational Interest Blank." *J Counsel Psychol* 12:182–5 su '65. * (*PA* 39:12374)

773. ALSIP, JONATHAN EDWARD. *Differential Responses of Veterinarians to the Revised Strong Vocational Interest Blank for Men.* Master's thesis, Iowa State University (Ames, Iowa), 1966.

774. APOSTAL, ROBERT A. "Interest Stability and the Interpretable Change Criterion." *Voc Guid Q* 14:209–10 sp '66. * (*PA* 40:10490)

775. ASHBY, JEFFERSON D.; WALL, HARVEY W.; AND OSIPOW, SAMUEL H. "Vocational Certainty and Indecision in College Freshmen." *Personnel & Guid J* 44:1037–41 Je '66. * (*PA* 40:12643)

776. ATHELSTAN, GARY THOMAS. *An Exploratory Investigation of Response Patterns Associated With Low Profiles on the Strong Vocational Interest Blank for Men.* Doctor's thesis, University of Minnesota (Minneapolis, Minn.), 1966. (*DA* 27:4546B)

777. BOHN, MARTIN J., JR. "Psychological Needs Related to Vocational Personality Types." *J Counsel Psychol* 13:306–9 f '66. * (*PA* 40:12644)

778. BOHN, MARTIN J., JR. "Vocational Maturity and Personality." *Voc Guid Q* 15:123–6 D '66. * (*PA* 41:12636)

779. BROWN, ROBERT A., AND POOL, DONALD A. "Psychological Needs and Self-Awareness." *J Counsel Psychol* 13:85–8 sp '66. * (*PA* 40:5459)

780. CAMPBELL, DAVID P. "The 1966 Revision of the Strong Vocational Interest Blank." *Personnel & Guid J* 44:744–9 Mr '66. *

781. CAMPBELL, DAVID P. "Occupations Ten Years Later of High School Seniors With High Scores on the SVIB Life Insurance Salesman Scale." *J Appl Psychol* 50:369–72 O '66. * (*PA* 40:13565)

782. CAMPBELL, DAVID P. "Stability of Interests Within an Occupation Over Thirty Years." *J Appl Psychol* 50:51–6 F '66. * (*PA* 40:4644)

783. CAMPBELL, DAVID P. "The Stability of Vocational Interests Within Occupations Over Long Time Spans." *Personnel & Guid J* 44:1012–9 Je '66. * (*PA* 40:12646)

784. CAMPBELL, DAVID P., AND JOHANSSON, CHARLES B. "Academic Interests, Scholastic Achievements and Eventual Occupations." *J Counsel Psychol* 13:416–24 w '66. * (*PA* 41:2247)

785. CLARK, ARTHUR B., III, AND GREGORIO, LEONARD J. "Graduate School Admissions Policies and the Counseling Use of the SVIB Student Personnel Scale." *J Col Stud Personnel* 7:176–9 My '66. *

786. DECENCIO, DOMINIC V. *Relationship Between Certain Interest and Personality Variables in a Sample of College Women.* Doctor's thesis, Temple University (Philadelphia, Pa.), 1966. (*DA* 27:1288B)

787. DEUTSCHER, JOHN CHARLES. *A Comparative Study of Selected Academic and Non-Academic Measures of College Males With High Intensity and Low Intensity Profiles on the Strong Vocational Interest Blank.* Doctor's thesis, University of North Dakota (Grand Forks, N.D.), 1966. (*DA* 27:1626A)

788. DICK, WILLIAM W., AND ISABELLE, LAURENT A. "Vocational Self-Concept in Terms of the Vocational Interests and Values of Seminarians and Ministers." *Can Psychologist* 7a:8–16 Ja '66. *

789. DOLLIVER, ROBERT HENRY. *The Relationship of Certain Variables to the Amount of Agreement in Inventoried and Expressed Vocational Interests.* Doctor's thesis, Ohio State University (Columbus, Ohio), 1966. (*DA* 27:2505B)

790. DUNTEMAN, GEORGE H. "Discriminant Analyses of the SVIB for Female Students in Five College Curricula." *J Appl Psychol* 50:509–15 D '66. * (*PA* 41:3333)

791. FALCK, FRANCES ELIZABETH. *An Analysis of Achievement and Attitudes of Freshman Participants in the Federal Work-Study Program at the University of Colorado.* Doctor's thesis, University of Colorado (Boulder, Colo.), 1966. (*DA* 28:1263A)

792. FEIST, JESS. "Predictive Value of SVIB Primary and Reject Patterns." *J Appl Psychol* 50:556–60 D '66. * (*PA* 41:3495)

793. FORREST, DONALD VINCENT. *A Comparative Study of Male Secondary School Underachievers Matriculating at the University of South Dakota.* Doctor's thesis, University of South Dakota (Vermillion, S.D.), 1966. (*DA* 27:671A)

Strong Vocational Interest Blank for Men

794. FREDERIKSEN, NORMAN. "Validation of a Simulation Technique." *Organiz Behav & Hum Perfor* 1:87-109 S '66. * (*PA* 41:862)

795. GASH, IRA ARNOLD. *The Stability of Measured Interests as Related to the Clinical Improvement of Hospitalized Psychiatric Patients.* Doctor's thesis, Temple University (Philadelphia, Pa.), 1966. (*DA* 27:1290B)

796. GRENFELL, JOHN ELLIOT. *The Effect of National Defense Education Act Counseling Institutes on the Measured Interests of Institute Enrollees.* Doctor's thesis, Oregon State University (Corvallis, Ore.), 1966. (*DA* 27:3692A)

797. HINTON, BERNARD LLOYD. *A Model of Creative Problem Solving Performance and the Effects of Frustration.* Doctor's thesis, Stanford University (Stanford, Calif.), 1966. (*DA* 27:2508B)

798. JOHNSON, DAVIS G., AND HUTCHINS, EDWIN B. "Doctor or Dropout? A Study of Medical Student Attrition: Chap. 4, 'The Student.'" *J Med Ed* 41:1139-56, 1263-5 D '66. *

799. KEARNEY, DOROTHY LUCILLE. *Selected Non-Intellectual Factors as Predictors of Academic Success in Junior College Intellectually Capable Students.* Doctor's thesis, University of Southern California (Los Angeles, Calif.), 1966. (*DA* 27:395A)

800. KINSLINGER, HOWARD JOSEPH. *The Interest, Self-Perception, and Life-History Correlates of Leadership.* Doctor's thesis, Purdue University (Lafayette, Ind.), 1966. (*DA* 27:4155B)

801. KNAPP, THOMAS R. "Interactive Versus Ipsative Measurement of Career Interest." *Personnel & Guid J* 44:482-6 Ja '66. * (*PA* 40:5971)

802. KOHLAN, RICHARD GEORGE. *Relationships Between Inventoried Interests and Inventoried Needs in a College Sample.* Doctor's thesis, University of Minnesota (Minneapolis, Minn.), 1966. (*DA* 27:2397A)

803. KUNCE, JOSEPH; STURMAN, JOHN; LONGHOFER, PAUL; AND CASTOR, MARVEL. "Psychological Factors in High School Accidents." *Personnel & Guid J* 45:140-3 O '66. * (*PA* 41:2147)

804. KUNCE, JOSEPH T., AND BREWER, BLAYNE. "Neuropsychiatric Patients, Accident Proneness, and Interest Patterns." *J Psychol* 63:287-90 Jl '66. * (*PA* 40:10379)

805. KUNCE, JOSEPH T., AND WORLEY, BERT H. "Interest Patterns, Accidents and Disability." *J Clin Psychol* 22:105-7 Ja '66. * (*PA* 40:4632)

806. MCCAMPBELL, MOLLY KELLY. *Differentiation of Engineers' Interests.* Doctor's thesis, University of Kansas (Lawrence, Kan.), 1966. (*DA* 27:1662A)

807. MEADOWS, MARK EUGENE. *A Comparative Study of Selected Characteristics of Counseled and Non-Counseled Students in a College Counseling Center.* Doctor's thesis, University of Georgia (Athens, Ga.), 1966. (*DA* 27:2404A)

808. MILLAR, ANDREW CRAIG. *The Suitability of Using Non-Intellectual Characteristics in the Selection of Honors Students at the University of North Dakota.* Doctor's thesis, University of North Dakota (Grand Forks, N.D.), 1966. (*DA* 27:1629A)

809. MILLER, C. DEAN, AND THOMAS, DONALD L. "Relationships Between Educational and Vocational Interests." *Voc Guid Q* 15:113-8 D '66. * (*PA* 41:12640)

810. NASH, ALLAN N. "Development of an SVIB Key for Selecting Managers." *J Appl Psychol* 50:250-4 Je '66. * (*PA* 40:8269)

811. ORTMEYER, DALE; WELKOWITZ, JOAN; AND COHEN, JACOB. "Interactional Effects of Value System Convergence: Investigation of Patient-Therapist Dyads." Abstract. *Proc 74th Ann Conv Am Psychol Assn* 1:193-4 '66. * (*PA* 41:6013)

812. PENFIELD, ROBERT VERDON. *The Psychological Characteristics of Effective First-Line Managers.* Doctor's thesis, Cornell University (Ithaca, N.Y.), 1966. (*DA* 27:1610B)

813. PETERSON, CHARLES A. *The Prediction of Students' Success in College Accounting.* Doctor's thesis, University of Minnesota (Minneapolis, Minn.), 1966. (*DA* 28:61A)

814. ROSEN, JULIUS. *The Predictive Value of Personal Characteristics Associated With Counselor Competency.* Doctor's thesis, New York University (New York, N.Y.), 1966. (*DA* 27:2408A)

815. SCHLETZER, VERA M. "SVIB as a Predictor of Job Satisfaction." *J Appl Psychol* 50:5-8 F '66. * (*PA* 40:4634)

816. SCHOFIELD, WILLIAM, AND MERWIN, JACK C. "The Use of Scholastic Aptitude, Personality, and Interest Test Data in the Selection of Medical Students." *J Med Ed* 41:502-9 Je '66. *

817. STOLER, NORTON. *The Relationship of Patient Likability and the A-B Psychiatric Resident Types.* Doctor's thesis, University of Wisconsin (Madison, Wis.), 1966. (*DA* 28:1213B)

818. STRICKER, LAWRENCE J. "Compulsivity as a Moderator Variable: A Replication and Extension." *J Appl Psychol* 50:331-5 Ag '66. * (*PA* 40:10639)

819. TAYLOR, RONALD G., AND BONDY, STEPHEN B. "Interest Patterns of Male Trade and Industrial and Collegiate Technical Graduates." *Voc Guid Q* 15:57-60 S '66. *

820. THOMAS, CAROLINE BEDELL. *An Atlas of Figure Drawings: Studies on the Psychological Characteristics of Medical Students, Volume 3.* Baltimore, Md.: Johns Hopkins Press, 1966. Pp. xvi, 922. *

821. THORESEN, CARL E. "Oral Non-Participation in College Students: A Study of Characteristics." *Am Ed-Res J* 3:198-210 My '66. *

822. WAGMAN, MORTON. "Interests and Values of Career and Homemaking Oriented Women." *Personnel & Guid J* 44:794-801 Ap '66. * (*PA* 40:8782)

823. WATLEY, DONIVAN J. "Counselor Variability in Making Accurate Predictions." *J Counsel Psychol* 13:53-62 sp '66. * (*PA* 40:5817)

824. WEISE, INGRID BERGSTROM. *Guidelines for a Supervisory Program Directed to Relating the Mathematics Programs of the Elementary and Junior High School.* Doctor's thesis, University of Maryland (College Park, Md.), 1966. (*DA* 27:3686A)

825. WILLIAMS, PHOEBE A., AND KIRK, BARBARA A. "Vocational Testing: How Valid?" *J Col Placement* 27:24-5+ O-N '66. *

826. YANIS, MARTIN. *"Full-Term Scholastic Survival" Empiric Keying of an Interest Inventory in the Prediction of Academic Performance.* Doctor's thesis, University of Houston (Houston, Tex.), 1966. (*DA* 27:1286B)

827. ABRAHAMS, NORMAN M. "SVIB Key Length: Dissident Data." *J Appl Psychol* 51:266-73 Je '67. * (*PA* 41:10991)

828. ANDERSON, WAYNE. "SVIB Interest Patterns of Agricultural Freshmen." *Voc Guid Q* 16:59-63 S '67. *

829. BENJAMIN, DARRELL RAYMOND. *A Thirty-One Year Longitudinal Study of Engineering Students' Interest Profiles and Career Patterns.* Doctor's thesis, Purdue University (Lafayette, Ind.), 1967. (*DA* 28:4441A)

830. BRANDT, JAMES E., AND HOOD, ALBERT B. "Predictive Validity of the SVIB as Related to Personality Adjustment." Abstract. *Proc 75th Ann Conv Am Psychol Assn* 2:355-6 '67. * (*PA* 41:14264)

831. BRANDT, JAMES EDWARD. *The Effect of Personality Adjustment on the Predictive Validity of the Strong Vocational Interest Blank.* Doctor's thesis, University of Iowa (Iowa City, Iowa), 1967. (*DA* 28:102A)

832. BREIMEIER, KENNETH H. *Relationship Between Various Psychological Measures in Use at Theological Seminaries.* Comments by James E. Dittes. Occasional Papers No. 1. Washington, D.C.: Ministry Studies Board, 1967. Pp. iii, 59. *

833. BROWN, F. G., AND SCOTT, D. A. "Differential Predictability in College Admissions Testing." *J Ed Meas* 4:163-6 f '67. *

834. BRUENING, JOSEPH HERBERT. *Midsouth Department Chairmen: A Study of Backgrounds and Interest Patterns Through the Use of the Strong Vocational Interest Blank.* Doctor's thesis, Mississippi State University (State College, Miss.), 1967. (*DA* 28:1908A)

835. CARSON, ROBERT C. "A and B Therapist 'Types': A Possible Critical Variable in Psychotherapy." *J Nerv & Mental Dis* 144:47-54 Ja '67. * (*PA* 41:11979)

836. CHAFFEE, GLENN ALBERT. *A Study of the Self Concepts, Occupational Personas, and Occupational Stereotypes of Engineering Students.* Doctor's thesis, Michigan State University (East Lansing, Mich.), 1967. (*DA* 28:3968A)

837. CHAPPELL, JOHN SINGLEHURST. *Multivariate Discrimination Among Selected Occupational Groups Utilizing Self Report Data.* Doctor's thesis, Purdue University (Lafayette, Ind.), 1967. (*DA* 28:2620B)

838. COBABE, TERRY ANDERSON. *The Strong Vocational Interest Blank as a Predictor of Success in Engineering.* Doctor's thesis, Purdue University (Lafayette, Ind.), 1967. (*DA* 28:4443A)

839. COHEN, TAMARA ROSE. *A-B Distinction and Therapist Expectancies in a Quasi-Therapeutic Situation.* Doctor's thesis, Syracuse University (Syracuse, N.Y.), 1967. (*DA* 28:1693B)

840. CRANNY, CHARLES JOSEPH. *Factor Analytically Derived Scales for the Strong Vocational Interest Blank.* Doctor's thesis, Iowa State University (Ames, Iowa), 1967. (*DA* 28:1717B)

841. DOLLIVER, ROBERT H. "The High Status SVIB-M Occupations." *Voc Guid Q* 16:118-24 D '67. *

842. DOMINO, GEORGE. *Personality Patterns and Choice of Medical Specialty.* Doctor's thesis, University of California (Berkeley, Calif.), 1967. (*DA* 28:1694B)

843. ELLIOTT, EARL S. *An Analysis of Similarities and Differences of Baccalaureate Degree Engineering Students and Associate Degree Engineering Students at the Pennsylvania State University.* Doctor's thesis, University of Kansas (Lawrence, Kan.), 1967. (*DA* 28:2438A)

844. FORREST, DONALD V. "High School Underachievers in College." *J Ed Res* 61:147-50 D '67. *

845. GARRISON, MARY LOU. *A Correlational Study of Factors Utilized in Counselor Candidate Selection at Western Michigan University.* Master's thesis, Western Michigan University (Kalamazoo, Mich.), 1967. (*Masters Abstracts* 6:125)

846. GAUBINGER, JOSEPH RUDOLPH. *The Relationship of Interpersonal Concerns to Inventoried Interests.* Doctor's thesis, Catholic University of America (Washington, D.C.), 1967. (*DA* 28:2622B)

847. GOLDSCHMID, MARCEL L. "Prediction of College Majors by Personality Tests." *J Counsel Psychol* 14:302-8 Jl '67. * (*PA* 41:12452)

Strong Vocational Interest Blank for Men

848. GREENWALD, ALLEN F. "Adjustment Patterns in First Year Theology Students." *R Relig* 26:483–8 My '67. *
849. GUTHRIE, GEORGE M., AND ZEKTICK, IDA N. "Predicting Performance in the Peace Corps." *J Social Psychol* 71: 11–21 F '67. * (*PA* 41:6319)
850. HARFORD, THOMAS C.; WILLIS, CONSTANCE H.; AND DEABLER, HERDIS L. "Personality Correlates of Masculinity-Femininity." *Psychol Rep* 21:881–4 D '67. * (*PA* 42:7316)
851. HARFORD, THOMAS C.; WILLIS, CONSTANCE H.; AND DEABLER, HERDIS L. "Personality, Values, and Intellectual Correlates of Masculinity-Femininity." *Newsl Res Psychol* 9:17–8 Ag '67. *
852. HEALY, CHARLES CHRISTOPHER. *The Relation of Occupational Choice to the Similarity Between Self and Occupational Ratings.* Doctor's thesis, Columbia University (New York, N.Y.), 1967. (*DA* 28:1683B)
853. HINMAN, SUSAN LEE. *A Predictive Validity Study of Creative Managerial Performance.* Greensboro, N.C.: Creativity Research Institute of The Richardson Foundation, Inc., November 1967. Pp. vi, 124. *
854. KARR, BENJAMIN. *A Proposed Method for Test Interpretation.* Doctor's thesis, University of Cincinnati (Cincinnati, Ohio), 1967. (*DA* 28:3473A)
855. KEMP, DAVID E., AND CARSON, ROBERT C. "AB Therapist-Type Distinction, Evaluation of Patient Characteristics, and Professional Training." Abstract. *Proc 75th Ann Conv Am Psychol Assn* 2:247–8 '67. * (*PA* 41:13719)
856. KROGER, ROLF O. "Effects of Role Demands and Test-Cue Properties Upon Personality Test Performance." *J Consult Psychol* 31:304–12 Je '67. * (*PA* 41:10466)
857. KUNCE, JOSEPH T. "Vocational Interests and Accident Proneness." *J Appl Psychol* 51:223–5 Je '67. * (*PA* 41:10998)
858. KUNCE, JOSEPH T., AND WORLEY, BERT. "Interest Scores and Accidents Among Students." *J Col Stud Personnel* 8:121–3 Mr '67. *
859. LONNER, WALTER JOSEPH. *Cross-Cultural Measurement of Vocational Interests.* Doctor's thesis, University of Minnesota (Minneapolis, Minn.), 1967. (*DA* 28:5226B)
860. MARGOLIS, VICTOR HERBERT. *Kuder-Strong Discrepancy in Relation to Conflict and Congruence of Vocational Preference.* Doctor's thesis, Columbia University (New York, N.Y.), 1967. (*DA* 28:1685B)
861. MARSDEN, RALPH DAVENPORT. *Topological Representation and Vector Analysis of Interest Patterns.* Doctor's thesis, Utah State University (Logan, Utah), 1967. (*DA* 28:4004A)
862. MARTYN, MARGARET M.; SHEEHAN, JOSEPH; AND HADLEY, ROBERT G. "Vocational Interest Patterns of Speech Pathologists and Audiologists." *ASHA* 9:207–13 Je '67. * (*PA* 41:12639)
863. MASIH, LALIT K. "Career Saliency and Its Relation to Certain Needs, Interests, and Job Values." *Personnel & Guid J* 45:653–8 Mr '67. * (*PA* 41:9470)
864. MAZAK, RUTH MARJORIE JOHNSON. *The Relationship of Selected Characteristics of Junior College Pre-Engineering Students to Their Success and Persistence in Upper-Division Professional Education for Engineering.* Doctor's thesis, University of California (Los Angeles, Calif.), 1967. (*DA* 28: 470A)
865. MENDOZA, BUENA FLOR H. *A Normative Analysis of Psychological Test Results of Graduate Students Selecting Counselor Education.* Master's thesis, Western Michigan University (Kalamazoo, Mich.), 1967. (*Masters Abstracts* 6:34)
866. MOFFIE, D. J., AND GOODNER, SUSAN. *A Predictive Validity Study of Creative and Effective Managerial Performance.* Greensboro, N.C.: Creativity Research Institute of The Richardson Foundation, Inc., December 1967. Pp. 80. *
867. MOWBRAY, JEAN K., AND TAYLOR, RAYMOND G. "Validity of Interest Inventories for the Prediction of Success in a School of Nursing." *Nursing Res* 16:78–81 w '67. * (*PA* 42: 4634)
868. OSIPOW, SAMUEL H., AND GOLD, JAMES A. "Factors Related to Inconsistent Career Preferences." *Personnel & Guid J* 46:346–9 D '67. * (*PA* 42:7922)
869. PERRY, DALLIS K. "Vocational Interests and Success of Computer Programmers." *Personnel Psychol* 20:517–24 w '67. * (*PA* 42:7923)
870. PERRY, DALLIS K., AND CANNON, WILLIAM M. "Vocational Interests of Computer Programmers." *J Appl Psychol* 51:28–34 F '67. * (*PA* 41:5103)
871. PETRIK, NORMAN D. "Socio-Economic Status, Vocational Interests, and Persistence in Selected College Curricula." *Voc Guid Q* 16:39–44 S '67. *
872. ROSEN, JULIUS. "Multiple-Regression Analysis of Counselor Characteristics and Competencies." *Psychol Rep* 20:1003–8 Je '67. * (*PA* 41:12734)
873. ROSSMANN, JACK E.; LIPS, ORVILLE; AND CAMPBELL, DAVID P. "Vocational Interests of Sociologists." *J Counsel Psychol* 14:497–502 N '67. * (*PA* 42:3136)
874. ROYS, KEITH B., SR. "Vocational Interests of Community Recreation Administrators Using the SVIB." *J Appl Psychol* 51:539–43 D '67. * (*PA* 42:3022)
875. SCHELLER, THOMAS GEORGE. *A Study of the Academic Aptitude, Occupations, and Occupational Satisfaction of a Sample of Men With Low Intensity Occupational Interests.* Doctor's thesis,

University of Minnesota (Minneapolis, Minn.), 1967. (*DA* 28:3040A)
876. SCHISSEL, ROBERT FRANCES. *Differential Interest Characteristics of Career Women.* Doctor's thesis, University of Nebraska (Lincoln, Neb.), 1967. (*DA* 28:2103A)
877. SIESS, THOMAS F., AND JACKSON, DOUGLAS N. "A Personological Approach to the Interpretation of Vocational Interests." Abstract. *Proc 75th Ann Conv Am Psychol Assn* 2:353–4 '67. * (*PA* 41:14261)
878. SINAY, RUTH DORIS. *Creative Aptitude Patterns of College Honors Students.* Doctor's thesis, University of Southern California (Los Angeles, Calif.), 1967. (*DA* 28:5212B)
879. TAYLOR, RONALD G.; LEZOTTE, LAWRENCE; AND BONDY, STEPHEN B. "Interest Patterns of Successful and Nonsuccessful Male Collegiate Technical Students." *J Ed Res* 60: 401–2 My–Je '67. *
880. THORNDIKE, ROBERT M.; WEISS, DAVID J.; AND DAWIS, RENE V. "Multiple Relationships Between Measured Vocational Interests and Measured Vocational Needs." Abstract. *Proc 75th Ann Conv Am Psychol Assn* 2:351–2 '67. * (*PA* 41:14262)
881. TORONTO, ROBERT SHARP. *The Strong Vocational Interest Blank and a Biographical Inventory as Predictors of Creativity and Academic Achievement in Engineering Students.* Master's thesis, University of Utah (Salt Lake City, Utah), 1967.
882. VOGEL, BRUCE S., AND SCHELL, ROBERT E. "Vocational Interest Patterns in Late Maturity and Retirement." *J Gerontol* 23:66–70 O '67. *
883. WALL, HARVEY W.; OSIPOW, SAMUEL H.; AND ASHBY, JEFFERSON D. "SVIB Scores, Occupational Choices, and Holland's Personality Types." *Voc Guid Q* 15:201–5 Mr '67. * (*PA* 42:9546)
884. WEISE, PHILLIP. *Sex-Role Identity, Self-Concept, and Vocational Interests of Adolescent Hemophiliacs.* Doctor's thesis, University of Southern California (Los Angeles, Calif.), 1967. (*DA* 28:3888B)
885. WELKOWITZ, JOAN; COHEN, JACOB; AND ORTMEYER, DALE. "Value System Similarity: Investigation of Patient-Therapist Dyads." *J Consult Psychol* 31:48–55 F '67. * (*PA* 41:4676)
886. WELKOWITZ, JOAN; ORTMEYER, DALE H.; AND COHEN, JACOB. "A Development of Value Profile Types of Psychotherapists." Abstract. *Proc 75th Ann Conv Am Psychol Assn* 2:249–50 '67. * (*PA* 41:13659)
887. WELSCH, LAWRENCE A. *The Supervisor's Employee Appraisal Heuristic: The Contribution of Selected Measures of Employee Aptitude, Intelligence and Personality.* Doctor's thesis, University of Pittsburgh (Pittsburgh, Pa.), 1967. (*DA* 28:4321A)
888. WELSH, GEORGE S. "Verbal Interests and Intelligence: Comparison of Strong VIB, Terman CMT, and D-48 Scores of Gifted Adolescents." *Ed & Psychol Meas* 27:349–52 su '67. * (*PA* 41:13633)
889. WHITTAKER, DAVID NEIL EATON. *Psychological Characteristics of Alienated, Nonconformist, College-Age Youth as Indicated by AVL, OPI, ACL and SVIB-M/W Group Profiles.* Doctor's thesis, University of California (Berkeley, Calif.), 1967. (*DA* 28:3055B)
890. WILSON, ROBERT NICHOLI. *A Comparison of Similar Scales on the Strong Vocational Interest Blank and the Kuder Occupational Interest Survey, Form DD.* Master's thesis, Kansas State University (Manhattan, Kan.), 1967.
891. ZAHN, JANE C. "Some Characteristics of Successful and Less Successful Overseas Community Development Advisers." *Adult Ed* 18:15–23 f '67. *
892. ZYTOWSKI, DONALD G. "Internal-External Control of Reinforcement and the Strong Vocational Interest Blank." *J Counsel Psychol* 14:177–9 Mr '67. * (*PA* 41:7353)
893. ZYTOWSKI, DONALD G., AND WALSH, JAMES A. "Response Tendencies in the SVIB: The Popular, the Rare, and the Socially Desirable." *J Appl Psychol* 51:491–6 D '67. * (*PA* 42:2594)
894. ANDERSON, WAYNE. "Predicting Graduation From a School of Nursing." *Voc Guid Q* 16:295–300 Je '68. *
895. APOSTAL, ROBERT A. "Interests of Engineering Graduates According to Undergraduate Curricula." *Personnel & Guid J* 46:909–13 My '68. *
896. ATKINSON, GILBERT, AND LUNNEBORG, CLIFFORD E. "Comparison of Oblique and Orthogonal Simple Structure Solutions for Personality and Interest Factors." *Multiv Behav Res* 3:21–35 Ja '68. * (*PA* 42:11349)
897. BAGGALEY, ANDREW R. "Congruent Validity of the Milwaukee Academic Interest Inventory." *Ed & Psychol Meas* 28:1207–11 w '68. * (*PA* 44:6786)
898. BAROCAS, RALPH, AND CHRISTENSEN, DONALD. "Impression Management, Fakeability, and Academic Performance." *J Counsel Psychol* 15:569–71 N '68. * (*PA* 43:1494)
899. BAUER, ROGER; MEHRENS, WILLIAM A.; AND VINSONHALER, JOHN F. "Predicting Performance in a Computer Programming Course." *Ed & Psychol Meas* 28:1159–64 w '68. * (*PA* 44:7333)
900. BERDIE, RALPH F., AND CAMPBELL, DAVID P. Chap II, "Measurement of Interest," pp. 367–92. In *Handbook of Measurement and Assessment in Behavioral Sciences.* Edited by

Strong Vocational Interest Blank for Men

Dean K. Whitla. Reading, Mass.: Addison-Wesley Publishing Co., Inc., 1968. Pp. xx, 508. *

901. BOHN, MARTIN J., JR. "Vocational Indecision and Interest Development in College Freshmen." *J Col Stud Personnel* 9:393–6 N '68. *

902. BRANDT, JAMES E., AND HOOD, ALBERT B. "Effect of Personality Adjustment on the Predictive Validity of the Strong Vocational Interest Blank." *J Counsel Psychol* 15:547–51 N '68. * (*PA* 43:126)

903. BROWN, THOMAS E. "Interest Satisfaction in the Minister's Search for Personal Integration." *Ministry Studies* 2:25–9 N '68. *

904. BRUNO, FRANK BARTOLO. *Life Values, Manifest Needs, and Vocational Interests as Factors Influencing Professional Career Satisfaction Among Teachers of Emotionally Disturbed Children.* Doctor's thesis, Wayne State University (Detroit, Mich.), 1968. (*DAI* 31:3999A)

905. BRYAN, WILLIAM EDWARD. *A Comparison of the Career Orientation of College Women in Contrasting Majors.* Doctor's thesis, Wayne State University (Detroit, Mich.), 1968. (*DAI* 30:980A)

906. CAMPBELL, DAVID P. "Changing Patterns of Interests Within the American Society." *Meas & Eval Guid* 1:36–49 sp '68. * (*PA* 44:7378)

907. CAMPBELL, DAVID P. Chap. 6, "The Strong Vocational Interest Blank: 1927–1967," pp. 105–30. In *Advances in Psychological Assessment, Vol. 1.* Edited by Paul McReynolds. Palo Alto, Calif.: Science & Behavior Books, Inc., 1968. Pp. xiii, 336. *

908. CAMPBELL, DAVID P.; BORGEN, FRED H.; EASTES, SUZANNE H.; JOHANSSON, CHARLES B.; AND PETERSON, ROBERT A. "A Set of Basic Interest Scales for the Strong Vocational Interest Blank for Men." *J Appl Psychol Monogr* 52(6, pt 2): 1–54 D '68. * (*PA* 43:3154)

909. CAMPBELL, DAVID P.; STEVENS, JOSEPH H.; UHLENHUTH, E. H.; AND JOHANSSON, CHARLES B. "An Extension of the Whitehorn-Betz A-B Scale." *J Nerv & Mental Dis* 146: 417–21 My '68. * (*PA* 42:15514)

910. CLEMANS, WILLIAM V. "Interest Measurement and the Concept of Ipsativity." *Meas & Eval Guid* 1:50–5 sp '68. * (*PA* 44:7280)

911. COTTLE, WILLIAM C. *Interest and Personality Inventories,* pp. 30–55. Guidance Monograph Series, Series 3, Testing, [No. 6]. Boston, Mass.: Houghton Mifflin Co., 1968. Pp. xi, 116. *

912. DAVIS, CLIFFORD E., AND WAGNER, PAULA D. *Evaluating and Counseling Prospective Church Workers: Supplement 1, Strong Vocational Interest Blank.* New York: Board of Christian Education, 1960. Pp. 19. *

913. DAVIS, SAMUEL EUGENE. *Predicting Probable Failure in College-Level Music Theory Courses.* Doctor's thesis, University of Montana (Missoula, Mont.), 1968. (*DAI* 30:354A)

914. DOLLIVER, ROBERT H. "Likes, Dislikes, and SVIB Scoring." *Meas & Eval Guid* 1:73–80 sp '68. * (*PA* 44:7282)

915. DOLLIVER, ROBERT H., AND NEAL, ROBERT G. "The SVIB-M: The Influence of an L-I-D Response Style." *Meas & Eval Guid* 1:202–4+ f '68. *

916. EKBLAD, ROBERT LINDY. *Effects of Client Expectations and Preferences for Counselor Behavior on Counseling Outcomes.* Doctor's thesis, University of California (Berkeley, Calif.), 1968. (*DA* 29:4279A)

917. ELDER, GLEN H., JR. "Achievement Motivation and Intelligence in Occupational Mobility: A Longitudinal Analysis." *Sociometry* 31:327–54 D '68. *

918. ELDER, GLEN H., JR. "Occupational Level, Achievement Motivation, and Social Mobility: A Longitudinal Analysis." *J Counsel Psychol* 15:1–7 Ja '68. * (*PA* 42:6186)

919. FAUNCE, PATRICIA SPENCER. "Personality Characteristics and Vocational Interests Related to the College Persistence of Academically Gifted Women." *J Counsel Psychol* 15:31–40 Ja '68. * (*PA* 42:6683)

920. FOSSHAGE, JAMES LEWIS. *Effect of Counselor-Client Interest Similarity on Counseling Relationship and Outcome.* Doctor's thesis, Columbia University (New York, N.Y.), 1968. (*DA* 29:3481B)

921. FREEBURN, PAUL PRICE. *A Comparison of Selected Characteristics of Men Who Stay in Teaching, Men Who Enter Teaching Then Withdraw, and Men Who Were Prepared for but Never Entered Teaching.* Doctor's thesis, University of South Dakota (Vermillion, S.D.), 1968. (*DA* 29:2433A)

922. GRANT, JOSEPH N. *The Appropriateness of the Science Curriculum in Nigerian Secondary Schools for the Country's Scientific Manpower Needs.* Doctor's thesis, University of Connecticut (Storrs, Conn.), 1968. (*DA* 29:4226A)

923. HARMON, LENORE W. "Optimum Criterion Group Size in Interest Measurement." *Meas & Eval Guid* 1:65–72 sp '68. * (*PA* 44:7287)

924. HARMON, LENORE W., AND CAMPBELL, DAVID P. "Use of Interest Inventories With Nonprofessional Women: Stewardesses Versus Dental Assistants." *J Counsel Psychol* 15:17–22 Ja '68. * (*PA* 42:6189)

925. HEALY, CHARLES C. "Relation of Occupational Choice to the Similarity Between Self-Ratings and Occupational Ratings." *J Counsel Psychol* 15:317–23 Jl '68. * (*PA* 42:16183)

926. HELMICK, KENNETH DALE. *A Comparative Study of*

Personality Characteristics of Elementary and Secondary Education Majors: Using the California Psychological Inventory and the Strong Vocational Interest Blank. Doctor's thesis, Oklahoma State University (Stillwater, Okla.), 1968. (*DAI* 30:1048A)

927. HELSON, RAVENNA. "Generality of Sex Differences in Creative Style." *J Personality* 36:33–48 Mr '68. *

928. HERSHENSON, DAVID B., AND SLOAN, CHARLES M. "Recent Students Using the SVIB With the Physically, Emotionally, and Culturally Handicapped." *Rehabil Counsel B* 12:23–8 S '68. *

929. HESCH, GEORGE PETER. *A Study of the Relationship Between Counselor Trainee Attitudes Towards Adolescents and Preferences for Client Characteristics and Counseling Effectiveness.* Doctor's thesis, Purdue University (Lafayette, Ind.), 1968. (*DA* 29:2523A)

930. JAMES, NEWTON E., AND BRONSON, LOUISE. "The OAIS—An Evaluation." *J Col Stud Personnel* 9:120–5 Mr '68. *

931. JOHNSON, JAMES C., AND DUNNETTE, MARVIN D. "Validity and Test-Retest Stability of the Nash Managerial Effectiveness Scale on the Revised Form of the Strong Vocational Interest Blank." *Personnel Psychol* 21:283–93 au '68. * (*PA* 43:4585)

932. JOSELYN, EDWIN GARY. *The Relationship of Selected Variables to the Stability of Measured Vocational Interest of High School Seniors.* Doctor's thesis, University of Minnesota (Minneapolis, Minn.), 1968. (*DA* 29:2526A)

933. KAHN, EDWIN MORRIS. *Socioeconomic Variables, Paternal Identification and Sons' Interests.* Doctor's thesis, Columbia University (New York, N.Y.), 1968. (*DA* 29:757B)

934. KELLOGG, RICHARD L. "The Strong Vocational Interest Blank as a Differential Predictor of Engineering Grades." *Ed & Psychol Meas* 28:1213–7 w '68. * (*PA* 44:7335)

935. KENWORTHY, JOY ANNE. *Personality Characteristics Associated With Effectiveness in Psychotherapy.* Doctor's thesis, Iowa State University (Ames, Iowa), 1968. (*DA* 29:3488B)

936. KOHLAN, RICHARD G. "Relationships Between Inventoried Interests and Inventoried Needs." *Personnel & Guid J* 46:592–8 F '68. * (*PA* 42:12126)

937. KROGER, ROLF O. "Effects of Implicit and Explicit Task Cues Upon Personality Test Performance." *J Consult & Clin Psychol* 32:498 Ag '68. * (*PA* 42:17201)

938. LEPAK, ROY C. "A Clergy Scale for the Revised Strong Vocational Interest Blank." *Ministry Studies* 2:6–24 N '68. *

939. LEPAK, ROY C. "Development of a 'Catholic Priest' Scale on the Strong Vocational Interest Blank." *Nat Cath Guid Conf J* 12:261–8 su '68. * (*PA* 44:3635)

940. LONNER, WALTER J. "The SVIB Visits German, Austrian, and Swiss Psychologists." *Am Psychologist* 23:164–79 Mr '68. * (*PA* 42:9723)

941. MARSHALL, JON C., AND MOWRER, GEORGE E. "Parents' Perceptions of Their Son's Interests." *Meas & Eval Guid* 1:190–201 f '68. * (*PA* 44:11271)

942. MARSHALL, JON C., AND MOWRER, GEORGE E. "Validity of Parents' Perceptions of Their Son's Interests." *J Counsel Psychol* 15:334–7 Jl '68. * (*PA* 42:16104)

943. MEADOWS, MARK E., AND OELKE, MERRITT C. "Characteristics of Clients and Non-Clients." *J Col Stud Personnel* 9:153–7 My '68. *

944. MEHRENS, WILLIAM A.; VINSONHALER, JOHN F.; AND BAUER, ROGER. "Predicting Computer Programming Performance." Abstract. *AERA Paper Abstr* 1968:31–2 '68. *

945. MENDOZA, BUENA FLOR H. *Predicting Counselor Effectiveness: A Multiple Regression Approach.* Doctor's thesis, Western Michigan University (Kalamazoo, Mich.), 1968. (*DAI* 30:552A)

946. MILLER, LELAND DALE. *A Research Study of the Interests of Occupational Therapists as Reflected on the Strong Vocational Interest Blank.* Doctor's thesis, University of Missouri (Columbia, Mo.), 1968. (*DA* 29:2964A)

947. MUNDAY, LEO A.; BRASKAMP, LARRY A.; AND BRANDT, JAMES E. "The Meaning of Unpatterned Vocational Interests." *Personnel & Guid J* 47:249–56 N '68. * (*PA* 43:6022)

948. OSIPOW, SAMUEL H., AND GOLD, JAMES A. "Personal Adjustment and Career Development." *J Counsel Psychol* 15: 439–43 S '68. * (*PA* 42:19334)

949. PASEWARK, R. A., AND SAWYER, R. N. "Changes in Interests Associated With an Undergraduate Summer Work-Study Program in Mental Health." *J Ed Res* 62:58–9 O '68. *

950. PERRY, DALLIS K., AND CANNON, WILLIAM M. "Vocational Interests of Female Computer Programmers." *J Appl Psychol* 52:31–5 F '68. * (*PA* 42:6194)

951. PRIEBE, DONALD WALTER. *An Interest Inventory of Minnesota Farmers.* Doctor's thesis, University of Minnesota (Minneapolis, Minn.), 1968. (*DA* 29:4293A)

952. RITCHIE, CLINTON MCCAY. *Vocational Interests as a Factor in the Academic Achievement of Male Students in a Teacher Education Institution.* Doctor's thesis, Rutgers—The State University (New Brunswick, N.J.), 1968. (*DA* 29: 3026A)

953. ROBERTS, BRUCE BEN. *The Leader, Group, and Task Variables of Leader Selection in College.* Doctor's thesis, Claremont Graduate School (Claremont, Calif.), 1968. (*DA* 29: 2360A)

Strong Vocational Interest Blank for Men

954. ROHLF, RICHARD JOHN. *A Higher-Order Alpha Factor Analysis of Interest, Personality, and Ability Variables, Including an Evaluation of the Effect of Scale Interdependency.* Doctor's thesis, University of Kansas (Lawrence, Kan.), 1968. *(DA* 29:1758A)

955. SALVA, DAVID MATTHEW. *Self-Actualization and Its Relationship to Intensity of Vocational Interests of Male College Freshmen.* Doctor's thesis, University of Kansas (Lawrence, Kan.), 1968. *(DAI* 30:837B)

956. SCHISSEL, ROBERT F. "Development of a Career-Orientation Scale for Women." *J Counsel Psychol* 15:257–62 My '68. * *(PA* 42:12865)

957. SHARDLOW, GEORGE WILLIAM. *The Whitehorn-Betz A-B Scale as Related to Differential Motivational Effectiveness and Interpersonal Perception.* Doctor's thesis, University of Minnesota (Minneapolis, Minn.), 1968. *(DA* 29:1181B)

958. THORNDIKE, ROBERT M.; WEISS, DAVID J.; AND DAWIS, RENÉ V. "Canonical Correlation of Vocational Interests and Vocational Needs." *J Counsel Psychol* 15:101–6 Mr '68. * *(PA* 42:9544)

959. TRENT, JAMES W., AND MEDSKER, LELAND L. *Beyond High School: A Psychosociological Study of 10,000 High School Graduates.* San Francisco, Calif.: Jossey-Bass Inc., Publishers, 1968. Pp. xxv, 333. *

960. WERTS, CHARLES E. "Paternal Influence on Career Choice." *J Counsel Psychol* 15:48–52 Ja '68. * *(PA* 42:6195)

961. WILLIAMS, PHOEBE A.; KIRK, BARBARA A.; AND FRANK, AUSTIN C. "New Men's SVIB: A Comparison With the Old." *J Counsel Psychol* 15:287–94 My '68. * *(PA* 42:12867)

962. WILSON, ROBERT N., AND KAISER, HERBERT E. "A Comparison of Similar Scales on the SVIB and the Kuder, Form DD." *J Counsel Psychol* 15:468–70 S '68. * *(PA* 42:19287)

963. ZYTOWSKI, DONALD G. "Relationships of Equivalent Scales on Three Interest Inventories." *Personnel & Guid J* 47:44–9 S '68. * *(PA* 43:5936)

964. *Predicting Job Success of MBA Graduates: Implications of a Study of Stanford MBA Graduates After Five Years.* Admission Test for Graduate Study in Business, Brief No. 1. Princeton, N.J.: Educational Testing Service, April 1969. Pp. 23. *

965. ABRAHAMS, N. M.; NEUMANN, IDELL; AND GITHENS, W. H. "Real-Life Versus Simulated Motivation to Fake the SVIB." Abstract. *Proc 77th Ann Conv Am Psychol Assn* 4(2):685–6 '69. * *(PA* 44:1251)

966. AGEE, KATHLEEN MACHREE. *Experienced Counselors: Attitude and Interest Patterns by Type of Work Setting.* Doctor's thesis, University of Alabama (University, Ala.), 1969. *(DAI* 30:3712A)

967. ALDAG, JEAN C. KERZ. *Male Nurse Interest and Personality Characteristics.* Doctor's thesis, Washington University (St. Louis, Mo.), 1969. *(DAI* 30:5672B)

968. ANDERSON, GILBERT WERNER. *The Characteristics of Voluntary and Involuntary Counselees at Thorton Junior College.* Doctor's thesis, University of Arizona (Tucson, Ariz.), 1969. *(DAI* 30:3713A)

969. BAZIK, ANNA MARIE. *Characteristics of Junior College Male Students Who Seek Counseling Services.* Doctor's thesis, Northwestern University (Evanston, Ill.), 1969. *(DAI* 30:2793A)

970. BODDEN, JACK LEO. *Cognitive Complexity as a Factor in Appropriate Vocational Choice.* Doctor's thesis, Ohio State University (Columbus, Ohio), 1969. *(DAI* 30:3380B)

971. BOYD, ROBERT EMMETT. *Counselor Interests as a Factor in Counselor Effectiveness.* Doctor's thesis, University of Minnesota (Minneapolis, Minn.), 1969. *(DAI* 30:4785B)

972. BREDEMEIER, RICHARD ALAN. *An Exploration of Factors Associated With Students Who Are Successful Following Their Readmission to Purdue University.* Doctor's thesis, Purdue University (Lafayette, Ind.), 1969. *(DAI* 30:3716A)

973. BUCK, CHARLES WARREN. *Crystallization of Vocational Interests as a Function of Exploratory Experience During the College Years.* Doctor's thesis, Columbia University (New York, N.Y.), 1969. *(DAI* 30:4823A)

974. CAMPBELL, DAVID P. "Comment on '3.5 to 1' on the Strong Vocational Interest Blank." *J Counsel Psychol* 16(2):175–6 Mr '69. * *(PA* 43:10466)

975. CAMPBELL, DAVID P. "SVIB Managerial Orientation Scores of Outstanding Men." *Personnel Psychol* 22(1):41–4 sp '69. * *(PA* 43:14917)

976. CAMPBELL, DAVID P. "The Vocational Interests of Dartmouth College Freshmen: 1947–67." *Personnel & Guid J* 47(6):521–30 F '69. * *(PA* 43:11954)

977. CARLSON, RAE. "Rorschach Prediction of Success in Clinical Training: A Second Look." *J Consult & Clin Psychol* 33(6):699–704 D '69. * *(PA* 44:3697)

978. CHRISTENSON, JEFFRY MILTON. *A Study of the Differences Between Seekers and Non-Seekers at a College Counseling Center.* Doctor's thesis, University of South Dakota (Vermillion, S.D.), 1969. *(DAI* 30:2326A)

979. CLEMENS, BRYAN TILLMAN. *Discriminant Function Analysis of Inventoried Interests Among Selected Engineering Groups.* Doctor's thesis, Purdue University (Lafayette, Ind.), 1969. *(DAI* 30:1394A)

980. DENISON, WALTER MARSHALL. *A Study of Three Interest Inventories Currently in Use at Central Virginia Community College.* Doctor's thesis, University of Virginia (Charlottesville, Va.), 1969. *(DAI* 31:996A)

981. DiGIORGIO, ANTHONY JOSEPH. *Discriminant Function Analysis of Measured Characteristics Among Committed Career Groups With Requisite Graduate Training.* Doctor's thesis, Purdue University (Lafayette, Ind.), 1969. *(DAI* 30:4769A)

982. DOLLIVER, ROBERT H. "Strong Vocational Interest Blank Versus Expressed Vocational Interests: A Review." *Psychol B* 72(2):95–107 Ag '69. * *(PA* 43:16491)

983. DOLLIVER, ROBERT H. "'3.5 to 1' on the Strong Vocational Interest Blank as a Pseudo-Event." *J Counsel Psychol* 16(2):172–4 Mr '69. * *(PA* 43:10467) For comments, see 975. *

984. DUBLIN, JAMES E.; ELTON, CHARLES F.; AND BERZINS, JURIS I. "Some Personality and Aptitudinal Correlates of the 'A-B' Therapist Scale." *J Consult & Clin Psychol* 33(6):739–45 D '69. * *(PA* 44:3595)

985. EIDE, LYLE JACOB. *Test Self-Estimates as Related to Needs, Vocational Interests, Ability, Achievement and Persistence of University Freshman Males.* Doctor's thesis, University of North Dakota (Grand Forks, N.D.), 1969. *(DAI* 30:1818A)

986. ENGEN, HAROLD B., AND MILLER, LEONARD A. "The Development of an SVIB Interest Scale for School Counselors." *Personnel & Guid J* 47(8):767–72 Ap '69. * *(PA* 43:14851)

987. FOREMAN, MILTON E., AND JAMES, LEONARD E. "Vocational Relevance and Estimated and Measured Test Scores." *J Counsel Psychol* 16(6):547–50 N '69. * *(PA* 44:4197)

988. FRANK, AUSTIN C., AND KIRK, BARBARA A. "Characteristics and Attributes of Prospective City and Regional Planners." *J Col Stud Personnel* 10(4):317–23 S '69. *

989. FULLERTON, JOHN REYNOLDS. *A Factor Analytic Study of Rehabilitation Role Perceptions Reported by Undergraduate Rehabilitation Students.* Doctor's thesis, Pennsylvania State University (University Park, Pa.), 1969. *(DAI* 31:607A)

990. GAHLHOFF, PETER ERIC. *An Analysis of the Personal and Situational Factors Influencing School Counselors' Career Patterns.* Doctor's thesis, Purdue University (Lafayette, Ind.), 1969. *(DAI* 30:4771A)

991. GALINSKY, M. DAVID, AND FAST, IRENE. "Use of the SVIB With Identity Problems." *J Col Stud Personnel* 10(3):177–81 My '69. *

992. GEHLHAUSEN, PAUL EDWARD. *An Exploration of Selected Factors Associated With Success of Beginning Engineering Students at Tri-State College.* Doctor's thesis, Purdue University (Lafayette, Ind.), 1969. *(DAI* 30:3724A)

993. GOLISCH, JOHN EDWARD WILLIAM. *Psychological Variables on Missouri Synod Lutheran Clergy.* Doctor's thesis, University of Minnesota (Minneapolis, Minn.), 1969. *(DAI* 30:1396A)

994. GORDON, JAMES HALE. *A Comparison of Selected Characteristics of Students Entering Five Campuses of Ohio University.* Doctor's thesis, Ohio University (Athens, Ohio), 1969. *(DAI* 30:2332A)

995. GRACE, EVELYN RANDALL. *The Relationship Between Personality Traits and Vocational Interests in the Choice of Field of Study of Selected Junior College Students in Business Administration.* Doctor's thesis, North Texas State University (Denton, Tex.), 1969. *(DAI* 30:4827A)

996. HAAG, RICHARD A., AND DAVID, KENNETH H. "The Latent Dimensionality of Several Measures of Creativity." *J General Psychol* 80(2):279–85 Ap '69. * *(PA* 43:11328)

997. HALL, WALLACE B., AND MacKINNON, DONALD W. "Personality Inventory Correlates of Creativity Among Architects." *J Appl Psychol* 53(4):322–6 Ag '69. * *(PA* 43:15815)

998. HARMON, LENORE W. "SVIB Patterning: A Comparison of Clients and Non-Clients." *Meas & Eval Guid* 2(1):32–6 sp '69. * *(PA* 44:13460)

999. HARRELL, THOMAS W. "The Personality of High Earning MBA's in Big Business." *Personnel Psychol* 22(4):457–62 w '69. * *(PA* 44:13525)

1000. HARRINGTON, CHARLES. "Forecasting College Performance From Biographical Data." *J Col Stud Personnel* 10(3):156–60 My '69. *

1001. HEILBRUN, ALFRED B., JR. "Parental Identification and the Patterning of Vocational Interests in College Males and Females." *J Counsel Psychol* 16(4):342–7 Jl '69. * *(PA* 43:14837)

1002. HERSCH, PAUL D.; KULIK, JAMES A.; AND SCHEIBE, KARL E. "Personal Characteristics of College Volunteers in Mental Hospitals." *J Consult & Clin Psychol* 33(1):30–4 F '69. * *(PA* 43:11408)

1003. HULL, JOSHUA SHELTON, III. *An Investigation of Identification of Male College Students With Their Fathers as a Variable Influencing Vocational Interests and Vocational Counseling.* Doctor's thesis, Michigan State University (East Lansing, Mich.), 1969. *(DAI* 30:4775A)

1004. IRVIN, FLOYD S. "The Relationship Between Manifest Anxiety and Measures of Aptitude, Achievement, and Interest." *Ed & Psychol Meas* 29(4):957–61 w '69. *

1005. ISABELLE, LAURENT A., AND DICK, WILLIAM. "Clarity of Self-Concepts in the Vocational Development of Male Liberal Arts Students (An Abstract)." *Can Psychologist* 10(1):20–31 Ja–F '69. * *(PA* 43:16396)

Strong Vocational Interest Blank for Men

1006. JOHANSSON, CHARLES BERTHIL. *Psychometric Characteristics of the Inventory of Interests.* Doctor's thesis, University of Minnesota (Minneapolis, Minn.), 1969. (*DAI* 31:1519B)

1007. JOHNSON, RICHARD W. "Effectiveness of SVIB Academic Interest Scales in Predicting College Achievement." *J Appl Psychol* 53(4):309–16 Ag '69. * (*PA* 43:16452)

1008. KATZ, MARTIN. "Interests and Values: A Comment." *J Counsel Psychol* 16(5):460–2 S '69. * (*PA* 43:18042)

1009. KISH, GEORGE B., AND DONNENWERTH, GREGORY V. "Business and Professional SVIB Interest Patterns Related to Sensation-Seeking in College Males." *Newsl Res Psychol* 11(1): 18–9 F '69. *

1010. KISH, GEORGE B., AND DONNENWERTH, GREGORY V. "Interests and Stimulus Seeking." *J Counsel Psychol* 16(6): 551–6 N '69. * (*PA* 44:4260)

1011. KOHLER, ADAM THOMAS. *Some Possible Effects of Leader-Member, Similarity-Dissimilarity in the Counseling Technique of Group Psychoevaluation.* Doctor's thesis, University of California (Los Angeles, Calif.), 1969. (*DAI* 30:5240B)

1012. KRIENKE, JOHN WALTER. *Cognitive Differentiation and Occupational—Profile Differentiation on the Strong Vocational Interest Blank.* Doctor's thesis, University of Florida (Gainesville, Fla.), 1969. (*DAI* 31:2961B)

1013. KUNCE, JOSEPH T. "Vocational Interest, Disability, and Rehabilitation." *Rehabil Counsel B* 12(4):204–10 Je '69. *

1014. KUNCE, JOSEPH T., AND CALLIS, ROBERT. "Vocational Interest and Personality." *Voc Guid Q* 18(1):34–40 S '69. *

1015. LEFKOWITZ, DAVID MICHAEL. *A Comparison of the SVIB and Kuder DD Scoring Procedures.* Doctor's thesis, University of Kansas (Lawrence, Kan.), 1969. (*DAI* 31:155A)

1016. LEIGH, KENT B. *A Validation and Investigation of the Academic Scale of the Strong Vocational Interest Blank.* Master's thesis, University of Utah (Salt Lake City, Utah), 1969.

1017. LINDSAY, CARL A., AND ALTHOUSE, RICHARD. "Comparative Validities of the Strong Vocational Interest Blank Academic Achievement Scale and the College Student Questionnaire Motivation for Grades Scale." *Ed & Psychol Meas* 29(2): 489–93 su '69. * (*PA* 44:17506)

1018. LIU, PHYLLIS YUNG-HOU. "Cluster Analysis of SVIB Profile Patterns of Adult Women and College Men." *Psychol & Ed* 3:1–9 D '69. *

1019. MILLER, PHYLLIS GENE. *Occupational Patterns of a Vocationally Counseled and a Nonvocationally Counseled Group of Washington State University Graduates.* Doctor's thesis, Washington State University (Pullman, Wash.), 1969. (*DAI* 30:4228A)

1020. NIELSON, CHARLES L. *A Study of the Relation Between Selected Academic Factors and Performance on the I-E Scale.* Doctor's thesis, University of North Dakota (Grand Forks, N.D.), 1969. (*DAI* 30:1402A)

1021. O'TOOLE, JAMES J. *Vocational Interests of Teaching Brothers in the United States as Measured by the 1966 Revision of the Strong Vocational Interest Blank.* Doctor's thesis, St. John's University (Jamaica, N.Y.), 1969. (*DAI* 30:3330A)

1022. PENNINGTON, ALLAN L., AND PETERSON, ROBERT A. "Interest Patterns and Product Preferences: An Exploratory Analysis." *J Marketing Res* 6(3):284–90 Ag '69. *

1023. PETERSON, ROBERT A., AND PENNINGTON, ALLAN L. "SVIB Interests and Product Preferences." *J Appl Psychol* 53(4):304–8 Ag '69. * (*PA* 44:16518)

1024. PETRIK, NORMAN D. "Test-Retest Reliability of the SVIB and Differing Curricular Experience." Abstract. *Proc 77th Ann Conv Am Psychol Assn* 4(2):687–8 '69. * (*PA* 44: 1257)

1025. PRIEBE, DONALD W. "New Occupational Interest Scale for Farmers." *Ag Ed Mag* 42(2):44 Ag '69. *

1026. REITZ, WILLARD E., AND McDOUGAL, LINDSAY. "Interest Items as Positive and Negative Reinforcements: Effects of Social Desirability and Extremity of Endorsement." *Psychon Sci* 17(2):97–8 O 25 '69. * (*PA* 44:3562)

1027. RHODE, JOHN GRANT. *The Vocational Interests of Business Administration Professors.* Doctor's thesis, University of Minnesota (Minneapolis, Minn.), 1969. (*DAI* 31:872A)

1028. ROBERTS, RALPH KENT. *A Study of Changes in Vocational Interest Inventory Patterns and Scores After Two Years for Male College Students Initially Having No Primary Interest Patterns.* Doctor's thesis, University of North Dakota (Grand Forks, N.D.), 1969. (*DAI* 31:162A)

1029. ROHILA, PRITAM KUMAR. *Multivariate Relationships Between Personality and Vocational Interests.* Doctor's thesis, University of Oregon (Eugene, Ore.), 1969. (*DAI* 31:1022A)

1030. ROSSMANN, JACK E., AND BENTLEY, JOSEPH C. "Vocational Interests of Future College Teachers." *Voc Guid Q* 17(3):206–11 Mr '69. *

1031. RUDLOFF, JOSEPH S. "Descriptive Profile of Teachers of Exceptional and Non-Exceptional Children With Implications for Recruitment." *J Ed Res* 63(3):130–5 N '69. *

1032. SPIEGEL, JOSEPH A. *Test Score Performance on Irish and Italian College Freshmen.* Doctor's thesis, Rutgers—The State University (New Brunswick, N.J.), 1969. (*DAI* 30: 3802A)

1033. TAYLOR, RONALD G., AND CAMPBELL, DAVID P. "A Comparison of the SVIB Basic Interest Scales With the Regular Occupational Scales." *Personnel & Guid J* 47(5):450–5 Ja '69. *

1034. THOMAS, SAMUEL DAVID. *A Study of Environmental Variables in the War Orphan Home and Their Effects on Occupational Interest Patterns and College Success.* Doctor's thesis, University of Southern Mississippi (Hattiesburg, Miss.), 1969. (*DAI* 30:2623A)

1035. VILLAVECES, HAROLD JOSE. *Comparison of the Vocational Interests of Over-, Expected, and Under-Achieving Engineering Graduates.* Doctor's thesis, University of Kansas (Lawrence, Kan.), 1969. (*DAI* 30:5356A)

1036. VINITSKY, MICHAEL HARLAN. *Changes in the Interests of Psychologists With Age and Critical Incidents in Their Careers.* Doctor's thesis, University of Minnesota (Minneapolis, Minn.), 1969. (*DAI* 31:1028A)

1037. WEIGEL, RICHARD G.; PHILLIPS, MARYANN; AND LEWIS, RAYMOND. "Machine-Scoring Consistency of the Strong Vocational Interest Blank." *J Ed Res* 62(5):200+ Ja '69. *

1038. WELSH, GEORGE S. *Gifted Adolescents: A Handbook of Test Results.* Greensboro, N.C.: Prediction Press, June 1969. Pp. viii, 89. *

1039. WHITNEY, DOUGLAS R. "Predicting From Expressed Vocational Choice: A Review." *Personnel & Guid J* 48(4): 279–86 D '69. * (*PA* 44:11457)

1040. ZYTOWSKI, DONALD G. "A Test of Criterion Group Sampling Error in Two Comparable Interest Inventories." *Meas & Eval Guid* 2(1):37–40 sp '69. * (*PA* 44:11612)

1041. ZYTOWSKI, DONALD G.; MILLS, DAVID H.; AND PAEPE, CLAUDE. "Psychological Differentiation and the Strong Vocational Interest Blank." *J Counsel Psychol* 16(1):41–4 Ja '69. *

1042. ADINOLFI, ALLEN A. "Characteristics of Highly Accepted, Highly Rejected, and Relatively Unknown University Freshmen." *J Counsel Psychol* 17(5):456–64 S '70. * (*PA* 45:2994)

1043. ADINOLFI, ALLEN ANDREW. *The Characteristics of Highly Accepted, Highly Rejected and Relatively Unknown University Freshmen.* Doctor's thesis, University of Rochester (Rochester, N.Y.), 1970. (*DAI* 31:2271B)

1044. ALDAG, JEAN C. "Occupational and Nonoccupational Interest Characteristics of Men Nurses." *Nursing Res* 19(6): 529–33 N–D '70. *

1045. BAILEY, ROGER LAWRENCE. *A Canonical Correlation Analysis of the Basic Interest Scales and the Edwards Personal Preference Schedule: A Test of Holland's Theory.* Doctor's thesis, University of Kansas (Lawrence, Kan.), 1970. (*DAI* 31:3259A)

1046. BEDNAR, RICHARD L. "Therapeutic Relationship of A-B Therapists as Perceived by Client and Therapist." *J Counsel Psychol* 17(2):119–22 Mr '70. * (*PA* 44:8608)

1047. BERDIE, RALPH F.; PILAPIL, BONIFACIO; AND IM, IN JAE. "Entrance Correlates of University Satisfaction." *Am Ed Res J* 7(2):251–66 Mr '70. *

1048. BERZINS, JURIS I.; SEIDMAN, EDWARD; AND WELCH, ROBERT D. "A-B Therapist 'Types' and Responses to Patient-Communicated Hostility: An Analogue Study." *J Consult & Clin Psychol* 34(1):27–32 F '70. * (44:6885)

1049. BIGGS, DONALD A.; ROTH, JOHN D.; AND STRONG, STANLEY R. "Self-Made Academic Predictions and Academic Performance." *Meas & Eval Guid* 3(2):81–5 su '70. * (*PA* 45:1357)

1050. BUCK, CHARLES W. "Crystallization of Vocational Interests as a Function of Vocational Exploration in College." *J Counsel Psychol* 17(4):347–51 Jl '70. * (*PA* 44:21550)

1051. BURTON, ROBERT L., AND HARTMANN, EUGENE L. "A Study of Post-Choice Vocational Counseling With the SVIB." *Voc Guid Q* 18(3):195–8 Mr '70. *

1052. CAMPBELL, DAVID P. "Report on Twenty Year Study of Dartmouth Freshmen Completing the Strong Vocational Interest Blank and Scholastic Aptitude Test." *Col & Univ* 45(4): 585–605 su '70. *

1053. CLEMENS, BRYAN; LINDEN, JAMES; AND SHERTZER, BRUCE. "Engineers' Interest Patterns: Then and Now." *Ed & Psychol Meas* 30(3):675–86 au '70. * (*PA* 45:5122)

1054. CLEMENS, BRYAN T. "Engineers' Interest Patterns After Thirty-One Years: Implications for SVIB Scale Revision?" *Meas & Eval Guid* 3(3):152–7 f '70. * (*PA* 45: 11064)

1055. COMBS, HARRISON TYLER, JR. *An Investigation of the Relationship Between the Academic Achievement Scale of the Strong Vocational Interest Blank and First Year Academic Achievement in College.* Doctor's thesis, University of South Carolina (Columbia, S.C.), 1970. (*DAI* 31:3262A)

1056. CRONBACH, LEE J. *Essentials of Psychological Testing, Third Edition,* pp. 460–86. New York: Harper & Row, Publishers, Inc., 1970. Pp. xxx, 752. *

1057. CURTIS, JOHN TAYLOR. *Inventoried Interests as Related to Persistence and Academic Achievement in an Engineering Program.* Doctor's thesis, Purdue University (Lafayette, Ind.), 1970. (*DAI* 31:1572A)

1058. DODD, W. E.; WOLLOWICK, H. B.; AND McNAMARA, W. J. "Task Difficulty as a Moderator of Long-Range Prediction." *J Appl Psychol* 54(3):265–70 Je '70. * (*PA* 44:13452)

1059. DORÉ, RUSSELL LEE. *Self Concept and Interests Related to Job Satisfaction of Managers.* Doctor's thesis, University of Washington (Seattle, Wash.), 1970. (*DAI* 31:2338B)

1060. DUNN, DAVID CAMERON. *Scholastic Aptitude and Vocational Interest as Factors in the Selection of Entering Stu-*

dents in the School of Hotel Administration at Cornell University. Doctor's thesis, Cornell University (Ithaca, N.Y.), 1970. (*DAI* 31:953A)

1061. ERICKSON, CLARA; GANTZ, BENJAMIN S.; AND STEPHENSON, ROBERT W. "Logical and Construct Validation of a Short-Form Biographical Inventory Predictor of Scientific Creativity." Abstract. *Proc 78th Ann Conv Am Psychol Assn* 5(1):151–2 '70. * (*PA* 44:18715)

1062. FRANK, AUSTIN C., AND KIRK, BARBARA A. "Forestry Students Today." *Voc Guid Q* 19(2):119–26 D '70. *

1063. FRANK, AUSTIN C., AND KIRK, BARBARA A. "Uncertainties About the New Strong Interest Blanks." Invited reply by David Campbell. *Personnel & Guid J* 49(1):41–53 S '70. *

1064. FRESCO, RICHARD. "Recent APA Presidents Score Higher." Letter. *Am Psychologist* 25(8):765 Ag '70. *

1065. GRIFFIN, JOHN J., JR. *An Investigation of the Work Satisfaction of Priests of the Archdiocese of Boston.* Doctor's thesis, Boston College (Chestnut Hill, Mass.), 1970. (*DAI* 31:3018A)

1066. GROSS, MICHAEL CARLON. *Interest Inventory Items as Attitude Eliciting Stimuli in Classical Conditioning: A Test of the A-R-D Theory.* Doctor's thesis, University of Hawaii (Honolulu, Hawaii), 1970. (*DAI* 31:3953A)

1067. HARRELL, THOMAS W. "The Personality of High Earning MBA's in Small Business." *Personnel Psychol* 23(3):369–75 au '70. * (*PA* 45:9041)

1068. HELSON, RAVENNA, AND CRUTCHFIELD, RICHARD S. "Creative Types in Mathematics." *J Personality* 38(2):177–97 Je '70. * (*PA* 44:18669)

1069. HELSON, RAVENNA, AND CRUTCHFIELD, RICHARD S. "Mathematicians: The Creative Researcher and the Average PhD." *J Consult & Clin Psychol* 34(2):250–7 Ap '70. * (*PA* 44:10374)

1070. HINTON, BERNARD L. "Personality Variables and Creative Potential." *J Creative Behav* 4(3):210–7 su '70. *

1071. HUDESMAN, JOHN. *Predictive Validity of the Strong Vocational Interest Blank Applied to Accounting Students in an Urban Two-Year College.* *J Counsel Psychol* 17(1):67–9 Ja '70. * (*PA* 44:4358)

1072. JOHANSSON, CHARLES B. "Strong Vocational Interest Blank Introversion-Extraversion and Occupational Membership." *J Counsel Psychol* 17(5):451–5 S '70. * (*PA* 45:3003)

1073. JOHANSSON, CHARLES B., AND CHAPMAN, CAROL B. "College Professors—Their Likes and Dislikes." Abstract. *Proc 78th Ann Conv Am Psychol Assn* 5(2):659–60 '70. * (*PA* 44:19468)

1074. KILBURN, KENT L.; McDOLE, GARY; AND SMITH, RUTH E. "The Strong Vocational Interest Blank as a Measure of Success in the Training of Psychiatric Technicians." *Psychol Rep* 26(3):883–6 Je '70. * (*PA* 45:764)

1075. KRAMER, HOWARD C. "Interpretation of CSQ Scales." *J Col Stud Personnel* 11(1):28–32 Ja '70. *

1076. KRIEGSFELD, MICHAEL. *An Investigation of the Relationship of Some Psychotherapist Variables to the Outcome of Treatment With Patients of Different Social Classes.* Doctor's thesis, New York University (New York, N.Y.), 1970. (*DAI* 31:4339B)

1077. KROGER, ROLF O., AND TURNBULL, WILLIAM. "Effects of Role Demands and Test-Cue Properties on Personality Test Performance: Replication and Extension." *J Consult & Clin Psychol* 35(3):381–7 D '70. * (*PA* 45:6353)

1078. LEFKOWITZ, DAVID M. "Comparison of the Strong Vocational Interest Blank and the Kuder Occupational Interest Survey Scoring Procedures." *J Counsel Psychol* 17(4):357–63 Jl '70. * (*PA* 44:19776)

1079. McNEELY, JAMES BRICE. *Discriminant Function Analysis of Measured Characteristics of Male Undergraduates in Short Term, Educational-Vocational Counseling.* Doctor's thesis, Purdue University (Lafayette, Ind.), 1970. (*DAI* 31:1577A)

1080. MORRIL, RICHARD ALLEN. *Harmony of Self-Concept as a Factor Influencing the Vocational Development of Upper-Class and Graduate Male College Students.* Doctor's thesis, Michigan State University (East Lansing, Mich.), 1970. (*DAI* 31:3880A)

1081. NAVRAN, LESLIE, AND POSTHUMA, ALLAN B. "A Factor Analysis of the Strong Vocational Interest Blank for Men Using the Method of Principal Factors." *J Counsel Psychol* 17(3):216–23 My '70. * (*PA* 44:11601)

1082. NICHOLSON, EVERARD. *Final Report of the Study of Success and Admission Criteria for Potentially Successful Risks.* Providence, R.I.: Brown University, 1970. Pp. iv, 264. *

1083. NORENBERG, CURTIS DUANE. *An Interest Inventory of Vocational Agriculture Teachers.* Doctor's thesis, University of Minnesota (Minneapolis, Minn.), 1970. (*DAI* 31:3439A)

1084. PESCI, MICHAEL LINDEN. *Psychological Differences Between Research, Development and Product Engineers and Their Implications for Placement Decisions.* Doctor's thesis, University of Minnesota (Minneapolis, Minn.), 1970. (*DAI* 31:3048B)

1085. POSTHUMA, ALLAN B., AND NAVRAN, LESLIE. "Relation of Congruence in Student-Faculty Interests to Achievement in College." *J Counsel Psychol* 17(4):352–6 Jl '70. * (*PA* 44:21606)

1086. ROBERTS, FANNIE M. *Relationships in Respect to Attitudes Toward Mathematics, Degree of Authoritarianism, Vocational Interests, Sex Differences, and Scholastic Achievement of College Juniors.* Doctor's thesis, New York University (New York, N.Y.), 1970. (*DAI* 31:2134A)

1087. ROSE, HARRIETT A., AND ELTON, CHARLES F. "Ask Him or Test Him?" *Voc Guid Q* 19(1):28–32 S '70. *

1088. SCHRADER, CHARLES HENRY. *Vocational Choice Problems: Indecision vs. Indecisiveness.* Doctor's thesis, University of Iowa (Iowa City, Iowa), 1970. (*DAI* 31:3694B)

1089. SEAQUIST, DAVID LOWELL. *An Investigation of the Effectiveness of a Programmed Interpretative Guide to the Strong Vocational Interest Blank.* Doctor's thesis, University of Minnesota (Minneapolis, Minn.), 1970. (*DAI* 31:3278A)

1090. SHAH, IFFAT. *A Cross-Cultural Comparative Study of Vocational Interests.* Doctor's thesis, University of Minnesota (Minneapolis, Minn.), 1970. (*DAI* 31:5049B)

1091. SIESS, THOMAS F., AND JACKSON, DOUGLAS N. "Vocational Interests and Personality: An Empirical Integration." *J Counsel Psychol* 17(1):27–35 Ja '70. * (*PA* 44:5695)

1092. STANFIEL, JAMES D. "Administration of the SVIB Men's Form to Women Counselors." *Voc Guid Q* 19(1):22–7 S '70. *

1093. STEINER, ARTHUR FREDERICK. *The Identification of Accident-Proneness in Junior College Vocational Students and Industrial Employees.* Doctor's thesis, University of Southern California (Los Angeles, Calif.), 1970. (*DAI* 31:2721A)

1094. STEPHENSON, NORMAN LESLIE. *Some Empirical Relationships of an Actuarial Pattern Analysis of Basic Scales of the Strong Vocational Interest Blank.* Doctor's thesis, University of Minnesota (Minneapolis, Minn.), 1970. (*DAI* 31:3011B)

1095. TAYLOR, RONALD G., AND HANSON, GARY R. "Interest and Persistence." *J Counsel Psychol* 17(6):506–9 N '70. * (*PA* 45:3051)

1096. WILLIS, CONSTANCE H.; HARFORD, THOMAS; AND EDDY, BARBARA. "Comparison of Samples of Amputee and Nonamputee Subjects on the Strong Vocational Interest Blank." *J Counsel Psychol* 17(4):310–2 Jl '70. * (*PA* 44:21664)

1097. WRIGHT, FRED H., AND L'ABATE, LUCIANO. "On the Meaning of the MMPI Mf and SVIB MF Scales." *Brit J Social & Clin Psychol* 9(2):171–4 Je '70. * (*PA* 44:16718)

1098. WYNNE, JOHN T., AND MURPHY, PATRICK S. "Using the Strong Vocational Interest Blank Diversity Scale Score as a Predictor of Freshman Academic Success." *Col Ed Rec* 55(9):203–6 Je '70. *

1099. CAMPBELL, DAVID P. *Handbook for the Strong Vocational Interest Blank.* Stanford, Calif.: Stanford University Press, 1971. Pp. xxv, 516. *

MARTIN R. KATZ, *Senior Research Psychologist, Educational Testing Service, Princeton, New Jersey.*[1]

The definitive review of the 1966–69 revision of the SVIB cannot be written until the Handbook (*1099*), which is said to contain the data necessary for use and evaluation, becomes available. This reviewer must join Frank and Kirk (*1063*) in their criticism of the authors and publisher for marketing the new forms prematurely; as the foreword to the 1969 supplement to the manual points out, the Handbook "should be required reading for anyone using the SVIB in any setting." In the absence of the Handbook, this review must be confined to comments on the changes and on one unresolved issue that seems to be of crucial importance in evaluating any interest inventory.

The revision has been handled with the circumspection that befits a highly respected institution. In a time when all established institutions are buffeted by winds of change, Campbell has apparently sought a middle course

1 This review was completed before the publication of the *Handbook for the Strong Vocational Interest Blank.*—The Editor.

Strong Vocational Interest Blank for Men

between orthodoxy and radicalism. He seems to be trying to preserve the structure of the instrument that Strong built, so that the hierophants can continue their comfortable reliance on accumulated data, personal experience, and familiar ritual. At the same time, he has modernized and streamlined the instrument, has made it more adaptable, and has laid a foundation for more extensive innovations in the future.

More specifically, many of the changes seem to represent direct, common-sense remedies for well-known defects. First, over 100 items in the 1938 form have been replaced. Some had become archaic (Street-car conductor, "Judge," Vaudeville, Repair auto) ; some had been recognized as offensive (Deaf mutes, People with hooked noses) ; and some were of marginal validity. (Cultural note : Repair auto has been replaced by Repaint auto.) The new items were selected, in general, to be more relevant to occupational activities than some of the so-called "personality-type" items that were deleted. The new items are not, however, presently scored for the occupational scales, which are now based only on the items retained from the old form. Presumably, data gathered through use of the new items will be available for the next revision. This evident plan for "rolling revision" is commendable. Meantime, the new items are not carried as dead weight, since they do contribute to scores on the new Basic Interest Scales.

The item weights for occupational scale scores on the old form had ranged from $+4$ to -4. Complaints against these cumbersome scoring weights had subsided to a low grumble in an era when everyone became resigned to dependence on machine-scoring services. Still, there no longer appeared any cogent reason to resist the proponents of unit weights. The reduction in the range of the item weights to ± 1 on the revised form considerably simplifies hand scoring and may also make the scale scores slightly more stable (diminishing the impact of a changed response to a single item).

A noteworthy revision has been made in the men-in-general (MIG) norms. In scales developed empirically to differentiate members of an occupational group from MIG, the definition of the respective reference groups is crucial. For example, Campbell found that recently tested people from a variety of occupations tended to obtain high scores on all newly developed scales. He attributed this phenom-

enon to a businessman bias in the old MIG group and to "shifts over time" in responses to some 20 items. To avoid this merely temporal differentiation between new occupational groups and MIG, he added to the MIG group people from nonbusiness occupations who had been tested over the span of years from 1925 to 1965. Has this maneuver been successful? Perhaps the Handbook will tell us. Unfortunately, it is still very difficult to characterize the MIG norms except in operational terms of the sort just indicated. One can say remarkably little about the population they presumably represent. The problem encountered in developing new scales may be ominous for the future, even if Campbell's ingenious diagnosis and pragmatic remedy work this time.

Meanwhile, however, the list of occupational scales has been augmented from time to time (modern additions include Computer Programmer and Community Recreation Worker). And the currency of occupational scales dating back to the 1920's and 1930's has been demonstrated in some nice studies which match scores obtained by old reference groups and those of people holding the same positions some 30 years later. So practitioners have been encouraged to continue in good conscience using the old occupational scales, along with more recently developed ones, for new generations of clients.

But Williams, Kirk, and Frank (*961*) have challenged the claim of continuity and comparability from old form to revision. They report sizable differences between scores obtained under the two procedures, "large enough across a significant number of scales to give rise to different counseling interpretations of old and new profiles for individuals." Their study does not, of course, answer the question of which set of scores is more valid. Obviously, there would be no point in making changes if the changes had *no* effects on scores and interpretations. Perhaps these critics misinterpreted the statement by Campbell (*780*) that "None of the revision work will create any major change in the use of the SVIB in counseling."

It seems clear, however, that Campbell has hedged his bets on the occupational scales, old and new, by adding the basic interest scales (BIS), comprised of clusters of items with high intercorrelations (based on Like responses only). There are 22 of these "homogeneous" scales : some include as few as five items, although one—Mechanical—has 28 ; in general, the number of items fluctuates around 11. These scales do not represent independent dimensions. For example, Agriculture and Nature share many of the same items, and the same four occupational groups are listed as scoring high on each scale. One wonders, therefore, why not fewer scales, with more items per scale? Score profile sheets permit an individual to compare his BIS scores with norms for adults (650 men tested at age 52) and for adolescents (the same persons tested when they were 16). Looking at "high" scores and "low" scores (.8 of a standard deviation above or below the mean) on the BIS is stated in the 1969 Supplement to be the "most important interpretive step" in discussing SVIB scores. Evidently, the emphasis on these scales reflects a desire to give a more "psychological" interpretation of interests than could be derived from the curious mixtures of items in the occupational scales. It also offers an escape from the endless labor of adding occupational scales without much hope of achieving a comprehensive array in the foreseeable future. (Even with recent additions, the occupational scales sample sparsely from the universe of middle- and upper-level occupations that the SVIB purports to cover.) Presumably, also, the BIS will not be so time-bound as the occupational scales. The brief rationale given for use of these scales in counseling, however, is not convincing. If they should turn out to have validity for predicting persistence, satisfaction, or interest in occupations, they are indeed likely to be more flexible for counseling use and more comprehensible psychologically than the occupational scales have been. But such flexibility and comprehensibility are adjuncts to predictive validity, not substitutes for it. Perhaps, again, we can look to the Handbook for evidence that .8 of a standard deviation above the mean score of 650 men on some BIS scale represents *enough* interest to warrant consideration of related occupational choices. In the absence of such data, there seems no reason to believe that BIS scores are any more useful for guidance than scores on the *Kuder Preference Record—Vocational* (see my review of the Kuder, 6:1063). In short, the justification for including the BIS must be for research, not for guidance. Indeed, in this reviewer's judgment, most of the items used in the SVIB (e.g., occupational titles) are less suitable for developing useful homogeneous interest scales than are items that describe activities.

The nonoccupational scales have been a source of perennial concern, and there is nothing in the revision to abate this concern. The number and nature of scales that might be developed empirically by contrasting responses of groups defined according to some psychological construct is rather terrifying. Such scales seem to proliferate faster than the research data necessary to explain their implications and to justify their use. For example, the original M-F scale was widely misinterpreted, and one wonders whether M-F II will be any more resistant to misuse. Perhaps the Handbook will define and describe the constructive uses that would make the risk more acceptable. Nothing of this sort appears in the 1969 Supplement, nor has anything ever appeared to support the publication of the earlier M-F scale. The track record for these nonoccupational scales in general has not been good, and perhaps the time has come to scratch them.

Finally, one trusts that the Handbook will deal with the most basic question of all, which should be addressed to every interest inventory: Is it worth the trouble? More specifically, is more valid and useful information obtained from having a student respond to some 400 items, with all the attendant cost and complexities of scoring, reporting, etc., than from having him rate his interest, simply and directly, once, for each scale (occupational or basic) represented by an array of items? This is the question of incremental validity: Does the inventory add significantly to what the student already knows? The way to find out is to pit the inventory against the direct rating of interests in longitudinal validity studies. This is readily done. The time required of students to record the ratings is only a small fraction of the time required for completing the inventory, and the addition to data processing is neither costly nor difficult. In a review of relevant studies, Dolliver (982) concluded, "The predictive validity of expressed interests is at least as great as the predictive validity of the SVIB. In no study where direct comparison was made....was the SVIB as accurate as the expressed interests in predicting occupation engaged in." Furthermore, although one might assume that the SVIB predicts best for students whose expressed interests are least valid, this assumption was not borne out; in the studies reviewed, the validity of the SVIB tended to vary directly with the validity of expressed interests. In a review that encompassed other inventories besides the SVIB, Whitney (*1039*) also concluded that expressed choice was as valid as inventories in predicting future occupation. (In these reviews, one may fault the criterion—occupational membership—although it has been widely accepted for judging the validity of the SVIB. This and such other criteria as success or persistence in an occupation are generally known to be affected by factors other than interests—by abilities, for example. Satisfaction also may be too inclusive a criterion, encompassing values besides interests. The criterion that an occupational interest measure should most reasonably be expected to predict is *interest* in the occupation—intrinsic activity interest.)

A study [2] of the predictive validities of academic interest measures found that students' simple ratings of interests in 12 subject fields were generally just as valid as their scale scores on a highly reliable 192-item inventory—regardless of whether the criterion was marks or differences between marks, interests (academic or occupational) or differences between interests—in grade 12 or first year after high school graduation. Furthermore, the factor structure of the ratings was virtually identical with that of the inventory scales. In short, by early adulthood, interests seem to occupy a rather well integrated and coherent territory in the individual's awareness, such that expressed interests "behave" in very much the same way as inventoried interests.

Until the scheduled Handbook [3] or future handbooks enlighten counselors on the advantages of the SVIB over expressed interests, this reviewer is reluctant to recommend the use of the SVIB—or any other interest inventory.

CHARLES J. KRAUSKOPF, *Professor of Psychology, and Associate Director of Testing and Counseling, University of Missouri, Columbia, Missouri.*

This is a paper-and-pencil inventory of interests applicable to late adolescents and young adults. It is clerically administered, requiring about 40 minutes. Scoring, although simplified from previous procedures, is still tedious enough to make most people use one of the scoring services listed in the entry above.

2 NORRIS, LILA, AND KATZ, MARTIN. *The Measurement of Academic Interests, Part II: The Predictive Validities of Academic Interest Measures.* College Board Research and Development Report 70-71, No. 5 and ETS Research Bulletin 70-58, Princeton, N.J.: Educational Testing Service, 1970. Pp. ix, 180.
3 Now published, see *1099.*—The Editor.

The extensive data available on the SVIB are not always conveniently presented for the user. The current forms are revisions, but the rationale and the large majority of items are identical to those for Strong's original instrument. The rationale is essentially that it is possible to differentiate men in a given occupation from men-in-general by asking questions about their likes and dislikes—and, further, that a person who likes and dislikes the same things as successful people in that occupation will be more likely to enter the occupation and be more likely to succeed in it. One could argue with this rationale, even use data presented by the author on American Psychological Association presidents who do not all look like psychologists on the test, but the validity evidence suggests that a large proportion of college trained people do seek out occupations consistent with the rationale.

The new form has replaced 109 items and somewhat changed 50 more. Occupational scales are constructed to maximize separation between people in the occupation and men-in-general. Both the occupational groups and the men-in-general groups are described in the manual and in the Handbook (*1099*). The original men-in-general group was biased, with too many men in business occupations. The new group makes some adjustment for this but still appears to have too many professional-technical-clerical occupations to be a real men-in-general group. Several new occupational groups have been added.

On the profile itself are several new features in addition to the new occupations. The grey area now represents the middle third of the men-in-general group rather than the "chance" scores obtained by throwing dice, as it did before. This should make interpretation easier. New scales called Basic Interest Scales are prominently featured. These are not mentioned in the 1966 manual but are presented in the 1969 manual supplement and in the Handbook. Although the items have good face validity, no empirical information is presented in either the manual or the supplement. One has to go to the Handbook. Here we find test-retest data for 17 samples over periods from two weeks to 36 years. Concurrent and predictive validity information are presented. The manual suggests that the Basic Interest Scales are to indicate possibilities for exploration. They should be good for this purpose, but the user should spend some time with the information in the Handbook, because the data are not always consistent with the expectations created by the labels. For example, Army Reserve personnel do not score as high on military activities as a sample of college freshmen. These scales look as if they might eventually provide information toward a better understanding of occupational interests, but for the present we cannot say. They have an additional disadvantage of being quite short, with a median length of 9.5 items. This can make the standard score misleading as to the magnitude of the difference.

With the mass of information available, users and interpreters of the test should have training in psychological testing and spend some time with the manuals and the Handbook. The Handbook appears to be the most complete document of its kind ever assembled. It is unfortunate that the Handbook or extensive journal reading is so necessary. A revision of the 1966 manual and 1969 supplement to give a clearer and better-referenced picture to the potential user might be helpful.

In the manual, reliability information is presented both over time and for internal consistency summarized for the whole instrument, but not for the individual scales. The occupational scales have a median odd-even reliability of approximately .80 and a test-retest reliability of approximately .90 over 30 days. The Basic Interest Scales are said to have higher internal consistency but slightly lower consistency over time. Complete information is presented on the intercorrelation of the occupational scales.

A related issue, faking, is discussed in the manual supplement. The summary of studies of faking indicates that people can raise their scores on specific scales from one to two standard deviations and that this causes other unknown changes in scores. Most uses of the SVIB are in situations where there is no apparent motivation to fake.

Concurrent validity information is presented on the new scales, predictive validity on the old forms, and a sort of postdictive validity on conversions of data from old forms to the new ones. It is assumed that the item changes are not great enough to cause radical departures from the characteristics of the previous forms. This is the best one can do to translate validity studies which covered 25 and more years. However, such studies should be interpreted with some caution. Campbell argues against cross-validation, saying that it is more advantageous to use all available data to construct the scales rather than holding out crossvalidation samples. He is probably right when he says that large changes will not occur, but his general argument loses force when studies he quotes in the manual show some shrinkage. Much of the predictive validity information is impressive, but one feature is misleading and often misused. Data are reported in the form of chances that one will be employed in the occupation named in the scale. The computational method assumes equal representation of occupations in the population, which is not the case. Worse, it is logically backwards. The method actually used gives the chances that one ending up in a given occupation will have a high score on that occupational scale. In addition he usually will have high scores on other scales. In one study reported, both accountants and lawyers had scored higher on Office Man and on Real Estate Salesman than they did on their own occupational scale when they were high school seniors. Also reported in the manual are more data related to the expression "chances in 100 of employment in that occupation." One study indicates that of 199 college students, 53 percent of those with A ratings and 21 percent of those with B+ ratings on the Physician scale became physicians. This is not meant to be damning criticism of the validity information presented. Compared to other psychological tests, this is one of the best, not only in amount of information but also in providing methodological information on how the validity evidence was obtained.

There are several new special scales added to this form, and the old Interest Maturity scale is gone. The new scales are divided into nonoccupational scales and administrative indices. Little information beyond the scale development procedure is presented for most of these scales. A notable exception is the Academic Achievement scale. The information presented is not the kind that should inspire much confidence. The scale has been criticized by Frank and Kirk (1063). In general, I would have to suggest caution in interpreting these scales. More data and references are available in the Handbook but unfortunately, especially for the references, are not in the manuals.

After some of the above criticism a final statement should be added. Both the original author, E. K. Strong, and the current authors, especially D. P. Campbell, have shown themselves willing to tackle the complex and frustrating task of providing as complete as possible information for their test. They have succeeded better than most. The authors are aware of the criticisms of their efforts and are to be complimented on their efforts to correct deficiencies where they agree and to make the rest of us understand where they do not agree.

J Counsel Psychol 14:187–9+ *Mr '67. John W. M. Rothney.* "Where does one get parts for a 1931 Model A?" asks an advertisement in one of the current issues of a popular magazine. The revisers of the Strong did not have trouble in answering that one. They used most of the old parts, added some new ones, discarded the real antiques, rearranged some arithmetic....and gave the product a new paint job. * this collection of items has been christened a vocational interest blank without evidence that it measures vocational interest. Having attached the label, the originator and the revisers write about "retesting of interests," "stability of vocational interests," and "vocational interest patterns" as if it were well established that the blank actually measures vocational interests. Validity by fiat might have been acceptable when the original model appeared. * the original MIG was dominated by businessmen, with only a relatively small number of individuals from scientific and cultural occupations (How many of the users of the old form knew that?), so a new group has been assembled. It has been done by sampling equally from, "most of the occupational groups that have been tested with the SVIB over the entire time span, 1925–1965." One notes, however, that the majority of the scales will be based on the criterion groups tested by Strong in the 1930's. The term men-in-general is really a misnomer since so few occupations were sampled. The revisers hope that they will have a better MIG group, but they admit that there are, and always have been, puzzles in the data. "Only time and further research will completely untangle the threads." Meanwhile, with validity established by fiat and the admission that the data are puzzling, one is encouraged to buy and use the instrument. * No comparison is ever given with the percentages of men who, having committed themselves to a field of graduate preparation, or who are well advanced in a university major, remain in the field. In fact, one just doesn't find any data on comparison groups or any concern for antecedent probabilities. The evidence is always offered as if the results were so much greater than zero—a condition that one rarely finds. Did anyone ever think to ask the men in the Stanford study just what field they planned to enter to see if their answers would be as predictive as the Strong scores? The new evidence of stability which is suggested very subtly as evidence of validity, and which those unwary of semantic traps may misinterpret, is presented in terms of median scale "test-retest" correlations of .91 for college sophomores over a 2-week period; .91 for young adults (unspecified further) over 30 days; .68 for college freshmen over 3 years; .61 for high school seniors over 8 years; .67 for college seniors over 22 years (old form); .56 for adults over 30 years. The last four of these are just not high enough for use in individual counseling. Additional evidence purporting to indicate "substantial stability in interest patterns" within four occupational groups was obtained by comparing scores of small numbers of men who hold the "same" jobs (school superintendents, ministers, bankers, corporation presidents) as men in the 1930 Strong criterion group. Specifics on "substantial" are not given, but it soon becomes apparent that what is termed substantial by a Strong enthusiast might be labeled something else by a skeptic. * The revisers seem to have decided that the many doubts and questions about the inventory technique raised by many persons over a long period of time are not worth their consideration. No attempt has been made to come to grips with the many problems inherent in the procedure. The matter of faking is ignored; the requiring of responses to items about which the individual may have little knowledge or concern is not discussed. The forced-choice procedure, requiring selection among items about which there may be uneven familiarity (Items 281–290, for example), is not defended. Such matters as lack of opportunity to express genuine enthusiasm or the opposite, difficulties in ipsative score interpretation, and inadequate interpretative data for low scores are simply ignored. The value of responses given under such directions as, "Show your interest in school subjects even though you have not studied them," and, "Do not think over various possibilities," and (in responding to lists of occupations) "Forget about how much money you could make or whether you could get ahead in it," seem not to be questioned. Several writers, including this reviewer, have raised additional questions but they are not given any consideration. The case for the blank must rest, then, on the data obtained. Since there are genuine problems in interpretation for persons who are not willing to accept that offered by the revisers and who try not to get lost in the verbiage, it would seem that a counselor who "believes in taking an active part in the advising process and in providing the individual with as much systematic evidence about himself as possible" could not find this a useful instrument. Since the blank lacks any theoretical structure and employs questionable techniques which have produced equivocal data, one must wonder now why the revision was undertaken. Would it not have been better to use the brains and the money to try to build a new model than to soup up the old Model A? * In reviewing these two inventories [see 1026 for my review of the *Minnesota Vocational Interest Inventory*], this writer has been forced to look back on interest measurement during the 32 years following a doctoral dissertation he did in that area at Harvard University. He finds that these reviews are not curmudgeon-like utterances but restatements of recurring problems that have not been solved. Why, during the past 30 years, has there been no real longitudinal study with, at least, annual appraisals of the development of vocational interests and enthusiasms as young people go through their educations, enter careers, and persist in or leave them? And why do we not have much more information about vocational interests that has not been obtained from structured inventories? Have the Strong and that other common one inhibited research rather than fostered it? Has it been too easy to assume that such inventories provide adequate information (with lots of scores to manipulate) and that study of interests by other techniques is not necessary? Why do the studies in this area seem more like advertisements than experiments? Why are there so few reports of comparisons of the inventory procedure with other techniques? The general attitude of the authors and revisers of these inventories and their many followers seems to be that it is unnecessary to make comparisons of results obtained from interviews, essays (in which the subject can tell about his interests in his own words and in the length and detail of his own choosing), autobiographies, and combinations of techniques that counselors use. If a counselor is to consider both validity and economy in the selection of his instruments he must have some comparative data. It is not enough for an inventory maker to dismiss all other approaches without additional information. * [See original review for additional critical comments not excerpted.]

J Counsel Psychol 14:192 Mr '67. David P. Campbell. "Reaction to Rothney's Review." This is not a review of the SVIB and MVII, it is a review of a philosophy. As John Rothney clearly states, he is opposed to inventories, ALL inventories, and it is hard to imagine any data that might change his opinions. Interest-inventory scales can separate occupations by more than four standard deviations (compare the mean scores of policemen and psychologists on the SVIB psychologist scale); students who score high on these scales enter quite different occupations than those who score low; within an occupation, men who score low on the occupational scale report less job satisfaction than those who score high; scores are stable over time, especially over short periods, and especially for adults. Given this body of knowledge, are interest inventories helpful to counselors? I think so; Rothney does not. Incisive, accurate criticism of the SVIB and MVII would be welcome, for it is certainly true that the researcher is too close to the instrument for proper perspective. However, Rothney's comments are so laced with errors that it is difficult to know how much attention should be given him. For example, in discussing the test-retest samples, he criticizes us for listing one sample as "young adults" by inserting the parenthetical comment "(unspecified further)." In the text under the table for this group, we have specifically said: "The 102 men composing the 30 day test-retest group were members of a U.S. Army Reserve unit from Fort Snelling, Minnesota. They were mostly college graduates, and their median age was about 25. They were spread throughout a wide range of civilian occupations, with mild concentrations in the advertising and newspaper fields." In a second example, Rothney criticizes us for failing to come to grips with many problems, for example, "The matter of faking is ignored...." On page 2 of the SVIB Manual is the statement: "practitioners should be cautious in the use of interest inventories in selection, both because of the lack of empirical data to support such practices, and because we know that these instruments can be faked." Further, on page 3, is the remark: "Students can fake their responses on interest inventories when instructed to do so (Longstaff, 1948). Though this is seldom a problem when students are completing the inventory for counseling purposes, it can be troublesome in employee selection situations." One last example: Rothney, in decrying the value of Strong's 18-year follow-up of 663 Stanford men, says that no alternative approaches are ever tried, and pleads, "Did anyone ever think to ask the men in the Stanford study just what field they planned to enter to see if their answers would be as predictive as the Strong scores?" Well, yes, Strong did that. The results were published in 1954 in *Educational and Psychological Measurement* in an article entitled, "Validity of Occupational Choice." Strong summarized the study: "Occupational choices of Stanford University freshmen in 1930 are compared with occupation-engaged-in in 1949. Anywhere from 38 to 61 per cent continued in the occupation of their early choice. The range....depends upon whether or not 'don't know' responses are included in the calculations and....how the term 'business' is interpreted." This information is not included in the new SVIB Manual and, all right—I confess—I did not include all of the results from the 800 studies of the SVIB, nor even all those from the 119 publications by Strong. * Though I am smarting from the criticism, I do believe the testing enterprise needs gadflies like John Rothney and the others, such as Banesh Hoffman and Martin Gross. They do, by their excesses, keep the rest of us more honest and careful in our work. In a way, it would be too bad if they ever began to read and understand the professional literature, for that might subdue their small, not-very-quiet voices from outside the establishment, and we periodically need that external clamor to broaden our perspectives.

For reviews by Alexander W. Astin and Edward J. Furst of earlier editions, see 6:1070; for reviews by Edward S. Bordin and Elmer D. Hinckley, see 4:747; for reviews by Harold D. Carter, John G. Darley, and N. W. Morton, see 2:1680; for a review by John G. Darley, see 1:1178.

[1037]

*Strong Vocational Interest Blank for Women. Ages 16 and over; 1933-71; SVIB-W; 81 scoring scales (19 basic interests, 58 occupational, 4 nonoccu-

pational) and 6 administrative indices; BASIC INTERESTS: art ('69), biological science ('69), homemaking ('69), law/politics ('69), mechanical ('69), medical service ('69), merchandising ('69), music ('69), numbers ('69), office practices ('69), outdoors ('69), performing arts ('69), physical science ('69), public speaking ('69), religious activities ('69), social service ('69), sports ('69), teaching ('69), writing ('69); OCCUPATIONAL: *group 1, music-performing:* music teacher ('54-69), entertainer ('69), musician performer ('54-69), model ('69); *group 2, art:* art teacher ('69), artist ('35-69), interior decorator ('69); *group 3, verbal-linguistic:* newswoman ('35-69, original scale titled author), English teacher ('35-69), language teacher ('69); *group 4, social service:* YWCA staff member ('35-69, original scale titled YWCA secretary), recreation leader ('69), director-Christian education ('69), nun-teacher ('62-69, original scale titled sister teacher by Sister Mary David Olheiser), guidance counselor ('69), social science teacher ('35-69), social worker ('35-69); *group 5, verbal-scientific:* speech pathologist ('66-69), psychologist ('46-69), librarian ('35-69), translator ('69); *group 6, scientific:* physician ('35-69), dentist ('35-69), medical technologist ('69), chemist ('69), mathematician ('69), computer programmer ('67-69), math-science teacher ('35-69), engineer ('54-69); *group 7, military-managerial:* army-enlisted ('69), navy-enlisted ('69), army-officer ('69), navy-officer ('69); *group 8, business:* lawyer ('35-69), accountant ('69), bankwoman ('69), life insurance underwriter ('35-69, original scale titled life insurance saleswoman), buyer ('46-69), business education teacher ('38-69, original scale by H. F. Koepke); *group 9, home economics:* home economics teacher ('46-69), dietician ('46-69); *group 10, health-related services:* physical education teacher ('41-69, original scale by Patricia Collins), occupational therapist ('46-69), physical therapist ('58-69), public health nurse ('35-69), registered nurse ('35-69), licensed practical nurse ('35-69), radiologic technologist ('69), dental assistant ('69); *group 11, nonprofessional:* executive housekeeper ('69), elementary teacher ('41-69, original scale by Ralph Bedell), secretary ('35-69, original scale titled stenographer-secretary), saleswoman ('69), telephone operator ('69), instrument assembler ('69), sewing machine operator ('69), beautician ('69), airline stewardess ('69); NONOCCUPATIONAL SCALES: academic achievement ('66-69), diversity of interests ('69), femininity-masculinity II ('35-69), occupational introversion-extroversion; ADMINISTRATIVE INDICES: total responses ('69), unpopular responses ('69), form check ('69), like percentage ('69), indifferent percentage ('69), dislike percentage ('69); 1 form; Form TW398 ('68, 8 pages); combined manual ('66, 79 pages) and supplement ('69, 25 pages) for tests for women and men; handbook ('71, 551 pages, see 167 below); separate answer sheets (Hankes, MRC, NCS) must be used; $6 per 25 tests; $3 per manual; $1.75 per supplement; $6 per specimen set of tests for women and men; postage extra; a test booklet, Form TW398R, in which responses are recorded and later transferred to answer sheets is available for research use; for special scoring services, see below; (30-60) minutes; Edward K. Strong, Jr. (except supplement) and David P. Campbell; Stanford University Press. *

a) HANKES (TESTSCOR) SCORING SERVICE. Hankes answer sheets: $2.25 per 50, $8.50 per 250; scoring service (duplicate profile report): first 10 tests within a month, $1.20 each; thereafter, $1.10 each or an 80¢ coupon ($40 per 50 coupons); telephone service available; cash and coupon orders postpaid; 1 day service on up to 50 tests; Testscor, Inc. *

b) MRC SCORING SERVICE. MRC answer sheets: $1.50 per 25, $4 per 100; scoring service (duplicate profile report): 1–25 tests, 75¢ each; 26–100 tests, 65¢ each; 101–1000 tests, 60¢ each; $1.50 handling charge; postage extra; 48 hour service; Measurement Research Center. *

c) NCS SCORING SERVICE. NCS answer sheets: $2 per 25, $7 per 100; scoring service (duplicate profile report): 1 day service (1–5 tests, $1.25 each; 6–24 tests, $1 each; 25 or more tests, 90¢ each); prepaid scoring certificates may be used for scoring tests in any quantity; 1 week service (25–99 tests, 80¢ each); optional statistical services also available; postage extra; National Computer Systems. *

REFERENCES

1–9. See 2:1681.
10–45. See 3:649.
46–64. See 5:869.
65–76. See 6:1071.
77. HUTCHINSON, JOHN CALDWELL, JR. *Vocational Interest and Job Satisfaction of Women Elementary Teachers.* Doctor's thesis, New York University (New York, N.Y.), 1952.
78. TANNER, WILLIAM C., JR. "Personality Bases in Teacher Selection." *Phi Delta Kappan* 35:271–4+ Ap '54. *
79. GLOTZBACH, CHARLES JEROME. *Intellectual and Non-intellectual Characteristics Associated With Persistence of Women in an Elementary and Nursery School Teacher-Education Program.* Doctor's thesis, University of Minnesota (Minneapolis, Minn.), 1957. (*DA* 18:146)
80. ISENBERGER, WILMA E. *Self-Attitudes of Women Physical Education Majors as Related to Measures of Interest and Success.* Doctor's thesis, State University of Iowa (Iowa City, Iowa), 1957. (*DA* 17:2911)
81. MEADOW, LLOYD. *Prediction of Success in Practical Nursing.* Doctor's thesis, Wayne State University (Detroit, Mich.), 1961. (*DA* 24:4801)
82. McCARTHY, M. KIERAN. *Masculinity Faking in a Validity Study of the Minnesota Multiphasic Personality Inventory (MMPI) and the FM Scale of the Strong Vocational Interest Blank for Women (SVIBW).* Master's thesis, Marquette University (Milwaukee, Wis.), 1962.
83. OLHEISER, MARY DAVID. *Development of a Sister-Teacher Interest Scale for the Strong Vocational Interest Blank for Women.* Doctor's thesis, Boston College (Chestnut Hill, Mass.), 1962.
84. ZISSIS, CECELIA. *The Relationship of Selected Variables to the Career-Marriage Plans of University Freshman Women.* Doctor's thesis, University of Michigan (Ann Arbor, Mich.), 1962. (*DA* 23:128)
85. BECKER, JAMES A. "Interest Pattern Faking by Female Job Applicants." *J Indus Psychol* 1:51–4 Je '63. * (*PA* 38:10455)
86. HALL, WILLIAM JOSEPH. *College Women's Identifications With Their Fathers in Relation to Vocational Interest Patterns.* Doctor's thesis, University of Texas (Austin, Tex.), 1963. (*DA* 24:5192)
87. McGANN, JOHN R. *Interests of a Group of Women Religious on the Strong Vocational Interest Blank.* Doctor's thesis, St. John's University (Jamaica, N.Y.), 1963.
88. ROSSMANN, JACK EUGENE. *An Investigation of Maternal Employment Among College Women—A Twenty-Five Year Follow-Up.* Doctor's thesis, University of Minnesota (Minneapolis, Minn.), 1963. (*DA* 25:2658)
89. MEADOW, LLOYD. "Assessment of Students for Schools of Practical Nursing." *Nursing Res* 13:222–9 su '64. *
90. TYLER, LEONA E. "The Antecedents of Two Varieties of Vocational Interests." *Genetic Psychol Monogr* 70:177–227 N '64. * (*PA* 39:10878)
91. VETTER, LOUISE, AND LEWIS, EDWIN C. "Some Correlates of Homemaking vs. Career Preference Among College Home Economics Students." *Personnel & Guid J* 42:593–8 F '64. * (*PA* 39:6057)
92. ANDERSON, HARRY E., JR. "A Factorial Study of the Female Form of the SVIB." *J Appl Psychol* 49:270–3 Ag '65. * (*PA* 39:15206)
93. GERSTEIN, ALVIN I. "Development of a Selection Program for Nursing Candidates." *Nursing Res* 14:254–7 su '65. *
94. GLICK, RUTH. *Practitioners and Non-Practitioners in a Group of Women Physicians.* Doctor's thesis, Western Reserve University (Cleveland, Ohio), 1965. (*DA* 26:6845)
95. HARMON, LENORE ANNETTE WHITE. *The Measurement of Women's Interests: The Effect of Using Married Women as Occupational Criterion Groups on the Women's Strong Vocational Interest Blank.* Doctor's thesis, University of Minnesota (Minneapolis, Minn.), 1965. (*DA* 26:5541)
96. MILLER, DORIS I. "Characteristics of Graduate Students in Four Clinical Nursing Specialties." *Nursing Res* 14:106–13 sp '65. *
97. BROWN, NORBERTA WILSON. *A Study of the Interests of Baccalaureate Registered Nurses in Relation to Aptitudes, Achievement, and Attitudes, and the Development of an Occupational Scale for the Strong Vocational Interest Blank.* Doctor's thesis, University of California (Los Angeles, Calif.), 1966. (*DA* 27:107A)
98. DUNTEMAN, GEORGE H. "A Note on the Factorial Invariance of the Female Form of the SVIB." *J Appl Psychol* 50:561–2 D '66. * (*PA* 41:2250)
99. FAUNCE, PATRICIA SPENCER. *Personality Characteristics and Vocational Interests Related to the College Persistence of Academically Gifted Women.* Doctor's thesis, University of Minnesota (Minneapolis, Minn.), 1966. (*DA* 28:338B)
100. GLOSSER, EARL ATWELL. *The Consistency of L I D Response Sets and Related Scales on the Strong Vocational Interest Blank for Women.* Doctor's thesis, Indiana University (Bloomington, Ind.), 1966. (*DA* 27:2068A)
101. GOLDEN, MARY CONSTANCE. *An Investigation of the Teaching Interests of Sisters, Their Personality Characteristics, and the Ratings of Their Supervisors.* Doctor's thesis, Fordham University (New York, N.Y.), 1966. (*DA* 27:2879A)
102. HELSON, RAVENNA. "Personality of Women With Imaginative and Artistic Interests: The Role of Masculinity, Originality, and Other Characteristics in Their Creativity." *J Personality* 34:1–25 Mr '66. * (*PA* 40:8830)
103. HERKENHOFF, LOUIS HENRY. *A Comparison of Older and Younger Women Students at San Jose City College With Implications for Curriculum and Student Personnel Services.* Doctor's thesis, University of California (Berkeley, Calif.), 1966. (*DA* 27:2443A)
104. KLAHN, JAMES EDWARD. *An Analysis of Selected Factors and Success of First Year Student Nurses.* Doctor's thesis, Washington State University (Pullman, Wash.), 1966. (*DA* 27:2888A)
105. MAYER, WILHELM KARL. *Vocational Interest Patterns of Teaching and Non-Teaching Female College Graduates.* Doctor's thesis, University of Florida (Gainesville, Fla.), 1966. (*DA* 27:2831A)
106. MILLER, DORIS I. "Characteristics of Graduate Students Preparing for Teaching or Supervision in a Nursing Specialty." *Nursing Res* 15:168–71 sp '66. *
107. O'NEIL, PATRICIA M., AND MADAUS, GEORGE F. "Differences in Interest Patterns Between Graduates of Diploma and Basic Collegiate Programs in Nursing." *J Counsel Psychol* 13:300–5 f '66. * (*PA* 40:12654)
108. PARKER, AILEEN W. "Career and Marriage Orientation in the Vocational Development of College Women." *J Appl Psychol* 50:232–5 Je '66. * (*PA* 40:9216)
109. RUDLOFF, JOSEPH STEPHEN. *A Descriptive Profile of Teachers of Hearing Handicapped Children With Implications for Teacher Recruitment.* Doctor's thesis, University of California (Los Angeles, Calif.), 1966. (*DA* 27:886A)
110. WILKINS, PHOEBE ELEANOR. *A Validity Study of Selected Scales of the Strong Vocational Interest Blank for Women.* Doctor's thesis, University of Iowa (Iowa City, Iowa), 1966. (*DA* 27:2835A)
111. CAMPBELL, DAVID P. "The Vocational Interests of Beautiful Women." *Personnel & Guid J* 45:968–72 Je '67. * (*PA* 42:4631)
112. CAMPBELL, DAVID P., AND SCHUELL, HILDRED. "The Vocational Interests of Women in Speech Pathology and Audiology." *ASHA* 9:67–72 Mr '67. * (*PA* 41:9465)
113. CAWLEY, ANNE. "Interest Changes in Elementary Teaching." *Cath Ed R* 65:396–403 S '67. *
114. DUNTEMAN, GEORGE H. "Gross Validities of Six SVIB Discriminant Equations for Female Students in Health and Education." *Ed & Psychol Meas* 27:1091–7 w '67. * (*PA* 42:8090)
115. DUNTEMAN, GEORGE H. "Validities of the Female Form of the Strong Vocational Interest Blank Occupational Therapy, Laboratory Technology, and Nursing Keys." *J Exp Ed* 35:53–7 su '67. *
116. DUNTEMAN, GEORGE H., AND BAILEY, JOHN P., JR. "A Canonical Correlational Analysis of the Strong Vocational Interest Blank and the Minnesota Multiphasic Personality Inventory for a Female College Population." *Ed & Psychol Meas* 27:631–42 au '67. * (*PA* 42:124)
117. HARMON, LENORE W. "Women's Interests—Fact or Fiction?" *Personnel & Guid J* 45:895–900 My '67. * (*PA* 41:17166)
118. HARMON, LENORE W. "Women's Working Patterns Related to Their SVIB Housewife and 'Own' Occupational Scores." *J Counsel Psychol* 14:299–301 Jl '67. * (*PA* 41:12622)
119. NOLTING, EARL, JR. *A Study of Female Vocational Interests: Pre-College to Post-Graduation.* Doctor's thesis, University of Minnesota (Minneapolis, Minn.), 1967. (*DA* 28:2074A)
120. SIEGEL, HILDEGARDE JULIA. *A Study of Professional Socialization in Two Baccalaureate Nursing Education Programs.* Doctor's thesis, University of Minnesota (Minneapolis, Minn.), 1967. (*DA* 28:3041A)
121. WERKMAN, SIDNEY L., AND GREENBERG, ELSA S. "Personality and Interest Patterns in Obese Adolescent Girls." *Psychosom Med* 29:72–80 Ja–F '67. * (*PA* 41:5990)
122. WHITTAKER, DAVID NEIL EATON. *Psychological Characteristics of Alienated, Nonconformist, College-Age Youth as*

Indicated by AVL, OPI, ACL and SVIB-M/W Group Profiles. Doctor's thesis, University of California (Berkeley, Calif.), 1967. (DA 28:3055B)

123. BOTT, MARGARET M. "Measuring the Mystique." *Personnel & Guid J* 46:967–70 Je '68. * (PA 43:3012)

124. BUCHANAN, BERNICE F. *Vocational Interest of Student Nurses in a Professional College Nursing Program.* Master's thesis, Catholic University of America (Washington, D.C.), 1968.

125. CAMPBELL, DAVID P., AND SOLIMAN, ABDALLA M. "The Vocational Interests of Women in Psychology: 1942–66." *Am Psychologist* 23:158–63 Mr '68. * (PA 42:11238)

126. FARNSWORTH, KIRK EDWIN. *The Vocational Interests of Women: A Factor Analysis of the Women's Form of the Strong Vocational Interest Blank.* Doctor's thesis, Iowa State University (Ames, Iowa), 1968. (DA 29:3481B)

127. GYSBERS, NORMAN C., AND JOHNSTON, JOSEPH A. "Characteristics of Homemaker- and Career-Oriented Women." *J Counsel Psychol* 15:541–6 N '68. * (PA 43:1552)

128. HAMMER, MAX. "Differentiating 'Good' and 'Bad' Officers in a Progressive Rehabilitative Women's Reformatory." *Correct Psychiatry & J Social Ther* 14:114–7 sp '68. *

129. HELSON, RAVENNA. "Generality of Sex Differences in Creative Style." *J Personality* 36:33–48 Mr '68. * (PA 42:15482)

130. JOSELYN, EDWIN GARY. *The Relationship of Selected Variables to the Stability of Measured Vocational Interest of High School Seniors.* Doctor's thesis, University of Minnesota (Minneapolis, Minn.), 1968. (DA 29:2526A)

131. KISH, GEORGE B., AND DONNENWERTH, GREGORY. "Traditional and Nontraditional Strong VIB Interest Patterns as Related to Sensation-Seeking in Women." *Newsl Res Psychol* 10:7–9 My '68. *

132. MATIS, EDWARD EUGENE. *An Analysis of Differences in Interests, Personality Needs, and Personality Structures Between College Women Majoring in Speech Pathology and College Women Majoring in Other Professional Areas.* Doctor's thesis, University of Alabama (University, Ala.), 1968. (DA 29:4290A)

133. MERKLE, RICHARD WILLIAM. *Actuarial Validation of a Psychometric Instrument.* Doctor's thesis, University of Missouri (Columbia, Mo.), 1968. (DA 29:3091B)

134. SEDLACEK, CAROLINE GLADYS. *Selected Factors Affecting Certainty and Persistence of Vocational Choice for College Women.* Doctor's thesis, University of North Dakota (Grand Forks, N.D.), 1968. (DA 29:3843A)

135. TAYLOR, RONALD G., AND BONDY, STEPHEN B. "Validation of Factor Analytic Classification of the Women's Form of the SVIB: Implications for College Counseling." *J Ed Res* 61:273–4 F '68. *

136. ALDAG, JEAN C. KERZ. *Male Nurse Interest and Personality Characteristics.* Doctor's thesis, Washington University (St. Louis, Mo.), 1969. (DAI 30:5672B)

137. BAILEY, JOHN P., JR.; JANTZEN, ALICE C.; AND DUNTEMAN, GEORGE H. "Relative Effectiveness of Personality, Achievement and Interest Measures in the Prediction of a Performance Criterion." *Am J Occup Ther* 23(1):27–9 Ja–F '69. * (PA 44:731)

138. CAMPBELL, DAVID P., AND HARMON, LENORE W. "Vocational Interests of WAC Officers and Enlisted Personnel." *Voc Guid Q* 17(4):267–74 Je '69. *

139. COMPTON, NORMA H. "Characteristics of Clothing and Textile Students Compared With Those of Women in Fashion Careers." *J Home Econ* 61(3):183–8 Mr '69. *

140. FARNSWORTH, KIRK E. "Vocational Interests of Women: A Factor Analysis of the Women's Form of the SVIB." *J Appl Psychol* 53(5):353–8 O '69. * (PA 44:1405)

141. FRANCE-KELLY, KENNETH ARCHIBALD. *An Investigation of the Relationship Between Score Interpretation of the Strong Vocational Interest Blank for Women and the Choice of a College Major of Freshmen College Women.* Master's thesis, Catholic University of America (Washington, D.C.), 1969.

142. FRIEDERSDORF, NANCY WHEELER. *A Comparative Study of Counselor Attitudes Toward the Further Educational and Vocational Plans of High School Girls.* Doctor's thesis, Purdue University (Lafayette, Ind.), 1969. (DAI 30:4220A)

143. HARMON, LENORE W. "Predictive Power Over Ten Years of Measured Social Service and Scientific Interests Among College Women." *J Appl Psychol* 53(3):193–8 Je '69. * (PA 43:11956)

144. HARMON, LENORE W. "SVIB Patterning: A Comparison of Clients and Non-Clients." *Meas & Eval Guid* 2(1):32–6 sp '69. * (PA 44:13460)

145. HERSCH, PAUL D.; KULIK, JAMES A.; AND SCHEIBE, KARL E. "Personal Characteristics of College Volunteers in Mental Hospitals." *J Consult & Clin Psychol* 33(1):30–4 F '69. * (PA 43:11408)

146. HORNUNG, PHILIP E. *The Association Among the Variables of the California Psychological Inventory and the Strong Vocational Interest Blank on an Eleventh Grade Female Population.* Master's thesis, Catholic University of America (Washington, D.C.), 1969.

147. KISH, GEORGE B., AND DONNENWERTH, GREGORY V. "Interests and Stimulus Seeking." *J Counsel Psychol* 16(6):551–6 N '69. * (PA 44:4260)

148. LINDSAY, CARL A., AND ALTHOUSE, RICHARD. "Comparative Validities of the Strong Vocational Interest Blank Academic Achievement Scale and the College Student Questionnaire Motivation for Grades Scale." *Ed & Psychol Meas* 29(2):489–93 su '69. *

149. PETRIK, NORMAN D. "Test-Retest Reliability of the SVIB and Differing Curricular Experience." Abstract. *Proc 77th Ann Conv Am Psychol Assn* 4(2):687–8 '69. * (PA 44:1257)

150. SHANKS, JAMES LOUIS. *Concept Achievement in Science and Its Relationship to Some Non-Intellectual Characteristics of Prospective Elementary Teachers.* Doctor's thesis, University of California (Berkeley, Calif.), 1969. (DAI 31:272A)

151. STEELE, CAROLYN IRENE. *Institutional Placement During Adolescence and Its Relationship to the Girl's Task of Sexual Identification.* Doctor's thesis, Smith College (Northampton, Mass.), 1969. (DAI 31:474A)

152. STONE, THOMAS H., AND ATHELSTAN, GARY T. "The SVIB for Women and Demographic Variables in the Prediction of Occupational Tenure." *J Appl Psychol* 53(5):408–12 O '69. * (PA 44:738)

153. ALDAG, JEAN C. "Occupational and Nonoccupational Interest Characteristics of Men Nurses." *Nursing Res* 19(6):529–33 N–D '70. *

154. DEWOLFE, ALAN S. "Dimensions of Young Women's Vocational Interest." *Newsl Res Psychol* 12(1):33–6 F '70. *

155. FARMER, HELEN S., AND BOHN, MARTIN J., JR. "Home-Career Conflict Reduction and the Level of Career Interest in Women." *J Counsel Psychol* 17(3):228–32 My '70. * (PA 44:13459)

156. FLINT, ROBERT THOMAS. *The Relationship of Women's Tenure in Occupational Therapy to Strong Vocational Interest Blank and Demographic Variables.* Doctor's thesis, University of Minnesota (Minneapolis, Minn.), 1970. (DAI 31:4379B)

157. FRANK, AUSTIN C., AND KIRK, BARBARA A. "Characteristics of Dental Hygiene Students." *Voc Guid Q* 18(3):207–11 Mr '70. *

158. FRANK, AUSTIN C., AND KIRK, BARBARA A. "Uncertainties About the New Strong Interest Blanks." Invited reply by David Campbell. *Personnel & Guid J* 49(1):41–53 S '70. *

159. HARMON, LENORE W. "Strong Vocational Interest Blank Profiles of Disadvantaged Women." *J Counsel Psychol* 17(6):519–21 N '70. * (PA 45:3131)

160. JOHNSON, RAY W. "Parental Identification and Vocational Interests of College Women." *Meas & Eval Guid* 3(3):147–51 f '70. * (PA 45:4977)

161. JOHNSON, RICHARD J., AND LEONARD, LOUISE C. "Psychological Test Characteristics and Performance of Nursing Students." *Nursing Res* 19(2):147–50 Mr–Ap '70. *

162. LIND, AMY I. "An Exploratory Study of Predictive Factors for Success in the Clinical Affiliation Experience." *Am J Occup Ther* 24(3):222–6 Ap '70. *

163. MORRILL, WESTON H.; MILLER, C. DEAN; AND THOMAS, LUCINDA E. "Educational and Vocational Interests of College Women." *Voc Guid Q* 19(2):85–9 D '70. *

164. NOLTING, EARL, JR. "Vocational Interests of Women: A Longitudinal Study of the Strong Vocational Interest Blank." *J Appl Psychol* 54(2):120–7 Ap '70. * (PA 44:11454)

165. NUZUM, ROBERT EDWARD. *Inferred Parental Identification and Perceived Parental Relationship as Related to Career- and Homemaking-Orientation in Above-Average Ability College Women.* Doctor's thesis, Washington State University (Pullman, Wash.), 1970. (DAI 31:2689A)

166. ROBERTS, FANNIE M. *Relationships in Respect to Attitudes Toward Mathematics, Degree of Authoritarianism, Vocational Interests, Sex Differences, and Scholastic Achievement of College Juniors.* Doctor's thesis, New York University (New York, N.Y.), 1970. (DAI 31:2134A)

167. CAMPBELL, DAVID P. *Handbook for the Strong Vocational Interest Blank.* Stanford, Calif.: Stanford University Press, 1971. Pp. xxv, 516. *

168. JOHNSON, RICHARD W. "Comparability of Old and Revised Forms of the Strong Vocational Interest Blank for Women." *J Appl Psychol* 55(1):50–6 F '71. * (PA 46:1926)

DOROTHY M. CLENDENEN, *Formerly Assistant Director, Test Division, The Psychological Corporation, New York, New York.*

It is to be hoped that this revision of the 1946 *Strong Vocational Interest Blank for Women* will not only be of immediate practical value to counselors but will also generate more research than did the earlier inventory and lead ultimately to more information on the structure of women's interests. The revised blank of 398 items maintains the original format and sections; 111 of the original items have been replaced and 2 items discarded and not replaced. The women's form has 249 items in common with the men's blank. As with the men's form, scoring has been simplified by using ±1 weights. The revision has 19 basic interest scales, 58 occupational scales, and 4 nonoccupational scales. The profile also shows 6 administrative indices, which provide for the detection of errors caused by incorrect scoring or mismarked answer sheets and misunderstood directions.

The basic interest scales have been constructed by grouping highly intercorrelated items to provide content areas. They are standardized so that 50 represents the average score of a sample of 1,000 women employed in a wide range of occupations; average scores for 906 high school senior girls are also shown on the profile. The number of items on a scale ranges from 6 (Music) or 7 (Biological Science) to 17 (Medical Service) or 18 (Office Practices). These scales are internally consistent, and although the scales are short, test-retest correlations are only a few points lower than those of the occupational scales, or .89 over short time spans and .65 over long time intervals for adults, and .56 for teenagers. The counselor and the examinee are urged to look at high and low scores, and to look at tables showing average scores of various occupations on each scale. In the Handbook a chapter is given to the basic interest scales of the SVIB-W. This includes tables of item intercorrelations; of means and standard deviations on the BIS for the normative sample of women and for a sample of high school seniors; of scale intercorrelations; and of test-retest reliability. One study of predictive validity is cited, with favorable results.

The introduction of basic interest scales is a commendable addition which provides information on the content of a person's interests, but the experienced counselor and the mature examinee will probably find the occupational scales of greater value. Most of the criterion groups are new. A few of the original groups had been tested recently and these were not retested. On the revised women's blank the 58 scales are clustered into 11 groups of related occupations based on their statistical relationship. In general, when criterion groups scored above 40 on each other's scales and the scales correlated .65 or higher with each other, the occupations were grouped. "Housewife" no

longer appears on the profile as one of the scales, nor does "Author," although in a table dealing with the basic interest scales, author is given as an example of an occupation scoring high on Writing, and low on eight scales: Homemaking, Medical Service, Merchandising, Numbers, Office Practices, Social Service, Sports, and Teaching. References to the author group appear elsewhere in the text and in tables, also. New scales include scientific occupations such as Chemist, and Mathematician, and such nonprofessional groups as Telephone Operator, Instrument Assembler, and Beautician. Nurse has been replaced by Public Health Nurse, Registered Nurse, and Licensed Practical Nurse.

One of the problems this reviewer faced was that of locating information dealing with the SVIB-W. The manual was prepared prior to the availability of the revised women's blank, and yet the 1969 manual supplement contained minimal information on the women's form and nothing on reliability or validity (other than a sentence on percent overlap in the occupational scales). Information on development was limited to one statement, that "Occupational Scales were developed analogously by using employed women, in the criterion samples, versus women-in-general." The manual does have information on reliability (using an interim version of the old profile), a table comparing mean scores of criterion groups and women-in-general, a table showing intercorrelation between scales, and a table of mean standard scores for all criterion groups. None of these, if one judges by the list of occupational scales, pertains to Women's Blank TW398. With the recent publication of the Handbook (167), some additional psychometric data became available. With the exception of the chapter on the BIS, the information on the women's blank is not consolidated, and the index of the Handbook has some notable gaps. A study of the predictive validity of the occupational scales, discussed on pages 59–60 and the sole such study for the women's blank, is not indexed under "Women," nor is the topic of "reliability." To be sure, one finds the reference under "Reliability," but for the potential user of the women's blank, the location of widely dispersed data would be facilitated by a more adequate index.

Occupational scales were developed by selecting items which differentiate a criterion group from a women-in-general group. The important statistic is the percent overlap. For the revision, the overlaps range from 14 to 52 percent, with a median of 36, five points higher than the median for the revised men's blank. This represents a separation of about two standard deviations and is satisfactory in. terms of concurrent validity. The women-in-general group is composed of a sample of 1,000, selected from 42 occupational groups to maximize diversity and supplemented by miscellaneous groups such as high school students. In the revision of the men's blank it was found that item statistics shift over time, and to make possible the continuing development of new scales while keeping the earlier scales, a considerable time spread in the reference group was desirable and necessary. This was not done for the women's blank, and it is not known yet whether this will prove unwise as new scales are developed.

Available test-retest groups are small, and the median correlation coefficients are .68 (for two groups tested first as college freshmen, with one group retested 4 years later and the other 15 years later) and .53 (for freshmen retested 26 years later). These are comparable to median test-retest correlations for the men's blank, but one hopes that additional data will be sought, since the samples are small.

Predictive validity for the women's blank is not discussed in the 1969 supplement and only briefly in the Handbook. The reviewer hopes that subsequent research will provide this. Such research might indicate whether more than one women-in-general group would have value, as some earlier research has suggested; whether criterion groups should include (as they now may) those who choose a job because of convenience and income rather than interest; whether larger percentage differences in item selection are required for women than for men; as well as other questions that have remained unanswered in the study of the measured interests of women.

The revised SVIB-W has four nonoccupational scales. Academic Achievement contrasts those who do well in school with those who do poorly, with women in occupations which require more schooling generally scoring higher than others. Diversity of Interests contains items that are statistically unrelated, and, as for men, breadth of interest was not found in such occupational groups as authors, artists,

and physicians. Femininity-Masculinity utilizes items that men and women in 18 occupations answered differently. A positive response to these items, many of which are aesthetic and cultural in nature, results in a "feminine" score. Occupational Introversion-Extroversion attempts to differentiate groups that are defined as "introverts" by responses to the *Minnesota Multiphasic Personality Inventory* from those defined as "extroverts." Beauticians, as well as mathematicians, score high (introverted) while in general those dealing with the public—e.g., guidance counselors and stewardesses—score low.

In general, this reviewer believes that in this revision major steps have been taken to improve differential measurement of women's interests. With increasing numbers of women, especially married and older women, in the labor force, this instrument should be a valuable tool for counselors and other personnel workers. The publication of the Handbook has made available data which permit the user to evaluate the current status of the women's blank, although these data are not always easily found in a book of over 500 pages. One has the feeling that the women's form is still, as the Handbook comments historically, a "slightly neglected little sister of the Men's Form." We are told that "working with the Women's Form was never one of Strong's favorite activities." Given the need to assist young women in making educational and vocational decisions, counselors would welcome an instrument of such proved validity as the men's blank. It is hoped that continuing research will provide more information on predictive validity and on the counselor use of the instrument.

BARBARA A. KIRK, *Director, Counseling Center, University of California, Berkeley, California.*

In 1969 the first major revision of the women's form of the *Strong Vocational Interest Blank* since 1946 was published. Now known as Form TW398, the inventory incorporates so many changes that it bears only a slight resemblance to the original Form W, initially published in 1933. The new form provides a total of 87 scales, which are divided as follows: 19 basic interest scales, each made up of from 6 to 18 similar (homogeneous) items; 58 of the familiar occupational scales, 29 of which are new; 4 nonoccupational scales; and

6 administrative indices. The basic interest scales consist of scales such as Merchandising, Office Practices, Teaching, and Homemaking, and are prominently displayed across the upper half of the profile with indicated norms for employed adult women and high school senior girls. They are intended to provide an indication of the test taker's core interests and to assist in explicating the scores on the occupational scales below.

The occupational scales include a refreshing array of new scales which much more thoroughly reflect the contemporary occupational and vocational opportunities available to women. Most of the criterion samples were tested or retested between 1966 and 1968, and quite a few scales have been developed for vocations below the professional level, such as Saleswoman, Telephone Operator, and Instrument Assembler. Along with a lowered reading level, this helps broaden the spectrum with which this new women's form may be used.

The nonoccupational scales attempt to assess Academic Achievement, Diversity of Interests, Occupational Introversion-Extroversion, and a modification of the previous Femininity-Masculinity of Interests, now called F-M II. The administrative indices, a welcome new addition, help the interpreter of the profile to evaluate some aspects of the way in which the inventory was completed: how many items were answered (unanswered), how many generally unpopular responses were given, whether there seems to have been confusion about which form of the test booklet was used, and what percentages of items are responded to as Like, Indifferent, and Dislike.

Other changes in the revision include replacing items considered obsolete, radically shortening the length of the occupational scales and regrouping them on the profile, simplifying the item weights, changing the shaded areas in the occupational scales to represent the middle third of the distribution of women-in-general on those scales instead of the former "chance" scores, and the redefinition and reconstitution of the "women-in-general" reference group. These changes have been reviewed elsewhere more extensively than is possible here (158).

The increased scope and sophistication of the new SVIB-W will be extremely attractive to counselors and researchers, and it can be expected to make an ongoing contribution to the complex problems of understanding women's interests and arriving at a more fully developed psychology of women in our society. Because of the instrument's appeal and the fact that revision has been needed for some years, it may be tempting to look past some of the visible shortcomings in the revision work to date, some of them serious. An important planning error resulted in the new women's form being released for general use in mid-1969 along with the publication of a supplement to the 1966 manual, but the supplement did not include the central reliability and validity data. Instead, these data did not appear until the 1971 Handbook was published, almost two years after the inventory was publicly distributed. The Handbook includes eight helpful case illustrations of the use of the SVIB-W in counseling, prepared by Lenore Harmon.

Not present in the Handbook or the 1969 manual supplement is any comparison of the new Form TW398 scores with scores on the old Form W. Without studies such as that by Johnson (168), users are left with the inference that similarly named new and old form scales have no psychologically significant differences worthy of interpretive concern or comment. But this is not invariably the case, and score levels on the two forms frequently differ, even when the correlations between corresponding scales are high. This is a serious deficiency, despite the fact that with the publication of the Handbook more useful and important information about the SVIB-W is available now than ever before. In view of the rising standards of reportage, the Handbook may also be criticized for not specifying the degree of cooperativeness of the occupational norm groups (the return rates of solicited inventories), a figure which would help the user to estimate the representativeness of norm group samples. Related to this, and more important, is the fact that the occupational scales are not crossvalidated but use the same occupational sample for both item selection and scale norming. This is a longstanding SVIB defect which seems increasingly less excusable. The Handbook reprints a great deal of previously published material, which some may find useful and others not, but it does not present an extensive, well-rounded, up-to-date working bibliography of publications about the SVIB. The 1969 supplement contains no bibliography whatever. Since the Handbook is the only author-publisher source of essential interpretive data for the new SVIB-W, the $20 cost of the volume may well reduce access to these data at the very time the inventory is being given broadened marketplace exposure as a fresh instrument which has an added set of "simple" scales (the basic interest scales), new subprofessional occupational scales, a lowered reading level, etc.

Additional attention and concern for the potential user of this instrument need to be focused on: (*a*) the lower concurrent and predictive validity of the basic interest scales in comparison with the occupational scales and the complex way in which these two different types of measurement relate and interact (The basic interest scales are built almost completely on "Like" responses, are made up of "obvious" items, and not infrequently will appear to conflict with occupational scales with which they seem logically to be associated, e.g., Art vs. Artist. From such discrepancies, where they occur, it may be possible for a knowledgeable counselor to develop a useful counseling dialogue on the relationship of stated to measured interests, but this cannot be counted upon to happen routinely.); (*b*) the radically shortened graphical display of the occupational scales in contrast to their previous presentation on the SVIB-W profile and the resulting possibility of overlooking or underestimating the importance of very low scores, which are of importance for counseling; (*c*) the relatively weak scale development procedures used for some nonoccupational scales and the need to evaluate them with particular caution. The Academic Achievement scale (AACH) for the men's SVIB has not been as successful as the 1966 manual expectations for it [1] (*148*), and the women's AACH scale was developed in the same fashion. In general, the inventory's reliability and concurrent validity data appear to range from excellent to adequate. The women's occupational scales are only slightly less differentiating than the men's (median overlap of 36 percent vs. 31 percent).

In summary, the 1969 revision of the SVIB-W, Form TW398, is an instrument which despite some shortcomings—one is almost tempted to say inevitable shortcomings—will be of major assistance to counselors and research workers.

1 FRANK, AUSTIN C. "Men's Strong Vocational Interest Blank Academic Achievement Scale: An Attempted Validation." *J Counsel Psychol* 18(4):324–31 Jl '71. *
JOHNSON, RICHARD W. "Effectiveness of SVIB Academic Achievement Scales in Predicting College Achievement." *J Appl Psychol* 53(4):309–16 Ag '69. *

Strong Vocational Interest Blank for Women

The inventory is of greatly increased complexity, and its best and most appropriate use will come only following cautious preliminary experience and ongoing research with it. The new content-homogeneous basic interest scales may help supplement the empirically derived and psychologically complex occupational scales, which must continue to be considered the core of the instrument. Overall, this is the best instrument available for measuring women's vocational interests. Its interpretation requires a considerable degree of sophistication and skill, and, at this early stage, caution.

For a review by Gwendolen Schneidler Dickson of an earlier edition, see 3:649; for a review by Ruth Strang, see 2:1681; for a review by John G. Darley, see 1:1179.

[1038]
★**Vocational Agriculture Interest Inventory.** Boys grade 8; 1965; VAII; Form A ['65, 4 pages]; manual ('65, 20 pages); student survey information sheet ['65, 1 page]; no data on reliability; separate answer sheets must be used; $1.25 per 20 tests; 75¢ per 20 answer sheets; 10¢ per set of scoring stencils; 25¢ per manual; $1 per specimen set; cash orders postpaid; (20–30) minutes; Robert W. Walker, Glenn Z. Stevens, and Norman K. Hoover; Interstate Printers & Publishers, Inc. *

REFERENCES
1. WALKER, ROBERT WILLIAM. *Development of a Vocational Agriculture Interest Inventory for Guidance of Eighth Grade Students.* Doctor's thesis, Pennsylvania State University (University Park, Pa.), 1962. (*DA* 23:3702)
2. WALKER, ROBERT W. "Interest Inventory Test Developed for Prospective Vo-Ag Students." *Ag Ed Mag* 36:235–6 Ap '64. *
3. ROBINSON, WILLIAM ALFRED. *Agriculture Interest Inventory Score and Other Characteristics of Eighth Grade Boys Related to High School Graduation Major and Employment.* Doctor's thesis, Pennsylvania State University (University Park, Pa.), 1967. (*DA* 29:819A)
4. MCCARLEY, WALTER WILLIAM. *An Experimental Study to Evaluate the Effectiveness of an Individualized Instructional Method and the Lecture-Discussion Method for Teaching Vocational Agriculture Classes.* Doctor's thesis, Michigan State University (East Lansing, Mich.), 1969. (*DAI* 30:5323A)

DAVID P. CAMPBELL, *Professor of Psychology and Director, Center for Interest Measurement Research, University of Minnesota, Minneapolis, Minnesota.*

This is an inventory constructed by three professional agriculture educators; this suggests that the authors have considerable knowledge of the field of vocational agriculture and the problems of occupational choice there, but relatively less background and fewer skills in psychological testing.

Their inventory reflects both factors. The items are sensible and useful for what they are asking, and the discussion of the use of the results, though limited, is relevant to the counselor working with boys considering agriculture as a career choice. On the other hand, their psychometric approach is naive, the normative data are pitifully few, and the general "hard data foundation" for the inventory is non-existent.

The inventory has 75 items, almost all concerned with agricultural topics. The student is asked to respond on a five-point scale, from "Strongly Like" to "Strongly Dislike." There is only one scale, "Interest in Agriculture," and the inventory can be easily hand scored with the stencils that are provided; the scoring weights were determined by contrasting a criterion group of "Successful Vo-Ag Students" with a norms group of all eighth grade boys from 20 schools. Item response positions with significant differences between these two groups are included in the scoring scale. Because the statistical significance was followed blindly, some peculiarities arose: e.g., the "Undecided" and "Strongly Dislike" responses to "Have a chance to own a farm" are both weighted negatively, but the intervening response "Dislike" receives a zero weight.

The manual reports the development in a sketchy manner and has no other psychometric information. The recommendations for use are minimal, but sensible—though I doubt that it is necessary to give the test to all eighth grade boys to find the few that will major in agriculture.

In summary, the inventory has the strengths of being developed by people who know their area and have some common sense; it has the weaknesses of sketchy psychometrics and hardly any research of developmental data. It would be better described as a systematic questionnaire, rather than as a test or inventory, and for those who need such a specific technique, it would be minimally adequate.

[1039]

★**Vocational Interest and Sophistication Assessment.** Retarded adolescents and young adults; 1967-68; VISA; individual; administration manual ('68, 51 pages); inquiry sheet ('68, 1 page); standardization report ('68, 71 pages, out of print); $2 per 50 inquiry sheets; $1 per 25 response sheets; $1 per 25 profiles; $2 per manual; $7 per specimen set; cash orders postpaid; [20-40] minutes; Joseph J. Parnicky, Harris Kahn, and Arthur D. Burdett; Joseph J. Parnicky. *
a) FORM FOR MALES. 1 form ('67, 86 pictures); interest and knowledge scores in each of 7 areas: garage, laundry, food service, maintenance, farm and grounds, materials handling, industry; response sheet ('68, 1 page); profile ('68, 2 pages); $3 per set of stimulus pictures.
b) FORM FOR FEMALES. 1 form ('67, 60 pictures); interest and knowledge scores in each of 4 areas: busi-

ness and clerical, housekeeping, food service, laundry and sewing; response sheet ('68, 1 page); profile ('68, 2 pages); $2 per set of stimulus pictures.

REFERENCES

1. PARNICKY, JOSEPH J.; KAHN, HARRIS; AND BURDETT, ARTHUR. "Preliminary Efforts at Determining the Significance of Retardates' Vocational Interests." *Am J Mental Def* 70: 393-8 N '65. * (*PA* 40:3316)
2. PARNICKY, JOSEPH J.; KAHN, HARRIS; AND BURDETT, ARTHUR D. "Standardization of the VISA (Vocational Interest and Sophistication Assessment) Technique." Abstract. *Proc 77th Ann Conv Am Psychol Assn* 4(1):165-6 '69. * (*PA* 43:16636)

[1040]

★**Vocational Interest Profile.** Ages 15 and over; 1960-66; VIP; 9 scores: numerical, mechanical, scientific, clerical, persuasive, musical, artistic, literary, service; 1 form ('66, 4 pages); user's guide ('60, 8 pages); technical manual ('66, 33 pages); mimeographed preliminary profile atlas ('66, 22 pages); Can $3 per 35 tests; 75¢ per 25 profile charts; 50¢ per profile atlas; $1.75 per technical manual; 35¢ per user's guide; $2.50 per specimen set; postage extra; (15-30) minutes; Robin N. Smith and J. R. McIntosh (test and user's guide); distributed by University of British Columbia Bookstore. *

REFERENCE

1. HENRY, SALLYANN. *A Comparison of the Factor Structures of Normative and Ipsative Interest Inventories.* Doctor's thesis, Columbia University (New York, N.Y.), 1969. (*DAI* 30:4777B)

[1041]

William, Lynde & Williams Analysis of Interest. Male adults; 1956-62; WLWAI; 8 scores: management, accounting, engineering, mechanical, sales, service, teaching, writing; 1 form ('60, 4 pages); mimeographed combined manual ('62, 8 pages) for this test and test 160; no data on reliability of present edition; no description of normative population; $12.50 per 100 tests, postpaid; [15] minutes; R. W. Henderson; William, Lynde & Williams. *

RALPH F. BERDIE, *Professor of Psychology and Director, Student Life Studies, University of Minnesota, Minneapolis, Minnesota.*

The relevant material on this test in the combined manual consists of less than a thousand words of text and a short table presenting quartile scores on six of the eight scales for related occupations. Although the author claims that each of the six occupational groups scores higher on its relevant scale than does the general population, no figures are presented in the manual for the general population. When the median scores for the occupational groups are plotted on the profile which appears at the end of the inventory, and which is based on norms derived from one thousand executives, managers, salesmen, clerks, etc., the occupational groups obtain percentile ranks ranging from 67 through 77.

The only evidence regarding validity that this reviewer found at all acceptable was the content validity. The items directly reflect the concepts defined by the eight interest scales, and when a respondent indicates that he prefers the occupation of accountant over those of plant manager, civil engineer, and master mechanic, one assumes that the item is related to the concept of accounting. Although the manual presents no information regarding this, it is relevant to question whether the respondent could not as well rate himself on eight separate rating scales, one for each of the interest dimensions, as well as express his preferences on each of the 40 items. When comparisons are made on the Strong or the Kuder inventories between scores and such self ratings, some relationship is apparent, as indicated by correlation coefficients varying around .50. With the WLWAI one well might expect correlation coefficients between self-rating and interest scores of .80 or higher.

The manual describes the reliabilities of the scores in terms of results based on earlier editions of the inventory. Reliability coefficients "in the .70's and .80's (split-half)" are reported, although the samples are not described, nor are the earlier forms of the inventory. Test-retest reliabilities are described as higher than the split-half reliabilities, but no further information is provided.

The manual provides no information regarding relationships with other interest scales; scores on personality, ability, or aptitude measurements, self-expressed or self-rated vocational interests or preferences; nor are curricular groups, age, and sex variations reported. The inventory presumably is developed for men, although nowhere in the manual is this mentioned.

The author does refer to the ipsative nature of the inventory, although this is mentioned in the section of the manual devoted to another inventory. A person may receive a high score on one of the interest scales not because he has an outstanding interest in that dimension but rather because he finds each of the other seven dimensions repellent.

The evidence available regarding this inventory does not justify its use. It requires little time of the examinee and little time to score. The manual provides no basis for saying more than this about the instrument.

[1042]

★Work Values Inventory. Grades 7–16 and adults; 1968–70; WVI; 15 scales: altruism, esthetics, creativity, intellectual stimulation, independence, achievement, prestige, management, economic returns, security, surroundings, supervisory relations, associates, variety, way of life; 1 form ('68, 4 pages, MRC scorable); manual ('70, 50 pages); reliability data for grade 10 only; norms for grades 7–12 only; $15 per 100 tests; 90¢ per specimen set; postage extra; scoring service, 36¢ per test; (10–20) minutes; Donald E. Super; Houghton Mifflin Co. *

REFERENCES

1. HANA, ATTIA MAHMOUD. Work Values in Relation to Age, Intelligence, Socioeconomic Level, and Occupational Interest Level. Doctor's thesis, Columbia University (New York, N.Y.), 1954. (DA 14:1454)
2. O'HARA, ROBERT P., AND TIEDEMAN, DAVID V. "The Vocational Self-Concept in Adolescence." J Counsel Psychol 6:292–301 w '59. * (PA 35:3279)
3. O'CONNOR, JAMES P., AND KINNANE, JOHN F. "A Factor Analysis of Work Values." J Counsel Psychol 8:263–7 f '61. * (PA 36:5LH630)
4. KINNANE, JOHN F., AND PABLE, MARTIN W. "Family Background and Work Value Orientation." J Counsel Psychol 9:320–5 w '62. * (PA 39:1378)
5. KINNANE, JOHN F., AND SUZIEDELIS, ANTANAS. "Work Value Orientation and Inventoried Interests." J Counsel Psychol 9:144–8 su '62. * (PA 37:7226)
6. SUPER, DONALD E. "The Structure of Work Values in Relation to Status, Achievement, Interests, and Adjustment." J Appl Psychol 46:231–9 Ag '62. * (PA 37:3949)
7. SUPER, DONALD E., AND MOWRY, JAMES G., JR. "Social and Personal Desirability in the Assessment of Work Values." Ed & Psychol Meas 22:715–9 w '62. * (PA 37:6736)
8. ANKER, JAMES M.; TOWNSEND, JOHN C.; AND O'CONNOR, JAMES P. "A Multivariate Analysis of Decision Making and Related Measures." J Psychol 55:211–21 Ja '63. * (PA 37:6186)
9. IVEY, ALLEN E. "Interests and Work Values." Voc Guid Q 11:121–4 w '63. * (PA 38:1441)
10. KINNANE, JOHN F., AND GAUBINGER, JOSEPH R. "Life Values and Work Values." Comment by Harry Beilin. J Counsel Psychol 10:362–7 w '63. * (PA 38:8278)
11. HARLAN, GRADY EDWARD. A Comparison of Differences in Selected Characteristics Among High School Seniors, College Freshmen, Trade School Students, Technical School Students, and Business School Students. Doctor's thesis, State University of Iowa (Iowa City, Iowa), 1964. (DA 25:5016)
12. KINNANE, JOHN F., AND BANNON, M. MARGARET. "Perceived Parental Influence and Work-Value Orientation." Personnel & Guid J 43:273–9 N '64. * (PA 39:10874)
13. DRAHOZAL, EDWARD CHARLES. A Study of Selected Characteristics of Senior High School Students and Their Perceptions of Their Counselor's Role in the Post High School Decision. Doctor's thesis, State University of Iowa (Iowa City, Iowa), 1965. (DA 26:2544)
14. HARRANGUE, M. DAMIAN. Developmental Changes in Vocational Interests and Work Values as Related to the Vocational Choices of College Women. Doctor's thesis, Catholic University of America (Washington, D.C.), 1965. (DA 26:2050)
15. SURETTE, RALPH FRANCIS. The Relationship of Personal and Work-Value Orientations to Career Versus Homemaking Preference Among Twelfth Grade Girls. Doctor's thesis, Catholic University of America (Washington, D.C.), 1965. (DA 26:4462)
16. GOSS, ALLEN, AND PATE, KENTON D. "Work Attitudes and Industrial Adjustment of Psychiatric Patients." Newsl Res Psychol 8:9–10 Ag '66. *
17. HUMBERT, JACK TERRILL. The Work Values of Male and Female Urban and Rural High School and Technical Institute Welfare Students in New Mexico. Doctor's thesis, University of New Mexico (Albuquerque, N.M.), 1966. (DA 27:1708A)
18. MALONE, FRANCIS EDWARD, JR. A Study of Students Enrolled in Post-High School Public Vocational Education Programs in Iowa During the 1964–1965 School Year. Doctor's thesis, University of Iowa (Iowa City, Iowa), 1966. (DA 27:678A)
19. GOSS, ALLEN M., AND PATE, KENTON D. "Predicting Vocational Rehabilitation Success for Psychiatric Patients With Psychological Tests." Psychol Rep 21:725–30 D '67. * (PA 42:7550)
20. MADAUS, GEORGE F., AND O'HARA, ROBERT P. "Contrasts Between High School Boys Choosing the Priesthood as Their Occupational Choice and Boys Choosing Eight Other Occupational Categories." Cath Psychol Rec 5:41–51 sp '67. *
21. NORMILE, RICHARD HENRY. Differentiating Among Known Occupational Groups by Means of the Work Values Inventory. Doctor's thesis, Catholic University of America (Washington, D.C.), 1967. (DA 28:2075A)
22. O'HARA, ROBERT P. "Vocational Self Concepts of Boys Choosing Science and Non-Science Careers." Ed & Psychol Meas 27:139–49 sp '67. * (PA 41:9476)
23. SUPER, DONALD E., AND KAPLAN, HERBERT H. "Work

Values of School Counselors Attending NDEA Summer Guidance Institutes." *Personnel & Guid J* 46:27–31 S '67. *

24. BERNSTEIN, BRUCE HARVEY. *A Study of the Work Values of a Group of Disadvantaged High School Boys in a Co-Operative Education Program.* Doctor's thesis, New York University (New York, N.Y.), 1968. (*DA* 29:2512A)

25. CARRUTHERS, T. E. "Work Values and Chosen Careers: Note on the Trial of an American Work Values Inventory With British Subjects." *Occup Psychol* 42:111–7 Ap–Jl '68. * (*PA* 43:13407)

26. GOSS, ALLEN M. "Importance of Diagnostic Categories in Evaluating Psychological Data." *J Counsel Psychol* 15:476–8 S '68. *

27. HENDRIX, VERNON L., AND SUPER, DONALD E. "Factor Dimensions and Reliability of the Work Values Inventory." *Voc Guid Q* 16:269–74 Je '68. *

28. COTNAM, JOHN DALE. *Variance in Self-Report Measures of Disadvantaged Young Adults as a Function of Race and Stated Purpose of Testing.* Doctor's thesis, University of Rochester (Rochester, N.Y.), 1969. (*DAI* 30:3719A)

29. MARGULIES, NEWTON. "Organizational Culture and Psychological Growth." *J Appl Behav Sci* 5(4):491–508 O–D '69. * (*PA* 44:10309)

30. MOSES, ROLAND GEORGE. *Perceived and Tested Value Similarities Between Client and Counselor and Their Relationship to Counseling Outcome Criteria.* Doctor's thesis, Columbia University (New York, N.Y.), 1969. (*DAI* 30:4378B)

31. SHAH, USHA DINESH. *Work Values and Job Satisfaction.* Doctor's thesis, Columbia University (New York, N.Y.), 1969.

32. PALLONE, N. J.; RICKARD, F. S.; HURLEY, R. B.; AND TIRMAN, R. J. "Work Values and Self-Meaning." *J Counsel Psychol* 17(4):3–6–7 Jl '70. * (*PA* 44:21559)

33. ZYTOWSKI, DONALD G. "The Concept of Work Values." *Voc Guide Q* 18(3):176–86 Mr '70. *

RALPH F. BERDIE, *Professor of Psychology and Director, Student Life Studies, University of Minnesota, Minneapolis, Minnesota.*

The section in the manual describing the validity of this inventory presents information about its construct validity, content or face validity, and concurrent validity. No attention is given to what might be called the pragmatic validity, or the practical usefulness of the inventory. What can the inventory contribute to the process of which it is a part? The author states, "Understanding the value structure of a student or client in educational and vocational counseling, or of an applicant for a position in business or industry, is thus important as an aid to clarifying goals and to determining the psychological appropriateness of a given type of training or employment." Are counseling, selection, and placement improved by incorporating the inventory into the process? To what extent do results of the inventory expand our knowledge of human behavior? Research similar to the early British evaluation of counseling with and without the use of tests is needed, not only to determine what the *Work Values Inventory* contributes, but also to determine the contributions of other tests and procedures.

The author presents in the manual little information about how the counselor, personnel worker, or research psychologist can use the inventory. Psychometric information regarding the instrument is presented and the development of the inventory is described. A bibliography refers to representative literature in vocational and occupational psychology but contains little, if any, reference to uses or possible uses of the inventory by counselors or others. The reviewer recognizes that similar comments can be made regarding most tests and inventories, but today the author who introduces a new instrument has particular responsibility for helping its potential user in light of the store of available experience relevant to the users of instruments with long histories of research and application.

The WVI has its source in Super's long and illustrious career in research on careers. The inventory consists of 45 brief items, each descriptive of a particular value referring to work and jobs. The respondent rates each value in terms of its importance to him, using a five-step rating scale. The 45 items are designed to assess the importance to the respondent of each of 15 values with three different items applying to each value. A factor analysis described in the manual and based only on 51 boys and 48 girls revealed four dimensions for each of the sex groups. For the men, these dimensions were labeled material or situational, goodness of life, self-expression, and behavior control, and for the women there were slight but not major differences. Earlier forms of the WVI have provided somewhat similar structures. The intercorrelations between the scales range up to .66, the Economic Returns and Security scales having this highest correlation. The decimal points have been omitted from the tables presenting the correlations and the reader is left to assume that a reported correlation of 275 really is a correlation of .275 insofar as most of the correlations are presented with two digits and only a few with three. Editors should be urged to round off decimals!

The manual is deficient in terms of the reliability information presented and in terms of comprehensiveness of norms. Reliability is reported only for 51 males and 48 females in the tenth grade. The test-retest reliabilities over a two-week period range from .74 to .88. The means are presented for 99 tenth graders and a comparison of these means to the percentiles presented in the norm tables suggests that the group on which the reliabilities were determined was not representative of the norm group. For example, the mean score on the creativity scale for the 51 tenth grade males used in the reliability study was 10.06, which corresponds to a percentile score of 32 on the norms for tenth grade boys. The norms for grades 7 through 12 appear adequate, although the reviewer is curious about the extent to which representatives from innercity schools were included in the norm group. Norms for other than secondary school students are not presented in the manual.

The present form of the *Work Values Inventory* is the most recent of previously developed forms and much of the supporting research has been done on earlier forms. As is always the case in such situations, the user must recognize the possibility that information obtained from early forms of a test may not apply to later forms, and inferences must be made cautiously.

The manual presents correlations between the WVI and other scales, and these also are reported in separate reports for various forms of the inventory. Work values are related to interests as measured by the Strong and Kuder but correlations are low.

The *Work Values Inventory* may be compared to another instrument, the *Minnesota Importance Questionnaire*. This latter inventory is presented only for research purposes but it is one of a series of carefully planned instruments designed to provide systematic information about job satisfaction, work values, and job success.

The research psychologist must decide for himself which of these instruments to use. The counseling psychologist, before he decides which instrument he will use, must determine first the way in which knowledge regarding an individual's work values will further counseling and placement. He will find as a most useful reference the paper by Zytowski (*33*), which reviews both the research and theory on work values. Zytowski states, "it seems reasonable to conclude that a concept of work values is a viable one in the description of vocational behavior, perhaps more so than interests or other conceptions of satisfaction. Despite its promises, the work values concept awaits considerably more empirical work before it can stand equally with constructs already established."

DAVID V. TIEDEMAN, *Professor of Education, Harvard University, Cambridge, Massachusetts.*

"Values are related to interests, but differ in that they are the qualities sought rather than the activities or objects which embody them: they are thus more fundamental." This quotation from the manual epitomizes the purpose of the *Work Values Inventory*. We perpetually

seek the reasons for our acts and desires. We try to capture those reasons in scales we call values since they should reveal our fundamental orientations to situations, people, and life in general.

The Allport-Vernon-Lindzey *Study of Values* currently enjoys high regard as a scale of general values. It has been widely studied and used. It was advanced in terms of a general theory which has proven itself. Super, therefore, launched his *Work Values Inventory* from the springboard of the *Study of Values*. He further extended its general context to the specific context of work and placed his *Work Values Inventory* in relation to both the *Strong Vocational Interest Blank* and the *Kuder Preference Record—Vocational*. The result is Super's inventory which has been under development for about 20 years. Longer forms of the inventory have been used in research throughout this period. The items in both these longer forms and the present short form were talked through with junior high school students. The result is an instrument which is understandable to junior high school youth but not offensive to adults.

The present inventory consists of but 45 items, three in each of the 15 scales detailed above. You expect that scores based on only three items in a scale would not be very reliable. However, the one set of test-retest reliability data available indicates that tenth graders after a two-week interval made scores on the 15 scales which had correlations ranging from .74 to .88, with the median being .83. The respectable size of these correlations for three-item tests suggests that the claimed selection of the items on the basis of their homogeneity indexes was actually quite adequately achieved.

The inventory has been around for two decades. Hence it is not surprising that there is quite a bit of validity data available in the manual. These data suggest that the values constructs sought have been reasonably approximated in the scales, that the items in the scale have content validity, and that the inventory offers concurrent results with outside criteria in accord with expectations, although results are not markedly different, merely statistically so.

Norms on the inventory were quite carefully developed. A representative sample of the nation was tested and norms were adjusted according to the proportions of cases in each of several categories, in accord with Project

Talent procedures. Although norms are available for only grades 7–12 as noted above, this may not be a factor against their use with college students and adults, since the grade differences in the known range are not at all marked. Work values do not seem to change overall with age to any marked degree.

In summary, the *Work Values Inventory* checks out in a number of important ways. It has a solid general base. It is aimed at an important specific departure from that general base, namely work. It has tolerable reliability. Throughout two decades several interesting things have been learned about the operation of work values in life space. However, users of the WVI are still going to face the nagging question, "What do these work value scores mean?"

One of the possible ways of lending meaning to the value scores, which is not set out in the manual, is to divide the score of each scale by three in order to give the scores the meaning which inheres in the definitions of numbers which the subject originally used as he completed the inventory. This procedure will tell how important the subject considered each value to be. But then what? The items composing each scale are noted in the manual. Hence, a second step could be to attach this import to the specific items of the WVI. One could then free associate in order to expand that meaning both to other items like the ones in the scales and to work situations in which the particular value might find satisfaction. But here is where the specific intent of the *Work Values Inventory* runs into difficulty. A good deal of work was put into obtaining norms for the inventory. However, the interpersonal context does not seem to help in offering meaning to vocational choice or development. The personal context seems to offer greater promise, but this context is not exploited in the manual. Hence counselors will be on their own in lending personal meaning to the inventory. So will those persons who complete it. But counselors and those who inventory their work values should not despair. The values are fairly clearly defined. It is possible from the raw scores to determine how a subject values each area. Some careful thought about the meaning of the values might well guide a person in his consideration of his work, vocation, and career. At about 50¢ for the test and its scoring, it seems worthwhile

to place one's values into this context. If you do, just don't worry about how stable your inventoried values will be or what they will predict. The major contribution of the exercise to your well-being will be in terms of what it teaches you about what you consider to be worthwhile about work at the present moment. This is really quite valuable if you stop to reflect on that value just a little!

J Ed Meas 8(1):53–4 sp '71. John W. French. * While many users will receive with enthusiasm this brief, easy-to-use instrument, it is not possible for a reviewer to endorse completely an inventory that claims to measure, in 10 to 15 minutes of testing time, 15 different values with sufficient reliability for individual counselling. The median reliability figure for 15 scales was found to be .83 when using retest after two weeks. This is adequate for only rough individual measurement. In addition, we might worry that the data may not be accurate, because they come from a mere 99 pupils in a single suburban high school. If this group of both sexes combined was an unusually diverse group, these reliability estimates could be inflated. However, judging from the mass of other correlational data that are presented, these reliability figures look reasonable and are, to be sure, excellent for 3-item scales. Both the test and the manual are written with a kind of straightforward, open, obvious approach. The items are clear and undisguised. It is easy to see which ones belong on the same scale; it would be easy to fake just about any pattern of values that one might wish. In discussing this possibility, the author winds up by observing that "the frequently demonstrated fact that subjects *can* distort does not prove that they *do* distort." Fortunately, the manual gives the user adequate warning that this test could be misleading unless the test taker is reasonably disposed toward honesty. This reviewer is inclined to agree that distortions are likely to be rare * In a full and frank discussion of this situation, the manual actually cites evidence that greater differentiating power is obtained with the forced-choice format. However, the author correctly points out that better reliability and better rapport with the test taker is gained from the easier, more pleasant rating technique that he uses. The forced-choice method also distorts correlations both among the test's own scales and with other test scores. This happens because a strong interest in one value requires the responder to deny the importance of other values. Perhaps the most important and most obvious fault of this manual is that research on the test has not yet been completed. The presently available evidence for each type of validity is clearly discussed. Construct validity is demonstrated through correlations with the Strong and Kuder interest inventories and with the Allport-Vernon-Lindzey Study of Values. Expected correlations are generally present, but they are somewhat spotty and not large. The discussion of content validity cites field studies that sound effective but presents no data on actual judges' agreement that the items are directed toward the values they are supposed to measure. Concurrent validity looks reasonable but is demonstrated merely by data from occupational groups who had taken earlier forms of the test, forms differing sharply from the present test by featuring forced choices. Data on occupational predictive validity have not yet been collected. This test is attractive and seems to this reviewer to be measuring what it is supposed to measure. The manual is unusually well written and seems to be of high quality as far as it goes. However, brevity and directness in the test have been achieved at the cost of questionable reliability and the choice of a format that may not adequately standardize test responses. The research that has been done seems well done and clearly presented, but adequate studies normally provided for a published test are not yet complete. While the tables of norms are good and interscale analyses are excellent, reliability needs further confirmation, correlations with other tests must be computed for the up-to-date form of the test, and no data have yet been collected for evaluating predictive validity. The completion of research is likely to lead to an unusually good manual for a test that is highly usable but overly simplified for precise measurement.

MANUAL DEXTERITY

[1043]
★**Crissey Dexterity Test.** Job applicants; 1964; CDT; individual; 1 form; manual (4 pages); $60 per set of pegboard and manual, postage extra; (5) minutes; Orlo L. Crissey; Psychological Services, Inc. *

REFERENCE

1. CRISSEY, ORLO L. "Test Predictive of Success in Occupation of Job-Setter." Abstract. *Psychol B* 39:436 Jl '42. *

LYLE F. SCHOENFELDT, *Associate Professor of Psychology, University of Georgia, Athens, Georgia.*

The author claims that this test "measures the ability to work with the hands in a coordinated manner" and that it is "recommended as a pre-employment screening test for assembly, packing, simple machine operation, and other jobs which require extensive use of the hands." The apparatus consists of a rectangular board with 128 wells in eight columns of 16 each and 64 cylindrical pegs.

The examinee is instructed to move pegs from the wells at one end of the board to the 64 wells closest to him, turning them in the process so that the end previously facing upward will be inserted in the well. The movement is in a prescribed pattern and is done two pegs at a time (one in each hand). The score is the number of pegs placed in the second and third trials.

The manual contains fewer than 1,000 words and is the briefest this reviewer has seen. The administration instructions are clear and succinct.

The only norms are based on a mixed sample of 243 male and female production workers—general assemblers, inspectors, packagers, and routine machine operators. A reliability of .91 was obtained on 163 cases using "separately timed halves."

The results of three validity studies are reported for waitresses (N = 39), kiln loaders (N = 17), and machine operators (N = 18). The results with these small groups were correlations with rated production in the .50's.

One expects that a test designed by the Director of Personnel Evaluation Services, General Motors Institute, would be backed by a galaxy of validity and normative data. The absence of data leads this reviewer to conclude that either the test was never tried or that it was tried and did not work, neither of which speaks well for the test.

On the other hand, this test would seem to merit consideration as a pre-employment screening test for jobs requiring a large amount of coordinated two-hand manipulatory movement. As with similar tests, the user should plan to collect job-specific norm and validity information. One of its principal competitors is the *Minnesota Rate of Manipulation Test,* a series of five tests, two of which involve using both hands simultaneously. The Crissey test seems to involve a greater component of coordination than would either of the Minnesota subtests. A disadvantage of the Crissey test is the fact that very little published research exists to attest to its utility.

[1044]

*Hand-Tool Dexterity Test. Adolescents and adults; 1946-65; HTDT; individual; 1 form ('46); revised manual ('65, 8 pages); $39 per set of testing materials including manual; 60¢ per manual; postage extra; (4-12) minutes; George K. Bennett; Psychological Corporation. *

REFERENCES

1-2. See 3:659.
3. LANEY, ARTHUR R., JR. "Validity of Employment Tests for Gas-Appliance Service Personnel." *Personnel Psychol* 4: 199-208 su '51. * (*PA* 26:1735)
4. RIM, Y. "The Predictive Validity of Seven Manual Dexterity Tests." *Psychologia* 5:52-5 Mr '62. * (*PA* 38:1417)
5. ELKIN, LORNE. "Predicting Performance of the Mentally Retarded on Sheltered Workshop and Non-Institutional Jobs." *Am J Mental Def* 72:533-9 Ja '68. * (*PA* 42:7638)
6. PAYTON, OTTO D. "A Study of the Dexterity and Coordination of Physical Therapy Students." *Physical Ther* 49(8):845 Ag '69. *

For reviews by C. H. Lawshe, Jr. and Neil D. Warren, see 3:659.

[1045]

★Manipulative Aptitude Test. Grades 9–12 and adults; 1967; MAT; 3 scores: left hand, right hand, total; 1 form; preliminary manual (14 pages); profile-record form (2 pages); no adult norms; $69.50 per set of testing materials including 10 record forms and manual; $5.50 per 25 record forms; $3.75 per manual; postpaid; 5(7) minutes; Wesley S. Roeder; distributed by Western Psychological Services. *

[1046]

*Minnesota Rate of Manipulation Test, 1969 Edition. "Grades 7 to adults"; 1931-69; MRMT; revision of *Minnesota Manual Dexterity Test* which is still available; 5 scores: placing, turning, displacing, 1-hand turning and placing, 2-hand turning and placing; formboard ('69, same as 1946 edition except for material and use of wells rather than holes); manual ('69, 21 pages); record form ('69, 1 page); all data on reliability and validity, originally reported in 1943 and 1945, based on earlier editions; no school norms; older adult norms based on 1933 testing, younger adult norms based on 1957 testing; $47 per set of testing materials, 50 record forms, and manual; $2 per manual; postage extra; (30-50) minutes; Minnesota Employment Stabilization Research Institute (test); American Guidance Service, Inc. *

REFERENCES

1-4. See 2:1662.
5-26. See 3:663.
27-50. See 6:1077.
51. SPRAGUE, ANN LEE. *The Relationship Between Selected Measures of Expressive Language and Motor Skill in Eight-Year-Old Boys.* Doctor's thesis, State University of Iowa (Iowa City, Iowa), 1961. (*DA* 21:3696)
52. RIM, Y. "The Predictive Validity of Seven Manual Dexterity Tests." *Psychologia* 5:52-5 Mr '62. * (*PA* 38:1417)
53. WINSCHEL, JAMES FRANCIS. *Performance of Normal and Mentally Retarded Children on Selected Motor and Intellectual Tasks as a Function of Incentive Conditions.* Doctor's thesis, University of Pittsburgh (Pittsburgh, Pa.), 1963. (*DA* 25: 6443)
54. FINLEY, PETER J. "Performance of Male Juvenile Delinquents on Four Psychological Tests." *Training Sch B* 60: 175-83 F '64. * (*PA* 39:5704)
55. PETERSON, FLOYD E. "Identification of Sub-Groups for Test Validation Research." *J Indus Psychol* 2:98-101 D '64. * (*PA* 40:10636)
56. CLAWSON, LAVERE EDWIN. *A Study of the Clawson Worksample Tests for Measuring Manual Dexterity of the Blind.* Doctor's thesis, University of Utah (Salt Lake City, Utah), 1967. (*DA* 28:2548A)
57. CLAWSON, LAVERE E. "A Study of the Clawson Worksample Tests for Measuring the Manual Dexterity of the Blind." *New Outl Blind* 62:182-7+ Je '68. *
58. McCOY, WESLEY LAWRENCE. *A Comparison of Select Psychomotor Abilities of a Sample of Undergraduate Instrumental Music Majors and a Sample of Undergraduate Non-Music Majors.* Doctor's thesis, Louisiana State University (Baton Rouge, La.), 1970. (*DAI* 31:1833A)
59. ROSEN, MARVIN; KIVITZ, MARVIN S.; CLARK, GERALD R.; AND FLOOR, LUCRETIA. "Prediction of Postinstitutional Adjustment of Mentally Retarded Adults." *Am J Mental Def* 74(6): 726-34 My '70. * (*PA* 44:17195)
60. STERNLICHT, M.; BIALER, I.; AND DEUTSCH, M. R. "Influence of External Incentives on Motor Performance on Institutionalized Retardates." *J Mental Def Res* 14(2):149-54 Je '70. *

LYLE F. SCHOENFELDT, *Associate Professor of Psychology, University of Georgia, Athens, Georgia.*

This series of tests, now serving a second generation of psychometricians, has established itself as a standard instrument for use in selecting applicants for jobs requiring gross arm-hand manipulatory movements. The basic apparatus consists of two rectangular boards, each with 60 wells arranged in four rows of 15, and 60 cylindrical blocks which fit into the wells. The major differences in the 1969 edition are the thicker, more durable boards with wells rather than holes, as in earlier versions (the dimensions of the receptacles are the same as previously).

The battery consists of the following five tests: Placing, Turning, Displacing, One-Hand Turning and Placing, and Two-Hand Turning and Placing. The first two were the only tests in the earlier versions of the battery and continue to be the most widely used of the five. The turning and displacing tests use only one board and require removing and replacing the blocks. Two hands are required in the turning test, the preferred hand in the displacing test. The other three tests require moving the blocks from one board to the second in prescribed patterns. For all tests, the score is the total seconds required to complete the sequence of manipulations during the second through fifth trials, the first being for practice.

The revised manual includes improved procedures for administering all five tests in individual and group sessions, as well as procedures for administering the turning and displacing tests to the blind. (The tasks performed by the subject and the instructions to him are the same as before.) For the displacing test the figure illustrating the sequence movement disagrees with the instructions to the subject. The latter is correct.

The technical data tend toward a somewhat disjointed assemblage of information collected during the thirties and forties. Even more unfortunate from the user's point of view, the major norms are unchanged since 1946 and no new technical data have been added since 1957.

Reliabilities, based on a single administration and given for all but the displacing test, average in the low to mid .90's depending on the number of trials. Although a number of validity studies have been reported, the publishers include only a 1943 study by Jurgensen (*13*), based on 60 paper mill employees.

The intercorrelations between the tests average .50, high enough to suggest that it would probably be unnecessary to administer more than two of the tests for any particular application. Norms are presented for two, three, and four trials. Although separate group norms are presented for the placing and turning tests, there is no reason to believe group administration scores would be different from those obtained during individual trials. No breakdown (age, sex, etc.) is given for the "depression era" sample on which the norms are based. Separate and less detailed norms based on young adults (average age, 19) are presented for three trials on the placing and turning tests. An average young adult on these tests would be at the 95th percentile when compared to the depression era sample.

In view of the inadequate norm and validity information, potential users would do well to heed the publisher's caveat concerning the importance of developing job-specific norms and validity information. In spite of the several deficiencies, this test should provide valuable quantitative data to aid in selection and placement decisions.

For reviews by Edwin E. Ghiselli and John R. Kinzer, see 3:663 (1 excerpt); for reviews by Lorene Teegarden and Morris S. Viteles, see 2:1662.

[1047]

★**Practical Dexterity Board.** Ages 8 and over; 1962; PDB; individual; 1 form; manual (4 pages); $29.95 per set of dexterity board, 50 record sheets, and manual; $1 per 50 record sheets; postage extra; (10–15) minutes; John G. Miller; SPECO Educational Systems. *

[1048]

★**Yarn Dexterity Test.** Textile workers and applicants; 1964–65; YDT; individual; 1 form ['64]; man-

ual ('65, 12 pages); $50 per set of testing materials including manual; $3 per manual; postage extra; (10) minutes; Robert L. Brown; Brown & Associates. *

MECHANICAL ABILITY

[1049]

*****Bennett Mechanical Comprehension Test.** Grades 9–12 and adults; 1940–70; BMCT; revision of *Tests of Mechanical Comprehension,* Forms AA, BB, WI; Form CC, for men in engineering schools, is still available; Forms S, T, ('69, 19 pages); manual ('69, 17 pages); supplement ('70, 2 pages) for tape administration; no norms for grades 9 and 10; separate answer sheets (NCS) must be used; $6.50 per 25 tests; $3.50 per 50 answer sheets; 50¢ per key; $7.50 per 3¾ ips tape recording; 50¢ per manual; $1 per specimen set; postage extra; Spanish edition available; 30(35) minutes; George K. Bennett; Psychological Corporation. *

REFERENCES

1–19. See 3:683.
20–47. See 4:766.
48–93. See 5:889.
94–108. See 6:1094.
109. BRUCE, MARTIN MARC. *The Importance of Certain Personality Characteristics, Skills and Abilities in Effectiveness as a Factory Foreman.* Doctor's thesis, New York University (New York, N.Y.), 1952. (*DA* 13:116)
110. HANES, BERNARD. *A Factor Analysis of the MMPI, Aptitude Test Data and Personal Information Using a Population of Criminals.* Doctor's thesis, Ohio State University (Columbus, Ohio), 1952. (*DA* 18:1483)
111. CHANDLER, ROBERT E. *Validation of Apprentice Screening Tests in an Oil Refinery.* Doctor's thesis, Purdue University (Lafayette, Ind.), 1956. (*DA* 27:325B)
112. BRADLEY, ARTHUR DICKINSON. *Estimating Success in Technical and Skilled Trade Courses Using a Multivariate Statistical Analysis.* Doctor's thesis, University of Minnesota (Minneapolis, Minn.), 1958. (*DA* 21:313)
113. SHUKLA, N. N. "The Relation of Intelligence and Ability to Scholastic Achievement of Pupils in the S.S.C. Class." *J Ed & Voc Guid* 5:38–44 Ag '58. *
114. TORRES, LEONARD. *A Study of the Relationship Between Selected Variables and the Achievement of Industrial Arts Students at Long Beach State College.* Doctor's research study No. 1, Colorado State College (Greeley, Colo.), 1963. (*DA* 25:316)
115. DREW, ALFRED S. "The Relationship of General Reading Ability and Other Factors to School and Job Performance of Machine Apprentices." *J Indus Teach Ed* 2:47–60 f '64. *
116. HODGSON, RICHARD W. "Personality Appraisal of Technical and Professional Applicants." *Personnel Psychol* 17:167–87 su '64. * (*PA* 39:6067)
117. MEADOW, LLOYD. "Assessment of Students for Schools of Practical Nursing." *Nursing Res* 13:222–9 su '64. *
118. RONAN, W. W. "Evaluation of Skilled Trades Performance Predictors." *Ed & Psychol Meas* 24:601–8 f '64. * (*PA* 39:6074)
119. DICKEN, CHARLES F., AND BLACK, JOHN D. "Predictive Validity of Psychometric Evaluations of Supervisors." *J Appl Psychol* 49:34–47 F '65. * (*PA* 39:8793)
120. PENFIELD, ROBERT VERDON. *The Psychological Characteristics of Effective First-Line Managers.* Doctor's thesis, Cornell University (Ithaca, N.Y.), 1966. (*DA* 27:1610B)
121. SORENSON, WAYNE W. "Test of Mechanical Principles as a Suppressor Variable for the Prediction of Effectiveness on a Mechanical Repair Job." *J Appl Psychol* 50:348–52 Ag '66. * (*PA* 40:11537)
122. HINMAN, SUSAN LEE. *A Predictive Validity Study of Creative Managerial Performance.* Greensboro, N.C.: Creativity Research Institute of The Richardson Foundation, Inc., November 1967. Pp. yi, 124. *
123. LIPSMAN, CLAIRE K. *The Relation of Socio-Economic Level and Occupational Choice to Needs and Vocational Behavior.* Doctor's thesis, Catholic University of America (Washington, D.C.), 1967. (*DA* 28:2073A)
124. MOFFIE, D. J., AND GOODNER, SUSAN. *A Predictive Validity Study of Creative and Effective Managerial Performance.* Greensboro, N.C.: Creativity Research Institute of The Richardson Foundation, Inc., December 1967. Pp. 80. *
125. WELSH, LAWRENCE A. *The Supervisor's Employee Appraisal Heuristic: The Contribution of Selected Measures of Employee Aptitude, Intelligence and Personality.* Doctor's

thesis, University of Pittsburgh (Pittsburgh, Pa.), 1967. (*DA* 28:4321A)

126. BRADSHAW, OTTIE LEON. *The Relationship of Selected Measures of Aptitude, Interest, and Personality to Academic Achievement in Engineering and Engineering Technology.* Doctor's thesis, Oklahoma State University (Stillwater, Okla.), 1968. (*DAI* 30:979A)

127. FINCH, CURTIS R. "Predicting Mathematics Achievement in Technical Training." *Voc Guid Q* 16:193–7 Mr '68. *

128. MOORE, CLAY L., JR.; MACNAUGHTON, JOHN F.; AND OSBURN, HOBART G. "Ethnic Differences Within an Industrial Selection Battery." *Personnel Psychol* 22(4):473–82 w '69. * (*PA* 44:13473)

129. CRONBACH, LEE J. *Essentials of Psychological Testing, Third Edition,* pp. 188–90. New York: Harper & Row, Publishers, Inc., 1970. Pp. xxx, 752. *

130. GRANT, DONALD L., AND BRAY, DOUGLAS W. "Validation of Employment Tests for Telephone Company Installation and Repair Occupations." *J Appl Psychol* 54(1):7–14 F '70. *

HAROLD P. BECHTOLDT, *Professor of Psychology, The University of Iowa, Iowa City, Iowa.*

In 1969, the new Forms S and T of the *Bennett Mechanical Comprehension Test,* formerly known as the *Tests of Mechanical Comprehension,* were made available. These new forms are to cover the age, sex, and skill ranges previously identified with the forms AA, BB, and WI of the *Tests of Mechanical Comprehension.* Information regarding the new forms is provided in a 14-page manual and by discussions of additional points by Cronbach in his text, *Essentials of Psychological Testing;* [1] both the manual and Cronbach's text also treat the Mechanical Reasoning Test of the *Differential Aptitude Tests* as an alternate form of the *Tests of Mechanical Comprehension.* The relatively large quantity of data developed since 1950 which deal with the different forms provides much of the material summarized so instructively by Cronbach.

In view of the extensive 1949 reviews of Forms AA, BB, and WI in the 3rd MMY (3:683), and later of these three forms plus Form CC in the 4th MMY (4:766), it is considered appropriate at this time to look at the new manual of this popular test from the viewpoint of the previously stated points of concern. Critical suggestions in the previous reviews dealt with the topics of validity and of selection of items. The previously published comments dealing with validity of this test noted the emphasis in the manual on indirect, rather than on direct, evidence of usefulness; the evidence of usefulness noted earlier was developed from studies using similar tests with military personnel working at military occupations. The previous comments regarding the test construction and item selection procedures deal largely with the failure of the manual to detail the item

1 CRONBACH, LEE J. *Essentials of Psychological Testing, Third Edition.* New York: Harper and Row, Publishers, Inc., 1970. Pp. xxx, 752. *

analysis procedures or to treat the adequacy of the criteria used in item selection and the effect of differential amounts of formal training in physics.

As was true of the earlier forms, Forms S and T rate high in terms of simplicity of instructions and responses required, legibility of type, adequacy of the drawings, and general acceptability by job applicants of the test items as relevant to the topic of mechanical comprehension (face validity). In addition, Forms S and T are characterized by four features representing desirable changes from the earlier forms: (*a*) two "parallel forms" (with respect both to content categories and to statistical properties) of the test are now available; (*b*) the number of items has been increased from 60 to 68 (but the wide range of difficulty values is associated with a wide range of item-test point-biserial coefficients); (*c*) the score is number right rather than right minus one-half wrongs; and (*d*) a time limit of 30 minutes, rather than unlimited time, is now indicated.

Relatively little technical information on the development of Forms S and T is given. While the manual claims "unusual care in item selection," the only supporting details provided consist of the mean values and the ranges of the difficulty and discrimination indices; the present manual is as inadequate as were the manuals of the other forms of the test on this point. Cronbach suggests that extreme splits of 27 percent were used in the selection of the items of the earlier forms. Since only 42 new items and 43 changed items were added to the item pool for the development of Forms S and T, the criticisms expressed in previous reviews regarding the criterion for item selection might still be a matter of concern to some test users. Rather than dealing with this criterion problem directly, the authors have emphasized in the new manual the reliability and comparability of the two forms of the test. Reliability in this case, however, is the internal consistency notion estimated by means of odd-even coefficients and the Spearman-Brown formula. The evidence in the manual of test-retest stability or parallel-form consistency is restricted to a short interval practice effect study (very stable results were found for 16 and 22 items) and correlations of Forms S and T with Form BB (correlations of .87 on samples of 50 cases). While the internal consistency coefficients vary from .81 to .93, the standard error of measurement tends to be approximately 3.5 points. More evidence of form-to-form stability of the Mechanical Reasoning form of the test is provided by the manual of the *Differential Aptitude Tests;* over a period of several months, the Mechanical Reasoning Test scores correlated about .70 across forms, with associated standard errors of measurement of around 4.4 points. Although no adequate direct evidence of stability based on the scores of Forms S and T is available, the general consistency of data from the several earlier forms obtained over a period of years indicates that the authors are probably on reasonably safe ground in emphasizing the relationships found with the earlier forms of the *Tests of Mechanical Comprehension.*

It is generally agreed among test "specialists" that the "validity" of a test is its most important characteristic; disagreement often arises, however, as to the definition of the word "validity." According to the manual of Forms S and T of the BMCT, the objective of the test is to "measure the ability to perceive and understand the relationship of physical forces and mechanical elements in practical situations"; the items do seem to have face validity for this objective. However, no direct evidence of accurate prediction of rate of acquisition of skill, or of change in performance with practice or training, is provided. The new forms of the test, however, are probably both predictive of future performances and definitive (in a trade test sense) of a low level of mechanical skill. The manual reports two correlations above .30 between test scores on Form S or T and job *ratings.* The review by Ghiselli [2] indicated that a test of mechanical principles usually was a useful predictor of training program success or current job proficiency for a variety of mechanics, machinists, and machine operators. In the earlier manuals, as well as in the present one, the evidence of predictive usefulness is very inadequate.

The results of the early (1940) investigation of the effect of formal physics training are repeated in the present manual; unfortunately, these data are not an acceptable basis for judging the effect of modern schooling on these new forms. The influence of informal relevant experience on test performances is emphasized and is clearly indicated in the variation in mean

2 GHISELLI, EDWIN E. *The Validity of Occupational Aptitude Tests.* New York: John Wiley & Sons, Inc., 1966. Pp. ix, 155. *

performance for the several groups used to provide norms for Forms S and T.

Perhaps the more interesting data for counselors would be evidence of the usefulness of the BMCT in differential prediction situations. The correlations of the scores of the several forms of the *Tests of Mechanical Comprehension* and of other aptitude tests are relatively high; these data, plus those presented by Cronbach, suggest that while a useful degree of differential prediction involving the BMCT can be expected for a few comparisons, other tests will probably be more generally useful for purposes of differential prediction.

In summary, the *Bennett Mechanical Comprehension Test,* Forms S and T, is probably the most acceptable and certainly one of the most popular tests of the special ability represented by the test title. However, it would seem to be of limited value to educational counselors and to those setting up test batteries for differential prediction objectives. The test may well be most useful either when used alone or when used with a few clerical aptitude and manual dexterity tests to predict current performance in a few relatively simple, mechanically oriented occupations.

A. OSCAR H. ROBERTS, *Senior Research Scientist, American Institutes for Research, Palo Alto, California.*

These tests were originally copyrighted in 1940. Since then they have been the models for similar tests all over the world. They have had additions, parallel forms, special forms for women, revisions (notably in 1951), more recently (1967) a renewal of copyright, and still more recently (1969), two new thoroughly modernized revised and extended parallel forms, intended to replace the others. There has always been debate as to just what these tests measure, but their perennial hardiness and long survival may be due in part to the principal author's modest claims and factual support. It is difficult to criticize a test called "Mechanical Comprehension"—*not* "Mechanical Aptitude," or "Interest," or "Skill," or "Ability"—when the content is principally pictures of mechanisms whose functions call for comprehension, especially when the results correlate significantly with criteria with which one would, a priori, have expected them to do so. Like some other famous tests, these appear to have had their christening under the fire of army and wartime use, and now have added a long history of civilian use.

All forms are similar in appearance to the oldest, Form AA, and consist of large, clear, simple drawings of mechanisms and contrivances. Nonessentials have been stripped from both illustration and the question which follows, e.g., A train of four gears of assorted sizes— "which gear will make the most turns in a minute?"; A spread-eagled stepladder and a prim one—"which stepladder is safer to climb on?" The introduction to the manual says of the test, it measures "the ability to perceive and understand the relationship of physical forces and mechanical elements in practical situations * is influenced by environmental factors, but not to an extent that introduces important difficulties in interpretation * The practical value....is enhanced....by its relatively low correlation with other tests."

The current Forms S and T drew 23 and 24 items, respectively, from the original Form AA, 16 and 21 from Form BB, 14 and 12 from Form W-1; 15 and 11 new items were added to give a total of 68 questions in each form. Of course, some of the benefits of the earlier item and other statistical analysis accrue to these new forms, but during the revision all older items were scrutinized, some being modernized in depiction, or changed in wording. The increased length of the tests (from 60 to 68 items) has resulted in slightly increased reliabilities and spreads of scores, as would have been expected. Difficulty ranges are from .16 to .96—unusually wide—and the point-biserial correlations range from .20 to .51.

Percentile norms are given for six industrial groups (e.g., process training jobs in an oil refinery) ranging in size from 100 to 906 and for four student groups (grades 11 and 12 in academic and technical schools in one city) ranging from 85 to 254. The two forms are held to be equivalent and alternate, with means differing by .5 and standard deviations by 1.4 (about 1 and 17 percent, respectively). No correlations between forms are reported. Odd-even reliabilities range from .81 to .93, with median .86; these reliabilities are satisfactory for most purposes. The five validity quotients reported for Forms S and T range from .12 to .52, with median .24.

In conclusion, the new forms represent a sufficiently energetic revision of the earlier ones to give the test a new lease of life.

J Ed Meas 8(1):55–6 sp '71. Ronald K. Hambleton. * The publisher reports that an attempt was made to update the illustrations. It is the reviewer's opinion, however, that many of the pictures still look old-fashioned, although the illustrations do depict appropriate mechanical principles clearly. * Very clear directions....are provided for the examiner. * It is unfortunate that the publisher chose not to give information in the test directions about the degree of speededness of the test and the scoring procedure. Confusion and uncertainty relating to these procedures on the part of the examinee could have an adverse effect on the test reliability and validity. Directions such as, "Work carefully but quickly through the test. Your score on this test will be the number of questions answered correctly," might clarify some potential questions raised by examinees. * Test reliability was estimated using the odd-even split-half correlation * Unfortunately, the publisher reports no other reliability data. Particularly useful would have been information on the stability of mechanical comprehension scores over various time intervals. On the matter of equivalence of the two forms, the publisher does report means and standard deviations for the forms (which, incidentally, could have been matched more closely on variability), but an unfortunate major omission is the correlation between scores on the two forms. * of the 32 predictive validity coefficients reported in the manual, only five pertain to the new forms S and T. The remaining 27 correlations refer to validity coefficients obtained with the other forms. Since the publisher reports high correlations between scores on the new forms and the earlier ones, these "inherited" validity coefficients do serve as indicators of the predictive power of the new forms in a wide variety of situations and with different criteria. The 32 predictive validities reported varied from .12 to .64 with a median of .36. Since the validities are only moderately high it is apparent that the test would be particularly useful when used in conjunction with a battery of tests. * Forms S and T....represent an improvement over the earlier forms of the test. Replacing three tests designed for different populations by one test with parallel forms should be appreciated by test users because of the convenience and added flexibility that it will allow. The publisher should be commended for the manual which is well organized, clear and complete, with only two (albeit extremely important) exceptions. Missing from the manual are essential reliability data (neither a coefficient of stability or a coefficient of equivalence are reported) and sufficient validity data using forms S and T. In conclusion, it is this reviewer's opinion that the BMCT will continue to be a very useful instrument in educational and vocational guidance, and along with other appropriate tests it can also be used very effectively by employers for selection purposes.

For a review by N. W. Morton of earlier forms, see 4:766; for reviews by Charles M. Harsh, Lloyd G. Humphreys, and George A. Satter, see 3:683.

[1050]

*College Placement Test in Spatial Relations. Entering college freshmen; 1962-70, c1954-70; CPTSR; irregularly scheduled reprintings of inactive forms of *College Board Special Aptitude Test in Spatial Relations;* Forms KPL1 ['62, reprint of 1955 test], KPL2 ['62, reprint of 1954 test] in a single booklet (27 pages); for more complete information, see 665; 60(70) minutes; program administered for the College Entrance Examination Board by Educational Testing Service. *

REFERENCES
1-4. See 6:1084.

For a review by Robert L. Thorndike of earlier forms, see 4:808. For a review of the testing program, see 665.

[1051]

★Form Perception Test. Illiterate and semiliterate adults; 1966-68; no reading by examinees; 1 form ('66, 11 pages); manual ('68, 25 pages); no data on validity; R6.60 per 25 tests; 30c per single copy; 50c per key; R2 per manual; 40c per demonstration poster set; postpaid within South Africa; 18(30) minutes; J. M. Schepers; National Institute for Personnel Research. *

[1052]

★Group Test 82. Ages 14.5 and over; 1959-70; subtest of *N.I.I.P. Engineering Apprentice Selection Test Battery;* spatial perception; 1 form ['59, 16 pages]; instructions ('68, 2 pages); no specific manual; mimeographed battery manual ['69, 19 pages, with 1970 revision]; separate answer sheets must be used; £1.50 per 10 tests; 30p per single copy; 15p per 10 answer sheets; 15p per scoring stencil; 7p per instructions; 20p per battery manual; postpaid within U.K.; 18(30) minutes; National Institute of Industrial Psychology. *

[1053]

★Mechanical Comprehension Test, Second Edition. Male technical apprentices and trainee engineer applicants; 1966-68; 1 form ('68, 29 pages, Afrikaans and English editions in 1 booklet); manual ('68, 17 pages); no norms or data on reliability and validity for the complete test; norms are available only for scores derived from items carried over from the original edition; separate answer sheets (IBM 1230) must be used; R16 per 25 tests; 75c per single copy; 40c per 25 answer sheets; 50c per scoring stencil; post-

Bennett Mechanical Comprehension Test

paid within South Africa; Afrikaans edition of manual available; 45(55) minutes; P. D. Griffiths (manual); National Institute for Personnel Research. *

[1054]

★Mechanical Information Test. Ages 15 and over; 1948-70; MIT; subtest of *N.I.I.P. Engineering Apprentice Selection Test Battery;* 1 form ['48, 2 pages]; instructions ('68, 1 page); no specific manual; mimeographed battery manual ['69, 19 pages, with 1970 revision]; no data on reliability; 20p per 10 tests; 4p per single copy; 3p per key; 7p per instructions; 20p per battery manual; postpaid within U.K.; 10(15) minutes; National Institute of Industrial Psychology. *

REFERENCE
1. FRISBY, C. B.; VINCENT, D. F.; AND LANCASHIRE, RUTH. *Tests for Engineering Apprentices: A Validation Study.* National Institute of Industrial Psychology, Report 14. London: the Institute, 1959. Pp. iii, 24. *

[1055]

★Perceptual Battery. Job applicants with at least 10 years of education; 1961-63; spatial relations; Forms A, B, ('61, 9 pages, Afrikaans and English editions in 1 booklet); no manual; mimeographed norms sheets: Forms A ('62, 1 page), B ('63, 1 page); no data on reliability and validity; norms for male college students only; separate answer sheets must be used; R15 per 25 tests; 75c per single copy; 50c per 25 answer sheets; 40c per key; 25c per norms sheet; postpaid within South Africa; 30(35) minutes; National Institute for Personnel Research. *

[1056]

*Revised Minnesota Paper Form Board Test. Grades 9-16 and adults; 1930-70; 2 forms; 2 editions; manual ('70, 32 pages); $1 per specimen set; postage extra; 20(25) minutes; original test by Donald G. Paterson, Richard M. Elliott, L. Dewey Anderson, Herbert A. Toops, and Edna Heidbreder; revision by Rensis Likert and William H. Quasha; Psychological Corporation. *

a) HAND SCORING EDITION. 1930-70; Forms AA, BB, ('41, 6 pages); $3 per 25 tests, manual, and scoring stencils.

b) MACHINE SCORABLE EDITION. 1941-70; Forms MA, MB, ('41, 6 pages); separate answer sheets (IBM 805) must be used; $4.50 per 25 tests; $2.50 per 50 answer sheets; 70¢ per set of manual and scoring stencils.

REFERENCES
1-9. See 2:1673.
10-57. See 3:677.
58-95. See 4:763.
96-124. See 5:884.
125-140. See 6:1092.
141. HANES, BERNARD. *A Factor Analysis of the MMPI, Aptitude Test Data and Personal Information Using a Population of Criminals.* Doctor's thesis, Ohio State University (Columbus, Ohio), 1952. (*DA* 18:1483)
142. BRANSON, BERNARD DAVID. *An Investigation of Manifest Anxiety and the Role of Discrimination of Self-Ideal Discrepancy and Complex Tasks.* Doctor's thesis, Syracuse University (Syracuse, N.Y.), 1957. (*DA* 17:2063)
143. LEBOLD, WILLIAM KERNS. *A Longitudinal Study of Purdue Engineering Students.* Doctor's thesis, Purdue University (Lafayette, Ind.), 1957. (*DA* 17:2057)
144. BRADLEY, ARTHUR DICKINSON. *Estimating Success in Technical and Skilled Trade Courses Using a Multivariate Statistical Analysis.* Doctor's thesis, University of Minnesota (Minneapolis, Minn.), 1958. (*DA* 21:313)
145. SHUKLA, N. N. "The Relation of Intelligence and Ability to Scholastic Achievement of Pupils in the S.S.C. Class." *J Ed & Voc Guid* 5:38-44 Ag '58. *
146. TORRES, LEONARD. *A Study of the Relationship Between Selected Variables and the Achievement of Industrial Arts Students at Long Beach State College.* Doctor's research study No. 1, Colorado State College (Greeley, Colo.), 1963. (*DA* 25:316)
147. PHILLIPS, G. R. "A Study of Psychological Tests for the Selection of Trainee Nurses: 1, General Approach." *Personnel Prac B* 20:28-32 D '64. * (*PA* 39:10886)

148. RONAN, W. W. "Evaluation of Skilled Trades Performance Predictors." *Ed & Psychol Meas* 24:601–8 f '64. * (*PA* 39:6074)

149. TANDON, R. K. "A Study of Revised Minnesota Paper Form Board Tests Series A Among Banaras Hindu University Students." *Manas* 11(1):35–40 '64. * (*PA* 39:1764)

150. MARTIN, BERNARD LOYAL. *Spatial Visualization Abilities of Central Washington State College Prospective ·Elementary and Secondary Teachers of Mathematics.* Doctor's thesis, Oregon State University (Corvallis, Ore.), 1966. (*DA* 27: 2427A)

151. MILLER, AARON JULIUS. *A Study of Engineering and Technical Institute Freshman Enrollees and Dropouts in Terms of Selected Intellective and Non-Intellective Factors.* Doctor's thesis,. Oklahoma State University (Stillwater, Okla.), 1966. (*DA* 27:4050A)

152. GAVURIN, EDWARD I. "Anagram Solving and Spatial Aptitude." *J Psychol* 65:65–8 Ja '67. * (*PA* 41:3954)

153. FINCH, CURTIS R. "Predicting Mathematics Achievement in Technical Training." *Voc Guid Q* 16:193–7 Mr '68. *

154. STERNE, DAVID M. "The Effect of Age and Intelligence on Minnesota Paper Form Board Scores of V.A. Hospital Patients." *Newsl Res Psychol* 10:37–8 My '68. *

155. DEE, HENRY LEE. *Visuoconstructive and Visuoperceptive Deficit in Patients With Unilateral Cerebral Lesions.* Doctor's thesis, University of Iowa (Iowa City, Iowa), 1969. (*DAI* 30:3383B)

156. FRANK, AUSTIN C., AND KIRK, BARBARA A. "Characteristics and Attributes of Prospective City and Regional Planners." *J Col Stud Personnel* 10(4):317–23 S '69. *

157. LORENCKI, STANLEY F. "Is Dexterity Predictable in Dental Students? Predicting Success in a Pre-Clinical Area at a California Dental School." *J Calif Dental Assn* 45(1): 11–2 sp '69. *

158. SHIH, WEI-TUN. *The Correlation Among Factors Related to Measuring Ability.* Doctor's thesis, Texas A & M University (College Station, Tex.), 1969. (*DAI* 30:4804A)

159. RONAN, W. W. "Evaluation of Three Criteria of Management Performance." *J Indus Psychol* 5(1):18–28 Mr '70. * (*PA* 45:7148)

For a review by D. W. McElwain, see 5:884; for reviews by Clifford E. Jurgensen and Raymond A. Katzell, see 4:763; for a review by Dewey B. Stuit, see 3:677; for a review by Alec Rodger, see 2:1673.

[1057]

*Spatial Tests 1, 2, and 3. Ages 11-0 to 13-11, 10-7 to 13-11, 10-0 to 11-11 and 15-0 to 18-0; 1950–63; 3 tests; distribution restricted to directors of education; postpaid within U.K.; published for the National Foundation for Educational Research in England and Wales; Ginn & Co. Ltd. *

a) SPATIAL TEST 1. Ages 11-0 to 13-11; 1950–59; 1 form ['50, 23 pages]; revised manual ('59, 24 pages); 12p per test; 17p per manual; 41(60) minutes; I. Macfarlane Smith.

b) SPATIAL TEST 2 (THREE-DIMENSIONAL). Ages 10-7 to 13-11; 1950–56; 1 form ['51, 20 pages]; manual ['51, 13 pages]; provisional norms ['56] for ages 10-7 to 11-6; norms ['55] for ages 13-0 to 13-11; no data on reliability and validity; no norms for ages 11-7 to 12-11; 10p per test; 10p per manual; norms free on request from NFER; 26.5(45) minutes; A. F. Watts with the assistance of D. A. Pidgeon and M. K. B. Richards.

c) SPATIAL TEST 3 (NEWCASTLE SPATIAL TEST). Ages 10-0 to 11-11 and 15-0 to 18-0; 1958–63; 1 form ['58, 23 pages); manual ('59, 11 pages); mimeographed instructions for colleges of further education ['63, 5 pages]; no norms for ages 11-4 to 11-11; 12p per test; 8p per manual; instructions free on request from NFER; 39(60) minutes for ages 10-1 to 11-11, 19(40) minutes for ages 15-0 to 18-0; I. Macfarlane Smith and J. S. Lawes.

REFERENCES

1–4. See 6:1093.
5. VANDENBERG, STEVEN G. "A Twin Study of Spatial Ability." *Multiv Behav Res* 4(3):273–94 Jl '69. * (*PA* 44:356)

For reviews by E. G. Chambers and Charles T. Myers of tests 1 and 2, see 5:885; for a review by E. A. Peel of test 1, see 4:753.

[1058]

★Vincent Mechanical Diagrams Test. Ages 15 and over; 1936–70; VMD; based upon *The Vincent Mechanical Models Test A;* subtest of *N.I.I.P. Engineering Apprentice Selection Test Battery;* 1 form ['51, 21 pages]; instructions ('68, 2 pages); no specific manual; mimeographed battery manual ['69, 19 pages, with 1970 revision]; separate answer sheets must be used; £1.80 per 10 tests; 36p per single copy; 15p per 10 answer sheets; 17p per scoring stencil; 7p per instructions; 20p per battery manual; postpaid within U.K.; 20(35) minutes; National Institute of Industrial Psychology. *

MISCELLANEOUS

[1059]

*Business Judgment Test, Revised. Adults; 1953–69; BJT; 1 form ('69, 4 pages, identical with test copyrighted in 1953); manual ('65, 12 pages); $6 per 20 tests; 35¢ per key; $1.75 per manual; $2.50 per specimen set; cash orders postpaid, 10% extra on charge orders; (10–20) minutes; Martin M. Bruce; Martin M. Bruce, Ph.D., Publishers. *

REFERENCES

1–4. See 6:1101.
5. WATLEY, DONIVAN J. "The Effectiveness of Intellectual and Non-Intellectual Factors in Predicting Achievement for Business Students." *J Ed Res* 57:402–7 Ap '64. *

JEROME E. DOPPELT, *Associate Director, Test Division, The Psychological Corporation, New York, New York.*

The 25 items in this test are offered as a small sampling of the interpersonal situations an individual might encounter in the business world. The items are of the multiple-choice type, presented in the first person; for example, "If the fellow working next to me on the job was loafing, I would . . . ," and "If I were setting up a new procedure in an office, I would. . . ." The scoring key assigns weights that range from 0 to 3 to each of the four possible responses. For some items, only one response receives a non-zero weight; for other items, as many as three of the four responses receive positive weights. The weights have been assigned in accordance with the proportion of a "general" business population, a group of 1,129 people, that chose each alternative. The author maintains that the test "assesses the examinee's appreciation of what the majority feels are the 'proper' courses of action" in the situations.

The test is printed in a four-page booklet in which the examinee records his answers. There is no time limit. The author estimates that "most subjects require between 10 and 15 minutes to complete all items." Only one answer is to be given to each question. However, if multiple responses to an item are found when scoring the test, the score for that item is the average of the weights for the two or more choices that have been given. A decision to omit multiple-marked items would probably have simplified the scoring without sacrificing any significant information.

The examinee is asked what he would do in particular circumstances and his range of alternatives for each question is, of course, limited to the four options presented. For questions of this type, the "correct" answer is frequently the answer chosen by experts in the field of the questions. There is an obvious logic to this procedure and an earlier form of the test was keyed accordingly. However, the author then decided to revise the key in anticipation of "enhanced validity and value for the instrument." Consequently, he weighted the answers in accordance with the proportions of the "general" business population that chose the particular alternative. The business population on which the revised key was established was a very heterogeneous group of employed persons, essentially male, whose ages ranged from 19 to 61 and whose education ranged from "less than complete grade school to completed doctorate." In the opinion of this reviewer, the change to the revised scoring key was unfortunate. There is more logic in using a key based on expert judgment than in taking the majority view of a very wide-range group.

The manual describes several studies of small groups in which the test correlated significantly with a criterion measure. The manual also reports two studies in which no predictive validity was found. The author quite properly reminds the reader that the research studies have limitations and that the test user must "remember that no one criterion is uniquely appropriate for measures in the field of interpersonal relationships." This might also be interpreted as a suggestion to the user that he conduct his own studies whenever possible.

A reliability coefficient of .81 is reported for 82 cases tested twice with the instrument and based on the old scoring procedure. For a sample of 126 cases, an odd-even reliability coefficient of .85 was found, again using the original scoring procedure. The persons tested ranged in age from 19 to 60 and in education from seventh grade through completion of college. A

test-retest reliability coefficient of .81 for the revised key is given for another sample of 200 cases that was quite diverse occupationally and ranged in age from 23 to 49. Means and standard deviations on the test are not reported. It is clear, however, that the groups were quite heterogeneous in respect to age, education, and occupation. For the test user who is concerned with a more homogeneous sample, the relevance of these reliability data is questionable.

Four norms groups are offered. Two of these, middle management and supervisors, each contain fewer than 100 cases. The other two comprise a sample of over 1,000 salesmen and a "general population" of more than 3,000 cases. The last group is an amazing collection of many kinds of people, also including the other three normative groups. The age range of the "general population" is 17 to 61 and the educational range is from six years of grade school to the doctorate. The sample was collected over 10 years from a variety of companies. Comparisons with such a diversified group are not very meaningful.

The author suggests two areas of potential use for the test: selection and training. This reviewer doubts that the instrument will be of much value as a selection device. In training it might have some usefulness as a springboard for discussion. The measurement of business judgment still remains a challenge.

J Ed Meas 3:335–6 w '66. Kenneth D. Orton.
* The explanation of the procedures for the development of....[this test] is, for the most part, sufficient and the procedures appear to be sound. * As in most tests which attempt to assess personality attributes,.....[this test] may be criticized because of the possibility of faking. The items appear to be rather transparent; the examinee should be able to improve his chances of being favorably judged if he can assume the proper set. * The majority of the evidence for validity is of the concurrent variety. Much of the evidence is in the form of comparisons of the mean differences of a group presumed to have more of the attribute in question. Few predictive studies are reported. This seems to be a rather critical omission since the primary use of the....[test] is for....prediction. The major criticism....is the lack of [a guide]....for the interpretation of the test results. Percentile norms are given for a variety of populations *
But what is the probability that a person mak-

ing a given score will be a success....in business in general? * little information is presented which would convince a prospective buyer that ....[this test is] useful for purposes of making decisions about individuals seeking jobs or promotions. Additional information of this type would be invaluable * [The test shows] promise of being useful in personnel selection, but additional information is needed for that promise to be realized. * [Its] use in appraising potentials of the previously designated personnel is questionable at this time.

For a review by Edward B. Greene, see 5:893.

[1060]

★**The Conference Evaluation.** Conference participants; 1969; CE; ratings by participants; 1 form (1 page); instruction card (2 pages); no data on reliability; no norms, publisher recommends use of local norms; $3.50 per 25 forms; $1 per specimen set; cash orders postpaid; (5–10) minutes; Psychologists and Educators Press. *

[1061]

★**Gullo Workshop and Seminar Evaluation.** Workshop and seminar participants; 1969; GWSE; ratings by participants; 1 form (2 pages); instructions (1 page); no data on reliability; no norms, publisher recommends use of local norms; $5 per 25 forms; $1 per specimen set; cash orders postpaid; (10–15) minutes; John M. Gullo; Psychologists and Educators Press. *

[1062]

The Jenkins Job Attitudes Survey. Industrial employees; 1959; JJAS; derived from an unpublished form of *How Well Do You Know Yourself?*; identification of accident-prone individuals; Form AR-11 (6 pages); manual (6 pages); no data on reliability; $2 per test (including scoring service), postage extra; (25–40) minutes; Thomas N. Jenkins, Harold T. Fagin (manual), and John H. Coleman (manual); Executive Analysis Corporation. *

REFERENCES

1. See 6:1106.
2. JENKINS, THOMAS N. "Identifying the Accident-Prone Employee." *Personnel* 38:56–62 Jl-Ag '61. *
3. JENKINS, THOMAS N. "Who Will Be Your Injury-Repeaters?" *Safety Maint* 121:9–11+ Ap '61. *
4. GODEC, FRANK. "Personality Characteristics of the Accident Repeater." *Safety Maint* 134:13–6 S '67. *

ARTHUR C. MacKINNEY, *Dean of Graduate Studies, Wright State University, Dayton, Ohio.*

This instrument is another of the personality-type inventories operated on an exclusive basis by a consulting firm, in this case the Executive Analysis Corporation. Apparently this firm retains exclusive rights to the instrument, acting as publisher as well as a scoring and interpretation service. Neither norms nor scoring procedures were available to this reviewer.

The instrument is said to have several pur-poses, all of which relate either directly or indirectly to industrial accidents and, of course, accident prevention. Specifically, it is said to be an aid in the placement of employees so as to reduce the probability of accident, for it purports to be a "practical measure of personality variables which identify potential injury-repeaters." In addition, it is said to be helpful in identifying persons most in need of safety training and safety supervision.

This is a rather standard-appearing personality inventory, 150 items in length. A scan through the item content (an intuitive cluster analysis) would seem to indicate dimensions devoted to neuroticism, masculinity-femininity, and degree of socialization (psychopathic tendencies). Understand that this is, of course, purely impressionistic on the part of the reviewer and is not so stated in the manual. In fact, the manual claims that the present instrument is a distillation of an original (presumably larger) item pool which measures "feelings and attitudes....which for descriptive convenience can be organized in the following syndromes: attentiveness, judiciousness, group-dissociative independence, personal-social sensitivity, attitude toward personal pain, presumptuous self-assurance and social orientation." Through some process not revealed, the instrument is scored to yield a general "safety index," a high score on which is thought to be indicative of the safe worker.

Of course, the real point in all of this is the quality of the instrument, and in this case this is extremely difficult to assess because of factors which will be mentioned below. The managing director of the Executive Analysis Corporation provided this reviewer with the reprints of research (*1–4*) done on this instrument. These, taken together with the manual, seem to boil down to reports on two validity studies done on the instrument, not counting some original item selection work. In addition, there are other studies alluded to, but the results are not reported. The validities which are reported, however, are unusually high, indeed: one validity coefficient referred to repeatedly is above .70. Other data based on different varieties of accident criteria show rather remarkable separation of criterion groups. The typical four-fold table shows about three-fourths of the frequency in the on-quadrant-cell. These kinds of validities are remarkable, and indeed, one article by Jenkins [1] indicates "this would be an unusually high relationship between test scores and criterion data *of any kind."*

An additional study (*4*) of the *Jenkins Job Attitudes Survey* should be acknowledged. It is a study not done by someone associated with the parent firm, although the researcher acknowledges the assistance of the Executive Analysis Corporation. This study assessed the instrument against accident rate as well as time lost. Validity (in terms of mean differences by predictor groups) looks to be acceptable for the group employed less than six months. The differences tend to wash out when based on total time worked, but this does not negate the possibility of gain based on the shorter-tenure group.

An overall summary ought to acknowledge that the evidence available seems to be preponderantly favorable. The prospective user of the instrument should, however, note the following facts: (*a*) Information about the predictive efficiency of this test is clearly incomplete. There are data available which have apparently not been reported. (*b*) The test manual and associated literature report only sketchy validity information and nothing about other characteristics ancillary to the validity data, such as reliability. (*c*) The instrument is very tightly controlled and hence independent scrutiny is made more difficult. (*d*) Finally, and this is the most difficult point of all, the available evidence regarding this instrument is atypically high to such an extent as to make the careful professional worker wonder what secret has been captured by the Executive Analysis Corporation which has thus far been hidden from the other reputable research and publishing houses in this business. It is entirely possible, of course, that this instrument is indeed as good as it appears. Similarly, quite the contrary is not beyond the realm of possibility. Unfortunately, this reviewer can do no better than to ask each prospective user of this inventory to judge for himself.

[1063]

★**Minnesota Importance Questionnaire, 1967 Revision.** Vocational counselees; 1967–69; MIQ; vocational needs; 21 scores: ability utilization, achievement, activity, advancement, authority, company policies and practices, compensation, coworkers, creativity, independence, moral values, recognition, responsibility, security, social service, social status, supervision—human

relations, supervision—technical, variety, working conditions, validity; 1 form ('67, 19 pages) ; mimeographed preliminary manual ('69, 54 pages) ; separate answer sheets must be used; $3 per 10 tests ; $5 per 100 answer sheets ; postpaid; specimen set free; scoring service, 75¢ per test; (30–40) minutes; David J. Weiss, Rene V. Dawis, Lloyd H. Lofquist, and Evan G. Gay; Vocational Psychology Research. *

REFERENCES

1. SHAPIRO, SOLOMON. *A Study of the Needs and Satisfactions of Social Workers as Perceived by College Students and Social Workers.* Doctor's thesis, University of Minnesota (Minneapolis, Minn.), 1964. (*DA* 26:1174)

2. WEISS, DAVID J.; DAWIS, RENE V.; ENGLAND, GEORGE W.; AND LOFQUIST, LLOYD H.; WITH THE ASSISTANCE OF LOIS L. ANDERSON, ROBERT E. CARLSON, AND RICHARD S. ELSTER. *The Measurement of Vocational Needs.* University of Minnesota, Industrial Relations Center Bulletin 39; Minnesota Studies in Vocational Rehabilitation 16. Minneapolis, Minn.: the Center, April 1964. Pp. vi, 101. *

3. WEISS, DAVID J.; DAWIS, RENE V.; ENGLAND, GEORGE W.; AND LOFQUIST, LLOYD H.; WITH THE ASSISTANCE OF RICHARD S. ELSTER. *Construct Validation Studies of the Minnesota Importance Questionnaire.* University of Minnesota, Industrial Relations Center Bulletin 41; Minnesota Studies in Vocational Rehabilitation 18. Minneapolis, Minn.: the Center, December 1964. Pp. vi, 75. * (*PA* 39:10166, 39:10506)

4. DAUW, DEAN CHARLES. *Life Experiences, Vocational Needs and Choices of Original Thinkers and Good Elaborators.* Doctor's thesis, University of Minnesota (Minneapolis, Minn.), 1965. (*DA* 26:5223)

5. WEISS, DAVID J.; DAWIS, RENE V.; ENGLAND, GEORGE W.; AND LOFQUIST, LLOYD H.; WITH THE ASSISTANCE OF RICHARD S. ELSTER. *An Inferential Approach to Occupational Reinforcement.* University of Minnesota, Industrial Relations Center Bulletin 19; Minnesota Studies in Vocational Rehabilitation 19. Minneapolis, Minn.: the Center, 1965. Pp. 39. * (*PA* 40:5799)

6. DAUW, DEAN C. "Scholastic Aptitudes and Vocational Needs of Original Thinkers and Good Elaborators." *Personnel & Guid J* 45:171–5 O '66. *

7. KOHLAN, RICHARD GEORGE. *Relationships Between Inventoried Interests and Inventoried Needs in a College Sample.* Doctor's thesis, University of Minnesota (Minneapolis, Minn.), 1966. (*DA* 27:2397A)

8. WEISS, DAVID J.; DAWIS, RENE V.; LOFQUIST, LLOYD H.; AND ENGLAND, GEORGE W. *Instrumentation for the Theory of Work Adjustment.* University of Minnesota, Industrial Relations Center Bulletin 44; Minnesota Studies in Vocational Rehabilitation 21. Minneapolis, Minn.: the Center, December 1966. Pp. viii, 85. *

9. THORNDIKE, ROBERT M.; WEISS, DAVID J.; AND DAWIS, RENE V. "Multiple Relationships Between Measured Vocational Interests and Measured Vocational Needs." Abstract. *Proc 75th Ann Conv Am Psychol Assn* 2:351–2 '67. * (*PA* 41:14262)

10. BETZ, ELLEN LANGENBACHER. *Occupational Reinforcer Patterns and Need-Reinforcer Correspondence in the Prediction of Job Satisfaction.* Doctor's thesis, University of Minnesota (Minneapolis, Minn.), 1968. (*DA* 29:4418B)

11. BORGEN, FRED H.; WEISS, DAVID J.; TINSLEY, HOWARD E. A.; DAWIS, RENE V.; AND LOFQUIST, LLOYD H. *Occupational Reinforcer Patterns (First Volume).* University of Minnesota, Industrial Relations Center Bulletin 48; Minnesota Studies in Vocational Rehabilitation 24. Minneapolis, Minn.: the Center, October 1968. Pp. x, 263. *

12. DRESSLER, RICHARD M. *Relationships Among Needs, Interests, and Curricular Choice in a Sample of College Men.* Doctor's thesis, Temple University (Philadelphia, Pa.), 1968. (*DAI* 30:1356B)

13. FISHER, STEPHEN T.; WEISS, DAVID J.; AND DAWIS, RENE V. "A Comparison of Likert and Pair Comparisons Techniques in Multivariate Attitude Scaling." *Ed & Psychol Meas* 28:81–94 sp '68. * (*PA* 42:11359)

14. GRAEN, GEORGE B.; DAWIS, RENE V.; AND WEISS, DAVID J. "Need Type and Job Satisfaction Among Industrial Scientists." *J Appl Psychol* 52:286–9 Ag '68. * (*PA* 42:16223)

15. HENDEL, DARWIN D., AND WEISS, DAVID J. "Individual Response Consistency and Stability of Measurement." Abstract. *Proc 76th Ann Conv Am Psychol Assn* 3:249–50 '68. *

16. KOHLAN, RICHARD G. "Relationships Between Inventoried Interests and Inventoried Needs." *Personnel & Guid J* 46:592–8 F '68. * (*PA* 42:12126)

17. SALOMONE, PAUL ROBERT. *Rehabilitation Counselor Job Behavior and Vocational Personality: Needs and Work Style.* Doctor's thesis, University of Iowa (Iowa City, Iowa), 1968. (*DA* 29:1759A)

18. THORNDIKE, ROBERT M.; WEISS, DAVID J.; AND DAWIS, RENE V. "Canonical Correlation of Vocational Interests and Vocational Needs." *J Counsel Psychol* 15:101–6 Mr '68. * (*PA* 42:9544)

[1] JENKINS, THOMAS N. "The Measurement of Behavior Tendencies in the Accident-Repeater." *Nat Safety Cong Trans* 11: 16–21 '60.

19. THORNDIKE, ROBERT M.; WEISS, DAVID J.; AND DAWIS, RENE V. "Multivariate Relationships Between a Measure of Vocational Interests and a Measure of Vocational Needs." *J Appl Psychol* 52:491–6 D '68. * (*PA* 43:3161)

20. BETZ, ELLEN L. "Need-Reinforcer Correspondence as a Predictor of Job Satisfaction." *Personnel & Guid J* 47(9): 878–83 My '69. *

21. KATZ, MARTIN. "Interests and Values: A Comment." *J Counsel Psychol* 16(5):460–2 S '69. * (*PA* 43:18042)

22. KAUPPI, DWIGHT R., AND WEISS, DAVID J. "Efficiency of Commonly Used Measures in Predicting Inventory Validity." Abstract. *Proc 77th Ann Conv Am Psychol Assn* 4(2):691–2 '69. * (*PA* 44:675)

23. MUTHARD, JOHN E., AND SALOMONE, PAUL R. "The Roles and Functions of Rehabilitation Counselors." *Rehabil Counsel B* 13(1-SP):81–165 O '69. *

24. RICHARDSON, BILLY K. *Prediction of Rehabilitation Counselor Effectiveness: The Relationship of Counselor Characteristics to Supervisors' Ratings.* Doctor's thesis, University of Iowa (Iowa City, Iowa), 1969. (*DAI* 30:3738A)

25. GAY, EVAN G., AND WEISS, DAVID J. "Relationship of Work Experience and Measured Vocational Needs." Abstract. *Proc 78th Ann Conv Am Psychol Assn* 5(2):663–4 '70. * (*PA* 44:19069)

26. HENDEL, DARWIN D., AND WEISS, DAVID J. "Individual Inconsistency and Reliability of Measurement." *Ed & Psychol Meas* 30(3):579–93 au '70. * (*PA* 45:3231)

27. HENDEL, DARWIN D., AND WEISS, DAVID J. "Relationship of Race and Demographic Characteristics to Vocational Needs Profiles." Abstract. *Proc 78th Ann Conv Am Psychol Assn* 5(1):351–2 '70. * (*PA* 44:18429)

28. STONE, GAYLE VAUGHN. *The Relationship Between Personality and Work Need-Reinforcer Correspondence.* Doctor's thesis, University of Minnesota (Minneapolis, Minn.), 1970. (*DAI* 31:4346B)

29. ZYTOWSKI, DONALD G. "The Concept of Work Values." *Voc Guide Q* 18(3):176–86 Mr '70. *

[1064]

★**Minnesota Satisfaction Questionnaire.** Business and industry; 1963–67; MSQ; work satisfaction; manual ('67, 130 pages, see 6 below); postpaid; manual free (from Work Adjustment Project, Industrial Relations Center, University of Minnesota); David J. Weiss, Rene V. Dawis, George W. England, and Lloyd H. Lofquist; Vocational Psychology Research. *

a) LONG FORM. 21 scores: ability utilization, achievement, activity, advancement, authority, company policies and practices, compensation, coworkers, creativity, independence, moral values, recognition, responsibility, security, social service, social status, supervision—human relations, supervision—technical, variety, working conditions, general satisfaction; 2 forms: original edition ('63, 7 pages), 1967 revision ('67, 7 pages, for research use only); no manual or data (norms, reliability, validity) for the 1967 revision, which has the same items but differs in the response options; $5 per 25 tests; (15–20) minutes.

b) SHORT FORM. 3 scores: intrinsic, extrinsic, general; 1 form ('63, 4 pages); $2.50 per 25 tests; (5) minutes.

REFERENCES

1. WEISS, DAVID J.; DAWIS, RENE V.; ENGLAND, GEORGE W.; AND LOFQUIST, LLOYD H.; WITH THE ASSISTANCE OF RICHARD S. ELSTER. *Construct Validation Studies of the Minnesota Importance Questionnaire.* University of Minnesota, Industrial Relations Center Bulletin 41; Minnesota Studies in Vocational Rehabilitation 18. Minneapolis, Minn.: the Center, December 1964. Pp. vi, 75. * (*PA* 39:10166, 39:10506)

2. HAMLIN, MARJORIE MABEL. *Relationships Between Organizational Climates of Elementary Schools and the Degree of Job Satisfaction of Teachers in the Schools.* Doctor's thesis, University of Minnesota (Minneapolis, Minn.), 1966. (*DA* 28:76A)

3. WEISS, DAVID J.; DAWIS, RENE V.; LOFQUIST, LLOYD H.; AND ENGLAND, GEORGE W. *Instrumentation for the Theory of Work Adjustment.* University of Minnesota, Industrial Relations Center Bulletin 44; Minnesota Studies in Vocational Rehabilitation 21. Minneapolis, Minn.: the Center, December 1966. Pp. viii, 85. *

4. DAWIS, RENE V.; WEISS, DAVID J.; LOFQUIST, LLOYD H.; AND BETZ, ELLEN. "Satisfaction as a Moderator in the Prediction of Satisfactoriness." Abstract. *Proc 75th Ann Conv Am Psychol Assn* 2:269–70 '67. * (*PA* 41:14281)

5. OLSON, HARRY, JR. *Relationships Between Certain Personality Characteristics of Distributive Education Teacher-Coordinators and Job Satisfaction.* Doctor's thesis, University of Minnesota (Minneapolis, Minn.), 1967. (*DA* 28:2909A)

6. WEISS, DAVID J.; DAWIS, RENE V.; ENGLAND, GEORGE W.; AND LOFQUIST, LLOYD H. *Manual for the Minnesota Satisfaction Questionnaire.* University of Minnesota, Industrial Relations Center Bulletin 45; Minnesota Studies in Vocational Rehabilitation 22. Minneapolis, Minn.: the Center, October 1967. Pp. x, 120. * (*PA* 42:8111)

7. BETZ, ELLEN LANGENBACHER. *Occupational Reinforcer Patterns and Need-Reinforcer Correspondence in the Prediction of Job Satisfaction.* Doctor's thesis, University of Minnesota (Minneapolis, Minn.), 1968. (*DA* 29:4418B)

8. GOLIE, BYRON NEIL. *A Study of the Effects of an Orientation Treatment on New Teacher Perceptions of Organizational Climate and Other Selected Variables.* Doctor's thesis, University of Minnesota (Minneapolis, Minn.), 1968. (*DAI* 30:1018A)

9. GRAEN, GEORGE B.; DAWIS, RENE V.; AND WEISS, DAVID J. "Need Type and Job Satisfaction Among Industrial Scientists." *J Appl Psychol* 52:286–9 Ag '68. * (*PA* 42:16223)

10. WEISS, DONALD JOSEPH. *A Study of the Relationship of Participation in Decision-Making Selected Personality Variables and Job Satisfaction of the Educational Research and Development Council Elementary School Principals.* Doctor's thesis, University of Minnesota (Minneapolis, Minn.), 1968. (*DA* 29: 3404A)

11. ANDERSON, LOIS MARILYN LEDIN. *Longitudinal Changes in Level of Work Adjustment.* Doctor's thesis, University of Minnesota (Minneapolis, Minn.), 1969. (*DAI* 30:2940B)

12. BATES, GORDON L. *The Relationship of Personality and Work Adjustment of Vocational Rehabilitants: A Test of Holland's Theory.* Doctor's thesis, University of Oklahoma (Norman, Okla.), 1969. (*DAI* 30:126A)

13. BECVAR, RAPHAEL JACOB. *Job Satisfaction of First-Year Teachers: A Study of Discrepancies Between Expectations and Experiences.* Doctor's thesis, University of Minnesota (Minneapolis, Minn.), 1969. (*DAI* 30:4298A)

14. BETZ, ELLEN L. "Need-Reinforcer Correspondence as a Predictor of Job Satisfaction." *Personnel & Guid J* 47(9):878–83 My '69. *

15. CARLSON, ROBERT E.; DAWIS, RENE V.; AND WEISS, DAVID J. "The Effect of Satisfaction on the Relationship Between Abilities and Satisfactoriness." *Occup Psychol* 43(1):39–46 '69. * (*PA* 44:17573)

16. OLSON, HARRY, JR. "Distributive Education Teacher-Coordinators: Relationship Between Personality and Job Satisfaction." *Delta Pi Epsilon J* 11(3):4–20 My '69. *

17. TAYLOR, KENNETH E., AND WEISS, DAVID J. "Prediction of Individual Job Turnover From Measured Job Satisfaction." Abstract. *Proc 77th Ann Conv Am Psychol Assn* 4(2):587–8 '69. * (*PA* 44:1430)

18. BATES, GORDON L.; PARKER, HARRY J.; AND McCOY, JOHN F. "Vocational Rehabilitants' Personality and Work Adjustment: A Test of Holland's Theory of Vocational Choice." *Psychol Rep* 26(2):511–6 Ap '70. * (*PA* 44:21319)

LEWIS E. ALBRIGHT, *Director, Organization and Management Development, Kaiser Aluminum & Chemical Corporation, Oakland, California.*

The *Minnesota Satisfaction Questionnaire* is one of the products of the Work Adjustment Project studies at the University of Minnesota's Industrial Relations Center. The conceptual framework for these studies, which have been underway since 1957, is entitled the Theory of Work Adjustment.[1] This theory proposes that job satisfaction is a function of the correspondence between the individual's vocational needs and the reinforcement in the work environment. The MSQ has been developed as a measure of satisfaction with a number of different aspects of the work environment and is considered potentially useful by the authors for evaluating vocational rehabilitation outcomes.

The long form of the questionnaire was

1 DAWIS, RENÉ V.; ENGLAND, GEORGE W.; AND LOFQUIST, LLOYD H. *A Theory of Work Adjustment.* University of Minnesota, Industrial Relations Center Bulletin 38; Minnesota Studies in Vocational Rehabilitation 15. Minneapolis, Minn.: the Center, University of Minnesota, 1964. Pp. v, 27. *

derived from earlier attitude measures used in this project and consists of 100 items, in a Likert-type response format, requiring about 15–20 minutes for administration. The short form is composed of the 20 items most highly correlated with the 20 scales making up the longer form; only about five minutes is needed for the short form. Scoring of the long form is accomplished with the aid of a hand-scoring format provided but appears to be a cumbersome clerical task if the number of cases is large.

For some unexplained reason, the MSQ manual does not describe the derivation of the 20 scales on the long form, although the reader is referred to an earlier publication where this subject is apparently covered. It is noted, though, that homogeneity of scale content was increased through item wording. Unfortunately, some item redundancy results, as with the three items from the Social Service scale in which the respondent is asked to rate his satisfaction with regard to the chance his job provides him "to be of service to others" (item 1), "to people" (item 21), or "to be of some small service to other people" (item 81). Admittedly, this is an extreme example, but it would seem that some amount of "homogeneity" could be sacrificed for more varied item content.

The data on reliability of the long form look quite satisfactory, although this should not be surprising in view of the repetitiveness of the item content. Regarding internal consistency, Hoyt reliability coefficients were computed for some 27 occupational groups for all 20 scales plus General Satisfaction. Of the 567 coefficients, 83 percent were .80 or higher and only 2.5 percent were lower than .70. Stability of the MSQ was determined by retesting students and employed persons at one-week and one-year intervals, respectively. For the one-week period, stability coefficients ranged from .66 for the Co-workers scale to .91 for Working Conditions, with a median of .83. One-year retest correlations were somewhat lower, ranging from .35 for Independence to .71 for Ability Utilization, median of .61. Canonical correlation analysis was also performed on the retest data and indicated that both the one-week and one-year coefficients (.97 and .89, respectively) were significant beyond the .001 level.

Regarding validity, the evidence is mainly in the form of construct validity resulting from attempts to use the MSQ to test various pre-dictions from the Theory of Work Adjustment. The results are less clearcut than in the case of reliability. Again, other publications must be consulted for details of these studies, but a summary in the manual and one recent unpublished report indicate that individuals who have high need levels which are reinforced by their job situations report, as predicted, a higher level of satisfaction than a high-need-low-reinforcement group. Not all 20 scales yielded significant differences, however, and even for those which were significant in the unpublished report, the authors acknowledge the possibility of contamination due to a methodological weakness: both reinforcer level and satisfaction level were measured by similar questionnaires, raising the suspicion of spuriously high correlations simply as a function of the method similarity.

Other evidence of validity is inferred from the ability of the MSQ to discriminate between occupational groups of varying social status levels and between disabled and nondisabled groups. Although these findings may be viewed as encouraging, it is likely that almost any other job satisfaction measure would show similar differences. One empirical predictive study done with the MSQ involves the comparison of a 27-scale MSQ with 11 biographical items in terms of the relative ability of the two types of information to predict subsequent turnover of discount store employees. It was concluded that only the MSQ achieved better than chance prediction in a crossvalidation group. Many observers might argue, however, that 11 items is hardly a sufficient or representative sampling of biographical information and that more penetrating self-description items might have resulted in equal or better predictions than those yielded by the MSQ.

Several factor analyses done on the MSQ have typically found that about half the common scale score variance is accounted for by an extrinsic satisfaction factor and the other half by an intrinsic factor. The extrinsic factor is "defined by the two Supervision scales, Company Policies and Practices, Working Conditions, Advancement, Compensation and Security." The resemblance of this factor to Herzberg's Hygiene dimension in his well known Motivation-Hygiene theory is obvious but is not discussed anywhere in the manual. The remaining scales constitute the intrinsic satisfaction factor. Again, the remarkable similarity to Herzberg's Motivators is not mentioned. These omissions are interesting because many critics have dismissed Herzberg's two-factor formulation as oversimplified, as well as technique-bound because of its reliance on the story-telling method. With the MSQ, it appears that a similar factor structure has emerged from analysis of a paper-and-pencil job attitude measure. Two-factor theories may not be completely demolished, after all!

A strength of the MSQ manual is its extensive norms for the long form. In addition to norms for 25 different occupational groups (plus a disabled and nondisabled group), demographic characteristics are given for each normative sample, including such variables as sex, age, education, and job tenure. This complete reporting could serve as a model for authors of other psychometric devices. For the short form, data are available on seven occupational groups.

The present form of the MSQ is undergoing continuing research and revision and it would, therefore, be premature to recommend this questionnaire for widespread use by nonprofessionals. New scales are being added, for example, and, in an attempt to minimize an overly favorable "ceiling effect," the response continuum has been modified to range from "Not Satisfied" to "Extremely Satisfied," rather than the present "Very Dissatisfied" to "Very Satisfied." Until the results of these changes have been assessed, the *Minnesota Satisfaction Questionnaire* can best be described as promising but not yet ready for commercial use.

JOHN P. FOLEY, JR., *President, J. P. Foley and Company, Inc., New York, New York.*

The MSQ can undoubtedly contribute to an evaluation of the degree and types of work satisfaction of employees in American business and industry. When one or more large groups are to be surveyed—and when there are practical time restrictions—the MSQ has much to recommend it. It attempts to survey major parameters of satisfaction, i.e., important different aspects of the work environment. Administration time is reasonable. The items are easy to read (fifth-grade reading level). And there is evidence of acceptable standards of reliability, as well as some evidence of validity.

The wording of most of the items makes the scale, or scoring parameter, all too obvious. Moreover, the use of a direct five-point interval further contributes to the transparency of the questionnaire with respect to its *intent*. Con-

sequently, voluntary or involuntary faking or dissembling should be relatively easy. In many situations, especially those in which the respondent is ego-involved in making a desirable score, the validity of results will thus be suspect. It might be added that the MSQ is more transparent—and hence more susceptible to falsification of results—than such a time-worn test as the *Study of Values*.

In the light of the above limitation, it would seem that the MSQ will probably yield more valid and meaningful results in situations in which the respondent is not ego-involved in making a socially-desirable score. Moreover, the atmosphere, instructions, and amount and type of "selling" surrounding questionnaire administration will undoubtedly have a marked influence on the validity of results.

In summary, the MSQ represents one of a number of techniques for surveying work satisfactions. As a rough screener or classifier, for use under group auspices, the MSQ can be recommended, assuming the user is aware of its limitations. But for more intensive study of an individual's attitude toward various aspects of his working environment, such a questionnaire will not replace the depth interview by a highly-skilled practitioner.

[1065]

The Tear Ballot for Industry. Employees in industry; 1944-62; TBI; job satisfaction questionnaire; 1 form ('44, 2 pages); revised manual ('62, 21 pages, hectographed); group profile ('56, 1 page); $2 per 25 tests; $1.50 per 25 profiles; $1 per manual; $5 per examiner's kit of 50 tests, profile, and manual; cash orders postpaid; specimen set not available; (3-5) minutes; Willard A. Kerr; Psychometric Affiliates. *

REFERENCES

1-4. See 4:783.
5-9. See 6:1108.

J Counsel Psychol 13:121 sp '66. John O. Crites. * Whether the items are representative of a universe of job attitudes is a question, since at least four (and possibly six) out of the ten pertain to company and management policies rather than other possible sources of satisfaction, e.g., job duties and tasks. In fact, there are no items which directly refer to the intrinsic satisfactions of work, which are usually the predominant ones at the upper occupational levels (Centers, 1948). For this reason, as Katzell (Buros, 1965, p. 1324) has noted, the applicability of the *Tear Ballot* may be limited to non-managerial and non-professional workers. Most of the norms given in the Manual, incidentally, are for such groups. * In some of the studies, the samples were quite small, and it is consequently questionable how stable some of the reported correlation coefficients are. Moreover, it is not clear in certain instances why a relationship between the *Tear Ballot* and another variable, such as hearing loss, is evidence for the validity of the satisfaction measure. But, in general, the data indicate that the *Tear Ballot* is related to other, relevant variables and that it is a potentially useful measure of satisfaction for research on counseling and personnel problems.

For a review by Raymond A. Katzell, see 6:1108; for a review by Brent Baxter, see 4:783.

[1066]

★**Test Orientation Procedure.** Job applicants and trainees ; 1967 ; TOP ; job applicants needing practice taking tests ; no scores ; how to take tests booklet (20 pages) and instructions tape (3¾ ips, 30 minutes) ; untimed practice tests booklet (20 pages) to be taken at home ; manual (2 pages) ; $17.50 per 25 sets of booklets, tape, and manual ; $4 per 25 booklets ; 60¢ per specimen set (without tape) ; postage extra ; George K. Bennett and Jerome E. Doppelt with the assistance of A. B. Madans and R. G. Buchanan ; Psychological Corporation. *

Lewis E. Albright, *Director, Organization and Management Development, Kaiser Aluminum & Chemical Corporation, Oakland, California.*

As the title implies, this is not a test, but rather a test-familiarization exercise. It is designed for job applicants with little or no experience in taking tests and is intended to reduce anxiety on the part of such individuals prior to their encounter with "real" employment testing situations. The materials are suitable for either individual or group administration. Those whom the manual suggests the exercises might benefit include (*a*) students in vocational, technical, and business courses who are soon to enter the labor market, (*b*) trainees in youth opportunity training programs, (*c*) adults in manpower development or retraining programs, (*d*) applicants who face retesting after having been rejected for prior poor performance on employment tests.

In a "teaching session" the examinees follow along with the 30-minute tape recording which is coordinated with the booklet, How to Take Tests. They are taught how to fill out simple employment forms correctly and are coached on taking five types of objective tests : clerical speed and accuracy, spelling, vocabulary, arith-

metic, and general information. The last test also provides practice in how to use a separate answer sheet of the type commonly scored by machine.

A second booklet, Practice Tests, is distributed at the conclusion of the teaching session and contains short tests of the type enumerated above. The chief difference in the two booklets is that the latter exercises are to be taken by the examinee at home under self-administration conditions.

An apparent oversight in the second booklet, however, is the omission of suggested time limits for any of the tests. This omission seems particularly curious because the announcer concludes the tape recording with a strong admonition that the examinees try to take the practice tests in the second book under timed conditions as a kind of dress rehearsal for the tests that count. On the tape, silences of generous length are allowed for completion of each exercise. Strange, then, that no suggested time limits are provided when the examinee is on his own.

This entire issue of timed tests is handled somewhat awkwardly by the authors. Generally, their instructions are well written in simple but businesslike language for an unsophisticated audience. In the discussion of the rationale for timed tests, however, a patronizing tone must be acknowledged in such statements as "if you are taking a timed test and you see that there's still a lot left to do when time is called, don't feel bad. Everyone is probably in the same boat." Obviously, everyone is *not* in the same boat if individual differences are allowed to manifest themselves !

Is the *Test Orientation Procedure* somewhat oversimplified for its intended beneficiaries ? If one is looking for an accurate simulation of an employment test situation, the answer is certainly "yes." The average difficulty of both the problems and the instructional material does not appear to be much above the fourth grade level. Most commonly-used tests have a much higher ceiling than this. Simulation, therefore, might be better accomplished by the simple expedient of administering an alternate form of the "real" test.

How good is the TOP, therefore, as a purely introductory exercise to various types of testing problems, particularly for poorly educated or so-called culturally deprived groups ? Depending on the level of education and the general familiarity of the examinees with verbal materials, the answer could be a qualified "O.K." Reading ability, some writing facility, knowledge of vocabulary, and computational skills are called for, although there are no problems in arithmetic reasoning, analogies, or other higher-level skills. Even so, illiterates and those of very low ability will obviously not be able to respond to this material. For individuals whose education is deficient but who are otherwise alert and capable, it would seem more beneficial to provide training in basic literacy rather than to give practice in how to take tests.

For those who do possess the minimal abilities called for but who happen to have little familiarity with testing procedures, the TOP could be quite useful. No doubt there are many such people and they would certainly comprise some of the trainee groups mentioned earlier. But even this tentatively favorable conclusion must await verification, because no data are presented in the brief manual to show that the TOP does, in fact, reduce test anxiety or lead to improved test performance in a "for keeps" situation. Until some validation efforts with TOP are performed, its real usefulness will remain a matter for speculation.

In summary, then, the *Test Orientation Procedure* could be of value as a test familiarization device for those who are likely to do poorly on employment tests because of excessive anxiety attributable to lack of acquaintance with testing procedures. Illiterates and those of very low mental ability probably will not be aided by TOP and some examinees might even be misled by TOP's easy problems into underestimating the difficulty of a later test which counts toward getting a job.

SELECTION & RATING FORMS

[1067]

★**Application Interview Screening Form.** Job applicants; 1965; 10 ratings by interviewer: work experience, previous education and training, job knowledge, intelligence, sociability, ambition, emotional stability, fluency, maturity, leadership capacity; 1 form (1 page); mimeographed manual (6 pages); no data on reliability and validity; $2.50 per 20 forms; $1 per single copy; $1 per manual; postage extra; (5-10) minutes; Psychological Publications Press. *

[1068]

★**Employee Competency Scale.** Employees; 1969; ECS; ratings by supervisors; 6 scores: communication,

dependability, attitude, job competence, leadership, total; 1 form (4 pages); instruction card (2 pages); no data on reliability; no description of normative population; publisher recommends use of local norms; $5.50 per 25 forms; $1 per instruction card; $1 per specimen set; cash orders postpaid; [10-20] minutes; William T. Martin; Psychologists and Educators Press. *

[1069]

★**[Job Application Forms.]** Job applicants and employees; 1957-68; 7 application forms; manual ['60, 16 pages]; graphic experience chart ['57, 1 page]; instructions for use of chart ['60, 3 pages]; pre-interview checklist ['60, 2 pages]; no data on reliability and validity; $2 per manual; $3 per 50 graphic experience charts and instructions for use; $2.75 per 35 pre-interview checklists; cash orders postpaid; specimen set not available; Shepherd Associates. *
a) JOB APPLICATION FORM. Job applicants; [1960]; Form B (4 pages); $7.50 per 50 copies; [30-60] minutes.
b) PERSONNEL INVENTORY FORM. Employees considered for transfer or promotion; [1960]; 1 form (4 pages); $7.50 per 50 copies; [30-60] minutes.
c) EMPLOYMENT APPLICATION FORM. Job applicants; [1966]; Form C (2 pages); $5 per 50 copies; [15-30] minutes.
d) PERSONNEL RECORD FOLDER. 1968; Form F (3 pages); $15 per 50 copies.
e) CONTENT CONTROL SHEET. 1968; 1 form (2 pages).
f) MEDICAL EMPLOYMENT FORM. Administrators, nurses, technologists; 1967; Form D (4 pages); $7.50 per 50 copies; [30-60] minutes.
g) EMPLOYMENT APPLICATION. Nonmedical personnel; 1967; Form E (2 pages); $5 per 50 copies; [15-30] minutes.

[1070]

★**The Martin Performance Appraisal.** Employees; 1966; MPA; ratings by supervisors; 1 form (4 pages); no manual or other accessories; no data on reliability; $5.50 per 25 forms, postpaid; [5-45] minutes; William T. Martin; Western Psychological Services. *

[1071]

★**Personnel Rating Scale.** Employees; 1965-66; 11 ratings by supervisors: cooperativeness, quality of work, adaptability, dependability, emotional stability, quantity of work, sociability, persistence, initiative, work knowledge, overall; 1 form ('66, 1 page); mimeographed manual ('65, 4 pages plus scale); no data on reliability and validity; $2.50 per 20 scales; $1 per manual; postage extra; [5-10] minutes; Psychological Publications Press. *

[1072]

*★**RBH Individual Background Survey.** Business and industry; 1949-69; 3 editions; no data on reliability; local validation for specific jobs recommended by publisher; postage extra; Richardson, Bellows, Henry & Co., Inc. *
a) FORM T. Business and industry; 1952-63; 4 scoring keys: female clerical, male clerical, male industrial, male sales-supervisory-professional; 1 form ('52, 5 pages); manual ['63, 15 pages]; directions (no date, 1 page); $4.50 per 25 tests; 50¢ per key; $1.50 per manual; $1.50 per specimen set; (20-25) minutes.
b) FORM M-E. Managers and executives; 1962; 1 form ['62, 16 pages]; no manual; directions (no date, 3 pages); no data on validity; no norms; $9 per 10 tests; 50¢ per key; $1.50 per specimen set; (40-50) minutes.
c) FORM W-E. Wage earner level applicants; 1965-69; 1 form ('65, 12 pages); manual ('69, 6 pages); direc-

tions (no date, 3 pages) ; no norms for females ; separate answer sheets must be used ; $9 per 10 tests ; 20¢ per answer sheet ; $1.50 per manual ; $2 per specimen set ; (20–25) minutes.

REFERENCES

1. HARRELL, THOMAS W. "The Personality of High Earning MBA's in Big Business." *Personnel Psychol* 22(4):457–63 w '69. * (*PA* 44:13525)
2. HARRELL, THOMAS W. "The Personality of High Earning MBA's in Small Business." *Personnel Psychol* 23(3):369–75 au '70. * (*PA* 45:9041)

[1073]

★San Francisco Vocational Competency Scale. Mentally retarded adults ; 1968 ; SFVCS ; for rating workers in "sheltered workshops" ; 1 form (4 pages) ; manual (7 pages) ; $2.60 per 25 tests ; 50¢ per specimen set ; postage extra ; Samuel Levine and Freeman F. Elzey ; Psychological Corporation. *

Clin Psychologist 22(3):154 sp '69. N. M. Downie. * should be useful to educators who work with mentally retarded adults. The items may be completed by an individual in daily contact with the vocational experiences of the ratees. Follow-up studies should be made on those placed on jobs in the community. In summary, the reviewer feels that a potentially useful scale has been added to the battery of tools used by the worker with the mentally retarded adult.

[1074]

★Speech-Appearance Record. Job applicants ; 1967 ; SAR ; evaluation of young adults for employability ; individual ; 2 forms, each consisting of 6 response cards ; manual (3 pages) ; no data on reliability and validity ; no norms ; $4.50 per set of cards, 25 record forms, and manual ; $2 per set of cards ; $2.50 per 25 record forms ; 60¢ per specimen set (without cards) ; postage extra ; use of tape recorder optional ; 10(15) minutes ; George K. Bennett and Jerome E. Doppelt with the assistance of A. B. Madans ; Psychological Corporation. *

[1075]

★Wonderlic Personnel Selection Procedure. Applicants for employment ; 1967–69 ; WPSP ; part 3 is *Wonderlic Personnel Test;* 8 parts ; manual ('69, 15 pages, identical with manual copyrighted in 1967 except for advertising and prices) ; $28.50 per 25 sets of forms, postage extra ; $7.50 per 5 sets of forms excluding P-3, postpaid ; E. F. Wonderlic & Associates. *
a) P-1 : INTRODUCTORY APPLICATION. 1 card ['67] ; (5–10) minutes.
b) P-2 : PERSONNEL APPLICATION. 1 form ('67, 4 pages) ; (35–40) minutes.
c) P-3 : WONDERLIC PERSONNEL TEST, FORM I.
d) P-4 : PERSONNEL INTERVIEWER'S GUIDE. Adaptation of *Diagnostic Interviewer Guide* ('42) ; 1 form ('67, 4 pages) ; manual ('67, 4 pages) ; no data on reliability ; (25–45) minutes.
e) P-5 : HEALTH QUESTIONNAIRE. 1 form ('67, 2 pages).
f) P-6 : [WRITTEN REFERENCE REPORTS]. 3 reply envelopes ('67) : P-6 Empl (former employer reference), P-6 Educ (educational reference), P-6 Pers (personal reference).
g) P-7 : TELEPHONE REFERENCE CHECK. 1 form ('67, 2 pages).
h) P-8 : PRE-EMPLOYMENT SUMMARY. 1 form ('67, 2 pages).

[1076]

★Work Reference Check. Job applicants ; 1965 ; information and ratings by former employer ; 1 form (1 page) ; mimeographed manual (5 pages) ; $2.50 per 20 forms ; $1 per single copy ; $1 per manual ; postage extra ; (10) minutes ; Psychological Publications Press. *

SPECIFIC VOCATIONS

ACCOUNTING

[1077]

★Account Clerk Test. Job applicants ; 1957–59 ; ACT ; form 70-A ('59, 17 pages) ; manual ['59, 4 pages] ; general PPA directions ['57, 7 pages] ; no norms ; 10–49 tests, $1.20 each ; $2 per specimen set ; postpaid ; 120(130) minutes ; Public Personnel Association. *

[1078]

Accounting Orientation Test, High School Level. Grades 10–12 ; 1953–67 ; AOT : 4 scores : vocabulary, arithmetic reasoning, accounting problems, total ; Forms S, T, ('65, 8 pages) ; manual ('67, 13 pages) ; score report form ('65, 1 page) ; no norms for grades 10–11 for Form T ; separate answer sheets (IBM 805) must be used ; $6 per 25 tests ; $1 per specimen set ; postage extra ; scoring service, 20¢ per test ; 40(45) minutes ; Testing Project Office, American Institute of Certified Public Accountants ; distributed by Psychological Corporation. *

REFERENCES

1–2. See 5:907.
3. McIFF, LYLE HATCH. *The Relationship of Certain Selected Factors to the Success or Failure of Second-Quarter Accounting Students at Utah State University.* Doctor's thesis, University of Southern California (Los Angeles, Calif.), 1965. (*DA* 26:5767)
4. BUTTS, FRANKLIN EUGENE, AND PRICKETT, GARY L. *The Effect of Audio-Tutorial and Programmed Instruction Laboratories on Achievement in Accounting Principles.* Joint doctor's thesis, University of Northern Colorado (Greeley, Colo.), 1969. (*DAI* 30:4060A)
5. DAILY, VICTORIA LEE DeFORE. *The Effect of Programmed Instruction in the Teaching of Principles of Accounting.* Doctor's thesis, Colorado State College (Greeley, Colo.), 1969. (*DAI* 30:4061A)

[1079]

★CLEP Subject Examination in Introductory Accounting. 1 year or equivalent ; 1970 ; for college accreditation of nontraditional study, advanced placement, or assessment of educational achievement ; 2 parallel editions : 90 and 45 minute tests ; for program accessories, see 664 ; program administered for the College Entrance Examination Board by Educational Testing Service. *
a) 90 MINUTE EDITION. Tests administered monthly at regional centers throughout the United States ; tests also available for institutional testing at any time ; Form SCT1 (20 pages) ; optional essay supplement : Form SCT1A (4 pages) ; separate answer sheets (SCRIBE) must be used ; rental and scoring fee, $5 per student ; 90(95) minutes.
b) 45 MINUTE EDITION. Available only for institutional testing ; Forms SSL1, SSL3, (10 pages) ; separate answer sheets (Digitek-IBM 805, IBM 1230) must be used ; rental fee, 75¢ per student ; scoring service not available ; 45(50) minutes.

For reviews of the testing program, see 664 (3 reviews).

BUSINESS

[1080]

*Admission Test for Graduate Study in Business. Business graduate students; 1954–70; ATGSB; test administered 5 times annually (February, April, June, August, November) at centers established by the publisher; 3 scores: quantitative, verbal, total; Form QBS$_{R11}$ ('69, 50 pages); supervisor's manual ('69, 22 pages); bulletin for candidates ('70, 51 pages); handbook for. deans and admissions officers ('66, 121 pages); separate answer sheets (SCRIBE) must be used; examination fee, $10 per student; fee includes reporting of scores to 3 schools designated at time of application; $1 per additional report; postpaid; 205(235) minutes; Educational Testing Service. *

REFERENCES

1. HARRELL, THOMAS W. *Managers' Performance and Personality,* pp. 61–6. Cincinnati, Ohio: South-Western Publishing Co., 1961. Pp. v, 218. *
2. GRUBER, EDWARD C. *Graduate Business Admission Test.* New York: Arco Publishing Co., Inc., 1963. Pp. 262. *
3. RUDMAN, JACK. *How to Pass the Admission Test for Graduate Study in Business.* Brooklyn, N.Y.: College Publishing Corporation, 1963. Pp. 308. *
4. LEWIS, JOHN W. "Caution About Using Test Composites as Predictors." *J Col Stud Personnel* 6:95–7 D '64. *
5. LEWIS, JOHN W. "The Relationship of Selected Variables to Achievement and Persistence in a Masters Program in Business Administration." *Ed & Psychol Meas* 24:951–4 w '64. * (*PA* 39:8702)
6. MITTMAN, ARTHUR, AND LEWIS, JOHN W. "Correlates of Achievement on the Admissions Test for Graduate Study in Business." *Ed & Psychol Meas* 25:585–8 su '65. * (*PA* 39: 15248)
7. HINTON, BERNARD LLOYD. *A Model of Creative Problem Solving Performance and the Effects of Frustration.* Doctor's thesis, Stanford University (Stanford, Calif.), 1966. (*DA* 27: 2508B)
8. *Moderator Variable Study: The Effect of Background Factors on the Prediction of Performance in Graduate Business School.* Admission Test for Graduate Study in Business, Brief No. 3. Princeton, N.J.: Educational Testing Service, July 1969. Pp. 19. *
9. CURTIS, KENNETH CLAUDE. *An Evaluation of Variables for the Prediction of Achievement in a Graduate Program in Business Administration.* Doctor's thesis, Colorado State College (Greeley, Colo.), 1969. (*DAI* 30:4069A)
10. POUNDERS, CEDRIC J. "The Admissions Test for Graduate Study in Business: A Factor Analytic Study." *Ed & Psychol Meas* 30(2):469–73 su '70. * (*PA* 45:2955)

JEROME E. DOPPELT, *Associate Director, Test Division, The Psychological Corporation, New York, New York.*

The *Admission Test for Graduate Study in Business* is the only test in a program of the same name administered by the Educational Testing Service. The test results are intended to supplement other information available on applicants to graduate schools of business and thereby improve the selection of entering classes. The program is under the direction of a Policy Committee composed of representatives from 30 graduate business schools. The test was first administered in 1954 and is now offered several times each year. Different forms, equated to each other, are in use and it may be assumed that more forms will be made. The instrument was developed to provide a measure of the academic abilities of applicants. It is not a measure of achievement in particular subject matter and is not dependent on specific undergraduate preparation.

The ATGSB is a long test; the student is given 205 minutes to work on it. Each section of the test is timed separately. The test booklet informs the student that there will be a penalty for incorrect answers as "a correction for haphazard guessing" and a caution in regard to guessing is given. The extent of the correction is not mentioned in the test booklet, but the student who reads the Bulletin of Information for Candidates will know that "you will lose one-fourth of a point for each wrong answer." It would be advisable to state the actual correction on the booklet cover as well, since it does appear in the bulletin. Three scores are obtained: verbal, quantitative, and total. The results are reported in standard scores. For the verbal and quantitative scores, the mean standard score was set at 30 and the standard deviation at 8. For the total score, the mean standard score was set at 500 and the standard deviation at 100. Some confusion may result from the use of different scale units for the part and total scores, but perhaps such troubles are short-lived.

The test questions and item styles are rather ponderous, and taking the examination is likely to be an exhausting experience. Each of two reading recall sections instructs the student to read three complex passages, then to answer questions about them without referring back to the passages. The handbook notes that the questions require the student "not only to recall in considerable detail the facts and ideas in the passages but also to arrive at conclusions not directly stated. The tasks he performs in this exercise....reproduce in miniature a kind of behavior in which he will be constantly engaged as a student." Although it is reasonable to expect the student to recall significant positions or conclusions from the passages he has just read, there is some doubt about his need to recall detailed facts and information. Some of the items refer to details that the student would ordinarily obtain by going back to the source document rather than by relying on his memory. The proscription on referring to the passage does, of course, put an added burden on the examiner and proctors who must enforce this rule.

In addition to questions based on reading passages, there are items dealing with recognition of antonyms, analogies, and the completion of sentences, as well as items based on numerous complex graphs, arithmetical and algebraic manipulation, data interpretation, and judgment of the sufficiency of presented data for answering particular questions. The variety provides a degree of interest but the length of the test calls for an even greater degree of endurance. There are fewer than 200 items, but the amount of reading and study of material is formidable.

The auxiliary documents include a very clear and helpful Bulletin of Information for Candidates, a Supervisor's Manual, and a Handbook for Deans and Admissions Officers. The latter document is a well-written presentation of the nature and purpose of the ATGSB Program and of technical information that has been collected over the years. A Memorandum Transmitting Scores to Business Schools, dated 1969–70, gives these figures for the reliability of scores on current forms : .93 for total score, .89 for verbal, and .91 for quantitative. These coefficients are very respectable. It has been recognized that the standard error of measurement is more useful than the reliability coefficient for estimating the extent of error in a test score. The user of the ATGSB will find that the standard errors of measurement of the reported scores are given, along with a clear discussion of their meaning.

The criterion for a large number of validity studies was first-year average grade in business school. The results confirm the claim that "while, in general, the test scores are as good as or somewhat better than undergraduate grade average for predicting average grades in the first year of graduate study, the best prediction may be obtained from the use of a combination of undergraduate grade average and test scores." For example, in a study of 19 graduate schools of business in 1962–63, the average correlation of the total score with first-year average grades was .36, and the undergraduate record (the measure of previous academic success used by the business school in its admissions program) correlated .30 with the criterion. The best weighted combination of total score and undergraduate record correlated .46 with the first-year average grade. The handbook informs the reader that the correlation between ATGSB scores and business school grades in individual school studies characteristically runs from .30 to .50. It is pointed out that such coefficients are low against a standard of perfect prediction and "anyone using the scores

for prediction should be prepared for many disappointments." This reflects commendable modesty and caution, but the test user should not overlook another sentence on the same page : "Moreover, the use of the test scores will result in the selection of a better class than if admissions are based on chance." Of course, students are not admitted to a school on the basis of chance. The point is that there is a useful relationship between test scores and subsequent grades.

Percentile norms, based on large numbers of candidates tested over a three-year period, are provided for the three reported scores. The comparison of an individual's scores with those of candidates in nationwide administrations can readily be made. One will also find, in the 1969–70 memorandum, the suggestion that schools develop their own normative tables as well, to permit the comparison of a candidate's test performance with the scores of other candidates to the particular school.

The ATGSB is described as an aptitude test designed to predict success in graduate business studies and nothing else. The method for determining the test's validity is specified as the extent to which it predicts future success in business school. The test achieves its purpose in terms of the framework that has been established. To admissions officers in graduate schools of business, the ATGSB offers useful supplementary information about a candidate's qualifications. This reviewer feels that the test is much longer and carries more of a reading load than is necessary to achieve the purpose. But, in the circumstances in which the ATGSB is administered, there may even be a point in having a long and perhaps exhausting examination. The candidate will have no doubt that he has been tested !

GARY R. HANSON, *Research Psychologist, The American College Testing Program, Iowa City, Iowa.*

The ATGSB is an aptitude test designed to predict success in graduate business education. In the tradition of the Educational Testing Service, the test measures verbal and quantitative academic skills. Specific knowledge from undergraduate business courses such as economics, accounting, or business law is not tested.

The 205-minute test is composed of five sections. Two reading recall sections, each composed of three rather difficult prose passages followed by a series of questions to be answered without referring to the passages, and a verbal omnibus section, composed of analogies, opposites, and sentence completion types of items, are combined to yield a verbal score. A data interpretation section, testing the candidate's facility to manipulate and extract relationships from quantitative information, and a data sufficiency section, requiring logical reasoning, are combined to yield a quantitative score.

Competent test construction leaves little room for criticism of the test content. The test items are appropriately difficult for the educational level of the students tested. Score distributions for verbal, quantitative, and total show excellent dispersion of scores, an adequate ceiling, and very little skewness. Although the test content is oriented to business-related problems, thus providing good face validity, ETS research has shown that, typically, students who majored in fields other than business and economics did better on the ATGSB (all three scores) than did those who majored in business and economics.

Only minor criticism can be made of the ATGSB test construction. The data interpretation section, consisting of 55 items, requires 75 minutes of testing time. Slightly more than one-fourth of the students finish the entire section, although nearly 90 percent finish three-fourths of it. While the reviewer does not object to the speeded nature of this section as such, the possibility of a fatigue effect in a test that is long and difficult may influence test scores. A better approach may be to split the one section into two and intersperse them between verbal sections of the test.

Extensive research, reported in the Handbook for Deans and Admissions Officers, provides a comprehensive summary of the reliability and validity of the ATGSB. The reliabilities for the total, verbal, and quantitative scales are .93, .89, and .91, respectively. Considering the number of items constituting each score, the relatively high reliabilities are not surprising. In fact, the tests could be reduced in length without seriously affecting the reliability. The time taken to obtain three pieces of information may not warrant the small increase in reliability obtained.

The primary purpose of the ATGSB is the prediction of grades in graduate business education. The extent to which the test fulfills that purpose has been investigated in a series of studies conducted by ETS. The results have been "typical." Studies conducted in 1954–55 and replicated in 1958–59 showed ATGSB total score and combined undergraduate record correlated .50 and .49, respectively, with first year business grades. ATGSB total score alone correlated .43 with first year grades in both studies. Because students in the 1958–59 study were selected on the basis of ATGSB scores, correlation coefficients were adjusted for restriction of range. The average adjusted correlation across the schools studied was .53. Later studies using the ATGSB showed declining validity coefficients. This finding, however, is a function of the effective use of the test in the admission process.

In most of the studies conducted, the ATGSB total score predicted first year grades somewhat better than undergraduate grade record, and the verbal and quantitative scores predicted less well than the undergraduate grade record. As expected, the combination of ATGSB total and undergraduate grade record predict better than either one alone. The relatively low validities of the verbal and quantitative scores do not support their use in the prediction of overall grades. The lack of evidence supporting differential validity of the verbal and quantitative scores further suggests that it is not particularly useful to report three scores. Only the total score provides an adequate index of general academic ability.

The supporting publication, mentioned previously, is well written and provides the college dean or admissions officer an excellent overview of the test, how to use it, and what the test scores measure. Research studies are cited throughout to substantiate the publisher's modest claims.

Test scores are reported to the appropriate school approximately three weeks after the test administration. Accompanying the score reports is a Memorandum Transmitting Scores to Business Schools which includes up-to-date norms tables and a brief description of the test characteristics (reliability and validity). Norms for the ATGSB total score are based on all students tested for the three previous years individually and combined. Norms for the verbal and quantitative scores are based only on the three combined years. Both publications for the ATGSB strongly recommend the development of local norms for the most effective use of the scores. Schools using the ATGSB for the first time may find the national norms of limited usefulness because of the lack of adequate sample description. If a particular school differs greatly from most schools in the norms samples, candidate score reports will have little meaning.

In summary, the ATGSB fulfills the purpose for which it was designed. When used appropriately, the test will provide an objective measure of the academic skills required in graduate business education. As recommended in the publications, the test is best used as one of several items of information about a prospective candidate.

[1081]

★CLEP Subject Examination in Introduction to Business Management. 1 semester or equivalent; 1969–70; for college accreditation of nontraditional study, advanced placement, or assessment of educational achievement; 2 parallel editions: 90 and 45 minute tests; for program accessories, see 664; program administered for the College Entrance Examination Board by Educational Testing Service. *
a) 90 MINUTE EDITION. Tests administered monthly at regional centers throughout the United States; tests also available for institutional testing at any time; Form SCT1 ('69, 14 pages); optional essay supplement; Form RCT2A ('69, 2 pages); separate answer sheets (SCRIBE) must be used; rental and scoring fee, $5 per student; 90(95) minutes.
b) 45 MINUTE EDITION. Available only for institutional testing; Forms RSL1, RSL3, ('69, 8 pages); separate answer sheets (Digitek-IBM 805, IBM 1230) must be used; rental fee, 75¢ per student; scoring service not available; 45(50) minutes.

For reviews of the testing program, see 664 (3 reviews).

[1082]

★CLEP Subject Examination in Introductory Business Law. 1 semester or equivalent; 1970; for college accreditation of nontraditional study, advanced placement, or assessment of educational achievement; 2 parallel editions: 90 and 45 minute tests; for program accessories, see 664; program administered for the College Entrance Examination Board by Educational Testing Service. *
a) 90 MINUTE EDITION. Tests administered monthly at regional centers throughout the United States; tests also available for institutional testing at any time; Form SCT1 (15 pages); optional essay supplement: Form SCT1A (2 pages); separate answer sheets (SCRIBE) must be used; rental and scoring fee, $5 per student; 90(95) minutes.
b) 45 MINUTE EDITION. Available only for institutional testing; Forms SSL1 (8 pages), SSL3 (9 pages); separate answer sheets (Digitek-IBM 805, IBM 1230) must be used; rental fee, 75¢ per student; scoring service not available; 45(50) minutes.

For reviews of the testing program, see 664 (3 reviews).

[1083]

★CLEP Subject Examination in Introductory Marketing. 1 semester or equivalent; 1968–70; for college accreditation of nontraditional study, advanced placement, or assessment of educational achievement; tests administered monthly at regional centers throughout the United States; tests also available for institutional testing at any time; Forms QCT1, QCT2, ('68, 12 pages); optional essay supplement: Form QCT2-A ('68, 2 pages); for program accessories, see 664; rental and scoring fee, $5 per student; postpaid; essay supplement scored by the college; 90(95) minutes, same for essay supplement; program administered for the College Entrance Examination Board by Educational Testing Service. *

For reviews of the testing program, see 664 (3 reviews).

[1084]

★CLEP Subject Examination in Money and Banking. 1 semester or equivalent; 1967–70; for college accreditation of nontraditional study, advanced placement, or assessment of educational achievement; tests administered monthly at regional centers throughout the United States; tests also available for institutional testing at any time; Forms PCT1, PCT2, ('67, 16 pages); optional essay supplement: Form K-PCT2-A ('67, 3 pages); for program accessories, see 664; rental and scoring fee, $5 per student; postpaid; essay supplement scored by the college; 90(95) minutes, same for essay supplement; program administered for the College Entrance Examination Board by Educational Testing Service. *

For reviews of the testing program, see 664 (3 reviews).

[1085]

★Organizational Value Dimensions Questionnaire: Business Form. Adults; 1965–66; OVDQ; for research use only; attitudes toward business and industrial firms in general; manual title is *Value Scale—The Business Firm;* 9 scores: organizational magnitude and structure, internal consideration, competition and strategy, social responsibility, quality, change, member identification and control, external political participation, member equality and participation; Form BBR-65 ('65, 4 pages); manual ('66, 7 pages); no data on reliability; no norms; separate answer sheets must be used; $2 per 25 tests; 2¢ per answer sheet; cash orders postpaid; specimen set free; (25) minutes; Carroll L. Shartle and Ralph M. Stogdill; University Publications Sales, Ohio State University. *

[1086]

★The Undergraduate Record Examinations: Business Test. College; 1969–70; Forms K-RUR ('69, 21 pages), SUR ('70, 23 pages); descriptive booklet ('70, 8 pages); for more complete information, see 671; 120(140) minutes; Educational Testing Service. *

For reviews of the testing program, see 671 (2 reviews).

COMPUTER PROGRAMMING

[1087]

★Aptitude Assessment Battery: Programming. Programmers and trainees; 1967–69; AABP; Form D ('69, 31 pages); no manual; no data on reliability and

validity; distribution restricted to employers of programmers, not available to school personnel; $15 per
applicant, fee includes scoring service; postpaid; specimen set not available; left-handed and French editions
available; (210–270) minutes; Jack M. Wolfe; Programming Specialists, Inc. *

REFERENCE

1. WOLFE, JACK M. "Testing for Programming Aptitude."
Datamation 15(4):67–72 Ap '69. *

[1088]

★CLEP Subject Examination in Computers and
Data Processing. 1–2 semesters or equivalent; 1968–
70; for college accreditation of nontraditional study,
advanced placement, or assessment of educational
achievement; 2 parallel editions: 90 and 45 minute
tests; for program accessories, see 664; program administered for the College Entrance Examination
Board by Educational Testing Service. *
a) 90 MINUTE EDITION. Tests administered monthly at
regional centers throughout the United States; tests
also available for institutional testing at any time;
Form RCT1 ('68, 14 pages); optional essay supplement: Form QCT2-A ('68, 2 pages); separate answer
sheets (SCRIBE) must be used; rental and scoring
fee, $5 per student; 90(95) minutes.
b) 45 MINUTE EDITION. Available only for institutional
testing; Forms QSL2, QSL3, ('68, 8 pages); separate
answer sheets (Digitek-IBM 805, IBM 1230) must be
used; rental fee, 75¢ per student; scoring service not
available; 45(50) minutes.

*For reviews of the testing program, see 664
(3 reviews).*

[1089]

★Computer Programmer Aptitude Battery. Applicants for computer training or employment; 1964–67;
CPAB; 6 scores: verbal meaning, reasoning, letter
series, number ability, diagramming, total; 1 form ('64,
25 pages); manual ('67, 20 pages); separate answer
sheets must be used; $1.82 per test; $4.55 per 25 self-
marking answer sheets; 75¢ per manual; $2.75 per
specimen set; postage extra; 79(90) minutes; Jean
Maier Palormo; Science Research Associates, Inc. *
(British edition: NFER Publishing Co. Ltd.)

REFERENCES

1. PALORMO, JEAN M. "The Computer Programmer Aptitude
Battery—A Description and Discussion." *Proc Ann Computer
Personnel Res Conf* 5:57–63 '67. *
2. CRONBACH, LEE J. *Essentials of Psychological Testing,
Third Edition,* pp. 417–21. New York: Harper & Row, Pub-
lishers, Inc., 1970. Pp. xxx, 752. *

RICHARD T. JOHNSON, *Senior Research Scientist, American Institutes for Research, Limbe,
Malawi.*

Almost all books written concerning the field
of electronic data processing include a section
on the abilities and duties of programmers. It
was from this base that the author of the *Computer Programmer Aptitude Battery* built the
test. Four of the five subtests show obvious
correspondence with the programming field;
the Letter Series seems tenuously related.

The Diagramming subtest, for instance, demands that the examinee analyze a flow chart
and choose appropriate steps to fill in blank por-

tions of the diagram. The flow chart applications cover such diverse fields as games and
acceptance sampling.

In the Reasoning subtest, the examinee must
translate word descriptions into mathematical
notation, a task very similar to that of programming. Similarly, on the Number Ability subtest,
he needs to estimate reasonable answers to
computations in a manner akin to debugging a
program or checking the quality of output. Verbal Meaning is simply a vocabulary test with
words chosen from data processing and related
fields.

With such obvious similarity between the
various tests and on-the-job behavior, it is surprising that the performance rating validities
are not higher. Although correlations of total
scores with grades in computer programming
training courses range from .46 to .71, which
would generally be considered adequate, the
correlations with job performance ratings were
only .03 and .31 in the two studies reported in
the manual.

The author discusses the problems of obtaining unbiased and uncontaminated job performance criteria in such a way that potential users
can easily appreciate her difficulties in constructing this test. The emphasis is placed on success
in training as a better interim criterion than the
ambiguous results of job ratings. One might
justify this criterion by mentioning that less
capable trainees are usually given more formal
course work at manufacturers' educational centers, a practice which would tend to reduce the
correlations between scores and job ratings.
However, since no information is given on the
extent of previous formal training, this supposition cannot be checked.

Although all three validity studies are based
upon scores of programmers, the manual claims
that the CPAB is also useful for selecting systems analysts. Since system analysis demands a
higher level and different type of ability, use of
the test for such selection should be approached
with caution.

Directions are refreshingly clear and uncomplicated, both in the manual and on the test.
Time limits are reasonable and clearly defined
for the examinee. Although no mention is made
of scratch paper, it could be useful in the Reasoning subtest, even if it were prohibited in the
Number Ability section.

The answer sheet is of the carbon-interleaved
type which is torn apart after use and scored

by counting the number of X's in the boxes. Item 22 is keyed incorrectly and item 62 has two correct answers since the stem does not specify if the answer is to be in octal or decimal. In the Number Ability section, an unwary examinee could miss a number of questions if he estimates answers by truncating rather than by rounding.

The interpretation section of the manual includes the valuable caveat: "All the evidence should be weighed in deciding whether to hire an applicant." And following this is such a convincing section on the necessity for conducting local research studies with the CPAB that one wishes the author had included for the novice a bibliographic reference to an acceptable approach for conducting such studies.

However, no matter how well done certain parts of the manual are, the author is not absolved from the necessity of describing the norm group with more than an N, mean, and standard deviation. With the large number of women in the programming field, some information concerning sex differences or lack thereof seems necessary. No reference to the age composition of the group is made—very likely one of the hazards of haphazard sampling.

Reliability is based on the experimental forms of the test, a practice that is inexcusable, since the separately timed halves and K-R 20 methods could as easily have been applied to the norm group tests. The obtained estimate of reliability for the total battery was .95. A different standard error of measurement is reported for the inexperienced and for the experienced norm groups, but it would have been much more accurate to use a single one based on the same group on which reliability was assessed.

The strength of the test lies in its close correspondence to the tasks of programming, the clarity of the directions, and the descriptive material concerning criteria and interpretation. The most serious weaknesses are the lack of information on the characteristics of the norm and validity groups and the technical errors committed in assessing standard error. Despite these weaknesses, the CPAB is probably the best device presently available for selection of computer programmers.

DONALD J. VELDMAN, *Professor of Educational Psychology, The University of Texas, Austin, Texas.*

The five sections of this instrument are independently timed, and scoring is a simple count of right answers. Special carbon-backed answer sheets allow rapid hand scoring without the use of templates. The manual includes a rather extensive discussion of the rationale and development of the test, along with a moderate amount of the usual reliability and validity data. Percentile norms, means, and standard deviations are provided for samples of 224 experienced programmers and 298 trainees and applicants.

The average correlations between items and their part scores ranged from .33 to .60. Split-half and K-R 20 reliabilities for part scores range from .67 to .94, and the estimate for the total score was .95. No retest correlations are reported in the manual, nor are any data concerning practice effects.

Correlations with IBM's *Revised Programmer Aptitude Test* in five small groups ranged from .55 to .86, but no comparative validity data are reported for the two instruments. With three small groups, validities of .52, .56, and .71 were obtained against a criterion of success in training. In another sample a correlation of .46 was obtained with this criterion. Two studies of the prediction of supervisor ratings among employed programmers yielded rather dismal results: correlations of .03 and .31.

Perhaps the most interesting material in the manual concerns the rationale for keeping the Verbal Meaning subtest when the seven-part experimental version was reduced to five subtests. This decision was based on anticipated changes in the job requirements of programmers: "The ability of the computer programmer to communicate with and understand the problems of specialists in a variety of fields will become increasingly important." This reviewer finds it hard to believe that things will *change* in this regard; the problem has been with us all along, no more or less severe than it ever was. The Verbal Meaning subtest is the only one of the five that does not substantially overlap the more economical IBM instrument, and there are no data reported in the manual to support the notion that it enhances the validity of the total test.

On the whole, this test seems to be useful for screening applicants to a training program. There is, however, little evidence that it predicts later job performance even as well as the cheaper, shorter IBM instrument.

Computer Programmer Aptitude Battery

[1090]

*IBM Aptitude Test for Programmer Personnel.
Applicants for programming training on IBM computers; 1955–64; ATPP; revision of still-in-print *Revised Programmer Aptitude Test;* 1 form ('64, 16 pages); manual ('64, 13 pages); separate answer sheets (IBM 1230) must be used; distribution restricted to IBM customers; 55(65) minutes; [Walter J. McNamara and George P. Hollenbeck]; distributed by International Business Machines Corporation. *

REFERENCES

1–2. See 6:1153.
3. REINSTEDT, ROBERT N.; HAMMIDI, BEAULAH C.; PERES, SHERWOOD H.; AND RICARD, EVELYN L. *Computer Personnel Research Group Programmer Performance Prediction Study.* Memorandum RM-4033-PR. Santa Monica, Calif.: Rand Corporation, 1964. Pp. vii, 64. *
4. HOLLENBECK, GEORGE P., AND MCNAMARA, WALTER J. "CUCPAT and Programming Aptitude." *Personnel Psychol* 18:101–6 sp '65. * (*PA* 39:16522)
5. DUGAN, ROBERT D. "The Industrial Psychologist: Selection and Equal Employment Opportunity (A Symposium): 4, Current Problems in Test Performance of Job Applicants: 2." *Personnel Psychol* 19:18–24 sp '66. * (*PA* 40:9275)
6. GORDON, BRUCE F., AND DENNIS, RICHARD A. "Characteristics and Performance Predictors of 7094 Computer Service Operators." *Proc Ann Computer Personnel Res Conf* 4:96–106 '66. *
7. HOWELL, MARGARET A.; VINCENT, JOHN W.; AND GAY, RICHARD A. "Testing Aptitude for Computer Programming." *Psychol Rep* 20:1251–6 Je '67. * (*PA* 41:15911)
8. MAYER, DAVID B., AND STALNAKER, ASHFORD W. "Computer Personnel Research—Issues and Progress in the 60's." *Proc Ann Computer Personnel Res Conf* 5:6–41 '67. *
9. SEILER, JOSEPH. "Survey of Validation Studies on Computer Personnel Selection Instruments." *Proc Ann Computer Personnel Res Conf* 5:43–51 '67. *
10. BAUER, ROGER; MEHRENS, WILLIAM A.; AND VINSONHALER, JOHN F. "Predicting Performance in a Computer Programming Course." *Ed & Psychol Meas* 28:1159–64 w '68. * (*PA* 44:7333)
11. CORRENTI, RICHARD J. *Predictors of Success in the Study of Computer Programming at Two-Year Institutions of Higher Education.* Doctor's thesis, Ohio University (Athens, Ohio), 1969. (*DAI* 30:3718A)
12. ALSPAUGH, CAROL ANN. *A Study of the Relationships Between Student Characteristics and Proficiency in Symbolic and Algebraic Computer Programming.* Doctor's thesis, University of Missouri (Columbia, Mo.), 1970. (*DAI* 31:4627B)
13. MILLER, ROBERT LOUIS. *A Study of the Relationship Which Exists Between Achievement in High School Vocational Data Processing Programs and the Programmer Aptitude Test.* Master's thesis, North Carolina State University (Raleigh, N.C.), 1970.
14. WALKER, ELAINE, AND MARKHAM, S. J. "Computer Programming Aptitude Tests." *Austral Psychologist* 5(1):52–8 Mr '70. * (*PA* 46:5840)

RICHARD T. JOHNSON, *Senior Research Scientist, American Institutes for Research, Limbe, Malawi.*

One of the trade journals in the electronic data processing field carries frequent advertisements concerning the care and feeding of programmers. Most installations would gladly care for and feed programmers well if they could find them. The *IBM Aptitude Test for Programmer Personnel* was designed to reduce the difficulties of their search.

Three subtests comprise the test: letter series, figure series, and arithmetical reasoning. The first subtest is similar to the reasoning test of the *SRA Primary Mental Abilities,* while the second is akin to the abstract reasoning subtest of the *Differential Aptitude Test.* The third subtest is an arithmetical word problem test with data processing applications.

The items are graded in difficulty within each subtest, and the time limits are short enough that most applicants will not finish (except perhaps the arithmetical reasoning section).

Although the manual recommends that the ATPP be used immediately in place of its predecessors, the *Programmer Aptitude Test* and *Revised Programmer Aptitude Test,* no reasons are given, nor is the nature of the revised revision indicated. No doubt even more frequent updating is necessary in such a volatile field, but it would be helpful to a potential user to know the nature of the changes.

Perhaps since the ATPP was developed primarily for IBM's customers, little is said about the qualifications or the duties of the examiner, except that he take and score the test himself before he administers it. Thus an improvement in the directions seems warranted. Rather than stating that the examiner "should make sure that the applicant understands the examples and how to use the separate answer sheet," the manual could specify exact directions to be used and demarcate them with italics. If the IBM 1230 answer sheet is to be corrected by machine, the directions should emphasize the necessity of careful erasure of changed answers.

Letter-grade norms are given: the top 30 percent are given A, the next 20 percent B, the next 34 percent C, and the remaining 16 percent D. The suggestion is then made that applicants with letter grades of A and B be considered for training if otherwise qualified. No mention is made of the influence of previous training, either in the norms or in any of the validity studies.

The norms were based on 407 students in IBM programming and basic computer systems classes at five of the IBM education centers. No information is given about the sex composition of the group, although mean age of 30.2 and educational level of 14.3 years are given. The section on reliability indicates that statistics were obtained from two administrations of the test to junior college students. Again, the sex composition is not mentioned and some doubt exists whether the age of the junior college students is comparable to that of the IBM students.

The statistics on the scores are adequate in that test-retest reliability coefficients are given for each subtest and total as well as means and standard deviations at each administration. Coefficients range from .57 to .79 for subtests, with a total score coefficient of .88. The standard error of measurement is also given, although no guidance in interpretation is offered.

A table of intercorrelations among subscores and the total score and correlations of total score with age and with educational level are given. There is also a section comparing the ATPP with its immediate predecessor on concurrent validity. With all this valuable information given, it is surprising that age or previous computer experience factors are not discussed or even implied in any part of the manual.

Both success in training and success on the job are taken as criteria in the validity section. For training, final class grades were used. Sadly enough, no information is given on how these were figured or on the type of performance required. Since IBM usually includes a practical exercise in their final tests, they would probably convert more potential users if they described the assessment procedure used. Means, standard deviations, and test-class grade correlations are given for 22 classes and the user can easily ascertain the range of coefficients (− .22 to .82).

Data for the training validity studies are also presented in expectancy tables. A surprising bit of information is gleaned from Figure 1, in which it appears that a high D score is better than a C score as far as expectation of success is concerned for one of the groups.

A single study of 27 programmers' success on the job compared with their scores on the ATPP is given. The programmers were ranked on ability to program; this skill correlated .54 with test scores. No mention is made of who ranked them.

The test has a number of good attributes: sufficient difficulty to assure a high ceiling, a clear presentation of test-retest scores and intercorrelations among parts, ease of scoring, and expectancy tables for ease of interpretation. On the other hand, information is sparse or nonexistent in regard to extent of revisions from earlier forms, influence of previous training, sex differences on norms, and the nature of the performance rated as criteria in the validity section.

DENTISTRY

[1091]

*Dental Admission Testing Program. Dental school applicants; 1946-70; DATP; formerly called *Dental Aptitude Testing Program;* tests administered 3 times annually (January, April, September or Oc-

tober) at centers established by the publisher ; 5 tests, 13 scores : academic average (average of *b, c,* and *e*), manual average (average of *a* and *d*) and 11 scores listed below ; examiner's manual ['70, 10 pages] ; score report explanation for examinees ['68, 2 pages] ; bulletin for applicants ('70, 19 pages) ; examination fee, $15 ; fee includes reporting of scores to any 5 schools designated at time of application ; $1 per additional report ($2 per report requested after examination) ; postpaid ; 290-310(355-375) minutes in 2 sessions ; Division of Educational Measurements, Council on Dental Education, American Dental Association. *

a) CARVING DEXTERITY TEST. 1946-68 ; Forms 64A ('65, 4 pages), 65 ('65, 4 pages), 68 ('68, 4 pages) ; 70(90) minutes.

b) COOPERATIVE SCHOOL AND COLLEGE ABILITY TESTS. 1961 ; 3 scores : quantitative reasoning, verbal reasoning, total ; Forms UA, UB, (14 pages) ; 60(70) minutes.

c) READING COMPREHENSION. 1953-69 ; 4 forms.

    1) *Reading Comprehension in the Natural Sciences.* 1953-65 ; Forms 54 ('65, 14 pages, identical with test copyrighted in 1954 except for directions), 55 ('65, 15 pages, identical with test copyrighted in 1955 except for directions) ; 80(90) minutes.

    2) *Reading Comprehension in the Basic Sciences.* 1968-69 ; Forms 68 ('68, 14 pages), 69 ('69, 14 pages) ; 60(70) minutes.

d) SPACE RELATIONS TEST. 1947-62 ; subtest of *Differential Aptitude Tests;* Forms L, M, ('62, 15 pages) ; 20(35) minutes.

e) SURVEY OF THE NATURAL SCIENCES. 1951-69 ; 5 scores : biology, chemistry, factual, application, total ; Forms 68, 69, 69A, ('69, 12 pages) ; 80(90) minutes.

REFERENCES

1-2. See 4:788.

3-8. See 5:916.

9. HUCK, FRANCIS TEDFORD. *The Predictive Efficiency of the American Dental Association Aptitude Tests and Predental Grades at the Dental School of the University of Pennsylvania.* Doctor's thesis, University of Pennsylvania (Philadelphia, Pa.), 1958.

10. PARKINS, GRACE L. "Report on the Results of the Aptitude Testing Program." *J Dental Ed* 22:9-32 Ja '58. *

11. TIMMONS, GERALD D. "History of the Development of the Aptitude Testing Program of the Council on Dental Education of the American Dental Association." *J Dental Ed* 22:5-9 Ja '58. *

12. WEBB, SAM C. "Evaluating Tests as Predictors of Dental School Grades." *J Dental Ed* 22:33-45 Ja '58. *

13. DEREVERE, ROBERT E. "Comparison of Dental Aptitude Results With Achievements in Operative Dentistry." *J Dental Ed* 25:50-6 Mr '61. *

14. TOCCHINI, JOHN J.; ENDEY, MARK W.; THOMASSEN, PAUL R.; AND REINKE, BENJAMIN C. "Correlation Study Between Aptitude Testing and Dental Student Performance." *J Dental Ed* 25:269-73 S '61. *

15. RUDMAN, JACK. *How to Pass Dental Aptitude Test: Questions and Answers.* Brooklyn, N.Y.: College Publishing Corporation, 1962. Pp. 301. *

16. GRUBER, EMANUEL C., AND GRUBER, EDWARD C. *Dental Aptitude Tests.* New York: Arco Publishing Co., Inc., 1963. Pp. vii, 184, 96. *

17. HOOD, ALBERT B. "Predicting Achievement in Dental School." *J Dental Ed* 27:148-55 Je '63. *

18. LAND, MELVIN. "Psychological Tests as Predictors for Scholastic Achievement of Dental Students." *J Dental Ed* 27:25-30 Mr '63. *

19. MANHOLD, JOHN H.; VINTON, PAUL W.; AND MANHOLD, BEVERLY S. "Preliminary Study of the Efficacy of the Dental Aptitude Test in Predicting Four-Year Performance in Dental School." *J Dental Ed* 27:84-7 Mr '63. *

20. HELLER, D. BRIAN; CARSON, R. LAWRENCE; AND DOUGLAS, BRUCE L. "Selection of Students for Dental School." *J Dental Ed* 29:202-7 Je '65. *

21. MANHOLD, JOHN H., JR., AND MANHOLD, BEVERLY S. "Final Report of an Eight-Year Study of the Efficacy of the Dental Aptitude Test in Predicting Four-Year Performance in a New Dental School." *J Dental Ed* 29:41-5 Mr '65. *

22. GINLEY, THOMAS J. "Present Status and Future Plans of the Dental Aptitude Testing Program." *J Dental Ed* 30: 163-74 Je '66. *

23. HALL, DAVID STANLEY. *Socio-Cultural and Personal Correlates of Differential Orientations of Dental Students to*

Dentistry. Doctor's thesis, University of Kentucky (Lexington, Ky.), 1966. (*DAI* 30:2166A)

24. CHEN, MARTIN K.; PODSHADLEY, DALE W.; AND SHROCK, JOHN G. "A Factorial Study of Some Psychological, Vocational Interest, and Mental Ability Variables as Predictors of Success in Dental School." *J Appl Psychol* 51:236–41 Je '67. * (*PA* 41:10970)

25. FERNÁNDEZ-PABÓN, JORGE J. "Prediction of Success in Dental School on the Basis of Dental Aptitude Test Scores and Other Variables." *J Dental Ed* 32:261–71 S '68. *

26. FREDERICKS, MARCEL A., AND MUNDY, PAUL. "Relations Between Social Class, Average Grade in College, Dental Aptitude Test Scores, and Academic Achievement of Dental Students." *J Dental Ed* 32:26–36 Mr '68. *

27. KREIT, LEONARD H., AND MCDONALD, RALPH E. "Preprofessional Grades and the Dental Aptitude Test as Predictors of Student Performance in Dental School." *J Dental Ed* 32:452–7 D '68. *

28. PHIPPS, GRANT T.; FISHMAN, ROSS; AND SCOTT, RUSSELL H. "Prediction of Success in a Dental School." *J Dental Ed* 32:161–84 Je '68. *

29. HUTTON, JACK G., JR. "Aptitude and Personality Correlates of Dental School Performance." *J Dental Ed* 33(4): 474–86 D '69. *

30. LORENCKI, STANLEY F. "Is Dexterity Predictable in Dental Students? Predicting Success in a Pre-Clinical Area at a California Dental School." *J Calif Dental Assn* 45(1): 11–2 sp '69. *

31. PHILLIP, P. JOSEPH. *A Comparison of the Relative Effectiveness of the Linear Discriminant Function and Bayesian Taxonomic Procedure: A Case Study of a Dental School.* Doctor's thesis, Wayne State University (Detroit, Mich.), 1969. (*DAI* 30:3735A)

32. PODSHADLEY, DALE W.; CHEN, MARTIN K.; AND SHROCK, JOHN G. "A Factor Analytic Approach to the Prediction of Student Performance." *J Dental Ed* 33(1, pt 2):105–11 Mr '69. *

33. ZIMMERMAN, JOHN JAMES. *Relationships Among Scholastic Aptitude, Attitudes Toward Various Facets of College Life, and Academic Performance of Students at Lycoming College.* Doctor's thesis, Pennsylvania State University (University Park, Pa.), 1969. (*DAI* 30:4792A)

34. DWORKIN, SAMUEL F. "Dental Aptitude Test as Performance Predictor Over Four Years of Dental School: Analyses and Interpretation." *J Dental Ed* 34(1):28–38 Mr '70. *

35. FERENCE, LYNN WAYNE. *Dental Student Selection Through Handwriting Analysis.* Doctor's thesis, University of Southern California (Los Angeles, Calif.), 1970. (*DAI* 31: 4378B)

36. GOUGH, HARRISON G., AND KIRK, BARBARA A. "Achievement in Dental School as Related to Personality and Aptitude Variables." *Meas & Eval Guid* 2(4):225–33 w '70. *

[1092]

*Dental Hygiene Aptitude Testing Program.** Dental hygiene school applicants; 1947–71; DHATP; tests administered 3 times annually (February, May, November) at centers established by the American Dental Hygienists' Association; 4 scores: numerical ability, study-reading, science, general information; 2 booklets: Part 1, Forms E ('55, 4 pages), F ('66, 4 pages); Parts 2–5, Forms E ('65, 19 pages), F ('67, 19 pages); manual ('71, 9 pages); handbook for admissions officers ('68, 33 pages); descriptive brochure ('70, 13 pages); separate answer sheets (Digitek) must be used; examination fee, $9 per student; fee includes reporting of scores to 3 schools designated on application; $1 per additional report; (140)155 minutes; prepared for the American Dental Hygienists' Association by Psychological Corporation. *

ENGINEERING

[1093]

★Garnett College Test in Engineering Science.** 1–2 years technical college; 1967; GCTES; 3 scores: mechanics, heat-electricity-magnetism, total; 1 form ['67, 11 pages]; manual ['67, 8 pages]; £1.70 per 25 tests; 50p per manual; £1 per specimen set; postage extra; 60(65) minutes; I. Macfarlane Smith; distributed by NFER Publishing Co. Ltd. *

[1094]

*The Graduate Record Examinations Advanced Engineering Test.** Graduate school candidates; 1939–

70; 6 current forms ('65–70, 32 pages); descriptive booklet ('70, 10 pages); for more complete information, see 667; 180(200) minutes; Educational Testing Service. *

For reviews of the testing program, see 667 (1 review) and 5:601 (1 review).

[1095]

*Minnesota Engineering Analogies Test.** Candidates for graduate school and industry; 1954–70; MEAT; Forms E, F, ('54, 4 pages); revised manual ('70, 17 pages); bulletin of information ('70, 61 pages); guide for testing center operation ['64, 8 pages]; distribution restricted and test administered at specified licensed university centers; separate answer sheets (IBM 805) must be used; scoring and reporting handled by the local center; examination fee to centers: $3 per examinee; fees to examinees are determined locally and include reporting of scores to the examinee and to 3 institutions or companies designated at the time of testing; additional score reports may be secured from the publisher at a fee of $1 each; (45–60) minutes; Marvin D. Dunnette; Psychological Corporation. *

REFERENCES

1–6. See 5:933.
7–8. See 6:1133.
9. DUNNETTE, MARVIN D.; WERNIMONT, PAUL; AND ABRAHAMS, NORMAN. "Further Research on Vocational Interest Differences Among Several Types of Engineers." *Personnel & Guid J* 42:484–93 Ja '64. * (*PA* 39:6040)
10. PESCI, MICHAEL LINDEN. *Psychological Differences Between Research, Development and Product Engineers and Their Implications for Placement Decisions.* Doctor's thesis, University of Minnesota (Minneapolis, Minn.), 1970. (*DAI* 31: 3048B)

For reviews by A. Pemberton Johnson and William B. Schrader, see 5:933.

[1096]

★N.I.I.P. Engineering Apprentice Selection Test Battery.** Engineering apprentices; 1942–70; 6 tests; 7 scores: 6 scores listed below and combined score for *a–e*; subtests available only as separates; mimeographed manual ['69, 19 pages, with 1970 revision]; profile ['70, 1 page]; no data on reliability for *d* and *f*; validity data presented in *1* below; 20p per 10 profiles; 20p per manual; postpaid within U.K.; specimen set not available; 116(180) minutes; National Institute of Industrial Psychology. *

a) GROUP TEST 82. Spatial perception; see 1052.
b) GROUP TEST 90A/B. Intelligence; see 357.
c) GROUP TEST 70/70B. Nonverbal intelligence; see 355.
d) TEST EA2. Ages 14.5 and over; 1947–70; arithmetic attainment; 1 form ['47, 5 pages]; instructions ('68, 1 page); 40p per 10 tests; 8p per single copy; 8p per key; 7p per instructions; 20(25) minutes.
e) VINCENT MECHANICAL DIAGRAMS TEST. Mechanical ability; see 1058.
f) MECHANICAL INFORMATION. See 1054.

REFERENCE

1. FRISBY, C. B.; VINCENT, D. F.; AND LANCASHIRE, RUTH. *Tests for Engineering Apprentices: A Validation Study.* National Institute of Industrial Psychology Report 14. London: the Institute, 1959. Pp. iii, 24. *

[1097]

★The Undergraduate Record Examinations: Engineering Test.** College; 1969–70; Form RUR ('69, 19 pages); descriptive booklet ('70, 12 pages); for more complete information, see 671; 120(140) minutes; Educational Testing Service. *

For reviews of the testing program, see 671 (2 reviews).

LAW

[1098]

*Law School Admission Test. Law school entrants; 1948–70; LSAT; 2 scores: aptitude (commonly referred to as the LSAT score), writing ability; test administered 5 times annually (February, April, July, October, December) at centers established by the publisher; supervisor's manual ('70, 31 pages); bulletin for candidates ('70, 63 pages); handbook for deans and admissions officers ('64, 74 pages); separate answer sheets (SCRIBE) must be used; examination fee, $13.50 per student; fee includes reporting of scores to 3 law schools designated at time of application; $1 per additional report; 340(420) minutes; Educational Testing Service. *

REFERENCES

1–6. See 4:815.
7–13. See 5:928.
14. DISTEFANO, M. K., JR., AND BASS, BERNARD M. "Prediction of an Ultimate Criterion of Success as a Lawyer." *J Appl Psychol* 43:40–1 F '59. * (*PA* 34:4886)
15. FRICKE, BENNO G. "Qualification for Law School and the Bar: How Should It Be Determined?" pp. 175–99. In *The Law Schools Look Ahead: 1959 Conference on Legal Education.* Ann Arbor, Mich.: University of Michigan Law School, 1959. Pp. xii, 328. *
16. RAMSEY, ROBERT R., JR. "Law School Admissions: Science, Art, or Hunch?" *J Legal Ed* 12(4):503–20 '60. *
17. RAMSEY, ROBERT R., JR. "Validity Patterns at Two Law Schools." *Ed & Psychol Meas* 21:489–91 su '61. * (*PA* 36:2KJ89R)
18. GRUBER, EDWARD C. *How to Score High on the Law School Admission Test.* New York: Arco Publishing Co., Inc., 1962. Pp. viii, 117, plus supplements. *
19. RUDMAN, JACK. *How to Pass Law School Admission Test: Questions and Answers.* Brooklyn, N.Y.: College Publishing Corporation, 1963. Pp. v, 295. *
20. SCHWEIKER, ROBERT F.; DEMAREE, ROBERT G.; AND SHAH, MAHENDRA. *The Law School Admission Test and Pre-Legal Record as Predictors of First Semester Grades in the College of Law.* Report No. 109. Champaign, Ill.: Office of Instructional Research, University of Illinois, [1963]. Pp. vii, 70. *
21. LEWIS, JOHN W.; BRASKAMP, LARRY; AND STATLER, CHARLES. "Predicting Achievement in a College of Law." *Ed & Psychol Meas* 24:947–9 w '64. * (*PA* 39:8703)
22. MILLER, PAUL VAN REED, JR. *The Contribution of Non-Cognitive Variables to the Prediction of Student Performance in Law School.* Doctor's thesis, University of Pennsylvania (Philadelphia, Pa.), 1965. (*DA* 26:7159)
23. REES, VIRGINIA M. *The Value of the Law School Admission Test and Other Variables in Predicting Performance in the University of Utah College of Law.* Master's thesis, University of Utah (Salt Lake City, Utah), 1965.
24. WARKOV, SEYMOUR. "Allocation to American Law Schools." *Sch R* 73:144–55 su '65. *
25. HALFTER, IRMA T. "Validity Studies: Law School." *J Ed Res* 59:307–9 Mr '66. * (*PA* 40:9434)
26. LUNNEBORG, CLIFFORD E., AND LUNNEBORG, PATRICIA W. "The Prediction of Different Criteria of Law School Performance." *Ed & Psychol Meas* 26:935–44 w '66. * (*PA* 41:4995)
27. LUNNEBORG, PATRICIA W., AND LUNNEBORG, CLIFFORD E. "Specificity of Undergraduate Preparation and Success in Law School." Abstract. *Proc 74th Ann Conv Am Psychol Assn* 1:291–2 '66. * (*PA* 41:6252)
28. LUNNEBORG, PATRICIA W., AND LUNNEBORG, CLIFFORD E. "Undergraduate Preparation and Success in Law School." *Voc Guid Q* 15:196–200 Mr '67. * (*PA* 42:9502)
29. PUGH, RICHARD C.; CHASE, CLINTON I.; AND LUDLOW, H. GLENN. *An Analysis of Achievement Behavior in the Law School.* Indiana University, Monograph of the Bureau of Educational Studies and Testing, Indiana Studies in Prediction, No. 9. Bloomington, Ind.: the Bureau, 1967. Pp. vii, 31. *
30. THOMSON, JACK EUGENE. *Two Prediction Methods That Correct for Bias: Their Accuracy and Their Utility.* Doctor's thesis, University of California (Los Angeles, Calif.), 1967. (*DA* 28:4497A)
31. ANDRULIS, RICHARD STANLEY. *Prediction of Scholastic Success in the University of Texas Law School.* Doctor's thesis, University of Texas (Austin, Tex.), 1968. (*DA* 29:1775A)
32. GOOLSBY, THOMAS M., JR. "Law School Selection and Performance and Subsequent Admission to Legal Practice." *Ed & Psychol Meas* 28:421–6 su '68. * (*PA* 42:19399)
33. KLEIN, STEPHEN P., AND EVANS, FRANKLIN R. "An Examination of the Validity of Nine Experimental Tests for Predicting Success in Law School." *Ed & Psychol Meas* 28:909–13 au '68. * (*PA* 43:4433)
34. KLEIN, STEPHEN P., AND HART, FREDERICK M. "Chance and Systematic Factors Affecting Essay Grades." *J Ed Meas* 5:197–206 f '68. *
35. KLEIN, STEPHEN P.; ROCK, DONALD A.; AND EVANS, FRANKLIN R. "The Use of Multiple Moderates in Academic Prediction." *J Ed Meas* 5:151–60 su '68. *
36. PUGH, RICHARD C. "Undergraduate Environment as an Aid in Predicting Law School Achievement." *J Ed Res* 62(6):271–4 F '69. *

LEO A. MUNDAY, *Vice President, Research and Development Division, The American College Testing Program, Iowa City, Iowa.* [Review of Forms LLS1 and K-JLP.]

Most of the applicants for admission to the nation's law schools write the *Law School Admission Test.* The LSAT is a program involving five national test dates, a registration procedure, security precautions, regular and controlled testing centers, and a council of law educators to set policy for the program.

The battery is administered on Saturday and takes all day. The morning is taken up with six tests which yield only one score. The morning test reviewed here is Form LLS1, copyrighted in 1963. The subtests are Reading Comprehension (25 items, 30 minutes), Data Interpretation (35 items, 45 minutes), Reading Recall (30 items, 30 minutes), Principles and Cases (40 items, 55 minutes), Figure Classification (20 items, 15 minutes), and a pretest section (30 items, 40 minutes). With the exception of Figure Classification, which looks like a spatial test or test of nonverbal reasoning, all of these tests involve reading and verbal facility. Principles and Cases has high content validity for legal education, and it seems that law school deans and admissions committees would quickly conclude that this kind of material is what is covered in law courses. The other tests do not appear to cover elements unique to legal education.

Since the fall of 1961, afternoon testing has been included. Though the additional tests were not expected to add to prediction of success in law school, they reflected concerns of the LSAT Council. The form reviewed here is K-JLP, copyright 1961. There are three parts to the test of Writing Ability, which yield one score. The subtests are Error Recognition (35 items, 20 minutes), Organization of Ideas (30 items, 20 minutes), and Editing (45 items, 30 minutes). The three English tests were added because the law educators felt candidates were frequently not sufficiently prepared in this important area.

In summary, after about six hours of testing time, we have two scores, one of which was not intended to add anything in a correlation sense to the first score but is part of an instrument designed primarily, if not exclusively, for selective admissions. It is appropriate to raise the issue of efficiency: Is all this time really necessary?

A high reliability for the score based on the morning test is expected, since it comes from 215 minutes of test time. The K-R 20 reliability is .92. Though subtest scores are not reported separately, K-R 20 reliabilities for some are given in an ETS report dated November 1963. The highest is .82 for Figure Classification and the lowest is .66 for Principles and Cases. Reliabilities are frequently lower on tests including reading passages and attempting to assess subtle and sophisticated reasoning, as the Principles and Cases test does. For the afternoon tests, a reliability figure was available only for the Editing subtest of the Test of Writing Ability, and this figure was .76.

The question of speededness in connection with reliabilities was raised by Wesman in his review for *The Fourth Mental Measurements Yearbook*. It appears from data available that a little better than 80 percent of the students finish the tests. While we would judge the tests as somewhat speeded, the use of K-R 20 does not appear contraindicated, though it may estimate the reliabilities a bit on the high side.

Intercorrelations among the first five tests administered in the morning range from .38 to .70, with median .59. As would be expected, the Figure Classification test correlated less with the other tests than the other tests did with each other. The afternoon subtests intercorrelated from .38 to .88, with median .64. Since both morning and afternoon subtests rely heavily on verbal skills, we would expect them to be at least moderately correlated. Intercorrelations range from .33 to .67, with median .52. Considering reliabilities from .66 to .82, these are substantial intercorrelations.

Evidence as to the validity of the tests is somewhat spotty. As has been pointed out, there is heavy emphasis on content validity in the Principles and Cases test and in the afternoon Test of Writing Ability. The latter is intended more as a test of proficiency than as a test for prediction. The prediction of first-year law school grades is usually based on the one score from the morning session combined with undergraduate grade point average. The LSAT Handbook describes multiple R's based on these two variables and law school grades as typically being .54. The handbook reports that validity studies were carried on at 20 law schools in the 1948–53 period, at 10 schools in 1959, and at 10 schools in 1963. The handbook reports correlations based on 4,138 students at 25 schools; apparently student records were pooled across schools. The year is not given. The correlation for undergraduate grades versus law school grades is .36; for LSAT scores versus law school grades, .45; and for LSAT scores plus undergraduate grades versus law school grades, .54. The point is made several times that the reason the R's are lower than at college admission is the restricted range. This seems like a reasonable supposition. No data are provided for subtest scores versus law school grades, or for the afternoon test scores versus school grades (although the publisher's statement that afternoon test scores do not usually add to prediction is credible). When we add together all the studies reported in the handbook (20 in 1948–53, 10 in 1959, 10 in 1963, and 25 date unknown), 65 studies in 23 years for a national testing program serving 98 schools does not seem to warrant the handbook statement: "Validity studies of the Law School Admission Test have become so frequent as to be virtually a routine part of the program." Undoubtedly some validity studies done locally are not reported in the handbook, but it is not likely that they are done in large numbers, since law school administrators and faculty are not particularly measurement-oriented.

In general, the supporting publications for the program are well done. The handbook is quite readable and describes the program and recommended uses of test results. The Bulletin of Information for Candidates is likewise a worthwhile publication. The test booklets are attractive and easy to read. The answer sheets, however, are printed in a light ink and over the period of testing time would likely get blurry for some candidates.

The weaknesses of the program may be described as follows: (*a*) In my opinion, the length of the test is such that it has to be justified by the LSAT Council and by the publisher. (*b*) The answer sheets are printed in light-colored ink and are hard to read. (*c*) More technical information should be provided. Very little is in the handbook, and the mimeographed

Law School Admission Test

test analysis supplement looks as though it were intended for ETS internal use. Even here the samples and procedures are not well defined (which they need not be in an internal document for staff who know what was done), and more data would be preferred. For example, reliability figures are not reported here or in the handbook (the only two publications that describe the test, other than the Bulletin of Information for Candidates) for the Test of Writing Ability. It is suggested that a technical supplement be prepared and added in the back of the handbook or distributed by itself. (*d*) No attention is given to success in a law career beyond training. Considerable evidence indicates that test scores will not be related to later life success. Schools exercising selective admissions may as profitably consider indices of success in legal practice or research as scores on proficiency tests that overlap the basic LSAT score. (*e*) Is a separate law test really needed? Would the GRE aptitude test predict success in legal education as well as the LSAT? If not, it would be nice to see the evidence. If so, law schools could use the GRE and not require a separate program with special tests, scoring programs, publications, and administration.

It is unnecessary to go into the matter of selective admissions based on a highly verbal test in the current social climate of greater awareness of the need for equal educational opportunity. In a selection situation where predictors possess no better than moderate validity, a black candidate below the artificial cutoff point in admissions now becomes attractive. Though the handbook is not recent (it was published in 1964), it appears that the LSAT Council and the publisher are not seriously recommending uses of the test beyond selection for admissions.

The strengths of the program may be described as follows: (*a*) The LSAT Handbook, intended for law school deans and admissions officers, is well done as far as it goes. The style of writing is informal, and recommended practices and cautions are appropriate. The booklet itself is attractive and easy to read. (*b*) The Bulletin of Information for Candidates should prove helpful to students preparing to register for and to write the test. Students always want to see sample items and this contains items of all the types included in the test. (*c*) The tests themselves are attractive and easy to read, and the items are interesting. I would consider them a very worthy accomplishment in test develop-

ment. (*d*) Clearly the publisher does well the administrative "dirty work" of seeing to registration, test security, scoring, maintenance of test centers, and so on, and thus relieves the law education profession of considerable bother. (*e*) The structure, including an LSAT Council of law school educators to set policy for the program, insures that the test and the program will be responsive to the changing needs of its constituency.

For a review by Alexander G. Wesman of an earlier form, see 4:815.

MEDICINE

[1099]

★**Colleges of Podiatry Admission Test.** Grades 14 and over; 1968–70; CPAT; tests administered 3 times annually (March, August, December) at centers established by the publisher; 4 scores: verbal aptitude, quantitative aptitude, natural science, spatial relationships; Form RPO ('69, 35 pages); supervisor's manual ('70, 21 pages); bulletin of information for candidates ('70, 16 pages); memorandum of transmitting scores ('70, 5 pages); publisher recommends use of local norms; separate answer sheets (SCRIBE) must be used; examination fee, $25 per student; fee includes reporting of scores to the candidate and 5 colleges of podiatry; 180(225) minutes; program administered for the American Association of Colleges of Podiatric Medicine by Educational Testing Service. *

[1100]

*Medical College Admission Test. Applicants for admission to member colleges of the Association of American Medical Colleges; 1946–70; MCAT; 4 scores: verbal, quantitative, general information, science; administered 2 times annually (spring, fall) at centers established by the publisher; examiner's manual ('63, 11 pages); handbook for admissions committees, second edition ('67, 97 pages); announcement ('70, 24 pages); examination fee, $20; fee includes reporting of scores to applicant and 6 schools designated at time of application; $2 per additional report; $2 per handbook for admissions committees (available postpaid from Association of American Medical Colleges); 210(255) minutes; Psychological Corporation. *

REFERENCES

1–11. See 4:817.
12–15. See 5:932.
16–58. See 6:1137.
59. Gee, Helen Hoffer, and Klinger, Eric. "The Study of Applicants: 1956–1957." *J Med Ed* 33:49–58 Ja '58. * (*PA* 34:2265)
60. Wilson, J. W. Dalton, and Dykman, Roscoe A. "Background Autonomic Activity in Medical Students." *J Comp & Physiol Psychol* 53:405–11 Ag '60. * (*PA* 36:1DJ05W)
61. Badgley, Robin F.; Hethrington, Robert W.; and Macleod, J. Wendell. "Social Characteristics and Prediction of Academic Performance of Saskatchewan Medical Students." *Can Med Assn J* 86:624–9 Ap 7 '62. *
62. Anderson, Donald O.; Riches, Eleanor; and Zickmantel, Rosalie. "Factors Relating to Academic Performance of Medical Students at the University of British Columbia." *Can Med Assn J* 89:881–8 O 26 '63. *
63. Peterson, Osler L.; Lyden, Fremont J.; Geiger, Jack; and Colten, Theodore. "Appraisal of Medical Students' Abilities as Related to Training and Careers After Graduation." *New Engl J Med* 269:1174–82 N 28 '63. *
64. "Applicants, Applications, Enrollment, and MCAT Data

for Entering Class 1963–64 in United States Medical Schools."
J Am Med Ed 39:974–5 O '64. *

65. BEISER, HELEN R., AND ALLENDER, JEROME S. "Personality Factors Influencing Medical School Achievement." *J Med Ed* 39:175–82 F '64. *

66. GOUGH, HARRISON G., AND HALL, WALLACE B. "Prediction of Performance in Medical School From the California Psychological Inventory." *J Appl Psychol* 48:218–26 Ag '64. * (*PA* 39:5980)

67. GRAVES, GRANT O., AND INGERSOLL, RALPH W. "Comparison of Learning Attitudes." *J Med Ed* 39:100–11 F '64. *

68. HUTCHINS, EDWIN B. "The AAMC Longitudinal Study: Implications for Medical Education." *J Med Ed* 39:265–77 Mr '64. *

69. KELLY, E. LOWELL. "Alternate Criteria in Medical Education and Their Correlates." *Proc Inv Conf Testing Probl* 1963:64–85 '64. *

70. McGUIRE, FREDERICK L., AND SCOTT, WYNELLE. "The Davis Reading Test, Hr Scale, MCAT, and Undergraduate Grades as Predictors of Success in Medical School." Abstract. *J Med Ed* 39:886 S '64. *

71. NETSKY, MARTIN G.; BANGHART, FRANK W.; AND HAIN, JACK D. "Seminar Versus Lecture and Prediction of Performance by Medical Students." *J Med Ed* 39:112–9 F '64. *

72. SCHUMACHER, CHARLES F. "Personal Characteristics of Students Choosing Different Types of Medical Careers." *J Med Ed* 39:278–88 Mr '64. *

73. "Application 'Activity and MCAT Data of Applicants to the Class of 1964–65.'" *J Med Ed* 40:1003–4 O '65. *

74. BUXBAUM, ROBERT C., AND PETERSON, OSLER L. "Medical College Admission Test Component Scores and Their Relationship to Postgraduate Training." Abstract. *J Med Ed* 40:892 S '65. *

75. FREDERICKS, MARCEL ANTHONY. *The Professionalization of Medical Students: Social Class, Attitude, and Academic Achievement.* Doctor's thesis, Loyola University (Chicago, Ill.), 1965. (*DA* 27:1939A)

76. FUNKENSTEIN, DANIEL H. "Current Problems in the Verbal and Quantitative Ability Subtests of the Medical College Admission Test." *J Med Ed* 40:1031–48 N '65. *

77. INGERSOLL, RALPH W., AND GRAVES, GRANT O. "Predictability of Success in the First Year of Medical School." *J Med Ed* 40:351–63 Ap '65. *

78. LIEF, VICTOR F.; LIEF, HAROLD I.; AND YOUNG, KATHLEEN M. "Academic Success: Intelligence and Personality." *J Med Ed* 40:114–24 F '65. *

79. ROEMER, R. E. "Nine Year Validity Study of Predictors of Medical School Success." *J Ed Res* 59:183–5 D '65. * (*PA* 40:5907)

80. WEITMAN, MORRIS, AND COISMAN, FREDERICK G. "Medical Student Pathways to Diagnosis." *J Med Ed* 40:166–79 F '65. *

81. "Physician Manpower: Medical School Applicants." *J Med Ed* 41:1001–2 O '66. *

82. EVANS, LLOYD R.; INGERSOLL, RALPH W.; AND SMITH, EDWIN JAY. "The Reliability, Validity, and Taxonomic Structure of the Oral Examination." *J Med Ed* 41:651–7 Jl '66. *

83. FUNKENSTEIN, DANIEL H. "Testing the Scientific Achievement and Ability of Applicants to a Medical School: The Problem and a Proposal." *J Med Ed* 41:120–34 F '66. *

84. GEERTSMA, ROBERT H., AND CHAPMAN, JOHN E. "Progress Through Medical School." *J Med Ed* 41:772–9 Ag '66. *

85. HUNKA, STEPHEN; GILBERT, JAMES A. L.; AND CAMERON, DONALD F. "The Prediction of Success in Medical School." *J Med Ed* 41:368–76 Ap '66. *

86. JOHNSON, DAVIS G., AND HUTCHINS, EDWIN B. "Doctor or Dropout? A Study of Medical Student Attrition: Chap. 4, 'The Student.'" *J Med Ed* 41:1139–56, 1263–5 D '66. *

87. MORRIS, W. W. "The MCAT-Science Survey." *J Med Ed* 41:817–25 S '66. *

88. SCHOFIELD, WILLIAM, AND MERWIN, JACK C. "The Use of Scholastic Aptitude, Personality, and Interest Test Data in the Selection of Medical Students." *J Med Ed* 41:502–9 Je '66. *

89. SEDLACEK, WILLIAM E., AND HUTCHINS, EDWIN B. "An Empirical Demonstration of Restriction of Range Artifacts in Validity Studies of the Medical College Admission Test." *J Med Ed* 41:222–9 Mr '66. *

90. "Application Activity and MCAT Data of Applicants to the Class of 1966–67." *J Med Ed* 42:1062–3 N '67. *

91. ANDERSON, DONALD O., AND RICHES, ELEANOR. "Some Observations on Attrition of Students From Canadian Medical Schools." *Can Med Assn J* 96:665–74 Mr 18 '67. *

92. BARTLETT, JAMES W. "Medical School and Career Performances of Medical Students With Low Medical College Admission Test Scores." *J Med Ed* 42:231–7 Mr '67. *

93. BEISER, HELEN R. "Personality Factors Influencing Medical School Achievement: A Follow-Up Study." *J Med Ed* 42:1087–95 D '67. * (*PA* 42:17981)

94. BRUHN, JOHN G.; ADSETT, C. ALEX; AND BIRD, HENRY B. "Social Profiles and Academic Standing: A Study of First Year Medical Students." *J Okla State Med Assn* 60:538–44 O '67. *

95. FREDERICKS, MARCEL A., AND MUNDY, PAUL. "The Relationship Between Social Class, Average Grade in College,

Medical College Admission Test Scores, and Academic Achievement of Students in a Medical School." *J Med Ed* 42:126–33 F '67. *

96. FREDERICKS, MARCEL A., AND MUNDY, PAUL. "The Relationship Between Social Class, Stress-Anxiety Responses, Academic Achievement, and Internalization of Professional Attitudes of Students in a Medical School." *J Med Ed* 42:1022–30 N '67. *

97. GRAVES, GRANT O.; INGERSOLL, RALPH W.; AND EVANS, LLOYD R. "The Creative Medical Student: A Descriptive Study." *J Creative Behav* 1:371–82 f '67. *

98. HOWELL, MARGARET A., AND VINCENT, JOHN W. "The Medical College Admission Test as Related to Achievement Tests in Medicine and to Supervisory Evaluations of Clinical Physicians." *J Med Ed* 42:1037–44 N '67. * (*PA* 43:11823)

99. MORRIS, W. W. "The MCAT-Science Survey: Interpreting the MCAT Science Subtest Scores of Repeaters." *J Med Ed* 42:918–25 O '67. *

100. POLLACK, SEYMOUR, AND MICHAEL, WILLIAM B. "The Predictive Validity of a Battery of Measures for Each of Four Different Classes of a Medical School." *Ed & Psychol Meas* 27:423–5 su '67. * (*PA* 41:12836)

101. SEDLACEK, WILLIAM E. *Medical College Admission Test: Handbook for Admissions Committees, Second Edition.* Evanston, Ill.: Association of American Medical Colleges, 1967. Pp. xi, 85. *

102. SEDLACEK, WILLIAM E. "The Study of Applicants, 1965–66." *J Med Ed* 42:28–46 Ja '67. *

103. SHATIN, LEO, AND OPDYKE, DAVID. "A Critical Thinking Appraisal and Its Correlates." *J Med Ed* 42:789–92 Ag '67. *

104. WOODS, BRYAN T.; JACOBSON, MILTON D.; AND NETSKY, MARTIN G. "Social Class and Academic Performance by Medical Students." *J Med Ed* 42:225–30 Mr '67. *

105. "Trends in Characteristics of MCAT Examinee Population, 1962–1967." *J Med Ed* 43:511–2 Ag '68. *

106. KORMAN, MAURICE; STUBBLEFIELD, ROBERT L.; AND MARTIN, LAWRENCE W. "Patterns of Success in Medical School and Their Correlates." *J Med Ed* 43:405–11 Mr '68. * (*PA* 43:12026)

107. MATTSON, DALE E.; JOHNSON, DAVIS G.; AND SEDLACEK, WILLIAM E. "The Study of Applicants, 1966–67." *J Med Ed* 43:1–13 Ja '68. *

108. SOLKOFF, NORMAN. "Application Activity and MCAT Data of Applicants to the Class of 1967–68." *J Med Ed* 43:1206–7 D '68. *

109. FATERSON, HANNA F.; MOLDOWSKI, EDWARD W.; AND MOLDOWSKI, LESLIE H. K. "The Human Figure Drawing Test and Academic Outcome in Medical School." *J Med Ed* 44(10):929–33 O '69. * (*PA* 45:3059)

110. "Application Activity and MCAT Data on Applicants Entering in 1968–69." *J Med Ed* 45(2):121–3 F '70. *

111. FREDERICKS, MARCEL A.; MUNDY, PAUL; ROBERTSON, LEON S.; AND KOSA, JOHN. "The National Board Examination and Academic Achievement in a Medical School." *J Ed Res* 63(6):274–8 F '70. *

112. JUAN, ISABEL R., AND HALEY, HAROLD B. "High and Low Levels of Dogmatism in Relation to Personality, Intellectual, and Environmental Characteristics of Medical Students." *Psychol Rep* 26(2):535–44 Ap '70. * (*PA* 44:20939)

113. NELSON-JONES, RICHARD, AND FISH, DAVID G. "MCAT Performance of Canadian and Landed Immigrant Applicants to Canadian Medical Schools, 1968–1969." *J Med Ed* 45(4):210–9 Ap '70. *

114. ROTHMAN, ARTHUR I., AND FLOWERS, JOHN F. "Personality Correlates of First-Year Medical School Achievement." *J Med Ed* 45(11, pt 1):901–5 N '70. *

115. SCHOFIELD, WILLIAM. "A Modified Actuarial Method in the Selection of Medical Students." *J Med Ed* 45(10):740–4 O '70. *

NANCY S. COLE, *Research Psychologist, The American College Testing Program, Iowa City, Iowa.*

The MCAT is required for admission to essentially all medical schools in the United States. In 1969, 28,880 students took the examination in the U.S. and Canada, most in either their junior or senior year of college.

DESCRIPTION. The MCAT is a four-part battery. The 75 items of the Verbal Ability subtest (20 minutes) are in the form of synonyms, antonyms, and analogies. The Quantitative Ability subtest (45 minutes) is a 50-item test

Medical College Admission Test

covering arithmetic, algebra, and geometry. The 75 items of the General Information subtest (25 minutes) are word recognition items from such diverse fields as history, music, and sports. The Science subtest (60 minutes) is made up of 86 items covering topics in chemistry, biology, and physics.

Scores on the MCAT range from 200 to 800, with the original 1951 norming group having a mean of 500. Since 1968, scores have been reported to the students, a change which I find commendable. In addition, the student is given a second score report for his undergraduate premedical advisor. The medical colleges specified by the student receive his report, but in addition all medical colleges in AAMC receive a so-called confidential publication containing all scores. This latter practice raises several questions concerning the confidentiality of a student's report and I cannot see what useful purpose it serves that score distributions without names would not serve. The student pays $20.00 to take the test, a price which seems high in light of the increasing number of students taking the test and in comparison with other similar tests.

TECHNICAL CHARACTERISTICS. In the technical aspects of test development, the test appears to be appropriately constructed. Most of the item statistics are within a suitable range. Typical reliabilities (K-R 20) from samples of 740 students tested in October 1968 for portions of several forms of the test were: Verbal, .90; Quantitative, .86; General Information, .80; and Science, .87. The tests have moderate intercorrelations, lower than in many academic batteries, which is likely achieved by the minimal verbal reading content in the short item formats of the test. The only exception is the intercorrelation between the Verbal and General Information subtests, which was .74 and .75 for two groups of over 6,000 each, tested in October 1969.

MISCELLANEOUS. There are several miscellaneous points to be mentioned. First, I found the MCAT Handbook for Admissions Committees a readable and useful publication. Second, the test booklet I received to review had the name "Test 42" on the front cover, along with directions for the test. Nowhere could I find a reference to MCAT. Further, the tests inside were labeled Part I, Part II, etc. As a student taking the test, I would be more comfortable first knowing I had the right test booklet (namely MCAT) and second knowing what

the tests were supposed to be measuring (by the title of the subtests, at least). Finally I found the MCAT policy of not correcting for guessing appropriate, time limits of the subtests adequate, and equating and norming procedures suitable.

CONTENT. The Verbal and Quantitative sections of the MCAT are typical of general tests of academic ability used frequently to predict academic performance in college and many postcollege fields of training. The Science subtest seems more related to medical training in content, but no effort is made to use medical examples or other material with a specified relation to medicine in any of the subtests. At present, a prospective medical student takes a test which would be equally appropriate for graduate training in a large number of fields. A test with more obvious relation in content to medicine would be more likely to relate statistically to success in medical training and certainly be more motivating for the student taking it.

The content of the General Information subtest deserves noting. Apparently, this subtest was originally included to broaden the MCAT so that science would not be overemphasized. Now, however, at a time in which doctors are sorely needed in rural areas and among minority groups, this subtest seems likely to serve a less appropriate function. I counted over 20 of the 75 items on Form U to be on topics of art, music, and literature. I would expect persons from other than the majority, urban (even "cultured") culture to have difficulty on this subtest, a difficulty which would not appear to correspond to any similar difficulty encountered in the process of medical education or practice. It would seem fruitful to replace this subtest with an experimental section in which an attempt is made to measure the kinds of nonacademic abilities and characteristics, currently untapped, which seem to be required in clinical training and eventual medical practice.

VALIDITY. Evaluating the validity of a standardized instrument used properly in conjunction with other information is most difficult. There are not only the problems of the reliability of the criterion and the restriction of range but also the problem that the only students with low MCAT scores admitted to medical school are those with offsetting qualifications in other areas, usually the MCAT "test misses." These situations all work to lower observed correlations and therefore a low correlation between

MCAT and an appropriate criterion is not conclusive evidence of lack of validity.

The median correlations for 73 medical schools using rank in class for each of the four years of medical school as the criteria were typically low, between .10 and .20, with the Science subtest the most predictive. Correlations with scores on the NBME were higher, with the best predictor, Science, having median correlations of .42 and .35, respectively, with the two parts of the NBME. Although modest, these correlations demonstrate at least some predictive validity of the MCAT for success in medical training. The best way to determine if the MCAT is actually more effective than these rather small correlations show would seem to be experimental not correlational. If one half of the admission selections at several medical colleges were made without use of the MCAT and the other half made using the MCAT along with other available data, then we could begin to evaluate the unique contribution of the MCAT to the prediction of success in medical school.

Predicting the success of practicing physicians is an even greater problem, but one that deserves as much attention. Undoubtedly there will be many factors in addition to academic ability involved. To be successful, the admissions process must select not only students who will successfully complete medical school but also students who will become good practicing physicians. At present we know little about the usefulness of the MCAT in this latter regard. Likely, some changes in and additions to the test would have to be made for it to have much validity for the prediction of successful practitioners. In an unpublished paper on MCAT by Mattson, Hutton, and Wallace, there is a suggestion that alternatives for broadening the MCAT in this direction are under consideration. Such a move should be encouraged.

CONCLUSION. The MCAT is a technically adequate instrument, typical of the many good standardized tests of academic ability. Its first limitation is its general academic nature without content specifically involving medicine or medical problems. Its second limitation (a limitation common to all of education and testing) is its neglect of the many important factors other than academic ability which need to be identified, efficiently measured, and rewarded in admissions as they will be in later medical practice. While we cannot expect quick and easy solutions to this second limitation, neither can we afford to rest on the only modest laurels of current testing practices. The MCAT is now useful, but it could be much better.

JAMES M. RICHARDS, JR., *Professor of Psychology, University of Missouri, Kansas City, Missouri.*

The authors of reviews of the *Medical College Admission Test* published in the *Fourth, Fifth,* and *Sixth Mental Measurements Yearbooks* have shown general agreement about a number of major points. The consensus of these reviewers is that the MCAT is a very carefully constructed test and an example of the best workmanship that current psychometric practice can offer. It is also generally agreed that the validity of the MCAT is disappointing, although a few of the reviewers make this point more through faint praise than through active indictment.

For the present review, the author was provided extensive materials, including the Second Edition (1967) of the Handbook for Admissions Committees; a copy of the MCAT consisting of Form U of the Verbal Ability, Science, and General Information subtests and Form W of the Quantitative Ability Subtest; copies of the materials sent to candidates; score report forms; and a staff paper by Dale E. Mattson, Jack G. Hutton, Jr. (both of the Association of American Medical Colleges), and Wimburn L. Wallace (of the Psychological Corporation), describing anticipated changes in the MCAT. There is nothing in these materials that would change the conclusions cited above that the MCAT is a very carefully and competently constructed instrument and that its validity is inadequate.

The content and item formats of current forms are essentially the same as those of the forms reviewed in *The Sixth Yearbook* as are the number of items and time limits for the subtests. The MCAT continues to display the features viewed favorably by earlier reviewers, such as clear instructions, precisely phrased item stems, four-choice items throughout the test, decoys that should be plausible to those who do not know the answer, generally appropriate time limits, and scores based simply on the number right. All of these characteristics do indeed deserve continued praise.

A substantial proportion of the items have short stems, in many cases a single word. Consequently, the items emphasize factual recall rather than more complex, or "higher," processes. Although there might be some difference of opinion, this reviewer would view use of such items as, in general, a favorable characteristic. There is little or no evidence of the superiority of more complex items in predicting important criteria, and it seems plausible that factual items would be more responsive to an *effective* program for preparing educationally disadvantaged groups for medical education. In this connection, however, it should be noted that the content of the General Information subtest is very heavily weighted toward Western and European culture. More diverse content would help meet some of the current criticisms of tests.

The test manual was prepared by the Association of American Medical Colleges. It is designed primarily for members of medical college admissions committees without training in testing, and secondarily for psychometricians. It is only marginally satisfactory for either audience. Very complete norms are provided, and their use in interpreting scores is explained in detail. Other advice about how to use the MCAT at particular medical colleges mentions all the correct points, such as using a statistical consultant when developing prediction equations. It would be a much better manual, however, if more emphasis were placed on this good advice and less on examples of use that are likely to be misunderstood. Certainly, examples of use should not be included that require a later disclaimer in the text stating that the illustrated practices distort information about the aptitude and achievement of candidates in important ways. Yet, just this was done in discussing a "Prediction Index" derived by combining, with unit weights, the candidate's percentile ranks on undergraduate GPA and the four MCAT scores. The reviewer sympathizes with the problems faced by the authors of this manual, for without such guidance many admissions committees almost certainly would use MCAT scores much more inappropriately. Nevertheless, only examples illustrating the best practices should be included in such a manual.

The data suggest that the reliability of the MCAT is satisfactory, but somewhat lower than the reliability of some tests used in admissions programs for other parts of higher education. K-R 20 subtest reliabilities for Forms A, B, and C range from .79 to .93, with a median of .88. Alternate-forms reliabilities for successive pairs from Forms A through G range from .80 to .92, with a median of .87. The intercorrelations of the subtests in general are much lower than the limits imposed by these reliabilities. This suggests that the separate subtest scores are potentially meaningful. It should be noted that generous time limits permit almost all candidates to finish all subtests except Quantitative Ability. Therefore, in contrast to data for many other tests, neither the reliabilities nor the intercorrelations are spuriously inflated by a substantial speed factor. The reliability data are incomplete, however, in that no information is presented for more recent forms. Because the tests are so carefully constructed, there is little reason to expect substantially lower reliabilities, but any revisions of the manual obviously should provide relevant information.

The most disappointing aspect of the MCAT, and the most persistently criticized, is its validity. The manual presents correlation coefficients between MCAT scores and rank in class (expressed as T scores) in each year of medical college for the graduating class of 1966 in approximately 72 medical colleges. Subtest validities for the preclinical years range from .06 to .22, with a median of .13, and for the clinical years from .09 to .14, with a median of approximately .11. There is considerable variation among colleges but very few really substantial validities. The median subtest validities across colleges are close to the subtest validities for all colleges combined. There are also data showing that the probability of academic failure decreases as MCAT scores increase, but again there seems to be only a low to moderate relationship. As would be expected, correlations with National Board Examinations are somewhat higher, and correlations with the *Miller Analogies Test* are substantially higher.

It is not sufficient, of course, to show that the MCAT is correlated with medical college grades; it must also be shown that the MCAT adds significantly to prediction from undergraduate grades alone. One of the major deficiencies of the manual is that no evidence is presented with respect to this point. On the basis of the evidence that is presented, however, one would expect the improvement to be minimal. Moreover, there are no data showing the relationship of MCAT scores to excellence in medical practice, surely the real criterion. This is not a minor point, for there is some evidence in the literature that grades are an inadequate and inappropriate substitute for measures of on-the-job performance.

Overall, the validity data suggest that the MCAT measures adequately what similar tests measure but that what is measured has little utility in the selection of medical students. Restriction of range is the explanation for such findings usually suggested by proponents of the MCAT. But, restriction of range in the simple sense does not seem to be a sufficient explanation, for medical student means and standard deviations on the MCAT are not that different from the corresponding values for medical college applicants. In a more complex sense, restriction of range may indeed be an important consideration. By the time they apply to medical school, students have already been stringently selected on academic aptitude through the procedures for selecting college students, admitting students to premedical programs, and evaluating the performance of students in premedical courses. Considerable self-selection on academic aptitude probably also takes place. As a consequence, medical colleges may be working with an applicant pool sufficiently restricted that it simply does not make sense to use yet another test of academic aptitude in selecting students. Certainly, as previous reviewers have noted, equivalent results could be obtained from a considerably shorter and less expensive test.

These or similar considerations appear to be guiding the plans for the future of the MCAT. The Association of American Medical Colleges staff paper suggests that the Science subtest may be expanded, the General Information subtest may be dropped, and the Verbal and Quantitative sections may be made optional. The testing time freed by these changes would be used to collect other sorts of information, such as measures of past accomplishment, that might be more useful in predicting performance as a physician. In view of general resistance throughout higher education to basic changes in existing programs, this reviewer is somewhat skeptical that *all* of these possible changes will actually transpire, but such changes should yield a much more appropriate instrument.

To summarize, the MCAT is a most competently developed test, and those responsible for it can justly be proud of their workmanship. Unfortunately, the validity of the MCAT does not appear to be commensurate with this workmanship, perhaps because of a restricted applicant pool. Therefore, a shorter, less costly test supplemented by measures of past accomplishment would probably be more appropriate for selecting medical students. Such changes in the MCAT are currently being discussed by the Association of American Medical Colleges.

For reviews by Robert L. Ebel and Philip H. DuBois, see 6:1137; for a review by Alexander G. Wesman of forms previously published by Educational Testing Service, see 5:932; for a review by Morey J. Wantman, see 4:817.

[1101]

*Veterinary Aptitude Test. Veterinary school applicants; 1951-70; VAT; tests administered at centers established by the publisher; 5 scores: reading comprehension, quantitative ability, science information, verbal memory, total; Form D ('68); 5 parts in 2 booklets: Parts 1-4 (27 pages), 5 (5 pages); norms ('70, 1 page); directions for administering ['70, 8 pages, mimeographed]; no data on reliability and validity; no description of normative population; separate answer sheets (NCS) must be used; examination fee, $15; fee includes reporting of scores to any 3 schools designated at time of application; $2 per additional report; scores not reported to examinees; 180(210) minutes; William A. Owens; Psychological Corporation. *

REFERENCES

1-3. See 5:957.
4-6. See 6:1139.

MISCELLANEOUS

[1102]

★Architectural School Aptitude Test. Candidates for admission to colleges of architecture; 1963-70; ASAT; tests administered 3 times annually (January, March, November) at centers established by the publisher; Form K-MRK ('65, 40 pages); supervisor's manual ('70, 22 pages); score interpretation guide ['64, 14 pages]; bulletin of information for candidates ('70, 20 pages); reliability and validity data based on 1956 experimental form; separate answer sheets (SCRIBE) must be used; examination fee, $12 per student; fee includes reporting of scores to all architectural schools; scores not reported to examinees; 125(180) minutes; program administered for the Association of Collegiate Schools of Architecture by Educational Testing Service. *

REFERENCES

1. LUNNEBORG, CLIFFORD E., AND LUNNEBORG, PATRICIA W. "Multiple Criteria of Architecture School Performance Predicted From ASAT, Intellective and Nonintellective Measures." Abstract. *Proc 76th Ann Conv Am Psychol Assn* 3:239-40 '68. *
2. LUNNEBORG, CLIFFORD E., AND LUNNEBORG, PATRICIA W. "Architecture School Performance Predicted From ASAT, Intellective, and Nonintellective Measures." *J Appl Psychol* 53(3):209-13 Je '69. * (*PA* 43:11928)

[1103]

Card Punch Operator Aptitude Test. Prospective trainees on IBM card punch equipment; 1952-60;

CPOAT; formerly called *Card Punch Aptitude Test*; 1 form ('52, 9 pages); revised manual ('60, 7 pages); no data on reliability; specimen sets and tests available to qualified research personnel on request; 12(20) minutes; distributed by International Business Machines Corporation. *

REFERENCES

1-2. See 6:1140.
3. KIRCHNER, WAYNE K., AND BANAS, PAUL. "Prediction of Key-Punch Operation Performance." *Personnel Adm* 24: 23-6 Ja-F '61. * (*PA* 38:9343)
4. KIRCHNER, WAYNE K. "Analysis Prediction of Performance of Experienced Key-Punch Operators." *J Indus Psychol* 4(2):48-52 '66. *

RICHARD T. JOHNSON, *Senior Research Scientist, American Institutes for Research, Limbe, Malawi.*

One of the most common positions open in any organization using electronic data processing is that of card punch operator. Selection of skilled key punch operators is relatively easy; all applicants are given a work sample. However, it often happens that applications from untrained personnel from both within and without the organization are solicited. In such cases a valid card punch operator aptitude test becomes necessary.

IBM's *Card Punch Operator Aptitude Test* is designed for trainee selection. There are two separately timed parts: an 80-item letter-digit substitution subtest and a 150-item name-checking subtest; the two are added for a single total score.

The CPOAT carries a 1952 copyright, although the manual claims a revision date of 1960. Neither the nature and extent of the revision nor the comparability of the data between the two forms is stated. Apparently the revision contains some new validity data and norms, but there are no dates of collection.

Directions for administration are scanty. The administrator reads aloud the instructions printed in the booklet and then tells the applicants to begin. No mention is made of an appropriate response to the sample items, so the administrator is on his own. The directions oscillate between instructions to the administrator and instructions to the applicant, with no clear demarcation between the two.

Strip keys are used for scoring, and the score is corrected by subtracting number wrong from number right. The applicant is told that accuracy is important, but he is not told the extent of the correction to be applied. The correction is the same for both subtests, although the possibility of guessing correctly in Part 1 is .0001 per item and in Part 2, .5 per item.

Norms are based on over 300 "applicants to the IBM card punch school in New York City," probably all female, although no information is given. No mention is made of level of education, age, or socioeconomic status in the norm group nor for any group in the validity section of the manual. For some of the validation groups, the sex is mentioned. The manual suggests considering all applicants with scores "above average test performance."

Six validity studies are presented. Four show correlations between the total test scores and either class letter grades or supervisory performance ratings. The remaining two show relationships with production standings, which is a laudable criterion. Unfortunately, no details are given on how performance was assessed in any of the studies.

Concurrent validities reported for the CPOAT range from correlations of .23 to .44 using course final letter grades, .50 to .73 using supervisory performance ratings, and .31 to .55 using production standing. One correlation of .45 is reported between test scores and supervisory ratings at a later time. However, no information is given on the number involved (although the maximum seems to be 37) nor the length of time elapsing before follow-up.

Two-way contingency tables showing the relationship between CPOAT grades and performance are presented, along with the correlation coefficients. The correlations seem to be neither tetrachoric nor phi coefficients, although the writeup suggests that they are.

No reliability estimates are given for the test; the only reliability figure mentioned in the entire manual is for a combination of two supervisors' ratings used as a criterion score in the validity section.

In general, the manual is inconsistent in level; detailed in presentation of scores in some of the validity studies and reporting of criterion validity, but sparse in details about the age, sex, and group composition; and entirely silent on the subject of test reliability. If an installation requires some unskilled trainees, the CPOAT may be useful despite these many defects.

DONALD J. VELDMAN, *Professor of Educational Psychology, The University of Texas, Austin, Texas.*

This instrument consists of two parts: 80 letter-digit substitution items with a seven-minute time limit, and 150 name-checking items with a five-minute time limit. Scoring is number right minus number wrong. Normative data provided in the manual were obtained from 306 applicants to an IBM card punch school in New York City; score ranges are indicated for four letter grades.

No reliability information is provided in the manual, but McNamara (1) reported two-week retest reliabilities of .86 and .83 for the parts and .85 for the total score (N = 52). He also found a correlation of .57 between the two parts (N = 100).

A variety of validity studies are reported in the manual, but almost no other evidence has appeared in the research literature during the 10 years since publication of the test. Validities reported in the manual for a criterion of success in training classes in four cities range from .23 to .44. Against supervisor ratings of job performance, validities range from .45 to .73 with four relatively small samples. Only one study used a standard key punching performance task as a criterion; the test correlated .54 with speed and .31 with accuracy, in a group of 36 operators. Perhaps the most serious omission in the manual concerns practice effects, since so many organizations use the instrument as a part of their job application procedures.

The instrument is the only one now on the market for this specific purpose and seems to be useful as a screening tool. With the gradual change from card-punching to direct keyboard entry to computer memories, one would hope for more research on the validity of the instrument for predicting performance in related jobs.

[1104]

*Chemical Operators Selection Test, Revised Edition. Chemical operators and applicants; 1958–71; Forms A ('60, 11 pages), B ('63, 12 pages); manual ('71, c1958, 11 pages); separate answer sheets must be used; 60¢ per test; 4¢ per answer sheet; $1 per scoring stencil; 50¢ per manual; $2.14 per specimen set; postpaid; (60–70) minutes; test by M. A. Storr, J. H. McPherson, P. A. Maschino, and R. G. Garner; manual by J. I. Wegener; Dow Chemical Co. *

REFERENCE

1. See 6:1141.

[1105]

★Fire Performance Rating System. Firemen; 1969; FPRS; ratings by immediate supervisors on 100 traits yielding 7 summary ratings: fire ground work, station work, personality traits and work habits, fire ground command, supervision, administration, total; individual trait rating sheet (2 pages); manual (29 pages); no data on reliability; $55 per set of 100 rating sheets and 10 manuals; specimen set loaned for rental fee of $10, which may be applied to purchase fee; postage extra; (60–120) minutes; McCann Associates. *

[1106]

*Fire Promotion Tests. Prospective firemen promotees; 1960–69; 5 tests; manual ('69, 17 pages); no data on reliability; separate answer sheets (IBM 805) must be used; tests rented only; rental fee: 5 or fewer examinees, $80 (additional candidates, $3 to $1 each); specimen set of any one test loaned for fee of $5, which may be applied to rental fee; postage extra; made-to-order test service available; 210(225) minutes; McCann Associates. *
a) LIEUTENANT. 1962–69; 4 scores: pre-fire practices, extinguishment practices, fire supervision, total; 1 form ('62, 22 pages).
b) CAPTAIN. 1962–69; 5 scores: pre-fire practices, extinguishment practices, overhaul-salvage-rescue, fire supervision, total; 1 form ('62, 22 pages).
c) ASSISTANT FIRE CHIEF. 1961–69; 5 scores: fire administration, firefighting knowledge, fire prevention, fire supervision, total; 1 form ('64, 22 pages).
d) DEPUTY FIRE CHIEF. 1967–69; test also used for battalion chief; 5 scores: same as for c; 1 form ('67, 22 pages).
e) FIRE CHIEF. 1969; 5 scores: same as for c; 1 form (22 pages).

[1107]

★General Municipal Employees Performance (Efficiency) Rating System. Municipal employees; 1967–69; ratings by immediate supervisors; 8 summary ratings: quality of work, quantity of work, work habits, personal traits, relationships with people, supervisory ability, administrative ability, total; performance rating sheet ('69, 1 page); manual ('67, 28 pages); no data on reliability; $50 per 100 rating sheets and 10 manuals; specimen set loaned for rental fee of $10, which may be applied to purchase fee; postage extra; (60–120) minutes; McCann Associates. *

[1108]

★Journalism Test. High school; 1957; 16 scores: news values, arrangement of facts, paragraphing, sentence variety, news source, sports, feature values, speech-interview, editorials, news style, columns, advertising, makeup, headlines, terminology, copyreading; 1 form (6 pages); no manual; no data on reliability; no norms; $1.50 per 10 tests, postage extra; specimen set not available; [60] minutes; Frances Miller and Kenneth Stratton; Stratton-Christian Press. *

[1109]

*Police Performance Rating System. Policemen; 1964–69; PPRS; ratings by immediate supervisors; 7 summary ratings: quality of work, interpersonal relationship traits, quantity of work, character traits, quality of supervision given, quality of administrative work, total; individual trait rating sheet ('69, 2 pages); manual ('69, 34 pages); no data on reliability; $55 per set of 100 rating sheets and 10 manuals; specimen set loaned for rental fee of $10, which may be applied to purchase fee; postage extra; "more than an hour"; McCann Associates. *

[1110]

*Police Promotion Tests. Prospective policemen promotees; 1960–69; 6 tests; manual ('69, 27 pages); no data on reliability; norms for Forms B low scores are estimates; separate answer sheets (IBM 805) must be used; tests rented only; rental fee: 5 or fewer examinees, $80 (additional candidates, $3 to $1 each); specimen set of any one test loaned for a fee of $5, which may be applied to rental fee; postage extra; made-to-order test service available; 210(235) minutes; McCann Associates. *

a) SERGEANT. 1962–69; 6 or 7 scores: patrol, other police knowledges, crime investigation, law, supervision, reading comprehension (Form B only), total; Forms A, B, ('68, 22–23 pages).
b) LIEUTENANT. 1962–69; 6 or 8 scores: same as for *a* plus administration (B); Forms A ('68, 23 pages), B ('69, 23 pages).
c) DETECTIVE. 1962–69; 4 scores: crime investigation, investigative judgment, law, total; Forms A, B, ('68, 24–25 pages); short forms also available for use with *Visual Comprehension Test*.
d) CAPTAIN. 1962–68; 6 scores: police supervision, police administration, crime investigation, other police knowledges, law (Form A only), reading comprehension (Form B only), total; Forms A, B, ('68, 22–23 pages).
e) ASSISTANT CHIEF. 1968–69; 6 scores: same as for *d*; Forms A ('69, 22 pages), B ('68, 22 pages).
f) CHIEF OF POLICE. 1960–69; 6 scores: same as for *d*; Forms A ('62, 22 pages), B ('68, 22 pages).

[1111]

*Policeman Test. Policemen and prospective policemen; 1953–65; PT; Forms 10-A ('53, 27 pages), 10-B ('56, 27 pages), 10-C ('60, 27 pages), 10-D ('65, 27 pages) plus fold-out answer sheets; observation and memory study sheet [dates as for tests, 3 pages] for each form; mimeographed manual ['60, 11 pages]; mimeographed general PPA directions ['57, 7 pages]; no data on reliability; no norms; 10–49 tests, $1.60 each; $2 per specimen set; postpaid; 95(105) minutes; Public Personnel Association. *

NURSING

[1112]

*Achievement Tests in Nursing. Students in schools of registered nursing; 1952–71; tests administered at any time by individual schools; 14 tests; directions: with Digitek answer sheets (no date, 3 pages), with IBM 805 answer sheets (no date, 2 pages); no data on reliability; separate answer sheets (Digitek with *a, b, f–n*, IBM 805 with *c–e*) must be used; no charge to schools requiring *Entrance Examination for Schools of Nursing;* $1 per test per student for other schools; fee includes scoring and reporting service; (40–50) minutes per test; Psychological Corporation. *
a) ANATOMY AND PHYSIOLOGY. 1953–68; Forms 21, 61, ('68, 6 pages).
b) CANCER NURSING. 1967; Forms A, B, (8 pages).
c) GENERAL CHEMISTRY. 1954–64; 1 form ('64, 8 pages).
d) ORGANIC AND INORGANIC CHEMISTRY. 1964; 1 form (9 pages).
e) COMMUNICABLE DISEASES. 1953–61; 1 form ('61, 10 pages).
f) MEDICAL NURSING. 1952–68; Forms 26, 66, ('68, 7 pages).
g) MICROBIOLOGY. 1952–68; Forms 27, 67, ('68, 5 pages).
h) NUTRITION AND DIET THERAPY. 1952–68; Forms 28, 68, ('68, 5 pages).
i) OBSTETRICAL NURSING. 1952–68; Form 29 ('68, 7 pages).
j) PEDIATRIC NURSING. 1952–68; Forms 30, 70, ('68, 7 pages).
k) PHARMACOLOGY. 1952–68; Forms 31, 71, ('68, 7 pages).
l) PSYCHIATRIC NURSING. 1952–71; Form 32 ('71, 8 pages).
m) PSYCHOLOGY AND SOCIOLOGY. 1957–68; Form 33 ('68, 6 pages).
n) SURGICAL NURSING. 1952–68; Forms 34, 74, ('68, 6 pages).

[1113]

*Achievement Tests in Practical Nursing. Practical nursing students; 1957–67; tests administered at any time by individual schools; Form A; parts 1 ('67, 7 pages), 2 ('67, 8 pages); directions (no date, 3 pages); no data on reliability; separate answer sheets (Digitek) must be used; no charge to schools requiring *Entrance Examination for Schools of Practical Nursing;* $1 per part per student for other schools; fee includes scoring and reporting service; (45–50) minutes per part; Psychological Corporation. *

REFERENCE

1. STERNLICHT, MANNY, AND CAVALLO, MARY. "Screening Techniques in the Selection of Practical Nursing Candidates." *Nursing Res* 14:170–2 sp '65. *

[1114]

★Empathy Inventory. Nursing instructors; 1966–70; EI; empathy for nursing school students; 1 form ('66, 8 pages); no specific manual; combined manual ('70, 159 pages) for this and tests 1117 and 1122; separate answer sheets must be used; $7 per 20 tests; $1.50 per 20 answer sheets; $6 per manual; $2.50 per specimen set (without manual); postpaid; scoring service, 25¢ per test; [15–30] minutes; John R. Thurston, Helen L. Brunclik, and John F. Feldhusen (manual); Nursing Research Associates. *

REFERENCES

1. BRUNCLIK, HELEN; THURSTON, JOHN R.; AND FELDHUSEN, JOHN. "The Empathy Inventory." *Nursing Outl* 15: 42–5 Je '67. *
2. THURSTON, JOHN R.; BRUNCLIK, HELEN L.; AND FELDHUSEN, JOHN F. *The Prediction of Success in Nursing Education: Phase III, 1967–1968.* An unpublished report to the Division of Nursing, National Institutes of Health, Research Grant NU 00018-09, Luther Hospital (Eau Claire, Wis.), 1968. Pp. x, 114. *

[1115]

*Entrance Examination for Schools of Nursing. Nursing school applicants; 1938–70; EESN; tests administered at centers established by the publisher; 13 scores: 7 ability scores (verbal, numerical, science, reading comprehension, arithmetic processes, general information, scholastic aptitude total) and 6 personality scores (achievement, orderliness, persistence, congeniality, altruism, respectfulness); Forms 1 ('62, 30 pages), 2 ('63, 30 pages); part 6, Personal Preference Schedule (formerly printed separately as *The Personal Preference Schedule for Student Nurses*) is an adaptation of *Edwards Personal Preference Schedule* and is common to both forms; manual ['62, 9 pages]; norms ['70, 1 page] for each form; interpretation leaflet ['62, 4 pages]; examination fee, $10 per student; fee includes reporting of scores to the school of nursing through which application for examination was made; $2 per additional report; scores not reported to examinees; 155(210) minutes; Psychological Corporation. *

REFERENCES

1–2. See 6:1156.
3. MEADOW, LLOYD. "Assessment of Students for Schools of Practical Nursing." *Nursing Res* 13:222–9 su '64. *
4. MUELLER, E. JANE. *The Pre-Entrance Prediction of Survival in a School of Nursing and Success on the Licensing Examination.* Doctor's thesis, University of Cincinnati (Cincinnati, Ohio), 1968. (*DA* 29:3335A)
5. MUELLER, E. JANE, AND LYMAN, HOWARD B. "The Prediction of Scores on the State Board Test Pool Examination." *Nursing Res* 18(3):263–6 My–Je '69. *

[1116]

*Entrance Examination for Schools of Practical Nursing. Practical nursing school applicants; 1942–69; tests administered at regional centers established by the publisher; 12 scores: 6 ability scores (verbal, numerical, science, reading, arithmetic fundamentals, total) and 6 personality scores (achievement, orderliness, persistence, congeniality, altruism, respectfulness) ; Forms 1 ('64, 22 pages), 2 ('66, 22 pages) ; Forms 3, 4, ('67, 22 pages) identical with tests published 1964–66 except for order of test items ; Personal Preference Schedule (c1955) is an adaptation of *Edwards Personal Preference Schedule* and is common to all forms ; manual ('64, 9 pages) ; norms for Forms 1 and 3, 2 and 4, ('69, 1 page) ; examination fee, $8 per student ; fee includes scoring service and reporting of scores to one school designated at time of application ; $2 per additional report ; scores not reported to examinees ; (210) minutes ; Psychological Corporation. *

REFERENCES

1. STERNLICHT, MANNY, AND CAVALLO, MARY. "Screening Techniques in the Selection of Practical Nursing Candidates." *Nursing Res* 14:170–2 sp '65. *
2. SITZMANN, M. ROSALIE. *A Study of the Predictive Validity of the Psychological Corporation's Pre-Entrance Examination for Schools of Practical Nursing.* Doctor's thesis, Catholic University of America (Washington, D.C.), 1970. (*DAI* 31: 1024A)

[1117]

★**Luther Hospital Sentence Completions.** Prospective nursing students ; 1959–70 ; LHSC ; nonquantitative interpretations of responses in 7 attitudinal areas : nursing, self, home-family, responsibility, others, classwork and studies, love and marriage ; an abbreviated edition, consisting of 40 of the 90 items, is also available under the title *Nursing Sentence Completions* (NSC) ; these 40 items may be scored quantitatively in either edition to obtain a score for predicting success in training, the authors refer to the scoring key as the *Nursing Education Scale* (NES) ; regular edition : 1 form ('59, 4 pages) ; abbreviated edition : 1 form ('64, 3 pages) ; no specific manual ; combined manual ('70, 159 pages) for this and tests 1114 and 1122 ; $4 per 25 tests ; $6 per manual ; $1.50 per specimen set (without manual) ; postpaid ; scoring service, $2 per individual ; (40–50) minutes for regular edition, (20–30) minutes for abbreviated edition ; John R. Thurston, Helen L. Brunclik, P. A. Finn (test), and John F. Feldhusen (manual) ; Nursing Research Associates. *

REFERENCES

1. THURSTON, JOHN R., AND BRUNCLIK, HELEN L. "The Prediction of Success in Schools of Nursing." *Nursing Outl* 13:69 Mr '65. *
2. THURSTON, JOHN R., AND BRUNCLIK, HELEN L. "The Relationship of Personality to Achievement in Nursing Education." *Nursing Res* 14:203–9 su '65. *
3. THURSTON, JOHN R.; BRUNCLIK, HELEN L.; AND FELDHUSEN, JOHN F. *The Prediction of Success in Nursing Education: Phase I and II, 1959–67; A Manual for the Luther Hospital Sentence Completions and the Nursing Sentence Completions.* An unpublished report to the Division of Nursing, National Institutes of Health, Research Grant NU 00018-07, Luther Hospital (Eau Claire, Wis.), 1967. Pp. xvi, 265. *
4. THURSTON, JOHN R.; BRUNCLIK, HELEN L.; AND FELDHUSEN, JOHN F. *The Prediction of Success in Nursing Education: Phase III, 1967–1968.* An unpublished report to the Division of Nursing, National Institutes of Health, Research Grant NU 00018-09, Luther Hospital (Eau Claire, Wis.), 1968. Pp. x, 114. *
5. THURSTON, JOHN R.; BRUNCLIK, HELEN L.; AND FELDHUSEN, JOHN F. "The Relationship of Personality to Achievement in Nursing Education, Phase 2." *Nursing Res* 17:265–8 My–Je '68. * (*PA* 42:17997)

[1118]

*****NLN Achievement Tests for Schools Preparing Registered Nurses.** Students in state-approved schools preparing registered nurses ; 1943–71 ; tests loaned to schools for their own use ; 1 form ; 2 levels ; mimeographed manual (no date, 26 pages) ; directions for administering (no date, 4 pages) ; interpretive manual for schools ('64, 45 pages, see 1 below) ; separate answer sheets (IBM 1230) must be used ; fees include reporting results to schools ; postpaid one way ; National League for Nursing, Inc. *

a) [BASIC ACHIEVEMENT TESTS.] Undergraduates completing courses in the subjects specified ; 1943–71 ; 10 tests ; (90–120) minutes per test.

1) *Anatomy and Physiology.* 1943–64 ; Form 464 ('64, 24 pages) ; rental fee, 75¢ per student.
2) *Chemistry.* 1943–64 ; 4 scores : inorganic, organic, biochemistry, total ; Form 963 ('63, 24 pages) ; rental fee, $1 per student.
3) *Microbiology.* 1943–71 ; Form 171 ('71, 17 pages) ; rental fee, 75¢ per student.
4) *Normal Nutrition.* 1946–64 ; formerly called *Nutrition and Diet Therapy;* Form 662 ('62, 23 pages) ; rental fee, 75¢ per student.
5) *Basic Pharmacology.* 1944–67 ; formerly called *Pharmacology and Therapeutics;* Form 267 ('67, 20 pages) ; rental fee, $1 per student.
6) *Medical-Surgical Nursing.* 1956–64 ; 4 scores : medical nursing, surgical nursing, medical-surgical nursing, total ; Form 862 ('62, 28 pages) ; rental fee, $1 per student.
7) *Public Health Nursing.* 1956–64 ; for baccalaureate programs only ; 3 scores : nursing practice and service, science and general information, total ; Form 661 ('61, 36 pages) ; rental fee, $1 per student.
8) *Obstetric Nursing.* 1945–68 ; 4 scores : antepartal care, partal and postpartal care of mothers, care of newborn, total ; Form 468 ('68, 29 pages) ; rental fee, $1.25 per student.
9) *Nursing of Children.* 1945–68 ; 3 scores : growth and development, care of the sick child, total ; Form 368 ('68, 27 pages) ; rental fee, $1.25 per student.
10) *Psychiatric Nursing.* 1945–65 ; 3 scores : psychiatric nursing practices, facts and principles, total ; Form 665 ('65, 32 pages) ; rental fee, $1 per student.

b) COMPREHENSIVE ACHIEVEMENT TESTS. Seniors about to graduate ; 1957–68 ; 11 tests ; (120–130) minutes per test (except 10 and 11).

1) *Diet Therapy and Applied Nutrition.* 1962–64 ; Form 762 ('62, 28 pages) ; rental fee, 75¢ per student.
2) *Pharmacology in Clinical Nursing (Application of Facts and Principles).* 1960–67 ; Form 767 ('67, 27 pages) ; rental fee, $1 per student.
3) *Natural Sciences in Nursing.* 1957–68 ; 3 scores : facts and principles (knowledge, application, total) ; Form 768 ('68, 29 pages) ; rental fee, $1 per student.
4) *Maternity and Child Nursing.* 1958–67 ; 3 scores : care of the normal pregnant woman and normal child, care of sick children, total ; Form 467 ('67, 32 pages) ; rental fee, $1.25 per student.
5) *Disaster Nursing.* 1961–64 ; 3 scores : general nursing applied to disasters, facts and principles of disasters and disaster nursing, total ; Form 261 ('61, 39 pages) ; rental fee, $1 per student.
6) *Medical-Surgical Nursing, Part 1.* 1961–64 ; 4 scores : orthopedic nursing, neurological-neurosurgical nursing, eye-ear-nose-and-throat nursing, total ; Form 262 ('61, 31 pages) ; rental fee, $1 per student.
7) *Medical-Surgical Nursing, Part 2.* 1962–64 ; 3 scores : medical nursing, surgical nursing, total ; Form 962 ('62, 35 pages) ; rental fee, $1 per student.
8) *Communicable Disease Nursing.* 1946–64 ; 3 scores : prevention and transmission, disease manifestations and other aspects, total ; Form 863 ('63, 31 pages) ; rental fee, $1 per student.
9) *Maternal-Child Nursing.* 1964 ; for baccalaureate programs only ; 4 scores : growth and development (including pregnancy), conditions and care of the sick child, other relevant aspects, total ; Form 964 (36 pages) ; rental fee, $1 per student.

10) *Medical-Surgical Nursing.* 1967; for baccalaureate programs only; 4 scores: part A, part B, knowledge, application; Form 967 (32 pages); rental fee, $1.25 per student; (150–180) minutes.

11) *Applied Natural Sciences.* 1967; for baccalaureate programs only; 4 scores: part A, part B, knowledge, application; Form 367 (29 pages); rental fee, $1.25 per student; (150–180) minutes.

REFERENCES

1. See 6:1157.
2. FLITTER, HESSEL. "Achievement Test in the Natural Sciences in Nursing." *Nursing Outl* 7:410–3 Jl '59. *
3. STERNLICHT, MANNY, AND CAVALLO, MARY. "Screening Techniques in the Selection of Practical Nursing Candidates." *Nursing Res* 14:170–2 sp '65. *
4. THOMAS, MARTHA J., AND WEINSTEIN, ABBOTT S. "Comparison of Test Scores in Psychiatric Nursing." *Nursing Outl* 13:38–41 My '65. *
5. BRANDT, EDNA MAE; HASTIE, BETTIMAE; AND SCHUMANN, DELORES. "Predicting Success on State Board Examinations: Relationships Between Course Grades, Selected Test Scores, and State Board Examination Results." *Nursing Res* 15:62–9 w '66. *
6. BALDWIN, JEAN P.; MOWBRAY, JEAN K.; AND TAYLOR, RAYMOND G. "Factors Influencing Performance on State Board Test Pool Examinations." *Nursing Res* 17:170–2 Mr-Ap '68. *
7. BAZIAK, ANNA T. "Developing Reliable Indices to Predict Success on Psychiatric Nursing State Board Examinations." *J Psychiatric Nursing* 6:79–85 Mr-Ap '68. *
8. LEDBETTER, PEGGY JEAN. *An Analysis of the Performance of Graduates of a Selected Baccalaureate Program in Nursing With Regard to Selected Standardized Examinations.* Doctor's thesis, University of Alabama (University, Ala.), 1968. (*DA* 29:3381A)
9. MUELLER, E. JANE, AND LYMAN, HOWARD B. "The Prediction of Scores on the State Board Test Pool Examination." *Nursing Res* 18(3):263–6 My-Je '69. *
10. NLN Measurement and Evaluation Services. "The Relationship of PNG and Achievement Test Scores." *Nursing Outl* 17(3):52 Mr '69. *
11. National League for Nursing. *A Validation Study of the NLN Pre-Nursing and Guidance Examination and Related Studies Emerging From Data Gathered From the Validation Study.* New York: the League, Inc., 1970. Pp. v, 58. *

[1119]

★**NLN Aide Selection Test.** Applicants for aide positions in hospitals and home health agencies; 1970; AST; 1 form (8 pages); manual (8 pages); $5 per set of 25 tests, key, and manual; 75¢ per specimen set; postpaid; 30(35) minutes; National League for Nursing, Inc. *

[1120]

*****NLN Practical Nursing Achievement Tests.** Students in state-approved schools of practical nursing; 1950–64; tests loaned to schools for their own use; 1 form; 3 tests; mimeographed manual (no date, 12 pages) for these tests and test 6:1161; directions for administering (no date, 4 pages); interpretive manual for schools ('64, 45 pages, see *1* below); separate answer sheets (IBM 1230) must be used; fees include reporting results to schools; postpaid one way; (90–120) minutes per test; National League for Nursing, Inc. *

a) THREE UNITS OF CONTENT. 1957–64; TUC; 4 scores: body structure and function, basic nursing procedures, nutrition and diet therapy, total; Form 764 ('64, 29 pages); rental fee, $1 per student.

b) NURSING INCLUDING ASPECTS OF PHARMACOLOGY. 1950–64; NIP; 4 scores: medical-surgical, maternal-child, pharmacology, total; Form 864 ('64, 34 pages); rental fee, $1 per student.

c) ELEMENTARY PSYCHIATRIC NURSING. 1958; for aide-training programs; Form 858 (22 pages); rental fee, 75¢ per student.

REFERENCE

1. NATIONAL LEAGUE FOR NURSING. *The NLN Achievement Test, Third Edition. The Use of Tests in Schools of Nursing* Pamphlet No. 2. New York: National League for Nursing, Inc., 1964. Pp. iv, 41. *

[1121]

★**Netherne Study Difficulties Battery for Student Nurses.** Student nurses; 1964–69; SDB; also called *Study Difficulties Battery;* 15 scores: understanding of words, use of words, scientific information, learning from a text, checking correctness of spelling, checking accuracy of numbers, checking accuracy of names, learning from a diagram, summarizing a paragraph, following directions, summarizing drawings and diagrams, speed of associations, speed and legibility of handwriting, speed and accuracy of freehand drawing, total; 1 form ('64, 77 pages, mimeographed); study sheets ['69, 2 pages] for 2 subtests; mimeographed manual ('69, 58 pages); profile ('69, 2 pages); separate answer sheets must be used; £2 per test; £4 per 100 sets of answer sheets; 50p per 10 sets of study sheets; 50p per profile; £2 per manual; postage extra; specimen set not available; 70(90–105) minutes; James Patrick S. Robertson; Psychological Research Department, Netherne Hospital; distributed by NFER Publishing Co. Ltd. *

[1122]

★**Nurse Attitudes Inventory.** Prospective nursing students; 1965–70; NAI; a multiple choice test based upon the *Luther Hospital Sentence Completions;* 9 scores: attitudes (nursing, self, home-family, responsibility, others-love-marriage, academic), verification (V-1, V-2), total; the authors refer to the scoring key used to obtain the total score as the *Nursing Education Scale,* abbreviated NES-NAI to distinguish it from the *Nursing Education Scale* based upon either the *Luther Hospital Sentence Completions* or the *Nursing Sentence Completions;* Forms 1, 2, ('65, 13 pages, 84 percent of the items have stems common to both forms); no specific manual; combined manual ('70, 159 pages) for this and tests 1114 and 1117; no data on reliability; separate answer sheets (IBM 805) must be used; $5 per 25 tests; $5 per key; $6 per manual; $1.50 per specimen set (without manual); postpaid; scoring service, $1.50 per test; [30–45] minutes; John R. Thurston, Helen L. Brunclik, and John F. Feldhusen (manual); Nursing Research Associates. *

REFERENCES

1. THURSTON, JOHN R., AND BRUNCLIK, HELEN L. *Nurse Attitudes Inventory (NAI).* An unpublished report to the Division of Nursing, National Institutes of Health, Research Grant NV 00018-06, Luther Hospital (Eau Claire, Wis.), 1965. Pp. 190. *
2. THURSTON, JOHN R.; BRUNCLIK, HELEN L.; AND FELDHUSEN, JOHN F. *The Prediction of Success in Nursing Education: Phase III, 1967–1968.* An unpublished report to the Division of Nursing, National Institutes of Health, Research Grant NU 00018-09, Luther Hospital (Eau Claire, Wis.), 1968. Pp. x, 114. *
3. BEHRING, DANIEL WILLIAM. *Adaptive Functioning: A Rationale for the Prediction of Achievement in Nursing Education.* Doctor's thesis, Ohio University (Athens, Ohio), 1969. (*DAI* 31:1065A)
4. THURSTON, JOHN R.; BRUNCLIK, HELEN L.; AND FELDHUSEN, JOHN F. "Personality and the Prediction of Success in Nursing Education." *Nursing Res* 18(3):258–62 My-Je '69. *
5. OWEN, STEVEN V.; FELDHUSEN, JOHN F.; AND THURSTON, JOHN R. "Achievement Prediction in Nursing Education With Cognitive, Attitudinal, and Divergent Thinking Variables." *Psychol Rep* 26(3):867–70 Je '70. * (*PA* 45:1361)

SELLING

[1123]

*****Combination Inventory, Form 2.** Prospective debit life insurance salesmen; 1954–66; CI; 6 scores: arithmetic, general knowledge, sales aptitude (interest, reaction, personal history, total); interest items selected from *Strong Vocational Interest Blank for Men,*

Revised; 1 form ('66, 33 pages); manual ('66, 8 pages); no data on reliability; norms available on request; distribution restricted to home offices of member life insurance companies; details may be obtained from publisher; separate answer sheets (Digitek) must be used; 90(120) minutes; Life Insurance Agency Management Association. *

REFERENCE

1. See 6:1170.

[1124]

*LIAMA Inventory of Job Attitudes. Life insurance field personnel; 1956–70; IJA; group measurement of company performance; job attitude scores in 10 areas; Forms 2-C ('70, 9 pages, for use by combination agents), 2-O ('70, 7 pages, for use by ordinary agents); manual, second edition ('70, 32 pages plus forms); no data on reliability; distribution restricted to home offices of member life insurance companies and research personnel; details may be obtained from publisher; [20–30] minutes; Life Insurance Agency Management Association. *

SKILLED TRADES

[1125]

★Electrical Sophistication Test. Job applicants; 1963–65; 1 form ('63, 2 pages); mimeographed manual ('65, 2 pages); $2.50 per 25 tests; $1 per specimen set; cash orders postpaid; (5–10) minutes; Stanley G. Ciesla; Psychometric Affiliates. *

CHARLES F. WARD, *Assistant Professor of Occupational Education and Research Associate, Center for Occupational Education, North Carolina State University, Raleigh, North Carolina.*

The test is multiple choice, consists of 14 items, and must be hand scored. There is no time limit, but many candidates finish within five minutes, according to the manual. The test is very rudimentary, covering a few basic concepts in electricity. The two-page mimeographed manual indicates that the test's purpose is to discriminate between persons with substantial knowledge of electricity and those with no, little, and merely chance knowledge, and to screen candidates for a wide variety of jobs and positions in which electrical knowledge is important to competent performance. The test was constructed from a pool of items which, as a result of library work and consultation with a university staff, appeared most likely to be known by persons "truly motivated in electrical achievement."

A .74 test-retest reliability coefficient was obtained on a sample of 238 college men after an interval of seven weeks. While a .74 reliability is good for a 14-item test, it indicates a large error score component.

The manual provides normative data for nine

classifications: random job applicants; liberal arts majors; math majors; civil engineers; mechanical engineers; chemical engineers; physics majors; electricians; and electrical engineers. Sample size for norming ranged from 59 to 340, and raw scores were converted to percentiles for each group. The only effort toward validation is to point out that the difference between scores of random job applicants and people in jobs presupposing electrical knowledge is highly significant.

The test has several weaknesses. Its brevity and the method of content sampling raise a question of the sufficiency and representativeness of the items. Sampling bias is in fact indicated in that four of the 14 items concern relays. None of the test items requires mathematical application or the use of equations. Only rote memory is required to answer most items. Test construction techniques are inadequate, lacking both preliminary testing of the pool of items and subsequent item analysis. Normative data, often predicated upon small samples, are available for only nine specific categories or occupations, and the overlap between distributions for occupations is often substantial.

By comparison, the *Short Occupational Knowledge Test for Electricians* appears to be superior to this test in method of construction, content validity, and normative data.

[1126]

★Mechanical Handyman Test. Maintenance workers; 1957–65; MHT; form 80-A ('65, 22 pages plus fold-out answer sheet); mimeographed manual ('65, 9 pages); mimeographed general PPA directions ['57, 7 pages]; no data on reliability; no norms; 10–49 tests, $1 each; $2 per specimen set; postpaid; 120(130) minutes; Public Personnel Association. *

[1127]

★Ohio Auto Body Achievement Test. Grades 11–12; 1969–70; OABAT; available only as a part of the Ohio Trade and Industrial Education Achievement Test Program (see 1134 for more complete information); 16 scores: welding, metal forming, body filler, refinishing, trim and hardware, parts replacement, alignment, glass replacement, fiber glass repair, frame and unit body, electrical system, cooling and conditioning, shop management, applied science, applied math, total; 1 form; parts 1 ('70, 13 pages), 2 ('70, 12 pages); Ohio norms for juniors, seniors, ('70, 1 page); course outline ['69, 66 pages]; (120) minutes for each part; Instructional Materials Laboratory, Ohio State University. *

[1128]

★Ohio Basic Electricity and Electronics Achievement Tests. Grades 11–12; 1962–70; OBEAT; available only as a part of the Ohio Trade and Industrial Education Achievement Test Program (see 1134 for more complete information); 2 tests either or both of which may be administered; Ohio norms for juniors, seniors, ('70, 1 page) for each test; course outline ('62, 92 pages); Instructional Materials Laboratory, Ohio State University. *

a) OHIO BASIC ELECTRICITY ACHIEVEMENT TEST. 10 scores: D.C. electricity, laws of magnetism, A.C. electricity, measurement, construction wiring, diagnosis and maintenance, circuit tracing, applied math, applied science, total; 1 form ('62, 16 pages); (190) minutes.

b) OHIO BASIC ELECTRONICS ACHIEVEMENT TEST. 9 scores: tuning circuits, vacuum tubes, semiconductor characteristics, power supplies, amplifiers, detector circuits, test equipment, oscillator circuits, total; 1 form ('62, 8 pages); (90) minutes.

[1129]

★**Ohio Cosmetology Achievement Test.** Grades 11–12; 1967–70; OCAT; available only as a part of the Ohio Trade and Industrial Education Achievement Test Program (see 1134 for more complete information); 14 scores: scalp, hands and feet, hair, hair tints and bleach, face information, facial, make-up, sanitation and bacteriology, applied science, anatomy and physiology, shop management, trade math, legal guidance, total; 1 form; parts 1 ('69, 15 pages), 2 ('69, 12 pages); Ohio norms for juniors, seniors, ('70, 1 page); course outline ('67, 31 pages); (120) minutes for each part; Instructional Materials Laboratory, Ohio State University. *

[1130]

★**Ohio Machine Trades Achievement Test.** Grades 11–12; 1958–70; OMTAT; available only as a part of the Ohio Trade and Industrial Education Achievement Test Program (see 1134 for more complete information); 18 scores: applied math, layout, hand tools, measuring, power sawing, drilling, shaping, heat treating, trade science, machining-lathe, milling, blueprint reading, grinding (bench, surface, tool and cutter, cylindrical, internal), total; 1 form; parts 1 ('60, 8 pages), 2 ('60, 12 pages); Ohio norms for juniors, seniors, ('70, 1 page); course outline ('58, 50 pages); (180) minutes for each part; Instructional Materials Laboratory, Ohio State University. *

[1131]

★**Ohio Mechanical Drafting Achievement Test.** Grades 11–12; 1962–70; OMDAT; available only as a part of the Ohio Trade and Industrial Education Achievement Test Program (see 1134 for more complete information); 19 scores: materials and equipment, dimensioning, auxiliary views, threads and fasteners, production or working drawings, machine elements, auxiliary information, industrial processes, materials of industry, applied science, orthographic projection, sectional views, pictorial drawings, intersections and developments, geometric drawing, lettering, reproduction of drawings, functions of mathematics, total; 1 form; parts 1 ('63, 14 pages), 2 ('63, 16 pages); Ohio norms for juniors, seniors, ('70, 1 page); course outline ['63, 18 pages]; (180) minutes for each part; Instructional Materials Laboratory, Ohio State University. *

[1132]

★**Ohio Printing Achievement Test.** Grades 11–12; 1963–70; OPAT; available only as a part of the Ohio Trade and Industrial Education Achievement Test Program (see 1134 for more complete information); 17 scores: orientation, printing planning, composition (hand, machine, photo), camera operation, film processing, letterpress (platemaking, presswork), applied science, lithograph (stripping and platemaking, presswork), bindery work, paper technology, ink technol-

ogy, applied math, total; 1 form; parts 1 ('63, 13 pages), 2 ('63, 8 pages); Ohio norms for juniors, seniors, ('70, 1 page); course outline ['63, 19 pages]; (150) minutes for part 1, (90) minutes for part 2; Instructional Materials Laboratory, Ohio State University. *

[1133]

★**Ohio Sheet Metal Achievement Test.** Grades 11–12; 1964–70; OSMAT; available only as a part of the Ohio Trade and Industrial Education Achievement Test Program (see 1134 for more complete information); 15 scores: blueprint reading, applied science, applied math, hand tool operations, machine operations, soldering, special operations, mechanical drawing, freehand sketching, metals, nonmetallic, layout, fabricating, welding, total; 1 form; parts 1 ('66, 13 pages), 2 ('64, 7 pages); Ohio norms for juniors, seniors, ('70, 1 page); course outline ['64, 8 pages]; (180) minutes for each part; Instructional Materials Laboratory, Ohio State University. *

[1134]

★**Ohio Trade and Industrial Education Achievement Test Program.** Grades 11–12; 1958–70; tests administered annually in March at participating schools; each student must take 3 tests: an intelligence test, an arithmetic test, and a trade test; 1 form; revised manual ('70, 65 pages); instructions for administration ['70, 53 pages]; separate answer cards (IBM) must be used; rental and scoring of tests, $1.50 per student; postage extra; individual state norms will be provided for minimum of 100 students and 5 or more schools per grade and trade; specimen set not available; (270–450) minutes in 3 sessions; Instructional Materials Laboratory, Ohio State University. *

a) INTELLIGENCE TEST. See *Survey of Mental Maturity,* Advanced Level; 3 scores: language, nonlanguage, total; 30(40) minutes.

b) ARITHMETIC TEST. See *Stanford Achievement Test: Arithmetic,* Advanced Level (Computation section only); 35(45) minutes.

c) TRADE TESTS. 1958–70; 10 tests based on course outlines prepared for use in Ohio; $1.25 per course outline, postpaid.

   1) *Ohio Machine Trades Achievement Test.* See 1130.
   2) *Ohio Automotive Mechanics Achievement Test. Out of print.*
   3) *Ohio Basic Electricity Achievement Test.* See 1128.
   4) *Ohio Basic Electronics Achievement Test.* See 1128.
   5) *Ohio Mechanical Drafting Achievement Test.* See 1131.
   6) *Ohio Printing Achievement Test.* See 1132.
   7) *Ohio Sheet Metal Achievement Test.* See 1133.
   8) *Ohio Cosmetology Achievement Test.* See 1129.
   9) *Ohio Auto Body Achievement Test.* See 1127.
   10) *Ohio Welding Achievement Test.* See 1135.

[1135]

★**Ohio Welding Achievement Test.** Grades 11–12; 1969–70; OWAT; available only as a part of the Ohio Trade and Industrial Education Achievement Test Program (see 1134 for more complete information); 12 scores: blueprint reading, flame cutting, oxy-acetylene, arc welding, resistance welding, gas tungsten—arc welding, gas metal arc welding, equipment, labor and management, applied math, applied science, total; 1 form; parts 1 ('70, 16 pages), 2 ('70, 11 pages); Ohio norms for juniors, seniors, ('70, 1 page); course outline ['69, 50 pages]; (180) minutes for part 1,

(150) minutes for part 2; Instructional Materials Laboratory, Ohio State University. *

[1136]

Purdue Test for Electricians. Industry and vocational schools; 1942; Forms A, B, (4 pages, self-scoring); preliminary manual (3 pages); $6.50 per 25 tests; 45¢ per manual; $1.08 per specimen set; postage extra; 25(30) minutes; C. W. Caldwell, H. R. Goppert, H. G. McComb, W. B. Hill, and Joseph Tiffin (manual); Science Research Associates, Inc. *

CHARLES F. WARD, *Assistant Professor of Occupational Education and Research, Associate, Center for Occupational Education, North Carolina State University, Raleigh, North Carolina.*

This test, designed to aid industry and vocational schools in determining the amount of knowledge of electricity and electrical operations possessed by applicants or students, was reviewed in *The Third Mental Measurements Yearbook* (3:701). The 65-item test is completely objective. Answers are punched and each test contains its own key, which provides for rapid scoring. Parallel-form reliability is an adequate .91 (time between administrations not specified), which rises to .96 when both forms are administered in succession. The only validity claimed in the still-preliminary manual is said to be predicated upon the thoroughness of the sampling of electricity and electrical operations in standard textbooks and upon the fact that particular industrial concepts were incorporated in the construction of the test. The sampling of the fundamentals of magnetism and direct current are good, but there are fewer items on alternating current fundamentals and industrial practices. Two norms have been developed, one based upon 434 students in vocational and industrial arts electricity classes, and one based upon 131 sales-and-service applicants of one electrical manufacturing company.

Two major weaknesses limit the use of the test: the lack of research on the instrument, and the absence of any attempt to update the material to reflect changes in subject matter content which have occurred since 1942. The same "preliminary manual" cited in the earlier review is still in use, leading one to conclude that the reliability figures cited date back almost 30 years, as do the two sets of norms. Since that time there has not been any effort either to validate the instrument in terms of predicting job performance or to update and expand the normative data. When the test was first published (as noted above), validity was said to rest largely on the thoroughness of the sampling from the then current textbooks and on the fact that particular industrial concepts were incorporated. The textbooks referenced were written in the 1930–37 era. While many of the items deal with fundamentals of electricity and are therefore still current, some dealing with industrial concepts are out of date. The most serious deficiency is the omission of basic electronic concepts which have evolved since the test was published. Today, a knowledge of basic electronic concepts is a requisite for most industrial electricians. Such concepts, found in most current basic textbooks and taught in introductory courses on electrical theory, should be incorporated in an updated version of the test.

In conclusion, because of the lack of recent normative data, validation studies, or any efforts to update the test to reflect current knowledge and industrial practices, the test is of questionable value in predicting the success of potential industrial electricians or in determining achievement in basic electricity courses as currently taught.

For a review by John W. French, see 3:701.

[1137]

★Short Occupational Knowledge Test for Auto Mechanics. Job applicants; 1969-70; score is pass, fail, or unclassifiable; 1 form ('69, 2 pages, self-marking); series manual ('70, 15 pages); $5.30 per 25 tests; 75¢ per manual; $3.30 per specimen set of the 12 tests in the series; postage extra; (10-15) minutes; Bruce A. Campbell and Suellen O. Johnson; Science Research Associates, Inc. *

EMORY E. WISEMAN, *Assistant Professor of Automotive and Power Technology, Illinois State University, Normal, Illinois.*

The purpose of the test is to assist in differentiating between knowledgeable applicants and those with limited knowledge of the occupation. The areas of information are highly comprehensive in the topics sampled: cooling, pollution control, steering geometry, suspension, brakes, drive train, electrical, diagnosis and tools.

The format, typing, and printing of the test material are such that the test is easily read. The directions for administration are clearly defined in regard to both the purpose and scoring procedure of the test. The test is primarily a power test.

Extensive analyses have been made of the test items to determine which questions discriminated between high and low scorers within each group sampled. As a result of item analyses of pretest performance, the present 20 questions were chosen from 82 pretested questions which were drawn from an original list of 100 items. Pretest data were established by selecting adequate samples from two groups.

K-R 20 reliabilities of .81 and .88 and alternate-forms reliabilities of .87 and .93 appear to assure a reasonably adequate test reliability.

The content validity appears to be adequate as a result of the method of question selection. The questions were obtained from experts in the field. Through administration of these questions and item analyses, the most appropriate questions were selected. The questions will not soon become obsolete, even though modifications in the automobile are frequently made.

In summary, one should have a reasonable degree of confidence in the value of this test to classify men into various experience levels. Since it can provide a quick objective estimate of an individual's knowledge, it may be used as one criterion in the total evaluation of an individual.

[1138]

★Short Occupational Knowledge Test for Carpenters. Job applicants; 1969–70; score is pass, fail, or unclassifiable; 1 form ('69, 2 pages, self-marking); series manual ('70, 15 pages); $5.30 per 25 tests; 75¢ per manual; $3.30 per specimen set of the 12 tests in the series; postage extra; (10–15) minutes; Bruce A. Campbell and Suellen O. Johnson; Science Research Associates, Inc. *

[1139]

★Short Occupational Knowledge Test for Draftsmen. Job applicants; 1969–70; score is pass, fail, or unclassifiable; 1 form ('69, 2 pages, self-marking); series manual ('70, 15 pages); $5.30 per 25 tests; 75¢ per manual; $3.30 per specimen set of the 12 tests in the series; postage extra; (10–15) minutes; Bruce A. Campbell and Suellen O. Johnson; Science Research Associates, Inc. *

[1140]

★Short Occupational Knowledge Test for Electricians. Job applicants; 1969–70; score is pass, fail, or unclassifiable; 1 form ('69, 2 pages, self-marking); series manual ('70, 15 pages); $5.30 per 25 tests; 75¢ per manual; $3.30 per specimen set of the 12 tests in the series; postage extra; (10–15) minutes; Bruce A. Campbell and Suellen O. Johnson; Science Research Associates, Inc. *

CHARLES F. WARD, *Assistant Professor of Occupational Education and Research Associate, Center for Occupational Education, North Carolina State University, Raleigh, North Carolina.*

This test, designed for use by employers to differentiate between knowledgeable applicants and those having only a smattering of knowledge in electricity, consists of 18 multiple choice, job-related items which are of a practical rather than theoretical orientation. The test is easily administered and is hand scored by use of a carbon-insert format. A cutoff method of scoring is used to yield scores which are either passing, failing, or unclassifiable. From a pretested item pool of 118 items constructed by persons working or teaching in the area covered by the test and reviewed by experts (unnamed) in the field, 18 items were selected for each form of the test. Reliability (internal consistency) based on K-R 20 is .75 for the pretest sample and .70 for the validation sample. Correlations between forms of .85 and .83 are reported for two groups, which is good for a test of this length. Predictive validity has yet to be determined. Concurrent validity was ascertained by administering the test to a sample comprised of a control group and specialists to determine the percentage correctly identified in each group. For the two forms of the test, the percentages of validation subjects making "unclassifiable" scores were 31.5 and 18.5.

This test for electricians appears adequate for an initial screening device of potential employees. It is not sufficiently long to provide an in-depth measure of achievement, nor does it claim to do so. The test has several features which commend its use. Test construction procedures were thorough. Test items have good face validity, are current in terms of subject matter content, require reasoning and mathematical ability as well as rote knowledge, and appear to provide a good sample of the subject matter content. Research on the instrument is adequate, and the manual is thorough in providing factual information. Conversely, the internal consistency is somewhat low, but this is probably attributable to the test's brevity. Also, further knowledge of its predictive validity is needed. Another weakness is the rather large proportion of testees making an "unclassifiable" score in the validation sample. This could necessitate the use of additional tests to preclude possible rejection of competent persons.

This test is superior to the *Electrical Sophistication Test* in terms of construction technique, content validity, currentness, and in the knowledge and understanding required to successfully respond to the items. Its manual is also more thorough in providing the information needed to use the test or to make professional judgments concerning its applications. Use of the test is recommended.

[1141]

★**Short Occupational Knowledge Test for Machinists.** Job applicants; 1969–70; score is pass, fail, or unclassifiable; 1 form ('69, 2 pages, self-marking); series manual ('70, 15 pages); $5.30 per 25 tests; 75¢ per manual; $3.30 per specimen set of the 12 tests in the series; postage extra; (10–15) minutes; Bruce A. Campbell and Suellen O. Johnson; Science Research Associates, Inc. *

[1142]

★**Short Occupational Knowledge Test for Plumbers.** Job applicants; 1970; score is pass, fail, or unclassifiable; 1 form (2 pages, self-marking); series manual (15 pages); $5.30 per 25 tests; 75¢ per manual; $3.30 per specimen set of the 12 tests in the series; postage extra; (10–15) minutes; Bruce A. Campbell and Suellen O. Johnson; Science Research Associates, Inc. *

[1143]

★**Short Occupational Knowledge Test for Tool and Die Makers.** Job applicants; 1970; score is pass, fail, or unclassifiable; 1 form (2 pages, self-marking); series manual (15 pages); $5.30 per 25 tests; 75¢ per manual; $3.30 per specimen set of the 12 tests in the series; postage extra; (10–15) minutes; Bruce A. Campbell and Suellen O. Johnson; Science Research Associates, Inc. *

[1144]

★**Short Occupational Knowledge Test for Welders.** Job applicants; 1969–70; score is pass, fail, or unclassifiable; 1 form ('69, 2 pages, self-marking); series manual ('70, 15 pages); $5.30 per 25 tests; 75¢ per manual; $3.30 per specimen set of the 12 tests in the series; postage extra; (10–15) minutes; Bruce A. Campbell and Suellen O. Johnson; Science Research Associates, Inc. *

SUPERVISION

[1145]

★**Ideal Leader Behavior Description Questionnaire.** Supervisors; 1957; ILBDQ; employee ratings of a supervisor; test booklet title is *Ideal Leader Behavior (What You Expect of Your Leader)*; same as *Leader Behavior Description Questionnaire* except that the responses indicate what a supervisor ought to be rather than what he is; 1 form (3 pages); no manual; no data on reliability; no norms; $2 per 25 tests, cash orders postpaid; specimen set free; (10) minutes; original edition by John K. Hemphill and Alvin E. Coons; current edition by Personnel Research Board, Ohio State University; University Publication Sales, Ohio State University. *

REFERENCES

1. HALPIN, ANDREW W. "The Leader Behavior and Leadership Ideology of Educational Administrators and Aircraft Commanders." *Harvard Ed R* 25:18–32 w '55. * (*PA* 30:2646)
2. HEMPHILL, JOHN K. "Leadership Behavior Associated With the Administrative Reputation of College Departments." *J Ed Psychol* 46:385–401 N '55. * (*PA* 31:3837)
3. HALPIN, ANDREW W. Chap. 5, "The Observed Leader Behavior and Ideal Leader Behavior of Aircraft Commanders and School Superintendents," pp. 65–8. In *Leader Behavior: Its Description and Measurement.* Edited by Ralph M. Stogdill and Alvin E. Coons. Ohio State University, Bureau of Business Research, Research Monograph No. 88. Columbus, Ohio: the Bureau, 1957. Pp. xv, 168. * (*PA* 32:1466)

4. HEMPHILL, JOHN K. Chap. 7, "Leader Behavior Associated With the Administrative Reputations of College Departments," pp. 74–85. In *Leader Behavior: Its Description and Measurement.* Edited by Ralph M. Stogdill and Alvin E. Coons. Ohio State University, Bureau of Business Research, Research Monograph No. 88. Columbus, Ohio: the Bureau, 1957. Pp. xv, 168. * (*PA* 32:1466)
5. LUCKIE, WILLIAM RONALD. *Leader Behavior of Directors of Instruction.* Doctor's thesis, University of Southern Mississippi (Hattiesburg, Miss.), 1963. (*DA* 25:1690)
6. BEER, MICHAEL. *Leadership, Employee Needs, and Motivation.* Ohio State University, Bureau of Business Research Monograph No. 129. Columbus, Ohio: the Bureau, 1966. Pp. xii, 100. *
7. GOTT, CLYDE MORRIS. *A Study of Perceptions and Expectations of Leadership Behavior of Principals of Texas Large Senior High Schools.* Doctor's thesis, University of Texas (Austin, Tex.), 1966. (*DA* 27:2025A)
8. BRYANT, GEORGE WENDELL. *Ideal Leader Behavior Descriptions of Appointed and Sociometrically Chosen Student Leaders.* Doctor's thesis, North Texas State University (Denton, Tex.), 1967. (*DA* 28:3497A)
9. BLACK, DELBERT OTIS. *Perceptions and Expectations of the Leadership Behavior of County Extension Directors in Oklahoma.* Doctor's thesis, Oklahoma State University (Stillwater, Okla.), 1969. (*DAI* 31:3800A)
10. STOGDILL, RALPH M., AND COADY, NICHOLAS P. "Preferences of Vocational Students for Different Styles of Supervisory Behavior." *Personnel Psychol* 23(3):309–12 au '70. * (*PA* 45:9117)

[1146]

★**Leader Behavior Description Questionnaire.** Supervisors; 1957; LBDQ; employee ratings of a supervisor; 2 scores: consideration, initiating structure; scores are based upon responses by 4 to 10 raters; 1 form (3 pages); manual (10 pages); $2 per 25 tests, cash orders postpaid; specimen set free; (10) minutes; original edition by John K. Hemphill and Alvin E. Coons; manual by Andrew W. Halpin; current edition by Personnel Research Board, Ohio State University; University Publications Sales, Ohio State University. *

REFERENCES

1. RUSH, CARL HARRISON, JR. *Group Dimensions of Aircrews.* Doctor's thesis, Ohio State University (Columbus, Ohio), 1953. (*DA* 19:1847)
2. HALPIN, ANDREW W. "The Leadership Behavior and Combat Performance of Airplane Commanders." *J Abn & Social Psychol* 49:19–22 Ja '54. * (*PA* 28:8211)
3. HALPIN, ANDREW W. "The Leader Behavior and Leadership Ideology of Educational Administrators and Aircraft Commanders." *Harvard Ed R* 25:18–32 w '55. * (*PA* 30:2646)
4. HALPIN, ANDREW W. "The Leadership Ideology of Aircraft Commanders." *J Appl Psychol* 39:82–4 Ap '55. * (*PA* 30:1740)
5. HEMPHILL, JOHN K. "Leadership Behavior Associated With the Administrative Reputation of College Departments." *J Ed Psychol* 46:385–401 N '55. * (*PA* 31:3837)
6. BENEVENTO, PHILIP. *Administrative Communication: A Study of Its Relationship to Administrative Leadership.* Doctor's thesis, Syracuse University (Syracuse, N.Y.), 1956. (*DA* 16:2357)
7. BASS, BERNARD M. 11, "Leadership Opinions and Related Characteristics of Salesmen and Sales Managers," pp. 134–9. In *Leader Behavior: Its Description and Measurement,* see *14*. *
8. HALPIN, ANDREW W. Chap. 4, "The Leader Behavior and Effectiveness of Aircraft Commanders," pp. 52–64. In *Leader Behavior: Its Description and Measurement,* see *14*. *
9. HALPIN, ANDREW W. Chap. 5, "The Observed Leader Behavior and Ideal Leader Behavior of Aircraft Commanders and School Superintendents," pp. 65–8. In *Leader Behavior: Its Description and Measurement,* see *14*. *
10. HEMPHILL, JOHN K. Chap. 7, "Leader Behavior Associated With the Administrative Reputations of College Departments," pp. 74–85. In *Leader Behavior: Its Description and Measurement,* see *14*. *
11. HEMPHILL, JOHN K., AND COONS, ALVIN E. Chap. 2, "Development of the Leader Behavior Description Questionnaire," pp. 6–38. In *Leader Behavior: Its Description and Measurement,* see *14*. *
12. RUSH, CARL H., JR. Chap. 6, "Leader Behavior and Group Characteristics," pp. 69–73. In *Leader Behavior: Its Description and Measurement,* see *14*. *
13. SEEMAN, MELVIN. Chap. 8, "A Comparison of General and Specific Leader Behavior Descriptions," pp. 86–102. In *Leader Behavior: Its Description and Measurement,* see *14*. *
14. STOGDILL, RALPH M., AND COONS, ALVIN E., EDITORS. *Leader Behavior: Its Description and Measurement.* Ohio State

University, Bureau of Business Research, Research Monograph No. 88. Columbus, Ohio: the Bureau, 1957. Pp. xv, 168. * (*PA* 32:1466)

15. BAILEY, BENJAMIN HASTING. *Personality Rigidity, Patterns of Operation, and Leadership Effectiveness of Secondary School Principals.* Doctor's thesis, University of Florida (Gainesville, Fla.), 1959. (*DA* 20:2650)

16. HARMES, HAROLD MYRON. *Personality Rigidity, Patterns of Operation, and Leadership Effectiveness of Elementary School Principals.* Doctor's thesis, University of Florida (Gainesville, Fla.), 1959. (*DA* 20:2657)

17. KEYS, SAMUEL ROBERT. *A Study of Expected and Described Leader Behavior of Principals of Senior High Schools in the State of Minnesota.* Doctor's thesis, University of Minnesota (Minneapolis, Minn.), 1959. (*DA* 20:4015)

18. CAMPBELL, ONA LEE. *The Relationships Between Eight Situational Factors and High and Low Scores on the Leadership Behavior Dimensions of Instructional Supervisors.* Doctor's thesis, North Texas State College (Denton, Tex.), 1961. (*DA* 22:786)

19. GREENFIELD, T. B., AND ANDREWS, J. H. M. "Teacher Leader Behavior and Its Relation to Effectiveness as Measured by Pupil Growth." *Alberta J Ed Res* 7:93–102 Mr '61. * (*PA* 36:3KM93G)

20. KEELER, BERNARD T. *Dimensions of Leader Behavior of Principals, Staff, Morale, and Productivity.* Doctor's thesis, University of Alberta (Edmonton, Alta., Canada), 1961.

21. NEWMAN, WILLIAM HENRY. *Factors Affecting Leadership.* Doctor's thesis, Stanford University (Stanford, Calif.), 1961. (*DA* 21:3329)

22. TAYLOR, MARVIN; CROOK, ROBERT; AND DROPKIN, STANLEY. "Assessing Emerging Leadership Behavior in Small Discussion Groups." *J Ed Psychol* 52:12–8 F '61. * (*PA* 36:2GF12T)

23. BARNHART, ALVIN ELBERT. *A Study of Teacher-Principal Perceptions of Superintendents in Selected School Districts.* Doctor's research study No. 1, Colorado State College (Greeley, Colo.), 1962. (*DA* 23:893)

24. CARSON, JOSEPH O'HARA, JR. *An Analysis of the Leader Behavior of Junior College Deans as Viewed by Student Leaders.* Doctor's thesis, Florida State University (Tallahassee, Fla.), 1962. (*DA* 23:1568)

25. CLAYE, CLIFTON M. "Leadership Behavior Among Negro School Principals." *J Negro Ed* 31:521–6 f '62. *

26. FEELEY, ARDELL LEE. *Administrative Leadership: A Study of Role Expectations and Perceptions in the Areas of Public Relations and Curriculum Development by Secondary School Principals and Staff Members.* Doctor's thesis, University of Pittsburgh (Pittsburgh, Pa.), 1962. (*DA* 23:1980)

27. LAW, LILLARD EUGENE. *The Identification of Informal Groups and Informal Group Leadership in Selected Schools in Ohio.* Doctor's thesis, Ohio State University (Columbus, Ohio), 1962. (*DA* 23:3207)

28. NEWPORT, GENE. "A Study of Attitudes and Leader Behavior." *Personnel Adm* 25:42–6 S–O '62. * (*PA* 38:5981)

29. ST. CLAIR, JAMES KENNETH. *An Evaluation of a Clinical Procedure for Predicting On-the-Job Administrative Behaviors of Elementary School Principals.* Doctor's thesis, University of Texas (Austin, Tex.), 1962. (*DA* 23:138)

30. WISCH, PAUL JOSEPH. *An Investigation of the Value Patterns and Perceptions Held by Superintendents, Principals, and Teachers in Selected School Districts.* Doctor's research study No. 1, Colorado State College (Greeley, Colo.), 1962. (*DA* 23:1259)

31. GREENFIELD, T. BARR. *Systems Analysis in Education: A Factor Analysis and Analysis of Variance of Pupil Achievement.* Doctor's thesis, University of Alberta (Edmonton, Alta., Canada), 1963.

32. HILLS, R. JEAN. "The Representative Function: Neglected Dimension of Leadership Behavior." *Adm Sci Q* 8:83–101 Je '63. *

33. KEELER, B. T., AND ANDREWS, J. H. M. "The Leader Behavior of Principals, Staff Morale and Productivity." *Alberta J Ed Res* 9:179–91 S '63. *

34. LUCKIE, WILLIAM RONALD. *Leader Behavior of Directors of Instruction.* Doctor's thesis, University of Southern Mississippi (Hattiesburg, Miss.), 1963. (*DA* 25:1690)

35. MATHEWS, JOHN EDWARD. *Leader Behavior of Elementary Principals and the Group Dimensions of Their Staffs.* Doctor's thesis, University of Pittsburgh (Pittsburgh, Pa.), 1963. (*DA* 25:2318)

36. PARSONS, GORDON ELLIOTT. *Assessment and Evaluation of the Administrative Behavior of Elementary School Administrators.* Doctor's thesis, University of Arizona (Tucson, Ariz.). 1963. (*DA* 25:245)

37. WEBER, ROBERT GENE. *Leadership Characteristics of Public School Business Administrators.* Doctor's research study No. 1, Colorado State College (Greeley, Colo.), 1963. (*DA* 25:259)

38. ANDERSON, RUTH M. "Activity Preferences and Leadership Behavior of Head Nurses." *Nursing Res* 13:239–42, 333–7 su, f '64. *

39. BOWMAN, HERMAN JAMES. *Perceived Leader Behavior Patterns and Their Relationships to Self-Perceived Variables-Responsibility, Authority and Delegation.* Doctor's thesis, State

University of New York (Buffalo, N.Y.), 1964. (*DA* 25:3340)

40. CARSON, J. O., JR., AND SCHULTZ, RAYMOND E. "A Comparative Analysis of the Junior College Dean's Leadership Behavior." *J Exp Ed* 32:355–62 su '64. * (*PA* 39:6000)

41. CROFT, JOHN CALVIN. *Open and Closed Mindedness and Perceptions of Leader Behavior.* Doctor's thesis, Pennsylvania State University (University Park, Penn.), 1964. (*DA* 25:4491)

42. FOGARTY, BRYCE MARTIN. *Characteristics of Superintendents of Schools and Centralization-Decentralization of Decision-Making.* Doctor's thesis, University of Wisconsin (Madison, Wis.), 1964. (*DA* 25:3928)

43. HATCH, ROBERT HERMAN. *A Study of the Leadership Ability of Negro High School Principals.* Doctor's research study No. 1, Colorado State College (Greeley, Colo.), 1964. (*DA* 25:6334)

44. OAKLANDER, HAROLD, AND FLEISHMAN, EDWIN A. "Patterns of Leadership Related to Organizational Stress in Hospital Settings." *Adm Sci Q* 8:520–32 Mr '64. *

45. SMITH, LOUIS M. "Classroom Social Systems and Pupil Personality." *Psychol Sch* 1:118–29 Ap '64. *

46. SPENCER, RALPH LEE. *The Leadership Behavior of Elementary-School Principals.* Doctor's thesis, Cornell University (Ithaca, N.Y.), 1964. (*DA* 25:1702)

47. WATTS, CHARLES B. *Problem-Attack Behavior and Its Relationship to Leadership Behavior and Effectiveness Among Selected High School Principals.* Doctor's thesis, University of Texas (Austin, Tex.), 1964. (*DA* 25:5080)

48. WELLS, WELDON STANLEY. *A Study of Personality Traits, Situational Factors, and Leadership Actions of Selected School Maintenance Supervisors.* Doctor's thesis, North Texas State University (Denton, Tex.), 1964. (*DA* 25:975)

49. COOK, EDWARD VANCE. *Leadership Behavior of Elementary School Principals and the Organizational Climate of the Schools Which They Administer.* Doctor's thesis, Rutgers—The State University (New Brunswick, N.J.), 1965. (*DA* 27:345A)

50. ANDERSON, LYNN R. "Leader Behavior, Member Attitudes, and Task Performance of Intercultural Discussion Groups." *J Social Psychol* 69:305–19 Ag '66. * (*PA* 40:12282)

51. BAILEY, HIGGINS DEE. *An Exploratory Study of Selected Components and Processes in Educational Organizations.* Doctor's thesis, University of California (Berkeley, Calif.), 1966. (*DA* 28:69A)

52. GOTT, CLYDE MORRIS. *A Study of Perceptions and Expectations of Leadership Behavior of Principals of Texas Large Senior High Schools.* Doctor's thesis, University of Texas (Austin, Tex.), 1966. (*DA* 27:2025A)

53. KORMAN, ABRAHAM K. "'Consideration,' 'Initiating Structure,' and Organizational Criteria—A Review." *Personnel Psychol* 19:349–61 w '66. * (*PA* 41:5147)

54. STROMBERG, ROBERT PHILIP. *Value Orientation and Leadership Behavior of School Principals.* Doctor's thesis, Pennsylvania State University (University Park, Pa.), 1966. (*DA* 27:2811A)

55. VERBEKE, MAURICE GEORGE. *The Junior College Academic Dean's Leadership Behavior as Viewed by Superiors and Faculty.* Doctor's thesis, Pennsylvania State University (University Park, Pa.), 1966. (*DA* 28:926A)

56. ANDERSON, JAMES WENDELL. *The Effect of Simulated Experiences Upon the Leadership Behavior of Elementary School Administrators.* Doctor's thesis, University of Minnesota (Minneapolis, Minn.), 1967. (*DA* 28:4840A)

57. CARTER, CECIL E., JR. *The Relation of Leader Behavior Dimensions and Group Characteristics to County Extension Advisory Committee Performance.* Doctor's thesis, Ohio State University (Columbus, Ohio), 1967. (*DA* 28:3450A)

58. GORDON, BILLY KENNETH. *Dogmatism, Philosophy, and Leader Behavior of School Administrators.* Doctor's thesis, University of Kentucky (Lexington, Ky.), 1967. (*DAI* 31:2051A)

59. HAYS, BOB BURK. *Student Teacher Expectations of the Leadership Role of the Principal.* Doctor's thesis, North Texas State University (Denton, Tex.), 1967. (*DA* 28:3557A)

60. HOLLOMAN, CHARLES R. "The Perceived Leadership Role of Military and Civilian Supervisors in a Military Setting." *Personnel Psychol* 20:199–210 su '67. * (*PA* 41:15905)

61. HUNT, JAMES EDMUND. *Expectations and Perceptions of the Leadership Behavior of Elementary School Principals.* Doctor's thesis, St. John's University (Jamaica, N.Y.), 1967. (*DA* 28:4852A)

62. INCARDONA, JOSEPH S. *Personal and Environmental Influences on School Principals' Pro-School and Pro-Teacher Decisions in Selected Conflict Situations.* Doctor's thesis, State University of New York (Buffalo, N.Y.), 1967. (*DA* 28:902A)

63. McDONALD, CLARENCE OTTO, JR. *Leader Behavior Dimensions of Central Office Personnel.* Doctor's thesis, University of Missouri (Columbia, Mo.), 1967. (*DA* 29:99A)

64. MANNHEIM, BILHA F.; RIM, YESHAYAHU; AND GRINBERG, GEULAH. "Instrumental Status of Supervisors as Related to Workers' Perceptions and Expectation." *Hum Relations* 20:387–97 N '67. * (*PA* 42:9530)

65. MOLONEY, MARY ANNETTA. *Leadership Behavior of Deans in University Schools of Nursing.* Doctor's thesis, Catholic University of America (Washington, D.C.), 1967. (*DA* 28:2036A)

66. NALDER, WALLACE KENLEY. *The Public High School Football Coach: A Study of Discrepancy in Perception of Behavior*

by Alter Groups. Doctor's thesis, University of Utah (Salt Lake City, Utah), 1967. (*DA* 28:2542A)

67. STOGDILL, RALPH M. "The Structure of Organization Behavior." *Multiv Behav Res* 2:47–61 Ja '67. * (*PA* 41:9500)

68. TRIMBLE, CLIFFORD. *Teachers' Conceptions of Leadership Behavior of Principals as Related to Principal's Perception of His Involvement in the Decision-Making Process.* Doctor's thesis, Purdue University (Lafayette, Ind.), 1967. (*DA* 28:4432A)

69. WRAY, JAMES FRANCIS. *Closed-Mindedness, Leader Behavior, and the Organizational Climate of the Christian Brothers Schools in the Midwest.* Doctor's thesis, University of Wisconsin (Madison, Wis.), 1967. (*DA* 28:2971A)

70. EVANS, MARTIN GRIFFITH. *The Effects of Supervisory Behavior Upon Worker Perception of Their Path-Goal Relationships.* Doctor's thesis, Yale University (New Haven, Conn.), 1968. (*DA* 29:4419B)

71. FLOCCO, EDWARD CARL. *An Examination of the Leader Behavior of School Business Administrators.* Doctor's thesis, New York University (New York, N.Y.), 1968. (*DAI* 30:84A)

72. GREENFIELD, T. B. "Research on the Behaviour of Educational Leaders: Critique of a Tradition." *Alberta J Ed Res* 14:55–76 Mr '68. * (*PA* 44:4210)

73. HEROD, JOYZELLE. *Characteristics of Leadership in an International Fraternity for Women and Influence on the Leaders' Attitudes of a Group Centered Leader Training Experience.* Doctor's thesis, University of Texas (Austin, Tex.), 1968. (*DA* 29:3461A)

74. HOUSE, ROBERT J., AND FILLEY, ALAN C. "Leadership Style, Hierarchical Influence and the Satisfaction of Subordinate Role Expectations." Abstract. *Proc 76th Ann Conv Am Psychol Assn* 3:557–8 '68. *

75. NEALY, STANLEY M., AND BLOOD, MILTON R. "Leadership Performance of Nursing Supervisors at Two Organizational Levels." *J Appl Psychol* 52:414–22 O '68. * (*PA* 42:19526)

76. NIEMEYER, KENNETH PAUL. *The Relationship of Selected Factors to the Upward Mobility of Male Elementary School Teachers.* Doctor's thesis, University of Wisconsin (Madison, Wis.), 1968. (*DAI* 30:104A)

77. PACINELLI, RALPH NICHOLAS. *Rehabilitation Counselor Job Satisfaction as It Relates to Perceived Leadership Behavior and Selected Background Factors.* Doctor's thesis, Pennsylvania State University (University Park, Pa.), 1968. (*DA* 29:1863B)

78. PETERSON, GARY DON. *Personality Authoritarianism and the Perceived Leadership Behavior of North Dakota School Administrators.* Doctor's thesis, University of North Dakota (Grand Fork, N.D.), 1968. (*DA* 29:3812A)

79. ROBINSON, HERBERT WILLIAM. *A Study of the Relationship Between Leader Behavior of Secondary School Principals in Georgia and Certain Selected Variables.* Doctor's thesis, University of Georgia (Athens, Ga.), 1968. (*DA* 29:4248A)

80. ROUSEY, NORMAN SCHUYLER. *An Investigation of the Relationship Between Decision Style and Leadership Behavior of the Chief School Official in the Southeastern Ohio, Kentucky and West Virginia School Study Council.* Doctor's thesis, Ohio University (Athens, Ohio), 1968. (*DAI* 30:113A)

81. SCHNEIDER, FRANK AUGUST, SR. *A Study of the Leadership Role of Directors of Public Libraries as Reported by Selected Public Library Directors.* Doctor's thesis, Arizona State University (Tempe, Ariz.), 1968. (*DA* 29:1552A)

82. WOODALL, MICHAEL VANCE. *An Investigation of the Relationship Between Certain Aspects of Experience and Leaders' Behavior.* Doctor's thesis, University of South Carolina (Columbia, S.C.), 1968. (*DA* 29:4263A)

83. BLACK, DELBERT OTIS. *Perceptions and Expectations of the Leadership Behavior of County Extension Directors in Oklahoma.* Doctor's thesis, Oklahoma State University (Stillwater, Okla.), 1969. (*DAI* 31:3800A)

84. CARLSON, JOHN WALLACE. *The Effects of an Iota In-Service Education Program on Teachers' Perceptions of Administrative Behavior.* Doctor's thesis, Arizona State University (Tempe, Ariz.), 1969. (*DAI* 30:2280A)

85. CROGHAN, JOHN HENRY. *A Study of the Relationships Between the Perceived Leadership Behavior of Elementary Principals and Informal Group Dimensions and Composition in Elementary Schools.* Doctor's thesis, Syracuse University (Syracuse, N.Y.), 1969. (*DAI* 30:3220A)

86. GARNER, WARREN KENNETH. *Leader Behavior Following Executive Succession in Selected California School Districts.* Doctor's thesis, Claremont Graduate School (Claremont, Calif.), 1969. (*DAI* 30:1358A)

87. GLOGAU, LILLIAN F. *A Study of the Relationship Between the Leadership Style of the Elementary School Principal and the Introduction of the Nongraded Organization.* Doctor's thesis, New York University (New York, N.Y.), 1969. (*DAI* 31:1535A)

88. HOBBS, PHILIP JESSE. *Perception of the Community Power Structure by the Public School Administrator as Related to His Effectiveness.* Doctor's thesis, Purdue University (Lafayette, Ind.), 1969. (*DAI* 30:3682A)

89. HUTTON, DUANE EDWARD. *A Study of the Relationship Among the Elementary Principal's Organizational Orientation and Two Leadership Dimensions.* Doctor's thesis, Syracuse University (Syracuse, N.Y.), 1969. (*DAI* 30:5197A)

90. KELADA, FOUAD S. *Comparative Study of Leadership Behavior of Selected High School Principals, Church Ministers and Business Executives in Indiana.* Doctor's thesis, Indiana University (Bloomington, Ind.), 1969. (*DAI* 30:3685A)

91. KLINE, CHARLES EWERT. *Leader Behavior, Curricular Implementation and Curricular Change.* Doctor's thesis, University of Wisconsin (Madison, Wis.), 1969. (*DAI* 30:957A)

92. KOKOVICH, STEVE, JR. *A Study of the Relationship Between Perceptions of Leader Behavior and Certain Dimensions of Teacher Morale.* Doctor's thesis, Ohio University (Athens, Ohio), 1969. (*DAI* 31:969A)

93. LINDEMUTH, MARVIN HERALD. *An Analysis of the Leader Behavior of Academic Deans as Related to the Campus Climate in Selected Colleges.* Doctor's thesis, University of Michigan (Ann Arbor, Mich.), 1969. (*DAI* 30:2765A)

94. MITCHELL, LEONARD LOUIS, JR. *The Expressed Perceptions and Expectations of Selected Prospective Secondary School Teachers as They View the Leader Behavior of the Secondary School Principal.* Doctor's thesis, Michigan State University (East Lansing, Mich.), 1969. (*DAI* 30:5201A)

95. MURPHY, MARCUS DEAN. *Some Dimensions of Leadership Behavior of School Superintendents in Selected Texas School Districts.* Doctor's thesis, North Texas State University (Denton, Tex.), 1969. (*DAI* 30:5203A)

96. PACINELLI, RALPH N., AND BRITTON, JEAN O. "Some Correlates of Rehabilitation Counselor Job Satisfaction." *Rehabil Counsel B* 12(4):212–20 Je '69. *

97. PATTERSON, JAMES WHITE. *An Exploratory Study of Selected Supervisory Interviews at the Secondary School Level.* Doctor's thesis, University of Texas (Austin, Tex.), 1969. (*DAI* 30:1374A)

98. SCHROEDER, GLENN BURNETT. *Leadership Behavior of Department Chairmen in Selected State Institutions of Higher Education.* Doctor's thesis, University of New Mexico (Albuquerque, N.M.), 1969. (*DAI* 30:5209A)

99. SOMMERS, NORMAN LOUIS. *Factors Influencing Teacher Morale in Selected Secondary Schools.* Doctor's thesis, Kent State University (Kent, Ohio), 1969. (*DAI* 31:986A)

100. STOGDILL, RALPH M. "Validity of Leader Behavior Descriptions." *Personnel Psychol* 22(2):153–8 su '69. * (*PA* 44:7419)

101. BARDEN, JOHN W. *Leader Behavior and Organizational Climate: Their Relation to School Change Movements.* Doctor's thesis, University of North Dakota (Grand Forks, N.D.), 1970. (*DAI* 31:2095A)

102. GLASGOW, ANN DUNCAN. *The Self-Perceptions of Leadership Behavior of the Black Secondary School Principal.* Doctor's thesis, Catholic University of America (Washington, D.C.), 1970. (*DAI* 31:2050A)

103. HILTENBRAND, ROBERT EDWIN. *The Relationship Between the Open and Closed Mindedness of the Chief School Officer and the Leadership Behavior Demonstrated by the Elementary Principal to His Faculty.* Doctor's thesis, State University of New York (Albany, N.Y.), 1970. (*DAI* 31:2641A)

104. HOWARD, JAMES MERLE. *The Relationship of Organizational and Leader Factors to Communication Effectiveness in Illinois Public Junior Colleges.* Doctor's thesis, Illinois State University (Normal, Ill.), 1970. (*DAI* 31:585A)

105. MITCHELL, TERENCE R. "The Construct Validity of Three Dimensions of Leadership Research." *J Social Psychol* 80(1):89–94 F '70. *

106. MOULLETTE, JOHN BRINKLEY. *Selected Leadership Dimensions of Management Personnel in Vocational Education, General Education, Industry, and the Military.* Doctor's thesis, Rutgers—The State University (New Brunswick, N.J.), 1970. (*DAI* 31:3224A)

107. PEIRCE, JERRY ROGER. *Effects of Selected Organizational Variables on the Behavioral Style of the Industrial Supervisor.* Doctor's thesis, University of Michigan (Ann Arbor, Mich.), 1970. (*DAI* 31:3047B)

108. YUKL, GARY. "Leader LPC Scores: Attitude Dimensions and Behavioral Correlates." *J Social Psychol* 80(2):207–12 Ap '70. * (*PA* 44:14539)

[1147]

★**Leader Behavior Description Questionnaire, Form 12.** Supervisors; 1957–63; LBDQ-12; revision of still-in-print *Leader Behavior Description Questionnaire* with 10 additional scores; for research use only; employee ratings of a supervisor; 12 scores: representation, demand reconciliation, tolerance of uncertainty, persuasiveness, initiation of structure, tolerance of freedom, role assumption, consideration, production emphasis, predictive accuracy, integration, superior orientation; scores are based upon responses of 4 to 10 raters; 1 form ('62, 6 pages); manual ('63, 15 pages); record sheet ('63, 1 page); no norms; $4 per 25 tests; cash orders postpaid; specimen set free; (20) minutes; original edition by John K. Hemphill and Alvin E. Coons; manual by Ralph M. Stogdill;

current edition by Bureau of Business Research, Ohio State University; University Publication Sales, Ohio State University. *

REFERENCES

1. CHRISTNER, CHARLOTTE A., AND HEMPHILL, JOHN K. "Leader Behavior of B-29 Commanders and Changes in Crew Members' Attitudes Toward the Crew." *Sociometry* 18:82–7 F '55. *

2. STOGDILL, RALPH M., AND SHARTLE, CARROLL L. Chap. 7, "Leader Behavior Descriptions," pp. 54–63. In their *Methods in the Study of Administrative Leadership.* Ohio State University, Bureau of Business Research, Research Monograph No. 80. Columbus, Ohio: the Bureau, 1955. Pp. xv, 77. *

3. CAMPBELL, DONALD T. Chap. 9, "Leader Behavior Description," pp. 54–64. In his *Leadership and Its Effects Upon the Group.* Ohio State University, Bureau of Business Research Monograph No. 83. Columbus, Ohio: the Bureau, 1956. Pp. xii, 92. *

4. STOGDILL, RALPH M.; SCOTT, ELLIS L.; AND JAYNES, WILLIAM E. *Leadership and Role Expectations.* Ohio State University, Bureau of Business Research Monograph No. 86. Columbus, Ohio: the Bureau, 1956. Pp. xvi, 168. *

5. STOGDILL, RALPH M.; WHERRY, ROBERT J.; AND JAYNES, WILLIAM E. Chap. 4, "A Factorial Study of Administrative Performance," pp. 39–104. In *Patterns of Administrative Performance.* By Ralph M. Stogdill, Carroll L. Shartle, and Associates. Ohio State University, Bureau of Business Research Monograph No. 81. Columbus, Ohio: the Bureau, 1956. Pp. xx, 108. *

6. HALPIN, ANDREW W., AND WINER, B. JAMES. Chap. 3, "A Factorial Study of the Leader Behavior Descriptions," pp. 39–51. In *Leader Behavior: Its Description and Measurement,* see 7. *

7. STOGDILL, RALPH M., AND COONS, ALVIN E., EDITORS. *Leader Behavior: Its Description and Measurement.* Ohio State University, Bureau of Business Research, Research Monograph No. 88. Columbus, Ohio: the Bureau, 1957. Pp. xv, 168. * (*PA* 32:1466)

8. STOGDILL, RALPH M.; SCOTT, ELLIS L.; AND JAYNES, WILLIAM E. Chap. 12, "A Factorial Study of Very Short Scales," pp. 140–9. In *Leader Behavior: Its Description and Measurement,* see 7. *

9. MARDER, EUGENE. *Leader Behavior as Perceived by Subordinates as a Function of Organizational Level.* Master's thesis, Ohio State University (Columbus, Ohio), 1960.

10. DAY, DAVID ROBERT. *Basic Dimensions of Leadership in a Selected Industrial Organization.* Doctor's thesis, Ohio State University (Columbus, Ohio), 1961. (*DA* 22:3760)

11. SINDWANI, KHAIRATI LALL. *Leader Behavior in Social Work Administration.* Doctor's thesis, Ohio State University (Columbus, Ohio), 1962. (*DA* 23:3017)

12. STOGDILL, RALPH M.; GOODE, OMAR S.; AND DAY, DAVID R. "New Leader Behavior Description Subscales." *J Psychol* 54:259–69 O '62. * (*PA* 37:6626)

13. HASTINGS, ROBERT EDWARD. *Leadership in University Research Teams.* Doctor's thesis, Ohio State University (Columbus, Ohio), 1963. (*DA* 24:2723)

14. STOGDILL, RALPH M.; GOODE, OMAR S.; AND DAY, DAVID R. "The Leader Behavior of Corporation Presidents." *Personnel Psychol* 16:127–32 su '63. *

15. STOGDILL, RALPH M.; GOODE, OMAR S.; AND DAY, DAVID R. "The Leader Behavior of United States Senators." *J Psychol* 56:3–8 Jl '63. * (*PA* 38:4206)

16. ASHBROOK, JAMES BARBOUR. *Protestant Ministerial Attributes and Their Implications for Church Organization.* Doctor's thesis, Ohio State University (Columbus, Ohio), 1964. (*DA* 25:7070)

17. ANDREWS, JOHN H. M. "School Organizational Climate: Some Validity Studies." *Can Ed & Res Dig* 5:317–34 D '65. *

18. JACOBS, JAN WAYNE. *Leadership, Size, and Wealth as Related to Curricular Innovations in the Junior High School.* Doctor's thesis, University of Michigan (Ann Arbor, Mich.), 1965. (*DA* 27:354A)

19. ANDERSON, BARRY DOUGLAS. *Leader Behavior Styles of Alberta School Principals.* Master's thesis, University of Calgary (Calgary, Alta., Canada), 1966.

20. BEER, MICHAEL. *Leadership, Employee Needs, and Motivation.* Ohio State University, Bureau of Business Research Monograph No. 129. Columbus, Ohio: the Bureau, 1966. Pp. xii, 100. *

21. BLATT, CALVIN ALFRED. *The Relationships Between In-Service Education Activities of Principals and Teacher Perceptions of Principals' Leader Behavior.* Doctor's thesis, University of Maryland (College Park, Md.), 1966. (*DA* 27:3649A)

22. LARSEN, JACK LYLE. *A Study of the Decision-Making Process in the High School and the Leader-Behavior Role of the Principal in the Process.* Doctor's thesis, University of Michigan (Ann Arbor, Mich.), 1966. (*DA* 27:3265A)

23. MORSINK, HELEN MURIEL. *A Comparative Study of the Leader Behavior of Men and Women Secondary School Principals.* Doctor's thesis, University of Michigan (Ann Arbor, Mich.), 1966. (*DA* 27:2793A)

24. PEAK, LLOYD NICHOLS. *The Internship in Educational Administration and Interpersonal Competency.* Doctor's thesis, University of Rochester (Rochester, N.Y.), 1966. (*DA* 27:1230A)

25. ASHBROOK, JAMES B. "Ministerial Leadership in Church Organization." Discussion by James D. Glasse. *Ministry Studies* 1:5–36 My '67. *

26. BROWN, ALLEN F. "Reactions to Leadership." *Ed Adm Q* 3:62–73 w '67. *

27. KELLEY, WILBUR ROBERT, JR. *The Relationship Between Cognitive Complexity and Leadership Style in School Superintendents.* Doctor's thesis, State University of New York (Albany, N.Y.), 1967. (*DA* 28:4910A)

28. NEARY, JOHN RUPERT. *Differential Perception of the Leader Behavior of Secondary School Principals.* Doctor's thesis, University of Maryland (College Park, Md.), 1967. (*DA* 28:3429A)

29. ROOKER, JAMES LEROY. *The Relationship of Need Achievement and Need Affiliation to Leader Behavior.* Doctor's thesis, University of Wisconsin (Madison, Wis.), 1967. (*DA* 28:4426A)

30. SCHMIDT, WERNER G. *The Relationship Between Certain Aspects of Teacher Behavior and Organizational Climate.* Master's thesis, University of Alberta (Edmonton, Alta., Canada), 1967.

31. GARRISON, JOE MAC. *The Leader Behavior of Oklahoma Secondary School Principals.* Doctor's thesis, University of Oklahoma (Norman, Okla.), 1968. (*DA* 29:88A)

32. GREENFIELD, T. B. "Research on the Behaviour of Educational Leaders: Critique of a Tradition." *Alberta J Ed Res* 14:55–76 Mr '68. * (*PA* 44:4210)

33. HARRIS, EVANS HOWELL. *Leader Behavior and Its Relationship to Compensatory Educational Programs.* Doctor's thesis, University of Oklahoma (Norman, Okla.), 1968. (*DA* 29:1709A)

34. MANSOUR, JOSEPH MIKAEL. *Leadership Behavior and Principal-Teacher Interpersonal Relations.* Doctor's thesis, University of Pittsburgh (Pittsburgh, Pa.), 1968. (*DAI* 30:526A)

35. SCHREINER, JERRY OWEN. *An Exploratory Investigation of Leader Behavior of Full-Time and Part-Time Elementary School Principals.* Doctor's thesis, Oklahoma State University (Stillwater, Okla.), 1968. (*DAI* 30:1381A)

36. STREUFERT, SIEGFRIED; STREUFERT, SUSAN C.; AND CASTORE, CARL H. "Leadership in Negotiations and the Complexity of Conceptual Structure." *J Appl Psychol* 52:218–23 Je '68. * (*PA* 42:12051)

37. TARALLO, JOSEPH JOHN. *The Relationships Between Pre-Principalship Activities of Secondary Principals and Teacher Perceptions of Principals' Leadership Behavior.* Doctor's thesis, University of Maryland (College Park, Md.), 1968. (*DA* 29:2500A)

38. ASH, WILLIAM EDWARD. *A Comparative Study of Leadership Behavior of Secondary School Principals Trained in the National Association of Secondary School Principals' Administrative Internship Project and Secondary School Principals Trained by Non-Internship Methods.* Doctor's thesis, Purdue University (Lafayette, Ind.), 1969. (*DAI* 30:4169A)

39. BOSTIC, CARROLL RAY. *The Effects of Perceived Leadership Climate in the State Rehabilitation Agency.* Doctor's thesis, University of Missouri (Columbia, Mo.), 1969. (*DAI* 31:141A)

40. GOOD, CECIL GRANVILLE. *A Study of the Internship as a Dimension of a Training Program for Urban Principals.* Doctor's thesis, University of Michigan (Ann Arbor, Mich.), 1969. (*DAI* 31:959A)

41. GRIMSLEY, WILLIAM GERALD. *The Relationship Between Creativity and Leader Behavior of School Superintendents.* Doctor's thesis, University of Missouri (Columbia, Mo.), 1969. (*DAI* 30:5193A)

42. HOLLOWAY, JOE EARL. *An Analysis of the Leadership Behavior of Selected High School Principals in Alabama, Louisiana, and Mississippi.* Doctor's thesis, University of Southern Mississippi (Hattiesburg, Miss.), 1969. (*DAI* 30:4722A)

43. OLAFSON, GORDON ALBERT ALEXANDER. *Leader Behavior of Junior College and University Physical Education Administrators.* Doctor's thesis, University of Illinois (Urbana, Ill.), 1969. (*DAI* 31:636A)

44. IGNATOVICH, FREDERICK RICHARD. *Types and Effects of Elementary School Principal-Leaders: A Q-Factor Analysis.* Doctor's thesis, University of Iowa (Iowa City, Iowa), 1970. (*DAI* 31:2644A)

45. PARKS, DAVID JOHN. *A Study of Relationships Between Interpersonal Relations Orientations and Leader Behaviors of Elementary Principals.* Doctor's thesis, Syracuse University (Syracuse, N.Y.), 1970. (*DAI* 31:2657A)

46. RAWLINGS, JOSEPH STANLEY. *A Comparative Study of the Self-Perceived Leadership Behavior of Public School Superintendents and Chamber of Commerce Executives.* Doctor's thesis, Michigan State University (East Lansing, Mich.), 1970. (*DAI* 31:3837A)

47. SARIS, RONALD JOHN. *The Development of a 13th Subscale to the Leader Behavior Description Questionnaire-Form XII Entitled: "Responsibility Deference."* Doctor's thesis, University of Idaho (Moscow, Idaho), 1970. (*DAI* 31:3236A)

Leader Behavior Description Questionnaire, Form 12

48. WALL, CHARLES CASWELL. *Perceived Leader Behavior of the Elementary School Principal as Related to Educational Goal Attainment.* Doctor's thesis, University of California (Los Angeles, Calif.), 1970. (*DAI* 31:3851A)

[1148]

★**Leadership Evaluation and Development Scale.** Prospective supervisors; 1964–65; LEADS; 1 form; 2 parts: casebook ('64, 11 pages), question booklet ('64, 8 pages); preliminary manual ('65, 4 pages, mimeographed); $12.50 per kit of 2 casebooks, 25 question booklets, scoring stencil, and manual; 50¢ per casebook; $17.50 per 50 question booklets; $2 per specimen set; postage extra; [40–50] minutes; Harley W. Mowry (question booklet and casebook, from materials prepared by the Armstrong Cork Company); Psychological Services, Inc. *

REFERENCE

1. TENOPYR, MARY L. "The Comparative Validity of Selected Leadership Scales Relative to Success in Production Management." *Personnel Psychol* 22(1):77–85 sp '69. * (PA 43:14924)

CECIL A. GIBB, *Professor of Psychology, Australian National University, Canberra City, Australia.*

The identification of men with "leadership ability" has been an aim and ambition of men throughout recorded history and, no doubt, before. Unfortunately, men of affairs have acquired faith in a great variety of devices, from measuring height or head shape to consulting horoscopes. Psychological research has never been able to identify or assess leadership ability. Mowry's scale is almost certainly just another forlorn chase in this elusive hunt. There is no evidence available to this reviewer that "by using the LEADS score in combination with everything else known about an employee, better promotion decisions can be made." Indeed, Tenopyr's paper,[1] though it does not directly compare the multiple correlations for all of her variables (temperament, intellectual and biographical) less LEADS with those obtainable with LEADS, leaves one with a pretty strong conviction that LEADS makes little or no significant contribution. In her 1969 paper, however, the evidence for LEADS is a little more positive (*1*). Here the criterion for 113 male production managers is salary corrected for age and seniority. LEADS correlates .36 with this criterion, while Verbal Comprehension shows .29 and the *Leadership Opinion Questionnaire* scores for Structure and Consideration produce correlations effectively zero. As Tenopyr points out, "The multiple regression analysis involving all four predictors and employing corrected salary as a criterion resulted

1 TENOPYR, MARY L. "Characteristics of Men Successful in the Labor-Relations Field." An unpublished paper presented at a meeting of the American Psychological Association, New York, September 1966. Pp. 13. *

in an R of .39 (p < .01). This is not appreciably higher than the validity of .36 for LEADS alone." These data are identical with those in the manual, authorship of which is not acknowledged.

LEADS consists of eight human relations cases, each followed by several multiple choice questions, to give 44 questions in all. There is one "right," or scoring, answer to each question. According to the manual and to Tenopyr's 1969 paper, the scale derives from earlier work by Mowry. The cases were selected and edited from a larger set which had proved successful as bases for discussion in training for human relations in supervision. The 44 questions were chosen on the basis of validity studies in which supervisors were rated by their immediate supervisors on the basis of overall success and ability to handle people. These are really the only clues to the basic intentions of the test. Tenopyr's 1966 paper suggests that LEADS measures "the ability to recognize subtler aspects of interpersonal situations in organization settings." Given the barest suggestion of human relations orientation, the subtlety is certainly open to question.

The manual claims a split-half reliability of .81. This again appears to be derived from Tenopyr's work with 113 production managers.

While the comments made above undoubtedly mean that this is not a scale which could be applied with confidence and honesty in a selection or promotion situation, and while this reviewer will not predict that further research would remove its shortcomings, LEADS may have some legitimate uses.

The cases are not bad ones, they do present real problems, the questions sometimes pose real and difficult choices. Used as a discussion starter in training for human relations, the scale may prove very successful. This reviewer would guess that such relevance would, however, be restricted to introductory human relations courses. With any degree of human relations sophistication, management personnel could be expected to identify the "right" answers here without necessarily giving any valid indication that in a like situation they would actually behave that way.

[1149]

***Leadership Opinion Questionnaire.** Supervisors and prospective supervisors; 1960–69; LOQ; 2 scores: consideration, structure; 1 form ('60, 4 pages, self-marking); manual ('69, 15 pages); $7.65 per 25 tests; $1.25 per specimen set; postage extra; (15–20) minutes; Edwin A. Fleishman; Science Research Associates, Inc. *

REFERENCES

1–6. See 6:1190.

7. HARRIS, EDWIN F., AND FLEISHMAN, EDWIN A. "Human Relations Training and the Stability of Leadership Patterns." *J Appl Psychol* 39:20–5 F '55. * (*PA* 30:1741)

8. BASS, BERNARD M. "Leadership Opinions as Forecasts of Supervisory Success." *J Appl Psychol* 40:345–6 O '56. * (*PA* 31:8981)

9. PARKER, TREADWAY CHISHOLM. *Some Relationships Among Measures of Supervisory Behavior, Group Behavior and Situational Characteristics in Industrial Work Groups.* Doctor's thesis, New York University (New York, N.Y.), 1962. (*DA* 23:2235)

10. KERNAN, JOHN PAUL. *Laboratory Human Relations Training—Its Effect on the "Personality" of Supervisory Engineers.* Doctor's thesis, New York University (New York, N.Y.), 1963. (*DA* 25:665)

11. LITZINGER, WILLIAM DAVID. *Entrepreneurial Prototype in Bank Management: A Comparative Study of Branch Bank Managers.* Doctor's thesis, University of Southern California (Los Angeles, Calif.), 1963. (*DA* 24:127)

12. PARKER, TREADWAY C. "Relationships Among Measures of Supervisory Behavior, Group Behavior, and Situational Characteristics." *Personnel Psychol* 16:319–34 w '63. * (*PA* 38:9380)

13. AYERS, A. W. "Effect of Knowledge of Results on Supervisors' Post-Training Test Scores." *Personnel Psychol* 17:189–92 su '64. * (*PA* 39:6017)

14. CARRON, THEODORE J. "Human Relations Training and Attitude Change: A Vector Analysis." *Personnel Psychol* 17:403–24 w '64. * (*PA* 39:10912)

15. HAY, JOHN EARL. *The Relationship of Certain Personality Variables to Managerial Level and Job Performance Among Engineering Managers.* Doctor's thesis, Temple University (Philadelphia, Pa.), 1964. (*DA* 25:3973)

16. OAKLANDER, HAROLD, AND FLEISHMAN, EDWIN A. "Patterns of Leadership Related to Organizational Stress in Hospital Settings." *Adm Sci Q* 8:520–32 Mr '64. *

17. SPITZER, MORTON EDWARD, AND MCNAMARA, WALTER J. "A Managerial Selection Study." *Personnel Psychol* 17:19–40 sp '64. * (*PA* 39:2945)

18. LITZINGER, WILLIAM D. "Interpersonal Values and Leadership Attitudes of Branch Bank Managers." *Personnel Psychol* 18:193–8 su '65. * (*PA* 39:16587)

19. RIM, Y. "Leadership Attitudes and Decisions Involving Risk." *Personnel Psychol* 18:423–30 w '65. * (*PA* 40:4660)

20. BIGGS, DONALD A.; HUNERYAGER, S. G.; AND DELANEY, JAMES J. "Leadership Behavior: Interpersonal Needs and Effective Supervisory Training." *Personnel Psychol* 19:311–20 au '66. * (*PA* 41:872)

21. CAPELLE, MACON HARSHAW. *Concurrent Validation of the Leadership Opinion Questionnaire for College Student Leadership.* Doctor's thesis, University of Maryland (College Park, Md.), 1966. (*DA* 27:3607A)

22. GRUENFELD, LEOPOLD W., AND WEISSENBERG, PETER. "Supervisory Characteristics and Attitudes Toward Performance Appraisals." *Personnel Psychol* 19:143–51 su '66. * (*PA* 40:11561)

23. KORMAN, ABRAHAM K. " 'Consideration,' 'Initiating Structure,' and Organizational Criteria—A Review." *Personnel Psychol* 19:349–61 w '66. * (*PA* 41:5147)

24. MCCLUNG, JAMES ALLEN. *Dynamics of Interaction Patterns Among Industrial Foremen.* Doctor's thesis, Michigan State University (East Lansing, Mich.), 1966. (*DA* 27:1449A)

25. PENFIELD, ROBERT VERDON. *The Psychological Characteristics of Effective First-Line Managers.* Doctor's thesis, Cornell University (Ithaca, N.Y.), 1966. (*DA* 27:1610B)

26. STEPHENSON, HARRIET BUCKMAN. *The Effect of a Management Training Program on Leadership Attitudes and on-the-Job Behavior.* Doctor's thesis, University of Washington (Seattle, Wash.), 1966. (*DA* 27:1512A)

27. WEISSENBERG, P., AND GRUENFELD, L. W. "Relationships Among Leadership Dimensions and Cognitive Style." *J Appl Psychol* 50:392–5 O '66. * (*PA* 40:13595)

28. AHNELL, INGEMAR V. *A Study of Relationships Between the Personal Characteristics of Elementary School Principals and Their Evaluations of Teachers.* Doctor's thesis, University of Kansas (Lawrence, Kan.), 1967. (*DA* 28:3395A)

29. HOOPER, DONALD BRUCE. *Differential Utility of Leadership Opinions in Classical and Moderator Models for the Prediction of Leadership Effectiveness.* Doctor's thesis, Ohio State University (Columbus, Ohio), 1968. (*DAI* 30:13A)

30. ROWLAND, KENDRITH M., AND SCOTT, WILLIAM E., JR. "Psychological Attributes of Effective Leadership in a Formal Organization." *Personnel Psychol* 21:365–77 au '68. *

31. SEILER, DALE ARNOLD. *Supervisors' Judged Importance of the Aspects of the Clerical Job.* Doctor's thesis, Colorado State University (Ft. Collins, Colo.), 1968. (*DA* 30:882B)

32. SIEGEL, JACOB P. *A Study of the Relationships Among Organizational Factors, Personality Traits, Job, and Leadership Attitudes.* Doctor's thesis, University of California (Berkeley, Calif.), 1968. (*DA* 29:2662B)

33. BERLFEIN, HAROLD PAUL. *Effects of Personal Values on Managerial Behavior and Attitudes.* Doctor's thesis, Colorado State University (Ft. Collins, Colo.), 1969. (*DAI* 30:2448B)

34. GREENWOOD, JOHN M., AND MCNAMARA, WALTER J. "Leadership Styles of Structure and Consideration and Managerial Effectiveness." *Personnel Psychol* 22(2):141–52 su '69. * (*PA* 44:7413)

35. HARRELL, THOMAS W. "The Personality of High Earning MBA's in Big Business." *Personnel Psychol* 22(4):457–63 w '69. * (*PA* 44:13525)

36. HINRICHS, J. R. "Comparison of 'Real Life' Assessments of Management Potential With Situational Exercises, Paper-and-Pencil Ability Tests, and Personality Inventories." *J Appl Psychol* 53(5):425–32 O '69. * (*PA* 44:1442)

37. JABS, MAX LEWIS. *An Experimental Study of the Comparative Effects of Initiating Structure and Consideration Leadership on the Educational Growth of College Structs.* Doctor's thesis, University of Connecticut (Storrs, Conn.), 1969. (*DAI* 30:2762A)

38. SCHENK, KATHERINE NIXON. *Factors Associated With Planned Change in Baccalaureate Nursing Programs.* Doctor's thesis, University of Florida (Gainesville, Fla.), 1969. (*DAI* 31:268B)

39. SKINNER, ELIZABETH W. "Relationships Between Leadership Behavior Patterns and Organizational-Situational Variables." *Personnel Psychol* 22(4):489–94 w '69. *

40. TENOPYR, MARY L. "The Comparative Validity of Selected Leadership Scales Relative to Success in Production Management." *Personnel Psychol* 22(1):77–85 sp '69. * (*PA* 43:14924)

41. WOLLOWICK, HERBERT B., AND MCNAMARA, W. J. "Relationship of the Components of an Assessment Center to Management Success." *J Appl Psychol* 53(5):348–52 O '69. * (*PA* 44:1448)

42. YEAGER, JOSEPH CORNELIUS. *The Effectiveness of a Training Program in Human Relations.* Doctor's thesis, University of Pittsburgh (Pittsburgh, Pa.), 1969. (*DAI* 31:2344B)

43. CUMMINS, ROBERT C. "An Investigation of a Model of Leadership Effectiveness." Abstract. *Proc 78th Ann Conv Am Psychol Assn* 5(2):599–600 '70. * (*PA* 44:19657)

44. GORHAM, WILLIAM A., AND MANN, WALTER G. "Validation, Moderation, and Clarification." Abstract. *Proc 78th Ann Conv Am Psychol Assn* 5(1):139–40 '70. * (*PA* 44:17772)

45. HARRELL, THOMAS W. "The Personality of High Earning MBA's in Small Business." *Personnel Psychol* 23(3):369–75 au '70. * (*PA* 45:9041)

46. HAWKINS, ROGER EVERETT. *Need-Press Interaction as Related to Managerial Styles Among Executives.* Doctor's thesis, Illinois Institute of Technology (Chicago, Ill.), 1970. (*DAI* 31:3044B)

47. PEIRCE, JERRY ROGER. *Effects of Selected Organizational Variables on the Behavioral Style of the Industrial Supervisor.* Doctor's thesis, University of Michigan (Ann Arbor, Mich.), 1970. (*DAI* 31:3047B)

CECIL A. GIBB, *Professor of Psychology, Australian National University, Canberra City, Australia.*

The analysis of leader behavior, of what leaders actually do, has proved to be the most rewarding research approach to the understanding of leadership. The most notable, and the most complete, research directed toward the determination of dimensions of leader behavior has been that of the Ohio State Leadership Studies.[1] Nine a priori dimensions of leader behavior postulated by Hemphill and assessed by means of the *Leader Behavior Description Questionnaire,* were shown by Halpin and Winer [2] to reduce to four factor-analytic dimensions. These were named Consideration, Struc-

1 STOGDILL, RALPH M., AND COONS, ALVIN E., EDITORS. *Leader Behavior: Its Description and Measurement.* Ohio State University, Bureau of Business Research, Research Monograph No. 88. Columbus, Ohio: the Bureau, 1957. Pp. xv, 168. *

2 HALPIN, ANDREW W., AND WINER, B. JAMES. *Studies in Aircrew Composition: 3, The Leadership Behavior of the Airplane Commander.* An unpublished study prepared for the Human Factors Operations Research Laboratories, Air Research and Development Command, 1952.

ture, Production Emphasis, and Sensitivity. Of these, Consideration and Structure were by far the most important, accounting for some 83 percent of the variance between them. A number of subsequent studies [3] have confirmed that Consideration and Structure may be regarded as two major dimensions of leader behavior. The task and social-emotional leadership differentiation of Bales [4] offers a parallel which is, in itself, a confirmation. Fiedler's observation that his differentiations in terms of interpersonal judgments are meaningfully related to the concepts of Structure and Consideration also, from a widely different approach, affords support. Fiedler [5] has shown that his high-LPC leaders, i.e., those who describe their least preferred coworkers in favorable terms, are in fact leaders who are described as more "considerate" as defined by the Ohio State Leadership Studies. On the other hand, Fiedler's low-LPC leaders are shown to be "more task- than relationship-oriented," more goal oriented, more punitive, and more directive in their behavior. In other words, these leaders display much "structuring" behavior.

The definitions of Consideration and Structure have been stated a little differently by the various authors of the Ohio State Leadership Studies but no better statements are available than those offered by Fleishman in the manual of the *Leadership Opinion Questionnaire:*

Consideration (*C*). Reflects the extent to which an individual is likely to have job relationships with his subordinates characterized by mutual trust, respect for their ideas, consideration of their feelings, and a certain warmth between himself and them. A high score is indicative of a climate of good rapport and two-way communication. A low score indicates the individual is likely to be more impersonal in his relations with group members.

Structure (*S*). Reflects the extent to which an individual is likely to define and structure his own role and those of his subordinates toward *goal attainment*. A high score on this dimension characterizes individuals who play a very active role in directing group activities through planning, communicating information, scheduling, criticizing, trying out new ideas, and so forth. A low score characterizes individuals who are likely to be relatively inactive in giving direction in these ways.

3 FLEISHMAN, EDWIN A.; HARRIS, EDWIN F.; AND BURTT, HAROLD E. *Leadership and Supervision in Industry: An Evaluation of a Supervisory Program.* Ohio State University, Bureau of Business Research Monograph No. 33. Columbus, Ohio: the Bureau, 1955. Pp. xiii, 110.
   HALPIN, ANDREW W. "The Leader Behavior and Leadership Ideology of Educational Administrators and Aircraft Commanders." *Harvard Ed R* 25:18–32 w '55. *
   4 BALES, ROBERT F. "The Equilibrium Problem in Small Groups," pp. 111–61. In *Working Papers in the Theory of Action.* Edited by Talcott Parsons, Robert F. Bales, and Edward A. Shils. Glencoe, Ill.: Free Press, 1953. Pp. 269.
   5 FIEDLER, FRED E. *A Theory of Leadership Effectiveness.* New York: McGraw-Hill Book Co., Inc., 1967. Pp. viii, 310. *

Such is the body of research relating to these dimensions of leader behavior that there could be little quarrel with Fleishman's assertion of meanings for high and low scores if these scores are obtained by leader *behavior* description. His confident assertion that the LOQ scores have these meanings does, however, demand cautious examination. This questionnaire asks the leader to indicate how he believes he *should* behave, rather than how he does behave. There is a need to establish a link between the attitude adopted by the leader and his behavior or between the attitude measures of the *Leadership Opinion Questionnaire* and the criterion performances for which leader behavior descriptions of Consideration and Structure have shown themselves valid. Fleishman is, of course, well aware of this need and refers to it directly in the manual. Indeed, the manual carries a good deal of information concerning the direct validities of the LOQ scales. Neither these validity coefficients nor the analysis of them made by Korman (*23*) will encourage much use of the LOQ for the prediction of criterion performance whatever the nature of the leadership criteria. On the other hand, as Fleishman says, "many significant validities have been obtained," and there is support for his claim that low Consideration scores on the test are often associated with an undesirable situation. And one cannot but notice that in a study of nursing supervisors (*16*) although samples were small, Structure scores, with some consistency, showed a meaningful relationship to measures of stress. High Structure was associated with high *intra*-departmental but with low *inter*-departmental stress, as any student of organizational behavior would expect.

Given some knowledge of recent research in leadership by Fleishman and Harris [6] and by Fiedler [7] and his associates, it is not at all surprising that direct validities of the LOQ scales should be low. Both of these research programs have emphasized the *contingent* nature of the relationships between leader attitudes and behavior and the effectiveness of the leadership. Fleishman and Harris have examined the interaction effects between Consideration and Structure in relation to both grievance and turnover rate. From this work it is clear that Consideration is the more critical of the two dimensions

6 FLEISHMAN, EDWIN A., AND HARRIS, EDWIN F. "Patterns of Leadership Behavior Related to Employee Grievances and Turnover." *Personnel Psychol* 15:43–56 sp '62. *
   7 FIEDLER, op. cit.

but that there is a significant interaction. While low-Consideration foremen were always in-effective, high-Consideration foremen were able to indulge in high levels of Structure on task emphasis without any significant changes in grievances or turnover. Since there is other evidence to suggest that in real hierarchical or-ganizations, at least, high levels of behavior on both dimensions are desirable, there is signifi-cant information here concerning management training. Programs which increase Considera-tion behavior of managers are very likely indeed to increase management efficiency.

This suggestion leads easily to a point that should be made in considering the validity and use of the *Leadership Opinion Questionnaire*. While its value for selection or for the predic-tion of criterion performance is severely limited by the contingent significance of other variables, there are other uses to be considered. The LOQ can be administered in ordinary circumstances in about 15 minutes; since it is self-scoring, both C and S scores can be obtained in a further five minutes. As a consequence, this is a con-venient training aid which may be usefully employed in training evaluation, especially if the vector analysis procedure described in the man-ual is followed.

Fleishman, the author of the present instru-ment, enjoys a high reputation as a truly pro-fessional psychologist. It is therefore not sur-prising that the LOQ manual is very good indeed. Inasmuch as the questionnaire is self-administering, self-scoring and very readily understood, its manual might have been very casual. On the contrary, Fleishman has been very thorough. Many estimates of reliability and validity are given from a variety of sources derived from an exhaustive consideration of the literature on the instrument. The independ-ence of LOQ scales from intelligence measures is explored, as are the correlations of LOQ scales with personality measures. Recent work by Tenopyr (*40*) has suggested that there may be a significant, though not large, negative corre-lation of LOQ Structure with verbal compre-hension. As against this, Greenwood and Mc-Namara (*34*) found both LOQ S and C scores generally unrelated to scores from other stand-ard pencil-and-paper tests of personality, in-telligence, and interests. By and large, the evi-dence is pretty clear that scores on these scales are not dependent on intelligence and such cor-relations as there are with personality measures

do not contradict the meanings given the two constructs but do confirm that these attitudes may be held independently of personality traits. The one modification of these facts that must be considered, and one surprisingly given no attention by Fleishman, is the pretty well established relation between Fiedler's LPC scores and these dimensions of leader behavior. That work must also call into question, at least to some extent, the important claim that Con-sideration and Structure, whether as dimen-sions of leader behavior or as LOQ scores, are completely independent. The question is not one which can be answered without a good deal of research employing both approaches, but from what is available about the *Leadership Opinion Questionnaire* it is fair to say that under many conditions the correlations between LOQ Con-sideration and Structure scores approximate zero. Tenopyr (*40*) adds to this evidence, but there are research studies—such as that of Gruenfeld and Weissenberg (*22*) who found a quite significant correlation of .40 between LOQ C and S—which suggest that under certain conditions common factors may affect both scores.

Despite difficulties and as yet incomplete in-formation, the LOQ is a well-made instrument. Its author's claims for it are cautious and modest and they rest upon research which he is ready to expose to users. It is an instrument with definite potential in training and training evaluation, and by its use in a variety of situa-tions and organizations there may be some prospect of elaborating the complex, contingent, and often curvilinear relationships which exist between the basic dimensions of Consideration and Structure and measures of leadership effectiveness.

For reviews by Jerome E. Doppelt and Wayne K. Kirchner, see 6:1190.

[1150]
★The RAD Scales. Supervisors; 1957; RAD; per-ceived responsibility, authority, and delegation of au-thority as reported by a supervisor; 3 scores: respon-sibility, authority, delegation; 1 form ('57, 4 pages); manual ['57, 7 pages]; no norms; $2 per 25 tests, cash orders postpaid; specimen set free; (5) minutes; Ralph M. Stogdill; University Publications Sales, Ohio State University. *

REFERENCES
1. BROWNE, CLARENCE GEORGE. *An Exploration Into the Use of Certain Methods for the Study of Executive Function in Business.* Doctor's thesis, Ohio State University (Columbus, Ohio). 1948.
2. STOGDILL, RALPH M., AND SHARTLE, CARROLL L. "Methods for Determining Patterns of Leadership Behavior in Relation

to Organization Structure and Objectives." *J Appl Psychol* 32:286–91 Je '48. * (*PA* 23:1239)

3. BROWNE, C. G. "Study of Executive Leadership in Business: I, The R, A, and D Scales." *J Appl Psychol* 33:521–6 D '49. * (*PA* 24:4321)

4. BROWNE, C. G., AND NEITZEL, BETTY J. "Communication, Supervision, and Morale." *J Appl Psychol* 36:86–91 Ap '52. * (*PA* 27:704)

5. STOGDILL, RALPH M., AND SHARTLE, CARROLL L. Chap. 5, "Responsibility, Authority and Delegation Scales (The RAD Scales)," pp. 33–43. In their *Methods in the Study of Administrative Leadership.* Ohio State University, Bureau of Business Research, Research Monograph No. 80. Columbus, Ohio: the Bureau, 1955. Pp. xv, 77. *

6. CAMPBELL, DONALD T. Chap. 10, "Responsibility, Authority, and Delegation," pp. 65–8. In his *Leadership and Its Effects Upon the Group.* Ohio State University, Bureau of Business Research Monograph No. 83. Columbus, Ohio: the Bureau, 1956. Pp. xii, 92. *

7. FLEISHMAN, EDWIN A. Chap. 3, "Differences Between Military and Industrial Organizations," pp. 31–8. In *Patterns of Administrative Performance.* By Ralph M. Stogdill, Carroll L. Shartle, and Associates. Ohio State University, Bureau of Business Research Monograph No. 81. Columbus, Ohio: the Bureau, 1956. Pp. xx, 108. *

8. SCOTT, ELLIS L. Chap. 7, "Perceptions of Organization and Leader Behavior," pp. 46–9. In his *Leadership and Perceptions of Organization.* Ohio State University, Bureau of Business Research Monograph No. 82. Columbus, Ohio: the Bureau, 1956. Pp. xvii, 122. *

9. STOGDILL, RALPH M., AND SHARTLE, CARROLL L. Chap. 1, "Performance Profiles of High Level Positions," pp. 1–15. In *Patterns of Administrative Performance.* By Ralph M. Stogdill, Carroll L. Shartle, and Associates. Ohio State University, Bureau of Business Research Monograph No. 81. Columbus, Ohio: the Bureau, 1956. Pp. xx, 108. *

10. STOGDILL, RALPH M.; SCOTT, ELLIS L.; AND JAYNES, WILLIAM E. *Leadership and Role Expectations.* Ohio State University, Bureau of Business Research Monograph No. 86. Columbus, Ohio: the Bureau, 1956. Pp. xvi, 168. *

11. STOGDILL, RALPH M.; SHARTLE, CARROLL L.; SCOTT, ELLIS L.; COONS, ALVIN E.; AND JAYNES, WILLIAM E. *A Predictive Study of Administrative Work Patterns.* Ohio State University, Bureau of Business Research Monograph No. 85. Columbus, Ohio: the Bureau, 1956. Pp. xii, 68. *

12. STOGDILL, RALPH M.; WHERRY, ROBERT J.; AND JAYNES, WILLIAM E. Chap. 4, "A Factorial Study of Administrative Performance," pp. 39–104. In *Patterns of Administrative Performance.* By Ralph M. Stogdill, Carroll L. Shartle, and Associates. Ohio State University, Bureau of Business Research Monograph No. 81. Columbus, Ohio: the Bureau, 1956. Pp. xx, 108. *

13. STOGDILL, RALPH M., AND SCOTT, ELLIS L. Part 2, "Responsibility and Authority Relationships," pp. 61–85. In *Leadership and Structures of Personal Interaction.* By Ralph M. Stogdill. Ohio State University, Bureau of Business Research Monograph No. 84. Columbus, Ohio: the Bureau, 1957. Pp. xiii, 90. *

14. BOWMAN, HERMAN JAMES. *Perceived Leader Behavior Patterns and Their Relationships to Self-Perceived Variables-Responsibility, Authority and Delegation.* Doctor's thesis, State University of New York (Buffalo, N.Y.), 1964. (*DA* 25:3340)

15. MORSINK, HELEN MURIEL. *A Comparative Study of the Leader Behavior of Men and Women Secondary School Principals.* Doctor's thesis, University of Michigan (Ann Arbor, Mich.), 1966. (*DA* 27:2793A)

16. ZINN, LAWRENCE ALFRED. *Role Dimensions of the Administrative Assistant to the Superintendent, Related to the Organizational Climate of the Central Office, in Selected Ohio School Districts.* Doctor's thesis, Ohio State University (Columbus, Ohio), 1966. (*DA* 27:1238A)

17. STOGDILL, RALPH M. "The Structure of Organization Behavior." *Multiv Behav Res* 2:47–61 Ja '67. * (*PA* 41:9500)

18. GLOGAU, LILLIAN F. *A Study of the Relationship Between the Leadership Style of the Elementary School Principal and the Introduction of the Nongraded Organization.* Doctor's thesis, New York University (New York, N.Y.), 1969. (*DAI* 31:1535A)

19. SCHROEDER, GLENN BURNETT. *Leadership Behavior of Department Chairmen in Selected State Institutions of Higher Education.* Doctor's thesis, University of New Mexico (Albuquerque, N.M.), 1969. (*DAI* 30:5209A)

20. TRIBBLE, JANET SIMES. *Perceptions of Elementary Principals, Teachers, and Curriculum Specialists Concerning Responsibility, Authority, and Competence in Curriculum and Instruction.* Doctor's thesis, New York University (New York, N.Y.), 1970. (*DAI* 31:3245A)

[1151]

*Supervisory Index. Supervisors; 1960–69; SI; 5 attitude scores: management, supervision, employees, human relations practices, total; 1 form ('60, 4 pages, self-marking); manual ('69, 15 pages); $7.65 per 25 tests; 50¢ per manual; $1.10 per specimen set; postage extra; (20–30) minutes; Norman Gekoski and Solomon L. Schwartz; Science Research Associates, Inc. *

REFERENCES

1. See 6:1192.
2. SCHWARTZ, SOLOMON L. *The Development of a Forced-Choice Scale for the Evaluation of Supervisory Attitude and Behavior in Industry.* Doctor's thesis, Temple University (Philadelphia, Pa.), 1957. (*DA* 17:3084)

For reviews by Arthur H. Brayfield and Albert K. Kurtz, see 6:1192.

[1152]

★Supervisory Inventory on Communication. Supervisors and prospective supervisors; 1965–69; SIC; 1 form ('65, 3 pages, self-marking); manual ('68, 11 pages); explanation of correct responses ('69, 4 pages); no data on reliability and validity; $5 per 20 tests; $2 per 20 explanations; 50¢ per specimen set; postage extra; (20) minutes; Donald L. Kirkpatrick; the Author. *

REFERENCE

1. KIRKPATRICK, DONALD L. "Development and Validation of a Communication Inventory for Supervisors." *J Commun* 18:404–11 D '68. * (*PA* 43:6861)

[1153]

★Supervisory Inventory on Safety. Supervisors and prospective supervisors; 1967–69; SIS; 1 form ('67, 3 pages, self-marking); manual ('69, 10 pages); explanation of correct responses ('69, 4 pages); no data on reliability; $5 per 20 tests; $2 per 20 explanations; 50¢ per specimen set; postage extra; (20) minutes; Donald L. Kirkpatrick; the Author. *

[1154]

★The WPS Supervisor-Executive Tri-Dimensional Evaluation Scales. Supervisors; 1966; TES; the same questions about the individual being rated are answered by 3 persons—his supervisor, a colleague, and himself; 12 scores obtained from each of the 3 forms: knowledge, planning, results, delegating, leadership, morale, training, adaptability, communication, emotionality, growth, total; 3 forms: self-rating, colleague-rating, supervisor-rating, (6 pages); manual (9 pages plus forms); no data on reliability; no description of normative population; $9.50 per manual and 10 sets of the 3 forms; $19.50 per 25 sets of the 3 forms; $3.50 per manual; postpaid; (30) minutes; Western Psychological Services. *

TRANSPORTATION

[1155]

★Short Occupational Test for Truckdrivers. Job applicants; 1970; score is pass, fail, or unclassifiable; 1 form (2 pages, self-marking); series manual (15 pages); $5.30 per 25 tests; 75¢ per manual; $3.30 per specimen set of the 12 tests in the series; postage extra; (10–15) minutes; Bruce A. Campbell and Suellen O. Johnson; Science Research Associates, Inc. *

TIP II SCANNING INDEX

This classified index of all tests in *Tests in Print II* can be used to determine what tests are available in areas besides vocations. Citations are to test entry numbers in TIP II. The population for which a test is intended is included. Stars indicate tests not previously listed in an MMY; asterisks indicate tests revised or supplemented since last listed. The vocations portion of this index, the only part relevant to this monograph, is repeated at the end of this volume.

ACHIEVEMENT BATTERIES

Academic Proficiency Battery [South Africa], college entrants, see 1

Adult Basic Education Student Survey, poorly educated adults in basic education classes, see 2

Adult Basic Learning Examination, adults with achievement levels grades 1–12, see 3

American School Achievement Tests, grades 1–9, see 4

Bristol Achievement Tests [England], ages 8–13, see 5

*CLEP General Examinations: Humanities, 1–2 years of college or equivalent, see 6

*California Achievement Tests, grades 1–14, see 7

Canadian Tests of Basic Skills [Canada], grades 3–8, see 8

Classification and Placement Examination, grade 8 and high school entrants, see 9

*College-Level Examination Program General Examinations, 1–2 years of college or equivalent, see 10

*Comprehensive Tests of Basic Skills, grades kgn–12, see 11

Cooperative Primary Tests, grades 1.5–3, see 12

★*Educational Skills Tests: College Edition*, open-door college entrants, see 13

General Tests of Language and Arithmetic [South Africa], standards 5–7, see 14

Gray-Votaw-Rogers General Achievement Tests, grades 1–9, see 15

★*Guidance Test for Junior Secondary Bantu Pupils in Form 3* [South Africa], see 16

High School Fundamentals Evaluation Test, grades 9–12, see 17

Iowa High School Content Examination, grades 11–13, see 18

*Iowa Tests of Basic Skills, grades 1.7–9, see 19

*Iowa Tests of Educational Development, grades 9–12, see 20

Ligondé Equivalence Test [Canada], adults who left elementary or secondary school 15–20 years ago, see 21

*Metropolitan Achievement Tests, grades kgn–9, see 22

National Achievement Tests, grades 4–9, see 23

*National Educational Development Tests, grades 7–10, see 24

*National Teacher Examinations: Common Examinations, college seniors and teachers, see 25

Peabody Individual Achievement Test, grades kgn–12, see 26

★*Primary Survey Tests*, grades 2–3, see 27

Public School Achievement Tests, grades 3–8, see 28

*SRA Achievement Series, grades 1–9, see 29

*SRA Assessment Survey, grades 1–12, see 30

*SRA High School Placement Test, grade 9 entrants, see 31

*STS Closed High School Placement Test, grade 9 entrants, see 32

*STS Educational Development Series, grades 2–12, see 33

*Scholastic Proficiency Battery [South Africa], standards 8–10, see 34

*Sequential Tests of Educational Progress, grades 4–14, see 35

*Stanford Achievement Test, grades 1.5–9, see 36

Stanford Achievement Test: High School Basic Battery, grades 9–12, see 37

*Stanford Early School Achievement Test, grades kgn–1.5, see 38

★*Stanford Test of Academic Skills*, grades 8–12 and first year junior/community college, see 39

Survey of College Achievement, grades 13–14, see 40

*Teacher Education Examination Program: General Professional Examinations, college seniors preparing to teach, see 41

*Test for High School Entrants, high school entrants, see 42

Test of Reading and Number: Inter-American Series, grade 4 entrants, see 43

*Tests of Academic Progress, grades 9–12, see 44

Tests of Adult Basic Education, adults at reading levels of children in grades 2–9, see 45
★*Tests of Arithmetic and Language for Indian South Africans* [South Africa], standards 6–8, see 46
Tests of Basic Experiences, prekgn–grade 1, see 47

Tests of General Educational Development, candidates for high school equivalency certificates, see 48
Undergraduate Program Area Tests, college, see 49
Wide Range Achievement Test, ages 5 and over, see 50

ENGLISH

Advanced Placement Examination in English, high school students desiring credit for college level courses or admission to advanced courses, see 51
American School Achievement Tests: Language and Spelling, grades 4–9, see 52
Analytical Survey Test in English Fundamentals, grades 9–13, see 53
Barrett-Ryan English Test, grades 7–13, see 54
★*Berry-Talbott Language Test: Comprehension of Grammar*, ages 5–8, see 55
Bristol Achievement Tests: English Language [England], ages 8–13, see 56
Business English Test: Dailey Vocational Tests, grades 8–12 and adults, see 57
CLEP General Examinations: English Composition, 1–2 years of college or equivalent, see 58
CLEP Subject Examination in English Composition, 1 year or equivalent, see 59
★*CLEP Subject Examination in Freshman English*, 1 year or equivalent, see 60
California Achievement Tests: Language, grades 1–14, see 61
Canadian Achievement Test in English [Canada], grade 10, see 62
Canadian English Achievement Test [Canada], grades 8.5–9, see 63
★*Canadian English Language Achievement Test* [Canada], candidates for college entrance, see 63A
College Board Achievement Test in English Composition, candidates for college entrance, see 64
College English Placement Test, college entrants, see 65
College English Test: National Achievement Tests, grades 12–13, see 66
College Placement Tests in English Composition, entering college freshmen, see 67
Comprehensive Tests of Basic Skills: Language, grades 2.5–12, see 68
Cooperative English Tests, grades 9–14, see 69
Cooperative Primary Tests: Writing Skills, grades 2.5–3, see 70
Cotswold Junior English Ability Test [Scotland], ages 8.5–10.5, see 71
Cotswold Measurement of Ability: English [Scotland], ages 10–12, see 72
English Expression: Cooperative English Tests, grades 9–14, see 73
English IX–XII: Achievement Examinations for Secondary Schools, grades 9–12, see 74
English Progress Tests [England], ages 7–3 to 15–6, see 75
English Test FG [England], ages 12–13, see 76
English Test: Municipal Tests, grades 3–8, see 77
English Test: National Achievement Tests, grades 3–12, see 78
English Tests (Adv.) [England], ages 12–13, see 79
English Tests 14–20 and 22 [England], ages 10–11, see 80
Essentials of English Tests, grades 7–13, see 81
★*Functional Grammar Test*, high school and college, see 82
Grammar and Usage Test Series, grades 7–12, see 83

Grammar, Usage, and Structure Test and Vocabulary Test, college entrants, see 84
Hoyum-Sanders English Tests, 1–2 semesters in grades 2–8, see 85
Iowa Placement Examinations: English Aptitude, grades 12–13, see 86
Iowa Placement Examinations: English Training, grades 12–13, see 87
Iowa Tests of Educational Development: Correctness and Appropriateness of Expression, grades 9–12, see 88
★*Language Arts Diagnostic Probes*, grades 3–9, see 89
Language Arts: Minnesota High School Achievement Examinations, grades 7–12, see 90
Language Arts Tests: Content Evaluation Series, grades 7–9, see 91
Language Perception Test, business and industry, see 92
Language Usage: Differential Aptitude Tests, grades 8–12 and adults, see 93–4
Moray House English Tests [England], ages 8.5–14, see 95
National Teacher Examinations: English Language and Literature, college seniors and teachers, see 96
Nationwide English Composition Examination, grades 4–12, see 97
Nationwide English Grammar Examination, grades 4–12, see 98
New Purdue Placement Test in English, grades 11–16, see 99
Objective Tests in Constructive English, grades 7–12, see 100
Objective Tests in Punctuation, grades 7–12, see 101
Pacific Tests of English Attainment and Skills: Pacific Test Series [Australia], job applicants in Papua New Guinea, see 102
Picture Story Language Test, ages 7–17, see 103
Pressey Diagnostic Tests in English Composition, grades 7–12, see 104
Purdue High School English Test, grades 9–12, see 105
RBH Spelling Test and Word Meaning Test, business and industry, see 106
RBH Test of Language Skills, business and industry, see 107
SRA Achievement Series: Language Arts, grades 2–9, see 108–9
Schonell Diagnostic English Tests [Scotland], ages 9.5–16, see 110
Senior English Test [England], technical college entrants, see 111
★*Sequential Tests of Educational Progress, Series 2: English Expression*, grades 4–14, see 112
Sequential Tests of Educational Progress: Writing, grades 4–14, see 113
Stanford Achievement Test: High School English and Spelling Tests, grades 9–12, see 114
Stanford Achievement Test: Spelling and Language Tests, grades 4–9, see 115
Survey Tests of English Usage, grades 9–13, see 116
Teacher Education Examination Program: English Language and Literature, college seniors preparing to teach secondary school, see 117

Test of English Usage [India], English-speaking high school and college students and adults, see 118

Tests of Academic Progress: Composition, grades 9–12, see 119

*Tests of Basic Experiences: Language, prekgn–grade 1, see 120

Tressler English Minimum Essentials Test, grades 8–12, see 121

Walton-Sanders English Test, 1–2 semesters in grades 9–13, see 122

Watson English Usage and Appreciation Test [Canada], grades 4–8, see 123

Writing Skills Test, grades 9–12, see 124

Writing Test: McGraw-Hill Basic Skills System, grades 11–14, see 125

LITERATURE

*American Literature Anthology Tests, high school, see 126

★CLEP Subject Examination in American Literature, 1 year or equivalent, see 127

*CLEP Subject Examination in Analysis and Interpretation of Literature, 1 year or equivalent, see 128

*CLEP Subject Examination in English Literature, 1 year or equivalent, see 129

*College Board Achievement Test in Literature, candidates for college entrance, see 130

*College Placement Test in Literature, entering college freshmen, see 131

★Cooperative Literature Tests, grades 9–12, see 132

*English Literature Anthology Tests, high school, see 133

English Tests for Outside Reading, grades 9–12, see 134

*Graduate Record Examinations Advanced Literature in English Test, graduate school candidates, see 135

Hollingsworth-Sanders Junior High School Literature Test, grades 7–8, see 136

Hoskins-Sanders Literature Test, 1–2 semesters in grades 9–13, see 137

*Iowa Tests of Educational Development: Ability to Interpret Literary Materials, grades 9–12, see 138

Literature Test: National Achievement Tests, grades 7–12, see 139

*Literature Tests/Objective, high school, see 140

Look at Literature: NCTE Cooperative Test of Critical Reading and Appreciation, grades 4–6, see 141

★Poetry Test/Objective, grades 7–12, see 142

Tests of Academic Progress: Literature, grades 9–12, see 143

*Undergraduate Program Field Tests: Literature Tests, college, see 144

★World Literature Anthology Tests, high school, see 145

SPELLING

Buckingham Extension of the Ayres Spelling Scale, grades 2–9, see 146

★Correct Spelling, grades 10–13, see 147

Group Diagnostic Spelling Test, grades 9–13, see 148

Iowa Spelling Scales, grades 2–8, see 149

Kansas Spelling Tests, grades 3–8, see 150

Kelvin Measurement of Spelling Ability [Scotland], ages 7–12, see 151

Lincoln Diagnostic Spelling Tests, grades 2–12, see 152

N.B. Spelling Tests [South Africa], standards 1–10 for English pupils and 3–10 for Afrikaans pupils, see 153

Nationwide Spelling Examination, grades 4–12, see 154

New Iowa Spelling Scale, grades 2–8, see 155

Sanders-Fletcher Spelling Test, 1–2 semesters in grades 9–13, see 156

*Spelling: Differential Aptitude Tests, grades 8–12 and adults, see 157

Spelling Errors Test, grades 2–8, see 158

Spelling Test for Clerical Workers, stenographic applicants and high school, see 159

Spelling Test: McGraw-Hill Basic Skills System, grades 11–14, see 160

Spelling Test: National Achievement Tests, grades 3–12, see 161

Traxler High School Spelling Test, grades 9–12, see 162

VOCABULARY

A.C.E.R. Word Knowledge Test [Australia], ages 18 and over, see 163

American Literacy Test, adults, see 164

Bruce Vocabulary Inventory, business and industry, see 165

*Iowa Tests of Educational Development: General Vocabulary, grades 9–12, see 166

Johnson O'Connor English Vocabulary Worksamples, ages 9 and over, see 167

Johnson O'Connor Vocabulary Tests, professionals, see 168

Nationwide English Vocabulary Examination, grades 4–12, see 169

Purdue Industrial Supervisors Word-Meaning Test, supervisors, see 170

RBH Vocabulary Test, applicants for clerical and stenographic positions, see 171

Sanders-Fletcher Vocabulary Test, 1–2 semesters in grades 9–13, see 172

Survey Test of Vocabulary, grades 3–12, see 173

Test of Active Vocabulary, grades 9–12, see 174

★Vocabulary Survey Test, grades kgn–1, see 175

Vocabulary Test for High School Students and College Freshmen, grades 9–13, see 176

Vocabulary Test: McGraw-Hill Basic Skills System, grades 11–14, see 177

Vocabulary Test: National Achievement Tests, grades 3–12, see 178

Wide Range Vocabulary Test, ages 8 and over, see 179

Word Clue Tests, grades 7–13 and adults, see 180

Word Dexterity Test, grades 7–16, see 181

Word Understanding, grades 6–12, see 182

FINE ARTS

ART

★Advanced Placement Examination in Art, high school students desiring credit for college level courses or admission to advanced courses, see 183

Art Vocabulary, grades 6–12, see 184

Graves Design Judgment Test, grades 7–16 and adults, see 185

Horn Art Aptitude Inventory, grades 12–16 and adults, see 186

Knauber Art Ability Test, grades 7–16, see 187
Knauber Art Vocabulary Test, grades 7–16, see 188
Meier Art Tests, grades 7–16 and adults, see 189
*National Teacher Examinations: Art Education, college seniors and teachers, see 190
★Teacher Education Examination Program: Art Education, college seniors preparing to teach secondary school, see 191
*Undergraduate Program Field Tests: Art History Test, college, see 192

MUSIC

★Advanced Placement Examination in Music, high school students desiring credit for college level courses or admission to advanced courses, see 193
Aliferis-Stecklein Music Achievement Tests, music students college level entrance and over, see 194
★Belwin-Mills Singing Achievement Test, grades 5–16, see 195
★Elementary Rhythm and Pitch Test, grades 4–8, see 196
*Graduate Record Examinations Advanced Music Test, graduate school candidates, see 197
Gretsch-Tilson Musical Aptitude Test, grades 4–12, see 198
*Iowa Tests of Music Literacy, grades 4–12, see 199
Jones Music Recognition Test, grades 4–16, see 200
Knuth Achievement Tests in Music, grades 3–12, see 201

Kwalwasser-Dykema Music Tests, grades 4–16 and adults, see 202
Kwalwasser Music Talent Test, grades 4–16 and adults, see 203
Kwalwasser-Ruch Test of Musical Accomplishment, grades 4–12, see 204
Kwalwasser Test of Music Information and Appreciation, high school and college, see 205
Measures of Musical Abilities [England], ages 7–14, see 206
Music Achievement Tests, grades 3–12, see 207
★Music Aptitude Test, grades 4–8, see 208
Musical Aptitude Profile, grades 4–12, see 209
*National Teacher Examinations: Music Education, college seniors and teachers, see 210
Seashore Measures of Musical Talents, grades 4–16 and adults, see 211
Snyder Knuth Music Achievement Test, elementary education and music majors, see 212
*Teacher Education Examination Program: Music Education, college seniors preparing to teach secondary school, see 213
Test of Musicality, grades 4–12, see 214
*Undergraduate Program Field Tests: Music Tests, college, see 215
Watkins-Farnum Performance Scale, music students, see 216
Wing Standardised Tests of Musical Intelligence [England], ages 8 and over, see 217

FOREIGN LANGUAGES

Foreign Language Prognosis Test, grades 8–9, see 218
*Graduate School Foreign Language Testing Program, graduate level degree candidates required to demonstrate foreign language reading proficiency, see 219
Iowa Placement Examinations: Foreign Language Aptitude, grades 12–13, see 220
Modern Language Aptitude Test, grades 9 and over, see 221
Modern Language Aptitude Test—Elementary, grades 3–6, see 222
Pimsleur Language Aptitude Battery, grades 6–12, see 223

ARABIC

*First Year Arabic Final Examination, 1 year college, see 224

CHINESE

Harvard-MLA Tests of Chinese Language Proficiency, college and adults, see 225

ENGLISH

Comprehensive English Language Test for Speakers of English as a Second Language, non-native speakers of English, see 226
Diagnostic Test for Students of English as a Second Language, applicants from non-English language countries for admission to American colleges, see 227
English Knowledge and Comprehension Test [India], high school, see 228

★English Placement Test, college entrants from non-English language countries, see 229
*English Usage Test for Non-Native Speakers of English, non-native speakers of English, see 230
Examination in Structure (English as a Foreign Language), college entrants from non-English language countries, see 231
★Michigan Test of Aural Comprehension, college applicants from non-English language countries, see 232
*Michigan Test of English Language Proficiency, college applicants from non-English language countries, see 233
Oral Rating Form for Rating Language Proficiency in Speaking and Understanding English, non-native speakers of English, see 234
★Test A/65: English Language Achievement Test [South Africa], matriculants and higher, see 235
Test of Aural Perception in English for Japanese Students, Japanese students in American colleges, see 236
Test of Aural Perception in English for Latin-American Students, Latin-American students of English, see 237
*Test of English as a Foreign Language, college applicants from non-English language countries, see 238
*Vocabulary and Reading Test for Students of English as a Second Language, non-native speakers of English, see 239

FRENCH

*Advanced Placement Examination in French, high school students desiring credit for college level courses or admission to advanced courses, see 240

Baltimore County French Test, 1 year high school, see 241

Canadian Achievement Test in French [Canada], grade 10, see 242

★*College Board Achievement Test in French Listening-Reading,* candidates for college entrance with 2–4 years high school French, see 243

College Board Achievement Test in French Reading, candidates for college entrance with 2–4 years high school French, see 244

College Placement Test in French Listening Comprehension, entering college freshmen, see 245

★*College Placement Test in French Listening-Reading,* entering college freshmen, see 246

College Placement Test in French Reading, entering college freshmen, see 247

Cooperative French Listening Comprehension Test, 2–5 semesters high school or college, see 248

First Year French Test, high school and college, see 249

Ford-Hicks French Grammar Completion Tests [Canada], high school, see 250

French I and II: Achievement Examinations for Secondary Schools, 1–2 years high school, see 251

Graduate Record Examinations Advanced French Test, graduate school candidates, see 252

Graduate School Foreign Language Test: French, graduate level degree candidates required to demonstrate reading proficiency in French, see 253

Iowa Placement Examinations: French Training, grades 12–13, see 254

MLA Cooperative Foreign Language Proficiency Tests: French, French majors and advanced students in college, see 255

MLA-Cooperative Foreign Language Tests: French, 1–4 years high school or 1–2 years college, see 256

National Teacher Examinations: French, college seniors and teachers, see 257

Pimsleur French Proficiency Tests, grades 7–16, see 258

Second Year French Test, high school and college, see 259

Teacher Education Examination Program: French, college seniors preparing to teach secondary school, see 260

Undergraduate Program Field Tests: French Test, college, see 261

GERMAN

Advanced Placement Examination in German, high school students desiring credit for college level courses or admission to advanced courses, see 262

★*College Board Achievement Test in German Listening-Reading,* candidates for college entrance with 2–4 years high school German, see 263

College Board Achievement Test in German Reading, candidates for college entrance with 2–4 years high school German, see 264

College Placement Test in German Listening Comprehension, entering college freshmen, see 265

★*College Placement Test in German Listening-Reading,* entering college freshmen, see 266

College Placement Test in German Reading, entering college freshmen, see 267

German I and II: Achievement Examinations for Secondary Schools, 1–2 years high school, see 268

Graduate Record Examinations Advanced German Test, graduate school candidates, see 269

Graduate School Foreign Language Test: German, graduate level degree candidates required to demonstrate reading proficiency in German, see 270

MLA Cooperative Foreign Language Proficiency Tests: German, German majors and advanced students in college, see 271

MLA-Cooperative Foreign Language Tests: German, 1–4 years high school or 1–2 years college, see 272

National German Examination for High School Students, 2–4 years high school, see 273

National Teacher Examinations: German, college seniors and teachers, see 274

Pimsleur German Proficiency Tests, grades 7–16, see 275

Undergraduate Program Field Tests: German Test, college, see 276

GREEK

College Placement Test in Greek Reading, entering college freshmen, see 277

HEBREW

★*Achievement Test—Hebrew Language,* grades 5–7, see 278

College Board Achievement Test in Hebrew, candidates for college entrance with 2–4 years high school Hebrew, see 279

College Placement Test in Hebrew Reading, entering college freshmen, see 280

NCRI Achievement Tests in Hebrew, grades 5–9, see 281

Test on the Fundamentals of Hebrew, grades 2–7, see 282

ITALIAN

College Placement Test in Italian Listening Comprehension, entering college freshmen, see 283

★*College Placement Test in Italian Listening-Reading,* entering college freshmen, see 284

College Placement Test in Italian Reading, entering college freshmen, see 285

MLA Cooperative Foreign Language Proficiency Tests: Italian, Italian majors and advanced students in college, see 286

MLA-Cooperative Foreign Language Tests: Italian, 1–4 years high school or 1–2 years college, see 287

LATIN

Advanced Placement Examination in Classics, high school students desiring credit for college level courses or admission to advanced courses, see 288

College Board Achievement Test in Latin, candidates for college entrance with 2–4 years high school Latin, see 289

College Placement Test in Latin Reading, entering college freshmen, see 290

Cooperative Latin Test: Elementary and Advanced Levels, grades 9–16, see 291

Emporia First Year Latin Test, 1 year high school, see 292

Emporia Second Year Latin Test, 2 years high school, see 293

Latin I and II: Achievement Examinations for Secondary Schools, 1–2 years high school, see 294

RUSSIAN

★*College Board Achievement Test in Russian Listening-Reading,* candidates for college entrance with 2–4 years high school Russian, see 295

College Placement Test in Russian Listening Comprehension, entering college freshmen, see 296

★*College Placement Test in Russian Listening-Reading*, entering college freshmen, see 297

College Placement Test in Russian Reading, entering college freshmen, see 298

Graduate School Foreign Language Test: Russian, graduate level degree candidates required to demonstrate reading proficiency in Russian, see 299

MLA Cooperative Foreign Language Proficiency Tests: Russian, Russian majors and advanced students in college, see 300

MLA-Cooperative Foreign Language Tests: Russian, 1–4 years high school or 1–2 years college, see 301

SPANISH

Advanced Placement Examination in Spanish, high school students desiring credit for college level courses or admission to advanced courses, see 302

Baltimore County Spanish Test, 1 year high school, see 303

★*College Board Achievement Test in Spanish Listening-Reading*, candidates for college entrance with 2–4 years high school Spanish, see 304

College Board Achievement Test in Spanish Reading, candidates for college entrance with 2–4 years high school Spanish, see 305

College Placement Test in Spanish Listening Comprehension, entering college freshmen, see 306

★*College Placement Test in Spanish Listening-Reading*, entering college freshmen, see 307

College Placement Test in Spanish Reading, entering college freshmen, see 308

First Year Spanish Test, high school and college, see 309

Furness Test of Aural Comprehension in Spanish, 1–3 years high school or 1–2 years college, see 310

Graduate Record Examinations Advanced Spanish Test, graduate school candidates, see 311

Graduate School Foreign Language Test: Spanish, graduate level degree candidates required to demonstrate reading proficiency in Spanish, see 312

Iowa Placement Examinations: Spanish Training, grades 12–13, see 313

MLA Cooperative Foreign Language Proficiency Tests: Spanish, Spanish majors and advanced students in college, see 314

MLA-Cooperative Foreign Language Tests: Spanish, 1–2 years high school or 1–2 years college, see 315

National Spanish Examination, 1–5 years junior high school and high school, see 316

National Teacher Examinations: Spanish, college seniors and teachers, see 317

Pimsleur Spanish Proficiency Tests, grades 7–16, see 318

Second Year Spanish Test, high school and college, see 319

Spanish I and II: Achievement Examinations for Secondary Schools, 1–2 years high school, see 320

Teacher Education Examination Program: Spanish, college seniors preparing to teach secondary school, see 321

Undergraduate Program Field Tests: Spanish Test, college, see 322

INTELLIGENCE

GROUP

A.C.E.R. Advanced Test B40 [Australia], ages 13 and over, see 323

A.C.E.R. Advanced Tests AL and AQ [Australia], college and superior adults, see 324

A.C.E.R. Higher Tests [Australia], ages 13 and over, see 325

A.C.E.R. Intermediate Test A [Australia], ages 10–13, see 326

A.C.E.R. Intermediate Tests C and D [Australia], ages 10–13, see 327

A.C.E.R. Junior Non-Verbal Test [Australia], ages 8.5–11, see 328

A.C.E.R. Junior Test A [Australia], ages 8.5–11, see 329

A.C.E.R. Lower Grades General Ability Scale [Australia], ages 6-6 to 9-1, see 330

AH4, AH5, and AH6 Tests [England], ages 10 and over, see 331

APT Performance Test, adults, see 332

Abstract Reasoning: Differential Aptitude Tests, grades 8–12 and adults, see 333

Academic Alertness "AA," adults, see 334

Academic Aptitude Test: Non-Verbal Intelligence: Acorn National Aptitude Tests, grades 7–16 and adults, see 335

Academic Aptitude Test: Verbal Intelligence: Acorn National Aptitude Tests, grades 7–16 and adults, see 336

Adaptability Test, job applicants, see 337

Advanced Test N [Australia], ages 15 and over, see 338

American School Intelligence Test, grades kgn–12, see 339

Analysis of Learning Potential, grades 1–12, see 340

Analysis of Relationships, grades 12–16 and industry, see 341

Army Alpha Examination: First Nebraska Revision, grades 6–16 and adults, see 341A

Army General Classification Test, First Civilian Edition, grades 9–16 and adults, see 342

★*BITCH Test (Black Intelligence Test of Cultural Homogeneity)*, adolescents and adults, see 343

Boehm Test of Basic Concepts, grades kgn–2, see 344

Business Test, clerical workers, see 345

CGA Mental Ability Tests [Canada], grades 6–12, see 346

★*C.P. 66 Test* [England], ages 13 and over, see 347

California Short-Form Test of Mental Maturity, grades kgn–16 and adults, see 348

California Test of Mental Maturity, grades kgn–16 and adults, see 349

Canadian Academic Aptitude Test [Canada], grades 8.5–9.0, see 350

Canadian Cognitive Abilities Test [Canada], grades kgn–3, see 351

Canadian Lorge-Thorndike Intelligence Tests [Canada], grades 3–9, see 352

★*Canadian Scholastic Aptitude Test* [Canada], candidates for college entrance, see 353

Cattell Intelligence Tests [England], mental ages 4 and over, see 354

Chicago Non-Verbal Examination, ages 6 and over, see 355

Cognitive Abilities Test, grades kgn–12, see 356

College Board Scholastic Aptitude Test, candidates for college entrance, see 357

College Qualification Tests, candidates for college entrance, see 358

Concept Mastery Test, grades 15–16 and graduate students and applicants for executive and research positions, see 359

Cooperative Academic Ability Test, superior grade 12 students, see 360

Cooperative School and College Ability Tests, grades 4–16, see 361

Cotswold Junior Ability Tests [Scotland], ages 8.5–10.5, see 362

Cotswold Measurement of 'Ability [Scotland], ages 10–12, see 363

Culture Fair Intelligence Test, ages 4 and over, see 364

D48 Test, grades 5 and over, see 365–6

Deeside Non-Verbal Reasoning Test [England], ages 10–12, see 367

Deeside Picture Puzzles [England], ages 6.5–8.5, see 368

Dennis Test of Scholastic Aptitude, grades 4–8, see 369

Detroit General Intelligence Examination, grades 7–12, see 370

Doppelt Mathematical Reasoning Test, grades 16–17 and employees, see 371

Draw-A-Man Test for Indian Children [India], ages 6–10, see 372

Essential Intelligence Test [Scotland], ages 8–12, see 373

Executive Employment Review, applicants for executive level positions, see 374

Figure Reasoning Test [England], ages 10 and over, see 375

Fundamental Achievement Series, semiliterate job applicants and employees, see 376–7

General Mental Ability Test, job applicants, see 378

General Verbal Practice Test G1–G3 [England], ages 10–11, see 379

Gilliland Learning Potential Examination, ages 6 and over, see 380

Goodenough-Harris Drawing Test, ages 3–15, see 381

Graduate Record Examinations Aptitude Test, graduate school candidates, see 382

★Group Test for Indian South Africans [South Africa], standards 4–10, see 383

Group Test 36 [England], ages 10–14, see 384

Group Test 75 [England], ages 12–13, see 385

Group Test 91 [England], industrial applicants, see 386

★Group Test 95 [England], ages 14 and over, see 386A

Group Test of Learning Capacity: Dominion Tests [Canada], grades kgn–1, 4–12 and adults, see 387

Group Tests 70 and 70B [England], ages 15 and over, see 388

Group Tests 72 and 73 [England], industrial applicants, see 389

Group Tests 90A and 90B [England], ages 15 and over, see 390

Henmon-Nelson Tests of Mental Ability, grades kgn–17, see 391

Illinois Index of Scholastic Aptitude, grades 9–12, see 392

Inventory No. 2, ages 16 and over, see 393

Junior Scholastic Aptitude Test, grades 7–9, see 394

Kelvin Measurement of Ability in Infant Classes [Scotland], ages 5–8, see 395

Kelvin Measurement of Mental Ability [Scotland], ages 8–12, see 396

Kingston Test of Intelligence [England], ages 10–12, see 397

Kuhlmann-Anderson Test, grades kgn–12, see 398

Kuhlmann-Finch Tests, grades 1–12, see 399

Lorge-Thorndike Intelligence Tests, grades kgn–13, see 400

Lorge-Thorndike Intelligence Tests, College Edition, grades 12–13, see 401

Mental Alertness: Tests A/1 and A/2 [South Africa], job applicants with 9 or more years of education, see 402

Mill Hill Vocabulary Scale [England], ages 4 and over, see 403

Miller Analogies Test, candidates for graduate school, see 404

★Minnesota Scholastic Aptitude Test, high school and college, see 405

Mitchell Vocabulary Test [England], adults, see 406

Modified Alpha Examination Form 9, grades 7–12 and adults, see 407

Moray House Picture Tests [England], ages 6.5–8.5, see 408

Moray House Verbal Reasoning Tests [England], ages 8.5 and over, see 409

N.B. Group Tests [South Africa], ages 5–8, see 410

New South African Group Test [South Africa], ages 8–17, see 411

★Non-Language Test of Verbal Intelligence [India], class 8 (ages 11–13), see 412

Non-Readers Intelligence Test [England], ages 6–8, see 413

Non-Verbal Reasoning Test, job applicants and industrial employees, see 414

Non-Verbal Tests [England], ages 8–15, see 415

Northumberland Mental Tests [England], ages 10–12.5, see 416

OISE Picture Reasoning Test: Primary [Canada], grades 1–2, see 417

Ohio Penal Classification Test, penal institutions, see 418

Ohio State University Psychological Test, grades 9–16 and adults, see 419

★Oral Verbal Intelligence Test [England], ages 7.5–14, see 419A

Oregon Academic Ranking Test, gifted children grades 3–7, see 420

O'Rourke General Classification Test, grades 12–13 and adults, see 421

"Orton" Intelligence Test, No. 4 [Scotland], ages 10–14, see 422

Otis Employment Tests, applicants for employment, see 423

Otis-Lennon Mental Ability Test, grades kgn–12, see 424

Otis Quick-Scoring Mental Ability Tests, grades 1–16, see 425

Otis Self-Administering Tests of Mental Ability, grades 4–16, see 426

Pacific Reasoning Series Tests [Australia], job applicants in Papua New Guinea, see 427

Pattern Perception Test [England], ages 6 and over, see 428

Performance Alertness "PA" (With Pictures), adults, see 429

Personal Classification Test, business and industry, see 430

Personnel Research Institute Classification Test, adults, see 431

Personnel Research Institute Factory Series Test, applicants for routine industrial positions, see 432

Personnel Tests for Industry, trade school and adults, see 433

Picture Test A [England], ages 7-0 to 8-1, see 434

Pintner-Cunningham Primary Test, grades kgn–2, see 435

Preliminary Scholastic Aptitude Test/National Merit Scholarship Qualifying Test, grades 10–12, see 436

★*Preschool and Early Primary Skill Survey*, ages 3-3 to 7-2, see 437

Pressey Classification and Verifying Tests, grades 1–12 and adults, see 438

Progressive Matrices [England], ages 5 and over, see 439

Proverbs Test, grades 5–16 and adults, see 440

Public School Primary Intelligence Test, grades 2–4, see 441

Purdue Non-Language Personnel Test, business and industry, see 442

Quantitative Evaluative Device, entering graduate students, see 443

RBH Test of Learning Ability, business and industry, see 444

RBH Test of Non-Verbal Reasoning, business and industry, see 445

Reasoning Tests for Higher Levels of Intelligence [Scotland], college entrants, see 446

Revised Beta Examination, ages 16–59, see 447

Ryburn Group Intelligence Tests [Scotland], ages 6.5–15.5, see 448

*SRA Nonverbal Form, ages 12 and over, see 449

*SRA Pictorial Reasoning Test, ages 14 and over, see 450

*SRA Short Test of Educational Ability, grades kgn–12, see 451

*SRA Verbal Form, grades 7–16 and adults, see 452

Safran Culture Reduced Intelligence Test [Canada], grades 1 and over, see 453

Scholastic Mental Ability Tests, grades kgn–8, see 454

Schubert General Ability Battery, grades 12–16 and adults, see 455

Scott Company Mental Alertness Test, applicants for office positions, see 456

Ship Destination Test, grades 9 and over, see 457

Short Form Test of Academic Aptitude, grades 1.5–12, see 458

Simplex GNV Intelligence Tests [England], ages 11–12, see 459

Simplex Group Intelligence Scale [England], ages 10 and over, see 460

Simplex Junior Intelligence Tests [England], ages 7–14, see 461

Sleight Non-Verbal Intelligence Test [England], ages 6–10, see 462

Southend Test of Intelligence [England], ages 10–12, see 463

Spiral Nines [South Africa], job applicants with 7–8 years of education, see 464

Test of Adult College Aptitude, evening college entrants, see 465

*Test of Perceptual Organization, ages 12 and over, see 466

Tests of General Ability, grades kgn–12, see 467

*Tests of General Ability: Inter-American Series, preschool and grades kgn–13.5, see 468

Thurstone Test of Mental Alertness, grades 9–12 and adults, see 469

*Undergraduate Program Aptitude Test, grades 15–16, see 470

Verbal Power Test of Concept Equivalence, ages 14 and over, see 471

Verbal Reasoning, job applicants and industrial employees, see 472

*Verbal Reasoning: Differential Aptitude Tests, grades 8–12 and adults, see 473

Verbal Tests (Adv.) [England], ages 12–13, see 474

Verbal Tests BC, CD, C, and D [England], ages 8–11, see 475

Verbal Tests EF and GH [England], ages 11–14, see 476

*Verbal Tests 15–23 and 69 [England], ages 10–12, see 477

★*WLW Employment Inventory III*, job applicants, see 478

★*WLW Mental Alertness Inventory*, job applicants, see 479

Wesman Personnel Classification Test, grades 8–16 and adults, see 480

Western Personnel Tests, college and adults, see 481

*Wonderlic Personnel Test, adults, see 482

INDIVIDUAL

Arthur Point Scale of Performance Tests, ages 4.5 to superior adults, see 483

Bayley Scales of Infant Development, ages 2–30 months, see 484

★*Bingham Button Test*, disadvantaged children ages 3–6, see 485

Canadian Intelligence Test [Canada], ages 3–16, see 486

Cattell Infant Intelligence Scale, ages 3–30 months, see 487

★*Classification Tasks* [Australia], ages 5–9, see 488

*Columbia Mental Maturity Scale, ages 3.5–9, see 489

Cooperative Preschool Inventory, ages 3–6, see 490

Crichton Vocabulary Scale [England], ages 4–11, see 491

Denver Developmental Screening Test, ages 2 weeks to 6 years, see 492

Detroit Tests of Learning Aptitude, ages 3 and over, see 493

Developmental Screening Inventory, ages 1–18 months, see 494

*English Picture Vocabulary Test [England], ages 5 and over, see 495

Full-Range Picture Vocabulary Test, ages 2 and over, see 496

Gesell Developmental Schedules, ages 4 weeks to 6 years, see 497

Haptic Intelligence Scale for Adult Blind, blind and partially sighted adults, see 498

Hiskey-Nebraska Test of Learning Aptitude, ages 3–17, see 499

Immediate Test: A Quick Verbal Intelligence Test, adults, see 500

★*Individual Scale for Indian South Africans* [South Africa], ages 8–17, see 501

Kahn Intelligence Tests, ages 1 month and over (particularly the verbally or culturally handicapped), see 502

Kent Series of Emergency Scales, ages 5–14, see. 503

*Leiter Adult Intelligence Scale, adults, see 504

Leiter International Performance Scale, ages 2–18, see 505

★*McCarthy Scales of Children's Abilities*, ages 2.5–8.5, see 506

Merrill-Palmer Scale of Mental Tests, ages 24–63 months, see 507

★*Minnesota Child Development Inventory*, ages 1–6, see 508

Minnesota Preschool Scale, ages 1.5–6.0, see 509

New Guinea Performance Scales [Papua New Guinea], pre-literates ages 17 and over, see 510

New South African Individual Scale [South Africa], ages 6–17, see 511

Non-Verbal Intelligence Tests for Deaf and Hearing Subjects [The Netherlands], ages 3–16, see 512

Ohwaki-Kohs Tactile Block Design Intelligence Test for the Blind, blind ages 6 and over, see 513

Pacific Design Construction Test [Australia], illiterates and semiliterates in Papua New Guinea, see 514

Passalong Test: A Performance Test of Intelligence, ages 8 and over, see 515

Peabody Picture Vocabulary Test, ages 2.5–18, see 516

Pictorial Test of Intelligence, ages 3–8, see 517

Porteus Maze Test, ages 3 and over, see 518

Preschool Attainment Record, ages 6 months to 7 years, see 519

Queensland Test [Australia], ages 7 and over, see 520

Quick Screening Scale of Mental Development, ages 6 months to 10 years, see 521

Quick Test, ages 2 and over, see 522

Ring and Peg Tests of Behavior Development, birth to age 6, see 523

Slosson Intelligence Test, ages 2 weeks and over, see 524

Stanford-Binet Intelligence Scale, ages 2 and over, see 525; *Clinical Profile for the Stanford Binet Intelligence Scale (L–M),* ages 5 and over, see 526

Stanford-Ohwaki-Kohs Block Design Intelligence Test for the Blind, blind and partially sighted ages 16 and over, see 527

Vane Kindergarten Test, ages 4–6, see 528

Wechsler Adult Intelligence Scale, ages 16 and over, see 529; *Rhodes WAIS Scatter Profile,* see 530; ★*WAIS Test Profile,* see 531

Wechsler-Bellevue Intelligence Scale, ages 10 and over, see 532

Wechsler Intelligence Scale for Children, ages 5–15, see 533; *California Abbreviated WISC,* educable mentally retarded ages 8–13.5 and intellectually gifted elementary school children, see 534; *Rhodes WISC Scatter Profile,* see 535; ★*WISC Mental Description Sheet,* see 536; ★*WISC Test Profile,* see 537

Wechsler Preschool and Primary Scale of Intelligence, ages 4–6.5, see 538; ★*WPPSI Test Profile,* see 539

Williams Intelligence Test for Children With Defective Vision [England], blind and partially sighted ages 5–15, see 540

SPECIFIC

★*Abstract Spatial Relations Test* [South Africa], Bantu industrial workers with 0–12 years of education, see 541

Alternate Uses, grades 6–16 and adults, see 542

Benton Visual Retention Test, ages 8 and over, see 543

★*Biographical Inventory—Creativity,* "adolescents and young adults," see 544

Block-Design Test, mental ages 5–20, see 545

Christensen-Guilford Fluency Tests, grades 7–16 and adults, see 546

Closure Flexibility (Concealed Figures), industrial employees, see 547

Closure Speed (Gestalt Completion), industrial employees, see 548

Concept Assessment Kit—Conservation, ages 4–7, see 549

★*Concept Attainment Test* [South Africa], college and adults, see 550

Consequences, grades 9–16 and adults, see 551

★*Consequences* [South Africa], ages 15 and over, see 552

★*Creativity Attitude Survey,* grades 4–6, see 553

★*Creativity Tests for Children,* grades 4–6, see 554

Decorations, grades 9–16 and adults, see 555

Feature Profile Test: Pintner-Paterson Modification, ages 4 and over, see 556

★*Gottschaldt Figures* [South Africa], job applicants with at least 10 years of education, see 557

Healy Pictorial Completion Tests, ages 5 and over, see 558

Hidden Figures Test, grades 6–16, see 559

Higgins-Wertman Test: Threshold of Visual Closure, ages 5–15, see 560

Jensen Alternation Board, ages 5 and over, see 560A

Kit of Reference Tests for Cognitive Factors, grades 6–16, see 561

Making Objects, grades 9–16 and adults, see 562

Manikin Test, ages 2 and over, see 563

Match Problems, grades 9–16 and adults, see 564

Match Problems 5, grades 9–16, see 565

★*Memory for Events,* grades 9–13, see 566

★*Memory for Meanings,* grades 7–16, see 567

New Uses, grades 10–16, see 568

★*Pattern Relations Test* [South Africa], college graduates, see 569

Perceptual Speed (Identical Forms), grades 9–16 and industrial employees, see 570

Pertinent Questions, grades 9–16 and adults, see 571

Plot Titles, grades 9–16, see 572

Possible Jobs, grades 6–16 and adults, see 573

Remote Associates Test, grades 9–16 and adults, see 574

Rutgers Drawing Test, ages 4–9, see 575

★*Seeing Faults* [South Africa], ages 15 and over, see 576

Seeing Problems, grades 9–16, see 577

Seguin-Goddard Formboard, ages 5–14, see 578

Simile Interpretations, grades 10–16, see 579

Similes Test, grades 4–16 and adults, see 580

★*Sketches,* grades 9 and over, see 581

Subsumed Abilities Test, ages 9 and over, see 582

★*Symbol Identities,* grades 10 and over, see 583

Symbol Series Test [South Africa], illiterate and semiliterate adults, see 584

★*Test of Concept Utilization,* ages 4.5–18.5, see 585

★*Test of Creative Potential,* grades 2–12 and adults, see 586

★*Thinking Creatively With Sounds and Words,* grades 3–12 and adults, see 587

Time Appreciation Test, ages 10 and over, see 588

Torrance Tests of Creative Thinking, kgn through graduate school, see 589

Two-Figure Formboard, ages 4 and over, see 590

Utility Test, grades 9–12, see 591

Wechsler Memory Scale, adults, see 592

★*Willner Instance Similarities Test,* adults, see 593

Word Fluency, industrial employees, see 594

MATHEMATICS

★*ACER Mathematics Tests* [Australia], grades 4–6, see 595

ACT Mathematics Placement Examination, college entrants, see 596

Advanced Mathematics (Including Trigonometry): Minnesota High School Achievement Examinations, high school, see 597

★*Annual High School Mathematics Examination,* high school students competing for individual and school awards, see 598

Basic Mathematics Tests [England], ages 7–14.5, see 599

Bristol Achievement Tests: Mathematics [England], ages 8–13, see 600

CLEP General Examinations: Mathematics, 1–2 years of college or equivalent, see 601

CLEP Subject Examination in College Algebra and Trigonometry, 1 semester or equivalent, see 602

California Achievement Tests: Mathematics, grades 1–14, see 603

Canadian Achievement Test in Mathematics [Canada], grade 10, see 604

Canadian Achievement Test in Technical and Commercial Mathematics [Canada], grade 10, see 605

Canadian Mathematics Achievement Test [Canada], grades 8.5–9.0, see 606

College Board Achievement Test in Mathematics, Level 1, candidates for college entrance, see 607

College Board Achievement Test in Mathematics, Level 2, candidates for college entrance, see 608

College Placement Test in Advanced Mathematics, entering college freshmen, see 609

College Placement Test in Intermediate Mathematics, entering college freshmen, see 610

College Placement Test in Mathematics, Level 1, entering college freshmen, see 611

College Placement Test in Mathematics, Level 2, entering college freshmen, see 612

Cooperative Mathematics Tests: Structure of the Number System, grades 7–8, see 613

Cooperative Primary Tests: Mathematics, grades 1.5–3, see 614

★*Diagnostic Test in Mathematics—Level 1* [Canada], grades 8–9, see 615

ERB Modern Mathematics Test, grades 7–8, see 616

General Mathematics III: Achievement Examinations for Secondary Schools, grade 9, see 617

Graded Arithmetic-Mathematics Test: Decimal Currency Edition [England], ages 7–21, see 618

Graduate Record Examinations Advanced Mathematics Test, graduate school candidates, see 619

★*Group Mathematics Test* [England], ages 6.5–8.5, see 620

Iowa Placement Examinations: Mathematics Aptitude, grades 12–13, see 621

Iowa Placement Examinations: Mathematics Training, grades 12–13, see 622

Iowa Tests of Educational Development: Ability to Do Quantitative Thinking, grades 9–12, see 623

Junior High School Mathematics Test: Acorn Achievement Tests, grades 7–9, see 624

★*Leicester Number Test* [England], ages 7-1 to 8-1, see 625

★*Mathematics Attainment Test EF* [England], ages 11–12, see 626

Mathematics Attainment Tests C1 and C3 [England], ages 9-3 to 10-8, see 627

Mathematics Attainment Tests DE1 and DE2 [England], ages 10–11, see 628

Mathematics Attainment Tests (Oral) [England], ages 7 to 9-8, see 629

★*Mathematics Inventory Tests*, grades 4–12, see 630

Mathematics: Minnesota High School Achievement Examinations, grades 7–9, see 631

Mathematics Test (Adv.) 6 [England], ages 12–13, see 632

Mathematics Test: Content Evaluation Series, grades 7–9, see 633

Mathematics Test for Grades Four, Five and Six, grades 4–6, see 634

Mathematics Test: McGraw-Hill Basic Skills System, grades 11–14, see 635

Mathematics Tests 20–22 [England], ages 10–11, see 636

Metropolitan Achievement Tests: Mathematics Tests, grades 3–9, see 637

Minimum Essentials for Modern Mathematics, grades 6–8, see 638

Modern Mathematics Supplement to the Iowa Tests of Basic Skills, grades 3–9, see 639

Moray House Mathematics Tests [England], ages 8.5–12, see 640

★*Moreton Mathematics Tests—Level 2* [Australia], grades 3–5, see 641

N.B. Mathematics Tests [South Africa], standards 7–8 (ages 14–15), see 642

National Teacher Examinations: Mathematics, college seniors and teachers, see 643

Numerical Ability: Differential Aptitude Tests, grades 8–12 and adults, see 644

★*Objective Tests in Mathematics: Arithmetic and Trigonometry* [England], ages 15 and over, see 645

Portland Prognostic Test for Mathematics, grades 6.9–8, see 646

★*Prescriptive Mathematics Inventory*, grades 4–8, see 647

★*Prescriptive Mathematics Inventory Interim Evaluation Tests*, grades 4–7, see 648

★*Primary Mathematics Survey Tests*, grades 2–3, see 649

Purdue Industrial Mathematics Test, adults, see 650

Senior Mathematics Test [England], technical college entrants, see 651

Sequential Tests of Educational Progress: Mathematics, grades 4–14, see 652

Stanford Achievement Test: High School Mathematics Test, grades 9–12, see 653

Stanford Achievement Test: High School Numerical Competence Test, grades 9–12, see 654

Stanford Achievement Test: Mathematics Tests, grades 1.5–9, see 655

Stanford Modern Mathematics Concepts Test, grades 5.5–9.5, see 656

Teacher Education Examination Program: Mathematics, college seniors preparing to teach secondary school, see 657

★*Test A/16: Mathematical Achievement Test* [South Africa], job applicants with at least 10 years of education, see 658

Tests of Academic Progress: Mathematics, grades 9–12, see 659

Tests of Achievement in Basic Skills: Mathematics, grades 4–12, see 660

Tests of Basic Experiences: Mathematics, prekgn–grade 1, see 661

Undergraduate Program Field Tests: Mathematics Tests, college, see 662

★*Watson Diagnostic Mathematics Test: Computation* [Canada], grades 1–10, see 663

ALGEBRA

Advanced Algebra: Achievement Examinations for Secondary Schools, high school, see 664

Algebra Readiness Test, grades 8–9, see 665

Algebra Test for Engineering and Science, college entrants, see 666–7

Blyth Second-Year Algebra Test, grades 9–12, see 668

Breslich Algebra Survey Test, 1–2 semesters high school, see 669

CLEP Subject Examination in College Algebra, 1 semester or equivalent, see 670

California Algebra Aptitude Test, high school, see 671

Cooperative Mathematics Tests: Algebra I and II, grades 8–12, see 672

Cooperative Mathematics Tests: Algebra III, high school and college, see 673

Diagnostic Test in Basic Algebra [Australia], 2–3 semesters high school, see 674

*ERB Modern Elementary Algebra Test, grades 8–9, see 675

ERB Modern Second Year Algebra Test, high school, see 676

Elementary Algebra: Achievement Examinations for Secondary Schools, high school, see 677

*Elementary Algebra: Minnesota High School Achievement Examinations, high school, see 678

First Year Algebra Test: National Achievement Tests, 1 year high school, see 679

Illinois Algebra Test, 1–2 semesters high school, see 680

Iowa Algebra Aptitude Test, grade 8, see 681

Kepner Mid-Year Algebra Achievement Tests, 1 semester high school, see 682

Lankton First-Year Algebra Test, grades 8–12, see 683

Lee Test of Algebraic Ability, grades 7–8, see 684

Mid-Year Algebra Test, high school, see 685

★Modern Algebra Test: Content Evaluation Series, 1 year high school, see 686

★Objective Tests in Mathematics: Algebra [England], ages 15 and over, see 687

Orleans-Hanna Algebra Prognosis Test, grades 7–11, see 688

Survey Test of Algebraic Aptitude, grade 8, see 689

ARITHMETIC

A.C.E.R. Arithmetic Tests: Standardized for Use in New Zealand [New Zealand], ages 9–12, see 690

A.C.E.R. Number Test [Australia], ages 13.5 and over, see 691

★Adston Diagnostic Instruments in Elementary School Mathematics: Whole Numbers, grades 4–8, see 692

American Numerical Test, adults in "that great middle and upper middle block of vocations which emphasize shop and white collar skills involving number competence," see 693

American School Achievement Tests: Arithmetic Readiness, grades kgn–1, see 694

American School Achievement Tests: Part 2, Arithmetic, grades 2–9, see 695

Analytical Survey Test in Computational Arithmetic, grades 7–12, see 696

Arithmetic Computation: Public School Achievement Tests, grades 3–8, see 697

Arithmetic Reasoning: Public School Achievement Tests, grades 3–8, see 698

Arithmetic Reasoning Test, clerical applicants and high school, see 699

Arithmetic Test (Fundamentals and Reasoning): Municipal Tests, grades 3–8, see 700

Arithmetic Test: National Achievement Tests, grades 3–8, see 701

*Arithmetic Tests EA2A and EA4 [England], ages 14.5 and over, see 702

*Arithmetical Problems: Test A/68 [South Africa], job applicants with at least 10 years of education, see 703

Basic Skills in Arithmetic Test, grades 6–12, see 704

Bobbs-Merrill Arithmetic Achievement Tests, grades 1–9, see 705

Brief Survey of Arithmetic Skills, grades 7–12, see 706

*Comprehensive Tests of Basic Skills: Arithmetic, grades 2.5–12, see 707

Computation Test A/67 [South Africa], job applicants with at least 6 years of education, see 708

Cooperative Mathematics Tests: Arithmetic, grades 7–9, see 709

*Cotswold Junior Arithmetic Ability Tests [Scotland], ages 8.5–10.5, see 710

*Cotswold Measurement of Ability: Arithmetic [Scotland], ages 10–12, see 711

*Diagnostic Arithmetic Tests [South Africa], standards 2–5 (ages 9–12), see 712

Diagnostic Chart for Fundamental Processes in Arithmetic, grades 2–8, see 713

★Diagnostic Decimal Tests 1–3 [Australia], ages 9–13, see 714

Diagnostic Fractions Test 3 [Australia], ages 7–11, see 715

Diagnostic Number Tests 1–2 [Australia], ages 8–12, see 716

Diagnostic Tests and Self-Helps in Arithmetic, grades 3–12, see 717

*ERB Modern Arithmetic Test, grades 5–6, see 718

Emporia Arithmetic Tests, grades 1–8, see 719

Kelvin Measurement of Ability in Arithmetic [Scotland], ages 7–12, see 720

★KeyMath Diagnostic Arithmetic Test, grades kgn–7, see 721

Moray House Arithmetic Test [England], ages 10–12, see 722

★Moreton Arithmetic Tests [Australia], grades 6–7, see 723

N.B. Arithmetic Tests [South Africa], standards 2–8 (ages 9–15), see 724

Number Test DE [England], ages 10.5–12.5, see 725

*Office Arithmetic Test, job applicants, see 726

RBH Arithmetic Fundamentals Test, business and industry, see 727

RBH Arithmetic Reasoning Test, business and industry, see 728

RBH Shop Arithmetic Test, industry, see 729

Revised Southend Attainment Test in Mechanical Arithmetic [England], ages 7–15, see 730

SRA Achievement Series: Arithmetic, grades 1–9, see 731

SRA Arithmetic Index, job applicants with poor educational backgrounds, see 732–3

Schonell Diagnostic Arithmetic Tests [Scotland], ages 7–13, see 734

*Seeing Through Arithmetic Tests, grades 1–6, see 735

Southend Attainment Test in Mechanical Arithmetic [England], ages 6–14, see 736

Staffordshire Arithmetic Test [England], ages 7–15, see 737

Stanford Diagnostic Arithmetic Test, grades 2.5–8.5, see 738

Survey Tests of Arithmetic Fundamentals [Canada], grades 3–8, see 739

Test A/8: Arithmetic [South Africa], technical college students and applicants for clerical and trade positions with 8–12 years of education, see 740

Watson Number-Readiness Test [Canada], grades kgn–1, see 741

CALCULUS

*Advanced Placement Examination in Mathematics: Calculus, high school students desiring credit for college level courses or admission to advanced courses, see 742

*CLEP Subject Examination in Introductory Calculus, 1 year or equivalent, see 743

Cooperative Mathematics Tests: Calculus, high school and college, see 744

GEOMETRY

Cooperative Mathematics Tests: Analytic Geometry, high school and college, see 745

Cooperative Mathematics Tests: Geometry, grades 10–12, see 746

Diagnostic Test in Basic Geometry [Australia], 1–2 years high school, see 747

Geometry (Including Plane and Solid Geometry): Minnesota High School Achievement Examinations, high school, see 748–9

Howell Geometry Test, grades 9–12, see 750

Iowa Geometry Aptitude Test, high school, see 751

Mid-Year Geometry Test, high school, see 752

★*Modern Geometry Test: Content Evaluation Series*, grades 10–12, see 753

★*Objective Tests in Mathematics: Geometry* [England], ages 15 and over, see 754

Orleans-Hanna Geometry Prognosis Test, grades 8–11, see 755

Plane Geometry: Achievement Examinations for Secondary Schools, high school, see 756

Plane Geometry: National Achievement Tests, high school, see 757

Solid Geometry: Achievement Examinations for Secondary Schools, high school, see 758

Solid Geometry: National Achievement Tests, high school, see 759

SPECIAL FIELDS

★*Decimal Currency Test* [England], primary and secondary school, see 760

★*NM Consumer Mathematics Test*, grades 9–12, see 761

TRIGONOMETRY

CLEP Subject Examination in Trigonometry, 1 semester or equivalent, see 762

Cooperative Mathematics Tests: Trigonometry, high school and college, see 763

Plane Trigonometry: National Achievement Tests, grades 10–16, see 764

Trigonometry: Minnesota High School Achievement Examinations, high school, see 765

MISCELLANEOUS

Modern Photography Comprehension Test, photography students, see 766

★*NM Consumer Rights and Responsibilities Test*, grades 9–12, see 767

AGRICULTURE

★*Agribusiness Achievement Test*, grades 9–12, see 768

BLIND

Colorado Braille Battery: Literary Code Tests, grades 1 and over, see 769

Colorado Braille Battery: Nemeth Code Tests, grades 4 and over, see 770

Lorimer Braille Recognition Test [England], students (ages 7–13) in grade 2 Braille, see 771

Roughness Discrimination Test, blind children in grades kgn–1, see 772

★*Stanford Multi-Modality Imagery Test*, blind and partially sighted ages 16 and over, see 773

Tooze Braille Speed Test [England], students (ages 7–13) in grades 1 or 2 Braille, see 774

BUSINESS EDUCATION

Bookkeeping: Achievement Examinations for Secondary Schools, high school, see 775

Bookkeeping: Minnesota High School Achievement Examinations, high school, see 776

Bookkeeping Test: National Business Entrance Tests, grades 11–16 and adults, see 777

Business Fundamentals and General Information Test: National Business Entrance Tests, grades 11–16 and adults, see 778

Business Relations and Occupations: Achievement Examinations for Secondary Schools, high school, see 779

Clerical Aptitude Test: Acorn National Aptitude Tests, grades 7–16 and adults, see 780

Clerical Speed and Accuracy: Differential Aptitude Tests, grades 8–12 and adults, see 781

Clerical Tests FG and 2 [England], ages 12–13, see 781A

Detroit Clerical Aptitudes Examination, grades 9–12, see 782

General Office Clerical Test: National Business Entrance Tests, grades 11–16 and adults, see 783

Hiett Simplified Shorthand Test (Gregg), 1–2 semesters high school, see 784

Machine Calculation Test: National Business Entrance Tests, grades 11–16 and adults, see 785

National Business Entrance Tests, grades 11–16 and adults, see 786

National Teacher Examinations: Business Education, college seniors and teachers, see 787

★*Office Information and Skills Test: Content Evaluation Series*, high school, see 788

Reicherter-Sanders Typewriting I and II, 1–2 semesters high school, see 789

Russell-Sanders Bookkeeping Test, 1–2 semesters high school, see 790

SRA Clerical Aptitudes, grades 9–12 and adults, see 791

SRA Typing Skills, grades 9–12 and adults, see 792

Shorthand Aptitude Test [Australia], high school, see 793

Stenographic Aptitude Test, grades 9–16, see 794

Stenographic Test: National Business Entrance Tests, grades 11–16 and adults, see 795

Tapping Test: A Predictor of Typing and Other Tapping Operations, high school, see 796

Teacher Education Examination Program: Business Education, college seniors preparing to teach secondary school, see 797

Turse Shorthand Aptitude Test, grades 8 and over, see 798

Typewriting Test: National Business Entrance Tests, grades 11–16 and adults, see 799

Undergraduate Program Field Tests: Business Test, college, see 800

United Students Typewriting Tests, 1–4 semesters, see 801

COMPUTATIONAL & TESTING DEVICES

★*Bowman Chronological Age Calculator*, see 802

Bowman M.A. and I.Q. Kalculator, see 803

**Chronological Age Computer*, ages 3-7 to 19-5, see 804

Dominion Table for Converting Mental Age to I.Q. [Canada], see 805

Grade Averaging Charts, see 806

I.Q. Calculator, see 807

★*Mental Age Calculator*, see 808

**Multiple Purpose Self Trainer*, high school and adults, see 809

Psychometric Research and Service Chart Showing the Davis Difficulty and Discrimination Indices for Item Analysis [India], see 810

Rapid-Rater, see 811

★*Ratio I.Q. Computer*, see 812

COURTSHIP & MARRIAGE

★*Albert Mate Selection Check List*, premarital counselees, see 813

California Marriage Readiness Evaluation, premarital counselees, see 814

Caring Relationship Inventory, marital counselees, see 815

Courtship Analysis, adults, see 816

Dating Problems Checklist, high school and college, see 817

El Senoussi Multiphasic Marital Inventory, premarital and marital counselees, see 818

★*I-Am Sentence Completion Test*, marital counselees, see 819

Individual and Family Developmental Review, counselees and therapy patients, see 820

★*Love Attitudes Inventory*, grades 12-16, see 821

Male Impotence Test, adult males, see 822

Marital Communication Inventory, adults, see 823

★*Marital Diagnostic Inventory*, marital counselees, see 824

Marital Roles Inventory, marital counselees, see 825

Marriage Adjustment Form, adults, see 826

Marriage Adjustment Inventory, marital counselees, see 827

Marriage Adjustment Sentence Completion Survey, marital counselees, see 828

Marriage Analysis, married couples in counseling, see 829

★*Marriage Expectation Inventories*, engaged and married couples, see 830

Marriage-Personality Inventory, individuals and couples, see 831

Marriage Prediction Schedule, adults, see 832

Marriage Role Expectation Inventory, adolescents and adults, see 833

**Marriage Scale (For Measuring Compatibility of Interests)*, premarital or married counselees, see 834

★*Marriage Skills Analysis*, marital counselees, see 835

Otto Pre-Marital Counseling Schedules, adult couples, see 836

★*Pair Attraction Inventory*, college and adults, see 837

Sex Knowledge Inventory, sex education classes in high school and college and adults, see 838

Sexual Development Scale for Females, adult females, see 839

**Taylor-Johnson Temperament Analysis*, grades 7-16 and adults, see 840

Thorman Family Relations Conference Situation Questionnaire, families receiving therapy, see 841

DRIVING & SAFETY EDUCATION

**American Automobile Association Driver Testing Apparatus*, drivers, see 842

**Bicycle Safety—Performance and Skill Tests*, ages 10-16, see 843

Driver Attitude Survey, drivers, see 844

★*Driving Skill Exercises*, automobile drivers, see 845

General Test on Traffic and Driving Knowledge, drivers, see 846

Hannaford Industrial Safety Attitude Scales, industry, see 847

McGlade Road Test for Use in Driver Licensing, Education and Employment, prospective drivers, see 848

Road Test Check List for Passenger Car Drivers, passenger car drivers, see 849

Siebrecht Attitude Scale, grades 9-16 and adults, see 850

★*Simplified Road Test*, drivers, see 851

EDUCATION

Academic Freedom Survey, college students and faculty, see 852

**CLEP Subject Examination in History of American Education*, 1 semester or equivalent, see 853

**CLEP Subject Examination in Tests and Measurements*, 1 semester or equivalent, see 854

★*Classroom Atmosphere Questionnaire*, grades 4-9, see 855

★*Comprehensive Teaching and Training Evaluation*, college and training programs, see 856

★*Counseling Services Assessment Blank*, college and adult counseling clients, see 857

★*Course Evaluation Questionnaire*, high school and college, see 858

Diagnostic Teacher-Rating Scale, grades 4-12, see 859

★*Educational Values Assessment Questionnaire*, adults, see 860

Faculty Morale Scale for Institutional Improvement, college faculty, see 861

★*General Tests of Language and Arithmetic for Students* [South Africa], first and second year Bantu candidates for primary teacher's certificate, see 862

**Graduate Record Examinations Advanced Education Test*, graduate school candidates, see 863

**Illinois Course Evaluation Questionnaire*, college, see 864

Illinois Ratings of Teacher Effectiveness, grades 9-12, see 865

Illinois Teacher Evaluation Questionnaire, grades 7-12, see 866

**Junior Index of Motivation*, grades 7-12, see 867

Minnesota Teacher Attitude Inventory, elementary and secondary school teachers and students in grades 12-17, see 868

**National Teacher Examinations*, college seniors and teachers, see 869

**National Teacher Examinations: Early Childhood Education*, college seniors and teachers, see 870

**National Teacher Examinations: Education in an Urban Setting*, college seniors and teachers, see 871

**National Teacher Examinations: Education in the Elementary School*, college seniors and teachers, see 872

**National Teacher Examinations: Education of Mentally Retarded*, college seniors and teachers, see 873

★*National Teacher Examinations: Educational Administration and Supervision*, prospective principals, see 874

★*National Teacher Examinations: Guidance Counselor*, prospective guidance counselors, see 875

National Teacher Examinations: Media Specialist—Library and Audio-Visual Services, college seniors and teachers, see 876

Ohio Teaching Record: Anecdotal Observation Form, teachers, see 877

★*Oral School Attitude Test,* grades kgn–3, see 878

Pictographic Self Rating Scale, high school and college, see 879

Purdue Instructor Performance Indicator, college teachers, see 880

Purdue Rating Scale for Instruction, college teachers, see 881

Purdue Student-Teacher Opinionaire, student teachers, see 882

Purdue Teacher Evaluation Scale, grades 7–12, see 883

Purdue Teacher Opinionaire, teachers, see 884

Remmlein's School Law Test, teacher education classes in school law, see 885

★*School Administration and Supervision,* prospective elementary school administrators and supervisors, see 886

★*School Atmosphere Questionnaire,* grades 7–12, see 887

★*School Attitude Test,* grades 4–6, see 888

★*School Personnel Research and Evaluation Services,* teachers and prospective administrators and supervisors, see 889

★*School Survey of Interpersonal Relationships,* teachers, see 890

★*Secondary School Administration,* prospective secondary school administrators, see 891

★*Secondary School Supervision,* prospective secondary school supervisors, see 892

Self Appraisal Scale for Teachers, teachers, see 893

★*Student Instructional Report,* college teachers, see 894

★*Student Reactions to College,* two-year college, see 895

Student's Rating Scale of an Instructor, high school and college, see 896

★*Survey of Educational Leadership Practices,* teachers and school administrators, see 897

Teacher Education Examination Program, college seniors preparing to teach, see 898

Teacher Education Examination Program: Early Childhood Education, college seniors preparing to teach kgn–grade 3, see 899

Teacher Education Examination Program: Elementary School Education, college seniors preparing to teach grades 1–8, see 900

Teacher Opinionaire on Democracy, teachers, see 901

Teacher Preference Schedule, elementary school teachers and prospective teachers, see 902

★*Teacher Self-Rating Inventory,* teachers, see 903

Teaching Aptitude Test, grades 12–16, see 904

Teaching Evaluation Record, teachers, see 905

Undergraduate Program Field Tests: Education Test, college, see 906

Wilson Teacher-Appraisal Scale, ratings by students in grades 7–16, see 907

HANDWRITING

Ayres Measuring Scale for Handwriting: Gettysburg Edition, grades 5–8, see 908

Expessional Growth Through Handwriting Evaluation Scale, grades 1–12, see 909

HEALTH & PHYSICAL EDUCATION

★*AAHPER Cooperative Health Education Test,* grades 5–9, see 910

AAHPER Cooperative Physical Education Tests, grades 4–12, see 911

AAHPER-Kennedy Foundation Special Fitness Test for the Mentally Retarded, ages 8–18, see 912

AAHPER Sport Skills Tests, ages 10–18, see 913

AAHPER Youth Fitness Test, ages 10–30 (grades 5–16), see 914

Action-Choice Tests for Competitive Sports Situations, high school and college, see 915

Attitude Inventory, college women, see 916

Basic Fitness Tests, ages 12–18, see 917

Belmont Measures of Athletic Performance, females grades 9–16, see 918

CAHPER Fitness-Performance Test [Canada], ages 7–44, see 919

CLEP Subject Examination in Human Growth and Development, 1 semester or equivalent, see 920

College Health Knowledge Test, college, see 921

★*Drug Abuse Knowledge Test,* grades 10–12, see 922

Drug Knowledge Inventory, grades 7–16 and adults, see 923

Emporia Elementary Health Test, grades 6–8, see 924

Emporia High School Health Test, high school and college, see 925

Health and Safety Education Test, grades 3–6, see 926

Health Behavior Inventory, grades 3–16, see 927

Health Education Test: Knowledge and Application, grades 7–13, see 928

Health Knowledge Test for College Freshmen, grade 13, see 929

Health Test: National Achievement Tests, grades 3–8, see 930

Illinois Ratings of Character in Physical Education, high school, see 931

Indiana Physical Fitness Test, grades 4–12, see 932

Information Test on Drugs and Drug Abuse, grades 9–16 and adults, see 933

Information Test on Human Reproduction, grades 9–16 and adults, see 934

Kilander-Leach Health Knowledge Test, grades 12–16, see 935

Modified Sjöstrand Physical Work Capacity Test [Canada], ages 7–44, see 936

National Teacher Examinations: Men's Physical Education, college seniors and teachers, see 937

National Teacher Examinations: Women's Physical Education, college seniors and teachers, see 938

Patient's Self-History Form, patients, see 939

★*Self Administered Health Questionnaire for Secondary School Students,* high school, see 940

Swimming Ability Scales for Boys in Secondary Schools: National Swimming Norms [England], boys ages 11–18, see 941

Teacher Education Examination Program: Physical Education, college seniors preparing to teach secondary school, see 942

★*Tests for Venereal Disease Education,* junior high school, high school and college, see 943

★*Thompson Smoking and Tobacco Knowledge Test,* grades 7–16, see 944

Undergraduate Program Field Tests: Physical Education Test, college, see 945

★*VD Knowledge Test,* grades 6 and over, see 946

Wetzel Grid Charts, ages birth–18, see 947

HOME ECONOMICS

Compton Fabric Preference Test, females in grades 7 and over, see 948

Emporia Clothing Test, high school, see 949

Emporia Foods Test, high school, see 950

Minnesota Check List for Food Preparation and Serving, grades 7–16 and adults, see 951

★*National Teacher Examinations: Home Economics Education*, college seniors and teachers, see 952

★*Nutrition Information Test*, grades 9–16 and adults, see 953

Scales for Appraising High School Homemaking Programs, pupils, teachers, community members, and administrators, see 954

★*Teacher Education Examination Program: Home Economics Education*, college seniors preparing to teach secondary school, see 955

★*Test of Family Life Knowledge and Attitudes*, grade 12 boys and girls seeking Betty Crocker college scholarships and awards, see 956–66

INDUSTRIAL ARTS

Drawing: Cooperative Industrial Arts Tests, 1 semester grades 7–9, see 967

Electricity/Electronics: Cooperative Industrial Arts Tests, 1 semester grades 7–9, see 968

Emporia Industrial Arts Test, high school, see 969

General Industrial Arts: Cooperative Industrial Arts Tests, 1 year grades 7–9, see 970

Metals: Cooperative Industrial Arts Tests, 1 semester grades 7–9, see 971

★*National Teacher Examinations: Industrial Arts Education*, college seniors and teachers, see 972

★*Teacher Education Examination Program: Industrial Arts*, college seniors preparing to teach secondary school, see 973

Technical and Scholastic Test: Dailey Vocational Tests, grades 8–12 and adults, see 974

Woods: Cooperative Industrial Arts Tests, 1 semester grades 7–9, see 975

LEARNING DISABILITIES

★*Automated Graphogestalt Technique*, grades 1–4, see 976

★*Basic Screening and Referral Form for Children With Suspected Learning and Behavioral Disabilities*, grades 1–12, see 977

★*Cutrona Child Study Profile of Psycho-Educational Abilities*, grades kgn–3, see 978

First Grade Screening Test, first grade entrants, see 979

★*Grassi Basic Cognitive Evaluation*, ages 3–9, see 980

Illinois Test of Psycholinguistic Abilities, ages 2–10, see 981; *Filmed Demonstration of the ITPA*, see 982

★*Individual Learning Disabilities Classroom Screening Instrument*, grades 1–3, see 983

Meeting Street School Screening Test, grades kgn–1, see 984

★*Psychoeducational Inventory of Basic Learning Abilities*, ages 5–12 with suspected learning disabilities, see 985

Psychoeducational Profile of Basic Learning Abilities, ages 2–14 with learning disabilities, see 986

★*Pupil Rating Scale: Screening for Learning Disabilities*, grades 3–4, see 987

Screening Test for the Assignment of Remedial Treatments, ages 4-6 to 6-5, see 988

Screening Tests for Identifying Children With Specific Language Disability, grades 1–4, see 989

Specific Language Disability Test, "average to high IQ" children in grades 6–8, see 990

Valett Developmental Survey of Basic Learning Abilities, ages 2–7, see 991

LISTENING COMPREHENSION

★*Assessment of Children's Language Comprehension*, ages 2–6, see 992

Brown-Carlsen Listening Comprehension Test, grades 9–16 and adults, see 993

Cooperative Primary Tests: Listening, grades 1.5–3, see 994

Orr-Graham Listening Test, junior high school boys, see 995

★*Progressive Achievement Tests of Listening Comprehension* [New Zealand], standards 1–4 and Forms I–IV (ages 7–14), see 996

Sequential Tests of Educational Progress: Listening, grades 4–14, see 997

★*Tests for Auditory Comprehension of Language*, ages 3–7, see 997A

PHILOSOPHY

★*Graduate Record Examinations Advanced Philosophy Test*, graduate school candidates, see 998

★*Undergraduate Program Field Tests: Philosophy Test*, college, see 999

★*Undergraduate Program Field Tests: Scholastic Philosophy Test*, college, see 1000

PSYCHOLOGY

Aden-Crosthwait Adolescent Psychology Achievement Test, college, see 1001

★*CLEP Subject Examination in Educational Psychology*, 1 semester or equivalent, see 1002

★*CLEP Subject Examination in General Psychology*, 1 semester or equivalent, see 1003

Cass-Sanders Psychology Test, high school and college, see 1004

★*Graduate Record Examinations Advanced Psychology Test*, graduate school candidates, see 1005

★*Undergraduate Program Field Tests: Psychology Test*, college, see 1006

RECORD & REPORT FORMS

★*A/9 Cumulative Record Folder*, grades kgn–12, see 1007

American Council on Education Cumulative Record Folders, grades 1–16, see 1008

California Cumulative Record and Health Insert, grades 1–12, see 1009

★*Cassel Developmental Record*, birth to death, see 1010

Florida Cumulative Guidance Record, grades 1–12, see 1011

G.C. Anecdotal Record Form [Canada], teachers' recordings of student actions, see 1012

★*Guidance Cumulative Folder and Record Forms*, grades kgn–12, see 1013

★*Height Weight Interpretation Folders*, ages 4–17, see 1014

Junior High School Record, grades 7–10, see 1015

★*Ontario School Record System* [Canada], grades kgn–13, see 1016

★*Permanent Record Folder*, exceptional children, see 1017

★*Psychodiagnostic Test Report Blank*, psychologists' test data on clients, see 1018

★*Secondary-School Record*, grades 9–12, see 1019

RELIGIOUS EDUCATION

Achievement Test in Jewish History, junior high school, see 1020

★*Achievement Test—Jewish Life and Observances,* grades 5–7, see 1021

★*Achievement Test—The State of Israel,* "pupils who have completed an organized course of study on the State of Israel," see 1022

★*Bible and You,* ages 13 and over, see 1023

★*Biblical Survey Test,* college, see 1024

Concordia Bible Information Inventory, grades 4–8, see 1025

Inventory of Religious Activities and Interests, high school and college students considering church-related occupations and theological school students, see 1025A

Religious Attitudes Inventory, religious counselees, see 1026

Standardized Bible Content Tests, Bible college, see 1027

Theological School Inventory, incoming seminary students, see 1028

Youth Research Survey, ages 13–19, see 1029

SCORING MACHINES & SERVICES

Automata EDT 1200 Educational Data Terminal, see 1030

Hankes Scoring Service, see 1031

IBM 1230 Optical Mark Scoring Reader, see 1032

★*IBM 3881 Optical Mark Reader,* see 1033

MRC Scoring and Reporting Services, see 1034

NCS Scoring and Reporting Services, see 1035

NCS Sentry 70, see 1036

OpScan Test Scoring and Document Scanning System, see 1037

Psychological Resources, see 1038

SOCIOECONOMIC STATUS

American Home Scale, grades 8–16, see 1039

Environmental Participation Index, culturally disadvantaged ages 12 and over, see 1040

Home Index, grades 4–12, see 1040A

Socio-Economic Status Scales [India], urban students, adults, and rural families, see 1041

STATISTICS

CLEP Subject Examination in Statistics, 1 semester or equivalent, see 1042

★*Objective Tests in Mathematics: Statistics* [England], ages 15 and over, see 1043

TEST PROGRAMS

ACT Assessment, candidates for college entrance, see 1044

Advanced Placement Examinations, high school students desiring credit for college level courses or admission to advanced courses, see 1045

Canadian Test Battery, Grade 10 [Canada], see 1046

Canadian Test Battery, Grades 8–9 [Canada], grades 8.5–9.0, see 1047

College Board Admissions Testing Program, candidates for college entrance, see 1048

★*College Guidance Program,* grade 11, see 1049

College-Level Examination Program, 1–2 years of college or equivalent, see 1050

College Placement Tests, entering college freshmen, see 1051

Comparative Guidance and Placement Program, entrants to two-year colleges and vocational-technical institutes, see 1052

Graduate Record Examinations: National Program for Graduate School Selection, graduate school candidates, see 1053

Junior College Placement Program, junior college entrants, see 1054

National Guidance Testing Program, grades 1.5–14, see 1055

National Science Foundation Graduate Fellowship Testing Program, applicants for N.S.F. fellowships for graduate study in the sciences, see 1056

★*Ohio Survey Tests,* grades 4, 6, 8, and 10, see 1057

Project Talent Test Battery, grades 9–12, see 1058

Secondary School Admission Test, grades 5–10, see 1059

★*Service for Admission to College and University Testing Program* [Canada], candidates for college entrance, see 1060

★*Testing Academic Achievement,* high school students desiring credit for college level courses or advanced placement, entering college freshmen, and 1–2 years of college or equivalent, see 1061

Undergraduate Program for Counseling and Evaluation, college, see 1062

MULTI-APTITUDE BATTERIES

Academic Promise Tests, grades 6–9, see 1063

★*Academic-Technical Aptitude Tests* [South Africa], "coloured pupils" in standards 6–8, see 1064

★*Aptitude Test for Junior Secondary Pupils* [South Africa], Bantus in Form I, see 1065

Aptitude Tests for Occupations, grades 9–13 and adults, see 1066

★*Armed Services Vocational Aptitude Battery,* high school, see 1067

Detroit General Aptitudes Examination, grades 6–12, see 1068

Differential Aptitude Tests, grades 8–12 and adults, see 1069

Differential Test Battery [England], ages 7 to "top university level," see 1070

Employee Aptitude Survey, ages 16 and over, see 1071

Flanagan Aptitude Classification Tests, grades 9–12 and adults, see 1072

General Aptitude Test Battery, grades 9–12 and adults, see 1073

Guilford-Zimmerman Aptitude Survey, grades 9–16 and adults, see 1074

High Level Battery: Test A/75 [South Africa], adults with at least 12 years of education, see 1075

★*International Primary Factors Test Battery,* grades 5 and over, see 1076

★*Jastak Test of Potential Ability and Behavior Stability,* ages 11.5–14.5, see 1077

Job-Tests Program, adults, see 1078

★*Junior Aptitude Tests for Indian South Africans* [South Africa], standards 6–8, see 1079

Measurement of Skill, adults, see 1080

Multi-Aptitude Test, college courses in testing, see 1081

Multiple Aptitude Tests, grades 7–13, see 1082

N.B. Aptitude Tests (Junior) [South Africa], standards 4–8, see 1083

National Institute for Personnel Research Intermediate Battery [South Africa], standards 7–10 and job applicants with 9–12 years of education, see 1084

National Institute for Personnel Research Normal Battery [South Africa], standards 6–10 and job applicants with 8–11 years of education, see 1085

Nonreading Aptitude Test Battery, disadvantaged grades 9–12 and adults, see 1086

SRA Primary Mental Abilities, grades kgn–12 and adults, see 1087

Senior Aptitude Tests [South Africa], standards 8–10 and college and adults, see 1088

PERSONALITY

NONPROJECTIVE

Ai3Q: A Measure of the Obsessional Personality or Anal Character [England], sixth form and intelligent adults, see 1089

A-S Reaction Study, college and adults, see 1090

Activity Vector Analysis, ages 16 and over, see 1091

Adaptive Behavior Scales, mentally retarded and emotionally maladjusted ages 3 and over, see 1092

Addiction Research Center Inventory, drug addicts, see 1093

Adjective Check List, grades 9–16 and adults, see 1094

Adjustment Inventory, grades 9–16 and adults, see 1095

Adolescent Alienation Index, ages 12–19, see 1096

Affect Scale, college, see 1097

Alcadd Test, adults, see 1098

Animal Crackers: A Test of Motivation to Achieve, grades kgn–1, see 1099

Anxiety Scale for the Blind, blind and partially sighted ages 13 and over, see 1100

Attitude-Interest Analysis Test, early adolescents and adults, see 1101

Attitudes Toward Industrialization, adults, see 1102

Attitudes Toward Parental Control of Children, adults, see 1103

Ayres Space Test, ages 3 and over, see 1104

Babcock Test of Mental Efficiency, ages 7 and over, see 1105

Baker-Schulberg Community Mental Health Ideology Scale, mental health professionals, see 1106

Balthazar Scales of Adaptive Behavior, "profoundly and severely mentally retarded adults and the younger less retarded," see 1107

Barclay Classroom Climate Inventory, grades 3–6, see 1108

Barron-Welsh Art Scale, ages 6 and over, see 1109

Behavior Cards, delinquents having a reading grade score 4.5 or higher, see 1110

Behavior Status Inventory, psychiatric inpatients, see 1111

Bristol Social Adjustment Guides [England], ages 5–15, see 1112

Brook Reaction Test [England], ages 13 and over, see 1113

Burks' Behavior Rating Scale for Organic Brain Dysfunction, grades kgn–6, see 1114

Burks' Behavior Rating Scales, preschool and grades kgn–8, see 1115

C-R Opinionaire, grades 11–16 and adults, see 1116

Cain-Levine Social Competency Scale, mentally retarded children ages 5–13, see 1117

California Life Goals Evaluation Schedules, ages 15 and over, see 1118

California Medical Survey, medical patients ages 10–18 and adults, see 1119

California Preschool Social Competency Scale, ages 2.5–5.5, see 1120

California Psychological Inventory, ages 13 and over, see 1121; *Behaviordyne Psychodiagnostic Lab Service,* see 1122

California Test of Personality, grades kgn–14 and adults, see 1123

Cassel Group Level of Aspiration Test, grades 5–16 and adults, see 1124

Chapin Social Insight Test, ages 13 and over, see 1125

Child Behavior Rating Scale, grades kgn–3, see 1126

Children's Embedded Figures Test, ages 5–12, see 1127

Children's Hypnotic Susceptibility Scale, ages 5–16, see 1128

Children's Personality Questionnaire [South Africa], ages 8–12, see 1129

Client-Centered Counseling Progress Record, adults and children undergoing psychotherapeutic counseling, see 1130

Clinical Analysis Questionnaire, ages 18 and over, see 1131

Clinical Behavior Check List and Rating Scale, clinical clients, see 1132

College and University Environment Scales, college, see 1133

College Inventory of Academic Adjustment, college, see 1134

College Student Questionnaires, college entrants and students, see 1135

College Student Satisfaction Questionnaire, college, see 1136

Community Adaptation Schedule, normals and psychiatric patients, see 1137

Community Improvement Scale, adults, see 1138

Comrey Personality Scales, ages 16 and over, see 1139

Concept Formation Test, normal and schizophrenic adults, see 1140

Concept-Specific Anxiety Scale, college and adults, see 1141

Conceptual Systems Test, grades 7 and over, see 1142

Conservatism Scale [England], ages 12 and over, see 1143

Cornell Index, ages 18 and over, see 1144

Cornell Medical Index, ages 14 and over, see 1145

Cornell Word Form 2, adults, see 1146

Cotswold Personality Assessment P.A.1 [Scotland], ages 11–16, see 1147

Crawford Psychological Adjustment Scale, psychiatric patients, see 1148

Cree Questionnaire, industrial employees, see 1149

Current and Past Psychopathology Scales, psychiatric patients and nonpatients, see 1150

DF Opinion Survey, grades 12–16 and adults, see 1151

Defense Mechanism Inventory, ages 16 and over, see 1152

Demos D Scale: An Attitude Scale for the Identification of Dropouts, grades 7–12, see 1153

Depression Adjective Check Lists, grades 9–16 and adults, see 1154

Detroit Adjustment Inventory, grades kgn–12, see 1155

Developmental Potential of Preschool Children, handicapped children ages 2–6, see 1156

Devereux Adolescent Behavior Rating Scale, normal and emotionally disturbed children ages 13–18, see 1157

Devereux Child Behavior Rating Scale, emotionally disturbed and mentally retarded children ages 8–12, see 1158

Devereux Elementary School Behavior Rating Scale, grades kgn–6, see 1159

Diplomacy Test of Empathy, business and industry, see 1160

★*Discharge Readiness Inventory*, psychiatric patients, see 1161

Dynamic Personality Inventory [England], ages 15 or 17 and over with IQ's of 80 and over, see 1162

Early School Personality Questionnaire, ages 6–8, see 1163

Edwards Personal Preference Schedule, college and adults, see 1164

Edwards Personality Inventory, grades 11–16 and adults, see 1165

Ego-Ideal and Conscience Development Test, ages 12–18, see 1166

Ego Strength Q-Sort Test, grades 9–16 and adults, see 1167

Elizur Test of Psycho-Organicity, ages 6 and over, see 1168

Embedded Figures Test, ages 10 and over, see 1169

Emo Questionnaire, adults, see 1170

Empathy Test, ages 13 and over, see 1171

Evaluation Modality Test, adults, see 1172

★*Experiential World Inventory*, disturbed adolescents and adults, see 1173

Eysenck Personality Inventory [England], grades 9–16 and adults, see 1174

Eysenck-Withers Personality Inventory [England], institutionalized subnormal adults, see 1175

FIRO Scales, grades 4–16 and adults, see 1176

★*Fairview Development Scale*, infirm mentally retarded, see 1177

★*Fairview Problem Behavior Record*, mentally retarded, see 1178

★*Fairview Self-Help Scale*, mentally retarded, see 1179

★*Fairview Social Skills Scale*, mentally retarded, see 1180

Family Adjustment Test, ages 12 and over, see 1181

Family Relations Test [England], ages 3 and over, see 1182

Famous Sayings, grades 9–16 and business and industry, see 1183

Fatigue Scales Kit, adults, see 1184

Fear Survey Schedule, college and adults, see 1185

Fels Parent Behavior Rating Scales, parents, see 1186

Forty-Eight Item Counseling Evaluation Test, adolescents and adults, see 1187

Freeman Anxiety Neurosis and Psychosomatic Test, mental patients, see 1188

★*Frost Self Description Questionnaire* [Canada], ages 8–14, see 1189

Getting Along, grades 7–9, see 1190

Gibson Spiral Maze [England], ages 8.5 and over, see 1191

Goldstein-Scheerer Tests of Abstract and Concrete Thinking, brain damaged adults, see 1192

Gordon Personal Inventory, grades 9–16 and adults, see 1193

Gordon Personal Profile, grades 9–16 and adults, see 1194

Gottschalk-Gleser Content Analysis Scales, ages 14 and over, see 1195

Grassi Block Substitution Test, mental patients, see 1196

Grayson Perceptualization Test, detection of cortical impairment, see 1197

Grid Test of Schizophrenic Thought Disorder [England], adults, see 1198

Group Cohesiveness: A Study of Group Morale, adults, see 1199

Group Dimensions Descriptions Questionnaire, college and adult groups, see 1200

★*Group Embedded Figures Test*, ages 10 and over, see 1201

Group Psychotherapy Suitability Evaluation Scale, patients in group therapy, see 1202

Guidance Inventory, high school, see 1203

Guilford-Holley L Inventory, college and adults, see 1204

Guilford-Martin Inventory of Factors GAMIN, grades 12–16 and adults, see 1205

Guilford-Martin Personnel Inventory, adults, see 1206

Guilford-Zimmerman Temperament Survey, grades 12–16 and adults, see 1207

★*Hahn Self Psychoevaluation Materials*, ages 40 and over, see 1208

★*Hahnemann High School Behavior Rating Scale*, grades 7–12, see 1209

Handicap Problems Inventory, ages 16 and over with physical disabilities, see 1210

Hartman Value Profile, ages 12 and over, see 1211

Harvard Group Scale of Hypnotic Susceptibility, college and adults, see 1212

Hellenic Affiliation Scale, college, see 1213

Hill Interaction Matrix, psychotherapy groups, see 1214

Hoffer-Osmond Diagnostic Test, mental patients, see 1215

Hooper Visual Organization Test, ages 14 and over, see 1216

Hospital Adjustment Scale, mental patients, see 1217

Hostility and Direction of Hostility Questionnaire [England], mental patients and normals, see 1218

★*How I See Myself Scale*, grades 3–12, see 1219

How Well Do You Know Yourself?, high school, college, office and factory workers, see 1220

Human Relations Inventory, grades 9–16 and adults, see 1221

Humm-Wadsworth Temperament Scale, adults, see 1222

Hunt-Minnesota Test for Organic Brain Damage, chronological ages 16–70 and mental ages 8 and over, see 1223

Hysteroid-Obsessoid Questionnaire [England], mental patients and normals, see 1224

IPAT Anxiety Scale Questionnaire, ages 14 and over, see 1225

IPAT Contact Personality Factor Test, high school and adults, see 1226

IPAT 8-Parallel-Form Anxiety Battery, ages 14 or 15 and over, see 1227

IPAT Humor Test of Personality, high school and adults, see 1228

IPAT Neurotic Personality Factor Test, grades 9–16 and adults, see 1229

Independent Activities Questionnaire, high school and college, see 1230

★*Inferred Self-Concept Scale*, grades 1–6, see 1231

Inpatient Multidimensional Psychiatric Scale, hospitalized mental patients, see 1232

Institute of Child Study Security Test [Canada], grades 1–8, see 1233

Institutional Functioning Inventory, college faculty and administrators, see 1234

★*Institutional Goals Inventory*, college faculty and students, see 1235

Institutional Self-Study Service Survey, college students, see 1236

Integration Level Test Series, adults, see 1237

Interest Inventory for Elementary Grades, grades 4–6, see 1238

Inter-Person Perception Test, ages 6 and over, see 1239

★Interpersonal Check List, adults, see 1240

★Interpersonal Communication Inventory, grades 9–16 and adults, see 1241

★Interpersonal Orientation Scale, college and adults, see 1242

Interpersonal Perception Method [England], married couples and other 2-person or 2-group situations, see 1243

★Inventory of College Activities, college, see 1244

Inventory of Factors STDCR, grades 9–16 and adults, see 1245

★"Is of Identity" Test, grades 4–16, see 1246

It Scale for Children, ages 5–6, see 1247

★Jesness Behavior Checklist, ages 10 and over, see 1248

★Jesness Inventory, disturbed children and adolescents ages 8–18 and adults, see 1249

★Job Analysis and Interest Measurement, adults, see 1250

Jones Personality Rating Scale, grades 9–12 and adults, see 1251

Junior Eysenck Personality Inventory [England], ages 7–15, see 1252

★Jr.-Sr. High School Personality Questionnaire, ages 12–18, see 1253

KD Proneness Scale and Check List, ages 7 and over, see 1254

Katz Adjustment Scales, normal and mentally disordered adults, see 1255

Kuder Preference Record—Personal, grades 9–16 and adults, see 1256

Kundu's Neurotic Personality Inventory [India], adults, see 1257

★Kupfer-Detre System, psychiatric patients, see 1258

Leadership Ability Evaluation, grades 9–16 and adults, see 1259

Leadership Q-Sort Test, adults, see 1260

Level of Aspiration Board, mental ages 12.5 and over, see 1261

Life Adjustment Inventory, high school, see 1262

Lüscher Color Test, adults, see 1263

★MACC Behavioral Adjustment Scale, psychiatric patients, see 1264

★M-B History Record, psychiatric patients and penal groups, see 1265

★M-Scale: An Inventory of Attitudes Toward Black/White Relations in the United States, college and adults, see 1266

★Maferr Inventory of Feminine Values, older adolescents and adults, see 1267

★Maferr Inventory of Masculine Values, older adolescents and adults, see 1268

Manchester Scales of Social Adaptation [England], ages 6–15, see 1269

Mandel Social Adjustment Scale, psychiatric patients and others, see 1270

Manson Evaluation, adults, see 1271

★Martin S-D Inventory, clients and patients, see 1272

Maryland Parent Attitude Survey, parents, see 1273

★Mathematics Anxiety Rating Scale, college and adults, see 1274

Maudsley Personality Inventory [England], college and adults, see 1275

Maxfield-Buchholz Scale of Social Maturity for Use With Preschool Blind Children, infancy–6 years, see 1276

Memory-For-Designs Test, ages 8.5 and over, see 1277

Mental Status Schedule, psychiatric patients and non-patients, see 1278

Middlesex Hospital Questionnaire [England], ages 18 and over, see 1279

Minnesota Counseling Inventory, high school, see 1280

Minnesota Multiphasic Personality Inventory, ages 16 and over, see 1281; *★Behaviordyne Psychodiagnostic Lab Service,* see 1282; *★MMPI-ICA Computer Report,* see 1283; *The Psychological Corporation MMPI Reporting Service,* see 1284; *★Roche MMPI Computerized Interpretation Service,* see 1285

Minnesota Rating Scale for Personal Qualities and Abilities, college and adults, see 1286

★Missouri Children's Picture Series, ages 5–16, see 1287

★Mood Altering Substances, high school and college, see 1288

Mooney Problem Check List, grades 7–16 and adults, see 1289

Mother-Child Relationship Evaluation, mothers, see 1290

Motivation Analysis Test, ages 17 and over, see 1291

Multidimensional Maturity Scale, grades kgn–12, see 1292

Multiple Affect Adjective Check List, grades 8–16 and adults, see 1293

Myers-Briggs Type Indicator, grades 9–16 and adults, see 1294

Neuroticism Scale Questionnaire, ages 13 and over, see 1295

New Junior Maudsley Inventory [England], ages 9–16, see 1296

Northampton Activity Rating Scale, mental patients, see 1297

Nurses' Observation Scale for Inpatient Evaluation, mental patients, see 1298

Object Sorting Scales [Australia], adults, see 1299

Objective-Analytic (O-A) Anxiety Battery, ages 14 and over, see 1300

Ohio College Association Rating Scale, high school, see 1301

Omnibus Personality Inventory, college, see 1302

Opinion, Attitude, and Interest Survey, high school seniors and college students, see 1303

★Opinions Toward Adolescents, college and adults, see 1304

Organic Integrity Test, ages 5 and over, see 1305

Orientation Inventory, college and industry, see 1306

★Ottawa School Behavior Check List [Canada], ages 6–12, see 1307

★PHSF Relations Questionnaire [South Africa], standards 6–10 and college and adults, see 1308

PRADI Autobiographical Form, clinical clients, see 1309

Parent-Adolescent Communication Inventory, high school and adults, see 1310

★Perceptual Maze Test [England], ages 6–16 and adults, see 1311

★Personal Adjustment Index, job applicants, see 1312

Personal Adjustment Inventory, ages 9–13, see 1313

Personal Audit, grades 9–16 and adults, see 1314

Personal Orientation Inventory, grades 9–16 and adults, see 1315

Personal Preference Scale, ages 15 and over, see 1316

★Personal Values Abstract, ages 13 and over, see 1317

Personal Values Inventory, grades 12–13, see 1318

Personality Evaluation Form, ages 2 and over, see 1319

Personality Inventory, grades 9–16 and adults, see 1320

Personality Rating Scale, grades 4–12, see 1321

Personality Research Form, college, see 1322

★Personnel Reaction Blank, adults, see 1323

Philo-Phobe, ages 10 and over, see 1324

Pictorial Study of Values, ages 14 and over, see 1325

Piers-Harris Children's Self Concept Scale, grades 3–12, see 1326

Polarity Scale, college and adults, see 1327

Polyfactorial Study of Personality, adults, see 1328

Power of Influence Test, grades 2–13, see 1329

Practical Policy Test, adults, see 1330

★*Preschool Embedded Figures Test,* ages 3–5, see 1331

Preschool Self-Concept Picture Test, ages 4–5, see 1332

Press Test, industrial employees, see 1333

★*Primary Self-Concept Inventory,* grades kgn–4, see 1334

Problem Check List: Form for Rural Young People, ages 16–30, see 1335

Process for In-School Screening of Children With Emotional Handicaps, grades kgn–12, see 1336

★*Profile of Mood States,* college and psychiatric outpatients, see 1337

Progress Assessment Chart of Social Development [England], mentally handicapped children and adults, see 1338

Psychiatric Evaluation Form, psychiatric patients and nonpatients, see 1339

Psychiatric Status Schedules, psychiatric patients and nonpatients, see 1340

Psychological Audit for Interpersonal Relations, marriage counselees and industrial personnel, see 1341

★*Psychological Screening Inventory,* ages 16 and over, see 1342

Psychometric Behavior Checklist, adults, see 1343

Psycho-Somatic Inventory, older adolescents and adults, see 1344

Psychotic Inpatient Profile, mental patients, see 1345

Psychotic Reaction Profile, mental patients, see 1346

Pupil Behavior Inventory, grades 7–12, see 1347

Purdue Master Attitude Scales, grades 7–16, see 1348

Purdue Rating Scale for Administrators and Executives, administrators and executives, see 1349

Purpose in Life Test, adults, see 1350

Q-Tags Test of Personality [Canada], ages 6 and over, see 1351

★*Reactions to Everyday Situations* [South Africa], ages 16 and over, see 1352

Reid Report, job applicants, see 1353

Richardson Emergency Psychodiagnostic Summary, mental patients, see 1354

★*Risk-Taking-Attitude-Values Inventory,* ages 3 and over, see 1354A

★*Rokeach Value Survey,* grades 7–16 and adults, see 1355

★*Runner Studies of Attitude Patterns,* job applicants, see 1356

Rutgers Social Attribute Inventory, adults, see 1357

SAQS Chicago Q Sort, college and adults, see 1358

S-D Proneness Checklist, clients and patients, see 1359

STS Junior Inventory, grades 4–8, see 1360

STS Youth Inventory, grades 7–12, see 1361

Scale of Socio-Egocentrism, grades 7–16, see 1362

Scale to Measure Attitudes Toward Disabled Persons, disabled and nondisabled adults, see 1363

★*School Attitude Survey,* grades 3–6, see 1364

School Interest Inventory, grades 7–12, see 1365

School Inventory, high school, see 1366

School Motivation Analysis Test, ages 12–17, see 1367

Science Research Temperament Scale, grades 12–16 and adults, see 1368

★*Secondary School Research Program,* high school students, teachers, and administrators, see 1369

Security-Insecurity Inventory, grades 9–16 and adults, see 1370

Self-Analysis Inventory, adults, see 1371

★*Self-Concept Adjective Checklist,* grades kgn–8, see 1372

★*Self-Concept and Motivation Inventory,* age 4 and grades kgn–12, see 1373

★*Self-Esteem Questionnaire,* ages 9 and over, see 1374

Self-Interview Inventory, adult males, see 1375

Self Perception Inventory, ages 12 and over, see 1376

Self-Rating Depression Scale, adults, see 1377

★*Self-Report Inventory,* college, see 1378

Sherman Mental Impairment Test, adults, see 1379

Shipley-Institute of Living Scale for Measuring Intellectual Impairment, adults, see 1380

★*Situational Attitude Scale,* college, see 1381

★*Situational Preference Inventory,* grades 9–16 and adults, see 1382

Sixteen Personality Factor Questionnaire, ages 16 and over, see 1383

Slosson Drawing Coordination Test for Children and Adults, ages 1.5 and over, see 1384

Social Competence Inventories, adults, see 1385

Social Intelligence Test, grades 9–16 and adults, see 1386

Spiral Aftereffect Test, ages 5 and over, see 1387

Stamp Behaviour Study Technique [Australia], preschool–kgn, see 1388

Stanford Hypnotic Susceptibility Scale, college and adults, see 1389

Stanford Profile Scales of Hypnotic Susceptibility, college and adults, see 1390

State-Trait Anxiety Inventory, grades 9–16 and adults, see 1391

★*State-Trait Anxiety Inventory for Children,* grades 4–8, see 1392

Stereopathy-Acquiescence Schedule, college, see 1393

Stern Activities Index, grades 7–16 and adults, see 1394

Stern Environment Indexes, grades 7 through graduate school, see 1395

Stockton Geriatric Rating Scale, hospital or nursing home patients aged 65 and over, see 1396

★*Structured and Scaled Interview to Assess Maladjustment,* mental patients, see 1397

Structured Clinical Interview, mental patients, see 1398

Student Attitude Inventory [Australia], college, see 1399

Student Description Form, grades 9–12, see 1400

★*Student Evaluation Scale,* grades 1–12, see 1401

Study of Choices, ages 16 and over, see 1402

Study of Values, grades 10–16 and adults, see 1403; British Edition [England], college and adults, see 1404

Style of Mind Inventory, college and adults, see 1405

★*Suinn Test Anxiety Behavior Scale,* college and adults, see 1406

Survey of Interpersonal Values, grades 9–16 and adults, see 1407

Survey of Personal Attitude "SPA" (With Pictures), adults, see 1408

Survey of Personal Values, grades 11–16 and adults, see 1409

Symptom Sign Inventory [England], mental patients, see 1410

Systematic Interview Guides [England], mothers, see 1411

★*T.M.R. Performance Profile for the Severely and Moderately Retarded,* ages 4 and over, see 1412

Temperament Comparator, adults, see 1413

★*Temperament Questionnaire* [South Africa], standards 8 and over, see 1414

Tennessee Self Concept Scale, ages 12 and over, see 1415

Test for Developmental Age in Girls, girls ages 8–18, see 1416

Test of Basic Assumptions, adults, see 1417

Test of Behavioral Rigidity, ages 21 and over, see 1418

Test of Social Insight, grades 6–16 and adults, see 1419

Test of Work Competency and Stability [Canada], ages 21 and over, see 1420

Tests of Social Intelligence, high school and adults, see 1421

Thorndike Dimensions of Temperament, grades 11–16 and adults, see 1422

Thurstone Temperament Schedule, grades 9–16 and adults, see 1423

Trait Evaluation Index, college and adults, see 1424

Triadal Equated Personality Inventory, adult males, see 1425

★*Tri-Cultural Attitude Scale*, grades kgn–6, see 1426

Tulane Factors of Liberalism-Conservatism, social science students, see 1427

Vineland Social Maturity Scale, birth to maturity, see 1428

Visual-Verbal Test, schizophrenic patients, see 1429

Vocational Preference Inventory, grades 12–16 and adults, see 1430

WLW Personal Attitude Inventory, business and industry, see 1431

★*Wahler Physical Symptoms Inventory*, psychiatric patients and counselees, see 1432

★*Wahler Self-Description Inventory*, grades 7 and over and psychiatric patients, see 1433

Walker Problem Behavior Identification Checklist, grades 4–6, see 1434

Ward Behavior Inventory, mental patients, see 1435

Weighted-Score Likability Rating Scale, ages 6 and over, see 1436

Welsh Figure Preference Test, ages 6 and over, see 1437

Western Personality Inventory, adults, see 1438

What I Like to Do, grades 4–7, see 1439

★*Whitaker Index of Schizophrenic Thinking*, mental patients, see 1440

William, Lynde & Williams Analysis of Personal Values, business and industry, see 1441

★*Work Environment Preference Schedule*, grades 11–16 and adults, see 1442

★*Y.E.M.R. Performance Profile for the Young Moderately and Mildly Retarded*, ages 5–9, see 1443

PROJECTIVE

African T.A.T. [South Africa], urban African adults, see 1444

Association Adjustment Inventory, normal and institutionalized adults, see 1445

Auditory Apperception Test, grades 9 and over, see 1446

Bender-Gestalt Test, ages 4 and over, see 1447

Blacky Pictures, ages 5 and over, see 1448

Braverman-Chevigny Auditory Projective Test, ages 4 and over, see 1449

Buttons, grades 7–9, see 1450

Children's Apperception Test, ages 3–10, see 1451

Color Pyramid Test [Switzerland], ages 6 and over, see 1452

Columbus: Picture Analysis of Growth Towards Maturity [Switzerland], ages 5–20, see 1453

Curtis Completion Form, grades 11–16 and adults, see 1454

Draw-A-Person, ages 5 and over, see 1455

Draw-A-Person Quality Scale, ages 16–25, see 1456

Driscoll Play Kit, ages 2–10, see 1457

★*Education Apperception Test*, preschool and elementary school, see 1458

Family Relations Indicator, emotionally disturbed children and their parents, see 1459

Five Task Test, ages 8 and over, see 1460

Forer Structured Sentence Completion Test, ages 10–18 and adults, see 1461

Forer Vocational Survey, adolescents and adults, see 1462

Franck Drawing Completion Test [Australia], ages 6 and over, see 1463

★*Gerontological Apperception Test*, ages 66 and over, see 1464

Graphoscopic Scale, ages 5–16 and over, see 1465

Group Personality Projective Test, ages 11 and over, see 1466

Group Projection Sketches for the Study of Small Groups, ages 16 and over, see 1467

HFD Test, ages 5–12, see 1468

H-T-P: House-Tree-Person Projective Technique, ages 3 and over, see 1469

Hand Test, ages 6 and over, see 1470

Holtzman Inkblot Technique, ages 5 and over, see 1471; *Computer Scoring Service for the Holtzman Inkblot Technique*, see 1472

Howard Ink Blot Test, adults, see 1473

Human Figure Drawing Techniques, see 1474

IES Test, ages 10 and over and latency period girls, see 1475

Incomplete Sentence Test, employees and college, see 1476

Industrial Sentence Completion Form, employee applicants, see 1477

Kahn Test of Symbol Arrangement, ages 6 and over, see 1478

Ka-Ro Inkblot Test [Japan], ages 3 and over, see 1479

Kent-Rosanoff Free Association Test, ages 4 and over, see 1480

Machover Draw-A-Person Test, ages 2 and over, see 1481

Make a Picture Story, ages 6 and over, see 1482

Measurement of Self Concept in Kindergarten Children, kgn, see 1483

Miner Sentence Completion Scale, managers and management trainees, see 1484

Minnesota Percepto-Diagnostic Test, ages 5–16, see 1485

Object Relations Technique [England], ages 11 and over, see 1486

PRADI Draw-A-Person Test, clinical clients, see 1487

Pain Apperception Test, adults, see 1488

Pickford Projective Pictures [England], ages 5–15, see 1489

Picture Identification Test, high school and college, see 1490

Picture Impressions Test, adolescents and adults, see 1491

★*Picture Situation Test* [South Africa], adult males, see 1492

Picture Story Test Blank, clinical clients, see 1493

Picture World Test, ages 6 and over, see 1494

★*Polite Sentence Completion Test*, grades 1–12, see 1495

Psychiatric Attitudes Battery, adults, see 1496

Rock-A-Bye, Baby, ages 5–10, see 1497

Rohde Sentence Completions Test, ages 12 and over, see 1498

Rorschach [Switzerland], ages 3 and over, see 1499

Rosenzweig Picture-Frustration Study, ages 4 and over, see 1500

Rotter Incomplete Sentences Blank, grades 9–16 and adults, see 1501

Ruth Fry Symbolic Profile, ages 14 and over, see 1502

School Apperception Method, grades kgn–9, see 1503

Self Explorations Inventory, college and adults, see 1504

Self Valuation Test [England], ages 7–15 and adults, see 1505

Sentence Completion Blank, college and adults, see 1506

★*Sentence Completion Test*, high school and college, see 1507

Seven Squares Technique [Sweden], ages 5 and over, see 1508

Social Relations Test [South Africa], adult males, see 1509

Sound-Apperception Test, ages 16 and over, see 1510

South African Picture Analysis Test [The Netherlands], ages 5–13, see 1511

Structured Doll Play Test, ages 2–6, see 1512

Structured-Objective Rorschach Test, adults, see 1513

Symbol Elaboration Test, ages 6 and over, see 1514

Symonds Picture-Story Test, grades 7–12, see 1515

Szondi Test [Switzerland], ages 5 and over, see 1516

*Tasks of Emotional Development Test, ages 6–11 and adolescents, see 1517

Test of Family Attitudes [Belgium], ages 6–12, see 1518

Thematic Apperception Test, ages 4 and over, see 1519

Thematic Apperception Test for African Subjects [South Africa], ages 10 and over, see 1520

★*This I Believe Test,* grades 9 and over, see 1521

Tomkins-Horn Picture Arrangement Test, ages 10 and over, see 1522

Toy World Test [France], ages 2 and over, see 1523

Tree Test [Switzerland], ages 9 and over, see 1524

Twitchell-Allen Three-Dimensional Personality Test, ages 3 and over (sighted and sightless), see 1525

Visual Apperception Test '60, ages 6 and over, see 1526

Washington University Sentence Completion Test, ages 12 and over, see 1527

Zulliger Individual and Group Test [Switzerland], ages 3 and over, see 1528

READING

A.C.E.R. Lower Grades Reading Test: Level 1 [Australia], grade 1, see 1529

★*ACER Primary Reading Survey Tests* [Australia], grades 3–6, see 1530

A.C.E.R. Silent Reading Tests: Standardized for Use in New Zealand [New Zealand], ages 9–12, see 1531

American School Achievement Tests: Reading, grades 2–9, see 1532

American School Reading Tests, grades 10–13, see 1533

Buffalo Reading Test for Speed and Comprehension, grades 9–16, see 1534

Burnett Reading Series: Survey Test, grades 1.5–12, see 1535

*California Achievement Tests: Reading, grades 1–14, see 1536

*Carver-Darby Chunked Reading Test, grades 9–16 and adults, see 1537

Commerce Reading Comprehension Test, grades 12–16 and adults, see 1538

Comprehension Test for Training College Students [England], training college students and applicants for admission, see 1539

Comprehensive Primary Reading Scales, grade 1, see 1540

Comprehensive Reading Scales, grades 4–12, see 1541

*Comprehensive Tests of Basic Skills: Reading, grades kgn–12, see 1542

Cooperative Primary Tests: Reading, grades 1.5–3, see 1543

Cooperative Reading Comprehension Test, Form Y [Australia], secondary forms 5–6 and university, see 1544

Cooperative Reading Comprehension Test, Forms L and M [Australia], secondary forms 2–4, see 1545

Davis Reading Test, grades 8–13, see 1546

Delaware County Silent Reading Test, grades 1.5–8, see 1547

★*Edinburgh Reading Tests* [England], ages 8.5–12.5, see 1548

Emporia Reading Tests, grades 1–8, see 1549

GAP Reading Comprehension Test [Australia], grades 2–7, see 1550

★*GAPADOL* [Australia], ages 10 and over, see 1551

*Gates-MacGinitie Reading Tests, grades 1–9, see 1552

Gates-MacGinitie Reading Tests: Survey F, grades 10–12, see 1553

Group Reading Assessment [England], end of first year junior school, see 1554

Group Reading Test [England], ages 6–10, see 1555

High School Reading Test: National Achievement Tests, grades 7–12, see 1556

Individual Reading Test [Australia], ages 6-0 to 9-9, see 1557

★*Informal Reading Assessment Tests* [Canada], grades 1–3, see 1558

★*Inventory-Survey Tests,* grades 4–8, see 1559

*Iowa Silent Reading Tests, grades 4–16, see 1560

Kelvin Measurement of Reading Ability [Scotland], ages 8–12, see 1561

Kingston Test of Silent Reading [England], ages 7–11, see 1562

Lee-Clark Reading Test, grades 1–2, see 1563

McGrath Test of Reading Skills, grades 1–13, see 1564

McMenemy Measure of Reading Ability, grades 3 and 5–8, see 1565

Maintaining Reading Efficiency Tests, grades 7–16 and adults, see 1566

*Metropolitan Achievement Tests: Reading Tests, grades 2–9, see 1567

Minnesota Reading Examination for College Students, grades 9–16, see 1568

Monroe's Standardized Silent Reading Test, grades 3–12, see 1569

N.B. Silent Reading Tests (Beginners): Reading Comprehension Test [South Africa], substandard B, see 1570

*National Teacher Examinations: Reading Specialist, college seniors and teachers, see 1571

Nelson-Denny Reading Test, grades 9–16 and adults, see 1572

Nelson Reading Test, grades 3–9, see 1573

New Developmental Reading Tests, grades 1–6, see 1574

OISE Achievement Tests in Silent Reading: Advanced Primary Battery [Canada], grade 2, see 1575

Pressey Diagnostic Reading Tests, grades 3–9, see 1576

★*Primary Reading Survey Tests,* grades 2–3, see 1577

Primary Reading Test: Acorn Achievement Tests, grades 2–3, see 1578

Progressive Achievement Tests of Reading [New Zealand], standards 2–4 and Forms I–IV (ages 8–14), see 1579

RBH Basic Reading and Word Test, disadvantaged adults, see 1580

RBH Test of Reading Comprehension, business and industry, see 1581

*Reading Comprehension: Canadian English Achievement Test [Canada], grades 8.5–9.0, see 1582

Reading Comprehension: Cooperative English Tests, grades 9–14, see 1583

Reading Comprehension Test, college entrants, see 1584

*Reading Comprehension Test DE [England], ages 10–12.5, see 1585

Reading Comprehension Test: National Achievement

Tests [Crow, Kuhlmann, and Crow], grades 4–9, see 1586

Reading Comprehension Test: National Achievement Tests [Speer and Smith], grades 3–8, see 1587

Reading for Understanding Placement Test, grades 3–16, see 1588

★*Reading Progress Scale*, grades 3–12, see 1589

Reading: Public School Achievement Tests, grades 3–8, see 1590

Reading Test AD [England], ages 7-6 to 11-1, see 1591

Reading Test (Comprehension and Speed): Municipal Tests, grades 3–8, see 1592

Reading Test: McGraw-Hill Basic Skills System, grades 11–14, see 1593

Reading Tests A and BD [England], 1–4 years primary school, see 1594

Reading Tests EH 1–3 [England], first 4 years of secondary school, see 1595

SRA Achievement Series: Reading, grades 1–9, see 1596

SRA Reading Record, grades 6–12, see 1597

Schrammel-Gray High School and College Reading Test, grades 7–16, see 1598

Sequential Tests of Educational Progress: Reading, grades 4–14, see 1599

Silent Reading Tests [South Africa], standards 1–10 (ages 7–17), see 1600

Southgate Group Reading Tests [England], ages 6–8, see 1601

Stanford Achievement Test: High School Reading Test, grades 9–12, see 1602

Stanford Achievement Test: Reading Tests, grades 1.5–9, see 1603

★*Sucher-Allred Reading Placement Inventory*, reading level grades 1–9, see 1604

Survey of Primary Reading Development, grades 1–4, see 1605

Survey of Reading Achievement, grades 7–12, see 1606

Survey Tests of Reading, grades 3–13, see 1607

Tests of Academic Progress: Reading, grades 9–12, see 1608

Tests of Reading: Inter-American Series, grades 1–13, see 1609

Traxler High School Reading Test, grades 10–12, see 1610

Traxler Silent Reading Test, grades 7–10, see 1611

Van Wagenen Analytical Reading Scales, grades 4–12, see 1612

W.A.L. English Comprehension Test [Australia], high school, see 1613

★*Wide-span Reading Test* [England], ages 7–15, see 1614

Williams Primary Reading Test, grades 1–3, see 1615

Williams Reading Test for Grades 4–9, see 1616

DIAGNOSTIC

California Phonics Survey, grades 7–12 and college, see 1617

Classroom Reading Inventory, grades 2–10, see 1618

★*Cooper-McGuire Diagnostic Word-Analysis Test*, grades 1 and over, see 1619

Cooperative Primary Tests: Word Analysis, grades 1.5–3, see 1620

Denver Public Schools Reading Inventory, grades 1–8, see 1621

Diagnostic Examination of Silent Reading Abilities, grades 4–12, see 1622

Diagnostic Reading Examination for Diagnosis of Special Difficulty in Reading, grades 1–4, see 1623

Diagnostic Reading Scales, grades 1–6 and retarded readers in grades 7–12, see 1624

Diagnostic Reading Test: Pupil Progress Series, grades 1.9–8, see 1625

Diagnostic Reading Tests, grades kgn–13, see 1626

Doren Diagnostic Reading Test of Word Recognition Skills, grades 1–4, see 1627

Durrell Analysis of Reading Difficulty, grades 1–6, see 1628

Gates-McKillop Reading Diagnostic Tests, grades 2–5, see 1629

★*Gillingham-Childs Phonics Proficiency Scales*, grades 1–12, see 1630

Group Diagnostic Reading Aptitude and Achievement Tests, grades 3–9, see 1631

★*Group Phonics Analysis*, reading level grades 1–3, see 1632

★*LRA Standard Mastery Tasks in Language*, grades 1–2, see 1633

McCullough Word-Analysis Tests, grades 4–6, see 1634

★*McGuire-Bumpus Diagnostic Comprehension Test*, reading levels grades 2.5–6, see 1635

★*Phonics Criterion Test*, reading level grades 1–3, see 1636

Phonics Knowledge Survey, grades 1–6, see 1637

Phonovisual Diagnostic Test, grades 3–12, see 1638

★*Prescriptive Reading Inventory*, grades 1.5–6.5, see 1639

★*Prescriptive Reading Inventory Interim Tests*, grades 1.5–6.5, see 1640

Primary Reading Profiles, grades 1–3, see 1641

★*Reading Diagnostic Probes*, grades 2–9, see 1642

Roswell-Chall Diagnostic Reading Test of Word Analysis Skills, grades 2–6, see 1643

Reading Skills Diagnostic Test, grades 2–8, see 1644

★*SPIRE Individual Reading Evaluation*, grades 1–10, see 1645

Schonell Reading Tests [Scotland], ages 5–15, see 1646

Silent Reading Diagnostic Tests, grades 2–6, see 1647

★*Sipay Word Analysis Tests*, grades 2–12, see 1648

Standard Reading Inventory, grades 1–7, see 1649

Standard Reading Tests [England], reading ages up to 9, see 1650

Stanford Diagnostic Reading Test, grades 2.5–8.5, see 1651

★*Swansea Test of Phonic Skills* [England], reading ages below 7.5, see 1652

Test of Individual Needs in Reading, grades 1–6, see 1653

★*Test of Phonic Skills*, reading level grades kgn–3, see 1654

★*Wisconsin Tests of Reading Skill Development: Word Attack*, grades kgn–6, see 1655

★*Woodcock Reading Mastery Tests*, grades kgn–12, see 1656

MISCELLANEOUS

Basic Sight Word Test, grades 1–2, see 1657

Botel Reading Inventory, grades 1–12, see 1658

Cumulative Reading Record, grades 9–12, see 1659

Durrell Listening-Reading Series, grades 1–9, see 1660

Durrell-Sullivan Reading Capacity and Achievement Tests, grades 2.5–6, see 1661

Dyslexia Schedule, children having reading difficulties and first grade entrants, see 1662

Individual Reading Placement Inventory, youth and adults with reading levels up to grade 7, see 1663

★*Instant Word Recognition Test*, reading level grades 1–4, see 1664

★*Inventory of Teacher Knowledge of Reading*, elementary school teachers and college students in methods courses, see 1665

Learning Methods Test, grades kgn–3, see 1666

★*National Test of Basic Words*, grades 1–5, see 1667

OC Diagnostic Syllabizing Test, grades 4–6, see 1668
Phonics Test for Teachers, reading methods courses, see 1669
Reader Rater With Self-Scoring Profile, ages 15 and over, see 1670
Reader's Inventory, entrants to a reading improvement course for secondary and college students and adults, see 1671
Reading Eye II, grades 1–16 and adults, see 1672
Reading Versatility Test, grades 5–16, see 1673
Roswell-Chall Auditory Blending Test, grades 1–4, see 1674
Word Discrimination Test, grades 1–8, see 1675
★*Word Recognition Test* [England], preschool to age 8.5, see 1676

ORAL

★*Concise Word Reading Tests* [Australia], ages 7–12, see 1677
Flash-X Sight Vocabulary Test, grades 1–2, see 1678
Gilmore Oral Reading Test, grades 1–8, see 1679
Graded Word Reading Test [England], ages 5 and over, see 1680
Gray Oral Reading Test, grades 1–16 and adults, see 1681
Holborn Reading Scale [England], ages 5.5–10, see 1682
Neale Analysis of Reading Ability [England], ages 6–13, see 1683
★*Oral Reading Criterion Test*, reading level grades 1–7, see 1684
Oral Word Reading Test [New Zealand], ages 7–11, see 1685
★*Reading Miscue Inventory*, grades 1–7, see 1686
★*St. Lucia Graded Word Reading Test* [Australia], grades 2–7, see 1687
Slosson Oral Reading Test, grades 1–8 and high school, see 1688
Standardized Oral Reading Check Tests, grades 1–8, see 1689
Standardized Oral Reading Paragraphs, grades 1–8, see 1690

READINESS

ABC Inventory to Determine Kindergarten and School Readiness, entrants to kgn and grade 1, see 1691
APELL Test, Assessment Program of Early Learning Levels, ages 4.5–7, see 1692
Academic Readiness and End of First Grade Progress Scales, grade 1, see 1693
American School Reading Readiness Test, first grade entrants, see 1694
★*Analysis of Readiness Skills: Reading and Mathematics*, grades kgn–1, see 1695
Anton Brenner Developmental Gestalt Test of School Readiness, ages 5–6, see 1696
Basic Concept Inventory, preschool and kgn, see 1697
Binion-Beck Reading Readiness Test for Kindergarten and First Grade, grades kgn–1, see 1698
Clymer-Barrett Prereading Battery, first grade entrants, see 1699
Contemporary School Readiness Test, first grade entrants, see 1700
★*Delco Readiness Test*, first grade entrants, see 1701
Gates-MacGinitie Reading Tests: Readiness Skills, grades kgn–1, see 1702
Gesell Developmental Tests, ages 5–10, see 1703
Group Test of Reading Readiness, grades kgn–1, see 1704
Harrison-Stroud Reading Readiness Profiles, grades kgn–1, see 1705

★*Initial Survey Test*, first grade entrants, see 1706
★*Inventory of Primary Skills*, grades kgn–1, see 1707
★*Kindergarten Behavioural Index* [Australia], grades kgn–1, see 1708
Kindergarten Evaluation of Learning Potential, kgn, see 1709
★*LRS Seriation Test*, ages 4–6, see 1710
Lee-Clark Reading Readiness Test, grades kgn–1, see 1711
Lippincott Reading Readiness Test, grades kgn–1, see 1712
McHugh-McParland Reading Readiness Test, grades kgn–1, see 1713
Macmillan Reading Readiness Test, first grade entrants, see 1714
Maturity Level for School Entrance and Reading Readiness, grades kgn–1, see 1715
Metropolitan Readiness Tests, grades kgn–1, see 1716
Murphy-Durrell Reading Readiness Analysis, first grade entrants, see 1717
Parent Readiness Evaluation of Preschoolers, ages 3–9 to 5–8, see 1718
★*Pre-Reading Assessment Kit* [Canada], grades kgn–1, see 1719
★*Prereading Expectancy Screening Scales*, first grade entrants, see 1720
Pre-Reading Screening Procedures, first grade entrants of average or superior intelligence, see 1721
★*Preschool and Kindergarten Performance Profile*, preschool and kgn, see 1722
Primary Academic Sentiment Scale, ages 4–4 to 7–3, see 1723
Reading Aptitude Tests, grades kgn–1, see 1724
★*Reading Inventory Probe 1*, grades 1–2, see 1725
Reversal Test [Sweden], grade 1 entrants, see 1726
Riley Preschool Developmental Screening Inventory, ages 3–5, see 1727
School Readiness Checklist, ages 5–6, see 1728
School Readiness Survey, ages 4–6, see 1729
Screening Test of Academic Readiness, ages 4–0 to 6–5, see 1730
Sprigle School Readiness Screening Test, ages 4–6 to 6–9, see 1731
Steinbach Test of Reading Readiness, grades kgn–1, see 1732
Van Wagenen Reading Readiness Scales, first grade entrants, see 1733
Watson Reading-Readiness Test [Canada], grades kgn–1, see 1734

SPECIAL FIELDS

ANPA Foundation Newspaper Test, grades 7–12, see 1735
Adult Basic Reading Inventory, functionally illiterate adolescents and adults, see 1736
Iowa Tests of Educational Development: Ability to Interpret Reading Materials in the Social Studies, grades 9–12, see 1737
Iowa Tests of Educational Development: Ability to Interpret Reading Materials in the Natural Sciences, grades 9–12, see 1738
Purdue Reading Test for Industrial Supervisors, supervisors, see 1739
RBH Scientific Reading Test, employees in technical companies, see 1740
Reading Adequacy "READ" Test: Individual Placement Series, adults in industry, see 1741
Reading: Adult Basic Education Student Survey, poorly educated adults, see 1742
Reading Comprehension Test for Personnel Selection [England], applicants for technical training programs with high verbal content, see 1743

★*Reading/Everyday Activities in Life,* high school and "adults at basic education levels," see 1744

Robinson-Hall Reading Tests, college, see 1745

SRA Reading Index, job applicants with poor educational backgrounds, see 1746

Understanding Communication (Verbal Comprehension), industrial employees at the skilled level or below, see 1747

SPEED

*Basic Reading Rate Scale, grades 3–12, see 1748

Minnesota Speed of Reading Test for College Students, grades 12–16, see 1749

STUDY SKILLS

Bristol Achievement Tests: Study Skills [England], ages 8–13, see 1750

College Adjustment and Study Skills Inventory, college, see 1751

*Comprehensive Tests of Basic Skills: Study Skills, grades 2.5–12, see 1752

★*Cornell Class-Reasoning Test,* grades 4–12, see 1753

★*Cornell Conditional-Reasoning Test,* grades 4–12, see 1754

Cornell Critical Thinking Test, grades 7–16, see 1755

★*Cornell Learning and Study Skills Inventory,* grades 7–16, see 1756

Evaluation Aptitude Test, candidates for college and graduate school entrance, see 1757

*Iowa Tests of Educational Development: Use of Sources of Information, grades 9–12, see 1758

Library Orientation Test for College Freshmen, grade 13, see 1759

★*Library Tests,* college, see 1760

Logical Reasoning, grades 9–16 and adults, see 1761

★*National Test of Library Skills,* grades 2–12, see 1762

Nationwide Library Skills Examination, grades 4–12, see 1763

OC Diagnostic Dictionary Test, grades 5–8, see 1764

SRA Achievement Series: Work-Study Skills, grades 4–9, see 1765

★*Study Attitudes and Methods Survey,* high school and college, see 1766

Study Habits Checklist, grades 9–14, see 1767

Study Habits Inventory, grades 12–16, see 1768

Study Performance Test, high school and college, see 1769

Study Skills Counseling Evaluation, high school and college, see 1770

Study Skills Test: McGraw-Hill Basic Skills System, grades 11–14, see 1771

Survey of Study Habits and Attitudes, grades 7–14, see 1772

Test on Use of the Dictionary, high school and college, see 1773

★*Uncritical Inference Test,* college, see 1774

Watson-Glaser Critical Thinking Appraisal, grades 9–16 and adults, see 1775

★*Wisconsin Tests of Reading Skill Development: Study Skills,* grades kgn–7, see 1776

SCIENCE

Adkins-McBride General Science Test, high school, see 1777

Borman-Sanders Elementary Science Test, grades 5–8, see 1778

*CLEP General Examinations: Natural Sciences, 1–2 years of college or equivalent, see 1779

Cooperative Science Tests: Advanced General Science, grades 8–9, see 1780

Cooperative Science Tests: General Science, grades 7–9, see 1781

Elementary Science Test: National Achievement Tests, grades 4–6, see 1782

Emporia General Science Test, 1–2 semesters high school, see 1783

★*General Science Test* [South Africa], matriculants and higher, see 1784

General Science Test: National Achievement Tests, grades 7–9, see 1785

General Science III: Achievement Examinations for Secondary Schools, high school, see 1786

*Iowa Tests of Educational Development: General Background in the Natural Sciences, grades 9–12, see 1787

*National Teacher Examinations: Biology and General Science, college seniors and teachers, see 1788

*National Teacher Examinations: Chemistry, Physics and General Science, college seniors and teachers, see 1789

SRA Achievement Series: Science, grades 4–9, see 1790

*Science: Minnesota High School Achievement Examinations, grades 7–9, see 1791

Science Tests: Content Evaluation Series, grades 8–9, see 1792

Scientific Knowledge and Aptitude Test [India], high school, see 1793

*Sequential Tests of Educational Progress: Science, grades 4–14, see 1794

Stanford Achievement Test: High School Science Test, grades 9–12, see 1795

Stanford Achievement Test: Science, grades 5.5–9.9, see 1796

*Teacher Education Examination Program: Biology and General Science, college seniors preparing to teach secondary school, see 1797

*Teacher Education Examination Program: Chemistry, Physics and General Science, college seniors preparing to teach secondary school, see 1798

Tests of Academic Progress: Science, grades 9–12, see 1799

BIOLOGY

*Advanced Placement Examination in Biology, high school students desiring credit for college level courses or admission to advanced courses, see 1800

*BSCS Achievement Tests, grade 10, see 1801

*Biological Science: Interaction of Experiments and Ideas, grades 10–12, see 1802

*Biology: Minnesota High School Achievement Examinations, high school, see 1803

*CLEP Subject Examination in Biology, 1 year or equivalent, see 1804

*College Board Achievement Test in Biology, candidates for college entrance, see 1805

*College Placement Test in Biology, entering college freshmen, see 1806

Cooperative Biology Test: Educational Records Bureau Edition, high school, see 1807

Cooperative Science Tests: Biology, grades 10–12, see 1808

Emporia Biology Test, 1–2 semesters high school, see 1809

General Biology Test: National Achievement Tests, high school, see 1810

Graduate Record Examinations Advanced Biology Test, graduate school candidates, see 1811

Nelson Biology Test, grades 9–13, see 1812

Undergraduate Program Field Tests: Biology Test, college, see 1813

CHEMISTRY

ACS Cooperative Examination Brief Course in Organic Chemistry, 1 semester college, see 1814

ACS Cooperative Examination in Analytical Chemistry, Graduate Level, entering graduate students, see 1815

ACS Cooperative Examination in Biochemistry, college, see 1816

ACS Cooperative Examination in Brief Physical Chemistry, 1 semester college, see 1817

ACS Cooperative Examination in Brief Qualitative Analysis, college, see 1818

ACS Cooperative Examination in General Chemistry, 1 year college, see 1819

ACS Cooperative Examination in Inorganic Chemistry, grades 15–16, see 1820

ACS Cooperative Examination in Inorganic Chemistry, Graduate Level, entering graduate students, see 1821

ACS Cooperative Examination in Inorganic-Organic-Biological Chemistry (for Paramedical Programs), 1–2 semesters of chemistry for nursing, home economics, and other paramedical students, see 1822

ACS Cooperative Examination in Instrumental Analysis, grades 15–16, see 1823

ACS Cooperative Examination in Organic Chemistry, 1 year college, see 1824

ACS Cooperative Examination in Organic Chemistry, Graduate Level, entering graduate students, see 1825

ACS Cooperative Examination in Physical Chemistry, 1 year college, see 1826

ACS Cooperative Examination in Physical Chemistry, Graduate Level, entering graduate students, see 1827

ACS Cooperative Examination in Qualitative Analysis, college, see 1828

ACS Cooperative Examination in Quantitative Analysis, college, see 1829

ACS-NSTA Cooperative Examination in High School Chemistry, 1 year high school, see 1830

ACS-NSTA Cooperative Examination in High School Chemistry: Advanced Level, advanced high school classes, see 1831

Advanced Placement Examination in Chemistry, high school students desiring credit for college level courses or admission to advanced courses, see 1832

CLEP Subject Examination in General Chemistry, 1 year or equivalent, see 1833

Chemistry: Achievement Examinations for Secondary Schools, high school, see 1834

Chemistry Achievement Test for CHEM Study or Equivalent, high school, see 1835

Chemistry: Minnesota High School Achievement Examinations, high school, see 1836

College Board Achievement Test in Chemistry, candidates for college entrance, see 1837

College Placement Test in Chemistry, entering college freshmen, see 1838

Cooperative Chemistry Test: Educational Records Bureau Edition, high school, see 1839

Cooperative Science Tests: Chemistry, grades 10–12, see 1840

Emporia Chemistry Test, 1–2 semesters high school, see 1841

General Chemistry Test: National Achievement Tests, grades 10–16, see 1842

Graduate Record Examinations Advanced Chemistry Test, graduate school candidates, see 1843

Iowa Placement Examinations: Chemistry Aptitude, grades 12–13, see 1844

Iowa Placement Examinations: Chemistry Training, grades 12–13, see 1845

RBH Test of Chemical Comprehension, employee applicants and applicants for nurses' training, see 1846

Toledo Chemistry Placement Examination, college entrants, see 1847

Undergraduate Program Field Tests: Chemistry Test, college, see 1848

GEOLOGY

CLEP Subject Examination in Geology, 1 year or equivalent, see 1849

Graduate Record Examinations Advanced Geology Test, graduate school candidates, see 1850

Undergraduate Program Field Tests: Geology Test, college, see 1851

MISCELLANEOUS

Butler Life Science Concept Test, grades 1–6, see 1852

Dubins Earth Science Test, grades 8–12, see 1853

★NM Concepts of Ecology Test, grades 6–8, see 1854

★Science Attitude Questionnaire [England], secondary school, see 1855

Test on Understanding Science, grades 9–12, see 1856

Tests of Basic Experiences: Science, prekgn–grade 1, see 1857

PHYSICS

Advanced Placement Examination in Physics, high school students desiring credit for college level courses or admission to advanced courses, see 1858

College Board Achievement Test in Physics, candidates for college entrance, see 1859

College Placement Test in Physics, entering college freshmen, see 1860

Cooperative Physics Test: Educational Records Bureau Edition, high school, see 1861

Cooperative Science Tests: Physics, grades 10–12, see 1862

Dunning-Abeles Physics Test, grades 10–13, see 1863

Emporia Physics Test, 1–2 semesters high school, see 1864

General Physics Test: National Achievement Tests, grades 10–16, see 1865

Graduate Record Examinations Advanced Physics Test, graduate school candidates, see 1866

Iowa Placement Examinations: Physics Aptitude, grades 12–13, see 1867

Iowa Placement Examinations: Physics Training, grades 12–13, see 1868

★Objective Tests in Physics, high school, see 1869

Physics: Achievement Examinations for Secondary Schools, high school, see 1870

Physics: Minnesota High School Achievement Examinations, high school, see 1871

Tests of the Physical Science Study Committee, high school, see 1872

Undergraduate Program Field Tests: Physics Test, college, see 1873

SENSORY-MOTOR

D-K Scale of Lateral Dominance, grades 2–6, see 1874
Developmental Test of Visual-Motor Integration, ages 2–15, see 1875
★*Frostig Movement Skills Test Battery,* ages 6–12, see 1876
Harris Tests of Lateral Dominance, ages 7 and over, see 1877
**Leavell Hand-Eye Coordinator Tests,* ages 8–14, see 1878
MKM Picture Arrangement Test, grades kgn–6, see 1879
**Moore Eye-Hand Coordination and Color-Matching Test,* ages 2 and over, see 1880
Perceptual Forms Test, ages 5–8, see 1881
Primary Visual Motor Test, ages 4–8, see 1882
Purdue Perceptual-Motor Survey, ages 6–10, see 1883
★*Rosner Perceptual Survey,* ages 5–12, see 1884
Southern California Kinesthesia and Tactile Perception Tests, ages 4–8, see 1885
Southern California Perceptual-Motor Tests, ages 4–8, see 1886
**Southern California Sensory Integration Tests,* ages 4–10 with learning problems, see 1887
★*Spatial Orientation Memory Test,* ages 5–8, see 1888
★*Symbol Digit Modalities Test,* ages 8 and over, see 1889
Trankell's Laterality Tests [Sweden], left-handed children in grades 1–2, see 1890
★*Wold Digit-Symbol Test,* ages 6–16, see 1891
★*Wold Sentence Copying Test,* grades 2–8, see 1892
★*Wold Visuo-Motor Test,* ages 6–16, see 1893

MOTOR

★*Devereux Test of Extremity Coordination,* emotionally handicapped and neurologically impaired ages 4–10, see 1894
Lincoln-Oseretsky Motor Development Scale, ages 6–14, see 1895
★*Manual Accuracy and Speed Test,* ages 4 and over, see 1896
★*Motor Problems Inventory,* preschool–grade 5, see 1897
Oseretsky Tests of Motor Proficiency: A Translation From the Portuguese Adaptation, ages 4–16, see 1898
Perrin Motor Coordination Test, adults, see 1899
Rail-Walking Test, ages 5 and over, see 1900
Smedley Hand Dynamometer, ages 6–18, see 1901
Southern California Motor Accuracy Test, ages 4–7 with nervous system dysfunction, see 1902
★*Teaching Research Motor-Development Scale,* moderately and severely retarded (preschool–grade 12), see 1903
★*Test of Motor Impairment* [Canada], ages 5–14, see 1904

VISION

A-B-C Vision Test for Ocular Dominance, ages 5 and over, see 1905
AO Sight Screener, adults, see 1906
Atlantic City Eye Test, grades 1 and over, see 1907
Basic Screen Test—Vision: Measurement of Skill Test 12, job applicants, see 1908
Burnham-Clark-Munsell Color Memory Test, adults, see 1909
Dennis Visual Perception Scale, grades 1–6, see 1910
Dvorine Pseudo-Isochromatic Plates, ages 3 and over, see 1911
Farnsworth Dichotomous Test for Color Blindness: Panel D-15, ages 12 and over, see 1912
Farnsworth-Munsell 100-Hue Test for the Examination of Color Discrimination, mental ages 12 and over, see 1913
★*Guy's Colour Vision Test for Young Children* [England], ages 3–5 and handicapped, see 1914
**Inter-Society Color Council Color Aptitude Test,* adults, see 1915
Keystone Ready-to-Read Tests, school entrants, see 1916
Keystone Tests of Binocular Skill, grades 1 and over, see 1917
**Keystone Visual Screening Tests,* preschool and over, see 1918
MKM Binocular Preschool Test, preschool, see 1919
MKM Monocular and Binocular Reading Test, grades 1 and over, see 1920
Marianne Frostig Developmental Test of Visual Perception, ages 3–8, see 1921
★*Motor-Free Visual Perception Test,* ages 4–8, see 1922
Ortho-Rater, adults, see 1923
**Pseudo-Isochromatic Plates for Testing Color Perception,* ages 7 and over, see 1924
School Vision Tester, grades kgn and over, see 1925
★*Sheridan Gardiner Test of Visual Acuity* [England], ages 5 and over, see 1926
★*Sloan Achromatopsia Test,* individuals suspected of total color blindness, see 1927
Southern California Figure-Ground Visual Perception Test, ages 4–10, see 1928
Spache Binocular Reading Test, nonreaders and grades 1 and over, see 1929
★*Speed of Color Discrimination Test,* college, see 1930
Stycar Vision Tests [England], ages 6 months to 7 years, see 1931
Test for Colour-Blindness [Japan], ages 4 and over, see 1932
★*3-D Test of Visualization Skill,* ages 3–8, see 1933
Titmus Vision Tester, ages 3 and over, see 1934
★*Visualization Test of Three Dimensional Orthographic Shape,* high school and college, see 1935

SOCIAL STUDIES

American History—Government—Problems of Democracy: Acorn Achievement Tests, grades 9–16, see 1936
American School Achievement Tests: Social Studies and Science, grades 4–9, see 1937
**CLEP General Examinations: Social Sciences and*
History, 1–2 years of college or equivalent, see 1938
**College Board Achievement Test in American History and Social Studies,* candidates for college entrance, see 1939
**College Board Achievement Test in European History*

and World Cultures, candidates for college entrance, see 1940

College Placement Test in American History and Social Studies, entering college freshmen, see 1941

College Placement Test in European History and World Cultures, entering college freshmen, see 1942

History and Civics Test: Municipal Tests, grades 3–8, see 1943

Iowa Tests of Educational Development: Understanding of Basic Social Concepts, grades 9–12, see 1944

National Teacher Examinations: Social Studies, college seniors and teachers, see 1945

Primary Social Studies Test, grades 1–3, see 1946

SRA Achievement Series: Social Studies, grades 4–9, see 1947

Sequential Tests of Educational Progress: Social Studies, grades 4–14, see 1948

Social Studies: Minnesota High School Achievement Examinations, grades 7–9, see 1949

Social Studies Test: Acorn National Achievement Tests, grades 7–9, see 1950

Social Studies Test: National Achievement Tests, grades 4–9, see 1951

Stanford Achievement Test: High School Social Studies Test, grades 9–12, see 1952

Stanford Achievement Test: Social Studies Tests, grades 5.5–9, see 1953

Teacher Education Examination Program: Social Studies, college seniors preparing to teach secondary school, see 1954

Tests of Academic Progress: Social Studies, grades 9–12, see 1955

Tests of Basic Experiences: Social Studies, prekgn-grade 1, see 1956

Zimmerman-Sanders Social Studies Test, grades 7–8, see 1957

CONTEMPORARY AFFAIRS

Current News Test, grades 9–12, see 1958

Newsweek NewsQuiz, grades 9–12, see 1959

School Weekly News Quiz, high school, see 1960

Time Current Affairs Test, grades 9–12 and adults, see 1961

★*Time Monthly News Quiz,* grades 9–12 and adults, see 1962

ECONOMICS

CLEP Subject Examination in Introductory Economics, 1 year or equivalent, see 1963

★*Economics/Objective Tests,* 1 semester high school, see 1964

Graduate Record Examinations Advanced Economics Test, graduate school candidates, see 1965

★*Modern Economics Test: Content Evaluation Series,* grades 10–12, see 1966

★*Primary Test of Economic Understanding,* grades 2–3, see 1967

Test of Economic Understanding, high school and college, see 1968

★*Test of Elementary Economics,* grades 4–6, see 1969

Test of Understanding in College Economics, 1–2 semesters college, see 1970

★*Test of Understanding in Personal Economics,* high school, see 1971

Undergraduate Program Field Tests: Economics Test, college, see 1972

GEOGRAPHY

Brandywine Achievement Test in Geography for Secondary Schools, grades 7–12, see 1973

Economic Geography: Achievement Examinations for Secondary Schools, high school, see 1974

Geography Test: Municipal Tests, grades 3–8, see 1975

Geography Test: National Achievement Tests, grades 6–8, see 1976

Graduate Record Examinations Advanced Geography Test, graduate school candidates, see 1977

Hollingsworth-Sanders Geography Test, grades 5–7, see 1978

Undergraduate Program Field Tests: Geography Test, college, see 1979

HISTORY

Advanced Placement Examination in American History, high school students desiring credit for college level courses or admission to advanced courses, see 1980

Advanced Placement Examination in European History, high school students desiring credit for college level courses or admission to advanced courses, see 1981

★*American History: Junior High—Objective,* grades 7–9, see 1982

American History: Senior High—Objective, 1–2 semesters high school, see 1983

American History Test: National Achievement Tests, grades 7–8, see 1984

★*CLEP Subject Examination in Afro-American History,* 1 semester or equivalent, see 1985

CLEP Subject Examination in American History, 1 year or equivalent, see 1986

CLEP Subject Examination in Western Civilization, 1 year or equivalent, see 1987

Cooperative Social Studies Tests: American History, grades 7–8, 10–12, see 1988

Cooperative Social Studies Tests: Modern European History, grades 10–12, see 1989

Cooperative Social Studies Tests: World History, grades 10–12, see 1990

Cooperative Topical Tests in American History, high school, see 1991

Crary American History Test, grades 10–13, see 1992

Emporia American History Test, 1–2 semesters high school, see 1993

Graduate Record Examinations Advanced History Test, graduate school candidates, see 1994

Hollingsworth-Sanders Intermediate History Test, grades 5–6, see 1995

Meares-Sanders Junior High School History Test, grades 7–8, see 1996

Modern World History: Achievement Examinations for Secondary Schools, high school, see 1997

Sanders-Buller World History Test, 1–2 semesters high school, see 1998

Social Studies Grade 10 (American History): Minnesota High School Achievement Examinations, grade 10, see 1999

Social Studies Grade 11 (World History): Minnesota High School Achievement Examinations, grade 11, see 2000

Undergraduate Program Field Tests: History Test, college, see 2001

World History/Objective Tests, 1–2 semesters high school, see 2002

World History Test: Acorn National Achievement Tests, high school and college, see 2003

POLITICAL SCIENCE

CLEP Subject Examination in American Government, 1 semester or equivalent, see 2004

Cooperative Social Studies Tests: American Government, grades 10–12, see 2005

Cooperative Social Studies Tests: Civics, grades 8–9, see 2006

Cooperative Social Studies Tests: Problems of Democracy, grades 10–12, see 2007

★*Government/Objective Tests,* 1 semester grades 11–12, see 2008

Graduate Record Examinations Advanced Political Science Test, graduate school candidates, see 2009

★*National Teacher Examinations: Texas Government,* college seniors and teachers, see 2010

Patterson Test or Study Exercises on the Constitution of the United States, grades 9–16 and adults, see 2011

Principles of Democracy Test, grades 9–12, see 2012

Sare-Sanders American Government Test, high school and college, see 2013

Sare-Sanders Constitution Test, high school and college, see 2014

Social Studies Grade 12 (American Problems): Minnesota High School Achievement Examinations, grade 12, see 2015

Undergraduate Program Field Tests: Political Science Test, college, see 2016

SOCIOLOGY

CLEP Subject Examination in Introductory Sociology, 1 year or equivalent, see 2017

Graduate Record Examinations Advanced Sociology Test, graduate school candidates, see 2018

Sare-Sanders Sociology Test, high school and college, see 2019

Undergraduate Program Field Tests: Sociology Test, college, see 2020

SPEECH AND HEARING

★*Diagnostic Test of Speechreading,* deaf children ages 4–9, see 2021

★*Multiple-Choice Intelligibility Test,* college, see 2022

★*Ohio Tests of Articulation and Perception of Sounds,* ages 5–8, see 2023

Preschool Language Scale, ages 2–6, see 2024

Reynell Developmental Language Scales [England], children ages 1–5 with delayed or deviant language development, see 2025

Undergraduate Program Field Tests: Speech Pathology and Audiology Test, college, see 2026

HEARING

Ambco Audiometers, ages 10 and over, see 2027

Ambco Speech Test Record, ages 3 and over, see 2027A

Auditory Discrimination Test, ages 5–8, see 2028

★*Auditory Memory Span Test,* ages 5–8, see 2029

★*Auditory Sequential Memory Test,* grades 5–8, see 2030

Auditory Tests, grades 2 and over, see 2031

Beltone Audiometers, grades kgn and over, see 2032

Comprehension of Oral Language: Inter-American Series, grade 1, see 2033

Eckstein Audiometers, grades kgn and over, see 2034

★*Flowers-Costello Tests of Central Auditory Abilities,* grades kgn–6, see 2035

★*Four Tone Screening for Older Children and Adults,* ages 8 and over, see 2036

Goldman-Fristoe-Woodcock Test of Auditory Discrimination, ages 4 and over, see 2037

Grason-Stadler Audiometers, ages 6 and over, see 2038

Hearing of Speech Tests, ages 3–12, see 2039

Hollien-Thompson Group Hearing Test, grades 1 and over, see 2040

★*Kindergarten Auditory Screening Test,* grades kgn–1, see 2041

★*Lindamood Auditory Conceptualization Test,* grades kgn–12, see 2042

Maico Audiometers, grades kgn and over, see 2043

Maico Hearing Impairment Calculator, see 2044

Massachusetts Hearing Test, grades 1–16 and adults, see 2045

Modified Rhyme Hearing Test, grades 4 and over, see 2046

National Teacher Examinations: Audiology, college seniors and teachers, see 2047

New Group Pure Tone Hearing Test, grades 1 and over, see 2048

★*Oliphant Auditory Discrimination Memory Test,* grades 2–6, see 2049

★*Oliphant Auditory Synthesizing Test,* grade 1, see 2050

Pritchard-Fox Phoneme Auditory Discrimination Tests: Test Four, kgn and over, see 2051

Robbins Speech Sound Discrimination and Verbal Imagery Type Tests, ages 4 and over, see 2052

Rush Hughes (PB 50): Phonetically Balanced Lists 5–12, grades 2 and over, see 2053

Screening Test for Auditory Perception, grades 2–6, see 2054

Stycar Hearing Tests [England], ages 6 months to 7 years, see 2055

Test of Listening Accuracy in Children, ages 5–9, see 2056

★*Test of Non-Verbal Auditory Discrimination,* ages 6–8, see 2057

★*Tracor Audiometers,* infants and older, see 2058

Verbal Auditory Screening for Children, ages 3–8, see 2059

★*Washington Speech Sound Discrimination Test,* ages 3–5, see 2060

★*Word Intelligibility by Picture Identification,* hearing impaired children ages 5–13, see 2061

★*ZECO Pure Tone Screening for Children,* ages 3–8, see 2062

Zenith Audiometers, preschool and over, see 2063–4

SPEECH

Arizona Articulation Proficiency Scale, mental ages 2–14 and over, see 2065

★*Boston Diagnostic Aphasia Examination,* aphasic patients, see 2066

★*Bzoch-League Receptive-Expressive Emergent Language Scale: For the Measurement of Language Skills in Infancy,* birth to age 3, see 2067

Communicative Evaluation Chart From Infancy to Five Years, see 2068

Deep Test of Articulation, all reading levels, see 2069

★*Edinburgh Articulation Test* [Scotland], ages 3–5, see 2070
Examining for Aphasia, adolescents and adults, see 2071
★*Fairview Language Evaluation Scale,* mentally retarded, see 2072
★*Fisher-Logemann Test of Articulation Competence,* preschool and over, see 2073
Forms From Diagnostic Methods in Speech Pathology, children and adults with speech problems, see 2074
Goldman-Fristoe Test of Articulation, ages 2 and over, see 2075
Halstead Aphasia Test, adults, see 2076
Houston Test for Language Development, ages 6 months to 6 years, see 2077
Language Facility Test, ages 3 and over, see 2078
Language Modalities Test for Aphasia, adults, see 2079
Minnesota Test for Differential Diagnosis of Aphasia, adults, see 2080
National Teacher Examinations: Speech-Communication and Theatre, college seniors and teachers, see 2081
National Teacher Examinations: Speech Pathology, college seniors and teachers, see 2082
Nationwide Speech Examination, grades 4–12, see 2083
★*Northwestern Syntax Screening Test,* ages 3–7, see 2084

Orzeck Aphasia Evaluation, mental and brain damaged patients, see 2085
Photo Articulation Test, ages 3–12, see 2086
Porch Index of Communicative Ability, adults, see 2087
Predictive Screening Test of Articulation, grade 1, see 2088
Riley Articulation and Language Test, grades kgn–2, see 2089
Screening Deep Test of Articulation, grades kgn and over, see 2090
Screening Speech Articulation Test, ages 3.5–8.5, see 2091
Sklar Aphasia Scale, brain damaged adults, see 2092
Speech Defect Questionnaire, ages 6 and over, see 2093
Speech Diagnostic Chart, grades 1–8, see 2094
Templin-Darley Tests of Articulation, ages 3 and over, see 2095
★*Undergraduate Program Field Tests: Drama and Theatre Test,* college, see 2096
Utah Test of Language Development, ages 1.5 to 14.5, see 2097
Verbal Language Development Scale, birth to age 15, see 2098
Weidner-Fensch Speech Screening Test, grades 1–3, see 2099

VOCATIONS

★*ACT Assessment of Career Development,* grades 8–11, see 2100
★*ACT Career Planning Program,* entrants to postsecondary educational institutions, see 2101
Aptitude Inventory, employee applicants, see 2102
★*Career Maturity Inventory,* grades 6–12, see 2103
★*Classification Test Battery* [South Africa], illiterate and semiliterate applicants for unskilled and semiskilled mining jobs, see 2104
Dailey Vocational Tests, grades 8–12 and adults, see 2105
ETSA Tests, job applicants, see 2106
Flanagan Industrial Tests, business and industry, see 2107
Individual Placement Series, high school and adults, see 2108
★*New Mexico Career Education Test Series,* grades 9–12, see 2109
Personal History Index, job applicants, see 2110
Steward Basic Factors Inventory, applicants for sales and office positions, see 2111
Steward Personnel Tests, applicants for sales and office positions, see 2112
TAV Selection System, adults, see 2113
Vocational Planning Inventory, vocational students in grades 8–12 and grade 13 entrants, see 2114
WLW Employment Inventory, adults, see 2115
★*Wide Range Employment Sample Test,* ages 16–35 (normal and handicapped), see 2116

CLERICAL

ACER Short Clerical Test—Form C [Australia], ages 13 and over, see 2117
A.C.E.R. Speed and Accuracy Tests [Australia], ages 13.5 and over, see 2118
APT Dictation Test, stenographers, see 2119
★*Appraisal of Occupational Aptitudes,* high school and adults, see 2120
Clerical Skills Series, clerical workers and applicants, see 2121

Clerical Tests, applicants for clerical positions, see 2122
Clerical Tests, Series N, applicants for clerical positions not involving frequent use of typewriter or verbal skill, see 2123
Clerical Tests, Series V, applicants for typing and stenographic positions, see 2124
Clerical Worker Examination, clerical workers, see 2125
Cross Reference Test, clerical job applicants, see 2126
Curtis Verbal-Clerical Skills Tests, applicants for clerical positions, see 2127
General Clerical Ability Test, job applicants, see 2128
General Clerical Test, grades 9–16 and clerical job applicants, see 2129
Group Test 20 [England], ages 15 and over, see 2130
Group Tests 61A, 64, and 66A [England], clerical applicants, see 2131
Hay Clerical Test Battery, applicants for clerical positions, see 2132
L & L Clerical Tests, applicants for office positions, see 2133
McCann Typing Tests, applicants for typing positions, see 2134
Minnesota Clerical Test, grades 8–12 and adults, see 2135
Office Skills Achievement Test, employees, see 2136
Office Worker Test, office workers, see 2137
O'Rourke Clerical Aptitude Test, Junior Grade, applicants for clerical positions, see 2138
Personnel Institute Clerical Tests, clerical personnel and typists-stenographers-secretaries, see 2139
Personnel Research Institute Clerical Battery, applicants for clerical positions, see 2140
Personnel Research Institute Test of Shorthand Skills, stenographers, see 2141
Purdue Clerical Adaptability Test, applicants for clerical positions, see 2142
RBH Checking Test, applicants for clerical and stenographic positions, see 2143
RBH Classifying Test, business and industry, see 2144
RBH Number Checking Test, business and industry, see 2145

RBH Test of Dictation Speed, stenographers, see 2146

RBH Test of Typing Speed, applicants for clerical positions, see 2147

Seashore-Bennett Stenographic Proficiency Test, adults, see 2148

Secretarial Performance Analysis, employees, see 2149

Selection Tests for Office Personnel, insurance office workers and applicants, see 2150

Short Employment Tests, applicants for clerical positions, see 2151

Short Occupational Knowledge Test for Bookkeepers, job applicants, see 2152

Short Occupational Knowledge Test for Office Machine Operators, job applicants, see 2153

Short Occupational Knowledge Test for Secretaries, job applicants, see 2154

Short Tests of Clerical Ability, applicants for office positions, see 2155

Shorthand Test: Individual Placement Series, adults, see 2156

Skill in Typing: Measurement of Skill Test 9, job applicants, see 2157

Stenographic Dictation Test, applicants for stenographic positions, see 2158

Stenographic Skill-Dictation Test, applicants for stenographic positions, see 2159

Stenographic Skills Test, job applicants, see 2160

Survey of Clerical Skills: Individual Placement Series, adults, see 2161

Thurstone Employment Tests, applicants for clerical and typing positions, see 2162

Typing Skill, typists, see 2163

Typing Test for Business, applicants for typing positions, see 2164

Typing Test: Individual Placement Series, adults, see 2165

USES Clerical Skills Tests, applicants for clerical positions, see 2166

INTERESTS

ACT Guidance Profile, junior college, see 2167

A.P.U. Occupational Interests Guide [England], ages 14–18, see 2168

Applied Biological and Agribusiness Interest Inventory, grade 8, see 2169

California Occupational Preference Survey, grades 9–16 and adults, see 2170

California Pre-Counseling Self-Analysis Protocol Booklet, student counselees, see 2171

★Career Guidance Inventory, grades 7–13 students interested in trades, services and technologies, see 2172

Chatterji's Non-Language Preference Record [India], ages 11–16, see 2173

College Interest Inventory, grades 11–16, see 2174

Connolly Occupational Interests Questionnaire [England], ages 15 and over, see 2175

Crowley Occupational Interests Blank [England], ages 13 and over of average ability or less, see 2176

Curtis Interest Scale, grades 9–16 and adults, see 2177

Educational Interest Inventory, grades 11–13 and adults, see 2178

Factorial Interest Blank [England], ages 11–16, see 2179

Geist Picture Interest Inventory, grades 8–16 and adults, see 2180

Geist Picture Interest Inventory: Deaf Form: Male, deaf and hard of hearing males (grades 7–16 and adults), see 2181

Gordon Occupational Check List, high school students not planning to enter college, see 2182

Gregory Academic Interest Inventory, grades 13–16, see 2183

Guilford-Shneidman-Zimmerman Interest Survey, grades 9–16 and adults, see 2184

Guilford-Zimmerman Interest Inventory, grades 10–16 and adults, see 2185

Hackman-Gaither Vocational Interest Inventory, grades 9–12 and adults, see 2186

Hall Occupational Orientation Inventory, grades 7–16 and adults, see 2187

Henderson Analysis of Interest, grades 9–16 and adults, see 2188

How Well Do You Know Your Interests, high school, college, adults, see 2189

Interest Check List, grades 9 and over, see 2190

★Interest Questionnaire for Indian South Africans [South Africa], standards 6–10, see 2191

Inventory of Vocational Interests: Acorn National Aptitude Tests, grades 7–16 and adults, see 2192

Kuder General Interest Survey, grades 6–12, see 2193

Kuder Occupational Interest Survey, grades 11–16 and adults, see 2194

Kuder Preference Record—Vocational, grades 9–16 and adults, see 2195

★Milwaukee Academic Interest Inventory, grades 12–14, see 2196

Minnesota Vocational Interest Inventory, males ages 15 and over not planning to attend college, see 2197

19 Field Interest Inventory [South Africa], standards 8–10 and college and adults, see 2198

Occupational Interest Inventory, grades 7–16 and adults, see 2199

Occupational Interest Survey (With Pictures), industrial applicants and employees, see 2200

Ohio Vocational Interest Survey, grades 8–12, see 2201

Phillips Occupational Preference Scale [Australia], ages 14 and over, see 2202

Pictorial Interest Inventory, adult males, particularly poor readers and nonreaders, see 2203

★Pictorial Inventory of Careers, grades 3–14 and disadvantaged adults, see 2204

Picture Interest Inventory, grades 7 and over, see 2205

Preference Analysis [South Africa], standards 8 and over, see 2206–7

Rothwell-Miller Interest Blank [Australia], ages 13 and over, see 2208

Rothwell-Miller Interest Blank, British Edition [England], ages 11 and over, see 2209

Safran Student's Interest Inventory [Canada], grades 8–12, see 2210

★Self Directed Search: A Guide to Educational and Vocational Planning, high school and college and adults, see 2211

Strong Vocational Interest Blank for Men, ages 16 and over, see 2212

Strong Vocational Interest Blank for Women, ages 16 and over, see 2213

Thurstone Interest Schedule, grades 9–16 and adults, see 2214

VALCAN Vocational Interest Profile [Canada], ages 15 and over, see 2215

Vocational Apperception Test, college, see 2216

Vocational Interest and Sophistication Assessment, retarded adolescents and young adults, see 2217

Vocational Interest Profile [Canada], ages 15 and over, see 2218

★Wide Range Interest-Opinion Test, grades 8–12 and adults, see 2219

William, Lynde & Williams Analysis of Interest, male adults, see 2220

Work Values Inventory, grades 7–16 and adults, see 2221

MANUAL DEXTERITY

APT Manual Dexterity Test, automobile and truck mechanics and mechanics' helpers, see 2222

Crawford Small Parts Dexterity Test, high school and adults, see 2223

Crissey Dexterity Test, job applicants, see 2224

Hand-Tool Dexterity Test, adolescents and adults, see 2225

Manipulative Aptitude Test, grades 9–16 and adults, see 2226

Minnesota Rate of Manipulation Test, grade 7 to adults, see 2227

O'Connor Finger Dexterity Test, ages 14 and over, see 2228

O'Connor Tweezer Dexterity Test, ages 14 and over, see 2229

★*One Hole Test*, job applicants, see 2230

Pennsylvania Bi-Manual Worksample, ages 16 and over, see 2231

Practical Dexterity Board, ages 8 and over, see 2232

Purdue Hand Precision Test, ages 17 and over, see 2233

Purdue Pegboard, grades 9–16 and adults, see 2234

Stromberg Dexterity Test, trade school and adults, see 2235

Yarn Dexterity Test, textile workers and applicants, see 2236

MECHANICAL ABILITY

A.C.E.R. Mechanical Comprehension Test [Australia], ages 13.5 and over, see 2237

A.C.E.R. Mechanical Reasoning Test [Australia], ages 13–9 and over, see 2238

Bennett Mechanical Comprehension Test, grades 9–12 and adults, see 2239

Chriswell Structural Dexterity Test, grades 7–9, see 2240

College Placement Test in Spatial Relations, entering college freshmen, see 2241

Cox Mechanical and Manual Tests [England], boys ages 10 and over, see 2242

Curtis Object Completion and Space Form Tests, applicants for mechanical and technical jobs, see 2243

Detroit Mechanical Aptitudes Examination, grades 7–16, see 2244

Flags: A Test of Space Thinking, industrial employees, see 2245

Form Perception Test [South Africa], illiterate and semiliterate adults, see 2246

Form Relations Group Test [England], ages 14 and over, see 2247

Group Test 80A [England], ages 15 and over, see 2248

Group Test 81 [England], ages 14 and over, see 2249

Group Test 82 [England], ages 14.5 and over, see 2250

MacQuarrie Test for Mechanical Ability, grades 7 and over, see 2251

Mechanical Aptitude Test: Acorn National Aptitude Tests, grades 7–16 and adults, see 2252

Mechanical Comprehension Test [South Africa], male technical apprentices and trainee engineer applicants, see 2253

Mechanical Information Test [England], ages 15 and over, see 2254

Mechanical Movements: A Test of Mechanical Comprehension, industrial employees, see 2255

Mechanical Reasoning: Differential Aptitude Tests, grades 8–12 and adults, see 2256

Mellenbruch Mechanical Motivation Test, grades 6–16 and adults, see 2257

Minnesota Spatial Relations Test, ages 11 and over, see 2258

O'Connor Wiggly Block, ages 16 and over, see 2259

O'Rourke Mechanical Aptitude Test, grades 7–12 and adults, see 2260

Perceptual Battery [South Africa], job applicants with at least 10 years of education, see 2261

Primary Mechanical Ability Tests, applicants for positions requiring mechanical ability, see 2262

Purdue Mechanical Adaptability Test, males ages 15 and over, see 2263

RBH Three-Dimensional Space Test, industrial workers in mechanical fields, see 2264

RBH Two-Dimensional Space Test, business and industry, see 2265

Revised Minnesota Paper Form Board Test, grades 9–16 and adults, see 2266

SRA Mechanical Aptitudes, grades 9–12 and adults, see 2267

Space Relations: Differential Aptitude Tests, grades 8–12 and adults, see 2268

Spatial Tests EG, 2, and 3 [England], ages 10–13 and 15–17, see 2269

Spatial Visualization Test: Dailey Vocational Tests, grades 8–12 and adults, see 2270

Vincent Mechanical Diagrams Test [England], ages 15 and over, see 2271

Weights and Pulleys: A Test of Intuitive Mechanics, engineering students and industrial employees, see 2272

MISCELLANEOUS

Alpha Biographical Inventory, grades 9–12, see 2273

Biographical Index, college and industry, see 2274

Business Judgment Test, adults, see 2275

Conference Evaluation, conference participants, see 2276

Conference Meeting Rating Scale, conference leaders and participants, see 2277

★*Continuous Letter Checking and Continuous Symbol Checking* [South Africa], ages 12 and over, see 2278–9

Gullo Workshop and Seminar Evaluation, workshop and seminar participants, see 2280

Job Attitude Analysis, production and clerical workers, see 2281

Mathematical and Technical Test [England], ages 11 and over, see 2282

Minnesota Importance Questionnaire, vocational counselees, see 2283

★*Minnesota Job Description Questionnaire*, employees and supervisors, see 2284

Minnesota Satisfaction Questionnaire, business and industry, see 2285

Per-Flu-Dex Tests, college and industry, see 2286

RBH Breadth of Information, business and industry, see 2287

Self-Rating Scale for Leadership Qualifications, adults, see 2288

Tear Ballot for Industry, employees in industry, see 2289

Test Orientation Procedure, job applicants and trainees, see 2290

Tests A/9 and A/10 [South Africa], applicants for technical and apprentice jobs, see 2291

Whisler Strategy Test, business and industry, see 2292

Work Information Inventory, employee groups in industry, see 2293

SELECTION & RATING FORMS

APT Controlled Interview, applicants for employment, see 2294

Application Interview Screening Form, job applicants, see 2295

Career Counseling Personal Data Form, vocational counselees, see 2296

Employee Competency Scale, employees, see 2297

Employee Evaluation Form for Interviewers, adults, see 2298

Employee Performance Appraisal, business and industry, see 2299

★*Employee Progress Appraisal Form,* rating of office employees, see 2300

Employee Rating and Development Forms, executive, industrial, office, and sales personnel, see 2301

Executive, Industrial, and Sales Personnel Forms, applicants for executive, industrial, office, or sales positions, see 2302

Job Application Forms, job applicants and employees, see 2303

Lawshe-Kephart Personnel Comparison System, for rating any aspect of employee performance by the paired comparison technique, see 2304

★*McCormick Job Performance Measurement "Rate-$-Scales,"* employees, see 2305

McQuaig Manpower Selection Series, applicants for office and sales positions, see 2306

Martin Performance Appraisal, employees, see 2307

Merit Rating Series, industry, see 2308

Nagel Personnel Interviewing and Screening Forms, job applicants, see 2309

Performance Review Forms, employees and managers, see 2310

Personal Data Blank, counselees ages 15 and over, see 2311

Personnel Interviewing Forms, business and industry, see 2312

Personnel Rating Scale, employees, see 2313

RBH Individual Background Survey, business and industry, see 2314

San Francisco Vocational Competency Scale, mentally retarded adults, see 2315

Selection Interview Forms, business and industry, see 2316

Speech-Appearance Record, job applicants, see 2317

Stevens-Thurow Personnel Forms, business and industry, see 2318

★*Tickmaster,* job applicants, see 2319

Wonderlic Personnel Selection Procedure, applicants for employment, see 2320

Work Reference Check, job applicants, see 2321

SPECIFIC VOCATIONS

ACCOUNTING

Account Clerk Test, job applicants, see 2322

American Institute of Certified Public Accountants Testing Programs, grades 13–16 and accountants, see 2323

CLEP Subject Examination in Introductory Accounting, 1 year or equivalent, see 2324

BUSINESS

Admission Test for Graduate Study in Business, business graduate students, see 2325

CLEP Subject Examination in Introduction to Business Management, 1 semester or equivalent, see 2326

CLEP Subject Examination in Introductory Business Law, 1 semester or equivalent, see 2327

CLEP Subject Examination in Introductory Marketing, 1 semester or equivalent, see 2328

CLEP Subject Examination in Money and Banking, 1 semester or equivalent, see 2329

Organizational Value Dimensions Questionnaire, adults, see 2330

COMPUTER PROGRAMMING

Aptitude Assessment Battery: Programming, programmers and trainees, see 2331

CLEP Subject Examination in Computers and Data Processing, 1–2 semesters or equivalent, see 2332

★*CLEP Subject Examination in Elementary Computer Programming—Fortran IV,* 1 semester or equivalent, see 2333

Computer Programmer Aptitude Battery, applicants for computer training or employment, see 2334

Diebold Personnel Tests, programmers and systems analysts for automatic data processing and computing installations, see 2335

★*Programmer Aptitude/Competence Test System,* computer programmers and applicants for programmer training, see 2336

DENTISTRY

Dental Admission Testing Program, dental school applicants, see 2337

Dental Hygiene Aptitude Testing Program, dental hygiene school applicants, see 2338

★*Ohio Dental Assisting Achievement Test,* grades 11–12, see 2339

ENGINEERING

AC Test of Creative Ability, engineers and supervisors, see 2340

Engineering Aide Test, engineering aides, see 2341

Garnett College Test in Engineering Science [England], 1–2 years technical college, see 2342

Graduate Record Examinations Advanced Engineering Test, graduate school candidates, see 2343

Minnesota Engineering Analogies Test, candidates for graduate school and industry, see 2344

N.I.I.P. Engineering Apprentice Selection Test Battery [England], engineering apprentices, see 2345

National Engineering Aptitude Search Test: The Junior Engineering Technical Society, grades 9–12, see 2346

Purdue Creativity Test, applicants for engineering positions, see 2347

Undergraduate Program Field Tests: Engineering Test, college, see 2348

LAW

Law School Admission Test, law school applicants, see 2349

MEDICINE

★*CLEP Subject Examination in Clinical Chemistry,* medical technologists, see 2350

★*CLEP Subject Examination in Hematology,* medical technologists, see 2351

★*CLEP Subject Examination in Immunohematology and Blood Banking,* medical technologists, see 2352

★*CLEP Subject Examination in Microbiology,* medical technologists, see 2353

Colleges of Podiatry Admission Test, grades 14 and over, see 2354

Medical College Admission Test, applicants for admission to member colleges of the Association of American Medical Colleges, see 2355

Medical School Instructor Attitude Inventory, medical school faculty members, see 2356

★*Optometry College Admission Test*, optometry college applicants, see 2357

Veterinary Aptitude Test, veterinary school applicants, see 2358

MISCELLANEOUS

Architectural School Aptitude Test, architectural school applicants, see 2359

Chemical Operators Selection Test, chemical operators and applicants, see 2360

Fire Promotion Tests, prospective firemen promotees, see 2361

Firefighter Test, prospective firemen, see 2362

Fireman Examination, prospective firemen, see 2363

General Municipal Employees Performance (Efficiency) Rating System, municipal employees, see 2364

Journalism Test, high school, see 2365

★*Law Enforcement Perception Questionnaire*, law enforcement personnel, see 2366

Memory and Observation Tests for Policeman, prospective policemen, see 2367

Police Performance Rating System, policemen, see 2368

Police Promotion Tests, prospective policemen promotees, see 2369

Policeman Examination, prospective policemen, see 2370

Policeman Test, policemen and prospective policemen, see 2371

Potter-Nash Aptitude Test for Lumber Inspectors and Other General Personnel Who Handle Lumber, employees in woodworking industries, see 2372

★*Test for Firefighter B-1*, firemen and prospective firemen, see 2373

★*Test for Police Officer A-1*, policemen and prospective policemen, see 2374

Visual Comprehension Test for Detective, prospective police detectives, see 2375

NURSING

Achievement Tests in Nursing, students in schools of registered nursing, see 2376

Achievement Tests in Practical Nursing, practical nursing students, see 2377

Empathy Inventory, nursing instructors, see 2378

Entrance Examination for Schools of Nursing, nursing school applicants, see 2379

Entrance Examination for Schools of Practical Nursing, practical nursing school applicants, see 2380

George Washington University Series Nursing Tests, prospective nurses, see 2381

Luther Hospital Sentence Completions, prospective nursing students, see 2382

NLN Achievement Tests for Schools Preparing Registered Nurses, students in state-approved schools preparing registered nurses, see 2383

NLN Aide Selection Test, applicants for aide positions in hospitals and home health agencies, see 2384

NLN Practical Nursing Achievement Tests, students in state-approved schools of practical nursing, see 2385

NLN Pre-Admission and Classification Examination, practical nursing school entrants, see 2386

NLN Pre-Nursing and Guidance Examination, applicants for admission to state-approved schools preparing registered nurses, see 2387

Netherne Study Difficulties Battery for Student Nurses [England], student nurses, see 2388

Nurse Attitudes Inventory, prospective nursing students, see 2389

PSB-Aptitude for Practical Nursing Examination, applicants for admission to practical nursing schools, see 2390

RESEARCH

Research Personnel Review Form, research and engineering and scientific firms, see 2391

Supervisor's Evaluation of Research Personnel, research personnel, see 2392

Surveys of Research Administration and Environment, research and engineering and scientific firms, see 2393

Technical Personnel Recruiting Inventory, research and engineering and scientific firms, see 2394

SELLING

Aptitudes Associates Test of Sales Aptitude, applicants for sales positions, see 2395

Combination Inventory, Form 2, prospective debit life insurance salesmen, see 2396

Detroit Retail Selling Inventory, candidates for training in retail selling, see 2397

Evaluation Record, prospective life insurance agency managers, see 2398

Hall Salespower Inventory, salesmen, see 2399

Hanes Sales Selection Inventory, insurance and printing salesmen, see 2400

Information Index, life and health insurance agents, see 2401

LIAMA Inventory of Job Attitudes, life insurance field personnel, see 2402

Personnel Institute Hiring Kit, applicants for sales positions, see 2403

SRA Sales Attitudes Check List, applicants for sales positions, see 2404

Sales Aptitude Test, job applicants, see 2405

Sales Comprehension Test, applicants for sales positions, see 2406

Sales Method Index, life insurance agents, see 2407

Sales Motivation Inventory, applicants for sales positions, see 2408

Sales Sentence Completion Blank, applicants for sales positions, see 2409

Steward Life Insurance Knowledge Test, applicants for life insurance agent or supervisory positions, see 2410

Steward Occupational Objectives Inventory, applicants for supervisory positions in life insurance companies or agencies, see 2411

Steward Personal Background Inventory, applicants for sales positions, see 2412

Test for Ability to Sell: George Washington University Series, grades 7–16 and adults, see 2413

★*Test of Retail Sales Insight*, retail clerks and students, see 2414

SKILLED TRADES

Electrical Sophistication Test, job applicants, see 2415

Fiesenheiser Test of Ability to Read Drawings, trade school and adults, see 2416

Mechanical Familiarity Test, job applicants, see 2417

Mechanical Handyman Test, maintenance workers, see 2418

Mechanical Knowledge Test, job applicants, see 2419

Ohio Auto Body Achievement Test, grades 11–12, see 2420

Ohio Automotive Mechanics Achievement Test, grades 11–12, see 2421

★*Ohio Carpentry Achievement Test,* grades 11–12, see 2422

★*Ohio Communication Products Electronics Achievement Test,* grades 11–12, see 2423

★*Ohio Construction Electricity Achievement Test,* grades 11–12, see 2424

Ohio Cosmetology Achievement Test, grades 11–12, see 2425

★*Ohio Industrial Electronics Achievement Test,* grades 11–12, see 2426

Ohio Machine Trades Achievement Test, grades 11–12, see 2427

Ohio Mechanical Drafting Achievement Test, grades 11–12, see 2428

Ohio Printing Achievement Test, grades 11–12, see 2429

Ohio Sheet Metal Achievement Test, grades 11–12, see 2430

Ohio Trade and Industrial Education Achievement Test Program, grades 11–12, see 2431

Ohio Welding Achievement Test, grades 11–12, see 2432

Purdue Industrial Training Classification Test, grades 9–12 and adults, see 2433

Purdue Interview Aids, applicants for industrial employment, see 2434

Purdue Trade Information Test for Sheetmetal Workers, sheetmetal workers, see 2435

Purdue Trade Information Test in Carpentry, vocational school and adults, see 2436

Purdue Trade Information Test in Engine Lathe Operation, vocational school and adults, see 2437

Purdue Trade Information Test in Welding, vocational school and adults, see 2438

Short Occupational Knowledge Test for Auto Mechanics, job applicants, see 2439

Short Occupational Knowledge Test for Carpenters, job applicants, see 2440

Short Occupational Knowledge Test for Draftsmen, job applicants, see 2441

Short Occupational Knowledge Test for Electricians, job applicants, see 2442

Short Occupational Knowledge Test for Machinists, job applicants, see 2443

Short Occupational Knowledge Test for Plumbers, job applicants, see 2444

Short Occupational Knowledge Test for Tool and Die Makers, job applicants, see 2445

Short Occupational Knowledge Test for Welders, job applicants, see 2446

Technical Tests [South Africa], standards 6–8 (ages 13–15), see 2447

SUPERVISION

How Supervise?, supervisors, see 2448

Ideal Leader Behavior Description Questionnaire, supervisors, see 2449

★*In-Basket Test* [South Africa], applicants for high level executive positions, see 2450

Leader Behavior Description Questionnaire, supervisors, see 2451

Leader Behavior Description Questionnaire, Form 12, supervisors, see 2452

Leadership Evaluation and Development Scale, prospective supervisors, see 2453

Leadership Opinion Questionnaire, supervisors and prospective supervisors, see 2454

★*Leadership Practices Inventory,* supervisors, see 2455

Managerial Scale for Enterprise Improvement, supervisors, see 2456

RAD Scales, supervisors, see 2457

RBH Test of Supervisory Judgment, business and industry, see 2458

Supervisory Index, supervisors, see 2459

Supervisory Inventory on Communication, supervisors and prospective supervisors, see 2460

★*Supervisory Inventory on Discipline,* supervisors, see 2461

★*Supervisory Inventory on Grievances,* supervisors, see 2462

Supervisory Inventory on Human Relations, supervisors and prospective supervisors, see 2463

★*Supervisory Inventory on Labor Relations,* supervisors in unionized firms, see 2464

Supervisory Inventory on Safety, supervisors and prospective supervisors, see 2465

Supervisory Practices Test, supervisors, see 2466

★*Survey of Management Perception,* supervisors, see 2467

WPS Supervisor-Executive Tri-Dimensional Evaluation Scales, supervisors, see 2468

TRANSPORTATION

American Transit Association Tests, transit operating personnel, see 2469

Driver Selection Forms and Tests, truck drivers, see 2470

McGuire Safe Driver Scale and Interview Guide, prospective motor vehicle operators, see 2471

Road Test Check List for Testing, Selecting, Rating, and Training Coach Operators, bus drivers, see 2472

Road Test in Traffic for Testing, Selecting, Rating and Training Truck Drivers, truck drivers, see 2473

Short Occupational Knowledge Test for Truck Drivers, job applicants, see 2474

Truck Driver Test, drivers of light and medium trucks, see 2475

Wilson Driver Selection Test, prospective motor vehicle operators, see 2476

PUBLISHERS DIRECTORY
AND INDEX

This directory and index gives the addresses and tests of all publishers represented in this volume. References are to entry numbers, not to page numbers. Stars indicate test publishers with test catalogs listing 10 or more tests. Tests not originating in the country of publication are identified by listing in brackets the country in which the test was originally prepared and published. All foreign tests distributed by United States publishers are listed; however, United States tests distributed by foreign publishers are listed only if the tests have been revised or supplemented for foreign use.

AVA Publications, Inc., 11 Dorrance St., Providence, R.I. 40510:
Measurement of Skill, 1080
Skill in Typing, 2157

American Automobile Association, 1712 G St. N.W., Washington, D.C. 20006:
Road Test Check List for Testing, Selecting, Rating, and Training Coach Operators, 2472
Road Test in Traffic for Testing, Selecting, Rating and Training Truck Drivers, 2473

American College Testing Program (The), P.O. Box 168, Iowa City, Iowa 52240:
ACT Assessment of Career Development, 2100
ACT Career Planning Program, 2101
ACT Guidance Profile, 2167
Medical College Admission Test, 2355

American Dental Association. *See* Division of Educational Measurements.

★American Guidance Service, Inc., Publishers' Bldg., Circle Pines, Minn. 55014:
Minnesota High School Achievement Examinations: Bookkeeping, 776
Minnesota Rate of Manipulation Test, 2227
Minnesota Spatial Relations Test, 2258
Pennsylvania Bi-Manual Worksample, 2231

American Transit Association, 465 L'Enfant Plaza West S.W., Washington, D.C. 20024:
Personal Reaction Test for Transit Employees, 2469b
Placement Interview for Transit Employees, 2469c
Standard Examination for Transit Employees, 2469a
Standardized Road Test for Bus Operators, 2469d

Aptitude Test Service, Inc., P.O. Box 16, Golf, Ill. 60029:
Hay Clerical Test Battery, 2132
Stenographic Skill-Dictation Test, 2159
Typing Skill, 2163

Armed Forces Vocational Testing Group, Randolph Air Force Base, Tex. 78148:
Armed Services Vocational Aptitude Battery, 1067

Associated Personnel Technicians, Inc., Box 1036, Wichita, Kan. 67201:
APT Controlled Interview, 2294
APT Dictation Test, 2119
APT Manual Dexterity Test, 2222

★Australian Council for Educational Research, P.O. Box 210, Hawthorn, Vic. 3122, Australia:
A.C.E.R. Mechanical Comprehension Test, 2237
A.C.E.R. Mechanical Reasoning Test, 2238
ACER Short Clerical Test—Form C, 2117
A.C.E.R. Speed and Accuracy Tests, 2118
How Supervise? [United States], 2448
Phillips Occupational Preference Scale, 2202
Rothwell-Miller Interest Blank, 2208
Shorthand Aptitude Test, 793

Ballen (Roland), P.O. Box 11209, Palo Alto, Calif. 94306:
Tickmaster, 2319

★Bobbs-Merrill Co., Inc. (The), 4300 West 62nd St., Indianapolis, Ind. 46268:
Achievement Examinations for Secondary Schools
Bookkeeping, 775
Business Relations and Occupations, 779
Detroit Clerical Aptitudes Examination, 782
Detroit General Aptitudes Examination, 1068
Detroit Mechanical Aptitudes Examination, 2244
Detroit Retail Selling Inventory, 2397

Brown & Associates, Inc., P.O. Box 5092, Station B, Greenville, S.C. 29606:
Yarn Dexterity Test, 2236

★Bruce (Martin M.), Ph.D., Publishers, 340 Oxford Road, New Rochelle, N.Y. 10804:
Aptitudes Associates Test of Sales Aptitude, 2395
Business Judgment Test, 2275
Career Counseling Personal Data Form, 2296
Clerical Skills Series, 2121
Employee Performance Appraisal, 2299
Performance Review Forms, 2310
Personnel Interviewing Forms, 2312
Sales Comprehension Test, 2406
Sales Motivation Inventory, 2408
Sales Sentence Completion Blank, 2409
Selection Interview Forms, 2316
Supervisory Practices Test, 2466
Wilson Driver Selection Test, 2476

★Bureau of Educational Measurements, Kansas State Teachers College, 1200 Commercial, Emporia, Kan. 66802:
Hiett Simplified Shorthand Test (Gregg), 784
Reicherter-Sanders Typewriting I and II, 789
Russell-Sanders Bookkeeping Test, 790

★CTB/McGraw-Hill, Del Monte Research Park, Monterey, Calif. 93940:
Aptitude Tests for Occupations, 1066
Career Maturity Inventory, 2103
MacQuarrie Test for Mechanical Ability, 2251
Multiple Aptitude Tests, 1082
Occupational Interest Inventory, 2199
Picture Interest Inventory, 2205

Careers Research and Advisory Centre, Bateman St., Cambridge, England:
Connolly Occupational Interests Questionnaire, 2175
Crowley Occupational Interests Blank, 2176

Case Western Reserve University. *See* Personnel Research Institute.

Center for Psychological Service, 1835 Eye St. N.W., Washington, D.C. 20006:
George Washington University Series Nursing Tests, 2381
Test for Ability to Sell, 2413

College Entrance Examination Board, 888 Seventh Ave., New York, N.Y. 10019:
CLEP Subject Examinations
Clinical Chemistry, 2350
Computers and Data Processing, 2332
Elementary Computer Programming—Fortran IV, 2333
Hematology, 2351
Immunohematology and Blood Banking, 2352
Introduction to Business Management, 2326
Introductory Accounting, 2324
Introductory Business Law, 2327
Introductory Marketing, 2328
Microbiology, 2353
Money and Banking, 2329
College Placement Test in Spatial Relations, 2241

★Consulting Psychologists Press, Inc., 577 College Ave., Palo Alto, Calif. 94306:
Personal Data Blank, 2311
Self Directed Search, 2211

Council on Dental Education. *See* Division of Educational Measurements.

Cox (Charles J.), Beaufort House, Marlborough Rd., Bowdon, Altrincham, Cheshire WA14 2RW, England:
Cox Mechanical and Manual Tests, 2242

Dartnell Corporation (The), 4660 Ravenswood Ave., Chicago, Ill. 60640:
Driver Selection Forms and Tests, 2470
Employee Rating and Development Forms, 2301
Executive, Industrial, and Sales Personnel Forms, 2302

Diebold (John) & Associates, 430 Park Ave., New York, N.Y. 10022:
Diebold Personnel Tests, 2335

Division of Educational Measurements, Council on Dental Education, American Dental Association, 211 East Chicago Ave., Chicago, Ill. 60611:
Dental Admission Testing Program, 2337

Dow Chemical Co. (The), Midland, Mich. 48640:
Chemical Operators Selection Test, 2360

Educational and Industrial Test Services, 83 High St., Hemel Hempstead, Herts, England:
Differential Test Battery, 1070

★Educational and Industrial Testing Service, P.O. Box 7234, San Diego, Calif. 92107:
California Occupational Preference Survey, 2170

Educational Guidance, Inc., P.O. Box 511, Main Station, Dearborn, Mich. 48120:
Career Guidance Inventory, 2172
Educational Interest Inventory, 2178

★Educational Testing Service, Princeton, N.J. 08540 (*See also* College Entrance Examination Board and Educational Testing Service [Midwest Office].):
Admission Test for Graduate Study in Business, 2325
Architectural School Aptitude Test, 2359
Graduate Record Examinations Advanced Engineering Test, 2343
Law School Admission Test, 2349
National Teacher Examinations: Business Education, 787
Teacher Education Examination Program: Business Education, 797
Undergraduate Program Field Tests
Business Test, 800
Engineering Test, 2348

Educational Testing Service (Midwest Office), 960 Grove St., Evanston, Ill. 60201:
Colleges of Podiatry Admission Test, 2354

Educators Assistance Institute, 2500 Colorado Ave., Santa Monica, Calif. 90406:
Pictorial Inventory of Careers, 2204

★Educators'-Employers' Tests & Services Associates, 120 Detzel Place, Cincinnati, Ohio 45219:
ESTA Tests, 2106
General Clerical Ability Test, 2128
Mechanical Familiarity Test, 2417
Mechanical Knowledge Test, 2419
Sales Aptitude Test, 2405
Stenographic Skills Test, 2160

Executive Analysis Corporation, 50 East 42nd St., New York, N.Y. 10017:
How Well Do You Know Your Interests? 2189

★Ginn & Co. Ltd., Elsinore House, Buckingham St., Aylesbury, Bucks, England:
Clerical Tests FG and 2, 781A
Spatial Tests EG, 2, and 3, 2269

Guidance Associates of Delaware, Inc., 1526 Gilpin Ave., Wilmington, Del. 19806:
Jastak Test of Potential Ability and Behavior Stability, 1077
Wide Range Employment Sample Test, 2116
Wide Range Interest-Opinion Test, 2219

Hall & Liles, 411 Sandra Drive, Oxford, Ohio 45056:
Hall Salespower Inventory, 2399

★Harcourt Brace Jovanovich, Inc., 757 Third Ave., New York, N.Y. 10017:
Gordon Occupational Check List, 2182
Ohio Vocational Interest Survey, 2201
Thurstone Employment Tests, 2162
Turse Shorthand Aptitude Test, 798

Harless (Byron), Schaffer, Reid & Associates, Inc., 3106 Morrison Ave., Tampa, Fla. 33609:
Supervisor's Evaluation of Research Personnel, 2392

★Harrap (George G.) & Co. Ltd., P.O. Box 70, 182/4 High Holborn, London WC1V 7AX, England:
Mathematical and Technical Test, 2282

Haverly Systems, Inc., 4 Second Ave., Denville, N.J. 07834:
Programmer Aptitude/Competence Test System, 2336

★Houghton Mifflin Co., 110 Tremont St., Boston, Mass. 02107:
Appraisal of Occupational Aptitudes, 2120
Dailey Vocational Tests, 2105; Spatial Visualization Test, 2270
Office Information and Skills Test: Content Evaluation Series, 788
Work Values Inventory, 2221

★Human Sciences Research Council, Private Bag 41, Pretoria, Republic of South Africa:
Academic-Technical Aptitude Tests, 1064
Aptitude Test for Junior Secondary Pupils, 1065
Interest Questionnaire for Indian South Africans, 2191
Junior Aptitude Tests for Indian South Africans, 1079
N.B. Aptitude Tests (Junior), 1083
19 Field Interest Inventory, 2198
Senior Aptitude Tests, 1088
Technical Tests, 2447

Industrial Psychology, Inc., 515 Madison Ave., New York, N.Y. 10022:
Job-Tests Program, 1078
Merit Rating Series, 2308

★Industrial Relations Center, University of Chicago, 1225 East 60th St., Chicago, Ill. 60637 (This publisher has not replied to our four requests to check the accuracy of the entries for the tests listed below. Entry 2110 was checked by one of the test authors.):
AC Test of Creative Ability, 2340
Flags: A Test of Space Thinking, 2245
Mechanical Movements: A Test of Mechanical Comprehension, 2255
Personal History Index, 2110
Weights and Pulleys: A Test of Intuitive Mechanics, 2272

Institute for Behavioral Research in Creativity, 1417 South 11th East, Salt Lake City, Utah 84105:
Alpha Biographical Inventory, 2273

Institute of Public Safety, Pennsylvania State University, University Park, Pa. 16802:
Road Test Check List for Testing, Selecting, Rating, and Training Coach Operators, 2472
Road Test in Traffic for Testing, Selecting, Rating and Training Truck Drivers, 2473

Instructional Materials Laboratory, Ohio State University, 1885 Neil Ave., Columbus, Ohio 43210:

Ohio Trade and Industrial Education Achievement Test Program, 2431
  Auto Body, 2420
  Automotive Mechanics, 2421
  Carpentry, 2422
  Communication Products Electronics, 2423
  Construction Electricity, 2424
  Cosmetology, 2425
  Dental Assisting, 2339
  Industrial Electronics, 2426
  Machine Trades, 2427
  Mechanical Drafting, 2428
  Printing, 2429
  Sheet Metal, 2430
  Welding, 2432

International Personnel Management Association, 1313 East 60th St., Chicago, Ill. 60637:
  Account Clerk Test, 2322
  Engineering Aide Test, 2341
  Firefighter Test, 2362
  Mechanical Handyman Test, 2418
  Office Worker Test, 2137
  Policeman Test, 2371
  Test for Firefighter B-1, 2373
  Test for Police Officer A-1, 2374
  Truck Driver Test, 2475

International Tests, Inc., Box 634, Stevens Point, Wis. 54481:
  International Primary Factors Test Battery, 1076

Interstate Printers & Publishers, Inc. (The), 19–27 North Jackson St., Danville, Ill. 61832:
  Applied Biological and Agribusiness Interest Inventory, 2169

K & W Products Co., Inc., 403 Salisbury Road, Wyncote, Pa. 19095:
  General Antitude Test Battery
    Finger Dexterity Board, 1073c5
    Pegboard, 1073c4
  Nonreading Aptitude Test Battery
    Finger Dexterity Board, 1086l
    Pegboard, 1086k

Kansas State Teachers College. *See* Bureau of Educational Measurements.

Kemper Psychological Services, Long Grove, Ill. 60049:
  Selection Tests for Office Personnel, 2150

Kirkpatrick (Donald L.), 4380 Continental Drive, Brookfield, Wis. 53005:
  Supervisory Inventory on Communication, 2460
  Supervisory Inventory on Human Relations, 2463
  Supervisory Inventory on Safety, 2465

L & L Associates, P.O. Box 20473, Charlotte, N.C. 28202:
  L & L Clerical Tests, 2133

Lafayette Instrument Co., P.O. Box 1279, North 9th St. Road and Sagamore Parkway, Lafayette, Ind. 47902:
  O'Connor Finger Dexterity Test, 2228
  O'Connor Tweezer Dexterity Test, 2229
  O'Connor Wiggly Block, 2259
  One Hole Test, 2230
  Purdue Hand Precision Test, 2233

Life Insurance Agency Management Association, 170 Sigourney St., Hartford, Conn. 06105:
  Combination Inventory, 2396
  Evaluation Record, 2398
  Information Index, 2401
  LIAMA Inventory of Job Attitudes, 2402
  Sales Method Index, 2407

★McCann Associates, 2755 Philmont Ave., Huntington Valley, Pa. 19006:
  Clerical Worker Examination, 2125
  Fire Promotion Tests, 2361
  Fireman Examination, 2363
  General Municipal Employees Performance (Efficiency) Rating System, 2364
  McCann Typing Tests, 2134
  Memory and Observation Tests for Policeman, 2367
  Police Performance Rating System, 2368
  Police Promotion Tests, 2369
  Policeman Examination, 2370
  Stenographic Dictation Test, 2158
  Visual Comprehension Test for Detective, 2375

McQuaig Institute of Executive Development, Suite 350, 541 Lexington Ave., New York, N.Y. 10022:
  McQuaig Manpower Selection Series, 2306

Management Research Associates, R.R. 25, Box 225, Terre Haute, Ind. 47802:
  Leadership Practices Inventory, 2455
  Survey of Management Perception, 2467

Manasayan, 32 Netaji Subhash Marg, Delhi 110006, India:
  Chatterji's Non-Language Preference Record, 2173

★Monitor, P.O. Box 2337, Hollywood, Calif. 90028:
  New Mexico Career Education Test Series, 2109

NCS Interpretive Scoring Systems, 4401 West 76th St., Minneapolis, Minn. 55435:
  Nonreading Aptitude Test Battery, 1086

★NFER Publishing Co. Ltd., 2 Jennings Bldgs., Thames Ave., Windsor, Berks SL4 1QS, England:
  Bennett Mechanical Comprehension Test [United States], 2239
  Computer Programmer Aptitude Battery [United States], 2334
  Factorial Interest Blank, 2179
  Form Relations Group Test, 2247
  Garnett College Test in Engineering Science, 2342
  General Clerical Test [United States], 2129
  Group Test 20, 2130
  Group Test 80A, 2248
  Group Test 81, 2249
  Group Test, 82, 2250
  Group Tests 61A, 64, and 66A, 2131
  Mechanical Information Test, 2254
  N.I.I.P. Engineering Apprentice Selection Test Battery, 2345
  Netherne Study Difficulties Battery for Student Nurses, 2388
  Rothwell-Miller Interest Blank [Australia], 2209
  Vincent Mechanical Diagrams Test, 2271

Nash (N.), Great Eastern Lumber Co., Inc., 2315 Broadway, New York, N.Y. 10024:
  Potter-Nash Aptitude Test for Lumber Inspectors and Other General Personnel Who Handle Lumber, 2372

National Business Education Association, 1201 Sixteenth St. N.W., Washington, D.C. 20036:
  National Business Entrance Tests, 786
    Bookkeeping Test, 777
    Business Fundamentals and General Information Test, 778
    General Office Clerical Test, 783
    Machine Calculation Test, 785
    Stenographic Test, 795
    Typewriting Test, 799
  United Students Typewriting Tests, 801

National Foremen's Institute, Inc., 24 Rope Ferry Road, Waterford, Conn. 06385:
  Employee Progress Appraisal Form, 2300
  Self-Rating Scale for Leadership Qualifications, 2288

★National Institute for Personnel Research, P.O. Box 10319, Johannesburg, Republic of South Africa:
  Classification Test Battery, 2104
  Continuous Letter Checking and Continuous Symbol Checking, 2278
  Form Perception Test, 2246
  High Level Battery: Test A/75, 1075
  In-Basket Test, 2450
  Mechanical Comprehension Test, 2253
  National Institute for Personnel Research Intermediate Battery, 1084
  National Institute for Personnel Research Normal Battery, 1085
  Perceptual Battery, 2261
  Preference Analysis, 2206
  Tests A/9 and A/10, 2291

National League for Nursing, Inc., 10 Columbus Circle, New York, N.Y. 10019:
  NLN Achievement Tests for Schools Preparing Registered Nurses, 2383
  NLN Aide Selection Test, 2384
  NLN Practical Nursing Achievement Tests, 2385
  NLN Pre-Admission and Classification Examination, 2386
  NLN Pre-Nursing and Guidance Examination, 2387

★Nelson (Thomas) & Sons (Canada) Ltd., 81 Curlew Drive, Don Mills 400, Ont., Canada:
  Safran Student's Interest Inventory, 2210

Nursing Research Associates, 3752 Cummings St., Eau Claire, Wis. 54701:
  Empathy Inventory, 2378
  Luther Hospital Sentence Completions, 2382
  Nurse Attitudes Inventory, 2389

Ohio State University. *See* Instructional Materials Laboratory and University Publications Sales.

O'Rourke Publications, P.O. Box 1118, Lake Alfred, Fla. 33850:
  O'Rourke Clerical Aptitude Test, 2138
  O'Rourke Mechanical Aptitude Test, 2260

Parnicky, (Joseph J.), Nisonger Center, Ohio State University, 1580 Cannon Drive, Columbus, Ohio 43210:
  Vocational Interest and Sophistication Assessment, 2217

Pennsylvania State University. *See* Institute of Public Safety.

Personal Growth Press, Inc., Box M, Berea, Ohio 44017:
College Interest Inventory, 2174
Henderson Analysis of Interest, 2188

Personnel Institute, Inc., 908 Fox Plaza, San Francisco, Calif. 94102:
Personnel Institute Clerical Tests, 2139
Personnel Institute Hiring Kit, 2403

Personnel Research Associates, Inc., 701 Metropolitan Bldg., 1407 Main St., Dallas, Tex. 75202:
Individual Placement Series, 2108
  Occupational Interest Survey, 2200
  Shorthand Test, 2156
  Survey of Clerical Skills, 2161
  Typing Test, 2165

Personnel Research Institute, Case Western Reserve University, 1695 Magnolia Drive, Cleveland, Ohio 44106:
Personnel Research Institute Clerical Battery, 2140
Personnel Research Institute Test of Shorthand Skills, 2141

Programming Specialists, Inc., P.O. Box 160, Brooklyn, N.Y. 11234:
Aptitude Assessment Battery: Programming, 2331

Psychological Business Research, 11000 Cedar Ave., Cleveland, Ohio 44106:
Employment Aptitude Inventory, 2102b
Management Aptitude Inventory, 2102a
Sales Aptitude Inventory, 2102c

★Psychological Corporation (The), 304 East 45th St., New York, N.Y. 10017:
Academic Promise Tests, 1063
Achievement Tests in Nursing, 2376
Achievement Tests in Practical Nursing, 2377
American Institute of Certified Public Accountants Testing Programs, 2323
Bennett Mechanical Comprehension Test, 2239
Crawford Small Parts Dexterity Test, 2223
Dental Hygiene Aptitude Testing Program, 2338
Differential Aptitude Tests, 1069
  Clerical Speed and Accuracy, 781
  Mechanical Reasoning, 2256
  Space Relations, 2268
Employee Evaluation Form for Interviewers, 2298
Entrance Examination for Schools of Nursing, 2379
Entrance Examination for Schools of Practical Nursing, 2380
General Clerical Test, 2129
Hand-Tool Dexterity Test, 2225
How Supervise?, 2448
Minnesota Clerical Test, 2135
Minnesota Engineering Analogies Test, 2344
Minnesota Vocational Interest Inventory, 2197
Multi-Aptitude Test, 1081
National Engineering Aptitude Search Test, 2346
Optometry College Admission Test, 2357
Revised Minnesota Paper Form Board Test, 2266
San Francisco Vocational Competency Scale, 2315
Seashore-Bennett Stenographic Proficiency Test, 2148
Short Employment Tests, 2151
Speech-Appearance Record, 2317
Stenographic Aptitude Test, 794
Stromberg Dexterity Test, 2235
Test Orientation Procedure, 2290
Thurstone Interest Schedule, 2214
Typing Test for Business, 2164
Veterinary Aptitude Test, 2358

Psychological Publications Press, 16040 West McNichols Road, Detroit, Mich. 48235:
Application Interview Screening Form, 2295
Personnel Rating Scale, 2313
Work Reference Check, 2321

Psychological Service Center of Philadelphia, Suite 904, 1422 Chestnut St., Philadelphia, Pa. 19102:
Hackman-Gaither Vocational Interest Inventory, 2186

Psychological Services, Inc., Suite 600, 4311 Wilshire Blvd., Los Angeles, Calif. 90010:
Crissey Dexterity Test, 2224
Employee Aptitude Survey, 1071
Leadership Evaluation and Development Scale, 2453

Psychological Services Bureau, P.O. Box 673, Indiana, Pa. 15701:
PSB-Aptitude for Practical Nursing Examination, 2390

Psychological Test Specialists, Box 1441, Missoula, Mont. 59801:
Vocational Apperception Test, 2216

★Psychologists and Educators, Inc., Suite 212, 211 West State St., Jacksonville, Ill. 62650:
Conference Evaluation, 2276
Employee Competency Scale, 2297
Gullo Workshop and Seminar Evaluation, 2280
Secretarial Performance Analysis, 2149
Test of Retail Sales Insight, 2414

★Psychometric Affiliates, Box 3167, Munster, Ind. 46321:
Acorn National Aptitude Tests
  Clerical Aptitude Test, 780
  Inventory of Vocational Interests, 2192
  Mechanical Aptitude Test, 2252
Biographical Index, 2274
Conference Meeting Rating Scale, 2277
Cross Reference Test, 2126
Curtis Interest Scale, 2177
Curtis Object Completion and Space Form Tests, 2243
Curtis Verbal-Clerical Skills Tests, 2127
Electrical Sophistication Test, 2415
Fiesenheiser Test of Ability to Read Drawings, 2416
Hanes Sales Selection Inventory, 2400
Job Attitude Analysis, 2281
Law Enforcement Perception Questionnaire, 2366
Managerial Scale for Enterprise Improvement, 2456
Mellenbruch Mechanical Motivation Test, 2257
Office Skills Achievement Test, 2136
Per-Flu-Dex Tests, 2286
Tear Ballot for Industry, 2289
Whisler Strategy Test, 2292
Work Information Inventory, 2293

Psychometric Techniques Associates, 710 Chatham Center Office Bldg., Pittsburgh, Pa. 15219:
Tapping Test, 796

Public Personnel Association. *See* International Personnel Management Association.

★Richardson, Bellows, Henry & Co., Inc., 1140 Connecticut Ave. N.W., Washington, D.C. 20036:
RBH Breadth of Information, 2287
RBH Checking Test, 2143
RBH Classifying Test, 2144
RBH Individual Background Survey, 2314
RBH Number Checking Test, 2145
RBH Test of Dictation Speed, 2146
RBH Test of Supervisory Judgment, 2458
RBH Test of Typing Speed, 2147
RBH Three-Dimensional Space Test, 2264
RBH Two-Dimensional Space Test, 2265

Rosinski (Edwin F.), School of Medicine, University of California, 50 Kirkham St., San Francisco, Calif. 94143:
Medical School Instructor Attitude Inventory, 2356

SPECO Educational Systems, 1230 North Industrial, Dallas, Tex. 75207:
Practical Dexterity Board, 2232

Scarborough (Barron B.), Florida State University, Tallahassee, Fla. 32306:
Pictorial Interest Inventory, 2203

★Scholastic Testing Service, Inc., 480 Meyer Road, Bensenville, Ill. 60106:
Hall Occupational Orientation Inventory, 2187

★Science Research Associates, Inc., 259 East Erie St., Chicago, Ill. 60611:
Computer Programmer Aptitude Battery, 2334
Flanagan Aptitude Classification Tests, 1072
Flanagan Industrial Tests, 2107
Kuder General Interest Survey, 2193
Kuder Occupational Interest Survey, 2194
Kuder Preference Record—Vocational, 2195
Leadership Opinion Questionnaire, 2454
Purdue Pegboard, 2234
SRA Clerical Aptitudes, 791
SRA Mechanical Aptitudes, 2267
SRA Primary Mental Abilities, 1087
SRA Sales Attitudes Check List, 2404
SRA Typing Skills, 792
Short Occupational Knowledge Tests
  Auto Mechanics, 2439
  Bookkeepers, 2152
  Carpenters, 2440
  Draftsmen, 2441
  Electricians, 2442
  Machinists, 2443
  Office Machine Operators, 2153
  Plumbers, 2444
  Secretaries, 2154
  Tool and Die Makers, 2445
  Truck Drivers, 2474
  Welders, 2446
Short Tests of Clerical Ability, 2155

Supervisory Index, 2459
Vocational Planning Inventory, 2114
Shepherd (Hilton) Co., Inc., P.O. Box 846, Fort Worth, Tex. 76101:
Job Application Forms, 2303
★Sheridan Psychological Services, Inc., P.O. Box 6101, Orange, Calif. 92667:
Gregory Academic Interest Inventory, 2183
Guilford-Shneidman-Zimmerman Interest Survey, 2184
Guilford-Zimmerman Aptitude Survey, 1074
Guilford-Zimmerman Interest Inventory, 2185
Specialty Case Manufacturing Co., P.O. Box 3067, Philadelphia, Pa. 19150:
General Aptitude Test Battery
  Finger Dexterity Board, 1073c5
  Pegboard, 1073c4
Nonreading Aptitude Test Battery
  Finger Dexterity Board, 10861
  Pegboard, 1086k
Stanford University Press, Stanford, Calif. 94305:
Strong Vocational Interest Blank for Men, 2212
Strong Vocational Interest Blank for Women, 2213
Stein (Morris I.), Department of Psychology, New York University, 4 Washington Place, New York, N.Y. 10003:
Research Personnel Review Form, 2391
Surveys of Research Administration and Environment, 2393
Technical Personnel Recruiting Inventory, 2394
Stevens, Thurow & Associates, Inc., 105 West Adams St., Chicago, Ill. 60603:
Clerical Tests, 2122
Clerical Tests, Series N, 2123
Clerical Tests, Series V, 2124
Primary Mechanical Ability Tests, 2262
Stevens-Thurow Personnel Forms, 2318
Steward-Mortensen & Associates, 232 North Lake Ave., Pasadena, Calif. 91101:
Steward Basic Factors Inventory, 2111
Steward Life Insurance Knowledge Test, 2410
Steward Occupational Objectives Inventory, 2411
Steward Personal Background Inventory, 2412
Steward Personnel Tests (Short Form), 2112
★Stoelting Co., 1350 South Kostner Ave., Chicago, Ill. 60623:
O'Connor Finger Dexterity Test, 2228
O'Connor Tweezer Dexterity Test, 2229
O'Connor Wiggly Block, 2259
Stratton-Christian Press, Box 1055, University Place Station, Des Moines, Iowa 50311:
Journalism Test, 2365
TAV Selection System, 12807 Arminta St., North Hollywood, Calif. 91605:
TAV Selection System, 2113
Trademark Design Products, Inc., P.O. Box 2010, Boca Raton, Fla. 33432:
McCormick Job Performance Measurement "Rate-$-Scales," 2305
United States Government Printing Office, Washington, D.C. 20402:
General Aptitude Test Battery, 1073
Interest Check List, 2190
Nonreading Aptitude Test Battery, 1086
USES Clerical Skills Tests, 2166
★University Book Store, 360 State St., West Lafayette, Ind. 47906:
Purdue Clerical Adaptability Test, 2142
Purdue Creativity Test, 2347
Purdue Industrial Training Classification Test, 2433

Purdue Interview Aids, 2434
Purdue Mechanical Adaptability Test, 2263
Purdue Trade Information Test for Sheetmetal Workers, 2435
Purdue Trade Information Test in Carpentry, 2436
Purdue Trade Information Test in Engine Lathe Operation, 2437
Purdue Trade Information Test in Welding, 2438
University of British Columbia Bookstore, Vancouver 8, B.C., Canada:
VALCAN Vocational Interest Profile, 2215
Vocational Interest Profile, 2218
University of Chicago. *See* Industrial Relations Center.
★University of London Press Ltd., St. Paul's House, Warwick Lane, London EC4P 4AH, England:
A.P.U. Occupational Interests Guide, 2168
University Publications Sales, Ohio State University, 20 Lord Hall, 124 West 17th Ave., Columbus, Ohio 43210:
Ideal Leader Behavior Description Questionnaire, 2449
Leader Behavior Description Questionnaire, 2451
Leader Behavior Description Questionnaire, Form 12, 2452
Organizational Value Dimensions Questionnaire, 2330
RAD Scales, 2457
Village Book Cellar, 308 West State St., West Lafayette, Ind. 47906:
Lawshe-Kephart Personnel Comparison System, 2304
Vocational Guidance Service, 8845 Sheridan Drive, Williamsville, N.Y. 14221:
Chriswell Structural Dexterity Test, 2240
Vocational Psychology Research, Elliott Hall, University of Minnesota, Minneapolis, Minn. 55455:
Minnesota Importance Questionnaire, 2283
Minnesota Job Description Questionnaire, 2284
Minnesota Satisfaction Questionnaire, 2285
Warwick Products Co., 7909 Rockside Road, Cleveland, Ohio 44131:
General Aptitude Test Battery
  Finger Dexterity Board, 1073c5
  Pegboard, 1073c4
Nonreading Aptitude Test Battery
  Finger Dexterity Board, 10861
  Pegboard, 1086k
★Western Psychological Services, 12031 Wilshire Blvd., Los Angeles, Calif. 90025:
California Pre-Counseling Self-Analysis Protocol Booklet, 2171
Geist Picture Interest Inventory, 2180
Geist Picture Interest Inventory: Deaf Form, 2181
McGuire Safe Driver Scale and Interview Guide, 2471
Manipulative Aptitude Test, 2226
Martin Performance Appraisal, 2307
Milwaukee Academic Interest Inventory, 2196
Nagel Personnel Interviewing and Screening Forms, 2309
WPS Supervisor-Executive Tri-Dimensional Evaluation Scales, 2468
William, Lynde & Williams, 153 East Erie St., Painesville, Ohio 44077:
WLW Employment Inventory, 2115
William, Lynde & Williams Analysis of Interest, 2220
Wonderlic (E. F.) & Associates, Inc., Box 7, Northfield, Ill. 60093:
Wonderlic Personnel Selection Procedure, 2320
Wyman (Earl J.), Box 200, Delafield, Wis. 53018:
Supervisory Inventory on Discipline, 2461
Supervisory Inventory on Grievances, 2462
Supervisory Inventory on Labor Relations, 2464

INDEX OF TITLES

In this monograph, "vocational tests" refers to all tests classified in the business education, multi-aptitude, and vocations sections of the *Mental Measurements Yearbooks* (MMY) and *Tests in Print II* (TIP II). This index lists (*a*) vocational tests in print as of February 1, 1974, and (*b*) vocational tests out of print, status unknown, or reclassified since last listed in a vocational section of an MMY. Citations are to test entries, not to pages. Numbers without colons refer to in print tests listed in this volume; numbers with colons refer to tests out of print, status unknown, or reclassified. Unless preceded by the word *"consult,"* all numbers containing colons refer to tests in this volume. The guide numbers next to the outside margins in the running heads of the reprint sections should be used to locate a particular test. The first reprint section, from TIP II, has guide numbers in the range 775 to 2476; the second reprint section, from the 1st MMY, 1:935 to 1:1181; the third reprint section, from the 2nd MMY, 2:1476 to 2:1684; etc. To obtain the latest information on a test no longer classified with vocational tests, the reader must consult either TIP II (if the test is in print) or an MMY (if the test is out of print). For example, "Minnesota Teacher Attitude Inventory, 4:801; reclassified, *consult* T2:868" indicates that the MTAI, test 801 in the 4th MMY, has since been reclassified and for the latest information, test 868 in TIP II must be consulted. Superseded titles are listed with cross references to the current title. Tests which are part of a series are listed under their individual titles and also their series titles. Acronyms for tests having 10 or more references are presented at the end of this title index.

ABC Occupational Inventory, 4:736
AC Test of Creative Ability, 2340
A.C.E.R. Mechanical Comprehension Test, 2237
A.C.E.R. Mechanical Reasoning Test, 2238
ACER Short Clerical Test, 2117
A.C.E.R. Speed and Accuracy Tests, 2118
ACT Assessment of Career Development, 2100
ACT Career Planning Program, 2101
ACT Guidance Profile, 2167
APT Controlled Interview, 2294
APT Dictation Test, 2119
APT Manual Dexterity Test, 2222
APT Quick Screening Interview, *see* APT Controlled Interview, 2294
A.P.U. Occupational Interests Guide, 2168
Academic Promise Tests, 1063
Academic-Technical Aptitude Tests, 1064
Account Clerk Test, 2322
Accounting Orientation Test, 7:1078
Achievement Examinations for Secondary Schools: Bookkeeping, 775; Business Relations and Occupations, 779
Achievement Tests in Nursing, 2376
Achievement Tests in Practical Nursing, 2377

Acorn National Aptitude Tests: Clerical Aptitude Test, 780; Inventory of Vocational Interests, 2192; Mechanical Aptitude Test, 2252
Addition and Multiplication: Clerical Tests, Series N, 2123c
Adjusted Graphic Analysis Chart, 2:1644
Admission Test for Graduate Study in Business, 2325
Aids to Self-Analysis and Vocational Planning Inventory, 2:1645
Airman Classification Battery, *see* Airman Qualifying Examination, 6:1023
Airman Qualifying Examination, 6:1023
Alpha Biographical Inventory, 2273
Alphabetical Filing: Clerical Tests, 2122e
Alphabetizing-Filing: Clerical Skills Series, 2121a
Alphabetizing Test: Personnel Research Institute Clerical Battery, 2140e
American Institute of Certified Public Accountants Testing Programs, 2323
American Transit Association Tests, 2469
Anatomy and Physiology: Achievement Tests in Nursing, 2376a
Anatomy and Physiology: NLN Achievement Tests, 2383a1

Application for Position: Clerical Tests, Series N, 2123f; Series V, 2124f
Application Interview Screening Form, 2295
Application-Interview Series, 5:892
Application-Interview Series: Job-Tests Program, 1078c
Applied Biological and Agribusiness Interest Inventory, 2169
Applied Natural Sciences: NLN Achievement Tests, 2383c3
Appraisal of Occupational Aptitudes, 2120
Aptitests, see ETSA Tests, 2106
Aptitude Assessment Battery: Program.ming, 2331
Aptitude Associates Test of Sales Aptitude, 2395
Aptitude Index, 6:1168b
Aptitude Index for Life Insurance Salesmen, see Aptitude Index Selection Procedure, 6:1168
Aptitude Index Selection Procedure, 6:1168
Aptitude-Intelligence Tests, see Factored Aptitude Series, 1078a
Aptitude Inventory, 2102
Aptitude Test for Elementary School Teachers-in-Training, 4:792
Aptitude Test for Junior Secondary Bantu Pupils in Form I, see Aptitude Test for Junior Secondary Pupils, 1065
Aptitude Test for Junior Secondary Pupils, 1065
Aptitude Test for Nursing, 2381a
Aptitude Tests for Occupations, 1066
Aptitudes Associates Test of Sales Aptitude, 2395
Architectural School Aptitude Test, 2359
Arithmetic: Clerical Skills Series, 2121b
Arithmetic: Flanagan Aptitude Classification Tests, 1072a9
Arithmetic: Flanagan Industrial Tests, 2107a1
Arithmetic Review: L & L Clerical Tests, 2133a
Arithmetic: Short Tests of Clerical Ability, 2155e
Arithmetic Test for Prospective Nurses, 2381b
Arithmetic Test: Personnel Institute Clerical Tests, 2139i
Arithmetic 3A: Selection Tests for Office Personnel, 2150c
Arithmetical Proficiency: Clerical Tests, 2122b
Arithmetical Reasoning: Clerical Tests, 2122a
Armed Services Vocational Aptitude Battery, 1067
Assembly: Flanagan Aptitude Classification Tests, 1072a5
Assembly: Flanagan Industrial Tests, 2107a2, 2107b1
Attitude Scale: Career Maturity Inventory, 2103a
Automotive Mechanic Test, 6:1185
B-B-ESS Inventory, 2403f6
Barr-Harris Teacher's Performance Record, 4:793
Basic Interest Questionnaire, 3:633
Basic Nursing Procedures and Elementary Nutrition, 6:1158b
Basic Pharmacology: NLN Achievement Tests, 2383a5
Beginner's Clerical Test, 6:1032
Benge Han-Dexterity Test (status unknown), 3:656
Benge Two Hand Coordination Test, 3:657
Bennett Mechanical Comprehension Test, 2239
Biographical Index, 2274
Biographical Inventory, Forms A–C, C–I, and J–O, see Alpha Biographical Inventory, 2273
Biographical Profile, 6:1168a
Blocks: Factored Aptitude Series, 1078a12
Bookkeeping Ability Test, see Bookkeeping Test: National Business Entrance Tests, 777
Bookkeeping: Achievement Examinations for Secondary Schools, 775; Minnesota High School Achievement Examinations, 776
Bookkeeping Achievement Test, 7:552
Bookkeeping: Every Pupil Scholarship Test, 6:34
Bookkeeping I: Every Pupil Test, see First Year Bookkeeping: Every Pupil Test, 6:37

Bookkeeping Test: National Business Entrance Tests, 777
Bookkeeping Test: State High School Tests for Indiana, 3:367
Bossboy Selection Tests, 6:1026b
Brainard Occupational Preference Inventory, 5:856
Breadth of Information, see RBH Breadth of Information, 2287
Breidenbaugh Bookkeeping Tests, 2:1477
Burke Inventory of Vocational Development, 6:1048
Business Backgrounds Test, 2:1478
Business Career Aptitude Test (status unknown), 7:987
Business Education Achievement Test Series: Bookkeeping Achievement Test, 7:552; General Business, 7:554; Typewriting, 7:559A
Business Education: National Teacher Examinations, 787; Teacher Education Examination Program, 797
Business Fundamentals and General Information Test: National Business Entrance Tests, 778
Business Judgment Test, 2275
Business Relations and Occupations: Achievement Examinations for Secondary Schools, 779
Business Test: Undergraduate Program Field Tests, 800
Business Vocabulary: Short Tests of Clerical Ability, 2155f
Byers' First-Year Shorthand Aptitude Tests, 6:41
CLEP Subject Examination in Clinical Chemistry, 2350; in Computer and Data Processing, 2332; in Elementary Computer Programming—Fortran IV, 2333; in Hematology, 2351; in Immunohematology and Blood Banking, 2352; in Introduction to Business Management, 2326; in Introductory Accounting, 2324; in Introductory Business Law, 2327; in Introductory Marketing, 2328; in Microbiology, 2353; in Money and Banking, 2329
California Occupational Preference Survey, 2170
California Pre-Counseling Self-Analysis Protocol Booklet, 2171
Can You Read a Micrometer?: Purdue Interview Aids, 2434b
Can You Read a Scale?: Purdue Interview Aids, 2434c
Can You Read a Working Drawing?: Purdue Interview Aids, 2434a
Cancellation Test, 5:894
Cancer Nursing: Achievement Tests in Nursing, 2376b
Card Punch Aptitude Test, see Card Punch Operator Aptitude Test, 7:1103
Card Punch Operator Aptitude Test, 7:1103
Cardall Interviewing Aids (status unknown), 6:1114
Cardall Test of Clerical Perception (status unknown), 6:1033
Cardall Test of Practical Judgment (status unknown), 6:1102
Career Counseling Personal Data Form, 2296
Career Finder (status unknown), 6:1049
Career Guidance Inventory, 2172
Career Incentive and Progress Blank, 2:1648
Career Maturity Inventory, 2103
Career Planning Profile, see ACT Career Planning Program, 2101
Carving Dexterity Test, 7:1091a
Case of Mickey Murphy, 4:794; reclassified, consult 5:533
Chart for the Rating of a Foreman, 5:915
Chatterji's Non-Language Preference Record, 2173
Check List for Self-Guidance in Choosing an Occupation, 2:1649
Check List of Occupations, 2:1650
Check List Review: L & L Clerical Tests, 2133b
Checking: Short Tests of Clerical Ability, 2155b
Checking Test, see RBH Checking Test, 2143
Chemical Operators Selection Test, 2360

Chemistry: NLN Achievement Tests, 2383a2
Chicago Tests of Primary Mental Abilities, *see* SRA Primary Mental Abilities, 1087
Chriswell Structural Dexterity Test, 2240
Circles Test: Classification Test Battery, 2104c
Classification Test Battery, 2104
Classifying Test, *see* RBH Classifying Test, 2144
Cleeton Vocational Interest Inventory, 3:635
Clerical Aptitude Test, 780
Clerical Perception Test, 3:624
Clerical Problems: O'Rourke Clerical Aptitude Test, 2138a
Clerical Routine Aptitude: Aptitude Tests for Occupations, 1066d
Clerical Skills Series, 2121
Clerical Speed and Accuracy: Clerical Skills Series, 2121c
Clerical Speed and Accuracy: Differential Aptitude Tests, 781
Clerical Test D (status unknown), 3:625
Clerical Tests, 2122
Clerical Tests FG and 2, 781A
Clerical Tests 1 and 2, *see* Clerical Tests FG and 2, 781A
Clerical Tests, Series N, 2123; Series V, 2124
Clerical Worker Examination, 2125
Clinton-LeMaster Commercial and Business Law Test, 2:1479
Coding: Clerical Skills Series, 2121d
Coding: Flanagan Aptitude Classification Tests, 1072a2
Coding 4A: Selection Tests for Office Personnel, 2150d
Coding: Short Tests of Clerical Ability, 2155a
College Entrance Examination Board Special Aptitude Test in Spatial Relations, 4:808
College Entrance Examination Board Test in Pre-Engineering Science Comprehension, 4:809
College Interest Inventory, 2174
College Placement Test in Spatial Relations, 2241
College Planning Inventory, 6:1051
Colleges of Podiatry Admission Test, 2354
Coloured Peg Board: Classification Test Battery, 2104a
Columbia-Southern Typing Test, *see* SRA Typing Adaptability Test, 5:518
Combination Inventory, 2396
Commercial Arithmetic Test: State High School Tests for Indiana, 4:448
Commercial Education Survey Tests: Junior and Senior Shorthand, 1:936; Junior and Senior Typewriting, 2:1480
Commercial Law: Every Pupil Scholarship Test, 6:38
Communicable Disease Nursing: NLN Achievement Tests, 2383b8
Communicable Diseases: Achievement Tests in Nursing, 2376e
Community Health Nursing: NLN Achievement Tests, 2383c4
Comparing Names and Numbers: Clerical Tests, Series N, 2123a
Comparing Names Test: Personnel Institute Clerical Tests, 2139g
Competence Test: Career Maturity Inventory, 2103b
Components: Flanagan Aptitude Classification Tests, 1072a11
Components: Flanagan Industrial Tests, 2107a3, 2107b2
Composite Inventory and Examination, *see* Steward Selection System, 4:828
Compound Series Test: Differential Test Battery, 1070a
Comprehensive Plan for Rating Employees, *see* Employee Merit Report, 4:771
Computational Aptitude: Aptitude Tests for Occupations, 1066e
Computer Programmer Aptitude Battery, 2334

Conference Evaluation, 2276
Conference Meeting Rating Scale, 2277
Confidential Personal History Inventory: Personnel Institute Clerical Tests, 2139b
Connolly Occupational Interests Questionnaire, 2175
Content Evaluation Series: Office Information and Skills Test, 788
Continuous Letter Checking and Continuous Symbol Checking, 2278
Cooperative Commercial Arithmetic Test, 4:449
Coordination: Flanagan Aptitude Classification Tests, 1072a7
Coordination: Flanagan Industrial Tests, 2107a4
Copying Names: Clerical Tests, Series N, 2123d
Copying Numbers: Clerical Tests, Series N, 2123b
Copying Numbers Test: Personnel Institute Clerical Tests, 2139h
Counseling Interview Summary, *see* Performance Review Forms, 2310
Cox Eyeboard Test No. 2, 2242d
Cox Mechanical and Manual Tests, 2242
Cox Mechanical Test M, 2242a
Cox Nailboard Test, 2242e
Cox Nailstick Test, 2242f
Crawford Small Parts Dexterity Test, 2223
Crawford Spatial Relations Test, 3:658
Crissey Dexterity Test, 2224
Cross Reference Test, 2126
Crowley Occupational Interests Blank, 2176
Curtis Interest Scale, 2177
Curtis Object Completion and Space Form Tests, 2243
Curtis Verbal-Clerical Skills Tests, 2127
Dailey Vocational Tests, 2105
Dailey Vocational Tests: Spatial Visualization Test, 2270
Dartnell Self-Administered Employee Opinion Unit, 6:1104
Data Perception 2A: Selection Tests for Office Personnel, 2150b
Dealer Inventory (status unknown), 6:1171
Dental Admission Testing Program, 2337
Dental Aptitude Testing Program, *see* Dental Admission Testing Program, 2337
Dental Hygiene Aptitude Testing Program, 2338
Detroit Clerical Aptitudes Examination, 782
Detroit General Aptitudes Examination, 1068
Detroit Mechanical Aptitudes Examination, 2244
Detroit Retail Selling Inventory, 2397
Devon Interest Test, 5:857
Dex-Aim Test, 2286g
Dex-Man Scale, 2286f
Dexterity: Factored Aptitude Series, 1078a14
Diagnostic Interviewer's Guide: Personnel Institute Clerical Tests, 2139c
Diagnostic Interviewer's Guide [Wonderlic], 6:1115
Diagnostic Teacher-Rating Scale, 4:795; reclassified, *consult* T2:859
Diagnostic Test of Letter-Writing Ability, 2:1481
Dictating Machine Transcription Test, 2:1482
Dictation Test: USES Clerical Skills Tests, 2166b
Diebold Personnel Tests, 2335
Diet Therapy and Applied Nutrition: NLN Achievement Tests, 2383b1
Differential Ability Tests, 5:604
Differential Aptitude Tests, 1069
Differential Aptitude Tests: Clerical Speed and Accuracy, 781; Mechanical Reasoning, 2256; Space Relations, 2268
Differential Test Battery, 1070
Dimension: Factored Aptitude Series, 1078a13
Directions—Oral and Written: Short Tests of Clerical Ability, 2155d
Disaster Nursing: NLN Achievement Tests, 2383b5
Driver Selection Forms and Tests, 2470

Dynamicube Test of Power to Visualize, 1:1167
EM-AY Inventory, 2403e1
E.R.C. Stenographic Aptitude Test, 3:372
ESS-AY Inventory, 2403e2
ESS-EYE Inventory, 2403f5
ETSA Tests, 2106
Edmiston Inventory of Interest, 4:738
Educational Guidance Test: Kefauver-Hand Guidance Tests and Inventories, 2:1661a
Educational Interest Inventory, 2178
Educational Progress Sheet: Michigan Adult Profile, 1:1171a
Electrical Sophistication Test, 2415
Electronics: Flanagan Industrial Tests, 2107a5, 2107b3
Elementary Psychiatric Nursing: NLN Practical Nursing Achievement Tests, 2385c
Empathy Inventory, 2378
Employee Aptitude Survey, 1071
Employee Attitude Series: Job-Tests Program, 1078b
Employee Competency Scale, 2297
Employee Evaluation Form for Interviewers, 2298
Employee Evaluation Series, *see* Merit Rating Series, 2308
Employee Merit Report, 4:771
Employee Opinion Survey, 6:1105
Employee Performance Appraisal, 2299
Employee Progress Appraisal Form, 2300
Employee Rating and Development Forms, 2301
Employee Rating Forms, 6:1118
Employee Selection Forms, 4:772
Employment Aptitude Inventory, 2102b
Engineering Aide Test, 2341
Engineering and Physical Science Aptitude Test, 4:810
Engineering Test: Undergraduate Program Field Tests, 2348
Entrance Examination for Schools of Nursing, 2379
Entrance Examination for Schools of Practical Nursing, 2380
Entrance Questionnaire and Experience Record, 2:1658
Evaluation Record, 2398
Every Pupil Scholarship Tests: Bookkeeping, 6:34; Commercial Law, 6:38; General Business, 6:31; Typewriting, 6:54
Every Pupil Tests: First Year Bookkeeping, 6:37; First Year Shorthand, 6:42; First Year Typewriting, 6:49; General Clerical, 1:937; Typewriting II, 1:944
Examination in Bookkeeping and Accounting, 3:373
Examination in Business Arithmetic, 3:374
Examination in Business English, 3:375
Examination in Clerical Work: Thurstone Employment Tests, 2162a
Examination in Commercial Correspondence, 3:376
Examination in Gregg Shorthand, 3:377
Examination in Typewriting, 3:378
Examination in Typing: Thurstone Employment Tests, 2162b
Exceptional Teacher Service Record, 4:796
Executive, Industrial, and Sales Personnel Forms, 2302
Experimental Comparative Prediction Batteries, 7:674
Expression: Flanagan Aptitude Classification Tests, 1072a14
Expression: Flanagan Industrial Tests, 2107a6
Eye-Hand Accuracy: Clerical Skills Series, 2121e
Factored Aptitude Series, 1078a
Factorial Interest Blank, 2179
Factory Terms: Factored Aptitude Series, 1078a3
Fiesenheiser Test of Ability to Read Drawings, 2416
Fife Tests of Ability, 4:713
Filing 7A: Selection Tests for Office Personnel, 2150g
Filing: Short Tests of Clerical Ability, 2155c
Filing Test: National Clerical Ability Tests, *see* Filing

Test: United-NOMA Business Entrance Tests, 3:379
Filing Test: Personnel Research Institute Clerical Battery, 2140d
Filing Test: United-NOMA Business Entrance Tests, 3:379
Finger Dexterity Board: General Aptitude Test Battery, 1073c5
Finger Dexterity Test, *see* O'Connor Finger Dexterity Test, 2228
Fire Performance Rating System, 7:1105
Fire Promotion Tests, 2361
Firefighter Test, 2362
Firefighting Promotion Tests, *see* Fire Promotion Tests, 2361
Fireman Examination, 2363
First-Year Bookkeeping: Every Pupil Test, 6:37
First Year Shorthand: Every Pupil Test, 6:42
First Year Typewriting: Every Pupil Test, 6:49
Flags: A Test of Space Thinking, 2245
Flanagan Aptitude Classification Tests, 1072
Flanagan Industrial Tests, 2107
Fluency: Factored Aptitude Series, 1078a9
Flu-Numb Test, 2286e
Flu-Verb Test, 2286d
Form Perception Test, 2246
Form Relations Group Test, 2247
Form Series Test: Classification Test Battery, 2104d
Fowler-Parmenter Self-Scoring Interest Record, 6:1053
Fundamental Achievement Series, 7:978; reclassified, *consult* T2:376
Fundamentals Test, *see* Business Fundamentals and General Information Test, 778
Fundamentals Test: National Clerical Ability Tests, 2:1484
GATB-NATB Screening Device, 1073a1, 1086a
G.C. Self-Scoring Interest Record, *see* Fowler-Parmenter Self-Scoring Interest Record, 6:1053
Garnett College Test in Engineering Science, 2342
Geist Picture Interest Inventory, 2180; Deaf Form: Male, 2181
General Ability Tests: Differential Test Battery, 1070b
General Adaptability Battery, 6:1026
General Aptitude Test Battery, 1073
General Business Achievement Test, 7:554
General Business: Every Pupil Scholarship Test, 6:31
General Chemistry: Achievement Tests in Nursing, 2376c
General Classification Battery, 6:1026a
General Clerical Ability Test: ETSA Test, 2128
General Clerical: Every Pupil Test, 1:937
General Clerical Test, 2129
General Clerical Test, PCI Selection Form 20, *see* General Clerical Test, 2129
General Information and Judgment Test: NLN Pre-Admission and Classification Examination, 2386a
General Information Test, *see* Business Fundamentals and General Information Test, 778
General Information Test: National Clerical Ability Tests, 2:1485
General Municipal Employees Performance (Efficiency) Rating System, 2364
General Office Clerical Test: National Business Entrance Tests, 783
General Reasoning, *see* Guilford-Zimmerman Aptitude Survey, 1074b
General Sales Aptitude: Aptitude Tests for Occupations, 1066c
General Science Test for Prospective Nurses, 2381d
General Test of Business Information, 3:380
General Test on Traffic and Driving Knowledge, 5:922; reclassified, *consult* T2:846

George Washington University Series: Aptitude Test for Nursing, 2381a; Arithmetic Test for Prospective Nurses, 2381b; General Science Test for Prospective Nurses, 2381d; Interest-Preference Test for Prospective Nurses, 2381e; Reading Comprehension Test for Prospective Nurses, 2381c; Test for Ability to Sell, 2413

George Washington University Series Nursing Tests, 2381

Gilbert Business Arithmetic, 4:450

Gordon-Douglass Fraction Test for Beginning Students of Nursing, 1:1168

Gordon Occupational Check List, 2182

Grading Scales for Typewriting Tests, 2:1486

Graduate Record Examinations Advanced Education Test, 4:797; reclassified, *consult* Graduate Record Examinations Advanced Education Test, T2:863

Graduate Record Examinations Advanced Engineering Test, 2343

Grammar and Punctuation: Clerical Skills Series, 2121f

Grammar: Clerical Tests, 2122f; Series V, 2124a

Grammar Test: Personnel Institute Clerical Tests, 2139j

Gregory Academic Interest Inventory, 2183

Group Test 20, 2130

Group Test 25 (Clerical), 4:724

Group Test 80A, 2248

Group Test 81, 2249

Group Test 82, 2250

Group Tests 61A, 64, and 66A, 2131

Guidance Questionnaire, 2:1659.1

Guide to Employment Decision, 4:828c

Guilford-Shneidman-Zimmerman Interest Survey, 2184

Guilford-Zimmerman Aptitude Survey, 1074

Guilford-Zimmerman Interest Inventory, 2185

Gullo Workshop and Seminar Evaluation, 2280

Hackman-Gaither Vocational Interest Inventory, 2186

Hall Occupational Orientation Inventory, 2187

Hall Salespower Inventory, 2399

Hand-Tool Dexterity Test, 2225

Hanes Sales Selection Inventory, 2400

Hankes' Answer Sheet for Vocational Interest Blank, 3:651

Hay Clerical Test Battery, 2132

Hay Tests for Clerical Aptitude, *see* Hay Clerical Test Battery, 2132

Hazlehurst Primary Mechanical Ability Tests, *see* Primary Mechanical Ability Tests, 2262

Health Guidance Test: Kefauver-Hand Guidance Tests and Inventories, 2:1661b

Henderson Analysis of Interest, 2188

Hiett Diamond Jubilee Shorthand Test, *see* Hiett Simplified Shorthand Test (Gregg), 784

Hiett Simplified Shorthand Test (Gregg), 784

Hiett Stenography Test (Gregg), 3:381

High Level Battery: Test A/75, 1075

High School Business and Economics Test: Stanford Achievement Test, 7:559

High School Prediction Program: Vocational Planning Inventory, 2114a

Hiring Kit (status unknown), 4:826

Hiring Summary Worksheet, 5:898

Holzinger-Crowder Uni-Factor Tests, 5:610

How I Counsel, 4:798

How I Teach, 4:799

How Supervise?, 2448

How Teach and Learn in College?, 4:800

How Well Do You Know Your Interests, 2189

IBM Aptitude Test for Programmer Personnel, 7:1090

Ideal Leader Behavior Description Questionnaire, 2449

Ideal Leader Behavior (What You Expect of Your Leader), *see* Ideal Leader Behavior Description Questionnaire, 2449

Identical Forms, 5:899

In-Basket Test, 2450

Individual Background Survey, *see* RBH Individual Background Survey, 2314

Individual Guidance Record, 2:1660

Individual Placement Series, 2108

Information Blank: For Obtaining Data About Vocational Plans and Problems of High School Students, 1:1169

Information Index, 2401

Ingenuity: Flanagan Aptitude Classification Tests, 1072a16

Ingenuity: Flanagan Industrial Tests, 2107a7, 2107b4

Inspection: Flanagan Aptitude Classification Tests, 1072a1

Inspection: Flanagan Industrial Tests, 2107a8, 2107b5

Interaction Chronograph, 3:688; reclassified, *consult* T2:76

Interest Check List, 2190

Interest-Preference Test for Prospective Nurses, 2381e

Interest Questionnaire for High School Students, 3:637

Interest Questionnaire for Indian South Africans, 2191

International Primary Factors Test Battery, 1076

Interpretation of Tabulated Material: Clerical Tests, 2122c–d

Interview Aids: Purdue Vocational Series, *see* Purdue Interview Aids, 2434

Interview Rating Scale for Prospective Employees, 4:776

Interviewer's Impressions—Sales Applicants (status unknown), 6:1175

Inventory of Religious Activities and Interests, 7:1023; reclassified, *consult* T2:1025A

Inventory of Student Plans: Kefauver-Hand Guidance Tests and Inventories, 2:1661c

Inventory of Student Self-Ratings: Kefauver-Hand Guidance Tests and Inventories, 2:1661d

Inventory of Vocational Interests: Acorn National Aptitude Tests, 2192

Iowa Legal Aptitude Test, 4:814

Jastak-King Work Samples, *see* Wide Range Employment Sample Test, 2116

Jastak Test of Potential Ability and Behavior Stability, 1077

Jenkins Job Attitudes Survey, 7:1062

Job Application Forms, 2303

Job Attitude Analysis, 2281

Job Choice Inventory, *see* RBH Job Choice Inventory, 7:1032

Job Description Questionnaire, 6:1121

Job Qualification Inventory, 3:639

Job Satisfaction Inquiry Blank, *see* Survey of Company Morale, 3:693

Job-Tests Program, 1078

Journalism Test, 2365

Judgment and Comprehension: Flanagan Aptitude Classification Tests, 1072a8

Judgment and Comprehension: Flanagan Industrial Tests, 2107a9

Judgment: Factored Aptitude Series, 1078a7

Junior Aptitude Tests for Indian South Africans, 1079

Kahn Career Orientation Questionnaire, 4:777

Kauzer Typewriting Test, 3:382

Kefauver-Hand Guidance Tests and Inventories, 2:1661

Kent-Shakow Formboard, 3:660

Kent-Shakow Spatial Relations Test, *see* Kent-Shakow Formboard, 3:660

Key-Driven Calculating Machine Ability Test, *see* Machine Calculation Test, 785

Kimberly-Clark Typing Ability Analysis, 5:513

Kuder B or C, *see* Kuder Preference Record—Vocational, 2195

Kuder D, *see* Kuder Preference Record—Occupational, 6:1062

Kuder DD, *see* Kuder Occupational Interest Survey, 2194

Kuder E, *see* Kuder General Interest Survey, 2193

Kuder General Interest Survey, 2193

Kuder Occupational Interest Survey, 2194

Kuder Preference Record—Occupational, 6:1062

Kuder Preference Record—Vocational, 2195

L & L Clerical Tests, 2133

LIAMA Inventory of Job Attitudes, 2402

Language: Short Tests of Clerical Ability, 2155g

Language Skills 1A: Selection Tests for Office Personnel, 2150a

Law Enforcement Perception Questionnaire, 2366

Law School Admission Test, 2349

Lawshe-Kephart Personnel Comparison System, 2304

Leader Behavior Description Questionnaire, 2451; Form 12, 2452

Leaderless Group Test, 6:1026b

Leadership Evaluation and Development Scale, 2453

Leadership Opinion Questionnaire, 2454

Leadership Practices Inventory, 2455

Legal Spelling Test: USES Clerical Skills Test, 2166f

Luther Hospital Sentence Completions, 2382

M-T Test, *see* Mathematical and Technical Test, 2282

McCann Typing Tests, 2134

McCormick Job Performance Measurement "Rate-$-Scales," 2305

McGuire Safe Driver Interview Guide, 2471b

McGuire Safe Driver Scale, 2471a

Machine Calculation Test: National Business Entrance Tests, 785

McQuaig Manpower Selection Series, 2306

MacQuarrie Test for Mechanical Ability, 2251

Management Aptitude Inventory, 2102a

Managerial Performance Review, *see* Performance Review Forms, 2310

Managerial Scale for Enterprise Improvement, 2456

Manipulative Aptitude Test, 2226

Manual Speed and Accuracy: Employee Aptitude Survey, 1071i

Martin Alphabetizing Test (status unknown), 4:726g

Martin Arithmetic Reasoning Test (status unknown), 4:726f

Martin Name Checking Test (status unknown), 4:726b

Martin Number Checking Test (status unknown), 4:726a

Martin Number Facility Test (status unknown), 4:726c

Martin Numerical Operations Test (status unknown), 4:726d

Martin Numerical Order Test (status unknown), 4:726h

Martin Office Aptitude Tests (status unknown), 4:726

Martin Peg Board (status unknown), 4:749

Martin Performance Appraisal, 2307

Martin Stenographic Test (status unknown), 4:726i

Martin Typing Test (status unknown), 4:726j

Martin Vocabulary Test (status unknown), 4:726e

Maternal-Child Nursing: NLN Achievement Tests, 2383c1

Maternity and Child Nursing: NLN Achievement Tests, 2383b4

Mathematical and Technical Test, 2282

Mathematics and Reasoning: Flanagan Industrial Tests, 2107a10

Measure of Consociative Tendency, 5:931

Measurement of Skill, 1080

Measurement of Skills Test 9, *see* Skill in Typing, 2157

Mechanical Ability Test: Differential Test Battery, 1070d

Mechanical Aptitude: Aptitude Tests for Occupations, 1066b

Mechanical Aptitude Test: Acorn National Aptitude Tests, 2252

Mechanical Comprehension Test [Bennett], *see* Bennett Mechanical Comprehension Test, 2239

Mechanical Comprehension Test [NIPR], 2253

Mechanical Diagrams Test, 2242b

Mechanical Explanation Test 1, 2242c

Mechanical Familiarity Test: ETSA Test, 2417

Mechanical Handyman Test, 2418

Mechanical Information Questionnaire (status unknown), 6:1088

Mechanical Information Test, 2254

Mechanical Knowledge, *see* Guilford-Zimmerman Aptitude Survey, 1074g

Mechanical Knowledge Test: ETSA Test, 2419

Mechanical Movements, 2255

Mechanical Reasoning: Differential Aptitude Tests, 2256

Mechanics: Flanagan Aptitude Classification Tests, 1072a13

Mechanics: Flanagan Industrial Tests, 2107a11

Medical College Admission Test, 2355

Medical Nursing: Achievement Tests in Nursing, 2376f

Medical School Instructor Attitude Inventory, 2356

Medical Spelling Test: USES Clerical Skills Test, 2166e

Medical-Surgical Nursing: NLN Achievement Tests, 2383a6; 2383b6-7, 2383c2

Mellenbruch Curve-Block Series, 3:662

Mellenbruch Mechanical Aptitude Test for Men and Women, *see* Mellenbruch Mechanical Motivation Test, 2257

Mellenbruch Mechanical Motivation Test, 2257

Memory and Observation Tests for Policeman, 2367

Memory: Factored Aptitude Series, 1078a10

Memory: Flanagan Aptitude Classification Tests, 1072a3

Memory: Flanagan Industrial Tests, 2107a12, 2107b6

Mental Alertness Test: Personnel Institute Clerical Tests, 2139e

Merit Rating Series, 2308

Miami-Oxford Curve-Block Series, *see* Mellenbruch Curve-Block Series, 3:662

Michigan Adult Profile, 1:1171

Michigan Nonverbal Series, 1:1171d

Michigan Occupational Preferences Check List, 1:1171b

Microbiology: Achievement Tests in Nursing, 2376g

Microbiology: NLN Achievement Tests, 2383a3

Miles Career Evaluation Inventory, 4:780

Milwaukee Academic Interest Inventory, 2196

Minnesota Assembly Test, 3:671

Minnesota Clerical Test, 2135

Minnesota Engineering Analogies Test, 2344

Minnesota High School Achievement Examinations: Bookkeeping, 776

Minnesota Importance Questionnaire, 2283

Minnesota Job Description Questionnaire, 2284

Minnesota Manual Dexterity Test, *see* Minnesota Rate of Manipulation Test, 2227

Minnesota Mechanical Assembly Test, *see* Minnesota Assembly Test, 3:671

Minnesota Occupational Rating Scales and Counseling Profile, 3:689

Minnesota Paper Form Board Test, *see* Revised Minnesota Paper Form Board Test, 2266

Minnesota Rate of Manipulation Test, 2227

Minnesota Satisfaction Questionnaire, 2285

Minnesota Spatial Relations Test, 2258

Minnesota Teacher Attitude Inventory, 4:801; reclassified, *consult* T2:868

Minnesota Vocational Interest Inventory, 2197

Minnesota Vocational Test for Clerical Workers, *see* Minnesota Clerical Test, 2135

Moore Eye-Hand Coordination and Color-Matching Test, 5:872; reclassified, *consult* T2:1880

Mooseheart Graphic Rating Scale for Housemothers and Housefathers, 1:1172

Moray House Space Test 2, 6:1090

Motivation Indicator, 3:641

Motor: Factored Aptitude Series, 1078a15

Multi-Aptitude Test, 1081

Multiple Aptitude Tests, 1082

Mutilated Cubes Test of Power to Visualize, 1:1173

N.B. Aptitude Tests (Junior), 1083

NCR Test Battery for Prospective Check-Out Cashiers (status unknown), 6:1147

N.I.I.P. Clerical Test, *see* National Institute of Industrial Psychology Clerical Test, 6:1041

N.I.I.P. Engineering Apprentice Selection Test Battery, 2345

N.I.I.P. Squares Test, 5:880

NLN Achievement Tests for Basic Professional Nursing Program, *see* NLN Achievement Tests for Schools Preparing Registered Nurses, 2383

NLN Achievement Test for Schools Preparing Registered Nurses, 2383

NLN Aide Selection Test, 2384

NLN Graduate Nurse Examination, 6:1159

NLN Graduate Nurse Qualifying Examination, *see* NLN Graduate Nurse Examination, 6:1159

NLN Practical Nurse Achievement Examinations, *see* NLN Practical Nursing Achievement Tests, 2385

NLN Practical Nursing Achievement Tests, 2385

NLN Pre-Admission and Classification Examination, 2386

NLN Pre-Nursing and Guidance Examination, 2387

NLN Reading Test: NLN Pre-Nursing and Guidance Examination, 2387b

NLN Science Test: NLN Pre-Nursing and Guidance Examination, 2387c

NLN Social Studies Test: NLN Pre-Nursing and Guidance Examination, 2387d

NLN Test of Academic Aptitude: NLN Pre-Nursing and Guidance Examination, 2387a

NM Attitude Toward Work Test, 2109a

NM Career Development Test, 2109f; Planning Test, 2109b; Oriented Activities Checklist, 2109c

NM Job Application Procedures Test, 2109e

NM Knowledge of Occupations Test, 2109d

Nagel Personnel Interviewing and Screening Forms, 2309

Name Comparison Test for Clerical and Industrial Inspection Operations, 2140b

Name Finding Test: Hay Clerical Test Battery, 2132c

National Business Entrance Tests, 786; Bookkeeping Test, 777; Business Fundamentals and General Information Test, 778; General Office Clerical Test, 783; Machine Calculation Test, 785; Stenographic Test, 795; Typewriting Test, 799

National Clerical Ability Tests, *see* National Business Entrance Tests, 786

National Engineering Aptitude Search Test, 2346

National Institute for Personnel Research High Level Battery, *see* High Level Battery: Test A/75, 1075

National Institute for Personnel Research Intermediate Battery, 1084; Normal Battery, 1085

National Institute of Industrial Psychology Clerical Test, 6:1041

National Teacher Examinations, 4:802; reclassified, *consult* T2:869

National Teacher Examinations: Business Education, 787

Natural Sciences in Nursing: NLN Achievement Tests, 2383b3

Navy Vocational Interest Inventory, *see* Minnesota Vocational Interest Inventory, 2197

Netherne Study Difficulties Battery for Student Nurses, 2388

New Mexico Career Education Test Series, 2109

Newcastle Spatial Test, *see* Spatial Test 3, 2269c

19 Field Interest Inventory, 2198

Nonreading Aptitude Test Battery, 1086

Normal Nutrition: NLN Achievement Tests, 2383a4

Number Checking Test, *see* RBH Number Checking Test, 2145

Number Comparison Test for Clerical and Industrial Inspection Operations, 2140a

Number Perception Test: Hay Clerical Test Battery, 2132b

Number Series Completion Test: Hay Clerical Test Battery, 2132d

Numbers: Factored Aptitude Series, 1078a5

Numerical Ability: Employee Aptitude Survey, 1071b

Numerical Operations, *see* Guilford-Zimmerman Aptitude Survey, 1074c

Numerical Reasoning: Employee Aptitude Survey, 1071f

Numerical Reasoning: Multiple Aptitude Tests, 1082c

Nurse Attitudes Inventory, 2389

Nursing Education Scale, *see* Luther Hospital Sentence Completions, 2382

Nursing Education Scale: NAI, *see* Nurse Attitudes Inventory, 2389

Nursing Including Aspects of Pharmacology: NLN Practical Nursing Achievement Tests, 2385b

Nursing of Children: NLN Achievement Tests, 2383a8

Nursing Sentence Completions, *see* Luther Hospital Sentence Completions, 2382

Nutrition and Diet Therapy: Achievement Tests in Nursing, 2376h

Object-Completion Test, 2243a

Obstetric Nursing: NLN Achievement Tests, 2383a7

Obstetrical Nursing: Achievement Tests in Nursing, 2376i

Occupational Analysis Form, 2:1665.1

Occupational Interest Blank, 2:1666

Occupational Interest Blank for Women, 3:642

Occupational Interest Inventory, 2199

Occupational Interest Survey (With Pictures), 2200

Occupational Interests: Self Analysis Scale (status unknown), 3:644

Occupational Orientation Inquiry, 2:1667

O'Connor Finger Dexterity Test, 2228

O'Connor Tweezer Dexterity Test, 2229

O'Connor Wiggly Block, 2259

Office Ability Review: L & L Clerical Tests, 2133c

Office Information and Skills Test, 788

Office Skills Achievement Test, 2136

Office Terms: Factored Aptitude Series, 1078a1

Office Worker Test, 2137

Ohio Auto Body Achievement Test, 2420

Ohio Automotive Mechanics Achievement Test, 2421

Ohio Basic Electricity Achievement Test, 7:1128a

Ohio Basic Electronics Achievement Test, 7:1128b

Ohio Carpentry Achievement Test, 2422

Ohio Communication Products Electronics Achievement Test, 2423

Ohio Construction Electricity Achievement Test, 2424

Ohio Cosmetology Achievement Test, 2425

Ohio Dental Assisting Achievement Test, 2339

Ohio Industrial Electronics Achievement Test, 2426

Ohio Machine Trades Achievement Test, 2427

Ohio Mechanical Drafting Achievement Test, 2428

Ohio Printing Achievement Test, 2429

Ohio Sheet Metal Achievement Test, 2430

Ohio Trade and Industrial Education Achievement Test Program, 2431

Ohio Vocational Interest Survey, 2201

Ohio Welding Achievement Test, 2432

One Hole Test, 2230

Optometry College Admission Test, 2357
Organic and Inorganic Chemistry: Achievement Tests in Nursing, 2376d
Organization Attitude Survey, *see* Organization Survey (status unknown), 6:1107
Organization Survey (status unknown), 6:1107
Organizational Value Dimensions Questionnaire, 2330
O'Rourke Clerical Aptitude Test, 2138
O'Rourke Mechanical Aptitude Test, 2260
Otis and Laurent Test of Shorthand Skills, *see* Personnel Research Institute of Shorthand Skills, 2141
Owens' Creativity Test for Machine Design, 6:1135
PSB-Aptitude for Practical Nursing Examination, 2390
PSB-Entrance Examination for Schools of Practical Nursing, *see* PSB-Aptitude for Practical Nursing Examination, 2390
PSYCAN Vocational Interest Profile, *see* VALCAN Vocational Interest Profile, 2215
Parke Commercial Law Test, 3:385
Parts: Factored Aptitude Series, 1078a11
Pattern Reproduction Test: Classification Test Battery, 2104b
Patterned Merit Review Form, *see* Executive, Industrial, and Sales Personnel Forms, 2302
Patterns: Flanagan Aptitude Classification Tests, 1072a10
Patterns: Flanagan Industrial Tests, 2107a13
Pediatric Nursing: Achievement Tests in Nursing, 2376j
Pegboard: General Aptitude Test Battery, 1073c4
Pennsylvania Bi-Manual Worksample, 2231
Perception: Factored Aptitude Series, 1078a6
Perceptual Battery, 2261
Perceptual Mechanics Test, 3:673
Perceptual-Motor Ability Test, 2337d
Perceptual Speed, *see* Guilford-Zimmerman Aptitude Survey, 1074d
Perceptual Speed: Multiple Aptitude Tests, 1082b
Per-Flu-Dex Tests, 2286
Performance Record, 5:902
Performance Review Forms, 2310
Per-Numb Test, 2286c
Personal Data Blank, 2311
Personal Data Form for Scientific, Engineering, and Technical Personnel, 2394b
Personal Development Record, 6:1191
Personal History, 2:1670
Personal History Index, 2110
Personal History Record, 6:1126
Personal Inventory of Background Factors, *see* Steward Personal Background Inventory, 2412
Personal Inventory of Basic Factors, 4:828a
Personal Reaction Test for Transit Employees, 2469b
Personal-Social Aptitude: Aptitude Tests for Occupations, 1066a
Personality 6A: Selection Tests for Office Personnel, 2150f
Personnel Institute Clerical Tests, 2139
Personnel Institute Hiring Kit, 2403
Personnel Interviewing Forms, 2312
Personnel Rating Scale, 2313
Personnel Research Institute Clerical Battery, 2140
Personnel Research Institute Test of Shorthand Skills, 2141
Personnel Selection and Classification Test, 3:690
Personnel Service Rating Report, 5:939
Per-Symb Test, 2286a
Per-Verb Test, 2286b
Pharmacology: Achievement Tests in Nursing, 2376k
Pharmacology in Clinical Nursing (Application of Facts and Principles): NLN Achievement Tests, 2383b2
Phillips Occupational Preference Scale, 2202
Pictorial Interest Inventory, 2203

Pictorial Inventory of Careers, 2204
Pictorial Inventory of Occupational Training Interest, *see* Pictorial Inventory of Careers, 2204
Picture Interest Inventory, 2205
Placement Examination in General Engineering Drawing, 1:1175
Placement Interview for Transit Employees, 2469c
Planning: Flanagan Industrial Tests, 2107a14
Police Performance Rating System, 2368
Police Promotion Examinations, *see* Police Promotion Tests, 2369
Police Promotion Tests, 2369
Policeman Examination, 2370
Policeman Test, 2371
Post-High School Prediction Program: Vocational Planning Inventory, 2114b
Potter-Nash Aptitude Test for Lumber Inspectors and Other General Personnel Who Handle Lumber, 2372
Practical Dexterity Board, 2232
Precision: Factored Aptitude Series, 1078a8; Flanagan Industrial Tests, 2107a15
Precision: Flanagan Aptitude Classification Tests, 1072a4
Pre-Engineering Ability Test, 4:812
Pre-Engineering Inventory, *see* Pre-Engineering Ability Test, 4:812
Preference Analysis, 2206
Preference Record, *see* Kuder Preference Record—Vocational, 2195
Preliminary Screening Interview: Personnel Institute Clerical Tests, 2139a
Primary Business Interests Test (status unknown), 6:1067
Primary Mechanical Ability Tests, 2262
Primary Mental Abilities, *see* SRA Primary Mental Abilities, 1087
Probst Rating System, 4:785
Prognostic Test of Mechanical Abilities, 4:761
Programmer Aptitude/Competence Test System, 2336
Programmers Aptitude Test, *see* Revised Programmer Aptitude Test, 6:1153, and IBM Aptitude Test for Programmer Personnel, 7:1090
Programming: Aptitude Assessment Battery, 2331
Psychiatric Nursing: Achievement Tests in Nursing, 2376l; NLN Achievement Tests, 2383a9, 2383c5
Psychological Corporation General Clerical Test, *see* General Clerical Test, 2129
Psychology and Sociology: Achievement Tests in Nursing, 2376m
Punched Card Machine Operator Aptitude Test, 5:941
Purdue Blueprint Reading Test, 4:782
Purdue Clerical Adaptability Test, 2142
Purdue Creativity Test, 2347
Purdue Hand Precision Test, 2233
Purdue Industrial Training Classification Test, 2433
Purdue Interview Aids, 2434
Purdue Mechanical Adaptability Test, 2263
Purdue Mechanical Performance Test, 5:883
Purdue Pegboard, 2234
Purdue Rating Scale for Instruction, 4:803; reclassified, *consult* T2:881
Purdue Teachers Examination, *see* How I Teach, 4:799
Purdue Test for Electricians, 7:1136
Purdue Test for Machinists and Machine Operators, 4:816
Purdue Trade Information Test for Sheetmetal Workers, 2435; in Carpentry, 2436; in Engine Lathe Operation, 2437; in Welding, 2438
Qualifications Record (status unknown), 6:1068
Qualifying Test for Ediphone Voice Writing, 2:1488
RAD Scales, 2457
RBH Breadth of Information, 2287
RBH Checking Test, 2143

RBH Classifying Test, 2144
RBH Coding Test, *see* RBH Checking Test, 2143
RBH Individual Background Survey, 2314
RBH Industrial Questionnaire, 7:982
RBH Job Choice Inventory, 7:1032
RBH Language Skills and Dictation Test, 7:996
RBH Number Checking Test, 2145
RBH Personal Development Record, *see* Personal Development Record, 6:1191
RBH Personal History Record, *see* Personal History Record, 6:1126
RBH Test of Dictation Speed, 2146
RBH Test of Supervisory Judgment, 2458
RBH Test of Typing Speed, 2147
RBH Three-Dimensional Space Test, 2264
RBH Tool Knowledge Test, 6:1096
RBH Tool Knowledge Test, *see* Tool Knowledge Test [Richardson, Bellows, Henry & Co., Inc.], 6:1096
RBH Two-Dimensional Space Test, 2265
Rating 5A: Selection Tests for Office Personnel, 2150e
Rating Form for Use of Interviewers and Oral Examiners, 3:691
Rating Scales of Vocational Values, Vocational Interests and Vocational Aptitudes, 7:1033
Reading Comprehension Test for Prospective Nurses, 2381c
Reasoning: Flanagan Aptitude Classification Tests, 1072a15
Reasoning Test: O'Rourke Clerical Aptitude Test, 2138b
Recreational Guidance Test: Kefauver-Hand Guidance Tests and Inventories, 2:1661e
Reicherter-Sanders Typewriting I and II, 789
Research Personnel Review Form, 2391
Revised Minnesota Paper Form Board Test, 2266
Revised Programmer Aptitude Test, 6:1153
Revised Programmer Aptitude Test, *see* IBM Aptitude Test for Programmer Personnel, 7:1090
Revised Standard Graded Tests for Stenographers, 6:44
Road Test Check List for Testing, Selecting, Rating and Training Coach Operators, 2472
Road Test in Traffic for Testing, Selecting, Rating, and Training Truck Drivers, 2470g, 2473
Rothwell Interest Blank, *see* Rothwell-Miller Interest Blank, 2208
Rothwell-Miller Interest Blank, 2208; British Edition, 2209
Russell-Sanders Bookkeeping Test, 790
SRA Clerical Aptitudes, 791
SRA Dictation Skills, 4:454
SRA Employee Inventory, 5:905
SRA Language Skills, 3:388c
SRA Mechanical Aptitudes, 2267
SRA Primary Mental Abilities, 1087
SRA Sales Attitudes Check List, 2404
SRA Tests of Primary Mental Abilities for Ages 5 and 6, *see* SRA Primary Mental Abilities, 1087
SRA Typing Adaptability Test, 5:518
SRA Typing Skills, 792
Safran Student's Interest Inventory, 2210
Safran Vocational Interest Test, *see* Safran Student's Interest Inventory, 2210
Sales Aptitude Inventory, 2102c
Sales Aptitude Test: ETSA Test, 2405
Sales Comprehension Test, 2406
Sales Employee Inventory (status unknown), 6:1179
Sales Method Index, 2407
Sales Motivation Inventory, 2408
Sales Personnel Description Form, 6:1180
Sales Questionnaire, 3:703
Sales Sentence Completion Blank, 2409
Sales Situation Test, 4:827
Sales Terms: Factored Aptitude Series, 1078a2

Salespower Inventory, *see* Hall Salespower Inventory, 2399
San Francisco Vocational Competency Scale, 2315
Scale for Rating Effective Teacher Behavior, 4:804
Scale of Problems in Commercial Arithmetic, 2:1489
Scales: Flanagan Aptitude Classification Tests, 1072a6
Scales: Flanagan Industrial Tests, 2107a16, 2107b7
Scientific Aptitude: Aptitude Tests for Occupations, 1066f
Screening Tests for Apprentices, 6:1028
Seashore-Bennett Stenographic Proficiency Test, 2148
Secretarial Performance Analysis, 2149
Selection Interview Forms, 2316
Selection Tests for Office Personnel, 2150
Self-Administering Vocational Interest Locator With Work Interest Picture, 4:744
Self Directed Search, 2211
Self-Rating Scale for Leadership Qualifications, 2288
Senior Aptitude Tests, 1088
Shapes Test: Differential Test Battery, 1070c
Shemwell-Whitcraft Bookkeeping Test, 3:387
Short Employment Tests, 2151
Short Occupational Knowledge Test for Auto Mechanics, 2439; for Bookkeepers, 2152; for Carpenters, 2440; for Draftsmen, 2441; for Electricians, 2442; for Machinists, 2443; for Office Machine Operators, 2153; for Plumbers, 2444; for Secretaries, 2154; for Tool and Die Makers, 2445; for Truck Drivers, 2474; for Welders, 2446
Short Tests of Clerical Ability, 2155
Shorthand Aptitude Test, 793
Shorthand I and II: Every Pupil Test, *see* First Year Shorthand: Every Pupil Test, 6:42
Shorthand Test: Individual Placement Series, 2156
Shorthand Test: State High School Tests for Indiana, 3:388
Simplified Shorthand: State High School Tests for Indiana, 4:457
Skill in Typing: Measurement of Skills Test 9, 2157
Small Parts Dexterity Test, *see* Crawford Small Parts Dexterity Test, 2223
Social-Civic Guidance Test: Kefauver-Hand Guidance Tests and Inventories, 2:1661f
Space Form Test, 2243b
Space Relations: Differential Aptitude Tests, 2268
Space Visualization: Employee Aptitude Survey, 1071e
Spatial Orientation, *see* Guilford-Zimmerman Aptitude Survey, 1074e
Spatial Relations Test, *see* Minnesota Spatial Relations Test, 2258
Spatial Test 1, *see* Spatial Test EG, 2269a
Spatial Tests EG, 2, and 3, 2269
Spatial Visualization, *see* Guilford-Zimmerman Aptitude Survey, 1074f
Spatial Visualization: Multiple Aptitude Tests, 1082d
Spatial Visualization Test: Dailey Vocational Tests, 2270
Specific Interest Inventory, *see* Brainard Occupational Preference Inventory, 5:856
Speech-Appearance Record, 2317
Speed and Accuracy, 1080d
Speed Tests: Differential Test Battery, 1070e
Spelling: Clerical Skills Series, 2121g
Spelling: Clerical Tests, Series V, 2124b
Spelling 9A: Selection Tests for Office Personnel, 2150i
Spelling Review: L & L Clerical Tests, 2133d
Spelling Test: Personnel Institute Clerical Tests, 2139k
Spelling Test: USES Clerical Skills Tests, 2166c
Spelling-Vocabulary: Clerical Skills Series, 2121h
Spot-the-Error Test, 7:1005
Standard Examination for Transit Employees, 2469a
Standardized Road Test for Bus Operators, 2469d

Standardized Test: Traffic and Driving Knowledge for Drivers of Motor Trucks, 2470f

Stanford Achievement Test: High School Business and Economics Test, 7:559

Stanford High School Business and Economics Test, *see* Stanford Achievement Test: High School Business and Economics Test, 7:559

Stanford Scientific Aptitude Test, 4:813

State High School Tests for Indiana: Bookkeeping, 3:367; Commercial Arithmetic, 4:448; Shorthand, 3:388; Simplified Shorthand, 4:457; Typewriting, 4:463

Staticube Test of Power to Visualize, 1:1177

Statistical Typing Test: USES Clerical Skills Tests, 2166d

Stein Research Environment Survey, 2393b

Stein Survey for Administrators, 2393a

Stenogauge (status unknown), 3:389

Stenographic Ability Tests, *see* Stenographic Test: National Business Entrance Tests, 795

Stenographic Aptitude Test, 794

Stenographic Dictation Test, 2158

Stenographic Skill-Dictation Test, 2159

Stenographic Skills Test: ETSA Test, 2160

Stenographic Test: National Business Entrance Tests, 795

Stenography 8A: Selection Tests for Office Personnel, 2150h

Stenquist Assembling Test, 3:679

Stenquist Mechanical Aptitude Test, 3:678

Stevens-Thurow Personnel Forms, 2318

Steward Basic Factors Inventory, 2111

Steward Life Insurance Knowledge Test, 2410

Steward Occupational Objectives Inventory, 2411

Steward Personal Background Inventory, 2412

Steward Personnel Tests (Short Form), 2112

Steward Sales Aptitude Inventory, *see* Steward Basic Factors Inventory, 2111

Steward Selection System, 4:828

Steward Supervisory Personnel Inventory, *see* Steward Occupational Objectives Inventory, 2411

Steward Vocational Fitness Inventory, *see* Steward Basic Factors Inventory, 2111

Store Personnel Test, 5:954

Stromberg Dexterity Test, 2235

Strong Vocational Interest Blank for Men, 2212; for Women, 2213

Structural Dexterity Test of Mechanical Ability, *see* Chriswell Structural Dexterity Test, 2240

Student Follow-Up Questionnaire, 2101

Student-Judgment Guidance Test: Kefauver-Hand Guidance Tests and Inventories, 2:1661g

Study Difficulties Battery, *see* Netherne Study Difficulties Battery for Student Nurses, 2388

Supervisor's Evaluation of Research Personnel, 2392

Supervisory Index, 2459

Supervisory Inventory on Communication, 2460

Supervisory Inventory on Discipline, 2461

Supervisory Inventory on Grievances, 2462

Supervisory Inventory on Human Relations, 2463

Supervisory Inventory on Labor Relations, 2464

Supervisory Inventory on Safety, 2465

Supervisory Practices Test, 2466

Surgical Nursing: Achievement Tests in Nursing, 2376n

Survey of Clerical Skills: Individual Placement Series, 2161

Survey of Company Morale: Job Satisfaction Blank No. 12, 3:693

Survey of Management Perception, 2467

Survey of Mechanical Insight, 5:886

Survey of Object Visualization, 5:887

Survey of Space Relations Ability, 5:888

Survey of Working Speed and Accuracy, 3:631

Surveys of Research Administration and Environment, 2393

Symbolic Reasoning: Employee Aptitude Survey, 1071j

TAV Adjective Checklist, 2113a; Judgments, 2113b; Mental Agility, 2113g; Personal Data, 2113c; Preferences, 2113d; Proverbs and Sayings, 2113e; Salesman Reactions, 2113f; Selection System, 2113

Tables: Flanagan Aptitude Classification Tests, 1072a12

Tables: Flanagan Industrial Tests, 2107a17

Tabulation Test: Personnel Research Institute Clerical Battery, 2140c

Tapping Test, 796

Teacher Education Examination Program: Business Education, 797

Teacher Opinionaire on Democracy, 4:805; reclassified, *consult* T2:901

Teaching Aptitude Test: George Washington University Series, 4:806; reclassified, *consult* T2:904

Tear Ballot for Industry, 2289

Technical Personnel Recruiting Inventory, 2394

Technical Tests, 2447

Test for Ability to Sell, 2413

Test for Firefighter B-1, 2373

Test for Police Officer A-1, 2374

Test for Stenographic Skill, *see* Stenographic Skill-Dictation Test, 2159

Test for Typing Skill, *see* Typing Skill, 2163

Test of Dictation Speed, *see* RBH Test of Dictation Speed, 2146

Test of Mechanical Comprehension, *see* Bennett Mechanical Comprehension Test, 2239

Test of Practical Judgment, *see* Cardall Test of Practical Judgment (status unknown), 6:1102

Test of Retail Sales Insight, 2414

Test of Sales Insight, *see* Test of Retail Sales Insight, 2414

Test of Sales Judgment (status unknown), 4:830

Test of Supervisory Judgment, *see* RBH Test of Supervisory Judgment, 2458

Test of Typewriting Ability: Clerical Tests, 2124d

Test of Typing Speed, *see* RBH Test of Typing Speed, 2147

Test Orientation Procedure, 2290

Tests A/9 and A/10, 2291

Tests for Primary Mental Abilities, *see* SRA Primary Mental Abilities, 1087

Tests of Mechanical Comprehension, *see* Bennett Mechanical Comprehension Test, 2239

Tests of Primary Mental Abilities, *see* SRA Primary Mental Abilities, 1087

Thompson Business Practice Test, 1:942

Three-Dimensional Space Test, *see* RBH Three-Dimensional Space Test, 2264

Three Units of Content: NLN Practical Nursing Achievement Tests, 2385a

Thurstone Employment Tests, 2162

Thurstone Examination in Clerical Work, *see* Thurstone Employment Tests: Examination in Clerical Work, 2162a

Thurstone Examination in Typing, *see* Thurstone Employment Tests: Examination in Typing, 2162b

Thurstone Interest Schedule, 2214

Tickmaster, 2319

Tool Knowledge Test [Australian Council for Educational Research], 5:890

Tool Knowledge Test [Richardson, Bellows, Henry & Co., Inc.], 6:1096

Tools: Factored Aptitude Series, 1078a4

Traffic and Driving Knowledge for Drivers of Motor Trucks, 2470f

Truck Driver Test, 2475

Turse Clerical Aptitudes Test, 5:855

Turse-Durost Shorthand Achievement Test (Gregg), 3:392

Turse Shorthand Aptitude Test, 798

Tweezer Dexterity Test, *see* O'Connor Tweezer Dexterity Test, 2229

Two-Dimensional Space Test, *see* RBH Two-Dimensional Space Test, 2265

Typewriting Achievement Test: Business Education Achievement Test Series, 7:559A

Typewriting I and II: Every Pupil Scholarship Test, 6:54

Typewriting I: Every Pupil Test, *see* First Year Typewriting: Every Pupil Test, 6:49

Typewriting Test: National Business Entrance Tests, 799

Typewriting Test: State High School Tests for Indiana, 4:463

Typewriting II: Every Pupil Test, 1:944

Typing Ability Test, *see* Typewriting Test: National Business Entrance Tests, 799

Typing Review: L & L Clerical Tests, 2133e

Typing Skill, 2163

Typing 10A: Selection Tests for Office Personnel, 2150j

Typing Test for Business, 2164

Typing Test: Individual Placement Series, 2165

Typing Test: Personnel Institute Clerical Tests, 2139l

Typing Test: USES Clerical Skills Tests, 2166a

USAFI Subject Examinations: Bookkeeping and Accounting, 3:373; Business Arithmetic, 3:374; Business English, 3:375; Commercial Correspondence, 3:376; Gregg Shorthand, 3:377; Typewriting, 3:378

USES Clerical Skills Tests, 2166

USES Pretesting Orientation Exercises: General Aptitude Test Battery, 1073a2

Undergraduate Program Field Tests: Business Test, 800

Undergraduate Program Field Tests: Engineering Test, 2348

United-NOMA Business Entrance Tests, *see* National Business Entrance Tests, 786

United States Employment Service Special Aptitude Tests, 4:717

United Students Typewriting Tests, 801

VALCAN Vocational Interest Profile, 2215

V.G.C. Clerical Indicator, 4:735

V.G.C. Object Visualization Indicator, 4:767

V.G.C. Space Relations Ability Indicator, 4:768

Verbal Comprehension, *see* Guilford-Zimmerman Aptitude Survey, 1074a

Verbal Comprehension: Employee Aptitude Survey, 1071a

Verbal Comprehension: Multiple Aptitude Tests, 1082a

Verbal Reasoning: Employee Aptitude Survey, 1071g

Veterinary Achievement Test, *see* Veterinary Aptitude Test, 2358

Veterinary Aptitude Test, 2358

Vincent Mechanical Diagrams Test, 2271

Vincent Mechanical Models Test A (Industrial), 4:769

Visual Comprehension Test for Detective, 2375

Visual Pursuit: Employee Aptitude Survey, 1071c

Visual Speed and Accuracy: Employee Aptitude Survey, 1071d

Vocabulary and Reading Test: NLN Pre-Admission and Classification Examination, 2386b

Vocabulary: Clerical Skills Series, 2121i

Vocabulary: Clerical Tests, 2124c

Vocabulary: Flanagan Industrial Tests, 2107a18

Vocabulary Test: Personnel Institute Clerical Tests, 2139f

Vocational Agriculture Interest Inventory, *see* Applied Biological and Agribusiness Interest Inventory, 2169

Vocational Apperception Test, 2216

Vocational Aptitude Examination, 3:695

Vocational Development Inventory, *see* Career Maturity Inventory, 2103

Vocational Guidance Program, 6:781

Vocational Guidance Questionnaire, 2:1679.1

Vocational Guidance Test: Kefauver-Hand Guidance Tests and Inventories, 2:1661h

Vocational Interest Analyses, 5:870

Vocational Interest and Sophistication Assessment, 2217

Vocational Interest Blank for Men, *see* Strong Vocational Interest Blank for Men, 2212; for Women, *see* Strong Vocational Interest Blank for Women, 2213

Vocational Interest Inventory, *see* Cleeton Vocational Interest Inventory, 3:635

Vocational Interest Profile: ACT Career Planning Program, 2101a

Vocational Interest Profile (Smith and McIntosh), 2218

Vocational Interest Schedule, 3:653

Vocational Interest Test for College Women, 3:654

Vocational Inventory, 3:655

Vocational Planning Inventory, 2114

Vocational Sentence Completion Blank, 6:1073

WIPCO Vocational Interest Profile, *see* VALCAN Vocational Interest Profile, 2215

WLW Employment Inventory, Short Form, 2115

WLW Supervisor Survey, 6:1196

WPS Supervisor-Executive Tri-Dimensional Evaluation Scales, 2468

Weights and Pulleys, 2272

Whisler Strategy Test, 2292

Wide Range Employment Sample Test, 2116

Wide Range Intelligence and Personality Test, *see* Jastak Test of Potential Ability and Behavior Stability, 1077

Wide Range Interest-Opinion Test, 2219

Wide-Range Scale, *see* GATB-NATB Screening Device, 1073a1, 1086a

William, Lynde & Williams Analysis of Interest, 2220

Wilson Driver Selection Test, 2476

Wilson Teacher-Appraisal Scale, 4:807; reclassified, *consult* T2:907

Wonderlic Personnel Selection Procedure, 2320

Worcester Formboard, *see* Kent-Shakow Formboard, 3:660

Word Check Forms (status unknown), 6:1184

Word Fluency: Clerical Skills Series, 2121j

Word Fluency: Employee Aptitude Survey, 1071h

Work Information Inventory, 2293

Work Reference Check, 2321

Work Reference Investigation, 2139d

Work Values Inventory, 2221

Written Trade Tests, 6:1188

Yale Educational Aptitude Test Battery, 5:615

Yarn Dexterity Test, 2236

Your Educational Plans, 6:1075

ACRONYMS

ABI, Alpha Biographical Inventory, 2273

ATGSB, Admission Test for Graduate Study in Business, 2325

BMCT, Bennett Mechanical Comprehension Test, 2239

CMI, Career Maturity Inventory, 2103

DAT, Differential Aptitude Tests, 1069

DATP, Dental Admission Testing Program, 2337

FACT, Flanagan Aptitude Classification Tests, 1072

GPII, Geist Picture Interest Inventory, 2180

HGVII, Hackman-Gaither Vocational Interest Inventory, 2186

ILBDQ, Ideal Leader Behavior Description Questionnaire, 2449

KOIS, Kuder Occupational Interest Survey, 2194

KPR-V, Kuder Preference Record—Vocational, 2195

LBDQ, Leader Behavior Description Questionnaire, 2451

LBDQ-12, Leader Behavior Description Questionnaire Form 12, 2452

LOQ, Leadership Opinion Questionnaire, 2454

LSAT, Law School Admission Test, 2349

MCAT, Medical College Admission Test, 2355

MEAT, Minnesota Engineering Analogies Test, 2344

MIQ, Minnesota Importance Questionnaire, 2283

MRMT, Minnesota Rate of Manipulation Test, 2227

MSQ, Minnesota Satisfaction Questionnaire, 2285

MVII, Minnesota Vocational Interest Inventory, 2197

PII, Picture Interest Inventory, 2205

PNG, NLN Pre-Nursing and Guidance Examination, 2387

PP, Purdue Pegboard, 2234

RAD, RAD Scales, 2457

SET, Short Employment Tests, 2151

SVIB, Strong Vocational Interest Blank for Men, 2212

SVIB-W, Strong Vocational Interest Blank for Women, 2213

TAV, TAV Selection System, 2113

TBI, Tear Ballot for Industry, 2289

WVI, Work Values Inventory, 2221

INDEX OF NAMES

This analytical index indicates whether a citation refers to authorship of a test, test review, excerpted review, or a reference for a specific test. Citations are to test numbers, not to page numbers. In the reprint sections, the numbers of the first and last tests on facing pages are given in the running heads next to the outside margins. Numbers without colons refer to in print tests presented in the section reprinted from TIP II. Interpret abbreviations and numbers for in print tests as follows: "*test, 2230*" indicates authorship of test 2230; "*rev, 780*," authorship of a review of test 780; "*exc, 1072*," authorship of an excerpted review of test 1072; and "*ref, 2383*," authorship of one or more references for test 2383. (The Cumulative Name Index for that test must be consulted to locate the references.) Numbers with colons (e.g., 4:749, test 749 in the 4th MMY) refer to out of print tests included in the material reprinted from the MMY's, unless otherwise indicated. In the reprint sections, the yearbook digit preceding the colon is given in the running head only.

ALA BOARD on Personnel Administration: *test,* 5:939
Abbatiello, A. A.: *test,* 2120
Abdel-Ghaffar, A. S. A. K.: *ref,* 2185
Abdel-Meguid, S. G. M.: *ref,* 2180
Abe, C.: *ref,* 2273
Abell, E. L.: *exc,* 1:936, 1:1170
Aboud, J.: *ref,* 2194
Abrahams, I.: *ref,* 2195
Abrahams, N.: *ref,* 2212, 2340, 2344
Abrahams, N. M.: *ref,* 2197, 2212
Abramowitz, E.: *ref,* 2212
Abrams, E. N.: *ref,* 1087
Abrams, P.: *ref,* 2292
Abramson, H. A.: *ref,* 2266
Achard, F. H.: *ref,* 2135, 2212, 2266
Achauer, M. P.: *ref,* 2213
Achilles, P. S.: *ref,* 2212
Ackerman, B. R.: *ref,* 2212
Acree, N. E.: *test,* 2212
Adams, F. J.: *ref,* 2195
Adams, J. F.: *ref,* 2212
Adams, M.: *test,* 4:814; *ref,* 4:814 (1, 4)
Adams, W. M.: *ref,* 4:814(2, 3)
Adamson, D.: *ref,* 2212
Adcock, C. J.: *rev,* 2107; *ref,* 1069
Adinolfi, A. A.: *ref,* 2212
Adjutant General's Office, Personnel Research Section: *ref,* 2195
Adkins, D. C.: *rev,* 785, 1071, 1080, 3:690; *exc,* 4:786; *ref,* 1087, 2195

Adsett, C. A.: *ref,* 2355
Aftanas, M. S.: *ref,* 2234
Aga, H.: *ref,* 2247
Agee, K. M.: *ref,* 2212
Ahnell, I. V.: *ref,* 2454
Ahola, V. I.: *ref,* 2323
Ahrens, J. B.: *test,* 2296
Aijaz, S. M.: *ref,* 1069
Aiken, L. R.: *ref,* 1069
Air Force Personnel Research Laboratory: *test,* 6:1023
Akerman, R. H.: *ref,* 1073
Alberts, N. F.: *test,* 1088, 2198
Albright, L. E.: *rev,* 2285, 2290; *ref,* 2229, 2234, 2239, 2266, 2392, 2406, 2448, 6:1140(2)
Aldag, J. C.: *ref,* 2212-3
Aldag, J. C. K.: *ref,* 2212-3
Alderfer, R. D.: *ref,* 2103
Alderman, E.: *ref,* 2234
Alexakos, C. E.: *ref,* 1073
Alexander, D.: *ref,* 1087
Alford, M. L.: *ref,* 1072
Allebach, N. L.: *ref,* 1087
Allen, B. V.: *ref,* 2212
Allen, C. L.: *ref,* 2195, 2212-3
Allen, G. E.: *ref,* 2212
Allen, R. J.: *ref,* 2195
Allender, J. S.: *ref,* 2355
Allmandinger, M. F.: *ref,* 1074
Alsip, J. E.: *ref,* 2212
Alspaugh, C. A.: *ref,* 7:1090(12)
Alteneder, L. E.: *ref,* 2212-3 2266

Althouse, R.: *ref,* 2212-3
Altman, J. W.: *ref,* 1072
Alvi, S. A.: *ref,* 1069
American Association of Colleges of Podiatric Medicine: *test,* 2354
American College Testing Program: *test,* 2101, 2167
American Dental Association: *test,* 2337
American Gas Association: *ref,* 2135, 2251, 5:888(2)
American Institute of Accountants: *ref,* 2323
American Institute of Certified Public Accountants: *test,* 2323, 7:1078
American Nurses' Association: *ref,* 2195
Amerson, V. M.: *rev,* 778, 3:380
Amicucci, E.: *ref,* 2212
Ammons, R. B.: *test,* 2216; *ref,* 2216
Amundson, G. J.: *ref,* 1087
Anant, S. S.: *ref,* 1069, 1087
Anastasi, A.: *rev,* 1074, 1077, 1087, 5:610, 5:615; *ref,* 1087, 2195, 2212
Anastasiow, N. J.: *ref,* 1087
Anderson, A. V.: *ref,* 2337
Anderson, B. D.: *ref,* 2452
Anderson, C. L.: *ref,* 2195
Anderson, D. O.: *ref,* 2355
Anderson, F. E.: *ref,* 2195

Anderson, G. V.: *exc*, 2189
Anderson, G. W.: *ref*, 2212
Anderson, H. C.: *ref*, 2212
Anderson, H. D.: *ref*, 2251
Anderson, H. E.: *ref*, 2212-3
Anderson, J. W.: *ref*, 2451
Anderson, L. D.: *test*, 2258, 2266, 3:671; *ref*, 2258, 2266, 3:671(1, 3), 3:678(5), 3:679(3)
Anderson, L. L.: *ref*, 2283
Anderson, L. M. L.: *ref*, 2285
Anderson, L. R.: *ref*, 2451
Anderson, M. E.: *ref*, 2195
Anderson, M. R.: *ref*, 1073, 2212-3
Anderson, P. K.: *ref*, 1073
Anderson, R.: *ref*, 1069
Anderson, R. C.: *ref*, 1072
Anderson, R. G.: *ref*, 2135, 2195, 2239, 2251, 2266, 5:856(9)
Anderson, R. J.: *ref*, 2212
Anderson, R. M.: *ref*, 2451
Anderson, R. N.: *ref*, 782, 2135, 2138, 2212, 2:1675(2)
Anderson, S. C.: *ref*, 2212-3
Anderson, T. E.: *ref*, 2194-5
Anderson, W.: *ref*, 2212
Andrew, D. M.: *test*, 2135; *ref*, 2135
Andrews, J. H. M.: *ref*, 2451-2
Andrews, M. E.: *ref*, 2213
Andrulis, R. S.: *ref*, 2349
Andruss, H. A.: *rev*, 777, 3:373
Angers, W. P.: *ref*, 2195, 2266
Anikeeff, A. M.: *ref*, 2195
Anker, J.: *ref*, 2212
Anker, J. M.: *ref*, 2212, 2221
Ankers, R. G.: *ref*, 2323
Ansbacher, H. L.: *ref*, 1087
Ansell, E. M.: *ref*, 2103
Anstey, E.: *rev*, 6:1090
Antley, E. M.: *ref*, 2340
Antoinetti, J. A.: *ref*, 2401
Apostal, R. A.: *ref*, 2212-3
Appelbaum, M.: *ref*, 2212
Arbuckle, D. S.: *ref*, 2195
Arden, W.: *ref*, 2212
Arkoff, A.: *ref*, 2454
Armatas, J. P.: *ref*, 2212
Armbrust, R.: *ref*, 1069
Armed Forces Vocational Testing Group: *test*, 1067
Armstrong, K. E.: *ref*, 1069, 1073
Armstrong, M. E.: *ref*, 2195
Armstrong Cork Co.: *test*, 2453
Arnold, D. L.: *ref*, 2195
Arnold, F. C.: *ref*, 2183
Arnold, J. N.: *test*, 4:782
Arnoldi, J.: *ref*, 2251
Arns, J.: *ref*, 2186
Aron, J.: *ref*, 2406
Arsenian, S.: *ref*, 2212, 3:635(3, 10)
Asbury, C. A.: *ref*, 1087
Ash, P.: *ref*, 792, 1078, 2151, 2239, 2266, 2406, 5:905(1)
Ash, W. E.: *ref*, 2452
Ashbrook, J. B.: *ref*, 2452
Ashbury, F. A.: *ref*, 2103
Ashby, J. D.: *ref*, 2212
Ashe, M. R.: *ref*, 1073
Asher, E. J.: *ref*, 2234
Asquith, R. H.: *ref*, 2454, 2459
Associated Personnel Technicians, Inc.: *test*, 2119, 2294

Association of American Medical Colleges: *test*, 2355
Association of Collegiate Schools of Architecture: *test*, 2359
Asta, P.: *ref*, 2408
Astin, A. W.: *rev*, 2212; *ref*, 2212
Athelstan, G. T.: *ref*, 2212-3
Atkinson, E.: *ref*, 2195
Atkinson, G.: *ref*, 2195, 2212
Atkinson, J. A.: *ref*, 2195
Attwell, A. A.: *ref*, 1087
Atty, J. C.: *ref*, 2195
Aucker, J. R.: *ref*, 1073
Auria, C.: *ref*, 1087
Aursand, I. M.: *ref*, 2214, 5:615(10)
Auston, C. A.: *ref*, 2195
Australian Council for Educational Research: *test*, 2117-8, 2237-8
Ausubel, D. P.: *ref*, 2195, 2199
Avakian, S. A.: *ref*, 1087
Ayers, A. W.: *ref*, 2454
Ayers, L. D.: *ref*, 1073
Aylward, M. S.: *ref*, 2212, 2344
Ayres, A. J.: *ref*, 1073

BAAS, M. L.: *ref*, 2195
Babcock, H.: *ref*, 2251
Bachner, V. M.: *ref*, 2195, 2392
Bacon, R. V.: *test*, 2212; *ref*, 2212
Badgley, R. F.: *ref*, 2355
Bae, A. Y.: *ref*, 1069
Baehr, M. E.: *test*, 2110, 5:905, 6:1107; *ref*, 2110, 2340, 5:905(2, 6)
Baer, B. S.: *ref*, 2195
Baggaley, A. R.: *test*, 2196; *ref*, 2195-6, 2212
Baier, D. E.: *ref*, 2195, 2401
Bailey, B. H.: *ref*, 2451
Bailey, H. C.: *ref*, 2195
Bailey, H. D.: *ref*, 2451
Bailey, J. P.: *ref*, 2213
Bailey, L. J.: *ref*, 2386
Bailey, R. L.: *ref*, 2212
Bailey, W. M. B.: *ref*, 1080
Bair, J. T.: *ref*, 780, 782, 1069, 1074, 2129, 2135, 2138, 2266
Baird, M. W.: *ref*, 786
Baird, R. G.: *ref*, 1073
Baker, E. H.: *ref*, 1087
Baker, H. J.: *test*, 782, 1068, 2244, 2397; *ref*, 2244
Baker, P. C.: *test*, 4:803
Baker, R. L.: *ref*, 2340, 6:1062(9-10)
Bakirdgis, I.: *ref*, 2135
Baldwin, E. F.: *ref*, 2266
Baldwin, G. B.: *test*, 3:624, 3:641
Baldwin, J. P.: *ref*, 2383
Baldwin, T. S.: *rev*, 2105
Balinsky, B.: *rev*, 2216; *test*, 2316; *ref*, 2227-9, 2251, 2258, 2266-7
Ball, F. J.: *ref*, 1087
Ball, J. M.: *ref*, 1074
Ball, M. K.: *ref*, 2195
Ballantyne, R. H.: *ref*, 1074
Ballen, R.: *test*, 2319
Ballou, S. I.: *ref*, 2212
Balsley, I. W.: *rev*, 2141
Baltes, P. B.: *ref*, 1087
Banas, P.: *ref*, 796, 2151, 7:1103(3)
Banas, P. A.: *ref*, 1073, 2212

Banerjee, C.: *ref*, 2173
Banghart, F. W.: *ref*, 2355
Banks, R. R.: *ref*, 2195
Bannochie, M. N.: *ref*, 1087
Bannon, M. M.: *ref*, 2221
Barbera, R. C.: *ref*, 2214
Barclay, J. R.: *ref*, 2197
Barden, H. E.: *ref*, 3:678(9)
Barden, J. W.: *ref*, 2451
Bare, C. E.: *ref*, 2195
Barksdale, A.: *ref*, 2199
Barnabas, B.: *test*, 2222; *ref*, 2212, 2239
Barnett, A.: *ref*, 2258, 2266
Barnett, G. J.: *ref*, 2212
Barnette, W. L.: *ref*, 2129, 2135, 2195, 2197, 2212, 2234, 2239, 2266, 4:810(3, 5)
Barnhart, A. E.: *ref*, 2451
Barocas, R.: *ref*, 2212
Baron, S.: *ref*, 2195
Baroya, G. M.: *ref*, 1069
Barr, A. S.: *test*, 4:793
Barr, F. E.: *ref*, 3:689(1)
Barratt, E. S.: *ref*, 1069, 1071, 1074, 2266
Barre, M. F.: *ref*, 2227
Barrett, A. M.: *ref*, 2180
Barrett, D. M.: *ref*, 794, 798, 2135, 2213, 2251, 2266, 3:392(3)
Barrett, R. E.: *ref*, 2195
Barrett, R. S.: *rev*, 2301; *ref*, 1069, 2151, 2195, 2239, 2266, 2387
Barrilleaux, L. E.: *ref*, 2195
Barrows, G. A.: *ref*, 2212
Barry, C. M.: *ref*, 2195
Barry, J. R.: *ref*, 1069, 2212, 2214
Barshay, H. B.: *ref*, 2195
Barthol, R. P.: *ref*, 2212, 2448
Bartlett, J. W.: *ref*, 2355
Bartlett, W. E.: *ref*, 2103
Barton, E. M.: *ref*, 6:1062(2)
Bashaw, W. L.: *ref*, 2199
Bass, A. R.: *ref*, 2454
Bass, B. M.: *ref*, 2234, 2275, 2325, 2349, 2406, 2448, 2451, 2454
Bateman, H. B.: *ref*, 2195
Bateman, R. M.: *ref*, 2195
Bates, C. O.: *ref*, 2212
Bates, G. L.: *ref*, 2285
Bates, J.: *ref*, 2258-9, 2266
Bates, W. T. G.: *test*, 2168; *ref*, 2168
Bath, J. A.: *ref*, 2195
Battle, E. S.: *ref*, 1087
Bauer, R.: *ref*, 2212, 7:1090(10)
Bauernfeind, R. H.: *exc*, 2170; *ref*, 2195
Baughman, E. E.: *ref*, 1087
Bauman, M. K.: *ref*, 2223, 2227, 2231
Baumgold, J.: *ref*, 2234
Baurer, H. T.: *ref*, 3:678(12)
Baxter, B.: *rev*, 2289, 2308, 2456
Baxter, J. L.: *ref*, 2195
Bayley, N.: *ref*, 2195
Bayroff, A. G.: *ref*, 1067
Bayti, J. L.: *ref*, 2173
Baziak, A. T.: *ref*, 2383, 2387
Bazik, A. M.: *ref*, 2212
Beal, L. E.: *ref*, 2197
Beamer, G. C.: *ref*, 1069, 1073, 2135, 2195, 2212, 2229, 2251, 2266, 2323
Bean, K. L.: *ref*, 2266

Beard, R. B.: *ref,* 1073
Beard, R. M.: *ref,* 1070
Beaton, M. A.: *ref,* 2195
Beattie, A. D.: *test,* 779
Beatty, R. W.: *ref,* 2451, 2454
Beaver, A. P.: *ref,* 2195
Bechtel, R.: *ref,* 1087
Bechtel, R. D.: *ref,* 2212
Bechtoldt, H.: *rev,* 1069, 1074
Bechtoldt, H. P.: *rev,* 1072-3, 1078, 2239
Beck, I. H. H.: *ref,* 1087
Becker, G. J.: *ref,* 1087
Becker, J. A.: *ref,* 2195, 2213
Becker, S. J.: *ref,* 2213
Becvar, R. J.: *ref,* 2285
Bedell, R.: *test,* 2213; *ref,* 2213
Bednar, R. L.: *ref,* 2212
Bedrosian, H.: *ref,* 2212
Beecher, D. E.: *test,* 4:796, 4:804; *ref,* 4:804(1)
Beer, M.: *ref,* 2449, 2452
Beery, K. E.: *ref,* 1087
Behring, D. W.: *ref,* 2389
Beilin, H.: *ref,* 2221
Beiser, H. R.: *ref,* 2355
Belcher, T. L.: *ref,* 2273
Beldo, L. A.: *ref,* 2135
Bell, E. L.: *ref,* 2195, 2199
Bell, F. O.: *ref,* 1073
Bell, M. L.: *ref,* 2195
Bellamy, R. Q.: *ref,* 1073
Bellows, R. M.: *ref,* 1087, 2135, 2212, 2227-9, 2251, 2258, 2266
Bellucci, J. T.: *ref,* 1073
Belman, H. S.: *ref,* 2195, 2263, 2448, 4:799(3-4)
Bemis, S.: *ref,* 1073, 1086
Bemis, S. F.: *ref,* 1073
Bender, L. D.: *ref,* 1073
Bender, W. R. G.: *ref,* 798, 2135
Bendig, A. W.: *ref,* 1087, 2195, 2212
Benevento, P.: *ref,* 2451
Benge, E. J.: *test,* 2288, 3:389, 3:625, 3:644, 3:656-7, 3:673, 3:703, 6:1088, 6:1175; *rcf,* 3:703 (1)
Benjamin, D. R.: *ref,* 2212
Benjamin, J. A.: *ref,* 2195
Bennett, E.: *ref,* 5:880(6)
Bennett, G. K.: *rev,* 2184, 3:645, 3:690; *test,* 781, 791, 1063, 1069, 2148, 2151, 2225, 2239, 2256, 2268, 2290, 2317; *ref,* 794, 1069, 2129, 2135, 2148, 2151, 2225, 2227-9, 2239, 2244, 2251, 2258-60, 2266, 3:658(3), 3:660(12), 3:671(10), 3:678(17), 3:679(10), 5:954(1)
Bennett, M. G.: *test,* 1063
Benson, D.: *ref,* 2212, 2463
Bentley, J. C.: *ref,* 2212
Benton, A. L.: *ref,* 2212, 2223, 4:813(4)
Bentz, V. J.: *ref,* 2195
Benz, S. C.: *test,* 4:798; *ref,* 4:798 (1-2)
Berdie, R. F.: *rev,* 1069, 1072, 1082, 1087, 2195, 2205, 2220-1, 3:639; *test,* 2212; *ref,* 1069, 1087, 2195, 2212, 2266
Berg, I. A.: *ref,* 2195, 2212, 2239, 2381, 5:886(2), 5:888(4)
Berg, O. D.: *ref,* 1069

Bergen, G. L.: *ref,* 2135, 2212, 2227-9, 2258
Berger, R. M.: *ref,* 1074, 2212
Berkshire, R.: *ref,* 2135
Berlfein, H. P.: *ref,* 2454
Berman, I. R.: *ref,* 2135, 2212-3, 2227-9, 2258, 3:642(4)
Bernard, J.: *ref,* 2195
Bernberg, R. E.: *test,* 2293
Bernreuter, R. G.: *rev,* 3:703; *ref,* 1087
Bernstein, A. J.: *ref,* 2212
Bernstein, B. H.: *ref,* 2221
Berrier, J. G.: *ref,* 2186
Berryessa, M. J.: *ref,* 2195
Bertness, H. J.: *ref,* 2212
Berzins, J. I.: *ref,* 2212
Best, W. R.: *ref,* 2355
Beswick, D. G.: *ref,* 2195
Betz, B. J.: *ref,* 2212
Betz, E.: *ref,* 2285
Betz, E. L.: *ref,* 1071, 2283-5
Beukes, D. P. M.: *test,* 1075
Beveridge, M. D.: *ref,* 1069
Beymer, C. L.: *ref,* 1063
Bhatt, L. J.: *ref,* 1069
Bialer, I.: *ref,* 2227
Bidlake, L. A.: *ref,* 2212
Bidwell, G. P.: *ref,* 1073, 2195
Biedenkapp, M. S.: *ref,* 2212
Bierbaum, W. B.: *ref,* 1073
Bigelow, B.: *test,* 4:826
Biggers, A. F.: *ref,* 1073
Biggs, D. A.: *ref,* 2212, 2454
Bilaski, I.: *ref,* 1078
Biles, D.: *ref,* 2118, 2238, 2266
Billing, P. S.: *ref,* 2195
Billings, E. L.: *ref,* 2:1675(3)
Bills, M. A.: *rev,* 780, 2192; *ref,* 2212, 5:913(20)
Binder, A.: *ref,* 1087
Bingham, W. V.: *rev,* 1:1174; *test,* 3:691; *ref,* 2135, 2212-3, 2227-9, 2251, 2258, 2260, 2266, 2:1676(3), 2:1683(2), 3:637(5), 3:642(5), 3:671(6), 3:678(10), 3:689(4), 3:691(1-2)
Bingman, R. M.: *ref,* 1069, 2195
Bininger, M. L.: *ref,* 4:718(3)
Bird, D. J.: *ref,* 2213
Bird, H. B.: *ref,* 2355
Bird, R. G.: *ref,* 1073
Bisbee, E. V.: *test,* 1:936; *rcf,* 1:936(1)
Bischof, L. J.: *ref,* 1073
Bissett, S. J.: *ref,* 2199
Bitner, H. M.: *ref,* 2195
Bittel, J.: *ref,* 2259
Bittner, R. H.: *rev,* 2132, 2159, 2252, 2304, 3:680
Bixler, H. H.: *rev,* 2140
Black, D. O.: *ref,* 2449, 2451
Black, J. D.: *ref,* 2129, 2135, 2212, 2239, 2448
Black, M. H.: *ref,* 2135
Blackburn, H. L.: *ref,* 1073
Blackburn, J. B.: *ref,* 1073
Blackburn, J. M.: *exc,* 2242
Blackburn, J. R.: *ref,* 1073
Blackstone, E. G.: *rev,* 799, 3:378, 3:382-3
Blade, M. F.: *ref,* 2241
Blake, R.: *ref,* 2180, 2205
Blake, R. H.: *ref,* 2180, 2205

Blakemore, A.: *ref,* 1074, 2132, 2135
Blakemore, A. M.: *ref,* 2135
Blanchard, H. L.: *ref,* 2135, 2266
Blanchard, R. E.: *ref,* 6:1062(3)
Blank, P. M.: *ref,* 2197
Blank, S. S.: *ref,* 2135, 2195, 2406
Blankenship, K. R.: *ref,* 2185
Blanton, W. L.: *ref,* 1069
Blatt, C. A.: *ref,* 2452
Blewett, D. B.: *ref,* 1087
Blocher, D. H.: *ref,* 2212
Block, V. L.: *test,* 2:1661
Blood, M. R.: *ref,* 2451
Bloom, T. K.: *ref,* 1069
Blosser, G. H.: *ref,* 1069
Bluett, C. G.: *ref,* 2212, 2234
Bluhm, H.: *ref,* 2195, 2212
Blum, L. P.: *ref,* 2212
Blum, M.: *ref,* 2135, 2227-9
Blum, M. L.: *rev,* 1073, 2190, 2258, 3:657, 3:660; *ref,* 2135, 2228-9, 2251
Blumenfeld, E. R.: *ref,* 1087
Blumenfeld, W. S.: *ref,* 1087
Boaz, J. A.: *ref,* 2213
Bobbitt, J. M.: *ref,* 2214, 2241, 2266
Bock, R. D.: *ref,* 1069
Bodden, J. L.: *rev,* 2170; *ref,* 2212
Bodley, E. A.: *ref,* 2227-8, 2266
Boernke, C.: *ref,* 792, 2151
Bohn, M. J.: *ref,* 2212-3
Bolanovich, D. J.: *ref,* 2195
Bolin, S. F.: *ref,* 2140, 2212, 2235, 2448
Bolton, B.: *ref,* 2181, 2234, 2266
Bolton, F. B.: *ref,* 1072
Bond, G. L.: *ref,* 1087, 2135, 2195, 2199, 2212, 2239
Bond, N. A.: *ref,* 2185, 2195
Bond, P. J.: *ref,* 2212
Bondy, S.: *ref,* 2212
Bondy, S. B.: *ref,* 2212-3
Bone, J. H.: *ref,* 2195
Boney, J. D.: *ref,* 1069
Bonfield, J.: *ref,* 2197
Bonfield, J. R.: *ref,* 1087
Bonney, W. C.: *ref,* 2199
Bons, P. A.: *ref,* 2454
Bookout, D. V. T.: *ref,* 1073
Booth, M. D.: *ref,* 2195
Bordin, E. S.: *rev,* 2192, 2195, 2199, 2212, 3:655, 5:862; *exc,* 1077; *rcf,* 2195, 2212
Borg, W. R.: *ref,* 2135, 2195, 2212, 2239
Borgen, F. H.: *test,* 2284; *ref,* 2212, 2283-4
Borko, H.: *ref,* 1074
Borow, H.: *test,* 4:810; *exc,* 6:1075; *ref,* 4:810(1)
Bose, U.: *ref,* 2173
Bostic, C. R.: *ref,* 2452
Botsford, F. R.: *test,* 3:367, 4:457, 4:463
Bott, M. M.: *ref,* 2213
Botterbusch, K. F.: *ref,* 1073
Bouck, W. C.: *ref,* 2397
Boulger, J. R.: *ref,* 1073
Bourassa, G. L.: *ref,* 2227-9, 2234
Bourdo, E. A.: *ref,* 2195
Bourne, R. K.: *ref,* 1069
Bouthilet, L.: *ref,* 1087
Bouton, A.: *ref,* 2195
Bouton, A. G.: *ref,* 2195

Bowen, C. W.: *ref,* 1069
Bowers, H.: *test,* 4:792; *ref,* 4:792 (1-2)
Bowers, O. R.: *ref,* 1082
Bowman, H. J.: *ref,* 2451, 2457
Bown, M. D.: *ref,* 2244, 2266
Boyce, E. M.: *ref,* 2212
Boyce, R. W.: *ref,* 6:1062(7)
Boyd, H. L.: *ref,* 1073
Boyd, J. B.: *ref,* 2212
Boyd, J. D.: *ref,* 2212
Boyd, R. E.: *ref,* 2212
Boykin, L. L.: *ref,* 2199
Boynton, P. L.: *ref,* 3:678(13)
Braasch, W. F.: *ref,* 2135, 2212
Braaten, L. J.: *ref,* 2214, 5:615(10)
Braden, G. D.: *ref,* 2349
Bradfield, A. F.: *ref,* 2195, 2212
Brading, P. L.: *ref,* 2355
Bradley, A. D.: *ref,* 2195, 2197, 2212, 2239, 2266
Bradley, R. W.: *ref,* 1069
Bradshaw, O. L.: *ref,* 2195, 2239
Brailey, L. B.: *ref,* 2140
Brainard, P. P.: *test,* 5:856; *ref,* 2:1675(1)
Brainard, R. T.: *test,* 5:856
Brainard, S. R.: *ref,* 2452
Bramos, I.: *ref,* 2135
Brams, J. M.: *ref,* 2212
Brandt, E. M.: *ref,* 2383
Brandt, J. E.: *ref,* 2212
Branson, B. D.: *ref,* 2266
Brasington, C. R.: *ref,* 2212
Braskamp, L.: *ref,* 2349
Braskamp, L. A.: *ref,* 2212
Braun, J. R.: *ref,* 2113, 2408
Bray, D. W.: *ref,* 1069, 2223, 2239
Brayfield, A. H.: *rev,* 2199, 2257, 2459, 5:886; *exc,* 2195, 3:655; *ref,* 1069, 2135, 2195, 2212, 5:905 (8)
Brazziel, W. F.: *ref,* 2199
Bredemeier, R. A.: *ref,* 2212
Breese, F. H.: *ref,* 1087
Breidenbaugh, B. E.: *ref,* 2195
Breidenbaugh, V. E.: *test,* 2:1477
Breimeier, K. H.: *ref,* 2212
Brendemuehl, F. L.: *ref,* 1087
Brenkus, P. M.: *ref,* 2355
Brenna, D. W.: *ref,* 1073
Brennan, J. T.: *ref,* 1087
Brennan, T. F.: *ref,* 2228
Brenner, D.: *ref,* 2227
Brentlinger, W. H.: *ref,* 2135
Breslow, E.: *ref,* 2349
Bretnall, E. P.: *ref,* 2212
Brewer, B.: *ref,* 2212
Brewer, J. M.: *ref,* 2195, 2212, 3:635(11)
Brewington, A.: *rev,* 795, 2148
Brickner, C. E.: *ref,* 2451
Bridge, L.: *ref,* 2199
Bridgman, C. S.: *ref,* 2195
Briggs, L.: *ref,* 3:653(10)
Briggs, P. F.: *ref,* 1073
Brigham, L. H.: *ref,* 786
Brim, C. W.: *ref,* 1069
Brimble, A. R.: *ref,* 1085
Brintle, S. L.: *ref,* 2212
Britton, J. H.: *ref,* 1087
Britton, J. O.: *ref,* 2451
Broadbent, L. A.: *ref,* 2195
Broadhurst, J. C.: *ref,* 2244, 2266

Brody, A. B.: *ref,* 1087
Brody, D.: *ref,* 2258
Brody, D. S.: *ref,* 2195
Broe, J. R.: *ref,* 1071
Brogden, H. E.: *ref,* 2195
Broman, H. J.: *ref,* 1073
Bromer, J. A.: *ref,* 1069
Bronson, L.: *ref,* 2212
Brooks, E.: *ref,* 2213
Brooks, G. W.: *ref,* 1073
Brooks, M. S.: *ref,* 2195
Broverman, D. M.: *ref,* 1087
Brown, A. F.: *ref,* 2452
Brown, C. M.: *ref,* 1073
Brown, D. J.: *ref,* 2212
Brown, F.: *ref,* 2228-9, 2258
Brown, F. G.: *exc,* 2194; *ref,* 2212, 2221, 2358
Brown, J. E.: *ref,* 2212
Brown, M. N.: *ref,* 2195, 2199, 2212
Brown, N. W.: *ref,* 2213
Brown, R. A.: *ref,* 2195, 2212
Brown, R. L.: *test,* 2236, 5:883; *ref,* 5:883(1)
Brown, T. E.: *ref,* 2195, 2212
Brown, W. E.: *ref,* 2195, 2199
Browne, C. G.: *ref,* 2457
Brownless, V.: *test,* 793
Brozek, J.: *ref,* 1087
Brozovich, R. W.: *ref,* 2195
Bruce, M. M.: *test,* 2121, 2275, 2395, 2406, 2408, 2466; *ref,* 1087, 2195, 2223, 2234, 2239, 2263, 2266, 2275, 2395, 2403, 2406, 2408, 2466, 5:905(9)
Bruce, R. L.: *ref,* 2466
Bruce (Martin M.), Ph.D., Publishers: *test,* 2299
Brue, E. J.: *ref,* 2167
Brueckner, L. J.: *rev,* 4:796, 4:804
Bruening, J. H.: *ref,* 2212
Bruhn, J. G.: *ref,* 2355
Bruininks, R. H.: *ref,* 1087
Brunclik, H.: *ref,* 2378
Brunclik, H. L.: *test,* 2378, 2382, 2389; *ref,* 2378, 2382, 2387, 2389
Bruno, F. B.: *ref,* 2212
Brush, E. N.: *ref,* 2242, 2258-9, 2266, 3:671(9)
Brussell, E. S.: *test,* 3:689
Bruton, F. E.: *ref,* 2387
Bryan, A. I.: *ref,* 2266
Bryan, J. G.: *ref,* 2195
Bryan, J. L.: *ref,* 2195
Bryan, W. E.: *ref,* 2212
Bryant, G. W.: *ref,* 2449
Bryant, J. H.: *ref,* 1082
Buchanan, B. F.: *ref,* 2213
Buchanan, P. C.: *ref,* 1074
Buchanan, R. G.: *test,* 2290
Buck, C. W.: *ref,* 2212
Buck, J. R.: *ref,* 2195
Buckalew, R. J.: *ref,* 2186, 2195
Buckeye, D. A.: *ref,* 2340
Bucklow, M.: *ref,* 2118
Buckton, L.: *ref,* 2349, 2355
Budd, T. A.: *ref,* 2323
Budd, W. C.: *ref,* 2195
Buegel, H. F.: *ref,* 2195
Buehler, J. A.: *ref,* 2355
Buel, W. D.: *test,* 2392; *ref,* 2151, 2195, 2392
Buikema, R. J.: *ref,* 1069
Bull, E. R.: *ref,* 2269

Bunch, R. H.: *ref,* 2259
Bundy, R. D.: *test,* 5:915
Bunker, C. S.: *ref,* 2194
Burack, B.: *ref,* 2212
Burden, L.: *ref,* 2452
Burdett, A.: *ref,* 2217
Burdett, A. D.: *test,* 2217; *ref,* 2217, 2234-5
Burdette, W. E.: *ref,* 2195
Burdock, E. I.: *ref,* 2212, 2234
Bureau of Business Research, Ohio State University: *test,* 2452
Bureau of Educational Measurements: *test,* 6:31, 6:34, 6:38, 6:54
Burg, B. W.: *ref,* 2180
Burgemeister, B. B.: *ref,* 2213
Burgess, E.: *ref,* 2212
Burgess, M. M.: *ref,* 2234
Burgess, T. C.: *ref,* 1087
Burk, K. W.: *ref,* 2212
Burke, C.: *test,* 6:1048, 6:1051
Burke, H. R.: *ref,* 2212
Burke, M.: *ref,* 1069
Burkhart, R.: *test,* 3:367, 4:457, 4:463
Burney, S. W.: *ref,* 1073
Burnham, P. S.: *rev,* 2183; *test,* 5:615; *ref,* 1087, 2212, 2349, 4:718(4), 5:615(8, 11)
Burnham, R. E.: *ref,* 1087
Burns, R. K.: *test,* 2110, 5:905, 6:1107, 6:1171; *ref,* 5:902(1)
Burr, M.: *ref,* 2251
Burrall, L.: *ref,* 1087
Bursch, C. W.: *ref,* 2195
Burt, C.: *rev,* 1087
Burt, S. M.: *ref,* 1073
Burton, R. L.: *ref,* 2212
Busby, W. A.: *ref,* 1069
Busch, A. C.: *ref,* 2251
Busse, T. V.: *ref,* 1087
Busse, W.: *ref,* 1073, 2195
Butcher, H. J.: *ref,* 1087, 2195
Butler, B. V.: *ref,* 2195
Butler, M. N.: *test,* 2216; *ref,* 2216
Buttenweiser, P.: *ref,* 2212
Butterfield, E. C.: *exc,* 1077
Butts, F. E.: *ref,* 7:1078(4)
Buxbaum, R. C.: *ref,* 2355
Byers, E. E.: *test,* 6:41; *ref,* 6:41 (1)
Byers, K.: *exc,* 2298
Byrne, K. M.: *ref,* 1087

CAFFYN, H. R.: *ref,* 2323
Cahoon, D. D.: *ref,* 2195
Cain, E. T.: *ref,* 2194
Cain, L. F.: *ref,* 1087
Cain, R. W.: *ref,* 1069
Caine, T. A.: *ref,* 2248
Caird, W. K.: *ref,* 1073
Caldwell, C. W.: *test,* 7:1136
Calia, V. F.: *ref,* 1069, 2195
Callahan, D. M.: *ref,* 2212
Callis, R.: *test,* 7:559; *exc,* 2212-3; *ref,* 2195, 2212
Cameron, A. R.: *ref,* 2212
Cameron, D. F.: *ref,* 2355
Campbell, B. A.: *test,* 2152-4, 2439-46, 2474
Campbell, D.: *ref,* 2197, 2212
Campbell, D. P.: *rev,* 2168-9, 2179, 6:1053, 6:1062, 7:1032; *test,* 2197,

2212–3; *exc,* 2197, 2212; *ref,* 2197, 2212–3

Campbell, D. T.: *ref,* 2452, 2457

Campbell, J.: *ref,* 2457

Campbell, J. F.: *ref,* 2195

Campbell, J. P.: *ref,* 2196

Campbell, J. T.: *ref,* 2140, 2239, 2263, 2448, 6:1062(8)

Campbell, M. G.: *ref,* 2195

Campbell, O. L.: *ref,* 2451

Campbell, R. E.: *ref,* 2195

Campbell, R. K.: *ref,* 2212

Candee, B.: *ref,* 2135, 2227–9

Canfield, A. A.: *ref,* 2195

Canisia, M.: *ref,* 1087

Canning, L.: *ref,* 2212

Canning, L. B.: *ref,* 2212–3

Cannon, D. J.: *ref,* 2195

Cannon, W. M.: *ref,* 2195, 2212

Canter, R. R.: *ref,* 2448

Cantoni, L. J.: *ref,* 2244, 2266

Cantor, G. N.: *ref,* 2227, 2234

Capelle, M. H.: *ref,* 2454

Caplan, S. W.: *ref,* 1082

Capwell, D. F.: *ref,* 2135, 2195

Carbuhn, W. M.: *ref,* 1073

Cardall, A. J.: *test,* 6:1033, 6: 1067, 6:1102, 6:1114; *ref,* 4:784 (1), 6:1067(1–2)

Cardon, B. W.: *ref,* 2197

Carey, J.: *ref,* 2195

Carkhuff, R. R.: *ref,* 2195, 2212

Carleton, F. O.: *ref,* 2340

Carley, J. W.: *ref,* 1074

Carlson, J. S.: *test,* 3:689

Carlson, J. W.: *ref,* 2451

Carlson, R.: *ref,* 2212

Carlson, R. E.: *ref,* 1071, 1073, 2283, 2285

Carlson, S. L.: *ref,* 2195

Carlton, S.: *ref,* 2212

Carman, P. M.: *ref,* 2195

Carmical, L.: *ref,* 1069, 2195

Carmical, L. L.: *ref,* 1069, 2195

Carmichael, V. H.: *test,* 3:367, 4: 457

Carnes, G. D.: *ref,* 2212

Carpenter, E. K.: *ref,* 2135

Carrett, P.: *ref,* 2193

Carrington, D. H.: *ref,* 4:784(3–4)

Carroll, D. L.: *ref,* 2212

Carroll, J. B.: *rev,* 1069, 1072–4, 1087

Carron, T. J.: *ref,* 1078, 2195, 2273, 2454

Carruth, M. S.: *ref,* 2379

Carruthers, J. B.: *ref,* 2135, 2162

Carruthers, T. E.: *ref,* 2221

Carse, D.: *ref,* 2195

Carson, J. O.: *ref,* 2451

Carson, R. C.: *ref,* 2212

Carson, R. L.: *ref,* 2337

Carter, C. E.: *ref,* 2451

Carter, G. C.: *ref,* 2195, 2239, 2448

Carter, H. D.: *rev,* 2192, 2195, 2212, 1:1170, 1:1180, 2:1679, 3: 655; *exc,* 2212–3; *ref,* 2195, 2212–3, 2266

Carter, L.: *ref,* 1087, 2135, 2195, 2239

Cartwright, L. K.: *ref,* 2355

Case, H. W.: *test,* 5:888; *ref,* 2195, 2239, 5:888(1, 3)

Casey, D. L.: *ref,* 2266

Casey, E. W.: *ref,* 2195

Casner, D.: *ref,* 2195

Cass, J. C.: *ref,* 2135, 2195, 2239, 2266

Cassel, R.: *test,* 2414

Cassel, R. H.: *ref,* 1087

Cassel, R. N.: *ref,* 1069, 1073, 2195, 2199, 2205

Casson, A. M.: *ref,* 2212

Castor, M.: *ref,* 2212

Castore, C. H.: *ref,* 2452

Castricone, N. R.: *ref,* 2195

Cattell, R. B.: *test,* 1078; *ref,* 1069, 1087

Cavallo, M.: *ref,* 2377, 2380, 2383

Cawley, A.: *ref,* 2213

Cawley, A. M.: *ref,* 2213

Cawley, J. F.: *ref,* 1087

Ceithaml, J.: *ref,* 2355

Celaschi, D. A.: *ref,* 2452

Celliers, C. P.: *test,* 1064

Center, W. R.: *ref,* 1087

Central Surveys, Inc.: *test,* 6: 1104

Cerf, A. Z.: *ref,* 2195, 2212

Chaffee, G. A.: *ref,* 2212

Chambers, E. G.: *rev,* 2130, 2195, 2248–9, 2269, 3:682, 4:724; *exc,* 1087

Chambers, J. A.: *ref,* 1087

Chambers, J. R.: *ref,* 1087

Chambers, R. M.: *ref,* 2212

Champion, J.: *ref,* 1073

Champion, J. M.: *ref,* 2135, 2195

Chancellor, G. A.: *ref,* 1069

Chandler, R. E.: *ref,* 2239

Chaney, F. B.: *ref,* 2212

Chansky, N. M.: *ref,* 1082, 1087, 2203, 2205

Chaplin, C. L.: *ref,* 2212

Chapman, C. B.: *ref,* 2212

Chapman, C. R.: *ref,* 2212

Chapman, J. E.: *ref,* 2355

Chapman, R. L.: *ref,* 2251

Chappel, S.: *ref,* 2238

Chappell, J. S.: *ref,* 2212

Chartier, G. M.: *ref,* 2212

Chase, C. I.: *ref,* 1069, 1082, 1087, 2349

Chase, J. B.: *ref,* 2195

Chatterji, S.: *test,* 2173; *ref,* 2173, 2195

Chaudhry, G. M.: *ref,* 1069

Cheek, F.: *ref,* 2212

Chen, M. K.: *ref,* 2337

Cheney, T. M.: *ref,* 1069, 1073

Cheong, G. S. C.: *ref,* 1069

Chesler, D. J.: *test,* 2140

Chille, R. A.: *ref,* 2212

Chothia, F. S.: *ref,* 1069, 2266

Christel, R. I.: *ref,* 1068

Christensen, C. M.: *ref,* 2195

Christensen, D.: *ref,* 2212

Christensen, L.: *ref,* 2199

Christensen, P. R.: *ref,* 1074, 2185, 2195

Christensen, T. E.: *ref,* 2195

Christenson, J. M.: *ref,* 2212

Christiansen, H. D.: *ref,* 2197

Christner, C. A.: *ref,* 2452

Chriswell, M. I.: *test,* 2240; *ref,* 2234, 2240

Church, J. J.: *ref,* 1063

Churchill, R. D.: *rev,* 5:615

Ciesla, S. G.: *test,* 2415

Cisney, H. N.: *test,* 3:689; *ref,* 2212–3, 3:689(2)

Clancy, E.: *test,* 2204

Clar, P. N.: *ref,* 2212

Clark, A. B.: *ref,* 2212

Clark, E. T.: *ref,* 2216

Clark, G. R.: *ref,* 2227, 2234

Clark, G. W.: *rev,* 784, 5:518

Clark, J. B.: *ref,* 6:1135(1)

Clark, J. F.: *rev,* 5:880, 5:890

Clark, J. P.: *ref,* 1069

Clark, J. V.: *ref,* 2199

Clark, J. W.: *ref,* 1087

Clark, K. E.: *test,* 2197, 2212; *ref,* 2195, 2197, 2212

Clark, M. L.: *ref,* 2234

Clark, M. P.: *ref,* 1087

Clark, P. J.: *ref,* 1087

Clark, P. N.: *ref,* 2212

Clark, W. W.: *test,* 3:690

Clarke, C. T.: *ref,* 2180

Clarke, F. H.: *ref,* 2135, 2212, 2266

Clarke, R. B.: *ref,* 1069

Clarke, W. V.: *ref,* 1069, 1080

Clarke (Walter V.) Associates, Inc.: *test,* 1080, 2157

Clausen, J.: *ref,* 1087, 2234

Clawson, L. E.: *ref,* 2227, 2234

Claye, C. M.: *ref,* 2451

Cleeton, G. U.: *rev,* 3:645, 3:694; *test,* 2469, 3:635, 3:695; *ref,* 2: 1679(2–3), 3:695(4)

Clegg, H. D.: *ref,* 2239

Cleland, D. L.: *ref,* 1087

Cleland, V.: *ref,* 6:1159(3)

Clem, J. E.: *test,* 2:1480

Clemans, W. V.: *ref,* 2194–5, 2212

Clemens, B.: *ref,* 2212

Clemens, B. T.: *ref,* 2212

Clendenen, D. M.: *rev,* 2213; *test,* 1063

Cline, V. B.: *ref,* 2273

Clinton, R. J.: *test,* 2:1479

Closs, S. J.: *test,* 2168

Clymer, T. W.: *ref,* 1087

Coady, N. P.: *ref,* 2449

Coats, J. E.: *ref,* 2195, 2360

CoBabe, T. A.: *ref,* 2212

Cobb, B. B.: *ref,* 1069

Cobb, K. C.: *ref,* 1073

Coblentz, I.: *ref,* 2212

Cochran, R.: *test,* 2437

Cockriel, I. W.: *ref,* 2213

Cockrum, L. V.: *ref,* 2195

Cofer, C. N.: *ref,* 2212

Coffield, W.: *ref,* 2212

Cohen, D.: *ref,* 2212

Cohen, J.: *ref,* 2212

Cohen, L. M.: *ref,* 2186, 2195

Cohen, R. M.: *ref,* 2239

Cohen, S. A.: *ref,* 1087

Cohen, T. R.: *ref,* 2212

Coisman, F. G.: *ref,* 2355

Cole, N. S.: *rev,* 2355; *ref,* 2101, 2194, 2197, 2212

Coleman, J. C.: *ref,* 1087

Coleman, J. H.: *test,* 2189, 7:1062

Coleman, W.: *ref,* 2239, 2266

College Entrance Examination Board: *test,* 2241, 2324, 2326–9, 2332–3, 2350–3, 4:808–9

Collier, B. N.: *ref,* 1074

Collins, C. C.: *ref,* 2212

Collins, J. A.: *ref,* 2212

Collins, P.: *test,* 2213
Collins, P. J.: *ref,* 2213
Collister, E. G.: *exc,* 2212; *ref,* 2212
Colmen, J. G.: *ref,* 1073
Colten, T.: *ref,* 2355
Combs, H. T.: *ref,* 2212
Comer, J. E.: *ref,* 2195
Commins, W. D.: *rev,* 2135; *ref,* 3:635(12)
Compton, N. H.: *ref,* 2213
Comrey, A. L.: *rev,* 1073, 2286; *ref,* 2195, 2234
Condell, J. F.: *ref,* 1077
Conduff, E.: *ref,* 2103
Congdon, N. A.: *exc,* 2:1682; *ref,* 3:635(1-2)
Congdon, R. G.: *ref,* 2199
Conger, J. J.: *ref,* 2355
Conner, H. T.: *ref,* 2195
Connery, T. F.: *ref,* 1087
Connolly, T. G.: *test,* 2175; *ref,* 2175
Connors, M.: *ref,* 2180
Conry, R.: *ref,* 1087
Cook, D. W.: *ref,* 2227
Cook, E. V.: *ref,* 2451
Cook, F. S.: *ref,* 782
Cook, G. L.: *ref,* 1073
Cook, J. M.: *ref,* 2448
Cook, K. L.: *ref,* 2186
Cook, R. P.: *ref,* 2451
Cooley, D. B.: *ref,* 1069
Cooley, W. W.: *ref,* 1069, 1072-3, 2212
Coomb, W. A.: *ref,* 2195
Coombs, C. H.: *rev,* 3:685; *ref,* 1087
Coons, A. E.: *test,* 2449, 2451-2; *ref,* 2451-2, 2457
Cooper, A. C.: *ref,* 2212
Cooper, C. E.: *ref,* 2212
Cooper, C. L.: *ref,* 2323
Cooper, I. S.: *ref,* 2266
Cooper, J. H.: *ref,* 2135, 2227-9, 2251, 2258, 2266
Cooper, M. N.: *ref,* 2195
Cooperative Tests and Services: *test,* 4:449
Cooprider, H. A.: *ref,* 4:810(2), 4:813(6)
Copeland, H. A.: *test,* 1:937; *ref,* 2135, 2138
Cordrey, L. J.: *ref,* 2212
Corey, D.: *ref,* 2195
Corey, D. Q.: *ref,* 2195
Corey, S. M.: *exc,* 2212-3
Corlett, E. N.: *ref,* 2228, 2230, 2234
Corpus, M. C.: *ref,* 2451
Correnti, R. J.: *ref,* 7:1090(11)
Corter, H. M.: *ref,* 1087
Costa, L. D.: *ref,* 2234
Costello, C. G.: *ref,* 2195
Cotnam, J. D.: *ref,* 2221
Cottingham, H. F.: *ref,* 2195, 2239, 2244, 2257
Cottle, W. C.: *rev,* 5:856; *exc,* 2212; *ref,* 1069, 1074, 2195, 2212
Cottrell, D. A.: *ref,* 2451
Coughlin, G. J.: *ref,* 1069
Coulson, R. W.: *ref,* 2195
Counts, P. D.: *ref,* 2273
Courtis, S. A.: *rev,* 1087
Coutts, R. L.: *ref,* 2195

Cowan, H. E.: *ref,* 786
Cowdery, K. M.: *ref,* 2212
Cowles, J. T.: *ref,* 2355, 4:812(10)
Cox, J. W.: *test,* 2242; *ref,* 2242
Cox, K. J.: *ref,* 2135, 2195
Cox, S. G.: *ref,* 2103, 2105
Coxford, L. M.: *ref,* 1069
Coyle, F. P.: *ref,* 2135
Craft, C. O.: *ref,* 2340
Crambert, A. C.: *ref,* 1073, 2166
Crandall, V. C.: *ref,* 1087
Crane, W. J.: *ref,* 2135, 2195, 2239
Crannell, C. W.: *ref,* 2239
Cranny, C. J.: *ref,* 2212
Crary, H. L.: *ref,* 1087
Craven, E. C.: *ref,* 2195
Cravens, D. W.: *ref,* 2325
Crawford, A. B.: *rev,* 2195, 2:1676; *test,* 5:615; *exc,* 1087; *ref,* 1087, 2212, 2349, 4:718(4), 5:615(8)
Crawford, D.: *test,* 3:658
Crawford, D. M.: *test,* 2223; *ref,* 2223
Crawford, J. E.: *test,* 2223, 3:658; *ref,* 2223, 2251, 2266, 3:658(1-2, 4)
Crawford, J. M.: *ref,* 1073
Crawford, L. E.: *ref,* 2195
Creamer, W.: *ref,* 2186
Crider, B.: *ref,* 2213
Crissey, O. L.: *test,* 2224; *ref,* 2135, 2212-3, 2224, 2229, 2258
Crissy, W. J.: *ref,* 786
Crissy, W. J. E.: *ref,* 2213
Crites, J. O.: *rev,* 2182, 2197; *test,* 2103; *exc,* 1071, 2113, 2289, 2409; *ref,* 1069, 1073, 1087, 2103, 2135, 2195, 2212, 2227-9, 2234, 2239, 2251, 2258, 2260, 2266
Crockett, A. C.: *test,* 1068, 2244
Croft, J. C.: *ref,* 2451
Croft, L. W.: *rev,* 2183, 3:637; *ref,* 2212, 2:1683(3)
Croftchik, V. P.: *ref,* 2212
Croghan, J. H.: *ref,* 2451
Cronbach, L. J.: *ref,* 1069, 1073, 2193, 2195, 2212, 2239, 2334, 5:880(9)
Cronholm, B.: *ref,* 1087
Crook, R.: *ref,* 2451
Cropley, A. J.: *ref,* 1087
Crosby, R. C.: *ref,* 2195
Cross, O. H.: *ref,* 2195
Cross, T. R.: *ref,* 2212
Crouch, M. S.: *ref,* 1069
Crowder, D. G.: *ref,* 2212, 2355
Crowder, N. A.: *test,* 5:610; *ref,* 5:610(2)
Crowell, O.: *ref,* 2195
Crowley, A. D.: *test,* 2176
Cruikshank, R. M.: *ref,* 2227-9, 2239, 2244, 2251, 2258-60, 2266, 3:658(3), 3:660(12), 3:671(10), 3:678(17), 3:679(10)
Crumrine, W. M.: *ref,* 2195
Crutchfield, R. S.: *ref,* 2212
Crutchlow, M. A.: *ref,* 2387
Csikszentmihalyi, M.: *ref,* 1074
Culhane, M. M.: *ref,* 1073
Cull, J. G.: *ref,* 2195
Cullum, F. W.: *ref,* 1073
Cumings, R.: *ref,* 2195
Cummings, I. M.: *ref,* 2195
Cummings, R. W.: *ref,* 2212

Cummins, R. C.: *ref,* 2454
Cuomo, S.: *ref,* 2239, 2266
Cureton, E. E.: *rev,* 2129, 2132; *test,* 1081; *ref,* 1066, 1069, 1072-4, 1078, 1082, 1087
Cureton, L. W.: *rev,* 2140; *test,* 1081
Curran, J. P.: *ref,* 2195
Currie, C.: *ref,* 1073, 2195
Curtis, H. S.: *ref,* 2251
Curtis, J. T.: *ref,* 2212
Curtis, J. W.: *test,* 2126-7, 2177, 2243; *ref,* 2234
Curtis, K. C.: *ref,* 2325
Cutler, T. H.: *ref,* 3:635(4)
Cynamon, M.: *ref,* 4:812(10)

DABAS, Z. S.: *ref,* 5:905(4, 10)
Dabelstein, D. H.: *ref,* 2195
Dahlstrom, W. G.: *ref,* 1087
Dailey, J. T.: *test,* 2105, 2270
Daily, V. L. D.: *ref,* 2323, 7:1078(5)
Daley, R. F.: *ref,* 2212
Dalton, S. L.: *ref,* 2449, 2451
Daly, J. M.: *ref,* 2195, 2214
D'Amico, L. A.: *ref,* 1082
Damm, V. J.: *ref,* 2273
Dane, M. W. A.: *test,* 1:1169
Danenhower, H. S.: *ref,* 1087
Daniel, W. J.: *ref,* 2213
D'Aoust, T.: *ref,* 1069, 2195
Darbes, A.: *ref,* 2251
D'Arcy, P. F.: *ref,* 2195, 2212
Darley, J. G.: *rev,* 2212-3, 1:1171; *exc,* 2212-3; *ref,* 2212-3, 2228-9, 3:642(4)
Darter, C. L.: *ref,* 2195
Das, A. K.: *ref,* 2103
Dauw, D. C.: *ref,* 2194, 2283
Davenport, K. S.: *ref,* 4:799(2)
David, K. H.: *ref,* 2212
Davids, A.: *ref,* 2227
Davidson, C. M.: *ref,* 2135, 2162, 2212
Davidson, K. S.: *ref,* 1087
Davis, A.: *ref,* 1087
Davis, C. E.: *ref,* 2212
Davis, E. W.: *rev,* 3:634
Davis, G. A.: *ref,* 2273
Davis, J. R.: *ref,* 2355
Davis, L. J.: *ref,* 2228, 2234
Davis, M. R.: *ref,* 1087
Davis, R. A.: *ref,* 798
Davis, S. E.: *ref,* 2212
Davis, S. P.: *ref,* 2190
Davis, S. S.: *ref,* 2195
Davis, W. A.: *ref,* 1087
Davis, W. E.: *ref,* 3:678(14)
Dawis, R. V.: *test,* 2283-5; *ref,* 1071, 1073, 2197, 2212, 2283-5
Dawson, J. L. M.: *ref,* 2266
Day, D. R.: *ref,* 2451-2, 2457
Day, J. F.: *ref,* 2195
Day, M. E.: *ref,* 2195
Dayal, P.: *ref,* 1069
Dayley, A. J.: *ref,* 2212
D'Costa, A.: *ref,* 2201
D'Costa, A. G.: *test,* 2201
D'Costa, A. G. J. E.: *ref,* 2201
Deabler, H. L.: *ref,* 1073, 2212
Dean, D. A.: *ref,* 1087
Dean, J. W.: *ref,* 2212
Deb, M.: *ref,* 2212

DeCencio, D. V.: *ref,* 2186, 2212
Decker, C. E.: *ref,* 2212
Decker, R. L.: *ref,* 2239, 2448
Dee, H. L.: *ref,* 2266
Deemer, W. L.: *test,* 3:372, 7:987
DeGideo, J.: *ref,* 2212
de Heus, J. H.: *ref,* 2244
Dejmek, F. W.: *ref,* 2266
Dekker, J. H.: *ref,* 2212
Delancy, E. O.: *ref,* 1087
Delaney, J. J.: *ref,* 2454
DeLisle, F. H.: *ref,* 2195
Delman, F.: *ref,* 1087
Demaree, R. G.: *ref,* 2349
De Martino, A. J.: *ref,* 1069
de Mille, R.: *ref,* 1074
Demos, G. D.: *test,* 2170-1, 7:1033
Dendaluce, I.: *ref,* 2221
Denenberg, V. H.: *ref,* 2212
Denison, W. M.: *ref,* 2212
Dennis, J. M.: *ref,* 2454, 2457
Dennis, R. A.: *ref,* 7:1090(6)
Densley, K. G.: *ref,* 1073
Dent, O. B.: *ref,* 2195
Denton, J. C.: *test,* 2102; *ref,* 2102
Denton, M. J.: *ref,* 2195
DeRevere, R. E.: *ref,* 2337
Derrick, M. W.: *ref,* 1087
Desbiens, B.: *ref,* 2212
DeSena, P. A.: *ref,* 2212
Deskin, G.: *ref,* 2234
Desmond, R. E.: *ref,* 1073
Detchen, L.: *ref,* 2195
Deutsch, M. R.: *ref,* 2227
Deutsch, S.: *ref,* 2212
Deutscher, J. C.: *ref,* 2212
Devadasan, K.: *ref,* 2229
Devlin, J. P.: *ref,* 1087
DeWitt, C. J.: *ref,* 2406, 2408
DeWitt, K. N.: *ref,* 2195
DeWolfe, A. S.: *ref,* 2213
Dharmangadan, B.: *ref,* 2266
Diamond, E. E.: *ref,* 2194
Diamond, S.: *ref,* 2195
Di Bona, L. J.: *ref,* 798
Dick, W.: *ref,* 2212, 2214
Dick, W. W.: *ref,* 2212
Dicken, C. F.: *ref,* 2129, 2135, 2212, 2239, 2448
Dickson, G. S.: *rev,* 2213, 3:642
Diebold (John) & Associates: *test,* 2335
Diekema, A. J.: *ref,* 2355
Dielman, T. E.: *ref,* 1087
Diener, C. L.: *ref,* 2195
DiGiorgio, A. J.: *ref,* 2212
DiMichael, S. G.: *ref,* 2195
Dingman, H. F.: *ref,* 1087, 2234
Dirr, P. M.: *ref,* 1069
Distefano, M. K.: *ref,* 2227, 2349, 2452
DiVesta, F. J.: *ref,* 2448
Dixon, A. S.: *ref,* 1069
Dixon, D. H.: *ref,* 2187
Dodd, W. E.: *ref,* 2212
Dodge, A. F.: *ref,* 2135
Doerr, J. J.: *ref,* 2105, 2197
Dohner, C. W.: *ref,* 2355
Dole, A. A.: *test,* 6:1073; *ref,* 1069, 6:1073(1, 3-4)
Doleys, E. J.: *ref,* 2195
Dolliver, R. H.: *rev,* 2194, 2200; *ref,* 2212

Domenichetti, M.: *ref,* 2103
Domino, G.: *ref,* 2212
Donahue, M. A.: *ref,* 2103, 2221
Donald, M. W.: *ref,* 1087
Donnenwerth, G.: *ref,* 2213
Donnenwerth, G. V.: *ref,* 2195, 2212-3
Doppelt, J. E.: *rev,* 2189, 2275, 2325, 2454, 4:812; *test,* 1063, 2164, 2290, 2317; *ref,* 1069, 2151, 2212, 2349, 2355, 5:954(1)
Dore, R. L.: *ref,* 2212
Dorris, C. W.: *ref,* 2195
Dosaijh, N. L.: *ref,* 1069
Doub, B. A.: *ref,* 2132
Doughty, P.: *ref,* 2118
Douglas, B. L.: *ref,* 2337
Douglass, H. R.: *test,* 1:1168; *ref,* 2228, 2381
Dow, J.: *ref,* 2452
Downey, R. D.: *ref,* 2451
Downie, N. M.: *exc,* 2315; *ref,* 2195
Drahozal, E. C.: *ref,* 2103, 2221
Drake, J. D.: *ref,* 1087, 2212
Drasgow, J.: *ref,* 2195, 2212
Dreffin, W. B.: *ref,* 2212-3, 2266
Dreger, R. M.: *ref,* 1069
Dreher, R. G.: *ref,* 2195
Dreiling, T. C.: *ref,* 1073
Dressel, P.: *ref,* 2199
Dressel, P. L.: *ref,* 1069, 2195
Dressler, R. M.: *ref,* 2186, 2283
Drevdahl, J. E.: *ref,* 1087
Drew, A. S.: *ref,* 2195, 2239, 2263
Drewes, D. W.: *ref,* 2227
Drewes, H. W.: *ref,* 1074
Driscoll, A. M.: *ref,* 1087
Driscoll, J.: *ref,* 2195
Droege, R. C.: *rev,* 2107; *ref,* 1073, 1086
Dropkin, S.: *ref,* 2451
Drucker, A. J.: *ref,* 4:798(4)
Drum, D. J.: *ref,* 2194
Drussell, R. D.: *ref,* 2227
Dube, W. F.: *ref,* 2355
Dubin, J. A.: *ref,* 1071
Dubin, W.: *ref,* 2212
Dublin, J. E.: *ref,* 2212
DuBois, P. H.: *rev,* 794, 798, 2355, 3:372; *ref,* 2212, 2239, 2266
Dubrow, M.: *ref,* 2212
Duda, W. B.: *ref,* 2212
Dudycha, G. J.: *ref,* 2135
Duffy, E.: *ref,* 2213
Dugan, R. D.: *ref,* 2401, 2406, 7:1090(5)
Dulsky, S. G.: *rev,* 2199, 2:1666, 3:639, 3:644; *ref,* 2195, 4:784(5)
Dunford, R. E.: *test,* 2:1644; *ref,* 2:1644(1)
Dungan, R. H.: *ref,* 1063
Dunham, P. R.: *ref,* 2195
Dunham, R. E.: *ref,* 1087, 2135, 2234, 2239, 2266
Dunkleberger, C. J.: *ref,* 2212
Dunlap, J. W.: *rev,* 2:1675; *ref,* 2195, 2212-3
Dunn, D. C.: *ref,* 2212
Dunn, F. E.: *ref,* 2199
Dunn, R. E.: *ref,* 2448
Dunn, S.: *test,* 793
Dunn, S. S.: *rev,* 1082

Dunnette, M. D.: *rev,* 2106; *test,* 2344; *ref,* 1069, 1078, 2151, 2212, 2340, 2344, 2448
Dunteman, G. H.: *ref,* 2212-4
Duran, J. C.: *ref,* 2251
Durflinger, G. W.: *ref,* 1066, 2212-3
Durkin, D.: *ref,* 1087
Durling, D.: *ref,* 1087
Durnall, E. J.: *ref,* 2195
Durost, W. N.: *test,* 3:392
Durrett, H. L.: *ref,* 2239
Dustan, L. C.: *ref,* 2195
du Toit, J. P.: *test,* 1065
Dutt, K. F.: *ref,* 1069, 1073
Dutta, A.: *ref,* 2173
Duvlick, J.: *ref,* 2113
Dvorak, B.: *ref,* 2242
Dvorak, B. J.: *rev,* 799, 3:389; *ref,* 1073, 1086, 2135, 2227-9, 2251, 2258, 2266
Dworkin, S. F.: *ref,* 1069, 2337
Dwyer, P. S.: *ref,* 2212
Dyer, D. T.: *ref,* 2212
Dyer, H. S.: *rev,* 2189; *test,* 2:1485
Dykman, R. A.: *ref,* 2355

EADDY, M. L.: *ref,* 2212
Earle, F. M.: *test,* 4:713; *exc,* 2242; *ref,* 4:713(1-2)
Eastern Commercial Teachers' Association: *ref,* 786
Eastes, S. H.: *ref,* 2212
Eastman, F.: *ref,* 2199
Easton, J. C.: *ref,* 2214
Ebel, R. L.: *rev,* 2355
Ebert, E.: *ref,* 2266, 3:660(15)
Echeverria, B. P.: *ref,* 1069, 1073, 2195
Eddins, E. L.: *ref,* 2186
Eddy, B.: *ref,* 2212
Eddy, R. T.: *ref,* 2212
Edens, L. W.: *ref,* 2195
Edgerton, H. A.: *ref,* 1087
Edington, E. D.: *ref,* 1069, 1073, 2135
Edmiston, R. W.: *test,* 4:738; *ref,* 4:738(1)
Edmonson, L. D.: *ref,* 2135, 2195, 2229, 2251, 2266
Educational Records Bureau: *ref,* 2212
Educational Testing Service: *test,* 787, 797, 800, 2325, 2343, 2348-9, 4:812
Edwards, K. D.: *ref,* 2266
Eells, K.: *ref,* 1069, 1087
Eells, W. C.: *ref,* 2251
Eggert, W. A.: *test,* 2150
Eichsteadt, A. C.: *ref,* 2212
Eide, L. J.: *ref,* 2212
Eidle, W. R.: *ref,* 2234
Eimicke, V. W.: *ref,* 2195
Eisen, I.: *ref,* 1073
Ekblad, R. L.: *ref,* 2212
El-Abd, H. A.: *ref,* 2245
Elberfeld, S.: *ref,* 2195
Eldeen, M. H.: *ref,* 2235
Elder, D.: *ref,* 2195, 2212
Elder, G. H.: *ref,* 2212
Elder, R. F.: *ref,* 2195
Elias, J. Z.: *ref,* 1087

Elkin, L.: *ref,* 2223, 2225, 2228, 2234
Elliott, D. N.: *ref,* 4:800(2-4)
Elliott, E. S.: *ref,* 2212
Elliott, M. H.: *rev,* 3:689
Elliott, R. M.: *test,* 2258, 2266, 3:671; *ref,* 2228-9, 2258, 2266, 3:671(3), 3:678(5), 3:679(3)
Ellis, B. W.: *exc,* 2105
Ellis, D. S.: *ref,* 2227
Ellis, N. R.: *ref,* 2227
Ellison, G. D.: *ref,* 2227-8, 2234
Ellison, M. L.: *ref,* 1087
Ellison, R. L.: *ref,* 2273
Elo, M. R.: *ref,* 2283, 2285
El-Sharkawy, M. K. L.: *ref,* 1070
Elster, R. S.: *ref,* 2283, 2285
Elton, C. F.: *ref,* 1069, 2212
Elzey, F. F.: *test,* 2315; *ref,* 2315
Embree, R. B.: *ref,* 1069
Emerson, M. R.: *ref,* 2251
Emm, M. E.: *ref,* 1087
Emmett, W. C.: *ref,* 6:1090(1)
Endey, M. W.: *ref,* 2337
Endler, O. L.: *ref,* 2135, 2227-9, 2251, 2258, 2266
Engel, I. M.: *ref,* 2212
Engelhardt, O. E. de C.: *ref,* 2135
Engen, H. B.: *ref,* 2167, 2212
England, G. W.: *test,* 2285; *ref,* 1073, 2212, 2283, 2285
Engram, W. C.: *ref,* 2195
Enneis, W. H.: *ref,* 1073
Enright, J. B.: *ref,* 2212
Enslein, K.: *ref,* 2212
Entwisle, F. N.: *ref,* 2195, 2266
Epstein, B.: *rev,* 4:449
Erdmann, J. B.: *ref,* 2355
Erickson, C.: *ref,* 2212, 2340
Erickson, I. P.: *ref,* 2135, 2266
Erickson, L. W.: *rev,* 789, 792, 799, 7:559A
Erickson, P.: *ref,* 2212
Erlandson, F. L.: *ref,* 2195, 2212
Ertl, J. P.: *ref,* 1087
Escalona, S. K.: *ref,* 2212
Esen, F. M.: *ref,* 1087
Espenschade, A.: *ref,* 2213
Estabrooks, G. H.: *ref,* 2212
Estenson, L. O.: *ref,* 2212
Estes, S. G.: *ref,* 2212, 2259, 2266, 3:658(5)
Evans, A. S.: *test,* 2390
Evans, C. E.: *ref,* 2195, 2212
Evans, F. R.: *ref,* 2349
Evans, L. R.: *ref,* 2355
Evans, M. C.: *ref,* 2195
Evans, M. G.: *ref,* 2451
Evans, R. K.: *ref,* 2355
Evans, R. N.: *ref,* 2195, 2263, 2448, 4:799(3-4)
Ewald, A. T.: *ref,* 2266
Ewald, H. H.: *ref,* 1069
Ewen, R. B.: *ref,* 1069, 2151, 2387
Ewens, W. P.: *ref,* 2195
Ewing, T. N.: *ref,* 2239
Eyde, L. D.: *ref,* 2212
Eyman, R. K.: *ref,* 2234
Eysenck, H. J.: *exc,* 1087

FAGIN, H. T.: *test,* 2189, 7:1062
Fagin, W. B.: *ref,* 2212
Fahrig, M. W.: *ref,* 2381
Fair, D. C.: *ref,* 2212

Falck, F. E.: *ref,* 2212
Fangman, E. G.: *ref,* 1069, 2195
Farber, N.: *ref,* 2234
Farber, R. H.: *ref,* 2195
Farbro, P. C.: *ref,* 2448
Fargo, R.: *ref,* 2212
Farmer, H. S.: *ref,* 2213
Farmer, T. A.: *ref,* 2355
Farnsworth, K. E.: *ref,* 2213
Farnsworth, P. R.: *ref,* 2212-3
Farrant, R. H.: *ref,* 1087
Farrell, M. L.: *ref,* 1087
Farrow, E. G.: *ref,* 2195
Fassett, K. K.: *ref,* 2212
Fast, I.: *ref,* 2212
Faterson, H. F.: *ref,* 2355
Fattu, N. A.: *ref,* 2195
Fatzinger, F. A.: *ref,* 1073
Faubion, R.: *ref,* 1087, 2251
Fauble, M. L.: *ref,* 2195
Faunce, P. S.: *ref,* 2212-3
Fauquier, W.: *ref,* 2199
Fear, R. A.: *test,* 2298; *ref,* 2225, 2239
Feather, D. B.: *ref,* 2195
Feder, D. D.: *ref,* 2195, 2212
Feeley, A. L.: *ref,* 2451
Feeney, B. J.: *ref,* 2349, 4:814(5)
Fehrer, E.: *rev,* 785, 795; *ref,* 2212
Feil, M. H.: *ref,* 2212
Fein, A.: *ref,* 2212
Feinberg, M. R.: *ref,* 2195
Feingold, W.: *ref,* 1073
Feist, J.: *ref,* 2212
Feitler, F. C.: *ref,* 2452
Feldhusen, J.: *ref,* 2378
Feldhusen, J. F.: *test,* 2378, 2382, 2389; *ref,* 2378, 2382, 2387, 2389
Ference, C.: *ref,* 2201, 2212
Ference, L. W.: *ref,* 2337
Ferguson, G. A.: *rev,* 3:645, 3:690, 4:735
Ferguson, L. R.: *ref,* 1087
Ferguson, L. W.: *rev,* 2102, 2151; *ref,* 2212, 2396, 4:825(19), 6:1168(21)
Ferguson, R. H.: *ref,* 2387
Fernald, L. D.: *ref,* 2234
Fernald, P. S.: *ref,* 2234
Fernandez-Pabon, J. J.: *ref,* 2337
Ferson, R. F.: *ref,* 2199, 2239, 2266-7
Fiedler, E. R.: *ref,* 1087
Fiedler, G. O.: *ref,* 1073
Field, L. W.: *ref,* 2212
Fielder, D. W.: *ref,* 2212
Fiesenheiser, E. I.: *test,* 2416
Fife, I. E.: *ref,* 2135, 2231, 2251
Filbeck, R. W.: *ref,* 2212
File, Q. W.: *test,* 2448; *ref,* 2448
Filella, J. F.: *ref,* 1069
Filley, A. C.: *ref,* 2451
Finch, C. R.: *ref,* 1073, 2239, 2266
Finch, F. H.: *ref,* 2212
Finco, A. A.: *ref,* 2195
Fine, S. A.: *ref,* 1073
Finegan, A. L.: *ref,* 2195
Fink, D. D.: *ref,* 1069
Finley, P. J.: *ref,* 1087, 2195, 2227, 2258
Finn, P. A.: *test,* 2382; *ref,* 2382
Firkins, C. J.: *ref,* 2195
Fish, D. G.: *ref,* 2355
Fisher, E. J.: *ref,* 2212

Fisher, L. A.: *ref,* 2355
Fisher, S.: *ref,* 2212, 2214
Fisher, S. T.: *ref,* 2283
Fishman, R.: *ref,* 2337
Fiske, D. W.: *ref,* 1087, 2195, 2212, 2239
Fiss, C. B.: *ref,* 2381
Fitz, R. H.: *ref,* 2355
Fitzpatrick, E. D.: *ref,* 2151, 2195, 2223, 2239
Fitzpatrick, R.: *rev,* 2121
Fitzpatrick, T. F.: *test,* 5:857; *ref,* 5:857(1-2)
Fivars, G.: *test,* 796; *ref,* 796
Flanagan, J.: *ref,* 1073
Flanagan, J. C.: *test,* 796, 1072, 2107, 5:902; *exc,* 2212, 1:1170; *ref,* 796, 1072, 5:902(1)
Flax, M. L.: *ref,* 2185
Fleet, D.: *ref,* 2135
Fleigler, L.: *ref,* 2214
Fleishman, E. A.: *test,* 2454; *ref,* 2227-8, 2234, 2451, 2454, 2457
Fleming, C. M.: *exc,* 4:792
Fleming, S. V.: *ref,* 1073
Fleming, W. G.: *ref,* 2195
Flemming, C. W.: *test,* 4:830; *ref,* 2212
Flemming, E. G.: *test,* 4:826, 4:830; *ref,* 2212
Fletcher, F. M.: *ref,* 2239, 6:1073(3)
Flinner, I. A.: *ref,* 2212
Flint, R. T.: *ref,* 2213
Flitter, H.: *ref,* 2383
Flocco, E. C.: *ref,* 2451
Flom, P. K.: *ref,* 2212, 2355
Floor, L.: *ref,* 2227, 2234
Florestano, T. E.: *ref,* 2454
Flowers, H. M.: *ref,* 2194
Flowers, J. F.: *ref,* 2355
Floyd, W. A.: *ref,* 1073
Flye, L. M.: *ref,* 1069, 2195
Fogarty, B. M.: *ref,* 2451
Foley, A. W.: *ref,* 2195
Foley, G. F.: *ref,* 2452
Foley, J.: *ref,* 2259
Foley, J. P.: *rev,* 2285, 2302, 2404
Foley, W. J.: *ref,* 2337
Foote, R. P.: *ref,* 1069, 2195, 2256, 2267
Force, R. C.: *ref,* 2195
Ford, A. B.: *ref,* 2195
Ford, A. H.: *ref,* 1087, 2195, 2381
Ford, G. C.: *ref,* 786
Ford, J. S.: *test,* 1071
Forehand, G. A.: *ref,* 2239
Foreman, M. E.: *ref,* 2195, 2212
Forer, B. R.: *ref,* 2195, 2212
Formica, L. A.: *ref,* 2212
Forness, S. R.: *ref,* 2195
Forrest, D. V.: *ref,* 2212
Forrest, G. M.: *ref,* 2195
Forster, C. R.: *ref,* 2135, 2195, 2239
Forster, M. C.: *ref,* 2212
Fosselius, E. E.: *ref,* 2195
Fosshage, J. L.: *ref,* 2212
Foster, J. A.: *ref,* 2212
Foster, K. E.: *ref,* 2184
Foster, P. B.: *ref,* 2325
Fouché, F. A.: *test,* 1088, 2198
Foulds, G. A.: *ref,* 2248
Fowler, H. M.: *rev,* 2195; *test,* 6:1053; *ref,* 6:1053(1-2)

Fox, D. G.: *ref,* 2273
Fox, F. C.: *ref,* 1073
Fox, J.: *test,* 2175
Fox, W. H.: *ref,* 2195
Foy, G. A.: *ref,* 1071
Fozard, J. L.: *ref,* 1073
France-Kelly, K. A.: *ref,* 2213
Francesco, E.: *ref,* 1074
Frandsen, A.: *ref,* 2195, 2212
Frandsen, A. N.: *ref,* 1069, 2195, 3:671(5)
Frank, A. C.: *ref,* 2212-3, 2266
Frank, H.: *ref,* 1087
Frankel, E.: *ref,* 1069, 2195
Frantz, T. T.: *rev,* 2201, 2210
Frary, R. B.: *ref,* 1069, 2349
Frederick, M. L.: *ref,* 2212, 2323
Fredericks, M. A.: *ref,* 2337, 2355
Frederiksen, N.: *rev,* 1069, 1072, 1087, 2214, 3:641, 3:698; *ref,* 2212
Freeberg, N. E.: *ref,* 2170, 2231, 2234
Freeburn, P. P.: *ref,* 2212
Freedman, M. H.: *ref,* 2349
Freedman, S.: *ref,* 2199, 2234
Freehill, M. F.: *ref,* 2195
Freeman, F. S.: *rev,* 4:794; *ref,* 2195, 2212
Freeman, J. A.: *ref,* 1087
French, J. L.: *ref,* 2195, 2197
French, J. W.: *rev,* 2170, 2174, 2192, 2286, 2392, 3:701, 4:810, 6:1053; *test,* 7:674; *exc,* 2221; *ref,* 2214, 2241, 2266, 7:674(1-3)
French, T. M.: *exc,* 1087
Fresco, R.: *ref,* 2212
Freyberg, P. S.: *ref,* 1087
Frick, J. W.: *ref,* 1074
Fricke, B. G.: *ref,* 2195, 2349
Friedersdorf, N. W.: *ref,* 2213
Friedl, F. P.: *ref,* 2212
Friedman, S.: *ref,* 2337
Friesen, D.: *ref,* 1069
Friesen, E. P.: *ref,* 2275, 2406
Frinsko, W.: *ref,* 2195, 2212
Frisby, C. B.: *ref,* 2247-8, 2254, 2345
Fritz, K. V.: *ref,* 2267
Fritz, M. F.: *ref,* 2267
Froehlich, C. P.: *rev,* 1066, 1073, 2195, 4:798; *ref,* 1069, 2195, 3:655(3)
Froemel, E. C.: *ref,* 2110, 2340
Fruchter, B.: *rev,* 1082, 5:610; *ref,* 1069, 1087
Frye, E. K.: *ref,* 2259, 3:679(9)
Frye, R. L.: *ref,* 1069
Frye, U. C.: *ref,* 1087
Fryer, D.: *rev,* 3:685, 3:691; *ref,* 2:1675(4), 3:642(1)
Fryer, D. H.: *rev,* 2298
Fryett, H. L.: *ref,* 1069
Fuchs, A. F.: *ref,* 1067
Fulkerson, S. C.: *ref,* 1069
Full, C. A.: *ref,* 2337
Fuller, F. D.: *ref,* 2251, 2266
Fullerton, J. R.: *ref,* 2212
Fultineer, J. D.: *ref,* 2452
Funkenstein, D. H.: *ref,* 2212, 2355
Funks, L. K.: *test,* 4:814
Furcon, J.: *ref,* 2340
Furcon, J. E.: *ref,* 2110, 2340

Furst, E. J.: *rev,* 2212, 7:1033; *ref,* 2195
Furuno, S.: *rev,* 1087

GAAL, D. A.: *ref,* 2452, 2457
Gable, R. K.: *ref,* 2195, 2221
Gadel, M. S.: *ref,* 2195
Gage, N. L.: *ref,* 2195
Gagni, A. O.: *ref,* 1073
Gahlhoff, P. E.: *ref,* 2212
Gaither, J. W.: *test,* 2186; *ref,* 2186
Gale, D. F.: *ref,* 1087
Galinsky, M. D.: *ref,* 2212
Gallagher, R. E.: *ref,* 2355
Gamble, A. O.: *exc,* 2212
Gantz, B. S.: *ref,* 2212, 2340
Garber, J. R.: *ref,* 1082, 2195
Gardner, E. F.: *test,* 7:559
Gardner, P. L.: *ref,* 2212
Gardner, R. C.: *ref,* 1087
Gareis, F. E.: *ref,* 2212
Garfield, S. L.: *ref,* 2355
Garland, K. E.: *ref,* 1069
Garman, G. D.: *ref,* 2212
Garman, L. W.: *test,* 2140
Garner, G. L.: *ref,* 781, 1069
Garner, R. G.: *test,* 2360; *ref,* 2195, 2360
Garner, W. K.: *ref,* 2451
Garretson, O. K.: *test,* 3:637; *ref,* 2251, 2266, 3:637(1, 3)
Garrett, G. A.: *ref,* 2195, 2212
Garrett, H. E.: *rev,* 1087; *exc,* 1087, 2242; *ref,* 2266
Garrett, J. B.: *ref,* 2212
Garrett, W. S.: *ref,* 2135, 2251, 2381
Garrison, J. M.: *ref,* 2452
Garrison, K. C.: *ref,* 2244
Garrison, M.: *ref,* 1087
Garrison, M. L.: *ref,* 2212
Garry, R.: *ref,* 2212
Garry, R. J.: *ref,* 2212
Gash, I. A.: *ref,* 2186, 2195, 2212
Gaubinger, J. R.: *ref,* 2212, 2221
Gavurin, E.: *ref,* 1073
Gavurin, E. I.: *ref,* 1069, 2266
Gay, E. G.: *test,* 2283; *ref,* 2283
Gay, R. A.: *ref,* 1073, 7:1090(7)
Gee, H. H.: *ref,* 2197, 2212, 2355
Geertsma, R. H.: *ref,* 2355
Gehlhausen, P. E.: *ref,* 2212
Gehlmann, F.: *ref,* 2212
Gehman, W. S.: *ref,* 2195, 2212
Geiger, J.: *ref,* 2355
Geist, H.: *test,* 2180-1; *exc,* 2180; *ref,* 2180-1, 2227, 2231, 2234, 2258
Gekoski, N.: *test,* 2409, 2459; *ref,* 2459
Gelatt, H. B.: *ref,* 1069
Gelink, M.: *test,* 2151; *ref,* 2151
Gengerelli, J. A.: *ref,* 2195
Gentry, C. G.: *test,* 3:655; *ref,* 3:655(1)
Georgas, J. G.: *ref,* 2135
George, C. E.: *ref,* 2195, 2199
George, E. I.: *ref,* 2229, 2266
George, N.: *ref,* 2452, 2457
George, R.: *test,* 2413
Gerber, V. R.: *ref,* 1073
Gericke, F. W.: *test,* 1065

Gerken, C. d'A.: *test,* 3:689
Gerlach, V. S.: *ref,* 2340
Gernes, E.: *ref,* 2213
Gershon, A.: *ref,* 1071
Gerstein, A. I.: *ref,* 2213
Gerstein, O. B.: *ref,* 2212
Gerum, E.: *ref,* 2212
Getzels, J. W.: *ref,* 1074, 2195
Gewirtz, H.: *ref,* 2212
Ghei, S.: *ref,* 2197
Ghiselli, E. E.: *rev,* 2227, 2231, 2234; *ref,* 2135, 2212, 2227-8, 2251, 2258, 2266
Ghosh, S. N.: *ref,* 2231
Gibb, C. A.: *rev,* 2453-4
Giblette, J. F.: *ref,* 2195
Gibney, E. F.: *ref,* 1087
Gibson, A. M.: *ref,* 1073
Giese, W. J.: *ref,* 2129, 2259, 5:513(2)
Gieseke, M.: *ref,* 1084
Giesz, W. G.: *ref,* 2212
Gikas, A. M.: *ref,* 6:1075(1)
Gilberg, R. L.: *ref,* 2199, 2212
Gilberstadt, H.: *ref,* 2234
Gilbert, A. C. F.: *ref,* 2212
Gilbert, H. B.: *ref,* 2239
Gilbert, J.: *ref,* 2195
Gilbert, J. A. L.: *ref,* 2355
Gilbert, M. D.: *test,* 4:450
Gilbert, W. M.: *ref,* 2239
Giles, G. C.: *ref,* 1069
Gilger, G. A.: *ref,* 3:635(5)
Gilkinson, H.: *ref,* 2212-3
Gillam, E. S.: *ref,* 1069
Gillespie, J. O.: *ref,* 2451
Gillett, A. N.: *test,* 2300
Ginley, T. J.: *ref,* 2337
Githens, W. H.: *ref,* 2212
Gitlin, S.: *ref,* 2185, 2195
Givens, P. R.: *ref,* 2195
Gjernes, O.: *ref,* 1073
Gladstone, R.: *ref,* 6:1102(7)
Glaser, R.: *ref,* 1069, 2199, 2268, 2355
Glaser, R. J.: *ref,* 2355
Glasgow, A. D.: *ref,* 2451
Glass, C. F.: *ref,* 2212
Glazer, S. H.: *ref,* 2195
Glennon, J. R.: *ref,* 2239, 2266, 2392, 2406, 2448, 6:1140(2)
Glick, R.: *ref,* 2213
Glick, W. P.: *ref,* 2212
Glogau, L. F.: *ref,* 2451, 2457
Glosser, E. A.: *ref,* 2213
Glotzbach, C. J.: *ref,* 2213
Gluskinos, U.: *ref,* 2228
Gluskinos, U. M.: *ref,* 2340, 2347
Gobetz, W.: *ref,* 2195
Goble, R. L.: *ref,* 1073
Goche, L. N.: *ref,* 2195
Godec, F.: *ref,* 7:1062(4)
Godin, M. A.: *ref,* 1087
Golburgh, S. J.: *ref,* 2195
Gold, J. A.: *ref,* 2212
Goldberg, L. R.: *ref,* 1087, 2212
Golden, J. F.: *ref,* 1073, 2195
Golden, M. C.: *ref,* 2213
Goldman, B. A.: *ref,* 2194
Goldman, L.: *rev,* 6:781, 6:1075; *ref,* 1069
Goldman, R. C.: *ref,* 1073
Goldman, S.: *ref,* 2151
Goldschmid, M. L.: *ref,* 2212

Goldstein, A. P.: *ref*, 2195, 2216
Goldwhite, M.: *ref*, 2113
Golie, B. N.: *ref*, 2285
Golisch, J. E. W.: *ref*, 2212
Good, C. G.: *ref*, 2452
Goode, O. S.: *ref*, 2451-2, 2457
Goodenough, F. L.: *rev*, 1087
Goodfellow, L. D.: *ref*, 2212
Goodfellow, R. C.: *test*, 2:1488
Goodish, N.: *ref*, 1069
Goodling, R. A.: *ref*, 2212
Goodman, C. H.: *ref*, 1087, 2195.
  2251, 3:635(7)
Goodman, C. M.: *ref*, 1087
Goodman, J. O.: *ref*, 1087
Goodman, P.: *ref*, 2340
Goodner, S.: *ref*, 2212, 2239, 2273
Goodrich, J. R.: *ref*, 2259
Goodstein, L. D.: *ref*, 2212
Goolsby, T. M.: *ref*, 1069, 2349
Goppert, H. R.: *test*, 7:1136
Gordon, B. F.: *ref*, 7:1090(6)
Gordon, B. J. A.: *ref*, 2195, 2212
Gordon, B. K.: *ref*, 2451
Gordon, H. C.: *ref*, 2195, 2212,
  3:635(6, 8), 3:637(6), 3:653(8,
  11), 3:655(2, 4)
Gordon, J. H.: *ref*, 2212
Gordon, L. V.: *rev*, 2111-2, 2412;
  test, 2182
Gordon, O. J.: *ref*, 1073
Gordon, P.: *test*, 1:1168
Gordon, T.: *ref*, 2239
Gorelick, J.: *ref*, 2234
Gorham, W. A.: *ref*, 2454
Gorman, J. R.: *ref*, 2195
Gorman, W. E.: *ref*, 2195
Gorseline, D. E.: *exc*, 3:639
Gory, A. E.: *ref*, 2212
Goshorn, W. M.: *ref*, 2195
Gosney, C. A.: *ref*, 2212
Goss, A.: *ref*, 2221
Goss, A. M.: *ref*, 2195, 2221
Goswitz, C. R.: *ref*, 2212
Gotsman, E.: *ref*, 6:1026(1)
Gott, C. M.: *ref*, 2449, 2451
Gotterer, M.: *ref*, 2212
Gough, H. G.: *ref*, 2337, 2355
Gowan, J. C.: *ref*, 2195
Grace, E. R.: *ref*, 2212
Graen, G. B.: *ref*, 2283, 2285
Graff, F.: *test*, 6:1051
Graff, F. A.: *ref*, 2212
Graham, H. B.: *test*, 1066
Graham, J.: *exc*, 2:1477, 2:1480-1,
  2:1489
Graham, L. F.: *ref*, 2266
Graham, W. R.: *ref*, 2135
Grant, B.: *test*, 2170-1, 7:1033
Grant, D. L.: *ref*, 1069, 2195, 2223,
  2239
Grant, G. V.: *test*, 1073
Grant, J. N.: *ref*, 2212
Grant, W. V.: *ref*, 1073
Grater, H.: *ref*, 2212
Graves, G. O.: *ref*, 2355
Gray, B.: *ref*, 1069
Gray, B. G.: *ref*, 2195
Gray, B. L.: *ref*, 2285
Gray, C. W.: *ref*, 2212
Gray, E. J.: *ref*, 2395
Green, H. B.: *ref*, 2212
Green, H. J.: *ref*, 2135, 2212,
  2227-9, 2258

Green, M. C.: *ref*, 2259
Green, P. C.: *ref*, 2451
Green, R. F.: *ref*, 2195
Green, S.: *ref*, 2212
Greenberg, E. S.: *ref*, 2213
Greenburg, H.: *ref*, 2234
Greene, E. B.: *rev*, 795, 1073,
  2275, 2456, 3:635, 5:518; *test*,
  1:1171; *exc*, 2212-3, 2242; *ref*,
  2258
Greene, J. E.: *ref*, 2195, 2212
Greene, R. R.: *ref*, 2239
Greenfield, T. B.: *ref*, 2451-2
Greenly, R. J.: *ref*, 2228
Greenwald, A. F.: *ref*, 2212
Greenwood, J. M.: *ref*, 2454
Greenwood, K. B.: *ref*, 2213
Gregg, G. W.: *ref*, 4:810(6)
Gregorio, L. J.: *ref*, 2212
Gregory, W. S.: *test*, 2183; *ref*,
  2183
Grenfell, J. E.: *ref*, 2212
Gresham, M.: *ref*, 2212
Griess, J. A.: *ref*, 1073
Griffin, C. H.: *test*, 4:810; *ref*,
  4:810(1)
Griffin, J. J.: *ref*, 2212
Griffin, J. V.: *ref*, 1069, 1073, 2195
Griffin, W. B.: *test*, 2435, 2438;
  ref, 2438
Griffith, J. W.: *ref*, 2289
Griffiths, D. E.: *ref*, 2212
Griffiths, P. D.: *test*, 2253
Griffitts, C. H.: *ref*, 2251
Griggs, S. A.: *ref*, 2189
Grimsley, G.: *test*, 1071
Grimsley, W. G.: *ref*, 2452
Grina, A. A.: *ref*, 1073
Grinberg, B.: *ref*, 2451
Grobman, H.: *ref*, 1069
Groff, M.: *ref*, 2355
Grohsmeyer, F. A.: *ref*, 2239
Gross, M. C.: *ref*, 2212
Grosz, R. D.: *ref*, 2212
Grove, B. A.: *ref*, 2289
Grove, W. R.: *rev*, 3:658, 3:662,
  3:671, 3:679; *ref*, 3:660(10-1)
Grover, V. M.: *ref*, 1087
Gruber, E. C.: *ref*, 2325, 2337, 2349,
  2355
Gruenfeld, L. W.: *ref*, 2454
Guazzo, E. J.: *ref*, 2195, 2266
Guba, E. G.: *ref*, 2195
Gubasta, J. L.: *ref*, 2452
Guest, L.: *ref*, 2135, 2212
Guest, T. A.: *ref*, 2401
Guetzkow, H.: *ref*, 1087
Guilford, J. P.: *test*, 1074, 2184;
  ref, 1069, 1074, 1087, 2184-5,
  2195, 2212, 4:761(1)
Guilford, J. S.: *test*, 2185
Guilliams, C. I.: *ref*, 1072
Guinn, M. P.: *ref*, 782, 2251
Guion, R. M.: *ref*, 1071, 2102,
  2227-9, 2234
Gujarata, D. N.: *ref*, 2451
Gulati, K.: *ref*, 2180
Gullo, J. M.: *test*, 2280
Gundlach, R. H.: *ref*, 2212
Gunnell, D. C.: *ref*, 2213
Gunter, L. M.: *ref*, 2195
Gustad, J. W.: *rev*, 5:862; *ref*,
  2212
Gutekunst, J. G.: *ref*, 2212

Guthrie, G. M.: *ref*, 2212
Guttman, I.: *ref*, 2197
Gwydir, R. R.: *ref*, 1069
Gysbers, N. C.: *ref*, 2212-3

HAAG, R. A.: *ref*, 2212
Haakenstad, K. W.: *ref*, 2212
Haase, R. F.: *ref*, 2212
Habegger, O. F.: *ref*, 2266
Haber, W.: *ref*, 2135, 2234
Haberman, H.: *test*, 775
Hackett, H. R.: *ref*, 2212
Hackman, R. B.: *test*, 2186
Hackman, R. C.: *ref*, 2135, 2227-9,
  2258, 2266
Hadley, J. M.: *ref*, 2195, 4:825
  (13-4)
Hadley, R. G.: *ref*, 2212
Hadley, S. T.: *test*, 2106, 2128,
  2160, 2405, 2417, 2419
Hafeez, A.: *ref*, 2135
Hagenah, T.: *ref*, 2212
Hager, C. W.: *ref*, 1069
Hager, P. C.: *ref*, 2212
Hahn, M. E.: *rev*, 2180, 2395,
  2397, 3:704, 4:798; *test*, 3:689;
  ref, 2135, 2195, 2212
Hahn, M. S.: *ref*, 1069
Hain, J. D.: *ref*, 2355
Haines, R. B.: *ref*, 1069
Hakanson, I. S.: *ref*, 2195
Hake, D. T.: *ref*, 2195
Hakkinen, S.: *ref*, 2266
Hale, P. P.: *ref*, 2195, 2197
Hales, W. M.: *ref*, 2135, 2162
Haley, H. B.: *ref*, 2355
Halfter, I. T.: *ref*, 2349
Hall, C. E.: *ref*, 1069, 1080
Hall, C. W.: *test*, 2399
Hall, D. H.: *ref*, 2212
Hall, D. S.: *ref*, 2337
Hall, D. W.: *exc*, 2197; *ref*, 2103
Hall, J. A.: *ref*, 2221
Hall, L. G.: *test*, 2187; *ref*, 2187
Hall, L. T.: *ref*, 1069
Hall, O. A.: *ref*, 2213
Hall, O. M.: *ref*, 2266
Hall, R. C.: *ref*, 1069
Hall, S. G.: *ref*, 2195
Hall, W. B.: *ref*, 2212, 2355
Hall, W. E.: *ref*, 1087
Hall, W. J.: *ref*, 2212-3
Halliday, R. W.: *ref*, 2239
Halpin, A. W.: *test*, 2451; *ref*,
  2449, 2451-2
Halsey, H.: *ref*, 1069
Halstead, H.: *ref*, 2239, 2258
Hamberg, R. L.: *ref*, 2355
Hambleton, R. K.: *exc*, 2239
Hamilton, H. A.: *ref*, 783
Hamlin, M. M.: *ref*, 2285
Hammer, R.: *ref*, 2213
Hammidi, B. C.: *ref*, 2212, 7:1090
  (3)
Hammill, D.: *ref*, 2195
Hampton, P. J.: *ref*, 2212
Hana, A. M.: *ref*, 2221
Hand, H. C.: *test*, 2:1661
Handelsman, I.: *ref*, 2212
Hanes, B.: *test*, 2400; *ref*, 2239,
  2266
Haney, R.: *ref*, 1071, 1074, 2251
Hankes, E. J.: *ref*, 2212
Hankey, R. O.: *ref*, 2113

Hanley, D. E.: *ref*, 2103
Hanman, B.: *ref*, 2260, 2266
Hanna, G. S.: *ref*, 1069, 2195
Hanna, J. V.: *ref*, 2129, 2195
Hannum, T. E.: *test*, 2212; *ref*, 2195, 2212
Hansen, J. C.: *ref*, 2103
Hanson, G. R.: *rev*, 2325; *ref*, 2101, 2194, 2197, 2212
Hanson, R.: *ref*, 2212, 2463
Hanson, R. N.: *ref*, 798
Harbilas, J. N.: *ref*, 1087
Hardaway, M.: *test*, 2:1478; *ref*, 2:1478(1)
Harding, D. W.: *ref*, 2247
Harding, W. T.: *ref*, 2195
Hardy, R. E.: *ref*, 2195
Harford, T.: *ref*, 2212
Harford, T. C.: *ref*, 1073, 2212
Harker, J. B.: *ref*, 2132, 2151, 2212
Harlan, G. E.: *ref*, 2103, 2221
Harless, B. B.: *ref*, 2395
Harmes, H. M.: *ref*, 2451
Harmon, J. B.: *ref*, 2258
Harmon, J. S.: *ref*, 1073
Harmon, L. A. W.: *ref*, 2213
Harmon, L. R.: *ref*, 2195, 2258
Harmon, L. W.: *ref*, 2212-3
Harootunian, B.: *ref*, 1069
Harper, B. P.: *exc*, 2212; *ref*, 2212-3
Harrangue, M. D.: *ref*, 2195, 2221
Harrell, T. W.: *rev*, 2231, 2234; *ref*, 2212, 2314, 2325, 2454
Harrell, W.: *ref*, 1087, 2212, 2227, 2251, 2258-9, 3:671(8), 3:678 (11, 15)
Harrington, C.: *ref*, 2212, 2273
Harrington, C. C.: *ref*, 2212
Harrington, J. A.: *ref*, 2195
Harrington, T. F.: *ref*, 2194, 2212
Harris, A. E.: *test*, 4:793
Harris, A. J.: *ref*, 2229, 2259
Harris, D.: *ref*, 2347
Harris, D. B.: *ref*, 1087
Harris, D. H.: *test*, 2347; *ref*, 2347
Harris, E. F.: *ref*, 2454
Harris, E. H.: *ref*, 2452
Harris, J. W.: *ref*, 2103
Harris, R. E.: *ref*, 2355
Harris, R. H.: *test*, 2340
Harris, Y. Y.: *ref*, 1069
Harrison, L.: *ref*, 2195
Harrison, M. T.: *rev*, 2164-5
Harrison, R.: *ref*, 1069, 2212, 2239, 2268
Harsh, C. M.: *rev*, 2239, 3:673, 3:681
Hart, F. M.: *ref*, 2349
Hartlage, L. C.: *ref*, 1069, 2268
Hartman, A. D.: *test*, 2164
Hartman, B. J.: *ref*, 2195
Hartmann, E. L.: *ref*, 2212
Hartmann, G. W.: *ref*, 2212
Hartshorn, H. H.: *ref*, 2212
Hartzell, M. D.: *ref*, 3:635(9)
Harvey, J.: *test*, 4:800
Harvey, L. J.: *ref*, 4:800(1)
Harvey, O. L.: *ref*, 2242, 2258, 3:671(4)
Hascall, E. O.: *ref*, 1069, 2195
Haselkorn, H.: *ref*, 2195, 2212

Hashmi, S. A.: *ref*, 1069
Hasler, K. R.: *ref*, 1073
Hassler, R. H.: *ref*, 2323
Hastie, B.: *ref*, 2383
Hastings, R. E.: *ref*, 2452
Hatch, R. H.: *ref*, 2451
Havens, J. M.: *ref*, 2194
Haverly Systems, Inc.: *test*, 2336
Havighurst, R. J.: *exc*, 2212-3; *ref*, 1087, 2266
Haviland, F. H.: *ref*, 4:825(7)
Havlicek, L. L.: *ref*, 2212
Hawk, J.: *ref*, 1073, 1086
Hawk, J. A.: *ref*, 1073
Hawkes, N. J.: *ref*, 1069
Hawkins, R. E.: *ref*, 2454
Hawkridge, D. G.: *rev*, 2168, 2175
Hay, E. N.: *rev*, 786, 791, 2129, 2142, 3:624, 3:631; *test*, 2132, 2159, 2163; *exc*, 1087; *ref*, 791, 2132, 2135
Hay, J. E.: *ref*, 1073, 2454
Hayes, A. B.: *ref*, 2212
Hayes, E. G.: *ref*, 2228
Hayes, M. P.: *ref*, 2180
Hayes, S. P.: *ref*, 2195
Hayes, W. G.: *ref*, 2448
Haynes, J. R.: *ref*, 1074
Haynes, L. M.: *rev*, 798
Hays, B. B.: *ref*, 2451
Hazelhurst, J. H.: *test*, 2262
Headlee, M. K.: *ref*, 2195
Healy, C. C.: *test*, 2109; *ref*, 2212
Healy, I.: *ref*, 2195
Heath, D. H.: *ref*, 2212
Heath, H. E.: *ref*, 2212
Hecht, R.: *ref*, 2406
Hedley, C. N.: *ref*, 2195
Hedlund, D. E.: *ref*, 2454, 2459
Heemstra, J. J.: *ref*, 798
Hefty, J. C.: *ref*, 2452
Heggen, J. R.: *ref*, 1073
Heiberg, D. A.: *ref*, 2195
Heidbreder, E.: *test*, 2258, 2266, 3:671; *ref*, 2258, 2266, 3:671(3), 3:678(5), 3:679(3)
Heilbrun, A. B.: *ref*, 2212
Heilman, H.: *ref*, 2195
Heim, A. W.: *rev*, 2209
Heimann, R. A.: *ref*, 2103, 2340
Heist, P.: *ref*, 2212
Hellebrandt, F. A.: *ref*, 2251
Heller, D. B.: *ref*, 2337
Helm, C. R.: *ref*, 1069
Helme, W. H.: *rev*, 1078
Helmick, K. D.: *ref*, 2212
Helper, M. M.: *ref*, 2212
Helson, R.: *ref*, 2212-3
Helton, W. B.: *ref*, 2199
Helwig, C.: *ref*, 1069
Hempel, W. E.: *ref*, 2227-8, 2234
Hemphill, J. K.: *rev*, 2110, 2273-4; *test*, 2449, 2451-2; *ref*, 2212, 2449, 2451-2
Hendel, D. D.: *test*, 2283; *ref*, 1073, 2283
Henderson, B.: *ref*, 2190
Henderson, C.: *test*, 4:448
Henderson, E. C.: *ref*, 2195
Henderson, H. L.: *ref*, 2212
Henderson, M. T.: *ref*, 2258-9, 2266
Henderson, R. W.: *test*, 2115, 2174, 2188, 2220, 6:1105, 6:1196

Hendrix, O. R.: *ref*, 2212, 2323
Hendrix, V. L.: *ref*, 2221
Hendsch, G.: *ref*, 2199, 2205
Henkin, J. B.: *ref*, 1073
Hennessy, T.: *ref*, 2195, 2212
Henry, S.: *ref*, 2218
Henry, W. E.: *rev*, 2216
Henry, W. O.: *ref*, 2195
Heriot, M. R.: *ref*, 1069
Herkenhoff, L. H.: *ref*, 2213
Herkness, W. W.: *ref*, 2195, 2212, 3:635(6, 8), 3:637(6), 3:653 (8, 11), 3:655(2, 4)
Herman, D. O.: *rev*, 2200, 6:1147, 7:1032
Herman, L. M.: *test*, 2212; *ref*, 2212
Herod, J.: *ref*, 2451
Heron, A.: *ref*, 1073
Herrick, V. E.: *ref*, 1087
Herrmann, W. C.: *ref*, 4:718(1)
Hersch, P. D.: *ref*, 2212-3
Hershenson, D. B.: *ref*, 2212
Hershey, C. F.: *test*, 796
Hershey, G. L.: *ref*, 2285
Herzberg, F.: *ref*, 1087, 2195
Herzig, S. A.: *test*, 2216; *ref*, 2216
Hesch, G. P.: *ref*, 2212
Heslin, P.: *ref*, 2386
Hess, A. W.: *ref*, 2186
Hessemer, M.: *ref*, 1087
Hester, E. J.: *ref*, 2448
Hester, R.: *ref*, 2195
Heston, J. C.: *ref*, 2195, 2212
Hetherington, R. W.: *ref*, 2355
Hewer, V. H.: *ref*, 2212
Hewick, W. E.: *ref*, 1069
Heyward, R. W.: *ref*, 2387
Heywood, H.: *ref*, 2113
Heywood, H. C.: *ref*, 2113
Heywood, H. L.: *ref*, 2113
Hiett, V. C.: *test*, 784, 3:381
Higginbottom, A. R.: *ref*, 2213
High, W. S.: *ref*, 2195
Hilgard, J. R.: *ref*, 2213
Hill, A. M.: *ref*, 4:784(6)
Hill, G. E.: *ref*, 2195
Hill, J.: *ref*, 2234
Hill, J. K.: *ref*, 2355
Hill, J. M.: *ref*, 2195
Hill, W. B.: *test*, 7:1136
Hillis, D. J.: *ref*, 2212
Hillman, C.: *ref*, 2195
Hills, J. R.: *rev*, 2189; *ref*, 1074, 2349
Hills, R. J.: *ref*, 2451
Hiltenbrand, R. E.: *ref*, 2451
Hilton, A. C.: *ref*, 2140, 2212, 2448, 6:1180(2)
Himmelweit, H. T.: *ref*, 1087
Hinckley, E. D.: *rev*, 2212, 4:737
Hinds, E.: *ref*, 2212
Hindsman, E.: *ref*, 1069
Hines, M.: *ref*, 2228
Hinman, S. L.: *ref*, 2212, 2239, 2273
Hinrichs, J. R.: *ref*, 2454
Hinton, B. L.: *ref*, 2212, 2325
Hirsch, M. W.: *ref*, 2266
Hirschhorn, B.: *ref*, 2234
Hirt, M.: *ref*, 1073, 2195
Hirt, M. L.: *ref*, 1073
Hittler, G. M.: *ref*, 786
Hoag, R. L.: *ref*, 2234

Hobbs, D. J.: *ref,* 1073
Hobbs, P. J.: *ref,* 2451
Hobson, J. R.: *rev,* 1087; *ref,* 1087
Hobson, R. L.: *test,* 4:800
Hodge, S. E.: *ref,* 2212
Hodges, J. M.: *ref,* 1069, 1087
Hodgson, R. W.: *ref,* 2239
Hoepfner, R.: *ref,* 1069
Hoff, A. L.: *ref,* 1073
Hoffman, E. G.: *ref,* 2212
Hoffman, E. L.: *ref,* 2212, 2355
Hoffman, P. J.: *ref,* 1071, 2266
Hoffman, S.: *ref,* 2227, 2231, 2234
Hofstaetter, P. R.: *ref,* 1087
Hogadone, E.: *ref,* 4:784(2)
Hogan, J.: *ref,* 2212
Hogg, M. I.: *ref,* 2212
Hohne, H. H.: *ref,* 2118, 2237, 2266, 5:880(8)
Holcomb, G. W.: *ref,* 2212, 2251, 3:678(7), 3:679(5)
Holden, R. H.: *ref,* 2234
Holder, J. R.: *ref,* 1069
Hole, R. M.: *ref,* 2195
Holland, J. L.: *test,* 2211; *ref,* 2195, 2211-2
Holland, P. L.: *ref,* 2212
Hollenbeck, G. P.: *test,* 7:1090; *ref,* 1069, 2195, 7:1090(4)
Hollender, J. W.: *ref,* 1073
Holliday, F.: *ref,* 2242, 2247, 2249, 4:769(1, 4-6), 5:880(1, 3)
Holloman, C. R.: *ref,* 2451
Holloway, H. D.: *ref,* 1087
Holloway, J. E.: *ref,* 2452
Holmen, M. G.: *test,* 2212; *ref,* 2212
Holmes, F. J.: *test,* 2286; *ref,* 2448
Holmes, J. A.: *ref,* 798, 1087, 2195
Holmes, J. L.: *ref,* 2239, 2266
Holt, R. R.: *ref,* 2212
Holtan, B.: *ref,* 2195
Holzberg, J. D.: *ref,* 2212
Holzinger, K. J.: *test,* 5:610
Hood, A. B.: *ref,* 2212, 2337
Hood, D.: *ref,* 1069
Hooper, D. B.: *ref,* 2454
Hoover, K. H.: *ref,* 2195
Hoover, N. K.: *test,* 7:1038
Hopkins, J. J.: *ref,* 4:825(19)
Hoppock, M. E.: *test,* 2:1650
Hoppock, R.: *test,* 2:1649, 3:693; *ref,* 3:693(1)
Horn, D.: *ref,* 2212
Horn, F. M.: *ref,* 1069, 2268
Horn, J. L.: *exc,* 2107
Horn, W. O.: *test,* 1076
Hornaday, J. A.: *ref,* 2194-5
Horne, R. R. C.: *test,* 1065
Horning, S. D.: *ref,* 2251
Hornung, P. E.: *ref,* 2213
Horsman, V. G.: *ref,* 2212
Horst, P.: *ref,* 1087
Horwitz, M.: *ref,* 2234
Hosford, P. M.: *ref,* 2195
Hosford, R. E.: *ref,* 1073
Hosler, R. J.: *ref,* 798, 3:372(1), 3:392(4)
Hotchkiss, S. M.: *ref,* 2195
Hountras, P. T.: *ref,* 1073
House, R. J.: *ref,* 2451
Housley, W. F.: *ref,* 2201
Houston, L. N.: *ref,* 2205

Houtz, S. J.: *ref,* 2251
Hovland, C. I.: *ref,* 6:1115(2)
Howard, J. M.: *ref,* 2451
Howard, J. T.: *ref,* 2251
Howard, L. H.: *ref,* 2212
Howell, M. A.: *ref,* 1073, 2355, 7:1090(7)
Howland, R. H.: *ref,* 2212
Hoyt, D. P.: *ref,* 2212-3
Hoyt, K. B.: *rev,* 2182, 2185; *test,* 2105, 2270; *ref,* 1073
Hrapchak, W. J.: *ref,* 2451
Huang, D. D.: *ref,* 2170
Huber, N. A.: *ref,* 2110
Huck, F. T.: *ref,* 2337
Huckabee, M. W.: *ref,* 2195
Huddy, J. A.: *ref,* 1073
Hudesman, J.: *ref,* 2212
Hudson, D. K.: *ref,* 1069
Hudson, H. H.: *ref,* 1087
Hueber, J.: *ref,* 2239, 2263, 2266
Huff, B.: *ref,* 1069
Huffman, W. J.: *ref,* 2195
Hughes, H. B.: *ref,* 2195
Hughes, H. H.: *ref,* 1069
Hughes, H. M.: *ref,* 2212
Hughes, J. B.: *ref,* 2195
Hughes, J. L.: *test,* 6:1153; *ref,* 2129, 2151, 2212, 6:1140(1), 6:1153(1)
Hughes, L. J.: *ref,* 2213
Hujsa, C.: *ref,* 2251, 2266-7
Hull, J. S.: *ref,* 2212
Hultgren, D. D.: *ref,* 2212
Human Sciences Research Council: *test,* 1083, 2447
Humbert, J. T.: *ref,* 2221
Hume, C. D.: *test,* 4:816
Humm, D. G.: *test,* 5:931
Humm, K. A.: *test,* 5:931
Hummel, R.: *ref,* 2212
Humphreys, L. G.: *rev,* 1066, 1069, 1073, 1080, 2239, 2244, 2257; *ref,* 1087, 2212
Hundleby, J. D.: *ref,* 1087
Huneryager, S. G.: *ref,* 2454
Hunka, S.: *rev,* 6:1032; *ref,* 2355
Hunt, J. E.: *ref,* 2451
Hunt, T.: *rev,* 2129, 2135; *test,* 2381, 2413
Hunt, W.: *ref,* 1069, 2212, 2239, 2268
Hunter, N. W.: *ref,* 1069, 1073
Hunter, R. C. A.: *ref,* 2355
Hurd, A. W.: *ref,* 2355
Hurley, R. B.: *ref,* 2221
Husek, T. R.: *exc,* 2193
Huston, B. M.: *ref,* 2195
Hutcheon, J. F.: *ref,* 1087
Hutcheon, N. B.: *ref,* 2214, 2242, 2247, 2:1683(4)
Hutchins, E. B.: *ref,* 2212, 2355
Hutchinson, J. C.: *ref,* 2213
Hutson, B. T.: *ref,* 2199
Huttner, L.: *ref,* 2212
Hutton, D. E.: *ref,* 2451
Hutton, J. G.: *ref,* 2337, 2355
Hyman, B.: *ref,* 2195

IANNACCONE, L.: *ref,* 2212
Ignatovich, F. R.: *ref,* 2452
Im, I. J.: *ref,* 2212
Impellitteri, J. T.: *ref,* 1073
Incardona, J. S.: *ref,* 2451

Industrial Relations Center: *test,* 2245, 2255, 2272, 2340
Ingersoll, R. W.: *ref,* 1073, 2355
Inglis, J.: *ref,* 1073
Inskeep, G. C.: *ref,* 2228
Institute for Behavioral Research in Creativity: *test,* 2273
Instructional Materials Laboratory, Ohio State University: *test,* 2339, 2420-32, 7:1128
International Personnel Management Association: *test,* 2137, 2322, 2341, 2362, 2371, 2373-4, 2418, 2475
Irvin, F. S.: *ref,* 2212
Irvine, F. R.: *ref,* 1069, 2256
Irvine, S. H.: *ref,* 1085
Irwin, I. A.: *ref,* 2199, 2212
Irwin, J. T.: *ref,* 1069
Irwin, T. J.: *ref,* 2212
Isaacson, L. E.: *ref,* 1073, 2195
Isabelle, L. A.: *ref,* 2212, 2214
Isenberger, W.: *ref,* 2213
Isenberger, W. E.: *ref,* 2213
Ivanoff, J. M.: *ref,* 2195
Ivers, K. J.: *ref,* 2212
Ivey, A. E.: *ref,* 2195, 2221
Izard, C. E.: *ref,* 2195

JABS, M. L.: *ref,* 2454
Jackson, A. M.: *ref,* 2199
Jackson, C. W.: *ref,* 1069, 2195
Jackson, D. N.: *ref,* 2212
Jackson, G. G.: *ref,* 2355
Jackson, J.: *ref,* 2135, 2195
Jackson, T. A.: *ref,* 1069, 2212, 2239, 2268
Jacobs, A. W.: *ref,* 2355
Jacobs, J. N.: *ref,* 1069
Jacobs, J. W.: *ref,* 2452
Jacobs, O.: *ref,* 1069, 2268
Jacobs, R.: *ref,* 1087, 2195, 2199, 2212, 2323, 4:718(5-6), 5:907(1)
Jacobs, R. E.: *ref,* 1087
Jacobsen, C. F.: *ref,* 2212
Jacobsen, E. E.: *ref,* 2228-9, 2239, 2266, 3:658(6)
Jacobsen, G.: *ref,* 1069, 1080
Jacobson, M. D.: *ref,* 2355
Jaeger, M.: *ref,* 2251
Jalkanen, A. W.: *ref,* 2103
James, F.: *ref,* 2355, 6:1062(4)
James, L. E.: *ref,* 2195, 2212
James, L. R.: *ref,* 2273
James, N. E.: *ref,* 2212
Jamieson, G. H.: *ref,* 2249
Janke, L. L.: *ref,* 2266
Jantzen, A. C.: *ref,* 2213
Janus, S.: *ref,* 2266
Jarecky, R. K.: *ref,* 2355
Jarvik, M. E.: *ref,* 2266
Jastak, J. F.: *test,* 1077, 2116, 2219
Jastak, S. R.: *test,* 2219
Jayalakshmi, G.: *ref,* 1069, 2227-8, 2256, 2268
Jaynes, W. E.: *ref,* 2452, 2457
Jeffrey, T. E.: *test,* 2245, 2255, 2272
Jeffries, L. A.: *ref,* 1087
Jenkins, F. T.: *ref,* 1069
Jenkins, J. J.: *ref,* 2135, 2266
Jenkins, T. N.: *test,* 2189, 7:1062; *ref,* 6:1106(1), 7:1062(2-3)
Jenkins, T. V.: *ref,* 1069

Jennings, E.: *ref,* 1069
Jennings, J. R.: *rev,* 2237–8
Jensen, G. L.: *ref,* 2195
Jensen, M. B.: *ref,* 2239, 3:653(12)
Jensen, V. H.: *ref,* 2195
Jenson, P. G.: *ref,* 2212
Jenson, R. E.: *ref,* 1069
Jenssen (Ward J.), Inc.: *test,* 6: 1147
Jerdee, T. H.: *ref,* 2212
Jeremias, H. I.: *ref,* 1073, 2186
Jervis, F. M.: *ref,* 2199
Jessee, B. E.: *ref,* 2103
Jex, F. B.: *ref,* 1069, 1072–3, 4:812(3, 11)
Joel, M. L.: *ref,* 2387
Jog, R. N.: *ref,* 2247
Johansen, A. N.: *ref,* 2195
Johansson, C. B.: *ref,* 2212
John, E. R.: *ref,* 2212
Johnson, A. P.: *rev,* 2240, 2344; *ref,* 1087, 2195, 2212, 2258, 2266, 2349, 4:812(9)
Johnson, B. R.: *ref,* 2212
Johnson, C. W.: *ref,* 2194
Johnson, D. E.: *ref,* 2212
Johnson, D. G.: *ref,* 2212, 2355
Johnson, D. L.: *ref,* 2227, 2239
Johnson, G. K.: *ref,* 2212
Johnson, H. S.: *ref,* 1063, 1069
Johnson, J. C.: *ref,* 2212
Johnson, J. M.: *ref,* 1069, 2195
Johnson, J. T.: *ref,* 1087
Johnson, M. M.: *ref,* 2449
Johnson, P. O.: *ref,* 2451
Johnson, R. H.: *ref,* 2135, 2195, 2199, 2212, 2228–9, 2239, 2258, 2266
Johnson, R. J.: *ref,* 2213, 2448
Johnson, R. T.: *rev,* 2334, 7:1090, 7:1103
Johnson, R. W.: *ref,* 1087, 2194, 2197, 2212–3
Johnson, S. O.: *test,* 2152–4, 2439–46, 2474
Johnson, T. G.: *ref,* 1087
Johnston, J. A.: *ref,* 2213
Joint Committee on Tests: *test,* 2:1482, 2:1484–5, 3:379; *ref,* 786
Jones, B. M.: *ref,* 2234
Jones, C.: *rev,* 2209
Jones, C. W.: *ref,* 1069, 2256, 2268, 6:1062(1)
Jones, D.: *ref,* 2223
Jones, E.: *ref,* 2113
Jones, E. M.: *ref,* 2113
Jones, E. S.: *rev,* 2311
Jones, J. B.: *ref,* 2195
Jones, K. J.: *ref,* 2195
Jones, M. C.: *ref,* 2212–3
Jones, P. P.: *ref,* 2195
Jones, R. A.: *rev,* 5:855; *ref,* 1074, 2251
Jones, R. L.: *ref,* 2212
Jones, R. D.: *ref,* 1073
Jones, W. J.: *exc,* 2397
Jordan, B.: *test,* 2298
Jordan, M. J.: *ref,* 2221
Jorgensen, C.: *ref,* 2162, 2251
Jose, A. B.: *ref,* 2214
Joselyn, E. G.: *ref,* 2212–3
Joseph, M. P.: *ref,* 2212, 6:1062(5)
Judd-Safian Associates: *test,* 2312
Juan, I. R.: *ref,* 2355

Juergenson, E. M.: *ref,* 2239
Junkala, J. B.: *ref,* 1087
Jurgensen, C. E.: *rev,* 799, 2102, 2159, 2266, 2466, 3:681–2; *test,* 5:513; *ref,* 2227, 2239, 2448, 5:513(1)

KACZKOWSKI, H. R.: *ref,* 1087
Kahn, D. F.: *ref,* 2195, 4:825(11, 13–4)
Kahn, E. M.: *ref,* 2212
Kahn, H.: *test,* 2217; *ref,* 2217, 2234–5
Kahn, T. C.: *test,* 4:777
Kaiser, H. E.: *ref,* 2194–5, 2212
Kaloger, J. H.: *ref,* 1069
Kamin, L. J.: *ref,* 1087
Kanderian, S. S.: *ref,* 1087
Kapes, J. T.: *ref,* 1073, 2103, 2427–31
Kaplan, H. A.: *ref,* 2234
Kaplan, H. H.: *ref,* 2221
Kaplan, H. K.: *ref,* 1087
Kaplon, M. D.: *ref,* 2212
Kapoor, K.: *ref,* 2229
Karasick, B. W.: *ref,* 2285
Karlson, L. A.: *ref,* 2201
Karn, H. W.: *rev,* 2301; *ref,* 2448
Karp, R. E.: *ref,* 1069
Karpoff, J. T.: *ref,* 1069, 2195
Karr, B.: *ref,* 2212
Kashiwagi, S.: *ref,* 1087
Kasl, S. V.: *ref,* 1073
Kassarjian, H. H.: *ref,* 2212
Kassarjian, W. M.: *ref,* 2212
Kates, S. L.: *ref,* 2212
Katz, M.: *rev,* 2195, 2199; *ref,* 2195, 2212, 2283
Katz, M. R.: *rev,* 2212
Katzell, M.: *ref,* 2386
Katzell, R. A.: *rev,* 2106, 2129, 2138, 2223, 2266, 2289, 2406, 3:624, 5:954, 6:1104; *ref,* 1069, 2151, 2387, 2448
Katzenmeyer, W. G.: *ref,* 2195
Kaufman, H. A.: *test,* 2456
Kauppi, D. R.: *ref,* 1073, 2197, 2283
Kauzer, A.: *test,* 3:382
Kavanagh, M. J.: *ref,* 2451
Kayani, M. R.: *ref,* 1069
Kazmier, L. J.: *ref,* 2239
Keane, F. L.: *ref,* 2259
Kearney, D. L.: *ref,* 2212
Keats, J. A.: *rev,* 1069
Kebbon, L.: *ref,* 1069, 1073, 1087, 2223, 2228
Kee, B. E.: *ref,* 2167
Keeler, B. T.: *ref,* 2451
Keeler, H. J.: *ref,* 2214
Kefauver, G. N.: *test,* 2:1661; *ref,* 2251, 3:678(4)
Kegan, E. O.: *ref,* 2195
Keim, L.: *ref,* 2195
Kelada, F. S.: *ref,* 2451
Kelleher, E. J.: *ref,* 2177, 2286
Kelley, E. P.: *ref,* 2195
Kelley, I. B.: *test,* 4:799; *ref,* 4:799(1)
Kelley, T. L.: *rev,* 1087; *ref,* 2212
Kelley, W. R.: *ref,* 2452
Kellogg, R. L.: *ref,* 2212
Kellow, W. F.: *ref,* 2355

Kelly, E. L.: *ref,* 1087, 2195, 2212, 2355
Kelly, J. G.: *ref,* 2195
Kelly, L.: *ref,* 2212
Kelso, D. F.: *ref,* 2212
Kelso, N. E.: *ref,* 2195, 2212
Kemp, C. G.: *ref,* 2195, 2212
Kemp, D. E.: *ref,* 2212
Kendall, L. M.: *ref,* 2212
Kendall, W. E.: *rev,* 2400, 2409; *ref,* 2135, 2195, 2212
Kennedy, C. E.: *ref,* 2212–3
Kennedy, E. C.: *ref,* 2195, 2212
Kennedy, L. T.: *ref,* 2180
Kennedy, P.: *ref,* 2113
Kennedy, P. K.: *ref,* 2113
Kenney, C. E.: *ref,* 2195
Kent, G. H.: *test,* 3:660
Kentz, M. J.: *ref,* 2213
Keough, M. A.: *ref,* 2195
Kephart, N. C.: *test,* 2304; *ref,* 2304
Kermeen, B. G.: *ref,* 1069, 2195
Kern, D. W.: *ref,* 2195
Kernan, J. P.: *ref,* 2129, 2454
Kerns, R. D.: *ref,* 2195
Kerr, G.: *ref,* 2130, 2242, 2247
Kerr, S.: *ref,* 2451
Kerr, W. A.: *rev,* 2471, 2475–6, 3:662, 4:761; *test,* 2274, 2289; *ref,* 2177, 2212, 2239, 2286, 2289, 2292
Kerr, W. D.: *ref,* 1087, 2195
Ketcham, W. A.: *ref,* 1087
Keys, S. R.: *ref,* 2451
Khan, H. I. A.: *ref,* 2259
Khan, L.: *ref,* 1082
Kidneigh, J. C.: *ref,* 2212–3
Kiessling, R. J.: *ref,* 2234
Kiev, A.: *ref,* 2212
Kilburn, K. L.: *ref,* 2212
Killcross, M. C.: *test,* 2168; *ref,* 2168
Killen, J. R.: *ref,* 1087
Kilman, M. D.: *ref,* 1087
Kimbell, F. T.: *ref,* 2195
Kimber, J. A. M.: *ref,* 2195
King, C. E.: *ref,* 1069
King, D. C.: *ref,* 1071, 2195
King, D. E.: *test,* 2116
King, F. J.: *ref,* 1069, 1087
King, H. E.: *ref,* 2234
King, J.: *ref,* 1069
King, J. E.: *rev,* 3:684; *test,* 1078, 2308, 5:892, 5:898, 6:781; *ref,* 1078, 2308
King, L. A.: *ref,* 2212
King, M.: *ref,* 1069
King, P.: *ref,* 2195, 2212
King, P. T.: *ref,* 2212
Kingsbury, F. A.: *rev,* 2:1682
Kingsley, R. F.: *ref,* 1087
Kingston, A. J.: *ref,* 2195, 2199
Kinnane, J. F.: *ref,* 2212, 2221
Kinney, L. B.: *test,* 2:1489; *ref,* 2:1489(1–3)
Kinsey, D. R.: *ref,* 1069
Kinslinger, H. J.: *ref,* 2212
Kinzer, J. R.: *rev,* 2227, 2251
Kirchner, W.: *ref,* 2212, 2463
Kirchner, W. K.: *rev,* 2454, 6: 1180; *ref,* 796, 1069, 1078, 2151, 2212, 2448, 7:1103(3–4)

Kirk, B. A.: *rev,* 2193, 2213; *exc,* 2212; *ref,* 2212–3, 2266, 2337
Kirk, D.: *ref,* 2212
Kirk, J. P.: *ref,* 2212
Kirk, K. W.: *ref,* 2212
Kirkpatrick, D. L.: *test,* 2460, 2462–3, 2465; *ref,* 2135, 2460
Kirkpatrick, J. J.: *ref,* 1069, 2151, 2239, 2387
Kish, G. B.: *ref,* 1073, 2195, 2212–3
Kivitz, M. S.: *ref,* 2227, 2234
Kjerland, R. N.: *ref,* 2259
Klahn, J. E.: *ref,* 2213
Klein, F.: *ref,* 1073
Klein, F. L.: *ref,* 2212
Klein, S. P.: *test,* 2109; *ref,* 2349
Kleinmuntz, B.: *rev,* 1077
Kleist, M.: *ref,* 2212–3
Kleist, M. E.: *ref,* 2212
Kline, C. E.: *ref,* 2451
Kline, G. R.: *ref,* 2186
Kline, M. V.: *ref,* 2195
Klinger, E.: *ref,* 2355
Kloster, C. G.: *ref,* 2212
Kluczny, R.: *ref,* 2195
Klugman, S. F.: *ref,* 1073, 2135, 2195, 2199, 2212–3, 2251, 2266
Knaak, N. K.: *ref,* 2195
Knapp, R. H.: *ref,* 2212
Knapp, R. R.: *test,* 2170
Knapp, T.: *ref,* 2212
Knauft, E. B.: *ref,* 2212
Knievel, W. R.: *ref,* 1078
Knower, F. H.: *ref,* 2212–3
Knowles, R. H.: *ref,* 2212
Knudsen, R. G.: *ref,* 2195
Kobal, A.: *test,* 780, 2192, 2252
Kobler, F. J.: *ref,* 2195
Koch, H. L.: *ref,* 1087
Kodama, H.: *ref,* 2212
Kodanaz, A.: *ref,* 2234
Koelling, J. A.: *ref,* 2213
Koepke, H. F.: *test,* 2213; *ref,* 2213
Kogan, K. L.: *ref,* 1068, 2212
Kogan, L.: *ref,* 2212
Kohlan, R. G.: *ref,* 2212, 2283
Kohler, A. T.: *ref,* 2212
Kohli, P. E.: *ref,* 1069
Kohn, H. A.: *test,* 1:1172
Kohn, N.: *ref,* 2195, 2212
Kokovich, S.: *ref,* 2451
Kolb, A.: *ref,* 2212
Kolbe, L. E.: *ref,* 2135, 2227–9, 2251, 2258, 2266
Kole, D. M.: *ref,* 2212
Kolpack, K. C.: *ref,* 2213
Kolstoe, O. P.: *ref,* 1087
Komorita, S. S.: *ref,* 2454
Konecny, P. W.: *ref,* 1073
Kooker, E. W.: *ref,* 1073
Koons, P. B.: *test,* 2201
Kopas, J. S.: *ref,* 2212
Kopp, T.: *ref,* 2195, 3:635(17)
Koppelmeier, G. J.: *ref,* 2289
Koprowski, E. J.: *ref,* 2212
Korman, A. K.: *ref,* 2451, 2454
Korman, M.: *ref,* 2355
Korn, H. A.: *ref,* 2212
Kornhaus, D. C.: *ref,* 1069
Kornhauser, S. I.: *ref,* 2212
Kosa, J.: *ref,* 2355
Kosai, J. H.: *ref,* 1069
Kosuth, T.: *test,* 2204
Kraft, L.: *ref,* 2381

Kraft, M. A.: *test,* 2469; *ref,* 2469
Kramer, H. C.: *ref,* 2212
Krathwohl, D. R.: *ref,* 2239, 5: 880(9)
Krause, A. H.: *ref,* 2195
Krauskopf, C. J.: *rev,* 2212; *ref,* 2195, 2212
Krawchick, F. B.: *test,* 2164
Kraybill, E. K.: *ref,* 2195
Krebs, E. G.: *ref,* 1087
Kreit, L. H.: *ref,* 2337
Kriedt, P. H.: *rev,* 2126, 2155; *test,* 2212; *ref,* 2195, 2212
Kriegsfeld, M.: *ref,* 2212
Krienke, J. W.: *ref,* 2212
Kroger, R. O.: *ref,* 2212
Kronenberger, E. J.: *ref,* 2180
Kropp, R. P.: *ref,* 1087, 2199
Krout, M. H.: *ref,* 2195, 4:784(5)
Krumm, R. L.: *ref,* 2195
Kubis, J. F.: *ref,* 1073
Kuder, F.: *ref,* 2194
Kuder, G. F.: *rev,* 1068; *test,* 2193–5, 6:1062; *exc,* 2212–3; *ref,* 1087, 2194–5, 2212, 6:1062(12)
Kulberg, G. E.: *ref,* 2212
Kulick, W.: *ref,* 2195
Kulik, J. A.: *ref,* 2212–3
Kumar, K.: *ref,* 2214
Kunce, J.: *ref,* 2212
Kunce, J. T.: *ref,* 2212
Kuntz, R. H.: *ref,* 1073
Kunze, K. R.: *test,* 780, 2192, 2252
Kunzler, H. G.: *ref,* 2195
Kurek, A.: *ref,* 1069
Kurtz, A. K.: *rev,* 1087, 2140, 2400, 2459, 5:902, 6:1115; *ref,* 2212, 2:1646(5), 2:1670(5), 4: 825(6, 8–9, 12)
Kutner, M.: *ref,* 2195, 2212–3

L & L ASSOCIATES: *test,* 2133
L'Abate, L.: *ref,* 2195, 2212
LaBue, A. C.: *ref,* 2195, 2212
Lackey, F. W.: *ref,* 2251
Lagan, A. E.: *ref,* 1087
LaGrone, C. W.: *ref,* 2195
Lahey, H. C.: *ref,* 2195
Laime, B. F.: *ref,* 2212–3
Laird, D. A.: *ref,* 6:1115(1)
Laird, J. T.: *ref,* 2195
Laleger, G. E.: *ref,* 2213, 3:642(6)
Lamb, M. M.: *exc,* 2:1486
Lambert, C. M.: *ref,* 4:769(7)
Lambert, W. E.: *ref,* 1087
Lampton, T. D.: *ref,* 2135
Lancashire, R.: *ref,* 2247–8, 2254, 2345
Land, M.: *ref,* 2337
Landry, H. A.: *rev,* 2260
Landswerk, D. R.: *ref,* 2451
Lane, G. G.: *ref,* 2239
Lane, P. A.: *ref,* 2195
Laney, A. R.: *ref,* 2225, 2228, 2239, 2251, 2258, 2266
Lang, H.: *ref,* 2227–9, 2258
Lange, H. M.: *ref,* 2195
Langmuir, C. R.: *rev,* 2282
Lanier, L. H.: *ref,* 2266
Lanna, M. G.: *ref,* 2195, 2212
Lansdell, H.: *ref,* 1069
Lantay, G. C. von W.: *ref,* 2212
Lapp, C. J.: *test,* 4:810; *ref,* 1087, 2266

Larose, M. J.: *ref,* 2197
Larsen, A. H.: *ref,* 2195
Larsen, J. L.: *ref,* 2452
Larson, A. A.: *ref,* 1087
Larson, D. N.: *test,* 6:1171, 6:1179
Lasch, H. A.: *ref,* 2212
Lasco, R. A.: *ref,* 1069, 2349
Laslett, H. R.: *ref,* 2212, 2251, 3:678(7), 3:679(5), 4:810(2), 4:813(6)
Latham, A. J.: *ref,* 1072
Latham, E. D.: *ref,* 1072
Lathrop, R. C.: *ref,* 2195
Lattin, G. W.: *ref,* 2195
Lau, A. W.: *ref,* 2197
Lauer, A. R.: *ref,* 2259, 2266
Launer, P. T.: *ref,* 2212
Laurent, H.: *test,* 2141
Lauro, L.: *ref,* 2195
Lavely, R. H.: *ref,* 1087
Law, L. E.: *ref,* 2451
Law, M. L.: *ref,* 1078
Lawes, J. S.: *test,* 2269; *ref,* 2269
Lawrence, R. M.: *ref,* 2195
Lawshe, C. H.: *rev,* 2225, 2251, 3:656; *test,* 2142, 2263, 2304, 2347, 2433–4; *ref,* 2142, 2212, 2260, 2263, 2304, 2433
Lawson, E. D.: *ref,* 2195
Lay, A. W.: *ref,* 2195
Laycock, S. R.: *ref,* 2214, 2242, 2247, 2:1683(4)
Layton, W. L.: *rev,* 2184, 2188, 2199, 5:870; *ref,* 1069, 2212, 2337, 2358, 5:887(2)
Leach, K. W.: *ref,* 2195
Leafgren, F.: *ref,* 2212
Leahy, D. M.: *ref,* 2213
Leahy, L.: *ref,* 2195
Learner, D. B.: *ref,* 2466
LeBlanc, C. R.: *ref,* 2195
LeBold, W. K.: *ref,* 1069, 2266
Ledbetter, E. W.: *ref,* 2195
Ledbetter, P. J.: *ref,* 2383
Ledgerwood, L. B.: *ref,* 2452
Ledgerwood, R.: *rev,* 1:1171
Lee, D. L.: *ref,* 2212
Lee, D. M.: *ref,* 1070
Lee, E. A.: *test,* 2199, 5:870
Lee, E. C.: *ref,* 2212
Lee, E. S.: *ref,* 1087, 2266
Lee, F.: *test,* 2366
Lee, L. J. W.: *ref,* 2285
Lee, M. C.: *ref,* 2135, 2195, 2239
Lee, P. J.: *ref,* 2135, 2195
Lee, R. J.: *ref,* 2212
Lee, T.: *ref,* 2130, 2229
Lefever, D. W.: *rev,* 1078, 2433, 2448, 3:695, 4:726
Lefkowitz, D. M.: *ref,* 2194, 2212
Lehman, R. T.: *ref,* 2195
Lehmann, I. J.: *ref,* 1073
Leigh, K. B.: *ref,* 2212
LeMaster, J. L.: *test,* 2:1479
Lentz, T. F.: *ref,* 3:653(5)
Leon, H.: *ref,* 2212–3
Leonard, L. C.: *ref,* 2213
Leonard, R. J.: *ref,* 2195
Lepak, R. C.: *ref,* 2212
Lepkin, M.: *ref,* 1087
Lepley, W. M.: *ref,* 2381
Leshner, S. S.: *ref,* 2195
Lessing, E. E.: *ref,* 2195
Lester, H.: *ref,* 2212

Lester, R. A.: *ref, 2212*
LeSuer, B. V.: *test, 2:1666*
LeUnes, A.: *ref, 2199*
Levine, H.: *ref, 2189*
Levine, P. R.: *ref, 2195*
Levine, S.: *test, 2315; ref, 1087, 2315*
Levinson, B. M.: *ref, 2195*
Levita, E.: *ref, 2234, 2266*
Levitt, E. E.: *ref, 2195, 2355*
Levy, P. M.: *ref, 1070*
Levy, S.: *rev, 2308, 2463; test, 2310*
Lewis, D. G.: *ref, 1070, 1087, 2249*
Lewis, E. C.: *ref, 2195, 2212-3*
Lewis, G.: *ref, 1073*
Lewis, H. J.: *ref, 1073*
Lewis, J. A.: *ref, 2195*
Lewis, J. W.: *ref, 2325, 2349*
Lewis, L.: *ref, 2195*
Lewis, L. H.: *ref, 1087*
Lewis, R.: *ref, 2212*
Lezotte, L.: *ref, 2212*
Lhota, B.: *ref, 2212*
Libby, B. C.: *ref, 2212*
Licht, M.: *ref, 2259*
Liddle, L. R.: *ref, 2113*
Lief, H. I.: *ref, 2212, 2355*
Lief, V. F.: *ref, 2212, 2355*
Lien, A. J.: *ref, 2199*
Life Insurance Agency Management Association: *test, 2396, 2398, 2401-2, 2407, 2:1670, 6: 1168; ref, 2:1646(1-4), 2:1670 (1-4)*
Liggett, J.: *rev, 2248*
Lighthall, F. K.: *ref, 1087*
Ligthelm, G. J.: *test, 1065*
Likert, R.: *test, 2266; ref, 2266*
Liles, P.: *ref, 786*
Lind, A.: *ref, 2212*
Lind, A. I.: *ref, 2213*
Lindeman, R. P.: *ref, 2195*
Lindemuth, M. H.: *ref, 2451*
Linden, J.: *ref, 2212*
Lindgren, H. C.: *ref, 2195, 2199, 2212*
Lindsay, C. A.: *test, 2212; ref, 2212-3*
Lindsey, T. T.: *ref, 2251, 2259*
Lingwood, J.: *ref, 2239, 5:880(7)*
Linn, M. R.: *ref, 2195*
Linnick, I.: *ref, 2213*
Lips, O.: *ref, 2212*
Lips, O. J.: *ref, 2212*
Lipsett, L.: *ref, 2195*
Lipsman, C. K.: *ref, 2239*
Lipton, L.: *ref, 2212*
Lipton, R. L.: *ref, 2251*
Liske, R. E.: *ref, 2195, 6:1062(8)*
Little, E. B.: *ref, 1072*
Little, J. M.: *ref, 2355*
Little, O. E.: *rev, 3:375-6*
Littleton, I. T.: *ref, 2239, 2266-7, 2433*
Littrell, R. T.: *ref, 1069*
Litzinger, W. D.: *ref, 2454*
Liu, P. Y. H.: *ref, 2212*
Livingston, C. D.: *ref, 2195*
Livingston, E.: *ref, 2195*
Llana, A.: *ref, 2186*
Llewellyn, H. C.: *ref, 2135*
Lloyd, C. J.: *ref, 1087*
Loadman, W. E.: *ref, 2194*
Locke, E. A.: *ref, 1074, 2135, 2340*

Lockman, R. F.: *ref, 1069, 1074, 2135, 2266*
Lodato, F. J.: *ref, 2195*
Loehlin, J. C.: *ref, 1087*
Loevinger, J.: *ref, 2135*
Lofgreen, J. C.: *ref, 1073*
Lofquist, L. H.: *test, 2283-5; ref, 1073, 2283-5*
Logue, J. J.: *ref, 2186*
Lohmann, V. L.: *test, 776*
Lohnes, P. R.: *rev, 2193*
Lohrenz, J. G.: *ref, 2355*
Loman, W.: *test, 2413*
Lomax, P. S.: *rev, 786*
Lombard, D. P.: *test, 1065*
LoMonaco, L. J.: *ref, 2195*
Long, C. D.: *ref, 2451*
Long, J. M.: *ref, 1074, 2195*
Long, J. R.: *ref, 1087*
Long, L.: *ref, 2195, 2212, 2234, 4:812(4), 4:813(5)*
Long, T. E.: *ref, 2427-31*
Longhofer, P.: *ref, 2212*
Longstaff, H. P.: *test, 2135; ref, 2135, 2195, 2212*
Lonner, W. J.: *ref, 2212*
Loo, C.: *ref, 1087*
Loos, F. M.: *ref, 2258*
Loper, R. G.: *exc, 2212-3*
Lopez, F. M.: *ref, 1069*
Loranger, A. W.: *ref, 1087*
Lord, F.: *ref, 4:812(10)*
Lorencki, S. F.: *ref, 2266, 2337*
Lorge, I.: *rev, 782, 1068, 2244; ref, 3:679(8)*
Lorimer, M. W.: *ref, 2212*
Lorr, M.: *ref, 2212*
Lothridge, C. D.: *ref, 1087, 2212, 2334, 2336*
Loudermilk, K. M.: *ref, 1073*
Loughridge, R. E.: *ref, 1069*
Lourens, P.: *test, 2206*
Love, B.: *ref, 2195*
Lovelass, H. D.: *ref, 2195*
Loveless, H. E.: *ref, 798, 2135*
Lowe, B. W.: *ref, 2382*
Lowe, L. M.: *ref, 2135*
Lowin, A.: *ref, 2451*
Lowman, C. L.: *ref, 2197*
Lowrie, K. H.: *ref, 2195, 2212, 3:689(5)*
Lubetkin, A. I.: *ref, 2186*
Lubin, B.: *ref, 2195*
Luborsky, L.: *ref, 2212*
Lucas, D. H.: *ref, 1073, 2195*
Lucas, J. R.: *ref, 2212*
Lucas, R. J.: *ref, 1069*
Luciano, W.: *ref, 2221*
Lucietto, L. L.: *ref, 2451*
Lucio, W. H.: *ref, 2195*
Luckie, W. R.: *ref, 2449, 2451*
Ludlow, H. G.: *ref, 1069, 2349*
Lufburrow, N. A.: *test, 2:1648, 4:736, 4:744*
Lumsden, J.: *rev, 793*
Lundberg, G. A.: *exc, 1087*
Lundgren, E. J.: *ref, 2213*
Lundquist, J. N.: *ref, 1069*
Lundy, C. T.: *ref, 1069*
Lunneborg, C. E.: *ref, 1071, 1073-4, 2195, 2212, 2273, 2349, 2359*
Lunneborg, P. W.: *ref, 1071, 1073-4, 2349, 2359*
Luton, J. N.: *ref, 2195*

Lutz, S. W.: *ref, 2167*
Lybarger, A. E.: *ref, 2283*
Lyden, F. J.: *ref, 2355*
Lyerly, S. B.: *ref, 2212*
Lyman, H. B.: *ref, 2379, 2383*
Lynch, B. L.: *ref, 5:887(3)*
Lynch, M. D.: *ref, 2194, 2212*
Lyon, J. B.: *ref, 2212*

MAAG, C. H.: *ref, 2234*
McArthur, C.: *ref, 2212-3*
MacArthur, R. S.: *ref, 1085*
McCall, J. N.: *rev, 2182, 2193; ref, 2195, 2197*
McCall, R. J.: *ref, 2213*
McCall, W. C.: *ref, 2195*
McCampbell, M. K.: *ref, 2212*
McCann Associates: *test, 2125, 2134, 2158, 2361, 2363-4, 2367-70, 2375, 6:1185, 6:1188, 7:1105*
McCarley, W. W.: *ref, 2169*
McCarthy, M. K.: *ref, 2213*
McCarthy, M. V.: *ref, 2184, 2195, 2213, 5:615(9)*
McCarthy, T. N.: *ref, 2195, 2212*
McCarty, J. J.: *ref, 2148, 2151, 2195, 2223, 2239*
McClelland, D. C.: *ref, 2212*
McClelland, W. A.: *ref, 4:798(3)*
McClintic, S. A.: *ref, 1069*
McClung, J. A.: *ref, 2454*
McClung, R. O.: *ref, 2167*
Maccoby, E. E.: *ref, 1087*
McCollum, E. L.: *ref, 2212*
McComb, H. G.: *test, 4:816, 7: 1136*
McConnell, T. R.: *ref, 2212*
McCormick, E. J.: *test, 5:883; ref, 2304, 2448*
McCormick, J. H.: *ref, 1087*
McCormick, R. R.: *test, 2305*
McCornack, R.: *ref, 2212-3*
McCornack, R. L.: *ref, 2212*
McCoy, J. F.: *ref, 1087, 2285*
McCoy, R. A.: *ref, 2195*
McCoy, W. L.: *ref, 2227, 2234, 2251*
McCullough, C. M.: *ref, 2228-9, 2381*
McCully, C. H.: *ref, 2195*
McCune, C. D.: *ref, 2212*
McDaniel, E. D.: *ref, 1073*
McDaniel, H. B.: *ref, 2180*
McDaniel, J. W.: *ref, 2239, 2251, 2260*
McDole, G.: *ref, 2212*
McDonagh, A. J.: *ref, 2195*
McDonald, B. W.: *ref, 2273*
McDonald, C. O.: *ref, 2451*
McDonald, K. L.: *ref, 1073*
McDonald, R. E.: *ref, 2337*
McDougal, L.: *ref, 2212*
Mace, R. E.: *ref, 2285*
McElheny, W. T.: *ref, 2239*
McElwain, D. W.: *rev, 2118, 2237, 2266, 5:888*
McElwee, A. R.: *ref, 1087*
McElwee, E. W.: *ref, 3:679(6)*
McFarland, R. L.: *ref, 1087*
McGann, J. R.: *ref, 2213*
McGehee, E. M.: *ref, 2286, 2292*
McGehee, W.: *ref, 2135, 2239, 2266*
McGhee, P. R.: *ref, 2451*

McGilligan, R. P.: *ref,* 1087
McGowan, J. F.: *ref,* 2195
McGuire, C.: *ref,* 1069, 2256
McGuire, F.: *ref,* 2471
McGuire, F. L.: *test,* 2471; *ref,* 2355, 2471
McGunnigal, J. V.: *ref,* 2195
McHale, K.: *test,* 3:654; *ref,* 3:654(1–2)
Machover, S.: *ref,* 2234
McIff, L. H.: *ref,* 2212, 7:1078(3)
McIntosh, A.: *ref,* 2212
McIntosh, J. R.: *test,* 2215, 2218
McIntosh, W. J.: *ref,* 2259
Mack, J. L.: *ref,* 2234
McKee, J. P.: *ref,* 1087
McKendry, M. S.: *ref,* 2212
MacKenzie, H.: *ref,* 2212
McKinley, M. M.: *ref,* 1073
MacKinney, A. C.: *rev,* 6:1049, 6:1068, 7:1062; *ref,* 1078, 2132, 2195, 2199, 2212, 2227, 2234, 2239, 2266–7
MacKinnon, D. W.: *ref,* 2212, 2344
MacLean, M. J.: *ref,* 2195
McLennan, T. D.: *ref,* 2449
Macleod, J. W.: *ref,* 2355
McMahon, D.: *test,* 2168; *ref,* 2168
McMahon, W. J.: *ref,* 2195
McMillen, D.: *ref,* 1069, 2256, 2268
McMillen, D. M.: *ref,* 2195
McMurray, R. M.: *ref,* 2227
McMurry, R. N.: *test,* 2110, 2301–2, 2470; *ref,* 2239, 2303
McMurry (Robert N.) & Co.: *test,* 4:772
McNair, D. M.: *ref,* 2212
McNamara, T. A.: *ref,* 1073
McNamara, W. J.: *test,* 5:941, 6:1140, 7:1090; *ref,* 2129, 2151, 2195, 2212, 2454, 2458, 6:1140(1), 6:1153(1), 7:1090(4)
MacNaughton, J. F.: *ref,* 2239
McNeely, J. B.: *ref,* 2212
McNeill, J. G.: *ref,* 2340
McNemar, Q.: *exc,* 1087; *ref,* 1069
MacPhail, A. H.: *ref,* 2195, 2199
McPherson, J. H.: *test,* 2360
McQuaig, J. H.: *test,* 2306
MacQuarrie, T. W.: *test,* 2251, 3:690; *ref,* 2251
McQuary, J. P.: *exc,* 1072
MacQueen, J. C.: *ref,* 2223
McQuitty, L. L.: *ref,* 2212, 2239
McRae, G. G.: *ref,* 2195
McRae, J. A.: *ref,* 2251
McTaggart, H. P.: *ref,* 1087
MacTaggert, D. S.: *ref,* 2285
Madans, A. B.: *test,* 2290, 2317
Madaus, G. F.: *ref,* 2195, 2213, 2221, 2387
Maday, D.: *ref,* 2190
Madden, G. J.: *ref,* 1073
Madden, R.: *test,* 7:559
Maddox, H.: *ref,* 1070
Maffia, L. A.: *ref,* 2212
Magary, J. F.: *ref,* 2180
Magee, P. C.: *ref,* 2195
Magill, J. W.: *ref,* 2195
Maglaras, T.: *ref,* 2451
Magoon, T. M.: *exc,* 2212–3
Magowan, R. E.: *ref,* 2340
Maher, H.: *ref,* 2135, 2231, 2251
Mahlman, R. W.: *ref,* 2197

Mahoney, S. C.: *ref,* 2195
Mahoney, T. A.: *ref,* 2212
Maier, G. E.: *ref,* 2195, 2212
Maier, J.: *test,* 2155, 7:987
Maizell, R. E.: *ref,* 2340
Malcolm, D. D.: *ref,* 2195, 2199, 2212
Malecki, H. R.: *ref,* 1073
Mallinson, G. G.: *ref,* 2195
Malloy, J. P.: *ref,* 2266
Malo, A. H.: *test,* 2150
Malone, F. E.: *ref,* 2103, 2105, 2221
Malone, J. H.: *ref,* 2212
Malone, R. L.: *ref,* 2212
Maloney, P. W.: *ref,* 2448
Mandell, M. M.: *rev,* 2448, 4:785
Mangan, G. L.: *ref,* 1087
Manhold, B. S.: *ref,* 2337
Manhold, J. H.: *ref,* 2337
Mann, C. V.: *test,* 1:1167, 1:1173, 1:1175, 1:1177; *ref,* 2212, 1:1173(1), 1:1175(1)
Mann, L.: *ref,* 1063
Mann, W. G.: *ref,* 2454
Mannheim, B. F.: *ref,* 2451
Manson, G. E.: *test,* 3:642; *ref,* 3:642(2)
Mansour, J. M.: *ref,* 2452
Manuel, H. T.: *rev,* 3:634
Manwiller, C. E.: *ref,* 2244
Manzano, I. B.: *ref,* 2195
Mapeli, D.: *ref,* 2195, 2212
Mapou, A.: *ref,* 1073
Marder, E.: *ref,* 2452
Margolis, V. H.: *ref,* 2195, 2212
Margulies, N.: *ref,* 2221
Maricle, L. R.: *ref,* 2212
Marita, M.: *ref,* 2195
Marjoribanks, K.: *ref,* 1087
Marjoribanks, K. M.: *ref,* 1087
Markham, S. J.: *ref,* 7:1090(14)
Marks, E.: *ref,* 2212
Marks, L. G.: *ref,* 2110
Marks, M. R.: *rev,* 786
Marks, P. A.: *ref,* 2212
Markwardt, F. C.: *ref,* 2212
Marles, L.: *ref,* 2337
Marquis, F. N.: *ref,* 1087
Marsden, R. D.: *ref,* 2195, 2199, 2212
Marsh, J. S.: *ref,* 2212
Marsh, M. M.: *ref,* 1069, 2195
Marsh, S. H.: *ref,* 2195
Marshall, J. C.: *ref,* 2212
Martens, W. L.: *ref,* 1069
Martin, A. H.: *exc,* 2242
Martin, A. M.: *ref,* 2212
Martin, B. L.: *ref,* 1069, 2266, 2268
Martin, F.: *ref,* 2135, 2151
Martin, G. C.: *ref,* 1074, 2195, 2251, 5:886(1)
Martin, G. E.: *ref,* 1073
Martin, G. R.: *ref,* 2197
Martin, H. G.: *test,* 4:726, 4:749
Martin, H. T.: *ref,* 2212, 2266, 2275, 2466
Martin, J. R.: *ref,* 2251
Martin, L. W.: *ref,* 2355
Martin, M. A.: *ref,* 2334
Martin, W. A.: *ref,* 1087
Martin, W. T.: *test,* 2149, 2297, 2307; *ref,* 1069
Martinson, F. M.: *ref,* 2195

Martoccia, C. T.: *ref,* 1069, 1074, 2135, 2266
Martucci, L. G.: *ref,* 2212
Martyn, M. M.: *ref,* 2212
Maschino, P. A.: *test,* 2360
Masih, L. K.: *ref,* 2212
Maslany, G. W.: *ref,* 1087
Mason, C. W.: *test,* 3:695; *ref,* 2:1679(1–3), 3:695(4)
Mason, P. L.: *ref,* 2266
Massey, H. W.: *ref,* 1069
Masten, F. D.: *ref,* 2199
Matarazzo, J. D.: *ref,* 2212
Mather, M. E.: *ref,* 2212
Mathews, J. E.: *ref,* 2451
Mathis, H. I.: *ref,* 1073
Matis, E. E.: *ref,* 2213
Matteson, R. W.: *rev,* 4:726; *ref,* 2195
Matthews, R. E.: *ref,* 2135
Mattson, D. E.: *ref,* 2251, 2355
Matzler, F.: *ref,* 2212
Maxey, E. J.: *ref,* 2167
Maxfield, K. E.: *ref,* 2234
Mayer, D. B.: *ref,* 2212, 7:1090(8)
Mayer, W. K.: *ref,* 2213
Mayeske, G. W.: *ref,* 2195
Mayfield, E. C.: *ref,* 2212
Mayhugh, J. C.: *ref,* 2234
Maynard, P. E.: *ref,* 2103
Mayo, G. D.: *ref,* 2197
Mayo, S. T.: *rev,* 2340, 2347, 6:1135
Mayo, T. B.: *ref,* 2289
Mazak, R. M. J.: *ref,* 2212
Mazer, G. E.: *ref,* 2340
Mazur, J. M.: *ref,* 1073
Mazurek, F. H.: *ref,* 2199
Meadow, A.: *ref,* 2340
Meadow, L.: *ref,* 1073, 2213, 2239, 2379, 2386
Meadows, M. E.: *ref,* 2212
Mearig, J. S.: *ref,* 1069, 1087
Meckler, R. S.: *ref,* 2223
Meddleton, I. G.: *rev,* 5:890
Medsker, L. L.: *ref,* 2212
Meek, C. R.: *ref,* 2195
Meeker, M.: *ref,* 1069
Meerbach, J. C.: *ref,* 2103
Mehenti, P. M.: *ref,* 2212
Mehrens, W. A.: *ref,* 1073, 2212, 7:1090(10)
Mehrotra, C. M. N.: *ref,* 2195
Mehrotra, S. N.: *ref,* 2247
Meigh, C.: *ref,* 1073
Meisgeier, C. H.: *ref,* 2178
Melberg, M. E.: *ref,* 2266
Meleika, L. K.: *ref,* 1069, 2195
Mellenbruch, P. L.: *rev,* 2151, 2436; *test,* 2136, 2257, 2281, 3:662; *ref,* 2281, 3:662(1)
Melton, R. S.: *rev,* 2243, 2274; *ref,* 1069, 1087, 2212
Melton, W. R.: *ref,* 5:870(1)
Melville, N. T.: *ref,* 2177, 2286
Melville, S. D.: *ref,* 2212
Mendelson, M. A.: *ref,* 2189
Mendenhall, G. V.: *ref,* 1082
Mendicino, L.: *ref,* 1069, 2256, 2268
Mendoza, B. F. H.: *ref,* 2212
Mengelkoch, R. F.: *test,* 2436; *ref,* 2436
Mensh, I. N.: *ref,* 2355
Mercer, M.: *ref,* 2213, 2251, 2266

Meredith, P.: *ref,* 1087
Merenda, P. F.: *exc,* 2212-3; *ref,* 1069, 1080
Merkle, R. W.: *ref,* 2213
Merrifield, P. R.: *rev,* 2340, 2347, 6:1135; *ref,* 1074
Merrill, K. E.: *ref,* 2212
Merrill, R. A.: *ref,* 2381
Merritt, C. B.: *ref,* 2212
Merwin, J. C.: *test,* 7:559; *exc,* 1069, 2105; *ref,* 1069, 2212, 2355
Messman, W. B.: *ref,* 2197
Metcalf, W. K.: *ref,* 2355
Metcalfe, Z. F.: *ref,* 3:679(8)
Metwally, A.: *ref,* 1073
Metzcus, R.: *ref,* 2452
Metzger, P. L.: *ref,* 2212
Meyer, B.: *rev,* 2163; *ref,* 2387
Meyer, C. A.: *exc,* 4:786
Meyer, H. H.: *ref,* 1087, 2239, 2266, 2448
Meyer, P. R.: *ref,* 2195
Meyer, W. J.: *ref,* 1087, 2195
Meyers, C. E.: *ref,* 1069, 1087
Meyers, E.: *ref,* 1087
Meyers, E. S.: *ref,* 2195
Michael, W. B.: *rev,* 1072; *ref,* 1071, 1074, 1087, 2251, 2355, 4:761(1)
Michal, R. D.: *ref,* 2195
Michaux, W.: *ref,* 2195
Micheels, W. J.: *rev,* 2437, 5:887
Micheli, G. S.: *ref,* 1087
Michels, A. M.: *ref,* 3:642(3)
Michie, J.: *ref,* 2197
Micka, H. K.: *ref,* 2195
Middaugh, R. W.: *ref,* 2448
Middleton, M.: *test,* 2413
Mihalka, J. A.: *ref,* 2205
Mikan, C. J.: *ref,* 2387
Milam, A. T.: *ref,* 2212
Miles, D. T.: *ref,* 2340
Miles, L. F.: *test,* 4:780; *ref,* 4:780(1)
Miles, R. W.: *ref,* 2195
Miles, W. R.: *ref,* 2223
Milholland, J. E.: *rev,* 1087; *ref,* 1069
Mill, C. R.: *ref,* 1087
Millar, A. C.: *ref,* 2212
Millard, K. A.: *ref,* 2448
Miller, A. D.: *ref,* 2195
Miller, A. J.: *ref,* 2244, 2266
Miller, A. W.: *ref,* 2195, 2212
Miller, C.: *ref,* 2259, 2266
Miller, C. D.: *ref,* 2178, 2212-3
Miller, C. H.: *ref,* 2199
Miller, C. W.: *ref,* 2212
Miller, D. G.: *ref,* 1073
Miller, D. I.: *ref,* 2213
Miller, D. R.: *test,* 5:886-7
Miller, E.: *ref,* 2247
Miller, F.: *test,* 2365
Miller, F. G.: *ref,* 2448
Miller, G. E.: *ref,* 2239
Miller, J.: *ref,* 2186
Miller, J. D.: *ref,* 1069
Miller, J. G.: *test,* 2232
Miller, K. M.: *test,* 2208-9; *ref,* 2209
Miller, L. A.: *ref,* 2212
Miller, L. D.: *ref,* 2212
Miller, M. M.: *ref,* 2151
Miller, P. G.: *ref,* 2212

Miller, P. V. R.: *ref,* 2349
Miller, R. B.: *test,* 5:902; *ref,* 2132, 2135
Miller, R. L.: *ref,* 7:1090(13)
Miller, R. S.: *ref,* 1074
Miller, W. G.: *ref,* 2195
Mills, D. H.: *ref,* 2212
Millsap, C. S.: *ref,* 2195
Milton, C. R.: *ref,* 2212, 2266
Milton, O.: *ref,* 1069
Mims, T. S.: *ref,* 2195
Miner, J. B.: *rev,* 2:1666, 2:1683; *ref,* 1082, 2195
Mink, O. G.: *ref,* 2195
Minnesota Employment Stabilization Research Institute: *test,* 2227
Minnesota State Employment Service: *ref,* 1073
Mirels, H. L.: *ref,* 2212
Misiak, H.: *ref,* 1087
Misko, A. E.: *ref,* 2129
Mitchell, B. C.: *ref,* 5:610(1)
Mitchell, J. V.: *ref,* 1087
Mitchell, L. L.: *ref,* 2451
Mitchell, T. R.: *ref,* 2451
Mitchell, W. M.: *ref,* 2212
Mitra, S.: *ref,* 2173
Mitrano, A. J.: *ref,* 2251, 2266
Mittman, A.: *ref,* 2325
Mitzel, H. E.: *ref,* 2213
Modisette, B. R.: *test,* 2435
Moffatt, D. J.: *ref,* 2355
Moffett, C. R.: *ref,* 2195
Moffie, D. J.: *ref,* 1087, 2135, 2212, 2234, 2239, 2266, 2273
Moldowski, E. W.: *ref,* 2355
Moldowski, L. H. K.: *ref,* 2355
Mollenkopf, W. G.: *ref,* 2239
Molomo, R. R-S.: *ref,* 1069, 2266
Moloney, M. A.: *ref,* 2451
Money, J.: *ref,* 1087
Monroe, G. D.: *ref,* 2195
Monroe, M. B.: *ref,* 2195
Montag, G. M.: *ref,* 1073
Montesano, N.: *ref,* 2180
Montesano, N. R.: *ref,* 2180
Montgomery, G. W. G.: *ref,* 2247
Montgomery, T.: *ref,* 1073
Moodie, M.: *ref,* 2251
Moody, C. B.: *ref,* 1087
Mooney, R. F.: *ref,* 2193
Moore, B. G. R.: *ref,* 2247
Moore, B. V.: *test,* 4:810; *ref,* 2212, 2239, 2266, 3:691(2)
Moore, C. L.: *ref,* 2239
Moore, C. W.: *ref,* 2195
Moore, D. G.: *test,* 5:905; *ref,* 5:905(5)
Moore, G. D.: *ref,* 2195
Moore, H.: *test,* 2142, 6:1032; *ref,* 2:1665(1-2)
Moore, J. E.: *rev,* 1080, 2142, 2223, 2416, 2470, 3:656, 4:813; *ref,* 2227
Moore, J. H.: *test,* 6:1041
Moore, R. A.: *ref,* 2355
Moore, T. I.: *ref,* 1069
Moorman, J. D.: *ref,* 2195
Morea, P. C.: *ref,* 2175
Morey, E. A.: *ref,* 2195, 2213
Morgan, A. B.: *test,* 4:776
Morgan, G. A. V.: *test,* 781A
Morgan, H. H.: *ref,* 2212

Morgan, J. P.: *ref,* 1073
Morgan, M.: *ref,* 1073
Morgan, W. J.: *test,* 4:776; *ref,* 2251, 2266
Morgart, H. S.: *ref,* 1072, 1074
Morici, A. R.: *ref,* 2323, 5:907(2)
Morman, R.: *ref,* 2113
Morman, R. R.: *test,* 2113; *ref,* 2113
Morril, R. A.: *ref,* 2212
Morrill, W. H.: *ref,* 2178, 2213
Morris, C. M.: *ref,* 2266
Morris, D.: *ref,* 1069
Morris, J. B.: *rev,* 2257, 5:954
Morris, J. L.: *ref,* 2180, 2195, 2212
Morris, R. P.: *ref,* 2199
Morris, W. W.: *ref,* 2355
Morrisby, J. R.: *test,* 1070; *ref,* 1070
Morrison, J. S.: *ref,* 2201, 2212
Morrison, J. W.: *ref,* 2195
Morrison, M. M.: *ref,* 1069
Morrison, W. E.: *ref,* 2135
Morrow, H. G.: *ref,* 2449, 2451
Morrow, R. S.: *ref,* 2135, 2228-9, 2258, 2266
Morrow, W. R.: *ref,* 2212
Morse, J. L.: *ref,* 1063
Morse, P. K.: *ref,* 2212
Morsink, H. M.: *ref,* 2452, 2457
Morson, M.: *ref,* 2199
Mortensen, D. G.: *ref,* 2212, 4:828(6)
Mortola, D. S.: *ref,* 2195
Morton, J.: *ref,* 2195
Morton, N. W.: *rev,* 2212, 2239, 1:1180, 2:1682
Mosel, J. N.: *ref,* 2448
Moser, H. P.: *ref,* 2212
Moser, W. E.: *ref,* 1069, 2195
Moses, R. G.: *ref,* 2221
Moshin, S. M.: *ref,* 1069
Mosier, C. I.: *rev,* 2433, 2448; *ref,* 2212
Moskovis, L. M.: *ref,* 2135
Moss, F. A.: *test,* 2381, 2413
Motto, J. J.: *ref,* 2195
Moul, E. C.: *ref,* 2195
Moullette, J. B.: *ref,* 2451
Mouly, G. J.: *ref,* 1073
Moutoux, A. C.: *test,* 2433
Mowbray, J. K.: *ref,* 2195, 2212, 2383
Mowrer, G. E.: *ref,* 2212
Mowry, H. W.: *test,* 2453; *ref,* 2448
Mowry, J. G.: *ref,* 2221
Mueller, D. E.: *ref,* 1069, 1073
Mueller, E. J.: *ref,* 2379, 2383
Mueller, M. W.: *ref,* 1087
Muenter, M. D.: *ref,* 2228, 2234
Mugaas, H. D.: *ref,* 2195
Muhlenkamp, A. F.: *ref,* 2383
Mukerjee, M.: *ref,* 2173, 2195
Mukherjee, B. N.: *ref,* 1069, 1087
Mulaik, S. A.: *ref,* 2273
Mulder, F.: *ref,* 2195
Mullen, R. A.: *ref,* 1073
Munday, L. A.: *rev,* 2349; *ref,* 2212
Mundy, P.: *ref,* 2337, 2355
Munson, H. R.: *ref,* 2195
Munson, P. J.: *ref,* 2103
Murphy, F. E.: *ref,* 3:635(9)

Murphy, H. D.: *exc,* 1072
Murphy, L. W.: *ref,* 2244, 2251, 2266
Murphy, M. D.: *ref,* 2451
Murphy, P. S.: *ref,* 2212
Murphy, R. O.: *ref,* 2212
Murray, J. B.: *ref,* 2212
Murray, J. E.: *ref,* 1087, 2266
Murray, L. E.: *ref,* 2406, 2408
Murray, S.: *ref,* 2212
Murtaugh, J. J.: *ref,* 2195
Mussen, P.: *ref,* 2212
Mussio, J. J.: *ref,* 1087, 2212, 2334
Muthard, J. E.: *ref,* 2283
Mydelle, E. K.: *ref,* 2213
Myers, C. S.: *exc,* 2212-3
Myers, C. T.: *rev,* 2269; *ref,* 2241
Myers, M.: *ref,* 1069
Myers, R. W.: *ref,* 1073
Myers, W. P.: *ref,* 2103
Myklebust, H. R.: *ref,* 1087, 2258, 2266, 3:671(11), 3:678(18)

NLN MEASUREMENT and Evaluation Service: *ref,* 2379, 2383, 2386-7
Nadel, R. S.: *ref,* 2199
Nagel (Jerome H.) Associates: *test,* 2309
Nair, R. K.: *ref,* 2199, 2239, 2244, 2266
Nalder, W. K.: *ref,* 2451
Namani, A. K.: *ref,* 2195, 2212
Nance, R. D.: *ref,* 2212
Naor, N. K.: *ref,* 2212
Nardi, A. H.: *ref,* 1087
Nash, A. N.: *ref,* 1073, 2195, 2212
Nash, M. J.: *ref,* 1069
Nash, N.: *test,* 2372
Nash, P. G.: *ref,* 2199
Natale, G. M.: *ref,* 795, 799
National Bureau of Educational and Social Research: *test,* 5:604, 6:1028
National Business Education Association: *test,* 777-8, 783, 785-6, 795, 799
National Institute for Personnel Research: *test,* 2104, 2261, 2291, 2450, 6:1026
National Institute of Industrial Psychology: *test,* 2130-1, 2247-50, 2254, 2271, 2345, 4:724, 5:880
National League for Nursing, Inc.: *test,* 2383-7, 6:1158b, 6:1159; *ref,* 2383, 2385, 2387, 6:1159(2, 4)
Naughton, J.: *ref,* 1069
Nauss, A. H.: *ref,* 2195, 2212
Navran, L.: *ref,* 2212-3
Neal, C. M.: *ref,* 2195
Neal, R. G.: *ref,* 2212
Nealy, S. M.: *ref,* 2451
Neary, J. R.: *ref,* 2452
Needham, W. E.: *ref,* 1074
Neel, R. G.: *ref,* 2448
Neeman, R. L.: *ref,* 2228, 2234
Neitzel, B. J.: *ref,* 2457
Nelson, A. G.: *exc,* 3:635; *ref,* 2194
Nelson, B. C.: *ref,* 2355
Nelson, C. L.: *ref,* 1087
Nelson, C. W.: *test,* 2455, 2467
Nelson, D. M.: *ref,* 2209
Nelson, H. F.: *ref,* 2197

Nelson, J. C.: *ref,* 1087
Nelson, J. H.: *ref,* 786, 795, 799
Nelson, K. G.: *ref,* 2212
Nelson, L. T.: *ref,* 1069, 2268
Nelson, W. H.: *ref,* 1069
Nelson-Jones, R.: *ref,* 2355
Nemzek, C. L.: *ref,* 2244
Nesbitt, J. D.: *ref,* 1073
Netsky, M. G.: *ref,* 2355
Neuhaus, J. O.: *ref,* 1087
Neumann, I.: *ref,* 2212
Neumann, T. M.: *ref,* 2195
Newall, K.: *ref,* 2266
Newman, B. H.: *rev,* 790, 7:552
Newman, J.: *ref,* 2195, 3:660(19)
Newman, S. H.: *ref,* 2214, 2241, 2266
Newman, W. H.: *ref,* 2451
Newport, G.: *ref,* 2451
Neyhart, A. E.: *test,* 2470, 2472-3
Neyhart, H. L.: *test,* 2470
Nichol, J. S.: *ref,* 2103
Nicholls, J. G.: *ref,* 1087
Nicholson, E.: *ref,* 2199, 2212
Nickels, J. B.: *ref,* 2212
Nicksick, T.: *ref,* 1073
Nicol, D. D.: *ref,* 2195
Nicolay, R. C.: *ref,* 2195
Niebuhr, H. E.: *ref,* 2454
Nielson, C. L.: *ref,* 2212
Niemeyer, K. P.: *ref,* 2451
Ninemeier, J. D.: *ref,* 1073
Nissley, W. W.: *ref,* 2323
Nitardy, J. R.: *ref,* 1073
Nixon, M.: *ref,* 1087, 2135, 2195, 2239
Nixon, M. E.: *ref,* 2195
Nolan, E. G.: *ref,* 2212
Nolen, D. R.: *ref,* 1073
Nolting, E.: *ref,* 2213
Nordén, K.: *ref,* 2223, 2228
Norenberg, C. D.: *ref,* 2212
Norman, J. H.: *test,* 2108, 2156, 2161, 2165, 2200
Norman, R. D.: *ref,* 3:639(2)
Norman, W. T.: *rev,* 2177; *ref,* 2197
Normile, R. H.: *ref,* 2221
Norrell, G.: *ref,* 2195, 2212
North, A. J.: *ref,* 2195, 2239
North, R. D.: *ref,* 2195, 2323, 5:610(3)
Norton, D. P.: *ref,* 1069
Norton, E. D.: *ref,* 2212
Nottingham, R. D.: *ref,* 2213
Novack, H. S.: *ref,* 1087
Novak, B. J.: *ref,* 2195, 2266
Novak, D. F.: *ref,* 2195
Novick, M. R.: *ref,* 2355
Nuckols, R.: *ref,* 2135
Nuckols, R. C.: *ref,* 2448
Nugent, F. A.: *ref,* 1069, 1074, 2195
Null, E. J.: *ref,* 2452
Nunnery, M. Y.: *ref,* 2195
Nuttall, R. L.: *ref,* 1073
Nutting, R. E.: *ref,* 2213
Nuzum, R. E.: *ref,* 2213

OAKES, F.: *ref,* 1069, 2195
Oaklander, H.: *ref,* 2451, 2454
Oakley, C. A.: *rev,* 2242, 2257, 3:635
Oberheim, G. M.: *ref,* 3:628(3-4, 6)

Oberlin, K. W.: *exc,* 2242
O'Block, F. R.: *ref,* 1077
Oborny, W. J.: *ref,* 2451
O'Brien, M. C.: *ref,* 1087
Obst, F.: *ref,* 2213
O'Connell, M. M.: *ref,* 798
O'Connor, G.: *ref,* 2251
O'Connor J.: *test,* 2228-9, 2259; *ref,* 2228-9, 2259
O'Connor, J. P.: *ref,* 1087, 2212, 2221
O'Connor, N.: *ref,* 1073
Odell, C. E.: *ref,* 1073
Odgers, J. G.: *test,* 2201; *ref,* 1069
Odoroff, M. E.: *ref,* 2212
Oelke, M. C.: *ref,* 2212
Ogawa, G. Y.: *test,* 6:1171, 6:1179
Ogden, M. H.: *ref,* 2212
Ogden, W. E.: *ref,* 2212
O'Hara, R. P.: *ref,* 1069, 2195, 2221
Ohio Employment Service, State Testing Staff: *ref,* 1073
Ohio Scholarship Tests: *test,* 6:37, 6:42, 6:49
Ohlsen, M. M.: *ref,* 2212
Ohvall, R. A.: *ref,* 2212
Ojha, J. M.: *ref,* 1069
Okun, B. F.: *ref,* 2213
Olafson, G. A. A.: *ref,* 2452
Older, H. J.: *ref,* 2212
Olheiser, M. D.: *test,* 2213; *ref,* 2212-3
Oliver, J. A.: *ref,* 2195, 2212
Oliver, J. E.: *test,* 2172, 2178
Oliver, R. A. C.: *ref,* 2212
Oliver, T. C.: *test,* 2178; *ref,* 6:1153(2)
Oliverio, M. E.: *rev,* 2142, 2466, 7:554, 7:559
Ollrich, A. H.: *ref,* 2223, 2235
O'Loughlin, D. R.: *ref,* 2195
Olsen, M. A.: *ref,* 2349
Olson, D. J.: *ref,* 1087
Olson, D. W.: *ref,* 2197
Olson, H.: *ref,* 2285
Onarheim, J.: *ref,* 2195, 2239
O'Neil, P. M.: *ref,* 2213
Ontario College of Education. See University of Toronto.
Ontario Commercial Teachers' Association: *ref,* 798
Oosthuizen, S.: *test,* 1079, 2191
Opdyke, D.: *ref,* 2355
Openshaw, J. M.: *ref,* 2168
Orbach, C. E.: *test,* 5:954
Orleans, J. S.: *rev,* 786, 792
O'Rourke, L. J.: *test,* 2138, 2260
Orpet, R. E.: *ref,* 1087
Orr, B.: *ref,* 1073
Ort, R. S.: *ref,* 2195
Ortenzi, A.: *ref,* 2212
Ortmeyer, D.: *ref,* 2212
Ortmeyer, D. H.: *ref,* 2212
Orton, K. D.: *exc,* 2275
Osborn, H. B.: *test,* 1078
Osborne, A. E.: *rev,* 3:377, 3:381; *ref,* 2266
Osborne, H. F.: *ref,* 2135, 2227-9, 2251, 2258, 2266
Osborne, R. T.: *ref,* 2195, 2212, 2223
Osburn, H.: *ref,* 1071
Osburn, H. G.: *ref,* 1069, 1087, 2239

O'Shea, A. J.: *ref,* 2194, 2212
Osipow, S. H.: *ref,* 2103, 2195, 2212
Ostlund, L. A.: *ref,* 2195
Ostrand, J. L.: *ref,* 2212
Ostrom, S. R.: *ref,* 2212
Ota, Y. K.: *ref,* 1069
Otis, J. L.: *rev,* 2260, 2263, 3:680, 4:776; *test,* 2140–1; *ref,* 2135, 2227–9, 2251, 2258, 2266, 2457, 6:1062(8)
O'Toole, C. E.: *test,* 4:761
O'Toole, J. J.: *ref,* 2212
Otterness, W. B.: *ref,* 2239, 2266
Ousley, J. M.: *ref,* 2451, 2454
Overall, J. E.: *ref,* 2195
Overley, H. M.: *test,* 6:44
Overton, E. C.: *ref,* 1087
Owen, H. F.: *test,* 4:782, 4:816
Owen, K.: *test,* 1064
Owen, M. L.: *ref,* 2344
Owen, S. V.: *ref,* 2389
Owens, C. D.: *ref,* 1087
Owens, W. A.: *rev,* 2255, 2272; *test,* 2239, 2358, 6:1135; *ref,* 2212, 2239, 2358, 6:1135(1)
Oxlade, M.: *ref,* 2237, 2242
Oxlade, M. N.: *ref,* 2227, 2266

PABLE, M. W.: *ref,* 2221
Pacinelli, R. N.: *ref,* 2451
Packard, A. G.: *rev,* 2231, 2234
Paepe, C.: *ref,* 2212
Page, A. N.: *ref,* 2325
Page, D. S.: *ref,* 2463, 2466
Page, M. J.: *ref,* 2212
Page, M. L.: *ref,* 2258
Page, R. M.: *test,* 2399
Paiva, R. E. A.: *ref,* 2355
Pallone, N. J.: *ref,* 2195, 2221
Palmer, D. H.: *ref,* 2195
Palormo, J. M.: *rev,* 2292, 2299; *test,* 2334; *ref,* 2334
Palubinskas, A. L.: *ref,* 2212
Pankaskie, M.: *ref,* 1087
Pappas, A. J.: *ref,* 2212
Paredes, A.: *ref,* 2234
Parke, L. A.: *test,* 3:385
Parker, A. D.: *ref,* 2195
Parker, A. W.: *ref,* 2213
Parker, C.: *test,* 6:1104
Parker, E. B.: *ref,* 2212
Parker, H. J.: *ref,* 1087, 2285
Parker, J. F.: *ref,* 2227–8, 2234
Parker, J. W.: *ref,* 2140, 2195, 2212, 2448
Parker, T. C.: *ref,* 2454
Parkins, G. L.: *ref,* 2337
Parkinson, M.: *ref,* 2180, 2195, 2212
Parks, D. J.: *ref,* 2452
Parmenter, M. D.: *test,* 6:1053
Parmenter, W. H.: *ref,* 1069, 2256, 2268
Parmon, R. E.: *ref,* 1069
Parnes, S. J.: *ref,* 2340
Parnicky, J. J.: *test,* 2217; *ref,* 2217
Parry, D. F.: *ref,* 2212
Parry, J. B.: *ref,* 4:724(1)
Parry, M. E.: *ref,* 2129, 2448
Parsons, G. E.: *ref,* 2451
Parsons, R. T.: *ref,* 2212–3
Parton, N. W.: *ref,* 1069, 2195
Pascale, A. C.: *ref,* 1069, 1080

Pasewark, R. A.: *ref,* 2212
Paskewitz, D. L.: *ref,* 1073
Pasricha, P.: *ref,* 1069
Passmore, J. L.: *ref,* 2105, 2197
Pate, K. D.: *ref,* 2195, 2221
Paterson, D. G.: *rev,* 780, 2311, 2395, 2:1665, 3:625, 3:631, 4:825, 4:828; *test,* 2135, 2258, 2266, 3:671, 3:689; *ref,* 2135, 2195, 2212–3, 2227–9, 2258, 2266, 3:642(4), 3:671(3), 3:678(5), 3:679(3)
Patinka, P. J.: *ref,* 2433
Patterson, C. H.: *ref,* 2195, 2212, 2239, 2266
Patterson, J. W.: *ref,* 2451
Patton, W. M.: *ref,* 2448
Pauk, W.: *ref,* 798
Pauk, W. J.: *ref,* 1069
Paul, G. J.: *ref,* 2212
Paulson, B. B.: *ref,* 2195
Payne, D. A.: *rev,* 2174
Payne, L. C.: *test,* 2358; *ref,* 2358
Payton, O. D.: *ref,* 2225
Peak, L. N.: *ref,* 2452
Peak, P.: *test,* 4:448
Pear, T. H.: *exc,* 2242
Pearlman, S.: *ref,* 2195
Pearson, D. T.: *ref,* 2195
Pearson, W. W.: *ref,* 2448
Peatman, J. G.: *rev,* 1068, 2:1667
Peck, R. F.: *ref,* 1069
Pedersen, D. M.: *ref,* 2195
Pedersen, E. C.: *ref,* 1069
Pedersen, R. A.: *test,* 792, 3:388c, 4:454; *ref,* 4:454(1)
Pedersen, T.: *ref,* 2251
Peel, E. A.: *rev,* 1070, 2269; *ref,* 2247
Peel, R. A.: *ref,* 1069
Pehrson, P. J.: *ref,* 798
Peirce, J. R.: *ref,* 2451, 2454
Pelosi, J. W.: *ref,* 2234
Pemberton, C. L.: *ref,* 2195
Pender, F. R.: *ref,* 1069, 2195
Pendergraph, A.: *ref,* 1069
Penfield, R. V.: *ref,* 2107, 2212, 2239, 2454
Pennington, A. L.: *ref,* 2212
Penzer, W. N.: *ref,* 2195
Peres, S. H.: *ref,* 2212, 7:1090(3)
Peretz, D.: *ref,* 2234
Perkins, K. J.: *test,* 4:799; *ref,* 4:799(1)
Perlman, R. M.: *ref,* 1087
Perrine, M. W.: *ref,* 1069, 2195, 2266
Perrone, P. A.: *ref,* 1073
Perry, D.: *ref,* 2212
Perry, D. K.: *ref,* 2197, 2212
Perry, J. D.: *ref,* 2195, 2212, 2234, 4:812(4), 4:813(4)
Perry, J. O.: *ref,* 1087, 2195
Perry, M. L.: *ref,* 2195
Perry, S. D.: *ref,* 2454
Person, G. A.: *ref,* 2212
Personnel Institute, Inc.: *test,* 2139, 2403, 6:1118, 6:1121
Personnel Research & Development Corporation: *test,* 2404
Personnel Research Board, Ohio State University: *test,* 2449, 2451
Personnel Research Institute: *test,* 6:1180

Pervin, D. W.: *ref,* 2195
Pesci, M. L.: *ref,* 2212, 2344
Peters, D. R.: *ref,* 2454
Peters, E. F.: *ref,* 2195, 2212
Peters, H. D.: *ref,* 1087
Peters, H. J.: *ref,* 1073
Petersen, D. F.: *ref,* 2212
Petersen, H.: *ref,* 1069
Petersen, L. P.: *ref,* 2195
Peterson, A. J.: *ref,* 1069
Peterson, B. M.: *ref,* 2212–3
Peterson, C. A.: *ref,* 2212
Peterson, C. D.: *ref,* 1073
Peterson, D. F.: *ref,* 1069, 1087
Peterson, F. E.: *ref,* 2223, 2227, 2229, 2235
Peterson, G. D.: *ref,* 2451
Peterson, J.: *ref,* 2266
Peterson, J. E.: *ref,* 1069
Peterson, L. R.: *ref,* 2239, 2266
Peterson, M. A.: *ref,* 1073, 2251
Peterson, M. B.: *ref,* 2195
Peterson, M. E.: *ref,* 2195, 2213
Peterson, O. L.: *ref,* 2355
Peterson, R. A.: *ref,* 2212
Peterson, S.: *rev,* 3:680–1; *ref,* 2337
Petit, J. L.: *ref,* 1069
Petrie, A.: *ref,* 2135, 2229
Petrik, N. D.: *ref,* 2212–3
Petro, P. K.: *ref,* 2135, 2195
Petty, G. C.: *ref,* 1073
Pfanstiel, E. E.: *ref,* 2457
Phelan, R. F.: *ref,* 2195
Phelps, H. R.: *ref,* 2212
Philbrick, B. B.: *ref,* 2234
Philip, B. R.: *ref,* 2259
Philippus, M. J.: *ref,* 2214
Phillip, P. J.: *ref,* 2337
Phillips, B. K.: *ref,* 2234
Phillips, G. R.: *test,* 2202; *ref,* 2266
Phillips, J. J.: *ref,* 2259
Phillips, L. W.: *ref,* 2195
Phillips, M.: *ref,* 2212
Phillips, W. S.: *ref,* 2195
Phipps, G. T.: *ref,* 1072, 1074, 2337
Pickett, L. M.: *ref,* 1073
Pidgeon, D. A.: *test,* 2269
Pierce-Jones, J.: *rev,* 2195; *ref,* 2195
Pierson, G. A.: *ref,* 2355, 4:812(11)
Pierson, J. S.: *ref,* 2212
Pierson, R. R.: *ref,* 2212
Pilapil, B.: *ref,* 2212
Pillay, P. G.: *ref,* 2266
Pimsleur, P.: *ref,* 1074
Pinneau, S. R.: *ref,* 2212
Piotrowski, Z. A.: *ref,* 2195
Pippert, R. R.: *ref,* 1069
Pittman, F. M.: *ref,* 2234, 2267
Plant, W. T.: *ref,* 1087
Planty, E.: *test,* 2463
Plata, M.: *ref,* 2194
Plotkin, A. L.: *ref,* 2193
Plummer, R. H.: *ref,* 1069, 2195
Pockell, N. E.: *ref,* 1073
Podshadley, D. W.: *ref,* 2337
Poe, C.: *ref,* 2212
Poe, W. A.: *ref,* 2212, 2239, 5:886(2), 5:888(4)
Poidevin, B.: *ref,* 2266
Poley, J. P.: *rev,* 2285
Pollack, I. W.: *ref,* 2212
Pollack, S.: *ref,* 2355

Pollan, W. D.: *ref,* 2195
Pomeroy, M. C.: *ref,* 1069
Pond, B. B.: *ref,* 2448
Pond, M.: *ref,* 2135
Pont, H. B.: *ref,* 1087, 2195
Pool, D. A.: *ref,* 2195, 2212
Pooler, M. H.: *ref,* 1087
Poor, F. A.: *ref,* 2195
Portenier, L. G.: *ref,* 2244
Porter, A.: *ref,* 2212
Porter, J. M.: *rev,* 2252, 3:678, 3:682
Porter, L. W.: *rev,* 2111-2, 2412
Posthuma, A. B.: *ref,* 2212
Poston, W. K.: *ref,* 2195
Poteet, J. A.: *ref,* 1087
Potter, F. T.: *test,* 2372
Pouncey, A. T.: *ref,* 1087
Pounders, C. J.: *ref,* 1071, 2325
Powell, F. V.: *ref,* 2212
Powell, J. O.: *ref,* 2195, 2212
Powell, M. B.: *ref,* 2135, 2229
Powers, G. P.: *ref,* 2195, 2212
Powers, M. K.: *ref,* 2212
Prado, W. M.: *ref,* 2195
Prahl, M. R.: *ref,* 1082
Prak, J. L.: *test,* 2282
Prakash, J. C.: *ref,* 2228-9
Pratt, A. B.: *ref,* 2213
Prediger, D.: *test,* 2100
Preische, W. A.: *ref,* 2244
Prescott, G. A.: *ref,* 5:855(1)
Pressel, G. L.: *ref,* 2289
Pressey, S. L.: *test,* 2:1667
Preston, L. R.: *ref,* 2168
Price, J. S.: *ref,* 2273
Price, P. B.: *ref,* 2355
Price, R. G.: *rev,* 2137, 3:385, 6:31, 7:554; *ref,* 777, 787, 796
Price, T. H.: *ref,* 1066, 2199
Prickett, G. L.: *ref,* 7:1078(4)
Prideaux, G. G.: *test,* 5:870; *ref,* 2199
Priebe, D. W.: *ref,* 2212
Prien, E.: *ref,* 2457
Prien, E. P.: *ref,* 2140, 2151, 6:1062 (8)
Priest, H. F.: *rev,* 2179
Primmer, R. D.: *ref,* 1073
Prince, R. H.: *ref,* 2355
Princenthal, H. H.: *ref,* 2195
Pritchard, M. C.: *ref,* 2258, 2266
Probst, J. B.: *test,* 4:785; *ref,* 4:785(1-2)
Proctor, C. H.: *ref,* 1087
Proctor, W. M.: *test,* 2:1661
Proger, B. B.: *ref,* 1063
Pruzek, R. M.: *ref,* 2221
Pryer, M. W.: *ref,* 2452
Psychological Corporation: ·*test,* 2129, 2164, 2338, 2346, 2357, 2376-7, 2379-80, 7:552, 7:554, 7:559A
Psychological Publications Press: *test,* 2295, 2313, 2321
Psychological Services Bureau: *test,* 2106, 2128, 2160, 2390, 2405, 2417, 2419
Psychologists and Educators, Inc.: *test,* 2276
Public Personnel Association: *test,* 6:1131
Pugh, L. A.: *ref,* 2234
Pugh, R. C.: *ref,* 1069, 1073, 2349

Purdue Research Foundation: *test,* 2234
Purdy, B. F.: *ref,* 2135
Purdy, R. D.: *test,* 1:943-4
Pyles, M. K.: *ref,* 2212
Pyskacek, R. A.: *ref,* 2337

QUASHA, W. H.: *test,* 2266; *ref,* 2266
Quasha, W. R.: *ref,* 2266
Quatman, G. L.: *ref,* 2180
Quayle, M. S.: *ref,* 2135
Queensland Department of Public Instruction: *test,* 793, 2238, 5:890
Quereshi, M. Y.: *rev,* 1069, 1087
Quidwai, A. A.: *ref,* 1069
Quimby, N. F.: *ref,* 2195
Quiring, R. G.: *ref,* 2212

RABE, A.: *ref,* 2266
Rabiner, A.: *ref,* 2234
Rabinowitz, W.: *ref,* 2212
Racky, D. J.: *ref,* 1087, 2195, 2251
Radcliffe, J. A.: *ref,* 2195
Radford, D.: *ref,* 2349
Radley, S.: *ref,* 2234
Raffel, S. C.: *ref,* 2135
Ragland, R.: *ref,* 2234
Ragland, R. E.: *ref,* 2234
Raine, W. J.: *ref,* 2349
Rainey, R. G.: *ref,* 1087
Raju, N. S.: *ref,* 2212
Raju, V.: *ref,* 1087
Raley, C. L.: *ref,* 2212
Ralph, R. B.: *ref,* 1073, 2355
Ralph, S.: *ref,* 1073
Ramamurthi, P. V.: *ref,* 1087
Ramaseshan, R. S.: *ref,* 1087
Ramey, W. S.: *ref,* 2199
Ramsey, R. R.: *ref,* 2349
Randecker, H.: *ref,* 1087
Rapaport, D.: *ref,* 2212
Rapin, I.: *ref,* 2234
Rapp, M. L.: *ref,* 2340
Raskin, E.: *test,* 1082
Rasmussen, O. M.: *test,* 4:450
Rau, G. N.: *ref,* 2427
Raubenheimer, A. S.: *ref,* 2251, 2260, 3:678(6), 3:679(4)
Raubenheimer, I. van W.: *ref,* 2142
Rausch, V. L.: *ref,* 2212
Ravensborg, M. R.: *ref,* 2195, 2197, 2205
Rawlings, J. S.: *ref,* 2452
Rawlings, T. D.: *ref,* 1073, 1087
Ray, D. K.: *ref,* 2358
Ray, T. S.: *ref,* 2234
Raygor, A. L.: *ref,* 2195
Razin, A. M.: *ref,* 2212
Razor, B. A. L.: *ref,* 1074
Recktenwald, L. N.: *ref,* 3:635 (14-5, 18)
Rector, A. P.: *ref,* 1069
Reddig, G. L.: *ref,* 1087
Redfearn, L.: *ref,* 3:678(13)
Redlener, J.: *ref,* 2195, 2212
Redmond, J. F.: *ref,* 2212
Reed, H. B.: *ref,* 3:653(6, 9), 3: 678(16)
Reed, R. L.: *ref,* 2449, 2451
Reed, W. W.: *ref,* 2195
Rees, V. M.: *ref,* 2349
Reese, H.: *ref,* 2340
Reese, H. W.: *ref,* 2340

Refice, R. J.: *ref,* 2195
Reichard, S.: *ref,* 2266
Reicherter, R. F.: *test,* 789
Reid, J.: *ref,* 795
Reid, J. W.: *ref,* 2195, 2266
Reier, G. W.: *ref,* 1073
Reilly, R. R.: *ref,* 2251
Reinhard, N. F.: *ref,* 2195
Reinhart, W. C.: *ref,* 1069
Reining, H.: *ref,* 1087
Reinke, B. C.: *ref,* 2337
Reinstedt, R. N.: *ref,* 2212, 7:1090 (3)
Reitan, H. M.: *ref,* 1073
Reiter, R. G.: *ref,* 2186
Reitz, W. E.: *ref,* 2212
Remmers, H. H.: *rev,* 1081; *test,* 2448, 4:798; *ref,* 2195, 2259, 2448, 4:798(4), 4:800(3)
Remmers, L. J.: *ref,* 2448
Renck, R.: *test,* 6:1107, 6:1171, 6:1179; *ref,* 5:905(5)
Renfer, M. E. F.: *ref,* 2195
Renick, C. P.: *ref,* 1073
Renke, W. W.: *ref,* 2195
Rennels, M. R.: *ref,* 1087
Replogle, J. R.: *ref,* 2193
Repovich, L. D.: *ref,* 2234
Resnick, H.: *ref,* 2195
Reuning, H.: *test,* 2278
Reymert, M. L.: *test,* 1:1172; *exc,* 2298
Reynolds, H. J.: *ref,* 2344
Reynolds, W. A.: *ref,* 2239, 2251, 2260
Rezler, A. G.: *ref,* 2195
Rhinehart, J. B.: *ref,* 2381
Rhode, J. G.: *ref,* 2212
Rhodes, G. S.: *exc,* 2216; *ref,* 2212
Ricard, E. L.: *ref,* 2212, 7:1090(3)
Rice, R. R.: *test,* 2:1481
Rice, V.: *ref,* 1069
Richard, J. T.: *ref,* 2194
Richard, W. A.: *ref,* 2183
Richards, J. M.: *rev,* 2355; *ref,* 2273, 2355
Richards, M. K. B.: *test,* 781A, 2269
Richardson, B. K.: *ref,* 2283
Richardson, Bellows, Henry & Co., Inc.: *test,* 791, 2143-7, 2264-5, 2267, 2287, 2314, 2458, 6:1096, 6:1126, 6:1191, 7:982, 7:996, 7: 1032
Richardson, H. D.: *test,* 2:1645, 2:1658, 2:1660; *ref,* 2:1645(1), 2:1658(1), 2:1660(1)
Richardson, J. F.: *ref,* 2195
Richardson, M. W.: *rev,* 782; *test,* 792, 3:388c, 4:454
Riches, E.: *ref,* 2355
Richman, J. T.: *ref,* 1069
Richmond, A. M.: *ref,* 2212
Rickard, F. S.: *ref,* 2221
Ricks, J. H.: *test,* 1063
Ricksecker, E. L.: *ref,* 2195, 2212
Riddle, C. W.: *ref,* 1069
Ridgway, R. W.: *ref,* 1087
Riedel, R. G.: *ref,* 2195
Riklan, M.: *ref,* 2266
Riland, L. H.: *ref,* 2239
Riley, G.: *ref,* 3:671(2)
Riley, R. C.: *ref,* 2323

Rim, Y.: *ref*, 2223, 2225, 2227–9, 2231, 2234–5, 2451, 2454
Rines, W. B.: *ref*, 2234
Rinsland, H. D.: *ref*, 2228, 2234, 2239, 2258, 2266
Ripka, G. E.: *test*, 788
Risch, F.: *ref*, 2195
Rishel, D. F.: *ref*, 2178, 2195, 2212
Risher, C. C.: *ref*, 2195
Ritchie, C. M.: *ref*, 2194, 2212
Rittenhouse, C. H.: *ref*, 2212–3
Ritter, W.: *ref*, 2234
Rivers, L. W.: *ref*, 1087
Roadman, H. E.: *ref*, 2212
Robb, G. P.: *ref*, 2195
Robbins, A.: *ref*, 2195
Robbins, J. E.: *ref*, 2195
Roberts, A. O. H.: *rev*, 2239
Roberts, B. B.: *ref*, 2212
Roberts, D.: *ref*, 1087
Roberts, F. M.: *ref*, 2212–3
Roberts, J. P.: *ref*, 2195
Roberts, J. R.: *test*, 2231, 5:894; *ref*, 2227, 2231
Roberts, R. K.: *ref*, 2212
Roberts, S. O.: *ref*, 1087, 2195
Roberts, W. H.: *ref*, 2195
Robertson, G. J.: *ref*, 1069
Robertson, J. P. S.: *test*, 2388
Robertson, L. S.: *ref*, 2355
Robertson, M. H.: *ref*, 1069
Robey, D. L.: *ref*, 1069
Robinson, F. K.: *ref*, 1069
Robinson, F. P.: *ref*, 1087
Robinson, H. A.: *exc*, 2212
Robinson, H. W.: *ref*, 2451
Robinson, J. B.: *ref*, 1087, 2212, 2251
Robinson, J. M.: *ref*, 1087
Robinson, L. G. M.: *ref*, 1073
Robinson, W. A.: *ref*, 2169
Robison, J. O.: *ref*, 1073
Rochlin, I.: *ref*, 1087
Rock, D. A.: *ref*, 2212, 2349
Rock, M. L.: *test*, 4:827; *ref*, 4:827(1)
Rock, R. T.: *ref*, 2212
Rodger, A.: *rev*, 2142, 2242, 2251–2, 2266–7
Rodgers, F. P.: *ref*, 2212
Rodgers, W. L.: *ref*, 1073
Roeber, E. C.: *test*, 5:870; *ref*, 2195, 2199, 2212, 2214, 4:73–(7)
Roeder, W. S.: *test*, 1066, 2226
Roehlke, A.: *ref*, 2212
Roemer, R. E.: *ref*, 2355
Rogers, C. A.: *ref*, 1087
Rogers, H. B.: *ref*, 2227, 2233
Rogge, H.: *ref*, 2195
Rogge, H. J.: *ref*, 2195
Rohila, P.: *ref*, 2173
Rohila, P. K.: *ref*, 2212
Rohlf, R. J.: *ref*, 2212
Rohrer, J. H.: *ref*, 2212, 2355
Rohrs, D. K.: *ref*, 2195
Rollins, R. W.: *ref*, 2195
Romero, T. D.: *ref*, 2212
Romney, A. K.: *ref*, 2195
Ronan, W. W.: *ref*, 1074, 1078, 1087, 2195, 2231, 2239, 2266, 2448
Rooker, J. L.: *ref*, 2452
Rooks, I.: *ref*, 2195
Rose, C. L.: *ref*, 1073
Rose, H. A.: *ref*, 2212

Rose, J.: *ref*, 2340
Rose, T.: *ref*, 1073, 2323
Rose, W.: *ref*, 2195
Rosen, E.: *ref*, 2212
Rosen, J.: *ref*, 2212, 2214
Rosen, J. C.: *ref*, 2395
Rosen, M.: *ref*, 2227, 2234
Rosen, M. H.: *ref*, 1073, 2195
Rosen, N. A.: *ref*, 2448
Rosenau, C. B.: *ref*, 1073
Rosenbaum, I.: *ref*, 2212
Rosenberg, N.: *ref*, 2195
Rosenberg, P.: *ref*, 2195
Rosenstein, I.: *ref*, 2212
Rosenthal, F.: *ref*, 1087
Rosenzweig, S.: *ref*, 1068, 2212
Rosinski, E. F.: *test*, 2356; *ref*, 1069, 2356
Ross, D. R.: *ref*, 1069, 2268
Ross, G. R.: *ref*, 2195
Ross, J.: *ref*, 2212, 2247
Ross, J. E.: *ref*, 1073
Ross, L. W.: *ref*, 2228, 2258, 2266
Ross, P. F.: *rev*, 1071, 2292
Ross, S.: *ref*, 2212
Rossi, A. M.: *ref*, 1087
Rossiter, C. M.: *ref*, 2340
Rossmann, J. E.: *ref*, 2212–3
Roth, J.: *test*, 2100
Roth, J. D.: *ref*, 2212
Roth, N. C.: *ref*, 2212
Rothe, H. F.: *rev*, 2148, 4:454; *ref*, 2263
Rothman, A. I.: *ref*, 2355
Rothney, J. W. M.: *rev*, 2201; *exc*, 2197, 2212; *ref*, 1069, 1087
Rothwell, J. W.: *test*, 2208–9
Rothwell, W. B.: *ref*, 795
Rotman, C. B.: *ref*, 1073
Rotter, J. B.: *ref*, 2239, 3:653(12)
Roudabush, G. E.: *ref*, 1087
Rousey, N. S.: *ref*, 2451
Rowan, T. C.: *ref*, 1087
Rowe, F. B.: *ref*, 2195
Rowe, H. R.: *ref*, 2387
Rowland, K. M.: *ref*, 2454
Royce, J. R.: *ref*, 2234
Royer, H. L.: *rev*, 776
Roys, K. B.: *ref*, 2212
Royse, A. B.: *rev*, 5:857
Royster, R. F.: *test*, 2469
Rozynko, V.: *ref*, 1073
Rozynko, V. V.: *ref*, 1073
Rubin, R. A.: *ref*, 1069
Rubin, S. I.: *rev*, 1078
Ruble, R. A.: *ref*, 1082
Ruch, F. L.: *rev*, 2301–2, 2397, 2413, 3:704; *test*, 1071, 3:631, 5:888; *ref*, 1071
Ruch, W. W.: *ref*, 1071
Rudd, J. P.: *ref*, 1069
Rude, H. N.: *ref*, 1071
Rudloff, J. S.: *ref*, 2212–3
Rudman, J.: *ref*, 2325, 2337, 2349, 2355
Ruebush, B. K.: *ref*, 1087
Ruedisili, C. H.: *rev*, 2298, 2448; *ref*, 2195
Ruggles, E. W.: *ref*, 2266
Rulon, P. J.: *test*, 2:1485; *ref*, 2212
Rundquist, E. A.: *rev*, 794, 3:372
Rupiper, O. J.: *ref*, 2195, 2212
Rush, C. H.: *ref*, 2451
Rush, H.: *ref*, 2195

Rusmore, J.: *ref*, 2135, 2151
Rusmore, J. T.: *ref*, 3:658(7), 6:1102(8, 10)
Russell, D.: *ref*, 2195
Russell, D. H.: *ref*, 1087
Russell, D. L.: *ref*, 2195
Russell, R. B.: *test*, 790
Russo, J. R.: *ref*, 1073, 6:1023(1)
Rust, R. M.: *ref*, 2212
Rutt, R. J.: *ref*, 1069
Ryan, F. J.: *ref*, 2212
Ryan, J. A.: *ref*, 2197
Ryan, T. A.: *exc*, 2212
Ryan, T. G.: *ref*, 2212
Ryden, E. R.: *ref*, 2212
Ryder, A. D.: *ref*, 2195

SACKETT, E. B.: *rev*, 1:1176
Saddler, L. E.: *ref*, 2212
Sadnavitch, J. M.: *ref*, 1073
Safran, C.: *test*, 2210; *ref*, 2210
Saguiguit, G. F.: *ref*, 2212
St. Clair, J. K.: *ref*, 2451
St. John, D. E.: *ref*, 2197
Sakalosky, J. C.: *ref*, 1069, 1073
Salomone, P. R.: *ref*, 2283
Saltiel, S.: *ref*, 1069
Salva, D. M.: *ref*, 2212
Salvendy, G.: *test*, 2230; *ref*, 2228, 2230, 2234
Salzinger, K.: *ref*, 2234
Salzinger, S.: *ref*, 2234
Sample, D.: *ref*, 2195
Samuelson, C. O.: *ref*, 1073, 2195
Sanazaro, P. J.: *ref*, 2355
Sanborn, M. P.: *ref*, 1069
Sandall, P. H.: *test*, 2179; *ref*, 2179
Sanders, J. R.: *ref*, 1087
Sanders, M. W.: *test*, 789–90
Sanders, R. M.: *ref*, 1087
Sanders, W. B.: *ref*, 2195, 2212, 2223
Sandmann, C. W.: *ref*, 1073
Sarason, S. B.: *ref*, 1087
Sarbin, T. R.: *ref*, 1073, 2212
Saris, R. J.: *ref*, 2452
Sartain, A. Q.: *ref*, 2195, 2227, 2234, 2239, 2251, 2260, 2266, 2379, 2448
Saslow, G.: *ref*, 2212
Sassenrath, J. M.: *ref*, 2195
Satlow, I. D.: *rev*, 776
Sattel, L.: *ref*, 1087
Satter, G.: *ref*, 1087
Satter, G. A.: *rev*, 791, 2129, 2239, 2260
Satterfield, A. E.: *ref*, 2212
Saunders, D. R.: *ref*, 1087, 2212
Saunders, W. J.: *ref*, 2239, 2448
Savastano, H.: *ref*, 2195
Saville, P.: *test*, 2239, 2334
Sawyer, J.: *ref*, 2135
Sawyer, R. N.: *ref*, 2212
Saxena, K. N.: *ref*, 2266
Scarborough, B. B.: *test*, 2203; *ref*, 2195, 2203
Scarola, L. M.: *ref*, 2234
Schaaf, W. L.: *rev*, 4:450
Schaefer, W. C.: *ref*, 1087
Schafer, E. W. P.: *ref*, 1087
Schaffer, M. C.: *ref*, 1087
Schaie, K. W.: *ref*, 1087
Schalling, D.: *ref*, 1087
Scheibe, K. E.: *ref*, 2212–3

Scheier, I. H.: *ref,* 1069
Schell, J. W.: *ref,* 2259
Schell, R. E.: *ref,* 2212
Scheller, T. G.: *ref,* 2212
Schenk, K. N.: *ref,* 2454
Schenkel, K. F.: *ref,* 1073, 2197
Schepers, J. M.: *test,* 2246; *ref,* 1075
Scheuhing, M. A.: *ref,* 2195, 2266
Schieffelin, B.: *ref,* 2258
Schiff, H. M.: *ref,* 2195, 2199
Schillinger, M.: *ref,* 2212-3
Schissel, R. F.: *ref,* 2212
Schletzer, V. M.: *ref,* 2212
Schmidt, L. A.: *ref,* 2323
Schmidt, L. G.: *ref,* 1087
Schmidt, W. G.: *ref,* 2452
Schmitt, J. R.: *ref,* 2273
Schmitz, R. M.: *ref,* 2239, 2266
Schnadt, F. W.: *ref,* 2195
Schnebly, L. M.: *ref,* 2195
Schneck, M. R.: *ref,* 2266
Schneider, A. E.: *rev,* 3:379, 3:387
Schneider, D. E.: *ref,* 2195, 6:1180 (1)
Schneider, D. L.: *ref,* 2193
Schneider, F. A.: *ref,* 2451
Schneidler, G. G.: *rev,* 1:1170; *test,* 3:689; *ref,* 2135, 2212-3, 2227-9, 2258, 2266
Schnell, W.: *test,* 2413
Schoenfeldt, L. F.: *rev,* 2224, 2227
Schofield, W.: *ref,* 2212, 2355
Scholl, C. E.: *ref,* 2212
Scholter, A. J.: *test,* 2:1659.1, 2: 1679.1
Schott, J. L.: *ref,* 2452
Schottstaedt, W. W.: *ref,* 2355
Schrader, C. H.: *ref,* 2103, 2212
Schrader, W. B.: *rev,* 2344; *ref,* 2349
Schrammel, H. E.: *test,* 784, 3: 381-2, 3:387
Schreck, T. C.: *ref,* 1069
Schreiner, J. O.: *ref,* 2452
Schroeder, G. B.: *ref,* 2451, 2457
Schroth, M. L.: *ref,* 1069, 2268
Schuell, H.: *ref,* 2213
Schuettler, A. K.: *test,* 1078
Schulman, J.: *ref,* 1069
Schultz, D. G.: *rev,* 2136-7, 2143-5, 2267, 4:761; *ref,* 2355
Schultz, R. E.: *ref,* 2212, 2451
Schultz, R. S.: *ref,* 2212, 2266
Schulzetenberge, A. C.: *ref,* 2212-3
Schumacher, C. F.: *ref,* 2212, 2355, 6:1135(1)
Schumann, D.: *ref,* 2383
Schusler, M. M.: *ref,* 1069
Schuster, D. H.: *rev,* 2471, 2475-6
Schutz, R. A.: *ref,* 2212
Schutz, R. E.: *rev,* 1069, 1087; *ref,* 2212, 2340, 6:1062(9-10)
Schwartz, A. H.: *ref,* 2234
Schwartz, M. M.: *ref,* 2189
Schwartz, S. L.: *test,* 2459; *ref,* 2459
Schwartzman, A. E.: *ref,* 2355
Schwebel, M.: *test,* 2212; *ref,* 2212
Schweiker, R. F.: *ref,* 2349
Schwesinger, G. C.: *ref,* 2258
Science Research Associates, Inc.: *test,* 2114, 7:987

Scott, D. A.: *ref,* 2212
Scott, E. L.: *ref,* 2452, 2457
Scott, J. A.: *ref,* 2355
Scott, R.: *ref,* 1087
Scott, R. H.: *ref,* 1072, 1074, 2337
Scott, T. B.: *ref,* 2197, 2212
Scott, W.: *ref,* 2355
Scott, W. E.: *ref,* 2454
Scudder, C. R.: *ref,* 2251, 2260, 3:678(6), 3:679(4)
Seagoe, M.: *ref,* 2195
Seagoe, M. V.: *rev,* 4:799; *ref,* 2212-3
Seaquist, D. L.: *ref,* 2212
Seashore, H.: *test,* 2148; *ref,* 1069
Seashore, H. G.: *rev,* 2469; *test,* 781, 1063, 1069, 2256, 2268, 5: 954; *ref,* 791, 794, 1069, 1087, 2129, 2132, 2135, 2148, 2227
Seder, M.: *ref,* 2212-3
Seder, R. W.: *ref,* 2170
Sedlacek, C. G.: *ref,* 2213
Sedlacek, W. E.: *ref,* 2355
Seeley, W. H. C.: *ref,* 2469
Seeman, M.: *ref,* 2451
Seeman, W.: *ref,* 2212
Segal, D.: *ref,* 2212
Segal, S. J.: *ref,* 2212
Segel, D.: *test,* 1082; *ref,* 1082, 2212
Seibert, E. W.: *ref,* 2195, 3:639(1, 3)
Seidman, E.: *ref,* 2212
Seiler, D. A.: *ref,* 2454
Seiler, J.: *ref,* 1073, 1086, 7:1090 (9)
Seiner, J. P.: *ref,* 2336
Seitz, M. J.: *ref,* 1073
Selover, R. B.: *rev,* 2135, 3:628
Semanek, I. A.: *ref,* 2263
Semler, I. J.: *ref,* 2103
Senior, N.: *ref,* 1073
Sergiovanni, T. J.: *ref,* 2452
Sessions, A. D.: *ref,* 2195
Sevransky, P.: *ref,* 1069
Seymour, J. H.: *ref,* 2234
Seymour, W. D.: *test,* 2230; *ref,* 2228, 2230, 2234
Shadeed, C. T.: *ref,* 1069
Shaffer, L. F.: *exc,* 1066, 1078, 2212, 2251
Shaffer, R. H.: *ref,* 2195
Shah, I.: *ref,* 2212
Shah, M.: *ref,* 2349
Shah, S. A.: *ref,* 2195
Shah, U. D.: *ref,* 2221
Shakow, D.: *test,* 3:660
Shalloe, M. P.: *ref,* 1087
Shankhdhar, S. C.: *ref,* 2173
Shanks, J. L.: *ref,* 2213
Shann, M. H.: *ref,* 2193
Shanner, W. M.: *ref,* 1087
Shapiro, R. M.: *ref,* 2193
Shapiro, S.: *ref,* 2283
Shappell, D. L.: *test,* 2187; *ref,* 1069, 2183, 2187
Shardlow, G. W.: *ref,* 2212
Sharf, R. S.: *ref,* 2213
Sharma, V.: *ref,* 2173
Sharp, H. C.: *ref,* 1073
Shartle, C. L.: *test,* 2330; *exc,* 2212-3; *ref,* 2135, 2227-9, 2251, 2258, 2266, 2452, 2457
Shatin, L.: *ref,* 2355

Shaw, C. E.: *ref,* 2195
Shaw, D. C.: *ref,* 1087
Shaw, J.: *ref,* 2212
Shay, J. B.: *ref,* 2135
Shaycoft, M. F.: *ref,* 2387
Shazo, D. D.: *ref,* 2212
Shea, P. D.: *test,* 6:1075
Shears, L. M.: *ref,* 2454
Sheehan, J.: *ref,* 2212
Sheehan, J. G.: *ref,* 2212
Sheldon, F. A.: *ref,* 1069
Shellow, S. M.: *ref,* 2212
Shemwell, E. C.: *test,* 3:387
Shepard, E. L.: *ref,* 2227, 2258, 2266
Shepherd (Hilton) Co., Inc.: *test,* 2303
Shepler, B. F.: *ref,* 2212-3
Sheppard, N. A.: *ref,* 2212, 2221
Sherman, E. C.: *ref,* 2195
Sherman, L. L.: *ref,* 2199
Sherr, R. D.: *ref,* 1073, 2186
Sherry, N. M.: *ref,* 2212
Shertzer, B.: *ref,* 1069, 2212
Shierson, H. E.: *ref,* 2195, 2199
Shih, W.: *ref,* 2234, 2266
Shimberg, B.: *rev,* 2105, 2180, 3:695
Shimota, H. E.: *ref,* 2234
Shinn, E. O.: *ref,* 1087, 2195
Shipman, V. C.: *ref,* 1073
Shirley, J. H.: *ref,* 2212
Shirts, R. G.: *ref,* 2103
Shlaudeman, K. W.: *ref,* 2212
Shneidman, E.: *test,* 2184
Shneidman, E. S.: *ref,* 2184, 2195, 2212
Shoemaker, H. A.: *ref,* 2212, 2355
Shoemaker, W. L.: *ref,* 2195
Shofstall, W. P.: *exc,* 1087
Shore, R. P.: *ref,* 1078, 2135, 2151, 2227, 2234, 2251
Shore, T. C.: *ref,* 1073
Shott, G. L.: *ref,* 6:1140(2)
Showler, W.: *ref,* 1073, 1086
Showler, W. K.: *ref,* 1073
Shrock, J. G.: *ref,* 1069, 2337
Shugert, J. M.: *ref,* 2234
Shukla, N. N.: *ref,* 1069, 2239, 2266
Shultz, I. T.: *ref,* 2195, 2212, 2239, 2251
Shuman, J. T.: *ref,* 2135, 2239, 2266
Shutterly, V.: *ref,* 3:634(5)
Shuttleworth, C. W.: *ref,* 2130, 2242, 2247, 2249, 4:769(3), 5: 880(5)
Shuttleworth, F. K.: *ref,* 2195
Sidney, G. P.: *ref,* 2195
Siegel, H. J.: *ref,* 2213
Siegel, J. P.: *ref,* 2454
Siegel, L.: *exc,* 1082, 2102, 2205, 2392
Siegel, M.: *ref,* 2234
Siess, T. F.: *ref,* 2212
Silver, H. A.: *ref,* 2197
Silver, R. J.: *ref,* 2195
Silverman, E. H.: *ref,* 2186
Silverman, R. H.: *ref,* 1082
Silverstein, A. B.: *ref,* 1087
Silvey, H. M.: *ref,* 2195
Simberg, A. L.: *test,* 2340
Simes, F. J.: *ref,* 2212
Simkevich, J. C.: *ref,* 2212
Simmons, K.: *ref,* 2266, 3:660(15)

Simms, J. T.: *ref,* 2185
Simon, G. B.: *test,* 2:1485
Simonian, K.: *ref,* 1087
Simpson, A. R.: *ref,* 2283
Simpson, D.: *ref,* 1069
Simpson, D. B.: *ref,* 2451
Simpson, R. M.: *ref,* 3:678(8)
Sinaiko, H. W.: *ref,* 4:798(3)
Sinay, R. D.: *ref,* 1074, 2212
Sinclair, G. R.: *ref,* 2142
Sindwani, K. L.: *ref,* 2452
Singer, H.: *ref,* 1087, 2195
Singer, S. L.: *ref,* 2199
Singh, N. P.: *ref,* 2195
Singh, R. P.: *ref,* 2195
Sinha, S.: *ref,* 2173
Sinick, D.: *ref,* 2251
Sininger, R. A.: *ref,* 1069, 2195
Sinnett, E. R.: *ref,* 2195, 2212
Sirota, L. M.: *ref,* 2212
Sitzmann, M. R.: *ref,* 2380
Skard, O.: *ref,* 2214, 5:615(10)
Skelly, C. G.: *ref,* 1069
Skinner, E. W.: *ref,* 2454
Skodak, M.: *ref,* 2212-3
Skolnicki, J.: *ref,* 2266
Skolnik, R. F.: *ref,* 2251
Skula, M.: *ref,* 792
Slater, P.: *rev,* 2192, 3:681; *ref,*
    2242, 2247, 2249, 2258, 3:628(5),
    4:769(2), 5:880(2, 4, 6)
Slaughter, K. B.: *ref,* 2195
Slaughter, R. E.: *ref,* 786
Slaymaker, R. R.: *ref,* 2195, 4:
    812(5)
Slayton, W. G.: *ref,* 2195
Slife, W. G.: *ref,* 2212
Slivinski, L. W.: *ref,* 2212
Sloan, C. M.: *ref,* 2212
Sloan, W.: *ref,* 2227
Sloane, B.: *ref,* 1073
Sloane, R. B.: *ref,* 1073
Slocombe, C. S.: *exc,* 2242; *ref,*
    2448
Smallenburg, H. W.: *ref,* 3:635
    (13)
Smead, W. H.: *ref,* 2452
Smith, A. E.: *ref,* 1087
Smith, C. E.: *exc,* 1087
Smith, D. D.: *ref,* 1069, 1087, 2195
Smith, D. E.: *ref,* 2195
Smith, E. J.: *ref,* 2355
Smith, G.: *ref,* 1069
Smith, G. R.: *ref,* 1087
Smith, H. C.: *ref,* 1087
Smith, I. M.: *rev,* 2243, 2245, 4:
    713; *test,* 2269, 2342; *ref,* 1070,
    2195, 2245, 2249, 2269, 6:1090(4)
Smith, J. A.: *ref,* 2186, 2199
Smith, J. M.: *ref,* 2259
Smith, L. F.: *ref,* 2266, 4:784(2)
Smith, L. M.: *ref,* 2212, 2451
Smith, N. E.: *ref,* 2355
Smith, O. B.: *ref,* 2239, 2266
Smith, R. E.: *ref,* 2212
Smith, R. L.: *ref,* 1069
Smith, R. N.: *test,* 2215, 2218; *ref,*
    2195
Smith, R. S.: *ref,* 1087
Smith, S. E.: *ref,* 2212
Smith, W. J.: *ref,* 2239, 2266, 2406,
    2448
Smith, W. R.: *ref,* 1073
Snyder, D. F.: *ref,* 2213

Solbach, M. T.: *ref,* 2452
Soliman, A. M.: *ref,* 2213
Solkoff, N.: *ref,* 2355
Sommerfeld, D.: *ref,* 1073
Sommers, N. L.: *ref,* 2451
Soper, M. E.: *ref,* 2234
Sorenson, A. G.: *ref,* 1073
Sorenson, G.: *ref,* 1073
Sorenson, H.: *ref,* 2266
Sorenson, M.: *ref,* 2195
Sorenson, W. W.: *ref,* 2197, 2239
Soueiff, M. I.: *ref,* 1073
Southall, B. J.: *ref,* 1069
Southern, J. A.: *ref,* 2195
Southwick, R. N.: *ref,* 1073
Souza, S. P.: *ref,* 6:1073(2)
Sparks, C. P.: *ref,* 2239
Spaulding, G.: *ref,* 1087
Spaulding, V. V.: *ref,* 2195
Spearman, C.: *rev,* 1087
Spearritt, D.: *rev,* 2142, 5:855;
    test, 5:890
Speer, G. S.: *ref,* 2195, 2223, 2266,
    2395
Spence, B. A.: *ref,* 2452
Spencer, G. M.: *ref,* 2344
Spencer, R. L.: *ref,* 2451
Spencer, S. J.: *ref,* 1073
Spergel, P.: *ref,* 1073, 2186
Speroff, B. J.: *test,* 2277; *ref,* 2289
Spiegel, J. A.: *ref,* 2212
Spiers, D. E.: *ref,* 2195
Spies, C. J.: *ref,* 2197
Spillane, R. F.: *ref,* 792
Spitzer, M. E.: *ref,* 2195, 2454, 2458
Spivey, G. M.: *ref,* 1087, 2195
Spoerl, D. T.: *ref,* 2212
Sprague, A. L.: *ref,* 2227
Springfield, F. B.: *ref,* 2214
Springob, H. K.: *ref,* 1069, 2195
Sprinkle, R. L.: *ref,* 2212
Sprinthall, N.: *ref,* 2212
Staats, A. W.: *ref,* 2212
Staats, C. K.: *ref,* 2212
Stacey, C. L.: *ref,* 2234
Stachniak, J. J.: *ref,* 2251
Stafford, R. E.: *ref,* 1069, 2197
Stagner, R.: *ref,* 2195
Stahmann, R. F.: *exc,* 2193-4; *ref,*
    2199
Stalans, V.: *ref,* 2195
Stallings, W. M.: *ref,* 2195
Stalnaker, A. W.: *ref,* 2212, 7:1090
    (8)
Stalnaker, J. M.: *rev,* 1:1171; *exc,*
    1087; *ref,* 1087, 2355
Stancik, E. J.: *ref,* 1069
Stanfiel, J. D.: *ref,* 2212
Stanley, J. C.: *rev,* 1063, 2235,
    4:746; *ref,* 2195
Stannard, C.: *ref,* 2251
Stanton, E. S.: *ref,* 2454
Stanton, M. B.: *ref,* 2258, 2266,
    3:671(7)
Staples, J. D.: *ref,* 2195
Starbuck, E. O.: *ref,* 2212
Statler, C.: *ref,* 2349
Stauffacher, J. C.: *ref,* 2195
Stauffer, E.: *ref,* 2195
Staveley, B.: *ref,* 1087, 2238
Stead, W. H.: *ref,* 2135, 2227-9,
    2251, 2258, 2266
Stedman, M. B.: *ref,* 2162, 2251
Steel, M.: *ref,* 2227-9, 2258

Steele, C. I.: *ref,* 2213
Steen, F. H.: *ref,* 2212
Stefanu, C.: *ref,* 2355
Steffen, H. H. J.: *ref,* 1073
Stefflre, B.: *ref,* 2195, 2199, 2212,
    3:634(6), 3:635(19)
Steigelman, G. W.: *ref,* 2135
Steimel, R. J.: *ref,* 2212
Stein, C. I.: *ref,* 1073
Stein, F.: *ref,* 2195
Stein, H. L.: *rev,* 6:1032, 6:1041
Stein, J.: *ref,* 2212
Stein, K. B.: *ref,* 2195
Stein, M. I.: *test,* 2391, 2393-4
Stein, M. L.: *ref,* 2251, 3:678(3)
Steinberg, A.: *ref,* 2195
Steinberg, M. D.: *ref,* 2142
Steiner, A. F.: *ref,* 2212
Steiner, B. J.: *ref,* 2195
Steinmetz, H. C.: *ref,* 2212
Stelter, M. W.: *ref,* 2454
Stempel, E. F.: *ref,* 1087
Stene, D. M.: *ref,* 1087, 2212
Stenquist, J. L.: *test,* 3:678-9; *ref,*
    3:678(1), 3:679(1)
Stenson, O. J.: *ref,* 2103
Stephan, E. E.: *ref,* 2195
Stephans, P.: *ref,* 2195
Stephens, D. H.: *ref,* 2212
Stephens, E. W.: *ref,* 2266
Stephens, J. H.: *ref,* 2212
Stephenson, H. B.: *ref,* 2454
Stephenson, H. W.: *ref,* 1073
Stephenson, N. L.: *ref,* 2212
Stephenson, P. M.: *ref,* 2212
Stephenson, R. R.: *ref,* 2212
Stephenson, R. W.: *ref,* 2212, 2340
Sternberg, C.: *ref,* 2195
Sterne, D. M.: *ref,* 2195, 2234,
    2251, 2266
Sternlicht, M.: *ref,* 2227, 2377, 2380,
    2383
Sternlof, R. E.: *ref,* 1087
Stevason, C. C.: *test,* 4:816
Stevens, G. Z.: *test,* 2169
Stevens, J. H.: *ref,* 2212
Stevens, L. B.: *ref,* 2212
Stevens, N. Y.: *ref,* 1069
Stevens, S. N.: *test,* 3:685; *ref,*
    2151
Stevens, Thurow and Associates,
    Inc.: *test,* 2122-4, 2318
Steward, V.: *test,* 2111-2, 2410-2,
    4:828; *ref,* 2:1651(1-3), 3:704
    (4-5), 4:828(7)
Stewart, B.: *ref,* 2195
Stewart, B. M.: *ref,* 2195
Stewart, F. G.: *test,* 2:1675
Stewart, H. Z.: *test,* 2:1486
Stewart, J. A.: *ref,* 2210
Stewart, L. H.: *exc,* 2212-3; *ref,*
    1069, 2195, 2212
Stice, G.: *ref,* 2212
Stier, L. D.: *ref,* 1087
Stilgebauer, L. K.: *ref,* 1069
Stillwell, D. J.: *ref,* 1069
Stinson, M. C.: *ref,* 2195
Stinson, P. J.: *ref,* 1069, 1074, 2195
Stock, W. H.: *ref,* 2251
Stockridge, H. C. W.: *ref,* 2168
Stockstill, K.: *ref,* 1069
Stogdill, R. M.: *test,* 2330, 2452,
    2457; *ref,* 2449, 2451-2, 2457
Stoker, H. W.: *ref,* 2199

Stoler, N.: *ref*, 2212
Stone, C. H.: *ref*, 2212
Stone, G. V.: *ref*, 2283-4
Stone, S.: *ref*, 2195
Stone, T. C.: *ref*, 1073, 2105
Stone, T. H.: *ref*, 2213
Stone, V. W.: *ref*, 2212
Stone, W. H.: *exc*, 2212-3
Stonesifer, F. A.: *ref*, 1087
Stonesifer, J. N.: *exc*, 1087
Stoops, J. A.: *ref*, 2195
Stordahl, K. E.: *ref*, 2212
Storey, J. S.: *ref*, 2135, 2195
Storr, M. A.: *test*, 2360
Storrs, S.: *ref*, 1073
Storrs, S. V.: *ref*, 1073
Stotsky, B. A.: *ref*, 2397
Stouffer, G. A. W.: *test*, 2106, 2128, 2160, 2390, 2405, 2417, 2419
Stouffer, S. A.: *test*, 6:1075
Stoughton, R. W.: *ref*, 1069
Stover, R. D.: *ref*, 2381
Stowe, E. W.: *ref*, 2195, 2216
Stoy, E. G.: *ref*, 2251, 2259, 2266
Strang, R.: *rev*, 2213, 2:1672
Strange, J. R.: *ref*, 2227, 2234
Strate, M. W.: *ref*, 5:905(8)
Stratton, H. B.: *ref*, 2199
Stratton, K.: *test*, 2365
Strauss, R. J.: *ref*, 2251
Stretch, L. B.: *ref*, 1077
Streufert, S.: *ref*, 2452
Streufert, S. C.: *ref*, 2452
Stricker, L. J.: *ref*, 2212
Strickland, E. H.: *ref*, 798
Stritch, T. M.: *ref*, 1069
Stritter, F. T.: *ref*, 2355
Stromberg, E. L.: *test*, 2235; *ref*, 2235
Stromberg, R. P.: *ref*, 2451
Stromsen, K. E.: *ref*, 1087
Strong, E. K.: *test*, 2212-3; *ref*, 2135, 2195, 2212-3, 2323
Strong, F. W.: *ref*, 2212
Strong, S. L.: *ref*, 2213
Stroops, S. L.: *ref*, 2213
Strother, C. R.: *ref*, 1087
Strother, G. B.: *ref*, 2135, 2195, 2229, 2251, 2266
Strowig, R. W.: *ref*, 1073
Strunk, O.: *ref*, 2212
Stubblefield, R. L.: *ref*, 2355
Stucki, R. E.: *ref*, 2234
Studebaker, M. E.: *test*, 3:367, 4: 457
Stufflebeam, D. L.: *ref*, 2212
Stuit, D. B.: *rev*, 2244, 2263, 2266, 4:812-3; *test*, 4:814; *ref*, 1087, 2212-3, 2266, 4:814(4)
Sturman, J.: *ref*, 2212
Subbert, D. C.: *ref*, 1073
Sullivan, B. A.: *ref*, 4:810(4)
Sullivan, B. D.: *ref*, 2451
Sullivan, E. T.: *test*, 3:690
Sullivan, J. J.: *ref*, 2289
Sullivan, J. W.: *ref*, 2186
Sullivan, T. W.: *ref*, 1073
Summerfield, A.: *ref*, 1087
Summers, B. L.: *ref*, 1069
Summers, G. F.: *ref*, 1069
Summers, M. D.: *ref*, 1073
Sumner, F. C.: *ref*, 2212
Sundberg, N. D.: *ref*, 2212
Super, D. E.: *rev*, 1070, 2135, 2188,

2195, 2205, 2214, 3:653, 3:655, 4:744; *test*, 2221; *exc*, 2212-3, 3:633, 6:1075; *ref*, 1069, 1073, 1078, 1087, 2135, 2195, 2199, 2212, 2221, 2227-9, 2234, 2239, 2251, 2258, 2260, 2263, 2266, 5:610(2)
Surette, R. F.: *ref*, 2212, 2221
Surgent, L. V.: *ref*, 2227-9, 2234
Sutherland, K.: *ref*, 1069
Sutherland, T. E.: *ref*, 1087
Sutter, C. R.: *ref*, 2195
Sutter, N. A.: *ref*, 2266
Sutton, M. A.: *ref*, 2185, 2195
Sutton, S.: *ref*, 2234
Suziedelis, A.: *ref*, 1087, 2212, 2221
Swanson, A. G.: *ref*, 2355
Swanson, E. O.: *rev*, 6:41; *ref*, 1069
Swanson, F. T.: *ref*, 2195
Swanson, R. A.: *ref*, 2199
Swanson, V. J.: *test*, 6:1184
Swanson, Z.: *ref*, 6:1090(2)
Sweeney, F. J.: *ref*, 2195
Sweeney, J. W.: *ref*, 4:812(7)
Sweeney, R. H.: *ref*, 2195
Swem, B. R.: *ref*, 2135
Swenson, J. K.: *ref*, 2449, 2451
Swinford, B. M.: *test*, 3:367, 4:457
Swink, R.: *ref*, 2135
Symonds, P. M.: *test*, 3:637; *ref*, 3:637(2)
Symons, N. A.: *ref*, 6:1180(1)

TABER, T.: *ref*, 1071, 2266
Tallent, N.: *ref*, 1087
Tallmadge, G. K.: *ref*, 2195
Tandon, R. K.: *ref*, 2266
Tanner, W. C.: *ref*, 2195, 2212-3
Tarallo, J. J.: *ref*, 2452
Tarpey, M. S.: *ref*, 2195
Tarrier, R. B.: *test*, 2187; *ref*, 2187, 2195
Tarter, R. E.: *ref*, 2234
Tarvin, J. C.: *ref*, 2235
Tate, F. E.: *ref*, 1073
Tate, J. R.: *ref*, 1073
Tate, M. W.: *ref*, 1069
Tavris, E. C.: *ref*, 2195
Taylor, A. L.: *ref*, 1069
Taylor, C. C.: *ref*, 2269
Taylor, C. W.: *ref*, 1073, 2273, 2355
Taylor, D. H.: *ref*, 2251, 2266
Taylor, D. W.: *ref*, 2212, 2239
Taylor, E. K.: *rev*, 1071, 2135, 3:624, 3:631, 5:905; *test*, 2404; *ref*, 2140, 2195, 2212, 2448, 6:1180 (1-2)
Taylor, E. S.: *ref*, 1073
Taylor, F. R.: *ref*, 1073
Taylor, G. J.: *ref*, 2212
Taylor, G. M.: *ref*, 2212
Taylor, H. R.: *rev*, 1073, 2190, 3:694
Taylor, J.: *ref*, 1069
Taylor, J. B.: *ref*, 2234-5, 2251
Taylor, J. G.: *ref*, 2212, 5:913(20)
Taylor, K. E.: *ref*, 2285
Taylor, K. V. F.: *ref*, 2212
Taylor, K. von F.: *ref*, 2213
Taylor, M.: *ref*, 2451
Taylor, P. L.: *ref*, 1087, 2195
Taylor, R. G.: *ref*, 1063, 2195, 2212-3, 2383
Tebo, J.: *ref*, 2221

Teegarden, L.: *rev*, 2227, 2258; *ref*, 2227, 2258, 3:660(13-4, 16)
Tellegen, A.: *ref*, 1073
Tenopyr, M. L.: *ref*, 1071, 2453-4
Terman, L. M.: *ref*, 2212
Terwilliger, J. S.: *ref*, 2195, 6:1062 (13)
Tharpe, F. D.: *ref*, 2195
Thayer, P. W.: *rev*, 2136, 2155; *ref*, 2401
Thiel, P. G.: *ref*, 1073
Thomas, C. B.: *ref*, 2212
Thomas, D. L.: *ref*, 2178, 2212
Thomas, D. S.: *ref*, 2197
Thomas, E. R.: *ref*, 2212
Thomas, L. E.: *ref*, 2178, 2213
Thomas, M. J.: *ref*, 2383, 2385
Thomas, P. L.: *ref*, 2195
Thomas, R. R.: *ref*, 2212
Thomas, S. D.: *ref*, 2212
Thomassen, P. R.: *ref*, 2337
Thompson, A. S.: *rev*, 2340, 1:1181, 4:825, 4:828, 5:902, 5:905
Thompson, C. E.: *ref*, 2195, 2228-9, 2251, 2266
Thompson, G. R.: *ref*, 2199
Thompson, J. M.: *test*, 1:942
Thompson, J. N.: *ref*, 2195
Thompson, J. S.: *ref*, 2212
Thompson, J. W.: *ref*, 1073
Thompson, P. O.: *ref*, 1074
Thompson, W. R.: *test*, 4:800
Thomson, G. H.: *rev*, 1087
Thomson, J. E.: *ref*, 2349
Thomson, R. W.: *ref*, 2212
Thomson, W. A.: *ref*, 2212
Thomson, W. D.: *ref*, 1069
Thoresen, C. E.: *ref*, 2212
Thorndike, R. L.: *rev*, 2241, 4:808
Thorndike, R. M.: *ref*, 2197, 2212, 2283
Thornton, G. R.: *ref*, 2260, 2433
Thornton, M. F.: *ref*, 2451
Thorpe, L. P.: *test*, 2199, 3:690, 5:870
Thrall, J. B.: *ref*, 2212
Thrall, J. R.: *ref*, 2212
Thrash, P. A.: *ref*, 2195
Thrush, R. S.: *ref*, 2212
Thumin, F.: *ref*, 2151
Thumin, F. J.: *ref*, 792, 1071, 2151, 2463, 2466
Thurman, C. G.: *ref*, 1073
Thurston, J. R.: *test*, 2378, 2382, 2389; *ref*, 2378, 2382, 2387, 2389
Thurstone, L. L.: *test*, 1087, 2162, 2214, 2245, 2255, 2272, 3:653, 5:899, 5:905; *ref*, 1087, 2162, 2195, 2212, 2214, 2:1683(1)
Thurstone, T. G.: *test*, 1087; *ref*, 1087
Tidey, W. J.: *ref*, 1063
Tiedeman, D. V.: *rev*, 2221, 7:1033; *exc*, 2180; *ref*, 1069, 2135, 2195, 2221, 2239, 2266
Tiegs, E. W.: *test*, 3:690
Tiffin, J.: *test*, 2142, 2233-4, 2263, 2435-8, 4:782, 4:816, 7:1136; *ref*, 2142, 2195, 2227-8, 2233-4, 2263
Tillinghast, B. S.: *ref*, 2193
Tillman, C. A.: *ref*, 2212
Tillman, K.: *ref*, 2195
Tillman, K. G.: *ref*, 2195
Timmons, G. D.: *ref*, 2337

Tinker, M. A.: *ref,* 2266
Tinsley, H. E. A.: *test,* 2284; *ref,* 2283-4
Tipton, R. M.: *ref,* 1073
Tirman, R. J.: *ref,* 2221
Tizard, J.: *ref,* 1073, 2258
Tobias, J.: *ref,* 2234
Tocchini, J. J.: *ref,* 2337
Todd, J. E.: *ref,* 2212
Toews, J. M.: *ref,* 2212
Toivainen, Y.: *ref,* 2266
Tollefson, N. F.: *ref,* 2212
Tomedy, F. J.: *ref,* 2213
Tomkins, S. S.: *ref,* 1074
Tonne, H. A.: *rev,* 1 :942, 3 :376, 3 :380, 5 :894
Toops, H. A.: *rev,* 2183; *test,* 2258, 2266, 3 :671; *ref,* 2258, 2266, 3 :671 (3), 3 :678(2, 5), 3 :679(2-3)
Topal, J. R.: *ref,* 2289
Topetzes, N. J.: *ref,* 2195, 2227, 2239, 6 :1102(9)
Toronto, R. S.: *ref,* 2212
Torr, D. V.: *ref,* 2199, 2212, 2214, 5 :856(8)
Torres, L.: *ref,* 2239, 2266
Tourk, L. M.: *ref,* 2234
Toussaint, I. H.: *ref,* 1087
Townsend, A.: *ref,* 1069, 1087, 2195, 2212
Townsend, J. C.: *ref,* 2212, 2221
Trabue, M. R.: *rev.* 1 :1170-1, 1 :1174, 1 :1181, 2 :1675, 2 :1679; *test,* 2258; *ref,* 2135, 2258, 3 :689 (3)
Traeger, C.: *ref,* 1073
Trainer, J. B.: *ref,* 2355
Trang, M. L.: *ref,* 2454
Traphagen, A. L.: *ref,* 2212
Trattner, M. H.: *ref,* 1073
Travers, K. J. D.: *ref,* 2195
Travers, R. M. W.: *rev,* 3 :698, 4 :792; *ref,* 2239, 2251, 2266
Traxler, A. E.: *rev,* 2195, 2311, 1 :1171, 3 :635, 3 :641, 4 :738, 4 : 777; *ref,* 1087, 2195, 2212, 2239, 2266, 2323, 5 :907(1)
Traxler, H. W.: *ref,* 1073
Tredick, V. D.: *ref,* 1087
Trembath, M. F.: *ref,* 2195
Tremel, J. G.: *ref,* 1069
Trent, J. W.: *ref,* 2212
Treumann, M. J.: *ref,* 4 :810(4)
Tribble, J. S.: *ref,* 2457
Triggs, F. O.: *rev,* 3 :642, 3 :654; *ref,* 2195, 2212-3, 3 :639(4)
Trimble, C.: *ref,* 2451
Trimble, J. T.: *ref,* 2212
Trinkhaus, W. K.: *ref,* 2212
Trione, V.: *ref,* 1073
Tripathi, R. C.: *ref,* 2231
Triplett, B.: *ref,* 1073
Trites, D. K.: *ref,* 1069
Trockman, R. W.: *ref,* 2197
Troxel, L. L.: *ref,* 2195
Trueblood, G. E.: *ref,* 2212
Trumbull, R.: *ref,* 1087
Tryon, R. C.: *rev,* 1087
Tsacnaris, H. J.: *ref,* 2448
Tsai, L. S.: *ref,* 1069
Tucker, A. C.: *ref,* 2212
Tucker, C. A.: *ref,* 2340
Tucker, M. F.: *ref,* 2273
Tucker, W. F.: *ref,* 1069

Tuckman, J.: *ref,* 798, 2195, 2227, 2251, 2260, 2266, 3 :392(2)
Tuel, J. K.: *ref,* 1087
Turille, S. J.: *test,* 3 :380
Turnbull, W.: *ref,* 2212
Turnbull, W. W.: *rev,* 1063
Turner, C. J.: *ref,* 1087
Turner, J. F.: *ref,* 1073
Turner, J. N.: *ref,* 2454
Turner, T. B.: *ref,* 2340
Turo, J. K.: *ref,* 2195
Turse, P. L.: *test,* 798, 3 :392, 5 : 855; *ref,* 798, 3 :392(1)
Tuska, S. A.: *test,* 796; *ref,* 796
Tussing, L.: *ref,* 2195, 2212, 3 :635 (17)
Tuthill, C. E.: *ref,* 2212
Tutt, M. L.: *ref,* 1087
Tutton, M. E.: *ref,* 2195
Twichell, C. M.: *ref,* 4 :825(18)
Twogood, A. P.: *test,* 2 :1665.1
Tydlaska, M.: *test,* 5 :518
Tyler, D. J.: *ref,* 2266
Tyler, E. A.: *ref,* 2355
Tyler, F. T.: *ref,* 2195
Tyler, L. E.: *rev,* 2177; *ref,* 1087, 2195, 2212-3
Tyler, R. W.: *ref,* 1087

UECKER, A. E.: *ref,* 2195
Uhlenhuth, E. H.: *ref,* 2212
Uhr, L.: *ref,* 2212
Uhrbrock, R. S.: *ref,* 2212, 4 :718 (7), 4 :813(7)
Underwood, K. L.: *ref,* 2221
United States Armed Forces Institute, Examinations Staff : *test,* 3 :373-8
United States Employment Service : *test,* 1073, 1086, 2166, 2190, 4 :717; *ref,* 1073, 2395
University of Edinburgh, Godfrey Thomson Unit : *test,* 6 :1090
University of Toronto, Ontario College of Education, Department of Educational Research : *ref,* 798
Unruh, L. D.: *ref,* 1069
Upchurch, W. B.: *ref,* 1087
Upshall, C. C.: *rev,* 778, 3 :379; *ref,* 2239
Uray, R. M.: *ref,* 2212
Urschalitz, M. O.: *ref,* 2195

VACCARO, J. J.: *ref,* 2199
Vairo, J. D.: *ref,* 2212
Van Allyn, K.: *test,* 3 :633, 3 :639, 4 :771, 6 :1049, 6 :1068; *ref,* 3 : 639(5)
van Biljon, I. J.: *ref,* 2234
Van Camp, S. S.: *ref,* 1087
Van Dalsem, E. L.: *ref,* 2195
Vandenberg, S. G.: *ref,* 1069, 1087, 2197, 2212, 2269
Vanden Boogert, A. W.: *ref,* 2258
Vander Woude, J. D.: *ref,* 2195
Van Dusen, A. C.: *ref,* 2212
Van Eastern, M. E.: *ref,* 3 :637(4)
Van Meier, E. J.: *ref,* 2452
van Staden, J. D.: *test,* 1065
Van Voorhis, W. R.: *ref,* 1087
Van Zelst, R.: *ref,* 2289
Varner, D. G.: *ref,* 1087
Vaughan, G. E.: *ref,* 2195

Vaughan, H. G.: *ref,* 2234
Vaughan, L. E.: *ref,* 2195
Vaughan, R. P.: *ref,* 2195
Vaughn, K. W.: *ref,* 2355, 4 :718 (2), 4 :812(1-2, 6)
Vega, A.: *ref,* 2234
Veldman, D. J.: *rev,* 2334, 7 :1103
Venables, E. C.: *ref,* 2247
Verbeke, M. G.: *ref,* 2451
Verburg, W. A.: *ref,* 2212
Verda, M. M.: *ref,* 2212
Verger, D. M.: *ref,* 2195
Vernon, L. N.: *ref,* 2212, 2239
Vernon, P. E.: *rev,* 1070, 1074, 1087, 5 :610; *exc,* 2242; *ref,* 2239, 2242, 4 :724(1)
Vernson, E. E.: *ref,* 2213
Very, P. S.: *ref,* 1074
Vetter, L.: *ref,* 2213
Vicinanza, P.: *ref,* 2194
Villaveces, H. J.: *ref,* 2212
Villeme, M. G.: *ref,* 2195
Vincent, D. F.: *test,* 4 :769; *ref,* 2247-8, 2254, 2345
Vincent, J. W.: *ref,* 1073, 2355, 7 : 1090(7)
Vincent, N. M.: *ref,* 2199
Vincent, W. J.: *ref,* 1074
Vineyard, E. E.: *ref,* 1069
Vinitsky, M. H.: *ref,* 2212
Vinsonhaler, J. F.: *ref,* 2212, 7 :1090 (10)
Vinton, P. W.: *ref,* 2337
Viswanathan, K.: *ref,* 2194
Viteles, M. S.: *rev,* 2227-9, 2469; *ref,* 2259, 2266, 3 :679(7)
Voas, R. B.: *ref,* 2195
Vocational Guidance Centre : *test,* 4 :735, 4 :767-8
Voelker, P. H.: *test,* 782, 1068, 2244, 2397
Vogel, B. S.: *ref,* 2212
Volkin, L. A.: *ref,* 1072
Vopatek, S. H.: *ref,* 2195, 2267
Vordenberg, W.: *ref,* 4 :738(1)
Vrooman, T. H.: *ref,* 2451

WAECHTER, R. H.: *test,* 6 :1107
Wagman, M.: *ref,* 2195, 2212
Wagner, E. E.: *ref,* 2195
Wagner, H. E.: *ref,* 2234
Wagner, P. D.: *ref,* 2212
Wagner, R. M.: *ref,* 1087
Wahlstrom, M. W.: *ref,* 1087, 2212, 2334
Waite, R. R.: *ref,* 1087
Waite, W. W.: *rev,* 2434, 3 :693, 3 : 702
Waits, J. V.: *rev,* 2469; *ref,* 2469
Wakeland, W. F.: *ref,* 1069
Walch, S. L.: *ref,* 1069, 2195
Waldrop, R. S.: *ref,* 2195
Walker, E.: *ref,* 7 :1090(14)
Walker, F. C.: *ref,* 2151, 2223, 2239
Walker, J. E.: *ref,* 2451
Walker, K. F.: *ref,* 2227, 2266
Walker, R. E.: *ref,* 2195
Walker, R. O.: *ref,* 2195
Walker, R. W.: *test,* 2169; *ref,* 2169, 6 :1062(11)
Walker, T. H.: *ref,* 2212
Walker, W. B.: *ref,* 2140, 2212, 2448
Wall, C. C.: *ref,* 2452

Wall, H. W.: *ref,* 2212
Wallace, M.: *ref,* 2258-9, 2266
Wallace, S. R.: *rev,* 1071, 2408, 2470, 4:776; *ref,* 2195, 4:825(10, 15-8)
Wallace, W. L.: *rev,* 786; *ref,* 2212, 2239, 2251, 2266, 2355
Wallar, G. A.: *test,* 2:1667; *ref,* 2212, 2:1667(1)
Wallen, R.: *ref,* 2195
Wallner, C. A.: *ref,* 1073
Walsh, J. A.: *ref,* 2212
Walsh, W. B.: *rev,* 2194
Walter, L.: *ref,* 2195
Walters, R. H.: *ref,* 1087
Walton, M. S.: *ref,* 2251
Wandt, E.: *rev,* 4:792, 4:796, 4:804
Wandzek, F. P.: *ref,* 2178
Wanger, R. S.: *ref,* 1073
Wantman, M. J.: *rev,* 2355; *ref,* 786
War Manpower Commission, Division of Occupational Analysis, Staff: *ref,* 1073, 2227, 2258, 2266
Warburton, F. W.: *rev,* 2282; *ref,* 2195
Ward, C. F.: *rev,* 2415, 2442, 7:1136
Ward, G.: *ref,* 2195, 2454
Ward, G. R.: *ref,* 6:1062(6)
Ward, L. B.: *ref,* 2323
Ward, L. W.: *ref,* 2212
Ward, R. S.: *ref,* 2135, 2227-9, 2251, 2258, 2266
Ward, W. C.: *rev,* 2273
Ward, W. P.: *ref,* 2212
Warkov, S.: *ref,* 2349
Warman, R. E.: *ref,* 1073, 2212
Warnath, C. F.: *rev,* 6:1049, 6:1068
Warren, L. W.: *ref,* 2283, 2285
Warren, N. D.: *rev,* 2223, 2225, 2231, 2234; *test,* 1071
Warren, P. A.: *ref,* 2213
Wasdyke, R. G.: *ref,* 2451
Wassenaar, G. M. C.: *ref,* 2227
Waterhouse, S. M. A.: *test,* 1085
Watkins, R. W.: *rev,* 2167; *ref,* 2195
Watley, D. J.: *ref,* 2195, 2212, 2266, 2275, 2466
Watson, C. G.: *ref,* 2195
Watson, G. E.: *ref,* 1073
Watson, R. I.: *ref,* 2212, 2239, 2266, 2355
Watson, W. S.: *ref,* 2241
Watts, A. F.: *test,* 2269
Watts, C. B.: *ref,* 2451
Watts, F. P.: *ref,* 2266
Wauck, L.: *ref,* 2195
Way, H. H.: *ref,* 2195
Weaver, S. J.: *ref,* 2199
Webb, M. W.: *ref,* 2214
Webb, S. C.: *ref,* 2212, 2337, 5:887(4)
Webberley, M.: *ref,* 1069
Weber, R. G.: *ref,* 2451
Weber, T. R.: *ref,* 1073
Webster, E. C.: *ref,* 2195, 2212
Weeks, W. R.: *ref,* 1069
Wegener, J. I.: *test,* 2360
Wegner, K. W.: *ref,* 2212-3
Weider, A.: *ref,* 2239
Weigel, R.: *ref,* 2212

Weigel, R. G.: *ref,* 2212
Weiner, M.: *ref,* 1073
Weinert, J. R.: *ref,* 2212
Weingarten, K. P.: *test,* 2205; *ref,* 2205
Weinstein, A. S.: *ref,* 2383, 2385
Weir, J. R.: *ref,* 2212
Weis, S. F.: *ref,* 2195
Weise, I. B.: *ref,* 2212
Weise, P.: *ref,* 1087, 2212
Weiser, J. C.: *ref,* 2178
Weiss, D. J.: *rev,* 1073; *test,* 2283-5; *ref,* 1071, 1073, 2197, 2212, 2283-5
Weiss, I.: *ref,* 2337, 5:887(1)
Weissenberg, P.: *ref,* 2454
Weissman, M. P.: *ref,* 2212
Weitman, M.: *ref,* 2355
Weitz, H.: *rev,* 780, 796, 2186
Weitz, J.: *ref,* 2448
Welch, R. D.: *ref,* 2212
Welford, A. T.: *rev,* 2247, 4:769
Welkowitz, J.: *ref,* 2212
Wellington, J. A.: *ref,* 1087
Wellman, F. E.: *ref,* 1087
Wells, F. L.: *rev,* 1087; *ref,* 2228-9, 2259
Wells, R. G.: *ref,* 2263
Wells, R. V.: *ref,* 5:905(8)
Wells, W. S.: *ref,* 2451
Welna, C. T.: *ref,* 2195
Welsch, L. A.: *ref,* 2212, 2239
Welsh, G. S.: *ref,* 2212
Wenar, C.: *ref,* 1087
Wenk, E.: *ref,* 1073
Wenk, E. A.: *ref,* 1073
Werkman, S. L.: *ref,* 2213
Werner, E. E.: *ref,* 1087
Werner, L. K.: *ref,* 2266
Wernimont, P.: *ref,* 2212, 2340, 2344
Werts, C. E.: *ref,* 2212
Wesley, S. M.: *ref,* 2195
Wesman, A.: *ref,* 1069
Wesman, A. G.: *rev,* 2349, 2355, 4:814; *test,* 781, 1063, 1069, 2256, 2268; *ref,* 1069, 1081, 1087, 2129, 2135, 2225, 2239
West, D. N.: *ref,* 2195, 2212
West, L. J.: *rev,* 2164, 7:559A
West, R. R.: *ref,* 2325
Westberg, W. C.: *ref,* 2151, 2195, 2239
Westbrook, B.: *test,* 2100
Westbrook, B. W.: *rev,* 2182, 2197
Western Psychological Services: *test,* 2468
Westmoreland, L.: *ref,* 2195
Weston, L. D.: *ref,* 1087
Westwood, D.: *ref,* 1073
Weynand, R. S.: *ref,* 2195
Wheatley, M. M.: *ref,* 1087
Wherry, R. J.: *ref,* 2212, 2452, 2457, 5:905(3, 7)
Whisler, L. D.: *test,* 2292
Whitcraft, J. E.: *test,* 3:387
White, A. J.: *ref,* 1072
White, B. J.: *ref,* 2213
White, C.: *test,* 5:518
White, G. R.: *ref,* 2212
White, H. G.: *ref,* 1087, 2195
White, I. W.: *ref,* 1087
White, J. G.: *test,* 2311
White, R. K.: *ref,* 2452

White, R. M.: *ref,* 2195
Whitehorn, J. C.: *ref,* 2212
Whitford, T. M.: *test,* 2118, 2238
Whitlock, G. E.: *ref,* 2212
Whitlock, J. B.: *ref,* 2239
Whitney, D. R.: *ref,* 2212
Whittaker, D.: *ref,* 2212
Whittaker, D. N. E.: *ref,* 2212-3
Whittemore, R. G.: *ref,* 1069, 1073, 2195, 2340
Whittock, J. M.: *ref,* 2195, 2212
Wickert, F.: *ref,* 3:653(7)
Wickert, F. R.: *ref,* 2448
Wiener, D. N.: *ref,* 2195, 2448
Wiens, A. N.: *ref,* 2212
Wientge, K. M.: *ref,* 2212
Wiesner, E. F.: *ref,* 2195
Wiggins, J. S.: *ref,* 2212
Wiggins, N.: *ref,* 1071, 2266
Wiggins, R. E.: *ref,* 2195
Wightwick, B.: *ref,* 794, 2135, 2266
Wightwick, M. I.: *ref,* 2213
Wilcocks, A. M.: *test,* 1084, 7:1005
Wiley, E. S.: *ref,* 796
Wiley, N. N.: *ref,* 2212
Wilhide, E. R.: *ref,* 1073
Wilkerson, C. D.: *ref,* 1069
Wilkins, M. F.: *ref,* 1087
Wilkins, P. E.: *ref,* 2213
Wilkinson, A. E.: *ref,* 2195
Wilkinson, B.: *ref,* 2151
Wilkinson, M. A.: *ref,* 2212
Willard, L. A.: *ref,* 1063
Wille, G. R.: *ref,* 2129
Williams, C. L.: *ref,* 2212
Williams, C. T.: *ref,* 2195
Williams, E. I.: *ref,* 2448
Williams, F. J.: *ref,* 2212
Williams, G. B.: *ref,* 2110
Williams, H. B.: *ref,* 2213
Williams, H. S.: *rev,* 2237-8
Williams, J. D.: *ref,* 1073
Williams, N.: *ref,* 1069
Williams, P.: *ref,* 2212
Williams, P. A.: *ref,* 2212
Williams, R.: *ref,* 1073
Williams, R. A.: *ref,* 2244
Williams, R. E.: *ref,* 2212
Williams, R. H.: *ref,* 2103
Williams, W. O.: *ref,* 2195
Williamson, E. G.: *rev,* 1:1181, 2:1661; *ref,* 2135, 2212-3, 2227-9, 2258, 2266, 2381
Willis, C. H.: *ref,* 1073, 2212
Willis, W. K.: *test,* 2178; *ref,* 1087, 2195, 6:1153(2)
Willits, J. M.: *rev,* 2162, 3:625
Willmarth, J. G.: *ref,* 2195
Willoughby, T. C.: *ref,* 2212, 2283-5
Wilson, A. W.: *ref,* 3:660(17)
Wilson, C. L.: *test,* 2476
Wilson, E.: *ref,* 2195
Wilson, E. H.: *ref,* 2195
Wilson, G. M.: *ref,* 2227
Wilson, J. A. R.: *ref,* 1087
Wilson, J. E.: *ref,* 1074
Wilson, J. T.: *ref,* 4:713(3)
Wilson, J. W.: *ref,* 2195
Wilson, J. W. D.: *ref,* 2355
Wilson, R. C.: *ref,* 1087
Wilson, R. N.: *ref,* 2194-5, 2212
Windholz, G.: *ref,* 2195
Windle, C.: *ref,* 2234

Winefordner, D.: *ref, 2201*
Winefordner, D. W.: *test,* 2201; *ref, 2201*
Winer, B. J.: *ref, 2452*
Wing, C. W.: *ref, 2355*
Winick, C.: *ref, 2195*
Winick, D. M.: *ref, 1071*
Winn, A.: *ref, 2195, 2212*
Winn, J. C.: *ref, 2195*
Winnett, W. L.: *rev, 7:552*
Winschel, J. F.: *ref, 2227*
Winsor, A. L.: *ref, 2195*
Winter, F.: *ref, 2212*
Winter, G. D.: *ref, 2195*
Winterbottom, J. A.: *ref, 2349*
Winters, J. S.: *ref, 2212*
Wisch, P. J.: *ref, 2451*
Wisdom, J. R.: *ref, 2195, 2212*
Wise, R. M.: *ref, 1073*
Wiseman, E. E.: *rev, 2439*
Wiseman, S.: *test,* 5:857; *ref,* 5:857 (2–3)
Witherspoon, R. P.: *ref, 2195*
Witherspoon, Y. T.: *ref, 2266*
Witkin, A. A.: *ref, 2212*
Wittenborn, J. R.: *ref, 2195, 2212, 2258, 2266*
Woehr, H. J.: *ref, 2212*
Woellner, R. C.: *exc,* 3:639
Wolfe, J. M.: *test,* 2331; *ref,* 2331
Wolff, W. M.: *ref, 2195, 2239*
Wolins, L.: *rev,* 1082; *ref,* 1078, 2132, 2195, 2199, 2212, 2227, 2234, 2239, 2266–7
Wolking, W. D.: *ref, 1069, 1087*
Wollowick, H. B.: *ref, 2212, 2454*
Wolpin, M.: *ref, 2355*
Womer, F. B.: *ref, 1069, 2195*
Wonderlic, E. F.: *rev,* 780, 782, 2129, 2135, 2162, 3:624; *test,* 6:1115; *ref,* 6:1115(2)
Wonderlic (E. F.) & Associates: *test,* 2320
Wong, J. C.: *ref, 2213*
Wood, B. D.: *ref, 2212, 2323*
Wood, D. A.: *ref, 1069*
Wood, M. H.: *ref, 1087*
Wood, P. L.: *ref, 2195*
Wood, S.: *ref, 1069*
Woodall, M. V.: *ref, 2451*
Woodbury, R. W.: *ref, 2221*
Woodhead, M. J.: *ref, 1073*
Woods, B. T.: *ref, 2355*
Woods, J. E.: *ref, 2212*

Woods, N. J.: *ref, 1073*
Woods, W. A.: *ref, 2195*
Woodward, C. L.: *ref, 2195, 2199, 2212*
Woodward, R. H.: *ref, 2251*
Woody, C.: *ref, 1068, 2138, 2195*
Woolf, J. A.: *ref, 2212*
Woolf, M. D.: *ref, 2212*
Woolington, J. M.: *ref, 1073*
Woo-Sam, J. M.: *ref, 2212*
Worcester, D. A.: *rev,* 4:799–800
Work, H. H.: *ref, 2355*
Worley, B.: *ref, 2212*
Worley, B. H.: *ref, 2212*
Worpell, D. F.: *ref,* 5:886(3), 5:887(5)
Wray, J. F.: *ref, 2451*
Wren, H. A.: *ref,* 4:812(8)
Wrenn, C. G.: *rev,* 2:1667; *ref,* 2212–3, 2266
Wright, E. N.: *test,* 2210
Wright, F. H.: *ref, 2195, 2212*
Wright, J. C.: *ref, 2195*
Wright, R. E.: *ref, 1087*
Wright, R. L.: *ref, 2195*
Wright, R. M.: *ref, 2212*
Wright, W.: *ref, 2212*
Wrightstone, J. W.: *test,* 780, 2192, 2252, 4:761; *exc,* 2244
Wrigley, C.: *ref, 1087*
Wrigley, J.: *ref,* 2249, 6:1090(3)
Wyland, R. R.: *ref.* 2448
Wyle, H.: *test,* 2413
Wylie, R. C.: *ref,* 3:660(18, 20)
Wyman, E. J.: *test,* 2461–2, 2464
Wyndham, A. J.: *ref, 2227*
Wynn, D. C.: *ref, 2195*
Wynne, J. T.: *ref, 2212*
Wysocki, B.: *ref, 2266*
Wysong, H. E.: *ref, 1073*

YAKUB, S.: *ref, 2135*
Yanis, M.: *ref, 2212*
Yanuzzi, J. R.: *test,* 2390
Yater, A. C.: *ref, 1073*
Yates, A.: *rev,* 5:857
Yates, L. G.: *ref, 1087*
Yeager, J. C.: *ref, 2454*
Yela, M.: *ref, 2242*
Yeslin, A. R.: *ref, 2212, 2239*
Yoder, D.: *rev,* 4:785
Young, C. R.: *ref, 1069*
Young, C. W.: *ref, 2212*

Young, D. M.: *ref, 1069*
Young, E. F.: *exc,* 1087
Young, G. W.: *ref, 2203*
Young, K. M.: *ref, 2212, 2355*
Young, M. B.: *ref, 2135*
Young, R. H.: *ref, 2355*
Younger, J. G.: *ref, 2187*
Yukl, G.: *ref, 2451*
Yum, K. S.: *ref, 1087, 2195*
Yura, M. T.: *ref, 2212*

ZAHN, J. C.: *ref, 2212*
Zahran, H. A. S.: *ref, 2179*
Zaidi, S. W. H.: *ref, 1087*
Zakolski, F. C.: *ref, 2251*
Zech, J. C.: *ref, 2195*
Zeigler, M.: *ref, 2448*
Zeigler, M. L.: *test,* 2212; *ref,* 2212
Zektick, I. N.: *ref, 2212*
Zeleny, M. P.: *ref, 2195, 2199*
Zenger, W. F.: *ref, 2195*
Zenti, R. N.: *ref, 2195*
Zerfoss, K. P.: *ref,* 3:635(16)
Zickmantel, R.: *ref, 2355*
Ziegler, D.: *ref, 2234*
Ziegler, D. J.: *ref, 2186*
Ziegler, D. K.: *ref, 2234*
Ziegler, E.: *ref, 1073*
Zimmer, J. H.: *ref, 1069*
Zimmerer, A. M.: *ref, 2195*
Zimmerman, J. J.: *ref,* 2223, 2227–9, 2234, 2258, 2337
Zimmerman, W. S.: *test,* 1074, 2184–5; *ref,* 1074, 1087, 2184, 4:761(1)
Zinn, L. A.: *ref, 2457*
Zintz, F. R.: *ref, 2289*
Zissis, C.: *ref, 2213*
Zubek, J. P.: *ref, 1078*
Zubin, J.: *exc,* 1087; *ref,* 1074, 2212, 2234
Zuckerman, M.: *ref, 2212*
Zuckman, L.: *ref, 1069*
Zullo, T. G.: *ref,* 2223, 2227–9, 2234, 2266, 2337
Zupka, A. J.: *ref, 1069*
Zurick, G. T.: *ref, 2203*
Zwilling, V. T.: *ref, 2195, 2214*
Zytowski, D. G.: *rev,* 2187; *ref,* 2194–5, 2197, 2212–3, 2221, 2283
Zyve, D. L.: *test,* 4:813; *ref,* 2:1676(1–2)

VOCATIONS
SCANNING INDEX

This scanning index is an expanded table of contents listing all tests in this volume. Foreign tests are identified by listing the country of origin in brackets immediately after the title. The population for which a test is intended is presented to facilitate the search for tests for use with a particular group. Stars indicate tests not previously listed in a *Mental Measurements Yearbook*; asterisks indicate tests revised or supplemented since last listed. Numbers refer to test entries, not to pages.

BUSINESS EDUCATION

Bookkeeping: Achievement Examinations for Secondary Schools, high school, see 775
Bookkeeping: Minnesota High School Achievement Examinations, high school, see 776
Bookkeeping Test: National Business Entrance Tests, grades 11–16 and adults, see 777
Business Fundamentals and General Information Test: National Business Entrance Tests, grades 11–16 and adults, see 778
Business Relations and Occupations: Achievement Examinations for Secondary Schools, high school, see 779
Clerical Aptitude Test: Acorn National Aptitude Tests, grades 7–16 and adults, see 780
Clerical Speed and Accuracy: Differential Aptitude Tests, grades 8–12 and adults, see 781
Clerical Tests FG and 2 [England], ages 12–13, see 781A
Detroit Clerical Aptitudes Examination, grades 9–12, see 782
General Office Clerical Test: National Business Entrance Tests, grades 11–16 and adults, see 783
Hiett Simplified Shorthand Test (Gregg), 1–2 semesters high school, see 784
Machine Calculation Test: National Business Entrance Tests, grades 11–16 and adults, see 785
National Business Entrance Tests, grades 11–16 and adults, see 786

National Teacher Examinations: Business Education, college seniors and teachers, see 787
★*Office Information and Skills Test: Content Evaluation Series*, high school, see 788
Reicherter-Sanders Typewriting I and II, 1–2 semesters high school, see 789
Russell-Sanders Bookkeeping Test, 1–2 semesters high school, see 790
SRA Clerical Aptitudes, grades 9–12 and adults, see 791
SRA Typing Skills, grades 9–12 and adults, see 792
Shorthand Aptitude Test [Australia], high school, see 793
Stenographic Aptitude Test, grades 9–16, see 794
Stenographic Test: National Business Entrance Tests, grades 11–16 and adults, see 795
Tapping Test: A Predictor of Typing and Other Tapping Operations, high school, see 796
Teacher Education Examination Program: Business Education, college seniors preparing to teach secondary school, see 797
Turse Shorthand Aptitude Test, grades 8 and over, see 798
Typewriting Test: National Business Entrance Tests, grades 11–16 and adults, see 799
Undergraduate Program Field Tests: Business Test, college, see 800
United Students Typewriting Tests, 1–4 semesters, see 801

MULTI-APTITUDE BATTERIES

Academic Promise Tests, grades 6–9, see 1063

★*Academic-Technical Aptitude Tests* [South Africa], "coloured pupils" in standards 6–8, see 1064

★*Aptitude Test for Junior Secondary Pupils* [South Africa], Bantus in Form I, see 1065

Aptitude Tests for Occupations, grades 9–13 and adults, see 1066

★*Armed Services Vocational Aptitude Battery,* high school, see 1067

Detroit General Aptitudes Examination, grades 6–12, see 1068

Differential Aptitude Tests, grades 8–12 and adults, see 1069

Differential Test Battery [England], ages 7 to "top university level," see 1070

Employee Aptitude Survey, ages 16 and over, see 1071

Flanagan Aptitude Classification Tests, grades 9–12 and adults, see 1072

General Aptitude Test Battery, grades 9–12 and adults, see 1073

Guilford-Zimmerman Aptitude Survey, grades 9–16 and adults, see 1074

High Level Battery: Test A/75 [South Africa], adults with at least 12 years of education, see 1075

★*International Primary Factors Test Battery,* grades 5 and over, see 1076

Jastak Test of Potential Ability and Behavior Stability, ages 11.5–14.5, see 1077

Job-Tests Program, adults, see 1078

★*Junior Aptitude Tests for Indian South Africans* [South Africa], standards 6–8, see 1079

Measurement of Skill, adults, see 1080

Multi-Aptitude Test, college courses in testing, see 1081

Multiple Aptitude Tests, grades 7–13, see 1082

N.B. Aptitude Tests (Junior) [South Africa], standards 4–8, see 1083

National Institute for Personnel Research Intermediate Battery [South Africa], standards 7–10 and job applicants with 9–12 years of education, see 1084

National Institute for Personnel Research Normal Battery [South Africa], standards 6–10 and job applicants with 8–11 years of education, see 1085

Nonreading Aptitude Test Battery, disadvantaged grades 9–12 and adults, see 1086

SRA Primary Mental Abilities, grades kgn–12 and adults, see 1087

Senior Aptitude Tests [South Africa], standards 8–10 and college and adults, see 1088

VOCATIONS

★*ACT Assessment of Career Development,* grades 8–11, see 2100

★*ACT Career Planning Program,* entrants to postsecondary educational institutions, see 2101

Aptitude Inventory, employee applicants, see 2102

★*Career Maturity Inventory,* grades 6–12, see 2103

★*Classification Test Battery* [South Africa], illiterate and semiliterate applicants for unskilled and semiskilled mining jobs, see 2104

Dailey Vocational Tests, grades 8–12 and adults, see 2105

ETSA Tests, job applicants, see 2106

Flanagan Industrial Tests, business and industry, see 2107

Individual Placement Series, high school and adults, see 2108

★*New Mexico Career Education Test Series,* grades 9–12, see 2109

Personal History Index, job applicants, see 2110

Steward Basic Factors Inventory, applicants for sales and office positions, see 2111

Steward Personnel Tests, applicants for sales and office positions, see 2112

TAV Selection System, adults, see 2113

Vocational Planning Inventory, vocational students in grades 8–12 and grade 13 entrants, see 2114

WLW Employment Inventory, adults, see 2115

★*Wide Range Employment Sample Test,* ages 16–35 (normal and handicapped), see 2116

A.C.E.R. Speed and Accuracy Tests [Australia], ages 13.5 and over, see 2118

APT Dictation Test, stenographers, see 2119

★*Appraisal of Occupational Aptitudes,* high school and adults, see 2120

Clerical Skills Series, clerical workers and applicants, see 2121

Clerical Tests, applicants for clerical positions, see 2122

Clerical Tests, Series N, applicants for clerical positions not involving frequent use of typewriter or verbal skill, see 2123

Clerical Tests, Series V, applicants for typing and stenographic positions, see 2124

Clerical Worker Examination, clerical workers, see 2125

Cross Reference Test, clerical job applicants, see 2126

Curtis Verbal-Clerical Skills Tests, applicants for clerical positions, see 2127

General Clerical Ability Test, job applicants, see 2128

General Clerical Test, grades 9–16 and clerical job applicants, see 2129

Group Test 20 [England], ages 15 and over, see 2130

Group Tests 61A, 64, and 66A [England], clerical applicants, see 2131

Hay Clerical Test Battery, applicants for clerical positions, see 2132

L & L Clerical Tests, applicants for office positions, see 2133

McCann Typing Tests, applicants for typing positions, see 2134

Minnesota Clerical Test, grades 8–12 and adults, see 2135

Office Skills Achievement Test, employees, see 2136

Office Worker Test, office workers, see 2137

O'Rourke Clerical Aptitude Test, Junior Grade, applicants for clerical positions, see 2138

CLERICAL

ACER Short Clerical Test—Form C [Australia], ages 13 and over, see 2117

Personnel Institute Clerical Tests, clerical personnel and typists-stenographers-secretaries, see 2139

Personnel Research Institute Clerical Battery, applicants for clerical positions, see 2140

Personnel Research Institute Test of Shorthand Skills, stenographers, see 2141

Purdue Clerical Adaptability Test, applicants for clerical positions, see 2142

RBH Checking Test, applicants for clerical and stenographic positions, see 2143

RBH Classifying Test, business and industry, see 2144

RBH Number Checking Test, business and industry, see 2145

RBH Test of Dictation Speed, stenographers, see 2146

RBH Test of Typing Speed, applicants for clerical positions, see 2147

Seashore-Bennett Stenographic Proficiency Test, adults, see 2148

Secretarial Performance Analysis, employees, see 2149

Selection Tests for Office Personnel, insurance office workers and applicants, see 2150

Short Employment Tests, applicants for clerical positions, see 2151

Short Occupational Knowledge Test for Bookkeepers, job applicants, see 2152

Short Occupational Knowledge Test for Office Machine Operators, job applicants, see 2153

Short Occupational Knowledge Test for Secretaries, job applicants, see 2154

Short Tests of Clerical Ability, applicants for office positions, see 2155

Shorthand Test: Individual Placement Series, adults, see 2156

Skill in Typing: Measurement of Skill Test 9, job applicants, see 2157

Stenographic Dictation Test, applicants for stenographic positions, see 2158

Stenographic Skill-Dictation Test, applicants for stenographic positions, see 2159

Stenographic Skills Test, job applicants, see 2160

Survey of Clerical Skills: Individual Placement Series, adults, see 2161

Thurstone Employment Tests, applicants for clerical and typing positions, see 2162

Typing Skill, typists, see 2163

Typing Test for Business, applicants for typing positions, see 2164

Typing Test: Individual Placement Series, adults, see 2165

USES Clerical Skills Tests, applicants for clerical positions, see 2166

INTERESTS

ACT Guidance Profile, junior college, see 2167

A.P.U. Occupational Interests Guide [England], ages 14–18, see 2168

Applied Biological and Agribusiness Interest Inventory, grade 8, see 2169

California Occupational Preference Survey, grades 9–16 and adults, see 2170

California Pre-Counseling Self-Analysis Protocol Booklet, student counselees, see 2171

Career Guidance Inventory, grades 7–13 students interested in trades, services and technologies, see 2172

Chatterji's Non-Language Preference Record [India], ages 11–16, see 2173

College Interest Inventory, grades 11–16, see 2174

Connolly Occupational Interests Questionnaire [England], ages 15 and over, see 2175

Crowley Occupational Interests Blank [England], ages 13 and over of average ability or less, see 2176

Curtis Interest Scale, grades 9–16 and adults, see 2177

Educational Interest Inventory, grades 11–13 and adults, see 2178

Factorial Interest Blank [England], ages 11–16, see 2179

Geist Picture Interest Inventory, grades 8–16 and adults, see 2180

Geist Picture Interest Inventory: Deaf Form: Male, deaf and hard of hearing males (grades 7–16 and adults), see 2181

Gordon Occupational Check List, high school students not planning to enter college, see 2182

Gregory Academic Interest Inventory, grades 13–16, see 2183

Guilford-Shneidman-Zimmerman Interest Survey, grades 9–16 and adults, see 2184

Guilford-Zimmerman Interest Inventory, grades 10–16 and adults, see 2185

Hackman-Gaither Vocational Interest Inventory, grades 9–12 and adults, see 2186

Hall Occupational Orientation Inventory, grades 7–16 and adults, see 2187

Henderson Analysis of Interest, grades 9–16 and adults, see 2188

How Well Do You Know Your Interests, high school, college, adults, see 2189

Interest Check List, grades 9 and over, see 2190

Interest Questionnaire for Indian South Africans [South Africa], standards 6–10, see 2191

Inventory of Vocational Interests: Acorn National Aptitude Tests, grades 7–16 and adults, see 2192

Kuder General Interest Survey, grades 6–12, see 2193

Kuder Occupational Interest Survey, grades 11–16 and adults, see 2194

Kuder Preference Record—Vocational, grades 9–16 and adults, see 2195

Milwaukee Academic Interest Inventory, grades 12–14, see 2196

Minnesota Vocational Interest Inventory, males ages 15 and over not planning to attend college, see 2197

19 Field Interest Inventory [South Africa], standards 8–10 and college and adults, see 2198

Occupational Interest Inventory, grades 7–16 and adults, see 2199

Occupational Interest Survey (With Pictures), industrial applicants and employees, see 2200

Ohio Vocational Interest Survey, grades 8–12, see 2201

Phillips Occupational Preference Scale [Australia], ages 14 and over, see 2202

Pictorial Interest Inventory, adult males, particularly poor readers and nonreaders, see 2203

Pictorial Inventory of Careers, grades 3–14 and disadvantaged adults, see 2204

Picture Interest Inventory, grades 7 and over, see 2205

Preference Analysis [South Africa], standards 8 and over, see 2206–7

Rothwell-Miller Interest Blank [Australia], ages 13 and over, see 2208

Rothwell-Miller Interest Blank, British Edition [England], ages 11 and over, see 2209

Safran Student's Interest Inventory [Canada], grades 8–12, see 2210

Self Directed Search: A Guide to Educational and Vocational Planning, high school and college and adults, see 2211

Strong Vocational Interest Blank for Men, ages 16 and over, see 2212

Strong Vocational Interest Blank for Women, ages 16 and over, see 2213

Thurstone Interest Schedule, grades 9–16 and adults, see 2214

VALCAN Vocational Interest Profile [Canada], ages 15 and over, see 2215

Vocational Apperception Test, college, see 2216

Vocational Interest and Sophistication Assessment, retarded adolescents and young adults, see 2217

Vocational Interest Profile [Canada], ages 15 and over, see 2218

★*Wide Range Interest-Opinion Test,* grades 8–12 and adults, see 2219

William, Lynde & Williams Analysis of Interest, male adults, see 2220

Work Values Inventory, grades 7–16 and adults, see 2221

MANUAL DEXTERITY

APT Manual Dexterity Test, automobile and truck mechanics and mechanics' helpers, see 2222

Crawford Small Parts Dexterity Test, high school and adults, see 2223

Crissey Dexterity Test, job applicants, see 2224

Hand-Tool Dexterity Test, adolescents and adults, see 2225

Manipulative Aptitude Test, grades 9–16 and adults, see 2226

Minnesota Rate of Manipulation Test, grade 7 to adults, see 2227

O'Connor Finger Dexterity Test, ages 14 and over, see 2228

O'Connor Tweezer Dexterity Test, ages 14 and over, see 2229

★*One Hole Test,* job applicants, see 2230

Pennsylvania Bi-Manual Worksample, ages 16 and over, see 2231

Practical Dexterity Board, ages 8 and over, see 2232

Purdue Hand Precision Test, ages 17 and over, see 2233

Purdue Pegboard, grades 9–16 and adults, see 2234

Stromberg Dexterity Test, trade school and adults, see 2235

Yarn Dexterity Test, textile workers and applicants, see 2236

MECHANICAL ABILITY

A.C.E.R. Mechanical Comprehension Test [Australia], ages 13.5 and over, see 2237

A.C.E.R. Mechanical Reasoning Test [Australia], ages 13–9 and over, see 2238

Bennett Mechanical Comprehension Test, grades 9–12 and adults, see 2239

Chriswell Structural Dexterity Test, grades 7–9, see 2240

College Placement Test in Spatial Relations, entering college freshmen, see 2241

Cox Mechanical and Manual Tests [England], boys ages 10 and over, see 2242

Curtis Object Completion and Space Form Tests, applicants for mechanical and technical jobs, see 2243

Detroit Mechanical Aptitudes Examination, grades 7–16, see 2244

Flags: A Test of Space Thinking, industrial employees, see 2245

Form Perception Test [South Africa], illiterate and semiliterate adults, see 2246

Form Relations Group Test [England], ages 14 and over, see 2247

Group Test 80A [England], ages 15 and over, see 2248

Group Test 81 [England], ages 14 and over, see 2249

Group Test 82 [England], ages 14.5 and over, see 2250

MacQuarrie Test for Mechanical Ability, grades 7 and over, see 2251

Mechanical Aptitude Test: Acorn National Aptitude Tests, grades 7–16 and adults, see 2252

Mechanical Comprehension Test [South Africa], male technical apprentices and trainee engineer applicants, see 2253

Mechanical Information Test [England], ages 15 and over, see 2254

Mechanical Movements: A Test of Mechanical Comprehension, industrial employees, see 2255

Mechanical Reasoning: Differential Aptitude Tests, grades 8–12 and adults, see 2256

Mellenbruch Mechanical Motivation Test, grades 6–16 and adults, see 2257

Minnesota Spatial Relations Test, ages 11 and over, see 2258

O'Connor Wiggly Block, ages 16 and over, see 2259

O'Rourke Mechanical Aptitude Test, grades 7–12 and adults, see 2260

Perceptual Battery [South Africa], job applicants with at least 10 years of education, see 2261

Primary Mechanical Ability Tests, applicants for positions requiring mechanical ability, see 2262

Purdue Mechanical Adaptability Test, males ages 15 and over, see 2263

RBH Three-Dimensional Space Test, industrial workers in mechanical fields, see 2264

RBH Two-Dimensional Space Test, business and industry, see 2265

Revised Minnesota Paper Form Board Test, grades 9–16 and adults, see 2266

SRA Mechanical Aptitudes, grades 9–12 and adults, see 2267

Space Relations: Differential Aptitude Tests, grades 8–12 and adults, see 2268

Spatial Tests EG, 2, and 3 [England], ages 10–13 and 15–17, see 2269

Spatial Visualization Test: Dailey Vocational Tests, grades 8–12 and adults, see 2270

Vincent Mechanical Diagrams Test [England], ages 15 and over, see 2271

Weights and Pulleys: A Test of Intuitive Mechanics, engineering students and industrial employees, see 2272

MISCELLANEOUS

Alpha Biographical Inventory, grades 9–12, see 2273

Biographical Index, college and industry, see 2274

Business Judgment Test, adults, see 2275

Conference Evaluation, conference participants, see 2276

Conference Meeting Rating Scale, conference leaders and participants, see 2277

★*Continuous Letter Checking and Continuous Symbol Checking* [South Africa], ages 12 and over, see 2278–9

Gullo Workshop and Seminar Evaluation, workshop and seminar participants, see 2280

Job Attitude Analysis, production and clerical workers, see 2281

Mathematical and Technical Test [England], ages 11 and over, see 2282

Minnesota Importance Questionnaire, vocational counselees, see 2283

★*Minnesota Job Description Questionnaire,* employees and supervisors, see 2284

Minnesota Satisfaction Questionnaire, business and industry, see 2285

Per-Flu-Dex Tests, college and industry, see 2286

RBH Breadth of Information, business and industry, see 2287

Self-Rating Scale for Leadership Qualifications, adults, see 2288

Tear Ballot for Industry, employees in industry, see 2289

Test Orientation Procedure, job applicants and trainees, see 2290

Tests A/9 and A/10 [South Africa], applicants for technical and apprentice jobs, see 2291

Whisler Strategy Test, business and industry, see 2292

Work Information Inventory, employee groups in industry, see 2293

SELECTION & RATING FORMS

APT Controlled Interview, applicants for employment, see 2294

Application Interview Screening Form, job applicants, see 2295

Career Counseling Personal Data Form, vocational counselees, see 2296

Employee Competency Scale, employees, see 2297

Employee Evaluation Form for Interviewers, adults, see 2298

Employee Performance Appraisal, business and industry, see 2299

★_Employee Progress Appraisal Form,_ rating of office employees, see 2300

*_Employee Rating and Development Forms,_ executive, industrial, office, and sales personnel, see 2301

*_Executive, Industrial, and Sales Personnel Forms,_ applicants for executive, industrial, office, or sales positions, see 2302

*_Job Application Forms,_ job applicants and employees, see 2303

Lawshe-Kephart Personnel Comparison System, for rating any aspect of employee performance by the paired comparison technique, see 2304

★_McCormick Job Performance Measurement "Rate-$-Scales,"_ employees, see 2305

McQuaig Manpower Selection Series, applicants for office and sales positions, see 2306

*_Martin Performance Appraisal,_ employees, see 2307

Merit Rating Series, industry, see 2308

Nagel Personnel Interviewing and Screening Forms, job applicants, see 2309

Performance Review Forms, employees and managers, see 2310

Personal Data Blank, counselees ages 15 and over, see 2311

Personnel Interviewing Forms, business and industry, see 2312

Personnel Rating Scale, employees, see 2313

RBH Individual Background Survey, business and industry, see 2314

San Francisco Vocational Competency Scale, mentally retarded adults, see 2315

Selection Interview Forms, business and industry, see 2316

Speech-Appearance Record, job applicants, see 2317

*_Stevens-Thurow Personnel Forms,_ business and industry, see 2318

★_Tickmaster,_ job applicants, see 2319

Wonderlic Personnel Selection Procedure, applicants for employment, see 2320

Work Reference Check, job applicants, see 2321

SPECIFIC VOCATIONS

ACCOUNTING

Account Clerk Test, job applicants, see 2322

*_American Institute of Certified Public Accountants_

Testing Programs, grades 13–16 and accountants, see 2323

*_CLEP Subject Examination in Introductory Accounting,_ 1 year or equivalent, see 2324

BUSINESS

*_Admission Test for Graduate Study in Business,_ business graduate students, see 2325

*_CLEP Subject Examination in Introduction to Business Management,_ 1 semester or equivalent, see 2326

*_CLEP Subject Examination in Introductory Business Law,_ 1 semester or equivalent, see 2327

*_CLEP Subject Examination in Introductory Marketing,_ 1 semester or equivalent, see 2328

*_CLEP Subject Examination in Money and Banking,_ 1 semester or equivalent, see 2329

Organizational Value Dimensions Questionnaire, adults, see 2330

COMPUTER PROGRAMMING

Aptitude Assessment Battery: Programming, programmers and trainees, see 2331

*_CLEP Subject Examination in Computers and Data Processing,_ 1–2 semesters or equivalent, see 2332

★_CLEP Subject Examination in Elementary Computer Programming—Fortran IV,_ 1 semester or equivalent, see 2333

*_Computer Programmer Aptitude Battery,_ applicants for computer training or employment, see 2334

Diebold Personnel Tests, programmers and systems analysts for automatic data processing and computing installations, see 2335

★_Programmer Aptitude/Competence Test System,_ computer programmers and applicants for programmer training, see 2336

DENTISTRY

*_Dental Admission Testing Program,_ dental school applicants, see 2337

Dental Hygiene Aptitude Testing Program, dental hygiene school applicants, see 2338

★_Ohio Dental Assisting Achievement Test,_ grades 11–12, see 2339

ENGINEERING

AC Test of Creative Ability, engineers and supervisors, see 2340

Engineering Aide Test, engineering aides, see 2341

*_Garnett College Test in Engineering Science_ [England], 1–2 years technical college, see 2342

*_Graduate Record Examinations Advanced Engineering Test,_ graduate school candidates, see 2343

Minnesota Engineering Analogies Test, candidates for graduate school and industry, see 2344

*_N.I.I.P. Engineering Apprentice Selection Test Battery_ [England], engineering apprentices, see 2345

*_National Engineering Aptitude Search Test: The Junior Engineering Technical Society,_ grades 9–12, see 2346

Purdue Creativity Test, applicants for engineering positions, see 2347

*_Undergraduate Program Field Tests: Engineering Test,_ college, see 2348

LAW

*_Law School Admission Test,_ law school applicants, see 2349

MEDICINE

★*CLEP Subject Examination in Clinical Chemistry*, medical technologists, see 2350

★*CLEP Subject Examination in Hematology*, medical technologists, see 2351

★*CLEP Subject Examination in Immunohematology and Blood Banking*, medical technologists, see 2352

★*CLEP Subject Examination in Microbiology*, medical technologists, see 2353

Colleges of Podiatry Admission Test, grades 14 and over, see 2354

Medical College Admission Test, applicants for admission to member colleges of the Association of American Medical Colleges, see 2355

Medical School Instructor Attitude Inventory, medical school faculty members, see 2356

★*Optometry College Admission Test*, optometry college applicants, see 2357

Veterinary Aptitude Test, veterinary school applicants, see 2358

MISCELLANEOUS

Architectural School Aptitude Test, architectural school applicants, see 2359

Chemical Operators Selection Test, chemical operators and applicants, see 2360

Fire Promotion Tests, prospective firemen promotees, see 2361

Firefighter Test, prospective firemen, see 2362

Fireman Examination, prospective firemen, see 2363

General Municipal Employees Performance (Efficiency) Rating System, municipal employees, see 2364

Journalism Test, high school, see 2365

★*Law Enforcement Perception Questionnaire*, law enforcement personnel, see 2366

Memory and Observation Tests for Policeman, prospective policemen, see 2367

Police Performance Rating System, policemen, see 2368

Police Promotion Tests, prospective policemen promotees, see 2369

Policeman Examination, prospective policemen, see 2370

Policeman Test, policemen and prospective policemen, see 2371

Potter-Nash Aptitude Test for Lumber Inspectors and Other General Personnel Who Handle Lumber, employees in woodworking industries, see 2372

★*Test for Firefighter B-1*, firemen and prospective firemen, see 2373

★*Test for Police Officer A-1*, policemen and prospective policemen, see 2374

Visual Comprehension Test for Detective, prospective police detectives, see 2375

NURSING

Achievement Tests in Nursing, students in schools of registered nursing, see 2376

Achievement Tests in Practical Nursing, practical nursing students, see 2377

Empathy Inventory, nursing instructors, see 2378

Entrance Examination for Schools of Nursing, nursing school applicants, see 2379

Entrance Examination for Schools of Practical Nursing, practical nursing school applicants, see 2380

George Washington University Series Nursing Tests, prospective nurses, see 2381

Luther Hospital Sentence Completions, prospective nursing students, see 2382

NLN Achievement Tests for Schools Preparing Registered Nurses, students in state-approved schools preparing registered nurses, see 2383

NLN Aide Selection Test, applicants for aide positions in hospitals and home health agencies, see 2384

NLN Practical Nursing Achievement Tests, students in state-approved schools of practical nursing, see 2385

NLN Pre-Admission and Classification Examination, practical nursing school entrants, see 2386

NLN Pre-Nursing and Guidance Examination, applicants for admission to state-approved schools preparing registered nurses, see 2387

Netherne Study Difficulties Battery for Student Nurses [England], student nurses, see 2388

Nurse Attitudes Inventory, prospective nursing students, see 2389

PSB-Aptitude for Practical Nursing Examination, applicants for admission to practical nursing schools, see 2390

RESEARCH

Research Personnel Review Form, research and engineering and scientific firms, see 2391

Supervisor's Evaluation of Research Personnel, research personnel, see 2392

Surveys of Research Administration and Environment, research and engineering and scientific firms, see 2393

Technical Personnel Recruiting Inventory, research and engineering and scientific firms, see 2394

SELLING

Aptitudes Associates Test of Sales Aptitude, applicants for sales positions, see 2395

Combination Inventory, Form 2, prospective debit life insurance salesmen, see 2396

Detroit Retail Selling Inventory, candidates for training in retail selling, see 2397

Evaluation Record, prospective life insurance agency managers, see 2398

Hall Salespower Inventory, salesmen, see 2399

Hanes Sales Selection Inventory, insurance and printing salesmen, see 2400

Information Index, life and health insurance agents, see 2401

LIAMA Inventory of Job Attitudes, life insurance field personnel, see 2402

Personnel Institute Hiring Kit, applicants for sales positions, see 2403

SRA Sales Attitudes Check List, applicants for sales positions, see 2404

Sales Aptitude Test, job applicants, see 2405

Sales Comprehension Test, applicants for sales positions, see 2406

Sales Method Index, life insurance agents, see 2407

Sales Motivation Inventory, applicants for sales positions, see 2408

Sales Sentence Completion Blank, applicants for sales positions, see 2409

Steward Life Insurance Knowledge Test, applicants for life insurance agent or supervisory positions, see 2410

Steward Occupational Objectives Inventory, applicants for supervisory positions in life insurance companies or agencies, see 2411

Steward Personal Background Inventory, applicants for sales positions, see 2412

Test for Ability to Sell: George Washington University Series, grades 7-16 and adults, see 2413

★*Test of Retail Sales Insight*, retail clerks and students, see 2414

SKILLED TRADES

Electrical Sophistication Test, job applicants, see 2415
Fiesenheiser Test of Ability to Read Drawings, trade school and adults, see 2416
Mechanical Familiarity Test, job applicants, see 2417
Mechanical Handyman Test, maintenance workers, see 2418
Mechanical Knowledge Test, job applicants, see 2419
Ohio Auto Body Achievement Test, grades 11–12, see 2420
Ohio Automotive Mechanics Achievement Test, grades 11–12, see 2421
★*Ohio Carpentry Achievement Test,* grades 11–12, see 2422
★*Ohio Communication Products Electronics Achievement Test,* grades 11–12, see 2423
★*Ohio Construction Electricity Achievement Test,* grades 11–12, see 2424
Ohio Cosmetology Achievement Test, grades 11–12, see 2425
★*Ohio Industrial Electronics Achievement Test,* grades 11–12, see 2426
Ohio Machine Trades Achievement Test, grades 11–12, see 2427
Ohio Mechanical Drafting Achievement Test, grades 11–12, see 2428
Ohio Printing Achievement Test, grades 11–12, see 2429
Ohio Sheet Metal Achievement Test, grades 11–12, see 2430
Ohio Trade and Industrial Education Achievement Test Program, grades 11–12, see 2431
Ohio Welding Achievement Test, grades 11–12, see 2432
Purdue Industrial Training Classification Test, grades 9–12 and adults, see 2433
Purdue Interview Aids, applicants for industrial employment, see 2434
Purdue Trade Information Test for Sheetmetal Workers, sheetmetal workers, see 2435
Purdue Trade Information Test in Carpentry, vocational school and adults, see 2436
Purdue Trade Information Test in Engine Lathe Operation, vocational school and adults, see 2437
Purdue Trade Information Test in Welding, vocational school and adults, see 2438
Short Occupational Knowledge Test for Auto Mechanics, job applicants, see 2439
Short Occupational Knowledge Test for Carpenters, job applicants, see 2440
Short Occupational Knowledge Test for Draftsmen, job applicants, see 2441
Short Occupational Knowledge Test for Electricians, job applicants, see 2442
Short Occupational Knowledge Test for Machinists, job applicants, see 2443
Short Occupational Knowledge Test for Plumbers, job applicants, see 2444
Short Occupational Knowledge Test for Tool and Die Makers, job applicants, see 2445
Short Occupational Knowledge Test for Welders, job applicants, see 2446

Technical Tests [South Africa], standards 6–8 (ages 13–15), see 2447

SUPERVISION

How Supervise?, supervisors, see 2448
Ideal Leader Behavior Description Questionnaire, supervisors, see 2449
★*In-Basket Test* [South Africa], applicants for high level executive positions, see 2450
Leader Behavior Description Questionnaire, supervisors, see 2451
Leader Behavior Description Questionnaire, Form 12, supervisors, see 2452
Leadership Evaluation and Development Scale, prospective supervisors, see 2453
Leadership Opinion Questionnaire, supervisors and prospective supervisors, see 2454
★*Leadership Practices Inventory,* supervisors, see 2455
Managerial Scale for Enterprise Improvement, supervisors, see 2456
RAD Scales, supervisors, see 2457
RBH Test of Supervisory Judgment, business and industry, see 2458
Supervisory Index, supervisors, see 2459
Supervisory Inventory on Communication, supervisors and prospective supervisors, see 2460
★*Supervisory Inventory on Discipline,* supervisors, see 2461
★*Supervisory Inventory on Grievances,* supervisors, see 2462
Supervisory Inventory on Human Relations, supervisors and prospective supervisors, see 2463
★*Supervisory Inventory on Labor Relations,* supervisors in unionized firms, see 2464
Supervisory Inventory on Safety, supervisors and prospective supervisors, see 2465
Supervisory Practices Test, supervisors, see 2466
★*Survey of Management Perception,* supervisors, see 2467
WPS Supervisor-Executive Tri-Dimensional Evaluation Scales, supervisors, see 2468

TRANSPORTATION

American Transit Association Tests, transit operating personnel, see 2469
Driver Selection Forms and Tests, truck drivers, see 2470
McGuire Safe Driver Scale and Interview Guide, prospective motor vehicle operators, see 2471
Road Test Check List for Testing, Selecting, Rating, and Training Coach Operators, bus drivers, see 2472
Road Test in Traffic for Testing, Selecting, Rating and Training Truck Drivers, truck drivers, see 2473
Short Occupational Knowledge Test for Truck Drivers, job applicants, see 2474
Truck Driver Test, drivers of light and medium trucks, see 2475
Wilson Driver Selection Test, prospective motor vehicle operators, see 2476